The African-American Experience

MACMILLAN

INFORMATION NOW ENCYCLOPEDIA

The African-American Experience

SELECTIONS FROM THE FIVE-VOLUME

Macmillan Encyclopedia of African-American Culture and History

Jack Salzman

Editor-in-Chief

MACMILLAN LIBRARY REFERENCE USA

New York

Designed by Kevin Hanek

Macmillan Library Reference USA
1633 Broadway, 7th Floor
New York, NY 10019

Manufactured in the United States of America

Printing number
1 2 3 4 5 6 7 8 9 10

Library of Congress Cataloging-in-Publication Data

The African-American experience : selections from the five-volume
    Macmillan encyclopedia of African-American culture and history /
Jack Salzman, editor-in-chief.
        p.   cm. — (Macmillan information now encyclopedia)
    Includes index.
    ISBN 0-02-865017-4 (alk. paper)
    1. Afro-Americans—Dictionaries.   2. Afro-Americans—History—
Dictionaries.   I. Salzman, Jack.   II. Series.
E185.E542   1998b
973′.0496073′003—dc21   98-43733
                                                                 CIP

This paper meets the requirements of ANSI/NISO Z39.48-1992 (Permanence of Paper).

Table of Contents

W

Y

Z

Preface

ORIGINS

The history of African Americans, beginning in 1619 with the arrival of the first slaves from Africa, is to a great extent the history of the United States. Yet, it was not until the end of the nineteenth century that artifacts related to the lives of African-Americans were systematically collected. Moreover, until the second half of the twentieth century too few historians made African-American culture and history their area of expertise. Because of this long neglect of a vital part of the nation's history, important knowledge about almost 15 percent of America's current population has gone unexamined or remained accessible only to a small group of scholars.

In 1989, when I was Director of the Center for American Culture Studies at Columbia University, I entered into an agreement with Macmillan Publishing Company to remedy this lack of accurate, easily available information by preparing a reference work that would present the lives and significance of African Americans in the broadest way possible. The result was the five-volume 1.8-million-word *Encyclopedia of African-American Culture and History*, published in 1996.

It was a massive undertaking, one that involved the cooperation of hundreds of scholars and innumerable hours of careful, painstaking work. It was, of course, well worth the effort. Students and scholars have learned to rely on this five-volume set, which provides more information about the history and culture of African Americans than any other single source. Yet, even as we neared completion of our monumental undertaking, we were aware of the need to make *The Encyclopedia of African-American Culture and History* available in a single volume. General readers, historians, and students have made it clear that a single-volume, consumer version of the larger work is most desirable. *The African-American Experience*, the latest volume in the *Information Now Encyclopedia* series, is designed to fulfill that need.

To be sure, all reference works are bounded by the practicalities of book publishing. Although *The Encyclopedia of African-American Culture and History* contains well over a million and half words, it could not possibly include all the entries we originally had in mind. So, too, difficult decisions had to made about articles selected for the *Information Now Encyclopedia*. But with *The African-American Experience* we have been able to make selections with the confidence that articles not included in this volume may well be found in the more comprehensive, five-volume set. Thus, although *The African-American Experience* does not include entries on individual states, ambassadors and diplomats, black identity, the presidency, insurance companies, and the

Postal Service, these subjects (and many more) are included in *The Encyclopedia of African-American Culture and History*. We urge you to consult that set whenever necessary.

Still, *The Information Now Encyclopedia of the African-American Experience* is grand in scope. The full range of African-American history and culture is covered. Moreover, all of the articles included in this volume were written for the parent volume, and as such are truly authoritative. Among the contributors you will find such outstanding scholars as Ira Berlin (University of Maryland), David Blight (Amherst College), Mary Schmidt Campbell (New York University), Clayborn Carson (Stanford University), Dan T. Carter (Emory University), James de Jongh (City College, CUNY), Gerald Early (Washington University), Eric Foner (Columbia University), Robert A. Hill (UCLA), Darlene Clark Hine (Michigan State University), Gerald Jaynes (Yale University), Robin D. G. Kelley (NYU), David Levering Lewis (Rutgers University), Nell Painter (Princeton University), Richard J. Powell (Duke University), and Arnold Rampersad (Princeton University).

To preserve the integrity of the original entries, all of the articles are presented in their entirety. The organization is alphabetical, and a system of margin cross-references makes it easy to find your way through the encyclopedia. By reading these additional articles, you become aware of the context in which the original article takes place. A comprehensive index at the end of the volume will provide further assistance.

FEATURES

To add visual appeal and enhance the usefulness of the volume, the page format was designed to include the following helpful features.

- **Cross-Reference Quotations:** These quotations, extracted from related articles in the volume and referenced with a specific page number, will lead to further exploration of the subject.
- **Cross-References:** Appearing at the base of many margins, "See also" cross-references cite related articles to encourage further research.
- **Notable Quotations:** Found throughout the text in the margin, these thought-provoking quotations will complement the topic under discussion.
- **Definitions:** Brief definitions of important terms in the main text can be found the margins of the book.

- **Sidebars:** Appearing in a gray box, these provocative asides relate to the text and amplify topics.
- **Index:** A thorough index provides thousands of additional points of entry into the work.

ACKNOWLEDGMENTS

The African-American Experience contains over one hundred illustrations. Acknowledgments of sources for illustrations can be found with the captions. Here I would like to acknowledge the cooperation of David H. Cohen, Vice President of Arts and Sciences and Dean of Faculty at Columbia University, for graciously allowing publication of this one-volume adaptation of the source encyclopedia. In addition I want to thank the staff of Macmillan Library Reference who made this work possible, Greg Robinson, who provided valuable research assistance, and the entire staff of the Center for American Culture—especially Lisa Hacken and Peter Eisenstadt—for the extraordinary work they did in preparing the original encyclopedia. Finally, while all this was happening, Jonah and Libby joined us and have added to the delight provided by Becca and Phoebe. Their grandmother, Cecily, remains the person on whom I most rely, and the one who most sustains me.

Jack Salzman
Director of Education Programs
New York Council for the Humanities

AARON, HENRY

LOUIS "HANK"

Henry Louis "Hank" Aaron (February 5, 1934–), baseball player. Henry Aaron grew up in relative poverty in Mobile, Ala. The third of eight children born to Herbert and Estella Aaron, he developed an early love for baseball, playing whenever possible on vacant lots and, later, at municipally owned, though racially restricted, diamonds in his neighborhood. He played semipro ball for the Mobile Black Bears before signing a contract in 1952 with the Indianapolis Clowns of the American Negro League. Aaron quickly attracted the attention of major league scouts, and in May 1952, he signed with the Boston Braves of the National League. The Braves sent him to their Northern League farm club in Eau Claire, Wis., where he won Rookie of the Year honors. In 1953, Aaron and two other black ball players were selected to integrate the South Atlantic League by playing for the Braves' Class A farm team in Jacksonville, Fla. In 1954 he was elevated to the Braves' major league club, which had moved to Milwaukee the previous year. Aaron rapidly became one of the mainstays for the Braves, both in Milwaukee and, from 1966 to 1974, in Atlanta, leading the Milwaukee club to World Series appearances in 1957 and 1958 and a world championship in 1957, and Atlanta to the National League championship series in 1969. In 1957, he was named the National League's most valuable player. In 1975, after twenty-one seasons with the Braves, Aaron was traded to the American League's Milwaukee Brewers, where he completed his playing career in 1976.

The most celebrated highlights of Aaron's major league career came on April 8, 1974, when he eclipsed the career home run record of Babe Ruth by connecting off the Los Angeles Dodgers' Al Downing at Fulton County Stadium in Atlanta. The home run, his 715th in the major leagues, climaxed a very difficult period in Aaron's life as he confronted various forms of abuse, including racial insults and death threats, from those who did not want an African American to surpass

Ruth's mark. "It should have been the happiest time of my life, the best year," Aaron has said. "But it was the worst year. It was hell. So many bad things happened. . . . Things I'm still trying to get over, and maybe never will. Things I know I'll never forget" (Capuzzo 1992).

Aaron's lifetime record of 3,771 base hits ranks behind only those of Pete Rose and Ty Cobb, and he is the all-time leader in home runs (755), runs batted in (2,297), extra-base hits (1,477), and total bases (6,856). His 2,174 runs scored tie him for second place (with Ruth) behind Cobb. These credentials, established over a twenty-three-year career, easily earned "Hammerin' Hank" induction into the Major League Baseball Hall of Fame at Cooperstown, N.Y., in his first year of eligibility, in 1982.

Following his retirement as a player, Aaron returned to the Braves' organization as director of player development and later was promoted to a vice presidency. In this capacity, he has been one of the most outspoken critics of major-league

**BASEBALL
LEGEND**

Hank Aaron of the Atlanta Braves appears in the on-deck circle in 1973, one year before he became the career leader in home runs.

AP/WIDE WORLD PHOTOS

baseball's sparse record of bringing minorities into executive leadership positions both on and off the playing field. In addition, he is a vice president of Turner Broadcasting Company and maintains a number of business and charitable interests in the Atlanta area.

—JAMES M. SORELLE

ABDUL-JABBAR, KAREEM

Kareem Abdul-Jabbar (April 16, 1947–), basketball player. Kareem Abdul-Jabbar was born Lewis Ferdinand Alcindor, the only child of Ferdinand Lewis and Cora Alcindor, in the Harlem district of New York City. His father took a degree in musicology from the Juilliard School of Music on the G.I. bill, but worked most of his life as a prison corrections officer and as a policeman for the New York Transit Authority. In 1950 the family moved to the Dyckman Street projects, city-owned middle-class housing in the Inwood section of Manhattan. Surrounded by books and jazz in his home, young Alcindor attended a parochial elementary school, Saint Jude's, and in 1961 he enrolled at another Roman Catholic school in Manhattan, Power Memorial Academy.

Alcindor began playing basketball competitively at age nine. Standing six feet, eight inches tall at fourteen years of age, he proceeded to lead Power Memorial High School to two New York City interscholastic basketball championships and to two national crowns; he made All-City and All-American three times each. Widely recruited by colleges, in 1965 he chose the University of California at Los Angeles (UCLA), whose basketball program thrived under coach John Wooden. Freshmen were then ineligible for varsity competition, but in all three of his varsity years Alcindor led the Bruins to National Collegiate Athletic Association (NCAA) championships. By now he was more than seven feet tall, making it virtually impossible for opponents to block his trademark shot, the skyhook. But another of his tactics proved to be more controversial. After his sophomore season, his awesome dunk shot (jamming the ball in the basket) provoked NCAA officials to establish a rule against dunking. The "Alcindor Rule" lasted for just ten years.

During his three varsity seasons, Alcindor scored 2,325 points, averaged 26.4 points per game, and achieved the rare distinction of making first-team All-American for all three years. Yet as a collegian he is probably best remembered for a single game he played in 1968, one of the most famous games in the history of college basketball. In the Houston Astrodome, a live audience of more than fifty thousand and a television audience of millions watched Elvin Hayes and the unbeaten Houston Cougars challenge Alcindor and unbeaten UCLA. Suffering double vision from an eye bruised in an earlier game, Alcindor still performed well, but Hayes's thirty-nine points led the Cougars to a two-point victory. Later, in the NCAA semifinals, UCLA with a healthy Alcindor demolished Houston, 101–69.

Never a mere athlete, Alcindor emerged in 1968 as a person of political and religious principles. In high school in the early 1960s, his racial consciousness had been raised by the civil rights movement, Birmingham church bombings, Harlem riots, and a racially insensitive coach. He wore his hair Afro-style, participated in the verbal and visible "revolt of the black athlete" led by California sociology professor Harry Edwards, and in 1968 effectively boycotted the Mexico City Olympics by refusing to compete for an assured place on the United States Olympic basketball team. For some time he had been studying Islam, and in 1968 he dispensed with his Catholic religion to become a Muslim. His Muslim mentor gave him a new name, Kareem Abdul-Jabbar, "generous and powerful servant of Allah"; three years later he legally changed his name.

In 1969 he launched his professional career with the Milwaukee Bucks, winning the Rookie of the Year award. In 1971, following the acquisition of veteran Oscar Robertson, the Bucks seized the National Basketball Association (NBA) championship. For six seasons with the Bucks, Abdul-Jabbar averaged more than thirty points per game and won three Most Valuable Player (MVP) trophies. Yet he was never really happy at Milwaukee, whose culture and climate were vastly different from anything he had ever known. Marriage and a child provided little solace. Burrowing deeper into his Islamic faith, in 1972 he studied Arabic at a Harvard summer school, and bought a house for the extended family of his Muslim teacher, Hamaas. Tragedy struck in January 1973, when rival Muslims massacred several members of that family; two years later, Hamaas and several comrades were sent to prison for their illegal activities in opposition to a public showing of a film that negatively portrayed Muhammad.

In that same year, 1975, Abdul-Jabbar went to the Los Angeles Lakers in a six-player exchange.

See also
Basketball

Within his first five years with the Lakers, he won three MVP awards. After a frustrating first year, he led the Lakers to the NBA playoffs thirteen consecutive times, and (teamed with Earvin "Magic" Johnson in the golden Laker decade of the 1980s) to three NBA championships. For a man seemingly always in search of inward peace, however, sad moments continued to intrude upon Abdul-Jabbar's personal life. In 1983, fire destroyed an expensive California home and an irreplaceable collection of jazz recordings; in 1987, Abdul-Jabbar lost $9 million in bad business deals. All the while, two sons and two daughters bounced back and forth from their mother, Habiba, to their father in an on-and-off marriage.

After thirty-three years of competitive basketball, Abdul-Jabbar retired in 1989, at the age of forty-two. His numerous NBA records included the most seasons, games, and minutes played; the most field goals attempted, the most made, and the most points scored; and the most personal fouls and blocked shots. In a total of 1,560 NBA outings, he averaged 24.6 points per game. Into retirement he carried six MVP awards, six championship rings, and memories from nineteen NBA All-Star games.

—WILLIAM J. BAKER

ABOLITION

Scholars often distinguish "abolitionism" from "antislavery," with the latter designating all movements aiming to curtail slavery, no matter how slowly or cautiously, and "abolitionism" reserved for the most immoderate opposition. This distinction echoes the usage of radical abolitionists, who described their goal as "immediate abolition" and disparaged other reformers' gradualism. The gradualists, for their part, labeled the radicals "ultraists," a term some immediatists embraced despite its intended derogatory connotations. As this war of labels suggests, controversies over methods and goals were recurrent in the history of organized opposition to slavery. In addition, rifts between black abolitionists and white abolitionists in the United States were at times so wide that some scholars speak of two abolitionisms.

If they cling to the radicals' narrow definitions, scholars may get a skewed perspective on the movement's progress: immediatism emerged only in the early 1830s and was submerged in broad-scale political movements in the 1840s and 1850s. To stress sectarian disagreements is to obscure the success of slavery's foes in winning allies and eliminating a mammoth institution during a remarkably brief period of history.

In a series of sardonic letters, "To Our Old Masters," published in Canada West (now Ontario) in 1851, Henry Walton Bibb, an ex-slave speaking for all the "self-emancipated"—those who had escaped from the American South's peculiar institution—placed abolitionism in a broader context. Improving the opportunities that freedom provided for the study of history, Bibb had learned "that ever since mankind formed themselves into communities, slavery, in various modifications, has had an existency." The master class's own ancestors had experienced subjugation in eras when Romans and Normans invaded England. History proved other lessons, too: "the individuals held in bondage never submitted to their yoke with cheerfulness," and in slavery's entire history no moral argument had ever been "adduced in its favor; it has invariably been the strong against the weak." Modern masters were crueler than any before, in Bibb's view, but they also were broadly despised—"you elicit the contempt of the whole civilized world." It was inevitable that they would have to "adopt one of the many proposed schemes which the benevolent have put forth for our emancipation," or they would reap the whirlwind. Bibb may have been wrong about past justifications for bondage, but his sense that slavery had lost legitimacy and was approaching its termination turned out to be accurate.

The economic historian Robert William Fogel points out, for example, "how rapidly, by historical standards, the institution of slavery gave way before the abolitionist onslaught." A small group of English reformers formed a society to abolish the Slave Trade in 1787; by 1807 they had won that fight, by 1833 the slave system in the British empire was toppled, and slavery was abolished in its last stronghold, Brazil, in 1888. "And so, within the span of little more than a century, a system that had stood above criticism for 3,000 years was outlawed everywhere in the Western world" (Fogel 1989, pp. 204–205). In the United States, where slavery was a deeply entrenched institution and antislavery coalitions looked comparatively weak, the period required to outlaw slavery was even shorter. Thus, discussion of abolitionist factionalism must be balanced by recognition of its triumph.

Early English and American Endeavors

In England, the Quakers, a small sect with little political influence, took most of the early steps against slavery. Alliances with other dissenting

Uncle Tom's Cabin *had a mighty and often radical cultural and social impact for over half a century.*

PAGE 705

See also
Civil War
Slave Trade

3

A

ABOLITION

*The Colonizationist
New Departure*

sects broadened support for antislavery in a political system increasingly responsive to popular agitation. When antislavery gained the support of William Wilberforce, Granville Sharp, and other Anglican evangelicals, it acquired respectable voices in Parliament. While advancing the view that slavery was obsolete and immoral, English leaders ensured that no fundamental threat to property rights was associated with abolition. Slave owners retained their human property during a six-year transitional "apprenticeship," and they received compensation for their losses. Having abolished its own immoral institution, England assumed responsibility for campaigns against the slave trade on the high seas, in the Islamic world, and in India. These campaigns had the effect of spreading British imperial influence and promoting British views of civilization.

As British antislavery approached its great triumphs, it began to send speakers, books and pamphlets, and some financial support to its American counterparts. Some Americans viewed British encouragement of American antislavery efforts as unwelcome meddling that endangered American independence and welfare. Both black and white abolitionists venerated names like Wilberforce and applauded the British example, but there was little resemblance between slavery in the two economies and political systems. American antislavery was compelled to address issues affecting a growing black population, a prosperous domestic economic institution, and sectional animosities in a federal political system for which England's experience offered little precedent. On the other hand, there was no existing English equivalent to the network of organizations among northern free blacks, who sought to embolden white reformers to pursue the cause of abolition more aggressively and to combat racial discrimination wherever it occurred.

As they had in England, Quakers took early leadership in American antislavery activities; and they were joined, sometimes, by insurgent evangelical movements to whom old institutions no longer seemed sacred and unchanging. Unlike England, the United States experienced a revolution that supplemented religious reform motivations with strong new reasons for opposing traditional inequalities. Slavery not only violated the law of God, but in an age of liberation and enlightenment, it contradicted the rights of man. Neither religious nor secular arguments necessarily obliged whites to combat racial prejudice or extend humanitarian aid to free blacks. Though black abolitionists would often accuse whites of

coldhearted bigotry it may be the case that the Revolution "doomed" slavery.

In the 1780s, abolitionist societies were formed in most states (including the upper South). A national abolitionist "convention" met annually from 1794 to 1806 and periodically thereafter. In the decades after the Revolution, northern states abolished slavery, often after organized antislavery campaigns. In 1808, Congress, which had previously prohibited slavery in the Northwest Territory, ended the foreign slave trade. This was assumed to be a blow to North American slavery (though some slave owners supported the measure, and later experience showed that the slave population grew rapidly without imports). Appeals to the great principles of republican government seemed ready to transform American society.

Those who believed in an optimistic scenario of revolutionary liberation underestimated the ways in which persistent white hostility to blacks would impede antislavery activity. They also overlooked obstacles imposed by the Constitution. Most abolitionists accepted the prevailing consensus that the federal government lacked any constitutional power over slavery in the states. While antislavery coalitions prevailed in states like New York and Pennsylvania, residents of a northern state had no way of influencing legislatures in South Carolina or Tennessee. When controversies over slavery arose in the U.S. Congress, as in debates over fugitive slave acts from 1793 to 1817, proslavery forces won repeated victories. With the elimination of slavery in northern states, abolition societies lost membership and purpose.

The Colonizationist New Departure

Only a change of direction, one that attracted support among southern slaveholders as well as black and white Northerners, revitalized antislavery commitments in the 1820s. Some Southerners had for years entertained hopes of deporting freed slaves (a solution to racial problems somewhat analogous to Indian removal). If ex-slaves could be relocated in the West, perhaps, or Africa, or Central America, slaveholders might be less reluctant to free them, nonslaveholding whites might be less anxious about competition for work, and northern and southern townspeople might show less fear of social consequences of emancipation. Some northern reformers believed that American society would never accept blacks as equals. Appealing simultaneously to those who hated or feared free blacks and those who deplored or regretted American racism, removal

See also
Slavery

schemes raised hopes of forging an irresistible coalition that might, once and for all, end slavery.

The premier organization advancing these schemes was the American Colonization Society (ACS), founded in 1816, which rapidly won the approval of prominent leaders of church and government in both the North and South. It sent only a few thousand blacks to its colony Liberia before 1830, however, and it failed to get federal funding for its efforts. Enthusiasm for the movement began to subside (though the ACS survived into the twentieth century) as doubts of its practicality grew. Modern scholars frequently dismiss its efforts as futile and its objectives as racist— both irrefutable charges. Less often pointed out are that slavery's most implacable champions hated the ACS; that with its decline, hopes for a national antislavery movement virtually disappeared; and that its predictions of enduring racism and misery for free blacks were realistic. If it included in its numbers slaveholders like Henry Clay, it also included many Northerners who would hold fast to abolitionist purposes for decades to come. It attracted the support of some northern blacks, including John B. Russwurm, a Bowdoin College graduate who spent much of his life in Liberia, and free southern blacks like those who appealed to Baltimore's white community in 1826 for help in leaving a republic where their inequality was "irremediable." Not only did they seek for themselves rights and respect that America seemed permanently to withhold, but they also upheld an antislavery vision: "Our absence will accelerate the liberation of such of our brethren as are in bondage."

Black support for colonization was undeniable. It was also extremely limited, while rejection of such schemes by prominent black abolitionists intensified during the 1820s. As early as 1817, a Philadelphia meeting had protested against the ACS's characterizations of blacks as a "dangerous and useless" class; linking manumission to colonization, the meeting continued, would only strengthen slavery. Even black leaders like James Forten, who privately favored emigration and believed African Americans would "never become a people until they come out from amongst the white people," joined in the protest. By 1829, militant documents like David Walker's Appeal denounced "the Colonizing Plan" as evidence of the pervasive racism that caused "Our Wretchedness."

The Immediatist New Direction

Anticolonizationist societies were launched in free black communities throughout the North, and several efforts were made to establish national newspapers to coordinate the movement. (Russwurm edited one before his conversion to colonizationism.) It was clear, however, that blacks could never sink the ACS without enlisting white allies. This meant, in practice, that blacks would have to speak in a less militant voice than Walker and other leaders might have preferred: they could not stress the virulence of racism or doubt the responsiveness of whites to conciliatory tactics. They could not advocate violent resistance to slavery or discrimination. They might also have to accept subsidiary roles in a coalition movement led by whites. These risks seemed tolerable, however, in light of the emergence in the early 1830s of a new, radical, and interracial antislavery movement that defined itself in opposition to the ACS. What for whites was a bold new departure was for blacks an episode in prudent compromise and coalition building.

Black abolitionists discovered a white champion in William Lloyd Garrison. It is likely that James Forten and other blacks influenced Garrison, at that time a colonizationist editor in Philadelphia and Baltimore, to embrace the idea of human equality. Black readers enabled Garrison in 1831 to launch his Boston-based newspaper, the *Liberator*, and they made up the great majority of subscribers to this weekly organ of immediate abolitionism throughout its early years. David Walker was one of several blacks who named children after Garrison; others gave him financial support or protected him as he walked home at night. Many viewed the *Liberator* as their voice in American public life. Maria Stewart was one of many blacks who contributed articles condemning slavery, prejudice, and colonizationism. Garrison adopted a style of denunciation thrilling to his friends and infuriating to those whom he opposed: "I will be as harsh as truth, and as uncompromising as justice. . . . I will not equivocate—I will not excuse—I will not retreat a single inch—AND I WILL BE HEARD," proclaimed his first issue. He took up the view of the ACS that blacks had urged in the previous decade and gave it powerful and influential expression. In its first year, the *Liberator* published ten times as many articles denouncing the ACS as explaining immediate abolition. Garrison's *Thoughts on African Colonization* (1832), a withering critique of racist and proslavery quotations from colonization leaders, was widely distributed and persuaded many young reformers to change loyalties and follow a new course.

This is *beautiful country.*

JOHN BROWN
ON HIS WAY TO THE
GALLOWS, DEC. 2, 1859

A

We first crush people to the earth, and then claim the right of trampling on them forever, because they are prostrate.

LYDIA MARIA CHILD
AN APPEAL ON BEHALF OF THAT CLASS OF AMERICANS CALLED AFRICANS, 1833

♦ **Nonresistence**
The principles or practice of passive submission to constituted authority even when unjust or oppressive

The attack on the ACS was a means of redefining antislavery strategy that appealed to a new generation of reformers in the early 1830s. Besides Garrison, the most influential of these was Theodore Dwight Weld, a restless and charismatic leader from upstate New York who had traveled extensively and worked for causes ranging from religious revivals to educational reform. As a student at Cincinnati's Lane Seminary in the early 1830s, he worked with blacks in the student body and local community, precipitating a crisis by forcing discussion of slavery and racial prejudice. He had no peer at a style of earnest, emotional antislavery lecturing, facing down mobs and winning converts to the cause, that he taught to other abolitionist speakers. Though Garrison and Weld were (in a not fully acknowledged sense) rivals, the former's uncompromising editorial stance and the latter's confrontational lecture style joined in shaping an exciting new era for abolitionism. Other important abolitionist leaders included the brothers Lewis and Arthur Tappan, merchants in New York City, well connected with prominent evangelical reform movements, who furnished a sober counterpoint to Weld's and Garrison's romantic outbursts. John Greenleaf Whittier, early in a career that led to great fame as a poet, was a valued new convert.

Despite condemnation by Andrew Jackson and other public figures, anticolonizationism spread with remarkable velocity. In 1832 eleven persons formed the New England Anti-Slavery Society, "the first society of this kind created on this side of the Atlantic," as the South Carolina political leader James Henry Hammond later recalled. Though slaveholders initially mocked this news, by 1837, Massachusetts had 145 societies, and New York and Ohio, where the Tappans and Weld held influence, had 274 and 213, respectively. In December 1833, sixty-three men (three of them black) formed the American Anti-Slavery Society (AASS). Earlier that year, interracial female antislavery societies were formed in Boston and Philadelphia, and in 1837 there occurred the first "national" (northern) women's antislavery convention. By 1838, the AASS claimed 1,350 affiliated societies, with membership approaching a quarter million. Important new voices, including those of ex-Southerners James G. Birney and Angelina and Sarah Moore Grimké, added to the excitement of the mid–1830s.

The positive meaning of the immediatist, anticolonizationist doctrines that stirred up so much commotion was never a simple matter to establish. For decades scholars have argued over which of two strategies—political coercion or nonviolent persuasion—was more consistent with the immediatist commitment of the early 1830s. The truth is that immediatism had more than two potential meanings, as it blended rather unrealistic expectations of religious transformation with cautious recognition of obstacles to reform. On the one hand, some abolitionists wished to persuade slaveholders to let their slaves go free, or they hoped, at least, to encourage antislavery majorities to form in southern states. Conceding the lack of federal authority to interfere with state institutions, founders of the AASS were obliged to adopt a conciliatory stance toward the South. In particular, they denied any intention to use coercion; slavery must end by "moral suasion." On the other hand, the harsh, categorical denunciations of slavery that distinguished the new movement from the ACS were hardly conciliatory. In letters of instruction and training sessions for antislavery lecturers, Weld (who injured his own voice and retired from the field) insisted that they should not get bogged down in political or economic issues: "the business of abolitionists is with the heart of the nation, rather than with its purse strings." Slavery was, he taught, "a *moral* question," and the conviction to drive home was simply that "*slavery is a sin.*" Once convinced of that, clergymen and other opinion leaders would exert pressure on slaveholders to give up their sin. The slaveholders, similarly convinced, would be impelled to change their lives. If they did not, morally awakened democratic majorities had to compel them.

Schism and Variation

By decade's end, it was obvious that slavery was not going to succumb to northern condemnation, no matter how conciliatory or intemperate. Disagreements among abolitionists, subdued during years of enthusiasm, took on new seriousness. The AASS split in two at its 1840 convention when the Tappans and other prominent reformers walked out after a woman, Abby Kelley, was elected to a committee. They protested that under Garrison's leadership the movement was too defiant of social conventions, thus offending the clergy and other respectable leaders of society, and too enthusiastic about new radical causes, especially a new form of nonviolent anarchism called "nonresistance." The departing abolitionists believed the cause could gain popular support by shunning "extraneous," controversial positions. Many on this side were moving toward more active participation in politics. For Garrison's loyal cadres in the AASS, including radical pacifists like Henry C. Wright, abolitionist commitments led toward broad condemnation of coercive behavior and institutions. The AASS survived as a separate organization, open to all who chose to join, while in the *Liberator* and in speeches and writings, Garrisonians gave increasing attention to nonviolence, utopian communities, women's rights, and other enthusiasms of the 1840s. (They showed less sympathy with working-class reforms.) They remained adamant in opposing political ventures, some out of anarchistic convictions, others out of dismayed assessment of the receptiveness of American politicians to antislavery principles.

Many black abolitionists continued to admire Garrison, but they, too, often criticized the lengths to which he carried the logic of moral suasion. Some agreed with the charge that he depleted antislavery energy by his romantic penchant for adopting new causes. But he, at least, was unwilling to compromise the principle of equality in order to appease northern majorities. Though blacks tended to favor political action, they appreciated Garrison's scorn when political abolitionism bowed to necessity by accepting slavery where it existed in the South and segregation as it worsened in the North. They complained repeatedly that all factions of white abolitionists rel-

THE ESCAPE ON SHIPBOARD.

ARREST IN BOSTON.

DEPARTURE FROM BOSTON.

THE SALE.

THE ADDRESS.

THE PRISON.

Anthony Burns.

The term "Middle
passage" refers to
the transit or
transportation of
African bondspeople
from the African
coast to the
Americas during
the slave trade.

PAGE 642

---

*I believe that to
have interfered as I
have done—as I
have always freely
admitted I have
done—in behalf
of His despised
poor, was not
wrong but right.*

JOHN BROWN
OCT. 31, 1859

---

egated blacks to subsidiary roles, at best, in their organizations. Such inability to accept blacks in visible leadership positions showed that white abolitionists had not really understood the links between bigotry and slavery. It was difficult, moreover, to interest whites in combating Jim Crow in northern streetcars with the zeal aroused by movements to keep slavery (and African Americans) out of the territories. After the schism of 1840, black abolitionists met more frequently in their own organizations, held their own conventions, and supported their own newspapers, like Samuel E. Cornish's *Colored American* and Frederick Douglass's paper.

In a powerful 1843 address to slaves, Henry Highland Garnet urged, *"Resistance! Resistance! Resistance!"* His controversial text was suppressed until 1848, but in the following years, similar militancy among other black leaders became increasingly noticeable. Talk of moral suasion gave way to insistence on the universal right of revolution. If whites did not concede to blacks the right to self-defense, some leaders asked, and if blacks never showed their willingness to fight, then how could southern slavery and northern injustice ever be ended? Blacks (with limited white support) engaged in civil disobedience against segregated schools and streetcars, and they used all available means to assist fugitives from slavery. But such militancy coincided with renewed interest in emigration, either to Canada, where tens of thousands of blacks, many of them fugitives, lived in constant rebuke to conditions in the northern and southern United States, or perhaps to Liberia (despite continuing black denunciation of the ACS), or Haiti, favored by Garnet as late as 1861. Douglass, James McCune Smith, and other black leaders deplored any possible abandonment of the cause of civil rights for free blacks and emancipation of the slaves.

After the war with Mexico from 1846 to 1848, a series of political events and court decisions—particularly events and decisions returning fugitives to bondage—struck abolitionists as calamities. Not only were some black leaders resigned to emigration, but many white Garrisonians denounced the political system dominated by proslavery leaders. Theodore Parker, Thomas Wentworth Higginson, and some others began to contemplate acts of violent resistance to proslavery legislation. Wendell Phillips advocated disunion: the northern states must sunder connections with southern sinfulness. At one public meeting in 1854, Garrison denounced the Fugitive Slave Act and burned the Constitution as "a covenant with Death and

an agreement with Hell." Southern extremists portrayed Garrisonians as men and women of enormous influence in the North. They had no such influence, but in taking positions of uncompromising moral purity, these skilled agitators created an atmosphere of escalating moral concern. While eschewing politics, they guaranteed that southern political victories brought the fate of slavery closer and closer to the center of national political debate.

Political abolitionists, meanwhile, tried various courses of action. Some, including many blacks, supported the Whigs; others experimented with third parties. During a period of confusing political realignment, skilled publicists like the journalist Horace Greeley and clergyman Henry Ward Beecher used newspapers, lecture platforms, and other popular institutions to disseminate selected elements of the abolitionist message—that the slave power jeopardized the liberty and prosperity of all workers and farmers—across the North and much of the West. In this endeavor they gained the cooperation of antislavery politicians, who were usually reluctant to confront racial prejudice or clarify the meanings of equality. An antislavery majority probably could not have been assembled without ambiguous appeals to expediency and prejudice as well as to principle. It is important to note, nevertheless, that as political abolitionism augmented its small shares of the electorate (the Liberty party garnered about 6,000 votes in the 1840 presidential election and 60,000 in 1844, and the Free Soil party polled about 290,000 in 1848), the clarity of its attacks on slavery blurred. Both Weld and Garrison had counseled abolitionists to stick to the moral high ground, to denounce the iniquity of slavery and racism. Antislavery opinion grew in the North and West, however, as slavery was seen as threatening to the economic welfare of whites. More often than not, antislavery public opinion of the kind that sustained the Republican party's slim majority in 1860 was saturated by racial prejudice. It would have been content to tolerate slavery where it already existed, if proslavery politicians had not repeatedly fueled northern fears and resentments.

The Triumph of Antislavery

Abolitionism existed in a tense love-hate relation with Abraham Lincoln and the Republicans in the 1860s. Abolitionists took credit for preparing the ground for the new party's success, but some sought to oust Lincoln in 1864. If anything, Garrisonians were more willing than other factions to excuse the Republicans' slow advance toward the goal of abolishing slavery, a goal promoted by all abolitionists throughout the war. Abolitionists did what they could to pressure the Union army to mobilize black soldiers and treat them fairly once in uniform. Black abolitionists worked at recruitment, and some, like Martin R. Delaney, as well as whites like Thomas Wentworth Higginson, served as officers. Pacifistic abolitionists volunteered for medical duties in hospitals and on the battlefield. Before slavery was abolished, abolitionist men and women went south to work among freedmen in areas occupied by Union armies, thus setting a pattern for educational and related endeavors during Reconstruction and afterward.

At the end of the Civil War, and with enactment of the Thirteenth Amendment, abolitionists were jubilant. The *Liberator* ceased publication, and the AASS disbanded. But abolitionists, especially younger ones who had entered the movement in the 1850s, continued to promote education for African Americans and condemn violations of their civil rights long after the war. As the century approached its end, such endeavors increasingly seemed futile, and many victories of Civil War and Reconstruction days were overturned. At the same time, ironically, some Northerners lauded abolitionists as an example of a principled minority who had led the nation to higher moral conceptions and practices.

Some of this glorification can be discounted as an expression of sectional pride and Republican partisanship. It was offset, for many decades, by scholarly condemnation of abolitionists as fanatics responsible, along with southern fire-eaters, for disrupting the union. Nevertheless, the merging of abolitionist principles, espoused by a zealous minority, with the concerns and interests of a majority of citizens, led to the destruction of slavery, for so long an accepted social institution, and this triumph has gained a prominent place in the history of American democracy. Abolitionists tested the openness of democratic politics to reform, and they agitated successfully for the extension of the nation's founding principles to groups who had formerly been left out. Their triumph has served as an inspiring model for subsequent movements, on both the left and right, from woman's suffrage before 1920 to the student movements of the 1960s and, most recently, to Operation Rescue and antiabortion activities.

—LEWIS PERRY

AFFIRMATIVE ACTION

Affirmative action is an act, policy, plan or program designed to remedy the negative effects of wrongful discrimination. "Affirmative action" can remedy the perceived injustice of discrimination on the basis of a person's race, national origin, ethnicity, language, sex, religion, disability, sexual orientation, or affiliation. As a civil rights policy affecting African Americans, "affirmative action" most often denotes race-conscious and result-oriented efforts undertaken by private entities and government officials to correct the unequal distribution of economic opportunity and education that many attribute to slavery, segregation and racism.

What counts as affirmative action varies from one field to the next. Affirmative action in employment has generally meant seeking to hire a racially mixed and balanced workforce that includes a representative number of Americans of African, Latin, Asian-Pacific, or native ancestry, using the distribution of minority groups in the national or local population to gauge adequate representation. Self-described "equal opportunity/affirmative action" employers may voluntarily seek to hire African Americans, sometimes with explicit numerical goals and timetables in mind. For example, an employer whose workforce is 2 percent African American begins to hire additional blacks aiming at a workforce that will eventually include 10 percent African Americans, 3 percent of whom will occupy management positions within three years.

Employers may base affirmative-action programs on the assumption that they can achieve racially balanced workforces through race-conscious hiring and promotion preferences. Preferential employment strategies involve affirmative action on behalf of a racial minority group when a person's minority race results in employment for which race is not otherwise a significant qualification. A person's race may sometimes be a bona fide job-related qualification (Fullinwider 1980). For instance, undercover police work in black neighborhoods may require black police officers; realistic filmmaking about African-American history may require black actors. In such instances, preferring black workers is not affirmative action.

Not all racial preferences involve affirmative action and not all affirmative action involves racial preferences. For example, to attract more African-American job applicants, an employer with a mainly white workforce begins to advertise job openings in the city's neighborhood newspapers,

♦ **Integration**
Incorporation as equals into society or an organization of individuals of different groups (as races)

A

AFFIRMATIVE ACTION

History

including newspapers circulated in black neighborhoods. This change in practice is potentially effective affirmative action, but it is not preferential treatment in the sense of according blacks employment advantages over whites or other groups (Greenawalt 1983). However, if the same employer committed itself to hiring blacks over similarly qualified or better qualified whites, or by exempting blacks from the adverse impact of seniority rules, one could describe the employer as according blacks preferential treatment as an affirmative-action measure.

Affirmative action in public and private education has focused on such race-conscious programs as "desegregation," "integration," "diversity," and "multiculturalism." Whether voluntarily or pursuant to court orders, to achieve desegregation in public primary and secondary schools formerly subject to state-imposed racial segregation, school officials have expressly mandated numerical goals, ratios and quotas for faculty hiring and pupil enrollment. At some schools, voluntary affirmative action has meant allocating financial resources to recruiting and retaining minority students with special scholarships, curricula, and social programs. At others, it has also meant admissions procedures that deemphasize standardized test scores and other traditional qualifications. Some colleges and universities have adopted legally controversial minority admissions quotas or diversity criteria aimed at enrolling a representative percentage of nonwhite students each year. In many schools the ideal of a diverse, multicultural student body is thought to require affirmative action to employ teachers and to enroll and retain students of varied racial and ethnic backgrounds.

Beyond employment and education, the distribution of public or private benefits on the basis of race for the remedial purpose of redressing group discrimination fits the definition of affirmative action. Hence, minority "set-aside" requirements that reserve a percentage of public contracts for minority businesses qualify as affirmative action. The concept also reaches special effort made by public and private scientific, humanistic, and arts organizations to disburse a share of their grants, awards, and prizes to members of once-neglected minority groups. The concept even reaches redistricting to aggregate minority voters into district that remedy a history of inadequate political representation. Telling evidence of the link some see between affirmative-action quotas and voting rights was exemplified in 1993 when University of Pennsylvania law professor Lani Guinier's scholarly explorations of cumulative voting and other

novel strategies to strengthen minority voting rights earned her the epithet "Quota Queen" among conservatives, who successfully thwarted her presidential appointment to head the Civil Rights Division of the Justice Department.

Viewing affirmative action goals as quotas is often designed to suggest "that they, like yesterday's quotas, serve an immoral end" (Erzorsky 1991). Indeed, the affirmative action practiced in employment, education and other fields has excited intense moral and legal debate. The debate centers on the charges that race-conscious remedies designed to redress invidious discrimination against some groups amount to wrongful "reverse discrimination" against others (Steele 1990). Opponents of affirmative action raise particular concern about any form of affirmative action that involves numerical mandates, especially goals and quotas. Although *goals* often connotes flexible guidelines for group inclusion and *quotas* often connote rigid limits with discriminatory intent, both entail optimal percentages or numbers of persons belonging to specific groups targeted to serve in specific capacities (Fullwinder 1980). The strongest proponents of affirmative action argue that numerical mandates, whether termed "goals" or "quotas," are just and effective remedies for persistent discrimination (Johnson 1992).

History

The idea that special effort is needed to remedy discrimination on the basis of race is as old as President Abraham Lincoln's Emancipation Proclamation and the Thirteenth Amendment to the Constitution ending slavery. However, affirmative action as a distinct race-relations policy did not come about until the crest of the Civil Rights Movement of the 1960s. The term "affirmative action" quietly made its debut in American law in 1935, the year Congress passed the Wagner Act, expressly requiring "affirmative action" of employers guilty of discrimination against workers on the basis of union membership.

In June 1941, President Franklin D. Roosevelt issued Executive Order 8802, a precursor of affirmative-action policies in the arena of race relations, which called for "special measures" and "certain action" to end "discrimination in the employment of workers in the defense industries or government [occurring] because of race, creed, color, or national origin." Roosevelt's historic move was intended to boost the wartime economy and reduce severe black unemployment, as urged by A. Philip Randolph and other leaders. Executive Order 8802 was not consistently enforced,

See also

Atlanta

Jesse Jackson

but in some states sudden black competition for traditionally white jobs prompted hostility and violence against blacks.

Internal White House discussions of employment policy during the presidency of Dwight D. Eisenhower included consideration of mandatory affirmative action. On March 8, 1961, President John F. Kennedy issued Executive Order 10925 establishing a President's Committee on Equal Employment Opportunity to expand and strengthen efforts to promote full equality of employment opportunity across racial lines. Order 10925 also required that all government contractors agree not to "discriminate against any employee or applicant for employment because of race, creed, color or national origin" and to "take affirmative action to ensure that applicants are employed, and that employees are treated during employment, without regard to their race, creed, color, or national origin."

The monumental Civil Rights Act of 1964 outlawed the most blatant forms of racial discrimination in employment, education, housing, public accommodations, and voting. The 1964 Act desegregated restaurants, cinemas, retail stores, hotels, transportation, and beaches. Building on Brown v. Board of Education (1954), the historic Supreme Court decision that ended legal racial segregation of public primary and secondary schools and pronounced that school desegregation should occur "with all deliberate speed," the Act blocked federal aid to segregated schools. The Act banned unequal application of the requirements of voter registration. The Voting Rights Act of 1965 went even further in protecting the franchise, restricting literacy tests and authorizing federal election supervision in the states. Title VII of the 1964 Act banned discrimination by employers of twenty-five or more, labor unions and employment agencies, and created the Equal Employment Opportunity Commission (EEOC). Title VII empowered the federal courts to order "affirmative action as may be appropriate" to remedy past workplace discrimination.

Finally, on September 28, 1965, in the wake of the Civil Rights Act of 1964, President Lyndon B. Johnson's Executive Order 11246 launched affirmative action as the centerpiece of national employment policy and race relations. Aimed at "the full realization of equal employment opportunity," Executive Order 11246, like Kennedy's earlier order, required that firms conducting business with the federal government and these firms' suppliers "take affirmative action to ensure that applicants are employed, and that employees are treated during employment, without regard to their race,

creed, color, or national origin." Order 11246 was amended by Executive Order 11375 and implemented by Labor Department Revised Order No. 4, requiring that government contractors in "good faith" set "goals" and "time-tables" for employing previously "underutilized" minority group members available and qualified for hire. The Labor Department's Office of Federal Contract Compliance, awarded responsibility for implementing Order 11246 and its amendments, developed regulations defining a program of "affirmative action" as "a set of specific and result-oriented procedures" undertaken with "every good faith effort" to bring about "equal employment opportunity." Vice President Hubert Humphrey coordinated the Johnson administration's civil rights and affirmative action policies. On August 20, 1965, at a White House conference on equal employment opportunity, Humphrey had revealed a broad understanding of the economic plight of blacks. Humphrey said America had "neglected the Negro too long" and that "government, business and labor must open more jobs to Negroes [and] must go out and affirmatively seek those persons who are qualified and begin to train those who are not."

In 1967, the Department of Health, Education and Welfare (HEW) began requiring colleges and universities receiving federal funds to establish affirmative-action goals for employing female and minority faculty members. In 1972, HEW issued guidelines for higher education requiring both nondiscrimination and efforts to recruit, employ, and promote members of formerly excluded groups "even if that exclusion cannot be traced to particular discriminatory actions on the part of the employer." The HEW guidelines also indicated that colleges and universities were not expected to lower their standards or employ less qualified job candidates. The HEW guidelines distinguished affirmative-action "goals," which its directives required as an indicator of probable compliance, from "quotas" which its directives expressly prohibited. Critics of HEW have argued that a firm distinction is untenable since "a positive 'goal' for one group must be a negative 'quota' for another" (Goldman 1977). Numerous efforts to distinguish goals from quotas have left some analysts unpersuaded: although the purpose of goals may be inclusion and quotas exclusion, "getting people in, where the shape of the 'in' is fixed, will be possible only by keeping others out" (Fullinwider 1980).

By the early 1970s affirmative action in employment became a full-fledged national policy. The EEOC had taken the stand that an obliga-

Political action is the highest responsibility of a citizen.

JOHN F. KENNEDY
SPEECH, OCTOBER 20, 1960

America is God's crucible, the great melting pot.

ISRAEL ZANGWILL
THE MELTING POT, 1908

See also
NAACP

tion of result-oriented affirmative action extended to all employers within its jurisdiction, not just federal contractors or educational institutions receiving federal funds. Political support for the federal government's affirmative action initiatives was initially strong and broad based. Some maintained that affirmative action utilizing numerical goals and timetables was a necessary complement to the 1964 Civil Rights statutes. A century after the formal abolition of slavery, African Americans as a group remained substantially poorer, less well educated, and politically less powerful than whites as a group. Legally enforced segregation had intensified black inequality.

The leadership of the NAACP, the Congress on Racial Equality, the NAACP Legal and Educational Defense Fund, and the National Urban League quickly endorsed affirmative action. Diverse sectors of the economy promptly responded to Washington's affirmative action programs. For example, in 1966, the city of New York, the Roman Catholic Church in Michigan, and the Texas-based retailer Neiman Marcus were among the organizations announcing voluntary plans requiring that their suppliers and other contractors to take affirmative steps toward hiring African Americans.

The political popularity of affirmative action during the Johnson administration subsequently yielded to controversy. An erosion of political support in Congress and the White House for higher education affirmative action programs was evident as early as 1972, seemingly prompted by opposition from faculty members and administrators fearing the demise of traditional standards of scholarly merit. In 1975, the United States Attorney General Edward H. Levi publicly stated that affirmative action constitutes "quotas" and is "not good government." After 1976 both during and after the one-term presidency of the pro-affirmative action Democrat Jimmy Carter, disagreements over the legality, morality, and efficacy of affirmative action strained African-Americans' relationships with labor unions, the Republican Party, and white liberal Democrats, including Jewish liberals who supported the Civil Rights Movement but who were suspicious of government-backed racial quotas that historically had been used to exclude Jews.

Ronald Reagan and George Bush campaigned for the presidency on opposition to affirmative-action "quotas." President Reagan spoke out against affirmative action's numerical goals and quotas, and this opposition became one of the cornerstones of his public policy agenda on issues affecting African Americans. High-profile conservatives defended the ideal of a colorblind society and characterized blacks as overly dependent upon welfare, affirmative action, and other government programs promulgated chiefly by liberal democrats. *Time* and *Newsweek* magazines, as well as other mainstream media, lavished more publicity on affirmative-action controversies than any other topic related to blacks, including unemployment, health, hunger, and homelessness (Daniel and Allen 1988). The NAACP and the National Urban League maintained their support for affirmative action and the civil rights laws. Consistent with the Reagan agenda, however, the federal government lessened its enforcement of federal contracts compliance programs in the 1980s and a number of Supreme Court cases curbed affirmative action in employment and other key fields.

In the 1990s some were prepared to attribute significant gains for blacks to affirmative action, including an increase in black employment and promotion at major corporations, in heavy industry, in police and fire departments, and in higher education (Erzorsky 1991). Yet, persistent critics converted "affirmative action" into a virtual pejorative, along with "preferential treatment," "reverse discrimination," and "quotas." Symbolic of the era, Democrat Bill Clinton, a supporter of affirmative-action policies, after election to the presidency in 1992 abruptly withdrew the nomination of Lani Guinier to the Justice Department after her critics labeled her affirmative-action policies as outside the mainstream.

Moral and Policy Debates

Reflecting ties to the Civil Rights Movement, the stated goals of affirmative action range from the forward-looking goal of improving society by remedying distributive inequities, to the backward-looking goal of righting historic wrongs (Erzorsky 1991; McGary 1977–78). Affirmative action on behalf of African Americans often was, and often is, defended by scholars as compensation or reparation owed to blacks by whites or a white-dominated society (Boxhill 1984; Thomson 1977). In particular, it is argued that after two centuries of legally enforced slavery, racial segregation, and racism, African Americans now deserve the jobs, education, and other benefits made possible through affirmative action. Beyond compensatory or reparative justice, goals ascribed to affirmative action include promoting economic opportunity for minority groups and individuals; eradicating racial subordination; neutralizing the competitive advantages many whites enjoy in education, business, and employment; educating a cadre of minority professionals for service in underserved minority communities; creating minority role models, intellectuals, artists, and civic leaders; and, finally, acknowledging society's cultural diversity (Goldberg 1994; Erzorsky 1991; Boxhill 1984; Greenawalt 1983).

African Americans widely support affirmative action-policies. To be sure, some African-American neoconservatives, such as Glen Loury, Thomas Sowell, and Clarence Thomas, have rejected affirmative action on the grounds that it is incompatible with a "colorblind" civil rights policy. Other African Americans sometimes have also criticized affirmative action, often on pragmatic grounds (Carter 1991; Steele 1990; Wilson 1987). They have joined those who argue that preferential treatment in education and employment mainly benefits middle-class blacks, leaving the problem of profound rural and urban black poverty untouched (Goldman 1979; Cohen 1980). Critics say affirmative action reinforces pervasive negative stereotypes of blacks as inferior to whites (Jencks, 1983). African Americans have noted this and have argued that racial preferences are demeaning or dispiriting to minorities; that they compromise African-Americans' self-esteem or self-respect (Sowell 1976). Some reject affirmative action because it has proven to be socially divisive, having bred resentment among white Americans (Nagel 1977).

As an antidote to simmering white resentments, William J. Wilson (1987) has proposed promoting race-neutral "universal policies" aimed at the health and employment problems of the poor rather than merely promoting affirmative action for racial minorities. The search for factors beyond race and racism to explain persistent black inequality in the post civil rights era has led some politically conservative opponents of affirmative action to advance the argument that minority economic inequality stems from a pervasive breakdown in work, family, and community values in minority communities.

Supporters of affirmative action offer pertinent replies to all of these arguments (Erzorsky 1991). To the contention that affirmative action does not help the poorest blacks, a reply has been that affirmative action nonetheless enhances the lives of some deserving blacks. To the argument that affirmative action lowers esteem for blacks and blacks' self-esteem, a reply is that blacks are held in very low esteem already and are vulnerable to low self-esteem due to their inferior education

and employment. To the argument that affirmative action is racially divisive and breeds resentment, a reply is that blacks should not be deprived of the benefits of affirmative action simply because of white resentment, unless that resentment can be shown to stem from genuine racial injustice. Finally, to the "fingerpointing" argument that blacks' problems result from lapses of individual responsibility, one reply is that communities of poverty, drugs, and violence result from decades of private and public decision making concerning legal, economic, and social policy.

Gertrude Erzorsky (1991), who supports affirmative action, has noted a libertarian argument against affirmative action: employers should be free to choose their own workers as a basic moral freedom, comparable to the freedom to choose one's own spouse. The more common libertarian argument asserts that social and economics benefits should be distributed solely in accordance with colorblind principles of entitlement, merit, and personal. In liberal academic and intellectual circles, opponents of affirmative action have questioned the coherence of the idea that blacks as a group are entitled to, merit or deserve affirmative action as compensation or reparations for past wrongdoing (Sher 1977). Corrective justice, some philosophers say, is both causal and relational. That is, when an injury occurs, the person who caused that injury must personally pay his or her victim. Yet affirmative action makes white males pay for societal injuries to women and minorities that they did not cause (Paul 1991). The ex-slaves wronged by slavery are dead, as are the people who wronged them. It is therefore illogical, the argument continues, to hold all current whites responsible for the evils of slavery that were perpetrated by the remote ancestors of some whites on the remote ancestors of some blacks (Sher 1977). In sum, set-asides and other preferential programs that fall under the rubric of affirmative action "reward an ill-defined class of victims, indiscriminately favor some in that class and leave others totally uncompensated, benefit groups whose members were never the victims of state imposed discrimination, and most importantly, do not concentrate recompense on those whose rights were most flagrantly violated, namely, the black slaves, now long dead" (Simon 1977).

Against the argument that African Americans who stand to benefit by affirmative action were never in bondage to whites and may have led lives free of egregious discrimination, some philosophers defend affirmative action as a moral right of persons belonging to groups that have been

The collapse of Reconstruction deeply affected the future course of American development.

PAGE 577

A

AFFIRMATIVE ACTION

*Endorsing
Race-Conscious Remedies*

*The problem of the
twentieth century is
the problem of the
color line.*

W.E.B. DU BOIS
TO THE NATIONS OF THE
WORLD, SPEECH,
PAN-AFRICAN CONFERENCE,
LONDON, 1900

uniquely harmed in the past by public law and that are disproportionately poor or otherwise disadvantaged today. Admitting that white citizens are not personally at fault for slavery and may not harbor racist sentiments, these advocates of affirmative action observe that white citizens benefit from the system of racial privilege and institutional racism that continued to pervade American institutions after blacks' emancipation from slavery and segregation (Thomson 1977). Whites have a competitive advantage over blacks that society may fairly seek to erase through affirmative action.

Endorsing Race-Conscious Remedies

The Supreme Court unanimously endorsed quotas and other race-conscious numerical requirements to achieve school desegregation in *United States* v. *Montgomery County Board of Education* (1969) and *Swann* v. *Charlotte-Mecklenburg Board of Education* (1971). In a different context, the Court again endorsed race-conscious remedies in *United Jewish Organizations* v. *Carey* (1977). Over Fourteenth Amendment and other constitutional objections, the Court upheld a New York redistricting plan that explicitly attempted to increase the voting strength of "nonwhite" voters—blacks and Puerto Ricans—seemingly at the expense of a community of Hasidic Jews, viewed as whites under the plan. Four justices agreed that the use of race as a factor in districting and apportionment is constitutionally permissible; that express findings of past discrimination were not required to justify race-conscious policies; and that racial quotas in electoral districting were not by definition unconstitutional. Chief Justice Warren Burger dissented from the judgment of the Court, stressing his discomfort with putting the "imprimatur of the State on the concept that race is a proper consideration in the electoral process."

Seniority Limits on Workplace Preferences

In 1977, the Court established a limitation on affirmative action that it would reiterate in subsequent cases. *International Brotherhood of Teamsters* v. *United States* (1977) held that a disparate impact on minorities alone does not make a seniority system illegal under Title VII. Justice Thurgood Marshall partly dissented from the majority, joined by Justice William Brennan. The Court's lone African-American justice, Marshall cited Federal Court of Appeals opinions, EEOC decisions, scholarly materials, and legislative history to attest to the broadness of the remedial goal of Title VII. Marshall admitted that Congress had expressed reservations about orders of retroactive seniority in a nonremedial context or based solely upon a showing of a policy's disparate impact on minorities without any evidence of discriminatory intent. But Marshall argued that Congress did not clearly intend to preserve seniority systems that perpetuate the effects of discrimination. Seven years after the teamsters came, *Firefighters Local Union No. 1784 v. Stotts* (1984) overturned a District Court's injunction prohibiting the city of Memphis from following its seniority system's "last hired, first fired" policy during layoffs. In *Wygant v. Jackson Board of Education* (1986), Justice Marshall again dissented from a ruling elevating seniority rules over affirmative action principles. Here the Court invalidated the provision of a collective bargaining agreement between a school board and the local teachers' union that would have preserved minority representations in teaching staff in the event of layoffs. Justice Powell applied strict scrutiny to the contested provision arguing for the Court that strict scrutiny applies to any racial classification, even when the classification "operates against a group that historically has not been subject to discrimination." Justices Sandra Day O'Connor and Justice Byron White concurred in the use of strict scrutiny review to assess the impact of affirmative action on whites.

Professional School Admissions: No Strict Quotas

Two cases involving affirmative action in law and medical school admissions evidence the Court's judgment of limited constitutional tolerance for affirmative-action plans involving numerical quotas: *Defunis v. Oregaard* (1977) and *Regents of the University of California v. Bakke* (1978). In *Defunis,* a law school applicant challenged the race-conscious admissions policies of the state-supported University of Washington Law School as a violation of his right to equal protection under the Fourteenth Amendment. The school had established a separate admissions process for minorities and a fifteen to twenty percent admissions goal for applicants who described their dominant ethnic origin as black, Chicano, American Indian, or Filipino. The Defunis case was not decided on its merits; the Court declared the case moot after Defunis matriculated in law school during the pendency of the suit. However, in a dissenting opinion, Justice William O. Douglas criticized conventional law school admissions criteria and stressed that schools can and should broaden their inquiries beyond test scores and grades. Douglas opined that race could be a factor in admissions,

consistent with the constitutional requirement of race neutral evaluation, so long as all persons are judged "on an individual basis, rather than according to racial classifications."

Decided fully on the merits, the highly publicized *Bakke* case struck down the special admissions program of the public Medical School of the University of California at Davis. The program featured a sixteen percent quota for "blacks, Chicanos, Asians, and American Indians." The purpose of the program was to increase minority representation in the medical field, to compensate minorities for past societal discrimination, to increase medical care in underserved communities, and to diversify the student body. Allen Bakke, a twice-rejected white applicant to the medical school, challenged its admissions program both under Title VI of the Civil Rights Act of 1964 and under the Equal Protection Clause of the Fourteenth Amendment.

The court issued a long and complex series of opinions to resolve Bakke's case. In the final analysis, the case declares minority admissions quotas unlawful at schools receiving federal dollars, but upholds the use of race as a factor in selecting a diverse student body. Five members of the Court affirmed the illegality of the Davis program and directed Bakke to be admitted to the school. Justice Powell affirmed the illegality of the school's admissions program, but voted with Justices Brennan, White, Marshall, and Blackmun to approve the use of race as a factor in higher education admissions. Justice Stevens and three others thought it unnecessary to decide the constitutional issues raised by the case, finding that the admissions policy was invalid under Title VI. They ascertained that the plain language of the statute prohibiting discrimination was sufficient justification for nullifying the program.

The dissenting opinion of Justices Brennan, White, Marshall, and Blackmun cautioned that the nation's "colorblind" values were purely aspirational. They argued that a reading of the history and purpose of Title VI did not rule out race-conscious remedies. Taking up the constitutional issues, these justices rejected strict scrutiny review in favor of a lower, "intermediate" level of scrutiny. They reasoned that intermediate scrutiny permits racial classification "substantially related to an important government objective" and concluded that the university's purpose of counteracting an actual or potential disparate racial impact stemming from discrimination was sufficiently important to justify race-conscious admissions. Justice Marshall also separately wrote a dissenting opin-

In 1982, Clarence Thomas was appointed chair of the Equal Employment Opportunity Commission.

PAGE 683

See also

Emancipation

> *The ground which
> a colored man
> occupies in this
> country is, every
> inch of it, sternly
> disputed.*
>
> FREDERICK DOUGLASS, 1853

See also
Education

ion expressing his sense of irony at the Court's reluctance to uphold race-conscious remedies: "[i]t is unnecessary in 20th century America to have individual Negroes demonstrate that they have been victims of racial discrimination; the racism of our society has been so pervasive that none, regardless of wealth or position, has managed to escape its impact."

In 1982 the Supreme Court again took up the subject of affirmative action in professional school admissions in *Mississippi University for Women* v. *Hogan.* The nursing school of the university denied full admission to male students (admitted only as auditors) on the grounds that the education of women was "educational affirmative action" intended to mitigate the adverse effects of discrimination on women. A man denied admission brought suit under the Equal Protection Clause. A five-justice majority that included Justices Marshall and O'Connor invalidated the single-sex policy on his behalf. Justice O'Connor wrote for the Court, applying the intermediate scrutiny standard of review. This same standard is the one the Court normally applies to gender classification cases brought under the Fourteenth Amendment's Equal Protection Clause. It is also the standard that Justice Marshall defended as appropriate for affirmative action cases involving *remedial* racial classifications. The Court required that Mississippi advance an "exceedingly persuasive justification" for its gender distinction in nursing education, that included a claim that the distinction was substantially related to an important government goal. Finding no such relationship or justification, the Court disparaged the ideal of a single-sex learning environment in nursing as a "self-fulfilling prophecy" based on the stereotype that nursing is "women's work." Dissenting Justices Powell, Blackmun, Rehnquist, and Chief Justice Burger denied that the case raised a serious question of gender discrimination. Powell stressed that no woman had complained about the school and that coed nursing education was available elsewhere in the state. Although the majority limited its holding to the nursing school, the dissenters raised concerns about the implication of the case for traditional same-sex higher education in the United States. It appears that affirmative action for women may not be used as a rationale for excluding men from women's traditional provinces.

Title VII Permits Voluntary Quotas

In a significant decision, the Supreme Court reconciled Title VII of the Civil Rights Act of 1964 with voluntary affirmative action programs in *United Steel Workers* v. *Weber* (1979). With a vote of 5 to 2 (two justices did not participate in the decision), the *Weber* case upheld an employer's affirmative-action plan that temporarily required a minimum of 50 percent African-American composition in a skill-training program established to increase African-American representation in skilled positions. The lower courts had ruled that *any* racial preferences violated Title VII, even if they were established in the context of an affirmative action plan. Importantly, the Court held that Title VII's ban on all racial discrimination did not apply to affirmative-action plans. Dissenting justices Burger and Rehnquist disagreed, arguing in separate opinions that the plain language of Title VII and its legislative history banned voluntary racial preferences, even those employed as affirmative-action remedies. *Newsweek* magazine reported the *Weber* decision as a "Victory for Quotas." Eleanor Holmes Norton, the African-American head of the EEOC, declared that "employers and unions no longer need fear that conscientious efforts to open job opportunities will be subjected to legal challenge." Senator Orrin Hatch responded differently, asserting that the purpose of the Civil Rights Act had not been to "guarantee any racial group a fixed proportion of the positions and perquisites available in American society" and that the "American dream" of true liberty was "in real danger."

In *Johnson* v. *Transportation Department* (1987) the court held (6 to 3) that Title VII permits affirmative consideration of employees' gender when awarding promotions. In *Johnson* the Court upheld the promotion of Diane Joyce, made according to the Transportation Agency of Santa Clara County's voluntarily adopted affirmative-action plan. Permitting the use of sex, minority status, and disability as factors for promotional consideration, the plan survived a challenge under Title VII by a man passed over for a "road dispatcher" position. In another case, *Local No. 93, International Association of Firefighters* v. *Cleveland* (1986), the Court held that parties to a consent decree may agree to relief that might not be within a court's ordering authority under Title VII. An African-American and Latino firefighters' organization, the Vanguards, had filed a complaint against the city of Cleveland for intentional discrimination in "hiring, assignment and promotion." Since the city had previously been unsuccessful in defending other discrimination suits, it sought to settle with the Vanguards. Local 93 (Union) intervened, not bringing any claims for or against either party, but voicing strenuous opposition to a settlement including any race-conscious action. When a consent decree, which provided for the action was agreed upon and entered, the Union filed its unsuccessful formal complaint that the decree exceeded a court's authority under Title VII.

Title VII permits affirmative action that includes numerical goals, and may permit courts to order it. In *Local 28 of the Sheet Metal Workers' International Association* v. *EEOC* (1986), the Supreme Court upheld a court-ordered membership plan for a trade union found guilty of racial discrimination violating Title VII. The plan included a membership goal of 29 percent African American and Latino. The Court was again willing to permit a numerically based affirmative-action remedy in *United States* v. *Paradise* (1987). There the Court validated a temporary affirmative-action plan ordered by a lower court that required a one-for-one promotion ratio of whites to qualified blacks in the Alabama Department of Public Safety. The department had been found guilty of discrimination in 1972, but had failed to adopt promotion procedure that did not have a disparate impact on blacks. Justice William Brennan wrote an opinion arguing that the affirmative-action order was a narrowly tailored means to achieve a compelling government purpose, and it therefore met the requirements of strict scrutiny imposed by Fourteenth Amendment equal protection.

Noncongressional Business Set-Asides Set Aside

A year after the *Weber* case, in *Fullilove* v. *Klutznick* (1980), the Court upheld a provision of the congressional Public Works Employment Act, which mandated that ten percent of $4 billion in federal funds allocated for local public construction projects go to "minority business enterprises," statutorily defined as at least 50 percent owned by citizens who are "Negroes, Spanish-speaking, Oriental, Indians, Eskimos, and Aleuts." The provision had been challenged under equal protection principles. Chief Justice Burger delivered the judgment of the Court, joined by Justices White and Powell. Justice Marshall, concurring in the judgment in *Fullilove* and joined in his opinion by Justices Brennan and Blackmun, argued that "Congress reasonably determined that race-conscious means were necessary to break down the barriers confronting participation by minority enterprises in federally funded public works projects." *Fullilove* survived contest in the Court at a time when critics of federal support for minority business enterprises argued that, in addition to raising questions of fairness raised by all affirmative action, the disbursal of funds under the 1977 Public Works Employment Act by the Commerce Department's Economic Development Administration was subject to abuse (Ross 1979). The Government Accounting Office uncovered hundreds of instances of federal dollars being awarded both to minority brokers serving as go-betweens for nonminority firms and government administrators; and to nonminority firms feigning minority ownership with the help of minority "fronts" installed as phony partners or owners.

Richmond v. *J. A. Croson Co.* (1989) successfully attacked an affirmative-action plan reserving specific numerical percentages of a public benefit for minorities. The invalidated "minority set-aside" plan required prime contractors with the city of Richmond to "subcontract at least 30 percent of the dollar amount of the contract to one or more Minority Business Enterprises." The plan was challenged under 42 U.S.C. §1983, a civil rights statute, by a nonminority firm who lost a contracting opportunity due to noncompliance with the program. The justices widely disagreed about the outcome and the reasoning of the case. Thus, Justice O'Connor delivered the opinion of the Court with respect to three of its parts, joined by Chief Justice Rehnquist and Justices Stevens, White, and Kennedy; Justices Stevens and Kennedy field separate partial concurrences; Justice Scalia field a concurring opinion; Justice Marshall dissented, joined in his opinion by Justices Brennan and Blackmun; finally, Justice Blackmun filed a dissenting opinion, joined by Justice Brennan. A major task for the majority was to explain how they could invalidate the set-aside in *Croson* when the Court had previously validated a similar set-aside in *Fullilove*. Justice O'Connor distinguished the *Fullilove* case on the ground that its set-aside had been created by Congress and involved an exercise of federal congressional power, whereas the set-aside in *Croson* was a creature of municipal government. Justice Thurgood Marshall dissented from the judgment in *Croson*, warning that the Court's ruling threatened all affirmative action plans not specifically enacted by Congress—virtually all plans.

Metro Broadcasting, Inc. v. *FCC* (1990) upheld two race-conscious Federal Communications Commission programs designed to enhance program diversity. The race-conscious set-asides were challenged under equal protection principles by a

Charged with investigating complaints of discrimination, Eleanor Holmes Norton was a visible and respected force within the Carter administration.

PAGE 524

*At the age of twenty,
only a few months
after buying his
freedom in Kent
County, Del.,
Richard Allen was
preaching to mostly
white audiences and
converting many of
his hearers to
Methodism.*

PAGE 28

nonminority broadcasting company that had lost its bid to acquire a broadcasting license to a minority-owned company. The Court argued that programming diversity, a goal both the FCC and Congress linked to ownership diversity, was derived from the public's First Amendment interest in hearing a wide spectrum of ideas and viewpoints. The interest was a sufficiently important one to justify race-conscious allocation policies. Justice O'Connor and three other justices dissented from what they considered excessive deference to Congress and a refusal to apply strict scrutiny to an instance of race-conscious thinking grounded in racial stereotypes.

Future Directions

Decided by the slimmest majority and largely on unusual First Amendment grounds, *Metro Broadcasting* leaves standing the basis for Justice Marshall's concerns about the future of all affirmative action. So, too, does *Shaw v. Reno* (1993). This case held that white voters stated a legitimate Fourteenth Amendment equal protection claim against North Carolina for creating a voter redistricting plan described as "so irrational on its face that it c[ould] be understood only as an effort to segregate voters" on the basis of race. Justices White, Souter, and Stevens dissented. In an attempt to comply with the Voting Rights Act, North Carolina had created a redistricting plan with two irregularly shaped "majority-minority" (majority Black and Native American) districts. In reversing the lower court, the Court invoked the ideal of a "colorblind" society and warned of the dangers of "political apartheid." Nonetheless, the constitutionality of the districts was subsequently upheld by a federal judicial panel.

The ideal of a colorblind society continues to vex proponents of race-conscious remedies to discrimination. The greatest consistency in the evolving law of affirmative action is that, at any given time, its precise contour mirrors the mix of perspectives represented on the Court concerning the deepest purposes and meaning of the 1964 Civil Rights Act and the Fourteenth Amendment of the Constitution. The Supreme Court has upheld key affirmative-action measures in the past, and may again in the future, although a series of rulings in the the spring and summer of 1995 have cast considerable doubt on the allowable scope of affirmative action. Notably, in the case of *Adarand Constructors* v. *Peña* (1995) the Court ruled, 5 to 4, that the federal government's affirmative-action programs must be able to meet the same strict standards for constitutional review

as had previously been applied by the Court to state and local programs. Outside the courts, controversy continues.

—ANITA LAFRANCE ALLEN

AFRICAN METHODIST EPISCOPAL CHURCH

Richard Allen (1760–1831), founder of the African Methodist Episcopal (AME) Church, was born a slave in Philadelphia, Pa., on February 14, 1760. Slaveholder Benjamin Chew sold Allen, his parents, and three siblings to Stokley Sturgis of Kent County, Del. Methodist church circuit riders frequently preached in the area, and Allen responded to their evangelism—perhaps also to their antislavery reputation—and joined the Wesleyan movement. His piety deepened because Sturgis permitted him to attend Methodist services regularly and to hold religious gatherings in the slave owner's own home. Sturgis also allowed Allen and his brother to buy their freedom, a task which was accomplished in 1783. For three years, Allen traveled through the Middle Atlantic as an itinerant Methodist preacher, then settled in Philadelphia to preach to blacks at the St. George Methodist Episcopal Church. The founding of the Free African Society of Philadelphia in 1787 and a racial altercation caused him to leave St. George, which in turn led to the building of Philadelphia's Bethel African Methodist Episcopal Church in 1794, often known as the Mother Bethel Church. In 1807, efforts by several pastors at St. George to control the congregation moved Allen to gain judicial recognition of Bethel's independence. A final attempt in 1815 by a St. George pastor to assert authority at Bethel Church induced Daniel Coker, the leader of Baltimore's black Methodists, to preach a sermon the following year commending Allen for his successful stand. Not long after, Allen drew Coker and other blacks from Baltimore; Salem, N.J.; and Attleborough, Pa., to meet with his Philadelphia followers to form the AME Church.

At the Philadelphia conference in 1816, Coker was elected bishop but declined the offer, perhaps because of his light skin color. Allen was then chosen bishop, and under his leadership the denomination rapidly expanded. African Methodism spread north to New York and New England; south through Maryland, the District of Columbia, and (for a time) South Carolina; and west to the Ohio Valley and the old Northwest Territory.

During the antebellum period, the denomination included congregations in the slave states of Kentucky, Missouri, and Louisiana. Missionaries such as William Paul Quinn 1788?–1873), an AME bishop after 1844, founded scores of congregations in the Midwest in the 1830s and 1840s. Along the Pacific Coast, the AME church spread from Sacramento and San Francisco in the early 1850s and to other locations in California and adjoining territories. AME loyalists also had success in Canada and made some inroads into Haiti. In 1864, thirty-three years after Allen's death, the AME church had a membership of 50,000 in 1,600 congregations.

During the antebellum period, while the AME Church was largely restricted to the northern states, numerous clergy and congregations gave direct aid to abolitionism. Morris Brown, who became the second bishop of the church after Allen's death, had been implicated in Denmark Vesey's abortive slave insurrection in South Carolina in 1822. Vesey himself was an AME preacher who, according to white authorities, planned the slave revolt during AME church services. The abolitionist stances of Allen, Quinn,

and Brown were reaffirmed at the 1840 Pittsburgh annual conference. Stating that "slavery pollutes the character of the church of God, and makes the Bible a sealed book to thousands of immortal beings," the delegates resolved that their denomination should use its "influence and energies" to destroy black bondage.

Daniel A. Payne, who became a bishop in 1852, greatly influenced the development of the AME church. Freeborn in 1811 in Charleston, S.C., Payne in his early adult years was a schoolteacher until a South Carolina state law forbade the education of blacks and forced him to close his school. In 1835 he moved north and matriculated at Gettysburg Theological Seminary in Pennsylvania. After his ordination into the AME ministry in 1843, Payne pastored in Baltimore, later serving the denomination as historiographer, and crusaded for an educated clergy. In 1863, Payne convinced reluctant AME leaders to commit to a daring venture in higher education by founding Wilberforce University, the first black college started by African Americans. Wilberforce was only the first of several colleges founded by the AME. Others include Allen University

AFRICAN METHODIST EPISCOPAL CHURCH

FOUNDING A TRADITION

Later AME Church bishops surround the image of their founder, Richard Allen, in this post-Civil War engraving. The vignettes in the corners depict the church's educational and missionary endeavors.
PRINTS AND PHOTOGRAPHS DIVISION, LIBRARY OF CONGRESS

(1880) in South Carolina, Morris Brown College (1881) in Georgia, Paul Quinn College (1881) in Texas, and Kittrell College (1886) in North Carolina.

The period of the Civil War and Reconstruction proved pivotal to AME church development. Recruitment of black soldiers occurred on the premises of AME congregations such as Israel Church in Washington, D.C. Four AME ministers—Henry M. Turner, William H. Hunter, David Stevens, and Garland H. White—served with ten other black chaplains in the Union Army. Additional AME clergy, including some who would become bishops, also fought on the Union side.

As northern victories liberated Confederate strongholds in Virginia and North Carolina, the Baltimore annual conference dispatched AME preachers in 1864 to those states to attract blacks into African Methodism. In 1865, Bishop Daniel A. Payne sailed from New York City to his hometown, Charleston, S.C., to establish the AME mission in the South. The rapid acquisition of members and congregations from Virginia to Texas swelled the denomination in 1880 to 387,566 persons in 2,051 churches.

The development of the AME church in Alabama is illustrative of the denomination's expansion in the postbellum South. Mobile had the first, though shortlived, AME congregation as early as 1820. The denomination revived when two AME ministers preached in the state in 1864. Formal organization of an annual conference occurred in Selma in 1868, a year after missionaries arrived from Georgia; it started with 6 churches, 31 missions, and 5,617 members. Preachers such as Winfield Henri Mixon played a large role in spearheading AME Church growth. Born a slave near Selma in 1859, Mixon in 1882 began a long career as a pastor and presiding elder until his death in 1932. As a presiding elder, he reported that between 1892 and 1895 he launched fourteen new congregations. When he started his ministry, the state comprised three annual conferences: the Alabama, the Central Alabama, and the North Alabama. As a result of his efforts and those of other church founders, Mixon mapped out three additional jurisdictions, including the East, South, and West Alabama annual conferences. In 1890, AME congregations in the state numbered 247 with 30,781 members; Mixon helped to increase these numbers in 1916 to 525 congregations and 42,658 members.

These evangelistic efforts paralleled the unprecedented political involvement of the AME

clergy in Reconstruction state governments and in the U.S. Congress. Approximately fifty-three AME ministers served as officeholders in the legislatures of South Carolina, Florida, Alabama, Georgia, and other states. Henry M. Turner, a Republican, was elected to the Georgia state legislature in 1868, only to be ousted that same year by triumphant Democrats. Richard H. Cain, then pastor of Emmanuel Church in Charleston, served in the South Carolina state Senate from 1868 through 1870 and then in the U.S. House of Representatives from 1873 through 1875. Turner and Cain became AME bishops in 1880.

Bishop Payne was unhappy about the ascent of Turner and Cain to the AME episcopacy. He and other northern-based bishops were wary of the new generation of denominational leaders whose followers came from the South. Many of these new leaders, among them Turner and Cain, had experiences in elective offices that Payne believed caused an unfortunate politicization of denominational affairs. In the late nineteenth century, regional backgrounds of ministers determined regional alliances and formed the bases of power within the AME church.

There was also increasing political involvement of AME clergy in the northern branch of the denomination. Ezekiel Gillespie, a lay founder of the St. Mark Church in Milwaukee, for example, initiated a state supreme court case that won the suffrage for Wisconsin blacks in 1866. Benjamin W. Arnett, who became a bishop in 1888, won an election in 1886 to the Ohio legislature, where he became a friend of future President William McKinley. He successfully pushed a repeal of Ohio's discriminatory Black Laws.

In the late nineteenth century, the denomination expanded outside of the United States. In 1884 the British Methodist Episcopal (BME) Church, in existence since 1856, reunited with the AME Church. Thereafter, BME congregations throughout Canada, Bermuda, and South America were part of the AME fold. In 1891, Bishop Turner, who was an influential African emigrationist, established annual conferences in West Africa, Sierra Leone, and Liberia. Five years later, Turner formally received the Ethiopian Church of South Africa into the denomination. This church was established in 1892, when dissident Africans led by M. M. Makone withdrew from the white-dominated Wesleyan Methodist church after experiencing the same kind of racial discrimination that had brought the AME church into existence in the United States. Turner invited an Ethiopian delegation to the United States, where they accepted membership. (In 1900, Bishop Levi J. Coppin became the first resident bishop in South Africa.)

Bishop Turner's missionary interests were not confined to Africa. Between 1896 and 1908 he presided as bishop of Georgia. He mobilized support and manpower from this jurisdiction for expansion into Cuba and Mexico. He commissioned presiding elders from Georgia to establish congregations among black Latinos in both countries, and several successful AME missions were instituted.

Whenever AME advocates for overseas expansion combined this perspective with black nationalism, ideological fissures surfaced in denominational affairs. Turner's espousal of emigration drew vehement opposition from Benjamin T. Tanner. Tanner, who in 1868 became editor of *The Christian Recorder,* a weekly founded in 1852, started the *AME Church Review* in 1884, and edited it until his election to the episcopacy in 1888. Concerning Turner's back-to-Africa efforts, Tanner asserted that those who wished to escape the fight for racial equality in the United States counseled "cowardice." He felt that blacks should remain in the United States to secure their full constitutional privileges. While Tanner opposed black emigration to Africa, he and other AME leaders did not fully disagree with all of Turner's nationalist views. Tanner, for example, authored *Is the Negro Cursed?* (1869) and *The Color of Solomon, What?* (1895), both of which challenged racist interpretations of scripture and argued that persons of color figured prominently in Biblical history. In 1893, Benjamin Arnett, who served as bishop with Turner and Tanner, told the World's Parliament of Religions in his speech "Christianity and the Negro" that St. Luke was black and so were other important figures in the early church.

Between 1890 and 1916 the AME Church grew from 494,777 members in 2,481 congregations to 548,355 members in 6,636 congregations. In 1926 the denomination included 545,814 members in 6,708 congregations. There was significant numerical strength in Georgia, for example, where 74,149 members worshipped in 1,173 congregations. Florida had 45,541 members in 694 churches. There was some decline in AME strength by 1936, however, when the church reported 4,578 congregations and 493,357 members.

While the AME Church in the South was growing, so was the church in the industrial North. The massive black migration from southern rural communities to industrial centers in the North and South during the two World Wars caused major growth in AME churches in New York, Philadelphia, Chicago, St. Louis, Atlanta, Birmingham, Los Angeles, and other major cities. In these settings, clergy fashioned a version of the social gospel which required their involvement with numerous issues in housing, social welfare, unionization, and politics. In the 1920s the Rev. Harrison G. Payne, pastor of Park Place Church in Homestead, a milltown near Pittsburgh, initiated an effort to supply housing to blacks newly arrived from the South; and during World War II, investigators with the federal Fair Employment Practices Committee found cooperative AME pastors in numerous cities. Many AME pastors worked with labor unions. Dwight V. Kyle of the Avory Chapel Church in Bluff City, Tenn., for example, sided with the efforts of the Congress of Industrial Organizations (CIO) to unionize black and white mass-production workers in a dangerous antiunion setting.

The burgeoning Civil Rights Movement of the late 1940s and early 1950s found substantive support within the AME clergy. J. A. Delaine, a pastor and school principal in Clarendon County, S.C., and Oliver Brown, the pastor of St. Mark Church in Topeka, Kans., filed suits against public school segregation. Their efforts culminated in the landmark Brown v. Board of Education of Topeka, Kansas (1954) decision in which the U.S. Supreme Court nullified the "separate but equal" doctrine. Threats against Delaine pushed him out of South Carolina to New York City. Activist AME clergy moved the denomination at the 1960 general conference to establish a social action department; Frederick C. James, a South Carolina pastor and future bishop, became its first director.

When Bishop Richard Allen authorized Jarena Lee in 1819 to function as an exhorter in the AME church, he opened the door to women in the ministry. For nearly 150 years unordained female evangelists played important roles as preachers, pastors, and founders of congregations. During the nineteenth and early twentieth centuries, Amanda Berry Smith, Sarah Hughes, and Lillian Thurman preached in AME pulpits. Smith, for example, evangelized widely in the United States and then preached abroad in the British Isles, India, and West Africa. Like many, Millie Wolfe, a woman preacher in Waycross, Ga., focused her efforts on the denomination's Women's Home and Foreign Missionary Society. She published a book of sermons that included her thoughts about "Scriptural Authority for Women's Work in the Christian Church." Female

Congress shall make no law respecting an establishment of religion, or prohibiting the free exercise thereof. . . .

THE CONSTITUTION,
AMENDMENT 1

See also
Brown v. Board of Education of Topeka, Kansas

AFROCENTRICITY

evangelists in the Rocky Mountain states in the early 1900s became crucial to AME Church expansion in Colorado, New Mexico, Arizona, Wyoming, and Montana. They established congregations and frequently supplied pulpits throughout this large region. While the gifted preaching of Martha Jayne Keys, Mary Watson Stewart, and others sustained the visibility of female ministers in the first half of the twentieth century, it was not until 1960 that the denomination allowed the full ordination of women. (An earlier attempt by Henry M. Turner to ordain women in 1885 had been promptly overturned by a church conference.)

Ecumenical efforts among African-American Christians also drew upon AME church leadership. In 1933, Bishop Reverdy C. Ransom called together black denominational leaders to establish in 1934 the Fraternal Council of Negro Churches. Similarly, in 1978 Bishop John Hurst Adams spearheaded the founding of the Congress of National Black Churches. Subsequently, Bishop Philip R. Cousin became president of the National Council of Churches in 1983 while Bishop Vinton R. Anderson became president of the World Council of Churches in 1991.

The Black Theology movement from the late 1960s into the 1980s drew AME participation through AME trained theologians Cecil W. Cone and James H. Cone. They respectively authored *The Identity Crisis in Black Theology* (1975) and *Black Theology and Black Power* (1969). Jacqueline Grant, another theologian out of the AME tradition, pioneered the development of feminist theology. Her ideas were explored in *White Women's Christ and Black Woman's Jesus* (1989).

Throughout its history, the AME church embraced congregations that crossed lines of class, culture, and geography. Several elements of Wesleyan worship remained in AME services regardless of location and demography. A standard order of worship, mainly consisting of hymn singing, remained a staple of AME worship. Baptismal practices and the communion service made the AME church virtually indistinguishable from white Methodist congregations. However, other practices rooted in African-American tradition—such as extemporaneous praying, singing of spirituals and gospels, and shouting—were observed depending on the cultural makeup of the congregation.

Since its formal founding in 1816, the AME Church's quadrennial general conference has remained the supreme authority in denominational governance. Annual conferences over which active bishops have presided cover particular geographical areas. During these yearly jurisdictional meetings, ministers receive their pastoral appointments. Within the annual conferences, districts have been established; these are superintended by presiding elders. The AME episcopacy from Richard Allen's election and consecration in 1816 to the present has been a lifetime position. General officers who administer such programs as publishing, pensions, Christian education, and evangelism serve for four years, but they can stand for reelection. Bishops and general officers are chosen at the general conference by elected ministerial and lay delegates. By 1993 the denomination had grown to 2,000,000 members in 7,000 congregations in the United States and 30 other countries in the Americas, Africa, and Europe. The AME has no central headquarters, although its publishing house is located in Nashville, Tenn. In 1993 twenty active bishops and twelve general officers made up the African Methodist Episcopal Church leadership.

—DENNIS C. DICKERSON

AFROCENTRICITY

Afrocentricity is a state of being in which consciousness is centered by and within the processes that maintain and perpetuate the historical continuity of African life and culture and establish the perspectives from which reality is interpreted or reinterpreted. Afrocentricity is an essential corollary to the African worldview (Asante 1980, 1987, 1990; Carruthers 1980; Azibo 1992; Ekwe-Ekwe and Nzegwu, 1994) and is worthy of serious consideration by all who study African-American culture and history. Senegalese multidisciplinary scholar Cheikh Anta Diop's (1959, 1978) theory of African cultural unity is regarded as fundamental to both concepts.

Diop's work emerged during the 1950s and '60s, when continental and diasporan African intellectuals were constructing paradigms based on theories of racial unity to guide their resistance to white supremacy (Spady 1978). These attempts to imbue "blackness" with the dynamic qualities required to serve as a theory of African commonality were capable of refuting white supremacy but inadequate to explain the uniqueness of the African way of life. Diop's work, in general, is credited with beginning a movement that extended the thinking of African intellectuals worldwide beyond the limitations of racial analy-

A

AFROCENTRICITY

Gospel-style singing, at least until the advent of rap music, dominated African-American popular music.

PAGE 302

22

ses by demonstrating the existence of particular qualities of African history, linguistics, and psychology that have endured as aspects of African culture since antiquity (Spady 1978; Ekwe-Ekwe and Nzegwu 1994).

While the Afrocentric worldview has existed from antiquity, Afrocentrism as a construct has not. In an essay entitled "Reflections on the History of the Afrocentric World View," Carruthers (1980) defines the concept of a worldview and distinguishes it from ideology. Unlike ideology, which he associates with class interests, a worldview "includes the way a people conceive of the fundamental questions of existence and organization of the universe" (p. 4). The Afrocentric world view, according to Carruthers, rests on two "basic truths": (1) It is distinct to and universal among African people throughout the world, and (2) its restoration is the only viable foundation for the liberation of all Africans worldwide. Conceptions of Afrocentric worldview consistent with that put forth by Carruthers have been articulated by Nobles (1974), Ani and Richards (1980, 1990, 1994), Azibo (1992), and others. Afrocentrism is a concept constructed to enable Africans to use the strengths of enduring cultural unity as weapons for liberation and as tools for building new social realities in which Africans understand themselves as subjects of their own experiences (Asante 1980). The need for such a concept was created by African experiences with invasion, conquest, enslavement, colonization, and neocolonization, and concomitant processes of cultural alienation.

Restoration of Afrocentric worldview exists as a project because African culture has been the target of systematic acts of destruction by proponents of Western (European) cultural imperialism and white nationalist supremacy (Williams 1974, Ani and Richards 1994). Frantz Fanon (1967), for instance, noted that racism's object is not the individual "but a certain form of existing" (p. 32). Ani argues that "the most effective weapon" against cultural destruction "is a strong national consciousness" (1994, p. 294). Clarke (1991) and Akoto (1993) as well as Ani and Richards (1994) emphasize nation building as the objective of African worldview restoration. We will conclude with three illustrations of the methodology of African worldview restoration.

In *Afrocentricity: The Theory of Social Change* (1980), Asante avers that Afrocentricity is a "transforming agent" for the restoration of the Afrocentric worldview. The process by which this transformation is to be effected is guided by "Afrology," a term coined by Asante to refer to a comprehensive Afrocentric "philosophical statement with attendant possibilities for a new logic, science, and rhetoric" (p. 65). He formally defines Astrology as "the science or study of all modalities related to people of African descent from an Afrocentric perspective" (p. 117). However, Asante in this book also offers an analysis of the personal transformation process that enables an individual to transcend a consciousness born out of "otherness" and to realize Afrocentricity. It is precisely this possibility of individual transformation that makes an Afrocentric collective consciousness viable.

Azibo (1992) argues that restoring the African worldview requires an understanding of and use of three approaches that may be described as (1) deconstructionist, (2) reconstructionist, and (3) constructionist. Non-African concepts, variables, and formulations must be deconstructed and reconstructed. The *deconstructionist* approach employs critical analysis in a fashion that corresponds to Ani's (1994) notion of "de-Europeanization." It isolates Eurocentric concepts from the mix of ideas and seeks to eliminate their influence. The *reconstructionist* approach "revises, revamps, and otherwise alters alien-centered formulations to better fit or jibe with African reality" (Azibo 1992, p. 86). It takes Eurocentric or other foreign concepts and "Africanizes" them. Lastly, the *constructionist* approach "proceeds with formulations and concepts derived from the African cultural deep-structure" (p. 86). It would seem that deconstruction and reconstruction must occur in tandem, although Azibo does not explicitly state this. The employment of constructionist approaches is necessarily preceded by simultaneous deconstruction and reconstruction.

Finally, Marimba Ani focuses on personal transformation facilitated by the de-Europeanization of the culture concept. In her book *Yurugu: An African-Centered Critique of European Cultural Thought and Behavior* (1994), she argues that the ideological function of culture can be understood through the systematic analysis of European culture's deep structure and the uses of its logic. This essentially means learning how to demystify the universalist claims of Western cultural imperialism by treating them as manifestations of a particular ideology. When culture is made "visible" in this way, it is possible for Africans to transcend the Europeanization of thought and to redefine their thinking in African-centered terms.

—MWALIMU J. SHUJAS AND KOFI LOMOTEY

♦ **Diaspora**
The breaking up and scattering of a people; people settled far from their ancestral homelands

See also
Civil Rights Movement

23

AILEY, ALVIN

Alvin Ailey (January 5, 1931–December 1, 1989), African-American dancer and choreographer. Born in Rogers, Tex., the only child of working-class parents who separated when he was two, Ailey moved to Los Angeles with his mother in 1942. Shy from his itinerant Texas life, Ailey reluctantly turned to dance when a high-school classmate introduced him to Lester Horton's Hollywood studio in 1949. He poured himself into study and developed a weighty, smoldering performance style that suited his athletic body. Ailey moved to New York in 1954 to dance with partner Carmen DeLavallade in the Broadway production of *House of Flowers.* Performing success and study with leading modern dance and ballet teachers Martha Graham, Doris Humphrey, Charles Weidman, and Karel Shook led Ailey to found his own dance theater company in 1958. The Alvin Ailey American Dance Theater (AAADT) began as a repertory company of seven dancers devoted to both modern dance classics and new works created by Ailey and other young artists. The critically successful first concerts in 1958 and 1960 marked the beginning of a new era of dance performance devoted to African-American theme. *Blues Suite* (1958), set in and around a barrelhouse, depicts the desperation and joys of life on the edge of poverty in the South. Highly theatrical and immediately accessible, the dance contains sections of early twentieth-century social dances, Horton dance technique, Jack Cole-inspired jazz dance, and ballet partnering. Early performances of *Revelations* (1960) established Ailey's company as the foremost dance interpreter of African-American experience. The dance quickly became the company's signature ballet, eclipsing previous concert attempts at dancing to sacred black music. Set to a series of spirituals and gospel selections arranged by Brother John Sellers, *Revelations* depicts a spectrum of black religious worship, including richly sculpted group prayer ("I've Been Buked"), a ceremony of ritual baptism ("Wade in the Water"), a moment of introverted, private communion ("I Wanna Be Ready"), a duet of trust and support for a minister and devotee ("Fix Me, Jesus"), and a final, celebratory gospel exclamation, "Rocka My Soul in the Bosom of Abraham."

Several Ailey dances established precedents for American dance. *Feast of Ashes* (1962), created for the Harkness Ballet, is acknowledged as the first successful *pointe* ballet choreographed by a modern dancer. In 1966 Ailey contributed dances for the New York Metropolitan Opera's inaugural production at Lincoln Center, Samuel Barber's *Antony and Cleopatra.* In 1970 he created *The River* for American Ballet Theatre. Set to an original score commissioned from Duke Ellington, this ballet convincingly fused theatrical jazz dancing and ballet technique. In 1971 Ailey created the staging for Leonard Bernstein's rock-influenced *Mass,* which opened the newly built Kennedy Center in Washington, D.C.

Major distinctions and honors followed Ailey throughout his choreographic career, which spanned the creation of more than fifty dances for his own company, American Ballet Theater, the Joffrey Ballet, the Paris Opera Ballet, the London Festival Ballet, and the Royal Danish Ballet. Among his many awards were honorary doctorates in fine arts from Princeton University, Bard College, Adelphi University, and Cedar Crest College; a United Nations Peace Medal, and an NAACP Spingarn Medal, in 1976. In 1988 he was celebrated by the president of the United States for a lifetime of achievement in the arts at the Kennedy Center Honors.

CUTTING-EDGE DANCE

Alvin Ailey emerged as one of the leading choreographers of his generation with the founding of the Alvin Ailey American Dance Theater. PRINTS AND PHOTOGRAPHS DIVISION, LIBRARY OF CONGRESS

Company and Repertory

In its earliest years, the AAADT spent much time on the road, touring and bringing dance to a large audience of people who had never heard of concert performance. This largely African-American audience has provided the wellspring of support essential to the Ailey enterprise. The AAADT established its vast international reputation through a series of tours begun in 1962 by a five-month engagement in Southeast Asia and Australia. Sponsored by the International Exchange Program under the Kennedy administration, this tour established a pattern of performance in foreign countries that continued with a trip to Rio de Janeiro (1963); a European tour including London, Hamburg, and Paris (1964); an engagement at the World Festival of Negro Arts in Dakar, Senegal (1966); a sixteen-week European tour, including the Holland Festival in Amsterdam (1967); a visit to Israel (August 1967); a U.S. State Department-sponsored nine-nation tour of Africa (1967); and a performance at the Edinburgh Festival in Scotland (1968). In 1970 the AAADT became the first American modern dance company to perform in the postwar Soviet Union. The company has retained peerless stature as a touring ambassador of goodwill since the 1970s; high points have included a prize-winning performance at the International Dance Festival in Paris (1970); a second Far East tour (1977); a Brazil tour (1978); and several command performances for heads of state and royalty. By 1989, the AAADT had been seen by some fifteen million people worldwide.

Active in the pursuit of dance history, the varied repertory of the AAADT has, in Ailey's words, sustained an "impulse to preserve modern dance to know where it's been in order to know where it's going, and to encourage the participation of the audience" in that process. The eclectic repertory has been provided by choreographers working in a variety of dance modes, including ballet, jazz dance, Graham modern, Horton, and Dunham technique. Important pieces danced by the company have included Donald McKayle's *Rainbow Round My Shoulder* (1959), Talley Beatty's *The Road of the Phoebe Snow* (1959), Anna Sokolow's *Rooms* (1965), Louis Johnson's *Lament* (1965), Geoffrey Holder's *Prodigal Prince* (1967), Ulysses Dove's *Vespers* (1986), Judith Jamison's *Forgotten Time* (1989), and Donald Byrd's *Dance at the Gym* (1991), as well as dances by venerable American choreographers Ted Shawn, Pearl Primus, Katherine Dunham, Joyce Trisler, and Lester Horton. In 1976 the AAADT celebrated composer Duke Ellington with a festival featuring fifteen new ballets set to his music, a project that highlighted Ellington's musical achievement.

Company Members

Ailey encouraged his dancers to present individualized and highly emotional performances, a strategy that created the first series of star personalities in American modern dance. Judith Jamison's electrifying performance of *Cry* presented a coherent relationship between the dancing body and the experience of living as a black woman in America. Created in 1971 as a birthday present for Ailey's mother, Lula Cooper, *Cry* has been successfully assumed by several dancers, most notably Donna Wood, Renee Robinson, Sara Yarborough, and Nasha Thomas. In 1972, Ailey created the elegiac solo *Love Songs* for dancer Dudley Williams, revived in 1993 by dancer Michael Joy. Dancer Gary DeLoatch, a longtime principal with the company, brought an eloquent intensity to his roles, especially as the pusher in Talley Beatty's *The Stack-Up* (1983) and as Charlie Parker in Ailey's *For "Bird"—With Love* (1984). Innumerable significant dance personalities have passed through the AAADT, including Marilyn Banks, Hope Clarke, Carmen DeLavallade, George Faison, Miguel Godreau, Dana Hash, Linda Kent, Desmond Richardson, Kelvin Rotardier, Elizabeth Roxas, Clive Thompson, James Truitte, Andre Tyson, and Sylvia Waters.

School and Outreach

In 1969 Ailey founded the Alvin Ailey American Dance Center School to educate dance students in the history and art of ballet and modern dance. Courses have been offered in dance technique and history, music for dancers, dance composition, and theatrical design. In 1974 the Alvin Ailey Repertory Ensemble, a professional performance ensemble, was formed under the direction of Sylvia Waters as a bridge between study and membership in professional dance companies. In 1984 the Alvin Ailey Student Performance Group was created under the direction of Kelvin Rotardier. The Student Performance Group has offered lecture-demonstrations to communities traditionally underserved by the arts. In 1989 Dance Foundation Inc., the umbrella organizations for the AAADT and the Ailey School, initiated the Ailey Camps program, an outreach program designed to "enhance the self-esteem, creative expression, and critical thinking skills of inner-city youth through dance." Success of the

AILEY, ALVIN

School and Outreach

Dance is the hidden language of the soul.

MARTHA GRAHAM
BLOOD MEMORY, 1991

Judith Jamison's electrifying performances of Ailey's fifteen-minute solo Cry *(1971) propelled her to an international stardom unprecedented among modern dance artists.*

PAGE 374

A

initial venture in Kansas City, Mo., led to similar programs begun in New York City (1990) and Baltimore, Md. (1992).

Ailey created the AAADT to feature the talents of his African-American colleagues, though the company was never exclusively black. Ailey integrated his company to counter the "reverse chauvinism in being an all-black anything." He told the *New York Times,* "I am trying to show the world that we are all human beings and that color is not important. What is important is the quality of our work." In the last interview conducted before his death, he commented that the essence of the Ailey enterprise was that "the dancers be fed, kept alive, interested" in the work. "We're trying to create a whole spectrum of experience for the dancer as well as the audience," he said, dramatically understating the realities of his achievements.

Ailey stopped dancing in 1965 and slowed his choreographic assignments in the 1970s to attend to the administrative and fund-raising operations associated with his ever expanding company. Upon Ailey's death, Judith Jamison was appointed artistic director of the company, to work closely with rehearsal director and longtime company member Masazumi Chaya. The AAADT finally emerged from financial difficulties in 1992, when *Dance Magazine* proclaimed it "recession-proof" due to powerful development efforts on the part of the Dance Foundation Inc.'s board of directors.

Although Ailey gave numerous interviews throughout his career, he was decidedly private about his personal life. He described himself as "a bachelor and a loner" to writer John Gruen and hardly ever allowed outsiders into his most private thoughts. In 1980 Ailey was briefly hospitalized for stress-related conditions. His death followed a long, solitary struggle that had taken him out of the limelight for some time. Ailey's legacy to the dance world was to foster a freedom of choice—from ballet, modern, and social dance performance—to best express humanity in movement terms suited to the theatrical moment.

—THOMAS F. DEFRANTZ

ALI, MUHAMMAD

Muhammad Ali (January 17, 1942–), boxer. Muhammad Ali was born Cassius Marcellus Clay, Jr. in Louisville, Ky. He began boxing at the age of twelve under the tutelage of Joe Martin, a Louisville policeman. Having little interest in school and little affinity for intellectual endeavors,

young Clay devoted himself wholeheartedly to boxing. He showed great promise early on and soon developed into one of the most impressive amateurs in the country. He became the National Amateur Athletic Union (AAU) champion in 1959 and in 1960, and also won a gold medal in the light-heavyweight division at the 1960 Olympics in Rome. As a result of his boyish good looks and his outgoing personality—his poetry recitations, his good-natured bragging, and his undeniable abilities—Clay became famous after the Olympics. Shortly after returning from Rome, he turned professional and was managed by a consortium of white Louisville businessmen. Carefully nurtured by veteran trainer Angelo Dundee, he accumulated a string of victories against relatively mediocre opponents and achieved a national following with his constant patter, his poetry, and his boyish antics. At 6'3" and a fighting weight of around 200 pounds, he astonished sportswriters with his blazing hand and foot speed, his unorthodox style of keeping his hands low, and his ability to avoid punches by moving his head back. No heavyweight in history possessed Clay's grace or speed.

On February 25, 1964, Clay fought as the underdog for the heavyweight title against Sonny Liston. Liston, an ex-convict, was thought by many to be virtually invincible because of his devastating one-round victories against former champion Floyd Patterson. An air of both the theater of the absurd and of ominousness surrounded the bout in Miami. Publicly, Clay taunted and comically berated Liston. He called him "the Bear," harassed him at his home, and almost turned the weigh-in ceremony into a shambles as he seemingly tried to attack Liston and appeared on the verge of being utterly out of control. Privately, however, Clay was seen with Malcolm X and members of the Nation of Islam (NOI). Rumors started that he had joined the militant, mysterious sect. Soon after, it was discovered that he had been secretly visiting NOI mosques for nearly three years and that he had indeed become a friend of Malcolm X, who sat ringside at the Liston fight.

Clay beat Liston fairly easily in seven rounds, shocking the world by becoming heavyweight champion. Immediately after the fight, he announced that he was a member of the NOI and that his name was no longer Cassius Clay but Muhammad Ali. The response from the white press, white America, and the boxing establishment generally was swift and intensely hostile. The NOI was seen, largely through the rhetoric of Malcolm X, its most stylish spokesman, as an antiwhite hate group. (When Malcolm X broke with the NOI, shortly after the Liston fight, Ali remained loyal to Elijah Muhammad and ended his friendship with Malcolm X.) Following his public conversion to Islam, Ali was publicly pilloried. Most publications and sports journalists refused to call him by his new name. Former champion Floyd Patterson nearly went on a personal and national crusade against the NOI in his fight against Ali on November 22, 1965, but Patterson later became one of the few fighters to defend Ali publicly during his years of exile. Indeed, not since the reign of Jack Johnson was the white public and a segment of the black population so enraged by the opinions and life of a black athlete.

After winning his rematch with Liston in Lewiston, Me., on May 25, 1965, in a bizarre fight that ended with Liston apparently being knocked out in the first round, Ali spent most of the next year fighting abroad, primarily because of his unpopularity in this country. Among his most important matches during this period were a fifteen-round decision over George Chuvalo in Toronto, a sixth-round knockout of Henry Cooper in London, and a fifteen-round decision over Ernest Terrell in Houston. While Ali was abroad American officials changed his draft status from 1−Y (unfit for Army services because of his low score on Army intelligence tests) to 1−A (qualified for induction). Many saw this change as a direct response to the negative public opinion concerning Ali's political views and the mounting war in Vietnam. Ali refused to serve in the Army on the grounds that it was a violation of his religious beliefs. (Elijah Muhammad, leader of the NOI, had served time in prison during World War II for refusing to serve in the armed services.) In 1967, Ali was convicted in federal court of violation of the Selective Service Act, sentenced to five years in prison, and immediately stripped of both his boxing title and his boxing license. For the next three and one-half years, Ali, free on bond while appealing his case (which he eventually won on appeal to the U.S. Supreme Court), was prohibited from boxing. Still, Ali had inspired black athletes to become more militant and more politically committed. Medal-winning track stars John Carlos and Tommie Smith gave a clenched-fist salute during the playing of the National Anthem at the Olympic Games in Mexico City in 1968, and Harry Edwards became one of the more outspoken leaders of a new cadre of young black athletes who saw Ali as a hero.

By 1970, with public opinion decidedly against the Vietnam War, and a growing black influence in several southern state governments, Ali was given a license to fight in Georgia. He returned to the ring on October 26 to knock out Jerry Quarry in the third round. Although he was still a brilliant fighter, the nearly four year lay-off had diminished some of Ali's abilities. He took far more punishment in the ring during the years of his return than he had taken before. This was to have dire consequences for him as he grew older.

In the early 1970s Ali fought several of his most memorable matches. On March 8, 1971, he faced the undefeated Philadelphian Joe Frazier in New York City. Frazier had become champion during Ali's exile. The fifteen-round fight, which Frazier won in a close decision, was so fierce that both boxers were hospitalized after it. Many have speculated that this fight initiated Ali's neurological deterioration. In July of that year Ali won the North American Boxing Federation (NABF) heavyweight title by knocking out Jimmy Ellis in twelve rounds. His next major boxing challenge came in March 1973, when Ken Norton captured the NABF title from Ali in a twelve-round decision. Ali regained the title six months later with a

Float like a butterfly, Sting like a bee! Rumble young man! Rumble! Waa!

MUHAMMAD ALI AND DREW "BUNDINI" BROWN THEIR "WAR CRY," *THE GREATEST: MY OWN STORY*

THE CHAMP

Muhammad Ali is as famous for his poetry recitations and good-natured bragging as he is for his superior boxing ability.
© JAMES PINEDA/ BLACK STAR

A

By 1933, Joe Louis compiled an amateur record of 50 wins, 43 by knockout, and only 4 losses.

PAGE 432

twelve-round decision over Norton. In January of the following year, Ali and Frazier staged their first rematch. This nontitle bout at Madison Square Garden ended with Ali victorious after twelve hard-fought rounds. Ali finally regained the World Heavyweight title in Kinshasa, Zaire, on October 30, 1974, when he knocked out a seemingly indestructible George Foreman in eight rounds. To counter Foreman's awesome punching power, Ali used what he called his "rope-a-dope" strategy, by which he leaned back against the ropes and covered his head, allowing Foreman to punch himself out. The next year, Ali and Frazier faced off one last time in what Ali dubbed "The Thrilla in Manila." Both boxers received tremendous punishment during this bludgeoning ordeal. Ali prevailed, however, when Frazier's trainer refused to let the boxer come out for the fifteenth round.

During the 1970s Ali was lionized. No longer seen as a race demon, he virtually became a national icon. He appeared in movies—including the film *The Greatest* (1977), based on his autobiography of the same name (1975). Like Jackie Robinson and Joe Louis before him, Ali played himself in the film—he also appeared in television programs and in commercials. He was one of the most photographed and interviewed men in the world. Indeed, Ali even beat Superman in the ring in a special issue of the comic devoted to him. Part of Ali's newfound popularity was a result of a shift in attitude by the white public and white sportswriters, but part of it was also a reflection of Ali's tempered approach to politics. Ali became a great deal less doctrinaire in the political aspects of his Islamic beliefs and he eventually embraced Wallace D. Muhammad's more ecumenical form of Islam when the NOI factionalized after the death of Elijah Muhammad in 1975. Finally, as befitting a major celebrity, Ali had one of the largest entourages of any sports personality in history, resembling that of a head of state.

On February 15, 1978, Ali again lost the title. His opponent this time was Leon Spinks, an ex-Marine and native of a north St. Louis housing project. Spinks fought in only eight professional bouts before he met Ali. Ali, however, became the first heavyweight in history to regain the title for a third time when he defeated Spinks on September 15 of the same year.

In 1979, Ali was aged and weary; his legs were shot, his reflexes had slowed, and his appetite for competition was waning as a result of the good life that he was enjoying. Ali retired from the ring at that time, only to do what so many other great champions have so unwisely done, namely, return to battle. His return to the ring included a savage ten-round beating on October 2, 1980, at the hands of Larry Holmes, a former sparring partner who had become champion after Ali's retirement. His next fight was a ten-round decision lost to Trevor Berbick on December 11 of the following year. After the Berbick fight, Ali retired for good. His professional record stands at: 56 wins, 37 of which were by knockout, and 5 losses. He was elected to the Boxing Hall of Fame in 1987.

During Ali's later years, his speech became noticeably more slurred, and after his retirement he became more aged: moving slowly, speaking with such a thick tongue that he was almost incomprehensible, and suffering from attacks of palsy. There is some question as to whether he has Parkinson's disease or a Parkinson's-like deterioration of the neurological system. Many believe that the deterioration of his neurological system is directly connected to the punishment he took in the ring. By the early 1990s, although his mind was still sound, Ali gave the appearance of being a good deal older and more infirm than he actually was. He found it difficult to write or talk, and often walked slowly. Despite this, he is living a full life, travels constantly, and seems to be at peace with himself.

His personal life has been turbulent. He has been married four times and has had several children as well as numerous affairs, especially during his heyday as a fighter. His oldest daughter, Maryum, is a rap artist, following in her father's footsteps as a poet—Ali made a poetry recording for Columbia Records in 1963 called *The Greatest*—Maryum has recorded a popular rap dedicated to her father.

It would be difficult to overestimate Ali's impact on boxing and on the United States as both a cultural and political figure. He became one of the most recognized men in the world, an enduring, if not always appropriate, stylistic influence on young boxers, and a man who showed the world that it was possible for a black to speak his mind publicly and live to tell the tale.

—GERALD EARLY

ALLEN, RICHARD

Richard Allen (February 14, 1760–March 26, 1831), minister and community leader. As a reformer and institution builder in the post-Revolutionary period, Richard Allen was matched in achievements by few of his white con-

See also

Boxing

Nation of Islam

Rap

DEBBIE ALLEN

A Performing Powerhouse Takes to the Stage

Debbie Allen (January 16, 1950–), dancer and television producer. Debbie Allen was born in Houston, Tex., where her father, Andrew Allen, was a dentist and her mother, Vivian Ayers Allen, was a Pulitzer Prize-nominated writer. Her sister, Phylicia Rashad, became well known for her role as Claire Huxtable on the television series *The Cosby Show.*

As a child, Allen tried to take ballet classes at the Houston Foundation for Ballet, but she was rejected for reasons her mother thought were discriminatory. Allen began learning dance by studying privately with a former dancer from the Ballet Russes and later by moving with her family to Mexico City where she danced with the Ballet Nacional de Mexico. Allen reauditioned for the Houston Foundation for Ballet in 1964, and this time was admitted on a full scholarship and became the company's first black dancer.

After high school, Allen hoped to attend North Carolina School of Arts, but when she was rejected she decided to pursue a B.A. at Howard University (1971) with a concentration in classical Greek literature, speech, and theater. During her college years, she continued to dance with students at the university and with choreographer Michael Malone's dance troupe. After graduating in 1971, Allen relocated to New York City where she would develop her talents as a dancer, actress, and singer in her appearances on Broadway, and eventually in television shows and movies.

Allen's Broadway experience began in 1971 when she became a member of the chorus in *Purlie,* the musical version of Ossie Davis's *Purlie Victorious.* The following year, when chorus member George Faison left the show to form the Universal

Dance Experience, Allen became his principal dancer and assistant. By 1973 Allen returned to Broadway and for two years she played the role of Beneatha Younger in *Raisin,* a musical adaptation of Lorraine Hansberry's *A Raisin in the Sun.*

Allen began receiving critical attention in 1980, when she appeared in the role of Anita in the Broadway revival of *West Side Story,* which earned her a Tony Award nomination and a Drama Desk Award. The next year she made her movie debut in the film version of E.L. Doctorow's novel *Ragtime,* and then appeared in the hit movie *Fame,* with a small part as the dance teacher Lydia Grant. When the movie was turned into a television series of the same name, Allen returned as Lydia Grant and developed the role which brought her recognition by international audiences. She remained on the show until it went off the air in 1987, serving as a choreographer, and eventually as a director and producer.

During the 1980s Allen also acted in the television movie *Women of San Quentin* (1983), appeared in Richard Pryor's movie *Jo Jo Dancer, Your Life Is Calling* (1985), and played Charity in the Broadway revival of *Sweet Charity* (1986). In 1988 she became director of *A Different World,* and helped turn it into a Top Twenty television hit. The next year Allen hosted her first television special on ABC, *The Debbie Allen Show,* and later that year she directed the television musical *Polly,* which was followed in 1990 by *Polly: One More Time.* During the 1990–1991 season Allen directed episodes of NBC's *Fresh Prince of Bel Air* and *Quantum Leap.* Allen was a choreographer for the Academy Awards show from 1991 to 1994, and in 1992 she produced and directed the television movie *Stompin' at the Savoy.*

—ZITA ALLEN

temporaries. At age twenty, only a few months after buying his freedom in Kent County, Del., Allen was preaching to mostly white audiences and converting many of his hearers to Methodism. At twenty-seven, he was a cofounder of the Free African Society of Philadelphia, probably the first autonomous organization of free blacks in the United States. Before he was thirty-five, he had become the minister of what would be Philadelphia's largest black congregation—Bethel African Methodist Episcopal Church. Over a long lifetime, he founded, presided over, or served as officer in a large number of other organizations

designed to improve the condition of life and expand the sphere of liberty for African Americans. Although he received no formal education, he became an accomplished writer, penning and publishing sermons, tracts, addresses, and remonstrances; compiling a hymnal for black Methodists; and drafting articles of organization and governance for various organizations.

Enslaved at birth in the family of the prominent Philadelphia lawyer and officeholder Benjamin Chew, Allen was sold with his family to Stokely Sturgis, a small farmer near Dover, Del., in about 1768. It was here, in 1777, that Allen ex-

See also
African Methodist
Episcopal Church

A

perienced a religious conversion, shortly after most of his family had been sold away from Dover, at the hands of the itinerant Methodist Freeborn Garretson. Three years later he and his brother contracted with their master to purchase their freedom.

For a short time, Allen drove a wagon carrying salt for the Revolutionary army. He also supported himself as a woodchopper, brickyard laborer, and shoemaker as he carried out a six-year religious sojourn as an itinerant Methodist preacher. In something akin to a biblical journey into the wilderness, Allen tested his mettle and proved his faith, traveling by foot over thousands of miles, from North Carolina to New York, and preaching the word to black and white audiences in dozens of villages, crossroads, and forest clearings. During this period of his life, it seems, Allen developed the essential attributes that would serve him the rest of his career: resilience, toughness, cosmopolitanism, an ability to confront rapidly changing circumstances, and skill in dealing with a wide variety of people and temperaments.

Allen's itinerant preaching brought him to the attention of white Methodist leaders, who in 1786 called him to Philadelphia to preach to black members of the Methodist flock that worshiped at Saint George's Methodist Church, a rude, dirt-floored building in the German part of the city. Allen would spend the rest of his life there.

In Philadelphia, Allen's career was marked by his founding of Mother Bethel, the black Methodist church that opened its doors in 1794, and by the subsequent creation, in 1816, of the independent African Methodist Episcopal Church (AME Church). Soon after his arrival in 1786, he began pressing for an independent black church. His fervent Methodism brought him into contention with other emerging black leaders who wished for a nondenominational or "union" church, and thus within a few years two black churches took form. Both were guided by the idea that African Americans needed "to worship God under our own vine and fig tree," as Allen put it in his autobiographical memoir. This was, in essence, a desire to stand apart from white society, avoiding both the paternalistic benevolence of its racially liberal members and the animosity of its racially intolerant members. Allen's Bethel church, after opening its doors in a converted blacksmith's shop in 1794, grew into a congregation of more than five hundred members by 1800.

Bethel's rise to the status of Philadelphia's largest black church was accomplished amid a twenty-year struggle with white Methodist leaders. White Methodists were determined to make the popular Allen knuckle under to their authority, and this ran directly counter to Allen's determination to lead a church in which black Methodists, while subscribing to the general doctrines of Methodism, were free to pursue their churchly affairs autonomously. The struggle even involved the ownership of the church building itself. The attempts of white Methodists to rein in Allen and his black parishioners reached a climax in 1815 that was resolved when the Pennsylvania Supreme Court ruled on January 1, 1816, that Bethel was legally an independent church. Just a few months later, African-American ministers from across the mid-Atlantic region gathered in Philadelphia to confederate their congregations into the African Methodist Episcopal Church, which was to spread across the United States and abroad in the nineteenth and twentieth centuries.

Allen's epic twenty-year battle with white Methodist authorities represents a vital phase of the African-American struggle in the North to get out from under the controlling hand of white religionists. The AME Church, with Allen as its first bishop, quickly became the most important of the autonomous institutions created by black Americans that allowed former slaves to forge an Afro-Christianity that spoke in the language and

REFORMER AND FOUNDER

Although he was enslaved at birth and received no formal education, Richard Allen founded and presided over many organizations designed to improve life for African Americans.

answered the needs of a growing number of northern—and, later, southern—blacks. For decades, the AME helped to heal the disabling scars of slavery and facilitated the adjustment of black southern migrants to life as citizens in the North. Allen's success at Bethel had much to do with the warmth, simplicity, and evangelical fervor of Methodism, which resonated with a special vibrancy among the manumitted and fugitive southern slaves reaching Philadelphia in the early nineteenth century.

Between the founding of Bethel in 1794 and the organization of the AME Church, Allen founded schools for black youths and mutual aid societies that would allow black Philadelphians to quash the idea that they were dependent upon white charity. A successful businessman and a considerable property owner, Allen also wrote pamphlets and sermons attacking the slave trade, slavery, and white racism. The most notable of them, coauthored with Absalom Jones in 1794, was *A Narrative of the Proceedings of the Black People, During the Late Awful Calamity in Philadelphia, in the year 1793*. In this pamphlet, Allen and Jones defended the work of black citizens who aided the sick and dying during the horrendous yellow fever epidemic of 1793, but they went on to condemn the oppression of African Americans, both enslaved and free. In the first quarter of the nineteenth century, almost every African-American institution formed in Philadelphia included Allen's name and benefited from his energy and vision.

In the later years of his life, Allen was drawn to the idea of colonization—to Africa, Haiti, and Canada—as an answer to the needs of African Americans who as freedpersons faced discrimination and exploitation. His son, John Allen, was one of the leaders of the Haitian immigrants in 1824. The capstone of Allen's career came six years later, when he presided over the first meeting of the National Negro Convention Movement—an umbrella organization that launched a coordinated reform movement among black Americans and provided an institutional structure for black abolitionism. When death came to Allen shortly thereafter, his funeral was attended by a vast concourse of black and white Philadelphians.

—GARY B. NASH

AMISTAD MUTINY

The *Amistad* mutiny was a rebellion of African captives that occurred off the northern coast of Cuba in July 1839. The mutineers had been seized in Africa, herded onto a Portuguese slave ship along with hundreds of others, and then transported illegally from the African island of Lombokor to Cuba (then a Spanish colony). Upon reaching Havana, the Africans were smuggled ashore under cover of night, in violation of an 1817 treaty between England and Spain that prohibited the slave trade. There, fifty-three captives—forty-nine adult males, three girls, and a boy—were sold to two Spaniards, José Ruiz and Pedro Montes; they were then shipped along the Cuban coast to Puerto Príncipe aboard the Spanish schooner *La Amistad*.

On July 1–2, 1839, just a few days after the *Amistad* set sail, the captured Africans rose up in revolt. Led by Sengbe Pieh (or Joseph Cinqué), they freed themselves from their irons and launched an armed assault against their captors, killing the ship's captain and cook. Several crew members disappeared, and one African was killed in the fray. The mutineers spared Ruiz and Montes, ordering them to sail back to Africa. The Spaniards, however, maintained a meandering northerly course that, by late August, brought the ship to New York state waters.

On August 25, the Africans, desperate from hunger and thirst, anchored the now-bedraggled *Amistad* off the coast of Long Island in New York to search for provisions. But they had been spotted by the crew of the U.S.S. *Washington;* after a show of resistance, they surrendered to the ship's commanders and were towed to New London, Conn. They were shortly afterward taken to New Haven, where they languished in jail while awaiting a hearing on their case. So began an ordeal for the "Mendians" (many of the Africans had come from Mende) that lasted for more than two years.

The *Amistad* case attracted widespread attention along the Atlantic seaboard and even on an international scale. Ruiz and Montes insisted that the Africans had already been slaves in Cuba at the time of purchase and were therefore legal property; as such, they could be tried on charges of piracy and murder. Cuban and Spanish authorities demanded the return of the ship and its surviving human "cargo"—thirty-nine adults and the four children. But abolitionists mobilized in defense of the mutineers, hoping to prove that they had been unlawfully enslaved and must be set free. Some antislavery advocates sought to use the case to demonstrate that the principle of natural rights applied to black people.

The *Amistad* Committee, composed of such prominent abolitonists as Lewis Tappan, Joshua

♦ **Mutiny**
Forcible or passive resistance to lawful authority; esp: concerted revolt (as of a naval crew) against discipline or a superior officer

See also
Slave Trade
Underground Railroad

Leavitt, and Simeon Jocelyn, launched a vigorous campaign to raise funds for the defense. They also succeeded in generating substantial public sympathy for the defendants, even among many who did not oppose the institution of slavery itself. Activists located two African-born seamen, James Covey and Charles Pratt, who were able to communicate with the prisoners, including the undisputed leader Cinqué. The Africans were sketched by artists and displayed on speaking tours; models of them were made and sent along to sites where they could not personally appear. They were taught English and instructed in Christianity. Throughout the prolonged period of litigation that followed their arrest, the case was hotly debated in the press.

Thousands of onlookers converged on Hartford, Conn., when the U.S. Circuit Court convened in September 1839. The court refused to release the captives and remanded the case to the U.S. District Court. It was not until January 1840 that a ruling was issued. Judge Andrew T. Judson determined that the Africans had indeed been illegally kidnapped and sold, and that they had legitimately rebelled to win back their freedom. At the same time, he upheld the institution of slavery by ordering the return to Cuba of Antonio, who actually had been a slave of the slain *Amistad* captain. Judson also ordered the return of the mutineers to Africa.

The U.S. government, under the administration of President Martin Van Buren, had been expecting a verdict that would uphold its own position: that the Africans should be returned to Spain under Pinckney's Treaty of 1795. A naval vessel, the U.S.S. *Grampus,* was anchored in New London harbor, waiting to spirit the Africans out of the country and back to Cuba before the abolitionist forces could appeal the ruling. But now, it was the government that filed an appeal. After Judson's decision was upheld in May 1840, the *Amistad* case was sent to the U.S. Supreme Court.

A majority of the Court were Southerners who had been slave owners at one time, including Chief Justice Roger B. Taney. The *Amistad* Committee was able to secure the services of John Quincy Adams, former president of the United States, who argued the case before the Court. In March 1841, the Court delivered its opinion, affirming the original ruling by an eight-to-one margin. The *Amistad* mutineers were free. Antonio, at risk of being sent back to Cuba, was transported secretly to Canada via the Underground Railroad. The *Amistad* Committee set about rais-

ing private funds to return the remaining Africans to their homeland.

On November 17, 1841, thirty-five Africans (the others had died while imprisoned in Connecticut), along with translator James Covey and five white missionaries, left New York for Sierra Leone. Traveling with protection from the British, they reached Africa in mid-January 1842. Little is known of Cinqué after his repatriation—according to some accounts, he died some time around 1879—but he remains one of the leading symbols of resistance to the Atlantic slave trade. Although the Spanish government demanded reparations, their effort was hampered by sectional divisions within the U.S. Congress and was eventually abandoned with the coming of the U.S. Civil War.

—ROBERT L. HALL

ANDERSON, EDDIE "ROCHESTER"

Eddie "Rochester" Anderson (Edmund Lincoln) (September 18, 1905–February 28, 1977), actor. Eddie Anderson, the actor who played "Rochester" for more than twenty years on Jack Benny's radio and television shows, was born in Oakland, Calif. The son of vaudevillians, Anderson started his career in show business at age fourteen in an all-black revue and later toured with his brother Cornelius in a song-and-dance act. Anderson's film career began in black "race" movies, but in the early 1930s he crossed over to the white studios, playing bit parts in Hollywood movies.

In 1936 Anderson was cast as Noah in the film *Green Pastures*, his first important comic role in a studio production. This led to a part on the Jack Benny radio show. Anderson's appearance as the Pullman porter Rochester was so successful that he was signed on as a full-time member of the cast. Eventually Rochester became the most popular character on the show, aside from Benny. With masterful sarcasm, characterized by his famous line "What's that, boss?" Anderson regularly punctured Benny's inflated ego. The camaraderie between them surpassed the standard portrayal of interracial master-servant relationships. Together they constituted an unusual domestic partnership that entertained audiences for over two decades.

This rapport carried over into films they appeared in together, including *Man About Town* (1939), *Buck Benny Rides Again* (1940), and *Love*

See also
Film

Thy Neighbor (1940). Anderson made other films during the 1930s and 1940s, including *Jezebel* (1938), *Gone With the Wind* (1939), *Birth of the Blues* (1941), and the black Hollywood musicals *Cabin in the Sky* (1943) and *Stormy Weather* (1943), starring in *Cabin*. In 1945 his film *Brewster's Millions* was banned in Memphis because it portrayed "too much social equality and racial mixture," typified by Anderson's easy familiarity with the white characters.

From 1950 to 1965 Anderson appeared on *The Jack Benny Show* on television. In 1962 he was listed by *Ebony* magazine as one of the one hundred wealthiest African Americans in the United States. He returned to film with *It's a Mad, Mad, Mad, Mad World* in 1963. On television he appeared in *Bachelor Father* (1962), *Dick Powell's Theatre* (1963), and *Love American Style* (1969). Anderson died in Los Angeles, at the Motion Picture Country Home and Hospital.

—ELIZABETH V. FOLEY

ANDERSON, MARIAN

Marian Anderson (February 17, 1897–May 19, 1993), opera and concert singer. Marian Anderson, a contralto of international repute, may be best remembered as the first African American to sing at the Metropolitan Opera Company. She grew up in Philadelphia, where her family members were active as musicians at the Union Baptist Church. An interest in singing was stimulated by her participation in the church choirs, and she began local solo performances by the age of ten, singing professionally while still in high school. Initial venues, in addition to her church, included the Philadelphia Choral Society, New York's Martin-Smith School of Music, the National Association of Negro Musicians (which in 1921 awarded her its first scholarship), the NAACP, the National Baptist Convention, schools, and various regional organizations.

Anderson's formal recital debut, at Town Hall in New York in 1922, was not a success, obligating further study. In 1925 she won a vocal competition that granted her a successful performance with the New York Philharmonic at Lewisohn Stadium, but the major appearances that followed were initially in Scandinavia. Her Parisian debut, in 1935, was attended by Sol Hurok, who then became her manager. That summer she won the notice of a distinguished audience at a private recital in Salzburg; in December, she presented a Town Hall recital, this one well received.

Anderson's international acclaim encouraged Howard University in 1939 to seek a recital for her in Washington, D.C. When she was denied access for racial reasons to Constitution Hall by the Daughters of the American Revolution, the public protest approached that of a scandal. Eleanor Roosevelt resigned her DAR membership and criticism came from opera singer Lawrence Tibbett, New York Mayor Fiorello La Guardia, conductor Leopold Stokowski, and other major figures. Secretary of the Interior Harold Ickes granted Anderson use of the Lincoln Memorial for an Easter Sunday concert as an alternative. Seventy-five thousand people heard her program, which began in subtle irony with "My Country 'Tis of Thee" and ended with "Nobody Knows the Trouble I've Seen." The location for this performance was not forgotten nearly a quarter of a century later by the Rev. Dr. Martin Luther King, Jr., who arranged for her to sing there again during the 1963 March on Washington.

Anderson's tour schedule intensified, and Metropolitan Opera manager Rudolph Bing determined that she would appear as Ulrica in Verdi's *Un Ballo in Maschera*. She sang the role eight times, starting on January 7, 1955, although she was no longer in her prime. (In 1958, RCA Victor issued a recording of highlights from the opera with Dimitri Mitropoulos conducting and Anderson in the role of Ulrica.) She retired from the stage at

GROUNDBREAKING VOCALIST

Marian Anderson (1897-1993) was the first African American to sing at New York's Metropolitan Opera Company. In 1939, she performed before an audience of 75,000 at the Lincoln Memorial.
AP/WIDE WORLD PHOTOS

*The needs of society
determine its ethics.*

MAYA ANGELOU
*I KNOW WHY THE
CAGED BIRD SINGS*, 1969

Carnegie Hall on Easter 1965, after presenting fifty-one farewell concerts across the country. Her repertory was centered on sacred arias by J. S. Bach and Handel, spirituals (especially Harry Burleigh's "Deep River"), lieder (Schubert's "Ave Maria" was a favorite), and some opera arias—notably "O Mio Fernando" from Donizetti's *La Favorita*, in which she demonstrated that she could have excelled in bel canto roles, given the chance. When granted the Bok Award in 1940, Anderson established a scholarship fund for vocalists whose awards have been granted to McHenry Boatwright, Grace Bumbry, Gloria Davy, Reri Grist, Bonia Hyman, Louise Parker, Rawn Spearman, Camellia Williams, and others.

Her primary voice teacher was Giuseppe Boghetti, although she worked in London with Amanda Aldridge, a daughter of the actor Ira Aldridge. Early in her career, she was accompanied by minstrel pianist William King, then by Kosti Vehanen from Finland, and later by Franz Rupp of Germany. Anderson was appointed in 1958 to the U.S. delegation to the United Nations, where she spoke on behalf of the independence of African nations. Although she denied playing an overt role in the Civil Rights Movement, Anderson's dignity and artistry brought about social change and opened the door for the many concert singers who followed her. In tribute on her seventy-fifth birthday in Carnegie Hall,

MAYA ANGELOU
A Versatile Writer Speaks with a Powerful Voice

Maya Angelou (1928–), writer. Born Marguerite Annie Johnson on April 4, 1928, to Vivian Baxter and Bailey Johnson in St. Louis, Mo., Angelou was raised in Stamps, Ark., by her grandmother, Anne Henderson. She related her experience of growing up in her popular autobiography *I Know Why the Caged Bird Sings* (1970), a title taken from the poetry of Paul Laurence Dunbar. It was nominated for a National Book Award. Like many African-American autobiographers, Angelou saw herself not only as an individual but as a representative of black people.

What *Caged Bird* contributed to the tradition of African-American autobiography was its emphasis on the effects of growing up black and female in the South. Angelou writes of the rape of the protagonist by her mother's boyfriend. Until recently, intragroup rape and incest were taboo subjects in African-American literature; *Caged Bird* helped to break that silence. Her second biography, *Gather Together In My Name* (1974), a title taken from the Bible, focuses on the vulnerable Angelou's entry into the harsh urban world of Los Angeles, while her third autobiography, *Singin' & Swinging & Getting Merry Like Christmas* (1976), relates the experience of her first marriage and of raising her son while pursuing her singing, dancing, and acting career.

The fourth autobiography, *The Heart of A Woman* (1981), a title taken from a poem by Georgia Douglas Johnson, the Harlem Renaissance poet, presents a mature Angelou who works with the Rev. Dr. Martin Luther King, Jr. and Malcolm X. Active in the Civil Rights Movement, she served as northern coordinator for the Southern Christian Leadership Conference in 1959–1960. In her fifth autobiography, *All God's Children Need Traveling Shoes* (1986), Angelou goes to Ghana, where she experiences the complexity of being an African American in Africa.

Angelou has also published many volumes of poetry: *Just Give Me a Cool Drink of Water 'fore I Diiie* (1971), which was nominated for a Pulitzer Prize; *Oh Pray My Wings Are Gonna Fit Me Well* (1975); *And Still I Rise* (1978); *Shaker Why Don't You Sing?* (1983); *Now Sheba Sings the Song* (1987); and *I Shall Not Be Moved* (1990). As these titles indicate, Angelou's poetry is deeply rooted in the African-American oral tradition and is uplifting in tone. Angelou says, "All my work is meant to say 'You may encounter many defeats but you *must* not be defeated.' "

A versatile writer, Angelou has written for television: the PBS ten-part series *Black, Blues, Blacks* (1968); a teleplay of *Caged Bird;* and for the screen; *Georgia Georgia* (1971) and *Sister, Sister* (1979). As well as being a prolific writer, Angelou has been a successful actress and received a Tony nomination for best supporting actress in the TV miniseries *Roots*. Angelou says of her creative diversity, "I believe all things are possible for a human being and I don't think there's anything in the world I can't do." On January 20, 1993, at the request of President Bill Clinton, Angelou concluded the president's inauguration by reading a poem composed for the occasion, "On the Pulse of Morning," which celebrates a new era of national unity.

—BARBARA T. CHRISTIAN

Leontyne Price paid her respects succinctly: "Dear Marian Anderson, because of you, I am."
—DOMINIQUE-RENÉ DE LERMA

APOLLO THEATER

The Apollo Theater has stood in the heart of Harlem, N.Y., as the single most important African-American theater for more than half a century, presenting major stars and launching the careers of previously unknown amateur musicians, dancers, and comics.

Located at 253 West 125th Street, the Apollo opened in 1913 as Hurtig and Seamon's Music Hall, presenting white vaudeville and burlesque theater to white audiences. As burlesque routines lost popularity and became incorporated into the downtown musical comedy revues, the theater was rechristened the Apollo by Sidney Cohen, who bought it in 1933. The inaugural show, billed as "Jazz à la Carte" and held on January 26, 1934, featured a film and several types of acts, including the Benny Carter Orchestra.

Under the direction of Frank Schiffman, the Apollo soon became famous for presenting top performers in lavish costumes on often exotic stage settings hosted by Ralph Cooper. The 1,600-seat auditorium hosted thirty shows each week, and was the site of regular live broadcasts on twenty-one radio stations across the country. The greatest jazz musicians of the era performed at the Apollo, including the Duke Ellington Orchestra, Lionel Hampton's band, and Louis Jordan. Perhaps the most famous of the Apollo's offerings was its Amateur Hour, held every Wednesday night from 11 P.M. until midnight, when the performances of seven or eight contestants would be judged by audience response. Those who failed to earn the audience's approval were booed off stage in mid-performance, but winners, including Ella Fitzgerald, Sarah Vaughan, and Pearl Bailey, were sometimes rewarded with recording and performance contracts. The thrilling experience of concerts at the Apollo during this period is captured on a recording of jazz broadcasts made at the Apollo in the mid-1940s, *Live at the Apollo* (1985), including performances by the Count Basie Orchestra, the Jimmie Lunceford Orchestra, and Marjorie Cooper, a singer who failed to gain the amateur hour audience's approval.

With the demise of the Swing Era, many of New York's grand black theaters and nightclubs closed, but the Apollo remained popular by embracing the new sounds of rhythm and blues. By the mid-1950s, the Apollo regularly featured rhythm and blues revues, as well as gospel stars, and comedians such as Moms Mabley and Pigmeat Markham. With the ascendance of soul music in the 1960s, the theater presented sold-out runs by soul singers such as James Brown, Sam Cooke, Jackie Wilson, and popular shows by Dionne Warwick, the Jackson 5, Gladys Knight, and Funkadelic. Brown's album *Live at the Apollo* (1963) captured not only one of the greatest performances by the "Godfather of Soul," but the extraordinary fervor that the discerning Apollo audience was capable of.

By the mid-1970s, black entertainers had gained access to better-paying stadium and arena venues, and the theater could no longer afford to draw top acts. The Apollo fell on hard times, presenting only a few dozen shows per year, and closed its doors in 1977. In 1981 an investment group headed by Percy Sutton bought the theater out of bankruptcy for $225,000. Despite being declared a national historic landmark in 1983, the reinstatement of amateur hour in 1985, and a guarantee of its mortgage by New York state, the theater failed to succeed. In 1988, the theater underwent a $20 million renovation, but it continued to lose money—$2 million a year until 1991, when it was taken over by a non-profit organization led by Leon Denmark and Congressman Charles Rangel. Since that time, the Apollo has led the revitalization of 125th Street by once again presenting both the stars and unknowns of black popular music, from B. B. King to Luther Vandross, hip-hop, and rap shows.

—IRA BERGER

ARMSTRONG, LOUIS "SATCHMO"

Louis "Satchmo" Armstrong (August 4, 1901–July 6, 1971), jazz trumpeter and singer. Although it is certain that Louis Armstrong was born in New Orleans in poverty, there has long been confusion concerning his exact birth date. During his lifetime, he claimed he was born on July 4, 1900, but a baptismal certificate discovered in the 1980s now establishes his real date of birth as August 4, 1901. He was raised in terrible poverty by his mother and grandmother, and he contributed to the family income from his earliest years. His first musical experience was singing in a barbershop quartet. In 1912 or 1913, according to legend, he celebrated the Fourth of July by firing a pistol; he

Confidence among African-American leaders in the power of the muses to heal social wrongs was the rule, rather than the exception, by 1927.

PAGE 326

See also
Harlem Renaissance
Rhythm and Blues

A

*"Man, if you gotta
ask, you'll never
know."*

LOUIS ARMSTRONG
WHEN ASKED WHAT JAZZ IS

was arrested and sent to the Colored Waifs' Home, where he remained for about two years.

There an already evident interest in music was encouraged, and he was given instruction on cornet and made a member of the band. Armstrong came to adulthood just as jazz was emerging as a distinct musical style in New Orleans, and the new music and Armstrong matured together. He played in local clubs called "tonks" and apprenticed in local bands, where he met most of New Orleans's early jazz musicians, and found a mentor in Joseph "King" Oliver. He soon developed a reputation as one of the best young brass musicians in the city. In 1919 he joined Fate Marable's band, playing on Mississippi riverboats, where he learned to read music. He returned to his hometown in 1921.

In 1923 King Oliver invited Armstrong to join his successful Creole Jazz Band in Chicago as second cornetist, and it was with Oliver that Armstrong made his first recordings. These records provide an invaluable document of early New Orleans jazz, and, while they contain much ensemble playing and collective improvisation, they also show that Armstrong was already a formidable soloist. The following year, encouraged by his second wife, Lil Hardin, Armstrong joined the jazz orchestra of Fletcher Henderson in New York City. Recordings such as Don Redman's arrange-

ment of the 1924 "Copenhagen" reveal an inventive melodist and improvisor. His big-band experience helped Armstrong fashion a new type of jazz playing, featuring extended improvised solos. In New York he also recorded as an accompanist to blues singers Bessie Smith, "Ma" Rainey, and Bertha "Chippie" Hill.

This new style was featured in the extraordinarily influential series of recordings made under Armstrong's leadership from 1925 to 1929 with ensembles called the Hot Fives and Hot Sevens. His collaborators on the early dates include Johnny Dodds on clarinet, Kid Ory on trombone, and pianist Lil Hardin, whom he married. Hardin played an important role at this time in furthering and supervising her husband's career.

His solos on "Big Butter and Egg Man" (1926), "Struttin' with Some Barbecue" (1927), "Potato Head Blues" (1927), and "Hotter Than That" (1927) are superb improvised melodies, and they showed that jazz was becoming a soloist's art. Every night on the bandstand, Armstrong found in pianist Earl "Fatha" Hines a musician who could not only function on his level but with whom he could exchange musical ideas. That collaboration did not produce recordings until 1928, but then it produced such masterpieces as "West End Blues," "Skip the Gutter," and the duet "Weather Bird."

In 1929 Armstrong returned to New York, which remained his home for much of the remainder of his life. That year he appeared in the Fats Waller/Andy Razaf Broadway Show *Hot Chocolates*. He was also the leader of his own orchestra, which featured popular tunes rather than the original blues and New Orleans songs he had previously favored. Increasingly prominent in his performances at this time was his singing, which in its use of scat (wordless syllables) and creative rhythmic reworking of a song's lyrics and melodies influenced all subsequent jazz singers. His recordings "Body and Soul," "Memories of You," "Sweethearts on Parade" (all 1930), and "Stardust" (1931), among many others, helped establish both the repertory and playing style of big-band jazz. In 1932, and again in 1933–1935, he toured Europe. On the first tour he acquired the nickname "Satchmo," short for "Satchelmouth," though his fellow musicians favored the sobriquet "Pops."

There were no real innovations in Armstrong's work after the early 1930s, but there were over three decades of this powerful trumpeter and grand and compelling entertainer's life still ahead. Extending the range of his instrument to F above

A TRUMPETING SUCCESS

Louis Armstrong (1901–1971) shook up the jazz world by introducing improvisation into his tunes. His gravelly voice is instantly recognizable.
AP/WIDE WORLD PHOTOS

high C, Armstrong recorded "Swing That Music" (1936) and two years later revisited "Struttin' with Some Barbecue," offering another classic solo on that piece. In addition to his purely musical accomplishments, Armstrong in the 1930s became an entertainment celebrity, the first African American to appear regularly on network radio programs and to be widely featured in motion pictures such as *Pennies from Heaven* (1936) and *Going Places* (1938).

By the early 1940s, Armstrong's popularity had waned somewhat. In 1947 his career was reinvigorated by his return to a small-group format under the name of Louis Armstrong and the All-Stars, which he continued to lead with varying personnel for the remainder of his life. In its early years, his fellow band members included pianist Earl Hines, trombonist Jack Teagarden, and clarinetist Barney Bigard. In his later years Armstrong made numerous tours of Europe, Asia, and Africa; in 1960 the United States government appointed him a special "ambassador of goodwill" for the positive feelings his travels abroad engendered.

Armstrong's genial and nonconfrontational personality, and his inclusion of some "coon" and plantation songs in his repertory (including his theme song "When It's Sleepy Time Down South"), were sometimes criticized by a younger, more militant generation of black entertainers. Though Armstrong was a product of the segregated South who learned early in his career not to discuss racial matters in performance, he cared deeply about racial injustice. In 1957 his uncharacteristically blunt comments about the inaction of the Eisenhower administration in the Little Rock incident ("The way they are treating my people in the South, the government can go to hell") created something of a furor, though such public statements by Armstrong were rare.

Armstrong was perhaps best known to the general public in the last years through popular recordings featuring his singing, including "Blueberry Hill" (1949), "Mack the Knife" (1955), and "Hello, Dolly" (1967). In 1988 his 1968 recording of "It's a Wonderful World" appeared on the popular charts after it was used in the film *Good Morning, Vietnam*.

As Albert Murray has remarked, Louis Armstrong had the innate ability to make people feel good simply by his presence. But that feeling was not a simple matter of cheering up his audiences. His music could encompass melancholy and sadness while at the same time expressing a compensating and equally profound joy. Armstrong was the first great improvisor in jazz, and his work not only changed that music but all subsequent popular music, vocal and instrumental. He expanded the range of his instrument and all its brass cousins in ways that have affected composers and players in all forms of music. In his progression from simple beginnings to international celebrity he became, arguably, both the most beloved and the most influential American musician of the twentieth century. Armstrong, whose career had slowed after a 1959 heart attack, died in Corona, Queens, where he had lived since 1942 with his fourth wife, Lucille Wilson.

—MARTIN WILLIAMS

ASHE, ARTHUR ROBERT, JR.

Arthur Robert Ashe, Jr. (July 10, 1943–February 6, 1993), tennis player and political activist. Born in Richmond, Va., Arthur Ashe traced his lineage back ten generations on his father's side to a woman who in 1735 was brought from West Africa to Yorktown, Va., by the slave ship *Doddington*. Ashe's mother, Mattie Cunningham, also of Richmond, taught him to read by the time he was four. She died when Arthur was six, one year after giving birth to her second son and last child, Johnnie.

Ashe, who was frail in his youth, was forbidden by his father, a police officer in Richmond's Department of Recreation and Parks, to play football on the segregated Brookfield playground adjacent to the Ashes' home. Instead, young Ashe took to playing tennis on the four hard courts of the playground. By the time he was ten, Ashe had attracted the keen eye of Dr. Walter Johnson, a Lynchburg, Va., physician and tennis enthusiast who had previously discovered and coached Althea Gibson, the first black woman to win Wimbledon.

Ashe's father and Dr. Johnson were both stern disciplinarians who insisted that Ashe cultivate self-discipline, good manners, forbearance, and self-effacing stoicism. These qualities would characterize Ashe throughout his entire life and, even in the midst of the most turbulent social conditions, would define him as a man of reason, conscience, integrity, and moral authority. His cool disposition enabled him not only to survive, but to distinguish himself in an overwhelmingly white tennis environment.

In 1960, Ashe was awarded a tennis scholarship to UCLA, where he earned All-American

Racism is not an excuse to not do the best you can.

ARTHUR ASHE
SPORTS ILLUSTRATED,
JULY 1991

See also
United Negro College Fund

37

A

status. Two years after Ashe graduated with a business degree, he became the first black man to win one of the preeminent Grand Slam titles, accomplishing that as an amateur and U.S. Army representative at the U.S. Open of 1968. Numerous titles would follow, highlighted by Ashe's place on three victorious Davis Cup squads and the addition of two more Grand Slam titles, one at the Australian Open in 1970, and the other, his *pièce de résistance,* at Wimbledon in 1975.

Throughout those years, Ashe devoted considerable time and energy to civil rights issues. In 1973, after three years of trying, he secured an invitation to play in the all-white South African Open. Although his participation was controversial, it personified Ashe's lifelong belief in constructive engagement—an attitude that he abandoned only on one noteworthy occasion in 1976, when he joined in the call for an international embargo of all sporting contact with South Africa.

In 1979, at age thirty-six, Ashe suffered a myocardial infarction, which forced him to have by-

pass surgery and retire from tennis. Nevertheless, over the ensuing years he served as the U.S. Davis Cup captain (1981–1985), he worked as a journalist and television commentator, and he served or helped create various foundations, ranging from the American Heart Association to the United Negro College Fund to his own Safe Passage Foundation.

Eighteen months after undergoing a second heart operation in 1983, Ashe learned that he had contracted the AIDS virus through blood transfusions. He immediately set to work on his definitive three-volume history of black athletes in America, *A Hard Road to Glory* (1988). Forced by the national newspaper *USA Today* to reveal that he was suffering from AIDS in April 1992, Ashe worked as an activist for the defeat of AIDS until he died of the disease in February 1993.

—PETER BODO

ATLANTA, GEORGIA

The origins and early growth of Atlanta can be directly traced to the railroads. In 1837, surveyors for the Western and Atlantic Railroad selected as a southern terminus for their line a spot seven miles southeast of the Chattahoochee River on a plateau formed by the eastern slope of the Allegheny Mountains. Here, a small settlement, aptly named Terminus, arose. While work was progressing on the Western and Atlantic, Terminus grew, changed its name twice (to Marthasville in 1843 and finally to Atlanta two years later), and linked up with two other Georgia railroads. The junction of these three railroads made Atlanta the center of a growing transportation network and hastened the city's development as a commercial center of the Southeast. By the eve of the Civil War, Atlanta, with a population of more than 9,000, was the fourth largest city in Georgia.

Fewer African Americans, either free or enslaved, were present in Atlanta during the antebellum period than in the older, more-established cities of the South. One Atlanta resident noted in 1847 that "there are not 100 Negroes in the place, and white men black their own shoes, and dust their own clothes, as independently as in the north." Between 1850 and 1860 the number of slaves in Atlanta increased from 493 to 1,914, and "free persons of color" grew slightly in number from 19 to 25. Slaves in both census years, however, made up only about one-fifth of the city's population. (By way of contrast, Savannah's 1850

TENNIS PRO

Arthur Ashe (1943-1993) accomplished feats both on and off the tennis court during his short life. The pro won two Grand Slam titles and was an outspoken civil rights activist.

AP/WIDE WORLD PHOTOS

38

slave population of 6,231 was about 40 percent of that city's population, and 686 free blacks resided in the city.) The relatively small number of slaves and free blacks in Atlanta and their dispersal throughout the city precluded the formation of any large black enclaves during the antebellum period.

Whatever biracial residential patterns had been established in Atlanta were disrupted by the siege and destruction of the city during the Civil War and the tremendous influx of blacks and whites following the war. Between 1865 and 1867 almost 9,000 African Americans and 10,000 whites migrated to the city. Three years later, blacks in Atlanta numbered over 12,000 and made up almost one half of the city's total population.

In the intense competition for living space that ensued, race and class were the prime determinants of residential location. The resulting patterns resembled those found in many preindustrial cities, with the upper class living near the center of the city and the poor (both black and white) on the urban periphery. Emerging black settlements in Atlanta, as in many other southern cities, were further relegated to the most undesirable areas of the city: back alleys; low-lying, flood-prone ground; industrial sites; and tracts of land adjacent to railroads, cemeteries, city dumps, and slaughter houses. These locations not only tended to separate black settlements from surrounding white neighborhoods, but also contributed in some cases to very high black-mortality rates.

By 1880, several large and distinctive black communities had emerged within the city limits—most notably, Jenningstown on the west side of Atlanta, Summer Hill to the south, Shermantown on the east side, and Mechanicsville in the southwestern quadrant of the city. Other smaller black communities were scattered throughout the city, and in some areas whites and blacks continued to live in close proximity. Nonetheless, the emerging pattern in the late nineteenth century was one of separation and increasing racial division as black settlements became more concentrated and well defined. W. E. B. Du Bois said that Atlanta's black population by the turn of the century "stretched like a great dumbbell across the city, with one great center in the east and a smaller one in the west, connected by a narrow belt."

For African Americans in Atlanta after the Civil War, employment opportunities were largely confined to unskilled labor, domestic service, or to jobs that whites did not want. Rural blacks migrating to the city tended to swell the ranks of un-skilled workers, and even those freedmen who enjoyed positions as craftsmen or artisans before the war were often denied the opportunity to use those skills by prevailing white prejudice and an increasingly specialized urban job market. As a result, the vast majority of the city's unskilled labor positions (over 76 percent in 1870 and almost 90 percent in 1890) were filled by African Americans.

The economic insecurity facing back Atlantans during this period was further reflected in the relative scarcity of African Americans who owned property and the number of black women employed in personal and domestic service. In 1870 only 311 black men and 27 black women (about 3 percent of the adult population) were property owners. Ten years later, the number of black property owners had almost doubled but still lagged far behind the total for whites. Because of the low average earning power of black males, black women worked in much larger numbers than their white counterparts. The vast majority of black working women (92 percent in 1890) were confined to low-paying domestic service positions.

On the few occasions in the nineteenth century that black workers in Atlanta organized to negotiate for more pay, better working conditions, or increased job security, their efforts were usually unsuccessful. In 1881 an estimated 3,000 of Atlanta's black washerwomen joined forces to strike for higher wages and the establishment of a city-wide charge of $1 per dozen pounds of wash. The city government and enraged white employers responded to these demands with arrests, fines, and threats of economic reprisals and incarceration. Under the weight of this government hostility and economic pressure, the strike eventually collapsed. Nine years later, protest by black firemen at the Georgia Pacific Railroad collapsed when the striking workers were replaced by white applicants.

Despite the considerable obstacles facing them, some black Atlantans did succeed during this period in establishing thriving businesses and accumulating wealth and property. Among these were undertaker David T. Howard, barbers Moses H. Bentley and Alonzo F. Herndon (who was also the founder of Atlanta Life Insurance Company), grocer James Tate, and hotel owner and grocer Moses Calhoun. These businessmen made their mark in a hostile economic environment in part by catering to black clients or by providing services to whites that were not in direct competition with white businesses.

Martin Luther King, Jr.'s maternal grandfather, the Rev. A. D. Williams, had transformed Ebenezer Baptist Church, a block down the street from his grandson's home, into one of Atlanta's most prominent black churches.

PAGE 401

See also
Civil War
Jim Crow

*In 1894 only one
black faculty
member was
employed at Fisk,
and none at
Atlanta University.*

PAGE 212

White Atlantans and the city government were equally unwilling to address the social and educational needs of the city's growing black population. It was not until 1908 that the city established its first social service agencies and programs for African Americans. In the interim, black community needs were met instead through the actions of individuals or the programs of a growing array of black self-help, fraternal, and religious organizations. Carrie Steele Logan founded the city's first black orphanage. Self-help agencies such as the mutual aid societies organized to provide medical and death benefits for their members. The Neighborhood Union (founded by Lugenia Hope, wife of a Morehouse College president) established health centers, boys' and girls' clubs, and vocational classes for children; it also lobbied for improved public facilities for blacks. Fraternal organizations such as the Odd Fellows and the Good Samaritans raised thousands of dollars for the poor and infirm of the city.

The black churches of Atlanta likewise organized programs to meet the pressing social and economic needs of their communities. The First Congregational Church of Atlanta under the leadership of the Reverend Henry Hugh Proctor, for example, sponsored a home for black working women, business and cooking schools, a kindergarten, and an employment bureau. Similar community services and programs were provided by the city's other prominent black churches such as Big Bethel A.M.E. Church and Wheat Street Baptist.

In the area of education, black churches and religious organizations also played a prominent role. Atlanta University, the first black institution of higher learning in the city, was founded by the American Missionary Association in 1865. Atlanta Baptist College for men (Morehouse College) followed two years later, and Clark University, supported by the Freedmen's Aid Society of the Methodist Episcopal Church, was established in 1870. The final two schools of what would later become the Atlanta University Center—Morris Brown College, affiliated with the African Methodist Episcopal Church (A.M.E.), and Spelman Seminary (Spelman College) for women, a Baptist school—opened in 1881. Although many of these schools were, at first, little more than advanced grammar or secondary schools, this nucleus of black higher education, unmatched in any other city in the United States, provided important educational and training opportunities for Atlanta's black

students and contributed to the growth of what would become a sizable and well-educated black middle class.

Black Atlantans were less successful in the nineteenth century in establishing public elementary and secondary schools for their children, partly because of a sudden decline in the political strength of the city's African-American population following a signal achievement. In 1870, Republicans in the Georgia state legislature succeeded in changing the election system in the state's cities from an at-large selection process to a ward system. In the elections that followed in Atlanta that year, two African Americans—William Finch and George Graham—won seats on the city council. Finch used this opportunity to push for the establishment of black public schools; despite strong Democratic opposition and obstruction, he succeeded in incorporating into the city's school system two schools for black children organized and run by the American Missionary Association.

The following year, however, Democrats regained control of the state legislature, repealed the election law, and swept Finch and other Republican leaders out of office. The city continued to maintain separate public schools for its black students until the 1960s, but these schools remained few in number, and were overcrowded and understaffed. For many years, blacks were limited to grammar schools; not until the 1920s did Atlanta construct its first black public high school.

Efforts in Atlanta to segregate African Americans and restrict their political rights intensified in the period from 1890 to 1920 as the city's black population more than doubled. In 1892, local Democratic officials enacted a "white primary" law, effectively limiting voting in primary elections to white males. That same year, the city passed its first segregation ordinance, which authorized and mandated the separation of black and white passengers on streetcars. In 1913, Atlanta became the first city in Georgia to try to extend segregation to housing patterns through use of a residential segregation ordinance. Although this law was struck down by the state supreme court two years later, the city council passed a similar statute in 1917 and in 1922 tried to institute and formalize segregated housing through use of a comprehensive zoning ordinance.

Violence or threats of violence often accompanied attempts in the South during this period to disfranchise and segregate African Americans. A dramatic example of the ever-present potential for racial violence occurred in the Atlanta Riot of

See also
Education

1906. Racial tensions that year were intensified by a long and bitter campaign for governor in which both candidates called for the complete exclusion of blacks from the political process. Following a series of unsubstantiated reports in the local newspapers of wanton black attacks on white females, a race riot erupted in the city. Spurred on by lurid newspaper accounts of black rapists and rumors of black insurrection, roving gangs of white males attacked African Americans wherever they could find them in the downtown area and in nearby black neighborhoods.

Estimations of the number of blacks and whites killed and wounded in this riot vary widely among contemporary accounts, but the impact of this disturbance on black housing and business patterns was more clear. The riot hastened the city's move toward the economic exclusion and residential segregation of African Americans. Following the riot, African Americans were more likely to settle in established black communities, particularly those located on the eastern fringe of downtown or on the west side of the city near Atlanta University. And black businesses, which had once been interspersed among white commercial concerns on Peachtree Street, were now increasingly located to the east on Auburn Avenue, where a thriving but separate black business district soon developed.

Modest efforts to promote biracial understanding followed in the wake of the riot, culminating in the formation of the Commission on Interracial Cooperation in 1919. Overtures such as this, however, remained the exception in the 1920s and 1930s, as white supremacist organizations made their presence felt in the city. The Ku Klux Klan, reborn on nearby Stone Mountain in 1915, designated Atlanta as its headquarters (renaming it the "Imperial City of the Invisible Empire"). By 1923 the city's Nathan Bedford Forrest Klan No. 1 had a membership of over 15,000, including many notable local businessmen, educators, clergy, and politicians. In 1930, in the midst of growing unemployment, another white supremacist organization—the "Order of the Black Shirts"—surfaced in the city and pushed for the replacement of all black workers with unemployed whites. Although the Black Shirts' influence was short-lived, the organization nonetheless helped contribute to a restriction of the opportunities for African Americans during the years of the Great Depression.

Amazingly, in the midst of this repressive Jim Crow system, Atlanta's African Americans still managed to register some impressive gains. In 1921, for example, blacks used their ability to vote in city bond referendums and negotiations with the Commission on Interracial Cooperation to gain a commitment from the board of education to build the city's first black high school. The school was eventually constructed on the west side of town, where pioneer black businessman, banker, realtor, and builder Heman Perry was already developing new homes for Atlanta's blacks. Though Perry's overextended business empire collapsed later in the decade, his efforts on the west side helped pave the way for subsequent residential expansion in that area.

Ironically, the economic exclusion of Atlanta's African Americans from white business transactions also contributed to the growth of the city's middle class and the development of a black business and cultural mecca on Auburn Avenue that *Fortune* magazine would later describe as "the richest black street in the world." By 1920, Auburn Avenue was already home to a wide range of black-owned and -operated businesses, such as insurance companies, banks, a newspaper, barber and beauty shops, restaurants, grocery stores, photo studios, and funeral homes that provided African Americans the services denied them in the larger urban community. Freed from competition with white businessmen and assured the patronage of Atlanta's black community, many black entrepreneurs and their businesses prospered under Jim Crow.

By 1930, Jim Crow and the color line had been firmly established in the city. In the period from 1940 to 1960, however, black leaders began negotiating with city hall and white business leaders to weaken Jim Crow's hold. That city hall and the white business elite were even willing to discuss the issue with black leaders was a reflection of two important post–World War II developments: increased black voting strength and a rapidly deteriorating housing situation.

The repeal of the poll tax by the Georgia legislature in 1945 and the invalidation of the white primary by the state supreme court the following year removed two important barriers to black political participation, and Atlanta's black community responded in 1946 with a voter registration drive that added almost 18,000 new black voters to the city's rolls in only fifty-one days. Three years later, in an effort to coordinate and concentrate their newfound political strength, black Republicans and Democrats joined together to form the Atlanta Negro Voters League—a body which was soon openly courted by the mayor and by white candidates for office.

No race can prosper till it learns there is as much dignity in tilling a field as in writing a poem.

BOOKER T. WASHINGTON
SPEECH,
ATLANTA EXPOSITION,
SEPTEMBER 18, 1895

*A course on the
Bible taught by
Morehouse professor
George Kelsey
exposed Martin
Luther King, Jr., to
theological
scholarship.*

PAGE 401

This increased black voting power and the severe housing shortage facing black Atlantans brought city hall, black leaders, and the white business elite together in behind-the-scenes meetings to negotiate such issues as the range and location of black residential expansion, redevelopment of the central business district, and city plans for annexation and growth. Each side succeeded in taking something away from the table. Mayor William Hartsfield gained important black electoral support for the city's 1951 annexation of northside suburbs (which added an estimated 100,000 residents, most of them white, to the city's population). White business leaders solicited general support for urban renewal plans that would remove low-income blacks and whites from the fringe of the central business district. They also received assurances that black residential expansion would not proceed into northside Atlanta. Black leaders got land for expansion and the construction of new housing and commitments from the city to build additional low-income housing. They also got promises from Mayor Hartsfield for a gradual phase-out of Jim Crow and increased protection against white violence.

The concessions gained on black housing were important for African Americans of all income levels, as dwelling units in most of the city's black neighborhoods were overcrowded and in poor condition. As late as 1959, blacks made up over one-third of the city's total population, yet occupied only about 16 percent of the developed residential land. Not surprisingly, almost three-fourths of the dilapidated housing in the city was found in black communities.

Yet as important as these negotiated agreements were, they did little to break the rigid color line in Atlanta. Interstate highway construction and urban renewal programs in the 1950s and 1960s, for example, wiped out many inner city neighborhoods, displacing thousands of black residents who then relocated in nearby, already overcrowded, black communities. Similarly, while low-income public housing in Atlanta was increased during these decades, facilities remained strictly segregated and most new public housing was located in existing black residential areas. As a result, public housing tended not to disperse the black population throughout the metropolitan area but instead to confine it to existing areas of black residential concentration. Finally, although the 1951 annexation held certain benefits for Atlanta's black population, it also initially diluted black voting strength by adding thousands of white voters.

The peaceful biracial negotiations of this era contributed to Atlanta's emerging image as the most racially progressive city in the South. In 1961, this national reputation was further enhanced by the peaceful desegregation of four of the city's white high schools. Atlanta, ever mindful of the value of a good image, promoted itself during this decade as "the city too busy to hate."

Signs were already emerging, however, that suggested that the era of backstage biracial negotiations and gentlemen's agreements was fast coming to a close. Sit-ins in 1961 by black students to desegregate Atlanta's downtown restaurants threatened to upset relationships and alliances forged between black leaders and the white business elite and exposed generational cleavages within the black community. Martin Luther King, Jr., who had personally led one of the sit-in demonstrations, soon found himself in the unenviable position of mediating between the more radical college students and older black leaders like his father, "Daddy" King.

One year later, changes in black leadership and tactics became even more apparent in the response of African Americans to the so-called "Peyton Road barricades." In that year, as blacks moved into the new white-only subdivision in southwest Atlanta, the city responded much as it had in the past by erecting barriers to slow and contain further black expansion (in this instance, by putting up street barricades). The resulting uproar in the black community and the accompanying national press coverage embarrassed the city and forced city hall to recognize that the days of a tightly segregated housing market in Atlanta, kept in place by overt discrimination and racial barriers, was over. While segregation practices would continue in more discreet forms—through the use of real estate tactics like blockbusting, racial steering, and discriminatory loan and mortgage policies—the right of African Americans to housing on an equal opportunity basis was now officially acknowledged.

This acknowledgment and the accelerated movement of African Americans into formerly all-white communities in south and east Atlanta contributed to a dramatic outmigration of white Atlantans in the 1960s. During this decade, the city's white population declined by 60,000 while its black population increased by 70,000. The result, as documented in the 1970 census, was that Atlanta had a black majority for the first time in its history.

This dramatic population change was reflected in black political gains in the city's 1973 elections. Not only was the city council evenly divided be-

See also
Martin Luther King, Jr.

tween whites and blacks for the first time, but the school board now had a slim African-American majority and Maynard Jackson was elected the city's first black mayor. One hundred and twenty-five years of white rule in Atlanta had come to an end.

In the years following Jackson's 1973 victory, significant gains have been made in minority participation in city government and business. Andrew Young and, most recently, Bill Campbell have continued Atlanta's black mayoral presence, and efforts have been instituted to encourage the city's black and white business elite's involvement in city planning and development.

Atlanta's population base has also changed dramatically in the last few decades with the infusion of a growing cultural and ethnic diversity in what has traditionally been a biracial society. Both the city and the larger metropolitan area, however, retain a high degree of racial segregation as the city remains over two-thirds black while the surrounding suburbs are over two-thirds white. The

increasing suburbanization of new jobs and business growth (particularly on the north side) has also left Atlanta, like many other cities, with a declining economic base and decreased job opportunities for those other than white-collar workers.

The growing multicultural nature of Atlanta's population, the presence of internationally recognized business concerns (e.g., CNN and Coca-Cola) and the city's selection as the site for the 1996 Olympics underlie Atlanta's current claims to being "the next great international city." How well the city succeeds at this task may be determined by Atlanta's success in overcoming the racial divisions, both social and geographical, that have historically divided the city.

—JOSEPHINE ALLEN

ATTICA UPRISING

On September 13, 1971, after more than 1,200 black and Latino inmates seized control of Attica

RACIAL TENSIONS ESCALATE

Inmates lie on the ground while others are strip-searched after a 1971 uprising at the Attica State Prison. Many raised questions about the racial tensions that contributed to the rebellion and the severity of the suppression.
AP / WIDE WORLD PHOTOS

*Returning violence
for violence
multiplies violence,
adding deeper
darkness to a night
already devoid
of stars.*

Correctional Facility, a state prison in Attica, N.Y., 211 state troopers and corrections officers retook the prison, killing ten hostages and twenty-nine prisoners. Four days earlier, the inmates had taken over the prison, held thirty-nine hostages, and issued a series of demands, including a minimum wage for prison labor, more educational opportunities, religious freedom, better medical treatment, balanced diets, and complete amnesty for those involved in the uprising.

Since the 1950s, Attica's prison population had included a large number of black and Latino inmates. With the intensification of radical protest in the 1960s, there were also a substantial number of political prisoners, some of whom were members of the Black Panther Party and others adherents of the Nation of Islam. In addition, many black prisoners had been radicalized by the killing of Black Panther leader Fred Hampton by Chicago police in December 1969 and the death two years later in a California prison of George Jackson, a black activist who spent much of his life fighting injustice in the prison system.

At the same time, prison conditions had deteriorated substantially, and overcrowding was a chronic problem. Since the summer of 1971, prisoners at Attica had organized and demanded changes in prison conditions. In July the inmates sent a list of their grievances to the warden. When little came of their efforts to effect changes within the facility, tension rose. On September 9, after a minor scuffle the previous day between inmates and guards, Attica prisoners rebelled. The riot spread quickly as guards were taken hostage and the inmates gathered together in one yard.

Inmates asked for and received an outside committee of politicians, journalists, and activists to help negotiate their cause. The committee drafted a proposal that included most of the inmates' demands, but New York State Corrections Commissioner Russell C. Oswald refused to consider amnesty for the protesting prisoners. One of the corrective officers who had been injured during the takeover died during the negotiations; the inmates could have been charged with murder.

REVOLUTIONARY MARTYR

First to Die in Boston Massacre

Crispus Attucks (c. 1723–March 5, 1770), patriot. Crispus Attucks is acclaimed as the first martyr of the American Revolution. Although not much is known about Attucks's early life, he was a tall, muscular mulatto of African and Native Indian ancestry, and a slave of William Brown of Framingham, Mass., before he ran away in November 1750. Attucks worked on whaling ships operating out of various New England ports over the next two decades. On the night of March 5, 1770, he was a leader of a crowd of twenty to thirty laborers and sailors who confronted a group of British soldiers, whose presence in Boston was deeply resented. Brandishing a club, Attucks allegedly struck one of the grenadiers, prompting several soldiers to fire into the crowd. Attucks fell instantly, becoming the first of five to die in the so-called Boston Massacre. His body was carried in its coffin to Faneuil Hall, where it lay for three days before he and the other victims of the massacre were given a public funeral. Ten thousand people marched in their funeral cortege. During the officers' trial, John Adams, acting as their defense attorney, ascribed to Attucks, whom Adams claimed had "undertaken to be the hero of the night," chief blame for instigating the massacre. The soldiers were acquitted.

The Boston Massacre was used by Revolutionary-era patriots to heighten opposition to the British, and March 5 was commemorated in Boston until the 1840s. In 1858, as a reaction to the Supreme Court's Dred Scott Decision, African-American historian William Cooper Nell revived Crispus Attucks Day, and Boston's blacks celebrated it until 1870. By the middle of the nineteenth century, Attucks's name graced numerous African-American schools and other institutions. In 1888, Boston authorities erected a monument to him on Boston Common.

Throughout the twentieth century, black leaders called for a national holiday on March 5. In 1965, blacks in Newark, N.J., revived Crispus Attucks Day with annual parades, and in 1967 the Newark school system began school closings to observe the holiday. By the 1970s, a few cities were celebrating Crispus Attucks Day. However, the interest in Crispus Attucks Day waned as agitation grew for the creation of a holiday for the Rev. Dr. Martin Luther King, Jr.

—ROY E. FINKENBINE

See also
Black Panther Party
Nation of Islam

The inmates, aware of the potential consequences they faced, did not want to accept a compromise without amnesty. After four days of negotiations, Gov. Nelson Rockefeller, who had refused to go to the prison or speak with the inmates, authorized a raid.

During the raid on September 13, tear gas was dropped by helicopter into the prison yard and members of the National Guard fired indiscriminately into the smoke-filled area. When the smoke cleared, thirty-nine people had been shot—including ten hostages. Once the prisoners were in custody, corrective officers and National Guard members continued the pattern of brutal behavior. Inmates were verbally abused, threatened, and mercilessly beaten. Their watches, wedding rings, and glasses were smashed, and other personal belongings were burned. In one instance, prisoners were forced to run through a tunnel lined with rows of state troopers who beat them with nightsticks.

Shortly after the raid, state and prison officials disclaimed responsibility and blamed the prisoners, who had no firearms, for the deaths of the hostages. Yet within a few days it was apparent that all the hostages had been killed by the police during the assault. The district attorney launched an investigation of the rebellion and retaking of the prison, but state police refused to cooperate and intentionally covered up their actions by withholding or destroying evidence such as photographs, videotapes, and testimony. Subsequent inquiries charged that the district attorney's investigation, which resulted in indictments of 62 inmates and one officer, was one-sided. By 1976 most of the inmates had been acquitted, pardoned, or had their charges dismissed. Charges against the one trooper were also dismissed. Although officials were never brought to trial by the state, all official investigations concurred that there was undoubtedly an excessive use of force on the part of the troopers.

In 1974, 1,281 prisoners who participated in the rebellion filed a lawsuit to hold the troopers accountable for their use of excessive force, but the case was stalled with the mass pardonings and dismissals in 1976. After years of appeals and delays, inmates who sought to hold four supervisory officials liable for the use of unnecessary force and abuse by state troopers were granted another trial in 1991. The court decided the next year that the inmates had suffered "cruel and unusual punishment" and that the state had failed to provide adequate medical care. However, only a deputy warden was found liable in the final resolution of the suit. Subsequently, inmates appealed under federal civil rights law for monetary compensation for personal damages in a case that was still pending at the end of 1993.

Attica is indelibly etched into the collective memory of the African-American community and is a symbol for all Americans of the potential for brutality by state and law-enforcement authorities. The state response showed the willingness of officials to sacrifice the lives of their employees for the sake of political posturing in a conflict that could have ended peacefully. In addition, Attica exhibited the ways in which governments can rely on force to quell dissent or opposition and demonstrated the difficulty of seeing justice served when the victims are poor black and Latino prisoners.

—JEANNE THEOHARIS

It is compassion rather than the principle of justice which can guard us against being unjust to our fellow men.

ERIC HOFFER,
THE PASSIONATE STATE OF MIND, 1954

B

BAKER, ELLA J.

Ella J. Baker (December 13, 1903–December 13, 1986), activist. Ella J. Baker was a leading figure in the struggle of African Americans for equality. In the 1960s she was regarded as the godmother of the Civil Rights Movement, or, as one activist put it, "a Shining Black Beacon." Though she was not accorded recognition by the media, Baker was affiliated with all the major civil rights organizations of her time, and she worked closely with all the better-known leaders of the movement.

Ella Baker was the daughter of a waiter on the Norfolk-Washington ferry, and was a grade-school teacher and the granddaughter of slaves. From the extended family of aunts, uncles, and cousins who lived on land her grandfather had purchased from owners of the plantation on which they had worked as slaves, Baker acquired a sense of community, a profound sense of the need for sharing, and a sense of history and of the continuity of struggle. She also gained a fierce sense of independence and a belief in the necessity of rebellion, which guided her work for the rest of her life.

After leaving Shaw University in Raleigh, N.C., from which she graduated as valedictorian, Baker immersed herself in the cause of social justice. She moved to New York, where she continued her education on the streets of the city, attending all kinds of political meetings to absorb the intellectual atmosphere. In the 1930s, while earning her living working in restaurants and as a correspondent for several black newspapers, Baker helped to found the Young Negroes Cooperative League, of which she became executive director. She worked for the Works Project (originally Works Progress) Administration (WPA), teaching consumer and labor education. During the depression, Baker learned that, in her words, "a society could break down, a social order could break down, and the individual is the victim of the breakdown, rather than the cause of it."

In 1940, Baker accepted a position as field secretary at the National Association for the Advancement of Colored People (NAACP). She soon established regional leadership-training conferences with the slogan "Give light and the people will find a way." While a national officer, Baker traveled for several months a year throughout the country (concentrating on the segregated South), building NAACP membership and working with the local people who would become the sustaining forces of the Civil Rights Movement. Her organizing strategy was to stress local issues rather than national ones and to take the NAACP to people, wherever they were. She ventured into beer gardens and nightclubs where she would address crowds and secure memberships and campaign workers. Baker was named director of branches in 1943, but, frustrated by the top-down approach of the NAACP leadership, resigned in 1946. In this period she married a former classmate, Thomas Roberts, and took on the responsibility of raising her sister's daughter, Jacqueline.

From 1946 to 1957, while working in New York City for the New York Cancer Society and the New York Urban League, Baker participated in campaigns to desegregate New York City schools. She was a founder of In Friendship, a group organized to support school desegregation in the South; a member of the zoning subcommittee of the New York City Board of Education's committee on integration; and president and later education director of the New York City branch of the NAACP.

In 1957 Bayard Rustin and Stanley Levison, advisers to the Rev. Dr. Martin Luther King, Jr., asked her to return south to set up the office of the newly organized Southern Christian Leadership Conference (SCLC), headed by King, and to organize the Crusade for Citizenship, a voter-registration drive. Intending to stay six weeks, she remained with the SCLC for two years, serving variously as acting director, associate director, and executive director.

In 1960 Baker mobilized SCLC support for a meeting to bring together the student sit-in protest groups that had sprung up across the South. A battle for control of the sit-in movement ensued. Older civil rights organizations, particularly the SCLC, sought to make the new move-

See also
Civil Rights Movement
NAACP
Southern Christian
Leadership Conference

ment a youth arm of their own operations. Baker, however, advocated an independent role for the student activists.

Baker resigned from the SCLC in 1960 to accept a part-time position as human-relations consultant to the Young Women's Christian Association (YWCA), working with colleges across the South to further integration. In 1963 she joined the staff of the Southern Conference Educational Fund (SCEF), a regionwide interracial organization that put special emphasis on developing white support for racial justice. While affiliated with the YWCA and SCEF, Baker devoted much of her time to the fledgling Student Nonviolent Coordinating Committee (SNCC), in which she found the embodiment of her belief in a "group-centered leadership, rather than a leadership-centered group."

SNCC was for Baker the "new community" she had sought. Her work was an inspiration for other activist movements of the 1960s and '70s: the anti-Vietnam War movement and the feminist movement. But Baker's greatest contribution was her counseling of SNCC. During one crisis she pointed out that both direct action and voter registration would lead to the same result—confrontation and resolution. Her support of confrontation was at variance with the Kennedy administration's policy, which advocated a "cooling-off" period. Baker also counseled the young mavericks of SNCC to work with the more conservative southern ministers, who, she advised, had resources that could help them.

In 1964, SNCC was instrumental in organizing the Mississippi Freedom Democratic Party (MFDP), which sent its own delegation to Atlantic City to challenge the seating of the segregationist Mississippi delegation at the Democratic National Convention. Baker, in the new party's Washington headquarters and later in Atlantic City, orchestrated the MFDP's fight for the support of other state delegations in its claim to Mississippi's seats. This challenge eventually resulted in the adoption of new Democratic party rules that guaranteed the inclusion of blacks and women in future delegations.

After the convention, Baker moved back to New York, where she remained active in human-rights affairs. Throughout her life she had been a speaker at hundreds of Women's Day church meetings across the country, a participant in tenants' associations, a consultant to the wartime Office of Price Administration, an adviser to the Harlem Youth Council, a founder and administrator of the Fund for Education and Legal Defense. In her later years she worked with such varied groups as the Puerto Rican Solidarity Committee, the Episcopal Church Center, and the Third World Women's Coordinating Committee.

While never professing a political ideology, Baker consistently held views far to the left of the established civil rights leadership. She was never a member of a political party, but she did run for the New York City Council on the Liberal party ticket in 1951. She acted within the constraints of a radical critique of society and was drawn toward "radical" rather than "safe" solutions to societal problems. Her credo was "a life that is important is a life of service."

—JOANNE GRANT

BAKER, JOSEPHINE

Josephine Baker (June 6, 1906–April 14, 1975), entertainer. Josephine Baker was born in St. Louis, Mo., the daughter of Carrie McDonald, an unmarried domestic worker, and Eddie Carson, a jazz drummer. At age eight she was working as a domestic. At age eleven she survived the East St. Louis race riots in which thirty-nine blacks were killed. Before she was fourteen, Baker had run away from a sadistic employer, and married and discarded a husband, Willie Wells. "I was cold, and I danced to keep warm, that's my childhood," she said. After entertaining locally, she joined a traveling show called the Dixie Steppers, where she developed as a dancer and mime.

In 1920 she married a jockey named Willie Baker, but quickly left him to try out for the new black musical, Noble Sissle and composer Eubie Blake's path-breaking *Shuffle Along*. She was turned down as too young, too thin, and too dark. At sixteen she was hired as end girl in a *Shuffle Along* road show chorus line, where she captivated audiences with her mugging. Sissle and Blake wrote her into their next show, *Chocolate Dandies* (1924), and the next year, Caroline Dudley invited her to join a troupe of "authentic" Negro performers she was taking to Paris in *La Revue Nègre*.

Baker was an overnight sensation and became the rage of Paris, a phenomenon whose style and presence outweighed her talents, and a black exotic jungle Venus. Everyone danced her version of the Charleston and Black Bottom. Women copied her hairdo. Couturiers saw a new ideal in her body. She took a series of lovers, including Paul Colin, who immortalized her on posters, and

Georges Simenon, who worked as her secretary. In 1927 "La Bakair" opened at the *Folies Bergère* in her famous costume of a few rhinestoned bananas.

That same year she met the café-society habitué "Count" Pepito de Abatino (actually a Sicilian stonemason). He became her lover and manager, taught her how to dress and act, trained her voice and body, and sculpted a highly sophisticated and marketable star. They toured Europe and South America. In Vienna, Baker was preached against for being the "impure incarnation of sex." She provoked hostility fueled by economic frustration, moral indignation, xenophobia, and racism.

When she returned to France, Abatino had done what he had promised: turned the diamond-in-the-rough of 1925 into the polished gem of 1930. There followed a ten-year reign of Baker in the music halls of Paris. Henri Varna of the Casino de Paris added to her image a baby leopard in a $20,000 diamond necklace and the song which would become her signature "J'ai deux amours, mon pays et Paris." Her name was linked with several Frenchmen, including singer Jacques Pills, and in 1934 she made her best motion picture, *Zouzou,* costarring Jean Gabin, followed by *Princess Tam Tam* in 1935.

Baker returned to New York to play in the 1936 *Ziegfield Follies,* but the show was a fiasco. She learned America would neither welcome her nor look on her with color-blind eyes as France did. Abatino died of cancer before she returned to Paris. Baker married Jean Lion, a wealthy sugar

broker, in 1937, and divorced him fourteen months later. By 1939, Baker had become a French citizen. When the Nazis occupied France during World War II, Baker joined the Resistance, recruited by the head of French intelligence. For her activities in counterintelligence, Baker received the Croix de Guerre and the Légion d'Honneur. After operating between Marseilles and Lisbon under cover of a revival of her operetta *La Creole,* she was sent to Casablanca in January of 1940 to continue intelligence activities.

In 1941 Baker delivered a stillborn child, the father unknown. Complications from this birth endangered her life for more than nineteen months, and at one point her obituary was published. She recovered and spent the last years of the war driving an ambulance and entertaining Allied troops in North Africa. After the war, she married orchestra leader Jo Bouillon and adopted four children of different races that she called her "Rainbow Tribe." She turned her château, Les Milandes, into her idea of a multiracial community. In 1951, she attracted wide attention in the United States, and was honored by the NAACP, which organized a Josephine Baker Day in Harlem.

She continued to be an outspoken civil rights advocate, refusing to perform before segregated audiences in Las Vegas and Miami, and instigating a notorious *cause célèbre* by accusing the Stork Club of New York of discrimination. Her controversial image hurt her career, and the U.S. State Department hinted they might cancel her visa. Baker continued to tour outside America as her

STEPPING OUT

Josephine Baker (1906–1975) lit up the Paris stage with her flashy performance in all-black musical revues of the 1920s.
© LIDHOFF / RAPHO /
BLACK STAR

Rainbow Tribe grew to twelve. Between 1953 and 1963, she spent more than $1.5 million on Les Milandes, her financial affairs degenerated into chaos, her fees diminished, and she and Bouillon separated.

In 1963, Baker appeared at the March on Washington, and after performing in Denmark, had her first heart attack. In the spring of 1969, she declared bankruptcy and Les Milandes was seized. Baker accepted a villa in Monaco from Princess Grace, began a long series of farewell performances, and begged in the streets when she couldn't work. In 1975, she summoned all her resources and professionalism for a last farewell performance at the Olympia Theatre in Paris. Baker died two days into her performance run on April 14. Her televised state funeral at the Madeleine Church drew thousands of people and included a twenty-one-gun salute.

—BARBARA CHASE-RIBOUD

BALDWIN, JAMES

James Baldwin (August 2, 1924–November 30, 1987), author and civil rights activist. Born in New York City's Harlem in 1924, James Baldwin, who started out as a writer during the late 1940s rose to international fame after the publication of his most famous essay, *The Fire Next Time,* in 1963. However, nearly two decades before its publication, he had already captured the attention of an assortment of writers, literary critics, and intellectuals in the United States and abroad. Writing to Langston Hughes in 1948, Arna Bontemps commented on Baldwin's "The Harlem Ghetto," which was published in the February 1948 issue of *Commentary* magazine. Referring to "that remarkable piece by that 24–year-old colored kid," Bontemps wrote, "What a kid! He has zoomed high among our writers with his first effort." Thus, from the beginning of his professional career, Baldwin was highly regarded and began publishing in magazines and journals such as the *Nation,* the *New Leader, Commentary,* and *Partisan Review.*

Much of Baldwin's writing, both fiction and nonfiction, has been autobiographical. The story of John Grimes, the traumatized son of a tyrannical, fundamentalist father in *Go Tell It on the Mountain,* closely resembles Baldwin's own childhood. His celebrated essay "Notes of a Native Son" describes the writer's painful relationship with his stepfather. Born out of wedlock before his mother met and married David Baldwin,

young Jimmy never fully gained his stern patriarch's approval. Raised in a strict Pentecostal household, Jimmy became a preacher at age fourteen, and his sermons drew larger crowds than his father's. When Jimmy left the church three years later, the tension with his father was exacerbated, and, as "Notes of a Native Son" reveals, even the impending death of David Baldwin in 1943 did not reconcile their mutual disaffection. In various forms, the problems of father-son conflict, with all of its Old Testament connotations, became a central preoccupation of Baldwin's writing.

Baldwin's career, which can be divided into two phases—up to *The Fire Next Time* (1963) and after—gained momentum after the publication of what were to become two of his more controversial essays. In 1948 and 1949, respectively, he wrote "Everybody's Protest Novel" and "Many Thousands Gone," which were published in *Partisan Review.* These two essays served as a forum from which he made pronouncements about the limitations of the protest tradition in American literature. He scathingly criticized Harriet Beecher Stowe's *Uncle Tom's Cabin* and Richard Wright's *Native Son* for being firmly rooted in the protest tradition. Each writer failed, in Baldwin's judgment, because the "power of revelation . . . is the business of the novelist, that journey toward a more vast reality which must take precedence over all other claims." He abhorred the idea of the writer as a kind of "congressman," embracing Jamesian ideas about the art of fiction. The writer, as Baldwin envisioned himself during this early period, should self-consciously seek a distance between himself and his subject.

Baldwin's criticisms of *Native Son* and the protest novel tradition precipitated a rift with his mentor, Richard Wright. Ironically, Wright had supported Baldwin's candidacy for the Rosenwald Fellowship in 1948, which allowed Baldwin to move to Paris, where he completed his first novel, *Go Tell It on the Mountain* (1953). Baldwin explored his conflicted relationship with Wright in a series of moving essays, including "Alas, Poor Richard," published in *Nobody Knows My Name.*

Baldwin left Harlem for Paris when he was twenty-four. Although he spoke little French at the time, he purchased a one-way ticket and later achieved success and fame as an expatriate. Writing about race and sexuality (including homosexuality), he published twenty-two books, among them six novels, a collection of short stories, two plays, several collections of essays, a children's book, a movie scenario, and *Jimmy's Blues* (1985), a chapbook of poems. Starting with his controversial *Another Country* (1962), many of his books, including *The Fire Next Time* (1963), *If Beale Street Could Talk* (1974), and *Just Above My Head* (1979), were best-sellers. His play *Blues for Mr. Charlie* (1964) was produced on Broadway. And his scenario *One Day When I Was Lost: A Scenario Based on Alex Haley's "The Autobiography of Malcolm X"* was used by the movie director Spike Lee in the production of his feature film on Malcolm X.

Baldwin credits Bessie Smith as the source of inspiration for the completion of his first novel *Go Tell It on the Mountain* (1953). In "The Discovery of What It Means to Be an American," he writes about his experience of living and writing in Switzerland: "There, in that alabaster landscape, armed with two Bessie Smith records and a typewriter, I began to re-create the life that I had first known as a child and from which I had spent so many years in flight . . . Bessie Smith, through her tone and cadence . . . helped me dig back to the way I myself must have spoken when I was a pickaninny, and to remember the things I had heard and seen and felt. I had buried them very deep."

Go Tell It on the Mountain recaptures in some definitive ways the spirit and circumstances of Baldwin's own boyhood and adolescence. John Grimes, the shy and intelligent protagonist of the novel, is remarkably reminiscent of Baldwin. Moreover, Baldwin succeeds at creating a web of relationships that reveals how a particular character has arrived at his or her situation. He had, after all, harshly criticized Stowe and Wright for what he considered their rather stereotypical depiction of characters and their circumstances. His belief that "revelation" was the novelist's ultimate goal persisted throughout his career. In his second and third novels—*Giovanni's Room* (1956) and *Another Country* (1962)—he explores the theme of a varying, if consistent, American search for identity.

In *Giovanni's Room* the theme is complicated by international and sexual dimensions. The main character is forced to learn a harsh lesson about another culture and country as he wrestles with his ambivalent sexuality. Similarly, in *Another Country* Baldwin sensationally calls into question many American taboos about race, sexuality, marriage, and infidelity. By presenting a stunning series of relationships—heterosexual, homosexual, interracial, bisexual—he creates a *tableau vivant* of American mores. In his remaining novels, *Tell Me How Long the Train's Been Gone* (1968), *If Beale Street Could Talk* (1974), and *Just Above My*

Head (1979), he also focuses on issues related to race and sexuality. Furthermore, he tries to reveal how racism and sexism are inextricably linked to deep-seated American assumptions. In Baldwin's view, race and sex are hopelessly entangled in America's collective psyche.

Around the time of *The Fire Next Time*'s publication and after the Broadway production of *Blues for Mr. Charlie,* Baldwin became known as a spokesperson for civil rights and a celebrity noted for championing the cause of black Americans. He was a prominent participant in the March on Washington at which the Rev. Dr. Martin Luther King, Jr., gave his famous "I Have a Dream" speech. He frequently appeared on television and delivered speeches on college campuses. Baldwin actually published two excellent collections of essays—*Notes of a Native Son* (1955) and *Nobody Knows My Name* (1961)—before *The Fire Next Time.* In fact, various critics and reviewers already considered him in a class of his own. However, it was his exhortative rhetoric in the latter essay, published on the one hundredth anniversary of the Emancipation Proclamation, an essay that anticipated the urban riots of the 1960s, which landed him on the cover of *Time* magazine. He concluded: "If we—and now I mean the relatively conscious whites and the relatively conscious blacks who must, like lovers, insist on or create the consciousness of the others—do not falter in our duty now, we may be able . . . to end the racial nightmare, and achieve our country, and change the history of the world."

After the publication of *The Fire Next Time,* several black nationalists criticized Baldwin for his conciliatory attitude. They questioned whether his message of love and understanding would do much to change race relations in America. Eldridge Cleaver, in his book *Soul on Ice,* was one of Baldwin's more outspoken critics. But Baldwin continued writing, becoming increasingly more dependent on his early life as a source of inspiration, accepting eagerly the role of the writer as "poet" whose "assignment" was to accept the "energy" of the folk and transform it into art. It is as though he was following the wisdom of his own words in his story "Sonny's Blues." Like Sonny and his band, Baldwin saw clearly as he matured that he was telling a tale based on the blues of his own life as a writer and a man in America and abroad: "Creole began to tell us what the blues were all about. They were not about anything very new. He and his boys up there were keeping it new at the risk of ruin, destruction, madness, and death, in order to find new ways to

I am far from certain that being released from the African witch doctor was worthwhile if I am now . . . expected to become dependent on the American psychiatrist.

JAMES BALDWIN
THE FIRE NEXT TIME, 1963

make us listen. For, while the tale of how we suffer, and how we are delighted, and how we may triumph is never new, it always must be heard. There isn't any other tale to tell, it's the only light we've got in all this darkness."

Several of his essays and interviews of the 1980s discuss homosexuality and homophobia with fervor and forthrightness, most notably "Here Be Dragons." Thus, just as he had been the leading literary voice of the civil rights movement, he became an inspirational figure for the emerging gay rights movement. Baldwin's nonfiction was collected in *The Price of the Ticket* (1985).

During the final decade of his life, Baldwin taught at a number of American colleges and universities—including the University of Massachusetts at Amherst and Hampshire College—frequently commuting back and forth between the United States and his home in St. Paul de Vence in the south of France. After his death in France on November 30, 1987, the *New York Times* reported on its front page for the following day: "James Baldwin, Eloquent Essayist in Behalf of Civil Rights, Is Dead."

—HORACE PORTER

BALTIMORE, MARYLAND

When Baltimore was established as a town in 1729, many African Americans already lived in the area which, like most of Maryland, was rural. As the town grew during the eighteenth century, its African-American population increased gradually. Both slaves and free blacks worked as house servants, laborers, and craftsmen. Trades such as barbering, blacksmithing, and coach driving came to be almost exclusively black.

In Baltimore, as elsewhere, African Americans fought on both sides of the American Revolution. Before free blacks were allowed to enlist in the Maryland militia, 250 black men helped build the batteries and mount the guns around Whetstone Point, where Fort McHenry is now located, at the entrance to the port of Baltimore. Many enslaved blacks manumitted during the Revolutionary era settled in Baltimore. In 1789 a group of prominent Baltimoreans formed the Society for the Abolition of Slavery and the Relief of Poor Negroes and Others Unlawfully Held in Bondage. Although these abolitionists did not win a legal end to slavery, by 1810 free blacks, their numbers

augmented by free black and mulatto refugees from Haiti, outnumbered slaves in the city 3,973 to 3,713. The city's most notable abolitionist in the nineteenth century was Benjamin Lundy, editor of the journal the *Genius of Universal Emancipation.* The famous abolitionist leader William Lloyd Garrison began his antislavery career in Baltimore as one of Lundy's assistants.

The African-American experience in Baltimore during the antebellum era was unique. Although Maryland was a slave state, slavery declined rapidly in urban areas. By 1820 Baltimore had the largest free black population of any city in the antebellum United States. The first independent black institutions in Baltimore were churches. In the 1780s African-American religious congregations began to separate from white-controlled churches. As early as 1787, blacks left white Methodist congregations and formed the Baltimore African Church on Sharp Street. In 1793 an African School opened on Sharp Street with financial help from local Quakers. A few years later, operation of the school was taken over by the African-American congregation of the Sharp Street African Methodist Church. An outstanding preacher from Sharp Street, Daniel Coker, formed the African Bethel Church (later Bethel African Methodist Episcopal Church), became its first ordained Methodist preacher in 1811, and helped form the African Methodist Episcopal (AME) Conference in 1816.

Other congregations, Sunday schools, and day schools were set up during the ensuing years. In 1824 a group of free and enslaved blacks led by William Levington, an Episcopal priest from New York City, founded St. James Episcopal Church. The church building, finished in 1827, is a landmark which still stands in Lafayette Square in West Baltimore, though it was damaged in a major fire in 1994. In 1829, a group of black Catholics led by Elizabeth Lange, an educated Haitian mulatto who had opened a school for black children, founded the Oblate Sisters of Providence, the first black women's Catholic order, with the assistance of Sulpician priest Father Jacques Hector Nicholas Joubert. That same year, the Oblate nuns established on Richmond Street the first black girls' school in the United States, Saint Frances of Rome Academy. Another school, the William Watkins Academy for Negro Youth, operated until 1850, and boasted Baltimore native Frances E. Watkins Harper as its most distinguished graduate. In 1860 the Madison Avenue Presbyterian Church had Hiram Revels, later a senator, as its pastor, and Henry McNeal Turner, later an AME bishop, was a deacon at Bethel AME Church.

Slavery continued in Baltimore, though on a small scale, throughout the antebellum period. By 1860 there were 25,680 free blacks, and only 2,218 slaves. Most slave owners owned one or two slaves, who served as domestic servants. Other slaves, notably Frederick Douglass, who came to Baltimore in the late 1820s and worked as a caulker in the city's shipyards, were hired out or charged to find skilled or unskilled labor by their masters.

There was a clear social difference between slaves and free blacks, although free blacks suffered the same discrimination the slaves did. Blacks were excluded from the interior of streetcars (until 1871 they could only ride on the outside platforms), theaters, and schools in the city, and most housing was segregated. Their always precarious social position was increasingly attacked in the years before the Civil War. Maryland slave owners disliked the example of freedom Baltimore's black community offered their slaves. Also, the city's economy underwent several convulsions. Many white immigrants settled in Baltimore, so that despite African-American population growth, the percentage of blacks in the city fell from 22 percent in 1810 to 13 percent in 1860. Job competition between black laborers and immigrant white laborers was intense, and violent conflicts often ensued. Pro-Confederate sentiment ran high in the city. In March 1861, a white mob stoned Union troops.

Following the end of slavery in 1864, African-American progress was dramatic, despite continued discrimination. In 1865 the Frederick Douglass Institute, a cultural center created to "promote the intellectual advancement of the colored portion of the community," opened in a former war hospital on Lexington Avenue near Monument Square. The building contained a concert/meeting hall, dining room, and offices of an African-American newspaper, the *Communicator*. The institute, white-owned but black-managed, remained open until 1888. In 1867 Centenary Biblical Institute (later Morgan State University) opened, and in 1871 "colored" public schools opened for the first time. In 1900 a Colored Training School for teachers, later named in honor of Fannie Jackson Coppin, was established. In 1894 African-American doctors William T. Carr and John Marcus Cargill opened Provident Hospital. The city's small black aristocracy, led by such figures as Francis Cardozo, settled on Druid Hall in the city's northwest section. There they

built charitable organizations, fraternities such as the Baltimore Assembly, and literary societies such as the Monumental Literary and Scientific Association, founded in 1885. The great lasting legacy of late nineteenth-century black Baltimore is the Baltimore Afro-American newspaper, founded in 1892, the oldest major black journal still in publication. The era's most famous black Baltimorean was explorer Matthew Henson, codiscoverer of the North Pole.

In 1866, following a strike by white caulkers attempting to exclude blacks, black workers led by Isaac Myers organized a successful cooperative shipyard and labor union. Myers later helped establish entrepreneurial associations such as the Colored Business Men's Association of Baltimore and the Colored Building and Loan Association of Baltimore. In 1890 a black Republican lawyer, Harry Sythe Cummings, was elected to the city council, and five more blacks served on the council over the following fifty years.

Black political influence in the city waned after 1900, and conditions for blacks worsened. In 1904 railroads and ships (but not trolley cars) were segregated. Soon, further ordinances followed, as Baltimore's caste lines hardened and the city belatedly sought to imitate its southern counterparts. For a short time after 1912, the city mandated separate black and white city blocks. During the 1920s, epidemic tuberculosis was rampant in the black community.

However bleak the political situation, the cultural picture was impressive. Baltimore natives such as Eubie Blake had long played a part in black theater and music. During the 1920s and '30s, Pennsylvania Avenue in West Baltimore emerged as the center of local African-American business and social life. Baltimore native Cab Calloway and other important musicians were featured in clubs, while the city gave birth to performers such as Billie Holiday, Chick Webb, John Kirby, and Joe Turner.

In 1935 the Baltimore NAACP, largely dormant since its founding in 1913, was revived by Lillie Mae Carroll Jackson, who built it into the largest NAACP chapter outside New York City. During the 1930s the NAACP organized a "Don't Buy Where You Can't Work" campaign that opened up job opportunities for blacks throughout Baltimore; arranged the hiring of black police officers, though initially without uniforms or arrest powers; registered large numbers of new voters; and, with the aid of Baltimore-born NAACP counsel Thurgood Marshall, pushed successfully for equalization of black and white

The relation subsisting between the white and colored people of this country is the great, paramount, imperative and all-commanding question for this age and nation to solve.

FREDERICK DOUGLASS SPEECH, CHURCH OF THE PURITANS, NEW YORK CITY, MAY 1863

See also
Eubie Blake
Billie Holiday

Congress of Racial Equality activists played a pivotal role in many of the leading events of the Civil Rights Movement.

PAGE 155

teachers' salaries. Jackson's daughter, Juanita Jackson Mitchell, became the NAACP's national youth director, and went on to gain a law degree, becoming a prominent civil rights lawyer.

World War II brought 33,000 new black migrants to Baltimore in two years, sparking racial tension. In April 1942, after a white policeman shot an African American in the back, thousands marched on Baltimore in protest, and intensified political action. The city's bureau of the Fair Employment Practices Commission, administered by Baltimore native Clarence Mitchell, succeeded in ending discriminatory policies in many firms.

In 1943, with the aid of heavy support in black areas, liberal Republican Theodore McKeldin was elected mayor of Baltimore. During his two terms, McKeldin named blacks to health, education, and recreation boards, and hired large numbers of black police and nurses. The first victory over black exclusion from public facilities occurred in 1946, when Willie Adams, a millionaire gambler and liquor industry tycoon, led a successful protest over segregated city golf courses. However, while Ford's Theater and downtown department stores began admitting blacks in the early 1950s, most of the city remained segregated until 1954, when the Supreme Court's Brown v. Board of Education of Topeka, Kansas ruling led to the integration of public schools (Catholic schools also became integrated). Further integration was slow. In 1956 the city passed an equal employment ordinance but without enforcement powers. In early 1960, students from Morgan State began lunch counter sit-ins aimed at desegregating city facilities. However, city authorities did not pass a civil rights statute until 1962.

Baltimore's economy worsened during the 1960s. Police brutality was a chronic problem, and job and union discrimination remained rampant. In February 1966, black women staff of the city's Lincoln Nursing Home staged a walkout. With help from organizers from the Congress of Racial Equality, (CORE), they formed the Maryland Freedom Union (MFU) to bring civil rights tactics and consciousness to unions. The MFU, whose leaders and membership were largely black and female, organized low-wage nursing home, retail, and service workers. The MFU organized boycotts of retail stores in black neighborhoods and won contracts from three large retailers. Leaders also attempted, with less success, to organize food stores and hospitals. Eventually, faced by financial restraints and the hostility of mainstream organized labor, the MFU dissolved.

On April 6, 1968, following the assassination of the Rev. Dr. Martin Luther King, Jr., rioting erupted in Baltimore. Looting broke out on Gay Street, then spread as blacks started fires and broke windows. The next day, as rioting grew more intense, Maryland Governor Spiro Agnew declared the riot an insurrection and called in National Guard troops. Violence continued for two more days. Altogether there were six deaths, dozens of injuries, 5,512 arrests, and 1,208 major fires. On Wednesday, April 10, Agnew met with a hundred moderate black leaders, but instead of promising to deal with conditions causing the riot, he blamed the disturbance on black radicals and denounced the moderates as "cowards" for not opposing them. Most of the group walked out, and Agnew refused to listen to the remaining leaders. (Later invited to tour black ghetto areas, he replied, "if you've seen one slum, you've seen them all.") Agnew's uncompromising stance soon led to his nomination and subsequent election as vice president of the United States.

Since 1968 Baltimore has followed the pattern of many urban areas in the United States. During the mid-1970s, Baltimore became a black majority city. The city's economy has declined in the face of deindustrialization and middle-class migration to nearby suburbs. Unemployment and crime have been recurring problems. In 1992 a Maryland Commission report found that over half of Baltimore's black men between eighteen and thirty-five were in trouble with the law.

At the same time, blacks have established political control of the city. In 1970 in a close election, Parren Mitchell became Baltimore's first African-American congressman from a district that had a white majority at the time. After retiring in 1986, he was succeeded by Kweisi Mfume. In 1987 Kurt Schmoke, a former Rhodes scholar and state's attorney, became the city's first black mayor. Schmoke has adopted various reforms to deal with the housing, health and safety problems of the city's African Americans and has focused his attention on improving education. He increased school funding in the city's budget, and in cooperation with city businesses, he set up the Commonwealth Agreement and the College Bound Foundation, which guaranteed jobs or college educations to qualifying high school graduates. His slogan is "Baltimore: the city that reads." In 1990 he approved the creation of three experimental all-black, all-male public schools as a way of promoting racial consciousness and self-esteem. He has also gained national attention through his controversial advocacy of drug legalization.

See also
NAACP

In 1991 Baltimore became the home of the Great Blacks in Wax museum, the nation's first wax museum devoted to African Americans, a fitting tribute to the important place blacks have occupied in the city's history.

—SUZANNE ELLERY GREENE CHAPELLE

BANNEKER, BENJAMIN

Benjamin Banneker (November 9, 1731–October 9, 1806), amateur astronomer. Banneker was the first African-American man of science. He was born free in Baltimore County, Md., the son of a freed slave from Guinea named Robert, and of Mary Banneky, the daughter of a formerly indentured English servant named Molly Welsh and her husband Bannka, a freed slave who claimed to be the son of a Gold Coast tribal chieftain.

Raised with three sisters in a log house built by his father on his 100–acre farm near the banks of the Patapsco River, Banneker received no formal schooling except for several weeks' attendance at a nearby Quaker one-room schoolhouse. Taught to read and write from a Bible by his white grandmother, he became a voracious reader, borrowing books when he could. He was skillful in mathematics and enjoyed creating mathematical puzzles

**SELF-TAUGHT
SCIENTIST**

Astronomer and mathematician Benjamin Banneker (1731–1806) published an annual almanac from 1792 to 1797. The almanac was supported by abolitionist groups in Pennsylvania and Maryland.
UPI / BETTMANN

B

To be black and an intellectual in America is to live in a box. . . . On the box is a label, not of my own choosing.

STEPHEN CARTER
*REFLECTIONS OF AN
AFFIRMATIVE ACTION BABY,*
1992

and solving others presented to him. At about the age of twenty-two, he successfully constructed a wooden striking clock without ever having seen one. He approached the project as a mathematical problem, working out relationships between toothed wheels and gears, painstakingly carving each from seasoned wood with a pocketknife. The clock continued telling and striking the hours until his death. Banneker cultivated tobacco, first with his parents and then alone until about the age of fifty-nine, when rheumatism forced his retirement. He was virtually self-sufficient, growing vegetables and cultivating orchards and bees.

It was during his retirement that Banneker became interested in astronomy after witnessing a neighbor observing the stars with a telescope. With borrowed instruments and texts and without any assistance from others, Banneker taught himself sufficient mathematics and astronomy to make observations and to be able to calculate an ephemeris for an almanac. His efforts to sell his calculations for 1791 to a printer were not successful, but he continued his celestial studies nonetheless.

Banneker's opportunity to apply what he had learned came in February 1791, when President Washington commissioned the survey of an area ten miles square in Virginia and Maryland in which to establish the national capital. Unable on such short notice to find an assistant capable of using the sophisticated instruments required, the surveyor Andrew Ellicott selected Banneker to assist him until others became available. During the first three months of the survey, Banneker occupied the field observatory tent, maintaining and correcting the regulator clock each day, and each night making observations of the transit of stars with the zenith sector, recording his nightly observations for Ellicott's use on the next day's surveying. During his leisure, he completed calculations for an ephemeris for 1792. Banneker was employed on the survey site from early February until late April 1791, then returned to his home in Baltimore County. Recently discovered records of the survey state that he was paid $60 for his participation and the costs of his travel.

Shortly after his return home, Banneker sent a handwritten copy of his ephemeris for 1792 to Secretary of State Thomas Jefferson, because, he wrote, Jefferson was considered "measurably friendly and well disposed towards us," the African-American race, "who have long laboured under the abuse and censure of the world . . . have long been looked upon with an eye of contempt, and . . . have long been considered rather as brutish than human, and scarcely capable of mental endowments." He submitted his calculations as evidence to the contrary, and urged that Jefferson work toward bringing an end to slavery. Jefferson responded promptly: "No body wished more than I do to see such proofs as you exhibit, that nature has given to our black brethren, talents equal to those of other colors of men, and that the appearance of a want of them is owing merely to the degraded condition of their existence, both in Africa & America. . . . no body wishes more ardently to see a good system commenced for raising the condition of both their body & mind to what it ought to be, as fast as the imbecility of their present existence, and other circumstances which cannot be neglected, will admit." Jefferson sent Banneker's calculations to the Marquis de Condorcet, secretary of the French Academy of Sciences, with an enthusiastic cover letter. There was no reply from Condorcet because at the time of the letter's arrival he was in hiding for having opposed the monarchy and having supported a republican form of government. The two letters, that from Banneker to Jefferson and the statesman's reply, were published in a widely distributed pamphlet and in at least one periodical during the following year.

Banneker's ephemeris for 1792 was published by the Baltimore printer Goddard & Angell with the title *Benjamin Banneker's Pennsylvania, Delaware, Maryland and Virginia Almanack and Ephemeris for the Year of Our Lord 1792*. It was also sold by printers in Philadelphia and Alexandria, Va. He continued to calculate ephemerides that were published in almanacs bearing his name for the next five years. Promoted by the abolitionist societies of Pennsylvania and Maryland, Banneker's almanacs were published by several printers and sold widely in the United States and England. Twenty-eight separate editions of his almanacs are known. A recent computerized analysis of Banneker's published ephemerides and those calculated by several contemporaries for the same years, including those by William Waring and Andrew Ellicott, has revealed that Banneker's calculations consistently reflect a high degree of comparative accuracy. Although he continued calculating ephemerides through the year 1802, they remained unpublished.

Banneker died in his sleep following a morning walk on October 9, 1806, one month short of his seventy-fifth birthday. He was buried several days later in the family graveyard within sight of his house. As his body was being lowered into the grave, his house burst into flames, the cause un-

See also
Science

known, and all of its contents were destroyed. Fortunately, the books and table he had borrowed, his commonplace book, and the astronomical journal in which he had copied all of his ephemerides had been given to his neighbor immediately following his death, and have been preserved. Although he espoused no particular religion or creed, Banneker was a very religious man, attending services and meetings of various denominations held in the region, preferring those of the Society of Friends.

—SILVIO A. BEDINI

BANNISTER, EDWARD MITCHELL

Edward Mitchell Bannister (c. 1826–January 9, 1901), painter. Edward Mitchell Bannister was born sometime between 1826 and 1828 in St. Andrews, a small seaport in New Brunswick, Canada. His father Edward Bannister, probably a native of Barbados, died in 1832, and Edward and his younger brother William were raised by their mother, Hannah Alexander Bannister, a native of St. Andrews. Bannister's artistic talent was encouraged by his mother, and he won a local reputation for clever crayon portraits of family and schoolmates.

By 1850, Bannister had moved to Boston with the intention of becoming a painter, but because of his race he was unable to find an established artist who would accept him as a student. He worked at a variety of jobs to support himself, and by 1853 was a barber in the salon of the successful African-American businesswoman Madame Christiana Carteaux, whom he married in 1857.

Bannister continued to study and paint, and began winning recognition and patronage in the African-American community. In 1854 he received his first commission for an oil painting, from African-American physician John V. DeGrasse, entitled *The Ship Outward Bound* (present whereabouts unknown). By 1863 Bannister was featured in William Wells Brown's book celebrating the accomplishments of prominent African-Americans (Brown, 1863). His earliest extant portrait, *Prudence Nelson Bell* (1864), was commissioned by an African-American Boston family.

Bannister was active in the social and political life of Boston's African-American community. He belonged to the Crispus Attucks Choir and the Histrionic Club. His colleagues included such leading black abolitionists as William Cooper Nell, Charles Lenox Remond, Lewis Hayden, and John Sweat Rock. He was an officer in two African-American abolitionist organizations (the Colored Citizens of Boston and the Union Progressive Association), added his name to antislavery petitions, and served as a delegate to the New England Colored Citizens Conventions, in 1859 and 1865. In 1864, Bannister donated his portrait of the late Col. Robert Gould Shaw (whereabouts unknown) to be raffled at the Solders' Relief fair organized by his wife to assist the families of soldiers from the Massachusetts Fifty-fourth Colored Regiment.

Bannister is said to have spent a year in New York City in the early 1860s apprenticed to a Broadway photographer; he advertised himself as a photographer from 1863 to 1866. An 1864 photograph of Bannister's early patron Dr. DeGrasse survives from that period. Bannister continued to paint and win commissions, and although he listed himself in city directories as a portrait painter until 1874, works like his *Untitled* [Rhode Island Seascape] and *Dorchester, Massachusetts,* both painted c. 1856, document his beginning interest in interpreting the New England landscape.

In the mid-1860s Bannister began to receive greater recognition in the Boston arts community. Sometime between 1863 and 1865 he received his only formal training, studying in the life-drawing classes given by physician and artist William Rimmer at the Lowell Institute. Bannister took a studio in the Studio Building from 1863 to 1866, where he was exposed to William Morris Hunt's promotion of the French Barbizon painters, and his paintings began receiving favorable notices from Boston critics. His growing confidence as an artist is indicated in two tightly painted monumental treatments of farmers and animals in the landscape, *Herdsman with Cows* and *Untitled* [Man with Two Oxen], both completed in 1869.

Bannister was part of a community of African-American artists in Boston in the 1860s. Sculptor Edmonia Lewis had a studio just two doors from him in the Studio Building; portraitist William H. Simpson was a neighbor and fellow member of the Attucks Choir and the Histrionic Club; and the young painter Nelson Primus sought out Bannister when he moved to Boston in the mid-1860s.

In 1869, the Bannisters moved to Providence, R.I., where Bannister was immediately recognized by its growing art community. His first exhibit included *Newspaper Boy* (1869), one of the earliest depictions of working-class African

Abolitionists tested the openness of democratic politics to reform, and they agitated successfully for the extension of the nation's founding principles to groups who had formerly been left out.

PAGE 9

Americans by an African-American artist, and a portrait of abolitionist William Lloyd Garrison (whereabouts unknown).

Bannister came to national attention in 1876, when his four-by-five-foot painting *Under the Oaks* (whereabouts unknown) won a first prize medal at the Philadelphia Centennial Exposition. This bucolic view of sheep and cows under a stand of oaks received widespread critical acclaim. But Bannister later remembered how, when he stepped forward to confirm his award, he was "just another inquisitive colored man" to the hostile awards committee.

Recognition for *Under the Oaks* brought Bannister increasing stature and success. By 1878 he sat on the board of the newly created Rhode Island School of Design, and he and fellow artists Charles Walter Stetson and George Whitaker founded the influential Providence Art Club. From 1877 to 1898, Bannister's studio was in the Woods Building, along with artists John Arnold, James Lincoln, George Whitaker, Sidney Burleigh, and Charles Walter Stetson. His Saturday art classes were well attended, and he won silver medals at exhibitions of the Boston Charitable Mechanics Association in 1881 and 1884. He exhibited throughout his career at the Boston and Providence Art Clubs, and also in Hartford, Conn.; New York City; New Orleans; and Detroit. His work was much in demand by New England galleries and collectors, and in 1891 the Providence Art Club featured thirty-three of his works in a retrospective exhibition, to favorable reviews.

A number of Bannister's paintings (including *Woman Walking Down a Path,* 1882; *Pastoral Landscape,* 1881; *Road to a House with a Red Roof,* 1889; *Seaweed Gatherers,* 1898) reflect his strong affinity for the style and philosophy of Barbizon artists like Jean-François Millet and Camille Corot. But Bannister drew from numerous sources throughout his career, producing work in a variety of styles and moods, from serene vistas like his *Palmer River* (1885), to the Turner-influenced dramatic skies of *Sunset* (c. 1875–1880) and *Untitled* [Landscape with Man on Horse] (1884), to free and lushly rendered views of woodland scenery like *Untitled* [Trees and Shrubbery] (1877), in order to express what he described as "the infinite, subtle qualities of the spiritual idea, centering in all created things."

Remembered primarily as a landscape painter, Bannister's subjects also included classical literature (*Leucothea Rescuing Ulysses,* 1891), still life (*Untitled* [Floral Still Life], n.d.), and religion

(*Portrait of Saint Luke,* n.d.). His prolific output as a marine painter is represented by numerous drawings and watercolors, and paintings like *Ocean Cliffs* (1884), *Sabin Point, Narragansett Bay* (1885), and *Untitled* [Rhode Island Seascape] (1893).

As in Boston, Bannister associated with, and his work was collected by, leaders of Rhode Island's African-American community. Bannister and his wife continued their involvement in the concerns of their church and community. In 1890 Christiana Carteaux Bannister led the efforts of African Americans to establish a Home for Aged Colored Women in Providence, which is today known as the Bannister Nursing Care Center.

Although he had been experiencing heart trouble in his later years, Bannister continued to paint. Indeed, his late works (*Street Scene,* c. 1895; *The Old Home,* 1899; *Untitled* [Plow in the Field], 1897) reveal an openness to experimentation and growth, with an increasingly abstract consideration of form and color on canvas.

On January 9, 1901, Bannister collapsed at an evening prayer meeting at the Elmwood Street Baptist Church and died shortly thereafter. Held in great esteem by Providence artists and patrons, he was the subject of lengthy tributes and eulogies. In May 1901, his friends in the Art Club organized a memorial exhibition of over one hundred Bannister paintings loaned by local collectors. Later that year, Providence artists erected a stone monument on his grave in North Burial Ground. Christiana Carteaux Bannister died two years later.

—JUANITA MARIE HOLLAND

BAPTISTS

African-American Baptists are Christians who trace their common descent to Africa and share similar Biblical doctrines and congregational policy. They share these values with the broader American Baptist religious tradition. African-American Baptists represent the largest and most diverse group of the many African-American denominations in the United States. They are known for their emphasis on emotional preaching and worship, educational institutions, economic leadership in the community, and sociopolitical activism.

The origin of African-American Baptists must be understood in the context of the interracial religious experiences of colonial American history and the African roots of the spirituality of slaves.

White Baptists were initially slow in their evangelistic efforts among African slaves. Language barriers and economic considerations militated against the rapid evangelization of transplanted Africans. However, by the second half of the eighteenth century, a few persistent Baptist evangelists eluded these barriers and converted growing numbers of slaves.

Antebellum Baptists

The movement began largely on plantations in the South where the vast majority of African slaves resided, and it spread to urban areas. Generally, the conversion of slaves tended to follow the denominational lines of white masters. Hence, the numbers of African-American Baptists tended to grow along with the remarkable expansion of Baptists in the South between 1750 and 1850. On occasion, Baptist evangelists were invited by masters belonging to local Baptist congregations to preach to their plantation slaves. On other occasions, masters would allow slaves to accompany them to church or hold devotional services in their own "big houses."

There were scattered instances of African Americans holding membership in biracial churches during the late colonial period. As early as 1772, Robert Stevens and eighteen other African Americans held membership in the First Baptist Church of Providence, R.I. By 1772, the First Baptist Church of Boston was also receiving blacks into its membership. Very likely, the Baptist churches of the South had received some into their membership prior to the 1770s. As a result of interracial evangelizing between 1773 and 1775, David George organized the first black Baptist church in North America, at Silver Bluff, S.C., near Savannah, Ga. At any rate, this increasing tendency to receive slaves into the Baptist churches created the interracial Baptist church experience in colonial American society.

By the early national period, the presence of slaves exceeded the numbers of whites in a few churches in the South. Whether they were the majority or minority presence in these churches, African-American Baptists were still limited in their membership privileges and responsibilities. Slavery and racism prevented the existence of authentic fellowship based on Christian principles within these early churches. These social pressures later resulted in the demise of racially mixed churches and the emergence of Baptist churches organized along racial lines.

Slave preachers were the first to verbalize the need for churches separate from the white Baptists. Some of them had been previously exposed to leadership roles, having served as religious leaders in Africa. They wanted a style of Baptist life and witness that would permit the free expression of spirituality and the involvement of African-American preachers in pastoral leadership. The first movement toward separate black Baptist churches took place when African Americans stole off to the woods, canebrakes, and remote cabins to have preaching and prayer meetings of their own. These meetings were usually held early in the morning when the patrols over the slaves would retire from night duty to sleep during the day. Hence, early morning prayer meetings were created out of necessity.

Among the early African-American Baptist preachers who pioneered the plantation missions and the movement toward separate churches were "Uncle Jack," who went from plantation to plantation in Virginia in the last quarter of the eighteenth century, preaching to whites as well as African Americans; "Uncle Harry" Cowan, who labored extensively in North Carolina; and George Liele, who preached on the plantations of South Carolina and Georgia and actually paved the way for the planting of the first separate churches among African-American Christians. Liele's evangelistic ministry inspired the founding of the Silver Bluff Baptist Church in Aikens County, S.C., by David George in the late 1700s and of the First Colored Baptist Church of Savannah, Ga., by Andrew Bryan in the 1780s. There were other African-American preachers who labored on plantations for the evangelization of slaves and the subsequent separate Baptist church movement, but most of their names are now lost.

Within a decade after the founding of African-American Baptist churches in South Carolina and Georgia, slaves and free blacks in other parts of the country began similar movements away from white-dominated churches and toward the creation of their own churches. During the American Revolution, the African-American Baptists of Petersburg, Va., organized the Gilfield Baptist Church and the Harrison Street Baptist Church in Petersburg, and the first Baptist churches in both Williamsburg and Richmond, Va.

African-American Baptist churches were soon organized in the north. The Joy Street Baptist Church, originally called the African Meeting House, was constituted in Boston in 1805. The Abyssinian Baptist Church of New York City was organized in 1808, presumably by a group of

The first documented reports of distinctive black religious singing date from the beginning of the nineteenth century.

PAGE 657

59

CIVIL WAR ERA

A Period of Rapid Reorganization for Baptists

The Civil War era and Reconstruction gave impetus to the organization of several cooperative movement bodies. The Baptists of the West and Southwest met in St. Louis in 1864 and organized the Northwestern and Southern Baptist Conventions. In 1866, these two regional conventions met in a special session in Richmond, Va., and organized the Consolidated American Baptist Convention, representing 100,000 black baptists and two hundred ministers. The new convention was an attempt to promote unity and discourage sectionalism, and to create a national spirit of cooperation. The work of the Consolidated Convention was fostered by the formation of district auxiliary conventions, state conventions, and associations.

In 1873 the African-American Baptists of the West organized the General Association of the Western States and Territories; and in 1874 those in the East organized the New England Baptist Missionary Convention. These two bodies soon overshadowed the spirit of unity expressed in the Consolidated American Baptist Convention. A persistent spirit of independence and sectionalism on the part of both eastern and western Baptists caused the decline of the Consolidated Baptist Convention, and resulted in its termination at the last meeting in Lexington, Ky., in 1878. A vacuum in the cooperative missionary movement resulted.

In response, William W. Colley, a missionary to Africa appointed by the Foreign Mission Board of the Southern Baptist Convention, returned to the United States with a determination to revive a cooperative spirit among African-American Baptists. He led the way for the organization of the Baptist Foreign Mission Convention on November 24, 1880, in Montgomery, Ala. This convention effectively revived an expanding interest in the evangelization of Africa.

The next steps toward separate denominational development were with the organization of the American National Baptist Convention (1893) and the Tripartite Union (1894). These organizations merged to form the first real denomination among African-American Baptists with the founding of the National Baptist Convention (NBC) U.S.A. on September 28, 1895. For the first time, the combined ministries of the churches throughout the nation were fostered by a separate national organization of African-American Baptists.

—LEROY FITTS

traders who came to New York City from Ethiopia. These were followed by Concord Baptist Church of Brooklyn, N.Y. (May 18, 1847); the First African Baptist Church, Philadelphia, Pa. (June 19, 1809); the First African Baptist Church, Trenton, N.J. (1812); the Middlerun Baptist Church, Xenia, Ohio (1822); and the First Colored Peoples' Baptist Church of Baltimore (1836). This lists only some of the more important churches.

The roots of the Baptist cooperative movement go back to the antebellum period. In the early 1830s, organizational consciousness emerged among black Baptists in Ohio with the evolution of the associational movement. Baptists began to see the need for united Christian ministries among churches in near proximity. Hence, local churches began the formation of associations to advance such causes as education, home missions, and foreign missions. In 1834, they organized the Providence Baptist Association in Berlin Cross Roads, Ohio. This was followed by the founding of a politically oriented movement called the Union Anti-Slavery Baptist Association, also organized in Ohio in 1843. Slowly, the associational

movement spread to other states. The organization of Baptist state conventions began in North Carolina with the founding of the General State Convention in 1866.

The cooperative efforts of African-American Baptists were prompted by a growing consciousness of an interest in doing missionary work in Africa. Lott Carey and other pioneer African-American missionaries inspired early church leaders to seek even greater cooperation among their separate churches. As early as 1840, black Baptists of New England and the Middle Atlantic states met in New York's Abyssinian Baptist Church to organize the American Baptist Missionary Convention, their first cooperative movement beyond state lines.

Primitive Baptists

A number of African-American baptists were opposed to the organization of missionary associations, in part because the Arminianism of the mid-nineteenth century revivals was in conflict with traditional notions of predestination. The major outgrowth of the anti-mission movement was the rise of the African-American Primitive

See also

Civil Rights Movement

Baptists. Initially, Primitive Baptists inherited their anti-mission spirit from white Baptists. As early as 1820, the St. Barley Primitive Baptist Church of Huntsville, Ala. (originally organized as the Huntsville African Baptist Church), evolved as one of the earliest separate Primitive Baptist churches. Subsequently, a number of churches joined with them.

By 1907 these churches had gained sufficient strength to organize themselves into the National Primitive Baptist Convention. However, their rate of growth was far below that of the National Baptists. Still smaller in numbers and influence are the United American Freewill Baptists. Both the Primitive and Freewill Baptists constitute a minority presence among African-American Baptists.

The question of missions also played a major role in a split at the National Baptist Convention, U. S. A. In 1897 a controversy erupted in the annual session of the convention convening in Boston. The major issues in dispute were the financial administration of foreign mission programs and cooperation with white Baptists. The majority opinion favored the fiscal policy of the convention and the exclusive operation of the denomination independent of white Baptist influence.

However, a minority of delegates from Virginia, North Carolina, and several other Atlantic seaboard states, as well as Washington, D.C., decided to organize a separate missionary society that, with white support, was designed exclusively to advance a foreign mission enterprise. They met at the Baptist Church, in Washington, D.C., and organized the Lott Carey Baptist Foreign Mission Convention. These leaders adopted a constitutional provision requiring at least 75 percent of all funds collected by the convention to be sent to foreign missions.

The great cleavage within the National Baptist Convention, U.S.A., during its formative years came in 1915. All effort to maintain unity and harmony within the convention had previously posed vexing challenges to the officials. Unlike the crisis which led to the Lott Carey Convention movement, the crisis of 1915 was primarily a legal problem regarding the ownership and management of the National Baptist Publishing Board, headquartered in Nashville. Signs of dissent within the leadership of the convention were apparent for almost a decade before the actual separation of 1915.

The crisis came to a head during the annual session in Chicago. It took the form of a legal struggle between two groups: the majority, who supported convention control of the publishing board, and those who favored the independence of the publishing board as a separate corporate entity. The court decided in favor of the majority, and unity between the factions could not be restored. The result was the organization of a new denomination. The majority faction incorporated as the National Baptist Convention U.S.A., Inc.; the minority group met at the Salem Baptist Church and organized the National Baptist Convention of America, on September 9, 1915. It is now called the National Baptist Convention of America. Members of the publishing board played the key role in the development of the new denomination. Its policies are similar to those of the National Baptist Convention.

Progressive National Baptist Convention

The Progressive National Baptist Convention of America, Inc., organized in 1961, grew out of a major crisis within the National Baptist Convention, U.S.A., relating to the issues of tenure and civil rights strategies. Joseph H. Jackson, the president of the National Baptist Convention, was opposed to the civil rights agenda of the Southern Christian Leadership Council (SCLC) and related organizations. He was opposed by Gardner C. Taylor, pastor of Concord Baptist Church, Brooklyn, N.Y., and the Rev. Martin Luther King, Jr., president of the SCLC.

The initial struggle erupted in 1961 when Taylor challenged Jackson's bid for reelection to the presidency on the grounds that Jackson had exceeded the tenure requirement. The challenge was marked by violence, controversy, and a legal battle. The "Taylor team" was determined to defeat Jackson and plan a new course for the convention. However, Jackson's popularity prevailed in the vote on the floor of the convention and was upheld in the civil court. The Taylor team did not accept this defeat since they were determined to lead African-American Baptists in a new and progressive direction, especially in the area of civil rights.

On September 11, 1961, a national news release invited progressive-minded leaders to join forces with the Taylor team and organize a new denomination named the Progressive National Baptist Convention of America, Inc. The new denomination promoted the civil rights program of Martin Luther King, Jr., and launched a program of cooperation with the largely white American Baptist Churches, U.S.A. The new program was called the Fund of Renewal, designed to promote

The National Baptist Convention, USA, Inc., constitutes the largest body of organized African-American Christians in the world.

PAGE 493

See also
Martin Luther King, Jr.
National Baptist Convention

specialized mission projects. Moreover, this program also engendered a new spirit of cooperation between African-American and white Baptists.

Black Baptism was one of the anchors of the Civil Rights Movement, with Baptist ministers such as Vernon Johns, Benjamin Mays, Adam Clayton Powell, Jr., Martin Luther King, Jr., David Abernathy, and Gardner Taylor in the forefront of the struggle for black equality. The contribution of black Baptists to the Civil Rights Movement, and the inspiration that it has provided to both Americans and oppressed people elsewhere, will no doubt prove to be one of the greatest legacies of twentieth-century African-American Baptists.

The vast majority of African-American Baptists have been strong supporters of foreign missions. Early pioneers of the missionary enterprise, besides Lott Carey and George Liele, were Prince Williams and W. W. Colley. These men set the stage for an aggressive missionary program in India, Africa, Central America, and the West Indies. With the rise of foreign missions boards

among the denominations, African-American Baptists developed a sophisticated approach to the evangelization of non-Christians. They developed schools, hospitals, clinics, and agricultural projects, and they planted new churches in various parts of the world. The Lott Carey Baptist Foreign Mission Convention pioneered the movement to utilize indigenous people in leadership positions on the foreign fields, a movement that facilitated the philosophy of self-help and independence among peoples in developing nations. Many of the leaders within these nations came out of the missionary agencies.

One of the important changes in the black Baptist church in recent decades has been the changing status of women. Nannie Helen Burroughs (1883–1961), through her longtime leadership of the Women's Convention Auxiliary of the National Baptist Convention, was a dominant figure in twentieth-century African-American Baptist life. For the most part, however, women were not allowed until recently to be preachers or take active roles in church leadership. The Bap-

WOMEN BAPTISTS ORGANIZE

Nannie Burroughs, holding the banner, ensured an important role for women in the governance of the National Baptist Convention by founding an auxiliary called the Women's Convention.

PRINTS AND PHOTOGRAPHS DIVISION, LIBRARY OF CONGRESS

tists were slow to ordain women for the ministry; black women were not ordained until the 1970s and even then in small numbers. Nor have women been allowed until recently other positions of leadership within the church, such as deacon. The bias against promoting women to positions of prominence in the Baptist church is changing, although too slowly for many.

Education

The ministry of education of African-American Baptists has been in the forefront of the cooperative programs of associations, state conventions, and national conventions. The Civil War marked the beginning of strong cooperative strides among local churches to advance the intellectual development of blacks. Many churches served as schools during the week and houses of worship on Sundays. Moreover, local associations organized schools in many of the rural areas and small towns of the South. With the rise of public education, most of the associational secondary schools closed.

The development of higher education for African Americans, however, has been among the lasting contributions of African-American Baptists. The magnitude of the task prompted African-American Baptists to cooperate with whites in the development of schools of higher learning. This evolution may be classified into two groups: cooperative schools with whites and independent African-American schools. There are a number of Historically Black Colleges and Universities (HBCU) that were founded with Baptist support. These colleges, most of which were created in the South in the postbellum years, had two main purposes. Some of these schools were seminaries and helped train young men for the ministry. An even more pressing task in the minds of many of the college founders was to create a cadre of teachers that in turn could educate freedmen in primary schools. However, due to funding problems, many of the Baptist HBCUs functioned as little more than secondary schools in their early decades.

Many Baptist HBCUs were founded by whites, one of the driving forces being the American Baptist Home Mission Society (ABHMS). Wayland Seminary, the first seminary for black Baptists, later incorporated into Virginia Union University, opened in Washington, D.C., in 1865. Another root of the Virginia Union University was the Richmond Theological Center, founded in Richmond, Va., also in 1865. Other HBCUs founded by white Baptists include Shaw University (originally Raleigh Institute, 1865) in

Raleigh, N.C.; Morehouse College (originally Augusta Institute, 1867) in Atlanta, Ga.; Spelman College (originally Atlanta Baptist Female Seminary, 1881) in Atlanta; Benedict College in Columbia, S.C. (1870); Jackson State University (originally Natchez Seminary, 1877) in Jackson, Miss.; and Florida Memorial College (originally Florida Baptist Institute, 1879) in Miami, Fla.

Many of these schools represent substantial efforts by white Baptists in the intellectual development of African Americans. They financed, administered, and staffed most of these schools. Only gradually did African-American Baptists assume responsibility for directing the schools. A number of schools also were founded by African-American Baptists, but because of problems with funding, they had severe operating difficulties and had to close. The first independent African Baptist school of higher learning founded by black Baptists was Guadelupe College in Seguin, Tex. Others appeared in rapid succession: Houston College at Houston, Tex. (1885); Walker Baptist Institute, Augusta, Ga. (1888); and Friendship Baptist College in Rock Hill, S.C. (1891). Only Morris College in Sumter, S.C. (1908) remained open in the 1990s.

In the early twentieth century, Baltimore became a center of Baptist seminaries. The Colored Baptist Convention of Maryland organized Clayton-Williams Academy and Biblical Institute in 1901; the Maryland Baptist Missionary Convention organized Lee and Hayes University in 1914; the Independent Colored Baptist Convention organized Williams and Jones University in 1928; and the United Baptist Missionary Convention organized Maryland Baptist Center and School of Religion in 1942. These Baltimore schools were largely the result of convention rivalry and survived only a few years. In 1921 two other schools were organized: Central Baptist Theological Seminary at Topeka, Kan., and Northern Baptist University, Rahway, N.J. Both schools provided educated leadership for blacks, and many of the graduates have helped to advance the social, political, economic, and religious progress of African Americans. The Interdenominational Theological Center in Atlanta, Ga., was formed in 1958 by a merger of a number of African-American seminaries, including the former Morehouse School of Religion.

Music and Liturgy

From the beginning of separate religious services, African-American Baptists utilized music in their worship. This music was an expression of the deep

Body and soul, Black America reveals the extreme questions of contemporary life, questions of freedom and identity: How can I be who I am?

JUNE JORDAN
IN *EVERGREEN REVIEW*, 1969

See also
Baltimore
Education

sentiment of the people as they reacted to the severe oppression of life in America. It grew out of the secular songs of plantation slave-labor gangs. As slaves were converted to Christianity, they incorporated their new religious beliefs into the songs of the plantations. The result was Negro Spirituals. These songs played a major role in church life until the postbellum era, when Protestant hymns from the white religious experience began to become more important in church serv-

AMIRI BARAKA
Leader of the Black Arts Movement

Amiri Baraka (LeRoi Jones) (October 7, 1934–), poet, playwright. Amiri Baraka, born Everett LeRoi Jones in 1934, first gained fame as a poet and playwright in New York's Greenwich Village and subsequently became the most prominent and influential writer of the black arts movement. Throughout his career, Baraka has been a controversial figure, noted for his caustic wit and fiery polemics. In his poems, plays, and essays, Baraka has addressed painful issues, turning his frank commentary upon himself and the world regarding personal, social, and political relations. As a stylist, Baraka has been a major influence on African-American poetry and drama since 1960; and as a public figure, he has epitomized the politically engaged black writer.

Raised in Newark, N.J., Baraka attended Howard University and served briefly in the U.S. Air Force: an episode that his autobiography describes as "Error/Farce." As Baraka explains, his subscriptions to *Partisan Review* and other literary magazines led authorities to suspect him of communist affiliations, and he was "undesirably discharged." He subsequently moved to Greenwich Village, where he met and married another young writer, Hettie Cohen. They had two daughters, Kellie and Lisa. Baraka, known as LeRoi Jones in this period, gained notoriety in the Village literary scene, frequently publishing, reading, and socializing alongside Diane di Prima, Allen Ginsberg, Jack Kerouac, and other Beat movement figures. He and Cohen edited *Yugen,* an avant-garde literary magazine, and his book *Preface to a Twenty Volume Suicide Note* (1961) established him as a major voice among the new poets.

During this period he published his celebrated essay "Cuba Libre," a New Journalistic travelogue about visiting Cuba shortly after the revolution. This essay marked the beginning of his movement toward radical politics and away from his bohemian associates. His early political essays were eventually collected in *Home* (1966). Similarly, his book *Blues People* (1963) introduced his continuing interest in jazz as a key to African-American culture. Baraka's plays of this period, emotionally intense and quasi-

autobiographical, culminate with *Dutchman* (1964), an Obie winner that remains his most famous and admired work. *Dutchman* explores the manic tension and doomed attraction between a black man and a white woman riding in the New York subway. Like *The Slave* (1965) and his second volume of poems, *The Dead Lecturer* (1965), this work reflects the racial anxieties that would soon estrange him from his white wife and Village friends.

After the assassination of Malcolm X on February 21, 1965, LeRoi Jones abandoned his family, moved to Harlem, and changed his name to Imamu Amiri Baraka (Blessed Priest and Warrior). Entering a period of intense black cultural nationalism, he directed the Black Arts Repertory Theater and School in Harlem while continuing to publish prolifically throughout the late 1960s. His important books of this period include *Black Magic Poetry* (1969), *Four Black Revolutionary Plays* (1969), *Raise Race Rays Raze* (1971), and *Black Music* (1968). Many of these works attack whites and assail Negro false consciousness, advocating an authentic black identity as the prerequisite to political liberation.

In the 1970s, Baraka renounced cultural nationalism, dropped "Imamu" from his name, and embraced what he called "Marxism/Leninism/ Mao Tse Tung Thought." His subsequent writing has remained in a Marxist mode, but with a strong African-American and Third World orientation. Some of these later works lapse into schematically pedantic social commentaries and crude, unimaginative polemics. At his best, however, in long poems such as "In the Tradition" and "Wailers," Baraka demonstrates his continuing brilliance, combining music, sports, and political struggle into a densely realized vision of African-American culture as a triumphant, complexly expressive tradition.

The most comprehensive collection of Baraka's work is *The LeRoi Jones/Amiri Baraka Reader,* edited by William J. Harris. Baraka lives in Newark with his wife and collaborator, Amina, and is a professor of African Studies at SUNY-Stony Brook.

—DAVID LIONEL SMITH

See also

Literature

ices. Groups such as the Fisk Jubilee Singers (1871) sustained the spiritual tradition in the late nineteenth century. Their concert tours of Europe and America introduced concert spirituals to a new and highly receptive audience.

Gospel music has been one of the most important innovations in church services in the twentieth century. Thomas A. Dorsey, a pioneer gospel music composer, exponent, and instructor, was largely responsible for the introduction of gospel music in the worship of these churches. In 1932, the National Convention of Gospel Choirs was organized to promote the work of Dorsey in the churches. This organization encouraged the introduction of contests of choirs, quartets, and soloists in local churches. Two other major individuals contributed to the development of music in the religious experience of African Americans; James A. Cleveland, through his National Workshop Choir, and Glenn T. Settle, originator of Wings Over Jordan, a nationally acclaimed chorus. Subsequently, most of the performing artists in the broader culture received training, inspiration, and exposure from serving in local church choirs and choruses. Currently, many African-American Baptist churches are influenced by recording artists on popular gospel music radio stations.

Similarly, drama has played a role in the development of African-American Baptist churches. African-American preaching itself emerged as a unique art form. The dramatic presentation of the sermon was characteristic of these churches; preachers literally acted out the contents of their messages to their congregations. Moreover, these churches served as the central stage for dramatic presentations of other performing artists in talent shows, plays, and pageants. The recitation of religious poetry became a component of the artistic expression of church programs.

Painting has been less influential in African-American Baptist churches, which have tended to accept white expressions of religious art. However, the Black Power and Black Theology movements altered the art works in the churches. Currently, some churches, like New Shiloh Baptist Church of Baltimore, are developing Afrocentric murals of the Last Supper, the Crucifixion, and scenes from African-American life and culture.

Because of the inherent autonomy of African-American Baptists, there remains much variety in size, political involvement, and religious practice of independent congregations. Some of the larger urban churches, such as Shiloh Baptist Church in Washington, D.C., Mount Olivet in Chicago,

Concord Baptist Church in Brooklyn, and the Abyssinian Baptist Church in Harlem, have long been centers of community activity and have also served as political bases for their pastors. On the other hand, small rural Baptist churches, while their numbers have declined somewhat in recent years, remain the backbone of numerous communities.

Since the 1930s, and with even more emphasis since the '60s, many black Baptist pastors have emphasized the social aspects of their ministry, and have stressed social outreach, working with disaffected teenagers and prison populations and discouraging drug use. Baptism remains the largest denominational group among African Americans and continues to shape black cultural, political, and spiritual life in countless ways. In 1990 there were approximately twelve million African-American Baptists. Black Baptists will likely continue to endure and change in response to the myriad challenges of contemporary African-American life.

—LEROY FITTS

BASEBALL

African Americans have been involved in baseball, or "base ball" as it was first known, since its earliest days. Some enslaved blacks on southern plantations played baseball during their time off from work, and there were scattered African-American amateur baseball players in the Northeast in the years before the Civil War. Games were played in Brooklyn between the Colored Union Club and the Unknown Club in 1860 and also between the Unknown Club and the Monitors in 1862. By 1867, the Philadelphia Pythians, a well-known team that included among its members the abolitionist William Still, a participant in the Underground Railroad, encountered the first known example of racial exclusion of all-black organized ballclubs. In that year, the Pythians applied to join the National Association of Base Ball Players, whose nominating committee, wishing to avoid "political subjects" and "division of feeling," unanimously voted to exclude "any club which may be composed of one or more colored persons."

The National Association of Professional Baseball Players, formed in 1871, never formally banned black teams and players. However, both it and its successor, the National League, formed in 1876, adhered to a tacit prohibition. Nevertheless, several black teams, which played both each other and white teams, sprang up. As among the white

The 1920s were a crucial time in the development of gospel music.

PAGE 303

See also
Hank Aaron

B

BASEBALL

Early Professional Baseball

Jackie Robinson's assault on baseball's color line captured the imagination of both black and white Americans.

PAGE 603

clubs of the time, the membership of these early clubs was overwhelmingly middle class. In 1869, the Pythians played and defeated the white Philadelphia City Items in a series of games. The same year, the Brooklyn Uniques and the Philadelphia Excelsiors were matched up in what was billed as the "Championship of Colored Clubs." The Washington Alerts, a powerful club, had as secretary Charles E. Douglass, son of Frederick Douglass. Even in New Orleans, where thirteen black clubs played a tournament in 1875, there were interracial games. By the late 1870s, various blacks, including Oberlin's Fleet and Weldy Walker, Marietta College's John L. Harrison, and Dartmouth's Julius P. Haynes, joined white college teams. In the 1890s, James Francis Gregory played for Amherst, becoming team captain, and his brother Eugene pitched for Harvard.

Early Professional Baseball

Within organized baseball, the minor leagues did not originally exclude African Americans, and a total of seventy-three blacks competed in various leagues during the nineteenth century. Bud Fowler was probably the first black professional ballplayer. Born John Jackson in upstate New York in 1858, he grew up, like most baseball players of the day, in the North. Some sources say he was paid by a club in Springfield, Mass., in 1872. He pitched in semipro leagues, beating the National League's Boston Red Stockings in one game, then switched to the infield and played in several minor leagues. In 1884 he signed with Stillwater, Minn., of the Northwestern League, and during the following two years, he played for Keokuk and Topeka of the Western League. He was released after pressure from white players led to the exclusion of blacks from the league. According to *Sporting Life,* a magazine of the time, "[Fowler] is one of the best general players in the country, and if he had a white face would be playing with the best of them . . . the poor fellow's color is against him. With his splendid abilities he would long ago have been on some good club had his color been white instead of black. Those who know say there is no better second baseman in the country."

The first professional all-black teams were the Philadelphia Orions, founded in 1882, and the St. Louis Black Stockings, founded soon after, but the best was the Cuban Giants, founded in 1885 by Frank Thompson, headwaiter at Babylon, N.Y.'s Argyle Hotel. The club, composed originally of hotel staff, called itself "Cuban" to alleviate prejudice (which was often less pronounced in the case of dark-skinned foreigners) and "Giants" after New York's National League team. The nickname became a common one among black teams, with ball clubs such as the Philadelphia Giants, the (New York) Lincoln Giants, the Chicago Giants, and the Leland Giants springing up later. The Cuban Giants were owned by Walter Cook, a white man, and managed by an African American, S. K. Govern. Players earned wages of $48 to $72 per month depending on their position (pitchers and catchers made the most, infielders the least). These were good wages in comparison to what other black workers earned. The Cuban Giants played other black "nines," college squads, and even minor and major league clubs, although the American Association champion St. Louis Browns backed out of a scheduled contest in 1887. In 1889, the Cuban Giants and another black team, the New York Gothams, spent a season playing white teams as part of the Middle States League. In 1886, black promoters in Jacksonville, Fla., formed the six-team Southern League of Colored Baseballists, but it only lasted a few games. The nine-team League of Colored Baseball Clubs was organized one year later, and was recognized by the National Association as an organized baseball league, but it was disbanded after only one week.

In 1883, the Toledo, Ohio, team of the minor Northwestern League hired a catcher, Moses Fleetwood "Fleet" Walker. Walker, who was a minister's son from Steubenville, Ohio, and had attended college at Oberlin and Michigan, played well. Adrian "Cap" Anson, player-manager of the National League's Chicago White Stockings, one of the game's biggest stars, threatened to cancel a planned exhibition game with Toledo if Walker played. Toledo's manager, who had been planning to rest the injured Walker, responded by putting him in the lineup, and the game proceeded without incident. The next year, Toledo joined the American Association, a rival of the National League, and Fleet Walker became the first black major leaguer.

Walker had to face enormous obstacles. Pitcher Tony Mullane later admitted that Walker "was the best catcher I ever worked with, but I disliked a Negro and whenever I had to pitch to him I used anything I wanted without looking at his signals." In Richmond, Va., six fans (using pseudonyms) wrote a letter threatening him with a beating by a mob of seventy-five men if he played. Walker was not on the team by then, and the threat went unchallenged. In fifty-one games, Walker batted .263, and he was praised for his catching. At the end of the season, his brother, Weldy Walker, joined Toledo for five games. The team folded at the end of the season. The two Walkers were the only African-American players to reach the major leagues during the nineteenth century.

In 1885 Fleet Walker played for Cleveland in the Western League and then Waterbury in the Eastern League. In 1887 he joined Newark of the International League (IL), which was then, as it is today, one step below the majors. There were seven African Americans in the IL, playing on six of the league's ten teams. The most notable were pitcher George Stovey of Newark, who set an all-time IL record with 34 wins, and second baseman Frank Grant of Buffalo, considered the best black player of the nineteenth century, who batted .366 and led the league in doubles, triples, and home runs.

However, black players in the IL faced the same widespread abuse Fleet Walker had experienced from white players, both teammates and opposition players, who were racists or who feared the presence of blacks would lower the status of their occupation and lower salary levels. Blacks had balls thrown at them, and spikings on the field from fellow players were common. Grant allegedly developed wooden shin guards to protect his legs from injury by white baserunners. White teammates gave wrong advice to blacks and shunned them off the field. Some white players even refused to pose with black teammates for pictures. The derogatory public image of black players was reinforced by the media. Pictures in *Harper's Weekly* depicted them as lazy and stupid, and *The Official Baseball Record* referred to them as "coons." In July 1887, the league's team owners bowed to pressure from white players, and agreed not to sign additional black players. They limited the seven existing players to two per team. The seven players soon left to join all-black teams. Fleet Walker was the last IL holdout, playing through 1889.

In 1887, the same year the International League restricted blacks, "Cap" Anson refused to schedule a game with the Newark team of the International League if their star African-American pitcher, George Stovey, played. Unlike Toledo four years previously, Newark complied, benching Stovey. The black baseball historian Sol White, himself a former professional baseball player, wrote in his landmark *History of Colored Baseball* (1906) that Anson was primarily responsible for pushing blacks out of organized baseball. However, without minimizing Anson's role, it seems

clear that he reflected widespread white opinion. As *Sporting News* commented in 1889, "Race prejudice exists in professional baseball to a marked degree, and the unfortunate son of Africa who makes his living as a member of a team of white professionals has a rocky road to travel."

Only three blacks played on white teams in the 1890s, and after 1898 whites refused to compete against all-black teams. By the end of the nineteenth century blacks were also excluded from most other major sports, including horse racing and bicycling. A few blacks may have "passed" as white during the 1890s, and in 1901 Baltimore Orioles manager John McGraw tried to pass off African-American Charlie Grant as an Indian during preseason games. The ruse was discovered, however, and Grant was released. When the Cincinnati Reds signed two Cuban players in 1911, they pledged that the players were Caucasian and that they would take no blacks. In 1916 Jimmy Claxton, a pitcher of mixed black and Indian ancestry, played two games for the Oakland Oaks of the Pacific Coast League before being released.

Black Baseball in the Jim Crow Era

Baseball prospered among blacks throughout the era of segregation. Countless young African-American boys and girls played. Black leaders, including such disparate figures as activist Ida B. Wells and poet James Weldon Johnson, were baseball players or fans. Chicago established itself as a leading black baseball center with several fine teams. Numerous black army teams sprouted up, including the team from the all-black 25th Infantry, later famous for its involvement in the Brownsville incident of 1906, which beat all comers in competition in the Philippines. On the amateur level, black college teams had existed at Howard University and elsewhere since the 1860s. In the 1890s, Atlanta became a center of college baseball with competing teams from Atlanta Baptist Seminary (now Morehouse College), Atlanta University, Clark University, and Morris Brown College.

Outside organized baseball, there was still interracial competition all during the first half of the twentieth century. Major and minor league teams and various "barnstorming" squads (*see* below) played black teams—who more than held their own—in exhibition games. Black American players starred in interracial competition in Cuba and Mexico. The success of African Americans against white competition gave the lie to any claim that blacks were not good enough for the

A ball player's got to be kept hungry to become a big leaguer. That's why no boy from a rich family ever made the big leagues.

JOE DIMAGGIO
IN *THE NEW YORK TIMES*,
APRIL 30, 1961

See also
Jesse Owens

major leagues. Also, white colleges featured various black players, such as Paul Robeson at Rutgers from 1915 to 1918, and northern neighborhoods sometimes featured matches between black and white teams. The most genuinely integrated teams, ironically, may have been prison baseball teams such as those at New York's Sing Sing and at San Quentin in California, both of which had numerous black inmates competing alongside whites.

Once excluded from organized competition with white clubs, black teams made their money by what were called "barnstorming" tours, playing each other, or taking on local or semipro teams. The Cuban Giants were joined by such teams as Philadelphia's Cuban X Giants, the Philadelphia Hilldales, and the Columbia (Page Fence) Giants, which had been started by Bud Fowler and which paraded through towns on bicycles. In 1903, the Cuban X Giants played the Philadelphia Giants in a series dubbed "The Colored Championship of the World."

During the first twenty years of the twentieth century, a few standout baseball players made a reputation for themselves. John Henry Lloyd, shortstop for the Indianapolis ABC's, was dubbed "the Black Honus Wagner," and "Smokey Joe" Williams of the Lincoln Giants compiled a 6–4–2 record against white major leaguers in exhibition games, including a three-hit shutout against the National League champion Philadelphia Phillies in 1915.

During this period, there were two attempts to form leagues. In 1906 the International League of Independent Baseball Clubs, with four black and two white teams, was organized, but played just one season. The National Negro Baseball League, founded in 1910 by Chicago Giants owner Frank Leland, did not last long enough for a single game. In 1911 star pitcher Andrew "Rube" Foster, so named for having outpitched the New York Giant pitcher Rube Marquard in unofficial competition, took a white partner, baseball promoter John Schorling, and founded the powerful

**STAR-STUDDED
LINEUP**

*The Pittsburgh Crawfords
were the dominant Negro
National League baseball team
of the 1930s, producing five
Hall of Fame Members.*
PHOTOGRAPHS AND PRINTS
DIVISION, SCHOMBURG CEN-
TER FOR RESEARCH IN BLACK
CULTURE, THE NEW YORK
PUBLIC LIBRARY, ASTOR,
LENOX AND TILDEN
FOUNDATIONS

Chicago American Giants. Three years later, J. K. Wilkinson, a white man, put together a powerful All-Nations team, which included African Americans, whites, Latinos, and Native Americans. In 1920, Wilkinson combined players from the All-Nations team with members of the black 25th Infantry Squad Army team to form the Kansas City Monarchs, one of the most important black teams.

The Negro Leagues

The first Negro National League (NNL), officially named the National Association of Professional Baseball Clubs, was founded in Kansas City in 1920. The guiding force behind it was Rube Foster, who had built his Chicago American Giants into a strong, financially successful team. Foster's organizational genius and astute understanding of the promotional possibilities inherent in league play, plus his desire to wrest economic power and leadership over black baseball from white booking agents, led him to put together the first lasting Negro league.

The league was composed of six teams located in midwestern cities with significant black populations. It was originally designed to be entirely black-owned, but the popular appeal of Wilkinson's Kansas City Monarchs led Foster, after much thought, to agree to their inclusion. The new league was an almost immediate success, with outfielders like Oscar Charleston of Indianapolis ("the Black Babe Ruth") and John Lloyd, who joined several teams; or pitchers like "Smokey Joe" Williams and Wilbur "Bullet" Rogan of the Kansas City Monarchs.

The Negro National League was challenged in 1923 by the white booking agent Nat Strong, who created the Eastern Colored League with six teams, four white-owned, in eastern cities. After a period of mutual bad feeling and raids on each other's players, the two leagues observed a truce and organized a structure similar to that of white leagues, with champions of the two leagues competing in a black World Series. However, since ballclubs sometimes preferred lucrative barnstorming exhibitions to scheduled league games, teams played uneven numbers of games, so league standings were hard to determine. There was a third league, the short-lived Southern Negro League, created around the same time, but it could not compete financially with the other leagues and it remained independent. A few independent teams, notably Pittsburgh's Homestead Grays, refused to join the Negro Leagues but played exhibition games with league teams. The Eastern Colored League folded in 1928, and some teams were absorbed into the NNL.

The Great Depression took a heavy toll on black baseball. The NNL, already weakened by Rube Foster's 1926 breakdown and his subsequent death in 1930, was unable to meet its debts and folded in 1931. During the following two years, teams disbanded or survived precariously as local semipro or touring barnstorming teams depended on white bookers for survival. Some players went to play in the Caribbean or Mexico.

In 1933, the Negro National League, containing six teams (later eight), was reformed under the guidance of Gus Greenlee. Greenlee was a prosperous "numbers" king in Pittsburgh who sought a legitimate outlet for his money. He organized the Pittsburgh Crawfords. Other black businessmen—including several gangsters—followed suit in putting together teams, and the league was recreated. The new NNL played two half-seasons. The winners of each portion met in the World Series. The Pittsburgh Crawfords were the dominant team in the early to mid 1930s, as the free-spending Gus Greenlee recruited LeRoy "Satchel" Paige, Josh Gibson, Oscar Charleston, James "Cool Papa" Bell, and Judy Johnson, all future Hall-of-Famers, to play on his team, but other clubs eventually evened the balance of power within the leagues. In 1937, the six-team Negro American League (NAL) was organized. This league was mainly white-owned and included the Kansas City Monarchs, who had previously declined to join the revamped NNL. The NNL now concentrated on eastern teams, while the NAL held western franchises. The two league champions met each other in the Colored World Series, either in September or October. However, the biggest event in black baseball was not the World Series but the East-West game, played in Chicago. Greenlee introduced the idea. In 1933 (the same year the first Major League All-Star Game was played, also in Chicago), a squad of the best players from the eastern teams met their western counterparts. The games, played yearly until 1950, routinely attracted crowds of 30,000 to 40,000. This showcase event was covered nationally in the increasingly important black press and became a national social event of significance in black America. Indeed, newspapers such as the the *Chicago Defender* and the *Pittsburgh Courier* had large national circulations in part because they were the only source of regular black baseball information.

The Negro League season began in the southern states in February with spring training. After

Jackie Robinson became a leading symbol and spokesperson of the postwar integration crusade, both within baseball and in broader society.

PAGE 603

See also
Washington, D.C.

69

a few days the teams began barnstorming, working their way north. The exhibition games not only furthered team development and strategy, but were also a necessary source of revenue, and helped cement the relationship between players and the local black populations. In April or May the teams arrived in their home cities and commenced league play, although they continued to play exhibitions throughout the season, sometimes playing three or four games per day. When the season ended in September, or after the Colored World Series, the better players went on to play in winter leagues in Mexico, Cuba, the Dominican Republic, and California.

As with the first NNL, the constant exhibition games played havoc with League schedules and standings. Because the big city black population could not sustain a major league schedule of 154 games, and because the white stadiums most teams rented when major or minor league teams were away were unavailable at times, the teams traveled much more than comparable white teams. Players normally traveled by bus, or in several cars, over bad rural roads. A few black teams

"SATCHEL" PAIGE
Independent Baseball's Premier Attraction

Leroy Robert "Satchel" Paige (July 7, 1906–June 8, 1982). By far the best known of those who played baseball in the relative obscurity of the Negro Leagues, pitcher and coach Satchel Paige became a legendary figure from Canada to the Caribbean basin. Born in a shotgun house (a railroad flat) in Mobile, Ala., to John Paige, a gardener, and Lulu Paige, a washerwoman, he combined athletic prowess and exceptional durability with a flair for showmanship. In 1971, the Baseball Hall of Fame made Paige—Negro League ball incarnate—its first-ever selection from the (by then defunct) institution.

Paige gained his nickname as a boy by carrying satchels from the Mobile train station. Sent to the Mount Meigs, Ala., reform school at age twelve for stealing a few toy rings from a store, he developed as a pitcher during his five years there. After joining the semipro Mobile Tigers in 1924, he pitched for a number of Negro League, white independent, and Caribbean teams until he joined the Cleveland Indians as a forty-two-year-old rookie in 1948. The first African-American pitcher in the American League, Paige achieved a 6–1 record that helped the Indians to the league pennant. His first three starts drew over 200,000 fans.

But it was in the Negro Leagues and Caribbean winter ball that Paige attained his status as independent baseball's premier attraction. During the 1920s and 1930s, he starred for the Birmingham Black Barons and the Pittsburgh Crawfords, where he teamed up with catcher Josh Gibson to form what was possibly baseball's greatest all-time battery. Between 1939 and 1947, Paige anchored the strong Kansas Monarchs staff, winning three of the Monarchs' four victories over the Homestead Grays in the 1942 Negro League World Series. Developing a reputation as a contract jumper, he led Ciudad Trujillo to the 1937 summer championship of the Dominican Republic and later pitched in Mexico, Cuba, and Venezuela.

Playing before an estimated 10 million fans in the United States, Canada, and the Caribbean, the "have arm—will pitch" Paige, according to his own estimates, threw 55 no-hitters and won over 2,000 of the 2,500 games in which he pitched.

The 6'3½" 180-pound Paige dazzled fans with his overpowering fastball (called the "bee ball"—you could hear it buzz, but you couldn't see it), his hesitation pitch, and unerring control. Stories of him intentionally walking the bases full of barnstorming white all-stars, telling his fielders to sit down, and then striking out the side became part of a shared black mythology. "I just could pitch!" he said in 1981. "The Master just gave me an arm. . . . You couldn't hardly beat me. . . . I wouldn't get tired 'cause I practiced every day. I had the suit on every day, pretty near 365 days out of the year."

Probably the most widely seen player ever (in person), Paige was a regular at the East-West Classic (the Negro League all-star game), and also appeared on the 1952 American League all-star squad. His 28 wins and 31 losses, 476 innings pitched, 3.29 earned run average in the majors represented only the penultimate chapter of a professional pitching career that spanned five decades.

Paige ended his working life as he began it, on the bus of a barnstorming black club, appearing for the Indianapolis Clowns in 1967. In 1971, after the Hall of Fame belatedly began to induct Negro Leaguers, he led the way. As his Pittsburgh Crawfords teammate Jimmie Crutchfield put it, when Paige appeared on the field "it was like the sun coming out from behind a cloud."

—ROB RUCK

See also
Jim Crow

had their own ballparks. Around 1932, the Kansas City Monarchs became one of the first teams to use portable lights for night baseball. Night games eased schedule conflicts with white teams, few of which had lights in their ballparks, and had a larger potential black worker audience than day games.

League play was exciting. While there were power hitters, the greatest being Josh Gibson of the Pittsburgh Crawfords and Homestead Grays, runs were scored slowly and games depended, more than in white leagues, on pitching, defense, and speed. Pitchers, the most famous being LeRoy "Satchel" Paige of the Kansas City Monarchs and other teams, worked frequently and were reliant not only on speed but on trick pitches to beat opposing teams. There was little money for equipment, so scuffed and loaded balls remained in play. The spitball and similar pitches, which had been banned in the major leagues in 1920, remained legal in the Negro Leagues. Running was also emphasized in Negro League play, and bunts, stolen bases, and hit-and-run plays were common strategies.

Another difference between white and black baseball was the amount of showmanship involved. Black baseball players were particularly conscious of their role as entertainers. Batters might begin their at-bat with their back to home plate, and then turn around to hit the ball. Pitchers such as Satchel Paige would call in the outfielders, and proceed to strike out the other side. Paige, in fact, was so popular and renowned for his exploits that his home club, the Kansas City Monarchs, raised revenue by loaning Paige out to minor league or semipro teams. The Indianapolis Clowns (previously the Ethiopian Clowns), an independent black team whose players clowned and pulled trick plays in the manner of basketball's Harlem Globetrotters, were such a financial attraction that despite their unserious reputation, they were invited to join the Negro American League in 1938.

Negro League baseball, in economic terms, was one of the most successful black businesses of the Jim Crow era. Not only were the leagues themselves profitable, but they also boosted related black-owned enterprises. As a cultural institution, Negro League baseball was ubiquitous throughout black America. The games provided an important source of recreation and local pride, and were choice social events. The barnstorming tradition meant that teams played wherever there was a sizeable black population, and indeed in many places, such as in the Dakotas or the Canadian prairie provinces, the local populace's only contact with blacks was via the black teams that came to town every summer.

Despite the hard life and the rigorous travel and play schedules players underwent, the leagues had a certain glamour. The players themselves were popular heroes of the first magnitude in the black communities of the North. They were acknowledged stars, of particular importance because of their victories over white players in exhibition games. They were also a particularly cosmopolitan group, akin to other black entertainers of the period. They were equally at home in the small-town rural world of the Deep South, staying in homes of local community members when they visited southern towns, and in the big cities of the North with their vibrant social and cultural life. Also, the many darker-skinned Latinos, such as Martin Dihigo and Luis Tiant, Sr., who played in the leagues gave them an international flavor, buttressed by the sojourns of Negro League stars in Latin America, where they mingled freely with the political and economic leadership of the countries like other celebrities.

The integration of organized baseball, beginning with Jackie Robinson in 1946, plus the coming of televised games, spelled the end of the Negro Leagues. Black fans made it clear that they preferred seeing their heroes compete in the newly integrated major leagues rather than in all-black leagues. As early as 1947, the Negro League teams on the eastern seaboard ("Jackie Robinson country") suffered severe financial losses as black fans deserted the Negro National League. The last East-West classic was played in 1950, and the NNL folded after the next season. The Negro American League, whose franchises tended to be in midwestern states, further from major league franchises, continued to play on a reduced level. In a move to increase attention, in 1953 the NAL's Indianapolis Clowns signed a woman, Toni Stone, who played 50 games at second base and hit .253. During the 1950s, major league teams moved west and NAL teams could not compete financially for talented players. The NAL folded in 1960, and the Indianapolis Clowns returned to their independent status, touring small towns and playing semipro teams through the 1980s.

During the 1970s, African American and white interest in the Negro Leagues was awakened, partly by the book and documentary film *Only the Ball Was White* (1969). The Baseball Hall of Fame created a Negro League Committee, and 11 players out of an estimated 2,600 who played

In 1957, Hank Aaron was named the Negro League's most valuable player.

PAGE I

Whoever wants to know the heart and mind of America had better learn baseball, the rules and realities of the game.

JACQUES BARZUN
QUOTED IN MICHAEL NOVAK,
THE JOY OF SPORTS, 1976

In 1965, African-American players staged a walkout at an American Football League All-Star game in New Orleans to protest racial discrimination in the city.

PAGE 513

During the 1920s and 1930s, Washington, D.C. had several sandlot baseball teams, as well as Negro League clubs such as the Washington Elite Giants.

PAGE 726

in the Negro Leagues were inducted at this time for their league efforts: Rube Foster, Satchel Paige, Josh Gibson, Cool Papa Bell, Judy Johnson, Buck Leonard, Oscar Charleston, Monte Irvin, Martin Dihigo, Ray Dandridge, and John Henry Lloyd. In 1990, the Negro League Baseball Museum was created in Kansas City, Mo., and the Negro Leagues Players Association was established in New York.

Integration

Little serious effort was made to integrate the major leagues until the postwar 1940s, despite the acknowledged skill of blacks in the Negro Leagues who performed at a high level against touring major leaguers. Baseball Commissioner Judge Kenesaw Mountain Landis, a midwesterner who served from 1920 to 1944, was a firm opponent of integration, although he disingenuously maintained that there was no rule against blacks in organized baseball. In 1943, at the annual baseball meetings, African Americans led by Paul Robeson were granted the opportunity to speak to owners about integration, but Landis was unmoved. The same year, entrepreneur Bill Veeck sought to purchase the Philadelphia Phillies, but Landis blocked the sale when he learned of Veeck's plans to stock the club with black players.

Baseball's owners accepted and rationalized the situation. Critics of integration claimed that fans would lose interest in the game, that black players would be opposed by their colleagues (while some players were racists, a poll of major leaguers in the late 1930s indicated that 80 percent did not object to integration), and that severe social problems would emerge, especially during spring training in the South. Larry MacPhail, president of the Brooklyn Dodgers, claimed in 1943 that integration would kill off the Negro Leagues. This assertion was challenged by white Newark Eagles owner Effa Manley, the only female owner in the Negro Leagues, but many Negro League owners opposed integration, fearing rightly that it would destroy their business.

The movement for integration was promoted in the 1930s by white journalists Westbrook Pegler, Jimmy Powers, and Shirley Povich, who recognized black talent in baseball and the accomplishments of other black sportsmen such as Joe Louis and Jesse Owens. Their black colleagues, including Wendell Smith of the *Pittsburgh Courier,* Sam Lacy of the *Baltimore Afro-American,* and Joe Bostic of the *People's Voice* (Harlem) campaigned for integration. Communists such as Lester Rodney, the white sports editor of the

Daily Worker, also played a role in publicizing the issue. They demanded tryouts for Negro Leaguers, collected petitions, and picketed ballparks. On opening day in 1945, one banner outside Yankee Stadium read, "If We Can Stop Bullets, Why Not Balls?" The demonstrations led to several tryouts for black players but no jobs.

Ultimately, World War II tipped the balance, causing Americans to reevaluate the meaning of democracy. It was difficult to fight for freedom overseas while neglecting it at home. Furthermore, when the major leagues, faced by a shortage of players, admitted players who would not normally be given a chance to compete, such as teenagers and handicapped players like one-armed Pete Gray, the exclusion of blacks seemed more glaring. Judge Landis's death in December 1944 removed an important obstacle to integration. The new commissioner, former Kentucky governor and senator Albert "Happy" Chandler, was subjected to pressure for integration from labor unions, civil rights leaders, and politicians.

In the summer of 1945, the crucial first step was taken by Branch Rickey, president of the Brooklyn Dodgers. He secretly investigated Negro League talent under the guise of scouting for a new Brooklyn Brown Dodgers Negro League team. Rickey knew that the first African American in the majors had to be an excellent all-around athlete who could maintain a high level of performance despite certain abuse and pressure, and decided that the best candidate was Jackie Robinson of the Kansas City Monarchs, a good player though hardly the best in the league. Robinson had grown up in an interracial community in California, had been an outstanding all-around athlete and a good student at UCLA, had been a noncommissioned officer in the Army, and was married. After a stressful interview with Rickey, in which he promised not to challenge racist attacks, Robinson was signed on October 33, 1945. Rickey's action was unanimously opposed by other club owners.

In 1946, Robinson played for the Montreal Royals, the Dodgers' top farm team. Spring training in Florida proved a trying experience, as Robinson had difficulty finding meals and accommodation and was once even ordered off the field by a local sheriff, but when the club moved north conditions eased. For a time, he was joined by John Wright and Roy Partlow, Negro League veterans, but they were eventually demoted to Trois Rivières, Quebec (Class C). Robinson was enormously successful, leading the Class AAA International League with a .349 batting average and in runs scored with 119. That year, the Dodgers also had two other African-American minor leaguers, catcher Roy Campanella and pitcher Don Newcombe, who played for Nashua, N.H. (Class B).

In 1947, Jackie Robinson joined the Brooklyn Dodgers following spring training in Cuba, where race relations were less hostile than in Florida. He encountered discrimination from teammates, who originally petitioned to keep him out. Rickey offered to trade any player who did not wish to play alongside Robinson. Opponents, particularly members of the Philadelphia Phillies and St. Louis Cardinals, threatened to strike, but were warned by Commissioner Chandler that any player who struck would be suspended. Robinson turned out to be a great gate attraction, and had a superb first year, despite being moved to an unfamiliar position, first base. He led the Dodgers to the National League pennant and won the first Rookie of the Year Award. A handful of other blacks also played that year, including pitcher Dan Bankhead for the Dodgers. Larry Doby, one of the Negro Leagues' top prospects, became the first African American in the American League when Cleveland Indians' owner Bill Veeck bought him for $10,000 from the Newark Eagles in mid 1947. This purchase was an exception to the general pattern of uncompensated raids that major league clubs were beginning to make on Negro League teams, whose players had no reserve clause binding them to their teams. Later in the season, Henry Thompson and Willard Brown were briefly brought up by the St. Louis Browns to increase attendance, but neither did well and they were demoted after a month.

In 1948, the Dodgers brought up Roy Campanella. The same year, at the age of at least forty-two, Satchel Paige, legendary among both white and black fans, joined the Indians after twenty-two years as a professional. He had been the highest paid Negro Leaguer, and like most other black players took a substantial salary cut to compete in the major leagues. His contribution, however, was less significant than that of Larry Doby, who batted .301 and helped lead the Indians to the World Championship.

The following year, Don Newcombe of the Dodgers was named Rookie of the Year, Jackie Robinson was named NL Most Valuable Player, and he, Doby, and Campanella made the All-Star teams. However, the major leagues had room only for stars and were not interested in older players, with the exception of Paige. There were blacks in every Class AAA and A league that year. Many,

such as Ray Dandridge, an all-time Negro League star who hit .364 for Minneapolis (of the Class AAA American Association), started in leagues beneath their ability.

Within the next few years, lower minor leagues and other areas of organized baseball outside the South also integrated. Even the All-American Girls Baseball League discussed integrating its teams in the years before its demise in 1954. Recruitment was too difficult to make gender integration successful, however. The integration of southern teams in the minors (there were no teams in the major leagues south of the border states until the 1960s) began in 1952 in Florida, the Upper South, and the Southwest, because of blacks' superior play and their ability to attract crowds. A major breakthrough occurred in 1953 when the Class A South Atlantic (Sally) League, which had teams in Florida, Georgia, and Alabama, integrated with three blacks, including Henry "Hank" Aaron with Jacksonville. The Cotton States League integrated in 1954, with blacks playing for Hot Springs, Ark., and Meridian, Miss. After the Brown v. Board of Education of Topeka, Kansas decision in 1954, race relations became more hostile in the South, and integrated baseball became a threat to white supremacy. Integration continued, however, though at a slowed pace. By 1955, the only high-level minor league without blacks was the Southern Association (AA). Nat Peeples, who appeared in two games for Atlanta, was the only African American to play in the league, which disbanded in 1961. In 1957 Texas League nines were barred by Louisiana law from playing their black players in Shreveport. African-American fans responded by boycotting the league, with the result that the league dropped the Louisiana franchise.

The pace of integration in the major leagues was slow, and as late as September 1953, only six teams had black players. Many whites undoubtedly felt like St. Louis Cardinals owner Sam Breadon, who in the late 1940s expressed his belief that only a handful of black players could be talented enough to make the major leagues. Teams avoided older blacks and sought only players with star potential and a clean image. Players who were considered too proud or "uppity," like Vic Power of the Cleveland Indians, faced great difficulties. Between September 1953 and early 1954, six more teams integrated, but the champion New York Yankees refused to integrate until 1955 when catcher Elston Howard joined the team, and it was not until July 21, 1959, that the last holdout, the Boston Red Sox, brought up Eli-

See also

New Orleans

jah "Pumpsie" Green to the majors. Teams did not go out of their way to assure blacks service at restaurants and hotels. Players of different races were rarely roommates, and teams with more than one African-American player always roomed them together.

African Americans in Contemporary Baseball

In the years since integration, African Americans have starred in major league baseball. In the National League, the first to integrate, African Americans soon won five straight Rookie of the Year Awards (1949–1953) and seven straight Most Valuable Player (MVP) Awards (1953–1959). Blacks and Latinos, most of whom had been too dark-skinned for the major leagues before integration, soon revolutionized the game, introducing an emphasis on speed and baserunning in addition to power hitting. Between 1947 and 1993, white players led the NL in stolen bases just twice, and in the AL only on two occasions

BASEBALL LEGEND
Willie Mays Sets the Standard

Willie Howard Mays (May 6, 1931–), baseball player. The son of steel-mill worker William Mays and Ann Mays, Willie Mays was born in Westfield, Ala. After his parents divorced soon after his birth, Mays was raised by an aunt in Fairfield, Ala. At Fairfield Industrial High School, Mays starred in basketball, football, and baseball.

At the age of seventeen, he began his professional career, joining the Birmingham Black Barons of the Negro National League. During three seasons with the Black Barons, he played 130 games in the outfield and compiled a batting average of .263. In 1950, he started the season with the Black Barons, but he was soon signed by the New York Giants. Mays played on the Giants' minor league teams until early in the 1951 season, when he joined the major league club. Mays was voted the NL Rookie of the Year, and acquired the nickname "the 'Say Hey' kid" when he forgot a Giants' teammate's name in 1951 and used the phrase.

In 1952 and 1953 Mays served in the U. S. Army, but he returned to baseball in 1954 to play one of his best seasons ever. He led the National League with a .345 batting average and had 41 home runs and 110 runs batted in. Mays led the Giants to the 1954 National League pennant and world championship. In the first game of the World Series with the Cleveland Indians at the Polo Grounds in New York City, Mays made one of the most famous catches in baseball history: With his back to home plate, he ran down Vic Wertz's 440-foot drive to center field, wheeled around, and fired a perfect throw to the infield, thus preventing the Indians from scoring. Mays was named the National League's Most Valuable Player for 1954. He won the award a second time in 1965.

Mays is often considered the most complete ballplayer of the postwar era, if not of all time. He excelled in every aspect of the game. He hit over .300 in ten seasons. His total of 660 career home runs is the third best to date. He was one of the game's great baserunners and a superlative fielder. (His fielding earned him twelve consecutive Gold Gloves, from 1957 to 1968). Mays played in every All-Star game from 1954 to 1973 and in four World Series (in 1951 and 1954 with the New York Giants; in 1962 with the San Francisco Giants; and in 1973 with the New York Mets).

Because of his formidable abilities, and because of racism, Mays was also the target of an inordinate number of "bean balls"—pitches thrown at the batter's head. However, Mays was one of the first black superstars to receive widespread adulation from white fans. In the 1960s, Mays was among the many black athletes who were criticized for not publicly supporting the Civil Rights Movement. As on most controversial issues, Mays projected a naive innocence when confronted about his political silence. "I don't picket in the streets of Birmingham," he said. "I'm not mad at the people who do. Maybe they shouldn't be mad at the people who don't."

Mays played with the Giants (the team moved to San Francisco in 1958) until 1972, when he was traded to the New York Mets. The following year he retired as a player but was retained by the Mets as a part-time coach. Mays was inducted into the National Baseball Hall of Fame in 1979. Three months later, he was ordered by Major League Baseball Commissioner Bowie Kuhn to choose between his job with the Mets and fulfilling a public relations contract with the Bally's Casino Hotel. Mays, along with Mickey Mantle, chose the latter and was banned from any affiliation with professional baseball. In 1985, the new Commissioner, Peter Ueberroth, lifted the ban.

—THADDEUS RUSSELL

See also
Arthur Ashe

from 1951–1993. Maury Wills broke Ty Cobb's forty-seven-year-old record by stealing 104 bases in 1962, before his total was exceeded by Lou Brock, who stole 118 in 1974 and a record 938 during his career which included 3,023 hits. Brock's record was exceeded in turn by Rickey Henderson's 130 in 1982 and 1,117 total stolen bases (through 1994).

Through 1993 blacks and Latinos have won forty-six batting titles, thirty-five home run championships, and forty-three MVP awards. They have included three of the top four lifetime home run leaders, including such greats as Henry Aaron, the all-time leader in home runs (755), runs batted in (2,297), and extra-base hits (1,477); Willie Mays (third in career home runs); and Roberto Clemente. Frank Robinson (fourth in lifetime home runs) was a Triple Crown Winner (1966) and the first player to win the Most Valuable Player award in both leagues. Among pitchers, in 1968 Bob Gibson attained a 1.12 ERA, by far the lowest since World War I, and is second in World Series wins and strikeouts (with the single-game record of 17). Ferguson Jenkins won 284 games and had 3,192 strikeouts. There are twenty-eight blacks and Latinos in the Hall of Fame, eleven chosen primarily for their performance in the Negro Leagues.

Among North American blacks, representation in the major leagues reached its proportionate share of the national population in the late 1950s (12 percent). The first all-black starting team played for the Pittsburgh Pirates in 1967. The percentage of black Americans in the major leagues peaked at 26 percent in 1974. In the early 1990s, blacks represented between 16 and 20 percent of all major leaguers. The current declining African-American presence in baseball mirrors reduced black interest in the sport. A 1986 survey found that blacks made up just 6.8 percent of baseball spectators, less than either football (7.5 percent) or basketball (17.0 percent), both of which are professional sports with higher average ticket prices, but sports whose players are predominantly African American.

Baseball, like other sports, has been an avenue of African-American social mobility. A study made during the late 1980s of major leaguers born since 1940 found that five-sixths of blacks (83.3 percent) had blue-collar backgrounds while three-fourths of white players came from white-collar backgrounds. Until the 1970s, black players generally earned less than white players of equal ability. By the mid-1980s, African-American players made more money per capita than white players,

and race was no longer considered a factor in their wages.

However, discrimination has continued in many areas. Blacks have long complained of informal team quotas and the fact that mediocre black players were removed from teams, while white nonstarters were retained. Blacks have also been slotted by position. Black pitchers and catchers (positions which are often considered centers of leadership and intellectual challenge) have been relatively rare. Conversely, in 1960, one-third of major league outfielders were black; by 1989, 58 percent of blacks were outfielders, while only 18 percent of black players (versus 45 percent of whites) were at the central positions of catcher, shortstop, and second base.

Many blacks still consider racism prevalent in the baseball world. In the early 1970s, when Henry Aaron was challenging Babe Ruth's home run record, he received hate mail and racial threats. In the 1980s, the Equal Employment Opportunity Commission found that Boston Red Sox coach Tommy Harper was fired after he complained that the Florida country club which served as the team's spring training headquarters excluded blacks. In 1993 Cincinnati Reds owner Marge Schott was suspended for racial slurs.

Off-the-field opportunities in baseball have remained limited. In 1966, Emmet Ashford became the first black umpire in the major leagues. The first black manager was Frank Robinson of Cleveland in 1975. Robinson later managed in Baltimore and San Francisco. There have been five other black managers, and in 1993, four out of twenty-eight teams had black managers. Also, few blacks—only 21 percent in 1993—had positions as coaches, especially at third base, the position that most often leads to a manager's spot. The issue of black underrepresentation in management got considerable attention in 1987 from an interview with Al Campanis, Los Angeles Dodgers vice president for player personnel, on the ABC-TV show *Nightline*, in which he questioned whether blacks had the character "necessities" to be managers. Only 9 percent of all front office employees of baseball clubs are black, including just 3 percent of vice presidents and general managers. In 1990, Ellen Weddington of the Boston Red Sox became the first black female assistant general manager; there are no black CEOs or owners. Bill White, an African American, became president of the National League in 1989, but he complained bitterly of the slowness of minority hiring in baseball. In the early 1990s, the Rainbow Commission for Fairness, led by Jesse

The determination of blacks to improve their position revolved largely around efforts to secure accommodations that equaled those provided the whites.

PAGE 384

Jackson, attempted to use demonstrations and boycotts of games to call attention to the problem of black employment in baseball. Meanwhile, the World Series victories of the Toronto Blue Jays in 1992 and 1993, led by African-American manager Cito Gaston, have served as an inspiring reminder of the possibilities for black leaders in baseball.

—STEVEN A. RIESS AND DONN ROGOSIN

*Jazz originated
during a time of
enormous oppression
and violence in the
South against
African Americans.*

PAGE 375

BASIE, WILLIAM JAMES "COUNT"

William James "Count" Basie (August 21, 1904–April 26, 1984), jazz pianist, bandleader. Born in Red Bank, N.J., Basie took up drums as a child, performing at informal neighborhood gatherings. He began to play piano before his teens, and in high school he formed a band with drummer Sonny Greer. In 1924 Basie moved to New York, where he was befriended by two of the greatest stride piano players of the day, Fats Waller and James P. Johnson. Basie himself became a fine stride pianist, as well as a proficient organist, learning that instrument while observing Waller's performances at the Lincoln Theater in Harlem. Basie left New York in the mid-1920s to work as a touring musician for bands led by June Clark and Elmer Snowden, and as accompanist to variety acts such as those led by Kate Crippen and Gonzelle White. When White's group broke up in Kansas City in 1927, Basie found himself stranded. He supported himself as a theater organist, but more important, also began performing with many of the Southwest "territory" bands. In 1928 he joined bassist Walter Page's Blue Devils, and the next year he joined Bennie Moten's band in Kansas City.

After Moten's death in 1935, Basie took over the group, now reorganized as Count Basie and the Barons of Rhythm. Producer John Hammond heard the band on a 1935 radio broadcast from the Reno Club in Kansas City, and the next year brought the band to New York City. During this time the Basie band became one of the country's best-known swing bands, performing at the Savoy Ballroom, at the Famous Door on 52nd Street, and at the Woodside Hotel in Harlem, a stay immortalized in "Jumpin' at the Woodside" (1938). The band's recordings from this time represent the best of the hard-driving, riff-based Kansas City style of big-band swing. Many of these recordings are "head" arrangements, in which the horns spontaneously set up a repeating motif behind the melody and solos. Memorable recordings from this period include "Good Morning Blues" (1937), "One O'Clock Jump" (1937), "Sent for You Yesterday" (1937), "Swinging the Blues" (1938), "Every Tub" (1938), and "Taxi War Dance" (1939). In 1941 the Basie band recorded "King Joe," a tribute to boxer Joe Louis, which had lyrics by Richard Wright and vocals by Paul Robeson. In 1943 the band appeared in two films, *Stage Door Canteen* and *Hit Parade of 1943*.

In the late 1930s and early '40s, the Basie group was primarily a band of soloists. The leading members included tenor saxophonists Herschel Evans and Lester Young, alto saxophonists Buster Smith and Earle Warren, trumpeters Harry "Sweets" Edison and Wilbur "Buck" Clayton, and trombonists Eddie Durham and William "Dicky" Wells. Jimmy Rushing, Helen Humes, and Billie Holiday provided vocals. In the 1940s Basie also added saxophonists Buddy Tate and Don Byas, trumpeters Clark Terry and Joe Newman, and trombonists Vic Dickenson and J. J. Johnson. Throughout, the band's "all-American rhythm section" consisted of Basie, drummer Jo Jones, bassist Walter Page, and guitarist Freddie Green, who remained with the band for more than fifty years. Together, they provided the sparse and precise, but also relaxed and understated, accompaniment. Basie himself was one of the first jazz pianists to "comp" behind soloists, providing accompaniment that was both supportive and prodding. His thoughtful solos, which became highly influential, were simple and rarefied, eschewing the extroverted runs of stride piano, but retaining a powerful swing. That style is on display on Basie's 1938–1939 trio recordings ("How Long, How Long Blues," "Oh! Red"). He also recorded on the organ in 1939.

With the rise of the bebop era, Basie had difficulty finding work for his big band, which he dissolved in 1949. However, after touring for a year with a bebop-oriented octet, Basie formed another big band, which lasted until his death. The "second" Basie band was very different from its predecessor. The first was famed for its simple and spontaneous "head" arrangements. In contrast, arrangers Neal Hefti, Johnny Mandel, and Ernie Wilkins, with their carefully notated arrangements and rhythmic precision, were the featured musicians of the second Basie band. The latter also had many fine instrumentalists, including saxophonists Eddie "Lockjaw" Davis and Paul Quinichette, Frank Wess and Frank Foster playing saxophone and flute, trombonist Al Grey, trumpeter Thad Jones, and vocalist Joe Williams.

Basie's second band toured extensively worldwide from the 1950s through the '70s. Basie had his first national hit in 1955 with "Every Day I Have the Blues." Other popular recordings from this time include *April in Paris* (1955, including "Corner Pocket" and "Shiny Stockings"), *The Atomic Basie* (1957, including "Whirly Bird" and "Lil' Darlin"), *Basie at Birdland* (1961), *Kansas City Seven* (1962), and *Basie Jam* (1973). During this period the Basie band's popularity eclipsed even that of Duke Ellington, with whom they made a record, *First Time*, in 1961. The Basie band became a household name, playing at the inaugural balls of both John F. Kennedy and Lyndon B. Johnson, and appearing in such films as *Cinderfella* (1959), *Sex and the Single Girl* (1964), and *Blazing Saddles* (1974).

In the 1980s, Basie continued to record, in solo, small-group, and big-band settings (*Farmer's Market Barbecue*, 1982; *88 Basie Street*, 1984). He lived for many years in the St. Albans section of Queens, N.Y., with Catherine Morgan, a former dancer he had married in 1942. Health problems induced him to move to the Bahamas in his later years. He died in 1984 in Hollywood, Fla. His autobiography, *Good Morning Blues*, appeared the next year. Basie's band has continued performing, led by Thad Jones until 1986 and since then by Frank Foster.

—MICHAEL D. SCOTT

BASKETBALL

Although basketball in the United States is now dominated by African Americans, their role in the sport was relatively unimportant in the early years of the game. Created in 1891 by James Naismith at a Springfield Mass., YMCA, basketball was originally played primarily at YMCAs. Black YMCAs produced the earliest African-American teams.

By the outbreak of World War I, a handful of blacks competed on white varsity basketball teams, mostly in small, remote midwestern colleges. Ironically a man who did not play varsity basketball, Edwin B. Henderson, opened the door for many others to compete at both the interscholastic and intercollegiate levels. In 1905, after a summer at Harvard, Henderson, who was a physical education instructor, returned home to Washington, D.C., to become a founding father of African-American basketball. As physical edu-

cation director for black schools in Washington, Henderson led in the organization and promotion of high school, club, and YMCA sports programs for African-American youths. In 1909 he became an instructor at Howard University, where he introduced basketball. Two years later he launched a varsity program, recruiting most of his players from the black YMCA in Washington.

A number of black colleges joined Howard in adopting basketball for intramural and intercollegiate purposes. During World War I, these colleges began forming conferences "in a common effort for athletic elevation," as a Howard professor put it, and "to train students in self-reliance and stimulate race-pride through athletic attainment." In 1916 Howard, Lincoln, Shaw, and Virginia Union universities joined Hampton Institute in forming the Central Interscholastic Athletic Association. Four years later, educators and coaches from several Deep South colleges convened at Morehouse College in Atlanta to form the Southeastern Athletic Conference. By 1928, four regional conferences covered most of the black institutions below the Mason-Dixon line. By codifying rules and clarifying terms of athletic eligibility, these new conferences benefited the game of basketball.

Historians have made much of the massive black migration northward in the 1920s, but there also was a reverse migration of black athletes from the North to such southern schools as Tuskegee Institute (later Tuskegee University) in Alabama and Tugaloo College in Mississippi. Basketball especially flourished at Morgan State University in Baltimore, which went undefeated in 1927; at Xavier University in New Orleans, whose entire starting team in the late 1930s came from a championship high school team in Chicago; and Virginia Union University, whose 42–2 record in 1939–1940 included two victories over the National Invitation Tournament (NIT) champions Long Island University.

During the period between World War I and World War II, some black students played basketball at integrated colleges. John Howard Johnson, the first black basketball player at Columbia University, graduated from there in 1921. Basketball players who later achieved fame in other endeavors included Ralph Bunche, a Nobel Peace Prize recipient who starred at UCLA in the mid-1920s, and Jackie Robinson, who, also playing for UCLA (1939–1941), led his conference in scoring two years in a row before he went on to become the first African American to play baseball in the modern major leagues.

On December 4, 1927, Duke Ellington's band debuted at Harlem's Cotton Club, an all-white nightclub.

PAGE 230

See also
Harlem Globetrotters

77

"DR. J"

A Slam Dunk On and Off the Court

Julius Winfield Erving, II (February 22, 1950–), basketball player. Born in East Meadow, N.Y., Julius Erving, popularly known as "Dr. J," was one of the most exciting players in professional basketball. His hallmark move was a slam dunk that began with a tremendous leap from the foul line. As a basketball player at Roosevelt High School, Erving made the All-County and All-Long Island teams while maintaining a high scholastic average. Offered many athletic scholarships on graduation, he chose the University of Massachusetts. Dropping out after his junior year, he signed a four-year contract with the Virginia Squires of the American Basketball Association (ABA) and was voted rookie of the year in 1972. The following year Erving was traded to the New York Nets, and in his first season with the Nets he led the league in scoring and helped his team capture the ABA championship.

In 1976 Erving was sold by the Nets to the Philadelphia 76ers of the National Basketball Association (NBA). He retired from professional basketball in 1987, the same year in which he became the third player in NBA history to score 30,000 points. During his career, Erving was named to the NBA All-Star First Team eleven times (every year from 1977 to 1987), and in 1977 and 1983 was voted the All-Star Game's most valuable player. He was voted the most valuable player twice in the ABA (1974 and 1976) and once in the NBA (1981), and in 1980 was named to the NBA thirty-fifth anniversary All-Time Team.

Upon his retirement from basketball, Erving began to devote his energies to numerous business enterprises, including the Erving Group, Inc., "Dr. J" Enterprises, the Philadelphia Coca-Cola Bottling Company, and Garden State Cable. For his athletic and civic activities, he has been the recipient of honorary degrees from Temple University (1983) and the University of Massachusetts (1986, the same year in which he completed his undergraduate degree). Other awards include *Ebony*'s Jackie Robinson Award for American Black Achievement (1983), American Express's Man of the Year Award (1985), and the Lupus Foundation of America Award (1985).

—KEITH ROONEY

Since basketball is less expensive than football and more centrally positioned in the academic year than baseball, it became popular in black high schools in the 1920s. The black state high school athletic associations of West Virginia were the first of many to begin sponsoring state basketball tournaments in 1924. By 1930 eight tournaments were established; by 1948 every racially segregated southern and midwestern state had African-American statewide athletic organizations that emphasized basketball. In May 1929, Charles H. Williams, the director of physical education at Hampton Institute, inaugurated the National Interscholastic Basketball Tournament, which was held annually until 1942.

Of the several professional basketball leagues that rose and fell during the interwar period, all excluded blacks, though given the weak and disorganized nature of professional basketball at this time, this ban had less impact than for other professional sports. Independent all-black teams such as the Smart Set in Brooklyn, St. Christopher's, Alphas, and the Spartans in New York City, and Loendi in Pittsburgh struggled to survive despite inadequate facilities, small turnouts, and uncertain schedules. The most successful teams hit the road, barnstorming from city to city on a trail blazed by the best all-white team of the interwar era, the Original Celtics. The two best African-American squads, the New York-based Renaissance Big Five ("Harlem Rens") and the Chicago-based Harlem Globetrotters, frequently played against the Original Celtics and other all-white touring teams, thus making basketball the only interwar professional team sport to allow interracial competition.

The Rens began in 1923, the creation of the St. Kitts native Robert L. Douglas, who immigrated as a child to the United States in 1888. For several years Douglas played with the New York Spartans, then decided to form his own team. He rented the Renaissance Casino ballroom in Harlem. The team took their name from that home site, but played most of their games on the road against any team—black or white, city or small town—that would take them on. Over a twenty-year span, the Rens averaged more than 100 victories annually. In their greatest season, 1932–1933, they won 88 consecutive games and finished with a 120–8 record. At Chicago in 1939 they won the first "world tournament" of professional basketball. Little wonder that all seven players who formed the core of the team during the 1930s—Charles T. "Tarzan" Cooper, John "Casey" Holt, Clarence "Fats" Jenkins, James

See also

Harlem

"Pappy" Ricks, Eyre "Bruiser" Satch, William "Wee Willie" Smith, William J. "Bill" Yancey—are in the Basketball Hall of Fame.

The Rens were already well established when the Harlem Globetrotters played their first game in January 1927. Initially called the Savoy Big Five because they played in the Savoy Ballroom in Chicago, the Globetrotters were the brainchild of a Jewish immigrant, Abraham Saperstein. The somewhat misleading Harlem tag was a public relations ploy, which provided a racial rather than a geographical reference. As a team of barnstorming professionals, they traveled far longer, more widely, and to consistently larger crowds than any sports team in history. In 1951 they appeared before 75,000 spectators in Berlin's Olympic Stadium. They have performed for literally millions of live spectators around the world, as well as to huge television and movie audiences.

Although best known in recent decades for their basketball comedy, the original Globetrotters were serious, highly skilled athletes. In 1940 they succeeded the Rens as "world champions" in the fiercely fought Chicago tournament. Earlier, during the Great Depression, they averaged nearly 200 games per year, winning more than 90 percent of them. Constant travel produced fatigue; large margins of victory made for boredom. For rest and relief from tedium, the Globetrotters began clowning, especially on those frequent occasions when they dramatically outmatched their opponents. Comedy proved contractually lucrative, so the Globetrotters developed funny skits and routines. Staged silliness swamped competitive play in the 1940s. Still, Reece "Goose" Tatum, Marques Haynes, Meadow George "Meadowlark" Lemon, Nat "Sweetwater" Clifton, Connie Hawkins, and Wilt Chamberlain are among the most famous of the many superb athletes who have worn the colorful Globetrotter uniform.

It was just as well that the Globetrotters shifted from serious basketball to comedy routines, because the racial integration of the National Basketball Association (NBA) in 1950 meant that the Globetrotters could no longer attract the best college athletes. (A forerunner of the NBA, the Basketball Association of America, signed black players as early as 1948.) For the 1950–1951 season, the Boston Celtics recruited Charles "Chuck" Cooper from Duquesne University, the Washington Capitals tapped Early Lloyd from West Virginia State College, and the New York Knicks bought Sweetwater Clifton from the Globetrotters.

Prior to World War II the abolition of the center jump, the introduction of an innovative one-handed shot, and the use of the fast break, served to streamline Naismith's slow and deliberate original game. In the early 1950s, the NBA responded to the market's demand for a faster, more attractive game by banning zone defenses, doubling the width of the foul lane (to twelve feet), and introducing a twenty-four-second shot clock. All these changes were completed by 1954 and worked to the great advantage of African-American newcomers who had mastered a more spontaneous, personalized style of play on the asphalt courts of urban playgrounds.

The first African American to become a dominant player in the NBA was William "Bill" Russell. Russell came from an extremely successful undergraduate career at the University of San Francisco where he and another gifted African American, K. C. Jones, led the San Francisco Dons to 55 straight victories and two National Collegiate Athletic Association (NCAA) championships. Rather than go into the NBA immediately, however, both men participated in the 1956 Summer Olympics in Melbourne, Australia, leading the United States basketball team to an easy gold medal. Then, while Jones fulfilled a two-year military obligation, Russell joined the Celtics at mid-season. The defensive, shot-blocking, and rebounding skills of Russell complemented those of several high-scoring Celtics. Together they produced their first NBA championship in Russell's first pro season.

Jones joined the Celtics in 1958–1959, and he and Russell helped the Celtics to an all-time record nine consecutive NBA crowns. In 1964 Boston fielded the first all-black starting lineup in the NBA: Russell, Jones, Sam Jones, Tom "Satch" Sanders, and Willie Naulls; John Thompson, the future coach of Georgetown University, backed up Russell. Russell's NBA nemesis was a high-scoring giant of a man, Wilton Norman "Wilt" Chamberlain. Over seven feet tall and weighing 265 pounds in his prime, Chamberlain earlier led Overbrook High School in Philadelphia to two city championships, once scoring 90 points in a single game. In his varsity debut at the University of Kansas in 1957, his 52 points set the Jayhawks on the path to the NCAA finals, where they narrowly lost in triple overtime to top-ranked North Carolina. After two All-American seasons at Kansas, Chamberlain toured for a year with the Harlem Globetrotters, then joined the Philadelphia Warriors in the NBA in 1959. In a fourteen-year NBA career, he played with four different

In 1969, Kareem Abdul-Jabbar launched his professional career with the Milwaukee Bucks, winning the Rookie of the Year award.

PAGE 2

The Globetrotters played the itinerant schedule of barnstorming basketball teams, taking on black and white squads of greatly varying levels of ability.

PAGE 324

teams and was selected for thirteen All-Star games, seven first-team All-NBA squads, and four Most Valuable Player awards. In a total of 1,045 NBA games, he averaged more than 30 points per game, and in 1962, he scored 100 points in a single game against the New York Knickerbockers. At his retirement in 1973, he held or shared forty-three NBA records.

In addition to Chamberlain and Russell, black athletes such as Elgin Baylor and Oscar Robertson achieved basketball renown in the late 1950s and '60s. Though they had their differences in talent and style, it is perhaps possible to see in their play elements of a shared athletic aesthetic that would dominate NBA basketball in the 1970s. Baylor, Chamberlain, Robertson, and Russell exhibited skills developed in playground competition best represented in the Rucker tournament (New York) and the Baker League (Philadelphia), both created in the postwar era. All four of these early NBA stars grew up in urban, not rural, America, and they developed their game in East Coast, industrial Midwest, and West Coast inner-city playgrounds. All four also attended white rather than traditionally black colleges. Other players from the early and mid 1960s who exemplified the playground style were Earl "the Pearl" Monroe, who attended Winston-Salem College in North Carolina, before beginning a successful career with the Baltimore Bullets and New York Knicks. Connie Hawkins, a consummate play-

ground basketball player from New York City, had his promising career derailed by his ambiguous involvement in a point-shaving scandal in 1960. After some years in basketball purgatory, he joined the Phoenix Suns in 1969.

In the period after World War II, blacks became prominent in college basketball. Two black players started for the City College of New York (CCNY) squad of 1950, the only team ever to win the NCAA and NIT tournaments in the same year. When the first significant cracks appeared in the armor of racially segregated universities in the 1950s, basketball coaches rushed to recruit blue-chip African-American athletes for traditionally all-white teams. Even the smallest of colleges sought to enhance their status through the basketball prowess of new black talent. With fewer than 1000 students, little St. Francis College of Loretto, Pa., wooed Maurice Stokes. He carried them from the obscure National Catholic Tournament to the more prestigious and lucrative National Invitational Tournament in 1955.

As integration undercut black college athletics, coach John B. McLendon's program at Tennessee A&I enjoyed a kind of last hurrah of basketball excellence. After successful stints at North Carolina College and Hampton Institute, McLendon in 1954 went to Tennessee A&I in Nashville. Employing a fast-break press-and-run game that he claimed to have learned years earlier from the aged Dr. Naismith at the University of Kansas, within five years McLendon won four league championships and three national titles in the newly integrated National Association for Intercollegiate Athletics (NAIA). The Most Valuable Player of the 1959 NAIA Tournament was Tennessee A&I's Richard "Dick" Barnett, a future New York Knickerbocker stalwart.

Strong racially integrated teams won NCAA titles for the University of Cincinnati and Loyola University of Chicago in the early 1960s. Building on a tradition of integration that dated back to the 1920s, UCLA attracted a number of African-American athletes during the eleven-year span (1964–1975) in which they won ten national titles. The person most identified with UCLA's reign was Lew Alcindor, later known was Kareem Abdul-Jabbar, a 7′2″ dominating center with a deft scoring touch, who later went on to a twenty-year career in the NBA with the Milwaukee Bucks and the Los Angeles Lakers.

The passing of the old era of segregated basketball was symbolized in the NCAA finals of 1966, in which an all-black squad from Texas Western University (now the University of Texas

LEGENDARY FACEOFF

Wilt Chamberlain of the Los Angeles Lakers takes a shot while Bill Russell—in 1969 during his last season with the Boston Celtics—defends.
AP/WIDE WORLD PHOTOS

at El Paso) defeated a highly favored all-white team from the University of Kentucky. Shortly thereafter, the color bar began crumbling in the segregated schools of the Southwest Conference, when James Cash became Texas Christian University's first black basketball player in 1966. In Maryland, Billy Jones became the first African-American basketball recruit in the Atlantic Coast Conference. Finally, Perry Wallace of Vanderbilt University broke the racial barrier in the Southeastern Conference in 1967, the same year the University of Alabama's new basketball coach, C. M. Newton, began recruiting African Americans. In 1974 Alabama became the first SEC team to field five black starters.

The growing dominance of African Americans in college basketball has not been without its share of problems, however. Many colleges recruit black players as athletes, with little regard for or interest in providing them with an education. For example, shortly after winning the 1966 NCAA title, members of the Texas Western team began dropping out of college. They had all been recruited from the New York City area, and the overwhelmingly white, southern campus environment provided a combination of academic and social pressure. Even today, dropout rates remain at unacceptably high levels. Between 1985 and 1991, the average graduation rate among black college athletes was 26.6 percent, as opposed to the rate of 45.7 percent for white athletes (the rate for each group was slightly higher for basketball players). Another problem that has ruined or seriously detoured many promising careers is drug addiction. Len Bias, a number one NBA draft choice from the University of Maryland, allegedly died of a drug overdose in 1988. Other talented black basketball players, such as the playground legends Earl "the Goat" Manigault or Herman "Helicopter" Knowings of New York City, or William "Chicken Breast" Lee, or Terry "Sweets" Matchett, from Washington, D.C., did not have the social skills to enable them to move beyond the milieu of their hometown neighborhoods.

The African-American player has simply transformed basketball at all levels, especially bringing extraordinary excitement, media exposure, and financial success to the NBA. The seamless web of connection between high school, college, and professional basketball is best seen in Baltimore's Dunbar High School squad of 1982–1983. Finishing with a 31–0 record, Dunbar was top-ranked among all high school teams by *USA Today*. Virtually the entire team went to college on basketball scholarships. In 1987, three of them were selected in the first round of the NBA draft: Tyrone "Mugsey" Bogues of Wake Forest, by the Washington Bullets; Reggie Lewis of Northeastern, by the Boston Celtics; and Reggie Williams of Georgetown, by the Los Angeles Lakers. As of 1992 three-quarters of all NBA players were black.

African Americans also play a prominent role in women's basketball. The 1984 Olympic women's basketball team included Cheryl Miller, who led her University of Southern California team to two NCAA championships, Pam McGee, and Lynette Woodard, who later became the first female player for the Harlem Globetrotters. C. Vivian Stringer, who became coach of the women's basketball team at Cheyney State College in 1972, led the team to a second-place victory in the NCAA Women's National Basketball Championship ten years later. When Stringer became coach of the University of Iowa's women's team in 1983, she became the first black female coach to lead a women's basketball team of national rank. Under her leadership, the Iowa team qualified to play in the NCAA national tournament for seven straight years, from 1986 to 1992. In 1992, Stringer became the NCAA delegate for the committee organizing the Barcelona Olympic Games.

Although African Americans are vastly underrepresented in the management and coaching ranks of the NBA, they are considerably more visible there than in major league baseball or in the National Football League. At the outset of the 1992–1993 season, the NBA had only two black head coaches, although three had been let go during the previous year; but fully one-third of the assistant coaches, five general managers, and one co-owner (of the Denver Nuggets) were African American.

In the collegiate ranks, African-American head coaches John Thompson of Georgetown, John Chaney of Temple, George Raveling of the University of Southern California, and Nolan Richardson of the University of Arkansas are the exceptions, not the rule, for NCAA Division I teams. Division II coach Clarence "Big House" Gaines is less well known, but he is by far the most successful of all African-American coaches. At the end of the 1992–1993 season, he retired after forty-seven years as coach of Winston-Salem State University. Gaines coached his teams to a record of 828–440, making him second only to Kentucky coach Adolph Rupp in career victories.

Georgetown's John Thompson is probably the most visible, and certainly the most controversial,

After World War II, professional all-white basketball leagues began slowly integrating.

PAGE 324

See also
Kareem Abdul-Jabbar

81

Standing six feet, eight inches tall at fourteen years of age, Kareem Abdul-Jabbar led Power Memorial High School to two New York City interscholastic basketball championships and to two national crowns.

PAGE 2

"MAGIC" STYLE

Earvin Johnson Becomes a National Icon

Earvin "Magic" Johnson, Jr. (August 14, 1959–), basketball player. "Magic" Johnson was born and raised in Lansing, Mich., where he soon demonstrated an unusual aptitude for basketball. Despite the flair suggested by his nickname (which was given to him in 1974 by Fred Stabley, Jr., a reporter for the *Lansing State Journal*), Johnson's playing style was crafted out of devotion to basketball fundamentals and endless hours of practice. After leading his high school team to the state championship in his senior year, Johnson chose to attend college at nearby Michigan State University. He electrified crowds with his dazzling playmaking and the enthusiasm he displayed on the court while leading the Spartans to a national collegiate championship as a sophomore in 1979. At 6'9", he was perhaps the most agile ball-handler for anyone of his size in the history of the game, and his combination of height, athletic skills, and passing ability brought a new dimension to the position of guard.

Johnson left Michigan State after his sophomore year, and at the age of twenty he joined the professional ranks, leading the Los Angeles Lakers to the National Basketball Association (NBA) Championship in 1980—a feat they achieved four more times during the decade (in 1982, 1985, 1987, and 1988). Though Johnson holds the NBA record for assists (9,921) and was named the league's MVP three times (1987, 1989, 1990), Playoff MVP three times (1980, 1982, 1987), and All-Star Game MVP twice (1990, 1992), his desire to win translated into an unselfish style of play that elevated passing to an art form and stressed teamwork over individual accolades. His charisma and court savvy helped to revive interest in the NBA, while his versatility transformed the game to one dominated by multitalented guards and forwards. Johnson's contributions on the court have been matched by his efforts and leadership away from it: He has worked for numerous charitable organizations and has raised several million dollars for the United Negro College Fund over the course of his career. With an engaging personality and smile, Johnson became one of the most famous and recognizable Americans in the 1980s.

He retired from professional basketball in November 1991 when he revealed that he had tested positive for the virus that causes AIDS (acquired immune deficiency syndrome). Following his announcement, Johnson assumed a leadership role once again in working to raise research funds for, and awareness of, the disease. In 1992 he was appointed to the President's National Commission on AIDS, but he resigned soon thereafter when he became disillusioned with the government's efforts on behalf of AIDS research. Johnson kept AIDS in the public eye when he resumed his career shortly after guiding the United States basketball team to a gold medal at the 1992 Olympics. He attempted a comeback with the Lakers in the fall of 1992, but after some players in the league expressed reservations about playing with him because of his infection, he retired again. In that same year, Johnson authored *What You Can Do to Avoid AIDS,* the net profits from which went to the Magic Johnson Foundation, which Johnson established for prevention, education, research, and care in the battle against AIDS.

—JILL DUPONT

African-American coach. After a brief, successful stint at St. Anthony's Catholic High School in Washington, D.C., Thompson moved to Georgetown in 1972. Emphasizing the tenacious defense and team play he had learned during his brief time as a Celtic, he steered the Georgetown Hoyas to three consecutive NCAA finals, from 1983 to 1985, and to the national championship in 1984. Four years later he coached the United States Olympic team to a bronze medal in Seoul. Always emphasizing the primacy of academics, he ably recruited African-American athletes for Georgetown. Patrick Ewing and Alonzo Mourning are two of the most famous among many players to whom Thompson directed his homilies of racial pride and achievement.

In the 1980s basketball soared to new heights of international popularity, as did African-American basketball players. Two players who stood out in particular are Earvin "Magic" Johnson and Michael Jordan. Johnson, an unusally tall guard at 6'8", led Michigan State University to an NCAA championship in his sophomore year in 1979, before turning pro and joining the Los Angeles Lakers. He helped the Lakers to an NBA championship in his rookie season and subsequently led his team to five championships during his career. In addition to his basketball skills, his effervescent and winning personality propelled him to media celebrity. His many admirers were shocked to learn of his early retirement in the fall of 1991 after he announced that he had contracted the HIV virus. In the second half of the 1980s and early 1990s the dominant basketball player was Michael Jordan. Jordan played for the University of North Carolina before joining the Chicago Bulls in 1984, where, as a shot maker of astounding versatility, he quickly became one of the most powerful players in league history. Jordan also became a media spokesman for a number of products and advertising campaigns. His widespread acceptance and popularity has been as remarkable as his outstanding on-court skills. The role of African Americans in basketball was underlined by the success of the so-called "Dream Team," an NBA All-Star team that romped against the best of the rest of the world in the 1992 Summer Olympics in Barcelona. Eight of the twelve players on the team were black, including Magic Johnson in his final competitive appearance before his retirement. Michael Jordan would himself retire in October 1993 but returned in spring 1995. New aspirants also began to rise. Seven-foot-tall Shaquille O'Neal of the Orlando Magic, who in February 1993 became the first rookie since 1985 to lead the NBA All-Star Game starting lineup, would become one of the most closely watched stars of professional basketball.

Yet, despite the increasing successes of individual black basketball players, the nature of collegiate basketball itself continues to be an issue of controversy in the African-American community. In late 1993 and early 1994 the NCAA considered the adoption of new rules for prospective players, setting minimum academic standards for team admittance (a grade of "C" or better) and limiting the number of college scholarships offered for basketball. The rules revived tensions between a number of interests: the need to attract more promising minority athletes, the need to maintain a quality team in order to attract alumni donations, the need for schools to maintain consistent academic standards, and the decrease in available scholarship funds. For prospective African-American student athletes, the proposed new rules meant the intensification of an already keen competition for a chance at professional status. The controversy highlighted the debate within the black community on whether basketball unduly dominated the activities of black teenagers, and the role of basketball as a means of upward mobility for inner-city youth.

—WILLIAM J. BAKER

BASQUIAT, JEAN-MICHEL

Jean-Michel Basquiat (December 22, 1960–August 12, 1988), artist. Jean-Michel Basquiat was one of the most prominent artists to gain worldwide recognition in the 1980s. He was born in Brooklyn, N.Y., of Haitian and Puerto Rican-American parentage. His parents were separated in 1968, and Basquiat and his two sisters grew up with their father in Brooklyn, except for a period from 1974 to 1976, when the family lived in Puerto Rico. At the age of seven, Basquiat was badly hurt when he was hit by a car. He spent a month in the hospital, where his spleen was removed. While he was recuperating, his mother gave him *Gray's Anatomy,* a reference work that led to a lifelong interest in images of human anatomy.

Basquiat dropped out of high school and left home at the age of seventeen, determined to become a star in the downtown art and club scene of the late 1970s, where his aphoristic graffiti writings and drawings signed "SAMO©;" soon earned wide underground recognition. In 1980 his art was exhibited for the first time and to critical acclaim in the Times Square Show in New York City. Other group shows followed, and in 1981 he had his first solo exhibition in Modena, Italy.

In New York, Basquiat began showing at the Annina Nosei Gallery in SoHo, using the gallery basement as his studio. His first one-man show there took place in 1982, and soon his work was being exhibited at prominent galleries worldwide. In 1982, Basquiat was the youngest artist to participate in Documenta 7 in Kassel, Germany, and one of the youngest ever to be included the following year in the Whitney Biennial. A close friendship with Andy Warhol was a significant force in his life until Warhol's death in 1987.

Within the space of a few years, Basquiat rose from an anonymous street graffitist to become a world-famous artist, a feat that—as much as his art itself—came to define his popular image and to epitomize the fast-paced art world of the 1980s. As a young black male, however, he was viewed with suspicion by people blind to the significance of his work. In addition, a growing drug problem exacerbated his difficult relations with dealers, family, and the people closest to him. Basquiat died of a heroine overdose in August 1988 at the age of twenty-seven.

Robert Duncanson progressed from being a humble housepainter to an artist of international stature.

PAGE 197

See also

Harlem Renaissance

*Within the space of
a few years,
Jean-Michel
Basquiat rose from
an anonymous street
graffitist to become
a world-famous
artist.*

PAGE 83

Since his death, the importance of Basquiat's work has come to be still more widely recognized. In only eight years his work evolved from a direct, highly energized, expressionistic vocabulary to a complex synthesis of African-American and European cultural traditions, incorporating elements of black history, music, and popular culture in an advanced visual language of painting, collage, photo-mechanical reproduction, and sculpture. In his hands a sometimes raucous world of boxing, jazz, TV, and political reality was expressed in the language of Picasso, Rauschenberg, Warhol, Twombly, Dubuffet, and Leonardo da Vinci. His syncopated and haunting juxtaposition of words with images created a kind of visual poetry that is one of his most distinctive contributions to twentieth-century painting.

The first full museum retrospective of Basquiat's work, organized by the Whitney Museum of American Art, opened in New York City in 1992.

—NATHAN KERNAN

BEARDEN, ROMARE

Romare Bearden (September 2, 1912–March 12, 1988), artist. In the last twenty-five years of Romare Bearden's life, collage was his principle medium. Through that medium, relying on memory, he recorded the rites of African-American life in all their historical and ceremonial complexity. In so doing, he joined the ranks of Picasso, Matisse, and Miró, artists who transformed collage into a quintessentially twentieth-century language. Working with a medium which by its very nature is fragmented and heterogeneous, where reality and illusion hang in a precarious balance, Bearden, as his friend the writer Ralph Ellison once noted in *Projections,* captures

> *the sharp breaks, leaps in consciousness, distortions, paradoxes, reversals, telescoping of time and surreal blending of styles, values, hopes and dreams which characterize much of Negro American history.*

Fred Howard Romare Bearden was a child of privilege. He was born in Charlotte, N.C., in the home of his great-grandparents, Rosa and Henry Kennedy. Former slaves, the Kennedys had become prosperous landowners, and Bearden spent the early years of his life in a spacious Victorian-style frame house surrounded by doting great-grandparents and grandparents. In spite of their comfortable life, however, Bearden's college-educated parents, Bessye and Howard, were dissatisfied with the limitations of the Jim Crow South. On the eve of World War I, like hundreds of thousands of black Americans throughout the South, they migrated north.

After traveling to Canada, Bessye and Howard finally settled in Harlem. Harlem, in the years following World War I, was the black cultural capital of the world, the home of the New Negro Movement, the site of the Harlem Renaissance. A flowering of poetry, painting, and music that marked the African American's first efforts to define himself as a distinctive cultural entity within the larger American culture, the Harlem Renaissance proved to be a rich crucible for Bearden.

Bessye, Bearden's beautiful and dynamic mother who was a New York editor for the Chicago Defender and a political organizer, was at the center of this cultural activity. Her Harlem apartments were always filled with writers and intellectuals such as W. E. B. Du Bois, Paul Robeson, Langston Hughes, and Zora Neale Hurston, as well as painters Aaron Douglas and Charles Alston. Musicians, too, were part of Bearden's circle, and young Romy, as he was called, was surrounded by such exciting jazz musicians and composers as Fats Waller, Andy Razaf, and Duke Ellington. Together, Bessye and Howard, who worked for the Department of Health, provided their only child with a remarkable upbringing.

During the summers Bearden often visited his great-grandparents and grandparents in Mecklenberg, a place which became a veritable paradise in his mind. During his high school years he lived in Pittsburgh with his maternal grandmother, Carrie Banks, who ran a boardinghouse for steelworkers. Like Charlotte and Harlem, Pittsburgh became part of a rich inventory of images for Bearden's mature art.

Bearden came of age as an artist during the depression. While in high school, he met the successful black cartoonist E. Simms Campbell. Campbell's success inspired Bearden to try his hand at cartooning. From 1931 to 1935 he did editorial cartoons for the *Baltimore Afro-American* and drawings for *Collier's* and the *Saturday Evening Post.* After short stays at Lincoln University and Boston University, Bearden enrolled at New York University where in 1935 he received a B.S. in education. He continued cartooning at NYU, contributing to the university's humor magazine, *The Medley.*

After he graduated, Bearden became interested in inserting a social message into his cartoons, which led him, as he said, "to the works of Daumier, Forain, and Käthe Kollwitz, to the Art Students League and to George Grosz." Grosz, a German satirist whose visual commentary on post–World War I society was unforgiving, instilled in Bearden the lifelong habit of studying the artists of the past even as he was trying to make contemporary social commentary. Bearden's stay at the Art Students League was his only formal art school training.

Formal training, however, was amply augmented for Bearden by the Harlem art scene of the 1930s and '40s. In spite of the depression, Harlem boasted a thriving community of visual artists. Many, supported by the New Deal's federally funded Works Progress Administration (WPA), worked on public art projects, taught, or worked on WPA easel projects. They were supported by a network of exhibition spaces and art centers: the federally supported art center at West 125th Street, sculptor Augusta Savage's art garage, Ad Bates's exhibiting space at 306 West 141st Street, local libraries, the YMCA, and upscale living rooms and salons. Though Bearden did not qualify for the WPA because his well-to-do parents supported him, he was active nonetheless in artistic activities uptown. He was one of the artists who organized uptown artists into the Harlem Artists Guild, and he wrote articles for *Opportunity*, the magazine of the Urban League, on black American art and social issues.

More important, Bearden and his artist friends—Norman Lewis, Roy DeCarava, and Ernest Crichlow—were devotees of jazz. They regularly made the rounds of nightclubs and cabarets where they heard firsthand the compositionally complex innovative music. Though it was many years before Bearden was able to recognize the esthetic importance of jazz to his painting—inspired by his mentor, Stuart Davis—the music became as important to him as the painting of the masters he studied with George Grosz.

During this time, 1937 to 1940, Bearden produced his first paintings, gouaches on brown paper, eighteen of which were exhibited along with some drawings at his first solo show held at Ad Bates's place on West 141st Street. Scenes of black life in Charlotte, and on the streets of Pittsburgh and Harlem, these early paintings, with their terra-cotta colors, bulky figures, and narrative, almost illustrational quality, were painted in the then fashionable social realist style.

Bearden's uptown art community disintegrated with the coming of World War II and the dismantling of the WPA. Bearden enlisted in the army, continued to exhibit, and came to the atten-

tion of Caresse Crosby, the flamboyant founder and publisher with her husband of Black Sun Press. Crosby exhibited Bearden's works at the G Place Gallery in Washington and introduced him to gallery dealer Samuel M. Kootz. Kootz invited Bearden to exhibit, and from 1945 until 1948, Bearden showed there along with such other leading avant-garde painters as Robert Motherwell, Adolph Gottlieb, William Baziotes, Carl Holty, and Byron Browne. During this period Bearden painted oils filled with abstract figures. His works were largely derived from epic literary sources—the Bible, Rabelais, Homer, García Lorca. The style, boldly drawn contours filled with vibrant stained-glass color, was derivative as well, reminiscent of analytical cubism.

During his time at the Kootz gallery, Bearden grew intellectually restless. He found the direction of his colleagues—who came to be known as abstract expressionists—unsatisfying, and he left the country in 1950 to study in Paris on the GI bill. Though he enrolled at the Sorbonne, Bearden spent most of his time enjoying the city. When he returned in 1951, he found that he had lost interest in painting and he took up songwriting. Without painting, however, he was disconnected. He had a nervous breakdown and recovered with the help of Nanette Rohan, whom he married in 1954.

With Bearden's recovery came a return to painting. To spur his return, he systematically copied the old masters, actually making large photostatic copies and tracing them. Starting with Duccio and Masaccio, he worked his way into the present, tracing Vermeer, Rembrandt, Delacroix, Matisse, and Picasso. Bearden's copying taught him well, and with Carl Holty he wrote a book on space, color, and composition entitled *The Painter's Mind: A Study of the Relations of Structure and Space in Painting* (1969). Once he had relearned painting, Bearden began to paint large abstract expressionist oils with mythopoeic titles such as "Blue Is the Smoke of War, White the Bones of Men" (1960).

Bearden's most noteworthy work did not come until he was over fifty years old. Galvanized by the Civil Rights Movement, Bearden, as he had done in the 1930s, organized a group of black artists. They took the name Spiral. The group wanted to do something to celebrate the movement, and Bearden thought that perhaps a group work, a collage, might be a vehicle. The group, however, was not interested, but he found himself engaged by the medium. As Bearden worked on these collages, allowing images of Charlotte, Pittsburgh,

A painting is a symbol for the universe.

CORITA KENT
IN *NEWSWEEK*,
DECEMBER 17, 1984

B

and Harlem to flood his memory, he captured the turbulence of the time with spacial distortions, abrupt juxtapositions, and vivid imagery.

Bearden's collages made use of a visual language seldom seen in American painting. His collages were populated by conjure women, trains, guitar players, birds, masked figures, winged creatures, and intense ritualistic activities: baptism, women bathing, families eating together at their dinner tables, funerals, parades, nightclub scenes. His representative works contain scenes of enduring ceremonies underscoring the beauty and densely complex cultural lineage of African-American life. Notable works include *Watching the Good Trains Go By* (1964); *At Connie's Inn* (1974), one of his many collages on the theme of jazz; *Maudell Sleet's Magic Garden* (1978) from his autobiographical series; *Calypso's Sacred Grove* (1977) from his series based on Homer's *Odyssey;* and lushly colored, late works like *In a Green Shade* (1984). Ralph Ellison referred to Bearden's images as "abiding rituals and ceremonies of affirmation." Bearden invented his own phrase—the "Prevalence of Ritual"—to underscore the continuity of a culture's ceremonies, marking the traditions and values that connect one generation to another.

In his earliest works Bearden painted genre scenes, but in his mature work he pierced the skin of those scenes to explore the interior lives of black people. Bearden's first collages were photomontages, that is, they were photographic blow-ups of collages. After a year he abandoned that technique and, as his collages matured, began to use color more sensuously, creating lush landscapes with layers upon layers of cut paper, photographs, and paint. By the time of his death in 1988, Bearden had won virtually every prize and accolade imaginable, including the Medal of Honor, countless honorary doctorates, cover stories in the leading art magazines, and several retrospectives of his work, including one at the Museum of Modern Art in 1971.

—MARY SCHMIDT CAMPBELL

JAZZ WIZARD

Sidney Bechet Makes Music

Sidney Joseph Bechet (May 14, 1897–May 14, 1959), jazz musician, saxophonist. Sidney Bechet was born in New Orleans. He first borrowed his brother's clarinet at age six and within a few years was performing with the city's most established musicians. In 1914 he began a lifetime of touring, settling in Chicago in 1917. There he purchased a soprano saxophone, which would become his favorite instrument. In 1919 he joined Will Marion Cook's Southern Syncopated Orchestra, with whom he toured Europe. In the fall of 1919, Swiss conductor Ernest Ansermet's glowing review of the orchestra, and Bechet in particular, marked the first time that a jazz artist was given serious consideration by an established classical musician. Bechet returned to New York in 1921 and made his first recording in 1923, establishing himself as one of jazz's premier soloists. Bechet went back to Europe in 1925 with Josephine Baker's *La Revue Nègre* and in 1928 began a ten-year association with Noble Sissle's orchestra. By the end of the 1930s Bechet was based in New York, where he performed and recorded regularly for the next decade. His 1939 interpretation of "Summertime" became his best known work. After three European tours Bechet permanently settled in France in 1951 and achieved a measure of celebrity reached by few jazz musicians. He died of cancer in 1959.

Bechet's playing was characterized by a wide vibrato and a passionate, commanding spirit. He was a unique stylist and was instrumental both in changing jazz from ensemble music to a soloist's art and spreading New Orleans jazz throughout America and the world. His autobiography, *Treat It Gentle* (1960), is a vivid portrait of his Louisiana Creole background and the formative period of New Orleans jazz.

—MARVA GRIFFIN CARTER

BELAFONTE, HAROLD GEORGE "HARRY"

Harold George "Harry" Belafonte (March 1, 1927–), singer, actor, and activist. The son of a Jamaican mother and a father from Martinique, Harry Belafonte was born in New York City and received his early education in the public schools in Jamaica. In 1940 he returned to the United States and attended high school in New York. After Navy service during World War II, he enrolled in Irwin Piscator's Dramatic Workshop in New York City and in 1948 became a member of the acting group of the American Negro Theater in New York. In September and October 1949 he appeared as a regular on CBS's black variety show, *Sugar Hill Times.*

Racial stereotyping greatly limited Belafonte's acting possibilities, and so he turned to singing.

See also

Television

He made his debut in 1949, singing pop songs at New York's Royal Roost nightclub. He signed a record contract with RCA in 1952; however, it was not until 1957 that he achieved major commercial success as a singer. In the meantime he turned again to acting, and his muscular body, good looks, and rich, husky voice made him one of the first interracial male sex symbols. He appeared in the Broadway show *Almanac*, for which he won a Tony Award (1952), and he shared billing with Marge and Gower Champion in the musical *Three for Tonight* (1954). Belafonte's first film role was in *Bright Road* (1953), and he drew critical acclaim for his performance the next year in *Carmen Jones*, a black version of George Bizet's opera *Carmen*. He also appeared in the films *Island in the Sun* (1957) and *The World, the Flesh, and the Devil* (1959).

In the mid-1950s Belafonte began singing calypso, a folk-song style popular in Trinidad and other Caribbean islands. His passionate, witty and suave renditions of such songs as "Matilda," "Jamaica Farewell," "Island in the Sun," "Brown Skin Girl," "Come Back Liza," and his signature tune, "The Banana Boat Song," ignited a calypso fad in the United States. Belafonte's album *Calypso* (1956) became the first solo album in history to sell a million copies. Over the next decade he recorded eleven more albums, including *Belafonte Sings of the Caribbean* (1957), *Belafonte at Carnegie Hall* (1957), *Porgy and Bess* (with Lena Horne, 1959), *Jump Up Calypso* (1961), *The Midnight Special* (1962), and *Belafonte on Campus* (1967).

In 1960 Belafonte became the first African American to star in a television special, which won him an Emmy Award. Belafonte also began a long association with African culture and politics at this time. In 1959 he brought to the United States two protégés, the South African musicians Miriam Makeba and Hugh Masekela.

Like his idol, Paul Robeson, Belafonte combined singing with civil rights activism. In part because of his friendship with Robeson, Belafonte was partially blacklisted during the early fifties and was refused television and other engagements. He, in turn, refused to appear in the South from 1954 to 1961. In 1956 Belafonte helped raise money to support the Montgomery bus boycott and met the Rev. Dr. Martin Luther King, Jr. The two became close friends, and by 1960 Belafonte was a major fund-raiser and strategist in the Civil Rights Movement. He helped raise funds to support freedom riders and voter-registration efforts and in 1963 helped establish the Southern Free Theater in Jackson, Miss., which was dedicated to the development of a black political

leader. Belafonte also served as an unofficial liaison between the Kennedy administration and black leaders. In 1961 he was named to the advisory committee of the Peace Corps.

He was an active film and television producer, and his company, Harbel, formed in 1959, was responsible for the first major television show produced by a black, *Strolling Twenties*, which featured such well-known black artists and performers as Duke Ellington, Sidney Poitier, Nipsey Russell, and Joe Williams. In 1959 the company also produced the film *Odds Against Tomorrow*, in which Belafonte appeared with Ed Begley and Robert Ryan. In the 1970s, following the death of Martin Luther King and the ebbing of the Civil Rights Movement, Belafonte resumed making films, appearing with Sidney Poitier in *Buck and the Preacher* (1971) and *Uptown Saturday Night* (1974). Toward the end of the 1970s, Belafonte, who had sung in nightclubs only sporadically in the past decade, resumed singing. He made major tours in 1976 and 1979. In 1984 Belafonte coproduced the hip-hop film *Beat Street*.

Through the 1980s and early 1990s Belafonte achieved a new renown for his intentional political activities. Most notable was his commitment to humanitarian efforts in Ethiopia. In 1985 he conceived the project that resulted in the recording "We Are the World," written by Lionel Richie and Michael Jackson and conducted by Quincy Jones, which raised over $70 million to aid victims of famine in Africa. For his humanitarian work he was awarded the position of goodwill ambassador for UNICEF in 1986. In 1988 he recorded an album of South African music, *Paradise in Gazankulu*. In 1990, Belafonte, a longtime opponent of apartheid, served as chair of the committee that welcomed African National Congress leader Nelson Mandela to America. The same year, New York Governor Mario Cuomo appointed Belafonte to lead the Martin Luther King, Jr., Commission to promote knowledge of nonviolence.

—JAMES E. MUMFORD

BERRY, CHARLES EDWARD ANDERSON "CHUCK"

Charles Edward Anderson "Chuck" Berry (October 18, 1926–), rock-and-roll singer. Berry was born in St. Louis, Mo., the third of four children. His parents were deeply religious Baptists, but

Handsome and blessed with a commanding physique and a voice of unusual resonance and charm, Paul Robeson might have capitalized on his stage and screen success and ignored politics altogether.

PAGE 601

See also
Paul Robeson

B

Berry became interested in secular music as a teenager. He was inspired to become a performer and guitarist after an enthusiastic reception of his rendition of "Confessin' the Blues" at Sumner High School, where he was a student. He attended Poro School of Beauty Culture in St. Louis during the 1940s and used his skills as a hairdresser and cosmetologist to support himself in the late 1940s and early '50s. Berry also performed at clubs around St. Louis with several groups in the early 1950s and became popular with both white and black audiences because he sang country songs and blues with equal zest.

In 1955, Berry relocated to Chicago, where Muddy Waters recommended him to Chess Records, which signed him to a recording contract. Berry's first recording, and his first hit tune, was "Maybelline" (1955), a reinterpretation of the traditional country song "Ida Red" named for the Maybelline line of hair creams. He performed the song with crisp rapid-fire delivery and introduced new lyrics on the subjects of teenage love and car racing.

Berry was a pioneer in rock and roll and helped transform the new music into a commercially successful genre. His greatest success was in the late 1950s with songs that were definitive expressions of the themes of teenage angst, rebelliousness, and the celebration of youthful vitality. His best-known recordings include "Roll Over, Beethoven" (1956), "School Days" (1957), "Rock-and-Roll Music" (1957), "Sweet Little Sixteen" (1958), "Memphis" (1958), and "Johnny B. Goode" (1958). His only number-one record was the crass and forgettable "My Ding-a-Ling" (1972), a salute to male teenage masturbation.

After 1959 Berry's career was interrupted when he was arrested for transporting a minor across state lines. Though the events are still contested, Berry allegedly took a fourteen-year-old prostitute from Texas to St. Louis to check hats for a nightclub where he was performing. When he fired her, she reported his actions to local police. Berry served a two-year prison sentence at the federal penitentiary at Terre Haute, Ind. from 1961 to 1963. While Berry never reached his former level of popularity, he became active in the rock and roll revival circle of the 1980s and early 1990s and performed widely.

Berry was arguably the central figure in the creation of the sound and style of rock and roll in the mid−1950s. He had a tremendous influence on rock performers who came after him, including Buddy Holly, the Beatles, the Beach Boys, the Rolling Stones, and Linda Ronstadt, who emulated both his guitar style and his highly energized stage presence. Berry's tune "Johnny B. Goode" was included in the payload of the Neptune-bound *Voyager 1,* a testimony to the original and representative nature of his work.

—DAVID HENDERSON

ROCK AND ROLL

Chuck Berry, pictured here in 1956, appealed to both white and black audiences because he sang country songs and blues with equal zest.

FRANK DRIGGS COLLECTION

BETHUNE, MARY MCLEOD

Mary McLeod Bethune (July 10, 1875−May 18, 1955), rights activist. "If I have a legacy to leave my people, it is my philosophy of living and serving. As I face tomorrow, I am content, for I think I have spent my life well. I pray now that my philosophy may be helpful to those who share my vision of a world of peace, progress, brotherhood, and love." With these words, Mary McLeod Bethune concluded her last will and testament outlining her legacy to African Americans. Bethune lived up to her stated philosophy throughout her long career as a gifted institution builder who focused on securing rights and opportunities for African American women and youth. Her stunning successes as a leader made her one of the most influential women of her day and, for many years, a premier African-American leader.

Mary McLeod was born in 1875, the thirteenth of fifteen children of Sam and Patsy (McIntosh) McLeod. The McLeod family, many of whom had been slaves before the Civil War, owned a farm near Mayesville, S.C., when Mary was growing up. Mary McLeod attended the Trinity Presbyterian Mission School near her home from 1885 until 1888, and with the help of her mentor, Emma Jane Wilson, moved on to Scotia Seminary (later Barber-Scotia College), a Presbyterian school in Concord, N.C.

McLeod set her sights on serving as a missionary in Africa and so entered the Bible Institute for Home and Foreign Missions (later known as the Moody Bible Institute) in Chicago. She was devastated when she was informed that the Presbyterian Church would not support African-American missionaries to Africa. Instead, McLeod turned her attentions and talents to the field of education at home.

From 1896 through 1897, McLeod taught at the Haines Institute, a Presbyterian-sponsored school in Augusta, Ga., an experience that proved meaningful for her future. At Haines, McLeod worked with Lucy Craft Laney, the school's founder and a pioneering African-American educator. McLeod took away examples and skills she would put into action throughout her life.

From Haines, McLeod moved on to another Presbyterian school, the Kendall Institute in Sumter, S.C., where she met and married Albertus Bethune in 1898. The couple moved to Savannah, Ga., and in 1899 their only child, Albert Bethune, was born. Although Albertus and Mary McLeod Bethune remained married until Albertus's death in 1918, they were no longer together by 1907. In 1900 Bethune moved to Palatka, Fla., where she founded a Presbyterian school and later an independent school that also offered social services to the community.

In 1904 Bethune settled in Daytona, Fla., in order to establish a school for African-American girls. She opened her Daytona Educational and Industrial Institute in a rented house with little furniture and a tiny group of students. Students at the school learned basic academic subjects, worked on homemaking skills, engaged in religious activities, and worked with Bethune in the fields of a farm she bought in 1910. Through the farm, Bethune and her students were able to feed the members of the school community, as well as sell the surplus to benefit the school. The Daytona

Institute also emphasized connections with the community, offering summer school, a playground for children, and other activities. All of this made Bethune an important voice in her local community.

The school's reputation began to grow at the national level through a visit by Booker T. Washington in 1912 and the addition of Frances Reynolds Keyser to the staff in the same year. Keyser had served as superintendent of the White Rose Mission in New York and was a well-known activist. After World War II, the school grew to include a high school and a nurses' training division. In 1923 the school merged with the failing Cookman Institute of Jacksonville, Fla., and embarked on a coeducational program. In 1929 it took the name Bethune-Cookman College. By 1935 Bethune's school, founded on a tiny budget, had become an accredited junior college and, by 1943, a fully accredited college, awarding bachelor's degrees. This success gained Bethune a national reputation and won her the NAACP's prestigious Spingarn Medal in 1935.

In addition to her success as an educator, Bethune also made a major mark on the black women's club movement in America. In 1917 she was elected president of the Florida Association of Colored Women, a post she retained until 1924. Under her leadership, the organization es-

B

BETHUNE, MARY MCLEOD

EDUCATION PIONEER

In 1904, Dr. Mary McLeod Bethune (1875-1955) founded an all-female industrial training school in Daytona Beach, Fla. Bethune-Cookman College later became a four-year institution.

PRINTS AND PHOTOGRAPHS DIVISION, LIBRARY OF CONGRESS

See also
Education

*The National
Council of Negro
Women has been
among the most
influential African-
American women's
organizations of the
twentieth century.*

PAGE 496

See also
Civil Rights Movement
Southern Christian
Leadership Conference

tablished a home for young women in Ocala. In 1920 Bethune organized the Southeastern Federation of Colored Women and guided this group through 1925. From 1924 to 1928, she served as president of the National Association of Colored Women (NACW), the most powerful organization of African-American women's clubs in the country. During this period, she toured Europe as the NACW's president and established the organization's headquarters in Washington, D.C., in 1928. Bethune's crowning achievement in the club movement was the 1935 founding of the National Council of Negro Women (NCNW). This organization served to coordinate and streamline the cooperative work of a wide variety of black women's organizations. During Bethune's fourteen years as president, the NCNW achieved this goal, began to work closely with the federal government on issues facing African Americans, and developed an international perspective on women's lives.

Bethune's influence with the Franklin D. Roosevelt administration led her to activities that made her an even greater public figure on behalf of African Americans. In 1936 she organized the Federal Council on Negro Affairs, popularly known as the Black Cabinet, a group of black advisers who helped coordinate government programs for African Americans. In this same period, she became deeply involved in the work of the National Youth Administration (NYA), serving on the advisory committee from its founding in 1935. In 1936 Bethune began functioning as director of the NYA's Division of Negro Affairs, a position which became official in 1939 and which she held until 1943. This appointment made her the highest ranking black woman in government up to that point. Bethune's goals in the NYA were to increase the representation of qualified African Americans in leadership in local and state programs and to ensure that NYA benefits distributed to whites and to blacks achieved parity.

In addition to Bethune's many other achievements, she served as the president of the Association for the Study of Negro Life and History from 1936 to 1951, established the Mary McLeod Bethune Foundation, and wrote a column for the *Pittsburgh Courier*. Bethune's career is testimony to her leadership skills, her commitment to justice and equality for African Americans, her unfailing dedication to the ideals of American democracy, and her philosophy of service.

—JUDITH WEISENFELD

BIRMINGHAM, ALABAMA

Birmingham's African-American community came into existence with the founding of the city in 1871. Its initial growth was rapid, but in 1873, the outbreak of cholera and a national economic panic substantially reduced both black and white populations. Recovery was slow.

In the early 1880s, with the advent of a viable coal and iron industry, came a revitalized economy and a renewal of population growth. Thousands of African Americans flocked to the Birmingham area to mine coal or work in the iron mills. In both the 1890 and 1900 censuses, African Americans constituted 43 percent of the total population. After a slight decline in the years between 1910 and 1940, the percentage of African Americans in the city's total population began a steady increase, reaching 55 percent in 1980 and 63 percent in 1990.

Most African-American immigrants in Birmingham came from cotton farms in south Alabama and from the virtual enslavement represented by the sharecropper system. The city's lure was the promise of regular wages paid in cash, but what these migrants found available were generally the most menial jobs or those that were lowest paying. For African-American males, who worked in the mines and mills, the jobs they received were invariably the most dangerous. For females, job opportunities meant domestic work as maids or cooks or employment as dishwashers, laundresses, seamstresses, waitresses, or in the kitchens.

Despite the hard work, low pay, and discrimination that African Americans experienced, however, life in Birmingham was generally an improvement over what they had known on the farm. They had more money, a more active social life, more freedom from white domination, and better education for their children. The best evidence of Birmingham's attractiveness to blacks exists in the census, which shows a reasonably sustained growth of the city's black population.

Most African Americans lived in the areas that were generally, but not strictly, segregated. New arrivals often moved into a "company house": a three- or four-room rental structure owned by a coal or steel company. Usually identical in design, company houses stood in rows; several rows made up a company "village." Blacks and whites were segregated by rows of houses, but a black row and a white row often stood back to back. Thus, company villages respected segregation in principal, but in reality they did not keep the races very far apart.

Until the 1960s the largest single concentration of blacks in one neighborhood was Birmingham's Southside, the area immediately south of the downtown business district. Before the mid-1960s urban renewal program, "shotgun" houses covered much of the area. Domestics, furnace and foundry workers, and a smattering of teachers occupied the houses, though few owned their homes.

Several large, predominantly white neighborhoods in Birmingham had distinct black sections that were sometimes considered—especially by their own residents—as separate neighborhoods. Tuxedo Junction in Ensley, Collegeville in North Birmingham, Zion City in Woodlawn, and Kingston in East Birmingham were all black enclaves in otherwise white neighborhoods.

Among the purely black neighborhoods were several that were middle class in character. Enon Ridge, just northwest of Interstates 59 and 65 near downtown, became the fashionable place for the few black professionals in the city in the 1890s. Shortly after the turn of the century, the neighborhood of Smithfield—southwest of Enon Ridge—was developed; large numbers of black teachers and some other professionals bought homes there. In the 1940s South Titusville, to the west of Southside, began to attract working-class African Americans who could afford to own their own homes.

Once settled in a job and a neighborhood, African Americans usually joined a church. Each black neighborhood had at least one, and usually several churches. By far the most popular denomination among African Americans was the Baptist, which had perhaps three times as many members as its nearest rival, the Methodist. The

AN INDUSTRIAL CENTER

Birmingham industries actively recruited blacks to work at facilities such as this steel mill, helping to shape a unique tradition of African-American political and union radicalism in the city.
PRINTS AND PHOTOGRAPHS DIVISION, LIBRARY OF CONGRESS

B

**BIRMINGHAM,
ALABAMA**

*Tuskegee Institute's
graduates primarily
became members of
the teaching
profession.*

PAGE 211

various Pentecostal sects had the next largest number of members. The Presbyterians, Catholics, Episcopalians, and Congregationalists each had at least one, but not more than four, black congregations in the Birmingham area.

The typical black church in Birmingham at the turn of the century closely resembled the country churches of rural south Alabama. Several larger churches had a somewhat different character from the smaller neighborhood ones, primarily because of the higher economic status of their congregations. The Sixteenth Street Baptist Church, the first black church downtown (1873), always had many professionals among its members. Its services, conducted by highly educated ministers, rarely had the emotionalism seen in many other black churches.

The Sixth Avenue Baptist Church on the Southside was for decades the largest working-class church in Birmingham. In recent decades, however, it has added many professional members, and in the early 1990s, was the largest black congregation in the state.

Birmingham's African Americans encountered both prejudice and discrimination from the time the city was first established, but they especially suffered in the years just before the turn of the century. The rapid growth of the black population in Birmingham frightened local whites at a time when racist fears were on the rise nationally. In 1901, all but a few blacks lost the right to vote when a new state constitution established a poll tax, literacy tests, and "good character"—as defined by whites—as prerequisites for voting.

In 1911, the city of Birmingham began the enactment of segregation ordinances, outlawing saloons in black neighborhoods and making ones owned by whites separate black and white customers by using partitions. Other ordinances followed, including an encompassing Jim Crow statute in the 1920s.

In the early years of Birmingham's African-American community, educational concerns centered less on professional degrees than on establishing grammar schools. The first black public grammar school in Birmingham was Lane School, founded in 1886 on the Southside. Carrie A. Tuggle built Tuggle Institute, a popular private school and orphanage, on Enon Ridge in 1903.

There was no black high school in Jefferson County before 1900. Parents who wanted to educate their children beyond grammar school sent them to Tuskegee Institute or Talladega College, which had high schools at the time. In 1899, however, a group led by William R. Pettiford, a local minister and businessman, requested that the city establish a public high school for blacks. The next year the board of education appointed Arthur Harold Parker as the first principal of "Industrial High School."

The local black community took great pride in the school for which Parker had responsibility, and justifiably so. In the 1930s, for example, Industrial was recognized as the largest black high school in the world. Nowhere, however, was discrimination against African Americans more evident than in education. In 1911 Birmingham spent $18.86 for each white child of school age but only $1.81 for each black child. White teachers had an average of thirty-six students per class. Black teachers, who earned much less than their white counterparts, had fifty-eight. Moreover, the school buildings provided for African Americans were grossly inferior to those for whites. Until 1925, for instance, the Industrial High School building was nothing more than two rows of shotgun houses connected by ramps.

Discrimination kept many African Americans from attempting business enterprises. Among those that did, a number located their businesses along Fourth Avenue North between Sixteenth and Eighteenth Streets, an area that became Birmingham's central black commercial district.

Most African-American businesses provided services to other black Americans not provided by white businessmen. For example, A. G. Gaston, Birmingham's wealthiest black businessman, began his career with the Smith and Gaston Funeral Homes in 1923; he then added the Booker T. Washington Insurance Company and, subsequently, a business college, a drug store, a motel, a radio station, and a bank—Citizen's Federal Savings and Loan. All of these businesses originally filled the needs of the black community in a way that whites either refused to do or did inadequately.

Fraternal organizations also originally performed for blacks some of the services that insurance companies did for whites. The Masons, the Knights of Pythias, the Elks, and the Oddfellows were all burial societies in addition to providing social activities for their male members.

African-American women formed social clubs for the same reasons that their male counterparts joined fraternal organizations. Membership in women's clubs like Sojourner Truth, founded in 1895, or Semper Fidelis, organized in 1900, carried with it status and opportunities for social activities.

Certain recreational activities have been particularly popular among Birmingham's African

Americans. Through the first half of this century, baseball attracted many talented athletes and thousands of avid fans. Many blacks played in industrial leagues, and a few made it to professional teams. The Birmingham Black Barons, whose roster from 1948 to 1950 included baseball Hall of Famer Willie Mays, drew large crowds of both African Americans and whites to Rickwood Field, though white attendance fell when the city commissioned enforced segregated seating in the 1940s.

Birmingham was also a center for jazz in the 1920s and 1930s. The growth of jazz in Birmingham must be traced to John T. "Fess" Whatley, band director at Industrial High School. A stern taskmaster, Whatley schooled his many students on the fundamentals of reading and performing music. One of Whatley's most famous students, Erskine Hawkins, brought fame to Birmingham jazz and its black neighborhoods in 1939 when he wrote a song entitled "Tuxedo Junction," which became a national hit.

The happy lyrics of "Tuxedo Junction" should not hide the misery felt by Birmingham's blacks in the 1930s. The depression hit Birmingham early and hard. Tens of thousands of black miners and steel workers were thrown out of work as the big steel companies virtually ceased operations. Getting food and fuel became a major problem for most black families in the city's industrial neighborhoods. The hard times brought a radical political response from some of Birmingham's African Americans, who joined the American Communist party. Unions, however, attracted far more blacks unhappy with their economic situation than the Communist party did. In the 1890s, they had responded enthusiastically to the United Mine Workers' organizing efforts among African-American miners. They remained loyal to the UMW despite several concerted efforts on the part of coal companies to break up the union by creating racial animosity between black and white workers.

Biracial organizing was used in the 1930s against the Mine, Mill, and Smelter Workers, an organization of iron ore miners that some whites called "the nigger union." In an effort to destroy the union, its opponents accused some Mine, Mill officials of being Communists and harassed white members about their close association with blacks. In the late 1940s Mine, Mill was absorbed by the Steelworkers Union, against the will of many black members.

Civil rights activism began to appear in the 1930s, especially in the area of voting discrimina-

tion. It was not, however, until the end of World War II that a confrontation between the races became pointed. Tension between blacks and whites increased markedly after World War II, as whites sensed that blacks intended to challenge segregation and other forms of discrimination. In addition to voting, residential patterns became a point of conflict. The need for more and better housing led blacks to build in sections of neighborhoods that had previously been all white.

In 1947 a local black man successfully challenged Birmingham's residential segregation law when the city attempted to prevent him from occupying his new home in North Smithfield, a neighborhood the city had designated as white. Two weeks later his home was blown apart by a dynamite bomb. Other blacks followed him to North Smithfield, but so did more trouble. Several new black homes were bombed in the late 1940s and early 1950s, apparently the work of local Klansmen angry at black encroachment into white neighborhoods. The violence happened with such regularity that this section of town became known as "Dynamite Hill."

In the late 1950s blacks began to challenge the segregation of public schools, but it was not until 1963 when, under federal court order, several all-white schools were desegregated despite bitter opposition from local whites.

In the 1960s the national Civil Rights Movement accelerated change in Birmingham. The sit-in movement in 1960 and the freedom-riders in 1961 challenged "Jim Crow" restaurants and waiting rooms and heightened the anxieties of segregationist whites. In the spring of 1963 the Rev. Dr. Martin Luther King, Jr., Birmingham minister Fred Shuttlesworth, and the Southern Christian Leadership Conference initiated a series of protests against all forms of discrimination in Birmingham.

Daily marches in downtown Birmingham exposed the protesters to the violent tactics of Birmingham Police Commissioner Eugene "Bull" Connor. When thousands of black school children joined the protest, Connor met the challenge with police dogs and firehoses. After King was arrested during the demonstrations, he wrote his "Letter from Birmingham Jail," one of the central statements of his political and spiritual convictions. After several weeks of conflict, business and civil rights leaders arranged a truce, and a settlement that broke down some of the segregation barriers soon followed.

The worst moment of racial turmoil in Birmingham, however, came a few months later, on

Birmingham is a new city in an old land.

CARL CARMER
STARS FELL ON ALABAMA,
1934

See also
Education

93

*After 1965 the Civil
Rights Movement
fragmented in the
absence of an
overriding goal to
unify and inspire it.*

PAGE 136

See also
Eldridge Cleaver

Sunday morning, September 15, when a bomb exploded in the Sixteenth Street Baptist Church. It killed four young girls—Cynthia Wesley, Addie Mae Collins, Carole Robertson, and Denise McNair.

After the spring demonstrations and the Sixteenth Street bombing, race relations in Birmingham improved. Many new doors were opened, literally and figuratively, to blacks. No achievement was more important than the gaining of the right to vote. Arthur Shores, a local black attorney, was elected to the Birmingham City Council in 1969, and blacks subsequently won other public offices. The election of Richard Arrington, Jr., a black educator and city council member, to the mayor's office in 1979 was the best evidence of black progress in politics.

The years since World War II have brought many changes in the black community not directly related to civil rights. Fewer African Americans work in the steel industry, but more have white-collar occupations. Fewer African Americans live on the Southside, but many more live in the western section of the city in what were all-white neighborhoods. Older neighborhoods like Ensley, Woodlawn, West End, and North Birmingham have gained black population and lost whites at a rapid rate since the mid-1960s.

In 1963 Birmingham was accurately characterized as the "most segregated city" in the United States. By the early 1990s, however, schools, playgrounds, parks, and other public facilities had been desegregated. All of the segregation ordinances have been repealed. Although vestiges of racial segregation remain, communication and cooperation between blacks and whites have greatly improved in an effort to make Birmingham "the Magic City."

—MARVIN Y. WHITING, OTIS DISMUKES,
AND ROBERT J. NORRELL

BLACK PANTHER
PARTY FOR
SELF-DEFENSE

Huey P. Newton and Bobby Seale founded the Black Panther Party for Self-Defense in October 1966, and despite periods of imprisonment, they remained leaders as the party expanded from its Oakland, Calif., base to become a national organization. Assuming the posts of defense minister and chairman, respectively, of the new group,

Newton and Seale drafted a ten-point program and platform that included a wide range of demands, summarized in the final point: "We want land, bread, housing, education, clothing, justice and peace." Rather than on its program, however, the party's appeal among young African Americans was based mainly on its brash militancy, often expressed in confrontations with police. Initially concentrated in the San Francisco Bay area and Los Angeles, by the end of 1968 the Black Panther party ("for Self-Defense" was dropped from its name) had formed chapters in dozens of cities throughout the United States, with additional support chapters abroad. Although most of its leaders were male, a substantial proportion of its rank-and-file members were female. Influenced by the ideas of Marx and Malcolm X, the Black Panther Party's ideology was not clearly defined, and the party experienced many internal disputes over its political orientation. The FBI's covert Counterintelligence Program (COINTELPRO) and raids by local police forces exacerbated leadership conflicts, resulted in the imprisonment or death of party members, and hastened the decline of the group after 1968.

After joining the party in 1967, Eldridge Cleaver, a former convict and author of a book of essays called *Soul on Ice*, became one of the party's main spokespersons and a link with white leftist supporters. Arrested in May 1967 during a protest at the California state capitol in Sacramento against pending legislation to restrict the carrying of weapons, Cleaver remained affiliated with the Panthers despite repeated efforts of authorities to return him to prison for parole violations. His caustic attacks on white authorities combined with media images of armed Panthers wearing black leather jackets attracted notoriety and many recruits during the summer of 1967. Cleaver's prominence in the Black Panther party increased after October 28, 1967, when Newton was arrested after an altercation that resulted in the death of an Oakland police officer. The Panthers immediately mobilized to free Newton, who faced a possible death sentence if convicted. As part of this support effort, Cleaver and Seale contacted Stokely Carmichael, former chairman of the Student Nonviolent Coordinating Committee (SNCC) and a nationally known proponent of black power. SNCC activists and representatives from other black militant groups participated in "Free Huey" rallies during February 1968, helping to transform the Panthers from a local group into a national organization. When Cleaver was arrested during an April 6 raid that resulted in the

BOBBY SEALE

Founder of the Black Panther Party

Robert George "Bobby" Seale (October 22, 1936–), activist. Bobby Seale was born to George and Thelma Seale in Dallas. Before he had reached the age of ten, his family moved to California, where his father continued in his profession as a building carpenter. At the age of eighteen, Bobby Seale was accepted into the Air Force and sent to Amarillo, Tex., for training as an aircraft sheet-metal mechanic. After training for six months, he graduated as an honor student from the Technical School Class of Air Force Training. He was then sent to Ellsworth Air Force Base in Rapid City, S. Dak., where he served for three and a half years and was discharged as a corporal. He attended Merrit College in Oakland, Calif., after his discharge.

When he enrolled in college in 1961, Seale intended to study engineering. He joined the Afro-American Association, an organization formed by young militant African Americans in Oakland to explore the various problems confronting the black community. Influenced by the association's regular book-discussion sessions, Seale became interested in the works of Mao Zedong and Kwame Nkrumah, and he also began to read W. E. B. Du Bois and Booker T. Washington. His awareness of and involvement in the Afro-American Association were shaped by a fellow student, Huey Newton, whose articulation of the social problems victimizing the black community attracted his interest.

With Newton, Seale formed the Soul Students Advisory Council; which was concerned with ending the drafting of black men into the service to fight in the Vietnam War. Fired by nationalist zeal, especially after he heard Malcolm X speak, Seale invited three friends, Kenny, Isaac, and Ernie, to create the Revolutionary Action Movement to organize African Americans on the West Coast for black liberation. In October of 1966, he and Huey Newton formed the Black Panther Party in Oakland. The party's objectives were reflected in its ten-point platform and program, which emphasized freedom, full employment, and equality of opportunity for African Americans. It called for an end to white racism and police brutality against black people. Although the FBI under J. Edgar Hoover's directorship declared Seale's party to be the greatest threat to the internal security of the United States, the party's programs for the poor won it broad support from the community as well as praise from civic groups. The Black Panther party also recognized the need for political participation by African Americans. To this end, it frequently organized voter-registration drives.

Three years after the formation of the party, Seale shifted his philosophical and ideological stance from race to class struggle, stressing the unity of the people and arguing that the Panthers would not "fight racism with more racism." In 1973 he ran for mayor of Oakland, forcing a runoff with John Reading, the incumbent, who defeated him. In 1974, he resigned as the chairman of the Black Panther party, perhaps in an effort to work within the mainstream political system. Since the late 1980s, Seale has been involved in an organization called Youth Employment Strategies, of which he was founder, and in encouraging black youth to enroll in doctoral programs. He is based in Philadelphia.

—LEVI A. NWACHUKU

killing of party treasurer Bobby Hutton, his parole was revoked, and his legal defense, as well as that of Newton, became a major focus of Panther activities.

Serious conflicts accompanied the party's rapid growth, however, for its leaders divided over ideological and tactical issues. Cleaver and Seale were unsuccessful in their effort to forge an alliance with SNCC, whose members distrusted the Panthers' hierarchical leadership style. When relations between the two groups soured during the summer of 1968, Carmichael decided to remain allied with the Panthers, but his advocacy of black unity and Pan-Africanism put him at odds with other Panther leaders, who advocated class unity and close ties with the white New Left. Although his presence helped the Panthers to establish strong chapters in the eastern United States, Carmichael severed ties with the party after he established residency in Africa in 1969. The party's relations with southern California followers of black nationalist Maulana Karenga also deteriorated, a result both of the FBI's COINTELPRO efforts and the Panthers' harsh criticisms of Karenga's cultural nationalist orientation. In January 1969, two members of Karenga's U.S. organization killed two Panthers during a clash at UCLA.

Although the Black Panther party gradually shifted its emphasis from revolutionary rhetoric

See also
Malcolm X

and armed confrontations with police to "survival programs," such as free breakfasts for children and educational projects, clashes with police and legal prosecutions decimated the party's leadership. Soon after finishing his 1968 presidential campaign as candidate of the Peace and Freedom party, Cleaver left for exile in Cuba and then Algeria to avoid returning to prison for parole viola-tion. In March 1969, Seale was arrested for conspiracy to incite rioting at the 1968 Democratic convention in Chicago, and in May, Connecticut officials charged Seale and seven other Panthers with murder in the slaying of party member Alex Rackley, who was believed to be a police inform-ant. In New York, twenty-one Panthers were charged with plotting to assassinate policemen

I criticize America because I love her. I want to see her stand as a moral example to the world.

MARTIN LUTHER KING, JR.

Civil rights activity quickened after World War II, in an increasingly open society that could not easily justify segregation after years of propaganda denouncing Nazi Germany for its vicious racial policies.

PAGE 133

ART BLAKEY
Champion of the Bop Tradition

Art Blakey (Abdullah Ibn Buhaina) (October 11, 1919–October 16, 1990), drummer and bandleader. Born in Pittsburgh, Pa., and or-phaned as an infant, Blakey learned enough piano in his foster home and school to organize a group and play a steady engagement at a local nightclub while in his early teens. He later taught himself to play drums, emulating the styles of Kenny Clarke, Chick Webb, and Sid Catlett. Blakey left Pittsburgh for New York City with Mary Lou Williams's band in the fall of 1942, leaving her band in 1943 to tour with the Fletcher Henderson Orchestra. After his stint with Henderson, he briefly formed his own big band in Boston before heading west to St. Louis to join Billy Eckstine's new big bebop band. Blakey remained with the band for its three-year duration, working with other modern jazz musicians including Dizzy Gillespie, Charlie Parker, Sarah Vaughan, Miles Davis, Dexter Gordon, and Fats Navarro.

After Eckstine disbanded the group in 1947, Blakey organized another big band, the Seventeen Messengers. At the end of the year, he took an octet including Kenny Dorham, Sahib Shihab, and Walter Bishop, Jr., into the studio to record for Blue Note Records as the Jazz Messengers. In the same year Blakey joined Thelonious Monk on his historic first recordings for Blue Note, recordings that document both performers as remarkably original artists. The next year Blakey went to Africa to learn more about Islamic culture and subsequently adopted the Arabic name Abdullah Ibn Buhaina. During the early 1950s Blakey continued to perform and record with the leading innovators of his generation, including Char-lie Parker, Miles Davis, and Clifford Brown. With his kindred musical spirit, Horace Silver, Blakey in 1955 formed a cooperative group with Kenny Dorham (trumpet), Doug Watkins (bass), and Hank Mobley (tenor saxophone), naming the quintet the Jazz Mes-sengers. When Silver left the group in 1956, Blakey assumed leadership of the seminal hard bop group,

renowned for combining solid, swinging jazz with rhythm and blues, gospel, and blues idioms.

Blakey's commitment to preserving the quintes-sence of the hard bop tradition lasted unflaggingly for over thirty-five years. His group toured widely, serving both as a school for young musicians and the definitive standard for what has become known as "straight-ahead jazz." Blakey's Jazz Messengers graduated from its ranks many of the most influential figures in jazz, including Wayne Shorter, Freddie Hubbard, Donald Byrd, Jackie McLean, Lee Morgan, Johnny Griffin, Woody Shaw, Keith Jarrett, JoAnn Brackeen, Branford, Delfayo, and Wynton Marsalis, Donald Harrison, and Terence Blanchard. A drum-mer famous for his forceful intensity, hard swinging grooves, and an inimitable press roll, Blakey also adopted several African drumming techniques—in-cluding rapping the sides of his drums and altering the pitch of the tom-toms with his elbow—which ex-panded the timbral and tonal vocabulary of jazz drumming. His drumming style as an accompanist is characterized by an unwavering cymbal beat punc-tuated by cross-rhythmic accents on the drums. A distinctive soloist, Blakey exploited the full dynamic potential of his instrument, often displaying a com-mand of rhythmic modulation and a powerful ex-pressiveness that incorporated polyrhythmic con-ceptual influences from West Africa and Cuba. In addition to his singular achievements as a drummer and bandleader, Blakey also served as a catalyst in bringing together percussionists from diverse tradi-tions to perform and record in a variety of ensem-bles. His versatility as a drummer outside of the con-text of his own group received global recognition during his 1971–1972 tour with the Giants of Jazz, which included Dizzy Gillespie, Sonny Stitt, Thelo-nious Monk, Kai Winding, and Al McKibbon. Blakey died in New York City in 1990.

—ANTHONY BROWN

and blow up buildings. Though nearly all charges brought against Panther members either did not result in convictions or were overturned on appeal, the prosecutions absorbed much of the party's resources. An effort during 1969 to purge members considered disloyal or unreliable only partly succeeded.

In 1970, when Newton's conviction on a lesser manslaughter charge was reversed on appeal, he returned to find the party in disarray. Seale still faced murder charges (they were dropped the following year). Chief of staff David Hilliard awaited trial on charges of threatening the life of President Richard Nixon. Some chapters, particularly those in the eastern United States, resisted direction from the Oakland headquarters. In 1971, Newton split with Cleaver, in exile in Algeria, charging that the latter's influence in the party had caused it to place too much emphasis on armed rebellion. In 1973, Seale ran an unsuccessful, though formidable, campaign for mayor of Oakland. The following year Newton, facing new criminal charges and allegations of drug use, fled to Cuba. After Newton's departure, Elaine Brown took over leadership of the ailing organization. The Black Panther party continued to decline, however, and, even after Newton returned in 1977 to resume control, the group never regained its former prominence.

—CLAYBORNE CARSON

BLAKE, JAMES HUBERT "EUBIE"

James Hubert "Eubie" Blake (February 7, 1883–February 12, 1983), jazz pianist, composer. Born in Baltimore, Md., the son of former slaves, Eubie Blake began organ lessons at the age of six and was soon syncopating the tunes he heard in his mother's Baptist church. While in his teens he began to play in the ragtime style then popular in Baltimore sporting houses and saloons. One of his first professional jobs was as a dancer in a minstrel show, *In Old Kentucky*. During this time Blake also began to compose music, with his first published piece, "Charleston Rag," appearing in 1899. While in his twenties Blake began performing each summer in Atlantic City, where he composed songs ("Tricky Fingers," 1904) and came in contact with such giants of ragtime and stride piano as Willie "The Lion" Smith, Luckey Roberts, and James P. Johnson. His melodic style and penchant for waltzes were influenced by the comic operettas of Victor Herbert, Franz Lehar, and Leslie Stuart. During this time Blake began to perform songs in his mature style, which was marked by broken-octave parts and arpeggiated figures, as well as sophisticated chord progressions and altered Blues chords. In 1910 Blake married Avis Lee, a classical pianist.

In 1916, with the encouragement of bandleader James Reese Europe, Blake began performing with Noble Sissle as "The Dixie Duo," a piano-vocal duet. Sissle and Blake performed together on the B. F. Keith vaudeville circuit, and also began writing songs together. In 1921 Sissle and Blake joined with the well-known comedy team of Flournoy Miller and Aubrey Lyles to write *Shuffle Along*, which became so popular in both its Broadway and touring versions that at one point three separate companies were crisscrossing the country performing it. In 1924 Sissle and Blake teamed up with Lew Payton to present *In Bamville*, which later was known as *The Chocolate Dandies*. After the closing of the show in 1925, Sissle and Blake returned to vaudeville, touring the United States, Great Britain, and France. In 1927 Sissle remained in Europe, and Blake teamed up with Henry Creamer to write cabaret shows. In 1928 Blake joined with Henry "Broadway" Jones and a cast of eleven performers to tour the United States on the Keith-Albee Orpheum

RAGTIME MAN

James Hubert "Eubie" Blake (1883–1983) was the son of former slaves. His musical career spanned the twentieth century and influenced several generations of musicians. PHOTOGRAPHS AND PRINTS DIVISION, SCHOMBURG CENTER FOR RESEARCH IN BLACK CULTURE, THE NEW YORK PUBLIC LIBRARY, ASTOR, LENOX AND TILDEN FOUNDATIONS

Ragtime was the first music of African-American origin to play a significant role in American popular culture.

PAGE 568

circuit with *Shuffle Along Jr.* In that year he also wrote "Tickle the Ivories." Two years later Blake set to music lyrics by Andy Razaf for Lew Leslie's *Blackbirds of 1930,* which included "Memories of You," which became one of the best known of Blake's many songs. In 1932, after the death of Lyles, Sissle and Blake reunited with Miller to present *Shuffle Along of 1933,* but the show closed after only fifteen performances. During the Great Depression, Blake wrote several shows with Milton Reddie. *Swing It,* which included the songs "Ain't We Got Love" and "Blues Why Don't You Leave Me Alone," was produced by the Works Progress Administration. During the war years Blake performed in U.S.O. shows and wrote *Tan Manhattan* (1943). When "I'm Just Wild About Harry," from *Shuffle Along,* became popular during the 1948 presidential campaign of Harry Truman, Sissle and Blake reunited to update the show. The new version failed to gain popularity, and Blake retired from public life.

In the 1960s there was a renewed public interest in ragtime, and Blake recorded *The Eighty-Six Years of Eubie Blake* (1969), an album that led to a resurgence in his career. Thereafter, Blake performed regularly in concert and on television, and continued to compose ("Eubie's Classic Rag," 1972). He performed at jazz festivals in New Orleans (1969) and Newport R.I. (1971). Even in his last years, he retained his remarkable virtuosity on piano, vigorously improvising melodic embellishments to a syncopated ragtime beat. In 1978 the musical revue *Eubie!* enjoyed a long run on Broadway. Blake also established a music publishing and recording company and received numerous honorary degrees and awards, including the Presidential Medal of Freedom in 1981. Blake, whose more than three hundred compositions brought a sophisticated sense of harmony to the conventions of ragtime-derived popular song, was active until his ninety-ninth year, and his centennial in 1983 was an occasion for many tributes. However, the 1982 death of his wife, Marion, to whom he had been married since 1945—his first marriage had ended with the death of his wife, Avis—led to a decline in his own health. He died on February 12, 1983 in Brooklyn, N.Y., only five days after his hundredth birthday.

—JOHN GRAZIANO

BLUES, THE

A type of African-American musical art that was first developed in the Mississippi Delta region of Louisiana at the end of the nineteenth century, the blues, like many musical expressions, is difficult to define. Some people think of the blues as an emotion; others regard it primarily as a musical genre characterized by a special blues scale, containing twelve bars and three chords in a particular order. Besides embodying a particular feeling (the "blues") and form, the blues also involves voice and movement: poetry set to dance music. It is vocal not only in the obvious sense that most blues songs have lyrics, but in that even in purely instrumental blues, the lead instrument models its expressivity on the singing voice; and it involves dance because it quite literally moves listeners—even when they are sitting down. Its influence on jazz, gospel music, theater music, rock, and almost every subsequent form of popular music in the twentieth century has been incalculable.

Early blues singers composed their own songs, inventing verses and borrowing from other singers, and they were among the first Americans to express feelings of *anomie* characteristic of modern life and to rise above it through art. By singing about frustration, mistreatment, and misfortune and often overcoming it with irony, blues singers helped themselves and their listeners to deal with the problems of life, whether frustrated and angered by cheating lovers, ignorant bosses, hypocritical churchgoers, crooked shopkeepers, an unjust legal system, racism and prejudice, police brutality, inadequate pay, unemployment, or the meaninglessness of menial labor. Blues singers fought adversity by asserting human creativity, by turning life into art through ironic signification, by linking themselves through their traditional art to others in the community, and by holding out a future hope for freedom and better times down the road. The blues as music and poetry can convey a tremendous range of emotions succinctly and powerfully. Blues lyrics represent an oral poetry of considerable merit, one of the finest genres of vernacular poetry in the English language.

The blues is a distinct musical type. It is an instrumentally accompanied song-type with identifying features in its verse, melodic, and harmonic structures, composition, and accompaniment. Most blues lyrics are set in three-line or quatrain-refrain verses. In the three-line verse shown below, the second line repeats the first, sometimes with slight variation, while the third completes the thought with a rhyme.

I'm gonna dig me a hole this morning, dig it deep down in the ground;

*I'm gonna dig me a hole this morning, dig it
deep down in the ground;
    So if it should happen to drop a bomb
around somewhere, I can't hear the echo when it
sound.*
    ("Lightnin'" Hopkins, "War News Blues")

In the quatrain-refrain verse shown below a rhymed quatrain is followed by a two-line refrain. Each verse form occupies twelve measures or bars of music; in the quatrain-refrain form the quatrain occupies the first four of the twelve.

*I got a job in a steel mill,
a-trucking steel like a slave.
For five long years every Friday
I went straight home with all my pay.
If you've ever been mistreated, you know just
what I'm talking about:
I worked five long years for one woman; she
had the nerve to throw me out.*
    (Eddie Boyd, "Five Long Years")

The tonal material in the blues scale (illustrated herewith) includes both major and minor thirds and sevenths and perfect and diminished fifths. Blues shares this tonal material with other African-American music such as work songs, lined hymnody, gospel music, and jazz. A sharp rise to the highest pitch followed by a gradual descent characterizes the melodic contour of most vocal lines in each verse. Blues shares this contour with the field holler, a type of work song.

Blues has a distinctive harmonic structure. The first line of the verse (or the quatrain in the quatrain-refrain form) is supported by the tonic chord (and sometimes the subdominant, resolving to the tonic at the end of the line), the second line by the subdominant (resolving to the tonic), and the third line by the dominant seventh and then the subdominant before resolving to the tonic. Urban blues and jazz musicians modify this harmonic structure with altered chords and chord substitutions. The blues also has characteristic contents and performance styles. Most blues lyrics are dramatic monologues sung in the first person; most protest mistreatment by lovers and express a desire for freedom. Early blues singers improvised songs by yoking together lines and verses from a storehouse in their memories; most of today's singers memorize entire songs.

Most early down-home blues singers accompanied themselves on piano or on guitar, on the latter supplying a bass part with the right-hand thumb and a treble part independently with the right-hand fingers. Early vaudeville or classic blues singers were accompanied by pianists and small jazz combos. In the 1930s or after, blues "shouters" were accompanied by jazz and rhythm 'n' blues bands, and this led in the 1940s to urban blues singers who played electric guitar and led their own bands. After World War II, most down-home blues singers played electric guitar, sometimes with a small combination of bass, drums, second guitar, harmonica, or piano.

The beginning of blues cannot be traced to a specific composer or date. The earliest appearance of music recognizable as the blues was the publication of W. C. Handy's "The Memphis Blues" (1912) and the "St. Louis Blues" (1914), but by his own testimony, Handy first heard the blues along the lower Mississippi River in the 1890s, and many historians agree with Handy that this was the likeliest environment for the origin of the blues. However, just when and where one locates the origin of blues depends upon what is considered sufficient to the genre. Some cultural historians locate the essence of the blues in resignation or in protest against mistreatment, and they believe that since slaves sung about their condition, these songs must have been blues, even though there is no evidence that they were called blues or that the verse or musical forms resembled later blues. Folklorists and musicologists, on the other hand, have constructed a narrower definition, essentializing structural aspects of the blues as well as their subject and relying for evidence on a combination of oral history, autobiography, and the first blues music recorded by the oldest generation of African Americans.

W. C. Handy and "Jelly Roll" Morton, well-known and accomplished African-American musicians who were very much involved in music before the turn of the twentieth century, recalled in their autobiographies that blues began along the Mississippi in the 1890s as a secular dance music, accompanied by guitars and other portable instruments or piano, with more or less improvised verses, among the river roustabouts in the juke joints and barrelhouses and at picnic and other roadside entertainments. About 1900, folklorists first collected this music, but did not realize they were witnessing the formation of a new genre. Verse patterns varied, the only standard feature being the repetition of the first line; sometimes once, sometimes twice, sometimes three times. The verses were aphoristic, and their subjects concerned lovers, traveling, and daily aspects of life. Harmonic support often was confined to the tonic. The collectors did not call those songs

*"Leadbelly"
Ledbetter's repertory
was huge and
included blues,
children's tunes,
cowboy and work
songs, ballads,
religious songs, and
popular songs.*

PAGE 410

blues, and we may suppose that the singers did not, either.

The first recordings of African Americans singing blues were not made until the 1920s, but it is clear that between 1890 and 1920 the blues developed into a named and recognizable musical genre. In this period the blues developed and diffused wherever there were African Americans in the United States, in the rural areas as well as the towns and cities and among the traveling stage shows. Ma rainey, the "mother of the blues," claimed to have begun singing blues from the stage in 1902, while "Jelly Roll" Morton identified a blues ballad, "Betty and Dupree," as popular fare in New Orleans during the last years of the nineteenth century. Handy's "Memphis Blues" was used in the 1912 mayoralty campaign, while "St.

Louis Blues" was a show tune designed to elevate blues to a higher class. Rural songs at country dance parties gradually consolidated toward three-line verse forms with twelve-measure stanzas and the typical harmonic pattern indicated above, while many of the stage songs featured two sections, an introduction followed by a section in recognizable blues form. The stage songs later became known as "classic" or "vaudeville" blues.

African Americans recorded vaudeville blues beginning with Mamie Smith in 1920. Women with stage-show backgrounds, accompanied by pianists and small combos, sang blues songs composed by professional tunesmiths. The best of the vaudeville blues singers, Ma Rainey and Bessie Smith, appealed across racial and class boundaries, and their singing styles revolutionized

BLUES PIONEER

W. C. Handy Brings Folk Blues to the Public

William Christopher "W. C." Handy (November 16, 1873–March 28, 1958), anthologist and composer. While a child in his native Alabama, W. C. Handy studied music in school; in his teens, he joined a traveling minstrel show as a cornetist. After returning to finish his basic schooling, Handy embarked on a varied career as a teacher, factory worker, college bandmaster, dance-orchestra leader, and minstrel musician. He eventually settled in Memphis in 1908, where he cofounded a music-publishing company with Harry Pace.

After moving to New York in 1918, the Pace and Handy Music Company became the leading publisher of music by African Americans. In 1920, the two owners discontinued their partnership and started separate enterprises, Pace his Black Swan Records, and Handy his Handy Brothers, Inc., and short-lived Handy Record Company. In addition, Handy served variously as a musical consultant, concert program producer, and booking agent. Meanwhile, he continued playing trumpet, composing, arranging, touring, and recording. During his life as a performer, Handy played with such popular groups as W. A. Mahara's minstrels, with Jelly Roll Morton and with other jazz and popular-music luminaries. He appeared at theaters, dance halls, and concert venues as an instrumentalist and as a bandleader.

Handy's first published blues, "Memphis Blues," in 1912, started a fad; by 1914 he had published the song for which he is best known, "St. Louis Blues."

Later he published "Beale Street Blues," making a third Handy "standard" in America's published blues canon. A consensus among jazz historians is that some compositions popularly attributed to Handy are derivative. Some esteem him more highly as a collector, publisher, and popularizer than as a creator of blues. His transcribing and arranging of blues and spirituals led to his books *Blues: An Anthology* (1926; reprinted as *Treasury of the Blues,* 1930), and *Book of Negro Spirituals* (1938).

Handy was a pioneer in bringing folk blues to the public. This led to his being called "the Father of the Blues," which was later used as the title of his autobiography. In 1928, Handy organized a concert at Carnegie Hall to present black music from plantation songs to concert compositions. During the 1930s he organized other concerts of black music for the Chicago World's Fair, the New York World's Fair, and the Golden Gate Exposition in San Francisco.

Handy's productivity declined after he was accidentally blinded in 1943. He died in New York in 1958 of bronchial pneumonia, having suffered an impairing stroke several years earlier. He was honored and memorialized by, among other things, all-Handy musical programs; a movie, *St. Louis Blues;* a 1957 birthday party attended by over eight hundred persons; W. C. Handy Park in Memphis; a postage stamp; and names of institutions and places, including a housing development in his hometown of Florence, Ala.

—THEODORE R. HUDSON

See also
Duke Ellington
Billie Holiday

American popular music. In some of their blues, Rainey and Smith sang about strong, independent women who put an end to mistreatment. Rainey in particular, who sang about such subjects as prostitution, lesbianism, and sadomasochistic relationships, may be viewed as a spokesperson for women's rights. Other vaudeville blues singers, such as Mamie Smith, Sippie Wallace, Ida Cox, and Alberta Hunter, were also very popular in the 1920s, but the era of vaudeville or "classic" blues came to an end during the Great Depression. The down-home or country-flavored blues was recorded beginning in 1926, when record companies took portable recording equipment to southern cities and recorded the local men who sang the blues and accompanied themselves on guitars and pianos in the juke joints and at the country dance parties. Some of the older singers like Charley Patton and Henry Thomas (1874–c. 1959) sang a variety of traditional songs, not all blues; others, like "Blind" Lemon Jefferson, specialized in blues; yet others, like Blind Blake, achieved instrumental virtuosity that has never been surpassed. The variety of traditional music recorded by the older generation reveals the proto-blues as well as the blues and helps to show how the form evolved.

Geographic regions featured their own particular instrumental guitar styles before World War II. The down-home blues of Florida, Georgia, and the Carolinas tended toward rapidly finger-picked accompaniments: "ragtime" styles in which the right-hand thumb imitated the stride pianist's left hand, while the right-hand fingers played melody. Blind Blake, Blind Boy Fuller (c. 1909–1941), and Blind Gary Davis (1896–1972) were among the first exponents of this East Coast style. In Mississippi, on the other hand, chord changes were not as pronounced, and accompaniments featured repeated figures, or riffs, rather than the melody of the verse. Charley Patton, "Son" House (1902–1988), Robert Johnson, and Muddy Waters (McKinley Morganfield) were outstanding guitarists in the Mississippi Delta style. Piano styles equally reflected regional differences. All embodied genuine innovations, such as bottleneck or slide guitar or imitating the expressiveness of the voice, and an inventiveness and technical accomplishment unparalleled in vernacular American music.

Down-home blues became so popular in the late 1920s that talent scouts arranged for singers to travel north to make recordings in the companies' home studios. Blues music was available on what were called "race records," 78-rpm records for African Americans, and they were advertised heavily in black newspapers like the Chicago *Defender.*

While early recordings offer the best evidence of the sound of blues music in its formative years, they can only begin to capture the feel of an actual performance. Because down-home blues usually was performed in barrelhouses, juke joints, at parties, and picnics where the bootleg whiskey flowed, gambling took place, fighting was not uncommon, and sexual liaisons were formed, the music became associated with those who frequented these places. Churchgoers shunned blues because it was associated with sin, while middle-class blacks kept blues at a distance. Most communities, whether rural or urban, had their local blues musicians and entertainments, however. In the 1920s, blues was the most popular African-American music.

The depression cut heavily into record sales and touring stage shows, and most of the classic blues singers' careers ended. The increasing popularity of jazz music provided an opportunity for their successors to tour and record with jazz bands. The down-home blues continued unabated in the rural South and in the cities. A small number of outstanding down-home singers, including Tommy McClennan (1908–1960) Memphis Minnie (McCoy), and Robert Johnson, made commercial recordings, but the big-band blues of Count Basie and other jazz bands, featuring blues "shouters" like Walter Brown, Jimmy Rushing, and "Hot Lips" Page, rode radio broadcasts and records to national popularity later in the 1930s. The blues form became a common ground for

"Jelly Roll" Morton was the first great jazz composer.
PAGE 465

THAT BLUES SOUND

Muddy Waters defined a classic Chicago blues sound that many think was the high point of the genre.
AP/WIDE WORLD PHOTOS

See also
John Coltrane
Miles Davis
Wynton Marsalis

jazz improvisors, and jazz artists of the highest stature, from Louis Armstrong through Duke Ellington, Billie Holiday, and Charlie Parker, Sarah Vaughn, Miles Davis, John Coltrane, and Wynton Marsalis, composed and improvised a great many blues. For Charles Mingus, one of the most important jazz innovators of the 1950s and 1960s, blues and church music were the twin African-American cornerstones of jazz, and much of his music successfully integrated these roots into contemporary "soul" music. Indeed, since the 1940s, periodic reinvigorations of jazz have taken blues for their basis, and it appears that they will continue to do so: bop, hard bop, funk, and other jazz movements all looked for inspiration in blues roots.

Besides the jazz bands, blues in the 1940s and '50s was featured in the urban and rhythm 'n' blues bands led by such guitarists-singers as (Aaron) "T-Bone" Walker and (Riley) B. B. [Blues Boy] King, whose spectacular instrumental innovations virtually defined the genre and influenced countless blues and rock guitarists. Electronic amplification of the guitar allowed it to be heard above the piano and brass and reed instruments; Walker's pioneering efforts virtually invented the modern blues band, the core of which is an electric guitar accompanied by a rhythm section. King's live performances combined instrumental virtuosity in the service of great feeling with a powerful, expressive voice that transformed daily experience into meaningful art, and he spoke to and for an entire generation. His album *B. B. King Live at the Regal* (1965) is often cited as the finest blues recording ever made.

Down-home blues was well served in the years just after World War II by a host of new recording companies. Among the outstanding singer-guitarists were Sam "Lightnin'" Hopkins from Houston and John Lee hooker from Mississippi (and later Detroit) who, along with West Helena and Arkansas harmonica-player "Sonny Boy Williamson" (Rice Miller), contributed a magnificent body of original blues lyric poetry. The Mississippi Delta connection led to such singers as Muddy Waters and Howlin' Wolf (Chester Burnett), who led small combos in Chicago after 1945 that helped create the Chicago blues style, basically a version of the Delta blues played on electrified and amplified instruments. Muddy Waters' band of the early 1950s, featuring "Little" Walter (Jacobs) on amplified harmonica, defined a classic Chicago blues sound that many think was the high point of the genre. With his horn-influenced, amplified harmonica solos, "Little"

Walter invented a completely new sound, and his work stands as another influential example in a music with a history of astonishing technological innovation in the service of greater expressivity. A cluster of post-World War II artists including Waters, Wolf, Jimmy Reed (1925–1976), John Lee Hooker, Elmore James, Little Walter, Sonny Boy Williamson (Rice Miller), and others greatly influenced rock 'n' roll in the 1960s, while a number of similar artists, relying heavily on blues, such as Fats Domino and Chuck Berry, helped to define rock 'n' roll in the 1950s.

In the 1960s, the African-American audience for blues declined, while the white audience increased and the first "blues revival" occurred. Young white musicians and researchers rediscovered older down-home blues singers such as Son House and Mississippi John Hurt, and blues singers and bands became featured acts in coffeehouses, clubs, and festivals that catered to a college-age white audience. Many blues singers' musical careers were extended by this attention. Young white musicians began to play and sing the music, and, along with traditional blues musicians, found a new audience. Earlier recordings were reissued for collectors, research magazines devoted to blues appeared, and cultural historians and scholars began writing about the music. Although black musicians continue to perform blues in traditional venues—bars, juke joints, etc.—particularly in Chicago and in the Mississippi Delta, since the 1960s, newer styles such as motown, soul music, disco, funk, rap, and hip-hop eclipsed blues as popular music among African Americans.

In the early 1990s, another blues revival began to take place. As a resurgence of interest in blues occurs, older blues recordings are being reissued on CD, and some recordings, such as those of Robert Johnson, sell extremely well, while younger singers and musicians, black and white, increasingly choose to perform and record blues. Blues radio shows, such as the one hosted on National Public Radio by Ruth Brown, have increased the music's visibility and popularity. Blues now appears as background music for ads on radio and television. Nightclubs featuring blues can now be found in many American cities, and older artists such as Robert Jr. Lockwood (1915–) and Buddy Guy (1936–) have had new careers, while younger artists such as the Holmes Brothers and Robert Cray have come to prominence. Some southern cities and states, such as Memphis and Mississippi, have set up a significant tourist industry around blues, and there are blues museums and monuments as well. Thirty years ago, it was a music in decline, known outside African-American culture only to a small number of aficionados; but today the blues is historicized, an official part of American and African-American culture. Thirty years ago, literary critics and cultural historians saw little use for the blues, viewing it as a music of slave-consciousness and resignation; but today a new generation of African-American writers, such as Henry Louis Gates, Jr., and Houston Baker, see blues as a source of black pride and a root tradition. As such, blues has had a profound effect upon African-American life and, lately, upon popular culture throughout the world where it and its musical offspring have spread.

—JEFF TODD TITON

BOND, HORACE MANN

Horace Mann Bond (November 8, 1904–December 21, 1972), teacher and administrator. Horace Mann Bond was born in Nashville, Tenn., the youngest of five sons of Jane Bond and James Bond, an educator and Methodist minister. Bond was named for Horace Mann, the nineteenth-century proponent of public education. When Bond was a young boy, the family traveled throughout the South, settling near educational institutions with which James Bond was affiliated, such as Berea College in Kentucky, Talladega College in Alabama, and Atlanta University. A precocious student, Bond was placed in high school when he was nine years old. While in high school, Bond moved with his family back to Kentucky, where his father served as chaplain during World War I at Camp Taylor.

In 1919, at the age of fourteen, Bond enrolled at Lincoln University, an African-American liberal arts college in southeastern Pennsylvania. After graduating from Lincoln in 1923, Bond entered the University of Chicago as a graduate student in education. While pursuing his Ph.D., Bond was a teacher and administrator at several African-American universities: Langston University in Oklahoma, Alabama Agricultural and Mechanical College, and Fisk University in Nashville.

In the early 1930s Bond gained a national reputation by publishing a number of articles in scholarly journals and popular magazines on black education in the South. In 1934 he published a major scholarly work, *The Education of the Negro in the American Social Order*, which argued that the poor quality of education among African Americans was directly linked to their lack of political and economic power. Bond did not recommend the abolition of segregated schools; instead, he called for the equalization of resources given to black and white children. Along the lines of W. E. B. Du Bois's theory of the "talented tenth," Bond's book also argued that young African Americans showing intellectual promise should be trained as future leaders.

While at Chicago, Bond developed a relationship with the Julius Rosenwald Fund, a philanthropic organization that provided funding for African-American scholars and universities. The fund supported Bond through most of his career, first with research fellowships that allowed him to publish widely and later with significant grants to the universities where he served as administrator.

In 1936, the same year he completed his dissertation on the development of public education in Alabama, Bond accepted the deanship of Dillard University, a newly reorganized black college in New Orleans. Bond remained at Dillard until 1939. That year he published his dissertation, *Negro Education in Alabama: A Study of Cotton and Steel*. The work was considered an important challenge to established scholarship on Reconstruction. Bond argued that Reconstruction was a significant step forward for black Americans, in

*If you don't like the
blues, you've got a
hole in your soul.*

ANONYMOUS SAYING

**RENOWNED
SCHOLAR**

Horace Bond, the author of several pathbreaking studies of black education in the 1930s, was later president of Fort Valley State College and Lincoln University.
PHOTOGRAPHS AND PRINTS DIVISION, SCHOMBURG CENTER FOR RESEARCH IN BLACK CULTURE, THE NEW YORK PUBLIC LIBRARY, ASTOR, LENOX AND TILDEN FOUNDATIONS

It would be difficult to overestimate Muhammad Ali's impact on boxing and on the United States as both a cultural icon and political figure.

PAGE 26

particular in the educational institutions established during that period.

Following the publication of *Negro Education in Alabama,* Bond devoted the rest of his career to administration at black colleges, serving as president of Fort Valley State Teachers College in Georgia from 1939 to 1945 and as the first black president of Lincoln University in Pennsylvania from 1945 to 1957. In large part his career was made by successfully lobbying for his institutions, often transforming them from underfunded colleges into comprehensive, well-respected research and teaching universities.

Bond had a variety of social involvements and intellectual interests. While at Lincoln University, he helped to direct research for a historical document supporting the NAACP's challenge to segregation in the *Brown v. Board of Education of Topeka, Kansas* Supreme Court case. In the 1950s and '60s Bond developed an interest in Africa. Through tours, lectures, and articles he attempted to raise support among African Americans for independence movements in African countries. He was a leader of the American Society for African Culture, an organization funded by the Central Intelligence Agency, which both encouraged interest in African culture and warned against the dangers of communism in the African independence movements.

After Bond left Lincoln in 1957, he spent the rest of his career as an administrator at Atlanta University, first as dean of the School of Education and then as the director of the Bureau of Educational and Social Research. During the summer before his first year at Atlanta, Bond delivered the Alexander Inglis Lectures at Harvard University, published in 1959 under the title *The Search for Talent,* in which he argued that social circumstances determine the outcome of mental testing. In the last half of his career Bond's scholarship focused primarily on social influences, and he often argued that IQ tests were biased against African Americans. He retired in 1971.

Horace Mann Bond, who died in Atlanta in 1972, was the father of Julian bond, the civil rights activist and politician.

—THADDEUS RUSSELL

BOXING

Despite the fact that professional prizefighters and sites for professional boxing matches are found all over the world, the origins of modern boxing can be traced to one country and era: late eighteenth- and early nineteenth-century England.

Although proto-forms of combat or blood sports existed in ancient Greece and Rome, they have little connection with the sport of boxing as practiced and understood today. The antecedent of modern boxing was bare-knuckle prizefighting, which sprang up in England almost simultaneously with that country's emergence as a major capitalist world power.

To be sure, the less restrictive moral atmosphere accompanying the decline of Puritanism in the mid-1600s permitted a revival of the rough sports of antiquity. Early on, boxing had close ties to the city, as it was supported by urban wealth when local squires migrated to the metropolis along with increasing numbers of working-class men. Boxing's rise came in large part from the growth of commercialized leisure and popular recreation.

Before the rules formulated by Jack Broughton, one of the earliest of the new breed of "scientific boxers" who appeared on the English sporting scene in the early 1730s, bare-knuckle fighting largely consisted of butting, scratching, wrestling, and kicking. Under the Broughton Rules, elements of wrestling remained, but there was more emphasis on the fists, on skilled defensive maneuvers, and on different styles of throwing a punch effectively. Broughton, for instance, developed the technique called "milling on the retreat," or moving backward while drawing one's opponent into punches, a technique Muhammad Ali used to great effect during his reign as heavyweight champion over two hundred years later. Broughton also used gloves or "mitts" for training his pupils, many of whom were among England's leading citizens.

Under the Broughton Rules, which were superseded by the London Prize Ring Rules in 1838, boxers fought for indeterminate lengths of time, a fight not being declared ended until one could not come up to the scratch mark in the center of the ring. A round lasted until one fighter was felled; both men then returned to their corners and were given thirty seconds to "make scratch" again. London Prize Ring Rules governed the sport of prizefighting as a bare-knuckle contest until the coming of gloves and the Marquis of Queensberry Rules. The first heavyweight championship fight under Queensberry Rules was held between the aging John L. Sullivan and James J. "Jim" Corbett on September 7, 1892. Not only did the fight usher in the age of Queensberry, it also ushered in the age of American domination of the sport, as both Sullivan and Corbett were Americans.

The golden age of bare-knuckle fighting in England, overlapping with the Regency period, occurred between 1800 and 1824, an era captured by Pierce Egan, one of the earliest boxing journalists, in his classic work *Boxiana*. It is during this era that there is record of the first black boxers of note. Bill Richmond was a slave who learned to box by sparring with British seamen. He was taken to England in 1777 by Gen. Earl Percy, a commander of British forces in New York during the American Revolution. Richmond, known as "the Black Terror," became the first American to achieve fame as a prizefighter. He stood about five feet tall and weighed between 155 and 170 pounds. Richmond beat such established British fighters as Paddy Green and Frank Mayers. Among his losses was one in 1805 to the British champion Tom Cribb, who was a title aspirant at the time. Richmond, who died in London, is probably best known not for his fighting but for being a second to the first black fighter to challenge for the championship.

That man, also an American ex-slave, made an even bigger name for himself as a prizefighter. Tom Molineaux apparently came from a boxing family, as it has been claimed that his father was an accomplished plantation scrapper. While there is no record of Molineaux's career before his arrival in England, it is well established that many planters engaged their more athletic slaves in sports. Since most young planters had taken the obligatory European tour and discovered boxing to be the rage among British gentlemen, it is little wonder they imported it to America.

Molineaux, who became known in England as "the Moor," arrived in England in 1809 and quickly defeated Bill Burrows and Tom Blake. Molineaux was matched with Tom Cribb, the champion, for the first time on December 18, 1810, a bitterly cold day (during the bare-knuckle era, most fights took place outdoors). It was one of the most talked-about and eagerly anticipated sports events in British history. Molineaux apparently won the fight, knocking Cribb out in the twenty-eighth round. However, Cribb's seconds accused Molineaux of illegal tactics. During the pandemonium that ensued, Cribb was able to recover, finish the fight, and beat Molineaux, largely because the black boxer had become chilled by the damp cold. The two men fought a rematch in 1811, with Cribb the easy winner, as Molineaux

had failed to train and had generally succumbed to dissipation. He went downhill rapidly after his second loss to Cribb and died in Ireland in 1818, a shell of the figure he had been in his prime.

Despite the impact of Richmond and Molineaux, blacks did not constitute a significant presence in boxing until the late nineteenth and early twentieth centuries, when the United States became the principal venue for professional matches. This era can be referred to as the pre-Jack Johnson age, as the coming of Johnson signified a new epoch not only in boxing but in American sports history. The years 1890 and 1905 are considered among the worst in American race relations, when blacks experienced Jim Crow and American racist practices in their most virulent, oppressive, and blatant forms. Life for black fighters was far from easy: They often were denied fights against whites or, if permitted, found they were expected to throw the fight. They were paid less and fought far more often than did their white counterparts.

Among the important black fighters of this era were Peter Jackson, George Dixon, Joe Gans, and Jersey Joe Walcott. The latter three were all champions in the lighter weight divisions. Boxing under the Queensberry Rules had evolved to the point where there were now firmly established weight divisions, unlike during the bare-knuckle days of Richmond and Molineaux, when boxers fought at "open weight," and there were sometimes great weight disparities between the contestants.

Peter Jackson was arguably the best heavyweight of his generation. Many experts felt he could have taken the measure of the then-champion, John L. Sullivan, had not Sullivan—in keeping with the intense racism of the times—drawn the color line and refused to meet Jackson. The "Black Prince," as Jackson was called, was born in St. Croix, Virgin Islands. His family emigrated to Australia when he was twelve years old and returned to the Virgin Islands three years later. Jackson did not come back with them, opting to seek his fortune as a sailor. During his years as a sailor, Jackson developed his boxing skills. He became the Australian heavyweight champion, but on discovering that America was a place to make one's name, he emigrated in 1888.

At the age of thirty, in 1891, Jackson fought contender Jim Corbett to a sixty-one-round draw, but it was Corbett who fought Sullivan for the title the following year. Although Jackson enjoyed success as a fighter, he left the ring for the stage, as

My business is hurting people.

SUGAR RAY ROBINSON
TESTIMONY, NEW YORK
STATE BOXING COMMISSION,
MAY 23, 1962

See also
Sugar Ray Robinson

he was unable to obtain a title match against either Sullivan or Corbett once Corbett defeated Sullivan for the championship. Jackson toured with a stage production of *Uncle Tom's Cabin* for several years. At thirty-seven, out of condition and well past his prime, he tried a comeback against Jim Jeffries, only to be knocked out in three rounds. Despite the frustration Jackson endured, he was widely admired by many white sports enthusiasts for his gentlemanly demeanor, and he was idolized by blacks. The abolitionist Frederick Douglass in his old age hung a portrait of Jackson in his home. Jackson died of consumption in Australia in 1901.

George Dixon, known to the world as "Little Chocolate," was a smooth and cagey boxer who began his professional career on November 1, 1886. He first became bantamweight champion, although there was dispute about the exact weight qualification for this division. He eventually became the world featherweight champion, a title he held from 1892 to 1900. Dixon was a popular fighter, often featured in white sporting publications such as the *National Police Gazette,* as well as being seen in the haunts of the black entertainment world. Life in the sporting world eventually dissipated Dixon, who was knocked out by Terry McGovern in New York in 1900. He lost his last fight to Monk Newsboy in 1906 and died penniless and broken in health in 1909.

HEAVYWEIGHT CHAMPION

Jack Johnson (left) defeated Tommy Burns in the 1908 heavyweight championship, becoming the first black heavyweight champion. Here he is introduced by Billy Jordan.
PRINTS AND PHOTOGRAPHS
DIVISION, LIBRARY OF
CONGRESS

Joe Gans, "the Old Master," is considered by many historians of boxing to be one of the greatest lightweights of all time. He was born in Baltimore on November 25, 1874, and launched his professional career in 1891. He reigned as lightweight champion from 1902 to 1908. Gans was plagued by ill health, eventually losing his title to Battling Nelson in a rematch. In 1909, he tried to win his title back in another battle against Nelson, but he was sick and aging and easily beaten. Gans died a year later of tuberculosis. It has been suggested that he became a follower of Father Divine before his death. Gans died in Baltimore, and Divine was living there at the time, although at this stage in his career, Divine was virtually unknown as a black religious leader. As Divine was known as a healer (it is not clear whether, at this stage, his followers believed he was God, as they later did) and Gans was afflicted with a disease with no known cure that ravaged the black community, he may have been drawn to Divine as a last-ditch effort to seek a cure.

Joe Walcott was born in Barbados on March 13, 1873. Called "the Barbados Demon" because of his whirlwind punching power and ability to endure punishment (a style that can be likened to that of the popular 1970s junior welterweight champion Aaron Pryor), Walcott held the welterweight title from 1898 to 1906. He retired from the ring in 1911 and worked for a time as a janitor, winding up, as many black fighters did, with no money from his ring efforts. He was killed in an automobile accident in 1935.

From 1908 to the present, the history of blacks in boxing can be divided into three periods: the Jack Johnson era (1908–1915), the Joe Louis era (1937–1949), and the Muhammad Ali era (1964–1978). There have been many impressive and important black fighters aside from these heavyweight champions: Henry Armstrong, a dominant force in the 1930s, who became champion of the featherweight, lightweight, and welterweight divisions simultaneously, the first fighter to achieve such a feat; Sugar Ray Robinson, welterweight champion and winner of the middleweight title on five different occasions, who dominated his weight division in the 1950s and was probably one of the most stylish and influential boxers in history; Archie Moore, "the Old Mongoose," who was champion of the light heavyweight division from 1952 and 1962; Floyd Patterson, Olympic champion in 1952, heavyweight champion from 1956 to 1962, one of the youngest men ever to hold that title; Sugar Ray Leonard, Olympic champion in 1976, champion in the welterweight, junior middleweight, middleweight, and super middleweight divisions, one of the most popular fighters in the 1980s; and the controversial Mike Tyson, who was imprisoned for rape, the youngest man ever to win the heavyweight championship when he won the belt in 1986, and one of the most ferocious and unrelenting fighters ever to enter the ring.

These are a few of the notable black fighters of the twentieth century. But none of these men exercised the social and political impact on American society that Johnson, Louis, and Ali did. These three not only changed boxing, but their presences reverberated throughout the world of sport and beyond. People who normally had no interest in either boxing or sport took an interest in the careers of these three.

Jack Johnson learned the craft of boxing as a child in the same manner many black youngsters were forced to: through participating in battles royal, where five, six, or seven black youngsters were blindfolded and fought against one another in a general melee. The toughest survived the ordeal and made the most money. It may be argued that battles royal were not necessarily more brutal than ordinary prizefights, but they were surely far more degrading.

Johnson fought his first professional fight at the age of nineteen, and the defensive skills he learned to survive the battle royal stood him in good stead when he challenged white fighters in the early twentieth century. Black fighters at this time were expected not to win many fights against white opponents; if they did win, they did so on points. Johnson was among three other black heavyweights who fought during this period: Joe Jeanette, Sam McVey, and Sam Langford, also known as "the Boston Tarbaby." Johnson became a leading contender for the title. After much wrangling and many concessions, he fought Tommy Burns for the heavyweight championship in December 1908 in Sydney, Australia.

Although the color line had been drawn against black challengers to the heavyweight title, Johnson succeeded in part because he was in the right place at the right time. Many in the white sporting public felt it was time to give a black a shot at the title, and Johnson was, at that point, well liked by the white sporting fraternity. Publications such as the *National Police Gazette*, not noted for any enlightened racial attitudes, campaigned vigorously for him to get a title fight. When Johnson defeated Burns, he became the first black heavyweight champion, the most prized title in professional sports.

Soon, however, the white sporting public soured on Johnson. His arrogance and his public preference for white women provoked a cry for "a great white hope" to win the title back for whites. In 1910, Jim Jeffries, a former champion, was lured out of a six-year retirement to take on Johnson in the Nevada desert, a fight that was the most publicized, most heatedly discussed, and most fervently anticipated sporting event in American history at that time. It was the first prizefight to take on significant political overtones, as many whites and blacks saw it as a battle of racial superiority. Johnson was easily the most famous, or the most notorious, black man in America, and the fight occurred at the height of American and Western imperialism, when racial segregation and oppression in this country were fiercely enforced and severely maintained. Johnson easily won the fight, although the victory caused race riots around the country as angry whites brutalized rejoicing blacks. This was Johnson's last great moment as a professional athlete.

In 1912, Johnson's first white wife, Etta Duryea, committed suicide at the champion's Chicago nightclub. In 1913, on the testimony of a white prostitute with whom Johnson had once been intimate, he was convicted under the Mann Act and sentenced to a year and a day in federal prison. Johnson's personal life was now in shambles, and he had no future as a fighter because he was thoroughly hated by the white public. He left the country for Paris.

Johnson lost the title to Kansan Jess Willard in Cuba in 1915, a fight Johnson claimed he threw in order to regain entry to the United States. In fact, he did not return until 1920, when he served his time in prison with little fanfare or notice. Johnson went on to become a museum raconteur, an autobiographer, a fight trainer, and an occasional participant in exhibitions. He died in an automobile accident in 1946.

When Joe Louis defeated Jim Braddock in June 1937 to win the heavyweight title, he was the second black to become heavyweight champion, the first permitted even to fight for the championship since the end of Johnson's tenure in 1915. During the ensuing twenty-two years, there were only three black champions of any division, and two had brief reigns: West African Battling Siki was light heavyweight champion from September 1922 to March 1923, Tiger Flowers was middleweight champion for six months in 1926, and Kid Chocolate was featherweight and junior lightweight champion from 1931 to 1933.

Joe Louis became a symbol of black aspirations in white America.

PAGE 432

See also
Joe Louis

Joe Louis's father was institutionalized for mental illness and his mother remarried. The family relocated from Alabama to Detroit because of job opportunities in the automobile industry. Louis had little interest in school and was attracted to boxing. He had a distinguished amateur career before turning professional in 1934 under the management of John Roxborough and Julian Black, both African Americans. Louis's trainer Jack Blackburn, a former fighter of considerable accomplishment, was also black. With Mike Jacobs, an influential New York promoter, serving as the entrée into big-time fights, Louis's career was carefully guided to the championship in three years.

Image was everything for Louis, or at least for his handlers. In order to be accepted by the white public, he had to be the antithesis of Johnson in every respect. Johnson had bragged and consorted with white women publicly; Louis was taciturn and seen only with black women. Louis went about his business with dispatch, never relishing his victories or belittling his opponents. This latter was an especially sensitive point, as all of Louis's opponents, before he won the championship, were white.

Louis came along at a time when blacks were more assertively pushing for their rights, unlike the era of Johnson. A. Philip Randolph scored a significant victory when he achieved recognition for his union from the Pullman Car Company and achieved further gains when his threatened March on Washington forced President Franklin D. Roosevelt to issue Federal Order 8802 in 1942, integrating defense industry jobs. Louis came of age after the Harlem Renaissance and after Marcus Garvey's Universal Negro Improvement Association movement, both of which signaled greater militancy and race awareness on the part of blacks.

Louis's most important fight was his rematch against German heavyweight Max Schmeling in 1938. Louis had lost to Schmeling in 1936 and for both personal and professional reasons wanted to fight him again. Because Schmeling was German and probably a Nazi, the fight took on both racial and political overtones. Louis became the representative of American democracy against German arrogance and totalitarianism, as well as of American racial fair play against Schmeling's image of racial superiority and intolerance.

Louis won the fight easily, smashing Schmeling in less than a single round. As a result, he became the first black hero in American popular culture. During World War II, he served in the U.S. Army and donated purses from his fights to the war effort. He retired in 1949, after holding the title longer than any other champion and defending it successfully more times than any other champion. Money problems, particularly back income taxes, forced him to make a comeback in 1950. He retired permanently after his loss to Rocky Marciano in 1951. In later years, Louis became a greeter in a Las Vegas hotel. He suffered from mental problems as well as a period of cocaine addiction. He died in Las Vegas in 1981, probably the most revered black boxer, arguably the most revered black athlete, in American history.

Muhammad Ali, born Cassius Clay, Jr., had a distinguished career as an amateur, culminating in a gold medal at the 1960 Olympic Games. Always outgoing with a warm but theatrical personality, the photogenic young boxer spouted poetry, threw punches with greater grace and speed than any heavyweight before him, and was generally well received by the public. Although many people disliked his showy, sometimes outrageous ways, others thought him a breath of fresh air in boxing. The young Clay fought an aging but still intimidating Sonny Liston for the championship in 1964, defeating the older man in a fight in which Clay was the decided underdog.

It was after this fight that Clay announced his conversion to the Nation of Islam. Shortly afterward, he changed his name to Muhammad Ali, probably one of the most widely and thoroughly discussed and damned name changes in American history. Ali's popularity among whites plummeted as a result of his conversion.

But he was not through provoking the white American public. In 1967 he refused induction into the armed services on religious grounds. His spiritual leader, Elijah Muhammad, had served time in prison during World War II for taking the same stand. Ali was stripped of his title, and his license to fight was revoked. Despite outcries from more liberal sections of the white public, Ali was, in effect, under a kind of house arrest for three and a half years, not permitted to fight in this country and not permitted to leave the country to fight abroad while his case was being appealed.

Ali was finally permitted to fight again in late 1970 in Georgia against journeyman heavyweight Jerry Quarry, whom he dispatched in a few rounds. During the interval of Ali's exile, the sentiments of the white public had changed significantly. Many turned against the Vietnam War. The deaths of Rev. Dr. Martin Luther King, Jr., and Robert Kennedy only two months apart in

SUGAR RAY ROBINSON
Boxing Finesse and Knockout Power

Sugar Ray Robinson (Walker Smith, Jr.) (May 3, 1921–April 12, 1989), boxer. Sugar Ray Robinson was born to Marie and Walker Smith in Detroit. He moved with his mother in 1933 to Harlem, where he attended DeWitt Clinton High School. Representing the Salem Athletic Club, he began boxing, using the identification card of a Ray Robinson. He won the New York Golden Gloves in 1939 and 1940 and turned professional late in 1940. A reporter described his technique as "sweet as sugar." Robinson won his first forty fights (twenty-six knockouts) until Jake LaMotta beat him on a decision in 1943. He served as a private during World War II, mainly boxing exhibitions on tour with his idol, Joe Louis. Robinson demanded fair treatment for blacks in the military, refusing to appear at one show until blacks were allowed into the audience, and getting into a fight with a military policeman (MP) who had threatened Louis for using a phone in a whites-only area.

Robinson won the vacant welterweight (147 pounds) championship on December 20, 1946, in a fifteen-round decision over Tommy Bell. In Robinson's first defense, Jimmy Doyle suffered fatal brain injuries in an eighth-round knockout. When questioned if he had intended to get Doyle into trouble, Robinson responded, "Mister, it's my business to get him in trouble." He moved up to the middleweight division (160 pounds), besting champion Jake LaMotta in the 1951 "St. Valentine's Day Massacre," which got its name from the punishment LaMotta took until the fight was stopped in the thirteenth round. Robinson lost the title on a decision five months later to Randy Turpin in London, making his record 128–1–2. Two months later he regained the title from Turpin with a dramatic tenth-round knockout in New York as he bled heavily from a cut above the left eye. In 1952 he fought Joey Maxim for the light

heavyweight championship at Yankee Stadium. He was far ahead on points, but he collapsed after the thirteenth round in 100–degree heat.

Robinson retired from the ring and worked two years as a tap dancer. He returned to boxing in 1955 and in his seventh bout regained the middleweight crown with a second-round knockout of Bobo Olson on December 9, 1955. He lost the title on January 2, 1956, to Gene Fullmer, regaining it in a rematch four months later, knocking Fullmer unconscious in the fifth. Carmen Basilio dethroned Robinson on September 23 but lost the rematch on March 25, 1958, by decision. Robinson held the middleweight title until defeated by Paul Pender on January 22, 1960. Robinson lost the rematch and two other title bouts, and he retired in 1965. He held the middleweight championship a record five times.

Robinson was renowned for his flashy living. He owned a night club, Sugar Ray's, and other Harlem properties and on tours took a large entourage, including a valet and barber. He appeared in television and films. Once he was well established, he acted as his own manager and was regarded as a tough negotiator. An IRS tax dispute led to a ruling that allowed income averaging. However, Robinson went through $4 million so fast he had to continue boxing well past his prime. In 1969 he moved to Los Angeles, where he established the Sugar Ray Robinson Youth Foundation for inner city youth. He lived there with his second wife, Millie Bruce, until he died of Alzheimer's disease and diabetes. Robinson had a record of 174 (with 109 KO's)–19–6–2. Renowned for his superb footwork, hand speed, and leverage, he was so powerful that he could knock out an opponent when moving backwards. He was elected to the Boxing Hall of Fame in 1967.

—STEVEN A. RIESS

1968, made many think the country was on the verge of collapse, and as a result there was a greater sense of tolerance and understanding. Ali's religious beliefs did not strike so many as being as bizarre and threatening as they had a few years earlier. Finally, blacks had achieved some political leverage in the South, and this was instrumental in getting Ali a license to box again. Ali eventually won his case in the U.S. Supreme Court when his conviction was overturned as one of a series of de-

cisions that broadened the allowable scope for conscientious objection to war.

Ali lost his claim to the title when he suffered his first professional defeat at the hands of Joe Frazier in March 1971, the first of three epic battles between the two great fighters. But Ali eventually regained his title in 1974 when he defeated George Foreman in a shocking upset in Zaire. He lost the title again in 1978 to Olympic champion Leon Spinks, but regained it a few months later in

See also
Muhammad Ali

*I have heard in the
voices of the wind
the voices of my dim
killed children. /
. . . Believe me, I
knew you, though
faintly, and I loved,
I loved you / All.*

a rematch, becoming the first heavyweight to win the championship three times.

Ali was by far the most popular champion in the history of boxing. His face was, and still is, recognized more readily in various parts of the world than that of virtually any other American. Ali has been particularly important in creating a stronger sense of kinship between American blacks and people of the Third World. He is the most renowned Muslim athlete in history.

Like many before him, Ali fought too long, disastrously trying a comeback in 1981 against champion Larry Holmes, who badly thrashed him over ten rounds. Ali's health deteriorated throughout the 1980s. It was finally revealed that he suffers from Parkinson's disease, induced by the heavy punishment he took in the ring. Although physically not what he once was, Ali remains a formidable physical presence, a man of great warmth and humor, and an athlete who is still honored around the world for his courage both in and out of the ring.

With Ali's departure from boxing, the heavyweight division was dominated for a considerable period by Holmes, a formidable fighter but a man of little personality, wit, or engagement. Although Holmes enjoyed considerable popularity during his reign, it was fighters from the lighter weight divisions who attracted media attention and huge purses during the late 1970s through the 1980s. Sugar Ray Leonard, Marvelous Marvin Hagler, Matthew Saad Muhammad, Aaron Pryor, Dwight Muhammad Qawi, Thomas "Hitman" Hearns, Marvin Johnson, Mike "the Body Snatcher" Mc-Callum, Livingstone Bramble, and Michael Spinks were among the best and most highly publicized fighters of the day.

Relying on the popularity of several highly skilled Latin American fighters, including the redoubtable Roberto Duran, Alexis Arguella, Pipino Cuevas, and Victor Galindez, which enabled fight promoters to once again use ethnic and cultural symbolism as a lure for a diverse and fragmented public, these black fighters were able to bring greater attention and larger sums of money to boxing arenas in the 1980s than ever before.

After Holmes, the heavyweight class fell into complete disarray, similar to the 1930s before the coming of Joe Louis. A succession of undistinguished champions paraded before the public. Not until the emergence of Mike Tyson did the category reclaim its position as the glamour division of the sport. Tyson enjoyed greater financial success than any other heavyweight in history.

However, he was poorly advised, surrounded by cronies who did not protect his interests or their own. Tyson pursued a self-destructive path of erratic, violent behavior and suspected substance abuse, and was finally imprisoned for an assault on a black beauty contestant.

—GERALD EARLY

BROOKS, GWENDOLYN ELIZABETH

Gwendolyn Elizabeth Brooks (June 7, 1917–), poet, novelist, teacher, and reader/lecturer. Taken to Topeka, Kans., to be born among family, Brooks was reared in Chicago, where she continues to reside. In her autobiography, *Report from Part One* (1972), she describes a happy childhood spent in black neighborhoods with her parents and younger brother, Raymond. "I had always felt that to be black was good," Brooks observes. School awakened her to preferences among blacks, the "black-and-tan motif" noted in her earlier works by critic Arthur P. Davis. Her father, David Anderson Brooks, was the son of a runaway slave, a janitor with "rich Artistic Abilities" who had spent a year at Fisk University, Nashville, hoping to become a doctor, and who sang, told stories, and responded compassionately to the poverty and misfortune around him; her mother, Keziah Wims Brooks, had been a fifth-grade teacher in Topeka and harbored a wish to write. They nurtured their daughter's precocious gifts. When the seven-year-old Gwendolyn began to write poetry, her mother predicted, "You are going to be the *lady* Paul Laurence Dunbar." Years later, Mrs. Brooks took her daughter to meet James Weldon Johnson and then Langston Hughes at church. Hughes became an inspiration, friend, and mentor to the young poet.

Brooks was graduated from Wilson Junior College (now Kennedy-King) in 1936. She was employed for a month as a maid in a North Shore home and spent four months as secretary to a spiritual adviser (see the "Prophet Williams" section of the story "In the Mecca"). In 1939, she married Henry Lowington Blakely II, a fellow member of Inez Cunningham Stark's poetry workshop in the South Side Community Art Center and himself a poet and writer. Motherhood (Henry, Jr., 1940; Nora, 1951), early publishing (*A Street in Bronzeville*, 1945), warm critical reception, careful supervision of her career by her editor at *Harper's,* and a succession of honors and prizes helped her overcome her reticence about public speaking. The first African American (or "Black," her articulated preference) to win a Pulitzer Prize, for poetry (*Annie Allen,* 1950), Brooks also received two Guggenheim Fellowships. Upon the death of Carl Sandburg (in 1968), she was named the poet laureate of Illinois. She was the first black woman to be elected to the National Institute of Arts and Letters (1976); to become consultant in poetry to the Library of Congress (1985–1986, just before the title was changed to poet laureate); to become an honorary fellow of the Modern Language Association; and to receive the Poetry Society of America's Shelley Memorial Award and its Frost Medal. She was elected to the National Women's Hall of Fame and given the National Endowment for the Arts Lifetime Achievement Award in 1989. In Illinois, the Junior High School at Harvey, the cultural center at Western Illinois University, and the center and a chair as Distinguished Professor of English at Chicago State University all bear her name. The number of her honorary doctorates already exceeds seventy.

Brooks's work is notable for its impeccable craft and its social dimension. It marks a confluence of a dual stream: the black sermonic tradition and black music, and white antecedents such as the ballad, the sonnet, and conventional and free-verse forms. Influenced early by Hughes, T. S. Eliot, Emily Dickinson, and Robert Frost, she was propelled by the Black Arts movement of the 1960s into black nationalist consciousness. Yet her poetry has always been infused with both humanism and heroism, the latter defined as extending the concept of leadership, by both personality and art. In 1969 she moved to Dudley Randall's nascent, historic Broadside Press for the publication of *Riot* and subsequent works.

Brooks's books span six decades of social and political changes. *A Street in Bronzeville* addresses the quotidian realities of segregation for black Americans at home and in World War II military service; *Annie Allen* ironically explores postwar antiromanticism; *Maud Martha,* her novel (1953), sketches a bildungsroman of black womanhood; *Bronzeville Boys and Girls* (1956) presents sturdy, home-oriented black children of the 1950s; *The Bean Eaters* (1960) and new poems in *Selected Poems* (1963) sound the urgencies of the Civil Rights Movement. In 1967, at the second Fisk University Writers' Conference at Nashville, Brooks was deeply impressed by the activist cli-

B

BROOKS, GWENDOLYN ELIZABETH

PULITZER PRIZE WINNER

Gwendolyn Brooks was the first African-American recipient of a Pulitzer prize, which she won in 1950 for her poetry. Her work is acclaimed for its impeccable craft and its social dimension.
AP/WIDE WORLD PHOTOS

mate, personified by Amiri Baraka. Though she had always experimented with conventional forms, her work subsequently opened more distinctly to free verse, a feature of the multiform *In the Mecca* (1968), which Haki R. Madhubuti calls "her epic of Black humanity" (*Report from Part One,* p. 22).

Upon returning to Chicago from the conference at Fisk, Brooks conducted a workshop with the Blackstone Rangers, a teenage gang, who were succeeded by young writers such as Carolyn M. Rodgers and Madhubuti (then don l. lee). Broadside published *Riot* (1969), *Family Pictures* (1970), *Aloneness* (1971), and *Beckonings* (1975). Madhubuti's Third World Press published *The Tiger Who Wore White Gloves* (1974) and *To Disembark* (1981). In 1971 Brooks began a literary annual, *The Black Position,* under her own aegis, and made the first of her two trips to Africa. Beginning with *Primer for Blacks* (1980), she published with her own company *The Near-Johannesburg Boy* (1986), the omnibus volume *Blacks* (1987), *Gottschalk and the Grande Tarantelle* (1988), and *Winnie* (1988, a poem honoring Winnie Mandela). Her books are also being reissued by Third World Press. The adult poems of

See also

Literature

Children Coming Home (1991) express the perspective of contemporary children, and may be contrasted with the benign ambience of *Bronzeville Boys and Girls* among her works for children.

Brooks supports and promotes the creativity of other writers. Her annual Poet Laureate Awards distribute considerable sums of her own money, chiefly to the schoolchildren of Illinois. She visits prisons, where her readings have inspired poets such as the late Ethridge Knight. Lauded with affectionate respect in two tribute anthologies, recognized nationally and internationally as a major literary figure, Brooks continues to claim and to vivify our democratic heritage.

—D. H. MELHEM

BROWN, JAMES JOE, JR.

James Joe Brown, Jr. (May 3, 1933–), singer and songwriter. Born near Barnwell, S.C., to Joe Brown, a turpentine worker, and Susan Behlings. After his mother left the family when the boy was four years of age, Brown spent his formative years in a brothel run by his aunt Handsome Washington in Augusta, Ga. After the authorities closed the brothel in 1943, he lived with his aunt Minnie Walker, receiving occasional tutoring on drums and piano from neighbors and showing early promise on harmonica and organ. He absorbed the music of the black church and of the minstrel shows that passed through Augusta; he heard the blues his father learned in the turpentine camps, and he listened to pop music on the radio. Fascinated by "soundies" (filmed musical numbers that preceded the feature at movie theaters), he paid close attention to those of Louis Jordan and His Tympany Five, who performed jump blues and novelty songs with great showmanship. Singing Jordan's "Caldonia," Brown entered and won local talent contests while not yet in his teens. At thirteen, he formed the Cremona Trio, his first musical group, performing the songs of such rhythm and blues artists as Jordan, Amos Milburn, Wynonie Harris, Charles Brown, and the Red Mildred Trio.

These early musical endeavors were cut short when Brown's habit of stealing clothes and other items from unlocked automobiles earned him a harsh eight-to-sixteen-year prison sentence, which he began serving at Georgia Juvenile Technical Institute (GJTI) in Rome, Ga., in 1949. In GJTI, he formed a gospel quartet with

See also

Literature

CLAUDE BROWN

Author Chronicles Harlem Youth

Claude Brown (February 23, 1937–), writer. Claude Brown was born in Harlem in New York City, one of four children of a railroad worker and a domestic. Brown displayed behavioral problems and at age eight was sent to Bellevue Hospital for observation. By the time he was ten, he had an extensive history of truancy and expulsion and was sent to the Wiltwyck School, a school for emotionally disturbed boys, and then to the Warwick reform school. After his release from reform school, Brown performed a series of odd jobs and enrolled in night courses at Washington Irving High School. He graduated in 1957 and returned to Harlem, where he sold cosmetics and played piano for a living. In 1959 he won a grant from the Metropolitan Community Methodist Church to study government at Howard University, which awarded him a B.A. in 1965. While in his last year of college, Brown was encouraged by a mentor from the Wiltwyck School to write an article about growing up in Harlem for *Dissent Magazine*. An editor at Macmillan Publishing Company saw the article and offered Brown an advance to write what would become his celebrated 1965 memoir *Manchild in the Promised Land*.

The book was an uncensored account of coming-of-age in the turbulent setting of Harlem and was praised by critics for its honesty in its depiction of his difficult childhood. The bestseller made Brown a celebrity and consequently interfered with his studies at Stanford University Law School. He transferred to Rutgers Law School, which he left in 1968 without obtaining his degree. In 1976, Brown's second book, *Children of Ham*, about a group of Harlem youths struggling to succeed, was published, but it failed to have the same impact as his first book.

Since the 1970s, Brown has worked as a freelance writer, commenting on the status of urban America. His articles have been published in a number of periodicals including the *New York Times*, the *Los Angeles Times*, *Esquire*, and the *New York Times Magazine*.

—KENYA DILDAY

three other inmates, including Johnny Terry, who would later become one of the original Famous Flames. After serving three years, he was paroled in Toccoa, the small town in northeast Georgia to which GJTI had been moved. He soon formed a gospel group with several youthful Toccoa musicians including Bobby Byrd, a talented keyboard player, who would remain a central figure in James Brown's musical endeavors into the early 1970s.

The fledgling gospel group soon began playing rhythm and blues and performed for dances and in small clubs throughout eastern Georgia and neighboring areas of South Carolina until Little Richard's manager induced them to come to the vital music scene centered in Macon, Ga. At a Macon radio station, the group, soon to be known as the Famous Flames, recorded a demo of "Please, Please, Please," which attracted the attention of Cincinnati-based King records. Rerecorded in Cincinnati and released in 1956, the song eventually climbed to number six on the rhythm and blues record chart. During the next two years, Brown sought to duplicate the success of "Please," essaying a number of rhythm and blues styles and occasionally imitating the differing approaches of Little Richard and King labelmates Hank Ballard and the Midnighters and the Five Royales. In 1958, with the recording of "Try Me," a pleading ballad steeped in gospel, he achieved the number one position on the rhythm-and-blues chart, and began to realize his own distinctive style.

Brown soon became a headliner at Harlem's Apollo Theater and toured tirelessly, playing as many as 300 dates annually and presenting a stage revue complete with comedians, warmup acts, dancers, and a full orchestra. As a singer, he developed a powerful shouting style that owed much to gospel, but his rhythmic grunts and expressive shrieks harked back farther still to ring shouts, work songs, and field cries. As a band leader, he developed one of the most disciplined bands in entertainment and maintained it for more than three decades. He reimported the rhythmic complexity from which rhythm and blues, under the dual pressure of rock 'n' roll and pop, had progressively fallen away since its birth from jazz and blues. As one of the greatest vernacular dancers in rhythm and blues, he integrated the latest dance crazes with older black popular dance styles and integrated them into a seamless whole that came to be known as "the James Brown." He became one of the most exciting live performers in popular music, capping his performances with a collapse-and-resurrection routine that became his trademark.

With the album *Live at the Apollo* (1963), Brown brought the excitement of his stage show to record buyers throughout the world. Through the mid-1960s, he enjoyed enormous success with such compositions as "Out of Sight" (1964), "I Feel Good (I Got You)" (1965), "Papa's Got a Brand New Bag" (1965), and "Cold Sweat" (1967). These infectious, rhythmically complex dance hits propelled him to international stardom and heralded funk, his most original and enduring contribution to popular music around the world. Dispensing almost entirely with chord changes, Brown, by the late 1960s, stripped the music to its rhythmic essence. Horns, guitars, and voices—including Brown's rich assortment of grunts, groans, shrieks, and shouts—were employed percussively. Rhythmic emphasis fell heavily on the downbeat at the beginning of each measure, imparting a sense of overwhelming propulsiveness to the music while leaving ample room for complex rhythmic interplay.

From the late 1960s through the mid 1970s, Brown and his band, assisted by gifted arrangers Pee Wee Ellis and Fred Wesley, produced powerful, polyrhythmic funk music that included inspired dance tracks as heard on albums such as *Sex Machine* (1970) and *Super Bad* (1971). He also wrote inspirational, political and social commentary such as the anthem of black pride "Say It Loud—I'm Black and I'm Proud" (1968). Brown also became something of a political figure; several presidential candidates sought his endorsement. Following the murder of the Rev. Dr. Martin Luther King, Jr. in April 1968, Brown helped quell riots in Boston and Washington, D.C. In 1971 he produced a single about the dangers of drug use, "King Heroin."

Although Brown's records sold well through the early 1970s, the magnitude of his accomplishment was obscured by the rise of disco. Plagued by personal problems, including the break-up of his second marriage, the death of his oldest son, a federal tax case, and troubles with his numerous business enterprises, he briefly went into semi-retirement, though he never entirely stopped performing, and he recorded numerous albums during this period, including *Hot* (1976) and *Bodyheat* (1976).

In the early 1980s he staged a successful comeback. He made cameo appearances in numerous motion pictures such as *The Blues Brothers* (1980). A series of retrospective albums, including *The Federal Years* (*Part 1 and 2*, 1984) and *Dead on the Heavy Funk* (1985) traced the development of his music from 1956 to 1976, and he returned to extensive recording and performing. His music was also widely sampled by rap artists. In 1986 he performed "Living in America" in the film *Rocky IV*

Say It Loud: I'm Black and Proud.

JAMES BROWN
SONG TITLE, 1979

See also
Blues
Motown

and that year became one of the first performers inducted into the Rock and Roll Hall of Fame.

In 1988, after leading police in Georgia and South Carolina on a high-speed chase that ended when the police fired some two dozen bullets into his truck, Brown was sentenced to six years in prison for failing to stop for a police officer and aggravated assault. Although the lengthy sentence sparked a national outcry for Brown's pardon, he remained incarcerated for more than two years, earning early release in 1991. Nevertheless, he re-emerged to be seen as one of the towering figures of popular music throughout the world. His musical innovations inform rock and jazz-funk hybrids, dance pop, reggae, hip-hop, and much African and Latin popular music. Critics, formerly ignoring him, now generally recognize him as one of the most influential American musicians of the past half century. His output has been prodigious, including more than seventy albums. In 1991 he released *Star Time,* a 71–song, 4–CD compilation of his greatest hits. He has also produced hundreds of recordings by other artists and continues to record (*Love Over-Due,* 1991).

—BRUCE TUCKER

BROWN, STERLING ALLEN

Sterling Allen Brown (May 1, 1901–January 13, 1989), poet, scholar. Sterling A. Brown, who expressed the humor and resilience of the black folk tradition in his poetry, teaching, and public persona, was born on the Howard University campus. Except for a few years spent elsewhere as student and teacher, he remained at Howard most of his life. His father, Sterling Nelson Brown, born a slave, became a distinguished clergyman in Washington, D.C., as pastor of the Lincoln Temple Congregational Church and professor of religion at Howard, beginning in the 1890s. Rev. Brown died shortly before his son followed his example by joining the Howard faculty in 1929, a post that he held until his retirement forty years later, in 1969.

As a youngster Brown attended the Lucretia Mott School and Dunbar High School, which was generally acknowledged as the finest black high school in the country. Upon graduation Brown accepted the scholarship that Williams College in Massachusetts offered to the Dunbar valedictorian each year. At Williams he joined the debating team, earned Phi Beta Kappa member-ship, and became the doubles tennis partner of Allison Davis, subsequently a distinguished social scientist and University of Chicago professor. After graduating from Williams in 1922, Brown earned his master's degree in English from Harvard University the following year. Before returning to Howard in 1929, he taught for three years at Virginia Seminary in Lynchburg, Va., for two years at Lincoln University in Missouri; and for a year at Fisk University in Nashville.

Brown achieved an enduring reputation as a poet, scholar, and teacher. His most celebrated volume of poems was *Southern Road* (1932). Unlike such Harlem Renaissance contemporaries as Claude McKay and Countee Cullen, who wrote sonnets imitating Keats and Shakespeare, Brown eschewed traditional high literary forms and subjects, preferring instead the folk-ballad form and taking common black people as his subjects. In this he was like Langston Hughes. Brown was influenced by realist and narrative poets such as A. E. Housman, Edwin Arlington Robinson, and Edgar Lee Masters, as well as by African-American folklore, blues, and work songs. The characters of Brown's poems, such as Slim Greer, Scrappy, and Old Lem, are tough, worldly, and courageous. Some are fighters and troublemakers; some are pleasure-seekers or hardworking farmers; and some are victims of racist mobs. At once unsentimental and unapologetic, these characters embody the strength and forthrightness that was typical of Brown's work in every genre.

As a scholar, Brown is best remembered for two books: *The Negro in American Fiction* (1937) and *Negro Poetry and Drama* (1937). These are both exhaustive works that document the African-American presence in American literature from the beginnings to the 1930s. The former book has been especially influential as the first and most thorough work of its kind, and has been a foundation for all subsequent studies of blacks in American fiction. From 1936 through 1940 Brown served as national editor of Negro affairs for the Federal Writers' Project (FWP). In this position he was involved with reviewing how African Americans were portrayed in the publications of the FWP, especially the series of state guidebooks. Although the task was frustrating—especially where the Deep South states were concerned—the appointment reflected how highly Brown, not yet forty, was regarded. During this same period, Brown also edited, along with Arthur P. Davis and Ulysses Lee, *The Negro Caravan* (1941), which remains one of the most useful and comprehensive anthologies of African-American writ-

See also

Literature

ing ever published. All in all, the 1930s was the most intensely productive decade of Brown's life.

As a teacher, Brown has been broadly influential. He was a pioneer in the teaching of African-American literature, and a startling number of black writers, scholars, and political figures have studied with him. Outside the classroom, Brown for many years held informal listening sessions, using his own massive record collection to introduce students to jazz, the blues, and other black musical forms. Alumni of those sessions include LeRoi Jones (Amiri Baraka) and A. B. Spellman, both of whom subsequently wrote important books about jazz. Similarly, Stokely Carmichael and Kwame Nkrumah were students of Brown who have often acknowledged their debt to him. His power as a teacher derived in part from his erudition but especially from his rare ability to combine the vernacular, scholarly, and literary traditions of the United States with progressive political values and a blunt, unpretentious personal style.

Brown's literary productivity decreased after the 1940s, partly due to recurrent illnesses. He nonetheless remained active as a guest lecturer and poetry recitalist, and taught at several universities during his forty-year tenure at Howard, including Vassar College, Atlanta University, and New York University. In 1980 Michael S. Harper edited Brown's *Collected Poems,* which was awarded the Lenore Marshall Prize for the oustanding volume of poetry published in the United States that year. Brown's memoir, "A Son's Return: 'Oh, Didn't He Ramble,'" published in *Chant of Saints* (1979), recounts his early years, especially his life at Williams College, and is, despite its short length, one of the most compelling of African-American literary memoirs. Brown died in Takoma Park, Md.

—DAVID LIONEL SMITH

BROWN V. BOARD OF EDUCATION OF TOPEKA, KANSAS

Brown, 347 U.S. 483 (1954), was the most important legal case affecting African Americans in the twentieth century and unquestionably one of the most important Supreme Court decisions in U.S. constitutional history. Although directly involving segregated public schools, the case became the legal underpinning for the Civil Rights Movement of the 1950s and 1960s and the dismantling of all forms of statutory segregation.

Brown combined separate cases from Kansas, South Carolina, Virginia, and Delaware that turned on the meaning of the Fourteenth Amendment's requirement that states not deny their citizens "equal protection of the law." The Court also heard a similar case from Washington, D.C., *Bolling* v. *Sharpe,* which involved the meaning of the Fifth Amendment's due process clause.

In 1954, laws in eighteen states plus the District of Columbia mandated segregated schools, while other states allowed school districts to maintain separate schools if they wanted to do so. Although theoretically guaranteeing blacks "separate-but-equal" education, segregated schools were never equal for blacks. Linda Brown, whose father, Rev. Oliver Brown, sued the Topeka, Kans., school system on her behalf, had to travel an hour and twenty minutes to school each way. If her bus was on time, she was dropped off at school a half hour before it opened. Her bus stop was six blocks from her home, across a hazardous railroad yard; her school was twenty-one blocks from her home. The neighborhood school her white playmates attended was only seven blocks from her home, and required neither bus nor hazardous crossings to reach. The *Brown* companion cases presented segregation at its worst. Statistics from Clarendon, S.C., where one of the cases began, illustrate the inequality of separate but equal. In 1949 and 1950, the average expenditure for white students was $179, but for blacks it was only $43. The county's 6,531 black students attended school in 61 buildings valued at $194,575; many of these schools lacked indoor plumbing or heating. The 2,375 white students in the county attended school in twelve buildings worth $673,850, with far superior facilities. Teachers in the black schools received, on average, salaries that were one-third less than those of teachers in the white schools. Finally, Clarendon provided school buses for white students in this rural county but refused to provide them for blacks.

The plaintiffs could easily have won orders requiring state officials to equalize the black schools, on the grounds that education was separate but *not* equal. Since the 1930s the Court had been chipping away at segregation in higher education, interstate transportation, housing, and voting. In *Brown* the NAACP Legal Defense Fund, led by Thurgood Marshall, decided to directly challenge the whole idea of segregation in schools.

We conclude that in the field of public education "separate but equal" has no place.

EARL WARREN
BROWN V. BOARD OF EDUCATION OF TOPEKA, KANSAS, MAY 17, 1954

See also
Education

Marshall's bold challenge of segregation per se led the Court to reconsider older cases, especially Plessy v. Ferguson, that had upheld segregation. The Court was also compelled to consider the meaning of the Fourteenth Amendment, which had been written at a time when most states allowed some forms of segregation and when public education was undeveloped in the South. The Court ordered attorneys for both sides to present briefs and reargument on these historical matters. In the end, the Court found the historical argument to be

> at best . . . inconclusive. The most avid proponents of the post-War Amendments undoubtedly intended them to remove all legal distinctions among "all persons born or naturalized in the United States." Their opponents, just as certainly, were antagonistic to both the letter and the spirit of the Amendments. . . . What others in Congress and the state legislatures had in mind cannot be determined with any degree of certainty.

After reviewing the histories of the Fourteenth Amendment, public education, and segregation, Chief Justice Earl Warren, speaking for a unanimous Court, concluded, "In approaching this problem, we cannot turn the clock back to 1868 when the Amendment was adopted, or even to 1896 when Plessy v. Ferguson was written. We must consider public education in the light of its full development and its present place in American life throughout the Nation." Warren found that "in the field of public education the doctrine of 'separate but equal' has no place. Separate education facilities are inherently unequal." *Brown* did not technically overturn *Plessy* (which involved seating on railroads) or the separate-but-equal doctrine. But that technicality was unimportant. *Brown* signaled the end to the legality of segregation. Within a dozen years the Supreme Court would strike down all vestiges of legalized segregation.

Brown did not, however, lead to an immediate end to segregated education. The Court instead ordered new arguments for the next year to determine how to begin the difficult social process of desegregating schools. The NAACP urged immediate desegregation. However, in a second case, known as *Brown II* (1955), the Court ordered its mandate implemented with "all deliberate speed," a process that turned out to be extraordinarily slow. Linda Brown, for example, did not attend integrated schools until junior high; none of the plaintiff children in the Clarendon County case ever attended integrated schools.

—PAUL FINKELMAN

BUNCHE, RALPH JOHNSON

Ralph Johnson Bunche (1904–1971), scholar, diplomat, and international civil servant. Ralph Bunche was born in Detroit, Mich., to Fred and Olive Johnson Bunch. His father, a barber, abandoned the family when his son was young. Bunche moved with his mother to Albuquerque, N. Mex., where she died in 1917. He then went to Los Angeles to be raised by his maternal grandmother, Lucy Taylor Jackson. During his teen years, he added a final "e" to his name to make it more distinguished. Bunche lived in a neighborhood with relatively few blacks, and he was one of only two blacks in his class at Jefferson High School, where he graduated first in his class, although Los Angeles school authorities barred him from the all-city honor roll because of his race. Bunche's valedictory address was his first public speech. Bunche entered the University of California at Los Angeles (UCLA) on scholarship, majoring in political science and philosophy. He was active on the debating team, wrestled, played football and baseball, and was a standout basketball player. In 1927, he graduated *summa cum laude* and again, first in his class.

Assisted by a tuition fellowship and a $1,000 scholarship provided by a group of African-American women in Los Angeles, Bunche enrolled at Harvard University in 1927 to pursue graduate study in political science. He received a master's degree in 1928, and then accepted an invitation to join the faculty of Howard University. Bunche was only twenty-five when he created and chaired Howard's political science department. His association with Howard continued until 1941, although he pursued graduate work at Harvard during leaves.

Bunche's graduate work combined his interest in government with a developing interest in Africa. He conducted field research in western Africa in 1932 and 1933, and wrote a dissertation on the contrast between European colonial and mandatory governments in Africa. The dissertation, completed in 1934, won a Harvard award as the best political science dissertation of the year, and Bunche was awarded the first Ph.D. in political science ever granted an African American by

See also
NAACP

an American university. Bunche undertook post-doctoral studies in 1936 and 1937, first at Northwestern University, then at the London School of Economics and at South Africa's University of Cape Town. In 1936 he published a pamphlet, *A World View of Race*. His notes, taken during fieldwork in South Africa and detailing the political and racial situation were published in 1992 under the title *An African American in South Africa*.

During Bunche's time at Howard in the 1930s, he was deeply involved in civil rights questions. He believed that black people's principal concerns were economic, and that race, though significant, was secondary. While he participated in civil rights actions—notably a protest he organized against segregation in Washington's National Theater in 1931—Bunche, a principled integrationist, warned that civil rights efforts founded on race would collapse over economic issues. He felt that the best hope for black progress lay in interracial working-class economic improvement, and he criticized Franklin Roosevelt both for his inattention to the needs of black people and for the New Deal's failure to attack existing political and economic structures. In 1936, Bunche and others founded the National Negro Congress, a broad-based coalition he later termed "the first sincere effort to bring together on an equal plane Negro leaders [and] professional and white-collar workers with the Negro manual workers and their leaders and organizers." The Congress was eventually taken over by Communist Party workers. Bunche, disillusioned, resigned in 1938.

In 1939, Bunche was hired by the Swedish sociologist Gunnar Myrdal to work on what would become the classic study of race relations in the United States, *An American Dilemma: The Negro Problem and Modern Democracy* (1944). Over the next two years Bunche wrote four long research memos for the project (one was published in 1973, after Bunche's death, as *The Negro in the Age of FDR*). The final report incorporated much of Bunche's research and thought. The unpublished memos, written for the Carnegie Corporation, have remained an important scholarly resource for researchers on black America, both for their exhaustive data and for Bunche's incisive conclusions.

In 1941, after the United States entered World War II, Bunche left Howard to work for the Office of the Coordinator of Information for the Armed Service, and later joined the newly formed Office of Strategic Services, the chief American intelligence organization during World War II, precursor of the Central Intelligence Agency.

Bunche headed the Africa section of the Research and Analysis Branch. In 1944, Bunche joined the U.S. Department of State's Postwar Planning Unit to deal with the future of colonial territories.

From this point forward, Bunche operated in the arena of international political affairs with an ever-increasing degree of policy-making power. In 1945, he was appointed to the Division of Dependent Area Affairs in the Office of Special Political Affairs, becoming in the process the first African American to head a State Department "desk."

In 1944, Bunche was a member of the U.S. delegation at the Dumbarton Oaks Conference in Washington, D.C., which laid the foundation for the United Nations. Appointed to the U.S. delegation in San Francisco in 1945 and in London in 1946, Bunche helped set up the U.N. Trusteeship system to prepare colonies for independence. His draft declaration of principles governing all dependent territories was the basis of Chapter XI, "Declaration Regarding Non-Self-Governing Territories," of the United Nations Charter.

Bunche went to work in the United Nations Secretariat in 1946 as head of the Trusteeship Department. In 1947, he was assigned to the U.N. Special Commission on Palestine which was a United Nations Trusteeship. The outbreak of the First Arab-Israeli War in 1948, and the assassination of U.N. mediator Folke Bernadotte by Jewish militants, propelled Bunche, Bernadotte's assistant, into the position of acting mediator. Bunche brought the two sides together, negotiating with each in turn, and succeeded in arranging an armistice. Bunche's actions earned him the 1950 Nobel Prize for Peace. He was the first United Nations figure, as well as the first African Ameri-

Martin Luther King, Jr., acquired a reputation as a powerful preacher, drawing ideas from African-American traditions as well as theological and philosophical writings.

PAGE 401

RALPH BUNCHE

The outspoken Bunche addresses a crowd during a civil rights march.

© IVAN MASSAR / BLACK STAR

can, to win a Nobel Prize. Bunche also won the NAACP's Spingarn Medal (1950), and other honors. In 1953 the American Political Science Association elected him its president, the first time an African American was so honored. In 1950, President Truman offered him the post of Assistant Secretary of State. Bunche declined it, and in a rare personal statement on racism, explained that he did not wish to raise his family in Washington, a segregated city.

Bunche remained at the United Nations until shortly before his death in 1971. In 1954, he was appointed United Nations Undersecretary General for Special Political Affairs, and served as a roving specialist in U.N. work. Bunche's most significant contribution at the United Nations was his role in designing and setting up U.N. peacekeeping forces, which supervise and enforce truces and armistices and have arguably been the U.N.'s most important contribution to global peace. Building on the truce supervising operation he put into place after the 1949 Middle East armistice, Bunche created a United Nations Emergency Force in 1956, after the Suez crisis. U.N. peacekeepers played a major role in Lebanon and Yemen, later in the Congo (now Zaire), in India and Pakistan, and in Cyprus. Sir Brian Urquhart, Bunche's assistant and successor as U.N. Undersecretary General for Special Political Affairs, said: "Bunche was unquestionably the original principal architect of [what] is now called peacekeeping . . . and he remained the principal

CHARLES BURNETT

His Films Chronicle African-American Experience

Charles Burnett (April 13, 1944–), filmmaker. Charles Burnett was born in Vicksburg, Miss. He moved with his family to Watts in South Central Los Angeles during World War II. In 1971 he received a B.A. in theater arts from the University of California at Los Angeles (UCLA), where he made his first film, *Several Friends* (1969), about a group of young African-American men who are unable to see or understand that something has gone wrong in their lives. Burnett completed his M.F.A. at UCLA as well. As a graduate student in 1977, he made a fourteen-minute film, *The Horse,* about a boy in the South who has to witness the death of an old horse. It won first prize at the fifteenth Westdeutsche Kurzfilmtage Oberhausen in West Germany.

Killer of Sheep, his first feature film, was made the same year as *The Horse,* at which time he not only satisfied his M.F.A. thesis requirement but was also awarded a Louis B. Mayer Grant, given to the thesis project at UCLA that shows the most promise. Touted for its neorealist approach, *Killer of Sheep* received critical praise and a life in the festival circuit. The film was a winner of the Berlin International Film Festival Critics Prize in 1981. In 1990, *Killer of Sheep* was selected for the National Film Registry at the Library of Congress. Each year twenty-five American films deemed culturally and historically significant are selected for the registry.

Finding inspiration outside the Hollywood formulaic aesthetic, Burnett's *Killer of Sheep, My Brother's Wedding* (1984), and *To Sleep with Anger* (1990) focus on the dynamics, tensions, and frustrations of urban black families, with a particular emphasis on the relationships between fathers, sons, and brothers. His films strive to reflect the black American culture and the black American experience he knows. According to Burnett, "To make filmmaking viable you need the support of the community; you have to become a part of its agenda, an aspect of its survival. A major concern of storytelling should be restoring values, reversing the erosion of all those things that make a better life."

In 1980, Burnett received a Guggenheim Fellowship to do preproduction work on *My Brother's Wedding.* In 1988, he was the recipient of one of the MacArthur Foundation's "Genius" Awards, which provided the resources for a production company and a professional cast, including Danny Glover, for *To Sleep with Anger,* his most critically acclaimed work. The film earned a special jury prize at the 1990 Sundance Film Festival in Park City, Utah. Following that film, Burnett began work on *America Becoming,* a documentary about new immigrants funded by the Ford Foundation. Burnett's film *The Glass Shield*, which depicts the travails of the first black cop in an all-white police squad, opened to enthusiastic reviews in 1995.

—FARAH JASMINE GRIFFIN

See also
Film

architect, coordinator, and director of United Nations peacekeeping operations until the end of his career at the U.N."

While Bunche remained primarily involved as an international civil servant with the United Nations, promoting international peace and aiding developing countries, he also remained interested in the civil rights struggle in America. Indeed, Bunche demanded and received special dispensation from the United Nations to speak out on racial issues in the United States. Bunche served on the board of the NAACP for many years, and served as an informal adviser to civil rights leaders. In 1963, he attended the March on Washington, and two years later, despite poor health, he traveled to Alabama and walked with the Rev. Dr. Martin Luther King, Jr., in the front row of the Selma-to-Montgomery Voting Rights March.

—C. GERALD FRASER

BUTLER, OCTAVIA ESTELLE

Octavia Estelle Butler (June 22, 1947–), novelist and short-story writer. Butler is one of a select number of African Americans whose writing deliberately discards the realistic tradition to embrace a specialized genre—science fiction. The only surviving child of Laurice and Octavia M. Guy Butler, she was raised in a racially and culturally diverse neighborhood of Pasadena, Calif., and educated in the city. College consisted of a two-year program at Pasadena City College and subsequent course work at both California State College and UCLA. Dyslexic, extremely shy, and therefore solitary, Butler began writing as a child, convinced she could write better science fiction stories than those she saw on television.

Respected by the science fiction community of writers, critics, and fans as an important author ever since her first books earned excellent reviews, Butler has produced many novels and several highly regarded short stories. Her first published novel (although plotwise the last in its series), *Patternmaster* (1976), is one of the five books in her past-and-future-history Patternist saga, a series of interrelated stories using genetic breeding and the development of "psionic" powers as a unifying motif. The saga reaches from precolonial Africa to a post-holocaust Earth of the distant future. In the proper reading order, the books in the tale are *Wild Seed* (1980), *Mind of My Mind* (1977), *Clay's Ark* (1984), and *Survivor* (1978).

In each of these novels, as in *Kindred* (1979)—her only novel outside a series—Butler conspicuously introduces issues of race and gender to science fiction. Her female protagonists are African, African-American, or mixed-race women operating principally in nontraditional modes. This depiction of women as powerful, self-sustaining, and capable, able either to adapt or to nurture and heal, equally equipped to fight or to compromise, gained Butler the critical approval of two additional audiences—black readers and scholars, and white feminists.

Butler's Xenogenesis series—*Dawn* (1987), *Adulthood Rites* (1988), and *Imago* (1989)—which was deemed "satisfying . . . hard science fiction" by Orson Scott Card, continues an examination of women in differing roles as it explores issues of human survival in another grim post-holocaust future where aliens have landed. Here Butler continues to explore her interest in genetics, anthropology, ecology, and sociobiology. Also central are issues of family, alliances or networks, power, control, and hierarchical structures fueling what Butler designates the "human contradiction," the capacity for self-destruction if humanity refuses to change.

Although she is primarily a novelist, Butler's short stories have won two coveted science fiction awards. "Speech Sounds" (1983) received a Hugo; "Bloodchild" (1984) earned both a Hugo and a Nebula. Each first appeared in *Isaac Asimov's Science Fiction Magazine*. "The Evening and the Morning and the Night" (1987) initially appeared in *Omni*. "Bloodchild" explores a forced human adaptation to change through the metaphor of male pregnancy; "Speech Sounds" examines a violent near-future cityscape whose inhabitants contract a sometimes deadly illness that dramatically affects language. "The Evening . . ." recounts the impact of a terrifying genetically based disease and the efforts of those affected to eradicate or control it.

—SANDRA Y. GOVAN

The Black Power, Black Arts, and Black Aesthetic movements left an indelible mark on the consciousness of the African-American writer.

PAGE 424

See also
Literature

C

CALLOWAY, CABELL "CAB"

Cabell "Cab" Calloway (December 25, 1907–November 18, 1994), jazz singer and bandleader. Born in Rochester, N.Y., Calloway was raised in Baltimore, Md. In high school he sang with a local vocal group called the Baltimore Melody Boys. The Calloway family, including Cab's sister, singer Blanche Calloway, then moved to Chicago, where he attended Crane College. Calloway began his career as a singer, drummer, and master of ceremonies at nightclubs in Chicago and other midwestern cities. In the late 1920s in Chicago, Calloway worked with the Missourians, a big band; in the male vocal quartet in *Plantation Days*; and as leader of the Alabamians. In 1929, he took the Alabamians to Harlem's Savoy Ballroom, and that same year was featured in Fats Waller and Andy Razaf's *Hot Chocolates* revue.

In 1929 Calloway began to lead the Missourians under his own name ("St. James Infirmary," 1930). In 1931, they replaced Duke Ellington as the Cotton Club's house band. During the 1930s Calloway became a household name, the country's prototypical "hipster," renowned for his infectious vocal histrionics, his frenzied dashing up and down the stage in a white satin zoot suit, and leading audience sing-a-longs, particularly on his biggest hit, "Minnie the Moocher" (1931). That song, with its "Hi-de-ho" chorus, was a million-copy seller and earned him the nickname "Hi-de-ho Man."

Calloway's talents were not limited to comic entertainment. During the swing era Calloway's band was one of the most popular in the country ("At the Clambake Carnival," 1938; "Jumpin' Jive," 1939; "Pickin' the Cabbage," 1940), and he nurtured some of the best instrumentalists of the day, including saxophonists Ben Webster and Chu Berry, trumpeters Jonah Jones and Dizzy Gillespie, bassist Milt Hinton, and drummer Cozy Cole. The orchestra held its own in competitions throughout the 1930s with the bands of Count Basie, Duke Ellington, Chick Webb, and Jimmy Lunceford. Calloway's orchestra left the Cotton Club in 1934 for a European tour. In addition to its success in nightclubs and on the concert stage, the Calloway orchestra also appeared in movies, including *The Big Broadcast* (1932), *The Singing Kid* (1936), *St. Louis Blues* (1939), and *Stormy Weather* (1943). Calloway disbanded the orchestra in 1948, and worked with a sextet before touring England as a solo.

Calloway returned to his roots in musical theater in 1952 for a two-year run in the role of Sportin' Life in a touring version of George Gershwin's *Porgy and Bess*. Throughout the 1950s and 1960s, Calloway continued to perform both as a solo act and as the leader of big bands. In the mid-1960s he toured with the Harlem Globetrotters comic basketball team. In 1974 Calloway appeared in an all-black version of *Hello, Dolly!*, and two years later he published his autobiography, *Of Minnie the Moocher and Me*. Calloway appeared on Broadway in *Bubbling Brown Sugar* in 1975, and his cameo in *The Blues Brothers* (1980) brought a revival of interest in him. In 1984 he sang with his vocalist daughter, Chris, in an engagement at New York's Blue Note nightclub. In 1987 he again appeared with Chris Calloway, this time in *His Royal Highness of Hi-de-ho* in New York.

—MICHAEL D. SCOTT

CARPETBAGGERS

Devised by opponents of Reconstruction as a term of abuse for Northerners who came to the South after the Civil War and joined the Republican Party, the word *carpetbagger* has remained part of the lexicon of American politics. Today it refers to those, regardless of region, who run for office in a district to which they have only recently moved.

During Reconstruction, the term implied that Republican newcomers were men from the lower echelons of northern society who had packed all their belongings in a suitcase and left their homes in order to reap the spoils of office in the South. This image was reinforced by anti-Reconstruction scholars early in the twentieth century, who

See also

Count Basie

Duke Ellington

Jazz

C

CARPETBAGGERS

Black responses to the outbreak of the war ranged from an ecstatic willingness to serve to caution and resistence.

PAGE 140

charged that carpetbaggers poisoned the South's allegedly harmonious race relations by turning gullible African Americans against their former masters and using them as stepping-stones to office.

Some carpetbaggers undoubtedly were corrupt adventurers. The large majority, however, hardly fit the traditional image. Most tended to be well educated and middle-class in origin. Some had been lawyers, businessmen, newspaper editors, and other pillars of northern communities. The majority (including fifty-two of the sixty who served in Congress during Reconstruction) were veterans of the Union army who simply decided to remain in the South when the war ended in 1865. At this time, blacks did not enjoy the right to vote, and the possibility of office for northern newcomers was remote.

For most carpetbaggers, the lure of the South was the same that drew thousands of Americans to settle in the West during the nineteenth century—economic opportunity. With cotton prices high and the South starved of capital, numerous army veterans purchased land or went into business with impoverished southern planters. They hoped to combine personal economic gain with a role in helping to mold the "backward" South in the image of the modern, industrializing North, substituting, as one wrote, "the civilization of freedom for that of slavery." Other groups of carpetbaggers were teachers, Freedmen's Bureau officers, and those who came to the region genuinely hoping to assist the former slaves.

A variety of motives led these Northerners to enter politics in 1867. Crop failures had wiped out many who had invested in cotton land, and politics offered a livelihood. Some had earned the former slaves' goodwill, or proved more willing to work politically with African Americans than were native-born white Southerners. Indeed, in some localities, carpetbaggers were the only Republicans with political experience, and a number ran for office because they had been asked to do so by the former slaves. Generally, carpetbaggers were more likely than white southern Republicans to support black aspirations for equality before the law, and laws prohibiting racial segregation in public accommodations. As proponents of the North's "free labor" ideology, they strongly favored Reconstruction programs promoting railroad development and economic modernization, and tended to oppose measures to use the power of the state to distribute land to the former slaves.

No accurate figures are available as to how many Northerners came to the South during Re-

construction, but in no state did those born in the North represent even 2 percent of the total population. Nonetheless, carpetbaggers played a major role in Republican politics. Generally representing Black Belt constituencies, they held a major share of Reconstruction offices in Florida, Louisiana, and South Carolina, whose Republican parties attracted little support from white Southerners. Their ranks included such Republican governors as Robert K. Scott (who came south from Ohio with the Army and directed the Freedmen's Bureau in South Carolina) and Henry C. Warmoth and William P. Kellogg of Louisiana (army veterans from Illinois). In Mississippi, when black leaders became dissatisfied with the moderate policies of "scalawag" Gov. James L. Alcorn, they turned to Maine native Adelbert Ames, who had demonstrated a commitment to equal rights when he commanded the fourth military district under the Reconstruction Act of 1867. Ames was elected governor in 1873. Another prominent carpetbagger was Albion W. Tourgée, who, as a judge in North Carolina, waged a courageous campaign against the Ku Klux Klan.

Although the term *carpetbagger* generally applies to whites, a considerable number of black Northerners also came south during this period. Reconstruction was one of the few occasions in American history when opportunities for black men of talent and ambition were greater in the South than in the North. The ranks of "black carpetbaggers" included veterans of the Union army, ministers and teachers who had come south to work for the Freedmen's Bureau or for northern aid societies, and the children of southern free blacks who had been sent north years before for an education. Quite a few were veterans of the antislavery struggle in the northern states or Canada.

Over 100 public officeholders after the Civil War were African Americans who had been born in the North or lived there for a substantial period before the war. Born in Philadelphia, Mifflin Gibbs and Jonathan Gibbs held major positions in Arkansas and Florida, respectively. Tunis G. Campbell, who had lived in New York before the Civil War, was the political "boss" of McIntosh County, Ga., during Reconstruction, and Stephen A. Swails, a veteran of the Fifty-fourth Regiment of Massachusetts Voluntary Infantry, became the most prominent political leader in Williamsburg County, S.C. A number of "black carpetbaggers" had been born abroad, including South Carolina congressman Robert B. Elliott, apparently a na-

See also
Civil War
Reconstruction

tive of Great Britain, and Martin F. Becker, a South Carolina constitutional convention delegate, who hailed from Dutch Guiana (now known as Suriname).

After the end of Reconstruction, most white carpetbaggers appear to have returned to the North, as did many of their black counterparts.

—ERIC FONER

CARVER, GEORGE WASHINGTON

George Washington Carver (c. 1864–January 5, 1943), scientist and educator. Born in Diamond, Mo., George Washington Carver did not remember his parents. His father was believed to be a slave killed accidentally before Carver's birth. His mother was Mary Carver, a slave apparently kidnapped by slave raiders soon after he was born. He and his older brother were raised by their mother's former owners, Moses and Susan Carver, on their small, largely self-sufficient farm.

Denied admission to the neighborhood school because of his color, Carver was privately tutored and then moved to nearby Neosho to enter school in the mid-1870s. He soon realized he knew more than the teacher and left with a family moving to Fort Scott, Kans. After witnessing a lynching there, he left that town and for over a decade roamed around the Midwest seeking an education while supporting himself by cooking, laundering, and homesteading.

In 1890 Carver enrolled in Simpson College in Indianola, Iowa, where he was an art major and the only African-American student. After his teacher convinced him that a black man could not make a living in art, Carver transferred to Iowa State College at Ames in 1891 to major in agriculture. Again the only black student on campus, Carver participated fully (except for dating) in extracurricular activities and compiled such an impressive academic record that he was hired as a botany assistant to pursue postgraduate work. Before he received his master of agriculture degree in 1896, he was placed in charge of the greenhouse and taught freshmen students.

An expert in mycology (the study of fungi) and plant cross-fertilization, Carver could have remained at Iowa and probably would have made significant contributions in one or both fields. However, he felt an obligation to share his knowledge with other African Americans and accepted Booker T. Washington's offer to become head of the agricultural department at Tuskegee Normal and Industrial Institute in 1896.

When he arrived at Tuskegee, Carver intended only to stay a few years and then pursue doctoral work. Instead, he spent his remaining forty-six years there. Although he once considered matrimony, he never married and instead "adopted" many Tuskegee students as his "children," to whom he provided loans and guidance. For the first half of his tenure, he worked long hours in administration, teaching, and research. The focus of his work reflected the needs of his constituents rather than his personal talents or interests. As director of the only all-black-staffed agricultural experiment station, he sought answers to the debt problems of small-scale farmers and landless sharecroppers. Thus, in his teaching, extension work (carried on with a wagon equipped as a movable school), and agricultural bulletins, Carver preached the use of available and renewable resources to replace expensive, purchased commodities. He especially advocated the growing of peanuts as a cheap source of protein and published several bulletins with peanut recipes.

After twenty years at Tuskegee, Carver was respected by agricultural researchers but largely unknown to the general public. His rise to fame began with his induction in 1916 into Great Britain's Royal Society for the Arts and the growing realization of his usefulness by the peanut industry. In 1921, a growers' association paid his way to testify at tariff hearings in Congress. There his showmanship in demonstrating peanut products drew national press coverage. Two years later,

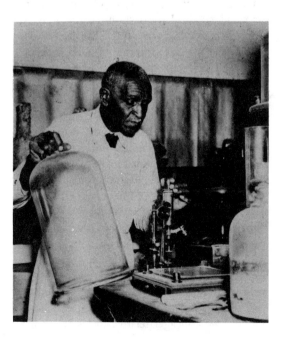

UNWITTING CELEBRITY

Because of his compelling personality, scientist and educator George Washington Carver (1864–1943) had a profound impact on almost everyone who came in contact with him. His research led to wide publicity in the 1920s and 1930s. PHOTOGRAPHS AND PRINTS DIVISION, SCHOMBURG CENTER FOR RESEARCH IN BLACK CULTURE, THE NEW YORK PUBLIC LIBRARY, ASTOR, LENOX AND TILDEN FOUNDATIONS

some Atlanta businessmen founded the Carver Products Company, and Carver won the Spingarn Medal of the NAACP. Although the company failed, it generated publicity. Then in 1933 an Associated Press release exaggerated Carver's success in rehabilitating polio patients with peanut-oil massages. Soon he was perhaps the best known African American of his generation.

The increasing publicity caught the attention of numerous people who found Carver's rise from slavery and his personality appealing. Articles began to appear describing the flowers in the lapels of his well-worn jackets and his rambles in the woods to commune with his "Creator," through which he expressed his devout but nonsectarian belief. Because he took no public stand on political or racial matters, many diverse groups could adopt him as a symbol of their causes. Thus he was appropriated by advocates of racial equality, the "New South," religion, the "American Dream," and even segregation. His significant work as an agricultural researcher and educator was obscured by the myth of the "peanut wizard."

Relishing the publicity, Carver did little to correct the public record, aside from general statements of his "unworthiness" of the honors that came with increasing frequency. Some symbolic uses of his life helped to perpetuate white stereotypes of African Americans, but most of the publicity had a positive impact on both white and black Americans. Indeed, Carver became a potent tool for racial tolerance after the Commission on Interracial Cooperation and the YMCA began to sponsor his lecture tours of white college campuses in the 1920s and 1930s. On these tours, Carver added dozens of whites to his adopted "family." To them he was no "token black" but a trusted father figure to whom they wrote their innermost thoughts. Many, such as white clergyman Howard Kester, became outspoken advocates of racial justice.

Because of his compelling personality, Carver had a profound impact on almost everyone—black or white—who came in contact with him. His "special friends" ranged from white sharecroppers to Henry Ford. Most of his major publicists were true disciples of Carver's vision of the interrelatedness of all human beings and their environment. Because of his extreme frugality, he was also able to leave a substantial legacy by giving about sixty thousand dollars to establish the George Washington Carver Foundation, which continues to support scientific research at Tuskegee University. Although his scientific contributions were meager relative to his fame, and

he could not single-handedly save the black family farm, Carver's work and warmth greatly enriched the lives of thousands.

—LINDA O. MCMURRY

CHAMBERLAIN, WILTON NORMAN "WILT"

Wilton Norman "Wilt" Chamberlain (August 21, 1936–), basketball player. Born in Philadelphia, Wilt Chamberlain was one of nine children of William Chamberlain, a custodian/handyman, and Olivia Chamberlain, a part-time domestic. Large even as a child, he grew to 7′1″ by the age of eighteen, and developed great running speed and endurance. At Overbrook High School, he starred in track and field. Dubbed "Wilt the Stilt" and "The Big Dipper" for his great height, he became the premier high school basketball player of his era. The Philadelphia Warriors of the National Basketball Association (NBA) drafted him before he finished high school, but Chamberlain elected to go to college. After fierce competition among colleges, he chose to attend the University of Kansas. While at Kansas, he starred in track, and his amazing basketball skills and dominance led to many changes in the college rule book including the widening of the foul lanes, in order to hamper him. Despite these impediments, in his first year with the varsity Chamberlain led Kansas to the National College Athletic Association (NCAA) finals. However, the constant harassment, fouling, and triple-teaming upset him, and after another year he left Kansas, saying basketball was no longer fun. Not yet eligible for the NBA, he spent a year touring with the Harlem Globetrotters (playing at guard!).

Chamberlain entered the NBA with the Philadelphia Warriors in 1959–1960 and was an immediate sensation. In his rookie year, he broke eight NBA scoring and rebounding records, and was named both Rookie of the Year and Most Valuable Player. In 1960 he made a record fifty-five rebounds in a game. The following season, Chamberlain had the greatest individual scoring performance the game has ever seen. He scored 4,029 points, an average of 50.4 points per game, and on March 2, 1962, scored 100 points in a game.

Chamberlain went on to play fourteen seasons with the Philadelphia/Golden State Warriors

See also
Booker T. Washington
Science

(1959–1965), the Philadelphia 76ers (1965–1968), and the Los Angeles Lakers (1968–1973). He won four MVP awards, and was named to the All-Star team thirteen times (every year he was in contention). He revolutionized professional basketball, ushering in the era of the dominant centers, usually seven feet or taller. A sensational scorer during his early years, he relied on a graceful jump shot and popularized the "dunk" shot. His lifetime scoring totals—31,419 points and an average of 30.1 points per game—stood for many years. He also excelled at shot blocking and defense. While Chamberlain led his teams to NBA championships in 1967 and 1972, his teams lost several times in playoff finals, and he was unfairly derided by fans as a "loser." A controversial figure, he complained at the lack of recognition of his talents, stating "nobody roots for Goliath." In 1973 he left the Lakers, and was hired as a player-coach by the San Diego Conquistadores of the American Basketball Association (ABA). The Lakers obtained an injunction in court forbidding him from playing, and he passed the year unhappily as a coach, leading the team to a 38–47 record, and then retired. He was elected to the Naismith Memorial Basketball Hall of Fame in Springfield, Mass., in 1978.

After his retirement, Chamberlain, a volleyball enthusiast, helped start the International Volleyball Association and also sponsored track-and-field meets. He has at various times pursued a performing career. He acted in the film *Conan the Destroyer* (1984) and appeared as himself in several commercials. During the 1960s he owned the Harlem nightspot Big Wilt's Small Paradise, and he now owns Wilt Chamberlain's Restaurants. He achieved considerable notoriety for his claims of extraordinary sexual promiscuity in his 1991 book, *A View from Above*. Whatever his exploits off the court, he remains one of the greatest basketball players of all time.

—GREG ROBINSON

CHARLES, RAY

Ray Charles (Ray Charles Robinson) (September 23, 1930–), musician. Ray Charles's achievement over the past forty-five years marks him as one of the most important and influential figures of American music in the postwar period. He is often called the "Father of Soul," both for his innovative blending of gospel, blues, and jazz, and his enormous versatility as a singer, pianist, songwriter, composer-arranger, saxophonist, and band leader.

Born into a poor family in Albany, Ga., Ray Charles was raised in Greenville, Fla. At the age of five he contracted glaucoma; left untreated, it soon blinded him. His mother, Aretha, sent him to the School for the Deaf and Blind in St. Augustine, where he spent the next eight years studying composition, learning to write musical scores in braille, and mastering various instruments (the trumpet, alto saxophone, clarinet, organ, and piano). After his mother died in 1945, he left school to form a combo; after he had saved enough money, he moved to Seattle, where he played in a number of jazz trios, gradually developing a piano and vocal style heavily influenced by Nat "King" Cole. At around this time, Ray Charles decided to drop his surname in order to avoid being confused with prizefighter Sugar Ray Robinson.

Charles developed a significant following in Seattle, and soon began to record for various labels. His first hits, "Baby Let Me Hold Your Hand" (1951) and "Kiss Me Baby" (1952) were recorded for the Swing Time label. In 1952 Charles began to record for Atlantic Records, where he made his first musical breakthrough with "I've Got a Woman" (1955), a blend, startlingly unconventional for the time, of a coarse bluesy sexuality with the intense emotionality of gospel. Many of his musical ideas in this period were taken from gospel music, but his adaptations provoked much criticism for their combination of the vocal techniques of "testifying" with sexually explicit lyrics. This style nevertheless provided Charles with some of his most successful songs, among them, "Hallelujah, I Love Her So" (1956), "The Right Time" (1959), and "What'd I Say" (1959).

As his fame increased, Charles increasingly found favor with white audiences. In 1959 he left Atlantic for ABC/Paramount; the move signaled a turn toward country-and-western music and popular standards. While his early recordings with ABC (such as "Georgia on My Mind," "Hit the Road Jack," and "I Can't Stop Loving You") are generally considered the equals of those of his Atlantic period, some critics charged that his music was gradually becoming conventional and uninspired. Nevertheless, throughout the 1960s Charles turned out scores of Top-Ten hits (including "You Are My Sunshine," "Let's Go Get Stoned," and "Here We Go Again"), and a number of successful LPs.

Charles's rise to fame was not without its struggles. Along the way he developed an addiction to heroin, and in 1955, 1961, and 1965, he

Drum on your drums, batter on your banjos, sob on the long cool winding saxophones. Go to it, O jazzmen.

CARL SANDBURG
JAZZ FANTASIA, 1920

See also
Blues
Gospel
Jazz

was arrested for the possession of narcotics. He never served a long prison term, but he stopped performing for a year after his last arrest, during which time he worked successfully to overcome the seventeen-year-long addiction. Since then the record shows a steady series of successes and honors. In 1966, the U.S. House of Representatives passed a special resolution honoring Charles for his musical achievement. In the late 1960s he founded his own record label and music publishing firm. In 1979, Hoagy Carmichael's "Georgia on My Mind," perhaps Charles's best-known recording, was adopted as the official song of Georgia. In 1986, Charles was among the first ten artists inducted into the Rock and Roll Hall of Fame.

During his career, Charles has appeared in several films, including *Blues for Lovers* (a.k.a. *Ballad in Blue,* 1965) and *The Blues Brothers* (1980), and has performed on the soundtracks of many more, including *The Cincinnati Kids* (1965) and *In the Heat of the Night* (1967); his song "What'd I Say" was the subject of *Cosmic Ray,* an experimental film by Bruce Conner, in 1961.

In recent years, Charles has been active in various social causes, including civil rights issues, African famine relief, and aid to the disabled. In 1985, he attributed the presence of several bombs found under a bandstand where he was to perform to his public statements opposing racism. In 1987 he made an appeal to Congress for federal aid for the deaf and established the Robinson Foundation for Hearing Disorders with an endowment of $1 million.

In addition to making frequent concert appearances and appearing in several popular commercials (most notably the phenomenally successful Diet Pepsi ads in the early 1990s), Charles has remained active in producing and recording his own albums. His LP *Friendship* rose to number one on the country-and-western charts in 1985. In 1990, he performed with B.B. King in the Philip Morris Superband, and released an album, *Would You Believe?* Charles's autobiography *Brother Ray* (1978, with David Ritz), was published in a revised and updated edition in 1992. Charles has won eleven Grammy Awards, the title of Commandeur de l'Ordre des Arts et des Lettres from the French Republic, an NAACP Hall of Fame Award (1983), and a Lifetime Achievement Award from the National Academy of Recording Arts and Sciences (1989).

—ROBERT W. STEPHENS

See also
Literature

CHESNUTT, CHARLES WADDELL

Charles Waddell Chesnutt (June 20, 1858–November 15, 1932), writer. Born in Cleveland, Ohio, to freeborn mulattoes, Chesnutt was raised mostly in Fayetteville, N.C., by his father, Andrew; his mother, Ann Maria, died when he was only thirteen. Though Chesnutt attended the Howard School and received a fairly sound general education, he proved to be a model autodidact, teaching himself advanced mathematics, ancient languages, history, and shorthand. His first teaching assignments in Charlotte, N.C., and Spartanburg, S.C., from 1875 to 1877, served as a proving ground for what he had learned. He rose in 1879 from being first assistant to the principal of the State Colored Normal School of North Carolina to become its principal, serving also as Sunday-school superintendent of the renowned Evans Chapel African Methodist Episcopal Zion Church. Despite his success, Chesnutt was determined to escape the harsh racism of the South. In 1883, peddling his shorthand skills, he sought work with northern newspapers, such as the *New York Mail and Express;* he stayed there only five months before moving on to Cleveland to try his luck in this city of his birth, soon to become his permanent place of residence. While working in the law offices of a railroad company, Chesnutt studied law, and in 1887 passed the Ohio bar examination. Pleased with his accomplishments, he began operating a stenographic service for the courts and was well rewarded for his efforts. Having secured a foothold on this trade, he sent for his wife, Susan, whom he married in 1878, and his children, who were left behind in Fayetteville while he traveled from the South to the North and back again—a pattern of departures and returns that would later play a subtle role in most of his fiction.

Rankled by racist or insensitive southern white writers and their depictions of miscegenation and the black experience, Chesnutt vowed to render a more accurate and faithful account of the issues. In 1887, his tale of magic, witchcraft, and slavery "The Goophered Grapevine," brought him to the nation's attention, though by now he had already published approximately sixteen short stories in a variety of magazines and newspapers. With the heavy-handed assistance of his publisher's editors, Chesnutt produced *The Conjure Woman* (1899), a

CRAFTING BLACK HISTORY

Chase-Riboud Creates Sculpture and Poetry

Barbara Dewayne Chase-Riboud (June 26, 1939–), sculptor, poet, and novelist. The only child of middle-class parents, Barbara Chase was born in Philadelphia and raised in that city. After earning a B.A. in fine arts from Temple University in 1957, Chase traveled to Rome, Italy on a John Hay Whitney Foundation fellowship. There she worked for the first time in bronze and entered her sculptures in exhibitions at the Spoleto Festival (1957) and at the American Academy in Rome and the Gallery L'Obeliso (1958). During the winter of 1957, Chase spent three months in Egypt, receiving what she later termed a "blast of Egyptian culture." The visit marked a turning point in her artistic career, as Chase, newly exposed to nonclassical art, was forced to reevaluate the academic training with which her works had previously been infused. "Though I didn't know it at the time," she said, "my own transformation was part of the historical transformation of the blacks that began in the '60s."

After receiving an M.F.A. from Yale University (1960), Chase traveled to London before finally settling in Paris. In 1961, she married the French photographer Marc Riboud; shortly thereafter, the couple journeyed to China, Chase-Riboud being one of the first American women to visit the country after the onset of the Cultural Revolution. Her notes from the trip, which also included visits to Nepal and Inner Mongolia, were later transformed into a collection of poems, issued under the title *From Memphis to Peking* (1974).

Although Chase-Riboud's interest in Asian art can be traced to sculptures dating from as early as 1960, it was not until the latter half of the decade that she began fully to incorporate this and African influences into her own work. She became known for using radically different materials—such as bronze and wool, steel and synthetics, and bronze and silk—in compositions that were both abstract and expressive, elegant and minimalist. Hemp, wood, raffia, leathers, metals, and feathers were also used in figures reminiscent of African masks. Chase-Riboud exhibited her work internationally at such festivals as the New York Architectural League Show (1965), the Festival of Negro Art in Dakar (1966), and the L'Oeil Ecoute Festival of Avignon (1969).

By the early 1970s, Chase-Riboud's work had achieved worldwide renown. She was awarded a National Endowment for the Humanities fellowship in 1973 and an outstanding alumni award from Temple University in 1975. In addition to participating in group shows at the Boston Museum of Fine Arts, the Smithsonian Institute of Washington, D.C. (National Gallery of Art), New York's Whitney Museum, the Centre Pompidou of Paris, and other museums, Chase-Riboud held solo exhibitions at the Betty Parsons Gallery in New York, the Museum of Modern Art in Paris, and the Kunstmuseum in Düsseldorf, among others.

Chase-Riboud came to prominence as an author in 1979 with the publication of her first novel, *Sally Hemings,* a historical work based on Thomas Jefferson's relationship with his slave mistress. She won the Janet Heidinger Kafka Prize for fiction for that volume. Her claim that Jefferson had fathered seven children with Hemings proved extremely controversial, and she was both widely commended and criticized for her endeavor. In 1981, Chase-Riboud divorced Marc Riboud and married Sergio G. Tosi, an Italian art dealer and publisher. Four years later, she published a second volume of poems, *Love Perfecting,* and another novel about slavery, *Valide,* in 1986. Two additional works followed, a collection of poems titled *Study of a Nude Woman as Cleopatra* (1988) and a novel, *Echo of Lions* (1989).

Chase-Riboud, who was awarded an honorary doctorate from Temple University in 1981, continued to exhibit her artwork throughout the 1980s, holding one-woman shows at the Musée Reattu in Arles (France), the Kunstmuseum in Freiburg, the Bronx Museum in New York, the Museum of Modern Art in Sydney (Australia), and the Studio Museum in Harlem. While maintaining permanent residences in Paris and Rome, she has continued to travel widely, to write, and to produce visual art. In the spring of 1990, she was artist-in-residence at Pasadena City College in California.

In 1994 Barbara Chase-Riboud returned to the subject of Thomas Jefferson and Sally Hemings with another novel, *The President's Daughter,* about Harriet Hemings, the slave daughter of Sally Hemings and Jefferson.

—PAMELA WILKINSON

C

CHESNUTT, CHARLES WADDELL

June Jordan contributed to black feminism with major essays and poems.

PAGE 419

See also
Jean-Michel Basquiat

collection of tales connected by their plots' depiction of magical events and unified by their portrayal of the horrors of slavery while raising troubling questions regarding the complex attachments that linked the ex-slaves to their slave forebears and to their masters. It was a stunning success, preceded a few months earlier by *The Wife of His Youth and Other Stories of the Color Line* (1899)—a collection of tales wherein irony and inexplicable coincidences, rather than magic, represent the controlling literary technique, and where blacks confront the lessons of the "color line": color prejudice among blacks, which is as much about race as it is about kinship and familial affiliation. This too was very well received.

Though Chesnutt appears to have been steadfast against any temptation to pass as white himself, he flirted very much with this topic in his fiction. Thus, the pathos aroused in his first novel, *The House Behind the Cedars* (1900), is created by the choice a young woman must make between passing as white, thereby enjoying the apparent benefits of white society, and remaining with her mother to live among those of the black race with whom she was raised, but among whom she would be forever blocked from enjoying the fruits due her as an American citizen.

In the wake of his early successes, Chesnutt closed his stenographic offices and devoted himself full-time to writing fiction. By now it appeared that he had joined that diverse group of regional writers called "local colorists"; but with a compulsory life of Frederick Douglass (1899) behind him, his next literary efforts proved too realistic and bitter for his newfound audience. Though readers may be moved by the sibling rivalry of two women, one black and one white, depicted in *The Marrow of Tradition* (1901), in his second novel, their kinship is eclipsed by the highly charged politics of the post-Civil War period, a polarized time that left little room for moderating sentiments in the North or the South. The plot depicts strange bedfellows brought together by political goals based more on postbellum fears than on any alliance they might have forged during the antebellum era or any indignity they might have suffered in common. Forced by poor sales, Chesnutt returned in 1901 to stenography, consequently remaining sorely underrated during his lifetime.

As a witness to events that took place in the South during the 1890s, Chesnutt could no longer believe that paternalistic, well-meaning whites were able or willing to do anything more for blacks. In his last published novel, *The Colonel's Dream* (1905), the white colonel returns to his southern home with the belief that he can forestall the return to slave conditions into which many blacks and poor whites are falling. Having failed, the colonel returns north with the belief that blacks cannot win the war of "Redemption," as this era was dubbed, with or without the assistance of white patrons. With Reconstruction over, blacks were, during this nadir of their odyssey in America, on their own.

Chesnutt's light complexion, erudition, sophistication, and accomplishments, however, gave him an entrée into the upper ranks of Cleveland society, where he observed activities satirized in that highly ironic short story "Baxter's Procrustes." As one of the wealthiest black men in the city, Chesnutt was among the most successful political forces in Cleveland, though he never held political office. He often took the middle ground in racial affairs, whether the issue was between blacks and whites or among blacks: He was a member of both the National Association for the Advancement of Colored People (NAACP), founded in part by the militant W. E. B. Du Bois,

and the Committee of Twelve, steered by the cautious and conciliatory Booker T. Washington.

Nevertheless, until his death, Chesnutt was so outspoken in defense of blacks against discrimination and illegal practices that in 1928 he was awarded the NAACP Spingarn Medal for the most "distinguished service" of any black person that year who had acted to advance the cause of blacks in America.

Besides his two published collections of short stories, Chesnutt wrote and/or published an additional twenty-nine short stories, sixteen "tales," ten "anecdotes," seven occasional poems, and numerous essays, articles, and book reviews. He continued to write and publish until 1930 ("Concerning Father" was his last short story), despite poor critical reception and sales, not to mention poor health. As Chesnutt's reputation grows, he will be seen as the first African-American master of the short story.

—GORDON THOMPSON

CHICAGO, ILLINOIS

Chicago's African-American community emerged in the 1840s, sixty-one years after the arrival of Jean Baptiste Pointe du Sable, an Afro-French immigrant and Chicago's first non-Native American settler. Excluded from most manufacturing and mercantile employment and lacking capital to establish businesses, black Chicagoans filled less promising and rewarding roles in the city's growing economy. Resisting marginalization, these African Americans agitated against slavery, formed vigilance committees to defend fugitives, lobbied for the repeal of the Illinois Black Laws, and developed a skeletal institutional life.

The implications of Reconstruction legislation forced state legislators to reconsider legal constraints on black citizens: Black men won the franchise (1870), while legislation overturned de jure school segregation (1874) and prohibited discrimination in public accommodations (1885). Integrationist in orientation, business and professional leaders had strong ties to white Chicagoans and established the legitimacy of black participation in civic life. They published Chicago's first black newspaper, built churches, and engineered the election of the city's first black public official in 1871.

Between 1890 and 1915, migration—largely from the upper South—tripled Chicago's black population to fifty thousand. Employers' assumptions regarding particular aptitudes of the various races relegated eastern and southern European immigrants to the least skilled jobs in the dynamic industrial sector; African Americans—supposedly incapable of regular, disciplined industrial work—were virtually excluded except as temporary strikebreakers. Black men overwhelmingly labored in service positions. Black women, more likely than other women to enter the paid labor force, were even more concentrated in these dead-end occupations.

African Americans earned less than their white counterparts, but paid higher housing prices in Chicago's increasingly rigid dual housing market. Racially distinct blocks gradually consolidated into enclaves during the late nineteenth century. Limited to residences in these areas, black Chicagoans concentrated in two emerging ghettos—a long thin sliver on the South Side and a smaller area on the West Side.

In response to exclusion coupled with population growth, Chicago's black male leadership turned inward. Between 1890 and 1915 a new generation of leaders focused its energies on developing black institutional life. Women were more likely than men to be active in interracial reform movements, but men occupied positions of power within the community. Oscar DePriest, the first black alderman in a city where power resided in the city council, won election in 1915. By then black Chicago had its own YMCA, settlement houses, hospital, military regiment, and bank, and a vital business and entertainment district along the State Street "Stroll."

Looking inward did not imply a retreat from nineteenth-century traditions of asserting citizenship rights. Chicago's black leadership honored both Booker T. Washington and W. E. B. Du Bois. George Cleveland Hall presided over the National Negro Business League one year and sat on the NAACP committee on grievances the next. Chicago Defender editor Robert Abbott venerated Tuskegee Institute and its founder, while advising black Southerners to answer white violence with armed opposition.

The economic and demographic dislocations of World War I transformed Chicago and other manufacturing centers. Industrial demand jumped while immigration dwindled, forcing industrialists to lay aside assumptions about black workers. To black Southerners, the North offered opportunities to fulfill aspirations for complete citizenship; the new jobs made the move possible. Approximately sixty thousand black Southerners—largely from the deep South—relocated in Chicago.

I have struck a city—a real city— and they call it Chicago. . . . I urgently desire never to see it again. It is inhabited by savages.

RUDYARD KIPLING
AMERICAN NOTES, 1891

See also
W.E.B. Du Bois
NAACP
Booker T. Washington

C

Chicago is the great American City.

NORMAN MAILER
MIAMI AND THE SIEGE OF CHICAGO, 1968

With men earning factory wages and women maintaining high rates of labor-force participation, the material base for a "black metropolis" complemented the existing South Side institutional infrastructure. Men worked in steel mills, packinghouses, other heavy industries, and traditional service niches. Women worked in light industry and domestic service. Postal workers and Pullman porters anchored a middle class defined more by lifestyle and institutional affiliation than by income. Chicago had more black-owned stores by the end of the 1920s than any other city in the United States. A thin professional and business elite occupied the top of an attenuated class structure. Black politicians sat in the city council, the state legislature, and, by 1929, the U.S. House of Representatives.

This community's rapid growth exacerbated tensions rooted in competition over neighborhood turf, political influence, and unionization. Middle- and upper-class white Chicagoans mobilized financial and legal resources to "protect" their neighborhoods from black "invasion"; the white working class looked to political clout and physical intimidation. Violence escalated during the Great Migration, erupting into a massive riot in 1919. Retaliating after whites attacked black citizens, first at a beach and subsequently on streetcars and in the streets, black Chicagoans suffered the brunt of both the attacks and the arrests.

The weight of the Great Depression fell with similarly unequal force. Last admitted through the factory gates, black workers were the first sacrificed to the business cycle. Eviction often followed unemployment. Little new housing opened for black Chicagoans until the first public-housing project was completed in 1940.

Black Chicagoans responded to the depression with renewed activism. Resurrecting "Don't Buy Where You Can't Work" campaigns initiated during the 1920s, ghetto residents successfully picketed stores and office buildings. Black politicians, however, found their clout diminished, as a dominant Democratic organization replaced competitive politics. No longer brokers between black voters and white factional leaders, a new generation of black politicians accepted places in William Dawson's "submachine." Eschewing confrontation, black politicians concentrated on expanding the community's niche in government employment.

The New Deal, industrial recovery during World War II, and the emergence of the Congress of Industrial Organization (CIO) opened new economic and political opportunities. By the end of the war, thousands of black Chicagoans held union jobs, and a new generation of black activists emerged from the CIO and, later, the Negro American Labor Council.

This energy had its counterpart in the arts, producing a cultural efflorescence often referred to as the "Chicago Renaissance." Extending beyond the jazz and blues innovations customarily associated with Chicago musicians like Muddy Waters and Dizzy Gillespie, this creative terrain included literature (Richard Wright, Arna Bontemps, Willard Motley, Margaret Walker, and Gwendolyn Brooks), dance (Katherine Dunham), and art (Archibald Motley, George Neal, Richmond Barthé, and Margaret Taylor Goss [Burroughs]).

Migration from the South surged during the 1940s and 1950s, with the ghetto expanding along its margins. Attempts to leapfrog across boundaries, whether by individuals or within the context of Chicago Housing Authority initiatives, attracted violent resistance. By the early 1950s a reconstructed housing authority had shifted from being a force for integration to becoming a developer of high-rise ghettos constructed in black neighborhoods. In 1959 the U.S. Commission on Civil Rights labeled Chicago "the most residentially segregated city in the nation."

Residential segregation combined with gerrymandered public-school districts to dominate the agenda of Chicago's postwar civil rights movement. The formation of the Coordinating Council of Community Organizations in 1962 established an institutional foundation for accelerated mobilization, focusing mainly on school desegregation and led by Albert Raby and Dick Gregory. The entrance of the Southern Christian Leadership Conference and the Rev. Dr. Martin Luther King, Jr., in 1965 and 1966 shifted the focus toward open housing. Marches through white neighborhoods encountered violent opposition, bringing Mayor Richard Daley to the bargaining table, but black leaders lacked the resources to secure more than rhetoric and promises. By 1967 only Jesse Jackson's employment-oriented Operation Breadbasket was winning tangible concessions. Riots in 1966 and 1968 articulated rage and provoked temporary civic concern about racial injustice and poverty, but left mainly devastation in their wake.

Continued organizing efforts paid dividends in 1983, with the election of Chicago's first African-American mayor, Harold Washington. Frequently stymied by an obstructionist city council, Washington had begun to wield effective power only two years before his death in 1988. Washington's coalition divided after his death, but its elements remained a force in city politics and within the black community into the 1990s.

In the 1990s, Chicago's African-American population remained largely on the South and West Sides. Block after block of working-class bungalows and apartment buildings housed families struggling to maintain their standard of living amid deteriorating public schools, a declining industrial base, and a vulnerable public sector. The implications of unemployment or low-wage service jobs were visible nearby, in neighborhoods characterized by deteriorated housing and dwindling business activity. Public-housing projects held a population skewed toward children and unemployed or underemployed women. But prosperous middle-class neighborhoods, while losing some residents to increasing opportunities in the suburbs, continued to include a black elite that has maintained its commitment to black institutions while taking its place among the city's power brokers.

—JAMES R. GROSSMAN

CHISHOLM, SHIRLEY

Shirley Chisholm (November 30, 1924–), politician. Shirley Chisholm's career places her among the most significant black politicians of the twentieth century. Born Shirley St. Hill in Brooklyn, she lived with her family in Barbados for some years before returning to the United States. She graduated cum laude from Brooklyn College in 1946 and then earned a master's degree from Columbia University's Teachers College. After her marriage to Conrad Chisholm in 1949, she taught nursery school and became involved in Democratic party work.

In 1960, Chisholm helped to form the Unity Democratic Club in New York, and in 1965 she ran a successful campaign for a seat in the New York State Assembly. During her tenure there she pressed her interest in education and helped to establish the Search for Education, Equity, and Knowledge (SEEK) program to assist poor students in New York. She also helped win a maternity-leave policy for teachers.

In 1969, Chisholm won a seat in the House of Representatives, becoming the first African-American woman to be elected to Congress. While in the House she served on a number of committees, including Veterans' Affairs, Educa-

tion and Labor, and House Rules. She was an outspoken opponent of the war in Vietnam, and continued to fight for economic justice and women's rights.

In January of 1972, Chisholm announced her candidacy for the Democratic party nomination for president. She was the first African American ever to do so. While her campaign was unable to gain the support of the Congressional Black Caucus or the major women's groups with which she had long worked, Chisholm's effort was nonetheless groundbreaking.

Shirley Chisholm retired from Congress in 1982. She has since taught at Mount Holyoke and Spelman colleges. She continues to be active in politics as the founder of the National Political Congress of Black Women and as its first president.

—JUDITH WEISENFELD

CIVIL RIGHTS MOVEMENT

The African-American Civil Rights Movement has roots in the earliest resistance by blacks to their involuntary arrival in America and their unequal treatment. As slaves in America, blacks protested through work slowdowns and sabotage, escapes, and rebellions; while free blacks in the North opposed racial discrimination through petitions, litigation, and more aggressive nonviolent tactics such as boycotts from 1844 to 1855 that pressured Boston authorities to desegregate public schools.

The South, where slavery endured until 1865 and where at least 90 percent of black Americans lived until 1910, posed the crucial testing ground for civil rights activism. The newly freed slaves asserted their rights in ways ranging from participation in southern electoral politics, as voters and public officials, to nonviolent protests against segregated horsecars. These protests triumphed in New Orleans, Richmond, Va., and Charleston, S.C., in 1867, in Louisville in 1871 (all involving confrontations with passengers and police), and in Savannah, Ga., in 1872 (through a boycott that placed economic pressure on the traction company).

The rise of Jim Crow laws throughout the South beginning in the late nineteenth century triggered black resistance in every state of the former Confederacy; most of this resistance centered on boycotts of segregated streetcars. These protests postponed the spread of segregation in

And this nation, for all its hopes and boasts, will not be fully free until all its citizens are free.

JOHN F. KENNEDY
CIVIL RIGHTS SPEECH TO
THE NATION, JUNE 11, 1963

some cities, but ultimately they failed everywhere amid a surge of white racial violence and legal repression, including disfranchisement of most southern blacks by 1900. Black civil rights activity also succumbed to a national resurgence of racism, evident in the Supreme Court verdict in *Plessy* v. *Ferguson* (1896) that sustained a Louisiana segregation statute for affording blacks separate-but-equal facilities. The preeminent southern black spokesman, Booker T. Washington, accommodated these bleak trends by appealing to whites for economic toleration and racial peace while publicly renouncing agitation for social and political rights.

Because of the long odds and mortal risks facing black dissidents in the South, civil rights militance in the early twentieth century remained chiefly the province of northern blacks such as the

Massachusetts natives William Monroe Trotter and W.E.B. Du Bois. In 1905 Du Bois began a movement in Niagara Falls, N.Y., to urge redress of racial injustices. Poorly attended and funded, the Niagara Movement lived four years in obscurity before dissolving into a new, interracial organization that formed in the wake of white racial rioting in Springfield, Ill., the city of Abraham Lincoln's youth. In 1910 the NAACP began its long crusade for racial equality, operating through the courts and the trenchant pen of Du Bois, the group's first black officer and the editor of a new journal for black rights, the *Crisis*.

In the 1915 case *Guinn* v. *United States,* attorneys for the NAACP persuaded a unanimous Supreme Court to declare unconstitutional the "grandfather clause," by which some states had disfranchised blacks through harsh registration

---

BREAKING SOCIAL BOUNDARIES
Emmett Till's Murder a Civil Rights Milestone

Emmett Louis Till (July 25, 1941–August 28, 1955). Emmett Till was born and raised in Chicago, Ill. When he was fourteen, his parents sent him to LeFlore County, Miss., to visit his uncle for the summer. That summer Till bragged to his friends about northern social freedoms and showed them pictures of a white girl he claimed was his girlfriend. His friends, schooled in the southern rules of caste based on black deference and white supremacy, were incredulous. One evening, they dared Till to enter a store and ask the white woman inside, Carolyn Bryant, for a date. Till entered the store, squeezed Bryant's hand, grabbed her around the waist, and propositioned her. When she fled and returned with a gun, he wolf-whistled at her before being hurried away by his friends.

Till's act of youthful brashness crossed southern social barriers that strictly governed contact between black men and white women. In Mississippi, where the Ku Klux Klan was newly revived and African Americans were impoverished and disfranchised, these barriers were strictly enforced by the threat of social violence. On August 28, 1955, Carolyn Bryant's husband, Roy, and his half brother, J. W. Milam, abducted Till from his uncle's home, brutally beat him, shot him in the head, and then dumped his naked body in the Tallahatchie river. Till's mangled and decomposed body was found three days later, and his uncle named both men as the assailants. Bryant and Milam were tried for murder. Despite the fact that the two men had admitted

abducting Till, they were acquitted on September 23 by an all-white jury because the body was too mangled to be definitively identified.

The verdict unleashed a storm of protest. Till's mother had insisted on an open-casket funeral, and pictures of Till's disfigured body featured in *Jet Magazine* had focused national attention on the trial. Till's age, the innocence of his act, and his killers' immunity from retribution represented a stark and definitive expression of southern racism to many African Americans. Demonstrations were organized by the National Association for the Advancement of Colored People (NAACP), and the Brotherhood of Sleeping Car Porters and black leaders like W. E. B. Du Bois demanded antilynching legislation and federal action on civil rights.

Emmett Till's lynching was a milestone in the emergent Civil Rights Movement. Outrage over his death was key to mobilizing black resistance in the deep South. In addition, black protest over the lack of federal intervention in the Till case was integral to the inclusion of legal mechanisms for federal investigation of civil rights violations in the Civil Rights Act of 1957.

In 1959, Roy and Carolyn Bryant and Milam told their stories to journalist William Bradford Huie. Only Milam spoke for the record, but what he revealed was tantamount to a confession. Huie's interviews were subsequently published in 1959 as a book entitled *Wolf Whistle*.

—ROBYN SPENCER

See also

Plessy v. *Ferguson*

tests while exempting citizens—almost invariably whites—whose grandfathers had voted. This ruling did not clearly exhaust the South's legal strategems for denying blacks the ballot, but it encouraged the NAACP's reliance on the courts—the branch of government best insulated from political pressures—and on constitutional appeals for colorblind justice.

During the 1930s the NAACP sued for equal school facilities for blacks, in accord with the Supreme Court sanction of separate-but-equal treatment. In this way the NAACP secured the desegregation of all-white law or graduate schools in Maryland, Missouri, and other states unable to convince federal courts of an equal commitment to black and white students. The NAACP also beat down the formal exclusion of blacks from party primary elections in the South, through litigation culminating with the Supreme Court case *Smith* v. *Allright* in 1944.

Beginning in the 1930s elected officials received increasingly vigorous tutoring from the NAACP and other black groups on the need for protection of civil rights. Strong federal anti-lynching bills passed the House of Representa-

tives in 1937 and again in 1940, though each time succumbing to southern filibusters in the Senate. In 1941 the black union leader A. Philip Randolph planned a march on Washington to protest racial discrimination in the armed forces and defense industries. To persuade Randolph to call off the march, President Franklin Roosevelt in July 1941 created an advisory committee, the Fair Employment Practices Committee, to promote racial integration in munitions factories. A limited step, it was also the first presidential order for civil rights since Reconstruction—and the first intended chiefly to quiet an emerging black mass movement.

Civil rights activity quickened after the end of World War II, in 1945, in an increasingly open society that could not easily justify segregation after years of propaganda denouncing Nazi Germany for its vicious racial policies. The registration of over two million blacks by the late 1940s, many of them migrants from the rural South to northern cities, further undermined the racial status quo. So did the growing numbers of religious, civil, labor, intellectual, and white minority leaders who termed racism a challenge to national

**GROUPS HALT
LYNCHINGS**

In 1936, Harlem demonstrators pushed for the passage of the Anti-Lynching bill. The NAACP provided increasingly vigorous civil rights tutoring for black groups beginning in the 1930s.

PHOTOGRAPHS AND PRINTS DIVISION, SCHOMBURG CENTER FOR RESEARCH IN BLACK CULTURE, THE NEW YORK PUBLIC LIBRARY, ASTOR, LENOX AND TILDEN FOUNDATIONS

*We shall overcome,
we shall overcome,
We shall overcome
some day,
Oh, deep in my
heart, I do believe
We shall overcome
some day.*

ANONYMOUS CIVIL RIGHTS
SONG OF THE 1960s

*In the 1960s Ella
Baker was regarded
as the godmother of
the Civil Rights
Movement.*

PAGE 47

democratic values. Their words gained added force from the competition between the United States and the Soviet Union for support from emerging nonwhite nations, which made evidence of American racism a damaging embarrassment.

In December 1946 President Harry Truman appointed a committee to investigate violations of black rights. Three months later he endorsed the resulting report, entitled "To Secure These Rights," which prescribed a comprehensive federal assault on Jim Crow. In 1948 Truman acceded to a strong civil rights plank that liberal delegates had inserted in the Democratic national platform. He then weathered defections by a minority of southern whites to win a second term, aided by 70 percent of the northern black vote. Two years later he began desegregation of the armed forces to heighten military efficiency for the Korean War and to quiet restive black leaders.

By the late 1940s the NAACP's chief legal counsel, Thurgood Marshall, felt emboldened to attack directly the principle of segregation in public education. In several cases before the Supreme Court, Marshall argued that segregation denied blacks "equal protection of the laws" as guaranteed by the Fourteenth Amendment to the Constitution. In 1954 Chief Justice Earl Warren wrote for a unanimous Court, in Brown v. Topeka, Kansas Board of Education, that in the area of public education "the doctrine of 'separate but equal' has no place."

By threatening white supremacy the Brown case intensified southern resistance to civil rights progress. The Ku Klux Klan and other fringe hate groups experienced overnight revivals, congressmen and governors vowed "massive resistance," and state district attorneys sought injunctions to ban NAACP branches (they were entirely successful in Alabama by 1957). In May 1955 the Supreme Court tempered its original ruling in *Brown* by requiring no timetable for school desegregation, only that school districts move "with all deliberate speed." Compliance proved minimal, and when President Dwight D. Eisenhower sent federal troops in 1957 to guard nine blacks attending a formerly all-white high school in Little Rock, Ark., the prolonged furor discouraged further national intervention for desegregation.

Despite its limited tangible impact, *Brown* did confer a symbol of legitimacy on black activists, who prepared bolder assaults on segregation in the South. In December 1955 blacks in Montgomery, Ala., organized a bus boycott after a former NAACP secretary, Rosa Parks, was arrested for refusing to yield her seat on a segregated bus to

a white man. The boycott leader was a twenty-six-year-old, northern-educated minister originally from Atlanta, the Rev. Dr. Martin Luther King, Jr. King gained national attention for the protest against segregation by invoking Christian morality, American ideals of liberty, and the ethic of nonviolent resistance to evil exemplified by Mohandas Gandhi of India in his campaign against British colonial rule. Like Gandhi, King advocated confronting authorities with a readiness to suffer rather than inflict harm, in order to expose injustice and impel those in power to end it. In November 1956, despite growing white violence, the boycott triumphed with aid from the NAACP, which secured a Supreme Court decision (in *Gayle* v. *Browder*) that overturned Montgomery's laws enforcing bus segregation.

The signs of growing black restiveness in the South encouraged new civil rights initiatives. In January 1957 King organized the Southern Christian Leadership Conference (SCLC), a network of nonviolent civil rights activists drawn mainly from the black church. In September of that year Congress passed the first Civil Rights Act since Reconstruction; the act created a commission to monitor civil rights violations and authorized the Justice Department to guard black voting rights through litigation against discriminatory registrars. This act (and a follow-up measure in April 1960) nonetheless failed to curb the widespread disfranchisement of southern blacks.

The failure to implement federal civil rights edicts increasingly spurred blacks to shift their struggle for equality from the courts and cloakrooms to the streets. During the late 1950s blacks, often affiliated with local NAACP youth chapters, conducted scattered, short-lived sit-ins at lunch counters that served whites only. On February 1, 1960, a sit-in by four students at the Woolworth's lunch counter in Greensboro, N.C., triggered a host of similar protests throughout the South, targeting Jim Crow public accommodations from theaters to swimming pools. Strict conformity to nonviolent Christian and Gandhian tenets characterized the demonstrators, many of whom courted arrest and even imprisonment in order to dramatize the evils of segregation.

In April 1960 several hundred student activists gathered in Raleigh, N.C., at the invitation of Ella Baker, the executive director of the Southern Christian Leadership Conference. Baker urged the students to preserve their grass-roots militancy by remaining independent of established civil rights groups, and they responded by forming the Student Nonviolent Coordinating Commit-

RACIAL FACE-OFF

James Meredith Enters University Amidst Opposition

James H. Meredith (June 25, 1933–), civil rights activist. Born in Kosciusko, Miss., James Meredith became the central figure in two major events of the civil rights movement. He had studied at Jackson State University in Jackson, Miss., when in September 1962 he sought to enroll in the University of Mississippi to complete his bachelor's degree. The state university system was segregated, and though a court order confirmed Meredith's right to enter the school, Mississippi Gov. Ross Barnett led the opposition and personally stood in the doorway of the registrar's office to block Meredith's enrollment. In response, the Kennedy administration dispatched federal marshals to escort Meredith to classes. To quell the subsequent rioting, U.S. troops policed the campus, where they remained until Meredith graduated in 1963.

During the next year, Meredith studied at Ibadan University in Nigeria, and on his return to the United States he began taking courses for a law degree at Columbia University. In the summer of 1966, Meredith announced he would set out on a sixteen-day "walk against fear," which would take him from Memphis to the Mississippi state capital in Jackson. He sought both to spur African-American voter registration for the upcoming primary election and to show that blacks could overcome the white violence that had so long stifled aspirations.

On the second day of the hike, an assailant shot Meredith with two shotgun blasts. His wounds were not serious, but the attack sparked great outrage and the major civil rights organizations carried on a march to Jackson from the place where Meredith had been shot. This procession was marked by Stokely Carmichael's call for black power and a resulting rift between the moderate and militant wings of the movement. Meredith left the hospital after several days and was able to join the marchers before they reached Jackson.

Later in 1966, Meredith published *Three Years in Mississippi* and lectured on racial justice. Returning to law school, Meredith received his degree from Columbia University in 1968. That same year he ran unsuccessfully for Adam Clayton Powell, Jr.'s Harlem seat in the U.S. House of Representatives, then returned to Mississippi, where he became involved in several business ventures. In 1984 and 1985 he taught a course on blacks and the law at the University of Mississippi. In September 1989, he joined the staff of North Carolina Sen. Jesse Helms, an arch-conservative, as domestic policy adviser.

—STEVEN J. LESLIE

tee (SNCC, pronounced "snick") to promote Gandhian resistance to Jim Crow. By the summer of 1960 the sit-ins, which were often reinforced by boycotts of offending stores, had desegregated dozens of lunch counters and other public accommodations, mainly in southern border states.

Black protests intensified during the presidency of John F. Kennedy, a Democrat elected in 1960 with heavy black support. Kennedy early directed the Justice Department to step up litigation for black rights, but he avoided bolder commitments that he feared would trigger southern white racial violence and political retaliation. Civil rights leaders therefore increasingly designed campaigns to pressure their reluctant ally in the White House. In May 1961 James Farmer, who had cofounded the Congress of Racial Equality (CORE) nearly two decades earlier, led fourteen white and black CORE volunteers on a freedom ride through the South, testing compliance with a Supreme Court order to desegregate interstate bus terminal facilities. White mobs abetted by police beat the riders in Birmingham, Ala., on May

14; six days later federal marshals saved the riders from a mob in Montgomery. As the freedom rides proliferated, Kennedy quietly persuaded southern communities to desegregate their bus terminals.

Although the Kennedy administration strove to balance the competing pressures of black activists and their southern white opponents, growing racial tensions impelled the president to take stronger civil rights initiatives. In October 1962 Kennedy sent federal marshals to protect a black student, James Meredith, who had registered at the all-white University of Mississippi at Oxford. After mobs killed two people at the campus and besieged the marshals, the president reluctantly troops to restore order.

Racial polarization worsened in 1963, as demonstrations throughout the South precipitated 15,000 arrests and widespread white violence. On May 3 and for several days afterward, police in Birmingham beat and unleashed attack dogs on nonviolent black followers of Dr. King, in full view of television news cameras. The resulting public revulsion spurred President Kennedy to ad-

*Our nation is
moving toward two
societies, one black,
one white—separate
and unequal.*

OTTO KERNER, JR.
*REPORT OF THE NATIONAL
ADVISORY COMMISSION ON
CIVIL DISORDERS,* 1968

*The NAACP's most
outstanding
contribution to
the Civil Rights
Movement
continued to be
its legal and
lobbying efforts.*

PAGE 479

dress the nation on June 11, to confront a "moral issue" that was "as old as the Scriptures" and "as clear as the American Constitution." He urged Congress to enact a strong civil rights law that would allow race "no place in American life."

A coalition of African-American groups and their white allies sponsored a march on Washington on August 28, 1963, to advance the civil rights bill then before Congress. Reflecting the growing national stature of the Civil Rights Movement, the rally secured the participation of diverse political, cultural, and religious figures. Standing before the Lincoln Memorial, Dr. King told several hundred thousand blacks and whites at this event of his "dream" for interracial brotherhood. Afterward President Kennedy praised the goals and peaceful character of the march.

When Lyndon B. Johnson succeeded to the presidency on November 22, 1963, he made passage of the civil rights bill his top priority and effectively linked this goal to the memory of the martyred President Kennedy. A broad-based federation called the Leadership Conference on Civil Rights coordinated the lobbying efforts of over a hundred groups on behalf of the legislation, centered on extraordinary activity by Protestant, Catholic, and Jewish ministers. On July 2, 1964, Johnson signed the omnibus Civil Rights Act, which barred segregation in public accommodations, ended federal aid to segregated institutions, outlawed racial discrimination in employment, sought to strengthen black voting rights, and extended the life of the United States Commission on Civil Rights.

SNCC remained in the vanguard of civil rights activism in 1964 by organizing rural blacks in Mississippi, a state whose history was pockmarked with the casual shootings of black people. About a thousand college students, most of them white, volunteered for the Freedom Summer project to further the nonviolent, integrationist ideals of the Civil Rights Movement. The project workers set up "Freedom Schools" to give black children a positive sense of their history and identity, and an interracial party, the "Freedom Democrats," to give otherwise disfranchised blacks a political voice. The project also exposed the extreme dangers daily facing civil rights workers, after a federal manhunt recovered the bodies of three volunteers—Michael Schwerner, Andrew Goodman, and James Chaney—who had been murdered by a mob led by the deputy sheriff of Philadelphia, Miss. In late August the project workers helped the Freedom Democrats try to unseat Mississippi's lily-white delegation at the

Democratic national convention. Despite considerable northern support, their challenge failed because of strong resistance by President Johnson, who feared the loss of southern white voters in an election year. This harsh coda to the Freedom Summer spurred younger black activists to question the wisdom of alliances with white liberals and to stress instead the importance of black solidarity.

The fraying civil rights coalition rallied in 1965 behind Dr. King's campaign in Selma, Ala., for equal voting rights. On March 7 black marchers setting out from Selma toward Montgomery suffered assaults by state and local police. The televised scenes of violence galvanized national support for protection of blacks seeking the ballot, a view that President Johnson reinforced in a special appearance before Congress on March 15. Ten days later twenty-five thousand black and white marchers reached Montgomery escorted by federal troops. On August 6, 1965, Johnson signed a strong Voting Rights Act, which authorized the attorney general to send federal examiners to supersede local registrars and regulations wherever discrimination occurred. The act also directed the attorney general to challenge poll taxes for state and local elections in the courts (the Twenty-fourth Amendment to the Constitution, adopted in 1964, had already banned such taxes in national elections).

After 1965 the Civil Rights Movement fragmented in the absence of an overriding goal to unify and inspire it. During a march with King through Mississippi in June 1966, SNCC's Stokely Carmichael ridiculed faith in nonviolence and white good will and demanded "black power," a militant slogan that alienated white liberals and divided blacks. As the focus of the Civil Rights Movement increasingly turned from de jure segregation, to economic inequality and patterns of de facto segregation in the North, agreement on a strategy for addressing and solving these problems became more elusive. Ghetto riots, including a six-day rampage in South Central Los Angeles in August 1965, further split the movement by harming its nonviolent image and by shifting its focus from constitutional rights to problems of slum housing and poverty, for which no reform consensus existed. On April 4, 1968, the assassination of King in Memphis, Tenn., touched off riots that left Washington, D.C., in flames for three days. The following week, partly in tribute to the slain King, Congress passed the Civil Rights Act of 1968, which banned discrimination in the sale and rental of most housing.

Bloody Sunday Veteran Initiates Civil Rights Changes

John Lewis (February 21, 1940–), civil rights activist, politician. John Lewis was born near the town of Troy, in Pike County, Ala. Growing up on a small farm, Lewis was one of ten children in a poor sharecropping family. Lewis had been drawn to the ministry since he was a child, and in fulfillment of his lifelong dream, he entered the American Baptist Theological Seminary in Nashville, Tenn., in 1957. He received his B.A. four years later. As a seminary student Lewis participated in nonviolence workshops and programs taught by James Lawson—a member of the Fellowship of Reconciliation (FOR), a pacifist civil rights organization. Lewis became a field secretary for FOR and attended Highlander Folk School, an interracial adult education center in Tennessee committed to social change, where he was deeply influenced by Septima Clark, the director of education at Highlander.

Lewis became an active participant in the growing Civil Rights Movement. He became a member of the Nashville Student Movement, and along with Diane Nash Bevel, James Bevel, and other African-American students he participated in the Nashville desegregation campaigns of 1960. Lewis was one of the founding members of the Student Nonviolent Coordinating Committee (SNCC) in 1960 and played a leading role in organizing SNCC participation in the Congress of Racial Equality's (CORE) freedom rides. He led freedom rides in South Carolina and Alabama, where he and the other protesters were violently attacked by southern whites.

Lewis rose to a leadership position within SNCC, serving as national chairman from 1963 to 1966. During the 1963 march on Washington, Lewis—representing SNCC—delivered a highly controversial speech that criticized the federal government's consistent failure to protect civil rights workers, condemned the civil rights bill as "too little, too late," and called on African Americans to participate actively in civil rights protests until "the unfinished revolution of 1776 is complete." Despite the fact that he had acceded to the march organizers and other participants and allowed his speech to be severely edited to tone down its militant rhetoric, it was still considered by most in attendance to be the most radical speech of the day.

In March 1965 Lewis marched with Rev. Dr. Martin Luther king, Jr., in Selma, Ala., to agitate for a voting rights act that would safeguard African Americans' access to the franchise. He was one of the many participants severely beaten by state troopers on what became known as Bloody Sunday. By 1966 Lewis's continued advocacy of nonviolence had made him an anachronism in the increasingly militant SNCC. He resigned from the organization in June of that year, to be succeeded by Stokely carmichael as SNCC's chairperson. Lewis continued his civil rights activities as part of the Field Foundation from 1966 to 1967 and worked as director of community organization projects for the Southern Regional Council. In 1970 he was appointed director of the Voter Education Project, which promoted black empowerment through greater participation in electoral politics.

Lewis became more directly involved in the political arena six years later when he was appointed by President Carter to serve on the staff of ACTION—a government agency that coordinated volunteer activities. From 1981 to 1986, he served on the Atlanta City Council. In 1986, in a bitter race, he challenged and defeated Julian Bond—another civil rights veteran—for the seat in Congress from an Atlanta district. In Congress Lewis became an influential member of the House Ways and Means Committee. He was an advocate of civil rights and drew much praise from political observers for his political acumen. In 1992 he was reelected from Georgia's Fifth Congressional District for a fourth term.

—MARSHALL HYATT

Jesse Jackson has been the most prominent civil rights leader and African-American national figure since the death of Martin Luther King, Jr.

PAGE 369

The 1970s witnessed the emergence of expressly race-conscious government programs to redress the legacy of racial discrimination. In the 1971 case *Swann* v. *Charlotte-Mecklenburg* the Supreme Court acknowledged the failures of earlier approaches to school desegregation by sanctioning the busing of children to other neighborhoods as a tool to achieve racial balance. The federal government also promoted Affirmative Action to afford blacks (and, increasingly, other minorities and women) preference in school admissions and employment. These developments reflected the limitations of civil rights legislation in affording access to the economic mainstream; but they provoked fierce opposition. Violence in Boston and other cities over racial busing confirmed that the race problem was truly national rather than southern. And in *Regents of University*

*Segregation now.
Segregation
tomorrow.
Segregation forever.*

GEORGE WALLACE
INAUGURATION SPEECH AS
GOVERNOR OF ALABAMA, 1963

*The Niagara
Movement, which
was organized in
1905, was the first
significant
organized black
protest movement in
the twentieth
century.*

PAGE 523

See also
Ku Klux Klan

of California v. *Bakke* in 1978 the Supreme Court reflected the national acrimony over affirmative action by ruling five to four to strike down racial quotas in medical school admissions while allowing (by an equally slim margin) some race-conscious selection to achieve educational "diversity."

During the 1980s a conservative shift in national politics frustrated civil rights leaders, especially in the NAACP and the Urban League, who relied on federal activism to overcome state, municipal, and private acts of discrimination. Ronald Reagan, a Republican who won the presidency for the first of two terms in 1980, sought to trim federal authority in racial matters. From 1981 to 1985 his administration reduced the number of lawyers in the Justice Department's Civil Rights Division from 210 to 57, and also vainly attempted to disband altogether the United States Commission on Civil Rights. On January 8, 1982, Reagan restored the federal tax exemptions for segregated private schools that had been ended in 1970. The following year the Supreme Court, by an eight-to-one vote, overturned this ruling as a violation of the Civil Rights Act of 1964; in 1986 Reagan appointed the lone dissenter, William Rehnquist, to be Chief Justice of the Supreme Court.

The Rehnquist Court increasingly chipped away at government safeguards of black rights, a pattern evident from several employment discrimination cases in 1989: in *Patterson* v. *McLean Credit Union* the Court ruled that the Civil Rights Act of 1866 protected blacks merely in contracting for jobs but did not protect them from racial harassment by employers; in *Wards Cove Packing Co.* v. *Atonio* the Court shifted the burden of proof from employers to employees regarding job discrimination; in *City of Richmond* v. *J. A. Croson Co.* the Court rejected a program setting aside 30 percent of city contracts for minority businesses in the absence of flagrant evidence of discrimination, although Richmond had a history of official segregation and although minority contractors held fewer than 1 percent of the city contracts in Richmond, where minorities constituted half the population; in *Price Waterhouse* v. *Hopkins* the Court exonerated an employer who had committed acts of racial discrimination but who also cited other, legitimate reasons for such actions. In October 1990 the Republican president, George Bush, vetoed a civil rights bill that expressly restored the earlier, tougher curbs on job discrimination, and the Senate sustained his veto by a single vote. In November 1991, President Bush signed a milder version of this same bill while re-

stating his opposition to quotas to promote minority hiring.

The central goal of the Civil Rights Movement—full equality between blacks and whites—remains a distant vision. Residential segregation, seen in the persistence of inner-city black ghettos and lily-white suburbs, has easily survived federal open-housing statutes. De facto segregation of churches, social centers, and private schools also remains routine; and wealth, too, is largely segregated along racial lines, with the median family income of blacks in 1990 barely three-fifths that of whites, and with blacks three times as likely to be poor. Many civil rights leaders have urged comprehensive government remedies; but black political power remains limited with regard to national office holding and access to the circles that make foreign and domestic policy.

Despite its limitations, the Civil Rights Movement has in key respects transformed American race relations. In communities throughout the South during the 1960s, "whites only" signs that had stood for generations suddenly came down from hotels, rest rooms, theaters, and other facilities. School desegregation by the mid-1970s had become fact as well as law in over 80 percent of all southern public schools (a better record than in the North, where residential segregation remains pronounced). The federal government has also vigorously checked groups promoting racial hatred: Beginning in 1964 the FBI infiltrated the Ku Klux Klan so thoroughly that by 1965 perhaps one in five members was an informant; federal indictments and encouragement of private lawsuits helped reduce Klan membership from 10,000 in 1981 to less than 5,500 in 1987.

Protection of the suffrage represents the Civil Rights Movement's greatest success: When Congress passed the Voting Rights Act in 1965 barely 100 blacks held elective office in the country; by 1989 there were more than 7,200, including 24 congressional representatives and some 300 mayors. Over 4,800 of these officials served in the South, and nearly every Black Belt county in Alabama had a black sheriff. Mississippi, long the most racially repressive state, experienced the most dramatic change, registering 74 percent of its voting-age blacks and leading the nation in the number of elected officials (646). The unexpectedly strong showing by the Reverend Jesse Jackson in seeking the Democratic presidential nomination in 1984 and 1988 reflected the growing participation by blacks in mainstream politics.

Having leveled the formal barriers of a legal caste system during the early 1960s, the Civil

Rights Movement has since expanded its aims to include substantive equality of opportunity in all areas of American life. The NAACP and the Urban League have for decades urged federal measures to reconstruct the inner cities, create jobs, extend job training to all poor Americans, and strengthen affirmative action to help minorities overcome a legacy of exclusion. Beginning in the 1980s, however, a growing minority of blacks have gained national influence (highlighted by the appointment of Clarence Thomas to the Supreme Court in 1991) by emphasizing private rather than government initiatives and by deploring quotas and other race-conscious programs as politically divisive. The movement for racial equality is now struggling to forge a program that can both unify black activists and also capture the nation's moral high ground and its reform impulses as convincingly as earlier civil rights campaigns.

—ROBERT WEISBROT

CIVIL WAR

On April 12, 1864, three years to the day after the Civil War began with the firing on Fort Sumter in Charleston harbor, George W. Hatton, a former slave who had risen to the rank of sergeant in Company C, First Regiment, United States Colored Troops, encamped near New Bern, N.C., sat down to write a letter and reflect upon the circumstance in which he found himself. Hatton, his fellow soldiers, and their families had lived generations as slaves in the American South. Now they were part of a liberating army and serving a government that, through a combination of intent and necessity, waged total war on the South in order to destroy slavery. Hatton struggled to find the right words for his sentiments. "Though the Government openly declared that it did not want the Negroes in this conflict," he wrote, "I look around me and see hundreds of colored men armed and ready to defend the Government at any moment; and such are my feelings, that I can only say, the fetters have fallen—our bondage is over."

A month later, Hatton's regiment was encamped close to Jamestown, Va., when several African-American freedwomen entered their lines showing evidence that they had been severely whipped. Members of Hatton's company managed to capture "a Mr. Clayton," the man who had allegedly administered the beatings. The white Virginian was stripped to the waist, tied to

a tree, and given twenty lashes by one of his own former slaves, a William Harris, now a member of the Union army. In turn, each of the women Clayton had beaten was given her chance to lay the lash on the slaveholder's back. The women were given leave to, in Sgt. Hatton's words, "remind him that they were no longer his, but safely housed in Abraham's bosom, and under the protection of the Star Spangled Banner, and guarded by their own patriotic, though once downtrodden race." Again Hatton felt almost lost for words to describe the transformations he witnessed. "Oh that I had the tongue to express my feelings," he declared, "while standing on the banks of the James River, on the soil of Virginia, the mother state of slavery, as a witness of such a sudden reverse! The day is clear, the fields of grain are beautiful, and the birds are singing sweet melodious songs, while poor Mr. C. is crying to his servants for mercy."

Such acts of violent retribution by ex-slaves against their former masters were rare in the wake of Emancipation. Most freedpeople simply sought a portion of land, freedom of movement, and security for their families in circumstances of hardship and uncertainty. But Hatton's eloquence allows us to see many elements in the meaning of the Civil War in African-American history. It was the extraordinary time when blacks, free and ex-slave alike, came to identify their own fate closely with the fate of the Union—the United States "Government" (blacks frequently capitalized the word as Hatton did) and its military and political fortunes. Because the war to save the Union became the war to free the slaves, and because so many southern blacks liberated themselves when the opportunity came, many thousands serving as soldiers and sailors in Union uniforms, the Civil War and black Emancipation became inextricable parts of the same epic event. Because the sectional balance of political and economic power was fundamentally altered for a century in great part out of the destruction of slavery, and because, simply put, the terrible conflict would not have happened were it not for the presence of over four million slaves and the array of contradictions they caused for the meaning of America, the Civil War may rightly be considered, as many historians now consider it, the "Second American Revolution."

The drama of Emancipation—four million people liberated from chattel slavery in the midst of the world's first total war—is all the more striking because for black leaders the 1850s had been a decade of discouragement and division combined with unpredictable political crisis. Some black

Fourscore and seven years ago, our fathers brought forth on this continent a new nation, conceived in liberty, and dedicated to the proposition that all men are created equal.

ABRAHAM LINCOLN
GETTYSBURG ADDRESS,
NOV. 19, 1863

abolitionists like Martin Delany, Henry Highland Garnet, and Mary Ann Shadd struggled to organize emigration plans by which free blacks could start life over again in Africa, the Caribbean, or Canada. Most antebellum free blacks living in the North (a quarter million in the 1850s) followed the lead of Frederick Douglass, James McCune Smith, or Sojourner Truth, who insisted that the future for African Americans lay in America. This was not an easy position to sustain by the late 1850s, especially in the wake of the Dred Scott Decision in 1857, wherein Chief Justice of the U.S. Supreme Court Roger B. Taney proclaimed that blacks were "beings of an inferior order . . . so far inferior, that they had no rights which the white man was bound to respect." But black and white abolitionists condemned such ideas, and hope could also be found in the mounting sectional conflict over the expansion of slavery into the West, and in the new antislavery Republican Party to which it gave birth. Blacks welcomed the news of John Brown's Raid on Harpers Ferry in 1859; some had actively participated in the ill-planned and ill-fated raid on a federal arsenal in northern Virginia. Plotting slave insurrections, however, had always been easier in theory than in practice, as many fugitive slaves in the North knew from experience. Larger hopes rested in the idea that somehow the conflict between North and South would boil into disunion and political confrontation sufficient enough to cause the federal government to move, militarily and legally, against slavery.

So, after the election of Abraham Lincoln in 1860, the secession crisis the following winter, and the outbreak of war in the spring of 1861, African Americans could take heart that the longed-for "jubilee" of black freedom that they had sung and written about for years might now happen. Although prophecy and reality would not meet easily, nor without ghastly bloodshed, most would have agreed with Douglass's editorial of March 1861. "The contest must now be decided, and decided forever," he wrote, "which of the two, Freedom or Slavery, shall give law to this Republic. Let the conflict come." In a few short years and through untold suffering, the rest of the American people, with differing degrees of satisfaction or resistance, would be forced to see in the war the same meaning that Douglass proclaimed. In the wake of the outbreak of war, Douglass captured the anxiety and the hopes of his people as well as their antislavery friends: "For this consummation we have watched and wished with fear and trembling. God be praised! that it has come at last."

Black responses to the outbreak of war ranged from an ecstatic willingness to serve to caution and resistance. Across the North, free black communities sent petitions to state legislatures, organized militia companies, and wrote to the secretary of war offering their services on the battlefield. Only two days after President Lincoln's call for volunteers, the Twelfth Baptist Church in Boston hosted a meeting that the abolitionist William Wells Brown called "crowded as I had never seen a meeting before." In one resolution after another, these black Bostonians declared their support. "Our feelings urge us to say to our countrymen," they announced, "that we are ready to stand by and defend the Government with our lives, our fortunes, and our sacred honor." From Pittsburgh came the offer of a black militia company called the "Hannibal Guards," who insisted on being considered "American citizens." Although "deprived of all our political rights," this group of eager soldiers understood the moment as a historic main chance: They wished "the government of the United States sustained against the tyranny of slavery." From Philadelphia came the news that the sizable black population of that city would raise two full regiments of infantry. In New York City, blacks rented a hall to hold meetings and drill their own militia in preparation for service. In Albany, Ohio, a militia company organized, calling itself the "Attucks Guards" and flying a handmade flag presented by the black women of the town. In Detroit a full black military band under the command of a Capt. O. C. Wood sought to enlist. And from Battle Creek, Mich., a black physician, G. P. Miller, wrote to the War Department asking for the privilege of "raising from 5,000 to 10,000 freemen to report in sixty days to take any position that may be assigned to us (sharpshooters preferred)."

But as promptly as blacks volunteered, their services were denied during the first year of the war. Most states explicitly prohibited black participation in their militias. The policy of the federal government reflected widespread white public opinion: that the war was for the restoration of the Union and not the destruction of slavery. On a deeper level, most white Northerners held the view that "this is a white man's war," as the police in Cincinnati told a large gathering of blacks attempting to find a hall in which to hold their patriotic meetings. Amid this fear, confusion, and bravado, the deep-seated racism of the mid-nineteenth century prevailed as the United States Congress and the War Department made it federal policy to deny enlistment to black soldiers.

A CHARISMATIC FIGURE

Persuasive John Brown Launches a Raid on Harper's Ferry

On his way to the gallows in 1859, John Brown handed a note to one of his attendants avowing that slavery "*will* never be purged *away*; but with Blood." The Connecticut-born abolitionist and Christian zealot held that the South would never voluntarily abandon slavery. Nearly three decades of abolitionist agitation had not, Brown maintained, moved the nation any closer to ending that "wicked" institution. His war against proslavery forces in the Kansas Territory and Missouri during the 1850s convinced him that only a direct attack on the South offered hope of destroying slavery.

Beginning in 1857, Brown used his extensive contacts in the antislavery community to raise funds for an astonishing scheme. Although he contacted scores of black and white abolitionists, he offered them few details and gave most only the broadest outline of his plan to invade Virginia. Blacks pledged their support, but some of his closest friends in the African-American community, such as Frederick Douglass, had no idea that Brown aimed to seize the federal arsenal at Harpers Ferry, Va. (now part of West Virginia), arm local slaves, and commence a war against the slaveholding South. Although northern blacks eagerly promised money and assistance, most feared retribution against their families and refused to join his small band. Others, with far more militant ideas than Brown's, simply did not trust the plans of whites.

Despite a disappointing response from blacks, Brown proceeded with his scheme and in May 1858 presented a draft constitution, an outline for a provisional government, and details of the plan to an interracial meeting of forty-six abolitionists in Chatham, Ontario. Many of his supporters doubted the advisability of launching a race war in the South, but nevertheless supported the charismatic figure. By July 1859, Brown had raised sufficient funds to purchase arms and supplies, and rented a farmhouse in Maryland, seven miles from Harpers Ferry, to serve as a staging ground. Frederick Douglass again met with him from August 19 to 21 in Chambersburg, Pa., but upon learning the details of the raid refused to join the venture. By October 15, 1859, however, twenty-one others—including five blacks, Osborne P. Anderson, Dangerfield Newby, Shields Green, John A. Copeland, Jr., and Lewis Leary—had pledged their lives to Brown and his cause. If he had exercised more patience and better organization, Brown might have been joined by black militia units from Ohio and Canada, but he believed that divine inspiration dictated action. On October 16 at 8:00 P.M., he assembled his small force and announced: "Men, get on your weapons; we will proceed to the ferry."

After quickly seizing the armory and engine house, Brown stalled and waited. He expected that word of the uprising would attract slaves eager for the opportunity to throw off their shackles and slay their oppressors. Instead, his inaction allowed militia forces to organize and the state to alert President James Buchanan, who promptly dispatched a detachment of marines under the command of Robert E. Lee and J. E. B. Stuart. After only thirty-six hours, Brown found himself cornered in the armory's engine house; ten of his men, including two of his own sons, lay dead; and nearly the entire western part of the state had been incited against him. Federal troops stormed the building, easily capturing Brown and his surviving comrades.

The outcome of Brown's trial, beginning on October 27, was never in doubt. Although some of his northern supporters prepared to free him, Brown rejected such schemes. He now sought the martyrdom that was assured him and turned the trial into a forum for his antislavery views. Newspapers across the country reported his speeches, winning him the admiration of thousands. Even his bitterest enemies could not deny Brown's courage and devotion to his principles. By the time of his execution for murder and treason against the state of Virginia on December 2, 1859, he had captured the attention of the entire North. The transcendentalist poet and author Ralph Waldo Emerson proclaimed that Brown "will make the gallows glorious like the cross." Brown's raid also radicalized northern blacks. "I believe in insurrections," the Boston black abolitionist John S. Rock exclaimed after Harpers Ferry, and most northern blacks hailed Brown and his men as martyrs in the cause of liberty. The attack became a watershed event in African-American history, convincing blacks that only violence would end slavery; more important, it convinced most Americans that compromise on the issue of slavery was impossible. Although the raid failed dismally in its immediate goals, Brown succeeded in riveting the nation's attention upon the issue of slavery and firmly put the country on the road to civil war.

—DONALD YACOVONE

Few events in American history can match the drama and the social significance of black emancipation in the midst of the Civil War.

PAGE 233

All of this occurred amid widespread assumptions in the North that secession and rebellion would be easily put down in one summer. But underneath all such social currents rested the fear that white men simply would not shoulder muskets next to black men. Soon, a tragically divided people would be forced to see how historical forces had been unleashed that would compel them to act both because of and above their prejudices.

A vigorous debate about support for the war ensued among blacks during the first year of the conflict. Stung by the rejection of their early enthusiasm for enlistment, some blacks turned away in anger, declaring—as did a man in Troy, N.Y.—that "we of the North must have all the rights which white men enjoy; until then we are in no condition to fight under the flag which gives us no protection." An "R.H.V." from New York City was even more explicit in opposing black participation. "No regiments of black troops," he said, "should leave their bodies to rot upon the battlefield beneath a Southern sun, to conquer a peace based upon the perpetuity of human bondage." Black newspaper editors divided over the issue. The *Anglo-African* (New York) vehemently urged support for the war as a crusade against the slaveholding South, and therefore in blacks' long-term interests. Frederick Douglass, in his *Douglass Monthly* (Rochester, N.Y.), demanded black enlistment from the first sounds of war. The exclusion policy angered him deeply, and by September 1861, he attacked the Lincoln administration's "spectacle of blind, unreasoning prejudice," accusing it of fighting with its "white hand" while allowing its "black hand to remain tied." The *Christian Recorder,* the African Methodist Episcopal Church newspaper in Philadelphia, dissented from Douglass's call for troops. "To offer ourselves now," wrote its editor Elisha Weaver, "is to abandon self-respect and invite insult." Blacks should not fight, said Weaver, in a war where "not only our citizenship, but our common humanity is denied." The war was not yet the social revolution it would become; and no black leader could see the end from the beginning.

In the South, the bulk of African Americans found themselves living in the Confederate States of America, a hastily created nation mobilizing for war on a scale no one had imagined, determined to preserve slavery as the basis of its socioeconomic system, and soon under siege and invasion. All of these circumstances made for what would eventually become—especially when the Yankee armies came in large numbers to Virginia, the coast of the Carolinas, the Mississippi River Valley, and the Tennessee-Georgia region—a mass exodus of both military and self-emancipation from 1862 to 1865. But at the outset of the war, motivated by local pride, protection of the home place, or fear of reprisal, some southern blacks actually offered their services to the Confederate armies. Two Louisiana regiments of blacks were enlisted in 1861, but were never allowed to serve in active duty.

In March 1861, in a speech in Savannah, Ga., Vice President of the Confederacy Alexander H. Stevens stated, at least implicitly, what all Southerners would come to know—that it was black Southerners who might have the most at stake in this war. Comparing the Confederacy to the federal government created in 1787, Stevens declared that the South's move for independence "is founded upon exactly the opposite ideas; its foundations are laid, its cornerstone rests, upon the great truth that the Negro is not equal to the white man; subordination to the superior race is his natural and moral condition." Stevens knew, as did the masses of slaves anticipating "de Kingdom comin' an' de year ob Jubilo," that the status of slavery was central to the war. Before it was over in 1865, that founding Constitution of 1787 would undergo the beginnings of a process of fundamental change.

One of the few economic strengths in the Confederacy's war-making capacity was its huge supply of black labor. Tens of thousands of slaves were pressed into service to build fortifications and to work as teamsters, cooks, boatmen, blacksmiths, laundresses, and nurses. Slaves had long performed these tasks in the South; so, as the massive mobilization took place all across the Confederacy, black forced labor became one of the primary means by which the South waged war. Blacks were "hired out" by their owners to work in ordnance factories, armories, hospitals, and many other sites of military production and transport. In Georgia alone, an estimated ten thousand blacks worked on Confederate defenses. In some twenty-nine hospitals across northern Georgia in 1863, blacks comprised 80 percent (nearly one thousand people) of the workers, especially the nurses, cooks, and laundresses. Early in the war many slaveholders were quite willing to offer the labor of their slaves to the South's cause. But as the conflict endured, and the displacement of people became ever more chaotic, many owners began to transfer (or, as this process became known, "refugee") their slaves to the interior.

Huge numbers of slaves were set in motion by these removals. Many blacks experienced separation of families as men were forced into Confederate labor gangs and women and children were often left to their own devices back on the home place, or themselves were eventually caught up in refugee movement in the face of advancing Union armies. But especially for males, this social flux, however great the hardship, provided enormous opportunity for escape to Union lines. Especially in the upper South and along the coasts, but eventually in the South's heartland as well, many slaves would find freedom by slipping away from Confederate railroad crews or joining Union forces after decisive battles.

Indeed, thousands of blacks were "employed" (not always with compensation) as military laborers on the Union side as well. Wherever Union forces advanced into the South, so important were blacks as foragers, wagon masters, construction workers for fortifications and bridges, and cooks and camp hands that a visitor to any Yankee army camp would see hundreds and sometimes thousands of black faces. Ex-slaves who were familiar with the southern countryside also served numerous Union officers as spies and sources of military intelligence. Harriet Tubman, famous for her earlier career as a "conductor" on the Underground Railroad, was one of the countless blacks who served the Union cause as guides and spies. She was formally commended by the secretary of war and at least five high-ranking Union officers for her two years' work in the Sea Islands as a nurse and a daring scout.

Driven by human will and military necessity, an enormous exodus of liberation ensued throughout the first three years of the war. The black Union soldier and later historian George Washington Williams observed both motivations. "Whenever a Negro appeared with a shovel in his hands," wrote Williams, "a white soldier took his gun and returned to the ranks." "It was an exodus whose Moses was multiple," wrote historian Benjamin Quarles, "an Odyssey whose Ulysses was legion."

Nothing so typified the eventual antislavery character of the Civil War as the black soldier in Union blue. As the war dragged on, events moved so quickly that Emancipation and black enlistment became inseparable realities. From the first designation of fugitive slaves as "contrabands" (confiscated property of war) in 1861, abolitionists demanded that blacks be recruited as soldiers. The initial exclusion policy proved untenable in the face of total war, and by 1862, due to mounting white casualties, northern public opinion was increasingly favorable to the employment of black

troops. That sentiment grew even stronger in the spring of 1863, when the federal government instituted a much-despised conscription law.

In the wake of the bloody and unsuccessful Peninsular campaign in July 1862, Congress enacted the Second Confiscation Act, empowering Lincoln to "employ . . . persons of African descent . . . for the suppression of the rebellion." Under vague authority, initial black regiments had already been organized by zealous Union commanders in Louisiana and Kansas. But by August 1862, the War Department authorized the recruitment of five regiments of black infantry in the Sea Islands of South Carolina and Georgia. By Thanksgiving Day, Thomas Wentworth Higginson, the commander of the First South Carolina Volunteers (the first regiment of ex-slaves), looked out of the broken windows of an abandoned plantation house in the Sea Islands, "through avenues of great live oaks," and observed that "all this is the universal Southern panorama; but five minutes walk beyond the hovels and the live oaks will bring one to something so un-Southern that the whole Southern coast at this moment trembles at the suggestion of such a thing—the camp of a regiment of freed slaves."

Following Lincoln's Emancipation Proclamation in January 1863, the governors of Massachusetts, Connecticut, and Rhode Island were authorized to raise black regiments. Gov. John Andrew of Massachusetts had been especially instrumental in convincing the Lincoln administration to make such moves. Abolitionist George L. Stearns was commissioned to organize black recruiters, and by April black abolitionists such as Douglass, Martin Delany, Henry Highland Garnet, John Mercer Langston, William Wells Brown, Charles Lenox Remond, and O. S. B. Wall were enlisting young free blacks from across the North and sending them to Readville, Mass., where they became part of the Fifty-fourth Massachusetts Colored Regiment. That spring, as a recruiting document, Douglass published his "Men of Color to Arms!," a pamphlet that captured the revolutionary character of the war now imagined in black communities. "I urge you to fly to arms and smite with death the power that would bury the government and your liberty in the same hopeless grave," Douglass demanded of young recruits, of whom his own first two were his sons Lewis and Charles.

The Fifty-fourth Massachusetts became the famous test case of what the northern press still viewed as the experiment with black troops. Its valorous assault on Fort Wagner on the sands

If slaves seem good soldiers, then our whole theory of slavery is wrong.

GENERAL HOWELL COBB

around Charleston harbor in South Carolina, July 18, 1863, where the regiment suffered 100 dead or missing and 146 wounded, served as a tragic but immensely symbolic demonstration of black courage. Indeed, many white Northerners, as well as Confederate soldiers, discovered that black men would and could fight. Blacks who served in the Union army and navy during the Civil War fought for many reasons. They fought for the simplest and deepest of causes: their own freedom and that of their families. They fought because events had seemed to provide an opening to a new future, to the achievement of the birthright of *citizenship* through military service. They also fought for the right to fight, for a sense of human dignity. They fought because they lived in a world that so often defined "manhood" as that recognition gained by the act of soldiering.

In May 1863 the War Department established the Bureau of Colored Troops, and from then until the end of the war, quartermasters and recruiting agents labored competitively to maximize the number of black soldiers throughout the South. The manpower needs of the Union armies were endless, and black enlistment became the most direct way to undermine and destroy slavery. By the end of the war in April 1865, the nearly

LEGENDARY RESCUER

An escaped slave, Harriet Tubman (1820–1913) freed more than two hundred others as a leader of rescue expeditions on the Underground Railroad. She became a legend among slaves and abolitionists.

PRINTS AND PHOTOGRAPHS DIVISION, LIBRARY OF CONGRESS

180,000 blacks in the Union forces included 33,000 from the northern free states. The border slaveholding states of Delaware, Maryland, Missouri, and Kentucky provided a total of 42,000, half that number from Kentucky alone. Tennessee sent 20,000; Louisiana, 24,000; Mississippi, nearly 18,000; and the remaining states of the Confederacy, almost 40,000. These statistics demonstrate that Emancipation and black enlistment became twin functions of the Union war effort. Wherever northern armies arrived first and stayed the longest, there the greatest numbers of black men became Yankee soldiers.

In desperation, some slaveholders offered wages and other privileges in order to induce their slaves to stay. As the war dragged on, some black men eagerly enlisted with the Union, but others were forced into service by impressment gangs— sometimes composed of black soldiers—as a means of filling the ranks. Like their white comrades, black soldiers suffered untold hardships. But they sometimes received inadequate medical care compared with white troops, faced possible re-enslavement or execution if captured, and encountered several overt forms of discrimination within the Union ranks. Virtually all commissioned officers in black units were white, and though promises had been made to the contrary during the early recruiting period, the federal government capitulated to racism with an explicitly unequal pay system for black soldiers. White privates in the Union army received $13 per month plus $3 for clothing, while black men received only $7 plus clothing. As a matter of both principle and dire hardship for their families, the unequal pay issue angered black soldiers and recruiters more than any other form of discrimination. During 1863 many black regiments resisted the policy, refusing to accept any pay until it was equalized. Open revolt resulted in at least one regiment, the Third South Carolina Volunteers, being led by black sergeant William Walker. Walker led his company in stacking their arms at their commanding officer's tent in protest of unequal pay. After a lengthy court-martial, Walker was convicted of mutiny, and in February 1864 he was executed by a firing squad before the audience of his own brigade. The strictures of military law, mixed with racism, made war in this instance an extremely unforgiving business.

Black families, especially women, suffered not only the dislocations of war, but tremendous physical and financial hardship as well. Many, like Rachel Ann Wicker of Piqua, Ohio, wrote in protest to governors and President Lincoln. In

September 1864, Wicker informed Governor Andrew of Massachusetts (her husband was in the Fifty-fifth Massachusetts) that "i speak for myself and Mother and i know of a great many others as well as ourselve are suffering for the want of money to live on." She demanded that Andrew explain "why it is that you Still insist upon them takeing 7 dollars a month when you give the Poorest White Regiment that has went out 16 dollars." Under pressure from such women, from black communities, abolitionists, and governors, Congress enacted equal pay for blacks and whites in June 1864.

In spite of ill treatment, black soldiers—motivated by their own sense of freedom, feeling a sense of dignity that perhaps only military life could offer, and politicized as never before—participated in some 39 major battles and 410 minor engagements during the last two years of the war. Many vocal white critics were silenced when black units fought heroically and suffered terrible casualties in such battles as Port Hudson, La., in May 1863; Milliken's Bend in June 1863; Fort Wagner the next month; and various stages during the siege of Petersburg, Va., in 1864. Sometimes Confederate troops gave no quarter to their captured black opponents. At Fort Pillow, Tennessee, in April 1864, Confederate general Nathan Bedford Forrest gave orders that led to the massacre of at least 200 black soldiers. In all, nearly 3,000 blacks died in battle during the Civil War, and another staggering 33,000 died of disease. Again and again, many of the white officers who led black units testified to the courage and devotion of their men. Higginson declared that he never had to "teach the principles of courage" to his regiment of freed slaves. And he especially marveled at one of his black sergeants, Prince Rivers, who had been a "crack coachman" in Beaufort, S.C., before Emancipation. "There is not a white officer in this regiment," wrote Higginson, "who has more administrative ability, or more absolute authority over the men; they do not love him, but his mere presence has controlling power over them. He writes well enough . . . if his education reached a higher point, I see no reason why he should not command the Army of the Potomac." By the time Abraham Lincoln spoke of a "new birth" of freedom at Gettysburg in November 1863, and called Emancipation the "result so fundamental and astounding" in his second inaugural address in March 1865, there was no better symbol emerging of that regeneration than the anguished sacrifices of black soldiers and their families in the crusade for their own freedom.

With the passage of the Thirteenth Amendment in February 1865, slavery was legally abolished in America; the institution from which all blacks had been forced to derive social identity had been destroyed. For blacks the ending of the Civil War was a season of great hope and anxiety. Freedom, and at least the promise of the right to vote and equality before the law, was now possible. Millions of ex-slaves dreamed of land ownership amid their ambiguous new status in the conquered and devastated South. The years ahead during Reconstruction and beyond would bring great advancement in black politics, civil rights, and institution-building, as well as great disappointment and betrayal. But Emancipation had come at last.

In its own context, the meaning of the Civil War for African Americans had no more poignant illustration than the fall of Richmond, the capital of the Confederacy, in the first week of April 1865. Black troops were among the first Union forces to triumphantly occupy the city, and the freed population welcomed them in what the black newspaper correspondent T. Morris Chester called "a spectacle of jubilee." Jubilant black folk also welcomed Lincoln when he visited Richmond on April 4, only two days after Confederate evacuation. There was "no describing the scene along the route," reported Chester. "The colored population was wild with enthusiasm." There were whites in the crowd, but "they were lost in the great concourse of American citizens of African descent." To the black soldiers, many of whom were recently slaves, as well as to the masses of freedpeople, such a revolutionary transformation, such an apocalyptic moment, could only be the work of God in union with his people. Garland H. White, a former Virginia slave who had escaped to Ohio before the war, now marched into Richmond as the chaplain of the Twenty-eighth United States Colored Troops. After making a triumphant speech "amid the shouts of ten thousand voices" on Broad Street, White, overcome by joyful tears, wandered the streets of Richmond, where later that day he found his mother, whom he had not seen in twenty years. Even more telling, though, was the liberation of Richmond's remaining slave pens and auction rooms. As the black troops approached the abandoned "Lumpkin's Jail" (owned by the notorious slave trader Robert Lumpkin), the prisoners behind the barred windows began to chant:

Slavery chain done broke at last!
Broke at last! Broke at last!

Those who deny freedom to others deserve it not for themselves.

ABRAHAM LINCOLN
LETTER TO
H. L. PIERCE ET AL.,
APRIL 6, 1859

Slavery chain done broke at last!
Gonna praise God till I die!

Now no more weary trav'lin',
'Cause my Jesus set me free,
An' there's no more auction block for me
Since he give me liberty.

—DAVID W. BLIGHT

CLEAVER, ELDRIDGE LEROY

Eldridge Leroy Cleaver (August 31, 1935–), writer, political activist. Eldridge Cleaver was born in Wabbaseka, Ark., where he attended a junior college. From 1954 to 1957 and again from 1958 to 1966 he was incarcerated on drug and rape charges, and furthered his education while in prison. In 1965, Cleaver became the most prominent "Black Muslim" prisoner to break with Elijah Muhammad's Nation of Islam after Malcolm X's assassination. Just as FBI director J. Edgar Hoover had begun to target the Black Panthers as the nation's "greatest threat," Cleaver became the party's minister of information in 1966, calling for an armed insurrection to overthrow the United States government and replace it with a black socialist government. During the late 1960s and early '70s, he also was an assistant editor and contributing writer to *Ramparts* magazine.

In 1968, Cleaver published *Soul on Ice*, which remains his primary claim to literary fame. A collection of autobiographical and political essays in the form of letters and meditations, *Soul on Ice* articulated the sense of alienation felt by many black nationalists who refused to work within an inherently corrupt system. Cleaver viewed his own crimes as political acts and spelled out how racism and oppression had forged his revolutionary consciousness.

Later that year, while on parole, Cleaver was involved in a shootout with Oakland police during which a seventeen-year-old Black Panther, Bobby Hutton, was killed; Cleaver and a police officer were wounded. Cleaver's parole was revoked and he was charged with assault and attempted murder. Although he received worldwide support and was chosen to run as the presidential candidate for the Peace and Freedom Party, Cleaver feared for his safety if he surrendered to the authorities. He fled the country, jumping a $50,000 bail, and lived for the next seven years in Cuba, France and Algiers. He also visited the So-

viet Union, China, North Vietnam, and North Korea during these years of exile. But in 1975 he returned to the United States and struck a deal with the FBI. Although he faced up to seventy-two years in prison, he was sentenced instead to 1,200 hours of community service.

In 1978, Cleaver published *Soul on Fire*, a collection of essays on his newly acquired conservative politics, and in 1979 he founded the Eldridge Cleaver Crusades, an evangelical organization. In 1984 he ran as an independent candidate for Congress in the eighth Congressional District in California. In the 1980s, he lectured on religion and politics, and published his own poetry and polemical writings. In March 1994, his struggle with drugs came to national attention when he underwent brain surgery after he had been arrested in Berkeley, Calif., late at night with a serious head injury, in a state of drunkenness and disorientation.

Cleaver has been a prolific writer and speaker and was seen by some in the late 1960s as a black leader capable of organizing and leading a mass movement. *Soul on Ice* won the Martin Luther King Memorial Prize in 1970. Most of his work consists of nonfiction writing: *Eldridge Cleaver: Post-Prison Writings and Speeches* (1969), *Eldridge Cleaver's Black Papers* (1969), the introduction to Jerry Rubin's *Do It!* (1970), and contributions to *The Black Panther Leaders Speak: Huey P. Newton, Bobby Seale, Eldridge Cleaver, and Company Speak Out Through the Black Panther Party's Official Newspaper* (1976) and to *War Within: Violence or Nonviolence in Black Revolution* (1971). He has also authored and coauthored numerous pamphlets for the Black Panther party and the People's Communication Network. Some of his work has also appeared in anthologies such as the *Prize Stories of 1971: The O. Henry Awards*.

Cleaver has had both his critics and his followers. There are those who felt that his commitment to violence and his use of rape as a political weapon in the 1960s had no place within society. Others have questioned the sincerity and credibility of his later *volte face* to right-wing politics and fundamentalist Christianity, and Cleaver has often felt compelled to explain and defend himself. According to him, combined with his growing disenchantment with communism and radical politics was a mystical vision resulting in his conversion to Christianity. When accused of having mellowed with age, Cleaver replied, "That implies that your ideas have changed because of age. I've changed because of new conclusions."

—AMRITJIT SINGH

See also
Literature

146

KING OF THE AIRWAVES

Nat "King" Cole Wins Acclaim for One-of-a-Kind Style

Nat "King" Cole (Nathaniel Adams Cole) (March 17, 1919–February 15, 1965), singer and pianist. Born in Montgomery, Ala., Nat Cole moved with his family to Chicago when he was two years old. His father, the Rev. Edward James Cole, Sr., was a pastor at the True Light Baptist Church. His parents encouraged the musical talents of young Cole and his four brothers. All but one eventually became professional musicians. Cole had his earliest musical experiences in his father's church, where he sang and played the organ. While in high school, he played in the Rogues of Rhythm, a band led by his brother Eddie, at a Chicago night spot called the Club Panama. In 1936 he played piano in a touring production of Noble Sissle and Eubie Blake's *Shuffle Along*. The tour ended in Long Beach, Calif., in 1937. Cole stayed in southern California, and played piano in Los Angeles-area clubs.

In 1938 he organized a trio with Oscar Moore on guitar and Wesley Prince on bass. About this time he adopted the name Nat "King" Cole. The trio began to gain popularity largely due to Cole's sophisticated, swinging piano style. In 1943 Cole signed a contract with the newly organized record company Capitol.

On his first hit recording "Straighten Up and Fly Right" (1943), Cole sang for the first time. The song, based on a sermon of his father's, was taken from a traditional black folktale. In 1944, Cole achieved a national reputation as a pianist, taking part in "Jazz at the Philharmonic," a series of touring jazz concerts.

Eventually, Cole's singing came to dominate his piano playing. His 1946 recording of "The Christmas Song," which added a string section to Cole's singing, was a turning point in the evolution of his career. By 1949 he was recording primarily with orchestral accompaniment, and his piano playing was relegated to a secondary role. Cole achieved great success with such vocal recordings as "Mona Lisa" (1950) and "Unforgettable" (1951). Cole's singing style was, like his piano playing, relaxed, disarming, and authoritative. His performances remained impressive even with the most banal material, and they always retained their integrity, shunning both pseudodramatic straining for effects and coy mannerisms. His singing had an immense popularity with both white and black audiences. Cole's was the first black jazz combo to have its own sponsored radio program (1948–1949), and in 1956 and 1957 he became the first black performer to have his own series on network television. (The program was canceled, however, because of the difficulty in finding sponsors for it.) Cole also made several films, including *St. Louis Blues* (1958, a life of W. C. Handy), and *Cat Ballou* (1965).

In the early 1960s Cole was sometimes criticized by black activists for his failure to actively participate in the struggle for civil rights. Cole resented the accusations, noting that he had made substantial financial contributions to civil rights organizations. By this time, Cole was a headliner at Las Vegas casinos and was one of the most financially successful performers in popular music. He died of lung cancer in 1965 at the height of his popularity. He was the most successful black performer of the postwar era. The appreciation of his contribution to popular music has increased since his death. His television show has been syndicated and many of his recordings have been reissued.

Cole's first marriage, to Nadine Robinson in 1937, ended in divorce. He married Maria Ellington (no relation to Duke Ellington) in 1948. They had four children, and also adopted Maria's niece. One of their children, Natalie Cole, has had a successful career as a pop singer. In 1991, Natalie Cole achieved considerable recognition for her album *Unforgettable*, an ingeniously recorded album of duets with her late father, which won Grammies for best album and best song.

—ROBERT W. STEPHENS

By the end of the 1960s, many of the television shows in which blacks could either demonstrate their decision-making abilities or investigate the complexities of their lives had been canceled.

PAGE 672

COLEMAN, BESSIE

Bessie Coleman (January 26, 1892–April 30, 1926), aviator. Bessie Coleman was the first African-American female aviator. She was born in Atlanta, Tex., but her family moved to Waxahachie, Tex., when she was still an infant. When she was 7, her parents separated. Her father, who was a Choctaw Indian, returned to the reservation in Oklahoma, and her mother supported the large family by picking cotton and doing laundry, jobs in which she was aided by her children. Because she wanted Coleman to attend college, her mother allowed her to keep her income from her laundry work, but this money only financed one semester at the Colored Agricultural and Normal University in Langston, Okla. (now Langston University). After this semester, she returned to

C

Waxahachie briefly; and between 1915 and 1917, she went to Chicago, where she took a course in manicuring and worked at the White Sox barbershop until the early years of World War I. She then managed a small restaurant.

Coleman became interested in the burgeoning field of aviation, which had entered the national consciousness as a consequence of its role in World War I, but all her applications to aviation schools were rejected on the basis of her race and/or gender, until Robert S. abbott, founder and editor of the *Chicago Defender,* advised her to study aviation abroad. She took a course in French, went to Paris in November 1920, and attended an aviation school in Le Crotoy. She returned to the United States in September 1921 with a pilot's license and went back to Europe in 1922, this time obtaining an international pilot's license, the first African-American woman to obtain these licenses. When she returned to the United States after her second sojourn in Europe, Coleman made a name for herself in exhibition flying, performing at shows attended by thousands. She barnstormed throughout the United States and became known as "Brave Bessie." She lectured in schools and churches on the opportunities in avi-

ation wherever she performed, and she saved the money she earned from these lectures and performances in the hope of opening an aviation school for African Americans. On April 30, 1926, during a practice run in Jacksonville. Fla., Coleman's plane somersaulted out of a nosedive, and Coleman fell 2,000 feet to her death.

—SIRAJ AHMED

COLEMAN, ORNETTE

Ornette Coleman (c. March 9, 1930–), jazz saxophonist and composer. Born in Fort Worth, Tex., on a date that remains in dispute, Ornette Coleman's early musical influences included gospel, rhythm and blues, and bebop. Coleman, whose father was a singer, began playing saxophone at age sixteen, and had little formal music instruction. His earliest performances were in local churches, and he was expelled from his high school band for improvising during a performance of John Philip Sousa's "Washington Post March." Coleman at first played tenor saxophone in a honking rhythm-and-blues style influenced by Illinois Jacquet and Big Jay McNeely. His first professional work came in 1949 with the Silas Green Minstrels, a tent show that toured the South and Midwest. Coleman also traveled with blues singer Clarence Samuels, and blues singer and guitarist "Pee Wee" Crayton. By this time, Coleman had been inspired by bebop to start playing with a coarse, crying tone, and a frantic, unrestrained sense of rhythm and harmony. The reception in the jazz community to his controversial style kept him from working for a decade.

In 1950 Coleman moved to Los Angeles and began to recruit a circle of associates, including drummers Edward Blackwell and Billy Higgins, trumpeters Don Cherry and Bobby Bradford, bassist Charlie Haden, and pianist Paul Bley. Coleman married poet Jayne Cortez in 1954; unable to support himself as a musician, he took a job as a stock boy and elevator operator at a Los Angeles department store. Despite his reputation as an eccentric who had unusually long hair, wore overcoats in the summer, and played a white saxophone, in 1958 Coleman was invited to make his first recording, *Something Else!* which included his compositions "Chippie" and "When Will the Blues Leave." Pianist John Lewis brought Coleman and Cherry to the Lenox (Mass.) School of Jazz in 1959, which led to a famous series of quartet performances at New York's Five Spot nightclub.

"FREE JAZZ" PIONEER

The avant-garde sound of tenor saxophonist Ornette Coleman challenged almost all conventional assumptions about jazz style. Coleman expanded the vocabulary of jazz for more than thirty years. PHOTOGRAPHS AND PRINTS DIVISION, SCHOMBURG CENTER FOR RESEARCH IN BLACK CULTURE, THE NEW YORK PUBLIC LIBRARY, ASTOR, LENOX AND TILDEN FOUNDATIONS

The albums Coleman made over the next two years, including *Tomorrow Is the Question, The Shape of Jazz to Come, This Is Our Music,* and *Free Jazz,* were vilified by traditionalists, who heard the long, loosely structured, collective improvisations and adventurous harmonies as worthless cacophony. However, among his admirers, those performances, which included his compositions "Focus on Sanity," "Peace," "Lonely Woman," and "Beauty Is a Rare Thing," were also recognized as the first significant development in jazz since bebop. Although modeled on the wit and irreverence of bebop, Coleman's pianoless quartets broke out of traditional harmonies, as well as rigid theme-and-improvisation structures. Coleman began to call this style "harmolodics," referring to a musical system, since developed in a vast, unpublished manuscript, in which improvised melodies need not obey fixed harmonies.

In the 1950s Coleman had been shunned by the jazz world, but in the 1960s he found himself hailed as one of the greatest and most influential figures in jazz. Yet Coleman, who was divorced from Cortez in 1964, scaled back his activities in order to study trumpet and violin. In the mid-1960s Coleman most frequently appeared in trio settings (*At the Golden Circle,* 1965–1966), often including bassist David Izenzon and drummer Charles Moffett. In 1967 Coleman became the first jazz musician to win a Guggenheim fellowship. During the late 1960s and early 1970s, Coleman often played with the members of his old quartet, plus tenor saxophonist Dewey Redman, with whom he had first become acquainted in Fort Worth (*Science Fiction,* 1971).

Coleman, who had been composing classical music since the early 1950s, also saw performances in the 1960s of his string quartet *Dedication to Poets and Writers* (1961), his woodwind quintet *Forms and Sounds* (1967), and *Saints and Soldiers* (1967), a chamber piece. Coleman's *Skies of America* symphony was recorded in 1972 with the London Symphony Orchestra. In 1973 he traveled to Morocco to record with folk musicians from the town of Joujouka.

Coleman's next breakthrough came in 1975, when he began to play a style of electric dance music that recalled his early career in rhythm-and-blues dance bands. Using Prime Time, a new core group of musicians that often included his son, Denardo, a drummer, born in 1956, Coleman recorded *Dancing in Your Head,* an album-length elaboration of a theme from *Skies of America* in 1975, and recorded *Of Human Feelings* in 1979. During this time Coleman also founded Artists House, a collective that helped introduce guitarists James "Blood" Ulmer and bassist Jamaaladeen Tacuma.

The mid-1980s brought a revival of interest in Coleman. His hometown, Fort Worth, honored him with a series of tributes and performances, including the chamber piece *Prime Design/Time Design* (1983). A documentary by Shirley Clarke, *Ornette: Made in America,* was released in 1984, and Coleman collaborated with jazz-rock guitarist Pat Metheny (*Song X,* 1985), and rock guitarist Jerry Garcia (*Virgin Beauty,* 1987). On *In All Languages* (1987) he reunited with his 1959 quartet, and in 1991 Coleman, who had composed and performed on the film soundtracks for *Chappaqua* (1965) and *Box Office* (1981), recorded the score for *Naked Lunch.* Coleman, who has lived in Manhattan since the early 1960s, continues to compose regularly, though performing and recording only sporadically with Prime Time.

—BILL DIXON

COLTRANE, JOHN WILLIAM

John William Coltrane (September 23, 1926–July 17, 1967), jazz tenor and soprano saxophonist. Born in Hamlet, N.C., Coltrane moved with his family to High Point, N.C., when he was only a few months old. His father was a tailor, and his mother was an amateur singer. Coltrane received his first instrument, a clarinet, when he was twelve, though he soon began to play the alto saxophone, which was his primary instrument for a number of years.

After high school, Coltrane moved to Philadelphia, where he studied at the Ornstein School of Music and the Granoff Studios, where he won scholarships for both performance and composition. He played in the Philadelphia area until 1945, when he entered the Navy for two years, playing in Navy bands. His exposure at this time to bebop and the playing of Charlie Parker proved a major and lasting influence on Coltrane's music. Coltrane was so awed by Parker's abilities on the alto saxophone that he switched to playing the tenor saxophone, on which he felt he wouldn't be intimidated by the comparison. When Coltrane returned to Philadelphia, he started playing in blues bands, and in 1948 he was hired by Dizzy Gillespie. But Coltrane began drinking heavily and using drugs, and in 1951 he lost his job with the Gillespie band.

Louis Armstrong was the first great improvisor in jazz, and his work not only changed that music but all subsequent popular music, vocal and instrumental.

PAGE 37

See also
Dizzy Gillespie
Jazz

The recognition of Coltrane as a major jazz figure dates from his joining the Miles Davis Quintet in 1955, an association that would last, on and off, until 1959. In 1957, Coltrane overcame his drinking and narcotics problem, and in the process underwent a spiritual rebirth. Also in 1957 he began to play with Thelonious Monk, and recorded his first album as a leader, *Blue Train*. Other important albums from this period include *Giant Steps* and *Coltrane Jazz,* both from 1959.

Coltrane left Davis in 1959 and thereafter led his own ensemble. The key personnel in Coltrane's definitive quartet of the period, which stayed together from 1961 to 1965, included McCoy Tyner on piano, Elvin Jones on the drums, and Reggie Worhman on bass. Alto saxophonist Eric Dolphy played regularly with the ensemble until his death in 1964. In 1959 Coltrane started playing the soprano saxophone (an instrument that, except for Sidney Bechet, had been rarely used by jazz musicians). He soon recorded his most famous soprano sax solo, "My Favorite Things." Coltrane developed a distinctive soprano style, different from the one he favored on the tenor saxophone. His best-known works of this period include *A Love Supreme* (1964) and the collective free jazz improvisation *Ascension* (1965). In 1965 Coltrane's band underwent another change. His regular band members included Rashied Ali on drums, Pharoah Sanders as a second tenor saxophone, and on the piano, his second wife, Alice Coltrane. With this ensemble, Coltrane explored free jazz improvisation until his death from cancer on July 17, 1967.

In the little more than ten years of his active career, Coltrane's music underwent a number of metamorphoses. He first achieved renown as bluesy hard-bop tenor saxophonist. After 1957 he began to develop a new approach in which his solos were filigreed with myriad broken scales and arpeggios played extremely rapidly—this became known as his "sheets of sound" approach. In 1961 Coltrane began to play solos of unprecedented length, often lasting twenty or thirty minutes. If some found these solos to be soporific and self-indulgent, others were mesmerized by their sweep and intensity, and Coltrane acquired a number of avid fans. His best solos in the early 1960s were often gentle and powerfully introspective. By the mid-1960s Coltrane was playing free jazz, where his former lyrical style was often replaced by a harsh and turbulent soloing.

Coltrane, often simply called "Trane," was by far the most popular jazz musician to emerge from the New York City jazz avant-garde of the late 1950s and 1960s. His personal and communicative style, his spiritual quest, and his early death, in addition to the virtuosity and grace of his solos, contributed to a Coltrane "cult" that has not abated in the decades since his passing. His influence on subsequent musicians, which has been immense, includes not only his musical ideas but his taking of extended solos and his view of jazz as an ongoing quest for spiritual knowledge and self-wisdom.

—WILLIAM S. COLE

CONGRESS OF RACIAL EQUALITY

Congress of Racial Equality (CORE), civil rights organization. With a political and ideological legacy that spans six decades from interracial nonviolent direct action in the 1940s and '50s, militant black nationalist separatism in the late '60s, and black capitalism in the '70s, '80s, and '90s, the Congress of Racial Equality (CORE) is one of the most important civil rights organizations in the history of the United States. It was founded in Chicago in 1942 as the Committee of Racial Equality (the name was changed to the present one in 1943) by a group of ten white and five black student activists who were influenced by the Christian Youth Movement, rising industrial unionism, and the antiracist political activism of black and white communists in the 1930s. The founders of CORE were staunch believers in pacifism. Many of them were members of the Chicago chapter of the Fellowship of Reconciliation (FOR), an interracial and pacifist civil rights organization committed to social change through the transformation of racist attitudes, led by A. J. Muste (1885–1967). Deeply influenced by the strategies of social change championed by Indian activist Mahatma Gandhi as described in Krishnalal Shridharani's *War Without Violence* (1939), CORE founders believed that through interracial organizing and nonviolent direct action they could attack racism at its "core."

CORE was an informal, decentralized organization. Members drafted a "Statement of Purpose" and "CORE Action Discipline," both of which served as a constitution for the organization and proclaimed the members' commitment to working for social change through nonviolent direct action in a democratic, nonhierarchical organization. Guidelines for new members de-

See also

Charlie Parker

SIT-INS

Nonviolent Actions Initiate Civil Rights Movement

Sit-ins are a form of nonviolent direct action that are credited with initiating the modern Civil Rights Movement. A lunch counter sit-in on February 1, 1960, by four African-American students from Greensboro Agricultural and Technical College in North Carolina is generally regarded as marking a new, more activist phase in the struggle to achieve racial justice.

The use of the sit-in as a confrontational political strategy actually began much earlier. During labor unrest in the 1930s, strikers used what was referred to as the "sit-down" as a technique for gaining leverage with employers. Since a number of the early civil rights activists of the 1940s had previously been engaged in economic struggles on behalf of workers, they were familiar with the use of the sit-down as a useful weapon. The sit-down was also one in a series of increasingly confrontational strategies employed by the Indian emancipator Mohandas K. Gandhi.

Gandhi's campaign to free India of British rule, a struggle against colonialism that many Americans believed had a parallel in African-American efforts to break free from the consequences of white discrimination, was reported with increasing frequency in American activist circles in the 1930s and later. Those who founded the Congress of Racial Equality (CORE) in the United States in 1942—creating the first modern civil rights organization—were in fact significantly influenced by Gandhi and his concept of satyagraha, or soul force. A complex spiritual and political ideology that was revealed in techniques of nonviolent direct action, satyagraha, including the sit-down, was adapted to American purposes in the 1940s by the pioneering leaders in the civil rights struggle.

Although the Howard University NAACP held the first successful sit-in of the twentieth-century civil rights campaign, in the spring of 1943 at a Washington, D.C., restaurant, it was CORE that perfected the tactic as a principal weapon in the fight for racial equality. Several weeks after the encounter by the Howard group, CORE members began a sit-in, in May 1943, at Jack Spratt's restaurant in Chicago. In line with Gandhian ideals and satyagraha, the sit-in had been preceded by weeks of less confrontational strategies designed to persuade Jack Spratt's owners to serve black and white customers on an equal basis. When the sit-in was finally implemented, white CORE members seated in the restaurant refused to eat their meal until their black colleagues were also seated and served. After sitting in, nonviolently, for several hours, the interracial group was finally served. A few weeks later, a similar protest occurred at Stoner's restaurant in the city, with similarly successful results.

CORE quickly recognized the value of using the sit-in as a means for achieving integration of public accommodations. The sit-in became an effective symbol of the challenge to the "separate but equal" notion of the *Plessy* v. *Ferguson* Supreme Court decision. Consequently, CORE leaders began holding workshops and training institutes around the country to prepare potential sit-in participants for the kinds of abuse and harassment they might experience as they attempted to raze the wall of segregation in public facilities.

CORE, however, was a small and limited operation in the civil rights campaign during the 1940s and '50s. When the four college students in Greensboro sat in at the department-store lunch counter reserved for whites in 1960, they revealed the usefulness of the strategy and launched a new phase in the modern Civil Rights Movement. The sit-in, in a variety of forms—as a swim-in in public pools, or a pray-in in segregated religious facilities—became a vital part of the struggle. Because they were challenging local laws and customs upholding segregation, the participants were often arrested for their actions. Their strategy was to sit quietly and ignore all forms of verbal and physical abuse directed toward them until they were removed, arrested, or served.

As the civil rights campaign moved into its more assertive phase of black power activism after 1963, the nonviolent sit-in was employed less frequently. Over the course of the previous two decades, it had been an effective strategy in achieving the integration of local facilities.

—CAROL V. R. GEORGE

manded familiarity with Gandhian ideas and active participation in the organization. Voluntary contributions from the members served as the organization's only source of funding. The leadership of CORE was shared by George Houser, a white student at the University of Chicago, and James Farmer, a black Methodist student activist. James Robinson, a white Catholic pacifist, and

Although the Black Panther party gradually shifted its emphasis from revolutionary rhetoric and armed confrontations with police to "survival programs," clashes with police and legal prosecutions decimated the party's leadership.

PAGE 94

See also
Civil Rights Movement

C

*The Freedom
Summer's most
enduring legacy
was the change of
consciousness
it engendered
among black
Mississippians.*

PAGE 285

*You do not wipe
away the scars of
centuries by saying,
"Now, you are free
to go where you
want, do what you
desire, and choose
the leaders you
please." You do not
take a man who, for
years, has been
hobbled by chains,
liberate him, bring
him to the starting
line of the race,
saying, "You are
free to compete with
the others."*

LYNDON B. JOHNSON
SPEECH, HOWARD
UNIVERSITY, 1965

Bernice Fisher, a white divinity student at the University of Chicago, also provided inspirational and organizational leadership.

In their first year, CORE activists organized sit-ins and other protests against segregation in public accommodations, but white recalcitrance and a weak membership base left them with few victories. In 1942, at a planning conference to discuss organizational growth, CORE activists declared their commitment to expanding nationally by forming alliances with local interracial groups working to defeat racism through nonviolent direct action. Farmer argued that CORE would not grow as a mass-based activist organization unless it severed its ties to FOR and disassociated itself from the organization's pacifism. Under the rubric of FOR's Department of Race Relations, he and Bayard Rustin, a black FOR field secretary, traveled around the country and met with activists sympathetic to Gandhian ideology, to foster interest in forming CORE chapters among those present at FOR events.

As a result of their efforts, CORE had seven affiliates by the end of 1942. Most chapters were located in the Midwest; they contained fifteen to thirty members who were usually middle-class college students and were predominantly white. Local groups retained primary membership affiliation and control over local funds. As a result, chapter activities varied widely and were not centrally coordinated. Chapters where pacifists dominated focused almost entirely on educating and converting racists, rather than on direct action. The repressive atmosphere of the South in the 1940s severely curtailed the activity of CORE's few southern affiliates. New York, Chicago, and Detroit were the most active and militant chapters, conducting training workshops in nonviolent direct action for volunteers in selected northern cities as well. They also organized sit-ins—a tactic pioneered by CORE activists—and picket lines at segregated restaurants, swimming pools, movie theaters, and department stores.

CORE had some success in integrating public accommodations and recreational areas, but it was clear to CORE's founders that to mount a sustained assault on racism they would have to create a stronger national structure. In 1943, Farmer was elected the first chairman of CORE and Bernice Fisher was elected secretary-treasurer. By 1946, due to both the reluctance of local chapters to relinquish their independence or share their funds and to the infrequency of national planning meetings, CORE faced an organizational crisis. After much debate, CORE revamped its national struc-

ture: Farmer resigned and George Houser occupied the newly created leadership position of executive secretary. Houser played a central role in defining the ideology of CORE as editor of the *CORE-lator,* the organizational newsletter, and author of almost all CORE literature. He focused CORE's organizational energy and limited resources on a closer coordination of local activities among its thirteen affiliates, with the ultimate goal of building a mass movement.

The culmination of Houser's efforts was CORE's first nationally coordinated action, the Journey of Reconciliation—a two-week trip into the upper South to test the 1946 *Morgan* decision by the U.S. Supreme Court outlawing segregation in interstate travel. In April of 1947, sixteen men—eight white and eight black—traveled by bus through the region challenging segregated seating arrangements that relegated blacks to the back of the bus. The protesters were confronted by some violence and overt hostility, but in general they were faced with apathy from most whites, who were unaware of the Morgan decision. In many instances, black passengers on the bus followed suit when they saw racial mores being successfully challenged. The arrest of four of the protesters in Chapel Hill, N.C.—with three of them, Bayard Rustin, Igal Roodenko, and Joe Felmet forced to serve thirty days on a chain gang—catapulted CORE and the Journey of Reconciliation to national attention.

In 1947, CORE took further steps to strengthen their organizational structure by creating an office of field secretaries to travel around the country to organize new CORE chapters. Two years later they created the National Council—a policy-making body with one representative from each local chapter—to improve communication between the local and the national chapters. In 1951, CORE hired James Robinson to coordinate fund-raising efforts. Despite these efforts, the early fifties marked another period of organizational decline for CORE, as the number of affiliated chapters dropped from a high of twenty at the end of the 1940s and fluctuated around eleven during the early 1950s.

Weakened by continuing debates over the role of pacifism and the national organizational structure, CORE's growth was further stunted by anticommunism. Although CORE's executive committee had drafted a "Statement on Communism" in 1948 saying that it would not work with communists, CORE's civil rights activities were attacked as "subversive" and "un-American" in the hostile racial climate of the 1950s. At this organizational nadir, Houser resigned and the national structure was once again reorganized to divide his duties among three people: Billie Ames, a white activist from CORE's St. Louis chapter, became group coordinator and took charge of organizational correspondence; James Peck, a white Journey of Reconciliation veteran, was in charge of editing the *CORE-lator;* and James Robinson continued to serve as treasurer. Wallace Nelson, who had held the salaried position of field secretary, was replaced by four volunteers.

CORE found a renewed sense of purpose in the mid-1950s. In 1954, the Brown v. Board of Education of Topeka, Kansas decision declared separate but equal educational facilities unconstitutional. One year later, the Montgomery bus boycott mobilized thousands of African Americans to challenge segregated buses. CORE activists—as pioneers of the strategy of nonviolent direct action—provided philosophical resources to the boycott and dispatched LeRoy Carter, a black field-secretary, to Montgomery to provide support. Electrified by rising black protest, CORE decided to channel the majority of the organization's energy into expanding into the South.

To facilitate this expansion, there was a revival of the national staff. In 1957, James Robinson, whose tireless fund-raising efforts had boosted organizational finances, was appointed executive secretary. He worked closely with the National Action Committee, comprising influential members based in New York who made policy decisions. CORE created a staff position for a public relations coordinator, who was in charge of promoting CORE as a major civil rights organization alongside the NAACP and the Southern Christian Leadership Conference (SCLC), which was founded after the Montgomery bus boycott. In addition, the *CORE-lator* was transformed from an organizational organ into an informative newsmagazine that reported on the social movements emerging in the South.

Most importantly, CORE directly confronted its relationship to the black community for the first time. Although its predominantly white leadership structure remained firmly in place, African Americans such as James McCain, who was appointed field secretary in 1957, were sought out for prominent and visible positions. Publicity for CORE also was sought in the black press. Nonetheless, CORE'S ideological commitment to interracialism continued to be unwavering. McCain, for example, worked closely with James Carey, a white field secretary, to demonstrate the viability of interracial organizing to potential new affiliates. However, the fundamental nature of the organization had begun to change. Interracialism—which had been defined since CORE's inception as racial diversity within chapters—was redefined on a regional level. To reflect the probability of minimal white support for CORE in the South, as well as the continued inability of majority white chapters on the West Coast to secure a black membership base, the interracial requirement for chapters was removed from the constitution. In addition, although CORE retained its base among white and black middle-class college students, its class and age composition was radically altered as many younger and poorer African Americans, with few ideological links to pacifism, joined its ranks.

By 1960, the number of CORE chapters had risen to twenty-four, with new chapters springing up in Virginia, Tennessee, South Carolina, Florida, Kentucky. With a stable national structure, growing income, new constituencies, and increased visibility, CORE finally seemed poised to join the ranks of the major civil rights organizations. In February 1960, when four college students sat in at a lunch counter in Greensboro, N.C., to protest segregation and ignited a wave of student protest that spread throughout the South, CORE activists scrambled to provide guidance. In Florida, CORE members pioneered the "jail-in" technique when five members chose to serve out their sentences rather than pay bail after being arrested for sitting in at a department store counter. One year later, CORE activists organized another "jail-in" in Rock Hill, S.C., which received national attention, helped galvanize the black community, and set a precedent of "jail-no bail" that became an important direct action strategy in the Civil Rights Movement. In the North, affiliates started sympathy demonstrations for the student demonstrators and called for nationwide boycotts to attempt to place economic pressure on national chains to desegregate their facilities.

In May 1961, CORE mounted its most militant challenge to segregation: the Freedom Rides. Modeled on the earlier Journey of Reconciliation, the Freedom Rides were protests against segregated interstate buses and terminals in the South. Seven white and six black activists, including James Farmer (who had been appointed CORE executive director earlier that year), participated in the Freedom Rides. After successfully challenging segregation in Virginia and North Carolina, the Freedom Riders faced harassment, intimidation, and violence from racist southern whites in the deep South. Two riders were at-

See also
New York City

CONGRESS OF RACIAL EQUALITY

tacked in Rock Hill, S.C.; two were arrested in Winnesboro, S.C.; and in a violent climax, riders were beaten and their bus bombed by a white mob near Birmingham, Ala. After this event, which was recorded by the press for a shocked nation to see, CORE terminated the rides. SNCC activists resumed the Freedom Rides in Mississippi, un-

leashing a white backlash so virulent that the Kennedy administration was forced to intervene with federal protection. Though SNCC activists—with some resentment on the part of CORE officials—took the leadership of the protest and received most of the credit for the remaining Freedom Rides, CORE continued to provide

---

ANDREW YOUNG

Trusted MLK Aide Forges His Own Path

Andrew Young (October 23, 1932–), civil rights activist and politician. Andrew Young was born in New Orleans. His father was an affluent, prominent dentist, and Young was raised in a middle-class black family in a racially mixed neighborhood. He attended Howard University in Washington, D.C., and graduated in 1951. Young pursued his growing commitment to religion at Hartford Theological Seminary in Connecticut and was awarded a bachelor of divinity degree in 1955. He was ordained a Congregational minister, and from 1955 to 1959, he preached in churches in Georgia and Alabama. In the course of this work, Young experienced firsthand the wrenching poverty that shaped the lives of African Americans in the rural South. He became active in challenging racial inequality, joined the local Civil Rights Movement and helped organize a voter-registration drive in Thomasville, Ga., one of the first of its kind in southern Georgia.

In 1959, Young went to New York to become an assistant director of the National Council of Churches and help channel New York City philanthropic money into southern civil rights activities. Two years later, he returned to Georgia and joined the Southern Christian Leadership Conference (SCLC), a civil rights organization headed by the Rev. Dr. Martin Luther King, Jr. Young became an active participant in the SCLC, building a reputation for coolness and rationality and often providing a moderating influence within the movement. From 1961 to 1964, he served as funding coordinator and administrator of the SCLC's Citizenship Education Program—a program aimed at increasing black voter registration among African Americans in the South.

Young grew to be one of King's most trusted aides. In 1964, he was named executive director of the SCLC and three years later took on additional responsibility as executive vice president. During his tenure, he focused on creating social and economic programs for African Americans to broaden the scope of SCLC's activism. In 1970, Young relinquished his executive positions. However, he continued his affiliation with SCLC—serving on the board of directors—until 1972.

In 1972, Young turned his energies to the political arena and launched a successful campaign to become the first African American elected to the House of Representatives from Georgia since 1870. In Congress, he served on the House Banking Committee and became familiar with the national and international business markets. In 1976, he vigorously supported the candidacy of fellow Georgian Jimmy Carter for president and vouched for Carter's commitment to black civil rights to many who were skeptical of supporting a white Democrat from the deep South. Upon Carter's election, Young resigned his congressional seat to accept an appointment as the United States Ambassador to the United Nations.

As ambassador, Young focused on strengthening the ties between the United States and the Third World. In 1979, he was forced to resign his position when it was revealed that he had engaged in secret negotiations with representatives of the Palestine Liberation Organization (PLO) in violation of U.S. policy. Young's supporters argued that Young was merely doing the job of a diplomat by speaking to all interested parties in sensitive negotiations. Many Jews and other

supporters of Israel, however, believed that Young's actions gave the PLO unwarranted legitimacy. The furor that surrounded his actions forced him to submit his resignation.

In 1982, Young mounted a successful campaign for mayor of Atlanta. During his administration, he faced the same urban problems that plagued other big-city mayors, including a shrinking tax base, rising unemployment, and rising costs—all of which required difficult decisions in fund allocation. Despite these constraints, he was able to increase business investment in Georgia. He successfully ran for reelection in 1986, despite growing criticism from some African-American critics who argued that black Atlantans had been hurt by his economic development programs. In 1990, after he ran unsuccessfully for the Democratic gubernatorial nomination, Young reentered private life. He served as chairman of Law International, Inc., until 1993, when he was appointed vice chairman of their parent company, Law Companies Group, an internationally respected engineering and environmental consulting company based in Atlanta.

During the course of his career, Young has received many awards, including the Presidential Medal of Freedom—America's highest civilian award—and more than thirty honorary degrees from universities such as Yale, Morehouse, and Emory. In 1994, his spiritual memoir, *A Way Out of No Way,* was published. Young lobbied successfully to bring the 1996 Summer Olympics to Atlanta and served as cochairman of the Atlanta Committee for the Olympic Games.

—CHRISTINE A. LUNARDINI

guidance to the freedom riders and stationed field secretaries in key southern cities to assist riders. Many CORE activists, including Farmer, rejoined the rides when SNCC continued them. The freedom riders finally triumphed in September 1961 when the Interstate Commerce Commission issued an order prohibiting segregated facilities in interstate travel.

The Freedom Rides placed CORE in the vanguard of the Civil Rights Movement. As a result of the national attention that the rides had generated, James Farmer joined SNCC's John Lewis and SCLC's Rev. Dr. Martin Luther King, Jr., as a national spokesperson for the Civil Rights Movement. By the end of 1961, CORE—with fifty-three affiliated chapters, rising income, and increased visibility—was able to mount new activities. CORE was an active participant in the wave of direct action protest that swept through the South in 1962 and 1963. In 1962, CORE worked closely with the local NAACP to launch the Freedom Highways project to desegregate Howard Johnson hotels along North Carolina highways. Faced with retaliatory white violence, and locked into increasingly contentious competition with the other civil rights organizations, CORE broadened the scope of its activities. In 1962, CORE joined the Voter Education Project (VEP) initiated by President John F. Kennedy and mounted vigorous voter registration campaigns in Louisiana, Florida, Mississippi, and South Carolina.

CORE activists played a pivotal role in many of the leading events of the Civil Rights Movement. In 1963, CORE joined the NAACP, SCLC, and SNCC in sponsoring the March on Washington. As a part of the Council of Federated Organizations (COFO), a statewide coalition of civil rights organizations engaged in voter registration, CORE played a crucial role in the Freedom Summer in 1964 in Mississippi. James Chaney and Michael Schwerner, two of three civil rights workers killed in June 1964 by racist whites in the infamous case that focused national attention on the South, were members of CORE.

By 1963, CORE activities—severely curtailed by arrests and racial violence—shifted from the South to the North. Two thirds of CORE's sixty-eight chapters were in the North and West, concentrated mainly in California and New York. In the North, CORE chapters directly confronted discrimination and segregation in housing and employment, using tactics such as picketing and the boycott. As they began to address some of the problems of economically disadvantaged African Americans in the North—among them, unem-

ployment, housing discrimination, and police brutality—they began to attract more working class African-American members. To strengthen their image as a black-protest organization, leadership of northern chapters was almost always black, and CORE chapters moved their headquarters into the black community. As member composition changed and CORE acquired a more militant image, CORE's deeply held ideological beliefs and tactics of social change were increasingly challenged by black working-class members. These members were willing to engage in more confrontational tactics, such as resisting arrest, obstructing traffic, all night sit-ins, and other forms of militant civil disobedience. Drawing on different ideological traditions, they viewed nonviolence as a tactic to be abandoned when no longer expedient—not as a deeply held philosophical belief. They often identified with Malcolm X, who preached racial pride and black separatism, rather than with Gandhian notions of a beloved community.

By 1964, the integrationist, southern-based civil rights coalition was splintering, and consensus over tactics and strategy within CORE was destroyed. Vigorous debates emerged within CORE about the roles of whites (by 1964 less than 50 percent of the membership) in the organization. Infused with heightened black pride and nationalism, angered by the paternalism of some white members, and believing that black people should lead in the liberation of the black community, many black CORE members pushed for the diminution of the role of whites within the organization; an increasingly vocal minority called for the expulsion of whites.

As CORE struggled for organizational and programmatic direction, old tensions between rank and file members of the national leadership resurfaced as local chapters, operating almost autonomously, turned to grass-roots activism in poor black communities. In the South, CORE activities centered on building self-supporting community organizations to meet the needs of local communities. Activists organized projects that ranged from job discrimination protests, to voter registration, to securing mail delivery for black neighborhoods. In the North, CORE activists continued in the tradition of direct action. They fostered neighborhood organizations with local leadership, started community centers and job placement centers, and organized rent strikes and welfare rights protests.

In 1966, the National CORE convention endorsed the slogan of Black Power. Under the lead-

C

CONGRESS OF RACIAL EQUALITY

The danger of a conflict between the white and the black inhabitants perpetually haunts the imagination of the Americans like a bad dream.

ALEXIS DE TOCQUEVILLE
DEMOCRACY IN AMERICA, 1835

See also

Malcolm X

NAACP

C

The 1970s witnessed the emergence of several television sitcoms featuring black family affairs.

PAGE 672

ership of Farmer and Floyd McKissick—elected in 1963 as CORE national chairman—CORE adopted a national position supporting black self-determination, local control of community institutions, and coalition politics. In 1967 the word "multiracial" was deleted from the constitution, and whites began an exodus from the organization. One year later, Roy Innis, a dynamic and outspoken leader of CORE's Harlem chapter, replaced Farmer and under the new title of national director took control of the organization. Innis staunchly believed in separatism and black self-determination and argued that blacks were a "nation within a nation." He barred whites from active membership in CORE and centralized decision-making authority to assert control over local chapter activities. By this point, however, CORE was a weakened organization with a handful of affiliated chapters and dwindling resources.

Innis's economic nationalism and support for black capitalism led to an extremely conservative political stance for CORE on issues ranging from civil rights legislation and foreign policy to gun control and welfare. In 1970 he met with southern whites to promote separate schools as a viable alternative to court imposed desegregation and busing. In the late 1970s and early '80s, almost all CORE activities ground to a halt as Innis and CORE came under increasing criticism. In 1976, Farmer severed all ties with CORE in protest of Innis's separatism and his attempt to recruit black Vietnam veterans to fight in Angola's civil war on the side of the South-African-backed National Union for the Total Independence of Angola (UNITA). In 1981, after being accused by the New York State attorney general's office of misusing charitable contributions, Innis agreed to contribute $35,000 to the organization over a three-year period in exchange for not admitting to any irregularities in handling funds. In the early 1980s, former CORE members, led by Farmer, attempted to transform CORE into a multiracial organization, but Innis remained firmly in command. In 1987, Innis supported Bernhard Goetz, a white man who shot black alleged muggers on the subways in New York; and Robert Bork, a conservative Supreme Court nominee.

CORE chapters have mounted only sporadic activities in the 1990s, but Innis—at this point, one of the leading black conservatives—has maintained visibility as national director of the organization.

—CAROL V. R. GEORGE

COSBY, WILLIAM HENRY, JR. "BILL"

William Henry "Bill" Cosby, Jr. (July 12, 1937–), comedian and philanthropist. Bill Cosby was born in Germantown, Pa., to William and Annie Pearle Cosby. After a stint in the Navy (1956–1960), Cosby studied at Temple University in Philadelphia, but dropped out to pursue a career as a stand-up comic.

During the 1960s, Cosby worked in network television as a comedian featured on late-night talk shows. In 1965 he became the first African-American network television star in a dramatic series when producers named him to costar with Robert Culp in *I Spy* (1965–1968). Cosby's character, Alexander Scott, did not usually address his blackness or another character's whiteness. As with other forms of popular entertainment with black characters at the time, Cosby's character was portrayed in a manner in which being black merely meant having slightly darker skin. He won Emmy awards for the role in 1966 and 1967.

From 1969 through 1971, Cosby appeared as Chet Kincaid, a bachelor high school coach, on the situation comedy series *The Bill Cosby Show.* Cosby portrayed Kincaid as a proud but not militant black man. The series was moderately successful. A few years later, Cosby and CBS joined forces in a television experiment, *Fat Albert and the Cosby Kids* (1972–1977), a cartoon series for children. The series set the course for television in the vital new area of ethics, values, judgment, and personal responsibility. By the end of its three-year run, *Fat Albert* had inspired a number of new directions in children's television.

In 1972 and 1973, Cosby starred in *The New Bill Cosby Show,* a comedy-variety series. Cosby's Jemmin Company, which he had recently established, produced the shows, allowing him to have more control over the productions. As he did in all his television series, Cosby made great use of other black artists who had had few opportunities to practice their craft elsewhere.

For a few months in late 1976, largely because of his success as a regular guest on the PBS educational series *The Electric Company,* where he demonstrated great skill at working with and entertaining youngsters, ABC hired Cosby to host a prime time hour-long variety series oriented toward children, *Cos.* It did not catch on with viewers, however, and was canceled after a few months.

In the fall of 1984, *The Cosby Show* began on NBC, featuring Cosby as Cliff Huxtable, an obstetrician living with his wife and four children in a New York City brownstone. Their fifth child, away at college most of the time, appeared sporadically in featured parts. The show put black images on the screen that many people admired. The characters on *The Cosby Show* represented a real African-American upper-middle-class family, rarely seen on American television. Cosby sought black artists who had not been seen on network television in years for cameo roles (Dizzy Gillespie and Judith Jamison, for example). He also included black writers among his creative staff, and by the third year, he insisted on using a black director for some of the episodes. In its first year, *The Cosby Show* finished third in the ratings; from the second season through the fourth season, it was the number-one-rated show in the United States.

Conscious of the need to lead the networks toward more equitable treatment of African Americans, Cosby used his position to require that more doors be opened. He had a presence in almost every area of television programming: He was a mass volume spokesman and star presenter for advertisements and public relations image campaigns that included Jello, Coca-Cola, Delmonte, Kodak, and E. F. Hutton. He appeared in drama, action-adventure stories, comedies, and children's programs. In 1992 he also entered into prime time syndication with Carsey-Werner Productions with a remake of the old Groucho Marx game series, *You Bet Your Life*. The show lasted only one season. That same year, however, Cosby made public his bid to purchase the National Broadcasting Corporation (NBC-TV), a television network worth $9 billion. Cosby was determined to call attention to the proliferation of negative images of black people and the titillation of viewers with sex and violence. All television viewers, he argued, were diminished by the spate of "drive-by-images" that reinforced shallow stereotypes.

Throughout his career, Cosby appeared at highly popular concert performances across the United States. His comedy focused on his own life as a reflection of universal human needs. He also produced more than twenty comedy/musical record albums, many of which have won Grammy awards, including *Bill Cosby Is a Very Funny Fellow* (1963), *I Started Out as a Child* (1964), *Why Is There Air?* (1965), *Wonderfulness* (1966), *Revenge* (1967), *To Russell, My Brother, Whom I Slept With* (1968), *Bill Cosby* (1969), *Bill Cosby Talks to Children About Drugs* (1971), and *Children, You'll Understand* (1986). Cosby has written many best-

COMEDIAN WITH HEART

Bill Cosby, shown here during a 1987 performance at New York's Radio City Music Hall, serves as a role model for many African Americans.
AP/WIDE WORLD PHOTOS

selling books, including *The Wit and Wisdom of Fat Albert* (1973), *You Are Somebody Special* (1978), *Fatherhood* (1986), *Time Flies* (1987), and *Love and Marriage* (1989). He has served on numerous boards, including the NAACP, Operation Push, the United Negro College Fund, and the National Sickle Cell Foundation.

Cosby, who in 1993 was listed in *Forbes* magazine as one of the 400 richest people in the world with a net worth of more than $315 million, has been one of the most important benefactors to African-American institutions. In 1986 he and his wife gave $1.3 million to Fisk University; the following year they gave another $1.3 million to be divided equally among four black universities—Central State, Howard, Florida A & M, and Shaw; in 1988 they divided $1.5 million between Meharry Medical College and Bethune Cookman College. In 1989 Bill and Camille Cosby announced that they were giving $20 million to Spelman College, the largest personal gift ever made to any of the historically black colleges and universities. In 1994 the couple donated a historic landmark building in downtown Washington, D.C. to the National Council of Negro Women to help them establish a National Center for African-American Women. Cosby himself has been the recipient of numerous awards, in-

See also
Television

cluding the NAACP's Spingarn Medal (1985). He holds an M.A. (1972) and a doctorate (1976) in education from the University of Massachusetts at Amherst. In 1976 he also finally received a B.A. from Temple University. Cosby, who married Camille Hanks in 1964, has lived in rural Massachusetts since the early 1970s. Beginning in 1996, Cosby produced and starred in a successful comedy series called *Cosby*. His life was disrupted the following year by the murder of his son, Ennis, and the charge by Autumn Jackson that she was Cosby's illegitimate daughter. Cosby's popularity continued unabated through this period.

—JANNETTE L. DATES

CULLEN, COUNTEE

Countee Cullen (March 30, 1903–January 9, 1946), poet, novelist, and playwright. It has been difficult to place exactly where Countee Cullen was born, with whom he spent the very earliest years of his childhood, and where he spent them. New York City and Baltimore have been given as birthplaces by several scholars. Cullen himself, on his college transcript at New York University, listed Louisville, Ky., as his place of birth. A few years later, when he had achieved considerable literary fame during the era known as the New Negro or Harlem Renaissance, he was to assert that his birthplace was New York City, a claim he continued to make for the rest of his life. Both Cullen's second wife, Ida, and some of his closest friends, including Langston Hughes and Harold Jackman, all said he was born in Louisville, although one Cullen scholar, Beulah Reimherr, in her M.A. thesis, claims that Ida Cullen gave her husband's place of birth as Baltimore. As James Weldon Johnson wrote in *The Book of American Negro Poetry* (revised edition, 1931), "There is not much to say about these earlier years of Cullen— unless he himself should say it." And Cullen—revealing a temperament that was not exactly secretive but private, less a matter of modesty than a tendency toward being encoded and tactful— never in his life said anything more clarifying.

What we know for certain is that he was born on March 30, 1903, and that sometime between his birth and 1918 he was adopted by the Rev. Frederick A. and Carolyn Belle (Mitchell) Cullen

JAZZ HOT SPOT
Cotton Club Headlines Stars, Incites Racial Controversy

First opened in 1920 as the Club Deluxe, the venue at Lenox Avenue and West 142nd Street in Harlem took on new ownership and its permanent name in 1922. Owney Madden, who bought the club from heavyweight boxing champion Jack Johnson, intended the name Cotton Club to appeal to whites, the only clientele permitted until 1928. The club made its name by featuring top-level black performers and an upscale, downtown audience. It soon became a leading attraction for white "tourists" from high society wanting to see the much publicized, risqué Harlem cultural life.

Following the death in 1927 of Andy Preer, leader of the house band, the Cotton Club Syncopators, Duke Ellington and his orchestra were brought in as replacements and began a four-year rise to prominence on the Cotton Club's stage. Soon after Ellington took over as bandleader, the Cotton Club Orchestra was broadcast nightly over a national radio network.

Responding to local protests, the club's management opened its doors to black patrons for the first time in the winter of 1928. Nonetheless, prices were kept prohibitively high and the club's audience remained virtually all white. The nightly revues, which were generally more popular than the orchestra, featured scantily clad, light-skinned women dancing to Ellington's "jungle music."

In 1931 Ellington and his orchestra left the club and were replaced by Cab Calloway's Missourians. Calloway, like Ellington, established himself as a major figure in mainstream jazz during his Cotton Club years. Calloway's Missourians remained the house band until 1934, when they were replaced by Jimmie Lunceford's acclaimed swing band. Most of the renowned jazz performers of the period appeared at the Cotton Club, including Louis Armstrong, Ethel Waters, and dancers Bill "Bojangles" Robinson and the Nicholas Brothers.

Following riots in Harlem in 1935, the club was forced to close due to a widespread perception among whites that the area was unsafe. It reopened in 1936 downtown at 200 West 48th Street, where it remained until its final closing in 1940.

—THADDEUS RUSSELL

See also

Harlem Renaissance

Literature

of the Salem Methodist Episcopal Church in Harlem. It is impossible to state with any degree of certainty how old Cullen was at the time, or how long he knew the Cullens before he was adopted. Apparently, he went by the name of Countee Porter until 1918. He became Countee P. Cullen by 1921, and eventually just Countee Cullen. According to Harold Jackman, the adoption was never really "official"; that is to say, it was never formally consummated through the proper state-agency channels. It is difficult, indeed, to know whether Cullen was ever legally an orphan at any stage in his childhood.

Frederick Cullen was one of the pioneer black activist-ministers; he moved his Salem Methodist Episcopal Church from a storefront mission— where it was in 1902, when he first arrived in New York City—to the site of a former white church in Harlem in 1924, where he could boast of a membership of over 2,500. Since Countee Cullen himself stated in his 1927 anthology of black American poetry. *Caroling Dusk*, that he was "reared in the conservative atmosphere of a Methodist parsonage," it is clear that his foster father, particularly, was a strong influence. The two men were very close, often traveling abroad together. But as Cullen evidences a decided unease in his poetry over his strong and conservative Christian training and the attraction of his pagan inclinations, his feelings about his father may have been somewhat ambivalent. Frederick Cullen was, on the one hand, a puritanical Christian patriarch, and Countee was never remotely that. On the other hand, it has been suggested that Frederick was also something of an effeminate man. (He was dressed in girl's clothing by his poverty-stricken mother well beyond the acceptable boyhood age for such a practice and was apparently effeminate in his manner as an adult.) Some scholars, especially Jean Wagner, have argued that Countee Cullen's homosexuality, or decidedly ambiguous sexual nature, may have been attributable to his foster father's contrary influence as both fire-breathing Christian and latent or covert transsexual. To be sure, in his poetry Cullen equated paganism with various sensual postures, including homosexuality. Cullen was a devoted and obedient son, and the fact that the Cullens had no other children made this attachment much easier to achieve.

Cullen was an outstanding student both at De-Witt Clinton High School (1918–1921)—where he not only edited the school's newspaper but also assisted in editing the literary magazine, *Magpie*, and wrote his first poetry that achieved notice—

and at New York University (1921–1925), where he wrote most of the major work that was to make up his first two volumes, *Color* (1925) and *Copper Sun* (1927). It was also while at NYU that he wrote *The Ballad of the Brown Girl* (1927). In high school Cullen won his first contest, a citywide competition, with the poem "I Have a Rendezvous with Life," a nonracial poem inspired by Alan Seeger's "I Have a Rendezvous with Death." If any event signaled the coming of the Harlem Renaissance, it was the precocious success of this rather shy black boy who, more than any other black literary figure of his generation, was being touted and bred to become a major crossover literary figure. Here was a black man with considerable academic training who could, in effect, write "white" verse—ballads, sonnets, quatrains, and the like—much in the manner of Keats and the British Romantics (albeit, on more than one occasion, tinged with racial concerns), with genuine skill and compelling power. He was certainly not the first African American to attempt to write such verse, but he was first to do so with such extensive education, with such a complete understanding of himself as a poet, and producing poetry that was not trite or inferior. Only two other black American poets before Cullen could be taken so seriously as self-consciously considered and proficient poets: Phillis Wheatley and Paul Laurence Dunbar.

If the aim of the Harlem Renaissance was, in part, the reinvention of the native-born African American as a being who could be assimilated while decidedly retaining something called a "racial self-consciousness," then Cullen fit the bill better than virtually any other Renaissance writer. And if "I Have a Rendezvous with Life" was the opening salvo in the making of Cullen's literary reputation, then the 1924 publication of "Shroud of Color" in H. L. Mencken's *American Mercury* confirmed the advent of the black boy wonder as one of the most exciting American poets on the scene. After graduating Phi Beta Kappa from NYU, Cullen earned a master's degree in English and French from Harvard (1927). Between high school and graduation from Harvard he had become the most popular black poet—virtually the most popular black literary figure—in America. It was after one of his poems and his popular column appeared in *Opportunity* magazine that A'Lelia Walker (heiress of Madame C. J. Walker's hair-care-products fortune) named her salon, where the black and white literati gathered in the late 1920s, the Dark Tower.

For whites, art was the means to change society before they would accept it. For blacks, art was the means to change society in order to be accepted into it.

PAGE 326

See also
Langston Hughes

Cullen won more major literary prizes than any other black writer of the 1920s: the first prize in the Witter Bynner Poetry Contest in 1925; *Poetry* magazine's John Reed Memorial Prize; the Amy Spingarn Award of *The Crisis* magazine; second prize in *Opportunity* magazine's first poetry contest; second prize in the poetry contest of *Palms*. He was the second African American to win a Guggenheim Fellowship. His first three books—*Color, Copper Sun,* and *The Ballad of the Brown Girl*—sold well and made him a hero for many blacks. Lines from Cullen's popular poems, such as "Heritage," "Incident," "From the Dark Tower," and "Yet Do I Marvel," were commonly quoted.

Cullen was also at the center of one of the major social events of the Harlem Renaissance; on April 9, 1928, he married Yolande Du Bois, only child of W. E. B. Du Bois, in one of the most lavish weddings in black New York history. This wedding was to symbolize the union of the grand black intellectual patriarch and the new breed of younger African Americans who were responsible for much of the excitement of the Renaissance. It was an apt meshing of personalities, as both Cullen and Du Bois *père* were conservative by nature and ardent traditionalists. That the marriage turned out so disastrously and ended so quickly—Yolande and Cullen divorced in 1930—probably adversely affected Cullen. (He remarried in 1940.) Cullen published *The Black Christ and Other Poems* in 1929, receiving lukewarm reviews from both black and white presses. He was bitterly disappointed that *The Black Christ*, his longest and in many respects his most complicated poem, the product of over two years' work, was considered by most critics to be his weakest and least distinguished.

From the 1930s until his death, Cullen wrote a great deal less, partly hampered by his job as a French teacher at Frederick Douglass Junior High (his most famous student was James Baldwin). But he wrote noteworthy, even significant work in a number of genres. His novel *One Way to Heaven,* published in 1934, rates among the better black satires, and is one of the three important fictional retrospectives of the Harlem Renaissance, the others being Wallace Thurman's *The Infants of the Spring* and George Schuyler's *Black No More;* his translation of *The Medea* is the first major translation of a classical work by a twentieth-century black American writer; the children's books *The Lost Zoo* and *My Lives and How I Lost Them* are among the more clever and engaging books of children's verse, written at a time when there was not much work published for children by black writers; and his poetry of the period includes perhaps some of his best, certainly some of his more darkly complex, sonnets. He was also working on a musical with Arna Bontemps called *St. Louis Woman* (based on Bontemps's novel, *God Sends Sunday*) at the time of his death from high blood pressure and uremic poisoning.

For many years after his death, Cullen's reputation was eclipsed by those of other Harlem Renaissance writers, particularly Langston Hughes and Zora Neale Hurston, and his work had gone out of print. More recently, however, there has been a resurgence of interest in his life and work, and his books are being reissued.

—GERALD EARLY

See also

Zora Neale Hurston

DANCE THEATER OF HARLEM

Dance Theater of Harlem, classical dance company. The Dance Theater of Harlem (DTH) was founded on August 15, 1969, by Arthur Mitchell and Karel Shook as the world's first permanent, professional, academy-rooted, predominantly black ballet troupe. Mitchell created DTH to address a threefold mission of social, educational, and artistic opportunity for the people of Harlem, and to prove that "there are black dancers with the physique, temperament and stamina, and everything else it takes to produce what we call the 'born' ballet dancer." During its official 1971 debut, DTH triumphantly debunked opinions that black people could not dance ballet. By 1993 DTH had become a world-renowned company with forty-nine dancers, seventy-five ballets in its repertory, an associated school, and an international touring schedule.

DTH's extensive repertory has included technically demanding neoclassic ballets (George Balanchine's 1946 *The Four Temperaments*); programmatic works (Mitchell's 1968 *Rhythmetron* and Alvin Ailey's 1970 *The River* to music by Duke Ellington); and pieces that explore the African-American experience (Louis Johnson's 1972 *Forces of Rhythm* and Geoffrey Holder's 1974 *Dougla* created in collaboration with DTH conductor-composer Tania Leon). DTH also excels in its own versions of classic ballets, including a sumptuous, Geoffrey Holder-designed production of Stravinsky's *Firebird* (1982) choreographed by John Taras, and a stunning Creole-inspired staging of *Giselle* (1984) created by Mitchell, designer Carl Mitchell, and artistic associate Frederic Franklin. This highly acclaimed *Giselle* set the Romantic-era story in the society of free black plantation owners in pre–Civil War Louisiana. DTH is perhaps best known for its revivals of dramatic ballets, including Agnes de Mille's 1948 *Fall River Legend* and Valerie Bettis's 1952 *A Streetcar Named Desire,* both of which have starred principal ballerina Virginia Johnson. Other important classical dance artists associated

with DTH include Lydia Arbaca, Karen Brown, Stephanie Dabney, Robert Garland, Lorraine Graves, Christina Johnson, Ronald Perry, Walter Raines, Judith Rotardier, Paul Russell, Eddie J. Shellman, Lowell Smith, Mel Tomlinson, and Donald Williams.

In 1972 the DTH school moved to its permanent home at 466 West 152nd Street, where training in dance, choreography, and music supplemented outreach programs bringing dance to senior citizens and children of the Harlem community with special needs. The international celebrity achieved by DTH began with a Caribbean performance tour in 1970, an engagement at the Spoleto Festival in 1971, and an auspicious 1974 London debut at Sadler's Wells. In 1988 DTH embarked on a five-week tour of the U.S.S.R., playing sold-out performances in Moscow, Tbilisi, and Leningrad, where the company received a standing ovation at the famed Kirov Theatre. In 1992, DTH successfully performed in Johannesburg, South Africa.

In 1990, faced with a $1.7 million dollar deficit, DTH was forced to cancel its New York season and lay off dancers, technicians, and administrative staff for a six-month period. Mitchell and the board of directors responded with increased efforts to enlarge corporate support and strengthen their African-American audience base. In 1994 DTH completed a $6 million expansion and renovation project, which doubled classroom and administrative space and confirmed the DTH commitment to provide access to the disciplined training necessary for a career in classical ballet.

—THOMAS F. DEFRANTZ

DANDRIDGE, DOROTHY

Dorothy Dandridge (c. November 1923– September 8, 1965), actor and singer. The daughter of a minister and a stage entertainer, Dorothy Dandridge was born in Cleveland, Ohio, and was groomed for a stage career by her mother, Ruby

See also
Alvin Ailey
Harlem Renaissance

*For African
Americans, the
combination of an
increasingly
factory-like
Hollywood system
and a lingering
economic depression
provided only scant
hope of improved
roles.*

PAGE 253

See also
Film

Dandridge, who separated from her husband and began touring the country as a performer shortly after her second daughter was born. While still a child, Dandridge sang, danced, and did comedy skits as part of her mother's show. When their mother settled in Los Angeles, she and her older sister Vivian—together they had been billed as "The Wonder Kids"— attended school and appeared in bit parts in films, including the Marx Brothers comedy *A Day at the Races* (1937). During the 1940s, Dorothy and Vivian joined with another young African-American woman, Etta Jones, to form an act called "The Dandridge Sisters," and embarked on a tour with the Jimmie Lunceford band. Dandridge met her first husband, Harold Nicholas (of the Nicholas Brothers dancing team), while she was performing at the Cotton Club in Harlem. A brain-damaged daughter, Harolyn, was born to the couple before they divorced.

During this time, Dandridge managed to secure a few minor Hollywood roles, and appeared in such films as *Drums of the Congo* (1942), *The Hit Parade of 1943, Moo Cow Boogie* (1943), *Atlantic City* (1944), *Pillow to Post* (1946), and *Flamingo* (1947). The early 1950s witnessed the flowering of her movie career, as she acquired leading roles in the low-budget films *Tarzan's Perils, The Harlem Globe-Trotters,* and *Jungle Queen* (all made in 1951). Dandridge, who was exceptionally beautiful, worked actively at cultivating a cosmopolitan, transracial persona, brimming with sexual allure. She also became increasingly well known as a nightclub singer. Indeed, Dandridge's performances at New York's La Vie En Rose (1952) were in such demand that the club—then on the brink of bankruptcy—was saved from financial collapse. She was one of the first African Americans to perform at the Waldorf-Astoria's Empire Room, and appeared at such prestigious clubs as Ciro's (Los Angeles), the Cafe de Paris (London), the Copacabana (Rio de Janeiro), and the Chi Chi (Palm Springs).

Dandridge's big break as a motion picture actress came in 1954, when she secured the title role in Otto Preminger's all-black production *Carmen Jones.* That year, she became the first black actor to be nominated for an Oscar for a leading role. That she had achieved celebrity stature was evidenced by her appearances on the cover of *Life,* as well as in feature articles in national and international magazines. However, three years were to pass before Dandridge made another film, largely because, in racist Hollywood, she was not offered roles commensurate with her talent and beauty,

and she could no longer settle for less. Her next film, *Island in the Sun* (1957), was the first to feature an interracial romance (between Dandridge and white actor John Justin); the film was poorly received, as were *The Decks Ran Red* (1958), *Tamango* (1959), and *Malaga* (1962), all of which touched on interracial themes. Although Dandridge won acclaim in 1959 for her portrayal of Bess (opposite Sidney Poitier) in Otto Preminger's film of *Porgy and Bess,* she received fewer and fewer film and nightclub offers as time passed. After divorcing her second husband, white restaurant-owner Jack Dennison, she was forced to file for bankruptcy and lost her Hollywood mansion. Her sudden death in 1965 was attributed to an overdose of antidepressants; she was forty-one years old. Dandridge's autobiography, *Everything and Nothing,* was published posthumously in 1970; in 1977, she was inducted into the Black Filmmakers Hall of Fame.

—PAMELA WILKINSON

DAVIS, BENJAMIN OLIVER, JR.

Benjamin Oliver Davis, Jr. (December 18, 1912–), general. Benjamin O. Davis, Jr., son of the first African-American general in the U.S. Army, had a long and distinguished career of his own in the U.S. Air Force. Following his long military service, he spent a number of years working as an important administrator in the Department of Transportation.

The younger Davis was born in Washington, D.C. He spent many of his early years watching or participating in his father's military activities. In the 1920s, he lived with his parents and attended school in Tuskegee, Ala., and Cleveland, Ohio. One of his most vivid memories from those days involved his father facing down a Ku Klux Klan march while the family lived at Tuskegee. As an adolescent, Davis, Jr., was an excellent scholar and displayed leadership qualities. He was one of the few African-American students at Central High School in Cleveland and was elected president of his graduating class. He attended college at Western Reserve University (Cleveland, Ohio) and the University of Chicago, but then decided on a military career. Despite the handicaps that had faced his father, he felt that it was a profession where he could advance on his merits. In 1932 his father asked the assistance of Oscar DePriest, congressman from Illinois, who nominated Davis,

ANGELA DAVIS

Activist the Target of Political Conspiracies

Angela Yvonne Davis (January 26, 1944–), political activist. Angela Davis lived in a section of Birmingham, Ala., known as "Dynamite Hill" because of the violent attacks by white nightriders intent on maintaining the residential demarcation line between blacks and whites. Both of her parents were educators, worked actively for the NAACP, and taught their children not to accept the socially segregated society that existed at the time. She attended Brandeis University, where she was influenced by the teachings of Marxist philosopher Herbert Marcuse. After graduating in 1961, she spent two years in Europe, where she was exposed to student political radicals. Her own radicalism, however, came into focus with the murder in 1963 of four young black Sunday school children in a Birmingham, Ala., church bombing. In California, where she went to pursue graduate study with Marcuse (who was now at the University of California, San Diego), Davis began working with the Student Nonviolent Coordinating Committee (SNCC), the Black Panthers, and the Communist party, of which she became a member in 1968.

Hired in 1969 by UCLA to teach philosophy, Davis not long after was fired by the Board of Regents and then-Governor Ronald Reagan because of her Communist party affiliation. Ultimately, her case went to the Supreme Court, which overturned the dismissal. By that time, however, Davis herself was in hiding as a result of an incident at the Soledad state prison. In August 1970, George Jackson, a prisoner and member of the Black Panthers, assisted by his brother Jonathan, attempted to escape using smuggled guns. Both brothers were killed, and some of the guns were traced to Davis. Fearful for her safety and distrustful of the judicial system, Davis went underground. For two months she was on the FBI's Ten Most Wanted list before being apprehended and incarcerated. She remained in jail for sixteen months before being tried for murder and conspiracy. In June 1972 she was acquitted of all charges against her. Davis resumed her academic career at San Francisco State University and again became politically active, running as the Communist party candidate for vice president in 1980 and 1984. In 1991 she joined the faculty of the University of California, Santa Cruz, as professor of the history of consciousness. She is the author of several books, including *If They Come in the Morning* (1971), *Women, Race, and Class* (1983), and *Women, Culture, and Politics* (1989). Her autobiography, *Angela Davis: An Autobiography*, originally published in 1974, was reissued in 1988.

—CHRISTINE A. LUNARDINI

Jr., to the United States Military Academy. Subsequently he passed the entrance examination and entered West Point in 1932.

Life at the military academy had changed little since the last African-American had graduated in the 1880s. The presence of blacks was resented, and almost all the cadets ignored Davis. The only time he had any companionship was when he was allowed to leave West Point. During his years at the academy he began to develop an interest in flying, an area the Army had closed to African Americans. When he graduated in 1936, ranking thirty-fifth in a class of 276, he requested assignment to the Army Air Corps. The Army refused because there were no African-American flying units and they would not assign a black officer to a white unit.

During the next few years he performed a variety of duties, similar to those of his father. In 1938 he received an appointment as Professor of Military Science at Tuskegee Institute. Two years later he was detached to work as an aide to his father, who was then commanding the 2nd Cavalry Brigade at Fort Riley, Kans.

His interest in flying never waned, and in 1941, he received his opportunity. Bowing to pressure, the Army decided to allow African Americans into the Army Air Corps, established a flight training program at Tuskegee Institute, and ordered Davis to command the first class. After he graduated in 1942, he was rapidly promoted to the rank of major and given command of the 99th Pursuit Squadron, the first African-American air unit. In April 1943, the unit was transferred to North Africa and in June flew its first combat mission. Most of the ensuing missions were rather routine, but not everyone was persuaded of their effectiveness. A number of white officers were convinced that no African-American air unit could ever measure up to the quality of the white units.

Later in the year Davis was ordered back to the United States and assigned command of the 332nd Fighter Group, a larger all-black flying

See also

Klu Klux Klan

*Thelonious Monk
stood at the center
of the emergent
Bebop movement
during World
War II.*

PAGE 459

See also
Jazz

unit. More important, he was able to answer the many questions that army staff officers posed about the effectiveness of the 99th Squadron. Enough of these officers were convinced to the extent that they decided to continue the African-American flying program and transferred the 332nd to the Italian theater. During the last year of the war, Davis was promoted to the rank of colonel, flew sixty combat missions, mainly escorting bombers, and received several awards, including the Distinguished Flying Cross. At the end of the war he returned to the United States and was placed in command of the 477th Composite Group. Among the problems he had to face in his new assignment were segregated base facilities, poor morale, and continued evidence of the detrimental impact of segregation.

During the next few years Davis continued to deal with those problems while advocating an end to segregation. When President Harry S. Truman issued Executive Order 9981 in 1948, ending racial discrimination in the armed forces, Davis became a key officer in the Air Force. He helped draft desegregation plans and put them into practice at Lockbourne Air Base. Subsequently he was assigned to the new Air War College. During the Korean War he served at the Pentagon as deputy for operations in the Fighter Branch. Later he was given a variety of command assignments throughout the world, including Formosa, Germany, and the Philippines. In 1965 he was promoted to lieutenant general, the first African American to reach that rank. He retired from the Air Force in 1970.

During the following years he served in a variety of positions within civilian government. For several months in 1970 he was director of public safety in Cleveland, Ohio, but found he could not work well with Mayor Carl Stokes. Adapting to the world of urban politics proved to be quite difficult for a man who had spent the previous thirty years in the military. In June 1970 Davis became a member of the President's Commission on Campus Unrest. From 1970 to 1975, he served as an administrator in the Department of Transportation. As assistant secretary of transportation, he headed the federal programs developed to deal with air hijacking and highway safety. In 1978 he became a member of the Battle Monuments Commission, a position his father had held twenty-five years earlier. During the next few years, he remained busy with a variety of activities, including programs designed to tell people about the role of African Americans in aviation, and the writing of his autobiography, which was eventually published in 1991.

—MARVIN E. FLETCHER

DAVIS, MILES DEWEY, III

Miles Dewey Davis, III (May 26, 1926–September 28, 1991), jazz trumpeter and composer. One of the most influential musicians in America in the 1950s and 1960s, Davis was a restlessly innovative performer, a central figure in several post-bebop jazz styles, including cool, hard-bop, modal, fusion, and electric jazz. Born in Alton, Ill., Davis grew up in East St. Louis. His mother was a classically trained pianist and violinist. Davis received his first trumpet at the age of thirteen from his father, a successful dentist. In high school he studied with Elwood Buchanan. Trumpeter Clark Terry also served as a mentor. Davis began playing dates in the St. Louis area in his mid-teens, and in 1943 and 1944 he played with Eddie Randle's Rhumboogie Orchestra. He also performed with Adam Lambert's Six Brown Cats in Chicago, and with Billy Eckstine in St. Louis, before moving to New York in 1944. Davis's ostensible reason for coming to New York was to study at the Juilliard School, but he gained his real education in the jazz clubs of Harlem and 52nd Street.

Once in New York, Davis began associating with the young musicians beginning to popularize bebop. He made his first recordings in 1945 with vocalist Rubberlegs Williams. Later that year he recorded with alto saxophonist Charlie Parker ("Billie's Bounce," "Now's the Time"). Parker became Davis's mentor and roommate, and over the next few years the two made many important and influential bebop recordings, including "Yardbird Suite," "Ornithology," "A Night in Tunisia," "Donna Lee," "Chasin' the Bird," and "Parker's Mood." On these recordings Davis distinguished himself by his intimate tone and sparse, hesitant style of improvisation. During this time Davis was a fixture on 52nd Street, performing and recording with pianist Tadd Dameron, pianists Bud Powell and Thelonious Monk, vocalist Billy Eckstine, and saxophonist Coleman Hawkins. He first recorded as a band leader in 1947 ("Milestones" and "Half Nelson," with Parker on tenor saxophone), and the next year left Parker to form an experimental nine-piece group in collaboration with arranger Gil Evans. The ensemble, which included a French horn and tuba and featured advanced harmonies and unusual compositional forms, was short-lived, performing at the Royal Roost nightclub for only two weeks. Nonetheless, its recordings from 1949–1950 ("Move," "Venus de Milo," "Boplicity," and "Israel") spawned the cool jazz movement of the 1950s, and became particularly popular upon their 1954 rerelease in LP form as *The Birth of the Cool*.

Despite a period of heroin addiction from 1949 to 1953, Davis continued to perform and record in a cool style, often with saxophonist Sonny Rollins ("Morpheus," "Dig," "The Serpent's Tooth," "Tune Up," and "Miles Ahead"). His career took another leap forward with the 1954 recording of "Walkin'." That recording, with its more extroverted approach, inaugurated hard bop, a rugged and bluesier version of bebop. In 1955 Davis formed his first significant quintet, including tenor saxophonist John Coltrane, bassist Paul Chambers, pianist Red Garland, and drummer Philly Joe Jones. They recorded the landmark *Round About Midnight* (1955) and performed and recorded until 1957, when Davis added alto saxophonist Cannonball Adderley to

OSSIE DAVIS

Writer/Performer Turns to Activism

Ossie Davis (December 18, 1917–), actor and playwright. Ossie Davis was born in Cogdell, Ga., to Kince Charles Davis, a railroad construction worker, and Laura Cooper Davis. After finishing high school in Waycross, Ga., he hitchhiked north and attended Howard University. In 1937, Davis left Howard and went to New York City, where he worked at odd jobs before joining Harlem's Rose McClendon Players in 1939.

Davis was drafted into the Army in 1942, and after his discharge in 1945, he again pursued his acting career. In 1946, he successfully auditioned for Robert Ardrey's *Jeb*, in which he starred opposite actress Ruby Dee. Davis and Dee were married in 1948.

In 1953, Davis wrote *Alice in Wonder*, a one-act play, produced in Harlem, that dealt with the politics of the McCarthy era. Blacklisted for left-wing associations, Davis and Dee supported themselves by staging readings at colleges. In 1955, Davis starred in a television production of Eugene O'Neill's *The Emperor Jones*, and two years later appeared on Broadway opposite Lena Horne in *Jamaica!*

In the 1960s, Davis achieved broad success in the performing arts. In 1960, he replaced Sidney Poitier and appeared with Ruby Dee in Lorraine Hansberry's play *A Raisin in the Sun*. The following year, his play *Purlie Victorious*, a satire on southern racism, opened on Broadway to an enthusiastic response. Davis also wrote and starred in the film version of *Purlie Victorious*, entitled *Gone Are the Days* (1963). He appeared in several other films during this period, including *The Cardinal* (1963), *The Hill* (1964), *The Scalphunters* (1968), and *Slaves* (1969). He also appeared on several television shows, wrote an episode for the popular series *East Side/West Side*, and narrated National Education Television's *History of the Negro People* (1965). In 1969, Davis was nominated for an Emmy award for his performance in the Hallmark Hall of Fame special *Teacher, Teacher*. That same year Davis directed, cowrote, and acted in the film *Cotton Comes to Harlem*, based on a novel by Chester Himes.

During these years, Davis continued his political activities. In 1962, he testified before Congress on racial discrimination in the theater, and joined the advisory board of the Congress of Racial Equality (CORE). The following year, he wrote a skit for the 1963 March on Washington, and in 1965 Davis delivered a eulogy at the funeral of his friend, Malcolm X. In 1972, he served as chairman of the Angela Davis Defense Fund. While Davis has strong affinities with black nationalism, he has nonetheless rejected black racism and separatism.

Through the 1970s, '80s, and early '90s, Davis continued his performing career, notably in a radio series, the *Ossie Davis and Ruby Dee Hour* (1974–1976); in the public television series *With Ossie and Ruby* (1981); in the role of Martin Luther King, Sr., in Abby Mann's television miniseries *King* (1977); and in the Spike Lee films *Do the Right Thing* (1989) and *Jungle Fever* (1991). Throughout the early 1990s, he was a semiregular on the television series *Evening Shade*. Davis also has written several children's books, which include plays based on the lives of Frederick Douglass and Langston Hughes, and a novel, *Just Like Martin* (1992), about a southern boy, inspired by the life of the Rev. Dr. Martin Luther King, Jr.

—SUSAN MCINTOSH AND GREG ROBINSON

See also
Literature

the group. In 1957 Davis went to France to record the soundtrack for Louis Malle's film *Elevator to the Gallows.* Back in the United States the next year, Davis recorded *Milestones,* which introduced the concept of modal jazz, in which modes or scales, as opposed to chord changes, determine a song's harmonies. In 1959 Davis recorded perhaps his greatest record, *Kind of Blue,* which included the modal compositions "So What," "All Blues," and "Freddie Freeloader," with an ensemble that included drummer Jimmy Cobb and pianists Wynton Kelly and Bill Evans. In the late 1950s Davis also renewed his association with arranger Gil Evans. They produced three acclaimed orchestral works, *Miles Ahead* (1957), *Porgy and Bess* (1958), and *Sketches of Spain* (1959–1960). During this time Davis achieved his mature instrumental style, delicate and tentative on ballads, boldly lyrical on up-tempo numbers.

Davis's trumpet style resembled, in a famous description, "a man walking on eggshells," but he was often belligerent and profane, on stage and off. He refused to announce titles, walked off the stage when sidemen soloed, and rarely acknowledged applause. Nonetheless, he openly demanded the respect he felt was appropriate to jazz musicians. During the 1950s Davis also became an internationally known public figure noted for his immaculate attire, his interest in sports cars, and for taking up boxing as a hobby.

In 1960, Adderley and Coltrane left the ensemble, which underwent a number of personnel shifts until 1963, when Davis hired pianist Herbie Hancock, bassist Ron Carter, and drummer Tony Williams. With saxophonist Wayne Shorter's arrival the next year, Davis began featuring churning, lengthy improvisations built around Shorter's quirky compositions (*E.S.P.,* 1965; *Miles Smiles,* 1966).

During the late 1960s Davis became disenchanted with the poor reception his music found among black audiences, and he began to search for a new, more commercially appealing style. He found inspiration in the funk rhythms of James Brown and Sly Stone, as well as in Karlheinz Stockhausen's vast electric-mystic soundscapes. Davis added Keith Jarrett and Chick Corea on electric pianos and John McLaughlin on electric guitar to his regular ensemble, and recorded *In a Silent Way* (1969) and the bestselling *Bitches Brew* (1969), albums that introduced the style that has become known as jazz-rock or "fusion," using loud rock instruments and funk rhythms to accompany extended solo and group improvisations. Davis continued in this vein on *Big Fun* (1969),

Live-Evil (1970), *On the Corner* (1972), *Agharta* (1975) and *Pangea* (1975). Although Davis gained many fans of rock music, jazz fans were perplexed and unsympathetic. Health problems due to drug abuse and a 1972 car accident convinced Davis to retire in 1975.

In 1980 Davis returned to music, but to the disappointment of many of his fans he continued using popular forms of electric instruments. In his best performances, Davis still communicated with the intensity and fire he had in the 1950s, but his recordings, including *The Man with the Horn* (1981), *Star People* (1982), *Tutu* (1986), and *Amandla* (1989), were largely panned by critics, who were particularly harsh on his undistinguished accompanists. Davis, who lived in New York and Malibu, continued to perform and record in the late 1980s and early 1990s. In 1982 Davis married his third wife, the actress Cicely Tyson; they were divorced in 1989.

He published an outspoken memoir, *Miles, the Autobiography,* in 1989. After many years of battling alcoholism, drug addiction, and circulatory and respiratory ailments, Davis died in 1991 in New York.

—WILLIAM S. COLE

DAVIS, SAMMY, JR.

Sammy Davis, Jr. (December 8, 1925–May 19, 1990), singer, dancer, and actor. Sammy Davis, Jr., was born in Harlem in New York and began performing with his father, a vaudeville entertainer, before his fourth birthday. Davis made his first film, *Rufus Jones for President* (1933) when he was eight years old. By the time he was fifteen, he had traveled widely throughout the United States as a full partner in the Will Mastin Trio, comprised of Davis, his father, and Davis's adopted "uncle" Will Mastin. Although they often played at white venues, the trio was compelled to eat and room at Negro establishments; yet Davis, who had received an informal education at the hands of family and friends, was unprepared for the virulent racism he encountered upon joining the Army in 1943. During his tenure in the military, he produced and performed in shows with other service personnel, including the singer and songwriter George M. Cohan, Jr.

Following World War II, Davis returned to the Will Mastin Trio. The group played to segregated audiences and, despite their rising popularity, were forbidden to sleep or socialize in the hotels and casinos where they worked. Davis began recording songs for Capitol Records in 1946; one of his first cuts, "The Way You Look Tonight," was named *Metronome*'s Record of the Year. An extremely versatile performer, adept at tap dancing, singing, impersonations, and comic and serious acting, he received his first big break when Frank Sinatra asked the trio to open for his show at Manhattan's Capitol Theater. Davis went on to perform at Slapsie Maxie's and Ciro's in Los Angeles and at the Copacabana in New York, in addition to appearing on *The Ed Sullivan Show* and Eddie Cantor's *The Colgate Comedy Hour.*

In November 1954, Davis, who had become a celebrity with white and black audiences alike, was involved in a near-fatal car accident while driving from Las Vegas to Los Angeles. He lost his left eye and was hospitalized for several months; during this time, he was visited by a rabbi, who urged him to reflect on the consequences of the accident and the meaning of his previous actions. After a period of intense study, Davis, who claimed to have found an "affinity" between blacks and Jews as oppressed peoples, converted to Judaism.

Davis's popularity was much enhanced by his brush with death. He performed in Philadelphia, Chicago, and Los Angeles, before taking the lead role in *Mr. Wonderful*, a musical comedy that opened on Broadway in 1956. Two years later, Davis, who had been nicknamed "Mr. Wonderful" after the Broadway show, was featured in a serious dramatic role in the movie *Anna Lucasta*. In the 1959 film of *Porgy and Bess*, Davis gave a memorable performance as the character Sportin' Life. That year, he married Loray White, an African-American dancer whom he later left for the Swedish actress Mai Britt. Davis's interracial romance with Britt was highly publicized, and the couple married in 1960.

Davis is perhaps best known for the films he made during the 1960s, when he worked and socialized with the "Rat Pack," a group of Hollywood actors that included Sinatra, Dean Martin, Peter Lawford, and Joey Bishop, who were featured, along with Davis, in such films as *Oceans Eleven* (1960), *Sergeants Three* (1962), *Robin and the Seven Hoods* (1964), *Salt and Pepper* (1968), and *One More Time* (1970). Davis also appeared in such films as *Johnny Cool* (1963), *A Man Called Adam* (1966), *Sweet Charity* (1969), and the German remake of *The Threepenny Opera* (1964), in which he sang "Mack the Knife." In addition, he continued to perform in clubs and on Broadway, where he was praised for his rendering of the title character in *Golden Boy*, Clifford Odets's play about an African-American

The Black Jews of Harlem is one of the oldest, largest, and best-known Hebrew Israelite groups in the United States.

PAGE 397

STAGE LEGEND

Sammy Davis Jr. (center) with James Baldwin (left) and Martin Luther King, Jr. (right), at the Majestic Theater, New York, 1964. Davis promoted civil rights and African-American/Jewish relations with benefit performances and donations.

(© GEORGE WEST)

boxer struggling to free himself from the constrictions of ghetto life. Davis appeared on television in numerous comic and guest-artist roles, as well as in serious dramatic series like the *Dick Powell Theatre* and *General Electric Theater.* In 1966, he hosted a television variety and talk show called *The Sammy Davis Jr. Show,* which ran for less than a year. He also continued to record albums and produced such hit songs as "Candy Man," "Hey There," "Mr. Bojangles," and "The Lady Is a Tramp."

Throughout the 1960s, Davis worked to promote civil rights and African-American/Jewish relations by giving benefit performances and substantial donations. His first autobiography, *Yes I Can,* was published in 1965; three years later, he was awarded the Spingarn Medal by the NAACP for his work in civil rights. Davis's marriage to Mai Britt ended in 1968, and two years later, he married the African-American actress Altovise Gore. In 1971, he was awarded an honorary doctorate of fine arts by Wilberforce University in Ohio. A controversy erupted the following year when Davis, a registered Democrat and supporter of left-wing causes, allowed himself to be photographed with President Richard Nixon at the 1972 Republican Convention; he publicly endorsed Nixon for a time but then renounced their affiliation in 1974.

During the early 1970s, Davis, by then almost as well known for his extravagant spending habits and hard-drinking lifestyle as for his stage presence and vitality, began to experience liver and kidney problems, for which he was eventually hospitalized in 1974. However, he rebounded fairly quickly and was back onstage a few months later in a revue called *Sammy on Broadway.* From 1975 to 1977, he starred in the television show *Sammy and Company.* He performed regularly on the Las Vegas club circuit, and in 1979, became the first recipient of *Ebony* magazine's Lifetime Achievement Award.

Davis's second autobiography, *Hollywood in a Suitcase,* was published in 1980; throughout the decade he continued to appear, albeit less frequently, in films, on television, and onstage. In 1986, he received an honorary degree from Howard University. Two years later, he embarked on a national tour with Frank Sinatra, Dean Martin, and Liza Minnelli. Davis was featured in the movie *Taps* (1989), a tribute to showbiz entertainers, and published a third autobiographical work, *Why Me?* (1989), before dying of throat cancer in spring 1990.

—JESSE RHINES

See also
Civil War
Frederick Douglass
Underground Railroad

DELANY, MARTIN ROBISON

Martin Robison Delany (May 6, 1812–June 24, 1885), abolitionist and writer. Delany was born in Charles Town, Va. (now Charleston, W. Va.); his mother was free, his father a slave. Delany grew up in Chambersburg, Pa., and was educated at the school of the Rev. Louis Woodson in Pittsburgh. His mentor was the well-to-do John B. Vashon. In 1843 he married Catherine Richards and began his career as a medical doctor and abolitionist. Between 1843 and 1847 Delany published the first African-American newspaper west of the Alleghenies, the *Mystery.* In 1847 he joined Frederick Douglass as coeditor of the newly founded *Rochester North Star,* in which his letters provide valuable commentary on antebellum free blacks.

In the 1840s Delany criticized colonizationists who advocated the emigration of free African Americans to Liberia, which he, like most blacks, saw as forcible exile. But as the decade ended, Delany and Douglass grew apart. Delany left the *North Star* in 1849, advocating more black self-reliance than Douglass, who welcomed the support of white reformers. The strengthening of the federal fugitive slave laws and his frustration with his fellow blacks prompted Delany to withdraw from reform in 1850 and attend the Harvard Medical School, until forced out in 1851.

The crisis of the 1850s distressed northern blacks, many of whom fled to Canada to avoid reenslavement and harassment. Four years before moving his family from Pittsburgh to Chatham, Canada West (now known as Ontario), Delany published the first book-length analysis of the economic and political situation of blacks in the United States: *The Condition, Elevation, Emigration, and Destiny of the Colored People of the United States, Politically Considered* (Philadelphia, 1852), which is cited for its nationalism and advocacy of emigration out of the United States. In 1859 the *Anglo-African Magazine* and in 1861–1862 the *Weekly Afro-American* published his only novel, *Blake, or the Huts of America,* in serial form.

During the 1850s Delany moved from cautious endorsement of emigration with the Americas to planning African-American colonies in West Africa. He organized emigration conferences in 1854, 1856, and 1858, and in 1854 published a pamphlet, *The Political Destiny of the Colored Race,* that recommended emigration. In late 1858 he sailed to West Africa; he visited Alexander Crummell in Liberia in 1859; in December of that year, in the company of Robert Campbell, a teacher at the Institute for Colored Youth in Philadelphia, he signed a treaty with the Alake of Abeokuta, in what is now western Nigeria, providing for the settlement of educated African Americans and the development of commercial production of cotton using free West African labor. Before the first group of settlers could leave for West Africa, however, the civil war broke out and changed everything.

Once the War Department reversed its refusal to enroll black volunteers in the Union Army, Delany became a full-time recruiter of black troops for the state of Massachusetts. One of the fifty-fourth regiment of massachusetts volunteer infantry's earliest volunteers was Toussaint Louverture Delany, his oldest son. (The Delanys had named each of their seven children after a famous black figure.) In early 1865 Martin Delany was commissioned a major in the Union Army, the first African American to be made a field officer. He ended the war in the South Carolina Low Country and began to work for the Bureau of Refugees, Freedmen, and Abandoned Lands (Freedmen's Bureau).

Immediately after the war, Delany was a popular speaker among the freedpeople, for he symbolized both freedom and blackness. But as the years passed and the South Carolina Republican party became the party of the poor and black, Delany also began to question its ability to govern the state of South Carolina as a whole. He went into the real estate business in Charleston and drifted into conservatism. By the mid–1870s he was criticizing South Carolina blacks and white carpetbaggers (he, too, was a carpetbagger) for demagoguery and corruption. In 1874 he ran unsuccessfully for lieutenant governor on the slate of the Independent Republicans, a coalition of conservative Republicans and moderate Democrats. By 1876 he was supporting the candidacy of the Democratic candidate for governor, Wade Hampton III, who had been the richest slave owner in the South before the war. Hampton and the Democrats were elected, and by 1879 had purged the state of all black officeholders, including Delany.

At sixty-seven, Delany once again dedicated himself to emigration, this time to Liberia, with the ill-fated Liberian Exodus Joint-Stock Steamship Company. His last acts were the publication of *Principia of Ethnology: The Origin of Races with an Archaeological Compendium of Ethiopian and Egyptian Civilization* and selling his book on a lecture tour. He died in Wilberforce, Ohio.

—NELL IRVIN PAINTER

MARTIN ROBISON DELANY

Delany was the first African American to become a commissioned officer in the United States Colored Troops during the War of the Rebellion.
PHOTOGRAPHS AND PRINTS DIVISION, SCHOMBURG CENTER FOR RESEARCH IN BLACK CULTURE, THE NEW YORK PUBLIC LIBRARY, ASTOR, LENOX AND TILDEN FOUNDATIONS

DELANY, SAMUEL R.

Samuel R. Delany (April 1, 1942–), science fiction writer and critic. Born in Harlem in comfortable circumstances, he graduated from the Bronx High School of Science and briefly attended City College of New York. Despite serious dyslexia, he embarked early on a literary career, publishing his first novel, *The Jewels of Aptor,* in 1962. Delany has been a rather prolific writer, and by the time of his eighth novel, *The Einstein Intersection* (1967), he had already achieved star status in science fiction. He was the first African American to devote his career to this genre. Delany won the Nebula—one of science fiction's two most prestigious awards—in 1967, twice in 1968, and again in 1969. He received the other major science fiction award, the Hugo, in 1968 and 1989 (the latter for his autobiography). Today, he is considered to be one of the wide-ranging masters of the field, having produced books of sword-and-sorcery fantasy as well as science fiction. In addition, he has established himself as a rigorous and erudite theorist and critic of what he calls "the science fiction enterprise."

See also
Civil War

From a perspective of African-American literary history, Delany is noteworthy in part because he was the first significant black figure in a field with which, previously, African Americans at best had had a tangential relationship. Still, he was not the first writer to introduce black themes or characters into science fiction; indeed, he has written of how startled he was to discover, deep into the novel, that the hero of Robert Heinlein's *Starship Troopers* (1959) was non-Caucasian. Early in his own career, in fact, Delany's blackness certainly was not evident to the majority of his readers. However, his real importance depends, first, upon the way his work has focused on the problematic aspects of desire, difference, and the nature of freedom. In his four-volume Nevèrÿon fantasy series (1983–1987), these themes are played out in a mythical past. In *The Tides of Lust* (1973) and *Dhalgren* (1975), the site is a kind of mythical present; and in *Triton* (1976) and *Stars in My Pocket Like Grains of Sand* (1984), the setting is the far future. Many of the same concerns found in his fiction are articulated in his autobiography, *The Motion of Light in Water* (1988). Delany's second major contribution is his successful meshing of postmodern critical thought with the discourses of science fiction and fantasy. He has brought to these often scorned forms a narrative depth and linguistic sophistication they had seldom previously displayed.

In 1961, Delany married the poet Marilyn Hacker. The two separated in 1975. They have a daughter, Iva Alyxander, born in 1974. Delany has taught at the State University of New York at Buffalo, the University of Wisconsin in Milwaukee, and Cornell University. Since 1988, he has been a professor of comparative literature at the University of Massachusetts at Amherst.

—ROBERT ELLIOT FOX

DETROIT, MICHIGAN

Detroit was founded in 1701 by Antoine de la Mothe Cadillac, as part of the French Empire in North America. Acquired by the British at the end of the French and Indian War in 1763, the city remained under English control until 1796, when after Jay's Treaty it was turned over to the United States. It is not clear when the first blacks arrived in Detroit, but they began migrating to Michigan in the early 1800s. White Detroiters owned slaves, although the Northwest Ordinance of 1787 officially banned slavery in the territories.

The 1810 census reported seventeen slaves in the city. In the 1820s there were sixty-seven blacks in town, 4.7 percent of the population.

In 1827 Michigan passed a Black Code that required all African Americans to have a valid, court-attested certificate of freedom and to register with the county clerk. Blacks were required to pay a $300 bond of good behavior, although most actually evaded paying. The law's ostensible purpose was to protect blacks from slavehunters, but its real purpose was to discourage black migration. In 1833 the city had its first major racial disturbance, called the Blackburn riot. After law enforcement officials arrested a fugitive slave couple, Thornton and Ruth Blackburn, in order to return them to Kentucky, blacks attacked the sheriff, who later died from his injuries, and a riot ensued. The Blackburns escaped to Canada. Although more than thirty blacks were arrested, some uninvolved in the conspiracy, none was convicted.

In 1837, the same year that Michigan became a state, its state legislature abolished slavery. The Detroit Anti-Slavery Society was founded that year. Detroit established itself as a major terminal of the Underground Railroad. Black abolitionists—such as Episcopal Rev. William Monroe, who eventually emigrated to Liberia; George DeBaptiste, a prominent businessman; William Lambert, later a supporter of John Brown; and Henry Bibby, a fugitive slave who eventually sought refuge in Canada—were active in the Colored Vigilance Committee, formed in 1840.

Black migration to Detroit was small until the mid-1840s, but by 1850 there were 587 blacks in the city. The first black community was located on the banks of the Detroit River, at the foot of Woodward Ave. The black area would expand north and a little east over time, but never west across Woodward. The first black church, Second Baptist, was established in 1836, in reaction to segregation in white churches. Bethel African Methodist Episcopal was organized in 1841, and St. Matthew's Episcopal, with Monroe in the pulpit, in 1846. In 1843 the community offered a Young Men's Debating Club, a reading room, a library, and a temperance society. An African-American Philharmonic Association opened in 1850. The churches also housed black schools and served as political halls. While blacks were denied suffrage, in 1855 they were given the right to vote in school board elections.

The Civil War was a turning point in Detroit's history. Many Michiganites opposed slavery, but many were also frankly racist. Detroit had pockets of immigrants from the South, and Confederate sympathizers, but the most hostile forces toward blacks in the city were the group of white immigrants from Ireland and Germany, who resented black labor competition. In 1863, Detroit had a race riot, the West's only major racial disturbance of the war. A black man, William Faulkner, was accused of molesting two nine-year-old girls, one white and one black. Convicted of rape, he was sentenced to life in prison, whereupon a white mob, mostly Irish and German, attempted to lynch him. Militia officers who came to protect Faulkner fired at the mob in self-defense, and one man was killed. The mob, frustrated in its lynch attempt, moved to the black area of Beaubien St., where they beat the residents, killing two and injuring over twenty, and burned down more than thirty of their houses. White Detroiters condemned the mob and reimbursed blacks for their losses, but Frederick Douglass used the defenselessness of Detroit blacks as an example of the need for black soldiers. After 1863, 895 black Michiganites, many from Detroit, joined the Union Army.

Between 1860 and 1870, Detroit's black population increased sevenfold, and continued to climb thereafter, due largely to migrants from Canada, rural Michigan, and elsewhere. Twenty-eight percent of the overall black population, representing the majority of the non-native-born Michiganites, came from Virginia and Kentucky. The migrants from Kentucky had generally been enslaved and had worked in agriculture. Mostly illiterate single people, they found jobs as unskilled laborers. The Virginians were free black family groups, among them a few professionals and many mechanics and tradespeople, who left the industrialized areas of Virginia to escape the state's harsh black codes. Between the two groups there were class tensions, and they frequented different churches.

By 1870, 85 percent of Detroit's blacks lived in the old quarter and an enclave called Kentucky, around Kentucky St., north of Jefferson Ave. Although the neighborhood was not majority black, blacks were confined to shabby tenements and dilapidated houses. Although blacks of mixed ancestry could vote as early as 1866, and some blacks did so illegally, black efforts to secure the vote were repeatedly voted down in Michigan until 1870, when the Fifteenth Amendment was passed. The public schools, despite orders of the state legislature, remained segregated until the following year. Once blacks were enfranchised, however, they immediately organized a Colored Republican Club at the ward level. In 1875 and 1876, Samuel Watson became Detroit's first African-American elected official when he was elected to the Board of Estimate, the city legislature's upper house. In 1884, Watson became the first northern black delegate to the Republican National Convention. In 1883, a group of blacks started the weekly *Plaindealer* as the voice of black protest, black business, and black Republicanism. It was one of the first organs to substitute the term "Afro-American" for "Negro." One of its founders, and the organizer of the protest group Afro-American League, was Robert Pelham, Jr., Detroit's leading black politician in the 1880s. After he left to take a position in the Federal Land Office in 1889, David Augustus Straker became Detroit's chief black leader. Straker, a former dean of Allen University Law School in South Carolina, argued civil rights cases and helped found the Detroit Industrial and Financial Cooperative Association and the National Federation of Colored Men. In 1892 he was elected Wayne County circuit court commissioner (judge). The same year, William W. Ferguson was elected to the Michigan legislature. The seat would be held by blacks until 1900.

After the turn of the century, the demography of black Detroit again shifted, as blacks from the deep South began to migrate. The southern-born population, which had been stable for thirty years, increased by 10 percent, relative to the Michigan-born population, between 1900 and 1910. The automobile and other industries, which hired few blacks, spurred the growth of secondary industries which used black labor. By 1915, increased industrial demand due to World War I, as well as a cut-off of immigration from Europe, induced Henry Ford and other industrialists to employ blacks in large numbers. The availability of jobs at $5 per day, advertised by handbills and by labor agents sent south by Ford, provoked a mass migration to Detroit. Black organizations like the Detroit Urban League were set up to find jobs and housing for the new arrivals. The city's black population, 5,000 in 1910, reached 120,000 in 1930.

While blacks toiled in the most difficult and unpleasant positions in industry, with abysmal housing conditions, the relatively high industrial wages they received, and their separation from white society made possible the growth of an independent black economy. Detroit's black middle class, built on the patronage of black workers, was one of the largest in the nation. Black Republicans, thanks partly to contributions by Henry Ford, were increasingly influential in the party. In 1930, Charles Roxborough was elected to the

Drawing on untrained recruits from the churches and projects of Detroit, Motown nurtured many prominent figures of postwar American popular music.

PAGE 469

See also
Nation of Islam

Michigan state senate, the first African American to serve there.

Competition for jobs and housing sparked widespread racial tension. Detroit was a center of the Ku Klux Klan in the 1920s. In 1925, when Dr. Ossian Sweet, an African American, bought a house in a white neighborhood, a white mob surrounded his house. Sweet fired out in self-defense and killed a white man. Defended by Clarence Darrow, Sweet and his relatives charged in the shooting were acquitted. During the 1930s, right-wing antiblack leaders Father Coughlin and Gerald L. K. Smith were based in the Detroit area.

The collapse of the economy during the 1930s left many blacks unemployed and ill-housed. Since the flow of friends and relatives from the South looking for work continued, conditions for Detroit blacks worsened. As competition for housing increased, many blacks were forced into the Black Bottom neighborhood, also known as Paradise Alley. The automobile industry cut down its hiring of blacks. Nevertheless, the black community continued to develop. In 1936, publisher/entrepreneur John Sengstacke, who later put together a chain of black newspapers, created the *Michigan Chronicle*, which became the major source of news for black Detroit. Both main-

stream and heterodox black religious denominations flourished in Detroit. The Rev. James Francis Marion Jones (Prophet Jones), who arrived in the city in 1938, became a popular cult leader/radio evangelist, although his claim of six million followers seems exaggerated. Of more lasting significance was the Nation of Islam, founded by W. D. Fard about 1930 and led after his death by Elijah Muhammad.

However, by far the best-known black Detroit resident in the first half of the twentieth century was Joe Louis, who moved to Detroit at the age of twelve. The heavyweight boxing champion from 1935 through 1949, Louis began his career in local Detroit clubs, and his swift rise to boxing eminence was aided by John Roxborough, a black Detroit businessman.

In 1938, the United Auto Workers (UAW) was able to get a contract with General Motors. Despite the hostility of white workers, the union promoted black unionists such as Horace Sheffield, Robert Battle, Coleman Young, and Sheldon Tappes to leadership positions. In part through union registration drives, blacks in Detroit, as elsewhere, became an important part of Franklin D. Roosevelt's New Deal coalition. In 1936, blacks elected their first Democratic state Representative, Charles Diggs, Sr.

RACIAL CONTROVERSY

Local white residents picket in February 1942 to prevent blacks from moving into the Sojourner Truth Homes, a newly opened federal housing project in Detroit. The disturbances were a grim foreshadowing of the massive Detroit riot of June 20, 1943, during which more than thirty people died.

PRINTS AND PHOTOGRAPHS DIVISION, LIBRARY OF CONGRESS

The coming of World War II and the awarding of lucrative defense contracts to Detroit industries sparked massive renewed migration to Detroit. Walter White of the NAACP estimated that 350,000 people, including 50,000 blacks, entered the city between March 1942 and June 1943. Hate strikes by white workers against blacks, and the past refusal of many blacks to join unions in strikes, had left great bitterness. In February 1942, blacks turned to protests and violence when the Sojourner Truth Homes, a federal housing project built for blacks, was suddenly reassigned to whites. The change was eventually canceled, but racial tensions grew as job competition and the housing crisis intensified. The tensions finally exploded into the Detroit Riot of 1943.

After the war, the African-American population of Detroit climbed, doubling again between 1940 and 1950, and reaching 482,000 in 1960, 29 percent of the city's population. The black middle class expanded. In 1959 Berry Gordy founded the Motown Record Corporation, which would become a cultural force, and the city's first black-owned multimillion dollar corporation. It created the "Motown sound," tuneful pop-oriented rhythm and blues, and features such groups as the Supremes, the Temptations, the Four Tops, and the Jackson Five. Black performers such as Diana Ross, Smokey Robinson, and Aretha Franklin became superstars in the music industry. Churches also expanded, and the Rev. C. L. Franklin and the Rev. Charles Hill became legends in their own time. The Rev. Albert Cleague also began the Black Messiah Movement in Detroit in 1952, turning his United Church of Christ into the Shrine of the Black Madonna. Detroit had the largest National Association for the Advancement of Colored People chapter in America, and blacks were key members of the Democratic Party coalition led by the UAW. In 1954, blacks elected Charles Diggs, Jr., to the U. S. House of Representatives, and in 1957 they elected the first black city councilman, William Patrick.

However, large-scale discrimination persisted. The Interracial Commission, renamed the Detroit Commission on Community Relations (CCR) in 1953, had no enforcement powers, and the UAW failed to win Fair Employment Practices clauses in its contracts. Decentralization in the auto industry led to rising unemployment. Detroit's police, segregated and almost all white, were notorious for bigotry. Only 3 percent of the 300,000 units of new housing built in the 1950s in Detroit were given to blacks. While large numbers of blacks moved into the formerly Jewish neighborhood on 12th Street, those who tried to move into other all-white neighborhoods were met by mobs and brick-throwers.

During the 1960s, Detroit achieved a somewhat undeserved reputation as a "model city" in terms of race relations. Reform Mayor Jerome Cavanaugh, whose 1961 campaign had been supported in large numbers by blacks angered at his incumbent opponent's policy of random police searches, installed a liberal police commissioner. In five years, Cavanaugh brought in an estimated $230 million in federal money for programs, some designed by city officials, for black Detroiters. Groups such as the Citizen's Committee for Equal Opportunity, founded by UAW head Walter Reuther, worked against discrimination. In June 1963, after black militants planned a civil rights protest march, Mayor Cavanaugh persuaded more moderate groups to participate, and invited the Rev. Dr. Martin Luther King, Jr., to speak. About 125,000 people participated in the Walk to Freedom, making it the largest civil rights protest up to that time. In 1964, a militant black lawyer, John Conyers, was elected to Congress.

Nevertheless, discrimination persisted. Whites resisted housing integration, and schools were chronically underfunded. Police bigotry proved resistant to change. Poor, unemployed inner-city blacks resented the high prices they faced in stores owned both by whites and by the black middle class, whom they felt were "collaborators" with an oppressive white power structure.

The Detroit Riot of 1967, a gigantic urban rebellion, scarred Detroit physically and destroyed its "model city" image. The alliance of African Americans and white liberals cut, the black community concentrated on electing African-American officials. In 1969, Richard Austin, an African American, ran unsuccessfully for mayor, but in 1973 Coleman Young was elected to the first of five terms as mayor. Mayor Young has reshaped the police force and brought blacks into city government.

Around 1975, Detroit became a black majority city. By 1990, the city had the largest percentage of African Americans of any big city in the United States, but it had lost one-third of its population in the previous twenty years as the auto industry and manufacturing sector declined and more affluent whites and blacks moved to nearby suburbs. Despite the mayor's efforts to stimulate development, symbolized by the Renaissance Center, and revive the local economy through job-

A riot is the language of the unheard.

MARTIN LUTHER KING, JR.
EPIGRAPH TO "RIOT,"
A POEM BY
GWENDOLYN BROOKS

See also
Elijah Muhammad

creating projects, 34 percent of Detroit's residents were receiving public assistance in 1987. Detroit's large black middle class gave it the highest black median household income in America in the 1980s. Nevertheless, the city experienced chronic double-digit unemployment through the early 1990s as crime rose and neighborhoods decayed.

—WILBUR C. RICH

DOUGLAS, AARON

Aaron Douglas (May 26, 1899–February 24, 1979), painter and educator. Born in Topeka, Kans., Aaron Douglas graduated from Topeka High School in 1917, then earned his B.F.A. from the University of Nebraska in 1922. While he taught art at Lincoln High School in Kansas City, Mo. (1923–1925), his social circle included future civil rights leader Roy Wilkins, future classical music composer William Levi Dawson, and Ethel Ray (Nance), who became Charles S. Johnson's assistant at *Opportunity* magazine. Ray and Johnson persuaded Douglas to postpone study in France to work in New York. Douglas soon became one of the leading artists of the New Negro movement, developing a geometric, monochromatic style of depicting African Americans in dynamic silhouettes by synthesizing formal and symbolic elements of West African sculpture with European-American traditions and modern design into a hard-edged, Art Deco-like style.

In 1925, Douglas earned three important distinctions that launched his career—first prize for a front cover illustration of *Opportunity,* first prize in drawing (for *The African Chieftain*) from *Crisis* magazine, and a commission to illustrate Alain Locke's anthology *The New Negro.* The following year, Douglas married his high school classmate, educator Alta Sawyer, and illustrated *The Emperor Jones* and the short-lived magazine of African-American art and literature *Fire!!* In 1927, he illustrated *Plays of Negro Life,* edited by Locke and Montgomery Gregory, and *God's Trombones: Seven Sermons in Negro Verse* by James Weldon Johnson. Six works in the latter book, along with a portrait, were exhibited at the Harmon Foundation in 1928. Over the next decade, Douglas would illustrate books by Charles S. Johnson, Claude McKay, Paul Morand, and Andre Salmon, as well as numerous magazine covers.

In the late 1920s, Douglas studied privately with Fritz Winold Reiss, a German-American artist whose modernist work Douglas had admired in the New Negro issue of *Survey Graphic*

(edited by Locke in March 1925). Reiss and Locke encouraged Douglas to look to African art for inspiration and develop his own racially representative work. Through their influence, Douglas received a one-year scholarship (1928–1929) to the Barnes Foundation in Merion, Pa., where he studied both African and modern European art.

In 1930, Douglas painted heroic murals of African-American culture and history in the library at Fisk University in Nashville, the Sherman Hotel in Chicago, and Bennett College in Greensboro, N.C. In 1931 he went to Paris for one year to study independently and with Charles Despiau and Othon Friesz at the Académie Scandinave. While Douglas worked diligently, only one piece from his time abroad is known: *Forge Foundry,* a black-and-white illustration published in the French journal *Revue du monde noir* (1931).

In the 1930s, Douglas based himself in New York as an arts leader and muralist. The year after he was elected president of the Harlem Artists' Guild (1935), he addressed the First American Artists Congress. With sponsorship from New Deal art programs and various grants, Douglas completed several murals, most notably *Aspects of Negro Life,* at the 135th Street Harlem Branch of the New York Public Library (1934); those for the Hall of Negro Life exhibited at the Texas Centennial Exposition (1936); and *Education of the Colored Man,* at the Atlanta City Housing Project (1938). In 1938, Douglas received a travel fellowship to the American South and Haiti from the Julius Rosenwald Fund. He exhibited his paintings of Haitian life at the American Contemporary Art Gallery in New York the following year.

In 1939, Douglas began teaching art at Fisk University, where he served as professor and chair of the Department of Art Education for nearly three decades. During this period, he often divided his time between Nashville and New York, where he completed his M.A. in Art Education at Columbia University Teachers College in 1944 (his fraternal affiliations included Sigma Pi Phi and Kappa Alpha Psi) and received a Carnegie teaching grant in 1951. From the 1930s until the '50s, the Douglases frequently entertained artists and writers at their home at 409 Edgecombe Avenue, known as "the White House of Harlem," because the building's residents included prominent intellectuals and civil rights leaders. Douglas painted many of their portraits, in addition to landscapes.

As founder of the Carl Van Vechten Gallery (1949) at Fisk, Douglas acquired a major gift

During the 1920s, the idea of the New Negro became an important symbol of racial progress.

PAGE 334

See also
Harlem Renaissance
Alain Locke

from Georgia O'Keefe, the Alfred Steiglitz Collection (1949), as well as an important series of portraits of African-Americans, the Winold Reiss Collection (1952), and he brought numerous artists to the university for lectures and exhibitions. Noted for these achievements and his art, Douglas was honored by President John F. Kennedy at a White House reception commemorating the centennial of the Emancipation Proclamation in 1963. In 1972 he became a fellow of the Black Academy of Arts and received its outstanding achievement award. The following year, Fisk University awarded Douglas an honorary degree of Doctor of Fine Arts. After retiring as professor emeritus in 1966, Douglas lectured widely and continued to paint until his death in 1979.

Douglas's work has appeared in many major American museums and galleries and in university and community center exhibitions. Additional solo exhibitions were held at D'Caz-Delbo Gallery (1933); University of Nebraska, Lincoln (1941); People's Art Center, St. Louis (1947); Chabot Gallery, Los Angeles (1948); Riley Art Galleries, New York (1955); University of California, Berkeley (1964); and Mulvane Art Center, Topeka (1970).

—THERESA LEININGER-MILLER
AND LINDA NIEMAN

DOUGLASS, FREDERICK

Frederick Douglass (February 1818–February 20, 1895), abolitionist, journalist, orator, and social reformer. Born Frederick Augustus Washington Bailey to Harriet Bailey, a slave, and an unacknowledged father (perhaps his master Aaron Anthony) in Tuckahoe, Md., Frederick Douglass—he assumed this name in 1838 when he escaped north to freedom—soon became the most famous African American of the nineteenth century. Separated from his family while young, he was a personal slave to several whites during his formative years. Consequently, he early learned self-reliance and began honing the arts of survival. At the same time, he found a sense of belonging through his relationships with various families and individuals, white and black, who liked and encouraged the bright and precocious youth. Ultimately, the lure of freedom and equality proved irresistible and propelled him on an extraordinary journey of both individual achievement and service to his people and his nation.

Taken in 1826 to Baltimore—where, as an urban slave, he could expand his horizons greatly—he taught himself how to read and write with the witting and unwitting assistance of many around him. Similarly, this more open urban environment, with its large and expanding free African-American population, further whetted his desire to learn as much as possible about freedom, including runaway slaves and the abolitionist movement.

Around the age of thirteen, he converted to Christianity, but over time he became increasingly disillusioned with a religious establishment that compromised with and supported evil and injustice, especially slavery and racial prejudice and discrimination. Also around that age, he purchased his first book, *The Columbian Orator*, which deepened not only his understanding of liberty and equality but also the enormous power of rhetoric, as well as literacy. Indeed, throughout his life he firmly believed in the power of the written and spoken word to capture and to change reality.

As a rapidly maturing eighteen-year-old, developing spiritually and intellectually as well as physically, he revealed an intensifying longing to be free that led him to plan an unsuccessful runaway scheme with several fellow slaves. Several months previously he fought Covey, the "Negro breaker"—one versed in subduing unruly slaves—another sign of the depth of that longing. He later

BREAKING RACIAL BARRIERS

When Frederick Douglass married Helen Pitts, his white secretary, in 1884, they endured much criticism from many blacks and whites. Douglass steadfastly articulated his allegiance to the human race.
PHOTOGRAPHS AND PRINTS DIVISION, SCHOMBURG CENTER FOR RESEARCH IN BLACK CULTURE, THE NEW YORK PUBLIC LIBRARY, ASTOR, LENOX AND TILDEN FOUNDATIONS

*We have to do with
the past only as we
can make it useful
to the present and
the future.*

FREDERICK DOUGLASS
*THE LIFE AND WRITINGS
OF FREDERICK DOUGLASS*

portrayed his triumph over Covey as a turning point in his struggle to become a free man. With the aid of Anna Murray, a free African-American woman in Baltimore with whom he had fallen in love, he escaped to freedom. They moved to New Bedford, Mass. (1838); Lynn, Mass. (1841); Rochester, N.Y. (1847); and Washington, D.C. (1872).

In the North, Douglass found it very hard to make a living as a caulker because of racial discrimination and often had to resort to menial jobs. Anna worked hard as well, creating a comfortable domestic niche for a family that eventually included five children: Rosetta, Lewis Henry, Frederick, Jr., Charles Remond, and Annie. Frederick's speeches within the local black communities brought him to the attention of the mostly white abolitionists allied with William Lloyd Garrison, and in 1841 they asked him to join them as a lecturer. An increasingly powerful lecturer and draw for the Garrisonian Massachusetts Anti-Slavery Society, Douglass learned a great deal from his work with such people as Garrison and Wendell Phillips. Most important, he adopted their pacifism and moral suasionist approach to ending slavery and was deeply influenced by their interrelated perfectionism and social reformism. As a good Garrisonian, he argued for disunion and rejected the political approach to ending slavery as a compromise with a proslavery Constitution.

Douglass also began to come into his own as an activist and a thinker. Drawing upon his experiences as a slave, he lambasted slavery and its notorious effects, most notably antiblack prejudice and discrimination in both North and South. As the living embodiment of a small measure of success in the enormous struggle against slavery, he spoke eloquently with uncommon authority. In 1845, his *Narrative of the Life of Frederick Douglass, an American Slave* was published and its huge success, followed by a successful speaking tour of Great Britain, heightened his celebrity immeasurably. Ever conscious of his public persona and his historical image, he carefully crafted both. *My Bondage and My Freedom* (1855) and *Life and Times of Frederick Douglass* (1881; revised 1892), fuller autobiographies, were likewise crucial in this regard.

His stirring narrative and equally stirring oratory derived much of their power and authenticity from Douglass's deep-seated engagement with the plethora of issues confronting blacks north and south, free and slave. His strong involvement in the national Negro convention movement, as

well as with various state and local black conferences, furthered his impact and by 1850 made him the principal spokesman for his race. His fierce commitment to egalitarianism, freedom, and justice similarly led him to embrace the women's-rights movement, notably women's suffrage, and to become one of the most important male feminists of the nineteenth century. He attended the first Women's Rights Convention, in Seneca Falls, N.Y., in 1848; on the day of his death, February 20, 1895, he had earlier attended a meeting of the National Council of Women.

Shortly after his return from Great Britain in 1847, Douglass embarked upon a distinguished career in journalism. He edited the *North Star* (1847–1851), *Frederick Douglass' Paper* (1851–1860), *Douglass' Monthly* (1859–1863), and, for a time, the *New National Era* (1870–1874). Complementing the other aspects of his varied public voice and extending its reach and influence, Douglass's work as a journalist furthered his use of the printed word as a tool for agitation and change. Stressing self-reliance, hard work, perseverance, education, and morality, Douglass exemplified the embrace by many African Americans of middle-class values and the American success ethic. Likewise, invoking America's revolutionary tradition, he emphasized the imperative of full black liberation within the confines of the American nation. After 1851, when he formally broke with the Garrisonians and accepted political action against slavery as viable and necessary, he became more politically engaged. By the outbreak of the Civil War, he supported the Republican Party.

The tumultuous events of the 1850s convinced Douglass, like untold numbers of his compatriots, that war was unavoidable, the Union cause just, and slave emancipation inevitable. He urged his audience, most notably President Abraham Lincoln, to further ennoble the Union cause by accepting black troops into the Union army and treating them fairly. He exhorted his people to support fully the Union cause and to struggle ceaselessly to ensure that Union victory would mean emancipation and the necessary conditions for black progress. His often arduous efforts to recruit black Union troops, who braved strong white hostility and mistreatment, showed him grappling intensely with the central and complex issue of African-American identity. African Americans, he cogently argued, honored their group as well as national heritage and mission through vigorous support of an abolitionist Union cause.

Douglass emerged from the war even more widely known and respected. He continued to urge his nation to deal justly and fairly with his people, even after the nation reneged on its insufficient and short-lived efforts to do so during Reconstruction. While many blacks questioned his continuing allegiance to the Republican party, Douglass valiantly—albeit unsuccessfully—endeavored to help the party rediscover its humanistic and moral moorings. Appointed to serve as the United States marshal for the District of Columbia (1877–1881), recorder of deeds for the District of Columbia (1881–1886), and chargé d'affaires for Santo Domingo and minister to Haiti (1889–1891), he remained a stalwart Republican.

Over the years, Douglass's status as a comfortable middle-class elder statesman tended on occasion to blind him to the harsh conditions confronting rural, impoverished, and migrant blacks. Still, as in his fiery condemnation of the alarming growth in the number of lynchings of black men in the 1880s and 1890s (often upon the false accusation of an attack on a white woman), it was clear that his commitment to justice never wavered. Likewise, while many women's-rights advocates criticized him for supporting the Fifteenth Amendment, which failed to enfranchise women as it enfranchised black men, Douglass contended that the greater urgency of the black male need for the vote and its greater likelihood of passage made support imperative. After its passage, he continued his efforts on behalf of women's rights and sought to heal the rift within the movement.

When Douglass married Helen Pitts, his white secretary, in January 1884, a year and a half after the death of his first wife, they endured much criticism from many blacks and whites, including close family members. Nonetheless, Douglass, the quintessential humanist, steadfastly articulated his commitment to a composite American nationality, transcending race, as an integral component of his vision of a democratic and egalitarian country. When others criticized him for a lack of race spirit, Douglass, refusing to be imprisoned within a racialist universe, claimed ultimate allegiance to the human race.

Yet he also fully understood and vividly personified his people's struggle from slavery to freedom, from obscurity and poverty to recognition and respectability. His enduring legacy to his people and all Americans is best captured in his lifelong and profound dedication to the imperative of agitation and concerted action: "If there is no struggle," he declared, "there is no progress."

—WALDO E. MARTIN, JR.

DOVE, RITA

Rita Dove (August 28, 1952–), poet. Rita Dove was born in Akron, Ohio. She graduated *summa cum laude* from Miami University in Oxford, Ohio in 1973, then spent the following year in Tubingen, Germany, as a Fulbright scholar. In 1975 she enrolled in the Writers' Workshop at the University of Iowa, where she received her Master's in Fine Arts degree two years later. In 1981 Dove joined the English Department at Arizona State University, where she continued to teach creative writing until 1989. In that year she accepted a position at the University of Virginia, which named her Commonwealth Professor of English in 1992.

Dove's first volume of poems, *Yellow House on the Corner,* was published in 1980. It was followed in 1983 by *Museum,* which displays a more conscious awareness of the conventions of artistic and historical practice. Three years later, Dove published *Thomas and Beulah* (1986), two versions of the story of two ordinary African Americans. The volume, which loosely narrates the lives of Dove's grandparents, was awarded the Pulitzer Prize in Poetry in 1957. *Thomas and Beulah* is a turning point in Dove's career for more reasons than its award-winning status. Not coincidentally, its narrative style emerges just after Dove's first published foray into fiction, *First Sunday* (1985), a collection of stories. Dove had also published one novel, *Through the Ivory Gate* (1992), the story of a black woman whose work as a puppeteer evokes painful childhood memories of disturbing cultural significance. What *First Sunday* and *Through the Ivory Gate* may lack in believable dialogue and depth of characterization is made up for in the echoes of *Grace Notes* (1989). In these poems, each moment is filled by the persistent ringing of carefully culled metaphor.

More public attention has fallen on Dove's career than on that of any other contemporary African American poet. Recognized for her virtuoso technical ability, Dove represents a generation of poets trained in university writers' workshops who are sometimes chastised for their formal competence at the expense of emotional depth. Dove has distinguished herself in her capacity to filter complex historical and personal information through precise selections of poetic form. In this, she is most closely allied to black poets such as Gwendolyn Brooks, Michael S. Harper, and Robert Hayden. Her unusual range of subject matter, thematically and geographically, has earned her a reputation as a black writer unafraid

The autobiographical narratives of former slaves comprise one of the most extensive and influential traditions in African-American literature and culture.

PAGE 625

See also

Gwendolyn Brooks

Literature

to set African-American culture within a global context. Dove's gifts as a poet were most fully acknowledged in 1993 when she was appointed Poet Laureate of the United States, the first black writer and the youngest poet ever to have been so honored.

—GINA DENT

DRAKE, ST. CLAIR

St. Clair Drake (January 2, 1911–June 14, 1990), sociologist. St. Clair Drake was born in Suffolk, Va., where his father was a Baptist pastor in small rural parishes. Although Drake knew his father only during his first thirteen years, the elder Drake had a decisive influence on his son's later development. John Gibbs St. Clair Drake had been born in Barbados, but studied for the Baptist ministry in Lynchberg, Va. During World War I, Reverend Drake followed his congregation to Pittsburgh, where many had migrated to work in the steel mills.

In Pittsburgh, the family lived in a "middle class" house, with access to a well-stocked library. There Drake formed his habit of wide reading on many subjects. He attended a school where he was the only African-American child, and listened, fascinated, to discussions of religion and race between his father and other preachers.

His parents were divorced in 1924, and Drake accompanied his mother back to Virginia. He attended Booker T. Washington High School in Staunton, Va., where he had his first encounters with southern segregation.

From 1927 through 1931, Drake attended Hampton Institute, in Virginia, where he was an outstanding student. Central to his subsequent career was the influence of a young professor, W. Allison Davis, who introduced him to anthropology. After graduating, Drake taught high school in rural Virginia, traveling to Philadelphia every summer and investing his small earnings in a few books on anthropology. During those summers, he worked and studied with the American Friends Service Committee, a Quaker organization.

In summer 1931, he demonstrated the quiet courage that remained characteristic of him. Some of the Friends initiated a "peace caravan," and Drake and his friend, Enoch Waters, traveled with it through the South, attempting to win support for disarmament and international cooperation. Remarkably, the trek did not terminate in disaster.

In 1935, while still teaching in Virginia, Drake became a member of a research team that was making a social survey of a Mississippi town. Davis had questioned whether the ideas of the white anthropologist, W. Lloyd Warner, concerning class and caste, were applicable to blacks and whites in the South. The outcome was Drake's earliest published research, which was incorporated into Davis's *Deep South*. Working with senior anthropologists, Drake conducted much of the research and prepared the manuscript for publication. After *Deep South*, Drake's closeness to those whom he studied caused him always to describe himself as a "participant-observer."

In 1937 Drake entered the University of Chicago on a Rosenwald Fellowship for further studies in anthropology. Intermittently, he continued to study there over the next fifteen years. In 1942 he married Elizabeth Johns, a white sociologist. *Black Metropolis,* his best-known work, appeared in 1945. Coauthored with Horace Cayton, it is a pathbreaking work of description and analysis of African-American life in Chicago.

In 1946, Drake joined the faculty of the newly established Roosevelt College (later University) in Chicago, where he remained until 1968. This college had been created as a protest against the racially restrictive Central YMCA College, its predecessor.

Drake was increasingly interested in Africa and the African diaspora. His doctoral dissertation for the University of Chicago, "Value Systems, Social Structure, and Race Relations in the British Isles," involved one year of research of the "colored" community of Cardiff, Wales, placing that community into the larger context of Africa and the South Atlantic. During that year in Britain, Drake became a close associate of George Padmore, the West Indian pan-Africanist and advisor to Kwame Nkrumah. After Ghana's independence, from 1958 to 1961, Drake became Professor of Sociology at the University of Ghana, while still holding his professorship at Roosevelt University.

In 1969 he accepted a long-standing invitation to become Professor of Sociology and Anthropology and Director of African and Afro-American Studies at Stanford University in California. The Stanford period was most notable for the publication of the vast and erudite *Black Folk Here and There* (two vols., 1987–1990). Using an enormous array of sources, it presents the thesis that prejudice against blacks is a relatively recent phenomenon, arising first during the Hellenistic period.

—FRANK UNTERMYER

See also

Education

DRAMA

Long before black men were allowed on American stages, a caricature stage Negro made an appearance. The English dramatist Isaac Bickerstaff introduced a lazy, rambunctious West Indian slave in *The Padlock* in 1769; in 1795 the white American James Murdoch followed suit with *The Triumph of Love*, in which a stupid buffoon known as Sambo delighted audiences and initiated a derogatory stereotype that the American public seemingly will not let die. To counter this representation with spectacles more pleasing to "ladies & gentlemen of color," a free black man named Mr. Brown (first name unknown) opened the African Grove Theatre in lower Manhattan in New York City in 1821. This first, professional black theater company mounted productions of Shakespeare, dance and pantomime interludes, and *King Shotaway* (1823), thought to be the first play written and performed by African Americans. Though no script remains today, records indicate that it concerned a slave insurrection in the Caribbean. Produced within a year of the Denmark Vesey slave insurrection in Virginia, the play roused the ire of white spectators to the extent that a group of rowdies intent on "wanton mischief" destroyed the theatre building and forced the company's closure in 1823. With its demise, Ira Aldridge, who had been inspired to join the group after seeing the West Indian actor James Hewlett in *Richard III*, left for Europe where he eventually won gold medals from the Prussian and Austrian heads of state for his superior artistry in Shakespearean tragedies as well as in popular comedies. Sadly, Aldridge became the first of a long line of African-American expatriate artists who found greater acceptance abroad than at home.

The Sambo stereotype would solidify in the 1840s into the minstrel show. According to conventional theater history, minstrelsy began in 1828 when a young white performer named Thomas D. Rice observed an old, deformed Negro singing and dancing. He is said to have borrowed the man's entire performance (including his clothing), thereby initiating what would become an extremely popular form of entertainment—and a pattern of exploitation repeated by many other white performers who reaped great profit from their imitations of black art. More recent scholarship, however, argues that minstrelsy originated not with Rice and his colleagues who claimed that they were accurately depicting real African-American customs, but with black people themselves. In gathering to sing and dance, enact stories, and mock the cultured pretensions of their masters, slaves were creating a form in which improvisation and ecstatic response based upon the interactions of those assembled were more important than a fixed or written text wherein all elements are related to each other by an inviolable logic that does not give any space to the unplanned or unexplained. They were pioneering a form in which language was treasured for its power to stimulate the imagination and emotions. Given slave conditions, they were projecting a metaphysical stance and style that enabled them to survive with their intelligence, humor, and dignity relatively intact. But in performing for white observers, these slaves masked their behavior so that the owners could interpret their efforts as black incompetence rather than as a critique of what appeared to the slaves as white ridiculousness. Thus, white minstrel performers were offering white audiences a parody of black behavior that was, unbeknownst to them, already a parody of white customs. By the 1860s when black men were allowed to perform onstage, audiences had grown so accustomed to the black-face image that African Americans had to black up—adding yet another layer of parody.

Because of its topicality, improvised quality, and general construction as entertainment aimed at the masses, the minstrel show is usually not considered drama. Yet, it was particularly significant for what would follow, because any playwright wishing to represent African Americans onstage would have to confront the enduring legacy of minstrelsy's grinning darky. Furthermore, it signaled that performance modes rooted in African-American culture were likely to be characterized by masking, evocative language, improvisation grounded in a mastery of technique, episodic structure shaped as much by performer-audience interactions as by logic, as well as by ecstasy, and an ethical/aesthetic stance that seeks to affirm the humane even while it holds opposites in balanced tension.

Masking is at the core of *The Escape; or a Leap for Freedom* by William Wells Brown, who is generally considered the first African American to have a play published. First read from Northern, abolitionist platforms in 1857 by Brown, who was a successful fugitive, this text appears double-voiced, offering contradictory representations to audience members. Undoubtedly, abolitionist attendees at a reading agreed with the representation of slave owners as exploitative and religiously hypocritical, and they sympathized with the mu-

A Great Actor always must act. . . . Every last second of his life must be pose and posture.

LIONEL BARRYMORE
GOOD NIGHT, SWEET PRINCE,
1943

♦ **Parody**
A literary or musical work in which the style of an author or work is closely imitated for comic effect or in ridicule

179

Man is least himself when he talks in his own person. Give him a mask, and he will tell you the truth.

OSCAR WILDE
THE CRITIC AS ARTIST, 1891

See also
Amiri Baraka

latto couple who, in fine diction, vow to seek freedom. They probably also found comic relief in Cato, the stereotypical buffoon who uses nonsensical words, pursues gluttonous pleasures, and apes white mannerisms. But Cato is also a trickster who, when beyond his owners' presence, sings freedom songs (in standard English) and cunningly schemes to turn every situation to his own advantage. Thus, when freedom is almost at hand, he jettisons the grinning mask, helps the runaway couple, and makes his own leap to freedom. In his trickstering, Cato seems to represent an independent spirit that will not be contained by social conventions not of his own making. That position could hardly have been a comforting prospect to those Northerners who, despite their antislavery convictions, believed in black inferiority, and yet, presumably it accurately reflected one attitude found among pre-Civil War blacks. Though the figure of the manipulative buffoon found no place in the theaters patronized by whites, its appearance in one of the earliest black plays identifies masking as an important African-American survival strategy. It is a representation to which African Americans have periodically returned in the musical comedies of Bert Williams and George Walker (*Abyssinia*, 1906; *Bandanna Land*, 1908), and in dramas as different as Garland Anderson's *Appearances* (1925), LeRoi Jones's (Amiri Baraka's) *The Slave* (1964), Douglas Turner Ward's *Day of Absence* (1965), and Ed Bullins's *The Gentleman Caller* (1969).

The use of theater as an arena for advancing social change continued in the first decades of the twentieth century, when W. E. B. Du Bois and others organized the pageant *The Star of Ethiopia*. Seeking to teach history to both blacks and whites, Du Bois and his pageant master Charles Burroughs crafted a series of tableaux linking Egyptian and Yoruba cultures with African-American heroes like Nat Turner and with the quest for freedom. Between 1913 and 1925, this pageant involved approximately three thousand people as performers and was performed in four cities before more than thirty thousand people. Not only did the pageant mobilize often competitive community energies, foster racial pride, and indulge a love of spectacle, but it also provided a model of nonprofessional, socially charged art that others would utilize. Thus, for example, inhabitants of Los Angeles mounted "50 Years of Freedom" in 1915 to combat the negative imagery of D. W. Griffith's film *The Clansman*, and in 1974, people dressed in Ku Klux Klan outfits appeared in San Francisco City Hall chambers as part of an effort to ban the display of regalia of groups advocating hate and genocide.

Angelina Weld Grimké's *Rachel* is the first twentieth-century full-length play written, performed, and produced by blacks. In this sometimes melodramatic coming-of-age play, a high-spirited young woman rejects marriage and the possibility of motherhood because she fears that future generations will be unable to escape the racism she has personally experienced. The production provoked a storm of controversy when sponsored by the District of Columbia branch of the National Association for the Advancement of Colored People (NAACP) in 1916, because it implicitly defied the NAACP philosophy of racial progress led by an educated, black elite, whom Du Bois had termed "the talented tenth." For some, the play reduced art to the level of propaganda. Thus, when Alain Locke, one of the leading theoreticians and promoters of the Harlem Renaissance, and educator Montgomery Gregory founded Howard University's dramatic art department in 1921, they explicitly espoused an aesthetic that privileged technical beauty or art over social concerns. W. E. B. Du Bois took a different position, arguing both in his writings and his organization of the amateur Krigwa Players that the two were not so easily separated. Though short-lived (1925–1927), this drama group was significant because it extended Du Bois's efforts and those of Charles Johnson to foster formal cultural production and increase readership through contests and publication in the NAACP and Urban League magazines, *Crisis* and *Opportunity*. Additionally, the theater's manifesto propounded a standard of evaluation that would be echoed in the militant sixties. Namely, an authentic black theater had to be "about us . . . by us . . . for us . . . and near us."

Also differing with Locke's and Montgomery's emphasis on art divorced from a strong social referent were a number of women who won most of the drama prizes in the *Crisis* and *Opportunity* contests sponsored between 1925 and 1927. Protest against lynching, the lack of birth-control information, and racial discrimination against returning black World War I veterans were some of the issues that women like Alice Dunbar Nelson, Georgia Douglas Johnson, Mary Burrill, and May Miller dramatized in plays like *Mine Eyes Have Seen* (1918), *Sunday Morning in the South* (1925), *Safe* (c. 1929), *Blue-Eyed Black Boy* (c. 1930), *Nails and Thorns* (1933), *They That Sit in Darkness* (1919), and *Aftermath* (1919). The antilynching dramas are of particular importance because these women, largely deprived of leadership roles in organizations like the NAACP or the Urban League, seemingly viewed the stage as an arena for advancing an important social agenda. Their work formed a continuum with the direct, antilynching campaigns launched by Ida B. Wells and other black women active in the Women's Club movement from the turn of the century to the early decades of the twentieth century. Additionally, the antilynch play was a genre in which black women predominated, producing more plays than either black men, white women, or white men.

The Great Depression of the 1930s largely stymied African-American efforts to establish their own theaters. One outlet for theatrical interests was the black church, where folk dramas such as "The Old Ship of Zion," "Heaven Bound," or "In the Rapture" began. Popular throughout the Midwest, East, and South, these dramas took their plots from the Bible. Often a given church would mount the same play over a number of years, so that novelty of story line was not an objective. Rather, dramatic appeal rested in the improvisational space allotted to comic byplay, the artistry with which spirituals were rendered, and the affirmation of a sense of communal solidarity in terms of both religious emotions aroused by the actual event and the creative energies marshalled in preparing costumes, sets, and participants for performance. The aesthetic evident in these folks dramas has parallels with such African traditions as festivals, for in both instances a community, sharing a set of beliefs and symbols, gathers to enact itself in a performance balancing fixed and fluid elements. That is, the broad parameters of a known plot, familiar spirituals, and performers whose personalities both onstage and offstage are known to the community are balanced against fluid performance specifics like the particular placement and rendition of individual songs and narrative episodes, the spontaneous extension of humorous moments, and the emotional dynamic between audience and performers. Through this symbolic practice, a value system is reaffirmed, and the individual is offered an opportunity to experience his or her relationship to a community. Started during the Great Depression, folk dramas like *Heaven Bound, Noah's Ark,* or *The Devil's Funeral* can still be witnessed in some black Baptist and fundamentalist churches.

The government inadvertently became another sponsor for dramatic activity during the Depression. Faced with the collapse of financial markets and the unemployment of millions of Americans, in 1935 the federal government established a relief program known as the Works Progress Administration. It included the Federal Theatre Project (FTP) that during its four years of operation annually employed some thirteen thousand theater workers who performed before approximately 65 million people in theaters, parks, schools, hospitals, and churches. With black units in twenty-two cities, FTP not only offered work to black performers, but also provided many of them with their first formal training in acting, directing, writing, and technical design. Offerings ran the gamut from adaptations of mainstream plays to musicals and dramas addressing contemporary social issues. One of its most popular shows with white and black audiences was a "voodoo" *Macbeth* directed by Orson Welles for the New York Negro unit of FTP. In setting this classic in the tropics, Welles was not only continuing the practice of making Shakespeare accessible to people with varying degrees of formal education, but he was also furthering a theatrical convention in which aspects of African-related culture are used to make mainstream fare more exotic or appealing. "Voodoo" *Macbeth* was soon followed by *Swing Mikado,* a jazz version of the Gilbert and Sullivan light opera; in more recent years, black "remakes" of white standards have resulted in such musicals as *The Wiz* (1975; adapted from *The Wizard of Oz*) and Lee Breuer's *The Gospel at Colonus* (1983; adapted from the fifth-century Greek drama *Oedipus at Colonus*).

In addition to delightful spectacles, the FTP also produced serious drama that questioned the fabric of American life. One such drama, *Big White Fog* by Theodore Ward, is a good example of a play that speaks simultaneously to both white and black audiences. Its realistic style with an immediately recognizable physical setting, operation of cause-and-effect within family relationships, and the hero's movement toward greater self-knowledge locates the text within the mainstream of American dramaturgy. The play's cultural specificity resides in its focus on the competing promises of Marcus Garvey's Back-to-Africa movement, a black capitalism derived from Booker T. Washington, and socialism within the context of the Depression. Furthermore, its dramatization of intraracial (as well as interracial) color prejudice adds powerful depth, because it captures a reality known painfully well by African Americans, but for the most part hidden from the view of the larger society. Produced first in 1938 by the FTP black unit in Chicago, it aroused a certain degree of controversy because of its seeming support of communism. It was subsequently

Amiri Baraka first gained fame as a poet and playwright in New York's Greenwich Village and subsequently became the most prominent and influential writer of the black arts movement.

PAGE 64

remounted in New York in 1940 by the short-lived Negro Playwrights Company, which Ward had helped to organize along with other playwrights like Langston Hughes and Abram Hill (*On Striver's Row,* 1940; *Walk Hard,* 1944). Theodore Ward subsequently found critical praise and limited audience success with his historical drama about Reconstruction, *Our Lan'.* Begun in 1941, it was first produced off-Broadway at the Henry Street Settlement Playhouse in 1946.

Further fueling conservative concern about art and politics was a form of experimental theater known as the Living Newspaper. The format was initially conceived by FTP director Hallie Flanagan, who, like many other white American artists had been impressed by the theatrical experimentation she witnessed in Germany and Russia in the 1920s. The Living Newspaper hired unemployed workers to research current events that were then enacted by large casts in an episodic, panoramic fashion with minimal sets or costumes, in effect producing a kind of theatricalized newsreel. One of the first Living Newspapers to run afoul of its government sponsors was *Ethiopia,* which was closed after an initial preview because of fears that its powerful dramatization of Benito Mussolini's invasion of the African nation of Ethiopia would provoke protests and jeopardize relations with the Italian government, with which the nation was then at peace. Politics also seems to have been the explanation for not producing Abram Hill and John Silvera's script *Liberty Deferred* (1938), which utilized many of the Living Newspaper techniques to dramatize the African-American history. Though FTP fare was very popular with the American public, it nonetheless drew the suspicions of congressmen who regarded this first attempt at subsidized public art as a haven for allegedly anti-American, communist sympathizers. With the economy improving as the nation moved toward active participation in World War II, the Dies Committee killed the Federal Theatre Program in 1939.

Langston Hughes's *Don't You Want to Be Free?* (1937) stands in marked contrast to Ward's *Big White Fog.* While Ward's play had been sponsored by the Federal Theatre, Hughes's was produced by his own leftist-affiliated Harlem Suitcase Theatre. Like much of the agitprop, or agitation-propaganda play writing of the Great Depression, his play utilizes minimal scenery, a small pool of actors to play a large number of roles, and direct address to the audience, designed to encourage them to undertake a specific action. In this case, the text argues for an acceptance of working-class

solidarity across racial barriers. The play's distinctiveness is marked by its use of poetry, gospel and blues songs, dance, and vignettes to suggestively chronicle black history from Africa to the United States. The validation of culture that Hughes had begun in experimenting with poetic form in *The Weary Blues* (1926) was here extended to the theater; his use of an episodic structure, knitted to-

GROUNDBREAKING PLAYWRIGHT

Lorraine Hansberry Wins Prestigious Drama Award

Lorraine Hansberry (May 19, 1930–January 12, 1965), playwright. Lorraine Hansberry was the youngest child of a nationally prominent African-American family. Houseguests during her childhood included Paul Robeson and Duke Ellington. Hansberry became interested in theater while in high school, and in 1948 she went on to study drama and stage design at the University of Wisconsin. Instead of completing her degree, however, she moved to New York, worked at odd jobs, and wrote. In 1959 her first play, *A Raisin in the Sun,* was produced and was both a critical and commercial success. It broke the record for longest-running play by a black author and won the New York Drama Critics Circle Award. Hansberry was the first African American and the youngest person ever to win that award. The play, based on an incident in the author's own life, tells the story of a black family that attempts to move into a white neighborhood in Chicago. Critics praised Hansberry's ability to deal with a racial issue and at the same time explore the American dream of freedom and the search for a better life. The play was turned into a film in 1961, and then was adapted as a musical, *Raisin,* which won a Tony Award in 1974.

Hansberry's second play, *The Sign in Sidney Brustein's Window,* focuses on white intellectual political involvement. Less successful than *A Raisin in the Sun,* it closed after a brief run at the time of Hansberry's death from cancer in 1965. After her death, Hansberry's former husband, Robert B. Nemiroff, whom she had married in 1953, edited her writings and plays, and produced two volumes: *To Be Young, Gifted and Black* (1969) and *Les Blancs: The Collected Last Plays of Lorraine Hansberry* (1972). *To Be Young, Gifted and Black* was presented as a play and became the longest-running Off-Broadway play of the 1968–1969 season.

— LILY PHILLIPS

gether and propelled by the emotional energy of black music as well as by the evocative intensity of language, provided a model that more contemporary playwrights like Amiri Baraka and Ntozake Shange would emulate in the 1970s. Hughes's later deployment of religious experience, which found commercial success in *Black Nativity* (1961), helped inaugurate the contemporary gospel drama genre, practiced by such artists as Vinnette Carroll with *Your Arms Too Short to Box with God* (1975) and Ken Wydro and Vi Higgensen with *Mama I Want to Sing* (1980).

World War II (1939–1945) brought in its wake increased militancy at home and abroad, as African Americans agitated for fair-employment practices, the elimination of restricted housing, and an end to segregated schools, and as Africans mobilized to gain their independence from colonial masters. This new aggressiveness was mirrored in Lorraine Hansberry's *A Raisin in the Sun* (1959). Using Langston Hughes's poetic query,

"What happens to a dream deferred?", the young playwright explored the conflicting aspirations of the Youngers, a Chicago tenement family eagerly awaiting the arrival of a $10,000 insurance check paid upon the death of the father. Thirty-year-old Walter Lee's dream of owning a liquor store and hence of functioning as a man in terms espoused by the American middle class clashes with Mama's desire to purchase a comfortable house with a small garden, while Beneatha's medical studies and humanist philosophy come into conflict with her brother's chauvinism and her mother's religiosity. Sister-in-law Ruth's decision to seek an illegal abortion marks the battering that the older generation's Southern, sharecropping values have taken in the industrial North. Paradoxically, Mama's spiritual faith, rooted in the American slave experience, is congruent with Asagai's progressive social commitment based in contemporary, African anticolonial movements, for in wooing Beneatha, this Nigerian student

D

DRAMA

Langston Hughes's play Mulatto *opened on Broadway in 1935 to hostile reviews, but enjoyed a long run.*

PAGE 357

GEORGE WOLFE

An Important Voice in Contemporary American Theater

George C. Wolfe (September 23, 1954–), playwright and director. Born in Frankfort, Ky., George Wolfe was the third of four children in a middle-class black family. His mother was the principal of a private black elementary school; his father worked for the state Department of Corrections. An introspective child, he soon became a voracious reader.

Wolfe was thirteen when, on a visit to New York, he saw his first professional play. The performance of *Hello, Dolly!*, starring Pearl Bailey, made Wolfe realize he wanted to work in the theater. He soon began directing plays in high school.

After earning a B.A. in theater from Pomona College in Claremont, Calif. (1977), Wolfe pursued an acting career in Los Angeles, while also teaching and directing at the Inner-City Cultural Center. In 1979 he came to New York City, where he earned an M.F.A. in dramatic writing and musical theater at New York University. He taught at City College and the Richard Allen Center for Cultural Art while pursuing a writing career.

In 1985, his musical about colonization, *Paradise*, was produced off-Broadway at Playwrights Horizons. But it was *The Colored Museum*, produced in 1986 at the New York Public Theater, that established him as an important voice in contemporary

American theater. The play, a satire of popular stereotypes from African-American culture, raised questions concerning the uses (by blacks as well as whites) and meanings of black cultural icons. It went on to major productions in London and Los Angeles; in 1991 it aired as part of the "Great Performances" series on public television.

In 1990, Wolfe was one of four artistic associates at the Public Theater. In this capacity he directed *Spunk*, his adaptation of three short stories by Zora Neale Hurston (for which he was given an Obie Award), and Bertolt Brecht's *The Caucasian Chalk Circle*, adapted by Thulani Davis. That same year he directed the Los Angeles premiere of *Jelly's Last Jam*, a musical based on the life of Jelly Roll Morton, for which Wolfe also wrote the book. It moved to Broadway in 1992 to considerable acclaim. Also in 1992 he directed the PBS "Great Performances" production of Anna Deavere Smith's *Fires in the Mirror*, about unrest between blacks and Jews in the Crown Heights section of Brooklyn in 1991. In 1993, he directed the Broadway production of Tony Kushner's *Angels in America: Millennium Approaches*, for which he won the Tony Award for Best Direction of a Play. That same year he was named producer of the New York Public Theater.

—MICHAEL PALLER

See also
Langston Hughes
Minstrels / Minstrelsy

speaks of the necessity of belief in human potential and the consequence struggle for human betterment.

Produced five years after the historic Brown v. Board of Education of Topeka, Kansas decision outlawing segregated schools, *A Raisin in the Sun* seemed to signal the nation's willingness to live up to its credo of equality. It constituted a number of landmarks: the first time that an African-American woman's work had been produced at the Ethel Barrymore Theatre on Broadway; the directorial debut of African-American Lloyd Richards in such a prestigious venue; widespread recognition for actors Claudia McNeil, Ruby Dee, Sidney Poitier, and Diana Sands; and encouragement for other artists to articulate their visions of black America. In addition, it won the New York Drama Critics Circle Award, beating out such mainstream competitors as Tennessee Williams's *Sweet Bird of Youth,* Eugene O'Neill's *A Touch of the Poet,* and Archibald MacLeish's *J.B.* Thus, the play's ending was interpreted, for the most part, as a ringing endorsement of integration. But at the time of its twenty-fifth-anniversary production in 1984, optimism had waned; the reinsertion of the character of the chatty neighbor, who brings news of a racial bombing, along with the final action of the play, namely Mama's retrieving her sickly plant for the family's move into a white neighborhood, clarified Hansberry's call for continued struggle for dignity.

In both its content and structure, *Raisin* speaks to the white mainstream and to black audiences. In fact, critics have compared this drama to the Depression-era *Awake and Sing* (1935), written by the white author Clifford Odets, because not only do both feature families dominated by women, but they also deploy ethnic slang and the metaphors of a cramped physical environment as a sign of moral constriction and of money from an insurance check as the vehicle for exercising personal integrity. Ephemeral, performance-based yet nonetheless significant elements, along with the written text, serve, however, to simultaneously locate this drama within an African matrix. Rather than arguing, as did critics influenced by the federally sponsored Moynihan Report on black families, that Mama is an emasculating matriarch because the Youngsters do not conform to the 1950s norm of the nuclear family, one can more profitably understand them as fitting the pattern of an extended African family in which great respect is due elders. At moments of extreme crisis, Mama and Walter Lee each evoke the dead patriarch's memory in halting, yet repetitive linguistic rhythms (that are merely suggested in the written script) seemingly to gain access to his moral support in their decision making. Their actions in these instances are akin to African customs of conjuring the spiritual energies of departed relatives in order to solve current, material problems. Similarly, Beneatha and Walter Lee's fanciful creation of a dance welcoming African warriors home from battle constitutes a writing of culture on the body that provides them a dignity denied them by the American environment; as such, it conforms to African assertions that knowledge is kinesthetic and subjective as well as cerebral.

If Hansberry's hero could be aligned with the southern Civil Rights Movement in his attempt to find a place within the American mainstream, then LeRoi Jones's (a.k.a. Amiri Baraka) protagonists in *Dutchman* and *The Slave* were related to the Nation of Islam and its fiery spokesman Malcolm X, for at the time of the plays' premieres in 1964, spectators saw these characters as determined to destroy the social system. In the former drama, a twentyish African-American man and older, white woman engage in a bizarre dating game on a subway car that never reaches its final destination. Claiming to know both everything and nothing concerning Clay's life history, this stranger named Lula alternately describes a tantalizing sexual liaison that they will enjoy and hurls racial taunts at the would-be poet until he sheds his polite, middle-class demeanor and acknowledges a deep hatred of white America. But Clay fails to act upon his murderous knowledge, preferring instead to use art as a safety valve that tempers rebellious impulses. Once Lula has exposed this rage, she kills Clay and enlists the aid of the hitherto passive onlookers in throwing his body off the train. Like the mythic captain of the *Flying Dutchman,* who was fated to sail the world looking for absolution for his crimes, Lula begins to seek out another young black male as the play closes. Seemingly, the play functioned as a cautionary tale demonstrating to blacks that death was the price for inaction upon their justifiable anger and warning whites of the rage they could expect if they continued to deny full citizenship to African Americans. Largely unnoted at the time was the text's gender politics, which accuses the white woman rather than fingering the actual holders of oppressive power in the United States.

In contrast, the black man is no longer the victim and the white man is visible in *The Slave.* Walker has invaded the home of his white former wife in order to take his daughters to safety behind the lines of his revolutionary army advancing on the city—or, so he alleges, because it seems as though Walker's real purpose is to exorcise those feelings that bind him to Grace and Easley, Grace's present (white) husband and Walker's former professor. In the ensuing literal and figurative battle, Walker kills Easley, a beam fatally hits Grace, and Walker departs, apparently leaving the children upstairs crying.

But social psychiatrist Frantz Fanon, whose writings on anticolonial struggles in Algeria provided intellectuals in the 1960s with an important framework for conceptualizing Black Power movements, has argued that it is easier to proclaim rejection than to reject. Fanon's analysis is pertinent to the Baraka text, for despite his aggressive stance, Walker agonizes that he has no language with which to construct a new world, his sole epistemology or frame of reference is a Western system that enforces hatred of black people.

The ambiguity of his position has, in fact, been signaled at the outset by a prologue in which an actor, dressed as a stereotypical old field slave, addresses viewers directly, arguing that whatever he and they understand as reality may be a lie told for survival purposes. What is needed, he suggests, is a superstructure that will enable communication among blacks and whites by ensuring that their common language has the same undeniable referents; otherwise, a black man's legitimate quest for control over his destiny may be understood by a white man as senseless terrorism. The rest of the play then argues that this enabling structure is violence, undertaken by the exploited black masses in defense, as Fanon argued, against the violence waged upon them by the state. But as a playwright, Baraka is caught in a problematic position, for his primary tool of communication with audiences is language itself, suspect because of its inherent capacity to simultaneously convey multiple references and values. Yet, given the *extra*-theatrical, social backdrop of armed confrontations waged by groups like the Black Panther Party, most spectators and readers at the time of the drama's initial productions focused their attention on the text's revolutionary rhetoric rather than its ambivalence.

At the heart of both these plays is an examination of hegemony or the power of a ruling class to enforce throughout the entire society perspectives that maintain its privileged status through noncoercive means like education, the arts, or certain everyday practices. In *Dutchman* the dominance of the elite, as embodied in Lula, is maintained in part because art functions as a passive mode of re-

sistance that deflects direct confrontation. In *The Slave* and subsequent dramatic works like *Four Black Revolutionary Plays, Arm Yrself or Harm Yrself* (1967), or *The Motion of History* (1977), art is defined as counterhegemonic; it is seen as a weapon that can be utilized to attack sociopolitical hierarchies. In rejecting, as Du Bois had done previously, the opposition of art to propaganda, Amiri Baraka became a major proponent of the Black Arts Movement (1964–1974), functioning as a role model for a younger generation eager to assert a positive sense of their black identity.

In an atmosphere of civil rights demonstrations and urban rebellions, entitlement programs designed to bring about what President Lyndon Johnson termed "the Great Society," Vietnam war protest, and the beginnings of a renewed feminism, African-American drama, with its implicit critique of the dominant social structure, briefly flourished. Playwrights like Ed Bullins, Richard Wesley, Clay Goss, Ron Milner, Ben Caldwell, Sonia Sanchez, and Marvin X followed Baraka's example. Artists like Robert Macbeth, Barbara Ann Teer, and Woodie King, Jr. established companies that advocated a black nationalist position (New York's the New Lafayette, National Black Theatre, and Concept East in Detroit respectively), while more moderate practitioners like Douglas Turner Ward, Hazel Bryant, C. Bernard Jackson, John Doyle, and Nora Vaughn, and such companies as the Negro Ensemble, the Richard Allen Cultural Center in New York, the Inner City Cultural Center in Los Angeles, and the Grassroots Experience and Black Repertory Group Theatre in the San Francisco Bay Area also found governmental funding and receptive audiences for their efforts.

Another of the most prolific playwrights of this period was Ed Bullins, who has written in a variety of styles, including comedy (*The Electronic Nigger*, 1968), theater of the Absurd (*How Do You Do?* 1965), fictionalized autobiography (*A Son Come Home*, 1968), and a realism whose seemingly photographic accuracy does not reveal the playwright's evaluation of his source material (*Clara's Ole Man*, 1965). Unlike virtually any other black dramatist before him, Ed Bullins placed onstage—and thereby validated—in plays like *Goin' a Buffalo* (1966), *In the Wine Time* (1968), and *The Taking of Miss Janie* (1975) lower-class hustlers, prostitutes, pimps, and unemployed teens as well as lower-middle-class community college students, veterans, musicians, and would-be artists and intellectuals, virtually all of whom aggressively pursue an individually-oriented ma-

Acting deals with very delicate emotions. It is not putting up a mask. Each time an actor acts he does not hide; he exposes himself.

JEANNE MOREAU
NEW YORK TIMES,
JUNE 30, 1976

See also

Brown v. Board of Education of Topeka, Kansas

Alain Locke

terialism shorn of any rhetoric of concern for a shared, common good.

In disavowing the espoused social values of the American mainstream, Bullins's playwriting style in his full-length dramas also demanded a mode of criticism that was outside the Aristotelian-derived, mainstream preference for tightly organized, linear dramatic structures. Thus, these dramas may be more productively analyzed in terms of jazz, a musical idiom that originated among African Americans and was until relatively recently held in low regard by the American public. Like a jazz composition in which individual musicians improvise a solo or "riff" off a shared melodic line, a play such as *The Fabulous Miss*

Marie (1971) has a basic narrative concerning a group of black Los Angelenos who party unconcernedly while a civil rights demonstration is being broadcast on television. The seemingly endless rounds of drinking, meandering conversations, verbal sparring, and sexual repartee function as a base line from which action is periodically stopped in order for individual characters to step from the shadows into a spotlight and address the audience directly with their own solos on the theme of trying to "make it" in the United States.

Adrienne Kennedy is another playwright whose work demanded different critical tools. Like Baraka, Kennedy confronts, in plays like *The Owl Answers* (1965) and *Rat's Mass* (1963), questions of representation and identity formation, offering a black woman's account of the cultural schizophrenia induced by American racial constructions. Thus, protagonists like Sarah in *Funnyhouse of a Negro* (1963) are paralyzed by devotion to European culture, symbolized in this text by Queen Elizabeth and the Duchess of Hapsburg, and by psychosexual confusion centered on a father figure, associated here with blackness, encroaching jungles, civilizing missions in Africa, and contradictorily, the anticolonialist Congolese hero Patrice Lumumba. Adding to the ambiguity is Kennedy's consistent decision to distribute the female protagonist's story amongst a number of different characters, thereby producing an identity or voice that does not come together in a single, coherent whole. Though her earliest plays were produced during the same time period as Baraka's, the ideological demand for positive valorization of "the black experience" in the sixties' Black Arts and Black Power movements meant that her frighteningly powerful dramatizations of the anguished sensibility Du Bois had termed "double consciousness" won a few supporters among African-American theatergoers. Notwithstanding, her highly abstract style found positive response within the limited circles of the white avant-garde in New York. Given subsequent critiques of identity and relationships of domination and marginality launched from theorists of feminism, literary deconstruction, postcoloniality, and postmodernism, a space has been cleared, and Kennedy's work is presently garnering from white and black critics alike the attention it deserves.

Exploding on the theatrical scene in 1976 with *for colored girls who have considered suicide/when the rainbow is enuf,* Ntozake Shange builds upon examples set by Hughes, Baraka, and Kennedy in black theater as well as those offered by Europe's

Antonin Artaud and Bertolt Brecht. Coining the term "choreopoem," Shange creates a total theater in which unscripted elements like music and dance become equal partners with the written word—i.e., poetry. Thus, in *for colored girls* . . . not only do the women talk about their encounters with men, but they also utilize 1960s Motown tunes, Afro-Cuban rhythms, nonsensical chants, and gospel cadences in order to break out of a social world in which they have been devalued as "a colored girl an evil woman a bitch or a nag." With this first text, Shange placed African-American women's experiences of rape, abortion, domestic abuse, sexual desire, and self-affirmation center stage, and she helped fuel an intense debate within black communities concerning the relevance of feminism—understood at that time as the preoccupation of white, middle-class women—to the lives of African Americans. Seeking in *Spell #7* (1979) to confront the power of the minstrel mask that has determined representations of blacks in American popular imagination she crafts a provocative theater whose implications refuse to remain within the illusionary space created by drama. Shange has continued in texts like *Boogie Woogie Landscapes* (1979), *From Okra to Greens/A Different Kinda Love Story* (1978), and *The Love Space Demands: A Continuing Saga* (1992) to utilize poetry, music, and dance in a nonlinear fashion to explore ways in which a sense of personal integrity and nobility can be harmonized with the realities of racist and sexist social constructions of black (female) identity. Playwrights like Alexis Deveaux, Aishah Rahman, and George C. Wolfe have followed Shange's lead in experimenting with dramatic form, while the last has parodied the feminist content of Shange's dramas in *The Colored Museum* (1986).

Closer to the American mainstream's penchant for realism is August Wilson, who has benefited from a virtually unique, creative collaboration with Lloyd Richards, the same director who brought Hansberry's *A Raisin in the Sun* to Broadway some thirty-five years earlier. Each of his plays has been "workshopped" (read aloud by professional actors and a director, critiqued, and rewritten) at the National Playwrights Conference of the Eugene O'Neill Theater, run by Richards, before receiving productions (and further revisions) and national media attention at various, mainstream regional theaters and on Broadway. A skilled storyteller, Wilson has taken on the challenge of writing a play for each decade of the twentieth century. Thus, *Ma Rainey's Black Bottom* (1984) focuses on the renowned 1920s blues

singer and her band, who, through their casual reminiscences, reveal a collective history of discrimination. *Fences* (1985) centers on an overbearing man's relationship to his son and other family members at the point in the 1950s when African Americans were being allowed entry into white, professional sports organizations; and *Joe Turner's Come and Gone* (1986) dramatizes the search by various boardinghouse occupants for a sense of wholeness and sustaining purpose in the first decade of the twentieth century, when thousands of rural black people moved north seeking employment in an industrializing economy. In *The Piano Lesson* (1987), set in the 1930s, a brother and sister fight for possession of the family's piano, which seems to symbolize conflicting ideas concerning uses of the past in charting present courses of action; while set against the backdrop of Malcolm X's militancy of the 1960s, *Two Trains Running* (1990) features the regular patrons of a modest diner who pursue their own dreams of advancement by playing the numbers (i.e., illegally betting on the outcome of horse races) or consulting Aunt Esther, a local fortune teller whose alleged, advanced age happens to correspond to the numbers of years African-Americans have lived in the United States.

Like the novelist Toni Morrison, August Wilson crafts a world in which the pedestrian often assumes grand, mythic proportions, nearly bursting in the process the neat, explanatory rationales implicit in the genre of dramatic realism. Characters regularly fight with ghosts, make pacts with the Devil, or talk to Death; seemingly, they quest for a spiritual center or standpoint from which to confront a material world hostile to their presence. Arguing the importance of blues music in shaping the identity of African Americans, Wilson seems to create characters whose very lives are a blues song: improvisatory, ironic, yet simultaneously affirmative, grounded in a bedrock of belief in the possibility of human integrity.

Seemingly with the post-sixties integration of some public school systems, (sub)urban neighborhoods, job sites, and mass media, the hybrid character of African-American—and indeed, American—culture has accelerated. Those comfortable with a postmodernism that often finds its inspirations in a global eclecticism of "high" and "low" cultures, can enjoy such African-American performance artists as Robbie McCauley (*My Father and the Wars,* 1985; *Sally's Rape,* 1991), and Laurie Carlos who, in the tradition of Ntozake Shange, work individually and collaboratively to fuse personal narratives with larger feminist issues. Also

The minstrel show was the first uniquely American form of stage entertainment.

PAGE 455

From the watershed of the Harlem Renaissance flowed a number of dramatic productions and musicals.

PAGE 330

AUGUST WILSON

Leading African-American Playwright of his Generation

August Wilson (April 27, 1945–), playwright. August Wilson was born Frederick August Kittel in Pittsburgh, the fourth of six children. Growing up in a neighborhood near the steel mills called the Hill, populated by poor African Americans, Italians, and Jews, he had a childhood of poverty and hardship. He rarely saw his father, a German baker who visited only occasionally, and the family subsisted on public assistance and on his mother's earnings as a janitor. Wilson adopted his mother's maiden name in the 1970s as a way of disavowing his father.

Wilson's stepfather, David Bedford, moved the family to a white suburb when Wilson was a teenager. This change, however, also proved difficult: Wilson was ostracized by his white schoolmates and frequently found notes on his desk reading "Nigger go home." When he was fourteen, he dropped out of school.

Wilson continued his education in the library, where he discovered the works of Ralph Ellison, Langston Hughes, Richard Wright, and other African-American writers, as well as the poetry of Dylan Thomas, which was to influence him greatly. About 1965 he heard recordings of the blues for the first time, and their lyrical expression of the hardships of life was to become another major influence on his work. Except for a one-year stint in the Army (1967), Wilson spent the middle sixties writing poetry at night while holding a series of menial jobs during the day.

In 1968 he returned to Pittsburgh, where he became caught up in the Black Arts Movement. Influenced now by the plays and polemical writings of Amiri Baraka, Wilson and his friend Rob Penny founded the Black Horizons Theatre in 1968—although he had no previous theater experience. Their aim was to use theater to provoke social change. His earliest one-act plays—*Recycle* (1973), *The Homecoming* (1976), and *The Coldest Day of the Year* (1977)—were written for this theater.

In 1977 Wilson moved to St. Paul, Minn., where he wrote a musical satire with a western theme, *Black Bart and the Sacred Hills,* which was staged a year later by the Inner City Cultural Center in Los Angeles. While supporting himself by writing educational dramas for the Minnesota Science Center, Wilson wrote *Jitney!* and *Fullerton Street* in 1982. Both were produced that year by the Minneapolis Playwrights' Center.

But it was *Ma Rainey's Black Bottom,* written in 1983 and first produced by the Eugene O'Neill National Playwrights Conference, that gained Wilson national attention. Produced at the Yale Repertory Theatre in 1984 under the direction of Lloyd Richards and later that year on Broadway, the play won the New York Drama Critics Circle Award for Best Play. *Ma Rainey,* which depicts a day in the life of the famous blues singer, explores not only the exploitation of black artists of the era but also the lack of knowledge that blacks had about one another. Wilson's next play, *Fences* (1985), is set in 1957 and focuses on the frustrations of Troy Maxon, a Pittsburgh garbage collector who had been a star ball player in the Negro Leagues before Jackie Robinson broke baseball's color line. The play was awarded the Pulitzer Prize and the Tony Award for best play of the year. After *Fences,* Wilson decided to make it and *Ma Rainey's Black Bottom* the opening plays of a ten-play cycle, each set in a different decade of the twentieth century and examining what Wilson considered to be the best important issues facing African Americans in that period. In *Joe Turner's Come and Gone* (1986), set in 1911, Wilson explored the emotional and physical displacement experienced by former slaves in the early twentieth century. Produced on Broadway in 1988, it won the New York Drama Critics Circle Award for Best Play.

The Piano Lesson (1987), set in 1936, concerns the ownership of a piano that had been built by the slave grandfather of a black brother and sister. This play perhaps best expresses Wilson's view of black history as something to be neither sold nor denied, but employed to create an ongoing, nurturing cultural identity. Produced on Broadway in 1990, the play received the Drama Desk Best Play award and the New York Drama Critics Circle Award, and won for Wilson his second Pulitzer Prize.

Wilson's play about the 1960s, *Two Trains Running* (1990), is again set in Pittsburgh, in 1968. It explores the allegiances and frictions among a group of friends who find themselves confronted with the era's radical social changes and by a sense that they will be swept along by large forces beyond their control. It was produced on Broadway in 1992 and won the New York Drama Critics Circle Award for Best Play.

Perhaps the leading African-American playwright of his generation, Wilson's view of black life in America is alternately affectionate and unsparing.

—SANDRA G. SHANNON

See also
Harlem Renaissance

termed a performance artist, Anna Deavere Smith offers in her *On the Road: A Search for American Change* series solo performances of edited interviews with people, both famous and obscure, on topics like gender and racial tensions in professional organizations, urban neighborhoods, and on university campuses. She has also focused on the increasingly multicultural, fractious character of American cities, for her *Fires in the Mirror: Crown Heights, Brooklyn and Other Identities* (1992) and *Twilight: Los Angeles, 1992* (1994), in which she performs the words of more than thirty women and men within an hour and a half, challenges audiences to grapple with notions of community in the context of competing demands for racial and economic justice. They can also sample dramas by Suzan-Lori Parks (*The Death of the Last Black Man in the Whole Entire World*, 1990; *Imperceptible Mutabilities in the Third Kingdom*, 1989), who cites the white, American expatriate writer Gertrude Stein and "The Wild Kingdom" television program among her influences; or work by Eric Gupton, Brian Freeman, and Bernard Branner (*Fierce Love: Stories from Black Gay Life*, 1991), collectively known as AfroPomoHomo, a shortening of the identificatory tags, African-American, postmodernist, and homosexual. Or, spectators can attend a concert by Urban Bush Women, Bill T. Jones/Arnie Zane Dance Company, or David Rousseve, whose mixture of modern dance choreography, pedestrian gestures, athleticism, and narrative communicated through both movement and spoken text blur conventional Western distinctions between drama and dance. What all these artists share is a sensibility that does not reach for some grand, master truth. Rather, juxtaposing elements as diverse as European high art, Georgia Sea Island chants, television programs, West African religions, and popular music, they recognize that African-American identity is varied, and no one can claim to represent black authenticity without doing violence to other perspectives found in these communities.

Indeed, for those theatergoers in the 1990s who find the choreopoem form of an Ntozake Shange, the mythic reach of an August Wilson, or the puzzling symbolism of a Suzan-Lori Parks not to their liking, other options are available. They can attend a performance of *Beauty Shop, Living Room,* or *Beauty Shop, Part 2,* all of which have been written, produced, and directed by Shelly Garrett. Starting in 1987 with the intention of simply creating dramatic pieces that would leave audiences exhausted with laughter, Garrett is said to have targeted his attentions primarily to-ward an underserved population of black women, ages 25 to 54 who watch soap operas and rarely frequent theater. Thus, his scripts are closer to TV sitcoms in their representations of everyday life; stereotypes abound, with the women portrayed as materialist, classist, sexually repressed or rapacious. Men are represented as self-centered sex objects, financially secure but dull, or flamboyant homosexuals outgossiping the most catty (yet hilarious) women. Seemingly, considerable advertising on black-oriented radio stations, the dramas' verbal play, the performers' zestful aura, a mixture of some recognizable truths, and cheerful confirmation of spectators' misogynist and homophobic attitudes have attracted thousands of spectators, enabling Garrett to tour at least fifty cities nationwide for more than two years with one show. But those disturbed by what they may perceive as rampant sexuality in these shows also have an option in the commercial arena, for producers have created a religious version, like Michael Mathews's *I Need a Man* (1993), wherein some of these lively stereotypes undergo spiritual conversion aided by the performance of Gospel music. As with much black art, the form is elastic, so that local, gospel radio personalities occasionally make guest appearances onstage during the performance; the predictability of plot and character types is offset by the dynamics of the performer-viewer interactions. Whether participants undergo a religious experience in this highly commercialized venue depends, as it does in church, upon their own belief systems and sensibilities.

In the early 1990s, approximately 200 companies were dedicated to the production of African-American theater and drama. As the foregoing account suggests, audiences can experience a wealth of themes, perspectives, and styles, all of which seek to articulate aspects of African-American culture.

—SANDRA L. RICHARDS

DRED SCOTT V. SANDFORD

In the Dred Scott decision of 1857 the Supreme Court ruled, in a 7–2 vote, that free blacks were not citizens of the United States and that Congress lacked the power to prohibit slavery in the western territories.

Scott was a Virginia slave, born around 1802, who moved with his master, Peter Blow, to St. Louis in 1830. Blow subsequently sold Scott to

Freedom is never voluntarily given by the oppressor; it must be demanded by the oppressed.

MARTIN LUTHER KING, JR.
LETTER FROM BIRMINGHAM
CITY JAIL, 1963

See also
Civil Rights Movement

Dr. John Emerson, an army surgeon, who took Scott to Fort Armstrong in Illinois, a free state, and Fort Snelling in the Wisconsin Territory, where slavery was prohibited by the Missouri Compromise. In 1846, after Emerson's death, Scott sued for his freedom (and that of his family). In 1850 a St. Louis court ruled that Scott became free by residing in Illinois and the Wisconsin Territory. In 1852 the Missouri Supreme Court, articulating the South's proslavery ideology, rejected precedents of its own that went back more than twenty-five years and reversed the lower court decision:

> *Times are not as they were when the former decisions on this subject were made. Since then not only individuals but States have been possessed of a dark and fell spirit in relation to slavery, whose gratification is sought in the pursuit of measures, whose inevitable consequence must be the overthrow and destruction of our government.*

Thus, Missouri would not recognize the freedom a slave might obtain by living in a free state.

In 1854 Scott began a new suit in United States District Court against John F. A. Sanford, a New Yorker who became the executor of Emerson's estate after Emerson's widow, the initial executor, remarried. Scott claimed he was a citizen of Missouri, suing Sanford in federal court because there was a diversity of state citizenship between the two parties. Sanford answered with a plea in abatement, arguing that no black, free or slave, could ever sue as a citizen in federal court. Federal District Judge Robert W. Wells ruled that *if* Scott was free, he was a citizen of Missouri for purposes of a diversity suit. However, Wells's ruling after the trial was that Scott was still a slave. Scott then appealed to the U.S. Supreme Court. At issue was more than his status: the Missouri Supreme Court's decision challenged the constitutionality of the Missouri Compromise. The central political issue of the 1850s—the power of the federal government to prohibit slavery in the territories—was now before the Supreme Court.

The ardently proslavery Chief Justice Roger B. Taney used *Dred Scott* v. *Sandford* to decide this pressing political issue in favor of the South. Taney asserted that (1) the Missouri Compromise was unconstitutional because Congress could not legislate for the territories; (2) freeing slaves in the territories violated the Fifth Amendment prohibition on taking of property without due process; and (3) blacks, even those in the North with full

state citizenship, could never be U.S. citizens. Taney asked: "Can a negro, whose ancestors were imported into this country, and sold as slaves, become a member of the political community formed and brought into existence by the Constitution of the United States, and as such become entitled to all the rights, privileges, and immunities guaranteed by that instrument to the citizens?" Taney answered his own question in the negative. He asserted that at the nation's founding blacks were considered "beings of an inferior order, and altogether unfit to associate with the white race, either in social or political relations; and so far inferior, that they had no rights which the white man was bound to respect; and that the negro might justly and lawfully be reduced to slavery for his benefit." Taney thought his lengthy decision would open all the territories to slavery and destroy the Republican party. In essence, he had constitutionalized racism and slavery. America, in Taney's view, was thoroughly a "white" nation.

Justice Benjamin Robbins Curtis of Massachusetts protested Taney's conclusions. Curtis noted: "At the time of the ratification of the Articles of Confederation [1781], all free native-born inhabitants of the States of New Hampshire, Massachusetts, New York, New Jersey, and North Carolina, though descended from African slaves, were not only citizens of those States, but such of them as had the other necessary qualifications possessed the franchises of electors, on equal terms with other citizens." Curtis concluded that when the Constitution was ratified, "these colored persons were not only included in the body of 'the people of the United States,' by whom the Constitution was ordained and established, but in at least five of the States they had the power to act, and doubtless did act, by their suffrages, upon the question of adoption." Curtis also argued that under a "reasonable interpretation of the language of the Constitution," Congress had the power to regulate slavery in the federal territories.

Northern Republicans and abolitionists were stunned and horrified. Horace Greeley, writing in the *New York Tribune*, called Taney's opinion "atrocious," "abominable," and a "detestable hypocrisy." The *Chicago Tribune* was repelled by its "inhuman dicta" and "the wicked consequences which may flow from it." Northern Democrats, on the other hand, hoped the decision would destroy the Republican party by undermining its "free soil" platform and by finally ending the national debate over slavery in the territories. The New York *Journal of Commerce* hopefully declared

See also
Slavery

that the decision was an "authoritative and final settlement of grievous sectional issues."

Ultimately, it was neither authoritative nor final. By 1858, northern Democrats faced a politically impossible dilemma. Their answer to the problem of slavery in the territories had been popular sovereignty —allowing the settlers to vote slavery up or down. But Taney's opinion denied both Congress and the settlers of a new territory the power to prohibit slavery. This made popular sovereignty meaningless. Stephen A. Douglas, the most prominent proponent of popular sovereignty, told his Illinois constituents that settlers could still keep slavery out of most of the territories by not passing laws that would protect slave property. This simply led to southern demands for a federal slave code for the territories and a split within the Democratic party in 1860.

Republicans made Taney and the decision the focus of their 1858 and 1860 campaigns. Abraham Lincoln argued in his "house divided" speech (1858) that Taney's opinion was part of a proslavery conspiracy to nationalize slavery. He predicted "another Supreme Court decision, declaring that the Constitution of the United States does not permit a *state* to exclude slavery from its limits." He told Illinois voters that "we shall *lie down* pleasantly dreaming that the people of Missouri are on the verge of making their state *free; and* we shall *awake* to the *reality*, instead, that the Supreme Court has made *Illinois* a *slave* state."

Such arguments helped lead to a Republican victory in 1860. During the Civil War the Lincoln administration gradually reversed many of Taney's assertions about the status of blacks. This Republican policy culminated with the adoption of the Fourteenth Amendment, which explicitly overruled *Dred Scott,* declaring, "All persons born or naturalized in the United States . . . are citizens of the United States and of the State wherein they reside."

—PAUL FINKELMAN

DREW, CHARLES RICHARD

Charles Richard Drew (December 6, 1904–April 1, 1950), surgeon. Born and raised in Washington, D.C., Charles Richard Drew graduated from Dunbar High School in 1922. In 1926 he received a B.A. from Amherst College. A first-rate basketball player, on graduation Drew was given an award as best athlete of the college. Between 1926 and 1928, he taught biology and chemistry at Morgan College (now Morgan State University) in Baltimore, where he also served as football coach and as director of athletics.

In 1928, Drew began medical studies at McGill University Medical School in Montreal, Canada. He excelled in medical science courses, won the annual prize in neuroanatomy, was elected to Alpha Phi Omega, the medical honorary scholastic fraternity, and received a prize for the top score in a medical exam competition. In 1933, Drew earned an M.D. and a master in surgery degree. He spent the next two years as an intern and as a resident in medicine at Royal Victoria and Montreal General Hospitals.

As a McGill medical student, Drew was introduced to research on the chemical composition of blood and blood groups by John Beattie, a British medical researcher. A major problem then facing medical science was that quantities of whole, fresh blood large enough to match blood group types between blood donor and blood receiver were not readily available. Drew was bothered by the deaths of seriously ill or injured patients due to blood loss. Learning more about blood and how to preserve it over long periods of time became a research interest that Drew carried with him as he left Montreal to assume a teaching position at Howard University's College of Medicine in 1935.

In 1938, Drew received a research fellowship from the Rockefeller Foundation for study at Columbia-Presbyterian Hospital in New York City. He and John Scudder undertook research that led to the finding that it was blood plasma (the liquid portion of the blood, devoid of blood cells) rather than whole blood that needed to be preserved for transfusions. Drew established an experimental blood bank at Columbia-Presbyterian Hospital. In 1940 Drew was awarded a doctorate at Columbia University with a thesis on "Banked Blood."

Returning to Howard University in 1940, Drew devoted himself to training its medical students in surgery. His teaching was abruptly interrupted, however, by a call for blood plasma needed by wounded soldiers on the battlefields of Europe during World War II. The Blood Transfusion Association in New York City asked Drew to return to help. He was given leave from his instructional duties at Howard University to accept an assignment in the fall of 1940 as Medical Director of the Blood for Britain Program, to supply blood for the British Red Cross. Under Drew's guidance, dried plasma was flown across the Atlantic Ocean to England. Once England had estab-

The history of blacks in science is as old as the history of science in America.

PAGE 616

See also
Basketball
Science

lished its own banks, a larger blood program for U.S. military forces was developed. The American Red Cross and the Blood Transfusion Association jointly conducted this program and Drew became its medical director.

In 1941 the military established a system of refusing blood donations from nonwhites to be used by whites. Blood donated by blacks was stored separately and given only to blacks. As director of the Red Cross Blood Bank Program, Drew took a strong stand against the racial separation of banked blood. As a result, he was asked to resign his directorship position. He did, and returned once again to teaching surgery at Howard University, where he became professor and head of the department of surgery and surgeon-in-chief at Freedmen's Hospital.

On March 31, 1950, after working a long day that included performing several operations, Drew agreed to drive with other colleagues to a medical conference in Tuskegee, Ala. He dozed at the wheel, and the car went off the road near Burlington, N.C., and overturned. Though stories abound that his medical emergency was ignored because of his race, he received prompt medical attention. He died on April 1, 1950 from injuries resulting from the accident.

Drew gained much recognition during his lifetime: He was named Diplomate of Surgery by the American Board of Surgery in 1941; was a recipient of the Spingarn Medal from the NAACP (1944); was granted honorary Doctor of Science degrees from Virginia State College (1945) and Amherst College (1947); and was elected as a Fellow of the International College of Surgery (1946).

—ROBERT C. HAYDEN

DU BOIS, WILLIAM EDWARD BURGHARDT

William Edward Burghardt Du Bois (February 23, 1869–August 27, 1963), historian, sociologist, novelist, and editor. W. E. B. Du Bois was born in Great Barrington, Mass. His mother, Mary Burghardt Du Bois, belonged to a tiny community of African Americans who had been settled in the area since before the Revolution; his father, Alfred Du Bois, was a visitor to the region who deserted the family in his son's infancy. In the predominantly white local schools and Congregational church, Du Bois absorbed ideas and values that left him "quite thoroughly New England."

From 1885 to 1888 he attended Fisk University in Nashville, where he first encountered the harsher forms of racism. After earning a B.A. (1888) at Fisk, he attended Harvard University, where he took another B.A. (1890) and a doctorate in history (1895). Among his teachers were the psychologist William James, the philosophers Josiah Royce and George Santayana, and the historian A. B. Hart. Between 1892 and 1894 he studied history and sociology at the University of Berlin. His dissertation, *The Suppression of the African Slave-Trade to the United States,* was published in 1896 as the first volume of the Harvard Historical Studies.

Between 1894 and 1896, Du Bois taught at Wilberforce University, Ohio, where he met and married Nina Gomer, a student, in 1896. The couple had two children, Burghardt and Yolande. In 1896, he accepted a position at the University of Pennsylvania to gather data for a commissioned study of blacks in Philadelphia. This work resulted in *The Philadelphia Negro* (1899), an acclaimed early example of empirical sociology. In 1897, he joined the faculty at Atlanta University and took over the annual Atlanta University Conference for the Study of the Negro Problems. From 1897 to 1914 he edited an annual study of one aspect or another of black life, such as education or the church.

Appalled by the conditions facing blacks nationally, Du Bois sought ways other than scholarship to effect change. The death of his young son from dysentery in 1899 also deeply affected him, as did the widely publicized lynching of a black man, Sam Hose, in Georgia the same year. In 1900, in London, he boldly asserted that "the problem of the Twentieth Century is the problem of the color line." He repeated this statement in *The Souls of Black Folk* (1903), mainly a collection of essays on African-American history, sociology, religion, and music, in which Du Bois wrote of an essential black double consciousness: the existence of twin souls ("an American, a Negro") warring in each black body. The book also attacked Booker T. Washington, the most powerful black American of the age, for advising blacks to surrender the right to vote and to a liberal education in return for white friendship and support. Du Bois was established as probably the premier intellectual in black America, and Washington's main rival.

His growing radicalism also led him to organize the Niagara Movement, a group of blacks who met in 1905 and 1906 to agitate for "manhood rights" for African Americans. He founded two journals, *Moon* (1905–1906) and *Horizon* (1907–

See also
NAACP
Universal Negro
Improvement Association

1910). In 1909 he published *John Brown,* a sympathetic biography of the white abolitionist martyr. Then, in 1910, he resigned his professorship to join the new National Association for the Advancement of Colored People (NAACP) in New York, which had been formed in response to growing concern about the treatment of blacks. As its director of research, Du Bois founded a monthly magazine, the *Crisis.* In 1911 he published his first novel, *The Quest of the Silver Fleece,* a study of the cotton industry seen through the fate of a young black couple struggling for a life of dignity and meaning.

The *Crisis* became a powerful forum for Du Bois's views on race and politics. Meanwhile, his developing interest in Africa led him to write *The Negro* (1915), a study offering historical and demographic information on peoples of African descent around the world. Hoping to affect colonialism in Africa after World War I, he also organized Pan-African Congresses in Europe in 1919, 1921, and 1923, and in New York in 1927. However, he clashed with the most popular black leader of the era, Marcus Garvey of the Universal Negro Improvement Association. Du Bois regarded Garvey's "back to Africa" scheme as ill-considered, and Garvey as impractical and disorganized.

Du Bois's second prose collection, *Darkwater: Voices from Within the Veil* (1920), did not repeat the success of *The Souls of Black Folk* but captured his increased militancy. In the 1920s, the *Crisis* played a major role in the Harlem Renaissance by publishing early work by Langston Hughes, Countee Cullen, and other writers. Eventually, Du Bois found some writers politically irresponsible; his essay "Criteria of Negro Art" (1926) insisted that all art is essentially propaganda. He pressed this point with a novel, *Dark Princess* (1928), about a plot by the darker races to overthrow European colonialism. In 1926 he visited the Soviet Union, then nine years old. Favorably impressed by what he saw, he boldly declared himself "a Bolshevik."

The Great Depression increased his interest in Socialism but also cut the circulation of the *Crisis* and weakened Du Bois's position with the leadership of the NAACP, with which he had fought from the beginning. In 1934, he resigned as editor and returned to teach at Atlanta University. His interest in Marxism, which had started with his student days in Berlin, dominated his next book, *Black Reconstruction in America* (1934), a massive and controversial revaluation of the role of the freedmen in the South after the Civil War. In

1936, Du Bois commenced a weekly column of opinion in various black newspapers, starting with the *Pittsburgh Courier.* He emphasized his continuing concern for Africa with *Black Folk: Then and Now* (1939), an expanded and updated revision of *The Negro.*

In 1940, Du Bois published his first full-length autobiography, *Dusk of Dawn: An Autobiography of a Concept of Race,* in which he examined modern racial theory against the major events and intellectual currents in his lifetime. In 1944, his life took another dramatic turn when he was suddenly retired by Atlanta University after growing tension between himself and certain administrators. When the NAACP rehired him that year, he returned to New York as director of special research. In 1945 he was honored at the Fifth Pan-African Congress in Manchester, England, and published a bristling polemic, *Color and Democracy: Colonies and Peace.* A year later, he produced a controversial pamphlet, "An Appeal to the World," submitted by the NAACP on behalf of black Americans to the United Nations Commission on Civil Rights. In 1947 came his *The World and Africa,* an examination of Africa's future following World War II.

One ever feels his twoness—an American, a Negro W.E.B. Du Bois; two souls, two thoughts, two unreconciled strivings, two warring ideals in one dark body, whose dogged strength alone keeps it from being torn asunder.

W.E.B. DU BOIS
THE SOULS OF BLACK FOLK,
1903

THINKER, WRITER, ACTIVIST

W.E.B. Du Bois, a Harvard-trained scholar and prolific writer, took on projects that reflected his passions: history, fiction, politics, and activism. PHOTOGRAPHS AND PRINTS DIVISION, SCHOMBURG CENTER FOR RESEARCH IN BLACK CULTURE, THE NEW YORK PUBLIC LIBRARY, ASTOR, LENOX AND TILDEN FOUNDATIONS

W.E.B. Du Bois's
The Philadelphia
Negro *examined the
history and present
condition of blacks
in Philadelphia.*

PAGE 541

*Abolitionism existed
in a tense love-hate
relation with
Abraham Lincoln
and the Republicans
in the 1860s.*

PAGE 3

By this time Du Bois had moved to the left, well beyond the interests of the NAACP, which generally supported the Democratic party. In 1948, when he endorsed the Progressive party and its presidential candidate, Henry Wallace, he was fired. He then joined Paul Robeson, who was by this time firmly identified with radical socialism, at the Council on African Affairs, which had been officially declared a "subversive" organization. In 1950, Du Bois ran unsuccessfully for the U.S. Senate from New York on the American Labor party ticket. Also that year, in another move applauded by communists, he accepted the chairmanship of the Peace Information Center, which circulated the Stockholm Peace Appeal against nuclear weapons.

Early in 1951, Du Bois and four colleagues from the Peace Information Center were indicted on the charge of violating the law that required agents of a foreign power to register. On bail and awaiting trial, he married Shirley Lola Graham, a fellow socialist and writer (his first wife had died in 1950). At the trial in November 1951, the judge heard testimony, then unexpectedly granted a motion by the defense for a directed acquittal. Du Bois was undeterred by his ordeal. In 1953, he recited the Twenty-third Psalm at the grave of Julius and Ethel Rosenberg, executed as spies for the Soviet Union. For such involvements, he found himself ostracized by some black leaders and organizations. "The colored children," he wrote, "ceased to hear my name."

Returning to fiction, he composed a trilogy, *The Black Flame,* about the life and times of a black educator seen against the backdrop of generations of black and white lives and national and international events (the trilogy comprised *The Ordeal of Mansart,* 1957; *Mansart Builds a School,* 1959; and *World of Color,* 1961). After the government lifted its ban on his foreign travel in 1958, Du Bois visited various countries, including the Soviet Union and China. In Moscow on May 1, 1959, he received the Lenin Peace Prize.

In 1960 Du Bois visited Ghana for the inauguration of Kwame Nkrumah as its first president. He then accepted an invitation from Nkrumah to return to Ghana and start work on an *Encyclopedia Africana,* a project in which he had long been interested. In October 1961, after applying (successfully) for membership in the Communist Party, he left the United States. He began work on the project in Ghana, but illness the following year caused him to go for treatment to Romania. Afterward, he visited Peking and Moscow. In

February 1963, he renounced his American citizenship and officially became a citizen of Ghana. He died in Accra, Ghana, and was buried there.

—ARNOLD RAMPERSAD

DUNBAR, PAUL LAURENCE

Paul Laurence Dunbar (June 27, 1872–February 9, 1906), writer. Dunbar, the child of ex-slaves, was the first African-American writer to attain widespread fame for his literary activities. Known chiefly for his dialect poetry, Dunbar also broke new ground in several ways for the further development of an African-American literary tradition.

Born and raised in Dayton, Ohio, Dunbar showed early signs of literary ambition. He served as editor of his high school newspaper, and at the same time began a short-lived newspaper of his own, the Dayton *Tattler,* focusing on matters of interest to the black community. Like most young black men, and despite a good school record, he confronted upon graduation a world with few opportunities, and had to take work as an elevator operator; but he also became increasingly dedicated to his literary activity, especially to poetry. Encouraged by several white friends in Dayton as well as by the noted popular poet James Whitcomb Riley, Dunbar published locally his first book of poetry, *Oak and Ivy,* in 1892. However, he achieved real fame in 1896, when an expanded and revised collection, *Majors and Minors*—also published mainly for a local audience—came to the attention of the prominent American writer William Dean Howells. Howells admired it and saw to the publication that year of a larger volume, *Lyrics of Lowly Life,* by the established American firm Dodd, Mead. It was the first of five major collections to be published by the company during Dunbar's lifetime.

Singled out for praise by Howells, and serving as the basis for Dunbar's fame, was his dialect verse. Fitting broadly into the popular, mainly white-authored, plantation-tradition literature of the time, Dunbar's dialect poetry created a sentimental portrait of African-American folklife in the antebellum South, treating a variety of themes, from love and courtship to social life and folk ideas. Although the dialect Dunbar used owed more to its literary antecedents than to actual folk speech, he also drew heavily on folk traditions for his own subjects and themes, and thus often succeeded in giving real life to the form, freeing it from the stereotypes that dominated the works of white practitioners. The publication of this work, together with successful public readings of it throughout the United States and abroad, made Dunbar among the most popular poets, regardless of race, in America at the turn of the twentieth century.

Dunbar's success with dialect poetry had a powerful impact on black American literature during its time. He had few black predecessors in the form—although such early black dialect writers as James Edwin Campbell and Daniel Webster Davis were his exact contemporaries—but as his fame grew, so did the volume of dialect poetry in African-American literature. It began to appear frequently in black newspapers and magazines, and few collections of African-American poetry over the next two decades lacked at least some examples of dialect verse. Many were dominated by it.

Dunbar himself was ambivalent about his success with the dialect form. He wrote a great deal of poetry in standard English, and felt that this was his most important work. Much of this verse is significant, especially for its time, as Dunbar not only addressed such contemporary issues as southern racial injustice and violence, but broke notably from conventions of piety and gentility that had earlier dominated poetry by black Americans. Still, it was the dialect poetry that critics, black and white, praised during Dunbar's lifetime, a fact that the poet found greatly frustrating. His frustration spilled over into a personal life marked by real difficulties, including problems in his marriage to the talented writer Alice Moore Dunbar, and the alcoholism and chronic ill health, culminating in tuberculosis, that led to his early death.

Although Dunbar made his reputation as a poet, his literary production during his brief life showed real diversity. It included a large number of short stories that appeared in popular magazines and in four major collections published by Dodd, Mead. Much of this short fiction complemented the popular dialect poetry, some of it written entirely in dialect and most of it featuring dialect-speaking folk characters. A few stories, however, moved in directions of protest, or of exploring issues of urbanization and cultural conflict. Dunbar also did some writing for the theater, including the highly popular musical comedy *Clorindy*, on which he collaborated with the composer William Marion Cook.

But some of his most important work, outside his poetry, lay in his novels. Dunbar published four novels; one, *The Love of Landry* (1900), was a sentimental work set in the American West, but the other three focused on questions of culture and identity in ways that allowed him to explore the issues affecting him as an individual and as an artist. These included *The Uncalled* (1899), tracing a young man's efforts to deal with pressures exerted on him to enter the ministry; *The Fanatics* (1901), a tale of Civil War-era Ohio; and *The Sport of the Gods* (1902), describing the travails of a black family forced to flee the South and to make its way in the more complex setting of urban New York. Only the last novel featured black protagonists, and it has often been considered the pioneering work in literary realism by a black writer. But all, excepting *The Love of Landry*, looked significantly and innovatively at the kinds of forces, cultural and psychological, that confront and constrain the individual in an effort to create a satisfying personal identity, and, at least implicitly, at the meaning of race in American life.

Dunbar's work has not always fared well in the hands of critics in the years after his death. Not without justification, many have found too much of the dialect work, despite the writer's efforts to the contrary, to be uncomfortably close to that of white plantation-tradition writers, contributing to the same stereotypes the plantation tradition helped to spread. But Dunbar's influence and originality remain important milestones in the subsequent evolution of an African-American literary tradition.

—DICKSON D. BRUCE, JR.

DUNBAR-NELSON, ALICE

Alice Dunbar-Nelson (July 19, 1875–September 18, 1935), writer. Alice Dunbar-Nelson was born Alice Ruth Moore in New Orleans, La. From her father, Joseph Moore, a sailor who never lived with the family, she inherited the light-colored skin and hair which enabled her to pass as white when she wished. Her mother, Patricia Wright Moore, an ex-slave who was part black and part Native American, supported the family as a seamstress. After attending public schools, Dunbar-Nelson graduated from the teachers' training program at Straight College (now Dillard University) in her hometown in 1892. In addition to her

See also

Literature

teaching, she worked as a stenographer and book-keeper for a black printing firm. She was interested in theater, played the piano and cello, and presided over a literary society. In 1895, *Violets and Other Tales,* her first collection of stories, essays, and poetry, was published.

In 1896 she moved with her family to West Medford, Mass. The following year she moved to New York, where she taught public school in Brooklyn while she helped her friend Victoria Earle Matthews found the White Rose Mission (later the White Rose Home for Girls in Harlem), where she also taught. On March 8, 1898, she married the poet Paul Laurence Dunbar, and moved to Washington, D.C., where he lived. Their romance had been conducted through letters. He first wrote to her after seeing her picture alongside one of her poems in a poetry review. At their first meeting they agreed to marry.

Although it was a stormy marriage, it significantly aided Dunbar-Nelson's literary career. In 1899 her husband's agent had her second collection, *The Goodness of St. Roque,* published as a companion book to Dunbar's *Poems of Cabin and Field.* The couple separated in 1902 and Dunbar-

DETERMINED EDUCATOR

After losing her job as a high school teacher for her political activity on behalf of women's and civil rights, Alice Dunbar-Nelson founded the Industrial School for Colored Girls in Marshalltown, Del., in 1920. PHOTOGRAPHS AND PRINTS DIVISION, SCHOMBURG CENTER FOR RESEARCH IN BLACK CULTURE, THE NEW YORK PUBLIC LIBRARY, ASTOR, LENOX AND TILDEN FOUNDATIONS

Nelson moved to Wilmington, Del., where she taught English at the Howard High School. Paul Dunbar died in 1906. In 1910 Dunbar-Nelson married a fellow teacher, Henry Arthur Callis, but that union soon dissolved. In 1916, she married Robert J. Nelson, a journalist with whom she remained until her death in 1935.

Dunbar-Nelson's writings, published continually throughout her life, displayed a wide variety of interests. After studying English literature as a special student at Cornell University, she published "Wordsworth's Use of Milton's Description of Pandemonium" in the April 1909 issue of *Modern Language Notes.* She also published several pedagogical articles, including "Is It Time for the Negro Colleges in the South To Be Put into the Hands of Negro Teachers?" (*Twentieth Century Negro Literature* 1902) and "Negro Literature for Negro Pupils" (*The Southern Workman* February 1922). The *Journal of Negro History* published her historical essay "People of Color in Louisiana" in two parts; the first appeared in October 1916 and the second in January 1917. From 1920 to 1922 she and Nelson published and edited the *Wilmington Advocate.* In addition, she wrote columns for the Pittsburgh *Courier* (1926, 1930) and the Washington *Eagle* (1926–1930) in which she reviewed contemporary literature and delivered political analyses.

In 1920, Dunbar-Nelson lost her job at Howard High School due to her political activity on behalf of women's and civil rights. That year she founded the Industrial School for Colored Girls in Marshalltown, Del., which she directed from 1924 to 1928. From 1929 to 1931 she served as Executive Secretary of the American Inter-Racial Peace Committee, a subsidiary of the American Friends (Quakers) Service Committee. She used this position to organize the National Negro Music Festival in 1929, and to engage in a ten-week cross-country speaking tour in 1930. In 1932 she moved to Philadelphia, where her husband was a governor appointee to the Pennsylvania Athletic Commission. Her lifelong interest in the African-American oral tradition prompted her to publish *Masterpieces of Negro Eloquence* in 1914 and *The Dunbar Speaker and Entertainer* in 1920. She was a member of the Delta Sigma Theta sorority and the Daughter Elks. Dunbar-Nelson is often considered a poet of the Harlem Renaissance. Her two most anthologized poems are "Sonnet" (often called "Violets"), and "I Sit and Sew." Her diary, published in 1984, is an invaluable source of information about her life.

—MICHEL FABRE

ROBERT S. DUNCANSON

Painter Transforms Landscape into Cultural Identity

Robert S. Duncanson (1821–December 21, 1872), painter. In this thirty-year career from the antebellum era through Reconstruction, Robert S. Duncanson progressed from being a humble housepainter to an artist of international stature who marked the emergence of the African-American practitioner into the Anglo-European art world. Duncanson was the first American artist of African descent to appropriate the landscape as an expression of his cultural identity. He was born into a family of mulatto freepeople who worked as painters, carpenters, and handymen in Fayette, N.Y. The family moved to Monroe, Mich., around 1830; there Duncanson apprenticed in the trade and then worked as a housepainter. By 1841 he had moved to Cincinnati, "the Athens of the West," to learn the art of painting. Throughout the 1840s he worked as an itinerant artist traveling between Cincinnati, Monroe, and Detroit painting portraits, historical subjects, and still lifes.

While working in Detroit, Duncanson received a commission to paint *The Cliff Mine, Lake Superior* (1848)—an event that altered the course of his career. The commission, from the Pittsburgh abolitionist Rev. Charles Avery, launched Duncanson's career as a landscape painter and established a lifelong relationship with abolitionist patrons. In this formative stage of his art, Duncanson was influenced by a group of Cincinnati landscape painters, including T. Worthington Whittredge (1820–1910) and William Louis Sonntag (1822–1900), to pursue the so-called Hudson River School style and create important early landscapes such as *Blue Hole, Flood Waters, Little Miami River* (1851; Cincinnati Art Museum). In 1853, he became the first African-American artist to take the traditional grand tour of Europe when abolitionist patron Nicholas Longworth sponsored his journey. Upon his return, Duncanson emerged as the principal landscape painter in the Ohio River Valley with such important pictures as *Landscape with Rainbow* (1859; National Museum of American Art).

At this time he and James Pressley Ball, a daguerreotypist, formed the nucleus of a group of African-American artists in Cincinnati who actively participated in the antislavery movement and created a monumental antislavery panorama that toured the United States.

In the months preceding the Civil War, Duncanson created the largest easel painting of his career, *The Land of the Lotus Eaters* (1861), which prophesied the imminent civil conflict. When he unveiled this vast tropical landscape, critics were moved to proclaim him "the best landscape painter in the West" (*Cincinnati Gazette*, May 30, 1862). Deeply troubled by the war, Duncanson exiled himself from the United States and traveled to Canada in 1863 on a journey to exhibit his "great picture" in England. Canadians warmly received the distinguished African-American painter without any reservations due to his race; he was therefore encouraged to remain there for two years, and contributed to founding a national landscape-painting school. He then toured the British Isles, where he was actively patronized by the aristocracy and where he extensively exhibited *The Lotus Eaters,* which English critics also praised as a "masterwork."

The success of Duncanson's second European tour crowned his career with international acclaim. Upon his return to Cincinnati in 1866, he began a series of Scottish landscapes inspired by English romantic literature, the finest being *Ellen's Isle, Loch Katrine* (1870). In his final years the artist suffered a tragic dementia, perhaps caused by lead poisoning, that led him to believe that he was possessed by the spirit of a master painter. His illness, combined with the pressures of racial oppression and his lofty artistic ambitions, proved too great for the artist to manage; he collapsed while hanging an exhibition in October 1872, dying in a Detroit sanatorium shortly thereafter.

—JOSEPH D. KETNER

DUNHAM, KATHERINE

Katherine Dunham (June 22, 1909–), choreographer and dancer. Born in Chicago, and raised in Joliet, Ill., Katherine Dunham did not begin formal dance training until her late teens. In Chicago she studied with Ludmilla Speranzeva and Mark Turbyfill, and danced her first leading role in Ruth Page's ballet *La Guiablesse* in 1933. She attended the University of Chicago on scholarship (B.A., Social Anthropology, 1936), where she was inspired by the work of anthropologists Robert Redfield and Melville Herskovits, who stressed the importance of the survival of African culture and ritual in understanding African-American culture. While in college she taught youngsters' dance classes and gave recitals in a Chicago storefront, calling her student company, founded in

See also
Jean-Michel Basquiat

197

1931, "Ballet Nègre." Awarded a Rosenwald Travel Fellowship in 1936 for her combined expertise in dance and anthropology, she departed after graduation for the West Indies (Jamaica, Trinidad, Cuba, Haiti, Martinique) to do field research in anthropology and dance. Combining her two interests, she linked the function and form of Caribbean dance and ritual to their African progenitors.

The West Indian experience changed forever the focus of Dunham's life (eventually she would live in Haiti half of the time and become a priestess in the *vodoun* religion), and caused a profound shift in her career. This initial fieldwork provided the nucleus for future researches and began a lifelong involvement with the people and dance of Haiti. From this Dunham generated her master's thesis (Northwestern University, 1947) and more fieldwork. She lectured widely, published numerous articles, and wrote three books about her observations: *Journey to Accompong* (1946), *The Dances of Haiti* (her master's thesis, published in 1947), and *Island Possessed* (1969), underscoring how African religions and rituals adapted to the New World.

And, importantly for the development of modern dance, her fieldwork began her investigations into a vocabulary of movement that would form the core of the Katherine Dunham Technique.

What Dunham gave modern dance was a coherent lexicon of African and Caribbean styles of movement—a flexible torso and spine, articulated pelvis and isolation of the limbs, a polyrhythmic strategy of moving—which she integrated with techniques of ballet and modern dance.

When she returned to Chicago in late 1937, Dunham founded the Negro Dance Group, a company of black artists dedicated to presenting aspects of African-American and African-Caribbean dance. Immediately she began incorporating the dances she had learned into her choreography. Invited in 1937 to be part of a notable New York City concert, *Negro Dance Evening*, she premiered "Haitian Suite," excerpted from choreography she was developing for the longer *L'Ag'Ya*. In 1937–1938 as dance director of the Negro Unit of the Federal Theater Project in Chicago, she made dances for *Emperor Jones* and *Run Lil' Chillun*, and presented her first version of *L'Ag'Ya* on January 27, 1938. Based on a Martinique folktale (ag'ya is a Martinique fighting dance), *L'Ag'Ya* is a seminal work, displaying Dunham's blend of exciting dance-drama and authentic African-Caribbean material.

Dunham moved her company to New York City in 1939, where she became dance director of the New York Labor Stage, choreographing the labor-union musical *Pins and Needles*. Simultane-

**KATHERINE
DUNHAM**

Katherine Dunham performs with the Stormy Weather dancers.
UPI/BETTMANN

ously she was preparing a new production, *Tropics and Le Jazz Hot: From Haiti to Harlem.* It opened February 18, 1939, in what was intended to be a single weekend's concert at the Windsor Theatre in New York City. Its instantaneous success, however, extended the run for ten consecutive weekends and catapulted Dunham into the limelight. In 1940 Dunham and her company appeared in the black Broadway musical, *Cabin in the Sky,* staged by George Balanchine, in which Dunham played the sultry siren Georgia Brown—a character related to Dunham's other seductress, "Woman with a Cigar," from her solo "Shore Excursion" in *Tropics.* That same year Dunham married John Pratt, a theatrical designer who worked with her in 1938 at the Chicago Federal Theater Project, and for the next forty-seven years, until his death in 1986, Pratt was Dunham's husband and her artistic collaborator.

With *L'Ag'Ya* and *Tropics and le Jazz Hot: From Haiti to Harlem,* Dunham revealed her magical mix of dance and theater—the essence of "the Dunham touch"—a savvy combination of authentic Caribbean dance and rhythms with the heady spice of American showbiz. Genuine folk material was presented with lavish costumes, plush settings, and the orchestral arrangements based on Caribbean rhythms and folk music. Dancers moved through fantastical tropical paradises or artistically designed juke-joints, while a loose storyline held together a succession of diverse dances. Dunham aptly called her spectacles "revues." She choreographed more than ninety individual dances, and produced five revues, four of which played on Broadway and toured worldwide. Her most critically acclaimed revue was her 1946 *Bal Nègre,* containing another Dunham dance favorite, *Shango,* based directly on *vodoun* ritual.

If her repertory was diverse, it was also coherent. *Tropics and le Jazz Hot: From Haiti to Harlem* incorporated dances from the West Indies as well as from Cuba and Mexico, while the "Le Jazz Hot" section featured early black American social dances, such as the Juba, Cake Walk, Ballin' the Jack, and Strut. The sequencing of dances, the theatrical journey from the tropics to urban black America implied—in the most entertaining terms—the ethnographic realities of cultural connections. In her 1943 *Tropical Revue,* she recycled material from the 1939 revue and added new dances, such as the balletic "Choros" (based on formal Brazilian quadrilles), and "Rites de Passage," which depicted puberty rituals so explicitly sexual that the dance was banned in Boston.

Beginning in the 1940s, the Katherine Dunham Dance Company appeared on Broadway and toured throughout the United States, Mexico, Latin America, and especially Europe, to enthusiastic reviews. In Europe Dunham was praised as a dancer and choreographer, recognized as a serious anthropologist and scholar, and admired as a glamorous beauty. Among her achievements was her resourcefulness in keeping her company going without any government funding. When short of money between engagements, Dunham and her troupe played in elegant nightclubs, such as Ciro's in Los Angeles. She also supplemented her income through film. Alone, or with her company, she appeared in nine Hollywood movies and in several foreign films between 1941 and 1959, among them *Carnival of Rhythm* (1939), *Star-Spangled Rhythm* (1942), *Stormy Weather* (1943), *Casbah* (1948), *Boote e Risposta* (1950), and *Mambo* (1954).

In 1945 Dunham opened the Dunham School of Dance and Theater (sometimes called the Dunham School of Arts and Research) in Manhattan. Although technique classes were the heart of the school, they were supplemented by courses in humanities, philosophy, languages, aesthetics, drama, and speech. For the next ten years many African-American dances of the next generation studied at her school, then passed on Dunham's technique to their students, situating it in dance mainstream (teachers such as Syvilla Fort, Talley Beatty, Lavinia Williams, Walter Nicks, Hope Clark, Vanoye Aikens, and Carmencita Romero; the Dunham technique has always been taught at the Alvin Ailey studios).

During the 1940s and '50s, Dunham kept up her brand of political activism. Fighting segregation in hotels, restaurants and theaters, she filed lawsuits and made public condemnations. In Hollywood, she refused to sign a lucrative studio contract when the producer said she would have to replace some of her darker-skinned company members. To an enthusiastic but all-white audience in the South, she made an after-performance speech, saying she could never play there again until it was integrated. In São Paulo, Brazil, she brought a discrimination suit against a hotel, eventually prompting the president of Brazil to apologize to her and to pass a law that forbade discrimination in public places. In 1951 Dunham premiered *Southland,* an hour-long ballet about lynching, though it was only performed in Chile and Paris.

Toward the end of the 1950s Dunham was forced to regroup, disband, and reform her com-

One becomes…an athlete of God.

MARTHA GRAHAM
ON DANCING

Several Alvin Ailey dances established precedents for American dance.

PAGE 24

In my honest and
unbiased judgment,
the good Lord will
place the Garden of
Eden in North
Carolina when he
restores it to earth.
He will do this
because he will have
so few changes to
make in order to
achieve perfection.

SAM J. ERVIN, JR.
*HUMOR OF A COUNTRY
LAWYER,* 1983

See also
Atlanta
Civil Rights Movement

pany, according to the exigencies of her financial and physical health (she suffered from crippling knee problems). Yet she remained undeterred. In 1962 she opened a Broadway production, *Bambouche,* featuring fourteen dancers, singers, and musicians of the Royal Troupe of Morocco, along with the Dunham company. The next year she choreographed the Metropolitan Opera's new production of *Aida*—thereby becoming the Met's first black choreographer. In 1965–1966, she was cultural adviser to the President of Senegal. She attended Senegal's First World Festival of Negro Arts as a representative from the United States.

Moved by the civil rights struggle and outraged by deprivations in the ghettos of East St. Louis, an area she knew from her visiting professorships at Southern Illinois University in the 1960s, Dunham decided to take action. In 1967 she opened the Performing Arts Training Center, a cultural program and school for the neighborhood children and youth, with programs in dance, drama, martial arts, and humanities. Soon thereafter she expanded the programs to include senior citizens. Then in 1977 she opened the Katherine Dunham Museum and Children's Workshop to house her collections of artifacts from her travels and research, as well as archival material from her personal life and professional career.

During the 1980s, Dunham received numerous awards acknowledging her contributions. These include the Albert Schweitzer Music Award for a life devoted to performing arts and service to humanity (1979); a Kennedy Center Honor's Award (1983); the Samuel H. Scripps American Dance Festival Award (1987); induction into the Hall of Fame of the National Museum of Dance in Saratoga Springs, N.Y. (1987). That same year Dunham directed the reconstruction of several of her works by the Alvin Ailey American Dance Theater and *The Magic of Katherine Dunham* opened Ailey's 1987–1988 season.

In February 1992, at the age of eighty-two, Dunham again became the subject of international attention when she began a forty-seven-day fast at her East St. Louis home. Because of her age, her involvement with Haiti, and the respect accorded her as an activist and artist, Dunham became the center of a movement that coalesced to protest the United States's deportations of Haitian boat-refugees fleeing to the U.S. after the military overthrow of Haiti's democratically elected President Jean-Bertrand Aristide. She agreed to end her fast only after Aristide visited her and personally requested her to stop.

Boldness has characterized Dunham's life and career. And, although she was not alone, Dunham is perhaps the best known and most influential pioneer of black dance. Her synthesis of scholarship and theatricality demonstrated, incontrovertibly and joyously, that African-American and African-Caribbean styles are related and powerful components of dance in America.

—SALLY SOMMER

DURHAM,
NORTH CAROLINA

Located in a north-central piedmont area of North Carolina, which includes much of the Research Triangle Park, Durham is the state's fifth largest city. In 1990 it had a population of 136,611, about 46 percent African American. A center of black enterprise, it is touted as a beacon of progressive race relations. Its significance is comparable to larger southern cities such as Richmond, Atlanta, and Nashville.

Durham was organized in the 1850s, in the middle of a slave-holding region, the antebellum hamlet boasting scarcely more than a post office and railroad station. Slaves and free people of color helped to cultivate its tobacco and other cash crops. Incorporated in 1866, it drew numerous black residents. Black life centered on the St. Joseph's African Methodist Episcopal and White Rock Baptist Churches.

By the 1880s, tobacco and textile factories and railroads began turning Durham into a model New South town. In 1890 the American Tobacco Company was formed. It soon controlled 75 percent of the national market. In 1898 blacks were hired in large numbers by tobacco factories. Soon after, black entrepreneurs established cotton mills, and in 1902 white tycoon Julian S. Carr opened a cotton mill with all black employees. Compared to many southern factory towns, which shunned black laborers, an unusual number of black Durhamites worked in factories.

A black middle class emerged. John Merrick, an ex-slave barber, bought the rights to the Royal Knights of King David, a fraternal order and used this framework to start an insurance business. After major white insurers like Prudential Life Insurance Company decided during the 1890s to stop accepting black policyholders, Merrick and several business partners formed a syndicate to develop the North Carolina Mutual and Provident Association, chartered in 1898. Mutual was unsuccessful at first, but under the leadership of Charles C. Spaulding it grew swiftly until it was the largest black-owned business in America. Its directors parlayed its capital and experience into other ventures, including drug stores, a real estate firm, textile mill, and the Mechanics and Farmers Bank, which opened in 1908. The black Durham elite was instrumental in founding North Carolina College (NCC) in 1910 (now North Carolina Central University). Commentators as diverse as Booker T. Washington and W. E. B. Du Bois wrote magazine articles hailing the development of black enterprise in Durham. By 1919, when Mutual declared itself the North Carolina Mutual Life Insurance Company, Durham had become virtually the "capital" of the black middle class, a term popularized by sociologist E. Franklin Frazier in *The New Negro* (1925). During the 1920s, the Bankers Fire Insurance Company, the Mutual Savings and Loan Association, and the National Negro Finance Corporation were founded there as well.

Despite Durham's reputation for interracial cooperation and economic backing from white businessmen, which buttressed black progress, Jim Crow remained strong in the city through the first half of the twentieth century. Health and labor conditions for black workers were poor. The Durham Committee on Negro Affairs (DCNA), a civil rights organization controlled by the black business elite, was launched in 1935. In 1942, the Durham NAACP, one of the state's oldest branches, joined the DCNA to support a meeting of southern black leaders at North Carolina College, out of which came the "Durham Manifesto" demanding the abolition of segregation in the South. Five years later, during the Journey of Reconciliation, an early effort by the Congress of Racial Equality (CORE) to test compliance with a Supreme Court decision against segregated interstate buses, Durham police beat and arrested freedom riders. In 1949, black parents won a school equalization suit against the city's board of education, although token school integration did not begin until 1959. The DCNA's voter registration efforts made it a political power.

In 1960, African-American students from NCC sat-in at lunch counters and forced city officials to take steps "quietly" to desegregate downtown stores. Student-led boycotts and mass demonstrations, assisted by Durham attorney Floyd B. McKissick, later head of CORE, led by 1963 to a fair hiring ordinance and nonracial admissions to policy at nearby Duke University. In 1968, Durham was swept by violent African-American protest after the assassination of the Rev. Dr. Martin Luther King, Jr. Black power advocates recruited hospital workers into unions and struggled to empower poor people. In 1981, black activists formed the National Black Independent Political Party. The DCNA, renamed the Durham Committee on Black Affairs, sponsored the election of blacks to various offices.

In the 1990s, one-fourth of Durham's black residents live in poverty. However, the city remains a hub of black capitalism. North Carolina Mutual is the largest black insurance company in America, while Mechanics and Farmers Bank and Mutual Savings and Loan are nationally prominent. Durham is also a cultural locus, home of the African American Dance Ensemble and the Thelonious Monk Institute of Jazz. In 1992, the predominantly black area of Durham was included in a newly drawn congressional district, and the city's first African-American Representative, Melvin L. Watt, was elected.

—RAYMOND GAVINS

See also
Franklin Frazier
Booker T. Washington

ECKSTINE, WILLIAM CLARENCE "BILLY"

William Clarence "Billy" Eckstine (July 8, 1914–March 8, 1993), popular singer and bandleader. Billy Eckstine was born in Pittsburgh, the youngest of three children. His family moved several times in his early childhood, and he attended high school in Washington, D.C., and later attended the St. Paul Normal and Industrial School in Lawrenceville, Va., and Howard University.

Eckstine began his career in show business as a singer and nightclub emcee in Buffalo, Detroit, and Chicago. In 1939 he was hired as the main vocalist for the big band of Earl "Fatha" Hines. While with Hines, he introduced Dizzy Gillespie, Charlie Parker, and Sarah Vaughan to the Hines band. After a number of hit recordings, including "Jelly, Jelly" (1940) and "Skylark" (1942), he left Hines in 1943.

In 1944 he organized his own big band, with personnel that included many up-and-coming bebop musicians, including Dizzy Gillespie, Miles Davis, Charlie Parker, Dexter Gordon, and Art Blakey. When, for financial reasons, he was obliged to abandon the band in 1947, he became a solo singer. His smooth baritone was particularly well suited for ballads. In the late 1940s and early '50s his popularity rivaled that of Frank Sinatra. He was one of the first black singers to transcend the race market and to become a national sex symbol.

Eckstine spent the next several decades as a performer in nightclubs, often accompanied by pianist Bobby Tucker. He also appeared in such films as *Skirts Ahoy* (1953), *Let's Do It Again* (1975), and *Jo Jo Dancer: Your Life is Calling* (1986). "Mr. B," as he was widely known, occasionally played the trumpet but was primarily known as a singer. He influenced several generations of African-American singers, including Joe Williams, Arthur Prysock, and Lou Rawls. He died in Pittsburgh.

—EDDIE S. MEADOWS

EDELMAN, MARIAN WRIGHT

Marian Wright Edelman (June 6, 1939–), attorney and founder of the Children's Defense Fund. The daughter of Arthur Jerome Wright, minister of Shiloh Baptist Church, and Maggie Leola Wright, a community activist, Marian Edelman was born and raised in Bennetsville, S.C. She attended Spelman College, from which she graduated as valedictorian in 1960. During her senior year, Edelman participated in a sit-in at City Hall in Atlanta. Responding to the need for civil rights lawyers, Edelman entered Yale Law School as a John Hay Whitney Fellow in 1960. After graduating from law school in 1963, she became the first black woman to pass the bar in Mississippi. From 1964 to 1968 she headed the NAACP Legal Defense and Education Fund in Mississippi, where she met her husband, Peter Edelman, a Harvard Law School graduate and political activist. In 1971, she became director of the Harvard University Center for Law and Education. She was also the first black woman elected to the Yale University Corporation, where she served from 1971 to 1977.

Edelman is best known for her work with the Children's Defense Fund (CDF), a nonprofit child advocacy organization that she founded in 1973. The CDF offers programs to prevent adolescent pregnancy, to provide health care, education, and employment for youth, and to promote family planning. In 1980, Edelman became the first black and the second woman to chair the Board of Trustees of Spelman College. She has been the recipient of numerous honors and awards for her contributions to child advocacy, women's rights, and civil rights, including the MacArthur Foundation Prize Fellowship (1985) and the Albert Schweitzer Humanitarian Prize from Johns Hopkins University (1988). Edelman has published numerous books and articles on the condition of black and white children in America, including *Children Out of School in America* (1974), *School Suspensions: Are They Helping Chil-*

See also

Jazz

203

EDUCATION

dren? (1975), *Portrait of Inequality: Black and White Children in America* (1980), *Families in Peril: An Agenda for Social Change* (1987), and *The Measure of Our Success: A Letter to My Children and Yours* (1992).

—SABRINA FUCHS

Before 1800, almost all slaves were largely self-taught. Free blacks—for example, the Maryland astronomer, surveyor, and almanac maker Benjamin Banneker—also acquired their knowledge from informal instruction and such printed matter as they were able to acquire. For many slaves, literacy began by finding a friendly white person, often a slave mistress or a generational cohort to the slave (and increasingly, after 1830, a fellow black) who was willing to give instructions in the rudiments of reading. This was usually followed by the careful and intense private reading and rereading of a selected text. At age twelve, Frederick Douglass purchased a copy of *The Columbian Orator* and proceeded to memorize its forms of speech in what was the first step toward his becoming perhaps the most gifted public speaker of his time. For slaves as for their white contemporaries, literacy began with the acquisition of a Bible or a copy of Noah Webster's "blue-black" speller, although the similarities between the ways in which slaves and other students acquired knowledge of reading (and of the even more dangerous art of writing) ended with these texts. For slaves the act was invariably covert. As a former slave related in an interview, many slaves could read but "de kep' dat up deir sleeve, dey played dumb lack dey couldn't read a bit till after surrender." Slaves developed elaborate strategies for hiding reading material from their masters; as Frederick Douglass noted, the fact that such knowledge was forbidden made its acquisition that much sweeter.

Religion

The dissemination of the Christian religion played a major role in providing both the motivation and the practical means for blacks, slave and free, to acquire an education. "The frequent hearing of my mistress reading the Bible aloud," Frederick Douglass wrote in his autobiography, ". . . awakened my curiosity with respect to this *mystery* of reading." In the Protestantism that most African Americans adopted during the antebellum period, great emphasis was placed on the

word of God and the biblical text as the center of the religious experience. Many slave owners questioned whether, given the admonitions against slavery in the Bible, a convert to Christianity could legally be owned. This problem was addressed in a number of colonial legislatures—in Maryland as early as 1644—and by various ministers throughout the succeeding two centuries; however, in every instance, a person's religious orientation was found to have no bearing on his or her status as a slave.

The conversion of Africans to Christianity did not take place on a large scale until the middle of the eighteenth century, when a movement known as the Great Awakening occurred. Many leaders of the Great Awakening, such as the white Virginian Presbyterian Samuel Davies, emphasized the need for black converts to read the word of God. Throughout the antebellum period a number of white religious leaders, including many staunch defenders of slavery, favored black literacy and the distribution of religious texts as a way of spreading the faith, and doubtless as a means of making slaves more tractable. White ministers, missionaries, and teachers initially believed that they could control the forms and purposes of black literacy; but the emergence of independent black congregations and denominations (which after the end of the eighteenth century usually had literate ministers) soon proved their hopes vain. Throughout and indeed beyond the antebellum period, the church remained a main arena for the advancement of African-American literacy. The ministry was a magnet for literate and ambitious young men, and most congregations tried to foster basic "Bible literacy" among its members.

Schools and Teachers

Not surprisingly, almost all formal education for African Americans in the North and South during the antebellum period was reserved for a small group of free blacks, comprising about 5 percent of the total black population. In New England and the mid-Atlantic colonies or states, schools for blacks became fairly common toward the end of the eighteenth century. Many were founded by abolitionist societies and Quakers. In New York City, the New York Manumission Society opened the New York African Free School in 1787. New Jersey Quakers had established schools for blacks in Burlington, Salem, and Trenton by 1800. Philadelphia had seven black schools by 1797. Schools stressing basic literacy were established over a wide range of places, including Newport, R.I.; Charleston, S.C.; Savannah, Ga.; Georgetown, Md.; Wilmington, Del.; Richmond, Alexandria, and Norfolk, Va.

Free blacks also opened a number of schools independently of abolitionist groups. In 1798, Primus Hall, son of the pioneer black Freemason Prince Hall, established a school in his Boston home. Catherine Ferguson, an ex-slave who had purchased her own freedom, opened a school in New York City in 1793. Maria Becraft opened the first boarding school for black girls, in Washington, D.C. Becraft later joined the Sisters of Providence, and by the 1830s, Roman Catholic teaching orders had established schools for black girls in Baltimore, Nashville, and New Orleans. Other late eighteenth-century and early nineteenth-century black mutual aid organizations, such as the African Union Society in Newport and the Free African Society of Philadelphia, also established schools. The elite mulatto Brown Fellowship Society in Charleston, S.C., supported two schools, one for the children of its members, another for darker free blacks and orphans. In Philadelphia in 1860, there were fixty-six private schools for blacks, only twelve of which were led by whites.

Schools for blacks were often underfunded, and faced other obstacles as well. In 1829 Daniel Payne, who later became the senior bishop of the African Methodist Episcopal Church, opened an innovative school in Charleston and charged his students fifty cents a month. But Payne was obliged to close the school in 1835, after South Carolina had tightened its restrictions against teaching blacks, and whites rioted against the free black community. In 1834 the building housing Noyes Academy in Canaan, N.H., was torn from its foundations and hauled into a swamp by local whites who objected to its integrated student body. Probably the most famous instance of racism of this sort was that encountered by the white Quaker operator of a boarding school in Canterbury, Conn., in 1833. Prudence Crandell lost all of her white students after she admitted a black girl. She then advertised for black girls to attend the school, and thereafter Crandell and the school faced violence by local residents and legal harassment by the state of Connecticut. Crandell refused to post bond and served time in jail. Though she was subsequently vindicated legally, Crandell abandoned the school after 1834.

The establishment of public funding for primary education raised a new series of questions concerning the funding and exclusion of blacks from public schools. Public funding for education began in the 1820s. In some states—as, for instance, Ohio in the 1830s—blacks were excluded altogether from common schools, and they had to fight for a share of tax revenue to establish their own schools in many cities and towns. From 1830 onward, black leaders were divided in their opinions as to whether African Americans should press for admission to the more prestigious and better-funded white schools, or establish public schools of their own. In 1847 Frederick Douglass led an unsuccessful fight for equal funding for a local black public school in Rochester, N.Y. Nine years later, the same black school was closed after the city fathers agreed to integrate the local school system. Lockport, a small New York State city on the Erie Canal, and the northern terminus of the Underground Railroad, chose to segregate its African-American population and the public schools in 1835. It was not until 1870 that the Rev. C. W. Mossell succeeded in renewing the black assault on Lockport's segregated schools. In a series of petitions to the Lockport school board, then to the New York State Superintendent, Mossell, joined by others in the black community, reminded the school board that it was "extravagant to continue the school."

In 1876 the black school "quietly closed its doors and blacks entered the public schools without a murmur of protest from the white community." The most publicized and protracted fight for educational integration of the antebellum period was carried out by prominent black and white abolitionists in Boston, who succeeded in integrating Massachusetts public schools in 1855, after a decade-long struggle.

The Civil War, Emancipation, and the First Schools

In the first half of the nineteenth century, the proliferation of numerous mutual aid societies, fraternal organizations, and black-owned libraries and reading rooms all promoted African-American literacy and education, as did the emergence of the black press and black publishing houses. The hundreds of slave narratives published in antebellum America, many proudly claiming "written by himself or herself," were, among other things, defiant assertions of the importance of literacy. These cultural developments, as well as the formal establishment of schools, contributed to the gathering sectional conflict over the status of slavery, which culminated in the Civil War.

So great was the need for literacy that efforts on behalf of African-American education persisted even after the country had erupted into war. Indeed, many of the roughly 180,000 black sol-

See also
Benjamin Banneker
Frederick Douglass

diers who served in the Union Army, a large number of them ex-slaves, saw army service as a way of acquiring reading skills. Classes were supervised by the army chaplain, and those who had some reading ability also served as instructors. A number of commanders reported a total reversal of illiteracy rates in their companies and regiments in a period of little more than a year.

The education of freed and runaway slaves who had not enlisted as soldiers also began almost immediately upon contact with the Union Army. Teachers worked in the many "contraband" camps that sprang up behind the Union lines. The earliest of these camps, established by Mary Chase in Alexandria, Va., on September 1, 1861, later became Hampton Institute. When a school for contrabands and freed slaves was established by the American Missionary Association (AMA) near Fortress Monroe at Hampton, Va. the AMA's Lewis Lockwood found that Mary S. Peake, a black Virginian educated in the private schools of Washington, D.C., already had begun a school for 45 children one month after Confederate forces had evacuated Hampton, Va., in September 1861.

Schools were created by the Union Army directly after taking control of rebel territory. One of the best-known examples is the school established on the Sea Islands of South Carolina, at Port Royal, which was captured by Union forces early in 1862. There, both white and black northern teachers—including Charlotte Forten, a black teacher from Philadelphia who wrote a widely circulated account of the aptitude of the freedmen as students—participated in what was termed a successful "rehearsal for Reconstruction."

In the aftermath of the Civil War, education emerged as one of the most prominent and basic concerns of the freed slaves. As Booker T. Washington wrote, "few people who were not right in the midst of the scenes can form any exact idea of the intense desire which the people of my race showed for education . . . it was a whole race trying to go to school. . . . Few were too young, and none too old, to make the attempt." Although many expressed a great interest in reading the Bible, students also saw literacy as the key to full citizenship. Their passion for education remained unchanged throughout the century after Emanci-

**CHURCHES
BECOME
SCHOOLROOMS**

This church in Gee's Bend, Ala., served as a classroom for pupils in 1937. Well into the twentieth century, churches were often transformed into classrooms because of inadequate funds for education and school construction.
PRINTS AND PHOTOGRAPHS
DIVISION, LIBRARY OF
CONGRESS

pation. It is striking how many African-American leaders in the succeeding century—Washington, W. E. B. Du Bois, Mary McLeod Bethune, Benjamin Mays, Alain Locke, and Anna Julia Cooper, to name a few—were educators. Perhaps the greatest tribute to the tenacity of African-American education is that by 1950, despite inadequate funding, the indifference or outright hostility of most government bodies, and the myriad indignities and injustices of southern segregation, 90 percent of African Americans in the South were literate.

The original Freedmen's Bureau Act of 1865 made no provision for education; however, the Civil Rights Act of 1866 enlarged the bureau's power in this area, and appropriated more than $500,000 for the building and repair of schoolhouses. The extensive educational system that the bureau then established became the framework for African-American common schools. By 1866 the percentage of ex-slaves attending schools in the South was equal to that of blacks in the North, and far above that of southern white students. There were 975 schools with more than 1,400 teachers for freedmen; the number of teachers jumped to 2,000 the following year. Most of the teachers were originally northern, female, and white; however, the Freedmen's Bureau devoted considerable energy to engaging African Americans, and by 1869 a majority of the instructors were black. Many of the whites involved in teaching had backgrounds in Abolition and church missionary work, and the underfunded educational efforts of the Freedmen's Bureau were supported by such secular abolitionist organizations as the National Freedmen's Relief Association of New York and the Indiana Emancipation League, as well as religious bodies such as the Scotch Convenanters Church and at least eight regional meetings of the Quakers. After 1868, reconstructed southern state governments also began to contribute to black education. Perhaps the most important alternative source of funding was the AMA, which supported the efforts of the Freedmen's Bureau in addition to establishing its own network of schools. Northern black denominations and organizations such as the African Civilization Society were also extremely active in sponsoring schools for the freedmen after emancipation.

However, many freed slaves, conscious of their lack of education and its relevance to their new status, founded schools without any prompting from outside authority. When John Alvord, the superintendent of schools for the Freedmen's Bu-

reau, conducted a survey trip to the South in 1865, he discovered that at least 500 schools had been independently established by the freed slaves. Not all of these schools were new; some served as continuations of schools that had operated secretly under slavery. In most areas, blacks were expected to supplement other sources with their own funds. By 1867, the direct and voluntary contributions of blacks greatly augmented, and in some cases far exceeded, the contributions of the Freedmen's Bureau in all southern states. Freed slaves also invested in their schools by purchasing schoolbooks, boarding and protecting teachers, and constructing school buildings.

Whereas the support of public or common schools through taxation had become a fixture of northern society, southern support of education was tenuous at best. Ex-slaves struggled to ensure the political survival of universal public education. As W. E. B. Du Bois wrote, "Public education for all at public expense was, in the South, a Negro idea." Numerous black Reconstruction era politicians made public education a key element in their political program, and joined with white members of the Republican Party to include a public school provision in the new state constitutions. Other literacy-related institutions, such as newspapers and printing operations, were established by southern African Americans at this time. "Freedom and school books and newspapers go hand in hand. Let us secure the freedom we have received by the intelligence that can maintain it," admonished an editorial in an 1865 edition of the *New Orleans Black Republican*.

Educating the newly freed slaves was a burden keenly felt by many northern missionaries who regarded education as a key means of regenerating the South. As one Illinois educator remarked in 1865, it was "now up to the teacher to finish the work the soldier had begun." Northern educators sought to inculcate in both white and black Southerners the Protestant values of hard work, sobriety, self-control, and piety. The schools they founded were based on the traditional New England model of liberal education. Arithmetic, reading, writing, Greek, Latin, history, geography, science, music, and philosophy were all included in the curriculum. In addition, missionary instruction was supplemented by moral teachings, biblical readings, prayer meetings, and other methods designed to shape the ethical as well as the intellectual development of black students.

Many of the missionary educators who went to the South to teach during this period did so at tremendous sacrifice. They frequently taught in

By the last decade of the twentieth century, African-American literature had become established as an important part of the curriculum in English departments.

PAGE 414

Without education, you are not going anywhere in this world.

MALCOLM X
SPEECH, MILITANT LABOR
FORUM, NEW YORK,
MAY 29, 1964

inadequate and dangerous conditions and faced indifference or hostility from most southern whites. Although they frequently showed a lack of understanding of the cultural background of their black students, most missionary teachers believed that African Americans were their spiritual equals, and considered education the first step toward achieving political and legal reform.

Colleges

Since the problem of secondary education for African Americans was largely ignored by the southern states, missionary societies concentrated increasingly on creating secondary schools. In the 1870s these societies began to address the need for institutions in which blacks could be trained as teachers; by 1895, more than forty colleges and sixty secondary schools for blacks, most of them supported by northern missionaries, had been established in the South.

Most of the so-called historically black colleges and universities (HBCUs) were founded in the years immediately following the Civil War, and almost all of these were founded by missionary organizations in the North. The American Missionary Association, affiliated with the Congregational Church, established Fisk University (1866), Straight University (1869), Talladega College (1867), Tougaloo College (1869), and Tillotson College (1875). The Freedmen's Aid Society of the Methodist Episcopal Church, North, sponsored Bennett College (1873), Clark University (1869), Claflin College (1869), Morgan College (1867), New Orleans University (1869), Philander Smith College (1877), and Meharry Medical College (1876). The mostly white American Baptist Home Mission Society was responsible for the founding of Benedict College (1870), Bishop College, Hartshorn Memorial College (1884), Morehouse College (1867), Shaw University (1865), and Spelman Seminary (1881) (now Spelman College). The Presbyterian-sponsored colleges were Biddle University (1867) (now Johnson C. Smith University), Knoxville College (1875), and Stillman Seminary (1876). Among the colleges founded by black denominations were Allen University (1880), Morris Brown College (1881), Wilberforce College (1856) (now Wilberforce University), Paul Quinn College (1881), Edward Waters College (1888), and Shorter College (1886), all organized by the African Methodist Episcopal Church. The African Methodist Episcopal Zion Church founded Livingstone College (1882), and the Colored Methodist Episcopal Church founded

Lane College (1879), Paine College (1884), Texas College (1895), and Miles Memorial College (1907). Black Baptists were responsible for the creation of Arkansas Baptist College (1885), Selma University (1878), and Virginia College and Seminary (1888). Three independent, nondenominational colleges were founded during this time: Atlanta University (1872), Howard University (1868), and Leland University (1870). Most African Americans received their higher education at the missionary colleges, despite the fact that these institutions acquiesced to segregation on campus and were controlled financially and administratively by whites.

Private, church-affiliated colleges were supplemented by state colleges and land-grant institutions. The first land-grant school, Alcorn Agricultural and Mining (A&M) College, was authorized in 1871. In 1890 the federal government passed the Second Morrill Act, which extended land-grant provisions to sixteen southern states. In many instances, black colleges were established solely to obtain funding for white colleges under the act. The financial resources of the state land-grant schools were even more limited than those of the private schools. However, unlike the missionary schools, the faculty and administration of the state land-grant institutions were predominantly black. By 1915, sixteen land-grant colleges for African Americans had been established, and almost every southern state supported some type of school for black higher education. Many of these institutions were normal schools, and had as their primary purpose the training of black teachers for a segregated primary education system.

Although this spate of college funding appears impressive, it gives a misleading impression of the state of black collegiate education in the post-emancipation period. Most of these colleges and universities were institutes of higher education in name only; very few actually taught courses at the college level. For the most part, these colleges were used for secondary and/or remedial instruction. Many white Southerners feared that higher education would increase the political and economic expectations of African Americans and did all they could to ensure that black colleges obtained as little support as possible from state governments.

As of 1915, only 33 of the nearly 100 black colleges were able to provide college-level courses for their students. A number of early twentieth-century surveys, undertaken by persons of varying ideological perspectives, concluded that the net-

See also

African Methodist
Episcopal Church

work of black colleges was overextended. In 1900, W. E. B. Du Bois found a total college-level enrollment of only 726 students. Ten years later, in his book *The College Bred Negro*, Du Bois recommended reducing the total number of black colleges from 100 to 32 to strengthen and improve black higher education. In his view, the only "first-grade colored colleges" were Fisk, Howard, Atlanta, Morehouse, and Virginia Union—while Lincoln, Talladega, and Wilberforce served as examples of "second-grade colored colleges." Those who were more skeptical of black higher education, and wished to replace it with industrial training, reached even more sweeping conclusions. Thomas Jesse Jones, the director of the Phelps-Stokes Fund, visited and studied black institutions over a period of two years, and in 1917 published a two-volume survey that claimed that the only colleges worth saving were Fisk and Howard.

While these debates over state-funded institutions were taking place, private black colleges were forced to seek new sources of funding. The missionary societies had fallen on hard times, and by the end of the century their finances had been greatly curtailed. Their resources were replaced with those of new philanthropies, such as the John T. Slater Fund (1881); the Anna T. Jeannes Foundation (1907); the Phelps-Stokes Fund (1910); and the Carnegie Foundation, Julius Rosenwald Fund, and Laura Spelman Rockefeller Fund (all founded between 1902 and 1917). Unlike the older missionary societies, the newer philanthropies were predominantly secular in their goals and skeptical of the need for, and possibilities within, black education. Like many northern whites of their era, these philanthropical societies wished to bring about a reconciliation with southern whites; and in their eagerness to be sensitive to southern white concerns, they gave scant consideration to the feelings, needs, and aspirations of southern blacks. To be sure, some northern philanthropies—in particular, the Rosenwald Fund—continued to support serious intellectual work by blacks. Whatever their biases, they performed a vitally needed function at a time when neither the state nor the federal government showed a serious interest in the education of African Americans.

Industrial vs. Academic Education

Chronic lack of funding provided the backdrop for the late nineteenth-century controversy between industrial and academic training, as exemplified by Booker T. Washington and W. E. B. Du Bois, respectively. The concept of industrial education for African Americans was not a new one. Vocational education for artisans had long been favored by both black and white educators. For blacks, the need to acquire an education outside the discriminatory influence of craft unions was a necessity. In 1853, Frederick Douglass had favored industrial schooling as a means of overcoming this problem, and during the post-Civil War period his solution was taken up by such prominent African-American leaders as T. Thomas Fortune.

The kind of industrial education favored by Douglass was related to, but differed significantly from, the model of industrial training that became associated with Booker T. Washington. Douglass favored an industrial education that would enable black laborers to become competent in any skill they chose, even if their skills placed them in direct competition with whites. Washington's method, by contrast, consisted primarily in training blacks for teaching in segregated schools and for working in traditionally black occupations (such as agriculture and domestic service).

One of the earliest industrial schools was Hampton Normal Agricultural Institute (now Hampton Institute), founded in 1868 by Gen. Samuel Chapman Armstrong, a Civil War officer who had spent his formative years in Hawaii as the son of missionary parents. There, future teachers worked six days a week to learn "the dignity of labor" before going out to preach the values of hard toil to the South's future labor force. Many white people viewed this form of education as a means of ensuring racial harmony, since it provided blacks with useful skills without challenging the existing racial order.

In 1881 Booker T. Washington, Armstrong's most illustrious pupil, founded Tuskegee Institute (now Tuskegee University) in Alabama. Washington's role in African-American education, like his role in black history in general, remains extremely controversial. His stated goal for his students was to enable them to become economically independent and self-sufficient. Washington advised the Tuskegee students against openly challenging the status quo, and suggested instead that they become responsible citizens by seeking to establish themselves in a job or a trade. Thereafter, he asserted, white society would concede equality. While Washington was not opposed to academic higher education as such, he looked on it as a secondary task. "It is well to remember," he claimed in a speech in 1904, ". . . that our teachers, ministers, lawyers, and doctors will prosper just in pro-

See also
Underground Railroad

EDUCATION

Industrial vs. Academic Education

portion as they have about them an intelligent and skillful producing class."

Washington's great opponent in educational philosophy was W. E. B. Du Bois, the author of *The Souls of Black Folk* (1903) and a Harvard Ph.D. Du Bois, who had begun his undergraduate career at Fisk, was a strong supporter of academic education and the missionary colleges. He placed great emphasis on the importance, within

the African-American tradition, of creating what he called "the Talented Tenth," college-educated blacks who would assume leadership roles in the community. For Du Bois, the missionary colleges, and the northern missionaries themselves, had played a critical role in creating educated black college undergraduates. In 1918 Du Bois described the northern missionaries as "men radical in their belief in Negro possibility" who by 1900

TUSKEGEE UNIVERSITY

Tuskegee University was founded in 1881 as the Normal School for colored teachers at Tuskegee in Alabama's Macon County, as the result of a political deal made between local white politicians and Lewis Adams, a leading black citizen. In exchange for black votes, Arthur Brooks and Col. Wilbur Foster, candidates for the Alabama legislature, promised to seek state appropriation for a black normal school in Tuskegee. Adams successfully rallied black support, and on February 10, 1881, House Bill No. 165 was passed, ap-

propriating $2,000 annually for a black state and normal school in Tuskegee. The act prohibited the charge of tuition and mandated a minimum of twenty-five students to open.

Booker T. Washington was recommended to organize the school by his mentor, Gen. Samuel Chapman Armstrong, the founder of Virginia's Hampton Institute, although Tuskegee's trustees had specifically requested a white man. Washington had been Armstrong's best student at Hampton, where he fully accepted Armstrong's philosophy that the first step for blacks was eco-

nomic and moral uplift.

When Booker T. Washington arrived at Tuskegee on June 24, 1881, there was no actual school to open, just an appropriation and authorization by the Alabama state legislature. Before selecting a location, Washington met with local white supporters, toured the area to recruit students, and investigated existing living and educational conditions for Tuskegee's black population. Washington selected a shack next to Butler Chapel, the African Methodist Episcopal church on Zion Hill, where Lewis Adams was

CHEMISTRY 101 *Laboratories such as this one formed the basis of a tradition of scientific instruction at Tuskegee University. Booker T. Washington organized the school in the 1880s.* (PRINTS AND PHOTOGRAPHS DIVISION, LIBRARY OF CONGRESS)

had "trained in Greek, Latin, and math 2,000 men, and these men trained fully 50,000 in morals and manners, and they in turn taught the alphabet to 9 million men." Du Bois believed that college-bred African Americans would lead all blacks to an awareness of their full capabilities, and ultimately to equal status with the white population. While he readily acknowledged the faults of the black colleges, he nevertheless insisted on weighing these faults against their potential for creating a black leadership class.

The difference between the philosophies of education for the Negro that were held by Du Bois and Washington became the major source of the debate and enmity between the two Negro educators. Du Bois's major objection to Washington's philosophy was Washington's, and the northern abolitionists', efforts to educate Negro

superintendent, as the site for the school. The school officially opened on July 4, 1881, as a secondary normal school with thirty students.

By July 14, 1881, Tuskegee Normal School had more than forty students ranging in age from sixteen to forty, most of whom were already public school teachers in Macon County. As enrollment increased, Washington recruited other Hampton and Fisk graduates to teach, including Olivia A. Davidson (who served as lady principal from 1881 until her death in 1889 and who married Washington in 1886). He decided that a larger facility would soon be needed. He wrote to J. F. B. Marshall, the treasurer of Hampton Institute, and requested a loan of $200 to purchase a new farm site. While the school could not make such loans, Marshall personally loaned Washington the money, enabling him to make a down payment on the Bowen estate.

The Bowen estate, owned by William B. Bowen, was located one mile south of town. The main house had been burned down during the Civil War, leaving two cabins, a stable, and a chicken house. In keeping with his philosophy of self-knowledge, self-help, and self-control, Washington required students to clean and rebuild the Bowen estate while attending classes. By requiring such manual labor of his students, Washington was attempting to demonstrate that others were willing to help them—provided that they help themselves.

The money acquired to complete the payments on the Bowen estate came from many sources, including northern philanthropy and student fundraisers, such as benefit suppers and student "literary entertainments," organized by Olivia Davidson. Payments on the Bowen estate were completed in April 1882.

Washington's philosophy of industrial education made Tuskegee Normal School a controversial model of black progress. Washington supported the use of manual labor as a moral training device, and he believed that manual labor would build students' character and improve their minds. In implementing a program of mandatory labor and industrial education, Washington had four basic objectives: to teach the dignity of labor, to teach the trades, to fulfill the demand for trained industrial leaders, and to offer students a way to pay expenses while attending the school (although no student, regardless of his or her economic standing was exempt from this labor requirement). Washington also considered industrial education to be valuable because it trained students in specific skills that would prepare them for jobs. However, Tuskegee's graduates primarily became members of the teaching profession. Instructors also offered academic and normal courses in botany, literature, rhetoric, astronomy, and geography in addition to the much publicized industrial courses.

On April 1, 1896, Booker T. Washington wrote to George Washington Carver, an agricultural chemist who had just completed his M.A. from Iowa State College of Agricultural and Mechanical Arts, and offered him a position as the head of the agriculture department at a salary of $1,500. Carver arrived shortly thereafter and established the Agriculture Experiment Station, where research was conducted in crop diversification. Carver taught Tuskegee's students, emphasizing the need for improved agricultural practices and self-reliance, and also made a great effort to educate Tuskegee's black residents. He garnered national and international fame in the 1920s for his experiments with sweet potatoes, cowpeas, and peanuts.

Both Carver and Washington left a powerful legacy of manual and agricultural training at Tuskegee. Their educational philosophies had a lasting impact upon Tuskegee's curriculum and continued to influence the school's direction. After Washington's death in 1915, it had become apparent to many that Tuskegee's industrial training was increasingly obsolete in the face of rapid technological transformation in American business. The school thus entered a new era, shifting its emphasis from industrial to vocational education.

—LISA MARIE MOORE

◆ **Accredit**

To recognize (an educational institution) as maintaining standards that qualify the graduates for admission to higher or more specialized institutions or for professional practice

See also
Civil War

young people for menial jobs and "to farm land that they would seldom own" (Levering Lewis, 1993).

Historian John Hendrik Clarke counsels against taking sides in the Washington–Du Bois debate, since black people were in need of workmen and technicians as well as educators and politicians accountable to the needs of black people.

After 1900, as the influence of missionary societies waned, Booker T. Washington's theories were championed by most of the northern philanthropists. Washington was also supported by an emerging group of white middle-class Southerners who became known as advocates of the "New South." Both groups sought to maintain white supremacy through the creation of a literate and skilled black workforce that would increase economic prosperity without threatening the existing social structure. Hampton and Tuskegee became the well-funded showcases for industrial education. It should be noted, however, that however popular industrial education might have been with white philanthropists, neither the concept nor the institutions were popular among black educators or among southern blacks as a whole. As James Anderson points out in *The Education of Blacks in the South, 1860–1935,* academic education was in greater demand, and it, rather than the few highly publicized examples of industrial education, became the model for almost all of the hundred colleges established in the South.

The controversy between Washington and Du Bois was fueled by the positive reactions of white philanthrophists to Washington's educational views. In a climate in which scientific racism, doubts about the intellectual ability of blacks, and the acceptance of blacks as an inferior, politically negligible caste were nearly universal among the whites in power, the prospect of academic education for blacks was discounted as threatening or irrelevant. Consequently, funding for black academic institutions (e.g., Atlanta University) was curtailed, while Hampton Institute and Tuskegee garnered the larger share of the philanthropists' money.

However, philanthropical discrimination against black colleges, and such criticisms as those expressed by Jones in his 1917 survey, did not force black colleges to close, but led instead to an upgrading of their academic programs. Starting in 1913, accreditation agencies pressured many schools either to eliminate or to separate higher education from their secondary programs of instruction in order to be considered full-fledged colleges or universities. State teaching examina-

tions also caused a number of black colleges—including Hampton and Tuskegee—to introduce a broader liberal arts curriculum so their graduates could pass the teacher certification tests.

The faculties of many black colleges remained predominantly, at times exclusively, white through the end of the nineteenth century. In 1894 only one black faculty member was employed at Fisk, and none at Atlanta University. By 1915, black professors made up 69 percent of the faculty at Howard University, 58 percent at Clark University, 93 percent at Meharry Medical College, and 31 percent at Fisk. Still, most of the presidents of the black colleges were white, and some—who owed their positions to northern philanthropists—were vehemently opposed to political activism and social change. Fayette McKenzie, the president of Fisk after 1915, eliminated the black educators and northern missionaries serving on the Board of Trustees, closed the student government and newspaper, and refused to allow a chapter of the National Association for the Advancement of Colored People (NAACP) on campus. In March 1925 a student strike supported by the alumni, the national black press, and local black leaders forced McKenzie to resign. At Hampton in 1929, students forced the president to resign and demanded an academic curriculum. The unrest at these and other black colleges in the 1920s marked a crucial transition in the history of the HBCUs. By the 1930s the colleges were predominantly staffed and administered by black educators and had become increasingly self-conscious with regard to their African-American orientation.

Primary and Secondary Education

Due to the controversy surrounding the Washington-Du Bois debate on black colleges, little attention was paid to primary and secondary education in the late nineteenth and early twentieth centuries. The commitment to African-American education by parents, teachers, and students was not matched by southern state governments, which discriminated against black schools by underfunding them on a regular basis. In 1900 only 36 percent of black children in the South attended school, and of these, 86 percent went for less than six months per year. The gains in school attendance and literacy were fewer for blacks than for whites. From 1876 to 1895 black enrollment increased 59 percent, while white enrollment was up 106 percent. About one-third of all southern blacks were literate by 1900—a sign of both how much had been achieved through black education (from a 90 percent illiteracy rate immediately after the Civil War) and how much was yet to be done.

Not until the first third of the twentieth century did the majority of black children have access to elementary school. The economic depression of the late nineteenth century and the increasingly virulent racism of most southern whites had prevented further developments in the educational programs initiated by the freedmen and northern missionaries right after the Civil War. What little money was available for public education was spent on the children of poor whites. After 1900, philanthropies such as the General Education Board frequently merged their programs for white and black education into a combined southern education directive—a process that resulted, as Booker T. Washington charged, in money "actually being taken from the colored people and given to the white schools."

Following 1915, a "public" primary education system emerged through the support of local governments, white philanthropies, and black communities. The philanthropies often demanded that black communities pay a large portion of the school costs, through the levying of special taxes and the donation of labor, materials, and land. This practice, documented by Richard R. Wright, Jr., in *Self-Help in Negro Education* (1909), demonstrated yet again the sacrifices African Americans were willing to make for education. Of all the philanthropies, the Rosenwald Fund was the most active in establishing common schools. Between 1913 and 1935, 15 percent of the total costs for school construction in the South were provided by the Rosenwald Fund, and 17 percent were covered by blacks themselves.

While state governments contributed, albeit meagerly and with reluctance, to primary schools, they made a concerted effort to prevent the building of high schools for African Americans. In 1934, 54 percent of southern white children attended high school, as compared to 18 percent of black youth in the South. There were almost no high schools in rural areas until 1915. That blacks were being denied educational opportunities was made clear in the case of *Cumming* v. *School Board of Richmond County, Georgia,* heard by the U.S. Supreme Court in 1899. Upon the closing of the only black high school in the county, local black residents sued for equal segregated facilities. The courts ruled against the plaintiffs, despite the precedent set by the 1896 *Plessy* v. *Ferguson* decision, which upheld the segregation of railway carriages on interstate lines but asserted that blacks

and whites should be accommodated on "separate but equal" terms. A black high school did not reopen in Richmond County until 1945.

In the South as a whole, the building of black high schools did not begin in earnest until 1920. Southern governments and northern philanthropists were determined to develop curricula that would train black youth to become laborers, although in many cases blacks managed to have an academic regimen included in the school programs. County normal schools, modeled on the Hampton and Tuskegee institutions, were cited as an alternative to academic normal schools by most philanthropies until 1930, after which these county normal schools either died out or were converted into public high schools.

Preparatory Elementary and Secondary Schools Founded by African-American Women

In the late nineteenth century and early twentieth century as blacks were migrating from the South to the North, four prominent African-American women founded elementary and secondary preparatory schools for black youths. The schools existed over long periods of time and successfully educated generations of black students.

The Haines Normal and Industrial Institute was chartered in 1886 and closed in 1949. It was founded by Lucy Craft Laney, the seventh of ten children in a slave family. Lucy Craft Laney was educated by a daughter of the Campbells, a slaveholding family. Later she graduated from Ballard Normal School and, aided by the American Missionary Association, entered Atlanta University, graduating in 1873. For the next ten years she taught in the public schools of several Georgia towns and cities, including Augusta and Savannah.

With the support and help of the Presbyterian Board of Missions, Lucy Craft Laney opened a school in a lecture room of the Christ Presbyterian Church in Augusta. In 1886, the school was chartered by the state of Georgia. By 1931, Haines Institute had grown to 27 teachers, 300 high school students, and 413 elementary school students. Mary McLeod Bethune began her teaching career at Haines Institute.

The Palmer Memorial Institute (1902–1971) was founded by Charlotte Hawkins Brown, an educator and civil rights activist. Charlotte Hawkins was born in rural Henderson, N.C., to parents who had lived with a part of a white family called Hawkins. When she was about seven years old, the family moved to Boston. Charlotte was edu-

Where the press is free and every man is able to read, all is safe.

THOMAS JEFFERSON
LETTER TO CHARLES YANCEY,
1816

*Education...is a
great equalizer of
the conditions of
men—the balance
wheel of the social
machinery.*

HORACE MANN
REPORT AS SECRETARY OF
THE MASSACHUSETTS BOARD
OF EDUCATION

cated in the public schools of Cambridge (the Allison Grammar School); she was an excellent student, and was chosen graduation speaker. She graduated from the Cambridge English High and Latin School, where the principal became one of her lifelong supporters. She wanted to attend Radcliffe College but her mother was not sympathetic toward Radcliffe, so she decided to prepare for a career in teaching and enrolled in the Massachusetts State Normal School at Salem.

Charlotte Hawkins began her career in teaching at Bethany Institute in McLeansville, N.C. She then returned north for further education at Harvard, Simmons College in Boston, and Temple University in Philadelphia. In 1902, seeking to help break down the walls of segregation in American life, she founded the Palmer Memorial Institute in Sedalia, N.C. The school became known for its emphasis on cultural education.

Charlotte Hawkins Brown also started the movement to establish the State Training School for Negro Girls in Rocky Mount, N.C. This school was organized into elementary, high school, and junior college instruction, with both cultural and academic courses. The campus was one of the first public interracial meeting places in North Carolina, in accordance with Brown's adamant opposition to racial segregation, which also resulted in her frequent ejection from Pullman berths and seats on southern trains.

The National Training School for Girls (1909–1961) was founded by Nannie Helen Burroughs, who had a long history of involvement in industrial education and throughout her life was associated with causes related to the African-American working woman.

In 1909 she founded the National Training School for Women and Girls in Washington, D.C. The school became well known for the emphasis Burroughs placed on spiritual training. She stressed the three "B's": the Bible, the bath, and the broom, which she regarded as tools for the advancement of the race.

The school continued to operate in its original format until after Burroughs's death in 1961, although in 1934 its name was changed to the National Trades and Professional School for Women. In 1964 the trade school curriculum was abandoned and the school was reestablished as the Nannie Helen Burroughs School, for students of elementary school age.

A tireless advocate of the education of African Americans, especially women, Burroughs also worked toward securing equality in the workplace for black women. She was a member of the National Association of Colored Women, which later became the National Council of Negro Women, under the leadership of Mary McLeod Bethune.

Mary McLeod Bethune founded the Daytona Normal and Industrial School in Daytona Beach, Fla., in 1904. The school is now called Bethune-Cookman College.

After serving in national positions under Presidents Calvin Coolidge and Herbert Hoover, Bethune became best known as an adviser to President Franklin D. Roosevelt, Eleanor Roosevelt, and President Harry Truman. Bethune was appointed by President Roosevelt to the directorship of the National Youth Administration. Well-known for her forceful speaking style, she became one of the most sought-after speakers of her day.

The Great Depression of the 1930s marked a turning point in the history of black education. The wholesale firing of blacks in menial positions in order to create work for unemployed whites demonstrated the futility of educating blacks for specifically "black" jobs. A growing militancy, which first found expression in the college disturbances of the previous decade, led blacks to demand control over the staffing and administrative policies of their institutions. In *The Mis-Education of the American Negro,* Carter Woodson criticized industrial education for shortchanging blacks and academic education for its failure to address the specific needs of black students, who were not offered courses in African-American history and culture.

The Educational Impact of the Great Migration

Beginning in the 1920s, blacks began migrating in large numbers to northern states and cities. In 1910, 90 percent of African Americans lived in the South; by 1970, only a bare majority resided in the southeastern and southern states. The movement north was part of a broader transformation from a largely rural into a largely urban population. Cities became the dominant dwelling places for southern as well as northern blacks. These two related migrations, from the South to the North and from the farm to the urban center, changed almost every aspect of African-American life. Migration from rural areas to southern and southwestern cities allowed many blacks to attend school for the first time. In 1910, 46.6 percent of all black children between ages ten and fifteen were working in agriculture, domestic employment, or industry, as compared to 14.3 percent of whites. By 1930, the figures for blacks had dropped to 16.1 percent. Not until 1930 did the percentage of fourteen- and fifteen-year-old blacks attending school reach 78.1 percent, a level approximating that which white children had reached (77.4 percent) two decades earlier. Southern educational authorities, fearful of rural depopulation, started more and somewhat better-funded schools in rural areas after 1915, in hopes of enticing African Americans to stay. (Nonetheless, these new schools remained segregated, underfunded, and were inferior to the schools established for whites.)

Integrated education was possible for those blacks who left the South for the North. By 1910, seven northern states prohibited segregated schools: Illinois, Massachusetts, Nevada, New Jersey, New York, Ohio, and Pennsylvania. Within these systems, differential treatment of black students was hardly a rarity. Nevertheless, there was far less likelihood that black children seeking a fair opportunity for education would be met with instant opposition. The centralization of public schools in northern urban, industrialized areas not only promised lower costs per pupil (as compared to costs in the South overall, and in rural areas in particular) but also precluded the maintenance of racially separate school systems (though not of racially isolated schools).

For African Americans, education in northern cities was in many ways a vast improvement over what was available in the South. Because most northern cities were formally integrated, black students could obtain funding and term lengths that were equal to those of whites, and many were able to excel in this new setting. However, in spite of the fact that segregation was not *de jure* (as it was in the South), segregated housing patterns often led to *de facto* segregation and consequently, to the inequitable distribution of funds for predominantly black schools. Blacks were frequently encouraged to take vocational rather than academic courses. In integrated schools they sometimes faced hostility from teachers and fellow students, and were discouraged from participating in extracurricular activities. High-school dropout rates remained higher for blacks than for whites, and quotas—if not outright bars—limited black entrance and matriculation in northern colleges.

By 1940 the percentage of black students between five and twenty years of age who were attending school had risen from 44.7 percent (in 1910) to 64.4 percent, while white attendance had climbed from 61.3 percent to 71.6 percent during those same years. The median schooling completed by persons aged 25 was 5.7 years for blacks

and 8.7 years for whites. This discrepancy was accounted for by the fact that 41.8 percent of blacks had spent fewer than five years in elementary school, as compared to 10.9 percent of whites. By 1950 the percentage of blacks with fewer than five years of primary schooling had dropped to 36.2 percent; not until 1980 would there be a rough parity in the median number of school years completed by blacks (12.2 years) and whites (12.5 years).

During the middle decades of the twentieth century, the federal government became increasingly involved in African-American education. As part of his 1930s New Deal, President Franklin D. Roosevelt created the Works Project Administration (WPA), which developed literacy programs and hired black writers to participate in such special projects as documenting the lives of former slaves. WPA classes were attended by more than 100,000 African Americans. From 1936 to 1943, the Division of Negro Affairs of the National Youth Administration (NYA), headed by noted black educator Mary McLeod Bethune, aided hundreds of thousands of black students both in the North and in the still-segregated South. Bethune's was the first federal program to address the needs of black students by providing direct aid, and as such served as an important precedent for later federal educational assistance programs. The federal government continued to voice its support for African-American education throughout the 1940s, and in 1947 the President's Commission on Higher Education issued a report calling for the full integration of all colleges and universities.

Perhaps the most significant indication of the government's commitment to creating educational opportunities for blacks was the appearance of the 1947 report by the Presidential Committee on Civil Rights. The report, titled *To Secure These Rights,* charged the government with failing to eliminate "prejudice and discrimination from the operation of either our public or our private schools and colleges." After examining the seventeen southern states and the District of Columbia, the committee concluded that "whatever test is used—expenditure per pupil, teachers' salaries, the number of pupils per teacher, transportation of students, adequacy of school buildings and educational equipment, length of school term, extent of curriculum—Negro students are invariably at a disadvantage." A single example of these inequities is the disparity in salaries between white and black teachers in Alabama and Mississippi for the school year 1943–44: In Alabama, white

EDUCATION

The Educational Impact of the Great Migration

Her stunning success as a leader made Mary McLeod Bethune one of the most influential women of her day and a premier African-American leader.

PAGE 88

See also
Emancipation
Alain Locke

THE SUPREME COURT

The Assault of Social Science and Law on "Separate but Equal" Education

The U.S. Supreme Court case of *Plessy* v. *Ferguson*, which upheld segregation by establishing the constitutionality of "separate but equal" facilities for whites and blacks, was decided in 1896, but it was not until the late 1930s that segregation became a legal issue in the South. In the subsequent assault on segregation, the great majority of cases involved education, primarily because this was the area in which state-provided facilities were most patently and grossly unequal. Starting with *Missouri ex. rel. Gaines* v. *Canada* (1938), the NAACP Legal Defense and Educational Fund (LDEF) began to chip away at the foundations of segregation on a case-by-case, aspect-by-aspect basis. The rulings in *Gaines* and such cases as *McLaurin* v. *Oklahoma State Regents for Higher Education* (1950) and *Sweatt* v. *Painter* (1950) forced white institutions to admit black students into their graduate and professional programs because no comparable institutions for blacks existed; however, it was the landmark case of *Brown* v. *Board of Education of Topeka* (1954) that challenged segregation both in principle and as social policy.

Brown v. Board of Education of Topeka

The case brought to the U.S. Supreme Court by the NAACP Legal Defense and Educational Fund in 1952 was a consolidation of five school cases from the states of South Carolina, Virginia, Kansas, Delaware, and the District of Columbia. Named for the litigants in the Kansas case, the case challenged the legality of segregated public schools, and in so doing, the validity of the ruling in *Plessy* v. *Ferguson* in 1896 (Kluger, *Simple Justice*, 1976; Franklin and Moss, *From Slavery to Freedom*, 1988).

On May 17, 1954, the Court ruled for the plaintiffs, writing, ". . . in the field of public education the doctrine of separate but equal has no place. Separate educational facilities are inherently unequal" (Kluger, *Simple Justice*, p. 707).

The following year, on May 7, 1955, the Court issued its implementation order, directing the desegregation of all public facilities and accommodations ". . . with all deliberate speed."

—THOMAS K. MINTER AND
ALFRED E. PRETTYMAN

teachers earned $1,158 to black teachers' $661; in Mississippi, white teachers earned $1,107 to black teachers' $342. As the report noted, relatively little had changed since Du Bois cited very similar statistics in his 1911 work *The Common School and the Negro American.*

Sharing Responsibility: A New Federal Role

Despite the *Brown* decision, and the telling need for massive improvement in elementary and secondary education, the federal government showed a great reluctance to intervene in school desegregation matters. Indeed, President Dwight D. Eisenhower failed to support the opinions expressed in *Brown,* and in so doing subtly encouraged the segregationists in their efforts to limit its impact on state and local policies. However, in 1957 a crisis was precipitated in Little Rock, Ark., when Gov. Orval Faubus openly defied a federal court order by using the Arkansas National Guard to prevent the desegregation of schools. Faubus finally backed down and withdrew the National Guard, but it was promptly replaced by white supremacist mobs, who gathered to stop nine black students from entering the all-white Central High School. Eisenhower responded by federalizing the National Guard and ordering them to protect those students. In the ensuing case, *Cooper* v. *Aaron* (1958), the Supreme Court ruled that state authorities must uphold the *Brown* decision.

The Little Rock incident spurred the passage of the Civil Rights Act of 1957, the first new civil rights legislation since Reconstruction. The 1957 act established the United States Commission on Civil Rights, whose duties included the investigation and appraisal of situations that denied blacks equal protection under the law. Although southern senators managed to strip the bill of almost all of its federal enforcement provisions, its enactment marked the first attempt by the federal government to take responsibility for the protection of civil rights.

The real turning point in the establishment of a federal civil rights policy occurred with the passage of the Civil Rights Act of 1964, which allowed the U.S. attorney general to take legal action in achieving school desegregation and authorized federal assistance for districts desegregating their schools.

See also
W.E.B. Du Bois

President Lyndon B. Johnson's energetic support of the act preceded his administration's landmark Elementary and Secondary Education Act of 1965, authorizing federal assistance in providing teaching materials and special services for school districts with large numbers of poor.

The Elementary and Secondary Education Act of 1965

The Elementary and Secondary Education Act (ESEA) of 1965 was a landmark piece of legislation because its enactment marked a major incursion into state prerogatives and responsibilities for providing elementary and secondary education.

Although the federal government had enacted several statutes affecting the preparation of teachers in elementary and secondary schools and the development of new curricula under the National Defense Education Act of 1958, it had left control of elementary and secondary education to the states.

The passage of the Elementary and Secondary Education Act of 1965 formally established the doctrine of equal educational opportunity as a national priority and gave millions of dollars to state education and local education authorities (SEAs and LEAs) to use in specified ways under the guidelines of the five titles of the act.

Title I made available an initial allocation of $775 million for the education of children of low-income families (Keppel, *The Necessary Revolution in Education,* 1966). Though allocation of the money was under federal control, it was administered through the states. Title I was changed to Chapter I by the 1981 reauthorization of ESEA. Of the poor children served by Chapter I, an estimated 47 percent have represented the black urban and rural poor. Though an insufficient amount of money was provided to alleviate the "savage inequalities" in local funding between wealthy white suburban school districts and largely black and poor urban school districts (Kozol, *Savage Inequalities,* 1991), Chapter I of ESEA has provided increased educational resources for poor children.

Funds also were provided to strengthen state departments of education (under Title V) in monitoring the spending of federal ESEA allocations by local school districts and to encourage states to provide additional monies for the education of poor pupils. State money was to be used to supplement, not supplant, federal funds.

With the passage of these acts, the federal government obtained the fiscal and legal leverage necessary to overcome the massive resistance to desegregation in the South and in other parts of the country. In 1964, 2.3 percent of southern black students attended integrated schools; percentages increased to 7.5 in 1965 and to 12.5 in 1966. The U.S. Supreme Court's ruling in *Green v. County School Board* (1968), ordering the immediate desegregation of schools, succeeded in greatly accelerating this process. Whereas in 1968–69 only 32 percent of southern black students were attending integrated schools, 79 percent were attending integrated schools in 1970–71.

As *de jure* segregation was being brought to an end in the South, civil rights activists turned their attention to the *de facto* segregation persisting elsewhere. While some legislators insisted that *de facto* segregation represented only residential ethnic clustering, and argued against applying civil rights legislation to the affected schools, civil rights advocates noted a more than passing resemblance between the quality of education in largely black inner city schools and the inferior schooling to which blacks were subjected in the segregated South.

Beginning in the mid-1960s, a number of studies were undertaken to assess the overall quality of African-American education. As a consequence of Section 402 of the Civil Rights Act of 1964, the U.S. commissioner of education was required to provide the president and Congress with a report on "the lack of availability of equal educational opportunities for individuals by reason of race, color, religion, or national origin in public educational institutions at all levels in the United States, its territories and possessions, and the District of Columbia." The report, titled *Equality of Educational Opportunity* and delivered on July 2, 1966, concluded that "American public education remains largely unequal in most regions of the country, including all those where Negroes form any significant part of the population." It had been shown that, among minority groups, blacks were subjected most frequently and in the greatest numbers to segregation; when all groups were taken into account, the same held true for white children. Eighty percent of white first-to-twelfth-grade pupils attended schools that were 90 percent to 100 percent white. Segregation also held for teaching staffs nationwide: Where the races of teachers and pupils were not matched, white teachers often taught black children, but black teachers seldom taught white children. Finally, where integration existed, it involved the enrollment of a few black pupils in predominantly white schools, almost never the enrollment of a few whites in predominantly black schools.

African-American fraternities and sororities have differed from their white counterparts in their stress on political involvement.

PAGE 279

Separate educational facilities are inherently unequal.

EARL WARREN
BROWN V. BOARD OF EDUCATION OF TOPEKA, KANSAS, MAY 17, 1954

*Booker T.
Washington
remained the
dominant African-
American leader in
the country until the
time of his death
from exhaustion
and overwork
in 1915.*

PAGE 720

The study, which came to be known as the Coleman Report—after James S. Coleman, the Johns Hopkins University professor who headed the research team—found that minority students scored "distinctly lower" than the average white student on tests that measured such basic skills as reading, writing, calculating, and problem-solving. Moreover, findings indicated that "the deficiency in achievement is progressively greater for minority pupils at higher grade levels." Little wonder, then, that in metropolitan areas of the North and West, 20 percent of black students sixteen and seventeen years of age dropped out of school.

In 1967, a year after the Coleman Report appeared, the Commission on Civil Rights issued a report titled *Racial Isolation in the Public Schools,* which stressed that redistricting would have little impact on the *de facto* segregation of housing and schools in large parts of the country. Studies showed that 83 percent of white elementary school students were enrolled in all-white schools, and 75 percent of black children were enrolled in all-black schools. The commission highlighted the liabilities of educating children in racial isolation. Not only did black students achieve less than white students, but also the longer they remained in school, the farther behind they fell. Black students were less likely to attend schools with adequate libraries, strong academic curricula, and competent teachers. Furthermore, black children who attended desegregated schools performed better than those attending racially segregated schools. The commission also recommended that the federal government take action by establishing a uniform standard of racial isolation in schools, and that schools with a black enrollment in excess of 60 percent be judged unsatisfactory.

As a solution to the problem of *de facto* segregation, the Commission on Civil Rights proposed the creation of "magnet schools," which would attract students from a wider area to inner-city schools, and "metropolitan school districts," which would draw on both urban and suburban student populations. Although, in the case of small cities, magnet schools proved successful as part of a citywide desegregation plan, their effectiveness was extremely limited in large cities such as New York, Chicago, Los Angeles, and Philadelphia. In these instances, federal funding was provided at the outset for desegregation planning, but that funding did not cover the costs of constructing new schools or converting large older schools, or of the special programs, equipment, and transportation needed to accommodate all the students who wished to attend. In addition, many poor and minority children lacked the preparation required to pass the entrance standards established for the magnet school programs. As a result, only middle-class children, or the most strongly motivated of the poor, were able to avail themselves of the magnet schools in their system.

The formation of metropolitan school systems has proven even more controversial, and has faced stiff resistance from those who insist on the primacy of neighborhood schools. The intensification of urban-suburban segregation following World War II, when federal programs such as those offered by the Federal Housing Administration (FHA) deliberately encouraged the development of all-white suburbs, presented an insuperable barrier to the establishment of integrated metropolitan districts. In *Milliken* v. *Bradley* (1974), the U.S. Supreme Court declared in a 5 to 4 vote that a metropolitan plan for Detroit could not be enforced, since to do so would be punitive to suburban whites, who could not be held responsible for the *de facto* segregation of inner-city schools. However, in *Milliken II* (1977), the Supreme Court overturned *Milliken I* and granted federal courts authority over metropolitan desegregation "when the plans were remedial in nature" and where suburban residents had directly influenced the distribution of races in a particular area. In the appeal of a Delaware case brought by the Delaware NAACP's Louis Redding (*Evans* v. *Buchannan*, 1969, 1978), the Court ruled that Delaware's Educational Advancement Act (1968) had limited school district consolidation to districts with fewer than 15,000 pupils, thereby excluding the possibility of merging Wilmington with any other suburban district. The U.S. District Court found that the state of Delaware and suburban real estate interests had colluded in preventing blacks from moving into the suburban districts bordering on Wilmington. It was impossible, therefore, for the Wilmington school district (which was 84 percent black, 4 percent Hispanic, and 12 percent white) to be desegregated within its own boundaries. The solution proposed by Wilmington for desegregating New Castle County schools resulted in the merging of ten of the eleven suburban school systems in that county with the Wilmington school system into a single consolidated school district.

In a county as small as New Castle County, busing was not too lengthy, since no school destination was more than forty minutes away. The same did not hold true for other states and communities, where busing was opposed on the basis of distance and length of the bus ride.

Gary Orfield and colleagues, in a 1993 study on school desegregation, *The Growth of Segregation in American Schools: Changing Patterns of Separation and Poverty Since 1968*, names Delaware (Wilmington), North Carolina (large county-city desegregation), Virginia (large county desegregation), Kentucky (Louisville), Nevada (Clark County), Indiana (Indianapolis), and Colorado (Denver) as states that have large proportions of African-American students attending integrated schools. He cites metropolitan desegregation orders—usually city with suburbs, or city with adjoining county—as being responsible factors. "When examining the most integrated states for African-American students, it is obvious that there have been long-term impacts of court orders, particularly those that provide for city-suburban desegregation."

In 1995, the U.S. Supreme Court ruled that the U.S. District Court was in error when it held that ". . . Missouri and the Kansas City school system were jointly liable for having run a segregated school system that they had failed to dismantle" (*New York Times*, June 13, 1995, p. 29). The case was remanded to the lower court for solution.

The effect of the ruling was to absolve the state of Missouri of the responsibility for paying for magnet schools and higher teachers' salaries in Kansas City, the remedy that the lower court had prescribed in order to attract white students to the Kansas City schools.

In 1982 the state of Delaware, with permission of the U.S. District Court, was allowed to divide the consolidated school district into four districts radiating from the center of the city of Wilmington, but did not relieve the state of Delaware of the obligation to maintain racial integration across the districts. Now, with the Kansas City

SCHOOL BUSING

Integration Plans Incite Controversy in 1970s

Busing, the means by which white and black students were transported from their home neighborhoods to outside schools, became the most popular, and at the same time the most controversial, means of creating integrated school settings in northern cities. In the 1971 case of *Swann v. Charlotte-Mecklenburg Board of Education*, the U.S. Supreme Court voted unanimously to direct school authorities in North Carolina to achieve "the greatest possible degree of actual desegregation" by redistributing 14,000 of the 24,000 black students remaining in all-black or nearly all-black schools. The *Swann* case affirmed the Court's pledge, previously articulated in *Green*, to enforce desegregation posthaste, even if—as in this instance—it meant forcing students to travel to schools outside their own district. In the aftermath of *Swann*, many who had been stalwart in their opposition to *de jure* segregation in the South reversed their position and argued against busing in the North by charging that busing was an infringement on the authority of local school districts and on the prerogatives of parents. Arguments against busing ranged from pragmatic worries about the length and cost of bus trips, to principled concerns as to its effect on the children themselves, since those who were bused had to struggle to adjust in an alien and often hostile environment. The public controversy over busing, which Richard M. Nixon invoked as a central issue in his successful 1968 and 1972 presi-

dential campaigns, peaked in the early 1970s. In 1974–75, a series of violent riots by white residents of South Boston who objected to the busing of blacks to their neighborhood high school attracted national attention and demonstrated the extent of racial animosity in the North.

For many blacks, the busing controversy highlighted the limitations of northern liberals with regard to their commitment to integration. As Carl Holman, president of the National Urban Coalition, observed, "racism comes much more naturally, and to a much broader spectrum of whites, than we could have imagined." Sen. Abraham Ribicoff of Connecticut charged the North with "monumental hypocrisy" in a speech on segregation that he delivered to the Senate in 1970. Senator Ribicoff's home state, Connecticut, did not adopt a comprehensive statewide school desegregation plan until 1993, when metropolitan school districts came into being under the forceful leadership of Gov. Lowell Weicker. Attempts to end *de facto* segregation in the North, once *de jure* segregation had been terminated in the South, had a curious result. Statistics from 1971 show a clear predominance of segregated education in northern schools: There, 57 percent of all black students attended largely black schools, while the same might be said of only 32 percent of black students in the South.

—THOMAS K. MINTER AND
ALFRED E. PRETTYMAN

See also
Mary McLeod Bethune

In 1954 Chief
Justice Earl Warren
wrote for a
unanimous Court,
in Brown v. Topeka,
Kansas Board of
Education, *that in
the area of public
education "the
doctrine of 'separate
but equal' has
no place."*

PAGE 115

See also
Civil Rights Movement

ruling, the future of metropolitan solutions (city-suburbs or city-county plans) to help desegregate city school systems looks increasingly dim.

Dilemmas of Isolation and Integration

Two major migratory waves following World War I and World War II brought more than one million African Americans to the major cities of the northern, north-central, and northeastern United States.

After World War II, the movement of blacks into such cities as New York, Boston, Detroit, and Seattle was accompanied by an exodus of whites to newly created suburbs. Because of racially discriminatory lending policies and restricted neighborhoods (Bradford, 1993), it was difficult for blacks to gain access to suburban housing. Neighborhood organizational patterns and the absence of whites in the cities caused urban school systems to become *de facto* racially segregated.

The opposition to school busing by the white majority and the difficulty of proving that *de facto* racial isolation in the North was caused by state or local governmental policies or action brought a growing disenchantment with busing as a means of improving the educational opportunities of black youth.

In the late 1960s and early '70s, a number of black and white liberal educators began to examine the research reporting on the dramatic gains that early childhood education could have on subsequent schooling, as a means of ensuring successful learning for poor urban and rural children, white and black.

Head Start

Head Start, begun in May 1965 and placed in the federal Office of Economic Opportunity, became one of the most durable and successful educational initiatives of President Johnson's administration. It was the most prominent component of Johnson's War on Poverty. Enrolling preschool children aged three to five years, Head Start is a program for poor children—a racially and ethnically diverse group—designed not only to motivate them and improve their conceptual and verbal skills but to motivate parents as well, by involving them in the educational process and educating them as to their children's health and nutritional needs.

Opponents of Head Start claimed it did not bring about the results its creators had supposed—namely, that it would raise IQ levels significantly in as brief a period as eight weeks. In addition, it was feared that the educational advantages of Head Start would tend to "fade out" if they were not reinforced in elementary and secondary education. However, numerous long-term studies have demonstrated Head Start's effectiveness as a preschool program, and despite past and present political opposition, it has been retained as a model for educational spending for successive administrations.

Another preschool program, the Perry Preschool Educational Project, beginning in 1962 with an original group of 123 African-American preschoolers from poor families in Benton Harbor, Mich., has developed a research paradigm that has allowed the project to track the progress of the original group through the twenty-seventh year of the program. The results show greatly reduced rates of delinquency and adolescent pregnancy and higher rates of school completion than those achieved in the nontreatment group.

Community Control of Local Schools

The call for community control of local schools is a more controversial, but not radical, approach to improving education in low-income urban neighborhoods.

When the parents and community called for control of a new intermediate school, I.S. 201, in the East Harlem community of New York City, in whose planning they had participated since 1958, the parents and community reflected the participatory political atmosphere of the 1960s.

As a precedent, parent advisory councils were mandated and had a defined participatory role with professional educators and planners in many federal education programs. Secondly, parents and community representatives were often members of community action agencies and corporations; therefore, while recognizing the professional roles of teachers and school administrators, the parents in the I.S. 201 community sought a similar participatory role in the operation of their new school.

A two-year study by Dr. Kenneth B. Clark, a professor of psychology at City College of New York—who, with his wife, Mamie Phipps Clark, completed social science research that contributed to the landmark decision in *Brown* v. *Board of Education of Topeka* (1954)—had produced evidence of the significant decrease in academic achievement in the schools in the Harlem Community (*Youth in the Ghetto*, 1964; *Dark Ghetto*, 1965).

Black parents and community members maintained that black schools and black students had suffered gravely under a centralized school system that was unsympathetic to their particular needs.

As a means of improving the performance of black students, they suggested placing schools under the community's jurisdiction and allowing parents, in concert with administrators and teachers, to exert a direct influence on school organization, curriculum, staffing, and policymaking.

In 1958, in one of a series of planning meetings with school officials about the building of a new intermediate school in the East Harlem community, the superintendent of schools, Bernard Donovan, promised parents a role in naming the school and selecting the principal; he said the school would be integrated and would function as a magnet school.

In the fall of 1966, I.S. 201 opened; however, it failed to draw white students from the Bronx or the West Side of Manhattan. When this failure became apparent, and other promises had been broken, the parents and community demanded "control of the school" (D. Jones, 1966). Black groups in New York City and in other parts of the country mobilized to support the East Harlem residents in their call for community action. Preston Wilcox, an assistant professor at the Columbia University School of Social Work, had worked with the parents for many years and suggested that the opening of I.S. 201 should be regarded as an opportunity to experiment with a new approach to relations between the community and the public educational system.

In the spring of 1967, in response to the crisis at I.S. 201, city officials, with planning grants and the help of consultants from the Ford Foundation, created seven demonstration projects designed to "improve the instruction programs for children in the schools concerned by bringing the parents and community into a more meaningful participation with the schools." Three of the projects (I.S. 201; Two Bridges, on Manhattan's Lower East Side; and Ocean Hill-Brownsville, in the East New York section of Brooklyn) included intermediate or junior high schools.

In the spring of 1968, Rhody McCoy, the supervisor of the Ocean Hill-Brownsville project, ordered nineteen teachers and supervisors to report to the city's central Board of Education offices for reassignment. McCoy claimed that these teachers were unsympathetic to the educational reforms advocated by the local school board. His action prompted a power struggle between the Ocean Hill-Brownsville school board and the city teachers' union—the United Federation of Teachers (UFT)—which escalated when the UFT's

president, Albert Shanker, called a citywide strike. During the strike, teachers opposed to the UFT tried to keep schools open in Brooklyn and in other parts of the city, with varying degrees of success. Race relations in the city suffered considerably over the next two months as the supporters of Ocean-Hill Brownsville accused their opponents of racism, while the UFT, which was predominantly Jewish, maintained that community control advocates were anti-Semitic. The strike ended after the central school board dismissed McCoy and the Ocean Hill-Brownsville board. It was decided that local schools should not be given the right to transfer teachers; at the same time, however, it was acknowledged that a centralized system could not meet the students' needs, and plans to decentralize New York City's schools were passed by the New York State legislature in the fall of 1969. The decentralization law allowed for the creation of thirty to thirty-three districts of approximately twenty thousand pupils each. The central board retained control over the high schools and citywide educational programs; the community boards were given control over the elementary, middle, and junior high schools within their boundaries. The chancellor was given limited authority over the community boards (N.Y. Education Law, chap. 2590, 1969).

New York City's school system became a model for other metropolitan school systems throughout the nation because decentralization conformed to the requirements of the Elementary and Secondary Education Act of 1965. Title I of the act required organized parental participation—distinct from that of the schools—in the allocation of more than $2.6 billion in funds designed to assist economically disadvantaged children of rural and urban, white and minority groups alike. Despite occasional instances of corruption on local boards and the periodic failure of some schools to lift performance levels (measured by the Board of Education, New York State Regents, and SAT tests), this form of governance, overseen by an active citywide chancellor, continues to be favored in New York City by many parents, community members, teachers, and politicians.

The action of the I.S. 201 parents and community must be evaluated in the political context of the times. This was a period of government-sanctioned, and -aided, community participation in quality of life areas by poor people, mainly black and Latino. The areas of health and education were targeted as those that would reduce crime and welfare dependency. The process was disrup-

The United Negro College Fund, an alliance of forty-one black colleges and institutions of higher education, is a philanthropic enterprise established to fund black education.

PAGE 223

*The NAACP Legal
Defense and
Educational Fund
has been the central
organization for
African-American
civil rights
advances through
the legal system.*

PAGE 477

*Mary McLeod
Bethune's career is
testimony to her
leadership skills,
her commitment
to justice and
equality for
African Americans,
her unfailing
dedication to the
ideals of American
democracy, and
her philosophy
of service.*

PAGE 90

tive to the established structure of the school system but resulted in a school system design that brought the system closer to the people it served.

Milwaukee and Chicago are examples of other cities for which New York was a model. The Milwaukee school system was partially decentralized in 1993.

In 1988, the Illinois state legislature enacted into law the School Reform Act, the first in a series of bills designed to decentralize the Chicago public schools. In 1991, the Illinois legislature passed a bill which originated in the State Senate as SB10 and was enacted into law as Public Act 87-454. The legislation determined the governance of the Chicago school system, decentralized the Chicago public schools into local attendance units, or multiattendance units, and designated each Local School Council, previously established, as the policymaking body for each school. The authority of the Local School Councils included responsibility for budget making, for allocation of federal funds to federal and state programs, and for special education and bilingual programs. The design of each school council, the council's authority, and a prescribed mode of operation is described in the publication *LSC Council Sourcebook: Basics for the Local School Council (1993)*.

A declining commitment to integration, evidenced by the controversy over decentralization, was also manifested in federal policy during the Nixon presidency. Presidential adviser Daniel Patrick Moynihan suggested that the administration pursue a policy of noninterference in local affairs and racial matters, which he termed "benign neglect." Nowhere was Nixon's lack of commitment to desegregation more apparent than in the wording of his statement of March 24, 1970, that announced the allocation of $1.5 billion "to mitigate the effects of segregated schools." Although the allocation provided financial assistance to segregated minority school districts or "racially impacted" areas, no effort was made to address the problem of their segregation per se. In 1972 Congress passed the Emergency School Aid Act, aimed at funding minority students according to their special needs. The act supported desegregation in principle; but the passage of the Equal Opportunity Act in 1974 sharply limited the initiatives the federal government could take in ending *de facto* segregation.

Higher Education Since 1954

The *Brown* ruling, which paved the way for drastic changes in public primary and secondary

school systems, did little to change the funding and structure of historically black colleges, which continued to subsist on meager funds from state, federal, and private sources. Four years prior to *Brown*, in *Sweatt v. Painter* and *McLaurin v. Oklahoma State Regents for Higher Education* (1950), two cases involving the admission of African Americans to all-white universities for graduate study, the U.S. Supreme Court ruled that blacks were not receiving the higher educational opportunities to which they were entitled under the "separate but equal" ruling of *Plessy v. Ferguson*. The Court's decisions, which ordered that Herman Sweatt be admitted to the all-white University of Texas Law School, and ruled unconstitutional the treatment of George W. McLaurin, who had been admitted to the University of Oklahoma's doctoral program in education on the condition that segregation be maintained (he was obliged to sit in a separate row "for Negroes" in class, eat at a separate table in the cafeteria, and study at a separate desk in the library), anticipated *Brown* insofar as they implied that equality for blacks could not be attained under the segregated state-supported system of higher education. However, the rulings were narrowly applied, and neither law schools nor graduate schools made haste to welcome black students.

During the 1950s and 1960s, HBCUs persisted in their dual function of providing students with a college-level education and offering secondary-level curricula to compensate for the incomplete preparation most graduates of southern public schools received. An emerging generation of well-trained academics, including some whites, brought a newly sustained level of college instruction to many of these institutions. However, only three HBCU's—Atlanta University, the Interdenominational Theological Center, and Meharry Medical College—were devoted solely to graduate study. Meharry and Howard University remained the primary academic institutions for training blacks as doctors, while Howard and Atlanta were the only institutions offering a Ph.D. degree.

Throughout the 1970s and '80s, HBCUs continued to confront the unique problems of providing substantial compensatory education, building and retaining highly trained faculty at salaries lower than the national norm, and attracting student bodies large enough to keep them in operation. Nevertheless, the importance of these institutions increased significantly with the dramatic rise in black college attendance during these two decades. In 1972 an estimated 727,000 black stu-

AN EDUCATIONAL ALLIANCE

United Negro College Fund Unites Black Colleges

The United Negro College Fund, an alliance of forty-one black colleges and institutions of higher education, is a philanthropic enterprise established to fund black education. It was created during World War II, at a time when almost all black colleges were in dangerously poor financial shape. The Great Depression and wartime shortages had cut deeply into charitable donations, and many students were unable to pay their own tuition. In 1943 Tuskegee Institute President Frederick Douglass Patterson wrote an article in the *Pittsburgh Courier*, proposing that black colleges streamline their fundraising by uniting in a joint funding appeal. The next year, presidents of twenty-seven colleges met and agreed to support a united mass fundraising campaign, the proceeds of which they would divide among themselves. With the aid of donations from the Julius Rosenwald Fund and by the Rockefeller-based General Education Board, the organization, named the United Negro College Fund (UNCF) and based in New York, was founded. It was composed of privately supported (largely southern) black colleges, which authorized the UNCF to raise all funds for operating expenses such as scholarships, teachers' salaries, and equipment. Each college president agreed to serve revolving thirty-day terms leading UNCF efforts. William Trent, a manager trained at the University of Pennsylvania's Wharton School, was its first executive director.

In 1944 the UNCF inaugurated its first national campaign. It was an enormous success: the organization raised $765,000, three times the combined amount that its member colleges had collected in the previous year. Fueled by its rapid success, the UNCF soon grew, hiring a permanent independent staff. In 1951 the UNCF began a separate capital campaign, the National Mobilization of Resources, for the United Negro Colleges to pay for building and endowment funds, and raised $18 million in four years with the help of John D. Rockefeller, Jr. In 1963 the UNCF, with the support of President John F. Kennedy and the Ford Foundation, began an additional appeal for funds for long-neglected maintenance and expansion of campus physical plants, and raised $30 million in a single year.

In 1964 Trent resigned. As it struggled to redefine its mission and to promote the legitimacy of black college education in the face of mainstream university desegregation, the UNCF went through six presidents, beginning with Patterson, in the next ten years. The turbulence of the Civil Rights Movement scared away potential donors, and funding levels dropped.

In 1972 the UNCF was accepted by the Advertising Council, and television and radio advertising became a major avenue for fundraising. The UNCF's slogan, "A mind is a terrible thing to waste," became so well known it was featured in *Bartlett's Familiar Quotations*. Under the leadership of Christopher Edley (president from 1973 to 1990), the UNCF's annual campaign receipts went from $11.1 million to $48.1 million; its membership grew to forty-one colleges. In 1978 the UNCF inaugurated a Capital Resources Development Program, which raised $60 million for its member institutions, and a College Endowment Funding Program, designed by Patterson to reduce college dependence on federal funding for permanent expenses. In 1980 the UNCF also began a yearly fundraising telethon, "The Lou Rawls Parade of Stars."

In 1990 Christopher Edley resigned, and the following year, U.S. House Majority Whip William Gray III left his seat in Congress to become the UNCF's new president, underlining its importance in the black community. That year, the UNCF started "Campaign 2000," a drive to raise $250 million by the year 2000. With the support of President George Bush and a $50 million gift from media magnate Walter Annenberg, it raised $86 million in its first year.

The United Negro College Fund remains the premier nongovernmental funding source for historically black colleges. Its narrow goal of endowment fundraising and appeal to donors across the political spectrum has brought it a certain amount of criticism as a politically "safe" charity. However, its defenders have emphasized that quality black colleges remain a necessary alternative for students seeking higher education, and the UNCF's efforts have assured the survival and growth of these institutions.

—GREG ROBINSON

dents were enrolled in college and graduate and professional schools. By 1984 this number had risen to 1,274,000, an increase of 75 percent. Black enrollment in higher education programs continued to rise, reaching 1,477,000 in 1991—more than doubling since 1972. At this time, African Americans constituted approximately 11 percent of the nation's total enrollment. Of the

See also
Carter Woodson

*Education makes a
people easy to lead,
but difficult to drive;
easy to govern
but impossible
to enslave.*

1,480,000 pursuing higher education, roughly 89,000 were in graduate programs and 17,000 in professional schools. Of the 1,330,000 undergraduates, roughly 16 percent (213,904) were attending HBCUs. Also attending HBCUs were 31,085 white, 2,131 Hispanic, 2,009 Asian-American, and 388 Native-American students. While African Americans constitute 8 percent of the total enrollment of non-black institutions of higher education, white students now make up 13 percent of the total enrollment at HBCUs.

In 1992 the U.S. Supreme Court found in *United States* v. *Fordice* that HBCUs had received unequal treatment in Mississippi because the state had not eliminated its dual system of public higher education, first established under segregation. The ruling, which affected eighteen other southern states, had the same impact on public higher education that *Brown* had had on secondary schools; but where *Brown* had been enthusiastically received, *Fordice* elicited widespread skepticism and dismay. According to the Supreme Court, the state of Mississippi had failed to abolish segregation by retaining a system of higher education that favored predominantly white colleges and universities over HBCUs. The state's admissions and funding policies were called into question, as was the number of its institutions, since it was found that programs were being duplicated at white colleges and HBCUs, and that such duplications perpetuated segregation.

The *Fordice* ruling required that action be taken to end *de facto* segregation by integrating Mississippi's eight state-sponsored colleges and universities. At the same time, the Court held that HBCUs should not be accorded preferential treatment in the desegregation process if they intended to remain exclusively black institutions. Many legislators and educators feared that instead of protecting the constitutional rights of African Americans, the Court's call for integration would result in the dismantling of HBCUs in favor of the larger, better-funded, and more "comprehensive" state-sponsored predominantly white schools. The lesson to be learned from *Brown*, opponents to the ruling claimed, was that integration had not been carried out as a two-way process; on the contrary, African Americans had had to bear the burden of adjusting to, and being educated in, white-majority schools. The loss of HBCUs, which African Americans had struggled for more than a century to maintain, would mean the loss of a crucial aspect of their education and history.

In response to the *Fordice* ruling, Mississippi's Board of Trustees of Institutions of Higher

Learning proposed closing Mississippi Valley State, a predominantly black university, and merging the other existing black schools. Previously, the Mississippi Black Legislative Caucus had sought a special appropriation of $55 million for academic programs and school renovation at Mississippi Valley State, Alcorn, and Jackson universities; but they were forced to settle for $11 million after failing to obtain legislative support. A similar battle ensued in the Alabama legislature, where internecine competition between Auburn University and the state's two public historically black colleges led to the killing of appropriations of $38 million in educational aid. Decisions regarding the funding and closure of HBCUs continue to be contested as plans for desegregation are decided in these and other states.

The 1990s controversy over desegregation and the budgetary disputes in state legislatures have brought to light the financial inequities against which HBCUs have been struggling since their inception. Reductions in the 1990s in federal as well as state educational budgets have also contributed to the financial difficulties with which HBCUs must contend. It has been shown that HBCUs lag behind other institutions in their reception of specialized funds. For example, in 1990 a study published by the President's Board of Advisers on Historically Black Colleges showed that more than $1.5 billion in research grants had been given to five predominantly white colleges, while $330 million had been divided among 117 predominantly black colleges during that one year. As a means of challenging these inequities, the fledgling Institute for College Research and Development was established by a consortium of six HBCUs. The purpose of the institute, which is supported by the Office of Minority Impact of the Department of Energy, is to increase the number of research grants and thereby diminish the operating costs for these six universities.

The Resegregation of Public Education

The impact of these years on African-American children in elementary and secondary schools was increasing isolation, whether in predominantly black schools or in desegregated schools, and a decline in the quality of educational opportunity available to them. A statistical analysis based on a 1985–1986 study of the nation's large urban school districts of 15,000 or more students confirms a resegregation in education through ability grouping, curriculum tracking, special education, and discipline. In every case these result in the placement of most black students in lower academic level groups and few black students in the higher level, "gifted" academic groups. Black students are nearly twice as likely to receive corporal punishment or suspension; they are three times more likely to be expelled. A black student is 18 percent more likely to drop out of school and 27 percent less likely to graduate. "This pattern," say the authors, "is consistent with a denial of equal educational opportunities for black students" (Meir, Steward, and England, 1989). As desegregation was being achieved in the South, segregation increased in the Northeast, now the most segregated region in the country. Studies have shown that because of their racial isolation, black and Hispanic students in urban areas are much less likely to become computer literate—a fact that has serious economic consequences. According to the National Bureau of Economic Research, the inability to use computers accounted for nearly one-third of the increase in the earnings gap between blacks and whites during the period from 1976 to 1990.

Such problems are rooted in early education. Statistics from 1990 show that black fourth graders scored 28.6 percent lower than white fourth graders in all areas of mathematics. In that same subject, blacks scored 31.3 percent lower in the eighth grade and 30.9 percent lower in the twelfth grade.

A similar disparity exists in tests reflecting their command of historical information: In 1988, black students scored 15.6 percent lower than whites in the fourth grade, and 31 and 15.4 percent lower in the eighth and twelfth grades, respectively.

Disproportionate Assignments to Special Education for Black and Latino Males: Classification/Placement of African-American and Latino Students

One very significant failing of America's big-city school systems to serve African-American children adequately is the disproportionate assignment of African-American male children to special education classes, especially those for the mentally retarded and for the emotionally disturbed. This pattern of assignment applies also to Latino males and is found in almost every big-city school system.

Many children are placed in special education classes because they perform below their grade in reading and/or for behavioral problems, rather than for organicity. For most children, placement in special education leads to permanent classification, despite state and federal regulations that mandate decertification examinations every three years.

According to a 1991 report (Walter Stafford et al., *Cause for Alarm: The Condition of Black and Latino Males in New York City*, pp. 13–14), "Black males accounted for 28 percent of special education students (33,787 black males, 27,668 Latino males, and 14,309 white males)." Within special education programs, black males (and Hispanic males) were enrolled in two programs: for those with learning disabilities and for those with emotional disturbance. These special education placements are especially damaging to the educational progress of black males, because return to the educational mainstream is virtually impossible; therefore, such placements often lead black male students to drop out of school without sufficient education or educational credentials.

Jay Gottlieb and colleagues, in a 1994 study of special education placements in urban school systems, "Special Education in Urban America: It's Not Justifiable for Many," find that "for children who reside in inner cities, the vast majority of whom are poor and members of minority groups, special education referral, evaluation, and placement practices are not more effective now than they were 25 years ago" (p. 453).

These findings, despite the passage of P.L. 94-142 (1975), legislation generated by the Civil Rights Movement giving people with handicaps the right to be educated in public education and in "the least restricted environment," indicate that urban public school systems continue to misdiagnose and mislabel minority children, black and Latino, and place them in special education classes, when analysis of the placements "reveals the powerful effects of poverty among the minority groups that predominate in urban schools."

Many of these children are classified as learning disabled, a medically oriented categorical designation, to ensure reimbursement for excess costs and special education services and programs. Such assignments are not in conformity with state and federal regulations and demonstrate the necessity for additional reforms in special education placement policies by urban school systems nationwide.

The Gottlieb study concludes:

. . . the vast majority of children who are classified as learning disabled and placed in special education in many urban school districts are not disabled in the sense demanded by legislation and regulation. Instead, they are children who suffer the many ravages of poverty, not the

E

EDUCATION

Disproportionate Assignments to Special Education for Black and Latino Males: Classification/Placement of African-American and Latino Students

The system—the American one, at least—is a vast and noble experiment.

PHYLLIS MCGINLEY
THE PROVINCE OF THE HEART,
1959

See also
Reconstruction

least of which is its effect on academic performance. (p. 456)

African-American Teachers

The publication of *A Nation at Risk* brought a new focus on the nation's teachers as a critical resource in the performance of the nation's schools and students. Two special studies, *A Nation Prepared: Teachers for the 21st Century,* by the Carnegie Forum on Education and the Economy (1986), and *Tomorrow's Teachers,* a 1986 report of the Holmes Group (a consortium of deans of schools of education in large universities), critically examined the preparation and practice of elementary and secondary teachers. Both reports spoke to the past roles of minority teachers educating children in the nation's public schools, and to the need for minority teachers in the future.

As noted in *A Nation Prepared* and *Teaching's Next Generation* (1993), there is a need to prepare a larger number of minority group members to become teachers. Minority students, mainly black and Latino, represent a majority in twenty-three of twenty-five of the nation's largest cities, but the number of black teachers in the United States is only 8.6 percent. The percentage is expected to decrease to 5 percent if drastic steps are not taken in training and recruitment of black teachers.

By the year 2000, black and Latino students will represent the majority of students in the 25 central cities and metropolitan areas of the United States. The present teaching force is predominantly Caucasian. Many teachers will retire within the next several years, and will have to be replaced with significant numbers of minority teachers.

As the number of minority public school students is rising, the minority teaching force is shrinking in number. The Carnegie Report recognized the role that the historically black colleges and state black colleges had performed over the years in the preparation of teachers and teacher educators and proposed collaborative relationships. Both the Carnegie and the Holmes Group reports noted the need to recruit and prepare bright minority students for teaching, now that desegregation had opened many other career choices for them.

A new emphasis now has been placed on teacher preparation. It requires a "knowledge base" in the liberal arts, with concomitant emphasis on the quantitative subjects, and the development of "pedagogical skills": studies in human development and theories of teaching and learning,

the knowledge of discrete teaching technologies appropriate to a given subject, as well as knowledge and recognition of a range of student needs.

Throughout the nation, teacher education is being strengthened to meet new state certification requirements by collaborations among education and liberal arts departments in their own colleges and universities and by participation in regional and national teacher education networks.

Preteaching programs and collaborations between and among colleges and high schools are being developed to encourage and recruit students to the teaching profession.

The DeWitt Wallace-Reader's Digest Fund is a major private sponsor of programs to prepare and recruit new minority teachers.

The federal government is providing funds to the states under Chapter V of ESEA, and in separate block grant programs, under Chapter II of the same legislation, for minority teacher education and recruitment.

To be successful, the programs will have to prepare recruits at every level to pass the state examination for certification or the National Teachers Examination from the Educational Testing Service. Failure to pass the required examinations has presented a major barrier to minority candidates in the past.

Bernard Watson and Fasha Traylor express concern about the reform movement in teaching, specifically about the outcome of greater professionalization of teachers. While having no doubt that individual teachers will benefit from the "professionalization" process that the Holmes Group recommends, they warn that greater professionalization of teachers may not necessarily "result in an educational system that is accessible, responsive, and responsible to all American children."

Watson and Traylor offer two bases for this conclusion. First, conceptualization of the National Board for Professional Teaching Standards does not indicate that the board will attend to the specific needs of individual local school districts. Second, given the certainty that the system of rewards for acquiring greater professionalization will find its way into collective bargaining agreements (as they already have in some school systems), it is questionable whether these superbly prepared teachers will seek positions in the schools of minority communities in urban centers or in rural America (Watson and Traylor, "Tomorrow's Teachers: Who Will They Be, What Will They Know?" 1988).

If either the board or the teachers fail to respond appropriately, minority students in the na-

See also

Plessy v. Ferguson

tion's big-city school systems will not benefit from the professionalization of the teaching profession.

Following World War II, large sections of New York City, Philadelphia, Chicago, Detroit, and Atlanta had school subdistricts that enrolled a majority of African-American students. In the late 1960s, the growing percentages of African-American pupils in urban school systems, plus the call for community control of schools, intensified the demand for black administrators in system-wide positions, including the general superintendency.

By March 1974 there were forty-four city or county African-American superintendents, a superintendent of the Virgin Islands (by presidential appointment), and two African-American state superintendents of public instruction, one in Michigan and the other in California (Scott, 1980).

By 1975 Detroit, Washington, D.C., Chicago, Atlanta, and Wilmington, Del., had black superintendents of public schools. New York City appointed its first black chancellor (the title of the system-wide superintendency), Richard Green, in 1985.

The graduate schools of education of Harvard, Columbia, Atlanta, and Fordham Universities, several aided by the Rockefeller and Ford Foundations, among others, recruited to their existing doctoral programs, or developed special programs for the academic and professional preparation of minority candidates for systemwide administrative positions.

Though well prepared, minority superintendents faced the same order of financial and educational problems as did their Caucasian colleagues and predecessors: shrinking budgets, municipal overburden, decaying and asbestos-filled school buildings; and the perpetual problems of racial balance and the underachievement of large numbers of minority pupils.

Afrocentrism and Multiculturalism

A resurgent interest in and support of Afrocentric studies, in part as one form of antidote to alienation from education, has been challenged by some educators as divisive, while the perpetuation of an emphasis on Eurocentric studies is not considered divisive in a culturally pluralistic nation such as ours. But neither an Afrocentric nor a Eurocentric education provides us with the "core around which a truly multicultural education can be developed," Gordon argues.

With increasing frequency we are required, as citizens of our national society, "to function in more than a single language, adapt to the demands of more than a single culture, meet the behavioral demands of more than a single situation, and understand the symbols and rituals of people other than those with whom most of us have been socialized." It is from these multidisciplinary, multiculturalist, multiperspectivist learning experiences that competencies in critical analysis, critical interpretation, and critical understanding will allow for responsibly discharging future decisions and judgments. Gordon concludes that "no matter what core knowledge is chosen as the vehicle . . . educators are beginning to realize that the teaching of dogma (either hegemonic or resistant) is no longer appropriate for the optimal development of learners." ("Conceptions of Africentrism and Multiculturalism in Education: A General Overview").

Where multiculturalism emphasizes the diversity of groups within a particular culture, Afrocentrism insists on the primacy of an African-based cultural tradition. Proponents of this method argue that black youngsters must develop a strong sense of their African heritage if they are to survive in a hostile, white-dominated environment.

One Afrocentric approach is the creation of all-male, Afrocentric schools. Advocates of such schools point to the high levels of violence, and low levels of education, among many black males, and stress the benefits of instilling in young black men a sense of pride in their cultural roots.

The prospect of creating these schools has been hotly debated, with critics charging that a segregated environment would damage students by further alienating them from the cultural mainstream. Not only would the gender exclusive schools be ineligible for federal funding, but evidence suggests that many black male and female students have succeeded academically and developed positive self-images in racially integrated public schools (Clark, *A Possible Reality*, 1972; Edmonds, *Educational Leadership*, 1982).

American blacks have long been divided between Afrocentrist and American nationalist philosophies. Perhaps the time has come for a rapprochement between these two philosophical positions.

W. E. B. Du Bois, in *Souls of Black Folk* (1903), stated the dilemma of the African American: "An American, a Negro; two souls, two thoughts, two unreconciled strivings. . . ."

The dilemma Du Bois described will be resolved when the African heritage of the African American takes its rightful and respected place

What sculpture is to a block of marble, education is to an human soul.

JOSEPH ADDISON
IN *SPECTATOR*,
NOVEMBER 6, 1711

See also
Benjamin Mays

alongside the other cultures of this intercontinental, international, multicultural nation.

School Choice

There has always been choice in American education, usually divided into three major sectors: public, parochial, and independent. Until choice became an issue in national efforts to improve the academic performance of poor children in public urban and rural schools, the sectors operated as separate islands, with the "separation clause" of the First Amendment to the U.S. Constitution as the arbiter.

The First Amendment to the U.S. Constitution prohibits funding religious schools with public monies. However, according to some legal experts, the "wall" between church and state, private and public schools, has been breached by the "child benefit theory," which was devised by the conceptualizers of the 1965 Elementary and Secondary Education Act to allow funding of poor children in parochial and nonpublic schools, under Title I, now Chapter I, of the act (Hughes and Hughes, 1972).

Under this theory, providing federal money to private schools is legal as long as the money follows the child who otherwise would be eligible in public school. The federal money, or program, therefore benefits the child, not the nonpublic school. A sizable proportion of the American public favors providing public money to private and parochial schools. Rather than equity and access, the battle is being based on quality of education.

There is a general consensus that public schools in city school systems are failing to give poor, racially isolated, language-different students the quality education that will prepare them for a future in the technologically oriented world-society of the twenty-first century. By contrast, suburban schools and private and parochial schools with smaller student bodies (and in the case of wealthy suburbs, different funding formulas) are providing such education.

The implications of choice plans, public and private, are grave for black parents and their children in urban school systems. There is usually an additional monetary cost for the family, if only for transportation to a school in another district or community. At the extreme, the costs are great if the parent has to make up the difference between the public voucher amount and the tuition of the private school.

This is particularly troubling to African Americans who remember that tuition grants for funding private education was the device resorted to in

1955 by Prince Edward County, Va., in defiance of the U.S. Supreme Court's 1954 *Brown* decision. Under this arrangement a system of private schools for white students was established, but none for blacks. Does "school choice" amount to nothing more than a present-day analogue for Prince Edward County's gambit of 1955?

Some educators regard tuition grants or vouchers as flawed policy for dealing with the problems of public education. They argue that school choice allows for winners and losers, and that a national policy that assures there will be losers is unacceptable, unconstitutional, and unsound.

School choice can be exercised within the public schools or outside of public education. The latter is the smaller sector, with a relatively stable 10 to 11 percent of the nation's school-age children in private schools. This sector is augmented slightly by such experiments as Whittle Schools, driven by an interest in both quality in education and the profit to be derived from such educational ventures. A similar experiment is being carried out by Educational Alternatives, Inc., for a group of privatized Baltimore schools and for the public schools of Hartford, Conn. Privatization of public schools raises questions about the equitable distribution of resources and funding among corporation-managed and non-corporation-managed schools. Another important concern is making students and teachers a captive audience for a commercial enterprise paid for with public monies.

Choice within the public sector includes special programs within schools, school pairing (a limited choice), magnet schools, examination schools, choice among schools within a district (a wider choice), choice among districts within a system, and schools funded by business.

Whatever the form of choice, considerations including accountability and governance, effectiveness, equity, and the allocation of resources are inescapable. In matters of accountability and governance, will private schools receiving public money be held to the same accreditation, affirmative action, open records requirements, health and safety statutes (including insurance), and accountability reporting required of the public sector? What is the meaning of claims that "choice works," as President Bush said, when experimental studies over the past twenty years have shown little evidence that choice brings educational improvement, greater parental involvement, or increased pupil learning? With a number of researchers finding that in New York, Chicago, Boston, and Philadelphia choice in education worked to the detriment of low-achieving students, what are the claims to be made for it on the basis of equity? Is it fair that students with learning problems or limited proficiency in English be excluded from magnet schools or that students who simply are average achievers are informally or formally returned to their neighborhood school without recourse? What is to be done about the failure of these schools to educate a student body representative of those cities? Since, according to a wide range of cost estimates and investigations, choice will not be low-cost school improvement, what are the benefits the new investments will bring as a result of choice, that is, benefits that could not be more readily achieved through the expenditure of these new investments on public education alone?

There are those who argue that any such new investments in choice, particularly if it involves public/private school vouchers, violate the long-held belief in the "American social contract," which, it is claimed, makes the entire society responsible for the elementary and secondary education of its children and youth.

There can be serious debits to school choice for black children—and others among the rising number of racial and ethnic minority children—and their parents in urban school systems if, in the name of excellence, better students are siphoned off to magnet and private schools and all other students are dumped into public education. This, as is evident from the history of other forms of tracking, will spawn a self-perpetuating vicious cycle erosive of effective public education.

A number of new academic models have proven to work effectively for black students. The College Board's Equity 2000 project, which has carried out pilot programs in California, Tennessee, Maryland, Rhode Island, Texas, and Wisconsin, trains teachers and guidance counselors to address the special needs of poor and minority students, and maintains a curriculum that emphasizes algebra and geometry as the "gatekeeper" subjects for all middle- and high-school students. A similar and more specialized mathematics program, called the Algebra Project, initiated by Robert P. Moses in the Roxbury neighborhood of Boston, Mass., has been carried out successfully in California and Mississippi.

One of the most celebrated and successful models for developing effective schools was instituted in the New Haven school system by Dr. James Comer, a member of the faculty of psychiatry at Yale University. The School Development Program is a comprehensive school program that involves parents, mental health professionals, teachers, and administrators in a mutually sup-portive relationship that in turn drives the academic program and assessment in an improved school climate (Comer, 1980).

Each of the programs is skills-based and provides students with the confidence to draw on their personal experiences to understand and resolve academic problems.

It should be noted, however, that successful models for public education are few, and many public school systems continue to struggle with increasing limitations in financial resources, lower academic standards, lack of discipline, and escalations of violence.

Perhaps the clearest indication of the nation's disillusionment with public education is the currency of school choice—a "public" system that would offer a better education to a select few. This will not respond to a pervasive concern among the nation's parents that their children gain the skills and assurance they will need to sustain themselves in the competitive multinational economy of their adulthood in the twenty-first century. For African Americans especially, the prospects of quality education remain a problem of equal educational rights.

In big cities across the nation attention is being focused on the improvement of public education at all levels. In New York, Chicago, and Philadelphia the Annenberg Foundation is helping principals, teachers, parents, communities, and boards of education to create smaller, theme-based, alternative primary and secondary schools.

Whatever the structure of the local school system, or the agreed-upon organizing theme of each school, however, preparation for a productive future in the modern world requires that students master the basic skills of English comprehension, writing and mathematics and an understanding of science and computer technology. Public education remains the most certain system for ensuring equity, quality, and personal empowerment. Federal, state, and local education officials, with the help of the private sector, must continue to be held responsible for the effective education of all of the nation's children, whatever their color or socioeconomic status.

—THOMAS K. MINTER AND ALFRED E. PRETTYMAN

ELLINGTON, EDWARD KENNEDY "DUKE"

Edward Kennedy "Duke" Ellington (April 29, 1899–May 24, 1974), composer, band leader, jazz pianist. One of the supreme composers of the

True education makes for inequality; the inequality of individuality, the inequality of success, the glorious inequality of talent, of genius; for inequality, not mediocrity, individual superiority, not standardization, is the measure of the progress of the world.

FELIX E. SCHELLING
PEDAGOGICALLY SPEAKING,
1929

See also
Ragtime

twentieth century, Edward Kennedy Ellington was born into a comfortable middle class family in Washington, D.C. The son of a butler, Ellington received the nickname "Duke" as a child because of the care and pride he took in his attire. As he grew older, his aristocratic bearing and sartorial elegance made the nickname stick. Although he took piano lessons starting in 1906, he was also a talented painter, and before he finished high school he was offered an NAACP-sponsored painting scholarship for college. By this time, however, his interests were again turning toward music, especially ragtime and stride piano. By 1918, when Ellington married Edna Thompson, he was leading a band that played popular tunes in a ragtime style at white "society" events. To support his wife and son, Mercer, who was born in 1919, Ellington also worked as a sign painter.

In 1923, Ellington, encouraged by pianist Fats Waller, moved to New York as pianist and arranger of the Washingtonians. When the leader of the ensemble, Elmer Snowden, left in 1924, Ellington took over and led the band in what were his first appearances on record. The Washingtonians had extensive stays at the Club Hollywood, later called the Kentucky Club, from 1924 to 1927. In this formative period, Ellington's key influence was trumpeter Bubber Miley, whose guttural, plunger-muted style added a robust, blues-tinged element to Ellington's previously genteel compositions and arrangements. Miley's growling, mournful solos inspired Ellington's most important compositions in the 1920s, including "East St. Louis Toodle-O" (1926), "Black and Tan Fantasy" (1927), and "The Mooche" (1928).

Another important composition from this period, "Creole Love Call" (1927), features a wordless obbligato by vocalist Adelaide Hall.

On December 4, 1927, Ellington's band debuted at Harlem's Cotton Club, an all-white nightclub. The engagement lasted on and off for four years, and gave Ellington a national radio audience, as well as the chance to accompany a variety of chorus and specialty dance numbers and vocalists, often portraying "primitive" and "exotic" aspects of African-American culture. It was in that environment that he perfected the style, marked by energetic climaxes and haunting sonorities, that became known as his "jungle music."

The Cotton Club engagement made Ellington one of the best-known musicians in jazz, famed not only for his eminently danceable tunes, but also for compositions that attracted the attention of the classical music world. During the 1930s the orchestra toured the U.S. extensively, and made trips to Europe in 1933 and 1939. Ellington's 1930s recordings, which achieved huge success among both white and black audiences, include "Ring Dem Bells" (1930), "Mood Indigo" (1930), "Rockin' in Rhythm" (1931), "It Don't Mean a Thing If It Ain't Got That Swing" (1932), "Sophisticated Lady" (1932), "Daybreak Express" (1933), "Solitude" (1934), "In a Sentimental Mood" (1935), trombonist Juan Tizol's "Caravan" (1937), "I Let a Song Go out of My Heart" (1938), and "Prelude to a Kiss" (1938). Ellington's early 1940s band is often considered the best he ever led. Bolstered by tenor saxophonist Ben Webster, bassist Jimmy Blanton, and Ellington's assistant, composer and arranger Billy Strayhorn,

**SUPREME
COMPOSER**

Duke Ellington jazzed up the American music scene with his danceable tunes and compositions that attracted the attention of classical music fans. Here his band performs in 1930 on the RKO lot in Culver City, Calif.

FRANK DRIGGS COLLECTION

the orchestra recorded a number of masterpieces, including "Ko-Ko" (1940), "Concerto for Cootie" (1940), "In a Mellotone" (1940), "Cotton Tail" (1940), "Perdido" (1942), and "C-Jam Blues" (1942), as well as Strayhorn's "Chelsea Bridge" (1941) and "Take the A Train" (1941). Ellington also recorded in groups led by clarinetist Barney Bigard, trumpeters Cootie Williams and Rex Stewart, and saxophonist Johnny Hodges.

In the 1940s Ellington became increasingly interested in extended composition. Though he was the greatest master of the four-minute jazz composition, he chafed against the limitations of the length of a 78-rpm record side. As early as 1934 he wrote the score for the short film *Symphony in Black,* and the next year recorded *Reminiscing in Tempo,* a contemplative work taking up four sides. His greatest extended composition was the fifty-minute *Black, Brown and Beige,* which premiered at Carnegie Hall on January 23, 1943. This work, which included the hymnlike "Come Sunday" passage, depicted African Americans at work and at prayer, with vignettes on aspects of history from emancipation to the development of Harlem as a black community. Other extended works from this period include *New World-a-Comin'* (1943), *The Liberian Suite* (1947), and *The Tattooed Bride* (1948). Ellington continued to issue shorter recordings, but there were fewer memorable short compositions after the mid-1940s, though "The Clothed Woman" (1947) and "Satin Doll" (1953) were notable exceptions. In addition to composing and conducting, Ellington was an excellent pianist in the Harlem stride tradition, and he made memorable duets with bassist Jimmy Blanton in 1940.

During the bebop era of the late 1940s and early '50s, Ellington's band declined in influence. However, their performance at the 1956 Newport Jazz Festival, featuring saxophonist Paul Gonsalves's electrifying solo on "Diminuendo and Crescendo in Blue," reaffirmed their reputation, and earned Ellington a cover article in *Time* magazine. Ellington thereafter took the orchestra to Europe, Japan, the Middle East, India, South America, and Africa. The orchestra also made albums with Louis Armstrong, Coleman Hawkins, Count Basie, Ella Fitzgerald, and John Coltrane, and as a member of a trio Ellington recorded with Max Roach and Charles Mingus. Among his many later extended compositions are *Harlem* (1951), *A Drum Is a Woman* (1956), *Such Sweet Thunder* (1957), *The Queen's Suite* (1959), *The Far East Suite* (1967), and *Afro-Eurasian Eclipse* (1971). Ellington also composed film scores for

Anatomy of a Murder (1959) and the Oscar-nominated *Paris Blues* (1961). He composed music for ballets by choreographer Alvin Ailey, *The River* (1970) and *Les Trois Rois Noirs,* including a section dedicated to the Rev. Dr. Martin Luther King, Jr., composed in Ellington's final years and premiered in 1976. In his last decade, Ellington also wrote religious music for three events he called "Sacred Concerts" (1965, 1968, 1973), vast productions that evoked his strong sense of spirituality through Gospel and choral music, dancing, and thankful hymns.

Starting with the 1943 *Black, Brown and Beige,* many of Ellington's extended works were tributes to his African-American heritage, and demonstrations of his pride in the accomplishments of African Americans. His many shorter depictions of Harlem range from the elegiac "Drop Me Off in Harlem" (1933) to the boisterous "Harlem Airshaft" (1940). Perhaps his most personal tributes are his two musicals, *Jump for Joy* (including "I Got It Bad and That Ain't Good," 1942), and *My People* (1963), both dealing with the theme of integration. The latter includes the song "King Fit the Battle of Alabam."

Ellington's music was collaborative. Many of his works were written by band members, and many more were written collectively, by synthesizing and expanding riffs and motifs into unified compositions. Ellington's compositions were almost always written with a particular band member's style and ability in mind, and his collaborator Strayhorn remarked that while Ellington played piano, his real instrument was his orchestra. Ellington was an exceptionally original musical thinker, whose orchestral sound was marked by instrumental doublings on reeds, ingenious combinations of instruments, and the carefully crafted use of a variety of muted brasses. The diversity of the band was remarkable, containing an extraordinary variety of masterful and distinctive soloists, ranging from the smooth, sensuous improvisations of saxophonist Johnny Hodges to the gut-bucket sounds of trumpeter Cootie Williams and trombonist "Tricky Sam" Nanton.

In the ever-changing world of the big bands, the Ellington orchestra's core roster seldom changed. The most important of his band members, with their tenures parenthetically noted, include trumpeters William "Cat" Anderson (1944–1947, 1950–1959, 1961–1971), Bubber Miley (1924–1929), Rex Stewart (1934–1945), Arthur Whetsol (1923–1924, 1928–1936), and Cootie Williams (1929–1940, 1962–1973); violinist and trumpeter Ray Nance (1940–1963);

"It Don't Mean a Thing If It Ain't Got That Swing"

DUKE ELLINGTON
SONG TITLE, 1932

See also
Cotton Club

trombonists Lawrence Brown (1932–1951, 1960–1970), Joe "Tricky Sam" Nanton (1926–1946), and Juan Tizol (1929–1944, 1951–1953); alto saxophonists Otto Hardwick (1923–1928, 1932–1946), Johnny Hodges (1928–1951, 1955–1970), and Russell Procope (1946–1974); tenor saxophonists Paul Gonsalves (1950–1970, 1972–1974) and Ben Webster (1940–1943, 1948–1949); baritone saxophonist Harry Carney (1927–1974); clarinetists Barney Bigard (1927–1942) and Jimmy Hamilton (1943–1968); vocalists Ivy Anderson (1931–1942) and Al Hibbler (1943–1951); drummer Sonny Greer (1923–1951); bassist Jimmy Blanton (1939–1941); and composer and arranger Billy Strayhorn (1939–1967).

During his lifetime Ellington was celebrated as a commanding figure in American culture. He cherished the many awards and honorary degrees he earned, including the Spingarn Medal (1959) and eleven Grammy Awards. Ellington remained gracious, though many were outraged by the refusal of a 1965 Pulitzer Prize committee, firmly opposed to recognizing "popular" music, to give him a special award for composition. In 1970 Ellington was awarded the Presidential Medal of Freedom by President Nixon and was feted with a seventieth-birthday celebration at the White House. He died of cancer on May 24, 1974.

Since Ellington's death, his orchestra has been led by his son, Mercer, himself a trumpeter and composer of note. In 1986, Duke Ellington became the first African-American jazz musician to appear on a U. S. postage stamp. The 1980s and '90s have witnessed a growing interest in Ellington among scholars who are increasingly interested in the extended compositions, and among jazz fans gaining access to a wealth of previously unreleased recordings. Such attention inevitably confirms Ellington's status not only as the greatest composer and bandleader in jazz, but as a figure unique in the history of twentieth-century music.

—MARTIN WILLIAMS

ELLISON, RALPH

Ralph Ellison (March 1, 1914–April 16, 1994), writer. Ralph Ellison was born to Lewis and Ida Millsap Ellison in Oklahoma City, Okla., a frontier town with a rich vernacular culture. As a child, he worked at Randolph's Pharmacy, where he heard animal tales and ghost stories. The local all-black high school provided rigorous training in music, and the Aldridge Theatre featured many of the leading blues, ragtime, and jazz musicians of the day. Ellison played in high school jazz bands and in 1933 enrolled as a music major at Tuskegee Institute, Ala. He involved himself in the other arts as well and on his own discovered T. S. Eliot's *Waste Land,* where he found a range of allusions "as mixed and varied as that of Louis Armstrong."

At the end of his third college year, Ellison went to New York to earn money. He never returned to Tuskegee. He met Langston Hughes, whose poetry he had read in high school, and Richard Wright, who urged him to write for *New Challenge,* which Wright was editing. Ellison wrote a review for the magazine in 1937, his first published work. In 1938 he took a Works Progress Administration job with the New York Writer's Project and worked at night on his own fiction. He read Hemingway to learn style.

Ellison wrote book reviews for the radical periodicals *Direction, Negro Quarterly,* and *New Masses,* which in 1940 printed at least one review by him every month. His first short stories were realistic in the manner of Richard Wright and presented fairly explicit political solutions to the dilemmas of Jim Crow. By 1940 he had begun to find his own direction with a series of stories in the Huck Finn/Tom Sawyer mold—tales of black youngsters who were not so much victims as playmakers in a land of possibility. "Flying Home" (1944) offers wise old Jefferson as a storyteller whose verbal art helps lessen the greenhorn Todd's isolation and teaches him a healthier attitude toward the divided world he must confront. That story set the stage for Ellison's monumental 1952 novel *Invisible Man,* which received the National Book Award the following year.

Set between 1930 and 1950, *Invisible Man* tells of the development of an ambitious young black man from the South, a naïf who goes to college and then to New York in search of advancement. At first Invisible Man, unnamed throughout the novel, wants to walk the narrow way of Booker T. Washington, whose words he speaks at his high school graduation as well as at a smoker for the town's leading white male citizens. At the smoker he is required to fight blindfolded in a free-for-all against the other black youths. In this key chapter, all the boys are turned blindly against one another in a danger-filled ritual staged for the amusement of their white patrons. That night the young man dreams of his grandfather, the novel's cryptic ancestor-wise man, who presents him with "an engraved document" that seems an ironic comment on his high school diploma and its costs.

"Read it," the old man tells him. "'To Whom It May Concern,' I intoned. 'Keep This Nigger Boy Running.'"

Whether a student in the southern college or a spokesman in New York for the radical political movement called the Brotherhood (modeled on the Communist party of the 1930s or some other American political organization that exploited blacks and then sold them out), Invisible Man is kept running. Quintessentially American in his confusion about who he is, he mad-dashes from scene to scene, letting others tell him what his experience means, who he is, what his name is. And he is not only blind, he is invisible—he is racially stereotyped and otherwise denied his individuality. "I am invisible," he discovers, "simply because people refuse to see me. Like the bodiless heads you see sometimes in circus sideshows, it is as though I have been surrounded by mirrors of hard, distorting glass. When they approach me they see only my surroundings, themselves, or figments of their imagination—indeed, everything and anything except me."

After encounters with remarkable adults—some wisely parental, some insane but brilliant, some sly con men—he learns to accept with equipoise the full ambiguity of his history and to see the world by his own lights. "It took me a long time," he says, "and much painful boomeranging of my expectations to achieve a realization everyone else appears to have been born with: That I am nobody but myself. But first I had to discover that I am an invisible man!" He had to find out that very few people would bother to understand his real motives and values; perhaps not all of these mysteries were knowable, even by himself. And yet in this novel of education and epiphany, Invisible Man decides he can nonetheless remain hopeful: "I was my experiences and my experiences were me," he says. "And no blind men, no matter how powerful they became, even if they conquered the world, could take that, or change one single itch, taunt, laugh, cry, scar, ache, rage or pain of it."

Rich in historical and literary allusions—from Columbus to World War II, from Oedipus and Br'er Rabbit to T. S. Eliot and Richard Wright—Invisible Man stands both as a novel about the history of the novel and as a meditation on the history of the United States. In doing so, it presents a metaphor for black American life in the twentieth century that transcends its particular focus. It names not only the modern American but the citizen of the contemporary world as tragicomically centerless (but somehow surviving and getting smarter): *Homo invisibilis*. It is Ellison's masterwork.

Shadow and Act (1964) and *Going to the Territory* (1987) are collections of Ellison's nonfiction prose. With these books he established himself as a preeminent man of letters—one whose driving purpose was to define African-American life and culture with precision and affirmation. The essays on African-American music are insider's reports that reflect Ellison's deep experience and long memory. Whether discussing literature, music, painting, psychology, or history, Ellison places strong emphases on vernacular culture—its art, rituals, and meanings—and on the power of the visionary individual, particularly the artist, to prevail. These books offer a strong challenge to social scientists and historians to consider African-American life in terms not just of its ills and pathologies but of its tested capacity to reinvent itself and to influence the nation and the world.

—ROBERT G. O'MEALLY

EMANCIPATION

Few events in American history can match the drama and the social significance of black Emancipation in the midst of the Civil War. Since the early seventeenth century, when African-born slaves were first brought ashore in Virginia, through the long development of the South's plantation economy and its dependence upon slave labor, Emancipation had been the dream of African-American people. Beyond the age of the American Revolution, when the northern states freed their relatively small numbers of slaves, and into the antebellum era of abolitionism, the writing of fugitive slave narratives, and increasing free black community development in the North, Emancipation became a matter of political and religious expectation. To be a black abolitionist, a fugitive slave desperately seeking his or her way through the mysterious realities of the Underground Railroad, or one of the millions of slaves cunningly surviving on southern cotton plantations was to be an actor in this long and agonizing drama. The agony and the hope embedded in the story of Emancipation is what black poet Francis Ellen Watkins tried to capture in a simple verse written in the wake of John Brown's execution in 1859 and only a little over a year before the outbreak of the Civil War:

Make me a grave where'er you will,
In a lowly plain, or a lofty hill,

Books which seldom, if ever, mentioned Negroes were to release me from whatever "segregated" idea I might have had of my human possibilities.

RALPH ELLISON
IN *JIM SLEEPER, THE CLOSEST OF STRANGERS*, 1990

See also
Dred Scott Decision

233

E

EMANCIPATION

See also
Reconstruction

The great ambition of the older people [after Emancipation] was to try to learn to read the Bible before they died.

BOOKER T. WASHINGTON
UP FROM SLAVERY, 1901

Make it among earth's humblest graves,
But not in a land where men are slaves.

Soon, by the forces of total war, which in turn opened opportunities for slaves to seize their own freedom, Emancipation became reality in America. Black freedom became the central event of nineteenth-century African-American history and, along with the preservation of the Union, the central result of the Civil War.

On Emancipation day, January 1, 1863 (when Abraham Lincoln's Emancipation Proclamation was to go into effect), "jubilee meetings" occurred all over black America. At Tremont Temple in Boston, a huge gathering of blacks and whites met from morning until night, awaiting the final news that Lincoln had signed the fateful document. Genuine concern still existed that something might go awry; the preliminary proclamation had been issued in September 1862, a mixture of what appeared to be military necessity and a desire to give the war a new moral purpose. Numerous luminaries from throughout antebellum free black leadership spoke during the day; the attorney John Rock, the minister and former slave John Sella Martin, the orator and women's suffragist Anna Dickinson, author William Wells Brown, and Boston's William Cooper Nell as presiding officer were among them. The most prominent of all black voices, Frederick Douglass, gave a concluding speech during the afternoon session punctuated by many cries of "Amen." In the evening, tension mounted and anxiety gripped the hall, as no news had arrived from Washington. Douglass and Brown provided more oratory to try to quell the changing mood of doubt. Then a runner arrived from the telegraph office with the news: "It is coming!" he shouted, "it is on the wires!" An attempt was made to read the text of the Emancipation Proclamation, but great jubilation engulfed the crowd. Unrestrained shouting and singing ensued. Douglass gained the throng's attention and led them in a chorus of his favorite hymn, "Blow Ye the Trumpet, Blow." Next an old black preacher named Rue led the group in "Sound the loud timbel o'er Egypt's dark sea, Jehovah has triumphed, his people are free!" The celebration lasted until midnight, when the crowd reassembled at pastor Leonard A. Grimes's Twelfth Baptist Church—an institution renowned among black Bostonians for its role in helping many fugitive slaves move along the road to liberty—to continue celebrating.

From Massachusetts to Ohio and Michigan, and in many Union-occupied places in the South where ex-slaves were now entering the Yankee army or beginning their first year as free people, such celebrations occurred. Full of praise songs, these celebrations demonstrated that whatever the fine print of the proclamation might say, black folks across the land knew that they had lived to see a new day, a transforming moment in their history. At a large "contraband camp" (center for refugee ex-slaves) in Washington, D.C., some six hundred black men, women, and children gathered at the superintendent's headquarters on New Year's Eve and sang through most of the night. In chorus after chorus of "Go Down, Moses" they announced the magnitude of their painful but beautiful exodus. One newly supplied verse concluded with "Go down, Abraham, away down in Dixie's land, tell Jeff Davis to let my people go!" Many years after the Tremont Temple celebration in Boston, Douglass may have best captured the meaning of Emancipation day for his people: "It was not logic, but the trump of jubilee, which everybody wanted to hear. We were waiting and listening as for a bolt from the sky, which should rend the fetters of four millions of slaves; we were watching as it were, by the dim light of stars, for the dawn of a new day; we were longing for the answer to the agonizing prayers of centuries. Remembering those in bonds as bound with them, we wanted to join in the shout for freedom, and in the anthem of the redeemed." For blacks the cruel and apocalyptic war finally had a holy cause.

The Emancipation policy of the Union government evolved with much less certitude than the music and poetry of jubilee day might imply. During the first year of the war, the Union military forces operated on an official policy of exclusion ("denial of asylum") to escaped slaves. The war was to restore the Union, but not to uproot slavery. But events overtook such a policy. Floods of fugitive slaves began to enter Union lines in Virginia, in Tennessee, and along the southern coasts. Thousands were eventually employed as military laborers, servants, camp hands, and even spies. Early in the war, at Fortress Monroe, Va., in May 1861, the ambitious politician-general Benjamin F. Butler declared the slaves who entered his lines "contraband of war." The idea of slaves as confiscated enemy property eventually caught on. In early August 1861, striking a balance between legality and military necessity, the federal Congress passed the First Confiscation Act, allowing for the seizure of all Confederate property used to aid the war effort. Although not yet technically freed by this law, the slaves of rebel masters came under its purview and an inexorable process to-

ward black freedom took root. Into 1862 the official stance of the Union armies toward slaves was a conflicted one: exclusion where the slaveholders were deemed "loyal," and employment as contrabands where the masters were judged "disloyal." Such an unworkable policy caused considerable dissension in the Union ranks, especially between abolitionist and proslavery officers. But wherever Union forces gained ground in the South, the institution of slavery began to crumble.

By the spring and summer of 1862, Congress took the lead on the issue of Emancipation policy. In April it abolished slavery in the District of Columbia, and a large sum of money was allocated for the possible colonization of freed blacks abroad. The Lincoln administration, indeed, pursued a variety of schemes for Central American and Caribbean colonization during the first three years of the war. The sheer impracticality of such plans and stiff black resistance notwithstanding, this old idea of black removal from America as the solution to the revolutionary implications of Emancipation died hard within the Lincoln administration and in the mind of the president himself. But Lincoln, as well as many other Americans, would be greatly educated by both the necessity and the larger meanings of Emancipation. A black newspaper in Union-occupied New Orleans declared that "history furnishes no such intensity of determination, on the part of any race, as that exhibited by these people to be free." And Frederick Douglass felt greatly encouraged by an evolving Emancipation movement in early 1862, whatever its contradictory motives. "It is really wonderful," he wrote, "how all efforts to evade, postpone, and prevent its coming, have been mocked and defied by the stupendous sweep of events."

In June 1862, Congress abolished slavery in the western territories, a marvelous irony when one remembers the tremendous political crisis over that issue in the decade before the war, as well as the alleged finality of the Dred Scott Decision of 1857. In July, Congress passed the Second Confiscation Act, which explicitly freed slaves of all persons "in rebellion," and excluded no parts of the slaveholding South. These measures provided a public and legal backdrop for President Lincoln's subsequent Emancipation Proclamation, issued in two parts, maneuvered through a recalcitrant cabinet, and politically calculated to shape northern morale, prevent foreign intervention (especially that of the British), and keep the remaining four slaveholding border states in the Union. During 1862, Lincoln had se-

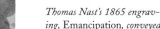

EMANCIPATION

Thomas Nast's 1865 engraving, Emancipation, *conveyed the hope of many Republicans that with the end of the Civil War, slavery's evil legacy would be overturned.*
PRINTS AND PHOTOGRAPHS DIVISION, LIBRARY OF CONGRESS

Acts of violent retribution by ex-slaves against their former owners were rare in the wake of Emancipation.

PAGE 139

cretly maneuvered to persuade Delaware and Kentucky to accept a plan of compensated, gradual Emancipation. But the deeply divided border states bluntly refused such notions. In the preliminary proclamation of September 21, 1862, issued in the aftermath of the bloody battle of Antietam (a Union military success for which Lincoln had desperately waited), the president offered a carrot to the rebellious South: in effect, stop the war, reenter the Union, and slavery would go largely untouched. In his State of the Union address in December, Lincoln dwelled on the idea of gradual, compensated Emancipation as the way to end the war and return a willful South to the Union. None of these offers had any chance of acceptance at this point in what had already become a revolutionary war for ends much larger and higher than most had imagined in 1861.

Lincoln had always considered slavery to be an evil that had to be eliminated in America. It was he who had committed the Republican party in the late 1850s to putting slavery "on a course of ultimate extinction." At the outset of the war, however, he valued saving the Union above all else, including whatever would happen to slavery. But after he signed the document that declared all slaves in the "states of rebellion . . . forever free," Lincoln's historical reputation, as often legendary and mythical as it is factual, became forever tied to his role in the Emancipation process. Emancipation did indeed require presidential leadership to commit America to a war to free slaves in the eyes of the world; in Lincoln's remarkable command of moral meaning and politics, he understood that this war had become a crucible in which the entire nation could receive a "new birth of freedom." The president ultimately commanded the armies, every forward step of which from 1863 to 1865 was a liberating step, soon by black soldiers as well. On one level, Emancipation had to be legal and moral, and, like all great matters in American history, it had to be finalized in the Constitution, in the Thirteenth Amendment (passed in early 1865). But black freedom was something both given and seized. Many factors made it possible for Lincoln to say by February 1865 that "the central act of my administration, and the greatest event of the nineteenth century," was Emancipation. But none more than the black exodus of self-Emancipation when the moment of truth came, the waves of freedpeople who "voted with their feet."

The actual process and timing of Emancipation across the South depended on at least three interrelated circumstances: one, the character of slave society in a given region; two, the course of the war itself; and three, the policies of the Union and Confederate governments. Southern geography, the chronology of the military campaigns, the character of total war with its massive forced movement of people, the personal disposition of slaveholders and Union commanders alike, and the advent of widespread recruitment of black soldiers were all combined factors in determining when, where, and how slaves became free. Thousands of slaves were "hired out" as fortification laborers, teamsters, nurses, and cooks in the Confederate armies, eventually providing many opportunities for escape to Union lines and an uncertain but freer future. Thousands were also "refugeed" to the interior by their owners in order to "protect" them from invading Yankee armies. Many more took to the forests and swamps to hide during the chaos of war, as Union forces swept over the sea islands of the Georgia or South Carolina coast, or the densely populated lower Mississippi Valley region. Many of those slaves eventually returned to their plantations, abandoned by their former masters, and took over agricultural production, sometimes under the supervision of an old driver, and sometimes by independently planting subsistence crops while the sugarcane rotted.

Many slaves waited and watched for their opportunity of escape, however uncertain their new fate might be. Octave Johnson was a slave on a plantation in St. James Parish, La., who ran away to the woods when the war came. He and a group of thirty, ten of whom were women, remained at large for a year and a half. Johnson's story, as he reported it to the American Freedmen's Inquiry Commission in 1864, provides a remarkable example of the social-military revolution under way across the South. "We were four miles in the rear of the plantation house," said Johnson. His band stole food and borrowed matches and other goods from slaves still on the plantation. "We slept on logs and burned cypress leaves to make a smoke and keep away mosquitoes." When hunted by bloodhounds, Johnson's group took to the deeper swamp. They "killed eight of the bloodhounds; then we jumped into Bayou Faupron; the dogs followed us and the alligators caught six of them; the alligators preferred dog flesh to personal flesh; we escaped and came to Camp Parapet, where I was first employed in the Commissary's office, then as a servant to Col. Hanks; then I joined his regiment." From "working on task" through survival in the bayous, Octave Johnson found his freedom as a corporal in Company C, Fifteenth Regiment, Corps d'Afrique.

For many slaves, the transition from bondage to freedom was not so clear and complete as it was for Octave Johnson. Emancipation was a matter of overt celebration in some places, especially in southern towns and cities, as well as in some slave quarters. But what freedom meant in 1863, how livelihood would change, how the war would progress, how the masters would react (perhaps with wages but perhaps with violent retribution), how freedpeople would find protection in the conquered and chaotic South, how they would meet the rent payments that might now be charged, how a peasant population of agricultural laborers deeply attached to the land might now become owners of the land as so many dreamed, and whether they would achieve citizenship rights were all urgent and unanswered questions during the season of Emancipation. Joy mixed with uncertainty, songs of deliverance with expressions of fear. The actual day on which masters gathered their slaves to announce that they were free was remembered by freedpeople with a wide range of feelings and experience. Some remembered hilarity and dancing, but many remembered it as a sobering, even solemn time. A former South Carolina slave recalled that on his plantation "some were sorry, some hurt, but a few were silent and glad." James Lucas, a former slave of Jefferson Davis in Mississippi, probed the depths of human nature and ambivalence in his description of the day of liberation: "Dey all had diffe'nt ways o' thinkin' 'bout it. Mos'ly though dey was jus' lak me, dey didn' know jus' zackly what it meant. It was jus' somp'n dat de white folks an' slaves all de time talk 'bout. Dat's all. Folks dat ain' never been free don' rightly know de *feel* of bein' free. Dey don' know de meanin' of it." And a former Virginia slave simply recalled "how wild and upset and *dreadful* everything was in them times."

But in time, confusion gave way to meaning, and the feel of freedom took many forms. For many ex-slaves who followed Union armies freedom meant, initially, life in contraband camps, where black families struggled to survive in the face of great hardship and occasional starvation. But by the end of 1862 and throughout the rest of the war, a string of contraband camps became the first homes in freedom for thousands of ex-slaves. At LaGrange, Bolivar, and Memphis in western Tennessee; at Corinth in northern Mississippi; in "contraband colonies" near New Orleans; at Cairo, Ill.; at Camp Barker in the District of Columbia; on Craney Island near Norfolk, Va.; and eventually in northern Georgia and various other places, the freedpeople forged a new life on government rations and through work on labor crews, and received a modicum of medical care, often provided by "grannies"—black women who employed home remedies from plantation life. For thousands the contraband camps became the initial entry into free labor practices, and a slow but certain embrace of the new sense of dignity, mobility, identity, and education that freedom now meant. Nearly all white Northerners who witnessed or supervised these camps, or who eventually administered private or government work programs on confiscated southern land, organized freedmen's aid societies and schools by the hundreds, or observed weddings and burials, were stunned by the determination of this exodus despite its hardships. In 1863, each superintendent of a contraband camp in the western theater of war was asked to respond to a series of interrogatives about the freedmen streaming into his facilities. To the question of the "motives" of the freedmen, the Corinth superintendent tried to find the range of what he saw: "Can't answer short of 100 pages. Bad treatment—hard times—lack of the comforts of life—prospect of being driven South; the more intelligent because they wished to be free. Generally speak kindly of their masters; none wish to return; many would die first. All delighted with the prospect of freedom, yet all have been kept constantly at some kind of work." All of the superintendents commented on what seemed to them the remarkable "intelligence" and "honesty" of the freedmen. As for their "notions of liberty," the Memphis superintendent answered: "Generally correct. They say they have no rights, nor own anything except as their master permits; but being freed, can make their own money and protect their families." Indeed, these responses demonstrate just what a fundamental revolution Emancipation had become.

Inexorably, Emancipation meant that black families would be both reunited and torn apart. In contraband camps, where women and children greatly outnumbered men, extended families sometimes found and cared for each other. But often, when the thousands of black men across the South entered the Union army they left women and children behind in great hardship, sometimes in sheer destitution, and eventually under new labor arrangements that required rent payments. Louisiana freedwoman Emily Waters wrote to her husband, who was still on duty with the Union army, in July 1865, begging him to get a furlough and "come home and find a place for us to live in." The joy of change mixed with terrible strain. "My children are going to school," she re-

I had reasoned this out in my mind: There was two things I had a right to, liberty and death. If I could not have one, I would have the other, for no man should take me alive.

HARRIET TUBMAN
DESCRIPTION OF HER FIRST
ESCAPE TO THE NORTH

See also
Slavery

*A peculiar
institution*

ON SLAVERY
ARTICLE IN THE
NEW YORK TRIBUNE,
OCTOBER 19, 1854

ported, "but I find it very hard to feed them all, and if you cannot come I hope you will send me something to help me get along. . . . Come home as soon as you can, and cherish me as ever." The same Louisiana soldier received a subsequent letter from Alsie Thomas, his sister, reporting that "we are in deep trouble—your wife has left Trepagnia and gone to the city and we don't know where or how she is, we have not heard a word from her in four weeks." The choices and the strains that Emancipation wrought are tenderly exhibited in a letter by John Boston, a Maryland fugitive slave, to his wife, Elizabeth, in January 1862, from Upton Hill, Va. "[I]t is with grate joy I take this time to let you know Whare I am i am now in Safety in the 14th regiment of Brooklyn this Day i can Adres you thank god as a free man I had a little truble in giting away But as the lord led the Children of Isrel to the land of Canon So he led me to a land Whare Fredom Will rain in spite Of earth and hell . . . i am free from al the Slavers Lash." Such were the joys of freedom and the agonies of separation. Boston concluded his letter: "Dear Wife i must Close rest yourself Contented i am free . . . Write my Dear Soon . . . Kiss Daniel For me." The rich sources on the freedmen's experience do not tell us whether Emily Waters ever saw her husband again, or whether the Bostons were reunited. But these letters demonstrate the depth with which freedom was embraced and the human pain through which it was achieved.

The freedpeople especially gave meaning to their freedom by their eagerness for education and land ownership. In the Sea Islands of South Carolina, the Port Royal Experiment was a large-scale attempt, led by northern philanthropists interested as much in profits as in freedmen's rights, to reorganize cotton production by paying wages to blacks. But amid this combination of abolitionists' good works and capitalist opportunity, thousands of blacks of all ages learned to read. So eager were the freedmen to learn that the teachers from the various freedmen's-aid societies were sometimes overwhelmed. "The Negroes will do anything for us," said one teacher, "if we will only teach them." Land ownership was an equally precious aim of the freedmen, and they claimed it as a right. No one ever stated the labor theory of value more clearly than Virginia freedman Bayley Wyat, in a speech protesting the eviction of blacks from a contraband camp in 1866: "We has a right to the land we are located. For Why? I tell you. Our wives, our children, our husbands, has been sold over and over again to purchase the lands we

now locates upon; for that reason we have a divine right to the land. . . . And den didn't we clear the land, and raise de crops ob corn, ob cotton, ob tobacco, ob rice, ob sugar, ob everything?" The redistribution of land and wealth in the South would remain a largely unrealized dream during Reconstruction, and perhaps its greatest unfinished legacy. But armed with literacy, and an unprecedented politicization, southern blacks accomplished much against great odds in the wake of Emancipation.

By the end of the war in 1865, the massive moving about of the freedpeople became a major factor in Confederate defeat. Thousands of white Union soldiers who witnessed this process of Emancipation became, despite earlier prejudices, avid supporters of the recruitment of black soldiers. And no one understood just what a transformation was under way better than the former slaveholders in the South, who now watched their world collapse around them. In August 1865, white Georgian John Jones described black freedom as the "dark, dissolving, disquieting wave of Emancipation." That wave would abate in the turbulent first years of Reconstruction, when the majority of freedmen would resettle on their old places, generally paid wages at first, but eventually working "on shares" (as sharecropping tenant farmers). Reconstruction would bring a political revolution to the South, a great experiment in racial democracy, led by radical Republicans in the federal government and by a new American phenomenon: scores of black politicians. This "disquieting wave" would launch black suffrage, citizenship rights, civil rights, and widespread black officeholding beyond what anyone could have imagined at the outset of the Civil War. That the great achievements in racial democracy of the period 1865–1870 were betrayed or lost by the late nineteenth century does not detract from the significance of such a passage in African-American history. Many of the twentieth-century triumphs in America's never-ending search for racial democracy have their deep roots in the story of Emancipation and its aftermath.

—DAVID W. BLIGHT

EQUIANO, OLAUDAH

Olaudah Equiano (c. 1750–April 30, 1797), autobiographer. Also known as Gustavus Vassa, Equiano was born the son of an Ibo chieftain in Benin, now part of Nigeria. He was eleven when he and his sister were kidnapped and sold to white slave traders on the coast. He was subsequently shipped to Barbados and later Virginia, where he was sold to a British naval officer whom he served for nearly seventeen years. On board ships and during brief intervals in England, he learned to read and write and converted to Christianity. His autobiography relates his several adventures at sea off the Canadian coast during the Seven Years' War and later with Admiral Boscawen's fleet in the Mediterranean. To his dismay, his master, who had promised him his freedom, sold him to an American shipowner who employed him in trading runs—sometimes with slaves as cargo—between the islands of the West Indies and the North American coast. Here Equiano records murders and cruel injustices inflicted on blacks, both free and enslaved.

In 1766, Equiano was at last able to purchase his freedom but elected to remain a seaman, although he passed some periods in England. Among other adventures, he sailed on the Phipps expedition to the Arctic in 1772–1773, and later worked as a manservant on a tour of the Mediterranean and as an assistant to a doctor with the Miskito Indians in Nicaragua. After 1777, he remained largely land-bound in the British Isles and assumed increasingly active roles in the antislavery movement. In 1787 he was appointed commissioner of stores for the resettlement of free Africans in Sierra Leone, but was dismissed after accusing a naval agent of mismanagement. His efforts to join an African expeditionary group or to do African missionary work also met with failure. In 1789 he published his autobiography under the title *The Interesting Narrative of Olaudah Equiano, or Gustavus Vassa the African, written by himself.* Three years later he married Susannah Cullen, an Englishwoman by whom he would have two children. Although several of his accounts have since been questioned, he saw nine editions of the book printed in his lifetime, thereby drawing invitations to lecture throughout the British Isles. Because Equiano infuses his autobiography with antislavery views and identifies enslaved blacks with biblical Hebrews, his work is generally regarded as a truer precursor of slave narratives written between 1830 and 1860 than other eighteenth-century Afro-American autobiographies.

—EDWARD MARGOLIES

EUROPE, JAMES REESE

James Reese Europe (February 22, 1881–May 9, 1919), composer and conductor. Born in Mobile,

Ala., Europe spent his formative years in Washington, D.C., where his father held a position with the U.S. Postal Service. The family was unusually musical; his brother, John, became a noted ragtime pianist, and his sister, Mary, was an accomplished concert pianist, choral director, and music teacher in the Washington public schools. James Europe attended M Street High School and studied violin, piano, and composition with Enrico Hurlie of the Marine Corps Band and Joseph Douglass, grandson of Frederick Douglass. Other musical influences included Harry T. Burleigh (especially his arrangements of African-American spirituals), organist Melville Charlton, and composer Will Marion Cook.

Like Cook and Burleigh—who had both studied with the celebrated Bohemian composer Antonín Dvořák while he was directing the Prague National Conservatory of Music—Europe accepted Dvořák's assessment of the importance of African-American folk music as a basis for an American national music. He did not believe, however, as did many at the time, that popular forms of musical expression were necessarily vulgar or "lowbrow" and therefore lacked potential musical value. He was a consistent champion of African-American music and musical artistry at every level and in any form, including those (like jazz) that had yet to emerge fully.

After moving to New York City in 1903, Europe established himself as a leading composer and music director in black musical theater, contributing to such productions as John Larkins's *A Trip to Africa* (1904), Ernest Hogan's *Memphis Students* (1905), Cole and Johnson's *Shoo-fly Regiment* (1906–1907) and *Red Moon* (1908–1909), S. H. Dudley's *Black Politician* (1907–1908), and Bert Williams's *Mr. Lode of Koal* (1910). In April 1910, Europe and several fellow professionals (including Ford Dabney, William Tyers, and Joe Jordan) formed the Clef Club, a union and booking agency that substantially improved the working conditions for black musicians in New York City. Europe was elected president and conductor of the club's concert orchestra, a 125-member ensemble whose unusual instrumentation (consisting primarily of plucked or strummed instruments) he felt to be better suited to the performance of authentic African-American music than that of the standard symphony orchestra. The orchestra's 1912 Concert of Negro Music at Carnegie Hall was a historic event, and Europe and the orchestra repeated their appearance on New York's most famous stage in 1913 and 1914.

Ragtime developed as both a solo-piano vehicle and as an ensemble style for virtually all instruments.

PAGE 568

See also

Duke Ellington

In addition to developing "an orchestra of Negroes which will be able to take its place among the serious musical organizations of the country," Europe realized the practical importance to black musicians of taking advantage of the increasing demand for popular music to support the expansion of nightlife. Between 1910 and 1914, he built the Clef Club (and later, the Tempo Club) into the greatest force for organizing and channeling the efforts of black musicians in New York, providing musicians for vaudeville orchestras, hotels, cabarets, and dance halls, as well as for private society parties and dances. In 1913, as a result of his success in providing dance orchestras for the eastern social elite, Europe was recruited as musical director for the legendary dance team of Vernon and Irene Castle. Between them, they revolutionized American social dancing by making the formerly objectionable "ragtime" dances (turkey trots, one-steps, etc., which had been derived from traditional African-American dance practice) widely acceptable to mainstream America. The most lasting of the Castle dances, the fox-trot, was conceived by Europe and Vernon Castle after a suggestion by W. C. Handy. Europe's association with the Castles led to a recording contract with Victor Records, the first ever for a black orchestra leader.

Late in 1916, Europe enlisted in the Fifteenth Infantry Regiment (Colored) of New York's National Guard and was commissioned as a lieutenant. Largely as an aid to recruitment, he organized a regimental brass band that became, when the Fifteenth was mobilized and sent overseas, one of the most celebrated musical organizations of World War I. As a machine-gun company commander, Europe also served in the front lines and was the first black American officer in the Great War to lead troops into combat. Upon his return to the United States in early 1919, he was hailed as America's "jazz king" for incorporating blues, ragtime, and jazz elements into his arrangements for the band. He received another recording contract and embarked upon a nationwide tour. During a performance in Boston, however, Europe was cut in a backstage altercation with a mentally disturbed member of the band. The injury did not appear serious at first, but his jugular vein had in fact been punctured, and he died before the bleeding could be stopped. Europe's funeral was the first public funeral ever held for an African American in New York City; he was buried with full military honors in Arlington National Cemetery.

Though Europe was not a composer of major concert works, his more than one hundred songs, rags, waltzes, and marches include several ("On the Gay Luneta," "Castle House Rag," "Castle Walk," "Hi There," "Mirandy") that exhibit unusual lyricism and rhythmic sophistication for their day. But it was as an organizer of musicians, as a conductor who championed the works of other African-American composers, and as an arranger and orchestrator that his genius was most pronounced and his influence the greatest. In this regard, Europe may properly be seen as an original catalyst in the development of orchestral jazz, initiating a line of development that would eventually lead to Fletcher Henderson and Duke Ellington. Among the many individuals who acknowledged his pioneering influence were Eubie Blake and Noble Sissle (whose epoch-making 1921 musical *Shuffle Along* helped restore black artistry to the mainstream of American musical theater) and composer George Gershwin.

—R. REID BADGER

See also
W. C. Handy

FARRAKHAN,

LOUIS ABDUL

Louis Abdul Farrakhan (May 17, 1933–). Louis Eugene Walcott was born in the Bronx, N.Y., but was raised in Boston by his West Indian mother. Deeply religious, Walcott faithfully attended the Episcopalian church in his neighborhood and became an altar boy. With the rigorous discipline provided by his mother and his church, he did fairly well academically and graduated with honors from the prestigious Boston English High School, where he also participated on the track team and played the violin in the school orchestra. In 1953, after two years at the Winston-Salem Teachers College in North Carolina, he dropped out to pursue his favorite avocation of music and made it his first career. An accomplished violinist, pianist, and vocalist, Walcott performed professionally on the Boston nightclub circuit as a singer of calypso and country songs. In 1955, at the age of twenty-two, Louis Walcott was recruited by Malcolm X for the Nation of Islam. Following its custom, he dropped his surname and took an *X,* which meant "undetermined." However, it was not until he had met Elijah Muhammad, the supreme leader of the Nation of Islam, on a visit to the Chicago headquarters that Louis X converted and dedicated his life to building the Nation. After proving himself for ten years, Elijah Muhammad gave Louis his Muslim name, "Abdul Farrakhan," in May 1965. As a rising star within the Nation, Farrakhan also wrote the only song, the popular "A White Man's Heaven is a Black Man's Hell," and the only dramatic play, *Orgena* ("A Negro" spelled backward), endorsed by Mr. Muhammad.

After a nine-month apprenticeship with Malcolm X at Temple No. 7 in Harlem, Minister Louis X was appointed as the head minister of the Boston Temple No. 11, which Malcolm founded. Later, after Malcolm X had split with the Nation, Farrakhan was awarded Malcolm's Temple No. 7, the most important pastorate in the Nation after the Chicago headquarters. He was also appointed National Spokesman or National Representative after Malcolm left the Nation in 1964 and began to introduce Elijah Muhammad at Savior Day rallies, a task that had once belonged to Malcolm. Like his predecessor, Farrakhan is a dynamic and charismatic leader and a powerful speaker with an ability to appeal to masses of black people.

In February 1975, when Elijah Muhammad died, the Nation of Islam experienced its largest schism. Wallace Dean Muhammad, the fifth of Elijah's six sons, was surprisingly chosen as supreme minister by the leadership hierarchy. In April 1975 Wallace, who later took the Muslim title and name of Imam Warith Deen Muhammad, made radical changes in the Nation of Islam, gradually moving the group toward orthodox Sunni Islam. In 1975 Farrakhan left the New York Mosque. Until 1978 Farrakhan, who had expected to be chosen as Elijah's successor, kept silent in public and traveled extensively in Muslim countries, where he found a need to recover the focus upon race and black nationalism that the Nation had emphasized. Other disaffected leaders and followers had already formed splinter Nation of Islam groups—Silas Muhammad in Atlanta, John Muhammad in Detroit, and Caliph in Baltimore. In 1978, Farrakhan formed a new organization, also called the Nation of Islam, resurrecting the teachings, ideology, and organizational structure of Elijah Muhammad, and he began to rebuild his base of followers by making extensive speaking tours in black communities. Farrakhan claimed it was his organization, not that of Wallace Muhammad, that was the legitimate successor to the old Nation of Islam.

In 1979, Farrakhan began printing editions of *The Final Call,* a name he resurrected from early copies of a newspaper that Elijah Muhammad had put out in Chicago in 1934. The "final call" was a call to black people to return to Allah as incarnated in Master Fard Muhammad or Master Fard and witnessed by his apostle Elijah Muhammad. For Farrakhan, the final call has an eschatological dimension; it is the last call, the last chance for black people to achieve their liberation.

See also
Malcolm X
Elijah Muhammad

Islam has had a much longer history in the United States, particularly among African Americans, than is commonly known.

PAGE 363

Farrakhan became known to the American public via a series of controversies which were stirred when he first supported the Rev. Jesse Jackson's 1984 presidential campaign. His Fruit of Islam guards provided security for Jackson. After Jackson's offhand, seemingly anti-Semitic remarks about New York City as "Hymietown" became a campaign issue, Farrakhan threatened to ostracize *Washington Post* reporter Milton Coleman, who had released the story in the black community. Farrakhan has also become embroiled in a continuing controversy with the American Jewish community by making anti-Semitic statements. Farrakhan has argued that his statements were misconstrued. Furthermore, he contends that a distorted media focus on this issue has not adequately covered the achievements of his movement.

Farrakhan's Nation of Islam has been successful in getting rid of drug dealers in a number of public housing projects and private apartment buildings; a national private security agency for hire, manned by the Fruit of Islam, has been established. The Nation has been at the forefront of organizing a peace pact between gang members in Los Angeles and several other cities. They have established a clinic for the treatment of AIDS patients in Washington, D.C. A cosmetics company, Clean and Fresh, has marketed its products in the black community. Moreover, they have continued to reach out to reform black people with the Nation's traditional dual emphases: self-identity, to know yourself; and economic independence, to do for yourself. Under Farrakhan's leadership, the Nation has allowed its members to participate in electoral politics and to run for office, actions that were forbidden under Elijah Muhammad. He has also allowed women to become ministers and public leaders in the Nation, which places his group ahead of all the orthodox Muslim groups in giving women equality. Although the core of Farrakhan's Nation of Islam continues to be about 20,000 members, his influence is much greater, attracting crowds of 40,000 or more in speeches across the country. His group is the fastest growing of the various Muslim movements, largely through the influence of rap groups like Public Enemy and Prince Akeem. International branches have been formed in Ghana, London, and the Caribbean. In the United States, however, Farrakhan has remained an immensely controversial figure, as was best exemplified by the response to the Million Man March held in Washington, D.C. on October 16, 1995.

—LAWRENCE H. MAMIYA

See also
Nation of Islam

FESTIVALS

From early colonial times to the present day, African Americans have created and observed an impressive calendar of celebratory and commemorative events: jubilees, festivals and anniversaries, "frolics" and seasonal feasts, fairs and markets, parades, and pilgrimages, not to speak of more private or secret ceremonies such as church meetings and revivals, family reunions, baptisms and funerals, and spiritual cults. These customs have received the casual or sustained attention of travelers, visitors, or local observers. They have been praised or disparaged, extolled as the epitome of a festive spirit that should prevail in any society and as the expression of an enduring, authentic culture, or dismissed as primitive, low-brow manifestations of a subculture, an unsophisticated, burlesque imitation of mainstream life, or, at best, an adaptation or appropriation of Euro-American customs.

This festive mood with which African Americans have been credited has encouraged the persistence of many prejudices and stereotypes fostered by the minstrel tradition, which represented blacks as a happy-go-lucky, careless, lighthearted people, prone to dancing and singing. This inclination for mirth has been interpreted as a sign that the predicament of slaves and their descendants should not be such a burden to the white mind and that their sufferings and the wrongs committed against them have been exaggerated.

Yet African-American celebrations, with all their unacknowledged complexities of forms and functions, are powerful symbolic acts that express, vehemently and with exuberance, not acquiescence to fate but needs, desires, and utopian will, disenchantment, anger, and rebelliousness. Communal, playful, or carnivalesque in character, they are events through which the community endeavors to build its identity, in self-reflective scrutiny and in constant confrontation with "the black image in the white mind," to question or challenge its basic assumptions. These feasts not only give the lie to and articulate the pain of certain truths, the ambivalence of a dream always deferred; they also define unexamined propositions in performances infused with subtle ironies and double entendre.

Among the "hallowdays" observed by northern slaves and free blacks, the coronation festivals or "negro elections" set the pattern for many civic feasts and festivals. Once a year in colonial New England, slaves were allowed to accompany their masters to election festivities where whites organized the election of their governors. In the 1750s, blacks started to organize their own similar celebrations, in which a leader, preferably African-born and of known royal ancestry, quick-witted and ready of speech, was elected king or governor, a title that endowed him with authority among both blacks and whites. (The title "king" or "governor" was used by blacks according to each New England colony's specific status: Governors were elected in colonies that were relatively autonomous, whereas kings were elected in colonies more closely tied to England. According to this custom, which endured through the 1850s, bondsmen confronted their African origin—the king was intermediary to the ancestors. Bondsmen also expressed their desire to have their separate institutions and to prove their ability for self-government.

Elections were prepared for by weeks of debates and meetings. A strong political message was conveyed to the community and to white rulers in a spirit that blended parodic intent and high seriousness. By ritually transferring power from the hands of the masters to those of one of their fellows, slaves were paving the way for their Emancipation. Election days were perhaps the first freedom celebrations that combined the memory of the freedom and power Africans enjoyed before their capture with an anticipation of the freedom to come. The official recognition of African royalty and gentility reversed old stereotypes, which associated Africanness with savagery and lack of culture. The king was regarded as a civilized "negro" (the term "black" was not in usage as a noun then), composed and refined. These elections, prompted by the desire to counter forces of fragmentation and to ease conflicts, sought a consensus and struck a note of unity.

Coronation festivals were also indicative of white-black relations. The elected was often the slave of a prominent master, and slaves devised strategies to gain the support of masters to organize their ceremonies. The wealthier the slave owner, the greater the chance of having a grand festival, and, conversely, the greater the display, the stronger the evidence of the master's influence. While these feasts increased antagonism between blacks and poor whites, they offered an occasion to redefine slave-master relations, based on mutual claims and obligations. Negro kings held many roles as opinion leaders, counselors, justice makers, and mediators who could placate black insurgency or white fearfulness when faced with such a display of autonomy and self-rule.

There were other occasions when blacks gathered around a self-appointed leader. Pinkster is another well-known festival. Derived originally from the Dutch Whitsuntide celebration "pfingster," which the "Africs" took over in the late eighteenth century, the pinkster reached its peak in the early 1800s in Albany, N.Y. There the choice of a hill as the site for the celebration had many symbolic meanings. From the top of this hill, the low could look down on the world—an interesting reversal of the usual situation and a mock imitation also of the hills on which rulers like to set their capitols. Pinkster Hill was close to the place where many executions of blacks (accused in 1793 of having set fire to the city) had been staged. It was also close to the burial grounds, a military cemetery, and an all-black cemetery.

Thus death presided over the festivities, reminding blacks of the limits set on their freedom, of punishments inflicted on black rebels, of the failure to acknowledge or reward the achievements of black soldiers who had participated in the nation's wars, and of the intricate game of integration and segregation. The epitaphs and names inscribed on the graves emphasized the enduring character of African customs and rites. Cemeteries may have been the ultimate freedom sites, since only in death could blacks reach the absolute freedom they were celebrating.

Coronations and the pinkster exemplify a significant trend in the role granted to feasts: the official recognition of blacks' special gift for creating festive performances and their capacity for infusing it into other groups. (Native Americans, Germans, Dutch, and French attended the pinkster.) Feasts thus offered an arena for interaction and for the dream of a utopian and pluralistic order in a society divided by many social and political conflicts. Feasts were also an ironic comment on a republic that claimed to be dedicated to freedom but could still enslave part of its population, on the indignity of those who dared establish their power through the subjugation of others, and on the resilience of victims whose spirits could not be crushed.

Through the postrevolutionary era and in the antebellum years, African Americans evolved a tradition of Emancipation celebrations that charted the different stages toward gradual, then complete liberation. This tradition, however, initiated at a time when blacks were experiencing a sense of betrayal and of the enduring precariousness of their situation, was conditional—the ought and the should prevailed. The future that was at stake was not only that of slaves and freed

See also
Emancipation

blacks, it was also the destiny of the nation and its aspiring democracy. These yearly occurrences were not marginal to black life; they were a political manifestation of jeremiad and claim making that was pursued deliberately, was announced and debated in the press, and involved major institutions, societies, and associations (churches, societies for mutual relief, temperance and benevolent societies, freemasons, etc.).

Emancipation celebrations were occasions for public appearances in marches and parades or at universal exhibitions. Many leaders, religious or political, seized these opportunities to address the world in sermons, speeches, orations, or harangues, developing race pride and race memory. There they assessed the contribution of black people in the building of the nation, their progress, their capacity for self-government, their commitment to liberty as a universal right. These feasts were not merely opportunities to celebrate on a large scale; they held out a promise to fashion new roles in a better world and wield new power, and they heralded a season of change, from enslavement and invisibility to liberation and recognition.

Both freedom and power were present in the ceremonies, not as mere allegorical figures but as fully developed ideas whose force needed to be

INDEPENDENCE DAY

Controversial Holiday for African Americans

In the black calendar of feasts, Independence Day was the most controversial as well as the bleakest celebration. The solemnities of the Fourth of July encouraged African Americans to organize their own separate ceremonies and formulate their own interpretation of the meaning of these national commemorations. One is reminded here of Frederick Douglass's famous 1852 address, "What Is to the American Slave Your Fourth of July?" Many black leaders urged their members not to observe that unholy day and proclaimed that persecution was not over and final emancipation still out of reach. July 4 thus became a menacing and perilous day, one on which blacks were more tempted to plan insurrection than to celebrate the republic, a day also when they were most exposed to violence, riots, arrests, and murder, as in New York in 1834 or New Hampshire in 1835. No wonder they looked for other sites and landmarks to construct an alternative memory.

—GENEVIÈVE FABRE

conveyed to large audiences. Images and symbols were evolved and played out—in words, gestures, movements, and visual forms, with much ado and the will to adorn. The talents and gifts of black folks were put to use in a collective effort to stir and arouse consciousness and encourage action.

After 1808, January 1 was adopted as a day of civic celebration. The time, New Year, coming right after the Christmas festivities, and the date, in commemoration of the official end of the slave trade, seemed most appropriate. Yet, as in similar feasts, thanksgiving was tempered by ardent protest, and rejoicing by mourning and memories of the hardships of the Middle Passage. January 1 induced a heightened consciousness of Africa, where the black odyssey had begun. Africa became the central symbol and the subject of heated debate, especially when the colonization movement encouraging free blacks to return to Africa divided the community.

Curiously, January 1 never became a black national holiday. It was celebrated as such for only eight years in New York, was abandoned in the 1830s in Philadelphia, and only after general Emancipation was proclaimed on January 1, 1863, did it assume new significance. The strengthening of the "peculiar institution," the development of the much dreaded domestic slave trade and its illegal perpetuation and that of the foreign trade, may explain the decline in popularity of this memorial celebration. Many states chose instead the days when Emancipation law was passed into their constitutions: July 14 was adopted in Massachusetts, while after 1827 New York institutionalized July 5 as its freedom day, setting it apart from the American Fourth of July.

The abolition of slavery in the British West Indies by an act of Parliament on August 1, 1834, brought new hopes, and henceforth this memorable date became a rallying point for all freedom celebrations and for the black abolitionist crusade. State Emancipations were indicted for having brought little improvement in the conditions of slaves and free blacks: The rights of blacks were trampled in the North, and racial violence and tensions continued to rise, while in the South slavery was entrenched more solidly than ever.

England and Canada became the symbols of the new celebration; the former (the perfidious and despotic tyrant at the time of the Revolutionary War) was praised for setting an example for the American republic, the latter was hailed as the land of the free and a refuge for the fugitives. Black orations became more fiery, urging the righting of wrongs and of all past errors. Orations also called for self-reliance, respectability, and exemplary conduct among blacks, for a distrust of whites, and for a stronger solidarity with the newly freed population of the West Indies and between the slaves and free blacks in the United States.

Increasingly, blacks sought sites that would commemorate events or figures more related to the African-American diaspora or to their community and its own distinctive history. Sometimes towns set the calendars—Baltimore for the Haitian Revolution, or Cleveland for Nat Turner's Rebellion, or Boston in the late 1850s for Crispus Attucks. In 1814, Wilmington, Del., created its own celebration, Big Quarterly, which has been observed until very recently. Held at the close of the harvest season, it honored the founder of the Union Church of Africa, Peter Spencer.

Similar to religious revivals and patterned after the early meetings of the Quakers, Big Quarterly celebrated the struggles endured by leaders to achieve full ecclesiastical autonomy. This feast can be seen as the prototype of many religious services: praying, singing, the clapping of hands and stomping of feet, the beating of drums and tambourines, the playing of guitars, violins, and banjos. There was a characteristic use of space at such gatherings: The feast began in the church, then moved outside on the church grounds, and finally moved out to the open—Baltimore's famous French Street, for instance—where late in the century, as the feast grew more popular (in Baltimore attendance reached 10,000 in 1892, 20,000 in 1912), revival preachers took their stands to urge repentance from sin, and wandering minstrel evangelists played spirituals on odd instruments.

It was then also that educated "colored people" criticized the celebrations for giving way to weird cult practices and worldly pleasures, and for being outdated relics of old slavery times. In antebellum days, this religious feast was closer to a freedom celebration. Occurring in a region where slave-catching activities were intense, where slaves—who had to have a pass from the master to attend—were tempted to escape to Philadelphia or to the free states, Big Quarterly became a "big excursion on the Underground Railroad," with the presence among the pilgrims, who became potential fugitives, of both vigilant spies and marshals in addition to helpful railroad conductors.

In Syracuse in 1851 another major festival emerged in protest against the 1850 Fugitive Slave Law and after the rescue of a slave named Jerry. Jerry Rescue Day, which established Syracuse as the slaves' City of Refuge, embodied the spirit of defiance, of bold resistance to "iniquitous power" and to an infamous act that prevailed in the prewar years. Significantly, black leaders, rebels, warriors, and fugitives became heroic figures in celebrations and were chosen as signs that could demonstrate the unending fight against tyranny and for freedom. The oratory became more exhortative, the mood more impatient and indignant.

Freedom celebrations culminated in the early 1860s in Emancipation Jubilees and in the famous "Juneteenth" still observed today in Texas and surrounding states. In Texas, Emancipation was announced to slaves eighteen months after its proclamation. This oddity of American history explains why Juneteenth and not January 1 became a popular celebration in those parts, in defiance of the official calendar and in reaction to the contempt in which part of the slave population had been held at a time when the proclamation event was a major breakthrough in the nation's history.

Thus, from Election Day to freedom celebrations, African Americans created a ritual tradition of religious and community life. Momentous appearances in public places became challenges to the established order, calling attention to the danger of overlooking or forgetting iniquities, setbacks, and sufferings as well as heroic acts. By reiterating a commonality of origin, goals, and strivings, feasts served to correct the inconsistencies of history and to cement a unity that was always in jeopardy.

Feasts also emphasized the necessary solidarity between the enslaved and the free, between African-born and American-born black people. Although most celebrations occurred in the North, they were symbolically and spiritually connected with slaves in the South, and a dense network of interaction was woven between various sites, places, and times. Former celebrations were often referred to and used as examples to follow or improve upon. The feasts themselves became memorable events to be passed on for generations to come and to be recorded in tales, song, and dance and in physical, verbal, kinetic, or musical images. The festive spirit became ingrained in African-American culture as something to celebrate in black speech, where it is inscribed in so many words, in the literature and the arts that bear incessant testimony to the tradition.

The tradition created by colonial and antebellum celebrations has continued well into the twentieth century, still in anticipation of a freedom and justice that general Emancipation failed

See also

Crispus Attucks

Kwanza, meaning "first fruits" in Swahili, is derived from the harvest time festival of East African agriculturalists.

PAGE 407

to accomplish. Numerous associations founded after the Civil War resorted to ceremonial and commemorative rites to continue to enforce the idea of freedom, and they patterned their meetings and conventions on earlier gatherings. Freedom celebrations remained a model for the great marches and demonstrations—the protest against the 1917 riots, or the parades of the Garvey movement, or the marches of the Civil Rights Movement. The persistence of the tradition attests to the participation of African Americans in the struggle for democracy and to the crucial significance of these ritual stagings in cultural, intellectual, and political life.

Yet civil celebrations underwent some dramatic changes. More and more they became occasions of popular rejoicings. Boisterous festivity, screened out at first, crept in. Abundance and plentifulness replaced the earlier sobriety. As they grew in scope (the most popular were in urban centers where the population was largest), they sometimes lost their original meaning and became essentially social occasions for convivial gatherings. It was the orator's and leader's duty and the role of the black press to remind participants of the seriousness of the purpose, and they did so with authority and eloquence. Nevertheless, the celebrations sometimes got out of control. With the changes brought by migration and demographic shifts, by the development of the media and of mass culture, and by the impunity of profit-seeking sponsors, some feasts turned into large commercial and popular events and lost their civil and political character, while others continued to meet white opposition and censure.

Rituals played an important role in celebrations and, whatever the occasion, shared certain features. They included the same speeches and addresses or sermons; parades and marches or processions; anthems, lyrics, and songs; banquets or picnics; dances and balls. They used all black people's skills—from the oratorical to the culinary, from the gift to adorn to polyrhythmic energy—to create their own modes, styles, and rhythms, always with an unfailing sense of improvisation and performance. And as they drew more people, many folkways, many rites of ordinary life (the habit of swapping songs, of cracking jokes, or "patting juba") found their way into the ceremonies, blending memories of Africa with New World customs and forms, in a mood that was both solemn and playful, sacred and secular, celebratory and satiric. In many respects also, feasts were a privileged space for the encounters between cultures, favoring reciprocal influences, mergings and combinations, syncretism and creolization.

Nowhere is the creolization of cultures more evident than in the carnivalesque tradition, which emerged in the New World in Brazil, Trinidad, Jamaica, and the other islands, is found in its earlier forms mostly in the South, and continues its modern forms in the great Caribbean festivals of Brooklyn and Toronto. These carnivals, perceived as bacchanalian revelry or weird saturnalia, were often associated with a special season and with rites of renewal, purification, or rebirth. Usually seen as more African, and therefore as more "primitive" and exotic, more tantalizing than the more familiar Anglo-European feasts, they have elicited ambiguous responses, ranging from outright disparagement on moral and aesthetic grounds (indecency and lewdness are judged horrid and hideous) to admiration for the exuberant display of so many skills and talents.

These "festivals of misrule" were often banned or strictly regulated by city ordinances and charged with bringing disturbances and misconduct—boisterous rioting and drunkenness, gambling and undue license of all sorts. The same criticism, phrased in similar words, was leveled by some members of the black community itself, especially those concerned with respectability and with the dignity of the "race," every time they suspected any feast of yielding too much to the carnivalesque propensity of their people.

Yet the carnivalesque is always present in festive rituals to correct excesses—of piety, fervor, power—and as an instrument of Emancipation from any form of authority. In the African-American quest for liberation, it became an essential means of expression, allying humor, wit, parody, and satire. It had ancient roots in African cultures; and in North American society, where the weight of puritanism was strong, where work, industriousness, sobriety, and gravity were highly valued and had become ideological tools to enforce servitude, the carnivalesque tradition became part of the political culture of the oppressed. Artistically it developed also as a subversive response to the Sambo image that later prevailed in the minstrel tradition: It created, as coronation festivals did, possibilities for the inversion of stereotypes and challenged a system of representation that was fraught with ideological misinterpretations. Paradoxically, black carnivalesque performances may have nourished white blackface minstrelsy, providing it with the artistic devices on which it thrived.

The most notorious manifestations of the tradition are perhaps to be found in the North Car-

See also

Kwanza

olina JonKonnu (John Canoe) Festival or in the Zulu and Mardi Gras parades of New Orleans. JonKonnu probably originated in Africa on the Guinea coast, was re-created in Jamaica in the late seventeenth century, spread through the Caribbean, where it was widely observed, and was introduced by slaves in the States in isolated places, on plantations like Somerset Place, or in city ports like Wilmington, N.C., or Key West, Fla. Meant to honor a Guinean folk hero, the festival became an elaborate satirical feast, ridiculing the white world with unparalleled inventiveness and magnificence.

The festival could last weeks, but it climaxed on Christmas Day and was attended by huge crowds. The procession, which took a ragman and his followers from house to house and through the streets, came to be known as a unique slave performance. "Coonering," as it was called, was characterized most of all by spectacular costumes and by extravagant dance steps to the music of "sinful" tunes. The rags and feathers, the fanciful headdress and masks, the use of ox or goat horns and cow and sheep bells, and the handmade instruments wove a complex web of symbolic structure, ritualization, and code building. The dressing in white skin encouraged slaves to claim certain prerogatives, even to organize revolts. In many feasts an implicit analogy was established between the "beaten" skin of the (often forbidden) drums and that of whipped slaves.

Christmas, the season of merrymaking and mobility that favored big gatherings and intense communication, became a dreaded time for planters who tried to stifle the subversive and rebellious spirit of Coonering and to change a disquieting performance into a harmless pageant. Still held today but now mostly controlled and observed by whites, it has lost part of its magnificence. In its heyday, in antebellum America, the carnival was an artistic and political response of the slave population to its situation; it echoed in its own mode the freedom celebrations of the North. The lampooning liberty and grotesque parody of southern festivals turned them into arenas in which to voice anger and protest.

In New Orleans, when the carnival came into existence in the late 1850s, blacks were not supposed to participate. The Zulu parade, which grew out of black social life, was created by a section of the population concerned about publicly asserting its status. It developed into a wholly separate street event, a parody of the white Krewes. The African Zulu, a new king of misrule, precedes Rex and mocks his regal splendor. The car-

nival figures—shrunken heads of jungle beasts, royal prognosticator or voodoo doctor—the masked or painted faces, and the coconuts emphasize both the African and minstrel motifs. Neither elite nor low-brow, neither genuinely African nor creole, the Zulu parade came under attack as too burlesque; later, in the 1960s, it was criticized as exemplifying an "Uncle Tom on Wheels" and not fitting the mood of the times.

Yet the Zulu is a complex ritual that brings together several traditions: satire and masking, minstrelsy and vaudeville, brass bands, song, and dance. Another version of the coronation festival, the Zulu fuses elements of the European carnival with African, Caribbean, and Latin American practices. It establishes African Americans' rights to participate in the city's pageant, not as mere onlookers or indispensable entertainers, whose various skills as musicians and jugglers had often been used to increase the glamor of white parades, but as creators and full-fledged citizens who could thus demonstrate both their role in the city's history and their potential role in its future.

The Mardi Gras Indians, consisting of ritual chiefs, each with a spy, flagboys, and followers, march in mock imitation of the king's court and follow secret routes through the city. They enact their own rituals of violent physical and verbal confrontations between tribes. These wild warriors chant disquieting songs and speak in tongues, accompanied by haunting drumbeats and an array of other percussive sounds, as old as ancestral memories (in preference and contrast to the orderly military music of the official bands). They dance weird dance steps (e.g., the famous spy dance) and wear elaborate costumes made of beads, sequins, rhinestones, ribbons, and lace.

The tradition of Indian masking is old; originally found in Brazil, it appeared in the Caribbean in 1847. Meant to celebrate the Indian's fighting spirit and resistance, it also relates to communal rites of ancestral worship and to Dahomean ceremonial dances found also in jazz funerals. It is no accident that Mardi Gras Indians perform in the same area of New Orleans where jazz emerged out of the brass bands of Congo Square dances. Their festival may be a resurgence of the early drum gatherings that started in 1730 near the marshes of Congo Square, a market site where slaves bought merchandise from Native Americans and danced to African beats.

Now, the black Indians also appear on another festive day, March 19, at the intermission of the Lenten season. St. Joseph Day, originally an Italian Catholic feast that stylized altar building,

FESTIVALS

See also
Nat Turner's Rebellion

Richard Pryor overcame a troubled life to become a preeminent comedian, film star, screenwriter, producer, and director.

PAGE 557

blends the cult of saints (St. Joseph, "Queen Esther") with that of Indian heroes (Black Hawk) as well as that of voodoo spirits. Thus religious and pagan rites, cult and carnival practices, indoor ceremonies and outdoor parades complement each other, converge, and merge.

Later in the year, Easter Rock, another feast that is still observed in rural Louisiana, celebrates the Resurrection and similarly blends pagan and Christian elements. Its hero and emblem is both son and sun. The Son of God's rise from the dead is likened to that of the sun "rocking from the earth." All night long, prayer, "the shout," and dance herald and accompany the rocking of the sun/son.

Although the South has been the cradle of a diverse black carnivalesque tradition, in the pre-jazz and jazz ages another form of carnival celebration found its way to the North. The modern West Indian festivals of Brooklyn, N.Y., and of Toronto, Canada, give further evidence of a process of Caribbeanization that has always been at work and that repeatedly intensified during periods of great migration. The importation of slaves from the Carib Basin, the arrival of many slaves from Santo Domingo after the Haitian Revolution in the early nineteenth century, and the late twentieth-century West Indian migration to the United States have all in various degrees brought many changes to "black" celebrations. They have intensified the creolization that brought together people of African, Hispanic, Indian, and French descent. The recent festivals are also generating a pan-West Indian consciousness that expresses itself artistically through costumes, masks, music, and dance. On a much-contested terrain they enact their own rituals of rebellion, resistance and protest, inclusion and exclusion. Chaotic, playful, or violent, carnivals offer a delicate balance between many complementary or contradictory elements.

African-American celebratory performances are special occasions to celebrate freedom; they consist of various cycles of ritualized events that have rich semantic and symbolic meaning, fully a part of African-American and American history and culture. They invite us to reconsider stereotyped representations of "the race" and to revise the assumptions upon which conceptions of important figures, events, and places have themselves become objects of celebration and commemorative fervor. They are potent weapons and arenas through which to voice anger, strivings, and desire. They are efficacious and eloquent tools to educate, exhort, or indict. They are witty paro-

dies and satires that help distance reality and change "mentalities." Crucial agents of change, celebratory performances demonstrate a people's faith in words and ideas, in the force of collective memory and imagination, in the necessity of finding powerful display. These entertaining and instructive ceremonies exhibit a gift for adornment and an inventiveness that emphatically proclaim the triumph of life over all the forces that tend to suppress or subdue "the souls of black folk."

—GENEVIÈVE FABRE

FILM

Motion pictures and large numbers of African Americans arrived in American cities simultaneously in the late nineteenth century. Black Americans came to cities in flight from the southern peonage that had replaced the institution of slavery after the Civil War. Their Great Migration in turn coincided with a similar migration from Europe. Movies, in their "primitive" days, when techniques of cutting and editing as a means of conveying a narrative had not yet been perfected, became the first medium of mass communications for the poor, teeming populations that filled northeastern cities toward the end of the nineteenth century.

Movies had played the Cotton States Exposition in Atlanta in 1895, and in the following year opened at Koster and Bial's music hall in New York. Strikingly, in these early years African Americans often appeared on the screen in unmediated, unedited form, and therefore devoid of some of the worst stereotypes with which they had been maligned by decades of southern novels, advertising logos, and popular songs. A shot of, for example, black soldiers watering their horses or dockers coaling a ship appeared on the screen untrammeled by the pejorative images of the past.

These topical vignettes were the result of a rage for news of events in the corners of the world. Thomas Edison filmed life in the Caribbean; others caught black "buffalo soldiers" on their way to the Spanish-American War, tribal ceremonies in Africa, and Theodore Roosevelt on safari.

Gradually after the turn of the century, the medium changed, both technically and economically. As the prospects for a profitable future opened up, producers began to cultivate more sophisticated techniques that allowed them to edit scenes into narratives along the lines set down by novelists and dramatists. The trend pointed toward a future cinema that would play to middle-class rather than poor audiences, in picture palaces rather than storefront nickelodeons, and at length rather than in the brief snippets with which the medium had begun its life.

For African Americans, this meant a resumption of many conventions inherited from the nineteenth-century melodramatic, comic, and musical stage. Indeed, in 1903 William S. Porter brought *Uncle Tom's Cabin* to the screen, complete with overambitious attempts at spectacle—cakewalks, pursuits across ice floes, and even a race between miniature steamboats. Tom himself was more a figure drawn from the sentimental stage than from Harriet Beecher Stowe's staunch hero.

Other restorations of familiar racial material gradually dominated the screen just as the medium began to emerge from a primitive, limited visual rhetoric. In *A Bucket of Cream Ale* (1904), a stock, obstreperous black-faced servant appeared; *The Fights of Nations* (1907) featured a razor fight; and comedies about chicken thieving and life in "coontown" became routine. From 1911 through 1915, movies sentimentalized the Civil War during the five years of its semicentennial. Rarely was there an opportunity for a genuine black portrayal to show through in *A Slave's Devotion* (1913), *Old Mammy's Secret Code* (1913), or *For the Cause of the South* (1914). Typical of the era was D. W. Griffith's *His Trust* (1911) and its sequel, a tale of the Civil War in which a slave is first entrusted with managing his master's estate while the latter is away fighting and then, after the master dies a hero's death, gives his own "savings" toward sending the master's daughter to finishing school so that she may meet and marry someone in her class.

It was at this moment that African Americans took their first steps toward an indigenous cinema. Local black entrepreneurs in Lexington, Ky., as early as the first decade of the century booked all-black films in their theaters. By 1912, William Foster in Kansas made *The Railroad Porter* with a black audience as his target. About the same time in Florida, James Weldon Johnson wrote two scripts for a company bent upon making films with an African-American angle.

Unfortunately for small-time entrepreneurs, the economic setting of moviemaking had begun to rationalize into competing oligopolies, even "trusts," in which ever-fewer sellers drove out competition for customers who gradually included more demanding middle-class, urbane tastemakers. Edison's Motion Picture Patents Trust, for example, formed a pool of patents through which it hoped to control the entire nation's film output by licensing the use of cameras and projectors. In such a richly capitalized economic field, African Americans only a half century removed from slavery had little chance.

The Birth of a Nation

Then in 1915, D. W. Griffith—after years spent learning filmmaking and extending its range into techniques unforeseen in the primitive years—released his Civil War epic *The Birth of a Nation*. An evocative combination of conventional racial attitudes, a celebration of the Civil War and of the forbearance of the white South during Reconstruction, and a genuinely avant-garde piece of filmmaking, *The Birth of a Nation* galvanized African Americans and their white allies into a nationwide protest campaign. At issue were two major factors: first, its depiction of Reconstruction as a tale of black cupidity, corruption, and vindictiveness toward the prostrate white South, and second, the unprecedented nationwide advertising campaign, which further heightened the film's impact. It was this *combination* that nettled blacks. Most literate Americans believed the account of Reconstruction as portrayed therein, complete with its venal freedmen who did the bidding of scalawags and carpetbaggers (Woodrow Wilson had retold it in his multivolume history of the nation), but the couching of it in a blaring ad campaign and in an emotionally charged movie made the difference.

The NAACP fruitlessly conducted a national campaign against the movie, demanding cuts of scenes that "slandered" blacks, advocating strict legal codes against maligning races and groups, and instigating a plan to make its own movie, to be titled *Lincoln's Dream*. But despite the protesters' best efforts, by the end of 1915 *The Birth of a Nation* could be seen almost anywhere its makers wished, and *Lincoln's Dream* foundered for want of an "angel."

Nonetheless, the struggle against Griffith's film confirmed a number of African Americans in their embracing of a strategy of making movies alternative to those of the mainstream. Even Booker T. Washington, the famous founder of Tuskegee Institute and a reputed accommodationist in racial matters, took up the idea of making black movies. At first he feared that the makers of *The Birth of a Nation* might profit from the notoriety that would follow from a vigorous black protest, but soon, through his secretary Emmett J. Scott, he committed resources to a film eventually titled *The Birth of a Race*.

Let's make a rule. Blacks don't direct Italian films. Italians don't direct Jewish films. Jews don't direct black American films.

AUGUST WILSON
"I WANT A BLACK DIRECTOR,"
NEW YORK TIMES,
SEPTEMBER 26, 1990

See also

Uncle Tom's Cabin
Booker T. Washington

Oscar Micheaux had a genius for negotiating around tight budgets, improvising with limited resources, and synchronizing production with distribution.

PAGE 453

See also

Paul Robeson

The Birth of a Race

Washington and Scott's movie seemed to possess everything: the endorsement of national worthies of the Republican Party; a script that traced the progress of humankind, while allocating a prominent place in it for African Americans; and a panel of rich angels led by Julius Rosenwald, a Sears and Roebuck vice president. But things fell apart. First, Washington died on November 15, 1915. Then, acting on rumors of unscrupulous practices among the project's Chicago fundraisers, Rosenwald and other prestigious figures withdrew. And finally, with the onset of World War I, the thrust of the already episodic movie veered wildly from a pacifist theme to its ideological opposite—a justification of the American entry into the war. Thus, after almost three years of scrabbling for money, shooting in Tampa, and cutting through the thicket of cross-purposed story lines, the project changed. And yet the completed movie reached a level of accomplishment never previously attained by black moviemakers. They had actually completed a feature-length film, albeit one burdened by seemingly endless title frames that slowed its pace and shouldered aside its African-American premise in favor of militaristic themes.

The Lincoln Company

Moreover, readers of the black press noticed. Indeed, one man in particular, a postman in Omaha named George P. Johnson, saw the film as more than a grand flop. Together with his brother Noble Johnson, a contract player at Universal, he assembled a circle of black investors in Los Angeles into the Lincoln Company. Between 1916 and 1922 they turned out an impressive string of films (of which only a fragment survives), all of them celebrations of the black aspiration embedded in one of the company's titles: *The Realization of a Negro's Ambition.*

Indeed, aspiration was emblazoned on the Johnsons' battleflags. It marked or guided everything they made, whether tales of black "buffalo soldiers" fighting Mexican *insurrectes* along the border or go-getters scoring successes in capitalist circles that few blacks would have had access to in the reality of American life. The Johnsons' rivals during the booming 1920s not only followed their example but extended their reach. Among these were the Frederick Douglass Company (with its Republican namesake on its letterhead), Sidney P. Dones's Democracy Company, and regional operations such as Gate City in Kansas, Ker-Mar in Baltimore, and Norman in Jacksonville and later Boley, Okla. In the pages of the African-American press there appeared dozens of announcements of additional companies, most of which did not survive long enough to see their first film to the screen.

Some studios, such as Norman, were conduits for the investments of white "angels" or were in fact white firms. Robert Levy's Reol Studio, for example, was a white-owned company that made films from well-known black classics such as Paul Laurence Dunbar's *The Sport of the Gods.* To some extent this rush of activity merely testified to the wealth that had reached even black strata of urban life during the 1920s. But it also suggested the presence of a maturing film culture, drawing in a sector of the black population that was not only well off enough to buy tickets but also literate enough to read the growing amount of advertising copy, reviews, and show-business gossip that had begun to fill the pages of the African-American press.

The Black Audience

In other words, an audience had been formed by the black migrations to the urban centers of America, both North and South. The names of the theaters signaled the identity of the audience. No Bijous, Criterions, or Paramounts there. But rather a Douglass or an Attucks to honor famous heroes, or a Lenox, Harlem, or Pekin to provide linkages to increasingly well-known centers of black urban culture. This sort of social, institutional, and cultural density suggested the nature of this newly arrived audience: urban, literate, employed, affiliated in a circle of lodges and clubs, and church members. In short, the audience constituted a thin layer of bourgeoisie to whom movies spoke of aspiration, racial pride, and heroism, and cautioned against the evils of drink and sloth—much like a Booker T. Washington commencement address with pictures.

We can sense these social traits not only from the themes of the movies themselves but also from the critics who wrote about them: D. Ireland Thomas in the Mississippi Valley, Lester Walton of the New York *Age,* Theophilus Lewis on several papers in the New York area, Billy Rowe on the *Pittsburgh Courier,* Romeo Daugherty in the *Amsterdam News,* Fay Jackson for Claude A. Barnett's Associated Negro Press service, and other regulars on the *Afro-American* chain and even smaller papers. Augmenting their own acute criticism that seemed to be maturing toward a genuine African-American posture toward cinema were the syndicated columnists, who wrote gossipy copy for the *Los Angeles Sentinel* and the *California Eagle*—Ruby Berkeley Goodwin, Harry Levette, and Lawrence LaMar.

Micheaux and the Colored Players

Playing to this emerging audience in the 1920s were the elite of "race" film companies, either staunchly black firms such as that of Oscar Micheaux or white firms with a feel for the audience, such as David Starkman's Colored Players in Philadelphia. Micheaux, a peripatetic author who sold his own novels from door to door, entered the movie business in 1919 after a failed negotiation with Lincoln to produce his autobiographical novel *The Homesteader*. For much of the ensuing quarter century and more, he audaciously if not always artfully reached for effects and messages left untouched by his forebears. In his *Body and Soul* (1924) he featured the singer Paul Robeson in his only appearance in a race movie. In *Within Our Gates* (1921) he put his own spin on the infamous Leo Frank murder case in Atlanta. And throughout his career Micheaux played on themes of racial identity, often hinging his plots upon revelations of mixed parentage.

The Colored Players differed from Micheaux's group in that they not only calculatedly played to urban, eastern audiences but seemed to have a capacity for putting every dollar on the screen, with handsomely—even densely—dressed sets and more polished levels of acting. They did Dunbar's *A Prince of His Race* (1926), a black version of the temperance tract *Ten Nights in a Bar Room* (1926), and an original screenplay entitled *The Scar of Shame* (1927).

More than any other race movie, *The Scar of Shame* addressed the concerns of the urban black middle class. Although it teased around the theme of color caste snobbery among African Americans, its most compelling argument was a call to rise above the lot that blacks had been given and to strive for "the finer things" despite adversity. But at the same time, as critic Jane Gaines has argued, their poor circumstances were given them not by a natural order but by a white-dominated system that blacks knew as the real puppeteer working the strings off camera.

Hollywood's Blacks

For its part, Hollywood in the 1920s rarely departed from conventions it had inherited from southern American racial lore. Its high moments

"RACE MOVIES"

During the 1920s, filmmaker Oscar Micheaux played on themes of racial identity. This scene comes from Within Our Gates, *which chronicled the infamous Leo Frank murder case in Atlanta.*

FILM

Hollywood's Blacks

included *In Old Kentucky* (1926), in which the black romance was in the hands of the enduring clown Stepin Fetchit. In most movies blacks merely lent an atmosphere to the sets: Sam Baker as a burly seaman in *Old Ironsides,* Carolynne Snowden as an exotic dancer in Erich von Stroheim's Ruritanian romances, and so on. The decade also produced its own obligatory version of *Uncle Tom's Cabin.*

But with the coming of the cultural crisis wrought by the Great Depression of 1929 and after, blacks and whites shared at least fragments of the same depths of despair and were thrust together in the same breadlines and federal programs such as the Works Progress Administration (WPA). In Hollywood the result was a run of socially and artistically interesting black roles, and even a couple of tolerable all-black homages to the hard life the race lived in the South: *Hallelujah!* and *Hearts in Dixie* (both in 1929).

At the same time, Hollywood had also matured into a corporate system that had rationalized moviemaking into a vertically integrated mode of production, distribution, and exhibition. The result was a manufactured product marked by so many family traits that it could be labeled by some historians "the classic Hollywood movie." Typically, such movies told an uncomplicated tale in which engaging characters embarked on a plot that obliged them to fill some lack, solve a mys-

---

STEPIN FETCHIT

Pioneering Actor of Profiteer?

Lincoln Theodore Monroe Andrew Perry (May 30, 1902–November 19, 1985), actor, named after four U.S. presidents, became a major star as Stepin Fetchit and the center of a still-ongoing controversy. His supporters see him as a pioneering black comic actor who had a pathbreaking Hollywood career; his detractors see him as one who profited through his demeaning depictions of African Americans.

Perry was born and raised in Key West, Fla. and left home in 1914, after a stint at St. Joseph's College (a Catholic boarding school) to pursue a career in show business, joining the Royal American Shows plantation minstrel revues. With comic Ed Lee, he developed a vaudeville act entitled "Step 'n' Fetchit: Two Dancing Fools from Dixie." When Perry and Lee split, he adopted the name "Stepin Fetchit" as his own.

Stepin Fetchit spent years on the TOBA (Theater Owners Booking Association) vaudeville circuit, developing his stage persona as a lazy, dim-witted, slow, shuffling black servant, where he performed for primarily black audiences to great success. Stepin Fetchit came to Hollywood in the 1920s, and his first appearance in the 1927 film *In Old Kentucky,* playing his stereotyped black persona, earned him a positive mention in *Variety.* The next two films in which he appeared—*Salute* (1929) and *Hearts of Dixie* (1929), the first all-black film musical—brought Stepin Fetchit considerable press attention.

Stepin Fetchit went on to make more than forty films between 1927 and 1976, becoming one of the first black Hollywood stars. He was a favorite of director John Ford, with whom he made five films: *Salute* (1929); *The World Moves On* (1934); *Judge Priest* (1934); *Steamboat Round the Bend* (1935); and *The Sun Shines Bright* (1954). In *Steamboat Round the Bend* and *Judge Priest,* Ford teamed him up with Will Rogers, with whom he had worked years earlier on the vaudeville circuit. The finale of *Judge Priest* consisted of Fetchit's leading a street parade in a top hat to the tune of "Dixie," and thereby stealing the show.

Nonetheless, Stepin Fetchit's main Hollywood career came to an end in the late 1930s. Black audiences were uncomfortable with the caricatures, and white audiences became tired of them. Stepin Fetchit left Hollywood in the early 1940s bankrupt, having reportedly squandered $1 million, and moved to Chicago where he made occasional nightclub appearances. In the 1950s he reemerged, appearing in *Bend of the River* (1952) and *The Sun Shines Bright* (1954), but neither film succeeded in reviving his career. It was not until the late 1960s that he resurfaced as a member of Muhammad Ali's entourage and as the litigant in a 1970 $3 million lawsuit against CBS for, Stepin Fetchit claimed, "taking me, a Negro hero, and converting me into a villain," in a television show on black history. The suit was eventually dismissed.

In 1972 Stepin Fetchit was awarded a Special Image Award by the Hollywood chapter of the NAACP. He also received the Bethune-Cookman Award for Black Leadership (1972), and in 1978 he was presented with the Black Film Makers' Hall of Fame Award. Stepin Fetchit died in Los Angeles in 1985.

—SUSAN MCINTOSH

---

tery, or complete a quest resulting in a closure that wrapped all the strands into a fulfilling denouement.

Unavoidably, the African-American roles that filled out these plots owed more to the conventions of the moviemaking system than to the authentic wellsprings of everyday black life. Moreover, supporting this industrial/aesthetic system were the proscriptions set forth by Hollywood's self-censorship system, the Production Code Administration or "the Hays Office." These dos and don'ts discouraged full black participation in any plot forbidding racial slander or miscegenation, so that almost no African-American "heavy" or villain could appear. Nor could any black person engage in any sort of close relationship other than that of master and servant.

Stepin Fetchit, for example, enjoyed a flourishing career during the Great Depression, but one severely limited in its range. In *The World Moves On* (1934) he had a rare opportunity to play a soldier in the French army, but only as a consequence of following his master into combat; in *Stand Up and Cheer* (1934) he joined the rest of the cast in fighting off the effects of the depression, but was absent from pivotal scenes that centered on the white principals; and in the middle of the decade he appeared in a brief string of rural fables as a sidekick to Will Rogers's folksy *Judge Priest* or *David Harum*. Women had their moments as wise or flippant servants, notably Louise Beavers in *Imitation of Life* (1934) and Hattie McDaniel in *Alice Adams* (1935). Such a role eventually won McDaniel the first Oscar ever won by an African American: her "Mammy" in *Gone with the Wind* (1939). Whenever the script called for a character of mixed heritage, such as Tondelayo in *White Cargo* or Zia in *Sundown*, the Hollywood self-censorship system, the Hays office, pressed the studios toward the cautious choice of casting white actors in the roles.

For African Americans, the combination of an increasingly factory-like Hollywood system and a lingering economic depression provided only scant hope of improved roles. And yet the coming of sound film technology opened a window of opportunity for black performers.

Already, theatrical audiences had been introduced to African-American musical performance in the form of rollicking revues such as the *Blackbirds* series and Marc Connelly's Pulitzer Prize fable *The Green Pastures*, which he had drawn from Roark Bradford's book of tales, *Ole Man Adam and His Chillun*. Fleetingly, two major Hollywood studios—Fox and Metro—had responded with *Hearts in Dixie* and *Hallelujah!* And both the majors and the independents offered hope for an African-American presence in sound films in the form of a rash of short musical films that lasted well past the decade.

The most famous of these one- or two-reel gems were Bessie Smith and Jimmy Mordecai's *St. Louis Blues* (1929)—which used not only W. C. Handy's title song but incidental choral arrangements by J. Rosamond Johnson, who, with his brother James Weldon, had written the "Negro national anthem," *Lift Ev'ry Voice and Sing*—and Duke Ellington's films *Black and Tan* and *The Symphony in Black* (1929 and 1935, respectively). Throughout the decade and beyond, stars of the jazz scene—Cab Calloway, Louis Armstrong, and the Nicholas Brothers, among others—appeared in these shorts, which culminated with Lena Horne, the duo pianists Albert Ammons and Pete Johnson, and the pianist Teddy Wilson in *Boogie Woogie Dream* (1944). By then such films had attracted the attention of white aesthetes such as the photographer Gjon Mili, who cast Illinois Jacquet, Sid Catlett, Marie Bryant, and others in his *Jammin' the Blues* (1946), which became a *Life* magazine Movie of the Week.

Late Race Movies

As for race-movie makers, the times were harder. Of the African Americans only their doyen, Oscar Micheaux, worked through the entire decade of the 1940s, albeit as a client of white capital sources such as Frank Schiffman, manager of the Apollo Theater. Now and again a newcomer such as William D. Alexander's All America firm or George Randol with his *Dark Manhattan* (1947) entered the field, but race movies too had matured into a system led mainly by white entrepreneurs such as Ted Toddy of Atlanta, Alfred Sack of Dallas, Bert and Jack Goldberg of New York, and Harry and Leo Popkin of Hollywood, whose loose federation was modeled on the classic Hollywood system.

As a result, race movies soon imitated Hollywood genres such as the gangster film and the Western. *Paradise in Harlem* (1940), for example, featured a tale of a black gang bent upon taking over Harlem. The community, led by an actor (Frank Wilson), mounts a jazz version of *Othello* as a fund-raiser, and the play is so compelling that even gangsters are won over by its seductive beat and a black-themed Shakespeare. Westerns—*Two Gun Man from Harlem, Bronze Buckaroo*, and *Harlem Rides the Range*—also borrowed their formulas from Hollywood, particularly their satisfy-

Spike Lee's most ambitious film to date has been Malcolm X.

PAGE 411

See also
Bessie Smith

Bessie Smith's single film, St. Louis Blues *(1929), immortalized her, although time and rough living had taken a toll on her voice and appearance.*

PAGE 651

ing closures that promised happy lives to the good people of the cast.

The Impact of World War II

No political event affected moviemaking more profoundly than did World War II. Even before the war reached America, Hollywood responded to it by forming an Anti-Nazi League and by cleansing its movies of the worst of racist traits, much as David O. Selznick tried to do when he told his writer to place African Americans "on the right side of the ledger during these Fascist-ridden times" as they began work on *Gone with the Wind.* Indeed, so successful was he that blacks were divided in their response to the Southern epic for which Hattie McDaniel became the first black ever to win an Oscar. In less splashy movies a similar impact of the war was felt. John Huston and Howard Koch included a strong black law student who stands up to a ne'er-do-well daughter of the southern gentry in their movie of Ellen Glasgow's Pulitzer Prize novel in *In This Our Life.* And Walter White of the National Association for the Advancement of Colored People (NAACP) helped to adapt Walter Wanger's *Sundown* (1941) to fit the changing politics brought on by the war.

The war provided a cultural crisis that weighed upon African Americans in several ways: The Allies' war aims included anticolonialism, the nation needed black soldiers and war workers, and black journalists campaigned to insist on such linkages, as the *Pittsburgh Courier* did in calling for a "Double V," a simultaneous victory over foreign fascism and domestic racism. Together with the NAACP, liberals within the Office of War Information and the Pentagon joined in a campaign to make appropriate movies. Two new trends resulted: government propaganda such as *The Negro Soldier, Wings for This Man,* and *Teamwork,* which asserted a black place in the war effort, and Hollywood films such as *Crash Dive, Sahara, Bataan,* and *Lifeboat,* which often integrated the armed forces before the services themselves acted to do so. Along with federal measures such as a Fair Employment Practices Commission, the movies contributed to a new political culture that reintroduced the issue of racism to the arena of national politics.

After the war, filmmakers emerged from their military experience to form a new documentary film culture bent upon making films of liberal advocacy, much as they had done during the war. The NAACP continued to lead this movement by urging wartime agencies to send their surplus films to schools, trade unions, and civil rights groups, constituting audiovisual aids for, as Roy Wilkins of the NAACP said, "educating white people now and in the future." Thus, informational films such as *The Negro Soldier* entered the civilian marketplace of ideas. In the same period, a wartime antiracist tract by Ruth Benedict and Gene Weltfish became *The Brotherhood of Man,* an animated cartoon endorsed and distributed by the United Auto Workers. Another film of the era was *The Quiet One,* an account of a black boy of the streets who enters Wiltwyck School, an agency charged with treating such children. The fact that it enjoyed an unprecedented run in urban theaters perhaps contributed to Hollywood's decision to resume attention to the racial issues it had taken up during the war.

By 1949, Hollywood majors and some independent companies that had sprung up following the war produced peacetime versions of the war movies. The results were mixed. Louis De-Rochemont's "message movie" *Lost Boundaries* focused on a New England village "black" family that had been passing as white, thereby blunting the main point, racial integration; Stanley Kramer's *Home of the Brave* did somewhat better by introducing a black soldier into an otherwise white platoon; Dore Schary's *Intruder in the Dust* faithfully rendered William Faulkner's book into film, including its portrayal of African Americans as icons of a sad past who could teach white people the lessons of history; Darryl F. Zanuck's *Pinky* provided a closure in which a black nurse learns the value of building specifically black social institutions; and Zanuck's *No Way Out* carried the genre into the 1950s, focusing tightly on a black family and neighborhood and their willingness to defend themselves against the threat of racism.

Postwar Hollywood

Taken as a lot, these message movies perpetuated the integrationist ideology that had emerged from the war and gave Sidney Poitier, James Edwards, Juano Hernandez, and others a foothold in Hollywood. Indeed, if anything, Hollywood only repeated itself in the ensuing decade, hobbling efforts to press on. Poitier, for example, after a few good films in the integrationist vein—*The Blackboard Jungle* (1954), *The Defiant Ones* (1959), and *Lilies of the Field* (1963)—was given few challenging scripts. Typical of the era was Alec Waugh's novel *Island in the Sun,* a book specifically about racial politics in the Caribbean, bought by Twen-

See also
Cab Calloway

OSCAR-WINNING ACTOR

Sidney Poitier Delivers Powerful On-Camera Presence

Sidney Poitier (February 20, 1927–), actor, director, and filmmaker. The youngest of eight children, Sidney Poitier was born in Miami and reared on Cat Island in the Bahamas. He was forced to leave school at fifteen in order to work on his parents' tomato farm, and then moved to Miami to live with his married brother Cyril. Shortly thereafter, Poitier left for New York City, enlisted in the U.S. Army, and served as a physiotherapist until World War II ended in 1945. Upon his return to New York, he supported himself with a series of menial jobs, while studying to become an actor. After an unsuccessful audition, he spent six months trying to rid himself of his West Indian accent and eventually became a member of the American Negro Theatre, for which he often played leading roles. He also won minor parts in the Broadway productions of *Lysistrata* (1946) and *Anna Lucasta* (1948), before trying his hand at film. In 1950 he married Juanita Hardy, a dancer, with whom he had three children; Poitier and Hardy were eventually divorced.

Poitier's big break came when he was cast as a young doctor in Twentieth Century Fox's "racial problem" film *No Way Out* (1950). Leading roles followed in such films as *Cry, the Beloved Country* (1951), *Go Man Go* (1954), *Blackboard Jungle* (1955), *Band of Angels, Edge of the City,* and *Something of Value* (the last three all released in 1957). With his performance as an escaped convict in *The Defiant Ones* (1958), Poitier became the first African American to be nominated for an Oscar in the best actor category; he also won the New York Film Critics and Berlin Film Festival awards for best actor. The next year, Poitier took on the title role in Otto Preminger's motion picture version of *Porgy and Bess* (1959), for which he was also critically acclaimed.

As an actor, Poitier was known for sensitive, versatile, and eloquent interpretations and powerful on-camera presence as well as his good looks. He was one of the first African Americans to become a major Hollywood star, and during the 1960s played leads in many influential and controversial films. After originating the role of Walter Lee Younger on Broadway in Lorraine Hansberry's *A Raisin in the Sun* (1959), Poitier was featured in such diverse films as *Paris Blue* (1960), *Pressure Point* (1961), *A Patch of Blue* (1965), *The Bedford Incident* (1965), *Duel at Diablo* (1966), *Guess Who's Coming to Dinner?, In the Heat of the Night,* and *To Sir, with Love* (all 1967). In 1963, he became the first African American to win an Academy Award for best actor for his performance in *Lilies of the Field.*

The late 1960s proved a transitional period for Poitier, who was accused of portraying unrealistic "noble Negro" or "ebony saint" characters by the militant black community. He confessed to feeling himself caught between the demands of white and black audiences, and attempted to diversify his roles by taking on such films as *They Call Me Mr. Tibbs!* (1970), *A Warm December* (1973), and *The Wilby Conspiracy* (1975), and applying his talents to directing. In 1968, Poitier joined with Paul Newman, Steve McQueen, Dustin Hoffman, and Barbra Streisand to form First Artists, an independent production company. The popular western *Buck and the Preacher* (1972) marked his debut as both director and star; *A Warm December* and the hit comedy *Uptown Saturday Night* (both 1974), *Let's Do It Again* (1975), and *A Piece of the Action* (1977) all featured him in this dual role. In 1975 he was elected to the Black Filmmakers Hall of Fame; his film *Let's Do It Again* earned him the NAACP Image Award in 1976. That year, Poitier married the actress Joanna Shimkus, with whom he had two children. His autobiography, *This Life,* was published in 1980.

Over the next decade, Poitier concentrated on directing such works as *Stir Crazy* (1980), *Hanky Panky* (1982), *Fast Forward* (1985), and *Ghost Dad* (1990). In 1982 he became the recipient of the Cecil B. DeMille Golden Globe Award and the Los Angeles Urban League Whitney M. Young Award. Poitier returned to acting briefly in 1988 for starring roles in *Shoot to Kill* and *Little Nikita,* both of which were released that year.

In addition to creative filmmaking, Poitier has produced a record album called *Sidney Poitier Reads the Poetry of the Black Man* and narrated two documentaries on Paul Robeson: *A Tribute to the Artist* (1979) and *Man of Conscience* (1986). In recognition of his artistic and humanitarian accomplishments, he was knighted by Queen Elizabeth II, and the NAACP honored him with its first Thurgood Marshall Lifetime Achievement Award in 1993.

—ED GUERRERO

See also
Duke Ellington

To create appeal for his films, Oscar Micheaux featured some of the most talented African Americans of his time.

PAGE 453

See also
Spike Lee

tieth Century Fox only to have its most compelling black spokesman written entirely out of the script. Black women fared little better, mainly because they were assigned only a narrow range of exotic figures, such as Dorothy Dandridge's title role in the all-black *Carmen Jones* (1954).

Not until the era of the Civil Rights Movement—when such events as the Greensboro, N.C., student sit-ins of 1960 became daily fare on national television—would Hollywood try to catch up with the pace of events and TV's treatment of them. Even then, the most socially challenging themes were in movies made outside the Hollywood system, on East Coast locations or even in foreign countries. These included Shirley Clarke's harsh film of Harlem's streets *The Cool World* (1964); Gene Persson and Anthony Harvey's London-made film of Amiri Baraka's *Dutchman* (1967); Larry Peerce's cautionary tale about the stresses of interracial marriage, *One Potato Two Potato* (1965); Marcel Camus's Afro-Brazilian movie of the myth of Orpheus and Eurydice, *Orfeo Negro* (1960); and Michael Roemer's *Nothing but a Man* (1964), a pastoral film that was named by *Black Creation* magazine as the "greatest" of black movies.

Parallel to the civil rights movement, Hollywood itself experienced key changes in its institutional structure. Its production system became less vertically integrated and more dependent on sound marketing; federal laws began to require the active recruiting of blacks into studio guilds and unions from which they had been excluded by "grandfather clauses"; the old Hays Office censorship gave way to legal challenges and eventually to a liberalized system of ratings; and television assumed the role of seeking the steady audiences that B movies once had done. All these factors would alter the ways Hollywood treated race, but television had a particular impact.

In the 1960s television shows *East Side/West Side, The Store Front Lawyers, Mod Squad,* and *Julia,* social workers, idealistic attorneys, dedicated cops, and self-sacrificing hospital workers struggled on behalf of their clients, often against the social order itself. Television news and documentaries provided a tougher image for Hollywood to strive to emulate. Daily camerawork from southern streets and courtrooms recorded the agony of the region as it resisted African-American challenges to the status quo. The documentaries, whether on commercial or public television, occasionally emerged from black origins, such as William Greave's black journal. "TV Is Black Man's Ally," said the *Los Angeles Sentinel,*

while *Variety* reported a new black stereotype: an "intensely brooding, beautiful black rebel."

"Blaxploitation" Films

Hollywood had little choice but to take the point, particularly since several studios were close to collapse. They stood on the verge of what came to be called the era of blaxploitation films. Black youth flocked to this cycle of jangling, violent, and shrilly political movies. Timidly at first, the majors fell to the task. But first, there were easily digestible crossover movies, such as the pastoral tales *Sounder* and *The Learning Tree* (both 1968), the latter an autobiography by the photographer Gordon Parks, Jr. Then came the urban, picaresque heroes most often thought of as "blaxploitation" icons, who combined the cynicism of 1940s film noir style with the kinetic yet cool mode of the black streets. The most famous and probably the highest earner of rentals was Parks's MGM film *Shaft* (1970). The movies that followed, such as Melvin Van Peebles's *Sweet Sweetback's Baadasssss Song* (1971), constituted calls for direct and sometimes violent retribution against brutal police and exploitative mobsters.

Other movies in the cycle tried to remake white classics by reinventing them in African-American settings—*Cool Breeze* (from *The Asphalt Jungle*), *Blacula* (*Dracula*), *The Lost Man* (*The Informer*). Some were derived from original material angled toward blacks, such as the cavalry Western *Soul Soldier.*

Still another genre—"crossover" movies—sought a wider sector of the market spectrum in the form of material, such as biographies of performers—Billie Holiday, Leadbelly (Huddie Ledbetter)—who had enjoyed followings among whites.

Yet whatever their uneven merits, the blaxploitation movies lost touch with the market. Their place was taken by Chinese martial-art fables, the work of purveyors such as Raymond Chow and Run Run Shaw, featuring impossibly adept warriors whose revenge motifs touched a nerve in the psyches of black urban youth. Soon the domestic makers of blaxploitation movies lost their market entirely, so that African Americans reached the screen only as functionaries in conventional Hollywood features—police, physicians, and the like—or in prestigious, even reverent treatments of classics or successes from other media, such as Eli Landau's movie of Kurt Weill and Maxwell Anderson's South African musical *Lost in the Stars,* Charles Fuller's *A Soldier's Story,* and E. L. Doctorow's *Ragtime.*

Nonetheless, the era had revealed a previously un-measured black marketplace that seemed ready for either the raffish or the political. Moreover, the combined impact of a thin wedge of black in the Hollywood guilds, an increase in African Americans' numbers in the university film schools, and the opening of television as a training ground resulted in a greater number of film-makers and, eventually, a steady flow of independently made black films. Madeleine Anderson's combination of journalism and advocacy; St. Clair Bourne's access to black institutions, as in *Let the Church Say Amen;* Haile Gerima's syncretism of the pace and rhythms of East African life and the stuff of African-American life, mediated by film school experience, resulting in his *Bush Mama;* and William Miles's classically styled histories such as *Men of Bronze* and *I Remember Harlem* reflected the catholicity of the movement.

In addition to this focused sort of journalism of advocacy, the 1980s also resulted in a black cinema of personal dimensions, represented by Ayoka Chenzira's *A Film for Nappy Headed People,* Charles Burnett's *Killer of Sheep,* Kathleen Collins's *The Cruz Brothers and Miss Malloy,* and Warrington Hudlin's *Streetcorner Stories* and *Black at Yale.*

By 1990 one of this generation of filmmakers, Spike Lee, had—most notably because of his flair for self-advertisement and for shrewd dealing with established Hollywood—crossed over into the mainstream system. A product of film school as well as the most famous African-American association of the craft, the Black Filmmakers Foundation, Lee managed to glaze his movies of black life with a certain universalist charm that earned the sort of rentals that kept Hollywood financing coming. Somehow he conveyed the urgency, extremity, and drama of the arcana of black life—courtship, Greek letter societies, neighborhood territoriality, the tensions of interracial marriage—into a crescendo of ringing cashboxes. From *She's Gotta Have It, School Daze, Do the Right Thing,* and *Jungle Fever,* he moved toward being entrusted with a Holy Grail of black filmmakers, a biography of Malcolm X that had been stalled for almost a quarter of a century by fears that its protagonist's memory and mission would be violated if placed in the wrong hands.

More than at any other moment in African-American film history, Lee's access to black life, classical training, black associations, and commercial theaters promised the continued presence and vision of African Americans in cinema, rather than a reprise of the peaks and troughs of faddishness that had marked all previous eras of the medium.

The most insidious threat to their work continued to be that which touched everyone in Hollywood, not only the latest generation of African-American moviemakers: the unyielding fact that Hollywood was a system, a way of doing business that obliged newcomers to learn its conventions and the rules of its game. This was how fads and cycles were made: an innovative spin placed upon a familiar genre revivified it, drew new patrons into the theaters, and inspired a round of sequels and imitators that survived until the next cycle drew attention to itself. After all, even the most dedicated outlaws, Oscar Micheaux and Melvin Van Peebles, either borrowed money from the system or used it to distribute their work. Unavoidably their benefactors expected to shape their products to conform to the codes of conduct by which all movies were made.

Spike Lee and his age-cohorts were particularly successful, since many of them had gone to film school where learning the trade meant in many ways learning the Hollywood system. Lee's *Malcolm X* was a case in point. In order to celebrate, render plausible, and retail his hero and his image, Lee was drawn into the dilemma of not only making a Hollywood "bioepic" but also marketing it as if it were a McDonald's hamburger. The result was remarkably faithful to its Hollywood model: its protagonist is carried along by his own ambition, revealing slightly clayed feet, as though more a charming flaw than a sin, faces implacable adversaries, is misunderstood by his friends and family, undergoes a revelatory conversion experience, is cast out by his coreligionists for having done it, and finally meets a martyr's death and a last-reel apotheosis. This formula, as stylized as a stanza of haiku poetry, in the hands of Lee was transformed into a vehicle for carrying a particularly reverential, yet engaging black political idiom to a crossover audience.

Could Lee's successors and age-mates not only endure but also prevail over their medium? Lee himself fretted over their future: "We seem to be in a rut," he told a black film conference at Yale in the spring of 1992. His concern was not so much directed at the Hollywood establishment but rather to the young African-American filmmakers who had followed him to Hollywood: John Singleton, who at age twenty-three had made *Boyz N the Hood;* Matty Rich, who while still a teenager had made *Straight Out of Brooklyn;* and

FILM

Black Independent Film

Paul Robeson's depictions of a black man contrasted starkly with the images of subservience, ignorance, criminality, or low comedy usually seen on the Hollywood screen.

PAGE 601

F

Lee's own cameraman, Ernest Dickerson, who had made *Juice*; each one of them set in a black ghetto, each centered on a protagonist at risk not so much from forces outside his circle but from within, and each marked by a fatalism that precluded tacking on a classic Hollywood happy ending.

Indeed, forces of daunting economic power seemed to hover over the new black filmmakers even as old-line Hollywood producing companies turned out attractive packages in which black themes and characters held a secure place. First, despite various gestures, the studios had hired woefully few black executives so that every project was pitched to persons uncommitted to its integrity. Second, the top-most owners of the system were more remote than ever, as in the case of the Japanese firm Sony which owned both Columbia Pictures and Tri-Star. Third, each new film, upon its release, faced a round of rumors of impending violence that would mar its opening. Fourth, some movies drawn from black material seemed lost in the welter of ghetto movies, much as Robert Townsend's chronicle of the careers of a black quintet of pop singers, *The Five Heartbeats,* sank from view without having reached the audience it deserved. Fifth, some black films, such as Julie Dash's *Daughters of the Dust,* a rose-tinted history of an African-American family in the Sea Islands of the Carolina low country, were so unique in texture, pace, and coloring that they were played off as esoteric art rather than popular culture. Sixth, Hollywood itself seemed ever more capable of portraying at least some aspects of black life or at least drawing black experiences into closer encounters with white. John Badham's *The Hard Way* (1992) featured the rapper LL Cool J as an undercover policeman of such depth that the actor felt "honored" to play him. Black critics almost universally admired the quiet depth of Danny Glover's role as a steady, rock-solid tow-truck driver in *Grand Canyon* (1992). And in the work of Eddie Murphy at Paramount (where he sponsored "fellowships" designed to add to the talent pool of minority writers) and in other movies such as *White Men Can't Jump,* the absurdities of race and racism in America were portrayed with arch humor.

At its height during the gestation period of Lee's *Malcolm X,* the trend toward a Hollywood-based African-American cinema seemed problematic and open either to a future of running itself into the ground as the moviemakers of the *Super Fly* era had done, falling prey to cooptation by the Hollywood system, or constantly searching

out new recruits who might be the answer to Susan Lehman's rhetorical query in her piece in *GQ* (February 1991): "Who Will Be the Next Spike Lee?"

—THOMAS CRIPPS

FISHER, RUDOLPH JOHN CHAUNCEY

Rudolph John Chauncey Fisher (1897–1934), fiction writer, dramatist, and essayist. The youngest child of a Baptist minister, Fisher was born in Washington, D.C. He lived briefly in New York City as a small boy but was raised and educated largely in Providence, R.I., where he graduated from Classical High School and Brown University. An undergraduate of many talents, he was chosen by fellow students to be Class Day orator and by the faculty to be commencement speaker. He wrote his first published short story, "The City of Refuge" (1925), in his final year at Howard Medical School, initiating simultaneous vocations in literature and science. When Fisher's internship ended at Freedman's Hospital in Washington, D.C., a National Research Council Fellowship brought him to New York City in 1925 to work in bacteriology with Dr. Frederick P. Gay at the College of Physicians and Surgeons of Columbia University. At the pivotal moment of Harlem Renaissance in the mid–1920s, he consolidated his medical and literary careers with scientific articles in the *Journal of Infectious Diseases* and *Proceedings of the Society of Experimental Biology and Medicine* and short stories in the *Atlantic Monthly, Survey Graphic,* and *McClure's* magazine. He married Jane Ryder in 1925, and their son Hugh was born in 1926.

One of the more prolific writers of the Harlem Renaissance, Fisher produced in less than a decade fifteen published and seven unpublished short stories, two novels, half a dozen book reviews, a magazine feature article, and a play—while maintaining a medical practice, administering a private X-ray laboratory, and chairing the department of roentgenology at the International Hospital in Manhattan. Harlem is at the center of his literary project. "I intended to write whatever interests me. But if I should be fortunate enough to be known as Harlem's interpreter," he said in response to a radio interviewer's question on WINS in 1933, "I should be very happy." *The Walls of Jericho* (1928), his first novel, interweaves genre elements of color-conscious 1920s Harlem

See also
Sterling Brown

fiction—country-rooted southern migrants, slick Harlemites, and West Indians with their distinctive dialects and repartee; block-busting scenarios; racist uplifters of the race; rival lovers and their Arcadian conflicts; passing—and brings it all together amid the converging vectors of social and racial distinction at a Harlem ball. His other novel, *The Conjure Man Dies* (1932), is regarded as the earliest example of a detective novel published in book form by an African-American author.

Fisher's place among the writers of the Harlem Renaissance rests, however, on the excellence of his short fiction. In short stories, focused on tensions between West Indians and native-born Americans ("Ringtail"); alienation and reconciliation ("Fire by Night" and "The Backslider"); divisions between youth and age, the modern and the traditional, spirituals and blues ("The Promised Land"); and black consciousness and jazz in a battle of the bands ("Common Meter"), he conveys what Arthur P. Davis called a "fuller" picture of Harlem life viewed with "an understanding and amused eye," and what Sterling Brown termed "a jaunty realism . . . less interested in that 'problem' than in the life and language of Harlem's poolrooms, cafes, and barbershops."

Two short stories in particular, "The City of Refuge" and "Miss Cynthie" (1933)—both anthologized in *The Best American Short Stories*—are Fisher's most highly regarded achievements. "The City of Refuge" concerns the arrival in Harlem of King Solomon Gillis, "a baby jess in from the land o' cotton . . . an' ripe f' the pluckin." Gillis is betrayed by everyone who seems to befriend him, yet when he is arrested by a black policeman, the symbol of Harlem's possibility he saw when he first arrived, Gillis, who "plodded flat-footedly" on "legs never quite straightened," can stand "erect" and "exhultant" as he submits to an icon of black authority. In "Miss Cynthie," Fisher's last published work, he matches his undisputed ability to evoke locale and character with what Robert Bone calls a newly discovered sense of "how to *interiorize* his dramatic conflicts, so that his protagonists have the ability to grow." Miss Cynthie struggles to embrace the success of the grandson she hopes is a doctor or at least an undertaker, but who turns out to be a song-and-dance virtuoso.

In 1934, Rudolph Fisher underwent a series of operations for an intestinal disorder—associated by some sources with his early work with X rays—and died on December 26 of that year.

—JAMES DE JONGH

FOLKLORE

African-American folklore is a mode of creative cultural production that manifests itself in expressive forms such as tales, songs, proverbs, greetings, gestures, rhymes, material artifacts, and other created products and performances. Although African-American folklore is most often thought of in terms of these expressive forms, it is in reality a dynamic process of creativity that arises in performative contexts characterized by face-to-face interaction. The performative aspects of this folklore is what distinguishes it from other modes of creative cultural production within an African-American context. In other words, unlike other modes of African-American creative cultural production, such as literary and popular culture, folklore gains its meaning and value as a form of expression within unmediated performances on an ongoing basis in African-American communities.

Although African-American folklore should be conceptualized as a performed medium, it has an important historical dimension as well. That is, its performance even in contemporary settings entails the creative manipulation of historical forms of indefinite temporal origin. As such, it is intricately linked to processes of black culture-building in that it has historically served as an important means of communicating shared cultural attitudes, beliefs, and values of and within an ever-changing African community in the United States. As interrelated phenomena, African folklore creation and culture-building are both dynamic creative processes with roots in the diverse African cultures from which contemporary African Americans originated.

Among scholars of African-American folklore, however, the existence of a dynamic relationship between African and African-American processes of folklore creation has historically been controversial. The controversy arose in large part from the intricate link that folklorists envisioned between folklore creation and culture-building. Early in the study of African-American culture and folklore, scholars postulated that African people were so traumatized by the process of enslavement that they arrived in the New World culturally bankrupt and, therefore, dependent on Europeans for new cultural capital. In early studies, this view of a lack of African cultural retention contributed to a conception of the products of African-American folklore as mere imitations of European expressive forms. Although this view has been challenged over the years by the discovery of African cultural forms in the United States,

FOLKLORE

Voodoo refers to traditional religious practices in Haiti and in Haitian-American communities.

PAGE 710

See also
Gospel Music

♦ Spiritual
*A religious song usually of a
deeply emotional character
that was developed
especially among blacks in
the southern United States.*

these cultural expressions have been disparaged
further by being identified as "Africanisms," isolated cases that somehow survived in the New
World despite the trauma of enslavement. In fact,
however, "Africanisms" represent the most obvious evidence that African culture and cultural
forms have had a profound influence on black
culture-building and folklore creation in the
United States.

Historically, the difficulty of appreciating and
recognizing the influence of African culture and
cultural forms on African-American folklore has
been exacerbated by the fact that Africans
brought to the United States as slaves did not
themselves share a coherent culture. Only recently
have scholars begun to realize the irrelevance of
this perspective to an understanding of black
culture-building in African communities throughout the New World. For example, Sidney Mintz
and Richard Price have suggested that although
Africans enslaved in the New World did not share
a common culture or folk tradition upon arrival,
they did share "certain common orientations to
reality which tended to focus the attention of individuals from West African cultures upon similar
kinds of events, even though the ways of handling
these events may seem quite diverse in formal
terms." While these "common orientations to reality" may not have been sufficient to support the
re-creation of African cultural institutions in their
pristine form, they could and did serve as a foundation for culture-building in a new environment.

African people who were forcibly uprooted
from their homelands and transplanted in America as slaves brought with them cherished memories of their traditional lifestyles and cultural
forms that served as the foundations of African-
American folk tradition. To understand the
dynamic processes that characterized the development over time of an African-American folk
tradition, we must recognize that both black
culture-building and folklore creation have proceeded as recursive rather than linear processes of
endlessly devising solutions to both old and new
problems of living under ever-changing social,
political, and economic conditions. While both
culture-building and folklore creation are dynamic and creative in that they adapt to social
needs and goals, they are also enduring in that
they change by building upon previous manifestations of themselves. Cultural transformation is a
normative process experienced and carried out by
all groups. In the process, the institutional and expressive forms by which a group communicates

and upholds the ideals by which it lives are equally
subject to transformation.

As James Snead has argued, however, the failure to recognize the dynamic and transforma-
tional properties of African cultures in the New
World has been influenced historically by the
view that African cultures are static. Only by recognizing that such cultures are and always have
been dynamic (i.e., capable of transforming themselves in response to the social needs and goals of
African people) is it possible to envision African-
American folklore as a continuous process of creativity intricately linked to a historical tradition of
black culture-building with roots in Africa. During the period of black slavery in the United
States, enslaved Africans began the process of
building a culture based on their "common orientations to reality." Despite their lack of a sense of
shared identity and values upon arrival, the similarity of the conditions and treatment that they
faced in the slave system facilitated their ability to
envision themselves as a community. To communicate their shared identity and value system, they
transformed many of their African cultural forms
by focusing on the common elements within
them. In the process, their creative efforts as well
as the final expressive products that they created
were greatly influenced by the differences in their
situations in the United States from those they
had known in Africa. In other words, the transformation of African cultural forms involved a
process of creating new forms based on common
elements from diverse African cultures and their
infusion with insights and meanings relevant to
contemporary situations in the United States.
That these new forms did not always resemble
some African original did not negate the debt
they owed to African cultural roots.

The beginnings of an African-American folk
tradition can be traced to the slavery period and to
the efforts of African people from diverse cultural
backgrounds to maintain a sense of continuity
with their past. Throughout the period of slavery,
scattered references to African-American folklore
appeared in written records. Systematic efforts to
collect and study such folklore, however, did not
begin until the late nineteenth century. The earliest efforts to collect it were carried out primarily
by white missionaries who flocked into the South
following Emancipation to assist black freedpeople. Although these early efforts were motivated in large part by a desire to use African
Americans' creative cultural production to demonstrate their humanity and fitness for freedom, such

activities nevertheless preserved for posterity a vast body of African-American oral tradition.

An equally important motive for early collectors of black folklore was the prevalent belief in the late nineteenth century that folklore as a mode of creative cultural production was rapidly disappearing. In the case of African Americans, many envisioned the growing rate of literacy among freedpeople as a sure sign that the African-American folk tradition would soon disappear. Although contemporary folklorists realize the falsity of this perspective, it nevertheless provided a primary impetus for the collection of African-American folklore in the late nineteenth century and influenced a concentration on those forms that had obvious roots in slavery. During this productive period of African-American folklore gathering, collectors focused most of their attention on three forms: spirituals, animal-trickster tales, and folk beliefs.

Spirituals received a great deal of attention, especially from northern missionaries, in the late nineteenth century. The first book-length collection of African-American folklore published was *Slave Songs of the United States* which primarily contained spirituals. The spiritual song tradition of African Americans developed during the late eighteenth and early nineteenth centuries with the conversion of large numbers of enslaved African-Americans to Christianity. Spirituals as a body of songs were developed primarily around the actions of Old Testament figures whose faith in God allowed them to be delivered from bondage and persecution in dramatic ways. The songs followed a pronounced leader/chorus pattern known as call and response, which in performance created a kind of communal dialogue about the power of faith and belief in an omnipotent God. While the songs often portrayed Heaven as the ultimate reward of faith in God, their primary focus was on earthly deliverance from bondage and persecution. Through analogy to Old Testament stories of persecution and divine deliverance, the songs constantly reiterated the power of God to deliver the faithful.

Spirituals provided enslaved Africans with an alternative expressive form for communicating their vision of the power of God and the rewards of faith in Christianity to that offered by the slavemasters. As enslaved Africans freely and often testified, the masters frequently attempted to use slaves' Christian conversion and participation in white religious services to reinforce the masters' view of enslavement. The dominant message that enslaved Africans received from white preachers was "Servants, obey your masters." In the spirituals, enslaved Africans were able to convey to members of their community a more empowering and liberating vision of God and the Christian religion. Of equal importance, the creation and performance of spirituals allowed them to incorporate more of their African cultural heritage into Christian worship. Despite general prohibitions against unsupervised worship, enslaved Africans created opportunities for separate worship in slave cabins, "hush harbors," and even their own churches, where they created and performed spirituals in a style and manner that incorporated African performance practices. These practices included the development of the "shout," a religious ritual characterized by a counterclockwise shuffling movement reminiscent of African ritual dancing. The primary purpose of the "shout" was to induce spirit possession, a form of communion with the supernatural valued by many people of African descent.

In the late nineteenth century, the collection of spirituals was rivaled only by the collection of animal-trickster tales. With the publication of Joel Chandler Harris's *Uncle Remus: His Songs and Sayings* in 1881, the collection of animal-trickster tales by various individuals escalated. By the end of the nineteenth century, literally hundreds of these tales had been collected and published. Early collectors of black folktales often expressed amazement over the variety of animal-trickster tales created by enslaved Africans. That tales of the animal trickster would become central in the narrative performances of enslaved Africans is not surprising, however. In the cultures from which enslaved Africans originated, folktales in which clever animals acted as humans to impart important lessons about survival were ubiquitous. Although various animals acted as tricksters in different African traditions, the tales of their exploits showed important similarities throughout sub-Saharan Africa. In fact, even the same plots could be found in the trickster-tale traditions of diverse African groups (Feldmann 1973, p. 15).

In the United States, the animal trickster was most often represented by Brer Rabbit, although other animals acted as tricksters in some tales. Although a number of trickster tales found in the repertory of enslaved Africans retained plots from African tradition, many transformed the African trickster in ways that reflected the situation of enslavement. The impetus for transforming the African trickster was not only the need to create a

FOLKLORE

Despite the publication of hymnals and the dissemination of individual songs in both print and by record, it was by word of mouth that gospel music spread.

PAGE 303

See also
Slavery

FOLKLORE

single tradition out of many but also the differences in the situations faced by Africans in the New World from those in Africa that had given the exploits of tricksters there meaning and value. In the trickster tales of enslaved Africans, the trickster was an actor particularly adept at obtaining the material means of survival within an atmosphere similar to that in which enslaved Africans lived. Unlike African tricksters, whose behavior was often conceptualized as a response to famine or other conditions in which material shortage existed, the trickster of enslaved African Americans acted in a situation of material plenty.

The primary obstacle to the acquisition of the material means of survival for the trickster of enslaved Africans was the physical power and control wielded by the dupe. This situation reflected the conditions under which enslaved Africans lived, in which the material means of survival were readily available but were denied by the control of the slavemasters. In these tales, the trickster was portrayed as developing clever strategies for obtaining material goods, especially food, despite the efforts of his dupes to deny access. As historians of the slave experience have noted, the concern with the acquisition of food was a common one during slavery (Blassingame 1972, p. 158; Genovese 1976, pp. 638–639). In tale after tale, Brer Rabbit proved to be a masterful manipulator of his dupes, who appeared most often in the guise of the wolf or the fox. The tales often portrayed situations in which cleverness, verbal dexterity, and native intelligence or wit allowed the trickster to triumph over the dupes. For enslaved Africans, this provided a model of behavior for dealing with the power and control of the slavemasters over the material means of survival.

Often reported as case studies, the folk beliefs of enslaved Africans also seemed widespread to collectors in the late nineteenth century. In many ways, the concerns of collectors reflected a stereotypical view of many white Americans that African Americans were inordinately superstitious. The collection of folk beliefs centered primarily around the practice of conjuration. At the core of this practice was the conjurer, a figure transformed by enslaved Africans but based on African religious leaders such as medicine men. While the conjurer in different parts of the South was known by different names, including root doctor, hoodooer, and two-heads, the practice of conjuration was remarkably similar wherever it was found (Bacon and Herron 1973, pp. 360–361). In most instances, conjurers were believed

to be individuals possessed of a special gift to both cause and cure illness. Although the source of the conjurer's powers was usually believed to be mysterious, some believed it came from an evil source, others believed it came from God, and still others believed it could be taught by those possessed of it.

During the period of slavery, conjurers played a prominent role among enslaved Africans, especially as healers. Although most slavemasters attempted to provide for the health needs of enslaved Africans, their efforts often fell short. In general, the state of scientific medicine during the period of slavery was so poorly developed that, even under ideal conditions, doctors were ineffective in treating many diseases. The importance of conjurers for enslaved Africans also had to do with beliefs about the causes of illness, beliefs deeply influenced by their African cultural heritage. Like their ancestors, many enslaved Africans continued to believe that illness was caused by the ill will of one individual against another through an act of conjuration. Individuals could induce illness either through their own action or by consulting a conjurer, who could be persuaded to "lay a spell." In these cases, only the power of a conjurer could alleviate the illness.

In their practices, conjurers used both material objects, such as charms and amulets, and verbal incantations in the form of curses and spells. However, theirs was primarily an herbal practice; hence, the common name of root doctor for these practitioners. The frequent use of verbal incantations derived from African beliefs about the power of the spoken word to influence forces in nature for good or ill. Although conjurers have often been associated with unrelieved evil, their role was a culturally sanctioned one. Within the belief and social system that supported the practice of conjuration, social strife, believed to be the dominant cause of illness, was seen as disruptive to the equilibrium and harmony of the community. The conjurer's role was to discover the identity of the individual responsible for the disruption and to restore harmony. For both the social and physical well-being of enslaved Africans, the conjurer's abilities in this regard proved beneficial. Not only did the presence of conjurers provide them with a means of tending to their own health needs, it also provided a mechanism for addressing issues of social strife within the group without the intervention of slavemasters.

Although spirituals, trickster tales, and folk beliefs were the focus of most early collecting, the folklore of enslaved Africans included more than these genres. Collectors seldom noted other vibrant genres that developed during slavery, including proverbs, courtship rituals, prayers, sermons, and forms of folktale other than trickster narratives. But while there was no concerted effort to collect these genres, examples sometimes found their way into collections. In addition, folklorists and other scholars have begun to utilize various kinds of records, including plantation journals, slave narratives, and diaries of various sorts in an effort to better understand the nature of black vernacular creativity during the slave period (Joyner 1984; Ferris 1983). These types of resources have proven particularly useful in the study of black material culture. Because slavemasters were generally responsible for the material needs of enslaved Africans, the importance of knowledge possessed by Africans and applied to the production of various material objects has generally been overlooked. However, African skill and knowledge were responsible for the production of many material objects used in everyday life on farms and plantations. It has become evident, for example, that African knowledge and skill in rice cultivation were responsible for the profitable rice industry that thrived along the coast of Georgia and South Carolina. In addition, African knowledge of basketry and textiles was responsible for the development of a unique tradition of basketry and quilting that continues to be practiced today (Ferris, 1983, pp. 63–110 and 235–274). Of equal importance, many enslaved Africans who served as blacksmiths, carpenters, cooks, and seamstresses on farms and plantations used African techniques in the production of the material products for which they were responsible.

Despite early predictions of the demise of an African-American folk tradition with the advent of freedom and literacy, African Americans have continued to create and perform various genres of folklore. In many ways, the success of early collectors was a testament to the vibrancy and importance of vernacular creativity among African Americans. Although Emancipation brought about important changes in lifestyle, it did not alter many of the conditions that had made the forms of folklore created by enslaved Africans meaningful. In the post-Emancipation era, the development of the sharecropping system and the imposition of Jim Crow laws created patterns of economic and social oppression similar to those that had existed during slavery. In fact, the similarities in the conditions of freedpeople in the late nineteenth and early twentieth centuries to those

endured by enslaved Africans allowed them to simply alter many of the forms they had created during slavery to reflect new realities.

As the conditions that would influence black culture-building in the post-Emancipation era became clear, African Americans began the process of both transforming existing forms and creating new ones to communicate their perceptions of the economic, social, and political realties that informed their lives as freedpeople. With the failure of Reconstruction and growing patterns of segregation following Emancipation, African Americans came to realize that conditions imposed on them that inhibited their progress in society had to be addressed differently. In a general sense, the powerful role that the law played in the lives of freedpeople made many of the strategies developed during slavery for dealing with white power and control no longer effective or in the best interest of African Americans. For example, the tales of the animal trickster, which had provided an important model of behavior for dealing with white economic exploitation and social oppression during slavery, gradually lost their effectiveness as the expressive embodiment of a strategy for freedpeople. In some animal-trickster tales collected in the late nineteenth century, contests between the animal trickster and dupe were settled in the courts.

Despite the decline of animal-trickster-tale narration, African Americans retained the trickster as a focus for folklore creation. In the late nineteenth and early twentieth centuries, the trickster was transformed into the badman, a character whose primary adversary was the law, personified by the white policeman or sheriff (Roberts 1989, pp. 171–220). The emergence of white lawmen as powerful and often brutal defenders of white privilege made it extremely problematic for African Americans to retaliate directly against whites for their exploitation. At the same time, the proliferation of patterns of segregation and economic exploitation and the rise of Jim Crow laws made the black community an arena for the actions of badmen. Therefore, although badmen spent much of their energy attempting to elude the law, they found their dupes in members of the black community. As tricksters, they attempted to dupe members of the black community into participating in illegal activities such as gambling, bootlegging, prostitution, numbers-running, and drug-dealing. That is, badmen as tricksters sought material gain by outwitting both African Americans and the law. In this sense, the black badmen of the post-Emancipation era faced

See also
Voodoo

a double bind not unknown to many African Americans.

Folklore creation surrounding black badmen in the late nineteenth and early twentieth centuries reflected changed conditions faced by African Americans in society. As the law in both its abstract and personified forms became a powerful force in maintaining white privilege, African Americans were forced to turn increasingly to their own communities for solutions to their economic and social oppression. Because the law was often brutal in its treatment of African Americans, they made avoidance of the law a virtue and attempted to keep the law out of their communities. In so doing, they assumed a great deal of responsibility for maintaining harmony and peace among themselves. In economically deprived black communities, however, the means of enhancing one's economic status were extremely limited. The rise of secular entertainment establishments such as jukes and bars served as a focus for many of the activities associated with black badmen. In these establishments, many African Americans found activities by which they had the potential to enhance their economic well-being, such as gambling and numbers-playing, as well as offering psychological escape in whiskey and drugs from the oppressive conditions of their lives. Despite their illegal nature, these activities posed little danger to the black community as long as individuals who participated in them played by the unwritten rules. However, the consumption of alcohol and the existence of games of chance created an environment in which violence often erupted and the law intervened.

The exploits of black badmen typically unfolded in jukes and bars. The badman emerged in folklore as an individual who, in defense of his trade, committed an act of murder. The badmen's exploits were celebrated in legends and ballads, narrative songs that told of their deeds. For example, the notorious gambling badman Stackolee purportedly shot Billy Lyons, who was cheating him in a card game. Duncan shot the white policeman, Brady, to end his bullying of patrons at Duncan's bar. Invariably caught and punished, the badman was treated sympathetically in folklore. The sympathy engendered by the badman derives from the importance to some members of the black community of the activities with which he became associated, as well as the individuals he killed. The badman's victims were usually cheaters or bullies whose actions threatened to bring the power and force of the law down on the community. In the late nineteenth and early twentieth centuries, many African Americans endured economic conditions that made the activities identified with black badmen important to their material well-being. At the same time, they recognized the potential and real consequences of participating in these activities.

In many ways, the focus of folklore creation surrounding black badmen reflects the nature of black folklore since Emancipation. In a profound sense, expressive celebration of the black badman reflected a general pattern of forms that focused on conditions faced by African Americans on a recurrent basis yet suggested that the solutions lie within the black community. The most common types of folktale performed by African Americans since Emancipation attempt to identify the origins of conditions that inhibit black progress in society. These often humorous narratives attempt through suggestion and persuasion to address intragroup attitudes and behaviors perceived as responsible for the conditions faced by African Americans. At the same time, they suggest that when African Americans recognize their own role in maintaining behaviors not in their best interest, they gain the ability and power to change them.

In many narratives the focus of the tales is on the origins of certain animal characteristics. These tales were developed during slavery and usually involved animals from the trickster cycle. In some instances, the animal trickster is made the dupe. The best known of these tales purport to explain why the rabbit has a short tail or the buzzard a bald head. While these tales often seem to be naive explanations for the physical characteristics of different animals in reality they impart useful lessons about African-American moral and social values. In most instances, the tales reveal that the acquisition of the physical characteristics came about as a result of obsessive pride and vanity, or a failure to evaluate the motives of one known to be an adversary.

The didactic intent of African-American origin tales is even more evident in those that involve human actors. Many of these tales, which also originated in slavery, continue to be performed in African-American communities today (Dance 1978, pp. 7–11). The focus is on the development of certain physical features associated with African Americans as a race. For example, the performer purports to explain why African Americans have big feet or hands, nappy hair, black skin, etc. The stories are invariably set at the beginning of time when God, a principal actor in the tales, gave out human traits. African Americans are envisioned as always getting the "worse"

See also
Film

characteristics because they arrived late, were playing cards and did not hear God calling them, or were too impatient to wait for God. Despite the humor often evoked in these tales, they speak to African Americans about certain negative patterns of behavior stereotypically associated with the race—laziness, tardiness, impatience, etc. Rather than being self-deprecating, as some scholars have suggested, these tales attempt in a humorous way to call attention to certain behavioral patterns perceived by some members of the black community as inhibitive to the advancement of African Americans. In addition, they reveal one of the ways in which African Americans have historically attempted to communicate in intragroup contexts the nature and consequences of negative stereotypes of them.

Closely associated with tales of origin is a large group of tales that revolves around the character of "Colored Man" (Dorson 1956, pp. 171–186). These tales often purport to explain the origins of conditions experienced by African Americans in society. From all internal evidence, Colored Man tales are a post-Emancipation invention that thrived in the early and mid-twentieth century. In this group of tales, Colored Man is pitted in a contest with White Man and a member of another racial or cultural group, either Jew or Mexican. In some instances, the three actors are given a task by God, usually involving the selection of packages of different sizes; in others, they are involved in a scheme of their own making. In the former case, Colored Man makes the wrong decision, whether he selects the largest or the smallest package. His choices are most often conceptualized as a result of his greed, his ability to be deceived by appearances of easy gain, his laziness, or even his efforts not to be outsmarted. The tales almost invariably revolve around some stereotype associated with African Americans. By portraying situations in which a generic African American acts out a stereotype, the performers of these tales implicitly call for critical self-examination. On the other hand, by setting these tales at the beginning of time, performers suggest that conditions experienced by African Americans in the present result from systemic sources.

Throughout the twentieth century, African Americans have created and performed folktales that deal realistically with their situation in society. Many function as jokes that revolve around stereotypes. However, these tales function to constantly remind African Americans that one of the most problematic aspects of their existence in American society derives from negative images of

them held by other groups. In many of these tales, the African American appears as the dupe of the nonblacks, who use stereotypes to manipulate him into making bad choices. In other tales, African-American performers celebrate certain stereotypical images that seem to allow them to gain an advantage over other groups. This type of narrative usually revolves around sexual stereotypes; blacks triumph over members of other groups because they demonstrate superior sexual prowess or larger sexual organs. In their celebration of an image of self generally evaluated negatively in society, African Americans reveal an interesting ambivalence about such images and possibly a different value orientation.

Besides narrative, other forms of African-American folklore created since Emancipation reveal an intimate concern with intragroup problems and solutions. Of the genres created and performed by African Americans, the blues is concerned directly with conditions and situations within the black community. As a body of song, the blues touches on various problematic areas of black life like unemployment, homelessness, sharecropping, police brutality, and economic exploitation (Titon 1977; Keil 1966; Oliver 1963). However, it concentrates primarily on the problems of black male/female relationships. Although the blues celebrates the joys of being in a successful relationship, it most often focuses on the problems involved in sustaining one. These problems often revolve around economic issues, especially the inability of black males to provide for the material well-being of lover, wife, or family.

In the late nineteenth century and the early decades of the twentieth, the blues served as an ongoing commentary on conditions faced by many African Americans. As an expressive form, the blues did not often propose solutions to the problems it identified but rather focused on defining the contours of situations shared by large numbers of African Americans. When the blues did offer a solution, it most often proposed mobility: either moving out of a troubled relationship or moving out of town. It might be suggested that the idea of mobility as a solution to problematic situations often found in the blues simply reflected a solution embraced by thousands of African Americans in the early twentieth century. During the heyday of the blues, African Americans witnessed the migration of thousands from the rural South into urban centers in search of better economic and social conditions.

For many African Americans, the blues reflected much about the nature of black culture-building

By the 1890s, spirituals had become widely popular, both in the United States and in Europe, in the versions sung by the college singers.

PAGE 658

See also
Blues

*Gospel, like the
blues, envisions a
diverse black
community.*

PAGE 266

in the early twentieth century. It emerged as the first solo form of musical expression created by African Americans and signaled the growing diversity of the black population. In the midst of the Great Migration and other changes in black life, the blues revealed the difficulty of speaking about a common African-American experience in post-Emancipation America. It envisioned a community beset by various problems of identity, values, and even beliefs arising from mobility as well as economic and social upheaval. Although blues performers spoke from a first-person point of view, their popularity derived from their ability to use personal experience as a metaphor for shared realities. Despite its popularity with a large segment of the black population, however, the blues was not valued by all members of the community. Due to its association with secular entertainment establishments in which drinking alcohol, dancing, gambling, and often violent crimes occurred, as well as to its often sexually explicit lyrics, it was sometimes strongly disparaged by religious and socially conscious members of the black community.

However, in the early twentieth century, the blues had its expressive and religious counterpart in the emergence of gospel music (Heilbut 1975; Allen 1991). The development of modern gospel can be attributed to two interrelated influences, which can be conceptualized as, on the one hand, musical and, on the other, social and religious. Although spirituals continued to be performed well after Emancipation, the message of deliverance from bondage and persecution through analogy to Old Testament figures and events lost much of its meaning for freedpeople. In addition, performance of spirituals in the post-Emancipation era was greatly influenced by efforts of some African-American religious leaders to make black religious practices more closely resemble those of white Americans. As a result, many black churches banned the "shout," an important context for spiritual song performance, and began to encourage the singing of European hymns to the neglect of spirituals. At the same time, the emergence of Europeanized arrangements and performances of spirituals proliferated, especially with touring college choirs such as those organized at Fisk University and Hampton Institute. The success of these choirs, as well as the barbershop-quartet craze of the nineteenth century, influenced the organization of hundreds of black harmonizing quartets that sang primarily arranged spirituals.

While these changes in the religious and musical life of African Americans in the South greatly influenced the attitude toward and performance of spirituals, the Great Migration confronted many African Americans with a new lifestyle and environment that threatened their ability to maintain the spiritual values that many had traditionally associated with black religion. In urban areas, many African Americans embraced not only new social and economic patterns but also modes of worship in churches that did not fulfill social and spiritual needs as southern churches had. In both South and North, many African Americans in the late nineteenth and early twentieth centuries turned to the newly developing Spiritual Church Movement and Holiness Movement and the storefront churches that arose to house them. In these churches, many African Americans found patterns of worship more conducive to their religious sensibilities, and an emerging musical style that came to be known as gospel. Unlike the spirituals of enslaved Africans, gospel songs tended to emphasize the New Testament message of love and faith in God as the solutions to human problems. As such, gospel relies less on analogy to Old Testament personalities and events and more on the abstract New Testament promise of rest and reward for the faithful.

In an important sense, gospel, like the blues, envisions a diverse black community, whereas spirituals relied on the existence of a coherent community sharing a single condition: slavery. As such, gospel songs tend to abstract the nature of the problems for which Christian faith provides a solution. In essence, the lyrics of gospel songs seldom identify specific conditions but, instead, speak of burdens, trials, and tribulations and offer faith in God as a solution. In this regard, gospel is genre that gains its meaning in performance. Through performance, its apparent abstract message is concretized in messages delivered as sermons, prayers, and testimonies, which provide numerous illustrations of the situations of which gospel music speaks. Although gospel songs are usually written by individuals and recorded by commercial companies, a development that goes back to the 1920s and 1930s, gospel remains a vernacular form performed in African-American communities in churches and concert halls throughout the United States on a regular basis.

The study of African-American folklore in the twentieth century remains vital. The focus of collection in recent years has turned from the rural South to urban communities in both North and South where viable traditions of African-American oral expressive culture continue to thrive. In the process, folklorists continue to produce important collections of African-American folklore reflective of both historical and contemporary concerns. For example, the toast tradition, which involves the recitation of long narrative poems revolving around the actions of black badmen, has been collected extensively (Jackson 1974; Wepman, Newman, and Binderman 1976). These poems, which have been collected in prisons and on the streets, chronicle the lives of individuals involved in criminal activities and warn of the consequences of their behavior. Although a large number of toast texts have been published, the toast as a genre is not widely known among African Americans. In fact, it seems to be known and performed primarily by individuals who participate in a criminal lifestyle or individuals who have connections with it. While toasts seem to celebrate criminality and the peculiar brand of "badness" associated with it, these poems tend to be highly moralistic and realistic in terms of the consequences of criminal activity. In addition—despite their often offensive language, violent imagery, and seeming disregard for legal and moral authority in the black community and society—toasts give expressive embodiment to behavioral and economic strategies and reflect attitudes embraced by some individuals in African-American communities with regard to drug-dealing, prostitution, gambling, and other so-called victimless crimes.

Although not primarily or exclusively an urban genre, the dozens has been the focus of much study in recent years (Abrahams 1970). The dozens is a generic name for a form of verbal artistry known variously in African-American communities as joning, wolfing, busting, breaking, and cracking, and by a host of other names. Although the art of playing the dozens is generally associated with adolescent males, the practice in different ways is one that knows no age limit or gender. Generally speaking, younger males tend to play more often and to rely more on formulaic rhymes and phrases in their performances. Often discussed as verbal exchanges that disparage the mother through implications of sexual impropriety, playing the dozens just as often involves apparent insults to one's opponent. While playing the dozens has been associated with the acquisition of verbal skill, especially among young African-American males, it also serves as an intragroup mechanism for communicating information with negative import for individuals. Regardless of who plays the dozens or how it is played, the content of the exchanges focuses on behaviors that violate certain norms generally ac-

cepted by African Americans, whether they relate to sexual activity, personal habits, physical characteristics, modes of dress, etc.

A concern with playing the dozens in recent years has been accompanied by a general focus on other forms of African-American folklore that reveal a rich tradition of verbal play. Forms such as signifying, marking, and loud-talking have been discussed as a reflection of the art of everyday life in African-American communities (Mitchell-Kernan 1972). The artistry of these forms derives from the ability of individuals to encode messages with serious import in humorous and witty forms. In addition, the rise of rap music, which transforms many African-American expressive forms into a flourishing narrative tradition, reflects the continuing verbal artistry in black communities. Rap, which exists as both a narrative and a musical tradition, reflects a continuing concern in African-American expressive culture with identifying conditions and situations that impact negatively on the black community. Though a diverse group, rap songs frequently point to the need for self-evaluation, criticism, and change in the black community itself without denying the impact of systemic causes for many of the conditions it identifies.

African-American folklore reflects many of the ways in which African Americans have historically communicated their attitudes, beliefs, and values in artistic forms in everyday life. Although the roots of the study of this folklore lie in beliefs about its ultimate demise, the African-American tradition of vernacular creativity and performance remains vital. While the genres that constitute the African-American folk tradition are too numerous to be examined in a short discussion, the basic categories of narrative, song, verbal artistry, and material culture suggest the tradition's contours. With African culture and cultural forms providing the tradition-rich source of African-American folklore, it has been endlessly transformed to both aid and reflect black culture-building in the United States. On an everyday basis, African-American folklore continues to provide individuals with a rich creative outlet for expression and performance.

—JOHN W. ROBERTS

FOOTBALL

American-style, intercollegiate football emerged from the English sport of rugby during the 1870s and 1880s. Almost immediately, African Ameri-

FOOTBALL

Salient features of a rap include metaphor, braggadocio, repetition, formulaic expressions, double entendre, mimicry, rhyme, and "signifyin' " (i.e., indirect references and allusions).

PAGE 573

See also
Literature

FOOTBALL

Black Pioneers at Predominantly White Colleges, 1889–1919

Football combines the two worst features of modern American life: it's violence punctuated by committee meetings.

GEORGE WILL
IN *BASEBALL*, PUBLIC
BROADCASTING SYSTEM, 1994

cans distinguished themselves on college grid-irons.

Black Pioneers at Predominantly White Colleges, 1889–1919

William Henry Lewis and William Tecumseh Sherman Jackson were two of the first blacks to play football at a predominantly white college. Both of these Virginians played for Amherst College from 1889 through 1891. Jackson was a running back, while Lewis was a blocker. In 1891 Lewis served as captain of the Amherst squad. After graduation, he attended Harvard Law School, and because of the lax eligibility rules of the time, played two years for Harvard. In 1892 and 1893, Yale coach Walter Camp named Lewis to the Collier's All-American team at the position of center. After his playing days, Lewis became an offensive line coach at Harvard, the first black coach at a predominantly white college. He left football when President William Howard Taft appointed him as United States Assistant Attorney General in 1903.

William Arthur Johnson, George Jewett, and George Flippin were other early black players. Johnson appeared as a running back for MIT in 1890. That same year, Jewett played running back, punter, and field-goal kicker for the University of Michigan. Flippin, who played running back for the University of Nebraska from 1892 to 1893, was an intense athlete who would not tolerate foul play. The press reported that in one game he "was kicked, slugged, and jumped on, but never knocked out, and gave as good as he received." Flippin went on to become a physician. Other African Americans who played in the 1890s included Charles Cook (Cornell), Howard J. Lee (Harvard), George Chadwell (Williams), William Washington (Oberlin), and Alton Washington (Northwestern).

After the turn of the century, numerous blacks played football for northern and midwestern schools. Two of the most talented stars were Edward B. Gray of Amherst and Robert Marshall of the University of Minnesota. A halfback and defensive end, Gray earned selection to Camp's All-American third team in 1906. Marshall was another skillful end and field-goal kicker who played from 1903 to 1906. In 1904, Minnesota defeated Grinnell College 146–0. Marshall scored 72 points in that contest, a record that still stands. He was named to the second All-American team in 1905 and 1906.

As intercollegiate football gained in popularity during World War I, two black players won na-

tional acclaim. Frederick Douglass "Fritz" Pollard entered Brown University in 1915. By mid-season, the 5′6″ freshman had excelled as a kicker, runner, and defensive back. He helped take his team to the second Rose Bowl game in 1916, a 14–0 loss to Washington State. The following year also proved successful. Pollard starred in games against Rutgers, Harvard, and Yale, scoring two touchdowns in each contest. In naming Pollard to the All-American team in 1916, Walter Camp described him as "the most elusive back of the year, or any year. He is a good sprinter and once loose is a veritable will-o'-the-wisp that no one can lay hands on."

The son of a Presbyterian minister, Paul Robeson of Princeton, N.J., enrolled at Rutgers University in 1915 on an academic scholarship. Tall and rugged (6′3″, 225 pounds), he played tackle and guard as a freshman and sophomore. In his final two seasons he was switched to end, where he gained All-American honors. Walter Camp described him in 1918 as "the greatest defensive end who ever trod a gridiron." Besides football, Robeson lettered in track, baseball, and basketball. He also excelled academically, earning election to Phi Beta Kappa. Although he was excluded from the college glee club for racial reasons, he was named to Cap and Skull, a senior society composed of four men "who most truly and fully represent the finest ideals and traditions of Rutgers." After graduation, he played professional football to finance his way through Columbia Law School. He also began an acting and singing career which brought him international recognition.

Almost all of the pioneer African-American players experienced both subtle and overt forms of discrimination. Pollard was forced to enroll at several universities before he found one willing to let him play football. Often black players were left off their squads at the request of segregated opponents. And football, a violent game at best, provided ample opportunities for players to vent racial animosities at black players. Paul Robeson, for example, suffered a broken nose and a dislocated shoulder as a result of deliberately brutal tactics by opposing players. Despite the drawbacks, there probably was no venue of major sporting competition of the era that had as few impediments to black participation as major collegiate football.

Pioneers at Black Colleges, 1889–1919

The first football game between black colleges occurred in North Carolina in 1892 when Biddle defeated Livingstone, 4–0. Owing to inadequate funding, it took nearly two decades for most black colleges to establish football programs. On New Year's Day in 1897, as a forerunner of the bowl games, Atlanta University and Tuskegee Institute met in what was billed as a "championship game." But major rivalries eventually developed between Fisk and Meharry in Tennessee, Livingstone and Biddle in North Carolina, Tuskegee and Talladega in Alabama, Atlanta University and Atlanta Baptist (Morehouse), and Virginia Union and Virginia State. By 1912, Howard and Lincoln in Pennsylvania, Hampton in Virginia, and Shaw in North Carolina had organized the Colored (later Central) Intercollegiate Athletic Association (CIAA).

The black press began to select All-American teams in 1911. Two of the players on that first team were Edward B. Gray, a running back from Howard who had played the same position from 1906 to 1908 at Amherst, and Leslie Pollard, older brother of Fritz, who had played halfback for one year at Dartmouth before resuming his career at Lincoln University. Two other standout athletes who played for black colleges were Floyd Wellman "Terrible" Terry of Talladega and Henry E. Barco of Virginia Union.

Pioneers: Black Professionals, 1889–1919

Charles Follis of Wooster, Ohio, is credited with being the first African-American professional football player. He was recruited by the Shelby, Ohio, Athletic Club, where he played professionally from 1902 to 1906. One of his teammates during the first two years was Branch Rickey, who would, as general manager and president of the Brooklyn Dodgers in 1947, desegregate major league baseball by signing Jackie Robinson. A darting halfback, Follis often experienced insults and dirty play. In one game in 1905 the Toledo captain urged fans to refrain from calling Follis a "nigger." By 1906 the abuse had become unendurable and Follis quit the game. He died of pneumonia in 1910, at the age of 31. Three other blacks appeared on professional club rosters prior to 1919. Charles "Doc" Baker ran halfback for the Akron Indians from 1906 to 1908, and again in 1911. Gideon "Charlie" Smith of Hampton Institute appeared as a tackle in one game in 1915 for the Canton Bulldogs. And Henry McDonald, probably the most talented black professional during the early years, played halfback for the Rochester Jeffersons from 1911 to 1917. In one game against Canton in 1917, Earle "Greasy" Neale hurled McDonald out-of-bounds and

snarled, "Black is black and white is white . . . and the two don't mix." Racial incidents and segregation would become even more severe in the interwar years.

Black Stars at Predominantly White Colleges, 1919–1945

Following World War I, a number of blacks gained national celebrity for their football skills. John Shelburne played fullback at Dartmouth from 1919 through 1921. During those same years, Fred "Duke" Slater was a dominant tackle at the University of Iowa. In the early 1920s, Charles West and Charles Drew played halfback for Washington and Jefferson (in Washington, Pa.) and Amherst, respectively. West became the second African American to appear in a Rose Bowl game. After their football careers, both men became medical doctors. Drew achieved international acclaim for perfecting the method of preserving blood plasma. Toward the end of the decade, David Myers appeared as a tackle and end for New York University and Ray Kemp played tackle for Duquesne.

Although scores of blacks played football for major colleges, they constantly faced racial prejudice. Some colleges denied blacks dormitory space, thus forcing them to live off campus. Others practiced a quota system by limiting the number of black players on a squad to one or two. Others benched minority athletes when they played segregated southern schools. In 1937, Boston College surrendered to southern custom when it asked Louis Montgomery to sit out the Cotton Bowl game against Clemson. One sportswriter complained that "even Hitler, to give the bum his due, didn't treat Jesse Owens the way the Cotton Bowl folk are treating Lou Montgomery—with the consent of the young Negro's alma mater. . . ." African Americans also encountered excessive roughness from white players. Jack Trice of Iowa State was deliberately maimed by Minnesota players in 1923 and died of internal bleeding. Finally, minority players were snubbed by white sportswriters. No blacks were named first-team All-Americans from 1918 to 1937, including Duke Slater, probably the best tackle of that era.

In the 1930s, dozens of black players had outstanding careers. The Big Ten Conference featured a number of gifted running backs, especially Oze Simmons of Iowa and Bernard Jefferson of Northwestern. Talented linemen included William Bell, a guard at Ohio State, and Homer Harris, a tackle at the University of Iowa. Two of

FOOTBALL

Black Stars at Predominantly White Colleges, 1919–1945

Paul Robeson was selected twice (1917 and 1918) as an All-American football player by the famed journalist Walter Camp.

PAGE 600

See also
Education

269

F

the best black athletes at eastern colleges were Wilmeth Sidat-Singh, a rifle-armed quarterback at Syracuse, and Jerome "Brud" Holland, an exceptional end at Cornell. Named first-team All-American in 1937 and 1938, Holland was the first black to be so honored since Robeson two decades earlier. In the West, Joe Lillard was a punishing running back at Oregon State in 1930 and 1931. And Woodrow "Woody" Strode and Kenny Washington starred for UCLA from 1937 to 1940. Strode was a 220–pound end with sure hands and quickness. Washington, a 195–pound halfback, was one of the nation's premier players. In 1939, he led all college players in total yardage with 1,370, but failed to win first-team All-American honors.

During the war years, there were five exceptional African-American college players. Marion Motley was a bruising 220–pound fullback at the University of Nevada. Two guards, Julius Franks of the University of Michigan and Bill Willis of Ohio State, were named to several All-American teams. And Claude "Buddy" Young was a brilliant running back at the University of Illinois. As a freshman in 1944, the diminutive, speedy halfback tied Harold "Red" Grange's single-season scoring record with 13 touchdowns. He spent the next year in the armed service, but continued his

career after the war. Finally, Joe Perry was a standout running back at Compton Junior College in southern California.

Black College Play, 1919–1945

Although black colleges lacked sufficient funds for equipment and stadiums, football grew in popularity after World War I. Black conferences sprang up throughout the South, but the CIAA, created in 1912, fielded the most talented teams. In the immediate postwar period, Franz Alfred "Jazz" Bird of Lincoln was the dominant player. A small but powerful running back, Bird was nicknamed "the black Red Grange."

Morgan State University was the dominant black college team of the 1930s and early 1940s. Coached by Edward Hurt, Morgan State won seven CIAA titles between 1930 and 1941. Running backs Otis Troupe and Thomas "Tank" Conrad were the star athletes for the Morgan State teams. In the deep South, Tuskegee Institute overwhelmed its opponents, winning nine Southern Intercollegiate Athletic Conference (SIAC) titles in ten years from 1924 through 1933. Tuskegee's team was led by Benjamin Franklin Stevenson, a skilled running back who played eight seasons from 1924 through 1931. (Eligibility rules were not enforced at the time.) In the more competitive Southwest Athletic Conference (SWAC), Wiley University boasted fullback Elza Odell and halfback Andrew Patterson. Langston College in Oklahoma, which won four championships in the 1930s, featured running back Tim Crisp. The Midwestern Athletic Conference (MWAC), started in 1932, was dominated by Kentucky State, which topped the conference four times in the 1930s. Its key players were ends William Reed and Robert Hardin, running back George "Big Bertha" Edwards, and quarterback Joseph "Tarzan" Kendall. During the war years, fullback John "Big Train" Moody of Morris Brown College and guard Herbert "Lord" Trawik of Kentucky State were consensus picks for the Black All-American team.

Black Professionals, 1919–1945

In 1919 several midwestern clubs organized the American Professional Football Association, the forerunner of the National Football League (NFL) created two years later. The first African Americans to play in the NFL were Robert "Rube" Marshall and Fritz Pollard. Over forty years old, Marshall performed as an end with the Rock Island Independents from 1919 through 1921. Pollard appeared as a running back with the

Akron Pros during those same years. Racial incidents were commonplace. Pollard recalled fans at away games taunting him with the song "Bye, Bye, Blackbird." Occasionally, they hurled stones at him. Even at home games, fans sometimes booed him. Besides playing, Pollard served as the first black NFL coach, directing Akron in 1920, Milwaukee in 1922, Hammond in 1923 and 1924, and Akron again in 1925 and 1926. Other blacks who performed in the NFL during the 1920s were Paul Robeson, Jay "Inky" Williams, John Shelbourne, James Turner, Edward "Sol" Butler, Dick Hudson, Harold Bradley, and David Myers. Those athletes did not compete without incident. In 1926, the New York Giants refused to take the field until the Canton Bulldogs removed their quarterback, Sol Butler, from the game. Canton obliged. The last three minority athletes to play in the desegregated NFL were Duke Slater, Joe Lillard, and Ray Kemp. An exceptional tackle who often played without a helmet, Slater performed for Milwaukee (1922), Rock Island (1922–1925), and the Chicago Cardinals (1926–1931). Joe Lillard also starred for the Cardinals from 1932 to 1933. He was a skillful punt returner, kicker, and runner, but his contract was not renewed after the 1933 season. Ray Kemp, a tackle with the Pittsburgh Pirates (later renamed the Steelers), met a similar fate.

In 1933, NFL owners established an informal racial ban that lasted until 1946. The reasons for the exclusionary policy are not entirely clear. Probably NFL moguls were attempting to please bigoted fans, players, and owners. In addition, professional football hoped to compete with baseball for fans and adopted that sport's winning formula on racial segregation. Southern-born George Preston Marshall, who owned the Boston franchise, was especially influential in the shaping of NFL policy. A powerful personality with a knack for innovation and organization, Marshall in 1933 spearheaded the reorganization of the NFL into two five-team divisions with a season-ending championship game. Four years later, he moved his Boston team to Washington, D.C., a segregated city. Marshall once vowed that he would never employ minority athletes. Indeed, the Redskins was in fact the last NFL team to desegregate, resisting until 1962.

Other owners implausibly attributed the absence of African-American athletes to the shortage of quality college players. The NFL draft was established in 1935, but owners overlooked such talented stars as Oze Simmons, Brud Holland, Wilmeth Sidat-Singh, Woody Strode, and Kenny

Washington. Owners also lamely argued that they purposely did not hire blacks in order to protect them from physical abuse by bigoted white players.

Denied an opportunity in the NFL, blacks formed their own professional teams. The New York Brown Bombers, organized in 1935 by Harlem sports promoter Hershel "Rip" Day, was one of the most talented squads. Taking their nickname from the popular heavyweight fighter Joe Louis, the Brown Bombers recruited Fritz Pollard as coach. Pollard agreed to coach, in part, to showcase minority athletes. He signed Tank Conrad, Joe Lillard, Dave Myers, Otis Troupe, Hallie Harding, and Howard "Dixie" Matthews. The Bombers competed mainly against semipro white teams such as the New Rochelle Bulldogs. Pollard coached the Bombers to three winning seasons, but he resigned in 1937 when the team was denied use of Dyckman Oval Field in the Bronx. The Brown Bombers continued for several more years as a road team and then disappeared.

During the war years, blacks played professionally on the West coast. In 1944 both the American Professional League and the Pacific Coast Professional Football League fielded integrated teams. Kenny Washington starred for the San Francisco Clippers and Ezzrett Anderson for the Los Angeles Mustangs. In the Pacific Coast League, Jackie Robinson, who would integrate major league baseball, represented the Los Angeles Bulldogs, and Mel Reid performed for the Oakland Giants. The following year the two leagues merged into the Pacific Coast League. The Hollywood Bears, with Washington, Anderson, and Woody Strode, won the title.

The Postwar Years: Blacks at Predominantly White Colleges

World War II and the Cold War proved instrumental in breaking down racial barriers. After all, how could Americans criticize Nazi Germany and then the Soviet Union for racism and totalitarianism when blacks were denied first-class citizenship in the United States? During the 1940s and 1950s, blacks worked diligently to topple segregation in all areas, including athletics. In football, their efforts met with considerable success.

During the postwar years, several minority athletes performed admirably at big-time schools. Buddy Young returned to the University of Illinois and helped lead his team to a Rose Bowl victory over UCLA. Levi Jackson, a fleet running back, became the first African American to play for Yale and was elected team captain for 1949.

It was hard to say, about football as about games in general, which was more impressive, the violence or the rationality.

HOWARD NEMEROV
THE HOMECOMING GAME,
1957

See also
Paul Robeson

FOOTBALL

The Postwar Years: Blacks at Predominantly White Colleges

♦ **Linebacker**

A defensive football player who lines up immediately behind the line of scrimmage to make tackles on running plays through the line or defend against short passes

See also
Jackie Robinson

Wally Triplett and Denny Hoggard became the first blacks to play in the Cotton Bowl when Penn State met Southern Methodist in 1948. And Bob Mann, Len Ford, and Gene Derricotte helped the University of Michigan trounce the University of Southern California in the 1949 Rose Bowl, 49–0.

Blacks continued to make their mark in intercollegiate football in the 1950s. Ollie Matson excelled as a running back at the University of San Francisco from 1949 through 1951. The following year he won two medals in track at the Olympics in Helsinki. Jim Parker was a dominant guard at Ohio State. In 1956 he became the first African American to win the Outland Trophy, awarded to the nation's foremost collegiate lineman. Bobby Mitchell and Lenny Moore starred at halfback for the University of Illinois and Penn State, respectively. Prentiss Gautt took to the gridiron for the University of Oklahoma in 1958, the first black to perform for a major, predominantly white southern school. And Jim Brown, perhaps the greatest running back in the history of the game, debuted at Syracuse University in 1954. There, Brown lettered in basketball, track, lacrosse, and football and was named All-American in the latter two sports. As a senior, he rushed for 986 yards, third highest in the nation. In the final regular season game he scored 43 points on 6 touchdowns and 7 conversions. In the 1957 Cotton Bowl game against Texas Christian University, he scored 21 points in a losing cause and was named MVP. Brown would go on to have a spectacular career in the NFL.

Literally and figuratively, African Americans made great strides on the gridiron in the 1950s. Yet barriers continued to exist. Dormitories at many colleges remained off-limits. Blacks were denied access to most major colleges in the South. They were virtually excluded from some football positions, especially quarterback. And they were not seriously considered for the Heisman Trophy, an award presented to the best collegiate player.

In the 1960s, a landmark decade in the advancement of civil rights, black gridiron stars abounded. Ernie Davis, Brown's successor at fullback for Syracuse, was an exciting and powerful runner who shattered most of Brown's records. As a sophomore in 1959, Davis averaged 7 yards per carry and helped lead Syracuse to its first undefeated season. Ranked first in the nation, Syracuse defeated Texas in the Cotton Bowl and Davis was named MVP. The following year, Davis gained 877 yards on 112 carries and scored 10 touchdowns. As a senior, he had another outstanding season and became the first African American to win the Heisman Trophy. Tragically, he was diagnosed with leukemia in 1962 and never played professional football. He died at the age of twenty-three.

The 1960s produced a number of sensational black running backs. Leroy Keyes of Purdue and Gale Sayers of Kansas twice earned All-American recognition. Floyd Little and Jim Nance proved worthy successors to Brown and Davis at Syracuse. And Mike Garrett and O. J. Simpson, both of USC, won Heisman awards. The decade's greatest breakaway runner, Simpson rushed for 3,295 yards and 22 touchdowns in only 22 games. Blacks also excelled as linemen, receivers, and defensive backs. Bobby Bell and Carl Eller both won All-American acclaim as tackles with the University of Minnesota. Bell also captured the Outland Trophy in 1962. Bob Brown of Nebraska and Joe Greene of North Texas State also were All-American tackles. Paul Warfield was a crafty wide receiver for Ohio State. And George Webster of Michigan State twice earned All-American distinction as a defensive back. Also from Michigan State was the feared defensive end Charles "Bubba" Smith, who joined the Baltimore Colts in 1967.

In the 1960s bastions of bigotry collapsed. The last three lily-white college conferences—the Southwest, Southeast, and Atlantic Coast—all desegregated. Blacks, too, put the lie to the stereotype that they lacked the intellectual necessities to perform as quarterbacks. Sandy Stephens was voted an All-American at Minnesota and Marlin Briscoe and Gene Washington called signals at the University of Omaha and Stanford, respectively. Yet the NFL showed little or no interest in Stephens, and the other two were converted to wide receivers.

During the 1970s, 1980s, and 1990s, major colleges actively recruited African-American athletes. Considered essential to the success of the football program, blacks at some schools were illegally offered monetary and material inducements. Meager grade point averages and low graduation rates also brought accusations that universities were exploiting minority athletes. After all, the vast majority of varsity players do not go on to enjoy lucrative professional athletic careers. To blunt the criticism, the NCAA instituted Proposition 48 in 1983. That directive required entering freshman varsity athletes to achieve a combined score of 700 on the Scholastic Aptitude Test (SAT) and to maintain at least a C average.

JIM BROWN

All-American Running Back Becomes a Legendary Athelete

James Nathaniel "Jim" Brown (February 17, 1936–), football player and actor. Born on St. Simons Island in Georgia, Jim Brown moved to Long Island, N.Y., with his mother when he was seven. He excelled in sports at Manhasset High School, where he won thirteen varsity letters. Named all-state in football, basketball, and track, he averaged 38 points a game on the basketball court, and 14.9 yards a carry on the football field. At Syracuse University (1954–1957), Brown received letters in football, track, basketball, and lacrosse. In 1957 he set a major college record for running backs when he scored 43 points in one football game against Colgate. In his final collegiate game, Syracuse played Texas Christian University in the Cotton Bowl. Though Syracuse lost, Brown rushed for 132 yards, scored 21 points, and was named most valuable player. He was Syracuse's first all-American running back.

Brown also had a successful college career in lacrosse, although he had never played the game before arriving at Syracuse. In 1957, he was the first black player in the North-South Game. Playing only half the game, he led the North to a 14–10 victory, scoring five goals and two assists. He was named all-American in the sport and was elected to the Lacrosse Hall of Fame. In addition, Brown helped Syracuse's basketball team by scoring 563 points in 43 games, and he competed in the decathlon for the track team.

In 1957, Brown turned down a three-year, $150,000 offer to become a professional fighter, and refused offers from the New York Yankees and the Boston Braves to play baseball, as well as an offer from the Syracuse Nationals to join their basketball team. Instead, Brown signed with the Cleveland Browns, who had chosen him in the first round of the National Football League draft. Generally regarded by sports journalists as the greatest NFL fullback of all time, Brown rushed for a lifetime total of 12,312 yards and scored 126 touchdowns in just nine seasons. In his NFL career he averaged 5.2 yards a carry, a record that still stands, and he averaged 102 yards rushing every game. Brown was named NFL Rookie of the Year in 1957. He was named to the Pro Bowl every year he played, and was elected to the Football Hall of Fame in 1971.

In 1965, a year after he appeared in *Rio Concho,*

Brown retired from the NFL at age twenty-nine to concentrate on his film career. He appeared in *The Dirty Dozen* (1967) and *Ice Station Zebra* (1968), as well as in a number of black action films such as *Black Gunn* (1972), *Slaughter* (1972), and *Slaughter's Big Rip-Off* (1973), and in *Take a Hard Ride,* a black western (1975). As head of his own independent movie production company, he was executive producer of *Richard Pryor Here and Now* (1983). He also made appearances on such television shows as "I Spy" (1965), "Chips" (1983), "T. J. Hooker" (1984), and "The A-Team" (1986).

Offscreen, Brown led a turbulent personal life, winding up in trouble with the police several times following violent altercations. In 1978, he was found guilty of a misdemeanor battery charge for punching a competitor in an argument during a golf match, and in 1986 he was arrested for assaulting his fiancée, but charges were never pressed.

Brown has always been outspoken in his involvement with civil rights and other political issues. Accordingly, when he retired from football, he founded the Black Economic Union to assist black-owned businesses. In February 1990, he threatened to have his name removed from the NFL Hall of Fame to protest "favoritism, good old boyism, cronyism, and racism" in the selection process, as he felt that some deserving black players had been bypassed. In the 1990s Brown created Amer-I-Can, a program to raise self-esteem among Los Angeles gang members. He arranged for transportation of the young men to his own home, where they participated in "life management skills" classes and support-group meetings, and had access to job-placement services. Brown also hosted benefits at his house for the widows of gang members. The program was designed to be sold to school administrators and state prison officials. In 1991, Amer-I-Can classes were being taught in ten California penal institutions, and in 1993, an Amer-I-Can representative was hired by the Chicago Housing Authority to develop a gang intervention program there.

Brown has written two autobiographies, *Off My Chest* (1964) and *Out of Bounds* (1989). As the Cleveland Browns' honorary captain for life, he is often involved in promotional events for the NFL.

—LYDIA MCNEILL

FOOTBALL

The Postwar Years: Blacks at Predominantly White Colleges

See also

FOOTBALL

Black College Play in the Postwar Era

Football isn't a contact sport, it's a collision sport. Dancing is a contact sport.

VINCE LOMBARDI
QUOTED BY
JAMES A. MICHENER,
SPORTS IN AMERICA, 1976

From 1970 through the 1993 season, blacks have won the Heisman Trophy 17 times. The vast majority of selectees have been running backs. Beginning with Ohio State's Archie Griffin in 1974 and 1975, minority athletes won the Heisman ten consecutive years: Tony Dorsett (1976), Earl Campbell (1977), Billy Sims (1978), Charles White (1979), George Rogers (1980), Marcus Allen (1981), Herschel Walker (1982), and Michael Rozier (1983). Running backs Bo Jackson (1985) and Barry Sanders (1988) also were recipients. The only non-running backs to capture the prize were receivers Johnny Rodgers (1972), Tim Brown (1987), and Desmond Howard (1991), and quarterbacks Andre Ware (1989) and Charlie Ward (1993). Outland trophy winners for the best interior lineman have included Rich Glover (1972), John Hicks (1973), Lee Roy Selmon (1975), Ross Browner (1976), Greg Roberts (1978), Mark May (1980), and Bruce Smith (1984).

Blacks have only slowly been hired as collegiate coaches. The first African-American head coach at a major college football program was Dennis Green, who was head coach at Northwestern (1981–1985) and at Stanford (1989–1991) before being named head coach of the Minnesota Vikings in the NFL. In the early 1990s the only African-American coaches at Division 1–A colleges were Ron Cooper at Eastern Michigan University, Ron Dickerson at Temple University, and Jim Caldwell at Wake Forest University.

Black College Play in the Postwar Era

Although football programs at black colleges continued to be strapped financially, they still produced some superb players and coaches. Eddie Robinson of Grambling, Ed Hurt and Earl Banks of Morgan State, and Jake Gaither of Florida A & M were four of the most successful black college coaches. Each won several conference titles and sent numerous players to the NFL. Morgan State produced three premier NFL players—Roosevelt Brown, a guard with the New York Giants in the mid-1950s, Leroy Kelly, a running back with the Cleveland Browns in the mid-1960s, and Willie Lanier, a linebacker with the Kansas City Chiefs from 1967 to 1977—among numerous other stars. Florida A & M yielded Willie Gallimore, a running back with the Chicago Bears (1957–1963), and Bob Hayes, a sprinter who played wide receiver for the Dallas Cowboys (1965–1974). Grambling has sent more than seventy players to the NFL, including quarterback James Harris, running backs Paul Younger and Sammy White,

wide receiver Charlie Joiner, defensive tackles Ernest Ladd and Junious "Buck" Buchanan, defensive backs Everson Walls, Roosevelt Taylor, and Willie Brown, and the outstanding defensive end for the Green Bay Packers, Willie Davis.

Two of the greatest offensive players in NFL history graduated from black colleges in Mississippi. NFL career rushing leader Walter Payton attended Jackson State before joining the Chicago Bears in 1975, and the San Francisco '49ers' Jerry Rice, the holder of the career record for touchdown receptions, graduated from Mississippi Valley State in 1985. Other notable products of black colleges include defensive specialists David "Deacon" Jones and Donnie Schell from South Carolina State, defensive end Elvin Bethea from North Carolina A & T, wide receivers John Stallworth and Harold Jackson of Alabama A & M and Jackson State, respectively, and guard Larry Little of Bethune Cookman. Prairie View A & M produced safety Ken Houston and wide receiver Otis Taylor. Maryland State delivered defensive back Johnny Sample and two dominant linemen, Roger Brown and Art Shell. Savannah State yielded tight end Shannon Sharpe.

The NFL in the Postwar Years

The democratic idealism of World War II and the emergence of a rival professional league, the All-America Football Conference (AAFC), proved instrumental in the toppling of the racial barrier in 1946. That year the Los Angeles Rams of the NFL hired Kenny Washington and Woody Strode, and the Cleveland Browns of the AAFC signed Marion Motley and Bill Willis. Washington and Strode were beyond their prime, but Motley and Willis were at their peak. They helped lead the Browns to the first of four consecutive league championships. Both athletes were named first-team All-Pros, an honor which became perennial. Both would also be inducted into the Pro Football Hall of Fame.

The success of the Browns prompted desegregation among other teams, especially in the AAFC, which lasted until 1949. The football New York Yankees signed Buddy Young and the gridiron Brooklyn Dodgers took Elmore Harris of Morgan State. The Los Angeles Dons recruited Len Ford, Ezzrett Anderson, and Bert Piggott. Ford would go on to star as a defensive end for the Cleveland Browns. The San Francisco '49ers, originally an AAFC team, in 1948 signed Joe Perry, who would, in his second season, lead the league in rushing. After the '49ers joined the NFL, he became the first back to amass back-to-back thousand-yard rushing seasons in 1953 and 1954.

Among NFL teams, only the Rams, the New York Giants, and the Detroit Lions took a chance on African-American athletes in the 1940s. The Lions signed Melvin Grooms and Bob Mann, and the Giants acquired Emlen Tunnell, one of the sport's greatest safeties. In the early 1950s, the Giants also obtained Roosevelt Brown, a superior tackle. The Baltimore Colts acquired Buddy Young from the Yankees, and the Chicago Cardinals signed Wally Triplett, Ollie Matson, and Dick "Night Train" Lane. Matson was a crafty runner and dangerous receiver who rushed for 5,173 yards and caught 222 passes in 14 NFL seasons. He was inducted into the Pro Football Hall of Fame in 1972. Dick Lane, another Hall of Fame inductee, excelled as a cornerback for the Cardinals and Lions. The Washington Redskins, the last NFL team to desegregate in 1962, acquired Bobby Mitchell from the Cleveland Browns for the draft rights to Ernie Davis. Mitchell was a gifted wide receiver and an explosive kick returner. He, too, was elected to the Pro Football Hall of Fame in 1983.

Jim Brown, Lenny Moore, and John Henry Johnson were all premier running backs in the 1950s and early 1960s. In nine seasons with Cleveland, Brown led the NFL in rushing eight times, amassing 12,312 yards and 126 touchdowns, a career record. He was selected Rookie of the Year in 1957, and MVP in 1958 and 1965. He was also voted to nine All-Pro teams. At 6′2″ and 230 pounds, Brown ideally combined power, speed, and endurance. Lenny Moore was the epitome of a runner-receiver. He gained 5,174 yards as a halfback and another 6,039 yards as a receiver. He was named Rookie of the Year in 1956 and helped propel the Baltimore Colts to NFL championships in 1958 and 1959. He was elected to the Pro Football Hall of Fame in 1975. John Henry Johnson, a powerful running back and ferocious blocker, played for San Francisco, Detroit, and Pittsburgh (1954–1966). In 13 seasons, he totaled 6,803 yards on 1,571 carries.

The formation of the American Football League (AFL) in 1959 presented opportunities on the new teams for scores of African Americans. Prior to its merger with the NFL in 1966, the AFL produced many exciting black players. Carlton "Cookie" Gilchrist of the Buffalo Bills became the league's first thousand-yard rusher in 1962. Other excellent running backs included Abner Haynes of the Dallas Texans, Paul Lowe of Oakland, Jim Nance of Boston, and Mike Garrett

of Kansas City. Lionel Taylor of Denver, Art Powell of Oakland, and Otis Taylor of Kansas City were all gifted receivers. Willie Brown and Dave Grayson were prominent defensive backs for Oakland. And three future Hall of Famers all played for Kansas City: Buck Buchanan, Bobby Bell, and Willie Lanier.

Minority athletes also excelled in the NFL during the 1960s. Roosevelt Brown of New York and Jim Parker of Baltimore were frequent All-Pros on the offensive line. The successful Green Bay teams were anchored on defense by Willie Davis at end, Herb Adderly at cornerback, and Willie Wood at safety. Other defensive standouts were Roger Brown and Dick Lane of Detroit, Abe Woodson of San Francisco, Roosevelt "Rosey" Grier of New York and Los Angeles, and Carl Eller and Alan Page of Minnesota.

Gale Sayers of the Chicago Bears was probably the most electrifying offensive star of the 1960s. A graceful back with breakaway speed, he won Rookie of the Year honors in 1965, scoring 22 touchdowns. The following year, he led the NFL in rushing with 1,231 yards. After leading the league in rushing for a second time in 1969, injuries ended his career. The decade also yielded two superior pass receivers: Paul Warfield and Charlie Taylor. Playing 13 seasons for Cleveland and Miami, Warfield caught 427 passes for 8,565 yards. Another Hall of Famer, Taylor played his entire thirteen-year career for Washington, totaling 649 passes for 9,140 yards.

The 1970 merger of the AFL and NFL set the stage for the emergence of professional football as America's most popular spectator sport. Since the merger, the NFL has been split into two divisions, the National Football Conference (NFC) and the American Football Conference (AFC). During the era of the unified league, African Americans have managed to topple virtually every existing sports barrier. In football, they have continued to dominate the skill positions of running back, receiver, and defensive back. In the 1970s, Orenthal James "O. J." Simpson became the dominant back. A slashing and darting runner for the Buffalo Bills, Simpson led the AFC in rushing in 1972, 1973, 1975, and 1976. In 1973 he shattered Jim Brown's single-season record by rushing for 2,003 yards. In eleven seasons he rushed for 11,236 yards and caught 232 passes for 2,142 yards. Walter "Sweetness" Payton became the game's most statistically accomplished running back, establishing an NFL record of 16,726 yards in 13 seasons with the Chicago Bears. A durable player who missed only four of 194 games, he also

At the University of Southern California, O. J. Simpson emerged as a national star, displaying tremendous speed and open-field running abilities.

PAGE 624

See also
Washington, D.C.

*Jackie Robinson
was an All-
American football
player, leading
scorer in basketball,
and record-setting
broad jumper, in
addition to his
baseball exploits.*

PAGE 603

holds the record for most thousand-yard seasons (10), most hundred-yard games (77), most yards rushing in a single game (275), and is second to Jim Brown for most touchdowns (125).

Erick Dickerson led the NFC in rushing with the Los Angeles Rams in 1983, 1984, 1986, and with the Indianapolis Colts in 1988. In 1984 he broke Simpson's record by gaining 2,007 yards in a single season. Earl Campbell, a barrel-thighed fullback with the Houston Oilers, led the AFC in rushing from 1978 to 1981. In 1978 he captured both the Rookie of the Year and the MVP awards. In eight seasons he gained 9,407 yards. Tony Dorsett of the Dallas Cowboys was another leading ground-gainer who accumulated more than 10,000 yards rushing. In a game against Minnesota in 1983 he sprinted for a 99-yard touchdown run, establishing an NFL record. In the 1970s, Franco Harris helped spark the Pittsburgh Steelers to four Super Bowl victories, and in the 1980s, Marcus Allen helped the Oakland Raiders win the Super Bowl in 1984. The following year Allen led the NFL in rushing and was named MVP. Ottis Anderson, Roger Craig, and Herschel Walker have been successful ground-gainers and pass receivers. Thurmond Thomas of the Buffalo Bills is another quality dual-purpose back. In the early 1990s, three of the NFL's most gifted runners were Thomas, Barry Sanders of Detroit, and Emmitt Smith of Dallas, who won rushing titles in 1991, 1992, and 1993.

A number of blacks have gained recognition as receivers. Possessing both blocking and pass-catching ability, Kellen Winslow, Ozzie Newsome, Shannon Sharpe, and John Mackey have served as model tight ends. Mackey was elected to the Pro Football Hall of Fame in 1991—an honor long overdue and probably denied him earlier because of his union fights against management and the NFL office. Notable wide receivers have included Otis Taylor, Paul Warfield, Harold Jackson, Cliff Branch, Drew Pearson, Mel Gray, Lynn Swann, John Stallworth, Isaac Curtis, James Lofton, Charlie Joiner, Mike Quick, Art Monk, Al Toon, Andre Rison, Andre Reed, John Taylor, Ahmad Rashad, Mark Duper, Mark Clayton, Michael Irvin, and Sterling Sharpe. In 1993, Sharpe of the Green Bay Packers caught 112 passes, surpassing his own single-season record established the year before. Sure hands, breath-taking quickness, and an incomparable ability to run with the ball make Jerry Rice of the '49ers a peerless receiver. In Super Bowl XXIII against Cincinnati, Rice won the MVP by catching 11 passes for a record 215 yards. The following year,

in Super Bowl XXIV against Denver, he caught 7 passes for 148 yards and 3 touchdowns. Barring injury, Rice seems certain to break Jim Brown's record for career touchdowns and Art Monk's record for career pass interceptions.

Blacks have also distinguished themselves as defensive backs, interior linemen, and linebackers. Art Shell, Gene Upshaw, Bob Brown, Leon Gray, Reggie McKenzie, Anthony Munoz, and Larry Little all have excelled on the offensive line. Little was selected to the Pro Football Hall of Fame in 1993. A frequent All-Pro selection, Dwight Stephenson of the Miami Dolphins became the first outstanding black center in the mid-1980s. Claude Humphrey, Leroy Selmon, Joe Greene, Bruce Smith, Reggie White, and Charlie Johnson have all been standout defensive linemen. Defensive backs include Ronnie Lott, Mel Blount, Lem Barney, Jimmy Johnson, Emmitt Thomas, Donnie Schell, Louis Wright, Mike Haynes, Albert Lewis, and Ron Woodson. And some of the best linebackers in the game have been minority athletes such as George Webster, David Robinson, Willie Lanier, Robert Brazille, Lawrence Taylor, Mike Singletary, Cornelius Bennett, Seth Joyner, Hugh Green, Andre Tippett, Derrik Thomas, Vincent Brown, Junior Seau, and Rickey Jackson.

Blacks, too, have dispelled the myth that they lack the intellectual gifts to play certain positions, especially quarterback. In 1953 the Chicago Bears signed a black Michigan State signal caller appropriately named Willie Thrower. He appeared in several games but did not distinguish himself and was released at the end of the year. George Taliaferro of Indiana University appeared as a quarterback for Baltimore in 1953, but he also failed to make an impression. Two years later, the Green Bay Packers signed Charlie Brackins from Prairie View A & M, but he was used sparingly. Marlin Briscoe of the University of Omaha quarterbacked several games for the Denver Broncos in 1968, but was released the following year and became a wide receiver for Buffalo. James Harris of Grambling took snaps for Buffalo in 1969, and led the Los Angeles Rams to a division title in 1974. Joe Gilliam played adequately for Pittsburgh in 1974, but lost the job to Terry Bradshaw, who became the offensive leader of the Super Bowl champions.

The performance of Doug Williams for the Washington Redskins in the 1988 Super Bowl against Denver demonstrated that a black possessed the athletic and intellectual necessities to direct an NFL football team. In Super Bowl XXII Williams captured the MVP award by completing 18 of 29 passes for a record 340 yards and 4 touchdowns. Nonetheless, within a year Williams was out of professional football, receiving little reward or lasting recognition for his accomplishment.

In 1988, Randall Cunningham demonstrated dazzling running and passing ability and directed the Philadelphia Eagles to their first division title since 1980. And in the early 1990s, Warren Moon, leader of the high-powered "run and shoot" Houston Oiler offense, was one of the most accomplished passers in football. In 1990, his receiving corps of Haywood Jeffries, Drew Hill, Ernest Givens, and Curtis Duncan each caught more than 65 passes, an unparalleled gridiron feat.

While distinguishing themselves at every playing position and earning salaries commensurate with their performances, blacks in football management positions are still a novelty. There are no black owners and few African Americans in NFL front office jobs. Minority head coaches are rare, even though by the 1990s sixty percent of the players were black. Art Shell was named head coach of the Los Angeles Raiders in 1989, becoming the first black NFL coach since Fritz Pollard. The Raiders also hired a minority candidate, Terry Robiskie, to become their offensive coordinator. In 1992, Minnesota appointed Dennis Green, formerly the coach of Northwestern and Stanford, to direct the team. Green named Tony Dungy as defensive coordinator. And that same year, the Green Bay Packers employed two black coordinators, Sherman Lewis and Ray Rhodes. Gene Upshaw was elected president of the NFL Players Union, but he came under fire when he led the membership in an unsuccessful one-game strike against the owners in 1987.

The status of African Americans in football in recent decades has been impressive, though many problems remain. Their entrance into leadership roles has been slow. The adjustment to the high-pressure world of top-level collegiate and professional football has proved difficult for many. Too many African Americans have developed drug problems, or have become burnt-out cases after their football careers have ended. For many, the adjustment to the largely white world of professional football has been jarring. In recent years football players have been more willing to speak out about racial problems. When the state of Arizona decided not to recognize the Martin Luther King, Jr., holiday, blacks helped persuade the NFL to transfer the site of the 1993 Super Bowl from Phoenix to Los Angeles.

In the past, high-salaried minority players have been criticized for being aloof. In part, blacks have been reluctant to speak out for fear of alienating the white majority. "A lot of people, myself included," Lawrence Taylor once observed, "don't want to give up their status in white America. You learn how to deal with certain situations, how to play the game." But Taylor and other highly visible minority athletes are increasingly speaking out on social issues in order to improve the human condition for athletes and nonathletes alike.

—THOMAS G. SMITH

FRANKLIN, ARETHA LOUISE

Aretha Louise Franklin (March 25, 1942–), singer. Known as "Lady Soul" and "The Queen of Soul," Aretha Franklin brought the undiluted power of black gospel singing to American popular music beginning in the late 1960s. Born March 25, 1942, in Memphis, Tenn., and raised in Detroit, Mich., she was the fourth of five children of Barbara Siggers Franklin and the well-known gospel preacher and singer, the Rev. C. L. Franklin of Detroit's New Bethel Baptist Church. Her mother, also a gospel singer, left her husband and children in 1948 when Aretha was six, and died shortly thereafter.

Aretha's formative years were spent singing in her father's church choir and traveling with him on the gospel circuit. Numerous jazz and gospel figures visited the Franklin's home, and James Cleveland boarded with the family and worked with Aretha as she practiced playing the piano and singing. Clara Ward sang at an aunt's funeral, and Franklin was so moved she decided to become a professional singer herself. At fourteen she recorded a selection of gospel songs including Thomas A. Dorsey's "Precious Lord, Take My Hand." She became pregnant at fifteen and dropped out of school.

At eighteen Franklin was brought to the attention of John Hammond, the producer at Columbia Records who had "discovered" Bessie Smith, Billie Holiday, and other African-American musicians. Hammond praised Franklin's voice as the best he had heard in twenty years. Franklin signed with Columbia and moved to New York but achieved only marginal success as a pop singer because of Columbia's material and arrangements, a confused hodgepodge of jazz, pop, and standards.

FRANKLIN, ARETHA LOUISE

Ray Charles is often called the "Father of Soul" for his innovative blending of gospel, blues, and jazz.

PAGE 125

See also
Ray Charles

Her breakthrough came in 1966 when her Columbia contract expired and she signed with Atlantic Records, where she was teamed with veteran producer Jerry Wexler. He constructed simple, gospel-influenced arrangements for her, often based on her own piano playing. In these comfortable musical settings her true voice emerged with intensity and emotion. Wexler said, "I took her to church, sat her down at the piano, and let her be herself." Franklin's first record with Wexler was "I Never Loved a Man (The Way I Love You)" in February 1967. It was an immediate success and topped *Billboard*'s charts. Her second hit, "Respect," was sung with such conviction it became a call for black and feminist pride and empowerment.

Often compared to Ray Charles for her fusion of sacred and secular styles, Franklin came to personify African-American "soul" music. She produced a series of top records including "Chain of Fools," "Think," and "Don't Play That Song." She has won fifteen Grammy Awards, three American Music Awards, and a Grammy Living Legend Award. With thirty-five albums, she has had seventeen number one rhythm-and-blues singles, and more million-selling singles than any other woman singer. In 1980 she switched to the Arista label.

Throughout her career, her dominant public voice has been contrasted with her private, even reclusive, personality, although she carefully monitors her career and the music industry. Her personal life has at times been difficult, with her mother's abandonment, her own pregnancy at age fifteen, several unsuccessful marriages, and, particularly, the fact that her father, to whom she was very close, spent five years in a coma from a gunshot wound in 1979 until his death in 1984.

—BUD KLIMENT

FRANKLIN, JOHN HOPE

John Hope Franklin (January 2, 1915–), historian and educator. John Hope Franklin was born in Rentiesville, Okla., an exclusively African-American town. At an early age he came to be introduced to white custom, law, and justice in the South. His father, a lawyer, was expelled from court by a white judge who told him that no black person could ever practice law in his court. Young Franklin was himself ejected, along with his mother (an elementary school teacher) and sister, from a train because his mother refused to move from the coach designated for whites. After moving to Tulsa in 1926, Franklin attended Booker T. Washington High School and learned the meaning of a "separate but equal" education—inferior facilities and a sharply limited curriculum. His avid interest in music introduced him to the Jim Crow seats in the local concert hall. He went on to receive his B.A. at Fisk University in 1935 and his Ph.D. in history at Harvard University in 1941.

Throughout his career, Franklin combined scholarship with social activism. As student body president at Fisk University, he protested the lynching of a local black man to the mayor, the governor, and President Franklin D. Roosevelt. Having once been barred from entering the University of Oklahoma to pursue graduate studies, he readily agreed to the NAACP's request that he be an expert witness for a black student seeking admission to the graduate program in history at the University of Kentucky. At the request of Thurgood Marshall, he served on the research team whose work led to the Supreme Court's *Brown* v. *Board of Education* decision outlawing school segregation. In 1965, he joined more than thirty other historians on the civil rights march into Montgomery, Ala.

Like Carter Woodson and W. E. B. Du Bois, Franklin demonstrated to a skeptical or indiffer-

John Hope Franklin demonstrated to a skeptical or indifferent profession that the history of black Americans was a legitimate field for scholarly research.
PHOTOGRAPHS AND PRINTS DIVISION, SCHOMBURG CENTER FOR RESEARCH IN BLACK CULTURE, THE NEW YORK PUBLIC LIBRARY, ASTOR, LENOX AND TILDEN FOUNDATIONS

ent profession that the history of black Americans was a legitimate field for scholarly research. His first book, *The Free Negro in North Carolina, 1790–1860* (1943), explored the anomalous position of free blacks in the slave South. *Reconstruction After the Civil War* (1961) was a revisionist treatment of the unique experiment in biracial democratic government in the postwar South, particularly in its depiction of blacks as active participants and leaders, not simply as victims or passive tools of white politicians. In *The Militant South* (1956) and *A Southern Odyssey* (1976), Franklin explored different facets of the southern experience and varieties of southern white expression. His Jefferson Lecture in the Humanities for 1976, *Racial Equality in America*, probed that troubled and elusive search. In a turn to biography, his *George Washington Williams* (1985) traced the life of a historian who wrote in the 1880s the first substantial and scholarly history of black Americans. For hundreds of thousands of students, Franklin's *From Slavery to Freedom* (first published in 1947) introduced them to African-American history. In *Race and History* (1989), he brought together his most important essays and lectures, including his autobiographical sketch and reflections, "A Life of Learning."

In his books, as in his teaching, Franklin transcends the distinction between African-American and American history. He has underscored the unique quality of the history of African Americans even as he has viewed that history as an intimate part of American history, inseparable from and a central theme in the national experience. Rejecting the need to replace old distortions with new myths and eulogistic sketches of heroes and heroines, he has demonstrated his full appreciation of the complexity and integrity of the American and African-American past.

His early teaching career included Fisk University, St. Augustine's College, North Carolina Central College, and Howard University. In 1956 he went to Brooklyn College as chairman of the department of history—a department of fifty-two white historians. (The appointment made the front page of the *New York Times;* Franklin's troubled search for housing did not.) In 1964, he joined the history faculty of the University of Chicago, serving as chair from 1967 to 1970 and as the John Matthews Manly Distinguished Service Professor from 1969 to 1982. Moving to Durham, N.C., he chose to diversify rather than retire, becoming the James B. Duke Professor of History and professor of legal history in the law school at Duke University.

Franklin has been elected to the presidencies of the American Studies Association, the Southern Historical Association, the United Chapters of Phi Beta Kappa, the Organization of American Historians, and the American Historical Association. More than seventy colleges and universities have awarded him an honorary degree. He has served on numerous national commissions, was chairman of the Advisory Board of President Bill Clinton's Initiative on Race, and in 1980 was a United States delegate to the 21st General Conference of UNESCO. In 1978 the state that initially forced John Hope Franklin to undergo the humiliating rites of racial passage elected him to the Oklahoma Hall of Fame.

—LEON F. LITWACK

FRATERNITIES AND SORORITIES

"Greek-letter" organizations, so called because each takes a series of three letters from the Greek alphabet for its name, have played an important role in African-American college life.

Devoted primarily to socializing among members (women in sororities and men in fraternities), campus chapters provide young people with a structured environment in which to adjust to college life and, often, to form lasting friendships. African-American fraternities and sororities share with similar white organizations a culture that features exclusiveness (members must be invited to join and meet both objective and subjective requirements regarding scholastic achievement and desirable personal and social qualities); secret rituals, grips, and passwords; humiliating and sometimes even physically dangerous initiation rites (though these have been discouraged by the national organizations at least since the 1930s); and an emphasis on parties and socializing for their own sake. However, they also encourage good scholarship, teach their members social skills, and instill a sense of character and service to society. In doing so these organizations have constituted one of the chief training grounds of what has been called the "community of striving blacks."

Moreover, many college graduates remain active in alumni chapters, swelling the ranks of the national organizations and giving them a central place in the institutional infrastructure of the black middle class. Graduate members usually provide the leadership of the national organiza-

◆ **Fraternity**

A group of people associated or formally organized for a common purpose, interest, or pleasure

See also
NAACP

Countee Cullen was an outstanding student at New York University (1921–1925), where he wrote most of the major work that was to make up his first two volumes of poetry.

PAGE 159

See also
Marian Anderson

tions, which over the years have distinguished themselves in both the provision of social services and the struggle for civil rights. Sorority and fraternity presidents have included such significant figures as Sadie T. M. Alexander and Dorothy I. Height (both of Delta Sigma Theta) and Charles Wesley, Rayford W. Logan, and Ernest Morial (all of Alpha Phi Alpha). Patricia Roberts Harris was Delta Sigma Theta's first executive director before she went on to become the first black woman cabinet secretary. Marian Anderson, Violette Anderson, Countee Cullen, W. E. B. Du Bois, John Hope Franklin, John Hope, Lena Horne, Barbara Jordan, Thurgood Marshall, Ralph Metcalfe, Jesse Owens, Adam Clayton Powell, Sr., Leontyne Price, Paul Robeson, Georgiana Simpson, and Walter White were just a few of the prominent blacks to join African-American fraternities and sororities.

Nevertheless, critics such as the eminent sociologist E. Franklin Frazier have taken the Greek-letter organizations to task for their elitism, social snobbishness, and frivolity, which, as Frazier charged in *Black Bourgeoisie,* "divert the students from a serious interest in education." Moreover, their detractors argue, black fraternities and sororities have at times reinforced pernicious class and color divisions within the black community. In particular, some have accused the Greek-letter organizations of favoring light-skinned candidates for membership. Those with darker complexions, they charge, are forced to demonstrate superior academic, athletic, or social prowess to gain admittance. The organizations themselves, however, have denied harboring this sort of prejudice.

Administrators at black colleges originally opposed the establishment of fraternities and sororities on their campuses, fearing that secret societies would divide student bodies and distract students from the Christian and literary activities preferred by the administrators. In 1910, for example, the trustees of Atlanta University voted to "disapprove entirely" of secret organizations and gave the administration and faculty the right to do whatever they deemed necessary to suppress such groups. Before 1925 Fisk University also prohibited fraternities. Both of these schools eventually lifted their bans on Greek-letter societies, but a similar prohibition remained in effect at Spelman College until at least 1964.

Despite their critics, however, Greek-letter organizations have provided many important benefits to their members. Although popular also at historically black colleges and universities, the social and cultural opportunities offered by fraternities and sororities were especially important for African Americans at predominantly white schools at a time when black students were few in number and excluded from general campus activities. Chapter houses provided housing for many students; at times this was the only adequate housing available to blacks barred from regular dormitories. On the campuses of black colleges, Greek-letter organizations often formed formidable political machines, dominating student government and controlling access to coveted positions in student clubs and publications. While this provoked the opposition of some, it also influenced others to seek membership.

The first African-American Greek-letter organization was not, strictly speaking, a college fraternity, though it was patterned after existing white societies. Sigma Pi Phi was founded in Philadelphia in 1904 by two physicians, a dentist, and a pharmacist. Open only to those with college degrees, it aimed to provide a space for social interaction for the most successful men in the African-American community. Self-consciously elitist, Sigma Pi Phi quickly spread to other cities, but its membership remained small—177 in 1920, 500 in 1954. Each chapter was called a *boulé,* a Greek term referring to a deliberative body, and the national organization soon also became known informally as Boulé. (Other sororities and fraternities use this word to describe their national conventions.) In 1992 Sigma Pi Phi claimed three thousand members in ninety-one chapters.

The years between 1906 and 1922 saw the founding of all of the eight major African-American Greek-letter student societies. Five of the eight were established at Howard University, though in most cases they quickly spread to white campuses as well. These were Alpha Kappa Alpha Sorority (1908), Omega Psi Phi Fraternity (1911), Delta Sigma Theta Sorority (1913), Phi Beta Sigma Fraternity (1914), and Zeta Phi Beta Sorority (1920). The other three, Alpha Phi Alpha Fraternity (1906), Kappa Alpha Psi Fraternity (1911), and Sigma Gamma Rho Sorority (1922), were established at Cornell (Ithaca, N.Y.), Indiana (Bloomington, Ind.), and Butler universities (Indianapolis), respectively.

Alpha Phi Alpha, the first black Greek-letter fraternity, was established by a group of seven students at Cornell University in 1906, emerging out of a literary society founded earlier. In 1907 students at Howard formed the fraternity's second chapter, and in 1908 a chapter at the University of

Toronto made Alpha Phi Alpha an international organization (the Toronto chapter lasted until 1912). Also in 1908, the fraternity held its first convention, adopting as its stated ideals, "manly deeds, scholarship, and love for all mankind."

Founded at Howard on January 15, 1908, Alpha Kappa Alpha became the first black sorority and the first Greek-letter organization established at a black school. The nine founders were all students in the university's School of Liberal Arts. Their leader, Ethel Hedgeman, was encouraged in this undertaking by Ethel Robinson, a graduate of Brown University who had been a sorority sister there. In its first year Alpha Kappa Alpha set standards for membership, requiring that candidates complete the first half of their sophomore year and maintain an average of 75 percent or better. The organization's early activities centered on concerts and cultural events, often relying on the talents of the members themselves.

Two fraternities were formed in 1911, Kappa Alpha Psi at Indiana University and Omega Psi Phi at Howard. The former typified the strength of fraternities and sororities among African-American students on predominantly white midwestern campuses, where they were greater in numbers than at eastern white schools but faced social isolation. The founders of Omega Psi Phi, on the other hand, received encouragement from Ernest E. Just, a biologist and prominent member of the Howard faculty.

By 1913 dissatisfaction had spread among some members of the Howard chapter of Alpha Kappa Alpha who wanted to put more emphasis on involvement in community affairs and building a national organization. They also opposed the pompous Greek titles given officers (basileus, anti-basileus, grammateus, epistoleus, tamiouchos). Based largely in Howard's Teachers College, many of the dissident members were also members of a circle of friends that included men in Omega Psi Phi. After an unsuccessful attempt to reform the older organization, twenty-two women left Kappa Alpha and founded a new sorority called Delta Sigma Theta.

The following year, Howard saw the founding of a new fraternity, Phi Beta Sigma, which adopted the motto "Culture for service and service for humanity." In 1920 members of Phi Beta Sigma played an important role in the establishment of a new sorority, Zeta Phi Beta, which became a sister organization to the fraternity from which it took part of its name and on whose constitution it based its own. Finally, in 1922 Sigma Gamma Rho Sorority became the last of the major black Greek-letter organizations to be founded. Originally established at Butler University as a professional sorority for teachers and students of education, Sigma Gamma Rho expanded beyond this constituency by the end of the decade. By the early 1920s the African-American fraternities and sororities claimed a total membership of several thousand in dozens of chapters.

Competition for members and honors characterized the interaction among the various Greek-letter societies on campus. The close relationship between Alpha Kappa Alpha and Delta Sigma Theta led to an especially heated rivalry that became part of the sororities' traditions. Attracting the boyfriend of a member of the other organization was considered a particular coup. Each group strove to best the other in academic pursuits as well; when Alpha Kappa Alpha established an award for the woman graduating from Howard with the highest grade point average, Deltas made a special effort to win the prize—and often did. Partly in an effort to control this sort of rivalry, black sororities and fraternities founded the National Interfraternal Council in 1922. The council also sought to develop common membership standards for the Greek-letter organizations. It was replaced in 1930 by the National Pan-Hellenic Council, which, in addition to setting academic standards for membership, worked to secure black representation in predominantly white interfraternal organizations and fought discrimination in dormitory housing.

Social service and the promotion of education have provided the national organizations with their main focus of activities. Together with both campus and graduate chapters, they have sponsored a variety of projects in the United States and abroad (especially in Africa).

Alpha Phi Alpha pioneered with its annual campaign to promote higher education among black youth. Inaugurated on a national level in 1916, this effort was broadened in 1919 under the title "Go to High School, Go to College." Carried out each year during the first week in June, this campaign featured the dissemination of literature, speeches by fraternity members, and counseling sessions with individual students and parents. Under the influence of its education director, the noted historian Rayford W. Logan, Alpha Phi Alpha replaced "Go to High School, Go to College" in 1933 with "Education for Citizenship." Designed to inform blacks of both the "rights" and the "responsibilities" of citizenship, Logan hoped that the campaign would help African Americans challenge their disfranchisement by

FRATERNITIES AND SORORITIES

See also
Countee Cullen

W.E.B. Du Bois attended Fisk University, where he first encountered the harsher forms of racism.

PAGE 192

preparing them to vote. Similarly, Kappa Alpha Psi established its "Guide Right Program" to help youth with "discovering and developing their potentials."

The sororities, in particular, initiated a number of notable social welfare programs. Alpha Kappa Alpha, for example, began its Mississippi Health Project in 1935. Continued for eight years, the project sent teams of doctors and nurses to rural areas of the state to provide treatment and education. In the 1940s and 1950s Sigma Gamma Rho sponsored "Teen Towns," where black youths ages thirteen to seventeen could spend their leisure time at "worthwhile activities." In 1937 Delta Sigma Theta initiated its National Library Program to send bookmobiles throughout the South. Ten years later the Detroit chapter of Delta Sigma Theta opened the Delta Home for Girls to provide a residential alternative to the local juvenile detention home.

Since 1965 Alpha Kappa Alpha has operated the Jobs Corps Center in Cleveland under contract with the government. In the 1970s Phi Beta Sigma initiated Project SAD (Sigma Attacks Defects) to promote infant health by educating men concerning the importance of proper prenatal and neonatal health care, as well as the dangers of tobacco, alcohol, drugs, and venereal disease. Both sororities and fraternities continued to sponsor a wide range of social welfare programs into the 1990s.

The sororities also took a particular interest in international affairs. In the late 1940s Alpha Kappa Alpha became an accredited observer at the United Nations. In Africa Sigma Gamma Rho started Project Africa to provide agricultural assistance to African women and ran several campaigns to send books to educational institutions on the continent. Alpha Kappa Alpha chapters "adopted" more than three hundred African villages in conjunction with the international-aid organization Africare. And in 1965 Zeta Phi Beta opened a Domestic Science Center in Monrovia, Liberia. Delta Sigma Theta has aided hospitals and other projects in Kenya and Uganda, as well as in India and Haiti.

All the Greek-letter organizations encouraged education among young African Americans by providing scholarships and fellowships to both members and nonmembers. They also sponsored essay contests and other competitions for high school and college students, ran tutoring, counseling, and placement programs and undertook leadership training seminars for college members and

TABLE 1

MAJOR AFRICAN-AMERICAN COLLEGE SORORITIES AND FRATERNITIES

Organization	Place and Date of Founding	Headquarters	Membership*	Number of Chapters‡
Alpha Kappa Alpha Sorority	Howard 1908	Chicago	110,000	Campus: 410 Alumnae: 420
Alpha Phi Alpha Fraternity	Cornell 1906	Chicago	100,000 (since founding)	Campus: 290 Alumni: 274
Delta Sigma Theta Sorority	Howard 1913	Washington, D.C.	175,000	Active: 760
Kappa Alpha Psi Fraternity	Indiana 1911	Philadelphia	80,000	Active: 323 Alumni: 308
Omega Psi Phi Fraternity	Howard 1911	Washington, D.C.	50,000	Active: 511 Alumni: 259
Phi Beta Sigma Fraternity	Howard 1914	Washington, D.C.	65,000	N.A.
Sigma Gamma Rho Sorority	Butler 1922	Chicago	50,000‡	Active: 350‡
Zeta Phi Beta Sorority	Howard 1920	Washington, D.C.	75,000	550 (College and alumnae)

* As reported in Julia C. Furtaw, ed., *Black Americans Information Directory 1992–93*, 2nd ed. (Detroit, 1992).

‡ As reported in Darren L. Smith, ed., *Black Americans Information Directory 1990–91*, (Detroit, 1990).

—DANIEL SOYER

graduates. Phi Beta Sigma had an affiliated Sigma Beta Club for young men in high school. Alpha Phi Alpha's Education Foundation encourages scholarship, promotes research, and aids the publication of works by African Americans. Over the years the fraternities and sororities have also contributed millions of dollars to educational, scientific, charitable, and civil rights causes, including the United Negro College Fund, and many individual black schools.

African-American fraternities and sororities have differed from their white counterparts in their stress on political involvement, particularly in support of civil rights. One of Delta Sigma Theta's first public activities after its founding in 1913 was to participate in the mass march on Washington for women's suffrage. (Later that year the sorority sent a delegate to the national conference of the Intercollegiate Socialist Society, where, as the only African-American present, she was called upon to comment on the question of civil rights for blacks.)

By the 1930s many of the organizations put considerable emphasis on civil rights work, lobbying for progressive legislation, participating in litigation, and working closely with such organizations as the National Association for the Advancement of Colored People (NAACP), the National Urban League, the Joint Council on National Recovery, and the National Council of Negro Women. Alpha Phi Alpha helped initiate Donald Murray's legal battle for admission to the law school of the University of Maryland. Following his court-ordered admission in 1936, the fraternity paid Murray's tuition and book costs. After campaigning actively for the Costigan-Wagner Anti-Lynching Bill, Alpha Kappa Alpha Sorority established a full-time civil rights lobby in 1938. In 1948 Alpha Kappa Alpha (which, ironically, had been viewed as too insular and conservative by the members who had split off to form Delta Sigma Theta in 1913) invited the seven other major African-American Greek-letter societies to join it in forming the American Council for Human Rights (ACHR), whose aim it was to eliminate racial discrimination and inequality. The ACHR pressed for fair employment legislation, desegregation in the armed forces, bans on poll taxes and lynching, and the integration of transportation and public accommodations in Washington, D.C. The council was dissolved in 1963.

In the late 1940s several of the organizations removed any reference to color or race from their membership requirements, enrolling a small number of students of non-African descent. Nevertheless, they remained overwhelmingly African-American and committed to work in the black community. The societies also continued to educate the public on the achievements of black men and women. In the 1940s Delta Sigma Theta produced a series of publications on black heroes, and in the 1960s Alpha Kappa Alpha published a series on black women in the judiciary, politics, business, medicine, and dentistry.

In the late-1960s, a period in which black and student militancy converged, sororities and fraternities suffered a decline in popularity among students who disdained their elitism and stress on purely social activities. Even within the organizations themselves, members advocated reforms that would de-emphasize their exclusive nature. Several societies, for example, did away with the minimum-grade-point-average requirements that had helped define their elite character. However, society members were often in the forefront of the black campus activism of the era. Cultural historian Paula Giddings, who joined Delta Sigma Theta at Howard University in 1967, recalls that most of the leaders of the student revolt there the following year were members of Greek-letter organizations.

By the early 1980s observers noted the resurgence of student interest in fraternities and sororities. To some extent, this was a consequence of collegians' increased concern for personal advancement and the realization that society membership could help them fulfill their aspirations in this regard. At the same time, however, organizational leaders, both on campus and among graduates, sought to reemphasize the societies' commitments to political action and social service within the black community and overcome their negative image as "noncaring, social-activity prone" groups. During this period Alpha Kappa Alpha carried out its "Black Faces in Public Places" campaign to build monuments to important African Americans in parks and government buildings. It also supported "Black Family Month" and "Black Dollar Day," the latter as part of an effort to encourage African Americans to patronize black-owned businesses.

Despite their temporary dip in popularity in the late 1960s and early 1970s, black sororities and fraternities have grown steadily since their inception, as more and more African Americans have attended college and as graduate members have accumulated. By 1990 the eight major black fraternities and sororities claimed a membership of more than 700,000 in thousands of campus and

Thurgood Marshall attended Lincoln University, where he shared classes with Cab Calloway, the entertainer; Kwame Nkrumah, who became president of Ghana; and Nnamdi Azikiwe, who became president of Nigeria.

PAGE 444

See also
W.E.B. Du Bois
E. Franklin Frazier
Lena Horne

EDWARD FRAZIER

Critic and Chronicler of Race Relations in America

Edward Franklin Frazier (September 24, 1894–May 17, 1962), essayist and activist. Born in Baltimore in 1894, the year in which W. E. B. Du Bois was completing his doctoral degree at Harvard and 135 blacks were lynched in the South, E. Franklin Frazier was encouraged in his formative years by his parents, especially his working-class father, to seek upward mobility and social justice through education. With a scholarship from Colored High School he went on to Howard University, where he graduated *cum laude* in 1916 after four years of rigorous education and political activism at the "capstone of Negro education." For the rest of his academic career, he taught primarily in segregated, African-American schools and colleges, first in the South in the 1920s and early '30s, then for most of his career in Howard's sociology department. In between teaching jobs, he received scholarships that enabled him to get a master's degree at Clark University (1920) and a Ph.D. in sociology from the University of Chicago (1931). Despite his election as the first African-American president of the American Sociological Association (1948) and his recognition by UNESCO in the 1950s as a leading international authority on race relations, Frazier was never offered a regular faculty appointment by a predominantly white university.

With minimal institutional and foundation support, Frazier managed to produce eight books and over one hundred articles. He is best known for his pioneering studies of African-American families, especially *The Negro Family in the United States* (1939), which demonstrated that the internal problems of black families were socially created within and by Western civilization, not by the failure of Africans to live up to American standards. Building upon Du Bois's 1908 essay, *The Negro American Family,* Frazier refuted the prevailing social scientific wisdom which, in his words, "most often dealt with the pathological side of [black] family life. . . ." In contrast, Frazier's family is a broad spectrum of households, constantly in a process of change and reorganization, sometimes disorganized and demoralized, sometimes tenacious and resourceful. To Frazier the serious problems within African-American families—"the waste of human life . . . delinquency, desertions, and broken homes"—was not due to cultural backwardness, but rather to economic exploitation and the social damage inflicted by racism.

Frazier also made a variety of other important intellectual contributions: as an ethnographer and historian of everyday life in black communities; as a trenchant and subtle critic of the dynamics and etiquette of racism; as an influential consultant to Gunnar Myrdal's *An American Dilemma* (1944); as the author of the first systematic textbook on *The Negro in the United States* (1949); and as a critic of overly specialized, narrowly conceived studies in the social sciences. Frazier's popular reputation was made by *Black Bourgeoisie* (first published in the United States in 1957), but he explored the controversial relationship between class, politics, and culture all his life, beginning with a polemical essay on "La Bourgeoisie Noire" in 1928 and ending with his scholarly assessment of *Race and Culture Contacts in the Modern World* (1957). In this body of work he challenged monolithic portraits of African-American communities and documented their socioeconomic diversity; in particular, he exposed the collaborative and opportunistic role played by the black middle class in holding back the struggle for social equality and ensuring that "bourgeois ideals are implanted in the Negro's mind." Instead of being "seduced by dreams of final assimilation," Frazier called upon black leaders to envision "a common humanity and a feeling of human solidarity" in which "racial and cultural differentiation without implications of superiority and inferiority will become the basic pattern of a world order."

Frazier was part of a cadre of activists, intellectuals, and artists who after World War I formed the cutting edge of the New Negro movement that irrevocably changed conceptions of race and the politics of race relations. Though a loner who distrusted organizations, Frazier had close and respectful relationships with civil rights leaders such as W. E. B. Du Bois, Paul Robeson, and A. Philip Randolph, as well as with scholars, such as Ralph Bunche and Abram Harris, who tried to bridge the gap between university and community, theory and practice. From his undergraduate days at Howard, when he was a vigorous opponent of U.S. entry into World War I, until his last years, when he welcomed a revitalized civil rights movement, Frazier was a politicized intellectual who believed that "a moral life is a life of activity in society."

—ANTHONY M. PLATT

alumni chapters. In 1981 the Council of Presidents was established to promote better relations among organizations on campus and augment its constituents' political influence.

In addition to the major college-based fraternities and sororities, there have been a number of much smaller Greek-letter societies recruiting from among practitioners and students of particular professions. These organizations provide their members with social activities, professional enrichment, and in some cases, scholarships and loan funds. They also sponsor charitable programs and recruit young people to their respective professions. These include Alpha Pi Chi Sorority (business and professional women, established in 1963), Chi Delta Mu Fraternity (physicians, dentists and pharmacists, est. 1913), Chi Eta Phi Sorority (registered and student nurses, est. 1932), Eta Phi Beta Sorority (businesswomen, est. 1942), Iota Phi Lambda Sorority (est. 1929), and the National Sorority of Phi Delta Kappa (women in education, est. 1923). In 1990 they ranged in membership from six hundred fifty to eight thousand.

—DANIEL SOYER

FREEDOM SUMMER

In the summer of 1964, the Council of Federated Organizations (COFO)— a Mississippi coalition of the Congress of Racial Equality (CORE), the Student Nonviolent Coordinating Committee (SNCC), and the National Association for the Advancement of Colored People (NAACP) invited Northern white college students to spearhead a massive black voter registration and education campaign aimed at challenging white supremacy in the deep South. This campaign, which became known as Freedom Summer, was the culmination of COFO's efforts to attack black disfranchisement in Mississippi. COFO had been formed in 1962 in response to the Kennedy administration's offer of tax-exempt status and funding from liberal philanthropies to civil rights organizations that focused their activities on increasing black voter registration. The considerable success of COFO activists in sparking the interest of black Mississippians in voter registration during the summer of 1963 prompted them to propose an entire summer of civil rights activities in 1964 to focus national attention on the disfranchisement of blacks in Mississippi, and to force the federal government to protect the civil rights of African Americans in the South.

SNCC played the largest role in the project and provided most of its funding. Robert Moses of SNCC was the guiding force behind the summer project, and the overwhelming majority of COFO staff workers were SNCC members who were veterans of the long fight for racial equality in Mississippi.

Approximately 1,000 northern white college students, committed to social change and imbued with liberal ideals, volunteered to participate in the Freedom Summer campaign. Under the direction of SNCC veterans, these volunteers created community centers that provided basic services such as health care to the black community, and initiated voter education activities and literacy classes aimed at encouraging black Mississippians to register to vote. SNCC activists also directly challenged the segregated policies of the all-white Mississippi Democratic party by supporting the efforts of local black leaders to run their own candidates under the party name Mississippi Freedom Democratic Party (MFDP). The MFDP efforts encouraged over 17,000 African Americans to vote for the sixty-eight delegates who attended the national Democratic Convention in Atlantic City in the summer of 1964 and demanded to be seated in replacement of the regular Democratic organization. The MFDP challenge, though unsuccessful, focused national attention on Mississippi and propelled Fannie Lou Hamer, a local activist, into the national spotlight.

Another focus of the Freedom Summer was institutionalized educational inequities in Mississippi. Thirty COFO project sites created "Freedom Schools," administered under the direction of Staughton Lynd, a white Spelman College history professor, to provide an alternative education to empower black children to challenge their oppression. These schools provided students with academic training in remedial topics, as well as in more specialized subjects like art and French. A key goal of the schools was to develop student leadership and foster activism through discussions about current events, black history, the philosophy behind the civil rights movement, and other cultural activities. Despite the overcrowding and the perennial lack of facilities, over 3,000 African-American students attended the Freedom schools.

Violence framed the context of all COFO activities and created a climate of tension and fear within the organization. White supremacists bombed or burned sixty-seven homes, churches, and black businesses over the course of the summer, and by the end of the project, at least three

I say violence is necessary. It is American as apple pie.

H. "RAP" BROWN
PRESS CONFERENCE AT THE
STUDENT NONVIOLENT
COORDINATING COMMITTEE
HEADQUARTERS,
WASHINGTON, D.C.,
JULY 27, 1967

See also
Civil Rights Movement
Congress of Racial Equality

civil rights workers—James Chaney, Michael Schwerner, and Andrew Goodman—had been killed by southern whites, four had been critically wounded, eight hundred had been beaten, and over a thousand had been arrested. The reluctance of the state government to prosecute the perpetrators of these acts of violence and the failure of the federal government to intervene to provide protection for civil rights workers left many activists disillusioned about the federal government's ability or desire to ensure racial justice.

The impact and legacy of the Freedom Summer stretched far beyond the borders of Mississippi. Many Freedom Summer programs lived on when the project ended and COFO disbanded. Freedom Summer community centers provided a model for federally funded clinics, Head Start programs, and other War on Poverty programs. Freedom schools served as models for nationwide projects in alternative schooling. The barriers to black voting uncovered and publicized during the summer project provided stark evidence of the need for the Voting Rights Act of 1965, which made literacy tests and poll taxes illegal.

The Freedom Summer facilitated the development of a radical new political consciousness among many white volunteers, who found the summer to be a powerful experience of political education and personal discovery. At least one-third of the volunteers stayed on in Mississippi to continue the struggle for black equality. Many volunteers who returned to the North were disillusioned with the promises of the federal government and became activists in the New Left and the antiwar movement. Mario Savio, a Freedom Summer veteran, emerged in the fall of 1964 as the principal spokesperson of the free speech movement at the University of California at Berkeley, a key event in the emergence of the New Left.

The Freedom Summer experience was also an important catalyst for the women's liberation movement. Group consciousness of gender oppression among white women grew markedly during the summer as male volunteers were assigned more visible organizing tasks. In November 1964, at a SNCC staff meeting in Waveland, Miss., Mary King and Casey Hayden, two white staff members, presented an anonymous position paper criticizing the enforced inferiority of women in the Freedom Summer project and their exclusion from the decision-making process. This memo was one of the first discussions of the issues that would form the basis of the emerging women's movement within the New Left.

The experience of the Freedom Summer also radicalized black civil rights workers—though in quite different ways from white radicals. The summer helped steer black radicals in SNCC

FREEDOM SUMMER, 1964

Freedom Summer combined the forces of several organizations in an effort to register and empower black Mississippians. Among its successful programs were freedom schools like the one shown here. PHOTOGRAPHS AND PRINTS DIVISION, SCHOMBURG CENTER FOR RESEARCH IN BLACK CULTURE, THE NEW YORK PUBLIC LIBRARY, ASTOR, LENOX AND TILDEN FOUNDATIONS

away from interracial movements and toward a suspicion of white participation that came to characterize the black power movement. Subsequent debates in the Civil Rights Movement about the doctrine of interracialism were fueled by what the Freedom Summer revealed about the successes, and inherent limitations, of interracial civil rights activity. From the inception of the project, some black SNCC activists contested the Freedom Summer's premise that national attention could only be garnered by exposing white people to the violence and brutality that black people faced daily. These blacks were veterans of the long battle with white racists that SNCC had waged in Mississippi since 1961, were increasingly skeptical of liberal politics, and believed that the presence of white volunteers—who often tended to appropriate leadership roles and interact with black people in a paternalistic manner— would undermine their goal of empowering Mississippi blacks and hamper their efforts to foster and support black-controlled institutions in Mississippi. Tensions and hostility between black and white COFO activists were further inflamed by interracial liaisons which were often premised on the very racial stereotypes and misconceptions that they sought to surmount.

However, the Freedom Summer's most enduring legacy was the change of consciousness it engendered among black Mississippians. The Freedom Summer succeeded in initiating thousands of African Americans into political action, providing thousands of black children with an antiracist education and creating black-led institutions like the Mississippi Freedom Democratic Party. Fannie Lou Hamer provided a fitting testament to the impact of the Freedom Summer when she stated in 1966, "Before the 1964 summer project there were people that wanted change, but they hadn't dared to come out. After 1964 people began moving. To me it's one of the greatest things that ever happened in Mississippi."

—ROBYN SPENCER

FUGITIVE SLAVE LAWS

From the colonial period to the adoption of the Thirteenth Amendment, African Americans sought to escape their bondage. Masters found the recovering of runaways to be time-consuming, expensive, and often impossible. Colonial governments occasionally agreed to help recover slaves from other jurisdictions, but generally such cooperation was ineffective.

During the American Revolution, those states dismantling slavery usually exempted fugitive slaves from their emancipatory schemes. The Articles of Confederation (1781) did not obligate the states to return fugitive slaves, but in 1787 the Confederation Congress adopted the first national fugitive slave law as part of the Northwest Ordinance. The ordinance prohibited slavery in the Northwest Territory but also provided that a fugitive slave "may be lawfully reclaimed and conveyed to the person claiming his or her labor or service."

Late in the Constitutional Convention of 1787, without serious debate or a recorded vote, the delegates adopted what became the fugitive slave clause, providing that "No Person held to Service or Labour in one State, under the Laws thereof, shall, in Consequence of any Law or Regulation therein, be discharged from such Service or Labour, but shall be delivered up on Claim of the Party to whom such Service or Labour may be due" (U.S. Constitution, Art. IV, Sec. 2, Par. 3). The framers apparently contemplated enforcement by state and local governments, or through individual action. The location of the clause in Article IV, with other clauses dealing with interstate relations, supports this analysis.

However, in the Fugitive Slave Act of 1793 Congress spelled out procedures for returning runaway slaves. This law emerged from a controversy between Pennsylvania and Virginia over the status of a black named John Davis. In 1788 three Virginians seized Davis in Pennsylvania, claiming him as a fugitive slave, and took him to Virginia. When Virginia's governor refused to extradite the three men charged with kidnapping in Pennsylvania, the governor of Pennsylvania complained to President Washington, who brought the problem to Congress. This eventually led to the 1793 law, which regulated both the extradition of fugitives from justice and the return of fugitive slaves.

Under this law, the slave owners or their agents (claimants) seized runaways and brought them to any federal, state, or local judge or magistrate and presented "proof to the satisfaction" of the judge that the person seized was the claimant's fugitive slave. A claimant could establish this proof orally or through a certified "affidavit taken before . . . a magistrate" of the claimant's home state. If the judge upheld the claim, he issued a certificate of removal to the claimant. Anyone interfering with the seizure or rendition of a fugitive slave was subject to a five-hundred-dollar penalty, plus the

You can't be Southern without being black, and you can't be a black Southerner without being white.

RALPH ELLISON
IN THE *NEW YORK TIMES*,
JULY 31, 1994

See also
Fannie Lou Hamer
NAACP
Nonviolent Coordinating Committee

value of any slaves lost and any costs a master incurred trying to reclaim the slave.

This law never worked well. All responsibility for capturing slaves rested with owners, who were not guaranteed any aid from police officials. Northern judges sometimes declined to participate in fugitive slave cases. In *Jack* v. *Martin* (1835), New York's highest court declared the federal law unconstitutional but returned Jack to slavery under the constitutional clause itself. In 1836, in an unpublished opinion, New Jersey's Chief Justice Joseph Hornblower declared the 1793 law unconstitutional and also freed the black before him.

Starting in the 1780s, northern legislatures passed "personal-liberty laws" to protect free blacks from kidnapping or mistaken seizure. These laws also provided state procedures to facilitate the return of bona fide fugitives. Laws passed after 1793 often added procedural and evidentiary requirements to the federal law. The northern states balanced protecting free blacks from kidnapping with fulfilling their constitutional obligation to return fugitive slaves.

In 1837 a local judge in Pennsylvania refused to take cognizance of a case involving an alleged fugitive slave named Margaret Morgan and her children. Edward Prigg, a professional slave-catcher, then acted on his own, taking Morgan and her children to Maryland in violation of Pennsylvania's 1826 personal-liberty law. In *Prigg* v. *Pennsylvania* (1842), United States Supreme Court justice Joseph Story held the 1793 law constitutional and determined that state personal-liberty laws interfering with rendition were unconstitutional. Story characterized the fugitive slave clause as "a fundamental article" of the Constitution necessary for its adoption, even though the history of the clause, by that time available to Story, shows this was not true. Story urged state officials to continue to enforce the 1793 law, but stated they could not be required to do so. A number of states soon passed new personal-liberty laws, prohibiting their officials from acting under the federal law.

Congress amended the 1793 law as part of the Compromise of 1850. Under this act, alleged fugitives could not testify on their own behalf or

CAUTION!!
COLORED PEOPLE
OF BOSTON, ONE & ALL,
You are hereby respectfully CAUTIONED and advised, to avoid conversing with the
Watchmen and Police Officers of Boston,
For since the recent ORDER OF THE MAYOR & ALDERMEN, they are empowered to act as
KIDNAPPERS
AND
Slave Catchers,
And they have already been actually employed in KIDNAPPING, CATCHING, AND KEEPING SLAVES. Therefore, if you value your LIBERTY, and the *Welfare of the Fugitives* among you, *Shun* them in every possible manner, as so many *HOUNDS* on the track of the most unfortunate of your race.
Keep a Sharp Look Out for KIDNAPPERS, and have TOP EYE open.
APRIL 24, 1851.

have a jury trial. In reaction to state refusals to participate in the rendition process, the Fugitive Slave Act of 1850 provided for enforcement by federal commissioners to be appointed in every county in the country. They received five dollars if they decided that the black before them was not a slave, but were paid ten dollars if they found in favor of the claimant. Popular opposition to the law increased after the publication of Harriet Beecher Stowe's fictional attack on slavery, *Uncle Tom's Cabin* (1852), which partially centered on the fugitive slave Eliza.

The 1850 law led to riots in Boston; Syracuse, N.Y.; Oberlin, Ohio; and elsewhere. Federal prosecutions of rescuers often failed. In Christiana, Pa., federal officials obtained treason indictments of over forty men after a group of fugitives fought their would-be captors and killed a slave owner. The prosecutions failed when United States Supreme Court justice Robert Grier ruled in *United States* v. *Hanway* (1851) that opposition to the fugitive slave law did not constitute treason. After these incidents, the Fugitive Slave Act was a dead letter in much of the North. In *Ableman* v. *Booth* (1859) the Supreme Court affirmed the constitutionality of the 1850 law and the supremacy of the federal courts.

Peaceful enforcement of the 1850 law was more common than violent opposition. Some removals required a show of federal force and the use of troops. Over nine hundred fugitives were returned under the act before 1862. However, Southerners estimated that as many as ten thousand slaves escaped during that period.

Ultimately, the fugitive slave laws did little to protect southern property, but did much to antagonize sectional feelings. Southerners saw the North as unwilling to fulfill its constitutional obligation. Northerners believed the South was trying to force them to become slavecatchers, and in the process undermining civil liberties in the nation. In 1864, after the issuance of the Emancipation Proclamation, Congress repealed both the 1793 and 1850 laws.

—PAUL FINKELMAN

FUGITIVE SLAVES

Many of the stories of fugitive slaves who managed to reach the free states in the antebellum period have entered the realm of legend. The dangers and sacrifice inherent in their efforts to reach free soil have been acknowledged and have become part of the historical record. Most scholars would agree, however, that only a small minority of the runaway slave population in any given year even attempted to reach the free states. Their stories are much more difficult to tell. This article will discuss the individual histories of fugitive slaves; a separate article discusses fugitive slave laws.

The principal source for the study of fugitive slaves is the advertisements published in local newspapers. (There is little reason to assume, however, that all slave runaways were advertised.) Information can also be gleaned from the diaries, logbooks, correspondence, and other personal papers of slave owners. Newspapers in both free states and slave states gave a great deal of attention to the more spectacular cases where violence or the threat of violence occurred in the recovery process. Newspapers also gave considerable coverage of efforts to subvert legal process in the return of fugitive slaves, particularly in the decade before the Civil War. Part of the record has also been preserved in legal documents and court records. The owners dispassionately, and in considerable detail, described the personal characteristics of the fugitives and noted whether or not they were habitual runaways, the names of their previous owners or employers, their motives for running away, and whether they were expected to be fleeing beyond state lines.

The advertisements provided elaborate descriptions noting age, height, date of running away, date of the advertisement, home county or city, any scarring, four or five gradations of skin color, marital status, literacy, speech impediments, whether the runaway had been charged with a crime, motivations, and work skills, along with the names of employers and previous owners by county. The advertisements of sheriffs and town jailers revealed the date and county of incarceration of those who had been "taken up."

The owners of fugitive slaves usually described their runaways with great care. Distinguishing marks were carefully noted. In the *Richmond Enquirer*, Robert Lewis, of Albemarle County, Va., described his runaway in the following manner:

Eighty dollars reward—Ran away from the Subscriber on the 4th of April, in the city of Richmond, a mulatto fellow, about 30 years of age, 5 feet 6 or 8 inches high; is remarkable on account of having red curly hair & grey eyes which generally appear to be sore; one of his legs somewhat shorter than the other, though scarcely to be perceived without nice observation; when standing, is very apt to stand fast

Harriet Tubman escaped from slavery in 1849, leaving behind her husband, who refused to accompany her.

PAGE 698

See also
Civil War

on his right leg, and rather extend the left. In pronouncing the word whiskey, which he is very fond of, and apt to call for at a public house, he pronounces it whisty. He is a very humble, obedient fellow, and when spoken to, has a downlook. It is not improbable that he may obtain free papers, to endeavor to pass as a free man, having absconded from his boat in the basin at Richmond, with about $120 in cash (June 24, 1817).

♦ **Fugitive**

A person who flees or tries to escape

Scholars have often noted the frequency of stuttering or other speech impediments in the runaway slave population. In the Virginia sample, the frequency was 7 percent, seven times greater than the norm for the population as a whole.

The interpretations of this phenomenon are controversial. Kenneth Stampp (1956) suggested that the "down look" and the speech impediments were caused by stress resulting from fear (pp. 381–382). While Eugene Genovese (1974) did not disagree that slaves had been conditioned to fear white men, he argued that the stuttering was also an expression of "smoldering anger and resentment" (p. 647). John W. Blassingame (1979) disagreed. He argued that the incidence of stuttering and other speech impediments may have resulted from the slaves' "unfamiliarity with European languages, missing teeth, and other physical infirmities" (p. 203). Another plausible explanation for the speech impediments is that stuttering was an acceptable form of aggression, a result of which was to make the listener suffer.

An analysis of the 1,433 fugitive advertisements in the Richmond *Enquirer* published between 1804 and 1830 revealed an interesting profile. In this record, 84.9 percent were males; 13.02 percent were females. Only 2 percent were children. James Benson Sellers, in *Slavery in Alabama* (1964), reported that of 562 fugitives advertised between 1820 and 1860, 84.1 percent were males; and 15.4 percent were females (p. 293). Eugene D. Genovese noted in *Roll, Jordan, Roll* that, between 1850 and 1860, the percentage of North Carolina runaways was 82 percent male (p. 798, note 2). The percentage of female runaways from New Orleans in 1850 was higher. Judith Kelleher Schafer reported in *The Journal of Southern History* that 31.7 percent were women (1981, pp. 33–56). All the sources seem to agree that the great majority of fugitives was made up of relatively young men. The average age in the Virginia sample was 27.

A possible explanation for the preponderance of males is suggested by the dangers inherent in

See also
Fugitive Slave Laws

running away. Successful flight demanded planning, ingenuity, bravery, and opportunity. In most southern states, the law provided that any black person could be stopped and checked for documentation of free status or possession of a "free pass." Any slave beyond a given distance from home without a "free pass" could be taken into custody and returned. The law also provided that the owner was obligated to pay a prescribed reward, based upon mileage, for the return of his slave. Even if those dangers were avoided, slave patrols had to be eluded and slave catchers frustrated. The rigor of successfully avoiding arrest and the fear of returning to face certain punishment were such that women, especially those with children, were discouraged from running away.

Although they were predominantly male, the runaways represented fieldhands, skilled artisans, the more privileged, and the less privileged. Roughly one-third of the fugitives were skilled or had some training and education. Fieldhands represented 70 percent of the Virginia slaves. Owners advertised for the return of runaways in Virginia every month, but the most popular months were between May and August. The least popular month was November. Owners demonstrated no hurry to advertise their runaways. A time lapse of six weeks to six months occurred between the date of running away and the date of advertisement. In January 1811, for example, Archer Hankins reported that his slave George had run away the previous July. In April 1811, John S. Payne of Campbell County reported that three of his slaves had absconded in January. The most plausible reason for the delay in advertising runaways was the assumption that the slaves would return of their own accord. Several instances on the record indicate that an owner knew where his slave was lurking; but rather than go after the fugitive himself, he offered a reward for someone else to return his slave to him, or "secure him in jail so that I get him again." Whatever the motivation for running away, large numbers returned of their own accord or were apprehended within days, or sometimes in weeks. Of 1,151 runaways advertised in Virginia, 831 were single men and 111 were single women. Married men numbered 154 and married women 55. The advertisements in the Richmond *Enquirer* also made a point of identifying fugitives by color: black, mulatto, tawny, yellow, and "pass for white." Only about 2.5 percent of the Virginia sample could read or write.

The motivations for running away discussed in the literature are complex. Gerald W. Mullin (1972) classified motives by objective. The first group were little more than truants who ran off to visit wives, friends, or family on other plantations. The second group included those slaves who absconded to the towns and cities to find employment and pass as free men. A third smaller group was made up of those slaves who preferred freedom to bondage and attempted, by whatever means, to reach the free states (p. 106). Stampp argued that slaves had a heightened sense of dignity that was easily insulted. Running away was a means of expressing a personal grievance (Stampp 1956, p. 112). There is general agreement on an extended list of reasons for running away that include fear of sale, loneliness resulting from sale out of state, the desire to reestablish family ties, to escape overwork, and simply to be free. In the Virginia advertisements, the single most important reason for running away was the desire not to be free, but to "pass as free."

Motivation for slaves who ran away was in many cases a great mystery to their owners. Kenneth Stampp (1956) reported several owners who stated that their slaves had run away for no apparent reason and without provocation (pp. 111–112). But William K. Scarborough has argued that a more common explanation was fear of the whip (Scarborough 1984, pp. 89–90). The cruelty of some masters and overseers in the treatment of slaves is well documented. While only a small minority of slaves in the Virginia sample were described as scarred, the scars were often noteworthy. Robert Dickenson of Nottoway County described the scars of Isaac, an "habitual" runaway. He had a scar "over his right eye and . . . a lump as large as the finger on the fore part of the right shoulder." The scars, he said, were "caused by whipping" (*Richmond Enquirer*, December 23, 1809). Many of the slaves had been scarred by smallpox. A few of the scars were inflicted with branding irons. A recently purchased slave of John Sanders had been "lately branded on the left hand" (*Richmond Enquirer*, March 12, 1814). Thomas Coleman of Lunenburg County branded his slave, Charles, on the forehead, on each cheek, and his chest with the letter C (*Richmond Enquirer*, July 1, 1823).

The treatment of runaway slaves was often callous; but occasionally the advertisements expressed concern for the welfare of the fugitive, especially the younger ones. Edmund Lewis had taken a thirteen-year-old boy into custody in Buckingham County. The boy told his captor that he had been stolen from his father, George Belew, when "very young" and thought he had been sold "about ten times." The object of the notice, said Lewis, was to notify "his parents or friends to attend to his case," which was pending before the court of Buckingham County (*Richmond Enquirer*, October 27, 1818). Samuel Carter of Halifax County expressed concern for a ten year old whom he had "taken up" after being lost from a slave-trading expedition. Carter did not place the boy in jail because he was too ill and too young (*Richmond Enquirer*, April 18, 1817).

A large category of fugitives comprised those who had been hired out. Because of the surplus of slave labor in Virginia, many slaveholders were forced either to sell their surplus slaves or to hire them out. The services of the slaves were usually rented for six months or a year, and many of them ran away during that time. Slaves were hired as boatmen on the river and laborers in the coal pits, brick yards, and rope walks. Some were hired because they had special skills. They worked as ostlers, carriage drivers, and house servants.

Those who hired slaves did not always find it a happy experience. P. V. Daniel of Richmond hired the services of John Brown, who was a "good house servant, ostler and driver, and a pretty good barber." One evening, Brown requested a pass to go into town and had not been heard from since (*Richmond Enquirer*, July 8, 1823). Nelson Patterson of Kanawha County hired John and Reuben from Thomas Logwood of Gloucester County. Patterson "carried them" to Buckingham County to make salt. At the first opportunity, they ran away (*Richmond Enquirer*, December 19, 1816).

The advertisements contain frequent expressions of fear that slaves had been "enticed off" by a white man or some other person. William B. Johnson could explain Isabella's elopement in no other way for "such was her attachment for her mistress and fellow-servants, that she would not have eloped had she not been taken off by some white man." Nathaniel Price believed that Kitty had been "inveigled off by her husband" (*Richmond Enquirer*, June 17, 1808).

A few African Americans engaged in an interesting racket. Lewis informed his owner William Fisher of Chesterfield County that a white man with whom Lewis had worked the previous year tried to decoy him off by promising to sell him and then later meet at some designated place, divide the money, and thus continue on (*Richmond Enquirer*, September 19, 1826). Jerman Baker in Cumberland County had a similar experience when a young fellow who called himself John Irvin came up to Baker's plantation on foot with two African-American men. He claimed that his horse had foundered on the road and that he was

When Sojourner Truth's master refused to keep his promise to give her her freedom in 1826, she fled with an infant child.

PAGE 696

on his way to Richmond to deliver one of the slaves. The other slave, he said, belonged to his father, a merchant in Campbell County. Baker bought this slave for $430. He gave Irvin a horse valued at $130, paid $100 in cash, and gave him a note for $200. The slave absconded shortly thereafter, and adding insult to injury, took a horse with him. Baker warned: "I forewarn all persons from trading for the note I executed to said John Irvin" (*Richmond Enquirer*, March 3, 1812).

White people aided and abetted relatively few slaves in their escapes. Some slaves received permission to visit their wives or families in other locations and never returned. Without help from other slaves, runaways could not remain away from their owners for long periods of time. Literate slaves provided forged passes that made it possible for fugitive slaves to lurk around the smaller towns or simply disappear in the larger cities. Owners could do little to prevent such aid. Free papers could be checked against the court records in the fugitive's home county; but if he was caught and returned to his master, another opportunity to escape usually presented itself.

The objective of the fugitives who remained within the state was usually the larger towns. Spencer Roane of Hanover complained that Betsy, one of his servants, "was so much pleased with Richmond, as to abscond, when his family returned from thence" (*Richmond Enquirer*, July 26, 1811). Joseph Ingraham sent Billy into Richmond with a load of wheat. Billy sold the wheat for $40 and disappeared (*Richmond Enquirer*, October 1, 1824). The chances of being detected in the cities were considerably reduced. In Virginia, Richmond, Manchester, Petersburg, Williamsburg, and Norfolk were the principal towns for which many fugitives aimed. Work could more readily be secured in the towns, and the townspeople were less suspicious of a strange black face. Hiding in the cities was easier and less dangerous than in the countryside.

Methods used to deter running away varied. William Scarborough has argued that overseers were more inclined to use harsh discipline in order to create fear. At least two overseers resorted to shooting their "recalcitrant" runaways (Scarborough 1984, pp. 90–91). A more common deterrent was the use of dogs. The practice of running away was so widespread that some men became professional slavecatchers who used hounds to hunt down fugitives. This practice was more likely to be used in the deep South than in the border states. Other methods were less violent. For example, in South Carolina, one planter

restricted the privileges of the slaves who did not run away in order to induce the runaways to return (Scarborough 1984, p. 92).

All slave states enacted laws both to deter and to aid in the recovery of fugitive slaves. The laws in Virginia were fairly typical. The laws to suppress runaway slaves before the Revolution were extremely harsh. In 1680 a law was passed making it lawful to kill any fugitive who resisted arrest. A 1723 law provided for punishment by "dismembering, or any other way not touching life." Laws designed to restrict the movement of slaves were amended very little over the years; only refinements were added. These laws required slaves who were away from the plantation to have written permission. The unfortunate slave without such permission was subject to punishment of ten lashes for every offense. In 1748, slave stealing was defined as a capital offense punishable by "death without benefit of clergy." Laws that made it a crime to transport a slave out of the colony or state without the consent of the owner were enacted and amended many times. A Virginia law enacted in 1805 prohibited a master of a vessel from taking any African American on board without checking his status. The penalties for violation of this law were severe. If the master of a vessel was convicted, his fine was to be $500 for every African American found on his vessel without a pass. The master was also liable for an additional $200 fine: "one third thereof shall go to the master or owner of such slave, one third to the informer, and one third to the overseers of the poor, for the use of the poor." Upon conviction of removing a slave out of the county, the master could be imprisoned for a period of up to four years.

Laws for the apprehension and return of fugitive slaves depended upon the goodwill and support of the white population. The function of these laws was to ensure, so far as possible, the return of the runaway to his master. A schedule of rewards was established by state legislatures to encourage compliance. Usually a basic fee was required, plus mileage. If a fugitive was caught in Maryland or Kentucky, the reward was to be $25 plus $0.25 per mile for traveling to the residence of the owner, or the jail to which the fugitive was committed. The reward for apprehending runaways in Delaware, New Jersey, New York, Pennsylvania, or Ohio was to be $50. Between 1800 and 1830 in Virginia, rewards offered for the return of fugitive slaves ranged from $3 to $150.

A system of confining and selling unclaimed runaways developed during the years preceding the American Revolution. After 1726, it was permissible to hire out such slaves with an iron collar around their necks stamped with the letter "P.G." (for "Public Gaol"). This procedure of confining slaves and hiring them out changed little except that after the Revolution, treatment of runaways became somewhat less stringent. After 1782, slaves were forbidden to hire themselves out in order to pay their masters money in lieu of services. After 1807, the owner became liable to a fine of $10 to $20 for permitting his slaves to hire themselves out.

Every free African American was forced to register with the county clerk and obtain a copy of the register certifying that he or she was free. This law facilitated the recognition of runaways and placed the burden of enforcement on the free population and not on the slaves. The fine for employing or harboring an African American without a pass was $5 for each offense, and the offender was liable to a suit for damages by the aggrieved party. The most severe penalties were reserved for those convicted of "enticing off" or stealing slaves. As late as 1799, the penalty was still death "without benefit of clergy." After 1805, however, the punishment for slave stealing was reduced to a fine of between $100 and $500 and imprisonment for not less than two years and not more than four. The convicted felon was also required to pay the owner an amount double the value of the slave, plus double the amount of costs.

The literature on fugitive slaves provides extended discussion of slave crime. Stampp (1956) argued that petty theft was almost universal. Other crimes discussed were arson, deliberate injury and self-mutilation, and acts of violence. The most frequent targets for arson were the slave quarters, cotton gins, and other farm buildings. Some slaves were willing to suffer personal injury and great pain rather than return to slavery. Attempts to arrest and return fugitive slaves frequently resulted in violence. A few slaves even resorted to murder (pp. 124–132). Genovese (1974) argued that some caution must be exercised concerning charges of arson. He asserted that in many cases, planters simply assumed that the arsonists were slaves. He further contended that arson committed by slaves was more likely to occur in the cities than on the plantations (pp. 613–615). Slaves were capable of the most violent crimes if provoked. A servant shot and killed Virginia Frost of Richmond, Va., when reproached for "insolent language" (Genovese 1974, pp. 361–362). In the period between 1710 and 1754, Mullin found evidence that only 2 slaves had been tried for murder before county courts

(Mullin 1972, p. 61). Only 26 fugitives were charged with crimes in the Virginia advertisements between 1800 and 1830: 17 for theft, 1 for arson, 6 for robbery, 1 for assault, and 1 for murder. In Richmond, a double murder was committed when a runaway name Jack broke into the home of Daniel Ford. Both Ford and his wife were shot and killed (*Richmond Enquirer*, October 17, 1820). However outrageous these crimes were perceived to be, the percentage of runaways charged with crime in Virginia was low. The number of crimes runaways committed after absconding is not known.

The fugitives who were believed by their owners in Virginia to be headed out of state were much more diligently pursued. The record indicates that, in many cases, the owners had a fairly clear idea of their runaway slaves' destinations. Mullin found a high correlation between the estimates of fugitives' destinations and the counties where they were intercepted and incarcerated (Mullin 1972, pp. 188–189). If the owners' estimates can be believed, only a small percentage of the runaways advertised in Virginia between 1800 and 1830 were headed north. In a sample of 1,253 fugitives, only 113, or 9 percent, were thought to be headed for the Mason-Dixon Line. During that period, 294, or 23.4 percent, were captured. Twelve northward-bound fugitives were advertised in 1823. Typical was an advertisement in January. John Taylor of Brunswick County, Va., advertised in the *Richmond Enquirer* for his runaway named Granderson. Granderson, "a first rate house and body servant," had been hired the previous year to Gen. Robert R. Johnson of Warrentown, N.C., from whom he had run away. Taylor believed that the slave was headed for Petersburg, "where it is feared he will attempt to procure a conveyance to the north" (January 14, 1823). Thirteen were thought to be headed north in 1826. Abner Mitchell of Richmond had hired a slave named Robin, alias Robert Chamberlayne, from his owner in New Kent County. Mitchell asserted that the fugitive "will endeavour to get to New-York, or some other Northern cities" (January 3, 1826). In 1826, 56 fugitives were advertised, and 20, or 35.7 percent, were captured and placed in jail. It must be understood that the 20 fugitives who were captured in 1826 had not necessarily run away that year.

Between the founding of the Republic and the Civil War, there is good reason to believe that many thousands of slaves slipped their shackles and successfully made their way to the free states; many went on to Canada. Despite the most strin-

The slaves' most dramatic response to the Civil War was to run away.

PAGE 642

See also
Slavery

gent efforts of both the state and national governments to deter the efforts of slaves to become free, the flow of fugitives to the North continued. The numbers of fugitives going north was only a small portion of the runaways. However, the impact of fugitive slaves on the African-American and white communities in the North and their role in shaping the antebellum antislavery discourse were out of proportion to their numbers.

—STANLEY W. CAMPBELL

FULLER, META VAUX WARRICK

Meta Vaux Warrick Fuller (June 9, 1877–March 18, 1968), sculptor. Named for one of her mother's clients (Meta, daughter of Pennsylvania senator Richard Vaux), Meta Vaux Warrick Fuller was born in Philadelphia, the youngest of three children of William and Emma (Jones) Warrick, prosperous hairstylists. She enjoyed a privileged childhood, with dancing and horseback-riding lessons. While attending Philadelphia public schools, Fuller took weekly courses at J. Liberty Tadd, an industrial arts school. At eighteen, she won a three-year scholarship to the Pennsylvania Museum and School for Industrial Art. In 1898 she graduated with honors, a prize in metalwork

for her *Crucifix of Christ in Anguish,* and a one-year graduate scholarship. The following year, she was awarded the Crozer (first) Prize in sculpture for *Procession of the Arts and Crafts,* a terra-cotta bas-relief of thirty-seven medieval costumed figures.

From 1899 to 1903, Fuller studied in Paris, at first privately with Raphael Collin, and then at the Colarossi Academy. Among her supporters in France were expatriate painter Henry O. Tanner and philosopher W. E. B. Du Bois, who encouraged her to depict her racial heritage. Fuller produced clay, painted-plaster, and bronze figurative works based on Egyptian history, Greek myths, French literature, and the Bible.

In 1901, sculptor Auguste Rodin praised Fuller's clay piece *Secret Sorrow* (or *Man Eating His Heart*). With his sponsorship, Fuller began to receive wider notice. Art dealer Samuel Bing exhibited twenty-two of her sculptures at his L'Art Nouveau Gallery in June 1902. *The Wretched,* a bronze group of seven figures suffering physical and mental disabilities (as well as other macabre pieces, such as *Carrying the Dead Body* and *Oedipus,* in the latter of which the figure is blinding himself), earned Fuller the title "delicate sculptor of horrors" from the French press. She later enlarged a plaster model of *The Impenitent Thief,* which she had shown at Bing's gallery. Although she never finished the piece, Rodin saw that it was

THE TALKING SKULL

Meta Fuller produced this acclaimed sculpture, The Talking Skull, *in 1937. Like many of her works, it conveys aspects of African-American culture, in this case an African fable.*

NATIONAL ARCHIVES

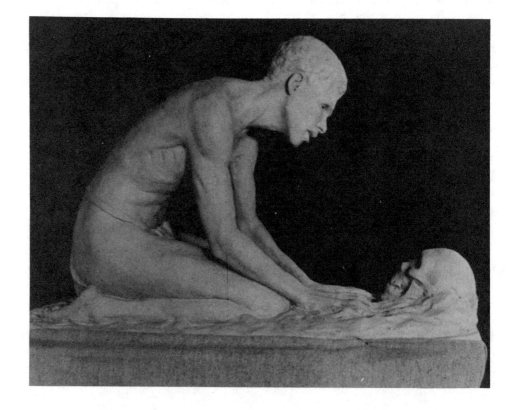

exhibited at the prestigious Société National des Beaux Arts Salon in April 1903.

Upon Fuller's return to Philadelphia, she established a studio on South Camac Street in a flourishing artistic neighborhood. Her sculptures were exhibited at the Pennsylvania Academy of Fine Arts in 1906, 1908, 1920, and 1928. In 1907 the Jamestown Tercentennial Exposition commissioned Fuller to create fifteen tableaux of 24-inch-high plaster figures depicting African-American progress since the Jamestown settlement in 1607. She received a gold medal for *The Warrick Tableaux,* a 10-foot-by-10-foot diorama.

The artist's career slowed considerably after her marriage in 1909 to the Liberian neurologist Solomon C. Fuller and a fire in 1910 that destroyed the bulk of her work in storage. By 1911, Fuller was the devoted mother of two sons (the last was born in 1916), an active member of Saint Andrew's Episcopal Church, and host to prominent guests who frequently visited the family in the quiet town of Framingham, Mass.

Fuller began to sculpt again in 1913, when Du Bois commissioned a piece for New York state's celebration of the fiftieth anniversary of the Emancipation Proclamation. *The Spirit of Emancipation* represented Humanity weeping for her freed children (a man and woman) as Fate tried to hold them back. Positive public response promoted Fuller to continue working. In 1914, the Boston Public Library exhibited twenty-two of her recent works. Among the numerous requests and awards that followed from African-American and women's groups were a plaster medallion commissioned by the Framingham Equal Suffrage League (1915); a plaster group, *Peace Halting the Ruthlessness of War* (for which she received second prize from the Massachusetts branch of the Women's Peace Party in 1917); and a portrait relief of the NAACP's first president, Moorfield Storey, commissioned by Du Bois in 1922. The same year, the New York Making of America Exposition displayed Fuller's *Ethiopia Awakening,* a one-foot-high bronze sculpture of a woman shedding mummy cloths. This Pan-Africanist work symbolized the strength of womanhood, the emergence of nationhood, and the birth of what Alain Locke would call three years later the "New Negro." One of Fuller's most poignant works, *Mary Turner: A Silent Protest against Mob Violence* (1919), commemorates both the silent parade of

ten thousand black New Yorkers against lynching in 1917 and the lynching of a Georgian woman and her unborn child in 1918. Fuller never finished the piece because she believed Northerners would find it too inflammatory and Southerners would not accept it. She created numerous other works that depicted symbolic and actual African and African-American culture, including her celebrated *Talking Skull* (1937), based on an African fable. She also produced portrait busts of friends, family members, and African-American abolitionists and other black leaders, such as educator Charlotte Hawkins Brown, composer Samuel Coleridge Taylor, and Menelik II of Abyssinia. The Harmon Foundation exhibited Fuller's work in 1931 and 1933. She later served as a Harmon juror.

Fuller participated in numerous local organizations; she was a member of the Boston Art Club, an honorary member of the Business and Professional Women's Club, chair of the Framingham Women's Club art committee, and the only African-American president of Zonta, a women's service club. Additionally, she designed costumes for theatrical groups and produced "living pictures": re-creations of artistic masterpieces with actors, costumes, sets, and lighting.

In the 1940s, Fuller's husband went blind and became increasingly ill. She nursed him until his death in 1953, then contracted tuberculosis herself and stayed at the Middlesex County Sanatorium for two years. She wrote poetry there, too, frail to create more than a few small sculptures.

By 1957, Fuller was strong enough to continue her work. She produced models of ten notable African-American women for the Afro-American Women's Council in Washington, D.C. She also created a number of sculptures for her community, including several religious pieces for Saint Andrew's Church, a plaque for the Framingham Union Hospital, and the bronze *Storytime* for the Framingham Public Library. For her achievements, Livingstone College (her husband's alma mater) awarded her an honorary doctorate of letters in 1962, and Framingham posthumously dedicated a public park in the honor of Meta and Solomon Fuller in 1973. Since then, Fuller's sculptures have been included in numerous exhibitions.

—THERESA LEININGER-MILLER

FULLER, META VAUX WARRICK

♦ **Tableau**
A striking or artistic grouping

See also
Alain Locke
New Negro
Henry O. Tanner

GABRIEL PROSSER CONSPIRACY

During 1800 Gabriel Prosser worked in secret to recruit and organize thousands of enslaved Virginians. He sketched out an elaborate plan to overthrow the slavery regime, and it came within hours of execution. But on the chosen day—Saturday, August 30—a hurricane destroyed bridges and flooded roads. The violent downpour washed out the proposed attack on the state capitol at Richmond, allowed time for word of the plan to leak to white authorities, and foiled what could have become a brilliant move in the dangerous chess game to force an end to slavery.

Gabriel was born into bondage about 1775 around the time that white Virginians declared their political independence. The authorities who executed him said he showed "courage and intellect above his rank in life." As the property of tavernkeeper Thomas Prosser, he worked regularly as a blacksmith in the Richmond area, where, inspired by stories of the recent Haitian Revolution, he framed his desperate plan. Aided by his wife and his brothers Martin and Solomon, he worked to procure weapons and rally recruits (Martin, a preacher, found recruits at funerals and secret religious gatherings, where he employed biblical accounts of the Israelites' escape from Egypt to inspire potential conspirators). According to testimony in subsequent trials, from two to ten thousand African Americans knew of the design and looked to Gabriel as their leader to, in Solomon's words, "conquer the white people and possess ourselves of their property." The insurrectionists intended to spare Methodists, Quakers, and local Frenchmen because of their emancipationist leanings, and they expected poor whites and nearby Catawba Indians to join their cause when it gathered strength.

The plan called for several hundred participants (advised by a veteran from the successful siege at Yorktown) to gather at a spot outside Richmond. Behind a banner invoking the American, French, and Haitian Revolutions with the words Death or Liberty, they would march on the city in three contingents. One group would light fires in the dockside warehouses to divert whites from the heart of the city, while the other two groups would seize the capitol armory and take Gov. James Monroe hostage. When the "white people agreed to their freedom," Gabriel "would dine and drink with the merchants of the city," and a white flag would be hoisted above the capitol, calling other blacks in the countryside to join them.

Betrayal by informers presented a huge danger, with so many persons approached about such an overwhelming plan. When torrential rains forced last-minute postponement of the march on Richmond, several slaves had already alerted whites to the impending action, and Gov. Monroe moved swiftly. The state militia arrested scores of suspects, and several dozen persons were executed. Prosser took refuge on the schooner *Mary,* captained by a sympathetic white Methodist. But in late September he was betrayed by two slave crewmen and captured in Norfolk. After a brief show trial in which the leader remained silent, he was hanged on October 7.

In the aftermath of the foiled insurrection, the Virginia Assembly acted to restrict the movement of all blacks—enslaved and free—and to set up a white public guard in Richmond. Such precautions proved ineffective, however. In 1802 authorities discovered further black plans to fight for freedom in Virginia and North Carolina. In 1936 the publication of Arna Bontemps's novel *Black Thunder* offered an interesting literary treatment of Prosser's revolt.

—PETER H. WOOD

GARVEY, MARCUS MOSIAH

Marcus Mosiah Garvey (August 17, 1887–June 10, 1940), founder and leader of the Universal Negro Improvement Association (UNIA), the largest organized mass movement in black history. Hailed in his own time as a redeemer, a "black Moses," Garvey is now best remembered as

See also
African Methodist
Episcopal Church
Slavery

champion of the Back-to-Africa movement that swept the United States in the aftermath of World War I.

Garvey was born on August 17, 1887, in the town of St. Ann's Bay on the north coast of the island of Jamaica. He left school at fourteen, worked as a printer's apprentice, and subsequently joined the protonationalist National Club, which advocated Jamaican self-rule. He participated in the printers' union strike of 1912, and following its collapse, he went to Central America, working in various capacities in Costa Rica, Honduras, and Panama. He spent over a year in England during 1913–14, where he teamed up for a time with the pan-Negro journalist and businessman Duse Mohamed Ali, publisher of the influential *African Times and Orient Review.* After a short tour of the European continent, he returned to England and lobbied the Colonial Office for assistance to return to Jamaica.

Garvey arrived back in Jamaica on the eve of the outbreak of World War I. He lost little time in organizing the UNIA, which he launched at a public meeting in Kingston on July 20, 1914. Content at first to offer a program of racial accommodation while professing strong patriotic support for British war aims, Garvey was a model

colonial. He soon aspired to establish a Tuskegee-type industrial training school in Jamaica. In spring 1916, however, after meeting with little success and feeling shut out from political influence, he came to America—ostensibly at Booker T. Washington's invitation, though Garvey arrived after Washington died.

Garvey's arrival in America was propitious. It coincided with the dawn of the militant New Negro era, the ideological precursor of the Harlem Renaissance of the 1920s. Propelled by America's entry into World War I in April 1917, the New Negro movement quickly gathered momentum from the outrage that African Americans felt in the aftermath of the infamous East St. Louis race riot of July 2, 1917. African-American disillusionment with the country's failure to make good on the professed democratic character of American war aims became widespread.

Shortly after his arrival in America, Garvey embarked upon a period of extensive travel and lecturing that provided him with a firsthand sense of conditions in African-American communities. After traveling for a year, he settled in Harlem, where he organized the first American branch of the UNIA in May 1917.

With the end of the war, Garvey's politics underwent a radical change. His principal political goal now became the redemption of Africa and its unification into a United States of Africa. To enrich and strengthen his movement, Garvey envisioned a black-owned and -run shipping line to foster economic independence, transport passengers between America, the Caribbean, and Africa, and serve as a symbol of black grandeur and enterprise.

Accordingly, the Black Star Line was launched and incorporated in 1919. The line's flagship, the SS *Yarmouth,* rechristened the SS *Frederick Douglass,* made its maiden voyage to the West Indies in November 1919; two other ships were acquired in 1920. The Black Star Line would prove to be the UNIA's most powerful recruiting and propaganda tool, but it ultimately sank under the accumulated weight of financial inexperience, mismanagement, expensive repairs, Garvey's own ill-advised business decisions, and ultimately, insufficient capital.

Meanwhile, by 1920 the UNIA had hundreds of divisions and chapters operating worldwide. It hosted elaborate annual conventions at its Liberty Hall headquarters in Harlem and published the *Negro World,* its internationally disseminated weekly organ that was soon banned in many parts of Africa and the Caribbean.

ORGANIZER AND FOUNDER

Within a decade of founding the Universal Negro Improvement Association (UNIA) in Jamaica in 1914, Marcus Garvey built the UNIA into the largest independent African-American political association.
PRINTS AND PHOTOGRAPHS DIVISION, LIBRARY OF CONGRESS

At the first UNIA convention in August 1920, Garvey was elected to the position of provisional president of Africa. In order to prepare the groundwork for launching his program of African redemption, Garvey sought to establish links with Liberia. In 1920 he sent a UNIA official to scout out prospects for a colony in that country. Following the official's report, in the winter of 1921 a group of UNIA technicians was sent to Liberia.

Starting in 1921, however, the movement began to unravel under the economic strain of the collapse of the Black Star Line, the failure of Garvey's Liberian program, opposition from black critics, defections caused by internal dissension, and official harassment. The most visible expression of the latter was the federal government's indictment of Garvey, in early 1922, on charges of mail fraud stemming from Garvey's stock promotion of the Black Star Line, though by the time the indictment was presented, the Black Star Line had already suspended all operations.

The pressure of his legal difficulties soon forced Garvey into an ill-advised effort to neutralize white opposition. In June 1922 he met secretly with the acting imperial wizard of the Ku Klux Klan in Atlanta, Ga., Edward Young Clarke. The revelation of Garvey's meeting with the KKK produced a major split within the UNIA, resulting in the ouster of the "American leader," Rev. J. W. H. Eason, at the August 1922 convention. In January 1923 Eason was assassinated in New Orleans, La., but his accused assailants, who were members of the local UNIA African Legion, were subsequently acquitted. Following this event and as part of the defense campaign in preparation for the mail fraud trial, Garvey's second wife, Amy Jacques Garvey (1896–1973), edited and published a small volume of Garvey's sayings and speeches under the title *Philosophy and Opinions of Marcus Garvey* (1923).

Shortly after his trial commenced, Garvey unwisely assumed his own legal defense. He was found guilty on a single count of fraud and sentenced to a five-year prison term, though his three Black Star Line codefendants were acquitted. (The year following his conviction, Garvey launched a second shipping line, the Black Cross Navigation and Trading Co., but it too failed.)

Thanks to an extensive petition campaign, Garvey's sentence was commuted after he had served thirty-three months in the Atlanta federal penitentiary. He was immediately deported to Jamaica upon release in November 1927 and never allowed to return to America. A second and expanded volume of *Philosophy and Opinions of Marcus Garvey* was edited and published by Amy Jacques Garvey in 1925 as part of Garvey's attempt to obtain a pardon.

Back in Jamaica, Garvey soon moved to reconstitute the UNIA under his direct control. This move precipitated a major split between the official New York parent body and the newly created Jamaican body. Although two conventions of the UNIA were held in Jamaica, Garvey was never able to reassert control over the various segments of his movement from his base in Jamaica.

Although he had high hopes of reforming Jamaican politics, Garvey went down to defeat in the general election of 1930 in his bid to win a seat on the colonial legislative council. He had to content himself with a seat on the municipal council of Kingston. Disheartened and bankrupt, Garvey abandoned Jamaica and relocated to London in 1935. A short time after arriving in England, however, fascist Italy invaded Ethiopia, producing a crisis that occasioned a massive upsurge of pro-Ethiopian solidarity throughout the black world, in which movement UNIA divisions and members were at the forefront. Garvey's loud defense of the Ethiopian emperor Haile Selassie soon changed to scathing public criticism, thus alienating many of Garvey's followers.

Throughout the thirties Garvey tried to rally his greatly diminished band of supporters with his monthly magazine, *Black Man*. Between 1936 and 1938 he convened a succession of annual meetings and conventions in Toronto, Canada, where he also launched a school of African philosophy as a UNIA training school. He undertook annual speaking tours of the Canadian maritime provinces and the eastern Caribbean.

In 1939 Garvey suffered a stroke that left him partly paralyzed. The indignity of reading his own obituary notice precipitated a further stroke that led to his death on June 10, 1940. Although his last years were spent in obscurity, in the decades between the two world wars, Garvey's ideology inspired millions of blacks worldwide with the vision of a redeemed and emancipated Africa. The importance of Garvey's political legacy was acknowledged by such African nationalists as Nnamdi Azikiwe of Nigeria and Kwame Nkrumah of Ghana. In 1964 Garvey was declared Jamaica's first national hero.

While he failed to realize his immediate objectives, Garvey's message represented a call for liberation from the psychological bondage of racial subordination. Drawing on a gift for spellbinding oratory and spectacle, Garvey melded black aspirations for economic and cultural independence

No race has the last word on culture and on civilization. You do not know what the black man is capable of; you do not know what he is thinking and therefore you do not know what the oppressed and suppressed Negro, by virtue of his condition and circumstance, may give to the world as a surprise.

MARCUS GARVEY
SPEECH, 6 JUNE 1928, ROYAL
ALBERT HALL, LONDON

See also
Universal Negro
Improvement Association

with the traditional American creed of success to create a new and distinctive black gospel of racial pride.

—ROBERT A. HILL

GILLESPIE, JOHN BIRKS "DIZZY"

John Birks "Dizzy" Gillespie (October 21, 1917– January 6, 1993), jazz trumpeter and composer. Born in Cheraw, S.C., John Birks Gillespie, or Dizzy, as he was later known, took up trombone in his early teens and began playing trumpet shortly thereafter. When he began to play trumpet, he puffed out his cheeks, a technical mistake that later became his visual trademark. Starting in 1932, Gillespie studied harmony and theory at Laurinburg Institute, in Laurinburg, N.C., but in 1935 he broke off studies to move with his family to Philadelphia. Frank Fairfax gave Gillespie his first important work, and it was in Fairfax's band that Gillespie earned his nickname, Dizzy, for his clowning onstage and off.

In 1937 Gillespie moved to New York and played for two years with Teddy Hill's band. Through the early 1940s his experience was mostly with big bands, including those of Cab Calloway, Ella Fitzgerald, Benny Carter, Charlie Barnet, Les Hite, Lucky Millinder, Earl Hines, Duke Ellington, and Billy Eckstine. Among his important early recordings were "Pickin' the Cabbage" (1940) with Calloway and "Little John Special" (1942) with Millinder. Gillespie, who married Lorraine Willis in 1940, began leading small ensembles in Philadelphia and New York shortly thereafter. In 1945 he joined with saxophonist Charlie Parker to lead a bebop ensemble that helped inaugurate the modern jazz era.

Although in the early 1940s younger jazz musicians had played in a bebop style in big bands and in after-hours jam sessions at clubs in Harlem, it was not until Parker and Gillespie's 1945 recordings, including "Dizzy Atmosphere," "Shaw 'Nuff," and "Groovin' High," that the new style's break from swing became clear. Bebop reacted to the at times stodgy tempos of the big bands and was instead characterized by adventurous harmonies and knotty, fast lines played in stunning unison by Gillespie and Parker, with solos that emphasized speed, subtlety, and wit.

Gillespie's trumpet style during this time was enormously influential. By the mid-1940s he had broken away from his earlier emulation of Roy Eldridge and arrived at a style of his own, one which he maintained for the next five decades. He had a crackling tone, and his endless flow of nimble ideas included astonishing runs and leaps into the instrument's highest registers. Although many of Gillespie's tunes were little more than phrases arrived at spontaneously with Parker, Gillespie composed many songs during this time that later became jazz standards, including "A Night in Tunisia" (1942), "Salt Peanuts" (1942), and "Woody 'n' You" (1943). In addition to his virtuosity on trumpet, Gillespie continued to display his masterful sense of humor and instinct for gleeful mischief both onstage and off. Starting in the mid-1940s he affected the role of the jazz intellectual, wearing a beret, horn-rimmed glasses, and a goatee. He popularized bebop slang and served as the hipster patriarch to the white beatniks.

After his initial successes with Parker in the mid-1940s, Gillespie went on to enormous success as the leader of a big band. He hired Tadd Dameron, George Russell, Gil Fuller, and John Lewis as composers and arrangers; some of the band's recordings include "Things to Come" (1946), "One Bass Hit" (1946), and "Our Delight" (1946). The band's celebrated appearance at the Salle Pleyel in Paris, France, in 1948 yielded recordings of "'Round About Midnight," "I Can't Get Started," and "Good Bait." The latter date included the Cuban percussionist Chano Pozo, and during this time Gillespie began to explore Afro-Cuban rhythms and melodies. Gillespie's composition "Manteca" (1947) and his performance of George Russell's "Cubana Be, Cubana Bop" (1947) were among the first successful integrations of jazz and Latin music, followed later by his composition "Con Alma" (1957). In the late 1940s and early '50s Gillespie also continued to work on small group dates, including reunions with Charlie Parker in 1950, 1951, and 1953 and a return to the Salle Pleyel as a leader in 1953.

Although Gillespie never lost his idiosyncratic charm and sense of humor—after 1953 he played a trumpet with an upturned bell, supposedly the result of someone having bent the instrument by sitting on it—he outgrew the role of practical joker and instead became a figure of respect and genial authority. He released "Love Me" and "Tin Tin Deo" in 1951 on his own short-lived Dee Gee record label and became a featured soloist on many performances by the popular traveling sessions known as Jazz at the Philharmonic (JATP). In 1956 Gillespie's integrated band became the first to tour overseas under the sponsorship of the U.S. State Department, and in the following years he took them on tours to the Middle East, South America, and Europe. In 1959 Gillespie, always an outspoken opponent of segregation, performed at the first integrated concert in a public school in his hometown of Cheraw, S.C. The next year he refused to back down when Tulane University in New Orleans threatened to cancel a concert unless he replaced his white pianist with an African American. Gillespie's political activities took another twist in 1964 when he went along with a tongue-in-cheek presidential campaign. During this time Gillespie continued to record, both with small groups (*Swing Low, Sweet Cadillac*, 1967) and with big bands (*Reunion Big Band*, 1968). He also worked extensively in film and television.

In the 1970s and '80s, Gillespie maintained his busy schedule of touring and recording both in the United States and abroad as a leader of small and large bands and as a guest soloist. He appeared with the Giants of Jazz tour (1971–72) and recorded with Mary Lou Williams (1971), Machito (1975), Count Basie (1977), Mongo Santamaria (1980), Max Roach (1989), and often with his trumpet protégé, John Faddis. During this time he also appeared on television shows such as *Sesame Street* and *The Cosby Show*. In 1979 he published his autobiography, *To BE or Not to BOP*, in which he explained his longstanding interest in Africa, which influenced his politics, music, and style of dress, and also recounted his involvement in the Baha'i faith, to which he had converted in the late 1960s.

By the late 1980s Gillespie had long been recognized as one of the founding figures of modern jazz. In 1989 he won the U.S. National Medal of the Arts and was made a French Commandeur d'Ordre des Arts et Lettres. Although his instrumental style was largely fixed by the mid-1940s, he won four Grammy Awards in the 1970s and '80s, and his career as a trumpeter ranked in influence and popularity with Louis Armstrong and Miles Davis; along with Armstrong he became jazz's unofficial ambassador and personification around the world. Gillespie, who lived in Queens, N.Y., and then in Camden, N.J., continued giving hundreds of concerts each year in dozens of countries until his death at the age of seventy-four.

—JONATHAN GILL

GIOVANNI, YOLANDA CORNELIA "NIKKI"

Yolanda Cornelia "Nikki" Giovanni (June 7, 1943–), poet. Nikki Giovanni was born in Knoxville, Tenn. Her father, Jones Giovanni, was a probation officer; her mother, Yolanda Cornelia Watson Giovanni, was a social worker. The Giovannis were a close-knit family, and Nikki felt a special bond with her younger sister, Gary, and her maternal grandmother, Louvenia Terrell Watson. Watson instilled in Giovanni a fierce pride in her African-American heritage.

After graduating from Fisk University in 1967, Giovanni was swept up by the Black Power and Black Arts movements. Between 1968 and 1970 she published three books of poetry reflecting her preoccupation with revolutionary politics: *Black Judgment* (1968), *Black Feeling, Black Talk* (1970), and *Re: Creation* (1970).

But *Re: Creation* also introduced more personal concerns. In the spring of 1969, Giovanni gave birth to a son, Tom. The experience, she said, caused her to reconsider her priorities. Her work through the middle 1970s concentrated less overtly on politics and confrontation and more on personal issues such as love and loneliness. Yet Giovanni would always deny any real separation between her "personal" and her "political" concerns. During this time she began writing poetry for children. *Spin a Soft Black Song: Poems for Children* appeared in 1971, *Ego-Tripping and Other Poems for Young People* in 1973, and *Vacation Time: Poems for Children* in 1980.

In the 1970s, Giovanni expanded her horizons in other ways. Between 1971 and 1978 she made a series of six records, speaking her poetry to an accompaniment of gospel music (the first in the series, *Truth Is on Its Way*, was the best-selling spoken-word album of 1971). She published essays and two books of conversations with major literary forebears: *A Dialogue: James Baldwin and Nikki Giovanni* (1973) and *A Poetic Equation: Conversations Between Nikki Giovanni and Margaret Walker* (1974). She was also a sought-after reader and lecturer.

Critical reaction to Giovanni's work has often been mixed. While some have praised her work for its vitality and immediacy, some have felt that her early popularity and high degree of visibility worked against her development as a poet. Others have criticized her work as politically naive, uneven, and erratic. Some of these reactions were due in part to Giovanni's very public growing up as a poet and the diversity of her interests. These criticisms have never bothered Giovanni, who believes that life is "inherently incoherent."

Other works of Giovanni's include *My House* (1972), *The Women and the Men* (1972), *Cotton Candy on a Rainy Day* (1978), *Those Who Ride the Night Winds* (1983), and a collection of essays, *Sacred Cows and Other Edibles* (1988).

—MICHAEL PALLER

Death is a slave's freedom.

NIKKI GIOVANNI
SPEECH AT THE FUNERAL OF
MARTIN LUTHER KING, JR.,
1968

See also

Literature

GOSPEL MUSIC

The African-American religious music known as gospel, originating in the field hollers, slave songs, spirituals, and Protestant hymns sung on southern plantations, and later at camp meetings and churches, has come to dominate not only music in black churches, but singing and instrumental styles across the spectrum of American popular music, including jazz, blues, rhythm and blues, soul, and country. Exemplified in songs such as "Take My Hand, Precious Lord" and "Move On Up a Little Higher," gospel music encourages emotional and jubilant improvisation on songs of thanksgiving and praise as well as sorrow and suffering.

Musically, gospel is distinguished by its vocal style, which in both male and female singers is characterized by a strained, full-throated sound, often pushed to guttural shrieks and rasps suited to the extremes of the emotion-laden lyrics. Melodies and harmonies are generally simple, allowing for spontaneity in devising repetitive, expressive fills and riffs. The syncopated rhythms of gospel are typically spare, with heavy, often hand-clapped accents.

The Founding Years

Although the roots of gospel can be traced to Africa, and the earliest arrival of Africans in the New World, the main antecedent was the "Dr. Watts" style of singing hymns, named for British poet and hymnist Isaac Watts (1674–1748), who emphasized a call-and-response approach to religious songs, with mournful but powerful rhythms. Thus, in the nineteenth century, African-American hymnody in mainstream denominations did not differ considerably from music performed in white churches. The earliest African-American religious denominations date back to the late eighteenth century, when black congregations split off from white church organizations in Philadelphia. In 1801 the minister Richard Allen, who later founded the African Methodist Episcopal (AME) denomination, published two collections of hymns designed for use in black churches. These collections were the forerunners of similar collections that formed the basis for the music performed in most nineteenth-century black churches, yet they were quite similar to the slow-tempo, restrained white Protestant hymnody. Around the middle of the nineteenth century a new type of music known as "gospel hymns" or "gospel songs" was being composed in a new style, lighter and more songlike than traditional hym-

nody, written by white composers such as Dwight Moody (1837–1899), Ira Sankey (1840–1908), Philip Paul Bliss (1838–1876), Robert Lowry (1826–1899), and William Batchelder Bradbury (1816–1868).

Another important nineteenth-century influence on gospel music was the idea, increasingly popular at a minority of nineteenth-century black churches, that spiritual progress required a deeper and more directly emotional relationship with God, often through the singing of white "gospel hymns," although gospel as an African-American form would not take that name for decades. These congregations, often led by charismatic ministers, began searching for a religion based on "Holiness or Hell" and were early participants in the Latter Rain movement, which sought to "irrigate the dry bones" of the church. The first congregation known to accept this doctrine, based on the activities of the Day of Pentecost (though, confusingly, this is *not* what is now called Pentecostalism) was the United Holy Church of Concord, S.C., which held its first meeting in 1886 and had its first convention in 1894 under the leadership of Brother L. M. Mason (1861–1930). Another early congregation to accept that doctrine and encourage early forms of gospel music was the Church of the Living God, in Wrightsville, Ark., under the leadership of William Christian (1856–1928) in 1889.

The Holiness doctrine proved controversial within black churches, as did the music associated with Holiness. In 1895 Charles Harrison Mason and Charles Price Jones were forced from the Baptist church, and together they proceeded to organize the Church of God in Christ in Lexington, Miss., where the music was heavily influenced by the performance style at Los Angeles's Azusa Street Revival, a black congregation that marked the beginning of Pentecostalism, under the leadership of William Joseph Seymour. The Azusa Street Revival featured highly charged services involving "speaking in tongues" as a manifestation of the Holy Ghost. Such activities were eventually integrated into the mainstream of black church activity, but around the turn of the century, Holiness-style services, and even the singing of spirituals, were strenuously opposed by conservative black church elders who had fought to "elevate" the musical standards of their congregations. Jones, for example, was opposed to the Azusa Street style, and eventually split from Mason to organize the Church of Christ, Holiness.

Early forms of gospel music such as sung or chanted testimonials and sermons were used to

See also
African Methodist Episcopal

complement prayers in Holiness churches. Drawing on the call-and-response tradition that dated back to slavery times, members of a congregation would take inspiration from a phrase from the sermon or testimony and out of it spontaneously compose a simple melody and text. A chorus of congregants would repeat the original phrase, while the leader interpolated brief extemporized choruses. For example, in Charles Harrison Mason's 1908 "I'm a Soldier," the leader and congregation begin by alternating the following lines: "I'm a soldier/In the army of the Lord/I'm a soldier/In the army." Succeeding choruses differ only in the lead line, with the leader interpolating such phrases as "I'm fighting for my life," "I'm a sanctified soldier," or "I'll live and I'll die," and the congregation repeating "In the army" as a refrain. The length of such songs often stretched to fifteen minutes or more. Along with simple "homemade" harmonies came hand-clapping, foot-stomping, and holy dancing, also known as "shouting."

Holiness, Sanctified, and Pentecostal congregations sprang up rapidly all over the South, particularly in rural, poor communities, starting around the turn of the century, and in less than a decade gospel music, then known as church music, was being sung in Baptist and Methodist congregations as well. During this time the most popular gospel hymns were by a new generation of black composers, including William Henry Sherwood; Jones, who composed "Where Shall I Be?" and "I'm Happy with Jesus Alone"; Mason, who in addition to "I'm a Soldier" wrote "My Soul Loves Jesus" and the chant "Yes, Lord"; and Charles Albert Tindley, who composed "What Are They Doing in Heaven," "Stand by Me," and "I'll Overcome Someday," which was the forerunner of the civil rights anthem "We Shall Overcome." Since at this time there were no publishing houses for black gospel, these composers began to establish their own. They also depended on recordings and traveling preachers to spread their music. Preachers who popularized their own songs included J. C. Burnett ("Drive and Go Forward," 1926), Ford Washington McGhee ("Lion of the Tribe of Judah," 1927), J. M. Gates ("Death's Black Train Is Coming," 1926), and A. W. Nix ("The Black Diamond Express to Hell," 1927).

The Birth of Gospel Music

The 1920s were a crucial time in the development of gospel music. In 1921 the National Baptist Convention, USA, the largest organization of black Christians in the world, not only formally recognized gospel as a legitimate sacred musical form but published a collection of hymns, spirituals, and gospel songs under the title *Gospel Pearls,* edited by Willa A. Townsend (1885–1963). That hymnal contained six songs by Tindley, the first gospel composer successfully to combine the conventions of white evangelical music with the simple, often sentimental melodies of black spirituals. The 1921 convention also marked the emergence of the composer Thomas A. Dorsey (1899–1993), who would go on to become the Father of Gospel because of his indefatigable songwriting, publishing, organizing, and teaching. Three years later the National Baptist Convention published the *Baptist Standard Hymnal,* another important step toward bringing gospel into the mainstream of African-American church worship. Other important gospel composers who came to prominence during this time were Lucie Campbell (1885–1963) and William Herbert Brewster (1897–1987).

Despite the publication of these hymnals and the dissemination of individual songs in both print and by record, it was by word of mouth that gospel spread, particularly in working-class communities in the rural South. In Jefferson County, Ala., workers in coal mines and factories used their lunch hours to organize quartets to sing this new type of religious song. In some respects these groups were inspired by the tradition of the secular Fisk Jubilee and Tuskegee vocal quartets, but the new groups emphasized the powerful emotional experiences of conversion and salvation. One of the first such groups, the Foster Singers, organized in 1916, stressed equality between the vocal parts. However, it was a Foster Singers spinoff group, the Birmingham Jubilee Singers, led by one of the members of the Foster Singers, that inspired gospel quartets that soon started all over the South. The Birmingham Jubilee Singers allowed the bass and tenor more prominence and freedom, raised tempos, and used more adventurous harmonies, including "blue" notes. The vocal quartets organized in this style in the 1920s include the Fairfield Four (1921), which as of 1992 still included one of its original members, the Rev. Samuel McCrary; the Blue Jay Singers (1926); the Harmonizing Four (1927); and the Dixie Hummingbirds (1928). In the 1930s, new quartets included the Golden Gate Quartet (1934), which went on to become the most popular group of the 1930s and '40s, and the Soul Stirrers (1936). The following year, Rebert H. Harris (b. 1916) joined the groups, and over the next fourteen years he became their most famous singer. In

G

GOSPEL MUSIC

The Birth of Gospel Music

From the beginning of separate religious services, African-American Baptists utilized music in their worship.

PAGE 58

See also

Richard Allen

James Brown

"GEORGIA TOM"

Author of "Precious Lord" Tranforms Gospel Music

Thomas Andrew "Georgia Tom" Dorsey (July 1, 1899–January 23, 1993), gospel composer. Born in Villa Rica, Ga., Thomas Dorsey was the oldest of three children of Rev. Thomas Madison and Etta Plant Dorsey.

After fourteen years as a jazz and blues musician, Dorsey renounced secular music in 1930 and became a full-time gospel musician, composing gospel pieces and peddling "song sheets" throughout Chicago. The response was discouraging and he was often the butt of jokes. Notwithstanding these initial rejections, Dorsey organized one of the first gospel choirs at Chicago's Pilgrim Baptist Church in 1931, where his accompanist was the young Roberta Martin, and whose future members included Eugene Smith, leader of the Roberta Martin Singers, and James Cleveland, later known as the "Crown Prince of Gospel." In the next year, Dorsey opened the first publishing house for the exclusive sale of gospel music by African-American composers in the country. The same year, along with Sallie Martin and others, he organized the National Convention of Gospel Choirs and Choruses, which, along with Cleveland's Gospel Music Workshop of America (organized in 1968), annually draws the largest number of gospel musicians and music lovers in the United States. In addition to Martin, Dorsey was aided in the early gospel movement by composers Theodore R. Frye and Kenneth Morris and singer Willie Mae Ford Smith.

In 1932, Dorsey and Frye traveled from Chicago to Indianapolis to organize a gospel choir. When Dorsey arrived in Indianapolis, a telegram informed him that his wife had given birth to a child, but had not survived. Dorsey returned to Chicago, only to find that his newly born daughter had died as well. In his grief, he sat alone in a dark room for three days, emerging to write the song that—after "Amazing Grace"—is the second most popular song in African-American Christendom:

Precious Lord, take my hand, lead me on, let me stand.
 I am tired, I am weak, I am worn;
 Through the storm, through the night, lead me on to the light.
 Take my hand, precious Lord, lead me on.

Dorsey taught this song to his choir at Pilgrim Baptist, and in less than a year it had moved into the folk category, with congregations singing all three stanzas without the benefit of sheet music. Since then, it has been translated into more than fifty languages, and Dorsey conducted it throughout the world.

"Precious Lord" is not unlike most of Dorsey's compositions, in that the text is that of the poor, disfranchised African-American Christian but also speaks to all people. He has a special penchant for imbuing his songs with catchy phrases, such as "I'm Going to Live the Life I Sing About in My Song," "If We Ever Needed the Lord Before, We Sure Do Need Him Now," and the song written for Mahalia Jackson, who served as his song demonstrator from 1935 to 1946, "There Will Be Peace in the Valley for Me." His melodies were simple, supported by harmonies that did not detract from the text. Dorsey was so instrumental in the development of gospel music that there was a period during the 1930s and '40s when gospel songs were referred to as "Dorseys." For his contributions he was, early on, dubbed the "Father of Gospel."

Though only a few of Dorsey's songs helped to initiate new trends in gospel music, he is nevertheless remembered as the most important person in gospel music to date. He organized gospel music's first chorus and its first annual national convention, founded its first publishing house, established the gospel-music concert tradition, and in recognition of this, he was celebrated in the 1982 documentary *Say Amen, Somebody.*

—HORACE CLARENCE BOYER

1938 Claude Jeter Harris (b. 1914) organized the Four Harmony Kings, who later changed their name to the Swan Silvertones to acknowledge their sponsorship by a bakery.

By the 1930s, gospel music had been firmly planted in northern cities. This was due not only to the Great Migration of rural blacks following World War I but also to the fact that, increasingly, record companies and publishing houses were lo-cated in northern cities, and particularly in Chicago, then the focal point for gospel music. Thomas Andrew Dorsey opened his publishing house in 1932, the same year he composed "Take My Hand, Precious Lord" (popularly known as "Precious Lord, Take My Hand"). Through composing, publishing, organizing, and teaching gospel choirs, Dorsey was given the sobriquet Father of Gospel.

See also
Ray Charles

Starting in the 1920s, gospel music was taken up by many different types of ensembles, in addition to vocal quartets. In urban areas, blind singers often came to prominence by performing on street corners and in churches. One of the most important of these was Connie Rosemond, for whom Lucie Campbell composed "Something Within Me." Others were Mamie Forehand and the guitarists and singers Blind Joe Taggard and Blind Willie Johnson. The blind Texan singer Arizona Dranes accompanied herself on piano and is credited with introducing that instrument to recorded gospel music. Among the gospel singers who sang with piano accompaniment as early as the 1920s were Willie Mae Ford Smith, Sallie Martin, Clara Hudmon (1900–1960), Madame Ernestine B. Washington (1914–1983), and guitarist and singer Sister Rosetta Tharpe, the first important performer to find a large audience outside the gospel circuit. Male-accompanied singers included Brother Joe May (1912–1973) and J. Robert Bradley (b. 1921). The greatest of the accompanied singers was Mahalia Jackson, who was born in New Orleans and found her calling in Chicago at age sixteen. Her 1947 recording of "Move On Up a Little Higher," by Herbert Brewster, featuring her soaring contralto, came to define the female gospel style.

In the late 1930s, accompanied gospel ensembles consisting of four to six women, four or five men, or a mixed group of four to six singers, became popular. Clara Ward (1924–1973) organized the earliest notable accompanied ensemble, the Ward Singers, in 1934. The year before, Roberta Martin had joined with composer Theodore Frye (1899–1963) to form the Martin-Frye Quartet, later known as the Roberta Martin Singers. Sallie Martin organized the Sallie Martin Singers in 1940. Three years later the Original Gospel Harmonettes were formed, with pianist Evelyn Stark. They later came to prominence when singer Dorothy Love Coates joined the group and introduced "hard" gospel techniques, such as singing beyond her range and straining the voice for dramatic effects. Other accompanied ensembles included the Angelic Gospel Singers and the Davis Sisters, with pianist Curtis Dublin.

During this time vocal quartets and quintets continued to be popular. Archie Brownlee (1925–1960) organized the Five Blind Boys of Mississippi in 1939, the same year that Johnny L. Fields (b. 1927) formed the Five Blind Boys of Alabama, featuring Clarence Fountain (b. 1929). James Woodie Alexander (b. 1916) began leading the Pilgrim Travelers in 1946.

In the years between the wars, women, who from the start had been pillars of African-American religious institutions, became increasingly involved as publishers and organizers. In 1932, Dorsey, Sallie Martin, and Willie Mae Ford Smith formed the National Convention of Gospel Choirs and Choruses. Roberta Martin, the composer of "God Is Still on the Throne," opened her own publishing house in 1939. Sallie Martin opened hers along with Kenneth Martin (1917–1989), the composer of "Yes, God Is Real," in 1940.

The Golden Age

By 1945, gospel was becoming recognized not only as a spiritual experience but also as a form of entertainment, and this became known as gospel's golden era. Singers, appearing on stage in attractive uniforms, had established and refined a popular and recognizable vocal sound. Gospel pianists such as Mildred Falls (1915–1975), Herbert Pickard, Mildred Gay, Edgar O'Neal, James Herndon, and James Washington and organists such as Little Lucy Smith, Gerald Spraggins, Louise Overall Weaver, and Herbert "Blind" Francis were working in exciting styles derived from ragtime, barrelhouse, and the blues, with chordal voicing, riffs, and complicated rhythms. Finally a group of composers including Doris Akers (b. 1923), Sammy Lewis, and Lucy Smith could be depended on to come up with fresh material. Just as early gospel composers relied on traveling from church to church to popularize their songs, so too did the first early popular gospel singers find it necessary to go on the road. Sister Rosetta Tharpe performed at nightclubs and dance halls, but far more typical was the experience of Mahalia Jackson, who by 1945 had quit her regular job and joined a growing number of traveling professional gospel singers performing in churches and schools, moving on to auditoriums and stadiums. These singers were able to support themselves, and some, like Jackson, were quite successful, especially in the context of touring companies.

After the war the recording industry and radio played a large part in popularizing gospel. At first, small companies such as King, Atlantic, Vee-Jay, Dot, Nashboro, and Peacock were the most active in seeking out gospel singers. Apollo Records recorded Jackson and Roberta Martin before they moved to larger labels. The Ward Sisters, the Angelic Gospel Singers, and the Davis Sisters first recorded for Gotham Records. The Original Gospel Harmonettes recorded first for RCA Vic-

Aretha Franklin's formative years were spent singing in her father's church choir and traveling with him on the gospel circuit.

PAGE 277

See also
Aretha Franklin

tor. With the proliferation of recordings, gospel radio programs became popular. In New York, the gospel disk jockey Joe Bostic was extraordinarily successful, as were Mary Manson in Philadelphia, Irene Joseph Ware in Chicago, Mary Dee in Baltimore, Goldie Thompson in Tampa, and John "Honeyboy" Hardy in New Orleans. Other cities with gospel shows in the postwar years included Atlanta, Los Angeles, Louisville, and Miami.

Among the more prominent performers and leaders who emerged during gospel's postwar golden era were Madame Edna Gallmon Cooke

MAHALIA JACKSON

"World's Greatest Gospel Singer"

Mahalia Jackson (October 26, 1911–January 27, 1972), gospel singer. When sixteen-year-old Mahala Jackson (as she was named at birth) arrived in Chicago in 1927, she had already developed the vocal style that was to win her the title of "world's greatest gospel singer." Though born into an extremely religious New Orleans family, she spent hours listening to the recordings of blues singers Bessie Smith and Ma Rainey, and could be found at every parade that passed her neighborhood of Pinching Town in New Orleans.

In later life she would admit that though she was a thoroughgoing Baptist, the Sanctified church next door to her house had had a powerful influence on her singing, for though the members had neither choir nor organ, they sang accompanied by a drum, tambourine, and steel triangle. They clapped and stomped their feet and sang with their whole bodies. She recalled that they had a powerful beat she believed was retained from slavery, and once stated, "I believe blues and jazz and even rock 'n' roll stuff got their beat from the Sanctified church."

Jackson's style was set early on: From Bessie Smith and Ma Rainey she borrowed a deep and dark resonance that complemented her own timbre; from the Baptist church she inherited the moaning and bending of final notes in phrases; and from the Sanctified church she adopted a full-throated tone, delivered with a holy beat. Surprisingly, though gospel in its early stages was being sung in New Orleans, none of her vocal influences came from gospel singers.

Upon arriving in Chicago with her Aunt Hannah, Jackson joined the Johnson Singers, an a cappella quartet. The group quickly established a reputation as one of Chicago's better gospel groups, appearing regularly in concerts and gospel-song plays with Jackson in the lead. In time, Mahalia, as she now chose to call herself, became exclusively a soloist. In 1935 Thomas A. Dorsey persuaded her to become his official song demonstrator, a position she held until 1945. Dorsey later stated that Jackson "had a lot of soul in her singing: she meant what she sang."

Though she made her first recordings in 1937 for Decca, it was not until 1946, when she switched to the small Apollo label, that Jackson established a national reputation in the African-American community. Her 1947 recording of "Move On Up a Little Higher" catapulted her to the rank of superstar and won her one of the first two Gold Records for record sales in gospel music. (Clara Ward won the other.) Accompanied on this recording by her longtime pianist, Mildred Falls, Jackson demonstrated her wide range and ability to improvise on melody and rhythm. As a result of this recording, she became the official soloist for the National Baptist Convention and began touring throughout the United States. She was the first gospel singer to be given a network radio show when, in 1954, CBS signed her for a weekly show on which she was the host and star. In the same year she moved to the Columbia label, becoming a crossover gospel singer through her first recording on that label, "Rusty Old Halo." Several triumphs followed in rapid succession. She appeared on the Ed Sullivan and Dinah Shore television shows, at Carnegie Hall, and in 1958 for the first time at the Newport Jazz Festival. Tours throughout the world began, with Jackson garnering accolades in France, Germany, and Italy.

A crowning achievement of Jackson's was the invitation to sing at one of the inaugural parties of President John F. Kennedy in 1961. In 1963 she was asked to sing just before Rev. Dr. Martin Luther King, Jr. was to deliver his famous "I Have a Dream" speech at the March on Washington. Her rendition of "I've Been Buked and I've Been Scorned" contributed to the success of King's speech. During her career, she appeared in such films as *Imitation of Life* (1959) and *Jazz on a Summer's Day* (1958), sang "Precious Lord, Take My Hand" at the funeral of Dr. King, and recorded with Duke Ellington. Toward the end of her life, she suffered from heart trouble but continued to sing. She died in Chicago on January 27, 1972.

—HORACE CLARENCE BOYER

See also

Fannie Lou Hamer

(1918–1967), Julius "June" Cheeks (1928–1981), who joined the Sensationales in 1946, "Professor" Alex Bradford (1927–1978), Robert Anderson (b. 1919), and Albertina Walker (b. 1930), who in 1952 formed the Caravans. Among the members of the Caravans were Shirley Caesar and Inez Andrews (b. 1928), who had a hit record with "Mary, Don't You Weep." Marion Williams left the Ward Singers in 1958 to form the Stars of Faith. Willie Joe Ligon (b. 1942) organized the Mighty Clouds of Joy in 1959. Perhaps the best-known singer to emerge from the golden era was Sam Cooke, who joined the Soul Stirrers in 1950 and revitalized the male gospel quartet movement with his hits "Nearer to Thee" and "Touch the Hem of His Garment" before going on to fame as a popular singer starting in 1956.

The most significant figure from this time was the Rev. James Cleveland, who began singing in Dorsey's children's choir at the age of eight. By the age of sixteen, Cleveland had composed his first hit for the Roberta Martin Singers. He accompanied the Caravans, formed his own group, and in 1963 began recording with the Angelic Choir of Nutley, N.J. Cleveland's recordings were so successful that they sparked a new phase in gospel music dominated by gospel choirs. Prominent choirs following Cleveland's lead included those led by Thurston Frazier, Mattie Moss Clark (b. 1928), and Jessy Dixon (b. 1938).

By the end of the 1950s, gospel was becoming ubiquitous, not only in black communities but as a part of mainstream American culture. Mahalia Jackson recorded "Come Sunday" as part of Duke Ellington's *Black, Brown and Beige* in 1958 and the next year appeared in the film *Imitation of Life.* Langston Hughes, who in 1956 wrote *Tambourines to Glory: A Play with Spirituals, Jubilees, and Gospel Songs,* wrote the gospel-song play *Black Nativity* in 1961, for a cast that included Marion Williams and Alex Bradford. In 1961, a gospel category was added to the Grammy awards, with Mahalia Jackson the first winner. During the 1960s, costumed groups and choirs began to appear on Broadway, at Carnegie Hall, and in Las Vegas, as well as on television shows. In addition to Sam Cooke, many singers trained in the gospel tradition helped popularize gospel-style delivery in popular music. Rhythm-and-blues doo-wop groups from the late 1940s and 1950s, such as the Ravens, the Orioles, and the Drifters, used close harmonies and a high-crooning-male-lead style borrowed from gospel. Singers such as Dinah Washington, Ray Charles, Al Green, Aretha Franklin, James Brown, Little Richard, and Stevie

Wonder used gospel techniques to cross over to enormous international popularity on the rock, soul, and rhythm-and-blues charts.

Gospel music was a crucial part of the Civil Rights Movement. There had been a political thrust in sacred black music since the abolitionist hymnody of the nineteenth century, and in the 1960s musicians such as Mahalia Jackson, Fannie Lou Hamer, Guy Carawan, the Montgomery Trio, the Nashville Quartet, the CORE Freedom Singers, the SNCC Freedom Singers, and Carlton Reese's Gospel Freedom Choir appeared at marches, rallies, and meetings. Gospel musicians had always reworked traditional material at will, and in the 1960s gospel songs and spirituals originally intended for religious purposes were changed to apply to secular struggles. For example, "If You Miss Me from Praying Down Here" became "If You Miss Me from the Back of the Bus." Other popular songs were "We Shall Overcome," "This Little Light of Mine," "We'll Never Turn Back," "Eyes on the Prize," "Ninety-Nine and a Half Won't Do," "O Freedom," and "Ain't Nobody Gonna Turn Me Around." For many leaders of the Civil Rights Movement, such as Hamer, the Rev. Dr. Martin Luther King, Jr., and the Rev. Wyatt Tee Walker, gospel music was an essential part of their organizing work. "Precious Lord" was a favorite of Martin Luther King, Jr., and Mahalia Jackson sang the song at his funeral.

The Contemporary Sound and Beyond

The next phase in the history of gospel music came in 1969, when Edwin Hawkins released his rendition of "Oh Happy Day," a white nineteenth-century hymn, in which he eschewed the gritty timbres of Cleveland in favor of smooth pop vocals, soul harmonies, and jazz rhythms, including a conga drum. The song, which became the number one song on Billboard's pop chart, represented a fusion of the traditional gospel style of Mahalia Jackson, Thomas Andrew Dorsey, and the Dixie Hummingbirds, with elements of jazz, rhythm and blues, and soul. Record producers, inspired by the crossover potential of what became known as contemporary gospel, began encouraging gospel groups toward a more contemporary sound, igniting a long-running controversy within the gospel community.

After Hawkins, one of the principal figures of contemporary gospel throughout the 1970s was the composer and pianist Andrae Crouch, the cousin of critic Stanley Crouch. Also important were Myrna Summers, Danniebell Hall, Douglas Miller, Bebe and Cece Winans, the Clark Sisters,

By the 1980s black Pentecostals such as Andrae Crouch, Edwin Hawkins, Walter Hawkins, Shirley Caesar, the Clark Sisters, and the Wynans dominated the gospel music movement.

PAGE 540

See also
Pentecostalism

307

EARL GILBERT GRAVES, JR.
Founder and Publisher of *Black Enterprise*

Earl Gilbert Graves, Jr. (January 9, 1935–), publisher. Born in Brooklyn, N.Y., Earl G. Graves attended Morgan State College in Baltimore, Md., receiving his B.A. in economics in 1958. Graves, who had been enrolled in the Reserve Officers' Training Corps, joined the U.S. Army immediately after graduation, and rose to the rank of captain. After leaving the Army in 1962, he sold houses and then worked for the Justice Department as a narcotics agent. In 1965 he was hired by New York Sen. Robert F. Kennedy as a staff assistant, charged with planning and supervising events. Graves occupied that position until Kennedy's death in 1968. That year he started his own business, Earl G. Graves Associates, a management consulting firm specializing in assistance to small businesses.

In 1970, using $150,000 borrowed from the Manhattan Capital Corporation, Graves became founder, editor, and publisher of *Black Enterprise,* the first African-American business magazine. An immediate success, the journal had sales of $900,000 by the end of its first year. By the beginning of the 1990s, the magazine had 250,000 subscribers and annual earnings of more than $15 million. *Black Enterprise* soon became a black community institution, widely known for its how-to advice on building minority business and its lists of the top 100 black-owned companies. Graves's monthly "publisher's page" served as a forum for examining politics and the black marketplace. The magazine developed two other special features. In 1975 Graves began the *Black Enterprise* Achievement Awards for successful African-American entrepreneurs. In 1982 he organized a board of economists to make periodic reports on the black economy.

While Earl G. Graves Publishing Company, Inc., which published *Black Enterprise,* remained the flagship property of Graves's company, Earl Graves, Ltd., Graves set up five other businesses over the following two decades: EGG Dallas Broadcasting, Inc.; B.C.I. Marketing, Inc.; a development firm; a market research firm; and a distribution firm. In 1990, in a notable deal, a limited partnership led by Graves and basketball star Earvin "Magic" Johnson acquired a $60 million Pepsi-Cola franchise in Washington, D.C. In addition to his business activities, Graves remained involved in social and political activism, and during the 1990s was active in the lobbying group TransAfrica, as national commissioner and member of the national board of the Boy Scouts of America, as a director of Howard University, and as a member on several corporate and foundation boards.

—GREG ROBINSON

and the ensemble Commissioned. At the same time, gospel came to Broadway again in the widely acclaimed musical *Your Arms Too Short to Box with God* (1976).

In 1983 *The Gospel at Colonus* was a popular stage production in New York, and in the 1980s and '90s gospel, particularly contemporary, has continued to attract large audiences. The unaccompanied vocal sextet Take 6 combined gospel-style harmonies with mainstream jazz rhythms to achieve huge popular success in the late 1980s. Other popular contemporary singers from this time included Richard Smallwood, who uses classical elements in his songs, Bobby Jones, Keith Pringle, and Daryl Coley. Walter Hawkins (b. 1949), the brother of Edwin Hawkins, combines elements of traditional and contemporary styles, especially on recordings with his wife, Tremaine (b. 1957). The Hawkins style was taken up by the Thompson Community Choir, the Charles Fold Singers, the Barrett Sisters, and the Rev. James Moore, as well as mass choirs in Florida, New Jersey, and Mississippi. The choral ensemble Sounds of Blackness has been popular in recent years, as have contemporary vocal quartets such as the Williams Brothers, the Jackson Southernaires, and the Pilgrim Jubilees. These groups often use synthesizers and drum machines in addition to traditional gospel instruments. Prominent contemporary gospel composers include Elbernita Clark, Jeffrey LeValle, Andrae Woods, and Rance Allen.

Gospel-style singing, at least until the advent of rap music, dominated African-American popular music. One indication of the importance of gospel to the music industry is the fact that as of 1993 there were six Grammy categories devoted to gospel music. Gospel, which started out as a marginal, almost blasphemous form of musical worship, now has a central place in African-American church activity. Not only Holiness and Pentecostal churches but Baptist and Methodist denominations have fully accepted gospel music. Its striking emotional power has enabled gospel music to remain a vital part of African-American culture.

—HORACE CLARENCE BOYER

GRAY, WILLIAM HERBERT, III

William Herbert Gray, III (August 20, 1941–), congressman and administrator. William H. Gray III was born in Baton Rouge, La., the son of William H. Gray, Jr., minister and president of Florida A&M University, and Hazel Yates, a high school teacher. In 1963 he received a B.A. from Franklin and Marshall College in Lancaster, Pa., in 1966 an M.Div. from Drew Theological Seminary in Madison, N.J., and an M.Th. from Princeton Theological Seminary in 1970. In 1964 he became pastor of Union Baptist Church, in Montclair, N.J., where he was active in helping to initiate low-income housing projects. In 1972, as both his father and grandfather before him, he became pastor of Bright Hope Baptist Church in Philadelphia where he developed a politically active ministry and continued his interest in housing and mortgage issues.

Gray was first elected to Congress from Pennsylvania's Second District as a Democrat in 1978. During his time in Congress, he served on the House Appropriations, Foreign Affairs, and District of Columbia committees. His most important post was chair of the House Budget Committee in 1985, from which he steered the passage of the country's first trillion-dollar budget through controversies and differences between Congress and President Ronald Reagan.

A centrist within the Democratic party, Gray's primary focus in domestic policy was federal support of black private-sector development. On foreign issues he served as a leading spokesman on U.S. policy toward Africa and was a congressional sponsor of the antiapartheid movement. Gray sponsored an emergency aid bill for Ethiopia in 1984 and helped secure passage of the Anti-Apartheid Acts of 1985 and 1986, overriding presidential vetoes.

Gray's mainstream domestic politics and energetic party politicking helped pave the way for his ascendance to the Democratic leadership. In 1985 he was elected chairman of the Democratic caucus in the House, and in 1989 he became majority whip, the number three leadership position in the House and the highest rank held by an African-American congressman.

In 1991 Gray resigned from Congress to become president of United Negro College Fund (UNCF) in New York City. That year he oversaw the inauguration of the UNCF's Campaign 2000, a drive to raise $250 million by the year 2000. With the support of President George Bush and a $50 million gift from media magnate Walter Annenberg, the campaign raised $86 million in its first year.

In May 1994 Gray was named temporary envoy to Haiti by President Bill Clinton but retained his position at the UNCF.

—RICHARD NEWMAN

GREAVES, WILLIAM

William Greaves (October 8, 1926–), actor, film director, writer, and TV producer. Born and raised in New York City, William Greaves attended Stuyvesant High School and later enrolled for a year as an engineering student at the City College of New York. Throughout the 1940s and early '50s, he worked in radio, television, and film and acted with the American Negro Theatre.

In 1950 Greaves was asked to play a stereotyped role in a Broadway revival and walked off the set, which led to an interest in studying film direction. He enrolled in film classes at the City College. Upon completion, he found most white studios unwilling to hire black apprentices, and in 1952 he left for work in Canada's more open film industry.

During his six years in Canada Greaves worked at the National Film Board (NFB), first in Ottawa and later in Montreal. He gained experience in both directing and editing. Yet, while the NFB afforded Greaves an opportunity to gain technical experience, it offered little chance for iconoclasm. After leaving the NFB Greaves founded and for two years directed a Canadian acting troupe. In 1960 he joined an agency of the United Nations, the International Civil Aviation Organization, as a public information officer. In 1963 Greaves moved back to New York.

The following year he took a position with the United States Information Agency (USIA). While there, he documented the historic summit of Pan-African artists and intellectuals in Dakar, Senegal, *The First World Festival of Negro Arts* (1966). In 1967 Greaves made a documentary entitled *Still a Brother: Inside the Negro Middle Class* for National Educational Television (NET). Around the same time, NET was developing *Black Journal*, a show with a magazine-type for-

Race movies of the 1940s soon imitated Hollywood genres such as the gangster film and the Western.

PAGE 253

See also
Film
Philadelphia, Pennsylvania

Its striking emotional power has enabled gospel music to remain a vital part of African-American culture.

PAGE 308

mat focusing on national black issues; Greaves became a cohost. After a power struggle between the program's white executive producer and its predominantly black staff, Greaves became the show's executive producer. In 1969 *Black Journal* received an Emmy Award.

While working on *Black Journal*, Greaves continued to operate William Greaves Productions, which he had established in 1964. Greaves's first independent feature-length film was the experimental *Symbipsycotaxiplasm: Take One* (1967), a movie within a movie depicting the creative and conflicting dynamics involved in acting and filmmaking. Though not commercially released at the time, the film enjoyed a critically praised release in the early 1990s. In 1970 Greaves left *Black Journal* to pursue his filmmaking interests. In 1971 he made the commercially successful "docutainment" *Ali the Fighter,* which was followed in 1972 by the lesser-known *Nationtime Gary* (about the National Black Political Convention in Gary, Ind.).

Greaves made several films for the Equal Employment Opportunity Commission, as well as *From These Roots* (1974), a documentary about the Harlem Renaissance that won twenty-two film festival awards. In 1981 he was executive producer for the Richard Pryor comedy *Bustin' Loose.* Throughout the 1980s he directed, wrote, and/or coproduced documentaries on black historical figures and black issues, including *Black Power in America: Myth or Reality* (1986) and the multi-award-winning *Ida B. Wells: A Passion for Justice* (1989), narrated by Toni Morrison, as well as works about Booker T. Washington (1982) and Frederick Douglass (1984). In all, Greaves has been involved in the production of more than three hundred documentary films.

—PETRA E. LEWIS AND SHIPHERD REED

GREEN, AL

Al Green (April 13, 1946–), singer and songwriter. Al Green was born in Forrest City, Ark., where at age nine he began singing in a family gospel quartet called the Green Brothers. For six years the group toured gospel circuits, first in the South and then in the Midwest when the family relocated to Grand Rapids, Mich., first recording in 1960. Green formed his own pop group, Al Green and the Creations, in 1964 after his father expelled him from the gospel quartet for listening to what he called the "profane music" of singer Jackie Wilson. The group toured for three years before changing their name in 1967 to Al Greene and the Soulmates (the "e" was briefly added to Green's name for commercial reasons). That year Green made his record debut with the single "Back Up Train," which went to number five on the national soul charts in 1968. However, there were no follow-up successes, and Green was plunged back into obscurity, playing small clubs again.

While touring in Midland, Tex., in 1969, Green met Willie Mitchell, vice president of Hi Records in Memphis, Tenn. Mitchell produced Green's version of "I Can't Get Next to You," which went to number one on the national soul charts in 1971. Continuing to collaborate with Mitchell and drummer Al Jackson, Jr. (of Booker T. and the MGs), Green went on to record a string of million-selling singles and LPs throughout the early 1970s. Combining sensuous, emotive vocals with strings, horns, and hard-driving backbeats, Green helped define the sound of soul music in the 1970s. His hits included "Let's Stay Together" (1971), "Look What You've Done for Me" (1972), "I'm Still in Love with You" (1972), and "You Ought to Be with Me" (1972).

At the height of his career, Green began to reconsider his pop music orientation and shifted back toward gospel music. A turning point was an incident in 1974 in which his girlfriend scalded him with a pot of boiling grits before killing herself with his gun. When Green recovered from his burns, he became a minister, and in 1976 he purchased a church in Memphis and was ordained pastor of the Full Gospel Tabernacle, where he would perform services nearly every Sunday. He did not immediately give up pop music, but his attempts to mix gospel themes with secular soul music fared poorly.

In 1979, Green decided to sing only gospel music, and the next year he released his first gospel album, *The Lord Will Make a Way*. In 1982 he costarred in a successful Broadway musical with Patti LaBelle, *Your Arms Too Short to Box with God.* The lines between gospel music and love songs remained somewhat blurred for Green, who in his shows would lose himself in religious ecstasy one moment and toss roses into the audience the next.

Throughout the 1980s and early '90s, Green continued to record gospel records and pastor the Full Gospel Tabernacle. In 1994 he rerecorded a duet, "(Ain't It Funny) How Time Slips Away," on the compilation disc *Rhythm, Country, and Blues* with country-pop singer Lyle Lovett.

—JOSEPH W. LOWNDES

See also

Literature

GRIGGS, SUTTON ELBERT

Sutton Elbert Griggs (1872–1933), novelist and preacher. Born in Chatfield, Tex., Sutton E. Griggs was raised in Dallas, and attended Bishop College in Marshall, Tex. Following the path of his father, the Rev. Allen R. Griggs, he studied for the Baptist ministry at the Richmond Theological Seminary (later part of Virginia Union University) and was ordained in 1893. Griggs's first pastorate was in Berkley, Va., and he went on to serve more than thirty years as a Baptist minister in Nashville and Memphis, Tenn. In addition to his career as a pastor, he soon established himself as an author of novels, political tracts, and religious pamphlets. In the period following Reconstruction, marked by a fierce resurgence of segregation, disfranchisement, and antiblack violence in the South, Griggs—along with such African-American writers as Charles W. Chesnutt, Paul Laurence Dunbar, W. E. B. Du Bois, and Frances Ellen Watkins Harper—responded with positive portrayals of black Americans and demands for civil rights.

Griggs wrote more than thirty books, most of which he published himself and vigorously promoted during preaching tours of the South, as he describes in *The Story of My Struggles* (1914). His

---

STALWART ABOLITIONIST
Charlotte Grimké Publishes Poetry in Antislavery Journals

Charlotte L. Forten Grimké (August 17, 1837–July 22, 1914), abolitionist, teacher, and writer. Charlotte Forten was born into one of Philadelphia's leading African-American families. Her grandfather, James Forten, was a well-to-do sail-maker and abolitionist. Her father, Robert Bridges Forten, maintained both the business and the abolitionism.

Charlotte Forten continued her family's traditions. As a teenager, having been sent to Salem, Mass., for her education, she actively joined that community of radical abolitionists identified with William Lloyd Garrison. She also entered enthusiastically into the literary and intellectual life of nearby Boston, and even embarked on a literary career of her own. Some of her earliest poetry was published in antislavery journals during her student years. And she began to keep a diary, published almost a century later, which remains one of the most valuable accounts of that era.

Completing her education, Forten became a teacher, initially in Salem, and later in Philadelphia. Unfortunately, she soon began to suffer from ill health, which would plague her for the rest of her life. Nevertheless, while unable to sustain her efforts in the classroom for any length of time, she did continue to write and to engage in antislavery activity. With the outbreak of the Civil War, she put both her convictions and her training to use, joining other abolitionists on the liberated islands off the South Carolina coast to teach and work with the newly emancipated slaves.

On the Sea Islands, she also kept a diary, later published. This second diary, and two essays she wrote at the time for the *Atlantic Monthly,* are among the most vivid accounts of the abolitionist experiment. Like many teachers, Forten felt a cultural distance from the freedpeople but worked with dedication to teach and to prove the value of emancipation. After the war, she continued her work for the freedpeople, accepting a position in Massachusetts with the Freedmen's Union Commission.

She also continued her literary efforts, which included a translation of the French novel *Madame Thérèse,* published by Scribner in 1869. In 1872, after a year spent teaching in South Carolina, Forten moved to Washington, D.C., where she worked first as a teacher and then in the Treasury Department. There she met the Rev. Francis Grimké, thirteen years her junior, and pastor of the elite Fifteenth Street Presbyterian Church. At the end of 1878, they married.

The marriage was long and happy, despite the death in infancy of their only child. Apart from a brief residence in Jacksonville, Fla., from 1885 to 1889, the Grimkés lived in Washington, D.C. and made their Washington home a center for the capital's social and intellectual life. Although Charlotte Grimké continued to suffer from poor health, she maintained something of her former activism, serving briefly as a member of the Washington school board and participating in such organizations as the National Association of Colored Women. She did a small amount of writing, although little published. Finally, after about 1909, her failing health led to her virtual retirement from active life.

—DICKSON D. BRUCE, JR.

See also
Charles W. Chesnutt
Paul Laurence Dunbar
W.E.B. Du Bois

five novels are technically unimpressive, weakened by stilted dialogue, flat characterizations, and sentimental and melodramatic plot lines. Even as flawed polemics, however, they are distinguished by their unprecedented investigation of politically charged themes of African-American life in the South, such as black nationalism, miscegenation, racial violence, and suffrage. Above all else a religious moralist, Griggs was critical of assimilationist projects, calling instead for social equality and black self-sufficiency, but he was equally impatient with radical militancy in the quest for civil rights.

His fiction often centers on such ethical concerns. In *Imperium in Imperio* (1899), Griggs's best-known work and one of the first African-American political novels, the integrationist Belton Piedmont chooses to die rather than support a militaristic plot to seize Texas and Louisiana from the United States as a haven for African-Americans. In *Overshadowed* (1901), Astral Herndon, discouraged by the "shadow" of racial prejudice both in the United States and in Africa, chooses exile as a "citizen of the ocean." Dorlan Worthell in *Unfettered* (1902) wins the hand of the beautiful Morlene only by offering a plan for African-American political organization. *The Hindered Hand* (1905) is pessimistic about the possibilities of reforming southern race relations: The Seabright family encounters violent tragedy in striving to "pass" in white society in order to transform white racist opinions, and their one dark-skinned daughter, Tiara, flees to Liberia with her husband, Ensal, who has refused to participate in a "Slavic" conspiracy to destroy the Anglo-Saxons of the United States through germ warfare. While Baug Peppers attempts inconclusively to fight for voting rights for southern blacks before the Supreme Court in *Pointing the Way* (1908), Letitia Gilbreth, who believes that "whitening" the race through assimilation is the only way to effect racial equality, is driven mad when her niece refuses the mulatto Peppers and marries a dark-skinned man.

Similar themes also appear in Griggs's political treatises, most notably *Wisdom's Call* (1909), an eloquent argument for civil rights in the South that comments on lynching, suffrage, and the rights of black women, and *Guide to Racial Greatness; or, The Science of Collective Efficiency* (1923), with a companion volume of biblical verses entitled *Kingdom Builders' Manual* (1924); these together offer a project for the political organization of the African-American southern population, stressing education, religious discipline, employ-

ment, and land ownership. At the end of his life, Griggs returned to Texas to assume the position his father had held, the pastorate of the Hopewell Baptist Church in Denison. He soon departed for Houston and, at the time of his death, was attempting to found a national religious and civic institute there.

—BRENT EDWARDS

GULLAH

The Gullah are a community of African Americans who have lived along the Atlantic coastal plain and on the Sea Islands off the coast of South Carolina and Georgia since the late seventeenth century. Comprised of the descendants of slaves who lived and worked on the Sea Islands, Gullah communities continue to exist in the late twentieth century, occupying small farming and fishing communities in South Carolina and Georgia. The Gullah are noted for their preservation of African cultural traditions, made possible by the community's geographic isolation and its inhabitants' strong community life. They speak an English-based Creole language also referred to as Gullah, or among Georgia Sea Islanders as Geechee.

The etymology of the term *Gullah* is uncertain. Among the most widely accepted theories is that it is a shortened form of Angola, a region of coastal central Africa (with different boundaries from the contemporary nation-state and former Portuguese colony of the same name). Many of South Carolina's slaves were imported from the older Angola. Equally plausible is the suggestion that the term is a derivation of the West African name *Golas* or *Goulah*, who were a large group of Africans occupying the hinterland of what is present-day Liberia. Large numbers of slaves were brought to South Carolina from both western and central Africa, lending both explanations credibility. The word *Geechee* is believed to have originated from *Gidzi*, the name of the language spoken in the Kissy country of present-day Liberia. Whatever the origins of these terms, it is clear that the Gullah community that developed in the Sea Islands embodied a mixture of influences from the coastal regions of West Africa.

The slave communities of the Sea Islands developed under unique geographic and demographic conditions that permitted them to maintain a degree of cohesion and autonomy denied slave communities in other regions of the South. A geographical shift in the production of rice within the South Carolina low country during the mid-1700s brought a major shift in population. South Carolina's slave population had been concentrated in the parishes surrounding Charleston, but in the 1750s, South Carolina rice planters abandoned the inland swamps for the tidal and river swamps of the coastal mainland. At the same time, new methods in the production of indigo stimulated settlement of the Sea Islands, where long-staple cotton also began to be produced in the late eighteenth century.

As a result, the coastal regions of South Carolina and the adjacent Sea Islands became the center of the plantation economy, and the demand for slave labor soared. Concurrent with this shift in agricultural production was a change in the African origins of the slaves imported into South Carolina. During the last half of the eighteenth century, imports from the Kongo-Angola region declined, and the majority of slaves introduced into the Sea Islands came from the Windward Coast (present-day Sierra Leone, and Senegal, and Gambia) and the Rice Coast (part of present-day Liberia). South Carolina planters apparently preferred slaves from these regions because of the Africans' familiarity with rice and indigo production. These African bondsmen and women brought with them the labor patterns and technical skills they had used in Africa. Their knowledge of rice planting had a major impact in transforming South Carolina's methods of rice production.

The geographic isolation of the Sea Islands and the frequency of disease in the swampy, semitropical climate of the region kept white settlement in the area to a minimum. Meanwhile, a constant, growing demand for slaves and their concentration on tremendous plantations created a black majority in the South Carolina coastal region. In 1770 the population in the South Carolina low country was 78 percent black, and the proportion of blacks along the coast and the Sea Islands probably was even higher.

The relative isolation and numerical strength of the slaves and their freedom from contact with white settlers permitted them to preserve many native African linguistic patterns and cultural traditions. The constant influx of African slaves into the region throughout the remainder of the eighteenth century, likewise permitted the Gullah to maintain a vital link to the customs and traditions of West Africa.

The end of slavery brought significant changes to the Gullahs' traditional way of life, but the unique geographic and demographic conditions on the Sea Islands ensured that the Gullah community would retain its distinctiveness well beyond the Civil War. Blacks remained a majority in the South Carolina low country. In 1870, the population was 67 percent black; by 1900 it had decreased only marginally.

The Gullahs' experiences during and after the Civil War differed from those of blacks across the South. While the Port Royal Experiment, established on the Sea Islands during the Union's wartime occupation to provide the Gullah with experience in independent farming, was ultimately a failure, many Gullah in the decades following the Civil War nevertheless were able to become independent farmers.

Due to the declining market for the Sea Islands' long-staple cotton, many white landowners began to desert the area shortly after the war's end. Agricultural production in the low country first suffered from war-related devastation of the land; then, in the early 1900s, competition from rice plantations in the western United States further crippled South Carolina's market position. As whites abandoned their former plantations and blacks took over the land, some cotton production for the market continued, but subsistence farming and fishing dominated the Sea Island economy.

Whites' abandonment of the coastal region and the Sea Islands left the Gullah even more isolated than before. While black residents of the Sea Islands during the first half of the twentieth century, like other African Americans across the South, were denied basic civil rights, they benefitted from their geographic isolation and numerical dominance. Unlike blacks in most other regions of the South, the Gullah were able to maintain cohesive, largely independent communities well into the twentieth century.

Most of what we know of the Gullah comes from studies conducted by anthropologists and linguists in the 1930s and '40s. The Gullah culture described by these observers reflects a blending of various African and American traditions. Gullah handicrafts such as basket weaving and wood carving demonstrate African roots, both in their design and their functionality. Wooden mortars and pestles, rice "fanners," and palm-leaf brooms were introduced into the Sea Islands by the Gullah and were used in ways that reflected African customs. The Gullah, for example, used their palm-leaf brooms to maintain grass-free dirt yards—a tradition they still maintain in the late twentieth century. The Gullah diet similarly reflects the African origins of the original Gullah slave community. Based heavily on rice, the Gul-

The heavy black presence that resulted from its rice plantation culture fundamentally altered Carolina slavery.

PAGE 631

See also
Civil War
Slavery

313

G

GULLAH

Slave narratives dominated the literary landscape of antebellum black America, far outnumbering the autobiographies of free people of color.

PAGE 625

See also

Slave Trade

lah make gumbos and stews similar to West African dishes such as *jollof* and *plasas*.

The distinctiveness of the Gullah community is perhaps best reflected in its language. Gullah, or Geechee, a predominantly oral language, is the offspring of the West African Pidgin English that developed along the African Coast during the peak of the slave trade. Pidgin languages developed in Africa as a merger of the English language and the native languages spoken on the African coast and served as a means of communication among Africans and British slave traders. Many of the slaves from the coastal regions of West Africa that were brought to South Carolina in the eighteenth century were familiar with pidgin language and used it to communicate with one another in the New World. Over time, the pidgin mixed with the language spoken by the South Carolina planter class and took on new form. Gullah, the creole language that developed, became the dominant and native language of the slave community of the Sea Islands. Like most unwritten creole languages, Gullah rapidly evolved, and by the time it was first seriously studied in the 1930s, it undoubtedly had more in common with standard English than antebellum or eighteenth-century Gullah.

The Gullah language derives most of its vocabulary from the English language, but it also incorporates a substantial number of African words, especially from the Krio language of present-day Sierra Leone. The Gullah used names, for example, that reflected personal and historical experiences and that carried specific African meanings. Naming practices of the Gullah served, as they do for West Africans, as symbols of power and control over the outside world. The pronunciation of Gullah and its sentence and grammatical structures, moreover, deviate from the rules of standard English, reflecting instead West African patterns. Gullah is spoken with a Caribbean cadence, reflecting the common African background of the Gullah and West Indian slaves.

Gullah, though less widely spoken in the late twentieth century, remains prevalent throughout the Sea Islands. Lorenzo Dow Turner, the first linguist to study Gullah speech in the 1940s, found a number of African words and phrases being used among the inhabitants of the Sea Islands in the 1940s. In 1993, William A. Stewart, a linguist at the City University of New York, estimated that 250,000 Sea Islanders still spoke Gullah and at least a tenth of this number spoke no other language. Gullah also has had a significant impact upon the language spoken among inhabi-

tants across the southeastern region of the United States. Such Gullah words as *buckra* (a white person), *goober* (peanut), and *juke* (disorderly) can be found in the vocabulary of black and white southerners.

Other aspects of Gullah language observed by Turner and such scholars as Ambrose E. Gonzales and Guy B. Johnson also exhibit African roots. Gullah proverbs demonstrate an adaptation of the African tradition of speaking in parables, and the oral tradition of storytelling among the Gullah also has been identified with African patterns. Trickster tales such as those about Brer Rabbit, which were popularized in the late nineteenth and early twentieth centuries by the white folklorist Joel Chandler Harris, are still part of Gullah and Geechee folklore. These tales, often moral in tone and content, are an important form of entertainment.

Religion played a dominant role within the Gullah slave community and continued to regulate community life into the twentieth century. Church membership predicated membership in the community at large, and one was not considered a member of the plantation community until one had joined the "Praise House." Praise Houses, originally erected by planters in the 1840s as meetinghouses and places of worship for slaves, functioned as town halls among the Gullah well into the late twentieth century, possibly as late as the 1970s. The Praise House essentially took the place of the white-controlled Baptist churches as the slave community's cultural center. Even after blacks assumed control of their churches during and after the war, the Praise House remained the locus of community power.

Everyone in the community was expected to abide by the Praise House customs and regulations, enforced by a Praise House Committee, which held them to certain standards of behavior and trust. This method of defining the borders of the community reinforced the Gullahs' close-knit community structure; some argue that it mirrored West African traditions of establishing secret societies.

This utilization of the Praise House to fit the needs of the Gullah community illustrates the adaptive nature of the Gullah's religious practices. Gullah slaves applied a mixture of African customs and beliefs to Christian principles introduced by their masters to create a religion that served a vital function within their community. The Gullah incorporated certain African religious traditions into their Christian beliefs. While accepting Christianity, for example, they maintained their belief in witchcraft, called *wudu, wanga, joso,* or *juju,* and continued to consult "root doctors" for protection and for their healing powers.

The Gullahs' physical forms of worship also continued to follow West African patterns. Gullah spirituals, both religious and secular in nature, for example, incorporated a West African pattern of call-and-response. In addition to being sung in church and at work, these highly emotional spirituals often were used as accompaniments to the Gullah "ring shout," a syncretic religious custom that combined Africanisms with Christian principles. During the ring shout, onlookers sung, clapped, and gesticulated, while others shuffled their heels in a circle. The performance started slowly but gained speed and intensity as it progressed. The ring shout, which has largely disappeared in the late twentieth century, served as a religious expression linked to natural and supernatural forces. While the trance-like atmosphere of the ring shout is believed to be of West African origin, the practice itself and the way it functioned within the community are Gullah creations.

The strength and endurance of the Gullah community and culture are evident in the cultural traditions of the Seminole Blacks, a group strongly tied to the original Sea Island Gullah community. From the late 1700s to the early nineteenth century, Gullah slaves escaped from the rice plantations and built settlements along the remote, wooded Florida frontier. Over time, these maroon communities joined with other escaped slaves and surrounding Native Americans to form a loosely organized tribe with shared customs, food, and clothing. Along with the Native Americans, the escaped slaves were removed from Florida in the nineteenth century and were resettled on reservations in the West. During the late twentieth century, groups of these Seminole Blacks were found throughout the West, especially in Oklahoma, Texas, and Mexico. Some of these groups, who have retained numerous African customs, continue to speak Afro-Seminole, a creole language descended from Gullah.

While Gullah communities still exist in the Sea Islands of Georgia and South Carolina, they have begun to disintegrate in recent decades. The social cohesion of the community was first threatened in the 1920s when bridges were built between the mainland and the islands. Outmigration from the Sea Islands accelerated during World War II as defense spending created new economic opportunities. During the 1950s and '60s, outside influence increased as wealthy developers began buying up land at cheap rates and building resorts on Hilton Head and other islands. While this development opened some job opportunities for black Sea Islanders, the openings tended to be in low-paying, service jobs with little opportunity for advancement.

One benefit of this development has been to break down the Gullah's isolation and to increase their awareness of trends within the larger African-American community. In the 1940s, Esau Jenkins, a native of Johns Island, led a movement to register voters, set up community centers, and provide legal aid to members of the island's African-American community. In an effort to register black voters, Jenkins, with the help of Septima Clark of Charleston, established the South's first Citizenship School on Johns Island in 1957. Jenkins' efforts helped break down the isolation of black Sea Islanders and involved them more directly in the struggle for civil rights among African Americans across the country.

The modernization of the Sea Islands and the Gullahs' subsequent loss of isolation, however, has caused the community to lose some of its cultural distinctiveness and cohesion. From a predominantly black population on Hilton Head in 1950, whites outnumbered blacks five to one by 1980. Many Gullah traditions, such as the ring shout, have largely disappeared, and many community members criticize the now predominantly white public schools for deemphasizing the history and culture of the Gullah people. In response to the negative impact of these modernizing changes, there have been efforts in recent years to increase public awareness of Gullah traditions and to preserve them.

In 1948, the Penn Center on St. Helena Island, S.C., formerly a school for freed slaves, was converted into a community resource center. It offers programs in academic and cultural enrichment and teaches Gullah to schoolchildren. In 1979, the Summer Institute of Linguistics, a professional society of linguists, and the nondenominational Wycliffe Bible Translators undertook projects on St. Helena Island to translate the Bible into Gullah, to develop a written system for recording Gullah, and to produce teaching aids for use in schools. The project director, Ervin Greene, a Baptist minister on nearby Daufuskie Island, estimated in 1993 that 75 percent of the New Testament already had been translated and that the New Testament would be completed by 1996, the Old Testament within five years of that date. In 1985, Beaufort, S.C., began an annual Gullah Festival to celebrate and bring recognition to the rich Gullah culture.

G

GULLAH

Increasingly, national attention has been focused on the Sea Islands. In 1989, "In Living Color," a dance-theater piece about Gullah culture on Johns Island, S.C., premiered in New York City at the Triplex Theater. Set in a rural prayer meeting, the piece offers a memoir of life among the Gullah during the late 1980s. *Daughters of the Dust,* a 1992 film about a Gullah family at the turn of the century, perhaps provided greatest national recognition for the Gullah. Written and directed by Julie Dash, whose father was raised in the Sea Islands, the film's dialogue is primarily in Gullah, with occasional English subtitles.

Such projects have helped increase public awareness of the importance of understanding and preserving Gullah traditions, and in 1994 the children's network, Nickelodeon, began work on a new animated series called *Gullah Gullah Island,* which focuses on a black couple who explore the culture of the Sea Islands. Black Sea Islanders hope that these efforts will bring the necessary national recognition to help protect the Gullah community from further cultural erosion.

—LOUISE P. MAXWELL

H

HALE, CLARA MCBRIDE "MOTHER"

Clara McBride "Mother" Hale (April 1, 1905–December 18, 1992), social activist. Clara McBride was born in Philadelphia. Her father died when she was an infant, and she and her three siblings were raised by their mother. After finishing high school, she married Thomas Hale and they moved to New York City. Her husband's floor-waxing business was not profitable, so Clara Hale worked nights as a domestic, cleaning theaters to help support their three children, Lorraine, Nathan, and Kenneth. Widowed at age twenty-seven, she began cleaning homes during the day to supplement her income. She abandoned this arrangement, however, since it forced her to leave her children alone all day, and she began to care for other people's children in her home. She also took in foster children and over the next two decades eventually raised forty children.

In 1968, Hale retired as a foster parent, but the following year, when she found a young heroin-addicted mother and baby on her doorstep, her career resumed. The mother and child had been sent to her by her daughter, Lorraine, who had discovered them on a park bench. Clara Hale agreed to care for the baby while the mother sought help for her addiction. News of her generosity spread, and within two months she was caring for twenty-two children, with only the financial support of her own children.

In the early 1970s New York City agreed to fund her, and in 1975 a federal grant made it possible for her to renovate an entire building in Harlem, which became the Hale House Center for the Promotion of Human Potential. By 1992 Hale House had cared for 1,000 children born with chemical dependencies, most of whom were returned to their mothers once the children had gone through withdrawal and their mothers were able to care for them.

Mother Hale, as Clara Hale came to be known, became a symbol for people of all political persuasions. She addressed the enduring problems of poverty and drug addiction, brought attention to the lack of services available to the needy, and exemplified the virtue of individual responsibility. In February 1985, President Ronald Reagan honored Clara Hale as "a true American hero" in his State of the Union Address. She was also awarded two of the highest distinctions given by the Salvation Army, the Leonard H. Carter Humanitarian Award in 1987 and the Booth Community Service Award in 1990. After Clara Hale's death in 1992, Hale House continued operating under the direction of her daughter, Lorraine Hale.

—LYDIA MCNEILL
AND PAM NADASEN

HALEY, ALEXANDER PALMER "ALEX"

Alexander Palmer "Alex" Haley (August 11, 1921–February 10, 1992), journalist and novelist. Alex Haley was born in Ithaca, N.Y., and raised in Henning, Tenn. He attended Elizabeth City State Teachers College in North Carolina from 1937 to 1939. At age seventeen he left college and enlisted in the Coast Guard, where he eventually served as editor of the official Coast Guard publication *The Outpost*. In 1959 he retired as chief journalist, a position that had been expressly created for him.

After leaving the Coast Guard, Haley became a freelance writer, contributing to *Reader's Digest, The New York Times Magazine, Harper's, Atlantic,* and *Playboy* (for which he inaugurated the "Playboy Interview" series). He first received widespread attention for *The Autobiography of Malcolm X* (1965). His collaboration with the black nationalist Malcolm X consisted of a series of extended interviews transcribed by Haley; the result was an autobiography related to Haley that was generally praised for vibrancy and fidelity to its subject. The book quickly achieved international success and was translated into many different languages, selling millions of copies in the United States and abroad. As a result, Haley received honorary doctorates in the early 1970s from

There's nothing I treasure more as a writer than being a Southerner.

ALEX HALEY
IN THE *NEW YORK TIMES*,
JULY 31, 1994

H

Martin Luther
King, Jr., acquired
a reputation as a
powerful preacher,
drawing ideas from
African-American
traditions as well as
theological and
philosophical
writings.

PAGE 401

See also
Civil Rights Movement

Simpson College, Howard University, Williams College, and Capitol University.

Haley is best known, however, for his epic novel *Roots: The Saga of an American Family* (1976). Based on Haley's family history as told to him by his maternal grandmother, *Roots* traces Haley's lineage to Kunta Kinte, an African youth who was abducted from his homeland and forced into slavery. Combining factual events with fiction, *Roots* depicts the African-American saga from its beginnings in Africa, through slavery, emancipation, and the continuing struggle for equality. The novel was an immediate bestseller, and two years after its publication had won 271 awards, including a citation from the judges of the 1977 National Book Awards, the NAACP's Spingarn Medal, and a special Pulitzer Prize. Presented as a television miniseries in 1977, *Roots* brought the African-American story into the homes of millions. The book and the series generated an unprecedented level of awareness of African-American heritage and served as a spur to black pride.

The reception of Haley's book, however, was not devoid of controversy. Two separate suits were brought against Haley for copyright infringement: one was dismissed, but the other, brought by Harold Courlander, was settled after Haley admitted that several passages from Courlander's book *The African* (1968) appeared verbatim in *Roots*. In addition, some reviewers expressed doubts about the reliability of the research that had gone into the book and voiced frustration at the blend of fact and fiction. After Haley's death, more evidence came to light to suggest that he had inflated the factual claims and plagiarized material for *Roots*.

The unparalleled success of *Roots* gave rise to a widespread interest in genealogy as well as to a proliferation of works dealing specifically with the African-American heritage. *Roots: The Next Generation* was produced as a miniseries in 1979. Haley formed the Kinte Corporation in California and became involved in the production of films and records, the first of which was *Alex Haley Speaks,* which included advice on how to research family histories. In 1980 Haley helped produce *Palmerstown U.S.A.,* a television series loosely based on his childhood experiences in the rural South in the 1930s. In the 1980s Haley lectured widely, made numerous radio and television appearances, and wrote prolifically for popular magazines.

In his last years he concentrated on writing a narrative of his paternal ancestry, *Queen: The Story of an American Family.* The book, which Haley intended to be a companion volume to *Roots,* was published and adapted for television the year following his 1992 death in Seattle. Since his death, Haley's reputation, which had suffered in the late 1970s due to previously mentioned charges of plagiarism, was again attacked, as information came to light that he may have invented parts of his story as presented in *Roots* and presented them as fact.

—ALEXIS WALKER

HAMER, FANNIE LOU

Fannie Lou Hamer (Townsend, Fannie Lou) (October 6, 1917–March 14, 1977), civil rights activist. Fannie Lou Townsend was born to Ella Bramlett and James Lee Townsend in Montgomery County, Miss., in 1917. Her parents were sharecroppers, and the family moved to Sunflower County, Miss., when she was two. Forced to spend most of her childhood and teenage years toiling in cotton fields for white landowners, Townsend was able to complete only six years of schooling. Despite wrenching rural poverty and the harsh economic conditions of the Mississippi Delta, she maintained an enduring optimism. She learned the value of self-respect and outspokenness through her close relationship with her mother. In 1944, she married Perry Hamer, moved with him to Ruleville, and worked as a sharecropper on a plantation owned by W. D. Marlowe.

During her years on the Marlowe plantation, Hamer rose to the position of time- and record-keeper. In this position she acquired a reputation for a sense of fairness and a willingness to speak to the landowner on behalf of aggrieved sharecroppers. She began to take steps to directly challenge the racial and economic inequality that had so circumscribed her life after meeting civil rights workers from the Student Nonviolent Coordinating Committee (SNCC) in 1962. In Mississippi, SNCC was mounting a massive voter registration and desegregation campaign aimed at empowering African Americans to change their own lives.

Inspired by the organization's commitment to challenging the racial status quo, Hamer and seventeen other black volunteers attempted to register to vote in Indianola, Miss., on August 31, 1962, but were unable to pass the necessary literacy test, which was designed to prevent blacks from voting. As a result of this action, she and her family were dismissed from the plantation, she was threatened with physical harm by Ruleville whites, and she was constantly harassed by local police. Eventually, she was forced to flee Ruleville and spent three months in Tallahatchie County, Miss., before returning in December.

In January 1963 Hamer passed the literacy test and became a registered voter. Despite the persistent hostility of local whites, she continued her commitment to civil rights activities and became a SNCC field secretary. By 1964, Hamer had fully immersed herself in a wide range of local civil rights activities, including SNCC-sponsored voter registration campaigns, and clothing- and food-distribution drives. At that time she was a central organizer and vice-chairperson of the Mississippi Freedom Democratic Party (MFDP), a parallel political party formed under the auspices of SNCC in response to black exclusion from the state Democratic Party. Hamer was one of the sixty-eight MFDP delegates elected at a state convention of the party to attend the Democratic National Convention in Atlantic City in the summer of 1964. At the convention the MFDP delegates demanded to be seated and argued that they were the only legitimate political representatives of the Mississippi Democratic Party because unlike the regular party which formed and operated at the exclusion of blacks, their party was open to all Mississippians of voting age.

Hamer's televised testimony to the convention on behalf of the MFDP propelled her into the national spotlight. A national audience watched as she described the economic reprisals that faced African Americans who attempted to register to vote and recounted the beating that she and five other activists had received in June 1963 in a Winona County, Miss., jail. Hamer's proud and unwavering commitment to American democracy and equality inspired hundreds of Americans to send telegrams supporting the MFDP's challenge to the southern political status quo. Although the MFDP delegates were not seated by the convention, Hamer and the party succeeded in mobilizing a massive black voter turnout and publicizing the racist exclusionary tactics of the state Democratic party.

By the mid-sixties, SNCC had become ideologically divided and Hamer's ties to the organization became more tenuous. However, she continued to focus her political work on black political empowerment and community development. Under her leadership, the MFDP continued to challenge the all-white state Democratic party. In 1964 Hamer unsuccessfully ran for Con-

SHE CHALLENGED INEQUALITY
Fannie Lou Hamer singing at a gathering at Enid Dam Campsite, MI, on June 12, 1966, during the march to Jackson, Miss., in the wake of the attack on James Meredith (© CHARMIAN READING)

gress on the MFDP ticket, and one year later spearheaded an intense lobbying effort to challenge the seating of Mississippi's five congressmen in the House of Representatives. She played an integral role in bringing the Head Start Program for children to Ruleville, and organized the Freedom Farm Cooperative for displaced agricultural workers. In 1969 she founded the Freedom Farm Corporation in Sunflower, a cooperative farming and landowning venture to help poor blacks become more self-sufficient. It fed well over 5,000 families before collapsing in 1974. Three years later, after over a decade of activism, she died from breast cancer and heart disease.

Fannie Lou Hamer was a symbol of defiance and indomitable black womanhood that inspired many in the Civil Rights Movement. Morehouse College and Howard University, among others, have honored her devotion to African-American civil rights with honorary doctoral degrees. Her words "I'm sick and tired of being sick and tired" bear testament to her lifelong struggle to challenge racial injustice and economic exploitation.

—CHANA KAI LEE

HARLEM, NEW YORK

Roughly bounded by 110th Street and running north to 155th Street, bordered on the west by Morningside Drive and St. Nicholas Avenue and on the east by the East River, Harlem during the twentieth century became the most famous African-American community in the United States. Prior to 1900, Harlem had been primarily

H

*O sweep of stars
over Harlem streets*

LANGSTON HUGHES
STARS, IN *FROM MY PEOPLE*

See also
Maya Angelou

a white neighborhood. In the 1870s it evolved from an isolated, impoverished village in the northern reaches of Manhattan into a wealthy residential suburb with the growth of commuter rail service.

With the opening of the Lenox Avenue subway line in the early years of the twentieth century, a flurry of real estate speculation contributed to a substantial increase in building. At the time the population of Harlem was largely English and German, with increasing numbers of Jewish immigrants. By 1904, however, the economic prosperity and expansion ceased as a result of high rental costs and excessive construction. In that same year, Phillip A. Payton, Jr., a black realtor, founded the Afro-American Realty Company with the intention of leasing vacant white-owned buildings and then renting them to African Americans. Although the Realty Company survived for only four years, due to Payton's unwise financial investments, it played a pivotal role in opening up the Harlem community to African Americans.

Coupled with this development, black migration from the South during the early years of the new century dramatically altered Harlem's composition, until by 1930 it had become a largely all-black enclave. In 1890 there were approximately 25,000 African Americans in Manhattan. By 1910 that number had more than tripled to 90,000. In the following decade the black population increased to approximately 150,000 and more than doubled by 1930 to over 325,000. In Harlem itself the black population rose from approximately 50,000 in 1914 to about 80,000 in 1920 to about 200,000 by 1930.

From a social perspective, Harlem was labeled a "city within a city," because it contained the normal gamut of classes, businesses, and cultural and recreational institutions traditionally identified with urban living. By the 1920s, moreover, Harlem's place in American intellectual and political history had progressed significantly. This transition was fueled on the cultural scene by the literary and artistic activity which is collectively called the Harlem Renaissance. Emerging after the promise of racial equality and egalitarianism in return for black military service in World War I had been squelched by renewed racism and a series of race riots during the Red Summer of 1919, the Renaissance reflected the evolution of a "New Negro" spirit and determination. As one of its acknowledged leaders, Alain Locke, explained, self-respect and self-dependence became characteristics of the New Negro movement, which were

exemplified in every facet of cultural, intellectual, and political life.

Represented by poets such as Claude McKay, Langston Hughes, and Countee Cullen; novelists like Zora Neale Hurston, Jean Toomer, and Jessie Fauset; artists like Aaron Douglas; photographers like James VanDerZee; and social scientists and philosophers like E. Franklin Frazier, Alain Locke, and W. E. B. Du Bois, the Renaissance was national in scope, but it came to be identified with the emerging African-American cultural capital, Harlem. The outpouring of literary and artistic production that comprised the Renaissance led as well to a number of social gatherings at which the black intelligentsia mingled and exchanged ideas. Many of the most celebrated of these events were held at the home of A'Lelia Walker Robinson, daughter of Madame C. J. Walker, who had moved the base of her multimillion-dollar beauty care industry to Harlem in 1913.

Also fostering Harlem's growth in the 1920s were a series of political developments. Both the National Association for the Advancement of Colored People (NAACP) and the National Urban League established offices in the area. Moreover, by 1920 two major New York black newspapers, *The New York Age* and *The New York Amsterdam News,* moved their printing operations and editorial offices to Harlem. Socialists A. Philip Randolph and Chandler Owen established their offices in Harlem as well and from there they edited and published their newspaper, the *Messenger,* after 1917. Nothing, however, caught the attention of Harlemites as quickly as the arrival in 1916 of Marcus Garvey, who established the headquarters of the Universal Negro Improvement Association (UNIA) in the district. Garvey's emphasis on race pride, the creation of black businesses and factories, and his appeal to the masses awakened and galvanized the Harlem community.

By 1915, in fact, Harlem had become the entertainment capital of black America. Performers gravitated to Harlem and New York City's entertainment industry. Musicians such as Willie "The Lion" Smith, Fats Waller, and James P. Johnson created a version of early jazz piano known as the Harlem Stride around the time of World War I. After 1920, bandleaders such as Fletcher Henderson, Duke Ellington, and Chick Webb laid the foundation for big-band jazz. (Early in the 1940s, at clubs such as Minton's Playhouse and Monroe's, a revolution would occur in jazz. Individuals such as Thelonious Monk, Charlie Parker, and Dizzy Gillespie moved away from swing, using advanced harmonies and substitute chords, creating be-bop jazz.)

Harlem also became a major center of popular dance. On the stage, Florence Mills was perhaps Harlem's most popular theatrical dancer in the 1920s; 150,000 people turned out for her funeral in 1927. Tap dance flourished in Harlem as well. The roster of well-known performers included the Whitman Sisters, Buck and Bubbles, the Nicholas Brothers, Earl "Snake Hips" Tucker, and Bill "Bojangles" Robinson, who carried the honorary title of "The Mayor of Harlem."

Theatrical life was also vibrant in Harlem. From the early years of the century through the Great Depression, the center of popular entertainment in Harlem was the Lincoln Theatre on 135th Street off Lenox Avenue. After 1934, the Lincoln was superseded by the Apollo Theater. Harlem attracted vaudevillians such as Bert Williams, George W. Walker, Flournoy Miller, and Aubrey Lyles, and a later generation of comedians including Dewey "Pigmeat" Markham and Dusty Fletcher, who popularized the "Open the Door, Richard" routine.

After 1917, the Lafayette Theater grew in prominence as a home of serious drama, due to the success of such actors as Paul Robeson, Richard B. Harrison (famous for his role as "De

FATHER DIVINE

Blend of Theology and Folk Religion Draws Thousands

Father Divine (c. 1880–September 10, 1965), minister. Born George Baker to ex-slaves in Rockville, Md., he endured poverty and segregation as a child. At age twenty he moved to Baltimore, where he taught Sunday school and preached in storefront churches. In 1912, he began an itinerant ministry, focusing on the South. He attracted a small following and, pooling his disciples' earnings, moved north and purchased a home in 1919 in the exclusively white Long Island community of Sayville, N.Y. He opened his doors to the unemployed and homeless.

By 1931, thousands were flocking to worship services in his home, and his white neighbors grew hostile. In November they summoned police, who arrested him for disturbing the peace and maintaining a public nuisance. Found guilty, he received the maximum fine and a sentence of one year in jail. Four days later, the sentencing judge died.

The judge's sudden death catapulted Father Divine into the limelight. Some saw it as evidence of his great powers; others viewed it as sinister retribution. Although Father Divine denied responsibility for the death, the incident aroused curiosity, and throughout the 1930s the news media continued to report on his activities.

Father Divine's Peace Mission Movement grew, establishing extensions throughout the United States and in major cities abroad. He relocated his headquarters to Harlem, where he guided the movement, conducted worship services, and ran an employment agency. During the Great Depression, the movement opened businesses and sponsored a national network of relief shelters, furnishing thousands of poor people with food, clothes, and jobs.

Father Divine's appeal derived from his unique theology, a mixture of African-American folk religion, Methodism, Catholicism, Pentecostalism, and the ideology based on the power of positive thinking, New Thought. He encouraged followers to believe that he was God, to channel his spirit to generate health, prosperity, and salvation. He demanded they adhere to a strict moral code, abstaining from sexual intercourse and alcohol. Disciples cut family ties and assumed new names. His worship services included a banquet of endless courses, symbolizing his access to abundance. His mind-power theology attracted many, especially those suffering from racism and economic dislocation, giving disciples a sense of control over their destinies in a time filled with chaos and confusion.

His social programs also drew followers. Although rigid rules governed the movement's shelters, they were heavily patronized. An integrationist, Father Divine campaigned for civil rights, attracting both African-American and Euramerican disciples. Challenging American racism, he required followers to live and work in integrated pairs.

With economic recovery in the 1940s, Father Divine's message lost much of its appeal; membership in the movement declined and Peace Missions closed. In 1946 he made headlines with his marriage to a white disciple named Sweet Angel. He spent his declining years grooming her for leadership. Upon his death in 1965, she assumed control of the movement, contending that Father Divine had not died but had surrendered his body, preferring to exist as a spirit. The movement perseveres with a small number of followers and businesses in the Philadelphia area.

—JILL M. WATTS

*Melting pot
Harlem—Harlem of
honey and
chocolate and
caramel and rum
and vinegar and
lemon and lime and
gall. Dusky dream
Harlem rumbling
into a nightmare
tunnel where the
subway from the
Bronx keeps right
on downtown.*

LANGSTON HUGHES
IN LOVE WITH HARLEM, 1963

See also
Duke Ellington

Lawd" in *Green Pastures*), and Abbie Mitchell. Harlem was also a center of nightclubs. The best known included the black-owned Smalls Paradise, the Cotton Club, and the mobster-connected and racially exclusive Connie's Inn. The best-known dance hall was the Savoy Ballroom, the "Home of Happy Feet," which presented the best in big-band jazz after 1926. Harlem's cultural vitality was celebrated in plays including Wallace Thurman's *Harlem* (1929), Langston Hughes's *Mulatto* (1935), *Little Ham* (1935), and *Don't You Want to be Free?* (1936–1937), and Abram Hill's *On Strivers' Row* (1939). Musical performers celebrated Harlem's social scene through such compositions as "The Joint is Jumping," "Stompin' at the Savoy," "Harlem Airshaft," "Drop Me Off in Harlem," and "Take the A Train."

As Harlem became a political and cultural center of black America, the community's black churches became more influential as well. Most were Protestant, particularly Baptist and Methodist, and the Abyssinian Baptist Church became the most famous during the interwar period. The Rev. Adam Clayton Powell, Sr. moved the church from West 40th Street in midtown Manhattan to West 138th Street in Harlem in 1923. He combatted prostitution, organized classes in home economics, built a home for the elderly, and organized soup kitchens and employment networks during the Great Depression. He was succeeded as senior pastor in 1937 by his son, Adam Clayton Powell, Jr., who expanded the scope of the Abyssinian church's community activism. Harlem's scores of storefront churches, many of which proliferated during the interwar period, imitated Abyssinian's community aid efforts on a smaller scale. Harlem's most famous heterodox religious leader of the 1930s, Father Divine, established a series of soup kitchens and stores in the community through his Peace Mission and his Righteous Government political organization.

The 1930s were a period of stagnation and decline in Harlem, as they were throughout the nation. Civil rights protest increased during the decade, and much of it originated in Harlem. In response to white businessmen's unwillingness to hire black workers for white-collar jobs in their Harlem stores, a series of "Don't Buy Where You Can't Work" boycott campaigns commenced in 1933 and became an effective method of protesting against racial bigotry throughout the decade. Harlem community leaders such as Adam Clayton Powell, Jr. often joined with the NAACP, the National Urban League, the Communist Party of the U.S.A., and the Citizens' League for Fair Play

(CLFP) in leading these protests. Under the aegis of the Communist party, major demonstrations were also held on Harlem streets in the early 1930s in support of the Scottsboro Boys and Angelo Herndon.

Major party politics thrived in Harlem as much as radical politics did during the first half of the century. In the 1920s the Republican Party (led in black communities by Charles Anderson) and the Democratic Party (led by Ferdinand Q. Morton under Tammany Hall's United Colored Democracy), competed fiercely for black votes. Within the black community itself, African Americans and Caribbean Americans competed for dominance over the few available instruments of political control. Caribbeans were particularly prominent in the struggle to integrate Harlem blacks into the main organization of the Democratic party; J. Raymond Jones (an immigrant from the Virgin Islands who would ultimately become head of Tammany Hall) led an insurgent group called the New Democrats in this effort during the early 1930s.

Civil disturbances played an important role in Harlem's growing political consciousness. In 1935 a riot, fueled by animosity toward white businesses and the police, left three dead, and caused over 200 million dollars in damage. New York City Mayor Fiorello LaGuardia later assigned his Mayor's Commission on Conditions in Harlem (led by E. Franklin Frazier) to study this uprising; the commission revealed a great number of underlying socioeconomic problems that were giving rise to racial animosities in Harlem. In 1943 Harlem experienced another major race riot, which left five dead. This second riot was fueled by race discrimination in war-related industries and continuing animosities between white police officers and Harlem's black citizens.

These events helped shape the emerging political career of Adam Clayton Powell, Jr., who was elected to the New York City Council in 1941 and to the United States Congress in 1944, representing Harlem's newly created Eighteenth District. Powell's intolerance of race discrimination, and his vocal and flamboyant style brought national attention to the community, and he remained a symbol of Harlem's strength and reputation until his expulsion from Congress in 1967. He was re-elected by his loyal Harlem constituency in 1968.

By the end of World War II, Harlem experienced another transition. The migration of middle-class blacks to more affluent neighborhoods destabilized the class balance of earlier decades. Many of the remaining businesses were owned not by black residents but by whites who lived far removed from the ghetto. At the same time, most of the literati associated with the Renaissance had left the district. However, Harlem's literary life was preserved by a number of dedicated authors, such as Ralph Ellison (whose 1952 novel *Invisible Man* was centered in Harlem) and Harlem native James Baldwin. The Harlem Writers Guild was founded in 1950 by John Killens, Maya Angelou, John Henrik Clarke, and others, and has for over four decades offered writers in the community a forum for the reading and discussion of their works. Photographers such as Austin Hansen and Gordon Parks, Sr. continued to capture and celebrate Harlem's community on film.

For most of those who remained in Harlem after the war, however, a sense of powerlessness set in, exacerbated by poverty and a lack of control over their community. The quality of Harlem housing continued to be an acute problem. Paradoxically, as the quality of Harlem's inadequately heated, rat-infested buildings continued to deteriorate, and as housing health ordinances were increasingly ignored, the rents on those units continued to rise. People were evicted for being unable to keep up with the costs, but having no other place to go, many either entered community shelters or joined the swelling ranks of the homeless.

Heroin addiction and street crime were increasingly serious problems. The 1950s saw Harlem deteriorate, both spiritually and physically. Dependent on welfare and other social services, many Harlemites longed for a chance to reassert some degree of hegemony over their community.

The 1964 Harlem Youth Opportunities Unlimited Act (HARYOU) represented an attempt to provide solutions. After an intensive study of the community from political, economic, and social perspectives, HARYOU proposed a combination of social action for the reacquisition of political power and the influx of federal funds to redress the increasing economic privation of the area. From the beginning, however, the project suffered from personnel conflicts at the leadership level. Social psychologist Dr. Kenneth B. Clark, who originally conceived and directed the project, resigned after a struggle with Congressman Adam Clayton Powell, Jr. Following Clark's tenure, a Powell ally, Livingston Wingate, led the project through a period of intensifying government scrutiny regarding its financial administration.

As a political attempt to increase local control through community action while remaining dependent upon government largess for funding, HARYOU failed. It was also unable to ameliorate the alienation and decline into delinquency that plagued Harlem's youth. Illustrative of its failure was the 1964 riot, ignited like its predecessors by an incident of alleged police brutality; this latest riot underscored the troubles that continued to plague the community.

By the late 1960s, Harlem precisely fit the conclusion reached by the 1968 National Commission of Civil Disorders report. It was a ghetto, created, maintained, and condoned by white society. Literary works of the postwar era, from Ann L. Petry's *The Street* (1946) to Claude Brown's *Manchild in the Promised Land* (1965), reflected this progressively deteriorating state of affairs as well.

It was in this period of decay that another charismatic organization emerged in the community, the Nation of Islam (NOI). Malcolm X, the head of Harlem's mosque, blended the intellectual acumen of the literati of the 1920s with the political sophistication and charisma of Garvey. Malcolm X galvanized the masses and rekindled in them a sense of black pride and self-determination, appealing to their sense of disgruntlement with a message that was far more angry and less conciliatory than that offered by other major civil rights leaders. He was assassinated on February 21, 1965, in the Audubon Ballroom in Upper Manhattan.

Harlem since the 1960s has been severely affected by the same external forces that plagued many other American urban centers. As the mainstay of the United States economy underwent a critical transition from heavy manufacturing to service and information technologies, large-scale industry left urban areas. Large numbers of the Harlem population followed this exodus from the community, settling in suburban areas in Queens, the Bronx, and other boroughs. The resultant unemployment among those who remained further eviscerated Harlem. The community had long lost its position as the population center of black New York to the Bedford-Stuyvesant area of Brooklyn. Community vital statistics have been no more encouraging; it was estimated in 1992 that the average African-American male born in Harlem would have a life expectancy of sixty-four years, dying before becoming eligible for most Social Security or retirement benefits.

The Harlem Commonwealth Council (HCC), a nonprofit corporation begun in 1967 and founded through the Office of Economic Opportunity and the private sector, sought to develop Harlem economically and empower its community leaders politically. Yet, in its first twenty-five years, bad investments and an uncertain economy have reduced its real estate holdings, and virtually all its large-scale enterprises have gone bankrupt.

See also
Islam

H

HARLEM GLOBETROTTERS

This is Harlem, where anything can happen.

CHESTER HIMES
THE CRAZY KILL, 1959

In 1989 David N. Dinkins, a product of Harlem's Democratic clubs, became the first African-American mayor of New York City. One of his biggest supporters was Charles Rangel, who in 1970 had succeeded Adam Clayton Powell, Jr., as Harlem's congressman. In his four years as mayor, Dinkins sought to reestablish an atmosphere of racial harmony and cooperation, to realize his vision of New York City as a "gorgeous mosaic" of diverse ethnicities.

Residents continued to reassert control over their community in the 1990s, as the Harlem Chamber of Commerce led efforts to revitalize Harlem's businesses and reclaim the community's physical infrastructure (a process sometimes referred to as "ghettocentrism"). A plan to spend over 170 million dollars to build permanent housing for the poor and homeless began early in the decade, and such landmark structures as the Astor Row houses on West 130th Street were rehabilitated as well. The Schomburg Center for Research in Black Culture, established in 1926 on 135th Street as a branch of the New York Public Library, remained the nation's leading resource of African-American scholarship, as well as the location of academic conferences and meetings of the Harlem Writers Guild. The Studio Museum of Harlem on 125th Street was a focus for African-American and Caribbean-American folk art. The Apollo Theater on 125th Street was reopened in 1989, and it continued to showcase the current and future leaders of black entertainment. The nearby Hotel Theresa no longer served as a hotel but continued as the Theresa Towers, a modern office center and community landmark.

Throughout Harlem's history there has been a wide gap between the social, intellectual, and artistic accomplishments of the community's elite and the poverty and neglect of its masses. At the same time, however, there remains in Harlem, as there has been in every decade of its existence, an inner energy and spirit.

—MARSHALL HYATT

HARLEM GLOBETROTTERS

The Harlem Globetrotters were founded in 1926. At that time, Abe Saperstein (1902–1966), an English-born Jewish Chicagoan who had coached semipro basketball in the Chicago area, took over coaching duties of an African-American team, the Savoy Big Five (formerly Giles Post American Legion). Saperstein decided the team would be more popular with better marketing. To emphasize its racial composition and its barnstorming, he renamed the team the Harlem Globetrotters, though they had no connection to the New York City neighborhood. The newly-renamed team debuted on January 7, 1927, in Hinckley, Ill., wearing red, white, and blue uniforms that Saperstein had sewn in his father's tailor shop. The first starting team consisted of Walter "Toots" Wright, Byron "Fat" Long, Willis "Kid" Oliver, Andy Washington, and Al "Runt" Pullins.

The Globetrotters played the itinerant schedule of barnstorming basketball teams, taking on black and white squads of greatly varying levels of ability, with many memorable games against their archrivals, the New York Rens. Players boosted the team's popularity by clowning—drop-kicking balls, spinning them on fingertips, and bouncing them off teammates' heads. In 1939, the Globetrotters finished third in the *Chicago Herald American*'s World Professional Tournament; in 1940, they became World Champions. In 1943, the team traveled to Mexico City (the first indication that the team would soon justify their "Globetrotter" name) and won the International Cup Tournament. During the mid-1940s, a white player, Bob Karstens, joined the Globetrotters (the team has briefly had two other white players).

After World War II, as professional all-white basketball leagues began slowly integrating, the Globetrotters, led by Marques Haynes, were so popular that rumors spread that Saperstein opposed integration in order to keep control of the market for black players. Meanwhile, they continued to hold their own against white teams in exhibition games. In February 1948, the Globetrotters, following a 52-game winning streak, played George Mikan and the Minneapolis Lakers evenly in two exhibition games in Chicago. The team's skill and popularity belied black exclusion policies.

By 1950, NBA teams had three black players, including ex-Globetrotter Nat "Sweetwater" Clifton. After the integration of professional basketball, the Globetrotters' playing style changed dramatically. Clowning now became predominant. Players such as Reece "Goose" Tatum, Meadowlark Lemon, and Fred "Curly" Neal were hired not only for playing ability but for trick shooting, dribbling, and comedic talent. The Globetrotters, now billed as "The Clown Princes of Basketball," became best known for already familiar routines, such as the pregame "Magic Circle." In this act, players stand in a loose circle and

See also
Malcolm X

display their skill and deftness with the ball, accompanied by the team's theme song, "Sweet Georgia Brown."

In 1950, the Globetrotters began annual coast-to-coast trips with squads of college All-Americans, which lasted until 1962. The same year, the team began annual European summer tours, playing to enormous crowds. In 1951, they played before 75,000 spectators in Berlin's Olympic Stadium, still one of the largest crowds ever to see a basketball game. During this period, they appeared in two movies, *Go Man Go* (1948) and *The Harlem Globetrotters* (1951). In the early 1950s, after the Globetrotters lost consecutive games to Red Klotz's Philadelphia Spas, Abe Saperstein decided to dispense with playing local teams and to barnstorm with the Spas (later renamed the Washington Generals), who play some 250 games with the Globetrotters each year, and serve as straight men for their stunts. The Generals, following an agreement with the Globetrotters, allow several trick-shot baskets per game. The last time the Generals beat their rivals was in 1971. In the 1950s, the Globetrotters split into two squads, one of which played on the East coast, while the other focused on the West. In 1958–1959, the same year that Wilt Chamberlain, after the end of his college career, spent playing with the team (often as a 7'1" guard!), the Globetrotters toured the Soviet Union as goodwill ambassadors. Other famous athletes who played with the team included Bob Gibson and Connie Hawkins. The team has retained its interracial popularity, though during the 1960s some blacks criticized team members for their clownish image, which reinforced racial stereotypes, and the team's silence on civil rights issues.

After Abe Saperstein's death in 1966, the team was sold to three Chicago businessmen for $3.7 million. In 1975, Metromedia purchased the team for $11 million. The Globetrotters remained popular into the 1970s, when they starred in cartoon and live-action TV series, but their popularity declined some years later, especially after stars such as Meadowlark Lemon left the team after contract disputes. In 1985, the first female Globetrotter, Lynette Woodward, was hired. In December 1986, Metromedia sold the team (as part of a package that included the Ice Capades) to International Broadcasting Corp. (IBC) for $30 million. In 1993, IBC entered bankruptcy and Mannie Johnson, a former Globetrotter, bought the team. It was another Globetrotter, Curly Neal, who best captured the team's appeal: "How do I know when we played a good 'game'?" he said. "When I look up at the crowd and I see all those

people laughing their heads off. It's a hard world and if we can lighten it up a little, we've done our job."

—GREG ROBINSON

HARLEM RENAISSANCE

Precisely why and how the Harlem Renaissance materialized, who molded it and who found it most meaningful, as well as what it symbolized and what it achieved, raise perennial American questions about race relations, class hegemony, cultural assimilation, generational-gender-lifestyle conflicts, and art versus propaganda. Notwithstanding its synoptic significance, the Harlem Renaissance was not, as some students have maintained, all-inclusive of the early twentieth-century African-American urban experience. There were important movements, influences, and people who were marginal or irrelevant to it, as well as those alien or opposed. Not everything that happened in Harlem from 1917 to 1934 was a Renaissance happening. The potent mass movement founded and led by the charismatic Marcus Garvey was to the Renaissance what nineteenth-century populism was to progressive reform: a parallel but socially different force, related primarily through dialectical confrontation. Equally different from the institutional ethos and purpose of the Renaissance was the black church. An occasional minister (such as the father of poet Countee Cullen) or exceptional Garveyites (such as Yale-Harvard man William H. Ferris) might move in both worlds, but black evangelism and its cultist manifestations, such as Black Zionism, represented emotional and cultural retrogression in the eyes of the principal actors in the Renaissance. If the leading intellectual of the race, W. E. B. Du Bois, publicly denigrated the personnel and preachings of the black church, his animadversions were merely more forthright than those of other New Negro notables like James Weldon Johnson, Charles S. Johnson, Jessie Redmon Fauset, Alain Locke, and Walter Francis White.

The relationship of music to the Harlem Renaissance was problematic, for reasons exactly analogous to its elitist aversions to Garveyism and evangelism. When Du Bois wrote, a few years after the beginning of the New Negro movement in arts and letters, that "until the art of the black folk compels recognition they will not be rated as human," he, like most of his Renaissance peers, fully intended to exclude the blues of Bessie Smith and the jazz of "King" Oliver. Spirituals sung like lieder by the disciplined Hall Johnson Choir—and, better yet, lieder sung by conservatory-trained Roland Hayes, recipient of the NAACP's prestigious Spingarn Medal—were deemed appropriate musical forms to present to mainstream America. The deans of the Renaissance were entirely content to leave discovery and celebration of Bessie, Clara, Trixie, and various other blues-singing Smiths to white music critic Carl Van Vechten's effusions in *Vanity Fair*. When the visiting film director Sergei Eisenstein enthused about new black musicals, Charles S. Johnson and Alain Locke expressed mild consternation in the Urban League's *Opportunity* magazine. They would have been no less displeased by Maurice Ravel's fascination with musicians in Chicago dives. As board members of the Pace Phonograph Company, Du Bois, James Weldon Johnson, and others banned "funky" artists from the Black Swan list of recordings, thereby contributing to the demise of the African-American-owned firm. But the wild Broadway success of Miller and Lyles's musical *Shuffle Along* (it helped to popularize the Charleston) or Florence Mills's *Blackbirds* revue flaunted such artistic fastidiousness.

The very centrality of music in black life, as well as of black musical stereotypes in white minds, caused popular musical forms to impinge inescapably on Renaissance high culture. Eventually, the Renaissance deans made a virtue out of necessity; they applauded the concert-hall ragtime of "Big Jim" Europe and the "educated" jazz of Atlanta University graduate and big-band leader Fletcher Henderson, and they hired a Duke Ellington or a Cab Calloway as drawing cards for fund-raising socials. Still, their relationship to music remained beset by paradox. New York ragtime, with its "Jelly Roll" Morton strides and Joplinesque elegance, had as much in common with Chicago jazz as Mozart with "Fats" Waller. The source of musical authenticity and the reservoir of musical abundance lay in those recently urbanized and economically beleaguered men and women whose chosen recreational environments were raucous, boozy, and lubricious. Yet these were the men and women whose culture and condition made Renaissance drillmasters (themselves only a generation and a modest wage removed) uncomfortable and ashamed, men and women whose musical pedigrees went back from Louis Armstrong and Sidney Bechet through Chicago to New Orleans's Storyville and its colonial-era Place Congo.

See also
Sterling Brown
Charles Waddell Chesnutt

The Renaissance relished virtuoso performances by baritone Jules Bledsoe or contralto Marian Anderson, and pined to see the classical works of William Grant Still performed in Aeolian Hall. It took exceeding pride in the classical repertory of the renowned Clef Club Orchestra. On the other hand, even if and when it saw some value in the music nurtured in prohibition joints and bleary rent parties, the movement found itself pushed aside by white ethnic commercial cooptation and exploitation—by Al Capone and the mob. Thus, what was musically vital was shunned or deplored in the Harlem Renaissance from racial sensitivity; what succeeded with mainstream audiences derived from those same shunned and deplored sources and was invariably hijacked; and what was esteemed as emblematic of racial sophistication was (even when well done) of no interest to whites and of not much more to the majority of blacks. Last, with the notable exception of Paul Robeson, most of the impresarios as well as the featured personalities of the Renaissance were more expert in literary and visual-arts matters than musical.

The purpose of emphasizing such negatives—of stressing whom and what the Harlem Renaissance excluded or undervalued—serves the better to characterize the essence of a movement that was an elitist response to a rapidly evolving set of social and economic conditions demographically driven by the Great Black Migration, beginning in the second decade of the twentieth century. The Harlem Renaissance began "as a somewhat forced phenomenon, a cultural nationalism of the parlor, institutionally encouraged and constrained by the leaders of the civil rights establishment for the paramount purpose of improving 'race relations' in a time of extreme national reaction to an annulment of economic gains won by Afro-Americans during the Great War" (Lewis 1981). This mobilizing elite emerged from the increasing national cohesion of the African-American bourgeoisie at the turn of the century, and of the migration of many of its most educated and enterprising to the North about a decade in advance of the epic working-class migration out of the South. Du Bois indelibly labeled this racially advantaged minority the "Talented Tenth" in a seminal 1903 essay. He fleshed out the concept biographically that same year in "The Advance Guard of the Race," a piece in *Booklover's Magazine:* "Widely different are these men in origin and method. Paul Laurence Dunbar sprang from slave parents and poverty; Charles Waddell Chesnutt from free

parents and thrift; while Henry O. Tanner was a bishop's son."

Students of the African-American bourgeoisie—from Joseph Willson in the mid-nineteenth century through Du Bois, Caroline Bond Day, and E. Franklin Frazier during the first half of the twentieth to Constance Green, August Meier, Carl Degler, Stephen Birmingham, and, most recently, Adele Alexander, Lois Benjamin, and Willard Gatewood—have differed about its defining elements, especially that of pigment. The generalization seems to hold that color was a greater determinant of upper-class status in the post–Civil War South than in the North. The phenotype preferences exercised by slaveholders for house slaves, in combination with the relative advantages enjoyed by illegitimate offspring of slavemasters, gave a decided spin to mulatto professional careers during Reconstruction and well beyond. Success in the North followed more various criteria, of which color was sometimes a factor. By the time of Booker T. Washington's death in 1915, however, a considerable amount of ideological cohesion existed among the African-American leadership classes in such key cities as Atlanta, Washington, Baltimore, Philadelphia, Boston, Chicago, and New York. A commitment to college preparation in liberal arts and the classics, in contrast to Washington's emphasis on vocational training, prevailed. Demands for civil and social equality were espoused again after a quietus of some fifteen years.

The once considerable power of the so-called Tuskegee Machine now receded before the force of Du Bois's propaganda, a coordinated civil rights militancy, and rapidly altering industrial and demographic conditions in the nation. The vocational training in crafts such as brickmaking, blacksmithing, carpentry, and sewing prescribed by Tuskegee and Hampton institutes was irrelevant in those parts of the South undergoing industrialization, yet industry in the South was largely proscribed to African Americans who for several decades had been deserting the dead end of sharecropping for the South's towns and cities. The Bookerites' sacrifice of civil rights for economic gain, therefore, lost its appeal not only to educated and enterprising African Americans but to many of those white philanthropists and public figures who had once solemnly commended it. The Talented Tenth formulated and propagated the new ideology being rapidly embraced by the physicians, dentists, educators, preachers, businesspeople, lawyers, and morticians comprising the bulk of the African-American affluent and in-

Harlem is the precious fruit in the Garden of Eden, the big apple.

ALAIN LOCKE
C. 1919

See also
Countee Cullen
Paul Laurence Dunbar

Throughout the first half of the twentieth century Harlem was the cultural and ideological capital of black America.

PAGE 514

See also
Jessie Redmon Fauset

fluential—some 10,000 men and women, out of a total population in 1920 of more than 10 million. (In 1917, traditionally cited as the natal year of the Harlem Renaissance, there were 2,132 African Americans in colleges and universities, probably no more than 30 of them attending "white" institutions.)

It was, then, the minuscule vanguard of a minority—0.02 percent of the racial total—that constituted the Talented Tenth that jump-started the New Negro Arts Movement. But what was extraordinary about the Harlem Renaissance was that its promotion and orchestration by the Talented Tenth were the consequence of masterful improvisation rather than of deliberate plan, of artifice imitating likelihood, of aesthetic deadpan disguising a racial blind alley. Between the 1905 "Declaration of Principles" of the Niagara Movement and the appearance in 1919 of Claude McKay's electrifying poem "If We Must Die," the principal agenda of the Talented Tenth called for investigation of and protest against discrimination in virtually every aspect of national life. It lobbied for racially enlightened employment policies in business and industry; the abolition through the courts of peonage, residential segregation ordinances, Jim Crow public transportation, and franchise restrictions; and enactment of federal sanctions against lynching. The vehicles for this agenda, the NAACP and the NUL, exposed, cajoled, and propagandized through their excellent journals, the Crisis and *Opportunity*, respectively. The rhetoric of protest was addressed to ballots, courts, legislatures, and the workplace: "We urge upon Congress the enactment of appropriate legislation for securing the proper enforcement of . . . the thirteenth, fourteenth and fifteenth amendments," the Niagara Movement had demanded and the NAACP continued to reiterate. Talented Tenth rhetoric was also strongly social-scientific: "We shall try to set down interestingly but without sugar-coating or generalizations the findings of careful scientific surveys and facts gathered from research," the first *Opportunity* editorial would proclaim in January 1923, echoing the objectives of Du Bois's famous Atlanta University Studies.

It is hardly surprising that many African Americans, the great majority of whom lived under the deadening cultural and economic weight of southern apartheid, had modest interest in literature and the arts during the first two decades of the twentieth century. Even outside the underdeveloped South, and irrespective of race, demotic America had scant aptitude for and much suspi-

cion of arts and letters. Culture in early twentieth-century America was paid for by a white minority probably not a great deal larger, by percentage, than the Talented Tenth. For those privileged few African Americans whose education or leisure inspired such tastes, therefore, appealing fiction, poetry, drama, paintings, and sculpture by or about African Americans had become so exiguous as to be practically nonexistent. With the rising hostility and indifference of the mainstream market, African-American discretionary resources were wholly inadequate by themselves to sustain even a handful of novelists, poets, and painters. A tubercular death had silenced poet-novelist Dunbar in 1906, and poor royalties had done the same for novelist Chesnutt after publication the previous year of *The Colonel's Dream*. Between that point and 1922, no more than five African Americans published significant works of fiction and verse. There was *Pointing the Way* in 1908, a flawed, fascinating civil rights novel by the Baptist preacher Sutton Griggs. Three years later, Du Bois's *The Quest of the Silver Fleece*, a sweeping sociological allegory, appeared. The following year came James Weldon Johnson's well-crafted *The Autobiography of an Ex-Colored Man*, but the author felt compelled to disguise his racial identity. A ten-year silence fell afterward, finally to be broken in 1922 by McKay's *Harlem Shadows*, the first book of poetry since Dunbar. In "Art for Nothing," a short, trenchant think piece in the May 1922 *Crisis*, Du Bois lamented the fall into oblivion of sculptors Meta Warrick Fuller and May Howard Jackson, and that of painters William E. Scott and Richard Brown.

Although the emergence of the Harlem Renaissance seems much more sudden and dramatic in retrospect than the historic reality, its institutional elaboration was, in fact, relatively quick. Altogether, it evolved through three stages. The first phase, ending in 1923 with the publication of Jean Toomer's unique prose poem *Cane*, was dominated by white artists and writers—bohemians and revolutionaries—fascinated for a variety of reasons with the life of black people. The second phase, from early 1924 to mid-1926, was presided over by the civil rights establishment of the NUL and the NAACP, a period of interracial collaboration between "Negrotarian" whites and the African-American Talented Tenth. The last phase, from mid-1926 to 1934, was increasingly dominated by African American artists themselves—the "Niggerati."

When Charles S. Johnson, new editor of *Opportunity*, sent invitations to some dozen African-

American poets and writers to attend an event at Manhattan's Civic Club on March 21, 1924, the movement had already shifted into high gear. At Johnson's request, William H. Baldwin III, white Tuskegee trustee, NUL board member, and heir to a railroad fortune, had persuaded *Harper's* editor Frederick Lewis Allen to corral a "small but representative group from his field," most of them unknown, to attend the Civic Club affair in celebration of the sudden outpouring of "Negro" writing. "A group of the younger writers, which includes Eric Walrond, Jessie Fauset, Gwendolyn Bennett, Countee Cullen, Langston Hughes, Alain Locke, and some others," would be present, Johnson promised each invitee. All told, in addition to the "younger writers," some fifty persons were expected: "Eugene O'Neill, H. L. Mencken, Oswald Garrison Villard, Mary Johnston, Zona Gale, Robert Morss Lovett, Carl Van Doren, Ridgely Torrence, and about twenty more of this type. I think you might find this group interesting enough to draw you away for a few hours from your work on your next book," Johnson wrote the recently published Jean Toomer almost coyly.

Although both Toomer and Langston Hughes were absent in Europe, approximately 110 celebrants and honorees assembled that evening, included among them Du Bois, James Weldon Johnson, and the young NAACP officer Walter Francis White, whose energies as a literary entrepreneur would soon excel even Charles Johnson's. Locke, professor of philosophy at Howard University and the first African-American Rhodes scholar, served as master of ceremonies. Fauset, literary editor of the *Crisis* and Phi Beta Kappa graduate of Cornell University, enjoyed the distinction of having written the second fiction (and first novel) of the Renaissance, *There Is Confusion,* just released by Horace Liveright. Liveright, who was present, rose to praise Fauset as well as Toomer, whom he had also published. Speeches followed in rapid succession—Du Bois, James Weldon Johnson, Fauset. White called attention to the next Renaissance novel: his own, *The Fire in the Flint,* shortly forthcoming from Knopf. Albert Barnes, the crusty Philadelphia pharmaceutical millionaire and art collector, described the decisive impact of African art on modern art. Poets and poems were commended—Hughes, Cullen, Georgia Douglas Johnson of Washington, D.C., and, finally, Gwendolyn Bennett's stilted yet appropriate "To Usward," punctuating the evening: "We claim no part with racial dearth, / We want to sing the songs of birth!" Charles Johnson wrote the vastly competent Ethel Ray Nance, his future

secretary, of his enormous gratification that Paul Kellogg, editor of the influential *Survey Graphic,* had proposed that evening to place a special number of his magazine at the service of "representatives of the group."

Two compelling messages emerged from the Civic Club gathering. Du Bois asserted that the literature of apology and the denial to his generation of its authentic voice were now ending; Van Doren said that African-American artists were developing at a uniquely propitious moment. They were "in a remarkable strategic position with reference to the new literary age which seems to be impending," Van Doren predicted. "What American literature decidedly needs at this moment is color, music, gusto, the free expression of gay or desperate moods. If the Negroes are not in a position to contribute these items," Van Doren could not imagine who else could. It was precisely this "new literary age" that a few Talented Tenth leaders had kept under sharp surveillance and about which they had soon reached a conclusion affecting civil rights strategy. Despite the baleful influence of D. W. Griffith's *The Birth of a Nation* and the robust persistence of Uncle Tom, "coon," and Noble Savage stereotypes, literary and dramatic presentations of African Americans by whites had begun, arguably, to change somewhat for the better.

The African American had indisputably moved to the center of mainstream imagination with the end of the Great War, a development crucially assisted by chrysalis of the Lost Generation—Greenwich Village bohemia. The first issue of Randolph Bourne's *Seven Arts* (November 1916), featuring, among others of the Lyrical Left, Waldo Frank, James Oppenheim, Paul Rosenfeld, Van Wyck Brooks, and the French intellectual Romain Rolland, incarnated the spirit that informed a generation without ever quite cohering into a doctrine. The inorganic state, the husk of a decaying capitalist order, was breaking down, these young white intellectuals believed. They professed contempt for "the people who actually run things" in America. Waldo Frank, Toomer's bosom friend and literary mentor, foresaw not a bloody social revolution in America but that "out of our terrifying welter or steel and scarlet, a design must come." There was another Village group decidedly more oriented toward politics: the Marxist radicals (John Reed, Floyd Dell, Helen Keller, Max Eastman) associated with *Masses* and its successor magazine, *Liberator,* edited by Max and Crystal Eastman. The inaugural March 1918 issue of *Liberator* announced that it

See also
Langston Hughes

*Ethel Waters
significantly
influenced the
sound of American
popular music.*

PAGE 728

would "fight for the ownership and control of industry by the workers."

Among the Lyrical Left writers gathered around *Broom, S4N,* and *Seven Arts,* and the political radicals associated with *Liberator,* there was a shared reaction against the ruling Anglo-Saxon cultural paradigm. Bourne's concept of a "transnational" America, democratically respectful of its ethnic, racial, and religious constituents, complemented Du Bois's earlier concept of divided racial identity in *The Souls of Black Folk.* Ready conversance with the essentials of Freud and Marx became the measure of serious conversation in MacDougal Street coffeehouses, Albert Boni's Washington Square Book Shop, or the Hotel Brevoort's restaurant. There Floyd Dell, Robert Minor, Matthew Josephson, Max Eastman, and other *enragés* denounced the social system, the Great War to which it had ineluctably led, and the soul-dead world created in its aftermath, with McKay and Toomer, two of the Renaissance's first stars, participating.

From such conceptions, the Village's discovery of Harlem followed logically and, even more, psychologically. For if the factory, campus, office, and corporation were dehumanizing, stultifying, or predatory, the African American—largely excluded from all of the above—was a perfect symbol of cultural innocence and regeneration. He was perceived as an integral, indispensable part of the hoped-for design, somehow destined to aid in the reclamation of a diseased, desiccated civilization. The writer Malcolm Cowley would recall in *Exile's Return* that "one heard it said that the Negroes had retained a direct virility that the whites had lost through being overeducated." Public annunciation of the rediscovered Negro came in the fall of 1917, with Emily Hapgood's production at the old Garden Street Theatre of three one-act plays by her husband, Ridgely Torrence. *The Rider of Dreams, Simon the Cyrenian,* and *Granny Maumee* were considered daring because the casts were black and the parts were dignified. The drama critic from *Theatre Magazine* enthused of one lead player that "nobody who saw Opal Cooper—and heard him as the dreamer, Madison Sparrow—will ever forget the lift his performance gave." Du Bois commended the playwright by letter, and James Weldon Johnson excitedly wrote his friend, the African-American literary critic Benjamin Brawley, that *The Smart Set*'s George Jean Nathan "spoke most highly about the work of these colored performers."

From this watershed flowed a number of dramatic productions, musicals, and several successful novels by whites, and also, with great significance, *Shuffle Along,* a cathartic musical by the African Americans Aubrey Lyles and Flournoy Miller. Theodore Dreiser grappled with the explosive subject of lynching in his 1918 short story "Nigger Jeff." Two years later, the magnetic African-American actor Charles Gilpin energized O'Neill's *The Emperor Jones* in the 150-seat theater in a MacDougal Street brownstone taken over by the Provincetown Players. *The Emperor Jones* (revived four years later with Paul Robeson in the lead part) showed civilization's pretensions being moved by forces from the dark subconscious. In 1921, *Shuffle Along* opened at the 63rd Street Theatre, with music, lyrics, choreography, cast, and production uniquely in African-American hands, and composer Eubie Blake's "I'm Just Wild About Harry" and "Love Will Find a Way" entering the list of all-time favorites. Mary Hoyt Wiborg's *Taboo* was also produced in 1921, with Robeson in his theatrical debut. Clement Wood's 1922 sociological novel *Nigger* sympathetically tracked a beleaguered African-American family from slavery through the Great War into urban adversity. T. S. Stribling's *Birthright,* that same year, was remarkable for its effort to portray an African-American male protagonist of superior education (a Harvard-educated physician) martyred for his ideals after returning to the South. "Jean Le Negre," the black character in e. e. cummings' *The Enormous Room,* was another Noble Savage paradigm observed through a Freudian prism.

But Village artists and intellectuals were aware and unhappy that they were theorizing about Afro-America and spinning out African-American fictional characters in a vacuum—that they knew almost nothing firsthand about these subjects. Sherwood Anderson's June 1922 letter to H. L. Mencken spoke for much of the Lost Generation: "Damn it, man, if I could really get inside the niggers and write about them with some intelligence, I'd be willing to be hanged later and perhaps would be." At least the first of Anderson's prayers was answered almost immediately, when he chanced to read a Jean Toomer short story in *Double-Dealer* magazine. With the novelist's assistance, Toomer's stories began to appear in the magazines of the Lyrical Left and the Marxists, *Diak, S4N, Broom,* and *Liberator.* Anderson's 1925 novel *Dark Laughter* bore unmistakable signs of indebtedness to Toomer, whose work, Anderson

See also

James Weldon Johnson

CLAUDE MCKAY

Writer Pens Controversial Portrayals of Black Heroes

Claude McKay (September 15, 1889–May 22, 1948), poet and novelist. Claude McKay was the child of independent small farmers. In 1912 he published two volumes of Jamaican dialect poetry, *Songs of Jamaica* and *Constab Ballads*. They reflect the British imperial influences of his youth and reveal that the rebellion that characterized McKay's American poetry lay in both his Jamaican experience and his later experience of white racism in the United States. His Jamaican poetry also contains early versions of his pastoral longing for childhood innocence and his primal faith in the self-sufficiency and enduring virtues of the rural black community of his childhood and youth.

McKay left Jamaica in 1912 to study agriculture at Tuskegee Institute and Kansas State University, but in 1914 he moved to New York City, where he began again to write poetry. In 1919, he became a regular contributor to the revolutionary literary monthly the *Liberator,* and he achieved fame among black Americans for his sonnet "If We Must Die," which exhorted African Americans to fight bravely against the violence directed against them in the reactionary aftermath of World War I. Although expressed in traditional sonnet form, McKay's post–World War I poetry heralded modern black expressions of anger, alienation, and rebellion, and he quickly became a disturbing, seminal voice in the Harlem Renaissance of the 1920s. His collected American poetry includes *Spring in New Hampshire and Other Poems* (1920) and *Harlem Shadows* (1922).

The years between 1919 and 1922 marked the height of McKay's political radicalism. In 1922 he journeyed to Moscow, where he attended the Fourth Congress of the Third Communist International, but his independence and his criticisms of American and British Communists led to his abandonment of communism. In the 1930s, he became a vocal critic of international communism because of its antidemocratic dominance by the Soviet Union.

From 1923 until 1934, McKay lived in western Europe and Tangiers. While abroad, he published three novels—*Home to Harlem* (1928), *Banjo* (1929), and *Banana Bottom* (1933)—plus one collection of short stories, *Gingertown* (1932). In his novels, McKay rebelled against the genteel traditions of older black writers, and he offended leaders of black protest by writing in *Home to Harlem* and *Banjo* of essentially leaderless rural black migrants and their predicaments in the modern, mechanistic, urban West. Both were picaresque novels that celebrated the natural resilience and ingenuity of "primitive" black heroes. To McKay's critics, his characters were irresponsible degenerates, not exemplary models of racial wisdom; black critics accused him of pandering to the worst white stereotypes of African Americans.

In *Gingertown* and *Banana Bottom*, McKay retreated to the Jamaica of his childhood to recapture a lost pastoral world of blacks governed by their own rural community values. Although critics still debate the merits of McKay's fiction, it provided encouragement to younger black writers. *Banjo,* in particular, by stressing that blacks should build upon their own cultural values, influenced the founding generation of the Francophone Négritude Movement.

In 1934, the Great Depression forced McKay back to the United States, and for the rest of his life he wrote primarily as a journalist critical of international communism, middle-class black integrationism, and white American racial and political hypocrisy. He continued to champion in his essays working-class African Americans, who he believed understood better than their leaders the necessity of community development. He published a memoir, *A Long Way from Home* (1937), and a collection of essays, *Harlem, Negro Metropolis* (1940), based largely on materials about Harlem folk life he collected as a member of New York City's Federal Writers Project. In 1944—ill, broke, and intellectually isolated—he joined the Roman Catholic church, and spent the last years of his life in Chicago working for the Catholic Youth Organization.

Although he is best known as a poet and novelist of the Harlem Renaissance, McKay's social criticism in the 1930s and 1940s was not negligible, but it was controversial, and has since remained hard to grasp because he was neither a black nationalist, an internationalist, nor a traditional integrationist. He instead believed deeply that blacks in their various American ethnicities had much to contribute as ethnic groups and as a race to the collective American life, and that in the future a recognition, acceptance, and celebration of differences between peoples—and not simply individual integration—would best strengthen and bring together the American populace.

—WAYNE F. COOPER

See also
Marcus Garvey

H

HARLEM RENAISSANCE

◆ **Miscegenation**

*A mixture of races;
especially marriage or
cohabitation between a
white person and a member
of another race*

See also
Alain Locke

stated, had given him a true insight into the cultural energies that could be harnessed to pull America back from the abyss of fatal materialism. Celebrity in the Village brought Toomer into Waldo Frank's circle, and with it criticism from Toomer about the omission of African Americans from Frank's sprawling work *Our America*. After a trip with Toomer to South Carolina in the fall of 1922, Frank published *Holiday* the following year, a somewhat overwrought treatment of the struggle between the races in the South, "each of which . . . needs what the other possesses."

Claude McKay, whose volume of poetry *Harlem Shadows* made him a Village celebrity also (he lived on Gay Street, then entirely inhabited by nonwhites), found his niche among the *Liberator* group, where he soon became coeditor of the magazine with Michael Gold. The Eastmans saw the Jamaican poet as the kind of writer who would deepen the magazine's proletarian voice. McKay increased the circulation of *Liberator* to 60,000, published the first poetry of e. e. cummings (over Gold's violent objections), introduced Garvey's Universal Negro Improvement Association (UNIA), and generally treated the readership to experimentation that had little to do with proletarian literature. "It was much easier to talk about real proletarians writing masterpieces than to find such masterpieces," McKay told the Eastmans and the exasperated hard-line Marxist Gold. McKay attempted to bring Harlem to the Village, as the actor Charlie Chaplin discovered when he dropped into the *Liberator* offices one day and found the editor deep in conversation with Hubert Harrison, Harlem's peerless soapbox orator and author of *When Africa Awakes*. Soon all manner of Harlem radicals began meeting at the West Thirteenth Street offices, while the Eastmans fretted about Justice Department surveillance. Richard B. Moore, Cyril Briggs, Otto Huiswood, Grace Campbell, W. A. Domingo, *inter alios*, represented Harlem movements ranging from Garvey's UNIA and Brigg's African Blood Brotherhood to the Communist party, with Huiswood and Campbell. McKay also attempted to bring the Village to Harlem, in one memorable sortie taking Eastman and another Villager to Ned's, his favorite Harlem cabaret. Ned's, notoriously antiwhite, expelled them.

This was part of the background to the Talented Tenth's abrupt, enthusiastic, and programmatic embrace of the arts after World War I. In 1924, as Charles Johnson was planning his Civic Club evening, extraordinary security precautions were in place around the Broadway theater where *All God's Chillun Got Wings*, O'Neill's drama about miscegenation, starring Paul Robeson, was playing. With white Broadway audiences flocking to O'Neill plays and shrieking with delight at *Liza, Runnin' Wild,* and other imitations of *Shuffle Along,* the two Johnsons, Du Bois, Fauset, White, Locke, and others saw a unique opportunity to tap into the attention span of white America. If they were adroit, African-American civil rights officials and intellectuals believed, they stood a fair chance of reshaping the images and repackaging the messages out of which mainstream racial behavior emerged.

Bohemia and the Lost Generation suggested to the Talented Tenth the new approach to the old problem of race relations, but their shared premise about art and society obscured the diametrically opposite conclusions white and black intellectuals and artists drew from it. Stearns's Lost Generation *révoltés* were lost in the sense that they professed to have no wish to find themselves in a materialistic, Mammon-mad, homogenizing America. Locke's New Negroes very much wanted full acceptance by mainstream America, even if some—Du Bois, McKay, and the future enfant terrible of the Renaissance, Wallace Thurman—might have immediately exercised the privilege of rejecting it. For the whites, art was the means to change society before they would accept it. For the blacks, art was the means to change society in order to be accepted into it.

For this reason, many of the Harlem intellectuals found the white vogue in Afro-Americana troubling, although they usually feigned enthusiasm about the new dramatic and literary themes. Most of them clearly understood that this popularity was due to persistent stereotypes, new Freudian notions about sexual dominion over reason, and the postwar release of collective emotional and moral tensions sweeping Europe and America. Cummings, Dreiser, O'Neill, and Frank may have been well intentioned, but the African-American elite was quietly rather infuriated that Talented Tenth lives were frequently reduced to music, libido, rustic manners, and an incapacity for logic. The consummate satirist of the Renaissance, George Schuyler, denounced the insistent white portrayal of the African American in which "it is only necessary to beat a tom tom or wave a rabbit's foot and he is ready to strip off his Hart, Schaffner & Marx suit, grab a spear and ride off wild-eyed on the back of a crocodile." Despite the insensitivity, burlesquing, and calumny, however, the Talented Tenth convinced itself that the civil rights dividends of such recognition were potentially greater than the liabilities were.

Benjamin Brawley put this potential straightforwardly to James Weldon Johnson: "We have a tremendous opportunity to boost the NAACP, letters, and art, and anything else that calls attention to our development along the higher lines." Brawley knew that he was preaching to the converted. Johnson's preface to his best-selling anthology *The Book of American Negro Poetry* (1922) proclaimed that nothing could "do more to change the mental attitude and raise his status than a demonstration of intellectual parity by the Negro through his production of literature and art." Reading Stribling's *Birthright,* an impressed Fauset nevertheless felt that she and her peers could do better. "We reasoned," she recalled later, " 'Here is an audience waiting to hear the truth about us. Let us who are better qualified to present that truth than any white writer, try to do so.' " The result was *There Is Confusion,* her novel about genteel life among Philadelphia's aristocrats of color. Walter Francis White, similarly troubled by *Birthright* and other two-dimensional or symbolically gross representations of African-American life, complained loudly to H. L. Mencken, who finally silenced him with the challenge, "Why don't you do the right kind of novel. You could do it, and it would create a sensation." White did. The sensation turned out to be *The Fire in the Flint* (1924), the second novel of the Renaissance, which he wrote in less than a month in a borrowed country house in the Berkshires.

Meanwhile, Langston Hughes, whose genius (like Toomer's) had been immediately recognized by Fauset, published several poems in the *Crisis* that would later appear in his collection *The Weary Blues.* The euphonious "The Negro Speaks of Rivers" (dedicated to Du Bois) ran in the *Crisis* in 1921. With the appearance of McKay's *Harlem Shadows* in 1922 and Toomer's *Cane* in 1923, the officers of the NAACP and the NUL saw how real the possibility of a theory being put into action could be. The young New York University prodigy Countee Cullen, already published in the *Crisis* and *Opportunity,* had his mainstream breakthrough in 1923 in *Harper's* and *Century* magazines. Two years later, Cullen won the prestigious Witter Bynner poetry prize, with Carl Sandburg as one of the three judges. Meanwhile, the *Survey Graphic* project moved apace under the editorship of Locke.

Two conditions made this unprecedented mobilization of talent and group support in the service of a racial arts and letters movement more than a conceit in the minds of its leaders: demog-

raphy and repression. The Great Black Migration produced the metropolitan dynamism undergirding the Renaissance. The Red Summer of 1919 produced the trauma that led to the cultural sublimation of civil rights. In pressure-cooker fashion, the increase in Harlem's African-American population caused it to pulsate as it pushed its racial boundaries south below 135th Street to Central Park and north beyond 139th ("Strivers' Row"). Despite the real estate success of the firms of Nail and Parker and the competition given by Smalls' Paradise to the Cotton Club and Connie's (both off-limits to African-American patrons), however, this dynamic community was never able to own much of its own real estate, sustain more than a handful of small, marginal merchants, or even control the profits from the illegal policy business perfected by one of its own, the literary Caspar Holstein. Still, both the appearance of and prospects for solid, broad-based prosperity belied the inevitable consequences of Harlem's comprador economy. The Negro Capital of the World filled up with successful bootleggers and racketeers, political and religious charlatans, cults of exotic character ("Black Jews"), street-corner pundits and health practitioners (Hubert Harrison, "Black Herman"), beauty culturists and distinguished professionals (Madame C. J. Walker, Louis T. Wright), religious and civil rights notables (Reverends Cullen and Powell, Du Bois, Johnson, White), and hard-pressed, hardworking families determined to make decent lives for their children. Memories of the nightspots in "The Jungle" (133rd Street), of Bill "Bojangles" Robinson demonstrating his footwork on Lenox Avenue, of raucous shows at the Lafayette that gave Florenz Ziegfeld some of his ideas, of the Tree of Hope outside Connie's Inn where musicians gathered as at a labor exchange, have been vividly set down by Arthur P. Davis, Regina Andrews, Arna Bontemps, and Hughes.

In the first flush of Harlem's realization and of general African-American exuberance, the Red Summer of 1919 had a cruelly decompressing impact on Harlem and Afro-America in general. The adage of peasants in Europe—"City air makes free"—was also true for sharecropping blacks, but not even the cities of the North made them equal or rich, or even physically secure. Charleston, S.C., erupted in riot in May, followed by Longview, Tex., and Washington, D.C., in July. Chicago exploded on July 27. Lynchings of returning African-American soldiers and expulsion of African-American workers from unions abounded. In the North, the white working

See also
Nella Larsen

NEW NEGRO

A Derogatory Term Turned Symbol of Racial Progress

The term *New Negro* was often used by whites in the colonial period to designate newly enslaved Africans. Ironically that same term began to be used at the end of the nineteenth century to measure and represent the distance that African Americans had come from the institution of slavery. Throughout the first three decades of this century, articles and books discussing the New Negro were commonplace. African-American leaders, journalists, artists, and some white Americans used the phrase to refer to a general sense of racial renewal among blacks that was characterized by a spirit of racial pride, cultural and economic self-assertion, and political militancy. William Pickens, in the *New Negro: His Political, Civil, and Mental Status, and Related Essays*, proclaimed the transformation of the "patient, unquestioning devoted semi-slave" into "the self-conscious, aspiring, proud young man" (Pickens, 1916, p. 236). While the notion of a New Negro was variously defined, it typically referred to the passing of an "old Negro," the "Uncle Tom" of racial stereotypes, and the emergence of an educated, politically and culturally aware generation of blacks.

A New Negro for a New Century (1900), a volume of historical and social essays, with chapters by Booker T. Washington and other prominent blacks, was one of earliest of several books that sought to define the new racial personality. In subsequent decades, many African Americans referred to Washington's political leadership and educational philosophy as symbolic of an accommodation that marked the "old Negro"; yet Washington's chapter, "Afro-American Education," stressed the role of education, "the grand army of school children" (p. 84), in remaking African-American consciousness. Fannie B. Williams's "Club Movement Among Colored Women in America" drew attention to the role of African-American women in the development of the "womanhood of a great nation and a great civilization," and she praised their organizations as the "beginning of self-respect and the respect" for the race (Washington, p. 404).

During the 1920s, the idea of the New Negro became an important symbol of racial progress, and different political groups vied with each other over who more properly represented the new racial consciousness. Most agreed that impact of black military service during World War I, the migration of blacks to the North, and the example of blacks fighting against racial violence during the race riots of 1919 provided clear evidence of a reinvigorated African-American sense of self. Political organizations like the National Association for the Advancement of Colored People, the National Urban League, and the Universal Negro Improvement Association of Marcus Garvey each felt that they represented an unquenchable political and racial militancy. The group of socialist and political radicals like A. Philip Randolph and Chandler Owen who were identified with the monthly journal *Messenger* and the Brotherhood of Sleeping Car Porters consistently argued that they represented the political ideas as the ideal of the New Negro.

In 1925, Alain L. Locke, a philosophy professor at Howard University and a leading promoter of black writers and artists, published an anthology *The New Negro, An Interpretation*. That volume proposed African-American creative artists as contenders with political spokesmen for the title of New Negro. The anthology contained contributions from leading political leaders like W. E. B. Du Bois, Jessie Fauset, James Weldon Johnson, and Walter White of the NAACP, and Charles H. Johnson of the National Urban League, yet Locke's essays, "Enter the New Negro" and "Negro Youth Speaks," focused exclusively on a group of young writers and artists: "Youth speaks and the voice of the New Negro is heard" (p. 47). Locke offered the drawings, poetry, and prose of Aaron Douglas, Countee Cullen, Langston Hughes, Zora Neale Hurston, Claude McKay, and Jean Toomer, artists who drew inspiration from the vernacular—blues, jazz, spirituals, and the folktale—as the voice of a vibrant "new psychology" (p. 3). Locke's anthology, and the subsequent work of the young artists included in it, tied the notion of the New Negro to the work of African-American artists and firmly bound the image of the New Negro to the artistic products of the Harlem Renaissance.

After the 1920s, the expression *New Negro* passed out of fashion, largely because the spirit that it referred to was taken for granted. Subsequent generations of scholars, however, still debate about which of the various political and artistic philosophies best represented the ideal of the New Negro.

See also
NAACP

classes struck out against perceived and manipulated threats to job security and unionism from blacks streaming north. In Helena, Ark., a pogrom was unleashed against black farmers organizing a cotton cooperative; outside Atlanta the Ku Klux Klan was reconstituted. The message of the white South to African Americans was that the racial *status quo ante bellum* was on again with a vengeance. Twenty-six race riots in towns, cities, and counties swept across the nation all the way to Nebraska. The "race problem" definitively became an American dilemma, and no longer a remote complexity in the exotic South.

The term "New Negro" entered the vocabulary in reaction to the Red Summer, along with McKay's poetic catechism: "Like men we'll face the murderous, cowardly pack / Pressed to the wall, dying, but fighting back!" There was a groundswell of support for Marcus Garvey's UNIA. Until his 1924 imprisonment for mail fraud, the Jamaican immigrant's message of African Zionism, anti-integrationism, working-class assertiveness, and Bookerite business enterprise increasingly threatened the hegemony of the Talented Tenth and its major organizations, the NAACP and NUL, among people of color in America (much of Garvey's support came from West Indians). The UNIA's phenomenal fundraising success, as well as its portrayal of the civil rights leadership as alienated by class and color from the mass of black people, delivered a jolt to the integrationist elite. "Garvey," wrote Mary White Ovington, one of the NAACP's white founders, "was the first Negro in the United States to capture the imagination of the masses." The *Negro World*, Garvey's multilingual newspaper, circulated throughout Latin America and the African empires of Britain and France. To the established leadership, then, the UNIA was a double threat because of its mass appeal among African Americans and because "respectable" civil rights organizations feared the spillover from the alarm Garveyism caused the white power structure. While Locke wrote in his introductory remarks to the special issue of *Survey Graphic* that "the thinking Negro has shifted a little to the left with the world trend," he clearly had Garveyism in mind when he said of black separatism, "this cannot be—even if it were desirable." Although the movement was its own worst enemy, the Talented Tenth was pleased to help the Justice Department speed its demise.

No less an apostle of high culture than Du Bois, initially a Renaissance enthusiast, vividly expressed the farfetched nature of the arts movement as early as 1923: "How is it that an organization of this kind [the NAACP] can turn aside to talk about art? After all, what have we who are slaves and black to do with art?" Slavery's legacy of cultural parochialism, the agrarian orientation of most African Americans, systematic underfunding of primary education, the emphasis on vocationalism at the expense of liberal arts in colleges, economic marginality, the extreme insecurity of middle-class status: all strongly militated against the flourishing of African-American artists, poets, and writers. It was the brilliant insight of the men and women of the NAACP and NUL that although the road to the ballot box, the union hall, the decent neighborhood, and the office was blocked, there were two paths that had not been barred, in part because of their very implausibility, as well as their irrelevancy to most Americans: arts and letters. These people saw the small cracks in the wall of racism that could, they anticipated, be widened through the production of exemplary racial images in collaboration with liberal white philanthropy, the robust culture industry located primarily in New York, and artists from white bohemia (like themselves, marginal and in tension with the status quo).

If in retrospect, then, the New Negro Arts Movement has been interpreted as a natural phase in the cultural evolution of another American group—a band in the literary continuum running from New England, Knickerbocker New York, and Hoosier Indiana to the Village's bohemia, East Side Yiddish drama and fiction, and the southern Agrarians—such an interpretation sacrifices causation to appearance. The other group traditions emerged out of the hieratic concerns, genteel leisure, privileged alienation, or transplanted learning of critical masses of independent men and women. The Renaissance represented much less an evolutionary part of a common experience than it did a generation-skipping phenomenon in which a vanguard of the Talented Tenth elite recruited, organized, subsidized, and guided an unevenly endowed cohort of artists and writers to make statements that advanced a certain conception of the race—a cohort of whom most would never have imagined the possibility of artistic and literary careers.

Toomer, McKay, Hughes, and Cullen possessed the rare ability combined with personal eccentricity that defined them as artists; the Renaissance needed not only more like them but a large cast of supporters and extras. American dropouts

Alain Locke was a leading spokesman for African-American humanist values during the second quarter of the twentieth century.

PAGE 427

See also
Niagara Movement

*While Madam
Walker is often said
to have invented the
"hot comb," it is
more likely that
she adapted
metal implements
popularized by the
French to suit black
women's hair.*

PAGE 718

See also
Charlie Parker

heading for seminars in garrets and cafés in Paris were invariably white, and descended from an older gentry displaced by new moneyed elites. Charles Johnson and his allies were able to make the critical Renaissance mass possible. Johnson assembled files on prospective recruits throughout the country, going so far as to cajole Aaron Douglas and others into coming to Harlem, where a network staffed by his secretary, Ethel Ray Nance, and her friends Regina Anderson and Louella Tucker (assisted by the gifted Trinidadian short story writer Eric Walrond) looked after them until a salary or fellowship was secured. White, the self-important assistant secretary of the NAACP, urged Robeson to abandon law for an acting career, encouraged Nella Larsen to follow his own example as a novelist, and passed the hat for artist Hale Woodruff. Fauset continued to discover and publish short stories and verse, such as those of Wallace Thurman and Arna Bontemps.

Shortly after the Civic Club evening, both the NAACP and the NUL announced the creation of annual awards ceremonies bearing the titles of their respective publications, *Crisis* and *Opportunity*. The award of the first *Opportunity* prizes came in May 1925 in an elaborate ceremony at the Fifth Avenue Restaurant with some 300 participants. Twenty-four judges in five categories had ruled on the worthiness of entries. Carl Van Doren, Zona Gale, Fannie Hurst, Dorothy Canfield Fisher, and Alain Locke, among others, judged short stories. Witter Bynner, John Farrar, Clement Wood, and James Weldon Johnson read the poetry entries. Eugene O'Neill, Alexander Woollcott, Thomas M. Gregory, and Robert Benchley appraised drama. The judges for essays were Van Wyck Brooks, John Macy, Henry Goodard Leach, and L. Hollingsworth Wood. The awards ceremony was interracial, but white capital and influence were crucial to success, and the white presence in the beginning was pervasive, setting the outer boundaries for what was creatively normative. Money to start the *Crisis* prizes had come from Amy Spingarn, an accomplished artist and poet and the wife of Joel Spingarn, chairman of the NAACP's board of directors. The wife of the influential attorney, Fisk University trustee, and Urban League board chairman L. Hollingsworth Wood had made a similar contribution to initiate the *Opportunity* prizes.

These were the whites Zora Neale Hurston, one of the first *Opportunity* prize winners, memorably dubbed "Negrotarians." These comprised several categories: political Negrotarians such as progressive journalist Ray Stannard Baker and maverick socialist types associated with *Modern Quarterly* (V. F. Calverton, Max Eastman, Lewis Mumford, Scott Nearing); salon Negrotarians such as Robert Chanler, Charles Studin, Carl and Fania (Marinoff) Van Vechten, and Elinor Wylie, for whom the Harlem artists were more exotics than talents; Lost Generation Negrotarians drawn to Harlem on their way to Paris by a need for personal nourishment and confirmation of cultural health, in which their romantic or revolutionary perceptions of African Americans played a key role—Anderson, O'Neill, Georgia O'Keeffe, Zona Gale, Frank, Louise Bryant, Sinclair Lewis, Hart Crane; commercial Negrotarians such as the Knopfs, the Gershwins, Rowena Jelliffe, Liveright, V. F. Calverton, and music impresario Sol Hurok, who scouted and mined Afro-America like prospectors.

The philanthropic Negrotarians, Protestant and Jewish, encouraged the Renaissance from similar motives of principled religious and social obligation and of class hegemony. Oswald Garrison Villard (grandson of William Lloyd Garrison, heir to a vast railroad fortune, owner of the New York *Evening Post* and the *Nation,* and cofounder of the NAACP), along with foundation controllers William E. Harmon and J. G. Phelps-Stokes, and Mary White Ovington of affluent abolitionist pedigree, looked on the Harlem Renaissance as a movement it was their Christian duty to sanction, as well as an efficacious mode of encouraging social change without risking dangerous tensions. Jewish philanthropy, notably represented by the Altmans, Rosenwalds, Spingarns, Lehmans, and Otto Kahn, had an additional motivation, as did the interest of such scholars as Franz Boas and Melville Herskovits, jurists Louis Brandeis, Louis Marshall, and Arthur Spingarn, and progressive reformers Martha Gruening and Jacob Billikopf. The tremendous increase after 1900 of Jewish immigrants from Slavic Europe had provoked nativist reactions and, with the 1915 lynching of Atlanta businessman Leo Frank, both an increasingly volatile anti-Semitism and an upsurge of Zionism. Redoubled victimization of African Americans, exacerbated by the tremendous out-migration from the South, portended a climate of national intolerance that wealthy, assimilated German-American Jews foresaw as inevitably menacing to all American Jews.

The May 1925 *Opportunity* gala showcased the steadily augmenting talent in the Renaissance— what Hurston pungently characterized as the

"Niggerati." Two laureates, Cullen and Hughes, had already won notice beyond Harlem. The latter had engineered his "discovery" as a Washington, D.C., bellhop by placing dinner and three poems on Vachel Lindsay's hotel table. Some prize winners were barely to be heard from again: Joseph Cotter, G. D. Lipscomb, Warren MacDonald, Fidelia Ripley. Others, such as John Matheus (first prize in the short story category) and Frank Horne (honorable mention), failed to achieve first-rank standing in the Renaissance. But most of those whose talent had staying power were also introduced that night: E. Franklin Frazier, winning the first prize for an essay on social equality; Sterling Brown, taking second prize for an essay on the singer Roland Hayes; Hurston, awarded second prize for a short story, "Spunk"; and Eric Walrond, third short-story prize for "Voodoo's Revenge." James Weldon Johnson read the poem taking first prize, "The Weary Blues," Hughes's turning-point poem combining the gift of a superior artist and the enduring, music-encased spirit of the black migrant. Comments from Negrotarian judges ranged from O'Neill's advice to "be yourselves" to novelist Edna Worthley Underwood's exultant anticipation of a "new epoch in American letters," and Clement Wood's judgment that the general standard "was higher than such contests usually bring out."

Whatever their criticisms and however dubious their enthusiasms, what mattered as far as Charles Johnson and his collaborators were concerned was success in mobilizing and institutionalizing a racially empowering crusade, and cementing an alliance between the wielders of influence and resources in the white and black communities, to which the caliber of literary output was a subordinate, though by no means irrelevant, concern. In the September 1924 issue of *Opportunity* inaugurating the magazine's departure from exclusive social-scientific concerns, Johnson had spelled out clearly the object of the prizes: they were to bring African-American writers "into contact with the general world of letters to which they have been for the most part timid and inarticulate strangers; to stimulate and foster a type of writing by Negroes which shakes itself free of deliberate propaganda and protest." The measures of Johnson's success were the announcement of a second *Opportunity* contest, to be underwritten by Harlem "businessman" (and numbers king) Caspar Holstein; former *Times* music critic Carl Van Vechten's enthusiasm over Hughes, and the subsequent arranging of a contract with Knopf for Hughes's first volume of po-

etry; and, one week after the awards ceremony, a prediction by the New York *Herald Tribune* that the country was "on the edge, if not already in the midst of, what might not improperly be called a Negro renaissance"—thereby giving the movement its name.

Priming the public for the Fifth Avenue Restaurant occasion, the special edition of *Survey Graphic* edited by Locke, "Harlem: Mecca of the New Negro," had reached an unprecedented 42,000 readers in March 1925. The ideology of cultural nationalism at the heart of the Renaissance was crisply delineated in Locke's opening essay, "Harlem": "Without pretense to their political significance, Harlem has the same role to play for the New Negro as Dublin has had for the New Ireland or Prague for the New Czechoslovakia." A vast racial formation was under way in the relocation of the peasant masses ("they stir, they move, they are more than physically restless"), the editor announced. "The challenge of the new intellectuals among them is clear enough." The migrating peasants from the South were the soil out of which all success would come, but soil must be tilled, and the Howard University philosopher reserved that task exclusively for the Talented Tenth in liaison with its mainstream analogues—in the "carefully maintained contacts of the enlightened minorities of both race groups." There was little amiss about America that interracial elitism could not set right, Locke and the others believed. Despite historical discrimination and the Red Summer, the Rhodes scholar assured readers that the increasing radicalism among African Americans was superficial. The African American was only a "forced radical," a radical "on race matters, conservative on others." In a surfeit of mainstream reassurance, Locke concluded, "The Negro mind reaches out as yet to nothing but American events, American ideas." At year's end, Albert and Charles Boni published Locke's *The New Negro,* an expanded and polished edition of the poetry and prose from the *Opportunity* contest and the special *Survey Graphic.*

The course of American letters was unchanged by the offerings in *The New Negro.* Still, the book carried several memorable works, such as the short story "The South Lingers On," by Brown University and Howard Medical School graduate Rudolph Fisher; the acid "White House(s)" and the euphonic "The Tropics in New York," poems by McKay, now in European self-exile, and several poetic vignettes from Toomer's *Cane.* Hughes's "Jazzonia," previously published in the *Crisis,* was so poignant as to be almost tactile as it

See also
Adam Clayton Powell

described "six long-headed jazzers" playing while a dancing woman "lifts high a dress of silken gold." In "Heritage," a poem previously unpublished, Cullen outdid himself in his grandest (if not his best) effort with its famous refrain, "What is Africa to me." The book carried distinctive silhouette drawings and Egyptian-influenced motifs by Aaron Douglas, whose work was to become the artistic signature of the Renaissance. With thirty-four African-American contributors—four were white—Locke's work included most of the Renaissance regulars. (The notable omissions were Asa Randolph, George Schuyler, and Wallace Thurman.) These were the gifted men and women who were to show by example what the potential of some African Americans could be and who proposed to lead their people into an era of opportunity and justice.

Deeply influenced, as were Du Bois and Fauset, by readings in German political philosophy and European nationalism (especially Herder and Fichte, Palacky and Synge, Herzl and Mazzini), Locke's notion of civil rights advancement was a "cell group" of intellectuals, artists, and writers "acting as the advance guard of the African peoples in their contact with Twentieth century civilization." By virtue of their symbolic achievements and their adroit collaboration with the philanthropic and reform-minded mainstream, their augmenting influence would ameliorate the socioeconomic conditions of their race over time and from the top downward. It was a Talented Tenth conceit, Schuyler snorted in Asa Randolph's *Messenger* magazine, worthy of a "high priest of the intellectual snobbocracy," and he awarded Locke the magazine's "elegantly embossed and beautifully lacquered dill pickle." Yet Locke's approach seemed to work, for although the objective conditions confronting most African Americans in Harlem and elsewhere were deteriorating, optimism remained high. Harlem recoiled from Garveyism and socialism to applaud Phi Beta Kappa poets, university-trained painters, concertizing musicians, and novel-writing officers of civil rights organizations. "Everywhere we heard the sighs of wonder, amazement and sometimes admiration when it was whispered or announced that here was one of the 'New Negroes,'" Bontemps recalled.

By the summer of 1926, Renaissance titles included the novels *Cane, There is Confusion, The Fire in the Flint,* and Walter White's *Flight* (1926), and the volumes of poetry *Harlem Shadows,* Cullen's *Color* (1924), and Hughes's *The Weary Blues* (1926). The second *Opportunity* awards banquet, in April 1926, was another artis-

GROUP PORTRAIT

Movers and shakers of the Harlem Renaissance included (back row, left to right) Ethel Ray (Nance), Langston Hughes, Helen Lanning, Pearl Fisher, Dr. Rudolf Fisher, Clarissa Scott, Hubert Delany; (front row, left to right) Regin M. Anderson (Andrews), Luella Tucker, Esther Popel, Jessie Fauset, Mrs. Charles S. Johnson, E. Franklin Frazier.

PHOTOGRAPHS AND PRINTS DIVISION, SCHOMBURG CENTER FOR RESEARCH IN BLACK CULTURE, THE NEW YORK PUBLIC LIBRARY, ASTOR, LENOX AND TILDEN FOUNDATIONS

tic and interracial success. Playwright Joseph Cotter was honored again, as was Hurston for a short story. Bontemps, a California-educated poet struggling in Harlem, won first prize for "Golgotha Is a Mountain," and Dorothy West, a Bostonian aspiring to make a name in fiction, made her debut, as did essayist Arthur Fauset, Jessie's able half-brother. The William E. Harmon Foundation transferred its attention at the beginning of 1926 from student loans and blind children to the Renaissance, announcing seven annual prizes for literature, music, fine arts, industry, science, education, and race relations, with George Edmund Haynes, African-American official in the Federal Council of Churches, and Locke as chief advisors. That same year, the publishers Boni & Liveright offered a $1,000 prize for the "best novel on Negro life" by an African American. Caspar Holstein contributed $1,000 that year to endow *Opportunity* prizes; Van Vechten made a smaller contribution to the same cause. Amy Spingarn provided $600 toward the *Crisis* awards. Otto Kahn underwrote two years in France for the young artist Hale Woodruff. There were the Louis Rodman Wanamaker prizes in music composition.

Both the Garland Fund (American Fund for Public Service) and the NAACP's coveted Spingarn Medal were intended to promote political and social change rather than creativity, but three of eight Spingarn medals were awarded to artists and writers between 1924 and 1931, and the Garland Fund was similarly responsive. The first of the Guggenheim Fellowships awarded to Renaissance applicants went to Walter White in 1927, to be followed by Eric Walrond, Nella Larsen (Imes), and Zora Neale Hurston. The Talented Tenth's more academically oriented members benefited from the generosity of the new Rosenwald Fund fellowships.

The third *Opportunity* awards dinner was a vintage one for poetry, with entries by Bontemps, Sterling Brown, Hughes, Helene Johnson, and Jonathan H. Brooks. In praising their general high quality, the white literary critic Robert T. Kerlin added the revealing comment that their effect would be "hostile to lynching and to jim-crowing." Walrond's lush, impressionistic collection of short stories, *Tropic Death*, appeared from Boni & Liveright at the end of 1926, the most probing exploration of the psychology of cultural underdevelopment since Toomer's *Cane*. If *Cane* recaptured in a string of glowing vignettes (most of them about women) the sunset beauty and agony of a preindustrial culture, *Tropic Death* did much the same for the Antilles. Hughes's second

volume of poetry, *Fine Clothes to the Jew* (1927), spiritedly portrayed the city life of ordinary men and women who had traded the hardscrabble of farming for the hardscrabble of domestic work and odd jobs. Hughes scanned the low-down pursuits of "Bad Man," "Ruby Brown," and "Beale Street," and shocked Brawley and other Talented Tenth elders with the bawdy "Red Silk Stockings." "Put on yo' red silk stockings, / Black gal," it began, urging her to show herself to white boys. It ended wickedly with "An' tomorrow's chile'll / Be a high yaller."

A melodrama of Harlem life that had opened in February 1926, *Lulu Belle*, produced by David Belasco, won the distinction for popularizing Harlem with masses of Jazz Age whites. But the part of Lulu Belle was played by Lenore Ulric in blackface. Drama quickened again in the fall of 1927 with Harlemite Frank Wilson (and, for one month, Robeson) in the lead role in Du Bose and Dorothy Heyward's hugely successful play *Porgy*. *Porgy* brought recognition and employment to Rose McClendon, Georgette Harvey, Evelyn Ellis, Jack Carter, Percy Verwayne, and Leigh Whipper. Richard Bruce Nugent, Harlem's most outrageous decadent, and Wallace Thurman, a Utah-born close second, newly arrived from Los Angeles, played members of the population of "Catfish Row." Frank Wilson of *Porgy* fame wrote a play himself, *Meek Mose*, which opened on Broadway in February 1928. Its distinction lay mainly in the employment it gave to Harlem actors, and secondarily in an opening-night audience containing Mayor James Walker, Tuskegee principal Robert Russa Moton, Alexander Woollcott, Harry T. Burleigh, Otto Kahn, and the Joel Spingarns. There was a spectacular Carnegie Hall concert in March 1928 by the ninety-voice Hampton Institute Choir, followed shortly by W. C. Handy's Carnegie Hall lecture on the origins and development of African-American music, accompanied by choir and orchestra.

Confidence among African-American leaders in the power of the muses to heal social wrongs was the rule, rather than the exception, by 1927. Every issue of *Opportunity*, the gossipy *Inter-State Tattler* newspaper, and, frequently, even the mass-circulation Chicago *Defender* or the *soi-disant* socialist *Messenger* trumpeted racial salvation through artistic excellence until the early 1930s. *Harper's* for November 1928 carried James Weldon Johnson's article reviewing the strategies employed in the past for African-American advancement: "religion, education, politics, industrial, ethical, economic, sociological." The executive

See also
Universal Negro
Improvement Association

secretary of the NAACP serenely concluded that "through his artistic efforts the Negro is smashing" racial barriers to his progress "faster than he has ever done through any other method." Charles Johnson, Jessie Fauset, Alain Locke, and Walter White fully agreed. Such was their influence with foundations, publishing houses, the Algonquin Round Table, and various godfathers and godmothers of the Renaissance (such as the mysterious, tyrannical, fabulously wealthy Mrs. Osgood Mason) that McKay, viewing the scene from abroad, spoke derisively of the artistic and literary autocracy of "that NAACP crowd."

A veritable ministry of culture now presided over African America. The ministry mounted a movable feast to which the anointed were invited, sometimes to Walter and Gladys White's apartment at 409 Edgecombe Avenue, where they might share cocktails with Sinclair Lewis or Mencken; often (after 1928) to the famous 136th Street "Dark Tower" salon maintained by beauty-culture heiress A'Lelia Walker, where guests might be Sir Osbert Sitwell, the crown prince of Sweden, or Lady Mountbatten; and very frequently to the West Side apartment of Carl and Fania Van Vechten, to imbibe the hosts' sidecars and listen to Robeson sing or Jim Johnson recite from "God's Trombones" or George Gershwin play the piano. Meanwhile, Harlem's appeal to white revelers inspired the young physician Rudolph Fisher to write a satiric piece in the August 1927 *American Mercury* called "The Caucasian Storms Harlem."

The third phase of the Harlem Renaissance began even as the second had just gotten under way. The second phase (1924 to mid-1926) was dominated by the officialdom of the two major civil rights organizations, with their ideology of the advancement of African Americans through the creation and mobilization of an artistic-literary movement. Its essence was summed up in blunt declarations by Du Bois that he didn't care "a damn for any art that is not used for propaganda," or in exalted formulations by Locke that the New Negro was "an augury of a new democracy in American culture." The third phase of the Renaissance, from mid-1926 to 1934, was marked by rebellion against the civil rights establishment on the part of many of the artists and writers whom that establishment had promoted. Three publications during 1926 formed a watershed between the genteel and the demotic Renaissance. Hughes's "The Negro Artist and the Racial Mountain," appearing in the June 1926 issue of the *Nation,* served as a manifesto of the break-

away from the arts and letters party line. Van Vechten's *Nigger Heaven,* released by Knopf that August, drove much of literate Afro-America into a dichotomy of approval and apoplexy over "authentic" versus "proper" cultural expression. Wallace Thurman's *Fire!!,* available in November, assembled the rebels for a major assault against the civil rights ministry of culture.

Hughes's turning-point essay had been provoked by Schuyler's *Nation* article "The Negro Art-Hokum," which ridiculed "eager apostles from Greenwich Village, Harlem, and environs" who made claims for a special African-American artistic vision distinctly different from that of white Americans. "The Aframerican is merely a lampblacked Anglo-Saxon," Schuyler had sneered. In a famous peroration, Hughes answered that he and his fellow artists intended to express their "individual dark-skinned selves without fear or shame. If white people are pleased we are glad. . . . If colored people are pleased we are glad. If they are not, their displeasure doesn't matter either." And there was considerable African-American displeasure. Much of the condemnation of the license for expression Hughes, Thurman, Hurston, and other artists arrogated to themselves was generational or puritanical, and usually both. "Vulgarity has been mistaken for art," Brawley spluttered after leafing the pages of *Fire!!* "I have just tossed the first issue of *Fire!!* into the fire," the book review critic for the Baltimore *Afro-American* snapped after reading Richard Bruce Nugent's extravagantly homoerotic short story "Smoke, Lillies and Jade." Du Bois was said to be deeply aggrieved.

But much of the condemnation stemmed from racial sensitivity, from sheer mortification at seeing uneducated, crude, and scrappy black men and women depicted without tinsel or soap. Thurman and associated editors John Davis, Aaron Douglas, Gwendolyn Bennett, Arthur Huff Fauset, Hughes, Hurston, and Nugent took the Renaissance out of the parlor, the editorial office, and the banquet room. *Fire!!* featured African motifs drawn by Douglas and Nordic-featured African Americans with exaggeratedly kinky hair by Nugent, poems to an elevator boy by Hughes, jungle themes by Edward Silvera; short stories about prostitution ("Cordelia the Crude") by Thurman, gender conflict between black men and women at the bottom of the economy ("Sweat") by Hurston, and a burly boxer's hatred of white people ("Wedding Day") by Bennett; and a short play about pigment complexes within the race (*Color Struck*) by Hurston, shifting the focus to Locke's "peasant

See also
Madam C. J. Walker

matrix," to the sorrows and joys of those outside the Talented Tenth. "Let the blare of Negro jazz bands and the bellowing voice of Bessie Smith . . . penetrate the closed ears of the colored near-intellectuals," Hughes exhorted in "The Negro Artist and the Racial Mountain."

Van Vechten's influence decidedly complicated the reactions of otherwise worldly critics such as Du Bois, Jessie Fauset, Locke, and Cullen. While his novel's title alone enraged many Harlemites who felt their trust and hospitality betrayed, the deeper objections of the sophisticated to *Nigger Heaven* lay in its message that the Talented Tenth's preoccupation with cultural improvement was a misguided affectation that would cost the race its vitality. It was the "archaic Negroes" who were at ease in their skins and capable of action, Van Vechten's characters demonstrated. Significantly, although Du Bois and Fauset found themselves in the majority among the Renaissance leadership (ordinary Harlemites burned Van Vechten in effigy at 135th Street and Lenox Avenue), Charles Johnson, James Weldon Johnson, Schuyler, White, and Hughes praised the novel's sociological verve and veracity and the service they believed it rendered to race relations.

The younger artists embraced Van Vechten's fiction as a worthy model because of its ribald iconoclasm and its iteration that the future of African-American arts lay in the culture of the working poor, and even of the underclass—in bottom-up drama, fiction, music, poetry, and painting. Regularly convening at the notorious "267 House," Thurman's rent-free apartment on 136th Street (alternately known as "Niggerati Manor"), the group that came to produce *Fire!!* saw art not as politics by other means—civil rights between book covers or from a stage or an easel—but as an expression of the intrinsic conditions most people of African descent were experiencing. They spoke of the need "for a truly Negroid note," for empathy with "those elements within the race which are still too potent for easy assimilation," and they openly mocked the premise of the civil rights establishment that (as a Hughes character says in *The Ways of White Folks*) "art would break down color lines, art would save the race and prevent lynchings! Bunk!" Finally, like creative agents in society from time immemorial, they were impelled to insult their patrons and to defy conventions.

To put the Renaissance back on track, Du Bois sponsored a symposium in late 1926, inviting a wide spectrum of views about the appropriate course the arts should take. His unhappiness was readily apparent, both with the overly literary tendencies of Locke and with the bottom-up school of Hughes and Thurman. The great danger was that politics was dropping out of the Renaissance, that the movement was turning into an evasion, sedulously encouraged by certain whites. "They are whispering, 'Here is a way out. Here is the real solution to the color problem. The recognition accorded Cullen, Hughes, Fauset, White, and others shows there is no real color line,' " Du Bois charged. He then announced that all *Crisis* literary prizes would henceforth be reserved for works encouraging "general knowledge of banking and insurance in modern life and specific knowledge of what American Negroes are doing in these fields." Neither James Weldon Johnson nor White (soon to be a Guggenheim fellow on leave from the NAACP to write another novel in France) approved of the withdrawal of the *Crisis* from the Renaissance, but they failed to change Du Bois's mind.

White's own effort to sustain the civil-rights-by-copyright strategy was the ambitious novel *Flight*, edited by his friend Sinclair Lewis and released by Knopf in 1926. A tale of near-white African Americans of unusual culture and professional accomplishment who prove their moral superiority to their oppressors, White's novel was considered somewhat flat even by kind critics. Unkind critics, such as Thurman and the young Frank Horne at *Opportunity*, savaged it. The reissue the following year of *The Autobiography of an Ex-Colored Man* (with Johnson's authorship finally acknowledged) and publication of a volume of Cullen's poetry, *Copper Sun*, continued the tradition of genteel, exemplary letters. In a further effort to restore direction, Du Bois's *Dark Princess* appeared in 1928 from Harcourt, Brace; it was a large, serious novel in which the "problem of the twentieth century" is taken in charge by a Talented Tenth International whose prime mover is a princess from India. But the momentum stayed firmly with the rebels.

Although Thurman's magazine died after one issue, respectable Afro-America was unable to ignore the novel that embodied the values of the Niggerati—the first Renaissance best-seller by a black author: McKay's *Home to Harlem*, released by Harper & Brothers in the spring of 1928. No graduates of Howard or Harvard discourse on literature at the Dark Tower or at Jessie Fauset's in this novel. It has no imitations of Du Bois, James Weldon Johnson, or Locke—and no whites at all. Its milieu is wholly plebeian. The protagonist,

Adam Clayton Powell was a natural for the political arena, and in 1941, he became the first black to win election to the New York City Council.

PAGE 553

See also
Booker T. Washington

*34*1

*Booker T.
Washington
remained the
dominant African-
American leader in
the country until
his death from
exhaustion and
overwork in 1915.*

PAGE 722

See also

Walter Francis White

Jake, is a Lenox Avenue Noble Savage who demonstrates (in marked contrast to the book-reading Ray) the superiority of the Negro mind uncorrupted by European learning. *Home to Harlem* finally shattered the enforced literary code of the civil rights establishment. The *Defender* disliked McKay's novel, and Du Bois, who confessed feeling "distinctly like needing a bath" after reading it, declared that *Home to Harlem* was about the "debauched tenth." Rudolph Fisher's *The Walls of Jericho*, appearing that year from Knopf, was a brilliant, deftly executed satire that upset Du Bois as much as it heartened Thurman. Fisher, a successful Harlem physician with solid Talented Tenth family credentials, satirized the NAACP, the Negrotarians, Harlem high society, and easily recognized Renaissance notables, while entering convincingly into the world of the working classes, organized crime, and romance across social strata.

Charles Johnson, preparing to leave the editorship of *Opportunity* for a professorship in sociology at Fisk University, now encouraged the young rebels. Before departing, he edited an anthology of Renaissance prose and poetry, *Ebony and Topaz*, in late 1927. The movement was over its birth pangs, his preface declared. Sounding the note of Hughes's manifesto, he declared that the period of extreme touchiness was behind. Renaissance artists were "now less self-conscious, less interested in proving that they are just like white people. . . . Relief from the stifling consciousness of being a problem has brought a certain superiority" to the Harlem Renaissance, Johnson asserted. Johnson left for Nashville in March 1928, four years to the month after his first Civic Club invitations.

Meanwhile, McKay's and Fisher's fiction inspired the Niggerati to publish an improved version of *Fire!!* The magazine, *Harlem*, appeared in November 1928. Editor Thurman announced portentously, "The time has now come when the Negro artist can be his true self and pander to the stupidities of no one, either white or black." While Brawley, Du Bois, and Fauset continued to grimace, *Harlem* benefited from significant defections. It won the collaboration of Locke and White; Roy de Coverly, George W. Little, and Schuyler signed on; and Hughes contributed one of his finest short stories, based on his travels down the west coast of Africa—"Luani of the Jungles," a polished genre piece on the seductions of the civilized and the primitive. Once again, Nugent was wicked, but this time more conventionally. The magazine lasted two issues.

The other Renaissance novel that year from Knopf, Nella Larsen's *Quicksand*, achieved the distinction of being praised by Du Bois, Locke, and Hughes. Larsen was born in the Danish Virgin Islands of mixed parentage. Trained in the sciences at Fisk and the University of Copenhagen, she would remain something of a mystery woman, helped in her career by Van Vechten and White but somehow always receding, and finally disappearing altogether from the Harlem scene. *Quicksand* was a triumph of vivid yet economical writing and rich allegory. Its very modern heroine experiences misfortunes and ultimate destruction from causes that are both racial and individual; she is not a tragic mulatto, but a mulatto who is tragic for both sociological and existential reasons. Roark Bradford, in the *Herald Tribune*, thought *Quicksand*'s first half very good, and Du Bois said it was the best fiction since Chesnutt.

There were reviews (*Crisis, New Republic, New York Times*) that were as laudatory about Jessie Fauset's *Plum Bun*, also a 1928 release, but they were primarily due to the novel's engrossing reconstruction of rarefied, upper-class African-American life in Philadelphia, rather than to special literary merit. If Helga Crane, the protagonist of *Quicksand*, was the Virginia Slim of Renaissance fiction, then Angela Murray (Angele, in her white persona), Fauset's heroine in her second novel, was its Gibson Girl. *Plum Bun* continued the second phase of the Renaissance, as did Cullen's second volume of poetry, *The Black Christ*, published in 1929. Ostensibly about a lynching, the lengthy title poem lost its way in mysticism, paganism, and religious remorse. The volume also lost the sympathies of most reviewers.

Thurman's *The Blacker the Berry*, published by Macaulay in early 1929, although talky and awkward in spots (Thurman had hoped to write the Great African-American Novel), was a breakthrough. The reviewer for the Chicago *Defender* enthused, "Here at last is the book for which I have been waiting, and for which you have been waiting." Hughes praised it as a "gorgeous book," mischievously writing Thurman that it would embarrass those who bestowed the "seal-of-high-and-holy approval of Harmon awards." The ministry of culture found the novel distinctly distasteful: *Opportunity* judged *The Blacker the Berry* to be fatally flawed by "immaturity and gaucherie." For the first time, color prejudice within the race was the central theme of an African-American novel. Emma Lou, its heroine (like the author, very dark and conventionally unattractive), is obsessed with respectability as well as tortured by her pigment.

Thurman makes the point on every page that Afro-America's aesthetic and spiritual center resides in the unaffected, unblended, noisome common folk and the liberated, unconventional artists.

With the unprecedented Broadway success of *Harlem*, Thurman's sensationalized romp through the underside of that area, the triumph of Niggerati aesthetics over civil rights arts and letters was impressively confirmed. The able theater critic for the *Messenger*, Theophilus Lewis, rejoiced at the "wholesome swing toward dramatic normalcy." George Jean Nathan lauded *Harlem* for its "sharp smell of reality." Another equally sharp smell of reality irritated establishment nostrils that same year with the publication of McKay's second novel, *Banjo*, appearing only weeks after *The Blacker the Berry*. "The Negroes are writing against themselves," lamented the reviewer for the *Amsterdam News*. Set among the human flotsam and jetsam of Marseilles and West Africa, McKay's novel again propounded the message that European civilization was inimical to Africans everywhere.

The stock market collapsed, but reverberations from the Harlem Renaissance seemed stronger than ever. Larsen's second novel, *Passing*, appeared. Its theme, like Fauset's, was the burden of mixed racial ancestry. But, although *Passing* was less successful than *Quicksand*, Larsen again evaded the trap of writing another tragic-mulatto novel by opposing the richness of African-American life to the material advantages afforded by the option of "passing." In February 1930, white playwright Marc Connelly's dramatization of Roark Bradford's book of short stories opened on Broadway as *The Green Pastures*. The Hall Johnson Choir sang in it, Richard Harrison played "De Lawd," and scores of Harlemites found parts during 557 performances at the Mansfield Theatre, and then on tour across the country. The demanding young critic and Howard University professor of English Sterling Brown pronounced the play a "miracle." The ministry of culture (increasingly run by White, after James Weldon Johnson followed Charles Johnson to a Fisk professorship) deemed *The Green Pastures* far more significant for civil rights than Thurman's *Harlem* and even than King Vidor's talking film *Hallelujah!* The NAACP's Spingarn Medal for 1930 was presented to Harrison by New York's lieutenant governor, Herbert Lehman.

After *The Green Pastures* came *Not Without Laughter*, Hughes's glowing novel from Knopf. Financed by Charlotte Osgood Mason ("Godmother") and Amy Spingarn, Hughes had resumed his college education at Lincoln University and completed *Not Without Laughter* his senior year. The beleaguered family at the center of the novel represents Afro-Americans in transition within white America. Hughes's young male protagonist learns that proving his equality means affirming his distinctive racial characteristics. Not only did Locke admire *Not Without Laughter*, the *New Masses* reviewer embraced it as "our novel." The ministry of culture decreed Hughes worthy of the Harmon gold medal for 1930. The year ended with Schuyler's ribald, sprawling satire *Black No More*, an unsparing demolition of every personality and institution in Afro-America. Little wonder that Locke titled his retrospective piece in the February 1931 *Opportunity* "The Year of Grace." Depression notwithstanding, the Renaissance appeared to be more robust than ever.

The first Rosenwald fellowships for African Americans had been secured, largely due to James Weldon Johnson's influence, the previous year. Beginning with Johnson himself in 1930, most of the African Americans who pursued cutting-edge postgraduate studies in the United States over the next fifteen years would be recipients of annual Rosenwald fellowships. Since 1928 the Harmon Foundation, advised by Locke, had mounted an annual traveling exhibition of drawings, paintings, and sculpture by African Americans. The 1930 installment introduced the generally unsuspected talent and genius of Palmer Hayden, William H. Johnson, Archibald Motley, Jr., James A. Porter, and Laura Wheeler Waring in painting. Sargent Johnson, Elizabeth Prophet, and Augusta Savage were the outstanding sculptors of the show. Both Aaron Douglas and Romare Bearden came to feel that the standards of the foundation were somewhat indulgent and therefore injurious to many young artists, which was undoubtedly true. Nevertheless, the Harmon made it possible for African-American artists to find markets previously wholly closed to them. In 1931, more than 200 works of art formed the Harmon Travelling Exhibition of the Work of Negro Artists, to be seen by more than 150,000 people.

Superficially, Harlem itself appeared to be in fair health well into 1931. James Weldon Johnson's celebration of the community's strengths, *Black Manhattan*, was published near the end of 1930. "Harlem is still in the process of making," the book proclaimed, and the author's confidence in the power of the "recent literary and artistic emergence" to ameliorate race relations was unshaken. In Johnson's Harlem, redcaps and cooks

Charlie Parker was the principal architect of the style of jazz called bebop, which revolutionized jazz, taking it from dance music to a black musical aesthetic and art form.

PAGE 533

343

cheered when Renaissance talents won Guggenheim and Rosenwald fellowships; they rushed to newsstands whenever the *American Mercury* or *New Republic* mentioned activities above Central Park. In this Harlem, dramatic productions unfolded weekly at the YMCA; poetry readings were held regularly at Ernestine Rose's 135th Street Public Library (today's Schomburg Center); and people came after work to try out for Du Bois's Krigwa Players in the library's basement. It was the Harlem of amateur historians such as J. A. Rogers, who made extraordinary claims about the achievements of persons of color, and of dogged bibliophiles such as Arthur Schomburg, who documented extraordinary claims. It was much too easy for Talented Tenth notables Johnson, White, and Locke not to notice in the second year of the Great Depression that for the vast majority of the population, Harlem was in the process of unmaking. Still, there was a definite prefiguration of its mortality when A'Lelia Walker suddenly died in August 1931, a doleful occurrence shortly followed by the sale of Villa Lewaro, her Hudson mansion, at public auction.

Meanwhile, the much-decorated Fifteenth Infantry Regiment (the 369th during World War I) took possession of a new headquarters, the largest National Guard armory in the state. The monopoly of white doctors and nurses at Harlem General Hospital had been effectively challenged by the NAACP and the brilliant young surgeon Louis T. Wright. There were two well-equipped private sanitariums in Harlem by the end of the 1920s: the Vincent, financed by numbers king Caspar Holstein, and the Wiley Wilson, equipped with divorce settlement funds by one of A'Lelia Walker's husbands. Rudolph Fisher's X-ray laboratory was one of the most photographed facilities in Harlem.

Decent housing was becoming increasingly scarce for most families; the affluent, however, had access to excellent accommodations. Talented Tenth visitors availed themselves of the Dumas or the Olga, two well-appointed hotels. By the end of 1929, African Americans lived in the 500 block of Edgecombe Avenue, known as "Sugar Hill." The famous "409" overlooking the Polo Grounds was home at one time or another to the Du Boises, the Fishers, and the Whites. Below Sugar Hill was the five-acre, Rockefeller-financed Dunbar Apartments complex, its 511 units fully occupied in mid-1928. The Dunbar eventually became home for the Du Boises, E. Simms Campbell (illustrator and cartoonist), Fletcher Henderson, the A. Philip Randolphs, Leigh Whipper (actor),

and, briefly, Paul and Essie Robeson. The complex published its own weekly bulletin, the *Dunbar News,* an even more valuable record of Talented Tenth activities during the Renaissance than the *Inter-State Tattler.*

The 1931 *Report on Negro Housing,* presented to President Hoover, was a document starkly in contrast to the optimism found in *Black Manhattan.* Nearly 50 percent of Harlem's families would be unemployed by the end of 1932. The syphilis rate was nine times higher than white Manhattan's; the tuberculosis rate was five times greater; those for pneumonia and typhoid were twice those of whites. Two African-American mothers and two babies died for every white mother and child. Harlem General Hospital, the area's single public facility, served 200,000 people with 273 beds. Twice as much of the income of a Harlem family went for rent as a white family's. Meanwhile, median family income in Harlem dropped 43.6 percent in two years by 1932. The ending of Prohibition would devastate scores of marginal speakeasies, as well as prove fatal to theaters such as the Lafayette. Connie's Inn would eventually migrate downtown. Until then, however, the clubs in "The Jungle," as 133rd Street was called (Bamville, Connor's, the Clam House, the Nest Club), and elsewhere (Pod's and Jerry's, Smalls' Paradise) continued to do a land-office business.

Because economic power was the Achilles' heel of the community, real political power also eluded Harlem. Harlem's Republican congressional candidates made unsuccessful runs in 1924 and 1928. Until the Twenty-first Congressional District was redrawn after the Second World War, African Americans were unable to overcome Irish, Italian, and Jewish voting patterns in order to elect one of their own. In state and city elections, black Harlem fared better. African-American aldermen had served on the City Council since 1919; black state assemblymen were first elected in 1917. Republican party patronage was funneled through the capable but aged Charles W. ("Charlie") Anderson, collector of Internal Revenue for the Third District. Although African Americans voted overwhelmingly for the Republican ticket at the national level, Harlemites readily voted for Democrats in city matters. Democratic patronage for Harlem was handled by Harvard-educated Ferdinand Q. Morton, chairman of the Municipal Civil Service Commission and head of the United Colored Democracy—"Black Tammany." In 1933, Morton would bolt the Democrats to help elect Fusion candidate Fiorello La Guardia mayor. Despite a growing sense of political con-

See also
Edward Franklin Frazier

sciousness, greatly intensified by the exigencies of the Depression, Harlem continued to be treated by City Hall and the municipal bureaucracies as though it were a colony.

The thin base of its economy and politics eventually began to undermine the Renaissance. Mainstream sponsorship, direct and indirect, was indispensable to the movement's momentum, and as white foundations, publishers, producers, readers, and audiences found their economic resources drastically curtailed (the reduced value of Sears, Roebuck stock chilled Rosenwald Fund philanthropy), interest in African Americans evaporated. With the repeal of the Eighteenth Amendment, ending Prohibition, honorary Harlemites such as Van Vechten sobered up and turned to other pursuits. Locke's letters to Charlotte Osgood Mason turned increasingly pessimistic in the winter of 1931. In June 1932, he perked up a bit to praise the choral ballet presented at the Eastman School of Music, *Sahdji*, with music by William Grant Still and scenario by Richard Bruce Nugent, but most of Locke's news was distinctly downbeat. The writing partnership of two of his protégés, Hughes and Hurston, their material needs underwritten in a New Jersey township by "Godmother," collapsed in acrimonious dispute. Each claimed principal authorship of the only dramatic comedy written during the Renaissance, *Mule Bone,* a three-act folk play that went unperformed (as a result of the dispute) until 1991. Locke took the side of Hurston, undermining the affective tie between Godmother and Hughes, and essentially ending his relationship with the latter. The part played in this controversy by their brilliant secretary, Louise Thompson, the strong-willed, estranged wife of Wallace Thurman, remains murky, but it seems clear that Thompson's Marxism had a deep influence on Hughes in the aftermath of his painful breakup with Godmother, Locke, and Hurston.

In any case, beginning with "Advertisement for the Waldorf-Astoria," published in the December 1931 *New Masses,* Hughes's poetry became markedly political. "Elderly Race Leaders" and "Goodbye Christ," as well as the play *Scottsboro, Limited,* were irreverent, staccato offerings to the coming triumph of the proletariat. The poet's departure in June 1932 for Moscow, along with Louise Thompson, Mollie Lewis, Henry Moon, Loren Miller, Theodore Poston, and thirteen others, ostensibly to act in a Soviet film about American race relations, *Black and White,* symbolized the shift in patronage and the accompanying politicization of Renaissance artists. If F. Scott Fitzgerald, golden boy of the Lost Generation, could predict that "it may be necessary to work inside the Communist party" to put things right again in America, no one should have been surprised that Cullen and Hughes united in 1932 to endorse the Communist party candidacy of William Z. Foster and the African American James W. Ford for president and vice-president of the United States, respectively. *One Way to Heaven,* Cullen's first novel—badly flawed and clearly influenced by *Nigger Heaven*—appeared in 1932, but it seemed already a baroque anachronism with its knife-wielding Lotharios and elaborately educated types. An impatient Du Bois, deeply alienated from the Renaissance, called for a second Amenia Conference to radicalize the ideology and renew the personnel of the organization.

Jessie Fauset remained oblivious to the profound artistic and political changes under way. Her final novel, *Comedy: American Style* (1933), was technically much the same as *Plum Bun.* Once again, her subject was skin pigment and the neuroses of those who had just enough of it to spend their lives obsessed by it. James Weldon Johnson's autobiography, *Along This Way,* was the publishing event of the year, an elegantly written review of his sui generis public career as archetypal Renaissance man in both meanings of the word. McKay's final novel also appeared that year. He worried familiar themes, but *Banana Bottom* represented a philosophical advance over *Home to Harlem* and *Banjo* in its reconciliation through the protagonist, Bita Plant, of the previously destructive tension in McKay's work between the natural and the artificial, soul and civilization.

The publication at the beginning of 1932 of Thurman's last novel, *Infants of the Spring,* had already announced the end of the Harlem Renaissance. The action of the book is in the characters' ideas, in their incessant talk about themselves, Booker T. Washington, W. E. B. Du Bois, racism, and the destiny of the race. Its prose is generally disappointing, but the ending is conceptually poignant. Paul Arbian (a stand-in for Richard Bruce Nugent) commits suicide in a full tub of water, which splashes over and obliterates the pages of Arbian's unfinished novel on the bathroom floor. A still legible page, however, contains this paragraph that was in effect an epitaph:

> *He had drawn a distorted, inky black skyscraper, modeled after Niggerati Manor, and on which were focused an array of blindingly white beams of light. The foundation of this*

Poems in journals such as the Crisis *and* Opportunity *led to Langston Hughes's recognition as perhaps the most striking new voice in African-American voice.*

PAGE 357

building was composed of crumbling stone. At first glance it could be ascertained that the skyscraper would soon crumple and fall, leaving the dominating white lights in full possession of the sky.

The literary energies of the Renaissance finally slumped. McKay returned to Harlem in February 1934 after a twelve-year sojourn abroad, but his creative powers were spent. The last novel of the movement, Hurston's beautifully written *Jonah's Gourd Vine*, went on sale in May 1934. Charles Johnson, James Weldon Johnson, and Locke applauded Hurston's allegorical story of her immediate family (especially her father) and the mores of an African-American town in Florida called Eatonville. Fisher and Thurman could have been expected to continue to write, but their fates were sealed by the former's professional carelessness and the latter's neurotic alcoholism. A few days before Christmas 1934, Thurman died, soon after his return from an abortive Hollywood film project. Ignoring his physician's strictures, he hemorrhaged after drinking to excess while hosting a party in the infamous house at 267 West 136th Street. Four days later, Fisher expired from intestinal cancer caused by repeated exposure to his own X-ray equipment. A grieving Locke wrote Charlotte Mason from Howard University, "It is hard to see the collapse of things you have labored to raise on a sound base."

Locke's anthology had been crucial to the formation of the Renaissance. As the movement ran down, another anthology, English heiress Nancy Cunard's *Negro*, far more massive in scope, recharged the Renaissance for a brief period. Enlisting the contributions of most of the principals (though McKay and Walrond refused, and Toomer no longer acknowledged his African-American roots), Cunard captured its essence, in the manner of expert taxidermy.

Arthur Fauset attempted to explain the collapse to Locke and the readers of *Opportunity* at the beginning of 1934. He foresaw "a sociopolitical-economic setback from which it may take decades to recover." The Renaissance had left the race unprepared, Fauset charged, because of its unrealistic belief "that social and economic recognition will be inevitable when once the race has produced a sufficiently large number of persons who have properly qualified themselves in the arts." James Weldon Johnson's philosophical *tour d'horizon* appearing that year, *Negro Americans, What Now?*, asked precisely the question of the decade. Most Harlemites were certain that

the riot exploding on the evening of March 19, 1935, taking three lives and causing $2 million in property damage, was not an answer. By then, the Works Progress Administration had become the major patron of African-American artists and writers. Writers like William Attaway, Ralph Ellison, Margaret Walker, Richard Wright, and Frank Yerby would emerge under its aegis, as would painters Romare Bearden, Jacob Lawrence, Charles Sebree, Lois Maillou Jones, and Charles White. The Communist Party was another patron, notably for Richard Wright, whose 1937 essay "Blueprint for Negro Writing" would materially contribute to the premise of Hughes's "The Negro Artist and the Racial Mountain." And for thousands of ordinary Harlemites who had looked to Garvey's UNIA for inspiration, then to the Renaissance, there was now Father Divine and his "heavens."

In the ensuing years much was renounced, more was lost or forgotten; yet the Renaissance, however artificial and overreaching, left a positive mark. Locke's *New Negro* anthology featured thirty of the movement's thirty-five stars. They and a small number of less gifted collaborators generated 26 novels, 10 volumes of poetry, 5 Broadway plays, countless essays and short stories, 3 performed ballets and concerti, and a considerable output of canvas and sculpture. If the achievement was less than the titanic expectations of the ministry of culture, it was an artistic legacy, nevertheless, of and by which a beleaguered Afro-America could be both proud and sustained. Though more by osmosis than by conscious attention, mainstream America was also richer for the color, emotion, humanity, and cautionary vision produced by Harlem during its golden age. "If I had supposed that all Negroes were illiterate brutes, I might be astonished to discover that they can write good third-rate poetry, readable and unreadable magazine fiction," was the flinty judgment of a contemporary white Marxist. That judgment was soon beyond controversy largely because the Harlem Renaissance finally, irrefutably, proved the once-controversial point during slightly more than a single decade.

—DAVID LEVERING LEWIS

HARPER, FRANCES ELLEN WATKINS

Frances Ellen Watkins Harper (September 24, 1825–February 20, 1911), writer and activist.

See also
Underground Railroad

One of the most prominent activist women of her time in the areas of abolition, temperance, and women's rights, Frances Ellen Watkins Harper also left an indelible mark on African-American literature. Frances Watkins was born in Baltimore and raised among the city's free black community. She was orphaned at an early age and her uncle, the Rev. William Watkins, took responsibility for her care and education, enrolling her in his prestigious school for free blacks, the Academy for Negro Youth. Here Watkins received a strict, classical education, studying the Bible, Greek, and Latin. Although she left school while in her early teens in order to take employment as a domestic, she never ceased her quest for additional education. She remained a voracious reader; her love of books contributed to her beginnings as a writer.

Frances Watkins published her first of several volumes of poetry in 1845. This early work, *Forest Leaves*, has been lost, however. From 1850 until 1852, Watkins taught embroidery and sewing at Union Seminary, an African Methodist Episcopal Church school near Columbus, Ohio. She then moved on to teach in Pennsylvania. Both teaching situations were difficult, since the schools were poor and the facilities overtaxed. During this period, she was moved by the increasing number of strictures placed on free people of color, especially in her home state of Maryland, a slave state. From this point, she became active in the antislavery movement.

In 1854, Watkins moved to Philadelphia and became associated with an influential circle of black and white abolitionists. Among her friends there were William Still and his daughter Mary, who operated the key Underground Railroad station in the city. The same year another collection of Watkins's verse, *Poems on Miscellaneous Subjects*, was published. Many of the pieces in this volume dealt with the horrors of slavery. The work received popular acclaim and was republished in numerous revised, enlarged editions. Watkins also published poems in prominent abolitionist papers such as *Frederick Douglass' Paper* and the *Liberator*. Later would come other collections—*Sketches of Southern Life* (1872), the narrative poem *Moses: A Story of the Nile* (1889), *Atlanta Offering: Poems* (1895), and *Martyr of Alabama and Other Poems* (1895).

With her literary career already on course, Watkins moved to Boston and joined the antislavery lecture circuit, securing a position with the Maine Anti-Slavery Society. She later toured with the Pennsylvania Anti-Slavery Society. Watkins immediately distinguished herself, making a reputation as a forceful and effective speaker, a difficult task for any woman at this time, especially an African American. Public speaking remained an important part of her career for the rest of her life, as she moved from antislavery work to other aspects of reform in the late nineteenth century.

In 1860, Frances Watkins married Fenton Harper and the two settled on a farm near Columbus, Ohio. Their daughter, Mary, was born there. Fenton Harper died four years later, and Frances Harper resumed her public career. With the close of the Civil War, she became increasingly involved in the struggle for suffrage, working with the American Equal Rights Association, the American Woman Suffrage Association, and the National Council of Women. Harper also became an active member of the Women's Christian Temperance Union. Despite her disagreements with many of the white women in these organizations and the racism she encountered, Harper remained steadfast in her commitment to the battle for women's rights. She refused to sacrifice any aspect of her commitment to African-American rights in seeking the rights of women, however. She was also a key member of the National Federation of Afro-American Women and the National Association of Colored Women.

In addition to the many poems, speeches, and essays she wrote, Frances Ellen Watkins Harper is probably best known for her novel, *Iola Leroy; or, Shadows Uplifted*, published in 1892. The work tells the story of a young octoroon woman who is sold into slavery when her African-American heritage is revealed. It is a story about the quest for family and for one's people. Through Iola Leroy and the characters around her, Harper addresses the issues of slavery, relations between African Americans and whites, feminist concerns, labor in freedom, and the development of black intellectual communities. In this book, she combined many of her lifelong interests and passions.

Harper's public career ended around the turn of the century. She died in Philadelphia in 1911, leaving an enduring legacy of literary and activist achievement.

—JUDITH WEISENFELD

HAYDEN, ROBERT EARL

Robert Earl Hayden (August 4, 1913–February 25, 1980), poet. Born in Detroit, Mich., he wrote

See also
National Association of Colored Women

COLEMAN HAWKINS

King of Swing and Bebop

Coleman Randolph Hawkins (November 21, 1904–May 19, 1969), jazz saxophonist. Hawkins was born and raised in St. Joseph, Mo. His mother, a schoolteacher and organist, introduced him to music. By the age of nine, he had studied piano, cello, and tenor saxophone, and by the age of fourteen he was playing frequently at dances in Kansas City. By 1921 he was performing with the orchestra of the 12th Street Theatre in Kansas City, and at the same time studying music theory both at the Industrial and Educational Institute, and at Washburn College, in Topeka, Kans.

In 1921, Hawkins quit school to tour with Mamie Smith's Jazz Hounds ("I'm Gonna Get You," 1922) and two years later he moved to New York City, where he played with clarinetist Wilbur Sweatman at Connie's Inn. That year he was hired by bandleader Fletcher Henderson. His eleven-year engagement with Henderson's orchestra made him a star. Through touring and frequent recording, both with Henderson, a Benny Carter-led group known as the Chocolate Dandies, and other ensembles ("Dicty Blues," 1923; "The Stampede," 1926; "Sugar Foot Stomp," 1931; and "New King Porter Stomp," 1932), Hawkins became one of the dominant tenor saxophonists in jazz, proving that the instrument could produce more than novelty effects. Hawkins was also a progressive composer, whose "Queer Notions" (1933), with Fletcher Henderson's orchestra, featured unusual harmonies.

In 1934, Hawkins took a six-month leave from the Henderson band, never to return. He went to England to work for British bandleader Jack Hylton, and toured Europe to tremendous acclaim. Hawkins spent five years touring Europe. "Honeysuckle Rose" and "Crazy Rhythm" document his 1937 collaborations with fellow expatriate saxophonist Benny Carter and French guitarist Django Reinhardt. With war threatening Europe, Hawkins returned to the United States in 1939 to lead a nine-piece band at Kelly's Stable. That engagement immediately reestablished his reputation as the preeminent saxophonist in jazz.

In October 1939 Hawkins recorded "Body and Soul," which became one of the great musical landmarks of the twentieth century, demonstrating the extent to which Hawkins had elevated the tenor saxophone to a central place in jazz. With its ripe tone, jagged rhythm, and arresting harmonies, "Body and Soul" remains his best known and most identifiable recording. The recording also caps a major shift that had taken place in Hawkins's solo style. Whereas his early recordings with Henderson feature his big, powerful sound, and the so-called "slap-tongue" technique, characterized by rapid syncopations and arpeggiations that produced a "herky-jerky" sound, by the late 1920s Hawkins was developing the more swaggering, legato execution of tones first heard on "One Hour" (1929), with the Mound City Blue Blowers. That mature style, with its rough tone and vertical or chordal approach to harmony, established one of the two major schools of saxophone playing; the other school was that of Lester Young, with his light, vibratoless tone, and melodic, or horizontal, style of improvisation.

Always a restless experimenter, Hawkins was one of the few swing era musicians to gain new distinction during the bebop era. In 1940 he organized his own big band, one of the first to record bebop, and during the next decade he performed with bebop musicians such as Thelonious Monk, Miles Davis, Max Roach, Kenny Clarke, and Dizzy Gillespie and with Fats Navarro. Hawkins's "Picasso" (1948) is thought to be the first unaccompanied saxophone recording in jazz.

In the late 1940s and '50s Hawkins used New York City as a base from which to tour the United States and Europe, often with trumpeter Roy Eldridge. He also toured with the "Jazz at the Philharmonic" all-star jam sessions organized by Norman Granz (1945), and appeared on the 1957 television program "The Sound of Jazz."

Although his own playing was always firmly rooted in the traditions of the swing era, Hawkins kept up with new developments. He recorded with Thelonious Monk and John Coltrane (1957), Bud Powell (1960), Duke Ellington (1962), and Sonny Rollins (1963). He also recorded prolifically as a leader, including on *Hawk Eyes* (1957), *Night Hawk* (1960), and *Wrapped Too Tight* (1965). In the late 1960s Hawkins continued to appear at major jazz festivals and to perform in jazz clubs in New York. However, liver problems due to alcoholism made his behavior increasingly erratic. He died in New York in 1969.

—EDDIE S. MEADOWS

See also

Jazz

nine volumes of poetry and taught literature at Fisk University and the University of Michigan. Although his career began in the 1930s during the realist and protest period of African-American writing and reached its height in the decade following the Black Arts Movement, Hayden consistently pursued his own unique poetic muse. Distinguished by complexity and precision, his poetry expresses the diversity of the American experience. In 1966, Hayden received the grand prize for poetry in English at the First World Festival of Negro Arts, and he became a fellow of the American Academy of Poets in 1975. One year later, he became the first African American to serve as poetry consultant to the Library of Congress.

Hayden's childhood and his complex relationship to his family and ancestry were often the subjects of his poems, as was his early life in the Detroit ghetto known as "Paradise Valley." His early love of literature won him a scholarship to attend Wayne City College (later Wayne State University), where he majored in Spanish and immersed himself in the theater, cultivating the dramatic instincts that shaped much of his later multi-voiced poetry. The depression forced him to leave college just before completing his studies, yet this abrupt move was crucial to his development as a poet. He joined the Federal Writers' Project (FWP), where he researched local history and black folklore, concentrating on the Underground Railroad and the antislavery movement in Michigan. Enrolling as a part-time student at the University of Michigan in 1938, he went on to work for the Federal Historical Records Survey for several months processing the correspondence of several abolitionists. His major contribution to the FWP was the manuscript "The Negro in Michigan." His historical research informed much of his work as a poet.

In 1941, Hayden and his wife, Erma, moved to Ann Arbor so that he could begin graduate study in English at the University of Michigan, where he worked with the poet W. H. Auden. After receiving an M.A. in 1944, Hayden moved to Nashville in 1946 to teach at Fisk University, where he remained for twenty-two years before returning to the University of Michigan as a professor of English. While Hayden authored three chapbooks in the 1940s and '50s, his mature work did not appear until 1962 with the publication of *A Ballad of Remembrance. Angle of Ascent,* his best-known volume, was published in 1975; his *Collected Poems* was published posthumously in 1985.

Hayden probed his craft in search of universal truths, only to find the forms of revelation in the voices of the African-American historical landscape. His major contribution to American literature is those poems that reach down in search of the obsidian of history, the smoky shards of the black experience. In these historical poems, which include "Middle Passage," "The Ballad of Nat Turner," "Runagate Runagate," "Frederick Douglass," "The Dream (1863)," and "John Brown," the subjects of African-American history give a thematic focus while allowing him the freedom to discover his own identity. Hayden most distinguishes himself as an artist of the African-American experience.

His poetry is also rich in its variety of aesthetic and intellectual concerns. In "The Night-Blooming Cereus," "For a Young Artist," "The Peacock Room," "Kodachromes of the Island," "The Diver," and " 'An Inference of Mexico,' " Hayden writes as a modern poet who commands a unique sense of the importance of the imagination in confronting and transforming everyday life. His religious poems constitute the final major grouping of his work. His poems on the Baha'i Faith, including "Dawnbreaker," "Bahá'u'lláh in the Garden of Ridwan," and "Words in the Mourning Time," help him to locate his spiritual bearings as an artist. As he reveals in his "Statement on Poetics," Hayden viewed the writing of poems as "one way of coming to grips with inner and outer realities—as a spiritual act, really, a sort of prayer for illumination and perfection." His poetry revels in the multiple possibilities of racial and spiritual identity.

—MARCELLUS BLOUNT

HAYES, ROLAND WILLSIE

Roland Willsie Hayes (June 3, 1887–December 31, 1976), concert singer. Roland Hayes was the first African-American singer in the classical tradition to receive international acclaim. Heralded as one of the great singers of the twentieth century, he was at the height of his career one of the world's most celebrated interpreters of German lieder. Born in a two-room log cabin near Curryville, Ga., Hayes lived on his parents' farm with six siblings. When he was eleven, his father died, forcing him to quit school to help support the family. He moved with his family to Chattanooga,

A lover of black folk culture as well as a trained ethnographer, Zora Neale Hurston wrote of a black woman's search for an independent sense of identity and self-fulfillment.

PAGE 420

Tenn., in 1900, and attracted the attention of Arthur Calhoun, who introduced him to the basics of music and singing.

In 1905, Hayes entered Fisk University. Although he had only a fifth-grade education, his determination and musical talent were enough to warrant a probationary admittance. He excelled in his studies and worked at odd jobs to support himself. In his fourth year, the director of music, a woman unsympathetic to Hayes's participation in the fisk jubilee singers, had him expelled from school on the grounds of neglect of his musical studies. Undaunted, he continued to pursue a professional career, and in 1911 moved to Boston, where he became a student of Arthur Hubbard (himself a pupil of Francesco Limpertie). For the next eight years he studied with Hubbard while establishing himself on the local concert circuit, particularly in black churches. Unable to acquire management with any white agency, he began in 1915 to manage his own concerts. Even in the face of adversity, Hayes remained a man of determination, humility, and compassion. Although he had financial losses, the success of a concert in Boston's Symphony Hall in 1917 enabled him to travel to Europe for further study.

In Europe, as in America, Hayes's success was not immediate. Despite difficulties, a recital in 1921 at London's Wigmore Hall settled him securely into an international career that lasted more than thirty years. Possessed of a voice of beauty and purity, Hayes was aware very early of the uniqueness his ethnicity brought to the music he performed. He studied intensely throughout his career, and not only excelled in the interpretation of European art songs, but was the preeminent force in bringing the African-American spiritual to recognition on the solo concert stage. In Europe, Hayes studied with Sir George Henschel, Theodore Lierhammer, and Gabriel Fauré. Having achieved acclaim in Europe, in 1923 Hayes returned to an enthusiastic American public. So great was his influence that he performed for a forcibly integrated audience at Washington's Constitution Hall many years prior to the indignity inflicted there upon Marian Anderson at the hands of the Daughters of the American Revolution.

The first African-American singer to perform with a major American orchestra, Hayes performed with all the major orchestras and conductors of his time, including Koussevitzky, Walter, Stokowski, Monteux, and Klemperer. Among his numerous awards were the Spingarn Medal, awarded in 1924, and the Purple Ribbon, awarded by the French government in 1949. The first of many honorary degrees was awarded him by Fisk University in 1932, the same year in which he married Helen Alzada Mann, with whom he had one child, Africa Franzada Hayes. A scholar and accomplished composer, Hayes accepted a professorship at Boston University in 1950, although he also continued to sing for many years afterward.

—MAURICE B. WHEELER

HEMINGS, SALLY

Sally Hemings (1773–1836), supposed mistress of Thomas Jefferson. Born a quadroon slave, Sally Hemings was the sixth child of John Wayles, of Bermuda Hundred, Va., and his slave concubine, Elizabeth Hemings. Wayles died the year Hemings was born, and she and her five brothers and sisters were inherited by her legitimate, white half-sister Martha Wayles Jefferson, wife of Thomas Jefferson, who would later become third president of the United States. Martha died in 1782, and two years later Thomas Jefferson left for France as ambassador, taking his oldest daughter, also named Martha. In 1787 he sent for

ROLAND HAYES

Hayes was the first African-American singer to perform with a major American orchestra.

PHOTOGRAPHS AND PRINTS DIVISION, SCHOMBURG CENTER FOR RESEARCH IN BLACK CULTURE, THE NEW YORK PUBLIC LIBRARY, ASTOR, LENOX AND TILDEN FOUNDATIONS

his youngest daughter, Maria, and Hemings accompanied her as her nurse. During her stay in France, where she was legally free, Hemings allegedly became Jefferson's mistress. In 1789 she returned with him to Virginia, thereby re-enslaving herself. She remained at Monticello for the rest of her life and between 1790 and 1808 gave birth to seven children, all presumably Jefferson's: Thomas, Edy, Harriet I, Beverly, Harriet II, Madison, and Eston.

In 1802, the journalist James T. Callender, who had worked as a political muckraker, published the story in the *Richmond Recorder*. This article instigated an international political scandal that made Hemings famous and accused Jefferson of hypocrisy, immorality, and miscegenation—the last a crime punishable by fine and imprisonment. Jefferson never refuted this story and did not exile Hemings or her children from Monticello; they were allowed to run away and pass for white at twenty-one. In 1826 he died and freed Madison and Eston in his will, although he never freed Hemings. She was, however, subsequently freed by his legitimate, white daughter Martha.

Jeffersonians, such as Virginius Dabney, deny this story, and the bitter controversy over it persists to the present.

—BARBARA CHASE-RIBOUD

HENDRIX, JAMES MARSHALL "JIMI"

James Marshall "Jimi" Hendrix (November 27, 1942–September 18, 1970), rock guitarist, singer, and songwriter. In a professional career that lasted less than a decade, Jimi Hendrix created music that would establish him as the most innovative and influential guitarist rock music produced.

Born in Seattle, Wash., Hendrix started to play the guitar at age eleven and was playing with local rock groups as a teenager. He left school at sixteen, and with his father's permission, joined the Army as a paratrooper a year later. While in the service he met bass player Billy Cox, with whom he would later join forces as a civilian. Hendrix's Army career ended when he was injured on a practice jump.

Once out of the Army, he hit the "chitlin" circuit as a backup guitarist for a host of popular rock and rhythm-and-blues artists including Little Richard, the Isley Brothers, Curtis Knight, Wilson Pickett, Ike and Tina Turner, King Cur-

tis, and James Brown. During this period, from 1962 to 1964, he began incorporating his trademark crowd-pleasers—playing his guitar with his teeth, behind his back, and between his legs. Early in his career, Hendrix played ambidextrously before he eventually settled on using a right-handed Fender Stratocaster, restrung upside down and played left-handed. He manipulated the tone and volume controls (which were now on top) to make unique effects and sounds. Hendrix's huge hands allowed him a phenomenal reach and range; his ability to play clean leads and distorted rhythm simultaneously remains a musical mystery.

In 1964 Hendrix came to New York, and using the name "Jimmy James," fronted his own band, called the Blue Flames. He became known in New York at the height of the folk music era in the mid-1960s. Holding forth as a solo act at the Cafe Wha?, a basement café on MacDougal Street in Greenwich Village, he also found time to play local venues as a sideman with a group called Curtis Knight and the Squires, and in Wilson Pickett's band, where he met young drummer Buddy Miles. In 1967, Chas Chandler (the bassist of the former Animals) convinced Hendrix to return with him to London. On the promise that he would meet Eric Clapton, Hendrix agreed. In just three weeks in England the Jimi Hendrix Experience was formed with Mitch Mitchell on drums and Noel Redding on bass. "Hey Joe," their first single, went all the way to number six on the British charts in 1967, and an appearance on the British television show "Ready, Steady, Go" attracted wide attention when Hendrix played their new single, "Purple Haze."

The same year, Paul McCartney persuaded the Monterey Pop Festival officials to book Hendrix, despite the fact that his first album had yet to be released. His riveting musical performance ended with his setting his guitar on fire. His action and his performance transformed the twenty-four year old into a rock superstar. Later that year (1967) his debut album *Are You Experienced?* was called by *Guitar Players'* Jas Obrecht "the most revolutionary debut album in rock guitar history."

In 1968 he released his second album, *Axis: Bold As Love*, which contained more of his distinctive sounds in such songs as "Little Wing," "If 6 was 9," and "Castles Made of Sand." His third album, a double set titled *Electric Ladyland*, was released just nine months later. Hendrix created a recording studio of the same name in Greenwich Village, a reflection of his belief that he was connected to a female spirit/muse of fire and electricity.

See also
Jazz

CHESTER HIMES

Novelist Lives Life in the Fast Lane

Chester Himes (July 29, 1909–November 12, 1984), novelist and short story writer. Born in Jefferson City, Mo., the youngest of three sons, he spent his first fourteen years in the South. His mother, née Estelle Bomar, the daughter of former slaves who had achieved considerable success in the construction business, was educated at a black Presbyterian finishing school in North Carolina and taught music from time to time at African-American colleges and academies. Her husband, Joseph Himes, also born of former slaves, grew up in North Carolina poverty but acquired a diploma at Claflin College in Orangeburg, S.C. A skilled blacksmith and wheelwright, he taught mechanical arts at black institutions in Georgia, Missouri, Mississippi, and Arkansas. Both parents appear as thinly disguised characters whose conflicting social and racial views bewilder the protagonist in Himes's autobiographical novel *The Third Generation* (1954).

In 1923 a freak accident blinded Himes's older brother, causing the family to move from Pine Bluff, Ark., to St. Louis to seek specialized medical treatment. Two years later they moved to Cleveland, where Chester graduated from East High School in January 1926. Following graduation he worked as a busboy at a Cleveland hotel, where he suffered a traumatic fall that left him with permanent back and shoulder injuries. In September 1926 he enrolled as a liberal arts student at Ohio State University, but he was expelled the following February for failing grades and unseemly behavior. Thereafter he drifted into a life of crime in the black ghettos of Cleveland and Columbus. In December 1927, he was sentenced to serve twenty years in the Ohio State Penitentiary for armed robbery.

While in prison, Himes began a lifelong career writing fiction; his first stories were printed in African-American publications in early 1932. In 1934 he reached a national audience in *Esquire* for "To What Red Hell," describing the 1930 fire that swept through the Ohio penitentiary, killing more than 330 convicts. He was paroled in 1936, and in August 1937 he married Jean Lucinda Johnson, a longtime friend. From 1936 to 1940 he worked mainly at manual jobs and for the Federal Writers' Project, departing for California in the fall of 1940 in hopes of writing for Hollywood. Repeated rejections at the studios, however, required him to seek work at racially tense California shipyards. These experiences are reflected in several articles he wrote in the 1940s, as well as in two bitter novels, *If He Hollers Let Him Go* (1946) and *Lonely Crusade* (1947). The interethnic, economic, social, and sexual consequences of racism are treated at some length in these books.

From 1945 to 1953 Himes lived mainly in New York and New England; he sailed for France several months after the publication of his prison novel *Cast the First Stone* (1952). For the rest of his life he lived mainly in France and Spain, making only occasional visits to the United States. Much of his subsequent fiction was published first in France before appearing elsewhere. Among his books written abroad were seven Harlem police thrillers involving Cotton Ed Johnson and Grave Digger Jones; one of these won a French literary award in 1958. Two incomplete novels, *Plan B,* dealing with a future race war, and *The Lunatic Fringe* have not yet been printed in the United States. Himes's own favorite among his works was *The Primitive* (1955), depicting an intense, troubled relationship between a black man and a white woman in post-World War II New York. Himes's only published novel with a non-American setting, *A Case of Rape* (1985), focuses on four black men being tried in Paris for the violation and death of a white woman. Because the fictional characters were modeled on well-known African Americans living in Europe, the book caused something of a stir in the expatriate community. Himes's other works written in Europe were *Pinktoes* (1961), an interracial sex comedy about the activities of a celebrated Harlem hostess, and *Run Man Run* (1966), a thriller telling of a black man's flight from a murderous New York policeman. In 1978, Himes obtained a divorce in absentia and married Lesley Packard, an English journalist.

While living in Spain, Himes wrote two volumes of an autobiography, *The Quality of Hurt* (1973) and *My Life of Absurdity* (1976). Toward the end of his life he came to view his writings as being in the absurdist tradition. Racism, he said, made blacks and whites behave absurdly. He envisioned organized violence as the only means of ending racial oppression in America. Because his literary reputation was never as high in the United States as it was in Europe, Himes lived precariously for most of his authorial years, but a resurgence of interest in his writings in the 1970s brought him a measure of financial security. Upon his death in Alicante, Spain, he left a number of unfinished projects.

—EDWARD MARGOLIES

In 1969 Hendrix performed at the Woodstock Festival, the only black performer of his time to penetrate the largely white world of hard and psychedelic rock. He was pressured by black groups to take a more political stance, but Hendrix took no part in formal politics; his political statement was in his music. His electric version of the "Star-Spangled Banner," played at Woodstock, was in itself a political statement.

Later that year Hendrix formed the all-black Band of Gypsys with former Army friend Bill Cox on bass and Buddy Miles on drums. Although the group lasted only a few months, a live performance was captured on the album *Band of Gypsys*. Hendrix's management believed it was a mistake for him to forsake his white rock side, and he was pressured to make an adjustment. Hendrix finally settled on Mitch Mitchell on drums with Billy Cox on bass. They performed at the club Isle of Fehmarn in West Germany on September 6, 1970. Twelve days later Hendrix died in London after complications resulting from barbiturate use.

Though Hendrix's period as a headline performer lasted only three years, his influence on popular music has been considerable. In helping to establish the prime role of the electric guitar soloist, he was an inspiration for several generations of heavy metal musicians. His improvisatory style has inspired both jazz musicians and practitioners of avant-garde "new music."

—DAVID HENDERSON

HINES, EARL
KENNETH "FATHA"

Earl Kenneth "Fatha" Hines (December 28, 1903–April 22, 1983), musician. Because of his influence on the styles of countless other jazz pianists, Earl "Fatha" Hines has often been called "the father of modern jazz piano." Working from a foundation of classical music, blues, novelty piano, and Harlem stride playing, Hines developed a style that combined a linear approach to melody with a stunning independence of the two hands. As a highly successful bandleader, he played an important role in the early careers of such notable jazz musicians as Charlie Parker, Dizzy Gillespie, Billy Eckstine, and Sarah Vaughan. Hines was classically trained as a youngster, and his first major employment came as accompanist for Pittsburgh vocalist Lois Deppe, with whose group he recorded in 1923. He moved to Chicago in early 1925, and for the next four years he played with

groups led by Carroll Dickerson, Erskine Tate, Jimmie Noone, and others. The recordings made by Hines during this period, especially those with trumpeter Louis Armstrong, are among the most celebrated in all of jazz.

In December 1928, Hines took his own band into Chicago's Grand Terrace Ballroom, where he appeared until 1940. He continued to lead his own band until 1947; then in 1948 he joined Louis Armstrong's All-Stars, touring extensively with this group until the autumn of 1951. During the 1950s, Hines worked in relative obscurity on the West Coast, where he played a long residency with a small group at San Francisco's Hangover Club. He moved to California permanently in 1960. In 1964, at the behest of his close friend Stanley Dance, Hines played a triumphant series of concerts at New York's Little Theater. During the 1960s and '70s, he toured Europe and recorded extensively. Playing mainly with a small group that featured vocalist Marva Josie, Hines continued performing regularly until the weekend before his death.

—JEFFREY TAYLOR

HINES, GREGORY

Gregory Hines (February 14, 1946–), tap dancer. Born in New York City, Gregory Hines began dancing at age three and turned professional when he was five. For fifteen years he performed with his older brother Maurice as "The Hines Kids," garnering success in the dwindling world of vaudeville and in night clubs. His father, Maurice, Sr., joined his sons' act as a drummer in 1964, changing the act's name to "Hines, Hines & Dad." Although Broadway teacher and choreographer Henry Letang created their first routines, they learned their technique from older tap masters, becoming the direct inheritors of the great black tap dance traditions. Hoofers like Howard "Sandman" Sims would tutor them between shows; these men became their heroes and mentors, their tap professors in the unofficial institutions that existed in theaters and clubs, as well as in such places as the alleyway of Harlem's Apollo Theater.

In the early 1970s, Hines decided to leave the family tap team, "retiring" (as he says) to Venice, Calif., where he turned his attention to guitar and formed the jazz-rock ensemble Severance in 1973. He released a record album of original songs, then returned to the New York stage and tap dance in the late 1970s. His Broadway debut

Many of tap's choreographic structures reflect the formal musical structures of blues, ragtime or dixieland, swing, bebop, and cool jazz.

PAGE 667

in *Eubie* (1978), his performance in *Comin' Up-town* (1979), and his starring role in *Sophisticated Ladies* (1980–1981) earned him three Tony nominations. He has received two Emmy awards for his performances in television specials and has appeared in the movies *Wolfen* (1981), *The Cotton Club* (1984), *White Nights* (1985), *Running Scared* (1986), *Off Limits* (1988), *Tap* (1989), *A Rage in Harlem* (1991), and *Eve of Destruction* (1991). In 1988 Hines released a well-received solo debut album, *That Girl Wants to Dance with Me.* In 1989 he hosted the documentary *Tap: Dance in America* on public television and appeared in a production of *Twelfth Night* performed in Central Park by New York's Public Theater. In 1992, Hines earned a Tony Award as best actor in a Broadway musical for his leading role as Jelly Roll Morton in *Jelly's Last Jam.*

Such fame has made Hines an especially important influence on the younger generation of male tap dancers. Like a jazz musician who ornaments a melody with improvisational riffs, Hines improvises within the frame of the dance. His "Improvography" demands the percussive phrasing of a composer, the rhythms of a drummer, and the lines of a dancer. Hines, like avant-garde jazz artists, purposely fractures normal tempos, breaking free of the regular rhythms of musical phrasing. He also updates tap by performing on a special acoustic stage where his taps are highly amplified. The leading tap dancer of his generation, Hines is a generous artist and teacher, conscious of his importance as a role model for the next generation of tap artists.

—CONSTANCE VALIS HILL

HOLDER, GEOFFREY

Geoffrey Holder (August 20, 1930–), dancer, choreographer, and painter. Born in Port-of-Spain, Trinidad, Geoffrey Holder was one of four children in a middle-class family. He attended Queens Royal College, a secondary school in Port-of-Spain, and received lessons in painting and dancing from his older brother Boscoe.

When Holder was seven, he debuted with his brother's dance troupe, the Holder Dance Company. When Boscoe moved to London a decade later, Geoffrey Holder took over direction of the company. In 1952, Agnes de Mille saw the group perform on the island of St. Thomas, U.S. Virgin Islands, and invited Holder to audition for impresario Sol Hurok in New York City. Already an accomplished painter, Holder sold twenty of his paintings to pay for passage for the company to New York City in 1954. When Hurok decided not to sponsor a tour for the company, Holder taught classes at the Katherine Dunham School to support himself. His impressive height (6′6″) and formal attire at a dance recital attracted the attention of producer Arnold Saint Subber who arranged for him to play Samedi, a Haitian conjurer, in Harold Arlen's 1954 Broadway musical *House of Flowers.* During the run, Holder met fellow dancer Carmen deLavallade, and the two married in 1955. During 1955 and 1956 Holder was a principal dancer with the Metropolitan Opera Ballet in New York. He also appeared with his troupe, Geoffrey Holder and Company, through 1960. The multitalented Holder continued to paint throughout this time, and in 1957 he was awarded a Guggenheim Fellowship in painting.

In 1957 Holder acted in an all-black production of *Waiting for Godot.* Although the show was short-lived, Holder continued to act, and in 1961 he had his first film role in the movie *All Night Long,* a modern retelling of *Othello.* His career as a

MULTITALENTED DANCER

Geoffrey Holder continued to paint while he was a principal dancer with the Metropolitan Opera Ballet in New York. PHOTOGRAPHS AND PRINTS DIVISION, SCHOMBURG CENTER FOR RESEARCH IN BLACK CULTURE, THE NEW YORK PUBLIC LIBRARY, ASTOR, LENOX AND TILDEN FOUNDATIONS

character actor flourished with appearances in *Everything You Always Wanted to Know About Sex* (1972), *Live and Let Die* (1973), and as Punjab in *Annie* (1982).

Holder has also been an active director. His direction of the Broadway musical *The Wiz* (1975), an all-black retelling of *The Wizard of Oz,* earned him Tony Awards for best director and best costume design. In 1978 he directed and choreographed the lavish Broadway musical *Timbuktu!*. He has choreographed pieces for many companies including the Alvin Ailey American Dance Theater, for which he choreographed *Prodigal Prince* (1967), a dance based on the life of a Haitian primitive painter. Dance Theater of Harlem has in its repertory Holder's 1957 piece *Bele,* which like most of his work combines African and European elements.

Holder cowrote (with Tom Harshman) and illustrated the book *Black Gods, Green Islands* (1959), a collection of Caribbean folklore; and *Geoffrey Holder's Caribbean Cookbook* was published in 1973. He also gained widespread recognition in the late 1970s and 1980s for his lively commercials. In 1992 Holder appeared in the film *Boomerang* with Eddie Murphy. He resides in New York, where he continues to paint, choreograph, and act.

—ZITA ALLEN

HOLIDAY, BILLIE

Billie Holiday (April 7, 1915–July 17, 1959), singer. Born Eleanora Fagan in Philadelphia, the daughter of Sadie Fagan and jazz guitarist Clarence Holiday, Billie Holiday grew up in Baltimore and endured a traumatic childhood of poverty and abuse. As a teenager, she changed her name (after screen star Billie Dove) and came to New York, where she began singing in speakeasies, influenced, she said, by Louis Armstrong and Bessie Smith. In 1933 she was spotted performing in Harlem by critic-producer John Hammond, who brought her to Columbia Records, where she recorded classic sessions with such jazz greats as pianist Teddy Wilson and tenor saxophonist Lester Young.

Following grueling tours with the big bands of Count Basie and Artie Shaw, Holiday became a solo act in 1938, achieving success with appearances at Cafe Society in Greenwich Village, and with her 1939 recording of the dramatic antilynching song "Strange Fruit." Performing regularly at intimate clubs along New York's Fifty-second Street, she gained a sizable income and a reputation as a peerless singer of torch songs. A heroin addict, she was arrested for narcotics possession in 1947 and spent ten months in prison, which subsequently made it illegal for her to work in New York clubs. Yet despite such hardships and her deteriorating health and voice, she continued to perform and make memorable, sometimes challenging recordings on Decca, Verve, and Columbia until her death in 1959.

Although riddled with inaccuracies, Holiday's 1956 autobiography, *Lady Sings the Blues,* remains a fascinating account of her mercurial personality. A 1972 film of the same title, starring pop singer Diana Ross, further distorted her life but introduced her to a new generation of listeners. Holiday was one of America's finest and most influen-

Played in every country of the globe, jazz is perhaps twentieth-century America's most influential cultural creation.

PAGE 378

WHAT A VOICE

Shown here in 1949, Billie Holiday was known for the fluttering timbre and rhythmic grace of her singing voice. PRINTS AND PHOTOGRAPHS DIVISION, LIBRARY OF CONGRESS

Lena Horne (June 30, 1917–), singer and actress. Born in New York, Lena Horne accompanied her mother on a tour of the Lafayette Stock Players as a child and appeared in a production of *Madame X* when she was six years old. She received her musical education in the preparatory school of Fort Valley College, Ga. and in the public schools of Brooklyn. Horne began her career at the age of sixteen as a dancer in the chorus line at the Cotton Club in Harlem. She also became a favorite at Harlem's Apollo Theatre, and was among the first African-American entertainers to perform in "high-class" nightclubs. Appearing on stages and ballrooms from the Fairmont in San Francisco to the Empire Room at the Waldorf-Astoria in New York, Horne was among the group of black stars—including Sammy Davis, Jr., Eartha Kitt, and Diahann Carroll—who had musicals especially fashioned for them on Broadway.

Horne made her first recording in 1936 with Noble Sissle and recorded extensively as a soloist and with others. She toured widely in the United States and Europe. In 1941 she became the first black performer to sign a contract with a major studio (MGM). Her first film role was in *Panama Hattie* (1942), which led to roles in *Cabin in the Sky* (1942), *Stormy Weather* (1943), *I Dood It* (1943), *Thousands Cheer* (1943), *Broadway Rhythm* (1944), *Two Girls and a Sailor* (1944), *Ziegfeld Follies of 1945* and *1946*, *The Duchess of Idaho* (1950), and *The Wiz* (1978). Horne was blacklisted during the McCarthy era of the early 1950s, when her friendship with Paul Robeson, her interracial marriage, and her interest in African freedom movements made her politically suspect. Her Broadway musicals include *Blackbirds of 1939*, *Jamaica* (1957), and the successful one-woman Broadway show *Lena Horne: The Lady and Her Music* (1981). The record album of the latter musical won her a Grammy Award as best female pop vocalist in 1981.

Horne's spectacular beauty and sultry voice helped to make her the first nationally celebrated black female vocalist. Her powerful and expressive voice is perhaps captured best in the title song of *Stormy Weather*. In 1984 she was a recipient of the Kennedy Center honors for lifetime achievement in the arts. She published two autobiographies: *In Person: Lena Horne* (1950) and *Lena* (1965).

—JAMES E. MUMFORD

tial jazz singers. Her voice was light, with a limited range, but her phrasing, in the manner of a jazz instrumentalist, places her among the most consummate of jazz musicians. She was distinguished by her impeccable timing, her ability to transform song melodies through improvisation, and her ability to render lyrics with absolute conviction. While she was not a blues singer, her performances were infused with the same stark depth of feeling that characterizes the blues.

—BUD KLIMENT

HUDSON, HOSEA

Hosea Hudson (1898–1988), union leader and communist activist. Born into an impoverished sharecropping family in Wilkes County in the eastern Georgia black belt, Hudson became a plowhand at ten, which sharply curtailed his schooling. The combination of a boll-weevil infestation and a violent altercation with his brother-in-law prompted Hudson in 1923 to move to Atlanta, where he worked as a common laborer in a railroad roundhouse. A year later he moved to Birmingham, Ala., and commenced his career as an iron molder.

Although he remained a faithful churchgoer, Hudson harbored persistent doubts about God's goodness and power, given the oppression of African Americans as workers and as Negroes. As a working-class black, however, he lacked a focus for his discontent until the Communist Party of the U.S.A. (CPUSA) began organizing in Birmingham in 1930. In the wake of the conviction of the Scottsboro boys and the Camp Hill massacre, both in Alabama in 1931, Hudson joined the CPUSA. Within a year he had lost his job at the Stockham foundry. Although he was able to earn irregular wages through odd jobs and iron molding under assumed names, much of the burden of family support in the 1930s fell on his wife, who never forgave him for putting the welfare of the Communist party before that of his wife and child.

During the Great Depression, Hudson was active with a series of organizations in and around the CPUSA. He helped the Unemployed Coun-

See also

Jazz

cils secure relief payments and fight evictions on behalf of the poor. In his first trip outside the South, he spent ten weeks in New York State at the CPUSA Party National Training School in 1934, during which he learned to read and write. As a party cadre in Atlanta from 1934 to 1936, he worked with neighborhood organizations and helped investigate the lynching of Lint Shaw. Returning to Birmingham in 1937, he worked on the Works Project Administration (WPA), served as vice president of the Birmingham and Jefferson County locals of the Workers Alliance, and founded the Right to Vote Club (which earned him a key to the city of Birmingham in 1980 as a pioneer in the struggle for black civil rights).

After the creation of the Congress of Industrial Organizations, Hudson joined the campaign to organize unorganized workers. As the demand for labor during World War II eased his way back into the foundries, he became recording secretary of Steel Local 1489, then organized United Steel Workers Local 2815. He remained president of that local from 1942 to 1947, when he was stripped of leadership and blacklisted for being a communist. He was underground in Atlanta and New York City from 1950 to 1956, during the height of the Cold War and McCarthyism. Imbued with a justified sense of the historical importance of his life, Hudson initiated two books on his experiences: *Black Worker in the Deep South* (New York, 1972) and *The Narrative of Hosea Hudson* (Cambridge, Mass., 1979). Active in the Coalition of Black Trades Unionists until his health failed in the mid-1980s, Hudson died in Gainesville, Fla., in 1988.

—NELL IRVIN PAINTER

HUGHES, LANGSTON

Langston Hughes (February 1, 1902–May 22, 1967), writer. James Langston Hughes was born in Joplin, Mo., and grew up in Lawrence, Kans., mainly with his grandmother, Mary Langston, whose first husband had died in John Brown's band at Harpers Ferry and whose second, Hughes's grandfather, had also been a radical abolitionist. Hughes's mother, Carrie Langston Hughes, occasionally wrote poetry and acted; his father, James Nathaniel Hughes, studied law, then emigrated to Mexico around 1903. After a year (1915–1916) in Lincoln, Ill., Hughes moved to Cleveland, where he attended high school (1916–1920). He then spent a year with his father in Mexico. In June 1921, he published a poem

that was to become celebrated, "The Negro Speaks of Rivers," in the *Crisis* magazine. Enrolling at Columbia University in New York in 1921, he withdrew after a year. He traveled down the west coast of Africa as a mess man on a ship (1923), washed dishes in a Paris nightclub (1924), and traveled in Italy and the Mediterranean before returning to spend a year (1925) in Washington, D.C.

Poems in journals such as the *Crisis* and *Opportunity* led to Hughes's recognition as perhaps the most striking new voice in African-American verse. Steeped in black American culture, his poems revealed his unswerving admiration for blacks, especially the poor. He was particularly inventive in fusing the rhythms of jazz and blues, as well as black speech, with traditional forms of poetry. In 1926 he published his first book of verse, *The Weary Blues,* followed by *Fine Clothes to the Jew* (1927), which was attacked in the black press for its emphasis on the blues culture. A major essay, "The Negro Artist and the Racial Mountain," expressed his determination to make black culture the foundation of his art. In 1926, he enrolled at historically black Lincoln University, and graduated in 1929. With the support of a wealthy but volatile patron, Mrs. Charlotte Osgood Mason (also known as "Godmother"), he wrote his first novel, *Not Without Laughter* (1930). The collapse of this relationship deeply disturbed Hughes, who evidently loved Mrs. Mason but resented her imperious demands on him. After several weeks in Haiti in 1931, he undertook a reading tour to mainly black audiences, starting in the South and ending in the West. He then spent a year (1932–1933) in the Soviet Union, where he wrote several poems influenced by radical socialism, including "Goodbye Christ," about religious hypocrisy. In Carmel, Calif. (1933–1934), he wrote most of the short stories in *The Ways of White Folks* (1934). After a few months in Mexico following the death of his father there, Hughes moved to Oberlin, Ohio.

In New York, his play *Mulatto,* about miscegenation in the South, opened on Broadway in 1935 to hostile reviews, but enjoyed a long run. Several other plays by Hughes were produced in the 1930s at the Karamu Playhouse in Cleveland. He spent several months as a war correspondent in Spain during 1937. Returning to New York in 1938, he founded the Harlem Suitcase Theater, which staged his radical drama *Don't You Want to Be Free?* In 1939, desperately needing money, he worked on a Hollywood film, *Way Down South,* which was criticized for its benign depiction of

*I swear to the Lord
I still can't see
Why Democracy
Means
Everybody but me.*

LANGSTON HUGHES
THE BLACK MAN SPEAKS, IN
JIM CROW'S LAST STAND, 1943

See also
Harlem Renaissance
Literature

357

slavery. However, he was able to settle various debts and write an autobiography, *The Big Sea* (1940).

In 1940, when a religious group picketed one of his appearances, Hughes repudiated "Goodbye Christ" and his main ties to the left. In *Shakespeare in Harlem* (1942) he returned to writing poems about blacks and the blues. After two years in California, he returned to New York. Late in 1942, in the *Chicago Defender,* he began a weekly newspaper column that ran for more than twenty years. In 1943 he introduced its most popular feature, a character called Jesse B. Semple, or Simple, an urban black everyman of intense racial consciousness but also with a delightfully offbeat sense of humor. In 1947, his work as lyricist with Kurt Weill and Elmer Rice on the Broadway musical play *Street Scene* enabled him finally to buy a home and settle down in Harlem. Hughes, who never married, lived there with an old family friend, Toy Harper, and her husband, Emerson Harper, a musician.

As a writer, Hughes worked in virtually all genres, though he saw himself mainly as a poet. In *Fields of Wonder* (1947), *One-Way Ticket* (1949), and *Montage of a Dream Deferred* (1951), he used the new bebop jazz rhythms in his poetry to capture the mood of an increasingly troubled Harlem. With Mercer Cook, he translated the novel *Gouverneurs de la Rosée* (*Masters of the Dew,* 1947) by Jacques Roumain of Haiti; he also translated poems by Nicolás Guillén of Cuba (*Cuba Libre,* 1948), Federico García Lorca of Spain (1951), and Gabriela Mistral of Chile (*Selected Poems,* 1957). The first of five collections of Simple sketches, *Simple Speaks His Mind,* appeared in 1950, and another collection of short stories, *Laughing to Keep from Crying,* came in 1952. Working first with composer William Grant Still and then with Jan Meyerowitz, Hughes composed opera libretti and other texts to be set to music.

Right-wing groups, which were anti-Communist and probably also motivated by racism, steadily attacked Hughes—despite his denials—for his alleged membership in the Communist party. In 1953, forced to appear before Sen. Joseph McCarthy's investigating committee, he conceded that some of his radical writing had been misguided. Criticized by some socialists, he pressed on with his career, and later toured Africa and elsewhere for the State Department. He published about a dozen books for children on a variety of topics, including jazz, Africa, and the

Caribbean. With the photographer Roy DeCarava he published an acclaimed book of pictures accompanied by a narrative, *The Sweet Flypaper of Life* (1955). His second volume of autobiography, *I Wonder as I Wander,* came in 1956.

Perhaps the most innovative of Hughes's later work came in drama, especially his gospel plays such as *Black Nativity* (1961) and *Jericho-Jim Crow* (1964). He was also an important editor. He published (with Arna Bontemps) *Poetry of the Negro, 1746–1949* (1949), as well as *An African Treasury* (1960), *New Negro Poets: U.S.A.* (1964), and *The Book of Negro Humor* (1966). Hughes was widely recognized as the most representative African-American writer and perhaps the most original of black poets. In 1961, he was admitted to the National Institute of Arts and Letters. He died in New York City.

—ARNOLD RAMPERSAD

HURSTON, ZORA NEALE

Zora Neale Hurston (c. 1891–January 28, 1960), folklorist. Zora Neale Hurston was born and grew up in Eatonville, Fla., the first black incorporated town in America. (Her exact date of birth is uncertain. She claimed to be born in either 1901 or 1910, but a brother thinks it was as early as 1891.) Her father, a carpenter and Baptist preacher and a signer of the town's charter, was elected mayor three terms in succession. Her mother, formerly a country schoolteacher, taught Sunday school but spent most of her time raising her eight children. In Eatonville, unlike most of the South at the turn of the century, African Americans were not demoralized by the constant bombardment of poverty and racial hatred, and Hurston grew up surrounded by a vibrant and creative secular and religious black culture. It was here she learned the dialect, songs, folktales, and superstitions that are at the center of her works. Her stories focus on the lives and relationships between black people within their communities.

The untimely death of Hurston's mother in 1904 disrupted her economically and emotionally stable home life, and a year later, at age fourteen, she left home for a job as a maid and wardrobe assistant in a traveling Gilbert and Sullivan company. She left the company in Baltimore, found other work, and attended high school there. In 1918 she graduated from Morgan Academy, the

RICHARD HUNT

Sculptor Experiments with Properties of Metal

Richard Hunt (September 12, 1935–), sculptor, graphic artist, educator. Born and raised in Chicago, Richard Hunt saw his talent nurtured early in children's classes at the Art Institute of Chicago (AIC), which he attended from age thirteen. That institution was central to his development as a sculptor. There in 1953 he saw the work of Julio Gonzalez, a Spanish sculptor of welded metal whose technique differed radically from the traditional western methods of cast sculpture. Gonzalez' impact was so great that Hunt, still a high school student, built a studio in the basement of his father's barbershop to begin sculpting. He later taught himself to weld in two years. Also at the AIC, Hunt encountered the work of Richmond Barthé, an African-American sculptor who had graduated from the School of the AIC in 1929. Although their styles differed—Barthé modeled naturalistic representations of the human figure, while Hunt was more abstract—Hunt found the older artist to be an inspiration. In 1953, Hunt enrolled in the School of the AIC on a scholarship from the Chicago Public School Art Society. Since the school had limited welding equipment, he taught himself by talking to professional metalworkers and by taking metalcraft classes where he made jewelry. He graduated four years later with a degree in art education and was awarded a travel grant to visit England, Spain, France, and Italy.

If the school taught him techniques, another institution prompted him with ideas that have informed his entire career. From 1951 to 1957, Hunt worked part-time in the zoological experimental laboratory at the University of Chicago. From his earliest work there is a propensity for images that are biomorphic, suggesting tentacles, bones, wings, thoraxes, antennae, and tendons. One of these early works, *Arachne*, was acquired for the permanent collection of the Museum of Modern Art (MoMA) in New York in 1957, while he was still a student. His first one-person show followed in the same city the next year. Exhibitions and purchases from major museums and universities in the years immediately following his graduation indicate his early aesthetic maturity.

This early work used discarded metal parts, which Hunt welded into small-scale zoomorphic and anthropomorphic shapes whose gestures paralleled the "drawing in space" that could be found among other sculptors of the period, including David Smith,

another of his influences. The angular armatures and calligraphic forms echoed the gestures of Abstract Expressionist painting. Other sources for this style were the metal African sculpture he had seen with his mother on childhood visits to the Field Museum of Natural History, as well as Greek, Roman, and Renaissance sculpture. By the late 1960s, Hunt's reputation led to numerous commissions for public sculpture. He resolved the resultant change to a larger scale by increasing the mass of his forms to give them a stronger visual presence in the out-of-doors (and to accommodate their being cast from bronze and brass as well as being welded from aluminum and cor-ten steel). Works appeared not as branch or limblike extensions, but as congealed extrusions from some geological source. The works are often designed to protrude from their own rectilinear bases as if they are being manipulated by some overwhelming force. Although different in style, this work maintains Hunt's interest in natural processes of growth and change presented, paradoxically, in the inert medium of metal. This second phase of Hunt's career has led to more than seventy commissions of public sculpture across the country in airports, schools and universities, plazas, hospitals, churches, and synagogues.

Hunt has been included in many national and international exhibitions since he began showing in 1955. Retrospectives of his career were held in 1967 at the Milwaukee Art Center and in 1971 at MoMA and at the AIC. His awards include a Guggenheim Fellowship in the year 1962–1963 and a fellowship at the Tamarind Lithography Workshop in Los Angeles in 1965. In 1964 he was a visiting professor at Yale University. In 1966 he was included in the First World Festival of Negro Arts in Dakar, Senegal. His appointments include the Illinois Arts Council (1970–1975); the National Council on the Arts (1968–1974); board of trustees, Museum of Contemporary Art (Chicago, 1975–1979); board of governors, Skowhegan School of Painting and Sculpture (1979–1984); commissioner, National Museum of American Art, Smithsonian Institution (1980–1988); advisory committee, Getty Center for Education in the Arts (1984–1988); director, International Sculpture Center, (1984–); president, founder, Chicago Sculpture Society (1985–1989); and board of governors, School of the Art Institute of Chicago (1985–1989).

—HELEN M. SHANNON

See also
Alice Walker

high school division of Morgan State University, and entered Howard University in Washington, D.C., where she took courses intermittently until 1924. She studied there with poet Georgia Douglas Johnson and philosopher Alain Locke. Her first story, "John Redding Goes to Sea" (1921), appeared in *Stylus*, Howard's literary magazine.

Hurston arrived in New York in 1925, at the height of the Harlem Renaissance. She soon became active among the group of painters, musicians, sculptors, entertainers, and writers who came from across the country to be there. She also studied at Barnard College under the anthropologist Franz Boas and graduated with a B.A. in 1928. Between 1929 and 1931, with support from a wealthy white patron, Mrs. Osgood Mason, Hurston returned south and began collecting folklore in Florida and Alabama. In 1934 she received a Rosenwald fellowship and in 1936 and 1937 Guggenheim fellowships that enabled her to study folk religions in Haiti and Jamaica. She was a member of the American Folklore Society, the Anthropological Society, the Ethnological Society, the New York Academy of Sciences, and the American Association for the Advancement of Science. From her extensive research Hurston published *Mules and Men* (1935), the first collection (seventy folktales) of black folklore to appear by a black American. *Tell My Horse* (1938), a second folklore volume, came after her travels to the Caribbean. Her most academic study, *The Florida Negro* (1938), written for the Florida Federal Workers Project, was never published.

While Franz Boas and Mrs. Mason stimulated Hurston's anthropological interests that gave her an analytical perspective on black culture that was unique among black writers of her time, she was fully vested in the creative life of the cultural movement as well. Her close friends included Carl Van Vechten, Alaine Locke, Langston Hughes, and Wallace Thurman, with whom she coedited and published the only issue of the journal *Fire!!* Appearing in November 1926, its supporters saw it as a forum for younger writers who wanted to break with traditional black ideas. Ironically, *Fire!!* was destroyed by a fire in Thurman's apartment.

Hurston's first novel, *Jonah's Gourd Vine* (1934), reveals the lyric quality of her writing, her skillfulness with and mastery of dialect. The story is about a Baptist preacher with a personal weakness that leads him to an unfortunate end. But Hurston's protagonist, modeled on her father, is a gifted poet/philosopher with an enviable imagination and speech filled with the imagery of black folk culture. He is also a vulnerable person who lacks the self-awareness to comprehend his dilemma; thus, his tragedy.

For its beauty and richness of language, *Their Eyes Were Watching God* (1937), the first novel by a black woman to explore the inner life of a black woman, is Hurston's art at its best. Her most popular work, it traces the development of the heroine from innocence to her realization that she has the power to control her own life. An acknowledged classic since its recovery in the 1970s, it has been applauded by both black and white women scholars as the first black feminist novel. *Moses, Man of the Mountain* (1939), Hurston's third and most ambitious novel, makes of the biblical Israelite deliverance from Egypt an exploration of the black transition from slavery to freedom. Taking advantage of the pervasiveness of the Moses mythology in African and diaspora folklore and culture, Hurston removes Moses from Scripture, demystifies him, and relocates him in African-American culture, where he is a conjure man possessed with magical powers and folk wisdom. The novel tells the story of a people struggling to liberate themselves from the heritage of bondage. In *Seraph on the Suwanee* (1948), Hurston's last and least successful work, she turns away from black folk culture to explore the lives of poor white Southerners. This story focuses on a husband and wife trapped in conventional sexual roles in a marriage that dooms to failure the wife's search for herself.

Dust Tracks on a Road (1942), Hurston's autobiography, is the most controversial of her books; some of her staunchest admirers consider it a failure. Critics who complain about this work focus on its lack of self-revelation, the inaccurate personal information Hurston gives about herself, and the significant roles that whites play in the text. Other critics praise it as Hurston's attempt to invent an alternative narrative self to the black identity inherited from the slave narrative tradition. Poised between the black and white worlds, not as victim of either but participant-observer in both, her narrative self in *Dust Tracks* presents positive and negative qualities of each. From this perspective, *Dust Tracks* is a revisionary text, a revolutionary alternative women's narrative inscribed into the discourse of black autobiography.

Reviews of Hurston's books in her time were mixed. White reviewers, often ignorant of black culture, praised the richness of her language but misunderstood the works and characterized them as simple and unpretentious. Black critics in the 1930s and 1940s, in journals like the Crisis, objected most to her focus on black folk life. Their most frequent criticism was the absence from her works of racial terror, exploitation, and misery. Richard Wright expressed anger at the "minstrel image" he claimed Hurston promoted in *Their Eyes Were Watching God.* None of her books sold well enough while she was alive to relieve her lifetime of financial stress.

Hurston and her writings disappeared from public view from the late 1940s until the early 1970s. Interest in her revived after writer Alice Walker went to Florida "in search of Zora" in 1973, and reassembled the puzzle of Hurston's later life. Walker discovered that Hurston returned to the South in the 1950s and, still trying to write, supported herself with menial jobs. Without resources and suffering a stroke, in 1959 she entered a welfare home in Fort Pierce, Fla., where she died in 1960 and was buried in an unmarked grave. On her pilgrimage, Walker marked a site where Hurston might be buried with a headstone that pays tribute to "a genius of the South." Following her rediscovery, a once-neglected Hurston rose into literary prominence and enjoys acclaim as the essential forerunner of black women writers who came after her.

—NELLIE Y. MCKAY

See also

Literature

I

ISLAM

Originating as a religion in the seventh century A.D. through the revelations, visions, and messages received by the prophet Muhammad in Arabia, Islam spread rapidly throughout North Africa. Black African converts to Islam were called "Moors," and not only helped conquer southern Spain but also gained a reputation as skilled navigators and sailors. The Moors who accompanied the Spanish explorers in the fifteenth and sixteenth centuries were among the first to introduce the Islamic religion to the Americas. However, the greater impact of Islam in British North America occurred with the arrival of African Muslims (adherents of Islam) from the Islamized parts of West Africa who had been captured in warfare and sold to the European traders of the Atlantic slave trade.

The presence of Muslim slaves has been ignored by most historians, who have tended to focus on the conversion of Africans to Christianity or on the attempts to preserve aspects of traditional African religions. Yet their presence has been attested to by narrative and documentary accounts, some of which were written in Arabic. Yarrow Mamout, Job Ben Solomon, and Lamine Jay arrived in colonial Maryland in the 1730s. Abdul Rahaman, Mohammed Kaba, Bilali, Salih Bilali, and "Benjamin Cochrane" were enslaved in the late eighteenth century. Omar ibn Said, Kebe, and Abu Bakr were brought to southern plantations in the early 1800s; two others, Mahommah Baquaqua and Mohammed Ali ben Said, came to the United States as freemen about 1850 (Austin 1984, p. 9). Abdul Rahaman, a Muslim prince of the Fula people in Timbo, Fouta Djallon, became a slave for close to twenty years in Natchez, Miss., before he was freed; he eventually returned to Africa through the aid of abolitionist groups.

Court records in South Carolina described African slaves who prayed to Allah and refused to eat pork. Missionaries in Georgia and South Carolina observed that some Muslim slaves attempted to blend Islam and Christianity by identifying God with Allah and Muhammad with Jesus. A conservative estimate is that there were close to 30,000 Muslim slaves who came from Islamic-dominated ethnic groups such as the Mandingo, Fula, Gambians, Senegambians, Senegalese, Cape Verdians, and Sierra Leoneans in West Africa (Austin 1984, p. 38). However, in spite of the much larger presence of African Muslims in North America than previously thought, the Islamic influence did not survive the impact of the slave period. Except for the documents left by the Muslims named above, only scattered traces and family memories of Islam remained among African Americans, such as Alex Haley's ancestral Muslim character, Kunta Kinte of the Senegambia, in his novel *Roots.*

By the late nineteenth century, black Christian churches had become so dominant in the religious and social life of black communities that only a few African-American leaders who had traveled to Africa knew anything about Islam. Contacts between immigrant Arab groups and African Americans were almost nonexistent at this time. After touring Liberia and South Africa, Bishop Henry McNeal Turner of the African Methodist Episcopal church recognized the "dignity, majesty, and consciousness of [the] worth of Muslims" (Austin 1984, p. 24; Hill and Kilson 1971, p. 63). But it was Edward Wilmot Blyden, the West Indian educator, Christian missionary, and minister for the government of Liberia, who became the most enthusiastic supporter of Islam for African Americans. Blyden, who began teaching Arabic in Liberia in 1867, wrote a book, *Christianity, Islam and the Negro Race* (1888), in which he concluded that Islam had a much better record of racial equality than Christianity did—a conclusion that struck him especially after he compared the racial attitudes of Christian and Muslim missionaries whom he had encountered in Africa. Islam, he felt, could also be a positive force in improving life conditions for African Americans in the United States. Though he lectured extensively, Blyden did not become a leader of a social movement that could establish Islam effectively in America. That task awaited the prophets and forceful personalities of the next century.

The massive rural-to-urban migrations by more than four million African Americans during

See also

Nation of Islam

the first decades of the twentieth century provided the conditions for the rise of a number of black militant and separatist movements, including a few that had a tangential relationship to Islam. These "proto-Islamic" movements combined the religious trappings of Islam—a few rituals, symbols, or items of dress—with a core message of black nationalism.

In 1913 Timothy Drew, a black deliveryman and street-corner preacher from North Carolina, founded the first Moorish Holy Temple of Science in Newark, N.J. Rejecting Christianity as the white man's religion, Drew took advantage of the widespread discontent among the newly arrived black migrants and rapidly established temples in Detroit, Harlem, Chicago, Pittsburgh, and cities across the South. Calling himself Prophet Noble Drew Ali, he constructed a message aimed at the confusion about names, national origins, and self-identity among black people. He declared that they were not "Negroes" but "Asiatics," or "Moors," or "Moorish Americans" whose true home was Morocco, and their true religion was Moorish Science, whose doctrines were elaborated in a sixty-page book, written by Ali, called the *Holy Koran* (which should not be confused with the Qur'an of orthodox Islam).

Prophet Ali issued "Nationality and Identification Cards" stamped with the Islamic symbol of the star and crescent. There was a belief that these identity cards would prevent harm from the white man, or European, who was in any case soon to be destroyed, with "Asiatics" then in control. As the movement spread from the East Coast to the Midwest, Ali's followers in Chicago practiced "bumping days," on which aggressive male members would accost whites on the sidewalks and surreptitiously bump them out of the way—a practice that reversed the Jim Crow custom of southern whites forcing blacks off the sidewalks. After numerous complaints to the police, Noble Drew Ali ordered a halt to the disorders and urged his followers to exercise restraint. "Stop flashing your cards before Europeans," he said, "as this only causes confusion. We did not come to cause confusion; our work is to uplift the nation" (Lincoln 1961, p. 54). The headquarters of the movement was moved to Chicago in 1925.

The growth of the Moorish Science movement was accelerated during the post–World War I years by the recruitment of better-educated but less dedicated members who quickly assumed leadership positions. These new leaders began to grow rich by exploiting the less educated membership of the movement and selling them herbs,

magical charms, potions, and literature. When Ali intervened to prevent further exploitation, he was pushed aside, and this interference eventually led to his mysterious death in 1929. Noble Drew Ali died of a beating; whether it was done by the police when he was in their custody or by dissident members of the movement is not known. After his death, the movement split into numerous smaller factions with rival leaders who claimed to be "reincarnations" of Noble Drew Ali.

The Moorish Science Temple movement has survived, with active temples in Chicago, Detroit, New York, and a few other cities. In present-day Moorish temples, membership is restricted to "Asiatics," or non-Caucasians, who have rejected their former identities as "colored" or "Negro." The term *el* or *bey* is attached to the name of each member as a sign of his or her Asiatic status and inward transformation. Friday is the Sabbath for the Moors, and they have adopted a mixture of Islamic and Christian rituals in worship. They face Mecca when they pray, three times a day, but they have also incorporated Jesus and the singing of transposed hymns into their services. The Moorish Science Temple movement was the first proto-Islamic group of African Americans, and helped to pave the way for more orthodox Islamic practices and beliefs. Many Moors were among the earliest converts to the Nation of Islam, or Black Muslim movement.

While the Moors were introducing aspects of Islam to black communities, sometime around 1920 the Ahmadiyyah movement sent missionaries to the United States, who began to proselytize among African Americans. Founded in India in 1889 by Mizra Ghulam Ahmad, a self-proclaimed Madhi, or Muslim messiah, the Ahmadiyyahs were a heterodox sect of Islam that was concerned with interpretations of the Christian gospel, including the Second Coming. The Ahmadiyyahs also emphasized some of the subtle criticisms of Christianity that were found in the Qur'an such as the view that Jesus did not really die on the cross (Surah 4:157–159).

As an energetic missionary movement, the Ahmadiyyah first sent missionaries to West Africa, then later to the diaspora in the United States. Sheik Deen of the Ahmadiyyah mission was influential in converting Walter Gregg, who became one of the first African-American converts to Islam and changed his name to Wali Akram. After a period of studying the Qur'an and Arabic with the sheik, Akram founded the First Cleveland Mosque in 1933. He taught Islam to several generations of Midwesterners, including

See also

Malcolm X

many African Americans. He also worked as a missionary in India. Although it was relatively unknown and unnoticed, the Ahmadiyyah mission movement is significant in that it provided one of the first contacts for African Americans with a worldwide sectarian Islamic group, whose traditions were more orthodox than the proto-Islamic black-nationalist movements.

About the same time that the Ahmadiyyah movement began its missionary work in the United States, another small group of orthodox Muslims, led by a West Indian named Sheik Dawud Hamed Faisal, established the Islamic Mission to America in 1923 on State Street in Brooklyn. At the State Street Mosque, Sheik Dawud taught a more authentic version of Islam than the Ahmadiyyahs because he followed the Sunna (practices) of the Prophet Muhammad; where the Ahmadiyyahs believed in the tradition of the Mahdi, or Islamic messianism, Dawud belonged to the tradition of Sunni orthodoxy. The sheik welcomed black Americans to mingle with immigrant Muslims. He taught Arabic, the Qur'an, the Sunna-Hadith tradition, and Sharia, or Islamic law, emphasizing the five "pillars" of Islam: the credo (*shahadah*) of Islam that emphasizes belief in one God and Muhammad as the messenger of Allah; prayer (*salat*) five times a day facing Mecca; charity tax (*zakat*); fasting (*saum*) during the month of Ramadan; pilgrimage to Mecca (*hajj*) if it is possible. Sheik Dawud's work was concentrated mainly in New York and New England. He became responsible for converting a number of African-American Muslims.

A smaller group and third source of African-American Sunni Muslims was the community in Buffalo, N.Y., that was taught orthodox Islam and Arabic by an immigrant Muslim, Prof. Muhammad EzalDeen, in 1933. EzalDeen formed several organizations, including a national one called Uniting Islamic Societies of America in the early 1940s.

The work of the Ahmadiyyah movement, Sheik Dawud's Islamic Mission to America and the State Street Mosque, Imam Wali Akram's First Cleveland Mosque, and Professor Ezal Deen's Islamic Societies of America was important in establishing a beachhead for a more orthodox and universal Sunni Islam in African-American communities.

During the turmoil of the 1960s, young African Americans traveled abroad and made contact with international Muslim movements such as the Tablighi Jamaat. The Darul Islam movement began in 1968 among dissatisfied African-American members of Sheik Dawud's State Street Mosque in Brooklyn, and was led by a charismatic black leader, Imam Yahya Abdul Karim. Sensing the disenchantment with the lack of leadership, organization, and community programs in Sheik Dawud's movement, Imam Karim instituted the Darul Islam, the call to establish the kingdom of Allah. The movement spread to Cleveland, Baltimore, Philadelphia, and Washington, D.C. A network of over forty mosques was developed between 1968 and 1982. After a schism in 1982, the Darul Islam movement declined in influence, but it is since being revived under the charismatic leadership of Imam Jamin Al-Amin of Atlanta (the former H. Rap Brown of the Student Nonviolent Coordinating Committee). Other smaller Sunni organizations also came into existence during the 1960s, such as the Islamic Party and the Mosque of the Islamic Brotherhood. It is ironic, however, that the greatest impact and influence of Islam among black people were exerted by another proto-Islamic movement called the Nation of Islam.

In 1930 a mysterious peddler of sundry goods, who called himself Wali Fard Muhammad, began to spread the word of a new religion, designed for the "Asiatic black man." He soon developed a following of several hundred people and established Temple No. 1 of the Nation of Islam. Focusing on knowledge of self as the path to individual and collective salvation, Master Fard explained that black people were members of the lost-found tribe of Shabazz and owed no allegiance to a white-dominated country, which had enslaved and continuously persecuted them. When Fard mysteriously disappeared in 1934, his chief lieu-

AN ASCETIC LIFESTYLE

Elijah Muhammad advocated that black Muslims eat one meal per day and abstain from tobacco, alcohol, drugs, and pork.

PHOTOGRAPHS AND PRINTS DIVISION, SCHOMBURG CENTER FOR RESEARCH IN BLACK CULTURE, THE NEW YORK PUBLIC LIBRARY, ASTOR, LENOX AND TILDEN FOUNDATIONS

ELIJAH MUHAMMAD

Nation of Islam Leader Advocated Separate Black Nation

Elijah Muhammad (October 10, 1897–February 25, 1975), religious leader. Born Robert Poole in Sandersville, Ga., Muhammad was one of thirteen children of an itinerant Baptist preacher and sharecropper. In 1919 he married Clara Evans and they joined the black migration to Detroit, where he worked in the auto plants. In 1931 he met Master Wallace Fard (or Wali Farad), founder of the Nation of Islam, who eventually chose this devoted disciple as his chief aide. Fard named him "Minister of Islam," dropped his slave name, Poole, and restored his true Muslim name, Muhammad. As the movement grew, a Temple of Islam was established in a Detroit storefront. It is estimated that Fard had close to 8,000 members in the Nation of Islam, consisting of poor black migrants and some former members from Marcus Garvey's United Negro Improvement Association and Noble Drew Ali's Moorish Science Temple.

After Fard mysteriously disappeared in 1934, the Nation of Islam was divided by internal schisms and Elijah Muhammad led a major faction to Chicago, where he established Temple of Islam No. 2 as the main headquarters for the Nation. He also instituted the worship of Master Fard as Allah and himself as the Messenger of Allah and head of the Nation of Islam, always addressed with the title "the Honourable." Muhammad built on the teachings of Fard and combined aspects of Islam and Christianity with the black nationalism of Marcus Garvey into a "proto-Islam," an unorthodox Islam with a strong racial slant. The Honorable Elijah Muhammad's message of racial separation focused on the recognition of true black identity and stressed economic independence. "Knowledge of self" and "do for self" were the rallying cries. The economic ethic of the Black Muslims has been described as a kind of black puritanism—hard work, frugality, the avoidance of debt, self-improvement, and a conservative lifestyle. Muhammad's followers sold the Nation's newspaper, *Muhammad Speaks,* and established their own educational system of Clara Muhammad schools and small businesses such as bakeries, grocery stores, and outlets selling fish and bean pies. More than 100 temples were founded. The disciples also followed strict dietary rules outlined in Muhammad's book *How to Eat to Live,* which enjoined one meal per day and complete abstention from pork, drugs, tobacco, and alcohol. The Nation itself owned farms in several states, a bank, trailer trucks for its fish and grocery businesses, an ultramodern printing press, and other assets.

Muhammad's ministers of Islam found the prisons and streets of the ghetto a fertile recruiting ground. His message of self-reclamation and black manifest destiny struck a responsive chord in the thousands of black men and women whose hope

tenant—the former Robert Poole, now called Elijah Muhammad—led a segment of followers to Chicago, where he established Muhammad's Temple No. 2 as the headquarters for the fledgling movement.

Elijah Muhammad deified Master Fard as Allah, or God incarnated in a black man, and called himself the Prophet or Apostle of Allah, frequently using the title "the Honorable" as a designation of his special status. Although the basic credo of the Nation of Islam stood in direct contradiction to the tenets of orthodox Islam, the movement's main interests were to spread the message of black nationalism and to develop a separate black nation. The Honorable Elijah Muhammad emphasized two basic principles: to know oneself, a development of true self-knowledge based on the teachings of the Nation of Islam; to do for self, an encouragement to become economically independent. He also advocated a strict ascetic lifestyle, which included one meal per day and a ban on tobacco, alcohol, drugs, and pork. From 1934 until his death in 1975, Muhammad and his followers established more than 100 temples and Clara Muhammad schools, and innumerable grocery stores, restaurants, bakeries, and other small businesses. During this period the Nation owned farms in several states, a bank, a fleet of trailer trucks for its fish and grocery businesses, and an ultramodern printing plant. Muhammad's empire was estimated to be worth more than $80 million.

Elijah Muhammad's message of a radical black nationalism, which included the belief that whites were devils, was brought to the American public by a charismatic young minister who had converted to the Nation of Islam after his incarceration in a Boston prison in 1946 for armed robbery. Upon his release from prison in 1952 and until his assassination in 1965, Minister Malcolm X, the former Malcolm Little, had an enormous impact on the growth of the movement.

See also

Student Nonviolent
Coordinating Committee

and self-respect had been all but defeated by racial abuse and denigration. As a consequence of where they recruited and the militancy of their beliefs, the Black Muslims have attracted many more young black males than any other black movement.

Muhammad had an uncanny sense of the vulnerabilities of the black psyche during the social transitions brought on by two world wars; his *Message to the Black Man in America* diagnosed the problem as a confusion of identity and self-hatred caused by white racism. The cure he prescribed was radical surgery through the formation of a separate black nation. Muhammad's 120 "degrees," or lessons, and the major doctrines and beliefs of the Nation of Islam all elaborated on aspects of this central message. The white man is a "devil by nature," absolutely unredeemable and incapable of caring about or respecting anyone who is not white. He is the historic, persistent source of harm and injury to black people. The Nation of Islam's central theological myth tells of Yakub, a black mad scientist who rebelled against Allah by creating the white race, a weak, hybrid people who were permitted temporary dominance of the world. Whites achieved their power and position through devious means and "tricknology." But, according to the Black Muslim apocalyptic view, there will come a time in the not-too-distant future when the forces of good and the forces of evil—that is to say, blacks versus whites—will clash in a "Battle of Armageddon," and the blacks will emerge victorious to recreate their original hegemony under Allah throughout the world.

After spending four years in a federal prison for encouraging draft refusal during World War II, Elijah Muhammad was assisted by his chief protégé, Minister Malcolm X, in building the movement and encouraging its rapid spread in the 1950s and 1960s. During its peak years, the Nation of Islam had more than half a million devoted followers, influencing millions more, and accumulated an economic empire worth an estimated $80 million. Besides his residence in Chicago, Muhammad also lived in a mansion outside of Phoenix, Arizona, since the climate helped to reduce his respiratory problems. He had eight children with his wife, Sister Clara Muhammad, but also fathered a number of illegitimate children with his secretaries, a circumstance that was one of the reasons for Malcolm X's final break with the Nation of Islam in 1964.

With only a third-grade education, Elijah Muhammad was the leader of the most enduring black militant movement in the United States. He died in Chicago and was succeeded by one of his six sons, Wallace Deen Muhammad. After his death, Muhammad's estate and the property of the Nation were involved in several lawsuits over the question of support for his illegitimate children.

—LAWRENCE H. MAMIYA

God is black. All black men belong to Islam; they have been chosen. And Islam shall rule the world.

JAMES BALDWIN
THE FIRE NEXT TIME, 1963

Extremely intelligent and articulate, Malcolm was an indefatigable proselytizer for the Nation, founding temples throughout the country and establishing the newspaper *Muhammad Speaks.* For his efforts, he was rewarded with the prestigious post of minister of Temple No. 7 in Harlem and appointed as the national representative by Elijah Muhammad. Malcolm led the Nation of Islam's attack on the use of the word *Negro* as depicting a slave mentality, and successfully laid the ideological basis for the emergence of the Black Consciousness and Black Power movements of the late 1960s. However, an internal dispute with Elijah Muhammad about future directions and personal moral conduct led Malcolm to leave the Nation in 1964. On his *hajj* to Mecca, Malcolm became convinced that orthodox Sunni Islam was a solution to the racism and discrimination that plagued American society. On February 21, 1965, the renamed El Hajj Malik El Shabazz was assassinated in the Audubon Ballroom in Harlem while delivering a lecture for his newly formed Organization for Afro-American Unity. Minister Louis Farrakhan, another charismatic speaker, replaced Malcolm as the national representative and head minister of Temple No. 7.

When Elijah Muhammad died a decade later, in February 1975, the fifth of his six sons, Wallace Deen Muhammad, was chosen as his father's successor as supreme minister of the Nation. In April 1975, Wallace shocked the movement by announcing an end to its racial doctrines and black-nationalist teachings. He disbanded the Fruit of Islam and the Muslim Girls Training, the elite internal organizations, and gradually moved his followers toward orthodox Sunni Islam. Wallace's moves led to a number of schisms, which produced several competing black-nationalist groups: Louis Farrakhan's resurrected Nation of Islam in Chicago, the largest and most well known of the groups; Silas Muhammad's Nation of Islam in Atlanta; and a Nation of Islam led by John Muhammad, brother of Elijah Muhammed, in Detroit.

In the evolution of his movement, Wallace took the Muslim title and name Imam Warith

I

Deen Muhammad (in 1991 the spelling of his surname was changed to the British *Mohammed*). The movement's name and the name of its newspaper also changed several times: from the World Community of Al-Islam in the West (*Bilalian News*) in 1976 to the American Muslim Mission (*American Muslim Mission Journal*) in 1980; then in 1985 Warith decentralized the movement into independent masjids (*Muslim Journal*). With several hundred thousand followers—predominantly African Americans—who identify with his teachings, Mohammed has continued to deepen their knowledge of the Arabic language, the Qur'an, and the Sunna, or practices of the Prophet. Immigrant Muslims from Africa, Pakistan, and Middle Eastern countries also participate in the Friday Jumuah prayer services.

Although it adheres to the basic tenets of orthodox Sunni Islam, the movement has not yet settled on a particular school of theological thought to follow. Since every significant culture in Islamic history has produced its own school of thought, it is Mohammed's conviction that eventually an American school of Islamic thought will emerge in the United States, comprising the views of African-American and immigrant Muslims. Imam Warith Deen Mohammed has been accepted by the World Muslim Council as a representative of Muslims in the United States, and has been given the responsibility of certifying Americans who desire to make the pilgrimage to Mecca.

In its varying forms, Islam has had a much longer history in the United States, particularly among African Americans, than is commonly known. In the last decade of the twentieth century, about one million African Americans belong to proto-Islamic and orthodox Islamic groups. It has become the fourth major religious tradition in American society, alongside Protestantism, Catholicism, and Judaism. In black communities, Islam has reemerged as the dominant religious alternative to Christianity.

—LAWRENCE H. MAMIYA

See also
Louis Farrakhan

J

JACKSON, JESSE LOUIS

Jesse Louis Jackson (October 8, 1941–), minister, politician, civil rights activist. Jesse Jackson was born Jesse Burns in Greenville, S.C., to Helen Burns and Noah Robinson, a married man who lived next door. In 1943, his mother married Charles Henry Jackson, who adopted Jesse in 1957. Jesse Jackson has recognized both men as his fathers. In 1959, Jackson graduated from Greenville's Sterling High School. A gifted athlete, Jackson was offered a professional baseball contract; instead, he accepted a scholarship to play football at the University of Illinois, at Champaign-Urbana. When he discovered, however, that African Americans were not allowed to play quarterback, he enrolled at North Carolina Agricultural and Technical College in Greensboro. There, besides being a star athlete, Jackson began his activist career as a participant in the student sit-in movement to integrate Greensboro's public facilities.

Jackson's leadership abilities and charisma earned him a considerable reputation by the time he graduated with a B.S. in sociology in 1964. After graduation he married Jacqueline Brown, whom he had met at the sit-in protests. During his senior year, he worked briefly with the Congress of Racial Equality (CORE), quickly being elevated to the position of director of southeastern operations. Jackson then moved north, eschewing law school at Duke University in order to attend the Chicago Theological Seminary in 1964. He was later ordained to the ministry by two renowned figures: gospel music star and pastor, Clay Evans, and legendary revivalist and pulpit orator, C. L. Franklin. Jackson left the seminary in 1965 and returned to the South to become a member of the Rev. Dr. Martin Luther King, Jr.'s staff of the Southern Christian Leadership Conference (SCLC).

Jackson initially became acquainted with SCLC during the famous march on Selma, Ala. in 1965. In 1966, King appointed him to head the Chicago branch of SCLC's Operation Breadbasket, which was formed in 1962 to force various businesses to employ more African Americans. In 1967, only a year after his first appointment, King made Jackson the national director of Operation Breadbasket. Jackson concentrated on businesses heavily patronized by blacks, including bakeries, milk companies, soft-drink bottlers, and soup companies. He arranged a number of boycotts of businesses refusing to comply with SCLC demands of fair employment practices, and successfully negotiated compromises that soon gained national attention.

Jackson was in King's entourage when King was assassinated in Memphis in 1968. After King's death, however, Jackson's relationship with SCLC became increasingly strained over disagreements about his independence and his penchant for taking what was considered to be undue initiative in both public relations and organizational planning. He was also criticized for the direction in which he was leading Operation Breadbasket. Finally, in 1971, Jackson left SCLC and founded Operation PUSH (People United to Serve Humanity), which he would lead for thirteen years. As head of PUSH, he continued an aggressive program of negotiating black employment agreements with white businesses, as well as promoting black educational excellence and self-esteem.

In 1980, Jackson had demanded that an African American step forward as a presidential candidate in the 1984 election. On October 30, 1983, after carefully weighing the chances and need for a candidate, he dramatically announced, on the television program, "60 Minutes," his own candidacy to capture the White House. Many African-American politicians and community leaders, such as Andrew Young, felt that Jackson's candidacy would only divide the Democrats and chose instead to support Walter Mondale, the favorite for the nomination. Jackson, waging a campaign stressing voter registration, carried a hopeful message of empowerment to African Americans, poor people, and other minorities. This constituency of the "voiceless and downtrodden" became the foundation for what Jackson termed a "Rainbow Coalition" of Americans—the poor, struggling farmers, feminists, gays, lesbians,

See also
Congress on Racial Equality
Southern Christian
Leadership Conference

J

and others who historically, according to Jackson, had lacked representation. Jackson, offering himself as an alternative to the mainstream Democratic party, called for, among other things, a defense budget freeze, programs to stimulate full employment, self-determination for the Palestinians, and political empowerment of African Americans through voter registration.

Jackson's campaign in 1984 was characterized by dramatic successes and equally serious political gaffes. In late 1983, U.S. military flyer Robert Goodman was shot down over Syrian-held territory in Lebanon, while conducting an assault. In a daring political gamble, Jackson made Goodman's release a personal mission, arguing that if the flyer had been white, the U.S. government would have worked more diligently towards his release. Traveling to Syria, Jackson managed to meet with President Hafez al-Assad and Goodman was released shortly afterwards; Jackson gained great political capital by appearing at the flyer's side as he made his way back to the United States.

The 1984 campaign, however, was plagued by political missteps. Jackson's offhand dubbing of New York as "Hymietown" while eating lunch with two reporters cost him much of his potential Jewish support and raised serious questions about his commitment to justice for all Americans. Though Jackson eventually apologized, the characterization continued to haunt him, and remains a symbol of strained relations between African Americans and Jews. Another issue galling to many Jews and others was Jackson's relationship with Louis Farrakhan, head of the Nation of Islam. Farrakhan had appeared with Jackson and stumped for him early in the campaign. Jackson, despite advice to the contrary, refused to repudiate Farrakhan; it was only after one speech, in which Farrakhan labeled Judaism a "dirty" religion, that the Jackson campaign issued a statement condemning both the speech and the minister. Another controversy, and a source of special concern to Jews, was Jackson's previous meetings with Yasir Arafat, head of the Palestine Liberation Organization (PLO), and his advocacy of self-determination for the Palestinians.

Jackson ended his historic first run with an eloquent speech before the Democratic National Convention in San Francisco, reminding black America that "our time has come." In a strong showing in a relatively weak primary field, Jackson garnered almost 3.3 million votes out of the approximately 18 million cast.

Even more impressive than Jackson's first bid for the presidency was his second run in 1988.

Jackson espoused a political vision built upon the themes he first advocated in 1984. His campaign once again touted voter registration drives and the Rainbow Coalition, which by this time had become a structured organization closely overseen by Jackson. His new platform, which included many of the planks from 1984, included the validity of "comparable worth" as a viable means of eradicating pay inequities based on gender, the restoration of a higher maximum tax rate, and the implementation of national health care. Jackson also urged policies to combat "factory flight" in the Sun Belt and to provide aid to farm workers in their fight to erode the negative effect of corporate agri-business on family farms. Further, he railed against the exploitative practices of U.S. and transnational corporations, urging the redirection of their profits from various foreign ventures to the development of local economies.

While he failed to secure the Democratic nomination, Jackson finished with a surprisingly large number of convention delegates and a strong finish in the primaries. In thirty-one of thirty-six primaries, Jackson won either first or second place, earning almost seven million votes out of the approximately 23 million cast. In 1988, Jackson won over many of the black leaders who had refused to support him during his first campaign. His performance also indicated a growing national respect for his oratorical skills and his willingness to remain faithful to politically progressive ideals.

In the 1992 presidential campaign, Jackson, who was not a candidate, was critical of Democratic front-runners Bill Clinton and Al Gore, and did not endorse them until the final weeks of the campaign. Since his last full-time political campaign in 1988, Jackson has remained highly visible in American public life. He has crusaded for various causes, including the institution of a democratic polity in South Africa, statehood for the District of Columbia, and the banishment of illegal drugs from American society.

Jackson has also been an outspoken critic of professional athletics, arguing that more African Americans need to be involved in the management and ownership of professional sports teams and that discrimination remains a large problem for many black athletes. Further, on the college level, the institution of the NCAA's Proposition 42 and Proposition 48 have earned criticism from Jackson as being discriminatory against young black athletes. Through the medium of a short-lived 1991 television talk show, Jackson sought to widen his audience, addressing pressing concerns faced by African Americans.

Jackson's various crusades against illegal drugs and racism, while often specifically targeted towards black teenagers, have exposed millions of Americans to his message. His powerful oratorical style—pulpit oratory which emphasizes repetition of key phrases like "I am somebody"—often impresses and challenges audiences regardless of their political beliefs. In late 1988, Jackson became president of the National Rainbow Coalition, Inc.; he remains involved in the activities of numerous other organizations.

Jackson has been the most prominent civil rights leader and African-American national figure since the death of Martin Luther King, Jr. The history of national black politics in the 1970s and 1980s was largely his story. He has shown a great ability for making alliances, as well as a talent for defining issues and generating controversy. The essential dilemma of Jackson's career, as with many of his peers, has been the search for a way to advance and further the agenda of the civil rights movement as a national movement at a time when the political temper of the country has been increasingly conservative.

—MICHAEL ERIC DYSON

JACKSON, MICHAEL, AND THE JACKSON FAMILY

Michael Jackson and the Jackson Family, pop singers and performers. A dominant influence on American popular music since the 1960s, the Jackson family consists of the nine children of Joseph and Katherine Jackson. The couple's first five sons, Sigmund "Jackie" (May 4, 1951–), Toriano "Tito" (October 15, 1953–), Jermaine (December 11, 1954–), Marlon (March 12, 1957–), and Michael (August 29, 1958–), began singing in 1962. Their other children, Maureen "Rebbie" (May 29, 1950–), LaToya (May 29, 1956–), Steven "Randy" (October 29, 1962–), and Janet (May 16, 1966–) began entertaining publicly with their siblings in the 1970s. By the 1980s, the Jackson family was generating a nonstop stream of recordings, music videos, movies, television shows, and concerts, that were hugely popular among both African-American and white audiences. In the 1990s, however, public attention increasingly turned to squabbles within the family, and focused on their public airing of grievances.

All of the Jackson children were born and raised in the midwestern industrial city of Gary, Ind., where they led a sheltered existence in a working-class neighborhood. The five oldest sons were driven by their father, a steel mill crane operator and one-time rhythm and blues guitarist, to practice music three hours a day. They began to perform in local talent contests in 1963, and rapidly advanced to amateur contests in Chicago. In 1967, Michael's lead soprano and irresistible dance moves, borrowed from James Brown, helped the brothers win the famed amateur night contest at Harlem's Apollo Theater. The next year, after two single records released on the Steeltown label failed to create a stir, the Jacksons signed with Motown, the black-owned Detroit recording company. Motown's owner Berry Gordy took complete control over the group, even concocting the story that the group had been discovered by Motown singer Diana Ross. Gordy chose their songs, managed their performances, and gained the rights to their name, then "The Jackson Five." The group's first singles, including "I Want You Back" (1969) and "ABC" (1970),

were popular, layering Michael's vocals over funky, stutter-step bass lines.

In 1970 the family moved to Los Angeles, and in the years that followed the Jacksons made numerous television appearances, including a cartoon series and a feature special, "Goin' Back to Indiana." Although their recordings from this time suffered from a sense of forced cuteness, their popularity never flagged, and the brothers continued to distinguish themselves by insisting on performing much of the instrumental backing themselves. Their recordings from this time include *Lookin' Through The Windows* (1972) and *Get It Together* (1973). Michael recorded his first solo album, *Got To Be There,* in 1971. His second solo recording, *Ben* (1972), a soundtrack single, went to number one and received an Academy Award nomination. In 1974 the Jacksons broke with the formulaic routine of Motown recordings and produced "Dancing Machine," a frenetic dance hit that presaged the disco era. The next year, Michael recorded another solo album, *Forever, Michael.* In 1975 the group broke with Motown, and signed with Epic, which offered them five times as much in royalties as Motown. Since Motown owned the name "The Jackson Five," they changed their name to "The Jacksons." However, Jermaine remained with Motown to pursue a solo career, having married Hazel Gordy, the daughter of Motown's founder.

Like Motown, Epic at first refused to let the Jacksons, who had replaced Jermaine with Randy, write or produce their own material. Instead, their densely layered pop hits, bridging the gap between soul and disco, were written by the Philadelphia-based team of Kenny Gamble and Leon Huff. It was only in 1977 that the Jacksons were finally allowed to fully control their own recordings. The resulting album, *Destiny,* mixed Michael's intense, gospel-style vocals with streamlined rhythms, and yielded the hit single "Shake Your Body (Down to the Ground)," written by Michael and Randy. In 1976 and 1977 Randy joined Michael, Jackie, Tito, and Marlon in a television variety show, "The Jacksons." Rebbie, LaToya, and Janet also joined the cast, performing in both musical and comedy sketches. In 1978 Michael appeared as the Scarecrow in the film *The Wiz.*

In 1979 Michael appeared resplendent in a tuxedo and glowing white socks in a photograph on the cover of *Off The Wall,* an album that announced his emergence as an adult entertainer. A collaboration with Quincy Jones, the album yielded four Top Ten singles, including scorching dance cuts such as "Don't Stop 'Til You Get Enough," as well as lush ballads, and sold eleven million copies. The next year Michael reunited with his brothers on *Triumph,* but by this time it was clear that his superstar status virtually relegated his brothers to a backing role. In 1982 Michael again teamed up with Jones to make *Thriller,* a rock-oriented album that yielded seven Top Ten singles, including "Wanna Be Startin' Somethin' "; a duet with Paul McCartney, "The Girl is Mine;" "Beat It"; "Billie Jean"; and the title track, with a witty rap by actor Vincent Price. *Thriller* sold more than 40 million copies, making it the best-selling album of all time. The music videos for *Thriller's* singles brought an end to MTV's refusal to feature African-American music. The "Beat It" video brought special acclaim, with its choreographed gang fight evoking the production numbers of a Broadway musical scored for rock and roll, and was called "Michael's *West Side Story.*"

During this time Michael, who had always been a witty and talented stage performer, began to attract attention as a dancer. In a 1983 television special celebrating Motown's twenty-fifth anniversary, Michael electrified a huge broadcast audience with his rendition of the African-American vernacular dance step known as "the creep." Michael's version, known as "the moonwalk," combined the traditional forward-stepping, back-sliding routine with James Brown's signature spins, which Michael had copied as a child, and the robotic "locking" motions long popular among street performers.

After recording *Triumph* in 1980, the Jacksons brought Michael back for the enormously successful *Victory* album and tour. Since then the Jacksons as a group have been less active, concentrating on solo careers, although Jackie, Marlon, Tito, and Randy did record *2300 Jackson Street* (1989). After Michael, Jermaine Jackson has been the most successful male singer in the family. He released *Jermaine* in 1972 and recorded almost a dozen more solo albums over the next decade. In recent years he has recorded *Precious Moments* (1986), *Be the One* (1989), and *Don't Take It Personal* (1990). In 1991 he recorded "You Said, You Said" and "Word to the Badd," a scalding attack on Michael. Marlon Jackson's solo album, *Baby Tonight,* was released in 1987. Randy Jackson, who was badly injured in a 1980 auto accident, recovered in time for the Jacksons' reunion in 1984. He released his first solo album in 1989.

The Jackson daughters have also had solo careers. The oldest, Rebbie, continued performing after the 1970s, but without the popularity of her two younger sisters. LaToya Jackson released four undistinguished solo albums, including *LaToya Jackson, My Special Love, Heart Don't Lie,* and *La-Toya* before bringing on the censure of her family and many members of the African-American community by posing nude in *Playboy* in 1989. Since then she has continued to record and perform, notably in a Paris revue. In 1991 she countered her mother's 1990 memoirs, *The Jacksons: My Family,* by publishing *LaToya: Growing Up in the Jackson Family,* which portrayed a childhood dominated by fear and abuse.

Janet Jackson appeared on several television shows and recorded two albums, *Janet Jackson* and *Dream Street,* before her graduation from high school in 1984. Her 1986 album *Control,* presenting a persona of steely independence against spare, mechanical rhythms, sold more than six million copies and yielded the hit single "What Have You Done For Me Lately?" In 1989 she released *Janet Jackson's Rhythm Nation 1814.* The album's plea for racial unity sits somewhat uneasily over its pulsating rhythms, but it sold eight million copies, won a Grammy Award, and led to a world tour in which Janet showed off her precisely choreographed ensemble dancing. In 1993 she starred in the film *Poetic Justice* and released *janet.,* an album that traded in the bitter, independent stance of her previous albums for more themes involving romantic and sexual love.

Since the mid-1980s, Michael Jackson has become less a pop superstar than an icon of American popular culture. He helped write and perform the charity song "We Are the World" in 1985. His 1987 album *Bad* and his 1991 album *Dangerous* sold well, but broke no new musical ground. Increasingly, he has been noted more for his eccentricity than for his music. At first his flamboyant wardrobe combined martial elegance with street toughness, and he became famous for wearing a single, sequined glove. Extensive plastic surgery on his nose, chin, eyes, and cheeks, and chemical skin peels, as well as heavy makeup, have led to accusations that he is attempting to erase his identity as an African American. Michael has answered by claiming that he has a rare skin disease that causes discoloration. His increasingly androgynous appearance has caused frequent speculation in the media regarding his sexual identity, but Michael, who aside from his 1988 autobiography *Moonwalker* and infrequent television interviews, has guarded his privacy, long proclaimed his celibacy. He lived with his mother until he was twenty-nine, and he subsequently moved to "Neverland," a fantasy estate that includes a ferris wheel and a zoo. He has long publicly befriended children, and has worked on behalf of children's charities. In 1993 Michael was accused of having sexual relations with a minor. Jackson vigorously denied the accusation, but reached a monetary settlement with the boy's family in January 1994. Later that year he announced his marriage to Lisa Marie Presley, the daughter of white superstar Elvis Presley. In June 1995, just before the release of Michael's album *HIStory,* he and Lisa Marie were interviewed on television, and insisted on his innocence of any sexual misconduct with minors. *HIStory* reached number 1 on the charts shortly after its release.

Despite internal family conflicts, the Jacksons remain, collectively and individually, the most prominent and productive family in African-American popular music.

—HARRIS FRIEDBERG

JACKSON, REBECCA COX

Rebecca Cox Jackson (February 15, 1795–May 24, 1871), preacher. Rebecca Cox Jackson was born into a free family in Horntown, Pa., and lived at different times with her maternal grandmother and with her mother, Jane Cox (who died when Rebecca was thirteen). In 1830, when her religious autobiography begins, she was living in the household of her older brother, Joseph Cox, a tanner and local preacher of the Bethel African Methodist Episcopal (AME) Church in Philadelphia. Married to Samuel S. Jackson, and childless herself, Jackson cared for her brother's four children while earning her own living as a seamstress.

As the result of a powerful religious awakening during a thunderstorm, Jackson became active in the early Holiness Movement. She moved from leadership of praying bands to public preaching, stirring up controversy within AME circles not only as a woman preacher but also because she had received the revelation that celibacy was necessary for a holy life, and she criticized the churches roundly for "carnality." Jackson's insistence on being guided entirely by the dictates of an inner voice ultimately led to her separation from husband, brother, and church.

After a period of itinerant preaching in the late 1830s and early 1840s, Jackson joined the United Society of Believers in Christ's Second Appear-

See also
Gospel Music

"CHAPPIE" JAMES

America's First Black Four-Star General

Daniel "Chappie" James, Jr. (February 11, 1920–February 25, 1978), the first black four-star general. In 1937 James joined Tuskegee's pioneer black Army Air Corps unit. He served in World War II and led a fighter group in Korea, inventing air tactics to support ground forces and receiving the Distinguished Service Medal. In Vietnam he was vice commander of the Eighth Tactical Fighter Wing, earning the Legion of Merit award. National attention accompanied his speeches supporting the war and black soldiers' reasons to fight.

Afterward he commanded Wheelus Air Force Base in Libya, then became Defense Department public affairs officer and a popular speaker. He received his fourth star with command of the crucial North American Air Defense, monitoring possible air and missile attacks.

Skills and overwhelming personality smoothed James's unprecedented ascent. Generally opposed to mass movements to improve blacks' situation, he cited his mother's dictum that personal excellence could overcome all barriers. He applauded peaceful demonstrations, however; indeed, the violence at Selma, Ala., made him consider resigning. He brushed off personal experiences with racism, though seldom wearing civilian clothes so his uniform might shield him. Blacks sometimes criticized him, but many Americans liked his support of the Vietnam War and his view of race relations that emphasized individualism.

—ELIZABETH FORTSON ARROYO

inantly African-American and female Shaker family survived her death in 1871 by at least a quarter of a century.

Rebecca Jackson's major legacy is her remarkable spiritual autobiography, *Gifts of Power*. Here Jackson records her receipt of a wide variety of visionary experiences, dreams, and supernatural gifts, and her spiritual journey as a woman with a divine calling. Her visionary writing has received growing recognition both as source material for African-American history and theology and as spiritual literature of great power. Alice Walker has described Jackson's autobiography as "an extraordinary document" that "tells us much about the spirituality of human beings, especially of the interior spiritual resources of our mothers" (Walker 1983, p. 78).

—JEAN MCMAHON HUMEZ

JAMISON, JUDITH

Judith Jamison (May 10, 1943–), dancer. Born the younger of two children in Philadelphia, Pa., Jamison studied piano and violin as a child. Tall by the age of six, Jamison was enrolled in dance classes by her parents in an effort to complement her exceptional height with grace. She received most of her early dance training in classical ballet with master teachers Marion Cuyjet, Delores Brown, and John Jones at the Judimar School of Dance. Jamison decided on a career in dance only after three semesters of coursework in psychology at Fisk University, and she completed her education at the Philadelphia Dance Academy. In 1964 she was spotted by choreographer Agnes de Mille and invited to appear in de Mille's *The Four Marys* at the New York-based American Ballet Theatre. Jamison moved to New York in 1965 and that same year joined the Alvin Ailey American Dance Theater (AAADT).

Jamison performed with AAADT on tours of Europe and Africa in 1966. When financial pressures forced Ailey to briefly disband his company later that year, Jamison joined the Harkness Ballet for several months and then returned to the reformed AAADT in 1967. She quickly became a principal dancer with that company, dancing a variety of roles that showcased her pliant technique, stunning beauty, and exceptional stature of five feet, ten inches. Jamison excelled as the goddess Erzulie in Geoffrey Holder's *The Prodigal Prince* (1967), as the Mother in a revised version of Ailey's *Knoxville: Summer of 1915* (1968), and as the Sun in the 1968 AAADT revival of Lucas Hov-

ance (Shakers), at Watervliet, N.Y., attracted by their religious celibacy, emphasis on spiritualistic experience, and dual-gender concept of deity. With her younger disciple and lifelong companion, Rebecca Perot, Rebecca Jackson lived there from June 1847 until July 1851.

Disappointed in the predominantly white Shaker community's failure to take the gospel of their founder, Ann Lee, to the African-American community, Jackson left Watervliet in 1851, on an unauthorized mission to Philadelphia. In 1857 she and Perot returned to Watervliet, and after a brief second residence Jackson won the right from Shaker leadership to found and head a new Shaker "outfamily" in Philadelphia. This predom-

See also

Duke Ellington

ing's *Icarus.* These larger-than-life roles fit neatly with Jamison's regal bearing and highly responsive emotional center, and critics praised her finely drawn dance interpretations that were imbued with power and grace. Jamison's and Ailey's collaboration deepened, and she created a brilliant solo in his *Masekela Language* (1969). Set to music of South African trumpeter Hugh Masekela, Jamison portrayed a frustrated and solitary woman dancing in a seedy saloon. Her electrifying performances of Ailey's fifteen-minute solo *Cry* (1971) propelled her to an international stardom unprecedented among modern dance artists. Dedicated by Ailey "to all black women everywhere—especially our mothers," the three sections of *Cry* successfully captured a broad range of movements, emotions, and images associated with black womanhood as mother, sister, lover, goddess, supplicant, confessor, and dancer.

In 1976 Jamison danced with ballet star Mikhail Baryshnikov in Ailey's *Pas de Duke* set to music by Duke Ellington. This duet emphasized the classical line behind Jamison's compelling modern dance technique and garnered her scores of new fans. Jamison's celebrity advanced, and she appeared as a guest artist with the San Francisco Ballet, the Swedish Royal Ballet, the Cullberg Ballet, and the Vienna State Ballet. In 1977 she created the role of Potiphar's Wife in John Neumeier's *Josephslegende* for the Vienna State Opera, and in 1978 she appeared in Maurice Béjart's updated version of *Le Spectre de la Rose* with the Ballet of the Twentieth Century. Several choreographers sought to work with Jamison as a solo artist, and important collaborations included John Parks's *Nubian Lady* (1972), John Butler's *Facets* (1976), and Ulysses Dove's *Inside* (1980).

In 1980 Jamison left the Ailey company to star in the Broadway musical *Sophisticated Ladies,* set to the music of Duke Ellington. She later turned her formidable talent to choreography, where her work has been marked by a detached sensuality and intensive responses to rhythm. Jamison founded her own dance company, the Jamison Project, "to explore the opportunities of getting a group of dancers together, for both my choreography [and] to commission works from others." Alvin Ailey's failing health caused Jamison to rejoin the AAADT as artistic associate for the 1988–1989 season. In December 1989 Ailey died, and Jamison was named artistic director of the company. She has continued to choreograph, and her ballets include *Divining* (1984), *Forgotten Time* (1989), and *Hymn* (1993), all performed by the AAADT.

Jamison has received numerous awards and honors, including a Presidential Appointment to the National Council of the Arts, the 1972 Dance Magazine Award, and the Candace Award from the National Coalition of One Hundred Black Women. Her greatest achievement as a dancer was an inspiring ability to seem supremely human and emotive within an elastic and powerful dance technique.

—THOMAS F. DEFRANTZ

JAZZ

Despite complex origins, the status of jazz as a distinctively African-American music is beyond question. Nonetheless, in its development from folk and popular sources in turn-of-the-century America, jazz has transcended boundaries of ethnicity and genre. Played in every country of the globe, it is perhaps twentieth-century America's most influential cultural creation, and its worldwide impact, on both popular and art music, has been enormous. Jazz has proved to be immensely protean, and has existed in a number of diverse though related styles, from New Orleans- and Chicago-style Dixieland jazz, big band or swing, bebop, funky cool jazz, hard bop, modal jazz, free jazz, and jazz rock. One reason for the variety in jazz is that it is basically a way of performing music rather than a particular repertory. It originated in blends of the folk music, popular music, and light classical music being created just prior to 1900, and now embraces a variety of popular musical styles from Latin America, the Caribbean, Asia, and Africa, as well as diverse modern, classical, and avant-garde performance traditions.

Jazz also has an inescapable political thrust. It originated during a time of enormous oppression and violence in the South against African Americans. The early African-American practitioners of jazz found racial discrimination in virtually every aspect of their lives, from segregated dance halls, cafes, and saloons to exploitative record companies. Like blackface minstrelsy, early jazz was popular with whites, in part because it reinforced "darkie" stereotypes of African Americans as happy-go-lucky and irrepressibly rhythmic. Nonetheless, many black jazz musicians used jazz as a vehicle for cultural, artistic, and economic advancement, and were able to shape their own destinies in an often hostile environment. African-American jazz was, from its earliest days, often performed for or by whites, and it was assimilated into the overall fabric of popular music, to the un-

The lively entertainment scene in New Orleans nurtured the growth of distinctive African-American musical forms, especially jazz.

PAGE 508

See also
Scott Joplin

See also
Blues

easiness of some on both sides of the racial divide. It has continued to mirror and exemplify the complexities and ironies of the changing status of African Americans within the broader culture and polity of the United States.

Early Jazz

Although its origins are obscure, early forms of jazz began to flourish around the turn of the century in cities such as New Orleans, Chicago, and Memphis. The long prehistory of jazz begins with the rhythmic music slaves brought to America in the sixteenth and seventeenth centuries and developed on southern plantations. Since the traditional drums, flutes, and horns of West Africa were largely forbidden, call-and-response singing and chanting, field hollers, foot stomping, and handclapping were common, especially in the context of fieldwork and church worship. Under those restrictions, among the earliest African-American instruments adopted were European string instruments such as the violin and guitar. The African-derived banjo was also a popular instrument. Eventually the publicly performed music that Reconstruction-era city-dwellers made an essential part of urban life demanded brass and woodwind instruments, not only for their volume, but to accompany the Spanish American War–era military marches, popular songs, and light classics that were so popular among all classes and races in the late nineteenth century.

While it is difficult to draw a precise line between jazz and its precursors, its immediate predecessors were two forms of African-American folk and popular music known as blues and ragtime. Ragtime is primarily piano music that integrates complex African-derived rhythmic practices with the harmonies of light classics, parlor music, show tunes, and popular songs. The virtuosic practice of "ragging"—altering rhythms to, in effect, "tease" variety and humor out of formal, strict patterns—was widespread by the 1880s, especially in towns along the Mississippi River like St. Louis and (eventually) New Orleans. Ragtime was also being played before the turn of the century in eastern cities such as New York and Baltimore. The greatest ragtime players, Scott Joplin, Eubie Blake, Tony Jackson, and Jelly Roll Morton also composed, and sheet music became a central feature of home entertainments among families, black and white, who could afford pianos. Ragtime was also played by instrumental ensembles; the syncopated orchestras led in New York City by James Reese Europe and Will Marion Cook during the first two decades of the century owed

much to the precise, contrapuntal style of piano rags. The ragtime-derived piano style proved influential on later jazz styles, especially since many of the best bandleaders of the swing era, including Duke Ellington, Earl "Fatha" Hines, and Count Basie, were heavily influenced by Harlem stride pianists such as James P. Johnson, Fats Waller, Willie "The Lion" Smith, and Luckey Roberts. Also deeply indebted to stride were later pianists such as Teddy Wilson, Art Tatum, and Thelonious Monk.

The blues similarly began along the Mississippi River in the 1880s and 1890s. Among the first published blues, "Memphis Blues" (1912), by W. C. Handy, was broadly derived from black rural folk music. The sexual frankness and suggestiveness, its recognition of suffering and hardship of all kinds, and the slow, insinuating melodies soon had an impact on popular music. The 1920s saw the rise of such blues singers as Ma Rainey, Bessie Smith, and Mamie Smith, but long before that the blues had a palpable influence on the music of early New Orleans jazz.

It was New Orleans that gave its name to the earliest and most enduring form of jazz, and bred its first masters. That Buddy Bolden, Bunk Johnson, Kid Ory, Jelly Roll Morton, King Oliver, Sidney Bechet, and Freddy Keppard all came from New Orleans attests to the extraordinary fertility of musical life in what was then the largest southern city. In New Orleans, blacks, whites, and the culturally distinct light-skinned African Americans known as creoles supported various kinds of musical ensembles by the mid-nineteenth century. Other influences included traveling cabaret and minstrel shows, funeral, carnival, and parade bands. A more or less direct African influence on New Orleans was also pervasive, no more so than in Congo Square, a one-time site of slave auctions that later became an important meeting place and open-air music hall for New Orleans blacks.

The various layers of French, Spanish, Haitian, creole, Indian, and African-American culture in New Orleans created a mixed social environment, and not only in Storyville, the legendary red-light district whose role in the birth of jazz has probably been overemphasized. Nonetheless, it was in Storyville that legalized prostitution encouraged a proliferation of brothels, gambling houses, and saloons where many of the early New Orleans jazz musicians first performed. Though many of the early New Orleans jazz bands and performers, including Sidney Bechet and Jelly Roll Morton, were creoles, very soon non-creoles such as King

Oliver and Louis Armstrong were integrated into creole ensembles.

By the end of the first decade of the twentieth century, these diverse musical styles had evolved into the style of music that was almost exclusively associated with New Orleans. Although there are no recordings of jazz from this period, what the music sounded like can be inferred from photographs of the period, later reminiscences, and later recordings. A typical early New Orleans jazz ensemble might include one or more cornets, trombone, clarinet, and a rhythm section of string or brass bass, piano, and guitar or banjo. The cornets, which were eventually replaced by the trumpets, took the melodic lead, while an elaborate countermelody was contributed by the clarinet, and the trombone provided a melodic bass line. The rhythm section filled in the harmonies and provided the beat. The typical repertory of these ensembles consisted largely of blues-based songs.

The two main types of improvisation in early jazz were solo and collective improvisation. Solo improvisation takes place when one musician at a time performs solo. In collective improvisation, which was the key feature of the New Orleans early jazz sound and later Chicago-related Dixieland style, more than one musician improvises simultaneously. This style can be heard in the early recordings of Kid Ory, King Oliver, and Jelly Roll Morton, as well as music made by whites such as the Original Dixieland Jazz Band, the New Orleans Rhythm Kings, the Wolverines, and Chicago's Austin High School Gang.

Jazz no doubt existed in some recognizable form from about 1905—the heyday of the legendary and never-recorded New Orleans cornetist Buddy Bolden—but the first recording by a group calling itself a "jazz" band was made in 1917, in New York, by the white, New Orleans–based ensemble the Original Dixieland Jazz Band. Though as early as 1913 James Reese Europe had recorded with his black syncopated orchestra, and by the early 1920s Johnny Dunn and Kid Ory had recorded, it was not until 1923 that the first representative and widely influential New Orleans–style jazz recordings by African Americans were made in the Midwest, by King Oliver and Jelly Roll Morton.

The movement of the best New Orleans musicians to Chicago is often linked to the closing of Storyville in 1917. Much more important was the Great Migration of southern blacks to northern cities during the World War I years. In Chicago, jazz found a receptive audience, and jazz musicians were able to develop profitable solo careers while enjoying a more hospitable racial climate than in the South.

Big Band Jazz

Jazz underwent significant changes on being transplanted to the North. By the early 1920s, when the New York–based band of Fletcher Henderson made its first recordings, jazz was being presented in a manner akin to the refined dance band orchestras of the time, with larger ensembles of ten pieces or more, working within carefully written arrangements. Whereas the early jazz repertory consisted largely of original blues, in the 1920s, jazz musicians began performing waltzes and popular songs. The style of playing changed as well. In place of the thrilling but often unwieldy polyphony of New Orleans jazz came the antiphonal big-band style, in which whole sections traded off unison or close-harmony riffs, often in a call-and-response format with a single soloist. In contrast to the instrumentation of the typical New Orleans early jazz ensemble of three horns and a rhythm section, big bands generally had a brass section consisting of three trumpets and one trombone, and three or four reeds (a variety of saxophones and clarinets). In the 1930s the size of big bands often grew to fifteen or more musicians. Providing the pulse for the swing big bands was a rhythm section, usually containing a piano, string bass and drums, and often an acoustic guitar.

If the big bands regimented and reined in the sounds of New Orleans jazz, it also permitted the emergence of the soloist, particularly on the saxophone and trumpet, probably the most important development of the era. Though featured soloists were not unknown in the New Orleans jazz style, big band jazz arrangements often used themes as mere preludes to extended solo improvisations, with both the rhythm section and the orchestra as a whole often served as accompanists to whoever was soloing. No figure exemplified this change better than Louis Armstrong. Although bred in New Orleans, his stay in Chicago taught him much about the theatrical possibilities of a well-constructed solo. During 1924 and 1925 he performed with the Henderson band in New York, where his majestic tone and unfailingly fresh phrasing almost singlehandedly turned that ensemble from a straitlaced dance band toward a New Orleans–influenced style that would eventually become known as swing. Armstrong's recordings with his own ensembles in the 1920s feature not only his brilliant trumpet, but his voice. By singing the same way that he played the trumpet,

Armstrong became the model for superb jazz phrasing and popularized scat singing—using nonsense syllables instead of words. In the 1930s, his recordings of such emerging standards as "Body and Soul" and "Stardust" proved that jazz could redefine pop tunes.

In 1929 Armstrong fronted a big band in New York, a move that signaled the decline of both Chicago and Chicago-style jazz in favor of Harlem as the new capital, and swing big bands as the dominant sound. By the mid-1930s, Harlem was the undisputed center of the jazz world, and the swing era coincided with the rise of Harlem as the focal point for African-American culture. The largest black community in the world made its home along 125th Street in Manhattan, attending elegant and inexpensive dance palaces, and buying recordings also made in New York. However, it would be a mistake to focus exclusively on New York or Chicago. Many of the greatest swing big bands, known as territory bands, came from elsewhere. The Southwest, in particular Kansas City, an important railroad switching station as well as host to an extensive collection of mob-owned after-hours nightclubs, was the most important center for territory bands. In the early 1920s Ben-

nie Moten's group had already inaugurated a Kansas City style, in its mature phase marked by looser, four-to-the-bar rhythms and freer styles of soloing. The pianist in the band, a student of Harlem stride named Count Basie, brought the core of that band to New York in 1936, and brought to prominence a whole new generation of hard-swinging soloists such as Lester Young, Herschel Evans and Buck Clayton, as well as vocalist Jimmy Rushing.

The big band era was the only time jazz was truly America's popular music. Starting in the late 1920s, the dance bands of Ellington, Henderson, Basie, Jimmie Lunceford, Andy Kirk, Teddy Hill, Earl "Fatha" Hines, as well as those of Chick Webb, Cab Calloway, and Lionel Hampton competed with white bands led by Benny Goodman, Paul Whiteman, Tommy Dorsey, and Artie Shaw. The prominence of the soloist during the swing era marks the emergence of celebrity jazz musicians like Louis Armstrong, who became "stars" almost on a par with the most popular white entertainers of the day, such as Bing Crosby, in both white and black communities, in Europe as well as in America. The big band era also marks the emergence of tenor saxophonist stars such as

BIG BAND STYLE

Louis Armstrong performing as a member of King Oliver's Creole Jazz Band, around 1923.

PHOTOGRAPHS AND PRINTS DIVISION, SCHOMBURG CENTER FOR RESEARCH IN BLACK CULTURE, THE NEW YORK PUBLIC LIBRARY, ASTOR, LENOX AND TILDEN FOUNDATIONS

Coleman Hawkins and Ben Webster, as well as vocalists such as Billie Holiday and Ella Fitzgerald.

Jazz in the swing era gave numerous African-American performers a largely unprecedented degree of acceptance, fame, and financial success. Still, these achievements occurred within a society that was uncomfortable at best with both public and private racial interaction in any but the most controlled settings. Although some dance halls and nightclubs were integrated, many others, including the most famous ones, such as the Cotton Club, were not. Musicians often appeared there in less than flattering contexts, and audiences clamored for Duke Ellington's "exotic" side, known as jungle music, and for the comic, minstrel side of performers such as Louis Armstrong and Fats Waller. Through the end of the 1930s almost all jazz bands were segregated, with white bands such as those led by the Dorsey brothers, Paul Whiteman, Benny Goodman, Glenn Miller, Woody Herman, and Artie Shaw making considerably more money than their African-American counterparts.

Goodman's ensemble was the first intergrated jazz band. He hired Fletcher Henderson as an arranger and in 1936 hired Teddy Wilson as pianist and Lionel Hampton on vibes for his quartet. Goodman, the most popular bandleader of the late 1930s, played in a style quite similar to the best of the black bands, and was unfairly crowned the "King of Swing" by critics. This raised the ire of many black musicians. Although Armstrong, Ellington, Basie, and Waller became genuine celebrities, the white musicians who played in a "black" style often captured a market unavailable to blacks. This would be a persistent grievance among black jazz musicians.

Bebop

In the early 1940s, one of the last major bands from the Southwest to reach prominence in New York was led by Jay McShann, whose band contained the seeds of the next development in jazz (primarily through the innovations of its own saxophonist, Charlie Parker). Although the emergence of the frenetic and rarified style of jazz that became known as "bebop"—so named because of the final, two-note phrase that often ended bebop solos—is frequently seen as a revolt against big band swing, all of the early bebop giants drew upon their experiences playing with swing musicians, often in big bands. Earl Hines, Billy Eckstine, Coleman Hawkins, and Cootie Williams nurtured many beboppers, and one of the first great bebop groups was a big band led by Dizzy

Gillespie in 1945 and 1946. After Parker left Jay McShann, he worked with Gillespie in bands led by Hines and Eckstine. Thelonious Monk worked with Cootie Williams, as did Bud Powell.

The very first stirrings of bebop had come in the late 1930s, when drummer Kenny Clarke, who had worked in big bands led by Teddy Hill and Roy Eldridge, began keeping time on the high-hat cymbal, rather than on the bass drum, which was reserved for rhythmic accents, a style adopted by young drummers such as Max Roach and Art Blakey. Just as timekeepers were experimenting with the rhythmical palate of the drum kit, so too were soloists extending the limits of the harmonies of standard popular songs and blues, and aspiring to a new and recondite tonal vocabulary. Inspired by the virtuosic playing and harmonic sophistication of pianist Art Tatum and tenor saxophonist Lester Young, in the early 1940s Gillespie and Parker were creating a music for musicians, noted for its complexity, with a whole new, difficult repertory. Trumpeter Fats Navarro, bassist Charles Mingus, and pianists Thelonious Monk and Bud Powell were also prime architects of bebop, as were such white musicians as pianists Lennie Tristano and Al Haig, and alto saxophonist Lee Konitz.

Disgruntled swing musicians complained that bebop was an elitist style that robbed jazz of its place as America's popular music. Certainly, the refusal of bebop musicians to adhere to a four-to-bar bass drum rhythm meant that the music was no longer suitable for dancing. As bebop lost its function as dance music, tempos quickened even more, and solos became more rhythmically adventurous. Bebop's quirky, sophisticated compositions and fleet, witty improvisations demanded the serious and more or less undivided attention that concert music requires. Bebop came of age and reached its height of popularity not in "high-toned" Harlem dance halls, but in the nightclubs and after-hours clubs of Harlem and 52nd Street, and often the audience consisted of a small coterie of white and black jazz fans and sympathetic jazz musicians. In retrospect, however, it was not bebop that dealt the death blow to jazz as a popular music. The big bands were struggling to survive long before the bebop era began, and by the 1950s, not even Count Basie and Duke Ellington's bands could keep up with the dance rhythms of rhythm and blues and early rock and roll.

Just as New Orleans–style jazz established the basic language for what is generally considered "classic jazz," so too did the beboppers define what is still considered modern jazz. Bebop was

Wynton Marsalis has won critical acclaim for his virtuosic technique, musical sensitivity, and gift for improvisation.

PAGE 443

See also
Count Basie
Duke Ellington

ELLA FITZGERALD

First Lady of Song Enjoys Long-lived Acclaim

Ella Fitzgerald (April 25, 1918–June 15, 1996), jazz vocalist. In a career lasting half a century, Ella Fitzgerald's superb pitch and diction, infallible sense of rhythm, and masterful scat singing have all become part of the fabric of American music, and she has been recognized as one "First Lady of Song." While her background and technique were rooted in jazz, she has always been a popular singer, with a soothing yet crystalline sound that brought wide acclaim. Born in Newport News, Va., she came north as a child to Yonkers, N.Y., with her mother. In 1934, on a dare, she entered a Harlem amateur-night contest as a dancer, but became immobile with stage fright when called on to perform. Instead, she sang two songs popularized by the Boswell Sisters, "Judy" and "The Object of My Affection," and won first prize.

After she had won several more amateur competitions, an opportunity came in February 1935, when she appeared at the Apollo and was spotted by Bardu Ali, the master of ceremonies for Chick Webb's band, who persuaded Webb to hire her. Fitzgerald began performing with Webb's band at the Savoy Club, and cut her first record, "Love and Kisses," with them in June 1935. Inspired by a nursery rhyme, Fitzgerald cowrote and recorded "A-Tisket, A-Tasket" with Webb's group in 1938; it became one of the most successful records of the swing era and transformed the young singer into a national celebrity.

When Webb died suddenly in 1939, Fitzgerald assumed nominal leadership of his band, which broke up two years later. During the 1940s she gained prominence as a solo performer through hit records that showcased her versatility. Influenced by Dizzy Gillespie and bebop, in 1947 Fitzgerald recorded, "Oh, Lady Be Good" and "How High the Moon," two songs that utilized her scat singing, the wordless vocal improvising that became her signature style. By the early 1950s, she had appeared around the world with the star-studded Jazz and the Philharmonic tours organized by Norman Granz, a record producer and impresario who became her manager in 1954. Under his supervision and on his Verve label, she recorded *The Cole Porter Songbook* in 1956, followed by anthologies devoted to George and Ira Gershwin, Duke Ellington, Irving Berlin, and other popular composers. Heavily arranged and cannily designed to promote both songwriter and performer, Fitzgerald's "songbooks" extended her appeal.

By the 1960s, she was one of the world's most respected and successful singers. In the following years, she became something of an institution, regularly honored. She was named "Best Female Vocalist" by *Down Beat* magazine several times, and she has more Grammy Awards than any other female jazz singer. Following heart bypass surgery in 1986, she suffered from erratic health, but she intermittently recorded and gave concerts.

—BUD KLIMENT

inherently music for small ensembles, which usually included a rhythm section of piano, bass, and drums, and two or three horns, playing a new repertory of jazz standards often derived from the chord changes of Ray Noble's "Cherokee" or George Gershwin's "I Got Rhythm." In the standard bebop ensemble, after the initial statement of the theme in unison, each soloist was given several choruses to improvise on that theme. The beboppers, ever restless innovators, also experimented with Latin music, string accompaniments, and the sonorities of twentieth-century European concert music.

The latter influenced pianist John Lewis and trumpeter Miles Davis, bebop pioneers who forged a new style known as "cool jazz." In the late 1940s, Davis began listening to and playing with white musicians, especially arranger Gil Evans, associated with Claude Thornhill's band. Davis formed an unusual nine-piece band, including "non-jazz" instruments such as tuba and French horn for club and record sessions later known as *Cool Jazz.* The ensemble's elegant, relaxed rhythms, complex and progressive harmonies, and intimate solo styles proved enormously influential to white musicians such as Gerry Mulligan, Chet Baker, Lennie Tristano, Dave Brubeck, George Shearing, and Stan Getz, as well as to Lewis's Modern Jazz Quartet.

Davis, a prodigious creator of jazz styles, helped launch the other major trend of the 1950s, "hard bop." Inaugurated by "Walkin'" (1954), hard bop was marked by longer, more emotional solos reminiscent of 1930s cutting contests, and reaffirmation of the gospel and blues. Charles Mingus, Sonny Rollins, Clifford Brown, Horace Silver, Art Blakey, and Thelonious Monk were all major exponents of hard bop, as were Cannonball

Adderley, Eric Dolphy, Mal Waldron, Jackie McLean, and Wes Montgomery later. During the late 1950s Davis led an ensemble that included some of the finest and most influential of all hard bop players, including John Coltrane, Cannonball Adderley, and white pianist Bill Evans. Davis's landmark *Kind of Blue* (1959) introduced a popular and influential style of playing known as modal, in which modes or scales, rather than chord changes, generate improvisation. Davis also never gave up his interest in large-ensemble, arranged music, and he experimented in the late 1950s, collaborating with Gil Evans, with orchestrations derived from modern European concert music. This music, which white composer Gunther Schuller dubbed as "Third Stream," was never popular among jazz audiences, although black jazz composers such as John Lewis and George Russell embraced its concepts.

Bebop, cool jazz, hard bop, Third Stream music, and "soul" or "funk" jazz, pioneered by Horace Silver, dominated jazz in the late 1950s. However, the giants of the previous decades, playing what was to be called "mainstream" jazz, had some of their greatest popular, if not musical, successes. During that decade Louis Armstrong toured regularly in small and large ensembles, and had several enormously popular records. Basie organized a new orchestra, and also had several hit records. Ellington, who had triumphantly introduced new extended works annually in the 1940s, continued to compose for his orchestra, and also had several hits.

Avant-Garde Jazz

By the early 1960s, jazz had reached a crucial turning point. Many of the jazz masters of the swing era, such as Lester Young and Billie Holiday, were dead. Many of the most important musicians, including Charlie Parker, Bud Powell, and Clifford Brown, had died tragically young or had been devastated by heroin addiction, mental illness, or accidents. Musicians had pushed the rhythmic and harmonic conventions that had been established during the swing era to their breaking point. During the 1960s, Coltrane, Ornett Coleman, and Cecil Taylor led the way in beginning to abandon the swinging rhythms and melodies of traditional jazz in favor of implied tempos and harmonies, drawing on the largely unexplored reaches of their instruments, often in epic-length solos. By the mid-1960s, a whole new generation of avant-garde or free jazz musicians, including Albert Ayler, Archie Shepp, Marion Brown, Bill Dixon, Sun Ra, and Don Cherry be-

gan to abandon even the bedrock jazz convention of theme and improvisation in favor of dissonant collective improvisations related to the energetic polyphony of New Orleans–style jazz. These musicians, inspired by the Civil Rrights Movement, also began to address politics, especially race problems and black nationalism, in their music. They were often joined by musicians from the previous generation, such as Max Roach and Charles Mingus. Also in the 1960s, many jazz musicians visited Africa, and some converted to Islam, although some musicians—for example, Sadik Hakim—had converted as early as the 1940s. Many figures in the Black Arts Movement, such as Amiri Baraka, hailed the extended solos of musicians such as John Coltrane as an authentic African-American art form. Ironically, at the same time, almost any connection to a large black audience in America was sundered.

The "further out" jazz became, the more harshly it was attacked by traditional musicians and listeners alike. In response, by the late 1960s many free jazz musicians were searching for ways to recapture a mass black audience. Once again, it was Miles Davis who led the way. Starting in the late 1960s, Davis began using electric instruments in his bands, and incorporating funk, rhythm and blues, and rock rhythms into his albums. Members of Davis's electric ensembles, such as Herbie Hancock, Wayne Shorter, and Chick Corea, later enjoyed tremendous popular success.

If the electric music Davis created, known as "fusion" or "jazz rock," inspired accusations that he was selling out, in the 1970s, the purist mantle would be carried by a group of musicians who had been playing in Chicago since the early 1960s. Striving toward the implicit racial pride and artistic and economic independence preached by Sun Ra, Mingus, and Taylor, the Association for the Advancement of Creative Musicians (AACM) was founded in 1965. The AACM, and its offshoot, the St. Louis–based Black Artists Group, have been responsible for many of the most important developments in jazz since the mid-1970s. The Art Ensemble of Chicago, pianist Muhal Richard Abrams, and saxophonist Anthony Braxton and Henry Threadgill have all been important exponents of what they term "creative music," which idiosyncratically and unpredictably draws upon everything from ragtime to free jazz.

Jazz in the 1990s

In the 1980s, the institutionalization of jazz accompanied the more general interest of universi-

Coltrane, often simply called "Trane," was by far the most popular jazz musician to emerge from the New York City jazz avant-garde of the late 1950s and 1960s.

PAGE 149

See also
Ella Fitzgerald
Dizzy Gillespie
Billie Holiday

ties, symphonies, and museums in many areas of African-American culture. Since the 1970s, many jazz musicians, including Mary Lou Williams, Archie Shepp, Jackie McLean, Bill Dixon, and Anthony Braxton have held university positions. Although there is a long history of formally trained jazz musicians, from Will Marion Cook to Miles Davis, a large proportion of the best young jazz musicians now come from conservatories. Such training has resulted not only in avant-gardists like Anthony Davis and David Murray, who have a healthy appreciation for the roots of jazz, but bebop-derived traditionalists like Wynton Marsalis, who have brought mainstream jazz to the public prominence it has lacked for forty years. Further, although independent scholars compiled discographies and wrote biographies as early as the 1930s, since the 1980s there has been a burst of institutional scholarly activity, accompanied by the integration of jazz into traditional symphony repertories, as well as the creation of jazz orchestras dedicated to preserving the repertory, and developing new compositions, at the Smithsonian Institution and Lincoln Center. Jazz, as perhaps the greatest of all African-American cultural contributions, always captured the imagination of great African-American writers like Langston Hughes and Ralph Ellison, and it continues to suffuse the work of contemporary writers like Ishmael Reed, Toni Morrison, Albert Murray, and Stanley Crouch.

As jazz approaches its second century, a new generation of musicians, including pianist Geri Allen and tenor saxophonist Joshua Redman, continue to improvise on the history of jazz to further address and define issues central to this particular African-American experience.

—LEONARD GOINES

JIM CROW

As a way of portraying African Americans, "Jim Crow" first appeared in the context of minstrelsy in the early nineteenth century. Thomas "Daddy" Rice, a white minstrel, popularized the term. Using burnt cork to blacken his face, attired in the ill-fitting, tattered garment of a beggar, and grinning broadly, Rice imitated the dancing, singing, and demeanor generally ascribed to Negro character. Calling it "Jump Jim Crow," he based the number on a routine he had seen performed in

---

MAE JEMISON

First African-American Woman in Space

Mae Carol Jemison (October 17, 1956–), astronaut. Mae C. Jemison was born in Decatur, Ala., but grew up in Chicago, Ill. In 1977, she graduated from Stanford University with a B.S. in Chemical Engineering and a B.A. in African and Afro-American Studies. She received an M.D. from Cornell University Medical College in 1981. After interning at the University of Southern California Medical Center in Los Angeles, she worked in private practice until January 1983, when she joined the Peace Corps. She served in Sierra Leone and Liberia as a Peace Corps medical officer for two and a half years, returning in 1985 to Los Angeles to work as a general practitioner.

In 1987, Jemison's application to NASA's astronaut training program was accepted, and she was named the first African-American woman astronaut. After completing the one-year program, she worked as an astronaut officer representative at the Kennedy Space Center in Florida. In September 1992, Jemison became the first black woman in space when she flew as a payload specialist aboard the space shuttle *Endeavor.* During the seven-day flight, Jemison conducted experiments to determine the effects of zero gravity on humans and animals.

In March 1993, Jemison resigned from NASA in order to form her own company, the Jemison Group, which specializes in adapting technology for use in underdeveloped nations. Her historic spaceflight brought her much adulation. In Detroit a school was named after her. And in the spring of 1993, a PBS special, *The New Explorers,* focused on her life story, while *People* named her one of the year's "50 Most Beautiful People in the World." Also in 1993, Jemison made a guest appearance as a transport operator named Lieutenant Palmer on the television series *Star Trek: The Next Generation.* This was fitting, as Jemison claimed that she was inspired to become an astronaut by the actress Nichelle Nichols, who portrayed the black Lieutenant Uhura on the original *Star Trek.*

Jemison received the CIBA Award for Student Involvement in 1979, the Essence Award in 1988, the Gamma Sigma Gamma Woman of the Year Award in 1989, and the Makeda Award for community contributions in 1993.

—LYDIA MCNEILL

See also

John Coltrane

1828 by an elderly and crippled Louisville stableman belonging to a Mr. Crow. "Weel about, and turn about / And do jis so; / Eb'ry time I weel about, / I jump Jim Crow." The public responded with enthusiasm to Rice's caricature of black life. By the 1830s, minstrelsy had become one of the most popular forms of mass entertainment, "Jim Crow" had entered the American vocabulary, and many whites, north and south, came away from minstrel shows reinforced in their distorted images of black life, character, and aspirations.

Less clear is how a dance created by a black stableman and imitated by a white man for the amusement of white audiences would become synonymous with a system designed by whites to segregate the races. The term "Jim Crow" as applied to separate accommodations for whites and blacks appears to have had its origins not in the South but in Massachusetts before the Civil War. Abolitionist newspapers employed the term in the 1840s to describe separate railroad cars for blacks and whites. Throughout the North, blacks, though legally free, found themselves largely the objects of scorn, ridicule, and discrimination.

Most northern whites shared with southern whites the conviction that blacks, as an inferior race, were incapable of assimilation as equals into American society. Racial integrity demanded that blacks, regardless of class, be segregated in public transportation—that they be excluded from the regular cabins and dining rooms on steamboats, compelled to ride on the outside of stagecoaches, and forced to travel in special Jim Crow coaches on the railroads. Only in New England, prior to the Civil War, did blacks manage to integrate transportation facilities, but only after prolonged agitation, during which blacks and white abolitionists deliberately violated Jim Crow rules and often had to be dragged from the trains.

Before the Civil War, enslavement determined the status of most black men and women in the South, and there was little need for legal segregation. During Reconstruction, the radical state governments, though several of them outlawed segregation in the new constitutions, did not try to force integration on unwilling whites. Custom, habit, and etiquette defined the social relations between the races and enforced separation. The

A DOUBLE STANDARD

Jim Crow restrictions mandated separate facilities for blacks and whites. Here, in 1939, a man drinks from a Jim Crow water fountain.
PRINTS AND PHOTOGRAPHS DIVISION, LIBRARY OF CONGRESS

See also
Plessy v. *Ferguson*
Reconstruction

*. . . and I am
waiting / for a
sweet desegregated
chariot / to swing
low / and carry
me back to Ole
Virginie . . .*

LAWRENCE FERLINGHETTI
I AM WAITING, 1958

determination of blacks to improve their position revolved largely around efforts to secure accommodations that equaled those provided the whites.

But in the 1890s, even as segregation became less rigid and pervasive in the North, the term "Jim Crow" took on additional force and meaning in the South. It came to represent an expanded apparatus of segregation sanctioned by law. Economic and social changes had multiplied the places and situations in which blacks and whites might come into contact, and whites had become alarmed over a new generation of blacks undisciplined by slavery, unschooled in racial etiquette, less fearful of whites, and more inclined to assert their rights as citizens.

Jim Crow, then, came to the South in an expanded and more rigid form in the 1890s and the early twentieth century, in response to white perceptions of a new generation of blacks and to growing doubts that this generation could be trusted to stay in its place without legal force. Some whites, caught up in the age of progressive reform, preferred to view legal segregation as reform rather than repression, as a way to resolve racial tensions and maintain the peace. For most whites, however, it was nothing less than racial self-preservation, deeply rooted in the white psyche. "If anything would make me kill my children," a white woman told a northern visitor, "it would be the possibility that niggers might sometime eat at the same table and associate with them as equals. That's the way we feel about it, and you might as well root up that big tree in front of the house and stand it the other way up and expect it to grow as to think we can feel any different."

Between 1890 and 1915, the racial creed of the white South manifested itself in the systematic disfranchisement of black men, in rigid patterns of racial segregation, in unprecedented racial violence and brutality, and in the dissemination of racial caricatures that reinforced and comforted whites in their racial beliefs and practices. The white South moved to segregate the races by law in practically every conceivable situation in which they might come into social contact. The signs "White Only" and "Colored" would henceforth punctuate the southern scenery: from public transportation to public parks and cemeteries, from the work place to hospitals, asylums, orphanages, and prisons, from the entrances and exits at theaters, movie houses, and boardinghouses to toilets and water fountains. Oftentimes, Jim Crow demanded exclusion rather than separation, as with municipal libraries and many sports and recreational facilities. Jim Crow legislation tended

to be thorough, far-reaching, even imaginative: from separate public school textbooks for black and white children to Jim Crow Bibles for black witnesses in court, from separate telephone booths to Jim Crow elevators. New Orleans adopted an ordinance segregating black and white prostitutes.

In *Plessy* v. *Ferguson* (1896) the United States Supreme Court employed the "separate-but-equal" principle to affirm the constitutionality of Jim Crow, confirming what most black southerners already knew from personal experience—that the quality of their life and freedom depended on the whims and will of a majority of whites in their locality or state. The court decision, along with the elaborate structure of Jim Crow, remained in force for more than half a century. In the 1950s and 1960s, a new climate of political necessity and a new generation of black Americans helped to restructure race relations. With an emboldened and enlarged Civil Rights Movement in the vanguard, the federal government and the courts struck down the legal barriers of racial segregation and ended Jim Crow. But a far more intractable and elusive kind of racism, reflected in dreary economic statistics and a pervasive poverty, lay beyond the reach of the law and the growing Civil Rights Movement.

—LEON F. LITWACK

JOHNSON, CHARLES RICHARD

Charles Richard Johnson (April 23, 1948–), novelist. Charles Johnson was born in Evanston, Ill., and studied at Southern Illinois University and SUNY at Stony Brook in New York, majoring in philosophy. As he writes in the essay "Where Philosophy and Fiction Meet" (1988), he was inspired by a campus appearance of LeRoi Jones (Amiri Baraka) to turn toward literary expression (after some work as a cartoonist). Johnson's flirtation with cultural nationalism was intense but brief: He came to recognize that its built-in danger "is the very tendency toward the provincialism, separatism, and essentialist modes of thought that characterize the Anglophilia it opposes." If the utopianism and the mix of social hope and colorful individual expression of the 1960s inspired him to become a writer, he was attracted to the tradition of the philosophical novel, in which he began to write at the postmodern moment when parody, comedy, and tongue-in-

See also
Amiri Baraka

cheek improvisation in the face of disaster came together. He worked under the supervision of novelist John Gardner and remained closely associated with him for many years. Johnson draws freely on Indian and Japanese Buddhist sources, Western philosophy, and literary precursors from Cervantes to Slave Narratives and from Saint Augustine to Hermann Hesse's *Siddhartha*. He has also been deeply influenced by the ways in which the African-American writers W. E. B. Du Bois, Jean Toomer, Richard Wright, and Ralph Ellison approached fundamental questions of culture and consciousness. Johnson traced their legacy in the essay "Being & Race: Black Writing Since 1970" (1988), a subtly yet firmly argued survey of the contemporary literary scene, for the title of which Martin Heidegger served as an inspiration.

After writing a number of increasingly accomplished short stories that were collected in *The Sorcerer's Apprentice* (1986) and publishing a first novel, *Faith and the Good Thing*, in 1974 (several others exist in manuscript but were never published), Johnson achieved an artistic breakthrough with his novel *Oxherding Tale* (1982). A meditation on the representation of the eighth of the "Oxherding Pictures" by Zen artist Kakuan-Shien (in which both the ox and herdsman are gone), the novel also continues the tradition of autobiographical fiction as embodied in James Weldon Johnson's *Autobiography of an Ex-Colored Man*. *Oxherding Tale* represents the education of Andrew Hawkins, who is raised by a transcendentalist tutor on a southern plantation—a plantation that is visited by Karl Marx in the novel. As Andrew (like Saint Augustine before him) learns to free himself from dualism, another figure, that of the Soulcatcher, grows in importance. Johnson draws the philosophical issues out of love, education, or enslavement. It is a stylistically brilliant novel, both comic and profound, picaresque and self-reflexive. It parodies the eighteenth-century novel and the genre of the slave narrative yet manages to remain faithful to both these inspirations. Johnson received the Governor's Award for Literature from the state of Washington for *Oxherding Tale* in 1983.

Johnson's novel *Middle Passage* (1990) continued the exploration of a nineteenth-century setting for unusual purposes. It is the tale of Rutherford, who eludes collectors of gambling debts and the offer of redemption by marriage in New Orleans when he takes the place of a sailor, only to find himself aboard a slave ship headed for Africa. Johnson manages to revitalize what have become fixtures in imagining the nineteenth century by concerning himself with the human issues he locates in particular spaces. The enslaved Almuseri add some elements of magical realism to the text, which may be the most imaginative modern thematization of the experience that the title refers to, free from the clichéd ways in which this historical period has sometimes been fictionalized. *Middle Passage* was awarded the National Book Award in 1990.

In 1998, Johnson published *Dream: A Novel*, a fictionalized account of the life of Martin Luther King, Jr. during the Civil Rights era. Told from the perspective of civil rights activist Matthew Bishop, the novel explores the relationship between King and Chaym Smith, a man who bears an uncanny physical resemblance to King.

—WERNER SOLLORS

JOHNSON, JAMES WELDON

James Weldon Johnson (July 17, 1871–June 17, 1938), writer and political leader. James William Johnson, who changed his middle name to Weldon in 1913, was born in Jacksonville, Fla. James, Sr., his father, the headwaiter at a local hotel, accumulated substantial real estate holdings and maintained a private library. Helen Dillet Johnson, his mother, a native of Nassau in the Bahamas, was the only African-American woman teaching in Jacksonville's public schools. Through his parents' example, the opportunity to travel, and his reading, Johnson developed the urbanity and the personal magnetism that characterized his later political and literary career.

Johnson graduated in 1894 from Atlanta University, an all-black institution that he credited with instilling in him the importance of striving to better the lives of his people. Returning to Jacksonville, he traveled many different roads to fulfill that sense of racial responsibility. Appointed principal of the largest school for African Americans in Florida, he developed a high-school curriculum. At the same time, he founded a short-lived newspaper, the *Daily American* (1895–1896); studied law; passed the bar examination; and wrote lyrics for the music of his brother, J. Rosamond Johnson. In 1900 the brothers collaborated on "Lift Ev'ry Voice and Sing," a song that is regarded as the Negro National Anthem.

Johnson moved to New York in 1902 to work with his brother and his brother's partner on the vaudeville circuit, Robert Cole. Called by one

"Lift Ev'ry Voice and Sing"

JAMES WELDON JOHNSON
POEM TITLE, 1900

critic the "ebony Offenbachs," the songwriting team of Cole, Johnson, and Johnson was one of the most successful in the country. (The 1902 song "Under the Bamboo Tree" was their greatest success.) The team tried to avoid stereotypical representations of blacks and tried to invest their songs with some dignity and humanity, as well as humor.

While his brother toured with Cole, James Weldon Johnson studied literature at Columbia University and became active in New York City politics. In 1904, in a political association dominated by Booker T. Washington, Johnson became the treasurer of the city's Colored Republican Club. The Republican party rewarded his service with an appointment to the United States Consular Service in 1906, and Johnson served first as United States consul at Porto Cabello, Venezuela, and then, from 1908 to 1913, in Corinto, Nicaragua.

In Venezuela he completed his first and only novel, *The Autobiography of an Ex-Coloured Man* (1913). Published anonymously, it was taken by many readers for a true autobiography. That realism marks an important transition from the nineteenth- to the twentieth-century African-American novel. Johnson brought modern literary techniques to his retelling of the popular nineteenth-century "tragic mulatto" theme.

JAMES WELDON JOHNSON

Johnson drew on African-American religious expressions for poetic inspiration.
PHOTOGRAPHS AND PRINTS DIVISION, SCHOMBURG CENTER FOR RESEARCH IN BLACK CULTURE, THE NEW YORK PUBLIC LIBRARY, ASTOR, LENOX AND TILDEN FOUNDATIONS

See also
Harlem Renaissance

The election of Woodrow Wilson, a Democrat, to the presidency blocked Johnson's advancement in the consular service. He returned to New York, where, in 1914, he joined the *New York Age* as an editorial writer. While he was associated with the politics of Booker T. Washington, Johnson's instincts were more radical and he gravitated toward the NAACP. In 1916, the NAACP hired him as a field secretary, charged with organizing or reviving local branches. In that post, he greatly expanded and solidified the still-fledgling organization's branch operations and helped to increase its membership, influence, and revenue. He also took an active role organizing protests against racial discrimination, including the racial violence of the "Red Summer" of 1919, a phrase he coined.

Shortly after he joined the staff of the NAACP, Johnson published his first collection of poetry, *Fifty Years and Other Poems* (1917). Like the work of Paul Laurence Dunbar, Johnson's poetry falls into two broad categories: poems in standard English and poems in a conventionalized African-American dialect. While he used dialect, he also argued that dialect verse possessed a limited range for racial expression. His poems in standard English include some of his most important early contributions to African-American letters. Poems like "Brothers" and "White Witch" are bitter protests against lynching that anticipate the poetry of Claude McKay in the 1920s and the fiction of Richard Wright in the 1930s and 1940s.

During the 1920s, Johnson's political and artistic activities came together. He was appointed secretary of the NAACP's national office in 1920. His tenure brought coherence and consistency to the day-to-day operations of the association and to his general political philosophy. He led the organization in its lobbying for the passage of the Dyer Anti-Lynching Bill and in its role in several legal cases; his report on the conditions of the American occupation of Haiti prompted a Senate investigation. Johnson's leadership helped to establish the association as a major national civil rights organization committed to accomplishing its goals through lobbying for legislation and seeking legal remedies through the courts. In 1927–1928 and again in 1929, he took a leave of absence from the NAACP. During the latter period he helped organize the consortium of Atlanta University and Spelman and Morehouse colleges.

Also in the 1920s, Johnson, with such colleagues at the NAACP as W. E. B. Du Bois, Walter White, and Jessie Fauset, maintained that the promotion of the artistic and literary creativity of African Americans went hand in hand with political activism, that the recognition of blacks in the arts broke down racial barriers. Their advocacy of black artists in the pages of *Crisis,* and with white writers, publishers, and critics, established an audience for the flourishing of African-American literature during the Harlem Renaissance. Johnson himself published an anthology of African-American poetry, *The Book of Negro Poetry* (1922, rev. 1931), and he and his brother edited two volumes of *The Book of American Negro Spirituals* (1925 and 1926). In his introductions to these anthologies and in critical essays, he argued for a distinct African-American creative voice that was expressed by both professional artists and the anonymous composers of the spirituals. *Black Manhattan* (1930) was a pioneering "cultural history" that promoted Harlem as the cultural capital of black America.

Johnson was not in the conventional sense either a pious or a religious man, but he consistently drew on African-American religious expressions for poetic inspiration. In early poems like "Lift Ev'ry Voice and Sing," "O Black and Unknown Bards," and "100 Years," he formulated a secular version of the vision of hope embodied in spirituals and gospel songs. His second volume of poetry, *God's Trombones* (1927), drew on the African-American vernacular sermon. Using the rhythms, syntax, and figurative language of the African-American preacher, Johnson devised a poetic expression that reproduced the richness of African-American language without succumbing to the stereotypes that limited his dialect verse.

In 1930, Johnson resigned as secretary of the NAACP to take up a teaching post at Fisk University and pursue his literary career. His autobiography, *Along This Way,* was published in 1933; his vision of racial politics, *Negro American, What Now?,* was published in 1934; and his third major collection of poetry, *St. Peter Relates an Incident,* was published in 1935. He was killed in an automobile accident on June 17, 1938.

—GEORGE P. CUNNINGHAM

JOHNSON, JOHN ARTHUR "JACK"

John Arthur "Jack" Johnson (March 31, 1878– June 10, 1946), boxer. The third of six surviving children, Jack Johnson was born in Galveston, Tex., to Henry Johnson, a laborer and ex-slave, and Tiny Johnson. He attended school for about five years, then worked as a stevedore, janitor, and cotton picker. He gained his initial fighting experience in battle royals, brutal competitions in which a group of African-American boys engaged in no-holds-barred brawls, with a few coins going to the last fighter standing. He turned professional in 1897. In his early years Johnson mainly fought other African-American men. His first big win was a sixth-round decision on January 17, 1902, over Frank Childs, one of the best black heavyweights of the day. The six-foot, 200-pound Johnson developed into a powerful defensive boxer who emphasized quickness, rhythm, style, and grace.

In 1903, Johnson defeated Denver Ed Martin in a twenty-round decision, thus capturing the championship of the unofficial Negro heavyweight division, which was created by West coast sportswriters to compensate for the prohibition on blacks fighting for the real crown. Johnson, who was then the de facto leading heavyweight challenger, sought a contest with champion Jim Jeffries but was rebuffed because of the color line. Racial barriers largely limited Johnson's opponents to black fighters like Joe Jeanette, whom he fought ten times. Johnson's first big fight against a white contender was in 1905, against Marvin Hart, which he lost by the referee's decision, despite having demonstrated his superior talent and ring mastery. Hart became champion three months later, knocking out Jack Root to win Jeffries's vacated title. Johnson's bid to get a title fight improved in 1906, when he hired Sam Fitzpatrick as his manager. Fitzpatrick knew the major promoters and could arrange fights that Johnson could not when he managed himself. Johnson enhanced his reputation with victories in Australia, a second-round knockout of forty-four-year-old

"JACK" JOHNSON

Behind this dapper, smiling façade lay a powerful boxing force.
PRINTS AND PHOTOGRAPHS DIVISION, LIBRARY OF CONGRESS

J

ex-champion Bob Fitzsimmons in Philadelphia, and two wins in England.

In 1908 Canadian Tommy Burns became champion, and Johnson stalked him to Australia, looking for a title bout. Promoter Hugh McIntosh signed Burns to a match in Sydney on December 26 for a $30,000 guarantee with $5,000 for Johnson. Burns was knocked down in the first round by Johnson, who thereafter verbally and physically punished Burns until the police stopped the fight in the fourteenth round. White reaction was extremely negative, with journalists describing Johnson as a "huge primordial ape." A search began for a "white hope" who would regain the title to restore to whites their sense of superiority and to punish Johnson's arrogant public behavior. To many whites, Johnson was a "bad nigger" who refused to accept restrictions placed upon him by white society. A proud, willful man, Johnson recklessly violated the taboos against the "proper place" for blacks, most notoriously in his relationships with white women. Though much of the black middle class viewed his lifestyle with some disquiet, he became a great hero to lower-class African Americans through his flouting of conventional social standards and his seeming lack of fear of white disapproval.

Johnson defended his title five times in 1909, most memorably against middleweight champion Stanley Ketchell, a tenacious 160-pound fighter. Johnson toyed with Ketchell for several rounds, rarely attacking. Ketchell struck the champion behind the ear in the twelfth round with a roundhouse right, knocking him to the canvas. An irate Johnson arose, caught the attacking challenger with a right uppercut, and knocked him out. Johnson's only defense in 1910 was against Jim Jeffries, who was encouraged to come out of retirement by an offer of a $101,000 guarantee, split 3:1 for the winner, plus profits from film rights. When moral reformers refused to allow the match to be held in San Francisco, it was moved to Reno, Nev. The former champion, well past his prime, was overmatched. Johnson taunted and humiliated him, ending the fight with a fifteenth-round knockout. Fears that a Johnson victory would unleash racial hostilities were quickly realized as gangs of whites randomly attacked blacks in cities across the country. Some states and most cities barred the fight film for fear of further exacerbating racial tensions. Overnight the national press raised an uproar over the "viciousness" of boxing and clamored for its prohibition. Even Theodore Roosevelt, himself an avid boxer, publicly hoped "that this is the last prizefight to take place in the United States." The reaction to Johnson's victory over a white champion proved a significant event in the history of American racism, as white fears of black male sexuality and power were manifested in a wave of repression and violence.

In 1910, Johnson settled in Chicago, where he enjoyed a fast lifestyle; he toured with vaudeville shows, drove racing cars, and in 1912 opened a short-lived nightclub, the Cafe de Champion. Johnson defended his title once during the two years following the Jeffries fight, beating "Fireman" Jim Flynn in nine rounds in a filmed fight in Las Vegas, N.M. Subsequently, in response to anti-Johnson and anti-boxing sentiment and concern about films showing a black man pummeling a white, the federal government banned the interstate transport of fight films.

In 1911, Johnson married white divorcee Etta Terry Duryea, but their life was turbulent and she committed suicide a year later. Johnson later married two other white women. His well-publicized love life caused much talk of expanding state antimiscegenation statutes. More important, the federal government pursued Johnson for violation of the Mann Act (1910), the so-called "white slavery act," which forbade the transportation of women across state lines for "immoral purposes." The law was seldom enforced, but the federal government chose to prosecute Johnson, even though he was not involved in procuring. Johnson was guilty only of flaunting his relationships with white women. He was convicted and sentenced to one year in the penitentiary, but fled the country to Europe through Canada. He spent several troubled years abroad, defending his title twice in Paris and once in Buenos Aires, and struggled to earn a living.

In 1915 a match was arranged with Jess Willard (6'6" and 250 pounds) in Havana. By then Johnson was old for a boxer and had not trained adequately for the fight; he tired and was knocked out in the twenty-sixth round. The result was gleefully received in the United States, and thereafter no African American was given a chance to fight for the heavyweight title until Joe Louis. Johnson had hoped to make a deal with the government to reduce his penalty, and four years later claimed that he threw the fight. Most boxing experts now discount Johnson's claim and believe it was an honest fight. Johnson returned to the United States in 1920 and served a year in Leavenworth Penitentiary in Kansas. He subsequently fought a few bouts, gave exhibitions, trained and managed fighters, appeared on stage, and lectured. His autobiography, *Jack Johnson: In the Ring*

See also
Paul Robeson

and Out, appeared in 1927; a new edition was published, with additional material, in 1969. Johnson died in 1946 when he drove his car off the road in North Carolina.

Johnson's life was memorialized by Howard Sackler's play *The Great White Hope* (1969), which was made into a motion picture in 1971. Johnson finished with a record of 78 wins (including 45 by knockout), 8 defeats, 12 draws, and 14 no-decisions in 112 bouts. He was elected to the Boxing Hall of Fame in 1954. In 1987 *Ring* magazine rated him the second greatest heavyweight of all time, behind Muhammad Ali.

—STEVEN A. RIESS

JOHNSON, JOHN HAROLD

John Harold Johnson (January 19, 1918–), publisher. John H. Johnson rose from humble origins to found the country's largest African-American publishing empire and become one of the wealthiest men in the United States. Johnson was the only child of Leroy Johnson and Gertrude Jenkins Johnson and was reared in the Mississippi River town of Arkansas City. His father was killed in a sawmill accident when young Johnny (the name with which he was christened) was eight years old. The following year, 1927, his mother married James Williams, who worked as a bakery shop deliveryman.

Because the public school curriculum for blacks in Arkansas City terminated at the eighth grade and because Johnson and his mother had heard of greater opportunities in Chicago, they became part of the African-American migration to that city in 1933. Johnson enrolled in DuSable High School and proved himself an able student. Perhaps the crucial event in his life occurred when he delivered an honors convocation speech heard by Harry H. Pace, president of the Supreme Liberty Life Insurance Company.

Pace, who often helped talented black youths (among them Paul Robeson), encouraged Johnson to attend college. Pace gave Johnson a part-time job at the insurance company that enabled his protégé to attend the University of Chicago. But Johnson's interest focused on the impressive operations of the black-owned insurance firm, and he eventually dropped his university studies, married Eunice Walker in 1941, and assumed full-time work at Supreme Liberty Life.

Among Johnson's duties at Supreme Liberty Life was to collect news and information about black Americans and prepare a weekly digest for Pace. Johnson thought that such a "Negro digest" could be marketed and sold. In 1942 he parlayed a $500 loan using his mother's furniture as collateral to publish the first issue of *Negro Digest,* a magazine patterned after *Reader's Digest.* Although there were format similarities between the two publications, Johnson noted in his 1989 autobiography, *Succeeding Against the Odds,* that *Reader's Digest* tended to be upbeat whereas *Negro Digest* spoke to an audience that was "angry, disillusioned and disappointed" with social inequalities in the United States. Within eight months *Negro Digest* reached $50,000 a month in sales.

In 1945 Johnson launched his second publication, *Ebony,* using the format made popular by the major picture magazine *Life.* Central to his philosophy was the concept that African Americans craved a publication that would focus on black achievement and portray them in a positive manner. Six years later he created *Jet,* a pocket-sized weekly carrying news, society, entertainment, and political information pertinent to African Americans. In ensuing years Johnson added other enterprises to his lucrative empire, including new magazine ventures, book publishing, Fashion Fair cosmetics, several radio stations, and majority ownership of Supreme Liberty Life Insurance Company.

Despite the wide range and diversity of his business holdings, Johnson admitted his management style to be hands-on and direct, with every detail of operations requiring his personal approval. While tasks may be delegated, Johnson believes that his staff requires daily monitoring and oversight to ensure performance. Although he named his daughter, Linda Johnson Rice, president and chief operating officer in the late 1980s, he clearly remained in charge but asked "her opinion on decisions I plan to make."

By 1990 Johnson's personal wealth was estimated at $150 million. He has been a confidant of several U.S. presidents of both political parties and served as a goodwill ambassador to various nations throughout the world, including those in Eastern Europe and Africa.

—CLINT C. WILSON II

JOHNSON, WILLIAM HENRY

William Henry Johnson (March 18, 1901–April 13, 1970), painter. For most African Americans,

See also
Literature

life in a small southern town after Reconstruction hardly promised more than a succession of menial jobs, a world of hard labor, and an insular, often fearful existence. As an artistically inclined but poverty-stricken black youth growing up in Florence, S.C., during the first two decades of the twentieth century, William H. Johnson followed this all-too-familiar pattern. There were very few options in his life other than running errands for his parents at the local YMCA and train depot, or working at the local steam laundry.

With the encouragement of a few teachers and his Pullman porter uncle, however, Johnson left South Carolina around 1918 in search of a better life and migrated to New York City. From 1921 until 1926, Johnson attended the School of the National Academy of Design, where he quickly became one of the school's most outstanding students. Johnson also worked for three summers (1924–1926) with artist and teacher Charles Webster Hawthorne at his Cape Cod School of Art in Provincetown, Mass.

After failing to win the Pulitzer Traveling Scholarship in his final year at the School of the National Academy of Design, Johnson (with the financial backing of Charles Webster Hawthorne and painter George B. Luks) traveled to Paris, where he continued his art studies and experienced a sense of personal freedom for the first time. After about a year in Paris, Johnson moved to Cagnes-sur-Mer on the French Riviera, where he inaugurated an expressive and rhythmic painting style, best seen in works like *Village Houses* or *Cagnes-sur-Mer* (c. 1928–1929), *Young Pastry Cook* (c. 1928–1930), and *Jacobia Hotel* (1930).

These French-inspired paintings earned Johnson the William E. Harmon gold medal for distinguished achievements in the field of fine arts (1929–1930). Although his European sojourn was interrupted by a brief (and, as a result of the Harmon gold medal, widely celebrated) return to the United States in 1929, Johnson again returned to Europe—specifically, Denmark—in 1930, and maintained this Scandinavian base until 1938. During this time, Johnson married a Danish textile artist, Holcha Krake, traveled throughout Europe and North Africa, and exhibited his bold, expressionistic paintings (e.g., *Old Salt, Denmark*, c. 1931–1932; *Bazaars Behind Church, Oslo*, c. 1935; and *Midnight Sun, Lofoten*, 1937) in galleries in Denmark, Norway, and Sweden.

With the rise of the National Socialist Party in Germany and the expansion of Adolf Hitler's political dominion throughout Europe, Johnson and his wife fled Denmark in 1938 and settled in New

York City. Johnson embarked on a new career in New York, based not on his European-inspired portraits and landscapes, but rather on African-American subjects and themes, all painted in a highly chromatic two-dimensional patchwork quilt-like technique.

Although he lived for much of this time (c. 1938–1946) in a humble manner (in poorly heated lofts in Greenwich Village), Johnson exhibited regularly in New York galleries as well as in all of the major "all-Negro" exhibitions that were organized around the country during this time. Johnson's paintings of rural life in the South (*Going to Church*, c. 1940–1941), Harlem's fashionable nightclubs and urban lifestyles (*Cafe*, c. 1939–1940), the black soldier during World War II (*K.P.*, c. 1942), and religious themes based on Negro spirituals (*Swing Low Sweet Chariot*, c. 1944) all reaped positive but limited critical notice in their day, and remain classic examples of an authentic African-American painting tradition during the war years.

In spite of Johnson's critical successes and personal satisfaction with his work, he sold very little during his lifetime and experienced numerous personal tragedies. In 1942, a fire broke out in his studio/loft, destroying many of his paintings and personal belongings, and forcing him and his wife to seek temporary housing in the middle of winter. In 1943, his wife was diagnosed as suffering from breast cancer, from which she died shortly thereafter, leaving Johnson profoundly bereft.

Works produced by Johnson from 1944 onward exhibit a strange, almost untutored look, stemming no doubt from these trials in his personal life and, moreover, from an encroaching paresis, brought on by a then undiagnosed case of advanced syphilis. Still, these late paintings, which examined black history (*Nat Turner*, c. 1945), the breaking down of colonial rule in the world (*Nehru and Gandhi*, c. 1945), and the major political conferences which led to the conclusion of World War II (*Three Allies in Cairo*, c. 1945), demonstrate a heightened political consciousness on Johnson's part, as well as his desire to connect the world's mid-century quest for political and economic independence with the African American's ongoing struggle for freedom.

Johnson's art career halted in 1947, when he suffered a mental breakdown and was committed to a New York State mental hospital in Central Islip, Long Island. While Johnson languished in the hospital, never to paint or lead a normal life again, his personal estate of more than a thousand paintings, drawings, and prints lay in a wooden

See also

Meta Fuller

storage bin in lower Manhattan, neglected and essentially forgotten for almost a decade. In 1956, the Harmon Foundation, a philanthropic organization that had supported Johnson earlier in his career, agreed to take possession of Johnson's estate just as it was about to be disposed of by Johnson's court-appointed lawyers.

After several years of organizing, conserving, and exhibiting Johnson's art, the Harmon Foundation ceased operation in 1966, and soon thereafter turned over the entire collection (still in need of further research and conservation) to the Smithsonian Institution's National Museum of American Art (then known as the National Collection of Fine Arts). On the eve of the opening of Johnson's first major retrospective at the Smithsonian Institution in November 1971, the exhibition organizers learned that Johnson had died at Central Islip Psychiatric Center in 1970, totally unaware that his work and extraordinary career were finally receiving the recognition and acclaim that he had sought so fervently during his active years.

The art and life of William H. Johnson, the subject of several retrospective exhibitions, numerous publications, and a film documentary, intrigue audiences who have an interest in American art produced between the Great Depression and the end of World War II, the issue of primitivism in modern art and intellectual thought, and the various modes and methods of representing African-American culture during the twentieth century.

—RICHARD J. POWELL

JONES, JAMES EARL

James Earl Jones (January 17, 1931–), actor. James Earl Jones, an actor renowned for his broad, powerful voice and acting range, was born in Arkabutla, Miss., the son of actor Robert Earl Jones. He was raised by his grandparents, who moved to Michigan when Jones was five. Soon afterwards, Jones developed a bad stutter, and remained largely speechless for the following eight years. When he was fourteen, a high school English teacher had him read aloud a poem he had written, and Jones gradually regained the use of his voice. He subsequently starred on the school's debating team. In 1949 Jones entered the University of Michigan as a premedical student, but soon switched to acting, and received his bachelor's degree in 1953. Two years later, he moved to New York City and studied at the American Theater Wing. He made his professional debut in 1957.

Jones first became well-known in the early 1960s. His first leading role was in Lionel Abel's *The Pretender* in 1960. That same year he became a member of Joseph Papp's New York Shakespeare Festival; he remained with the company until 1967, performing on and off Broadway in numerous theatrical productions. He also played several small parts on Broadway. Between 1961 and 1963 he appeared in eighteen different plays Off-Broadway. His most notable performances came in Shakespeare Festival productions, as well as in an all-black production of Jean Genet's *The Blacks,* in Josh Greenfield's *Clandestine on the Morning Line* and in Jack Gelber's *The Apple.* In 1962 Jones won an Obie Award for best actor of the season based on his performances in the latter two productions and in Errol John's *Moon on a Rainbow Shawl.* He subsequently won both a Drama Desk Award (1964) and a second Obie (1965) for his performance in the title role of *Othello* at the New York Shakespeare Festival. Jones also made his screen debut at this time, in a small role in Stanley Kubrick's *Dr. Strangelove* (1964).

In 1967 Jones received his first widespread critical and public recognition when he was cast as the boxer Jack Jefferson (a fictionalized version of heavyweight champion Jack Johnson) in a Washington, D.C. production of Howard Sackler's play

The Great White Hope. In 1968 the play moved to Broadway. The following year, it won a Pulitzer Prize and Jones received a Tony Award. He also starred in the 1970 film based on the play and was nominated that year for an Oscar.

During the 1970s Jones appeared in a variety of stage and screen roles, including such movies as *The Man* (1972), *Claudine* (1974)—for which he was nominated for a Golden Globe Award, *The River Niger* (1975), *The Bingo Long Travelling All-Stars and Motor Kings* (1976), and *A Piece of the Action* (1977); he also provided the voice of Darth Vader in *Star Wars* (1977) and its sequels. On stage, Jones starred in Lorraine Hansberry's *Les Blancs* (1970), in Athol Fugard's *Boesman and Lena* (1970), in an adaptation of John Steinbeck's *Of Mice and Men* (1974), and in various Shakespearean roles.

In 1977 Jones appeared on Broadway in a one-man show in which he portrayed singer/activist Paul Robeson. The show (which opened soon after Robeson's death) was denounced as a distortion of Robeson's life by Paul Robeson, Jr., and was picketed by a committee of black artists and intellectuals who complained that the play had soft-pedalled Robeson's political radicalism. Jones countered that the committee was engaged in censorship. The play's Broadway run and subsequent appearance on public television served to revive public interest in Robeson's life and career.

During the 1980s and early '90s, Jones continued to act in various media. On stage, he starred on Broadway in 1981–82 in a highly acclaimed production of *Othello* with Christopher Plummer as Iago and Cecilia Hart (Jones's wife) as Desdemona, in Athol Fugard's *A Lesson From Aloes* (1980) and *Master Harold . . . and the Boys* (1982), and in August Wilson's *Fences,* for which he received a second Tony award in 1987. He also appeared in more than thirty films during this period, including such movies as *Matewan* (1984), *Soul Man* (1985), *Gardens of Stone* (1985), *Coming to America* (1988), *Field of Dreams* (1989), *The Hunt for Red October* (1990), *Sommersby* (1993), and the animated feature *The Lion King* (1994).

Jones also has had considerable experience in television. He appeared in several episodes of such dramatic series as *East Side, West Side* in the early 1960s. In 1965 his role on *As the World Turns* made him one of the first African Americans to regularly appear in a daytime drama. In 1973 he hosted the variety series *Black Omnibus.* In 1978 Jones played author Alex Haley in the television miniseries *Roots: The Next Generations.* He also has starred in two short-lived dramatic series,

Paris (1979–80) and *Gabriel's Fire* (1990–1992), and has made many television movies, including *The Cay* (1974), *The Atlanta Child Murders* (1984), and *The Vernon Johns Story* (1994). In 1993 Jones published a memoir, *Voices and Silences.*

—SABRINA FUCHS

JONES, M. SISSIERETTA "BLACK PATTI"

M. Sissieretta "Black Patti" Jones (January 5, 1869–June 24, 1933), dramatic concert soprano. Born in Portsmouth, Va., she moved around 1876 with her family to Providence, R.I., where she began formal music training. She studied voice at the Providence Academy of Music and the New England Conservatory of Music, and privately with Louisa Capianni and Mme. Scongia. Her public debut occurred on April 5, 1888, at Steinway Hall, New York. That July she embarked on a six-month tour of the West Indies with the Tennessee Jubilee Singers. On that tour she acquired the sobriquet "Black Patti" (derived from the name of Spanish soprano Adelina Patti), which she retained for the rest of her career.

Jones sang widely as a soloist from 1890 to 1895 in the United States, Canada, the West Indies, and Europe. She attracted considerable national attention from well-publicized performances at the Grand Negro Jubilee at Madison Square Garden and the White House in 1892 and the Pittsburgh Exposition and World's Columbian Exposition in Chicago in 1893. Her career as a soloist ended abruptly in 1896, when she became the leading soprano of Black Patti's Troubadours, a newly organized company managed by Rudolf Voelckel and James Nolan. This company attracted such established entertainers as Robert ("Bob") Cole, the De Wolfe Sisters, Ernest Hogan, and Aida Overton Walker. The show combined elements of vaudeville, minstrelsy, skits, and popular songs, and featured a special classical finale, called an "operatic kaleidoscope," which starred Jones with a supporting cast of soloists, chorus, and orchestra performing staged scenes from operas and musical comedies.

Jones emerged as a singer during the short-lived vogue of black prima donnas that flourished between 1870 and about 1895. She enjoyed celebrity status when most blacks with classical

See also

Marian Anderson

training found professional opportunities limited in American music because of racial prejudices. Endowed with a natural voice of phenomenal range and power, she brought musicality, artistry, and dramatic flair to the stage. Her repertory included classical songs, sentimental ballads, popular tunes, and roles in such operas as *Carmen, Lucia di Lammermoor, La Traviata,* and *Il Trovatore.*

—JOSEPHINE WRIGHT

JONES, QUINCY DELIGHT, JR.

Quincy Delight Jones, Jr. (March 14, 1933–), music producer and composer. Born in Chicago, Quincy Jones learned to play trumpet in the public schools in the Seattle, Wash., area, where his family moved in 1945. Jones sang in church groups from an early age, and wrote his first composition at the age of sixteen. While in high school he played trumpet in rhythm and blues groups with his friend Ray Charles. After graduating from high school, Jones attended Seattle University, and then Berklee School of Music in Boston. He traveled with Jay McShann's band before being hired by Lionel Hampton in 1951. Jones toured Europe with Hampton, and soloed on the band's recording of his own composition, "Kingfish" (1951).

After leaving Hampton in 1953, Jones, who had an undistinguished solo style on trumpet, turned to studio composing and arranging, working with Ray Anthony, Tommy Dorsey, and Hampton. During the 1950s Jones also led his own big bands on albums such as *This Is How I Feel About Jazz* (1956). In 1956 Jones helped Dizzy Gillespie organize his first state department big band. From 1956 to 1960 he worked as the music director for Barclay Records in Paris, and while there he studied arranging with Nadia Boulanger. He also worked with Count Basie, Charles Aznavour, Billy Eckstine, Sarah Vaughan, Dinah Washington, and Horace Silver, and led a big band for recording sessions such as *The Birth of a Band* (1959). Jones served as music director for Harold Arlen's blues opera *Free and Easy* on its European tour. Back in the U.S. in the early 1960s, Jones devoted his time to studio work, attaining an almost ubiquitous presence in the Los Angeles and New York music scenes.

Jones began working as a producer at Mercury Records in 1961. After producing Leslie Gore's hit record "It's My Party" (1963), he became Mercury's first African-American vice president in 1964. He increasingly made use of popular dance rhythms and electric instruments. In 1964 he also scored and conducted an album for Frank Sinatra and Count Basie, *It Might As Well Be Swing.* He recorded with his own ensembles, often in a rhythm and blues or pop jazz idiom, on albums such as *The Quintessence* (1961), *Golden Boy* (1964), *Walking in Space* (1969), and *Smackwater Jack* (1971). Jones also branched into concert music with his *Black Requiem,* a work for orchestra (1971). Jones was the first African-American film composer to be widely accepted in Hollywood, and he scored dozens of films, including *The Pawnbroker* (1963), *Walk, Don't Run* (1966), and *In Cold Blood* (1967).

In 1974, shortly after recording *Body Heat,* Jones suffered a cerebral stroke. He underwent brain surgery, and after recovering he formed his own record company, Qwest Productions. Throughout the 1970s Jones remained in demand as an arranger and composer. He also wrote or arranged music for television shows (*Ironside, The Bill Cosby Show,* the miniseries *Roots,* and *Sanford and Son*), and for films (*The Wiz,* 1978). During the 1980s Jones expanded his role in the film business. In 1985 he coproduced and wrote the music for the film *The Color Purple,* and served as executive music producer for Sidney Poitier's film *Fast Forward* (1985).

Jones's eclectic approach to music, and his ability to combine gritty rhythms with elegant urban textures is perhaps best exemplified by his long association with Michael Jackson. Their collaborations on *Off The Wall* (1979) and *Thriller* (1984) resulted in two of the most popular recordings of

RISE TO THE TOP

Some of Quincy Jones's twenty Grammy awards adorn the wall of his study in this 1974 photo.

AP/WIDE WORLD PHOTOS

See also

Count Basie

Ray Charles

all time. Jones also produced Jackson's 1987 *Bad.* During this time, Jones epitomized the crossover phenomenon by maintaining connections with many types of music. His eclectic 1982 album *The Dude* won a Grammy award, and in 1983 he conducted a big band as part of a tribute to Miles Davis at Radio City Music Hall. The next year he produced and conducted on Frank Sinatra's *L.A. Is My Lady.* He conceived of USA for Africa, a famine relief organization that produced the album and video *We Are The World* (1985). In 1991 Jones appeared with Davis at one of the trumpeter's last major concerts, in Montreux, Switzerland, a performance that was released on album and video in 1993 as *Miles and Quincy Live at Montreux.* During this time Jones also continued to work with classical music, and in 1992 he released *Handel's Messiah: A Soulful Celebration.*

By 1994, with twenty-two Grammy awards to his credit, Jones was the most honored popular musician in the history of the awards. He also wielded enormous artistic and financial power and influence in the entertainment industry, and was a masterful discoverer of new talent. In 1990 his album *Back on the Block,* which included Miles Davis and Ella Fitzgerald in addition to younger African-American musicians such as Ice-T and Kool Moe Dee, won six Grammy awards. He continued to expand his activities into the print media, including the magazine *Vibe,* aimed primarily at a youthful African-American readership. He also produced the hit television series "Fresh Prince of Bel Air," which began in 1990. That same year Jones was the subject of a video biography, *Listen Up: The Lives of Quincy Jones* (1990).

—JONATHAN GILL

JORDAN, BARBARA CHARLINE

Barbara Charline Jordan (February 21, 1936–January 17, 1996), congresswoman and professor. Barbara Jordan was born in Houston, Tex., the daughter of Arlyne Jordan and Benjamin M. Jordan, a Baptist minister. She spent her childhood in Houston, and graduated from Texas Southern University in Houston in 1956. Jordan received a law degree from Boston University in 1959. She was engaged briefly in private practice in Houston before becoming the administrative assistant for the county judge of Harris County, Tex., a post she held until 1966.

In 1962, and again in 1964, Jordan ran unsuccessfully for the Texas State Senate. In 1966, helped by the marked increase in African-American registered voters, she became the first black since 1883 elected to the Texas State Senate. The following year she became the first woman president of the Texas Senate. That year, redistricting opened a new district in Houston with a black majority. Jordan ran a strong campaign, and in 1972 she was elected to the House of Representatives from the district, becoming the first African-American woman elected to Congress from the South.

Jordan's short career as a high-profile congresswoman took her to a leadership role on the national level. In her first term, she received an appointment to the House Judiciary Committee, where she achieved national recognition during the Watergate scandal, when in 1974 she voted for articles of impeachment against President Richard M. Nixon. A powerful public speaker, Jordan eloquently conveyed to the country the serious constitutional nature of the charges and the gravity with which the Judiciary Committee was duty-bound to address the issues. "My faith in the Constitution is whole, it is complete, it is total," she declared. "I am not going to sit here and be an idle spectator to the diminution, the subversion, the destruction of the Constitution."

Jordan spent six years in Congress, where she spoke out against the Vietnam War and high military expenditures, particularly those earmarked for support of the war. She supported environmental reform as well as measures to aid blacks, the poor, the elderly, and other groups on the margins of society. Jordan was a passionate campaigner for the Equal Rights Amendment, and for grassroots citizen political action. Central to all of her concerns was a commitment to realizing the ideals of the Constitution.

Public recognition of her integrity, her legislative ability, and her oratorical excellence came from several quarters. Beginning in 1974, and for ten consecutive years, the *World Almanac* named her one of the twenty-five most influential women in America. *Time* magazine named Jordan one of the Women of the Year in 1976. Her electrifying keynote address at the Democratic National Convention that year helped to solidify her stature as a national figure.

In 1978, feeling she needed a wider forum for her views than her congressional district, Jordan chose not to seek reelection. Returning to her native Texas, Jordan accepted a professorship in the School of Public Affairs at the University of Texas

See also

Michael Jackson and the
Jackson Family

at Austin in 1979, and beginning in 1982 she held the Lyndon B. Johnson Centennial Chair in Public Policy. Reflecting her interest in minority rights, in 1985 Jordan was appointed by the secretary-general of the United Nations to serve on an eleven-member commission charged with investigating the role of transnational corporations in South Africa and Namibia. In 1991, Texas Gov. Ann Richards appointed her "ethics guru," charged with monitoring ethics in the state's government. In 1992, although confined to a wheelchair by a degenerative disease, Jordan gave a keynote speech at the Democratic National Convention, again displaying the passion, eloquence, and integrity that had first brought her to public attention nearly two decades earlier.

—CHRISTINE A. LUNARDINI

JORDAN, MICHAEL JEFFREY

Michael Jeffrey Jordan (February 17, 1963–), basketball player. Widely acknowledged as the most exciting player ever to pick up a basketball, Michael Jordan was born in Brooklyn, N.Y., the fourth of James and Deloris Jordan's five children and the last of their three boys. He grew up in North Carolina, first in rural Wallace and later in Wilmington.

A late bloomer in athletic terms, Jordan was released from the Laney High School varsity basketball team in his sophomore year. Even after an impressive junior season, he received only modest attention from major college basketball programs and chose to attend the University of North Carolina.

On March 29, 1982, the nineteen-year-old freshman sank the shot that gave his school a 63–62 victory over Georgetown and its first NCAA men's basketball championship in twenty-five years. Jordan followed that by winning the college Player of the Year award from the *Sporting News* in each of the next two seasons. After announcing that he would enter the NBA draft after his junior season, he capped his amateur career by captaining the U.S. men's basketball team to a gold medal at the 1984 Olympic Games in Los Angeles.

Jordan was the third pick in the 1984 NBA draft, chosen by the woeful Chicago Bulls. The six-foot-six-inch guard immediately set about reversing their fortunes and was named the NBA Rookie of the Year after leading the team in scoring, rebounding, and assists.

After sitting out most of his second season with a broken foot, Jordan put on one of the greatest individual performances in postseason history, scoring 63 points in a playoff loss to the Boston Celtics in 1986. The following season he scored 3,041 points—the most ever by a guard—and won the first of his six successive scoring titles with a 37.1 average. In 1987–1988 he became the first player ever to win the Most Valuable Player and Defensive Player of the Year awards in the same season.

Jordan's brilliance on the basketball court, however, was almost eclipsed by his success as a commercial spokesperson. Before his rookie season he signed with the Nike sneaker company to promote a signature shoe—the Air Jordan. The shoe was an instant smash, establishing Jordan as a viable spokesperson. The commercials in which he starred with filmmaker Spike Lee helped make him a pop icon as well.

Basketball purists have criticized Jordan for indulging his individual brilliance at the expense of his teammates. But he and the Bulls shook the one-man-team tag in 1990–1991 by defeating Earvin "Magic" Johnson and the Los Angeles

Chicago Bulls guard Michael Jordan slam-dunks the ball while forward Stacey King (right) and Sacramento Kings center Ralph Sampson (left) look on, February, 1991.
AP/WIDE WORLD PHOTO

See also
Spike Lee

Lakers in five games to win the franchise's first NBA championship. The following season, they defeated the Portland Trailblazers in six games to clinch another title, and in 1993 they again won the championship when they defeated the Phoenix Suns in six games.

Jordan was named the NBA's Most Valuable Player three times between 1988 and 1992. During that period he became the most successfully marketed player in the history of team sports, earning roughly sixteen million dollars in commercial endorsements in 1992 alone from such corporations as Nike, McDonald's, Quaker Oats (Gatorade), and General Mills (Wheaties). Even when controversy surrounded Jordan, as it did during the 1992 Olympic Games when he refused to wear a competing sponsor's uniform, or when he incurred sizable debts gambling on golf and poker, he regularly registered as one of the nation's most admired men and one of young peoples' most revered role models. Jordan's basketball career came to a sudden halt in October 1993 when he announced his retirement in a nationally tele-vised news conference. He said a diminishing love for the game, the pressures of celebrity, and the murder of his father three months earlier contributed to his decision. In February 1994 he signed with the Chicago White Sox of the American League, hoping to work his way up through the White Sox farm system to major league baseball. Unhappy with the progress he was making, Jordan subsequently elected to drop out of the White Sox organization, and in the spring of 1995, he resumed his basketball career by returning to the Bulls. After his return to basketball, Jordan led the Bulls to NBA championships in 1996, 1997, and 1998. He was named the NBA's Most Valuable Player in 1996 and 1998.

—JIM NAUGHTON

JUDAISM

Estimates of the number of black people in the United States who consider themselves Jews or Hebrews range from 40,000 to 500,000. These

See also
Florence Griffith-Joyner

people can be divided into three groups: individuals, such as Sammy Davis, Jr., and Julius Lester, who convert to Judaism and join predominantly white congregations—often as a result of intermarriage; African Americans who trace their Jewish heritage back to slavery and who worship in either black or white synagogues; and blacks whose attraction to Judaism is based on a racial identification with the biblical Hebrews.

The third group is by far the largest, but it is made up of many independent denominations that have a wide variety of beliefs and practices. The best known are the Black Jews of Harlem, the Temple Beth-El congregations, the Nation of Yahweh, the Original Hebrew Israelite Nation, the Israeli School of Universal Practical Knowledge, the Church of God, and the Nubian Islamic Hebrews. Reconstructionist Black Jews and Rastafarians are two groups whose relationship to Judaism or Hebrewism is so limited that they are best thought of as movements basically rooted in Christianity that have an affinity to the Old Testament and Jewish symbols.

Each of the major groups is unique, but they generally have the following characteristics in common: They believe that the ancient Hebrews were black people, that they are their descendants, and that their immediate ancestors were forcibly converted from Judaism to Christianity during slavery. In addition, they believe that they are not converts to Judaism but have discovered or returned to their true religion. On the other hand, they believe that white Jews are either converts to their way of life, descendants of one of the biblical people whom they believe started the white race (Edomites, Canaanites, Japhites, or lepers), or that they are imposters altogether. This is the principle reason why some groups consider the term "Jew" anathema and insist on the biblical terms Hebrew or Israelite, or more commonly, Hebrew Israelite. They believe that the enslavement of and discrimination against African Americans were predicted in the Bible and are therefore a combination of divine punishment upon the children of Israel for their sins and the result of the blatant aggression of white people. Hebrew Israelites are messianic and believe that when the messiah comes, retribution will be handed down upon all sinners—but particularly upon white people for their oppression of people of color. Beyond these similarities—which a few Hebrew Israelites strongly oppose—the groups can differ widely according to the degree to which they follow rabbinic traditions, use Hebrew, conduct services, follow dress codes, and

incorporate Christian or Islamic beliefs into their theology.

There have been three main phases in the use of elements of the Jewish religion in African-American worship. From exposure to evangelical Protestantism in the early nineteenth century, many African Americans identified with the enslavement, emancipation, and nation-building of the Hebrews as depicted in the Bible. Old Testament imagery was a staple of sermons and spirituals. The best-known of the latter is undoubtedly "Go Down, Moses," in which the release of the Hebrews from Egyptian captivity is seen as a sign of the redemption of blacks from slavery. This connection to the Jewish people, often strengthened by connections to Pan-African movements such as the one led by Marcus Garvey, provided the impetus for more formal identification as Jews, often outside of a Christian context, in the late nineteenth and early twentieth centuries. Since the 1960s, another period of active black nationalism, there has been renewed identification with elements of the Jewish religion by a number of African-American religious groups. Many of these groups are quite eclectic in their theology and religious borrowings, and are often hostile to mainstream Judaism.

—SHOLOMO BEN LEVY

JULIAN, PERCY LAVON

Percy Lavon Julian (April 11, 1899–April 21, 1975), chemist. The grandson of a former slave, Percy L. Julian was born in Montgomery, Ala. His father, James Sumner Julian, a railway mail clerk, and his mother, Elizabeth Adams Julian, stressed academic achievement. His two brothers earned M.D.'s. while his three sisters all received master's degrees.

Julian began his formal education in a public elementary school in Montgomery. Because the state of Alabama had only one public high school for African Americans, he was sent to a private school, the State Normal School for Negroes, in Montgomery. Upon graduating from high school in 1916, Julian was admitted to DePauw University in Greencastle, Ind. Because of the poor quality of his secondary education, he was admitted on a conditional basis, as a subfreshman. As a result, he was required to take, simultaneously, both high school and college courses during his first two years of college. In 1920, he graduated as

See also
Science

valedictorian of his class, earning membership in both the Phi Beta Kappa and Sigma Xi honorary societies.

It was the tradition at DePauw for the head of the chemistry department to find fellowships for students planning to pursue the Ph.D. degree. Julian was the top student; therefore, his classmates assumed he would get the award to attend Harvard. After all of his classmates received graduate fellowships, Julian became concerned that he not been informed of his fellowship. He approached the department head, who informed him that because of his race no graduate school had granted him a fellowship. In fact, graduate advisers at some of the country's leading departments had advised DePauw's department head to encourage Julian to forget about a Ph.D. and to pursue a teaching career at one of the predominantly black colleges. Left with few options, Julian took a position as a chemistry teacher at Fisk University in Nashville.

After two years at Fisk, Julian received an Austin Fellowship to attend Harvard, where he earned a M.A. in 1923. He returned to teach at West Virginia State College for Negroes. The following year, he took a position at Howard University, where he taught chemistry for two years. While at Howard, he received a General Education Board Fellowship to pursue his Ph.D. at the University of Vienna. After earning his doctorate in 1931, Julian resumed his teaching duties at Howard. He left Howard in 1932 to teach organic chemistry at his alma mater, De Pauw. It was at DePauw that he became internationally known for his research on the structure and synthesis of physostigmine, a drug that was effective in the treatment of glaucoma.

Julian's research success at DePauw led to employment opportunities in private industry. He was offered a research position at the Institute of Paper Chemistry in Appleton, Wis., until company officials allegedly discovered that the city had an old statute on the books prohibiting the housing of an African American overnight. Fortunately, W. J. O'Brien, a vice president of the Glidden Company, was president at the institute

and heard of the incident. He offered Julian the position of chief chemist and director of research at the company; and Julian joined the staff of Glidden in 1936. His appointment is considered the turning point in the hiring of African-American scientists in industry in the United States; it opened opportunities for other talented African-American scientists who had been denied industrial employment because of their race.

At Glidden, Julian directed the company's study of soybeans. The study involved developing a new process for isolating and commercially preparing soybean protein to be used in coating and sizing paper, in cold-water paints, and in textile sizing. This new process was cheaper than the existing one, and of equal quality. It was a huge commercial success for Glidden. The soybean protein was also used to develop a product for extinguishing gasoline and oil fires, which was credited with saving the lives of numerous sailors and airmen during World War II.

In 1953, Julian founded his own companies—Julian Laboratories, Inc., in Chicago and Julian Laboratorios de Mexico in Mexico City. These firms grew to be among the world's largest producers of drugs processed from wild yams. By the early 1960s, Julian had sold his laboratories for a considerable profit. At the time of his retirement, he held more than 130 chemical patents.

Julian was also a prominent civil rights leader. In 1967, he and Asa T. Spaulding, president of the black-owned North Carolina Mutual Life Insurance Company, cochaired a group of influential African Americans recruited by the NAACP's Legal Defense and Education Fund to raise a million dollars to finance lawsuits to enforce civil rights legislation. He was the recipient of numerous awards, including honorary degrees from twelve colleges and universities, the NAACP's prestigious Spingarn Medal, and Sigma Xi's Proctor Prize. Julian was a fellow of the National Academy of Science, American Chemical Society, American Institute of Chemists, Chemical Society of London, and New York Academy of Science.

—WILLIE J. PEARSON, JR.

See also

Booker T. Washington

K

KILLENS, JOHN OLIVER

John Oliver Killens (January 14, 1916–October 27, 1987), novelist. Born in Macon, Ga., to Charles Myles, Sr., and Willie Lee (Coleman) Killens, John Killens credits his relatives with fostering in him cultural pride and literary values: his father had him read a weekly column by Langston Hughes; his mother, president of the Dunbar Literary Club, introduced him to poetry; and his great-grandmother filled his boyhood with the hardships and tales of slavery. Such early exposure to criticism, art, and folklore is evident in his fiction, which is noted for its accurate depictions of social classes, its engaging narratives, and its successful layering of African-American history, legends, songs, and jokes.

Killens originally planned to be a lawyer. After attending Edward Waters College in Jacksonville, Fla. (1934–1935) and Morris Brown College in Atlanta, Ga. (c. 1935–1936), he moved to Washington, D.C., became a staff member of the National Labor Relations Board, and completed his B.A. through evening classes at Howard University. He studied at the Robert Terrel Law School from 1939 until 1942, when he abandoned his pursuit of a degree and joined the army. His second novel, *And Then We Heard the Thunder* (1963), concerning racism in the military, was based on his service in the South Pacific. It was nominated for the Pulitzer Prize.

In 1946 Killens returned briefly to his office job at the National Labor Relations Board. In 1947–1948, he organized black and white workers for the Congress of Industrial Organizations (CIO) and was an active member of the Progressive Party. But he soon became convinced that leading intellectuals, the white working class, and the U.S. government were not truly committed to creating a more inclusive society.

Killens moved to New York in 1948, attended writing classes at Columbia University and New York University, and met such influential figures as Langston Hughes, Paul Robeson, and W. E. B. Du Bois. While working on his fiction, he wrote regularly for the leftist newspaper *Freedom* (1951–1955). His views at the time, closely aligned to the Communist Party, were evident in his 1952 review of Ralph Ellison's *Invisible Man*. He attacked the novel as a "decadent mixture . . . a vicious distortion of Negro life." Killens believed that literature should be judged on its potential for improving society: "Art is functional. A Black work of art helps the liberation or hinders it."

Fortunately, Killens had already found some young writers, many with close ties to left-wing or black nationalist organizations, committed to the idea of writing as a vehicle of social protest. With Rosa Guy, John Henrik Clarke, and Walter Christmas, he founded a workshop that became known as the Harlem Writers Guild in the early 1950s.

Killens's *Youngblood* (1954), the first novel published by a guild member, treats the struggles of a southern black family in early twentieth-century Georgia. Following the critical praise of this book, Killens toured the country to speak on subjects concerning African Americans. In 1955 he went to Alabama to research a screenplay on the Montgomery Bus Boycott and to visit with the Rev. Dr. Martin Luther King, Jr. Killens also became close friends with Malcolm X, and with him founded the Organization for Afro-American Unity in 1964. *Black Man's Burden,* a 1965 collection of political essays, documents his shift from a socialist philosophy to one that promotes black nationalism.

Killens's major subject is the violence and racism of American society, how it hinders black manhood and family. *'Sippi* (1967) is a protest novel about struggle over voting rights in the 1960s. *The Cotillion; or, One Good Bull Is Half the Herd,* published in 1971 and nominated for the Pulitzer Prize, satirizes middle-class African-American values, and was the basis for *Cotillion,* a play produced in New York City in 1975. Killens's other plays include *Ballad of the Winter Soldiers* (1964, with Loften Mitchell) and *Lower Than the Angels* (1965). He wrote two screenplays, *Odds Against Tomorrow* (1959, with Nelson Gidding) and *Slaves* (1969, with Herbert J. Biberman and Alida Sherman). He also edited *The Trial Record of Denmark Vesey* (1970) and authored two juvenile novels, *Great Gittin' Up Morning: A Biography*

See also

Literature

K

of Denmark Vesey (1972) and *A Man Ain't Nothin' but a Man: The Adventures of John Henry* (1975).

By the mid–1960s, Killens had already started a string of positions as a writer-in-residence: at Fisk University (1965–1968), Columbia University (1970–1973), Howard University (1971–1972), Bronx Community College (1979–1981), and Medgar Evers College in the City University of New York (1981–1987). Other awards included a fellowship from the National Endowment for the Arts (1980) and a Lifetime Achievement Award from the Before Columbus Foundation (1986). Until his death, Killens continued to contribute articles to leading magazines such as *Ebony, Black World, The Black Aesthetic,* and *African Forum. The Great Black Russian: a Novel on the Life and Times of Alexander Pushkin* was published posthumously in 1988.

—DEREK SCHEIPS

KING, CORETTA SCOTT

Coretta Scott King (April 27, 1927–), civil rights activist. Born in Marion, Ala., a rural farming community, Coretta Scott attended Lincoln High School, a local private school for black students run by the American Missionary Association. After graduating in 1945, she received a scholarship to study music and education at Antioch College in Yellow Springs, Ohio. Trained in voice and piano, she made her concert debut in 1948 in Springfield, Ohio, as a soloist at the Second Baptist Church. Scott officially withdrew from Antioch in 1952 after entering the New England Conservatory of Music in 1951 to continue her music studies.

During her first year at the conservatory, she met the Rev. Dr. Martin Luther King, Jr., who was a doctoral candidate at Boston University's school of theology. The two were married on June 18, 1953, despite Martin Luther King, Sr.'s opposition to the match because of his disapproval of the Scott family's rural background and his hope that his son would marry into one of Atlanta's elite black families. The couple returned to Boston to continue their studies. The following year, Coretta Scott King received a bachelor's degree in music (Mus.B.) from the New England Conservatory of Music, and in September the two moved to Montgomery, Ala., despite Coretta King's misgivings about returning to the racial hostility of Alabama.

Although Coretta King aspired to become a professional singer, she devoted most of her time to raising her children and working closely with her husband after he had assumed the presidency of the Montgomery Improvement Association in 1955. She participated in many major events of the Civil Rights Movement along with her husband, both in the United States and overseas, as well as having to endure the hardships resulting from her husband's position, including his frequent arrests and the bombing of their Montgomery home in 1956.

Early in 1960, the King family moved to Atlanta when King became co-pastor of Ebenezer Baptist Church with his father. Later that year, Coretta King aided in her husband's release from a Georgia prison by appealing to presidential candidate John F. Kennedy to intervene on his behalf. In 1962, Coretta King became a voice instructor at Morris Brown College in Atlanta, but she remained primarily involved in sharing the helm of the civil rights struggle with her husband. She led marches, directed fund raising for the Southern Christian Leadership Conference and gave a series of "freedom concerts" that combined singing, lecturing, and poetry reading. A strong proponent of disarmament, King served as a delegate to the Disarmament Conference in Geneva, Switzerland, in 1962, and in 1966 and 1967 was a cosponsor of the Mobilization to End the War in Vietnam. In 1967, after an extended leave of absence, she received her bachelor of arts degree in

**CORETTA SCOTT
KING**

Coretta Scott King speaks at a rally during the Peace March on Washington, D.C., in 1963.
DENNIS BRACK/BLACK STAR

See also
Civil Rights Movement
Southern Christian
Leadership Conference

music and elementary education from Antioch College.

On April 8, 1968, only four days after the Rev. Dr. Martin Luther King, Jr., was assassinated in Memphis, Coretta King substituted for her deceased husband in a march on behalf of sanitation workers that he had been scheduled to lead. Focusing her energies on preserving her husband's memory and continuing his struggle, Coretta King also took part in the Poor People's Washington Campaign in the nation's capital during June 1968, serving as the keynote speaker at the main rally at the Lincoln Memorial. In 1969 she helped found and served as president of the Atlanta-based Martin Luther King, Jr. Center for Nonviolent Social Change, a center devoted to teaching young people the importance of nonviolence and to preserving the memory of her husband. In 1969 she also published her autobiography, *My Life with Martin Luther King, Jr.,* and in 1971 she received an honorary doctorate in music from the New England Conservatory.

In 1983 Coretta King led the twentieth-anniversary march on Washington and the following year was elected chairperson of the commission to declare King's birthday a national holiday, which was observed for the first time in 1986. She was active in the struggle to end apartheid, touring South Africa and meeting with Winnie Mandela in 1986 and returning there in 1990 to meet the recently released African National Congress leader, Nelson Mandela.

Coretta King has received numerous awards for her participation in the struggle for civil rights, including the outstanding citizenship award from the Montgomery Improvement Association in 1959 and the Distinguished Achievement Award from the National Organization of Colored Women's Clubs in 1962. As of 1993, she retained her position as chief executive officer of the Martin Luther King, Jr. Center for Nonviolent Change, having resigned the presidency to her son, Dexter Scott King, in 1989. As she has done for many years, Coretta Scott King continues to press for the worldwide recognition of civil rights and human rights.

—LOUISE P. MAXWELL

KING, MARTIN LUTHER, JR.

Martin Luther King, Jr. (January 15, 1929–April 4, 1968), minister and civil rights leader. Born Michael King, Jr., in Atlanta on January 15, 1929, he was the first son of a Baptist minister and the grandson of a Baptist minister, and his forebears exemplified the African-American social gospel tradition that would shape his career as a reformer. King's maternal grandfather, the Rev. A. D. Williams, had transformed Ebenezer Baptist Church, a block down the street from his grandson's childhood home, into one of Atlanta's most prominent black churches. In 1906, Williams had joined such figures as Atlanta University scholar W. E. B. Du Bois and African Methodist Episcopal (AME) bishop Henry McNeal Turner to form the Georgia Equal Rights League, an organization that condemned lynching, segregation in public transportation, and the exclusion of black men from juries and state militia. In 1917, Williams helped found the Atlanta branch of the NAACP, later serving as the chapter's president. Williams's subsequent campaign to register and mobilize black voters prodded white leaders to agree to construct new public schools for black children.

After Williams's death in 1931, his son-in-law, Michael King, Sr., also combined religious and political leadership. He became president of Atlanta's NAACP, led voter-registration marches during the 1930s, and spearheaded a movement to equalize the salaries of black public school teachers with those of their white counterparts. In 1934, King, Sr.—perhaps inspired by a visit to the birthplace of Protestantism in Germany—changed his name and that of his son to Martin Luther King.

Despite the younger King's admiration for his father's politically active ministry, he was initially reluctant to accept his inherited calling. Experiencing religious doubts during his early teenage years, he decided to become a minister only after he came into contact with religious leaders who combined theological sophistication with social gospel advocacy. At Morehouse College, which King attended from 1944 to 1948, the college's president, Benjamin E. Mays, encouraged him to believe that Christianity should become a force for progressive social change. A course on the Bible taught by Morehouse professor George Kelsey exposed King to theological scholarship. After deciding to become a minister, King increased his understanding of liberal Christian thought while attending Crozer Theological Seminary in Pennsylvania. Compiling an outstanding academic record at Crozer, he deepened his understanding of modern religious scholarship and eventually identified himself with theological

Say that I was a drum major for justice; say that I was a drum major for peace; I was a drum major for righteousness.

MARTIN LUTHER KING, JR.
SUGGESTIONS FOR HIS OWN
FUNERAL SERMON,
FEB. 4, 1968

See also
Birmingham, Alabama
W.E.B. Du Bois

K

personalism. King later wrote that this philosophical position strengthened his belief in a personal God and provided him with a "metaphysical basis for the dignity and worth of all human personality."

At Boston University, where King began doctoral studies in systematic theology in 1951, his exploration of theological scholarship was combined with extensive interactions with the Boston African-American community. He met regularly with other black students in an informal group called the Dialectical Society. Often invited to give sermons in Boston-area churches, he acquired a reputation as a powerful preacher, drawing ideas from African-American Baptist traditions as well as theological and philosophical writings. The academic papers he wrote at Boston displayed little originality, but King's scholarly training provided him with a talent that would prove useful in his future leadership activities: an exceptional ability to draw upon a wide range of theological and philosophical texts to express his views with force and precision. During his stay in Boston, King also met and began dating Coretta Scott, then a student at the New England Con-

servatory of Music. On June 18, 1953, the two students were married in Marion, Ala., where Scott's family lived. During the following academic year, King began work on his dissertation, which was completed during the spring of 1955.

Soon after King accepted his first pastorate at Dexter Avenue Baptist Church in Montgomery, Ala., he had an unexpected opportunity to utilize the insights he had gained from his childhood experiences and academic training. After NAACP official Rosa Parks was jailed for refusing to give up her bus seat to a white passenger, King accepted the post of president of the Montgomery Improvement Association, which was formed to coordinate a boycott of Montgomery's buses. In his role as the primary spokesman of the boycott, King gradually forged a distinctive protest strategy that involved the mobilization of black churches, utilization of Gandhian methods of nonviolent protest, and skillful appeals for white support.

After the U. S. Supreme Court outlawed Alabama bus segregation laws in late 1956, King quickly rose to national prominence as a result of his leadership role in a successful boycott movement. In 1957, he became the founding president of the Southern Christian Leadership Conference (SCLC), formed to coordinate civil rights activities throughout the South. Publication of King's *Stride Toward Freedom: The Montgomery Story* (1958) further contributed to his rapid emergence as a nationally known civil rights leader. Seeking to forestall the fears of NAACP leaders that his organization might draw away followers and financial support, King acted cautiously during the late 1950s. Instead of immediately seeking to stimulate mass desegregation protests in the South, he stressed the goal of achieving black voting rights when he addressed an audience at the 1957 Prayer Pilgrimage for Freedom. During 1959, he increased his understanding of Gandhian ideas during a month-long visit to India as a guest of Prime Minister Jawaharlal Nehru. Early in 1960, King moved his family—which now included two children, Yolanda Denise (born 1955) and Martin Luther III (born 1957)—to Atlanta in order to be nearer SCLC's headquarters in that city and to become copastor, with his father, of Ebenezer Baptist Church. The Kings' third child, Dexter Scott, was born in 1961; their fourth, Bernice Albertine, was born in 1963.

Soon after King's arrival in Atlanta, the lunch counter sit-in movement, led by students, spread throughout the South and brought into existence a new organization, the Student Nonviolent Co-

CIVIL RIGHTS LEGEND

Martin Luther King, Jr., walks with schoolchildren in Grenada, Miss., in the fall of 1966.

© BOB FITCH / BLACK STAR

ordinating Committee (SNCC). SNCC activists admired King but also pushed him toward greater militancy. In October 1960, his arrest during a student-initiated protest in Atlanta became an issue in the national presidential campaign when Democratic candidate John F. Kennedy intervened to secure his release from jail. Kennedy's action contributed to his narrow victory in the November election. During 1961 and 1962, King's differences with SNCC activists widened during a sustained protest movement in Albany, Georgia. King was arrested twice during demonstrations organized by the Albany Movement, but when he left jail and ultimately left Albany without achieving a victory, his standing among activists declined.

King reasserted his preeminence within the African-American freedom struggle through his leadership of the Birmingham, Alabama campaign of 1963. Initiated by the SCLC in January, the Birmingham demonstrations were the most massive civil rights protests that had occurred up to that time. With the assistance of Fred Shuttlesworth and other local black leaders, and without much competition from SNCC or other civil rights groups, SCLC officials were able to orchestrate the Birmingham protests to achieve maximum national impact. During May, televised pictures of police using dogs and fire hoses against demonstrators aroused a national outcry. This vivid evidence of the obstinacy of Birmingham officials, combined with Alabama Governor George C. Wallace's attempt to block the entry of black students at the University of Alabama, prompted President John F. Kennedy to introduce major new civil rights legislation. King's unique ability to appropriate ideas from the Bible, the Constitution, and other canonical texts manifested itself when he defended the black protests in a widely quoted letter, written while he was jailed in Birmingham.

King's speech at the August 28, 1963, March on Washington, attended by over 200,000 people, provides another powerful demonstration of his singular ability to draw on widely accepted American ideals in order to promote black objectives. At the end of his prepared remarks, which announced that African Americans wished to cash the "promissory note" signified in the words of the Constitution and the Declaration of Independence, King began his most quoted oration: "So I say to you, my friends, that even though we must face the difficulties of today and tomorrow, I still have a dream. It is a dream deeply rooted in the American dream that one day this nation will rise up and live out the true meaning of its creed—we hold these truths to be self-evident, that all men are created equal." He appropriated the familiar words of the song "My Country 'Tis of Thee" before concluding: "And when we allow freedom to ring, when we let it ring from every village and hamlet, from every state and city, we will be able to speed up that day when all of God's children—black men and white men, Jews and Gentiles, Catholics and Protestants—will be able to join hands and to sing in the words of the old Negro spiritual, 'Free at last, free at last, thank God Almighty, we are free at last.'"

After the march on Washington, King's fame and popularity were at their height. Named *Time* magazine's Man of the Year at the end of 1963, he was awarded the Nobel Peace Prize in December 1964. The acclaim he received prompted FBI director J. Edgar Hoover to step up his effort to damage King's reputation by leaking information gained through surreptitious means about King's ties with former communists and his extramarital affairs.

King's last successful civil rights campaign was a series of demonstrations in Alabama that were intended to dramatize the denial of black voting rights in the deep South. Demonstrations began in Selma, Ala., early in 1965 and reached a turning point on March 7, when a group of demonstrators began a march from Selma to the state capitol in Montgomery. King was in Atlanta when state policemen, carrying out Governor Wallace's order to stop the march, attacked with tear gas and clubs soon after the procession crossed the Edmund Pettus Bridge on the outskirts of Selma. The police assault on the marchers quickly increased national support for the voting rights campaign. King arrived in Selma to join several thousand movement sympathizers, black and white. President Lyndon B. Johnson reacted to the Alabama protests by introducing new voting rights legislation, which would become the Voting Rights Act of 1965. Demonstrators were finally able to obtain a court order allowing the march to take place, and on March 25 King addressed the arriving protestors from the steps of the capitol in Montgomery.

After the successful voting rights campaign, King was unable to garner similar support for his effort to confront the problems of northern urban blacks. Early in 1966 he launched a major campaign in Chicago, moving into an apartment in the black ghetto. As he shifted the focus of his activities north, however, he discovered that the tactics used in the South were not as effective else-

I have a dream that one day on the red hills of Georgia, the sons of former slaves and the sons of former slaveowners will be able to sit down together at the table of brotherhood.

MARTIN LUTHER KING, JR.
SPEECH AT THE LINCOLN
MEMORIAL IN WASHINGTON,
D.C., AUGUST 28, 1963

See also
Benjamin E. Mays
Southern Christian
Leadership Conference

where. He encountered formidable opposition from Mayor Richard Daley, and was unable to mobilize Chicago's economically and ideologically diverse black populace. He was stoned by angry whites in the suburb of Cicero when he led a march against racial discrimination in housing. Despite numerous well-publicized protests, the Chicago campaign resulted in no significant gains and undermined King's reputation as an effective leader.

His status was further damaged when his strategy of nonviolence came under renewed attack from blacks following a major outbreak of urban racial violence in Los Angeles during August 1965. When civil rights activists reacted to the shooting of James Meredith by organizing a March against Fear through Mississippi, King was forced on the defensive as Stokely Carmichael and other militants put forward the Black Power slogan. Although King refused to condemn the militants who opposed him, he criticized the new slogan as vague and divisive. As his influence among blacks lessened, he also alienated many white moderate supporters by publicly opposing United States intervention in the Vietnam War. After he delivered a major antiwar speech at New York's Riverside Church on April 4, 1967, many of the northern newspapers that had once supported his civil rights efforts condemned his attempt to link civil rights to the war issue.

In November 1967, King announced the formation of a Poor People's Campaign designed to prod the nation's leaders to deal with the problem of poverty. Early in 1968, he and other SCLC workers began to recruit poor people and antipoverty activists to come to Washington, D.C., to lobby on behalf of improved antipoverty programs. This effort was in its early stages when King became involved in a sanitation workers' strike in Memphis. On March 28, as he led thousands of sanitation workers and sympathizers on a march through downtown Memphis, violence broke out and black youngsters looted stores. The violent outbreak led to more criticisms of King's entire antipoverty strategy. He returned to Memphis for the last time early in April. Addressing an audience at Bishop Charles H. Mason Temple on April 3, he sought to revive his flagging movement by acknowledging: "We've got some difficult days ahead. But it doesn't matter with me now. Because I've been to the mountaintop. . . . And I've seen the promised land. I may not get there with you. But I want you to know tonight that we, as a people, will get to the promised land."

The following evening, King was assassinated as he stood on a balcony of the Lorraine Motel in Memphis. A white segregationist, James Earl Ray, was later convicted of the crime. The Poor People's Campaign continued for a few months but did not achieve its objectives. King became an increasingly revered figure after his death, however, and many of his critics ultimately acknowledged his considerable accomplishments. In 1969 his widow, Coretta Scott King, established the Martin Luther King, Jr., Center for Nonviolent Social Change, in Atlanta, to carry on his work. In 1986, a national holiday was established to honor his birth.

—CLAYBORNE CARSON

KU KLUX KLAN

To most people the words *Ku Klux Klan* mean a southern terrorist movement organized after the Civil War, with active chapters still in existence, that seeks forcibly to deny African Americans their rights. Such a perception mistakes the Klan as a monolithic movement with a continuous history. Similarities in name, costume, and ritual have hidden from view the Ku Klux Klan's separate incarnations. In four distinct movements differing in geographical base, tactics, targets, and purpose, Klansmen have organized their resources to claim power.

Confederate army veterans formed the first Klan movement in 1866 in Pulaski, Tenn. Manipulating the Greek word for circle, *kuklos,* they alliteratively created "Ku Klux Klan" as the name of what was initially designed to be only a fraternal body. Members, however, quickly became aware of the social-control power of a secret organization of armed white men. The Klan, under former Confederate General and now Imperial Wizard Nathan Bedford Forrest, soon spread throughout the South, emerging as a vehicle to combat Reconstruction and subordinate recently emancipated blacks and their white Republican allies. Masked and robed Klansmen threatened, flogged, and killed those who sought black rights and a more just distribution of wealth and power. Congress, with the support of President Ulysses S. Grant, responded to these outrages in 1870–1871 with laws protecting black voters and outlawing Klan activities. In 1871, under these laws, Grant suspended habeas corpus in parts of Klan-dominated South Carolina and ordered mass arrests and prosecutions of Klansmen. White Southerners, with the Klan's usefulness at an end, resorted to political activism and the more subtle and "acceptable" means of economic coercion inherent in their control of credit, land, and jobs to reassert influence.

See also

Student Nonviolent Coordinating Committee

Nearly half a century later, the second Ku Klux Klan appeared. On Thanksgiving Day in 1915, William Joseph Simmons, a former Methodist circuit rider and fraternal organizer and the son of a Reconstruction Klansman, convinced fifteen of his friends to follow him to the summit of Stone Mountain in Georgia. There, under an American flag and a burning cross, the men knelt and dedicated themselves to the revival of the Knights of the Ku Klux Klan. As early as 1898, Simmons had planned to re-create the Klan to honor the men of the first hooded order and to pioneer a new fraternal group. The interest generated by the fiftieth anniversary in 1915 of the end of the Civil War, and the premiere in Atlanta of the motion-picture masterpiece *Birth of a Nation,* enticed Simmons to reify his dream.

The second Klan grew slowly. By 1920, it counted only four or five thousand members in scattered chapters in Georgia and Alabama. To revitalize his dream, Simmons turned for help in promoting the Klan to E. Y. Clarke and Elizabeth Tyler of the Southern Publicity Association. They signed a contract with Simmons stipulating that the Association, henceforth the Propagation Department of the Invisible Empire, would promote and enlarge the Klan in exchange for eight dollars of every ten-dollar membership fee, or klectoken. Clarke and Tyler enlisted more than 200 organizers, known as kleagles, and directed them to exploit any issue or prejudice that could be useful in recruiting men for the movement. The kleagles fanned out across the United States. Working on a commission basis, they sought to secure as many new members for the Klan as they possibly could. The sharp rise in the secret order's membership reflected their success, for between June 1920 and October 1921, 85,000 men joined.

Directed from Atlanta by the new imperial wizard, Hiram Wesley Evans, but tuned to the local environment, the kleagles preached a multifaceted program. They portrayed the Klan as a patriotic movement determined to safeguard endangered American institutions and values. The Klan posed as the champion of the "old-time religion" and promised to unite all Protestants under a sin-

POWERFUL SYMBOLISM

Cross burnings like this one in 1950 in Jacksonville, Fla., intensified after World War II with the growing strength of the civil rights movement.
AP / WIDE WORLD PHOTOS

K

KU KLUX KLAN

gle banner. Law and order was another rallying cry. A sharp upsurge in crime in the postwar years, primarily fueled by Prohibition law violations, alarmed Americans. Many of those impatient with the police and courts turned to the Klan to enforce the laws and restore order to their communities.

The message of Americanism, Protestantism, and law enforcement was not aimed at all Americans. The Klan accused Catholics of placing their allegiance to the pope above their loyalty to the United States. Vowing to eliminate "papist power," the Klan boycotted Catholic businesses, burned crosses before churches, fired Catholic public school teachers, and defeated Catholic candidates for public office. Anti-Semitism was also a plank in the Klan program. The Jews, declared the kleagles, dominated the American economy and led those who sought to commercialize the Sabbath and exclude the Bible from the public schools. White supremacy was another tenet: Klan leaders exploited white fears of change and offered the movement as a means to maintain the racial status quo. Finally, the Klan beckoned lodge joiners by providing the fellowship, festivity, and mystery that these men craved. Simmons's creation of rituals and his titles for movement officers—kleagle, kludd, exalted cyclops—were intended to appeal to these men's imaginations.

The Klan advanced quickly in the early 1920s. In Texas, 200,000 men joined, and a Klansman was elected to the United States Senate. California's 50,000 Klansmen helped capture the statehouse for their candidate. Colorado Klan organizers counted 35,000 recruits, and elected members as governor and U.S. senator. Twenty local chapters were organized for Chicago's 50,000 Klansmen, while 35,000 wore the hood and robe in Detroit. The Klan citadel of Indiana claimed 240,000 knights, who succeeded in electing two governors and two United States senators. New York added 200,000 more Klansmen, and Pennsylvania 225,000. Only 16 percent of the membership lived in the South. The Klan population was higher in New Jersey than in Alabama; Indianapolis Klan membership was nearly double that in South Carolina and Mississippi combined. At its height in 1924, the national movement drew an estimated 3 million to 6 million men from throughout the United States.

The impact of the Ku Klux Klan on the 1924 presidential election is difficult to judge. Klan leaders' unyielding opposition at the Democratic National Convention to the presidential ambitions of New York governor Al Smith, a Catholic and antiprohibitionist, and to a platform plank specifically condemning their organization deepened divisions that the party would not bridge for years.

The Klan's response to community problems was usually political. By electing trusted officials, Klansmen would be assured that crime would be suppressed, minorities regulated, and community improvements initiated. In many cities and towns across America, Klan and government merged. Mayors, city councilmen, and police officials consulted with Klan leaders about policy, legislative agendas, and appointments. Such relationships also existed on the state level in Indiana, Oregon and Colorado. Violence, which occurred in isolated instances, was mainly perpetrated by independent bands of radicals, usually in the early days of Klan building.

The second Klan's fall was as rapid as its rise. The reasons for decline were varied: the movement's inability to fulfill its promises; members' demoralization in the face of their leaders' financial or moral corruption; and a failure to respond as the salience of past issues faded and new concerns came to the fore. By the end of the 1920s the Klan was discredited and without influence. Anti–New Deal rhetoric and a flirtation with the pro-Nazi American Bund in the 1930s did not revive the movement. In 1944, the Internal Revenue Service revoked its designation of the Klan as a charitable organization and forced William Simmons's Invisible Empire out of business with a demand for $685,000 in back taxes.

Burning crosses of the third Klan movement appeared in 1946; by 1949 over 200 chapters, holding 20,000 Klansmen, had been organized. Additional growth spurts followed the Supreme Court's *Brown* v. *Topeka, Kansas, Board of Education* decision in 1954 and school desegregation in Little Rock in 1957, for this was a southern campaign, focused upon African Americans' quest for racial and economic equality. Splintering early into more than a dozen separate groups, the secret order resorted to bombing, arson, and murder to stop the black challenge. The Klans competed unsuccessfully with the more respectable urban and middle-class White Citizens Councils for members and funds, and remained a secondary impulse in the 1950s and 1960s. Still, the organization became the center of national attention. In 1961, Klansmen assaulted freedom riders. In 1963, members bombed a Birmingham church, killing four black children. The following year, Klansmen murdered three civil rights workers in Mississippi.

In response, the Federal Bureau of Investigation (FBI) targeted seventeen Klan groups in

1964. Agents infiltrated chapters and paid Klansmen to disrupt activities by sowing discord among fellow members. By the early 1970s, one of every six Klansmen was on the FBI payroll. Repression was effective. Klan membership, which had grown to 50,000 in the mid-1960s, declined to 6,500 by 1975.

New Ku Klux Klans emerged in the late 1970s. College-educated leaders, proficient in their use of the media, offered a "modern" movement that rejected terrorism. Welcoming Catholics for the first time and accepting women as equal partners, the Klans opposed busing to remedy school segregation, affirmative action programs, and illegal immigration from Mexico. Klansmen spread north and west, aligning with neo-Nazi groups such as Aryan Nations and the White Aryan Resistance in a United Racist Front. Adopting the slogans of the Christian Identity movement that proclaimed white Christians as the true chosen people of God, Klansmen assailed blacks, Asians, and Hispanics as "mud people" under the rule of Satan's offspring, the Jews. Leaders, predicting a coming race war, established military training camps in the West and Midwest and organized a computer network linking members throughout the United States.

By the late 1980s, the Klan was again in retreat. Federal prosecutors brought Klansmen and their leaders to trial for violent acts, sedition, and conspiracy to overthrow the government. Groups such as the National Association for the Advancement of Colored People (NAACP), the Anti-Defamation League, and the Southern Poverty Law Center monitored hooded activities and filed civil lawsuits on behalf of Klan victims to collect damages and drain the movement of funds. Within the decade, the Klans had lost over half of their members, leaving approximately 5,000 men and women beneath hood and robe.

Yet the Klan's hold on America's mind has not loosened. The history of the Ku Klux Klan is a history of resurrection, and the observant search for the spark that will ignite another revival. Thus Louisiana state legislator David Duke, a former member of the American Nazi party and sometime imperial wizard of a Klan splinter group, drew the national spotlight when he ran for governor in 1991. His defeat did not ease concern, for he captured a majority of white votes. America's long history of racial and religious conflict, the eerie sight of the flaming cross, and the menacing imagery of hooded and robed men ensure that the Invisible Empire of the Ku Klux Klan will retain its powerful symbolism for friend and foe alike into the next century.

—ROBERT ALAN GOLDBERG

KU KLUX KLAN

Everyone is a prisoner of his own prejudices. No one can eliminate prejudices—just recognize them.

EDWARD R. MURROW
DEC. 31, 1955

KWANZA

Holiday Honors Communal Heritage

In 1966, at the height of the black self-awareness and pride that characterized the Black Power movement, cultural nationalist Maulana Karenga created the holiday of Kwanza. Kwanza, meaning "first fruits" in Swahili, is derived from the harvest time festival of East African agriculturalists. Karenga believed that black people in the diaspora should set aside time to celebrate their African cultural heritage and affirm their commitment to black liberation. His philosophy, called Kawaida, formed the ideological basis of Kwanza. The holiday was intended to provide a nonmaterialistic alternative to Christmas, and is celebrated from December 26 through January 1. Each day is devoted to one of the seven principles on which kawaida is based: *umoja* (unity), *kujichagulia* (self-determination), *ujima* (collective work and responsibility), *ujamaa* (cooperative economics), *nia* (purpose), *kuumba* (creativity), and *imani* (faith).

The attempt to honor communal heritage through ceremony is central to Kwanza. On each evening of the celebration, family and friends gather to share food and drink. The hosts adorn the table with the various symbols of Kwanza, and explain their significance to their guests. First a mkeka (straw mat) representing the African-American heritage in traditional African culture is laid down. Upon the mat, a kinara (candleholder) is lit with seven candles in memory of African ancestors. Each of the seven candles represents one of the seven values being celebrated. A kikomba (cup) is placed on the mat to symbolize the unity of all African peoples, and finally, tropical fruits and nuts are laid out to represent the yield of the first harvest.

Although Kwanza was at first limited in practice to cultural nationalists, as more African Americans came to heightened awareness and appreciation of their African heritage, the holiday gained wider and more mainstream acceptance. In the 1990s, Kwanza is celebrated internationally, but has gained its widest acceptance and popularity among African Americans.

—NANCY YOUSEF AND ROBYN SPENCER

LAWRENCE, JACOB ARMSTEAD

Jacob Armstead Lawrence (September 7, 1917–), painter and draftsman. Born in Atlantic City, N.J., Lawrence grew up in Harlem during the Great Depression, and his career owes much to that heritage. Soon after the births of his sister, Geraldine, and brother, William, in Pennsylvania, his parents separated. Seeking domestic work, Lawrence's mother brought her three children to Harlem around 1930. She enrolled them in a day-care program at Utopia House, a settlement house offering children hot lunches and after-school arts and crafts activities at nominal cost. The arts program was run by painter Charles Alston, who encouraged the young Jacob Lawrence, recognizing his talent.

Lawrence's mother was often on welfare, so Jake, as he was called, took on several jobs as a young teenager to help support the family: he had a paper route, and he worked in a printer's shop and in a laundry. But in the evenings he continued to attend art classes, and he committed himself to painting.

Between 1932 and 1937, Lawrence received training in the Harlem Art Workshops, which were supported first by the College Art Association and then by the government under the Federal Art Project of the Works Progress Administration. He attended the American Artists School in New York City on scholarship between 1937 and 1939. He was still a student when he had his first one-person exhibition at the Harlem YMCA in February 1938. At twenty-one and twenty-two years of age, he served as an easel painter on "the Project" in Harlem. Swept up in the vigorous social and cultural milieu of the era following the Harlem Renaissance, Lawrence drew upon Harlem scenes and black history for his subjects, portraying the lives and aspirations of African Americans.

By 1936, Lawrence had established work space in the studio of Charles Alston at 306 West 141st Street—the renowned "306" studio that was a gathering place for people in the arts. There Lawrence worked for several years, meeting and learning from such African-American intellectuals as philosopher Alain Locke, writers Langston Hughes and Claude McKay, and painter Aaron Douglas.

Lawrence's first paintings assumed the character of Social Realism, a popular style of the 1930s. His earliest works date from around 1936, and are typically interior scenes or outdoor views of Harlem activity (e.g., *Street Orator,* 1936; *Interior,* 1937). He was primarily influenced by the other community artists, such as Alston, sculptor Augusta Savage, and sculptor Henry Bannarn, who believed in him and inspired him by their interest in themes of ethnic origin and social injustice.

Lawrence's general awareness of art came from his teachers as well as from books, local exhibitions, and frequent trips to the Metropolitan Museum. When he was a youth, he met painter Gwendolyn Knight, originally from Barbados, and their friendship led to marriage in 1941. Their long relationship has been a vital factor in Lawrence's career.

Lawrence's art has remained remarkably consistent throughout the decades. His content is presented through either genre (scenes of everyday life) or historical narrative, and always by means of simplified, representational forms. He uses water-based media applied in vivid color. Lawrence is an expressionist: he tries to convey the feeling he gets from his subject through the use of expressionistic distortion and color choice, and often through cubist treatment of form and space.

A distinctive feature of Lawrence's work is his frequent use of the series format to render narrative content. Stimulated by the Harlem community's interest in the stories of legendary black leaders, he created several historical series about these heroic figures, including *Toussaint L'Ouverture* (1937–1938), *Frederick Douglass* (1938–1939), and *Harriet Tubman* (1939–1940). Some of his fifteen series are based on nonhistorical themes, such as *Theater* (1951–1952).

Jacob Lawrence received almost overnight acclaim when his *Migration of the Negro* series was shown at New York's prestigious Downtown

See also
Aaron Douglas
Langston Hughes

Gallery in November 1941. With this exhibition, he became the first African-American artist to be represented by a major New York gallery. By the time he was thirty, he had become widely known as the foremost African-American artist in the country. In 1960, the Brooklyn Museum mounted his first retrospective exhibition, and it traveled throughout the country. In 1974, the Whitney Museum of American Art in New York held a major retrospective of Lawrence's work, which toured nationally. In December 1983, he was elected to the American Academy of Arts and Letters. His third retrospective exhibition, originated by the Seattle Art Museum in 1986, drew record-breaking crowds when it toured the country. For more than forty years, Lawrence also distinguished himself as a teacher of drawing, painting, and design, first at Black Mountain College, North Carolina, in the summer of 1946, then at schools such as Pratt Institute in Saragota Springs, N.Y. (1955–1970), Brandeis University (spring 1965), and the New School for Social Research, New York (1966–1969).

During World War II, Lawrence served in the U.S. Coast Guard (then part of the Navy), first as a steward's mate and then as a combat artist. On coming out of the service, he received a Guggenheim Fellowship to paint a series about his war experiences (*War,* 1946–1947).

Lawrence and his wife spent eight months in Nigeria in 1964, an experience that resulted in his *Nigerian* series (1964). Also in the 1960s, he produced powerfully strident works in response to the civil rights conflicts in America (e.g., *Wounded Man,* 1968). When he was appointed professor of art at the University of Washington in 1971, he and his wife moved to Seattle. He retired from teaching in 1987. Since around 1968, Lawrence has concentrated on works with a *Builders* theme, which place a symbolic emphasis on humanity's aspirations and constructive potential. In 1979, he created the first of his several murals, *Games,* for the Kingdome Stadium in Seattle.

Lawrence's work is full of humor, compassion, and pictorial intensity. His central theme is human struggle. Always a social observer with a critical sensibility, he approaches his subjects with a quiet didacticism. Although his work is always emotionally autobiographical, his imagery has universal appeal. Lawrence's greatest contribution to the history of art may be his reassertion of painting's narrative function. In his art's ability to speak to us through time of the often neglected episodes of African-American history and the black experience, Lawrence offers a significant link in the traditions of American history painting, American scene painting, and American figural art.

—ELLEN HARKINS WHEAT

LEDBETTER, HUDSON WILLIAM "LEADBELLY"

Hudson William "Leadbelly" Ledbetter (c. January 15, 1888–December 6, 1949), blues singer and guitarist. Born Hudson William Ledbetter and raised near Mooringsport, La., on a date that is subject to dispute (January 21, 1885, and January 29, 1889, are also often given), Leadbelly, as he was known later in life, was still a child when he began to work in the cotton fields of his share-cropper parents. Later, they bought land across the border in Leigh, Tex. and "Huddie," as he was called, learned to read and write at a local school. During this time he also began to play the windjammer, a Cajun accordion. He also danced and performed music for pay at parties. Ledbetter learned to play twelve-string guitar as well as shoot a revolver in his early teens, and he began to frequent the red-light district of Fannin Street in Shreveport, La., where he performed for both black and white audiences. By the time he left home for good in 1906, Ledbetter had a reputation for hard work, womanizing, violence and musical talent. In 1908 Ledbetter, who had already fathered two children with Margaret Coleman, married Aletta Henderson, and settled down in Harrison County, Tex., where he worked on farms and became a song leader in the local Baptist church. Ledbetter also claimed to have attended Bishop College, in Marshall, Tex., during this time. In 1910 Ledbetter and his family moved to Dallas, and Ledbetter began to frequent the Deep Ellum neighborhood, where he began playing professionally with Blind Lemon Jefferson. The two were inseparable for five years.

In 1915 Ledbetter was jailed and sentenced to a chain gang for possessing a weapon. He escaped, and for several years lived under the pseudonym Walter Boyd. In 1917 he shot and killed a man in a fight, and the next year was sentenced to up to thirty years for murder and assault with intent to kill. He served at the Shaw State Farm Prison, in Huntsville, Tex., from 1918 to 1925. That year, when Texas Gov. Pat Neff visited the prison, Leadbelly made up a song on the spot ask-

See also
Blues

ing to be released and convinced Neff to set him free. By this time Ledbetter was known as "Leadbelly," a corruption of his last name that also referred to his physical toughness. In the late 1920s Leadbelly supported himself by working as a driver and maintenance worker in Houston and around Shreveport. He also continued to perform professionally. In 1930 Leadbelly was again jailed, this time for attempted homicide in Mooringsport. He had served three years when John Lomax came to the notorious Louisiana State Penitentiary at Angola to record music by the prisoners. Lomax, impressed by Leadbelly's musicianship, lobbied for his release, which came in 1934. Lomax hired him as a driver and set him on a career as a musician. In 1935 Leadbelly married Martha Promise.

Leadbelly made his first commercial recordings in 1935, performing "C.C. Rider," "Bull Cow," "Roberta Parts I and II," and "New Black Snake Moan." Thereafter, aside from another prison term in 1939–1940 for assault, Leadbelly enjoyed enormous success as a professional musician, performing and recording to consistent acclaim. In the late 1930s and throughout the 1940s he appeared at universities and political rallies on both the East and West coasts, as well as on radio and film, and was a key element and influence in the growth of American folk and blues music. He became a fixture of the folk music scene in Greenwich Village, near his home on New York's Lower East Side, and was often associated with left-wing politics.

Leadbelly was best known for his songs about prison and rural life in the South. However, his repertory was huge and included blues, children's tunes, cowboy and work songs, ballads, religious songs, and popular songs. Although his audiences were generally white, and Leadbelly made only a few recordings for the "race" market of African-American record buyers, he addressed matters of race in songs such as "Scottsboro Boys" (1938) and "Bourgeois Blues" (1938). His powerful voice was capable of considerable sensitivity and nuance, and his twelve-string guitar playing was simple, yet vigorous and percussive. Among his most popular and enduring songs, some of which were recorded by Lomax for the Library of Congress, are "Goodnight Irene" (1934), "The Midnight Special" (1934), "Rock Island Line" (1937), "Good Morning Blues" (1940), and "Take This Hammer" (1940). He recorded in 1940 with the Golden Gate Quartet, a gospel vocal group. From 1941 to 1943 Leadbelly performed regularly on the U.S. Office of War Information's radio pro-

grams, and in 1945 he appeared in Pete Seeger's short documentary film *Leadbelly*. He made a trip to Paris shortly before his death in New York City at the age of sixty-one from amyotrophic lateral sclerosis (Lou Gehrig's disease). The 1976 film *Leadbelly* was based on his life story. In 1988 Leadbelly was inducted into the Rock and Roll Hall of Fame.

—JONATHAN GILL

LEE, SHELTON JACKSON "SPIKE"

Shelton Jackson "Spike" Lee (March 20, 1957–), filmmaker. Spike Lee was born in Atlanta, Ga., to William Lee, a jazz musician and composer, and Jacqueline Shelton Lee, a teacher of art and literature. The oldest of five children, Lee grew up in Brooklyn, N.Y., with brothers David, Chris, and Cinque, and sister Joie. Lee's family environment was imbued with a strong sense of black history. Like his father and grandfather, Lee attended Morehouse College, and graduated with a B.A. in 1979. Upon graduating, Lee enrolled in New York University's Tisch School of the Arts, where he received an M.F.A. in film production in 1983. While at New York University Lee produced several student films: *The Answer* (1980), *Sarah* (1981), and *Joe's Bed-Stuy Barbershop: We Cut Heads* (1982). *Joe's Bed-Stuy Barbershop*, his M.F.A. thesis film, was awarded a Student Academy Award by the Academy of Motion Picture Arts and Sciences in 1982, was broadcast by some public television stations, and received critical notice in *Variety* and the *New York Times*.

Lee's first feature-length film was the highly acclaimed comedy *She's Gotta Have It* (1986), which he shot in twelve days on location in Brooklyn at a cost of $175,000. The film eventually grossed $8 million. The action of the film centers on a sexually liberated young black woman who is having affairs simultaneously with three men. Interspersed with these scenes, she and the film's characters debate her conduct from ideological perspectives then current in the black community; such topics as hip-hop, color differences, sexual codes, and interracial relationships are raised. This debate spilled over into the national media. Controversy was to become a hallmark of Lee's work.

She's Gotta Have It is characterized by disjointed narrative syntax, mock–cinéma vérité

See also

Bill Cosby

Michael Jordan

Malcolm X

technique, active camera movement, and disregard for autonomy of text. Lee has often employed the same actors and film technicians in many films, giving them a repertory effect.

Lee's second film, *School Daze* (1988), was financed by Columbia Pictures for $6.5 million and grossed more than $15 million. It also dealt with a controversial topic, the conflict at a southern black college between light-skinned students who seek assimilation into mainstream America and dark-skinned students who identify with Africa.

In 1989 Lee produced *Do the Right Thing*, which was set in Brooklyn. The film was produced for $6 million and grossed $30 million. *Do the Right Thing* focused on the relationship between an Italian-American family that operates a pizzeria in the Bedford-Stuyvesant neighborhood and the depressed black community that patronizes it. The film chronicles the racial tensions and events over a period of one day, climaxes in a riot in which one black youth is killed, and ends with the complete destruction of the pizzeria.

This highly successful film was followed by *Mo' Better Blues* (1990), the story of the love affairs, personal growth, and development of a jazz musician in New York City. *Jungle Fever* (1991), also set in New York, was Lee's treatment of interracial relationships, centering on an affair between a married black architect and his Italian-American secretary.

Lee's most ambitious film to date has been *Malcolm X*, which was released in November 1992. In this film Lee departed from his earlier technique and employed the traditional style and approach of the Hollywood epic biography. Produced by Warner Brothers, *Malcolm X* was three hours long and cost $34 million, though it had originally been budgeted for $28 million. By the end of 1994 it had grossed $48.1 million. In a highly publicized initiative Lee raised part of the additional funds needed from black celebrities Bill Cosby, Oprah Winfrey, Earvin "Magic" Johnson, Michael Jordan, Janet Jackson, and Prince, among others. Denzel Washington, who portrayed Malcolm X, was nominated for an Academy Award as best actor. Lee based his film on an original screenplay, written by James Baldwin and Arnold Perl in 1968, that was based on *The Autobiography of Malcolm X* as told to Alex Haley.

In 1994 Lee collaborated with his siblings Joie and Cinque Lee in the production of *Crooklyn*, the story of a large, working-class black family growing up in Brooklyn.

Lee's other films include *Clockers* (1995), about an inner city boy who becomes involved with drug dealers, and *Girl 6* (1996), about a woman employed as a phone sex operator. Lee's 1996 film *Get on the Bus* tells the story of a group of men who travel by bus to Washington, D.C. for the Million Man March in 1995. In 1998, Lee re-

SAY CHEESE

Spike Lee poses for photographers at the 1991 Cannes Film Festival. Lee's films explore the complexities of black-white relations in America.

AP/WIDE WORLD PHOTOS

leased *He Got Game*, his third film starring Denzel Washington. Washington appears as a convict who is released from prison to convince his son, a high school basketball star, to attend college.

Spike Lee's film career has generated a film company, Forty Acres and a Mule; a chain of retail outlets that sell paraphernalia from his films; and a series of television commercials, ten of them with basketball star Michael Jordan.

—ROBERT CHRISMAN

LEWIS, CARL

Carl Lewis (July 1, 1961–), track-and-field athlete. Born in Birmingham, Ala., and raised in Willingboro, N.J., Lewis was reared in a family with a rich athletic tradition. His parents, both former athletes, founded and coached the Willingboro Track Club, where the young Lewis's athletic achievements were frequently overshadowed by the accomplishments of his older, multitalented brothers and precocious younger sister. It was not until high school that Lewis came into his own, displaying both the speed and long-jumping ability that enabled him to dominate track and field throughout the 1980s and early 1990s. As a collegian at the University of Houston, Lewis became the first athlete in the twentieth century to win both the long jump and 100–meter dash at consecutive national championships. Lewis drew comparisons to Jesse Owens at the 1984 Olympic Games when he equaled the latter's feats of 1936 by winning gold medals in the long jump, 100-meter dash, 200-meter dash, and 4 × 100-meter relay. He repeated as long-jump champion at the 1988 Games and was awarded the gold medal in the 100 when Canadian Ben Johnson, the apparent victor, was disqualified after testing positive for steroid use. Lewis won the long jump again at the 1992 Olympics in Barcelona and captured his eighth career gold medal by anchoring the United States 4 × 100 relay team to a world record time of 37.40.

In a sport defined by youth and specialization, Lewis achieved an unusual blend of versatility and longevity while maintaining a standard of excellence. In 1991, at the age of thirty, he established a world record of 9.86 in the 100, and it took a world-record long jump by Mike Powell at that same meet to halt Lewis's string of 65 victories—a streak dating back to 1981.

Despite his consistently superior performances of the 1980s, Lewis seldom received public acclaim equal to his accomplishments. His businesslike approach to competition, perceived aloofness or arrogance, and outspokenness on certain controversial issues—ranging from the use of performance-enhancing drugs by Ben Johnson and others to the compensation of athletes in a sport reluctant to make the transition from amateur to professional standing—sometimes overshadowed his athletic achievements and meant that Lewis himself often met with an ambivalent response from the American public. That track and field is largely invisible—made accessible and meaningful to a large audience in the United States only with the Olympic Games every four years—also contributed to Lewis's difficulty in gaining the widespread popular appeal granted other athletic figures.

Interestingly, Lewis did begin to receive the appreciation and recognition merited by his lengthy, remarkable career only when he no longer appeared unbeatable. For while Lewis sustained his overall level of performance into the 1990s, his competition grew stronger and sometimes overtook him. The most dramatic example of this came at the United States Olympic Trials in 1992, when he failed to qualify in the event he had dominated perennially: the 100–meter dash. In defeat, Lewis became a more "human" figure—occasionally vulnerable to younger, talented challengers—and his achievements appeared all the more extraordinary.

—JILL DUPONT

LEWIS, REGINALD F.

Reginald F. Lewis (December 7, 1942–January 19, 1993), attorney and financier. Born in Baltimore, Md., Reginald F. Lewis received a B.A. in 1965 from Virginia State College, and an L.L.B. in 1968 from Harvard Law School. After graduating, he accepted a position at the law firm of Paul Weiss Rifkind Wharton & Garrison in New York. In 1973, he founded the first black law firm on Wall Street, Lewis & Clarkson, concentrating on corporate law and venture capital business.

During the early 1980s, Lewis served on the board of New York's Offtrack Betting Corporation. In 1983, he established and became CEO of a successful investment firm, the TLC Group. TLC (The Lewis Company) made headlines in 1984 when it bought the 117–year-old McCall Pattern Company, revitalized it, and sold it three years later at an eighty-to-one return on its investment. In 1987, with financing help from

See also

Jacqueline Joyner-Kersee

Charles Richard Johnson's Middle Passage *was awarded the National Book Award in 1990.*

PAGE 384

Michael Milken at Drexel Burnham Lambert, TLC bought Beatrice International Foods, a collection of sixty-four companies in thirty-one countries. This was the largest leveraged purchase ever of a non-American company, and it made TLC the largest black-owned company in the United States.

In 1992, Lewis was one of six executives inducted into the National Sales Hall of Fame by the Sales and Marketing Executives of Greater New York. In that same year, he was named by New York City Mayor David N. Dinkins to the nine-member Municipal Assistance Corporation.

At the time of his death from brain cancer on January 19, 1993, his personal fortune was estimated at $400 million. Through his philanthropic organization, The Lewis Foundation, Lewis donated approximately $10 million in four years to various institutions, charities, and artistic organizations, including the Abyssinian Baptist Church in Harlem, Howard University, and Virginia State University. His $3 million donation to his alma mater, Harvard Law School, establishing the Reginald F. Lewis Fund for International Study and Research, was the largest the school ever received from a single donor. The Lewis Center at Harvard was the first such facility there named in honor of an African American.

—LYDIA MCNEILL

LITERATURE

The earliest black writing reveals a combination of factors and influences that set African-American literature on its way. The desire for freedom and power was shaped at the start by religious rather than secular rhetoric, so that the Bible was the most important text in founding the new literature. Gradually, religious arguments and images gave way in the nineteenth century to political and social protest that eschewed appeals to scriptural authority. As blacks, increasingly estranged from their African cultural identities, sought to understand and represent themselves in the New World, they drew more and more on the wide range of European literatures to find the models and characters which they would adapt to tell their own stories. Rich forms of culture developed in folktales and other works of the imagination, as well as in music, dance, and the other arts. A major aspect of African-American literature, broadly defined, is the persisting influence of oral traditions rooted in the African cultural heritage; these traditions have probably affected virtually all significant artistic meditations by African Americans on their social and political realities and aspirations.

The first significant black American writing emerged toward the end of the eighteenth century with the poet Phillis Wheatley. Born in Africa but reared as a slave in Boston, Wheatley was anomalous in that she was encouraged by her white owners not only to read and write but also to compose literature. Like the other black poet of note writing about the same time, Jupiter Hammon, Wheatley was strongly influenced by Methodism. Unlike Hammon, however, she responded to secular themes as, for example, in celebrating George Washington and the American struggle for independence. Her volume *Poems on Various Subjects, Religious and Moral* (London, 1773) was the first book published by a black American and only the second volume of poetry published by any American woman.

One consequence of the religious emphasis in early black American writing was a tendency to deny, in the face of God's omnipotence, the authenticity of the individual self and the importance of earthly freedom and economic power. In *Autobiography*, the first literary assertion of the emerging African-American identity came in the eighteenth century from a writer ultimately committed to religion—Olaudah Equiano, born in Africa and sold into slavery in the West Indies, North America, and Great Britain. His volume *The Interesting Narrative of the Life of Olaudah Equiano, or Gustavus Vassa, the African* (London, 1789) became the model for what would emerge as the most important single kind of African-American writing: the slave narrative.

Also in the eighteenth century appeared the first of another significant strain—the essay devoted primarily to the exposition of the wrongs visited on blacks in the New World and to the demand for an end to slavery and racial discrimination. In 1791, the gifted astronomer and almanac maker Benjamin Banneker addressed an elegant letter of protest to Thomas Jefferson, then secretary of state and later president of the United States. Banneker appealed to Jefferson, as a man of genius who had opposed slavery (even as he continued to own slaves) and as a signer of the Declaration of Independence, to acknowledge the claims of blacks to equal status with white Americans.

Although the United States formally abolished the importation of slaves in 1807, the first half of the nineteenth century paradoxically saw the deepening of the hold of slavery on American life,

LEON FORREST

Writer Examines Contemporary African-American Life

Leon Forrest (1937–), novelist and educator. Leon Forrest was born in Chicago to Leon and Adeline Forrest, who came from two different African-American traditions—the Protestant deep South (Mississippi) and the Creole Catholic heritage of New Orleans, respectively. Both these traditions helped shape Forrest's imagination and are strongly reflected in his novels. His own experiences growing up in the city of Chicago, and his study of modern literature, particularly the fiction of Dostoyevsky, Joyce, and Faulkner and the drama of Eugene O'Neill, were additional influences on his development. Like Ralph Ellison and Toni Morrison, Forrest was one of those African-American writers of the second half of the twentieth century who adapted the forms and techniques of modern literature to the traditions of African-American fiction.

Forrest went to elementary and secondary schools on the South Side of Chicago and attended Roosevelt University and the University of Chicago before entering the U.S. Army in 1960. His army service in Germany as a public-information specialist from 1960 to 1962 helped launch him on a journalistic career. Beginning as a reporter on a small Chicago neighborhood paper, the *Woodlawn Observer,* he became an associate editor of *Muhammad Speaks,* the newspaper of the Black Muslim movement, in 1969, rising to managing editor in 1972. In 1973 he was appointed associate professor of African-American studies at Northwestern University, where he later became professor and director of the African-American studies program.

Forrest's most important literary creation is the Forest County series, which consists of four novels published from 1973 to 1992. These novels, like those of William Faulkner's Yoknapatawpha saga,

are quite different in form and style from each other, yet are interrelated in setting, characters, and themes. As a whole, the Forest County novels express a rich vision of African-American life, history, and culture in the United States as influences on the lives of characters in Forest County, an imaginative transformation of Chicago, during the 1960s and 1970s.

The first three Forest County novels—*There Is a Tree More Ancient Than Eden* (1973), *The Bloodworth Orphans* (1977), and *Two Wings to Veil My Face* (1983)—deal with a young African American's confrontation with his heritage. In *There Is a Tree,* Nathaniel Witherspoon faces the knowledge of loss and suffering in both his personal life and the consciousness of his heritage as an African American. In *The Bloodworth Orphans,* the same character learns about the tragic doom of a family whose history of miscegenation, incest, and orphanhood exemplifies the African-American heritage of racism and oppression and its catastrophic consequences. Finally, in *Two Wings to Veil My Face,* Nathaniel learns of his family's history in slavery from his adoptive grandmother, Sweetie Reed, who is one of Forrest's most memorable creations.

Forrest's most recent novel in the series, *Divine Days* (1992), is a comic epic of considerable range and variety that describes a crucial week and a day in which the aspiring young dramatist Joubert Jones encounters characters and experiences that reveal to him his true vocation as a writer.

In addition to his novels, Forrest has written a number of plays and librettos, as well as a collection of essays on such topics as William Faulkner, Billie Holiday, and Elijah Muhammad.

—JOHN G. CAWELTI

---

primarily because the invention of the cotton gin revived slavery as an economic force in the South. In response, African-American writers increasingly made the quest for social justice their principal theme. In 1829, George Moses Horton of North Carolina, who enjoyed unusual freedom for a slave, became the first black American to protest against slavery in verse when he published his volume *The Hope of Liberty.* Far more significant, however, was *David Walker's Appeal, in Four Articles* (1829), in which David Walker aggressively expounded arguments against slavery and racism

and attacked white claims to civilization even as that civilization upheld slavery. Walker's writing may have encouraged the most famous of all slave insurrections, led by Nat Turner in Virginia the following year, when some sixty whites were killed.

The founding by the white radical William Lloyd Garrison of the antislavery newspaper the *Liberator* in 1831 helped to galvanize abolitionism as a force among both whites and blacks. In particular, abolitionism stimulated the growth in popularity of slave narratives. A major early example was *A Narrative of the Adventures and Es-*

See also
James Baldwin

*In 1993 Toni
Morrison became
the first black
woman in history to
be awarded the
Nobel Prize for
literature.*

PAGE 463

cape of Moses Roper (1837), but the most powerful and effective was undoubtedly *Narrative of the Life of Frederick Douglass, an American Slave* (1845), which enjoyed international success and made Frederick Douglass a leader in the anti-slavery crusade. One New England observer, Ephraim Peabody, hailed the narratives as representing a "new department" in literature; another, Theodore Parker, declared that they were the only native American form of writing and that "all the original romance of Americans is in them, not in the white man's novel." Slave narratives were certainly a major source of material and inspiration for the white writer Harriet Beecher Stowe when she published, in the wake of the Fugitive Slave Act of 1850, her epochal novel *Uncle Tom's Cabin* (1852). This novel, which offered the most expansive treatment of black character and culture seen to that point in American literature, would itself have a profound effect on black writing.

One autobiography largely ignored in its time, but later hailed as a major work, was Harriet Jacobs's *Incidents in the Life of a Slave Girl* (1861), published under the pseudonym Linda Brent. In its concern for the fate of black women during and after slavery, and its emphasis on personal relationships rather than on the acquisition of power, *Incidents in the Life* anticipated many of the concerns that would distinguish the subsequent writing of African-American women.

Other important writers of the antebellum period who sounded notes of protest against social injustice were escaped slaves such as William Wells Brown and Henry Highland Garnet, as well as the freeborn John Brown Russwurm (from Jamaica, West Indies) and Martin R. Delany. Of these writers, the most versatile was certainly Brown, who published as a poet, fugitive slave narrator, essayist, travel writer, dramatist, historian, and novelist. Responding to the implicit challenge of *Uncle Tom's Cabin,* Brown published the first novel by an African American, *Clotel; or, The President's Daughter* (London, 1853), in which he drew on the rumor of a long-standing affair between Thomas Jefferson and a slave. *Uncle Tom's Cabin* and *Clotel* helped to establish the main features of the black novel in the nineteenth century. These include an emphasis on the question of social justice for African Americans, on light-skinned heroes and heroines, and on plots marked by melodrama and sentimentality rather than realism.

Almost as versatile as Brown, and in some respects the representative African-American writer of the second half of the nineteenth century, was the social reformer Frances Ellen Watkins Harper. As with the vast majority of black writers before and after the Civil War and the heyday of the abolitionist movement, Harper maintained her career by printing and distributing her own texts, almost entirely without the opportunities and rewards that came from white publishers. Her major source of her fame was her poetry, although she depended technically on the lead of traditional American poets of the age, such as Longfellow and Whittier. Antislavery sentiment formed the core of her first book, *Poems on Miscellaneous Subjects* (1854), which went through almost two dozen editions in twenty years. Harper also published the first short story by an African American, "The Two Offers," in 1859; the biblical narrative *Moses, a Story of the Nile* (1869); and a novel about an octoroon heroine, *Iola Leroy, or Shadows Uplifted* (1892). Although Harper's limitations as a novelist are clear, *Iola Leroy* raises significant questions about the place of women in African-American culture.

While opposition to slavery was an enormous stimulus to African-American writing of the time, the Civil War itself went largely unreflected in black poetry, fiction, or drama. William Wells Brown published *The Negro in the American Rebellion: His Heroism and His Fidelity* (1867), and a generation later the historian George Washington Williams offered his *History of the Negro Troops in the War of Rebellion* (1888). In some respects, however, the most powerful document to emerge from that watershed event in African-American history is the *Journal of Charlotte Forten* [1854–1892] (published in abridged form in 1953) by Charlotte Forten Grimké. The journal records events in Forten's life from her school days in Salem, Mass. (she was born in Philadelphia, the granddaughter of a wealthy black sail-maker active in the abolitionist cause), through her two years as a volunteer teacher in the Sea Islands off South Carolina during the war. Also illuminating is the autobiography of Elizabeth Keckley, *Behind the Scenes; or Thirty Years a Slave, and Four Years in the White House* (1868), which culminates in an account of her service as a seamstress to Mary Todd Lincoln, when Keckley strove to use her insider's position to assist other blacks and the war effort in general.

Although it is possible to see black literature of the 1850s as constituting a flowering or even a renaissance of writing, the two decades after the Civil War saw no rich development of the field. Reconstruction was a period of promise but also of disillusionment for blacks. It was followed by a dramatic worsening in their social, economic, and political status, culminating in the U.S. Supreme Court decisions *Williams* v. *Mississippi* (1895) and *Plessy* v. *Ferguson* (1896). These and other decisions effectively nullified the Fifteenth Amendment to the U.S. Constitution, which gave black freedmen the right to vote. Soon, black Americans had also essentially lost the right to associate freely with whites in virtually the entire public sphere.

The rise of segregation and of vigilante repression after Reconstruction diminished, but did not destroy, black American literature. With the rise of black newspapers and journals (as exemplified at the turn of the century by *The Voice of the Negro* and *The Colored American*), formed in response to the barriers to integration, there was another upsurge in literary creativity. In 1884, the poet Albery A. Whitman published probably his finest work, *Rape of Florida,* a long narrative poem in Spenserian stanzas that showed off his considerable lyrical gift. In 1899, Sutton Griggs published *Imperium in Imperio,* the first of five privately printed novels that gave expression to Griggs's startlingly nationalistic ideas about the future of black America. Another important figure was Pauline Hopkins, who served as editor of *The Colored American.* However, the major new talents of the age were the fiction writer Charles W. Chesnutt and the poet and novelist Paul Laurence Dunbar.

Between 1887 and 1900, Chesnutt kept his racial identity a secret from his readers while he built his reputation as a gifted writer of poems, articles, and short stories in magazines (including the prestigious *Atlantic Monthly*) and newspapers that served mainly whites. Several of his short stories, including "The Goophered Grapevine," drew on the black folklore of the antebellum South, which Chesnutt treated with imagination and sympathy but also with a shrewd awareness of the harsh realities of slavery. In 1900 came the first of his three novels, *The House Behind the Cedars,* followed by *The Marrow of Tradition* (1901) and *The Colonel's Dream* (1905). Folklore dominated his collection of stories *The Conjure Woman* (1899), but Chesnutt also boldly explored in realist fashion the racial tensions of his day, as in his use of the infamous Wilmington, N.C., riot of 1898 in *The Marrow of Tradition.*

Dunbar, on the other hand, published from the start as an African-American writer. Starting out with the collection *Majors and Minors* (1895), he achieved national fame as a poet—the first black American to do so—with his volume *Lyrics of Lowly Life* (1896). This volume sported a glowing introduction by William Dean Howells, the distinguished white novelist, critic, and editor. In 1899 came another collection, *Lyrics from the Hearthside.* Drawing on the stereotypes of black life formed by the black minstrel tradition, as well as on the so-called plantation tradition, which sought to glorify the antebellum culture of the South, Dunbar was an acknowledged master of dialect verse. Such poems found a ready audience among whites and, perhaps more uneasily, among blacks. Unwittingly, Howells had pointed to the essential lack of authenticity of black dialect verse. He praised Dunbar for writing poetry that explored the range of African-American character, which Howells saw as being "between appetite and emotion, with certain lifts far beyond and above it." Eventually Dunbar regretted Howells's endorsement. In his brief poem "The Poet," he seemed to deplore the fact that for all his valiant attempts to compose dignified poems in standard English, the world had "turned to praise / A jingle in a broken tongue."

Nevertheless, dialect poems became a staple of black literature, especially in the hands of writers such as John Wesley Holloway and James D. Corrothers; Dunbar's verse, in both dialect and standard English, became enshrined within African-American culture as beloved recitation pieces. He also published four volumes of short stories and four novels, few of which are memorable. Genial collections of stories such as *Folks from Dixie* (1898) and *In Old Plantation Days* mainly gave comfort to those Americans who would remember the "good old days" of slavery. His novels, too, were rather weakly constructed—except for the last, *The Sport of the Gods* (1902). Here Dunbar, emphasizing black characters in his novels for the first time, helped to break new ground in black fiction by dwelling on the subject of urban blight in the North.

Dunbar was admired and imitated by many black poets of the age, but his misgivings about dialect verse came to be widely shared. One of his most gifted admirers, James Weldon Johnson, himself later an influential poet, anthologist, novelist, and autobiographer, credited a reading of Whitman's *Leaves of Grass* around 1900 with alerting him to the limitations of dialect verse. However, by far the most influential publication for the future of African-American literature to appear in Dunbar's day was W. E. B. Du Bois's epochal *The Souls of Black Folk* (1903). With essays on black history and culture, as well as a short story and a prose elegy on the death of his

L

LITERATURE

Langston Hughes was widely recognized as the most representative African-American writer and perhaps the most original of black poets.

PAGE 357

The Souls of
Black Folk *fused a
denunciation
of racism with
detailed
descriptions of the
heroism of blacks.*

PAGE 418

young son, Du Bois virtually revolutionized Afro-American self-portrayal in literature.

Du Bois directly challenged the most popular recent book by a black American, Booker T. Washington's autobiography, *Up from Slavery* (1901). Washington's story tells of his rise from slavery to his acknowledged position as a powerful black American (he was the major consultant on black public opinion for most of the leading whites of his day). The autobiography comforted whites, especially white Southerners, by urging blacks to concede the right to vote and to associate freely with whites. Criticizing Washington, *The Souls of Black Folk* offered a far more complex definition of black American history, culture, and character. In elegant prose, it fused a denunciation of slavery and racism with equally detailed descriptions of the heroism of blacks in facing the vicissitudes of American life. The most striking passage of Du Bois's book was probably his identification of an essential "double consciousness" in the African American—"an American, a Negro; two souls, two thoughts, two unreconciled strivings; two warring ideals in one dark body, whose dogged strength alone keeps it from being torn asunder."

Along with his other books of history, sociology, biography, and fiction between 1897 and 1920, Du Bois's work as editor of the *Crisis* (founded in 1910), the official magazine of the newly formed NAACP, unquestionably helped to pave the way for the flowering of African-American writing in the 1920s. Influenced by *The Souls of Black Folk*, James Weldon Johnson explored the question of "double consciousness" in his novel *The Autobiography of an Ex-Coloured Man* (1912), which has been described as the first significantly psychological novel in African-American fiction. He also published an influential volume of verse, *Fifty Years and Other Poems* (1917, celebrating the anniversary of the Emancipation Proclamation in 1913), and an even more significant anthology, *Book of American Negro Poetry* (1922), which included dialect verse but consciously set new standards for younger writers. Another important anticipatory figure was the poet Fenton Johnson of Chicago, with his modernist compositions that deplored the pieties and hypocrisy of western civilization. The Jamaican-born Claude McKay, in a body of poetry highlighted by his *Spring in New Hampshire* (1920) and *Harlem Shadows* (1922), combined conventional lyricism with racial assertiveness. His best-known poem, the 1919 sonnet "If We Must Die," was widely read by blacks as a brave call to strike back at white brutality, especially at the bloody antiblack riots that year in

Chicago and elsewhere. Jean Toomer's *Cane* (1923), an avant-garde pastiche of fiction, poetry, and drama, captivated the younger writers and intellectuals with its intensely lyrical dramatization of the psychology of blacks at a major turning point in their American history.

The *Crisis,* the *Messenger* (founded in 1917 by the socialists A. Philip Randolph and Chandler Owen), and *Opportunity* (founded in 1923 by Charles S. Johnson for the National Urban League) consciously sought to stimulate literature as an adjunct to a more aggressive political and cultural sense among blacks. Marcus Garvey's *Negro World,* with its "back-to-Africa" slogan, also added to the sense of excitement among black Americans at the coming of a new day, especially with the mass migration to the North from the segregated South. In some respects, the culmination of these efforts was Alain Locke's *The New Negro* (1925). A revised version of a special Harlem number of the national magazine *Survey Graphic* (March 1925), this collection of essays, verse, and fiction by a variety of writers announced the arrival of a new generation and a new spirit within black America.

Among writers born in the twentieth century, the poets Countee Cullen, starting with *Color* (1925), and Langston Hughes, with *The Weary Blues* (1926) and *Fine Clothes to the Jew* (1927), set new standards in verse. Cullen offered highly polished poems that combined his reverence for traditional forms (he was influenced by the English poets John Keats and A. E. Housman, in particular) with his deep resentment of racism. Less reverential about literary tradition, and guided by the American examples of Whitman and Carl Sandburg, Hughes experimented with fusions of traditional verse and blues and jazz forms native to black culture. Also during what is often called the Harlem Renaissance (although the literary movement was certainly felt elsewhere) came the work of poets such as Georgia Douglas Johnson, Anne Spencer, Gwendolyn Bennett, and Arna Bontemps, as well as Sterling A. Brown, who also rooted his poetry in the lives of the southern black folk and in the blues idiom. Several of these writers were reticent about race as a subject in verse, let alone forms influenced by blues and jazz. For the others, however, the new spirit was perhaps captured best by Hughes in his essay "The Negro Artist and the Racial Mountain" (*Nation,* 1926). Dismissing the reservations of both blacks and whites, Hughes declared that "we younger Negro artists who create now intend to express our individual dark-skinned selves without fear or

JUNE JORDAN

June Jordan (July 9, 1936–), writer. Born in Harlem to Jamaican immigrants Granville and Mildred Jordan, June Jordan grew up in Brooklyn's Bedford Stuyvesant, where poverty and racism were rampant. She absorbed quite early, as she records in the introduction to her first collection of essays, *Civil Wars* (1981), her community's belief in the power of the word. In her family, literature was important, so that by age seven she was writing poetry. She attended an exclusive New England white high school and went to Barnard College in 1953, both of which she found alienating experiences.

In college she met Michael Meyer, a student at Columbia, whom she married in 1955. They had a son, Christopher David, in 1958 and were divorced by 1965, experiences she explores in later essays. In the 1960s, Jordan, now a single working mother, actively participated in and wrote about African-American political movements in New York City. Her first book-length publication, *Who Look at Me* (1969); her poems collected in *Some Changes* (1971); and her essays in *Civil Wars* exemplify her illumination of the political as intimate, the personal as political change, poetry as action—concepts central to all Jordan's work.

Jordan's writing workshop for Brooklyn children in 1965 resulted in the anthology *Voice of the Children* (1970), and anticipated her many books for children: *His Own Where* (1971), written in black English; *Dry Victories* (1972); *Fannie Lou Hamer* (1972); *New Life: New Room;* and *Kimako's Story* (1981), while her organizing of poets in the 1960s resulted in the anthology *SoulScript* Poetry. Her collaboration with Buckminster Fuller in 1964 to create an architectural design for Harlem indicates her concern with black urban environments, a theme evident in *His Own Where* and *New Life: New Room.* Her work as an architect won Jordan a Prix de Rome in 1970, a year she spent in Rome and Greece, geographical points for many poems in *New Days: Poems of Exile & Return* (1974).

Jordan's teaching at City College, New York City, and the State University of New York at Stony Brook is a starting point for theoretical essays on black English, of which she is a major analyst. Her reflections on her mother's suicide in 1966 are the genesis for black feminist poems such as "Getting Down to Get Over," in *Things That I Do in the Dark: Selected Poems* (1977). In the 1970s, Jordan contributed to black feminism with major essays and poems. Her "Poem about My Rights" in *Passion: New Poems, 1977–80* also indicates her growing internationalism, as she relates the rape of women to the rape of Third World countries by developed nations.

In the 1980s, through poetry in *Living Room* (1985) and *Naming Our Destiny* (1989), as well as in *On Call: Political Essays,* Jordan writes about oppression in South Africa, Lebanon, Palestine, and Nicaragua as she widens her personal vision as an African-American woman to include more of the struggling world. The growth of her international audience is indicated by the translation of her work into many languages (including Arabic and Japanese), by British publications of *Lyrical Campaigns: Poems* (1985) and *Moving towards Home: Political Essays* (1989), and by recordings of her poems as sung by Sweet Honey in the Rock.

In 1978 and 1980, Jordan recorded her own poems, and in the 1980s she began writing plays, a genre she calls "a living forum." Her play *The Issue* was produced in 1981; *Bang Bang über Alles,* in 1986, and *All These Blessings,* in 1990, had staged readings. Jordan has also widened her audience by being a regular columnist for the *Progressive* magazine. In her poetry, prose, and plays, Jordan continues to dramatize how life seems to be an increasing revelation of the "intimate face of universal struggle," a truth she offers to those who would hear her.

—BARBARA T. CHRISTIAN

shame. . . . We know we are beautiful. And ugly too."

Later in the 1920s and in the early 1930s, fiction supplanted poetry as the most powerful genre among black writers. In 1924, Jessie Fauset, the literary editor of the *Crisis* and ultimately the most prolific black novelist of the period, published her first book, *There Is Confusion,* set in the refined, educated black middle class from which she had come. The same year also saw Walter White's *The Fire in Flint,* on the subject of lynching. In 1928, Claude McKay published *Home to Harlem,* which antagonized some older blacks by emphasizing what they saw as hedonism. Nella Larsen's *Quicksand* (1928) and *Passing* (1929) sensitively treated the consciousness of African-American women teased and taxed by conflicts about color, class, and gender. Du Bois's *Dark*

See also
Nikki Giovanni

Dove's gifts as a poet were most fully acknowledged in 1993 when she was appointed Poet Laureate of the united States, the first black writer ever to have been so honored.

PAGE 177

Princess (1928) sought to examine some of the global political implications of contemporary black culture. Wallace Thurman's *The Blacker the Berry* (1929) probed color consciousness within the black world, and in *Infants of the Spring* (1932) he satirized aspects of the new movement. Langston Hughes's *Not without Laughter* (1930) told of a young black boy growing up with his grandmother and her daughters in the Midwest. Other noteworthy novels include Bontemps's *God Sends Sunday* (1931), George Schuyler's *Black No More* (1931), and Cullen's *One Way to Heaven* (1932).

A major feature of the New York flowering had been the close dependence of the younger black writers on personal relationships with whites—not only editors but wealthy patrons. If the role of white patronage in the movement would remain a much-debated matter, the financial collapse of Wall Street in 1929 and the onset of the Great Depression certainly helped to end the renaissance. Many black writers, like their white counterparts, began to find radical socialism and the Communist party appealing. Setting aside the blues, Langston Hughes, who lived in the Soviet Union for a year (1932–1933), wrote a series of propaganda poems for the radical cause; and even Countee Cullen found the Communist party attractive.

On the other hand, probably the greatest single work of this decade—Zora Neale Hurston's second novel, *Their Eyes Were Watching God* (1937)—went against the grain of radical socialism or the overt assertion of racial pride. A lover of black folk culture as well as a trained ethnographer, Hurston set in the rural South her highly poetic story of a black woman's search for an independent sense of identity and self-fulfillment; the narrative abounds in examples of folk sayings, humor, and wisdom. Ignored in its day, her novel would eventually be hailed as a masterpiece.

In poetry, both Margaret Walker's *For My People* (1942) and Melvin B. Tolson's *Rendezvous with America* (1944) reflected the radical populism and socialist influence of the 1930s, when both began to write seriously. Again, however, the outstanding work came in fiction. In Chicago, Richard Wright, not long from Mississippi and Tennessee, had started out as a propaganda poet for the Communist party, then turned to fiction. In 1938, his first collection of short stories, *Uncle Tom's Children*, set in the South, showed great promise that was realized two years later, when *Native Son* appeared. A Book-of-the-Month Club main selection, the novel became a national best-seller (the first by an African-American writer). *Native Son* was unprecedented in American literature. Its bleak picture of black life in an urban setting—Chicago—and the brutishness and violence of its central character, Bigger Thomas, who kills two young women, drew on extreme realism and naturalism to express Wright's sense of a crisis in American—and African-American—culture. His brilliant autobiography, *Black Boy* (1945), also a bestseller, set his individual determination to be an artist against the backdrop of almost unrelieved hostility from both whites and blacks in the South; it confirmed Wright's status as the most renowned black American writer.

In 1947, Wright emigrated with his family to Paris, where he lived until his death in 1960. However, *Native Son*, with its emphasis on black fear, rage, and violence in an urban, northern setting, left its mark on the next generation of African-American novelists. William Attaway's *Blood on the Forge* (1941), Chester Himes's *If He Hollers Let Him Go* (1945), Anne Petry's *The Street* (1946), and Willard Motley's *Knock on Any Door* (1947) all showed Wright's influence. On the other hand, the most successful (at least in terms of book sales) of African-American writers, the novelist Frank Yerby, also started his career in the 1940s, but on a completely different footing. Eschewing black culture and the idea of racial protest as sources of inspiration, Yerby established his reputation mainly with romances of the South, starting with his enormously popular *The Foxes of Harrow* (1946).

In a sense, Wright and his admirers, on the one hand, and Yerby, on the other, were enacting the latest stage of the essential political and aesthetic debate among African-American intellectuals, which pitted the merits of racial awareness and protest against the allure of integration within white America as the major goal. Yerby represented one extreme response to this question; the career of the gifted poet Gwendolyn Brooks illustrated a more moderate position. She won the Pulitzer Prize in 1950 for her volume *Annie Allen* (1949), which appeared to confirm not only the unprecedented degree of acceptability of black literature by whites but also Brooks's wisdom and insight in mixing, as she did, "high" or learned modernist technique with a commitment to African-American subject matter. Her first volume, *A Street in Bronzeville* (1945), in which she drew on the same Chicago setting on which *Native Son* is based, exemplifies this strategy.

In fiction, an even more acclaimed fusion of modernism and black material came with Ralph

See also
Lorraine Hansberry

Ellison's novel *Invisible Man* (1952), which won the prestigious National Book Award for fiction. Ellison had attended Tuskegee Institute for two years. There he had been drawn to modernist literature, especially as epitomized by T. S. Eliot's epochal poem *The Waste Land* and James Joyce's *Ulysses*. In New York, he had become friends with Richard Wright. In the following years, Ellison schooled himself in virtually all aspects of modernist literary criticism and technique, including advanced uses of folk material, and deepened his understanding of his relationship to the mainstream American literary tradition going back to Emerson, Melville, and Whitman. In *Invisible Man*, his unnamed hero struggles with fundamental questions of identity as a naive young black man making his way in the American world. At times baffled and confused, hurt and alienated, Ellison's hero nevertheless is sustained by a recognizably American vivaciousness and optimism. This last quality perhaps accounted in part for the success of the book among many white critics, as well as with many blacks, when it appeared.

Another pivotal figure in the late 1940s and the early 1950s was James Baldwin, who more clearly than Brooks or Ellison defined himself in opposition to earlier writers, and in particular to the master figure of Wright. Deploring what he saw as the commitment of black writing to forms of protest, Baldwin attacked *Native Son* in the celebrated essay "Everybody's Protest Novel" (*Partisan Review,* 1949), which is ostensibly concerned mainly with Harriet Beecher Stowe's *Uncle Tom's Cabin*. According to Baldwin, both novels dehumanize their black characters; art must rise, he argued, above questions of race and politics if it is to be successful. In his own first novel, *Go Tell It on the Mountain* (1953), set almost entirely within a black American community, a troubled adolescent struggles against a repressive background of storefront Pentecostal religion to assert himself in the face of his brutal, insensitive father and passive, victimized mother. Baldwin's second novel, *Giovanni's Room* (1956), on the individual's search for identity in the face of homophobia, included no black characters at all.

In 1954, the U.S. Supreme Court decision *Brown* v. *Board of Education* appeared to signal the end of segregation across the United States. Instead, it set in motion sharpening conflicts over the standing questions concerning race, identity, and art as the civil rights movement carried the struggle to the strongholds of segregation in the South. These conflicts in the 1950s and the early

1960s (in the era before the distinctive rise of Black Power as a philosophy, with its attendant Black Arts Movement) certainly stimulated the growth of African-American literature. Some older black writers, such as Hughes, Wright, Tolson, and Brooks, published effectively in this period. Hughes brought out five collections of stories based on his popular character "Simple," drawn from his columns in the weekly Chicago *Defender,* as well as several other books, including his second volume of autobiography, *I Wonder as I Wander* (1956). Ellison's collection of essays, *Shadow and Act* (1964), on the interplay between race and culture, consolidated his reputation as a leading intellectual. Baldwin became celebrated as an essayist with dazzling collections such as *Notes of a Native Son* (1956) and *Nobody Knows My Name* (1961). His novel *Another Country* (1962), with its exploration of the themes of miscegenation and bisexuality among blacks and whites, was a bestseller. In focusing primarily on whites, however, *Another Country* perhaps epitomized the integrationist impulse that was soon to pass from African-American writing.

In the theater, Lorraine Hansberry's *A Raisin in the Sun* (1959) dramatized in timely fashion the conflicts of integration within a black family rising in the world. This play became the longest-running drama by an African American in the history of Broadway, as well as an acclaimed motion picture. When Hansberry won the New York Drama Critics Circle Award, she became the first black American and the youngest woman to do so. Other playwrights of the 1950s included the indefatigable Langston Hughes, who broke ground with gospel plays such as *Black Nativity* and *Jericho-Jim Crow,* as well as younger writers such as Alice Childress (*Mojo, a Black Love Story;* 1971), William Branch (*In Splendid Error;* 1953), Loften Mitchell (*A Land beyond the River;* 1957), and the actor-dramatist Ossie Davis, whose *Purlie Victorious* (1961) was a solid commercial success.

Although the civil rights struggle was being waged mainly in the South, a major disquieting voice boldly challenging racism in the United States was that of Malcolm X. *The Autobiography of Malcolm X,* cowritten with Alex Haley and published in the year of Malcolm's assassination (1965), was hailed almost at once as a classic work that combined spiritual autobiography with racial and political polemic. The work tells of Malcolm's rise from a life of crime and sin to deliverance through his conversion to the Nation of Islam, then his repudiation of that sect in favor of a more

Following her rediscovery, a once-neglected Hurston rose into literary prominence and enjoys acclaim as the essential forerunner of black women writers who came after her.

PAGE 358

See also
Ellen Watkins Harper

inclusive vision of world and racial unity. Malcolm's work appeared to stimulate a series of highly significant autobiographies that demonstrated once again the centrality of this genre to black culture. Claude Brown's *Manchild in the Promised Land* (1965) is an often harrowing account of its author's determination to climb from a life of juvenile delinquency in Harlem. Anne Moody's autobiography, *Coming of Age in Mississippi* (1969), chronicles her troubled evolution from a small-town southern girlhood into a life as a militant worker in the tumultuous civil rights movement; it illuminates both her individual growth and some of the weaknesses of the movement as it affected many idealistic young blacks. Maya Angelou's *I Know Why the Caged Bird Sings* (1970) is a lyrical but also realistic autobiography of a woman whose indomitable human spirit triumphs over adversity, including her rape as a child.

Although Malcolm's *Autobiography* appeared finally to repudiate racial separation, it had a major impact on the separatist ideal that informed the next major stage in the evolution of African-American culture. In 1965, in a break with the integrationist ideal of all the major civil rights organizations, younger black leaders began to rally around the cry of Black Power. In this move, they were supported brilliantly by certain writers and artists. In 1964, LeRoi Jones, soon to be known as Amiri Baraka, had staged *Dutchman* and *The Slave*, two plays that anticipated this turnabout. A graduate of Howard University, Jones had begun his career as a bohemian poet in Greenwich Village, where he had edited the magazine *Yugen* and helped to edit *The Floating Bear* and *Kulchur*. All of these journals featured the work of avant-garde poets, almost all of them white. Exploring the sensibility of a bohemian poet, his first volume of verse, *Preface to a Twenty-Volume Suicide Note* (1961), touched only lightly on the theme of race. *Dutchman* and *The Slave*, however, laid bare Jones's deepening hatred of white culture and of African-American artists and intellectuals who resisted the evidence of white villainy. He soon left Greenwich Village for Harlem, where he founded the Black Arts Repertory Theatre School. Barring whites, he transformed himself into an ultraradical black artist, an extreme cultural nationalist whose art would be determined almost entirely by the conflicts of race and by the connection between blacks and Africa.

Vividly expounded by Baraka and by other theorists (several of them poets) such as Ron Karenga and Larry Neal, radical cultural nationalism became the dominant aesthetic among younger blacks. Baraka's collection of new poems, *Black Magic* (1969), defined the artistic temper of the movement. These and other poems of the age voiced their radical opinions in blunt, often profane and even obscene language inspired by an easy familiarity with black street idioms and jazz rhythms, conveyed through typographic and other stylistic innovations. A spurning of all persons and things white and a romantic questing for kinship with Africa—the proclaimed fountainhead of all genuine spirituality—characterized the writing of these cultural nationalists. Addison Gayle, Jr.'s *The Black Aesthetic* (1971), an edited collection of essays on literature and the other arts by black writers, gave another name and another degree of focus to the movement, even though several of the essays did not readily endorse the new radical nationalist position. Undoubtedly the most respected journal sympathetic to the new movement, imaginatively edited by Hoyt Fuller, was the monthly *Black World* (formerly called *Negro Digest,* and published by the parent company of *Ebony* magazine).

Baraka's attempt to form a theater committed to the politically purposeful expression of African-American values encouraged black playwrights to be bolder than ever. However, the existence Off-Broadway of the Negro Ensemble Company, led by Douglas Turner Ward, with a vision often in conflict with Baraka's, ensured variety among the writers. The result was probably the most prolific period in the history of African-American theater. Baldwin's *Blues for Mister Charlie* (1964) and *The Amen Corner* (staged on Broadway in 1965) reflected the new militancy and cynicism of black artists as they viewed the American landscape. Hansberry's *The Sign in Sidney Brustein's Window* (first staged in 1964) explored the minds and reactions of white liberals in contemporary New York. Adrienne Kennedy's *Funnyhouse of a Negro* (1964–1969) revealed her interest in expressionism and violence as she pursued questions of identity and personality. Charles Gordone's realist *No Place to Be Somebody* (1969) won a Pulitzer Prize for drama, the first by a black American. Other playwrights included Ted Shine, Douglas Turner Ward, Ed Bullins, Philip Hayes Dean, Ron Milner, and Richard Wesley. Lonnie Elder III wrote the acclaimed *Ceremonies in Dark Old Men* (1969), and Charles Fuller later enjoyed a commercial hit with *A Soldier's Play* (1981) about blacks in the military. In 1975, Ntozake Shange's brilliant staging of her "choreopoem" *For Colored Girls Who Have Considered Suicide / When the Rainbow Is Enuf* captivated audiences as it anticipated a theme of rising importance, the feminist

See also
Chester Himes
Langston Hughes

ERNEST J. GAINES

Writer Examines Caste and Class in Black America

Ernest J. Gaines (1933–), writer. The oldest son of a large family, Ernest Gaines was born on January 15, 1933, on the River Lake Plantation in Point Coupée Parish, La. His parents separated when he was young, and his father's absence led to a permanent estrangement. More important than his parents in his childhood was a maternal great-aunt who provided love and served as an example of strength and survival under extreme adversity. The older people in the close-knit community of the plantation "quarters" exemplified similar qualities, passing on to the child the rich oral tradition that figures prominently in his fiction.

At the age of fifteen Gaines moved from this familiar environment to Vallejo, Calif., where he could receive a better education. Lonely in these new surroundings, he spent much of his time in the town's public library and began to write. After high school he spent time in a junior college and the military before matriculating at San Francisco State College. An English major, he continued to write stories and graduated in 1957. Encouraged by his agent, Dorothea Oppenheimer, and (while in the creative writing program at Stanford) by Malcolm Cowley, Gaines committed himself to a literary career. In 1964 he published his first novel, *Catherine Carmier.* His subsequent books are *Of Love and Dust* (1967), *Bloodline* (1968), *The Autobiography of Miss Jane Pittman* (1971), *In My Father's House* (1978), and *A Gathering of Old Men* (1983). In a collection of interviews published as *Porch Talk with Ernest Gaines* (1990), he discussed his work in progress, a novel about an uneducated black man on death row and a black teacher in a Louisiana plantation school titled *A Lesson Before Dying.*

In the 1960s and '70s, except for a year at Denison University, Gaines lived and wrote in San Francisco. Since the early 1980s he has been associated with the University of Southwestern Louisiana, although he has continued to summer in San Francisco.

South Louisiana, the region of Gaines's youth and literary imagination, is beautiful and distinctive with unique cultural, linguistic, and social patterns. Like George Washington Cable and Kate Chopin before him, Gaines has been fascinated by the interplay of caste and class among the ethnic groups of the area: blacks, mixed-race Creoles, Cajuns, white Creoles, and Anglo whites. Once fairly stable as subsistence farmers, blacks and mixed-race Creoles have been dispossessed of the best land or displaced altogether by Cajuns, who are favored by the plantation lords because they are white and use mechanized agricultural methods. Under such socioeconomic conditions, young blacks leave, as Gaines himself did, though they often find themselves drawn back to Louisiana.

Such is the case in *Catherine Carmier.* In this novel the protagonist is the educated and alienated Jackson Bradley, who returns to his native parish to claim the love of the title character, daughter of a mixed-race Creole whose racial exclusivism, attachment to the land, and semi-incestuous feelings toward her cannot condone such an alliance. Nor do Jackson's fellow blacks approve. Jackson cannot recapture his love or his homeland because, for all its pastoral charm, the world of his childhood is anachronistic. In *Of Love and Dust* Gaines moves from Arcadian nostalgia to a tragic mode. Marcus Payne, the rebellious protagonist, defies social and racial taboos by making love to the wife of a Cajun plantation overseer, Sidney Bonbon, after being rejected by Bonbon's black mistress. As Marcus and Louise Bonbon prepare to run away together, the Cajun, a grim embodiment of fate, kills him with a scythe.

If *Catherine Carmier* is a failed pastoral and *Of Love and Dust* a tragedy, *The Autobiography of Miss Jane Pittman* is a near-epic account of a centenarian whose life has spanned slavery, Reconstruction, Jim Crow, and the Civil Rights Movement. Her individual story reflects the experience of oppression, resistance, survival, and dignity of an entire people. Although the protagonist of *In My Father's House* is a minister and civil rights leader in Louisiana and his unacknowledged son is an urban militant, this work's central theme is more private than public—the search for a father who has abdicated parental responsibility. In this grim tale, the son commits suicide and the father survives but without dignity. The mood of *A Gathering of Old Men,* on the other hand, is more comic than grim, but the old men who gather with shotguns to protect one of their own from unjust arrest achieve in this act of resistance the dignity that has been missing from their lives. White characters, too, achieve moral growth as social and racial change finally catches up with the bayou country. It is Gaines's most hopeful novel and in some ways his best.

In 1972 Gaines received the Black Academy of Arts and Letters Award. He was given the annual literary award of the American Academy and Institute of Arts and Letters in 1987.

—KENNETH KINNAMON

See also
Zora Neale Hurston

revaluation by women of their role in American and African-American culture.

In spite of successes on stage and in fiction, poetry became the most popular genre of the new black writers of the late 1960s. One encouraging development was the rise of small black-owned publishing houses, especially Dudley Randall's Broadside Press and Naomi Long Madgett's Lotus Press, which brought out the work of several poets in cheap editions that reached a wide audience among blacks. In this way, Sonia Sanchez, Nikki Giovanni, Don L. Lee (later known as Haki Madhubuti), Mari Evans, Lucille Clifton, Jayne Cortez, Etheridge Knight, Conrad Kent Rivers, Samuel Allen, June Jordan, Carolyn Rodgers, Ted Joans, Audre Lorde, and other writers acquired relatively large followings. Indeed, the relationship of poets to the black population in general had virtually no counterpart in the white world, where poetry had long passed almost entirely into the hands of academics. Among black poets less committed to populist and nationalist expression, the most outstanding were probably Jay Wright and Robert Hayden. Hayden's first volume had appeared in 1940; his *Selected Poems* (1966) showed his commitment to an allusive poetry of reflection and painstaking art, even as he probed subjects as disparate as the African slave trade, the Holocaust, and the landscapes of Mexico. Somewhere between the populist poets and the gravely meditative Hayden was Michael S. Harper, in whose several books of verse, such as *Dear John, Dear Coltrane* (1970) and *Nightmare Becomes Responsibility* (1975), one finds a lively interest in contemporary black culture, including jazz, as well as a deeply humane cosmopolitanism in the face of personal tragedy and the brutalities of racism.

With the exception of the work of a few poets, however, fiction by black writers exhibited a more sophisticated impulse than did poetry. Novelists such as Ishmael Reed and William Melvin Kelley broke relatively new ground in black fiction with work that often satirized whites and their culture, aspirations, and pretensions. Reed's *Yellow Back Radio Broke-Down* (1969) and *Mumbo Jumbo* (1972) are rich in diverse forms of parody, as are Kelley's *dem* (1967) and *Dunfords Travels Everywheres* (1970). Novelists such as William Demby, Jane Phillips, Charlene H. Polite, and Clarence Major also represented the commitment to narrative experimentalism that coexisted, sometimes uneasily, with the realist tradition in black American literature. More traditional in technique but equally rooted in an affection for black American

culture is the fiction of Ernest Gaines, notably *The Autobiography of Miss Jane Pittman* (1971).

John A. Williams, with ten novels (as well as other books) published so far, was the most prolific black novelist of the era. Emphasizing the travails of blacks in white America but often with reference to international conspiracy, espionage, and genocide, his books include *The Man Who Cried I Am* (1967), *Sons of Darkness, Sons of Light* (1969), and *!Click Song* (1982). Another major figure, but one with different concerns, was Paule Marshall, whose publishing career spanned more than three decades. Born in Brooklyn but keenly aware of her Caribbean ancestry, she has explored her experience between these worlds in *Brown Girl, Brownstones* (1959), *The Chosen Place, the Timeless People* (1969), and *Praisesong for the Widow* (1983). The poet Margaret Walker's historical novel *Jubilee* (1966) was probably the single most popular work of fiction published by a black woman in the 1960s. Other fiction writers of the age include John Oliver Killens, Al Young, and Cecil Brown. Gayl Jones's novel *Corregidora* (1975) was praised for its lyrical examination of sexual fear and rage, and Toni Cade Bambara's collection of stories *Gorilla, My Love* (1972) richly reflected the wide range of personalities and styles within black America. Writers who established themselves as urban realists included Nathan Heard, Robert D. Pharr, Louise Meriwether, and George Cain.

By the late 1970s, the high point of the Black Power, Black Arts, and Black Aesthetic movements had clearly passed. However, all had left an indelible mark on the consciousness of the African-American writer. Virtually no significant black writer in any major form now defined him or herself without explicit, extensive reference in some form to race and the history of race relations in the United States. On the other hand, gender began to rival race as a rallying point for an increasing number of women writers, most of whom addressed their concern for the black woman as a figure doubly imperiled on the American scene. Zora Neale Hurston's *Their Eyes Were Watching God* and, to a lesser extent, Harriet Jacobs's *Incidents in the Life of a Slave Girl* became recognized as fountainhead texts for black women, who were finally seen as having their own distinct line within the greater tradition of American writing.

The most influential black feminist fiction writer of this period was Alice Walker, who gained critical attention with her poetry and with her novels *The Third Life of Grange Copeland*

See also

Charles Johnson

Alain Locke

(1970) and *Meridian* (1976). However, *The Color Purple* (1981), with its exploration of the role of incest, male brutality against women, black "womanist" feeling (Walker's chosen term, in contrast to "feminist"), and lesbianism as a liberating force, against a backdrop covering both the United States and Africa, became an international success. The novel, which won Walker the Pulitzer Prize for fiction, appealed to black and white women alike, as well as to many men, although its critical portraiture of black men led some to see it as divisive. Gloria Naylor's *The Women of Brewster Place* (1982), the interrelated stories of seven black women living in a decaying urban housing project, was also hailed as a striking work of fiction; her *Linden Hills* (1985) and *Mama Day* (1988) brought her further recognition. Audre Lorde also contributed to black feminist literature, and expanded her considerable reputation as a poet with her autobiography, or "biomythography," *Zami: A New Spelling of My Name* (1982), which dealt frankly with her commitment to lesbianism as well as to black culture. With poetry, literary criticism, and her widely admired historical novel *Dessa Rose* (1986), Sherley Anne Williams established herself as a versatile literary artist. Earlier fiction writers, such as Toni Cade Bambara and Paule Marshall, also published with distinction in a new climate of interest in women's writing. Bambara's *The Salt Eaters* (1980) and Marshall's *Daughters* (1991) found receptive audiences.

The most critically acclaimed black American writer of the 1980s, however, was Toni Morrison. Without being drawn personally into the increasingly acrimonious debate over feminism, she nevertheless produced perhaps the most accomplished body of fiction yet produced by an African-American woman. Starting with *The Bluest Eye* (1970), then with *Sula* (1973), *Song of Solomon* (1977), *Tar Baby* (1981), and—garnering enormous praise—*Beloved* (1987), Morrison's works consistently find their emotional and artistic center in the consciousness of black women. *Beloved*, based on an incident in the nineteenth century in which a black mother killed her child rather than allow her to grow up as a slave, won Morrison the Pulitzer Prize for fiction in 1988. Her sixth novel, *Jazz*, appeared in 1992. In 1993 Morrison became the first black woman to be awarded the Nobel Prize for literature.

In some respects, the existence of a chasm between black female and male novelists was more illusion than reality. Certainly they were all participants in a maturing of the African-American tradition in fiction, marked by versatility and range, in the 1980s. In science fiction, for example, Samuel R. Delany, Octavia Butler, and Steven Barnes produced notable work, as did Virginia Hamilton in the area of children's literature.

NOBEL PRIZE WINNER

Novelist Toni Morrison (left) receives the Nobel Prize for Literature in 1993 from Swedish King Carl XVI Gustaf. Morrison was the first black woman to receive the prize.
AP/WIDE WORLD PHOTOS

David Bradley in the vivid historical novel *The Chaneysville Incident* (1981), and John Edgar Wideman in a succession of novels and stories set in the black Homewood section of Pittsburgh where he grew up, rivaled the women novelists in critical acclaim. Charles Johnson's novels *Oxherding Tale* (1982) and *Middle Passage* (1990; winner of the National Book Award) exuberantly challenged the more restrictive forms of cultural nationalism. Without didacticism, and with comic brilliance, Johnson's work reflects his abiding interests in Hindu and Buddhist religious and philosophical forms as well as in the full American literary tradition, including the slave narrative and the works of mid-nineteenth-century American writers.

The shift away from fundamental black cultural nationalism to more complex forms of expression was strongly reflected in the waning popularity of poetry. Most of the black-owned presses either went out of business or were forced by a worsening economic climate to cut back severely on their lists. The work of the most acclaimed new poet of the 1980s, Rita Dove, showed virtually no debt to the cultural-nationalist poets of the previous generation. While Dove's verse indicated her interest in and even commitment to the exploration of aspects of black culture, it also indicated a conscious desire to explore more cosmopolitan themes; from the start, her art acknowledged formalist standards and her sense of kinship with the broad tradition of American and European poetry. In 1987, she won the Pulitzer Prize for poetry (the first African American to do so since Gwendolyn Brooks in 1950) with *Thomas and Beulah,* a volume that drew much of its inspiration from her family history in Ohio. She was named U.S. poet laureate in 1993.

Sealing the wide prestige enjoyed by African-American writers late in the twentieth century, a major playwright appeared in the 1980s to match the recognition gained by writers such as Morrison and Walker. August Wilson, with *Fences* (1986), *Ma Rainey's Black Bottom* (1988), *The Piano Lesson* (Pulitzer Prize, 1990), and *Two Trains Running* (1992), was hailed for the power and richness of his dramas of black life. George C. Wolfe, especially with *The Colored Museum* and *Jelly's Last Jam* (1992), also enjoyed significant critical success as a dramatist.

By the last decade of the twentieth century, the study of African-American literature had become established across the United States as an important part of the curriculum in English departments and programs of African-American studies. This place had been created in part by the merit of the literature, but more clearly in response to demands by black students starting in the 1960s. Still later, the prestige of black literature was reinforced in the academic community through widespread acceptance of the idea that race, class, and gender played a far greater role in the production of culture than had been acknowledged. The academic study and criticism of African-American writing also flourished. In addition to the work of anthologists, who had helped to popularize black writers since the 1920s, certain essays and books had helped to chart the way for later critics. Notable among these had been the work of the poet-scholar Sterling Brown in the 1920s and '30s, especially his ground-breaking analysis of the stereotypes of black character in American literature. More comprehensively, a white scholar, Vernon Loggins, had brought out a study of remarkable astuteness and sympathy, *The Negro Author: His Development in America to 1900* (1931).

In 1939, J. Saunders Redding, himself a novelist and autobiographer of note, published a landmark critical study, *To Make a Poet Black;* with Arthur P. Davis, he also edited *Cavalcade,* one of the more important of African-American anthologies. Later, Robert Bone's *The Negro Novel in America* (1958; revised edition, 1965) laid the foundation for the future study of African-American fiction. In the 1960s and 1970s, academics such as Darwin Turner, Addison Gayle, Jr., Houston A. Baker, Jr., Mary Helen Washington, George Kent, Stephen Henderson, and Richard Barksdale led the reevaluation of black American literature in the context of the more radical nationalist movement. In biography, the French scholar Michel Fabre and Robert Hemenway contributed outstanding studies of Richard Wright and Zora Neale Hurston, respectively. Another French scholar, Jean Wagner, published the most ambitious study of black verse, *Black Poets of the United States* (1973). Still later, other academics such as Barbara Christian, Hortense Spillers, Frances Smith Foster, Donald Gibson, Thadious Davis, Trudier Harris, Robert B. Stepto, Robert G. O'Meally, Richard Yarborough, Deborah McDowell, Hazel V. Carby, William L. Andrews, Nellie Y. McKay, Gloria Hull, and Henry Louis Gates, Jr., provided an often rich and imaginative counterpart in criticism and scholarship to the achievement of African-American creative writers of the past and present. Gates's *The Signifying Monkey* (1988), which explores the relationship between the African and

See also
Claude McKay
Jean Toomer

African-American vernacular traditions and literature, became perhaps the most frequently cited text in African-American literary criticism. In 1991, Houston A. Baker, Jr., became the first African American to serve as president of the Modern Language Association, the most important organization of scholars and critics of literature and language in the United States.

—ARNOLD RAMPERSAD

LITTLE RICHARD (PENNIMAN, RICHARD)

Little Richard (Richard Penniman) (December 25, 1935–), singer. Born to a devout Seventh-Day Adventist family, Richard Penniman began singing and playing piano in the church. He left home at thirteen to start a musical career. In 1951 he made some recordings with various jump-blues bands but with little success. Shortly thereafter, however, he began recording for Specialty Records, where he was to have six hits, beginning with "Tutti Frutti" (1954), that outlined the style that became rock and roll. In 1957 he left his music career behind and enrolled at Oakwood College in Huntsville, Ala., following an "apocalyptic vision." He received a B.A. and became a minister in the Seventh-Day Adventist church. Inspired by the "British invasion," he returned to rock and roll in 1964, but he was unable to recapture his early success. During the 1970s he brought his flamboyant act to the Las Vegas showroom circuit, billing himself as the "bronze Liberace." He returned to the church in the early 1980s, but his influence on rock and roll was not forgotten. In 1986 he was among the first artists inducted into the newly established Rock and Roll Hall of Fame, an honor that helped restore his celebrity status in the late 1980s.

Little Richard's style, defined by his Specialty recordings, featured frenetic, shrieking vocals, suggestive lyrics, and boogie-woogie-style piano performed at a remarkably fast tempo. His flamboyant stage persona and extravagant costumes also became a significant part of his act.

—DANIEL THOM

LOCKE, ALAIN LEROY

Alain Leroy Locke (September 13, 1885–June 9, 1954), philosopher. Best known for his literary promotion of the Harlem Renaissance of the 1920s, Alain Locke was a leading spokesman for African-American humanist values during the second quarter of the twentieth century. Born into what he called the "smug gentility" and "frantic respectability" of Philadelphia's black middle class, Locke found himself propelled toward a "mandatory" professional career that led to his becoming the first African-American Rhodes scholar, a Howard University professor for over forty years, a self-confessed "philosophical midwife" to a generation of black artists and writers between the world wars, and the author of a multifaceted array of books, essays, and reviews.

Locke was descended from formally educated free black ancestors on both maternal and paternal sides. Mary and Pliny Locke provided their only child with an extraordinarily cultivated environment, partly to provide "compensatory satisfactions" for the permanently limiting effects that a childhood bout with rheumatic fever imposed. His mother's attraction to the ideas of Felix Adler brought about Locke's entry into one of the early Ethical Culture schools; his early study of the piano and violin complemented the brilliant scholarship that won him entry to Harvard College in 1904 and a magna cum laude citation and election to Phi Beta Kappa upon graduation three years later.

Locke's undergraduate years, during Harvard's "golden age of philosophy," culminated with his being selected a Rhodes scholar from Pennsylvania (the only African American so honored during his lifetime) and studying philosophy, Greek, and humane letters at Oxford and Berlin from 1907 to 1911. There Locke developed his lasting "modernist" interests in the creative and performing arts, and close relationships with African and West Indian students that gave him an international perspective on racial issues. Locke's singular distinction as a black Rhodes scholar kept a national focus on his progress when he returned to the United States in 1912 to begin his long professional career at Howard University. His novitiate there as a teacher of English and philosophy was coupled with an early dedication to fostering Howard's development as an "incubator of Negro intellectuals" and as a center for research on worldwide racial and cultural contacts and colonialism. He managed simultaneously to complete a philosophy dissertation in the field of axiology on "The Problem of Classification in Theory of Value," which brought him a Ph.D. from Harvard in 1918. In 1924, he spent a sabbatical year in Egypt collaborating with the French Oriental Archeological Society for the opening at Luxor of the tomb of Tutankhamen.

See also

Harlem Renaissance

The New Negro

On his return in 1925, Locke encountered the cycle of student protests then convulsing African-American colleges and universities, including Hampton, Fisk, and Lincoln, as well as Howard. Subsequently dismissed from Howard because of his allegiances with the protestors, he took advantage of the three-year hiatus in his Howard career to assume a leadership role in the emerging Harlem Renaissance by first editing the March 1925 special "Harlem number" of *Survey Graphic* magazine. Its immediate success led him to expand it into book form later that year in the stunning anthology The New Negro, which—with its cornucopia of literature, the arts, and social commentary—gave coherent shape to the New Negro movement and gave Locke the role of a primary interpreter.

More than just an interpreter, mediator, or "liaison officer" of the New Negro movement, however, Locke became its leading theoretician and strategist. Over the following fifteen years, and from a staggering diversity of sources in traditional and contemporary philosophy, literature, art, religion, and social thought, he synthesized an optimistic, idealistic cultural credo, a "New Negro formulation" of racial values and imperatives that he insisted was neither a formula nor a program, but that confronted the paradoxes of African-American culture, charting what he thought was a unifying strategy for achieving freedom in art and in American life.

Locke's formulation was rooted, like the complex and sometimes competing ideological stances of W. E. B. Du Bois, in the drive to apply the methods of philosophy to the problems of race. It fused Locke's increasingly sophisticated "cultural racialism" with the new cultural pluralism advocated by Jewish-American philosopher Horace Kallen (a colleague during Locke's Harvard and Oxford years) and by Anglo-American literary radicals such as Randolph Bourne and V. F. Calverton. Locke adapted Van Wyck Brooks's and H. L. Mencken's genteel critical revolt against Puritanism and Philistinism to analogous problems facing the emergent but precarious African-American elite; and he incorporated into his outlook the Whitmanesque folk ideology of the 1930s and 1940s "new regionalism." Finally, Locke's credo attempted to turn the primitivist fascination with the art and culture of Africa to aesthetic and political advantage, by discovering in it a "useable past" or "ancestral legacy" that was both classical and modern, and by urging an African-American cultural mission "apropos of Africa" that would combine the strengths of both Garveyism and Du Bois's Pan-African congresses.

In the course of doing so, Alain Locke became a leading American collector and critic of African art, clarifying both its dramatic influence on modernist aesthetics in the West and its import as "perhaps the ultimate key for the interpretation of the African mind." In conjunction with the Harmon Foundation, he organized a series of African-American art exhibitions; in conjunction with Montgomery Gregory and Marie Moore-Forrest, he played a pioneering role in the developing national black theater movement by promoting the Howard University Players, and by coediting with Gregory the 1927 watershed volume *Plays of Negro Life: A Source-Book of Native American Drama.* From the late 1920s to mid-century, Locke published annual *Opportunity* magazine reviews of scholarship and creative expression that constitute in microcosm an intellectual history of the New Negro era.

With the onset of the worldwide Depression in 1929 and the end of the 1920s "vogue for things Negro," Locke viewed the New Negro movement to be shifting, in lockstep, from a "Renaissance" phase to a "Reformation." His commitment to adult-education programs led him to publish, for the Associates in Negro Folk Education, *The Negro and His Music* and *Negro Art: Past and Present* in 1936 and a lavish art-history volume, *The Negro in Art: A Pictorial Record of the Negro Artists and the Negro Theme in Art,* in 1940. A return to formal work in philosophy found him producing a series of essays in the 1930s and 1940s on cultural pluralism. And his early interest in the scientific study of global race relations was revived in his coediting with Bernhard Stern of *When Peoples Meet: A Study in Race and Culture Contacts* (1942). During a year as an exchange professor in Haiti, Locke had begun a potential magnum opus on the cultural contributions of African Americans, which occupied the last decade of his life, when his preeminence as a scholar and the lessening of segregation in American higher education kept him in demand as a visiting professor and lecturer within the United States and abroad. The effects of his lifelong heart ailments led to Locke's death in June 1954. His uncompleted opus, *The Negro in American Culture,* was completed and published posthumously by Margaret Just Butcher, daughter of a Howard colleague.

—JOHN S. WRIGHT

AUDRE GERALDINE LORDE

Widely Respected Poet

Audre Geraldine Lorde (February 18, 1934–November 17, 1992), poet, novelist, and teacher. Born in Harlem to West Indian parents, Audre Lorde described herself as "a black lesbian feminist mother lover poet." The exploration of pain, rage, and love in personal and political realms pervades her writing. Perhaps because Lorde did not speak until she was nearly five years old and also suffered from impaired vision, her passions were equally divided between a love of words and imagery and a devotion to speaking the truth, no matter how painful. Her objective, she stated, was to empower and encourage toward speech and action those in society who are often silenced and disfranchised.

Lorde published her first poem while in high school, in *Seventeen* magazine. She studied for a year (1954) at the National University of Mexico, before returning to the United States to earn a bachelor of arts degree in literature and philosophy from Hunter College in 1959. She went on to receive a master's degree from the Columbia School of Library Science in 1960. During this time she married attorney Edward Ashley Rollins and had two children, Elizabeth and Jonathan. Lorde and Rollins divorced in 1970. Juggling her roles as black woman, lesbian, mother, and poet, she was actively involved in causes for social justice. Throughout this period she was a member of the Harlem Writers Guild.

An important juncture in Lorde's life occurred in 1968. She published her first collection of poetry, *The First Cities,* and also received a National Endowment for the Arts Residency Grant, which took her to Tougaloo College in Mississippi. This appointment represented the beginning of Lorde's career as a full-time writer and teacher. Returning to New York, she continued to teach and publish. In 1973, her third book, *From a Land Where Other People Live,* was nominated for the National Book Award for Poetry. It was praised for its attention to racial oppression and injustice around the world. She spent ten years on the faculty of John Jay College of Criminal Justice and then became professor of English at her alma mater, Hunter College, in 1980. She wrote three more books of poetry before the appearance of *The Black Unicorn* (1978), for which she received the widest acclaim and recognition. It fuses themes of motherhood and feminism while placing African spiritual awakening and black pride at its center.

Lorde's devotion to honesty and outspokenness is evident in the works she produced in the 1980s. She published her first nonpoetry work, *The Cancer Journals* (1980), so she could share the experience of her cancer diagnosis, partial mastectomy, and apparent triumph over the disease with as wide an audience as possible. *Zami: A New Spelling of My Name* (1982) was enthusiastically received as her first prose fiction work. Self-described as a "biomythography," it is considered a lyrical and evocative autobiographical novel. She was a founding member of Women of Color Press and Sisters in Support of Sisters in South Africa.

Sister Outsider (1984), a collection of speeches and essays spanning the years 1976 to 1984, details Lorde's evolution as a black feminist thinker and writer. In 1986, she returned to poetry with *Our Dead behind Us. Burst of Light* (1988), which won an American Book Award, chronicles the spread of Lorde's cancer to her liver, and presents a less hopeful vision of the future than *The Cancer Journals.* Lorde's work appeared regularly in magazines and journals and has been widely anthologized. In 1991 she became the poet laureate of New York State. She died in St. Croix, U.S. Virgin Islands.

—NICOLE R. KING

LOS ANGELES, CALIFORNIA

The experiences of African Americans in Los Angeles have differed from those of black people in most other large American cities. Los Angeles has always been characterized by cultural diversity. This diversity has shaped the history of African Americans in Los Angeles: African Americans have frequently compared themselves to Latinos and Asian Americans, and patterns of cooperation and competition among these groups have left indelible marks on the city's politics and culture.

The first black people in Los Angeles spoke Spanish. Twenty-nine of the 46 people who established the pueblo in September 1781 could trace some ancestors to Africa. Throughout the Spanish (1781–1821) and Mexican (1821–1848)

See also
Fugitive Slaves

*Thought is barred
in this City of
Dreadful Joy, and
conversation is
unknown.*

ALDOUS HUXLEY
JESTING PILATE, 1926

See also
Nat King Cole
Paul Robeson

eras, black residents participated in social, cultural, and political activities. Several black men or mulattoes held positions in the pueblo's government.

The U.S. conquest of northern Mexico and the Gold Rush of 1848–1849 scarcely affected Los Angeles, which remained a small, largely Mexican town. In the 1850s and '60s, Southern California's remoteness attracted some fugitive slaves. Biddy Mason, for example, came to Los Angeles in the 1850s. She acquired a fortune through shrewd investments in real estate, and she used some of her money to establish and support the first black community organizations. Reports of Mason's success helped Southern California to develop a reputation as a land of economic opportunity for African Americans.

The completion of railroad lines and harbor improvements in the 1870s and '80s sparked explosive growth in Southern California. Los Angeles' population grew from 11,000 in 1880 to nearly 320,000 in 1910 and to more than 1.2 million in 1930. Among the new residents were small but significant numbers of African Americans. The black population grew from under 100 in 1870 to 7,500 in 1910 and to nearly 50,000 by 1930. In 1940, the census counted 75,000 African Americans in the area.

New black residents moved into a segregated city. The first black neighborhood, labeled "Nigger Alley" by white residents, developed in the 1870s on Alameda Street, near Chinatown. By 1910 a ghetto had formed around the Central Avenue Hotel in downtown Los Angeles. This ghetto expanded south along Central Avenue toward Watts, a community that attracted African Americans from the rural South. By 1930, some 70 percent of the city's black residents lived in the Central Avenue neighborhood. Significant numbers of African Americans also settled in the West Adams district, west of downtown.

The Central Avenue district became the center of African-American culture. Businesses, entertainment houses, restaurants, and churches served the expanding community. Notable musicians such as tenor saxophonist Dexter Gordon emerged from the jazz clubs of Central Avenue. The district's theaters regularly drew celebrated black performers such as Nat King Cole, Duke Ellington, and Paul Robeson to Los Angeles in the 1930s and '40s.

Prior to World War II, black residents were routinely denied access to public swimming pools and parks. They were also excluded from many theaters and restaurants. Employers refused to hire black people for clerical or white-collar jobs, and skilled black workers found few openings in the city's small industrial sector. Most black men worked as manual laborers, and most black women worked as domestic servants.

Despite the pervasive housing and employment discrimination, the city's African Americans were able to exercise some political power. Frederick Roberts, a black Republican, represented the "East Side" in the State Assembly from 1919 until 1933. Democrat Augustus Hawkins defeated Roberts in the 1932 election and served in the Assembly from 1933 until his election to Congress in 1962.

The growth of the Mexican-American and Asian-American communities in the 1910s and '20s led African-American leaders to conclude that black residents might achieve greater political and economic power through cooperation with other minority groups. The black "East Side" abutted "Little Tokyo" and the Mexican-American barrio of East Los Angeles, and all of these communities confronted racial prejudice and discrimination.

World War II offered African-American leaders the opportunity to test their theories about multicultural cooperation. Federal propaganda fueled the desire of African and Mexican Americans to destroy racial discrimination in the United States. The federal government's decision to incarcerate Japanese Americans also haunted minority community leaders. Thousands of African Americans moved into the vacant houses and storefronts of Little Tokyo.

During the war years, black and Mexican-American civil rights organizations cooperated in their efforts to combat discrimination. Peaceful demonstrations and formal complaints to the President's Fair Employment Practices Committee (FEPC), which Franklin Roosevelt had created in 1941, succeeded in placing many black and Mexican-American workers in high-paying jobs in war industries. By 1945 black workers held 14 percent of the shipyard jobs in Los Angeles, even though African Americans comprised only 6.5 percent of the city's population.

The "Zoot-Suit Riots" further encouraged cooperation among African Americans and Mexican Americans. In response to rumors that gangs of young Mexican Americans had initiated a war against military men, hundreds of sailors and soldiers converged on downtown and east Los Angeles in early June 1943. Although the soldiers and sailors ostensibly sought gang members dressed in "zoot suits"—flashy outfits comprised of long, broad-shouldered jackets and pants that were baggy at the hips but tight around the ankle—their victims also included young Mexican-American and black men who were not wearing zoot suits. The sailors and soldiers dragged these young men from theaters and stores, stripped them of their clothing, beat them, and left them naked in the streets. After four nights of violence, military authorities ordered soldiers and sailors not to go downtown, and the rioting dissipated. In the wake of the riots, concerned activists and elected officials created several organizations which, along with the National Association for the Advancement of Colored People (NAACP) and the National Urban League, were the backbone of an emerging multiracial civil rights coalition.

This coalition's strength peaked in 1945 and 1946, when Japanese Americans returned to the city. The War Relocation Authority (WRA), which operated the concentration camps during the war, later worked to reestablish the Japanese-American community in Los Angeles. In this process, WRA employees recognized the similarities between discrimination against Japanese Americans and discrimination against African Americans and Mexican Americans. WRA employees then began to combat all forms of racial discrimination. The War Relocation Authority lent strong governmental support to the civil rights coalition, which mounted successful legal challenges to housing and school segregation.

After the war ended, however, civil rights activists found it difficult to reform local institutions. Many African Americans lost their jobs, and financial support for the NAACP and other organizations diminished. Politicians and newspaper publishers attached the "communist" label on all civil rights activism. The fears of white residents dominated the 1946 election: two-thirds of Los Angeles's voters rejected an initiative that would have outlawed employment discrimination in California.

Southern California's mild climate and its image as a land of opportunity continued to attract black people from the East and the South after World War II. The area's African-American population grew from 75,000 in 1940 to 200,000 in 1950 and to approximately 650,000 by 1965. The population growth promised greater political power. Tom Bradley, a retired police officer, put together a coalition of African Americans and liberal white voters—many of them Jews—and won a seat on the City Council in 1963.

Bradley's election lifted the hopes of many of Los Angeles's black residents, but conditions in the ghetto did not improve in the 1950s and '60s. Unemployment was higher in African-American districts than in the rest of the city, and police officers routinely harassed black people, often using excessive force in arresting black suspects.

An arrest on August 11, 1965, turned into a confrontation between police and Watts residents and ignited a six-day rebellion. As many as 30,000 African Americans looted and burned hundreds of businesses. State officials mobilized more than 15,000 National Guard troops and police officers to quell the rebellion. The violence left thirty-four people—thirty-one of whom were black—dead and hundreds injured. The police arrested more than 4,000 people.

After the rebellion, government officials and community leaders called for sweeping reforms, including programs to train and employ the thousands of unemployed African Americans in south central Los Angeles. Local, state, and federal agencies, however, never fully implemented these reforms.

While unemployment and other social problems continued to fester in the ghetto, changes within U.S society helped to open new opportunities for some African Americans. Access to good schools and colleges led to the emergence of a new black middle class in Los Angeles. Pressure from the NAACP and other civil rights organizations created new opportunities for black performers in film and television. Black superstars such as Eddie Murphy and Michael Jackson began to wield power within the entertainment industry in the 1980s. The wealth and power of these stars, however, put them out of touch with the hundreds of thousands of people trapped by poverty and discrimination in South Central Los Angeles.

Although African Americans were divided economically, they were able to unite politically. Bradley's electoral coalition expanded in the late 1960s and came to power in 1973, when Bradley was elected mayor. Bradley eliminated racial discrimination in municipal employment and encouraged interracial cooperation. Despite Bradley's popularity—he was reelected four times—he was unable to end police brutality or to improve conditions in the ghetto. By the 1980s, black unemployment reached 40 percent in some areas, more than three times the white jobless rate. Poor schools, inadequate health care, AIDS, crime, and drug abuse plagued South Central Los Angeles. These conditions threatened intercultural cooperation: African Americans increasingly blamed the community's problems on outsiders.

See also
Duke Ellington
Michael Jackson

In the mid- to late 1980s, some young African Americans began to address ghetto conditions in their art and music. South Central Los Angeles and the surrounding black suburbs produced a number of influential filmmakers and musical artists. Motion picture director John Singleton received an Oscar nomination for *Boyz N the Hood* (1991), which explored life in the ghetto. Musicians such as NWA and Ice Cube sold millions of copies of their releases. Many of these artists succeeded in appealing to a large, diverse audience while retaining their base in Los Angeles's black community.

Race relations in Los Angeles reached a critical point in the early 1990s. On March 3, 1991, police officers stopped a car driven by an African American named Rodney King. Before the police handcuffed King, four officers kicked him and beat him with clubs, fracturing his skull and one of his legs. A witness recorded King's beating on videotape. When the news media broadcast the tape, there was a national uproar. Less than two weeks after the beating, the police officers were indicted on charges that included assault with a deadly weapon.

More than a year after the beating, the police officers stood trial. On April 29, 1992, a mostly white jury acquitted the defendants on all but one of the charges. Within hours of the verdict's announcement, South Central Los Angeles exploded in violence. Angry people pelted cars with rocks and bottles and set fire to hundreds of buildings. African Americans and Latinos—many of them Central American refugees who had moved into South Central Los Angeles in the late 1980s—looted many of the stores in the area. Looters and arsonists spared some businesses belonging to African Americans. Stores owned by recent Asian immigrants, especially Koreans, were frequent targets.

Local, state, and federal officials responded rapidly to the riot. Within three days of the verdict's announcement, nearly 20,000 armed soldiers and peace officers patrolled the city's streets. Despite the quick response, 51 people were killed in the violence, and more than 2,000 were injured. The police arrested approximately 10,000 people.

The 1992 rebellion transformed racial politics in Los Angeles. Police Chief Daryl Gates resigned shortly after the rebellion. Mayor Bradley chose not to run for a sixth term. Before Bradley left office, however, he did succeed in convincing the voters to give the mayor greater power over the police department, a move that signaled a commitment to effect a decrease in police brutality toward African Americans. In the mayoral election of 1993, voters rejected Bradley's multicultural coalition, represented by City Council member Michael Woo, in favor of Richard Riordan, a white multimillionaire who promised to unite the divided city.

The bleak conditions in the ghetto in the late 1980s and the rebellion of 1992 changed black perceptions of Los Angeles. To most African Americans the city no longer symbolized hope and opportunity. Los Angeles's black population stopped growing in the 1980s; some black residents turned to the South. The stable number of black and white people in Los Angeles presages more change as the growing Latino and Asian-American communities demand greater political representation. In these political struggles, African Americans may lose some of the power they enjoyed between the 1960s and the early '90s.

Los Angeles was one of the first cities to experience the demographic changes that will continue to shape U.S society in the twenty-first century. Most cities will attract greater numbers of Latinos and Asian Americans. The lessons that other cities' officials can learn from Los Angeles are not clear, but the history of Southern California suggests that governments and community leaders must be committed to equality and intolerant of discrimination if cities are to escape bloodshed and fulfill the promise of multiethnic cooperation.

—KEVIN ALLEN LEONARD

LOUIS, JOE

Joe Louis (Joe Louis Barrow) (May 13, 1914–April 12, 1981), boxer. Joe Louis Barrow was born to a sharecropping couple in Chambers County, Ala., the seventh of eight children. Louis's father, Munroe Barrow, was placed in a mental institution when Louis was two, apparently unable to cope with the strain of the dirt farming life. (It has been suggested by a few observers that Louis's mental and emotional problems in later life may have resulted from congenital causes rather than blows in the prize ring.) Louis's father died in Searcy State Hospital for the Colored Insane nearly twenty years later, never having learned that his son had become a famous athlete.

Lillie Barrow, Louis's mother, remarried a widower with a large family of his own named Pat Brooks who, in 1920, moved the family to Mt. Sinai, Ala. In 1926 Brooks migrated north to Detroit to work for the Ford Motor Company. The

See also

Boxing

Jack Johnson

family, like many other African-American families of this period of the Great Migration, followed suit soon after, settling in Detroit's burgeoning black ghetto.

At the time of the move to Detroit, Louis was twelve years old. He was big for his age, but because of his inadequate education in the South and his lack of interest in and affinity for school, he was placed in a lower grade than his age would have dictated. Consequently, he continued to be an indifferent student and eventually went to work when his stepfather was laid off by Ford at the beginning of the Depression.

Like many poor, unskilled, undereducated, ethnic urban boys of the period, Louis drifted into boxing largely as an opportunity to make money and to release his aggression in an organized, socially acceptable way. Although his stepfather was opposed to his entry into athletics, his mother supported and encouraged him.

Competing as a light heavyweight, Louis started his amateur career in 1932 but lost badly in his first fight and did not return to the ring until the following year. Following this brief hiatus, however, Louis quickly rose to prominence in boxing and African-American or "race" circles. By 1933 he compiled an amateur record of 50 wins, 43 by knockout, and only 4 losses. In 1934, shortly after winning the light heavyweight championship of the Amateur Athletic Union, Louis turned professional and moved up to the heavyweight division. His managers were two black numbers runners, John Roxborough and Julian Black. Louis's trainer was a white man, the former lightweight fighter Jack Blackburn.

Thanks to generous coverage by the black press, Louis was already a familiar figure in the black neighborhoods of northern cities by 1934. At a time when color bars prohibited blacks from competing with whites in every major professional sport other than boxing, Louis became a symbol of black aspirations in white America. Through the prime of his career, Louis's fights were major social events for African Americans, and spontaneous celebrations would erupt in urban ghettos after his victories.

At the start of his professional career, Louis faced a number of obstacles in trying to obtain the heavyweight title. First, under a "gentlemen's agreement," no black fighter had been permitted to fight for that title since Jack Johnson, the first black heavyweight champion. Johnson lost the title in Havana, Cuba, to Jess Willard in 1915. Second, Louis had an entirely black support and management team, making it difficult for him to

break into the big market for the fight game in New York City and to get a crack at the name fighters against whom he had to compete if he were to make a name for himself.

Louis's managers overcame the first problem by making sure that Louis did not in any way act like or remind his white audience or white sportswriters of Johnson, who scandalized white public opinion with his marriages to white women and other breaches of prevailing racial mores. Louis was not permitted to be seen in the company of white women, never gloated over his opponents, was quiet and respectful, and generally was made to project an image of cleanliness and high moral character. The second problem was solved when Mike Jacobs, a fight promoter in New York City, decided to take on Madison Square Garden's monopoly on boxing with his 20th Century Sporting Club and formed a partnership with Louis's managers to promote him with the intention of guiding him to the championship.

Louis, 6'1", with a fighting weight around 200 pounds, soon amassed a glittering record. Starting in his first professional bout, a first-round knockout of Jack Kracken on July 4, 1934, to his winning the heavyweight title, in an eighth-round knockout of Jim Braddock on June 22, 1937,

PACKING A PUNCH

Joe Louis became an American icon and hero in and out of the boxing ring. He captured the heavyweight title in 1937.
PRINTS AND PHOTOGRAPHS DIVISION, LIBRARY OF CONGRESS

Louis recorded a record of 30 wins, 25 by knockout, and 1 loss. The most memorable of his fights during this period included the easy knockouts of former heavyweight champions Max Baer and Primo Carnera in 1935. Louis's one loss during this period was critically important in his career and in American cultural history. On June 19, 1936, the German Max Schmeling knocked out Louis, then a world-class challenger to the heavyweight crown, in twelve rounds, giving the highly touted black fighter his first severe beating as a professional. This loss greatly reduced Louis's standing with white sportswriters, who had previously built him up almost to the point of invincibility. (The writers had given him a string of alliterative nicknames, including the "Tan Tornado" and the "Dark Destroyer," but it was the "Brown Bomber" that stuck.) However, Louis's loss was also a watershed as it marked a slow change on the part of white sportswriters, who began to stop patronizing him and slowly grew to treat him more fully as a human being.

The loss also set up a rematch with Schmeling on June 22, 1938, after Louis had become champion by defeating Braddock the previous year. The second bout with Schmeling was to become one of the most important fights in American history. It was not Louis's first fight with political overtones. He had fought the Italian heavyweight Primo Carnera (beating him easily) as Italy was beginning its invasion of Ethiopia, and both fighters became emblems of their respective ethnicities; Louis, oddly enough, became both a nationalistic hero for blacks while being a kind of crossover hero for non-Italian, antifascist whites. By 1938, Hitler was rapidly taking over Europe and Nazism had clearly become a threat to both the United States and the world generally. Schmeling was seen as the symbol of Nazism, an identification against which he did not fight very hard. Indeed, Schmeling seemed eager to exploit the racial overtones of the fight as a way of getting a psychological edge on Louis. Louis became an emblem not simply of black America, but, like Jesse Owens in Berlin a few years earlier, a symbol of antitotalitarian America itself, of its ideology of opportunity and freedom. Perhaps in some sense no one could better bear the burden of America's utopian vision of itself as an egalitarian paradise than a champion black prizefighter, combining both the myths of class mobility with racial uplift. Under the scrutiny of both their countries and most of the rest of the world, Louis knocked out Schmeling in two minutes of the first round.

Following the second Schmeling bout, Louis embarked on a remarkable string of title defenses, winning seventeen fights over four years, fifteen by knockout. Because of the general lack of talent in the heavyweight division at the time and the ease of Louis's victories, his opponents were popularly referred to as "The Bum of the Month Club." The only serious challenge came from Billy Conn in 1941, who outboxed the champion for twelve rounds before succumbing to Louis's knockout punch in the thirteenth.

During World War II, Louis in some ways matured deeply as a man and came into his own as an American icon and hero. When the war began, he was twenty-seven and at his prime as a fighter. When it ended, he was thirty-one, beginning to slip as a champion athlete, and, probably, was not as interested in boxing as he had been. However, he had become something of an elder statesman among blacks who were also prominent in popular culture. Younger black athletes such as Jackie Robinson and Sugar Ray Robinson looked up to and respected him. Both men had served in the segregated armed forces with him, and he helped them bear with dignity the hostilities and humiliations that were often visited upon them as black soldiers. Louis became self-consciously political at that time; he campaigned for Republican presidential candidate Wendell Wilkie in 1940.

Louis was drafted January 12, 1942, but remained active as a boxer, continuing to fight professionally during the war. He contributed his earnings to both the Army and the Navy Relief Funds. While this was a wise move politically, it was disastrous for Louis financially. (In fact, even before he joined the service, he contributed the purse from his Buddy Baer fight on January 9, 1942, to the Navy Relief Fund.)

"We're going to do our part, and we will win," Louis intoned at a Navy Relief Society dinner on March 10, 1942, "because we are on God's side." This moment, perhaps more than any other in Louis's career, signaled the complete transformation of the image of the man in the mind of the white public. Louis rose from being the sullen, uneasy "colored boy" from black Detroit who was considered in 1935 the *wunderkind* of boxing, to become in seven years, the mature, patriotic American who could speak both to and for his country. Louis could now not simply address his audience but command it. He could, as one pundit put it, "name the war." Louis's phrase, "We're on God's side," became one of the most famous phrases in American oratory during the Second World War. Ironically, however, Louis had misre-

See also
Jackie Robinson

membered his lines. He was supposed to say the more commonplace, "God's on our side," yet it is this cunning combination of the inadvertent and the opportunistic, the serendipitous and the intentional, that marks Louis's career in its later phase.

After the war, Louis's abilities as a fighter diminished as his earnings evaporated in a mist of high living and alleged tax evasion. After winning a rematch against Jersey Joe Walcott on June 25, 1948—only the second black fighter against whom Louis defended his title, indicating how much of a presence white fighters were in the sport well into the twentieth century—on the heels of winning an earlier controversial match on December 5, 1947, that most observers felt he had lost, Louis retired from the ring in 1949. At that time he made a deal with the unsavory Jim Norris and the International Boxing Club, which re-sulted in the removal of an old, sick Mike Jacobs from the professional boxing scene. Louis's deal with Norris created an entity called Joe Louis Enterprises that would sign up all the leading contenders for the heavyweight championship and have them exclusively promoted by Norris's International Boxing Club. Louis received $150,000 and became a stockholder in the IBC. He was paid $15,000 annually to promote boxing generally and the IBC bout specifically. In effect, Louis sold his title to a gangster-controlled outfit that wanted and eventually obtained for a period in the 1950s virtual control over both the management and promotion of all notable professional fighters in the United States. By 1950, however, an aged Louis, reflexes shot and legs gimpy, was forced back into the ring because of money problems. He lost to Ezzard Charles in a fifteen-round decision on September 27. On October 26, 1951, his ca-

SLAVE TURNED COWBOY

Nat "Deadwood Dick" Love Won a Horse in a Raffle

Nat "Deadwood Dick" Love (June 1854–1921), cowboy. Born into slavery, Nat Love was the youngest child and second son of a slave foreman and a cook on the Davidson County, Tenn., plantation of Robert Love. After the Civil War, Nat's father farmed twenty acres he rented from his former master. At age fifteen, Nat became responsible for the family's meager finances after his father and brother-in-law died and his older brother left home.

Love worked briefly for a nearby farmer for $1.50 a month but returned to the family farm after the farmer tried to cheat him out of his pay. Love began supplementing his income by breaking horses for a neighbor. He also proved to be clever and lucky. In early 1869 Love won a horse in a raffle, sold it back to the owner for fifty dollars, and then rewon the horse when the owner raffled it off again. Love sold the horse again for fifty dollars, split his winnings with his mother, and like one of thousands of African Americans seeking opportunity, set off for the West.

Soon after going west, Love's horse-breaking skills won him a job with the cowboys from the Duval Ranch in the Texas panhandle. Love described himself in those days as "wild, reckless and free, afraid of nothing, that is nothing I ever saw, with a wide knowledge of the cattle country and the cattle business and of my guns with which I was getting better acquainted with every day, and not above taking my whisky straight or returning bullet for bullet in a scrimmage."

In July 1876 Love was in Deadwood, S.Dak., delivering three thousand head of three-year-old steers for his new ranch, the Pete Gallinger company from Arizona. The cowboys' route had taken them past Little Bighorn, Wyo., only two days behind Gen. George Armstrong Custer; they arrived in Deadwood on July 3, 1876, eight days after the Battle of Little Bighorn. The next day Love won the annual cowboy competition in Deadwood by roping, throwing, tying, bridling, saddling, and mounting an untamed bronco in nine minutes flat. This feat, along with his marksmanship, earned him the name Deadwood Dick. With his long hair, he cut a striking figure as an archetypal rough-and-tumble cowboy.

In 1890 Love left the range. He believed that the railroads had made his job obsolete, and he saw them as the wave of the future. Love became one of the first Pullman porters, working the Denver and Rio Grande Western Railroad. He published his autobiography, *The Life and Adventures of Nat Love, Better Known in Cattle Country as Deadwood Dick,* in 1907. By that time he had left the railroad and moved to Los Angeles, where he worked for the General Securities Company. Love died in Los Angeles in 1921.

—NANCY YOUSEF

See also
Muhammad Ali

reer ended for good when he was knocked out in eight rounds by the up-and-coming Rocky Marciano.

In 66 professional bouts, Louis lost only 3 times (twice in the last two years of his career) and knocked out 49 of his opponents. He was elected to the Boxing Hall of Fame in 1954.

After his career, Louis, like many famous athletes who followed him, lived off of his reputation. He certainly never considered the idea of returning to the ordinary work world he left in the early 1930s when he became a fighter. He was hounded by the IRS for back taxes, began taking drugs, particularly cocaine, suffered a number of nervous breakdowns, and seemed often at loose ends, despite a third marriage to a woman of considerable maturity and substance, Martha Jefferson. Eventually, in part as a result of his second marriage (his second wife Marva Trotter was a lawyer for Teamster boss Jimmy Hoffa), Louis wound up working in Las Vegas as a casino greeter, playing golf with high-rolling customers, and serving as a companion for men who remembered him in his glory years.

On April 12, 1981, the day after he attended a heavyweight championship match between Larry Holmes and Trevor Berbick, Louis collapsed at his home in Las Vegas and died of a massive heart attack. He was, without question, one of the most popular sports figures of this century. In 1993 Louis appeared on a U.S. postage stamp.

—GERALD EARLY

LOVING, ALVIN

Alvin Loving (September 19, 1935–), artist. Al Loving was born in Detroit, Mich. His mother, a Canadian, was a descendant of an underground railroad survivor. His father, Alvin Demar Loving, was associate dean at the University of Michigan and an important figure in international education who established universities in Nigeria and India, and served as a consultant to the Indian government on the reorganization of their secondary school system. When young Loving traveled to India in 1955 with his father, he observed an artist working on large-scale murals and decided to become a painter. From 1958 to 1960, Loving served in the U.S. Army as a propaganda illustrator. He graduated from the University of Illinois with a B.F.A. in 1963, and taught at Eastern Michigan University from 1964 to 1965 while pursuing his M.F.A. in painting at the University of Michigan, which he completed in 1965.

During his years at Michigan, Loving developed many technical interests—in geometry, the illusionistic manipulation of space, and the organization of color—which became trademarks of his style by the 1970s. When he moved to New York City in 1968, geometric shapes, particularly the square, became the central subjects of his paintings, allowing him to experiment with abstract problems in perspective while maintaining an interest in representational form. Images from this early period were known for their crisp geometric lines and their three-dimensional appearance (*Rational Irrationalism*, 1969; *Untitled*, 1970; *Time Trip I*, 1971; *Wyn . . . Time Trip II*, 1972).

Loving presented his first solo exhibition in 1969 at the Gertrude Kasle Gallery in Detroit, and Kasle helped him establish connections at the Whitney Museum of American Art, where Loving was invited to organize a solo show in the same year. In 1972, Loving was commissioned to paint a seventeen-story mural for the First National Bank Building in Detroit (*New Morning Detroit: Message to Damar and Laurie*). When a worker was seriously injured during construction of the piece, Loving shifted away from large-scale geometric painting and began to create smaller pieces using strips of cut, dyed, and sewn material. Loving's interest in the manipulation of canvas and cloth was influenced by his grandmother's work as a quilter, and he was captivated by the stylistic potential of strip painting over a ten-year period, creating his best known work in this genre in the early 1980s (*Self-Portrait*, series initiated in 1980; *Shades of '73: Composition for 1980*, 1980).

In the mid-1970s, Loving expanded his interest in manipulation of material by working with paper and cardboard to create large-scale corrugated collages (*Untitled* 1975; *Shelly, Fran, Susie, and Andrea*, 1976). During this period, he also created a series of works inspired by water lilies and some figurative compositions based on erotic subjects. From 1981 to 1985, after studying with lithographer Robert Blackburn, Loving created a number of monoprints (*Tropical Rain Forest*, 1985), and he also experimented with handmade paper works, including the production of paper pulp (*Mercer Street Series*, 1983–84).

Loving's work has been shown in solo exhibitions at William Zierler in New York (1971, 1972, 1973), the Fischbach Gallery in New York (1974, 1976), the Studio Museum in Harlem (1977, 1986), the Diane Brewer Gallery in New York (1980, 1983), and the Bronx Museum (1989). He has received grants from the National Endowment for the Arts, a CAPS grant, and a

See also

Jean-Michel Basquiat

Guggenheim Fellowship. Loving has been associate professor of art at City College, City University of New York, since 1988.

—APRIL KINGSLEY

LYNCHING

Although rooted in an older and broader tradition of vigilantism, the term "lynching" is primarily associated with the killing of African Americans by white mobs in the period from the Civil War to the middle of the twentieth century. By most accounts, the practice originated on the Revolutionary War frontier when Colonel Charles Lynch and other prominent citizens of Bedford County, Va., organized informally to apprehend and punish Tories and other lawless elements throughout the community.

"Lynch law" subsequently spread to other parts of the country, but became especially prevalent in less settled frontier areas with poorly developed legal institutions. Initially, lynch mobs punished alleged lawbreakers and enforced community mores through whippings, tarring and feathering, and, on occasion, extralegal executions by hanging or shooting. Victims were mostly white and ranged from outlaws and horse thieves in frontier areas to Catholics, immigrants, and abolitionists in northern cities.

Blacks were by no means immune to mob action and sometimes received harsher treatment than white victims, but lynching had not yet attained its special association with race. Even under slavery, the lynching of blacks was relatively infrequent. The economic self-interest and paternalistic attitudes of masters, combined with a rigid system of slave control, normally militated

LYNCH MOB

The lynching of Tom Shipp and Abe Smith at Marion, Ind., on August 7, 1930. Between 1882 and 1968, an estimated 4,742 people died at the hands of lynch mobs.

PHOTOGRAPHS AND PRINTS DIVISION, SCHOMBURG CENTER FOR RESEARCH IN BLACK CULTURE, THE NEW YORK PUBLIC LIBRARY, ASTOR, LENOX AND TILDEN FOUNDATIONS

♦ **Lynch**

To put to death (as by hanging) by mob action without legal sanction

against widespread mob violence against slaves, although in the aftermath of slave rebellions, mobs sought out and ruthlessly punished suspected conspirators.

After the Civil War, lynching spread rapidly and became a systematic feature of the southern system of white supremacy. Mob-inflicted deaths increased during Reconstruction as southern whites resorted to violence to restore white control over ex-slaves. The practice reached epidemic proportions in the late 1880s and 1890s, averaging more than 150 incidents per year in the latter decade, then began to decline after the turn of the century.

Overall, between 1882, when the *Chicago Tribune* began recording lynchings, and 1968, an estimated 4,742 persons died at the hands of lynch mobs. Although whites continued to be victimized on occasion, African-American men and women accounted for the overwhelming majority (some 72 percent) of known lynchings after 1882. By the 1920s, 90 percent of all victims were black, and 95 percent of all lynchings occurred in southern states.

Southern whites justified lynching as a necessary response to black crime and an inefficient legal system, but virtually any perceived transgression of the racial boundaries or threat to the system of white supremacy could provoke mob action. The alleged offenses of lynching victims ranged from such actual crimes as murder, assault, theft, arson, and rape to such trivial breaches of the informal etiquette of race as "disrespect" toward whites and failing to give way to whites on the sidewalks.

The most frequent justification, however, was the charge of rape or sexual assault of white women by black men. Although fewer than 26 percent of all lynchings involved even the allegation of sexual assault, the mythology of rape and images of the "black beast" despoiling white womanhood dominated the southern rationale for lynching by the 1890s and inflamed mobs to ever-increasing brutality.

Lynchings took various forms ranging from hangings and shootings administered by small groups of men in secret, to posses meting out summary justice at the conclusion of a manhunt, to large public spectacles with broad community participation. The classic public lynchings for which the South became so notorious always involved torture and mutilation and ended in death for the victim, either by hanging, or, increasingly, by being burned alive. The lynching ritual characteristically included prior notice of the event, the selection of a symbolically significant location, and the gathering of a large crowd of onlookers, including women and children.

Mobs typically sought to elicit confessions from their victims and frequently allowed them to pray before the final act of the drama. Lynchers often left the bullet-ridden bodies of hanging victims on public display as a warning to other potential transgressors. In both hangings and burnings, mobs tortured, mutilated, castrated (in the case of males), and even dismembered their victims. The victim of the alleged crime or a victim's close relative often played a prominent role in the ritual. A particularly gruesome feature of lynchings was the taking of souvenirs in the form of body pieces, bone fragments salvaged from the ashes, or photographs.

The social composition of southern mobs remains obscure. Some have argued that lynch mobs were composed primarily of lower-class whites, but most scholars agree that the upper class and community leaders at the very least condoned the mob's actions and not uncommonly were themselves participants. Police were rarely effective in preventing lynchings, even when they tried, and mob members were almost never identified and prosecuted. Authorities typically attributed lynchings to "persons unknown."

Lynching was ultimately a product of racism and the caste system it sustained, but social, economic, and political conditions shaped the rhythms and geographical distribution of the practice. Early twentieth-century investigators linked lynchings to such factors as rural isolation, poorly developed legal institutions, broad economic fluctuations, the price of cotton, the ratio of blacks to whites in the population, the structure of county government, revivalism, and the seasonality of southern crops. In his classic study *The Tragedy of Lynching*, Arthur Raper concluded that lynchings were most likely to occur in the poorest, most sparsely populated southern counties, and especially in recently settled ones where blacks constituted less than 25 percent of the population.

Extending these earlier findings, modern social scientists have viewed lynching variously as a form of "scapegoating" in which white aggression and frustration was displaced onto blacks during periods of economic decline, as a consequence of direct economic competition between whites and blacks, or as a manifestation of repressive justice in response to a "boundary crisis" precipitated by Populist Party efforts to unite lower-class whites and blacks in the 1890s.

See also

Civil War

While acknowledging some connection between lynching and populism, historians generally attribute the sudden emergence of lynching as a prominent feature of race relations in the 1880s and 1890s to broader and more complex forces. Jacquelyn Dowd Hall has argued that in addition to being a form of "repressive justice" designed to preserve the caste system, lynching served to dramatize "hierarchical power relationships based on gender and race" (Hall 1979, p. 156). It reinforced racial boundaries for black men and helped maintain caste solidarity for whites generally, but it also reinforced notions of female vulnerability and subordination in a patriarchal society. Joel Williamson (1984) also stressed the association between lynching and sex roles, but he attributed the growth of lynching in the late nineteenth century to the convergence of a radical strain of racism, deep-seated economic trouble, and white male anxiety over the perceived erosion of their ability to provide materially for their women and families. The pathological obsession with the black rapist, and the firestorm of lynchings it produced in the 1890s, thus constituted a kind of "psychic compensation" for male feelings of inadequacy (Williamson 1984, p. 115). Edward L. Ayers traced the epidemic of lynchings to a "widespread and multifaceted crisis" rooted in the economic depression of the 1890s. That depression contributed to the growth of crime and vagrancy, particularly among blacks, thereby feeding the submerged fears and anxieties of southern whites (Ayers 1984, pp. 250–253).

The number of lynchings declined gradually in the first three decades of the twentieth century, dropped dramatically after the early 1930s, but continued sporadically well into the 1950s. The emergence of vocal opposition to lynching, both inside and outside the South, contributed to its demise, as did fundamental changes in southern society and in race relations. Some blacks, and a few white liberals, spoke out against the horrors of lynching in the late nineteenth century, most notably Ida B. Wells, a black woman activist from Memphis who sought to mobilize public opinion against mob violence through newspaper editorials and lectures. After 1909, the National Association for the Advancement of Colored People (NAACP), under the leadership of W. E. B. Du Bois, James Weldon Johnson, Walter White, and others, investigated and publicized lynchings, pressured political leaders to speak out, and lobbied for antilynching legislation. Some states passed laws against lynching, but they were largely ineffective. Despite decades of effort, and near success in 1922, 1937, and 1940, no federal antilynching legislation was ever enacted. Within the South, opposition to lynching centered on two interracial organizations: the Commission on Interracial Cooperation, founded in 1919, and the Association of Southern Women for the Prevention of Lynching, founded by Jessie Daniel Ames in 1930.

The modernization of southern society and the institutionalization of other forms of repression also hastened the decline of lynching. New roads, electricity, telephones, automobiles, and other social changes transformed the most isolated and lynching-prone areas of the South. Business leaders worked to change the violent image of the region to encourage investment and economic development. And law enforcement officials became more effective in preventing lynchings. Beginning in the late nineteenth century, furthermore, the emergence of alternative forms of racial control—segregation, disfranchisement, and tenant farming—made lynching less essential to the preservation of white supremacy.

There is also evidence that the decline of lynching was accompanied by an increase in "legal" executions of blacks in the South, often with the mere formality of a trial, and that other forms of violence against blacks increased as the incidence of lynching waned in the twentieth century. African Americans would continue to be killed in the name of white supremacy, particularly at the height of the Civil Rights Movement, but lynching, in the classic sense of the earlier era, appears to have ended with the murder of Emmet Till in 1955 and of Mack Charles Parker in 1959.

—L. RAY GUNN

See also
NAACP

M

MALCOLM X

Malcolm X (May 19, 1925–February 21, 1965), nationalist leader. Malcolm X, born Malcolm Little and also known by his religious name, El-Hajj Malik El-Shabbazz, was the national representative of Elijah Muhammad's Nation of Islam, a prominent black nationalist, and the founder of the Organization of Afro-American Unity. He was born in Omaha, Nebr. His father, J. Early Little, was a Georgia-born Baptist preacher and an organizer for Marcus Garvey's Universal Negro Improvement Association. His mother, M. Louise Norton, also a Garveyite, was from Grenada. At J. Early Little's murder, Malcolm's mother broke under the emotional and economic strain, and the children became wards of the state. Malcolm's delinquent behavior landed him in a detention home in Mason, Mich.

Malcolm journeyed to Boston and then to New York, where, as "Detroit Red," he became involved in a life of crime—numbers, peddling dope, con games of many kinds, and thievery of all sorts, including armed robbery. A few months before his twenty-first birthday, Malcolm was sentenced to a Massachusetts prison for burglary. While in prison, his life was transformed when he discovered through the influence of an inmate the liberating value of education, and through his family the empowering religious/cultural message of Elijah Muhammad's nation of Islam. Both gave him what he did not have: self-respect as a black person.

After honing his reading and debating skills, Malcolm was released from prison in 1952. He soon became a minister in the Nation of Islam and its most effective recruiter and apologist, speaking against black self-hate and on behalf of black self-esteem. In June 1954, Elijah Muhammad appointed him minister of Temple Number 7 in Harlem. In the temple and from the platform on street corner rallies, Malcolm told Harlemites, "we are black first and everything else second." Initially his black nationalist message was unpopular in the African-American community. The media, both white and black, portrayed him as a teacher of hate and a promoter of violence. It was an age of integration, and love and nonviolence were advocated as the only way to achieve it.

Malcolm did not share the optimism of the Civil Rights Movement and found himself speaking to unsympathetic audiences. "If you are afraid to tell truth," he told his audience, "why, you don't deserve freedom." Malcolm relished the odds against him; he saw his task as waking up "dead Negroes" by revealing the truth about America and about themselves.

The enormity of this challenge motivated Malcolm to attack the philosophy of the Rev. Dr. Martin Luther King, Jr. and the Civil Rights Movement head-on. He rejected integration: "An integrated cup of coffee is insufficient pay for 400 years of slave labor." He denounced nonviolence as "the philosophy of a fool": "There is no philosophy more befitting to the white man's tactics for keeping his foot on the black man's neck." He ridiculed King's 1963 "I Have a Dream" speech: "While King was having a dream, the rest of us Negroes are having a nightmare." He also rejected King's command to love the enemy: "It is not possible to love a man whose chief purpose in life is to humiliate you and still be considered a normal human being." To blacks who accused Malcolm of teaching hate, he retorted: "It is the man who has made a slave out of you who is teaching hate."

As long as Malcolm stayed in the Black Muslim movement, he was not free to speak his own mind. He had to represent the "Messenger," Elijah Muhammad, who was the sole and absolute authority in the Nation of Islam. When Malcolm disobeyed Muhammad in December 1963 and described President John F. Kennedy's assassination as an instance of "chickens coming home to roost," Muhammad rebuked him and used the incident as an opportunity to silence his star pupil. Malcolm realized that more was involved in his silence than what he had said about the assassination. Jealousy and envy in Muhammad's family circle were the primary reasons for his silence and why it would never be lifted.

Malcolm reluctantly declared his independence in March 1964. His break with the Black Muslim movement represented another important turning point in his life. No longer bound by

See also

Elijah Muhammad

M

Muhammad's religious structures, he was free to develop his own philosophy of the black freedom struggle.

Malcolm had already begun to show independent thinking in his "Message to the Grass Roots" speech, given in Detroit three weeks before his silence. In that speech he endorsed black nationalism as his political philosophy, thereby separating himself not only from the Civil Rights Movement, but more important, from Muhammad, who had defined the Nation as strictly religious and apolitical. Malcolm contrasted "the black revolution" with "the Negro revolution." The black revolution, he said, is international in scope, and it is "bloody" and "hostile" and "knows no compromise." But the so-called "Negro revolution," the Civil Rights Movement, is not even a revolution. Malcolm mocked it: "The only revolution in which the goal is loving your enemy is the Negro revolution. It's the only revolution in which the goal is a desegregated lunch counter, a desegregated theater, a desegregated public park, a desegregated public toilet; you can sit down next to white folks on the toilet."

MALCOLM X

Alfred Duckett called Malcolm X "our sage and our saint." Here the cultural revolutionary sits in a New York restaurant in 1961 before a poster of Elijah Muhammad.
© HENRI CARTIER-BRESSON/
MAGNUM PHOTOS

After his break, Malcolm developed his cultural and political philosophy of black nationalism in "The Ballot or the Bullet." Before audiences in New York, Cleveland, and Detroit, he urged blacks to acquire their constitutional right to vote, and move toward King and the Civil Rights Movement. Later he became more explicit: "Dr. King wants the same thing I want—freedom." Malcolm went to Selma, Ala., while King was in jail in support of King's efforts to secure voting rights. Malcolm wanted to join the Civil Rights Movement in order to expand it into a human rights movement, thereby internationalizing the black freedom struggle, making it more radical and more militant.

During his independence, which lasted for approximately one year before he was assassinated, nothing influenced Malcolm more than his travel abroad. His pilgrimage to Mecca transformed his theology. Malcolm became a Sunni Muslim, acquired the religious name El-Hajj Malik El-Shabbazz, and concluded that "Orthodox Islam" was incompatible with the racist teachings of Elijah Muhammad. The sight of "people of all races, colors, from all over the world coming together as one" had a profound effect upon him. "Brotherhood," and not racism, was seen as the essence of Islam.

Malcolm's experiences in Africa also transformed his political philosophy. He discovered the limitations of skin-nationalism, since he met whites who were creative participants in liberation struggles in African countries. In his travels abroad, Malcolm focused on explaining the black struggle for justice in the United States and linking it with other liberation struggles throughout the world. "Our problem is your problem," he told African heads of state: "It is not a Negro problem, nor an American problem. This is a world problem; a problem of humanity. It is not a problem of civil rights but a problem of human rights."

When Malcolm returned to the United States, he told blacks: "You can't understand what is going on in Mississippi, if you don't know what is going on in the Congo. They are both the same. The same interests are at stake." He founded the Organization of Afro-American Unity, patterned after the Organization of African Unity, in order to implement his ideas. He was hopeful of influencing African leaders "to recommend an immediate investigation into our problem by the United Nations Commission on Human Rights."

Malcolm X was not successful. On February 21, 1965, he was shot down by assassins as he spoke at the Audubon Ballroom in Harlem. He was thirty-nine years old.

No one made a greater impact upon the cultural consciousness of the African-American community during the second half of the twentieth century than Malcolm X. More than anyone else, he revolutionized the black mind, transforming docile Negroes and self-effacing colored people into proud blacks and self-confident African Americans. Preachers and religious scholars created a black theology and proclaimed God as liberator and Jesus Christ as black. College students demanded and got black studies. Artists created a new black esthetic and proclaimed, "Black is beautiful."

No area of the African-American community escaped Malcolm's influence. Even mainstream black leaders who first dismissed him as a rabble-rouser, embraced his cultural philosophy following his death. Malcolm's most far-reaching influence, however, was among the masses of African Americans in the ghettos of American cities. Malcolm loved black people deeply and taught them much about themselves. Before Malcolm, most blacks did not want to have anything to do with Africa. But he reminded them that "you can't hate the roots of the tree and not hate the tree; you can't hate your origin and not end up hating yourself; you can't hate Africa and not hate yourself."

Malcolm X was a cultural revolutionary. Poet Maya Angelou called him a "charismatic speaker who could play an audience as great musicians play instruments." Disciple Peter Bailey said he was a "master teacher." Writer Alfred Duckett called him "our sage and our saint." In his eulogy, actor Ossie Davis bestowed upon Malcolm the title "our shining black prince." Malcolm can be best understood as a cultural prophet of blackness. African Americans who are proud to be black should thank Malcolm X. Few have played as central a role as he in making it possible for African Americans to claim their African heritage.

—JAMES H. CONE

MARSHALL,

HARRIET GIBBS

Harriet Gibbs Marshall (February 18, 1869– February 25, 1941), music educator. Harriet Gibbs Marshall was born in Vancouver, British Columbia, the daughter of Marie A. Alexander

VIRTUOSO PERFORMER

Wynton Marsalis Displays Gift for Improvisation

Wynton Marsalis (October 18, 1961–), jazz trumpeter and composer. Born in New Orleans, Wynton Marsalis grew up in a musical family. His father, Ellis (pianist), and brothers, Branford (tenor and soprano saxophonist), Delfeayo (trombonist), and Jason (drummer), are themselves well-known jazz artists. From an early age, he studied privately and played in a children's marching band directed by the eminent New Orleans musician/scholar Danny Barker. As a youngster, Marsalis made notable contributions in both classical and jazz genres. He performed at the New Orleans Jazz and Heritage Festival, and at the age of fourteen he performed Haydn's *Trumpet Concerto in E-flat* with the New Orleans Philharmonic Orchestra. He attended the Berkshire Music Center at Tanglewood and enrolled at Juilliard in 1980. While a student at Juilliard, he joined Art Blakey's Jazz Messengers (1980) and toured in a quartet with former Miles Davis personnel Herbie Hancock, Ron Carter, and Tony Williams. He recorded his first album as a leader, *Wynton Marsalis,* in 1981.

After leaving Blakey in 1982, Marsalis formed his first group, a quintet that included several young and extremely talented musicians—his brother Branford (tenor saxophone), Kenny Kirkland (piano), Charles Fambrough (bass), and Jeff Watts (drums). In addition to performing with his own group, Marsalis replaced Freddie Hubbard for the V.S.O.P. II tour (1983). In 1984, he became the first musician to win Grammy Awards for both jazz (*Think of One,* 1982) and classical (Haydn, Hummel, and Leopold Mozart trumpet concertos, 1984) recordings. Since the late 1980s, Marsalis has concentrated on jazz performance with a group consisting of Wes Anderson and Todd Williams (saxophones), Reginald Veal (bass), Wycliffe Gordon (trombone), Herlin Riley (drums), and Eric Reed (piano). Marsalis has won critical acclaim for his virtuosic technique, musical sensitivity, and gift for improvisation. He has become an articulate spokesperson for the preservation of "mainstream" jazz (a style rooted in bop and hard bop) through his performances and writings, and, beginning in 1991, as artistic director of the classical jazz program at Lincoln Center in New York.

—EDDIE S. MEADOWS

I firmly believe that Negroes have the right to fight against these racists by any means that are necessary.

MALCOLM X
THE AUTOBIOGRAPHY OF MALCOLM X, 1965

M

and Judge Mifflin W. Gibbs. The first African American to complete the course in piano at the Oberlin Conservatory of Music in Ohio (1889), she gave piano recitals and began her teaching career as director of music at Eckstein-Norton College in Cane Springs, Ky. In Washington, D.C., she served as music supervisor of black students in the public schools beginning in 1900, and in 1903 she established the Washington Conservatory of Music. Under her management and, from 1941 to 1960, that of her cousin Victoria Muse, the institution stood out as the country's most successful black-owned and -operated music school offering conservatory-level training. The conservatory drew students from all parts of the country as well as from the Washington area and, in addition, made an important contribution to the community through an annual concert series that presented nationally known artists. In keeping with the philosophy of the Harlem Renaissance, Marshall promoted the African-American musical heritage by opening a National Negro Music Center (1936), for which she collected published works by African-American composers. During a leave of absence spent in Haiti with her husband, she cofounded an industrial school and completed research for *A Story of Haiti*, published in 1930.

—DORIS EVANS MCGINTY

My Daddy told me it doesn't matter if it's a white snake or a black snake, it can still bite you.

THURGOOD MARSHALL

MARSHALL,

THURGOOD

Thurgood Marshall (July 2, 1908–January 24, 1993), civil rights lawyer, associate justice of U. S. Supreme Court. Thurgood Marshall distinguished himself as a jurist in a wide array of settings. As the leading attorney for the National Association for the Advancement of Colored People (NAACP) between 1938 and 1961, he pioneered the role of professional civil rights advocate. As the principal architect of the legal attack against *de jure* racial segregation, Marshall oversaw the most successful campaign of social reform litigation in American history. As a judge on the United States Court of Appeals, solicitor general of the United States, and associate justice of the Supreme Court, he amassed a remarkable record as a public servant. Given the influence of his achievements over a long span of time, one can reasonably argue that Thurgood Marshall may have been the outstanding attorney of twentieth-century America.

Marshall was born in Baltimore, Md., where his father was a steward at an exclusive, all-white boat club, and his mother was an elementary school teacher. He attended public schools in Baltimore before proceeding to Lincoln University in Pennsylvania where he shared classes with, among others, Cabell "Cab" Calloway, the entertainer, Kwame Nkrumah, who became president of Ghana, and Nnamdi Azikiwe, who became president of Nigeria. After graduating, he was excluded from the University of Maryland School of Law because of racial segregation. Marshall attended the Howard University School of Law, where he fell under the tutelage of Charles Hamilton Houston. Houston elevated academic standards at Howard, turning it into a veritable hothouse of legal education, where he trained many of those who would later play important roles in the campaign against racial discrimination. Marshall graduated in 1933, first in his class.

After engaging in a general law practice for a brief period, Marshall was persuaded by Houston to pursue a career working as an attorney on behalf of the NAACP. Initially he worked as Houston's deputy and then, in 1939, he took over from his mentor as the NAACP's special counsel. In that position, Marshall confronted an extraordinary array of legal problems that took him from local courthouses, where he served as a trial attorney, to the Supreme Court of the United States, where he developed his skills as an appellate advocate. Over a span of two decades, he argued thirty-two cases before the Supreme Court, winning twenty-nine of them. He convinced the Court to invalidate practices that excluded blacks from primary elections (*Smith* v. *Allwright*, 1944), to prohibit segregation in interstate transportation (*Morgan* v. *Virginia*, 1946), to nullify convictions obtained from juries from which African Americans had been barred on the basis of their race (*Patton* v. *Mississippi*, 1947), and to prohibit state courts from enforcing racially restrictive real estate covenants (*Shelley* v. *Kraemer*, 1948).

Marshall's greatest triumphs arose, however, in the context of struggles against racial discrimination in public education. In 1950, in *Sweatt* v. *Painter*, he successfully argued that a state could not fulfill its federal constitutional obligation by hurriedly constructing a "Negro" law school that was inferior in tangible and intangible ways to the state's "white" law school. That same year he successfully argued in *McLaurin* v. *Oklahoma State Regents* that a state university violated the federal constitution by admitting an African-American

See also
NAACP

444

student and then confining that student, on the basis of his race, to a specified seat in classrooms and a specified table in the school cafeteria. In 1954, in *Brown v. Board of Education*, Marshall culminated his campaign by convincing the Court to rule that racial segregation is invidious racial discrimination and thus invalid under the Fourteenth Amendment to the federal constitution.

In 1961, over the objections of white supremacist southern politicians, President John F. Kennedy nominated Marshall to a seat on the United States Court of Appeals for the Second Circuit in New York. Later, President Lyndon B. Johnson appointed Marshall to two positions that had never previously been occupied by an African American. In 1965, President Johnson appointed Marshall as Solicitor General, and in 1967 he nominated him to a seat on the Supreme Court.

Throughout his twenty-four years on the Court, Marshall was the most insistently liberal of the Justices, a stance that often drove him into dissent. His judgments gave broad scope to individual liberties (except in cases involving asserted claims to rights of property). Typically he supported claims of freedom of expression over competing concerns and scrutinized skeptically the claims of law enforcement officers in cases implicating federal constitutional provisions that limit the police powers of government. In the context of civil liberties, the most controversial positions that Marshall took involved rights over reproductive capacities and the death penalty. He viewed as unconstitutional laws that prohibit women from exercising considerable discretion over the choice to continue a pregnancy or to terminate it through abortion. Marshall also viewed as unconstitutional all laws permitting the imposition of capital punishment.

The other side of Marshall's jurisprudential liberalism was manifested by an approach to statutory and constitutional interpretation that generally advanced egalitarian policies. His judgments displayed an unstinting solicitude for the rights of labor, the interests of women, the struggles of oppressed minorities, and the condition of the poor. One particularly memorable expression of Marshall's empathy for the indigent is his dissent in *United States v. Kras* (1973), a case in which the Court held that a federal statute did not violate the Constitution by requiring a $50 fee of persons seeking the protection of bankruptcy. Objecting to the Court's assumption that, with a little self-discipline, the petitioner could readily accumulate the required fee, Marshall wrote that

It may be easy for some people to think that weekly savings of less than $2 are no burden. But no one who has had close contact with poor people can fail to understand how close to the margin of survival many of them are . . . It is perfectly proper for judges to disagree about what the Constitution requires. But it is disgraceful for an interpretation of the Constitution to be premised upon unfounded assumptions about how people live.

Marshall retired from the Court in 1991, precipitating the most contentious confirmation battle in the nation's history when President George Bush nominated as Marshall's successor Clarence Thomas, an ultraconservative African-American jurist.

Marshall died on January 24, 1993. His extraordinary contributions to American life were memorialized in an outpouring of popular grief and adulation greater than that expressed for any previous justice.

—RANDALL KENNEDY

MAYNOR, DOROTHY LEIGH

Dorothy Leigh Maynor (September 3, 1910–), concert singer. Born in Norfolk, Va., soprano Dorothy Maynor was one of the most successful singers of the 1940s and 1950s. She attended Hampton Institute College Preparatory School (where she was under the guidance of R. Nathaniel Dett) from 1924 until her college graduation (B.S., 1933). She later attended Westminster Choir School in Princeton, N.J. (B.M., 1935). In the summer of 1939 at the Berkshire Music Festival in Massachusetts, she sang for Serge Koussevitzky, who commented, "Her voice is a miracle, a musical revelation that the world must hear," and immediately arranged concerts and a recording with the Boston Symphony.

In the fall of 1939, Maynor had a critically acclaimed New York Town Hall debut. The success of that performance launched a twenty-five-year career that included extensive tours and recordings, radio and television shows, and appearances with major orchestras. In 1945, she became the director of Bennett College in Greensboro, N.C.; in 1959 she received an honorary doctor of music degree from Howard University. Upon her retirement from singing in 1965, she started a music-

SCIENCE ADVOCATE

Walter E. Massey (1938–), physicist and scientific administrator. In March 1991 this theoretical physicist began a six-year term as director of the National Science Foundation (NSF). Previous to this appointment he served as vice president for research at the University of Chicago and the Argonne National Laboratory. Prior to this he was director of the laboratory and professor of Physics at the University of Chicago.

Born in Hattiesburg, Miss., Massey received a bachelor's degree in physics and mathematics from Morehouse College in 1958, and completed graduate studies there for a master's degree in 1959. He received his doctoral degree in 1966 from Washington University in St. Louis. Following seven years of research at the Argonne National Laboratory—operated by the University of Chicago for the U.S. Department of Energy—he was professor of physics and later a college dean at Brown University in Providence, R.I. His own research has focused on the many-body theories of quantum liquids and solids—more specifically, examining the behavior of various substances at very low temperatures.

Upon his return to the Argonne National Laboratory as its director in 1979, he was responsible for overseeing a wide array of basic and applied energy research projects, involving nuclear fission, solar energy, fossil fuels, and the effects of energy production on the environment. As Argonne's director he managed a staff of 5,000, including 2,000 scientists and engineers, with an annual budget of $233 million.

Walter Massey has lectured and written widely on the teaching of science and mathematics in the nation's public schools and colleges and on the role of science and technology in society. He is an ardent advocate of African-American involvement in science. "More and more, science and technology will influence our life, and people who are not able to deal with or understand such issues will not be able to play meaningful roles in society," says Dr. Massey.

In 1974 he received the Outstanding Educator in America award; the next year, the Distinguished Service Citation of the American Association of Physics Teachers was bestowed upon him.

—ROBERT C. HAYDEN

education program for children at Saint James Presbyterian Church in Harlem, where her husband, Shelby Rooks, was the minister. This program expanded into the Harlem School for the Arts, and she began a new career as its first director (1964–1979). About her work in Harlem, Maynor said, "What I dream of is changing the image held by the children. We have made them believe that everything beautiful is outside the community. I want them to make beauty *in* this community!" Since her retirement in 1992 Dorothy Maynor has lived in Pennsylvania.

—A. LOUISE TOPPIN

MAYS, BENJAMIN ELIJAH

Benjamin Elijah Mays (August 1, 1894–March 28, 1984), educator, clergyman. Benjamin Mays was born in Ninety-Six, S.C., the eighth and youngest child of Hezekiah and Louvenia Carter Mays. His father supported the family as a sharecropper. A year at Virginia Union University in Richmond preceded Mays's matriculation at Bates College in Maine, from which he graduated with honors in 1920. At the Divinity School of the University of Chicago, he earned an M.A. degree in 1925. Ten years later, while engaged in teaching, social work, and educational administration, Mays received a Ph.D. from the Divinity School.

Mays lived in Tampa, Fla., in the early 1920s, where he was active in social work in the Tampa Urban League, exposing police brutality and attacking discrimination in public places. However, higher education soon became his principal vocation. Teaching stints at Morehouse College in Atlanta and South Carolina State College in Orangeburg between 1921 and 1926 put Mays in the classroom as an instructor in mathematics, psychology, religious education, and English.

In 1934, with his Ph.D. nearly finished, Mays went to Howard University in Washington, D.C., as dean of the School of Religion. He served for six years, and during that time graduate enrollment increased, the quality of the faculty improved, and its library was substantially augmented. During his tenure the seminary gained accreditation from the American Association of Theological Schools.

Mays's administrative successes at Howard University convinced the trustees of Morehouse College to elect him in 1940 as the new president

See also
W.E.B. Du Bois

of their institution. He served until 1967. During his tenure the percentage of faculty with Ph.D.s increased from 8.7 percent to 54 percent and the physical plant and campus underwent numerous improvements. One of Mays's proteges at Morehouse was Martin Luther King, Jr., who attended the college from 1944—when he entered as a fifteen-year-old—through 1948. Mays, both by example and personal influence, helped persuade young King to seek a career in the ministry. Mays remained a friend of King throughout his career, urging King to persevere in the Montgomery Bus Boycott. In 1965, Mays was instrumental in the election of King to the Morehouse Board of Trustees.

In addition to his activities in higher education, Mays remained involved in religious affairs. Though he was active as a pastor for only a few years in the early 1920s, he became a familiar presence in the affairs of the National Baptist Convention Inc. and in several ecumenical organizations. In 1944 he became vice president of the Federal Council of Churches of Christ, a national organization of mainline Protestant denominations. In 1948 Mays helped to organize the World Council of Churches (WCC) in Amsterdam, Holland, where he successfully pushed a resolution to acknowledge racism as a divisive force among Christians. When a delegate from the Dutch Reformed Church proposed that an all-white delegation from the WCC investigate apartheid in South Africa, Mays argued convincingly for an interracial team to report on race relations in that country.

Mays was a distinguished scholar of the black church and black religion. In 1930 the Institute of Social and Religious Research in New York City requested Mays and Joseph W. Nicholson, a minister in the Colored Methodist Episcopal Church, to survey black churches in twelve cities and four rural areas. In their study, *The Negro's Church* (1933), they argued that black churches represented "the failure of American Christianity." They found that there was an oversupply of black churches, too many with untrained clergy, and too much indebtedness. These shortcomings deprived the members and the communities that they served of adequate programs to deal with the broad range of social and economic ills they faced. Nonetheless, Mays and Nicholson praised the autonomy of black churches and their promotion of education, economic development, and leadership opportunities for African Americans.

In 1938 Mays produced a second important volume. *The Negro's God as Reflected in His Litera-* ture, a study of how blacks conceptualized God and related the deity to their temporal circumstances. Mays argued that many blacks believed God to be intimately involved in and mindful of their condition as an oppressed group. Even those who doubted or rejected either the notion of God or the social dimension of the deity, Mays argued, were still influenced by their understanding of the social purpose of God. In later years Mays wrote an autobiography, *Born to Rebel* (1971), which was published in an abridged version in 1981 as *Lord, the People Have Driven Me On.*

After his retirement in 1967, Mays won election to the Atlanta Board of Education in 1969. He also became president of that body in 1970.

Mays married twice. His first wife, Ellen Harvin Mays, died in 1923. His second wife, whom he married in 1926, was Sadie Gray Mays. She died on October 11, 1969. In 1982 Mays was awarded the NAACP's Spingarn Medal. Benjamin E. Mays died in Atlanta, Ga., on March 28, 1984.

—DENNIS C. DICKERSON

DISTINGUISHED SCHOLAR

Benjamin E. Mays argued that blacks believed God to be intimately involved in and mindful of their condition as an oppressed group. PHOTOGRAPHS AND PRINTS DIVISION, SCHOMBURG CENTER FOR RESEARCH IN BLACK CULTURE, THE NEW YORK PUBLIC LIBRARY, ASTOR, LENOX AND TILDEN FOUNDATIONS

See also

Jazz

MCDANIEL, HATTIE

Hattie McDaniel (June 10, 1895–October 26, 1952), singer and actress. Hattie McDaniel was born in Wichita, Kans. Her father, Henry McDaniel, was a Baptist preacher and an entertainer, and her mother, Susan (Holbert) McDaniel, was a choir singer. McDaniel was one of thirteen children. Soon after her birth the family moved to Colorado, and in 1901 they settled in Denver. In 1910, at the age of fifteen, she was awarded a gold medal by the Women's Christian Temperance Union for excellence in "the dramatic art" for her recital of "Convict Joe," which reportedly "moved the house to tears." On the strength of this success, McDaniel persuaded her family to allow her to leave school and to join her brothers in her father's newly formed traveling company, the Henry McDaniel Minstrel Show. Over the next decade she traveled and performed on the West coast, mostly with her father's company, and she began at this time to develop her abilities as a songwriter and singer.

Around 1920 McDaniel came to the notice of George Morrison, one of Denver's notable popular musicians. Taken on as a singer with Morrison's orchestra, McDaniel became increasingly well known throughout the West coast vaudeville circuit. She also appeared with the orchestra on Denver radio during this time, and she is reputed to be the first black woman soloist to sing on the radio. In 1929 she secured a place with a traveling production of *Show Boat*, but the stock market crash of October 1929 eliminated the show's financing.

After the crash, McDaniel moved to Milwaukee, where she worked in the coat room of the Club Madrid and eventually got an opportunity to perform. Encouraged by her success, McDaniel moved to Hollywood in 1931 and soon began working regularly in radio and film. Over the course of the next two decades she appeared in more than three hundred films, though mostly in minor, uncredited roles. Her debut was in *The Golden West* (1932). The first film for which she received screen credit was *Blonde Venus* (1932), in which she played the affectionate, loyal, but willful domestic, a type character that was virtually the only role available at the time to large black women in Hollywood. Over the course of the next two decades McDaniel successfully established herself in this role, gaining substantial, credited parts in over fifty films, including *Alice Adams* (1935), *The Mad Miss Manton* (1935), *Show Boat* (1936, with Paul Robeson), *Affectionately Yours* (1941), *Since You Went Away* (1944), and Walt Disney's animated *Song of the South* (1946).

McDaniel's career reached its high point in 1939 when she won an Academy Award, the first ever given to a black performer, for her portrayal of Mammy in *Gone with the Wind*. Praised by some and maligned by others for the image she portrayed, McDaniel in her Oscar acceptance speech (said to have been written by her studio) announced that she hoped always to be a credit to her race and to her industry. Despite Hollywood's evident self-satisfaction with this award, it is important to note that McDaniel (along with the other black cast members) had been excluded from the Atlanta premiere of the film and that her portrait was removed from the promotional programs that the studio distributed in the South.

McDaniel continued to play similar roles throughout the 1940s despite increased criticism from the NAACP, which felt that McDaniel and the other black actors who played servile stereotypes were helping to perpetuate them. In 1947, after the controversy with the NAACP had passed, McDaniel signed her first contract for the radio show *Beulah*, in which she once again played a southern maid. In the contract McDaniel insisted that she would not use dialect, and she demanded the right to alter any script that did not meet her approval. Both of her demands were met.

McDaniel died in Los Angeles in 1952, after completing the first six episodes of the television version of *Beulah*.

—MATTHEW BUCKLEY

MCFERRIN, ROBERT, JR., "BOBBY"

Robert "Bobby" McFerrin, Jr. (March 11, 1950–), jazz vocalist. Bobby McFerrin was born in New York City, the son of two distinguished opera singers, Sara and Robert McFerrin. He began his musical studies on piano at the preparatory division of the Juilliard School of Music, in New York City, and later studied at California State University, in Sacramento. Before attending college, he played piano in several local bands in Fullerton, Calif. Beginning in 1977, McFerrin concentrated on singing. His repertory is eclectic, ranging from the Top 10 hit "Don't Worry, Be Happy" (1988) to jazz classics like " 'Round Midnight."

McFerrin's ability to emulate jazz giants like Miles Davis and Wayne Shorter in his vocal improvisations was the most important factor contributing to his winning a 1984 and 1985 *Downbeat* "Best Male Vocalist" poll. He also received the 1985 and 1986 Grammy Award for "Best Male Jazz Vocalist." Since 1983, McFerrin's vocal improvisations have focused on timbre differences, a musical repertory that encompasses classical, jazz, and popular genres, and a vocal range that extends over three octaves. In addition, he likes to involve his audience in improvised performance, and uses a variety of vocal and body-percussion sounds in his recordings and live performances. In unaccompanied songs, McFerrin performs all the musical parts, in a multilayered texture.

McFerrin has organized an a cappella vocal group entitled "Voicestra," a group that ranges from eight to fourteen voices. The group generates its musical ideas from melodies, harmonies, and rhythms that are fed to it by McFerrin. McFerrin has explored many performance avenues. He has recorded *Hush* (1992), an album with classical cellist Yo-Yo Ma, and in 1990 McFerrin made his conducting debut with the San Francisco Symphony. His most successful albums include *Simple Pleasures* (1988), *Medicine Man* (1990), and *Hugs* (1992).

—EDDIE S. MEADOWS

MEMPHIS, TENNESSEE

Located on a bluff overlooking the Mississippi River, Memphis, Tenn., received its first African-American settlers shortly after its founding in 1819. Its early black population was largely free, and Shelby County's state representatives opposed slavery. African Americans worked as domestics, stevedores, draymen, blacksmiths, and artisans.

As the town grew into a major port city, racial attitudes began to change. In 1834 Tennessee enacted a new state constitution, which stripped blacks of citizenship rights. The town's African-American population, which previously had enjoyed voting rights, was disenfranchised and forced to observe a curfew. Black clergymen were not allowed to preach. In the 1840s, Tennessee repealed its ban—adopted in 1812—on the domestic slave trade. Memphis, with its large port, became a center for slave trading. Nevertheless, Memphis was more cosmopolitan than most southern cities in that a large number of immi-

grants—mostly Irish, Italians, and Germans—had settled there. By 1860 the city's population was 17 percent black and more than 36 percent foreign-born.

As the Civil War lurked on the horizon, Memphis initially did not endorse secession, and even though local support for the Confederacy built once the war began, the city fell to advancing Union troops in 1862 and remained occupied and largely undamaged throughout the war. The Union Army established a large freedpeople's camp near Memphis, and many blacks migrated there, remaining after the end of the war. Yet, emancipation spawned economic competition between black and white immigrants; and despite efforts by the Freedmens' Bureau, interracial strife developed, particularly between the blacks and Irish who resided in many of the same neighborhoods. In 1866, for instance, struggling Irish residents turned their frustrations on many of their newly arrived black neighbors in a riot that left forty-six blacks dead, nearly twice that many injured, five women raped, approximately 100 blacks robbed, and ninety-one homes, four churches, and all twelve black schools destroyed.

Once the United States Congress enacted civil rights laws in 1866, the political situation improved. By 1875, a coalition of blacks, Irish, and Italians dominated Memphis politics. The blacks were led by the likes of militant saloon-keeper Ed Shaw and the more conciliatory Hezekiah Henley. African Americans held seats on both the elected city council and school board as well as appointed positions such as wharfmaster and coal inspector. Yet, as the Jim Crow era dawned, no African American would hold elective office from 1888 until 1960. As a matter of fact, with the exception of a few Republican primaries, no black would even seek an elected position until 1951.

Due to black in-migration as well as successive yellow fever epidemics, which took a heavy toll on the white population of Memphis and caused a white out-migration, blacks remained a significant voting bloc. Although blocked from holding public office, black suffrage was never formally restricted except by selective enforcement of a poll tax. Thus, even after southern Democrats regained political control of Tennessee, they were compelled to court black votes. Furthermore, black Republican leaders retained influence over policy and the awarding of city and federal patronage jobs.

Despite this limited political power, the social conditions of blacks in Memphis grew steadily worse as the nineteenth century drew to a close.

Don't worry, be happy

BOBBY MCFERRIN
SONG LYRIC

See also
Emancipation
Jim Crow

The better-off, more cosmopolitan whites had fled the yellow fever epidemics of the 1880s and been replaced by poorer, more parochial whites from surrounding areas of rural Tennessee, Mississippi, and Arkansas. Blacks' civil and property rights were violated, and the city became increasingly segregated. In 1892, for instance, a white grocery storekeeper facing competition from the black-owned Peoples' Grocery tried to intimidate its owners, claiming a white mob would attack their neighborhood that evening. He then warned the police that blacks were intent on causing trouble. When the black store owners, their homes barricaded, were visited that evening by deputy sheriffs, they mistook the deputies for a mob and fired, fatally wounding them. Arrested the next day, they were taken from prison by a white mob and brutally lynched. When Ida B. Wells denounced the lynching in her newspaper, the *Memphis Free Speech*, a mob burned her press and forced her to flee the city, providing the impetus for her subsequent career as a crusader for African-American rights.

Memphis blacks were anything but passive in the face of the encroachment of segregation. A number of Memphis blacks resisted the day-to-day degradations of Jim Crow. In 1881, for example, prominent musician and schoolteacher Julia Hooks was arrested for her vociferous protest over not being seated in the theater's white section. And, beyond protest, when Mary Morrison was arrested for resisting streetcar segregation in 1905, a huge rally followed in Church Park and several thousand dollars was raised for her legal defense.

There were also forms of even more direct resistance. The following incidents occurred in 1915 and 1916 alone. When white men tried physically to remove Charley Park and John Knox from their trolley seats, Park stabbed one, and Knox ended up in a gun battle with another. A white trolley conductor was stabbed when he tried to collect extra fare from a black rider. Retaliatory ambush shootings and arson took place on occasion. Furthermore, lower-class blacks used a variety of physical means to resist local white police officers.

Meanwhile, despite such turmoil, Beale Street became known as the "Main Street of Negro America." The size and segregation of the black community early on had created a need for a number of black professionals and businesspersons. Black doctors, lawyers, and teachers provided essential services; while black entrepreneurs owned many of the groceries, barbershops, hair salons, funeral parlors, and even banks, open for black patronage. Beale Street, the black commercial center in its Jim Crow heyday, was lined with real estate and baking offices, dry goods and clothing stores, theaters, saloons, gambling joints, and a variety of other small shops (in the 1970s and 1980s, after decades of decline and neglect, city officials began to renovate the Beale Street area as an historic district and tourist attraction.)

In the business realm, in the early twentieth century, Bert Roddy founded the city's first black grocery chain and subsequently organized the Supreme Liberty Life Insurance Company. Included in his effort was an attempt to build on W. E. B. Du Bois's notion of developing community cooperative businesses, in this case Roddy's "Citizens' Coop" grocery stores. Roddy also was the first head of the Memphis branch of the NAACP. Thomas H. Hayes, another example, was a successful grocer who also started the T. H. Hayes and Sons Funeral Home, the longest continuously running black business in Memphis. Other prominent black businessmen included James Clouston, Clarence Gilliss, Phillip Nicholson, David Woodruff, and N. J. Ford.

Robert Church, Sr., however, was the best known. A former slave, he arrived in Memphis in 1863. By the time of his death in 1912, he had amassed more than $1 million dollars' worth of real estate and other holdings. He was most likely the nation's first black millionaire. His Solvent Savings Bank, founded in 1906, was the first black-owned bank in the city's history; and his donations of Church Park and the adjacent Church Auditorium provided major focal points for black social and cultural life, especially during the Jim Crow period.

Memphis gradually became an African-American cultural center. The city boasted several black theaters; concerts were held in the Church Auditorium. Memphis also contained the Julia Hooks Music School, a black-owned, interracial institution. Beale Street's saloons and gambling clubs were known for their "blues" music, and bands such as John R. Love's Letter Carrier's Band and Jim Turner's Band popularized the sound. Turner's pupil, W. C. Handy, wrote down much of this music and brought it to the rest of the country. His "Memphis Blues," originally written as a campaign song, became the city's unofficial anthem. In more recent years, the Beale Street milieu has fostered many leading blues musicians such as B. B. King and Memphis Slim.

The Mississippi-born Irishman, Edward H. "Boss" Crump, first won city office in 1905. Al-

See also

W.E.B. Du Bois

Martin Luther King, Jr.

NAACP

though an avowed segregationist, he successfully registered large numbers of black voters, and he turned them out to vote with the help of prominent blacks such as W. C. Handy. By the late 1920s, Crump had consolidated his political power. Thereafter, although no longer actually holding the mayor's office himself, he proceeded to dominate Memphis politics until his death in 1954. Between 1928 and 1948, for instance, his mayoral candidates lost a total of two precincts, which were subsequently abolished upon redistricting. Crump's base of support was an odd mix of blacks and Irish; like most bosses of the day, he held his coalition together with selective patronage.

Blacks, then, although not allowed to rise to positions of authority within the party structure or the bureaucracy, still were marshalled to the polls and, in return, received a share of the city's largesse for delivering a critical voting bloc for the Crump machine. Black leaders such as Harry Pace, Robert Church Jr., J. B. Martin, and Matthew Thornton brokered black political support for patronage benefits. Although Republicans, as were many of the businessmen and professionals in the black leadership elite, they were able to work effectively with Boss Crump—especially while the large majority of blacks apparently remained loyal to the "Party of Lincoln."

Then, as a combination of Crump's efforts and Franklin Roosevelt's emerging coalition lured many blacks from their traditional allegiance to the Republican party, Dr. J. E. Walker organized the Shelby County Democratic Club as an independent political base for black Memphians. Although organizationally separate from the Crump machine, Walker worked with Crump until the early 1950s, when the two had a falling-out over the issue of social segregation. This drove Walker into the camp of a number of white "reformers" who emerged around the successful machine-challenging senatorial bid of Estes Kefauver.

In 1951 Walker challenged the machine himself by running for a position on the school board. In the course of the campaign, the first of many aggressive voter-registration drives was launched within the black community. Although Walker was soundly defeated, he was the first black candidate in decades, and black voter registration nearly tripled in 1951 alone. Then, as Crump died, the poll tax was eliminated and registration drives continued in earnest, and the percentage of registered blacks would triple again over the course of this decade, leaving more than 60 percent of the city's African Americans registered by

1960. By 1963, as blacks struggled for the right to vote across the South, black Memphians were already registered at the same rate as white Memphians.

Two additional pieces of the electoral puzzle were George W. Lee and O. Z. Evers. Lee, a prominent black Republican who led a local group called the "Lincoln League," was helpful in rallying black Republicans, mostly businessmen and ministers. Evers, on the other hand, headed a small group of independents, calling themselves the "Unity League." In addition, none of this should be seen as understating the central political role played by local black churches from Emancipation to the present day. In 1955, as just one example, dozens of churchmen representing every black denomination came together to form the "Ministers and Citizens League." They adopted a $2,000 registration budget, hired three full-time secretaries, and pledged themselves to utilizing other resources at their disposal to increase black voter registration. The black ministers used the pulpit to preach the need to register; they held mass meetings; and they even drove unregistered voters to the courthouse.

Throughout the 1950s, black candidates ran unsuccessfully for citywide and statewide office. Then, in 1959, Russell Sugarmon led a field of black candidates, pulling together black Republicans, Democrats and independents to support a "Volunteer Ticket." His campaign manager was law partner and emerging political leader A. W. Willis. Along with others like Benjamin Hooks, they represented a new political generation. As it turned out, this became a racially divisive election marred by much uncharacteristically overt racist rhetoric. For example, the white "Citizens for Progress" ran under the banner "Keep Memphis Down in Dixie." Meanwhile, prominent African Americans such as the Rev. Dr. Martin Luther King, Jr. and Mahalia Jackson appeared to help rally the black vote. Although all black candidates were defeated, Sugarmon had made a strong run for a seat on the city commission. In addition, each of the Volunteer candidates finished second, and nearly two-thirds of black voters were now registered. Sugarmon concluded, "We won everything but the election."

Finally, in 1960, Jesse Turner, also head of the Memphis NAACP, became the first African American since Reconstruction to win an elective post, winning a seat on the Democratic Executive Committee. In the same year, a number of student sit-ins took place, and a successful boycott was launched against downtown retailers. By the mid-

W. C. Handy settled in Memphis in 1908, where he cofounded a music-publishing company with Harry Pace.

PAGE 100

*Dr. Martin Luther
King, Jr., was
assassinated in
Memphis on
April 4, 1968.*

PAGE 403

1960s, the city of Memphis had a population that was approximately 34 percent black, and two-thirds of them were registered. Then, in 1964, A. W. Williss won a seat in the state legislature, and Charles Ware won a constable position—both plurality votes. Thus, it was not long before a runoff provision was added in order to preclude such developments. In addition, other forms of racial discrimination persisted. For example, Republican "election challenges" focused on the black community, where registrations were reviewed carefully, and this obviously intimidated some legitimately registered blacks. Or, extra field wages would be offered on election day, with the field hands being brought back from the fields too late to vote.

Nevertheless, despite the fact that Memphis elections remained exceptionally polarized by race—especially because whites so seldom voted for black candidates—victories began to occur in districts with large black constituencies. From 1963 onward, as the black voting bloc increased to nearly 100,000 voters, prospects for success increased. They increased despite fairly regular annexations of predominantly white suburbs, a practice that had begun as early as 1909. In 1974, for example, Harold Ford became the first black Tennessean ever elected to the United States Congress, while seats also were being won on the city council, school board, and the judiciary.

Since his election to Congress, Ford has developed the reputation of having the most effective political operation in Memphis. Besides personally paying overdue rents, distributing food at Christmas, contributing to church bazaars, giving graduation presents, and so on, his local congressional staff is also quite proficient at helping constituents through the maze of the federal bureaucracy. In addition, his congressional seniority and consequent committee assignments put him in a position to bring a respectable share of federal funds to Memphis. The word is that "Harold delivers," and his "deliveries" are well chronicled both in his newsletters and in the *Tri-State Defender*. Such service has helped build a core of very loyal supporters; they remained loyal to Ford during his protracted trials and eventual vindication on charges of bank fraud in the 1990s. In addition, the congressman, his staff, and a small group of loyalists regularly compose and distribute a sample ballot endorsing a variety of candidacies. Such endorsements, which often appear to require a financial contribution to the congressman's campaign fund, are believed to generate a

sizable number of votes for the endorsed candidates.

Still, it has been the norm for black leaders to split—especially over which mayoral candidate to support. Over the years, these splits have been based on a variety of issues such as gender and intergenerational differences as well as personal rivalries. Such disunity has diluted the influence of the black community. This has been particularly problematic in a city where whites have managed to remain a majority, much of the black population has remained exceptionally poor and consequently difficult to mobilize, and where white allies have been few and far between.

Following the 1987 election, black union leader James Smith called for a leadership summit before the next mayoral election. In the spring of 1991, two "unity conferences" were held, one at the grass-roots level led by City Councilman Shep Wilbun and one at the leadership level led by Rep. Harold Ford. The result was a consensus black candidate, W. W. Herenton, whose Herenton campaign succeeded in uniting the various elite and mass groups under the banner of an uncompromising black political crusade. For the Memphis African-American community, Herenton's election—albeit by an extremely narrow margin of less than 200 votes—marked a high point in a political struggle that has spanned generations. That same year, blacks won a majority of seats on the city's school board and ended up only one vote shy of a majority on the city council.

Yet, despite political victories, the city's commerce and service-oriented economy has offered African Americans far more low-wage positions than higher-paying ones. This has left Memphis with arguably the poorest black underclass of any large U.S. city. By 1990, more than a third of that population was still impoverished; and as for the intensity of the poverty, six Census tracts had a median household income below $5,500. Consequently, a sizable number of black Memphians have ended up disproportionately poor, disillusioned, and militant as well as suspicious of political leaders, including many of their own black leaders.

Labor activism by black Memphians, protesting both their poverty and maltreatment, led to the best-remembered and most tragic event in the recent history of Memphis, the assassination of the Rev. Dr. Martin Luther King, Jr., on April 4, 1968. King was in Memphis to support a strike by the city's largely black staff of sanitation workers. The strikers' grievances went beyond economic issues and involved claims of maltreatment by white supervisors. The strike, which began in February 1968, became bitter and protracted. King encountered much hostility during his stay in Memphis, and the night before he died, in the city's largest black church, the Mason Temple, he seemed to publicly contemplate his own mortality. On the evening of April 4, King was fatally wounded by a rifle shot at the Lorraine Motel. In 1991 the motel reopened as a civil rights museum, dedicated to the memory of Dr. King.

—MARCUS D. POHLMANN

MICHEAUX, OSCAR

Oscar Micheaux (January 2, 1884–March 25, 1951), novelist and filmmaker. Oscar Micheaux was born in Metropolis, Ill., one of thirteen children of former slaves. The early events of his life are not clear and must be gleaned from several fictionalized versions he published. He evidently worked as a Pullman porter, acquiring enough capital to buy two 160-acre tracts of land in South Dakota, where he homesteaded. Micheaux's homesteading experiences were the basis of his first novel, *The Conquest: The Story of a Negro Pioneer* (1913). In order to publicize the book, Micheaux established the Western Book Supply Company and toured the Midwest. He sold most of the books and stock in his first company to white farmers, although his later ventures were financed by African-American entrepreneurs. From his bookselling experiences, he wrote a second novel, *The Forged Note: A Romance of the Darker Races* (1915). Micheaux's third novel, *The Homesteader* (1917), attracted the attention of George P. Johnson, who, with his Hollywood actor brother Noble, owned the Lincoln Film Company, with offices in Los Angeles and Omaha. The Johnson brothers were part of the first wave of African-American independent filmmakers to take up the challenge to D. W. Griffith's white supremacist version of American History, *Birth of a Nation* (1915), and to produce their own stories of African-American life. Fascinated by the new medium, Micheaux offered to sell the Johnson Brothers film rights to his novel, on the condition that he direct the motion picture version. When they refused, Micheaux decided to produce and direct the film himself, financing it through what became the Micheaux Book and Film Company, with offices located in New York, Chicago, and Sioux City, Iowa.

The film version of Micheaux's third novel, *The Homesteader* (1918), was the first of about fifty films he directed. He distributed the films himself, carrying the prints from town to town, often for one-night stands. His films played mostly in white-owned (but often black-managed) black theaters in the North and in the South. He even had some luck convincing southern white cinema owners to let him show his films at all-black matinees and interracial midnight shows in white theaters. While the black press at the time sometimes criticized Micheaux for projecting a rich black fantasy world and ignoring ghetto problems, he dealt frankly with such social themes as interracial relationships, "passing," intraracial as well as interracial prejudice, and the intimidation of African Americans by the Ku Klux Klan. Micheaux's second film, *Within Our Gates* (1919), contains a disturbing sequence representing a white lynch mob hanging an innocent black man and his wife. When Micheaux tried to exhibit the film in Chicago, less than a year after a major race riot in the city, both black and white groups urged city authorities to ban the film. Micheaux's response to such censorship was to cut and reedit his films from town to town. Showman and entrepreneur that he was, he would promote a film that had been banned in one town by indicating in the next town that it contained "censored" footage. Produced on a shoestring, his films earned him just enough money to continue his filmmaking.

Some twelve of Micheaux's films are extant, and they give an idea, though incomplete, of his style. His interior scenes are often dimly lit, but his location scenes of urban streets are usually crisp and clear, providing a documentary-like glimpse of the period. He seldom had money for more than one take, with the result that the actors' mistakes are sometimes left on screen. However, Micheaux had a genius for negotiating around tight budgets, improvising with limited resources, and synchronizing production with distribution. In the early 1920s, in order to purchase the rights to African-American author Charles Waddell Chesnutt's *The House Behind the Cedars* (1900), he offered the author shares in his film company.

To create appeal for his films, Micheaux features some of the most talented African-American actors of his time: Andrew Bishop, Lawrence-Chenault, A. B. Comithiere, Lawrence Criner, Shingzie Howard, and Evelyn Preer, many of whom were associated with the Lafayette Players stock company. Actor and singer Paul Robeson made his first motion picture appearance in Micheaux's *Body and Soul* (1924), in a dual role as both a venal preacher and his virtuous brother. Micheaux returned often to the theme of the

See also

Paul Robeson

hypocritical preacher, a portrait inspired by the betrayal of his father-in-law, a Chicago minister. Of the actors Micheaux made celebrities in the black community, the most notable was Lorenzo Tucker, a handsome, light-skinned actor, dubbed "the colored Valentino." Micheaux's films also featured cabaret scenes and chorus line dancers, and, after the coming of sound, jazz musicians and comedians.

Although his company went bankrupt in 1928, Micheaux managed to survive the early Depression, continuing to produce silent films. Although *Daughter of the Congo* (1930) featured some songs and a musical score, *The Exile* (1931) was thought to be the first African-American-produced all-talking picture. Micheaux went on to make a number of sound films, but many moments in these films are undercut because his technicians could not surmount the challenges produced by the new sound-recording technology. In the late 1930s, after the brief notoriety of *God's Stepchildren* (1937), Micheaux's film activities began to wind down and he returned to writing novels. He published *The Wind from Nowhere* (1941), a reworking of *The Homesteader,* and three other novels during the next five years. In 1948, he produced a large-budget version of *The Wind from Nowhere,* titled *The Betrayal* and billed as the first African-American motion picture to play in major white theaters. However, the film received unfavorable reviews in the press, including *The New York Times.* At a time of his decline in popularity as both novelist and filmmaker, Micheaux died during a promotional tour in 1951 in Charlotte, N.C.

Micheaux's work was first rediscovered by film scholars in the early 1970s. However, these critics still disdained the wooden acting and unmatched shots in his films and decried what they thought to be the escapist nature of his stories. More recent critics, however, have hailed Micheaux as a maverick stylist who understood but was not bound by classical Hollywood cutting style, who used precious footage economically, who was adept in his use of the flashback device, and whose "rough draft" films were vaguely avant-garde. Similarly, Micheaux is not recognized for his "protest" films and his use of social types to oppose caricature rather than to reinforce stereotype.

Largely ignored during his lifetime, Micheaux has received recognition in recent years. The Black Filmmakers Hall of Fame inaugurated an annual Oscar Micheaux Award in 1974. In 1985, the Directors' Guild presented Micheaux with a special Golden Jubilee Award, and in 1987, he re-ceived a star on the Hollywood Walk of Fame. The recent discovery of prints of two silent films, *Within Our Gates* (1919) and *Symbol of the Uncon-quered* (1920) in archives in Spain and Belgium, respectively, has increased the interest in his work.

—JANE GAINES AND CHARLENE REGESTER

MINGUS, CHARLES, JR.

Charles Mingus, Jr. (April 22, 1922–January 5, 1979), jazz musician. Born in Nogales, Ariz., Charles Mingus straddled the bebop and free jazz eras. Although he became a virtuoso bassist early in his career, his main contribution to jazz was as a composer and bandleader. For over thirty years Mingus created a body of compositions matched in quality and variety only by Duke Ellington and Thelonious Monk, and ranging from somber but gritty tributes to Lester Young, Charlie Parker, and Eric Dolphy to roaring evocations of African-American gospel prayer meetings. Taking a cue from Ellington, Mingus generally wrote music for particular individuals in his superb ensembles, and such compositions were developed or "work-shopped" through in-concert rehearsals rather than from fixed and polished scores prior to per-formance and recording. Mingus's mercurial per-sonality thrived in these improvisational settings, but this process often made for chaos and disaster as well. He was notorious for berating audiences and musicians from the bandstand, even firing and rehiring band members during the course of performances. However, the workshops also achieved a spontaneity and musical passion un-matched in the history of jazz, as Mingus con-ducted and shouted instructions and comments from the piano or bass, at times in a wheelchair at the end of his life, even improvising speeches on civil rights.

Mingus grew up in the Watts section of Los Angeles, and in his youth studied trombone and cello before switching at age sixteen to the bass. He studied with Britt Woodman, Red Callender, Lloyd Reese, and Herman Rheinschagen, and began performing professionally while still a teenager. He played in the rhythm sections of the bands of Lee Young (1940), Louis Armstrong (1941–1943), Barney Bigard (1942), and Lionel Hampton (1947–1948). He made his first recordings with Hampton in 1947, a session that included Mingus's first recorded composition, "Mingus Fingers." Mingus played in Red Norvo's

See also

Jazz

trio from 1950 to 1951, quitting in anger after Mingus, who was not a member of the local musicians' union, was replaced by a white bassist for a television performance. Mingus settled in New York in 1951, and played stints with Duke Ellington, Billy Taylor, Stan Getz, and Art Tatum. His most important work in his early period was a single concert he organized and recorded for his own record label, Debut Records, at Toronto's Massey Hall in May 1953, featuring pianist Bud Powell, drummer Max Roach, and the reunited team of Charlie Parker and Dizzy Gillespie—the definitive bebop quintet.

Mingus formed his own music workshop in 1955 in order to develop compositions for a core of performers, and it is from this point that his mature style dates. He had played in the cooperative Jazz Composers' Workshop from 1953 to 1955, but it was as the tempestuous leader of his own group that he created his most famous works, which in concerts often became long, brooding performances, building to aggressive, even savage climaxes. His compositions used folk elements such as blues shouts, field hollers, call and response, and gospel-style improvised accompanying riffs. In this middle period, which lasted from 1955 to 1966, Mingus employed a number of notable musicians, including saxophonists Eric Dolphy, Rahsaan Roland Kirk, Jackie McLean, Booker Ervin, John Handy, Clifford Jordan, and Charles McPherson; drummer Dannie Richmond; pianists Mal Waldron and Jaki Byard; trombonist Jimmy Knepper; and trumpeter Ted Curson. He produced numerous albums that are considered classics, including *Tijuana Moods* (1957), *Mingus Ah-Um* (1959), the orchestral *Pre-Bird* (1960), *Mingus Oh Yeah* (1961), *Town Hall Concerts* (1962, 1964), and *Mingus Mingus Mingus* (1963), and notable compositions such as "Love Chant" (1955), "Foggy Day" (1955), "Percussion Discussion" (1955), "Pithecanthropus Erectus" (1956), "Reincarnation of a Lovebird" (1957), "Haitian Fight Song" (1957), and "The Black Saint and the Sinner Lady" (1963).

Politics also began to enter Mingus's music in the 1950s, and the two eventually became inseparable, with Mingus issuing explicit musical attacks against segregation and racism. "Meditations on Integration" (1964) was written in response to the segregation and mistreatment of black prisoners in the American South and recorded live at the Monterey Jazz Festival, while "Fables of Faubus" (1959) protested Orval Faubus, the segregationist governor of Arkansas. Mingus's activism also extended to attempts at having jazz musicians wrest

control of their careers out of the hands of club owners and recording executives. He twice organized his own record companies, Debut Records in 1952 and Charles Mingus Records in 1963. In 1960 he helped lead a musical revolt against the staid Newport Jazz Festival, and along with Ornett Coleman, Coleman Hawkins, and Max Roach, he formed a group known as the Newport Rebels, which held a counter-festival.

In his peak years Mingus often performed in settings outside the workshops. In 1958 he led a quintet accompanying Langston Hughes reciting his poetry on *The Weary Blues of Langston Hughes*. Further, though he gained fame early as a bassist in the tradition of Jimmy Blanton and Oscar Pettiford, he also on occasion hired a bassist and performed at the piano, and he released *Mingus Plays Piano* in 1963. In 1962 he recorded *Money Jungle*, a trio album with Duke Ellington and Max Roach.

In 1966 Mingus stopped performing, largely as a result of the psychological problems that had always plagued him. In 1969 financial problems forced him out of retirement, and despite his deteriorating physical condition due to amyotrophic lateral sclerosis, a progressive degenerative disease of the nervous system (also known as Lou Gehrig's disease), he experienced a new burst of creativity in the 1970s. He published his picaresque, fictionalized autobiography, *Beneath the Underdog*, and was awarded a Guggenheim fellowship in 1971. He thereafter worked regularly, recording *Mingus Moves* (1973), until 1977, when he fell ill after recording *Three or Four Shades of Blue*. He released his last albums, *Me, Myself an Eye* and *Something like a Bird*, in 1978. His last appearance on record was on *Mingus*, an album by the singer Joni Mitchell, in 1978. He died in Cuernavaca, Mexico.

—EDDIE S. MEADOWS

MINSTRELS/ MINSTRELSY

The minstrel show was the first uniquely American form of stage entertainment. Begun by white performers using black makeup and dialect to portray African Americans, the minstrel show was a popular sensation in the 1840s, dominated American show business until the 1890s, and had profound and enduring impacts on show business, racial stereotypes, and African Americans in the performing arts.

Jazz gave numerous African-American performers a largely unprecedented degree of acceptance, fame, and financial success.

PAGE 379

White men in blackface had portrayed black people almost since the first contact of the races. But in the 1820s—when American show business was in its infancy, and audiences demanded stage shows about American, not European, characters and themes—some white performers began to specialize in blackfaced acts they called "Ethiopian Delineation." In 1828 in Louisville, Ky., one of these "Delineators," Thomas D. Rice, saw a crippled African-American stablehand named Jim Crow doing an unusual song and dance. Rice bought the man's clothes, learned the routine, and became a stage star with his "Jump Jim Crow" act. After that, blackfaced whites became more and more popular on America's stages.

In 1843 in New York City, four of these blackfaced entertainers, calling themselves the Virginia Minstrels, staged the first full evening of what they billed as "the oddities, peculiarities, eccentricities, and comicalities of that Sable Genus of Humanity." The Virginia Minstrels were a great hit. Within a year, the minstrel show became a separate entertainment form that audiences loved. Although it was centered in the big cities of the North, it was performed almost everywhere, from frontier camps to the White House. In fact, when Commodore Perry's fleet entered Japan in 1853–1854, the sailors put on a blackfaced minstrel show for the Japanese.

Minstrel shows had three distinct parts. The first opened with a rousing group song and dance. Then the minstrels sat in a semicircle facing the audience. The dignified man in the middle, the interlocutor, used a commanding voice and precise, pompous language as the master of ceremonies. Flanking him, holding instruments such as banjos and fiddles, were entertainers who performed the musical numbers, most notably the songs of Stephen Foster. In his string of minstrel hits, including "Old Folks at Home," "Oh Susanna," "My Old Kentucky Home," and "Old Black Joe," Foster was a pioneer of a new eclectic American popular music, blending European parlor music he heard at home, frontier music he heard in Cincinnati theaters, and African-American music he heard in a servant's church. On the ends of the semicircle sat the most popular minstrels, the comedians, "Mr. Tambo" and "Mr. Bones," who were named after their instruments, the tambourine and the rhythm clacker bones. (Various performers assumed these two roles.) Wearing flashy clothes and exaggerated black makeup and speaking in heavy dialects laden with humorous malapropisms, the endmen traded puns, riddles, and jokes with the interlocu-

tor (the man in the middle between them). This new fast-paced verbal humor later matured in vaudeville and radio. The first part ended with an upbeat song and dance.

The second part, the olio, was essentially a variety show with performers coming on stage one at a time to do their specialties, everything from acrobatics to animal acts. This was again a forerunner of vaudeville and of radio and television variety shows.

The third part, a one-act production with costumes, props, and a set, was at times a parody of a popular play or a current event. But in the early years, it was usually a happy plantation scene with dances, banjo playing, sentimentalism, slapstick, and songs such as "Dixie," a minstrel hit first introduced in New York City. These productions mixing music, comedy, and dance provided the seeds for the later development of the musical comedy.

Minstrelsy was not just precedent-setting entertainment. It was entertainment in blackface. It was about race and slavery, and it was born when those issues threatened to plunge America into civil war. During that period of rising tensions northern whites, with little knowledge of African Americans, packed into theaters to watch white men in blackface act out images of slavery and black people that the white public wanted to see. From its inception, in every part of the show, minstrelsy used makeup, props, gestures, and descriptions to create grotesque physical caricatures of African Americans—big mouths and lips, pop eyes, huge feet, woolly hair, and literally black skin. Minstrels also evolved sharp contrasts between African Americans in the North and in the South. In the show's first part, some of the olio, and the nonplantation farces, northern minstrel blacks were either lazy, ignorant good-for-nothings or flashy, preening dandies. Southern minstrel blacks, in first-part songs and plantation finales, were happy, frolicking "darkies" or nostalgic "old uncles" and loving "mammies" devoted to their kind, doting masters and mistresses. In the 1850s, as political conflicts grew, minstrelsy often portrayed unhappy plantation runaways who longed to be back in the land of cotton. It even converted the powerful antislavery messages of *Uncle Tom's Cabin* into closing plantation farces of "Happy Uncle Tom."

Minstrelsy never pretended to be anything but escapist entertainment, but its racial caricatures and stereotypes allowed its huge northern white audiences to believe that African Americans were inferior people who did not belong in the North

See also

New York City

Uncle Tom's Cabin

and were happy and secure only on southern plantations. So there was no need for a civil war over slavery or for acceptance of African Americans as equals. Even after the Civil War and the abolition of slavery, minstrelsy continued these stereotypes, as if to support the racial caste system that replaced slavery and kept African Americans "in their place" in the South.

After the Civil War, for the first time a large number of African Americans themselves became minstrels. Realizing that the popularity of blackfaced whites gave them a unique wedge into show business, early African-American minstrels emphasized their race. They billed themselves as "genuine," "bona fide" "colored" people who were untrained ex-slaves re-creating their lives on the plantation. Except for the endmen, they rarely wore blackface. Northern white audiences were astonished by the variety of African Americans' skin colors and delighted by their shows. Although African-American minstrels did modify and diversify their material in subtle ways, the bulk of their shows reproduced and in effect added credibility to ingrained minstrel stereotypes. African-American minstrel troupes were so popular that they performed all over the United States, in Europe, and in the South Pacific, and forced white minstrels to cut back their plantation material to avoid the new competition. One "Minstrel Wanted" ad in 1883 even warned, "Non-colored performers need not apply."

By the 1880s, as a result of minstrelsy, African Americans were established in all phases of show business as performers, composers, managers, and owners, though the most successful troupes were owned by whites. But the successes of African-American minstrels came at great expense. Personally, they faced discrimination daily. Professionally, they did not get the credit they deserved as performing artists because of their image as untrained, natural entertainers. Creatively, they had to stay within restrictive roles. Racially, they appeared to confirm negative stereotypes of African Americans. But for decades, there were no other real choices for blacks in show business. For instance, Sam Lucas, a top minstrel composer and star by 1873, repeatedly tried to break free of minstrelsy. In 1875, he costarred in *Out of Bondage*, a serious musical drama about blacks' progress from slavery to the "attainment of education and refinement," and in 1878, he was the first of his race to star in a serious production of *Uncle Tom's Cabin*, a role long considered too difficult for an African American. But each time, he had to return to minstrelsy to make a living. Still, he and the other

pioneers laid the foundation for future generations.

Although minstrelsy as an entertainment institution was originally created and shaped by white performers playing to white audiences, African-American culture was part of its appeal from the beginning. Some blackfaced stars, like Thomas D. Rice, admitted copying their acts directly from individual African Americans. More often, touring white minstrels bragged in general of learning new material and performance styles from black people, and there is considerable evidence in early minstrelsy that they did. Hans Nathan has identified African-derived syncopated rhythms in early banjo tunes that were the forerunners of ragtime and jazz. Robert C. Toll has found characteristically African-American folklore and humor in the early shows. And minstrelsy's biggest debts to African-American culture were in dance. In fact, the only African-American star in early minstrelsy was the dancer William Henry "Juba" Lane. Before emigrating to England in 1848, he repeatedly outdanced whites with "the manner in which he beats time with his feet." Virtually the father of American tap dance, Lane was, according to dance historian Marian Hannah Winter, the "most influential single performer of nineteenth century American dance." Most African-American influence on minstrel dance was less direct but no less real, as Marshall Stearns and Jean Stearns have demonstrated, with everything from the "buck and wing" to the "soft shoe."

When a number of black people became minstrels, they brought a new infusion of African-American culture. For the first time, spirituals were part of minstrelsy. Black composers drew on traditional culture, as black dancers did with African-American steps and styles. Comedians, such as Billy Kersands, used the double-edged wit and guile of the black folk to get the African Americans seated in segregated sections laughing *with* them at the same time that whites laughed *at* them.

Since these examples have to be gleaned from the few studies of the sparse nineteenth-century sources, they are probably the tip of the iceberg. Still, they do indicate that minstrelsy was the first example of the enormous influence that African-American culture would have on the performing arts in America. It was also the first example of white Americans exploiting and profiting from the creativity of African Americans.

By the 1890s, as public interest shifted from plantations and ex-slaves to big cities and new European immigrants, minstrelsy's national pop-

See also
Jim Crow

M

ularity faded, though it survived in some areas for a long time. For white minstrels, the blackface that was once such an asset became a handicap, limiting their ability to compete with vaudeville—which could make race just one part of its shows—and with nonracial musicals. Ultimately, the blackfaced dialect act moved into vaudeville, musicals, movies, and radio. For African Americans, though minstrelsy remained a limited possibility, more promising opportunities opened up in musicals, popular music, and vaudeville. But the struggles against bias, restrictions, and discrimination had only begun. Long after minstrelsy was gone, its negative stereotypes and caricatures of African Americans remained deeply embedded in American show business and popular culture.

—ROBERT C. TOLL

MITCHELL, ARTHUR ADAMS, JR.

Arthur Adams Mitchell, Jr. (March 27, 1934–), dancer and choreographer. Born in New York City, the oldest son of five children, Mitchell began tap-dance lessons at the age of ten, sang in the Police Athletic League Glee Club and attended the High School of Performing Arts, where he progressed quickly through a modern dance major. He began his professional career while still a senior in high school when he appeared in the 1952 Paris revival of Virgil Thomson and Gertrude Stein's opera *Four Saints in Three Acts.* Upon graduation from high school he was the first male to receive the school's prestigious Dance Award.

Mitchell was accepted as a scholarship student at the School of American Ballet in 1952. Determined to overcome a late start in classical ballet technique, he also studied with ballet master Karel Shook at the Studio of Dance Arts in New York. His vibrant, agile performance style made him highly sought by contemporary modern dance choreographers; and during this period he performed with the Donald Mckayle Company, Sophie Maslow and the New Dance Group, Louis Johnson, and Anna Sokolow. In 1955, after only three years of concentrated ballet study, Mitchell joined the John Butler Company for a brief European tour. He returned to New York to join the New York City Ballet (NYCB) in November 1955.

Within his first week with NYCB, Mitchell danced a featured role in George Balanchine's *Western Symphony.* He became the first African-American principal dancer permanently associated with that company, but asked that there be no publicity about breaking a color barrier. In 1957 Balanchine created the centerpiece pas de deux of *Agon* for Mitchell and ballerina Diana Adams. Performances of this technically demanding, modernist work gained Mitchell international recognition as a principal dancer imbued with supple control and precise partnering skills. Mitchell stayed with the NYCB for fifteen years, dancing a range of leading roles that included spare, sensual works (Jerome Robbins's *Afternoon of a Faun*), neoclassic works (Balanchine's *Four Temperaments*), and pure classical ballets (Balanchine's *Allegro Brillante*). In 1962 Mitchell created the role of Puck in Balanchine's version of *A Midsummer Night's Dream,* winning critical and audience praise for his dramatic abilities and charismatic warmth.

Mitchell also performed in the Broadway productions of *House of Flowers* (1954), *Shinbone Alley* (1957), and *Noel Coward's Sweet Potato* (1968). He choreographed for Eartha Kitt at the Newport Jazz Festival in 1957, and appeared at the 1960 and 1961 Festival of Two Worlds in Spoleto, Italy. He danced as a guest artist with the Metropolitan Opera (1962), the Munich Ballet Festival (1963), the Stuttgart Opera Ballet (1963), and the National Ballet of Canada (1964). In 1967, at the invitation of the United States government, he helped organize the National Ballet Company of Brazil.

Well aware of his role as a trailblazer, Mitchell encouraged others to follow his example of excellence in classical ballet. He taught at the Katherine Dunham School, the Karel Shook Studio, and the Harlem School of the Arts, as well as the Jones-Hayward School in Washington, D.C. In 1968 Mitchell and Shook reacted to the assassination of the Rev. Dr. Martin Luther King, Jr., by forming the school that became the Dance Theatre of Harlem (DTH), although Mitchell "never actually started out to have a company. I wanted to start a school to get kids off the streets. But I couldn't tell the young people in the school to be the best they could when they had no place to go." DTH was cofounded in February 1969 by Mitchell and Shook to "prove that there is no difference, except color, between a black ballet dancer and a white ballet dancer."

Mitchell has received numerous honors and awards, including the 1975 Capezio Dance Award, the New York Public Library "Lion of the Performing Arts" Award for outstanding contri-

See also

Alvin Ailey

butions to the performing arts, the NAACP's Image Award of Fame, and numerous honorary doctorates including ones from Harvard, Princeton, and Williams College. In 1993 Mitchell was honored by David Dinkins, mayor of New York City, with a Handel Medallion Award, and by President Bill Clinton at the Kennedy Center Honors for lifetime contribution to American culture. In June 1994 he was awarded a MacArthur Fellowship.

—THOMAS F. DEFRANTZ

MONK, THELONIOUS SPHERE

Thelonious Sphere Monk (October 10, 1917–February 17, 1982), jazz pianist and composer. Thelonious Monk was born in Rocky Mount, N.C., but moved with his family to New York at age four and grew up in the San Juan Hill district of Manhattan. He began a career as a professional pianist in the mid-1930s, playing at house rent parties and touring for two years as the accompanist to a female evangelist. By 1940, he was a member of the house rhythm section at Minton's Playhouse, a nightclub in Harlem well known among musicians for its nightly jam sessions. Surviving live recordings from this period document a piano style firmly rooted in the stride-piano tradition, as well as a penchant for unusual reharmonizations of standard songs.

Monk had already written several of his best-known compositions by this period: "Epistrophy" and "'Round Midnight" were performed and recorded by the Cootie Williams big band as early as 1944, while "Hackensack" (under the name "Rifftide") was recorded in Monk's professional recording debut with the Coleman Hawkins Quartet in the same year. With their astringent and highly original approach to harmony, these compositions attracted the attention of the most adventurous jazz musicians, and placed Monk at the center of the emergent bebop movement during World War II.

Although well known within the inner circle of bebop musicians, Monk did not come to more general attention until later in the 1940s. Beginning in 1947, he made a series of recordings for the Blue Note label, documenting a wide range of his compositions. These recordings, which include "Criss Cross," "Ruby, My Dear," and "Straight, No Chaser," feature him as both improviser and composer.

While Monk was admired as a composer, his unusual approach to the piano keyboard, lacking the overt virtuosity of such bebop pianists as Bud Powell and bristling with dissonant combinations that could easily be misinterpreted as "wrong notes," led many to dismiss him initially as a pianist. An incident in 1951 in which he was accused of drug possession led to the loss of his cabaret card, precluding further performances in New York City until 1957. But he continued to record for the Prestige label, including the famous "Bags Groove" session with Miles Davis in 1954, and he began making a series of recordings for Riverside, including *Brilliant Corners* (1956).

An extended residency at the Five Spot, a New York night club, in the summer of 1957 with John Coltrane finally drew attention to Monk as one of the most important figures in modern jazz. From the late 1950s through the 1960s, Monk worked primarily with his quartet, featuring tenor saxophonist Charlie Rouse, touring both in this country and abroad and recording prolifically for Columbia. Increasingly, he turned to the solo piano, recording idiosyncratic performances not only of his own compositions but also of such decades-old popular songs as "Just a Gigolo." The feature-length film *Straight, No Chaser* (1988; directed by Charlotte Zwerin) documents Monk's music and

MONK, THELONIOUS
SPHERE

THELONIOUS MONK

Monk's compositions caught the attention of the most adventurous jazz musicians during the bebop movement.
PHOTOGRAPHS AND PRINTS DIVISION, SCHOMBURG CENTER FOR RESEARCH IN BLACK CULTURE, THE NEW YORK PUBLIC LIBRARY, ASTOR, LENOX AND TILDEN FOUNDATIONS

See also
Miles Davis
John Coltrane
Coleman Hawkins

459

life in the late 1960s. After 1971, he virtually re-tired from public life. But his reputation contin-ued to grow, as a younger generation of musicians discovered his compositions and responded to the challenge of improvising within their distinctive melodic and harmonic framework.

—SCOTT DEVEAUX

MONTGOMERY, ALA., BUS BOYCOTT

The Montgomery, Ala., Bus Boycott began on December 5, 1955, as an effort by black residents to protest the trial that day in the Montgomery Recorder's Court of Rosa McCauley Parks. She had been arrested on December 1 for violating the city's ordinance requiring racial segregation of seating on buses. The boycott had initially been intended to last only for the single day of the trial, but local black support of the strike proved so great that, at a meeting that afternoon, black community leaders decided to continue the boy-cott until city and bus company authorities met black demands: the adoption by the bus company in Montgomery of the pattern of seating segrega-tion used by the same company in Mobile; the hiring of black bus drivers on predominantly black routes, and greater courtesy by drivers to-ward passengers. The leaders formed the Mont-gomery Improvement Association (MIA) to run the extended boycott. At a mass meeting that evening, several thousand blacks ratified these de-cisions.

The Mobile plan sought by the boycott dif-fered from the Montgomery pattern in that pas-sengers, once seated, could not be unseated by drivers. In Mobile, blacks seated from the back and whites from the front, but after the bus was full, the racial division could be adjusted only when riders disembarked. On Montgomery's buses, the front ten seats were irrevocably reserved for whites, whether or not there were any whites aboard, and the rear ten seats were in theory sim-ilarly reserved for blacks. The racial designation of the middle sixteen seats, however, was adjusted by the drivers to accord with the changing racial composition of the ridership as the bus proceeded along its route. In Rosa Parks's case, when she had taken her seat, it had been in the black section of the bus. Two blocks farther on, all white seats and standing room were taken, but some standing room remained in the rear. Bus driver J. Fred

Blake then ordered the row of seats in which Parks was sitting cleared to make room for board-ing whites. Three blacks complied, but Mrs. Parks refused and was arrested. She was fined fourteen dollars.

Black Montgomerians had long been dissatis-fied with the form of bus segregation used in their city. It had originally been adopted, for streetcars, in August 1900, and had provoked a boycott that had lasted for almost two years. In October 1952 a delegation from the black Women's Political Council had urged the city commission to permit the use of the Mobile seating plan. In a special election in the fall of 1953, a racial liberal with strong black support, Dave Birmingham, was elected to the three-member city commission. Following his inauguration, blacks again pressed the seating proposal at meetings in December 1953 and March 1954. In May 1954, the presi-dent of the Women's Political Council, JoAnn G. Robinson, a professor of English at Alabama State College for Negroes, wrote to the mayor to warn that blacks might launch a boycott if white authorities continued adamant. During the mu-nicipal election in the spring of 1955, black lead-ers held a candidates' forum at which they posed questions about issues of interest to the black community. At the head of the list was the adop-tion of the Mobile seating pattern.

On March 2, only weeks before the election, a black teenager, Claudette Colvin, was arrested for violation of the bus segregation ordinance. Fol-lowing this incident, representatives of the city and the bus company promised black negotiators that a seating policy more favorable to African Americans would be adopted. However, Birming-ham, the racially liberal city commissioner elected in 1953, had integrated the city police force in 1954. As a result of hostility to this action and other similar ones, he was defeated for reelection in 1955 by an outspoken segregationist, Clyde Sellers. The other commissioners at once became less accommodating. By the time that Rosa Parks was arrested in December, the discussions had come to a standstill. Mrs. Parks, the secretary of the Montgomery branch of the National Associa-tion for the Advancement of Colored People (NAACP), shared with other black leaders the frustration that grew out of the negotiations with municipal authorities. This frustration produced her refusal to vacate her seat.

From the city jail, Parks telephoned Edgar D. Nixon, a Pullman porter who was a former presi-dent of the Montgomery NAACP branch. After

See also
Ralph D. Abernathy
Ku Klux Klan
NAACP

ROSA PARKS

Quiet Woman Starts a Race Revolution on the Bus

Rosa Louise McCauley Parks (February 4, 1913–), civil rights leader. Rosa McCauley was born in Tuskegee, Ala. She lived with relatives in Montgomery, where she finished high school in 1933 and attended Alabama State College. She met her husband, Raymond Parks, a barber, and they married in 1932. Rosa Parks worked as a clerk, an insurance salesperson, and a tailor's assistant at a department store. She was also employed at the time as a part-time seamstress by Virginia and Clifford Durr, two white residents of Montgomery who were staunch supporters of the black freedom struggle.

Parks had been active in civil rights work since the 1930s. She and her husband supported the Scottsboro defendants, a notorious case in which nine young black men were convicted in 1931 on questionable evidence for raping two white women. In 1943, Parks became one of the first women to join the Montgomery NAACP. She worked as a youth adviser, served as secretary for the local group from 1943 to 1956, and helped operate the joint office of the NAACP and the Brotherhood of Sleeping Car Porters. In addition, she worked with the Montgomery Voters League to increase black voter registration. During the summer of 1955, with the encouragement of the Durrs, Parks accepted a scholarship for a workshop for community leaders on school integration at the Highlander Folk School in Tennessee. It was an important experience for Parks, not only for the practical skills of organizing and mobilizing she learned, but because the racial harmony she experienced there nurtured and sustained her activism.

Popularly known as the Mother of the Civil Rights Movement, Parks is best known for her refusal to give up her seat for a white man on a segregated bus in Montgomery on December 1, 1955, an incident which sparked the Montgomery Bus Boycott. Contrary to popular belief, Parks was not simply a tired woman who wanted to rest her feet, unaware of the chain of events she was about to trigger. As she wrote in *Rosa Parks: My Story,* "the only tired I was, was tired of giving in." Parks was a veteran of civil rights activity and was aware of efforts by the Women's Political Council and the local NAACP to find an incident with which they could address segregation in Montgomery.

Parks was actively involved in sustaining the boycott and for a time served on the executive committee of the Montgomery Improvement Association, an organization created to direct the boycott. The intransigence of the city council was met by conviction and fortitude on the part of African Americans. For over a year, black people in Montgomery car-pooled, took taxis, and walked to work. The result was a ruling by the United States Supreme Court that segregation on city buses was unconstitutional.

As a result of her involvement in the bus boycott, Parks lost her job at the department store in Montgomery. In 1957, she and her husband moved to Detroit, where she worked as a seamstress for eight years before becoming administrative assistant for Congressman John Conyers, a position she held until 1988. After she moved to Detroit, Parks continued to be active in the Civil Rights Movement and joined the Southern Christian Leadership Conference (SCLC). She participated in numerous marches and rallies, including the 1965 march from Selma to Montgomery.

In the mid-1980s she was a supporter of the free South Africa movement and walked the picket lines in Washington, D.C., with other antiapartheid activists. She has made countless public appearances, speaking out on political issues as well as giving oral history lessons about the Civil Rights Movement. In 1987, ten years after the death of her husband, she founded the Rosa and Raymond Parks Institute for Self-Development in Detroit, a center committed to career training for black youth. The institute, a dream of hers, was created to address the dropout rate of black youth.

Parks, an international symbol of African-American strength, has been given numerous awards and distinctions, including ten honorary degrees. In 1979, she was awarded the NAACP's prestigious Spingarn Medal. In 1980, she was chosen by *Ebony* readers as the living black woman who had done the most to advance the cause of black America. In the same year she was awarded the Martin Luther King, Jr., Nonviolent Peace Prize by the Martin Luther King, Jr., Center for Nonviolent Social Change. In addition, the SCLC has honored her by sponsoring the annual Rosa Parks Freedom award.

—PAM NADASEN

See also
Civil Rights Movement

Nixon had posted bail for Parks, he called other prominent blacks to propose the one-day boycott. The response was generally positive. At JoAnn Robinson's suggestion, the Women's Political Council immediately began distributing leaflets urging the action. It was then endorsed by the city's black ministers and other leaders at a meeting at the Dexter Avenue Baptist Church. The result was almost universal black participation.

At the December 5 meeting, when it was decided to continue the boycott and to form the Montgomery Improvement Association (MIA), the Rev. Dr. Martin Luther King, Jr., was chosen as the MIA's president, principally because, as a young man who had lived in the city only fifteen months, he was not as yet involved in the bitter rivalry for leadership of the black community between Nixon and funeral director Rufus A. Lewis. Nixon was elected the MIA's treasurer, and Lewis was appointed to organize car pools to transport blacks to their jobs without having to use buses. The Rev. Ralph D. Abernathy was named to head the committee designated to reopen negotiations with the city and the bus company.

Initially, the renewed negotiations seemed promising. Mayor William A. Gayle asked a committee of white community leaders to meet with the MIA's delegates. But by January 1956, these discussions had reached a stalemate. The MIA's attorney, Fred D. Gray, urged that the MIA abandon its request for the Mobile plan in favor of filing a federal court lawsuit seeking to declare unconstitutional all forms of seating segregation. The MIA's executive board resisted this proposal until January 30, when Martin Luther King's home was bombed. One day thereafter, the executive board voted to authorize the suit, which was filed as *Browder* v. *Gayle* on February 1.

Meanwhile, similar strains were at work in the white community. A group of moderate businessmen, the Men of Montgomery, was attempting to mediate between the MIA and the city commission. But segregationists were pressing authorities to seek the indictment of the boycott's leaders in state court for violating the Alabama Anti-Boycott Act of 1921, which made it a misdemeanor to conspire to hinder any person from carrying on a lawful business. On February 20, an MIA mass meeting rejected the compromise proposals of the Men of Montgomery, and on February 21, the county grand jury returned indictments of eighty-nine blacks, twenty-four of whom were ministers, under the Anti-Boycott Act.

Martin Luther King, the first to be brought to trial, was convicted by Judge Eugene Carter at the end of March and was fined $500. King appealed, and the remainder of the prosecutions were suspended while the appellate courts considered his case. On May 11, a three-judge federal court heard *Browder* v. *Gayle* and on June 5, it ruled 2–1, in an opinion by Circuit Judge Richard Rives, that any law requiring racially segregated seating on buses violated the equal protection clause of the Constitution's Fourteenth Amendment. The city appealed to the U.S. Supreme Court. Both segregation and the boycott continued while the appeal was pending.

Throughout the thirteen months of negotiations and legal maneuvers, the boycott was sustained by mass meetings and its car-pool operation. The weekly mass meetings, rotated among the city's black churches, continually reinforced the high level of emotional commitment to the movement among the black population. Initially the car pool, modeled on one used during a brief bus boycott in Baton Rouge in 1953, consisted of private cars whose owners volunteered to participate. But as contributions flowed in from sympathetic Northerners, the MIA eventually purchased a fleet of station wagons, assigned ownership of them to the various black churches, hired drivers and established regular routes. Rufus Lewis administered the car pool until May 1956, when he was succeeded by the Rev. B. J. Simms.

White authorities eventually realized that the MIA's ability to perpetuate the boycott depended on its successful organization of the car pool. In November the city sued in state court for an injunction to forbid the car-pool operation on the ground that it was infringing on the bus company's exclusive franchise. On November 13, Judge Eugene Carter granted the injunction, and the car pool ceased operation the next day. But on that same day, the U.S. Supreme Court summarily affirmed the previous ruling of the lower federal court that bus segregation was unconstitutional. The city petitioned the Supreme Court for rehearing, and a final order was delayed until December 20. On December 21, 1956, the buses were integrated and the boycott ended.

The city was at once plunged into violence. Snipers fired into the buses; one of the shots shattered the leg of a pregnant black passenger, Rosa Jordan. The city commission ordered the suspension of night bus service. On January 10, 1957, four black churches and the homes of the Rev. Ralph Abernathy and of the MIA's only white board member, the Rev. Robert Graetz, were bombed and heavily damaged. All bus service was then suspended. On January 27, a home near that

See also

Martin Luther King, Jr.

of Martin Luther King, was bombed and destroyed, and a bomb at King's own home was defused. On January 30, Montgomery police arrested seven bombers, all of whom were members of the Ku Klux Klan.

The arrests ended the violence, and in March full bus service resumed. However, the first two of the bombers to come to trial were acquitted in May 1957, despite their confessions and the irrefutable evidence against them. Meanwhile, in April, the Alabama Court of Appeals had affirmed on technical grounds King's conviction under the Anti-Boycott Act. Because it was now clear that the other bombing prosecutions would be unsuccessful and because the boycott had ended in any case, prosecutors in November agreed to dismiss all the remaining bombing and antiboycott-law indictments in return for King's payment of his $500 fine.

The Montgomery Bus Boycott marked the beginning of the Civil Rights Movement's direct action phase, and it made the Rev. Dr. Martin Luther King, Jr., a national figure. Although the integration of the buses was actually produced by the federal court injunction rather than by the boycott, it was the boycott that began the process of moving the civil rights movement out of the courtroom by demonstrating that ordinary African Americans possessed the power to control their own destiny.

—J. MILLS THORNTON III

MORRISON, TONI

Toni Morrison (February 18, 1931–), writer. By the 1980s, Toni Morrison was considered by the literary world to be one of the major American novelists. In 1992—five years after she received the Pulitzer Prize for *Beloved* and the year of publication both for her sixth novel, *Jazz,* and for a series of lectures on American literature, *Playing in the Dark*—Morrison was being referred to internationally as one of the greatest American writers of all time. In 1993 she became the first black woman in history to be awarded the Nobel Prize for literature.

The road to prominence began with Morrison's birth into a family she describes as a group of storytellers. Born Chloe Anthony Wofford in Lorain, Ohio, she was the second of four children of George Wofford (a steel-mill welder, car washer, and construction and shipyard worker) and Ramah Willis Wofford (who worked at home and sang in church).

Her grandparents came to the North from Alabama to escape poverty and racism. Her father's and mother's experiences with and responses to racial violence and economic inequality, as well as what Morrison learned about living in an economically cooperative neighborhood, have influenced the political edge of her art. Her early understanding of the "recognized and verifiable principles of Black art," principles she heard demonstrated in her family's stories and saw demonstrated in the art and play of black people around her, has also had its effect. Morrison's ability to manipulate the linguistic qualities of both black art and conventional literary form manifests itself in a prose that some critics have described as lyrical and vernacular at the same time.

After earning a B.A. from Howard University in 1953, Morrison moved to Cornell University for graduate work in English and received an M.A. in 1955. She taught at Texas Southern University from 1955 to 1957 and then at Howard University (until 1964), where she met and married Harold Morrison, a Jamaican architect, and gave birth to two sons. Those were years that Morrison has described as a period of almost complete powerlessness, when she wrote quietly and participated in a writers' workshop, creating the story that would become *The Bluest Eye.*

In 1964, Morrison divorced her husband and moved to Syracuse, N.Y., where she began work for Random House. She later moved to a senior editor's position at the Random House headquarters in New York City—continuing to teach, along the way, at various universities. Since 1988, she has been Robert F. Goheen Professor of the Humanities at Princeton University.

Morrison's first novel, *The Bluest Eye* (1970), is a text that combines formal "play" between literary aesthetics and pastoral imagery with criticism of the effects of racialized personal aesthetics. *Sula* (1973) takes the pattern of the heroic quest and the artist-outsider theme and disrupts both in a novel that juxtaposes those figurations with societal gender restrictions amid the historical constraint of racism. *Song of Solomon* (1977), *Tar Baby* (1981), and *Beloved* (1987) are engagements with the relation to history of culturally specific political dynamics, aesthetics, and ritualized cultural practices.

Song of Solomon sets group history within the parameters of a family romance; *Tar Baby* interweaves the effects of colonialism and multiple family interrelationships that are stand-ins for history with surreal descriptions of landscape; and *Beloved* negotiates narrative battles over story and

See also

Literature

history produced as a result of the imagination's inability to make sense of slavery. In *Jazz*, Morrison continues her engagement with the problems and productiveness of individual storytelling's relation to larger, public history.

Morrison's seventh novel, *Paradise* (1998), concerns an all-black township in Oklahoma and the interaction of its residents with four troubled women who live in an abandoned school nearby.

The lectures published as *Playing in the Dark* continue Morrison's interest in history and narrative. The collection abstracts her ongoing dialogue with literary criticism and history around manifestations of race and racism as narrative forms themselves produced by (and producers of) the social effects of racism in the larger public imagination.

Morrison's work sets its own unique imprimatur on that public imagination as much as it docs on the literary world. A consensus has emerged that articulates the importance of Morrison to the world of letters and demonstrates the permeability of the boundary between specific cultural production—the cultural production that comes out of living as part of the African-American group—and the realm of cultural production that critics perceive as having crossed boundaries between groups and nation-states.

Morrison's ability to cross the boundaries as cultural commentator is reflected in *Race-ing Justice and Engendering Power: Essays on Anita Hill, Clarence Thomas, and the Construction of Social Reality*, a collection of essays about the nomination of Supreme Court Justice Clarence Thomas and the accusations of sexual harassment brought against him by law professor Anita Hill. The essays in the collection were written by scholars from various fields, then edited and introduced by Morrison.

—WAHNEEMA LUBIANO

MORTON, FERDINAND JOSEPH "JELLY ROLL"

Ferdinand Joseph "Jelly Roll" Morton (October 20, 1890–July 10, 1941), jazz pianist and composer. Although the facts concerning his early life remain in dispute, along with his claim to have singlehandedly invented jazz in the early years of the twentieth century, Jelly Roll Morton nonetheless remains the crucial figure in bridging nineteenth-century blues, vaudeville songs, and ragtime with the small jazz ensembles of the

1920s. He was born Ferdinand Joseph LaMothe in Gulfport, Miss. His father, a Creole carpenter and trombonist schooled in classical music, whose name has also been spelled "LeMenthe" and "Lemott," left the family when Ferdinand was a child. Ferdinand was raised in New Orleans, and took the last name of Ed Morton, his stepfather, who was a porter and trombonist. Jelly Roll played guitar and trombone before taking up piano as a teenager, performing at "sporting houses," which were bordellos in the red-light district of New Orleans known as Storyville. He also learned from pianists during his travels along the Gulf Coast as far as Florida. Morton studied with a professor of music from St. Joseph's Seminary College in Saint Benedict, La., but it was his 1902 meeting in New Orleans with the elegant ragtime pianist Tony Jackson, the composer of "Pretty Baby" and "The Naked Dance," that determined the direction of his career.

Morton left New Orleans around 1906, working in Louisiana and Mississippi as a pianist and as a small-time pool hustler, card shark, gambler, and pimp. In 1908 he moved to Memphis to work in a vaudeville show, and the next year he went on the road again, playing with vaudeville shows throughout the South, and possibly in New York, Chicago, and California. In 1911, he was performing as a pianist and comedian with McCabe's Minstrel Troubadours in St. Louis and Kansas City, and he eventually went to Chicago, where he settled for three years, leading his own band and managing a cabaret. He also published his first composition, "Jelly Roll Blues" (1915), the title referring to Morton's self-bestowed nickname, a slang term for the female genitals and sex in general. In 1915 he traveled to San Francisco, Chicago, and Detroit, and the next year he performed in and ran a hotel and nightclub in Los Angeles. Between 1917 and 1923 Morton traveled and worked up and down the West Coast, from Tijuana, Mexico, to Vancouver and Alaska, as well as to Colorado and Wyoming, and finally back to Los Angeles, where he worked for a time as a boxing promoter.

In 1923, Morton returned to Chicago for five years, working as a staff arranger for the Melrose Publishing House. But much more important, it was during this time that he took advantage of the growing market for "hot" records and made the recordings upon which his reputation rests. He recorded as a solo pianist in Richmond, Ind., in 1923 and 1924 ("London Blues," "Grandpa's Spell," "Milenburg Joys," "Wolverine Blues," "The Pearls"), and also with a white group called

See also

Jazz

the New Orleans Rhythm Kings. Even better known are recordings he made from 1926 to 1930 in Chicago and New York ("Kansas City Stomps," "Sidewalk Blues," "Smokehouse Blues," "The Chant," "Mournful Serenade," "Shreveport Stomp," "Ponchartrain Blues") with his Red Hot Peppers, an ensemble which included trombonist Kid Ory, clarinetists Johnny Dodds and Omer Simeon, and drummer Baby Dodds. During this time Morton continued to perform, touring the Midwest with W. C. Handy, playing second piano in Fate Marable's riverboat band, and fronting pianist Henry Crowder's band.

Morton was the first great jazz composer. In addition to those works already mentioned, notable compositions include "New Orleans Blues," "King Porter Stomp," "Frog-i-more Rag," "Mamanita," and "Black Bottom Stomp." Morton was also the most important pianist to emerge from early New Orleans jazz, playing in an artful blend of ornamental nineteenth-century salon music and stomping blues. His arranging provided a model for small jazz ensembles, allowing raw improvisational passages to animate sophisticated composed sections, always within the conventions of New Orleans instrumental ragtime. As an arranger and composer, Morton paid careful attention to instrumentation and ensemble effects. In this he was the prime forerunner of subsequent jazz composers.

In 1928 Morton moved to New York, where in addition to continuing recording with the Red Hot Peppers, he played for two months at Harlem's Rose Danceland, and in 1929 he led an all-girl revue in Chicago. In 1931 he again led his own ensemble in Harlem, and in 1932 he served as the accompanist for Harlem musical shows. In 1934 he worked as the house pianist at the Red Apple Club in Harlem, and recorded with the white trumpeter Wingy Manone. Despite his busy schedule, Morton found both his health and his career beginning to decline by the early 1930s. Interest in New Orleans jazz had ebbed in general, the Great Depression had caused a collapse of the record industry, and Morton was virtually financially ruined by investments in a cosmetics company.

In 1935 Morton moved to Washington, D.C., and played a two-year engagement at the Jungle Club. He worked as a nightclub manager in 1937. In 1938 he recorded eight hours of music and anecdotal reminiscences for John Lomax at the Library of Congress. While they are pioneering and indispensable as oral history, because of Morton's boastful obfuscations they raise as many historical questions as they answer. In addition to the dubious claim that he invented jazz in New Orleans in 1902 by playing four beats to the bar instead of ragtime's two, Morton, whose arrogant personality had earned him many enemies, bitterly complained that numerous famous jazz tunes had been stolen from him. Nevertheless, the interviews provide an unequaled glimpse into the creation of New Orleans jazz, along with Morton's often quite perceptive insights into the workings of his music. Alan Lomax's *Mister Jelly Roll* (1950) is a condensed version of the Library of Congress interviews.

In 1938 Morton also moved back to New York, organized a music publishing company, and began performing and recording again, just in time for a revival of interest in New Orleans jazz. In 1939 he performed solo, but a heart attack forced him into the hospital. The following year, with his health still in decline, Morton moved to Los Angeles, hoping to claim an inheritance from his godmother. There he formed a new music company and led a new group of musicians, but he was too sick to work, and died of heart disease in 1941. In 1992 Morton was the subject of a loosely biographical Broadway musical by George C. Wolfe, *Jelly's Last Jam,* which attracted national attention.

—LAWRENCE GUSHEE

MOSELEY-BRAUN, CAROL

Carol Moseley-Braun (August 16, 1947–), politician. Carol Moseley was born and raised in Chicago, the daughter of a Chicago police officer. She was educated at public schools in Chicago and the University of Illinois at Chicago, and received a law degree from the University of Chicago in 1972. Although now divorced, she has used her married name throughout her public career but hyphenated it after joining the Senate.

Moseley-Braun worked for three years as a prosecutor in the U.S. Attorney's office in Chicago. For her work there she won the U.S. Attorney General's Special Achievement Award. She began her career in politics in 1978, when she successfully campaigned for a seat in the Illinois House of Representatives. While in the Illinois House she was an advocate for public education funding, particularly for schools in Chicago. She also sponsored a number of bills banning discrimination in housing and private clubs. After two

Early jazz in New Orleans in the first years of the twentieth century developed from a melange of ragtime, marching bands, and the music of popular entertainment halls.

PAGE 511

465

M

terms Moseley-Braun became the first woman and first African American elected assistant majority leader in the Illinois legislature.

In 1987 Moseley-Braun again set a precedent by becoming the first woman and first African American to hold executive office in Cook County government when she was elected to the office of Cook County Recorder of Deeds. She held the office through 1992, when she waged a campaign for the U.S. Senate. When she defeated two-term incumbent Alan Dixon and wealthy Chicago attorney Al Hofeld in the Democratic primary, Moseley-Braun became the first black woman nominated for the Senate by a major party in American history. Moseley-Braun then went on to defeat Republican nominee Rich Williamson in a close general election, becoming the first black woman to hold a seat in the U.S. Senate.

During her first year in the Senate Moseley-Braun sponsored several pieces of civil rights legislation, including the Gender Equity in Education Act and the 1993 Violence Against Women Act, and reintroduced the Equal Rights Amendment.

—THADDEUS RUSSELL

MOSES, ROBERT PARRIS

Robert Parris Moses (January 23, 1935–), civil rights activist, educator. Bob Moses was born in New York City and raised in Harlem. He graduated from Hamilton College in 1956 and began graduate work in philosophy at Harvard University, receiving his M.A. one year later. Forced to leave school due to his mother's death, Moses taught mathematics at a private school in New York City. He first became active in the Civil Rights Movement in 1959, when he worked with Bayard Rustin, a prominent Southern Christian Leadership Conference (SCLC) activist, on organizing a youth march for integrated schools. A meeting with civil rights activist Ella Baker inspired Moses to immerse himself in the Civil Rights Movement that was sweeping the South. In 1960 Moses joined the Student Nonviolent Coordinating Committee (SNCC) and became the fledgling organization's first full-time voter registration worker in the deep south.

Moses, who often worked alone facing many dangerous situations, was arrested and jailed numerous times. In McComb, Miss., he spearheaded black voter registration drives and organized Freedom Schools. He grew to play a more central role in SNCC, and in 1962 he became the strategical coordinator and project director of the Congress of Federated Organizations (COFO)—a statewide coalition of the Congress of Racial Equality (CORE), SNCC, and the National Association for the Advancement of Colored People (NAACP). In 1963, COFO, with Moses as the guiding force, launched a successful mock gubernatorial election campaign—"the Freedom Ballot"—in which black voters were allowed to vote for candidates of their choosing for the first time. Its success led Moses to champion an entire summer of voter registration and educational activities to challenge racism and segregation in 1964, the Freedom Summer, with the purpose of capturing national attention forcing federal intervention in Mississippi.

During the Freedom Summer, Moses played an integral role in organizing and advising the Mississippi Freedom Democratic Party (MFDP)—an alternative third party which challenged the legitimacy of the all-white Democratic party delegation at the Democratic national convention in Atlantic City. After the 1964 summer project came to an end, SNCC erupted in factionalism. Moses's staunch belief in the Christian idea of a beloved community, nonhierarchical leadership, grassroots struggle, local initiative, and pacifism made him the leading ideologue in the early years of SNCC. Finding himself unwillingly drawn into the factional struggle, Moses left the organization and ended all involvement in civil rights activities. Later that year, he adopted Parris—his middle name—as his new last name, to elude his growing celebrity.

A conscientious objector to the Vietnam War, Moses fled to Canada to avoid the draft in 1966. Two years later he traveled with his family to Tanzania, where he taught mathematics. In 1976 Moses returned to the United States and resumed his graduate studies at Harvard University. Supplementing his children's math education at home, however, led him away from the pursuit of his doctorate and back into the classroom. In 1980 he founded the Algebra Project, with grants received from a MacArthur Fellowship, to help underprivileged children get an early grounding in mathematics to better their job opportunities in the future.

Moses viewed the Algebra Project—whose classes were directly modeled on Freedom Schools and Citizenship Schools from the early

See also
Civil Rights Movement

1960s—as an integral continuation of his civil rights work. He personally oversaw all teacher training to insure that the emphasis was placed on student empowerment, rather than dependence on the teachers. Creating a five-step learning method to help children translate their concrete experiences into complex mathematical concepts, Moses pioneered innovative methods designed to help children become independent thinkers. After proven success in raising students' standardized test scores in Massachusetts public schools, the project branched out to schools in Chicago, Milwaukee, Oakland, and Los Angeles, and Moses was once again propelled into the public eye. In 1992, in what he saw as a spiritual homecoming, Moses returned to the same areas of Mississippi where he had registered African-American voters three decades earlier, and launched the Delta Algebra project to help ensure a brighter future for children of that impoverished region.

—MARSHALL HYATT

MOTLEY, ARCHIBALD JOHN, JR.

Archibald John Motley, Jr. (1891–1981), painter. Archibald John Motley, Jr., was born in New Orleans. In 1894, he and his family, who were Roman Catholic and of Creole ancestry, settled on Chicago's South Side. Motley graduated from Englewood High School in 1914, receiving his initial art training there, and then began four years of study at the School of the Art Institute of Chicago, from which he graduated in 1918.

During his study at the School of the Art Institute, Motley executed highly accomplished figure studies. In their subdued coloring, careful attention to modeling, and slightly broken brushwork, these works reflect the academic nature of the training he received at that institution. In the late 1910s and 1920s, as racial barriers thwarted his ambition to be a professional portraitist, Mot-

The academic study and criticism of African-American writing has flourished in the last half of the twentieth century.

PAGE 416

WALTER MOSLEY

Prolific Writer Finds Success in New York Literary World

Walter Mosley (January 12, 1952–), novelist. The son of an African-American janitor and a Jewish clerk, Walter Mosley was born in Los Angeles, Calif., and raised in the South Central section of that city. After graduating from high school on the west coast, he attended Goddard College and later Johnson State University, both in Vermont. Upon receiving his B.A. in 1975 from Johnson State, Mosley worked at various jobs, including that of potter and caterer. Mosley moved to New York City in 1981 and enrolled in a graduate writing program at City College, while supporting himself as a computer programmer. It was during this time that he wrote his first novel, *Gone Fishing,* for which he was unable to find a publisher. Shortly thereafter, he completed *Devil in a Blue Dress,* the first of his "Easy Rawlins" detective novels. Mosley waited for six months to show the book to his mentor, novelist Frederic Tuten. Within a week of submitting the manuscript, Mosley signed a publishing contract with the publishing company Norton, quit his job, and began writing full time.

Mosley's hero, Ezekiel "Easy" Rawlins, is an African-American detective working the South Central section of Los Angeles with his sidekick "Mouse." *Devil in a Blue Dress* (1990) finds him in his late thirties, struggling to make his way in the often violent and racist, yet colorful and endearing, working-class world of South Central just after World War II. Mosley's subsequent novels—*A Red Death* (1991), *A White Butterfly* (1992), and *Black Betty* (1994)—see Rawlins through the McCarthy era and into the early 1960s. From the outset, the series was praised by critics and sold relatively well, but it became exceptionally popular after President Bill Clinton mentioned Mosley as one of his favorite authors during his 1992 campaign. Three of the books were nominated for Gold Dagger Awards by the British Crime Writers Association; *A White Butterfly* was nominated for the Edgar Award by the Mystery Writers of America. A film version of *Devil in a Blue Dress*—directed by Jonathan Demme and featuring Denzel Washington, Eddie Murphy, and Wesley Snipes—was released in 1995. Mosley's fifth Rawlins novel, *The Little Yellow Dog,* was published in 1996. *Always Outnumbered, Always Outgunned* (1998) introduces Socrates Fortlow, a brooding ex-convict who has just completed 27 years of hard labor.

—PAMELA WILKINSON

M

ley hired models and asked family members to pose for him. His sensitive, highly naturalistic portraits show his strong feeling for composition and color.

The young painter was honored in a commercially successful one-man exhibition of his work at New York City's New Gallery in 1928, and he spent the following year in Paris on a Guggenheim Fellowship. For this show Motley painted several imaginative depictions of African ethnic myths. Following the exhibition, he visited family members in rural Arkansas, where he created portraits and genre scenes, as well as landscapes of the region.

During his stay in Paris in 1929–1930, Motley portrayed the streets and cabarets of the French capital. In *Blues,* perhaps his best-known painting, he captured the vibrant and energetic mood of nightlife among Paris's African community.

After finding little outlet for his ambitions as a portraitist, Motley at an early point in his career turned his talents to the subject of everyday life in Chicago's Black Belt. Deeply influenced by the syncopated rhythms, vibrant colors, and dissonant and melodic harmonies of jazz, his paintings evoke the streets, bars, dance halls, and outdoor gathering spots of Chicago's Bronzeville during its heyday of the 1920s and 1930s. He treated these subjects in a broad, simplified abstract style distinct from that of his portraits. Motley's Bronzeville views are informed by a modernist aesthetic.

A figure in Chicago's creative Renaissance known as the new negro movement and a participant in such mainstream artistic endeavors as the WPA Federal Arts Project, Motley applied a modernist sense of color and composition to images whose subjects and spirit drew on his ethnic roots. Between 1938 and 1941, he joined numerous other Illinois artists as an employee of the federally sponsored arts projects of the depression era. For institutions in Chicago and other parts of the state he painted easel pictures and murals, the latter often on historical or allegorical themes.

Motley visited Mexico several times in the 1950s, where he joined his nephew Willard Motley, the writer, and a host of expatriate artists. His Mexican work ranges from brightly colored, small-scale landscapes to large, mural-like works that were influenced in style and subject by the social realism of modern Mexican art.

At the end of his career, Motley experimented in several new directions. In his long lifetime he produced a relatively small number of works, of which the most important, *The First One Hundred*

Years, is his only painting with an overt political message. Today Motley is recognized as one of the founding figures of twentieth-century African-American art.

—JONTYLE THERESA ROBINSON

MOTLEY, CONSTANCE BAKER

Constance Baker Motley (September 14, 1921–), lawyer and judge. Constance Baker Motley was the first African-American woman to be elected to the New York State Senate, the first woman to be elected Manhattan borough president, and the first black woman to be appointed a federal judge. She was born in New Haven, Conn., to immigrants from the Caribbean island of Nevis. She graduated from high school with honors in 1939, but could not afford college. Impressed by her participation in a public discussion and by her high school record, Clarence Blakeslee, a local white businessman, offered to pay her college expenses.

Motley enrolled at Fisk University in February 1941, transferred to New York University, and received a bachelor's degree in economics in October 1943. She enrolled at Columbia Law School in February 1944 and graduated in 1946. In 1945, during her final year at Columbia, she began to work part-time as a law clerk for Thurgood Marshall at the NAACP Legal Defense and Educational Fund, and continued full-time after graduation, eventually becoming one of its associate counsels. Because Marshall's staff was small and there was little work being done in civil rights, Motley had the unusual opportunity to try major cases before circuit courts of appeal and the United States Supreme Court. From 1949 to 1964, she tried cases, primarily involving desegregation, in eleven southern states and the District of Columbia, including cases that desegregated the University of Mississippi (*Meredith* v. *Fair,* 1962) and the University of Georgia (*Homes* v. *Danner,* 1961). She helped write the briefs for the landmark desegregation case *Brown* v. *Board of Education* (1954), and won nine of the ten cases she argued before the Supreme Court.

She left the NAACP in 1964 to run for the New York State Senate, to which she was elected in February 1964, becoming only the second woman elected to that body. She left the Senate in February 1965, when she was elected Manhattan borough president, becoming only the third black

See also
NAACP

to hold this office. On January 25, 1966, President Lyndon B. Johnson appointed her to the bench of the United States District Court for the Southern District of New York. She was confirmed in August 1966, becoming both the first black and the first woman to be a federal judge in that district. On June 1, 1982, she became the chief judge of her court, serving in this position until October 1, 1986, when she became a senior judge.

—SIRAJ AHMED

MOTOWN

Motown, which was founded in 1959 in the basement of Berry Gordy, Jr.'s Detroit home and grew to become the largest black-owned company in the United States, virtually defines the style of African-American popular music known as soul. Integrating the unrestrained vocals, hand claps, and tambourine accents of black gospel music, the strong backbeat of rhythm and blues, the heavily produced sound of white popular music, and the detailed, narrative-style love lyrics of doo-wop and vocal group songs, Motown has always signified a range of African-American pop music styles. Drawing on untrained recruits from the churches and projects of Detroit, Motown nurtured many prominent figures of postwar American popular music, including Smokey Robinson, Marvin Gaye, The Temptations, The Four Tops, Diana Ross, Stevie Wonder, the Jackson 5, and the Commodores.

Gordy, a former boxer and record store owner who had worked on the assembly line at Ford and had written several of Jackie Wilson's hits, started his musical empire with two small record labels, Tamla Records and Gordy Records. At first, Gordy worked with his brothers, sisters, and friends to produce Motown's records. By 1962 Gordy was comparing Motown with the Detroit auto industry that gave the label its name, a contraction of "Motor Town." At the height of Motown's fame starting in 1963, the production schedules at "Detroit's other assembly line," were indeed arduous, but consistently successful.

Gordy and his producers created dozens of classic soul records in Motown's cramped basement studio. Even after 1963, when the Motown sound became more elaborate, recordings were largely improvised on the spot. Motown's house band of Joe Hunter or Earl Van Dyke on piano, drummer Benny Benjamin, and electric bassist James Jamerson (1938–1983) was provided with sketchy lead sheets of chords. They responded with the inventive figures behind hits like the Temptations' "My Girl" and Martha and the Vandellas' "Nowhere to Run," on which Jamerson is virtually the lead player.

Gordy also prepared his acts for performances on traveling tours known as the Motown Revue. In 1964 Gordy hired a consultant, Maxine Powell, to teach Motown's artists everything from makeup to deportment, readying them for audiences as racially diverse as those at Harlem's Apollo Theater, Las Vegas, and prime time television. In 1965 Motown hired the tap dancer Cholly Atkins to choreograph its acts. Atkins perfected the "Temptations' Walk" and taught The Supremes their demure half-turns and dance steps.

Smokey Robinson was the first of Motown's songwriter-producers, writing and producing six of Motown's first ten Top Ten hits. He specialized in wistful tunes and surprising lyrics, such as "I don't like you/But I love you," from the Miracles' "You Really Got a Hold on Me" (1963), and "I've got sunshine on a cloudy day," from the Temptations' "My Girl" (1965). His other songs included "The One Who Really Loves You," "You Beat Me to the Punch," "Two Lovers," and "My Guy." Starting in 1964 Robinson took over the direction of the Temptations. He gave them a song he had written for himself, "The Way You Do the Things You Do," and picked Eddie Kendricks (1939–1992), whose falsetto resembled Robinson's, to sing lead. A year later he wrote "My Girl," but instead of Kendricks he chose David Ruffin (1941–1992), a gruff, raspy gospel-styled baritone, to sing lead. Robinson also had hits with Marvin Gaye and with the Marvelettes.

The most famous version of the "Motown Sound" was largely the creation of two brothers, Eddie and Brian Holland, and Lamont Dozier, usually known as Holland-Dozier-Holland, or H-D-H. Starting in 1963, while writing for and producing Martha and the Vandellas, the Four Tops, and the Supremes, they created an instantly recognizable style: drums and tambourines on all the beats, vibraphone in tandem with piano, a throaty baritone saxophone, Jamerson's pulsating bass lines, and melodic riffs that counterpointed the melody of the lyrics instead of merely marking time. H-D-H cut thirty top-ten pop hits, among them five straight number ones for the Supremes in 1964 and 1965: "Where Did Our Love Go?" "Baby Love," "Come See About Me," "Stop! In the Name of Love," and "Back in My Arms Again."

Although black-owned, many top financial positions at the cluster of companies that made up

The Supremes were one of Motown's most successful rhythm and blues acts and one of the most successful recording groups of all time.

PAGE 663

See also

Michael Jackson

Literature

MOTOWN

Motown—including Tamla Records, Gordy Records, Motown Records, Jobete Music Publishing, Hitsville USA, and International Talent Management—were eventually filled by whites. Gordy was often accused of mistreating his performers financially. Motown lawyers wrote contracts that performers often never saw and paid them royalties that were well below industry standards. Motown also used the money performers made from live shows and songwriting to subsidize production costs for their next recordings, a practice known as cross-collateralization. By the end of the decade, Mary Wells, H-D-H, David Ruffin of the Temptations, and others had sued the company for keeping them in what Ruffin's lawyers called "economic peonage." Still, Motown

---

BERRY GORDY, JR.
Music Man Founds Legendary Motown Records

Berry Gordy, Jr. (November 28, 1929–), music executive. Born in Detroit, Berry Gordy, Jr., the third in his family to carry that name, was attracted to music as a child, winning a talent contest with his song "Berry's Boogie." He also took up boxing, often training with his friend, Jackie Wilson. Gordy quit high school to turn professional; however, he soon gave up that career at the urging of his mother. After spending 1951 to 1953 in the Army, Gordy married Thelma Louise Coleman and began to work in the Gordy family printing and construction business.

In 1953 Gordy opened a jazz record store in Detroit. However, since rhythm and blues records were more in demand, the business closed after only two years. Gordy then began working at a Ford Motor Co. assembly line, writing and publishing pop songs on the side, including "Money, That's What I Want" (1959). During this time Gordy, who had separated from his wife, wrote some of Jackie Wilson's biggest hits, including "Lonely Teardrops" (1958), "That Is Why I Love You So" (1959), and "I'll Be Satisfied" (1959). He also sang with his new wife, Raynoma Liles, whom he had married in 1959, on a number of records by the Detroit singer Marv Johnson. In the late 1950s Gordy met and worked with Smokey Robinson and the Matadors, who at Gordy's suggestion became the Miracles. Gordy recorded them on their first record, "Got a Job" (1958).

During this period Gordy became increasingly dissatisfied with leasing his recordings to larger record companies, who often would take over distribution. At the urging of Robinson, Gordy borrowed $800 and founded Tamla Records and Gordy Records, the first companies in what would become the Motown empire. He released "Way Over There" (1959) and "Shop Around" (1961) by the Miracles. Gordy began hiring friends and family members to work for him, and he began to attract young unknown singers, including Diana Ross, Marvin Gaye, Mary Wells, and Stevie Wonder. The songwriting team of Eddie Holland, his brother Brian, and Lamont Dozier began to write songs for Gordy, who had formed a base of operations at 2648 Grand Boulevard in Detroit. From that address Gordy also formed the publishing and management companies that would constitute the larger enterprise known more generally as Motown. Over the next ten years, Motown, with Gordy as chief executive and chief shareholder, and often producer and songwriter as well, produced dozens of pop and rhythm-and-blues hits that dominated the new style known as soul music.

In the mid–1960s Gordy began to distance himself from the company's day-to-day music operations, spending more and more time in Los Angeles, where he was growing interested in the film and television industries. He divorced Raynoma in 1964, and married Margaret Norton, whom he also later divorced. (Gordy again married in 1990, but that marriage, to Grace Eton, ended in divorce three years later.)

In the late 1960s, many Motown performers, writers, and producers complained about Gordy's paternalistic and heavy-handed management of their finances. Some of them—including the Jackson 5, Holland-Dozier-Holland, and the Temptations—left the company, claiming that Gordy had misled and mistreated them. By this time he was also quite wealthy, living in a Los Angeles mansion that contained a portrait of himself dressed as Napoleon Bonaparte. He resigned as president of the Motown Records subsidiary in 1973 in order to assume the chair of Motown Industries, a new parent corporation. The following year he completed what had been a gradual move of Motown to Los Angeles and produced several successful television specials. His film ventures—including the Diana Ross vehicles *Lady Sings the Blues* (1973), *Mahogany* (1975), and *The Wiz* (1978)—were not as successful.

Despite the departure of its core personnel over the years, the company Gordy presided over in the 1980s remained successful, with more than $100 million in annual sales in 1983, making it the largest black-owned company in the United States. In 1984 Gordy allowed MCA to begin distributing Motown's records, and the company bought Motown in 1988 for $61 million. Gordy kept control of Gordy Industries, Motown's music publishing, film, and television subsidiaries. His net worth in 1986, as estimated by *Forbes*, was more than $180 million, making him one of the wealthiest people in the United States. In the late 1980s and '90s Gordy branched out into other fields, including sports management and the ownership and training of racehorses.

Although Gordy, who was inducted into the Rock and Roll Hall of Fame in 1988, began his career as a successful songwriter and producer, his greatest achievement was selling soul music to white pop audiences, thus helping to shape America's youth into a single, huge, multiracial audience.

—JONATHAN GILL

grew steadily, and by 1965 the company was grossing $8 million a year, and had 100 employees in Detroit, New York, and Los Angeles.

By 1967, Motown was undergoing personnel and musical changes. Norman Whitfield (1943–) took charge of the Motown production line. Writing with his partner Barrett Strong (1941–) and producing by himself, he took over the Temptations in 1966 with "Ain't Too Proud to Beg." Whitfield highlighted the raspy gospel sound of David Ruffin's voice and the increasing influence of funk. New sounds like stutter-step polyrhythms, one-chord vamps, and fuzztone lead guitars all challenged the old Motown Sound, and resulted in the Temptations' "Cloud Nine" (1968), "Psychedelic Shack" (1969), and the eleven-minute "Papa Was a Rolling Stone" (1972).

The early 1970s saw important career changes for several musicians who had been with Motown almost from the start. Marvin Gaye's conceptual album, *What's Going On* (1971), originally rejected by Gordy, spawned three top-ten hits: "What's Going On," "Mercy, Mercy, Me," and "Inner City Blues." In the same year, 1971, Stevie Wonder turned twenty-one, and altered his contract with Motown in order to begin a series of albums which included *Where I'm Coming From* (1971), *Music of My Mind* (1972), *Talking Book* (1972) and *Innervisions* (1973). Wonder wrote and produced these records and played virtually every instrument himself. Motown's last discovery of the 1960s was the Jackson 5. Cut with musicians from Los Angeles, the Jackson's first four singles went to number one. Sizzling, danceable pop, the first two releases, "I Want You Back" (1969) and "ABC" (1970), featured vocals by Motown's new boy star, Michael Jackson.

As early as 1963, Gordy involved Motown in the Civil Rights Movement, releasing *The Great March to Freedom* containing the Rev. Dr. Martin Luther King, Jr.'s "I Have a Dream" speech. In the early 1970s Motown started a new spoken word label, Black Forum, which produced King's Grammy Award-winning *Why I Oppose the War in Vietnam* (1970), as well as *Guess Who's Coming Home: Black Fighting Men Recorded Live in Vietnam* (1970), and albums by Langston Hughes and Margaret Danner (1970), Stokely Carmichael (1970), Amiri Baraka (1972), Ossie Davis and Bill Cosby (1972), and Elaine Brown (1973).

In the early 1970s Gordy moved Motown to Los Angeles, where he became increasingly involved in television specials, which were quite successful, and films, which were not. In 1973 Motown was the biggest black-owned company in the United States, and Gordy helped finance and produce *Lady Sings the Blues* (1972), *Mahogany* (1975), and *The Wiz* (1978), all of which starred Diana Ross. Despite the departure of many of Motown's key musical and financial figures, the company remained strong. Diana Ross, Stevie Wonder, the Commodores, and Rick James, continued to put Motown's records on the charts.

By the 1970s, Motown had become a financial giant as well as a dominant musical influence. In 1973 the company had grossed $40 million. Five years later, that figure was up to $60 million. In 1981 Gordy made Suzanne De Passe president of Motown Productions. She concentrated on television specials, with great success, and in 1983 the company grossed $104 million. The next year, Gordy signed a distribution agreement with MCA, an ironic return to the corporate involvement that had inspired him to start his own record company. Further ventures in television and film, including *The Last Dragon* (1985), proved largely unsuccessful. Consequently, Gordy was soon entertaining offers for Motown, and in 1988 he sold the company—then the fifth largest black-owned business in the country, with $100 million in sales and 257 employees—to MCA for $61 million. Gordy remained in control of Motown's music publishing and television and film subsidiaries. However, in 1993, MCA in turn sold the company to Polygram for $325 million. Polygram revitalized Motown, developing several major pop acts, including the singer Johnny Gill, and the vocal group Boyz II Men. Since 1985 Motown's original headquarters, the house at 2468 West Grand Boulevard in Detroit, has been a museum dedicated to the history of the company.

—HARRIS FRIEDBERG

MUDDY WATERS (MORGANFIELD, MCKINLEY)

Muddy Waters (McKinley Morganfield) (April 4, 1915–April 30, 1983), blues singer and guitarist. Muddy Waters grew up in Clarksdale, Miss., and took up the harmonica at age seven. He switched to the guitar at seventeen and soon began playing at local gatherings. He recorded both as a soloist and with a string band in 1941–1942 for a Library of Congress field-recording project. Moving to Chicago in 1943, he began playing the electric

Black Pentecostalism became the carrier of black religious folk music, noted for its call-and-response, improvisation, polyrhythms, and diatonic harmonies.

PAGE 537

See also
Amiri Baraka
Stokely Carmichael
Ossie Davis

471

guitar, recording for the Aristocrat label (later Chess Records) by 1947 under the name Muddy Waters. He began performing with a band that featured harmonica player Little Walter; their recording "Louisiana Blues," made late in 1950, became a nationwide hit, entering the rhythm and blues Top Ten. The band, which also included Otis Spencer (pianist) and Jimmy Rogers (guitar), had many Top Ten hits in the 1950s, including "I'm Your Hoochie Coochie Man" (1953) and "I'm Ready" (1954). Muddy Waters continued to tour throughout the United States and Europe in the 1960s and received much acclaim as a primary influence on many "British Invasion" musicians. He remained active as a performer for the rest of his life, winning Grammy awards for several later recordings. He was inducted into the Rock and Roll Hall of Fame in 1987.

Muddy Waters retained a style that evoked the sound of the Delta blues in a band contest. His Library of Congress recordings illustrate the influence of Son House through their searing slide guitar playing, which he maintained throughout his band recordings in the 1950s. In contrast to the smoother Chicago blues of Big Bill Broonzy, Muddy Waters brought a tough, aggressive edge to the urban blues, making him a seminal figure in the development of the style and establishing him among the most important post–World War II blues singers.

—DANIEL THOM

MURPHY, ISAAC

Isaac Murphy (April 16, 1861–February 12, 1896), jockey. Isaac Murphy was born a slave in Fayette County, Ky. After emancipation, his family moved to Lexington, where Murphy apprenticed as a jockey. In 1878, he rode in his first horse race, and in 1879 he attracted national attention by riding to first place in the Phoenix Hotel Stakes and Clark Handicap and placed second in the Kentucky Derby. Over the next four years, Murphy emerged as a leading jockey on the national circuit and in 1883 won a remarkable 51 out of 133 races.

Murphy's greatest successes came in the 1884 and 1885 seasons, when he rode with the Corrigan Stable of New York City. In 1884, he took first place in the American Derby at Chicago and then rode Buchanon to the first of Murphy's three victories in the Kentucky Derby. Murphy's most famous race came in 1890, in a match with Snapper Garrison, the top white jockey of the time. A

great deal of excitement surrounded the race, as horseracing enthusiasts had debated for a decade over who was the better jockey. Murphy rode Salvator to a tight, half-head decision over Garrison's mount, Tenny. In the same year, Murphy again took the Kentucky Derby crown aboard Riley, and in 1891 he won his third crown aboard Kingman.

Although they are virtually nonexistent today, black jockeys were prominent in horseracing until the end of the nineteenth century, when the emergence of Jim Crow laws forced virtually every African American from the sport. Creeping segregation, combined with Murphy's weight problems and alcoholism, essentially ended his career after 1891. He died of pneumonia in 1896.

Murphy's record is one of the greatest in the history of horseracing. He won a remarkable 44 percent of his races, was the first jockey to win three Kentucky Derbys, and in 1955 was the first jockey elected to the National Museum of Racing Hall of Fame.

—THADDEUS RUSSELL AND LINDA SALZMAN

MUSICAL THEATER

Musical theater—formal, staged entertainments combining songs, skits, instrumental interludes, and dances—was relatively uncommon in America before the middle of the eighteenth century. It is very likely that slave musicians occasionally took part in the earliest colonial period musical theatricals, called ballad operas, at least in the orchestra pit, since many slaves were known to be musically accomplished. Less than fully developed theatrical shows that involved satirical skits by slaves about white masters are recorded in the late eighteenth century. These skits, related to African story-telling traditions, were the seeds from which black American theatricality sprang. "Negro songs" or "Negro jigs" are also recorded in the shows of this period, suggesting the impact of an unnotated tradition of black music making on the musical theater song repertory (Southern 1983, p. 89).

Up to the Civil War

The opening of the African Grove theater in 1821 near lower Broadway in New York inaugurated the staging of plays with music "agreeable to Ladies and Gentlemen of Colour" (Southern 1983, 119). Led by playwright Henry Brown, the African Grove players produced Shakespeare's *Hamlet, Othello,* and *Richard III* (including inserted songs), popular potpourris such as *Tom and*

See also

Slavery

Jerry; or Life in London, and the pantomime *Obi; or, Three Finger'd Jack.* James Hewlett was the company's principal singer and actor. Ira Aldridge, who later made his career in Europe, sang songs at the Grove. Despite the theater's popularity, it was plagued by hooligans and closed in 1829.

Various musical shows were produced with black performers periodically in Philadelphia and New Orleans, though very little information survives about these shows. New Orleans could command orchestral forces (as opposed to the modest pit band of violin, clarinet, and double bass at the African Grove) for theatricals, and it engaged black players in the 1840s. In the 1850s and '60s African-American actors became traveling entertainers or joined minstrel shows.

The Late Nineteenth Century

The Hyers Sisters touring company, founded in 1876, became the first established African-American musical comedy troupe. Managed by Sam Hyers, the company featured his two daughters, Emma Louise and Anna Madah, and a string of male comedy singer/actors: Fred Lyon, Sam Lucas, Billy Kersands, Wallace King, and John and Alexander Luca. The Hyers began as a concert-giving group but moved on to fully staged musical plays that often dealt with racial themes: *Out of Bondage* (1876); *Urlina, or The African Princess* (1879); *Peculiar Sam; or, The Underground Railroad* (1879); and *Plum Pudding* (1887). The music they presented included jubilee songs, spirituals, operatic excerpts, and new popular songs and dances.

By the 1890s a few specific plays regularly toured and featured parts for black singers, usually in the guise of "plantation slaves." Bucolic scenes or other scenarios in the cotton field, on the levee, or in a camp meeting were meant to evoke an idyllic antebellum South. Turner Dazey's *In Old Kentucky* (1892) and *The South before the War* (1893) included black singers and dancers, as did the most famous of all shows of this type, *Uncle Tom's Cabin* (based on Harriet Beecher Stowe's novel of 1852). The huge number and variety of staged versions of this powerful work made it a unique dramatic vehicle in American culture. Many African-American "jubilee" singing groups, typically male quartets, took part in the play, although early performances rarely used black actors. It served the careers of solo banjo virtuoso Horace Weston in 1877 and vaudevillian Sam Lucas, who played the role of Uncle Tom in the 1880s.

At least a half-dozen all-black companies, as well as some integrated ones, appeared before the end of the century. Black choral singers and supernumeraries, including children, brought literally hundreds of people to the stage in productions in the 1880s and 1890s. Other festivals featuring black vaudeville acts, musical specialties, and historical tableaux, with titles like *Black America* (1895) and *Darkest America* (1897), were well-attended showcases but did not present complete plays.

The most widely acclaimed operatic singer of the period to become involved with traveling musical theatrical companies was Sissieretta Jones, known as the Black Patti (after the renowned soprano Adelina Patti). In 1896 she formed the Black Patti Troubadours and remained an important presence on the road for two decades, eventually mounting full-fledged musical comedies.

White burlesque entrepreneur Sam T. Jack formed the Creole Company in 1890 to do the skit *The Beauty of the Nile; or, Doomed by Fire,* using the novelty of black women in a minstrel line that emphasized glittery, revealing costumes and diverse musical acts. John Isham, Jack's advance man, developed his own potpourri shows presented by mixed male and female companies known as the Octoroons (1895), one of which toured in Europe. All of Isham's shows exploited the popularity of exotic costumes, operatic excerpts, musical specialties, spectacular scenery, and attractive women, while avoiding farcical minstrel show caricatures.

The First Black Musicals and the Growth of Black Vaudeville, 1897–1920

Within this world of extravagant eclecticism, full-length musical comedies—plays in which songs were frequent and newly composed if not integral—became more and more common. The first musical written by and for African Americans, "Bob" Cole and Billy Johnson's *A Trip to Coontown* (1897), was built up from Cole's songs and vaudeville turns with the Black Patti Troubadours (Cole had also managed her show in its first season) and other elements: a trio from Verdi's opera *Attila,* Sousa's new march "The Stars and Stripes Forever," a tune by Cole that was later stolen to become Yale University's fight song "Boola Boola," energetic dancing, topical humor, and social commentary. The show eschewed the Old South nostalgia typical of the earlier touring shows. Minstrel tunes were replaced by snappy up-tempo, occasionally syncopated songs written by different composers.

See also
Minstrels and Minstrelsy

At the same time, cakewalk dancers/comedians Bert Williams and George Walker, in the course of several productions from 1898 to 1908, expanded their routines to even more ambitious dimensions, with elaborate plots and often African settings: *The Policy Players* (1899); *The Sons of Ham* (1900); *In Dahomey* (1902); *Abyssinia* (1905); and *Bandanna Land* (1907). Will Marion Cook, classical violinist and European-trained composer, wrote most of the music for these landmark shows in a unique syncopated style. Cook's sensational Broadway debut—his musical skit *Clorindy* was produced at the Casino Theatre Roof Garden in 1898—established him as a leading figure, along with its dancing star, Ernest Hogan.

In 1899 Bob Cole formed a partnership with the brothers J. Rosamond Johnson and James Weldon Johnson. This young trio wrote songs for many shows and performers, black and white, to great success, and later composed comic operettas for all-black casts entitled *The Shoo-Fly Regiment* (1906) and *The Red Moon* (1908); they also starred in the shows themselves. Black, white, and mixed audiences found these many early twentieth-century efforts attractive, but any hope for sustained development was dashed by the premature deaths of the leaders, Ernest Hogan, George Walker, and Bob Cole, around 1910 and the un-remitting financial burden of mounting and touring with a large cast. Racism and professional jealousies among competing companies also limited the success of these shows.

Black-owned theaters rapidly increased in number in the early twentieth century, providing sites for a wide variety of musical-theater activities. Following the opening of the Pekin Theatre in Chicago in 1905, many black-owned or black-managed houses were built. By 1920 some 300 theaters around the country were serving black patrons (approximately one-third of these theaters were black-run). This in turn led to the formation of resident stock companies that provided a regular menu of musical plays and developed loyal audiences. Many short-lived shows of the 1920s and '30s filled the Lafayette, Lincoln, and Alhambra theaters in Harlem, the Howard in Washington, D.C., the Regal in Baltimore, Md., the Monogram in Chicago, the 81 in Atlanta, Ga., and the Booker T. Washington in St. Louis, Mo., among others.

A few large companies continued to tour—J. Leubrie Hill's Darktown Follies (from 1911 to 1916) and the various Smart Set shows run by S. H. Dudley, H. Tutt, and S. T. Whitney—but many acts appeared in vaudeville as well. By 1920 the Theatre Owners' Booking Association (TOBA) was formed to facilitate the booking of black acts into theaters that served black audiences exclusively. The TOBA circuit of theaters eventually embraced houses all over the South and survived until the Great Depression.

Vaudeville acts and musicals of the first decades of the twentieth century served as apprenticeships for many young ragtime pianists and composers who wanted to break into the business. J. Tim Brymn, James Vaughan, Charles "Luckey" Roberts, James Price Johnson, and "Will" Vodery played, wrote songs for, and directed forgotten shows with titles like *George Washington Bullion Abroad* (1915) and *Baby Blues* (1919) before going on to arrange, perform, and write for military bands, Broadway shows, and films.

"Shuffle Along" and Its Successors, 1921–1939

Eubie Blake and Noble Sissle's *Shuffle Along* kicked off a major revival of black musical comedies in New York in 1921. Light, fast-moving, and filled with catchy melodies, it captured crowds for over 500 Broadway performances and spent two years on the road. Its lead comedians, still in blackface, were Aubrey Lyles and Flournoy

Miller, who wrote the book, developing material that they had been using for years. Many members of the cast later found individual stardom: Florence Mills, Josephine Baker, Caterina Yarboro, Ethel Waters, Adelaide Hall, Paul Robeson, William Grant Still, and Hall Johnson.

The upsurge in black shows in the wake of *Shuffle Along* has not been equaled since. Their number paralleled the high-water mark of new productions of all kinds on Broadway in the late 1920s. Many were close imitations of *Shuffle Along*, but a few broke new ground, with respect to both characters and music: *Put and Take* (1921); *Liza* (1922); *Strut Miss Lizzie* (1922); *Plantation Days* (1923); *Runnin' Wild* (1923); *Bottomland* (1927); *Africana* (1927); *Rang Tang* (1927); and five shows produced by Lew Leslie called *Blackbirds* (of 1926, 1928, 1930, 1933, and 1939).

Hot Chocolates (1929), by Andy Razaf and Fats Waller, epitomized the successful post-*Shuffle Along* show of the late 1920s: a revue (i.e., a string of topical acts and songs rather than a plotted story show) filled with new dance steps—the Black Bottom, the Lindy, the Shimmy, and the Charleston all appeared in these shows—with an attractive chorus line, blues songs, and repartee closer to the real speech of Harlem than either the pseudo-dialect of minstrelsy or the clean, cute shows of white Broadway. James P. Johnson, Tom Lemonier, Donald Heyward, Maceo Pinkard, Joe Jordan, Henry Creamer, Ford Dabney, and Perry Bradford emerged as songwriters with these shows.

The spirituals arranged by Hall Johnson and sung by his choir helped to make *The Green Pastures* the hit play of 1930. Weaving humor and gentleness together to create a naive picture of a black heaven, the superb cast was well received. Ironically, its very success led to bookings in exclusionary theaters where no blacks were admitted to the auditorium. Both this show and its successor, *Run Little Chillun* (1933), helped to ensure the continued employment of black players and singers during the general decline of the 1930s.

The Works Progress Administration (WPA) Negro Theatre Project (1935–1939) brought African Americans into all aspects of theater production, and a few musicals were performed: *Did Adam Sin?* (1936), using African-American folklore themes and music; Theodore Brown's *Natural Man* (1937), a retelling of the John Henry legend; *Swing It* (1937), by Cecil Mack (a.k.a. R. Cecil McPherson); and *Swing Mikado* (1939), a jazz transformation of Gilbert and Sullivan.

Developments since World War II

The only major shows featuring black stars in the 1940s were *Cabin in the Sky* (1940) with Ethel Waters and *St. Louis Woman* (1946) with Pearl Bailey and the Nicholas Brothers. Otherwise, opportunities for blacks in the New York musical theater scene through the 1940s, 1950s, and 1960s were few. A desire to eliminate stereotyped roles for black actors and the problem of dealing with serious race-related social issues in the normally lighthearted style of musicals resulted in the temporary elimination of nearly all black participation. No all-black-cast shows were staged in the early 1950s, nor were more than a handful of African Americans employed on- or offstage during this period. A small group of shows with integrated casts or a single black star did well at the box office, notably *Jamaica* (1957) with Lena Horne and *Golden Boy* (1964) with Sammy Davis, Jr.

In the wake of the Civil Rights Movement, via the revival of older black musical styles and the folk songs that had always found an audience, African Americans returned to Broadway and touring companies. The plays of Langston Hughes with various musical collaborators, *Simply Heavenly* (1957), *Black Nativity* (1961), *Tambourines to Glory* (1963), and *The Prodigal Son* (1965), embraced black culture and ignored the politics of integration. Vinnette Carroll adapted James Weldon Johnson's verse sermons for *Trumpets of the Lord* (1963). Gospel songs, spirituals, and folk songs also infused *A Hand Is at the Gate* (1966), *Don't Bother Me, I Can't Cope* (1972), and *Your Arms Too Short to Box with God* (1976).

More direct social criticism was offered in the calypso musical *Ballad for Bimshire* (1963) and in Melvin van Peebles's angry and challenging plays *Ain't Supposed to Die a Natural Death* (1971) and *Don't Play Us Cheap* (1972). Blues, jazz, and the special styles of famous artists in earlier eras of black music added a nostalgic aura to the shows of the rest of the 1970s and 1980s: *Me and Bessie* (1975), *One Mo' Time* (1979), *Eubie* (1979), *Sophisticated Ladies* (1981), *Blues in the Night* (1982), *Dreamgirls* (1982), *Williams and Walker* (1986), and *Black and Blue* (1989).

The same decades saw the successful conversion of straight plays by black playwrights (Ossie Davis, Lorraine Hansberry, and James Baldwin) into musicals: *Purlie* (1970), *Raisin* (1973), *The Amen Corner* (1983), as well as the improbable remake of Sophocles into the fervid gospel music show *The Gospel at Colonus* (1988). A uniquely whimsical and tuneful adaptation of L. Frank Baum's *Wizard of Oz*, with music by Charles

When a number of black people became minstrels, they brought a new infusion of African-American culture.

PAGE 457

Smalls, became *The Wiz* (1975, revived in 1984), and black-cast versions of white shows *Hello Dolly* (1963 and 1975) and *Guys and Dolls* (1976) and self-conscious historical song summaries like *Bubbling Brown Sugar* (1976) and *Black Broadway* (1980) also appeared. As in the 1930s, the revue format succeeded best with audiences and critics. *Ain't Misbehavin'*, using the tunes of "Fats" Waller, won the Tony Award for Best Musical in 1978.

One of the most interesting and impassioned imports at the end of the 1980s was the anti-apartheid South African show *Sarafina!* (1987), featuring native song styles and enjoying a long run. This show was striking for its dramatic content, but in the main the homegrown shows of the most recent decades have not been such. Shows high on energy, retrospection, and dance numbers but less apt to be driven by a powerful book have been the norm. *Jelly's Last Jam* (1992) attempted to address some serious issues surrounding the life of the famous Creole jazzman "Jelly Roll" Morton on his deathbed and portrayed the protagonist as a dancer to his own music; Gregory Hines starred. Part biography, part historical re-creation, and part satire (complete with a blackface chorus of Pullman porters) this ambitious and brilliantly produced show—*Variety* called it "original, outrageous, and exuberant"—received eleven Tony Award nominations.

—THOMAS L. RIIS

See also

Jazz

NAACP LEGAL DEFENSE AND EDUCATIONAL FUND

Created by the National Association for the Advancement of Colored People in 1940 as a tax-exempt fund for litigation and education, the NAACP Legal Defense and Educational Fund, (LDF), based in New York, has been the central organization for African-American civil rights advances through the legal system. While the LDF, popularly known as the "Inc. Fund," had from the beginning a board of directors and a separate fundraising apparatus from those of the NAACP, it was planned as an integrated component of the larger organization, designed to carry out Charles H. Houston's plan for a legal assault on segregation in public education. The LDF's leadership was represented on the NAACP board, and helped design organizational strategy. The LDF was set up with a loose administrative structure, with a director-counsel as the chief officer. The first LDF director-counsel, former NAACP Counsel Thurgood Marshall, hired a staff of five lawyers.

During the 1940s and 1950s, such lawyers as Robert Carter, Franklin Williams, and Constance Baker Motley joined the staff. Marshall made the LDF the main locus of civil rights law, and the LDF litigated a variety of landmark civil rights cases before the Supreme Court. In 1944, the LDF successfully argued in *Smith* v. *Allwright* that primaries which legally excluded blacks were unconstitutional. In 1946, *Morgan* v. *the Commonwealth of Virginia* outlawed segregation on interstate bus lines. In 1948 the LDF brought *Shelley* v. *Kramer* to the U.S. Supreme Court. The Court ruled that racially restrictive housing covenants that prohibited sales of homes to blacks were unenforceable.

However, much of the LDF's work was done not at the Supreme Court, but in small southern towns, fighting lawsuits or defending arrested blacks under adverse and dangerous conditions. LDF lawyers, forced to work on a shoestring budget, received death threats and ran from lynch mobs. While they frequently lost cases, their presence helped assure fair trials. In 1950, the Supreme Court ruling in *Shepard and Irvin* v. *Florida* helped establish the now-familiar doctrine that defendants must be tried in a venue free of prejudice against them.

Education cases were the centerpiece of LDF legal efforts. Following the NAACP's successful strategy in *Mississippi* ex rel *Gaines* v. *Canada* (1938), the LDF attacked discrimination in graduate education. Beginning in 1946, the LDF brought a series of cases before the Supreme Court, culminating in *Sipuel* v. *Board of Regents of the University of Oklahoma* (1948); *McLaurin* v. *Oklahoma State Regents* (1950); and *Sweatt* v. *Painter* (1950). In the latter, the Court ruled that segregated facilities led to discrimination, though the case did not directly challenge the principle of "separate but equal" in primary education. LDF lawyers also brought suit to eliminate pay differentials between white and black teachers, in part to demonstrate the enormous expense of a dual school system. By 1951, the LDF, preparing for a direct challenge to segregation, was working on twenty elementary and high school cases and a dozen higher-education cases. The LDF's efforts were crowned with success in 1954 with the decision in *Brown* v. *Board of Education of Topeka, Kansas*, argued by Thurgood Marshall.

By 1954, however, personal differences among staff members and disagreements over organizational mission led to a total split with the NAACP. The NAACP considered the LDF a vehicle for arguing civil rights cases. LDF leaders considered achieving educational equality their prime responsibility. The LDF and the NAACP formally parted in 1956, establishing separate boards of directors.

After the implementation ruling in *Brown* v. *Board of Education*, which ordered desegregation "with all deliberate speed," was announced in 1955, the LDF began designing desegregation plans and fighting court cases to force compliance, notably *Cooper* v. *Aaron* (1958), in which the Court mandated the integration of Arkansas's Little Rock Central High School. LDF lawyers

See also

Brown v. *Board of Education of Topeka, Kansas*

Thurgood Marshall

N

*The Montgomery
Bus Boycott marked
the beginning of
the Civil Rights
Movement's direct
action phase,
and it made the
Rev. Dr. Martin
Luther King, Jr.,
a national figure.*

PAGE 460

See also
Black Panther Party
Civil Rights Movement

continued to work to combat segregation in other fields. In 1956, the LDF began a central involvement in the Civil Rights Movement when it won *Gayle* v. *Browder*, the case of the Montgomery Bus Boycott led by the Rev. Dr. Martin Luther King, Jr.

At the same time, Southerners determined to keep the LDF from operating. Legislatures charged the LDF created cases in which it had no legitimate interest or standing. The Supreme Court finally ruled in 1963 that LDF litigation was constitutionally protected. By 1965, LDF lawyers had taken school cases as they had arisen in every southern state. Eventually, in *Griffin* v. *County School Board of Prince Edward County* (1964), the Court renounced "all deliberate speed," and in *Green* v. *County School Board of New Kent County* (1968) ordered immediate and total desegregation.

In 1961, Thurgood Marshall was appointed a federal judge by President John F. Kennedy, and left the LDF. Jack Greenberg, his white assistant, who had come to the LDF in 1949, succeeded him as the new director-counsel, a position he would hold for the next twenty-three years. During the 1960s, the LDF continued as an active force in the Civil Rights Movement, defending sit-in protesters in cases such as *Boynton* v. *Virginia* (1961) and *Shuttlesworth* v. *Alabama* (1964), as well as defending Freedom Riders and providing bail funds for the many activists who were arrested during the struggle.

The Black Power movement of the late 1960s and early '70s brought about tensions within the LDF, over its white leadership and its refusal to defend black radicals except in those few cases where civil rights issues were involved, such as exorbitant bail fees for incarcerated Black Panther Party members. In 1970, several LDF lawyers pressed the organization to take up the defense of black radical Angela Davis after she was implicated in a courthouse shootout, but the LDF Board of Directors and Director-Counsel Greenberg vetoed the idea. The same year, when Julian Bond was refused his seat in the Georgia Legislature because he opposed the Vietnam War, the LDF refused his case on the grounds that a white antiwar legislator would have suffered the same fate.

In recent decades, the LDF has concentrated on other pressing civil rights areas. In *Griggs* v. *Duke Power* (1971), the LDF persuaded the Supreme Court to strike down discriminatory educational or testing requirements irrelevant to job performance. The LDF then argued numerous

affirmative action cases based on *Griggs* in the following years. The most important of these was *Regents of the University of California* v. *Bakke* (1979), in which the LDF worked largely successfully in contributing to opposing Allan Bakke's "reverse discrimination" suit.

Capital punishment was a particular focus of LDF's efforts. In preparation for the Supreme Court case *Maxwell* v. *Bishop* (1970), which involved an Arkansas African American convicted of the rape of a white woman, the LDF organized a study which showed that 89 percent of defendants around the country given the death penalty for rape between 1930 and 1962 were black, and demonstrated patterns of racial discrimination in death sentences given for rape in Arkansas between 1945 and 1965. While the Court declined to rule on the LDF's statistics, Jack Greenberg continued to lead the campaign against the death penalty, which achieved temporary victory in *Furman* v. *Georgia* (1972). Capital punishment was reinstated in 1976, but the death penalty in cases of rape, a special concern of blacks, was declared unconstitutional in *Coker* v. *Georgia* (1977). The LDF continued to appeal death penalty sentences for African Americans. In the early 1980s it commissioned the so-called "Baldus Study," a mammoth study of the influence of race on death penalty sentencing, following which lawyers argued *McCleskey* v. *Kemp* (1987). However, the Supreme Court refused to rule solely on the basis of this statistical evidence that the death penalty was arbitrary or racially discriminatory.

In 1984, Julius LeVonne Chambers took over as director-counsel and continued to concentrate on litigation in the areas of poverty law, education, fair housing, capital punishment, fair employment, environmental justice, and voting rights. A housing discrimination suit the LDF brought in the San Fernando Valley in 1992 was settled for $300,000, one of the largest awards ever granted victims of racial bias in housing.

In 1992, Chambers resigned and was replaced by Elaine Ruth Jones. Jones had previously been head of the LDF's regional office in Washington, D.C., where she had helped draft and implement civil rights legislation, notably the Civil Rights Restoration Act (1988), the 1988 Fair Housing Act, and the Civil Rights Act of 1991. Jones redirected LDF's focus toward cases of environmental and health care discrimination. Environmental activism covers suits to ensure equal treatment of blacks victimized by toxic wastes, and cases enforcing federal laws mandating free lead-poisoning exams for poor children. Examples of health care cases include a suit filed in Contra Costa, Calif., charging with violation of civil rights statutes officials who built a county hospital largely inaccessible to the district's African-American population. The LDF continues involvement in poverty law, such as its suit to block New Jersey from stopping welfare payments to women who have additional children while on welfare; education, through its attempts to preserve the University of Maryland's special scholarship program for African Americans, among other matters; criminal justice, through the Capital Punishment Project; and voting rights, by its efforts to enforce the Voting Rights Act in judicial elections and to support black majority districts. The LDF also offers four scholarship programs to aid African-American law students. In the early 1990s, the LDF had twenty-eight staff lawyers in its New York, Washington, and Los Angeles offices, and a total annual budget of almost $8 million.

—GREG ROBINSON

NATIONAL ASSOCIATION FOR THE ADVANCEMENT OF COLORED PEOPLE

Founding and Early Days

Since its organization in 1909, the National Association for the Advancement of Colored People (NAACP) has been the premier civil rights organization in the United States. It has been in the forefront of numerous successful campaigns on behalf of African-American rights, from the effort to suppress lynching, to the long struggle to overturn legal segregation, to the still ongoing effort to secure the implementation of racial justice.

The NAACP owes its origins to the coalescence of two political movements of the early twentieth century, the group of black intellectuals,

MARCH AGAINST SEGREGATION

In Baltimore, Paul Robeson joins the NAACP picket line in front of Ford's Theatre protesting its policy of racial segregation.

PHOTOGRAPHS AND PRINTS DIVISION, SCHOMBURG CENTER FOR RESEARCH IN BLACK CULTURE, THE NEW YORK PUBLIC LIBRARY, ASTOR, LENOX AND TILDEN FOUNDATIONS

NATIONAL ASSOCIATION FOR THE ADVANCEMENT OF COLORED PEOPLE

Founding and Early Days

I have a dream that four little children will one day live in a nation where they will not be judged by the color of their skin but by the content of their character.

MARTIN LUTHER KING, JR.
SPEECH AT
THE LINCOLN MEMORIAL IN
WASHINGTON, D.C.,
AUGUST 28, 1963

See also
Vietnam War

led by William Monroe Trotter and W.E.B. Du Bois, who opposed the accommodationism of Booker T. Washington, and a small circle of white "neo-abolitionists," many of them descended from those who had led the antebellum fight against slavery, who were increasingly distressed by the deterioration in the legal rights and social status of African Americans.

The Niagara Movement, formed by Du Bois, Trotter, and twenty-eight other African American men at a conference on the Canadian side of Niagara Falls in August 1905, was the spiritual precursor of the NAACP. The movement was forthright in its opposition to Washingtonian accommodationism, and in its commitment to civil equality. Despite the inspiration provided by the Niagara Movement, the organization soon became dormant in the face of poor funding and Bookerite hostility.

Meanwhile, a violent race riot in Springfield, Illinois (Abraham Lincoln's home town) in August 1908 aroused the attention of William English Walling (1877–1936), a white socialist and labor activist, who graphically described the violence he had witnessed in an article in *The Independent*. Walling called for citizens to come to the assistance of blacks, and to fight for racial equality.

Walling's article was read by Mary White Ovington (1865–1951), a white journalist and social worker from a well-to-do abolitionist family who worked and lived in a black tenement in New York, doing research for her landmark sociological work *Half a Man: The Status of the Negro in New York* (1911). She responded to his plea and invited Dr. Henry Moskowitz (1879–1936), a labor reformer and social worker among New York immigrants, to join her in meeting with Walling in his New York apartment to discuss "the Negro Question." The three were the principal founders of the NAACP. Two other members of the core group were Charles Edward Russell (1860–1941), another socialist whose father had been the abolitionist editor of a small newspaper in Iowa, and Oswald Garrison Villard (1872–1949), grandson of the abolitionist William Lloyd Garrison, and publisher of the liberal *New York Evening Post* journal and later the *Nation*.

Ovington invited two prominent black New York clergymen, Bishop Alexander Walters of the African Methodist Episcopal Zion Church, a former president of the National Afro-American Council, and the Rev. William Henry Brooks, minister of St. Mark's Methodist Episcopal Church, to join the continuing discussions. The expanded group agreed to issue a call, written by Villard, for a conference in New York on February 12th, 1909, Lincoln's 100th birthday. Sixty people, seven of whom were black (Prof. William L. Bulkley, a New York school principal; Du Bois; Rev. Francis J. Grimké; Mary Church Terrell; Dr. Milton Waldron; Bishop Walters; and Ida B. Wells) signed the call.

As a result of the Call, The National Negro Conference met at the Charity Organization Hall in New York City on May 31 and June 1, 1909. The Conference created the National Committee for the Advancement of the Negro, or the Committee of Forty on permanent organization, to develop plans for an effective organization. The Committee's plans were implemented a year later at a second meeting in New York, when the organization's permanent name, the National Association for the Advancement of Colored People was adopted. The NAACP was organized as a small elite organization which would rely on agitation and legal action against racial discrimination. The organization chose to include the phrase "colored people" in its title to emphasize the broad and anti-imperialist concerns of its founders. Its structure and mission inspired the formation of several other civil rights groups, such as South Africa's African National Congress, formed in 1912.

In its first year, the new NAACP launched programs to increase industrial opportunities for blacks, and to obtain greater protection for them in the South by crusading against lynching and other forms of violence. Throughout its early years, the NAACP devoted most of its resources to seeking an end to lynchings and other forms of mob violence through press publicity campaigns, as well as with pamphlets, in-depth studies, and other educational activities; the organization's protest campaign after a lynching in Coatesville, Pennsylvania in 1911 gave it its first substantial publicity.

The new organization's most important act by far was the hiring of Du Bois as director of publications and research. Du Bois's visionary ideas and militant program were his primary contributions to the NAACP. His hiring also signalled the final demise of the Niagara Movement; while Du Bois brought its central vision to the new organization, the NAACP had better funding and a much more rigid structure and program than the Niagara Movement. In November 1910, Du Bois launched *The Crisis* as the NAACP's house journal. *The Crisis*, which mixed political articles with works by African-American writers, poets, and artists, soon became the principal philosophical instrument of the black freedom struggle. From an initial publication of 1,000 copies in November 1910 the magazine's circulation increased to 100,000 a month in 1918. While formally part of the NAACP, *The Crisis* had its own staff of eight to ten people (led by business manager Augustus Dill, one of the NAACP's only black staff members).

The NAACP's organizers created a formal, institutional structure headed by an executive committee composed largely of members of the Committee of Forty. While Du Bois and a handful of other black men, largely moderates, were included, black women—notably Ida B. Wells—were excluded from the Committee. Kathryn Johnson served as field secretary from 1910 through 1916

(on a volunteer basis for the first four years), becoming the first of many black women to serve as in that position, but black women were not offered leadership roles in the NAACP for several decades. Moorfield Storey (1845–1929), a former secretary to antislavery senator Charles Sumner, and one of the country's foremost constitutional lawyers, was named the organization's president. In addition to Storey and Du Bois, the only black and only salaried staffer, its officers were Walling, chairman; John E. Milholland, treasurer; Villard, assistant treasurer; and Ovington, secretary.

To ensure that the movement spread as quickly as possibly, the committee authorized mass meetings in Chicago, Cleveland, and Buffalo. The first local NAACP branch was organized in New York

JESSIE REDMON FAUSET
Literary Editor of *Crisis* also an Acclaimed Novelist

Jessie Redmon Fauset (April 27, 1884–April 30, 1961), writer and teacher. As literary editor of the *Crisis,* the official journal of the National Association for the Advancement of Colored People (NAACP), Fauset published the early writings of Arna Bontemps, Langston Hughes, and Jean Toomer. She promoted the work of poets Georgia Douglas Johnson and Anne Spencer. But, although she is more often remembered for her encouragement of other writers, she was herself among the most prolific authors of the Harlem Renaissance. In addition to her poems, reportage, reviews, short stories, and translations that appeared regularly in the *Crisis,* she published four novels in less than ten years.

Born in what is now Lawnside, N.J., Fauset grew up in Philadelphia. Her widowed father, a minister, was the primary influence on her childhood. Her outstanding academic record won her admission to Cornell University, where she was elected to Phi Beta Kappa; she graduated in 1905. She taught high school French and earned an M.A. from the University of Pennsylvania, before W. E. B. Du Bois hired her for the *Crisis* in 1919.

Her contributions to the *Crisis* were numerous and diverse: biographical sketches of blacks across the diaspora, essays on drama and other cultural subjects, and reports on black women activists and political causes. One of the few women to participate in the 1921 Pan-African Congress, Fauset recorded her vivid impressions of that meeting. Several of her best essays describe her travel to Europe and North Africa during 1925 and 1926. She reviewed and translated works by Francophone writers from Africa and the Caribbean.

Although she subtitled one of them "A Novel without a Moral," all of Fauset's books convey strong messages. *There Is Confusion* (1924) depicts the struggle of an educated, idealistic young woman to achieve her professional goal of becoming a concert singer without compromising her personal and racial pride. Fauset's best novel, *Plum Bun* (1929), uses the subject of "passing" to explore issues of race and gender identity. Its protagonist, another aspiring artist, learns that no success is worth betraying one's selfhood. In the foreword to *The Chinaberry Tree* (1931), Fauset explains that her purpose is to write about the "breathing-spells, in-between spaces where colored men and women work and love and go their ways with no thought of the 'problem.'" Blacks and whites were not so different after all. But as her final novel, ironically titled *Comedy: American Style* (1934), demonstrates, she did not ignore the problems of racism and sexism endemic to early twentieth-century American life. In general, however, Fauset's novels present sentimental resolutions to the complex problems they raise.

After resigning from the *Crisis* in 1926, Fauset returned to teaching. In 1929 she married businessman Herbert Harris and later moved to Montclair, N.J. She ceased thereafter to play a public role. Yet even after her death in 1961, her example continued to inspire. Not only had she probably published more than any black American woman before her, her fiction confirmed that not all the drama in African-American life revolved around interracial conflict.

—CHERYL A. WALL

See also
W.E.B. Du Bois

N

No democracy can long survive which does not accept as a fundamental to its very existence the recognition of the rights of minorities.

FRANKLIN D. ROOSEVELT,
LETTER TO THE NATIONAL
ASSOCIATION FOR THE
ADVANCEMENT OF COLORED
PEOPLE, JUNE 25, 1938

in January 1911. Its officers were Ovington and Joel E. Spingarn (1874–1939), a former chairman of the Department of Comparative Literature at Columbia University who later became a leading contributor of both money and ideas to the organization. Spingarn's brother Arthur, a lawyer, also became active in the branch. The following year, branches were created in Boston, Baltimore, Detroit, Indianapolis, St. Louis, and Quincy, Ill., and in 1913, others were created in Chicago, Kansas City, Tacoma and Washington, D.C. Membership in the organization was contingent upon acceptance of its philosophy and programs.

While the local branches had heavily African American staffs, the National NAACP was a largely white group during its early days. Whites had the financial resources to devote themselves to NAACP work; throughout the NAACP's early days, all of the board members contributed a considerable amount of time to the organization. Arthur Spingarn, for example, estimated that he devoted "half and probably more" of his time to the NAACP. Whites had the education, the administrative experience, and the access to money that were required to build the organization. For example, Villard initially provided office space for the NAACP in his *New York Post* building (it moved to its longtime home of 70 5th Avenue a few years later). He also gave his personal funds to save the infant organization from imminent collapse. Joel Spingarn paid for his own travel from city to city, soliciting memberships and funds during what were called the New Abolition tours, and he donated funds to establish the annual Spingarn Medal, first awarded in 1915, which rapidly became the most prestigious African-American award.

Despite the essential contributions of white activists, blacks were increasingly uneasy about their control of an organization that was meant for African Americans. Those differences had surfaced at the founding conference, when Ida B. Wells openly expressed concern over the leading roles that whites were playing in the movement. She and William Monroe Trotter shied away from involvement in the new organization because of its domination by whites.

In 1914, Villard resigned as chairman of the board, following clashes with Du Bois, and Joel Spingarn became chairman of the board. Even after Villard's departure, the issue of white control continued, and it caused considerable conflicts between Du Bois and Joel Spingarn, his longtime friend. Though, as Du Bois admitted, his haughty personality contributed to the problem,

he also interpreted his role within a racial context and felt that he could not accept even the appearance of inferiority or subservience to whites without betraying the race ideals for which he stood. At the same time, he feared that whites would refuse to aid a black dominated organization, and that it would compromise the NAACP's integrationist program. Spingarn and Ovington both acknowledged the difficulties inherent in white leadership, but felt it was a necessary evil until blacks had sufficient resources to run organizations without assistance.

In 1916 NAACP secretary Mae Nerney resigned. She recommended that the board choose a black person to succeed her as secretary, but the board chose a white man, Roy Nash. It could not, however, escape the pressure to hire another black executive, so it chose James Weldon Johnson, a writer for the *New York Age* and a highly respected man of letters, as field secretary.

Several events in the NAACP's first years combined to define and unite the fledgling organization. The first was the NAACP's ten-year protest campaign for the withdrawal of the D. W. Griffith film *The Birth of a Nation*, beginning in 1915. The NAACP charged that the film "assassinated" the character of black Americans and undermined the very basis of the struggle for racial equality. The organization organized pickets of movie theaters, and lobbied local governments to ban showings of the film.

The following year, upon the death of Booker T. Washington and the end of effective opposition by advocates of accommodation with the South's Jim Crow policies, the NAACP established itself as the primary black organization. Consolidating the NAACP's power, in 1916 Du Bois initiated the first Amenia Conference, a meeting of black leaders which included Washington's men and their friends. The fifty or so participants adopted resolutions on civil rights, education, and unity that were aimed at breaching the division between the Washington group and the NAACP.

World War I and related events combined to set the NAACP on its primary mission, a two-pronged legal and political course against racial violence. During the war, Du Bois instituted a controversial policy of black support for American military efforts, with the goal of greater recognition of civil rights afterward. However, the migration of southern blacks to Northern urban areas during and after the war led to racial tension and violent episodes, which climaxed during the postwar "Red Summer" of 1919. In 1917 the NAACP led a celebrated silent protest parade of 15,000 people through Harlem with muffled drums to protest the violent riots that year against blacks in East St. Louis, Illinois, and discrimination in general.

The strengthening of the branch structure heightened NAACP influence. James Weldon Johnson was charged with increasing significantly the number of NAACP branches in the South. Johnson began by organizing a branch in Richmond, Virginia in 1917. Initially, his progress was slow, but by the end of 1919, the NAACP had 310 branches, including 31 in the South. The Atlanta branch, founded in late 1916, became one of the organization's strongest, with a membership of more than 1,000. The NAACP's total membership jumped from 9,282 in 1917 to 91,203 in 1919.

In 1921 Johnson became NAACP secretary, charged with coordinating the branches and developing the strategy for implementing the organization's programs. Johnson's assumption of this power reflected the clearer administrative lines that were developing within the NAACP, and signalled the rising influence of paid African-American staff members within the organization.

The NAACP During the "New Negro" Era

Despite its promising beginnings, by 1919 it was clear that the NAACP's reliance on agitation and education had proved largely ineffective against racial violence. The most promising avenue of redress was by political challenge. Walter White, a young insurance salesman from Atlanta who Johnson met during an organizing trip, and who joined the national staff in 1918, was named assistant secretary with responsibility for investigating lynchings. White's effectiveness with this mission won him national respect.

In 1919, based on White's research, the NAACP published its report, *Thirty Years of Lynching in the United States, 1889–1918*. The book provided documentation for the campaign against the crime that White was leading. Two years later, through Johnson's extraordinary effort, the House passed an antilynching bill introduced by Congressman L.C. Dyer of Missouri, but southerners in the Senate killed it with a fillibuster. In 1924, the NAACP succeeded in persuading the Republican Party to pledge in its platform to seek legislation against lynching, but Congress failed to pass antilynching legislation during the Coolidge and Hoover administrations. During the Roosevelt administration, the NAACP continued pressing for the passage of antilynching laws in Congress. Two more bills were introduced

in this period, but one died in the House and the other in the Senate.

Despite its preeminent position in the black community, the NAACP was not without its critics during the 1920s. Proponents of radical protest, such as A. Philip Randolph and Chandler Owen of the journal *The Messenger*, criticized the NAACP for excessive legalism, claiming the organization should support self-defense efforts against racial violence. Furthermore, the NAACP engaged in a strong rivalry with Marcus Garvey's Universal Negro Improvement Association. Garvey scorned the NAACP's interracial, integrationist philosophy and its predominantly light-skinned, middle-class leadership. The NAACP, meanwhile, feared Garvey's Back-to-Africa movement as chauvinist and overly visionary. Du Bois called Garvey "the most dangerous man in America," while Robert Bagnall, the NAACP's Director of Branches, claimed that Garvey was "insane" and collaborated with United States government officials in their successful attempt to deport Garvey.

In 1930, James Weldon Johnson retired from the NAACP, and Walter White was appointed secretary. White, in turn, hired Roy Wilkins, a former managing editor of the *Kansas City Call*, as his assistant. The NAACP began the 1930s with 325 branches, which were located in every state of the Union except Maine, New Hampshire, Vermont, Idaho, and North Dakota. The branches served as information bureaus for the national office and stimulated the cultural life of African Americans. The broad organizational independence of the branches enabled them to put together actions, such as mass demonstrations, that differed strongly from national office policy.

The NAACP's growing influence was demonstrated by Walter White's successful campaign in 1930 to defeat President Herbert Hoover's nomination of Judge John J. Parker to the Supreme Court. Parker was a Southerner from North Carolina who had previously spoken against black suffrage as a gubernatorial candidate. While he had opposition from labor unions and other groups, the NAACP was largely influential in forming coalitions and lobbying senators against Parker's confirmation.

The NAACP Law Campaign

Alongside its political efforts, the NAACP had a long history of attempts to improve the status of blacks through the courts. Its first significant court action was the legal struggle to save the life of Pink Franklin, an illiterate farmhand in South

Emmett Till's lynching was a milestone in the emergent Civil Rights Movement.

PAGE 132

Carolina, which led the NAACP to establish a Legal Redress department in 1910. Franklin had been sentenced to death for killing a law officer attempting to arrest him for leaving his employer after he had received advances on his wages. While the U.S. Supreme Court affirmed the decision of the lower courts, the NAACP got the South Carolina governor to commute Franklin's sentence to life imprisonment.

An important victory came in 1915, when Moorfield Storey wrote an *amicus curiae* brief for the NAACP in *Guinn* v. *United States,* challenging the constitutionality of the Oklahoma "grandfather clause." The U.S. Supreme Court ruled that the clause violated the Fifteenth Amendment, giving the NAACP its first legal victory and incentive to seek redress in the courts.

Through the early part of century, the NAACP won some significant cases. In 1917 the NAACP struck a strong, though not final, blow against residential segregation when the U.S. Supreme Court ruled in *Buchanan* v. *Warley* that Louisville, Kentucky's residential segregation ordinance was unconstitutional. The case resulted in the striking down of mandatory housing segregation in Norfolk, Baltimore, St. Louis, and other cities. In 1919, the NAACP conducted an investigation of the convictions of 12 black Elaine, Arkansas, farmers arrested during a riot in 1919 and sentenced to death, and took their case to the U.S. Supreme Court, which threw out the convictions in *Moore* v. *Dempsey* (1923), ruling that the trial had been dominated by a mob atmosphere. In 1935, in the Court's ruling in *Hollins* v. *Oklahoma,* the NAACP won the reversal of two death penalty convictions due to racial discrimination in jury selection. The acquittal of Dr. Ossian Sweet of Detroit capped the legal and educational efforts of the NAACP. In 1925, Sweet moved his family into a house he had purchased in a middle-class white neighborhood. The house was surrounded by a white mob. Sweet shot at the mob in self defense, and killed one of its members. The NAACP hired Clarence Darrow, the greatest trial lawyer of the day, and he successfully defended the Sweets.

One notable area of NAACP interest was the "White Primary," which effectively disenfranchised southern blacks. In 1927, the Supreme Court declared in a unanimous decision *Nixon* v. *Herndon* that a Texas state primary law that excluded blacks from voting was unconstitutional. Soon afterward, a special session of the Texas legislature passed a new statute authorizing the Democratic State Committee to make it own de-

cisions on the eligibility of voters in party primaries. The NAACP appealed, and in 1932 the Supreme Court ruled in *Nixon* v. *Condon* that the Fourteenth Amendment forbade such distinctions. (Despite NAACP efforts, however, in 1935, the U.S. Supreme Court ruled in *Grovey* v. *Townshend* that a party was a private body and could exclude blacks from primary elections; the white primary was finally struck down in 1944).

Such victories led the NAACP to declare that "for the present the avenue to affirmation and defense of the Negro's fundamental rights in America lies through the courts." In 1929, Arthur Spingarn organized the NAACP Legal Committee, and served as its chair until 1939, when he succeeded his deceased brother Joel as president of the NAACP. The first members of the legal committee included the distinguished labor lawyer Clarence Darrow, Harvard Law Professor and Future U.S. Supreme Court justice Felix Frankfurter, liberal Michigan governor and future U.S. Supreme Court justice Frank Murphy, and American Civil Liberties Union lawyer Arthur Garfield Hays.

Darrow and Hays represented the NAACP on the Sweet case, as well as the "Scottsboro" case, which involved nine young black men who were convicted of raping two white women on a train passing through Scottsboro, Alabama in 1931. Eight of the Scottsboro defendants were sentenced to death. The NAACP, which lacked a regular legal department, was unable to move quickly into action, and the Communist Party took over control of the case. In 1933, the NAACP, spurred by black community criticism of its inaction on the famous case, formed the Scottsboro Defense Committee in an uneasy alliance with the Communist Party and its allied group, the International Labor Defense. After a series of protracted legal battles, the defendants' lives were saved.

NAACP in the Depression

The frustrations of the Scottsboro case were the beginning of a contentious and difficult period for the NAACP. The collapse of the national economy in 1929 brought disproportionate hardship to the masses of African Americans. The Communist Party and allied groups such as the League of Struggle for Negro Rights set up in black areas as rivals to the NAACP, while a generation of younger intellectuals, such as economist Abram Harris and political scientist Ralph Bunche of Howard University, brought pressure on the organization to make radical shifts in its elite reformist strategy and interracial character to meet the needs of impoverished blacks.

The organization did respond to economic discrimination during the early 1930s. For example, in 1933, Roy Wilkins and George S. Schuyler, a former Socialist and writer for the *Messenger*, disguised themselves as laborers in order to investigate the deplorable, peonage-like conditions under which blacks on the project were working. White officials discovered their identities, and both men barely escaped with their lives, but the Wilkins and Schuyler investigations enabled the NAACP to get the Secretary of War to quadruple the hourly pay for unskilled laborers and shorten their work week to 30 hours.

Although not everyone within the organization subscribed to the young activists' overriding focus on race pride or their focus on building greater solidarity between the black and white working class, there was nevertheless general agreement on the need for the NAACP to develop a comprehensive economic program. In the face of the criticisms, in August 1933 the NAACP held a second Amenia Conference. After significant prodding by Joel Spingarn, the NAACP created a Committee on Future Plan

GEORGE S. SCHUYLER

Considered One of the Best Journalists of His Time

George S. Schuyler (1895–1977), journalist. George S. Schuyler, often considered a political gadfly because of his move from young radical socialist to arch conservative later in life, was born in Providence, R.I., in 1895. Raised in Syracuse, N.Y., he attended school until he was seventeen, when he dropped out to enter the U.S. Army. He spent seven years in the service and saw action in France during World War I as a first lieutenant.

After the service, Schuyler was active in the labor movement, sometimes moving between Syracuse and New York City. He finally settled in New York as the Harlem Renaissance began. Although never a star of the Renaissance, he served as its goad. It was Schuyler's essay, "The Negro-Art Hokum," for example, that spurred Langston Hughes's now classic 1926 response, "The Negro Artist and the Racial Mountain." Both essays appeared in the *Nation*. In 1923 Schuyler joined A. Philip Randolph's *Messenger* as a columnist and assistant editor and later became its managing editor. The publication was considered so fiery that several southern members of Congress brought it under House investigation.

Schuyler moved on to do publicity for the NAACP, whose publication the *Crisis*, under the editorship of W. E. B. Du Bois, had opposed the radicalism of Randolph, Schuyler, and others. Schuyler's first book, *Racial Intermarriage in the United States*, was published in 1929.

In 1931 Schuyler published two novels—*Black No More* and *Slaves Today: A Story of Liberia*. The first was a scathing satire of black people enabled to become white by taking a chemical and so to vanish from Harlem and reappear elsewhere as whites. The second described the slavelike labor conditions in Liberia. A third novel, *Black Empire*, assembled from fiction serialized from 1936 through mid-1937 in the *Pittsburgh Courier*, a black weekly newspaper, was posthumously published in book form in 1991. The novel told of a black elite, headed by a fascistlike black genius, which revenges wrongs done by whites in the United States, gathers an army and air force, and heads to Africa, where the genius of black scientists carves out a black empire. It defeats all incursions by European whites. Schuyler wrote this work under the pen name of Samuel I. Brooks. (He also used Brooks and other pseudonyms while publishing fiction in the *Courier* until 1939.)

From 1927 to 1933 Schuyler published nine essays in H. L. Mencken's *American Mercury*. Eugene Gordon, a black communist of the period, wrote in 1934 in Nancy Cunard's *Negro* that Schuyler was "an opportunist of the most odious sort," which indicated that to some he had already distanced himself from socialism. Shortly thereafter, Schuyler began a forty-year sojourn with the *Courier*. While he published furiously, he noted that his primary interest was in "having enough money to live on properly." He supplemented his $60 weekly *Courier* salary by publishing in several white journals, including the *Nation, Plain Talk*, and *Common Ground*.

Schuyler during his prime was considered to be one of the best journalists working. His satire was called Rabelaisian, and he frequently played devil's advocate. He and his wife Josephine had a daughter, Philippa, in 1931. A prodigy who had grown to become a noted concert pianist, she was killed at age 35 in a helicopter crash while on tour in Vietnam in 1967. Schuyler himself died in 1977.

—JOHN A. WILLIAMS

See also
Jim Crow

and Program in 1935 to consider the concerns raised by the Amenia Conference. The Committee forced the organization to declare that its interests were "inextricably intertwined with those of white workers." This new approach was crystallized with the NAACP's alliance with a developing interracial labor union, the Congress of Industrial Organizations (CIO), with whom it negotiated on behalf of black automobile workers in Detroit. The NAACP was one of the 24 civil rights and religious organizations supporting the Joint Committee on National Recovery, a Washington-based economic lobbying and information group founded by Robert C. Weaver and John P. Davis in 1935. However, White redoubled the organization's efforts in its traditional areas of education, agitation and court litigation.

The Depression also sparked a schism in the NAACP between White and Du Bois, who had grown impatient with the pace of the NAACP's achievements. Openly challenging White (with whom he had deep, personal differences) and the NAACP, Du Bois shifted from his long-held position of urging integration to support for independent black economic development. Du Bois's stand made his departure from *The Crisis* and the NAACP board inevitable, and he resigned in 1934. Wilkins, in addition to being in charge of the organization's administration, succeeded him as editor of *The Crisis*.

As the 1930s progressed, the paid staff exercised control of the organization. In effect, White made the executive secretary the Association's chief executive officer as well as its chief spokesman. White was able to effect such changes because the bulk of the organization's strength and finances now came from its vastly expanded branch structure. Between 1927 and 1931, the NAACP raised $545,407 in general funds, of which $374,896 came from the branches. Despite the severe hardships of the depression, the branches in 1936 contributed $26,288 toward the total income of $47,724 (most of the remaining income came from contributions and from the Life Membership program, created in 1927).

Throughout the late 1930s, much of the NAACP's activism was organized by individual branches. For example, in such places Baltimore and Boston, NAACP Youth Council leaders formed "don't-buy-where-you-can't-work" boycotts and pickets to protest job discrimination in black community stores. In New Orleans, the NAACP paid residents' poll taxes to fight voting restrictions. In Kansas City, an NAACP-led protest campaign desegregated municipal golf courses. In New York, NAACP officials joined a committee to improve conditions in Harlem after a riot broke out in 1935.

The national NAACP also engaged in several campaigns during the 1930s, lobbying Congress for antilynching legislation and struggling against discrimination in New Deal programs. One important NAACP action was its protest against the Italian invasion of Ethiopia. The organization collected donations for war relief, sent official protests to the League of Nations and U.S. State Department, and lobbied against pro-Italian Amendments in the 1935 Neutrality Act. Another important struggle dealt with media stereotypes. NAACP representatives met with newspaper editors to persuade them to offer positive coverage of African Americans and to cease the practice of discussing the race of alleged criminals. The NAACP also launched a campaign to end stereotypes in Hollywood films and radio programs, notably the popular radio series "Amos 'n' Andy," which the organization claimed presented demeaning stereotypes of blacks. NAACP lobbying helped secure the signing of black performers such as Lena Horne to film studio contracts.

The Legal Assault on Segregation

To end its dependence on volunteer lawyers, which had proved a large handicap in the Scottsboro case, as well as to wage an all-out fight against segregation, the NAACP in 1935 created its legal department. The creation of the NAACP Legal Department resulted from a comprehensive study of the Association's legal program that Nathan Ross Margold, a white public service lawyer in New York, conducted in 1930 under a grant from the American Fund for Public Service (Garland Fund). Margold suggested that the NAACP "strike directly at the most prolific sources of discrimination" by boldly challenging "the constitutional validity of segregation if and when accompanied irremediably by discrimination" and that the organization concentrate on racial disparities in education.

The NAACP hired Charles H. Houston, the highly respected dean of Howard University School of Law, as its first special counsel. Houston followed the Margold report in a broad sense, but implemented an incremental approach.

Houston's first line of attack was graduate and professional schools. He successfully tested this strategy in the Maryland Supreme Court case *Murray* v. *Maryland* in 1935, the first of a series of challenges that would lead to the Supreme

See also

Marcus Garvey
Universal Negro
Improvement Association

Court's landmark *Brown* v. *Board of Education* decision in 1954. Houston left the NAACP in 1938 to return to private law practice in Washington, and was succeeded by Marshall, a graduate of Howard University Law School who had been working with the Baltimore NAACP branch.

Continuing to attack racial inequalities in education, the NAACP filed its first teacher's discrimination pay case in behalf of William Gibbs against the Montgomery County Board of Education in Maryland. The county was paying Gibbs $612 a year, whereas a white school principal with comparable qualifications was receiving $1,475. In 1938 the court ordered the county to equalize teacher's salaries, setting a precedent for similar NAACP challenges in other parts of the country. The same year, the NAACP won in *Missouri ex rel Gaines* v. *Canada,* in which the Supreme Court ruled that Missouri's offer of tuition aid to Lloyd Gaines to attend an out-of-state university law school did not constitute equal treatment under the Constitution. In 1939, the NAACP Legal Defense and Educational Fund, Inc. was incorporated to receive tax deductible contributions for those areas of the NAACP's work that met the Internal Revenue Service's guidelines. The LDF, dubbed the "Inc. Fund" and headed by Thurgood Marshall, was tied to the parent NAACP by interlocking boards.

As in the earlier years, the NAACP's cases covered four major areas: disfranchisement, segregation ordinances, restrictive covenants and due process, and equal protection for blacks accused of crimes. Among the fundamental victories won before the Supreme Court were *Smith* v. *Allwright* (1944), in which the all-white Texas Democratic primary was declared unconstitutional; *Morgan* v. *Virginia* (1946), in which it was declared that state laws requiring segregated travel could not be enforced in interstate travel; and *Shelley* v. *Kraemer* and *McGhee* v. *Sipes* (1948), in which it was declared that restrictive housing convenants could not be legally enforced.

World War II and Postwar Periods

World War II brought new challenges and enormous growth to the NAACP. During the War, the NAACP made an enormous effort to secure equal treatment for blacks in the military and in war industries. For example, NAACP officials lobbied successfully for a navy officer training program for African Americans, and investigated reports of discrimination against black GIs; Walter White personally conducted investigations of discrimination complaints in the European and

Pacific Theaters. White also championed A. Philip Randolph's 1941 March on Washington Movement, and was an advisor in the creation of the Fair Employment Practices Committee (FEPC). In 1942, NAACP investigators reported on living and working conditions in overcrowded cities, although they were largely ignored. After rioting broke out in Detroit and New York's Harlem in 1943, the NAACP backed interracial committee efforts. With the aid of such staffers as Ella Baker, Director of Branches from 1943 through 1946, the NAACP grew from 355 branches and 50,556 members in 1940 to 1073 branches and some 450,000 members by 1946.

After the end of the war, the NAACP redoubled its efforts to pass antilynching legislation. In the face of rising racial violence, such as an anti-black riot in Columbia, Tennessee, the NAACP called for federal civil rights protection. In 1946, Walter White organized a National Emergency Committee against Mob Violence, and met with President Truman to demand action. In 1947, the NAACP provided financial and logistical support for CORE's Journey of Reconciliation, a series of interracial bus rides to challenge discrimination in interstate travel. NAACP official Clarence Mitchell led the unsuccessful fight for a permanent FEPC. In a show of support, in 1947 Harry Truman became the first president to attend an NAACP convention.

Even as the NAACP solidified its antidiscrimination program and tactics, it was weakened during the late 1940s by the same Cold War tensions which struck other reform groups. Since the Communists had long been involved in civil rights efforts, the NAACP made an easy target for red-baiting by white conservatives. In response, the organization adopted a strict anticommunist membership policy, moderated its anticolonialist stance and rejected any cooperation with the Communist party in civil rights efforts. In 1948, W.E.B. Du Bois, who had rejoined the NAACP four years previously as Director of Special Research, and remained a symbol of its history, was expelled from the Association due to his left-wing sympathies. The following year, Roy Wilkins wrote an editorial in *The Crisis* strongly attacking black activist Paul Robeson, who was accused of pro-Soviet sentiments. The fear of radicalism and the resulting internal investigations, which aggravated chronic tensions over centralization and organizational democracy, brought about a temporary decline in NAACP membership during the late 1940s, although by 1951, the Association had 1,253 branches, youth councils

One of the things that makes a Negro unpleasant to white folk is the fact that he suffers from their injustice. He is thus a standing rebuke to them.

H. L. MENCKEN
NOTEBOOKS, 1930, IN
MINORITY REPORT: H. L. MENCKEN'S NOTEBOOKS [1956]

See also
Civil Rights Movement

It is never too late to give up our prejudices.

HENRY DAVID THOREAU
"ECONOMY," *WALDEN*, 1854

and college chapters, and a membership of 210,000.

The core of the NAACP's struggle for the passage of antiviolence and other civil rights laws was waged through its Washington bureau, which was created in 1942, as well as its branches. In addition to being executive secretary, Walter White served as the bureau's first director from its creation until 1950, when he relinquished the position to Clarence Mitchell, who also served as legislative chairman of the LCCR. Mitchell's function in developing the organization's political strategy and legislative program was similar to Thurgood Marshall's in the legal area. Both men served a notch under the executive secretary.

Since southerners in Congress continued to block passage of civil rights laws, the NAACP continued to concentrate its efforts on the courts. In 1950, the Supreme Court took decisive steps toward ending the "separate but equal" doctrine in *Sweatt* v. *Painter* and *McLaurin* v. *Oklahoma,* two cases which concerned discrimination in graduate education. In 1953, Dr. Channing H. Tobias, the newly elected chairman of the NAACP board of directors, launched a "Fight for Freedom Fund" campaign and a goal of "Free by '63." This slogan was designed to mobilize all of the organization's resources for what the NAACP saw as the final phase of the struggle to eliminate all state-imposed discrimination in celebration of the Centennial of Lincoln's Emancipation Proclamation. Reinforcing the climate of great anticipation within the civil rights community, President Eisenhower on May 10 addressed the NAACP's "Freedom Fulfillment" conference in Washington. He pledged that wherever the federal authority extended he would do his utmost to bring about racial equality. By 1954, the NAACP's membership had grown to 240,000.

Implementing Brown

On May 17, 1954, the Supreme Court handed down its landmark ruling in *Brown* v. *Board of Education,* which brought about an end to legalized segregation in the United States. Less than a year after he had led the celebrations of the school desegregation case victory, Walter White died. *Brown* v. *Board of Education* was his crowning achievement as much as it was Thurgood Marshall's. However, in his last years, White was an increasingly embattled figure. His autocratic style and overinvolvement in outside activities had made him many enemies on the NAACP board, and his marriage to a white woman in 1949 catalyzed anti-White sentiment. White took a leave

of absence, and found his policy-making power sharply restricted on his return.

Roy Wilkins, who was elected in April 1955 to succeed White as NAACP executive director, faced internal disorganization and enormous challenges. Wilkins's first problem was pressing for the enforcement of the *Brown* decision. NAACP lawyers participated in the formation of desegregation plans, and monitored compliance. In 1956, under NAACP sponsorship, Autherine Lucy, an African American, won a court ruling admitting her to the University of Alabama. However, university officials expelled her on the pretext of preventing violence.

At the same time, the organization was forced to expend effort combatting the onslaught of "massive resistance" to *Brown* unleashed by the white South. The organization's victories in the courts made it a main target of both legal and extralegal intimidation by the Ku Klux Klan, the White Citizen's Councils, and by Southern state governments. For example, on Christmas night of 1951, the home of Harry T. Moore, the NAACP's field secretary in Mims, Florida, was bombed. Moore died in the blast and his wife a few days later from injuries she received that night. In 1955, NAACP officials Rev. George W. Lee and Lamar Smith of Belzoni, Mississippi were shot to death, and Gus Courts, president of the Belzoni NAACP branch, was shot, wounded, and later forced to abandon his store and flee to Chicago. Despite the violence, the NAACP continued to grow. The number of branches in Mississippi increased from ten to twenty-one during 1955, while membership jumped 100 percent.

Meanwhile, Louisiana, Alabama, Texas, Georgia undertook a more deliberate assault on the NAACP. State officials or investigating committees demanded that the Association's branches produce their membership lists, and when the NAACP refused to do so, the states obtained injunctions barring the organization from operating in Louisiana. In 1958, the NAACP won a verdict lifting the Alabama injunction in the U.S. Supreme Court case *National Association for the Advancement of Colored People* v. *Alabama ex rel Patterson,* and enabling the NAACP to resume its activities (though other state action kept it out of Alabama until 1963). Virginia passed a statute for use against NAACP lawyers bringing civil rights suits. Not until the U.S. Supreme Court's 1963 decision in *National Association for the Advancement of Colored People* v. *Button,* would the NAACP's right to bring test cases to court be upheld.

See also

James Weldon Johnson

One casualty of the southern crusade against the NAACP and the *Brown* decision was the splitting off of the NAACP Legal Defense and Educational Fund, Inc. in 1956. The split was caused by personal and strategic differences within the NAACP, and threats from the southerners to rescind the LDF's tax-exempt status.

During this period, the NAACP repeatedly called on President Eisenhower to enforce *Brown* and support civil rights legislation. Eisenhower, sensitive to state's rights, opposed federal action to enforce *Brown*. In 1956, responding to election year domestic considerations as well as international pressure, President Eisenhower called for civil rights legislation in his State of the Union Address. The next year, under the leadership of Senate Majority leader Lyndon Johnson, a Southern filibuster was broken and the 1957 Civil Rights Act passed, handing the NAACP a major victory. While it was a weak voting rights law, it was the first such bill passed by Congress in 82 years and it broke the psychological barrier to civil rights measures. The passage of the Act was somewhat overshadowed that September by the Little Rock crisis, in which Governor Orval Faubus used the Arkansas National Guard to block implementation of a court order, obtained by Daisy Bates, president of the NAACP State Conference of Branches, desegregating Central High School. President Eisenhower was forced to federalize the Arkansas National Guard and order 1,000 members of the 101st Airborne Division into Little Rock in order to enable nine black children to desegregate the school.

The Civil Rights Movement

The NAACP's mastery of civil rights efforts was to be challenged in the 1960s by a new generation of more militant activists. The first sign of the tensions the NAACP would face appeared in 1955 and 1956, when blacks in Montgomery, Alabama, led by the Rev. Martin Luther King, Jr. led a boycott against segregated city buses. Although the movement was sparked by NAACP legal victories against segregation, the principal leaders of the boycott were also local NAACP leaders, and NAACP lawyers successfully argued the U.S. Supreme Court case *Gayle* v. *Browder*, which handed victory to the boycotters, the strategy of direct action they adopted was a radical departure from the Association's well-defined legal and political program.

Inspired by the tactics of nonviolent protest, NAACP Youth Council chapters in Wichita, Kansas, and Oklahoma City further successfully tested a new confrontation strategy in 1958 by staging "sit-downs" at lunch counters to protest segregation. In 1959, the NAACP chapter at Washington University in St. Louis conducted sit-ins to end segregation at local lunch counters. The same year the NAACP hired former CORE activist James Farmer as Program Director in order to set up direct action plans, but he was unable to move the Association's bureaucracy toward support for mass demonstrations, and he returned to CORE after less than two years.

As important as the Youth Council demonstrations were, however, they did not capture national media attention because they were not conducted in the Deep South. On February 1, 1960, four students from North Carolina Agricultural and Technical College sat at a segregated store lunch counter in Greensboro and refused to leave until they were served. Two of the students, Ezell Blair and Joseph McNeil, were former officers of the NAACP's college chapter. The NAACP was heavily involved—the "sit-in" was conducted in consultation with Dr. George Simpkins, president of the Greensboro NAACP branch, and Ralph Jones, president of the branch's executive committee. The Greensboro actions set the stage for the sit-in movement, which spread like brush fire through the South.

While the NAACP supported the sit-ins and NAACP branch officials, notably Mississippi field secretary Medgar Evers, coordinated protest campaigns, the students' confrontations with Jim Crow was an expression of impatience with the NAACP's carefully executed legal and political programs. (Differences over strategy were aggravated by questions of organizational discipline in 1959, when Wilkins suspended Robert Williams, president of the NAACP's Monroe, North Carolina branch, for advocating violent self-defense efforts). Despite the ideological clash, and the intense competition from the young activists for financial contributions, media attention and historical recognition, the strategy of King and the young activists complemented the NAACP's. Furthermore, the NAACP provided large sums for bail money and legal support for the demonstrators, and joined more militant movement groups in local alliances, such as the Council of Federated Organizations.

Despite the media attention that the demonstrations in the South drew, the NAACP's 388,347 members in 46 states and the District of Columbia by 1962 helped it to remain the leader in civil rights. That growth was especially significant, given that repeated court injunctions, state

Roy Ottoway Wilkins served as the NAACP's executive secretary / director for twenty-two years, longer than any other NAACP leader.

PAGE 737

N

**NATIONAL
ASSOCIATION FOR
THE ADVANCEMENT
OF COLORED PEOPLE**

*The Civil Rights
Movement*

*When hope is taken
away from a people,
moral degeneration
follows swiftly after.*

PEARL S. BUCK
LETTER TO *THE NEW YORK
TIMES*, NOV. 15, 1941

MEDGAR EVERS
Martyr of the Civil Rights Movement

Medgar Wylie Evers (July 2, 1925–June 12, 1963), civil rights activist. Born in Decatur, Miss., Medgar Evers served in World War II, graduated from Alcorn Agricultural and Mechanical College, and became an insurance agent. Refused admission to the University of Mississippi's law school, he became the first Mississippi field director of the National Association for the Advancement of Colored People.

Evers's job entailed investigating murders of blacks, including that of Emmett Till; local police generally dismissed such cases as "accidents." A clear target for violence, Evers bought a car big enough to resist being forced off the road, roomy enough to sleep in where motels were segregated, and powerful enough for quick escapes. His family owned guns and kept their window blinds drawn. Evers received daily death threats, but always tried reasoning with callers.

He led voter registration drives and fought segregation; organized consumer boycotts to integrate Leake County schools and the Mississippi State Fair; assisted James Meredith in entering the University of Mississippi; and won a lawsuit integrating Jackson's privately owned buses. He also began a similar effort with Jackson's public parks.

In May 1963, Evers's house was bombed. At a June NAACP rally he declared, "Freedom has never been free . . . I would die, and die gladly, if that would make a better life for [my family]."

In the middle of the night on June 12, Evers arrived home. His wife heard his car door slam, then gunshots. He died that night; his accused murderer was acquitted, despite compelling evidence. Evers was buried at Arlington National Cemetery.

—ELIZABETH FORTSON ARROYO

administrative regulations, punitive legislation, and other intimidating actions prevented many people from working with the NAACP in the South. The restrictions on the NAACP opened a window of opportunity for action by groups such as the Southern Christian Leadership Conference and the Student Nonviolent Coordinating Committee (organized with the aid of NAACP veteran Ella Baker), as well as NAACP spinoffs such as the Alabama Christian Movement for Human Rights.

The NAACP's most outstanding contribution to the Civil Rights Movement continued to be its legal and lobbying efforts. In 1958, the NAACP forced the University of Florida to desegregate. A similar law suit was pending against the University of Georgia when it desegregated in 1961. In 1962, Constance Baker Motley, of the LDF staff directed an NAACP-led battle to desegregate the University of Mississippi.

The NAACP also redoubled its lobbying campaign for passage of a meaningful civil rights law. In February 1963, President John F. Kennedy submitted a weak civil rights bill to Congress. Mobilizing a historic coalition through the LCCR, the NAACP began an all-out struggle for passage of the bill as well as the strengthening of its provisions. NAACP pickets in Lawrence, Kans., New York City, Newark, and Philadelphia helped highlight the struggle for such provisions as a national fair employment practice law.

Events in 1963 reshaped the civil rights bill and the struggle. The demonstrations in Birmingham that King led during the spring provoked national outrage. On June 11th, in response to the demonstrations, President Kennedy delivered a televised civil rights address. The following night, Medgar Evers was assassinated in Jackson, Mississippi. On June 19, the day Evers was buried, Kennedy sent Congress a revised civil rights bill that was much stronger than one he had submitted in February.

The climactic event of 1963 was the August 28 March On Washington. While A. Philip Randolph initiated the call for a march, the NAACP led in organizing it and got the march to broaden its focus to include the legislative struggle.

Following the assassination of President Kennedy in November 1963, Lyndon Johnson vowed to ensure passage of his predecessor's civil rights bill and provided the leadership that the NAACP had demanded from the Executive Branch. Passage of the Civil Rights Act of 1964 was an immense victory for the NAACP. The organization thereafter began the struggle in Congress for passage of legislation to protect the right to vote, and the NAACP helped secure passage of the 1965 Voting Rights Act. Following passage of the civil rights laws, the NAACP switched its attention to getting them enforced, particularly in the areas of public school desegregation, employment and housing. It also sought and won passage

See also
Thurgood Marshall

of strengthening provisions. It won the first extension of the 1965 Voting Rights Act in 1970 with a provision extending protection for the right to vote, as well as subsequent ones.

Despite the NAACP's crucial contribution to legislation which ended state-sponsored racial discrimination, the organization was scorned by increasing numbers of young blacks during the late 1960s as old-fashioned and overly cautious. The cycle of urban racial violence during the 1960s displayed the limits of the NAACP's program in appealing to frustrated urban blacks. Although President Johnson appointed Roy Wilkins a member of the National Advisory Commission on Civil Disorders, and the Commission's well-known 1968 report reflected fully the NAACP's concerns, the NAACP was largely unsuccessful at transforming the report into legislation.

Despite the radical criticism of the NAACP's program, the vitality of the organization's legal strategy was manifest by its continued success in passing legislation, notably its largely single-handed effort to securing the passage of the Fair Housing Act of 1968. Fearing the failure of a legislative struggle for fair housing legislation, many black leaders asked President Johnson to issue an comprehensive executive order barring discrimination in government-sponsored housing programs and federally insured mortgages instead. Johnson, however, did not want to deal with the problem piecemeal, and the NAACP supported him. The final days of this struggle were overshadowed by the assassination of Rev. King in Memphis on April 4. The following day, at a meeting of civil rights leaders at the White House, the NAACP agreed to a suggestion that Congress be urged to pass the fair housing bill as a tribute to the slain leader, and the Civil Rights Act of 1968 passed easily on April 11.

During the late 1960s and early 1970s, the NAACP faced new and sometimes more difficult challenges than in the past. These problems now resulted from systemic or endemic discrimination, which were more difficult to identify than state-imposed segregation and required the development of new strategies to correct. One of the organization's most important functions became the designing and implementing of Affirmative Action and minority hiring programs with government and private business. The NAACP brought suits or sent *amicus curaie* briefs in many notable affirmative action cases, notably the Supreme Court case *Regents of the University of California* v. *Bakke* in 1978.

Another aspect of the NAACP's legal struggle was the campaign against the death penalty. The organization monitored death penalty cases and compiled statistics demonstrating racial disproportions in death penalty sentencing outcomes. As a result, in *Furman* v. *Georgia* (1972), the U.S. Supreme Court temporarily struck down the death penalty.

Among the NAACP's other achievements was a double victory against the confirmation in 1969 of Judge Clement F. Haynsworth of South Carolina and in 1970 of Judge G. Harrold Carswell of Florida as Supreme Court justices, because of their records on racial issues. The NAACP would continue to be influential in Senate voting on executive appointments—for example in 1987, the organization led the successful opposition to the Supreme Court nomination of Robert Bork, and in 1990 helped defeat the confirmation of William Lucas, an African-American conservative, as Assistant Attorney for Civil Rights.

Still another focus of NAACP efforts was its ongoing campaign against media stereotypes. NAACP pressure succeeded in removing "Amos 'n' Andy" from television in the early 1950s, and in the 1960s, NAACP pressure was partly responsible for the creation of the TV series "Julia," the first series with a positive African-American leading character. In the 1980s, the NAACP organized protests of Steven Spielberg's film *The Color Purple* due to its white direction and negative portrayal of black men.

The Search for New Direction

In 1976, Roy Wilkins retired as NAACP executive director. Around the same time, NAACP stalwarts such as Clarence Mitchell and Henry Lee Moon retired. Meanwhile, in a sign of the growing influence of women in the organization and the Civil Rights Movement, in 1975 Margaret Bush Wilson, a St. Louis, Missouri lawyer, was elected chairman of the NAACP Board of Directors, and Hazel Dukes was named president of the organization's powerful New York State chapter.

Along with problems connected with the change in administration, the NAACP faced grave financial problems and some opposition to its program among blacks, who criticized the NAACP as irrelevant to black needs. This opposition was an important challenge facing Benjamin L. Hooks, a minister, lawyer, and member of the Federal Communications Commission, when he became executive director of the Association in January 1977. Hooks assumed command

See also
Martin Luther King, Jr.

N

**NATIONAL
ASSOCIATION FOR
THE ADVANCEMENT
OF COLORED PEOPLE**

*The Search for New
Direction*

JULIAN BOND

Democrat and Activist

Julian Bond (January 14, 1940–), activist, elected official. Julian Bond was born in Nashville, Tenn., of a prominent family of educators and authors. He grew up in the town of Lincoln University, Pa., where his father, Horace Mann Bond, was then president of the university, and later in Atlanta, when his father became president of Atlanta University. While attending Morehouse College in the early 1960s, Julian Bond helped found the Committee on Appeal for Human Rights. He dropped out of Morehouse to join the Student Nonviolent Coordinating Committee (SNCC), of which he became communications director in 1962. In 1964 he traveled to Africa and upon his return became a feature writer for the *Atlanta Inquirer*. Later he was named its managing editor. He eventually received his B.A. from Morehouse in 1981.

Bond won election to the Georgia House of Representatives in 1965, triggering controversy. On January 10, 1966, fellow legislators voted to prevent him from taking his seat in the house when he refused to retract his widely publicized support of draft evasion and anti-Vietnam activism. Protest in defense of Bond's right to expression was strong and widespread. Both SNCC and the Southern Christian Leadership Conference (SCLC) sought mass support for Bond through community meetings, where discussion and ferment strengthened African-American awareness of the relationship between peace activism and the civil rights struggle. The Rev. Dr. Martin Luther King, Jr., rallied to Bond's defense, Vice President Hubert Humphrey publicly supported Bond, and noted cultural figures took out ads for pro-Bond campaigns.

After nearly a year of litigation, the U.S. Supreme Court ruled that Bond's disqualification was unconstitutional. The Georgia house was forced to seat Bond, and he remained in the house until 1975. In 1968 Bond was presented as a possible vice presidential candidate by opposition Democrats at the Democratic Convention in Chicago. He was too young, however, to qualify for the office, and his name was withdrawn. In 1972 he published *A Time to Speak, a Time to Act: The Movement in Politics*, in which he discussed ways of channeling civil rights activism into the electoral system. In 1975 Bond was elected to the Georgia state senate, where he served for twelve years. His activities during this period included the presidency of the Atlanta NAACP, where he served until 1989, and service as the narrator of both parts of the popular PBS documentary series about the Civil Rights Movement, "Eyes on the Prize" (1985–1986, 1988–1989).

In 1986 Bond ran for U.S. Congress from Georgia and narrowly lost in a bitter contest with John Lewis, his former civil rights colleague. In the early 1990s Bond served as visiting professor and fellow at various colleges, including the University of Pennsylvania, Drexel University, Harvard University, and the University of Virginia, and was a frequent essayist and commentator on political issues. He also was, in the early 1990s, the host of a syndicated television program, *TV's Black Forum*. In 1996 Bond was elected Chair of the Board of the NAACP.

—EVAN A. SHORE AND GREG ROBINSON

of the NAACP at a time when it was not only struggling to devise an effective strategy for new civil rights challenges but battling for its very existence. Two adverse judgements in lawsuits against the NAACP in Mississippi presented it with the worst crisis in its lifetime. In 1976, a court awarded Robert Moody, a state highway patrolman, $250,000 as a result of a libel and slander lawsuit that he had filed against the NAACP after local NAACP officials and its state field director had charged him with police brutality. Also, in 1976 the Hinds County Chancery Court in Jackson, Mississippi, handed down a $1.25 million judgment against the NAACP as a result of a lawsuit that local businessmen had filed against the organization following a boycott of their stores. While these judgments were ulti-

mately overturned by higher courts, the NAACP was strapped for money and forced to borrow money in order to bond the judgments on appeal.

The election of Ronald Reagan as President in 1980, at a time when the NAACP was still groping for effective programs to meet new challenges, was an even more ominous development. The Reagan Administration all but destroyed the effectiveness of the U.S. Civil Rights Commission, the Civil Rights Division of the Justice Department, and the Equal Employment Commission. In 1984, Benjamin Hooks led a 125,000 person March on Washington to protest the "legal lynching" of civil rights by the Reagan Administration.

Questions concerning Hooks's leadership gained national attention in 1983 when Wilson unilaterally suspended him. Outraged that Wil-

See also
Malcolm X

son had reprimanded Hooks without its approval, the board ousted her and elected Kelly Alexander, Sr., a North Carolina mortician, chairman. Following Alexander's death in 1986, the board elected Dr. William F. Gibson, a South Carolina dentist, chairman. Under Gibson's leadership, in 1986 the NAACP relocated its national headquarters to Baltimore.

Despite those setbacks, Hooks led the NAACP in winning several promising agreements from corporations, such as $1 billion from the American Gas Association, to provide jobs and other economic opportunities for blacks under a fair share program he inaugurated. Among his other accomplishments was the ACT-SO (Afro-Academic Cultural Technological Scientific Olympics) program he created to promote excellence among minority youth through local, regional and national competition.

In April 1993, Hooks retired as NAACP executive director. The board of directors had considerable difficulty deciding on a successor. Candidates included the Rev. Jesse Jackson. The board finally selected the Rev. Benjamin F. Chavis, Jr., and official of the United Church of Christ in Cleveland. Chavis, much younger than his predecessor, was chosen in an attempt to revitalize the NAACP by attracting new sources of funding and reaching out to young African Americans.

Chavis' first year proved extremely controversial. In accord with his policy of attracting young African Americans, Chavis shifted NAACP policy in a more nationalistic direction. Chavis succeeded in increasing youth interest in the NAACP and was praised for his meetings with gang leaders, but he was widely criticized for inviting black radicals such as Nation of Islam chair Louis Farrakhan to a black leadership conference, and for refusing to disassociate himself from the Nation's anti-Semitic policies. The NAACP's membership dropped significantly as a result.

Chavis also attracted opposition to his administrative policies. Board members were angered by his unauthorized policy statements, such as his approval of the North American Free Trade Agreement. Chavis was blamed for running up the NAACP's deficit, already swelled by declining memberships, to $1.2 million through staff salary increases, and by using organization money to settle a sex discrimination suit filed by a female staffer.

The schism over Chavis' policies provided a forum for fundamental disagreements between blacks over the role of civil rights organizations.

With full legal equality substantially achieved, the NAACP continued to face troubling questions regarding the best use of its leadership and its traditional strategy in attacking the problems of African Americans. The departure of Chavis resulted in an invigorated NAACP. First, in 1995 Myrlie Evers-Williams replaced William F. Gibson as chair of the board, and the following year she was succeeded in the position by Julian Bond. That same year, 1996, Kweisi Mfume became President and CEO of the NAACP.

—DENTON L. WATSON

NATIONAL BAPTIST CONVENTION, U.S.A.

The National Baptist Convention, U.S.A., Inc., founded on September 24, 1895, constitutes the largest body of organized African-American Christians in the world. With over 7.5 million members, this influential body's roots go deep into the early religious and cooperative efforts of free blacks and slaves in antebellum America.

As early as 1834, African Americans in Ohio organized the Providence Baptist Association to strengthen the work of local Baptist churches. The formation of this association established a trend for other local churches, resulting in the organization of other associations, state conventions, regional conventions, and national bodies. The first significant trend toward a national body was the organization in 1894 of the Tripartite Union, consisting of the New England Baptist Foreign Missionary Convention, the African Foreign Mission Convention, and the Foreign Mission Convention of America. Although this Tripartite Union attempt failed by 1895, the spirit of national cooperation eventually prevailed.

In 1895, Revs. S. E. Griggs, L. M. Luke, and A. W. Pegues, former leaders of the Tripartite Union movement, led another attempt at national unity among African-American Baptists. They successfully encouraged the Foreign Mission Convention, the National Baptist Educational Convention, and the American National Baptist Convention to merge into the National Baptist Convention, U.S.A.

The purpose of the newly formed national convention was multipartite. The former work of the National Baptist Educational Convention was increased through the new convention's aggressive involvement in the education of the race. Local

I'm grateful to God that, through the Negro church, the dimension of nonviolence entered our struggle.

MARTIN LUTHER KING, JR.
LETTER FROM A
BIRMINGHAM JAIL, 1963

See also
Sutton Griggs

churches were encouraged to increase their support of secondary schools and colleges throughout the southern region of the United States. Internationally, the National Baptist Convention, U.S.A., advanced foreign missionary projects in Africa, Central America, and the West Indies. Schools, churches, and medical institutions were expanded in various mission stations on these foreign fields. A large number of the leaders among Africans on the developing continent as well as Africans of the diaspora were trained by these institutions.

In order to facilitate practical operations in the National Baptist Convention, U.S.A., the leadership was careful to develop comprehensive plans for a viable structure. The basic strategy was to organize the work of the convention through specialized boards. The leadership organized a Foreign Mission Board, Home Mission Board, Educational Board, Baptist Young People's Union, and Publishing Board. These were designed to carry out the mandates of the convention as articulated by Rev. Elias Camp Morris, the organization's first president. The pattern of specialized boards was continued by the subsequent leadership of the convention, but proved problematic in practice.

Problem areas developed within two of the strongest boards, Foreign Mission and Publishing. By 1897 there was enough internal disturbance in the convention to threaten the unity of the denomination. When the annual session was convened at Ebenezer Baptist Church in Boston, a group of ministers of national prominence led a debate over several key emotion-laden issues: (1) the advisability of moving the Foreign Mission Board from Richmond to Louisville; (2) the use of American Baptist literature and cooperation with white Baptists in general; and (3) a greater emphasis on foreign missions as a primary policy of the convention. The leadership was not able to resolve the conflicts, especially the last. Consequently, several clergymen from Virginia and North Carolina who were in favor of stronger foreign missions issued a call to like-minded ministers to meet at Shiloh Baptist Church in Washington, D.C., on December 11, 1897, for the purpose of developing a new convention strategy. Out of this movement emerged the Lott Carey Baptist Home and Foreign Mission Convention, specializing in foreign missions.

The second problem area was the Publishing Board. The National Baptist Publishing Board, under the leadership of Revs. Henry Allen Boyd and C. H. Clark, was given the exclusive right to publish all church and Sunday-school literature for local Baptist churches. With a significant increase in its financial holdings, the National Baptist Publishing Board tended to act independently of the general leadership of the convention. This resulted in a split within the leadership and the formation of the National Baptist Convention of America in 1915.

The National Baptist Convention, U.S.A., Inc., emerged from these splits, however, as the majority convention among African-American Baptists. Its scheme of organizational structure through major boards remained intact. Morris, the national president, was careful to require responsibility and accountability from the specialized boards' leadership. This policy facilitated unity within the convention until the middle of the twentieth century.

In 1956, a serious debate erupted over the question of tenure. Rev. Joseph H. Jackson, president of the convention, had risen to a position of such power and prestige that a majority of the convention's leaders and delegates desired the continuation of his leadership beyond the tenure limits of the constitution. Tensions increased, resulting in a strong challenge to Jackson's leadership by a group favoring the election of Rev. Gardner C. Taylor of Brooklyn to the presidency. The 1961 presidential election became a crisis that resulted in a civil court battle between Jackson and "the Taylor team." Jackson's position was confirmed by the court.

The Jackson victory did not calm the troubled waters, however. On September 11, 1961, a national call was issued for the organization of the Progressive National Baptist Convention. The rationale for creating a new convention was a protest against Jackson's policy of "gradualism" in civil rights issues, as well as a demonstration of support for Taylor's election bid for the presidency. Moreover, the new convention rallied to give stronger support to the Civil Rights Movement under the leadership of the Rev. Dr. Martin Luther King, Jr.

The National Baptist Convention remained the largest convention of African-American Baptists. But the advance of the civil rights revolution and the growth in power and influence of Martin Luther King, Jr., seriously challenged the moral and racial leadership of the majority convention. This trend continued until King's assassination and the rise of Rev. T. J. Jemison to the presidency of the convention. The new president, a veteran

See also
Martin Luther King, Jr.

civil rights leader, made efforts to restore the convention to its previous leadership role.

—LEROY FITTS

NATIONAL BLACK EVANGELICAL ASSOCIATION

Founded in 1963 as the National Negro Evangelical Association, the National Black Evangelical Association (NBEA) functions as an umbrella association of individuals, organizations, and churches. A theologically conservative organization, the NBEA is one of the same theological genus as the larger, modern, white American fundamentalist movement. This modern American fundamentalist movement had its beginning in the late nineteenth and early twentieth century with the fundamentalist-versus-modernist religious controversy. The National Association of Evangelicals (NAE), founded in 1942 as an outgrowth of this controversy, brought together evangelicals from a variety of theological positions, including fundamentalist, dispensational, Calvinist, Reformed, covenantal, pentecostal, and charismatic. These all hold in common the belief in the historic "fundamentals" of the Protestant tradition: the Reformation and Arminian doctrine of complete reliability and final authority of the Bible in matters of faith and practice; the real, historical character of God's saving work recorded in Scripture; personal eternal salvation only through belief in Jesus Christ; evidence of a spiritually transformed life; and the importance of sharing this belief and experience with others through evangelism and mission works.

In the early twentieth century, a distinct group of Christians within the African-American community aligned themselves with the fundamentalist movement and developed separately from traditional African-American churches. Traditional African-American churches, some of whose history dated back to the seventeenth century, emphasized moral and social reform in the areas of personal piety, slavery, and discrimination. They generally saw themselves as "Bible believers." Black fundamentalists, on the other hand, placed more emphasis on conservative, propositional, and doctrinal aspects of faith. The black fundamentalist charged that African-American churches were one of two types: poor congregations, who were "otherworldly" and emotionally focused in worship; or middle-class congregations, who were theological liberals and embraced modern science. This history caused some strains between these two movements. Some black evangelicals characterized the historic black church as "apostate and un-Biblical," and some in mainline black churches labeled black evangelicals as doctrinaire and schismatic "fanatics." This history led to the presence of African Americans in white fundamentalist and evangelical Bible schools and seminaries in the late 1940s and 1950s. Black alumni from these institutions helped to develop the NBEA.

At the time of its founding, the NBEA did not view itself as racially separatist but as an association focused on developing African-American leadership to minister with clear evangelical emphasis to the black community. During this early stage, many black evangelicals were also frustrated with the white evangelical movement. This tension focused on what blacks perceived as white evangelicals' indifference to and lack of sympathy for the evangelistic needs of the African-American community. This frustration eventually led some black evangelicals to charge their white counterparts with a spiritual "benign neglect." Eventually the charge of neglect evolved into a stronger allegation of racism. From the beginning its social-action commission raised social issues within the NBEA, yet major social concerns were not in the forefront of its work. Instead the NBEA concentrated on strategies for effectively communicating its particular brand of evangelicalism within the African-American community.

Like all social movements, black evangelicalism has not always been unified in its efforts. The movement could not avoid confronting the civil rights and Black Power movements and their attendant black theology movements of the late 1960s and early '70s. The challenges of these new movements, with their emphasis on social justice and self-determination, created anxiety, ambivalence, and dissension within the black evangelical movement. These rifts became evident in several of the annual NBEA conventions.

The Civil Rights Movement forced black evangelicals, in several NBEA conferences between 1968 and 1970, to look at the issues of social justice and racial discrimination and their relationship to presenting the gospel. The conservatives in the movement felt that their first priority was the promulgation of personal salvation rather than attacking social injustice. If society

♦ **Evangelical**
Emphasizing salvation by faith in the atoning death of Jesus Christ through personal conversion, the authority of Scripture, and the importance of preaching, as contrasted with ritual

See also
Civil Rights Movement

was to be changed, it would be through the changing of human hearts rather than through altering the individual person's social condition. The activists within the black evangelical movement argued that social action and the verbal proclamation of the gospel were equal tasks in evangelical missions. The whole truth of the gospel could be received only when the social concerns of the individual were met.

The Black Power movement challenged the black evangelical movement with issues of self-determination. This was reflected in several NBEA conferences from 1970 through 1975. Activist black evangelicals, drawing from Black Power advocates, believed that white evangelicals were too paternalistic in their support and that blacks were too dependent upon whites. The activists argued that African Americans should develop institutions and support within their own communities. They were not completely opposed to white support, however. Whites could contribute to the cause, but without any conditions attached. The conservative wing countered that this stance smacked of divisiveness within the body of Christ. They argued for a more conciliatory role with their white evangelical counterparts, emphasizing Christian reconciliation. This debate forced the movement to look anew at its historical links to the black church as a source of strength and self-determination. These discussions led to another major debate within the black evangelical movement revolving around the role of black theology and African-American culture in the movement as interpretative tools.

Black theology as a movement and the challenge of African-American history and culture were the catalysts of a major debate within the movement. This rift surfaced in several of the NBEA conferences in the late 1970s. Some within the black evangelical movement, such as William Bentley and Columbus Salley, closely followed the writings of black theologians. They disagreed with some black theologians' liberal assumptions regarding biblical authority. Yet these activist black evangelicals agreed with black theologians' interpretative critique of both the liberal and conservative European and white American theologians' claim of universality and, therefore, repudiated the appropriateness and normativeness of white theology in all situations. To these black critics, all theology was culturally bound and, therefore, culturally specific. Theology, then, had to be culturally relevant, and this was especially so for the African-American community. The conservatives countered that what was at

stake in the activists' critique of conservative white theology was the very essence of the theological foundation of this movement. They felt that the use of black theology, with its liberal theological foundation, compromised too much. It contradicted the very basis of their faith. The conservatives also feared that the activists placed too much emphasis on the importance of black culture at the expense of the gospel message.

These issues drove the NBEA to examine the historic role of the black church as an institution and its relationship to social issues. This was evident in the 1990 convention in which the delegates discussed the viability of dropping the term *evangelical* because it conjured images of political conservatism, which, some felt, further alienated the movement from the historic African-American church.

The NBEA's numerical strength is unknown, but its leadership estimates its mailing list at 5,000, with a larger black-evangelical constituency of between 30,000 and 40,000. Its annual convention draws several hundred participants, and smaller numbers participate in the meetings sponsored by local chapters. The NBEA has been an arena in which the differing factions of the black evangelical movement have been able to dialog, to discuss disagreements, and to reach compromise. It has been a delicate balancing act over the years. It remains to be seen whether the movement, and especially the NBEA as an organization, can continue to hold its various camps under its umbrella and simultaneously continue to stretch the canvas to include and win favor with the historic black church community as well.

—ALBERT G. MILLER

NATIONAL COUNCIL OF NEGRO WOMEN

The National Council of Negro Women (NCNW) has been among the most influential African-American women's organizations of the twentieth century, particularly under the guidance of its founder, Mary McLeod Bethune, and its later president Dorothy Height. Bethune seized on the idea of an umbrella organization to bring together the skills and experience of black women in a variety of organizations. This national council would provide leadership and guidance in order to make African-American women's voices heard in every arena of social and political life. When Bethune began to pursue this goal in 1929, she

See also
Mary McLeod Bethune

met with some resistance from the leadership of other national organizations, particularly the National Association of Colored Women. But she was successful in convincing the skeptics that a National Council of Negro Women would respect the achievements and strengths of other groups and streamline the cooperative operations of black women's organizations, rather than supersede existing groups.

The NCNW was founded in New York City on December 5, 1935, after five years of planning. The true signs of Bethune's diplomatic ability were the presence at the founding meeting of representatives of twenty-nine organizations and the election of such important figures as Mary Church Terrell and Charlotte Hawkins Brown to leadership positions. Bethune was elected president by a unanimous vote. The effectiveness of the council and its leadership was immediately apparent. One of its areas of greatest success was labor issues. With Bethune's influence in the federal government, the NCNW, in conjunction with other organizations, pressed for federal jobs for African Americans, and was one of the forces behind the founding of the Fair Employment Practices Committee. Under Bethune's leadership the NCNW also established an important journal, the *Aframerican Woman's Journal,* which in 1949 became *Women United.* The council expressed an interest in international affairs, supporting the founding of the United Nations. From its founding, the United Nations has had an NCNW official observer at its proceedings.

Bethune retired from the presidency of the NCNW in 1949 and was succeeded by Dorothy Boulding Ferebee, the grandniece of Josephine St. Pierre Ruffin and former NCNW treasurer. During Ferebee's tenure, the council continued to press the issues with which it had always been concerned—civil rights, education, jobs, and health care, among others. However, the organization experienced a crisis as it moved beyond merely defining goals and issues toward providing more tangible services to its constituency. This issue carried over to the term of its third president, Vivian Carter Mason, elected in 1953. During her four years in office, Mason employed administrative skills to improve the operation of the national headquarters and to forge closer ties between the local and national councils. Under Mason, the NCNW continued to develop as a force in the struggle for civil rights. Just as Bethune led the organization to fight for the integration of the military, Mason fought for swift implementation of school desegregation.

In 1957, the NCNW elected Dorothy I. Height to be the organization's fourth president. Height came to her work at the council with experience on the national board of the Young Women's Christian Association, eight years as president of Delta Sigma Theta, and involvement in a host of organizations and institutions. Height set out to place the NCNW on firm financial ground through gaining tax-exempt status (accomplished in 1966) and through grants from foundations. She was successful in garnering support from the Ford Foundation and the U.S. Department of Health, Education, and Welfare to expand the scope of the NCNW's work.

Among Height's other major accomplishments as president was the construction of the Bethune Memorial Statue, unveiled in Lincoln Park, Washington, D.C., in 1974. The memorial pays tribute to the contributions of an extraordinary woman. The NCNW continued its commitment to preserve the history of black women through the founding of the National Archives for Black Women's History. Although the council desired such an institution from its founding, the archives did not become a reality until 1979. This collection preserves the papers of the NCNW, the National Committee on Household Employment, and the National Association of Fashion and Accessory Designers. The personal papers of a number of women are also housed there. Through this collection and through conferences sponsored by the archives, the NCNW has become an important force in preserving the records and achievements of black women in the twentieth century.

The list of organizations affiliated with the National Council of Negro Women is long and varied, reflecting the council's commitment to building bridges to create a united voice for black women. Affiliated groups include ten national sororities, the National Association of Negro Business and Professional Women's Clubs, Inc., the Auxiliary of the National Medical Association, women's missionary societies of the National Baptist Convention and the African Methodist Episcopal Church, and Trade Union Women of African Heritage. The NCNW has also developed an international component to its work. In addition to maintaining a presence at the United Nations, it has worked with women in Africa (in Togo and Senegal, for example) and other areas of the diaspora, such as Cuba.

The NCNW has been successful in creating a national organization through which African-American women can address the issues facing

See also
Washington, D.C.

them and their families. It has enabled black women from a variety of backgrounds to design and implement programs and develop themselves as community leaders. The longevity and effectiveness of the council are due to the willingness of its leadership to change and to shape programs and methods to the emerging needs of African-American communities.

—JUDITH WEISENFELD

NATIONAL URBAN LEAGUE

Founded in New York City in 1911 through the consolidation of the Committee for Improving the Industrial Condition of Negroes in New York (1906), the National League for the Protection of Colored Women (1906), and the Committee on Urban Conditions Among Negroes (1910), the National Urban League quickly established itself as the principal organization then dealing with the economic and social problems of blacks in American cities.

The league divided with its contemporary, the National Association for the Advancement of Colored People, the work of the emerging struggle for racial advancement. Securing the legal rights of black Americans was the principal business of the NAACP; promoting economic opportunity and social welfare was the responsibility of the Urban League.

MAKING HEADWAY

The National Urban League improved educational and career opportunities for blacks. The leaders of the organization gather for a photo in 1920. PHOTOGRAPHS AND PRINTS DIVISION, SCHOMBURG CENTER FOR RESEARCH IN BLACK CULTURE, THE NEW YORK PUBLIC LIBRARY, ASTOR, LENOX AND TILDEN FOUNDATIONS

Committed to improving employment opportunities for blacks, the Urban League placed workers in the private sector, attacked the color line in organized labor, and sponsored programs of vocational guidance and job training. While it first concentrated on changing discriminatory employment practices in the private sector, it became involved increasingly over time in trying to influence the development of public policy. During the Great Depression, it lobbied for the inclusion of blacks in federal relief and recovery programs; in the 1940s, it pressed for an end to discrimination in defense industries and for the desegregation of the armed forces.

In the 1950s the league still measured its accomplishments in terms of pilot placements of blacks in jobs previously closed to them because of race. In the 1960s, with the passage of civil rights legislation and the pressures of urban violence, the climate changed. Now the league reported tens of thousands of placements annually in new or upgraded jobs. It sponsored an array of new projects to improve employment opportunities: a national skills bank, for example, which matched blacks who had marketable skills with positions that utilized their talents, and an on-the-job-training program that placed unskilled workers in training slots in private industry. In the 1970s and 1980s, the league pioneered a range of other employment programs providing skills training, apprenticeships, and job placements.

The league grounded its work in social welfare in scientific investigations of conditions among urban blacks which provided the basis for practical reform. Its studies—some published independently, some reported in the league's magazine, *Opportunity: Journal of Negro Life* (1923–1949)—contributed importantly to the development of a body of reliable literature on aspects of black urban life and helped to shape public and private policy with respect to race.

The Urban League pioneered professional social service training for blacks. The agency encouraged black colleges to incorporate instruction in economics, sociology, and urban problems in their curricula, and it cooperated in establishing the first training center for black social workers. An Urban League fellowship program enabled promising blacks to pursue advanced studies at designated schools of social work while gaining some practical experience at the Urban League or similar agencies. The result was a corps of professional black social workers, whom the League placed in a wide range of social service agencies.

The Urban League adapted for blacks the welfare services already offered to whites by settlement houses, charitable agencies, and immigrant aid societies. Working principally through a network of local affiliates, the league counseled blacks new to the cities on behavior, dress, sanitation, health, and homemaking, and sponsored community centers, clinics, kindergartens and day nurseries, and summer camps. League staff members engaged in casework to deal with individual problems including juvenile delinquency, truancy, and marital adjustment.

In the 1960s the Urban League supplemented its traditional social service approach with a more activist commitment to civil rights. It embraced direct action and community organization, sponsored leadership development and voter education and registration projects, helped organize the March on Washington of 1963 and the Poor People's Washington Campaign of 1968, called for a domestic Marshall Plan, and began to concentrate on building economic and political power in inner cities. The agency's services reflected a combination of new activism and the traditional Urban League concerns: assistance to black veterans, campaigns for open housing, consumer protection, efforts to find adoptive families for hard-to-place black children, as well as tutoring programs for ghetto youngsters and street academies to prepare high school dropouts to go to college.

In the 1970s the league became a major subcontractor for government employment and social welfare programs and worked increasingly closely with Congress, the executive departments, and the regulatory agencies as an advocate of the interests of black Americans. It significantly expanded its research capacity, with a range of new monographs and special studies, a policy research journal, *The Urban League Review* (1975–), and a widely publicized annual report, *The State of Black America* (1976–). In the 1980s, as federal social programs were cut back, the organization looked increasingly to black self-help, seeking to mobilize the institutions of the black community to address some of the most persistent problems of the ghetto—the crisis in the public schools, and the high incidence of teenage pregnancy, single female-headed households, and crime.

Guided in its earliest years by George Edmund Haynes, a sociologist who was the first black to earn a Ph.D. from Columbia University, in 1917 the National Urban League came under the direction of his assistant, Eugene Kinckle Jones, a former high school teacher who also held an advanced degree in sociology. Jones was succeeded

as executive secretary in 1941 by Lester B. Granger, a social worker who had been secretary of the league's Workers' Bureau. Granger stepped down in 1961, turning the League's leadership over to Whitney M. Young, Jr., dean of the Atlanta School of Social Work, who served until his death in 1971. Vernon E. Jordan, a lawyer then serving as executive director of the United Negro College Fund, was named president of the National Urban League in 1972. Jordan was succeeded in 1982 by John E. Jacob, also a social worker, who had spent his professional career in a number of Urban League posts, including that of executive vice president of the national organization.

—NANCY J. WEISS

NATION OF ISLAM

In the midsummer of 1930, a friendly but mysterious peddler appeared among rural southern immigrants in a black ghetto of Detroit called "Paradise Valley," selling raincoats, silks, and other sundries but also giving advice to the poor residents about their health and spiritual development. He told them about their "true religion," not Christianity but the "religion of the Black Men" of Asia and Africa. Using both the Bible and the Qur'an in his messages, he taught at first in the private homes of his followers, then rented a hall that was called the Temple of Islam. This mysterious stranger often referred to himself as Mr. Farrad Mohammed, or sometimes as Mr. Wali Farrad, W. D. Fard, or Professor Ford.

Master Fard, as he came to be called, taught his followers about a period of temporary domination and persecution by white "blue-eyed devils," who had achieved their power by brutality, murder, and trickery. But as a prerequisite for black liberation, he stressed the importance of attaining "knowledge of self." He told his followers that they were not Americans and therefore owed no allegiance to the American flag. He wrote two manuals for the movement—*The Secret Ritual of the Nation of Islam*, which is transmitted orally to members, and *Teaching for the Lost-Found Nation of Islam in a Mathematical Way*, which is written in symbolic language and requires special interpretation. Fard established several organizations: the University of Islam, to propagate his teachings; the Muslim Girls Training, to teach female members home economics and how to be a proper Muslim woman; and the Fruit of Islam, consisting of selected male members, to provide security for

With only a third-grade education, Elijah Muhammad was the leader of the most enduring black militant movement in the United States.

PAGE 363

See also
NAACP

WALLACE D. FARD

Mysterious Founder of the Nation of Islam

Wallace D. Fard (?-c. 1934), religious and political leader. Little is known about the mysterious Wallace D. Fard, credited with founding the Nation of Islam. Only the years of 1930 to 1934 are clearly documented. He claimed to have been born in Mecca, a member of the tribe of Kureish, to which the Prophet Muhammad belonged, and to have been educated in England and at the University of California. His detractors claimed he had been jailed in California for dealing in narcotics. Neither of these accounts of his life was ever confirmed.

Fard appeared in Detroit some time before 1930, peddling silks and raincoats and declaring that he was on a mission to secure justice, freedom, and equality for American blacks. He professed that he was an Islamic prophet and that redemption would come through Islam. Fard quickly gained a following, especially among recent immigrants from the South who were undergoing severe economic hardship. In 1930, he set up permanent headquarters for what he called the "Lost-Found Nation of Islam" in the Temple of Islam. He also organized the Fruit of Islam, a defense corps; the Muslim Girls Training Corps Class; and the University of Islam, a radically unconventional elementary and high school that Muslim children attended instead of public schools. Fard began the practice of substituting X for black Muslims' last names—disavowing their identities as slaves. The names were intended to be replaced later by their "original" Arabic names.

Fard asserted that blacks were the first people on Earth, indicating their superiority to whites, whom he castigated as devils. Fard was a reputed nationalist, calling for racial separatism and self-determination in the form of an independent black republic within current U.S. borders.

The Nation of Islam gained mainstream public attention in Detroit in November 1932 when one of its members, Robert Karriem, "sacrificed" his boarder by plunging a knife into his heart. Press reports tried to link this crime to his involvement in the Nation of Islam. The movement, however, continued. After converting an estimated 8,000 Detroit blacks to the Nation of Islam, Fard disappeared in late 1933 or 1934. His followers used the mysterious circumstances of Fard's disappearance to deify him further, maintaining that he was God, although his successor as the Nation's head, Elijah Muhammad, claimed to have accompanied him to the airport when he was deported.

While Wallace Fard clearly was important in the 1930s, his legacy in the large and influential Nation of Islam is most significant. Although his tenure with the organization was short, he continued to be revered as its spiritual leader. The Nation of Islam stated in an official publication in 1942, "We believe that Allah appeared in the person of Master W. Fard Muhammad, July 1930; the long-awaited 'Messiah' of the Christians and the 'Mahdi' of the Muslims."

—SIRAJ AHMED

Muslim leaders and to enforce the disciplinary rules.

One of the earliest officers of the movement and Fard's most trusted lieutenant was Robert Poole, alias Elijah Poole, who was given the Muslim name Elijah Muhammad. The son of a rural Baptist minister and sharecropper from Sandersville, Ga., Poole had immigrated with his family to Detroit in 1923; he and several of his brothers joined the Nation of Islam in 1931. Although he had only a third-grade education, Elijah Muhammad's shrewd native intelligence and hard work enabled him to rise through the ranks rapidly, and he was chosen by Fard as the chief minister of Islam to preside over the daily affairs of the organization.

Fard's mysterious disappearance in 1934 led to an internal struggle for the leadership of the Na-

tion of Islam. As a result of this strife, Muhammad eventually moved his family and close followers, settling on the south side of Chicago in 1936. There they established Temple of Islam No. 2, which eventually became the national headquarters of the movement. Throughout the 1940s, Muhammad reshaped the Nation and gave it his own imprimatur. He firmly established the doctrine that Master Fard was "Allah," and that God is a black man, proclaiming that he, the "Honorable" Elijah Muhammad, knew Allah personally and was anointed his "Messenger." Prior to 1961, members of the Nation of Islam were called "Voodoo People" or "People of the Temple"; Professor C. Eric Lincoln's study *The Black Muslims in America* (1961) established the usage of the phrase "Black Muslims" in referring to the Nation of Islam.

See also

Louis Farrakhan

Under Muhammad's guidance, the Nation developed a two-pronged attack on the problems of the black masses: the development of economic independence and the recovery of an acceptable identity. "Do for Self" became the rallying cry of the movement, which encouraged economic self-reliance for individuals and the black community. The economic ethic of the Black Muslims was a kind of black puritanism—hard work, frugality and the avoidance of debt, self-improvement, and a conservative lifestyle. During the forty-one-year period of his leadership, Muhammad and his followers established more than one hundred temples nationwide and innumerable grocery stores, restaurants, bakeries, and other small businesses. The Nation of Islam also became famous for the foods—bean pies and whiting—it peddled in black communities to improve the nutrition and physical health of African Americans. It strictly forbade alcohol, drugs, pork, and an unhealthy diet. Elijah Muhammad was prescient in his advice on nutrition: "You are what you eat," he often said.

In his *Message to the Black Man in America* (1965), Muhammad diagnosed the vulnerabilities of the black psyche as stemming from a confusion of identity and self-hatred caused by white racism; the cure he prescribed was radical surgery, the formation of a separate black nation. Muhammad's 120 "degrees," or lessons, and the major doctrines and beliefs of the Nation of Islam elaborated on aspects of this central message. The white man is a "devil by nature," unable to respect anyone who is not white and the historical and persistent source of harm and injury to black people. The central theological myth of the Nation tells of Yakub, a black mad scientist who rebelled against Allah by creating the white race, a weak hybrid people who were permitted temporary dominance of the world. But according to the apocalyptic beliefs of the Black Muslims, there will be a clash between the forces of good (blacks) and the forces of evil (whites) in the not-too-distant future, an Armageddon from which black people will emerge victorious and re-create their original hegemony under Allah throughout the world.

All these myths and doctrines have functioned as a theodicy for the Black Muslims, as an explanation and rationalization for the pain and suffering inflicted on black people in America. For example, Malcolm Little described the powerful, jarring impact that the revelation of religious truth had on him in the Norfolk State Prison in Massachusetts after his brother Reginald told

him, "The white man is the Devil." The doctrines of the Nation transformed the chaos of the world behind prison bars into a cosmos, an ordered reality. Malcolm finally had an explanation for the extreme poverty and tragedies his family suffered, and for all the years he had spent hustling and pimping on the streets of Roxbury and Harlem as "Detroit Red." The conversion and total transformation of Malcolm Little into Malcolm X in prison in 1947 is a story of the effectiveness of Elijah Muhammad's message, one that was repeated thousands of times during the period of Muhammad's leadership. Dropping one's surname and taking on an X, standard practice in the movement, was an outward symbol of inward changes: it meant ex-Christian, ex-Negro, ex-slave.

The years between Malcolm's release from prison and his assassination, 1952 to 1965, mark the period of the greatest growth and influence of the Nation of Islam. After meeting Elijah Muhammad in 1952, Malcolm began organizing Muslim temples in New York, Philadelphia, and Boston, and in the South and on the West Coast as well. He founded the Nation's newspaper, *Muhammad Speaks,* in the basement of his home and initiated the practice of requiring every male Muslim to sell an assigned quota of newspapers on the street as a recruiting and fund-raising device. He rose rapidly through the ranks to become minister of Boston Temple No. 11 and was later rewarded with the post of minister of Temple No. 7 in Harlem, the largest and most prestigious of the temples after the Chicago headquarters. The Honorable Elijah Muhammad recognized his organizational talents, enormous charismatic appeal, and forensic abilities by naming Malcolm national representative of the Nation of Islam, second in rank to the Messenger himself. Under his lieutenancy, the Nation achieved a membership estimated at 500,000. But as in other movements of this kind, the numbers involved were quite fluid and the Nation's influence, refracted through the public charisma of Malcolm X, greatly exceeded its actual numbers.

Malcolm's keen intellect, incisive wit, and ardent radicalism made him a formidable critic of American society, including the Civil Rights Movement. As a favorite media personality, he challenged the Rev. Dr. Martin Luther King, Jr.'s central notions of "integration" and "nonviolence." Malcolm felt that what was at stake, at a deeper level than the civil right to sit in a restaurant or even to vote, was the integrity of black selfhood and its independence. His biting critique of the "so-called Negro" and his emphasis on the recov-

See also

Islam

Malcolm X

*No one made a
greater impact upon
the cultural
consciousness of the
African-American
community during
the second half of
the twentieth
century than
Malcolm X.*

PAGE 441

ery of black self-identity and independence provided the intellectual foundations for the American Black Power Movement and black-consciousness movement of the late 1960s and 1970s. In contrast to King's nonviolence, Malcolm urged his followers to defend themselves "by any means possible." He articulated the pent-up frustration, bitterness, and rage felt by the dispossessed black masses, the "grass roots."

As the result of a dispute on political philosophy and morality with Elijah Muhammad, Malcolm left the Nation of Islam in March 1964 in order to form his own organizations, the Muslim Mosque Inc. and the Organization for Afro-American Unity. He took the Muslim name el-Hajj Malik el-Shabazz after converting to orthodox Sunni Islam and participating in the hajj, the annual pilgrimage to Mecca. Malcolm was assassinated on February 21, 1965, while he was delivering a lecture at the Audubon Ballroom in Harlem.

From 1965 until Elijah Muhammad's death in February 1975, the Nation of Islam prospered economically, but its membership never surged again. Minister Louis X of Boston, also called Louis Abdul Farrakhan, replaced Malcolm as the national representative and the head minister of Temple No. 7 in New York. During this period, the Nation acquired an ultramodern printing press, cattle farms in Georgia and Alabama, and a bank in Chicago.

After a bout of illness, Muhammad died in Chicago and one of his six sons, Wallace Deen Muhammad (later Imam Warith Deen Muhammad), was named supreme minister of the Nation of Islam. However, two months later Wallace shocked his followers and the world by declaring that whites were no longer viewed as devils and they could join the movement. He began to make radical changes in the doctrines and the structure of the Nation, moving it in the direction of orthodox Sunni Islam.

The changes introduced by Imam Warith Deen Muhammad led to a splintering of the movement, especially among the hard-core black-nationalist followers. In 1978, Louis Farrakhan led a schismatic group that succeeded in resurrecting the old Nation of Islam. Farrakhan's Nation, which is also based in Chicago, retains the black-nationalist and separatist beliefs and doctrines that were central to the teachings of Elijah Muhammad. Farrakhan displays much of the charisma and forensic candor of Malcolm X, and his message of black nationalism is again directed to those mired in the underclass, as well as to dis-

illusioned intellectuals, via the Nation's *Final Call* newspaper and popular rap-music groups such as Public Enemy.

Through more than sixty years, the Nation of Islam in its various forms has become the longest-lasting and most enduring of the black militant and separatist movements that have appeared in the history of black people in the United States. Besides its crucial role in the development of the black-consciousness movement, the Nation is important for having introduced Islam as a fourth major religious tradition in American society, alongside Protestantism, Catholicism, and Judaism.

—LAWRENCE H. MAMIYA AND C. ERIC LINCOLN

NAT TURNER'S REBELLION

Nat Turner (October 2, 1800–November 11, 1831) led the most significant slave revolt in U.S. history. Undertaken in 1831 in Virginia, Turner's Rebellion claimed more lives than any similar uprising. It had repercussions throughout the South, redrawing the lines of the American debate over slavery in ways that led toward all-out civil war within a generation. Indeed, some suggest that it represented the first major battle of the long war to end slavery.

In 1831 Virginia's Southampton County, bordering on North Carolina, contained roughly 6,500 whites and 9,500 blacks. Almost all of the latter, whether young or old, lived in perpetual bondage, including Nat Turner, a slave of Joseph Travis. Turner had been born in Southampton on October 2, 1800, only five days before the execution of black revolutionary Gabriel Prosser in Richmond, and as a boy he must have heard stories of Prosser's intended insurrection. Tradition suggests his mother was born and raised in Africa. She told her son at an early age that, on the basis of his quick intelligence and the distinctive lumps on his head, he seemed "intended for some great purpose."

Turner learned to read as a small boy, and he built a strong and composite faith from listening to the African beliefs retained within his family and the Christian values of his first master, Benjamin Turner. Confident from childhood that he had a special role to play, Nat Turner found outward confirmations for his messianic thoughts and eventually determined that his personal calling coincided with the most pressing public issue of the day—the termination of racial enslavement.

Most of what we know about the man must be drawn from his *Confessions*, a remarkable autobiographical statement taken down by a young lawyer named Thomas Ruffin Gray during the rebel's final days in jail. While one can question the validity of Turner's recollections and the motivations of the disillusioned and desperate Gray (who rapidly published his lurid transcript at a profit), the confession has an underlying ring of truth and represents one of the most extraordinary firsthand texts in American history.

According to this account, Turner experienced a powerful vision in 1825 in which he "saw white spirits and black spirits engaged in battle, and the sun was darkened—the thunder rolled in the Heavens, and blood flowed in streams. . . ." Three years later, another vision told him to prepare to slay his "enemies with their own weapons." But it was not until February 1831 that a solar eclipse signaled to Turner that he must begin. He laid plans with others to act on the holiday of July 4, but when he fell ill, the date was allowed to pass. Then, on August 13, he awoke to find the sun a dim reflection of itself, changing from one hazy color to another. Taking this as another sign, he brought together a handful of collaborators on Sunday, August 21, and told them of his plan for a terrorist attack.

His intention, Turner explained, was to move through the countryside from household to household, killing whites regardless of age or sex. He hoped that this brutal show of force would be so swift as to prevent any warning and so compelling as to convince others to join in the cause. Having rallied supporters and gathered up more horses and weapons, they could march on Jerusalem, the county seat, and take the arsenal, which would give them a substantial beachhead of resistance. From there the rebellion could spread, aided by a network of enslaved black Christians, and perhaps by divine intervention as well. Turner made clear, according to the *Richmond Enquirer*, that "indiscriminate slaughter was not their intention after they obtained a foothold, and was resorted to in the first instance to strike terror and alarm. Women and children would afterwards have been spared, and men too who ceased to resist."

Shortly after midnight, Turner and five others launched their violent offensive, attacking the home of Turner's master and killing the Travis household, then proceeding on to other farmsteads to wreak similar vengeance. As their ranks grew, the band became more disorderly and the element of surprise was lost, but the first militiamen who offered resistance on Monday afternoon beat a hasty retreat. By Monday night, as many as sixty or seventy African Americans had joined the cause, and on Tuesday morning Turner's army set out for Jerusalem. Behind them at least fifty-seven whites of all ages had been killed in a stretch of twenty miles.

When some rebels stopped at James Parker's farm, within three miles of Jerusalem, to win recruits and refresh themselves, the pause proved fatal, for the local militia had regrouped. They managed to attack and disperse the insurgents, who were off guard and poorly armed. Although Turner attempted to rally his followers, he never regained the initiative, and on Tuesday, white reinforcements launched a harsh and indiscriminate counteroffensive that took well over a hundred lives. One cavalry company slaughtered forty blacks in two days, mounting more than a dozen severed heads atop poles as public warnings. Turner, his force destroyed, eluded authorities for six weeks—during which time another black preacher known as David attempted to ignite an uprising in North Carolina, fueling white fears of widespread rebellion. After an enormous manhunt, authorities captured Turner in a swamp on October 30 and hanged him publicly twelve days later.

Turner's unprecedented insurgency had a complex impact. It forced Virginia's legislature to consider openly, if briefly, the prospect of gradual emancipation. It also attracted proslavery whites to the colonization movement, since many saw African resettlement as a way to remove dangerous bondsmen and reduce the free black community. For black and white abolitionists in the North, Turner's Rebellion reinforced the idea, later espoused by John Brown, that enslaved Southerners were willing and able to engage in armed revolt if only weapons and outside support could be arranged. Among churchgoing slaveholders, the uprising prompted tighter restrictions on black preaching and greater caution regarding slave access to the Gospel. Among African Americans, Turner became and has remained both a martyr and a folk hero never to be forgotten. As recently as 1969, one black Southampton resident could recall what his mother had learned in her childhood: that Nat Turner "was a man of war, and for legal rights, and for freedom."

—PETER H. WOOD

See also
Civil War
Slavery

NAYLOR, GLORIA

Gloria Naylor (January 25, 1950–), writer. Gloria Naylor was born in New York City to Roosevelt and Alberta Naylor. After traveling through New York, Florida, and North Carolina as a missionary for the Jehovah's Witnesses (1968–1975) she returned to New York, where she worked as a telephone operator at various hotels while she attended Brooklyn College (B.A., 1981). She received an M.A. in Afro-American Studies from Yale University in 1983.

Naylor's first published work, *The Women of Brewster Place* (1982), won the American Book Award for best first novel in 1983. Dealing with the lives of seven black women who live on one ghetto street, the novel conveys the oppression and spiritual strength that African-American women share. At the same time, by exploring the characters' differences, it emphasizes the variety of their experience. Naylor wrote a television screenplay adaptation of the novel which starred Oprah Winfrey and appeared on *American Playhouse* in 1984. Her next novel, *Linden Hills* (1985), is concerned with the spiritual decay of a group of black Americans who live in an affluent community, having forsaken their heritage in favor of material gain. *Mama Day*, published in 1988, tells of an elderly lady with magical powers. The bestselling *Bailey's Cafe* (1992) takes place in a 1940s American diner where neighborhood prostitutes congregate. Naylor wrote a play based on the novel which was produced and performed by the Hartford Stage Company in 1994. She also wrote the screenplay for the PBS presentation *In Our Own Words* (1985).

Naylor has said that she writes because her perspective, that of the black American woman, has been "underrepresented in American literature." Her goal is to present the diversity of the black experience. Although she reworks traditional Western sources in her novels, borrowing the structure of Dante's *Inferno* for *Linden Hills*, and elements of Shakespeare's *The Tempest* for *Mama Day*, Naylor utilizes black vernacular and other aspects of her own heritage in her writing.

Naylor has taught at George Washington University, New York University, Princeton, Cornell, and Boston University. She has received a National Endowment for the Arts Fellowship (1985), the Distinguished Writer Award from the Mid-Atlantic Writers Association (1983), the Candace Award from the National Coalition of 100 Black Women (1986), and a Guggenheim Fellowship (1988).

—LILY PHILLIPS AND LYDIA MCNEILL

See also

Literature

NEAL, LARRY

Larry Neal (September 5, 1937–January 6, 1981), writer. Larry Neal, one of the most prominent figures of the Black Arts Movement of the 1960s and 1970s, was born in Atlanta and graduated from Lincoln University in Pennsylvania in 1961, receiving an M.A. from the University of Pennsylvania in 1963. Neal soon became one of the most prominent of the African-American writers that emerged in the early 1960s championing the search for a distinctive African-American aesthetic. His early articles, including "The Negro in the Theatre" (1964) and "Cultural Front" (1965), were among the earliest to assert the need for separate cultural forms as necessary to the development of black artists in a racist society.

Neal developed his perspective on black art in the influential anthology *Black Fire* (1968), coedited with Amiri Baraka, and the essay "The Black Arts Movement" (1968), which helped give a name and direction to the nascent artistic trend. Neal argued that the purpose of black arts was to effect a "radical reordering of the Western cultural aesthetic" in part through a purging of the external European and white American cultural influences from black artistic expression. His critical thinking was further developed in a series of books: *Black Boogaloo: Notes on Black Liberation* (1969); *Trippin' a Need for Change* (1969), coauthored with Amiri Baraka and journalist A. B. Spellman; and *Hoodoo Hollerin Bebop Ghosts* (1971). Neal also authored plays (*The Glorious Monster in the Bell of the Horn*, 1976), screenplays (*Holler S.O.S.*, [1971]; *Moving on Up*, [1973]), and television scripts (*Lenox Avenue Sunday*, [1966]; *Deep River* [1967]).

Neal was an instructor at the City College of New York from 1968 to 1969, and subsequently taught at Wesleyan University (1969–1970) and Yale University (1970–1975). By the mid-1970s Neal was reconsidering his view of black culture. In "The Black Contribution to American Letters" (1976), he argued that while all African-American writers and literature must be in some sense political, it was important to separate the public persona of black writers from their specific private experiences, which are often wider and more inclusive than the polemical rejection of nonblack influences that characterized the Black Arts Movement. Other late works of Neal include a play, *In an Upstate Motel*, which premiered in New York in 1981. Neal died of a heart attack in Hamilton, N.Y., in 1981.

—REGINALD MARTIN

NEWARK, NEW JERSEY

Situated on the Passaic River in northern New Jersey, Newark was founded in 1666. It remained largely agricultural for the next 150 years, and slavery was practiced on a small scale in the area through the beginning of the nineteenth century. Starting in the 1830s, industrialization caused a spurt in local economic and population growth. In 1832 the town of Newark received its charter, and four years later was incorporated as a city. As German and Irish immigrants came to Newark, the population increased almost tenfold in forty years. Slavery in Newark and New Jersey finally ended in the 1840s, though the city remained sympathetic to Southern interests and largely free of abolitionist activity.

The city's modest free black community of poor laborers and servants, which never exceeded 2,000, was molded during this period. The Baxter School, a private black school, was founded in 1828. In 1832 the city's first black church, the Thirteenth Street Presbyterian Church, was founded. St. James African Methodist Episcopal Church was founded in 1842, and St. Phillip's Episcopal Church followed not long after.

In the decades following the Civil War, small numbers of African Americans migrated to Newark, and the town's black population grew to 10,000 by World War I, an overflow from the larger migration to nearby New York City. The thousands of immigrants from southern and eastern Europe who poured into Newark provided competition for labor and for scarce housing resources (one-fifth of the city's area was marshlands, and there was a chronic land and housing shortage). Meanwhile, the city's increasingly powerful industrial unions excluded black workers: In 1903, only six of the city's twenty-two major unions accepted black laborers.

During these decades, the city's black population remained almost exclusively trapped at the bottom of the economic ladder. In 1890 almost two-thirds of all male African Americans were engaged in unskilled labor or as servants, and 88 percent of women were maids or laundresses. Twenty years later, the picture was substantially the same. A few African Americans were able to found successful businesses. C. M. "Chicken" Brown operated a poultry stand, and Mary and Frank Anderson were the proprietors of a hotel with mostly white patrons. John S. Pinkman, who ran a furniture moving concern, became relatively wealthy.

At the same time, Newark was mostly free of overt racial tension, and the city's blacks were relatively integrated into community affairs. Housing stock, while poor, was open to blacks, and African Americans lived in integrated working-class areas throughout the city. The only all-black enclave was a district on the northern side of the downtown area. Public accommodations remained largely segregated, but schools integrated peacefully after the New Jersey Supreme Court's 1884 decision in *Pierce* v. *School Board of Burlington County,* which declared school segregation unconstitutional. In 1909, city authorities closed the all-black Baxter school, claiming separate schools were unnecessary.

The black community fostered several lasting institutions during this period. In 1871 the Bethany Baptist Church (later the city's largest black church) was founded. Bethany Church members also founded the Bethany Lodge, a masonic fraternity; the Sunday Afternoon Lyceum, a literary circle; and the Coloured Home for Aged and Orphans in nearby Montclair. In 1902, the *Appeal,* the city's first black newspaper, was founded. It was published through 1910. During the early 1900s, the Frederick Douglass Republican Club was organized to promote voting.

The Great Migration altered the face of black Newark. As the coming of World War I opened up jobs for African Americans in the city's steel mills and in war industries such as munitions plants, brickyards, and wire factories, southeastern blacks, the largest number from Georgia, poured into the city. The Negro Welfare League, an interracial group of black ministers and professionals and white businessmen founded in 1910 (transformed into the Newark branch of the National Urban League in 1919) and led by African-American Thomas Puryear, attempted to find jobs and housing for the migrants, some of whom were forced into shantytowns and tent cities. The league obtained employment for black workers, who were largely excluded from white unions, often through the use of no-strike pledges. The only large protest by black workers during the period was that of the dockworkers, led by Prosper Brewer (later a political leader and the black ward's Republican ward committeeman), who struck successfully for higher wages in 1916.

By the end of the 1920s, Newark's economy was already depressed, and its white population began to decline. Many large industrial firms left the crowded city for larger sites. Business flight cost the city well-paid jobs and tax revenue for city services, and the city's commission system of

Like China, New Jersey absorbs the invader.

FEDERAL WRITERS' PROJECT
NEW JERSEY: A GUIDE TO ITS PRESENT AND PAST, 1939

See also
National Urban League

government led to unresponsive and notoriously corrupt rule. Within such an environment, racial tension grew. Downtown stores, swimming pools, and theaters continued to exclude black patrons, who were forced into segregated neighborhoods in the old downtown areas. The Third Ward, better known as the "Hill District" and considered by many commentators "the worst slum in America," was the center of Newark's black community. By 1930, 30 percent of the city's 38,880 African-American residents lived there. Antiquated zoning laws, which prevented construction of new housing, meant that few blacks owned their homes, and most were forced to settle in overcrowded dilapidated, expensive, old, white-owned housing. Sanitation was primitive, and black residents were plagued by tuberculosis and venereal disease. In 1923, the city's Board of Health tried to use the tuberculosis epidemic as a pretext for deporting black migrants. In 1927, Dr. John Kenney founded Kenney Memorial Hospital to care for poor citizens. Police harassment was a chronic

problem. In 1928, police Captain George Fohs prohibited interracial contact after midnight in the district. In 1930 white city residents vetoed a proposal by the Prudential Insurance Corporation to build a black housing development in the Hill district.

Despite the depressing living conditions, a thriving black culture grew up within the "Roaring Third" Ward during the 1920s and 1930s. Religious institutions flourished, including heterodox denominations such as Father Divine's movement and Noble Drew Ali's Moorish Science Temple, founded in 1915, a black nationalist religious group that prefigured the Nation of Islam. An active jazz scene, loosely connected with New York City's, arose in the ward. It was centered on the core intersection of Spruce Street (the "Colored Broadway") and Broome Street. There, theaters such as the Orpheum and Paramount, and such nightclubs as the Kinney Club and the Skateland Club, featured New York performers and hopefuls such as Jimmy Lunceford

MAJOR LEAGUE PLAYER

A Varied Career for Larry Doby

Lawrence Eugene "Larry" Doby (December 13, 1923–), baseball player. Larry Doby was the second African American to play major league baseball and the second to manage a major league team. Born and raised in Camden, S.C. Doby moved to Paterson, N.J., in 1938, where he starred in three sports at Eastside High. During his high school years, he also played semipro baseball. In 1942, after graduation, Doby joined the Newark Eagles of the Negro National League, playing under the name "Larry Walker" to protect his amateur status. During the off-season, Doby attended Long Island University and Virginia Union University. Doby's career was interrupted by naval service from 1944 to 1945. In 1946, he returned to the Eagles, made the league all-star team, and helped lead them to the NNL pennant. According to surviving statistics, Doby hit .378 in the NNL, with 25 home runs in 139 games.

Doby played during the winter of 1946 and '47 with the San Juan Senators in Puerto Rico. In spring 1947, while Doby was playing with the Eagles, the Cleveland Indians of the American League recruited him for their outfield and purchased his contract. Doby joined the team on July 4, 1947, several months after Jackie Robinson had broken the color line of major league baseball with the Brooklyn

Dodgers of the National League. Although he faced much of the same brutal racist treatment from fans and other players that Robinson did, Doby received little media attention playing in Cleveland. He batted .301 in 1948, and .318 in that season's World Series. In eleven seasons, playing for Cleveland, Chicago, and Detroit, he batted .283, twice led the league in home runs (1952 and 1954, with 32), and made the all-star team six times. In 1962, at age 38, after retiring briefly, Doby went to Japan to play two seasons for the Chunichi Dragons. He was the second American to play in Japan.

After returning from Japan, Doby worked in Cleveland's Center Field Lounge, and operated a liquor store. In 1967, he was appointed Director of Bicycle Safety for Essex County, N.J. When the Montreal Expos were organized in 1969, Doby joined them as a scout and batting coach. In the winter of 1971 and in 1972, Doby managed a team in Venezuela, but lost his job when he refused to throw a game. In 1978 Doby was named manager of the Chicago White Sox, but he held that position for only 87 games, winning 37 and losing 50. In 1980, Doby became director of community relations with the National Basketball League's New Jersey Nets.

—GREG ROBINSON

See also
Baseball

and Ella Fitzgerald. Newark also has been the home of many important musicians in various genres, such as Willie "The Lion" Smith, Sarah Vaughan, Wayne Shorter, Babs Gonzales, Larry Young, Woody Shaw, James Moody, Hank Mobley, and Dave Thomas. Another focus of black community interest during the period was Ruppert Stadium, home of the Newark Eagles of the Negro National League, who featured such players as Larry Doby and future Hall-of-Famers Monte Irvin, Ray Dandridge, and (briefly) Satchel Paige.

The Great Depression devastated Newark. In the face of white competition, many blacks were unable to find work. By 1931 there were 20,000 African Americans on relief, one-third of the city's total. Although almost all welfare recipients were longtime Newark residents, in 1932 city officials organized a movement to send back all newly arrived southern blacks in order to reduce welfare rolls. Black ministers and leaders campaigned successfully against the project, and Newark Urban League president Thomas Puryear, who collaborated on it, was forced to resign.

The Depression and the struggle to remain in the city radicalized many young black Newark residents. In 1934, activist Harold Lett became director of the Newark Urban League and led protests over black job exclusion. The same year, Guy Moorehead organized the Essex County Worker's League, and in 1936 became New Jersey's first black Democratic state representative. In 1938 black community forces led by the Newark branch of the National Negro Congress successfully picketed chain stores to obtain jobs for African Americans. In 1939 Fred and Richard Martin bought the *Newark Herald* newspaper, renamed it the *Newark Herald-News,* and made it a powerful voice for civil rights during the 1940s.

The economic boom that followed the outbreak of World War II brought renewed black mass migration to Newark. African Americans, who had represented just 10 percent of the city's 1940 population, tripled over the next twenty years, growing to one-third of the city's total. Although black protesters won token access to public places, the rise in population was not accompanied by a rise in status. Indeed, whites actively opposed black equality. In 1949 the city Board of Education approved a policy of free transfers for white students from black majority schools, and by 1951, some 3,200 white students were attending schools outside their districts. In 1953 a reform city government was elected and replaced the corrupt city commission regime, which had systematically discriminated against blacks, with a mayor and city council.

The next year, Newark African Americans finally got their first voice in government, when former NAACP president Harry Hazelwood was named city magistrate, and newspaperman Irvine Turner was elected to the new city council, where he remained until 1970. Even so, the reform movement proved ephemeral, and Newark's Democratic machine soon regained control. Poor city services and police brutality remained chronic problems. Meanwhile, Turner became a corrupt and powerful "boss" in the black community. Famous for his fiery rhetorical denunciations of "slumlords" and racist practices, he tried to curtail efforts at reform by other blacks. The Newark NAACP, whose leaders were dependent on the machine, failed to press strongly for city action in support of black equality.

During the 1950s, even as the white population was reduced, the black population began to decline, as middle-class blacks moved to nearby suburbs. By the beginning of the 1960s, Newark was, in an often-used phrase, a "terminal case"—a city with little industry, high unemployment, corrupt government, and racial unrest. Its high crime rate and poor city services foreshadowed the problems of many urban areas in the United States at the end of the twentieth century.

Within the city, black residents unwilling to put up with discrimination began organizing civil rights efforts. In 1961 a chapter of the Congress of Racial Equality (CORE) was formed, and members protested police brutality, housing discrimination, and began negotiations with employers for jobs. In 1963 CORE joined with other groups to form the Newark Coordination Council (NCC). When the NCC protested discrimination in hiring for city school construction projects, Mayor Hugh Addonizio, supported by Turner and NAACP leader Carlton Norris, refused to act or meet with "irresponsible" protesters. Police harassment of NCC members weakened the group.

Despite official opposition, the African-American community was growing more powerful in Newark. White flight led to an African-American majority population by mid-decade, and federal antipoverty projects designed to bypass the city machine and encourage community participation fostered such black organizations as the Newark Community Union Project. Post and community organizer Imamu Amiri Baraka (formerly LeRoi Jones) returned to his native Newark, founded the community arts center Spirit House, and established the Temple of

See also
Nation of Islam

Kawaida as a center of African-American religion and culture. In 1966 Kenneth A. Gibson ran for Mayor. Though he was defeated, his strong showing clearly demonstrated the rise of African American political power in Newark. Meanwhile, radical protest groups were created. In 1967 Abdul-Jerud Hassan formed the Blackman's Liberation Army, and Baraka formed the Committee for a Unified Newark. The following year, Newark was the location of the first Black Power Conference. Black community groups organized successfully to oppose the granting of land in a black neighborhood to a state medical college, and blocked the appointment of an unqualified white city councilman, James Callaghan, to the school board, though they were unable to secure the appointment of City Budget Director Wilbur Parker, an African American.

On July 12, 1967, John Smith, a black cabdriver, attempted to speed past a police car and was arrested, beaten, and taken to a police station. Rumors of his death spread through the black community. The next night, after a "Police Brutality Protest Rally" downtown, rioting broke out, and crowds began looting and setting fires throughout the city. National Guard troops arrived to arrest rioters and looters, but the violence continued for three nights. Twenty-one African Americans died, 1,600 were arrested, and over $10,000,000 in property was destroyed. In 1968, following the assassination of the Rev. Dr. Martin Luther King, Jr., rioting broke out again.

The riots scarred Newark both physically and emotionally. During the following years, as whites continued to move out of the city, blacks concentrated on political organizing. In 1968 Mayor Addonizio was forced out of office after being convicted on criminal corruption charges. In 1970 Kenneth A. Gibson again ran for mayor. He received almost no white votes, but was elected by a coalition of black and Hispanic voters. Gibson was elected as a reformer, but was largely unable to dismantle existing police and educational structures. In 1971 Gibson appointed several new members to the city Board of Education in order to assure a nonwhite majority. The white-led city teacher's union went on strike for eleven weeks to protest the appointments, the longest teacher's strike ever in a large city in the United States.

Gibson remained in office for four terms. He attracted large amounts of federal money for improvements at Newark airport and the Port of Newark. He also was successful in persuading businesses such as Prudential Insurance to remain in Newark and secured funds to revive the downtown area. With the aid of federal grants, the city soon had the nation's largest percentage of families in public housing projects, including the Kawaida Towers development. Still, Newark remained a poor city, with high unemployment, crime, and homicide rates, dilapidated schools and housing, and poor city services. Gibson was increasingly criticized as ineffective in improving conditions, and in 1986 he was challenged and defeated in the Democratic mayoral primary by City Councilman Sharpe James. James was elected mayor and was reelected in 1990. By the early 1990s, blacks dominated the city's political scene. In 1988 Newark's Donald Payne became New Jersey's first black congressperson.

African-American life in Newark remained difficult in the early 1990s. The frustrations of the period were symbolized by an epidemic of car theft. Many young black men without jobs turned to stealing cars for joyrides as a form of excitement. Still, Newark's African-American residents have continued to struggle to improve conditions and enrich their lives. Institutions such as the Newark Museum and the Institute of Jazz Studies at Rutgers University-Newark (one of the city's two colleges) were particularly notable for their efforts to promote black culture. Newark also has been the home base of a large number of successful black business and professional people, as well as such entertainers as Dionne Warwick, Melba Moore, and Cissy and Whitney Houston.

—GREG ROBINSON

NEW ORLEANS, LOUISIANA

New Orleans was founded in 1718 by Jean Baptiste, Sieur de Bienville, governor of the French Colony of Louisiana, and was made the capital of the colony in 1722. By 1721 the town contained 145 white men, 65 white women, 38 children, 29 white servants, 172 black slaves, and 21 Indian slaves. The first imported slaves, five hundred Africans bought on credit from the St. Domingue colony (now Haiti), came in 1719. In the following twelve years, twenty-three slave ships arrived in Louisiana.

While only a few slaves were imported in the following forty years, the black inhabitants, mainly Senegalese (brought directly from Africa, unlike most blacks in British North America) helped build a distinct Afro-French culture in New Orleans. The enslaved black community

See also
Amiri Baraka
National Negro Congress

soon included most of the town's skilled laborers, and the "donated" labor of blacks built much of the city. Black Creoles—the term usually refers to native Louisianian francophones—borrowed heavily in their cuisine and art from African models, and passed them along to whites. Africans contributed words to the creole dialect. The first *code noir* (Black Code), passed in 1724, prohibited mixed-race marriage, provided for Roman Catholic religious training, outlawed Sunday labor, and allowed slaves to own property and marry. Many slave owners ignored the code.

New Orleans grew slowly into a major port. In 1763, along with the rest of the Louisiana Territory, it was ceded to Spain in the Treaty of Paris. In 1791, slave revolts in St. Domingue, plus smaller ones in rural Louisiana, brought large numbers of whites, free mulattos, and enslaved blacks, to New Orleans. Further immigrants from St. Domingue entered in 1809, when they were expelled from Spanish Cuba. In 1795, Spain granted the United States free navigation of the Mississippi River, and use of the large depot at New Orleans. Americans began to settle in the city. In 1800 France regained Louisiana in a secret treaty, though three years later, New Orleans and the Louisiana Territory were sold by Napoleon to the United States.

Throughout the years of Spanish rule, New Orleans remained largely French in culture. However, while slavery continued, the nature of the town's African-American population began to change, as a new, free colored community, mostly composed of mulattos, came into being. In 1769, the town contained 1,225 slaves, but only 100 free persons of color. The latter number would grow to 1,200 by the end of the Spanish era, against a slave population of 3,000, as a result of natural increase plus a huge Caribbean influx. The Spanish encouraged the growth of a free colored community as a buffer between blacks and whites. Spanish law made manumission easy and slaves worked to purchase their own freedom. Some earned their freedom by serving in militia units. Though most free blacks had enslaved relatives, authorities made use of them as city guards, in slave patrols, and as informers.

Under American rule, New Orleans became the most important city in the South, and a major port and banking center for the Mississippi River region. The city's French character, and its large black and immigrant population, highlighted its distinctiveness. Gen. Andrew Jackson recruited black troops from the city for the Battle of New Orleans in 1815, and in the mid-1840s black contingents fought in the *Mexican War*. Antebellum African-American culture in New Orleans took diverse forms. Congo Square in the center of the city, which took its name from the slaves who established a market there for their own produce, was the scene of funerals and public dances, with dances such as the *carabiné* and music provided by African instruments. The Voodoo religion, a syncretic combination of African snake worship, Haitian rituals, and Christian elements, attracted followers of all races and religions. Dr. John was dubbed the "king" of his voodoo, while his rival, Madame Marie Laveau, was acclaimed the "queen." Even the dominant Catholic religion was affected by African traditions. The famous Mardi Gras, the carnival preceding Lent, is adapted in part from African festivals. Blacks offered for sale at the slave auctions under the giant rotunda of the St. Louis Hotel often were presented in Mardi Gras-style costumes.

Although the Louisiana Civil Code of 1808 forbade mulattos from marrying either whites or black slaves, New Orleans became famous for its quadroon balls where white men trysted with mixed-race women. Mulatto women were kept under the arrangement known as *plaçage*. Under this system, white men took mulatto mistresses as "second wives," buying houses for the women and any children that resulted from their union. Mulatto children often legally inherited their parents' money and property, including slaves, and frequently traveled to France to vacation or be educated. Prominent mulatto citizens included Bastile Croquière, who instructed elite whites in fencing; Norbert Rillieux, inventor of the vacuum pump for sugar refining; Aristide Mary, philanthropist and real estate tycoon; Victor Sejour, a playwright; the doctors Louis Charles Roundanez, James Derham, and Alexandre Chaumette; the composer/conductor Edmond Dédé, who later led the Alcazar Orchestra in France; and the sculptor Eugene Warbourg. In 1845, a circle of writers, led by Armand Lanusse, published a volume of verse, entitled *Les Cenelles.*

The free black community prospered and continued to grow. Job opportunities for skilled black laborers were reasonably plentiful, since few white immigrants were trained artisans. Legal manumission remained simple. Free Anglo-American blacks continued to migrate to the city, although they remained largely separate from the creole community. They formed Baptist and Methodist churches, and joined several Masonic groups.

Despite New Orleans's reputation for tolerance, segregation and discrimination hindered the

> *New Orleans is the unique American place.*
>
> CHARLES KURAULT
> *CHARLES KURALT'S AMERICA,*
> 1995

See also

Jazz

*The first publicized
exhibition of a
work by a black
photographer was
held on March 15,
1840, in the hall of
the St. Charles
Museum in the city
of New Orleans.*

PAGE 546

lives of free people of color. Blacks were officially excluded when the New Orleans public school system was established in 1841, although some white fathers enrolled their mulatto children. Roman Catholic schools were established for blacks, such as the Couvent Institute. The Institute, funded by a legacy from an ex-slave, was established in 1847. As the city's Anglo-American population became dominant, and whites aligned themselves with the other southern states, prejudice against free people of color increased. By the 1850s black organizations such as churches and fraternal societies were forced to lead increasingly clandestine existences. The French *code noir* was officially abrogated in the mid-1850s. Laws against free black migration were enforced, and manumission became difficult.

The coming of the Civil War in 1861 dramatically changed the situation of African Americans in the city. When the war began, some 1,400 free people of color (eventually 3,000), acting variously out of southern patriotism, slaveholder interest, and/or fear of white wrath, entered the Confederate Army as an unarmed unit, the New Orleans Home Guards. The Union takeover of New Orleans in 1862 galvanized the city's black population and that of the surrounding area. Slavery became almost extinct in the area, as slaves left their masters and poured into the city. Union Army Gen. Benjamin Butler, commanding the city, originally opposed efforts by blacks to enlist in the Union Army. By September 1862 this policy was reversed, and eventually three black New Orleans units, including the Corps D'Afrique, were established.

Despite the military ability of African Americans, and the creoles' evident dignity and social standing, civil rights efforts lagged. The Union occupation forces retained the harsh Black Codes of the 1850s. Since President Abraham Lincoln had exempted Louisiana from the Emancipation Proclamation, free people of color began to lobby to formally end slavery throughout the United States, and in March, 1864, two creole delegates, E. Arnold Bertonneau and Jean-Baptiste Roudanez, went to Washington to press Congress and President Lincoln to extend suffrage rights to Louisiana's blacks. Their efforts were unsuccessful. Black creole opinion had as its major forum *L'Union*, a French (later bilingual) biweekly journal that became the major black newspaper. It folded in mid-1864, but Paul Trévigne, its editor, quickly began the bilingual *Tribune*, which in fall 1864 became the first African-American daily newspaper. The creole elite and black Americans

joined together at that time to form the National Equal Rights League of Louisiana. In 1864, league members lobbied in Congress against the bill readmitting Louisiana to the Union, since the government denied blacks suffrage. The end of the war brought fresh conflict to New Orleans.

In July 1866, a Radical Republican convention, organized to consider changing the 1864 state constitution to grant black suffrage, was held at the mechanics' Institute, Louisiana's capitol building. A group of freed blacks, led by a marching band, attempted to cross Canal Street, the city's wide main artery, to protest outside the convention. They were jeered by a white mob, organized by conservatives trying to break up the convention. A white protester shot at the blacks, who fired back. Police opened fire into the crowd of black marchers. Antiblack violence spread across the city. Neither the Union Army nor the Freedmen's Bureau intervened. By the time order was restored, 37 people were dead, 34 of them black; 136 people were wounded, 119 of them black; and police had made 293 arrests. Outrage over the violence in Congress led in part to the Civil Rights Act of 1866.

The following year, 1867, after African American William Nichols was thrown off a streetcar, New Orleans black leaders organized a successful sit-in campaign, and a mob of 500 blacks stoned segregated "star cars." Gen. Philip Sheridan, commanding the region, refused to support segregated facilities, and desegregation was achieved. The same year, Congress passed the Reconstruction Act, which dissolved the Louisiana government. The interim government enfranchised blacks. The next year, 1868, Sheridan organized a "Black and Tan" Radical Republican constitutional convention, of which two-thirds of the delegates were African-American. The new constitution provided for racial equality and integrated public schools, which opened in 1869. That same year, the Republican legislature passed a public accommodations law, which creoles and others enforced through large damage suits against violators.

In 1868, however, the race for the Republican nomination for governor, then tantamount to election, destroyed the fragile creole-American black alliance. That year, the black creole Francis Dumas, a Union army veteran and former slaveholder, ran for the gubernatorial nomination with the support of the *Tribune*, which refused to back a white candidate, Henry Warmoth. Warmoth, with the support of P.B.S. Pinchback, a powerful army veteran and political broker who had recently come to New Orleans, won a very close

See also
Civil War

race. Warmoth named the black Oscar Dunn his lieutenant governor, but broke with the creoles, ending the public subsidies that kept the *Tribune* afloat. His ally, Pinchback, named lieutenant governor in 1871, briefly became the first African-American state governor after Warmoth's impeachment in 1872. Pinchback was later elected to the U.S. Senate.

New black and creole institutions were set up in the post-bellum era. Blacks formed their own churches and Scots rite Masonic lodges and benevolent societies, although creoles generally stayed in interracial Catholic churches and French rite Masonic lodges. Three colleges opened in New Orleans: Straight University (1869), founded under the aegis of the American Missionary Association; Leland University (1869), a private college; and New Orleans University (1873), a state-funded institution. Originally integrated, eight of the ten graduates of its first Law School class in 1878 were white. Another college, Southern University, opened in 1879 (after it moved in 1914, its buildings housed Xavier University). The colleges remained intellectual centers through the Jim Crow era, and helped take the place of city high schools, which excluded blacks from 1879 to 1917 and segregated them afterwards.

Reconstruction also brought a cultural flowering in African-American New Orleans. Theaters opened, and public lectures—especially those of the African-American female suffragist and poet, Frances E. W. Harper—were popular among creoles. Dance halls such as the Brown, the Natural, the Economy, and the Union were popular among blacks. There were even large dances held at the state capitol. Many people enjoyed horse races and regattas, often organized through the city's many social clubs. Baseball had a wide following in the city. There were interracial games in the 1870s.

Perhaps most importantly, music was played throughout the city: A New Orleans University group gave concerts of spirituals; minstrel shows and vaudeville were popular, as were many brass bands, the most famous of them Sylvester Decker's Excelsior Brass Band; and Professor Louis Martin's Negro Symphony Orchestra and black concert performers, such as Victor Eugene Macarthy, played classical music. When a French opera company was stranded in the city in 1875, the black creole community sponsored a season of performances.

In 1874, white rioters rose up against Louisiana's biracial government in the so-called Battle of Liberty Place. In 1876 white Democrats won a disputed election and immediately started "redeeming" the state. City schools and public accommodations were resegregated almost immediately, although public transportation remained integrated. Most blacks were now restricted to older, squalid and segregated residential areas. During the 1880s, the creole élite, led by real estate tycoon and philanthropist Aristide Mary and lawyer/journalist Rodolphe Desdunes, began new efforts against discriminatory legislation. In 1887, Desdunes formed *L'Union Louisianaise,* which with creole financial support, grew into a newspaper, the New Orleans *Crusader,* for a time the nation's only African-American daily. In 1890, after the passage of a law segregating railroad transportation, the creoles formed a *Comité des Citoyens* to challenge the law in court, and raised money to defer legal expenses. A member of the *Comité,* Homer Plessy, agreed to serve as defendant. In 1896, however, the U.S. Supreme Court ruled in the *Plessy* v. *Ferguson* decision that "separate but equal" facilities were constitutional. The turn of the century brought the final decline of the creole community. The strict color bar eliminated the vestiges of their privileges, and promoted assimilation with blacks.

Despite official segregation and continuing racial tension, which broke into a major riot in 1900, New Orleans remained a culturally interracial city. One locus of interracial contact in these years, though clandestine and exploitative, was Storyville, the legal red-light district. Despite the romantic aura of Storyville, it played only a small part in African-American life in the city. The prostitutes, the majority African Americans, ranged in their pigmentation. The most expensive houses, which attracted an exclusively white clientele, usually featured light-skinned women. The owners of the larger brothels, except for "Miss Lulu" White, were all white.

The lively entertainment scene in New Orleans—of which Storyville was only one aspect—nurtured the growth of distinctive African-American musical forms, especially jazz. Early jazz, as played in the first years of the twentieth century by pioneers such as Buddy Bolden, Jelly Roll Morton and King Oliver, developed from a melange of ragtime, marching bands, and the music of popular entertainment halls. New Orleans' unusual multiracial culture promoted its development. Early jazz was primarily collectively improvised polyphonic versions of rags and of blues melodies. After 1915, with the emergence of the white Original Dixieland Jazz Band (who made

See also

Jim Crow

A city of sin and
gayety unique on
the North American
continent.

HERBERT ASBURY
*THE FRENCH QUARTER: AN
INFORMAL HISTORY OF THE
NEW ORLEANS UNDERWORLD,*
1936

"KING" OLIVER

Pioneering Jazz Trumpeter a New Orleans Legend

Joseph "King" Oliver (May 11, 1885–April 8, 1938), cornetist and bandleader. Joseph Oliver was born in Donaldsville, La., and raised in New Orleans. He began his music studies on trombone, and eventually switched to cornet and trumpet. While still a teen he began performing at dances, at parades, and in brass bands, although he made his living at times as a butler. Oliver's first important work (1916–1919) came with bandleader Edward "Kid" Ory, who gave him his nickname. Oliver moved to Chicago in 1919 to play in bassist Bill Johnson's band. He also co-led a band with clarinetist Lawrence Duhé. In 1921 Oliver performed in San Francisco.

The next year found him back in Chicago, where he led the enormously influential "hot" style Creole Jazz Band, including clarinetist Jimmie Noone, at the Royal Gardens Cafe, later known as the Lincoln Gardens. In 1922 Oliver called on trumpeter Louis Armstrong, who had substituted for him in Ory's group, to join the band. Oliver's classic 1923–1924 ensemble, which also included clarinetist Johnny Dodds, his brother drummer Baby Dodds, pianist Lil Hardin, trombonist Honore Dutrey, and Bill Johnson on banjo and double bass, is among the first great jazz ensembles, and is certainly the greatest authentic New Orleans-style ensemble to record. The group's 1923–1924 recordings, with their spontaneous polyphony and surging, four-to-the-beat rhythmic attack on "Riverside Blues," "Tears," "Weatherbird Rag," "Dipper Mouth Blues," "Chimes Blues," and "Canal Street Blues," rank with recordings by Jelly Roll Morton the same year as among the earliest African-American New Orleans-style jazz recordings.

Armstrong left the Oliver band after a tour of the Midwest in 1924, and in that year Oliver disbanded the Creole Jazz Band and recorded duos with Jelly Roll Morton. From 1924–1927 Oliver led a larger group called the Dixie Syncopators, including tenor saxophonist and clarinetist Barney Bigard, and also played again with Ory. In the late 1920s and early 1930s he led his own groups, with a somewhat sweeter, more bluesy sound ("Someday Sweetheart," 1927, "Too Late," 1929, "Sweet Like This," 1929). During these years Oliver also served as a sensitive accompanist for blues singers such as Sippi Wallace and Victoria Spivey.

Oliver was a pioneering jazz trumpeter, with an unadorned but highly expressive style. The recorded solo breaks he traded with Louis Armstrong in 1923–1924 show that his talent and influence also lay in straight and plunger-muted voicelike passages. In his final years Oliver was plagued by financial setbacks and failing health, including the gum disease that would make performing on cornet difficult. In the early and mid–1930s he toured with his own ensembles in the South and Southwest. In 1937 he quit music, and thereafter worked at a fruit stand and as a pool hall attendant. He died in Savannah, Ga., in 1938.

—LAWRENCE GUSHEE

the first jazz recordings in 1917), and after 1920, with King Oliver and Louis Armstrong, jazz soon became successively a national and international craze. However, the lure of larger entertainment markets elsewhere, such as Chicago and New York City, led to an exodus of jazz musicians to the North. By 1925, New Orleans was largely depleted of its first-rank jazz musicians, and the dominance of "New Orleans Jazz" was essentially over.

The depression of 1893 brought conflict and rioting by whites over apportionment of labor on the docks, and destroyed the uneasy decade-long alliance between black and white unionized labor. The two sides recognized their interest in alliance, though, and by 1901 made fresh agreements, which held through a general strike in 1907, and lasted until the decline of the unions in 1923.

During the following years, a few blacks were promoted to supervisory positions, but eventually the absence of union work rules and wage scales led to a steep decline in wages and working conditions. Beginning in 1929, the Great Depression further eroded black labor influence in the port.

Meanwhile, the city continued as a musical center. Traditional jazz remained a mainstay of New Orleans culture. In places such as Preservation Hall, early New Orleans jazz was lovingly preserved, primarily for the benefit of tourists. In 1969, the popular New Orleans Jazz and Heritage Festival was inaugurated. New Orleans also helped spawn other popular African-American musical forms. The great gospel singer Mahalia Jackson came from New Orleans, though the bulk of her career was spent in Chicago. In the 1930s and '40s local musicians, influenced by Latin and

Caribbean rhythms, developed an infectious, fast-paced, piano-centered blues style generally known as New Orleans rhythm and blues. The pioneers include Professor Longhair, Lloyd Price, and Dave Bartholomew, though the best-known exponent in the style was Fats Domino, one of the leading rock-and-roll performers of the 1950s. The Neville Brothers had a successful rhythm and blues career stretching from the 1950s through the 1990s. New Orleans is the hometown of a number of contemporary black musicians; avant-garde drummer Ed Blackwell hailed from New Orleans, and in the 1980s, natives Branford and Wynton Marsalis came to national prominence as jazz artists. In tribute to its musical heritage, in the 1990s the city was selected as the home of the Black Music Hall of Fame and Museum.

The movement for black equality never completely died in New Orleans. During the 1920s the black Federation of Civic Leagues, an organization of social clubs led by creole activist A. P. Tureaud, sponsored a New Orleans branch of the NAACP. The NAACP successfully challenged a 1924 residential segregation ordinance in the U.S. Supreme Court, won salary equalization for African-American teachers in the early 1940s, and paid residents' poll taxes to further an unsuccessful electoral challenge to voter registration laws. In 1946, Tureaud sponsored a lawsuit, *Hall* v. *Nagel,* which eased white interference with black voter registration. In 1953, after another lawsuit, *Tureaud* v. *Board of Supervisors,* Tureaud opened the doors of Louisiana State University to blacks.

During the 1950s, a moderate mayor, Chep Morrison, eased police harassment of blacks. However, only a few small gains were made in desegregation. Blacks remained largely excluded from downtown areas. The NAACP, led by Ernest "Dutch" Morial, faced constant white opposition, although white harassment increased the NAACP's prestige in the black community. In 1958, following a suit in court, Judge Skelly Wright voided streetcar/bus segregation, and in 1960, despite Morrison's strong opposition, the first schools were desegregated. The same year, activists from the Congress of Racial Equality (CORE) sponsored sit-ins and direct action on Canal St. White storeowners challenged the legality of the sit-ins, but the U.S. Supreme Court ruled in *Garner* v. *Louisiana* (1960) that they were constitutionally protected. The sit-ins eventually brought about the desegregation of city lunch counters in 1962. The NAACP joined CORE and other black groups in a short-lived Citizen's Committee, which sponsored a march on City Hall in

September 1963. Nevertheless, the process of desegregation was slow. In 1965, African-American players staged a walkout at an American Football League All-Star game in New Orleans to protest racial discrimination in the city.

The U.S. Voting Rights Act of 1965 altered the city's political landscape. In 1967, Dutch Morial won a seat in the Louisiana legislature, and two years later, almost won a seat as councilman-at-large. The same year, with his support and that of two important black political clubs, Community Organization for Urban Politics (COUP) and Southern Organization for Unified Leadership (SOUL), the moderate liberal Moon Landrieu was elected mayor. Landrieu ended discrimination in public accommodations and awarded city patronage to black allies in COUP and SOUL, particularly jobs connected with the Superdome, the city's giant new sports arena. During the early 1970s, a combination of white flight and new economic opportunity, transformed New Orleans into an African-American majority city.

In 1978, Dutch Morial ran for mayor and won by a narrow margin, mostly on the strength of the black vote. Ironically, due to past personal and political disagreements, Morial was opposed or only halfheartedly supported by COUP and SOUL, whose leaders he proceeded to prosecute for corruption once in office. Morial served two terms, retaining popularity among his black constituency despite opposition from both whites and black leaders over his independent policy-making, including color-blind merit hiring. In 1985, Sidney Barthelemy of COUP, running as a moderate against another black candidate, became New Orleans' second African-American mayor. Ironically, he received barely 25 percent of the black vote, but won 85 percent of the white vote.

While racial divisions continue to plague New Orleans, there has been progress in certain areas. In 1989, city officials voted to store the Liberty Monument, an obelisk commemorating the Battle of Liberty Place, on the grounds that it commemorated prejudice and served as a rallying point for the Ku Klux Klan. White supremacists led by gubernatorial candidate David Duke challenged the removal. In 1993, after a court ordered the monument restored, the city's Human Rights Commission voted unanimously that it be removed. The same year, under pressure from the city council, the Rex organization, one of the four prestigious secret societies that plan the city's annual Mardi Gras festival, invited its first three blacks to become members.

—CHARLES VINCENT

Zydeco is a style of popular dance music played by African Americans of Francophone descent in the bayou country of southwestern Louisiana.

PAGE 753

NEW YORK CITY

The founding by the Dutch of the colony of New Netherland in 1624 and its principal city, New Amsterdam, was soon followed by the importation of African slaves in 1626. Africans were an integral part of the economic development of the colony as the Dutch West India Company enslaved Africans for use on public works. Unlike other colonies in the New World, those in bondage to the company had certain basic rights such as baptism, marriage, and some legal standing afforded by the courts in a colony that operated without a formal slave code. Indeed, some Africans occupied a status termed "half-freedom," which released them from bondage for an annual payment to the company and the use of their labor at unspecified times. The precise extent of African slavery is unclear during this period, but it was increasing in the late 1650s.

A more restrictive form of bondage was introduced with the English conquest of New Netherland in 1664. Under the English, the colony became New York and the main city was renamed New York City. By 1741, blacks numbered 20 percent of the city's 11,000 population. English fears of a slave uprising became quite pronounced after the April 6, 1712 insurrection of approximately two dozen slaves. The hysteria following the insurrection resulted in the temporary closing of Elias Neau's Catechism School for Negroes, the first school for blacks in British North America, opened in 1704. In March of 1741 a rash of ten fires occurred (eight in six days) which many residents construed to be the beginning of a slave rebellion. Whether a form of protest against slavery or a revolt to overthrow slavery, some thirteen blacks were burned at the stake, sixteen hung along with four whites, and seventy-one deported.

Since the area's early settlement by the Dutch in the seventeenth century, blacks resided not only on Manhattan Island, or the city itself, but also lived in Brooklyn. A 1698 census of the province revealed no free blacks in Kings County (then a collection of independent villages that included Brooklyn), but indicated that there were 296 slaves, which constituted 15 percent of the county's population of 2,017. By 1738, Kings County was the leading slave holding county in New York, and by 1790 blacks accounted for more than one-third of the population. The agricultural economy of King's County accounts for the small number of free blacks—only 46—and the large number of slaves, 1,482. In comparison, 33 per-

cent, or 1,036, of New York City's black population was free. By 1820, only seven years before mandatory emancipation in the state, half of Kings County's black population remained enslaved. In 1820, more than 60 percent of white families in Kings County owned slaves, compared to 18 percent in New York City.

Slavery in New York City was not overthrown by overt rebellion, but by those in the state who recognized the contradiction between a slave society and the democratic rhetoric of the Revolutionary War; this recognition culminated in the passage of the gradual abolition law of 1799. In the final years of the institution in New York City most slave holding units were of small size. In 1790, 75 percent of slave holders in the city owned only one or two slaves.

The gradual emergence of a free black population led to the formation of a separate black institutional life in the 1790s and early nineteenth century. Black members dissatisfied with the discriminatory treatment they received within white churches left to form their own churches. African Americans attended segregated schools since they were excluded from most white schools. The best known school in early New York City was the African Free School, founded by the largely white New York Manumission Society in 1787. Blacks also started their own schools and formed mutual aid societies like the New York African Society for Mutual Relief in 1810, which was designed to aid the poor, widows, orphans, and disabled. The creation in 1827 of the nation's first black newspaper, *Freedom's Journal,* by John Russwurm and Samuel Cornish, provided a means of communication and discussion relevant to free blacks and the antislavery movement. In 1800 black Methodists in New York City, led by Peter Williams, consecrated the Zion Church, which in time became the founding congregation of the African Methodist Episcopal Zion Church. His son, Peter Williams, Jr., founded the first black Episcopal church in New York City, St. Phillips African Church in 1819. Other leading antebellum figures raised in New York City included abolitionists Henry Highland Garnet and Alexander Crummell. New York City also had some immigration of persons of African descent from the Caribbean in the late eighteenth century. Haiti was the largest source of emigrants, of whom the best known was the prominent lay Roman Catholic Pierre Toussaint.

Some free blacks prospered in this period of transition from slavery to freedom which occurred simultaneously with the movement of New York

See also

Claude McKay

National Urban League

City's economy toward "metropolitan industrialization." In 1800 more than one in three free male blacks worked as artisans, and by 1810, despite the economic hardships wrought by the Embargo Act of 1807, which prohibited exports from the United States to any foreign country, nearly three in ten male blacks were still classified as artisan. The embargo, which had been instituted to avoid war with British and French warships seizing American neutral vessels, did not reverse black economic opportunities in New York. These opportunities, however, decreased over the next decades as prejudice and discrimination from employers, the consuming public, native workers, and a poor competitive immigrant working class combined to drive blacks out of recently acquired skilled jobs and exclude them from newly developing industrial jobs. The economic position of blacks was fragile in the early nineteenth century. Attacks on individual black property owners by poor whites had begun during the first two decades of the nineteenth century and foreshad-

owed the antiabolitionist and antiblack riots of 1834 and 1835.

The position of African Americans was threatened by restrictions on their right to vote and an erosion of their economic status in the antebellum era. New York City blacks were affected after 1821 by the revised state constitution which retained a prohibitive $250 property qualification for voting for black males while eliminating property qualifications for white male voters. Occupational opportunities for free blacks also declined as they were forced out of many unskilled jobs due to competition from the increasing immigrant Irish population.

The perception of blacks as a racially inferior and degraded people coupled with the animosities fueled by economic competition resulted in numerous attacks on blacks, perhaps the most notable being the infamous Civil War draft riot of 1863 in which the Colored Orphan Asylum was burned down, almost one hundred persons were killed, and many blacks fled the city. Lincoln's

DEMONSTRATION MARCH

The streets of New York fill with early twentieth-century blacks marching in the name of equal rights.
PRINTS AND PHOTOGRAPHS DIVISION, LIBRARY OF CONGRESS

Emancipation Proclamation of 1862 had turned the war from one to preserve the Union to one to end slavery. Immigrant workers unable to pay the $300 "commutation fee" to avoid the draft and fearful of the job competition from emancipated blacks much prophesied by Democratic party propaganda ventilated their racial prejudices and economic fears upon the city's small black population.

Blacks fleeing the draft riots in 1863 were driven from downtown Brooklyn and New York City. Some found refuge in the Weeksville-Carrsville area of Kings County, named after local blacks. This area is located in present-day Bedford-Stuyvesant. The Weeksville-Carrsville area dates from the 1830s and was an acknowledged neighborhood by the 1840s. A sense of racial solidarity and assertiveness existed in the neighborhood; Weeksville blacks petitioned, albeit unsuccessfully, in 1869 to have a black ap-

pointed to the Brooklyn Board of Education so that they could have a say in the governance of the five "colored" schools. (In 1882 Phillip A. White became the first black on the Brooklyn Board of Education.) The distinctive black character of Weeksville and other parts of the Ninth Ward (which included part of present-day Bedford-Stuyvesant) was lost by 1870 as whites purchased property and moved into the area touted as excellent for "genteel suburban residences." However, more was lost than the character of the neighborhood, for as immigrants came to Brooklyn and New York City they and their offspring forced blacks out of skilled and semiskilled jobs.

Despite the contributions of black New Yorkers to the Union victory, including the formation of the Twentieth United States Colored Infantry, the referendum in New York State advocating equal suffrage was defeated. Equal suffrage for black New Yorkers would not come until the pas-

VIOLENT INSURRECTION
New York City Draft Riot of 1863 Intensifies Racism

The New York City Draft Riot of 1863 was the most violent of several urban insurrections that occurred during the Civil War. In Detroit, Toledo, Harrisburg, and Cincinnati the economic and social disruption caused by the war provoked violent protests and intensified the racism directed against northern free blacks. The violence in New York City was a direct response to federal implementation of the military-conscription act, but other conditions contributed to the magnitude of the insurrection. Longstanding economic competition between working-class whites and African Americans, particularly between Irish immigrants and blacks on the city's wharves, had strained race relations. A strong local Democratic party organization nurtured anti-Republican sentiment, and an inflammatory pro-Confederate and racist press fueled racial hatred and popular resentment against federal government policies.

Beginning on July 13, white mobs paralyzed the city. Numbering in the thousands and scattered throughout the city, the rioters overwhelmed the city's meager police force. They besieged the *New York Tribune* offices in search of the paper's Unionist editor, Horace Greeley. They ravaged the home of the city's provost marshal, and threatened the lives of other prominent Union sympathizers. But the mobs directed much of their wrath on the city's black community. Black New Yorkers were harassed, bru-

tally beaten in the streets, and driven from their homes. The mobs singled out black institutions, symbols of racial progress, for destruction. They burned the Colored Orphan Asylum and looted the Colored Seamen's Home. Black residents fled their homes in terror and took refuge outside the city. Some, in desperation, sought protection under police custody in the municipal jails. The rioters murdered at least eleven blacks and injured hundreds of others. Union army regiments, some recent arrivals from the Gettysburg battlefield, were brought in to restore order.

The rioting and the government's forceful response resulted in at least 105 deaths and hundreds of other casualties. Most of the dead and wounded were rioters. Property damage was extensive; in some cases the mobs razed entire city blocks. Losses exceeded $1.5 million, or about $16 million by present standards. Black residents and businesses suffered several thousand dollars in property losses. A special committee of New York City merchants raised over $50,000 to compensate many of the black victims and to rebuild the Colored Orphan Asylum. But no monetary reparations could relieve the psychological devastation or remove the specter of the mob's lynch law. Broken and dispirited by the five days of terror, many blacks left the city. By 1865, New York City had lost 20 percent of its black population.

—MICHAEL F. HEMBREE

See also

Jazz

NAACP

sage of the Fifteenth Amendment to the U.S. Constitution in 1870. Between 1870 and the turn of the century African Americans continued to contribute to the establishment of new institutions and organizations in their community. The *New York Age,* founded in 1887 under the editorship of T. Thomas Fortune, became one of the leading black newspapers in the nation. In the early years of the twentieth century Charles Anderson, a close ally of Booker T. Washington, was a leading black Republican politician. During the same years Tammany Hall organized the United Colored Democracy, its black auxiliary. During these years, the city's black population rose significantly from 17,580 in 1860 to 33,888 by 1890. Nevertheless, blacks remained less than 2 percent of the total population as southern and eastern European immigrants swelled the city's population.

In 1900, after the 1898 consolidation of the five boroughs (Manhattan, Brooklyn, Queens, the Bronx, and Staten Island), New York City had 60,000 black residents. By 1920, it had the largest black population of any city in the country, though less than 3 percent of the population was black. The city's ethnic diversification was accompanied by considerable social upheaval as groups contended for jobs and living space. African Americans, who had lived in the Greenwich Village area of Manhattan, were slowly moving northward and by the 1890s were residing in substantial numbers in the infamous San Juan Hill area (centered on the West Side of Manhattan between Sixtieth and Sixty-sixth Streets on Tenth and Eleventh Avenues), so named because of the frequent interracial battles there. The worst disturbance during these years was the August 1900 antiblack riot when policemen joined the white mobs in attacking blacks all along Eighth Avenue between Twenty-seventh and Forty-second Streets.

Seeking the security of new neighborhoods, better housing stock, and the concomitant status, blacks took the opportunity to move into the middle-class community of Harlem, created by vacant apartments in an overbuilt housing market, and the entrepreneurial skills of a black realtor, Philip A. Payton, and his Afro-American Realty Company organized in 1904. Many of the major African-American social, fraternal, and religious institutions relocated from their downtown quarters to Harlem by the early 1920s. The African Methodist Episcopal Zion ("Mother Zion"), St. Philip's Protestant Episcopal Church, and Abyssinian Baptist Church were some of the prominent churches that reestablished themselves in Harlem. The "Great Migration" of blacks from the South and the Caribbean was intensified by the demand for labor in the North during the World War I years. The black population of New York City increased from 60,666 in 1900 to 152,407 in 1920. Of Manhattan's black population of 109,133 in 1920, two-thirds lived in Harlem.

New York City also became the center of increased Caribbean immigration. Approximately 25 percent of Harlem's black population were foreign-born by the mid-1920s, with the vast majority of the foreign-born composed of Caribbean immigrants. Although the foreign-born percentage decreased 16.7 percent by 1930 due to restrictive immigration laws, West Indian immigrants continued to play an important role in the economic, intellectual, and political life of New York City. By 1930, an estimated one-third of New York City's black professionals were from the Caribbean. Harlem was home to many prominent Caribbean intellectuals such as journalist and African Blood Brotherhood leader Cyril Briggs, socialist organizers Frank Crosswaith and H. H. Harrison, and nationalist leaders W. A. Domingo and Ethelred Brown. In 1919 Caribbean immigrants founded New York City's leading black newspaper, the *Amsterdam News.*

By this time, Harlem had become the center of New York's black life, containing not only the working class, but also the small but influential black middle class. In 1919, the Equitable Life Assurance Society placed on the market the beautiful brownstones on W. 139th Street designed by Stanford White which had been off limits to black buyers. Within eight months, members of the black bourgeoisie had purchased them and they became known as "Striver's Row." Other streets, such as Edgecomb Avenue and St. Nicholas Place, became middle- and upper-income black enclaves. The diverse black nationalities and artistic communities of Harlem contributed to its heterogeneous class composition and cosmopolitan reputation in the 1920s.

Throughout the first half of the twentieth century Harlem was the cultural and ideological capital of black America. In the 1920s, it became the center of both a literary renaissance and the black nationalistic movement of Marcus Garvey—another Caribbean immigrant—and his Universal Negro Improvement Association (UNIA). From his Harlem headquarters, Garvey instilled a new racial pride while advocating the decolonization of Africa from European rule. The UNIA established several businesses, including the ill-fated

New York is the most fatally fascinating thing in America.

JAMES WELDON JOHNSON
O, BLACK AND UNKNOWN BARDS, 1917

See also
Cotton Club
Harlem Renaissance

*New York was
heaven to me. And
Harlem was
Seventh Heaven.*

MALCOLM X
*THE AUTOBIOGRAPHY OF
MALCOLM X*, 1965

Black Star Line of ships, which was intended to facilitate commerce between Africa and African-Americans. Its promoters hoped the UNIA would play a role in the repatriation of blacks from the racially repressive climate of the United States to freedom in an independent Africa. Garveyism was the nationalistic manifestation of the New Negro movement's search for racial pride and assertiveness in the struggle for freedom.

The literary ferment of the Harlem Renaissance produced numerous authors and poets who celebrated their African and African-American heritage. In such works as Langston Hughes's *Weary Blues* (1926), Jean Toomer's *Cane* (1923), and Countee Cullen's poem "Heritage" (1925), black writers extolled the culture and character of Africa. The cosmopolitan nature of the Renaissance is seen in the number of West Indian artists who played an instrumental role in the literature, such as Claude McKay and Eric Walrond. Artists and their literary promoters, such as the black sociologist and editor of the National Urban League magazine *Opportunity,* (1923–1944), Charles S. Johnson, sought to create a new and more positive image for African Americans through the arts which might be absorbed by the larger society. The National Association for the Advancement of Colored People, the leading civil rights organization in the United States, had its offices in Harlem, as did its journal, the Crisis (1910–).

Harlem had a vibrant nightlife which was soon discovered by white theatergoers, critics, publishers, and intellectuals. The dominant form of black popular music was jazz. One of the roots of jazz was locally-based ragtime and Harlem stride piano, as performed by musicians such as Eubie Blake, Fats Waller, and James P. Johnson. Another root of jazz was found in New Orleans and other southern cities. Southern jazz followed black migrants north and became the popular dance music of the 1920s through the 1940s. New York City soon became a music center for jazz. White New Yorkers found black music and entertainers readily available in Harlem nightclubs. Connie's Inn and the Cotton Club were two of the most famous clubs in Harlem in the twenties. Owned by white underworld figures, they featured black bands, singers, and chorus-line dancers. Duke Ellington and his band, and singer Lena Horne were among the major attractions at the Harlem clubs. The appreciation of black music did not carry over into the human sphere, however, and many of the white-owned clubs excluded black patrons.

The period of the twenties and thirties was one in which the city's black population demanded greater participation or control of the institutions in their communities. In Harlem, blacks demanded positions at Harlem Hospital from which they had been excluded, as well as control of Harlem's district leaderships, clubhouses, and representation. In 1929, Charles Fillmore, a Republican, became the city's first black district leader. In 1935, Herbert Bruce, a West Indian immigrant, became the Democratic Party's first black district leader. In the first five years of the Great Depression, West Indian politicians made significant gains in the Democratic party. By 1952, four of the five Democratic district leaders in Harlem were West Indians. Four of the five founding members of the Harlem branch of the Communist Party were West Indians. In part these trends were the result of African-American domination of the black posts within the Republican party and the greater accessibility of the Democratic party, which had far less black involvement until the New Deal. West Indians cooperated with African-American Democrats in attempts to gain black control over the Harlem Nineteenth and Twenty-first Assembly Districts. Despite some degree of tension between African Americans and West Indians, race far more than nationality determined the condition of blacks in the city and nation. By the 1930s, the first wave of West Indian immigrants that entered the country at the beginning of the twentieth century lived in neighborhoods segregated by race but not divided by black ethnic or class differences.

By the latter half of the 1920s the Garvey movement had collapsed with his imprisonment and deportation. The stock market crash of 1929 and accompanying Depression eroded interest in the Renaissance. Still, Harlem remained dynamic, as the struggle for equality intensified as the black unemployment rate in the city grew to nearly double that of whites and threw nearly half of Harlem's families onto relief. The injustice of employment discrimination in Harlem retail and chain stores in the midst of the Depression added insult to injury. Blacks initiated successful boycotts in Harlem in the 1930s, forcing department stores, utilities, and transportation companies to reverse their policies and hire blacks. Boycotts and protest marches were important weapons in breaking down the prejudice-induced barriers that existed during the Great Depression. The 1935 riot in Harlem and the accompanying violence directed at white businesses helped sensitize political and civic leaders to the need for change.

See also

Nation of Islam

With the onset of the preparedness drive for World War II, New York City became the headquarters for A. Philip Randolph's movement for the March on Washington in 1941 to protest discrimination in the armed forces and among federal contractors. This led to the creation of a Federal Fair Employment Practices Committee in 1941 to insure blacks their fair share of jobs in defense industries.

World War II ended the Depression and illustrated the contradiction of a country fighting against racist Nazi ideology with two armies, one white and one black. The shooting of a black soldier by a white policeman in the Hotel Braddock in Harlem touched off another riot on August 1, 1943. A critical factor contributing to the outbreak of the riot was the erroneous rumor that the soldier had been killed by the policeman. As the evening progressed crowds gathered at the local precinct, the Braddock Hotel, and at Sydenham Hospital, where he supposedly died. Rioting broke out around 10:30 P.M. with the breaking of store windows centering on 125th Street and continued for two days. The human cost of the riot was significant, with 6 people killed, all black, and 185 people injured, mostly black. Arrests of blacks numbered more than 550, with most in custody for burglary and reception of stolen goods. Estimates were that some 1,450 stores were damaged.

In comparison to the Detroit riot of June 21 of the same year, the loss of life and physical injury were considerably less, but the events of August 1st and 2nd came as a surprise in America's most cosmopolitan city in which the mayor, Fiorello La Guardia, was popular in the black community. Frustration with the continuation of racism was the underlying cause of the riot. Pictures of the earlier Detroit riot showing black victims of white mobs and police were carried by New York newspapers along with numerous articles on white violence and discrimination against black servicemen. On the local level the riot was in part sparked by black discontent with employment discrimination, with police brutality, and La Guardia's apparent retreat from liberal policies (such as his approval of the Navy's use of Hunter College as a segregated training facility for its WAVES [Women's Reserves]). La Guardia's subsequent approval of the Metropolitan Life Insurance Company's plan to build a tax-exempt quasi-public housing project (Stuyvesant Town) also incurred the wrath of blacks familiar with Metropolitan Life's policy of black exclusion and residential segregation.

Following the riot, La Guardia moved to implement policies that the black community had advocated. Within one week of the riot, the Office of Price Administration announced the opening of an office to investigate food price-gouging in Harlem. Within two weeks, La Guardia inaugurated a series of radio broadcasts to promote racial harmony. The New York City Board of Education created a course on Intercultural Relations for teachers which emphasized African-American contributions. The mayor also announced that any discrimination in tenant selection for Stuyvesant Town was illegal. The riot stimulated greater efforts at improving race relations.

World War II had a salutary effect upon the black condition, stimulating African-American migration to the North and the acquisition of industrial jobs. In 1944, the election of Adam Clayton Powell, Jr. to the United States Congress, and the election of Powell's successor to the New York City Council, Communist party member Benjamin J. Davis, contributed to the growth of militant black political leadership in Harlem.

In the post-World War II era, the black population grew, heavily augmented by migration from the South and the Caribbean. The passage of state and federal discrimination legislation in housing and employment aided the expansion of the black middle class and black outmigration to other boroughs and suburbs. Between 1940 and 1950, Bedford-Stuyvesant emerged as an overwhelmingly black ghetto and by 1960 black residents had expanded into the contiguous parts of Crown Heights and Brownsville. The Greater Bedford-Stuyvesant area developed into the largest black community in New York City. Nearly 40 percent of the city's blacks made their home in Brooklyn by 1970. The South Jamaica-St. Albans-Cambria Heights area of Queens also blossomed as a large area of black settlement after World War II. The black populations in other boroughs were significantly augmented by the increase in black immigration from the Caribbean following the reform of immigration laws in 1965. The 1980 census indicated that 300,000 New Yorkers were born in the non-Hispanic Caribbean, 80 percent of whom had arrived since 1965. The center of the Caribbean black community shifted in the 1970s from the Harlem and Bedford-Stuyvesant neighborhoods to Crown Heights, East Flatbush, and the Flatbush sections of central Brooklyn. In 1980, 54.8 percent of the city's West Indian population lived in Brooklyn, with only 7.4 percent living in Manhattan. Large West Indian settlements have developed in southeastern Queens

Throughout Harlem's history there has been a wide gap between the social, intellectual, and artistic accomplishments of the community's elite and the poverty and neglect of its masses.

PAGE 318

and the northeast Bronx. By the mid-1980s, many of the more prosperous West Indians had moved to the Springfield Gardens, Cambria Heights, and Laurelton sections of Queens. The rise of West Indians to national prominence was evidenced in the careers of former congresswoman, presidential candidate, and daughter of Barbadian immigrants, Shirley Chisholm, and Colin Powell, the first black chairman of the Joint Chiefs of Staff and son of Jamaican immigrants.

Postwar New York City continued to serve as a beacon for black immigrants from the South and Caribbean immigrants alike, but many did not find northern cities to be the urban promised land. Employment discrimination, housing segregation, periodic instances of police brutality, and inadequate education served to disillusion some with life in New York. In the 1950s, the Nation of Islam had sent its most talented organizer, minister, and spokesman, Malcolm X, to New York City. Malcolm X not only built the Harlem Mosque into a major force in the city, but he also significantly increased the national following of the Nation of Islam through his vehement condemnations of America's history of virulent racism. His assassination in upper Manhattan in 1965 was a major setback to the advocates of black nationalism and black empowerment.

Despite their disillusionment, blacks continued their quest for empowerment in the city. The expanding black population helped elect black politicians to many new offices. Hulan Jack, an immigrant from Guyana, became the first black Manhattan borough president in 1953. Anna Arnold Hedgeman became a high-ranking aide to Mayor Robert Wagner in the 1950s. J. Raymond Jones, a native of St. Thomas in the Virgin Islands, was selected to the leadership of Tammany

SPEAKING OF EMPOWERMENT

Malcolm X addresses an attentive crowd at a rally in Harlem on June 29, 1963.
AP / WIDE WORLD PHOTO

Hall (the regular Democratic organization of Manhattan) in 1964. Other prominent politicians include Charles Rangel, who replaced Adam Clayton Powell, Jr., as Harlem's congressman in 1970, and Percy Sutton, who was Manhattan borough president from 1966 to 1977.

In 1989, the greatest triumph of black political power in New York City was the election of David Dinkins, a product of Harlem's vital political scene, to the mayor's office. The administration of Dinkins, however, was plagued with the problems troubling all major cities. Some of these problems included the continuation of crime at unacceptable levels, an overburdened educational system, a growing underclass, a deteriorating physical infrastructure, poor minority-community relations with the police, and stagnating black impoverishment.

Despite its many problems, New York City continues to be the center of African-American cultural life in the United States. In almost every area of the arts, New York City remains one of the centers for innovations, and black New Yorkers, both native and transplanted, continue to make enduring contributions. The city has a long history of black classical and theatrical music, dating back to the early decades of the century, when Will Marion Cook, Harry T. Burleigh, J. Rosamund Johnson, Scott Joplin, and Eubie Blake composed for the theater and concert hall. In the second half of the century, musicians such as William Grant Still, Paul Robeson, Leontyne Price, Martina Arroyo, and André Watts have had significant associations with New York.

New York City has both been a home of numerous jazz movements and the place of residence for musicians such as Bud Powell, Charlie Parker, Sonny Rollins, Max Roach, Miles Davis, Ornett Coleman, and Cecil Taylor. Popular rhythm and blues groups such as Frankie Lymon and the Teenagers and Little Anthony, starting as street corner harmonists, were formed in New York City. Folk musicians associated with New York City include Leadbelly, Josh White, Sonny Terry, Brownie McGhee, and calypso and popular singer Harry Belafonte. There have also been a number of important dancers in New York City, including Florence Mills, Pearl Primus, and Asadata Dafora, along with more recent performers such as Arthur Mitchell and the Dance Theater of Harlem, Alvin Ailey, and his successor Judith Jamison, and modern dancer Bill T. Jones. New York City has also been home to tap dancers such as Bill "Bojangles" Robinson and Charles "Honi" Coles.

Beginning in the late 1970s, the most significant contribution of black New Yorkers to popular music was the creation and development of rap music, which originated in the housing projects of the Bronx, Manhattan, and Queens. Among the first important rap artists were Afrika Bambaata, Grand Master Flash and the Furious Five, the Sugar Hill Gang, and Run-DMC. Other important New York City rappers include LL Cool J, Kool Moe Dee, Krs-One, and Public Enemy.

There have also been a number of important black writers and artists associated with New York City since the Harlem Renaissance. James Baldwin, a native of Harlem, used the city for the setting of several of his novels, including *Go Tell It on the Mountain* (1953). Ralph Ellison lived in New York for most of his adult life, and much of his novel *Invisible Man* (1952) is set in the city. Other writers associated with New York City for significant portions of their careers include Zora Neale Hurston, Nella Larsen, John O. Killens, Lorraine Hansberry, Samuel R. Delany, Paule Marshall, Audre Lorde, Albert Murray, Gloria Naylor, Melvin Tolson, and Ann Petry.

African-American painters and sculptors from New York City include Romare Bearden, Jacob Lawrence, Richmond Barthe, Augusta Savage, and Jean-Michel Basquiat.

The racial divide prevalent in New York City was perhaps highlighted by the electoral defeat of Mayor Dinkins by former U.S. District Attorney Rudolph Giuliani in 1993. An important factor in the election was the criticism directed at Dinkins by those who believed he excessively restrained the police when rioting broke out in Crown Heights in August 1991 between blacks and Jews after the accidental death of a black youth hit by a Hasidic driver and the subsequent murder of a Jewish rabbinical student. The event polarized the city, and brought militant community-based black protest, largely led by Brooklyn minister Rev. Al Sharpton, to public attention. In the 1993 election, 76 percent of the white vote went for Republican candidate Giuliani in a city with a five-to-one Democratic majority in registered voters, while 95 percent of the black vote went to Dinkins. In 1989, when the city was less intensely divided than four years later, Giuliani had received 71 percent of the white vote and Dinkins had received 91 percent of the black vote. Given these figures, it is difficult not to sense the increasing racial polarization in the city and to feel uneasy about New York City's future.

—LARRY GREENE

See also

Ralph Ellison

Malcolm X

NEWTON, HUEY P.

Huey P. Newton (February 17, 1942–August 22, 1989), political activist. Huey Newton was born in Monroe, La. His family moved to Oakland, Calif., when he was young. Newton was the youngest of seven siblings. He attended Merritt College in Oakland and participated in the groundswell of political activities that were erupting on college campuses nationwide. He joined the increasing number of blacks who questioned the ability of the Civil Rights Movement to deal with the problems of housing, unemployment, poverty, and police brutality that plagued urban African Americans.

In college, Newton and his friend Bobby Seale were active in the effort to diversify the curriculum at Merritt, as well as lobbying for more black instructors. Newton joined the Afro-American Association but soon became a vocal critic of the organization's advocacy of capitalism. Instead, he sought inspiration from Robert Williams, a former head of the Monroe, N.C., NAACP, who advocated guerilla warfare, and from Third World revolutionaries such as Cuba's Fidel Castro, China's Mao Ze Dong, and Algeria's Franz Fanon. Newton believed that blacks were an oppressed colony being exploited economically and disfranchised politically within U.S. borders and argued that blacks should launch a liberation movement for self-empowerment.

In 1966, Newton and Seale founded the Black Panther Party for Self-defense. Newton took on the title of minister of defense and acted as leader of the organization. Among the points raised in their initial program was the right to bear arms to defend their community from police repression.

In November, Newton and Seale, armed with shotguns—which was legal at the time as long as they were not concealed—instituted "justice patrols" to monitor the actions of the police and inform blacks of their rights when stopped by the police. The police responded with resentment and harassment. On October 28, 1967, in culmination of a year of hostile and antagonistic relations between the Panthers and the police, Newton was arrested and charged in the shooting of one police officer and the murder of another. Events of this incident are unclear and conflicting. Newton claimed to be unconscious after being shot by one of the policemen.

Newton's arrest heightened the awareness of police brutality in the black community. While in prison Newton was considered a political prisoner; rallies and speeches focused attention on his plight. His trial became a cause célèbre, and "Free Huey" became a slogan that galvanized thousands of people on the New Left. Massive rallies and demonstrations at the courthouse demanding his release were organized by BPP members.

Newton remained active in prison, issuing speeches and directives. He was convicted in September 1968 of voluntary manslaughter, and was sentenced to two to fifteen years in prison. His conviction was overturned by the Court of Appeals, because of procedural errors during his first trial. Newton, after being released from prison, tried to revive the organization. However, during the early 1970s, the BPP had declined due to legal problems, internal tensions, and a factional split among BPP members on the East and West Coast. This division was fostered by the disinformation campaign launched by the FBI, which created a climate of distrust and suspicion within the BPP. Many on the East Coast believed the ideology of Eldridge Cleaver—who had become the public spokesperson for the BPP during Newton's incarceration and who advocated politically motivated armed actions. Newton articulated the feelings of many on the West Coast by arguing that the BPP, by becoming too militant, had moved onto a plane with which average blacks could no longer identify. He wanted to focus more on community programs and political education. Newton ordered a series of purges, which debilitated the party further.

Although Newton remained publicly identified with the party, many people no longer looked to him as leader. Increasingly isolated, Newton cultivated a small band of supporters. In 1974 Newton was accused of murder in the killing of a woman. The circumstances of this incident are unclear. Newton fled to Cuba, feeling that he would not get a fair trial here. In 1977 he returned to the United States to resume leadership of the weakened and splintering party. In his absence, Elaine Brown had assumed leadership of the organization and taken it in new directions. Newton's role in the organization continued to diminish. He was retried in the 1967 killing of the policeman and convicted, but that conviction was later overturned. He also faced trial for the murder of the woman, but the charge was dropped after two hung juries.

In 1980 Newton received a Ph.D. from the University of California. His thesis was "War Against the Panthers—A Study of Repression in America." While Newton remained politically active, his visibility as a public figure was waning. He was arrested in 1985 for embezzling funds

See also

Black Panther Party

from a nutritional program he headed. Three years later, he was convicted of possessing firearms. Increasingly addicted to drugs and involved in the drug trade, he was killed in a drug-related incident on the streets of Oakland in 1989.

—ROBYN SPENCER

NIAGARA MOVEMENT

The Niagara Movement, which was organized in 1905, was the first significant organized black protest movement in the twentieth century, and represented the attempt of a small but articulate group of radicals to challenge the then-dominant accommodationist ideas of Booker T. Washington.

The Niagara Movement developed after failed attempts at reconciling the two factions in African-American political life: the accommodationists, led by Booker T. Washington, and the more militant faction, led by W. E. B. Du Bois and William Monroe Trotter. A closed-door meeting of representatives of the two groups at Carnegie Hall in New York City in 1904 led to an organization, the Committee of Twelve for the Advancement of the Interests of the Negro Race, but the committee fell apart due to the belief of Du Bois and Trotter that Washington was controlling the organization.

In February 1905, Du Bois and Trotter devised a plan for a "strategy board" which would fight for civil rights and serve as a counterpoint to Washington's ideas. Since they knew Washington was most popular among whites, they resolved to form an all-black organization. Along with two allies, F. L. McGhee and C. E. Bentley, they set a meeting for that summer in western New York, to which they invited fifty-nine businessmen and professionals who were known to be anti-Washingtonites.

In mid-July 1905, Du Bois went to Buffalo. He had difficulty arranging hotel reservations, and crossed to the Canadian side of Niagara Falls. Fearing reprisals by Washington, who had sent spies to Buffalo, the radicals kept their conference secret. On July 11–14, 1905, twenty-nine men met and formed a group they called the Niagara Movement, both for the conference location and for the "mighty current" of protest they wished to unleash. Du Bois was named general secretary, and the group split into various committees, of which the most important was Trotter's Press and Public Opinion Committee. The founders agreed to divide the work among state chapters, which would "cooperate with congressmen and legislators to secure just legislation for the colored people," and pursue educational and informational programs. Movement members would meet annually.

The Niagara Movement's "Declaration of Principles," drafted by Du Bois and Trotter and adopted at the close of the conference, was a powerful and clear statement of the rights of African Americans: "We believe that this class of American citizens should protest emphatically and continually against the curtailment of their political rights." The declaration went on to urge African Americans to protest the curtailment of civil rights, the denial of equal economic opportunity, and denial of education; and the authors decried unhealthy living conditions, discrimination in the military, discrimination in the justice system, Jim Crow railroad cars, and other injustices. "Of the above grievances we do not hesitate to complain, and to complain loudly and insistently," they stated. "Persistent manly agitation is the way to liberty, and toward this goal the Niagara Movement has started. . . ."

At the end of its first year, the organization had only 170 members and was poorly funded. Nevertheless, the Niagarites pursued their activities, distributing pamphlets, lobbying against Jim Crow, and sending a circular protest letter to President Theodore Roosevelt after the Brownsville Incident in 1906. That summer the movement had its second annual conference, at Harpers Ferry, W.Va. This was an open meeting, and the conference speeches, and the tribute to John Brown, aroused much publicity.

The Niagara Movement, despite its impressive start, did not enjoy a long life. There was, from the start, determined opposition by Booker T. Washington—he prevented sympathetic white newspapers, and even many black ones, from printing the declaration—which dissuaded many blacks from joining or contributing funds. The loose organization, with only token communication between state chapters, and the radical nature, for the time, of such forthright protest, also contributed to the movement's decline. Not long after the Harpers Ferry Conference, factional struggles broke out between Du Bois and Trotter, as well as disagreements over the role of women in the movement. By the end of the summer of 1907, Trotter had been replaced as head of the Press Committee, and his supporters grew disenchanted with the movement. Du Bois tried to keep it going, guiding the movement through annual conferences in 1908 and 1909, after which it largely ceased to exist.

See also
W.E.B. Du Bois
NAACP
Booker T. Washington

However, even in its decline, the movement left a lasting legacy. In 1908, Du Bois had invited Mary White Ovington, a settlement worker and socialist, to be the movement's first white member; by 1910 he had turned to the search for white allies by joining the newly organized NAACP. Despite its predominantly white leadership and centralized structure, the NAACP was really the successor to the Niagara Movement, whose remaining members Du Bois urged to join the NAACP. (However, William Monroe Trotter and his faction of the Niagara Movement never affiliated with the new organization.) The NAACP inherited many of the goals and tactics of the Niagara Movement, including the cultivation of a black elite which would defend the rights of African Americans through protest and lobbying against oppression and the publicizing of injustice.

—GREG ROBINSON

NORMAN, JESSYE

Jessye Norman (September 15, 1945–), opera singer. Born in Augusta, Ga., Jessye Norman was a soprano of promise from an early age. At sixteen she entered the Marian Anderson competitions, and although she did not win, she auditioned at Howard University with Carolyn Grant. Her acceptance was delayed until she completed high school. She followed her undergraduate training at Howard (B. Music., 1967) with summer study at the Peabody Conservatory under Alice Duschak before enrolling at the University of Michigan for study with Elizabeth Mannion and Pierre Bernac.

A travel grant allowed Norman to enter the International Music Competition in Munich in 1968, where she won first place with performances of Dido's Lament (Henry Purcell) and "Voi lo sapete" from Pietro Mascagni's *Cavalleria rusticana*. She was immediately engaged for her operatic debut as Elisabeth in Richard Wagner's *Tannhäuser* by the Deutsche Oper (1969), with which she later appeared in Giuseppe Verdi's *Aida* and *Don Carlo*, Meyerbeer's *L'africaine*, and as the Countess in Mozart's *Le nozze di Figaro*. In 1972 she sang Aida at La Scala and Cassandre in Covent Garden's production of Berlioz' *Les troyens*, making her recital debuts in London and New York the next year.

Norman's American stage debut came on November 22, 1982, when she appeared as both Jocasta in *Oedipus Rex* (Stravinsky) and Dido in Purcell's *Dido and Aeneas* with the Opera Company of Philadelphia. The following year, she made her debut with the Metropolitan Opera as Cassandre in Berlioz' *Les troyens*, subsequently offering a performance as Didon in the same opera, as well as the Prima Donna and Ariadne in *Ariadne auf Naxos* (Richard Strauss).

As recitalist, guest orchestral soloist, presenter of master classes, and recording artist, Norman was acknowledged as a musician of the highest rank. She was heard in nearly every major American city by 1990 and appeared frequently in telecasts starting in 1979 when she gave a concert version of the first act of Wagner's *Die Walküre* with the Boston Symphony Orchestra conducted by Seiji Ozawa.

Norman has excelled in French and German repertories, stylistically and linguistically, while remaining faithful to her roots in the spiritual. With a voice ranging from a dark mezzo-soprano to a dramatic soprano, she has not hesitated to reintroduce works outside of the mainstream repertory (e.g., Gluck and Haydn operas), or to perform songs of the musical theater. She has appeared on numerous recordings, including Beethoven's *Fidelio*; Berlioz' *Mort de Cléopatre*; Bizet's *Carmen*; Gluck's *Alceste*; Mahler's *Das Lied von der Erde*; Offenbach's *Tales of Hoffmann*; Purcell's *Dido and Aeneas*; Schoenberg's *Gurre-Lieder*; Strauss's *Four Last Songs* and *Ariadne auf Naxos*; Verdi's *Aida*, Wagner's *Lohengrin* and *Die Walküre*; and Weber's *Euryanthe*. Other notable recordings include *Spirituals*, *Spirituals in Concert* (with Kathleen Battle), and *Jessye Norman at Notre-Dame*.

—DOMINIQUE-RENÉ DE LERMA

NORTON, ELEANOR HOLMES

Eleanor Holmes Norton (June 13, 1937–), civil rights leader. Born in Washington, D.C., Eleanor Holmes graduated from Antioch College in 1960, received an M.A. in American history from Yale University in 1963, and a law degree from Yale in 1965. Norton was a leader of the Student Nonviolent Coordinating Committee (SNCC), and was a participant in the Mississippi Freedom Democratic Party. In 1965, Holmes joined the American Civil Liberties Union (ACLU), where she served as a civil rights lawyer for five years. In 1967, she married Edward Norton, also a lawyer. The couple, who were separated in 1992, had two children. In 1968, Eleanor Holmes Norton gained

See also

Marian Anderson

attention for her active defense of freedom of speech when she represented segregationist presidential candidate George Wallace in his struggle to obtain permission from the City of New York for a rally at Shea Stadium. Keenly interested in fighting both race and gender discrimination, Norton published an article on black women in the well-known anthology *Sisterhood Is Powerful* (1970). "If women were suddenly to achieve equality with men tomorrow," she wrote, "black women would continue to carry the entire array of utterly oppressive handicaps associated with race. . . . Yet black women cannot—must not—avoid the truth about their special subservence. They are women with all that that implies."

In 1970, Norton was appointed chair of the New York City Commission on Human Rights by Mayor John Lindsay. Her achievement in detailing and correcting discriminatory practices led to a position as cohost of a weekly local television program on civil rights. In 1973, Norton helped organize a National Conference of Black Feminists, and in 1975 she cowrote *Sex Discrimination and the Law: Cases and Remedies,* a law textbook dealing with legal remedies to gender inequality.

In 1977, President Jimmy Carter appointed Norton as chair of the Equal Employment Opportunity Commission, a post she held until 1981. Charged with investigating complaints of discrimination, Norton was a visible and respected force within the Administration. In 1982,

she accepted a post as professor of labor law at Georgetown University. Throughout the 1980s, she was also a regular media commentator on civil rights and affirmative action issues.

In 1990, Norton announced her candidacy for the position of District of Columbia delegate to the U.S. House of Representatives. Despite the revelation during the campaign that she owed back taxes, she was elected to Congress. She soon won praise even from her opponents for her involvement in community affairs as well as for her work in assuring Washington's fiscal viability and cutting the District's budget. She also lobbied in Congress for District statehood. In 1992, the same year Norton won reelection, she won attention for her offer to escort women seeking abortion information at clinics past antiabortion picketers, and later for her denunciation of the verdict in the Rodney King trial, which she contended was as shameful as the actual beating of King. Since the House vote in 1993 to give delegates limited voting privileges on the floor, Norton has become the first District representative to vote in Congress. In recognition of her prestige, President Bill Clinton agreed that as chair of the District of Columbia Subcommittee on Judiciary and Education, Norton would be responsible for the nomination of candidates for local U.S. Attorney and federal judgeships, the first elected District of Columbia official to be privileged.

—EVAN A. SHORE AND GREG ROBINSON

See also
Student Nonviolent Coordinating Committee

OLYMPIC MOVEMENT, THE

The first modern Olympic Games were held in 1896, in Athens, Greece, the homeland of the ancient Olympic competitions, traditionally dated as beginning in 776 B.C. Since 1896 the Olympic Games have been held every four years, except for interruptions caused by the two world wars. The first Winter Olympiad was held at Chamonix, France, in 1924, and, like the summer games, the winter games have been held quadrennially. Starting with the Winter Olympics in Lillehammer, Norway, in 1994, the Winter Olympics will be held in even-numbered years in between the years of the Summer Olympics. Relatively few persons of African descent have participated in the Winter Olympics. The only African-American medalist has been figure skater Debi Thomas, holder of the 1986 U.S. and world titles, who won a bronze medal in figure skating at the 1988 Calgary games. The professional football player Herschel Walker was a member of the American bobsledding team at the 1992 Albertville Winter Games.

Despite the scarcity of African Americans in the Winter Olympics, black Americans have been involved in the Olympic movement almost from the beginning. It has been the scene of some of the greatest triumphs and most controversial moments in the history of African-American athletic competition. Though there has never been a "color line" barring African Americans from participating on American Olympics teams, there were subtle forms of racism present in the early years of the Olympic movement. The International Olympic Committee (IOC) and the founder of the Olympic movement, the French baron Pierre de Coubertin (1863–1937), were sympathetic to European colonialism and comfortable with invidious distinctions between European civilization and the peoples and cultures of the colonized world. An example of the sort of racism the Olympic movement endorsed were the so-called Anthropology Days, held at the 1904 St. Louis games, the first Olympic competition held in the United States. This was little more than a racial sideshow in which Africans, Asians, and American Indians engaged in mock athletic competition to the amusement of the spectators.

Nonetheless, Coubertin believed that Olympic competition could produce an "aristocracy of sport," which could serve as a basis for enhanced cooperation between nations and races. Coubertin attempted to stage "African games" in 1925 and 1929; he blamed the failure of these abortive competitions to take place on the efforts of colonialists. But Coubertin and the IOC had little interest in the participation of black Africans in the regular Olympics. No black sub-Saharan team competed in the Olympics until Nigeria and the Gold Coast (later Ghana) sent small contingents to the 1952 Helsinki games. Since the 1960s black Africans have excelled in many summer Olympic sports, especially distance events. Abebe Bikila of Ethiopia won the Olympic Marathons in 1960 and 1964, and several Kenyans won other distance events at Mexico City in 1968. At the 1988 Seoul games, Kenyan men won the events at 800 meters, 1,500 meters, 3,000-meter steeplechase, and at the 5,000 meters.

African-American runners began to make their mark early in the Olympic movement and have since become the dominant performers among American track-and-field Olympians. The first African-American Olympian medalist was George C. Poage, who won a bronze medal in the 400-meter hurdles race at the 1904 St. Louis games, representing the Milwaukee Athletic Club. The first African-American gold medalist was John Baxter Taylor, who ran on the winning 1600-meter relay team at the 1908 London games. Between 1924 (Paris) and 1936 (Berlin) fifteen African-American men won Olympic medals in track-and-field events (track-and-field events for women were initiated at the 1928 Amsterdam Games).

The first African-American athlete to attain worldwide fame through Olympic competition was Jesse Owens (1913–1980), a remarkable track-and-field performer who had already set a number of world records before his four-gold-medal performances at the 1936 Berlin games.

See also

Jacqueline Joyner-Kersee

The 1936 games are remembered both as a victory for Nazi propaganda and as Jesse Owens's personal triumph in the face of Nazi racism. Nazis, who treated blacks as subhumans not fit to compete with Aryans, were disdainful of black athletes. Owens won gold medals in the 100- and 200-meter races, the 4 × 100-meter relay, and the long jump. One of the most enduring stories of the Olympics is the refusal of Nazi dictator Adolf Hitler to shake Owens's hand after his victory in the 100 meters. Although there are different explanations for Hitler's snub, the most likely account holds that Nazi racial ideology was a large factor in Hitler's act. In his victory in the face of Nazi contempt, Owens served as a surrogate for all Americans opposed to Hitler and Nazism. But when Owens returned to the United States, racism of another kind denied Owens certain honors he surely deserved. President Franklin Delano Roosevelt neither invited him to the White House nor conveyed his congratulations, while the Amateur Athletic Union suspended him for an imagined act of insubordination and denied him the Sullivan award that was given annually to the outstanding amateur athlete. These acts of racial discrimination, however, should not obscure the fact that Olympic competition was among the most integrated venues for African-American athletes in the 1920s and 1930s.

African-American athletes continued to distinguish themselves in track-and-field competition at postwar Olympiads. Among the most important figures of the quarter-century following World War II were Harrison Dillard (gold medals in the 100-meter dash and 110-meter high hurdles in 1948 and 1952, respectively), Wilma Rudolph (gold medals in the 100- and 200-meter dash and the 4 × 100 relay in 1960); Rafer Johnson (gold medal in the decathlon in 1960 and lighter of the Olympic torch in the opening ceremonies of the 1984 Los Angeles Olympics); Bob Hayes (gold medal in the 100-meter dash in 1964); and Bob Beamon, whose long jump of 29′ 2½″—almost two feet longer than the existing record—was the single most spectacular achievement of the 1968 Mexico City games.

African-American participation in the Summer Olympic Games has long extended beyond the track-and-field events. The first sport other than track and field which included black athletes was weightlifting. John Terry was a member of the 1936 team, John Davis was the Olympic champion in the heavyweight division at both the London (1948) and Helsinki (1952) games, and James Bradford won silver medals in that division

at both the Helsinki and Rome (1960) games. In the sport of judo George Harris was the first African American to make an American Olympic team, competing at the 1964 Tokyo games. Allen Coage won a bronze medal as a heavyweight at Montreal (1976), and Edward Liddie won a bronze in the extra-lightweght class at the 1984 Los Angeles games.

African Americans have won medals in almost every Olympic sport. Anita DeFrantz won a bronze medal at the 1976 Montreal games as a member of the rowing team. In 1980 she was awarded the Olympic Order medal for opposing President Jimmy Carter's ordered boycott of the 1980 Moscow games (because of the Russian invasion of Afghanistan), and in 1986 she was elected a member of the IOC. In wrestling, Lloyd Keaser won a silver medal in the lightweight division in 1976, and Greg Gibson won a silver medal as a heavyweight in 1984. In the sport of cycling, Oliver "Butch" Martin, Jr., was a member of the 1964 American Olympic team, and Nelson Vails won a silver medal in the 1984 Olympic sprint competition. The first African-American member of an American Olympic fencing committee was Uriah Jones, who participated in the 1968 Mexico City games. Black fencers earned positions on American Olympic teams in 1972, 1976, 1980, and 1984, and Peter Westbrook won a bronze medal in the saber competition at the Los Angeles Games. The silver-medal winning women's volleyball team at the Los Angeles games included three African-American players, including the team's star player, Flo Hyman. Americans have dominated basketball competition since it was first held in 1936. African Americans who have won gold medals include Don Barksdale (1948), Bill Russell (1950), K. C. Jones (1956), Oscar Robertson (1960), Walt Hazzard (1964), Spencer Haywood (1968), JoJo White (1968), Phil Ford (1976), Quinn Buckner (1976), Michael Jordan (1984), and Patrick Ewing (1992). Jordan and Ewing, along with Charles Barkley and Earvin "Magic" Johnson, were among the professional National Basketball Association all-stars who overwhelmingly defeated their opposition in the largely African-American "dream team" at the 1992 Barcelona Olympics.

Olympic gold medals have launched several African-American boxers into successful careers as professional champions. Floyd Patterson, who won the Olympic middleweight championship at the 1952 games, eventually became heavyweight champion of the world. Joe Frazier and George Foreman won gold medals in the heavyweight

See also

Track and Field

(now super heavyweight) division in 1964 and 1968 respectively, and both went on to become professional heavyweight champions. Sugar Ray Leonard, who won a gold medal as a light welterweight in 1976, later won several world championships as a professional. The most famous African-American boxing champion was probably Muhammad Ali, who as Cassius Clay won an Olympic gold medal in the light heavyweight division in 1960 and went on to an extraordinary career as both a pugilist and black nationalist activist.

The politics of race and South Africa's policy of apartheid were central issues in the Olympic movement in the 1960s and 1970s. The IOC was reluctant to ban South Africa from the Olympic movement, and South Africa was allowed to participate in the 1960 Olympics because Avery Brundage, the president of the IOC, believed the claims of the South African representative that racial discrimination played no role in the selection of athletes. This was a transparent fiction, and by 1964, in part through pressure from the Organization of African Unity (OAU), South Africa was suspended from participation. In 1968 the IOC voted to admit a racially mixed South African team. This led to a proposed boycott, and the IOC bowed to massive pressure and excluded the South African team just as the competition was about to begin. Under pressure from black African nations, the IOC also banned a Rhodesian team from the 1972 Olympics. A team from Zimbabwe was admitted in 1980. Following significant changes in the apartheid laws, South Africa was readmitted to the 1992 Olympic games at Barcelona.

The proposed return of South Africa to the Olympics for 1968 led Harry Edwards, a young sociology professor at San Jose State University, to call for a boycott of the games by African Americans, in protest against South African apartheid and racial conditions in the United States. Among those who chose not to participate in the Olympics were basketball players Elvin Hayes, Bob Lanier, Wes Unseld, and Lew Alcindor (later known as Kareem Abdul-Jabbar). Some of those athletes who chose to take part in the games found themselves embroiled in even bigger controversy. The African-American sprinters Tommie Smith and John Carlos, gold and bronze medal winners respectively in the 200-meter dash, raised black-gloved fists above their heads during the medals ceremony. This Black Power demonstration resulted in their expulsion from the Olympic village, since the IOC saw their

symbolic protest as an unacceptable form of political interference in the games. George Foreman's flag-waving demonstration after his gold-medal victory was seized upon by critics as evidence that Smith and Carlos were misguided rebels.

There have been a number of outstanding African-American performers in recent Olympics. In 1984 Carl Lewis became the first Olympic performer since Jesse Owens in 1936 to win four track and field medals in one Olympiad (gold medals in the 100- and 200-meter dash, the long jump, and the 4 × 100 meter relay). Lewis won the 100-meter-dash at the 1988 Seoul games after the apparent winner, Ben Johnson of Canada, was stripped of his medal for steroid use. Lewis was awarded the gold medal, as well as also winning a gold in the long jump and a silver in the 200-meters. At the 1992 Barcelona games, Lewis won gold medals in the long jump and in the 4 × 400-meters. Lewis's eight gold medals are the most earned by any track and field athlete since the early years of the century.

At the 1988 Seoul games Florence Griffith-Joyner, or "Flo Jo" as she was popularly known, tied Wilma Rudolph's 1960 record of three gold

MEDALISTS

Sprinters Tommie Smith (center) and John Carlos (right) offered the Black Power salute—a black glove on a clenched and upraised fist— during the 1968 Summer Olympics in Mexico City. AP/WIDE WORLD PHOTOS

medals by winning gold medals in the 100- and 200-meter races and the 4 × 100-meter relay. Her striking appearance and dazzling track outfits were as much discussed as her track accomplishments. Jackie Joyner-Kersee (whose brother, Al Joyner, also an Olympic gold medal champion, married Florence Griffith in 1987) was acknowledged as "America's best all-around female athlete" after the 1988 Seoul games, where she won the heptathlon, the most demanding event in women's track and field. Joyner-Kersee went on to become the first woman to win two Olympic gold medals in the heptathlon after a repeat victory in the 1992 Barcelona games. In 1992 Dr. Leroy Walker became the first African American to be elected president of the United States Olympic Committee. The visibility of Olympic competition will continue to attract the most talented athletes from around the world, including African Americans, and in all likelihood the games will draw various forms of symbolic political protests as well.

—JOHN M. HOBERMAN

OWENS, JAMES CLEVELAND "JESSE"

James Cleveland "Jesse" Owens (September 12, 1913–March 31, 1980), athlete. Born in 1913, the tenth surviving child of sharecroppers Henry and Emma Owens, in Oakville, Ala., Jesse Owens moved with his family to Cleveland, Ohio, for better economic and educational opportunities in the early 1920s. His athletic ability was first noticed by a junior high school teacher of physical education, Charles Riley, who coached him to break several interscholastic records and even to make a bold but futile attempt to win a place on the U.S. Olympic team. In 1933 Owens matriculated at Ohio State University on a work-study arrangement and immediately began setting Big Ten records. In Ann Arbor, Mich., on May 25, 1935, he set new world records in the 220-yard sprint, the 220-yard hurdles, and the long jump and tied the world record in the 100-yard dash.

In the racially segregated sports world of 1936, Owens and Joe Louis were the most visible

**SPEEDING
BULLET**

Jesse Owens was a one-man refutation of the athletic inferiority of blacks. His four gold medals in the 1936 Berlin Olympics discomforted racists.
AP/WIDE WORLD PHOTOS

African-American athletes. In late June, however, Louis lost to German boxer Max Schmeling, making Owens's Olympic feats all the more dramatic. At Berlin in early August 1936, he stole the Olympic show with gold-medal, record-making performances in the 100 meters, 200 meters, long jump, and relays. All this occurred against a backdrop of Nazi pageantry and Adolf Hitler's daily presence and in an international scene of tension and fear. Out of that dramatic moment came one of the most enduring of all sports myths: Hitler's supposed "snub" in refusing to shake Owens's hand after the victories. (Morally satisfying but untrue, the yarn was largely created by American sportswriters.)

Business and entertainment offers flooded Owens's way in the wake of the Berlin games, but he quickly found most of them were bogus. Republican presidential candidate Alf Landon paid him to stump for black votes in the autumn of 1936. After that futile effort, Owens bounced from one demeaning and low-paying job to another, including races against horses. He went bankrupt in a dry-cleaning business. By 1940, with a wife and three daughters to support (he had married Ruth Solomon in 1935), Owens returned to Ohio State to complete the degree he had abandoned in 1936. However, his grades were too low and his educational background too thin

for him to graduate. For most of World War II, Owens supervised the black labor force at Ford Motor Company in Detroit.

In the era of the cold war, Owens became a fervent American patriot, hailing the United States as the land of opportunity. Working out of Chicago, he frequently addressed interracial school and civic groups, linking patriotism and athletics. In 1955 the U.S. State Department sent him to conduct athletic clinics, make speeches, and grant interviews as means of winning friends for America in India, Malaya, and the Philippines.

In 1956 President Dwight D. Eisenhower sent him to the Melbourne Olympics as one of the president's personal goodwill ambassadors. Refusing to join the Civil Rights Movement, Owens became so politically conservative that angry young blacks denounced him as an "Uncle Tom" on the occasion of the famous black-power salutes by Olympic athletes Tommie Smith and John Carlos at Mexico City in 1968. Before he died of lung cancer in 1980, however, Owens received two of the nation's highest awards: the Medal of Freedom Award in 1976, for his "inspirational" life, and the Living Legends Award in 1979, for his "dedicated but modest" example of greatness.

—WILLIAM J. BAKER

**OWENS, JAMES
CLEVELAND "JESSE"**

P

PARKER, CHARLES CHRISTOPHER "CHARLIE"

Charles Christopher "Charlie" Parker (August 29, 1920–March 23, 1955), jazz alto saxophonist. Charlie Parker, often known as "Bird" or "Yardbird," was the primary architect of the style of jazz called bebop, which revolutionized jazz, taking it from dance music to a black musical aesthetic and art form. He accomplished this as performer, composer, and theorist.

Parker was born in Kansas City, Mo. When he was eleven his mother bought him an alto saxophone. By the time he was fifteen he had become a professional musician, leaving school at the same time. At first his playing was ridiculed, but after he spent some time at a retreat in the Ozark Mountains of Missouri his technique grew immensely, and during the next couple of years he played in and around the Kansas City area. During this period he learned his craft mainly by sitting in and playing in bands, where he absorbed all he could about music.

In 1939 Parker made his first visit to New York. He stayed about a year, playing mostly in jam sessions. After that he began playing in the band of Jay McShann, touring in the Southwest, Midwest, and East. It was with this band that Parker made his first recording, in Dallas in 1941. At the end of 1942 he joined the Earl Hines orchestra, which featured trumpeter "Dizzy" Gillespie. Bird and Dizzy began an informal partnership that launched the beginning of bebop. A strike by the American Federation of Musicians made it impossible to make records for several years, and the early period of bebop's development is largely undocumented. In 1944 Parker, along with Gillespie and other modern players, joined the Billy Eckstine band. This band was one of the first to introduce the innovations being developed in the music, and it provided a platform for Parker's new improvisations.

In 1945 Parker began to record extensively with small groups that included Gillespie. His playing became more familiar to a larger audience and to other musicians, even though the new music was criticized harshly by critics. At the end of 1945 he took a quintet to California for what turned out to be an ill-fated trip. Audiences and musicians in the West were not familiar with bebop innovations, and Parker's addiction to heroin and alcohol finally forced him into the Camarillo State Hospital. He stayed there during the second half of 1946 and was released in January 1947. He did make several important recordings for the Dial record company before and after his stay at the hospital.

Parker returned to New York in April 1947 and formed a quintet featuring his protégé Miles Davis on trumpet, Duke Jordan on piano, Tommy Potter on bass, and Max Roach on drums. Between 1947 and 1951 Parker left a permanent imprint on jazz. With the quintet he recorded some of his most innovative compositions: "Now's the Time," "Koko," "Anthropology," "Ornithology," "Scrapple from the Apple," "Yardbird Suite," "Moose the Mooche," "Billie's Bounce," "Confirmation," and others. In addition to playing in his own quintet, Parker worked in a variety of other musical groups, including Afro-Cuban bands and a string chorus, which he led during 1950. He was featured soloist in the Jazz at the Philharmonic series, produced by Norman Granz. Parker's main venue continued to be his quintet, which changed members several times but still was vital. Within his quintet he worked in nightclubs, recording studios, and radio broadcasts, and made his first trip to Europe in 1949, returning there the next year for an extensive stay in Sweden, where he worked with Swedish musicians.

Parker's lifestyle continued to create problems for himself and his family. In 1951 he lost his cabaret card in New York because of his constant confrontations with narcotics police. This kept him from playing in New York clubs for over two years. His alcohol and drug use precipitated a downward financial spiral from which he never recovered. In 1953 he presented a landmark concert in Toronto with Gillespie, Bud Powell on piano, Charles Mingus on bass, and Max Roach on drums. The concert was at Massey Hall and fea-

See also
John Coltrane

533

tured many of the pieces Bird and Dizzy had created during the 1940s: "Night in Tunisia," "Hot House," "Wee," and others. This was Parker's last great musical statement. After the Toronto concert his physical and mental health deteriorated to the point where he attempted suicide several times, finally committing himself to Bellevue Hospital in New York. His last public performance was early in March 1955 at Birdland, the New York City club named after him. On March 23 he died of heart seizure in the New York apartment of his friend Baroness Pannonica de Koenigswarter.

Parker's contributions to jazz are extensive. He took saxophone playing to a level never reached before and in so doing led the way for others, not only saxophonists but all instrumentalists. He was able to weld prodigious skill with poetic content, and he left hours and hours of recordings of wondrous improvisations. Parker's playing struck fear in the hearts of many musicians and made some put down their instruments. John Coltrane, the gifted performer of the 1950s and 1960s, moved from alto to tenor saxophone because he felt that Parker had played all that was going to be played on the alto. Parker frequently composed using the harmonic structures of established melodies as the basis of his works. He did not invent this technique but used it more than anyone else before or since. In his improvisations he used all the intervals of the scales. In his harmonic structures he consistently used chords made up of eleventh and thirteenth intervals in order to take harmony out of the diatonic system and into chromaticism. Parker was clearly one of America's most innovative and prolific artists.

—WILLIAM S. COLE

PARKS, GORDON, SR.

Gordon Parks, Sr. (November 30, 1912–), photographer. A true Renaissance man, *Life* magazine photographer Gordon Parks has achieved international recognition in a wide variety of other fields including filmmaking, letters, and music. He has also pioneered as the first mainstream African-American photojournalist and as the first African American to direct a major Hollywood film.

Gordon Parks was born in Fort Scott, Kans., the youngest in a farming family of fifteen children. His mother's death when Parks was sixteen, along with his aged father's rapidly failing ability to manage a household, led to the family's

See also

Jazz

Charles Mingus

break-up, and Parks moved north to live with a married sister in Minneapolis. Unwelcome in his brother-in-law's home, the teenager was soon on his own, struggling to attend high school and support himself.

The Great Depression ended his formal education, but Parks seized every opportunity to learn by reading and attending closely to the talented individuals he encountered in his various jobs. As a teenager and later as a young husband and father, he worked as a bellhop, musician, semipro basketball player, and member of the Civilian Conservation Corps, primarily in the Midwest but also for a brief time in Harlem, New York. Relative security came with a position as a railroad dining car waiter. All the while Parks wrote, composed, and read, absorbing on his own what he had been unable to study in school.

The picture magazines of the day—*Vogue, Harper's Bazaar,* and especially the brand new *Life* magazine (first issued in November 1936)—caught Parks's imagination. A newsreel cameraman's in-person presentation of his latest battle-action footage in a Chicago movie theater inspired Parks to take up photography himself, and in 1937 he acquired his first camera. Largely self-taught, he took his earliest photographs with only a few pointers from the camera salesman. Quickly mastering technique, he intuitively found the subjects most meaningful to him. The same local Minneapolis camera store soon gave him his first exhibition.

A successful fashion assignment for a stylish Minneapolis department store caught the attention of Marva (Mrs. Joe) Louis, who encouraged Parks to establish himself in Chicago. His fashion background served him well there (as it would later throughout his years at *Life*) photographing Gold Coast socialites. In his spare time, he documented the grim poverty of the city's South Side, the fast-growing Chicago enclave of African Americans displaced from the rural South who came north for jobs in the heavy industries surrounding the Great Lakes.

This socially conscious camera work won for the young photographer, now responsible for a growing family of his own, the very first Julius Rosenwald Fellowship in photography. The 1942–1943 stipend enabled Parks to work with photographic mentor Roy Stryker in Washington, D.C., at the Farm Security Administration. This was the closing years of the influential New Deal agency that had undertaken a pioneering photo documentation of depression conditions in urban and rural America.

Parks continued with Stryker until 1947, first as a correspondent for the Office of War Information, and later at the Standard Oil Company of New Jersey, photographing the face of America for the company's public relations campaign. In the brief months before he began to work for *Life* magazine in 1948, Parks photographed for *Vogue* and *Glamour* and also authored two books on photographic technique: *Flash Photography* (1947) and *Camera Portraits: The Techniques and Principles of Documentary Portraiture* (1948).

Early in his more than two decades at *Life,* Parks spent two influential years assigned to the magazine's Paris office, where he covered fashion, the arts, celebrities, and political figures. The experience was seminal, providing a rich window on the diversity of contemporary creative expression as well as an opportunity for international recognition. Moreover, like other African Americans, he found the European experience, with its relative lack of racial barriers, especially liberating.

Back in the United States during the 1950s and early '60s, Parks executed hundreds of photographic assignments for *Life* that reflect the magazine's far-ranging coverage: popular culture, high fashion, arts, entertainment, sports, national events, and the personalities of business, labor and politics. Parks's direct, realistic style of photographing life in America and abroad won him international renown as the first African-American photojournalist.

Parks's longest assignment began in 1961, when he traveled to Brazil to photograph the slums of Rio de Janeiro. His story of Flavio da Silvia, a poverty-stricken Brazilian boy whom Parks found dying of asthma, attracted international attention that resulted in Flavio and his family receiving gifts, medical treatment, and, finally, a new home. At the same time, with the emerging Civil Rights Movement, Parks undertook a new role at *Life:* interpreting the activities and personalities of the movement, in words as well as pictures, from a personal perspective. His 1971 anthology *Born Black* is a collection of these essays and images.

A gifted storyteller, Parks began his chronological autobiographical book cycle in 1963 with *The Learning Tree,* a well-received novel that drew on the author's own childhood experiences and memories. This was followed in 1966 by *A Choice of Weapons,* a powerful first-person narrative that recounted the events and influences that enabled Parks to overcome societal prejudice and personal hardship. It is the most insightful of the series, illuminating the development of a sensitive and self-confident young man as he grows into what he will become, an artist of universal conscience and compassion.

Parks also gained distinction as a poet, composer, and filmmaker, becoming in 1969 the first African American to direct a major Hollywood film. He also produced and wrote the script for *The Learning Tree* and directed a number of other films, including the highly popular *Shaft* (1971), *Leadbelly* (1976), and *The Odyssey of Solomon Northup* (1984), about a free black sold into slavery. In addition, Parks has completed the music for a ballet about the Rev. Dr. Martin Luther King, Jr., and has worked on a novel based on the life of J. M. W. Turner, the English nineteenth-century landscape painter.

Parks is the recipient of numerous professional awards, organization citations, and honorary degrees, among them Photographer of the Year from the American Society of Magazine Photographers (1960) and the Spingarn Medal from the NAACP (1972).

His greatest satisfaction and motivation is expressed in his prologue to *Moments Without Proper Names,* one of his three books of poems accompanied by his photographs:

PHOTOGRAPHER CHRONICLES LIFE

Gordon Parks, Sr., executed hundreds of photographic assignments for Life *that reflect the magazine's far-ranging coverage.*

I hope always to feel the responsibility to communicate the plight of others less fortunate than myself, to show the abused and those who administer the abuses, to point up the pain of the underprivileged as well as the pleasures of the privileged—somehow to evoke the same response from a housewife in Harlem as I would from a seamstress in Paris or a butcher in Vladivostok.

In helping one another we can ultimately save ourselves. We must give up silent watching and put our commitments into practice.

—JULIA VAN HAAFTEN

PEETE, CALVIN

Calvin Peete (July 18, 1943–), golfer. Peete is the most accomplished African American to compete on the Professional Golfers' Association (PGA) tour through the 1990s. He achieved this distinction despite an unlikely personal background for professional golf. Born in Detroit, one of nineteen children, Peete moved with his family to Pahokee, Florida, where he grew up. After dropping out of high school, he made his living selling trinkets and wares to migrating farm workers who followed the seasonal crops of fruits and vegetables from northern Florida. On one of his trips north to Rochester, N.Y., Peete was lured out by a group of friends who told him they were going to a party. Instead they took him to a golf course where he agreed to follow them around, and eventually took some shots. After playing that day, he subsequently devoted all his spare time to golf. His game quickly improved, even though he was hampered with a deformed left arm—he could not fully straighten it—as a result of a childhood accident. Most golf experts consider a straight left arm essential for a good swing.

Within two years Peete was playing scratch golf (zero handicap), but he had no aspirations to become a professional, since he did not think that a black man could earn a living playing golf. He remembers the Sunday afternoon when he was watching a televised tournament (it was the 1968 American Golf Classic), and Lee Elder—at the time the most promising black professional on the PGA Tour—was in a playoff with Jack Nicklaus, the most renowned golfer of all time. Elder didn't win the playoff, but the fact that he was in it, competing for thousands of dollars, prompted Peete to renew his commitment to golf.

Peete didn't earn his PGA playing card until 1971, and in the next three years he struggled to maintain his eligibility to compete on the PGA Tour, finishing 96th, 105th, and 108th, respectively, on the PGA Tour earnings list. It was in 1978 that the thirty-five-year-old Peete won his first tournament, the Greater Milwaukee Open. In 1982 he became the second black multiple winner on the PGA tour when he won the Greater Milwaukee Open, the Anheuser-Busch Classic, the BC Open, and the Pensacola Open. His third-place finish in the 1982 PGA Championship, one of the tour's major events (the others are the Masters, the U.S. Open, and the British Open), demonstrated his ability to compete at the highest level of the sport. He won the Georgia-Pacific Atlanta Classic and the Anheuser-Busch Classic again in 1983, and the Texas Open in 1984.

By 1984, Peete had earned almost $1.25 million, by far the most money earned playing golf in such a short period by an African American. He was honored by *Golf Digest* magazine as the Most Improved Player of 1983, and named to its All-American Team. The Golf Writers' Association awarded him the prestigious Ben Hogan Award.

Despite his unorthodox swing, Peete distinguished himself as the most consistent striker of the golf ball in the sport, regularly leading all other professionals in the category of driving accuracy (the ability to land the first shot on the fairway) and greens in regulation (landing the ball on the green on the first shot for par 3s, the second shot for par 4s, and the third shot for par 5s).

The PGA requires its members to have graduated from high school in order to compete in the Ryder Cup match (the prestigious biennial competition pitting the best American professionals against the best European professionals). Peete passed the test for his high school equivalency in 1982, and was selected as a member of the 1983 U.S. Ryder Cup team. Peete and Lee Elder remain the only African Americans to have competed on the team.

Despite his accomplishments on the professional golf tour, Peete did not convert his success into significant commercial gain. Unlike white golf professionals with similar tour statistics, he received no major national commercial endorsement offers or advertising contracts. Thus, despite the significant liberalization in other areas of opportunity for African-American golfers, a subtle form of discrimination continues to exist.

—LAWRENCE LONDINO

See also

Track and Field

PENTECOSTALISM

Among scholars of Pentecostalism there are two schools of thought as to the emergence of this religious phenomenon. The first school, identified with Vinson Synan, William Menzies, and James Goff, argues that Charles Parham (1873–1929) was the founder of the Pentecostal movement and that it began in Kansas in 1901. The competing school, which includes Walter Hollenweger, James Tinney, J. Douglas Nelson, Cecil R. Robeck, and Edith Blumhofer, argues that the Azusa Street Revival in Los Angeles from 1906 to 1913 was the true beginning and William J. Seymour the pivotal person.

The second school focuses on Azusa Street and Seymour because they were the originating center of Pentecostalism throughout the United States and in Scandinavia, Great Britain, Brazil, Egypt, and India, where it spread. The revival defined Pentecostalism, shaped its interracial relations, and gave it its multicultural character. The first school designates Parham because he was the first proponent to link glossolalia with the biblical Pentecost event recounted in several chapters in the Book of Acts and to define this experience as the baptism of the Holy Spirit.

In 1901 Charles Parham operated the Bethel Bible School in Topeka, Kans. A major religious experience for him was the baptism of the Holy Spirit as described in the Bible, the Book of Acts, chapter 2. The Holiness Movement during the 1800s identified this experience as sanctification. The Wesleyan wing of the Holiness Movement defined the experience in terms of cleansing, while the Calvinist or Reformed wing saw it as empowerment for Christian living. Both positions understood the experience as subsequent to justification. The Reformed advocates described sanctification as a progressive process, while the Wesleyan advocates described it as an instantaneous event.

In the late 1890s Parham joined those who sought to categorize discrete experience beyond justification and sanctification. In January 1901 Parham identified glossolalia with the third experience and linked this experience instead of sanctification with Acts 2. He began preaching this new doctrine within Holiness circles in the Midwest.

In 1905 William J. Seymour, who was black, enrolled in Parham's school in Houston despite the white man Parham's enforcement of segregation laws that prevented Seymour from sitting

INSPIRED CONGREGATION

A group of devout followers celebrates Easter Sunday, April, 1941, at a Pentecostal service. PRINTS AND PHOTOGRAPHS DIVISION, LIBRARY OF CONGRESS

◆ **Pentecostal**

*Of, relating to, or
constituting any of various
Christian religious bodies
that emphasize individual
experiences of grace,
spiritual gifts (as glossolalia
and faith healing),
expressive worship,
and evangelism*

with the white students. While Seymour adopted the new doctrine, he failed at the time to have the actual experience himself. In 1906 he carried the new doctrine to California in response to an invitation to become pastor of a small black Holiness congregation in Los Angeles headed by Julia Hutchins. Hutchins and the other members established a congregation of Evening Light Saints after withdrawing from the Second Baptist Church, which had refused to embrace their Holiness message. Hutchins, however, rejected Seymour's addition to Holiness teaching and barred him from the pulpit. Edward Lee and, later, Richard Asberry invited Seymour to resume preaching at their homes.

After Seymour and others began speaking in tongues, they outgrew the "house church," and Seymour secured larger facilities at 312 Azusa Street, the former sanctuary of First African Methodist Episcopal Church (AME). Seymour's revival on Azusa Street attracted the attention first of local whites and blacks, especially those involved in the Holiness community. But soon participants from the Holiness Movement across the United States converged by the thousands on Azusa Street to observe events, examine the new doctrine, and experience glossolalia. Within twelve months the Azusa Street Mission spawned an international movement and began a journal, *Apostolic Faith*. From 1906 to 1908, *Apostolic Faith,* the Azusa Street Mission, and Seymour held the loosely bound movement together and provided it with a center and leadership.

Like its Holiness counterpart, Pentecostalism was basically local and regional and headed by both blacks and whites, as well as both women and men. In many places local and regional movements took over entire Holiness congregations and institutions. African-American Holiness leaders who embraced Pentecostalism along with all or some of their associated congregations included W. H. Fulford (d. 1916), William Fuller (1875–1958), Charles Harrison Mason (1866–1961), and Magdalena Tate (1871–1930).

Early Pentecostalism emerged as a strongly interracial movement and struggled with its interracial identity at a time when American society was segregated. Frank Bartleman, a white Azusa Street participant and reporter, stated that at the revival "the color line was washed away in the blood [of Jesus Christ]." While Baptist, Methodist, Presbyterian, and Holiness people lived in racially segregated congregations, associations, and denominational structures, the black and white Pentecostals pastored and preached to and

fellowshipped and worshipped with each other between 1906 and 1914, and many joined the predominantly black Pentecostal-Holiness group, the Church of God in Christ. The Pentecostal leadership was strongly anti-Ku Klux Klan and was often the targets of Klan terrorism because of their interracial sympathies.

But racism came to counter the interracial nature of early Pentecostalism. Parham exhibited racist behavior and a patronizing attitude toward his black counterparts, especially Seymour; in 1908 blacks withdrew from the Fire-Baptized Holiness Church (later called Pentecostal Holiness Church); in 1913 another black group withdrew from the Pentecostal Holiness Church; in 1914 a white group withdrew from the Church of God in Christ; and in 1924 a white group withdrew from the half-black Pentecostal Assemblies of the World, which was led by a black minister, Garfield Thomas Haywood.

While segregation among Pentecostals came to follow the pattern of American Christianity after the Civil War, there were exceptions. Blacks and whites continued to struggle together to structure their interracial relationships during the height of segregation in the United States. In 1924 the Church of God in Christ adopted the Methodist model of establishing a minority transgeographical conference, specifically a white conference to unite the white congregations across the United States that belonged to the predominantly black denomination. In 1907 and 1931 several different groups of blacks and whites entered and withdrew from the Pentecostal Assemblies of the World.

Theologically, Pentecostalism split early into two camps over the doctrine of God: Trinitarian and Oneness. The Oneness doctrine, as opposed to the classic Christian doctrine of the Trinity, claimed that Jesus was the name of God and that God expressed Godself in the form of the Father, Son, and Holy Spirit but was not three persons in one. The Trinitarians confessed the traditional Christian doctrine of the Trinity and rejected the Oneness interpretation. While the existing black Pentecostal denominations, such as the Church of God in Christ, United Holy Church, and Church of the Living God, remained Trinitarian, many independent black Pentecostal congregations in the Midwest, especially those associated with Haywood, rejected Trinitarianism. Oneness denominations identified themselves as Apostolic churches.

Haywood and the Pentecostal Assemblies of the World are the parents of most black Apostolic

See also
African Methodist
Episcopal Church

denominations in the United States. Significant leaders of the movement included Robert C. Lawson (1881–1961), who organized the Church of Our Lord Jesus Christ of the Apostolic Faith in 1919, Sherrod C. Johnson (1897–1961), who organized the Church of the Lord Jesus Christ of the Apostolic Faith in 1930, and Smallwood Williams, who organized Bible Way Churches of Our Lord Jesus Christ Worldwide in 1957.

While Pentecostal denominations opened more forms of ministry to women than other Protestant denominations, only a few granted women equality with men. Among black Pentecostals, full male-female equality existed only in denominations founded by black women. Magdalena Tate's denomination, the oldest Pentecostal denomination founded by a black woman, was among the Holiness groups that joined Pentecostalism after their establishment. During 1903 she founded in Tennessee the Church of Living God, Pillar and Ground of the Truth. The other major grouping of Pentecostal denominations founded by black women withdrew from the United Holy Church of America, which ordained women to the ministry but denied them the bishopric. In 1924 Ida Robinson founded the Mt. Sinai Holy Church to rectify this inequality. In 1944 Beulah Counts (d. 1968), an associate of Robinson, organized the Greater Mt. Zion Pentecostal Church of America.

Crossing Trinitarian and Apostolic divisions is a stream within Pentecostalism called the deliverance movement. The deliverance movement grew out of the white healing movement of the 1940s associated with William Branham that produced Oral Roberts, Gordon Lindsay, and A. A. Allen. The deliverance movement among black Pentecostals is related to Arturo Skinner (1924–1975), who expanded the traditional black Pentecostal emphasis on healing to include exorcisms and heightened the accent on the miraculous. In 1956 he established the Deliverance Evangelistic Centers, with headquarters in Newark, N.J. Deliverance ministries emerged in traditional Pentecostal congregations such as Faith Temple Church of God in Christ under Harry Willis Goldsberry (1895–1986) in Chicago. In urban centers there emerged new independent congregations that competed with traditional black Pentecostals; Benjamin Smith (b. 1926), who founded the Deliverance Evangelistic Center in Philadelphia in 1960, and Richard Hinton, who founded Monument of Faith Evangelistic Center in Chicago in 1963, were two of the best-known leaders of these congregations.

Although Pentecostals are stereotyped as otherworldly, studies have shown a social activist stream within black Pentecostalism. A number of black Pentecostal denominations and leaders joined the Fraternal Council of Negro Churches and participated in the marches for black employment during the 1930s. Robert C. Lawson cooperated with Adam Clayton Powell, Jr., and other leading Harlem ministers in campaigns for black employment. J. O. Patterson (1912–1990) of the Church of God in Christ and other ministers participated in local civil rights campaigns in Memphis, Tenn., and other southern cities and towns in the late 1950s. Smallwood Williams led the legal battle against segregated public schools during the 1950s in Washington, D.C. Arthur Brazier (b. 1921), Louis Henry Ford (b. 1914) and other Pentecostal clergy were active in the Civil Rights Movement in Chicago and other northern cities in the 1960s.

Studies of the black Pentecostal leadership note the occurrence of a cadre of black Pentecostals who identify with twentieth-century theological liberalism. Relations between liberal Protestantism and black Pentecostalism occur on a number of levels. A significant number of Pentecostals are graduates of liberal seminaries, some as early as the 1940s. They are graduates of schools such as Temple University, Oberlin, Union Theological Seminary (New York City), Duke, Emory, and McCormick. And the first accredited Pentecostal, and only African-American, seminary, Charles Harrison Mason Theological Seminary, is a member of Interdenominational Theological Center (ITC), a consortium of African-American seminaries affiliated with mainline denominations. The Church of God in Christ, the sponsor of Mason Seminary at ITC, embraces theological liberalism from a black perspective in the preparation of an educated clergy. A number of black Pentecostal leaders are also involved in the ecumenical movement that liberal Protestantism embraces: Herbert Daughtry (b. 1931) participates in some World Council of Churches programs, and Ithiel Clemmons (b. 1921) participates in regional and local ecumenical councils.

Black Pentecostalism also includes leaders who identify with evangelicalism. Black Pentecostals associated with the evangelical movement are often graduates of evangelical seminaries such as Fuller, Gordon-Conwell, and Trinity Evangelical Divinity School. Leaders such as William Bentley (b. 1926) and George McKinney (b. 1932) are active members of the National Association of

See also
Civil Rights Movement
Ku Klux Klan

Evangelicals along with the National Black Association of Evangelicals.

During the 1970s black Pentecostalism intersected with the "Word of Faith" movement spurred by Kenneth Hagin and his message of healing, prosperity, and positive confession. Fredrick Price (b. 1932) emerged as the Word of Faith leader among black Christians after establishing Crenshaw Christian Center of Los Angeles in 1973.

During the 1970s Pentecostalism influenced the historic black denominations, especially the AME Church. Neo-Pentecostal ministers occupy some major AME pulpits. The focal point for the movement during the early 1970s was St. Paul AME Church in Cambridge, Mass., under the pastorate of John Bryant (b. 1948). During the period, college campuses became centers for the growth of Pentecostalism among black students, particularly through the college gospel choir movement.

Black Pentecostals have been leaders within the black religious music movement since the early 1900s. Black Pentecostalism became the carrier of black religious folk music, noted for its call-and-response, improvisation, polyrhythms, and diatonic harmonies. By the 1920s Arizona Juanita Dranes (b. 1905) and Sallie Sanders were popular gospel singers. Dranes and Sanders began the tradition of the Baptist and Pentecostal leadership of the gospel music movement. By the 1980s black Pentecostals such as Andrae Crouch, Edwin Hawkins, Walter Hawkins, Shirley Caesar, the Clark Sisters, and the Wynans dominated the gospel music movement.

From its beginning at the Azusa Street Revival in 1906, black Pentecostalism has grown to become the second-largest religious movement among African Americans and one of the fastest-growing religious movements in the United States and around the globe, especially in the Third World.

—DAVID D. DANIELS III

PETRY, ANN LANE

Ann Lane Petry (October 12, 1908–), writer. Anne Lane was born to middle-class parents in Saybrook, Conn. The daughter of a pharmacist, she graduated from the University of Connecticut School of Pharmacy (formerly the Connecticut College of Pharmacy) in 1931 and worked for a while in her father's drugstore. Yet from the time she created a slogan for a perfume advertisement while still in high school, she was convinced she

could be a writer. In 1938 she married George D. Petry and moved to New York City.

In New York, Petry began serving a kind of writer's apprenticeship as a journalist for two Harlem newspapers, the *Amsterdam News* and *The People's Voice*. (From 1944 to 1946, she would also study creative writing at Columbia University.) This experience exposed her to the gritty world of Harlem's poverty, violence, crime, and economic exploitation that gave her early fiction its absorbing cast and distinctive signature. Her first published story, "On Saturday the Siren Sounds at Noon," appeared in the *Crisis* in 1943. Finding the story "Like a Winding Sheet" similarly engaging, *Crisis* published it in 1945. Collected in Martha Foley's *Best American Stories of 1946*, "Like a Winding Sheet" brought Petry national attention and a Houghton Mifflin Literary Fellowship Award to complete what became her best known and most celebrated novel, *The Street* (1946), the first by a black woman to sell more than one million copies.

In *The Street*, Petry focuses on the thwarted and naive efforts of a young black woman to secure a decent living for herself and her son. Petry closely documents the defeating conditions of the ghetto on a woman. She shows an especially critical sensitivity to the notion of the woman as a spectacle, as a body to be looked at and made the object of male sexual desire and exploitation. In her second novel, *Country Place* (1947), Petry shifts her focus from Harlem to Monmouth, Conn. Here she uses the effect that a violent storm has on the people who live in a small town to intricately weave strands of class conflict, bloodlines, and social responsibility. Many of these themes are reworked in Petry's next work, *The Narrows* (1953), a novel about the taboo and ultimately tragic relationship between a black man and a white woman. Petry does not skirt the history of sexual and racial politics that weighs on their relationship, a history that makes the white woman's cry of rape and the black man's subsequent lynching inevitable.

Petry joins urban and rural scenes in her only collection of short stories, *Miss Muriel and Other Stories* (1971). Of the stories in this diverse collection, standing out are those in which Petry experiments with the point of view of precocious, introspective child narrators. Set variously in Harlem, small-town upstate New York, and Connecticut, these stories show geography to be the dominant factor in Petry's writing. Other works include four children's books: *The Drugstore Cat* (1949), *Harriet Tubman, Conductor of the Underground Rail-*

See also

Literature

road (1955), *Tituba of Salem Village* (1964), and *Legends of the Saints* (1970).

—DEBORAH MCDOWELL

PHILADELPHIA, PENNSYLVANIA

When William Penn arrived on the shores of the Delaware River in 1682 to establish the Pennsylvania Colony, the area was inhabited by Delaware Indians, Dutch, Swedes, British settlers, and free and enslaved Africans. Penn selected and named Philadelphia to be the capital of the colony. The early city was small: 1,200 acres, two miles in length from east to west between the Delaware and Schuylkill rivers, and one mile in width from north to south. The boundaries remained unchanged until the consolidation of 1854, which made the county of Philadelphia coterminous with the city, incorporating many districts and townships, including Northern Liberties, Spring Garden, Southwark, Moyamensing, Passyunk, and Blockley into the city of Philadelphia.

Scant references exist to the early presence of blacks in the colony; however, by 1720 they numbered at least 2,500 in Pennsylvania. Many were slaves. There is evidence of their collective activities by various acts of proposed and enacted legislation. The first restriction imposed in 1693 required that Africans carry passes. Later, other acts prohibited their assembly and determined where and when they could meet. The 1790 Census recorded 210 slaves in the city and 384 in the county, but Pennsylvania's Gradual Abolition of Slavery Act of 1780 applied only to children born after the act, freeing them after service to their enslaved mothers' owners for twenty-eight years. Therefore, in addition to apprenticeship, a number of black children were indentured servants, adding an additional element of separation and rendering them still not free.

Despite these limitations, Philadelphia blacks developed a community in the eighteenth century. In 1786 a petition for a burial ground was presented. A year later, the Free African Society was formed. This was the first beneficial society, established by Richard Allen and Absalom Jones in Philadelphia and comprised blacks and a few white Quakers. Some members of the Society were part of the group that had petitioned for a burial ground.

Richard Allen recorded that the beginning of the African Church in Philadelphia occurred in 1787. Though there is considerable scholarly disagreement on the precise sequence of events, and the date of the famous incident when Allen, Jones, and their fellow black congregants were ejected from St. George's Church, by the late 1780s a number of blacks who had previously worshipped with whites began leaving those churches to establish their own places of worship. At first they worshipped in private dwellings. Later they were able to formally dedicate their own buildings.

The African Church, later the First African Church of St. Thomas (Protestant Episcopal), was dedicated in 1794. Jones was its first pastor. Bethel Methodist Church, the oldest real estate continuously owned by blacks in the United States, was dedicated in 1796. Allen was its first pastor. In 1816 Allen and others organized the African Methodist Episcopal Church, the first black denomination. African Zoar Methodist Church was formed in 1794 by another group of blacks who left St. George's and worshipped for some time in their homes in Campingtown, an area in Northern Liberties. Later, in 1796, on ground adjacent to property owned by Lunar Brown, a member and trustee, they formally dedicated their church. Methodists and Episcopalians were not the only groups to lose black parishioners. In 1809 nine black men and women received a letter of dismission from the First Baptist Church of Philadelphia. They established the First African Baptist Church in that year in the Spring Garden district, near Northern Liberties. The First African Presbyterian Church was established in 1811 by men and women led by John Gloucester. These and many more black churches came into existence providing for the growing black population, schools, burial grounds, and meeting places. Not only do census figures indicate an increase in the black population, but the proliferation of institutions also attests to the population's increase and potential influence. Perhaps the most notable event in the early history of black Philadelphia was the yellow fever epidemic of the summer of 1793, which claimed about one-tenth of the city's 50,000 residents. Under the mistaken belief that African Americans had natural immunity to the disease, city leaders appealed to blacks to help treat and bury the dead. Some whites criticized blacks for trying to profit from the crisis. Jones and Allen rebutted the accusations in their jointly written *Narrative of the Proceedings of the Black People During the Late Awful Calamity in Philadelphia* (1794).

There were nineteen black churches in the city and county of Philadelphia by 1847. Eighty-four

Philadelphia, the home of respectability, and the city of respectable homes.

ANONYMOUS
SAYING QUOTED IN
NATHANIEL BURT, *THE
PERENNIAL PHILADELPHIANS*,
1963

See also
Black Panther Party
W.E.B. Du Bois

percent of black persons living in the city who were surveyed that year by the Pennsylvania Abolition Society indicated church membership. In addition to the denominations mentioned, a large percentage of blacks were members of various other denominations: Roman Catholic, African Methodist Episcopal Zion, and Society of Friends.

Later, some black Philadelphians were members of the Shaker community established in Philadelphia by Rebecca Cox Jackson. Few blacks, however, attended interracial churches.

Literary and secret societies also came into existence in the 1800s. Beneficial society membership increased in every area in the city and county

ABSALOM JONES

Founder of the Free African Society of Philadelphia

Absalom Jones (1746–1818), minister and community leader. Among the enslaved African Americans who gained their freedom in the era of the American Revolution, Absalom Jones made some of the most important contributions to black community building at a time when the first urban free black communities of the United States were taking form. Enslaved from his birth in Sussex County, Del., Jones served on the estate of the merchant-planter Benjamin Wynkoop. Taken from the fields into his master's house as a young boy, he gained an opportunity for learning. When his master moved to Philadelphia in 1762, Jones, at age sixteen, worked in his master's store but continued his education in a night school for blacks. In 1770 he married, and through unstinting labor he was able to buy his wife's freedom in about 1778 and his own in 1784.

After gaining his freedom, Jones rapidly became one of the main leaders of the growing free black community in Philadelphia—the largest urban gathering of emancipated slaves in the post-Revolutionary period. Worshiping at Saint George's Methodist Episcopal Church, Jones soon began to discuss a separate black religious society with other black Methodists such as Richard Allen and William White. From these tentative steps toward community-based institutions came the Free African Society of Philadelphia, probably the first independent black organization in the United States. Although mutual aid was its purported goal, the Free African Society was quasi-religious in character; beyond that, it was an organization where people emerging from the house of bondage could gather strength, develop their own leaders, and explore independent strategies for hammering out a postslavery existence that went beyond formal legal release from thralldom.

Once established, the Free African Society became a vehicle for Jones to establish the African Church of Philadelphia, the first independent black church in North America. Planned in conjunction with Richard Allen and launched with the assistance of Benjamin Rush and several Philadelphia Quakers, the African Church of Philadelphia was designed as a racially separate, nondenominational, and socially oriented church. But in order to gain state recognition of its corporate status, it affiliated with the Protestant Episcopal Church of North America and later took the name Saint Thomas's African Episcopal Church. Jones became its minister when it opened in 1794, and served in that capacity until his death in 1818. For decades, Saint Thomas's was emblematic of the striving for dignity, self-improvement, and autonomy of a generation of African Americans released or self-released from bondage, mostly in the North. In his first sermon at the African Church of Philadelphia, Jones put out the call to his fellow African Americans to "arise out of the dust and shake ourselves, and throw off that servile fear, that the habit of oppression and bondage trained us up in." Jones's church, like many others that emerged in the early nineteenth century, became a center of social and political as well as religious activities, and a fortress from which to struggle against white racial hostility.

From his position as the spiritual leader at Saint Thomas's, Jones became a leading educator and reformer in the black community. Although even-tempered and known for his ability to quiet controversy and reconcile differences, he did not shrink from the work of promoting the rights of African Americans. He coauthored, with Richard Allen, *A Narrative of the Proceedings of the Black People, During the Late Awful Calamity in Philadelphia, in the year 1793*, a resounding defense of black contributions in the yellow fever epidemic of 1793—Jones himself assisted Benjamin Rush in ministering to the sick and dying in the ghastly three-month epidemic—and a powerful attack on slavery and white racial hostility. In 1797, he helped organize the first petition of African Americans against slavery, the slave trade, and the federal Fugitive Slave Law of 1793. Three years later, he organized another petition to President Jefferson and the Congress deploring slavery and the slave trade. From his pulpit he orated against slavery, and he was responsible in 1808 for informally establishing January 1 (the date on which the slave trade ended) as a day of thanksgiving and celebration, in effect an alternative holiday to the Fourth of July for black Americans.

Typical of black clergymen of the nineteenth century, Jones functioned far beyond his pulpit. Teaching in schools established by the Pennsylvania Abolition Society and by his church, he helped train a generation of black youth in Philadelphia. As Grand Master of Philadelphia's Black Masons, one of the founders of the Society for the Suppression of Vice and Immorality (1809), and a founder of the literary Augustine Society (1817), he struggled to advance the self-respect and enhance the skills of the North's largest free African-American community. By the end of Jones's career, Saint Thomas's was beginning to acquire a reputation as the church of the emerging black middle class in Philadelphia. But he would long be remembered for his ministry among the generation emerging from slavery.

—GARY B. NASH

from 1837 to 1847. Their purpose was the relief of members who were unable to work, the interments of deceased members, and the relief of widows and orphans. Occupational organizations such as Humane Mechanics, Coachman's Benevolent Society, Union Sons of Industry, and African Porter's Benevolent Society also were formed. These institutions and real property owned by blacks were seen by whites as symbols of upward mobility and power and were targeted for violence and destruction.

Prominent black Philadelphians such as sail maker James Forten, the aforementioned ministers Richard Allen and Absalom Jones, educator Sarah Douglass, dentist Jacob White, and members of the Bowser and the Bustill families were well known. Indeed, they were influential in the formation, growth, and development of Philadelphia's black community. Many also raised their voices against slavery and became prominent early abolitionists. In 1830, with Allen as president, the first National Negro Convention was held in Philadelphia. Other Philadelphia abolitionists included the three granddaughters of James Forten: Margaretta, Sarah, and Harriet Forten, and leader of the Underground Railroad, William Still.

Individual and collective economic enterprises began as early as 1810 with the founding of the African Insurance Company. Joseph Randolph was president, and Cyrus Porter and William Coleman, were treasurer and secretary, respectively. The company had capital in the amount of $5,000 in $50 shares. A financial panic in 1814 and a subsequent depression caused its failure. Two young black men, Derrick Johnson and Joseph Allen, initiated the African Fire Association (AFA) in 1818. There were more than 7,000 blacks in the city at that time, and its formation caused a "great excitement among the members of the [white] fire and hose companies." Whites successfully argued that black fire companies were unnecessary and would be unproductive. Thereafter the founders of the AFA, a potentially powerful political organization, were persuaded and encouraged to desist by some members of the black community.

Pennsylvania's Constitution in 1790 declared that a "freeman" 21 years of age who had resided in Pennsylvania for two years and paid a state or county tax "shall enjoy the rights of an elector." Though there was some African-American suffrage in the late eighteenth century and early nineteenth century in Pennsylvania, it was on a very small scale. The increasing black population in the city and county, along with their ownership of property valued at more than $300,000, caused the Pennsylvania Supreme Court in 1837 to declare that the Negro was not a "freeman" within the context of the Constitution. Revised a year later, Pennsylvania's Constitution prohibited black property owners from voting, stipulating that the vote belonged to every "white freeman," regardless of realty holdings. In 1848, blacks again petitioned for the right to vote, and in 1849, there was an election-day riot. Blacks regained the vote in 1871, and another riot ensued after that election, resulting in the murder of political leader Octavious V. Catto. The years 1829, 1835, 1838, and 1849 were tumultuous and in 1838 there were major riots against the black community which destroyed their churches, meeting halls, residences, the African Grand Lodge of Masons Hall (Pennsylvania Hall), and the Shelter for Colored Orphans.

Despite these setbacks, black Philadelphia's institutional life grew in the second half of the nineteenth century. Businessmen and philanthropists such as Stephen Smith (1797?–1873) helped found the Institute for Colored Youth, the Home for Destitute Colored Children, the House for the Aged and Infirm Colored Persons, Mercy Hospital, and the House of Refuge. Many prominent black Philadelphians such as Robert Bogle, James LeCount, James Prosser, Jeremia Bowser, and Peter Augustine made their fortunes in the catering industry. The black community supported a number of newspapers—five by the end of the nineteenth century—including the *Philadelphia Tribune*, founded in 1884, the oldest continually published black newspaper in the United States. The artistic and intellectual attainments of Philadelphia's black middle class were considerable. Benjamin T. Tanner, a bishop in the A.M.E. Church, edited the *Christian Recorder* and *AME Church Review* and made them into important forums for black intellectual and religious thought. His son, Henry Ossawa Tanner, became the leading black artist of his generation. In the middle decades of the twentieth century, the granddaughter of Bishop Tanner, Sadie Tanner Mossell Alexander and her husband, Raymond Pace Alexander, became lawyers and leaders in the civil rights struggle for Philadelphians. Arthur Huff Fauset, a distinguished folklorist and urban sociologist, also was an advocate for improving housing conditions for black Philadelphians. His sister, Jessie Redmon Fauset, was a leading novelist of the Harlem Renaissance, and in novels such as *The Chinaberry Tree* (1931) provided a sensitive portrait of Philadelphia's black elite. Though

See also
John Coltrane
Dizzy Gillespie

P

originally from a poor background, Marian Anderson became active at an early age in the middle-class musical culture of her local church, and the Philadelphia community financially supported her training and early career. By the 1930s, she was one of the leading concert performers of her generation.

In 1899 W. E. B. Du Bois's work, *The Philadelphia Negro*, was published. The monumental sociological study examined the history and present condition of blacks in Philadelphia.

After 1900 there were considerable changes in Philadelphia's black community. Between 1900 and 1960, Philadelphia's black population increased more than 800 percent. Conditions were often difficult for the new migrants. There were jobs, but new migrants met much hostility. In 1918 there was a riot that resulted in the deaths of four blacks and many injuries. Philadelphia was not prepared to house the multitude of people who came seeking refuge. Overcrowded slums

quickly developed in North and South Philadelphia, and residential segregation began. Although public housing had been available to whites, it was not until 1943 that public housing became available for blacks in North Philadelphia. In response to the increase in population, neighborhoods changed, the number of public and parochial schools increased and became more segregated, and more black churches came into existence. East Calvary Methodist Church, pastored by the charismatic Charles A. Tindley, attracted a large number of migrants from the South. Purchasing property on affluent Broad Street (circa 1924), East Calvary continued to grow and later became Tindley Temple (1925).

Although many black Philadelphians registered Republican, the New Deal attracted the loyalty of many who were less affluent, and the majority of black voters soon became Democrats. Philadelphia has long been a city of machine politics. Blacks benefited from political patronage,

BLACK PANTHERS IN PHILADELPHIA

Huey P. Newton speaks before an estimated 5,000 people at Temple University in 1970.
AP/WIDE WORLD PHOTOS

were elected ward leaders, and eventually won seats on city council and the courts. In 1938 Crystal Bird Fauset, running as a Democrat from a Philadelphia district, became the first black woman in the United States elected to a state legislature. The population continued to increase because of wartime employment opportunities. The many government installations, including the Philadelphia Navy Shipyard, provided jobs for migrants.

The 1960s and '70s were turbulent times for black Philadelphians. The emergence of a new militancy among them was evidenced by community protest meetings, race riots, and Black Panther Party rallies. Many of the rallies occurred, with the encouragement of Father Paul Washington, at the Church of the Advocate, an Episcopal church in the heart of North Philadelphia. Again, churches were influential in community improvement as evidenced by Opportunities Industrialization Center (OIC), a self-help organization founded by the Rev. Leon Sullivan.

Girard College, a segregated school in North Philadelphia, was established by the will of Stephen Girard for white male orphans and administered by the Board of City Trusts. Initial litigation to invalidate the will was begun in 1954 by attorney Raymond Pace Alexander. Later, another black attorney, Cecil B. Moore, not only renewed legal action, but rallied blacks to march around the wall of the college until it figuratively "came down." Moore was a criminal attorney known for representing indigent defendants *pro bono*. Moore increased the membership of the NAACP and eventually won election to city council. The combination of litigation and continued community pressure and moral outrage succeeded in the school's integration in 1968. (Even after the end of legal segregation, however, residential segregation patterns left the de facto segregation of Philadelphia's schools largely intact.)

With more blacks in influential positions and a large, black voting population, W. Wilson Goode was elected Philadelphia's first black mayor in 1983, with 91 percent of the black vote. Although reelected four years later, his political career was marred by the bombing of the Move compound in May 1985. After years of sparring with a black nationalist organization, MOVE, that rejected most contact with outsiders, Philadelphia police dropped bombs into its compound, killing six, and started a fire that burned down fifty adjoining homes and left 200 people homeless. All of black Philadelphia—and, indeed, most of the city's residents—were devastated at the loss of innocent lives and the destruction of a stable, black neighborhood in West Philadelphia.

Despite these difficulties, Philadelphia's black community is proud of its history as one of the centers of African-American institutional life for more than three centuries. Some of the leading monuments to black Philadelphia are the Afro-American Historical and Cultural Museum, opened in 1976, the All-Wars Memorial to Black Soldiers, unveiled in 1934, and the homes of the writer Frances Ellen Watkins Harper and the painter Henry O. Tanner. Philadelphia has been home to a number of prominent jazz musicians, including Dizzy Gillespie, John Coltrane, and the three Heath brothers: Percy, Al, and Jimmy. It also has been a center for black popular music. Other black Philadelphians who have achieved renown in recent decades include comedian Bill Cosby, and William Gray III, former congressman, ambassador to Haiti, and president of the United Negro College Fund.

—JANET HARRISON SHANNON

PHOTOGRAPHY

African Americans shaped the practice of photography from its origin in 1840 and have participated in its history as practitioners and subjects. The larger American public was fascinated with the daguerreotype as soon as Louis Jacques Mandé Daguerre (1787–1851) publicized the process in France in 1839. The French inventor Nicéphore Niepce (1765–1833) produced the earliest extant photographic image made by a camera obscura in 1827. After the death of Niepce, Daguerre successfully fixed an image and in January 1839 announced to the Paris press his discovery, which he named the Daguerreotype. Six months after the public announcement of the process in Paris, Jules Lion, a free man of color, a lithographer, and portrait painter, exhibited the first successful daguerreotypes in New Orleans.

The African-American public was enthusiastic about Daguerre's process of making likenesses (which we now call photographs). These were numerous free black men and women who established themselves as daguerreans, photographers, inventors, artists, and artisans who had gained local and national recognition in their respective cities. Portraits of prominent and lesser-known African Americans were produced regularly in galleries and studios throughout the country. The portraits of well-known African Americans soon became popular, and the practice of private pho-

See also

Jazz
United Negro College Fund

tography—the photographing of individuals for personal collections and albums—became more and more the artistic method for creating a likeness. Most of the photographs taken at this time were not intended for publication or public presentation, but noted citizens and other families from all walks of life thought it important to have their likenesses preserved for posterity.

During most of photography's early history, images produced by African-American photographers presented idealized glimpses of family members in romanticized or dramatic settings. Photographers such as C.M. Battey and James VanDerZee sought to integrate elements of romanticism and classicism, as did the painters of the previous centuries. Most photographs taken in the early years were made to commemorate a special occasion in the sitter's life—such as marriage, birth, graduation, confirmation, and anniversaries—or the achievement of a particular social or political success.

One of the earliest known photographical studies in America of African-American physiognomy was conducted in 1850 by Harvard scientist Louis Agassiz and J. T. Zealy, a white daguerreotypist in Columbia, S.C. The latter was hired to take a series of portraits of African-born slaves on nearby plantations. The daguerreotypes were anatomical studies of the faces and the nude upper bodies of African men and women. The photographs were to give visual evidence of the "natural difference in size of limbs, heads, and configurations of muscles," thereby establishing a theory that blacks were different and inferior. Much of the work of the nineteenth-century black photographers was in sharp contrast to these scientific and stereotypical images.

The first publicized exhibition of a work by a black photographer was held on March 15, 1840, in the Hall of the St. Charles Museum in the city of New Orleans. The exhibition, reported to have drawn a large crowd, was organized and sponsored by the artist, Jules Lion. In 1854, Glenalvin Goodridge, a black photographer from York, Pa., won the prize for "best ambrotypes" (a process using a wet plate) at the York County fair. Other black photographers who won distinction in the nineteenth century at exhibitions and expositions include James Presley Ball, who exhibited his daguerreotypes in 1855 at the Ohio Mechanics Annual Exhibition, and Harry Shepherd, who won the first prize at the 1891 Minnesota State fair and later exhibited photographs of the Tuskegee Institute (now University) at the Paris Exposition in 1900. In 1895, Daniel Freeman, known as the

first black photographer in Washington, D.C., exhibited his works in the Negro Building at the 1895 Atlanta Exposition.

Between the end of the Civil War and the turn of the nineteenth century, numerous itinerant photographers flourished in the North. But even earlier, several African-American photographers were able to open their own studios. In the 1840s and '50s, James Ball and Augustus Washington (1820–?) operated galleries in Cincinnati, Ohio, and Hartford, Conn.; Jules Lion had his own studio in New Orleans. (Ball and Washington were active abolitionists who often used their photographic skills to expose the inhumane institution of slavery and promote the abolitionist movement.) Harry Shepherd opened his first portrait gallery in St. Paul, Minn., in 1887, where he employed eight attendants. He advertised that "his patrons are among all classes—from the millionaires to day wage workers." Shepherd was one of the few African-American members of the National Photographers Association of America.

Fanny J. Thompson, a musician and composer living in Memphis, Tenn., in the 1880s, studied photography and was one of the first to record African-American women working in the field. The Goodridge brothers—Glenalvin, Wallace, and William—began their careers in York, Pa., in the 1850s, before settling in East Saginaw, Mich., in 1866. They opened their first studio the following year. In 1884 they were commissioned by the U.S. Department of Forestry to photograph views of the Saginaw Valley woodlands.

At the turn of the century, photography expanded in a variety of ways. Newspapers, journals, and books published photographic images. Courses in photography were offered in schools and colleges, and correspondence courses were also available. C. M. Battey, an accomplished portraitist and fine-art photographer, was a noted educator in photography. Battey founded the Photography Division at Tuskegee Institute in Alabama in 1916. In 1917, *Crisis* magazine highlighted Battey in the "Men of the Month" column as "one of the few colored photographers who has gained real artistic success." The most extensive portrait series of African-American leaders produced in the nineteenth century and early twentieth century was done by Battey. His photographic portraits of John Mercer Langston, Frederick Douglass, W. E. B. Du Bois, Booker T. Washington, and Paul Laurence Dunbar were sold nationally and were reproduced on postcards and posters.

Between 1900 and 1919, African-American photographers flourished in larger cities, produc-

See also
Countee Cullen
Claude McKay

ing images of both rural and urban experiences. They included Arthur Bedou (1882–1966) of New Orleans; King Daniel Ganaway (1883–?) of Chicago, who in 1918 received first prize in the John Wanamaker Annual Exhibition of photographers; and Arthur Laidler Macbeth (1864–?) of Charlestown, S.C., Baltimore, and Norfolk. Macbeth won many awards and citations for his photographs and was among the pioneers in motion pictures. He invented "Macbeth's Daylight Projecting Screen" for showing stereopticon and moving pictures in the daytime.

In 1911, Addison Scurlock, who was Howard University's official photographer, opened a studio in Washington, D.C., which he operated with his wife and sons, Robert and George, until 1964; after that time, his sons continued to operate the studio. In New York City, James VanDerZee, undoubtedly the best known of black studio photographers, began capturing the spirit and life of New York's Harlem in the 1920s and continued to do so for more than fifty years.

During the period of the Harlem Renaissance through the Great Depression and the New Deal, photographers began to exhibit their work widely in their communities. In the 1920s, young black photographers who viewed themselves as artists moved to the larger cities in search of education, patronage, and support for their art. Harlem was a cultural mecca for many of these photographers. In 1921 the New York Public Library's 135th Street branch in Manhattan (now known as the Schomburg Center for Research in Black Culture) organized its first exhibition of work by black artists, entitled "The Negro Artists." Two photographers, C. M. Battey and Lucy Calloway of New York, displayed six photographs in this exhibition of over sixty-five works of art. The Harmon Foundation was one of the first philanthropic organizations to give attention, cash awards, and exhibition opportunities to black photographers. These awards came to be known as the William E. Harmon Awards for Distinguished Achievement Among Negroes. In 1930, a special prize of $50 for photographic work was added in the name of the Commission on Race Relations.

A year earlier, James Latimer Allen (1907–1977) exhibited his portraits of African-American men, women, and children in a Harmon Foundation exhibition. Allen also photographed such writers of the period as Alain Locke, Langston Hughes, Countee Cullen, and Claude McKay. Other photographers active between 1920 and '40 included several students of C. M. Battey, among

them Elise Forrest Harleston (1891–1970) of Charleston, S.C., and P. H. Polk (1898–1985) of Tuskegee, Ala. Harleston opened a photography studio with her painter husband, Edwin Harleston, after studying with Battey in 1922. Polk opened his first studio at Tuskegee in 1927. The following year he was appointed to the faculty of Tuskegee Institute's photography department, photographed prominent visitors such as Mary McLeod Bethune and Paul Robeson, and made extensive portraits of scientist-inventor George Washington Carver. Richard S. Roberts (1881–1936) of Columbia, S.C., began studying photography through correspondence courses and specialist journals, and opened his studio in the early 1920s. According to Roberts's advertisements, his studio took superior photographs by day or night. Twin brothers Morgan (1910–1993) and Marvin Smith (1910–) were prolific photographers in Harlem in the 1930s and early '40s. They photographed members of the community, as well as political rallies, breadlines during the Great Depression, families, and "Lindy Hoppers" in the Savoy Ballroom.

During the Depression, numerous images were taken of the lives of African-Americans. The Resettlement Administration, later known as the Farm Security Administration (FSA), was created in 1935 as an independent coordinating agency; it inherited rural relief activities and land-use administration from the Department of the Interior, the Federal Emergency Relief Administration, and the Agricultural Adjustment Administration. Between 1935 and '43, the FSA photography project generated 270,000 images of rural, urban, and industrial America. Many of the heavily documented activities of the FSA were of black migrant workers in the South. In 1937, Gordon Parks, Sr. decided that he wanted to be a photographer after viewing the work of the Farm Security Administration photographers. He was hired by the FSA in 1941, and during World War II he worked as an Office of War Information correspondent. After the war, he was a photographer for Standard Oil Company. In 1949 he became the first African-American photographer to work on the staff of *Life* magazine.

Roy DeCarava is the forerunner of contemporary urban photography. He studied art at Cooper Union in New York City, the Works Progress Administration's Harlem Art Center, and the George Washington Carver Art School. In 1955, DeCarava collaborated with Langston Hughes in producing a book entitled *The Sweet Flypaper of Life,* which depicted the life of a black family in

See also

Langston Hughes

Alain Locke

ROY DECARAVA

Photographer Views African Americans through Lens of Art

Roy DeCarava (December 9, 1919–), photographer. Born and raised by his mother in Harlem, Roy DeCarava graduated with a major in art from the Straubenmuller Textile High School in 1938. While still in high school he worked as a sign painter and display artist and in the poster division of the Works Progress Administration (WPA) project in New York City. In his senior year he won a competition to design a medal for the National Tuberculosis Association's high school essay contest and upon graduation received a scholarship for excellence in art.

Supporting himself as a commercial artist, DeCarava studied painting at Cooper Union with Byron Thomas and Morris Kantor from 1938 to 1940, and lithography and drawing at the Harlem Art Center from 1940 to 1942. He attended the George Washington Carver Art School in 1944 and 1945, studying painting with Charles White. In 1946 his serigraph won the print award at the Atlanta University Fifth Annual Exhibition of Painting and Sculpture (a national juried exhibition for black artists), and the following year he had a one-man show at the Serigraph Gallery in New York.

In 1946, DeCarava began to use photography as a means to sketch ideas for paintings, and by 1947 he had decided to concentrate exclusively on it. Although he lacked formal training, DeCarava approached photography as "just another medium that an artist would use"; he quickly established a distinctive style and chose a subject—the people of Harlem—that engaged him deeply and productively. Some of his strongest work dates from the late 1940s and early 1950s, such as *Graduation* (1949) and *Gittel* (1950). His first photographic exhibition was in 1950 at New York's Forty-fourth Street Gallery, and that year he sold three prints to the Museum of Modern Art. In 1952, DeCarava became the tenth photographer and among the earliest black artists to be awarded a Guggenheim Fellowship. Continuing his work in Harlem during the fellowship year, DeCarava produced over 2,000 images; he wanted to show, he has said, "[African Americans'] beauty and the image that we presented in our being." In 1955 four of his photographs appeared in the Museum of Modern Art's famous *Family of Man* exhibition and best-selling book. In the same year, 141 photographs were published with a text by Langston Hughes in their much-acclaimed classic *The Sweet Flypaper of Life* (1955), a tale of everyday events in the lives of a fictional yet representative Harlem family.

DeCarava formed his style at a time in photographic history when the social documentary ethos of the 1930s was giving way to a more formalist aesthetic which especially appreciated a photographer's manipulation of the unique qualities of the medium. He was influenced by the French photographer Henri Cartier-Bresson, whose theory of the "decisive moment" credits formal organization equally with factual content in conveying essential meaning in a photograph. Like Cartier-Bresson, DeCarava uses a small camera, avoids contrived settings, often shooting in the street, and achieves important, often metaphorical, effects through composition, as in *Sun and Shade* (1952) and *Boy Playing, Man Walking* (1966). Indeed, DeCarava has taken pains throughout his career to foster interpretations that see more in his style than literal and programmatic documentary. His titles are always brief and uninflected, and he insists that his work is not political and that "the definition of truth is a personal one." Dismayed that so few galleries showed photography as a fine art, DeCarava operated the Photographer's Gallery from 1954 to 1956, exhibiting work by such artists as Berenice Abbott, Harry Callahan, and Minor White.

DeCarava felt keenly that black people were not seen as "worthy subject matter" for art; he was determined that African Americans be portrayed in ways that were "serious," "artistic," and "human." His dual commitment—to content representing the beauty and diversity of the African-American experience and to full formal mastery of his medium—has deeply influenced younger photographers, who have seen him as the first to develop "the black aesthetic" in photography. From 1963 to 1966, he directed the Kamoinge Workshop for black photographers and chaired the Committee to End Discrimination Against Black Photographers of the American Society of Magazine Photographers. In 1968 DeCarava picketed the Metropolitan Museum of Art's controversial *Harlem on My Mind* exhibition, protesting its emphasis on documentary, rather than artistic, representation of the Harlem Community. In 1972 DeCarava received the Benin Award for contributions to the black community.

—MAREN STANGE

See also
George Washington Carver
Harlem Renaissance

Harlem. In 1952, DeCarava received a Guggenheim Fellowship; he was one of the first black photographers to win the award. In 1954, he founded a photography gallery that became one of the first galleries in the United States devoted to the exhibition and sale of photography as a fine art. DeCarava founded the Kamoinge Workshop for black photographers in 1963.

From the 1930s through the '60s, photographers began working as photojournalists for local newspapers and national magazines marketed to African-American audiences, including *Our World,* Ebony, *Jet, Sepia,* and *Flash,* among others. Only a few African-American photojournalists, most notably Gordon Parks, Sr., Richard Saunders, Bert Miles, and Roy DeCarava, were employed for the larger picture magazines such as *Life, Look, Time, Newsweek,* and *Sports Illustrated.* Most of them learned photography while in the military and studied photography in schools of journalism.

This period also encompassed the beginning of reportage and the documentation of public pageantry and events. In the 1930s smaller hand-held cameras and faster films aided photographers in expressing their frustration and discontent with social and political conditions within their communities. The Civil Rights Movement was well documented by photographers such as Moneta Sleet, Jr. (New York and Chicago); Jack T. Franklin (Philadelphia); Charles "Teenie" Harris (Pittsburgh); Howard Morehead (Los Angeles); Bertrand Miles (New York); Austin Hansen (New York); and U.S. Information Service Agency photographers Richard Saunders and Griffith Davis.

Between 1935 and the early 1990s, musical pioneers were the frequent subjects of Chuck Stewart (1927–), Milt Hinton, Roy DeCarava, and Bert Andrews (1931–1993), who photographed performing artists in the studio, on stage, and in nightclubs. Milt Hinton received his first camera in 1935 while he was playing in Cab Calloway's band. As a jazz bassist and photographer, Hinton photographed his musician friends and colleagues. In 1950, Chuck Stewart, who studied photography at Ohio University, began photographing jazz musicians and vocalists on stage and in his studio in New York City. His photographs were used for album covers, publicity stills, and illustrations for books and articles of jazz. Stewart photographed virtually every well-known musician and vocalist between 1950 and '90; his coverage includes blues, bebop, fusion, salsa, and popular music. Bert Andrews photographed black theatrical productions on and off-Broadway from the early 1960s through the early 1990s. Among the production companies whose plays he photographed are the Negro Ensemble Company, the New Federal Theatre, and the Frank Silvera Writers' Workshop.

During the active years of the civil rights and Black Power movements—the early 1960s through the 1970s—a significant number of socially committed men and women became photographers, documenting the struggles, achievements, and tragedies of the freedom movement. Student Non-violent Coordinating Committee (SNCC) photographers Doug Harris, Elaine Tomlin, and Bob Fletcher were in the forefront in documenting the voter registration drives in the South; Robert Sengstacke, Howard Bingham, Jeffrey Scales, and Brent Jones photographed the North and West Coast activities of the Black Panther Party and desegregation rallies. Between 1969 and 1986, six African-American photographers received the coveted Pulitzer Prize in photography. The first to win the award was Moneta Sleet, Jr., in 1969 for his photograph of Coretta Scott King and her daughter at the funeral of the Rev. Dr. Martin Luther King, Jr. Following in subsequent years were Ovie Carter (1975) for international reporting for his photographs of famine in Africa and India; Matthew Lewis (1975) for his portrait studies of Washingtonians; John White (1982) for work published in the *Chicago Sun Times;* Michel Du Cille (1985) for the photographs of the Colombian earthquake; and Ozier Muhammad (1985) for international reporting for the photographic essay "Africa: The Desperate Continent."

In the 1970s, universities and art colleges began to offer undergraduate and graduate degrees in photography, and African-American photographers began studying photography and creating works for exhibition purposes. Others studied in community centers and workshops. The symbolic and expressive images of the works produced in the 1980s and '90s offer sociological and psychological insights into the past, as well as examinations of contemporary social themes, such as racism, unemployment, child and sexual abuse, death and dying. Most of these works are informed by personal experience. Significant contributors to the development of this genre are Albert Chong, Sulaiman Ellison, Roland Freeman, Todd Gray, Chester Higgins, Lynn Marshall-Linnemeier, Willie Middlebrook, Jeffrey Scales, Coreen Simpson, Lorna Simpson, Elisabeth Sunday, Christian Walker, Carrie Mae Weems, Carla Williams, and Pat Ward Williams.

—DEBORAH WILLIS-THOMAS

See also

Student Nonviolent
Coordinating Commitee

PIPPIN, HORACE

Horace Pippin (February 22, 1888–July 6, 1946), painter. One of the foremost self-taught painters of the twentieth century, Horace Pippin was born in West Chester, Pa. A disabled World War I veteran, he initially took up art in the 1920s to strengthen his wounded right arm. By the late 1930s Pippin's distinctive and diverse images of his childhood memories and war experiences, scenes of everyday life, landscapes, portraits, biblical subjects, and American historical events had found enthusiastic local supporters such as critic Christian Brinton, artists N. C. Wyeth and John McCoy, collector Albert C. Barnes, and dealer Robert Carlen.

In the eight years between his national debut in a 1938 group exhibition at New York's Museum of Modern Art and his death at the age of fifty-eight, Pippin's productivity increased and his paintings entered major private and museum collections on the East and West Coasts. In 1947 Alain Locke described Pippin as "a real and rare genius, combining folk quality with artistic maturity so uniquely as almost to defy classification."

A descendant of former slaves, the artist was raised by Harriet Pippin (1834–1908). It is unknown today if Harriet was his mother or grandmother. Her eyewitness account of the 1859 hanging of the abolitionist John Brown provided the basis for Pippin's 1942 painting on that subject, which depicted her as the sole African-American woman in the crowd of onlookers.

In 1891, the family relocated to the resort town of Goshen, N.Y., where they worked as domestic servants. As a boy, Pippin showed a strong interest in drawing, winning his first set of crayons and a box of watercolors for his response to an advertising contest for an art supply company. Pippin rendered the warm family circle of his boyhood in the memory picture *Domino Players* (1943; Phillips Collection).

He attended a segregated one-room school until 1902. After working as a porter at the St. Elmo Hotel for seven years he relocated to Paterson, N.J., finding employment crating oil paintings with a moving and storage company. Prior to his service in World War I, Pippin variously toiled in a coal yard, in an iron foundry, and as a used-clothing peddler.

In 1917, the twenty-nine-year-old Pippin enlisted in the New York National Guard, serving as a corporal in what would subsequently become the 369th Colored Infantry Regiment of the 93rd Division of the United States Army. Landing in Brest in December 1917, Pippin and his regiment first worked laying railroad track for two months prior to serving at the front lines in the Argonne Forest under French command.

While in the trenches, Pippin kept illustrated journals of his military service, but only six drawings from this period survive. He later wrote that World War I "brought out all the art in me." In October 1918 Pippin was shot through the right shoulder by a German sniper and was honorably discharged the following year. Awarded the French Croix de Guerre in 1919, he received a retroactive Purple Heart in 1945.

In 1920 Pippin married the twice-widowed Ora Fetherstone Wade, who had a six-year-old son. Supporting themselves on his disability check and her work as a laundress, they settled in West Chester, where she owned a home. A community-spirited man, Pippin helped organize a black Boy Scouts troop and served as commander of the local American Legion for black veterans. As therapy for his injured arm, he began making pictures in 1925 by burning images on wood panels using a hot iron poker. At the age of forty he expanded to oil paints, completing his first painting, *End of the War: Starting Home,* in 1930 (Philadelphia Museum of Art).

Pippin first received public attention when he exhibited two paintings in the Chester County Art Association annual of 1937. Immediately following this debut, John McCoy and Christian Brinton facilitated an exhibition for Pippin at the West Chester Community Center, a hub of local black activities. Within a year Pippin was included in Holger Cahill's "Masters of Popular Painting" at New York's Museum of Modern Art.

Art dealer Robert Carlen of Philadelphia mounted Pippin's first gallery show in 1940, comprising twenty-seven works including *Abraham Lincoln and His Father Building Their Cabin on Pigeon Creek* (Barnes Foundation), *Buffalo Hunt* (Whitney Museum of American Art), and *Cabin in the Cotton* (Art Institute of Chicago). Introduced to Pippin's work by Carlen, the renowned art collector Albert Barnes wrote two catalog essays on the artist. At his invitation, Pippin visited Barnes's Foundation to see his world-famous painting collection and to attend art appreciation lectures. This exposure did not alter his characteristic approach to his art, although from then on Pippin added still-life compositions to his repertory, of which there are many examples in Barnes's collection.

In the years between his first Philadelphia show in 1940 and his death in 1946, Pippin had

See also
Alain Locke

solo exhibitions at New York's Bignou Gallery (1940), the Arts Club of Chicago (1941), the San Francisco Museum of Art (1942), and New York's Downtown Gallery (1944). Among the museums that purchased his work during his lifetime were the Pennsylvania Academy of Fine Arts (*John Brown Going to His Hanging*); Buffalo's Albright Knox Gallery (*Self-Portrait*); and Washington's Phillips Collection (*Domino Players*). Early collectors included Philadelphia's Main Line society and such well-known actors and writers as Edward G. Robinson, Charles Laughton, Claude Rains, John Garfield, Ruth Gordon, S. J. Perelman, and Clifford Odets.

Pippin's commissioned works were varied. For the Capehart Collection in 1943 he executed a painting inspired by Stephen Foster's "Old Black Joe" (private collection); in 1944 *Vogue* magazine requested him to paint an image on the theme of cotton (Brady Museum, Cuernavaca); his painting *The Temptation of Saint Anthony* (1945; private collection) was created for an invited competition sponsored by the film producers David L. Loew and Albert Lewin, who also asked Salvador Dali, Marc Chagall, and Giorgio de Chirico, among others, to respond to a Guy de Maupassant short story.

Mrs. Pippin was hospitalized with mental problems in March 1946. She died four months later, two weeks after the artist himself had succumbed to a stroke on July 6, 1946. Of the 137 works on paper, fabric, and wood that Pippin was known to have created, approximately ten percent are today unlocated. He once summed up his approach to paintings: "Pictures just come to my mind. I think my pictures out with my brain, and then I tell my heart to go ahead."

—JUDITH E. STEIN

PLESSY V. FERGUSON

In *Plessy* v. *Ferguson*, 163 U.S. 537 (1896), the Supreme Court upheld an 1890 Louisiana statute that required railroads to provide separate but equal accommodations for blacks and whites, and forbade persons from riding in cars not assigned to their race. It gave constitutional sanction to virtually all forms of racial segregation in the United States until after World War II.

Plessy arose as part of a careful strategy to test the legality of the new Louisiana law. In September 1891, elite "persons of color" in New Orleans formed the "Citizens Committee to Test the Constitutionality of the Separate Car Law." They raised three thousand dollars for the costs of a test case. Albion Tourgee, the nation's leading white advocate of black rights, agreed to take the case without fee. Tourgee, a former judge, was a nationally prominent writer most noted for his novel about Reconstruction, *A Fool's Errand*.

In June 1892, Homer A. Plessy purchased a first-class ticket on the East Louisiana Railroad, sat in the "white" car, and was promptly arrested and arraigned before Judge John H. Ferguson. Plessy then sued to prevent Ferguson from conducting any further proceedings against him. Eventually his challenge reached the United States Supreme Court.

Before the Court, Tourgee argued that segregation violated the Thirteenth Amendment's prohibition of involuntary servitude and denied blacks equal protection of the laws, which was guaranteed by the Fourteenth Amendment. These amendments, along with the Declaration of Independence, Tourgee asserted, gave Americans affirmative rights against invidious discrimination. He asserted that the Fourteenth Amendment gave constitutional life to the Declaration of Independence, "which is not a fable as some of our modern theorists would have us believe, but [is] the all-embracing formula of personal rights on which our government is based." Joining Tourgee in these arguments was Samuel F. Phillips, a former solicitor general of the United States, who in 1883 had unsuccessfully argued the *Civil Rights Cases*.

The Court rejected Tourgee's arguments by a vote of 7 to 1. In his majority opinion, Justice Henry Billings Brown conceded that the Fourteenth Amendment was adopted "to enforce the absolute equality of the two races before the law," but asserted that the amendment "could not have been intended to abolish distinctions based upon color, or to enforce social, as distinguished from political equality, or a commingling of the two races." Ignoring the reality of the emerging Jim Crow South, the Court denied that "the enforced separation of the two races stamps the colored race with a badge of inferiority." Brown believed that segregation was not discriminatory because whites were also segregated from blacks. Thus, if segregation created a perception of inferiority "it is not by reason of anything found in the act, but solely because the colored race chooses to put that construction upon it." Reflecting the accepted social science and popular prejudices of his age, Brown argued:

> *Legislation is powerless to eradicate racial instincts or to abolish distinctions based upon*

After the implementation ruling in Brown v. Board of Education of Topeka, Kansas *was announced in 1955, the NAACP Legal Defense and Educational Fund began fighting court cases to force compliance.*

PAGE 477

See also
Marcus Garvey
Martin Luther King, Jr.
NAACP

physical differences, and the attempt to do so can only result in accentuating the difficulties of the present situation. If the civil and political rights of both races be equal, one cannot be inferior to the other civilly or politically. If one race be inferior to the other socially, the Constitution of the United States cannot put them upon the same plane.

Thus, as long as segregated facilities were "equal" they were permissible. Segregation had now received the sanction and blessing of the Supreme Court.

In a bitter, lone dissent, Justice John Marshall Harlan, a former slave owner, acknowledged that the "white race" was "the dominant race in this country." But, as Harlan read the Constitution,

in the eye of the law, there is in this country no superior, dominant, ruling class of citizens. There is no caste here. Our Constitution is color-blind, and neither knows nor tolerates classes among citizens. In respect of civil rights, all citizens are equal before the law. The humblest is the peer of the most powerful. The law regards man as man, and takes no account of his surroundings or his color when his civil rights as guaranteed by the supreme law of the land are involved.

Harlan protested that the Court's decision would "stimulate aggressions, more or less brutal and irritating, upon the admitted rights of colored citizens" and "encourage the belief that it is possible, by means of state enactments, to defeat the beneficent purposes which the people of the United States had in view when they adopted the recent amendments to the Constitution." In prophetic language, Harlan asserted, "The thin disguise of 'equal' accommodations for passengers in railroad coaches will not mislead any one, nor atone for the wrong this day done." Harlan argued that the Louisiana law was "inconsistent with the personal liberty of citizens, white and black" and "hostile to both the spirit and letter of the Constitution of the United States."

Harlan's voice was that of a prophet ignored by his own age. More than five decades would pass before the Supreme Court recognized the fundamental truth of his dissent. Meanwhile, the South built a social and legal system rooted in racial segregation. In January 1897, Homer Plessy pled guilty to attempting to board a "white" railroad car and paid a twenty-five-dollar fine.

—PAUL FINKELMAN

See also
Thurgood Marshall

POWELL, ADAM CLAYTON, JR.

Adam Clayton Powell, Jr. (November 29, 1908–April 4, 1972), congressman, civil rights activist, and clergyman. Adam Clayton Powell, Jr., was born in 1908 in New Haven, Conn. Shortly thereafter his father, Adam Clayton Powell, Sr., left New Haven for New York City to assume the pastorship of the Abyssinian Baptist Church in Harlem. The elder Powell, a prominent minister, sought the best for his only son, educating him at the elite Townsend Harris High School, then sending him to Colgate University, a largely white school in Hamilton, N.Y. In 1932 Powell received an M.A. in religious education from Columbia University Teachers College. By the time Powell had graduated from Colgate in 1930 and returned home, the United States was mired in the Great Depression. Young Powell was named an assistant pastor at the Abyssinian Church. Powell was not content, however, to concern himself exclusively with pastoral matters. With the Depression as backdrop, young Powell rallied for help for Harlemites from City Hall, and goaded the residents of Harlem to protest second-class treatment of African Americans. He declaimed from both pulpit and streetcorner, leading marchers not only to City Hall, but to the doorsteps of the ill-staffed and racially discriminatory Harlem Hospital. Older Abyssinian deacons considered him unpredictable, even impatient. But the younger members of the church adored him, and were eager to follow his lead. In the winter of 1937 Powell was named minister of the Abyssinian Baptist Church to succeed his father. He was twenty-nine years old. The congregation boasted more than 10,000 members and was probably the largest Protestant Church in the United States. During the next few years, Powell, in his forceful and flamboyant manner, became the most visible leader of the boycott campaign to break the bottleneck of discrimination that existed in stores. Melding together the often factious groups that comprised the "Don't Buy Where You Can't Work" campaign, Powell's tactics were hugely successful and emulated in other cities. He pressured New York utilities, including Consolidated Edison, to hire blacks. His boycotting tactics forced the New York City private bus companies for the first time to hire black drivers. Liberals and progressives from the world of politics were invited to appear in the Abyssinian pulpit. The mix was eclectic. They were animated by the spirit of progressive reform in the manner of Robert LaFollette and Franklin D. Roosevelt, as well as black nationalist sentiments inspired by Marcus Garvey. Powell turned the church stage into a personal bully pulpit.

Powell was a natural for the political arena, and in 1941, running as an Independent, he became the first black to win election to the New York City Council. Although he would thereafter usually run as a Democrat, he always maintained his independence from the Democratic machine. Before his first term was over, he decided to run for Congress from a newly created district that would, for the first time, enable a black to be elected from Harlem. With help from the left-wing East Harlem Congressman Vito Marcantonio, the powerful Abyssinian church, and the vibrant artistic community of Harlem, Powell launched a two-year campaign that saw him elected the first black in 1944 to Congress from the Northeast. His Washington debut was typically controversial. In fall 1945, when the Daughters of the American Revolution (DAR) refused to allow jazz pianist Hazel Scott, the second of his three wives, to perform on the stage of Constitution Hall, Powell assailed First Lady Bess Truman in the press because of her continued connections with the DAR. President Truman was livid, and Powell was never invited to the White House while Truman was President.

Powell's talent for attracting attention and making enemies soon made him the congressional leader in the fight for civil rights legislation. Working closely with Clarence Mitchell, Jr. and the NAACP in 1950 he offered an amendment to current legislation, which came to be known as the Powell Amendment, forbidding any federal support for segregated facilities. Powell would repeatedly introduce this amendment over the next several years. Politically he was liberal, but he was also a shrewd opportunist. In 1956 Powell backed President Eisenhower's reelection bid, a move that angered Democrats. Four years later, however, Powell heartily campaigned for the Kennedy-Johnson ticket. Coinciding with Kennedy's victory, Powell had gained sufficient seniority to become chairman of the powerful House Education and Labor Committee. The influence of his powerful position, however, would not be felt until 1964, when President Johnson's heightened domestic agenda went into full action. Powell was instrumental in passage of the war on poverty legislation, on which he and Johnson collaborated. These included increased federal aid to school programs, increasing the minimum wage, and the Head Start Program for preschool children. Bil-

lions of dollars flowed through the Powell committee. In 1964 the Civil Rights Act finally saw the core of the Powell Amendment enacted into law. From 1961 to 1967 Powell was one of the most powerful politicians in the United States, and certainly the most powerful African American. He was both an American insider and outsider, working inside the halls of Congress, and identifying with the masses who remained on the outside as one of the most riveting stump speakers in the country. He often engaged in one-upmanship with Martin Luther King, Jr. By the time his congressional career ended there would be more than sixty pieces of major legislation with his imprimatur.

Powell's political downfall began when, in 1960, he accused Esther James, a Harlem woman, of corruption. James successfully sued for libel. Powell refused to pay, and before he finally agreed to settle in 1966 Powell had accumulated enormous amounts of bad publicity because of his sometimes mercurial and sybaritic behavior. In January 1967 House members, led by southern Democrats and Republicans, refused to seat Powell until a committee could investigate his conduct, citing his indiscretions and personal

POWERFUL SPEAKER

Adam Clayton Powell, Jr., shown here in 1967, was a congressional leader in the fight for civil rights legislation. PRINTS AND PHOTOGRAPHS DIVISION, LIBRARY OF CONGRESS

lifestyle. The House committee set up to investigate Powell's conduct, the Celler Committee, chaired by New York Republican Emanuel Celler, decided to fine Powell, strip away his seniority, and have him repay money that had gone to his third wife, Yvette Diago Powell, while she had been on his payroll. The full House, however, ignored the recommendations of the Celler Committee and voted to expel Powell from Congress in March 1967. It was the first time since 1919 that the House had expelled one of its members. Powell vowed to fight the case all the way to the Supreme Court. He won a special election in March 1967 to fill his own vacant seat, and was re-elected in 1968, though he remained outside of Congress. In 1968 he barnstormed the United States, rallying black and white students on college campuses to fight for equality and end American involvement in Vietnam, peppering his defense with his catchphrase, "Keep the faith, baby." He was mentioned in 1968 as a favorite-son presidential candidate from New York. In 1969, in his last decision from the Supreme Court, Chief Justice Earl Warren ruled that Adam Clayton Powell had been unconstitutionally expelled from Congress. Back in Congress, however, Powell was without the power he had once yielded, returning as a freshman, because the Court had not ruled on the matter of his seniority and lost back pay. In 1970 he lost his last reelection bid to Charles Rangel by 150 votes. He spent the last two years of his life on the island of Bimini, in the Bahamas, where he said he was working on his memoirs, which never were published. He died of cancer in a Miami hospital on April 4, 1972, four years to the day from Martin Luther King's death.

—WIL HAYGOOD

POWELL, COLIN LUTHER

Colin Luther Powell (April 5, 1937–), Army officer, chair of the Joint Chiefs of Staff. Born and raised in New York City, Colin Powell grew up in a close-knit family of Jamaican immigrants in the Hunts Point section of the Bronx. After attending public schools, Powell graduated from the City College of New York (CCNY) in 1958. Although his grades were mediocre, he discovered an affinity for the military. Participating in CCNY's Reserve Officer Training Corps (ROTC) program, he finished as a cadet colonel, the highest rank attainable. Like all ROTC graduates, Powell was commissioned as a second lieutenant after completing college.

Powell served for two years in West Germany and two years in Massachusetts, where he met his wife, Alma. In 1962, already a captain, Powell received orders to report to Vietnam. He was one of the second wave of more than 15,000 military advisers sent by the United States to Vietnam and was posted with a South Vietnamese Army unit for most of his tenure. During his first tour of duty, from 1962 to 1963, he was decorated with the Purple Heart after being wounded by a Viet Cong booby trap near the Laotian border.

After returning to the United States, Powell spent almost four years at Fort Benning in Georgia, serving as, among other things, an instructor at Fort Benning's Army Infantry School. In 1967, now a major, he attended an officers' training course at the United States Army Command and General Staff College at Fort Leavenworth, Kans., finishing second in a class of more than twelve hundred. In the summer of 1968, Powell was ordered back to Vietnam. On his second tour, Powell primarily served as a liaison to Gen. Charles Gettys of the Americal Division and received the Soldier's Medal for his role in rescuing injured soldiers, including Gen. Gettys, from a downed helicopter.

Powell returned to the United States in mid-1969 and began moving between military field postings and political appointments, a process that would become characteristic of his career. In 1971, after working in the Pentagon for the assistant vice chief of the Army, he earned an M.B.A. from George Washington University in Washington, D.C. Shortly thereafter, Powell was accepted as a White House Fellow during the Nixon administration and was attached to the Office of Management and Budget (OMB), headed by Caspar Weinberger. In 1973, after a year at OMB, Powell received command of an infantry battalion in South Korea; his mission was to raise morale and restore order in a unit plagued by drug abuse and racial problems. He then attended a nine-month course at the National War College and was promoted to full colonel in February 1976, taking command of the 2nd Brigade, 101st Airborne Division, located at Fort Campbell, Ky.

In 1979 Powell was an aide to Secretary of Energy Charles Duncan during the crisis of the nuclear accident at Three Mile Island in Pennsylvania and the oil shortage caused by the overthrow of the shah of Iran. In June of that year, while working at the Department of Energy (DOE), he became a brigadier general. Powell returned to the field from 1981 until 1983, serving as assistant division commander of the Fourth Infantry (mechanized) in Colorado and then as the deputy commanding general of an Army research facility at Fort Leavenworth. In mid-1983, he became military assistant to Secretary of Defense Caspar Weinberger. In 1986, Powell, by then a lieutenant general, returned to the field as the commander of V Corps, a unit of 75,000 troops in West Germany. The following year, in the wake of the Iran-Contra scandal, he returned to serve as President Ronald Reagan's national security adviser. During the Intermediate Nuclear Forces (INF) arms-control negotiations with the Soviet Union, Powell was heralded as being a major factor in their success.

In July 1989, Powell, a newly promoted four-star general, was nominated by President George Bush to become the first black chairman of the Joint Chiefs of Staff, the highest military position in the armed forces. As chairman, Powell was responsible for overseeing Operation Desert Storm, the 1991 international response to the 1990 Iraqi invasion of Kuwait. Through his commanding and reassuring television presence during the successful Persian Gulf War, Powell became one of the most popular figures in the Bush administration. Reappointed chairman in 1991, he was the recipient of various military decorations as well as a Presidential Medal of Freedom from Bush. In the same year, the NAACP gave Powell the Spingarn Medal, its highest award for African-American achievement.

When Bill Clinton was elected president in 1992, he and Powell had differences over Clinton's plan to substantially reduce the defense budget. Powell also disagreed with Clinton's proposal to end the ban on homosexuals in the military and was instrumental in limiting the scope of the change. Powell retired from the Army in September 1993 at the end of his second term as chairman of the Joint Chiefs. Upon his departure, President Clinton awarded him his second Presidential Medal of Freedom.

—JOHN C. STONER

PRICE, MARY VIOLET

LEONTYNE

Mary Violet Leontyne Price (February 10, 1927–), opera singer. Born in Laurel, Miss., the soprano Leontyne Price came to be regarded as a *prima donna assoluta* during her exceptionally long operatic career (1952–1985).

Her parents had been involved in the musical life of Laurel, and provided her with piano lessons from the age of four. Soon thereafter, she joined her mother in the church choir and, after attending a recital by Marian Anderson in Jackson, Miss., in 1936, she resolved on a career in music. At that time, African-American women could aspire in music only for roles in education, and it was with that major in mind that Price enrolled at Central State College in Ohio. Before she graduated in 1949, however, her vocal talent was manifest and she was encouraged to enter the Juilliard School of Music, where she studied with Florence Kimball. As Mistress Ford in a school production of Verdi's *Falstaff*, she attracted the attention of American composer Virgil Thomson, who enlisted her for the role of Cecilia in a 1952 revival of his *Four Saints in Three Acts* (1934), a work calling for an all-black cast, thus initiating her professional career and terminating her formal study.

Following this production in New York and performances at the Paris International Arts Festival, she was engaged for the role of Bess in George Gershwin's *Porgy and Bess,* with which she toured in Berlin, Paris, and Vienna into 1954. In November of that year, she made her New York debut at Town Hall. The following February she appeared in the title role of Puccini's *Tosca* on television, later adding Mozart's *Die Zauberflöte* and *Don Giovanni,* and Poulenc's *Dialogues des Carmélites* to her NBC telecasts. In 1956, she sang the role of Cleopatra in Handel's *Giulio Cesare*.

It was in the Poulenc opera as Madame Lidoine that she made her debut with the San Francisco Opera in 1957, following this with the leading soprano roles with that company in Verdi's *Il Trovatore* and Puccini's *Madama Butterfly* and debuts that year at the Arena di Verona, Covent Garden, and the Vienna Staatsoper (*Aida*). Her debut with the Lyric Opera of Chicago was as Liù in Puccini's *Turandot* (1959).

The Metropolitan Opera had only begun adding black singers to its roster in 1955 with Marian Anderson and Robert McFerrin, followed by the debuts of African-American artists Mattiwilda Dobbs (1956), Gloria Davy (1958), and Martina Arroyo (1959). Actually, Price had already appeared in the Metropolitan Opera Jamboree, a fund-raising broadcast from the Manhattan Ritz Theater, April 6, 1953, when she performed "Summertime" from *Porgy and Bess,* but her formal debut was as Leonora in Verdi's *Il Trovatore* on January 27, 1961, when she won an

See also
Marian Anderson

unprecedented forty-two-minute ovation, fully justifying her selection as the leading lady to open the next Met season (as Puccini's Minnie in *La Fanciulla del West*) and that of the next year (repeating her 1957 Vienna role of Aida, in which she was heard each season for the following five years). During the last six years of the "old Met," she particularly excelled in the Italian repertory (as Liù in Puccini's *Turandot*, Cio-Cio-San in Puccini's *Madama Butterfly*, and Elvira in Verdi's *Ernani*, which she had sung for Herbert von Karajan at the 1962 Salzburg Festival).

The new home of the Metropolitan Opera at Lincoln Center was inaugurated in 1966 with a new opera by Samuel Barber, *Antony and Cleopatra*, written specifically for her. When she concluded her career in opera performances on January 3, 1985, with *Aida* at the Metropolitan Opera, she had proved her interpretive leadership in the Italian repertories of Verdi and Puccini, but she has expanded the previously practiced limits to move far past any stereotypes, excelling in German, Spanish, French, and Slavic works, as well as in spirituals and other American literature. Her

SPORTS AND ACADEMICS
Propositions 48 and 42 Test NCAA Racial Bias

Whether freshmen should compete in American intercollegiate athletics has been debated for a century. The issue, however, acquired distinct racial overtones only in 1983, when the National Collegiate Athletic Association (NCAA), the country's governing body for major intercollegiate athletics, adopted Proposition 48. Effective in 1986, the NCAA required that in order to be eligible to compete as a freshman, a student-athlete must have a 2.0 grade point average on a scale of 4.0 in eleven "core" courses (four English, three mathematics, and two each in social sciences and natural sciences), as well as either a 700 total score on the Scholastic Aptitude Test (SAT) or a 15 total score on the American College Test (ACT).

Historically black colleges in particular opposed Proposition 48, contending that the test scores were arbitrary and the tests themselves discriminated against lower-income minorities, often in neglected inner-city schools. Athletic grants-in-aid could still be received by "partial qualifiers"—those who had the requisite grades but not the test scores—but they could not play or practice their sport during the freshman year and lost one of their four years of eligibility.

Proposition 48, lobbied by the American Council on Education, was a reaction to the low academic standards of the previous decade, when only a 2.0 high school grade point average was required for athletic aid, without regard for the nature of the courses taken. Many athletes, often African Americans, were recruited for their athletic ability, were maintained in college while playing and then discarded upon completing their eligibility, without receiving meaningful higher education. Tony Rice, a Notre Dame quarterback among the first made ineli-

gible under Proposition 48, expressed its rationale: "It was tough, not being able to play. . . . But . . . I was able to get a foot down on my classes."

The NCAA commenced research on the effects of Proposition 48, but before meaningful data were available, its 1989 convention passed Proposition 42, barring athletic aid to partial qualifiers. While 85 percent of the African-American athletes entering Division I schools between 1987 and 1990 qualified, African Americans constituted two-thirds of the partial qualifiers. Half of all partial qualifiers play football or men's basketball, sports in which America's colleges serve as professional development teams.

The emotional protest of Georgetown basketball coach John Thompson, who walked off the court before his team's next two games, brought massive publicity to the issue, and led to a change by the 1990 convention, prior to the effective date. While Proposition 42's bar to athletic aid was retained, need-based aid was approved. Two years later, after a prestigious commission created by the Knight Foundation refocused public attention on the commercialization of college revenue sports, additional changes were made, sponsored by a newly powerful President's Commission within the NCAA. Effective August 1995, a 2.5 average in thirteen core courses will be required, though indexing could bring it as low as 2.0 if an SAT combined score of 900 or an ACT score of 21 is achieved. More significant in terms of minimizing exploitation of major college athletes, 25 percent of whom are African-American, is requiring that athletes meet the minimum grade point average requirements throughout their college careers and complete a steadily increasing portion of their degree requirements in order to remain eligible.

—GORDON A. MARTIN, JR.

See also
Track and Field

principal opera roles, in addition to those mentioned, were the Prima Donna and Ariadne (*Ariadne auf Naxos*), Amelia (*Un Ballo in Maschera*), Fiordiligi (*Così fan tutte*), Donna Anna (*Don Giovanni*), Tatiana (*Eugene Onegin*), Minnie (*La Fanciulla del West*), Leonora (*La Forza del Destino*), Manon (*Manon Lescaut*), and the title role in *Tosca*.

Her recorded legacy is extensive. In addition to many of the operatic roles in which she appeared on stage—Bizet's *Carmen*, Mozart's *Don Giovanni* and *Così fan tutte*, Puccini's *Madama Butterfly* and *Tosca*, Verdi's *Aida, Un Ballo in Maschera, Ernani, La Forza del Destino*, and *Il Trovatore*—she has recorded Samuel Barber's *Hermit Songs* and music of Fauré, Poulenc, Wolf, and R. Strauss, as well as Verdi's *Requiem* and Beethoven's *Ninth Symphony*. She has also recorded excerpts from *Porgy and Bess* (with her then-husband William Warfield), an album of popular songs with André Previn (*Right as Rain*), and *Swing Low, Sweet Chariot*, a collection of fourteen spirituals. In 1992 RCA reissued on compact disc forty-seven arias by Price under the title *Leontyne Price: The Prima Donna Collection*, arias which had been recorded between 1965 and 1979.

—DOMINIQUE-RENÈ DE LERMA

PRYOR, RICHARD FRANKLIN LENOX THOMAS

Richard Franklin Lenox Thomas Pryor (December 1, 1940–), comedian. Born in Peoria, Ill., Richard Pryor overcame a troubled life in an extended family headed by his grandmother, Marie Carter, to become a preeminent comedian, film star, screenwriter, producer, and director, beginning in the early 1960s.

During Pryor's boyhood, Peoria was like the Deep South. Segregation and discrimination in housing, employment, and places of public accommodation were deeply embedded in southern Illinois. Forty percent of the black population of Peoria was unemployed, while 32 percent worked for the Works Progress Administration (WPA). Odd jobs supported the rest, including the Pryor family, which ran small carting firms, pool halls, and, Pryor claimed, houses of prostitution. Peoria remained segregated for a time even after the 1954 Supreme Court decision that forbade it.

At eleven, Pryor, the son of Gertrude Thomas and Leroy "Buck" Carter Pryor, and, he once said, the seventh of twelve "Pryor kids," began acting at the Carver Community Center under the guidance of the drama teacher, Juliette Whittaker. Over the years she became the recipient of some of Pryor's performing awards; he also contributed to the private school she later founded, the Learning Tree.

After dropping out of school, Pryor joined the army in 1958, where his life was no less troublesome. After military service, he worked for his father's carting firm and the Caterpillar factory in Peoria. He also haunted the local clubs and watched television for the appearances of African-American entertainers such as Sammy Davis, Jr., and Bill Cosby, personalities he wanted to emulate and eventually replace.

Within a few years Pryor was playing small clubs in East St. Louis, Chicago, Windsor (Canada), Buffalo, Youngstown, and Cleveland. Much of his comic material was drawn from his army service and the early Cosby comedy routines. By 1964 he had attracted enough attention to be booked for his first national television appearance, on Rudy Vallee's *Broadway Tonight* show. Three years later, after stops on the Ed Sullivan, Merv Griffin, and Johnny Carson shows, Pryor appeared in the film *The Busy Body* with Sid Caesar and other comedians—the first of more than forty films he acted in, wrote, produced, and/or directed into the early 1990s. His first major role was in *Lady Sings the Blues* (1972), with Diana Ross, in which Pryor played a character called Piano Man.

The Richard Pryor Show ran briefly on NBC-TV for part of 1977. It was innovative and conveyed a wide range of both comedy and tenderness, but it was too daring for the executives of NBC. Amid legal wrangling, the show went off the air and, typically, Pryor laid the blame on NBC. In 1984, he played himself as a boy in *Pryor's Place*, a children's show that aired on Saturday mornings. It too was short-lived, this time without recrimination.

From 1970 through 1979, Pryor starred or costarred in twenty-one films. He contributed to the script of *Blazing Saddles* (1973), and in the same year wrote for and appeared on *The Flip Wilson Show* and was a cowriter for Lily Tomlin's television specials, for which he won Emmy Awards in 1973 and 1974. He continued to perform in clubs and theaters around the country; these performances provided material for his two *Richard Pryor Live in Concert* films (both in 1979).

The more realistic television genres that evolved as a result of the Civil Rights Movement served as powerful mechanisms for sensitizing audiences to the predicaments of those affected by racism.

PAGE 676

Since his death, the importance of Jean-Michel Basquiat's work has come to be more widely recognized.

PAGE 83

The recordings of his performances earned him three Grammy Awards: *That Nigger's Crazy,* 1974; *Is It Something I Said,* 1975; and *Bicentennial Nigger,* 1976. *That Nigger's Crazy* also became a certified gold and platinum album.

In 1980 he produced his first film, *Bustin' Loose,* starring himself and Cicely Tyson. Two years later he produced and wrote *Richard Pryor: Live on the Sunset Strip. Jo Jo Dancer, Your Life Is Calling,* which Pryor produced, directed, and helped write, was based upon his near-fatal self-immolation that occurred when he was freebasing cocaine in 1980. In 1986, Pryor, who had also survived two heart attacks, discovered that he had multiple sclerosis, but he continued to perform onstage.

Pryor was known as a "crossover" star: one who appealed to both black and white moviegoers. This label resulted from the "buddy" films he made with Gene Wilder—*Silver Streak* (1976), *Stir Crazy* (1980), and *See No Evil, Hear No Evil* (1989)—although he had starred with white actors in sixteen other movies. Few of Pryor's films during the 1980s were memorable, not even the concert film *Richard Pryor: Here and Now* (1983). But *Richard Pryor: Live on the Sunset Strip,* released only the year before, most typified his pungent, raunchy comedy that echoed the African-American man in the street, which was precisely what made Pryor the great comedian he was.

When he was at his peak, few comedians could match Pryor's popularity. Most contemporary comedy is said to be "post-Pryor," because of the standards he set. His life was his act, but he shaped his personal experiences into rollicking comedy. His major themes were racism in its several forms and the battle of the sexes. Usually, the women bested the men. His topics were current and to the point, and his favorite character was an old, foul-mouthed, wise black man named Mudbone from Mississippi.

—JOHN A. WILLIAMS

PURYEAR, MARTIN

Martin Puryear (1937–), sculptor. The oldest of seven children, sculptor Martin Puryear attended both elementary and secondary school in Washington, D.C. His father, Reginald, worked as a postal service employee, and his mother, Martina, taught elementary school. He developed strong interests in biology and art, and aspired to be a wildlife illustrator. Always interested in working with his hands, Puryear as a young man made numerous objects, including guitars, chairs, and canoes.

Puryear entered Catholic University in Washington in 1959. Although initially a biology major, he shifted in his junior year to the study of painting and sculpture. Following graduation in 1963, Puryear entered the Peace Corps and served for two years in Sierra Leone, where he taught English, French, art, and biology. In addition to his teaching, he studied the craftsmen of West Africa, particularly the carpenters, from whom he learned a wide variety of traditional techniques. In 1966 he moved to Stockholm, where he enrolled at the Swedish Royal Academy. In addition to his formal studies in printmaking, Puryear pursued an interest in Scandinavian woodworking and began to work independently, making wood sculptures in the studios of the academy. He traveled widely during his two years in Stockholm, visiting the Soviet Union and western Europe, as well as the region of Lapland in northern Scandinavia.

In 1968 Puryear returned to the United States, and the following year he entered Yale University to study sculpture at the graduate level. In addition to his exposure to the part- and full-time faculty (including James Rosati, Robert Morris, Richard Serra, and Salvatore Scarpitta) at Yale, Puryear visited New York often, familiarizing himself with recent developments in contemporary art. Following receipt of his master of fine arts degree in 1971, he taught at Fisk University in Nashville for two years. His first important sculptures were made in the early 1970s, and these were shown in a solo exhibition held in 1973 at the Henri Gallery in Washington and at Fisk.

In 1973 Puryear left Fisk and established a studio in Brooklyn. The following year he accepted a teaching position at the University of Maryland, and he commuted between New York and College Park, Md., from 1974 to 1978. It was during this period that his work became known to a larger audience. In 1977 the Corcoran Gallery of Art in Washington, D.C., organized the first museum exhibition of his work; this show included *Cedar Lodge* (1977), a large, quasi-architectural sculpture, as well as *Some Tales* (1977), a wall-mounted sculpture consisting of six linear wooden elements. In the same year, Puryear created *Box and Pole* for Art Park in Lewiston, N.Y. For this first outdoor commission, the sculptor constructed a wooden box made of milled wood with dovetailed corners, and a hundred-foot-tall pole, thereby contrasting the concentrated strength of the former with the upward, seemingly infinite reach of the latter.

If 1977 found Puryear being accorded increasing attention in the art world, it was also a time of great loss. On February 1, 1977, his apartment and studio—including virtually all of the sculptor's work to date—were lost in a fire. The following year he left the East Coast to accept a teaching position at the University of Illinois, Chicago; he lived in Chicago until 1991. During this period, Puryear achieved ever-increasing recognition and was included in numerous important group exhibitions (including the Whitney Biennial in 1979, 1981, and 1989; the Museum of Modern Art's International Survey of Recent Painting and Sculpture, in 1984; and the Walker Art Center's Sculpture Inside Outside, in 1988). In 1989 he was selected as the sole American representative to exhibit in the twentieth São Paulo Bienal in Brazil, and he received the grand prize for his installation of eight works. The same year, he received a John D. and Catherine T. MacArthur Foundation Fellowship. In the fall of 1991, a large retrospective of Puryear's work opened at the Art Institute of Chicago. This exhibition of some forty sculptures toured to the Hirshhorn Museum and Sculpture Garden, Washington, D.C.; the Museum of Contemporary Art, Los Angeles; and the Philadelphia Museum of Art.

During the 1980s, Puryear's work grew to full maturity. He has pursued a number of different sculptural directions simultaneously, including approximately forty wall-mounted sculptures, many in the form of nearly circular "rings"; increasingly large-scale, three-dimensional sculptures, most made principally of wood but often incorporating new materials such as wire mesh and tar; and, finally, several outdoor commissions, some of which were sited permanently.

Puryear concentrated on the "ring" sculptures between 1978 and 1985. Constructed primarily of thin wood strips laminated in place and often painted, the "rings" are the sculptor's most refined work to date. Around 1984 they evolved into larger, more imposing wall-mounted works that grew increasingly independent of the supporting wall. A sculpture such as *Greed's Trophy* (1984), in the collection of New York's Museum of Modern Art, suggests an enormous hunting trap, its wire-mesh shape projecting nearly five feet from the wall. At this time Puryear also began to apply tar to his wire-mesh surfaces—in a work such as *Sanctum* (1985), in the collection of the Whitney Museum of American Art—and this new element grants the undulating surface of the sculpture a sense of spatial enclosure as well as a tremendous physical presence. Since the mid–1980s, Puryear's sculpture has grown in new directions, as the artist has pressed the boundaries of abstraction to include allusions to living forms as well as objects. Finally, throughout the 1980s Puryear worked with distinction and great range in public, completing *Bodark Arc* (1982), commissioned for the Nathan Manilow Sculpture Park, south of Chicago, and *Ampersand* (1987–1988), commissioned for the Minneapolis Sculpture Garden. Throughout his work, Puryear has demonstrated a remarkable ability to create sculpture with multiple references, in which viewers discover images, memories, and allusions through their experience of the works.

—NEAL BENEZRA

See also
Meta Fuller

QUARLES, BENJAMIN

Benjamin Quarles (January 28, 1904–), historian. Born in Boston, Mass., in 1904, the son of a subway porter, Benjamin Quarles entered college at the age of twenty-three and received degrees from Shaw University (B.A., 1931) and the University of Wisconsin (M.A., 1933; Ph.D., 1940). He taught at Shaw, served as dean at Dillard University, and has chaired the history department at Morgan State University.

Quarles began his scholarly career at a time when racist assumptions hampered research and writing on African-American history. White historians questioned whether blacks could write objective history; and they believed that African-American history lacked sufficient primary sources for serious research and writing. Quarles proved both notions were false. Building on the pioneering research of Carger G. Woodson and other black historians of the previous generation, Quarles confirmed the existence of a rich documentary record of African-American life and culture. His early writings demonstrated both his careful research and his ability to present a balanced historical narrative. His essays in *Mississippi Valley Historical Review* in 1945 and 1959 were the first from a black historian to appear in a major historical journal.

Quarles's first scholarly article, "The Breach Between Douglass and Garrison," appeared in the *Journal of Negro History* in 1938 and revealed his interest in race relations. Many of his subsequent studies have explored the way in which blacks and whites have helped shape each other's identity on individual and collective levels. In *Lincoln and the Negro* (1962) and *Allies for Freedom: Blacks and John Brown* (1974), Quarles investigated the relationship between blacks and two notable whites in American history. Quarles focused on the eighteenth and nineteenth centuries, particularly the collective contribution of African Americans in two dramatic events in *The Negro in the Civil War* (1953) and *The Negro in the American Revolution* (1961). In *Black Abolitionists* (1969), he highlighted their participation in the nation's most important social reform movement.

Quarles has shared with his contemporary John Hope Franklin an optimistic appraisal of racial progress in American history. He has brought his scholarship to the classroom through two textbooks, *The Negro in the Making of America* and *The Negro American: A Documentary History*, and he has advanced African-American history as a contributing editor of *Phylon* and as associate editor of the *Journal of Negro History*.

—MICHAEL F. HEMBREE

GROUNDBREAKING HISTORIAN

Benjamin Quarles proved to his colleagues that African-American history was worthy of study, and he advanced the field with his careful research.
PRINTS AND PHOTOGRAPHS DIVISION, SCHOMBURG CENTER FOR RESEARCH IN BLACK CULTURE, THE NEW YORK PUBLIC LIBRARY, ASTOR, LENOX AND TILDEN FOUNDATIONS

See also
John Hope Franklin
Carger G. Woodson

R

RADIO

African-American radio can be divided into three general periods of historical development: black-face radio (1920–1941), black-appeal radio (1942–1969), and black-controlled radio (1970 to the present). Blackface radio was characterized by the appropriation of African-American music and humor by white entertainers, who performed their secondhand imitations for a predominantly white listening audience. During this period, black people were essentially outside of the commercial broadcasting loop; they were marginal as both radio entertainers and consumers. In the era of black-appeal radio, African Americans entered into the industry as entertainers and consumers, but the ownership and management of the stations targeting the black radio market remained mostly in the hands of white businessmen. This situation constrained the development of independent black radio operations, while the radio industry in general prospered from it. During the most recent period, African Americans have striven to own and operate their own radio stations, both commercial and public. In addition, they have established black-controlled radio networks and trade organizations. However, the percentage of African American-owned stations still lags far behind the percentage of black listeners.

The appropriation of black song, dance, and humor by white entertainers who blackened their faces with charcoal goes back to the early days of slavery. The resulting radical stereotypes were embedded in the blackface minstrel tradition, which dominated American popular entertainment in the antebellum period, and remained resilient enough in the postbellum years to reappear in film and radio in the early decades of the twentieth century. Popular black music styles like blues and jazz were first performed on the radio by white performers like Sophie Tucker, the first singer to popularize W. C. Handy's "Saint Louis Blues," and Paul Whiteman, the so-called king of jazz in the 1920s. A parallel trend developed with respect to black humor with the emergence of *Amos 'n' Andy* (starring Freeman Gosden and Charles Correll) as radio's most popular comedy series.

Indeed, *Amos 'n' Andy* was radio's first mass phenomenon: a supershow that attracted 53 percent of the national audience, or 40 million listeners, during its peak years on the NBC network in the early 1930s. In addition, the series provoked the black community's first national radio controversy. Robert Abbot, editor of the Chicago Defender, defended Gosden and Correll's caricatures of black urban life as inoffensive and even humane. Robert Vann, editor of the Pittsburgh Courier, countered by criticizing the series as racist in its portrayal of African Americans. He also launched a petition campaign to have the program taken off the air that amassed 740,000 signatures—but to no avail. The petition was ignored by the Federal Radio Commission. Meanwhile, *Amos 'n' Andy* dominated black comedy on radio throughout its heyday as the "national pastime" in the 1930s. In addition to Gosden and Correll, the other major blackface radio entertainers of the era included George Mack and Charles Moran, known as the Two Black Crows on the CBS network, as well as Marlin Hunt, who created and portrayed the radio maid Beulah on the series of the same name.

During the period when blackface comedy performed by whites dominated the portrayal of African Americans over the airways, its audience was mostly white; fewer than one in ten black households owned a radio receiver. There were black entertainers and actors who managed to get hired by the radio industry in the pre-World War II era, and for the most part they were restricted to playing stereotyped roles. The renowned black comedian Bert Williams was the first important black performer to be linked to commercial broadcasting, in the 1920s; he was featured on a New York station doing the same routines he popularized while performing in blackface on the Broadway stage. During the Great Depression, as if to add insult to injury, a number of black actors and actresses who auditioned for radio parts were told that they needed to be coached in the art of black dialect by white coaches if they wanted the jobs. This perverse chain of events happened to at least three African-American performers: Lillian Randolph (*Lulu and Leander Show*), Johnny Lee

See also
Civil Rights Movement

AMOS 'N' ANDY

Radio's Most Popular Comedy Series

Amos 'n' Andy, radio and television series. As a radio series that ran from 1928 until 1960, *Amos 'n' Andy* gave twentieth-century America its most popular and longest-lived comic depiction of black characters.

Freeman Gosden (1899–1982) and Charles Correll (1890–1972), two white men who had met as itinerant directors of amateur minstrel shows, wrote and broadcast *Amos 'n' Andy.* Their daily radio serial, introduced as *Sam 'n' Henry* in Chicago in 1926, featured two black characters who—like many real African Americans of the time—had left the rural South to seek a better life in the northern city. In 1929, the National Broadcasting Company (NBC) Blue network picked up the show, whose title characters had been renamed Amos and Andy the previous year. The series set off a national craze. *Amos 'n' Andy* was played nightly in restaurants, hotel lobbies, and cinemas; sales of radio sets soared, and radio's "golden age" was launched.

Amos 'n' Andy abounded with comic racial stereotypes. Lazy, pretentious Andy and meek, earnest Amos were ignorant, often bumbling figures; the show's dialogue, though truer than that of most other white performers, caricatured black vernacular English and bristled with malapropisms. The series gave no hint that race affected one's fortunes in life. Yet Gosden and Correll skillfully used the daily serial format to build suspense and to flesh out relatively complex characters who aroused empathy in many listeners. The team also pioneered by presenting secondary and incidental black characters who were bright and accomplished, most notably Ruby Taylor, a young Chicago woman who eventually married Amos.

The multifaceted *Amos 'n' Andy* won fans ranging from white racists to outspoken white liberals and African Americans of all social classes. Other blacks, however, complained that *Amos 'n' Andy*— whose maladroit title characters operated a "taxicab company" consisting of a single jalopy—mocked the struggle of African Americans to build a dignified life in a modern capitalistic society. In 1931 the *Pitts-*

burgh Courier, a black weekly newspaper, claimed to have gathered nearly 750,000 signatures on a petition demanding *Amos 'n' Andy*'s cancellation. Gosden and Correll drew heavily from the work of African-American comedians; the black debate over *Amos 'n' Andy* thus partook of a broader controversy over which aspects of black culture—including jazz, the blues, and ethnic comedy—should be exhibited to whites, which were better kept within the group, and which ought to be disowned altogether.

In 1943 Gosden and Correll converted their show from a daily serial story into a weekly half-hour comedy revolving more than ever around outlandish situations and verbal gags. The Kingfish, larcenous leader of Amos 'n' Andy's fraternal lodge, had long since become a central character of the show. The Columbia Broadcasting System (CBS) brought this version of *Amos 'n' Andy* to television in 1951. Veteran African-American performers—including Tim Moore, a former vaudevillian, as the Kingfish; Alvin Childress, a classically trained actor, as Amos; and Spencer Williams, Jr., a retired film director, writer, and actor, as Andy—took over the lead roles.

The new show dashed the hopes of Walter White, leader of the NAACP, that television would avoid the racial caricaturing that had pervaded radio and movies. A strenuous protest by the NAACP's leadership in 1951 resurrected the *Amos 'n' Andy* controversy of 1930–1931 and helped dissuade sponsors for some years afterward from supporting TV comedies featuring blacks.

Nonetheless, many black viewers joined whites to make *Amos 'n' Andy* a hit in its first season on television. Declining ratings led to the show's network cancellation after a second year, but *Amos 'n' Andy* thrived in syndication to local TV stations until 1966. Meanwhile, Gosden and Correll continued to broadcast new material on the radio until *Amos 'n' Andy* finally left the air in 1960. With the show died the American tradition, well over a century old, of white men playing black comic characters.

—MELVIN PATRICK ELY

(*Slick and Slim Show*), and Wonderful Smith (*Red Skelton Show*). The most famous black comic to appear regularly on network radio in the 1930s was Eddie Anderson, who played the role of the butler and chauffeur Rochester on the *Jack Benny Show.* Anderson was often criticized in the black

press for playing a stereotypical "faithful servant" role, even as he was being praised for his economic success and celebrity.

After blackface comedy, the African-American dance music called jazz was the next most popular expression of black culture broadcast over the air-

See also
Duke Ellington

ways in the 1920s and 1930s. As was the case with humor, the major radio jazz bands were made up of white musicians, and were directed by white bandleaders like Paul Whiteman, B. A. Rolfe, and Ben Bernie. The first black musicians to be broadcast with some regularity on network radio were New York bandleaders Duke Ellington and Noble Sissle. A number of influential white radio producers like Frank and Ann Hummert, the king and queen of network soap operas, began to routinely include black doctors, teachers, and soldiers in their scripts. In addition, the federal government produced its own radio series, entitled *Freedom's People,* to dramatize the participation of African Americans in past wars, and it recruited Paul Robeson as a national and then international radio spokesman for the U.S. war effort. But at the end of the war, the government withdrew from the domestic broadcasting sphere, allowing the logic of the marketplace to reassert itself. Then with the advent of the new television networks, and their subsequent domination of the national broadcasting market, radio was forced to turn to local markets in order to survive as a commercial enterprise. Inadvertently, this led to the discovery of a "new Negro market" in regions where African Americans' numbers could no longer be ignored by broadcasters. This was especially the case in large urban centers, where nine out of ten black families owned radios by the late 1940s. The result of this convergence of economic necessity and a mushrooming listening audience was the emergence of black-appeal radio stations and the rise of the African-American disc jockey—two interrelated developments that transformed the landscape of commercial radio in the postwar era.

A few black DJs were playing records over the airways in the 1930s; they worked through a brokerage system that charged them an hourly fee for airtime. The disc jockeys, in turn, solicited advertising aimed at the local black community and broadcast it in conjunction with recorded "race" music. Jack L. Cooper pioneered this approach in Chicago on his radio show *The All Negro Hour,* which first aired on WSBC in 1929. At first, he developed a live variety show with local black talent, but within two years he had switched to recorded music in order to cut costs. He played jazz discs, hosted a popular "missing persons" show, pitched ads, made community-service announcements, and also developed a series of weekend religious programs. This format was successful enough to make him into a millionaire; by the end of the 1930s, he had a stable of African-

American DJs working for him on a series of black-appeal programs broadcast on two stations. In the 1940s, Cooper was challenged as Chicago's premier black disc jockey by Al Benson, who also built up a small radio empire on local outlets with his own style of black-appeal programming. Cooper targeted the middle-class African-American audience; he played the popular big-band jazz recordings of the day and prided himself in speaking proper English over the air. Benson played the down-home blues of the era and spoke in the vernacular of the new ghetto populace, most of whom were working-class southern migrants. A new era of black radio was at hand.

By the end of the 1940s, there was a growing number of aspiring DJs in urban black communities ready to take advantage of the new "Negro-appeal" formats springing up on stations throughout the country. In Memphis, Nat D. Williams was responsible for broadcasting the first African-American radio show there, on WDIA in 1948; he also created the station's new black-appeal format and launched the careers of numerous first-generation African-American DJs over WDIA's airways. Two of the most important were Maurice "Hot Rod" Hulbert, who moved on to become the dean of black disc jockeys in Baltimore, on WBEE; and Martha Jean "the Queen" Stienburg, who later became the most popular black DJ in Detroit, on WCHB. In 1950, WERD, in Atlanta, became the first African-American-owned radio station in the country when it was purchased by J. B. Blayton, Jr. He appointed his son as station manager and then hired Jack "the Rapper" Gibson as program director. Other black-appeal stations that came into prominence during the early 1950s included WEDR in Birmingham, Ala.; WOOK in Washington, D.C.; WCIN in Cincinnati; WABQ in Cleveland; KXLW in St. Louis; and KCKA in Kansas City, which became the second African American-owned radio outlet in the nation in 1952. By 1956 there were over four hundred radio stations in the United States broadcasting black-appeal programming. Each of these operations showcased its own homegrown African-American disc jockeys, who were the centerpiece of the on-air sound.

The powerful presence and influence of the African-American DJs on the airways in urban America in the 1950s stemmed from two sources. On the one hand, they were the supreme arbiters of black musical tastes; they could make or break a new record release, depending on how much they played and promoted it. On the other hand, the black disc jockeys were also the new electronic

See also

Blues

griots of the black oral tradition, posturing as social rappers and cultural rebels. As such, they collectively constituted a social grapevine that was integral not just to the promotion of rhythm and blues, but also to the empowerment of the growing Civil Rights Movement in the South. Black-appeal radio stations like WERD in Atlanta and WDIA in Memphis, as well as Al Benson's shows in Chicago, played a vital role in informing people about the early civil rights struggles. In a speech to black broadcasters late in his life, civil rights leader the Rev. Dr. Martin Luther King, Jr., paid special tribute to disc jockeys Tall Paul White (WEDR, Birmingham), Purvis Spann (WVON, Chicago), and Georgie Woods (WHAT, Philadelphia) for their important contributions to the civil rights efforts in their respective cities.

During the 1950s, African-American radio DJs also had a profound effect on commercial radio in general. Some stations—such as WLAC in Nashville, a high-powered AM outlet heard at night throughout the South—devoted a hefty amount of their evening schedules to rhythm and blues records. In addition, the white disc jockeys at WLAC (John R., Gene Noble, Hoss Allen, and Wolfman Jack) adopted the on-air styles, and even dialect, of the black DJs. Many of their listeners, both black and white, thought that WLAC's disc jockeys were African Americans. This was also the case on WJMR in New Orleans, where the white DJs who hosted the popular *Poppa Stoppa Show* were actually trained to speak in black dialect by the creator of the show, an African-American college professor named Vernon Winslow. Other white DJs who became popular by emulating the broadcast styles of their black counterparts included Dewey Phillips in Memphis; Zenas "Daddy" Sears in Atlanta; Phil Mckernan in Oakland, Calif.; George "Hound Dog" Lorenz in Buffalo, N.Y.; and Allen Freed in Cleveland. Freed moved on to become New York City's most famous rock and roll disc jockey, before his fall from grace as the result of payola scandals in the early 1960s.

Payola, the exchange of money for record airplay, was a common practice throughout the radio industry. It was an easy way for disc jockeys to supplement the low wages they were paid by their employers. Hence, many well-known black DJs were adversely affected by the payola exposés. Some lost their jobs when their names were linked to the ongoing investigations, and an unfortunate few were even the targets of income-tax-evasion indictments. The industry's solution to the payola problem was the creation of the "top forty" radio format, which in effect gave management complete control over the playlists of records to be aired on their stations. Formerly, the playlists had been determined by the individual DJs. This change led to the demise of both the white rock-and-roll disc jockeys and the black "personality" DJs associated with rhythm and blues, and then "soul" music. Black-appeal stations were centralized even further by the emergence of five soul radio chains in the 1960s, all of which were white-owned and -managed. By the end of the decade, these corporations controlled a total of twenty stations in key urban markets with large African-American populations like New York, Chicago, Memphis, and Washington, D.C. The chain operations not only established standardized top forty soul formats at their respective outlets, thus limiting the independence of the black DJs they employed, but they also eliminated most of the local African-American news and public-affairs offerings on the stations.

In spite of the trend toward top forty soul formats, a number of black personality DJs managed to survive and even prosper in the 1960s. The most important were Sid McCoy (WGES, WCFL), Purvis Spann (WVON), and Herb Kent (WVON) in Chicago; LeBaron Taylor and Georgie Woods (both WDAS) in Philadelphia; Eddie O'Jay in Cleveland (WABQ) and Buffalo (WUFO); Skipper Lee Frazier (KCOH) in Houston; the Magnificent Montegue (KGFJ) in Los Angeles; and Sly Stone (KSOL) in San Francisco. LeBaron Taylor and Sly Stone went on to successful careers in the music industry—Taylor as a CBS record executive and Stone as a pioneering pop musician. The Magnificent Montegue's familiar invocation, "Burn, baby, burn," used to introduce the "hot" records he featured on his show, inadvertently became the unofficial battle cry of the 1967 Watts rebellion. The new mood of black militancy sweeping the nation also found its way into the ranks of the African-American DJs, especially among the younger generation just entering the radio industry. Two of the more influential members of this "new breed," as they came to be known, were Del Shields (WLIB) in New York and Roland Young (KSAN, KMPX) in San Francisco. Both men independently pioneered innovative black music formats, mixing together jazz, soul, and salsa recordings.

The 1970s ushered in the current era of black-owned and -controlled radio operations, both stations and networks. In 1970, of the more than three hundred black-formatted stations, only sixteen were owned by African-Americans. During

See also

Jazz

the next decade, the number of black-owned stations rose to 88, while the number of formatted stations surpassed 450. Some of the more prominent African Americans who became radio station owners during this era included entertainers James Brown and Stevie Wonder, Chicago publisher John Johnson, and New York City politician Percy Sutton. In particular, Sutton's Harlem-based Inner City Broadcasting (WLIB-AM, WBLS-FM) has been the national trendsetter in a black-owned-and-operated radio from the early 1970s to the present. In 1977, African-American broadcasters organized their own trade organization, the National Association of Black-Owned Broadcasters. By 1990 there were 206 black-owned radio stations—138 AM and 68 FM—in the country.

It was also during the 1970s that two successful black radio networks were launched: the Mutual Black Network, founded in 1972, which became the Sheridan Broadcasting Network in 1979; and the National Black Network, started in 1973. Both of these operations provide news, talk shows, public affairs, and cultural features to their affiliate stations throughout the nation. In the 1980s, the Sheridan network had over one hundred affiliates and 6.2 million weekly listeners; in addition to news and public affairs, it offered a wide range of sports programming, including live broadcasts of black college football and basketball games. The National network averaged close to one hundred affiliates and four million weekly listeners in the 1980s; its most popular programs, in addition to its news reports, were journalist Roy Woods's *One Man's Opinion* and Bob Law's *Night Talk*.

Two major formats have dominated black-owned commercial radio in the 1970s and 1980s—"talk" and "urban contemporary." Talk radio formats emerged on African-American AM stations in the early 1970s; in essence, they featured news, public affairs, and live listener call-in shows. By this time, the FM stations dominated the broadcasting of recorded music due to their superior reproduction of high fidelity and stereo signals. The AM stations were left with talk by default. Inner City Broadcasting initiated the move toward talk radio formats among African-American stations when it turned WLIG-AM, which it purchased in New York City in 1972, into "your total news and information station" that same year. The logic of the commercial radio market encouraged many of the other black AM operations, such as WOL-AM in Washington, D.C., to follow suit. Likewise, Inner City Broadcasting also pioneered the urban contemporary format on WBLS-FM during this same period. Much of the credit for the new format is given to Frankie Crocker, who was the station's program director at the time. In order to build up WBLS's ratings in the most competitive radio market in the country, Crocker scuttled the station's established jazz programming in favor of a crossover format featuring black music currently on the pop charts along with popular white artists with a black sound. The idea was to appeal to an upscale black and white audience. The formula worked to perfection; WBLS became the top station in the New York market, and scores of other stations around the country switched to the new urban contemporary format. One example was WHUR-FM, owned by Howard University in Washington, D.C. The station's original jazz and black-community-affairs format was sacked in favor of the urban contemporary approach in the mid-1970s. The new format allowed WHUR to become one of the top-rated stations in the Washington market. In the process, it gave birth to an innovative new nighttime urban contemporary style called "quiet storm," after the Smokey Robinson song of the same name. The architect of this novel format was Melvin Lindsey, a former Howard student and WHUR intern.

The 1970s and 1980s also marked the entrance of African Americans into the public broadcasting sphere. By 1990, there were thirty-two public FM stations owned and operated by black colleges around the country, and another twelve controlled by black community boards of directors. These stations are not subject to the pervasive ratings pressures of commercial radio, giving them more leeway in programming news, public affairs, talk, and unusual cultural features. Many of these stations—such as WCLK-FM, owned by Clarke College in Atlanta; WSHA-FM, owned by Shaw College in Raleigh, N.C., and WVAS-FM, from Alabama State University in Montgomery—have adopted the jazz formats abandoned by African-American-owned commercial FM stations. Others, like WPFW-FM in Washington, D.C. (the number one black public radio outlet in the country), have developed a more ambitious "world rhythms" format embracing the many musics of the African diaspora. In general, the growth of black public radio has expanded the variety and diversity of African-American programming found on the airwaves, while also increasing the numbers of African Americans working in radio.

—WILLIAM BARLOW

Amos 'n' Andy *dominated black comedy on radio throughout its heyday as the "national pastime" in the 1930s.*

PAGE 564

RAGTIME

Ragtime was the first music of African-American origin to play a significant role in American popular culture. It had both vocal and instrumental forms, flourished from the late 1890s until the late 1910s, and had important exponents among both black and white composers.

A major element of antebellum black music in the public mind was syncopated rhythm. This and similar rhythms were used to caricature black music and were widely heard in minstrel shows that toured the nation, bringing an incipient ragtime to public consciousness. Ragtime as a distinct genre came to public notice at the 1893 World's Fair in Chicago, one piece that was played there reportedly being Jesse Pickett's "Dream Rag." The term "ragtime" first appeared in print on song publications of 1896, possibly the earliest being Ernest Hogan's "All Coons Look Alike to Me," which included a syncopated "Choice Chorus, with Negro 'Rag,' Accompaniment." As this quotation indicates, the black roots of ragtime were acknowledged from the very beginning.

Vocal Ragtime

Most early ragtime songs were known as "coon songs," "coon" being a then-widely used contemptuous term for blacks. These songs typically had lyrics in stereotypical black dialect and played upon such negative themes as black men being shiftless, lazy, thieving, gambling, and violent; of black women being mercenary and sexually promiscuous. A typical song lyric would be "I don't like no cheap man / Dat spends his money on de 'stallment plan." (Bert Williams and George Walker, 1897). Adding to the songs' negative impressions were sheet music covers that usually portrayed African Americans in grotesquely exaggerated caricatures. With the relatively insensitive ethnic climate of the time, there was little protest from the black community; black artists—including such sophisticated individuals as composer Will Marion Cook and poet-lyricist Paul Laurence Dunbar—contributed to the genre.

Not all early ragtime songs were abusive, even though they retained racial stereotypes. Among those whose popularity outlived the ragtime years was Howard and Emerson's "Hello! Ma Baby" (1899), which celebrates courtship over the telephone. "Bob" Cole and J. Rosamond Johnson, black artists who were sensitive to the stigma of demeaning lyrics, wrote their enormously successful "Under the Bamboo Tree" (1902) to demonstrate that a racial song could express tasteful and universally appreciated sentiments.

Around 1905, the ragtime song began to lose its overtly racial quality and came to include any popular song of a strongly hic character. Typical examples were "Some of These Days" (1910) and "Waiting for the Robert E. Lee" (1913). Irving Berlin's hit song "Alexander's Ragtime Band" (1911) which was regarded by many as the high point of ragtime, retains only slight racial suggestions in its lyrics and these are nonderogatory.

Instrumental Ragtime

Ragtime developed both as a solo-piano vehicle and as an ensemble style for virtually all instruments. Ensemble ragtime was played by marching and concert bands, by dance orchestras, and in such diverse combinations as xylophone-marimba duos and trios, piano-violin duos, and mandolin-banjo groupings. Solo-piano ragtime was heard on the vaudeville stage, in salons and brothels, in the home parlor, and on the mechanical player piano.

Ragtime was closely associated with dance. In the early days, the two-step was most common, along with such variants as the slow-drag. The cakewalk remained popular throughout the ragtime years but was a specialty dance reserved mostly for exhibitions and contests. In the 1910s many new dances joined the ragtime category, including the one-step, fox-trot, turkey trot, grizzly bear, and such waltz variants as the Boston, hesitation, and half-and-half. The tango and maxixe, though Latin-American rather than ragtime dances, were performed to syncopated music and became part of the ragtime scene in the mid-1910s.

Piano Ragtime

Ragtime was published primarily for the piano and contributed significantly to the development of American popular music and jazz piano. Piano ragtime, like the ragtime song, flourished as published sheet music, but it also existed as an improvised art, giving it a direct link to early jazz. However, since improvised ragtime was not preserved on sound recordings, we have little detailed knowledge of it.

The defining elements of ragtime were established by 1897, when the earliest piano rag sheet music appeared. Of primary importance was the syncopation, for it was from this uneven, ragged rhythmic effect that the term "ragtime" was de-

While in his teens Eubie Blake began to play in the ragtime style then popular in Baltimore sporting houses and saloons.

PAGE 97

See also
Scott Joplin

rived. As applied to piano music, syncopation typically appeared as a right-hand pattern played against an even, metric bass. Around 1906 a new pattern, known as secondary ragtime, gained acceptance. This is not true syncopation, but the shifting accents within a three-note pattern create a polyrhythmic effect that was successfully integrated with the other ragtime gestures. After 1911, dotted rhythms made inroads into ragtime, further diluting the distinctiveness of the early ragtime syncopations.

The form into which ragtime was cast, though not a defining element, was consistent. The form followed that of the march and consisted of a succession of sixteen-measure thematic sections, each section being evenly divided into four phrases. Typically the two opening thematic sections were in the tonic key and were followed by one or two sections (known as the "trio") in the subdominant key. (As an example of the key relationships, if the tonic key were C, the subdominant key would be F.) Diagrammatically, with each section depicted with an upper-case letter, the form with repeats might appear as AA BB A CC or AA BB CC DD. To these patterns might be added four-measure introductions to A and to C and interludes between repeats of C or between C and D. Though these patterns were typical, they were not invariable; many rags used different numbers of sections and different key relationships.

Blues, another style that emerged from the African-American community, had some influence on the rags of a few composers, particularly in the use of so-called blue notes. What in later years was to become known as the classic twelve-bar blues form made its earliest appearances in piano rags. The first known example was in "One O' Them Things?" (James Chapman and Leroy Smith, 1904), in which a twelve-bar blues replaces the usual A section. Both the form and the term appear in a New Orleans ragtime publication of 1908, A. Maggio's "I Got the Blues." The first blues to achieve popularity was W. C. Handy's "Memphis Blues" (1912), which combines twelve-bar blues and sixteen-bar ragtime sections and was subtitled "A Southern Rag." Through the rest of the ragtime era, the term "blues" was applied indiscriminately to many rags.

Though instrumental ragtime lacked the direct verbal communication possible with the lyrics of ragtime songs, early published rags conveyed a racial connotation with cover pictures that caricatured blacks, frequently in an offensive manner.

As with the songs, piano ragtime's gradual acceptance as American music rather than as an exclusively racial expression was matched with the discontinuance of racial depictions.

The Composers and Performers

The first ragtime performer to acquire fame was vaudeville pianist, singer, and composer Ben Harney, who appeared in New York in 1896 with "plantation negro imitations." Though he was known as "the first white man to play ragtime," his racial origins remain uncertain.

The publication of piano ragtime began in 1897 with "Mississippi Rag," by white bandmaster William Krell. Several months later, Tom Turpin, with his "Harlem Rag," became the first black composer to have a piano rag published. Turpin, a St. Louis saloon keeper, was an important figure in the development of ragtime in that city and reportedly had composed this piece as early as 1892. The most prominent ragtime success of 1897 was Kerry Mills's "At a Georgia Campmeeting," known in both song and instrumental versions and recorded by the Sousa Band, among others.

Piano ragtime quickly caught on, and in the years 1897–1899 more than 150 piano rags were published, the most important and influential being Scott Joplin's "Maple Leaf Rag" (1899). Joplin was a composer with serious aspirations, and his frequent publisher John Stark adopted the term "classic ragtime" to describe the music of Joplin and others he published. These included black Missourians James Scott, Arthur Marshall, Louis Chauvin, Artie Matthews, and such white composers as J. Russel Robinson, Paul Pratt, and Joseph Lamb. Though virtually all classic rags are superior examples of the genre, the term did not embrace any single style. Nor were classic rags the best known. More popular were the easier and more accessible rags of such composers as Ted Snyder, Charles Johnson, Percy Wenrich, and George Botsford.

New York City, with its flourishing entertainment centers and music publishing industry (Tin Pan Alley), naturally attracted many ragtimers. Because of the competition and high musical standards in the city, some of the more adept ragtime pianists developed a virtuosic style known as "stride." Among the leaders of this style were Eubie Blake, James P. Johnson, and Luckey Roberts. These musicians—along with such figures as Joe Jordan, Will Marion Cook, Bob Cole, and J. Rosamond Johnson—also became involved in

See also
St. Louis, Missouri

SCOTT JOPLIN

"King of Ragtime Composers" Revered for Piano Rags

Scott Joplin (c. 1867/68–April 1, 1917), ragtime composer. Born in eastern Texas, some 35 miles south of present-day Texarkana, to an ex-slave father and a freeborn mother, Joplin rose from humble circumstances to be widely regarded as the "King of Ragtime Composers." (Formerly thought to have been born on November 24, 1868, he is now known to have been born in late 1867 or early 1868.) In the early years of his career he worked with minstrel companies and vocal quartets, in bands as a cornetist, and as a pianist. His earliest published compositions (1895–1896) were conventional songs and marches. In 1894 he settled in Sedalia, Mo., where he attended the George R. Smith College. His "Maple Leaf Rag" (1899), which memorializes a black social club in Sedalia, became the most popular piano rag of the era. By 1901 he was famous and moved to St. Louis, where he worked primarily as a composer. Despite his success in ragtime, he wanted to compose for the theater. In 1903 he formed a company to stage his first opera, *A Guest of Honor* (now lost). He spent all his money on the unsuccessful opera tour and then returned to composing piano rags. In 1907 he moved to New York, where major music publishers were eager to issue his rags, but he still aspired to be a "serious" composer. In 1911 he completed and self-published his second opera, *Treemonisha,* in which he expressed the view that his race's problems were exacerbated by ignorance and superstition and could be overcome by education. He never succeeded in mounting a full production of this work.

Despite his efforts with larger musical forms,

Scott Joplin is today revered for his piano rags, these being the most sophisticated examples of the genre. His published output includes fifty-two piano pieces, of which forty-two are rags (including seven collaborations with younger colleagues); twelve songs; one instructional piece; and one opera. Several songs, rags, a symphony, and several stage works—his first opera, a musical, and a vaudeville—were never published and are lost.

A Scott Joplin revival began in late 1970 when Nonesuch Records, a classical music label, issued a recording of Joplin rags played by Joshua Rifkin. For the record industry, this recording gave Joplin the status of a classical composer. This status was enhanced a year later when the New York Public Library issued the two-volume *Collected Works of Scott Joplin.* Thereafter, classical concert artists began including Joplin's music in their recitals. In 1972, his opera *Treemonisha* received its first full performance, staged in Atlanta in conjunction with an Afro-American Music Workshop at Morehouse College, and in 1975 the opera reached Broadway. (There have been three orchestrations of the work—by T. J. Anderson, William Bolcom, and Gunther Schuller.) In 1974, the award-winning movie *The Sting* used several Joplin rags in its musical score, bringing Joplin to the attention of an even wider public. "The Entertainer" (1902), the film's main theme, became one of the most popular pieces of the mid-1970s. Further recognition of Joplin as an artist came in 1976 with a special Pulitzer Prize, and in 1983 with a U.S. postage stamp bearing his image.

—EDWARD A. BERLIN

black musical theater, which made extensive use of ragtime.

Bandleader James Reese Europe, disliked the term "ragtime" but became one of the most influential musicians on the late ragtime scene in New York. In 1910 he formed the Clef Club, an organization that functioned both as a union and booking agency for New York's black musicians. As music director for the popular white dance team of Irene and Vernon Castle, beginning in 1914, Europe created a demand both for black music and for black dance-band musicians.

Many who were admired during the ragtime years left little or no record of their music. Among these were "One-Leg" Willie Joseph, Abba Labba (Richard McLean), and "Jack the Bear" (John

Wilson). "Jelly Roll" Morton was active from the early ragtime years but did most of his publishing and recording in the 1920s and 1930s. Tony Jackson was widely praised as a performer and composer but is remembered today primarily for his song "Pretty Baby." There were many black women active as performers, but they are now forgotten because they did not publish or record. Thus, the history of ragtime is slanted in favor of those who can be documented.

Reaction to Ragtime

Within the context of the genteel parlor music of the 1890s, ragtime was shockingly new. Nothing like it had ever been heard. For some, ragtime became America's statement of musical indepen-

See also

Tap Dance

"MA" RAINEY

Beloved Vaudeville Singer

Gertrude Pridgett "Ma" Rainey (April 26, 1886–December 22, 1939), singer. One of the most beloved blues and vaudeville singers of the first three decades in the twentieth century, Ma Rainey—"Mother of the Blues"—was born Gertrude Pridgett in Columbus, Ga. Rainey was the second of five children born to Thomas and Ella Pridgett. She performed in a local show, "A Bunch of Blackberries," at fourteen and married a tent showman, Will Rainey, when she was eighteen. They performed together for several years as a comedy song and dance act, billed as the "Assassinators of the Blues," with the Rabbit Foot Minstrels.

Supposedly, Rainey coined the term "blues" after she began singing the mournful songs that she had heard sung by a young woman along the tent show's route. Rainey left her husband after twelve years but continued to follow the TOBA (Theater Owner's Booking Association) circuit as a solo act because she was so popular with country folk, white and black. She sang with jug bands as well as small jazz bands, which included at times Tommy Ladnier, Joe Smith, and Coleman Hawkins. She was a seasoned performer who sang about the worries and tribulations of country folk in the traditional style of the rural South. Her subject matter was earthy, her renditions were often comedic, yet she did not resort to trivia.

Rainey's first recording, "Moonshine Blues," was produced by Paramount Records in 1923. She recorded a total of ninety-three songs, which included traditional country/folk blues, vaudeville songs, and popular songs. Rainey wrote many of her songs, addressing topics as diverse as the impact of the boll weevil on cotton crops to homosexuality, prostitution, and jail. Although she was overshadowed by her younger counterpart, Bessie Smith, Rainey had a loyal following until her last days on the tent show circuit in the 1930s. She handled her business affairs well and retired to her native city of Columbus, Ga., where she opened her own theater. She died there on December 22, 1939.

—DAPHNE DUVAL HARRISON

dence from Europe; it was hailed as a new expression, reflecting this nation's exuberance and restlessness. American youth, regardless of race, embraced the music as its own.

Inevitably, opposition to ragtime emerged. One sector of opposition was generational—the ever-present syndrome of the older generations rejecting the music of the younger. There was also opposition from musical elitists, those who objected to a music that lacked a proper pedigree and feared it would drive out "good music." Some denied that ragtime was at all innovative; they argued that the ragtime rhythms had been used by the European "old masters" and in various European folk musics. Then there were the blatant racists, who rejected the idea that an American music could have black origins and denied that African Americans were capable of creating anything original. Most of all, they feared that white youth was being "infected" by this developing black music.

Certain parts of African-American society also objected to ragtime. Church groups, noting that ragtime was played in saloons and brothels and used for dancing, concluded that the music contributed to sinfulness. Blacks striving for middle-class respectability were also wary of ragtime because of its lower-class associations. The *Negro Music Journal* (1902–1903), which encouraged blacks to cultivate tastes for classical music, denounced ragtime and denied that it was an African-American expression.

Despite such opposition, ragtime thrived and evolved. During the mid- to late 1910s jazz emerged as an offshoot of ragtime. At first there was little distinctiveness between the two, but by the end of World War I jazz had replaced ragtime as the most important vernacular music in America.

—EDWARD A. BERLIN

RANDOLPH, ASA PHILIP

Asa Philip Randolph (1889–1979), labor and civil rights leader. The younger son of James William Randolph (a minister in the African Methodist Episcopal Church), A. Philip Randolph was born in Crescent City, Fla., and raised in Jacksonville. In 1911, after graduating from the Cookman Institute in Jacksonville, the twenty-two-year-old Randolph migrated to New York City and settled in Harlem, then in an early stage of its development as the "Negro capital of the world." While working at odd jobs to support himself, he attended the City College of New

See also
Civil Rights Movement

R

RANDOLPH, ASA PHILIP

Freedom is never given; it is won.

A. PHILIP RANDOLPH
KEYNOTE SPEECH, SECOND
NATIONAL NEGRO CONGRESS,
1937

See also
Martin Luther King, Jr.

York (adjoining Harlem), where he took courses in history, philosophy, economics, and political science. During his enrollment at CCNY, he also became active in the Socialist party, whose leader, Eugene Debs, was one of his political heroes.

Between 1914 and the early 1920s, Randolph belonged to a group of young African-American militants in New York, the "Harlem radicals," who regarded themselves as the New Negro political avant-garde in American life. Some of them, including Randolph, combined race radicalism with socialism. Others, such as Marcus Garvey, who arrived in Harlem in 1916, emphasized an Africa-oriented black nationalism—they were averse to movements that advocated social reform or racial integration within the mainstream of American society. But all Harlem radicals defied the old establishment of African-American leadership, though it included so distinguished a member as W. E. B. Du Bois.

To race radicalism and socialism Randolph soon added an interest in trade unionism, which was to form a basic part of his approach to the struggle for black progress. In 1917, he and his closest socialist comrade in Harlem, Chandler Owen, founded and began coediting the messenger, a monthly journal that subtitled itself "The Only Radical Magazine Published by Negroes." The *Messenger* campaigned against lynchings in the South; opposed America's participation in World War I; counseled African Americans to resist the military draft; proposed an economic solution to the "Negro problem"; and urged blacks to ally themselves with the socialist and trade-union movements. For its irreverent editorial stands, the *Messenger* came under the close surveillance of the federal government. In 1918, Postmaster General Albert Burleson revoked the magazine's second-class mailing privileges; and in 1919, a Justice Department report ordered by Attorney General A. Mitchell Palmer described the *Messenger* as being "by long odds the most able and most dangerous of the Negro publications."

In 1917, Randolph also helped to organize the Socialist party's first black political club in New York, located in Harlem's Twenty-first Assembly District. And in 1920, the party recognized his growing importance as a spokesman by naming him its candidate for New York State comptroller, one of the highest positions to which a black socialist had been named. He lost in the November elections but polled an impressive 202,361 votes, about a thousand fewer than Eugene Debs polled in New York that year as the Socialist party's candidate for president.

In the early 1920s, Randolph began dissolving his formal ties to the party when it became clear to him that the black masses were not as responsive to the socialist message as he had hoped. This was partly because of their traditional distrust for ideologies they deemed to be un-American; partly because black nationalism was, emotionally and psychologically, more appealing to them; and partly because the Socialist party failed to address the special problems of black exclusion from the trade-union movement. But despite his retirement from formal party activities, Randolph was always to consider himself a democratic socialist.

In 1925, a delegation of Pullman porters approached him with a request that he organize their work force into a legitimate labor union, independent of employer participation and influence. Randolph undertook the task—a decision that launched his career as a national leader in the fields of labor and civil rights. But establishing the Brotherhood of Sleeping Car Porters was a far more difficult task than he had anticipated. The Pullman Company had crushed a number of earlier efforts at organizing its porters, and for the next twelve years it remained contemptuous of Randolph's. Not until 1937, after Congress had passed enabling labor legislation, did the Pullman executives recognize the Brotherhood of Sleeping Car Porters as a certified bargaining agent.

This victory gained the brotherhood full membership in the American Federation of Labor (AFL). It also gave Randolph—as the brotherhood's chief delegate to annual AFL conventions—an opportunity to answer intellectuals in Harlem who had criticized him for urging blacks to ally themselves with the trade-union movement. The black intelligentsia then regarded the AFL as a racist institution, most of whose craft unions barred nonwhite membership. How then (his critics argued) could Randolph call on blacks to invest their economic aspirations in organized labor? Randolph maintained, however, that trade unionism was the main engine of economic advancement for the working class, the class to which a majority of the black population belonged. He believed, moreover, that the achievement of political rights, for which all blacks were struggling, would be meaningless without comparable economic gains.

Throughout his tenure as a delegate to the annual conventions of organized labor (in 1955 he became a vice-president of the merged AFL-CIO), Randolph campaigned relentlessly against unions that excluded black workers. When he retired as a vice-president in 1968, the AFL-CIO had become the most integrated public institution in American life, though pockets of resistance remained. Randolph was not the sole instrument of that revolution, but he was its opening wedge, and much of it was owed to his unyielding agitation.

The brotherhood's victory in 1937 also inaugurated Randolph's career as a national civil rights leader; he emerged from the struggle with Pullman as one of the more respected figures in black America. In 1937, the recently formed National Negro Congress (NNC), recognizing Randolph's potential as a mass leader, invited him to be its president. In accepting, he himself saw the NNC as a potential mass movement. But he was obliged to resign the NNC's presidency in 1940, when he discovered that much of the organization had fallen under communist control. He was to be a resolute anti-communist for the rest of his life. He wrote to a colleague in 1959:

> They [communists] are not only undemocratic but anti-democratic. They are opposed to our concept of the dignity of the human personality, the heritage of the Judeo-Christian philosophy, and hence they represent a totalitarian system in which civil liberties cannot live.

Randolph's withdrawal from the NNC freed him to organize, early in 1941, the March on Washington Movement based on the Gandhian method of nonviolent direct action. It achieved its first major victory in June of that year. Faced with Randolph's threat to lead a massive invasion of the nation's capital, President Franklin D. Roosevelt issued an executive order banning the exclusion of blacks from employment in defense plants—the federal government's earliest commitment to the policy of fair employment. That breakthrough brought Randolph to the forefront of black mass leadership, making him "the towering civil rights figure of the period," according to James Farmer, one of his younger admirers. The March on Washington Movement disintegrated by the end of the 1940s. But by then Randolph had secured another historic executive order—this one from President Harry S. Truman, in 1948, outlawing segregation in the armed services. Scholars were to see his movement as one of the most remarkable in American history. Aspects of its influence went into the formation of Farmer's Congress of Racial Equality (1942) and Rev. Dr. Martin Luther King's Southern Christian Leadership Conference (1957), both of which helped to lead the great nonviolent protest movement of the 1960s.

Randolph was the elder statesman of that movement, a unifying center of the civil rights coalition that composed it. His collaboration with its various leaders culminated in the 1963 March on Washington, the largest demonstration for racial redress in the nation's history. Randolph had conceived that event. And it is appropriate that he should have called it a March for Jobs and Freedom; it represented his two-pronged approach, political and economic, to the black struggle.

After 1963, Randolph the architect of black mass pressure on the federal government faded gradually from the scene. In 1964, President Lyndon B. Johnson awarded him the Presidential Medal of Freedom, the nation's highest civilian honor. He spent the remaining years of his active life chiefly as a vice president of the AFL-CIO. He died in 1979, at the age of ninety.

—JERVIS ANDERSON

RAP

Rap is an African-American term that describes a stylized way of speaking. Salient features of a rap include metaphor, braggadocio, repetition, formulaic expressions, double entendre, mimicry, rhyme, and "signifyin' " (i.e., indirect references and allusions). Folklorists have credited the term to the 1960s black nationalist "H. Rap" Brown, whose praise name "rap" depicted his mastery of a "hip" way of speaking, aptly called rappin'. Although Brown is lauded for the name of this genre, the roots of rap can be traced from southern oral secular traditions such as toasts, folktales, blues, game songs (e.g., "hambone") to northern urban street jive—all of which make use of many of the same features.

While rap's southern antecedents (such as the blues) developed during the antebellum period and the turn of the century, jive emerged in inner city communities as the prototype of rap. Dan Burley, a scholar of jive, discovered that jive initially emerged among black Chicagoans around 1921. The primary context of its development was in secular environs remote from the home and religious centers, such as street corners, taverns, and parks, known among urban habitats as "the streets." Jive can be defined as a metaphorical style of communicating, using words and phrases from American mainstream English but reinterpreted from an African-American perspective. For example, in rap lingo, man becomes "cat," woman becomes "chick," and house becomes "crib." The art of jive resided in its ability to remain witty and

See also

Jazz

original, hence its constant fluctuation in vocabulary over the years.

Between the 1920s and 1950s, jive proliferated on all levels in the urban milieu—from the church to the street corner; but it also was incorporated in the literary works of noted black writers of the time, like Langston Hughes. Alongside its use by writers, jive became the parlance of jazz musicians. "Jam" (having a good time), "bad" (good), and "axe" (instrument) are some jive words commonplace in the jazz vernacular. By the late 1940s and 1950s, this urban style of speaking was introduced over radio airwaves by two Chicago disc jockeys, Holmes "Daddy-O" Daylie and Al Benson, who utilized jive in rhyme over music. Even the boastful poetry of former heavyweight champion boxer Muhammad Ali as well as comedian Rudy Ray Moore, known for popularizing audio recordings of toasts like "Dolemite" and "The Signifying Monkey," moved jive further into the American mainstream.

By the 1960s, jive was redefined and given a newer meaning by black nationalist "H. Rap" Brown, who laced his political speeches with signifyin', rhyme, and metaphor. Although his way of speaking inaugurated the shift from jive to rap, Brown's stylized speech soon gained popular acceptance among young urban admirers as rappin'. It was not, however, until the late 1960s that Brown's speaking style was set to a musical accompaniment by such political poets as the Watts Prophets of Los Angeles, the last poets of Harlem, and singer-pianist poet Gil Scott-Heron, who recited rhyming couplets over an African percussion accompaniment.

In the late 1960s and the 1970s, rappin' to music emerged as two distinct song styles: the soul rap and the funk-style rap. The soul rap, a rappin' monologue celebrating the feats and woes of love, was popularized by Isaac Hayes and further developed by Barry White and Millie Jackson. The funk-style rap, introduced by George Clinton and his group Parliament, consisted of rappin' monologues on topics about partying. Unlike the music of the political poets, the love and funk-style raps were not in rhyme but rather loosely chanted over a repetitive instrumental accompaniment. These artists nonetheless laid the foundation for a type of musical poetry begun primarily by African-American youth of the Bronx called rap music: a quasi-song with rhyme and rhythmic speech that draws on black street language and is recited over an instrumental soundtrack.

There are basically two factors that gave rise to rap music. With the overcommercialization of popular dance forms of the 1970s, particularly disco, and the ongoing club gang violence, African-American youth, particularly in New York City, left the indoor scene and returned to neighborhood city parks, where they created outdoor discotheques, featuring a disc jockey and an emcee. These circumstances were an impetus for the development of rap music, which is marked by four distinct phases: the mobile deejay (c. 1972–1978); the rappin' emcee and the emergence of the rap music genre (1976–1978); the early commercial years of rap music (1979–1985); and the explosive sound of rap in the musical mainstream (1986–1990s).

During the first phase, music performed in neighborhood city parks was provided by an itinerant disc jockey, the mobile deejay. Mobile jockeys were evaluated by the type of music they played as well as by the size of their sound systems. Similar to radio jockeys, mobile deejays occasionally spoke to their audiences in raps while simultaneously dovetailing one record after the other, a feat facilitated by two turntables. They were well known in their own boroughs and were supported by local followers. Popular jockeys included Pete "DJ" Jones of the Bronx and Grandmaster Flowers and Maboya of Brooklyn. The most innovative of mobile deejays, whose mixing technique immensely influenced the future sound direction and production of rap music, was Jamaican-born Clive Campbell, known as DJ Kool Herc. He tailored his disc jockeying style after the dub music jockeys of Jamaica, like Duke Reid and U Roy, by mixing collages of musical fragments, referred to as "break beats," from various recordings in order to create an entire new sound track.

Contemporaries of Kool Herc included Grandmaster Flash, Grand Wizard Theodore, and Afrika Bambaataa. Flash extended the Jamaican deejaying style with a mixing technique called backspinning (rotating one record counterclockwise to the desired beat then rotating the second record counterclockwise to the same location, thus creating an echo effect) and "phasing" (repeating a word or phrase in a rhythmic fashion on one turntable during or in between another recording). Grand Wizard Theodore popularized another mixing technique called "scratching" (the rhythmic movement of the tone arm needle of a turntable back and forth on a record). Bambaataa, on the other hand, perfected Herc's style of mixing by extending his break beats to include a variety of musical styles ranging from soul, funk, and disco to commercial jingle and television themes. But, more important, he is credited with starting a nonviolent organization called the Zulu Nation—a youth organization composed of local inner-city breakdancers, graffiti artists, and rappers—which laid the foundation for a youth mass art movement that came to be known as hip-hop.

Hip-hop not only encompassed street art forms, it also denoted an attitude rendered in the form of dress, gestures, and language associated with street culture.

The second phase of rap music began around the mid-1970s. Since mixing records had become an art in itself, some deejays felt the need for an emcee. For example, with the hiring of Clark Kent and Jay Cee, DJ Kool Herc became the Herculords, a three-man team. At many of his performances, Bambaataa was also accompanied by three emcees, Cowboy (not to be mistaken with Cowboy of the Furious Five), Mr. Biggs, and Queen Kenya. Other noted emcees during this phase were DJ Hollywood, Sweet G, Busy Bee, Kurtis Blow, Grandmaster Caz, and Lovebug Starski (the latter credited with the term "hip-hop"). Emcees talked intermittently, using phrases like "Get up," and "Jam to the beat," and recited rhyming couplets to motivate the audience to dance while the deejay mixed records. However, it was Grandmaster Flash's emcees, the Furious Five (Melle Mel, Cowboy, Raheim, Kid Creole, Mr. Ness), who set the precedent for rappin' in rhythm to music through a concept called "trading phrases"—the exchange of rhyming couplets or phrases between emcees in a percussive, witty fashion, and in synchrony with the deejay's music—as best illustrated by their hit "Freedom" (1980).

During rap's third phase, the early commercial years from 1979 to 1985, rap music was initially recorded by independent record companies like Winley, Enjoy, and Sugar Hill Records. Of the three, Sugar Hill Records, cofounded by Sylvia and Joe Robinson, succeeded in becoming the first international rap record company, producing such artists and groups as Sequence, Spoonie G., Lady B., Grandmaster Flash and the Furious Five, and Sugarhill Gang (best known for recording the first commercial rap song "Rapper's Delight"). Other modes of commercialization included Bambaataa's introduction of "techno-pop"—music created on synthesizers and drum machines—in rap music with "Planet Rock" (1982), recorded by his group, Soul Sonic Force. By the mid-1980s, techno-pop or the electronic influence in rap gave rise to sampling, the digital reproduction of prerecorded sounds—musical or vocal—in whole or fragmentary units anywhere throughout an entire sound track. Among the most popular styles of music sampled by rap deejays is funk, primarily the music of James Brown.

Bambaataa's musical innovation also provided the transition from the early commercial sound of rap, known as the "old school," to the "new school" rap. The former refers to earlier innovators and performers of rap music—for example, Kool Moe Dee, Melle Mel, Fat Boys, and Whodini, some of whom have continued to perform well into the 1990s. The "new school" performers are basically protégés of the pioneers; they comprise performers in the fourth phase.

In the fourth phase (1986–1990s), rap music gradually moved from the inner city into mainstream popular culture. Although independent record companies continued to dominate (e.g., Tommy Boy, Priority, Def Jam, Next Plateau), major record companies including MCA, Columbia, and Atlantic began recording rap and in some instances distributed for the independent labels. In addition, rap artists from areas outside of New York, Philadelphia, Los Angeles, Oakland, Miami, Atlanta, Houston, and Seattle, emerged as vital forces in the musical mainstream. Another factor that contributed to its growth was the fusion of rap music with hard rock, popularized by the group Run-DMC with their recording of "Rock Box" (1984) and their rendition of Aerosmith's "Walk This Way" (1986). The rap-rock fusion further evolved the new school techno-pop style through its extensive use of electronic instruments such as drum machines and samplers. However, it was the music of Public Enemy, masterminded by producer Hank Shocklee, that became the quintessence of sampling sounds, from James Brown's music and vocal stylings to black nationalists' speech excerpts. Furthermore, the use of sampling, funk-style drum rhythms with heavy bass drum, boisterous-aggressive vocal style of delivery, and/or moderate to excessive application of expletives in the text contributed to what rap artists refer to as a "hardcore" or street-style aesthetic.

See also
Gospel Music

Other factors that broadened the appeal of rap in popular culture were the rise of female rap artists (e.g., Roxanne Shante, the Real Roxanne, Salt-N-Pepa, MC Lyte, Queen Latifah, Yo-Yo); and the diversified sound of rap: party rap (e.g., Digital Underground, Kid 'N' Play, Hammer, De La Soul, Biz Markie, Tone Loc, and Young MC); political rap (e.g., KRS-One/BDP, Public Enemy, Sister Souljah, Arrested Development, X-Clan); "gangsta" rap (e.g., Ice-T, Ice Cube, Geto Boys, Schoolly-D, Too Short); and eclectic rap, a cross between party and hardcore (e.g., LL Cool J, Eric B & Rakim, Naughty by Nature, EPMD, Heavy D, Kriss Kross, Das Efx); and rap/jazz fusion (e.g., Digable Planets, Us3, and Guru).

By the late 1980s, rap music had not only become musically diverse but culturally diverse as well. While a few white rap artists existed in the shadows of their African-American counterparts (e.g., Vanilla Ice), others, like the Beastie Boys, Third Bass, and House of Pain, crossed over into wider acceptance in the 1990s. Also by the late 1980s, the rap scene expanded to include Spanish-speaking performers (whose raps are aptly called Spanglish): Mellow Man Ace, Kid Frost, and Gerardo. Rap music also gained international prominence in places like England, France, Denmark, Germany, and Canada. Much of rap's popularity in these countries was due to the establishment of Zulu Nation chapters abroad and the multimedia exposure of rap artists, from recordings to the silver screen.

By the beginning of the 1990s, rap had achieved unprecedented success in the American mainstream as evidenced by its use in advertising, fashion, and other musical genres. But despite its popularity, rap had created much controversy among critics who considered its lyrics to be too hardcore and sexually explicit. Among rap's most controversial artists have been 2 Live Crew and gangsta rappers. Although much of rap's controversy remains unresolved, it continues to appeal to listeners because of its artful use of street jive and funky beats.

—CHERYL L. KEYES

RAZAF, ANDY

Andy Razaf (Razafkeriefo, Andreamentania Paul) (December 15, 1895–February 3, 1973), lyricist. The exact spelling of Andy Razaf's real name is often disputed, but the above is generally ac-

cepted. Razaf was descended from the royal family of Madagascar. His grandfather, John Louis Waller, a former slave, became consul to that country, where Razaf's mother, Jennie Maria Waller, married Henry Razafkeriefo, the nephew of Queen Ranavalona III, before moving to Washington, D.C., where Razaf was born. His father's political activities took the family to Baltimore, Kansas City, Cuba, and New York around the turn of the century.

Razaf quit school at sixteen to help support the family, working as an elevator operator, butler, and custodian before moving to Cleveland to become a pitcher for a semiprofessional Negro team there. He also wrote newspaper articles, political speeches, and poems, as well as ragtime songs; he wrote his first song at the age of thirteen, and in 1913 sold his song "Baltimo'" to be performed in *The Passing Show*. In 1921 he returned to New York to play briefly for the New York Black Sox, but was soon able to make a living as a songwriter. His first important success was with *Joe Hurtig's Social Maids* show, for which he wrote lyrics in 1922.

In the early 1920s Razaf was a fixture of Harlem's nightclub scene, where he met many of the musicians with whom he would collaborate, including Willie "The Lion" Smith, Eubie Blake (with whom Razaf wrote "Memories of You" in 1930), and James P. Johnson. During this time Razaf also met Fats Waller, who would become his best friend and coauthor of some of the most beloved popular songs of the twentieth century (Waller was unrelated to Razaf's grandfather). Among their compositions were "Honeysuckle Rose" (1928), "My Fate Is in Your Hands" (1928), "Ain't Misbehavin'" (1929), "Blue Turning Grey over You" (1929), "Keeping Out of Mischief Now" (1932), and "The Joint Is Jumpin'" (1938). One of the duo's most famous songs, "What Did I Do to Be So Black and Blue" (1929), displayed Razaf's longstanding concern with racial injustice. Although Louis Armstrong's influential 1929 version interpreted the song in terms of white racism towards African Americans, Razaf's original lyrics were also directed at intraracial bias against darker-skinned blacks. Many of Razaf's songs first appeared in the Harlem shows that epitomized urban black popular culture in the 1920s. These shows included *Keep Shufflin'* (1928), *Hot Chocolates* (1929), *Blackbirds of 1930* (1930), *Hot Harlem* (1932), and *Rhythm for Sale* (1934).

The greatest vocalists and instrumentalists of jazz and popular music of the 1920s and '30s per-

See also
Harlem Renaissance

formed Razaf's music. Among his earliest champions were Louis Armstrong, Mildred Bailey, and Ethel Waters. Although Razaf was best known for his lyrics, he also made many recordings, including "Yes Sir! That's My Baby" (1925), "Back in Your Own Backyard" (1928), "Go Harlem" (1931) and "Lost Love" (1937).

In the mid-to-late 1930s, Razaf's estrangement from Waller and the diminished popularity of Harlem stage shows sent his career into decline. After *Tan Manhattan* (1940), which he wrote with Blake, Razaf moved to Englewood, N.J., where he failed in an attempt to enter local politics. In 1948 he moved to Los Angeles and lived the remainder of his life in illness and obscurity. Razaf, who married four times, died of kidney failure in North Hollywood at 77.

—BUD KLIMENT

RECONSTRUCTION

Reconstruction, period that began during the Civil War and ended in 1877. One of the most controversial and misunderstood eras in American history, it witnessed far-reaching changes in the country's political and social life. For the first time, the national government assumed the basic responsibility for defining and protecting Americans' civil rights. In the South, African-American men were for the first time given the right to vote and hold office, and a politically mobilized black community joined with white allies to bring the Republican Party—temporarily, as it turned out—to power. Reconstruction was America's first experiment in interracial democracy.

For much of the twentieth century, both scholarly and popular writing presented Reconstruction as an era of unrelieved sordidness in political and social life. According to this view, Abraham Lincoln, before his death, had embarked on a course of sectional reconciliation that was continued by his successor, Andrew Johnson. Their magnanimous efforts were thwarted by vindictive Radical Republicans in Congress, who fastened black supremacy upon the defeated Confederacy. An orgy of corruption and misgovernment soon followed, presided over by unscrupulous Carpetbaggers (Northerners who ventured south to reap the spoils of office), Scalawags (southern whites who cooperated with the Republican party for personal gain), and ignorant and childlike freedpeople, who were incapable of responsibly exercising the political power that had been thrust upon them. After much needless suffering—so the interpretation goes—the South's white community banded together in patriotic organizations such as the Ku Klux Klan to overthrow these "black" governments and restore "home rule" (their euphemism for white supremacy). Popularized through films such as *The Birth of a Nation*, this interpretation rested on the assumption that black suffrage was the gravest error of the Civil War period. It helped to justify the South's system of racial segregation and disfranchisement of black voters.

Although significant criticisms of the traditional interpretation were advanced earlier in the twentieth century, it was not until the 1960s that the older view was finally interred. The "second Reconstruction"—the Civil Rights Movement—inspired a new conception of the first, and in rapid sequence virtually every assumption of the old viewpoint was swept away. In the new scholarship, Andrew Johnson, yesterday's high-minded defender of constitutional principles, was revealed as a racist politician too stubborn to compromise with his critics. Commitment to racial equality, not vindictiveness or mere partisanship, motivated his Radical Republican critics. The period of Radical Reconstruction in the South was shown to be a time of progress for African Americans and the region as a whole. The Ku Klux Klan, whose campaign of violence had been minimized by earlier historians, was revealed as a terrorist organization that beat and killed its opponents in order to deprive blacks of their newly won rights. Most strikingly, African Americans were now shown to be active agents in shaping the era's history, rather than passive recipients of the actions of others, or simply a "problem" confronting white society. Today, scholars differ among themselves on many issues, but all agree that the traditional view of the period is dead, and unlamented, and that blacks must be considered central actors in the drama of Reconstruction.

Reconstruction During the Civil War

Reconstruction began not with the Confederacy's surrender in 1865 but during the Civil War. Long before the conflict ended, Americans were debating the questions that came to form the essence of Reconstruction: On what terms should the southern states be reunited with the Union? Who should establish these terms, Congress or the

All I ask for the Negro is that if you do not like him, let him alone. If God gave him but little, that little let him enjoy.

ABRAHAM LINCOLN
SPEECH, JULY 17, 1858

See also
Carpetbaggers

577

president? What system of labor should replace plantation slavery? What should be the place of blacks in the political and social life of the South and the nation? One definitive conclusion emerged from the Civil War: The reconstructed South would be a society without slavery.

The destruction of slavery, begun by blacks who fled the plantations in 1861 and 1862, and made into a national war aim by the Emancipation Proclamation of January 1, 1863, powerfully shaped the course of the war and the debate over Reconstruction. No longer could the Lincoln administration speak of allowing the South to return with its prewar institutions and leadership intact.

In December 1863, Lincoln announced a program for Reconstruction. He offered a pardon to all supporters of the Confederacy (except high-ranking officials) who took an oath of loyalty and pledged to accept the end of slavery. When 10 percent of a state's prewar voters took the oath, they could establish a state government and apply for readmission to the Union. New state constitutions would have to prohibit slavery, but otherwise Lincoln gave southern leaders a free hand in legislation. Voting and officeholding were limited to whites. The president, complained abolitionist Wendell Phillips, "frees the slave and ignores the Negro."

Lincoln attempted to implement his Reconstruction plan in Louisiana, portions of which had been occupied by Union troops in 1862. Two years later, elections were held for a constitutional convention, which abolished slavery and sought Louisiana's readmission to the Union. At the same time, the free African Americans of New Orleans—a self-conscious community that included many highly educated, economically successful individuals—pressed for the right to participate in Reconstruction. After meeting with two free black representatives, Lincoln in March 1864 private, and unsuccessfully, urged Louisiana's governor to allow at least some blacks to vote.

As Reconstruction proceeded in Louisiana, it became clear that many northern Republicans were unhappy with Lincoln's program. Foremost among them were the Radicals, a group that had led the opposition to slavery's expansion before the Civil War and had long favored granting equal civil and political rights to free blacks in the North. The most prominent were Rep. Thaddeus Stevens of Pennsylvania and Sen. Charles Sumner of Massachusetts, both longtime proponents of the rights of African Americans. The Radicals now insisted that the federal government had a responsibility to protect the basic rights of the former slaves. By 1864 some went further, announcing that Reconstruction could not be secure without black suffrage. Their stance combined principle and political advantage. The Radicals believed that without the right to vote, blacks would be vulnerable to domination by their former owners; they also understood that unless blacks voted, the Republican party would find it very difficult to win elections in the postwar South.

During 1864, the Radicals became convinced that Lincoln's 10-percent plan was too lenient to "rebels" and did too little to protect African Americans' rights. Enough moderate Republicans agreed that Congress passed the Wade-Davis Bill, which proposed to delay the start of Reconstruction until a majority of a state's white males—not just 10 percent—had taken an oath of loyalty. The new state governments were required to guarantee the equality before the law of black Southerners. Black suffrage, which most Republicans did not at this point support, was not mentioned. Not wishing to abandon his own approach, Lincoln pocket vetoed the bill.

Lincoln and the Radicals differed over Reconstruction, but their breach was not irreparable. Early in 1865, they worked together to secure congressional approval of the Thirteenth Amendment, which irrevocably abolished slavery throughout the nation. Shortly thereafter Congress passed, and Lincoln signed, a bill creating the Freedmen's Bureau, an agency empowered to protect the legal rights of the former slaves, provide education and medical care, oversee labor contracts between emancipated blacks and their employers, and lease land to black families.

As the act establishing the Freedmen's Bureau suggested, there was far more to Reconstruction than the problem of forming new state governments and determining who should vote. During the Civil War, the first steps were taken toward addressing the interrelated problems of access to land and control of labor. The most famous of these "rehearsals for Reconstruction" took place on the Sea Islands of South Carolina. When the Union navy occupied the area in 1861, virtually all the white inhabitants fled to the mainland, leaving behind some 10,000 slaves, who sacked the big houses, destroyed cotton gins, and commenced planting corn and potatoes for their own consumption.

Sea Island blacks, however, were not to chart their own course to "free labor." In the navy's wake

See also
Civil Rights Movement

came whites from the North—military officers, Treasury agents, northern investors eager to resume plantation agriculture, and a group of young teachers and missionaries known as Gideon's Band. Many of the reformers sympathized with African Americans' desire to acquire land. Most government officials and northern investors, however, believed the Sea Island experiment provided a golden opportunity to prove that blacks would work more efficiently and profitably as free laborers than as slaves. Rather than immediately acquiring land, they believed, the former slaves should work for wages and learn the discipline of the free market. The Sea Island experiment produced many improvements in the lives of the area's black population, including access to schools and a rise in their standard of living. However, it also brought disappointment, for when plantations abandoned by their owners were auctioned off by the federal government, only a small amount of land found its way into the hands of the former slaves.

The Sea Island experiment involved a far smaller area and far fewer persons than another rehearsal for Reconstruction, which took place in the Mississippi Valley. Here many slave owners remained on their plantations, declared their loyalty to the Union, and demanded that the army compel their black laborers to remain at work. Military officials, who established "contraband camps" for black refugees, had no desire to care permanently for large numbers of former slaves. They decreed that the former slaves sign labor contracts either with planters who took an oath of loyalty or with investors from the North. They would be paid wages and guaranteed access to schools, and corporal punishment would be prohibited, but they could not leave the plantations without permission of their employers.

Inaugurated in Louisiana, this system of "compulsory free labor" was extended to the entire Mississippi Valley, the home of over half a million slaves, after the Union capture of Vicksburg in 1863. A halfway house between slavery and freedom, the system satisfied no one. Planters disliked not being able to use the whip to enforce discipline, and complained that the former slaves were unruly and refused to obey orders. The freedpeople, for their part, resented being forced to work for white employers, often their former owners, rather than being allowed access to land.

Only occasionally did glimmerings of a different policy appear. In 1863, Gen. Ulysses S. Grant directed that Davis Bend, which contained the plantations of Confederate president Jefferson Davis, be set aside for the settlement of freedpeople. By 1865, Davis Bend had become a remarkable example of self-reliance, with successful cotton farming, a series of schools, and its own system of government.

Early in 1865, a new dimension to the questions of land and labor was added by Gen. William T. Sherman. After capturing Savannah at the conclusion of his famous march to the sea, Sherman met with a group of the city's black leaders. The best guarantee of freedom, they told him, was "to have land, and turn it and till it by our own labor." Four days later, Sherman issued Field Order No. 15, setting aside the Sea Islands and a portion of the South Carolina and Georgia coasts, extending thirty miles inland, for black settlement. Each family would receive forty acres of land, and Sherman later provided that the army could loan them mules. (Thus the phrase "forty acres and a mule," which would echo throughout the South.) By June, some 40,000 freedpeople had been settled on 400,000 acres of "Sherman land."

In the spring of 1865, as the Civil War drew to a close, it was apparent that the federal government had not yet worked out its Reconstruction policy. In March, in his second inaugural address, Lincoln called on the nation to bind up its wounds "with malice toward none and charity toward all." But leniency to whites, for Lincoln, did not mean abandoning concern for the rights of blacks. In his last speech, just a few days before his assassination, the president endorsed the idea of limited black suffrage for the Reconstruction South. He singled out former soldiers and those with some education as particularly deserving of the right to vote. This was the first time an American president had called for granting African Americans suffrage, and it illustrated the capacity for growth that had always been the hallmark of Lincoln's leadership.

The Meaning of Freedom

Critical to the debate over Reconstruction were the complex reactions of Southerners, black and white alike, to the end of slavery. That event led inevitably to conflict between blacks seeking to bring substantive meaning to their freedom and planters seeking to retain as much as possible of the old order. Rather than being a predetermined category or static concept, "freedom" itself became a terrain of conflict during Reconstruction, its definition open to different, often contradictory

If the Negro be a soul, if the woman be a soul, apparelled in flesh, to one master only are they accountable.

MARGARET FULLER
THE GREAT LAWSUIT: MAN VERSUS MEN, WOMAN VERSUS WOMEN, IN *THE DIAL,*
JULY 1843

See also
Ku Klux Klan

THE FREEDMEN'S BUREAU

The Origins of "Forty Acres and a Mule"

After the Civil War, many freedmen expected the federal government to provide them with enough land (forty acres) to establish themselves as independent farmers. This, they felt, was owed to them as restitution for their past labor. The hope for land redistribution sprung from a number of sources, including the wartime experiments at the Sea Islands of South Carolina and at Davis Bend. Expectations were also sparked by Union Gen. William T. Sherman's victorious march through Georgia. On January 12, 1865, Sherman and Secretary of War Edwin Stanton met with twenty leaders of the black community in Savannah, Ga. Four days after the meeting, Sherman issued Special Field Order No. 15, which set aside a thirty-mile portion of the low-country rice coast from South Carolina to Georgia for settlement by blacks. Families of freedmen would receive forty acres and, possibly, the loan of a mule—many historians claim this to be the origin of the phrase. Further indication that the government would assist blacks in their effort to become independent farmers came with the formation of the Freedmen's Bureau in March 1865. Along with distributing food and clothing, the bureau was authorized to divide abandoned and confiscated land into forty-acre plots for rental to freedmen and loyal refugees. Complicating these efforts was the fact that the federal government's legal title to southern land was still not clear.

In the summer of 1865, President Andrew Johnson ordered land in federal hands to be returned to former owners. Thaddeus Stevens, Charles Sumner, and other Radical Republican congressmen tried to pass a bill upholding the Sherman land titles; however, it was vetoed by Johnson. In July 1866 Congress ratified another attempt at land redistribution, with the Southern Homestead Act. Unfortunately, this, too, proved to be of little help to the freedmen. Many blacks had signed long-term restrictive labor contracts, and others were unable to afford the implements, seed, and rations needed to work the land. By mid-1867, Radical Republican congressmen had limited their focus to securing political rights for blacks (in particular the right to vote), rather than sweeping land reform.

The phrase "forty acres and a mule" has been used since the nineteenth century for a number of black causes. It suggests that African Americans deserve restitution for the work of black slaves. More generally, the term suggests empty promises made by the U.S. government and the debt owed to its black citizens.

—WALTER FRIEDMAN

interpretations, its content changing for whites as well as for blacks.

To African Americans, freedom meant independence from white control, autonomy both as individuals and as members of a community that was itself being transformed as a result of emancipation. Blacks relished the opportunity to flaunt their liberation from the innumerable regulations, significant and trivial, associated with slavery. They openly held mass meetings and religious services free of white oversight; they acquired dogs, guns, and liquor (all barred under slavery); they refused to yield the sidewalks to whites. No longer required to obtain a pass from their owners to travel, former slaves throughout the South left the plantations in search of better jobs, family members, or simply a taste of personal freedom. Many moved to southern towns and cities, where, it seemed, "freedom was free-er."

Before the war, free blacks had created a network of churches, schools, and mutual-benefit societies, and slaves had forged a semiautonomous culture centered on the family and church. With freedom, these institutions were consolidated, expanded, and liberated from white supervision.

The family stood as the main pillar of the postemancipation black community. Under slavery, most blacks had lived in nuclear family units, although they faced the constant threat of separation from loved ones by sale. Reconstruction provided the opportunity to solidify their family ties. Freedpeople made remarkable efforts to locate loved ones from whom they had been separated under slavery. One northern reporter in 1865 encountered a freedman who had actually walked more than six hundred miles from Georgia to North Carolina, searching for the wife and children from whom he had been sold away.

Control over their family life was essential to the former slaves' definition of freedom. Many freedwomen, preferring to devote more time to

See also

Slavery

their families, and wishing to be free from the supervision of white employers (which under slavery often led to sexual exploitation), refused to work any longer in the cotton fields. Black parents strenuously resisted efforts by many planters to force their children into involuntary labor through court-ordered apprenticeships, insisting that they, rather than the employer, would decide when children went to school and when they labored in the fields.

At the same time, African Americans withdrew almost entirely from white-controlled religious institutions, where they had been excluded from a role in church governance and had often been required to sit in the back pews during services. The rise of the independent black church, with Methodists and Baptists commanding the largest followings, redrew the religious map of the South. The church played a central role in the black community; a place of worship, it also housed schools, social events, and political gatherings, and sponsored many of the fraternal and benevolent societies that sprang up during Reconstruction. Inevitably, black ministers came to play a role in politics. Over two hundred held public office during Reconstruction.

Another striking example of the freedpeople's effort to breathe meaning into freedom was their thirst for education. Before the war, virtually every southern state had prohibited the instruction of slaves. Now, adults as well as children thronged the schools established during and after the Civil War. Northern benevolent societies, the Freedmen's Bureau, and, after 1868, state governments provided most of the funding for black education, but the initiative often lay with African Americans, who pooled their meager resources and voluntarily taxed themselves to purchase land, construct buildings, and hire teachers.

The desire for autonomy and self-improvement also shaped African Americans' economic definition of freedom. Blacks wished to take control of the conditions under which they labored and to carve out the greatest degree of economic independence. Most refused to work any longer in gangs under the direction of an overseer, and generally preferred renting land to working for wages. Above all, economic freedom meant owning land of their own. In some parts of the South, blacks in 1865 seized abandoned land, or refused to leave plantations, insisting that the property belonged to them. Many expected the federal government to guarantee them access to land.

If the goal of autonomy inspired African Americans to withdraw from social institutions controlled by whites, and attempt to work out their economic destinies by themselves, in political life "freedom" meant inclusion rather than separation. Recognition of their equal rights as citizens quickly emerged as the animating impulse of black politics. Throughout 1865, blacks organized mass meetings, parades, petitions, and conventions demanding equality before the law and the right to vote. The end of slavery, they insisted, enabled America for the first time to live up to the full implications of its democratic creed by abandoning racial proscription and absorbing blacks fully into the civil and political order.

If former slaves saw Reconstruction as heralding a new era of autonomy and equality, most southern whites reacted to military defeat and emancipation with dismay. Needing to borrow money to resume farming, many small farmers fell into debt and were forced to take up the growing of cotton. By the mid-1870s white farmers, who had cultivated only one-tenth of the South's cotton crop in 1860, were growing 40 percent, and many who had owned their land were tenants.

Planter families also faced profound changes in the aftermath of the war. In a sense, the most arduous task facing former slave owners was adjusting to the world of free labor. Planters understood that the questions of land and labor were intimately interrelated. Many were convinced, a northern visitor reported, that "so long as they retain possession of their lands they can oblige the negroes to work on such terms as they please." Between the planters' need for a disciplined labor force and the freedpeople's quest for autonomy, conflict was inevitable. Blacks, planters complained, insisted on setting their own hours of labor, worked at their own pace, and insisted on the right to conduct their personal lives as they saw fit.

With such polarized forces at work, it fell to the Freedmen's Bureau to attempt to mediate between the contending parties. The bureau's myriad responsibilities included establishing schools for freedmen, adjudicating disputes among blacks and between the races, and attempting to secure for blacks and for white Unionists equal justice from southern courts. Much to the bureau's activity, however, centered on overseeing the transition from slave to free labor.

Some bureau officials believed that the former slaves had to sign labor contracts and go back to work on the plantations. Others—such as Gen. Rufus Saxton, who directed the agency's activities in South Carolina in 1865—sympathized strongly with blacks' aspiration to own land. In

*Free at last!
Free at last!
Thank God
Almighty, we are
free at last!*

MARTIN LUTHER KING, JR.
TO CONCLUDE HIS SPEECH AT
THE LINCOLN MEMORIAL
IN THE MARCH ON
WASHINGTON IN 1963

R

After the Civil War, lynching became a systematic feature of the southern system of white supremacy.

PAGE 437

See also
Slave Trade

the summer of 1865, however, President Andrew Johnson, who had succeeded Lincoln, ordered land in federal hands returned to its former owners. A series of confrontations followed, notably in South Carolina and Georgia, where blacks were forcibly evicted from the land they had been settled on by Sherman. In the end, the vast majority of rural freedpeople remained propertyless and poor, with no alternative but to work as laborers on white-owned plantations. The Freedmen's Bureau attempted to ensure that labor contracts were equitable, and that the former slaves were free to leave their jobs once the contracts had expired. But the ideal of forty acres and a mule was dead. The result was a deep sense of betrayal, which survived among the freedpeople and their descendants long after the end of Reconstruction.

Out of the conflict on the plantations, and with black landownership all but precluded, new systems of labor emerged in the different regions of the South. Sharecropping came to dominate the cotton South and much of the tobacco belt of Virginia and North Carolina. In the Louisiana sugar region, an influx of northern capital allowed for the repair of equipment and the resumption of production. Gang labor survived the end of slavery, with blacks working for wages and allowed access to garden plots to grow their own food. In the rice kingdom of coastal South Carolina and Georgia, planters were unable to acquire the large amounts of capital necessary to repair irrigation systems and threshing machinery destroyed by the war, and blacks continued to demand access to land they had occupied in 1865. In the end, the plantations in this region fell to pieces, and blacks were able to acquire land and take up self-sufficient farming.

The Politics of Presidential Reconstruction

To Andrew Johnson fell the task of overseeing the restoration of the Union. Johnson was ill suited for the responsibilities he now shouldered. A lonely, stubborn man, he was intolerant of criticism and unable to compromise. He lacked Lincoln's political skills and keen sense of northern public opinion. Moreover, while Johnson had supported emancipation during the war, he held deeply racist views. A self-proclaimed spokesman for the poor white farmers of the South, he condemned the old planter aristocracy, but believed African Americans had no role to play in Reconstruction.

With Congress out of session until December, Johnson in May 1865 outlined his plan for reunit-

ing the nation. He issued a series of proclamations that inaugurated the period of Presidential Reconstruction (1865–1867). Johnson offered a pardon to all southern whites, except Confederate leaders and wealthy planters (and most of these soon received individual pardons) who took an oath of allegiance. He also appointed provisional governors and ordered conventions held, to which delegates were elected by whites alone. Apart from the requirement that they abolish slavery, repudiate secession, and abrogate the Confederate debt, the new governments were granted a free hand in managing their affairs.

The conduct of the southern governments elected under Johnson's program turned most of the Republican North against the president. White voters by and large returned members of the old elite to power. Alarmed by the apparent ascendancy of "rebels," Republicans were further outraged by reports of violence against former slaves and against northern visitors in the South. But what aroused the most opposition were laws of the new southern governments that attempted to regulate the lives of the former slaves. Known as the Black Codes, these did grant the freedpeople certain rights, such as owning property and suing in court. African Americans could not, however, testify against whites, serve on juries or in state militias, or vote.

Responding to planters' demands that the freedpeople be forced back to work on the plantations, the Black Codes required blacks to sign yearly labor contracts. The unemployed were declared vagrants, and could be arrested, fined and hired out to white landowners. Some states limited the occupations open to blacks and tried to prevent them from acquiring land. African Americans strongly resisted the implementation of these measures, and the apparent inability of the white South's leaders to accept the reality of emancipation fatally undermined northern support for Johnson's policies.

When Congress assembled in December 1865, Johnson announced that with loyal governments functioning in all the southern states, Reconstruction was over. In response, Radical Republicans, who had grown increasingly estranged from Johnson during the summer and fall, called for the establishment of new governments with "rebels" excluded from power and black men granted the right to vote.

Most Republicans, however, were moderates, not Radicals. They believed Johnson's plan flawed but desired to work with the president in modifying it, and did not believe that either southern or northern whites would accept black suffrage. Radicals and moderates joined together in refusing to seat the Southerners recently elected to Congress. Early in 1866, Sen. Lyman Trumbull of Illinois proposed two bills, reflecting the moderates' belief that Johnson's policy required modification. The first extended the life of the Freedmen's Bureau, which had been established for only one year. The second, the Civil Rights Bill, defined all persons born in the United States as citizens and spelled out rights they were to enjoy without regard to race—making contracts, bringing lawsuits, and enjoying "full and equal benefit of all laws and proceedings for the security of person and property." The bill left the new southern governments in place, but required them to accord blacks the same civil rights as whites. It made no mention of the right to vote.

Passed by overwhelming majorities in both houses of Congress, the Civil Rights Bill represented the first attempt to define in legislative terms the essence of freedom and the rights of American citizenship. In empowering the federal government to guarantee the principle of equality before the law, regardless of race, against violations by the states, it embodied a profound change in federal-state relations.

To the surprise of Congress, Johnson vetoed both bills. Both, he said, threatened to centralize power in the national government and deprive the states of their authority to regulate their own affairs. Moreover, he believed, blacks did not deserve the rights of citizenship. The vetoes made a complete breach between Congress and the president inevitable. In April 1866, the Civil Rights Bill became the first major law in American history to be passed over a presidential veto.

Johnson had united moderate and Radical Republicans against him. Congress now proceeded to adopt its own plan of Reconstruction. In June 1866, it approved the Fourteenth Amendment, which broadened the federal government's power to protect the rights of all Americans. It forbade states from abridging the "privileges and immunities" of American citizens or depriving any citizen of the "equal protection of the laws." In a compromise between Radical and moderate positions on black suffrage, it did not expressly give blacks the right to vote, but threatened to reduce the South's representation in Congress if black men continued to be denied the ballot. The amendment also empowered Congress to take further steps to enforce its provisions.

The most important change in the Constitution since the adoption of the Bill of Rights, the Fourteenth Amendment established equality before the law as a fundamental right of American citizens. It shifted the balance of power within the nation by making the federal government, not the states, the ultimate protector of citizens' rights. The Fourteenth Amendment, and the congressional policy of guaranteeing civil rights for blacks, became the central issue of the political campaign of 1866. Riots that broke out in Memphis and New Orleans, in which white policemen and citizens killed scores of blacks further undermined public support for Johnson's policies.

In the northern congressional elections, Republicans opposed to Johnson's policies won a sweeping victory. Nonetheless, every southern state but Tennessee, egged on by Johnson, refused to ratify the Fourteenth Amendment. The intransigence of Johnson and the bulk of the white South pushed moderate Republicans toward the proposals of the Radicals. In March 1867, over Johnson's veto, Congress adopted the Reconstruction Act, which divided the South into five military districts, temporarily barred many Confederates from voting or holding office, and called for the creation of new governments in the South with suffrage no longer restricted because of race.

The conflict between President Johnson and Congress did not end with the passage of the Reconstruction Act. In 1868 the House of Representatives impeached the president for violating the Tenure of Office Act of 1867, and the Senate came within a single vote of removing him from office. Shortly thereafter, the Republicans nominated Ulysses S. Grant as the party's presidential candidate. Reconstruction was the central issue of the 1868 campaign. Democrats denounced it as unconstitutional, and condemned black suffrage as a violation of America's political traditions. Grant's victory was a vindication of Republican Reconstruction, and it inspired Congress to adopt the era's third constitutional amendment. In February 1869, Congress approved the Fifteenth Amendment, prohibiting the federal and state governments from depriving any citizen of the right to vote because of race.

Although it left the door open to suffrage restrictions not explicitly based on race—literacy tests, property qualifications, poll taxes—and did nothing to extend voting rights to women, the Fifteenth Amendment marked the culmination of four decades of agitation on behalf of the slave. As late as 1868, only eight northern states had allowed black men to vote. "Nothing in all history," exclaimed veteran abolitionist William Lloyd Garrison, equaled "this wonderful, quiet, sudden

Hold fast to dreams for if dreams die, life is a broken bird that cannot fly.

LANGSTON HUGHES

*The most influential
publication for the
future of African-
American literature
was W.E.B. Du
Bois's epochal*
The Souls of Black
Folk *(1903).*

PAGE 417

transformation of four millions of human beings from . . . the auction-block to the ballot-box."

Radical Reconstruction in the South

Among the former slaves, the coming of black suffrage in 1867 caused an outburst of political organization. Determined to exercise their new rights as citizens, thousands joined the Union League, an organization closely linked to the Republican party, and the vast majority of eligible African Americans registered to vote. "You never saw a people more excited on the subject of politics than are the Negroes of the South," wrote a plantation manager.

By 1870, all the former confederate states had been readmitted to the Union, nearly all under the control of the Republican party. Their new constitutions, drafted in 1868 and 1869 by the first public bodies in American history with substantial black representation (of about 1,000 delegates throughout the South, over one-quarter were black), represented a considerable improvement over those they replaced. They made the structure of southern government more democratic, modernized the tax system, and guaranteed the civil and political rights of black citizens. A few states initially barred former Confederates from voting, but this policy was quickly abandoned by the new state governments.

Throughout Reconstruction, black voters provided the bulk of the Republican party's support. Although Democrats charged that "Negro rule" had come to the South, nowhere did blacks control the workings of state government, or hold office in numbers equal to their proportion of the total population (which ranged from about 60 percent in South Carolina to around one-third in Arkansas, North Carolina, Tennessee, and Texas). In nearly every state, whites (the much-maligned "carpetbaggers" and "scalawags") controlled the machinery of the Republican party and all but monopolized the top offices—governor, U.S. senator, and major patronage positions. Nonetheless, the fact that well over fifteen hundred African Americans occupied positions of political power in the Reconstruction South represented a stunning departure from past American government.

During Reconstruction, African Americans were represented at every level of government. Fourteen sat in the House of Representatives, and two, Hiram Revels and Blanche K. Bruce, represented Mississippi in the Senate. P. B. S. Pinchback of Louisiana served briefly as America's first black governor. Other blacks held major state

executive positions, including lieutenant governor, treasurer, and superintendent of education. Nearly 700 sat in state legislatures during Reconstruction, and there were scores of black local officials, ranging from justice of the peace to sheriff, tax assessor, and policeman. The presence of black officeholders and their white allies made a real difference in southern life, ensuring that those accused of crimes would be tried before juries of their peers, and enforcing fairness in such prosaic aspects of local government as road repair, tax assessment, and poor relief.

Many of these officeholders had been born free, and around fifty had gained their liberty before the Civil War by manumission, purchase, or escape. In South Carolina and Louisiana, homes of the South's wealthiest and best-educated free black communities, most prominent Reconstruction officeholders had never experienced slavery. A number of black officials had come from the North after the Civil War. But the majority were former slaves who had established their leadership in the black community by serving in the Union army, working as ministers, teachers, or skilled craftsmen, or engaging in Union League organizing.

Given the fact that many of the Reconstruction governors and legislators lacked previous experience in government, their record of accomplishment is remarkable. In many ways, Reconstruction at the state level profoundly altered traditions of southern government. The new governments established the region's first state-supported public school systems, as well as numerous hospitals and asylums for orphans and the insane. These institutions were provided for both blacks and whites, although they were generally segregated by race. Only in New Orleans were the public schools integrated during Reconstruction, and only in South Carolina did the state university admit black students (elsewhere, separate colleges were established for blacks). By the 1870s, in a region whose prewar leaders had made it illegal for blacks to learn and had done little to promote education among poorer whites, over half the children were attending public schools.

In assuming public responsibility for education, Reconstruction governments in a sense were following a path blazed by the North. Their efforts to guarantee African Americans equal treatment in transportation and places of public accommodation, however, launched them into an area all but unknown in American law. Racial segregation—or, indeed, the complete exclusion of

See also
Slave Narratives

blacks from both public and private facilities—was widespread throughout the country. Black demands for the outlawing of such discrimination produced deep divisions in the Republican party. But in the Deep South, where blacks made up the vast majority of the Republican voting population, laws were enacted making it illegal for railroads, hotels, and other institutions to discriminate on the basis of race. Enforcement of these laws varied considerably by locality, but Reconstruction established for the first time at the state level a standard of equal citizenship.

Republican governments also took steps to assist the poor of both races, and to promote the South's economic recovery. The black codes were repealed, the property of small farmers protected against being seized for debt, and the tax system revised to shift the burden from propertyless blacks to planters and other landowners. Little was done, however, to assist the former slaves in acquiring land. Only South Carolina took effective action, establishing a commission to purchase land for resale on long-term credit to poor families. In general, African-American officeholders tended to place more emphasis on issues relating to civil rights than on the land hunger of the black community.

Rather than on land distribution, the Reconstruction governments pinned their hopes for southern economic growth and opportunity for African Americans on a program of regional economic development. Every state affected by Reconstruction helped to finance the building of railroads, and through tax reductions and other incentives tried to attract northern manufacturers to invest in the region. The program had mixed results. A few states witnessed significant new railroad construction between 1868 and 1872, but economic development in general still remained weak.

Thus, to their supporters, the governments of Radical Reconstruction presented a complex pattern of achievement and disappointment. The economic vision of a modernizing, revitalized southern economy failed to materialize, and most African Americans remained locked in poverty. On the other hand, biracial democratic government, a thing unknown in American history, for the first time functioned effectively in many parts of the South. The conservative oligarchy that had run the South from colonial times to 1867 found itself largely excluded from political power, while those who had previously been outsiders—poorer white Southerners, men from the North, and es-

pecially former slaves—cast ballots, sat on juries, and enacted and administered laws.

The Overthrow of Reconstruction

The South's traditional leaders—planters, merchants, and Democratic politicians—bitterly opposed the new governments, denouncing them as corrupt, inefficient, and embodiments of wartime defeat and "black supremacy." There was corruption during Reconstruction, but it was confined to no race, region, or party. Frauds that existed in some southern states, associated primarily with the new programs of railroad aid, were dwarfed by those practiced in the same years by the Whiskey Rings, which involved high officials of the Grant administration and by New York's Tweed Ring, whose depredations ran into the tens of millions of dollars.

The rising taxes needed to pay for schools and other new public facilities, and to assist railroad development, were another cause of antagonism to Reconstruction. The most basic reason for opposition, however, was that most white Southerners could not accept the idea of former slaves voting, holding office, and enjoying equality before the law. Reconstruction, they believed, had to be overthrown in order to restore white supremacy in southern government, and to ensure planters a disciplined, reliable labor force.

In 1869 and 1870, Democrats joined with dissident Republicans to win control of Tennessee

WORSE THAN SLAVERY

This cartoon by Thomas Nast appeared in Harper's Weekly *in 1874.*
PRINTS AND PHOTOGRAPHS DIVISION, LIBRARY OF CONGRESS

and Virginia, effectively ending Reconstruction there. Elsewhere in the South, however, with Reconstruction governments securely entrenched, their opponents turned to a campaign of widespread violence in an effort to end Republican rule. In wide areas of the South, Reconstruction's opponents resorted to terror to secure their aim of restoring Democratic rule and white supremacy. Secret societies sprang up, whose purposes were to prevent blacks from voting and to destroy the infrastructure of the Republican party by assassinating local leaders and public officials.

The most notorious such group was the Ku Klux Klan, an organization of terrorist criminals that in effect served as a military arm of the Democratic party. Led by planters, merchants, and Democratic politicians, the Klan committed some of the most brutal acts of violence in American history. During the 1868 presidential election, Klansmen in Georgia and Louisiana established a reign of terror so complete that blacks were unable to go to the polls to vote, and Democrats carried both states.

Grant's election did not end the Klan's activities; indeed, in some parts of the South they accelerated in 1869 and 1870. The Klan singled out for assault Reconstruction's local leadership. White Republicans—local officeholders, teachers, and party organizers—were often victimized, but blacks bore the brunt of the violence. One black leader in Monroe County, Mississippi, had his throat cut because he was "president of a republican club" and was known as a man who "would speak his mind." In York County, S.C., where nearly the entire white male population joined the Klan (and women participated by sewing the robes the Klansmen wore as disguises), the organization committed eleven murders and hundreds of whippings.

Occasionally, violence escalated from attacks on individuals to wholesale assaults on the local African-American community. Institutions such as black churches and schools, symbols of black autonomy, frequently became targets. In Meridian, Miss., in 1871, some thirty blacks were murdered in cold blood, along with a white Republican judge. At Colfax, La., two years later, scores of African-American militiamen were killed after surrendering to armed whites who were intent on seizing control of the local government.

When the new southern governments proved unable to restore order or suppress the Klan, Congress in 1870 and 1871 adopted three Enforcement Acts, outlawing terrorist societies and allowing the president to use the army against

them. These laws continued the expansion of national authority during Reconstruction by defining certain crimes—those aimed at depriving citizens of their civil and political rights—as federal offenses. In 1871, President Grant authorized federal marshals, backed up by troops in some areas, to arrest hundreds of accused Klansmen. After a series of well-publicized trials, in which many of the organization's leaders were jailed, the Klan went out of existence.

Despite the Grant administration's effective response to Klan terrorism, the North's commitment to Reconstruction waned during the 1870s. Many Radical leaders, among them Thaddeus Stevens, had passed from the scene. Within the Republican party, their place was taken by politicians less committed to the ideal of equal rights for blacks. The federal government had freed the slaves, made them citizens, given them the right to vote, and crushed the Ku Klux Klan. Now, it was said, blacks should rely on their own resources, not demand further assistance from the North.

In 1872 a group of Republicans, alienated by corruption within the Grant administration, bolted the party. The Liberal Republicans, as they called themselves, believed that unrestrained democracy, in which "ignorant" voters such as the Irish immigrants of New York City could dominate politics in some locales, was responsible for such instances of corruption as the Tweed Ring. Democratic criticisms of Reconstruction found a receptive audience among the Liberals. As in the North, Liberals believed, the "best men" of the South had been excluded from power while "ignorant" voters controlled politics. The result was corruption and misgovernment. Government in the South should be returned to the region's "natural leaders."

The Liberals nominated Horace Greeley, editor of the New York *Tribune,* to run against Grant in 1872. The Democrats endorsed Greeley as well, and the continuation of Reconstruction became a major issue in the campaign. Grant overwhelmingly won reelection, but the Liberal attack on Reconstruction continued, contributing to a resurgence of racism in the North. Journalist James S. Pike, a leading Greeley supporter, in 1874 published *The Prostrate State,* an influential account of a visit to South Carolina. He depicted a state engulfed by corruption and extravagance, under the control of "a mass of black barbarism." "Negro government," he insisted, was the cause of the South's problems; the solution was to see leading whites restored to political power.

EXODUS TO KANSAS

Exodusters Begin Mass Movement Northward in 1879

The exodusters were about 20,000 southern African Americans who migrated spontaneously to Kansas from Mississippi, Louisiana, Texas, Kentucky, and Tennessee in the spring of 1879 in fear that they would be reenslaved when Democrats consolidated control as Reconstruction ended. The Exodus to Kansas was the most spectacular manifestation of a widespread anxiety among southern freedpeople who sought bodily safety, personal autonomy, and their rights as citizens. They had seen enough of their former masters' conception of freedom to realize they were in danger.

Even before the violent campaigns that ended Reconstruction made hundreds of former slaves into refugees, white supremacists had inflicted frightful injustices upon freedpeople; farming arrangements and credit practices kept black families poor and landless. Political violence subverted attempts to engender meaningful democracy in state that had been run as oligarchies by the rich. The rights to vote, hold office, and send children to school all came under intense pressure—much of it blatantly illegal. The withdrawal of federal support, after the Panic of 1873, signaled to white supremacists that the freedpeople were fair game. Thus began a process, called "Redemption," that wrested control of southern states from blacks and Republicans by any means necessary.

To overthrow Reconstruction, white supremacists used murder, rape, arson, fraud, and intimidation. These terrorist campaigns indicated that after Reconstruction, not only would black men not be able to vote, but black people generally would lose the relative autonomy they had come to identify with freedom. Many blacks saw only one alternative to literal or virtual reenslavement: migration. In the late 1870s, black Southerners began a process of interstate migration that would eventually take one-half of the African-American population out of the South.

Exodusters headed to Kansas, which they knew as the quintessential free state, in hopes of homesteading on free government land and becoming independent farmers. To people who vividly recalled the oppression of slavery, farming their own land meant being their own masters. Although few of the migrants of the Kansas Fever Exodus (as it was called at the time) were able to claim and keep land as homesteaders in the long term, as Kansans they were able to achieve much more economic and political autonomy than they would have in the South. Given that Kansas eventually became a segregated state (one of the five U.S. Supreme Court cases that together are known as *Brown* v. *Board of Education*, which paved the way for the desegregation of American life after 1954, originated in Topeka, Kans.), the Exodus to Kansas was qualified, though a real success.

After Reconstruction, blacks throughout the South sought sanctuary in Kansas, Indiana, and West Africa. The spectacular, millenarian Exodus of 1879 was merely the most visible indication that black Southerners had no faith in the self-designated "wealth and intelligence," the would-be natural leaders of the southern states.

In 1879, black and white observers divided over whether to support the Exodus to Kansas. In general, old abolitionists and radical Republicans of both races supported the exodusters' bid for freedom, but often with reservations. Blacks, especially, approved of migration out of the South, given the facts of political violence and economic exploitation, yet many would have preferred a carefully planned movement with educated leadership. While Henry Highland Garnet, Wendell Phillips, Sojourner Truth, William Lloyd Garrison, George T. Downing, John Mercer Langston, and Richard T. Greener supported the Exodus, the grand old man among black statesmen, Frederick Douglass, was its unbending critic. Douglass had fled Maryland as a fugitive slave in 1838, but by 1879 he had become a high-ranking federal official; he excoriated the Exodusters for acting out of cowardice. Former confederates first denigrated the exodusters as dupes, then attempted to persuade them to come back home and work. In general, the exodusters' supporters were most concerned with what happened to black people. Critics thought in terms of the interests of the South as an economic whole that depended on the very low wage labor of black families who had no political rights.

—NELL IRVIN PAINTER

See also
Sojourner Truth

Other factors also weakened northern support for Reconstruction. In 1873, the country plunged into a severe economic depression. Distracted by national economic problems, Republicans were in no mood to devote further attention to the South. Congress did enact one final piece of civil rights legislation, the Civil Rights Act of 1875, which outlawed racial discrimination in places of public accommodation. This was a tribute to Charles Sumner, who had devoted his career to promoting the principle of equality before the law, and who died in 1874.

Nonetheless, it was clear that the northern public was retreating from Reconstruction. Meanwhile, the Supreme Court began whittling away at the guarantees of black rights Congress had adopted. In the *Slaughterhouse* cases (1873), the Court decreed that the Fourteenth Amendment had not altered traditional federalism; most of the rights of citizens remained under state control. Three years later, in *U.S.* v. *Cruikshank,* the Court gutted the Enforcement Acts by throwing out convictions of some of those responsible for the Colfax Massacre.

By the mid-1870s, Reconstruction was on the defensive. The Depression dealt the South a severe economic blow, and further weakened the possibility that Republicans could create a revitalized southern economy. Factionalism between blacks and whites and between carpetbaggers and scalawags remained a serious problem among southern Republicans. In those states where Reconstruction survived, violence again reared its head, and this time the Grant administration showed no desire to intervene. In contrast to the Klan's activities—which had been conducted at night by disguised men—the violence of 1875 and 1876 took place in broad daylight, as if to flaunt Democrats' conviction that they had nothing to fear from Washington. In Mississippi in 1875, white rifle clubs drilled in public, and Republicans were openly assaulted and murdered. When Gov. Adelbert Ames frantically appealed to the federal government for assistance, President Grant responded that the northern public was "tired out" by southern problems and would condemn any interference from Washington. On election day in 1875, armed Democrats destroyed ballot boxes and drove former slaves from the polls. The result was a Democratic landslide and the end of Reconstruction in Mississippi. "A revolution has taken place," wrote Ames, "and a race are disfranchised—they are to be returned to . . . an era of second slavery."

Similar events took place in South Carolina in 1876. Here, where blacks made up 60 percent of the population, Democrats nominated for governor Wade Hampton, one of the state's most popular Confederate veterans. Hampton promised to respect the rights of all citizens, but his supporters launched a wave of intimidation, with rifle clubs disrupting Republican meetings, and freedmen assaulted and sometimes murdered.

Events in South Carolina directly affected the outcome of the presidential campaign of 1876. To succeed Grant, the Republicans nominated Governor Rutherford B. Hayes of Ohio. His Democratic opponent was New York's governor, Samuel J. Tilden. By this time, only South Carolina, Florida, and Louisiana remained under Republican control. The election was so close that whoever captured these states (and both candidates claimed to have carried them) would become the next president. In January 1877, unable to resolve the crisis on its own, Congress appointed an electoral commission composed of senators, congressmen, and Supreme Court justices. Republicans enjoyed an 8–7 majority on the commission; the members decided that Hayes had carried the disputed southern states, and he was elected.

Democrats, who controlled the House of Representatives, could still obstruct Hayes's inauguration, but after secret discussions with representatives of the incoming president they decided not to do so. This was the famous "Bargain of 1877": Hayes would recognize Democratic control of the remaining southern states and Democrats would not block the certification of his election. Hayes became president, promised to end federal intervention in the South, and ordered United States troops, who had been guarding the statehouses in South Carolina and Louisiana, to return to their barracks (but not to leave the region entirely, as is widely believed). Reconstruction was at an end.

The collapse of Reconstruction deeply affected the future course of American development. The South long remained a bastion of one-party Democratic rule, under the control of a reactionary elite who used the same violence and fraud that had helped defeat Reconstruction to stifle internal dissent. The federal government stood by indifferently as the southern states effectively nullified the Fourteenth and Fifteenth amendments and, beginning in the 1890s, stripped African Americans of the right to vote. By the turn of the twentieth century, southern blacks found themselves enmeshed in a complex system of oppression, each of whose components—segregation, economic inequality, political disempowerment, and the pervasive threat of violence—reinforced the others. Although the black

See also
Memphis, Tennessee

institutions created or strengthened after the Civil War—the family, church, and schools—survived the end of Reconstruction, southern governments fell far behind the rest of the nation in meeting their public responsibilities. Long into the twentieth century, the South would remain the nation's foremost economic problem, a region of low wages, stunted economic development, and widespread poverty. Not until the 1960s would the nation again attempt to come to terms with the political and social agenda of Reconstruction.

—ERIC FONER

REED, ISHMAEL

Ishmael Reed (February 22, 1938–), author. Ishmael Reed was born in Chattanooga, Tenn., but was raised and educated in Buffalo, N.Y. In high school he discovered the writings of Nathanael West, whose black comedy influenced his own distinctive expressionistic style, and later, at the University of Buffalo (1956–1960), he discovered the works of William Butler Yeats and William Blake, who taught him the importance of creating personal mythological systems. In 1962 he moved to New York City to become a writer. While living on the Lower East Side he encountered a group of young black writers, including Calvin Hernton, David Henderson, and Askia Muhammad Toure, from *Umbra* magazine and workshop, who convinced him of the importance of black literature. His first novel, *Free-Lance Pallbearers* (1967), a parody of Ralph Ellison's *Invisible Man,* is a savage satire of the United States during the Vietnam War years, personified by the President, Harry Sam, who literally eats American children.

In 1967, Reed moved to Berkeley, Calif., where he cofounded and published *The Yardbird Reader* (1972–1976), which reflected his new multiethnic spirit, engendered by his move to the multicultural West Coast. His second novel, *Yellow Back Radio Broke-Down* (1969), a surreal western, introduces the theme of the repressive forces of western culture embattled against the life-affirming forces of black culture, which have survived the Middle Passage from Africa to the New World. In this novel Reed presents voodoo religion as a source of authentic black folk culture and values. His next novel, *Mumbo Jumbo* (1972), initiates his countermythology. He argues that there is a conspiracy at the core of the western tradition: Its mythology preaches the glory of the West at the expense of all other cultures. Therefore it is imperative, for Reed, to revise this mythology so that he can expose the lies of the western tradition and affirm the virtues of African civilizations, including Egypt. In later creative works his countermythology, which he usually calls Neo-HooDooism, will draw on many non-European cultures, including Haitian, Black-American, and Native-American. In 1976 Reed cofounded the Before Columbus Foundation, devoted to the dissemination of multicultural literature. *Flight to Canada* (1976), his fifth novel, is a modern slave narrative, defining freedom as the ability to tell one's own story instead of allowing it to be appropriated by alien and hostile cultures. With *Reckless Eyeballing* (1986) Reed continues his exploration of freedom in the explosive area of sexual politics, where he argues against white feminist hegemony. In 1993 he published his ninth novel *Japanese by Spring,* which parodies black neoconservatism and multiethnic abuse of power by the powerful whether they are white, black or yellow.

Even though Reed is known primarily as a novelist, he has produced a number of books of poetry and essays. (He also has had several plays produced, including *Mother Hubbard* (1981) and *Savage Wilds* (1989).) Among his poetry collections are *Conjure* (1972), *Chattanooga* (1974), *A Secretary to the Spirits* (1978), and *New and Collected Poems* (1988). Mostly in free verse, these poems are experimental, humorous, and satiric. In his poetry, as in his fiction, he creates a countermythology, drawing on many non-European cultures for its symbolism. Reed's four books of essays are *Shrovetide in Old New Orleans* (1978), *God Made Alaska for the Indians* (1982), *Writin' Is Fightin': Thirty-Seven Years of Boxing on Paper* (1988), and *Airing Dirty Laundry* (1993). In his essays he tries to refute false and pernicious myths about black people. In recent years he has focused more on black men than on African Americans in general, arguing that they are in a particularly precarious position in American society: that indeed, they are everybody's scapegoat for the evils of the civilization. Reed's impassioned polemics in defense of black men have catapulted him into the center of many heated debates with both black and white feminists. Since all of Reed's works spring from the same individual vision, both the poems and essays help the reader clarify the more significant novels.

Reed is a major innovative writer who relentlessly uses comedy and satire to show the myopia, egotism, and brutality of eurocentric culture. Yet he does not let black culture off scot-free; he criticizes individual blacks when they do not live up

R

See also

Literature

to the ideals of freedom and creativity that he finds inherent in the African-American tradition. His critique of the West is often more subtle and penetrating than that of many scholars and is always much more amusing.

—WILLIAM J. HARRIS

REGGAE

A type of popular music that originated in Jamaica and became successful worldwide, reggae is characterized by a loping yet insistent bass rhythm. Performed largely by black musicians, reggae's appeal in America has traditionally been colorblind, finding favor originally with white listeners and then, more recently, with a core black audience.

Origins

Besides such local musical influences as calypso and mento, reggae has roots in American rhythm and blues, particularly those records made in New Orleans in the 1950s, which Jamaicans enjoyed via U. S. radio broadcasts and on "sound systems," mobile discos where records were played for dancing. To satisfy local demand, competitive sound system promoters such as Duke Reid and Clement Dodd began using primitive equipment to cut their own records, featuring island singers and musicians. Regional playing styles worked a kind of musical alchemy: the local musicians' attempts to simulate American R&B repeatedly came out skewed—they accented the second and fourth beats each measure rather than the first and third. The result, however, was no less appealing to island listeners, and the characteristic reggae rhythm was born. On the first records, released in the early 1960s, this rhythm was accelerated and the music was called "ska," after the scratchy guitar sound which propelled the songs. In subsequent years the rhythm grew slower: at medium tempo, it was called "rock steady"; then, finally, at its slowest, "reggae," after the 1968 release "Do the Reggay" by Toots and the Maytals.

Evolution

As in most popular music, the general term "reggae" actually encompasses many different styles. Two of the most distinctive, "dub reggae" and "deejaying" (also called "toasting"), began to flourish in the late 1960s and early '70s and became synonymous with the music, contributing

significantly to its subsequent success, particularly in America. "Dub" refers to versions of reggae songs that have been doctored in the recording studio with echo and other sounds, records on which the vocal and instrumental tracks drop in and out suddenly and the booming bass and percussion tracks dominate. Originating on the "B" sides of reggae 45s, dub evolved considerably through the efforts of such innovative producers as Lee Perry and Augustus Pablo, who in primitive recording studios transformed existing songs into unusual aural collages.

"Toasting," on the other hand, originated live with sound systems, when disk jockeys began to chant boastfully and rhythmically over records to encourage dancers, imitating the staccato chatter of American radio DJs. While remarkably similar to rap music, toasting actually emerged and was recorded years earlier, the specialty of such flamboyant reggae stars as U-Roy and Big Youth. It has even been speculated that records of toasting reggae DJs, played, sold, and heard in the 1970s in American cities with large concentrations of West Indian immigrants (such as New York City) directly influenced the birth of domestic Rap.

The Rastafarian Influence

Paralleling its musical development, certain reggae lyrics began reflecting specific aspects of Jamaican life and culture. By the late 1960s, besides the songs of sex and romance common to all pop music, reggae performers sang about "rude boys" (local street toughs), the harsh lives of the local underclass, and, most notably, the Rastafarian religious sect. Followers of the sect, called Rastas, wore their uncut hair in thick, matted dreadlocks, smoked marijuana as a sacrament, and revered Emperor Haile Selassie of Ethiopia as a god, because of a prediction attributed to back-to-Africa advocate Marcus Garvey—that a black king, crowned in Africa, would be the Redeemer. Elusively complicated, with roots in mysticism as well as the Bible, Rastafarianism had been present in Jamaica since the 1930s, offering impoverished believers spiritual identity and solace by reaffirming that Africa was their true homeland, and that the captor Babylon (the ruling class or material world) must inevitably fall. Since many Jamaican musicians were Rastafarian, its terminology and beliefs were often incorporated into reggae songs. While uniquely characteristic of the music, reggae's use of Rastafarianism corresponds on a basic level to the message of heavenly deliverance found in American spirituals, and to the earthly transcendence and catharsis provided by the blues.

From Jamaica to the United States

Most of the Americans who discovered reggae in the 1970s were introduced to it in one of two forms. The first, *The Harder They Come,* was a

1972 Jamaican feature film directed by Perry Henzell that starred singer Jimmy Cliff as Ivan Martin, a country boy turned pop star and outlaw. Part comic book and part western, with a perco-

REGGAE

RASTAFARIANS

Movement Provides Religious, Cultural, and Political Vehicle

The Rastafarian movement originated in the early twentieth century in Jamaica as a black nationalist religious phenomenon. However, its influence in the United States has been less religious and more as a cultural vehicle for a more general Afrocentrism, a political critique of colonialism, and a staple of popular music.

The first Rastafarians came together around Christian preachers in Kingston, Jamaica, who were heavily influenced by the teachings of Marcus Mosiah Garvey. Garvey was a Jamaican labor organizer, black nationalist, and founder of the Universal Negro Improvement Association who came to the United States in 1916 to develop a repatriation plan for Africans in the Diaspora. That same year, Garvey predicted the rise of a powerful black king in Africa, citing from the Biblical passage that predicts that "Ethiopia shall soon stretch out her hands unto God" (Psalms 68: 31). When Prince Ras Tafari was crowned king of Ethiopia on November 2, 1930, these Garveyite Christians welcomed his coronation as a fulfillment of Garvey's prophesy. The movement became popular in some of Kingston's poorest neighborhoods among people who welcomed a promised alternative to Jamaican society.

The new king's family name, Ras Tafari (literally "Lion's Head" in the Ethiopian language of Amharic), and his royal title, Haile Selassie ("Might of the Trinity"), became significant religious symbols for these Jamaicans, who began calling themselves Rastafarians. Selassie, employing the traditional symbols and ideological supports for Ethiopian kingship, referred to himself as "the King of Kings, Lord of Lords, Conquering Lion of the Tribe of Judah"—a reference to the coming of the Messiah in the Book of Revelation—and he claimed to be a direct descendant of King Solomon and the Queen of Sheba. To the Rastafarians, this was proof of the divinity of the man they began referring to as Jah Rastari. Haile Selassie's popularity was furthered by his defiant stance in opposing the invasion of his country by Italy during the Italo-Ethiopian War of 1935–1941.

Central to Rastafarian belief are the notions that the legacy of African slavery is a reincarnation of the Biblical narrative of Exodus and that the political, social, and economic structures of Western society constitute "Babylon," the Biblical society of sin and evil that is to burn in a coming Apocalypse. Freedom and redemption for people of African descent, according to them, can only be achieved through repatriation to Africa, or more specifically Ethiopia or "Zion." For some Rastafarians, this means physical repatriation, while others interpret it as a spiritual destination. The influence of Rastafarianism was enhanced by the state visit of Haile Selassie to Jamaica in April 1966.

Rastafarians generally let their hair grow into "dreadlocks"—long, matted tresses worn both in deference to the Nazarite code in the Book of Numbers forbidding the cutting of hair and in partial imitation of the braids worn by some Ethiopian tribal warriors and priests. They openly endorse the smoking of cannabis (marijuana) as a sacrament, believing that the trancelike state induced by its ritual use creates a communion with God. The colors of the Ethiopian flag—red, gold, and green—are significant to Rastafarians, who don the color in knitted caps or "tams," belts, and badges. Rastafarians are also vegetarian and shun food that is processed or cooked with salt, a process known as "I-tal," and stress the eating of fruits and drinking of homemade juices.

In the late 1960s and early 1970s, Rastafarian culture began gaining popularity among "rude boys," rebellious youth in Kingston's ghettos. However, this was often adopted more as a style by these youths, who grew dreadlocks and danced to the increasingly Rasta-influenced Jamaican popular music, Reggae. Referred to as "dreads," some of these young Jamaicans came to the United States in the 1970s to take part in gang warfare over the drug trade and over their allegiances to one of the two major political parties in Jamaica, the People's National Party and the Jamaican Labor Party. Throughout the decade there were a number of shootouts, murders, and bank robberies in the United States, especially in Brooklyn and the Bronx, by Jamaican dreads, giving Rastafarians a reputation among the police for extreme violence.

The Rastafarian movement began gaining adherents among African Americans and others in the United States beginning in the 1970s due to the growing popularity of reggae. Jamaican singer Desmond Dekker had a minor hit in the United States in 1972 with the American release of the 1968 song "Israelites," and the next year the film *The Harder They Come* was released, which depicted the ghettos of Kingston, Jamaica, and urban Rastafarian culture there. Reggae musicians such as Bob Marley and the Wailers and Peter Tosh toured the United States repeatedly during that decade, breathing new cultural life into black nationalism while turning dreadlocks into both a political and cultural statement.

In 1990 Rastafarians in the United States received exposure when the U.S. Supreme Court upheld the right of religious expression for Rastafarians, ruling that Rastafarians could not be required to cut their hair in prison. In 1994, Miami, Fla., was host to the International Nyahbinghi Gathering (*nyahbinghi* is Swahili for "Death to white oppressors and their black allies"), a Rastafarian meeting that brought more than 200 delegates from several countries.

—WINSTON THOMPSON

lating reggae sound track, the film found a niche at midnight showings in college towns and art cinemas around the country, where it ran for several years, giving domestic viewers a vibrant first glimpse of the gritty, vibrant world of Jamaican pop. At about the same time, Americans also discovered reggae in the person of Bob Marley and the Wailers. In a career that extended from 1964 until his death from cancer in 1981, Marley was the key individual in the popularization of reggae. Through his many brilliant albums of protest and love songs (including *Catch a Fire, Natty Dread,* and *Exodus*) and his highly charged concert tours, the singer-songwriter became the face, voice, and symbol of reggae for most of the world.

The Changing American Audience

Ironically, reggae's core audience in America was at first comprised largely of white rock fans, who responded to its exoticism, its rocklike drive, and its messages of alienation. They had also heard it first: reggae's earliest inroads beyond Jamaica had been via rock-oriented radio, first in the guise of novelties like the ska song "My Boy Lollipop" or the rock-steady classic "Israelites," hits during the 1960s, and later as audible influences in the work of such premier rock artists as Paul Simon and Eric Clapton. Rock's fascination with reggae reached an apex in the late 1970s, with the international emergence of the new wave-punk rock movement. While many punks voiced solidarity with the inflammatory and apocalyptic aspects of Rastafarianism, reggae's influence was most audible in the new-style rock, which adopted many of its rhythms and recording techniques, especially dub.

In the 1980s and '90s, reggae's black audience in the United States began to increase sizably, due in part to the country's escalating West Indian immigrant population and also to a growing interest in the Afrocentric ideals the music often expresses and reflects. But the primary reason for reggae's catching on with African-American listeners is a musical one: the dominance on the charts of "dancehall style," fast-talking toasting that rose concurrently and intersects considerably with rap music, spawning such intercultural stars as Shabba Ranks.

As reggae's audience shifts and grows, developments in the music have paralleled those in other forms of pop—traditional instrumentation, for instance, has been increasingly replaced by electronic keyboards and percussion. Nevertheless, reggae's widespread popularity in America seems secure, buoyed by the growing interest in all international musics (called "World Beat") that it anticipated.

—BUD KLIMENT

RHYTHM AND BLUES

The term *rhythm and blues* was a product of the post-World War II music industry's effort to find a new word to replace the category that had been known for several decades as "race records." First used by *Billboard* magazine in 1949, rhythm and blues was intended to describe blues and dance music produced by black musicians for black listeners, so that rhythm and blues—often abbreviated to R&B—was more a marketing category than a well-defined musical style. In effect, R&B reflected the confluence of jazz, Blues, Gospel, and vocal harmony group music that took place in cities such as New York, Detroit, Chicago, Memphis, Philadelphia, and New Orleans after World War II. In the 1950s successful marketing efforts that targeted white listeners made rhythm and blues, and the related category of rock and roll, the most popular music not only in the United States but in the rest of the world as well. Although much rhythm and blues music was produced by small, white-owned record labels such as Savoy, Atlantic, and Chess—in the 1960s Motown would be an exception—and was aimed at a multiracial market, rhythm and blues has always drawn its core influences from African-American culture.

The Roots of Rhythm and Blues: Jazz

The most obvious ancestor of rhythm and blues was jazz, which in the 1920s and '30s was black America's popular music, produced mostly to accompany dancing. In the 1940s many big bands featured "honking" tenor saxophonists who played in a bluesy, at times histrionic style that drove dancers to ever more frenzied steps and tempos. Lionel Hampton's "Flyin' Home" (1943), with its famous solo by Illinois Jacquet (1922–), was the model for such performances. Many tenor saxophonists followed Jacquet's model, including Bill Doggett (1916–), Arnett Cobb (1918–1989), Ike Quebec (1918–1963), Hal "Cornbread" Singer (1919–), and Willis "Gatortail" Jackson (1928–1987). Important recordings in this style include "Juice Head Baby" (1944) and "Deacon's Hop" (1948) by Big Jay McNeely (1929–) and "The Hucklebuck" (1949) by Paul Williams.

Another jazz influence on rhythm and blues was the jump bands that were popular starting in the mid-1940s. These midsized ensembles, named for their buoyant tempos, combined the extroverted solo style of the honking tenors with the relentless momentum of shuffle and boogie-woogie rhythms of pianists Albert Ammons, Meade "Lux" Lewis, and Pete Johnson (1904–1967), whose "Roll 'Em Pete" (1938) with vocalist Big Joe Turner was one of the first great rhythm-and-blues performances. Tiny Bradshaw (1905–1958), Slim Gaillard (1916–1991), and Johnny Otis (1921–1984), the latter a white musician whose bands were largely black, all led jump ensembles. The greatest of the jump band leaders was saxophonist and vocalist Louis Jordan. His biggest hits, including "Is You Is or Is You Ain't My Baby?" (1944), "Let the Good Times Roll" (1945), "Caldonia" (1945), "Choo Choo Ch'Boogie" (1946), and "Saturday Night Fish Fry" (1940), were novelty numbers suffused with earthy humor. Jordan was a masterful saxophonist in the jazz tradition, yet most of his records were carefully composed, and his rejection of jazz improvisation became a major characteristic of rhythm and blues.

In the late 1950s and '60s, the relationship between jazz and rhythm and blues was sometimes reversed, with musicians—especially the pianist Horace Silver, who recorded "Opus de Funk" in 1953—drawing inspiration from rhythm and blues. In the 1960s, Jimmy Smith (1925–), Cannonball Adderley, David "Fathead" Newman (1933–), Eddie Harris (1934–), King Curtis (1934–1971), Stanley Turrentine (1934–), and Ramsey Lewis (1935–) all performed in the bluesy, funky style known as soul jazz. Herbie Hancock, a groundbreaking avant-garde jazz pianist in the 1960s, went on to experiment with funk music in the 1970s and rap in the '80s.

Vocal Groups

The vocal harmonizing groups of the 1940s helped develop the heavily rhythmic backing of passionate vocals that characterize rhythm and blues. Some of these groups were called "doo-wop" groups, after the wordless, nonsense-syllable accompaniments they often sang. The Ink Spots, formed in 1934, were among the earliest important rhythm-and-blues vocal groups, although the group's smooth approach on songs such as "If I Didn't Care" (1939), "To Each His Own" (1946), and "The Gypsy" (1946) was less influential in the development of rhythm and blues than the more heavily rhythmic performances of the Mills Brothers, who had hits with "Paper Doll" (1942) and "You Always Hurt the One You Love" (1944).

After World War II, dozens of important vocal groups, starting with the "bird groups," drew heavily from the gospel tradition and dominated black popular music. Groups such as the Ravens ("Ol' Man River," 1946), the Orioles ("Crying in the Chapel," 1953), The Platters ("Only You," 1955, "The Great Pretender," 1956), the Dominoes ("Sixty Minute Man," 1951), and the Clovers ("Fool, Fool, Fool," 1951; "Good Lovin'," 1953; and "Love Potion Number Nine," 1959), and the 5 Satins ("In the Still of the Night," 1956) used simple arrangements and minimal instrumental accompaniment to highlight their passionate, gospel-style vocals. The Penguins ("Earth Angel," 1954) were notable for their juxtaposition of high falsetto with deep bass voices. The Coasters had a more raucous and humorous style than other doo-wop groups, evidenced on "Riot in Cell Block No. 9" (1954) and "Charlie Brown" (1959). The Drifters were hugely popular throughout the 1950s and early '60s ("Money Honey," 1953; "Save the Last Dance for Me," 1960; "Up on the Roof," 1962; "On Broadway," 1963; and "Under the Boardwalk," 1964).

In the 1950s and '60s impromptu, street-corner doo-wop-style singing was an essential part of African-American urban life. Solo rhythm-and-blues singers who drew on gospel, vocal harmony, and doo-wop traditions were among the most popular recording artists of the era. An early member of the Drifters, Clyde Mcphatter, topped the R&B and pop charts with "Without Love" (1956), "Long Lonely Nights" (1957), and "A Lover's Question" (1958). Jackie Wilson, another falsetto tenor and Drifters' alumnus, had a huge following for his "To Be Loved" (1958), "Lonely Teardrops" (1958), and "Higher and Higher" (1959). Ben E. King (1938–) also worked with the Drifters before recording "Spanish Harlem" (1960) and "Stand by Me" (1960). Frankie Lymon (1942–1968) and the Teenagers achieved great popularity with songs such as "Why Do Fools Fall in Love?" (1956), "The ABCs of Love" (1956), and "I'm Not a Juvenile Delinquent" (1956). A doo-wop group that came to prominence relatively late was Little Anthony Gourdine (1940–) and the Imperials, whose "Tears on My Pillow" was a hit record in 1958.

Gospel music was a direct influence on many important R&B singers. Sam Cooke sang gospel with the Soul Stirrers starting in 1950 and eventually recorded such secular songs as "You Send Me" (1957), "Chain Gang" (1960), and "Another Saturday Night" (1963). Solomon Burke (1936–), who recorded "Just Out of Reach"

Besides such local musical influences as calypso and mento, reggae has roots in American rhythm and blues.

PAGE 590

See also
Blues

(1960) and "Got to Get You off My Mind" (1965), also sang in a gospel-influenced R&B style. The vocals and even the themes of Curtis Mayfield and the Impressions' "I'm So Proud" (1964) and "People Get Ready" (1965) both have strong connections to black sacred music. Al Green, a child gospel sensation later known for soul recordings such as "Let's Stay Together" (1972) and "Take Me to the River" (1973), returned to the church in the late 1970s and has since concentrated solely on gospel music.

Blues

The urban blues styles of the late 1940s and early '50s, with loud, amplified guitars, anguished vocals, and churning rhythms, are also direct descendants of rhythm and blues. Perhaps the best examples of this influence are Muddy Waters, Howlin' Wolf, and B. B. King, all of whom were prominent on the rhythm and blues charts in the 1950s. Bo diddley ("Who Do You Love," 1955; "Bo Diddley," 1955, "I'm a Man," 1955) and Screamin' Jay Hawkins (1929–), who had a 1956 hit with "I Put a Spell on You," represent a less pure blues style that was nonetheless equally influential in creating rhythm and blues. Big Joe Turner, whose "Roll 'Em Pete" with pianist Pete Johnson is considered one of the founding songs of rhythm and blues, was known in the 1950s for his shouting renditions of "Chains of Love" (1951) and "Shake, Rattle and Roll" (1954), both of which are considered classic examples of a time when rock and roll was virtually synonymous with rhythm and blues. Another early rhythm and blues figure was Arthur "Big Boy" Crudup (1905–1974), a guitarist and singer who was popular throughout the 1940s but was best known for writing "That's All Right" (1946), which became a hit for Elvis Presley in 1954.

Along with the Chicago blues style, a different kind of blues, at once more derived from jazz and country music but with the same reliance on electric instruments, exerted a strong influence on early rhythm and blues. T-Bone Walker, a singer and guitarist who successfully negotiated the boundary between blues and jazz on "Stormy Monday" (1945), had several hit rhythm and blues-influenced records in the early 1950s, including "Strolling with Bones" (1950) and "Street Walkin' Woman" (1951). Wynonie Harris (1915–1969), a blues shouter with a strong Louis Jordan influence, wrote "Good Rocking Tonight" and had several hits in the mid-1940s. A mellower approach was represented by Roy Brown (1925–1981), Amos Milburn (1926–1980), and Lowell

RILEY "B.B." KING
Blues Giant

Riley B. "B. B." King (September 16, 1925–), blues singer and guitarist. Born Riley B. King in Itta Bena, Miss., B. B. King grew up on a plantation, working as a farmhand. He sang in choirs at school and church before teaching himself to play the guitar. He moved to Memphis in 1947 and began singing blues in bars. Following a radio appearance with Sonny Boy Williamson (Alex Miller), King began working on Memphis radio station WDIA as "the Pepticon Boy," advertising Pepticon tonic. He later became a disc jockey for WDIA, being billed as "the Blues Boy from Beale Street," gradually becoming "B. B." He began recording in 1949 and had a few local hits. His recording of "Three O'Clock Blues" (1952) was a national hit and allowed him to begin touring the country as a blues singer. By the mid-1960s he had become known as one of the country's greatest blues performers and a leading figure in the urban blues scene, thanks to the praise of many "British invasion" rock musicians, including Eric Clapton and Mick Jagger, who cited his influence. He has continued to record and perform, earning many industry awards, including a Grammy for his 1981 album *There Must Be a Better World Somewhere* and induction into the Rock and Roll Hall of Fame in 1987.

The focus of King's music remains his powerful, commanding voice and guitar playing, through which he maintains an emotional urgency while supporting his performance with a full band. Traditional blues arrangements form the backbone of his songs, featuring prominent call-and-response sequences between the guitar and vocals. His guitar playing is characterized by warm, clear tone and lyrical phrases punctuated by a quick, stinging vibrato.

—DANIEL THOM

Fulson (1921–), whose "Every Day I Have the Blues" (1950) later became B. B. King's signature tune.

An even more restrained, elegant blues vocal style, used by the "Sepia Sinatras," also gained a large following among rhythm and blues audiences in the 1940s and '50s. Nat "King" Cole started out as a jazz pianist but achieved his greatest acclaim as a singer, starting in 1950 with "Mona Lisa." Other singers in this genre included

See also
Aretha Franklin

Cecil Gant (1915–1951) and Charles Brown (1922–).

Ray Charles is often grouped with blues singers, but his synthesis of many early rhythm and blues influences, in particular the melding of sacred and secular black music traditions, is unique. Starting in the mid-1950s, he combined a smooth, almost country singing style on ballads with infectious gospel inflection and solid jazz rhythms on both slow and up-tempo numbers, including "I Got a Woman" (1955), "Drown in My Tears" (1955), "What'd I Say?" (1959), "Georgia on My Mind" (1960), and "Hit the Road, Jack" (1961).

Female blues singers often landed on the rhythm and blues charts in the 1950s. Ruth Brown (1928–), who worked with Lucky Millinder (1900–1966) and Blanche Calloway (1902–1978) in the late 1940s, sang in a jump blues style on "Teardrops from My Eyes" (1950), "Mama He Treats Your Daughter Mean" (1952), and "Wild Wild Young Men" (1954). LaVern Baker (1928–), a niece of the blues singer Memphis Minnie, recorded "Jim Dandy" (1956) and "I Cried a Tear" (1958), both of which were hits on the R&B chart. Etta James, who sang blues on Chess Records, recorded "Something's Got a Hold on Me" in 1962, a song that made her reputation in a rhythm and blues vein. Dinah Washington had considerable success as a jazz singer before entering the rhythm and blues market with records such as "Baby Get Lost" (1949). Washington later crossed over into the pop field with the ballad "What a Difference a Day Makes" (1959).

New Orleans rhythm and blues almost constitutes its own genre, no doubt because of the city's unique confluence of African-American and creole cultures. Fats Domino, whose first hit was "The Fat Man" (1949), became an archetypal crossover success, whose gently rocking voice and piano playing on "Ain't That a Shame" (1955), "Blueberry Hill" (1956), "I'm Walkin'" (1957), "I Hear You Knockin'" (1958), and "I'm Ready" (1959) appealed to a large white audience. Other important New Orleans rhythm and blues musicians include Dave Bartholomew (1920–), Huey "Piano" Smith (1934–), Allen Toussaint (1938–), the Meters, Irma Thomas (1941–), and the Neville Brothers.

Rock and Roll

In the early 1950s, rock and roll—originally a euphemism for sex—was virtually synonymous with rhythm and blues. By the mid-1950s, as more and more white teenagers began to listen to rhythm and blues, the scope of the term *rock and roll* expanded and was primarily applied to white musicians such as Elvis Presley, Buddy Holly (1936–1959), Roy Orbison (1936–1988), or Bill Haley (1925–1981), whose music copied aspects of rhythm and blues styles but was aimed at white audiences. However, black musicians remained crucial to the development of rock and roll even after the term was being applied mostly to white musicians. Chuck Berry, whose country-influenced, bluesy tunes were extraordinarily successful with white audiences, exemplified the adolescent themes, rebellious sound and look, and aggressive guitar playing of early rock and roll. His "Maybellene" (1955), "Johnny B. Goode" (1958), and "Sweet Little Sixteen" (1958) became rock standards almost immediately. This was also true of Little Richard, whose "Tutti Frutti" (1955), "Long Tall Sally" (1956), and "Good Golly Miss Molly" (1958) brought to early rock and roll a frenetic, updated version of New Orleans piano styles. Chuck Berry and Little Richard were enormously influential in England. In fact, the biggest rock groups of the 1960s, including the Beatles and the Rolling Stones, rebelled against the bland, staid sounds of white pop-rockers like Pat Boone and Paul Anka and began their careers by performing mostly cover versions of black rock-and-roll songs. Other rhythm-and-blues musicians who played an important role in the development of rock and roll include Junior Parker (1927–1971), who recorded "Mystery Train" (1953), "Next Time You See Me" (1957), and "Sweet Home Chicago" (1958), as well as Ike Turner (1931–), Jackie Brenston (1930–1979), Big Mama Thornton ("Hound Dog," 1953), the Isley Brothers ("Shout," 1959; "Twist and Shout," 1962), and Chubby Checker ("The Twist," 1960). During the late 1960s, relatively few black musicians remained involved in rock and roll, notable exceptions being Richie Havens and Jimi Hendrix, who had performed as an accompanist with Little Richard, the Isley Brothers, and Ike and Tina Turner before leading a popular rock ensemble.

Soul

By 1964 black popular music had acquired a new name: soul music. There is no clear chronological or stylistic division between rhythm and blues and soul music, but there are some important differences. Soul music displayed a more pronounced gospel influence, whether in up-tempo, unrestrained shouting or in slower, more plaintive

Dizzy Gillespie had a crackling tone and his endless flow of nimble ideas included astonishing runs and leaps into the instrument's highest registers.

PAGE 300

See also
Gospel Music

styles. Furthermore, soul's general rejection of extended instrumental soloing marked the continuing retreat of jazz as the popular music of the black middle class. Finally, even though most soul music consisted of solo singing with vocal backgrounds, the influence of carefully arranged close harmonies also waned.

It is no coincidence that soul flourished alongside the black pride movement. The music was made almost exclusively by blacks, at first almost exclusively for blacks, and was part of a rising black middle-class culture that celebrated black values and black styles in hair and clothing. In addition, soul's secular stance allowed the music to directly confront political issues central to African-American culture in the 1960s. James Brown, who had been a successful recording artist throughout the 1950s and achieved great popularity in the '60s with live performances and recordings of songs such as "I Got You" (1965) and "I

Feel Good" (1965), forever linked soul music and the Black Power Movement with "Say It Loud, I'm Black and Proud" (1968).

Two record companies, Atlantic and Motown, dominated the soul-style rhythm and blues markets starting in the late 1950s and defined two major approaches. Atlantic and its Stax subsidiary often concentrated on funky instrumentals. Wilson Pickett sang with a thrilling gospel feeling on songs such as "In the Midnight Hour" (1965) and "Mustang Sally" (1966). Otis Redding's brief career included "These Arms of Mine" (1962), "I've Been Loving You Too Long" (1965), "Try a Little Tenderness" (1966), and "Sittin' on the Dock of the Bay" (1967). Ballad singer Percy Sledge (1941–) recorded "When a Man Loves a Woman" (1966) for Stax. Sam and Dave specialized in energetic, shouting vocals on hits such as "Hold On, I'm Coming" (1966), "Soul Man" (1967), and "I Thank You" (1968). Booker T. Jones (1944–) and the MG's personified the Memphis rhythm and blues sound on their instrumental hits for the Stax label, including "Green Onions" (1962) and "Hip Hug-Her" (1967). Aretha Franklin reached her prime at Atlantic in the mid-1960s, when her white producer, Jerry Wexler (1917–), encouraged her to return to her gospel roots. She responded by creating perhaps the defining performances of the soul genre. Her majestic, emotional voice made songs such as "I Never Loved a Man the Way I Love You" (1967), "Respect" (1967), "Chain of Fools" (1967), and "Think" (1968) bona fide soul masterpieces.

If Stax and Atlantic musicians cultivated a funky, gritty sound, the founder of Motown, Berry Gordy, encouraged a sweeter sound, one that came to represent the classic soul sound even more than Atlantic or Stax. Those efforts produced dozens of hits during Motown's peak years in the 1960s by figures such as Marvin Gaye, Stevie Wonder, Mary Wells, and Gladys Knight. Important vocal groups included Smokey Robinson and the Miracles, the Jacksons, The Four Tops, The Temptations, and The Supremes.

Atlantic and Motown were by no means the only producers of soul music. Aside from James Brown, perhaps the most important, independent soul musicians of the 1960s were Tina Turner and her husband, Ike Turner, who had led his own groups and backed the blues guitarist Elmore James in the early 1950s. The duo had a string of influential hits in the 1960s, including "A Fool in Love" (1960), "It's Gonna Work Out Fine" (1961), and "River Deep, Mountain High" (1966).

LITTLE RICHARD

Little Richard brought a unique sense of hectic abandon and propulsion to the rock and roll of the 1950s.

AP/WIDE WORLD PHOTOS

TINA TURNER

Known for Strutting Dances and Powerful Voice

Tina Turner (November 26, 1939–), pop singer. Tina Turner was born Anna Mae Bullock in Brownsville, Tenn., where she lived until the age of eleven when her parents separated. As a child she sang and danced with Bootsie Whitelaw, a local trombonist. She lived with her grandmother until the age of sixteen, and then moved to St. Louis to live again with her mother. With her older sister Alline, she frequented night clubs across the river in East St. Louis to see the popular Kings of Rhythm band, led by the rhythm and blues singer, guitarist, producer, and disc jockey Ike Turner. One night Anna Mae took the stage and sang with Turner, and, soon after, she joined the group and went on tour with Ike and the Kings of Rhythm.

In 1960 Ike Turner declared that Anna Mae Bullock would be publicly known as "Tina" and announced that her first lead-vocal debut, "A Fool in Love" (1960), would be credited to Ike and Tina Turner. In 1962 Ike and Tina were married. The couple toured and recorded until 1974 as the "Ike and Tina Turner Revue" which featured Tina with her flamboyant back-up singers and dancers, the Ikettes, accompanied by the Kings of Rhythm. They became one of the foremost rhythm and blues groups of the 1960s, distinguished by Ike's hard-driving accompaniment and Tina's hard-edged singing and seductive dancing. Their most important and popular recordings from the 1960s include "It's Gonna Work Out Fine" (1961) and "River Deep, Mountain High" (1966). A tour of the United States with the Rolling Stones in 1969 launched Ike and Tina Turner into the rock mainstream, and in 1970, they recorded Sly Stone's "I Want to Take You Higher." The next year they won a Grammy Award for "Proud Mary." Their other hits from this period include "Nutbush City Limits" (1973) and "Sweet Rhode Island Red" (1974). In 1974 Tina Turner embarked upon an acting career, starring in the movie version of the Who's rock opera, *Tommy.*

Ike and Tina Turner separated in 1975, with Tina claiming she was the victim of frequent domestic abuse. Their divorce came in 1978, and Tina built her solo career. Her appearances with Rod Stewart and the Rolling Stones led to her signing with Capitol Records in 1983. Her 1984 album *Private Dancer,* including a revival of Al Green's "Let's Stay Together," marked her arrival as a solo performer. Turner won three Grammys for *Private Dancer* (1984) which included, "What's Love Got to Do with It?"

By the mid-1980s Turner had become a major pop singer in her own right, and was famed for her towering mane of hair, revealing costumes, and sexually charged strutting dances. In 1985 she resumed her acting career with the film *Mad Max 3: Beyond Thunderdome* whose soundtrack included her performances of "We Don't Need Another Hero" and the Grammy-winning "One of the Living." After publishing her autobiography, *I, Tina,* in 1986, Turner released *Break Every Rule,* a best-selling album that also won another Grammy. Turner then went on a 145-city tour, parts of which were released as *Tina Live in Europe!* (1988). In 1988, Turner announced that she was retiring from touring to focus on her acting career, but the following year she toured to promote her *Foreign Affair* album (1989). She continues to tour and record and has also remained involved in film, serving as consultant for the feature film *What's Love Got to Do with It?* (1993) which was based on her autobiography.

—KYRA D. GAUNT

In the 1970s, soul-style vocal groups remained popular, although the high lead vocals of the early vocal-harmony groups were backed with sleek, electrified rhythms. These groups included the Chi-Lites, the Stylistics, Harold Melvin (1941–) and the Bluenotes, the O'Jays, Earth, Wind and Fire, and the Spinners. Solo singers in the soul idiom in the 1970s included Roberta Flack, Barry White (1944–), Al Green, and Teddy Pendergrass (1950–), all of whom created slow, emotional ballads and love songs. In the 1980s and '90s, Whitney Houston (1963–) and Luther Vandross (1951–) have continued the tradition of the gospel-influenced singing style that characterizes soul.

Funk

In the mid-to-late 1960s a new style known as "funk," derived from the black vernacular term for anything with a coarse, earthy smell, began to dominate the rhythm and blues charts. James Brown, who had been so influential in the 1950s and early '60s in pioneering soul music, once again broke new ground, this time with stripped-down, forceful rhythms and simple, melodic riffs on "Papa's Got a Brand New Bag" (1965). This

See also

Jazz

Nicknamed "Sassy"
and "the Divine
One," Sarah
Vaughan is
considered one of
America's greatest
jazz vocalists.

PAGE 709

FAITH RINGGOLD

Story Quilts Brought her Acclaim

Faith Ringgold (October 8, 1930–), painter and sculptor. Born in Harlem, Faith Ringgold was one of three children of Andrew Louis Jones, Sr., and Willi Posey Jones, a fashion designer. She was married to Robert Earl Wallace, a pianist, from 1950 to 1956 and had two daughters in 1952: Michele, an author, and Barbara, a linguist. Ringgold graduated from City College, New York, in 1955, and taught art in New York public schools until 1973. In 1959 she received a master's degree, also from City College. She began spending summers in Provincetown, Mass., in 1957, took her first trip to Europe in 1961, and married Burdette Ringgold in 1962.

Ringgold's work and life exemplify her interests in civil rights and feminism. Some of her early paintings, such as *The Flag Is Bleeding* (1967) are large with stylized figures; others are abstract, like *Flag for the Moon, Die Nigger* (1969). Her radical use of potent national symbols, such as the flag and, later, postage stamps and maps, fiercely counterpointed American values with their ingrained racism. To achieve greater recognition for blacks and women in the mainstream art world, Ringgold participated in demonstrations at the Whitney Museum (1968, 1970) and at the Museum of Modern Art (1968). She was a cofounder in 1971 of Where We At, a group of black women artists. The following year she created a mural at the Women's House of Detention in New York that used only images of women.

The women's movement and Ringgold's close relationship with her mother influenced her to begin using fabrics, traditionally a women's medium, to express her art. She began to make masks and dolls—soft sculptures. Her mother made the dolls' clothes. They portray, among others, the Rev. Dr. Martin Luther King, Jr., the murdered children of Atlanta (the Atlanta child murder cases of 1979–1982), and vari-

ous people in the community. Some of Ringgold's paintings were bordered in tankas, cloth frames made by her mother. Ringgold and her mother also collaborated on the production of Sew Real doll kits in 1979.

Ringgold then began working in the medium that brought her acclaim, story quilts. The first, *Who's Afraid of Aunt Jemima?* (1983), is a visual narrative of a woman restaurateur in painting, text, and patchwork. The quilts' stories vividly raise the issues of racism and feminism. As the stories became more complex, Ringgold began to create multiple quilts to encompass them. Each consists of a large painted panel bordered by printed patches pieced together, with text at the bottom. The quilt series are *The Bitter Nest* (1988), *Woman on the Bridge* (1988), and *The French Connection* (1991). Ringgold used one of her quilts as the basis for a children's book, *Tar Beach*, which was a Caldecott Honor Book and received the Coretta Scott King award in 1992. The original quilt was acquired by the Guggenheim Museum.

Ringgold's awards include a grant from the National Endowment for the Arts (1989), Warner Communications' Wonder Woman (1983), and the National Coalition of 100 Black Women's Candace (1986). She holds honorary degrees from Moore College of Art and the College of Wooster, Ohio. A twenty-five-year retrospective of her work traveled between 1990 and 1993. Ringgold has taught at the University of California at San Diego since 1984, spending half the year there. Her designs from *Street Story Quilt* were selected by Judith Lieber for a limited edition of jeweled evening bags. Some of Ringgold's works are in the High, Metropolitan, Newark, and Modern Art museums, as well as in private collections.

—BETTY KAPLAN GUBERT

style was picked up by Sly Stone on "Dance to the Music" (1968), "Everyday People" (1968), "Hot Fun in the Summertime" (1969), and by George Clinton's work with his groups Parliament and Funkadelic in the 1970s. Other R&B musicians who adopted the funk style included Isaac Hayes (1938–), who recorded the soundtrack for *Shaft* in 1971, and Curtis Mayfield, who recorded *Super Fly* in 1972. Disco music by 1970s figures such as Donna Summer (1948–), Gloria Gaynor (1949–), Kool and the Gang, and Rick James

drew directly on funk's interpretation of rhythm and blues.

Although the category of rhythm and blues, created by white music-industry executives to describe a range of musical styles, has undergone dramatic transformations, the term continues to express the essential characteristics of African-American popular music. In the 1980s and '90s, musicians such as Prince (c. 1958–), Lenny Kravitz (1964–), and Living Color have taken inspiration from Little Richard, James Brown, and Jimi Hendrix, while younger musicians such as the group Boyz II Men have updated the close-harmony vocal ensemble sound of the 1940s and '50s. Black popular music—including funk, rock, rap, and pop-gospel ballads—continues to freely borrow and mix jazz, blues, and gospel, validating rhythm and blues as the common ground of modern African-American popular music.

—PETER EISENSTADT AND JONATHAN GILL

ROACH, MAXWELL LEMUEL "MAX"

Maxwell Lemuel "Max" Roach (January 10, 1924–), jazz drummer and bandleader. Born in Elizabeth City, N.C., and raised in Brooklyn, N.Y., Roach studied music as a child with his mother, a gospel singer, and received piano lessons from his aunt. He also received music lessons in public school, and by age ten was playing drums in church bands. He performed in Coney Island sideshows such as *Darktown Follies* while in high school. During this time he also began frequenting Minton's Playhouse in Harlem, where he met some of the leading jazz musicians of the day. In 1941 Roach graduated with honors from Brooklyn's Boys' High School. Soon after, he started performing regularly with Charlie Parker at Clark Monroe's Uptown House in Harlem, and by the next year he had a strong enough reputation to fill in for Sonny Greer for several nights with Duke Ellington's orchestra. In 1943–44 he recorded and performed with Coleman Hawkins at Kelly's Stable as a replacement for Kenny Clarke ("Woody 'n' You," 1944; "Bu-Dee-Daht," 1944). In 1944 he also joined Dizzy Gillespie's quintet at the Onyx Club, becoming a member of the first bebop band to open on 52nd Street, which had become the central location for New York jazz nightclubs. The next year Roach began working with Charlie Parker, an association that would last more than five years. On Roach's first important recording with Parker, the uptempo "Ko-Ko" (1945), Roach has already left swing drumming behind for a bebop style that keeps time on the cymbal, reserving the drums themselves for accents.

Together with Kenny Clarke, Roach redefined the rhythmical and structural architecture of jazz drumming, and created a new solo role for modern jazz drum performance. Initially influenced by the imaginative "melodic" solo style of Sid Catlett, the driving intensity of Chick Webb, and the fluid swing and finesse of Jo Jones, Roach distilled their stylistic characteristics through Clarke's polyrhythmic innovations. By the end of the 1940s, Roach was recognized as one of the leading drummers in jazz. He performed on Miles Davis's "Birth of the Cool" recordings (1949), and on Bud Powell's "Un Poco Loco" (1951). In the early 1950s he continued his prolific career while pursuing studies in composition and tympani at the Manhattan School of Music. From 1954 to 1956 he co-led the Clifford Brown-Max Roach Quintet, which pioneered the hard-driving style known as hard hop (*Study in Brown*, 1955; *At Basin Street*, 1956).

In the 1960s Roach began to combine his music with his politics, with a particular emphasis on racial oppression in both the United States and South Africa. His 1960 recording of *We Insist: Freedom Now Suite* used free-form musical structures, including an emotionally charged interplay between the drummer and his then-wife, vocalist Abbey Lincoln, to explore the theme of racial oppression in America. That work also used West African drumming and Afro-Cuban percussion to draw parallels between slavery in the U.S., segregation, and apartheid in South Africa.

In the 1960s Roach began to move away from appearing solely in strict jazz contexts. He began performing solo drum compositions as independent pieces, an effort dating back to his "Drum Conversation" (1953). He also recorded original works for vocal choruses and pianoless quartets. In the 1960s Roach taught at the Lenox School of Jazz, and in 1972 he assumed a faculty position at the University of Massachusetts, Amherst. Among Roach's most significant work from the 1970s are duet recordings he made with some of the leading figures from the post-bebop avant garde, including Archie Shepp, Anthony Braxton, Abdullah Ibrahim, and Cecil Taylor. In the 1980s, Roach's astoundingly protean career included performances and recordings with a jazz quartet, the percussion ensemble M'Boom, the Uptown String Quartet (with his daughter Maxine on viola), rap and hip hop musicians and dancers. In 1980 Roach recorded an interactive drum solo with a tape recording of the Rev. Dr. Martin Luther King, Jr.'s 1963 "I Have A Dream" speech (*Chattahoochee Red*), and in 1989 he recorded duets with Dizzy Gillespie. Roach, who wrote music as early as 1946 ("Coppin' The Bop"), has in recent years dedicated more and more of his time to composition. His *Shepardsets*, a work for the theater, received an Obie award in 1985, and he has also composed for film and television, and symphony orchestra.

R

Louis Armstrong was the first great improviser in jazz, and his work not only changed that music but all subsequent popular music, vocal and instrumental.

PAGE 35

See also
Motown

Roach, who has lived in New York all of his life, has in recent years been recognized not only as one of the most important drummers in the history of jazz, but as one of the leading African-American cultural figures of the twentieth century, with a decades-long commitment to fighting racial injustice. In addition to the several honorary doctorates he has received throughout his career, in 1988 Roach became the first jazz musician to receive a MacArthur Foundation "genius award."

—ANTHONY BROWN

ROBESON, PAUL

Paul Robeson (April 9, 1898–January 23, 1976), actor, singer, and political activist. Paul Robeson was born in Princeton, N.J., where his father, William Drew Robeson, was the minister of a local Presbyterian church, and his mother, Maria Louisa Bustill, was a schoolteacher. His childhood was happy, but marred by two defining events. His mother died when he was six, after she was accidentally set on fire at home; and his father lost his church following a fierce dispute among his congregation. After working at menial jobs in Princeton, his father moved first to Westfield and then to Somerville, both in New Jersey, where he again led churches affiliated with the African Methodist Episcopal Zion Denomination.

An uncommonly brilliant student and athlete, Paul Robeson entered Rutgers College (later Rutgers University) in New Brunswick in 1916. Although he was the only black student there, he became immensely popular. He was elected to Phi Beta Kappa as a junior and selected twice (1917 and 1918) as an All-American football player by the famed journalist Walter Camp. After graduating in 1919, he moved to Harlem, and in 1920 entered the law school of Columbia University in New York. To support himself he played professional football on weekends, then turned to acting after winning a role in *Simon the Cyrenian* at the Harlem YMCA in 1921.

Graduating from law school in 1923, he was admitted to the bar and served briefly in a law firm. Then, chafing at restrictions on him as a black, and urged on by his wife, Eslanda Cardoza Goode (a fellow student, in chemistry, at Columbia), he left the law for the stage. He enjoyed immediate success, particularly with the Greenwich Village-based Provincetown Players in Eugene O'Neill's *The Emperor Jones* (1923) and *All God's Chillun Got Wings* (1925). In 1925, with his longtime accompanist Lawrence Brown, he launched his celebrated career as an interpreter of African-American spirituals and of folk songs from around the world with a concert of the former in New York. He then traveled to Europe and Great Britain (where in 1922 he had been well received

A TIRELESS VOICE

Paul Robeson used his powerful voice to wow concert audiences and to spread anti-discrimination messages around the world.
AP/WORLD WIDE PHOTO

See also
NAACP

as an individual and as an actor in the play *Voodoo*). Critics hailed his acting in the 1925 London production of *The Emperor Jones*.

In the 1928 London production of Jerome Kern and Oscar Hammerstein II's musical *Show Boat*, his stirring rendition of "Ol' Man River" took his popularity to new heights. Although he triumphed again when *Show Boat* opened in New York in 1930, Great Britain was the scene of many of his greatest achievements. In the following years he starred there in a number of plays, including *Othello* (1930), *The Hairy Ape* (1931), and *Stevedore* (1933). Robeson also had prominent roles in almost a dozen films, such as *Sanders of the River* (1935), *Show Boat* (1936), *King Solomon's Mines* (1935), and *Proud Valley* (1941). In most of these efforts, his depictions of a black man contrasted starkly with the images of subservience, ignorance, criminality, or low comedy usually seen on the Hollywood screen.

Handsome and blessed with a commanding physique and a voice of unusual resonance and charm, Robeson might have capitalized on his stage and screen success and ignored politics altogether. However, his resentment of racism and his attraction to radical socialism, especially after an outstanding welcome in the Soviet Union in 1934, set him on a leftward course. A frequent visitor to the U.S.S.R. thereafter, Robeson learned to speak Russian (and eventually almost two dozen other languages, in which he recorded many songs). His son, Paul, Jr., attended school there for several years. Robeson became a dependable supporter of progressive causes, including the rights of oppressed Jews and of antifascist forces in Spain. In London, he befriended several students and other intellectuals, such as Kwame Nkrumah, George Padmore, and Jomo Kenyatta, who would later be prominent in the anticolonialist movements in Africa.

Resettling in the United States in 1939, Robeson joined enthusiastically in the war effort and maintained his stellar position as an entertainer—although racism, including that on Broadway and in Hollywood, still disturbed him. In 1943, his critically acclaimed portrayal of Othello, in the first Broadway production of Shakespeare's play with an otherwise white cast, created a sensation. He was awarded the NAACP's Spingarn Medal in 1945. He fared less well after the war, when the Cold War intensified. In 1946, he vowed to a special committee of the California State Legislature that he had never been a member of the Communist party. However, when accusations continued, he resolutely refused to cooperate with the authorities. Despite his protests, he was identified as a communist by the House Committee on Un-American Activities. Such opposition hampered his career as a recording artist and actor.

In 1949, in a major controversy, he told a gathering in Paris that it was "unthinkable" to him that African Americans would to go war against the Soviet Union, whose fair treatment of blacks was a rebuke to racist American laws and conventions. Later that year, the announcement of his participation in a musical festival sponsored by liberals and leftists in Peekskill, N.Y., led to rioting in the town that left scores of attendees injured. The next year, the State Department impounded his passport. With Robeson refusing to sign an oath disavowing communism, his singing and acting career in effect came to an end. He was widely ostracized by whites and blacks, except those among the far left.

In 1958, the Supreme Court declared the oath and other government rules unconstitutional. That year, Robeson published *Here I Stand*, which combined autobiography with a considered statement of his political concerns and other beliefs. He sang at Carnegie Hall in what was billed as a farewell concert, and also performed in California. Leaving the United States, he was welcomed as a hero in the Soviet Union, which had awarded him the Stalin Peace Prize in 1952, but he fell ill there. Complaining of chronic exhaustion and other ailments, he entered a series of hospitals in the Soviet Union, Europe, and Britain.

In 1963, when he and his wife returned to the United States, to a home in Harlem, he announced his formal retirement. In 1965, Eslanda Robeson died. With a further deterioration in health, including a nervous breakdown, Robeson moved to Philadelphia to live with his sister. A seventy-fifth birthday celebration at Carnegie Hall in 1973 found Robeson (whose illness kept him away) saluted, in a more liberal age, by prominent blacks, liberals, and socialists as one of the towering figures of the twentieth century. In a message to the gathering, Robeson described himself as "dedicated as ever to the worldwide cause of humanity for freedom, peace, and brotherhood." He died in Philadelphia in 1976.

—ARNOLD RAMPERSAD

ROBINSON, BILL "BOJANGLES"

Bill "Bojangles" Robinson (Luther Robinson) (May 25, 1878–November 25, 1949), tap dancer.

I saw no reason my convictions should change with the weather.

PAUL ROBESON
HERE I STAND, 1958

Like his idol, Paul Robeson, Harry Belafonte combined singing with civil rights activism.

PAGE 86

R

The most famous of all African-American tap dancers, Bill Robinson demonstrated an exacting yet light footwork that was said to have brought tap "up on its toes" from the flat-footed shuffling style prevalent in the previous era. Born Luther Robinson in Richmond, Va., he was orphaned when both his parents, Maria and Maxwell Robinson, died in 1885; he and his brothers were subsequently reared by his grandmother, Bedilia Robinson.

Robinson gained his nickname, "Bojangles"—possibly from the slang term *jangle*, meaning "to quarrel or fight,"—while still in Richmond. It was also in Richmond that Robinson is said to have coined the phrase "Everything's copasetic," meaning "fine, better than all right." He ran away to Washington, D.C., earning nickels and dimes by dancing and singing, and then got his first professional job in 1892, performing in the "pickaninny" chorus (in vaudeville, a chorus of young African-American children performing as backup for the featured performer) in Mayme Remington's *The South Before the War*. When Robinson arrived in New York City around 1900, he challenged tap dancer Harry Swinton, the star dancer in *Old Kentucky*, to a buck-dancing contest, and won.

From 1902 to 1914, Robinson teamed up with George W. Cooper. Bound by the "two-colored" rule in vaudeville, which restricted blacks to performing in pairs, Cooper and Robinson performed as a duo on the Keith and Orpheum circuits. They did not, however, wear the blackface makeup performers customarily used. Robinson, who carried a gold-plated revolver, was a gambler with a quick temper. He was involved in a series of off-stage scrapes; it was allegedly his arrest for assault in 1914 that finally put an end to the partnership with Cooper.

After the split, Robinson convinced his manager, Marty Forkins, to promote him as a soloist. Forkins managed to book him at the Marigold Gardens Theater in Chicago by promising its star and producer, Gertrude Hoffman, Robinson's services as dance instructor; Robinson therewith launched his solo career and eventually became one of the first black performers to headline at New York's prestigious Palace Theatre.

Hailed as "the Dark Cloud of Joy" on the Orpheum circuit, Robinson performed in vaudeville from 1914 to 1927. Onstage, Robinson's open face, flashing eyes, infectious smile, easygoing patter, and air of surprise at what his feet were doing made him irresistible to audiences. His tapping was delicate, articulate, and intelligible. He usually wore a hat cocked to one side, and often exited with a Chaplinesque waddle, or with another signature step, a kind of syncopated "camel walk" (which would later be called the "moon walk" by Michael Jackson). Robinson always danced in split-clog shoes, in which the wooden sole was attached from the toe to the ball of the foot and the rest was left loose, allowing for greater flexibility and tonality. Dancing upright and swinging to clean six-bar phrases, followed by a two-bar break, Robinson set new standards of performance, despite the fact that he invented few new steps.

In 1922, Robinson married Fannie Clay, who became his business manager and secretary. (The marriage was his second: in 1907, he had married Lena Chase, from whom he was divorced in 1922.) After twenty-one years he divorced Fannie and married a young dancer, Elaine Plaines.

Broadway fame came with an all-black revue, *Blackbirds of 1928*, in which he sang "Doin' the New Low Down" while dancing up and down a flight of five steps. Success was immediate: Robinson's performance was acclaimed by the major New York newspapers, and he was heralded by several as the greatest of all tap dancers. The dance Robinson performed in *Blackbirds* developed into his signature "stair dance"; notable for the clarity of Robinson's taps and for its unusual tonalities—each step yielded a different pitch—Robinson's appealing showmanship made it seem effortless. *Brown Buddies* (1930) was kept alive by Robinson's performance, as were *Blackbirds of 1933*, *The Hot Mikado* (1939), *All in Fun* (1940), and *Memphis Bound* (1945). Largely in recognition of his Broadway success, Robinson was named honorary "Mayor of Harlem" by Mayor Fiorello LaGuardia. In 1939, he celebrated his sixty-first birthday by tapping down Broadway, one block for each year.

Robinson turned to Hollywood, a venue largely closed to blacks, in the 1930s. His films included, *Dixiana* (1930), which had a predominantly white cast, and *Harlem Is Heaven* (1933), with an all-black cast. Robinson also appeared in the films *Hooray for Love* (1935), *In Old Kentucky* (1935), *The Big Broadcast of 1937* (1936), *One Mile from Heaven* (1937), *Road Demon* (1938), *Up the River* (1938), *By an Old Southern River* (1941), and *Let's Shuffle* (1941); in a newsreel about the 1939 World's Fair in Chicago, *It's Swing Ho! Come to the Fair;* and in a short, *Broadway Brevities* (1934). But of all his many stage and film performances, those that brought him the most fame were his appearances with child star Shirley Temple, in *The Littlest Colonel* (1935), *The Littlest*

See also
Gregory Hines

Rebel (1935), *Just Around the Corner* (1938), and *Rebecca of Sunnybrook Farm* (1938). In 1943, the all-black film *Stormy Weather,* with Robinson, Cab Calloway, Lena Horne, and Katherine Dunham's dance troupe, met with some success.

A founding member of the Negro Actors Guild of America, Robinson performed in thousands of benefits in the course of his career and made generous contributions to charities and individuals. Substantially, however, Robinson's career had peaked in the late 1930s, and when he died in 1949 he was in debt. According to contemporary accounts, nearly a hundred thousand people turned out to watch his funeral procession; the numbers testify to the esteem in which he was still held by his community and by the audiences who loved him. The founding of the Copasetics Club in the year that Robinson died ensured that his brilliance as a performer would not be forgotten.

—CONSTANCE VALIS HILL

ROBINSON, JACK ROOSEVELT "JACKIE"

Jack Roosevelt "Jackie" Robinson (January 31, 1919–October 24, 1972), baseball player, civil rights leader, businessman. Born in Georgia, the youngest of five children of sharecrop farmers Jerry and Mallie Robinson, Jackie Robinson was raised in Pasadena, Calif., where the Robinson family confronted the West Coast variety of American racism. White neighbors tried to drive the family out of their home; segregation reigned in public and private facilities. Robinson became an outstanding athlete at Pasadena Junior College, before transferring to U.C.L.A. in 1940, where he won renown as the "Jim Thorpe of his race," the nation's finest all-around athlete. Robinson was an All-American football player, leading scorer in basketball, and record-setting broad jumper, in addition to his baseball exploits.

Drafted into the Army in the spring of 1942 Robinson embarked on a stormy military career. Denied access to Officers' Candidate School, Robinson protested to heavyweight champion Joe Louis, who intervened with officials in Washington on Robinson's behalf. Once commissioned, Robinson fought for improved conditions for blacks at Camp Riley, Kans., leading to his transfer to Fort Hood, Tex. At Fort Hood, Robinson was court-martialed and acquitted for refusing to move to the back of a bus. Robinson's Army career demonstrated the proud, combative personality that would characterize his postwar life.

After his discharge from the Army in 1944, Robinson signed to play with the Kansas City Monarchs of the Negro American League. After several months of discontent in the Jim Crow league, Robinson was approached by Branch Rickey of the Brooklyn Dodgers, who offered him the opportunity to become the first black player in major league baseball since the 1890s. Robinson gladly accepted the opportunity and responsibility of this pioneering role in "baseball's great experiment."

In 1946 Robinson joined the Montreal Royals of the International League, the top farm club in the Dodger system. Following a spectacular debut in which he stroked four hits including a three-run home run, Robinson proceeded to lead the league with a .349 batting average. An immediate fan favorite, Robinson enabled the Royals to set new attendance records while winning the International League and Little World Series championships. Robinson's imminent promotion to the Dodgers in 1947 triggered an unsuccessful petition drive on the part of southern players to keep him off the team. In the early months of the season, beanballs, death threats, and rumors of a strike by opposing players swirled about Robinson. Through it all, Robinson paraded his excellence. An electrifying fielder and baserunner as well as an outstanding hitter, Robinson's assault on baseball's color line captured the imagination of both black and white Americans. He batted .297 and won the Rookie of the Year Award (since renamed the Jackie Robinson Award in his honor) en route to leading the Dodgers to the pennant.

Over the next decade Robinson emerged as one of the most dominant players and foremost gate attractions in the history of the major leagues. In 1949 he batted .342 and won the National League Most Valuable Player Award. During his ten years with the Dodgers the team won six pennants and one World Championship. Upon his retirement in 1956 Robinson had compiled a .311 lifetime batting average. He was elected to the Baseball Hall of Fame on the first ballot in 1961.

But Robinson's significance transcended his achievements on the baseball diamond. He became a leading symbol and spokesperson of the postwar integration crusade, both within baseball and in broader society. During his early years in Montreal and Brooklyn, Robinson had adhered to his promise to Branch Rickey to "turn the other cheek" and avoid controversies. After establishing

The integration of organized baseball, beginning with Jackie Robinson in 1946, spelled the end of the Negro Leagues.

PAGE 65

See also
Baseball
Joe Louis
NAACP

himself in the major leagues, however, Robinson's more combative and outspoken personality re-asserted itself. Robinson repeatedly pressed for baseball to desegregate more rapidly and to re-move discriminatory barriers in Florida training camps and cities like St. Louis and Cincinnati. He also demanded opportunities for black players to become coaches, managers, and front office personnel. Baseball officials and many sportswrit-ers branded Robinson an ingrate as controversies marked his career.

Upon retirement Robinson remained in the public eye. He continued to voice his opinions as speaker, newspaper columnist, and fundraiser for the NAACP. A believer in "black capitalism" through which blacks could "become producers, manufacturers, developers and creators of busi-nesses, providers of jobs," Robinson engaged in many successful business ventures in the black community. He became an executive in the Chock Full O' Nuts restaurant chain and later helped develop Harlem's Freedom National Bank and the Jackie Robinson Construction Company. Robinson also became active in Republican Party politics, supporting Richard Nixon in 1960, and working closely with New York Gov. Nelson Rockefeller, who appointed him Special Assistant for Community Affairs in 1966. These activities brought criticism from young black militants in the late 1960s. Ironically, at this same time Robinson had also parted ways with the NAACP, criticizing its failure to include "younger, more progressive voices."

By the late 1960s Robinson had become "bit-terly disillusioned" with both baseball and Amer-ican society. He refused to attend baseball events in protest of the failure to hire blacks in nonplay-ing capacities. In his 1972 autobiography, *I Never Had It Made,* he attacked the nation's waning commitment to racial equality. Later that year the commemoration of his major league debut led him to lift his boycott of baseball games. "I'd like to live to see a black manager," he told a nation-wide television audience at the World Series on October 15, 1972. Nine days later he died of a heart attack.

—JULES TYGIEL

ROOSEVELT'S
BLACK CABINET

Disaffected by Republican party politics in the decades following the Civil War, victimized by racism, and ravaged by the Great Depression, African Americans transferred their allegiance to Franklin D. Roosevelt and the Democratic party during the New Deal when they perceived that his efforts to improve conditions for all citizens included them as well. While Roosevelt did not propose specific civil rights legislation during his administrations, he did move to repeal particu-larly egregious racial restrictions within the fed-eral government bureaucracy, many of which had been initiated by his Democratic predecessor, Woodrow Wilson. Moreover, the First Lady, Eleanor Roosevelt, remained a vocal and active champion of racial equality. As a consequence of Mrs. Roosevelt's lobbying, of the concerns and in-terest of former Chicago NAACP president Harold Ickes, a key figure in the Roosevelt ad-ministration, and, most important, of concen-trated efforts to secure political appointments for blacks, Roosevelt was made aware of the plight of black Americans. In response, African Americans came to view the Democratic party as a haven.

Two seminal events in 1933 helped to set the stage for the appointment of a number of blacks to second-level positions within the administra-tion. The first was the Second Amenia Confer-ence, hosted by Joel Spingarn, the chairman of the board of the NAACP. The second was the Julius Rosenwald Fund meeting to discuss the economic status of blacks. Out of both of these meetings grew a determination to seek and secure appoint-ments of racial advisers in the administration in order to ensure that blacks would not be excluded from New Deal programs. An Interracial Inter-departmental Group (IIG), supported by the Rosenwald Fund, was set up to promote black ap-pointees. Working closely with Ickes and Eleanor Roosevelt, the IIG helped to secure the appoint-ment of at least one black adviser in all but five of some two dozen New Deal agencies by 1937. This network of officeholders became known as the "Black Cabinet."

Appointees included people such as Robert Weaver, later appointed by Lyndon B. Johnson to serve as the secretary of Housing and Urban Devel-opment; Mary McLeod Bethune, director of Negro affairs, National Youth Organization; Henry Hunt and Charles Hall, who, along with Weaver, were original members of the IIG; Joseph H. B. Evans, Farm Security Administration; Lawrence A. Axley, Department of Labor; Edgar G. Brown, Civilian Conservation Corps; N. Robinson, Agriculture; and Alfred E. Smith, Works Project Administra-tion. Bethune convened the members of this un-official Black Cabinet in 1935. Thereafter, they met

See also
Baseball

DIANA ROSS

Artist Hits Number One on the Pop Charts

Diana Ross (March 26, 1944–), pop singer, actress. Born Diane Ross in a low-income housing project in Detroit, Ross's interest in music began at an early age, when she sang with her parents in a church choir. In high school she studied dress design, illustration, and cosmetology, spending her free time singing on Detroit street corners with her friends Mary Wilson and Florence Ballard. Betty McGlowan was soon added to the group, and the quartet became known as the Primettes. They came to the attention of Motown Records founder Berry Gordy, who used them as background singers for Mary Wells, Marvin Gaye, and the Shirelles. The group was renamed the Supremes, and from the mid-1960s until 1970 they were one of the most popular groups in pop music, with a string of influential hits. In 1970, however, Ross, who had always sought to dominate what was nominally a balanced trio, left to pursue a solo career.

After leaving the Supremes, Ross's popularity continued ("Ain't No Mountain High Enough," 1970), and she also began a career as a film actress. Ross was nominated for an Academy Award for her performance as Billie Holiday in *Lady Sings the Blues* (1972), and starred in *Mahagony* (1975), which yielded the hit ballad "Do You Know Where You're Going To?" the next year. By the mid-1970s Ross was also considered a top disco diva, recording "Love Hangover" (1976) and "Upside Down" (1980). During this time she also had a starring role in the musical film *The Wiz* (1978). Ross reached the top of the pop charts again in 1981 with "Endless Love," a duet with Lionel Ritchie. Since then she has recorded less frequently (*Muscles,* 1982; *Eaten Alive,* 1985; and *Workin' Overtime,* 1989). Ross, who was married from 1971 to 1975 to Robert Silberstine, was remarried in 1985 to the Norwegian shipping tycoon and mountaineer Arne Naess. They have two sons and live in Norway and Connecticut. Ross has had nineteen number-one recordings on the pop charts—the most to date for a solo performer—and continues to perform sporadically in concert and on television.

—KAREN BENNETT HARMON

regularly (although unofficially), remaining in constant touch with one another, and creating a network whose purpose and goal was to promote the interests of black Americans. With a greater direct access to power than they had ever had before, they lobbied actively throughout the administration. Although their achievements were limited, they did realize some success. The Black Cabinet helped to ensure that, by 1935, approximately 30 percent of all black Americans participated in New Deal relief programs.

—CHRISTINE A. LUNARDINI

RUDOLPH, WILMA GLODEAN

Wilma Glodean Rudolph (June 23, 1940– November 12, 1994), athlete. Wilma Rudolph, the twentieth of twenty-two children, was born in Bethlehem, Tenn., and raised in Clarksville. As a child, she suffered from scarlet fever and pneumonia and was stricken with polio, which left her without the use of her left leg. She wore a leg brace until the age of nine, when she was able to regain the strength in her legs. By age twelve, Rudolph was the fastest runner in her school. She entered Cobb Elementary School in 1947 and then attended Burt High School in Clarksville, Tenn., where she played basketball and ran track.

Rudolph met Edward Temple, track coach at Tennessee State University, while at Burt. After her sophomore year, Temple invited Rudolph to a summer training camp and began to cultivate her running abilities. In 1956, at age 16, she participated in the Olympics in Melbourne, Australia, where her team won the bronze medal in the 4 × 100-meter relay race. Two years later, Rudolph entered Tennessee State to run track and study elementary education and psychology. She was determined to return to the Rome Olympics in 1960. She trained and ran with the Tigerbelles, the Tennessee State University team, which was one of the premier teams in the country. In 1960, Rudolph became the first woman to receive three gold medals, which she won for the 100-meter race, the 200-meter race, and the 4 × 100-meter relay. She instantly became a celebrity, drawing large crowds wherever she went. The French press called her "La Gazelle." Rudolph retired from amateur running at the height of her career, in 1962.

See also
Track and Field

Rudolph graduated from Tennessee State in 1963 and accepted a job as teacher and track coach at Cobb Elementary School. Although she has lived in many places and has held a number of different jobs, she has invariably dedicated herself to youth programs and education. She worked as the director of a community center in Evansville, Ind., with the Job Corps program in Boston and St. Louis, with the Watts Community Action Committee in California, and as a teacher at a high school in Detroit. In 1981, she started the Wilma Rudolph Foundation, a nonprofit organization which nurtures young athletes.

Wilma Rudolph has received many awards and distinctions. She was chosen in 1960 as the United Press Athlete of the Year, and the next year she was designated Woman Athlete of the Year by the Associated Press. She was inducted in 1973 into the Black Sports Hall of Fame, seven years later into the Women's Sports Hall of Fame, and in 1983 into the U.S. Olympic Hall of Fame. In 1993, she became the only woman to be

We don't have to be what you want us to be.

BILL RUSSELL
QUOTED BY GEORGE VECSEY,
NEW YORK TIMES, 1985

HOOPS STAR

William Felton "Bill" Russell

William Felton "Bill" Russell (February 12, 1934–), basketball player. Born in 1934, the second son of a laborer in a paper bag factory in Monroe, La., at age nine Russell moved with his family to Oakland, Calif. His parents separated and his mother died while he was still in elementary school, leaving Russell to grow up in "the projects" under the tutelage of an athletically gifted brother and a strong-willed, racially proud father. Young Russell failed in early attempts at both basketball and football, but by his senior year at McClymonds High School his wiry frame, leaping skills, and uncanny sense of timing marked him as a potentially great defensive basketball player and team leader.

Those strengths blossomed at the University of San Francisco (USF), where Russell enrolled in 1952 on an athletic scholarship. He and roommate K. C. Jones led USF to fifty-five consecutive victories and successive National Collegiate Athletic Association (NCAA) championships in 1955 and 1956. They then joined the United States Olympic basketball team at the summer Olympic Games in Melbourne, Australia. Shortly after the Americans defeated the Soviet Union in the finals 89–55 to win the gold medal, Russell rushed back home to marry his college sweetheart, Rose Swisher, and to sign a professional contract with the Boston Celtics.

For the next thirteen years, the six-foot, ten-inch Russell towered over a professional basketball dynasty, with the Celtics winning eleven of thirteen NBA championships, including eight consecutive crowns from 1958 to 1966. He regularly controlled the tempo, intimidated opponents driving for the basket, and triggered the Celtics' fast break; in almost a thousand games, he averaged 22.4 rebounds and 15.1 points per game, and five times won the Most Valuable Player award. Yet all was not athleticism and awards. On southern exhibition tours with the Celtics, Russell in the late 1950s and early 1960s hated having to stay in segregated hotels and eating places. At the height of his athletic prowess in 1966, he teamed with William McSweeny to produce a strong public assertion of black pride and an angry protest against racism in the form of an autobiography, *Go Up for Glory*.

In 1966, coach Harold "Red" Auerbach became the Celtics' general manager and asked Russell to coach as well as play, making him the NBA's first black coach. That season the Celtics had their string of NBA crowns broken by Wilt Chamberlain and the Philadelphia 76ers, but the Celtics recovered to take the next two championships under player-coach Russell. In 1969 Russell abruptly retired with a year still remaining on his contract. Welcomed on the college lecture and talk show circuits, he worked as a color commentator for televised NBA games. Never one to avoid a challenge, from 1973 to 1977 he enjoyed moderate success (162 games won, 166 lost) as coach and general manager for a young NBA club, the Seattle Supersonics; ten years later he signed a ten-year contract to coach yet another new, struggling NBA franchise, the Sacramento Kings. After a disastrous beginning record of 18–41, however, he relinquished the coaching reins to become the Kings' vice president.

In 1975 Russell was inducted into the Basketball Hall of Fame, and in 1980, the Professional Basketball Writers' Association voted him the outstanding player in the history of the NBA. *Second Wind: The Memoirs of an Opinionated Man* (1979), written with Taylor Branch, is Russell's frankly recounted autobiography.

—WILLIAM J. BAKER

See also
Basketball

awarded the National Sports Award. In addition, her autobiography, *Wilma: The Story of Wilma Rudolph*, published in 1977, was made into a television movie. Rudolph's achievements as a runner gave a boost to women's track in the United States and heightened awareness about racial and sexual barriers within sports. In addition, Rudolph has served as a role model and inspiration to thousands of African-American and female athletes, as well as people trying to overcome physical disabilities.

—PAM NADASEN

RUSTIN, BAYARD

Bayard Rustin (March 17, 1910–August 24, 1987), activist. Bayard Rustin was a civil rights leader, pacifist, political organizer, and controversial public figure. He was born in West Chester, Pa., in 1910, the last of nine children. He accumulated a colorful personal history, beginning with his youthful discovery that the woman he had assumed was his older sister was actually his mother. Reared by his mother and grandparents, local caterers, he grew up in the relatively privileged setting of a large mansion in town. Like the rest of his family, Rustin became a Quaker, maintaining an enduring commitment to personal pacifism as a way of life. Tall, thin, usually bushyhaired, and with an acquired West Indian accent, Rustin was noticed wherever he appeared.

He attended college at West Chester State, then moved to Harlem during the 1930s, where he cultivated a bohemian lifestyle, attending classes at City College, singing with jazz groups and at night clubs, and gaining a reputation as a chef. His most notable activity, however, was aligning with the Communist Party through the Young Communist League, a decision based on the party's position on race issues. In 1941 when asked by the party to abandon his program to gain young black recruits in favor of a singular emphasis on the European war effort, Rustin quit the party.

His public personality and organizing skills subsequently brought him to the attention of A. Philip Randolph, who recruited him to help develop his plans for a massive March on Washington to secure equal access to defense jobs. The two men, despite brief skirmishes, remained lifelong friends. When President Franklin D. Roosevelt capitulated to Randolph's threat to hold the march—though Rustin believed that Randolph should not have canceled the march—Randolph

arranged for Rustin to meet with A. J. Muste, the head of the radical pacifist Fellowship of Reconciliation (FOR). Muste came to regard the younger man almost as a son, naming him in 1941 as a field staff member for FOR while Rustin also continued as a youth organizer for the March on Washington Movement.

Now possessed of a reputation as an activist in the politics of race, Rustin was able to offer advice to the members of the FOR cell who became the nucleus for a new nonviolent action organization, the Congress of Racial Equality (CORE). Until 1955 Rustin remained a vital figure in the FOR/CORE alliance, holding a variety of offices within both groups, conducting weekend and summer institutes on nonviolent direct action in race relations, and serving as a conduit to the March on Washington Movement for ideas and techniques on nonviolence. In 1947 he worked closely with Randolph again in a movement opposing universal military training and a segregated military, and once again believed Randolph wrong in abandoning his strategies when met with a presidential executive order intended to correct the injustice. They argued briefly and publicly, then reconciled. Rustin is sometimes credited with persuading Randolph to accept nonviolence as a strategy.

Rustin's dual commitment to nonviolence and racial equality cost him dearly. In the summer of 1942, refusing to sit in the Jim Crow section of a bus going from Louisville, Ky., to Nashville, Tenn., he was beaten and arrested. The following year, unwilling to accept either the validity of the draft or conscientious objector status—though his Quaker affiliation made that option possible—he was jailed as a draft resister and spent twentyeight months in prison. Following his release, in 1947 he proposed that a racially integrated group of sixteen CORE/FOR activists undertake a bus trip through the Upper South to test a recent Supreme Court decision on interstate travel.

Termed the Journey of Reconciliation, the trip was essentially peaceful, although participants encountered violence outside Chapel Hill, N.C., where Rustin and three others were charged with violating the segregation laws. In a sham trial, Rustin and the others were convicted and sentenced to thirty days hard labor on a chain gang. His continuing visible role in racial policies brought him additional arrests and beatings.

After his release from the chain gang, Rustin traveled to India, where he was received by Mohandas K. Gandhi's sons. He had earlier blended strands of Gandhian nonviolence into his conception of pacifism. When the bus boycott developed

See also

Congress of Racial Equality

in Montgomery, Ala., Rustin appeared on the scene to offer support, advice, and information on nonviolence. Martin Luther King, Jr., accepted his help. But when word leaked of Rustin's former ties to the Communist party and his 1953 conviction on a morals charge—allegedly for homosexual activity—he was rushed out of town. The gossip led to Rustin's resignation from both CORE and FOR in 1955, although he continued the pacifist struggle in the War Resisters League.

A 1952 visit to countries in north and west Africa convinced him of the need to assist Africans in their independence struggle. And he continued to be an active though less visible force in the effort to achieve racial justice, invited by King to assist in the creation of the Southern Christian Leadership Conference and to serve as a publicist for the group. Conservative members, however, eventually sought his ouster, and from 1960 until 1963 Rustin had little contact with King.

In 1963, as Randolph renewed his plans for a massive March on Washington, he proposed Rustin as the coordinator for the national event. Though initially opposed by some major civil rights leaders and under surveillance by the FBI, Rustin successfully managed the complex planning for the event and avoided violence. He was named executive director of the A. Philip Randolph Institute in 1964, while continuing to lead protests against militarism and segregation.

—CAROL V. R. GEORGE

See also
Southern Christian
Leadership Conference

ST. LOUIS, MISSOURI

St. Louis, Mo., was founded in 1764 by French trader Pierre Laclade as a settlement and fur trading post in the Louisiana territory, then owned by Spain. African Americans, both slave and free, were present in the city virtually from the date of its creation. Few population figures are available for blacks during the colonial period. In 1772, a Spanish pastor, Father Valentine, arrived in the settlement, and in three years baptized twenty-four blacks into the Roman Catholic faith. By 1776, blacks formed about 30 percent of the rapidly growing settlement. Slaves and free blacks were employed as domestics, agricultural laborers, ship pilots, hunters, dockworkers, and craftspeople. Some free blacks, such as Jeannette Fourchet, became successful farmers.

In 1803, following the Louisana Purchase, the district of St. Louis, with its 667 slaves and 70 free black residents, became part of the United States. The number of slaves grew to 740 in St. Louis County by 1810, about 20 percent of the area's growing population. This large slave force frightened the district authorities, who passed several ordinances between 1808 and 1818 to prevent slaves from gathering in public, drinking, or associating with free blacks or whites. An 1818 ordinance prescribed jail or whipping for slaves found in public between 9:00 P.M. and daylight. The development of the steamboat and the increase in river traffic sparked sustained expansion of the settlement. In 1823, three years after Missouri became a state, and six years after the first steamboat docked at St. Louis, the city was incorporated with a population of 5,000.

Slavery continued in St. Louis throughout the antebellum period, but its rate of growth was soon checked by labor competition from white northern and European immigrants. Furthermore, some slaves—the most famous was future abolitionist William Wells Brown—escaped to free states across the Mississippi, or purchased their freedom by "hiring out" their time. In 1830, slaves still made up a fourth of the city's residents, but their numbers remained virtually static from then on, and slaves fell from 9 percent to 1 percent of the population during those years, mainly personal servants of wealthy whites in the city's third and fourth wards. The city remained solidly proslavery in its politics, and abolitionists stayed out of the area. When St. Louis slave Dred Scott tried to buy his freedom in 1846, his owner, who was part of a committee to defend slave-owner interests, refused. Forced to seek his freedom in court, with the help of white lawyers he won his freedom in 1850, before the case was overturned in the notorious 1857 U.S. Supreme Court decision, *Dred Scott* v. *Sanford*. (Soon after the case was decided, Scott was manumitted by a subsequent owner.) Even as slavery declined in St. Louis, the city remained a major slave market and was a major depot for slaves shipped to the deep South, home to such important slavetrading firms as Blakey and McAfee, and Bolton, Dickens and Company. Although the city enjoyed an unwarranted reputation, even among some abolitionists, for mild slavemasters, treatment and punishment of slaves was as cruel in St. Louis as elsewhere. Slaves were often whipped in public and sometimes beaten to death.

As economic opportunity grew during the antebellum years, a local free black class sprang up in St. Louis, whose numbers surpassed those of slaves by 1860. Free blacks occupied an uncertain place in society between slaves and whites. Life for St. Louis free blacks was better than for plantation slaves, though the free black Henry Clay Bruce (older brother of Blanche K. Bruce, St. Louis school teacher and later U.S. senator) claimed that while elite free blacks looked down on slaves, they faced so many legal restrictions that their status was hardly better. Most whites despised them and made their presence difficult in numerous ways. After 1835, all free blacks had to register with county courts and have white guarantors or pay large sums as bonds of good behavior. In 1847, laws were passed prohibiting free blacks from entering Missouri and forbidding the teaching of blacks to read or write. City ordinances and state laws prohibited blacks from assembling publicly, traveling without permits, or testifying against whites in court. Their precarious position was underlined by white violence. In

See also

Brown v. Board of Education of Topeka, Kansas

1836, a white mob lynched Francis McIntosh, a free black cook accused of the fatal stabbing of a constable. McIntosh's trial judge refused to intervene, saying that the lynching was justified by "a higher law." In 1846, Charles Lyons was summarily expelled from the state for not having a license. When he protested that his constitutional rights had been violated, Circuit Judge James Krum ruled that blacks were not citizens and had no right to trial by jury. Even sympathetic white leaders such as Francis Blair favored African colonization as the best solution to racial problems.

Within the free black community, there were marked social differences. Most were poor laborers, who lived on the waterfront and attended Baptist churches with slaves, with whom they often retained family ties. At the top was "the Colored Aristocracy," as Cyprian Clamorgan termed it in an 1858 pamphlet. Largely made up of light-skinned mulattos, educated merchants, and professionals, many owning substantial property (up to $500,000 worth in one case). The "aristocrats" attended their own churches, usually either Roman Catholic or Methodist Episcopal, and sent their children to be educated in exclusive northern schools. They largely refused to socialize with the other members of the community.

Large numbers of African Americans in St. Louis, whatever their social disdain for slaves, were involved in abolitionist and racial uplift efforts. The Rev. Moses Dickson founded a secret abolitionist fraternity, the Twelve Knights of Tabor, in 1846. Several black churches and schools opened during the antebellum era. In 1845, the Roman Catholic Sisters of St. Joseph of Carandolet opened a Sunday school for one hundred black girls, but it soon closed following attacks by a white mob. In 1856, other nuns established a clandestine school. In 1858, the Jesuit priest Father Peter Loning opened a chapel and school for blacks in the upper gallery of St. Francis Xavier Church. Blacks such as Elizabeth Keckley, a mulatto seamstress and later an employee and confidante of First Lady Mary Todd Lincoln, began schools, at times using the label "sewing schools" as a front. Hiram Revels and Blanche K. Bruce, the two Reconstruction-era black U.S. senators, both taught school in St. Louis during the 1860s.

The city's most outstanding leader was John Berry Meachum, a free black from Virginia. Meachum assisted John Mason Peck, a white missionary, in establishing religious services for blacks. In 1825, following his ordination by Peck, Meachum founded and became minister of the First African Baptist (later First Baptist) Church on Third and Almond streets, probably the first independent black religious congregation west of the Mississippi River. He also established a church school in defiance of the state's ban on black literacy. In the meantime, he prospered as a carpenter and barrelmaker, and set up his shop as a training ground for enslaved blacks, whom he would buy and instruct and who would purchase their freedom from him out of their wages. After 1847, Meachum evaded the laws banning black assembly and literacy by establishing a "school for freedom" on his steamboat moored on the Mississippi River, beyond Missouri jurisdiction.

The coming of the Civil War polarized opinion on slavery. By 1860, Republican Party and pro-Union sentiment, nurtured by economic as well as ideological ties, was ascendant. A small abolitionist movement set up in the city. On January 1, 1861, a slave auction was interrupted by a crowd of 2,000 men who forced the end of public sales, though newspaper advertisements for slaves continued to appear. When war broke out, St. Louis became a Union outpost. Refugees poured in, swelling the black population. They found employment in building levees and other laboring activities. In May 1863, blacks were recruited into the Army, and a Bureau of Colored Troops was set up in St. Louis. Blacks eventually volunteered in large numbers for the war effort. The American Missionary Association established a freedom school in the Missouri Hotel and in 1864 set up a Colored Board of Education to raise money for black schools.

An important partner in education was the Western Sanitary Commission (WSC), established during the war by liberal whites. Originally intended to care for wounded Union soldiers, the WSC soon devoted itself to relief efforts and the uplift of the black community. The WSC set up five tuition-supported schools, including a high school, and established a Freedmen's Orphan Home. Its members were mostly paternalistic in spirit and were unwilling to allow much black involvement in leadership. The WSC ceased operation in 1865.

The same year, following the end of the Civil War, slavery was outlawed and the ban on education was ended. St. Louis's population ballooned to 311,000 by 1870, making it the third largest city in the United States. The black population, however, grew even faster, rising from 2 percent of the 1860 population to 6 percent by 1870. Most had fled the oppressive atmosphere of the deep South and agreed with the popular adage, "Better a lamppost on Targee Street [the main street of

See also
Civil Rights Movement

the heavily black Near South Side] than the mayor of Dixie." They welcomed the jobs and educational opportunity available in St. Louis. In 1868, local officials successfully lobbied for the creation of a branch of the ill-fated Freedman's Bank in St. Louis to encourage black business. The black WSC schools, taken over by the St. Louis Board of Education, were funded by the city. By 1875, there were twelve black schools, although they were dilapidated, irregularly spaced in districts, and staffed by poorly paid teachers. The city did not hire its first black teacher, the Rev. Richard Cole, until 1877.

Although racial segregation was widespread, there were exceptions. Libraries and streetcars remained open to blacks throughout the century. There were even occasional incidences of interracial action. After the depression of 1873 brought widespread unemployment, an unsuccessful general strike was called to restore jobs and end wage cuts. Black levee workers marched and participated equally. The end of the Reconstruction era limited black opportunity. Outside of a few post office positions, blacks received few government jobs. When thousands of Exodusters fleeing to Kansas from the South were stranded in St. Louis in spring 1879, city authorities refused to provide relief or aid for passage beyond the city. The African-American community raised three thousand dollars to support travel expenses. In response to the prejudice, blacks united politically, although they remained divided along class and occupational lines, with old-time free black St. Louisans scorning newcomers. In 1880, the *St. Louis Advance*, the city's first black newspaper, was started by publisher P. H. Murray. John W. Wheeler's successful *St. Louis Palladium* followed in 1884.

By the turn of the century, the outline of the black community in St. Louis had been clearly established. A few successful businessmen grew up, many blacks, such as future entertainer Josephine Baker, lived in great poverty in Mill Creek Valley in the Near South Side. Others lived in "Chestnut Valley," the entertainment and vice district surrounding Chestnut, Market, and 20th streets.

There, in such establishments as Honest John Turpin's Silver Dollar Saloon, and the Hurrah Sporting Club, ragtime music was popularized by musicians led by Scott Joplin, "the King of Ragtime." In 1900, the year after he wrote the bestselling "Maple Leaf Rag," Joplin and his white publisher, John Stark, moved to St. Louis. Ragtime soon became a nationwide craze, with St. Louis its mecca. Joplin's house at 2658A Mor-

gan Street (later Delmar Boulevard) is today a ragtime museum and center. Other ragtime artists included Tom Turpin, composer of the "St. Louis Rag" and proprietor of the Rosebud Café, and Louis Chauvin.

In the early twentieth century, blacks organized politically into the Negro Civic League, led by attorney Homer G. Phillips, which leaned toward the Republicans, and the Democratic Negro Jefferson League. The two combined to elect black candidates such as Constable Charles Turpin in 1902 and delivered black votes in exchange for patronage and protection from legal discrimination.

Even so, the political influence blacks exercised on white elites did not change their essential powerlessness in the city. In 1916 white voters easily passed a residential segregation initiative, despite a heavy campaign against it by blacks and white officials. Although the measure was annulled following legal action by the fledgling St. Louis NAACP, restrictive covenants in much of the city kept blacks from moving into white areas until the U.S. Supreme Court's 1948 *Shelley* v. *Kraemer* decision.

The city soon improved its tattered reputation for racial harmony. After 1915, during the beginning months of the Great Migration, large numbers of southern blacks arrived in the area. Many were lured by false promises of high wages to the industrial suburb of East St. Louis, Ill., an oppressive company-dominated town whose businesses were shielded from taxes and regulation. Racial tensions grew following a failed labor strike and race baiting by Democrats fearful that the new blacks would swell the Republican vote. In July 1917, East St. Louis exploded in an enormous and bloody race riot. St. Louis, in contrast, seemed a haven for blacks; as the city's newspapers denounced the rioting, city residents organized relief efforts, and St. Louis police protected African Americans fleeing from East St. Louis.

The Great Migration transformed and revitalized St. Louis. In 1920, new voters helped elect the city's (and state's) first black legislator, Walthall Moore, and soon there were a handful of black municipal officials. Business expanded also. In 1919, the Douglass Life Insurance Company was founded. It was soon the largest insurer of Missouri blacks. Annie Malone, a beautician, established a very successful beauty business, and may have been the richest black woman in the United States during the 1920s. She founded the Poro Beauty College to teach her system and set up the Poro Music College and a black orphans'

See also
Civil War
Congress of Racial Equality
Exodusters

*Meet me in
St. Louis, Louis
Meet me at the fair.*

ANDREW B. STERLING
MEET ME IN ST. LOUIS, 1904

home on the proceeds of her business. The *St. Louis Argus* and the *St. Louis American* were the major African-American newspapers. While blacks continued to be excluded from white areas, two new black neighborhoods, the "Ville" and "Grove" sections, sprang up. Black commercial activity was concentrated near the shopping district of Chouteau, Franklin, and Vanderventer avenues.

Although St. Louis, musically immortalized in W. C. Handy's 1914 "St. Louis Blues," was never to regain the central place in American music it had held in the ragtime era, the city remained enormously important to African-American music. Along with Chicago and Memphis, the greater St. Louis area, including East St. Louis, Ill., was a major midwestern center for blues and jazz before World War II. Some of its leading blues musicians were Lonnie Johnson, "St. Louis Jimmy" Oden, Roosevelt Sykes, and "Peetie Wheatstraw." Big band jazz also became quite popular after the turn of the century, especially the riverboat bands led by Fate Marable, Charlie Creath, and Dewey Jackson. Later, Nightclubs such as the Jazzland, the Plantation, and the Hummingbird were the places to find big bands, such as the Jeters-Pillars Orchestra and Cab Calloway's band. Two of the most important jazz trumpeters of all time, Clark Terry and Miles Davis, came from the St. Louis area.

The mass of blacks remained poor during the 1920s and were made even poorer by the Great Depression. Works Project Administration contractors in St. Louis routinely discriminated against unemployed blacks until a formal appeal was made to Washington. Still, when city leaders authorized the use of federal funds to construct Homer Phillips Hospital, a $1.3 million black hospital, black labor was excluded from the project. The hospital filled a glaring need both for health care and for graduate medical and nursing training for blacks, but it long remained underfunded, overcrowded, and unsafe.

After World War II, blacks made the first successful challenges to discrimination in St. Louis. By 1949, city swimming pools and parks were opened to blacks, and Washington University integrated, although courts refused to order city schools to desegregate. The same year, students began a nine-year campaign of sit-ins that desegregated downtown stores and lunch counters.

In the 1950s, the Civil Rights Movement, led by students and labor activists mobilized by the Congress of Racial Equality (CORE), hit St. Louis in force. In the late 1950s, St. Louis CORE also joined with the NAACP Youth Council, led by William Clay (who would become Missouri's first black congressman in 1969) to form the Job Opportunities Council, which inaugurated strikes and sit-ins against discriminatory hiring practices.

During the early 1960s, CORE activists expanded the use of civil disobedience to obtain jobs for blacks and made dramatic peaceful takeovers of buildings to gain attention. They also protested to improve schooling for blacks. Even after the U.S. Supreme Court's 1954 *Brown v. Board of Education of Topeka, Kansas* ended legal school segregation, integration lagged due to almost total residential segregation. CORE activists lay in front of school buses to end the segregation of black students bused into white schools. Despite attempted busing, in 1965 91 percent of black children were still in mostly black schools.

After civil rights protest declined, NAACP and CORE members, such as Ivory Perry, shifted toward a concentration on tenants' rights and ward electoral politics as successful strategies for change. Urban renewal projects in St. Louis not only had failed to change residential segregation patterns, but had created new problems. The Pruitt-Igoe houses, a federal housing project for blacks opened in 1954, was badly planned, with few jobs available nearby and limited transportation, play, and shopping facilities. The project (home during the 1960s to future champion boxers Leon and Michael Spinks) eventually deteriorated so badly that in 1971 officials ordered it torn down, a national symbol of the failure of urban renewal.

Since the 1960s, blacks have made many gains in St. Louis. Educational opportunities have opened up, businessmen such as David B. Price, Jr., and Wayman F. Smith III have risen to prominence, and African Americans have entered the government. In 1993, St. Louis narrowly elected its first black mayor, former circuit court clerk Freeman Bosley, Jr.

Still, black St. Louisans face enormous difficulties. As a result of continued deindustrialization, by 1990 the city had less than half its 1950 residents, and its population had become almost half African American, despite a 25 percent drop in the black population over the previous twenty years. A school desegregation plan adopted in 1976 was still not complete fifteen years later. In 1991, Project HOPE estimated black unemployment in the city at 34 percent, and black youth unemployment at 96 percent.

See also
Jazz
Ragtime

Despite its troubles, St. Louis has remained an important incubator of musical talent. In the 1950s many significant blues and rock and roll musicians were based in St. Louis, including Ike Turner, Tina Turner, Chuck Berry, Albert King, and J. B. Hutto. The St. Louis-based Black Artists Group, formed in 1968 and disbanded in 1972, produced a number of extraordinary talents in avant-garde jazz, including Hamiett Bluiett, Joseph and Lester Bowie, Julius Hemphill, and Oliver Lake. The city has also been the home of such varied talents as entertainer Redd Foxx, comedian/activist Dick Gregory, and opera singers Grace Bumbry and Felicia Weathers.

—GREG ROBINSON

SAVAGE, AUGUSTA CHRISTINE FELLS

Augusta Christine Fells Savage (February 29, 1892–March 26, 1962), portrait sculptor and educator. The seventh of fourteen children, Augusta Savage was born in Green Cove Springs, Fla., to Cornelia and Edward Fells. Fells, a Methodist minister, initially punished his young daughter for making figurines in the local red clay, then came to accept her talent. Augusta attended public schools and the state normal school in Tallahassee (now Florida A&M) briefly. At sixteen, she married John T. Moore, who died within a few years of the birth of their only child. In the mid-1910s, she married James Savage, a laborer and carpenter; the two divorced in the early 1920s. In 1915, Savage moved to West Palm Beach, where one of her clay pieces won twenty-five dollars at a county fair. Public support encouraged Savage to move north in the Great Migration to New York, where she arrived in 1921 with just $4.60 and a letter of recommendation from the superintendent of the county fair to sculptor Solon Borglum, director of the School of American Sculpture.

Through Borglum's influence, Savage was admitted to the tuition-free college Cooper Union ahead of 142 women on the waiting list. She completed the four-year program in three years, specializing in portraiture. In the early 1920s, she sculpted realistic busts of W. E. B. Du Bois, Frederick Douglass, W. C. Handy, and Marcus Garvey. In 1923, Savage married Robert L. Poston, a Garveyite journalist who died five months later. The same year, Savage was one of a hundred American women who received a $500 scholarship from the French government for summer study at the palace of Fontainebleau. However, when the American committee of seven white men discovered her racial identity, they withdrew the offer. One committee member, Hermon A. MacNeil, gave her private instruction instead. Two years later, Countess Irene Di Robilant of the Italian-American Society gave Savage a scholarship for study at the Royal Academy of Fine Arts in Rome, but Savage was unable to raise money for expenses abroad as she struggled to support her parents while working at a laundry.

In 1926, Savage exhibited her work in three locations—at the New York Public Library, at the Frederick Douglass High School in Baltimore, and at the sesquicentennial exhibition in Philadelphia. The following year, she studied privately with sculptor Onorio Ruotolo, former dean of the Leonardo da Vinci Art School. She also worked with sculptor Antonio Salemme and taught soap sculpture classes to children at Procter & Gamble.

In 1928, recognition from the Harmon Foundation, which exhibited her *Evening* and *Head of a Negro,* brought Savage sales. Eugene Kinckle Jones, executive secretary of the National Urban League, was so impressed with his purchase of a baby's bust that Savage had sculpted that he asked the Carnegie Corporation to sponsor her training. Through the Carnegie, Savage began study with sculptor Victor Salvatore, who urged her to continue her studies in France.

STORIES IN CLAY

Augusta Savage created realistic portrait busts throughout her prolific career. Her most notable works are black female nudes.
PHOTOGRAPHS AND PRINTS DIVISION, SCHOMBURG CENTER FOR RESEARCH IN BLACK CULTURE, THE NEW YORK PUBLIC LIBRARY, ASTOR, LENOX AND TILDEN FOUNDATION

In fall 1929, Savage went to Paris with funds from both Carnegie and the Julius Rosenwald Fund. There, she studied privately with Felix Benneteau and created realistic portrait busts in plaster and clay. The most notable works Savage created abroad are of black female nudes, such as *Amazon* (a female warrior holding a spear) and *Mourning Victory* (a standing nude who gazes at a decapitated head on the ground) and works that celebrate her African heritage, such as *The Call* (in response to Alain Locke's call for racially representative art) and *Divinité nègre* (a female figurine with four faces, arms, and legs). In 1930, *La dépêche africaine*, a French journal, ran a cover story on Savage, and three of her figurative works were exhibited at the Salon d'Automne. Savage also sent works to the United States for display; the Harmon Foundation exhibited *Gamin* in 1930 and *Bust* and *The Chase* (in palm wood) in 1931. In 1931 Savage won a gold medal for a piece at the Colonial Exposition and exhibited two female nudes (*Nu* in bronze, and *Martiniquaise* in plaster) at the Société des Artistes Français.

After her return to New York, Savage exhibited three works (*Gamin, Envy,* and *Woman of Martinique*) at the American Art-Anderson Galleries in 1932. That same year, she opened the Savage School of Arts and Crafts. Some of her students, who included Jacob Lawrence, Norman Lewis, William Artis, and Ernest Crichlow, participated in Vanguard, a group Savage founded in 1933 to discuss art and progressive causes. She disbanded the group the following year when membership became communist-controlled.

In 1934, Argent Galleries and the Architectural League exhibited Savage's work, and she became the first African American elected to the National Association of Women Painters and Sculptors. Two years later, Savage supervised artists in the WPA's Federal Arts Project and organized classes and exhibitions at the Uptown Art Laboratory. In 1937, she became the first director of the Harlem Community Art Center. After receiving a commission from the New York World's Fair Board of Design, she left that position in 1938 to sculpt a sixteen-foot plaster harp, the strings of which were the folds of choir robes on singing black youths. Named after James Weldon Johnson's poem/song (also called the Negro National Anthem), *Lift Every Voice and Sing* was ex-

ARTHUR SCHOMBURG
Leading Spirit of the Harlem Renaissance

Arthur Alfonso Schomburg (January 24, 1874–June 10, 1938), bibliophile. Arthur Schomburg was born in San Juan, Puerto Rico, to a German merchant and an unmarried black laundress who was a native of St. Thomas, Virgin Islands. He received some formal education, but was largely self-taught. He emigrated to the United States in 1891, moving to New York City. Schomburg worked in a law office, was active in the "Porto [sic] Rican Revolutionary Party," and began his lifelong quest to amass a collection of African-American books and other materials in order to demonstrate the existence and significance of black history. In 1906 he went to work at Bankers Trust Company, where he eventually became head of the mail room, staying with the company for twenty-three years.

With his broad knowledge and passion for African-American history, Schomburg became a leading spirit in the Harlem Renaissance and an inspiration to a generation of historians. He was an active Prince Hall Mason, he cofounded with John Edward Bruce in 1911 the Negro Society for Historical Research, and in 1922 he became president of the soon-to-be moribund American Negro Academy. Schomburg wrote numerous pamphlets and bibliographical studies. His best-known essay is "The Negro Digs Up His Past," in Alain Locke's *The New Negro* (1925), a call to the important task of careful scholarly research into African and African-American history.

In 1925 the New York Public Library established a special Negro Division at the 135th Street Branch, and the next year the Carnegie Corporation purchased for $10,000 Schomburg's vast and unequalled collection of books, manuscripts, and art works, and donated it to the library. Schomburg, who was a librarian at Fisk University from 1930 to 1932, became curator of his own collection with another Carnegie grant, which he received in 1932. His collection forms the core of the present Schomburg Center for Research in Black Culture, the largest collection of materials by and about people of African descent. Schomburg died in New York City on June 10, 1938.

—RICHARD NEWMAN

See also
W.E.B. Du Bois

hibited at the New York World's Fair of 1939 but was bulldozed afterward. (Savage could not afford to have it cast in bronze.)

In June 1939, Savage opened the Salon of Contemporary Art, the first gallery devoted to the exhibition and sale of works by African-American artists. It folded within a few months for lack of funds. The same year, Savage exhibited fifteen works in a solo show at Argent Galleries; among them were *Green Apples, Sisters in the Rain, Creation, Envy, Martyr, The Cat,* and a bust of James Weldon Johnson. She also exhibited at the American Negro Exposition and at Perrin Hall in Chicago in 1940.

About 1945, Savage retired to Saugerties, N.Y., where she taught children in nearby summer camps, occasionally sold her work, and wrote children's stories and murder mysteries. She died of cancer in New York City.

—THERESA LEININGER-MILLER

SCIENCE

As a race, people of African origin have been the object of scientific scrutiny and analysis in America since the colonial period. The practice of science—and the perspectives of its practitioners—were shaped to a large extent by prevailing social and theological notions of racial hierarchy. Science operated on the assumption that the Negro race was inferior; it helped define race and was subsequently abused in the promotion of racism in America.

Racial Concepts

Models of racial classification had roots in the work of the eighteenth-century Swedish naturalist Carl Linnaeus. Linnaeus's framework was adopted by nineteenth-century naturalists and broadened by Georges Cuvier, Charles Lyell, Charles Darwin, and others to include analysis of hair, skull, and facial features. Lyell and Darwin thought of the Negro as an intermediate step on the ladder of evolution, somewhere between monkey and Caucasian. Cuvier held that blacks were "the most degraded of human races, whose form approaches that of the beast." Louis Agassiz, the Swiss-born American naturalist and professor at Harvard University, considered the Negro almost a separate species. It was difficult, he said, in observing "their black faces with their thick lips and grimacing teeth . . . to repress the feeling that they are not of the same blood as us."

The racially charged views of these and other scientists became part of the legacy passed on to succeeding generations. Nineteenth-century America, for example, saw the rise of craniometry (measurement of the brain) and anthropometry (the taking of anatomical measurements in general) as methods of exploring and comparing the physical, mental, and moral condition of the races. This work was carried out, during the Civil War and afterward, largely by white physicians in the service of governmental bodies such as the U.S. Sanitary Commission, a predecessor of the U.S. Public Health Service.

Physicians played a vital role in developing a science-based analysis of the Negro. The condition of the American Negro (often referred to as "the other race") was a common topic of discussion in professional journals, at conferences, and in articles on health topics for popular newspapers and magazines during the nineteenth century. White physicians portrayed African Americans as constitutionally weak—more prone to disease than whites, with a higher mortality rate, and exhibiting signs that pointed toward eventual extinction. Data and statistics, generally void of appropriate context, were used to buttress this thesis. The low rate of suicide among blacks, for example, was interpreted as a reflection of limited intellectual capacity—an indication that blacks lived only for the moment and, unlike whites, lacked the conceptual skills necessary to plan and shape the future.

Nineteenth-century black physicians remained more or less silent about the racial dogmas advanced by their white counterparts for several reasons. First, since white organizations generally refused to admit them to membership, black physicians were kept busy developing alternative forums—their own professional societies, discussion groups, journals—to provide opportunities for shared learning and experience. The National Medical Association, the black counterpart of the American Medical Association, was founded in 1895 through the efforts of prominent physicians such as Miles Vandahurst Lynk and Robert Fulton Boyd. Second, black physicians recognized that generating racial or political controversy risked a backlash that could undermine efforts to place their own professional role and community on a solid foundation. And third, some black professionals accepted the truth of racial stereotypes and distanced themselves from the perceived taint of their race by thinking of themselves as unique, as somehow different from the "typical" African American.

Louis Tompkins Wright and his researchers pioneered the use of chemotherapy to destroy cancerous cells.

PAGE 746

Eugenics and Other Movements

In the early twentieth century, activities pursued under the guise of science continued to point to the alleged inferiority of African Americans. The eugenics movement is a good example. While it had always been present in some form (in spirit if not in name), eugenics assumed formal standing as a science with the rediscovery of Mendel's seminal paper on genetics in 1900 and the establishment in 1910 of the Eugenics Records Office at Cold Spring Harbor, Long Island. Defined as the science of improving the hereditary qualities of particular races or breeds, eugenics found devotees among geneticists and reputable practitioners in other branches of the biological sciences. It captured the public imagination, bringing issues of racial inferiority into focus not only in the realm of natural science, but in the social arena as well. Eugenics, with its growing stock of data on what were termed "weak races," fed into regressive social policies such as the anti-immigration movement and programs of coercive sterilization aimed at "purifying" the nation's population stocks. Its ideas permeated American society, promoting racial fear among whites and self-antipathy among some blacks. Although eugenics slipped out of the mainstream of American science in the 1930s following its adoption by the Germans as a social-engineering tool, its assumptions remained firmly embedded in the American social fabric.

The racial thrust underlying the work of the craniometrists, anthropometrists, physician-scientists, and eugenicists persisted past the middle of the twentieth century—in spite of the rise of the Civil Rights Movement. In some respects, it persists down to the present day. Examples are numerous. From 1932 to 1972, the United States Public Health Service carried out the Tuskegee Study of Untreated Syphilis in the Negro Male (popularly known as the Tuskegee Syphilis Experiment). This project gathered together four hundred African-American "guinea pigs"; misled them about the nature of their illness by reinforcing the subjects' belief that they were suffering from vague ailments related to "bad blood"; and withheld treatment from them in order to observe the progress of the disease. One rationale underlying the project was the need to assess racial differences in the impact of the disease. Then there was the segregation of blood in the armed services during World War II. Still later, during the 1960s and '70s, Arthur Jensen, Richard Herrnstein, and William Shockley applied IQ and other data in studies of racial differences. These scientists drew broad conclusions, for example, about the genetic inferiority—and, in particular, the inherently lower intelligence—of blacks as compared to whites. Since the 1980s, some work in sociobiology and genetic engineering has attempted to identify genes with behavioral traits. In 1992, the National Institutes of Health awarded funds for a conference on heredity and criminal behavior but later withdrew support to placate critics who felt that linking genetics and crime in this way could add renewed authority to theories that blacks (represented disproportionately in U.S. crime statistics) were biologically inferior.

African Americans in Science

Science may have been used and abused in racially motivated ways, but this did not stop African Americans from being drawn to careers in the field. The history of blacks in American science is as old as the history of science in America. In colonial America, free blacks were known for their inventive, scientific, and technical skills. The first to achieve a national reputation in science was Benjamin Banneker (1731–1806), known in the latter part of the eighteenth century as a mathematician, astronomer, and compiler and publisher of almanacs. In 1791, Banneker served as part of a team of surveyors and engineers who contributed to planning the city of Washington, D.C. Other free blacks, including Thomas L. Jennings (1791–1859) and Norbert Rillieux, developed and patented technical devices in the years leading up to the Civil War. Some slaves were known for their inventive abilities, but their legal status prevented them from holding patents and from receiving widespread public recognition of their achievement.

After the Civil War, the number of blacks undertaking scientific work increased slowly. The establishment of black institutions of higher learning—necessary because white institutions did not routinely admit African-American students—provided an essential start. Nevertheless, black colleges and universities tended to focus on curricula in theology, education, medicine, and other fields that were more practical (or technical) than scientific, geared primarily toward creating a niche or foothold for African-American professionals in the social and economic mainstream. Science, in the sense of an activity devoted to pure or basic research, did not fit readily into this framework. As a result, African Americans wanting specialized science education or training were obliged to seek out programs at white institutions. It was a difficult proposition that only a few tackled successfully before the end of the nineteenth century. One of the earliest was Edward Alexander Bouchet (1852–1918), who earned a Ph.D. in physics from Yale University in 1876. Bouchet was said to have been the first African American to earn a Ph.D. from an American university. His subsequent career did not, however, include research in the sciences. He became a high-school science teacher at the Institute for Colored Youth, Philadelphia. Because of his race, professional op-

ERNEST JUST

Academic Pioneer Broke Scientific and Racial Barriers

Ernest Everett Just (August 14, 1883–October 27, 1941), zoologist and educator. Ernest Just was born in Charleston, S.C., the son of Charles Fraser Just, a carpenter and wharf-builder, and his wife, Mary Mathews Cooper Just, a teacher and civic leader. His early education was received at a school run by his mother, the Frederick Deming, Jr. Industrial School. In 1896, he entered the teacher-training program of the Colored Normal, Industrial, Agricultural and Mechanical College (South Carolina State College) in Orangeburg, S.C. After graduating in 1899, he attended Kimball Union Academy in Meriden, N.H. (1900–1903), before proceeding to Dartmouth College. At Dartmouth he majored in biology and minored in Greek and history. He received an A.B., graduating magna cum laude, in 1907.

Essentially, there were two career options available to an African American with Just's academic background: teaching in a black institution or preaching in a black church. Just chose the former, beginning his career in the fall of 1907 as an instructor in English and rhetoric at Howard University. In 1909, he taught English and biology, and a year later assumed a permanent full-time commitment in zoology as part of a general revitalization of the science curriculum at Howard. He also taught physiology in the medical school. A devoted teacher, he served as faculty adviser to a group that was trying to establish a nationwide fraternity of black students. The Alpha chapter of Omega Psi Phi was organized at Howard in 1911, and Just became its first honorary member. In 1912, he married a fellow Howard faculty member, Ethel Highwarden. They had three children—Margaret, Highwarden, and Maribel.

Meanwhile, Just laid plans to pursue scientific research. In 1909, he started studying at the Marine Biological Laboratory (MBL) in Woods Hole, Mass., under the eminent scientist Frank Rattray Lillie, MBL director and head of the zoology department at the University of Chicago. He also served as Lillie's research assistant. Their relationship quickly blossomed into a full and equal scientific collaboration. By the time Just earned a Ph.D. in zoology at the University of Chicago in 1916, he had already coauthored a paper with Lillie and written several on his own.

The two worked on fertilization in marine animals. Just's first paper, "The Relation of the First Cleavage Plane to the Entrance Point of the Sperm," appeared in *Biological Bulletin* in 1912, and was cited frequently as a classic and authoritative study. He went on to champion a theory—the fertilizin theory—first proposed by Lillie, who postulated the existence of a substance called "fertilizin" as the essential biochemical catalyst in the fertilization of the egg by the sperm. In 1915, Just was awarded the NAACP's first Spin-

garn Medal in recognition of his scientific contributions and "foremost service to his race."

Science was for Just a deeply felt avocation, an activity he looked forward to doing each summer at the MBL as a welcome respite from his heavy teaching and administrative responsibilities at Howard. Under the circumstances, his productivity was extraordinary. Within ten years (1919–1928), he published thirty-five articles, mostly relating to his studies on fertilization. Though proud of his output, he yearned for a position or environment in which he could pursue his research full-time.

In 1928, Just received a substantial grant from the Julius Rosenwald Fund that allowed him a change of environment and longer stretches of time for his research. His first excursion, in 1929, took him to Italy, where he worked for seven months at the Stazione Zoologica in Naples. He traveled to Europe ten times over the course of the next decade, staying for periods ranging from three weeks to two years. He worked primarily at the Stazione Zoologica; the Kaiser-Wilhelm Institut für Biologie in Berlin; and the Station Biologique in Roscoff, France.

In Europe, Just wrote a book synthesizing many of the scientific theories, philosophical ideas, and experimental results of his career. The book was published under the title *Biology of the Cell Surface* in 1939. Its thesis, that the ectoplasm or cell surface has a fundamental role in development, did not receive much attention at the time but later became a major focus of scientific investigation. Also in 1939, he published a compendium of experimental advice under the title *Basic Methods for Experiments on Eggs of Marine Animals*. In 1940, Just was interned briefly in France following the German invasion and then released to return to America, where he died a year later.

—KENNETH R. MANNING

DEDICATED SCHOLAR

For Ernest Just, science was a deeply felt avocation.
PHOTOGRAPHS AND PRINTS DIVISION, SCHOMBURG CENTER FOR RESEARCH IN BLACK CULTURE, THE NEW YORK PUBLIC LIBRARY, ASTOR, LENOX AND TILDEN FOUNDATION

*Benjamin Banneker
was the first
African-American
man of science.*

PAGE 55

portunities in science were essentially closed to him. Bouchet's was nonetheless an important accomplishment, a counterexample to the widespread mythology about the mental inferiority of blacks.

The number of blacks entering scientific fields increased markedly after the turn of the twentieth century. Among these were Charles Henry Turner, zoologist; George Washington Carver, agricultural botanist; Ernest Everett Just, embryologist; St. Elmo Brady, chemist; Elmer Samuel Imes, physicist; William Augustus Hinton, bacteriologist; and Julian Herman Lewis, pathologist. Percy Lavon Julian, chemist, and Charles Richard Drew, a surgeon and pioneer of the blood banking system, followed a couple of decades later. This cohort represents the first group of black scientists to receive graduate degrees from major white universities, pursue science at the research level, and publish in leading scientific journals.

World War II brought African-American scientists, as a distinct group, to public attention for the first time. Prior to this, they had worked primarily as teachers at black colleges and universities, and had not—with the notable exception, perhaps, of Ernest Just—exerted their influence widely or made their presence felt in the larger scientific community. As part of the war mobilization effort at Los Alamos and in the various branches of the Manhattan Project attached to laboratories at the University of Chicago, Columbia University, and other universities, some white scientists witnessed for the first time a sizable number of black physicists and chemists entering their world. African Americans who worked on the atom bomb project included Edwin Roberts Russell (b. 1913), Benjamin Franklin Scott (b. 1922), J. Ernest Wilkins, Jr., Jasper Brown Jeffries (b. 1912), George Warren Reed, Jr. (b. 1920), Moddie Daniel Taylor (1912–1976), and the brothers Lawrence Howland Knox (b. 1907) and William Jacob Knox, Jr. (b. 1904). At a postwar conference in 1946, one eminent white scientist, Arthur Holly Compton, remarked on how the bomb project had brought races and religions together for a common purpose.

After the war, even though a few white universities began to open up faculty appointments and graduate fellowships to blacks, racial discrimination continued to operate at many levels within the professional world of science. It was common for major associations, including the American Association for the Advancement of Science, to hold conventions in cities where segregation was

both customary and legally enforced, and where hotels serving as convention sites denied accommodation to anyone of African-American origin. Blacks often relied on their own scientific associations, such as the National Institute of Science (founded in 1942) and Beta Kappa Chi Scientific Society (incorporated in 1929), to share ideas and foster collegial ties. Furthermore, most science education for African Americans—certainly at the undergraduate level—continued to take place within the confines of historically black colleges and universities.

Following passage of the 1964 U.S. Civil Rights Bill, new educational opportunities gradually opened up for blacks, and scientific careers—in both academia and industry—became more of a tangible, realistic goal. Rosters of noteworthy scientists from the 1960s to the 1990s mention a number of African Americans, including Harold Amos, bacteriologist; Shirley Ann Jackson, physicist; Edward William Hawthorne (1921–1986), physiologist; Marie Maynard Daly (b. 1921), biochemist; and Ronald Erwin McNair, astronautical physicist. Scientific organizations, learned societies, and educational institutions grew more inclusive during this period. David Harold Blackwell, a mathematician, was elected to the National Academy of Sciences in 1965. The physicist Walter Eugene Massey became the first African-American president of the American Association for the Advancement of Science in 1988 and the first African-American director of the National Science Foundation in 1990. Nevertheless, statistics indicate that African Americans continue to be underrepresented in science. Only 2 to 3 percent of American scientists are black, while African Americans constitute around 12 percent of the total U.S. population.

—KENNETH R. MANNING

SCOTTSBORO CASE

On April 9, 1931, an Alabama judge sentenced eight black teenagers to death: Haywood Patterson, Olen Montgomery, Clarence Norris, Willie Roberson, Andrew Wright, Ozie Powell, Eugene Williams and Charley Weems. After perfunctory trials in the mountain town of Scottsboro, all-white juries convicted the youths of raping two white women (Victoria Price and Ruby Bates) aboard a freight train as it moved across northern Alabama on March 25. The case of the ninth defendant—thirteen-year-old Leroy Wright—ended in a mistrial after a majority of the jury re-

See also
Tuskegee Syphillis
Experiment

fused to accept the prosecution's recommendation for life imprisonment because of his extreme youth.

The repercussions of the Scottsboro case were felt throughout the 1930s; by the end of the decade, it had become one of the great civil rights cases of the twentieth century.

After the quick conviction and draconian verdict, the Communist party's legal affiliate, the International Labor Defense (ILD), took over the case from the National Association for the Advancement of Colored People. Using both propaganda and aggressive legal action, the ILD succeeded in obtaining a new trial for the eight defendants. In a landmark case, *Powell* v. *Alabama* (1932), the U.S. Supreme Court ruled that defendants in capital cases had to receive more than a pro forma defense. (One Scottsboro attorney had been drunk at the original trial; the other was elderly and incompetent.)

The April 1933 retrial of Haywood Patterson was moved to Decatur, Ala. Defense attorney Samuel Leibowitz introduced extensive evidence that the two women had concocted the charge of rape in order to avoid prosecution for prostitution and vagrancy. The highlight of the trial came when Ruby Bates—who had disappeared in 1932—dramatically renounced her earlier accusations and testified on behalf of Patterson and the other Scottsboro defendants.

But the jurors—reflecting the belief of the local white community that Bates was bribed by communist agitators ("Jew money from New York" in the words of one prosecutor)—ignored her testimony. They were particularly incensed by the willingness of Alabama's African-American population to join the defense in attacking the state's all-white jury system. (In pretrial hearings before Judge James E. Horton, Jr., ten members of Decatur's black community defied Klan cross burnings and threats to insist that they were qualified to serve as jurors but had never been called.) The jury convicted Patterson and mandated the judge to order the death penalty.

To the surprise of almost everyone, Judge Horton—convinced that Patterson and the other defendants were innocent—set aside the verdict, pointing out that the evidence "overwhelmingly preponderated" in favor of the Scottsboro defendants. He ordered a new trial and announced that the nine defendants would never be convicted in his court. In the next election, however, voters defeated Horton and elected a judge more amenable to the prosecution's case to preside over the trial of Patterson and Clarence Norris.

Many in Alabama had come to see the Scottsboro Case as a test of white Southerners' resolve against the forces of "communism" and "racial amalgamation." The guilt or innocence of the defendants thus seemed irrelevant.

The trials that followed were travesties of justice. Horton's replacement, Judge William Washington Callahan, barred critical defense evidence, bullied and belittled defense attorneys and witnesses, effectively acted as coprosecutor. In the fall of 1933, all-white juries convicted both Patterson and Clarence Norris.

ILD attorneys once again successfully appealed to the Supreme Court, this time on the grounds that African Americans had been systematically excluded from Alabama juries. In *Norris* v. *Alabama* (1935), the court accepted the defense argument, overturned the Norris and Patterson verdicts, and returned the case to Alabama for retrial. The decision, though not ending all-white juries, marked another step in the Supreme Court's willingness to chip away at the legal system of the South.

In 1936, oversight of the case passed from the Communist party to a coalition of mainline civil rights organizations. This shift gave Alabama officials—by now embarrassed over the continuing judicial rebukes—an opportunity to compromise. The state dropped the charges against the four youngest defendants, and the other five received prison sentences from twenty years to life with the understanding that once publicity in the case had subsided, they would be quietly released. Despite the intense lobbying of national civil rights leaders (and the secret intervention of President Franklin Roosevelt), Alabama officials blocked their release. It was 1950 before the last of the Scottsboro defendants, Andrew Wright, received his parole.

For a generation of African Americans who came of age in the 1930s, the Scottsboro Case was a vivid reminder of white legal oppression, and it helped further their resolve to mobilize against Jim Crow.

—DAN T. CARTER

SCURLOCK, ADDISON

Addison Scurlock (June 19, 1883–1964), photographer. Addison Scurlock was the patriarch of a family of photographers who documented the cultural, social, and political history of Washington, D.C., and adjacent communities from the early 1900s to the present. Born in Fayetteville,

See also

Jim Crow

S

N.C., Scurlock was the son of George Clay Scurlock, a local politician. The family moved to Washington in 1900, shortly after Addison's graduation from high school. George Clay Scurlock worked for the U.S. Treasury Department as a messenger while he studied law. On passing the bar examination, he opened a law office on U Street.

In 1900 young Addison Scurlock became an apprentice to Moses P. Rice, a local photographer of some prominence who had a studio on Pennsylvania Avenue. By 1904, Scurlock was sufficiently confident of his newly acquired skills to strike out on his own. His first photographic studio was located in the home of his parents, in the 500 block of Florida Avenue, N.W.

In 1911, he opened the Scurlock Studio of 900 U Street. He had garnered a reputation for his portraiture among the vibrant African-American intelligentsia and burgeoning middle-class communities in the District and counted many of Washington's most celebrated citizens, both black and white, as his customers. He was the official photographer for Howard University, and was frequently called on to document the visits of prominent black Americans to the nation's capital. His mastery of the panorama camera made him the photographer of choice for large socially

SECESSION
Southern Slaveholding States Seek Autonomy

The secession of eleven slaveholding states occurred in response to the election of Abraham Lincoln to the presidency in 1860. As Alexander H. Stephens, the vice president of the Confederacy, stated, the "cornerstone" of the new government rested "upon the great truth that the negro is not equal to the white man."

The idea of secession has a long history among disaffected Americans. The Constitution does not directly address the issue, so proponents could argue that secession was legal rather than revolutionary. New England Federalists during the War of 1812 openly threatened secession, and, ironically, Garrisonian abolitionists recommended the same course in the 1840s as a protest against slavery. But proslavery Southerners supported the idea of secession as being consistent with the dominant Jeffersonian-Jacksonian belief in "states' rights."

Most southern whites viewed secession as inexpedient as long as slavery was relatively safe in the Union; but the escalating sectional tension after the Mexican War undermined that confidence. The growing northern determination that the new western territories should be "free soil" appeared ominous, and the attempt to admit California as a free state provoked serious discussion of secession. The Compromise of 1850 briefly quieted the threat, but the rise of the Republican Party later in the decade added impetus to the movement. The Republican party's triumph in 1860 allowed outright secessionists to argue that the federal government now threatened slavery. Lincoln had pledged that he would not attack the institution of slavery in the southern states, but he also hoped for its "ultimate extinction."

South Carolina forced the issue, electing a se-

cession convention that voted to dissolve the state's relation to the Union on December 20, 1860. Over the next two months, the other Deep South states voted to secede, first Mississippi, then Alabama, Florida, Georgia, Louisiana, and, finally, Texas. There was substantial resistance to immediate secession, with opponents generally campaigning under the title of "Cooperationists" or "Cooperative Secessionists." Resistance to immediate secession tended to be strongest in the areas outside the plantation belt, particularly in the mountain areas populated by white small farmers. There was also a tendency for some of the wealthiest plantation counties to vote against immediate secession.

In the eight states of the upper South, the larger concentration of nonslaveholders prevented immediate action. Most whites hoped reconciliation was possible. Only the Confederate attack on Fort Sumter in April 1861, commencing the Civil War, and President Lincoln's subsequent call for troops forced these states to choose sides. Four states—Virginia, Tennessee, Arkansas, and North Carolina—seceded, but opposition remained strong in the mountain enclaves. The northwestern part of Virginia remained in the Union, becoming West Virginia. Four other slave states, termed "border states"—Kentucky, Delaware, Missouri, and Maryland—stayed with the Union or declared neutrality.

After Fort Sumter, a wave of enthusiasm swept through the white South, and many initially dubious Southerners reconciled themselves to the breakup of the Union. The limited support for immediate secession, however, points to the later social divisions that weakened the Confederacy.

—MICHAEL W. FITZGERALD

See also
Gordon Parks, Sr.

and historically significant community gatherings—such as weddings, cotillions, and banquets—throughout the District of Columbia. His clients included schools, churches, and social and civic organizations. According to historian Michael Winston, "The agencies of the Federal Government, though riddled with discrimination, offered [him] stable employment."

Scurlock was respected as a businessman, and was often described by those who knew him as a man who "didn't need a calling card." He made his clients feel comfortable with their own images: according to his son Robert Scurlock, "He wanted it to look like the person in their Sunday best, their best face forward." He was astute at lighting his subjects, and often touched up photographs so that he might achieve an image he could take pride in and his clients would value. *Washington Post* reporter Peter Perl stated that "for decade after decade, thousands of Washingtonians have wanted the Scurlock face."

Scurlock's accomplishments as a still photographer were well recognized and appreciated during his lifetime. Carter G. Woodson, the black historian and founder of the Association for the Study of Afro-American Life and History (first known as the Association for the Study of Negro Life and History), distributed a series of Scurlock portraits of black leaders to schools throughout the nation. In the 1930s, Scurlock was able to reach a broad audience through the publication of his work in books and newspapers. He also produced a weekly newsreel of Washington events, which was shown in local movie theaters.

From the beginning, the Scurlock photographic business was a family endeavor. His wife, Mamie, managed his studios; by 1940 his sons Robert and George, both graduates of Howard University, had joined the business. The Scurlock brothers worked as photojournalists, supplying photographs to the black press, and George handled the studio's nonportrait work. In 1948 the brothers opened the Capital School of Photography, where they trained many aspiring photographers.

In 1952, the school closed and Robert Scurlock opened Custom Craft Studios, introducing color photography to the Scurlock customers. Addison Scurlock died at the age of eighty-one in 1964. The Scurlock Studios on Connecticut Avenue closed in the early 1970s; the Ninth Street studio was demolished in 1983. Robert Scurlock continues to operate the Custom Craft Studio in the tradition of his father. His clients include local and national politicians, scholars, artists, and social activists. While the family goal of creating photographs that communicate the dignity of their subjects persists today, the historical significance of their work continues to be of importance.

—CLAUDINE BROWN

SENGSTACKE, ROBERT ABBOTT

Robert Abbott Sengstacke (May 29, 1943–), photographer, newspaper editor, and publisher. By the time he was two years old, Robert Sengstacke was interested in drawing. Sengstacke concentrated on painting until he turned fourteen, when his father, John Sengstacke, who was publisher of the *Chicago Defender* and president of Sengstacke Newspaper Enterprise, gave him a box camera, and his aunt gave him a developing set. In 1959, Sengstacke purchased another camera and an enlarger and organized a photography studio in his parents' basement. He took pictures of local high school students and worked as a freelance photographer for the *Defender*.

In 1962, Sengstacke moved to Los Angeles to attend Los Angles City College, where he studied business administration and art. He left school in 1964 and returned to Chicago to work as staff photographer for the *Defender*. Sengstacke was the first non-Muslim appointed as a staff photographer for *Muhammad Speaks* (1966–1968), the newspaper of the Nation of Islam, where he recorded significant public events and private encounters within the Nation of Islam. He also worked with the Visual Arts Workshop and the Organization of Black American Culture (OBAC) to create the *Wall of Respect* (1967), an outdoor mural located on Chicago's South Side that commemorated significant figures in African-American history.

During the 1960s, Sengstacke began to view photography as an art and as a powerful tool that African Americans could use to document their own history. The Civil Rights Movement became the central subject of Sengstacke's photographs, and he became known for his images of such civil rights leaders as the Rev. Dr. Martin Luther King, Jr., Jessie Jackson, and Ralph Abernathy. Sengstacke also photographed demonstrators at various civil rights marches, most notably in his series on the march from Selma to Montgomery in 1965. Sengstacke was known for his ability to record intimate moments within large-scale political events.

See also
Civil Rights Movement

In the summer of 1969, Sengstacke returned to school at the University of Southern California to study filmmaking. He was artist-in-residence at Fisk University from 1969 to 1971, and in 1971 he became vice president of Sengstacke Newspaper Enterprise. During that year he also worked as a photographer on assignment in Mississippi for *Ebony* magazine. In the mid to late 1970s, he photographed in Syria, Egypt, Lebanon, Jordan, and Israel for the Black Press and in Jamaica for the Jamaican Board of Tourism (1974). Sengstacke received the National Newspaper Association Best News Photography Award in 1974. He became general manager of the *Tri-State Defender* in Memphis, Tenn., in 1975, and four years later was appointed editor and publisher.

During the 1980s, Sengstacke began working commercially for Eastman Kodak and the *Phil Donahue Show;* he also took on assignments for *Essence, Jet* magazine, *Negro Digest, Life Magazine,* the *Washington Post,* and the *New York Times.* Sengstacke became the president of Sengstacke Newspaper Enterprise in 1988.

Since the mid-1960s, Sengstacke has exhibited in colleges throughout the United States, as well as in small public exhibits in Chicago and New York. He was the first African-American photographer from Chicago to exhibit work at the main branch of the Chicago Public Library (1969). His work also has been shown at Morehouse College in Atlanta (1970), the Chicago City Hall (1973), the University of Minnesota (1977), the William Grant Still Community Arts Center in Los Angeles (1979), the Kenkeleba House in New York (1986), and the Studio Museum in Harlem (1986). He was appointed executive editor of the *Chicago Daily Defender* in 1993.

—MELISSA RACHLEFF

SHANGE, NTOZAKE

Ntozake Shange (October 18, 1948–), playwright and performer. Ntozake Shange was born Paulette Williams in Trenton, N.J. She took the Zulu name Ntozake ("she who comes with her own things") Shange ("she who walks like a lion") in 1971. Shange grew up in an upper-middle-class family, very involved in political and cultural activities. She earned degrees in American studies from Barnard (1970) and the University of Southern California (1973). She lives in Philadelphia with her daughter.

Shange's writing is marked by unique spelling and punctuation, partly to establish a recognizable style, like that of a musician, but also as a reaction against Western culture. Much of her work is in the form of a "choreopoem," blending music, drama, and dance. Her work is brutally honest, reflective, and intense. She writes for those whose voices have often been ignored, especially young African-American women.

Her best-known work is the play *for colored girls who have considered suicide/when the rainbow is enuf* (1976). Despite many harrowing scenes the work is essentially optimistic, showing the "infinite beauty" of black women. The play's conception took place over many years; it opened on Broadway in September 1976, and played there for almost two years before going on national and international tour.

Shange is a highly prolific author whose other published plays include *a photograph: lovers in motion, boogie woogie landscapes,* and *spell #7,* which were collected in *three pieces* (1981). Many other plays have not been published as yet, including a powerful adaptation of Bertolt Brecht's *Mother Courage* (1980).

Her volumes of poetry include *Nappy Edges* (1978), *A Daughter's Geography* (1983), *from okra to greens* (1984), *Ridin' the Moon in Texas: Word Paintings* (1987), and *The Love Space Demands: A Continuing Saga* (1991). She has written two nov-

MULTITALENTED WRITER

Playwright, poet, and novelist Ntozake Shange's best-known work is for colored girls who have considered suicide / when the rainbow is enuf. SHAWN WALKER

els, *Sassafrass, Cypress & Indigo* (1982), and *Betsey Brown* (1985). Many of these works have also been adapted into theatrical form. Her prose is collected in *See No Evil: Prefaces, Essays, and Accounts, 1976–1983* (1984).

Shange has received many awards, including the Obie and the Outer Critics Circle awards.

—LOUIS J. PARASCANDOLA

SHEPP, ARCHIBALD VERNON "ARCHIE"

Archibald Vernon "Archie" Shepp (May 24, 1937–), tenor and soprano saxophonist and composer. Born in Fort Lauderdale, Fla., Shepp grew up in Philadelphia and began performing as a saxophonist and clarinetist while a teenager. He studied drama at Goddard College in Vermont and, after graduating, moved to New York City. Unable to support himself as an actor, he taught junior high school (1961–1963) and became active in the burgeoning avant-garde jazz and drama scenes. His raucous early style on tenor saxophone combined the stylings of hardbopper Sonny Rollins and swing era giant Ben Webster while pushing the harmonic and melodic limitations of improvisation. His uniquely rugged solos demonstrate his debt to the pantheon of traditional tenor players. Shepp also helped introduce a militant political activism to avant-garde jazz in the 1960s, advocating black nationalism in poems and essays, both in print ("An Artist Speaks Bluntly," *Downbeat* 32, 1965; "A View from the Inside," *Downbeat Yearbook*, 1966) and in performances during which he delivered impromptu lectures.

Shepp made his first recordings with Cecil Taylor in 1960 (*The World of Cecil Taylor;* reissued as *Air*) and in 1961 (*Into the Hot,* also with Gil Evans). That year he also performed onstage with Taylor's quartet in Jack Gelber's play *The Connection* at the Living Theater. He recorded with trumpeter Bill Dixon in 1962 and with saxophonist John Tchicai in 1963 on a series of albums as the New York Contemporary Five, including a composition dedicated to Medgar evers. In 1964 he played second tenor on a now-lost recording for John Coltrane's *A Love Supreme* and in that year recorded *Four for Trane,* an album produced by Coltrane. The next year Shepp led a sextet and a trio on *Fire Music,* which included "Malcolm, Malcolm, Semper Malcolm," dedicated to Malcolm X. In 1967 Shepp wrote and produced a

play, *Junebug Graduates Tonight!* In 1969 a group he led on a French and Algerian tour resulted in a series of controversial recordings for the Actuel series of BYG Records; with Rhasaan Roland Kirk and others he interrupted the taping of the Merv Griffin television show to demand that networks hire more black musicians. In the early 1970s, Shepp began teaching at the State University of New York at Buffalo, and in 1974 he became a member of the Afro-American Studies Department at the University of Massachusetts at Amherst.

Starting in the mid-1970s, Shepp's style became more overtly refined by his reverence for the jazz tradition. Always a lover of Ellingtonia, he also has recorded several tributes to traditional musicians and historical periods, including *Bird Fire: Tribute to Charlie Parker* (1979) and a series of spirituals in duet with pianist Horace Parlan. Shepp played piano on *Doodling* (1976) and *Maple Leaf Rag* (1978). In addition to teaching, Shepp continues to perform and record, as a leader of his own group on *Little Red Moon* (1986) as well as with vocalist Jeanne Lee on *African Moods* (1984) and duets with Dutch pianist Jasper van't Hof (1987) and bassist Richard Davis (*Body and Soul,* 1991).

—RON WELBURN

SICKLE-CELL DISEASE

Sickle-cell disease is a genetically acquired disorder of the red blood cells. A person who inherits the sickle-cell gene from both parents is born with the disease; a person inheriting the gene from only one parent is a sickle-cell carrier. Sickling disorders in the United States are concentrated in areas where there are large groups of African Americans, such as the Northeast, Midwest, and rural South. Sickle-cell disease (a term preferred to the older "sickle-cell anemia") can also be found among the populations of West Africa, the Caribbean, Guyana, Panama, Brazil, Italy, Greece, and India. Eight percent of African Americans are heterozygous for the sickling gene or trait. These carriers may become ill at high altitudes, and some unexpected deaths have occurred to soldiers during extreme maneuvers. The gene for sickle-cell hemoglobin was first introduced to the Americas through the slave trade. Carriers of the disease have some immunity to the fatal form of malaria, something that proved useful to African

See also
John Coltrane
Jazz

slaves in swampy tidal regions, as in the Chesapeake and South Carolina.

The sickle cell, so called because of its bent shape, was not named until 1910, when J. B. Herrick described the blood cells of an anemic patient. In 1949 Linus Pauling discovered the chemical abnormality that causes red blood cells to become misshapen and also found the link between the sickle cell and malaria. Although the attention given the disease has increased substantially since World War II, misinformation about the illness persists and often causes discrimination against sickle-cell carriers in the insurance industry and the job market. In the 1970s the prevalence and consequences of sickle-cell disease became widely publicized in both the African-American and mainstream media.

Several organizations have been established for education and research about the disease, including the National Association for Sickle-Cell Disease, founded in 1971 in Los Angeles. Numerous hospitals have centers for the study of sickle-cell disease, including the Columbia University Comprehensive Sickle-Cell Center at Harlem Hospital in New York City, founded in 1972, and the Center for Sickle-Cell Disease at Howard University, founded by Ronald B. Scott in 1972. These organizations have undertaken extensive fund-raising campaigns for research and treatment of the illness. Government funding for research has risen since the early 1970s. Attempts to cut federal research support in the 1980s drew vehement opposition from many black organizations. In 1993 thirty-eight states and the District of Columbia required testing of newborns for sickle-cell traits.

In persons with sickle-cell disease, deoxygenated hemoglobin S causes the red blood cells in the body to assume the sickle shape. These cells cannot carry oxygen as normal red blood cells do, and they lodge in small blood vessels, causing ischemia (oxygen deficiency) and necrosis. This blockage of vessels is called vaso-occlusive crisis and gives rise to intense pain.

Symptoms of sickle-cell disease usually appear after six months of age when the last of the fetal hemoglobin, which increases oxygen supply in the blood, leaves the infant's body. Untreated, a patient may develop circulatory collapse. Such a patient is given large amounts of intravenous fluids to support circulation and prevent shock. Older patients may have pain in the larger bones, chest, back, joints, and abdomen and can develop hemorrhages into the eye and brain.

Treatment for sickle-cell patients commonly calls for pain medication ranging from oral analgesics to the injectable narcotics for pain management. Intravenous fluids are prescribed to prevent dehydration and flood the vasculature with the intention of floating the sickling cells from occluded vessels. Antibiotics are ordered for infections, and prophylactic penicillin is suggested for infants to prevent infections. Blood transfusions are not routinely recommended for short-term crises but may be indicated during prolonged episodes and when lung and central nervous system involvement is evident.

Experimental treatment for sickle-cell patients includes the use of hydroxyurea, which can increase the level of fetal hemoglobin circulating in the body. Bone-marrow transplants have been performed on some children. This remains a risky procedure, however, carrying a 5 to 10 percent mortality rate. Though no cure exists, methods of treating chronic sickle-cell patients have improved in the past twenty years. Conservative treatment methods offer a prudent course of disease management. People with sickle-cell disease, once expected to live only to their forties, now live longer and healthier lives.

—JANE M. DELUCA

SIMPSON, ORENTHAL JAMES "O. J."

Orenthal James "O. J." Simpson (July 9, 1947–), football player. O. J. Simpson was born in San Francisco and starred in football, baseball, and track at Galileo High School. After graduating in 1965, Simpson enrolled at City College of San Francisco, where he set several junior-college football rushing records in two seasons. In 1967 the highly recruited halfback transferred to the University of Southern California (USC).

At USC, Simpson emerged as a national star, displaying tremendous speed and open-field running abilities. In two seasons he carried the ball 649 times for 3,295 yards and 34 touchdowns, led USC to a national championship in 1967, and won the Heisman Memorial Trophy in 1968.

Simpson was selected first overall by the American Football League's Buffalo Bills in the 1969 professional football draft. He failed to live up to expectations in his first three years with Buffalo, but in 1972 he rushed for 1,251 yards and established himself as one of the National Football League's best running backs. The following season Simpson rushed for 2,003 yards, becoming the first player to rush for more than 2,000 yards

See also

Football

624

in one season. He rushed for more than 1,000 yards in each of his next four seasons with Buffalo, and in 1976 he set a single-game rushing record with 273 yards gained against the Detroit Lions. After that year, Simpson's statistics declined, and following the 1977 season he was traded to the San Francisco Forty-niners, where he spent the final two years of his football career. Simpson retired in 1979 with a professional rushing record of 2,404 carries for 11,236 yards and 61 touchdowns. He was inducted into the NFL Hall of Fame in 1985.

Following his retirement from football, Simpson lived in Los Angeles and capitalized on his good looks and polished public persona by launching a successful career in television, film, and advertising. He appeared in several made-for-television and feature films, including *Roots* (1977) and three *Naked Gun* films (1988, 1991, 1993), served as a network sports commentator, and was featured in commercials.

Simpson became the center of a sensational murder case when his former wife, Nicole Brown, and a male friend of hers were stabbed to death in Los Angeles on June 12, 1994. Suspicion focused on Simpson, who led the police on a nationally televised car chase before surrendering at his home in a Los Angeles suburb. He was subsequently indicted and pleaded not guilty to both counts of murder. In the avalanche of publicity surrounding the case, some disquieting information about Simpson was revealed, including a pattern of wife abuse that included a little-publicized 1989 conviction for spousal battery. Information also surfaced later about possible police misconduct in the investigation of the case. After a lengthy pretrial hearing, a protracted jury selection process, and an eight-month trial, he was acquitted of all charges on October 3, 1995.

A wrongful-death suit was then filed in civil court, and in February 1997 Simpson was found liable in the deaths of Nicole Brown Simpson and Ronald Goldman. He was ordered to pay $8.5 million in compensatory damages and $25 million in punitive damages.

—THADDEUS RUSSELL

SLAVE NARRATIVES

The autobiographical narratives of former slaves comprise one of the most extensive and influential traditions in African-American literature and culture. The best-known slave narratives were authored by fugitives from slavery who used their personal histories to illustrate the horrors of America's "peculiar institution." But a large number of former slaves who either purchased their freedom or endured their bondage until emancipation also recounted their experiences under slavery. Most of the major authors of African-American literature before 1900, including Frederick Douglass, William Wells Brown, Harriet Jacobs, and Booker T. Washington, launched their writing careers via the slave narrative.

During the formative era of African-American autobiography, from 1760 to the end of the Civil War in the United States, approximately seventy narratives of fugitive or former slaves were published as discrete entities, some in formats as brief as the broadside, others in bulky, sometimes multivolume texts. Slave narratives dominated the literary landscape of antebellum black America, far outnumbering the autobiographies of free people of color, not to mention the handful of novels published by American blacks during this time. After slavery was abolished in North America, ex-slaves continued to produce narratives of their bondage and freedom in substantial numbers. From 1865 to 1930, during which time at least fifty former slaves wrote or dictated book-length accounts of their lives, the ex-slave narrative remained the preponderant subgenre of African-American autobiography. During the Great Depression of the 1930s, the federal writers' project gathered oral personal histories and testimony about slavery from 2,500 former slaves in seventeen states, generating roughly 10,000 pages of interviews that were eventually published in a "composite autobiography" of eighteen volumes. One of the slave narratives' most reliable historians has estimated that a grand total of all contributions to this genre, including separately published texts, materials that appeared in periodicals, and oral histories and interviews, numbers approximately six thousand.

The earliest slave narratives have strong affinities with popular white American accounts of Indian captivity and Christian conversion in the New World. But with the rise of the antislavery movement in the early nineteenth century came a new demand for slave narratives that would highlight the harsh realities of slavery itself. White abolitionists were convinced that the eyewitness testimony of former slaves against slavery would touch the hearts and change the minds of many in the northern population of the United States who were either ignorant of or indifferent to the plight of African Americans in the South. In the late 1830s and early 1840s, the first of this new brand

Boys on and about the plantation inevitably learned to use [the Negro woman], and having acquired the habit, often continued it into manhood and even after marriage.

W.J. CASH
THE MIND OF THE SOUTH,
1941

BEFORE HER TIME
Author First to Chronicle Sexual Abuse of Slaves

Harriet Ann Jacobs (1813–March 7, 1897), slave narrator and reformer. She was born a slave in Edenton, N.C. Jacobs's major contribution is her narrative, *Incidents in the Life of a Slave Girl: Written by Herself* (1861). The most comprehensive antebellum autobiography by an African-American woman, *Incidents* is the first-person account of Jacobs's pseudonymous narrator "Linda Brent," who writes of her sexual oppression and her struggle for freedom. After publishing her book, Jacobs devoted her life to providing relief for black Civil War refugees in Alexandria, Va.; Savannah, Ga.; and Washington, D.C.

Writing as "Linda Brent," Jacobs tells the story of her life in the South as slave and as fugitive, and of her life as a fugitive slave in the North. Breaking the taboos forbidding women to discuss their sexuality, she writes of the abuse she suffered from her licentious master, Dr. James Norcom, whom she calls "Dr. Flint." She confesses that to prevent him from making her his concubine, at sixteen she became sexually involved with a white neighbor. Their alliance produced two children, Joseph (c. 1829–?), whom she calls "Benny," and Louisa Matilda (1833–1917), called "Ellen." Jacobs describes her 1835 flight from Norcom and the almost seven years she spent in hiding, in a tiny crawl space above a porch in her grandmother's Edenton home.

She further recounts her 1842 escape to New York City; her reunion with her children, who had been sent north; and her subsequent move to Rochester, N.Y., where she became part of the circle of abolitionists around Frederick Douglass's newspaper the *North Star.* Condemning the compliance of the North in the slave system, she describes her North Carolina master's attempts to catch her in New York after passage of the 1850 Fugitive Slave Law. Jacobs explains that despite her principled decision not to bow to the slave system by being purchased, in 1853 her New York employer, Nathaniel Parker Willis (called "Mr. Bruce"), bought her from Norcom's family. Like other slave narrators, she ends her book with her freedom and the freedom of her children.

Most of the extraordinary events that "Linda Brent" narrates have been documented as having occurred in Jacobs's life. In addition, a group of letters that Jacobs wrote while composing her book present a unique glimpse of its inception, composition, and publication, and recount her complex relationships with black abolitionist William C. Nell and white abolitionists Amy Post and Lydia Maria Child. They also make an interesting commentary on Jacobs's northern employer, the litterateur Nathaniel Parker Willis, and on Harriet Beecher Stowe, the author of *Uncle Tom's Cabin,* whom Jacobs tried to interest in her narrative.

Although *Incidents* was published anonymously, Jacobs's name was connected with her book from the first; only in the twentieth century were its authorship and its autobiographical status disputed. *Incidents* made Jacobs known to the northern abolitionists, and with the outbreak of the Civil War she used this newfound celebrity to establish a new career for herself. She collected money and supplies for the "contrabands"—black refugees crowding behind the lines of the Union Army in Washington, D.C., and in occupied Alexandria, Va.—and returned south.

Supported by Quaker groups and the newly formed New England Freedmen's Aid Society, in 1863 Jacobs and her daughter moved to Alexandria, where they provided emergency relief supplies, organized primary medical care, and established the Jacobs Free School—a black-led institution providing black teachers for the refugees. In 1865, mother and daughter moved to Savannah, where they continued their relief work. Throughout the war years, Harriet and Louisa Jacobs reported on their southern relief efforts in the northern press and in newspapers in England, where Jacobs's book had appeared as *The Deeper Wrong: Incidents in the Life of a Slave Girl: Written by Herself* (1862). In 1868, they sailed to England, and successfully raised money for Savannah's black orphans and aged.

But in the face of increasing violence in the South, Jacobs and her daughter then retreated to Massachusetts. At Boston, they were connected with the newly formed New England Women's Club, then moved to Cambridge, where for several years Jacobs ran a boardinghouse for Harvard faculty and students. She and Louisa later moved to Washington, D.C., where the mother continued to work among the destitute freedpeople and the daughter was employed in the new "colored schools" and at Howard University. In 1896, when the National Association of Colored Women held its organizing meetings in Washington, Harriet Jacobs was confined to a wheelchair, but it seems likely that Louisa was in attendance. The following spring, Harriet Jacobs died at her Washington home. She is buried in Mount Auburn Cemetery, Cambridge, Mass.

—JEAN FAGAN YELLIN

See also
Sojourner Truth

of outspokenly antislavery slave narratives found their way into print. These set the mold for what would become by mid-century a standardized form of autobiography and abolitionist propaganda.

Typically, the antebellum slave narrative carries a black message inside a white envelope. Prefatory (and sometimes appended) matter by whites attests to the reliability and good character of the narrator, and calls attention to what the narrative will reveal about the moral abominations of slavery. The former slave's contribution to the text centers on his or her rite of passage from slavery in the South to freedom in the North. Usually the antebellum slave narrator portrays slavery as a condition of extreme physical, intellectual, emotional, and spiritual deprivation, a kind of hell on earth. Precipitating the narrator's decision to escape is some sort of personal crisis, such as the sale of a loved one or a dark night of the soul in which hope contends with despair for the spirit of the slave. Impelled by faith in God and a commitment to liberty and human dignity comparable (the slave narrative often stresses) to that of America's Founding Fathers, the slave undertakes an arduous quest for freedom that climaxes in his or her arrival in the North. In many antebellum narratives, the attainment of freedom is signaled not simply by reaching the free states but by renaming oneself and dedicating one's future to antislavery activism.

Advertised in the abolitionist press and sold at antislavery meetings throughout the English-speaking world, a significant number of antebellum slave narratives went through multiple editions and sold in the tens of thousands. This popularity was not solely attributable to the publicity the narratives received from antislavery movement. Readers could see that, as one reviewer put it, "the slave who endeavours to recover his freedom is associating with himself no small part of the romance of the time." To the noted transcendentalist clergyman Theodore Parker, slave narratives qualified as America's only indigenous literary form, for "all the original romance of Americans is in them, not in the white man's novel." The most widely read and hotly debated American novel of the nineteenth century, Harriet Beecher Stowe's *Uncle Tom's Cabin* (1852), was profoundly influenced by its author's reading of a number of slave narratives, to which she owed many graphic incidents and the models for some of her most memorable characters.

In 1845 the slave narrative reached its epitome with the publication of the *Narrative of the Life of Frederick Douglass, an American Slave, Written by Himself.* Selling more then 30,000 copies in the first five years of its existence, Douglass's *Narrative* became an international bestseller, its contemporary readership far outstripping that of such classic white autobiographies as Henry David Thoreau's *Walden* (1854). The abolitionist leader William Lloyd Garrison introduced Douglass's *Narrative* by stressing how representative Douglass's experience of slavery had been. But Garrison could not help but note the extraordinary individuality of the black author's manner of rendering that experience. It is Douglass's style of self-presentation, through which he recreated the slave as an evolving self bound for mental as well as physical freedom, that makes his autobiography so important. After Douglass's *Narrative,* the presence of the subtitle, *Written by Himself,* on a slave narrative bore increasing political and literary significance as an indicator of a narrator's self-determination independent of external expectations and conventions. In the late 1840s well-known fugitive slaves such as William Wells Brown, Henry W. Bibb, and James W. C. Pennington reinforced the rhetorical self-consciousness of the slave narrative by incorporating into their stories trickster motifs from African-American folk culture, extensive literary and biblical allusion, and a picaresque perspective on the meaning of the slave's flight from bondage to freedom.

As the slave narrative evolved in the crisis years of the 1850s and early 1860s, it addressed the problem of slavery with unprecedented candor, unmasking as never before the moral and social complexities of the American caste and class system in the North as well as the South. In *My Bondage and My Freedom* (1855), Douglass revealed that his search for freedom had not reached its fulfillment among the abolitionists, although this had been the implication of his *Narrative*'s conclusion. Having discovered in Garrison and his cohorts some of the same paternalistic attitudes that had characterized his former masters in the South, Douglass could see in 1855 that the struggle for full liberation would be much more difficult and uncertain than he had previously imagined. Harriet Jacobs, the first African-American female slave to author her own narrative, also challenged conventional ideas about slavery and freedom in her strikingly original *Incidents in the Life of a Slave Girl* (1861). Jacobs's autobiography shows how sexual exploitation made slavery especially oppressive for black women. But in demonstrating how she fought back and ultimately gained both her own freedom and that of her two children, Jacobs proved the inadequacy of the image of vic-

See also

Uncle Tom's Cabin

Booker T. Washington

tim that had been pervasively applied to female slaves in the male-authored slave narrative.

In most post-emancipation slave narratives, slavery is depicted as a kind of crucible in which the resilience, industry, and ingenuity of the slave was tested and ultimately validated. Thus the slave narrative argued that readiness of the freedman and freedwoman for full participation in the post-Civil War social and economic order. The biggest-selling of the late nineteenth- and early twentieth-century slave narratives was Booker T. Washington's *Up from Slavery* (1901), a classic American success story. Because *Up from Slavery* extolled black progress and interracial cooperation since emancipation, it won a much greater hearing from whites than was accorded those former slaves whose autobiographies detailed the legacy of injustices burdening blacks in the postwar South. Washington could not dictate the agenda of the slave narrative indefinitely, however. Modern black autobiographies, such as Richard Wright's *Black Boy* (1945), and contemporary African-American novels, such as Ernest J. Gaines's *The Autobiography of Miss Jane Pittman* (1971) and Toni Morrison's *Beloved* (1989), display unmistakable formal and thematic allegiances to the antebellum slave narrative, particularly in their determination to probe the origins of psychological as well as social oppression and in their searching critique of the meaning of freedom for twentieth-century blacks and whites alike.

—WILLIAM L. ANDREWS

SLAVERY

Slavery in the United States evolved over two centuries, from the middle of the seventeenth century through the 1860s. It varied from place to place and changed over time. A host of local factors shaped the institution and the lives of blacks and whites entangled in it. Such factors included the cultivation of particular crops, the size of the slaveholding unit, the local density of white and black populations, the laws of the colony or state, and even the personalities of individual slaveholders and slaves. At the same time, certain general features framed the common experience of slavery regardless of location. Foremost, throughout the New World, was the racial basis of enslavement. In the British North American mainland colonies, and then in the United States, bondage also was characterized by the definition of slaves as chattel property and by slavery's constant ex-

pansion westward, from tidewater to piedmont during the colonial period and across the lower South during the nineteenth century. That continuous expansion brought with it both an increasingly vigorous antislavery movement and an ever more assertive political and ideological defense by the slaveholders, so that the institution of slavery in the United States was clothed in controversy from the late eighteenth century through the secession crisis of 1860–1861. All the while, a vibrant African-American culture grew up in the slave quarters that somewhat protected slaves from the masters' demands even as the slaveholders attempted to impose more order on the institution of slavery.

Slavery was more than a labor system. It formed the economic, political, and social matrix from which developed a way of life unique in America at the locus of the clash and mixture of European and African cultures. Slavery also forced Americans to confront their true selves. In a republic born of liberty but prospering from bondage, the expansive energy of freedom collided with that of slavery. Such tensions led to civil war and, finally, to emancipation. But slavery's importance to the American identity did not end at Appomattox or even with the ratification of the Thirteenth Amendment in 1865. The cultural worlds of blacks and whites endured, and the economic and political legacies of slavery and the war that came from it burned deep into the American psyche. The historical memory of all that had been wrought by human bondage in the land of the free has made slavery a lasting point of reference for American self-identity.

For that reason alone, the subject has commanded much attention from historians and other scholars. Especially from the days of the modern Civil Rights Movement and the "coming apart" of the United States during the social protests of the 1960s, American scholarship has turned from considering slavery solely from the perspective of planters or abolitionists toward viewing the experience of bondage from the slaves' perspective. The principal shift in focus has been away from the political and institutional aspects of slavery toward the social and cultural ones. Historians now spend less time studying the profitability of slavery than they do the slaves' resistance to masters, less time on the management and marketing of crops than on the rhythms of work, less time in the fields than in the slave quarters.

In trying to reconstruct the world the slaves made, historians increasingly have relied on testimony left by the slaves themselves. Earlier gener-

See also
Civil War

ations of scholars chose to collect and read travel accounts, laws, petitions to legislatures, court cases, newspapers, planters' papers (daybooks, diaries, letters, and business records), and other documents written primarily by whites. Since the 1960s, historians have looked to the slaves' own material culture (the quilts stitched, baskets wo-ven, pots made) and have studied the slaves' folk-lore, music, speech, naming and kinship patterns, and remembrances of bondage. To do so, the modern student of slavery borrows from archaeology, anthropology, folklore, linguistics, musicology, and other social sciences, as well as reading closely the slave narratives an earlier generation of

BY
HEWLETT & BRIGHT.

SALE OF

VALUABLE
SLAVES,

(On account of departure)

The Owner of the following named and valuable Slaves, being on the eve of departure for Europe, will cause the same to be offered for sale, at the NEW EXCHANGE, corner of St. Louis and Chartres streets, on *Saturday,* May 16, at Twelve o'Clock, *viz.*

1. SARAH, a mulatress, aged 45 years, a **good cook** and accustomed to house work in general, is an excellent and faithful nurse for sick persons, and in every respect a first rate character.

2. DENNIS, her son, a mulatto, aged 24 years, a **first rate cook** and stew-ard for a vessel, having been in that capacity for many years on board one of the Mobile packets; is strictly honest, temperate, and a first rate subject.

3. CHOLE, a mulatress, aged 36 years, she is, without execption, one of the most competent servants in the country, a first rate washer and ironer, does up lace, a good cook, and for a bachelor who wishes a house-keeper she would be invaluable; she is also a good ladies' maid, having travelled to the North in that capac-ity.

4. FANNY, her daughter, a mulatress, aged 16 years, speaks French and English, is a superior hair-dresser, (pupil of Guilliac,) a good seamstress and ladies' maid, is smart, intelligent, and a first rate character.

5. DANDRIDGE, a mulatoo, aged 26 years, a first rate dining-room ser-vant, a good painter and rough carpenter, and has but few equals for honesty and sobriety.

6. NANCY, his wife, aged about 24 years, a confidential house servant, good seamstress, mantuamaker and tailoress, a good cook, washer and ironer, etc.

7. MARY ANN, her child, a creole, aged 7 years, speaks French and English, is smart, active and intelligent.

8. FANNY or FRANCES, a mulatress, aged 22 years, is a first rate washer and ironer, good cook and house servant, and has an excellent character.

9. EMMA, an orphan, aged 10 or 11 years, speaks French and English, has been in the country 7 years, has been accustomed to waiting on table, sewing etc.; is intelligent and active.

10. FRANK, a mulatto, aged about 32 years speaks French and English, is a first rate hostler and coachman, understands perfectly well the management of horses, and is, in every respect, a first rate character, with the exception that he will occasionally drink, though not an habitual drunkard.

☞ All the above named Slaves are acclimated and excellent subjects; they were purchased by their present vendor many years ago, and will, therefore, be severally warranted against all vices and maladies prescribed by law, save and except FRANK, who is fully guaranteed in every other respect but the one above mentioned.

TERMS:—One-half Cash, and the other half in notes at Six months, drawn and endorsed to the satisfaction of the Vendor, with special mortgage on the Slaves until final payment. The Acts of Sale to be passed before WILLIAM BOS-WELL, *Notary Public,* at the expense of the Purchaser.

New-Orleans, May 13, 1835.

PRINTED BY BENJAMIN LEVY.

SLAVES FOR SALE

This notice, posted by the com-pany Hewlett & Bright, advertises ten slaves for sale in 1835.
PHOTOGRAPHS AND PRINTS DIVISION, SCHOMBURG CEN-TER FOR RESEARCH IN BLACK CULTURE, THE NEW YORK PUBLIC LIBRARY, ASTOR, LENOX AND TILDEN FOUNDATIONS

*When Israel was in
Egypt's land,
Let my people go;
Oppressed so
hard they could
not stand,
Let my people go.*

ANONYMOUS,
GO DOWN, MOSES,
EARLY 19TH CENTURY

historians dismissed as propagandistic and irrelevant to the questions they thought important.

The reprinting of numerous narratives originally written or related by fugitive slaves such as Frederick Douglass during the antebellum period has made available a large cache of slave testimony. So, too, has the publication of the Slave Narrative Collection interviews, which participants in the New Deal's federal writers' project conducted with some two thousand ex-slaves during the 1930s. The abundance of slave-authored autobiographies and narratives, as well as the interviews and folklore handed down by former slaves, has altered forever the way historians approach slavery. The willingness of historians to examine slave-authored sources and to view the experience from the slaves' perspective has inverted the question of slavery's impact on the slaves and their culture. In the words of historian Eugene Genovese, the question now is not so much what was done to the slaves but "what did the slaves do for themselves?"

Answering that question has proved easier when studying the last generation of slaves than the first. No narrative accounts from slaves have survived from the seventeenth century, and the material cultural record for that formative period is fragmentary and sparse. More sources exist for the eighteenth and many for the nineteenth century, when slavery had become a mature institution. But, as historian Willie Lee Rose has reminded scholars, much of that evidence is colored by the political debates swirling about slavery—debates that eventually led to civil war. The richness, abundance, and variety of evidence from the last generation of slaves have fueled an intense examination of every facet of slave life. Adopting the perspectives of anthropology and the "new social history," both of which emphasize case studies, students of slavery have shifted the focus away from national or regional contexts toward studies of specific localities. At the same time, an earlier interest in comparing slave systems between North and South America has given way to comparing slave cultures in different U.S. settings—urban and rural, low-country and up-country, seaboard and Gulf South. In such work, the recognition that slaves were actors rather than objects in the story, struggling to define their own lives amid their travail, has been the underpinning assumption and the point of departure for discussions about the origins, evolution, and nature of slavery in the United States.

Slavery came slowly to British North America. Like so much else, it was imported and then adapted to local conditions. The first black slaves in the mainland British colonies arrived amid the boom years of Virginia tobacco growing. Because land was abundant and labor scarce in early Virginia, planters scrambled for workers to grow "the weed." In August 1619, "twenty and odd Negroes" were bartered for provisions by sailors from a Dutch ship anchored off Point Comfort, downstream from the Jamestown settlement. The status of these first blacks in the English colony is unclear. No doubt some were sold as slaves, although slavery as an institution had no legal standing in the young colony and had been unknown in England for centuries. Others likely entered indentured servitude, a labor arrangement whereby individuals sold their labor but not their person for a fixed term. By 1625, according to the first Virginia census, at least several of the blacks in the colony were free. Ominously, however, most remained locked in some form of bonded labor and, alone of those persons listed in the census, blacks were noted by color as well as condition.

For the next half-century, the number of blacks in the Chesapeake region increased to only a few hundred. While slavery became entrenched in the British West Indian sugar islands, it hardly grew in the British tobacco colonies. Disease and rough handling kept life short and mean for all workers in the tobacco colonies. Planters thus were unwilling to bid high for the lifetime labor of a slave who would most likely die within a few years when the temporary labor of an English servant was both available and quite cheap.

Englishmen in the Chesapeake region were reluctant at first to introduce large numbers of non-Englishmen into their midst. According to historian Winthrop Jordan, the English "discovered" the black African in the mid-sixteenth century, a time when the English were engaged in a process of discovering themselves as a separate people. To English eyes, the black African seemed the antithesis of Englishness. The English recoiled from the Africans' supposed savagery and heathenism, but especially from their color, which was associated with dirt, death, and the Devil in English parlance. The self-conscious English thus approached the black Africans cautiously, unsure whether they could be made over into Englishmen or if the English would be "corrupted" by mingling with them. Such attitudes did not cause the English to enslave black Africans, but once slavery did become established in the New World plantation colonies, such attitudes combined with the status of slaves as chattel property to reinforce the idea of blacks' racial inferiority.

See also
Gullah

Still, the small number of black slaves in early Chesapeake society initially blurred distinctions between slave and servant and black and white. Free blacks owned property (including slaves), bought and sold the indentures of white servants, sued in courts, served on juries, and participated in a wide range of public activities. Black slaves and white servants worked alongside one another and generally ate, slept, and caroused together. Scattered in ones and twos across farms and plantations separated by thick woods and rivers, the few blacks lost their African ways in the Chesapeake. With few women among them, they entered a male servant culture where racial distinctions mattered little. No rigid system of racial discrimination yet existed in either law or custom.

This began to change by the late seventeenth century. A declining birthrate in England and growing opportunities elsewhere curtailed the supply of white indentured servants. Meanwhile, life spans were lengthening in the Chesapeake region as physical conditions improved and people acclimated. More servants now survived to claim their freedom and the land due them—land planters tried not to grant to new tobacco competitors. Tensions between greedy planters and their angry former servants erupted in Bacon's Rebellion in Virginia in 1676, during which the new "freemen" combined with servants to drive the governor and his planter allies from the capital and threatened to overthrow Virginia altogether before finally disbanding. The shock of the rebellion of lower-class blacks and whites together forced planters to consider the implications of their labor policy. Their abuses of English indentured servants seemed to threaten the rights of all Englishmen. With indentured-servant labor less available and more unruly, and with African slave labor becoming more available and less expensive due to increased English involvement in the African slave trade, planters began to buy Africans in larger numbers.

The improved life expectancy of workers made investment in a permanent labor force of black slaves practical. So, too, did the clarification of the legal definition of slaves as chattel property during the 1660s and 1670s. After 1660, slavery was written into law in Virginia and Maryland. The status of the slave became both perpetual and hereditary. The shift from white indentured labor to black slave labor also promised to relieve class tensions among whites by binding all whites together on the basis of race. By the turn of the eighteenth century, slavery had become the normal condition for blacks in the Chesapeake. The

distinctions between servant and slave sharpened as slavery acquired a racial definition and as it came to mean a condition for life as chattel property.

Farther south, slavery took a different course. South Carolina's first permanent English settlers came from Barbados, where slavery was an established institution, bringing with them both their slaves and their expectations of building a plantation colony in South Carolina. After a brief diversion while they engaged in a lucrative deerskin trade with the Indians, in the 1690s the planters turned to rice to make their fortunes. African slaves taught the English planters rice cultivation, cattle herding, and riverboating techniques suitable to the Carolina environment. Possession of these skills, relative immunity to malaria, and adaptability to the humid low-country climate all conspired to make the Africans an attractive labor source to planters eager for profit but loath to stay in Sea Island and Tidewater plantations during the summer "sickly" season.

For a time, Carolina planters supported an Indian slave trade, which peaked in the mid-1720s before the supply gave out due to Indian population declines from disease and warfare. When Indian slavery and white indentured servitude failed to meet the planters' labor needs, they imported large numbers of African slaves. As early as 1708, blacks made up a majority of the South Carolina population. By the 1730s, much of the low country had been converted to a rice culture of large plantations, with blacks outnumbering whites by almost two to one and with newly imported Africans making up a significant proportion of the black slave population.

Early on, whites and blacks in Carolina lived and worked together on small farms and stock-raising plantations, or "cow pens." To defend the colony against Indians and Spaniards, whites had even armed blacks and enlisted them in the militia. Blacks enjoyed considerable autonomy and worked in a wide variety of employments. Rice changed all that.

The heavy black presence that resulted from rice plantation culture fundamentally altered Carolina slavery. The races increasingly lived apart, and nervous whites disarmed blacks and tried to circumscribe their activities with repressive laws borrowed from Caribbean slave codes. Blacks responded with repeated individual acts of resistance and several failed uprisings. Then, in the Stono Rebellion of 1739, nearly one hundred slaves seeking to escape to Spanish Florida seized weapons and killed a score of whites before being

Absalom Jones made some of the most important contributions to black community building at a time when the first urban free black communities of the United States were taking form.

PAGE 542

The Stono Rebellion of 1739 was the largest uprising of enslaved African Americans to take place in Britain's mainland colonies before the American Revolution.

PAGE 660

See also

Nat Turner's Rebellion

defeated by white militia. Whites clamped down hard. The colony's government curtailed African importations for a time afterward and passed the Negro Act of 1740, which imposed the harshest slave code in the British mainland colonies.

By insisting on greater white vigilance and patrols, the slave codes in Carolina and elsewhere discouraged mass uprisings, but they did not end slave resistance or autonomy. Stono was the largest mass slave insurrection during the colonial period—and the last—although smaller rumblings occurred in South Carolina and Georgia, which instituted slavery in 1750; New York City (which had experienced a slave uprising in 1712 during which blacks had killed several whites) panicked in 1741 amid a rumor of revolt. Instead, slave resistance became more localized and individual, though no less violent at times, as slaves cultivated a new culture of their own in the quarters away from the master.

By the time of the American Revolution, slavery was firmly rooted in British North America. Every colony had slaves, and even those colonies, such as Massachusetts, with little need for mass slave labor found slaves useful in maritime trades, craft occupations, and domestic service and as common laborers. New York City and environs were especially tied to slavery, where slaves constituted over 30 percent of the city's laborers by the mid-eighteenth century and the majority of unfree workers on farms along the Hudson River, on Long Island, and in northern New Jersey. Northern colonies were further implicated in slavery by the profits their merchants earned provisioning the sugar islands and trading in slaves. Slavery's principal foothold, however, remained in the southern staple-producing colonies. There, from the Chesapeake Tidewater to the Piedmont and in the Carolinas and Georgia, American slavery acquired the character that would distinguish it thereafter.

More than anything else, dramatic slave-population growth fixed the character of British North American slavery during the eighteenth century. Several hundred thousand African slaves were brought into North America, many through the principal slave entry point of Charleston, S.C., but others to the wharves of Chesapeake planters and such ports as Philadelphia. The largest number of African-born slaves arrived at mid-century, at the same time that the native- (or "country"-) born slave population was forming families and reproducing.

The arrival of so many Africans infused African cultural identities into "country"-born

slaves at a critical moment. Because the life cycles of marriage and childbirth demanded ritual, the "country"-born slaves readily adapted West African customs to New World conditions. Despite differences in language, sex ratio (the majority of African slaves imported were males), and culture, slaves in America starting families or burying their dead looked toward Africa and themselves rather than to the masters for ritual and meaning. Most slaves were native-born by mid-century, but the African influx between 1740 and 1760 made them more African and less European than they otherwise might have been.

By the early eighteenth century the construction of roads and bridges, the increased number of slaves, and larger plantation sizes all had brought slaves in closer physical contact with one another in the Chesapeake region. More significant, they had broken down language barriers that at one time had separated them. The first generation created a "pidgin" language, and the next incorporated European vocabulary into a "creole" English that retained an underlying West African grammar. Wherever large numbers of African-born slaves congregated, however, African-based language forms grew and persisted. In low-country Georgia and South Carolina, the Gullah dialect is spoken even today. But an Afro-English had developed virtually everywhere by the mid-eighteenth century, if not earlier, providing a common tongue for slaves across British North America and smoothing the way toward building slave families and community.

The timing varied. The sexual imbalance in the Carolina and Georgia low country, where men outnumbered women two to one as late as the 1770s, retarded the process of family formation there, and the sparse slave populations in New England and the mid-Atlantic region (except for New York City) left many slave men without wives or forced them to postpone marriage. But by the time of the American Revolution, native-born slaves principally defined themselves by their family identities. Therein lay the seeds of the African-American slave community.

Slave family culture grew from West African roots, but largely in response to the demands of bondage. Demography and the strictures of Christianity worked against the transplantation of West African traditions of polygamy to British North America. More telling over the long run was the slave family's lack of security. Slave marriages had no legal standing anywhere in British North America or, later, in the United States. Prevailing norms about masters' duties to slaves and slaves' own insistence on living in and protecting their families became increasingly important factors influencing the strength and inviolability of slave families, especially during the nineteenth century. But more than anything else, the custom of the plantation and the fortunes and interests of the master determined the fate of the slave family.

Masters who fell on hard times might break up slave families by sale—a prospect so feared by slaves that they understood among themselves that they had to work hard enough to ensure the minimum solvency of the master so as to prevent the sale of family members. Slaves were sold to pay debts and to settle estates when masters died. They also were sent to develop new farms farther west or south, were sometimes rented out for years to another master, and were given away as wedding presents or to set up the master's children on a new site.

The vulnerability of slave families to disruption by sale, migration, or death led slaves to create extensive kinship networks, reviving West African cultural traditions that emphasized wide kin connections. Among the slaves on farms and plantations, aunts, uncles, cousins, and grandparents shared child-rearing duties with the slave parents or took over altogether if the parents died or were separated from their children. Women especially developed highly elaborated networks to make up, to some extent, for the absence of menfolk who lived on or had been sold to another farm or plantation.

Parents or related elders taught children crafts, proper work habits, and survival skills, later referred to by slaves as "puttin' on massa." Working in the family garden outside the slave cabin and sharing chores inside it further bound children to the family. Naming patterns identified and reinforced family ties. Boys often were named for fathers who could be sold or who lived off the plantation, while girls commonly were named for aunts or other female relatives. Kin networks stretched across neighborhoods and even states. From the mid-eighteenth century to the end of slavery, native-born slaves lived and learned within a family context, variously as members of a nuclear slave family, as individuals connected to a kinship network, and as heads of their own family households.

Two-parent households were typical for native-born slaves on plantations of twenty or more slaves. On farms with ten or fewer slaves, women usually lived with their children while their husbands lived "abroad"—that is, off the farm but nearby—visiting on Sundays and holidays or at night whenever possible. Out of self-interest alone, masters sought to keep mothers and children under the age of six or seven together. Slave fathers who lived or worked off the plantation had much less opportunity to rear their children and could not prevent their wives and children from being abused and beaten, though many of them tried to do so with individual acts of bravery. Fathers hunted, fished, tended garden, and even stole to supplement the family diet and taught their children how to do likewise, but the peculiar and persistent demands of slavery strained traditional roles and sometimes relationships within the household. Although these dynamics of family formation and interaction persisted to the last days of slavery, men quickly asserted their authority as heads of household within the black family during Reconstruction.

The rise of slave families contributed to a dramatic natural increase of population and gave it a distinctly African-American and less African cast from the mid-eighteenth century on. Slave importations virtually halted during the French and Indian War and the Revolutionary War from the 1760s through the 1780s, but South Carolina and Georgia made a burst of African slave purchases between the ratification of the U.S. Constitution and the closing of the African slave trade to the United States by law, effective January 1, 1808. Roughly forty thousand Africans were brought illegally into the United States between 1808 and 1861. Such legal and illegal importations reinvigorated African identities in the South Carolina low country and Louisiana sugar parishes where the Africans were sold, but for American slavery generally, the immediate and powerful infusion of Africans into North America had ceased by the time of the American Revolution.

As the proportion of native-born to African-born slaves went up, the male-female ratio evened out, making it easier for slaves to find partners. By the early nineteenth century the United States had the only slave population in the New World that was reproducing itself. That demographic fact made all the difference for the kind of slavery and African-American culture that developed here. Slaveholders would depend on natural increase within the context of slave families to sustain and spread their plantation interests, and slaves would look to their own families to define and defend their emerging African-American identities.

American-born slaves responded to bondage differently than did unacculturated African-born ones. Masters sought to acculturate slaves to make

♦ **Manumission**
Formal emancipation from slavery

them work better and be more responsive to the masters' demands. The slave who could speak English, handle farm or artisans' tools, and understand planting and craft work was more valuable than the slave who could not. Yet the more knowledge the slave acquired about the master's ways, the more independent he or she became and the more dependent the master on the slave. African-born slave resistance generally was sudden, violent, and collective; groups of African-born slaves tended to run away and try to establish maroon colonies in the interior. Colonial governments sent militia and even Indian allies to destroy such settlements and return runaways to their masters. By contrast, acculturated slaves, who were more subtle in their subversion, were less easily detected and stopped.

A slave's place in the plantation hierarchy strongly influenced his or her resistance strategies. Artisans familiar with local customs and geography from having worked off the plantation escaped to towns and seaports where they could find work. Their understanding of the whites' economy, culture, and society and their tendency to run away as individuals rather than in groups allowed them to slip into an urban anonymity that made it difficult for masters to recapture them. Field hands and domestic servants largely confined their resistance to the plantation—feigning stupidity and illness, stealing from plantation stores, and absconding to the woods for a time to escape a punishment or protest an injustice. Field hands broke tools and shirked work, and house servants pilfered from the master's larder and liquor cabinet, inflicted a host of petty nuisances when the master's eyes were turned, and on rare occasions even poisoned the master's food, but both field hands and house servants tended to stay home rather than try to flee to freedom.

Slave drivers often protected their fellow slaves in ways that kept them on the plantation. Serving as foremen on large plantations, drivers ran the day-to-day operations under the direction of an overseer or master and meted out tasks and punishment as necessary. Many drivers set work rules that allowed the weakest slaves to avoid a whipping, ignored minor lapses in the work rhythms, hid runaways, and settled quarrels among slaves so the master would not intrude.

The more the slave became like the master, the more tenuous became the "logic" of a system of bondage based on difference. For that reason, colonial masters opposed efforts by such missionary groups as the Anglican-led Society for the Propagation of the Gospel in Foreign Parts to try to convert the slaves in the early eighteenth century. Masters who did not want to be bound by Christian obligation also had reason to worry that Christian slaves would prove more restive than "heathen" ones. Only when colonial legislatures made clear that the slaves' religious status did not affect their legal one did it become possible to bring the Gospel to the slaves.

From the Great Awakening of the 1740s through the Great Revival of 1800–1805, many American-born blacks accepted the promise of salvation that evangelical preachers offered to all people regardless of color, condition, or circumstance. The impact of Baptist and Methodist preachers by the early nineteenth century was particularly decisive. The evangelical Protestant emphasis on grace and an enthusiastic "felt," as opposed to an abstract learned, religion appealed to African-American sensibilities. For the slaves, the revivalists' emphasis on being seized by the spirit recalled common West African beliefs in spirit possession, and the symbolic importance evangelicals attached to baptism as a rite of spiritual rebirth paralleled West African religious rites involving water. The laying on of hands, baptism by immersion, religious trances, and the theology of the holy Trinity also corresponded with African ancestral rituals and beliefs. Because African-American slaves could interpret evangelical religious symbols, practices, and theology within an African context, they could and did claim evangelical religion as their own.

The entry of black slaves into white churches challenged the master's absolute authority. As fellow Christians, master and slave were alike in God's eyes and, in many cases, in church discipline. The full implications of Christianizing slaves did not become evident until the nineteenth century (see below), but the antiauthoritarian, and even antislavery, thrust of early evangelicalism shook the planters' power during the eighteenth century.

By the time of the American Revolution, then, the basic contours of an African-American slave culture had been formed. Indeed, the half-century from 1740 on was probably the single most important time for the formation of African-American slave culture.

The American Revolution drastically changed the political and ideological context of slavery. In proclaiming the "rights of man," white patriots used radical language that pointed up the contradiction between slavery and their own cries for freedom. Indeed, the Enlightenment thinkers from whom the patriots drew their emphasis on natural rights already had condemned slavery as incompatible with the idea of progress. Also, slavery based on color stressed differentness, but natural rights stressed sameness, the inalienable rights of "all men." The irony was not lost on slaves, such as a group who marched through Charleston in 1766 chanting "Liberty, liberty." At the same time, the evangelical thrust that challenged the political and social assumptions underpinning the hierarchical order the planters had made brought all authority into question.

Influenced by the new political currents as well as by the Great Awakening, some white religious groups worried that slavery was corroding their own piety. Quakers sought to cleanse themselves of the sin of slaveholding, which they equated with kidnapping and avarice, and during the 1770s and 1780s they extended their antislavery witness outward by organizing antislavery societies. As historian David Brion Davis argues, slavery, which in Western thought had been linked with progress since the days of classical Greece, now was on the ideological and moral defensive.

Slaves seized the moment to assert their own independence. Thousands of slaves fled to freedom amid the confusion and upheavals of the Revolutionary War, seeking refuge in towns in the Chesapeake and among Indians in Georgia and South Carolina. Others responded to the 1775 proclamation of Lord Dunmore, royal governor of Virginia, promising freedom to any slave who bore arms against his rebel master. In the Chesapeake region virtually every slaveholding family reported at least one slave "lost to the war." Farther south, up-country Loyalists encouraged slave rebellions against low-country "patriots," and British commanders also offered slaves freedom in exchange for service. Such actions did not transform revolts into revolution. As historian Sylvia Frey has observed, the high incidence of escapes and the British commanders' own policy of restricting blacks to support rather than military roles likely "lessened the possibility of organized rebellion." Although the British often reneged on the promise of freedom, thousands of black refugees left with the British armies in 1783 to be resettled in Canada and later Sierra Leone. Desperate for men, the American armies also recruited blacks. States of the lower South resisted the call, but Maryland rewarded slaves who served with Manumission and northern states eagerly met their recruitment quotas by enlisting blacks. About five thousand blacks, slave and free, served in the American armies and navy and helped lay

claim to the freedom promised by the American Revolution.

Whatever blacks' claims to freedom, American political leaders remained ambivalent about slavery. Concerns about property rights, racial and social order, and political stability led the Revolutionary War generation to try to contain slavery in the hope it would die a natural death. Hating slavery but fearing any precipitous action against it, the Revolutionary War generation moved indirectly. They abolished slavery only where it was weak or thinly rooted and even then adopted policies that minimized disruption of established labor patterns and property rights. The process was slow and sometimes bitterly contested by slaveholders. Indeed, slavery was so entrenched in the Hudson River valley, where slaves made up 20 percent or more of the population, as well as in northern New Jersey and in New York City and Philadelphia, that its abolition was no foregone conclusion. But the concentration of slaves in wealthy households in cities, where it functioned as a status symbol as much as an important labor source, weakened the institution's support among artisan and laboring classes. Slavery was on the decline in Philadelphia after 1770; only in New York City, where one in five households owned at least one slave as late as 1790, and on the iron plantations in rural Pennsylvania did the institution continue to grow in the region.

Prodded by Quaker example and Revolution-era thought, Pennsylvania led the way to emancipation in 1780 with a plan for a gradual, compensated abolition that allowed slaveholders to retain control over slaves until they reached their age of majority. Likewise, other states freed only the children of slaves born after specific dates—for example, 1799 in New York and 1804 in New Jersey—so that small numbers of slaves continued to labor in several northern states into the antebellum era. In the Northwest Ordinance of 1787, however, the Revolutionary War generation moved more forthrightly to prohibit the *expansion* of slavery outright by barring it from the Northwest Territory. Slavery, which had been a "national" institution in 1776, thus became a regional one, distinguishing "North" from "South" by the early nineteenth century.

The Revolutionary War generation also closed the United States to the African slave trade, and it even raised the issue of abolition in the Chesapeake states. During the 1780s the Virginia and Maryland legislatures openly debated antislavery proposals and passed laws making manumissions easier. Between 1782 and 1790, more than ten

Slave owners were generally made extremely uneasy by the prospect of literate slaves.

PAGE 204

MISSOURI COMPROMISE

The Missouri Compromise of 1820 directly affected African Americans by prohibiting slavery in the land acquired in the Louisiana Purchase north of the 36° 30' line, but allowing slavery in Missouri itself. At the time the American Southwest belonged to Mexico. Thus the Missouri Compromise implied that the nation would eventually have more free states than slave states. Congressional debates over it signaled the beginning of public discourse over the place of slavery and the rights of free blacks in the United States.

The Missouri Compromise also allowed Maine, previously part of Massachusetts, to enter the Union as a free state. The new state of Maine had few blacks, but those who did live there had almost total equality. The state allowed blacks to vote on the same basis as whites and did not segregate its schools or any other institutions.

At the same time, Missouri would come into the Union as a slave state. When it entered the Union, Missouri adopted a constitution that prohibited the state legislature from ending slavery without the consent of slaveholders and required the legislature to prohibit the migration of free blacks into the state. Northern congressmen opposed these constitutional provisions—especially the one requiring a prohibition on the migration of free blacks. In the resolution admitting Missouri, Congress declared that the state constitution "shall never be construed to authorize the passage of any law" denying a citizen of "the privileges and immunities" of an American citizen. Despite this provision, in 1848 Missouri prohibited free blacks from entering the state.

The provisions of the Missouri Compromise were not to last. The Kansas-Nebraska Act of 1854 effectively superceded the Missouri Compromise by allowing popular sovereignty to determine the fate of slavery in the Nebraska territories. In the Dred Scott Decision (1857), Chief Justice Taney declared that the entire provision violated the Constitution.

—PAUL FINKELMAN

During the Revolutionary War era, blacks laid the foundations for African-American freedom. Most important in that regard was the increase in the population of Free Blacks through escape, manumission, self-purchase, and the immigration of refugees from the revolutionary struggles in Haiti during the 1790s. By 1800, for example, more than 10 percent of all blacks in the Chesapeake region were free. Most of the new free black population gravitated toward towns, where they found work and community. The new free population was darker in complexion and more varied in skill than the small pre-Revolutionary War free black population, which had tended to be lighter-skinned, more highly acculturated, and more skilled than the slave population. As a result, runaway rural slaves were no longer conspicuously different in appearance and skill from the urban free black population. The recentness of their "freedom," however gained, also tied free blacks to slaves more closely than in earlier generations. Free blacks usually had family or friends in bondage.

From Charleston to New York, as the numbers of free blacks grew to critical masses large enough to form distinct African-American cultural and social institutions, blacks established their own churches, mutual-aid societies, and schools, often under the name "African." These institutions formed the matrix from which flowed black leadership during the nineteenth century.

The independence of blacks in towns and the blurring of distinctions between slaves and free blacks drove whites to reassert their control. Virginia imposed strict new rules on manumission in 1792, but such action did not prevent the Gabriel Prosser Rebellion of 1800 that finally shocked the upper South to recant its antislavery interest. The Bible-quoting Prosser, a slave from Henrico County, Va., organized a three-pronged attack on Richmond in order to arm slaves for a general rebellion and kidnap Gov. James Monroe as a hostage. The plot failed when two slaves betrayed the scheme and a severe rainstorm made streams impassable. Haunted by accounts of the Haitian slave rebellion of the 1790s, whites executed Prosser, stepped up slave patrols, restricted slave movements, and further tightened manumission procedures. Prosser's rebellion reverberated throughout the slave states, hastening a general retreat from Revolution-era antislavery sympathy. In those states where slavery counted, the chains tightened even before the Revolutionary War generation had passed away.

The Revolutionary War generation's reluctance to kill slavery outright ensured its growth

thousand slaves in Virginia were freed by masters responding to the idea of natural rights or to Christian impulses. Many other slaves used the new laws to purchase their own freedom and that of their spouses or children.

and expansion rather than its natural death. The lower South had resisted all antislavery urgings. Whites there believed slavery was a necessary instrument for controlling the substantial black population. Delegates from South Carolina and Georgia had threatened to bolt the Constitutional Convention in 1787 unless the new constitution being drafted satisfied their demands to protect slavery's interest. The Founding Fathers obliged by respecting slavery as a local institution in law, providing for the return of fugitives, and counting slaves for purposes of congressional representation. That calculation gave the slaveholding interest a disproportionate power in national government until the Civil War, and the new government enacted a federal fugitive slave law in 1793. Property rights thus superseded human ones, as the interests of political union overrode considerations of human liberty. Southern politicians in the 1840s and 1850s would summon the proslavery tradition of the Constitution and early government in their own defense of slavery's expansion.

The Revolutionary War generation thus bequeathed to America a contradictory legacy of protecting slavery's interest while seeking to limit its growth. During the debate over admitting Missouri to the Union as a slave state in 1819–1821, the Revolutionary War generation made its last bequest by drawing the Missouri Compromise line across the rest of the Louisiana Purchase territory and barring slavery north of that line. Thereafter, by reference to the Missouri Compromise as well as the Northwest Ordinance, the Revolutionary War heritage could be invoked to justify opposition to slavery's advance. Ironically, though, such opposition finally broke up the Union that the Founding Fathers had so desperately sought to preserve by accommodating slavery while trying to contain it. Rather than remain in a union that limited slavery's expansion in the hopes of speeding its demise, the slaveholder-dominated southern states seceded in 1860–1861.

Even during the Revolutionary War era, far from falling into decline, slavery was advancing geographically westward into the southern Piedmont and economically into a host of new activities. Planters in the upper South were restoring depleted soils with new agricultural techniques financed by selling surplus slaves southward and westward. From the first days of the republic to the last days of American slavery, the revitalization of the upper South hinged on the expansion of the lower South and thereby strengthened the institution everywhere. Slaveholders also sent slaves to work in lumbering and turpentine production, in coal and gold mining, in iron foundries and textile mills, and in a variety of mechanical and industrial trades in cities and in the countryside. Even though only about 10 percent of the slave population lived in cities or towns and only about 5 percent worked in industrial pursuits by 1860, the diversity of occupations and locations attested to the dynamism and flexibility of slavery.

The chief demand for slave labor, however, always came from agriculture. Although slaves grew tobacco and wheat in the Chesapeake region, hemp in Kentucky, rice in the Carolina-Georgia low country, and sugar in Louisiana, cotton became the principal southern staple during the nineteenth century. Cotton reigned from the eastern seaboard to Texas. The great cotton boom, spurred by European and northern demand, pushed slavery deep into the Old Southwest. Slave prices rose with cotton prices, and by 1860 slavery's center of gravity had shifted from Virginia and South Carolina to Alabama and Mississippi. From the 1830s through the 1850s the steady shuffle of slave coffles southward and westward uprooted roughly six hundred thousand slaves. Such a mass migration disrupted slave families and taxed slaves with the onerous work of cutting canebrake, draining swamps, building levees, and planting corn and cotton in frontier conditions. Although the slaves, and the plantations, spread across the South, they remained largely concentrated in the tidewater regions of the eastern coast and the deltas in the Gulf states.

Slavery grew because it was a very profitable, flexible labor system. It generated wealth for slaveholders in the form of new lands developed and of the increased value of land and slaves. Planters generally earned a return on their investment in slaves that was equal to the returns on money Northerners invested in manufacturing or railroads, and if they scrimped on food and maintenance for their slaves and drove them harder than the norm, the slaveholders gained even higher returns. By 1860 the huge capital investment in slaves exceeded in value all other capital worth in the South, including land.

The opening of the lower South also bolstered the southern nonslaveholders' allegiance to the system by keeping alive the prospect that they, too, might acquire slaves as new lands came under the plow. Rising slave prices and growing plantation sizes made acquiring slaves more difficult during the 1850s, but slaveholding remained widespread. In 1860 roughly two million whites,

Gospel, like the blues, envisions a diverse black community, whereas spirituals relied on the existence of a coherent community sharing a single condition: slavery.

PAGE 302

out of a total southern white population of eight million, owned slaves or were members of a slave-holding family; others rented slaves or had owned some at one time. Only ten thousand families owned at least fifty slaves; most slaveholders had few. The desire to own slaves for reasons of profit and social prestige consumed the white South and made the protection and expansion of slavery the dominant political concern there.

The size and location of the farming unit influenced the organization and character of the slaves' work. According to the 1860 federal census, about one-quarter of the nearly four million slaves in the agricultural South lived on farms with ten or fewer slaves. There they toiled alongside their master in the fields and did a host of other farm chores, rarely outside the master's pervasive and persistent presence. About half the slaves lived on plantations with twenty to forty-nine slaves, and about one-quarter of the slaves in 1860 were on plantations of fifty or more slaves, where field hands spent most of their time away from direct contact with the master.

Slaves labored from sunup to sundown, year in and year out, with only the Sabbath and the Christmas holidays off, but each crop set a particular work pace and pattern. In rice cultivation slaves worked at prescribed tasks, and when they completed their daily assignments to the satisfaction of the overseer or driver, they could spend as much as half a day tending their own garden, fishing, hunting, or in any other useful activity. In sugar and cotton cultivation, by contrast, masters organized the slaves into work gangs to plow, hoe, and harvest the crops. Such collective work was highly regimented, but also rhythmic. Consequently, slaves often were able to resist attempts to increase the work load or pace, except during harvest, when the crops had to be picked or cut in time to avoid spoilage from rain or frost. Picking cotton, more than any other activity, engaged the whole family, from children to elderly slaves. House servants, too, were drafted into the picking force, so that slaves on cotton plantations shared a common work experience regardless of age or position. Yet perhaps no more than half of the plantation slaves were full-time field hands. Large plantations functioned as almost self-sufficient enterprises, requiring their own handymen, carpenters, blacksmiths, millers, gardeners, and domestics. On large plantations slaves entered all areas of production, even management, and thereby gained a measure of control over their own work.

The physical conditions of bondage improved over time. By the 1850s many slaveholders had become more aware of the need to increase food allotments, maintain more sanitary living conditions, and provide adequate clothing and shelter for their slaves. Agricultural reformers pointed up the benefits in increased productivity, lengthened life spans, and the control such improvements might bring, and a general interest in bringing "modern" business practices to plantation agriculture, as evidenced in the neatly ruled account books used by many planters during the 1850s, encouraged the trend toward "reform." So, too, paradoxically, did the southern churches' proslavery argument that defended the practice by invoking scriptural passages while reminding masters of their duty toward the slaves. One of the reasons Southerners so tenaciously fought off antislavery criticism and demanded federal protection for slavery in the territories during the 1850s was their belief that they had evolved a more Christian, paternalistic labor system than the "wage slavery" being practiced in the industrializing North. Southerners pointed to the rootlessness and instability of northern society, where countless wage earners groaned under the lords of the loom, and praised the organic South, where the slaves enjoyed the "blessings" of being part of the master's "family." The southern emphasis on maintaining one's honor, which Southerners equated with liberty, demanded public responses to any criticism of one's person or family. The increasingly violent verbal and even physical confrontations in national politics during the 1850s derived in part from Southerners' honor-bound need to respond to what they considered the hypocritical, and fanatical, criticisms leveled against them and from their growing conviction that Northerners could not be trusted. Convinced of the "positive good" of slavery and their own benevolence, slaveholders tightened slave codes, increased efforts to recover fugitive slaves (with the help of the controversial federal Fugitive Slave Act of 1850), closed avenues for slaves to be manumitted or to purchase their own freedom, circumscribed the activities of free blacks, and even debated the wisdom of reopening the African slave trade during the 1850s.

The day-to-day realities of slave management belied the public face slaveholders assumed as the "good massa." Masters sometimes rewarded slaves with extra rations and favors for good work and even paid them for extra work, but violence more than incentive made slavery pay. To punish slaves for real or imagined failings, masters withheld privileges, denied passes to visit relatives off the plantation, cut food allowances—but, mostly, they whipped. Although the frequency of whipping varied from plantation to plantation, few slaves escaped the lash during their lifetimes.

The regular, regimented nature of staple crop production established standards of performance for the slaves. Masters knew what the slaves could do, and the slaves knew what they must do. But both the regularity and the variety of work allowed them some room for social maneuvering. Some jobs took slaves away from whites' supervision. Field hands in gangs talked, sang, and courted among themselves. The regularity of work set time boundaries for slaves, usually fifteen hours a day with a midday break for a meal. From sunup to sundown they adopted the public poses necessary to keep the lash off their backs and the masters out of their lives. From sundown to sunup, however, they were left to themselves. Only house servants had almost continuous association with the masters throughout the day, and they suffered for it in isolation from the regular camaraderie of the field hands and in the constant demands from the master and mistress of the plantation.

African-American culture grew especially in those areas of life where masters rarely intruded. Masters did not recognize the African aesthetic in coiled or plaited baskets, irregular rectangular designs on quilts, or the physiognomic shapes of pottery, nor did they understand the social implications of slaves' imposing their own artistic styles on the materials and social space available. Slaves not only played the fiddle—a European instrument—they also made fiddles of their own from gourds, producing an African-American instrument with its own distinctive sound. They crafted banjos from sheep hides, flute quills from willow stalks, and "bones" from bones. When they were not allowed to make drums, they kept alive complex West African syncopated percussion rhythms with hand-clapping, body-slapping, and foot-tapping known as "playin' Jubba." Slaves received food rations from the master, but they made corn into hoecakes or cornbread, mixed peas with rice, and added fish and game from hunting to create African-American dishes spiced with seasonings that recalled West African tastes. In building their slave cabins they converted the master's material into their own space. Folk architecture varied according to place, with cruder structures more prevalent as one proceeded west into frontier areas such as Texas, but African-American influences were present everywhere. Many slaves, for example, preferred pounded-dirt floors to plank ones because dirt floors harked back to African styles.

Inside the cabins and on the "street"—the row of cabins in the slave quarters—slaves asserted their own identity through story and song. Proverbs employed African styles of speaking by indirection but also provided instruction on how to survive in the New World. Slaves narrated tall tales and especially trickster tales about small, sly animals such as Brer Rabbit outwitting more powerful foes such as Brer Fox or Brer Bear. "John tales" featured John the human trickster, who bested his master with deft wordplay. Whether borrowed from African trickster tales or from the slaves' own experience, such folklore made language a means of resistance.

Likewise, in their songs slaves expressed their feelings about work and life. Singing regulated the rate of work, from hoeing to husking corn, and celebrated the rituals of the life cycle, from birth to death. Sacred songs, or spirituals, appeared during the slaves' gradual conversion to Christianity. Along with the "shout," or dance, slave sacred songs imparted a distinctly African-American character to sacred music. Polyrhythms, blue notes, and especially the call-and-response style, which was ideally suited to the singing and preaching of the evangelical camp meeting, marked slave sacred song. Such songs also were a form of protest, laced with double meanings for such common words and phrases as "Canaan" (as both a scriptural reference and a promise of freedom), "crossing the river Jordan," "stealing away with Jesus," and "deliverance." Slaves also sang lullabies and doleful tunes to quiet their children and lament life's travails.

Slave religion became the crucible of African-American slave culture. While oblivious or indifferent to the development of an African-American folk culture, masters cared about slave religion. In the 1830s, amid a general religious awakening in the South, many masters sought to bring the Gospel to the quarters, both as an instrument of social control and as a way to convert their slaves. The "mission to the slaves" contributed to increases in slave conversions. By 1860, roughly 15 percent of the slaves were members of a church. The normative church experience for slaves was biracial by 1860, with most "churched" slaves in Baptist or Methodist congregations, where they heard the same sermons as whites, submitted to the same discipline as white members, shared the communion table with whites, and experienced a kind of equality between the races nowhere else possible in slave society.

Religion for slaves was not, however, confined to churches and formal proceedings. Slaves lis-

See also
Civil War

639

tened to their own black preachers and exhorters translate the Bible in such ways as to claim that the slaves were God's chosen people and that Judgment Day would bring God's wrath down upon the sinful masters. Their message emphasized themes of judgment and deliverance and commingled Moses and Jesus as saviors of people and souls. Slaves converted Christianity into their own terms. They assumed a degree of moral superiority over masters who did not conform to common Christian standards of behavior. Breaking up a slave family violated Christian precepts, whatever the local law might otherwise allow.

In the quarters or off in the woods, slaves gathered at night to sing and dance in a rhythmic style reminiscent of the ring shout of many West African religions. Other religious practices mixed with Christian ones. In the lower Gulf area in and around Louisiana, some slaves followed voodoo; in places that still received illegal slave importations from Africa, a few practiced Islam. Many slaves subscribed to no formal religion at all. Conjurers tapped West African spiritual roots to find followers everywhere in the South, promising that their incantations, spells, and talismans could bring relief from daily torments, outmatch rivals,

PATRIOT OR AGITATOR?
Freed Slave Denmark Vesey Sparks Revolts in Charleston

Denmark Vesey (c. 1767–1822), born in Africa or the Caribbean, was an enslaved carpenter in Charleston when he won $1,500 in a lottery in 1799 and bought his freedom for $600 from slave trader Joseph Vesey. Passing up a chance to return to Africa, he opened a woodworking shop in Charleston and committed himself to the African-American freedom struggle. Vesey was an avid Bible reader, fluent in several languages, and he continually preached to his friends that blacks should be equal to whites. In the winter of 1821–1822 he began organizing for an armed revolt. He recruited enslaved artisans from diverse occupations—carters, sawyers, mechanics, lumberyard workers—and blacks from different religious, ethnic, and language groups within the area's varied community.

Vesey met with his recruits in the carpentry shop and in the local African church, formed several years earlier after whites had expelled blacks from the Methodist Church. He exhorted them to action, using the Bible, the French and Haitian revolutions, and the U.S. congressional debates about slavery in Missouri to support his argument. The planners apparently wrote several letters to Saint-Dominique requesting assistance in the uprising scheduled for mid-July. They planned to take the arsenal and guardhouse in Charleston and then start several fires. As whites left their homes, Vesey and his lieutenants would kill them before they could assemble.

But one recruit approached by Vesey's allies informed his master on May 30, and white authorities, disbelieving at first, questioned suspects until the full outline emerged. When word leaked out, Vesey moved the date forward to the night of Sunday,

June 16. The organizers destroyed all papers regarding their design, but it was too late. Further slave confessions and testimony of a black spy in the African Church soon revealed details of the revolt, and arrests began.

During the summer of 1822, the authorities executed thirty-seven black Carolinians and deported forty-three more. Vesey was captured on July 2, after refusing to confess. Gullah Jack Pritchard, the respected conjure man responsible for mobilizing less acculturated African newcomers in the countryside, tried to continue the revolt and free the jailed rebels, but he, too, was captured and hanged. Officials also imposed fines and short prison terms on four white participants found guilty of "inciting slaves to insurrection."

In the year following the revolt, frightened South Carolina legislators passed a series of laws restricting the movement of African Americans, including a Negro Seamen Act ordering all free black sailors to be jailed while their ships were in port. Other southern states followed suit, and when federal courts eventually ruled such laws unconstitutional, it only fueled the debate over states' rights. The fearful white reaction to Vesey's plot has led a few historians to suggest that the conspiracy was imaginary—entirely the product of paranoia among slaveholders. While white hysteria cannot be discounted, neither can the evidence and logic for a well-planned revolt. Some Americans have recalled Vesey as a patriot and martyr; others portray him as a dangerous agitator. Not surprisingly, a proposal in modern Charleston to commemorate Denmark Vesey with a public portrait aroused heated debate.

—PETER H. WOOD

See also

Reconstruction

and undo curses. African-American slave religion was varied and complex, and beyond the master's knowledge or observation. It could produce contradictory behavior, inspiring rebellion as well as justifying submission, but ultimately it was subversive—for, in the words of Willie Lee Rose, religion encouraged slaves to ponder their human condition, to think for themselves.

The danger of slave religion was made strikingly evident in Nat Turner's rebellion of 1831, the most important uprising in the nineteenth century. There had been earlier revolts or conspiracies, such as the 1811 Pointe Coupee revolt in Louisiana, in which between 150 and 500 slaves marched from their Mississippi Delta plantations toward New Orleans before being defeated, with 65 blacks losing their lives; and the Denmark Vesey conspiracy of 1822, in Charleston, S.C., in which as many as several thousand potential rebels were enlisted before the conspiracy was discovered and Vesey and 34 other conspirators were hanged. But these had not been messianic in character or even principally religious in motivation. The leaders of the Pointe Coupee revolt were from Haiti and built on a long period of slave violence in the Pointe Coupee area dating back to a revolt in 1795; Vesey was a free black, born in Africa or St. Thomas, who acted from a mix of ideas, including the principle of the rights of man, the Haitian revolution of 1800, and, to a lesser extent, religious conviction. Nat Turner, a slave in Southampton County, Va., however, believed he was called by God in a religious vision to deliver his people from bondage. Literate, highly articulate, and driven by a messianic impulse, Turner used preaching, conjuring, and cajoling to convince others to join his plan to strike one night following an eclipse of the sun. His original band of six swelled to eighty as it marched to Jerusalem, in Southampton County, killing fifty-seven men, women, and children until white authorities crushed the revolt. Turner avoided capture for over two months before he was caught and executed in November 1831.

Turner's revolt shocked the South. Hysterical white Southerners saw rebellion looming everywhere and killed as many as two hundred slaves in fits of reprisal and fear. Southern states tightened slave codes and muzzled criticism of slavery. Whites also sought to reassert their authority through closer supervision and religious instruction, even as the slaves were whispering Nat Turner's name in the same breath with those of the biblical prophets who foretold of Judgment Day and deliverance. The Turner revolt and its aftermath revealed how little the whites knew the slaves.

Deliverance came with the Civil War and the end of slavery. Once northern public opinion recognized that slavery helped sustain the Confederacy's ability to fight, the war for the Union became a war against slavery, the root cause of the conflict. From the slaves' perspective, the war meant both hardship and opportunity. By enduring the hardship and seizing the opportunity, they hastened their own liberation.

The war made burdensome physical demands on slaves. The Confederate impressment policy of 1863, for example, forced many slaves to work away from their homes building fortifications, hauling supplies, or performing other heavy tasks under debilitating conditions that often sent them home sick or injured and sometimes killed them. However coarse and spare, the quality and quantity of food, clothes, and shoes available to slaves had improved before the war, but wartime shortages cost them the modest material "gains" they had earned in the 1850s. It also cost them their own property, as Union and Confederate "bummers" alike looted slave cabins and took the produce of slave gardens and the crops from the fields. Whatever their attitudes toward the masters and the Confederate cause, slaves had a proprietary interest in the crops they planted, the livestock and fowl they raised, and the land they tilled. The failure of Union soldiers, especially, to respect that interest sowed seeds of distrust among blacks that would make them as wary of their "liberators" as they were of their masters.

The war also created opportunities. With so many white men away from home, the masters' control over the slaves eroded steadily. Some masters entrusted slaves with running plantations; many masters relied on "faithful" slaves, such as house servants and drivers, to assist plantation mistresses in doing so. There were enough instances of slaves hiding the white family's silver from the Yankees and sharing their own produce with the master's family to fuel the postwar myth of the slaves' loyalty. In fact, trusted slaves generally joined the field hands in pursuing their own common interest. During and after the war, masters railed against the "betrayal" by their "black family," thereby acknowledging that they had never known the slaves at all. Slaves dropped their masks during the war, revealing their true feelings and selves. Everywhere they became more openly disobedient and reduced their work. Slaves spied for and gave invading Union armies information about Confederate movements and the where-

In the Dred Scott decision of 1857 the Supreme Court ruled that free blacks were not citizens of the United States and that Congress lacked the power to prohibit Slavery in the western territories.

PAGE 189

See also
Dred Scott v. Sandford

abouts of the slaveholders' personal property. Even though no outright rebellions occurred, many individual acts of violence against white authority and property, especially in the sugar parishes of Louisiana, reminded whites that the slaves were a restive people. Most bided their time looking for the right moment to seize freedom.

The slaves' most dramatic response to the war was to run away. On the Sea Islands of South Carolina, as elsewhere where the masters fled from Union forces, slaves ran away by staying behind, refusing to follow their masters inland. They then took over the abandoned plantations. Wherever federal troops approached, slaves ran to them. The rush of slaves toward Union armies grew so large that it forced the Union generals to establish a policy of identifying the runaway slaves as "contraband" of war—that is, property that need not be returned to the enemy. By mid-1862 Congress had passed a confiscation act, freeing slaves who entered Union lines, but it excepted those belonging to Unionists. Slaves did not wait for Lincoln to issue his Emancipation Proclamation to seal slavery's doom. During the war, approximately one-seventh of the total slave population crossed over to Union lines. Old and young walked, swam, rode, and were carried over, pressing the issue of emancipation on the Lincoln administration more forcefully than abolitionist criticism had.

Understanding that each Union advance quickened slavery's end, many slaves joined the Union army. Almost a thousand from Florida, Georgia, and South Carolina joined a Union regiment that was formed at Port Royal, S.C., in late 1861, well before it was official government policy to recruit or accept black troops. Over 180,000 blacks, many of them newly escaped slaves, served in the Union army and navy during the war. They fought, and 37,000 of them died, so that emancipation was not something given to slaves but something earned by their own sweat and blood. And that made all the difference in what freedom meant to blacks after the war.

Blacks emerged from the war with a vibrant African-American culture and, in their own preachers and churches, the beginnings of black leadership and institutions that provided the foundations for a successful adjustment to freedom. They readily claimed in freedom what had been denied in slavery—legal recognition of marriages, access to education, and the right to own property and keep what they produced. More important, through folklore, crafts, food, language, music, family, and religion, blacks had developed a culture in bondage that had freed them from the debasement and self-condemnation that chattel slavery encouraged. They knew where they wanted to go in freedom because they had come to know who they were as a people.

—RANDALL M. MILLER

SLAVE TRADE

The Middle Passage

The term "Middle Passage" refers to the transit or transportation of African bondspeople from the African coast to the Americas during the slave trade. It was the middle phase of the three-step passage of Africans from the interior of Africa to the coast, across the Atlantic, and then to their place of servitude in the Americas. The hellish conditions of the passage have long made it a byword for horror and a metaphor for human suffering and cruelty.

There has long been considerable debate on the numbers involved in the Middle Passage. Older estimates, influenced by moral fervor and indignant outrage, projected estimates as high as fifty million Africans transported. The actual figure is probably considerably lower. Philip Curtin's influential *The Atlantic Slave Trade: A Census* (1969) argued that about ten million people survived the passage. The subsequent twenty-five years has seen no scholarly consensus, but many scholars believe between twelve and fifteen million Africans were brought across the ocean during the four-hundred-year history of the African slave trade. There has also been debate on the effects of the slave trade on the regional population of western and central Africa. Patrick Manning (1990) has argued that without the trade, the population of Africa in 1850 would have been 100 million rather than 50 million. Joseph C. Miller (1988), by contrast, argued that high rates of reproduction offset losses taken by slave ships. The dimensions and consequences of the slave trade on African society will likely be debated for some time to come.

The slave trader was part of the commerce between Europeans and Africans. Outside of Angola, where the Portuguese began in the sixteenth century to establish a colonial preserve, Africans controlled their western coast. The cost of slaves, which rose almost steadily over the course of the trade, was determined in negotiations between Africans and Europeans. First of all, Europeans paid ground rent for the use of land in those places where they had trading posts. Monopoly

See also
Civil War

companies, granted exclusive rights of trade by European imperial powers, normally absorbed these costs. In Upper Guinea, European ships paid tolls to use rivers en route to these posts. Individual traders had to hire "linguisters" to translate or act as go-betweens, and to arrange the "palavers" or conferences at which slave prices were determined. Before these conferences could be arranged, a "dash," or bribe, might have to be paid. These charges were part of the cost of doing business and had to be calculated in the accounting of profit and loss.

Part of the greatest cost of slaves, however, involved the prices of European and Asian goods used in trade and the mix of goods comprising the standard unit of account. Europeans adopted African account formulas or standards of equivalence, derived from the barter principle. Slaves were priced in various units of account—bars (based on the iron bar), ounces (form the ounce of gold), cowries (a type of shell), or manillas (copper bracelets)—depending on the region and local practice. Traders would determine slaves' prices (for a prime male, with women and children in proportion) in bars, say, after considerable discussion. They paid for slaves in "bundles," or "assortments," of goods equal to the determined price. Not all European goods were acceptable, nor were all equally desirable. Traders spent considerable time and effort before agreeing on the composition of bundles because the mix of goods could well make the difference between a successful voyage and a failing one. Traders with better or more attractive wares had an advantage over those whose merchandise had less demand. Competition among Europeans in port increased Africans' normal advantage.

Prices differed with time and place. During the height of the trade in the eighteenth century, slave prices were higher in Upper Guinea than in Angola. Portuguese colonization efforts permitted her merchants, often Afro-Portuguese pombeiros, to control every aspect of the trade, from the movement of slaves from the interior to their landing in Brazil. They took part in traditional African commerce and sold "everything from salt and palm cloth to sea shells" (Klein 1978, p. 38), together with the usual goods produced in Europe, Asia, or the Americas. This exclusive control brought them enormous profits, but also subjected them to the risk of loss on the Middle Passage, and they relinquished their interest in that part of the enterprise at the end of the century. In other regions, Africans brought slaves from the interior and sold them to Europeans on the coast.

Europeans could earn substantial profits in the Middle Passage, but there could also be great loss. Depending on the cost of goods dispensed (including their selling price in Europe and their value as part of a bundle), the rate of mortality in passage, and the demand in America, slave voyages could be hazardous. A 10 percent return rate seemed to be average for the century.

Slave mortality was the most striking aspect of the Middle Passage. Crowded and unsanitary conditions, poor food, inadequate supplies, insufficient drinking water, epidemic diseases, and long voyages conspired to make slave ships legendary for their foul smell and high death rate. Seventeenth-century ships of the Royal British African Company averaged a death rate as high as 24 percent. These rates decreased in the eighteenth and nineteenth centuries, reaching an average range of from 10 to 15 percent. The death rate for European sailors involved in the trade was also high, greater even than that of slaves during some periods: in the second half of the eighteenth century, white sailors died at the rate of 169 per thousand, in contrast to a mortality rate for black slaves at 152 per thousand. European immigrants suffered death rates comparable to those of slaves during the sea voyage, and their ships had an equal stench. They normally had more space, however, and contained a wider age spread. African slaves consisted of people in their prime whose life expectancy was greater; their mortality consequently was disproportionate.

In the early days of trade, slaving interests used regular merchant vessels and had carpenters insert platforms to hold the human cargo. By the eighteenth century, however, vessels were especially constructed for the trade. They were sleek, narrow vessels, with special grates and portholes to direct air below deck. The space between decks was normally four to five feet and slaves could not stand, and occasionally could not even sit, upright.

In one, presumably atypical, case, the space between decks was only fourteen inches. Under the worst conditions, slaves could be packed like sardines in stifling compartments with inadequate ventilation, little room for movement, and little or no provision for the exigencies of bodily functions or the effects of sea- or other sickness; in sum, they could be transported in pestilential tubs of unimaginable squalor. But the economics of trade encouraged ship captains and their employers to exercise care, as often the captain's wages and commissions and the employer's success depended on the number delivered safely to port. They tried to obtain sufficient food and of

See also
Emancipation

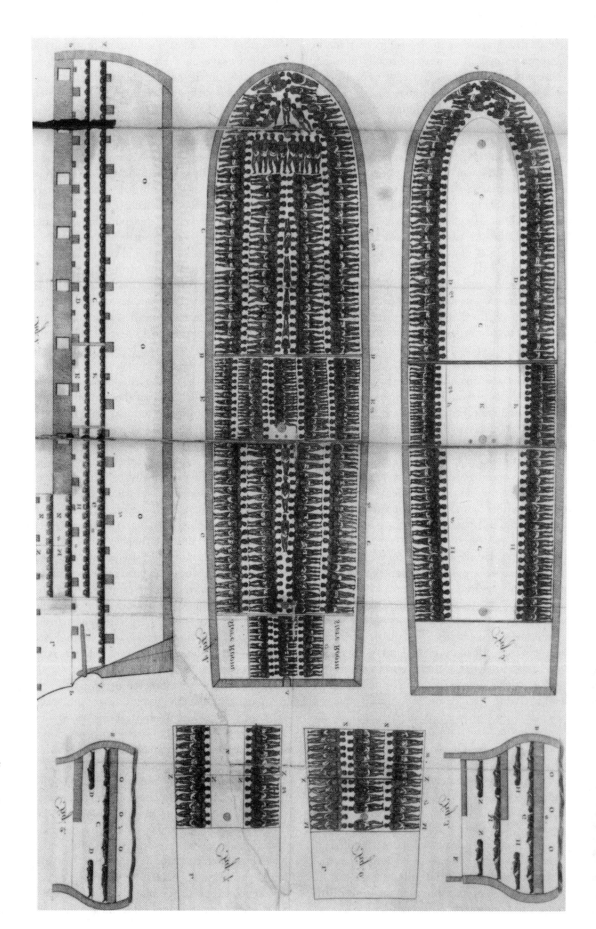

MIDDLE PASSAGE

"Middle Passage," which refers to the transportation of African bondspeople from Africa to the Americas, included horrific, overcrowded conditions aboard ship. This sectional view is from Thomas Clarkson's History of the Abolition of the Slave Trade *(Philadelphia, 1808).*
PRINTS AND PHOTOGRAPHS DIVISION, LIBRARY OF CONGRESS

the type preferred by the particular African ethnic groups aboard. They sometimes carried peas and beans from the home port, but usually secured food on the African coast: rice and corn in Upper Guinea and Angola; yams in the Niger Delta.

Scholars differ over the relationship between "tight-packing"—carrying an unusually high number of slaves relative to the capacity of the ship—and mortality. Klein (1978, p. 66) argues for little statistical correlation between the two, while Miller (1988, p. 338) suggests the practice increased deaths though "only moderately." But immigrant ships, which allowed more space per passenger, still suffered mortality rates comparable to those of slave ships. Unique among slaving nations, Portugal regulated the carrying capacity of slavers from the end of the seventeenth century, fixed at between 2.5 to 3.5 slaves per ton, depending on vessel construction. At the beginning of the nineteenth century these strictures were tightened to the lower figure, regardless of vessel construction.

At the end of the eighteenth century Britain attempted similar regulations (Dolben's Law, 1788), specifying five slaves per three tons up to two hundred tons, then one slave for each additional ton. An act in 1799 further restricted carrying capacity. It regulated space rather than tonnage and decreed a minimum of eight square feet for each slave, with five feet as the minimum height for a slave deck. These acts reduced the British ratio of slaves to tonnage from 2.6 before 1788 to 1.5 until 1798 and 1.0 thereafter until the abolition of the trade in 1807. The figures for pre-1799 British ships work out to five to six square feet of deck space for each slave. Although British tonnage measurements changed in the 1780s and although European nations used various methods of construction and measurement, clearly ships operating under less stringent regulations—all ships before 1788 and all except the British thereafter—alloted slaves less than five square feet of deck space.

Conditions deteriorated in the nineteenth century as illegal traders placed themselves beyond effective regulation. Steamships, used by mid-century, increased portage but did not immediately reduce sailing time or achieve a better ratio of slaves to tons. These larger ships carried more slaves—a thousand or more compared to four hundred or more in sailing ships—but did not provide them extra room and often carried them too close to the boiler, adding burning or scalding to other threats of mortality. At that period, observers perceived conditions to be as bad as they had ever been.

Herbert Klein indicates that the greatest single determinant of mortality was time at sea. David Eltis, to the contrary, suggests that, within limits, even that variable was not as important as disease. Dysentery among the shackled voyagers, whether amoebic or bacillary, was the most lethal killer, and its effects seemed to be unrelated to the length of voyage. But the length of voyage, including time spent on the coast, undeniably influenced mortality, and ships traveling from East Africa consistently recorded higher death rates related to their longer passage.

Mortality varied with African region, suggesting that diet, the rigors of travel to the coast, famine, or other factors in Africa had some influence on whether a slave was likely to survive the passage. The rainy season, generally from June to August, but changing with location, was equally hard on blacks and whites, and captives contracted diseases that might flower during the Middle Passage with disastrous consequences. Indeed, the melancholy attrition that began at capture matured on the coast as slaves were kept in unhealthy holding pens—damp dungeons or "trunks" in posts on the Gold Coast; floating ship hulks or "barracoons" in the Niger Delta; open stockades, exposed to the elements, in Angola. Chained, branded, and often subjected to inadequate care, they endured the physical and psychological trauma that mistreatment and uncertainty induced, and the winnowing process that the grim rule of the survival of the fittest obliged.

Individual captains set the tone of the voyage and determined whether slaves got needless abuse or minimal consideration. Taken aboard ship, men were chained together below deck, women above. Pregnant women and children roamed free once the ship cleared the coast. Sailors took great care at leavetaking, however, as slaves were most likely to rise as they departed African shores. At sea, they fed slaves twice a day, and they allowed a period of exercise on deck unless the weather forbade. The crew occasionally washed slave platforms with vinegar and water for sanitation. African women assisted in preparing the food, making it as palatable as possible, and carrying African tastes and culinary practices to the Americas.

In the midst of these deplorable conditions began the formation of new cultures and relationships. The shipmate relationship became one that endured among those who survived transport and formed the basis for relationships ashore. Cultural

See also
Slavery

*The black man
occupied the
position of a mere
domestic animal,
without will or right
of his own. The lash
lurked always in the
background.*

W.J. CASH
THE MIND OF THE SOUTH,
1941

transformation also began, establishing the foundations for New World social reorganization even before the Africans had landed. Along with their capacity for labor and their ability to last, survivors brought an abiding optimism and sense of self-worth that transcended physical and psychological scarring. Therein is found a moving story of human resilience and creativity.

Abolition of the Slave Trade in the United States

While the first efforts to suppress the slave trade in North America came nearly a century after the trade began, the beginning of anti-slave-trade agitation among Quakers and others paralleled the flowering of the trade in the 1680s. The first legal attempts at regulation came in the North. In 1705, Massachusetts laid a four-pound duty on slaves, which had the stated purpose of preventing "a spurious and mixt issue," and may or may not have been intended to drive the trade out of business. In any case, imports continued into Massachusetts. The first attempt to stop slave trading in the plantation colonies came in 1710, when Virginia's House of Burgesses voted a five-pound duty on slave imports. Royal Governor Spotswood vetoed the measure. In South Carolina, the other main colonial slave importer, the first slave trade regulation came in 1717, in the form of a forty-pound duty on slaves. This duty, meant to slow the rate of slave imports, shut them off so completely that it was lowered to ten pounds two years later. In 1740, on the heels of the Stono Rebellion, South Carolinians fearing slave insurrection laid a prohibitive duty of one hundred pounds, in order to build up a fund to encourage white immigration. In 1760, South Carolina outlawed the trade entirely. The Board of Trade in London nullified the prohibition. Despite official attempts at regulation, Africans poured into South Carolina during the entire Colonial period.

By the beginning of the 1770s, almost all of the American colonies had at least contemplated action against the slave trade at one time or another. However, northern and southern lawmakers had widely differing motives. In the North, anti-slave-trade sentiment was primarily moral; Quakers and other opponents of the trade were primarily interested in limiting the institution of slavery. However, Northerners had few scruples about participating in the trade, an important sector of the New England economy. Northerners built and opened their harbors to slave ships. Southerners, on the other hand, whatever their moral feelings about slavery, were primarily moti-

vated by other considerations. Planters wished to regulate competition by slavers by controlling imports, and their fear of slave insurrection made them uneasy about importing large numbers of Africans. Northern and southern attempts to limit the trade were, in any case, largely ineffective; the trade was too profitable, both for slaveholders and for the northern merchants and others who made money through shipping. Taxes were avoided through smuggling, and antislavery laws were laxly enforced. England, concerned with Colonial profits, also made use of its veto power to ensure a continuous flow of trade. When Virginia petitioned Parliament to halt the slave trade in 1772, the English declined to act.

During the era of the American Revolution, the slave trade was interrupted. The Americans' nonimportation "associations," and then the war itself, effectively stopped maritime commerce with England and with the British West Indies, source of most American slaves. In many revolutionaries' minds, slavery violated the same natural rights principles they were fighting for, and the slave trade seemed its cruelest and most horrible. The trade was also associated with the hated English authorities, who had vetoed all attempts to control it. A section of Thomas Jefferson's draft of the Declaration of Independence, not included in the final version, shifted blame for the slave trade onto the English, declaring that King George III had "waged cruel war against human nature itself, violating its most sacred rights of life and liberty in the persons of a distant people who never offended him, captivating and carrying them into slavery in another hemisphere. . . ." Neither Northerners nor Southerners were willing to renounce completely the "execrable commerce," though, and the passage was removed from the final product. After the end of the war in 1783, northern states definitively banned the trade, but southern planters whose labor force had declined during the previous years again began importing slaves in large numbers.

The Constitutional Convention of 1787 featured a strong debate on abolishing the slave trade. Few Americans approved of the trade, but since there had never previously been a self-sustaining slave population, slaveholders and opponents, both ignoring American slave demographics, equally considered the slave trade vital to the survival of the institution. Northerners demanded an end to the trade. Southerners advocated legal importation of slaves, free from prohibitive duties. The final compromise was to put off the possible prohibition of the slave trade until 1808, by which time, many delegates believed, the trade would have come to a natural end, and to limit import duties to ten dollars on what they termed a "person held to service."

In fact, by 1800 almost all the states, even South Carolina, usually the strongest supporter of the trade, had prohibited the trade or taxed it out of existence. In 1807, Great Britain ended its own slave trade. The next year, on President Jefferson's recommendation, the U.S. Congress formally closed the trade. Slaveholders, hopeful of a rise in slave values and fearful of a Haitian-style slave rebellion, offered no unified opposition. In 1818 and 1820, supplementary acts were passed against the trade to pay informers and punish slave buyers. The colony of Liberia was founded in part to resettle rescued Africans.

By 1808, however, it had become clear that the institution of slavery in the United States was flourishing and expanding to the new southern territories. South Carolina had acknowledged the futility of attempting to enforce its own ban on slave trading, and had reopened the trade in 1803. There was no special enforcement machinery set up by the federal legislation, and naval facilities were primitive. Smuggling of slaves became a lucrative and widespread field. Americans had a long history of countenancing smuggling, and even many Northerners saw nothing wrong in trading slaves. Bristol, R.I., was a notorious center of outfitting slave traders in the first years after 1808. While figures vary, at least one thousand slaves on average were illegally brought into the United States during the antebellum years. Before they became states of the Union, Florida and Texas were the chief points of origin for smugglers. St. Augustine and Galveston were, respectively, the major ports.

Throughout the first half of the nineteenth century, the government halfheartedly enforced its ban. Great Britain, starting in 1818, suggested reciprocal search agreements on ships plying the African coast, in order to catch smugglers. American Secretary of State John Quincy Adams, who opposed slavery, was suspicious of British intentions in the wake of English impressment of American sailors before the War of 1812, and he refused to agree.

Throughout the antebellum years, the United States hampered interdiction efforts off the African coast. Even after the Webster-Ashburton Treaty of 1842, in which the United States and Britain agreed to joint patrols, Americans refused to allow boarding by British authorities, whom Americans claimed misconstrued the treaty. Since America refused to permit its ships to be searched, smugglers used the American flag as a flag of convenience when carrying illegal cargoes. Americans, suspicious of British intentions, thwarted international efforts to secure right of search on naval vessels, declined to work jointly in anti-slave-trade efforts and refused to use British bases such as Freetown, Sierra Leone. The American Navy's own interdiction forces, a half-dozen old, slow, overgunned ships, were based in the Cape Verde Islands, far north of slave waters. Judges adopted hairsplitting definitions of illegality. The presence of manacles and other slaving paraphernalia on a ship were insufficient proof of smuggling; ships had to be caught with captives aboard. After a few wrongful arrest suits by ship captains, for a time the Navy stayed away from the areas commonly plied by slave ships. Despite congressional apathy and refusal to strengthen interdiction efforts, and the resulting drop in naval morale, the forces did manage to catch some thirty-eight ships between 1837 and 1862. However, American juries often acquitted smugglers. One of the last illegal slave ship journeys, that of the *Wanderer* in 1858, became well known. Finally, in 1862, during the Civil War, the Union government, anxious to remove American warships from Africa and to placate the British, agreed to reciprocal searches. This policy effectively shut off the illegal trade.

Despite widespread evasions of the law, it was not until the 1850s that the question of reopening the trade was seriously posed. Southern radicals such as Gov. James Adams of South Carolina proposed reopening the trade as a panacea for southern ills. Importing new slaves, Adams and his allies claimed, would bring down the inflated price of labor, halt the erosion of slavery in the upper South resulting from African-Americans being sold further south, make farming labor-intensive crops such as cotton easier, increase the population of the southern states, and increase poor white farmers' prestige and stake in the slave system by making it possible for them to own slaves. The contentious question of reopening the trade would add to sectional tensions, but radicals and secessionists were delighted by such a prospect.

Notwithstanding the logical contradictions inherent in such a position, most Southerners despised the slave trade, and most influential politicians opposed reopening. While they supported slavery, and thus did not dwell so much on the immorality of the trade, they argued that legalization would split the Union and leave the South divided. Slave property values would plummet, and

See also
Frederick Douglass

economic chaos would result. The upper South would still be unable to compete economically with its neighbors, and would lose the income it received from breeding and selling slaves. Increased slave competition might wipe out free white farms entirely. Adams's proposal was defeated in both houses of the South Carolina legislature. While proponents of legalization did win the backing of the powerful Southern Commercial Convention at Vicksburg in 1859, most politicians saw that the issue was not popular. Even after secession, in 1861, the Confederate congress voted to retain the ban, and the issue was eventually buried.

As the Atlantic slave trade petered to its end during the middle decades of the nineteenth century, it had already profoundly shaped three continents. It altered and likely stunted the developments of African society and political institutions in ways that are still being debated. It was the most significant population transfer of all time, creating an enormous and enduring African diaspora in the Caribbean, South America, and North America. It remains, above all, a monument to the cruelty that humans perpetrate upon their own kind. If there is any consolation to be found in its sad history, the abolition of the slave trade was the first great humanitarian reform movement. The slave trade, and later slavery itself, was ended by the combined efforts of Europeans, Africans, and Americans to redress and eliminate an enormous evil.

—DANIEL C. LITTLEFIELD AND GREG ROBINSON
—PETRA E. LEWIS

SLEET, MONETA J., JR.

Moneta J. Sleet, Jr. (February 14, 1926–), photographer. In 1969 Moneta J. Sleet, Jr., became the first African American to win a Pulitzer Prize in photography, for his now world-renowned image of Coretta Scott King at her husband's funeral, her upturned face shielded by a heavy veil as she embraced her young daughter Bernice. Sleet, although employed by the monthly *Ebony* magazine, became eligible for the prestigious newspaper award when his black-and-white film containing the image was let into a pool for wire-service use and subsequently published in daily newspapers throughout the country.

Moneta Sleet's major contribution to photojournalism has been his extensive documentation of the marches, meetings, and rallies of the Civil Rights Movement. He also has a special talent for photographing people. Over the years, he produced sensitive, humanistic, and, on occasion, humorous portraits of celebrities as well as ordinary men, women, and children of America, Africa, and the Caribbean. His photographs are powerful and direct and show a genuine respect for his subjects.

Moneta Sleet was born in Owensboro, Ky., where he grew up attending the local segregated public schools. His career as a photographer began in boyhood, when his parents gave him a box camera, and continued into high school. Sleet studied photography at Kentucky State College under the tutelage of John Williams, a family friend who was dean of the college and an accomplished photographer. When Sleet interrupted his studies as a business major to serve in World War II, he resolved to enter photography as a profession, though he returned and finished his degree. His mentor moved on to Maryland State College, and in 1948 invited Sleet to set up a photography department there. After a short time in Maryland, Sleet moved to New York, studying at the School of Modern Photography before attending New York University where he obtained a masters degree in journalism in 1950.

After a brief stint as a sportswriter for the *Amsterdam News,* Sleet joined the staff of *Our World,* a popular black picture magazine. His five years there were training for his photojournalistic sensibility. He and the other staff photographers and writers were subject to the high editorial standards of the publisher, John Davis. It was under Davis's auspices that Sleet produced one of his most engaging stories, a 1953 series on the coal-mining town of Superior, W.Va.

Our World ceased publication two years later, and Sleet joined the Johnson Publishing Company's New York-based illustrated monthly magazine *Ebony,* where he continued as staff photographer. Publisher John H. Johnson sent him to the far corners of the world on stories. In addition, coverage of the fledgling Civil Rights Movement established the reputation of *Ebony*'s sister publication *Jet,* and in the early years Sleet's photographs appeared in both.

On assignment in 1956, Sleet first met the Rev. Dr. Martin Luther King, Jr., then a twenty-seven-year-old Atlanta minister, emerging as the leader of the Civil Rights Movement. Their association flourished as the movement dominated the black press, with Sleet covering King's receiving the Nobel Peace Prize in Sweden in 1964, his

See also
Gordon Parks, Sr.

marching from Selma to Montgomery in 1965, and his funeral in Atlanta following his assassination in April 1968.

Sleet's recollection of the circumstances leading to his memorable Pulitzer Prize-winning photograph of Coretta Scott King was still vivid:

There was complete pandemonium—nothing was yet organized because the people from SCLC [the Southern Christian Leadership Conference] were all in a state of shock. We had the world press descending upon Atlanta, plus the FBI, who were there investigating.

We were trying to get an arrangement to shoot in the church. They said they were going to "pool it." Normally, the pool meant news services, Life, Time, *and* Newsweek. *When the pool was selected, there were no black photographers from the black media in it. Lerone Bennett and I got in touch with Mrs. King through Andy Young. She said, "If somebody from Johnson Publishing is not on the pool, there will be no pool." Since I was with Johnson Publishing, I became part of the pool. In those days there weren't many blacks [in journalism], whether writers or photographers.*

The day of the funeral, Bob Johnson, the executive editor of Jet, *had gotten in the church and he beckoned for me and said, Here's a spot right here. It was a wonderful spot. It was then a matter of photographing what was going on. It was so dramatic; everywhere you turned the camera—Daddy King, Vice President Humphrey, Nixon, Jackie Kennedy, Bobby Kennedy, Thurgood Marshall, Dr. Ralph Bunche reading the program with a magnifying glass. I considered myself fortunate to be there documenting everything. If I wasn't there I knew I would be somewhere crying.*

We had made arrangements with AP [the Associated Press] that they would process the black-and-white film immediately after the service and put it on the wire. Later I found out which shot they sent out. (Taped interview, New York, 1986)

Moneta Sleet's career has also encompassed the great period of African independence, when in the 1950s autonomous nations emerged from former colonies. His first experience in "pack" journalism abroad came on Vice President Richard Nixon's 1957 trip through Africa, where Sleet photographed in Liberia, Libya, and the Sudan. It was on this trip he photographed Kwame Nkrumah at the moment of Ghana's indepen-

dence. The results of the trip gained Sleet an Overseas Press Club citation in 1957.

Sleet's long career as a photojournalist has taken him all over the United States and Africa; he has also visited and photographed on assignment in South America, Russia, the West Indies, and Europe. While photo essays and portrait profiles make up the majority of his output, he has also photographed the children who tagged alongside him as he worked. To Sleet, the father of three grown children, these personal portraits have been the most rewarding.

In addition to winning a Pulitzer Prize in feature photography and a citation for excellence from the Overseas Press Club of America, Sleet has received awards from the National Urban League (1969) and the National Association of Black Journalists (1978). Over the years, his work has appeared in several group exhibitions at museums, including the Studio Museum in Harlem and the Metropolitan Museum of Art. In 1970, solo exhibitions were held at the City Art Museum of St. Louis and the Detroit Public Library. A retrospective exhibition organized by the New York Public Library in 1986 toured nationally for three years.

—JULIA VAN HAAFTEN

SLIGH, CLARISSA

Clarissa Sligh (August 30, 1939–), photographer. Clarissa Sligh was born in Washington, D.C., and attended school in Arlington, Virginia. In 1956 she became the lead plaintiff in the first successful school desegregation case in the state of Virginia, *Clarissa Thompson et al* v. *The Arlington County School Board et al.* Sligh's educational pursuits spanned several areas of interest. In 1963, the year that she married Thomas Sligh (they divorced several years later), she received a B.S. in mathematics from Hampton Institute. In 1972 Sligh earned her B.F.A. in painting from Howard University and a year later she completed her M.B.A. from the University of Pennsylvania. Sligh began her formal education as a photographer at the International Center for Photography from 1979 to 1980.

Sligh's photographic works featured images from family photo albums, often with several snapshots juxtaposed against each other, and framed by Sligh's handwritten passages drawn from overheard conversations (*Ted on Women* 1990; *Bill on Men,* 1990). The bulk of her work explored relationships between men and women,

See also
Roy Decarava
New Orleans

649

and Sligh often used her compositions to restage events from childhood. One of Sligh's best-known works, *What's Happening with Mamma?* (1988), was a book of photographs and text that explored the fear and disorientation a young girl felt while hearing the sounds of her mother giving birth to a child. She also created a book of photographs and text, *Reading Dick and Jane with Me* (1990), that used the children's primer to comment on how black children are educated in the United States. Sligh's other well-known works included *Kill or Be Killed* (1990), *Exposure* (1990), and *Work Yourself to Death* (1990).

Sligh's images have been shown at Williams College Museum of Art in Massachusetts, Nexus Gallery in Philadelphia (1989); INTAR Latin American Gallery in New York City (1990), and the Newport Art Museum in Rhode Island (1990). Her exhibit on the civil rights movement, "Witness to Dissent: Memory, Yearning, and Struggle," was shown at the Art in General Gallery in New York City in 1992. In 1987, Sligh joined artists Faith Ringgold and Margaret Gallegos to cofound Coast to Coast: Women of Color

Artists' Project, for which Sligh has served as national coordinator.

—NASHORMEH N. R. LINDO

SMITH, BESSIE

Bessie Smith (April 15, 1894–September 26, 1937), blues singer. Bessie Smith, "Empress of the Blues," was the greatest woman singer of urban blues and, to many, the greatest of all blues singers. She was born in Chattanooga, Tenn., the youngest of seven children of Laura and William Smith. Her father, a part-time Baptist preacher, died while she was a baby, and her early childhood, during which her mother and two brothers died, was spent in extreme poverty. Bessie and her brother Andrew earned coins on street corners with Bessie singing and dancing to the guitar playing of her brother.

The involvement of her favorite brother Clarence in the Moses Stokes Show was the impetus for Smith's departure from home in 1912. Having won local amateur shows, she was prepared for the move to vaudeville and tent shows, where her initial role was as a dancer. She came in contact with Gertrude "Ma" Rainey, who was also with the Stokes troupe, but there is no evidence to support the legend that Rainey taught her how to sing the blues. They did develop a friendship, however, that lasted through Smith's lifetime.

Smith's stint with Stokes ended in 1913, when she moved to Atlanta and established herself as a regular performer at the infamous Charles Bailey's 81 Theatre. By then the Theater Owners Booking Association (TOBA) consortium was developing into a major force in the lives and careers of African-American entertainers, and managers/owners often made the lives of performers miserable through low pay, poor working and living conditions, and curfews. Bailey's reputation in this regard was notorious. Smith became one of his most popular singers, although she was paid only ten dollars a week.

Smith's singing was rough and unrefined, but she possessed a magnificent vocal style and commanding stage presence, which resulted in additional money in tips. With the 81 Theatre as a home base, Smith traveled on the TOBA circuit throughout the South and up and down the eastern seaboard. By 1918 she was part of a duo-specialty act with Hazel Green but soon moved to her own show as a headliner.

Smith attracted a growing number of black followers in the rural South as well as recent im-

BESSIE SMITH

Smith sang with passion and authenticity about everyday problems, natural disasters, and the longing for someone to love. PHOTOGRAPHS AND PRINTS DIVISION, SCHOMBURG CENTER FOR RESEARCH IN BLACK CULTURE, THE NEW YORK PUBLIC LIBRARY, ASTOR, LENOX AND TILDEN FOUNDATIONS

migrants to northern urban ghettos who missed the down-home style and sound. She was too raw and vulgar, however, for the Tin Pan Alley black songwriters attempting to move into the lucrative world of phonograph recordings. White record company executives found Smith's (and Ma Rainey's) brand of blues too alien and unrefined to consider her for employment. As a result, Smith was not recorded until 1923, when the black buying public had already demonstrated that there was a market for blues songs and the companies became eager to exploit it.

Fortunately, Smith was recorded by the Columbia Gramophone Company, which had equipment and technology superior to any other manufacturer at the time. Columbia touted itself in black newspapers as having more "race" artists than other companies. Into this milieu came Bessie Smith singing "Down Hearted Blues" and "Gulf Coast Blues," the former written and previously performed by Alberta Hunter and the latter by Clarence Williams, studio musician for Columbia. Sales were astronomical. Advertisements in the black newspapers reported her latest releases, and Smith was able to expand her touring range to include black theaters in all of the major northern cities. By 1924, she was the highest-paid African American in the country.

Smith sang with passion and authenticity about everyday problems, natural disasters, the horrors of the workhouse, abuse and violence, unfaithful lovers, and the longing for someone, anyone, to love. She performed these songs with a conviction and dramatic style that reflected the memory of her own suffering, captured the mood of black people who had experienced pain and anguish, and drew listeners to her with empathy and intimacy. Langston Hughes said Smith's blues were the essence of "sadness . . . not softened with tears, but hardened with laughter, the absurd, incongruous laughter of a sadness without even a god to appeal to."

Smith connected with her listeners in the same manner as the southern preacher: They were her flock who came seeking relief from the burdens of oppression, poverty, endless labor, injustice, alienation, loneliness, and love gone awry. She was their spiritual leader who sang away the pain by pulling it forth in a direct, honest manner, weaving the notes into a tapestry of moans, wails, and slides. She addressed the vagaries of city life and its mistreatment of women, the depletion of the little respect women tried to maintain. She sanctioned the power of women to be their own independent selves, to love freely, to drink and party and enjoy life to its fullest, to wail, scream, and lambaste anyone who overstepped boundaries in relationships—all of which characterized Smith's own spirit and life.

Columbia was grateful for an artist who filled its coffers and helped move it to supremacy in the recording industry. Smith recorded regularly for Columbia until 1929, producing 150 selections, of which at least two dozen were her own compositions. By the end of the 1920s, women blues singers were fading in popularity, largely because urban audiences were becoming more sophisticated. Smith appeared in an ill-fated Broadway show, *Pansy*, and received good reviews, but the show itself was weak and she left almost immediately. Her single film, *St. Louis Blues* (1929), immortalized her, although time and rough living had taken a toll on her voice and appearance.

Because of the Great Depression, the recording industry was in disarray by 1931. Columbia dismantled its race catalog and dropped Smith along with others. She had already begun to shift to popular ballads and swing tunes in an attempt to keep up with changing public taste. Okeh Records issued four of her selections in 1933. She altered her act and costumes in an attempt to appeal to club patrons, but she did not live to fulfill her hope of a new success with the emerging swing ensembles. On a tour of southern towns, Smith died in an automobile accident.

—DAPHNE DUVAL HARRISON

SMITH, MARVIN PENTZ, AND SMITH, MORGAN SPARKS

Marvin Pentz Smith (February 16, 1910–), and Morgan Sparks Smith (February 16, 1910– February 17, 1993), photographers. Born in Nicholsville, Ky., Marvin and Morgan Smith were the twin sons of tenant farmers. They grew up in Lexington, Ky., and their creative activity started with painting and drawing in the late 1920s. In 1933, they moved to New York, where they studied art under sculptor Augusta Savage who ran a work space and studio in the basement of her Harlem home. They took full-time jobs as gardeners for New York's Parks Department, and also began working with other artists in the Harlem branch of the Works Project Administration (WPA). Assigned to work as artists for the Federal Arts Project, they assisted muralists Vertis

See also

Blues

Hayes and Charles Alston on such projects as that for the Harlem Hospital Nurses Residence.

The Smith brothers had owned cameras since childhood, and during the mid-1930s they began to concentrate on photography. In 1937, they were hired as staff photographers by the New York *Amsterdam News,* and in 1939, they traveled to France to study art. Soon after their return, they opened the M & M photographic studio on Harlem's 125th Street, next door to the famed Apollo Theater. Their studio was frequented by performing artists, writers, historians, and families in the Harlem community. Their cameras captured the political rallies, street demonstrations, and lindy hoppers in the Savoy Ballroom as well as street orators and the breadlines during the Great Depression. Some of their more famous subjects included Adam Clayton Powell, Jr., Adam Clayton Powell, Sr., Nat "King" Cole, Father Divine, Billie Holiday, Langston Hughes, and Romare Bearden. They also operated the Pictorial News Service, a short-lived newspaper picture service. Their photos were shown in books such as Claude McKay's *Harlem: Negro Metropolis,* in newspapers and magazines, and later in gallery exhibitions. In the 1960s, the Smith brothers gave some 2,000 photos to New York's Schomburg Center for Research in Black Culture.

During World War II, Marvin Smith served as a chief photographer's mate in the Navy, and was the first African American to attend the Naval Air Station School of Photography and Motion Pictures in Pensacola, Fla. In the years after World War II, the Smith brothers began creating in other fields. Both brothers spent the next several years as cameramen and recording engineers working on documentaries, and they worked for some years for ABC television, before retiring in 1968. Morgan Smith died of cancer in 1993.

—DEBORAH WILLIS-THOMAS

SMITH, "WILLIE THE LION"

"Willie the Lion" Smith (Bertholoff, William Henry Joseph Bonaparte) (November 25, 1897–April 18, 1973), jazz pianist and composer. Born in Goshen, N.Y., Smith grew up in Newark, N.J., with his mother and stepfather. (His mother had remarried after the death of her first husband.) Smith began studying piano at the age of six, inspired both by his grandmother, who played organ and banjo, and by the Christian and Jewish reli-

gious music he heard in Harlem and Newark. By age fifteen, he had begun to play in clubs and at parties in New York and New Jersey. He married Blanche Merrill in 1916, served in the armed forces in World War I from 1917 to 1918, and played regularly in New York City after his discharge in 1919. However, because he did not record as a soloist until the mid-1930s, he was at first somewhat less well known to the public than his contemporaries James P. Johnson and Thomas "Fats" Waller (although he was Waller's senior by a few years). In the late 1930s, Smith toured in United States and Europe. Duke Ellington, who had heard Smith in the 1920s, acknowledged him as an important influence, and paid tribute to him with the composition "Portrait of the Lion" (1939). Smith returned the compliment a decade later with "Portrait of the Duke." Between 1934 and 1949 Smith recorded only intermittently, but in the 1950s and '60s Smith's career experienced a resurgence, and he made numerous LPs of his playing, singing, and, in some cases, talking, on a variety of labels. An impressive quantity of his music was thus made available to the jazz public for the first time in the post-bop era, despite the fact that Smith's style had remained firmly rooted in the 1930s language of stride piano.

Although regarded highly by the major stride pianists of his generation (James P. Johnson noted, "Willie Smith was one of the sharpest ticklers I ever met—and I met most of them"), Smith's playing as revealed in his recordings appears somewhat less exuberant and extroverted than theirs. His left hand in particular occasionally lacks the aggressive rhythmic propulsion of Waller's or Johnson's, and his solos are less charged with syncopation as a result. But Smith infuses melodic lines with lyricism and unexpected rhapsodic turns of phrases ("Between the Devil and the Deep Blue Sea," recorded March 18, 1958), and he can juxtapose contemplative passages with sections of robust stride ("Echoes of Spring," the 1939 version on Commodore, and "Honeysuckle Rose," recorded November 30, 1965). Smith composed several piano vignettes, which he recorded as a set on the Commodore label (January 10, 1939). They demonstrated his mastery of popular song form, an ability to produce imaginative pianistic effects, and an understated but swinging stride.

Smith, whose father was said to be Jewish, claimed inspiration from music he heard in synagogues as a child. He was bar mitzvahed in 1910 and in the 1940s became the cantor of an African-American synagogue in Harlem. Smith published his autobiography, *Music on My Mind,* in 1964, and in 1969 he performed at the White House for Duke Ellington's seventieth birthday celebration. He died in New York City.

—PAUL S. MACHLIN

SOUTHERN CHRISTIAN LEADERSHIP CONFERENCE

Initially founded in January 1957 by the Rev. Dr. Martin Luther King, Jr., and other young ministers who were active in local civil rights protest efforts across the South, the Southern Christian Leadership Conference (SCLC) soon became the primary organization through which the southern black church made significant contributions to the black freedom struggle of the 1960s.

Viewed by many as simply the institutional reflection of King's individual role as the Civil Rights Movement's principal symbolic leader, SCLC in fact served a somewhat larger function. First, beginning in the late 1950s, SCLC drew together southern ministers who believed that the black church had a responsibility to act in the political arena and who sought an organizational vehicle for coordinating their activism. Second, in the years after 1961, when SCLC possessed a significant full-time staff, the organization pulled together important protest campaigns in Birmingham (1963) and Selma, Ala. (1965), that brought the southern struggle to the forefront of national attention and helped win passage of the landmark Civil Rights Act of 1964 and the Voting Rights Act of 1965. Third, between 1965 and 1968, SCLC provided the means by which King extended his own national agenda for economic change to include protest campaigns in northern cities such as Chicago (1966) and Cleveland (1967), as well as supplying the institutional basis for the Poor People's Campaign of 1968.

Three principal influences shaped SCLC's founding. The first was the Montgomery, Alabama Bus Boycott of 1955 and 1956, a successful local protest effort that brought King to national attention and made him the symbol of new black activism in the South. Second, young ministers in other cities seeking to emulate the Montgomery example launched bus protests in cities such as Birmingham, Tallahassee, New Orleans, and At-

lanta, and sought a forum for exchanging ideas and experiences. Third, New York-based civil rights activists Bayard Rustin, Ella Baker, and Stanley Levison, who already had helped garner northern funds and publicity for the Montgomery protest, began advocating the formation of a region-wide organization in the South that could spread the influence of Montgomery's mass movement and provide King a larger platform.

Initially labeled the "Southern Negro Leaders Conference on Transportation and Nonviolent Integration" by King and Rustin, the conference met three times in 1957 before finally adopting Southern Christian Leadership Conference (SCLC) as its actual name. Seeking to avoid competition and conflict with the NAACP, SCLC chose to be composed not of individual members but of local organization "affiliates," such as civic leagues, ministerial alliances, and individual churches. Looking for a goal beyond that of desegregating city bus lines, King and the other ministers leading the conference—C. K. Steele of Tallahassee, Fred L. Shuttlesworth of Birmingham, Joseph E. Lowery of Mobile, and Ralph D. Abernathy of Montgomery—focused on the right to vote and sought to develop a program, staff, and financial resources with which to pursue it. Until 1960, however, their efforts largely floundered, in part because of other demands upon King's time and energy, but also because of personnel problems and relatively meager finances.

Transformation of SCLC into an aggressive, protest-oriented organization began in 1960 with King's own move from Montgomery to Atlanta and his appointment of the energetic Rev. Wyatt Tee Walker as SCLC's new executive director. The coupling of Walker's organizational skills

CIVIL RIGHTS CENTER

The Rev. Ralph Abernathy stands in front of the Southern Christian Leadership Conference headquarters in Atlanta in 1970.

AP/WIDE WORLD PHOTO

RALPH ABERNATHY

Successor to Dr. Martin Luther King, Jr.

Ralph David Abernathy (March 11, 1926–April 17, 1990), clergyman, civil rights leader. Born in Linden, Ala., initially among family members he was called only "David"; later, through the inspiration a teacher gave one of his sisters, the appellation "Ralph" was added. After serving in the U.S. Army during World War II, Abernathy seized the opportunity offered by the G.I. Bill and earned a B.S. degree in 1950 from Alabama State College (now Alabama State University). In 1951 he earned an M.A. in sociology from Atlanta University.

In his formative years Abernathy was deeply influenced by his hardworking father, William L. Abernathy, who was a Baptist deacon and a farmer who owned 500 acres of choice real estate. The son's admiration for his father was a major factor in his work in public life.

In 1948 Abernathy was ordained a Baptist minister. He served as pastor of the following congregations: Eastern Star Baptist Church, Demopolis, Ala., 1950–1951; First Baptist Church, Montgomery, Ala., 1951–1961; West Hunter Street Baptist Church, Atlanta, Ga., 1961–1990.

While a student at Alabama State, Abernathy had two experiences that would prepare him for his later role as a civil rights leader: He was urged to contribute to the freedom struggle of African Americans by such professors as J. E. Pierce and Emma Payne Howard: and, as president of the student council, he led two campus protests, for improved cafeteria services and dormitory conditions. Due to his dignified protests, Abernathy won the respect of the institution's administration. As a result, in 1951 he returned to his alma mater to become dean of men.

While pastor of First Baptist, he became a close friend of Dexter Avenue Baptist Church's courageous pastor Vernon Johns. Johns as an older, seasoned pulpiteer displayed extraordinary boldness in his personal defiance of Montgomery's oppressive Jim Crow climate.

When Johns's ties with Dexter were severed, Abernathy developed an even closer friendship with his successor, Martin Luther King, Jr. The two young pastors' families became intertwined in a fast friendship that prompted alternating dinners between the two households. At these social meetings numerous conversations were held that frequently centered around civil rights.

In 1955 the two friends' ideas were propelled into action by the arrest of Rosa Parks a black seamstress. After a long day of toil, Parks refused to yield her seat on a public bus for a white passenger who boarded after her. This refusal by Parks was in violation of the city's segregationist laws. Her action was not the first of its kind by African Americans in Montgomery. However, when Parks was arrested, her quiet, admirable demeanor coupled with her service as secretary of the local NAACP branch helped to stir the black community to protest.

King and Abernathy became leaders of what came to be known as the Montgomery Improvement Association (MIA). Through meetings in churches, the two men spearheaded a mass boycott of Montgomery's buses. While King served as head of the MIA, Abernathy functioned as program chief. Nonviolence was the method with which the protest was implemented. Despite having been a soldier, Abernathy, like King, was convinced that nonviolence was the only acceptable means of dissent. Both had read and accepted the philosophies of Henry David Thoreau and Mahatma Gandhi.

The boycott persisted for more than a year. Despite the inordinate length of the struggle, the black community was consolidated in its refusal to ride segregated buses. Finally, in June 1956 a federal court upheld an injunction against the bus company's Jim Crow policy.

This successful boycott inspired the two young clergymen to expand their efforts to win civil rights for American's black citizens. As a result, in January 1957 the Southern Christian Leadership Conference (SCLC) was born in Atlanta. King was elected president of the new organization, and Abernathy became its secretary-treasurer. While he attended this meeting, Abernathy's home and church were bombed in Montgomery. Although it was a close call, Abernathy's family were spared any physical harm.

King moved to Atlanta in 1960, and a year later persuaded Abernathy to follow him and take on the pastorate of West Hunter Street Baptist Church. In the years that followed, the two men under the auspices of SCLC led nonviolent protests in cities such as Birmingham and Selma, Ala.; Albany, Ga.; Greensboro, N.C.; and St. Augustine, Fla. As a consequence, both were arrested many times, and experienced violence and threats of violence. In 1965 Abernathy became vice president at large of SCLC. When King was assassinated in Memphis, Tenn., in

See also
Civil Rights Movement

1968, Abernathy was unanimously elected his successor. Soon after, Abernathy launched King's planned Poor People's Campaign. He led other protests until he resigned as head of SCLC in 1977.

After Abernathy assumed the leadership of SCLC, many compared him to King. Unfortunately, he was often perceived as lacking the charisma and poise of his friend. Some even accused Abernathy of being cross or crude in his leadership style. Perhaps the best historical defense of Abernathy's reputation came from himself in the publishing of his autobiography, *And the Walls Came Tumbling Down* (1989). However, its content and literary style were unappreciated by many because of the book's revelations about King's extramarital affairs. The critics accused Abernathy of betraying his long-deceased friend.

—RANDOLPH MEADE WALKER

with King's inspirational prowess as a speaker soon brought about a sevenfold expansion of SCLC's staff, budget, and program. While some staff members concentrated on voter registration efforts and citizenship training programs funded by northern foundations, Walker and King set out to design a frontal assault on southern segregation. Stymied initially in 1961 and 1962 in the southwest Georgia city of Albany, Walker and King chose the notorious segregation stronghold of Birmingham, Ala., as their next target. In a series of aggressive demonstrations throughout April and May of 1963, SCLC put the violent excesses of racist southern lawmen on the front pages of newspapers throughout the world. Civil rights rose as never before to the top of America's national agenda, and within little more than a year's time, the Civil Rights Act of 1964 began fundamentally altering southern race relations.

Following King's much-heralded success at the 1963 March on Washington and his receipt of the 1964 Nobel Peace Prize, SCLC repeated the Birmingham scenario with an even more successful protest campaign in early 1965 in Selma, focusing on the still widely denied right to register and vote. Out of that heavily publicized campaign emerged quick congressional passage of the Voting Rights Act of 1965. With King deeply convinced that the civil rights agenda required an expansion of the southern struggle into the North so as to directly confront nationwide issues of housing discrimination and inadequate education and jobs, SCLC in early 1966 shifted much of its staff and energies to an intensive organizing campaign in Chicago. Although the "Chicago Freedom Movement" eventually garnered a negotiated accord with Chicago Mayor Richard J. Daley, promising new city efforts to root out racially biased housing practices, most observers—and some participants—adjudged SCLC's Chicago campaign as less than successful.

Following limited 1967 efforts in both Cleveland and Louisville, SCLC late that year at King's insistent behest began planning a massive "Poor People's Campaign" aimed at forcing the country's political elite to confront the issue of poverty in the United States. Following King's assassination on April 4, 1968, however, SCLC's efforts to proceed with the campaign were marred by widespread organizational confusion. Although SCLC played an important role in a successful 1969 strike by hospital workers in Charleston, S.C., the organization's resources and staff shrank precipitously in the years after King's death. Internal tensions surrounding King's designated successor, the Rev. Ralph D. Abernathy, as well as wider changes in the Civil Rights Movement, both contributed significantly to SCLC's decline. Only in the late 1970s, when another of the original founders, Joseph E. Lowery, assumed SCLC's presidency, did the conference regain organizational stability. But throughout the 1980s and into the early 1990s, SCLC continued to exist only as a faint shadow of the organization that had played such a crucially important role in the civil rights struggle between 1963 and 1968.

—DAVID J. GARROW

SPINGARN MEDAL

The Spingarn Medal is awarded annually by the National Association for the Advancement of Colored People (NAACP) for "the highest or noblest achievement by an American Negro." It is awarded by a nine-member committee selected by the NAACP board of directors. Nominations are open, and the awards ceremony has traditionally been part of the NAACP annual convention. First awarded in 1915, the Spingarn Medal has gone to African Americans who have made significant contributions in different fields of endeavor. It was for many years considered the highest honor in black America, although its prestige has declined somewhat in recent years, due to the NAACP's institution of the Image Awards and

See also

Martin Luther King, Jr.

Montgomery, Alabama Bus Boycott

SPINGARN MEDAL WINNERS

1915	Ernest E. Just	1944	Charles Drew	1969	Clarence Mitchell, Jr.
1916	Charles Young	1945	Paul Robeson	1970	Jacob Lawrence
1917	Harry T. Burleigh	1946	Thurgood Marshall	1971	Leon Howard Sullivan
1918	William S. Braithwhite	1947	Percy Julian	1972	Gordon Parks
1919	Archibald H. Grimké	1948	Channing H. Tobias	1973	Wilson C. Riles
1920	William E. B. [W. E. B.] Du Bois	1949	Ralph J. Bunche	1974	Damon J. Keith
		1950	Charles Hamilton Houston	1975	Henry Aaron
1921	Charles S. Gilpin			1976	Alvin Ailey
1922	Mary B. Talbert	1951	Mabel Keaton Staupers	1977	Alexander Palmer (Alex) Haley
1923	George Washington Carver	1952	Harry T. Moore (posthumous award)		
1924	Roland Hayes			1978	Andrew Jackson Young
1925	James Weldon Johnson	1953	Paul R. Williams	1979	Rosa L. Parks
1926	Carter G. Woodson	1954	Theodore K. Lawless	1980	Rayford W. Logan
1927	Anthony Overton	1955	Carl Murphy	1981	Coleman Alexander Young
1928	Charles W. Chesnutt	1956	Jack Roosevelt (Jackie) Robinson		
1929	Mordecai Wyatt Johnson			1982	Benjamin E. Mays
1930	Henry A. Hunt	1957	Martin Luther King, Jr.	1983	Lena Horne
1931	Richard Berry Harrison	1958	Daisy Bates and the Little Rock Nine	1984	Tom Bradley
1932	Robert Russa Moton			1985	William H. (Bill) Cosby, Jr.
1933	Max Yergan	1959	Edward Kennedy (Duke) Ellington		
1934	William Taylor Burwell Williams	1960	Langston Hughes	1986	Benjamin Lawson Hooks
		1961	Kenneth B. Clark	1987	Percy Ellis Sutton
1935	Mary McLeod Bethune	1962	Robert C. Weaver	1988	Frederick Douglass Patterson
1936	John Hope	1963	Medgar Wiley Evers (posthumous award)		
1937	Walter White			1989	Jesse Jackson
1938	no award given	1964	Roy Wilkins	1990	Lawrence Douglas Wilder
1939	Marian Anderson	1965	Leontyne Price	1991	Colin Powell
1940	Louis T. Wright	1966	John H. Johnson	1992	Barbara Jordan
1941	Richard Wright	1967	Edward W. Brooke III	1993	Dorothy I. Height
1942	A. Philip Randolph	1968	Sammy Davis, Jr.	1994	Oprah Winfrey
1943	William H. Hastie				—GREG ROBINSON

perhaps because of the fragmenting of black institutional leadership.

The Spingarn Medal is named for Joel E. Spingarn (1874–1939), who originated the idea of it. Spingarn, who was white, was professor and chair of the Department of Comparative Literature at Columbia University from 1909 until 1911, when he resigned over free-speech issues. He became involved in the NAACP because of civil rights abuses in the South. Spingarn joined the NAACP's board of directors in 1913, and helped establish the NAACP's New York office. In 1913 and 1914, while traveling throughout the country, organizing the association and speaking for the rights of black people, he noticed that newspaper coverage of African Americans tended to be negative, focusing on black murderers and other criminals. A close collaborator of W. E. B. Du Bois, Spingarn was sensitive to media portrayal of blacks. Independently wealthy, he en-

dowed an award, a medal to be made of gold "not exceeding $100" in value, that would pinpoint black achievement, strengthen racial pride, and publicize the NAACP. To assure that white attention would be directed toward the award, Spingarn set up an award committee consisting of prominent men, including Oswald Garrison Villard (grandson of abolitionist William Lloyd Garrison) and ex-president William Howard Taft. There were thirty nominations for the first medal, which was awarded to biologist Ernest E. Just and presented by the first of the celebrity presenters Spingarn would arrange, New York Gov. Charles S. Whitman.

By 1992, the Spingarn Medal winners included five ministers; eight educators; eleven performers, including five classical musicians and one jazz musician, two popular entertainers, and one dancer; two baseball players; two military officers; one labor leader; two historians; and one ar-

See also

NAACP

chitect. Beginning with Mary B. Talbert in 1922, nine women have won the Springarn Medal. The award has twice been given posthumously.

—GREG ROBINSON

SPIRITUALS

African-American sacred folk songs are known as anthems, hymns, spiritual songs, jubilees, gospel songs, or spirituals; the distinctions among these terms are not precise. "Spiritual song" was widely used in English and American tune books from the eighteenth century, but "spiritual" has not been found in print before the Civil War. Descriptions of songs that came to be known by that name appeared at least twenty-five years earlier, and African-American distinctive religious singing was described as early as 1819.

Travelers and traders in Africa in the early seventeenth century described the musical elements that later distinguished African-American songs from European folk song: strong, syncopated rhythms reinforced by bodily movement, gapped scales, improvised texts, and the universal call-and-response form in which the leader and responding chorus overlapped. To white contemporaries, the music seemed wholly exotic and barbaric, although later analysts identified elements common also to European music, such as the diatonic scale. The performance style of African music, quite distinct from familiar European styles, has persisted in many forms of African-American music to the present day.

Although the music of Africans has been documented in the West Indies and the North American mainland from the seventeenth century, conversion to Christianity was a necessary precondition for the emergence of the spiritual, a distinctive form of African-American religious music. Conversion proceeded slowly. Individual slaves were converted by the families with whom they lived in the seventeenth century, but on southern plantations, where most of the slaves lived, some planters opposed the baptism of their slaves in the belief that baptism would bring freedom. Moreover, plantations were widely separated, missionaries were few, and travel was difficult. Where religious instruction was permitted, the slaves responded with enthusiasm.

In the mid-eighteenth century a few Presbyterian ministers, led by Samuel Davies of Hanover County, Va., made special efforts to convert blacks within their neighborhoods, teaching them Isaac Watts's hymns from books sent from England.

Davies wrote in 1751, "The Negroes, above all the Human Species that I ever knew, have an Ear for Musick, and a kind of extatic Delight in *Psalmody*" (Epstein 1977, p. 104). Whether the blacks injected a distinctive performance style he did not say.

Toward the end of the century, Methodist itinerants like Bishop Francis Asbury, together with his black exhorter, Harry Hosier, held protracted meetings lasting several days that drew large crowds of blacks and whites. After 1800 the camp meeting developed on the frontier, where settlements were widely scattered. From the first camp meeting, black worshipers were present, sometimes seated separately, but in close proximity to whites. In an atmosphere highly charged with emotion, both groups shared songs, parts of songs, and styles of singing in participatory services where large numbers of people needed musical responses they could learn at once. The call-and-response style of the Africans resembled the whites' time-honored practice of "lining out."

The first documented reports of distinctive black religious singing date from the beginning of the nineteenth century, about twenty years before the first organized missions to plantation slaves. Throughout the antebellum period, spirituals were mentioned in letters, diaries, and magazine articles written by Southerners, but to most Northerners they were quite unknown. As northern men and women went south during the Civil War, they heard spirituals for the first time. Newspaper reporters included song texts in their stories from the front. Individual songs were published as sheet music, although some editors were well aware that their transcriptions failed to reproduce the music fully. Lucy McKim wrote to the editor of *Dwight's Journal of Music:* "The odd turns made in the throat; and the curious rhythmic effect produced by single voices chiming in at different irregular intervals, seem almost as impossible to place on score, as the singing of birds, or the tones of an Æolian Harp" (21 [November 8, 1862]: 254–255).

When a comprehensive collection of songs, *Slave Songs of the United States,* was published in 1867, the senior editor, William Francis Allen, wrote in the introduction: "The best we can do, however, with paper and types . . . will convey but a faint shadow of the original. . . . [T]he intonations and delicate variations of even one singer cannot be reproduced on paper. And I despair of conveying any notion of the effect of a number singing together" (Allen 1867, pp. iv–v). In effect, the notational system filtered out most of the

In 1925, Paul Robeson launched his celebrated career as an interpreter of African-American spirituals and of folk songs from around the world.

PAGE 600

characteristic African elements, leaving versions that looked like European music. These collectors had heard the music sung by its creators, and they fully realized how defective their transcriptions were. But they feared that the music would be lost forever if the transcriptions, however unsatisfactory, were not made.

The pattern of transcribing the music in conventional notation was followed in more popular collections of songs transcribed in the 1870s from the singing of the Fisk Jubilee Singers, the Hampton Singers, and other touring groups from black schools in the South. These tours of carefully rehearsed ensembles of well-trained singers introduced audiences in the North and Europe to versions of the spirituals that eliminated many of those characteristic elements that had so attracted Lucy McKim and William Allen. The singers had been trained in European music and felt a responsibility to reflect credit on the rising black population.

By the 1890s, spirituals had become widely popular, both in the United States and in Europe,

in the versions sung by the college singers. In 1892 a Viennese professor of jurisprudence, Richard Wallaschek, in a book entitled *Primitive Music*, advanced the theory that the spirituals were "mere limitations of European compositions which the negroes have picked up and served up again with slight variations" (p. 60). He never visited the United States or Africa, and his knowledge of the music was wholly derived from the defective transcriptions in *Slave Songs of the United States* and minstrel songs (p. 61). Never having heard the music, Wallaschek was unaware that there were elements that could not be transcribed, but his ideas were taken seriously by several generations of scholars.

The strongest statement of the white-origins school was made by George Pullen Jackson, a professor of German at Vanderbilt University, who explored with enthusiasm the so-called white spiritual. In his book *White Spirituals of the Southern Uplands* (1933), his discussion of black spirituals was based primarily on an analysis of transcribed versions. He cited priority in publication

WILLIAM GRANT STILL

Composer Developed Nationalist Style

William Grant Still (May 11, 1895–December 3, 1978), composer. Although he was born in Woodville, Miss., William Grant Still grew up in Little Rock, Ark. He attended Wilberforce University and Oberlin College. His private studies in composition were with George Whitefield Chadwick in Boston and Edgard Varèse in New York.

Still's musical style is perhaps best described as nationalist, successfully blending indigenous American musical elements, African-American folk materials, and the blues idiom into a range of musical genres: symphonic and operatic compositions, chamber music, and art songs. Many of his compositions were inspired by the black experience in America. Over the years, he developed an eloquent musical expressiveness in his works. An outstanding achievement was his handling of melody in his strongly lyrical pieces.

Because he was an excellent orchestrator, he was engaged by such celebrities as Paul Whiteman, Don Voorhees, Sophie Tucker, Willard Robison, and Artie Shaw to prepare orchestral arrangements. In his early years, he played in various dance orchestras and pit orchestras for musicals. Still was associated in the music industry with W. C. Handy, Harry Pace and his Black Swan Phonograph Company, the

Deep River Hour on CBS Radio, and Columbia Pictures.

Still composed over 150 musical works. His most significant symphonic compositions are the *Afro-American Symphony* (1930), *Symphony No. 2 in G Minor* (1937), *Festive Overture* (1944), *Plain-Chant for America* (1941, revised 1968), *From the Black Belt* (1926), *And They Lynched Him on a Tree* (1940), and *Darker America* (1924). Still composed ten operas, including *Highway 1, U.S.A* (1962), *Troubled Island* (1941), and *A Bayou Legend* (1941). His ballets include *Sadhji* (1930), *Lenox Avenue* (1937), and *La Guiablesse* (1927). Verna Arvey, his wife, collaborated as a librettist in the writing of many works.

Still received many commissions, awards, prizes, and honorary degrees, as well as Guggenheim and Rosenwald fellowships. His contributions to African-American music are significant: He was the first African-American composer to have a symphony played by a major American orchestra (*Afro-American Symphony*), the first to have an opera performed by a major company, the first black American to conduct a major orchestra, and one of the first African-American composers to write for radio, films, and television.

—LUCIUS R. WYATT

See also
James Weldon Johnson

as certain proof of origin, overlooking the irrelevance of this fact for folk music, most especially for the music of a population kept illiterate by force of law. The white-origins theory is no longer widely accepted. Not until the advent of sound recordings was it possible to preserve the performance itself, including improvised details and performance style, for later study and analysis.

Concert arrangements of spirituals for solo singers and choirs have been made, most notably by Harry T. Burleigh, James Weldon Johnson and J. Rosamund Johnson, and William Levi Dawson. Spiritual thematic materials have permeated diverse genres of American music in the twentieth century.

The musical elements that distinguished African-American spirituals from Euro-American hymnody were virtually impossible to reproduce in standard musical notation. Variable pitches; irregular strong, syncopated rhythms; and freely improvised melodic lines presented insoluble problems to the collector before the age of recording. The performance style also included humming or "moaning" in response to the solo performer (whether singer or preacher), responsive interjections, and ceaseless physical movement in response to the music—patting, hand-clapping, foot-tapping, and swaying. The overlapping of leader and responding chorus provided a complex interplay of voice qualities and rhythms. Slurs and slides modified pitch, while turns in the throat, blue notes, microtones, and sighs were equally impossible to notate. Pentatonic scales, however, and flattened fourth or seventh notes could be captured in notation.

Textual elements covered a whole spectrum of concepts, from trials and suffering, sorrow and tribulations, to hope and affirmation. Events from both the Old and the New Testaments were described, including Elijah's chariot and Ezekiel's wheel, along with more common images such as trains, shoes, wings, harps, robes, and ships. Hypocritical preachers and sinners were scorned, while death, heaven, resurrection, and triumph were often invoked.

Besides the purely religious message, there were also hidden meanings in some spirituals, exhorting the singers to resistance or freedom. Songs such as "Steal Away," "Follow the Drinking Gourd," and "Go Down, Moses"—with its refrain, "Let my people go"—could be interpreted in at least two ways. References to crossing Jordan and the trumpet blast could have both religious and secular interpretations.

—DENA J. EPSTEIN

STONE, SLY

Sly Stone (March 15, 1944–), musician. Sly Stone was born Sylvester Stewart in Dallas. He first recorded at the age of four, playing drums and guitar in "On the Battlefield for My Lord," by the Stewart Four, a family ensemble. His family moved to the San Francisco area in the 1950s. There he sang in vocal groups and performed with Joe Piazza and the Continentals. At the age of sixteen he recorded "Long Time Away."

In 1964 Stewart began to work as a producer and songwriter for Autumn Records, which recorded the Beau Brummels, the Great Society, and Bobby "The Swim" Freeman. In 1966 he worked as a disc jockey at radio stations KSOL and KDIA, both in San Francisco. In the mid–1960s he was also playing with his own group, the Stoners, which eventually changed its name to the Family Stone. Stewart began calling himself Sly Stone, and his group, a groundbreaking interracial rhythm-and-blues ensemble with male and female musicians and singers, rapidly gained popularity for its psychedelic, funky, soul-rock approach on albums such as *A Whole New Thing* (1967), *Dance to the Music* (1968), and *Life!* (1968), which included "Everyday People." In 1969 Sly and the Family Stone performed at Woodstock and released *Stand!* which included "Hot Fun in the Summertime." That was to be the height of Sly Stone's achievement. In the early 1970s his career began to falter. His offstage excesses, marked by a flamboyant, drug-fueled lifestyle, led to numerous show cancelations or late appearances. He was arrested on drug charges several times in the early 1970s, and on his next album, *There's a Riot Going On* (1971), his music took on a darker, more pessimistic tone. Stone's next two albums, *Fresh!* (1973) and *Small Talk* (1974), failed to sell. In June 1974 Stone married Kathy Silva on stage at Madison Square Garden, but they divorced before the year was out.

In the late 1970s Stone's albums, including *Heard Ya Missed Me, Well I'm Back* (1976) and *Back on the Right Track* (1979) were influential among musicians, but failed to gain a wider audience. In 1981 Stone performed on Funkadelic's *The Electric Spanking of War Babies*. The following year he entered a drug treatment program in Florida and attempted a comeback. Stone released *Ain't But the One Way* in 1983, and performed in concert in 1984 with Bobby Womack. In 1985 he performed on George Clinton's album *Some of My Best Jokes Are Friends*. However, Stone soon found himself again in trouble with the law. In 1985 he pleaded

By 1945, gospel was becoming recognized not only as a spiritual experience but also as a form of entertainment.

PAGE 302

guilty to failing to provide child support and was placed on parole for three years. He was jailed the next year in Los Angeles for the same offense and in Florida in 1987 for parole violation. He was held by police in Connecticut on a drug charge in 1989. Despite the brevity of his commercial success, Stone has remained a major influence on African-American popular music and is considered to be one of the founders of funk and disco music. In 1993 Stone was inducted into the Rock 'n' Roll Hall of Fame.

—JONATHAN GILL

STONO REBELLION

The Stono Rebellion of 1739 was the largest uprising of enslaved African Americans to take place in Britain's mainland colonies before the American Revolution. South Carolina's black majority outnumbered whites by nearly two to one and by far more in the coastal low country where West African rice-growing skills were providing planters with enormous profits. Though suppressed by local authorities, the revolt came close to succeeding in ways that could have made it a dramatic turning point in American history.

Despite harsh conditions and diverse languages, underground information networks allowed black Carolinians to communicate. Many were aware of recent resistance in other colonies and knew of the Spanish crown's 1733 offer of freedom to fugitive slaves reaching Florida. Harvest pressures upon blacks and seasonal sickness among whites made September a likely time to rebel, and planners selected Sunday morning, since most whites still attended church unarmed and most slaves were released from work on the Sabbath. Much of the leadership came from Angolans, who represented the largest proportion of recently arrived slaves and who brought military experience from Africa.

Led by a man named Jemmy and no doubt spurred by news that the so-called War of Jenkins' Ear had erupted between England and Spain, a score of black Carolinians met near the west branch of the Stono River about twenty miles southwest of Charleston early on Sunday, September 9, 1739. At Stono Bridge they broke into Hutcheson's store, killing the two storekeepers and taking guns and powder. With cries of "Liberty" and beating of drums, the rebels raised a standard and headed south toward Spanish St. Augustine, where escaping Carolina slaves had been granted freedom at Fort Mose. Along the road they gathered black recruits, burned houses, and killed white opponents, sparing one innkeeper who was "kind to his slaves."

By chance, Lt. Gov. William Bull glimpsed the insurgents and alerted white parishioners. Late Sunday afternoon, planters on horseback caught up with the band of sixty to one hundred rebels in an open field, where they had paused hoping news of their action would inspire further support. In the ensuing encounter, some rebels surrendered or were captured; others were wounded or killed. Several dozen managed to escape, but the organized march southward had been broken up. In the next two days, by one account, militiamen and Indians "kill'd twenty odd more, and took about 40; who were immediately some shot, some hang'd, and some Gibbeted alive." Others remained at large for months.

Over twenty whites and nearly twice as many blacks were killed in the uprising, which led quickly to a harsher slave code and a moratorium on slave imports, as the white minority debated their precarious situation. Had the rebels managed to travel farther, spread word faster, and delay a confrontation a bit longer, their brave attempt might have spiraled into a successful rebellion that challenged the logic and stability of the emerging slave system. But the tide flowed the other way. By the 1750s the neighboring colony of Georgia had legalized African slavery, and a decade later the English had taken over Florida from the Spanish. Occupants of the Carolina gulag would have to wait generations for a plausible opportunity to strike a blow for their release from bondage.

—PETER H. WOOD

STRAYHORN, WILLIAM THOMAS "BILLY"

William Thomas "Billy" Strayhorn (November 29, 1915–May 30, 1967), composer and jazz pianist. Born in Dayton, Ohio, and raised in early childhood in Hillsborough, N.C., Billy Strayhorn gained most of his schooling, including private piano instruction, in Pittsburgh. He sought out Duke Ellington in December 1938, hoping to work with him as a lyricist, introducing himself with his songs "Lush Life" and "Something to Live For." By 1939, Strayhorn had become a regular associate of the Ellington orchestra, contributing themes like "Day Dream" and "Passion Flower" for the alto saxophonist Johnny Hodges, and soon thereafter a melody and arrangement that became the orchestra's theme, "Take the A Train." Strayhorn regularly contributed fully realized instrumental works like "Raincheck," "Chelsea Bridge," and "Johnny Come Lately" (all 1941). Thereafter, Ellington and Strayhorn frequently worked collaboratively, and they said in later years that they were unsure, once a work was completed, which one of them had contributed what.

Strayhorn came to the orchestra with a sophisticated knowledge of chromatic harmony, much of which he had worked out on his own. Ellington himself had evolved from a very different point of departure, beginning with a knowledge only of basic harmony as practiced in ragtime and of blue notes (the lowered, "flatted," third, fifth, and seventh intervals), but he had been headed in a similar direction.

From the middle 1950s until his death, Strayhorn's collaborations with Ellington markedly intensified. There were several extended works such as *Such Sweet Thunder, Suite Thursday,* and the *Far East Suite.* One of Strayhorn's final short works, the compelling "Blood Count," was written for the orchestra's alto saxophonist, Hodges.

—MARTIN WILLIAMS

STUDENT NONVIOLENT COORDINATING COMMITTEE

After an initial protest on February 1, 1960, that attempted to integrate a Woolworth lunch counter in Greensboro, N.C., black college students spearheaded a sit-in movement that spread rapidly through the South. Reacting to this upsurge of student activism, Southern Christian Leadership Conference (SCLC) official Ella Baker invited student protest leaders to an Easter weekend conference in Raleigh, N.C. The student leaders, believing that existing civil rights organizations were overly cautious, agreed to form a new group, the Student Nonviolent Coordinating Committee (SNCC, or "Snick"), and elected Fisk University graduate student Marion Barry as chairman.

Originally a means of communication among autonomous local student protest groups, SNCC gradually assumed a more assertive role in the southern Civil Rights Movement. In February 1961, four students affiliated with SNCC traveled to Rock Hill, S.C., to join a group of protesters arrested at a segregated lunch counter. The arrested students utilized a "jail-no-bail" strategy that was designed to demonstrate their militancy and independence from the NAACP and its legal-assistance staff. In May 1961, after a group of Freedom Riders organized by the Congress of Racial Equality (CORE) encountered violence in Alabama, SNCC activists insisted on continuing the protests against segregated transportation facilities. Dozens of black students rode buses from Alabama to Jackson, Miss., where they were arrested, quickly convicted of violating segregation norms, and then incarcerated in Parchman Prison.

From the fall of 1961 through the spring of 1966, SNCC shifted its focus from nonviolent desegregation protests to long-term voting rights campaigns in the deep South. Full-time SNCC field secretaries—many of them veterans of the Mississippi Freedom Rides—gradually displaced representatives of local protest groups as the organization's principal policymakers. Initially dominated by advocates of Christian Gandhianism, SNCC became increasingly composed of secular community organizers devoted to the development of indigenous black leaders and local institutions.

SNCC's ability to work closely with local leaders was evident in the Albany, Ga., protests of 1961 and 1962. Under the leadership of former Virginia Union University student Charles Sherrod, SNCC workers in Albany mobilized black student protesters and spearheaded marches that resulted in hundreds of arrests. Neither the group's brash militancy nor the more cautious leadership of the Rev. Dr. Martin Luther King, Jr., overcame segregationist opposition in Albany, however, and SNCC's voter-registration campaign in nearby rural areas also achieved few gains in the face of violent white resistance. By 1963, SNCC staff members in southwest Georgia and elsewhere had become dissatisfied with the failure of the federal government to protect them. John Lewis, who replaced Barry as chairman, expressed this growing disillusionment in his controversial speech given at the massive 1963 March on Washington.

By the time of the march, SNCC's most substantial projects were in Mississippi, where its community-organizing efforts encountered fierce white resistance. After launching the Mississippi effort in McComb in 1961, Bob Moses, a former

Black power . . . is a call for black people in this country to unite, to recognize their heritage, to build a sense of community. . . . It is a call to reject the racist institutions and values of this society.

STOKELY CARMICHAEL AND CHARLES VERNON HAMILTON
BLACK POWER!, 1967

See also
Black Panther Party

STOKELY CARMICHAEL

Outspoken Leadership Makes an Impact

Stokely Carmichael (July 29, 1941–), activist. Born in Port of Spain, Trinidad, Stokely Carmichael graduated from the Bronx High School of Science in 1960 and Howard University in 1964. During his college years, he participated in a variety of civil rights demonstrations sponsored by the Congress of Racial Equality (CORE), the Nonviolent Action Group (NAG), and the Student Nonviolent Coordinating Committee (SNCC). As a freedom rider, he was arrested in 1961 for violating Mississippi segregation laws and spent seven weeks in Parchman Penitentiary. After college, he worked with the Mississippi Summer Project, directed SNCC voter-registration efforts in Lowndes County, Ala., and helped organize black voters through the Lowndes County Freedom Organization.

Elected SNCC chairman in 1966, he proffered an outspoken, militant stance that helped distance SNCC from the moderate leadership of competing civil rights organizations. A chief architect and spokesperson for the new Black Power ideology, Carmichael coauthored (with Charles V. Hamilton) *Black Power* (1967) and published a collection of his essays and addresses, *Stokely Speaks* (1971). He left his SNCC post in 1967. The next year he was made prime minister of the Black Panther Party; in 1969, he quit the Black Panthers and became an organizer for Kwame Nkrumah's All-African People's Revolutionary Party. Studies with Nkrumah of Ghana and Sékou Touré of Guinea confirmed his Pan-Africanism and, in 1978, moved him to change his name to Kwame Toure. Since 1969, he has made Conakry, Guinea, his home. He has continued his work in political education, condemning Western imperialism, and promoting the goal of a unified socialist Africa.

—WILLIAM L. VAN DEBURG

Harvard University graduate student, became voter-registration director of the Council of Federated Organizations (COFO), a SNCC-dominated coalition of civil rights groups. Although SNCC's staff was composed mainly of native Mississippians, the campaign for voting rights in the state attracted increasing support from northern whites. Acknowledging the need for more outside support, COFO sponsored a summer project in 1964 that was designed to bring hundreds of white students to Mississippi. The murder of three civil rights workers, two of them white, during the early days of the project brought unprecedented national attention to the suppression of black voting rights in the deep South. SNCC staff members, however, became ever more disillusioned with their conventional liberal allies. In August, this disillusionment increased when leaders at the Democratic National Convention refused to back the Mississippi Freedom Democratic Party's effort to take the seats of the all-white regular Democratic party delegation.

During 1965 and 1966, the gulf grew larger between SNCC and its former liberal allies. A major series of voting rights protests in Alabama during the spring of 1965 exposed the group's increasing tactical differences with the SCLC. After the killing of Jimmy Lee Jackson in Marion, and a brutal police attack in March on a group marching from Selma to the state capitol in Montgomery, SNCC militants severed many of their ties to the political mainstream. Stokely Carmichael and other SNCC organizers helped establish an independent political entity, the Lowndes County Freedom Organization, better known as the Black Panther Party. In May 1966, SNCC workers' growing willingness to advocate racial separatism and radical social change led to a shift in the group's leadership, with Carmichael replacing Lewis as chairman. The following month, Carmichael publicly expressed SNCC's new political orientation when he began using the Black Power slogan on a voting rights march through Mississippi. The national controversy surrounding his Black Power speeches further separated SNCC from the SCLC, the NAACP, and other elements of the coalition that had supported civil rights reform.

Confronting increasing external opposition and police repression, SNCC also endured serious internal conflicts that made it more vulnerable to external attack. In 1967, executive director Ruby Doris Robinson's death from illness further weakened the organization. After H. Rap Brown became the new chairman in June 1967, Carmichael traveled extensively to build ties with revolutionary movements in Africa and Asia. Upon his return to the United States, he led an abortive effort to establish an alliance between SNCC and the California-based Black Panther party. The two groups broke their ties in the summer of 1968, and Carmichael remained with the Panthers, leaving

James Forman as SNCC's dominant figure. By this time, however, SNCC's Black Power rhetoric and support for the Palestinian struggle against Israel had alienated many former supporters. In addition, its leaders' emphasis on ideological issues detracted from long-term community-organizing efforts. SNCC did not have much impact on African-American politics after 1967, although it remained in existence until the early 1970s.

—CLAYBORNE CARSON

THE SUPREMES

Soul Vocal Trio Tops the Charts

The female soul vocal trio called the Supremes was one of Motown's most successful rhythm and blues acts and one of the most successful recorded groups of all time. They earned twelve number-one hits and sold over twenty million records; their rise to national fame signaled the elimination of the color barrier in the pop market.

Originally a quartet known as the Primettes, the Detroit-based group had several personnel changes during its eighteen-year history. At the height of its popularity (1962–1967), the group included Diana Ross, Florence Ballard, and Mary Wilson. Their hits included "Where Did Our Love Go," "Baby Love," "Come See About Me," "Stop! In the Name of Love" (no. 1, *Billboard* charts 1965), "Back in My Arms Again" (no. 1, 1965), and "I Hear a Symphony" (no. 1, 1965), written by Motown's Holland-Dozier-Holland songwriting team. The Supremes' earliest recordings featured Ballard's strong lead vocals (produced by Smokey Robinson), but the hits from 1964 and 1965 featured Ross's bright, cooing vocals.

In 1967 Cindy Birdsong (formerly with Patti Labelle and the Blue Belles) replaced Ballard, and the group was billed as Diana Ross and the Supremes. Their hits included "Love Child" (no. 1, 1968), "Someday We'll Be Together" (no. 1, 1969), and, with The Temptations, "I'm Gonna Make You Love Me" (no. 2, 1968). In 1970, Ross departed for a solo career and Jean Terrell led the trio, but their popularity declined by 1973. The 1981 Broadway show *Dreamgirls* supposedly depicts Ballard's perspective on the group, and in 1984 Wilson published her own memoir, *Dreamgirl: My Life as a Supreme.*

—KYRA D. GAUNT

SUTTON, PERCY ELLIS

Percy Ellis Sutton (November 24, 1920–), politician and media businessman. Percy Ellis Sutton was born in San Antonio, Tex. His parents, Samuel J. Sutton and Lillian Smith, were educators and philanthropists. Percy Sutton graduated from Phillis Wheatley High School in San Antonio, and subsequently attended Prairie View Agricultural and Mechanical College, Tuskegee Institute, and Hampton Institute. When he attempted to join the Army Air Force in Texas during World War II, he was rejected (for reasons having to do with his racial background). He then successfully enlisted in New York City. As an intelligence officer with the black ninety-ninth Fighter Squadron serving in the Italian and Mediterranean theaters, Sutton earned combat stars and rose to the rank of captain.

After the war, Sutton completed his education under the G.I. Bill, graduating from Brooklyn Law School in 1950. During the Korean War, Sutton reentered the Air Force as an intelligence officer and trial judge advocate. When the war ended in 1953, Sutton opened a law partnership in Harlem with his brother, Oliver, and George Covington and worked with the NAACP on several civil rights cases throughout the 1950s. In addition to its work with the NAACP, the firm served other clients such as Malcolm X and the Baptist Ministers Conference of Greater New York.

From 1961 to 1962 Sutton served as branch president of the New York City NAACP, participating in demonstrations and freedom rides in the South. During the winter of 1963–1964, Sutton and Charles Rangel cofounded the John F. Kennedy Democratic Club, later known as the Martin Luther King, Jr., Club. Sutton was elected to the New York State Assembly in 1964. In 1966, after Manhattan borough president Constance Baker Motley accepted an appointment as a federal judge, the New York City Council chose Sutton to finish Motley's term. Sutton was reelected in his own right later that year, and was subsequently reelected in 1969 and 1973. As borough president, Sutton focused on decentralizing the municipal bureaucracy, cutting city spending, and addressing the broader social causes of urban crime and poverty.

In 1970 Sutton endorsed Rangel's campaign to replace Adam Clayton Powell, Jr., as congressman from Harlem. Rangel's victory marked the ascen-

See also
NAACP

dancy of a new black political coalition in Harlem, a coalition that included not only Percy Sutton but also future New York City mayor David Dinkins. In 1971, while still Manhattan borough president, Sutton set out to purchase several black-owned media enterprises, beginning with the New York *Amsterdam News* (which he sold in 1975) and radio station WLIB-AM. In 1977 Sutton became owner and board chairman of the Inner-City Broadcasting Company, a nationwide media corporation, and through the corporation he subsequently purchased radio stations in New York, California, and Michigan. He also formed Percy Sutton International, Inc., the investments of which encouraged the agricultural, manufacturing, and trade industries in Africa, Southeast Asia, and Brazil.

In September 1977 Sutton was an unsuccessful candidate for the nomination for mayor. He retired from public office after finishing his second full term as borough president in December 1977, but he continued to advise Rangel, Dinkins, and other black politicians on electoral strategy and urban policy. In 1981 he acquired Harlem's Apollo Theater as a base for producing cable television programs. By the end of the decade Sutton's estimated net worth was $170 million. In 1990 he was succeeded as head of Inner-City Broadcasting by his son, Pierre Montea ("PePe"), who raised the company's net worth to $28 million by 1992.

Sutton has been a guest lecturer at many universities and corporations and has held leadership positions in the Association for a Better New York, the National Urban League, the Congressional Black Caucus Foundation, and several other civil rights organizations. A founding member and director of Operation PUSH (People United to Save Humanity), Sutton was also a close adviser to the Rev. Jesse Jackson. He was awarded the NAACP's Spingarn Medal in 1987 at the Apollo Theater, which under Sutton's management had been restored as a major Harlem cultural center and landmark.

—DURAHN TAYLOR

See also

Harlem

T

TANNER, HENRY OSSAWA

Henry Ossawa Tanner (June 21, 1859–May 25, 1937), painter and illustrator. Tanner's father, Benjamin Tucker Tanner (1835–1923) and his mother, Sarah Elizabeth Miller (1840–1914), lived in Pittsburgh at the time of Henry's birth. They gave their son the middle name Ossawa, after the Kansas town of Osawatomie, where white abolitionist John Brown had started an antislavery campaign in 1856. After entering the ministry in 1863, Tanner's father rose to the rank of bishop in the African Methodist Episcopal Church by 1888. The Rev. Tanner relocated the family to Philadelphia in 1868 so that he could serve as editor of the Christian Recorder. Tanner attended Lombard Street School for Colored Students in 1868. The next year he enrolled at the Robert Vaux Consolidated School for Colored Students, then the only secondary school for black students in Philadelphia, which was renamed Robert Vaux Grammar School the year before Tanner graduated as valedictorian in 1877.

Tanner began painting when he was thirteen years old, and although his parents supported his early efforts, he did not receive formal training until 1880, studying with Thomas Eakins at the Pennsylvania Academy of the Fine Arts. He remained a student with Eakins until 1885. During his academy years and through 1890, Tanner was primarily a painter of seascapes, landscapes, and animal life. Many of his paintings engaged a particular technical challenge in representing natural phenomena such as waves breaking on rocks in stormy seas (*Seascape-Jetty*, 1876–1879), rippling autumn foliage (*Fauna*, 1878–1879), or the light in a lion's mane at the Philadelphia Zoo (*Lion Licking Its Paw*, 1886). While his work in each genre was influenced by numerous, lesser-known local artists, Tanner was developing his own style and becoming skilled at controlling effects of light, giving objects form through a subdued color scheme and a subtle sense of tonality, and creating decorative effects with tiny flecks of color. Tanner strategically organized space by surrounding central figures with vast areas of opaque color—representing grass or sky, for example—and using the emptiness to draw the viewer's attention to the locus of dramatic activity.

While Tanner met with some critical success as a landscape painter during his academy years, he was unable to support himself by painting and worked for a flour business owned by friends of his family. In 1889 he relocated to Atlanta, where he taught at Clark University and worked for a year as a photographer. There was a lull in Tanner's painting from 1889 to 1890, but he used some photographs from this year, taken on a trip to North Carolina, as studies for paintings such as his well-known work *The Banjo Lesson* (1893).

In Atlanta, Tanner met Joseph Crane Hartzell, a white Methodist Episcopal bishop, and his wife. They became his patrons, sponsoring the first exhibition of his work in Cincinnati in 1890. They supported Tanner when he traveled to Europe in 1891 and set up a studio in Paris, where he began studying with Jean-Joseph Benjamin Constant and Jean-Paul Laurens. Tanner returned to Philadelphia in 1893, though he found the racial restrictions onerous and soon returned to Paris. In 1899 he married Jessie Macauley Olssen (1873–1925), a white American of Swedish descent who was living abroad in Paris. The two remained happily married and lived in France for most of their lives, except for the years Tanner spent at an artists' colony in Mount Kisco, N.Y., from 1901 to 1904. Tanner's Paris studio became a hub of activity for visiting African-American artists and other visitors from abroad in the early part of twentieth century.

During the 1890s, Tanner's work shifted from landscape painting to genre scenes depicting black life in America. The change has been attributed to Tanner's 1893 participation as a speaker in the Columbian Exposition's Congress on Africa, where he asserted the achievements of African-American artists and listened to speakers give an overview of post-Emancipation black leadership across the nation. With his thoughts focused on issues of black identity and productivity, Tanner began depicting genre scenes of African-

See also

African Methodist Episcopal Church

American life. While he painted relatively few genre scenes, some of them, such as *The Banjo Lesson* and *The Thankful Poor* (1894), are among his best-known paintings. *The Banjo Lesson* depicted one of the acclaimed themes in American genre painting, an older musician teaching his art to a young boy. *The Thankful Poor* also featured an old man and a boy to show how the black family passed on moral and spiritual lessons to its children.

Tanner's style during his genre period had several influences. In 1889 Tanner spent time in the Brittany region of France, involved in the impressionist and postimpressionist movements, particularly those in the circle of Gaugin. While some critics have noted that Tanner borrowed the impressionists' techniques and was influenced by their use of color and spatial organization to communicate mood, the overall character of his work was shaped by academic romantic realism.

Tanner's illustrations appeared in American journals such as *Harper's Young People* and *Our Continent,* as well as in exhibition catalogs at the Pennsylvania Academy of the Fine Arts. His work was seen in exhibitions at the academy in 1888, 1889, 1898, and 1906, and was frequently shown at the prestigious Salon de la Société des Artistes Français in Paris during the period 1894 to 1914.

In the later stages of his career, Tanner was most active as a religious painter, and while these works were based on biblical stories and did not directly address issues of black life, they were continually concerned with broad themes of social justice in the earthly world, using the stories as metaphors for more contemporary issues such as slavery and emancipation in America. An early representation of *Daniel in the Lions' Den* (1896), one of his two known paintings of this well-known religious theme, was exhibited at the salon, where it received honorable mention. In 1897, shortly after he painted *Daniel in the Lions' Den,* Tanner traveled to the Middle East to observe the people and geography of the ancient lands, and to enhance the historical accuracy of his paintings with biblical themes. Among the most celebrated religious compositions was *The Raising of Lazarus* (1896), now located at the Musée d'Orsay in Paris. Other paintings on sacred subjects included *Nicodemus Visiting Jesus* (1899), *Flight into Egypt* (1899), *Mary* (1900), *Return of the Holy Women* (1904), *Christ at the Home of Mary and Martha* (1905), *Two Disciples at the Tomb* (1906), *The Holy Family* (1909–1910), *Christ Learning to Read* (1910), *The Disciples on the Sea of Galilee* (1910), and *The Good Shepherd* (1922).

Tanner's religious work went through multiple stylistic phases and had diverse influences, including Velazquez's portraiture, El Greco's elongated figures, David's scale of historical paintings, and Georges Rouault's use of color in contemporary religious paintings. The style of his paintings after 1920 was marked by an overall conservatism. He remained uninfluenced by contemporary developments. Despite some brilliant coloristic effects, the overall impact of his religious compositions, with their limited range of tonality and virtually absent source of light, is a brooding, somber, and contemplative mood.

He exhibited widely in the United States after 1900, with paintings appearing at the Pan-American Exposition (Buffalo) in 1901, the Louisiana Purchase Exposition in 1904, the St. Louis Exposition in 1904, the Carnegie Institute Annual Exhibition in Pittsburgh in 1906, the Anglo-American Art Exhibition (London) in 1914, the Panama-Pacific Exposition (San Francisco) in 1915, the Los Angeles County Museum in 1920, and the Grand Central Art Galleries in New York in 1920. Since 1968, Tanner's works have been shown in major United States exhibitions celebrating the accomplishments of American artists of African descent.

Tanner served his country during World War I as a lieutenant in the American Red Cross in the Farm Service Bureau. In 1918 he worked in the Bureau of Publicity as resident artist. Though his academic style was increasingly out of fashion, in his later years he was given many honors. He received the coveted Legion of Honor from the French Government in 1923. Tanner's son Jesse graduated from Cambridge University in 1924 and became an engineer upon his return to France. In 1927 Tanner became the first African American elected to full membership in the National Academy of Design. He continued to work as a painter until his death in Paris.

—DAVID C. DRISKELL

TAP DANCE

Tap is a form of American percussive dance that emphasizes the interplay of rhythms produced by the feet. Fused from African and European music and dance styles, tap evolved over hundreds of years, shaped by the constant exchanges and imitations that occurred between the black and white cultures as they converged in America. However, since it is jazz syncopations that distinguish tap's rhythms and define its inflections, the heritage of

African percussive sensibilities has exerted the strongest influence on tap's evolution.

Unlike ballet, whose techniques were codified and taught in the academies, tap developed informally from black and white vernacular social dances, from people watching each other dance in the streets and dance halls. As a result of the offstage challenges and onstage competitions where steps were shared, stolen, and reinvented, tap gradually got fashioned into a virtuosic stage dance. Because tap must be *heard,* it must be considered a musical form—as well as a dance form—that evolved as a unique percussive expression of American jazz music. Tappers consider themselves musicians and describe their feet as a set of drums—the heels playing the bass, the toes the melody. Like jazz, tap uses improvisation, polyrhythms, and a pattern of rhythmic accenting to give it a propulsive, or swinging, quality. Many of tap's choreographic structures reflect the formal musical structures of blues, ragtime or dixieland, swing, bebop, and cool jazz.

Perhaps the most distinguishing characteristic of tap is the amplification of the feet's rhythms. Early styles of tapping utilized boards laid across barrels, sawhorses, or cobblestones; hard-soled shoes, wooden clogs, hobnailed boots, hollow-heeled shoes, as well as soft-soled shoes (and even heavily calloused feet) played against a wooden, oily, or abrasive surface, such as sand. Specially made metal plates attached to the heel and toe of the shoes did not commonly appear until the early 1910s, in chorus lines of Broadway shows and revues.

Opportunities for whites and blacks to watch each other dance began in the early 1500s when enslaved Africans were shipped to the West Indies. During the infamous "middle passage" across the Atlantic, slaves were brought to the upper decks and forced to dance ("exercise"). Without traditional drums, slaves played on upturned buckets and tubs, and thus, the rattle and restriction of chains, the metallic thunk of buckets, were some of the first changes in African dance as it evolved toward an African-American style. Sailors witnessing these events set an early precedent of the white observers who would serve as social arbiters, onlookers, and participants at urban slave dances and plantation slave "frolicks." Upon arriving in North and South America and the West Indies, Africans, and African-Americans exposed to European court dances like the quadrille, cotillion, and contredanse adopted those dances, keeping the patterns and figures, but retaining their African rhythms.

Slaves purchased on the stopover in the Caribbean islands came into contact with thousands of Irishmen and Scotsmen who were deported, exiled, or sold in the new English plantation islands. The cultural exchange between first-generation enslaved Africans and indentured Irishmen, which had Ibo men playing fiddles and Kerrymen learning how to play jubi drums, continued through the late 1600s on plantations and in urban centers during the transition from white indentured servitude to African slave labor.

In colonial America a new percussive dance began to fuse from a stylistic meld of two great dance traditions. The African-American style tended to center movement in the hips and favored flat-footed, gliding, dragging, stamping, shuffling steps, with a relaxed torso gently bent at the waist and spine remaining flexible. Gradually that style blended with the British-European style, which centered movement in dexterous footwork that favored bounding, hopping, precisely placed toe-and-heel work, and complicated patterns, with carefully placed arms, an upright torso and erect spine, and little if any hip action.

Between 1600 and 1800, the new American tap-hybrid slowly emerged from British step dances and a variety of secular and religious African step dances labeled "juba" dances and "ring-shouts." The Irish jig, with its rapid toe and heelwork, and the Lancashire clog, which was danced in wooden-soled shoes, developed quickly. The clog invented faster and more complex percussive techniques while the jig developed a range of styles and functions that extended from a ballroom dance of articulate footwork and formal figures to a fast-stomping competitive solo performed by men on the frontier.

By contrast, the African-American juba (derived from the African *djouba*), moved in a counterclockwise circle and was distinguished by its rhythmically shuffling footwork, the clapping of hands and "patting" or "hamboning" (the hands rhythmically slap the thighs, arms, torso, cheeks, playing the body as if it were a large drum), the use of call-and-response patterning (vocal and physical), and solo or couple improvisation within the circle. The religious ring-shout, a similar countercircle dance driven by singing, stomping, and clapping, became an acceptable mode of worship in the Baptist church as long as dancers did not defy the ban against the crossing of the legs. With the arrival of the slave laws of 1740 prohibiting the beating of drums came substitutes for the forbidden drum: bone clappers, jawbones, tambourines, hand-clapping, hamboning, and the

See also
Duke Ellington

percussive footwork that was so crucial in the evolution of tap.

By 1800, "jigging" was a term applied to any black style of dancing in which the dancer, with relaxed and responsive torso, emphasized movement from the hips down with quickly shuffling feet beating tempos as fast as trip-hammers. Jigging competitions which featured buck-and-wing, shuffling ring dances, and breakdowns abounded on plantations and urban centers where freedmen and slave congregated.

Though African-Americans and European-Americans both utilized a solo, vernacular style of dancing, there was a stronger and earlier draw of African-American folk material by white performers. By the 1750s "Ethiopian delineators," most of them English and Irish actors, arrived in America. John Durang's 1789 "Hornpipe," a clog dance that mixed ballet steps with African-American shuffle-and-wings, was performed in blackface. By 1810 the singing-dancing "Negro boy" was an established stage character of blackface impersonators who performed jigs and clogs to popular songs. Thomas Dartmouth Rice's "Jump Jim Crow," which was less a copy of an African-American dance than it was Rice's "black" version of the Irish jig that appropriated a Negro worksong and dance, was a phenomenal success in 1829. After Rice, Irishmen George Churty and Dan Emmett organized troupes of blackface minstrelmen who brought their Irish-American interpretations of African-American song and dance styles to the minstrel stage. By 1840, the minstrel show as a blackface act of songs, fast-talking repartee in black dialects, and shuffle-and-wing tap dancing became the most popular form of entertainment in America.

That the oddly cross-bred and newly emerging percussive dance was able to retain its African-American integrity is due, in large measure, to William Henry Lane (c. 1825–1852). Known as Master Juba, he was perhaps the most influential single performer in nineteenth-century American dance. Born a free man in Rhode Island, Lane grew up in the Five Points district of Manhattan (now South Street Seaport). An accomplished Irish jig dancer, Lane was unsurpassed in grace and technique, popular for his imitations of famous minstrel dancers, and famous as the undisputed champion of fierce dance competitions. This African-American dancer broke the whites-only barrier of the major minstrel companies, and as a young teenager, Lane toured as featured dancer with four of the biggest troupes. Lane was an innovator who grafted authentic African-American performance styles and rhythms onto the exacting techniques of jig and clog dancing. Because of his excellence, he influenced the direction of tap, and, because he was so admired and imitated during his life and after his death, it fostered the spread of this new dance style.

When black performers finally gained access to the minstrel stage after the Civil War, the tap vocabulary was infused with a variety of fresh new steps and choreographic structures that jolted its growth. The "Essence of Old Virginia," originally a rapid, pigeon-toed sliding step, got slowed down and popularized in the 1870s by Billy Kersands, then refined by George Primrose in the 1890s to a graceful soft shoe, or song and dance. From the minstrel show came the walk-around finale, dances that included competitive and improvisatory sections, and a format of performance that combined songs, jokes, and specialty dances. By the late 1800s big touring shows such as *Sam T. Jack's Creole Company* and *South Before the War* brought black vernacular dance to audiences across America. With the success of *Clorindy* (1898), which featured a small chorus line of elegantly dancing women, fashionably dressed, and the *Creole Show* (1889), which replaced the usual blackface comedians with stylish cakewalk teams like Johnson and Dean, the stereotypes set by minstrelsy began to be displaced, and new images of the black performer were formed.

Turn-of-the-century medicine shows, gillies, carnivals and circuses helped establish the black dancer in show business and provided seeds for the growth of professional dancing. During the late 1890s touring roadshows like *In Old Kentucky* featured Friday night "buck dance" contests (another early term for "tap dancing"). *Black Patti's Troubadours* featured cakewalkers and buck-and-wing specialists, while the "jig top" circus tent had chorus lines and comedians dancing an early jazz style that combined shuffles, twists, grinds, struts, flat-footed buck and eccentric dancing. Tap dance incorporated rubber-legging, the shimmy and animal dances (peckin', camel-walk, scratchin') from social dance, as well as an entire vocabulary of wings, slides, chugs, and drags.

Performing opportunities increased with the rise of vaudeville (a kind of variety show). Vaudeville, which began in the 1880s, was the most popular stage form in America by 1900. It was controlled by syndicates that brought together large numbers of theaters under a single management, which hired and toured the various acts. Because of racist policies, however, two separate vaudevilles developed, one black and one white.

See also

Jazz

Ragtime

668

Because of the nature of vaudeville, where performers spent years perfecting their acts before audiences, tap artists were able to refine the steps and styles that expanded tap's vocabulary. The black vaudeville syndicate, Theatre Owners Booking Association (TOBA), offered grueling

SHOW-STOPPERS

The Nicholas Brothers Bring New Vitality to Tap Dancing

Nicholas Brothers, dancers. Fayard (1914–) and Harold (c. 1921–) Nicholas were born and reared in Philadelphia, where their parents played in a pit band called the Nicholas Collegians, which performed regularly at the Standard Theater. Fayard gravitated toward show business at a young age, claiming that the live performances and shows he saw as a child (such as Leonard Reed and his partner, Willie Bryant), were his first great influences. The children began their own professional career as the Nicholas Kids and for a short time danced with their sister Dorothy in different East Coast venues.

In 1930, the brothers danced on a popular Philadelphia radio show called the "Horn and Hardart Kiddie Hour." However, it was during an appearance at the Pearl Theater in Philadelphia that Frank Schiffman, the manager of the Lafayette Theater in Harlem, recruited the brothers to dance in New York. When they opened in New York, their name was changed to the Nicholas Brothers, and they joined the ranks of the famous "brothers" tap acts of the twentieth century.

On April 10, 1932, they moved to the Cotton Club, where they performed with the top bands of the period such as Jimmie Lunceford, Lucky Millinder, Duke Ellington, and Cab Calloway. Harold, who had a good soprano voice, did an impression of Cab Calloway that the club broadcast each night on a coast-to-coast radio show. Throughout the 1930s the Cotton Club was their "home." The Nicholas Brothers were known as "the Show Stoppers" because they literally stopped the show each night as the closing act. Perhaps because Fayard and Harold were children, they were the only African-American performers permitted to mingle with the exclusively white patrons of the club. The elegant rhythms of the young stars quickly propelled them to fame.

Fayard and Harold frequently left their regular act at the Cotton Club to tour with in-

THE NICHOLAS BROTHERS

From the time they were small, both Fayard (left) and Harold (right) danced with agility, grace, and sophistication.

PHOTOGRAPHS AND PRINTS DIVISION, SCHOMBURG CENTER FOR RESEARCH IN BLACK CULTURE, THE NEW YORK PUBLIC LIBRARY, ASTOR, LENOX AND TILDEN FOUNDATIONS

ternational shows such as Lew Leslie's *Blackbirds of 1936,* which had a successful run in London, or to perform in films. Their first film, *Pie, Pie Blackbirds* (1932), featured them in an appearance with Eubie Blake and his orchestra. During their career they appeared in more than fifty films including *Kid Millions* (1934), *Big Broadcast of 1936, Calling All Stars* (1937), *Down Argentine Way* (1940), *Tin Pan Alley* (1940), *Great American Broadcast* (1941), *Sun Valley Serenade* (1941), and *The Pirate* (1948). The brothers were among the select few who dubbed their own taps for film.

From the time they were small both Fayard and Harold danced with agility, grace, and sophistication. Even when they dis-

played their astonishing acrobatic ability, they managed to do so with elegance. They choreographed many of their own dance routines and improvised on stage with assurance and flair. The full use of their limber bodies and the exceptional use of their hands distinguished their dancing. The Nicholas Brothers perfected the innovative technique of doing *full* splits (as opposed to jazz or half splits), and they popularized acrobatic moves such as alternately jumping over each other's heads in splits while descending a staircase, as they did in the finale of *Stormy Weather* (1943). Their "classic" tap style flawlessly blended ballet, eccentric dancing, flash, and acrobatics.

When they worked with George Balanchine on the Broadway show *Babes in Arms* (1937), the great choreographer incorporated the brothers' own moves into their routine. In the show, Harold executed a sliding split through the legs of eight lined-up chorus girls while Fayard did a flying leap over them. In 1940 they worked with choreographer Nick Castle to develop a stunt that involved climbing up a wall, doing a back flip, landing in a split and returning to their feet—all on the beat.

During their nearly five decades in show business, Fayard and Harold toured the world from Africa to Europe. In the 1960s they appeared as guests on numerous TV shows and in 1965 performed as part of Bob Hope's Christmas special for the troops in Vietnam. In the 1970s, Fayard won a Tony Award for his choreography in the Broadway hit *Black and Blue,* and in 1980 both he and Harold received an award as part of a celebration honoring fifty years of men in dance. Their Lifetime Achievement Award, presented at the Kennedy Center in 1991, crowned the brothers' career as one of the best and most popular tap acts of the twentieth century.

—JENNIFER DEVERE BRODY

schedules and hard-earned but widespread exposure for such artists as the Whitman Sisters and the Four Covans. Although many black artists—such as "Covan and Ruffin," "Reed and Bryant" and "Greenlee and Drayton"—crossed over to appear on the white vaudeville circuits, they were bound by the "two colored" rule, which restricted blacks to pairs.

Rising from the minstrel show and vaudeville, "Williams and Walker" (Burt Williams and George Walker) introduced a black vernacular dance style to Broadway that was an eccentric blend of the shuffle, strut-turned cakewalk and grind, or mooch; other important contributions were made by younger tap stylists, such as Ulysses "Slow Kid" Thompson and Bill Bailey, whose styles were descendants of the flat-footed hoofing of King Rastus Brown. All together the combined contributions of many such artists added to tap's endowment and, as importantly, helped shape another stage dance, Broadway jazz.

The *Darktown Follies* (1913) serves as an example of how black shows disseminated African-American dance styles to the wider culture. Opening in Harlem's Lafayette Theater, *Darktown Follies* introduced the Texas Tommy, forerunner of the lindy hop, and tap dancer Eddie

Rector's smooth style of "stage dancing," Toots Davis's "over-the-top" and "through-the-trenches" (high-flying air steps that would become the tap act's traditional flash finale). Then the black musicals *Shuffle Along* (1921) and *Runnin' Wild* (1923) on Broadway created rapid-fire tapping by chorus lines dancing to ragtime jazz, combining tap and stylish vernacular dances, such as the Charleston, while the speciality solo and duo tappers blended tap with flips, somersaults and twisting shimmies.

Bill "Bojangles" Robinson gained wide public attention on Broadway in Lew Leslie's *Blackbirds of 1928* at the age of fifty, although he had performed in vaudeville houses since 1921. Wearing wooden, split-soled shoes that gave mellow tones to his tapping, Robinson was known for bringing tap up on its toes, dancing upright and swinging. The 1920s also saw the rise of John "Bubbles" Sublett, credited with inventing "rhythm tap," a fuller and more dimensional rhythmic concept that utilized the dropping of the heels as bass accents and added more taps to the bar. The team of "Buck and Bubbles," formed with Ford Lee "Buck" Washington, was a sensation in the *Ziegfield Follies of 1931*. White Broadway stars had African-American dance directors, like Clarence "Buddy" Bradley, who created routines that blended easy tap with black vernacular dance and jazz accenting. Bradley coached such stars as Ruby Keeler, Adele and Fred Astaire, Eleanor Powell and Paul Draper.

While white dancers learned tap in the classroom, black dancers developed on their own, often on street corners where dance challenges were hotly contested events. If tap had an institution of learning and apprenticeship, it was the Hoofers Club, next to the Lafayette Theatre in Harlem, where rookie and veteran tappers assembled to share, steal and compete with each other. During the 1930s, tap dancers were often featured performing in front of swing bands in dance halls like Harlem's Savoy Ballroom. The swinging 4/4 bounce of the music of bands like Count Basie's and Duke Ellington's proved ideal for hoofers, while the smaller vaudeville houses and intimate nightclubs, such as the Cotton Club, featured excellent tap and specialty dancers and small (six to eight-member) tap chorus lines like the Cotton Club Boys.

Tap was immortalized in the Hollywood film musicals of the 1930s and '40s, which featured Bill Robinson, Robinson and Shirley Temple, Buck and Bubbles, the Nicholas Brothers and the Berry Brothers. However, these were exceptions, and for the most part, black dancers were denied access to the white film industry. Because of continued segregation and different budgets, a distinction in tap styles developed. In general, black artists like John Bubbles kept the tradition of rhythm-jazz tapping with its flights of percussive improvisation, while white artists like Fred Astaire polished the high style of tapping seen on films, where rhythms were often less important than the integration of choreography with scenography.

As tap became the favorite form of American theatrical dance, its many stylistic genres got bunched into loose categories: The *Eccentric* style was comedic, virtuosic and idiosyncratic, exemplified by the routines (progenitors of later breakdancing moves) of Jigsaw Jackson, who circled and tapped while keeping his face against the floor; or the tapping of Alberta Whitman, who executed high-kicking legomania as a male impersonator. A *Russian* style, pioneered by Ida Forsyne in the teens, popularized Russian "kazotsky" kicks; then it was taken to Broadway by Dewey Weinglass and Ulysses "Slow Kid" Thompson. (A profusion of similar kicks and twisting, rubbery legs is reemerging in new style hip-hop dance).

The *Acrobatic* style made famous by Willie Covan, Three Little Words, and the Four Step Brothers, specialized in flips, somersaults, cartwheels, and splits. A cousin of this form, the *Flash Act,* brought to a peak of perfection by the Nicholas Brothers (Harold and Fayard), combined elegant tap dancing with highly stylized acrobatics and precision-timed stunts.

Comedy Dance teams such as Slap and Happy, Stump and Stumpy, Chuck and Chuckles, and Cook and Brown inculcated their tap routines with jokes, knockabout acrobatics, grassroots characterizations, and rambunctious translations of vernacular dance in a physically robust style.

The *Class Act* brought the art of elegance and nuance, complexity and musicality to tap. From the first decades of the century, the debonair song-and-dance teams of Johnson and Cole and Greenlee and Drayton and soloists such as Maxie McCree, Aaron Palmer and Jack Wiggins traversed the stage, creating beautiful pictures with each motion. Eddie Rector dovetailed one step into another in a graceful flow of sound and movement, while the act of Pete, Peaches and Duke brought precision and unison work to a peak. (Charles "Honi") Coles and (Cholly) Atkins, certainly the most famous of the Class Act tappers of the 1930s to '60s, combined flawless, high-speed rhythm-tapping with the slowest

soft shoe in the business. Lena Horne said that "Honi" Coles made butterflies seem clumsy.

By the mid-1940s big bands were being replaced by smaller, streamlined bebop groups whose racing tempos and complex rhythms were too challenging for most tappers accustomed to the clear rhythms of swing. However, led by the greatly admired "Baby" Laurence, who meshed into bop combos by improvising and using tap as another percussive voice within the combo, many younger tappers took flight with bop and made the transition. From a current perspective, these early tap bopsters of the 1940s and '50s broke ground for the rapid and dense tap style that is gaining popularity in the 1990s.

By the 1950s tap was in a sharp decline that has been attributed to various causes: the demise of vaudeville and the variety act; the devaluing of tap dance on film; the shift toward ballet and modern dance on the Broadway stage; the imposition of a federal tax on dance floors which closed ballrooms and eclipsed the big bands; and the advent of the jazz combo and the desire of musicians to play in a more intimate and concertized format. "Tap didn't die," says tap dancer Howard "Sandman" Sims. "It was just neglected." In fact the neglect was so thorough that this indigenous American dance form was almost lost, except for television reruns of old Hollywood musicals.

Those hoofers who lived through tap's lean years reveled in tap's resurgence. Jazz and tap historian Marshall Stearns, recognizing the danger of tap's imminent demise, arranged for a group of tap masters to perform at the 1962 Newport Jazz Festival. It was viewed as the last farewell, but it actually marked a rebirth that continued with Leticia Jay's historic *Tap Happening* (1969) at the Hotel Dixie in New York.

By the mid-1970s young dancers began to seek out elder tap masters to teach them. Tap dance—previously ignored as art and dismissed as popular entertainment—now made one of the biggest shifts of its long history and moved to the concert stage. The African-American aesthetic fit the postmodern dance taste: it was a minimalist art that fused musician and dancer; it celebrated pedestrian movement and improvisation; its art seemed casual and democratic; and tap could be performed in any venue, from the street to the stage. Enthusiastic critical and public response placed tap firmly within the larger context of dance as art, fueling the flames of its renaissance.

The 1970s produced video documentaries *Jazz Hoofer: The Legendary Baby Laurence, Great Feats of Feet* and *No Maps On My Taps* while the 1980s

See also
Bill "Bojangles" Robinson

exploded with the films *White Nights*, *The Cotton Club* and *Tap*, tap festivals across the country and *Black and Blue* on Broadway. On television, *Tap Dance in America*, hosted by Gregory Hines and featuring tap masters and young virtuosos such as Savion Glover, bridged the gap between tap and mainstream entertainment.

In the 1990s tap dance is a concertized art form danced, though not exclusively, to jazz music, infused with upper-body shapes of jazz dance and new spatial forms from modern dance. Incorporating new technologies for amplifying sounds and embellishing rhythms, new generations of tap artists are not only continuing tap's heritage, but forging new styles for the future.

—CONSTANCE VALIS HILL AND SALLY SOMMER

TELEVISION

In the early years of television, African Americans appeared most often as occasional guests on variety shows. Music entertainment artists, sports personalities, comedians, and political figures of the stature of Ella Fitzgerald, Lena Horne, Sarah Vaughan, Louis Armstrong, Duke Ellington, Cab

---

ART TATUM

Gifted Jazz Pianist Influences a Generation of Musicians

Arthur "Art" Tatum, Jr. (October 13, 1909–November 5, 1956), jazz pianist. Tatum was born in Toledo, Ohio, partially blind because of cataracts in both eyes. Encouraged by his mother, who played piano, and his father, who played guitar, Tatum began playing piano as a child. At first he learned songs from the radio and from piano rolls and recordings by stride pianists James P. Johnson and Fats Waller. Tatum, who also learned guitar, violin, and accordion, continued his musical education at Cousino School for the Blind in Columbus, Ohio. He then studied classical piano at the Toledo School of Music. By 1926 Tatum was performing with local bands led by Speed Webb and Milton Senior. By the late 1920s, Tatum's prodigious technique had earned him a local reputation, and in 1929 he was hired to play daily radio spots on a Toledo radio station. Singer Adelaide Hall hired him in 1930. Two years later she brought him to New York. There he went solo, making his reputation by publicly defeating his idols, Johnson, Waller, and Willie "The Lion" Smith, in a traditional Harlem "cutting" contest. Thereafter Tatum began playing to a cultlike following at the after-hours clubs that lined 52nd Street. Tatum first recorded in 1933 ("Tea for Two," "Tiger Rag"). Over the next decade he also performed at nightclubs in Cleveland, Chicago, and Los Angeles, and in 1938 he toured England. He also continued to record, both solo ("Sweet Lorraine," 1940; "Rosetta," 1940) and as a leader ("Body and Soul," 1937). He also recorded with tenor saxophonist Coleman Hawkins in 1943 ("Esquire Blues").

Starting in 1944, Tatum worked with guitarist Tiny Grimes and bassist Slam Stewart, and it was with a trio that he gained popular success over the next decade. But it was as a solo artist that he earned the almost unanimous critical judgment that he was the greatest pianist in jazz. Waller, his one-time idol, once announced during a Tatum set that "I play piano, but God is in the house tonight." Tatum established new standards for virtuosity among jazz musicians, and his magnificent technique proved enormously influential to the early bebop musicians, particularly saxophonist Charlie Parker and pianists Bud Powell and Oscar Peterson. Although Tatum was renowned for his astonishing speed, he also experimented with exotic harmonies within his headlong, stop-time runs. That style is perhaps best on display on a series of recordings he made for Capitol Records in 1949 ("Willow Weep for Me," "Nice Work If You Can Get It"). Tatum was most widely known as an interpreter of jazz standards and show tunes, but he also integrated classical music into his repertory, particularly pieces that showed off his technique, such as Dvořák's "Humoresque" and Massenet's "Elégie." Tatum rarely played the blues, and he composed few songs, both of which tendencies were unusual for pianists of his generation.

Despite health problems caused by years of overindulgence of food and alcohol, from 1953 to 1955 Tatum recorded more than 100 solo performances. In the years before his death, Tatum also made a variety of small ensemble recordings with some of the finest soloists of the day, including alto saxophonist Benny Carter, tenor saxophonist Ben Webster, vibraphonist Lionel Hampton, trumpeter Roy Eldridge, and clarinetist Buddy DeFranco. In 1956 he played at the Hollywood Bowl for almost nineteen thousand people. Tatum died later that year of kidney disease in Los Angeles.

—DOUGLAS J. CORBIN

See also

Louis Armstrong

Ralph Bunche

Calloway, Pearl Bailey, Eartha Kitt, the Harlem Globetrotters, Dewey "Pigmeat" Markham, Bill "Bojangles" Robinson, Ethel Waters, Joe Louis, Sammy Davis, Jr., Ralph Bunche, and Paul Robeson appeared in such shows as Milton Berle's *Texaco Star Theater* (1948–1953), Ed Sullivan's *Toast of the Town* (1948–1955), the *Steve Allen Show* (1950–1952; 1956–1961), and *Cavalcade of Stars* (1949–1952). Quiz shows like *Strike It Rich* (1951–1958), amateur talent contests like *Chance of a Lifetime* (1950–1953; 1955–1956), and shows concentrating on sporting events (particularly boxing matches), like *The Gillette Cavalcade of Sports* (1948–1960), provided another venue in which prominent blacks occasionally took part.

Rarely did African Americans host their own shows. Short-run exceptions included *The Bob Howard Show* (1948–1950); *Sugar Hill Times* (1949), an all-black variety show featuring Willie Bryant and Harry Belafonte; the *Hazel Scott Show* (1950), the first show featuring a black female host; the *Billy Daniels Show* (1952); and the *Nat "King" Cole Show* (1956–1957). There were even fewer all-black shows designed to appeal to all-black audiences or shows directed and produced by blacks. Short-lived local productions constituted the bulk of the latter category. In the early 1950s, a black amateur show called *Spotlight on Harlem* was broadcast on WJZ-TV in New York City; in 1955, the religious *Mahalia Jackson Show* appeared on Chicago's WBBM-TV.

Comedy was the only fiction-oriented genre in which African Americans were visible participants. Comedy linked television with the deeply entrenched cultural tradition of minstrelsy and blackface practices dating back to the antebellum period. In this cultural tradition, the representation of African Americans was confined either to degrading stereotypes of questionable intelligence and integrity (such as coons, mammies, Uncle Toms, or Stepin Fetchits) or to characterizations of people in willingly subservient positions (maids, chauffeurs, elevator operators, train conductors, shoeshine boys, handypeople, and the like). Beginning in the 1920s, radio comedies had perpetuated this cultural tradition, tailored to the needs of the medium.

The dominant television genre, the situation comedy, was invented on the radio. Like its television successor, the radio comedy—self-contained fifteen-minute or half-hour episodes, with a fixed set of characters, usually involving minor domestic or familial disputes, and painlessly resolved in the allotted time period—lent itself to caricature. Since all radio comedy was verbal, it relied for much of its humor on the misuse of language, such as malapropisms or syntax error; and jokes made at the expense of African Americans (and their supposed difficulties with the English language) were a staple of radio comedies.

The first successful radio comedy, and the series that in many ways defined the genre, was *Amos 'n' Andy* (1929–1960), which employed white actors to depict unflattering black characters. *Amos 'n' Andy* featured two white comedians, Freeman Gosden and Charles Correll, working in the style of minstrelsy and vaudeville. Another radio show that was successfully transferred to television was *Beulah* (1950–1953). The character Beulah was originally created for a radio show called *Fibber McGee and Molly* (1935–1957), in which she was played by Marlin Hurt, a white man. These two shows, which adopted an attitude of contempt and condescending sympathy toward the black persona, were re-created on television with few changes, except that the verisimilitude of the genre demanded the use of black actors rather than whites in blackface and "blackvoice." As with *Amos 'n' Andy* (1951–1953)—in its first season the thirteenth most-watched show on television—the creators of *Beulah* had no trouble securing commercial support; both television shows turned out to be as popular as their radio predecessors, though both were short-lived in their network television incarnations.

Beulah (played first by Ethel Waters, then by Louise Beavers) developed the story of the faithful, complacent Aunt Jemima, who worked for a white suburban middle-class nuclear family. Her unquestioning devotion to solving familial problems in the household of her white employers, the Hendersons, validated a social structure that forced black domestic workers to profess unconditional fidelity to white families, while neglecting their personal relations to their own kin. When blacks were included in Beulah's personal world, they appeared only as stereotypes. For instance, the neighbor's maid, Oriole (played by Butterfly McQueen), was an even more pronounced Aunt Jemima character; and Beulah's boyfriend, Bill Jackson (played by Percy Harris and Dooley Wilson), the Henderson's handyperson, was a coon. The dynamics between the white world of the Hendersons and Beulah's black world were those of the perfect object with a defective mirror image. The Hendersons represented a well-adjusted family, supported by a strong yet loving working father whose sizable income made it possible for the mother to remain at home. In contrast, Beulah was condemned to chasing after an idealized version of the family because her boyfriend did not seem too interested in a stable relationship; and she was destined to work forever because Bill Jackson did not seem capable of taking full financial responsibility in the event of a marriage. As the show could only exist as long as Beulah was a maid, it was evident that her desires were never to be fulfilled. If Beulah seemed to enjoy channeling all her energy toward the solution of a white family's conflicts, it was because her own problems deserved no solution.

Amos 'n' Andy, on the other hand, belonged to the category of folkish programs that focused on the daily life and family affairs of various ethnic groups. Several such programs, among them *Mama* (1949–1956), *The Goldbergs* (1949–1955), and *Life with Luigi* (1952–1953)—depicting the lives of Norwegians, Jews, and Italians, respectively—were popularized in the early 1950s. In *Amos 'n' Andy,* the main roles comprised an assortment of stereotypical black characters. Amos Jones (played by Alvin Childress) and his wife, Ruby (played by Jane Adams), were passive Uncle Toms, while Andrew "Andy" Hogg Brown (played by Spencer Williams) was gullible and half-witted. George "Kingfish" Stevens (played by

Tim Moore) was a deceiving, unemployed coon, whose authority was constantly being undermined by his shrewd wife Sapphire (played by Ernestine Wade) and overbearing mother-in-law "Mama" (played by Amanda Randolph). "Lightnin' " (played by Horace Stewart) was a janitor; and Algonquin J. Calhoun (played by Johnny Lee) was a fast-talking lawyer. These stereotypical characters were contrasted, in turn, with serious, level-headed black supporting characters, such as doctors, business people, judges, law enforcers, and so forth. The humorous situations created by the juxtapositions of these two types of characters—stereotypical and realistic—made *Amos 'n' Andy* an exceptionally intricate comedy and the first all-black television comedy that opened a window for white audiences on the everyday lives of African-American families in Harlem.

Having an all-black cast made it possible for *Amos 'n' Andy* to neglect relevant but controversial issues like race relations. The Harlem of this show was a world of separate but equal contentment, where happy losers, always ready to make fools of themselves, coexisted with regular people. Furthermore, the show's reliance on stereotypes precluded both the full-fledged development of its characters and the possibility of an authentic investigation into the pathos of black daily life. Even though the performers often showed themselves to be masters of comedy and vaudeville, it is unfortunate that someone like Spencer Williams, who was also a prolific maker of all-black films, would only be remembered by the general public as Andy.

While a number of African Americans were able to enjoy shows like *Beulah* and *Amos 'n' Andy,* many were offended by their portrayal of stereotypes, as well as by the marked absence of African Americans from other fictional genres. Black opposition had rallied without success to protest the airing of this kind of show on the radio in the 1930s. Before *Amos 'n' Andy* aired in 1951, the National Association for the Advancement of Colored People (NAACP) began suing CBS for the show's demeaning depiction of blacks, and the organization did not rest until the show was canceled in 1953. Yet the viewership of white and black audiences alike kept *Amos 'n' Andy* in syndication until 1966. The NAACP's victory in terminating *Amos 'n' Andy* and *Beulah* also proved somewhat pyrrhic, since during the subsequent decade, the networks produced no dramatic series with African Americans as central characters, while stereotyped portrayals of minor characters continued.

TV LEGEND

Bill Cosby appears in a publicity photograph for his 1972 series, Fat Albert and the Cosby Kids.

AP/WIDE WORLD PHOTO

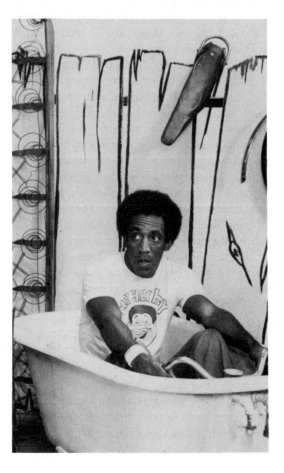

Many secondary comic characters from the radio and cinema found a niche for themselves in television. In the *Jack Benny Show* (1950–1965), Rochester Van Jones (played by Eddie "Rochester" Anderson) appeared as Benny's valet and chauffeur. For Anderson, whose Rochester had amounted to a combination of the coon and the faithful servant in the radio show, the shift to television proved advantageous, as he was able to give his character greater depth on the television screen. Indeed, through their outlandish employer-employee relationship, Benny and Anderson established one of the first interracial on-screen partnerships in which the deployment of power alternated evenly from one character to the other. The same may not be said of Willie Best's characterizations in shows like *The Stu Erwin Show* (1950–1955) and *My Little Margie* (1952–1955). Best tended to confine his antics to the Stepin Fetchit style and thereby reinforced the worst aspects of the master-slave dynamic.

African-American participation in dramatic series was confined to supporting roles in specific episodes in which the color-line tradition was maintained, such as the *Philco Television Playhouse* (1948–1955), which featured a young Sidney Poitier in "A Man Is Ten Feet Tall" in 1955; the *General Electric Theater* (1953–1962), which featured Ethel Waters and Harry Belafonte in "Winner by Decision" in 1955; and *The Hallmark Hall of Fame* (1952–) productions in 1957 and 1959 of Marc Connelly's "Green Pastures," a biblical retelling performed by an all-black cast. African Americans also appeared as jungle savages in such shows as *Ramar of the Jungle* (1952–1953), *Jungle Jim* (1955), and *Sheena, Queen of the Jungle* (1955–1956). The television western, one of the most important dramatic genres of the time, almost entirely excluded African Americans, despite their importance to the real American West. In the case of those narratives set in contemporary cities, if African Americans were ever included, it was only as props signifying urban deviance and decay. A rare exception to this was *Harlem Detective* (1953–1954), an extremely low-budget, local program about an interracial pair of detectives (with William Marshall and William Harriston playing the roles of the black and white detectives, respectively) produced by New York's WOR-TV.

Despite the sporadic opening of white households to exceptional African Americans and the effectiveness of the NAACP's action in canceling *Amos 'n' Andy*, the networks succumbed to the growing political conservatism and racial antagonism of the mid-1950s. The cancellation of the *Nat "King" Cole Show* (1956–1957) exemplifies the attitude that prevailed among programmers during that time. Nat "King" Cole had an impeccable record: his excellent musical and vocal training complemented his noncontroversial, delicate, and urbane delivery; he had a nationally successful radio show on NBC in the 1940s; and over forty of his recordings had been listed for their top sales by *Billboard* magazine between 1940 and 1955. Cole's great popularity was demonstrated in his frequent appearances as guest or host on the most important television variety shows. NBC first backed Cole completely, as is evidenced by the network's willingness to pour money into the show's budget, to increase the show's format from fifteen to thirty minutes, and to experiment with different time slots. Cole also had the support of reputable musicians and singers who were willing to perform for nominal fees. His guests included Count Basie, Mahalia Jackson, Pearl Bailey, and all-star musicians from "Jazz at the Philharmonic." Yet the *Nat "King" Cole Show* did not gain enough popularity among white audiences to survive the competition for top ratings; nor was it able to secure a stable national sponsor. After little more than fifty performances, the show was canceled.

African Americans exhibited great courage in these early years of television by supporting some shows and boycotting others. Organizations such as the Committee on Employment Opportunities for Negroes, the Coordinating Council for Negro Performers, and the Committee for the Negro in the Arts constantly fought for greater and fairer inclusion.

During the height of the Civil Rights Movement, the participation of African Americans in television intensified. Both Africans and African Americans became the object of scrutiny for daily news shows and network documentaries. The profound effects of the radical recomposition of race relations in the United States and the independence movement in Africa could not go unreported. "The Red and the Black" (January 1961), a segment of the *Close Up!* documentary series, analyzed the potential encroachment of the Soviet Union in Africa as European nations withdrew from the continent; "Robert Ruark's Africa" (May 1962), a documentary special shot on location in Kenya, defended the colonial presence in the continent. The series *See It Now* (1951–1958) started reporting on the Civil Rights Movement as early as 1954, when the Supreme Court had ruled to desegregate public schools, and exposed the measures that had been taken to hinder deseg-

See also
Duke Ellington
Ella Fitzgerald

regation in Norfolk high schools in an episode titled "The Lost Class of '59," aired in January 1959. *CBS Reports* (1959–) examined, among other matters, the living conditions of blacks in the rural South in specials such as "Harvest of Shame" (November 1960). *NBC White Paper* aired "Sit-In" in December 1960, a special report on desegregation conflicts in Nashville. "Crucial Summer" (which started airing in August 1963) was a five-part series of half-hour reports on discrimination practices in housing, education, and employment. It was followed by "The American Revolution of '63" (which started airing in September 1963), a three-hour documentary on discrimination in different areas of daily life across the nation.

However, the gains made by the airing of these programs were offset by the effects of poor scheduling, and they were often made to compete with popular series programs and variety and game shows from which blacks had been virtually erased. As the Civil Rights Movement gained momentum, some southern local stations preempted programming that focused on racial issues, while other southern stations served as a means for the propagation of segregationist propaganda.

As black issues came to be scrutinized in news reports and documentaries, African Americans began to appear in the growing genre of socially relevant dramas, such as *The Naked City* (1958–1963), *Dr. Kildare* (1961–1966), *Ben Casey* (1961–1966), *The Defenders* (1961–1965), *The Nurses* (1962–1965), *Channing* (1963–1964), *The Fugitive* (1963–1967), and *Slattery's People* (1963–1965). These shows, which usually relied on news stories for their dramatic material, explored social problems from the perspective of white doctors, nurses, educators, social workers, or lawyers. Although social issues were seriously treated, their impact was much diminished by the easy and felicitous resolution with which each episode was brought to a close. Furthermore, the African Americans who appeared in these programs—Ruby Dee, Louis Gossett, Jr., Ossie Davis, and others—were given roles in episodes where topics were racially defined, and the color line was strictly maintained.

The short-lived social drama *East Side/West Side* (1963–1964) proved an exception to this rule. It was the first noncomedy in the history of television to cast an African American (Cicely Tyson) as a regular character. The program portrayed the dreary realities of urban America without supplying artificial happy endings; on occasion, parts of the show were censored because of their liberal treatment of interracial relations. *East Side/West Side* ran into difficulties when programmers tried to obtain commercial sponsors for the hour during which it was aired; eventually, despite changes in format, it was canceled after little more than twenty episodes.

Unquestionably, the more realistic television genres that evolved as a result of the Civil Rights Movement served as powerful mechanisms for sensitizing audiences to the predicaments of those affected by racism. But as television grew to occupy center stage in American popular entertainment, the gains of the Civil Rights Movement came to be ambiguously manifested. By 1965, a profusion of top-rated programs had begun casting African Americans both in leading and supporting roles. The networks and commercial sponsors became aware of the purchasing power of African-American audiences, and at the same time they discovered that products could be advertised to African-American consumers without necessarily offending white tastes. Arguably the growing inclusion of African Americans in fiction-oriented genres was premised on a radical inversion of previous patterns. If blacks were to be freed from stereotypical and subservient representation, they were nevertheless portrayed in ways designed to please white audiences. Their emergence as a presence in television was to be facilitated by a thorough cleansing.

A sign of the changing times was the popular police comedy *Car 54, Where Are You?* (1961–1963). Set in a run-down part of the Bronx, this comedy featured black officers in secondary roles (played by Nipsey Russell and Frederick O'Neal). However, the real turning point in characterizations came with *I Spy* (1965–1968), a dramatic series featuring Bill Cosby and Robert Culp as Alexander Scott and Kelly Robinson, two secret agents whose adventures took them to the world's most sophisticated spots, where racial tensions did not exist. In this role, Cosby played an immaculate, disciplined, intelligent, highly educated, and cultured black man who engaged in occasional romances but did not appear sexually threatening and whose sense of humor was neither eccentric nor vulgar. While inverting stereotypical roles, *I Spy* also created a one-to-one harmonious interracial friendship between two men.

I Spy was followed by other top-rated programs. In *Mission Impossible* (1966–1973), Greg Morris played Barney Collier, a mechanic and electronics expert and member of the espionage team; in *Mannix* (1967–1975), a crime series about a private eye, Gail Fisher played Peggy Fair,

Mannix's secretary; in *Ironside* (1967–1975), Don Mitchell played Mark Sanger, Ironside's personal assistant and bodyguard; and in the crime show *Mod Squad* (1968–1973), Clarence Williams III played Linc Hayes, one of the three undercover police officers working for the Los Angeles Police Department. This trend was manifested in other top-ranked shows: *Peyton Place* (1964–1969), the first prime-time soap opera, featured Ruby Dee, Percy Rodriguez, and Glynn Turman as the Miles Family; in *Hogan's Heroes* (1965–1971), a sitcom about U.S. World War II prisoners in a German POW camp, Ivan Dixon played Sergeant Kinchloe; in *Daktari* (1966–1969), Hari Rhodes played an African zoologist; in *Batman* (1966–1968), Eartha Kitt appeared as Catwoman; in *Star Trek* (1966–1969), Nichelle Nichols was Lieutenant Uhura; in the variety show *Rowan and Martin's Laugh-In* (1966–1973), Chelsea Brown, Johnny Brown, and Teresa Graves appeared regularly; and in the soap opera *The Guiding Light* (1952–), Cicely Tyson started appearing regularly after 1967.

Julia (1968–1971) was the first sitcom in over fifteen years to feature African Americans in the main roles. It placed seventh in its first season, thereby becoming as popular as *Amos 'n' Andy* had been in its time. Julia Baker (played by Diahann Carroll) was a middle-class, cultured widow who spoke standard English. Her occupation as a nurse suggested that she had attended college. She was economically and emotionally self-sufficient; a caring parent to her little son Corey (played by Marc Copage); and equipped with enough sophistication and wit to solve the typical comic dilemmas presented in the series. However, many African Americans criticized the show for neglecting the more pressing social issues of their day. In Julia's suburban world, it was not so much that racism did not matter, but that integration had been accomplished at the expense of black culture. Julia's cast of black friends and relatives (played by Virginia Capers, Diana Sands, Paul Winfield, and Fred Williamson) appeared equally sanitized. Ironically, *Julia* perpetuated some of the same misrepresentations of the black family as *Beulah*—for despite its elegant trappings, Julia's was yet another female-headed African-American household.

As successful as *Julia* was the *Bill Cosby Show* (1969–1971), which featured Bill Cosby as Chet Kincaid, a single, middle-class high school gym teacher. In contrast to *Julia*, however, this comedy series presented narrative conflicts that involved Cosby in the affairs of black relatives and inner-

city friends as well as in those of white associates and suburban students. The *Bill Cosby Show* sought to integrate the elements of African-American culture through the use of sound, setting, and character: African-American music played in the background, props reminded one of contemporary political events, Jackie "Moms" Mabley and Mantan Moreland appeared frequently as Cosby's aunt and uncle, and Cosby's jokes often invested events from black everyday life with comic pathos. A less provocative but long-running sitcom, *Room 222* (1969–1974), concerned an integrated school in Los Angeles. Pete Dixon (played by Lloyd Haynes), a black history teacher, combined the recounting of important events of black history with attempts to address his students' daily problems. Another comic series, *Barefoot in the Park* (1970–1971)—with Scoey Mitchell, Tracey Reed, Thelma Carpenter, and Nipsey Russell—was attempted, but failed after thirteen episodes; it was an adaptation of the film by the same name but with African Americans playing the leading roles.

By the end of the 1960s, many of the shows in which blacks could either demonstrate their decision-making abilities or investigate the complexities of their lives had been canceled. Two black variety shows failed due to poor scheduling and lack of white viewer support: The *Sammy Davis, Jr., Show*, the first variety show hosted by a black since the *Nat "King" Cole Show* (1966); and *The Leslie Uggams Show* (1969), the first variety show hosted by a woman since Hazel Scott. A similar fate befell *The Outcasts* (1968–1969), an unusual western set in the period immediately following the Civil War. The show, which featured two bounty hunters, a former slave and a former slave owner, and addressed without qualms many of the same controversial themes associated with the Civil Rights Movement, was canceled due to poor ratings. Equally short-lived was *Hawk* (1966), a police drama shot on location in New York City, which featured a full-blooded Native American detective (played by Burt Reynolds) and his black partner (played by Wayne Grice). An interracial friendship was also featured in the series *Gentle Ben* (1967–1969), which concerned the adventures of a white boy and his pet bear; Angelo Rutherford played Willie, the boy's close friend. While interracial friendships were cautiously permitted, the slightest indication of romance was instantly suppressed: The musical variety show *Petula* (1968) was canceled because it showed Harry Belafonte and Petula Clark touching hands.

Presented as a television miniseries in 1977, Roots *brought the African-American story into the homes of millions.*

PAGE 318

See also
Lena Horne

GODFREY CAMBRIDGE
Broadway and TV were his Stage

Godfrey MacArthur Cambridge (February 26, 1933–November 29, 1976), actor. Godfrey Cambridge was born in New York City in 1933 and grew up in Harlem with his parents, Sarah and Alexander. He attended Flushing High School, where he excelled as both a student and a leader of extracurricular activities. Cambridge won a scholarship to Hofstra College (now Hofstra University) on Long Island, where he majored in English and had his first acting experience, appearing in a school production of *Macbeth*. After racial threats forced him to leave Hofstra during his junior year, Cambridge attended City College in New York City. Upon graduating, he worked at a number of jobs including stints as an airplane wing cleaner, a judo instructor, a cab driver, and clerk for the New York City Housing Authority.

In 1956 Cambridge landed his first professional role, as a bartender in an Off-Broadway revival of Louis Peterson's *Take a Giant Step*. The play ran for nine months and led to television appearances in shows such as *The United States Steel Hour*, *Naked City*, and *You'll Never Get Rich* (with Phil Silvers as Sergeant Bilko). In 1961 Cambridge appeared in Jean Genet's *The Blacks*, a savage drama about racial hatred, and for his efforts received the *Village Voice*'s Obie Award for best performer of 1961. The following year he appeared in Ossie Davis's *Purlie Victorious*, for which he earned a Tony nomination. Cambridge went on to perform in other plays, including *A Funny Thing Happened on the Way to the Forum* (1962), *The Living Promise* (1963), and *How to Be a Jewish Mother* (1967), in which he played every part but the title role.

After a successful appearance on *The Jack Paar Program* in 1964, Cambridge was able to choose his roles and began turning down film parts which stereotyped him. Instead he played a wide variety of movie characters, including a reprise of his role in the film version of *Purlie Victorious*, entitled *Gone Are the Days* (1963), an Irishman in *The Troublemaker* (1964), a Jewish cab driver in *Bye, Bye, Braverman* (1968), and a concert violinist in *The Biggest Bundle of Them All* (1968). Cambridge is probably best known for his leading roles in the popular films *Watermelon Man* (1970) and *Cotton Comes to Harlem* (1970).

In addition to his film appearances, Cambridge was a successful stand-up comedian. His sense of humor, while not alienating to white audiences, did not lack bite. Essentially a social satirist, his comedy often dealt with ordinary people, black and white, struggling with the problems of everyday life.

During the Civil Rights Movement, Cambridge performed at rallies and organized support for the employment of more African Americans in the entertainment industry. A compulsive eater who at times weighed as much as 300 pounds, in 1976 Cambridge collapsed and died on the set of the TV movie *Victory at Entebbe*, in which he played the Ugandan dictator Idi Amin.

—THADDEUS RUSSELL

Despite these limitations, the programs of the 1960s, '70s, and '80s represented a drastic departure from the racial landscape of early television. In the late 1940s, African Americans were typically confined to occasional guest roles; by the end of the 1980s, most top-rated shows featured at least one black person. It had become possible for television shows to violate racial taboos without completely losing commercial and viewer sponsorship. However, greater visibility in front of the camera did not necessarily translate into equal opportunity for all in all branches of television: the question remained as to whether discriminatory practices had in fact been curtailed, or had simply survived in more sophisticated ways. It was true that the presence of blacks had increased in many areas of television, including, for example, the national news: Bryant Gumbel began coanchoring *Today* (1952–) in 1983; Ed Bradley joined *60 Minutes* (1968–) in1981; Carole Simpson became a weekend anchor for *ABC World News Tonight*, where she had started as a correspondent in 1982. Nevertheless, comedy remained the dominant form for expressing black lifestyles. Dramatic shows centering on the African-American experience have had to struggle to obtain high enough ratings to remain on the air—the majority of the successful dramas have been those where blacks share the leading roles with other white protagonists.

During the 1970s and '80s, the number of social dramas, crime shows, or police stories centering on African Americans or featuring an African American in a major role steadily increased. Most of the series were canceled within a year. These included *The Young Lawyers* (1970–1971), *The*

See also
NAACP

Young Rebels (1970–1971), *The Interns* (1970–1971), *The Silent Force* (1970–1971), *Tenafly* (1973–1974), *Get Christie Love!* (1974–1975), *Shaft* (1977), *Paris* (1979–1980), *The Lazarus Syndrome* (1979), *Harris & Co.* (1979), *Palmerstown, USA* (1980–1981), *Double Dare* (1985), *Fortune Dane* (1986), *The Insiders* (1986), *Gideon Oliver* (1989), *A Man Called Hawk* (1989), and *Sonny Spoon* (1988). The most popular dramatic series with African-American leads were *Miami Vice* (1984–1989), *In the Heat of the Night* (1988–), and *The A-Team* (1983–1987). On *Miami Vice* and *In the Heat of the Night*, Philip Michael Thomas and Howard Rollins, the black leads, were partnered with better-known white actors who became the most identifiable character for each series. Perhaps the most popular actor on a dramatic series was the somewhat cartoonish Mr. T, who played Sgt. Bosco "B.A." Baracus on *The A-Team*, an action-adventure series in which soldiers of fortune set out to eradicate crime. Although, in the comedy *Barney Miller* (1975–1980), Ron Glass played an ambitious middle-class black detective, the guest spots or supporting roles in police series generally portrayed African Americans as sleazy informants, such as Rooster (Michael D. Roberts) on *Baretta* (1975–1978), or Huggy Bear (Antonio Fargas) on *Starsky and Hutch* (1975–1979).

In prime-time serials, African Americans appeared to have been unproblematically assimilated into a middle-class lifestyle. *Dynasty* (1981–1989) featured Diahann Carroll as one of the series' innumerable variations on the "rich bitch" persona; while *Knots Landing* (1979–1993), *L.A. Law* (1986–1994), *China Beach* (1988–1990), and *The Trials of Rosie O'Neal* (1991–1992) developed story lines with leading black roles as well as interracial romance themes.

MTM Enterprises produced some of the most successful treatments of African Americans in the 1980s. In their programs, which often combined drama and satire, characters of different ethnic backgrounds were accorded full magnitude. *Fame* (1982–1983) was an important drama about teenagers of different ethnicities coping with the complexities of contemporary life. *Frank's Place* (1987–1988), an offbeat and imaginative show about a professor who inherits a restaurant in a black neighborhood in New Orleans, provided viewers with a realistic treatment of black family affairs. Though acclaimed by critics, *Frank's Place* did not manage to gain a large audience, and the show was canceled after having been assigned four different time slots in one year.

African Americans have been featured in relatively minor roles on science fiction series. *Star Trek*'s communications officer Lt. Uhura (played by Nichelle Nichols) was little more than a glorified telephone operator. *Star Trek: The Next Generation* (1987–1994) featured LeVar Burton as Lt. Geordi La Forge, a blind engineer who can see through a visor. A heavily made-up Michael Dorn was cast as Lt. Worf, a horny-headed Klingon officer, and Whoopi Goldberg appeared frequently as the supremely empathetic, long-lived bartender Guinan. In *Deep Space 9* (1993–), the third *Star Trek* series, a major role was given to Avery Brooks as Commander Sisko, head of the space station on which much of the show's action takes place.

Until recently, blacks played an extremely marginal role in daytime soap operas. In 1966, *Another World* became the first daytime soap opera to introduce a story line about a black character, a nurse named Peggy Harris Nolan (played by Micki Grant). In 1968, the character of Carla Hall was introduced as the daughter of housekeeper Sadie Gray (played by Lillian Hayman). Embarrassed by her social and ethnic origins, Carla was passing for a white in order to be engaged to a successful white doctor. Some network affiliates canceled the show after Carla appeared. Since then, many more African Americans have appeared in soap operas, including Al Freeman, Jr., Darnell Williams, Phylicia Rashad, Jackée, Blair Underwood, Nell Carter, Billy Dee Williams, Cicely Tyson, and Ruby Dee. However, in most cases, character development has been minor, with blacks subsisting on the margins of activity, not at the centers of power. An exception was the interracial marriage between a black woman pediatrician and a white male psychiatrist on *General Hospital* in 1987. *Generations,* the only soap opera which focused exclusively on African-American family affairs, was canceled in 1990 after a year-long run.

The dramatic miniseries, *Roots* (1977) and *Roots: The Next Generation* (1979)—more commonly known as "Roots II"—were unusually successful. For the first time in the history of television, close to 130 million Americans dedicated almost twenty-four hours to following a 300-year saga chronicling the tribulations of African Americans in their sojourn from Africa to slavery and, finally, to emancipation. Yet *Roots* and "Roots II" were constrained by the requirements of linear narrative, and characters were seldom placed in situations where they could explore the full range of their historical involvement in the struggle against slavery. The miniseries *Beulah Land*

See also

Bill "Bojangles" Robinson

(1980), a reconstruction of the southern experience during the Civil War, attempted to recapture the success of *Roots,* but ended up doing no more than reviving some of the worst aspects of *Gone with the Wind.* Other important but less commercially successful dramatic historical reconstructions include *The Autobiography of Miss Jane Pittman* (1973), *King* (1978), *One in a Million: The Ron LeFlore Story* (1978), *A Woman Called Moses* (1978), *Backstairs at the White House* (1979), *Freedom Road* (1979), *Sadat* (1983), and *Mandela* (1987).

A number of miniseries and made-for-television movies about black family affairs and romance were broadcast in the 1980s. *Crisis at Central High* (1981) was based on the desegregation dispute in Little Rock, Ark.; while *Benny's Place* (1982), *Sister, Sister* (1982), *The Defiant Ones* (1985), and *The Women of Brewster Place* (1989) were set in various African-American communities.

The 1970s witnessed the emergence of several television sitcoms featuring black family affairs. In these shows, grave issues such as poverty and upward mobility were embedded in racially centered jokes. A source of inspiration for these sitcoms may have been *The Flip Wilson Show* (1970–1974), the first successful variety show hosted by an African American. The show, which featured celebrity guests like Lucille Ball, Johnny Cash, Muhammad Ali, Sammy Davis, Jr., Bill Cosby, Richard Pryor, and B.B. King, was perhaps best known for the skits Wilson performed. The skits were about black characters (Geraldine Jones, Reverend Leroy, Sonny the janitor, Freddy Johnson the playboy, and Charley the chef) who flaunted their outlandishness to such a degree that most viewers were unable to determine whether they were meant to be cruel reminders of minstrelsy or parodies of stereotypes.

A number of family comedies, mostly produced by Tandem Productions (Norman Lear and Bud Yoking), became popular around the same time as *The Flip Wilson Show: All in the Family* (1971–1983), *Sanford and Son* (1972–1977), *Maude* (1972–1978), *That's My Mama* (1974–1975), *The Jeffersons* (1975–1985), *Good Times* (1974–1979), and *What's Happening* (1976–1979). On *Sanford and Son,* Redd Foxx and Demond Wilson played father-and-son Los Angeles junk dealers. *Good Times,* set in a housing development on the South Side of Chicago, portrayed a working-class black family. Jimmie Walker, who played J.J., became an overnight celebrity with his "jive-talking" and use of catchphrases like "Dy-No-Mite." On *The Jeffersons,* Sherman Hemsley

played George Jefferson, an obnoxious and upwardly mobile owner of a dry-cleaning business. As with *Amos 'n' Andy,* these comedies relied principally on stereotypes—the bigot, the screaming woman, the grinning idiot, and so on—for their humor. However, unlike their predecessor of the 1950s, the comedies of the 1970s integrated social commentary into the joke situations. Many of the situations reflected contemporary discussions in a country divided by, among other things, the Vietnam War. And because of the serialized form of the episodes, most characters were able to grow and learn from experience.

By the late 1970s and early '80s, the focus of sitcoms had shifted from family affairs to nontraditional familial arrangements. *The Cop and the Kid* (1975–1976), *Diff'rent Strokes* (1978–1986), *The Facts of Life* (1979–1988), and *Webster* (1983–1987) were about white families and their adopted black children. Several comic formulas were also reworked, as a sassy maid (played by Nell Carter) raised several white children in *Gimme a Break!* (1981–1987), and a wise-cracking and strong-willed butler (played by Robert Guillaume) dominated the parody "Soap" (1977–1981). Guillaume played an equally daring budget-director for a state governor in *Benson* (1979–1986). Several less successful comedies were also developed during this time, including *The Sanford Arms* (1976), *The New Odd Couple* (1982–1983), *One in a Million* (1980), and *The Red Foxx Show* (1986).

The most significant comedies of the 1980s were those in which black culture was explored on its own terms. The extraordinarily successful *Cosby Show,* the first African-American series to top the annual Nielsen ratings, featured Bill Cosby as Cliff Huxtable, a comfortable middle-class paterfamilias to his Brooklyn family, which included his successful lawyer wife Clair Huxtable (played by Phylicia Rashad) and their six children. The long-running show *227* (1985–1990) starred Marla Gibbs, who had previously played a sassy maid on *The Jeffersons,* in a family comedy set in a black section of Washington, D.C. *A Different World* (1987–1993), a spin-off of *The Cosby Show,* was set in a black college in the South. *Amen* (1986–1991), featuring Sherman Hemsley as Deacon Ernest Frye, was centered on a black church in Philadelphia. In all of these series, the black-white confrontations that had been the staple of African-American television comedy were replaced by situations in which the humor was provided by the diversity and difference within the African-American community.

See also

Sarah Vaughan

Some of the most recent black comedies—*Charlie & Company* (1986), *Family Matters* (1989–), *Fresh Prince of Bel Air* (1990–), and *True Colors* (1990–)—have followed the style set by *The Cosby Show*. Others like *In Living Color* (1990–) have taken the route of reworking a combination of variety show and skits in a manner reminiscent of *The Flip Wilson Show*. Much of the originality and freshness of these comedies is due to the fact that some of them have been produced by African Americans (*The Cosby Show, A Different World, Fresh Prince of Bel Air,* and *In Living Color*). *Carter Country* (1977–1979), a sitcom which pitted a redneck police chief against his black deputy (played by Kene Holliday), inspired several programs with similar plot lines: *Just Our Luck* (1983) *He's the Mayor* (1986), *The Powers of Matthew Star* (1982–1983), *Stir Crazy* (1985), *Tenspeed and Brown Shoe* (1980), and *Enos* (1980–1981).

Alternatives

Local stations, public television outlets, syndication, and cable networks have provided important alternatives for the production of authentic African-American programming. In the late 1960s, local television stations began opening their doors to the production of all-black shows and the training of African-American actors, commentators, and crews. Examples of these efforts include *Black Journal*—later known as *Tony Brown's Journal*—(1968–), a national public affairs program; *Soul* (1970–1975), a variety show produced by Ellis Haizlip at WNET in New York; *Inside Bedford-Stuyvesant* (1968–1973), a public affairs program serving the black communities in New York City; and *Like It Is*, a public affairs show featuring Gil Noble as the outspoken host.

At the national level, public television has also addressed African-American everyday life and culture in such series and special programs as *History of the Negro People* (1965), *Black Omnibus* (1973), *The Righteous Apples* (1979–1981), *With Ossie and Ruby* (1980–1981), *Gotta Make This Journey: Sweet Honey and the Rock* (1984), *The Africans* (1986), *Eyes on the Prize* (1987), and *Eyes on the Prize II* (1990).

Syndication, the system of selling programming to individual stations on a one-to-one basis, has been crucial for the distribution of shows such as *Soul Train* (1971–), *Solid Gold* (1980–1988), *The Arsenio Hall Show* (1989–1994), *The Oprah Winfrey Show* (1986–), and *The Montel Williams Show* (1992–). A wider range of programming

has also been made possible by the growth and proliferation of cable services. Robert Johnson took a personal loan for $15,000 in the early 1980s to start a cable business—Black Entertainment Television (BET)—catering to the African Americans living in the Washington, D.C., area. At that time BET consisted of a few hours a day of music videos. By the early 1990s, the network had expanded across the country, servicing about 25 million subscribers, and had a net worth of more than $150 million. (Its programming had expanded to include black collegiate sports, music videos, public affairs programs, and reruns of, among others, *The Cosby Show* and *Frank's Place*.)

Children's Programming

As late as 1969, children's programming did not include African Americans. The first exceptions were *Sesame Street* (1969–) and *Fat Albert and the Cosby Kids* (1972–1989). These two shows were ground-breaking in content and format; they emphasized altruistic themes, the solution of everyday problems, and the development of reading skills and basic arithmetic. Other children's shows which have focused on or incorporated African Americans include *The Jackson Five* (1971), *ABC After-School Specials* (1972–), *The Harlem Globetrotters Popcorn Machine* (1974–1976), *Rebop* (1976–1979), *30 Minutes* (1978–1982); *Reading Rainbow* (1983–), *Pee-Wee's Playhouse* (1986–1991); *Saved by the Bell* (1989–), *Kid's Play* (1990–), and *Carmen San Diego* (1991–).

Although African Americans have had to struggle against both racial tension and the inherent limitations of television, they have become prominent in all aspects of the television industry. As we progress toward the twenty-first century, the format and impact of television programming will undergo some radical changes, and the potential to provoke and inform audiences will grow. Television programs are thus likely to become more controversial than ever, but they will also become an even richer medium for effecting social change. Perhaps African Americans will be able to use these technical changes to allay the racial discord and prejudice that persists off-camera in America.

—CHARLES HOBSON

TEMPTATIONS, THE

The Temptations, vocal group. During their more than three decades of entertaining, the Temptation's rhythm and blues quintet has included El-

Smokey Robinson was the first of Motown's songwriter-producers, writing and producing six of Motown's first Top Ten hits.

PAGE 469

T

dridge Bryant (replaced by David Ruffin in 1963; Ruffin was replaced by Dennis Edwards in 1967, Edwards by Louis Price in 1976, Price by Ali-Ollie Woodson in the 1980s), Eddie Kendricks (replaced by Damon Harris in 1971; Harris was replaced by Glenn Leonard in 1975, Leonard by Ron Tyson in the 1980s), Paul Williams (replaced by Richard Street in 1971), Otis Williams, and Melvin Franklin. First called the Elgins, the original quintet of Bryant (lead), Otis Williams (baritone), Franklin (bass), Paul Williams (lead), and Kendricks (tenor/falsetto) was signed by Berry Gordy to Motown in 1960.

The group's success in the 1960s and early 1970s was marked by two distinct styles. First, a polished gospel-inspired pop style resulted in several hit singles: "The Way You Do the Things You Do" (number eleven, 1964), "My Girl" (number one, 1965), "Since I Lost My Baby" (number seventeen, 1965), "Ain't Too Proud to Beg" (number thirteen, 1966), and "I Know I'm Losing You'" (number eight, 1966). These early successes were marked by Kendricks's creamy falsetto and David Ruffin's rugged baritone. After Dennis Edwards replaced Ruffin in 1967, producer Norman Whitfield gave the group a new sound—"psychedelic

soul," characterized by loud, brassy arrangements and lyrics containing moralizing social commentary. This style produced another string of hits, including "Cloud Nine" (number six, 1969), "Psychedelic Shack" (number seven, 1970), and "Ball of Confusion" (number three, 1970). After Damon Harris and Richard Street replaced Kendricks and Paul Williams, respectively, the new group created one of its most important hits, "Papa Was a Rolling Stone" (number one, 1972), a powerful piece that depicted the chilling despair of black family life. In 1989 the group was inducted into the Rock and Roll Hall of Fame.

—KYRA D. GAUNT

TERRY, SONNY

Sonny Terry (Saunders Terrell) (October 24, 1911–March 12, 1986), blues musician. Born Saunders Terrell in Greensboro, Ga., this influential harmonica player adopted the name Sonny Terry in the late 1920s. He was raised on a farm and tutored on the harp by his father, Reuben Terrell. Two separate accidents in 1927 left him totally blind. By 1929 he had moved to Shelby,

---

"SISTER" ROSETTA THARPE
Gospel Singer Performed at New York's Cotton Club

"Sister" Rosetta Tharpe (March 20, 1915–October 9, 1973), gospel singer and guitarist. Sister Rosetta Tharpe was born Rosetta Nubin in Cotton Plant, Ark. She began her musical apprenticeship playing guitar and singing in the Church of God in Christ, a Pentecostal church, and gained professional experience traveling with her mother, Katie Bell Nubin, a missionary. In her teens she followed her mother to Chicago. It is not clear whether she took a new last name as the result of a marriage, but it was as Sister Rosetta Tharpe that she came to prominence in 1938 in New York. At first she was known for performing in secular venues, a controversial practice for a gospel singer. In that year she performed at Harlem's Cotton Club with bandleader Cab Calloway and at the famous "Spirituals to Swing" concert at Carnegie Hall. Those performances helped her land a contract with Decca, making her the first gospel singer to record for a major label. In 1943 she performed at the Apollo Theater, the first time that a major gospel singer had appeared there. Her 1944 rendition of "Strange Things Happen Every Day" was widely popular.

Starting in the 1940s, Tharpe performed in churches, concert halls, nightclubs, on the radio, and later even on television. She gained fame not only because of her practice of playing secular venues, a practice she defended by calling all of her music evangelical, but also because of her jazz and blues-influenced guitar playing. Tharpe, who recorded "Daniel in the Lion's Den" in 1949 with her mother, eventually toured with such jazz and blues groups as those led by Benny Goodman, Count Basie, Muddy Waters, Sammy Price, and Lucky Millinder, as well as with gospel groups such as the Caravans, the James Cleveland Singers, the Dixie Hummingbirds, the Richmond Harmonizing Four, and the Sally Jenkins Singers, with whom she recorded "I Have Good News to Bring" in 1960. Tharpe, who was the first major gospel singer to tour Europe, was also widely known for her live performances and recordings of "That's All," "I Looked Down the Line," "Up Above My Head," and "This Train." She died in Philadelphia.

—IRENE V. JACKSON

See also

Blues

N.C., playing for local dances and at tobacco houses. He supported himself through music for the rest of his life.

Terry wandered throughout central North Carolina during the 1930s and early 1940s, working and recording with "Piedmont"-style blues guitarists Blind Boy Fuller and Brownie McGhee. In 1942, Terry joined the Great Migration to New York City, along with McGhee. They recorded prolifically, and worked at house parties, on radio programs, and for nearly four years on the stage, in the casts of *Finian's Rainbow* (1947–1948) and *Cat on a Hot Tin Roof* (1955–1957). By 1958, at the beginning of the folk revival, they worked the first of their overseas tours. Around 1970 this long-standing duo split up due to personality conflicts, though they later occasionally reunited for concerts, and Terry performed solo or as leader of a small band. He died in 1986, following a heart attack.

Terry is best known for his virtuosic "cross-note" playing technique (playing in a key other than the key of the harmonica) and his skill in executing special effects, such as train whistles, animal cries, and vocal moans, by simultaneously using his voice while he played. By controlling his breath and cupping his hands over the harmonica, Terry developed a particular skill in modulating from key to key and pitch blending.

—KIP LORNELL

THOMAS, CLARENCE

Clarence Thomas (June 23, 1948–), justice of U.S. Supreme Court. Born in Pin Point, Ga., Clarence Thomas was the second of three children of M. C. and Leola (Anderson) Thomas. M. C. Thomas left when his son was two, and Leola Thomas supported the family. They had little money, and after the family house burned down, Clarence Thomas went to live with grandparents in Savannah, Ga. Thomas attended Catholic schools, whose teachers he later credited with giving him hope and self-confidence.

In 1967, Thomas entered the Immaculate Conception Seminary in Conception, Mo., intending to become a Catholic priest. He decided to leave after hearing white classmates happily report the assassination of the Reverend Dr. Martin Luther King, Jr. Thomas transferred to Holy Cross College in Worcester, Mass., on the school's first Martin Luther King Scholarship. At Holy Cross, Thomas majored in English literature, graduating cum laude in 1971. An admirer of Malcolm X, Thomas helped form the Black Students League, joined the Black Panther Party, and ran a free-breakfast program for black children.

Rejected for military service on medical grounds, Thomas entered Yale University Law School in fall 1971 under the university's affirmative action program. He was admitted to the bar in 1974, then accepted a position as an aide to John Danforth, Missouri's attorney general. Shortly thereafter, he read the conservative African-American economist Thomas Sowell's book *Race and Economics* (1975), which he later claimed as his intellectual "salvation." Thomas adopted Sowell's pro-market, anti-affirmative action theories. In 1977, Thomas became a staff attorney for the Monsanto Company in St. Louis. In 1979, he joined Danforth, by that time a U.S. senator, as an energy and environmental specialist on his staff.

In 1980, Thomas spoke at the Fairmount Conference in San Francisco, a meeting of black conservatives. He denounced the social welfare system for fostering dependency. The publicity Thomas's conservative views received won him the interest of the Reagan administration. In 1981, despite his reluctance to be "typed" as a civil rights specialist, Thomas was named Assistant Secretary for Civil Rights in the Department of Education, where he drew criticism for refusing to push integration orders on southern colleges. In 1982, Thomas was appointed chair of the Equal Employment Opportunity Commission. Reappointed in 1986, he served until 1990. His tenure was controversial. An opponent of activist judicial action, he refused to press pending class-action suits, and opposed the use of comparable-worth guidelines in gender discrimination cases. The commission allowed thousands of age-discrimination lawsuits to lapse, through what he claimed was "bad management." Yet Thomas opposed efforts to secure tax-exempt status for racially discriminatory colleges, and in 1983 he secured an important affirmative action agreement with General Motors.

In 1989, President George Bush nominated Thomas for a seat on the U.S. Circuit Court of Appeals for the District of Columbia. The appointment was widely understood as preliminary to a possible Supreme Court appointment, as a replacement for aging African-American Justice Thurgood Marshall. Thomas was easily confirmed for the district court in February 1990. In July 1991, Marshall retired, and Bush nominated Thomas as his successor. Bush claimed race had

See also

Martin Luther King, Jr.

T

HILL-THOMAS HEARINGS

Confirmation Process Stirs Public Controversy

In September 1991, U.S. District Judge Clarence Thomas, nominated to the U.S. Supreme Court by President George Bush, began his confirmation hearing by the Senate Judiciary Committee. On September 27, the committee, tied in its vote on the nomination, sent the nomination to the floor without a recommendation. Despite the committee's failure to issue a recommendation, most commentators believed the Senate would confirm Thomas. On October 6, 1991, National Public Radio and *New York Newsday* ran a story about Anita Faye Hill (b. 1956), a law professor at the University of Oklahoma. Hill, who had been a staff attorney under Thomas at the Department of Education and the Equal Employment Opportunity Commission in the early 1980s, had told FBI investigators that Thomas had sexually harassed her during her tenure. The story was based on the leak of a confidential affidavit Hill had provided the committee on September 23. Her story made public, Hill openly repeated her accusations. In a comment later echoed by many women, Hill claimed the all-male Judiciary Committee had been insensitive to the importance of sexual harassment and had not questioned Thomas about it. Meanwhile, Thomas categorically denied any such conduct. On October 8, following a long debate in the Senate, the vote on Thomas's confirmation was delayed. Committee Chair Joseph R. Biden scheduled further hearings in order to provide Hill and Thomas an opportunity to testify publicly on the issue.

On October 11, 1991, before a nationwide television audience, the hearings on Thomas's conduct began. Hill described Thomas's repeated sexual overtures to her, charging that he had boasted of his sexual prowess, frequently used prurient sexual innuendos, and had insisted on describing to her the plots of pornographic movies he had seen. When asked why, if Thomas had harassed her in such a fashion, Hill had accepted a position under him at the EEOC, she explained that the harassment had

stopped for a period, and she feared she would be unable to find another job without his recommendation.

Thomas's testimony flatly contradicted that of Hill. While Thomas asserted he had not listened to Hill's testimony, which he angrily referred to as "lies," he denied any wrongdoing and repeatedly refused to discuss his private life. He denounced the committee's confirmation process as "un-American" and assailed it for staging what he called a "high-tech lynching" of him as an independent conservative black intellectual.

During the following days, as the Senate debated the hearings, Senate Republicans launched a furious assault on Hill's character and truthfulness in order to discredit her. Senators charged her with "fantasizing" about Thomas's interest in her. At the same time, many observers felt the Judiciary Committee had not investigated Thomas's veracity with equal zeal. Nationwide argument, which crossed ideological and gender lines, raged over whether Thomas or Hill was telling the truth, and whether Thomas's alleged sexual harassment was relevant to his confirmation.

On October 15, the Senate confirmed Thomas, 52–48, the second narrowest winning margin in history. Public opinion polls published at the time showed the majority of Americans believed Thomas and suspected Hill's allegations. Still, many women were politically energized by the hearings, and many women were elected to public office in 1992 with the support of their campaign contributions and activism. Within a year after the hearings, however, new opinion polls suggested that a majority of Americans now believed Anita Hill had told the truth. By that time, continuing public interest in the affair had been reflected in the publication of several books on the trials, including two notable anthologies of essays written by African Americans.

—GREG ROBINSON

nothing to do with the nomination and that Thomas was the "most qualified candidate" to succeed Marshall, an assertion widely viewed as disingenuous. Nevertheless, many blacks who opposed Thomas's conservative ideas initially felt torn by the nomination and supported him or remained neutral on racial grounds.

Thomas's confirmation hearings were acrimonious. He denounced the reasoning of the Court's

Brown v. *Board of Education* (1954) desegregation case as "dubious social engineering." He refused to take a position on the *Roe* v. *Wade* (1973) abortion decision and aroused doubts by his assertion that he had never discussed it, even in private conversation. On September 27, 1991, the Senate Judiciary Committee deadlocked on Thomas's nomination, and sent it to the Senate floor without recommendation. Shortly thereafter, testimony by

See also
Thurgood Marshall

Anita Hill, Thomas's former assistant who claimed he had sexually harassed her, was leaked to media sources. The committee reopened hearings in order to discuss the issue. The questioning of Hill and Thomas became a national television event and a source of universal debate over issues of sexual harassment and Hill's truthfulness. Despite the damaging allegations, on October 15, Thomas was confirmed, 52–48.

In his first years on the Supreme Court, Thomas voted consistently with the Court's conservative wing. His decisions narrowed the scope of the 1965 Voting Rights Act, upheld new limits on abortion rights (he pronounced himself ready to overturn *Roe* v. *Wade*), and curbed affirmative action policies. In *Hudson* v. *McMillian* (1992), perhaps his most controversial opinion, Thomas held that the Eighth Amendment did not proscribe beating of prison inmates by guards. Thomas remained bitter about the treatment he had received during his confirmation process. In 1993 he gave a controversial speech linking society's treatment of conservative African-American intellectuals to lynching.

—CLARENCE E. WALKER

THOMAS, DEBRA J. "DEBI"

Debra J. "Debi" Thomas (March 25, 1967–), ice skater. A native of Poughkeepsie, N.Y., Debi Thomas moved to northern California with her family when she was a small child. Fascinated by an ice show she watched at the age of three, Thomas became a competitive skater by the time she was in junior high school.

Thomas began to achieve national honors as a skater while a student at San Mateo High School and moved quickly to the senior women's division before graduating. She excelled academically as well as on the ice and became the first prominent female skater to attend college since Tenley Albright in the 1950s; Thomas graduated from Stanford in 1991.

At 5′ 6″, Thomas was taller than most of her competitors, with extra height on her double and triple jumps. She thrilled audiences and pleased judges with her graceful choreography blended with a powerful athleticism. She also excelled in the mandatory school figures required during her years of competition. In 1985 she was named Figure Skater of the Year, and in 1986 she became the first black woman to win the United States and Women's World Figure Championships. That same year she was named Amateur Female Athlete of the Year and Wide World of Sports Athlete of the Year. She developed tendonitis in 1987 but managed to place second in the U.S. and World Championships. In 1988 she placed third in both the World Championships and at the Winter Olympics in Calgary, Alberta.

Thomas turned professional in 1988, winning the World Professional Championships in 1988, 1989, and 1991. In 1991 she also won the World Challenge of Champions and entered Northwestern University Medical School that same year to study orthopedic and sports medicine.

—GAYLE PEMBERTON

THORNTON, WILLIE MAE "BIG MAMA"

Willie Mae "Big Mama" Thornton (December 11, 1926–July 25, 1984), blues singer. Born in Montgomery, Ala., the daughter of a minister, Willie Mae Thornton left home after her mother died. She joined Sammy Green's Hot Harlem Revue at the age of fourteen. In 1948 she moved to Houston, where Peacock Records owner Don Robey arranged for her to sing with the Johnny Otis Rhythm and Blues Caravan. Her 250-pound size earned her the nickname "Big Mama," and she became popular for her boisterous, shouting style. "Hound Dog" (1953), a blues song later made famous by Elvis Presley, was her only hit, but it enabled her to tour nationally with Johnny Ace as the "reigning king and queen of the blues" until Ace's Russian roulette death in 1954. Thornton's career never recovered from that event.

Thornton struggled in the San Francisco Bay area until the blues revival of the mid-1960s created a demand for older blues singers after which time she performed at jazz, folk, and blues festivals in the United States and abroad. The rock singer Janis Joplin remade Thornton's "Ball and Chain" into her signature song in 1968, but Thornton had signed away the copyright to the tune years before, and she earned no money for Joplin's version. Thornton's recordings include *In Europe* (1965), *Ball and Chain* (1968), *Stronger Than Dirt* (1969), *Saved* (1973), *Jail* (1975), and *Mama's Pride* (1978).

Throughout her career, Thornton drank heavily and dressed in men's clothing, sometimes wearing a dress over trousers and brogans. Her audiences, however, forgave the eccentricity. She

In the 1920s, blues was the most popular African-American music.

PAGE 101

685

WALLACE THURMAN

Writer of Critical Studies of African-American Life

Wallace Thurman (August 16, 1902–December 22, 1934), writer. Born in Salt Lake City, Utah, Wallace Thurman's literary career began shortly after he left the University of Utah to begin studies at the University of Southern California. Although his intent was to study medicine, Thurman soon rediscovered an earlier enthusiasm for writing. According to Arna Bontemps, whom he first met during this period, Thurman "lost sight of degrees" and began to pursue courses related to his interest in literature and writing at the University of Southern California. In Los Angeles he also wrote a column called "Inklings" for a local black newspaper. Having heard about the New Negro movement in New York, Thurman attempted to establish a West Coast counterpart to the Harlem Renaissance and began editing his own literary magazine, the *Outlet*. The publication lasted for only six months but was described by his friend Theophilus Lewis, the Harlem theater critic, as Thurman's "first and most successful venture at the editorial desk."

Dissatisfied, Thurman left for New York where, as he put it, he "began to live on Labor Day, 1925." Later, he became known for his declaration that he was a man who hated "every damned spot in these United States outside of Manhattan Island." In New York Thurman secured his first position, an editorial assistant at the *Looking Glass,* another small, short-lived review magazine. His first important position was as temporary editor for the leftist-oriented *Messenger,* published by A. Phillip Randolph and Chandler Owen. When the managing editor, George Schuyler, went on leave, Thurman's role provided him with a forum not only for his own work but for that of other nascent Renaissance talent, including Langston Hughes, Arna Bontemps, Zora Neale Hurston, and Dorothy West.

When Schuyler returned, Thurman became associated with a white publication, *The World Tomorrow,* and at the same time joined a group of young black writers and artists—Hurston, Hughes, Aaron Douglas, John P. Davis, Bruce Nugent, and Gwendolyn Bennett—to launch "a new experimental quarterly," *Fire,* in 1926. The purpose of *Fire,* according to its founders, was to "burn up a lot of the old, dead conventional Negro-white ideas of the past, *épater la bourgeoisie* into the realization of the existence of the younger Negro writers and artists." Yet Thurman's enduring ambition to become editor of "a fi-

nancially secure magazine" seemed ill fated. *Fire* itself became a casualty of a real fire in a basement where several hundred copies had been stored, and the disaster led to its demise after only the first issue. Thurman's next editorial venture came two years later when he began publishing *Harlem, a Forum of Negro Life.* Although this magazine lasted a little longer than its predecessor, it too folded due to a lack of funds.

Thurman also wrote critical articles on African-American life and culture for such magazines as the *New Republic,* the *Independent,* the *Bookman,* and *Dance Magazine.* The black writer, he contended, had left a "great deal of fresh, vital material untouched" because of his tendency to view his own people as "sociological problems rather than as human beings." Like Hughes, he also criticized those writers who felt "that they must always exhibit specimens from the college rather than from the kindergarten, specimens from the parlor rather than from the pantry." He exhorted black writers to exploit those authentic and unique aspects of black life and culture ignored by writers who suppressed the seamy or sordid or low-down, common aspects of black existence.

Thurman published his first novel, *The Blacker the Berry* (1929) while working for the staff of MacFadden Publications. Although the book was acclaimed by the critics, the author remained characteristically skeptical of his own efforts. Doubtlessly invoking some of his own experiences, Thurman's novel deals with the problems of a dark-skinned woman who struggles with intraracial schisms caused by colorism. Later that same year Thurman collaborated with a white writer, William Jourdan Rapp, on the play *Harlem,* which opened at the Apollo Theater. Thurman based the plot and dialogue on his short story "Cordelia the Crude," which was originally published in *Fire.* The play was described by Hughes as "a compelling study . . . of the impact of Harlem on a Negro family fresh from the south." After its production Thurman continued to write prolifically, sometimes ghostwriting popular "true confessions" fiction.

In 1932 Thurman published his second novel, *Infants of the Spring,* an autobiographical roman à clef, documenting the period from a contemporary and fictionalized perspective. It also constitutes a biting satire and poignant critique of the Harlem Renaissance. For Thurman the failure of the movement lay in the race consciousness emanating from the literary propagandists on the one hand and the assimilationists on the other, both undermining any expression of racial authenticity and individuality.

His final novel, *The Interne,* written in collaboration with Abraham L. Furman, was also published in 1932. It was a muckraking novel exposing the corrupt conditions of City Hospital in New York. Both of these novels were published by Macaulay, where Thurman became editor in chief in 1932. Two years later he negotiated a contract with Foy Productions Ltd. to write scenarios for two films, *High School Girl* and *Tomorrow's Children.* But the strain of life in Hollywood took its toll on Thurman, who became ill and returned to New York in the spring of 1934. Not only had he been marked by a certain physical fragility, he had also been plagued with chronic alcoholism. Shortly after his return Thurman was taken to City Hospital, ironically the very institution he had written about in *The Interne.* After remaining for six months in the incurable ward, he died of consumption on December 22, 1934.

Thurman had arrived in New York in 1925 at the peak of the Harlem Renaissance, whose rise and ebb paralleled his own life and career. Thurman early became one of the leading critics of the older bourgeoisie, both black and white; his lifestyle and literary criticism were calculated to outrage their sensibilities and articulate a New Negro attitude toward the black arts. His importance to the Harlem Renaissance can be measured in terms of both his literary contributions and his influence on younger and perhaps more successful writers of the period. His criticism also set a standard of judgment for subsequent scholars of the Harlem Renaissance. Perhaps his evaluation of Alain Locke's *The New Negro* (1925), a collection inaugurating the movement, best summarizes his own life and contribution: "In [*The New Negro*] are exemplified all the virtues and all the faults of this new movement." Thurman's life itself became a symbol of the possibilities and limitations of the Harlem Renaissance.

—MAE G. HENDERSON

was frail from cirrhosis and weighed only ninety-five pounds when she died of a heart attack at the age of fifty-seven in a Los Angeles boarding house. At a funeral conducted by the Rev. Johnny Otis, money was raised to pay for her burial expenses.

—JAMES M. SALEM

THURMAN, HOWARD

Howard Thurman (November 18, 1900–April 10, 1981), minister and educator. Howard Thurman, whose career as pastor, scholar, teacher, and university chaplain extended over fifty years, was the author of over twenty books. One of the most creative religious minds of the twentieth century, Thurman touched the lives of many cultural leaders within and beyond the modern Civil Rights Movement, including Martin Luther King, Jr., A. Philip Randolph, Alan Paton, Eleanor Roosevelt, Mary McLeod Bethune, Mordecai Wyatt Johnson, Rabbi Alvin Fine, and Arthur Ashe. "The search for common ground" was the defining motif of Thurman's life and thought. This vision of the kinship of all peoples, born of Thurman's own personal struggles with the prohibitions of race, religion, and culture, propelled him into the mainstream of American Christianity as a dis-

tinctive interpreter of the church's role in a pluralistic society.

The grandson of slaves, Thurman was born in Daytona, Fla., and raised in the segregated black community of Daytona. He was educated in the local black school, where he was the first African American to complete the eighth grade. He attended high school at Florida Baptist Academy (1915–1919), one of only three public high schools for blacks in the state. Upon graduation, Thurman attended Morehouse College (1919–1923) and Rochester Theological Seminary (1923–1926). After serving as pastor of Mt. Zion Baptist Church in Oberlin, Ohio, for two years (1926–1928), he studied with the Quaker mystic Rufus Jones in the spring of 1929. He served as Director of Religious Life and Professor of Religion at Morehouse and Spelman Colleges (1929–1930), and Dean of Rankin Chapel and Professor of Religion at Howard University (1932–1944).

Thurman was cofounder and copastor of the pioneering interracial, interfaith Fellowship Church for All Peoples in San Francisco from 1944 to 1953. In 1953, he assumed the dual appointment of Professor of Spiritual Resources and Disciplines and Dean of Marsh Chapel at Boston University. He founded the Howard Thurman Educational Trust in San Francisco in 1961,

Black Baptism was one of the anchors of the Civil Rights Movement, with Baptist ministers in the forefront of the struggle for black equality.

PAGE 62

See also
Baptists

T

which he administered after his retirement in 1965 until his death in 1981.

—WALTER EARL FLUKER

TOLSON, MELVIN BEAUNORUS

Melvin Beaunorus Tolson (February 6, 1898–August 29, 1966), poet and educator. Tolson was born in Howard County, Mo., to Alonzo, a Methodist minister, and Lera Tolson. He attended Lincoln High School in Kansas City, Mo., spent a year (1918) at Fisk University in Nashville, and then transferred to Lincoln University in Pennsylvania, where he received his B.A. With his wife, Ruth, whom he married in 1922, he would raise several highly successful children. In 1923, Tolson secured a post at Wiley College in Marshall, Tex., where he taught English literature and coached one of the country's most successful debating teams.

As early as 1917, Tolson had begun to write poems and short tales that reveal and foreshadow the intensity of his intellectual life and his preoccupation with esoteric knowledge. His poetic interests took off, however, while he was attending Columbia University on a Rockefeller Foundation scholarship during 1931 and 1932, the dimming of the so-called Harlem Renaissance. His M.A. thesis presents a somewhat brief but accurate portrait of some of the leading figures of the Renaissance, including Langston Hughes, whom he knew fairly well. The fervor and ferment of the Harlem community inspired Tolson in 1932 to write a sonnet about Harlem's denizens. This sonnet was the germ of an extended poetic work, which was published posthumously as *A Gallery of Harlem Portraits* (1979). Lyrics from the blues and spirituals freely intermix with conventional poetic language to create stylized "portraits" of Harlemites of the 1930s and 1940s. Several years after his return to Wiley College, Tolson's enormous success as a debating coach prompted the *Washington Tribune* in 1938 to request that he write a guest column, which for almost seven years flourished as a regular feature entitled "Caviar and Cabbages."

With the publication of "Dark Symphony" in the *Atlantic Monthly* (1941), Tolson demonstrates his earliest preoccupation with, and mastery of, the poetic sequence. Constructed around the personalities of major historical black figures, the poem won first prize at the American Negro Ex-

position in Chicago in 1940. The award assisted Tolson in getting *Rendezvous with America* (1944)—his first major poetic composition—published.

In his early phase Tolson's poems, which appeared in magazines such as the *Atlantic Monthly* and *Prairie Schooner,* were fairly accessible and transparent. But the poems of his second phase became more esoteric and highly allusive. His work then began appearing in magazines such as the *Modern Quarterly,* the *Arts Quarterly,* and *Poetry.* In the intervening years, Tolson was elected four times as mayor of Langston, Okla. And in 1947, the government of Liberia commissioned him to write a work to be read at the International Exposition in Liberia, commemorating the country's centennial, and simultaneously made him their poet laureate. To celebrate the ideals upon which Liberia was founded, Tolson wrote *Libretto for the Republic of Liberia* (1953), a difficult and enormously complex work about intellectual freedom and international brotherhood—a virtual constant in his writings. The primary work upon which Tolson's fame rests, however, is *Harlem Gallery* (1965), a lengthy poetic sequence of portraits or odes devoted as much to the modern Anglo-American poetic tradition as to African-American culture. *Harlem Gallery* is primarily concerned, for example, with the integrity of the black artist and his cultural allegiances.

Although Tolson is often grouped with the major poetic figures of the 1950s and early 1960s such as Gwendolyn Brooks and Robert Hayden, his reputation remains far behind those of his peers, and readers and scholars alike are kept at bay by the erudition and monumentality of his work.

—GORDON THOMPSON

TOOMER, JEAN

Jean Toomer (December 26, 1894–March 30, 1967), writer. Jean Toomer was born Nathan Pinchback Toomer in Washington, D.C. (He changed his name to Jean Toomer in 1920.) His maternal grandfather, Pinckney Benton Stewart Pinchback, a dominant figure in Toomer's childhood and adolescence, was acting governor of Louisiana for about five weeks in 1872 and 1873. Because Toomer's father, Nathan, deserted his wife and child in 1895, and his mother, Nina, died in 1909, Toomer spent much of his youth in the home of his Pinchback grandparents in Washington, D.C. After graduating from Dunbar High

See also
Harlem Renaissance

School in 1914, Toomer spent about six months studying agriculture at the University of Wisconsin. During 1916 and 1917, he attended classes at various colleges, among them the American College of Physical Training in Chicago, New York University, and the City College of New York.

By 1918, Toomer had written "Bona and Paul," a story that became part of *Cane*, his masterpiece. This early story signaled a theme that Toomer was preoccupied with in most of his subsequent writing: the search for and development of personal identity and harmony with other people. Throughout his life, Toomer, who had light skin, felt uncomfortable with the rigid racial and ethnic classifications in the United States. He felt such classifications limited the individual and inhibited personal psychic development. Having lived in both white and black neighborhoods in Washington, D.C., and having various racial and ethnic strains within him, he thought it ridiculous to define himself simplistically.

Two events early in Toomer's literary career were of great importance to his development as a writer. In 1920, he met the novelist and essayist Waldo Frank, and in 1921, he was a substitute principal at the Sparta Agricultural and Industrial Institute in Georgia. Toomer and Frank became close friends, sharing their ideas about writing, and Frank, the established writer, encouraged Toomer in his fledgling work. However, it was in Georgia that Toomer became most inspired. He was moved and excited by the rural black people and their land. He felt he had found a part of himself that he had not known well, and perhaps for the first time in his life truly identified with his black heritage. The result was an outpouring of writing, bringing forth most of the southern pieces that would be in *Cane*.

Cane, stylistically avant-garde, an impressionistic collection of stories, sketches, and poems, some of which had been previously published in *Crisis, Double Dealer, Liberator, Modern Review,* and *Broom*, was published in 1923. While only about 1,000 copies were sold, it received mostly good reviews and was proclaimed an important book by the writers who were then establishing what was to become the Harlem Renaissance. Alain Locke praised *Cane*'s "musical folk-lilt" and "glamorous sensuous ecstasy." William Stanley Braithwaite called Toomer "the very first artist of the race, who . . . can write about the Negro without the surrender of compromise of the artist's vision. . . . Toomer is a bright morning star of a new day of the race in literature." A review in *The New Republic* lauded *Cane* for its unstereotyped picture of the South, and Allen Tate compared Toomer's avant-garde style favorably to other modern works.

However, despite the critical praise for *Cane*, by 1924 Toomer was feeling restless and unhappy with himself. His struggle with personal identity continued. He went to France to study at Georges I. Gurdjieff's Institute for the Harmonious Development of Man at Fontainebleau. Gurdjieff believed that human beings were made up of two parts: "personality" and "essence." Personality is superficial, created by our social environment. It usually obscures our essence, which is our true nature and the core of our being. Gurdjieff claimed that he could help people discover their essence. Toomer soon embraced Gurdjieff's ideas of personal development, and when he returned to the United States, he became an advocate of Gurdjieff's philosophy, leading Gurdjieff workshops at first briefly in Harlem and then in Chicago until 1930.

Due to Gurdjieff's influence and Toomer's continuing search for a meaningful identity, after 1923 he largely abandoned the style and subject matter he had used in *Cane*. To a great extent he abandoned black writing. From 1924 until his death, he wrote voluminously, but with little critical or publishing success. He wrote in all genres: plays, poems, essays, stories, novels, and autobi-

JEAN TOOMER

Toomer was one of the most highly regarded writers of the Harlem Renaissance, and was only twenty-eight when he published Cane *in 1923.*
MOORLAND-SPINGARN
RESEARCH CENTER,
HOWARD UNIVERSITY

T

ographies. While his writing became noticeably more didactic, some of it was not without interesting stylistic experimentation, especially his expressionistic drama, most notably *The Sacred Factory*, published posthumously in 1980. During this period, Toomer also wrote a number of autobiographies and provocative social, political, and personal essays, some of which were published posthumously. Works that Toomer did publish after *Cane* include: *Balo* (1927), a play of Southern rural black life, written during the *Cane* period; "Mr. Costyve Duditch" and "Winter on Earth," stories published in 1928; "Race Problems and Modern Society" (1929), an important essay on the racial situation in the United States that complements "The Negro Emergent," published posthumously in 1993; and "Blue Meridian" (1936), a long poem in which Toomer depicts the development of the American race as the coming together of the black, red, and white races.

A decade after the publication of *Cane*, Toomer had dropped into relative obscurity. It was not until the 1960s and the renewed interest in earlier African-American writing and the republication of *Cane* that Toomer began to have a large readership and an influence on the young black writers of the day. Since then, four posthumous collections of mostly previously unpublished material have appeared: *The Wayward and the Seeking* (ed. Darwin T. Turner, 1980); *The Collected Poems of Jean Toomer* (ed. Robert B. Jones and Margery Toomer Latimer, 1988); *Essentials* (ed. Rudolph P. Byrd, 1991, a republication of a collection of aphorisms originally privately printed in 1931); and *A Jean Toomer Reader: Selected Unpublished Writings* (ed. Frederik L. Rusch, 1993).

Toomer had two wives. He married Margery Latimer in 1931, and she died the following year giving birth to their daughter, also named Margery. In 1934, he married Marjorie Content. From 1936 to his death, Toomer resided in Bucks County, Pa.

—FREDERIK L. RUSCH

TOUSSAINT, PIERRE

Pierre Toussaint (c. 1766–1853), businessman, philanthropist, candidate for canonization. Pierre Toussaint was probably born in Haiti in 1766, the slave of a planter, Jean Berard. Toussaint, a house servant, was looked upon affectionately by the Berards and treated as a member of the family. His grandmother taught him to read and his mas-

ter permitted him use of the home library. In 1787, during the early stages of a slave revolt, the Berards fled Haiti to go to New York City, taking Toussaint and his sister with them. Toussaint remained loyal to his masters throughout the unrest and rebellion. After arriving in New York, he was apprenticed to a hairdresser and, while still a slave, was able to set up a successful business of his own. His services were desired by many of the wealthiest and most distinguished women in the city. As a hairdresser he earned enough to become quite wealthy and to support his mistress after his master died. Although he had the means to purchase his own freedom, he chose to remain with his mistress even after she remarried.

In 1809, upon her deathbed, Madame Berard granted Toussaint his freedom. His loyalty did not end with his manumission, however, and he continued to support Madame Berard's daughter for several years. With his considerable wealth he was able to purchase the freedom of his sister, Rosalie, and his future wife, Juliette Noel, in 1811. Three years later he purchased the freedom of his niece, Euphemia, and cared for and educated her. Following Euphemia's death of tuberculosis in 1829, the grief-stricken Toussaint turned to benevolent activities.

Toussaint had been a devout Roman Catholic since he was a child, and after arriving in New York he attended mass every day for sixty-six years at Saint Peter's Roman Catholic Church in lower Manhattan. He was the most notable black layperson in the antebellum Roman Catholic church in New York City. The kindhearted Toussaint was also generous and charitable. He and his wife took black orphans into their home and raised money in support of the Catholic Orphan Asylum for white children. In 1841 he was the first person to respond to the request of Monsignor de Forbin-Jasson for donations to erect a Roman Catholic church for French-speakers (now Saint Vincent de Paul's) with what was then a considerable contribution of one hundred dollars. When Toussaint died in 1853, he was buried beside his wife in Saint Patrick's Cemetery.

In response to the many voices that called for recognition of Toussaint's exemplary piety, in the early 1990s the New York archdiocese began the process of his canonization. This effort led to some conflict and disagreement within the church. New York's John Cardinal O'Connor and other Catholics, black and white, regarded Toussaint as a model of faith and charity who deserved the honor of sainthood. Others saw his career as marked by passivity and servility and therefore

Clarence Thomas entered the Immaculate Conception Seminary in Conception, Mo., intending to become a Catholic priest.

PAGE 683

See also
Literature

unworthy of veneration. The canonization is to be decided by a commission in Rome. Despite the controversy surrounding Toussaint's legacy, he remains an important figure within nineteenth-century African-American history.

—WILLIAM J. MOSES

TRACK AND FIELD

African-American men and women have played a significant role in track and field. They have won an impressive number of championships, set numerous Olympic and world records, and contributed enormously to American success in international competition. These achievements have been especially prominent in the 100-meter and 200-meter dashes and in the long jump.

Track and field competition in the United States emerged in the late nineteenth century as a popular amateur sport for men. Women did not participate extensively until the 1930s. Prior to World War I, only a few black athletes won major honors. William Tecumseh Sherman Jackson of Amherst College was the first notable black runner. Jackson regularly won the 880-yard run at collegiate meets in the Northeast from 1890 to 1892. George C. Poage was another early champion. The first African American to receive an Olympic medal, Poage captured third place in the 400-meter hurdles at the 1904 games in St. Louis. The first international star was the University of Pennsylvania's John B. Taylor, the collegiate champion and record holder in the 440-yard run. In 1908 he became the first African-American gold medalist at the Olympics, running a leg on the winning 1600-meter relay team. Howard Porter Drew was the first famous black sprinter. From 1912 to 1916 Drew dominated the sprints in the U.S. and set world records in the 100-meter and 220-yard dashes.

After World War I, African-American competitors gained increased respect. The new willingness of predominantly white northern colleges and elite track clubs to recruit and train promising black athletes greatly expanded their opportunities. Probably the most gifted black track athlete of the 1920s was William DeHart Hubbard, a graduate of the University of Michigan. During his illustrious career as a long jumper, Hubbard earned the gold medal in the 1924 Olympics, captured two NCAA titles, won six consecutive Amateur Athletic Union (AAU) championships, and held the world record. Distance runner Earl Johnson also enjoyed considerable success. Johnson

won a bronze medal in the 1924 Olympics in the 10,000-meter run and claimed three AAU titles in the event.

The 1930s were a golden age for African-American sprinters, especially Eddie Tolan (Michigan), Ralph Metcalfe (Marquette), and Jesse Owens (Ohio State). Tolan won one NCAA spring championship and four AAU titles. Metcalf swept both the 100- and 220-yard NCAA championships for three straight years, and he also won seven AAU titles. But at the 1932 Olympics in Los Angeles, it was Tolan who won the head-to-head showdown, earning gold medals in both the 100- and 200-meter dashes in record time.

Owens, an Alabama native, burst onto the world scene in 1935. On May 25, at the Big Ten Championships, he delivered the greatest one-day performance in track and field history. Within the span of two hours he set three world records (long jump, 220-yard dash, and 220-yard low hurdles) and tied a fourth (100-yard dash). Owens's accomplishments at the so-called Nazi Olympics in Berlin the following year were only slightly less spectacular, as he became the first runner to earn four gold medals. He won the 100- and 200-meter dashes and the long jump, setting Olympic records in the latter two events. Owens earned his final gold medal as a late addition to the 400-meter relay squad, after U.S. coaches dropped two Jewish runners from the team. Four additional African-Americans also claimed gold medals in Berlin: Archie Williams in the 400-meter run, John Woodruff in the 800, Ralph Metcalfe in the 400-meter relay, and Cornelius Johnson in the high jump. When Johnson went to receive his award, Adolph Hitler abruptly left the stadium to avoid congratulating him, an apparent racial snub which journalists later erroneously reported to have been aimed at Owens.

Opportunities for African-American women still lagged far behind those for men. Only in the mid-1930s did black women finally gain the opportunity to demonstrate their potential. Tuskegee Institute captured its first AAU team title in 1937 and dominated national competition for a decade. Leading Tuskegee's rise to prominence was Lula Hymes, who won the AAU long jump in 1937 and 1938 and the 100-meter dash in 1938. Another Tuskegee product, Alice Coachman, became the first African-American female superstar. Coachman won three AAU 100-meter dash titles, but even more impressively she captured the AAU high jump championship every year from 1939 to 1948. She also became the first

Jacqueline Joyner-Kersee entered her first track and field competition at age nine.

PAGE 396

See also
Wilma Rudolph

African-American woman to receive an Olympic gold medal, winning the high jump in 1948.

During the late 1940s and '50s, two black champions dominated their events—William Harrison Dillard and Mal Whitfield. The premier hurdler of his day, Dillard won two gold medals at the 1948 Olympics and two more in 1952. Whitfield was an amazingly consistent 800-meter runner and earned Olympic gold medals in both 1948 and 1952. During the 1950s African-American athletes also excelled in the decathlon. Milton Campbell took the silver medal in the event at the 1952 summer games and the gold in 1956. Rafer Johnson finished second behind Campbell in 1956 and claimed first place in 1960, setting both Olympic and world records during the year. In 1956 Charlie Dumas became the first high jumper to clear the seven-foot barrier, and later in the year he won the Olympic gold medal in the event.

During the 1950s Tennessee State University replaced Tuskegee as the women's track power-house. The most successful of the school's famous Tigerbelle runners was Wilma Rudolph. Born into a family of twenty-two children, Rudolph overcame a childhood bout with polio that forced her to wear a leg brace for several years. In 1960 she became the first American woman ever to earn three gold medals at one Olympics, winning the 100-meter and 200-meter dashes and running a leg on the champion 400-meter relay team. Her athletic success and her inspiring personal story stimulated new interest in women's track. Randolph's successor as a Tigerbelle star and queen of the sprints was Wyomia Tyus, who won the 100-meter dash in both the 1964 and 1968 Olympics, establishing a world record of 11.0 seconds in her 1968 victory.

The late 1960s were a time of widespread social protests, and sports were not exempt. The 1968 summer games in Mexico City, which sociologist Harry Edwards and other black activists had urged African Americans to boycott, combined memorable athletic achievements with po-

MEDAL WINNERS

Gold medal winner Vincent Matthews (second from left) and silver medal winner Wayne Collett (left) are honored during the 1972 Munich Olympics.

PHOTOGRAPHS AND PRINTS DIVISION, SCHOMBURG CENTER FOR RESEARCH IN BLACK CULTURE, THE NEW YORK PUBLIC LIBRARY, ASTOR, LENOX AND TILDEN FOUNDATIONS

litical protest. Bob Beamon delivered the most spectacular individual performance, setting a world record of 29 feet, 2½ inches in the long jump. His leap, arguably the greatest single effort in track and field history, surpassed the previous mark by almost two feet and stood for twenty-four years. Three African-American sprinters also won individual gold medals while setting or tying world records at Mexico City: James Hines in the 100-meter dash, Tommie Smith in the 200-meter dash, and Lee Evans in the 400-meter run. Evans's outstanding mark of 43.8 seconds lasted for almost two decades. Also attracting considerable attention were several protests against racism by African-American athletes, especially one at the awards ceremony for the 200-meter dash winners. Standing on the victory stand during the American national anthem, Smith and John Carlos, the bronze medalist, each bowed their heads and raised one clenched fist inside a black glove in a "black power" salute, a controversial gesture for which they were suspended from the U.S. team.

The leading track superstar of the 1970s was hurdler Edwin Moses. A physics major at Morehouse College in Atlanta, Moses dominated the 400-meter hurdles, winning 122 consecutive races from 1977 to 1987. He set the world record for the event on several occasions and won gold medals in the 1976 and 1984 Olympics (the United States boycotted the 1980 Moscow games). The 1984 summer games in Los Angeles witnessed the emergence of another superstar—Carl Lewis. In a brilliant performance reminiscent of Jesse Owens at Berlin in 1936, Lewis became only the second male track competitor in history to claim four gold medals, winning individual titles in the 100-meter dash, the 200-meter dash, and the long jump, and sharing the 400-meter relay team's victory. Lewis successfully defended his 100-meter and long jump championships in 1988, and in 1992 he claimed an unprecedented third gold medal in the long jump. To do so he outdueled Mike Powell, who one month earlier had beaten Lewis and broken Bob Beamon's old long jump record with a leap of 29 feet 4½ inches.

The top women stars of the 1980s included Florence Griffith Joyner, Jackie Joyner-Kersee, and Valerie Brisco-Hooks. At the Los Angeles games Brisco-Hooks set Olympic records in winning the 200-meter dash and the 400-meter run, adding a third gold medal with the American 1600-meter relay team. Known for her colorful running attire, Griffith-Joyner earned three gold medals (100-meter dash, 200-meter dash, and

EDWIN MOSES

Record-Breaking Athlete Wins Most Consecutive Victories

Edwin Corley Moses (August 31, 1955–), track and field athlete. Born and raised in Dayton, Ohio, Edwin Moses began running hurdles at Dayton Fairview High School. An excellent student, Moses accepted an academic scholarship at Morehouse College in Atlanta after he failed to secure a college athletic scholarship. In his junior year at Morehouse, he began to compete in the 400–meter hurdles and qualified for the United States Olympic Team. Moses was the first hurdler to perfect a thirteen-step approach between each hurdle (most runners required fourteen or fifteen steps). At the 1976 Montreal Summer Olympics, he won the 400–meter hurdles in the world-record time of 47.64 seconds. Following the Olympics, Moses returned to Morehouse to finish his degree in aerospace engineering. He graduated in 1978.

Beginning in 1977, Moses won 122 consecutive races, establishing a record for the most consecutive victories in track and field competition. In 1983, he set a new world record in the 400–meter hurdles (47.02 second) and won the Sullivan award, given to the top amateur athlete in the United States. The following year, he won his second Olympic gold medal at the Los Angeles Games and was named Sportsman of the Year by both the U.S. Olympic Committee and *Sports Illustrated*. In 1985, Moses was elected to the U.S. Olympic Hall of Fame. He retired from competition in 1988 and subsequently served as chairman of substance abuse committees for the Athletic Congress and the United States Olympic Committee. Moses was one of several track and football stars who joined the United States Olympic bobsled program in the early 1990s. A brakeman for the top two-man sled for the United States, he won a bronze medal at a 1990 World Cup event in Winterberg, Germany. Moses attempted to return to track and field competition for the 1992 Summer Games in Barcelona, but was hampered by injuries and did not qualify. He maintained his ties to the United States Olympic movement, however, through his involvement with the U.S. Olympic Committee's Athletes' Advisory Council.

—BENJAMIN K. SCOTT

Wilma Rudolph's achievements as a runner gave a boost to women's track in the United States and heightened awareness about racial and sexual barriers within sports.

PAGE 607

*Whether freshmen
should compete
in American
intercollegiate
athletics has
been debated
for a century.*

PAGE 556

FLORENCE GRIFFITH-JOYNER

Outstanding Runner Takes Home the Gold in Seoul

Florence Delorez Griffith-Joyner (December 21, 1959–September 21, 1998) athlete. Florence Griffith was born in Los Angeles, the seventh of eleven children of an electronics technician and a garment worker. When she was four, her parents separated and she moved with her mother and siblings to the Jordan Downs housing project in the Watts section of Los Angeles. Griffith began running at age seven in competitions sponsored by the Jesse Owens National Youth Games for underprivileged youth and won races at ages fourteen and fifteen. She became a member of the track team at Jordan High School, where she set two school records before graduating in 1978.

In 1979 Griffith enrolled at California State University at Northridge, where she met assistant track coach Bob Kersee. However, she was forced to drop out of college the next year due to lack of funds. With the help of Kersee, who had moved to the University of California at Los Angeles (UCLA), Griffith won an athletic scholarship to UCLA and returned to college in 1981. Griffith competed on the track team, and in 1982 she won the NCAA championships in the two hundred meters. In 1983 she won the NCAA championships in the four hundred meters and graduated from UCLA with a major in psychology. In the 1984 Olympics in Los Angeles, she finished second to fellow American Valerie Brisco-Hooks in the two hundred meters.

After the Olympics Griffith worked as a customer-service representative for a bank during the day and as a beautician at night. In early 1987, however, she decided to train full-time for the 1988 Olympics. In October 1987 she married Al Joyner, brother of athlete Jackie Joyner-Kersee.

After strong showings in the world championships and the U.S. trials, Griffith-Joyner was a favorite for the 1988 Olympics in Seoul, Korea. Flo-Jo, as she was dubbed by the media, did not disappoint, winning three gold medals and one silver medal. Griffith-Joyner set an Olympic record in the one hundred meters and a world record in the two hundred meters. She ran the third leg for the American winning team in the four-by-one-hundred meter relay and the anchor leg for the American silver-medal winners in the four-by-four-hundred meter relay. Griffith-Joyner's outstanding performance and striking appearance (including long, extravagantly decorated fingernails and brightly colored one-legged running outfits) earned her worldwide media attention. She won the 1988 Jesse Owens Award and the 1988 Sullivan Award, given annually to the best amateur athlete.

Griffith-Joyner settled comfortably into post-Olympic life with numerous endorsements and projects, including designing her own sportswear line and a brief acting stint on the television soap opera *Santa Barbara* (1992). In 1993 President Bill Clinton named her cochairwoman of the President's Council on Physical Fitness and Sports.

—CINDY HIMES GISSENDANNER

400-meter relay) and one silver (1600-meter relay) at the 1988 Olympics and held world records in the first two events. Joyner-Kersee won the Olympic long jump competition in 1988, captured the heptathlon in 1988 and 1992, and set a new world record in the latter event.

The remarkable achievements of African-American athletes in the sprints, long jump, and hurdles, and their limited success in the distance and weight events, have perpetuated an old debate over whether sociological and cultural forces or physical tendencies help explain their success. Scholars continue to disagree vigorously over these issues. Nonetheless, they all concur that African-American men and women have made an impressive contribution to international track and field.

—CHARLES H. MARTIN

TROTTER, WILLIAM MONROE

William Monroe Trotter (April 7, 1872–April 7, 1934), newspaper editor and civil rights activist. William Monroe Trotter was born in 1872 in Chillicothe, Ohio, the son of James Monroe Trotter and Virginia Isaacs Trotter. Raised in a well-to-do white Boston neighborhood, young Trotter absorbed the militant integrationism of his politically active father, a tradition that he carried on throughout his own life.

Elected president of his senior class by his white high school classmates, Trotter worked briefly as a clerk and entered Harvard College in the fall of 1891. He graduated *magna cum laude* in

June 1895, and moved easily into Boston's elite black social set. In June 1899, he married Geraldine Louise Pindell. That same year he opened his own real estate firm.

By the turn of the century, Trotter and his peers were deeply concerned about worsening race relations in the South and signs of growing racial antagonism in the North. In March 1901, Trotter helped form the Boston Literary and Historical Association, which fostered intellectual debate among prosperous African Americans; he also joined the more politically active Massachusetts Racial Protective Association (MRPA). These organizations served as early forums for his denunciation of the virtually undisputed accommodationist leadership of Booker T. Washington. In contrast to Washington, Trotter defended liberal arts education for black people, championed electoral participation as a means of securing basic rights, and counseled agitation on behalf of racial justice. With fellow MRPA member George W. Forbes, Trotter embarked on what became his life work: the uncompromising advocacy of civil and political equality for African Americans, through the pages of the Boston *Guardian*.

The *Guardian* newspaper, which began weekly publication in November 1901, offered news and analysis of the African-American condition. At the same time, it served as a base for independent political organizing led by Trotter himself. The "Trotterites" not only vilified their enemies in the pages of the *Guardian*, they also resorted to direct confrontation. On several occasions, Trotter and his supporters attempted (without success) to wrest control of the Afro-American Council from the pro-Booker T. Washington camp. More effective was their disruption of a speech Washington himself was scheduled to deliver in July 1903. Amid the fracas, Trotter delivered a litany of accusations and demanded of Washington, "Are the rope and the torch all the race is to get under your leadership?" He served a month in jail for his role in what was dubbed the "Boston Riot." After the incident, Trotter founded the Boston Suffrage League and the New England Suffrage League, through which he called for federal antilynching legislation, enforcement of the Fifteenth Amendment, and the end of racial segregation.

While Trotter's editorial belligerence and unorthodox tactics were often disapproved of, many nonetheless respected his unswerving commitment to the cause of racial equality. They rose to Trotter's defense in the aftermath of the "riot" when Washington launched a malicious campaign—including surveillance, threats of libel,

and the secret financing of competing publications—to intimidate and silence the *Guardian* and its editor. In this sense, Trotter's actions, and Washington's heavy-handed efforts to squelch them, helped crystallize the growing disaffection with Washington into an organizational alternative. Trotter was able to forge a successful, if temporary, alliance with W. E. B. Du Bois and other proponents of racial integration, and he participated in founding the Niagara Movement in 1905.

Trotter's political independence and confrontational style went beyond the fight against Booker T. Washington, however. He clashed repeatedly with the Niagara Movement over questions of personality and leadership, and he resolved to wage the fight for racial justice under the auspices of his own virtually all-black organization, the National Equal Rights League, or NERL (originally founded as the Negro-American Political League in April 1908). While Trotter attended the founding convention of the NAACP in May 1909, he kept his distance from the white-dominated association; relations between NERL and the NAACP remained cool over the years, with occasional instances of cooperation to achieve common goals.

Trotter's zeal for direct action remained undiminished through the 1910s and 1920s. In a much-celebrated audience with Woodrow Wilson in 1914, Trotter challenged the president's segregationist policies; Wilson, viewing his adversary's candor as insolent and offensive, ordered the meeting to a close. The following year, Trotter led public protests against the showing of the film *The Birth of a Nation;* as a result of his renewed efforts in 1921, the movie was banned in Boston. In early 1919, denied a passport to travel to the Paris Peace Conference, he made his way to France disguised as a ship's cook, hoping to ensure that the Treaty of Versailles contained guarantees of racial equality; unable to influence the proceedings, he later testified against the treaty before the U.S. Congress. In 1926 Trotter again visited the White House to make the case against segregation in the federal government, this time before President Calvin Coolidge.

The *Guardian*, however, remained the primary outlet for Trotter's political convictions. Dependent largely on the contributions of black subscribers, the paper had often been on shaky financial ground. It not only absorbed Trotter's time and energy, it also drained his assets: Having abandoned the real estate business early on in order to devote himself entirely to the *Guardian*, he

See also
W.E.B. Du Bois
Marcus Garvey
NAACP

gradually sold off his property to keep the enterprise afloat. By 1920, with Trotter's standing as a national figure eclipsed by both the NAACP and the Garvey movement, publication of the *Guardian* became even more difficult to sustain.

Over the years, the impassioned advocacy of militant integrationism remained the hallmark of Trotter's *Guardian.* Back in 1908, Trotter, rather than supporting the black community's creation of its own hospital, had called for integration of Boston's medical training facilities. He had insisted that short-term benefits could not outweigh the "far more ultimate harm in causing the Jim Crow lines to be drawn about us." Trotter was driven by that philosophy throughout his life, even in the face of opposition from other African Americans.

On April 7, 1934, Trotter either fell or jumped to his death from the roof of his apartment building. Although he no longer enjoyed a mass following, he was remembered as one who had made enormous personal sacrifices for the cause of racial equality.

—TAMI J. FRIEDMAN

TRUTH, SOJOURNER

Sojourner Truth (c. 1797–November 26, 1883), abolitionist, suffragist, and spiritualist. Sojourner Truth was born Isabella Bomefree in Ulster County, N.Y., the second youngest of thirteen children born in slavery to Elizabeth (usually called Mau-Mau Bett) and James Bomefree. The other siblings were either sold or given away before her birth. The family was owned by Johannes Hardenbergh, a patroon and Revolutionary War patriot, the head of one of the most prominent Dutch families in late eighteenth-century New York.

Mau-Mau Bett was mystical and unlettered but imparted to her daughter strong faith, filial devotion, and a strong sense of individual integrity. Isabella Bomefree, whose first language was Dutch, was taken from her parents and sold to an English-speaking owner in 1808, who maltreated her because of her inability to understand English. Through her own defiance—what she later called her "talks with God"—and her father's intercession, a Dutch tavern keeper soon purchased her. Kindly treated but surrounded by the rough tavern culture and probably sexually abused, the girl prayed for a new master. In 1810 John I. Dumont of New Paltz, N.Y., purchased Isabella Bomefree for three hundred dollars.

Isabella remained Dumont's slave for eighteen years. Dumont boasted that Belle, as he called her, was "better to me than a man." She planted, plowed, cultivated, and harvested crops. She milked the farm animals, sewed, weaved, cooked, and cleaned house. But Mrs. Dumont despised and tormented her, possibly because Dumont fathered one of her children.

Isabella had two relationships with slave men. Bob, her first love, a man from a neighboring estate, was beaten senseless for "taking up" with her and was forced to take another woman. She later became associated with Thomas, with whom she remained until her freedom. Four of her five children survived to adulthood.

Although New York slavery ended for adults in 1827, Dumont promised Isabella her freedom a year earlier. When he refused to keep his promise, she fled with an infant child, guided by "the word of God" as she later related. She took refuge with Isaac Van Wagenen, who purchased her for the remainder of her time as a slave. She later adopted his family name.

Isabella Van Wagenen was profoundly shaped by a religious experience she underwent in 1827 at Pinkster time, the popular early summer African-Dutch slave holiday. As she recounted it, she forgot God's deliverance of his people from bondage and prepared to return to Dumont's farm for Pinkster: "I looked back in Egypt," she said, "and everything seemed so pleasant there." But she felt the mighty, luminous, and wrathful presence of an angry God blocking her path. Stalemated and momentarily blinded and suffocated under "God's breath," she claimed in her *Narrative,* Jesus mercifully intervened and proclaimed her salvation. This conversion enabled Isabella Van Wagenen to claim direct and special communication with Jesus and the Trinity for the remainder of her life, and she subsequently became involved with a number of highly spiritual religious groups.

A major test of faith followed Isabella Van Wagenen's conversion when she discovered that Dumont had illegally sold her son, Peter. Armed with spiritual assurance and a mother's rage, she scoured the countryside, gaining moral and financial support from prominent Dutch residents, antislavery Quakers, and local Methodists. She brought suit, and Peter was eventually returned from Alabama and freed.

In 1829 Isabella, now a Methodist, moved to New York City. She joined the African Methodist Episcopal Zion Church, where she discovered a brother and two sisters. She also began to attract attention for her extraordinary preaching, praying, and singing, though these talents were mainly employed among the Perfectionists (a sect of white radical mystics emerging from the Second Great Awakening who championed millennial doctrines, equated spiritual piety with morality, and social justice with true Christianity). As housekeeper for Perfectionist Elijah Pierson, Isabella was involved in "the Kingdom," a sect organized by the spiritual zealot, Robert Matthias. Among other practices he engaged in "spirit-matching," or wife swapping, with Ann Folger, wife of Pierson's business partner. Elijah Pierson's unexplained death brought public outcries of foul play. To conceal Ann Pierson's promiscuity, the Folgers suggested that there had been an erotic attachment between Matthias and Isabella Van Wagenen and that they murdered Pierson with poisoned blackberries. Challenging her accusers, Isabella Van Wagenen vowed to "crush them with the truth." Lack of evidence and prejudice about blacks testifying against whites led to dismissal of the case. Isabella Van Wagenen triumphed by successfully suing the Folgers for slander. Though chastened by this experience with religious extremism, the association with New York Perfectionists enhanced her biblical knowledge, oratorical skills, and commitment to reform.

Isabella Van Wagenen encouraged her beloved son Peter to take up seafaring to avoid the pitfalls of urban crime. In 1843 his vessel returned without him. Devastated by this loss, facing (at forty-six) a bleak future in domestic service, and influenced by the millennarian (known as the Millerite movement) ferment sweeping the Northeast at the time, she decided to radically change her life. She became an itinerant preacher and adopted the name Sojourner Truth because voices directed her to sojourn the countryside and speak God's truth. In the fall of 1843 she became ill and was taken to the Northampton utopian community in Florence, Mass., where black abolitionist David Ruggles nursed her at his water-cure establishment. Sojourner Truth impressed residents, who included a number of abolitionists, with her slavery accounts, scriptural interpretations, wit, and simple oral eloquence.

By 1846 Sojourner Truth had joined the antislavery circuit, traveling with Abby Kelly Foster, Frederick Douglass, William Lloyd Garrison, and British M.P. George Thompson. An electrifying public orator, she soon became one of the most popular speakers for the abolitionist cause. Her fame was heightened by the publication of her *Narrative* in 1850, related and transcribed by Olive Gilbert. With proceeds from its sale she purchased a Northampton home. In 1851, speaking before a National Women's Convention in Akron, Ohio, Sojourner Truth defended the physical and spiritual strength of women, in her famous "Ain't I a Woman?" speech. In 1853 Sojourner's antislavery, spiritualist, and temperance advocacy took her to the Midwest, where she settled among spiritualists in Harmonia, Mich.

"I cannot read a book," said Sojourner Truth, "but I can read the people." She dissected political and social issues through parables of everyday life. The Constitution, silent on black rights, had a "little weevil in it." She was known for her captivating one-line retorts. An Indiana audience threatened to torch the building if she spoke. Sojourner Truth replied, "Then I will speak to the ashes." In the late 1840s, grounded in faith that God and moral suasion would eradicate bondage, she challenged her despairing friend Douglass with "Frederick, is God dead?" In 1858, when a group of men questioned her gender, claiming she wasn't properly feminine in her demeanor, Sojourner Truth, a bold early feminist, exposed her bosom to the entire assembly, proclaiming that shame was not hers but theirs.

During the Civil War Sojourner Truth recruited and supported Michigan's black regiment, counseled freedwomen, set up employment operations for freedpeople willing to relocate, and initiated desegregation of streetcars in Washington, D.C. In 1864 she had an audience with Abraham Lincoln. Following the war, Sojourner Truth moved to Michigan, settling in Battle Creek, but remained active in numerous reform causes. She supported the Fifteenth Amendment and women's suffrage.

Disillusioned by the failure of Reconstruction, Sojourner Truth devoted her last years to the support of a black western homeland. In her later years, despite decades of interracial cooperation, she became skeptical of collaboration with whites and became an advocate of racial separation. She died in 1883 in Battle Creek, attended by the famous physician and breakfast cereal founder John Harvey Kellogg.

—MARGARET WASHINGTON

TUBMAN, HARRIET ROSS

Harriet Ross Tubman (c. 1820–March 10, 1913), abolitionist, nurse, and feminist. Harriet Ross, one of eleven children born to slaves Benjamin

Now the war begun.

SOJOURNER TRUTH
ON BEING SOLD TO
A HARSH MASTER,
*NARRATIVE OF
SOJOURNER TRUTH,*
1878

Ross and Harriet Green, was born about 1820 in Dorchester County in Maryland. Although she was known on the plantation as Harriet Ross, her family called her Araminta, or "Minty," a name given to her by her mother.

Like most slaves, Ross had no formal education and began work on the plantation as a child. When she was five years old, her master rented her out to a neighboring family, the Cooks, as a domestic servant. At age thirteen, Ross suffered permanent neurological damage after either her overseer or owner struck her in the head with a two-pound lead weight when she placed herself between her master and a fleeing slave. For the rest of her life, she experienced sudden blackouts.

In 1844, she married John Tubman, a free black who lived on a nearby plantation. Her husband's free status, however, did not transfer to Harriet upon their marriage. Between 1847 and 1849, after the death of her master, Tubman worked in the household of Anthony Thompson, a physician and preacher. Thompson was the legal guardian of Tubman's new master, who was still too young to operate the plantation. When the young master died, Tubman faced an uncertain future, and rumors circulated that Thompson would sell slaves out of the state.

In response, Tubman escaped from slavery in 1849, leaving behind her husband, who refused to

ESCAPED SLAVE

Harriet Tubman became the best-known leader of rescue expeditions on the Underground Railroad, bringing more than two hundred persons to freedom on at least fifteen trips to the South.
PRINTS AND PHOTOGRAPHS DIVISION, LIBRARY OF CONGRESS

accompany her. She settled in Philadelphia, where she found work as a scrubwoman. She returned to Maryland for her husband two years later, but John Tubman had remarried.

Tubman's successful escape to the free state of Pennsylvania, however, did not guarantee her safety, particularly after the passage of the Fugitive Slave Law of 1850, which facilitated southern slaveholding efforts to recover runaway slaves. Shortly after her escape from slavery, Tubman became involved in the Abolition movement, forming friendships with one of the black leaders of the Underground Railroad, William Still, and white abolitionist Thomas Garrett. While many of her abolitionist colleagues organized antislavery societies, wrote and spoke against slavery, and raised money for the cause, Tubman's abolitionist activities were more directly related to the actual freeing of slaves on the Underground Railroad. She worked as an agent on the railroad, assuming different disguises to assist runaways in obtaining food, shelter, clothing, cash, and transportation. Tubman might appear as a feeble, old woman or as a demented, impoverished man, and she was known for the rifle she carried on rescue missions, both for her own protection and to intimidate fugitives who might become fainthearted along the journey.

Tubman traveled to the South nineteen times to rescue approximately three hundred African-American men, women, and children from bondage. Her first rescue mission was to Baltimore, Md., in 1850 to help her sister and two children escape from slavery. Her noteriety as a leader of the Underground Railroad led some Maryland planters to offer a $40,000 bounty for her capture. Having relocated many runaways to Canada, Tubman herself settled in the village of St. Catharines, Canada West (now Ontario), in the early 1850s. She traveled to the South in 1851 to rescue her brother and his wife, and returned in 1857 to rescue her parents, with whom she resettled in Auburn, N.Y., shortly thereafter.

Tubman's involvement in the abolitionist movement placed her in contact with many progressive social leaders in the North, including John Brown, whom she met in 1858. She helped Brown plan his raid on Harpers Ferry, Va., in 1859, but illness prevented her from participating. Tubman's last trip to the South took place in 1860, after which she returned to Canada. In 1861, she moved back to the United States as the last of eleven southern states seceded from the Union.

When the Civil War broke out, Tubman served in the Union Army as a scout, spy, and nurse. In 1862, she went to Beaufort, S.C., where she nursed both white soldiers and black refugees from neighboring southern plantations. Tubman traveled from camp to camp in the coastal regions of South Carolina, Georgia, and Florida, administering her nursing skills wherever they were needed. Tubman also worked as a scout for the Union Army, traveling behind enemy lines to gather information and recruit slaves. She supported herself by selling chickens, eggs, root beer, and pies. After returning briefly to Beaufort, Tubman worked during the spring and summer of 1865 at a freedman's hospital in Fortress Monroe, Va.

After the war's end, Tubman eventually returned to Auburn to care for her elderly parents. Penniless, she helped support her family by farming. In 1869, Tubman married Nelson Davis, a Civil War veteran. That same year, she published *Scenes in the Life of Harriet Tubman,* written for her by Sarah H. Bradford and printed and circulated by Gerrit Smith and Wendall Phillips. Tubman received some royalties from the book, but she was less successful in her effort to obtain financial compensation for her war work. She agitated for nearly thirty years for $1,800 compensation for her service as a Civil War nurse and cook. In 1890, Congress finally awarded Tubman a monthly pension of $20 as a widow of a war veteran.

Tubman's activism continued on many fronts after the Civil War ended. She was an ardent supporter of women's suffrage and regularly attended women's rights meetings. To Tubman, racial liberation and women's rights were inextricably linked. Tubman formed close relationships with Susan B. Anthony and other feminists. She was a delegate to the first convention of the National Federation of Afro-American Women in 1896 (later called the National Association of Colored Women). The following year, the New England Women's Suffrage Association held a reception in Tubman's honor.

While living in Auburn, Tubman continued her work in the black community by taking in orphans and the elderly, often receiving assistance from wealthier neighbors. She helped establish schools for former slaves and wanted to establish a permanent home for poor and sick blacks. Tubman secured twenty-five acres in Auburn through a bank loan, but lacked the necessary funds to build on the land. In 1903, she deeded the land to the African Methodist Episcopal Zion Church, and five years later, the congregation built the Harriet Tubman Home for Indigent and Aged Negroes, which continued to operate for several

years after Tubman's death and was declared a National Historic Landmark in 1974.

Tubman died on March 10, 1913, at the age of ninety-three. Local Civil War veterans led the funeral march. The National Association of Colored Women later paid for the funeral and for the marble tombstone over Tubman's grave. A year after her death, black educator Booker T. Washington delivered a memorial address in celebration of Tubman's life and labors and on behalf of freedom. In 1978, the United States Postal Service issued the first stamp in its Black Heritage USA Series to honor Tubman.

Tubman, dubbed "the Moses of her people," had obtained legendary status in the African-American community within ten years of her escape to freedom. Perhaps more than any other figure of her time, Tubman personified resistance to slavery, and she became a symbol of courage and strength to African Americans—slave and free. The secrecy surrounding Tubman's activities on the Underground Railroad and her own reticence to talk about her role contributed to her mythic status. Heroic images of the rifle-carrying Tubman have persisted well into the twentieth century as Tubman has become the leading symbol of the Underground Railroad.

—LOUISE P. MAXWELL

TUSKEGEE SYPHILIS EXPERIMENT

In the early twentieth century, African Americans in the South faced numerous public health problems, including tuberculosis, hookworm, pellagra, and rickets; their death rates far exceeded those of whites. The public health problems of blacks had several causes—poverty, ignorance of proper health procedures, and inadequate medical care—all compounded by racism that systematically denied African Americans equal services. In an effort to alleviate these problems, in 1912 the federal government united all of its health-related activities under the Public Health Service (PHS). One of the primary concerns of the PHS was syphilis, a disease that was thought to have a moral as well as a physiological dimension. In 1918 a special Division of Venereal Diseases of PHS was created.

In the late 1920s, the PHS joined forces with the Rosenwald fund (a private philanthropic foundation based in Chicago) to develop a syphilis control program for blacks in the South.

The autobiographical narratives of former slaves comprise one of the most extensive and influential traditions in African-American literature.

PAGE 625

When I found I had crossed that line, I looked at my hands to see if I was the same person. There was such a glory over everything.

HARRIET TUBMAN
DESCRIPTION OF HER FIRST
ESCAPE TO THE NORTH,
QUOTED IN SARAH H.
BRADFORD, *HARRIET, THE
MOSES OF HER PEOPLE,* 1869

Most doctors assumed that blacks suffered a much higher infection rate than whites because blacks abandoned themselves to promiscuity. And once infected, the argument went, blacks remained infected because they were too poor and too ignorant to seek medical care. To test these theories, PHS officers selected communities in six different southern states, examined the local black populations to ascertain the incidence of syphilis, and offered free treatment to those who were infected. This pilot program had hardly gotten underway, however, when the stock market collapse in 1929 forced the Rosenwald Fund to terminate its support, and the PHS was left without sufficient funds to follow up its syphilis control work among blacks in the South.

Macon County, Ala., was the site of one of those original pilot programs. Its county seat, Tuskegee, was the home of the famed Tuskegee Institute. It was in and around Tuskegee that the PHS had discovered an infection rate of 35 percent among those tested, the highest incidence in the six communities studied. In fact, despite the presence of the Tuskegee Institute, which boasted a well-equipped hospital that might have provided low-cost health care to blacks in the region, Macon County was home not only to the worst poverty but the most sickly residents the PHS uncovered anywhere in the South. It was precisely this ready-made laboratory of human suffering that prompted the PHS to return to Macon County in 1932. Since they could not afford to treat syphilis, the PHS officers decided to document the damage to its victims by launching a study of the effects of untreated syphilis on black males. Many white Southerners (including physicians) believed that although practically all blacks had syphilis, it did not harm them as severely as it did whites. PHS officials knew that syphilis was a serious threat to the health of black Americans, and they intended to use the results of the study to pressure southern state legislatures into appropriating funds for syphilis control work among rural blacks.

Armed with these good motives, the PHS launched the Tuskegee Study in 1932. It involved approximately four hundred black males, who tested positive for the disease, and two hundred nonsyphilitic black males to serve as controls. In order to secure cooperation, the PHS told the local residents that they had returned to Macon County to treat people who were ill. The PHS did not inform them that they had syphilis. Instead, the men were told they had "bad blood," a catchall phrase rural blacks used to describe a host of ailments.

While the PHS had not intended to treat the men, state health officials demanded, as the price of their cooperation, that the men be given at least enough medication to render them noninfectious. Consequently, all of the men received a little treatment. No one worried much about the glaring contradiction of offering treatment in a study of untreated syphilis because the men had not received enough treatment to cure them. Thus, the experiment was scientifically flawed from the outset.

Although the original plan called for a one-year experiment, the Tuskegee Study continued until 1972 partly because many of the health officers became fascinated by the scientific potential of a long-range study of syphilis. No doubt others rationalized the study by telling themselves that the men were too poor to afford proper treatment, or that too much time had passed for treatment to be of any benefit. The health officials, in some cases, may have seen the men as clinical material rather than human beings.

At any rate, as a result of the Tuskegee Study approximately one hundred black men died of untreated syphilis, scores went blind or insane, and still others endured lives of chronic ill health from syphilis-related complications. Throughout this suffering, the PHS made no effort to treat the men and on several occasions took steps to prevent them from getting treatment on their own. As a result, the men did not receive penicillin when it became widely available after World War II.

During those same four decades, civil protests raised America's concern for the rights of black people, and the ethical standards of the medical profession regarding the treatment of nonwhite patients changed dramatically. These changes had no impact, however, on the Tuskegee Study. PHS officials published no fewer than 13 scientific papers on the experiment (several of which appeared in the nation's leading medical journals), and the PHS routinely presented sessions on it at medical conventions. The Tuskegee Study ended in 1972 because a whistle-blower in the PHS, Peter Buxtun, leaked the story to the press. At first health officials tried to defend their actions, but public outrage quickly silenced them, and they agreed to end the experiment. As part of an out-of-court settlement, the survivors were finally treated for syphilis. In addition, the men, and the families of the deceased, received small cash payments.

See also
Education

The forty-year deathwatch had finally ended, but its legacy can still be felt. In the wake of its hearings, Congress enacted new legislation to protect the subjects of human experiments. The Tuskegee Study left behind a host of unanswered questions about the social and racial attitudes of the medical establishment in the United States. It served as a cruel reminder of how class distinctions and racism could negate ethical and scientific standards.

—JAMES H. JONES

See also
Booker T. Washington

UNCLE TOM'S CABIN

Harriet Beecher Stowe's fiery abolitionist novel was published in 1852. Stowe came from a prominent family of public figures that included her father, clergyman Lyman Beecher; her sister, author Catharine Beecher; and her brother, clergyman Henry Ward Beecher. The wife of clergyman Calvin Stowe, Harriet was outraged by the Compromise of 1850, the group of legislative measures that effected a compromise between North and South on the increasingly divisive issue of slavery. The most notorious article of the compromise was the provision for the legal return to their owners of escaped slaves (the Fugitive Slave Law, enacted in 1851), which effectively legitimized the rule of slavery in the North and South. This measure, as well as the passionate advocacy of the compromise by trusted Vermont Sen. Daniel Webster, particularly infuriated Stowe and other New England intellectuals such as Ralph Waldo Emerson and John Greenleaf Whittier (whose poem "Ichabod" excoriates Webster). Stowe's first literary response to the legislation was a story called "The Freeman's Dream" (1850), about the divine retribution that visits a man who refuses to aid a group of slaves being led to market in a coffle (i.e., fastened together to form a train). Her literary career thus launched, Stowe experienced a vision, she later said, of an old black male slave being whipped to death. This image sparked the composition of *Uncle Tom's Cabin; or, Life Among the Lowly,* which was serialized in the antislavery newspaper *National Era* in 1851–1852 and published in book form on March 20, 1852.

Uncle Tom's Cabin so swarms with character, action, voice, and social detail that it defies adequate synopsis. Its multiple, intertwining plots begin with the imminent sale of the beautiful slave Eliza Harris. Her owner, Arthur Shelby, is in debt and must sell his slaves for money. Hearing of this, Eliza, with her small son and slave husband, George Harris, decides to escape, and before going informs the other slaves of Mr. Shelby's predicament. Uncle Tom, a slave on the Shelby plantation, bids Eliza to go but refuses to join her, preferring to sacrifice himself in sale for the possible preservation of the other slaves. Eliza's vividly ren-

dered escape with her son Harry across the ice floes of the Ohio River allows Stowe to elicit sympathy for the slaves and hatred for the slave traders, even though relatively kindly masters such as Shelby are spared neither the moral taint of slavery nor Stowe's disdain. Eliza's husband George escapes separately in disguise, while Eliza is sheltered by Ohio Quakers; George and Eliza reunite at the Quaker settlement. There they fight off the slave traders who have pursued them, whereupon George makes an impassioned defense of his right to freedom. Soon, George, Eliza, and Harry escape to Canada. Meanwhile Uncle Tom is indeed sold down the river, and upon the boat of transport he meets Evangeline (Little Eva) St.

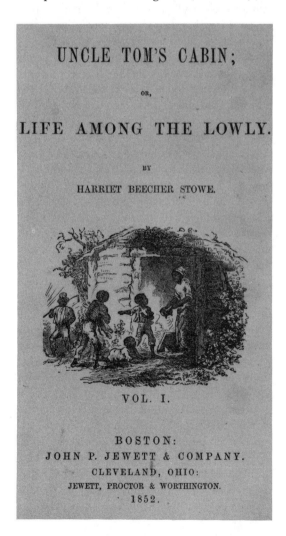

UNCLE TOM'S CABIN

In her novel, Harriet Beecher Stowe combined a skilled handling of conventions of nineteenth-century sentimental fiction with her abolitionist convictions to produce a masterpiece of political protest literature.
PRINTS AND PHOTOGRAPHS DIVISION, LIBRARY OF CONGRESS

Clare and her father, a New Orleans slaveowner, who buys Tom at Little Eva's behest. St. Clare is gentle, passive, but sharply reflective on the social system of slavery; he airs himself on a variety of subjects in conversation with the Vermonter Aunt Ophelia, who brings to the plantation her aid (St. Claire's wife, Marie, is perennially languid and abed) and her liberal northern perspective (some of the hypocrisies of which—for instance, advocating freedom yet feeling repulsed by slaves like Topsy—Stowe tellingly punctures). St. Clare is subject to Tom's religious influence, and under it, as well as that of the death of Little Eva, who suffers from her knowledge of slavery's oppression, decides to reform his life and to set Tom free. Before he is able to do this, however, St. Clare is killed attempting to mediate a bar fight, and once again, Tom is sold. He is purchased by Simon Legree, another Vermonter by origin, who abuses Uncle Tom the more the slave passively resists. Legree is at the same time haunted by Cassy, a slave woman on his plantation who exploits Legree's guilt over his abandonment of his mother. Cassy and another slave, Emmeline, pretend to escape but stay in an attic and drive Legree to distraction impersonating the ghosts that he believes dwell there. Legree ultimately kills Uncle Tom as young George Shelby, the son of Tom's former master, arrives; George superintends the burial of Tom and knocks Legree to the ground. He also helps Cassy and Emmeline escape, and in doing so learns that Cassy is in fact Eliza's mother. At the novel's end, everyone reunites in Canada, where they decide to voyage to Africa and establish a black Christian homeland in Liberia. George Shelby returns to Kentucky and sets all the Shelby slaves free; refusing to leave, the slaves stay to work as free people. The novel concludes with the kind of hectoring condemnations of slavery that lace the rest of the text.

So told, the novel is clearly rife with contradictions that both enrich and hobble it. For one thing the novel is misnamed, since we only see Uncle Tom's cabin briefly and most of the novel recounts Tom's painful longing to return to his family from whom he has been sold. This tale of the horrors of slavery is animated by a passion for and belief in the redemptive capacities of women. It presents a protofeminist orientation that vivifies the stories of slave and disempowered white women, and advances a feminized ethic of the antislavery struggle—most notably in the piously submissive Tom himself—even as it somewhat exploitatively uses the predicament of slaves to meditate on the oppression of women. What is more, this quite rad-

ical novel by the standards of 1852, depends on black stereotypes and seems to accept a long-discredited notion of innate racial traits (however positively rendered); thus, the blacker Uncle Tom submits while the lighter-skinned George Harris asserts the fighting spirit of his partial Anglo-Saxon blood. Finally, this story, so often accused of revolutionary intent by most of the South, is not only as hard on the North's apologists for slavery as it is on the South, it is also a fundamentally Christian novel whose social prescriptions revolve around transformations of individual feeling rather than collective struggle.

Contradictory or not, these sentimental, women-centered, radical Christian emphases achieved for *Uncle Tom's Cabin* an immediate and sustained success and influence. It sold 300,000 copies in its first year alone and inspired novelistic rebuttals and documentary defenses (one of them, *The Key to Uncle Tom's Cabin,* [1853], by Stowe herself), stage dramatizations and minstrel-show parodies, commercial take-offs, and popular-cultural iconography. The novel made national struggles over slavery—a dangerous social issue subject to persistent denial—henceforth an acknowledged fact of everyday life. Yet it was probably *Uncle Tom's Cabin*'s long stage presence in the form of the "Tom show" that was ultimately responsible for the enormity of its influence. As popularly written as the novel was, for every person who read it, very many more saw the stage play. The competing ideological inflections of *Uncle Tom*'s many dramatizations amplified the novel's political impact. With nonexistent copyright laws for stage adaptations, and Stowe declining participation in or permission for an authorized stage version, the field was open to the lowest bidder. In January 1852, attending to the novel's serialization, an anti-Tom play called *Uncle Tom's Cabin as It Is; The Southern Uncle Tom* appeared at the Baltimore Museum; in late August 1852, C. W. Taylor's crude and foreshortened version of the recently published novel ran briefly at New York's National Theatre—inspiring *New York Herald* editor James Gordon Bennett to denounce the advent of abolitionist drama. This pattern of dramatic conflict—a kind of prelude to the Civil War on stage—characterized productions of *Uncle Tom's Cabin* not only in the 1850s, but well into the 1870s.

The chief competing productions in the 1850s were those of George Aiken and H. J. Conway. Aiken's relatively faithful version of *Uncle Tom* gestated for a year in Troy, N.Y., first recounting only Little Eva's story, then only Uncle Tom's,

See also
Fugitive Slave Law

then combining the two into the first full-length, night-long theatrical production in history. This version, which vents many of Stowe's criticisms of slavery, opened at New York's National Theatre on July 18, 1853. Conway's much more ambiguous rendition took shape in Boston, and takes away with minstrel parody or outright racism that it occasionally renders with accuracy to Stowe's novel. P. T. Barnum heard of Conway's Compromise politics and the impressive Boston run of the show and booked this version for his American Museum beginning November 7, 1853. These adaptations, to be sure, appeared amid a dizzying array of offshoots, thefts, reworkings, rebuttals, and parodies, including (in New York alone) a "magic lantern" version (tableaux from the play) at New York's Franklin Museum; a Bowery Theatre version starring blackface originator T. D. Rice (not so outrageous as it appears, since even the "respectable" adaptations featured blackface performers in black roles); blackface lampoons such as Charles White's *Uncle Dad's Cabin* (1855), and Christy and Wood's Minstrels' *Uncle Tom's Cabin, or, Hearts and Homes* (1854); Irish parodies such as *Uncle Pat's Cabin* (by H. J. Conway) and *Uncle Mike's Cabin* (1853); and scores of others. But all this could not obscure the great theatrical rivalry that existed between the Aiken and Conway versions, encompassing everything from journalistic debate to street fights and making inescapably evident—in fact institutionalizing—the sectional conflicts that would soon eventuate in civil war. Perhaps this accounts for what Lincoln is supposed to have said upon meeting Stowe: "So this is the little lady who made this great war." Even after the war, Tom shows (which continued to be produced well into the twentieth century) and films (the first of many film versions of *Uncle Tom's Cabin* appeared in 1903) effortlessly invoked ongoing American political debate and upheavals over race and the legacy of slavery. While the novel's aesthetic and politics now seem obsolete, *Uncle Tom's Cabin* had a mighty and often radical cultural and social impact for over half a century.

—ERIC LOTT

UNDERGROUND RAILROAD

Few aspects of the antislavery movement have been more shrouded in myth and misunderstanding than the Underground Railroad. Although white abolitionists, including Quakers, played an important role in helping to free thousands of African Americans, the degree of their involvement has been overemphasized. In the years before the Civil War, the Underground Railroad was primarily run, maintained, and funded by African Americans. Black working-class men and women collected the bulk of money, food, and clothing, and provided the shelter and transportation for the fugitives. Wealthier, better educated blacks such as Pennsylvania's Robert Purvis and William Whipper arranged for legal assistance and offered leadership, financial support, and indispensable contacts among sympathetic and influential white political leaders. Philadelphia's William Still, who ran the city's vigilance committee and later recorded the stories of many of the people he helped, managed the pivotal point in the North's most successful underground system. He personally assisted thousands of escaping slaves and helped settle them in northern African-American communities or in Canada. As one white abolitionist leader admitted about the Underground Railroad in 1837, "Such matters are almost uniformly managed by the colored people."

Although the origins of the term are uncertain, by 1850 both those who participated in the Underground Railroad and those who sought to destroy it freely employed metaphors from the railroad business to describe its activities. More important, Northerners and Southerners understood both its symbolic and its real meanings. The numbers of African Americans who fled or were smuggled out of the South were never large enough to threaten the institutional stability of slavery. Yet the number actually freed was, in a way, less important than what such activities said about the institution of slavery and the true character of southern slaves. Apologists for slavery described blacks as inferior, incapable of living in freedom, and content in their bondage. Those who escaped from the South, and the free African Americans who assisted them, undermined slavery by irrefutably disproving its racist ideology.

Most slaves who reached freedom in the North initiated their own escapes. After their initial flight, however, fugitives needed guidance and assistance to keep their hard-won liberty. Many did not have to travel far before finding help. Although the black underground's effectiveness varied over time and place, there was an astonishingly large number of semiautonomous networks that operated across the North and upper South. They were best organized in Ohio, Pennsylvania, and New York, but surprisingly efficient net-

Caged birds accept each other but flight is what they long for.

TENNESSEE WILLIAMS
CAMINO REAL, 1953

See also
Slavery

*Thenceforward, and
forever free.*

ABRAHAM LINCOLN
PRELIMINARY EMANCIPATION
PROCLAMATION,
NOV. 22, 1862

works, often centered in local black churches, existed in most northern and border states, and even in Virginia. At hundreds of locations along the Ohio River, where many former slaves lived, fugitives encountered networks of black underground laborers who offered sanctuary and passed them progressively northward to other black communities. African-American settlements from New Jersey to Missouri served as asylums for fugitive slaves and provided contacts along well-established routes to Michigan, Ohio, Pennsylvania, and New York for easy transit to Canada.

Urban vigilance committees served as the hub for most of the black undergrounds. Along the East Coast, where the black underground was most effective, the Philadelphia and New York vigilance committees operated as central distribution points for many underground routes. Committee leaders such as William Still and David Ruggles directed fugitives to smaller black "stations," such as that of Stephen A. Myers in Albany, N.Y., who in turn provided transportation direct to Canada or further west to Syracuse. Vigilance committees also warned local blacks of kidnapping rings, and members hazarded their lives in searching vessels for illegal slaves. Such black leaders also maintained contacts among influential whites who covertly warned of the movement of slave owners and federal marshals. Where formal committees did not exist, ad hoc ones functioned, supplied with information from, for example, black clerks who worked in hotels frequented by slavecatchers. Black leaders such as William Still, who helped finance the famous exploits of Harriet Tubman, employed the latest technology to facilitate their work; during the 1850s these committees regularly used the telegraph to communicate with far-flung "stations."

The most daring and best-organized "station" toiled in the very shadow of the U.S. Capitol. Run by free blacks from Washington, D.C., and Baltimore, this underground network rescued slaves from plantations in Maryland and Virginia, supplied them with free papers, and sent them north by a variety of land and water routes. These free blacks used their good standing among whites—as craftsmen, porters, and federal marshals' assistants—to facilitate their work. One free black used his painting business as a cover to visit plantations and arrange escapes; another employed his carriage service to transport slaves; others sustained the charges of slave owners and used their positions as plantation preachers and exhorters to pass escape plans to their "parishioners." When stealth and secrecy failed, heroic members of the

Washington, D.C., "station" successfully attacked a slave pen to free some of its captives.

Members of this eastern network occasionally worked with white abolitionists such as Charles T. Torrey and the Quaker leader Thomas Garrett. But they primarily worked with other blacks, sending fugitives to Philadelphia where, either singly or in large groups, the escapees were directed to New York City and dispersed along many routes reaching into New England and Canada, or toward western New York. This network was temporarily disrupted during the 1840s, when race riots in northern cities and escalated southern surveillance forced the removal of Washington's most active agents. Nevertheless, by one estimate, between 1830 and 1860 over 9,000 fugitive slaves passed through Philadelphia alone on their way to freedom.

The Underground Railroad never freed as many slaves as its most vocal supporters claimed, and far fewer whites helped than the mythology suggests. Undeniably, however, the existence and history of the system reflect the African-American quest for freedom and equality.

—DONALD YACOVONE

UNIVERSAL NEGRO IMPROVEMENT ASSOCIATION

The Universal Negro Improvement Association (UNIA), with its motto "One God, One Aim, One Destiny" stands as one of the most important political and social organizations in African American history. It was founded by Marcus Garvey in July 1914, in Kingston, Jamaica, West Indies.

At the time of its establishment, its full name was the Universal Negro Improvement and Conservation Association and African Communities (Imperial) League (ACL). Originally organized as a mutual benefit and reform association dedicated to racial uplift, the UNIA and ACL migrated with Garvey to the United States in 1916. Incorporated in New York in 1918, the UNIA gradually began to give voice to the rising mood of New Negro radicalism that emerged within the African-American population following the signing of the Armistice ending World War I in November 1918.

The UNIA experienced a sudden, massive expansion of membership beginning in the spring of

See also
Harriet Tubman

1919, spearheaded by the spectacular success of the stock-selling promotion of the Black Star Line, Inc. (BSL). Together with the Negro Factories Corporation and other commercial endeavors, all of which were constituted under the ACL, the BSL represented the heart of the economic program of the movement.

Outfitted with its own flag, national anthem, Universal African Legion and other uniformed ranks, official organ (*The Negro World*), African repatriation and resettlement scheme in Liberia, constitution, and laws, the UNIA attempted to function as a sort of provisional government of Africa. The result was that by 1920–1921, the UNIA became the dominant voice advocating black self-determination, under its irredentist program of African Redemption. Accompanied by spectacular parades, annual month-long conventions were held at Liberty Hall in Harlem in New York City between 1920 and 1924, at all of which Garvey presided. The document with the greatest lasting significance to emerge was the "Declaration of the Rights of the Negro Peoples of the World," passed at the first UNIA convention in August 1920.

Nearly a thousand local divisions and chapters of the UNIA were established by the mid-twenties in the United States, Canada, the West Indies, Central and South America, Africa, and the United Kingdom, causing the influence of the UNIA to be felt wherever peoples of African descent lived. With actual membership running into the hundreds of thousands, if not millions, the UNIA is reputed to have been the largest political organization in African-American history.

After Garvey's conviction on charges of mail fraud in 1923, following the ill-fated collapse of the Black Star Line, and his incarceration in the Atlanta Federal Penitentiary starting in 1925, membership in the UNIA declined rapidly. When President Calvin Coolidge commuted Garvey's sentence and he was deported from the United States in 1927, the organization found itself racked by increasing factionalization.

A new UNIA and ACL of the World was incorporated by Garvey in Jamaica at the August 1929 convention, competing with the New York-based UNIA parent body headed at the time by Fred A. Toote, who was succeeded by Lionel Francis in 1931. With the worldwide economic collapse following the 1929 stockmarket crash, however, the UNIA went into further decline, as members' resources dwindled, making it difficult to support two separate wings of the movement. Demoralization also set in as a result of the increasing fragmentation of the UNIA leadership. Garvey was able to retain the loyalty of only a part of the movement, notably the Garvey Club and the Tiger division of the New York UNIA.

When Garvey moved his headquarters in 1935 from Jamaica to London, he tried once again to revive the movement, but soon found himself confronting considerable opposition by members who were in the forefront of the pro-Ethiopian support campaign during the Italo-Ethiopian War of 1935. These members repudiated the criticisms leveled by Garvey against Ethiopia's Emperor Haile Selassie I, following invasion by Mussolini and the Fascist Italian Army.

After Garvey's death in 1940, loyalists moved the headquarters of the organization to Cleveland, Ohio, under the leadership of the new president general, James Stewart, who thereafter relocated with it to Liberia. By the 1940s and '50s, the UNIA was a mere shadow of its former strength, but it still continues to function today.

—ROBERT A. HILL

See also
NAACP

V

VAUGHAN, SARAH

Sarah Vaughan (March 29, 1924–April 3, 1990), jazz singer. Nicknamed "Sassy" and "the Divine One," Sarah Vaughan is considered one of America's greatest vocalists and part of the triumvirate of women jazz singers that includes Ella Fitzgerald and Billie Holiday. A unique stylist, she possessed vocal capabilities—lush tones, perfect pitch, and a range exceeding three octaves—that were matched by her adventurous, sometimes radical sense of improvisation. Born in Newark, N.J., she began singing and playing organ in the Mount Zion Baptist Church when she was twelve.

In October 1942, she sang "Body and Soul" to win an amateur-night contest at Harlem's Apollo Theater. Billy Eckstine, the singer for Earl "Fatha" Hines's big band, happened to hear her and was so impressed that he persuaded Hines to hire Vaughan as a second pianist and singer in early 1943. Later that year, when Eckstine left Hines to organize his own big band, she went with him. In his group, one of the incubators of bebop jazz, Vaughan was influenced by Eckstine's vibrato-laced baritone, and by the innovations of such fellow musicians as Dizzy Gillespie and Charlie Parker. Besides inspiring her to forge a personal style, they instilled in her a lifelong desire to improvise. ("It was just like going to school," she said.)

Vaughan made her first records for the Continental label on New Year's Eve 1944, and began working as a solo act the following year at New York's Cafe Society. At the club she met trumpeter George Treadwell, who became her manager and the first of her four husbands. Treadwell promoted Vaughan and helped create her glamorous image. Following hits on Musicraft (including "It's Magic" and "If They Could See Me Now") and Columbia ("Black Coffee"), her success was assured. From 1947 through 1952, she was voted top female vocalist in polls in *Down Beat* and *Metronome* jazz magazines.

Throughout the 1950s, Vaughan recorded pop material for Mercury records, including such hits as "Make Yourself Comfortable" and "Broken-Hearted Melody" and songbooks (like those made by Ella Fitzgerald) of classic American songs by George Gershwin and Irving Berlin; she also recorded jazz sessions on the EmArcy label (Mercury's jazz label) with trumpeter Clifford Brown, the Count Basie Orchestra, and other jazz musicians. By the mid-1960s, frustrated by the tactics of record companies trying to sustain her commercially, Vaughan took a five-year hiatus from recording. By the 1970s, her voice had become darker and richer.

Vaughan was noted for a style in which she treated her voice like a jazz instrument rather than as a conduit for the lyrics. A contralto, she sang

SARAH VAUGHAN

The accomplished vocalist was known for her improvisational skills.

PHOTOGRAPHS AND PRINTS DIVISION, SCHOMBURG CENTER FOR RESEARCH IN BLACK CULTURE, THE NEW YORK PUBLIC LIBRARY, ASTOR, LENOX AND TILDEN FOUNDATIONS

wide leaps easily, improvised sometimes subtle, sometimes dramatic melodic and rhythmic lines, and made full use of timbral expressiveness—from clear tones to bluesy growls with vibrato. By the end of her career, she had performed in more than sixty countries, in small boîtes and in football stadiums, with jazz trios as well as symphony orchestras. Her signature songs, featured at almost all of her shows, included "Misty," "Tenderly," and "Send In the Clowns." She died of cancer in 1990, survived by one daughter.

—BUD KLIMENT

VOODOO

Voodoo, also spelled Vodou (following the official Haitian Creole orthography) or vodoun, refers to traditional religious practices in Haiti and in Haitian-American communities such as the sizable ones in New York City and Miami. New Orleans has the oldest Haitian immigrant community; it dates from the eighteenth century. In New Orleans priests and priestesses are sometimes called "voodoos," and throughout the southern United States the term is also used as a verb, to "voodoo" someone, meaning to bewitch or punish by magical means. More frequently "voodoo," or "hoodoo"—as well as "conjure," "rootwork," and "witchcraft"—is a term used to refer to a diverse collection of traditional spiritual practices among descendants of African slaves in the United States.

Haiti, a small, mountainous, and impoverished West Indian country, was a French slave colony and a major sugar producer during the eighteenth century. The strongest African influences on Haitian vodou came from the Fon and Mahi peoples of old Dahomey (now the Republic of Benin); the Yoruba peoples, mostly in Nigeria; and the Kongo peoples of Angola and Zaire. The term *vodun* is West African, probably Ewe, in origin and came to the Western Hemisphere with Dahomean slaves. Today, "vodun" is the most common Fon term for a traditional spirit or deity.

Haitian Vodou is said to have played a key role in the only successful slave revolution in the history of trans-Atlantic slavery, the plotters being bound to one another by a blood oath taken during a Vodou ceremony. The ceremony, conducted by the legendary priest Makandal, took place in Bois Cayman in northern Haiti. It is also claimed that word of the uprising spread via Vodou talking drums, and Vodou charms gave strength and courage to the rebels.

Haiti declared its independence in 1804, when the United States and much of Europe still held slaves. For approximately fifty years the Catholic church refused to send priests to Haiti, and for nearly a century the struggling black republic was economically isolated from the larger world. Political concerns played a major role in shaping the negative image of Haitian Vodou in the West. Vodou has been caricatured as a religion obsessed with sex, blood, death, and evil. The reality of Haitian Vodou, a religion that blends African traditions with Catholicism, is strikingly different from the stereotypes.

Following independence, large numbers of Haitians acquired small plots of land and became subsistence farmers. This agricultural base distinguishes Vodou from other New World African religions. Central to Vodou are three loyalties: to land (even urban practitioners return to conduct ceremonies on ancestral land), to family (including the dead), and to the Vodou spirits. Most Haitians do not call their religion Vodou, a word that more precisely refers to one style of drumming and dancing. Haitians prefer a verbal form. "Li sevi lwa-yo," they say, he (or she) serves the spirits. Most spirits have two names, a Catholic saint's name and an African name. Daily acts of devotion include lighting candles and pouring libations. Devotees wear a favored spirit's color and observe food and behavior prohibitions the spirits request. When there are special problems, they make pilgrimages to Catholic shrines and churches and undertake other trials. Most important, they stage elaborate ceremonies that include singing, drumming, dancing, and sumptuous meals, the most prestigious of which necessitate killing an animal. Possession, central in Vodou, provides direct communication with the *lwa*, or spirits. A devotee who becomes a "horse" of one of the spirits turns over body and voice to that lwa. The spirit can then sing and dance with the faithful, bless them, chastise them, and give advice. In Vodou persons are defined by webs of relationship with family, friends, ancestors, and spirits. The central work of Vodou ritual, whether performed in a community setting or one-on-one, is enhancing and healing relationships. Gifts of praise, food, song and dance are necessary to sustain spirits and ancestors and to enable them to reciprocate by providing wisdom and protection to the living.

The large Haitian immigrant communities that have grown up in the United States over the last forty years are thriving centers for Vodou practice. Hundreds of Vodou healers serve thousands of clients who are taxi drivers, restaurant workers, and nurse's aides. Most of the rituals performed in Haiti are now also staged, albeit in truncated form, in living rooms and basements in New York and Miami. Vodou "families" provide struggling immigrants with connections to Haitian roots and an alternative to American individualism.

Voodoo in New Orleans is more distant from its Haitian roots. Scholars believe there were three generations of women called Marie Laveau who worked as spiritual counselors in New Orleans. The first was a slave brought from Haiti to Louisiana during the time of the slave revolution. The most famous Marie Laveau, the "voodoo queen of New Orleans," born in 1827, was the granddaughter of this slave woman. Her religion was a distillation of Haitian Vodou. She kept a large snake on her altar (a representative of the spirit Danbala Wedo), went into possession while dancing in Congo Square, presided over an elaborate annual ceremony on the banks of Lake Pontchartrain on St. John's Eve (June 24), and above all, worked with individual clients as a spiritual adviser, healer, and supplier of charms, or gris-gris. Contemporary New Orleans voodoo is largely limited to these last activities.

Hoodoo, or voodoo as practiced throughout the American South, is similarly limited to discrete client/practitioner interactions. This type of voodoo is not a child of Haiti but the legacy of Dahomean and Kongo persons among North American slaves. As with Haitian Vodou, engagement with hoodoo has typically worked as a supplement to Christianity, most likely because hoodoo addresses issues Christianity ignores—issues of spiritual protection, romantic love, and luck. Harry M. Hyatt said it well: "To catch a spirit or to protect your spirit against the catching or to release your caught spirit—this is the complete theory and practice of hoodoo." The spiritual powers used in voodoo or hoodoo are morally neutral (e.g., souls of persons not properly buried) and can therefore be used constructively or destructively. Yet clear moral distinctions in how they are used are not always easy to make.

In hoodoo the illness in one person may be traced to an emotion in another, jealousy being the most destructive. In such a case, attacking the jealous person may be the only way to a cure. A related dynamic emerges in love magic, a very common type of healing that inevitably tries to control another's will. Zora Neale Hurston collected this cure for a restless husband: "Take sugar, cinnamon and mix together: Write name of a husband and wife nine times. Roll paper . . . and put in a bottle of holy water with sugar and honey. Lay it under the back step." There have been root doctors— conjure men and women—who have used their powers unethically and maliciously, but hoodoo's fear-provoking reputation is unmerited. Most hoodoo or voodoo is of the type described in Hurston's example.

—KAREN MCCARTHY BROWN

V

VOODOO

See also
Zora Neale Hurston

WALCOTT, DEREK ALTON

Derek Alton Walcott (January 23, 1930–), poet, playwright, and essayist. The son of Warwick Walcott, a civil servant and skilled painter in watercolor who wrote verse, and Alix Walcott, a school teacher who took part in amateur theater, Derek Walcott was born along with a twin brother in Castries, Saint Lucia, a small island in the Lesser Antilles of the West Indies. He grew up in a house he describes as haunted by the absence of a father who had died quite young, because all around the drawing room were his father's watercolors. His beginnings as an artist, he regards, therefore, as a natural and direct inheritance: "I feel that I have continued where my father left off." After completing St. Mary's College in his native Saint Lucia, he continued his education at the University of the West Indies in Kingston, Jamaica.

His literary career began in 1948 with his first book of verse, *25 Poems* (1948), followed not long thereafter by *Epitaph for the Young, XII Cantos* (1949), and *Poems* (1951), all privately published in the Caribbean. The decade of the 1950s, however, marked the emergence of his reputation as a playwright-director in Trinidad. His first theater piece, *Henri Cristophe* (1950), a historical play about the tyrant-liberator of Haiti, was followed by a series of well-received folk-dramas in verse. *The Sea at Dauphin* (1954), *Ione* (1957), and *Ti-Jean and His Brothers* (1958) are usually cited among the most noteworthy, along with his most celebrated dramatic work, *Dream on Monkey Mountain*, awarded an Obie, which he began in the late 1950s but did not produce until 1967 in Toronto. After a brief stay in the United States as a Rockefeller Fellow, Walcott returned to Trinidad in 1959 to become founding director of the Trinidad Theatre Workshop. He continues to work as a dramatist, and he is still more likely to be identified by a West Indian audience as a playwright.

Walcott's international debut as a poet came with *In a Green Night: Poems 1948–1960* (1962), followed shortly thereafter by *Selected Poems* (1964), established the qualities usually identified with his verse: virtuosity in traditional, particularly European literary forms; enthusiasm for allegory and classical allusion for which he is both praised and criticized; and the struggle within himself over the cruel history and layered cultural legacy of Africa and Europe reflected in the Caribbean landscape which some critics have interpreted as the divided consciousness of a Caribbean ex-colonial in the twilight of empire. A prolific quarter-century of work has been shaped by recurrent patterns of departure, wandering, and return, in his life as well as in his poetry, and a powerful preoccupation with the visual imagery of the sea, beginning with *Castaway and Other Poems* (1965), in which he establishes an imaginative topography (e.g., of "seas and coasts as white pages"), and a repertory of myths, themes, and motifs (e.g., of "words like migrating birds") for the titular exile, a repertory that recurs in later volumes.

In *The Gulf and Other Poems* (1969), reprinted with *Castaway and Other Poems* in a single volume as *The Gulf* (1970) in the United States, he sounds an ever more personal note as he considers the Caribbean from the alienating perspective of the political turbulence of the late 1960s in the southern and Gulf states of the United States. In *Another Life* (1973), his book-length self-portrait both as a young man and at forty-one, he contemplates the suicide of his mentor and alter-ego with whom he discovered the promise, and the disappointment, of their lives dedicated to art. In *Seagrapes* (1976) he identifies the Caribbean wanderer as caught up in the same ancient and unresolved dilemmas as the exiles Adam and Odysseus, whose pain the poems of a West Indian artist, like the language of the Old Testament and the Greek and Latin classics, can console but never cure.

At his most eloquent in *The Star-Apple Kingdom* (1979), Walcott fingers the rosary of the Antilles in the title poem in order to expose the inhumanity and corruption belied by the gilt-framed Caribbean pastoral of the colonialist's star-apple kingdom, and in the volume's other verse narrative, "The Schooner Flight," he finds a powerful voice in the West Indian vernacular of

See also

Literature

*Phillis Wheatley
was the first
African-American to
publish a book, the
first woman writer
whose publication
was nurtured by a
community of
women, and the
first American
woman author who
tried to earn a
living by writing.*

PAGE 733

the common man endowed with "no weapon but poetry and the lances of palms of the sea's shiny shields." In *The Fortunate Traveler* (1981) he sounds repeated and painful notes of exhaustion, isolation, and disappointment of the peripatetic poet in exile and at home, perhaps most sharply in the satirical mode of the *kaiso* vernacular of "The Spoiler Returns."

In *Midsummer* (1984), published in his fifty-fourth year, he probes the situation of the poet as prodigal *nel mezzo del camin* of exile in fifty-four untitled stanzas of elegiac meter. In *The Arkansas Testament* (1987), divided into sections "Here" and "Elsewhere" recalling the divisions of "North" and "South" of *The Fortunate Traveler,* he succumbs once again to pangs of art's estrangement. However, in *Omeros* (1990), his overlay of his problematic but richly figured Caribbean environment with Homer's transformative Mediterranean domain in his most ambitious verse narrative yet, he weaves together the myths, themes, motifs, and imaginary geography of a prolific career to attempt a consummation and reconciliation of the psychic divisions and the spiritual and moral wounds of history and exile in the visionary and restorative middle passage of Achilles, the West Indian fisherman, to the ancestral slave coast of Africa and back to the island, once named for Helen, where he was born.

Although he has described himself as a citizen of "no nation but the imagination," and has lived as an international bard, directing plays, creating poetry, and teaching at a number of colleges and universities, he has remained faithful to the Caribbean as his normative landscape. His affirmation of identity and of the significance of myth over history for the poetic imagination is inseparable from a discussion of the historic drama played out over recent centuries across the islands of the Caribbean and from which the odyssean wayfarer ventures in a lifelong cycle of escape and return. This profound engagement with the Caribbean, explored in a series of early essays, "What the Twilight Says: An Overture," "Meanings," and "The Muse of History," and restated in his Nobel lecture "The Antilles: Fragments of Epic Memory," is summed up in a particularly poignant credo: "I accept this archipelago of the Americas. I say to the ancestor who sold me, and to the ancestor who bought me . . . and also you, father in the filth-ridden gut of the slave ship . . . to you inwardly forgiven grandfathers, I like the more honest of my race, give a strange thanks. I give the strange and bitter and yet ennobling thanks for the monumental groaning and soldering of two great worlds, like

the halves of a fruit seamed by its own bitter juices, that exiled from your own Edens you have placed me in the wonder of another, that was my inheritance and your gift."

Since 1981 Walcott has been a professor of English and creative writing at Boston University. In 1992 he was awarded the Nobel Prize for literature.

—JAMES DE JONGH

WALKER, AIDA OVERTON

Aida Overton Walker (1880–1914), entertainer. Aida Overton Walker was the leading African-American female performing artist at the turn of the twentieth century. Unsurpassed as a ragtime singer and cakewalk dancer, she became a national, then international, star at a time when authentic black folk culture was replacing minstrelsy and making a powerful and permanent impact on American vernacular entertainment. Born in New York City, Walker began her career in the chorus of "Black Patti's Troubadours." She married George William Walker, of the vaudeville comedy team Williams and Walker, and soon became the female lead in their series of major musical comedies: *The Policy Players, Sons of Ham, In Dahomey, Abyssinia,* and *Bandanna Land.*

In Dahomey played London in 1903, including a command performance before the royal family on the lawn of Buckingham Palace. Walker also choreographed these shows, perhaps the first woman to receive program credit for doing so. Among her best-known songs were "Miss Hannah from Savannah," "A Rich Coon's Babe," and "Why Adam Sinned." At George Walker's death she continued in musical theater and vaudeville, playing the best houses, including Hammerstein's Victoria Theater in New York, where she performed *Salome* in 1912. She died in New York in 1914, at the age of thirty-four. Critics considered Walker a singer and dancer superior to both her better-known successors, Florence Mills and Josephine Baker.

—RICHARD NEWMAN

WALKER, A'LELIA

A'Lelia Walker (June 6, 1885–August 17, 1931), entrepreneur. Through the lavish parties she hosted, A'Lelia Walker made herself the center of

ALICE WALKER

Author Challenges Readers' Views on Race and Gender

Alice Walker (February 9, 1944–), novelist. Alice Walker was born in Eatonton, Ga., the eighth child of sharecroppers Willie Lee and Minnie Lou Grant Walker. The vision in Walker's right eye was destroyed when she was eight years old by a brother's BB gun shot, an event that caused her to become an introverted child. Six years later, Walker's self-confidence and commitment to school increased dramatically after a minor surgical procedure removed disfiguring scar tissue from around her injured eye. Encouraged by her family and community, Walker won a scholarship for the handicapped and matriculated at Spelman College in 1961.

After two years, Walker transferred to Sarah Lawrence College because she felt that Spelman stifled the intellectual growth and maturation of its students, an issue she explores in the novel *Meridian*. At Sarah Lawrence, Walker studied works by European and white American writers, but the school failed to provide her with an opportunity to explore the intellectual and cultural traditions of black people. Walker sought to broaden her education by traveling to Africa during the summer before her senior year. During her stay there, Walker became pregnant, and the urgency of her desire to terminate the pregnancy (she was prepared to commit suicide had she not been able to get an abortion), along with her experiences in Africa and as a participant in the Civil Rights Movement, became the subject of her first book, a collection of poems entitled *Once* (1968).

Walker moved to Mississippi in 1965, where she taught, worked with Head Start programs, and helped to register voters. There she met and married Melvyn Leventhal, a civil rights lawyer whom she subsequently divorced (a daughter, Rebecca, was born in 1969), and wrote her first novel, *The Third Life of Grange Copeland* (1970), a chilling exploration of the causes and consequences of black intrafamilial violence. While doing research on black folk medicine for a story that became "The Revenge of Hannah Kemhuff," collected in *In Love and Trouble* (1973), Walker first learned of Zora Neale Hurston.

In Hurston, Walker discovered a figure who had been virtually erased from American literary history in large part because she held views—on the beauty and complexity of black southern rural culture; on the necessity of what Walker termed a "womanist" critique of sexism; and on racism and sexism as intersecting forms of oppression—for which she had herself been condemned. In Hurston, Walker found legitimacy for her own literary project. Walker obtained a tombstone for Hurston's grave, which proclaimed her "A Genius of the South," and focused public attention on her neglected work, including the novel *Their Eyes Were Watching God*.

In her influential essay "In Search of Our Mothers' Gardens" Walker asked, with Hurston and other marginalized women in mind, "How was the creativity of the black woman kept alive, year after year and century after century?" Some of the most celebrated of Walker's works—from the short stories "Everyday Use" and "1955" to the novel *The Color Purple* (1982)—explore this question. By acknowledging her artistic debt to writers like Phillis Wheatley, Virginia Woolf, and Hurston, as well as to her own verbally and horticulturally adept mother, Walker encouraged a generation of readers and scholars to question traditional evaluative norms.

After *In Love and Trouble,* Walker published several novels (including *Meridian, The Temple of My Familiar,* and *Possessing the Secret of Joy*), volumes of poetry (including *Horses Make a Landscape Look More Beautiful*), collections of essays, and another short story collection, *You Can't Keep a Good Woman Down* (1981). In all these works, she examined the racial and gendered inequities that affect black Americans generally and black women in particular. The most celebrated and controversial of these works is her Pulitzer Prize- and National Book Award-winning epistolary novel, *The Color Purple*, which explores, among other matters, incest, marital violence, lesbianism, alternative religious practices, and black attitudes about gender. Since the early 1980s, Walker has lived in northern California and continues to produce work that challenges and inspires its readers.

—MICHAEL AWKWARD

elite social life during the Harlem Renaissance. She was born Lelia Walker to Sarah and Moses McWilliams in Vicksburg, Miss. (She changed her name to "A'Lelia" as an adult.) After her father died when she was two, her mother took her to St. Louis. She attended public schools there and graduated from Knoxville College, a private black school in Knoxville, Tenn.

See also
Literature

She and her mother then moved to Denver, where her mother married C. J. Walker, from whom they took their surnames. A'Lelia also married, but while she took the surname Robinson from her husband, she only occasionally used it, and the marriage was as short-lived as two subsequent unions. While in Denver, the Walkers began their hair care business. Madam C. J. Walker developed products that straightened and softened African-American women's hair, and assisted by her daughter, she quickly created a vast empire. She moved parts of her operations and her residence to Pittsburgh and Indianapolis before finally settling in New York. In 1917, the Walkers built a thirty-four-room mansion in Irvington-on-Hudson, N.Y., which A'Lelia's friend, the opera singer Enrico Caruso, dubbed "Villa Lewaro" (short for Lelia Walker Robinson).

With her mother's death on May 25, 1919, A'Lelia inherited the bulk of her mother's estate, including Villa Lewaro and two twin brownstones at 108–110 West 136th St. in Harlem. Soon after her mother's death, Walker also bought an apartment at 80 Edgecombe Avenue, in Harlem. While she was the titular director of the Walker business interests, A'Lelia Walker devoted most of her money and attention to social life. She threw parties at Villa Lewaro and in Harlem. She established "at-homes" at which she introduced African-American writers, artists, and performers to each other and to such white celebrities as Carl Van Vechten. Her "salon" was regarded as a place where artistic people, particularly male and female homosexuals, could go to eat and drink, and hear music. In 1927 and 1928, she turned part of the brownstones into a nightclub, which she named "The Dark Tower."

When the depression came, Walker experienced grave financial difficulties. She was forced to close her nightclub, and she mortgaged Villa Lewaro. When she died suddenly on August 17, 1931, Langston Hughes wrote that this "was really the end of the gay times of the New Negro era in Harlem." The NAACP, to whom Walker had willed Villa Lewaro, was unable to keep up the payments on the estate and ended up putting it on the auction block.

—SIRAJ AHMED

WALKER, DAVID

David Walker (c. 1785–June 28, 1830), civil rights activist and pamphleteer. Born free in Wilmington, N.C., the son of a free white mother and a slave father, David Walker traveled extensively in the South and observed the cruelty of slavery firsthand. Little is known about his life until he settled in Boston, where he was living as early as 1826. A tall, dark-complexioned mulatto, he operated a clothing store, selling both new and secondhand clothes, and became a leader in Boston's black community. Walker was a member of Father Snowden's Methodist Church, and was active in the Massachusetts General Colored Association formed in 1826. He was a contributor of funds to emancipate George M. Horton, a slave poet in North Carolina, and also served as an agent for *Freedom's Journal* (New York), established in 1827. Walker and his wife, Eliza, had one son, Edwin G. Walker, who later became the first black elected to the Massachusetts legislature.

Walker represented a new generation of black leaders forged by the experience of creating the first extensive free black communities in urban centers of the United States in the half-century after the American Revolution. The achievement of African Americans in establishing institutions (churches, schools, and mutual aid and fraternal societies) and in producing leaders (ministers, educators, businessmen) emboldened some in Walker's generation to challenge the reigning view among whites that African Americans, even if freed, were destined to remain a degraded people, a caste apart, better served by the removal of free blacks to Africa, which became the objective of the American Colonization Society (ACS), formed in 1817 by leading statesmen and clergy.

In an address in 1828 delivered before the Massachusetts General Colored Association, Walker laid out a strategy of opposition. Overcoming resistance to organization from within the black community, Walker and others recognized the need for a formal association to advance the race by uniting "the colored population, so far, through the United States of America, as may be practicable and expedient; forming societies, opening, extending, and keeping up correspondences" (*Freedom's Journal,* December 19, 1828). Presaging his famous *Appeal to the Colored Citizens of the World,* Walker sought to arouse blacks to mutual aid and self-help, to cast off passive acquiescence in injustice, and to persuade his people of the potential power that hundreds of thousands of free blacks possessed once mobilized.

Published in 1829, Walker's *Appeal* aimed at encouraging black organization and individual activism. It went through three editions in two years, each one longer than the previous one, the

See also

Civil Rights Movement

final version reaching eighty-eight pages. For many readers, the most startling aspect of the *Appeal* was its call for the violent revolt of slaves against their masters. But Walker was also vitally concerned with the institutions of free blacks in the North. Walker understood that the formation of organizations such as the Massachusetts General Colored Association and the appearance of *Freedom's Journal* in 1827 were evidence of a rising tide of black opposition to slavery and racism. Walker, along with many African-American activists of his era, was profoundly opposed to the African colonization schemes of the American Colonization Society. Colonizationists ignored and suppressed the prevailing black opposition and sought support among African Americans. For Walker, colonization represented an immediate threat to any long-term hopes of black advancement since its cardinal assumption was that such advancement was impossible.

Walker's *Appeal* was thus much more than a cry of conscience, for all its impassioned rhetoric. Despite its rambling organization, its prophetic denunciations of injustice and apocalyptic predictions, the *Appeal* forms a complex, cogent argument with political purpose: to persuade blacks to struggle with whites to abandon colonization and to strive toward racial equality. The essay culminates in an attack on colonization and concludes with an affirmation of the *Declaration of Independence*.

Walker aimed the *Appeal* at two audiences simultaneously. His first target was blacks, whose achievements in history, Walker argued, rebutted the degraded view popularized by colonizationists and the "suspicion" of Thomas Jefferson of inherent black intellectual inferiority. Walker insisted on the importance of black self-help through rigorous education and occupational training to refute Jefferson and others. He was also unsparing in his condemnation of the ignorance and passivity of free blacks and the complicity of the enslaved, their acquiescence in helping to sustain the American racial regime. Yet in justifying physical resistance—the element which most alarmed many readers in his own day and since—Walker carefully qualified his views. He relied primarily on the power of persuasion to convince white people to recognize that slavery and racism perverted Christianity and republicanism, though his apocalyptic warnings undoubtedly were designed to stir fear in the hearts of tyrants.

Walker succeeded. He circulated copies of the *Appeal* through the mails and via black and white seamen who carried them to southern ports in Virginia, North Carolina, Georgia, and Louisiana. Southern leaders became alarmed and adopted new laws against teaching free blacks to read or write and demanded that Mayor Harrison Gray Otis of Boston take action against Walker. Otis gave assurances that Walker's was an isolated voice, without sympathy in the white community, but Walker had violated no laws. Georgians, however, placed a large sum on Walker's head. In 1830, Walker died from causes unknown amid suspicion, never confirmed, of foul play.

Few documents in American history have elicited such diverse contemporary and historical evaluations as Walker's *Appeal*. Benjamin Lundy, the pioneer abolitionist, condemned it as incendiary. William Lloyd Garrison admired the *Appeal's* "impassioned and determined spirit," and its "bravery and intelligence," but thought it "a most injudicious publication, yet warranted by the creed of an independent people." The black leader Henry Highland Garnet in 1848 proclaimed it "among the first, and . . . the boldest and most direct appeals in behalf of freedom, which was made in the early part of the Antislavery Reformation." In 1908 a modern white historian, Alice D. Adams, deemed it "a most bloodthirsty document," while in 1950 the African-American scholar Saunders Redding thought "it was scurrilous, ranting, mad—but these were the temper of the times." In their biography of their father, the Garrison children probably came closest to the truth about Walker: "his noble intensity, pride, disgust, fierceness, his eloquence, and his general intellectual ability have not been commemorated as they deserve."

—PAUL GOODMAN

WALKER, MADAM C. J.

Madam C. J. Walker (December 23, 1867–May 25, 1919), entrepreneur, hair-care industry pioneer, philanthropist, and political activist. Born Sarah Breedlove to ex-slaves Owen and Minerva Breedlove on a Delta, La., cotton plantation, she was orphaned by age seven. She lived with her sister, Louvenia, in Vicksburg, Miss., until 1882, when she married Moses McWilliams, in part to escape Louvenia's cruel husband. In 1887, when her daughter, Lelia (later known as A'Lelia Walker), was two years old, Moses McWilliams died. For the next eighteen years she worked as a laundress in St. Louis. But in 1905, with $1.50 in

Live free or die.

MOTTO FOR THE STATE OF
NEW HAMPSHIRE

***

See also
NAACP

717

The first African-American magazine to have a lasting impact was the Crisis, *which was the brainchild of W.E.B. Du Bois.*

PAGE 192

savings, the thirty-seven-year-old McWilliams moved to Denver to start her own business after developing a formula to treat her problem with baldness—an ailment common among African-American women at the time, brought on by poor diet, stress, illness, damaging hair-care treatments, and scalp disease. In January 1906 she married Charles Joseph Walker, a newspaper sales agent, who helped design her advertisements and mail-order operation.

While Madam Walker is often said to have invented the "hot comb," it is more likely that she adapted metal implements popularized by the French to suit black women's hair. Acutely aware of the debate about whether black women should alter the appearance of their natural hair texture, she insisted years later that her Walker System was not intended as a hair "straightener," but rather as a grooming method to heal and condition the scalp to promote hair growth and prevent baldness.

From 1906 to 1916 Madam Walker traveled throughout the United States, Central America, and the West Indies promoting her business. She settled briefly in Pittsburgh, establishing the first Lelia College of Hair Culture there in 1908, then moved the company to Indianapolis in 1910, building a factory and vastly increasing her annual sales. Her reputation as a philanthropist was solidified in 1911, when she contributed one thousand dollars to the building fund of the Indianapolis YMCA. In 1912 she and C. J. Walker divorced, but she retained his name. Madam Walker joined her daughter, A'Lelia, and A'Lelia's adopted daughter, Mae (later Mae Walker Perry), in Harlem in 1916. She left the daily management of her manufacturing operation in Indianapolis to her longtime attorney and general manager, Freeman B. Ransom, factory forewoman Alice Kelly, and assistant general manager Robert L. Brokenburr.

Madam Walker's business philosophy stressed economic independence for the 20,000 former maids, farm laborers, housewives, and schoolteachers she employed as agents and factory and office workers. To further strengthen her company, she created the Madam C. J. Walker Hair Culturists Union of America and held annual conventions.

During World War I, she was among those who supported the government's black recruitment efforts and War Bond drives. But after the bloody 1917 East St. Louis riot, she joined the planning committee of the Negro Silent Protest Parade, traveling to Washington to present a petition urging President Wilson to support legislation that would make lynching a federal crime. As her wealth and visibility grew, Walker became increasingly outspoken, joining those blacks who advocated an alternative peace conference at Versailles after the war to monitor proceedings affecting the world's people of color. She intended her estate in Irvington-on-Hudson, N.Y.—Villa Lewaro, which was designed by black architect Vertner W. Tandy—not only as a showplace but as an inspiration to other blacks.

During the spring of 1919, aware that her long battle with hypertension was taking its final toll, Madam Walker revamped her will, directing her attorney to donate five thousand dollars to the National Association for the Advancement of Colored People's antilynching campaign and to contribute thousands of dollars to black educational, civic, and social institutions and organizations.

When she died at age fifty-one, at Villa Lewaro, she was widely considered the wealthiest black woman in America and was reputed to be the first African-American woman millionaire. Her daughter, A'Lelia Walker—a central figure of the Harlem Renaissance—succeeded her as president of the Mme. C. J. Walker Manufacturing Company.

Walker's significance is rooted not only in her innovative (and sometimes controversial) hair-care system, but also in her advocacy of black women's economic independence and her creation of business opportunities at a time when most black women worked as servants and sharecroppers. Her entrepreneurial strategies and organizational skills revolutionized what would become a multibillion-dollar ethnic hair-care and cosmetics industry by the last decade of the twentieth century. Having led an early life of hardship, she became a trailblazer of black philanthropy, using her wealth and influence to leverage social, political, and economic rights for women and blacks. In 1992 Madam Walker was elected to the National Business Hall of Fame.

—A'LELIA PERRY BUNDLES

WALKER, MARGARET

Margaret Walker (July 7, 1915–), writer. Margaret Abigail Walker was born in Birmingham, Ala. She received her early education in New Orleans, and completed undergraduate work at Northwestern University at the age of nineteen. Although Walker had published some of her po-

"FATS" WALLER

Prolific Composer of Songs and Musical Comedy Scores

Thomas Wright "Fats" Waller (May 21, 1904–December 15, 1943), jazz pianist, organist, and composer. The most ebullient and popular of the Harlem stride pianists, Waller was also an accomplished performer on the pipe organ, a prolific composer of songs and musical comedy scores, and a gifted comic. Waller, whose father was a lay preacher and member of Harlem's Abyssinian Baptist Church, was born in New York City in 1904, and lived most of his life there. He learned the rudiments of piano in his childhood, won a talent contest in 1918 playing James P. Johnson's "Carolina Shout" at the Roosevelt Theater, and eventually studied stride piano with Russell Brooks after leaving home in 1920. Thereafter he studied privately with Johnson, from whom he acquired further knowledge of the techniques and gestures of the stride style. Fascinated by the sound of the pipe organ, he secured occasional employment in his teens as an organist to accompany silent movies at Harlem's Lincoln Theater and later at the Lafayette Theater. In 1920 he married Edith Hatchett. They were divorced three years later, and in 1926 he married Anita Rutherford.

Waller gained local fame in New York early in the 1920s on the Harlem rent party circuit, but before 1927 he recorded only very occasionally as a soloist, accompanist for singers, or (even more rarely) with other groups. In 1927 and 1929, however, he recorded numerous sides at Victor's Camden, N.J., studio (a converted church), often playing his own compositions. These included organ solos ("Rusty Pail"), piano solos ("Gladyse," "Ain't Misbehavin' "), and small ensemble sessions ("Fats Waller Stomp," "The Minor Drag"). On April 27, 1928, Waller premiered James P. Johnson's *Yamekraw: Negro Rhapsody* (1928) at Carnegie Hall in New York City, and during the last half of the decade he composed music for shows and revues (*Tan Town Topics*, 1925, with Spencer Williams; *Keep Shufflin'*, 1928, with James P. Johnson; *Load of Coal* and *Hot Chocolates*, 1929, both with lyricist Andy Razaf).

In the 1930s, Waller became one of the most well-known and well-loved figures in jazz, through the hundreds of sides he recorded for Victor as well as through frequent appearances on radio and at night clubs; he also performed in films (*Hooray For Love*, 1935; *The King of Burlesque*, 1935), on European and domestic tours, and composed numerous popular songs on the Tin Pan Alley model. Usually, he worked from a given text; his most frequent collaborator was lyricist Andy Razaf. As a composer, Waller was as efficient as his fund of ideas was fertile. The elegance and sophistication of the majority of his songs (from "Ain't Misbehavin,' " 1929, to "Stayin' at Home," 1940) attest to a high level of craft in his composition.

Waller developed a flawless technique ("Gladyse," "Numb Fumblin'," both recorded in 1929), aided by exceptionally large hands, a physical characteristic he shared with both James P. Johnson and Luckey Roberts. Unlike most stride pianists, however, Waller occasionally exhibited a genuinely lyrical, introspective quality in both melodic line and accompaniment ("Inside This Heart of Mine," 1938). He was also the only stride pianist to play the pipe organ as a jazz instrument and to produce a substantial body of recorded jazz on this seemingly cumbersome instrument. As a singer, Waller's loose, energetic vocal style contributed to the sense of immediacy in his performances, and he often (but not always) indulged a penchant for satire, savaging mawkish or nonsensical lyrics by using exaggerated timbres, affected pronunciation, and rhythmic displacement. In addition, he would interpolate devastating asides, mocking the original intent of the text ("I'm Crazy 'Bout My Baby," 1931; "It's a Sin to Tell a Lie," 1936). He also created sophisticated African-American musical tropes on a style of piano technique one might loosely term "European virtuoso"; his most extensive effort in this type of parody may be found in his 1941 recording of "Honeysuckle Rose (à la Bach, Beethoven, Brahms, and Waller)."

Waller contracted a bronchial infection during an engagement at the Club Zanzibar in Los Angeles in December 1943; he died in the early hours of December 15 in or near Kansas City, Mo., while returning to New York aboard the Santa Fe Super Chief train.

—PAUL S. MACHLIN

ems before she moved to Chicago, it was there her talent matured. She wrote as a college student and as a member of the federal government's Works Project Administration, and she shared cultural and professional interests with black and white intellectuals in Chicago, the best known of whom was Richard Wright. Wright and Walker were close friends until Walker left Chicago for gradu-

See also
Literature

W

Science may have been used and abused in racially motivated ways, but this did not stop African Americans from being drawn to careers in the field.

PAGE 615

ate work at the University of Iowa in 1939, by which time she was on her way to becoming a major poet.

In 1942 Walker completed the manuscript of a collection of poems entitled *For My People,* the title poem of which she had written and published in Chicago in 1937. The book served as her master's thesis at the Iowa Writers Workshop, and won a measure of national literary prominence. In 1942 *For My People* won the Yale Younger Poets Award. About the same time, Walker began work on a historical novel based on the life of her grandmother, Elvira Dozier Ware, a work she did not finish until she returned to Iowa in the 1960s to complete her Ph.D. In the interim, she joined the faculty at Jackson State University in Jackson, Miss., where she and her husband, Firnist James Alexander, raised their four children.

Walker played an active role in the civil rights movement in Mississippi, and continued to write. The novel she created from her grandmother's stories was published in 1966 as *Jubilee,* and received the Houghton Mifflin Literary Award. It was translated into seven languages and enjoyed popularity as one of the first modern novels of slavery and the Reconstruction South told from an African-American perspective. Other books followed: *Prophets for a New Day* (1970), *How I Wrote Jubilee* (1972), *October Journey* (1973), and *A Poetic Equation: Conversations Between Nikki Giovanni and Margaret Walker* (1974). Throughout her long career, Walker received numerous awards and honors for her contribution to American letters. She holds several honorary degrees and in 1991 received a Senior Fellowship from the National Endowment for the Arts.

Walker retired from full-time teaching in 1979, remained in Jackson, and worked on several projects, especially a controversial biography of Richard Wright, published in 1988 as *Richard Wright: Daemonic Genius.* In 1989 Walker brought together new and earlier poems in *This Is My Century: New and Collected Poems.* A year later she published her first volume of essays, *How I Wrote Jubilee and Other Essays on Life and Literature.*

Throughout her work, Walker incorporates a strong sense of her own humanistic vision together with an autobiographical recall of her own past and cogent themes from black history. Her artistic vision recognizes the distinctiveness of black cultural life and the values associated with it. She is outspoken on matters of political justice and social equality, for women as well as for men.

Jubilee tells the story of Vyry, a slave on an antebellum Georgia plantation, the unacknowl-

edged daughter of the master, who aspires to freedom. She marries a fellow slave, and assumes responsibility for the plantation during the Civil War. After the war she moves away and discovers that her courage and determination make it possible for her to triumph over numerous adversities. In a 1992 interview Walker stated, "The body of my work springs from my interest in the historical point of view that is central to the development of black people as we approach the twenty-first century."

—MARYEMMA GRAHAM

WASHINGTON, BOOKER TALIAFERRO

Booker Taliaferro Washington (c. 1856–November 14, 1915), educator. Founder of Tuskegee Institute in Alabama and prominent race leader of the late nineteenth and early twentieth centuries, Booker T. Washington was born a slave on the plantation of James Burroughs near Hale's Ford, Va. He spent his childhood as a houseboy and servant. His mother was a cook on the Burroughs plantation, and he never knew his white father. With Emancipation in 1865, he moved with his family—consisting of his mother, Jane; his stepfather, Washington Ferguson; a half-brother, John; and a half-sister, Amanda—to West Virginia, where he worked briefly in the salt furnaces and coal mines near Malden. Quickly, however, he obtained work as a houseboy in the mansion of the wealthiest white man in Malden, Gen. Lewis Ruffner. There, under the tutelage of the general's wife, Viola Ruffner, a former New England schoolteacher, he learned to read. He also attended a local school for African Americans in Malden.

From 1872 to 1875 Washington attended Hampton Institute, in Hampton, Va., where he came under the influence of the school's founder, Gen. Samuel Chapman Armstrong, who inculcated in Washington the work ethic that would stay with him his entire life and that became a hallmark of his educational philosophy. Washington was an outstanding pupil during his tenure at Hampton and was placed in charge of the Native American students there. After graduation he returned to Malden, where he taught school for several years and became active as a public speaker on local matters, including the issue of the removal of the capital of West Virginia to Charleston.

See also

Jim Crow

Niagara Movement

In 1881, Washington founded a school of his own in Tuskegee, Ala. Beginning with a few ramshackle buildings and a small sum from the state of Alabama, he built Tuskegee Institute into the best-known African-American school in the nation. While not neglecting academic training entirely, the school's curriculum stressed industrial education, training in specific skills and crafts that would prepare students for jobs. Washington built his school and his influence by tapping the generosity of northern philanthropists, receiving donations from wealthy New Englanders and some of the leading industrialists and businessmen of his time, such as Andrew Carnegie, William H. Baldwin, Jr., Julius Rosenwald, and Robert C. Ogden.

In 1882 Washington married his childhood sweetheart from Malden, Fanny Norton Smith, a graduate of Hampton Institute, who died two years later as a result of injuries suffered in a fall from a wagon. Subsequently Washington married Olivia A. Davidson, a graduate of Hampton and the Framingham State Normal School in Massachusetts, who held the title of lady principal of Tuskegee. She was a tireless worker for the school and an effective fund-raiser in her own right. Always in rather frail health, Davidson died in 1889. Washington's third wife, Margaret James Murray, a graduate of Fisk University, also held the title of lady principal and was a leader of the National Association of Colored Women's Clubs and the Southern Federation of Colored Women's Clubs.

Washington's reputation as the principal of Tuskegee Institute grew through the late 1880s and the 1890s; his school was considered the exemplar of industrial education, viewed as the best method of training the generations of African Americans who were either born in slavery or were the sons and daughters of freed slaves. His control of the purse strings of many of the northern donors to his school increased his influence with other African-American schools in the South. His fame and recognition as a national race leader, however, resulted from the impact of a single speech he delivered before the Cotton States and International Exposition in Atlanta, in 1895. This important speech, often called the Atlanta Compromise, is the best single statement of Washington's philosophy of racial advancement and his political accommodation with the predominant racial ideology of his time. For the next twenty years, until the end of his life, Washington seldom deviated publicly from the positions taken in the Atlanta address.

In his speech, Washington urged African Americans to "cast down your bucket where you are"—that is, in the South—and to accommodate to the segregation and discrimination imposed upon them by custom and by state and local laws. He said the races could exist separately from the standpoint of social relationships but should work together for mutual economic advancement. He advocated a gradualist advancement of the race, through hard work, economic improvement, and self-help. This message found instant acceptance from white Americans, north and south, and almost universal approval among African Americans. Even W. E. B. Du Bois, later one of Washington's harshest critics, wrote to him immediately after the Atlanta address that the speech was "a word fitly spoken."

While Washington's public stance on racial matters seldom varied from the Atlanta Compromise, privately he was a more complicated individual. His voluminous private papers, housed at the Library of Congress, document an elaborate secret life that contradicted many of his public utterances. He secretly financed test cases to challenge Jim Crow laws. He held great power over the African-American press, both north and south, and secretly owned stock in several newspapers. While Washington himself never held political office of any kind, he became the most powerful African-American politician of his time as an adviser to presidents Theodore Roosevelt and William Howard Taft and as a dispenser of Republican party patronage.

Washington's biographer, Louis R. Harlan, called the Tuskegean's extensive political network "the Tuskegee Machine" for its resemblance to the machines established by big-city political bosses of the era. With his network of informants and access to both northern philanthropy and political patronage, Washington could make or break careers, and he was the central figure in African-American public life during his heyday. Arguably no other black leader, before or since, has exerted similar dominance. He founded the National Negro Business League in 1900, to foster African-American business and create a loyal corps of supporters throughout the country. Indirectly he influenced the National Afro American Council, the leading African-American civil rights group of his day. The publication of his autobiography, *Up from Slavery*, in 1901 spread his fame even more in the United States and abroad. In this classic American tale, Washington portrayed his life in terms of a Horatio Alger success story. Its great popularity in the first decade of the twenti-

WASHINGTON, BOOKER TALIAFERRO

The slave system on our place, in large measure, took the spirit of self-reliance and self-help out of the white people.

BOOKER T. WASHINGTON
UP FROM SLAVERY, 1901

W

When war was begun between the North and the South, every slave on our plantation felt and knew that, though other issues were discussed, the primal one was that of slavery.

BOOKER T. WASHINGTON
UP FROM SLAVERY, 1901

See also
Science
William Monroe Trotter

eth century won many new financial supporters for Tuskegee Institute and for Washington personally.

Washington remained the dominant African-American leader in the country until the time of his death from exhaustion and overwork in 1915. But other voices rose to challenge his conservative, accommodationist leadership. William Monroe Trotter, the editor of the *Boston Guardian,* was a persistent gadfly. Beginning in 1903 with the publication of Du Bois's *The Souls of Black Folk,* and continuing for the rest of his life, Washington was criticized for his failure to be more publicly aggressive in fighting the deterioration of race relations in the United States, for his avoidance of direct public support for civil rights legislation, and for his single-minded emphasis on industrial education as opposed to academic training for a "talented tenth" of the race. Washington, however, was adept at outmaneuvering his critics, even resorting to the use of spies to infiltrate organizations critical of his leadership, such as the Niagara Movement, led by Du Bois. His intimate friends called Washington "the Wizard" for his mastery of political intrigue and his exercise of power.

Washington's leadership ultimately gave way to new forces in the twentieth century, which placed less emphasis on individual leadership and more on organizational power. The founding of the National Association for the Advancement of Colored People (NAACP) in 1909 and of the National Urban League in 1911 challenged Washington in the areas of civil rights and for his failure to address problems related to the growth of an urban black population. The defeat of the Republican party in the presidential election of 1912 also spelled the end of Washington's power as a dispenser of political patronage. Nevertheless, he remained active as a speaker and public figure until his death, in 1915, at Tuskegee.

Washington's place in the pantheon of African-American leaders is unclear. He was the first African American to appear on a United States postage stamp (1940) and commemorative coin (1946). While he was eulogized by friend and foe alike at the time of his death, his outmoded philosophy of accommodation to segregation and racism in American society caused his historical reputation to suffer. New generations of Americans, who took their inspiration from those who were more outspoken critics of segregation and the second-class status endured by African Americans, rejected Washington's leadership role. While much recent scholarship has explored his racial philosophy and political activity in consid-

erable depth, he remains a largely forgotten man in the consciousness of the general public, both black and white. In recent years, however, there has been some revival of interest in his economic thought by those who seek to develop African-American businesses and entrepreneurial skills. Indeed, no serious student of the African-American experience in the United States can afford to ignore the lessons that can be gleaned from Washington's life and from the manner in which he exercised power.

—RAYMOND W. SMOCK

WASHINGTON, D.C.

The ten-mile-square District of Columbia, carved from Maryland and Virginia, the two most populous slave states in the United States, was created in 1791. (The Virginia portion reverted to Virginia early in the nineteenth century.) Blacks were the largest population group in the area when the site was selected for a federal district, and their labor supported the region's plantation economy. The black mathematician and almanac-maker Benjamin Banneker helped survey the land for the planned city. In 1800, when the nation's capital was moved there, more than a quarter of its population was black, and about a quarter of those were free. In 1814, when Washington was attacked by British troops, free blacks helped build barricades, and several volunteered as soldiers to defend the city.

As the district's population grew, slavery remained common. While there were plantations in its outlying areas as well as estates such as those of Robert E. Lee in Alexandria and Arlington, most slaves worked as skilled and unskilled laborers—as domestics, coachmen, carpenters, barbers, and teamsters and in other trades—in the capital city. Washington's central location and position as a port made it an important nucleus of the domestic slave trade. Slave jails, known as "Georgia pens," dotted the city, Kephart, Armfield and Franklin, and other large traders were established in the area.

The city of Washington developed into an entrenched slave society. Slaves and free blacks were tightly restricted by a series of black codes more restrictive than those of either of the surrounding states. Free blacks had a curfew, were required to post good behavior bonds, forbidden to operate businesses, and, after Nat Turner's Rebellion in 1831, banned from preaching. Slavenapping and antiblack violence were chronic problems. For example, in 1835, white mobs at the Washington Navy Yard rioted. Mobs broke into and burned several homes and tore down schools, forcing dozens of black residents to flee. The same year, blacks in Georgetown were set upon by an antiabolitionist lynch mob, and Ben Snow's restaurant was burned down by a group of white workers.

Despite the restrictions, a vibrant free black community, led by such figures as merchant Absalom Shadd, stablekeeper James Wormley, and feed dealer Alfred Lee, grew up in Washington in the years before the Civil War. Blacks in Washington managed to provide for many of their own community needs. No institution played a more significant role in the community's viability than did the church. When segregated by white churches, blacks built their own. The first independent congregation, Mount Zion Negro Church of Georgetown, was formed in 1814. Several important churches, such as Union Bethel Church (later Metropolitan African Methodist Episcopal Church) in 1838, the First Negro Baptist Church in 1839, and First Colored (later Fifteenth Street) Presbyterian Church in 1841 were established during the period; all continue to form a large part of the backbone of the community's social and political infrastructure. Under the guidance of John F. Cook, a former slave who was pastor of the Fifteenth Street Church, and founder of its Union Seminary school, a strong District of Columbia chapter of the Negro Convention movement was founded. Blacks also organized fraternal societies, notably the Resolute Beneficial Society, and developed cultural institutions. In 1853, for example, Anthony Bower organized a black branch of the Young Men's Christian Association.

Educational institutions were a primary concern of black Washingtonians. In 1807, former slaves George Bell, Moses Liverpool, and Nicholas Franklin founded a school. Several schools were later set up by African-American women, such as Louise Parke Costin; Maria Becroft, who founded a short-lived school in 1820 and seven years later cofounded what may have been the nation's first black girl's school; and Mary Wormley, who founded a school in 1830 with donations from her well-to-do brother. In 1851, Myrtilla Miner, a white woman, set up a black women's academy, which grew into the Miner Normal School after the Civil War and became the University of the District of Columbia in the 1970s.

As abolitionist activity increased, Washington became a symbol and a battleground in the struggle for freedom and equality. Its slaves served as an embarrassing reminder of the hold of the institution of slavery on the federal government. Congress had the power to abolish slavery in the district, and many congressmen (including Abraham Lincoln during his term in the House) called for gradual, compensated emancipation, but southern influence prevented passage of such a measure, though the slave trade was restricted in the city as part of the compromise of 1850.

The Civil War radically transformed Washington. Slavery was abolished in the District of Columbia with compensation to loyal slaveholders in the spring of 1862. With the freeing of the district's slaves and the Emancipation Proclamation in the following year, blacks volunteered en masse for the Union Army, and some 3,000 black District of Columbia troops saw action in the Civil War. Meanwhile, the city and its surrounding forts became a haven for blacks seeking to escape slavery and the ravages of war. The government considered various schemes to colonize the black residents. Several hundred freed slaves were transported to a short-lived colony at Ile de Vache, Haiti, before returning to "Freedmen's Village" on the Arlington estate of Maria Syphax, an African American. Despite such efforts, housing resources were strained by the migration, and many newcomers were housed in tents or barracks. "Alleys" were hastily constructed in back of existing houses to provide makeshift housing. Though badly lit and unsanitary, they housed the majority of blacks in the city for decades.

By the end of the Civil War, some 40,000 contrabands and emancipated slaves had settled in the nation's capital, and more followed in subsequent years. By 1870, the black population had tripled in ten years and represented one-third of the total. The newcomers came primarily from Maryland and Virginia, had little education and few skills to aid them in adapting to an urban environment, and were largely unable to secure employment. Several black charitable organizations sprang up to aid them. The first was the Contraband Relief Association, established by White House seamstress Elizabeth Keckley in 1862. The following year, the Freedman's Hospital was created under the leadership of African-American physician Alexander Augusta. Other private philanthropy coupled with national efforts—such as the Association for the Relief of Destitute Colored Women and Children, the National Freedmen's Relief Association of the District of Co-

WASHINGTON, D.C.

It is not healthy when a nation lives within a nation, as colored Americans are living inside America. A nation cannot live confident of its tomorrow if its refugees are among its own citizens.

PEARL S. BUCK
WHAT AMERICA MEANS TO ME,
1942

lumbia, and the Freedmen's Bureau—contributed much to the survival of Washington's fast-growing black population during and after the war.

During reconstruction, Washington became the center of African-American life. The area became a focus of activity as the federal government became the benefactor of black Americans. Federal government organizations such as the Freedmen's Bureau and the Freedman's Bank were created in the city. Meanwhile, the government became the city's largest employer, and black workers found jobs as clerks, messengers, and laborers in government facilities. Notable blacks, among them Alexander Crummell, Frederick Douglass, John Mercer Langston, and Francis J. Grimke, settled in the city, and formed the core of a growing black elite. Black politicians, notably Mississippi Sen. Blanche K. Bruce, arrived to serve their terms. Bruce was among the many of this group who settled in Washington after leaving office and occupied patronage positions. Others, such as elite hotelkeeper William Wormley, entered business.

A vibrant press developed to serve this highly literate black community, starting with Frederick Douglass's *New National Era* (1870–1874) and continuing with the founding of the *Washington Bee* by William Calvin Chase in 1882. Chase edited and published the journal until his death in 1922. Unswerving in his advocacy on behalf of his people, Chase was often caustic in his indictment of those aligned against the best interests of blacks as he saw them, and the paper lived up to its slogan, "Stings for Our Enemies—Honey for Our Friends." While E. E. Cooper's *Colored American* (1898–1904), the *Tatler*, the *Washington Tribune*, and the Washington edition of the *Baltimore Afro-American* would also contribute to a lively black press through the years, no paper was as bold, or as historically and politically important, as the *Bee*.

An important focus of community effort was education. Segregated public education was provided as early as 1862, and a black school board was created in 1865. Equal school funding was obtained in 1868. That year, George Cook became superintendent, and he remained in the post until 1900. In 1865, Wayland Seminary (later part of the Richmond, Va.-based Virginia Union University) was established.

In 1867, Howard University was established with the support of the Freedmen's Bureau, members of the First Congregational Church, and the federal government; it offered a wide range of ed-

ucational programs, including the country's first and most important black law school. In many ways its Preparatory Department was the first essentially public black high school in the city. However, the Colored Preparatory High School, created out of the 15th Street Presbyterian Church's Union Seminary in 1870, is generally credited as the first such school in the city. In 1891, it became the renowned M Street (later Dunbar) High School.

In Washington, as in other southern cities, most of the gains blacks made during Reconstruction were quickly overcome. The most significant reverse was in political power. In 1866, suffrage was extended to black males and in 1868, John F. Cook, Jr., and Stewart Barber were elected to the board of aldermen. Many conservative whites, fearing the influence enfranchised blacks might have in elections, formed the Citizens Reform Association in opposition to liberal mayor Sayles Bowen and in 1870 submitted to the Congress a plan for territorial government, which was adopted in a revised form in 1871. In 1874, with the support of the majority white population, Congress abolished all local suffrage and established an appointive three-commissioner system. The board remained all-white until 1961.

Blacks in Washington were stifled by discrimination in the last quarter of the nineteenth century and first quarter of the twentieth. Some prominent blacks such as Frederick Douglass continued to occupy patronage positions in government. Douglass and Blanche Bruce were recorders of deeds for the District, while others such as Andrew Hillyer served as register of the Treasury. Still, most black people remained in low-level positions regardless of their education or skills. Although black professionals contributed to Washington's stable, influential middle class, they also often found too few opportunities to use their talents. The black community, isolated from mainstream white society, developed an elaborate pecking order based upon education, economic status, social standing, and in some instances color consciousness. Differences among blacks were generally ignored in relations with whites, who made little distinction between classes of blacks. In any case, while this color and class consciousness has often served to divide Washington's black community, it never prevented the established black community from assisting its less fortunate brethren wherever possible.

In the face of discrimination, blacks built their own institutions. They would achieve a level of

See also

Abolition

Baseball

attainment that was envied by those in regions where such achievement was more difficult and often impossible. Whatever was lacking in physical resources and fiscal commitment was offset by the efforts of well-qualified and talented black teachers. Both the M Street High School and Howard University attracted faculties representing the highest quality of academic attainment. Under the leadership of its longtime dean Kelly Miller, Howard hired large numbers of black faculty and became a leading center for African-American thought. Meanwhile, in 1884 former South Carolina Secretary of State Francis Cardozo became the M Street High School's first black principal. He was succeeded by Robert Terrell, a future District of Columbia municipal judge. He was followed by writer-educator Anna Julia Cooper, who was ousted as principal in 1906 after leading the effort to maintain the school's strong academic curriculum in the face of a Booker T. Washington-influenced attempt to focus the school's courses primarily upon industrial and manual arts. In 1929, Cooper became the president of Frelinghuysen University, a pioneer night school for working adult African Americans.

Between the end of Reconstruction and the end of World War I, several important social and fraternal organizations were established in the city. These included the Colored American Opera Company (1879); Bethel Literary and Historical Association (1881); Medico-Chirurgical Society (1884); Colored Women's League (1892); Mu-SoLit Club (1905); Second Baptist Lyceum and Congressional Lyceum; and local branches of the Elks, Oddfellows, Masons, and Knights of Pythias. In addition, the Twelfth Street YMCA (1912) and the Phillis Wheatley YWCA (1905) were important additions to the city's community life. Music was ubiquitous in the city. In 1903, Andrew and Mamie Hillyer founded the Samuel Coleridge-Taylor Choral Society. The Amphion Glee Club and the Washington Folk-Song Singers, led by composer Will Marion Cook, were also popular.

During the period, such important national groups as the American Negro Academy (1897) and Carter G. Woodson's Association for the Study of Negro Life and History (1915) were founded in Washington. Omega Psi Phi fraternity and Alpha Kappa Alpha and Delta Sigma Theta sororities were developed at Howard University. In 1912 the NAACP established a Washington branch.

While Washington's black elites coalesced around issues important to the uplift of the race during the first part of the twentieth century, the city's masses of poor, undereducated residents attempted merely to survive. Washington continued to be a magnet attracting black migrants. By 1920, it had the third largest urban black population (110,000) in the country and was one-fourth black.

While well-to-do blacks, such as Robert and Mary Church Terrell, Anna Julia Cooper, and Paul Laurence Dunbar, settled in Le Droit Park, an exclusive, originally white enclave near Howard University, the migrants settled largely in Southwest Washington, as well as Capitol Hill and the northwest parts of the city, where they were plagued by disease, poor housing, and crime. In 1891, the black mortality rate was nearly twice the white rate. The overcrowded and underfunded Freedmen's Hospital was the only city facility open to blacks. Housing and public facilities were largely segregated. Racially restrictive housing covenants were strictly enforced. As early as 1914 the Congress outlawed alley housing, and the Alley Dwelling Act of 1934 provided that the worst areas be razed and inhabitants relocated. However, little was done during the first half of the century.

Black employment opportunity declined significantly during the period, even though many craftsmen were able to use their skills in the development of various large city projects. Union Station, which opened in 1907, was a notable instance. (Its snack bar long remained the only restaurant in the Capitol area open to blacks.) Because most unions remained closed to blacks, however, service trades offered the main opportunity to enter business. A large percentage of blacks worked as unskilled laborers and domestics. Blacks in the federal service, who numbered some 10 percent of the work force in 1891 (almost all in the lowest-paying and least responsible positions), found fewer jobs under presidents Theodore Roosevelt and William Howard Taft, partly as a result of civil service reform. Jobs open to blacks were further reduced under Woodrow Wilson, who approved the segregation of the workforce and signed a bill segregating public transportation in the city.

The period after World War I changed black Washington forever. During the Red Summer of 1919, exaggerated reports by the city's white press created a climate of discord among thousands of white troops stationed in Washington, while many blacks were inflamed by the failure of the

Look to the city of Washington, and let the virtuous patriots of the country weep at the spectacle. There corruption is springing into existence, and fast flourishing.

ANONYMOUS
LETTERS OF WYOMING...IN FAVOUR OF ANDREW JACKSON,
1824

city to include the city's First Separate Battalion—a highly decorated black unit—in the local victory parade. In July two black men allegedly attacking a white woman were set upon by an unruly mob of sailors and marines armed with clubs and guns, who then proceeded to attack blacks throughout the city indiscriminately. Many black servicemen responded with armed violence in self-defense.

The riot continued for two days and focused national attention on race relations in Washington. It also catalyzed black civil rights efforts. A Parents League, formed that year to protest the treatment of blacks in the public schools, campaigned unsuccessfully for the dismissal of Roscoe Conkling Bruce, an African American, as the assistant superintendent for colored schools. The league was an important development in the city's race relations; it provided a unifying influence and helped restore calm after the riots. In 1920, Community Services, an organization of civic volunteers, and the Council of Social Workers were established to improve race relations. Neither effort lasted; segregation persisted. The dedication ceremony in 1922 of the Lincoln Memorial was held under segregated conditions. A decade later, the Community Chest was founded to provide much needed cooperation among blacks and whites in tackling community problems.

Washington's black community played a significant role in the formation of the New Negro during the 1920s and '30s. Alain Locke and Sterling A. Brown were important teachers and writers contributing to the period's flowering of black culture. Washington natives Duke Ellington, Florence Mills, and Jean Toomer were among those who sought the more enlightened atmosphere of New York. The poet Georgia Douglas Johnson held gatherings known as Saturday Nighters, which attracted a large group of writers and intellectuals.

Black culture continued to thrive. U Street became the center of a vibrant entertainment district. The Howard Theater presented movies and shows; cabarets and dance halls proliferated; and jazz musicians such as Ellington, Sonny Greer, and Otto Hardwick got their start in the city's clubs. Sports were also popular. The city had several sandlot baseball teams, as well as Negro League clubs such as the Washington Elite Giants. The American Tennis Association was formed by local tennis enthusiasts.

During the Great Depression, blacks in Washington were as affected as those in other areas. Black community sources were mobilized to aid the needy. Elder Lightfoot Michaux's Church of God provided significant relief, while Sweet Daddy Grace created a pension plan for his Apostolic church members. The coming of Franklin Roosevelt and the New Deal raised the hopes of black Americans everywhere, and Roosevelt's Black Cabinet of African-American advisers drew heavily on local black talent. Public works such as the Langston Terrace projects were built for blacks. However, government aid was hardly enough to stem the effects of the depression.

Civil rights efforts increased during the era. The New Negro Alliance (NNA) was formed in 1933 to fight against rampant discrimination in the city. The NNA's "Don't Buy Where You Can't Work" protest and boycott campaign was instrumental in reducing employment exclusion. Walter E. Washington, Charles H. Houston, William Hastie, Robert C. Weaver, Mary Church Terrell, Nannie Helen Burroughs, and Mary McLeod Bethune were among those who played an important role in its efforts. National organizations such as the Joint Committee on National Recovery and the National Negro Congress were also founded in the city. In 1935, Howard University students picketed the segregated National Theater. In 1939, after being denied the use of Constitution Hall, Marian Anderson sang before 75,000 at the Lincoln Memorial, where blacks had earlier been second-class citizens. Two years later, A. Philip Randolph's threat of a march on Washington forced the Roosevelt administration to create the Fair Employment Practices Committee (FEPC). In 1942, the NAACP opened a powerful Washington bureau to lobby for civil rights legislation.

The coming of World War II led to an influx of black workers, which strained the city's limited black housing resources. While Foggy Bottom and Southwest remained large black areas, the greatest number of blacks settled around U Street, and others were scattered among the city's Ivy City, Barry Farm, Deanwood, Fort Reno, Kingman Park, and Capitol View districts.

Discrimination remained widespread. In 1945, FEPC advisor Charles H. Houston resigned when President Truman refused to press an anti-discrimination suit against the city's Capital Transport Company. In 1949, Nobel laureate Ralph Bunche, a former Howard University professor, publicly declined Truman's offer to name him assistant secretary of state, refusing to raise his family in segregated Washington. In 1949, the Co-ordinating Committee for the Enforcement of the District of Columbia Anti-Discrimination Laws, led by the venerable Mary Church Terrell,

See also

Benjamin Banneker

Mary McLeod Bethune

was formed, and began boycotting and picketing department stores that refused service to blacks. In 1950, the committee brought suit against the Thompson Restaurant, based on two civil rights ordinances passed in 1872 and 1873 and long unenforced. In 1953, the U.S. Supreme Court upheld the laws. The protests, capped by the legal victory, led to the end of Jim Crow in the city. Meanwhile, the Consolidated Parents Group formed to fight school segregation. In 1954, in *Bolling* v. *Sharpe* (one of the *Brown* v. *Board of Education* cases), the U.S. Supreme Court integrated District schools.

The early years of desegregation witnessed the migration of whites from the city and their virtual abandonment of the public school system. By the late 1950s, Washington was a black majority city—the first such large city in the nation. Housing remained an enormous problem. The city's slums became the targets of urban renewal, which resulted in the removal of many blacks. Banks refused to make loans to blacks for houses outside black areas, and owners, builders, and realtors all hindered black housing mobility. Even after the courts outlawed such practices, generations of discrimination in housing and economic opportunity limited black urban residential migration.

The Civil Rights Movement focused attention on the nation's capital with the Prayer Pilgrimage in 1957; the Youth March for Integrated Schools in 1958; the great March on Washington in 1963; and the Poor People's Washington Campaign of 1968, during which Resurrection City, a tent city, was set up in the capital. In 1968, after the assassination of the Reverend Dr. Martin Luther King, Jr., the city was shaken by rioting.

Since 1960, Washington has changed significantly. Black outmigration has increased the suburban population dramatically, while the city's population has fallen. The most important gain for blacks has been in political power. In 1961, John Duncan was appointed to the district board of commissioners. The same year, ratification of the Twenty-third Amendment gave district residents the right to vote in presidential elections. In 1967, after pressure by the "Free D.C." home rule movement, the board of commissioners was abolished, and Walter Washington was appointed as the city's first black mayor; he was elected in 1974. Although Congress continues to wield an important degree of power, blacks and the city in general made great strides in self-determination during the 1970s and '80s. In 1971, Walter Fauntroy was elected the district's nonvoting delegate to Congress. Although a constitutional amendment to give Washington representation in the Senate and House failed to achieve ratification in 1985, in 1991 the District House delegate, Eleanor Holmes Norton, received limited voting powers.

Despite these gains, many problems remain. While African Americans are employed throughout the city's agencies and private institutions, and numerous black professionals have obtained important private and government positions, many blacks continue to be employed in the lower-paying and least-responsible positions. Many blacks remain in decrepit housing, and the gentrification of black areas has increased housing costs. Health services and education continue to be uneven. Drugs and crime remain blots upon the reputation of the city and its residents. Mayor Marion Barry's conviction on drug charges in 1989 led to embarrassing revelations of corruption and drug use in his administration. In 1993, Barry's successor, Sharon Pratt Dixon (the first African-American woman mayor of a city of over 500,000 residents) called unsuccessfully for federal troops to help fight crime.

Washington remains a black cultural center, with such notable institutions as Howard's Moorland-Spingarn Research Center and the

A WASHINGTON INSTITUTION

Government charwoman Ella Watson stands before the American flag in 1942, in a photograph by Gordon Parks. PRINTS AND PHOTOGRAPHS DIVISION, LIBRARY OF CONGRESS

Smithsonian Institution's National Museum of African-American Art. The city has been the birthplace in recent decades to many distinguished blacks, including singer Marvin Gaye; basketball star Elgin Baylor; U.S. Sen. Edward Brooke; educator Allison Davis; writer and artist Richard Bruce Nugent; poet Dudley Randall; and writer John Edgar Wideman. It has also become the home of government officials and of such figures as activist Marian Wright Edelman, poet Essex Hemphill, journalists Carl Rowan and Roger Wilkins, and basketball coach John Thompson.

—THOMAS C. BATTLE

WASHINGTON, DENZEL

Denzel Washington (December 28, 1954–), actor. Born into a middle class family in Mount Vernon, N.Y., Denzel Washington is one of three children of a Pentecostal minister and a beauty shop owner. His parents divorced when he was fourteen, and Washington went through a rebellious period. Consequently, his mother sent him to boarding school at Oakland Academy in Windsor, N.Y. He went on to matriculate at Fordham University in New York City.

Washington became interested in acting while at college. When he was a senior at Fordham, he won a small role in the television film *Wilma*, the story of Olympic track star Wilma Rudolph. After graduating with a B.A. in journalism in 1978, Washington spent a year at San Francisco's American Conservatory Theater.

Washington's first film, *Carbon Copy* (1981), received little notice. However, his portrayals of Malcolm X in *When the Chickens Come Home to Roost* by Laurence Holder (Audelco Award, 1980) and Private Peterson in *A Soldier's Play* by Charles Fuller (Obie Award, 1981) brought him to the attention of New York's theater critics. After refusing to take roles that he deemed degrading, Washington took the part of the idealistic surgeon Dr. Philip Chandler on the popular hospital television drama series *St. Elsewhere* (1982–1988). In 1984, accompanied by most of the original stage cast, Washington reprised his role as Private Peterson in *A Soldier's Story*, the film version of *A Soldier's Play*.

Despite his consistently powerful performances, it was not until the end of the 1980s that Washington was acknowledged as one of America's leading actors. He appeared as martyred South African activist Stephen Biko in *Cry Freedom* (1987), a policeman in *The Mighty Quinn*, and the embittered ex-slave and Union soldier Trip in *Glory*, both in 1989. Washington received an Academy Award nomination for his work in *Cry Freedom* and in 1990 won an Academy Award for best supporting actor for his performance in *Glory*. That same year he played the title role of *Richard III* in the New York Shakespeare Festival.

In 1990 Washington starred as a jazz musician in director Spike Lee's film *Mo' Better Blues*. He teamed with Lee again in 1992 playing the title role in the controversial film *Malcolm X*. The film received mixed reviews, but Washington's performance as the black nationalist was a critical success, and he received an Oscar nomination as best actor. The following year he appeared in leading roles in three films to much acclaim. He portrayed Don Pedro, Prince of Aragon, in Kenneth Branagh's version of the Shakespearean comedy *Much Ado About Nothing*, an investigative reporter in the thriller *The Pelican Brief*, and a trial lawyer in *Philadelphia*. In 1995 he starred with Gene Hackman in *Crimson Tide*.

—JANE LUSAKA

WATERS, ETHEL

Ethel Waters (October 31, 1896?–September 1, 1977), singer and actress. Ethel Waters was born in Chester, Pa. She came from a musical family; her father played piano, and her mother and maternal relatives sang. Her first public performance was as a five-year-old billed as Baby Star in a church program. Waters began her singing career in Baltimore with a small vaudeville company where she sang W. C. Handy's "St. Louis Blues," becoming, apparently, the first woman to sing the song professionally. She was billed as Sweet Mama Stringbean.

About 1919 Waters moved to New York and became a leading entertainer in Harlem, where her first engagement was at a small black club, Edmond's Cellar. As an entertainer, she reached stardom during the Harlem Renaissance of the 1920s. In 1924, Earl Dancer, later the producer of the Broadway musical *Africana*, got her a booking in the Plantation Club as a replacement for Florence Mills, who was on tour. When Mills returned, Waters toured in Dancer's *Miss Calico*. By then, Waters had begun to establish herself as an interpreter of the blues with such songs as Perry Bradford's "Messin' Around." In 1921, she recorded "Down Home Blues" and "Oh Daddy"

See also

Film

for Black Swan Records. The success of her first recording led her to embark on one of the first personal promotion tours in the United States.

In 1932 and 1933 Waters recorded with Duke Ellington and Benny Goodman, respectively. Her renditions of "Stormy Weather," "Taking a Chance on Love," and "Lady Be Good" were closer stylistically to jazz than to popular music. She sang with the swing orchestra of Fletcher Henderson, who was her conductor on the Black Swan tours. Though her performances were unquestionably potent, many critics did not consider her a real jazz performer but rather a singer who possessed a style that was more dramatic and histrionic than jazz-oriented. However, Waters, along with Billie Holiday and Louis Armstrong, significantly influenced the sound of American popular music. Though generally regarded as blues or jazz singers, all of them sang the popular songs of their day like no other singers of the period.

"Dinah" (first performed in 1925), "Stormy Weather," and "Miss Otis Regrets" were among Waters's most popular songs. Later she recorded with Russell Wooding and Eddie Mallory, among others. Beginning in 1927 she appeared in Broadway musicals, including *Africana* (1927), Lew Leslie's *Blackbirds of 1930, Rhapsody in Black* (1931), *As Thousands Cheer* (1933), *At Home Abroad* (1936), and *Cabin in the Sky* (1940). All these roles primarily involved singing.

It was not until the Federal Theatre Project (FTP) that she had the chance to do more serious and dramatic roles. Waters received excellent reviews for her performance in Shaw's *Androcles and the Lion*, which led to her being cast as Hagar in Dubose and Dorothy Heyward's *Mamba's Daughters* (1939), for which she again received good notices. Ten years later, she was acclaimed for her performance as Berenice in Carson McCullers' *The Member of the Wedding* (which won the Drama Critics Circle Award for Best American Play of the Year in 1950).

Waters appeared in nine films between 1929 and 1959, the most popular being *Pinky*, which garnered her an Academy Award nomination as Best Supporting Actress (1949). From 1957 to 1976 she toured with evangelist Billy Graham's religious crusades in the United States and abroad and became celebrated for singing "His Eye Is on the Sparrow." This song became the title of her first autobiography, which was published in 1951. A second autobiography, *To Me It's Wonderful*, was published in 1972. Waters died in 1977, following a long bout with cancer.

—JAMES E. MUMFORD

ANDRE WATTS

Accomplished Concert Pianist

André Watts (June 20, 1946–), concert pianist. Born in Nuremberg, West Germany, at an army base, the son of a Hungarian mother and African-American soldier father, André Watts started piano study at age six with his mother. As a young man he studied at the Philadelphia Academy of Music and at Peabody Institute in Baltimore, Maryland. During this period he had the opportunity to perform as a soloist several times with the Philadelphia Orchestra, performing concerted piano works by Haydn, Mendelssohn, and Franck. In 1962, at sixteen, he achieved instant star status with his performance of the Liszt E-flat Piano Concerto with the New York Philharmonic Orchestra under Leonard Bernstein when the scheduled performer, Glenn Gould, became ill. During this period and until 1974, he studied with Leon Fleisher. His European debut dates from 1966 with the London Symphony Orchestra, and his solo tours have included the United States, Europe, Japan, Israel, and the former U.S.S.R. Watts's performances and recordings, known for their vitality and energy, range from Haydn to Debussy, though he is best known for his interpretations of the Romantic repertory, especially Liszt. In January 1988 he celebrated the twenty-fifth anniversary of his New York Philharmonic debut with a nationally televised concert. His honors include a 1964 Grammy for Most Promising Classical Artist, the Lincoln Center Medallion (1974), and honorary doctorates from Yale University (1973) and Albright College (1975).

—OTHA DAY

WEAVER, ROBERT CLIFTON

Robert Clifton Weaver (December 29, 1907–July 17, 1997), economist. Robert Weaver's maternal grandfather, Robert Tanner Freeman, the son of a slave who bought freedom for himself and his wife in 1830 and took his surname as the badge of his liberty, graduated from Harvard University in 1869 with a degree in dentistry, the first African American to do so. His daughter Florence attended Virginia Union University, then married Mortimer Grover Weaver, a Washington, D.C., postal clerk, and gave birth to Robert Weaver. Raising Robert and his older brother, Mortimer,

See also

Louis Armstrong

Harlem Renaissance

Billie Holiday

WEAVER, ROBERT CLIFTON

One of the NAACP's most important acts was the hiring of W.E.B. Du Bois as director of publications and research.

PAGE 480

Jr., in a mostly white Washington neighborhood, Florence Weaver repeatedly emphasized to her sons that "the way to offset color prejudice is to be awfully good at whatever you do."

The Weaver boys did exceptionally well in Washington's segregated school system: Mortimer went on to Williams College and then to Harvard for advanced study in English; Robert joined him at Harvard as a freshman, and when refused a room in the dormitory because he was African-American, lived with his brother off-campus. Robert Weaver graduated cum laude in 1929, the year his brother died of an unexplained illness, and stayed at Harvard to earn his master's degree in 1931 and doctorate in economics in 1934. In 1933, with the advent of the New Deal, Weaver was hired by Secretary of the Interior Harold Ickes to be the race-relations adviser in the Housing Division. While holding that post, Weaver helped desegregate the cafeteria of the Interior Department and became an active member of the "Black Cabinet," an influential group of African Americans in the Roosevelt administration who met regularly to combat racial discrimination and segregation in New Deal programs and within the government itself.

In 1935, Weaver married Ella V. Haith, a graduate of Carnegie Tech, and from 1937 to 1940 served as the special assistant to the administrator of the U.S. Housing Authority. During World War II he held positions on the National Defense Advisory Committee, the War Manpower Commission, and the War Production Board. In 1944, Weaver left the government to direct the Mayor's Committee on Race Relations, in Chicago, and then the American Council on Race Relations. After the war, he worked for the United Nations Relief and Rehabilitation Administration, headed a fellowship program for the John Hay Whitney Foundation, and published two critical studies of discrimination against African Americans—*Negro Labor: A National Problem* (1946) and *The Negro Ghetto* (1948)—before being chosen by New York's Democratic governor, Averell Harriman, in 1955 as the state rent commissioner, the first African American to hold a Cabinet office in the state's history.

This was followed by Weaver's appointment by President John F. Kennedy after the 1960 election to be director of the U.S. Housing and Home Finance Agency, at the time the highest federal position ever held by an African American. While heading what he termed an "administrative monstrosity," Weaver authored the acclaimed *The Urban Complex* (1964) and *Dilemmas of Urban America* (1965), which focused attention on the inadequate public services and the inferior schools in lower-class inner cities, but he achieved only minor successes in his endeavors to stimulate better-designed public housing, provide housing for families of low or moderate incomes, and institute federal rent subsidies for the ailing and the elderly.

Kennedy had promised in 1960 to launch a comprehensive program to assist cities, run by a Cabinet-level department. But because of his intention to select Weaver as department secretary, and thus the first African-American Cabinet member, Congress twice rebuffed Kennedy's plan. Southern Democrats opposed Weaver because of his race and his strong support of racially integrated housing. Following the landslide election of Lyndon B. Johnson in 1964, however, Congress approved a bill to establish a new Department of Housing and Urban Development (HUD) in 1965, and, because of Johnson's influence, confirmed his choice of Weaver to head it. By then, Weaver's moderation and reputation for being professionally cautious had won over even southern Democrats who had formerly voted against him, like Sen. A. Willis Robertson of Virginia, who claimed: "I thought he was going to be prejudiced. But I have seen no evidence of prejudice."

Weaver ably administered HUD's diffuse federal programs and the billions of dollars spent to attack urban blight, but innovative policies and plans, such as those in the Demonstration Cities and Metropolitan Development Act, soon fell victim to the escalating expenditures for the Vietnam War and to the conservative backlash fueled by ghetto rioting from 1965 to 1968. In 1969, after more than a third of a century of government service, Weaver left Washington to preside over the City University of New York's Baruch College for two years and then to be Distinguished Professor of Urban Affairs at CUNY's Hunter College until 1978, when he became professor emeritus.

Although never an active frontline fighter in the Civil Rights Movement, Weaver chaired the board of directors of the NAACP in 1960, served on the executive committee of the NAACP Legal Defense Fund from 1973 to 1990, and was president of the National Committee against Discrimination in Housing from 1973 to 1987. He has received numerous awards, including the Spingarn Medal of the NAACP (1962), the New York City Urban League's Frederick Douglass Award (1977), the Schomburg Collection Award (1978),

See also
NAACP

and the Equal Opportunity Day Award of the National Urban League (1987), and has been the recipient of some thirty honorary degrees from colleges and universities. He died July 17, 1997 in New York City.

—HARVARD SITKOFF

WELLS-BARNETT, IDA BELL

Ida Bell Wells-Barnett (July 6, 1862–March 25, 1931), journalist and civil rights activist. Ida Bell Wells was born to Jim and Elizabeth Wells in Holly Springs, Miss., the first of eight children. Her father, the son of his master and a slave woman, worked on a plantation as a carpenter. There he met his future wife, who served as a cook. After emancipation, Jim Wells was active in local Reconstruction politics.

Young Ida Wells received her early education in the grammar school of Shaw University (now Rust College) in Holly Springs, where her father served on the original board of trustees. Her schooling was halted, however, when a yellow fever epidemic claimed the lives of both her parents in 1878 and she assumed responsibility for her siblings. The next year, the family moved to Memphis, Tenn. with an aunt. There Ida found work as a teacher. She later studied at Fisk University and Lemoyne Institute.

A turning point in Wells's life occurred on May 4, 1884. While riding a train to a teaching assignment, she was asked to leave her seat and move to a segregated car. Wells refused, and she was physically ejected from the railway car. She sued the railroad, and though she was awarded $500 by a lower court, the Tennessee Supreme Court reversed the decision in 1887. In the same year, she launched her career in journalism, writing of her experiences in an African-American weekly called *The Living Way*. In 1892, she became the co-owner of a small black newspaper in Memphis, the *Free Speech*. Her articles on the injustices faced by southern blacks, written under the pen name "Iola," were reprinted in a number of black newspapers, including the *New York Age*, the *Detroit Plain-Dealer*, and the *Indianapolis Freeman*.

In March 1892, the lynching of three young black businessmen, Thomas Moss, Calvin McDowell, and Henry Steward, in a suburb of Memphis focused Wells's attention on the pressing need to address the increasing prevalence of this terrible crime in the post-Reconstruction South.

Her approach was characteristically forthright. She argued that though most lynchings were fueled by accusations of rape, they actually were prompted by economic competition between whites and blacks. Wells infuriated most whites by asserting that many sexual liaisons between black men and white women were not rape but mutually consensual.

She urged African Americans in Memphis to move to the West (where, presumably, conditions were more favorable) and to boycott segregated streetcars and discriminatory merchants. Her challenges to the preventing racial orthodoxy of the South were met by mob violence, and in May 1892, while she was out of town, the offices of the *Free Speech* were destroyed by an angry throng of whites.

After her press was destroyed, Wells began to work for the *New York Age*. There, Wells continued to write extensively on lynching and other African-American issues. She penned exposés of southern injustice and decried the situation before European audiences in 1893 and 1894. During these European tours, she criticized some white American supporters of black causes for their halfhearted opposition to lynching. Wells's most extended treatment of the subject, *A Red Record: Tabulated Statistics and Alleged Causes of Lynchings in the United States,* appeared in 1895. This was the first serious statistical study of lynchings in the post-emancipation South. She continued this work for the rest of her life. Some of her more widely read articles in this area include "Lynching and the Excuse for It" (1901) and "Our Country's Lynching Record" (1913). Perhaps her greatest effort in this arena was her tireless campaign for national antilynching legislation. In 1901, she met with President McKinley to convince him of the importance of such legislation. Her appeal was to no avail.

Another issue that provoked Wells's ire was the decision not to permit an African-American pavilion at the 1893 World's Fair. Wells, with the financial support of Frederick Douglass, among others, published a widely circulated booklet entitled *The Reason Why the Colored American Is Not in the World's Exposition* (1893).

In 1895, Wells married Chicago lawyer-editor Ferdinand L. Barnett, who was appointed assistant state attorney for Cook County in 1896. The couple had four children. Chicago would remain their home for the rest of their lives, and though she was a devoted mother and homemaker, Wells-Barnett's political and reform activities were unceasing. She served as Secretary of the National

See also
Frederick Douglass
Marcus Garvey
NAACP

Afro-American Council from 1898 to 1902 and headed its Antilynching Speakers Bureau. She organized, and played an important role in, the founding of the National Association of Colored Women in 1896. In 1910 she founded the Negro Fellowship League in Chicago, which provided housing and employment for black male migrants. As early as 1901, the Barnetts challenged restrictive housing covenants when they moved to the all-white East Side of Chicago. Her concern for the welfare of Chicago's black community led her to become, in 1913, the first black woman probation officer in the nation. She lost her appointment in 1916, when a new city administration came to power.

Wells-Barnett was also active in the fight for women's suffrage. In 1913, she organized the Alpha Suffrage Club, the first black women's suffrage club in Illinois. That year, and again in 1918, she marched with suffragists in Washington, D.C. On the former occasion she insisted on marching with the Illinois contingent, integrating it over the objection of many white women marchers.

Wells-Barnett's militant opposition to the southern status quo placed her at odds with Booker T. Washington and his strategy of accommodationism. She was much more sympathetic to the ideology of W. E. B. Du Bois and in 1906 she attended the founding meeting of the Niagara Movement. She was a member of the original Executive Committee of the National Association for the Advancement of Colored People (NAACP) in 1910. She was, however, uneasy about the integrated hierarchy at the organization and felt their public stance was too tempered, and she ceased active participation in 1912.

In 1916 Wells-Barnett began an affiliation with Marcus Garvey's Universal Negro Improvement Association (UNIA). In December 1918, at a UNIA meeting in New York, Wells-Barnett was chosen along with A. Philip Randolph to represent the organization as a delegate to the upcoming Versailles Conference. Both representatives were repeatedly denied U.S. State Department clearance, however, so they never attended the meeting. Wells-Barnett, however, did speak on behalf of the UNIA at Bethel AME Church in Baltimore at the end of December 1918. Her continued affiliation with the organization after this was less public.

In the last decades of her life, Wells-Barnett continued to write about racial issues and American injustice. The East St. Louis race riot of July 1917 and the Chicago riot of July and August 1919 provided the impetus for impassioned de-

nunciations of the treatment of African Americans in the United States. She wrote *The Arkansas Race Riot* in 1922 in response to the accusation of murder aimed at several black farmers, an accusation that was said to have instigated the disturbance. Most of her later work targeted social and political issues in Chicago. In 1930, Wells-Barnett ran, unsuccessfully as an independent candidate for the Senate from Illinois.

She died the next year, on March 25, 1931. In 1941, the Chicago Housing Authority named one of its first low-rent housing developments the Ida B. Wells Homes. In 1990 the U.S. Postal Service issued an Ida B. Wells stamp.

—MARGARET L. DWIGHT

WEST, DOROTHY

Dorothy West (1912–), writer. Dorothy West was born to Rachel Pease West and Isaac Christopher West in Boston, where she attended Girls' Latin School and Boston University. Hers has been a long and varied writing career that spans over seventy years, beginning with a short story she wrote at age seven. When she was barely fifteen, she was selling short stories to the *Boston Post*. And before she was eighteen, already living in New York, West had won second place in the national competition sponsored by *Opportunity* magazine, an honor she shared with Zora Neale Hurston. The winning story, "The Typewriter," was later included in Edward O'Brien's *The Best Short Stories of 1926*.

As friend of such luminaries as Countee Cullen, Langston Hughes, Claude McKay, and Wallace Thurman, Dorothy West judged them and herself harshly for "degenerat[ing] through [their] vices" and for failing, in general, to live up to their promise. Thus, in what many consider the waning days of the Harlem Renaissance and in the lean years of the depression, West used personal funds to start *Challenge,* a literary quarterly, hoping to recapture some of this failed promise. She served as its editor from 1934 until the last issue appeared in the spring of 1937. It was succeeded in the fall of that year by *New Challenge*. The renamed journal listed West and Marian Minus as coeditors and Richard Wright as associate editor, but West's involvement with the new project was short-lived.

The shift from *Challenge* to *New Challenge* is variously explained but can perhaps be summed up in Wallace Thurman's observation to West that *Challenge* had been too "high schoolish" and "pink

See also
Toni Morrison

tea." Whether *Challenge* was to *New Challenge* what "pink tea" was to "red" is debatable, but West has admitted that *New Challenge* turned resolutely toward a strict Communist party line that she found increasingly difficult to toe. Despite her resistance to this turn in the journal's emphasis, *Challenge,* under West's editorship, succeeded in encouraging and publishing submissions that explored the desperate conditions of the black working class.

Because of her involvement with *Challenge* and her early associations with the figures and events that gave the period its singular status and acclaim, West is now generally designated the "last surviving member of the Harlem Renaissance." The bulk of her writing, however, actually began to be published long after what most literary historians consider the height of the movement.

In the more than sixty short stories written throughout her career, West has shown that form to be her forte. Many of these stories were published in the *New York Daily News.* The first to appear there was "Jack in the Pot" (retitled "Jackpot" by the editors), which won the Blue Ribbon Fiction contest and was anthologized in John Henrik Clarke's 1970 collection *Harlem: Voices from the Soul of Black America.* Another story, "For Richer, for Poorer," has been widely anthologized in textbooks and various collections.

Although the short story has been the mainstay of her career, West is best known for her novel, *The Living Is Easy.* Published in 1948, the novel has been praised for its engaging portrayal of Cleo Judson, the unscrupulous and manipulative woman who brings ruin on herself as well as on family members who fall under her domination and control. But the novel has also earned West high marks for its treatment of the class snobbery, insularity, and all-around shallowness of the New England black bourgeoisie, whom West has termed the "genteel poor." While Mary Helen Washington commends *The Living Is Easy* for its array of feminist themes—"the silencing of women, the need for female community, anger over the limitations and restrictions of women's lives"—in the final analysis she faults it for silencing the mother's voice.

For the past forty years and more, Dorothy West has lived on Martha's Vineyard, contributing since 1968 a generous sampling of occasional pieces and columns to its newspaper, the *Vineyard Gazette.* She is currently at work on a number of projects and recently published a novel titled *The Wedding.*

—DEBORAH MCDOWELL

WHEATLEY, PHILLIS

Phillis Wheatley (c. 1753–December 5, 1784), poet. Phillis Wheatley was born, according to her own testimony, in Gambia, West Africa, along the fertile lowlands of the Gambia River. She was abducted as a small child of seven or eight, and sold in Boston to John and Susanna Wheatley on July 11, 1761. The horrors of the middle passage very likely contributed to the persistent asthma that plagued her throughout her short life. The Wheatleys apparently named the girl, who had nothing but a piece of dirty carpet to conceal her nakedness, after the slaver, the *Phillis*, that transported her. Nonetheless, unlike most slave owners of the time, the Wheatleys permitted Phillis to learn to read, and her poetic talent soon began to emerge.

Her earliest known piece of writing was an undated letter from 1765 (no known copy now exists) to Samson Occom, the Native American Mohegan minister and one of Dartmouth College's first graduates. The budding poet first appeared in print on December 21, 1767, in the *Newport Mercury* newspaper, when the author was about fourteen. The poem, "On Messrs. Hussey and Coffin," relates how the two gentlemen of the title narrowly escaped being drowned off Cape Cod in Massachusetts. Much of her subsequent poetry deals, as well, with events occurring close to her Boston circle. Of her fifty-five extant poems, for example, nineteen are elegies; all but the last of these are devoted to commemorating someone known by the poet. Her last elegy is written about herself and her career.

In early October 1770, Wheatley published an elegy that was pivotal to her career. The subject of the elegy was George Whitefield, an evangelical Methodist minister and privy chaplain to Selina Hastings, countess of Huntingdon. Whitefield made seven journeys to the American colonies, where he was known as "the Voice of the Great Awakening" and "the Great Awakener." Only a week before his death in Newburyport, Mass., on September 30, 1770, Whitefield preached in Boston, where Wheatley very likely heard him. As Susanna Wheatley regularly corresponded with the countess, she and the Wheatley household may well have entertained the Great Awakener. Wheatley's vivid, ostensibly firsthand account in the elegy, replete with quotations, may have been based on an actual acquaintance with Whitefield. In any case, Wheatley's deft elegy became an overnight sensation and was often reprinted.

See also

Literature

It is almost certain that the ship that carried news of Whitefield's death to the countess also carried a copy of Wheatley's elegy, which brought Wheatley to the sympathetic attention of the countess. Such an acquaintance ensured that Wheatley's elegy was also reprinted many times in London, giving the young poet the distinction of an international reputation. When Wheatley's *Poems* was denied publication in Boston for racist reasons, the countess of Huntingdon generously financed its publication in London by Archibald Bell.

Wheatley's support by Selina Hastings and her rejection by male-dominated Boston signal her nourishment as a literary artist by a community of women. All these women—the countess, who encouraged and financed the publication of her *Poems* in 1773; Mary and Susanna Wheatley, who taught her the rudiments of reading and writing; and Obour Tanner, who could empathize probably better than anyone with her condition as a slave—were much older than Wheatley and obviously nurtured her creative development.

During the summer of 1772, Wheatley actually journeyed to England, where she assisted in the preparation of her volume for the press. While in London she enjoyed considerable recognition by such dignitaries as Lord Dartmouth, Lord Lincoln, Granville Sharp (who escorted Wheatley on several tours about London), Benjamin Franklin, and Brook Watson, a wealthy merchant who presented Wheatley with a folio edition of John Milton's *Paradise Lost* and who would later become lord mayor of London. Wheatley was to have been presented at court when Susanna Wheatley became ill. Wheatley was summoned to return to Boston in early August 1773. Sometime before October 18, 1773, she was granted her freedom, according to her own testimony, "at the desire of my friends in England." It seems likely, then, that if Selina Hastings had not agreed to finance Wheatley's *Poems* and if the poet had not journeyed to London, she would never have been manumitted.

As the American Revolution erupted, Wheatley's patriotic feelings began to separate her even more from the Wheatleys, who were loyalists. Her patriotism is clearly underscored in her two most famous Revolutionary War poems. "To His Excellency General Washington" (1775) closes with this justly famous encomium: "A crown, a mansion, and a throne that shine, / With gold unfading WASHINGTON! be thine." "Liberty and Peace" (1784), written to celebrate the Treaty of Paris (September 1783), declares: "And new-born Rome [i.e., America] shall give *Britannia* Law."

Phillis Wheatley's attitude toward slavery has also been misunderstood. Because some of her antislavery statements have been recovered only in the 1970s and '80s, she has often been criticized for ignoring the issue. But her position was clear: In February 1774, for example, Wheatley wrote to Samson Occom that "in every human breast, God has implanted a Principle, which we call Love of Freedom; it is impatient of Oppression, and pants for Deliverance." This letter was reprinted a dozen times in American newspapers over the course of the next twelve months. Certainly Americans of Wheatley's time never questioned her attitude toward slavery after the publication of this letter.

In 1778 Wheatley married John Peters, a free African American who was a jack-of-all-trades, serving in various capacities from storekeeper to advocate for African Americans before the courts. But given the turbulent conditions of a nation caught up in the Revolution, Wheatley's fortunes began to decline steadily. In 1779 she published a set of *Proposals* for a new volume of poems. While the *Proposals* failed to attract subscribers, these *Proposals* attest that the poet had been diligent with her pen since the 1773 *Poems* and that she had indeed produced some 300 pages of new poetry. This volume never appeared, however, and most of its poems are now lost.

Phillis Wheatley Peters and her newborn child died in a shack on the edge of Boston on December 5, 1784. Preceded in death by two other young children, Wheatley's tragic end resembles her beginning in America. Yet Wheatley has left to her largely unappreciative country a legacy of firsts: She was the first African American to publish a book, the first woman writer whose publication was urged and nurtured by a community of women, and the first American woman author who tried to earn a living by means of her writing.

—JOHN C. SHIELDS

WHITE, WALTER FRANCIS

Walter Francis White (July 1, 1893–March 21, 1955), civil rights leader. Walter White, executive secretary of the National Association for the Advancement of Colored People (NAACP) from 1931 to 1955, was born in Atlanta, Ga. Blond and blue-eyed, he was an African American by choice

See also

Civil Rights Movement

NAACP

and social circumstance. In 1906, at age thirteen, he stood, rifle in hand, with his father to protect their home and faced down a mob of whites who had invaded their neighborhood in search of "nigger" blood. He later explained: "I knew then who I was. I was a Negro, a human being with an invisible pigmentation which marked me a person to be hunted, hanged, abused, discriminated against, kept in poverty and ignorance, in order that those whose skin was white would have readily at hand a proof of their superiority, a proof patent and inclusive, accessible to the moron and the idiot as well as to the wise man and the genius."

In 1918, when the NAACP hired him as assistant executive secretary to investigate lynchings, there were sixty-seven such crimes committed that year in sixteen states. By 1955, when he died, there were only three lynchings, all in Mississippi, and the NAACP no longer regarded the problem as its top priority. White investigated forty-two lynchings mostly in the deep South and eight race riots in the North that developed between World War I and after World War II in such cities as Chicago, Philadelphia, Washington, D.C., Omaha, and Detroit.

In August 1946 he helped to create a National Emergency Committee Against Mob Violence. The following month, he led a delegation of labor and civil leaders in a visit with President Harry S. Truman to demand federal action to end the problem. Truman responded by creating the President's Committee on Civil Rights, headed by Charles E. Wilson, chairman and president of General Electric. The committee's report, *To Secure These Rights,* provided the blueprint for the NAACP legislative struggle.

The NAACP's successful struggle against segregation in the armed services was one of White's major achievements. In 1940, as a result of the NAACP's intense protests, President Franklin D. Roosevelt appointed Judge William H. Hastie as civilian aide to the secretary of war, promoted Colonel Benjamin O. Davis, the highest-ranking black officer in the Army, to brigadier general, and appointed Colonel Campbell Johnson special aide to the director of Selective Service. As significant as these steps were, they did not satisfy White because they were woefully inadequate. So he increasingly intensified the NAACP's efforts in this area.

White then attempted to get the U.S. Senate to investigate employment discrimination and segregation in the armed services, but the effort failed. He therefore persuaded the NAACP board

to express its support for the threat by A. Philip Randolph, president of the Brotherhood of Sleeping Car Porters, to lead a march on Washington in demand for jobs for blacks in the defense industries and an end to segregation in the military. To avoid the protest, President Roosevelt on June 25, 1941, issued Executive Order 8802, barring discrimination in the defense industries and creating the Fair Employment Practice Committee. That was the first time a U.S. president acted to end racial discrimination, and the date marked the launching of the modern Civil Rights Movement. Subsequently, the NAACP made the quest for presidential leadership in protecting the rights of blacks central to its programs.

As a special war correspondent for the *New York Post* in 1943 and 1945, White visited the European, Mediterranean, Middle Eastern, and Pacific theaters of operations and provided the War Department with extensive recommendations for ending racial discrimination in the military. His book *A Rising Wind* reported on the status of black troops in the European and Mediterranean theaters.

White was as much an internationalist as a civil rights leader. In 1921 he attended the second Pan-African Congress sessions in England, Belgium, and France, which were sponsored by the NAACP and led by W. E. B. Du Bois. While on a year's leave of absence from the NAACP in

WALTER WHITE

White, who became executive director of the NAACP in 1931, managed the organization's legal and political challenge to racial inequality for a quarter century.
PRINTS AND PHOTOGRAPHS DIVISION, LIBRARY OF CONGRESS

1949 and 1950, he participated in the "Round the World Town Meeting of the Air," visiting Europe, Israel, Egypt, India, and Japan.

In 1945 White, Du Bois, and Mary McLeod Bethune represented the NAACP as consultants to the American delegation at the founding of the United Nations in San Francisco. They urged that the colonial system be abolished; that the United Nations recognize equality of the races; that it adopt a bill of rights for all people; and that an international agency be established to replace the colonial system. Many of their recommendations were adopted by the United Nations.

White similarly protested the menial roles that blacks were forced to play in Hollywood films and sought an end to the harmful and dangerous stereotypes of the race that the industry was spreading. He enlisted the aid of Wendell Willkie, the Republican presidential candidate who was defeated in 1940 and who had become counsel to the motion picture industry, in appealing to Twentieth Century Fox, Warner Brothers, Metro-Goldwyn-Mayer, and other major studios and producers for more representative roles for blacks in films. He then contemplated creating an NAACP bureau in Hollywood to implement the organization's programs there. Although the bureau's idea fizzled, the NAACP did create a Beverly Hills-Hollywood branch in addition to others in California.

During White's tenure as executive secretary, the NAACP won the right to vote for blacks in the South by getting the Supreme Court to declare the white Democratic primary unconstitutional; opposed the poll tax and other devices that were used to discriminate against blacks at the polls; forged an alliance between the organization and the industrial trade unions; removed constitutional roadblocks to residential integration; equalized teachers' salaries in the South; and ended segregation in higher education institutions in addition to winning the landmark *Brown* v. *Board of Education* decision in 1954, overturning the Supreme Court's "separate but equal" doctrine. Overall, White led the NAACP to become the nation's dominant force in the struggle to get the national government to uphold the Constitution and protect the rights of African Americans.

White was a gregarious, sociable man who courted on a first-name basis a vast variety of people of accomplishment and influence like Willkie, Eleanor Roosevelt, Harold Ickes, and Governor Averell Harriman of New York. In 1949 he created a furor by divorcing his first wife, Gladys, and marrying Poppy Cannon, a white woman who was a magazine food editor.

In addition to his many articles, White wrote two weekly newspaper columns. One was for the *Chicago Defender,* a respected black newspaper, and the other for white newspapers like the Sunday *Herald Tribune.* He wrote two novels, *The Fire in the Flint* (1924) and *Flight* (1926); *Rope and Faggot* (1929, reprint 1969), an exhaustive study of lynchings; *A Man Called White* (1948), an autobiography; and *A Rising Wind* (1945). An assessment of civil rights progress, *How Far the Promised Land?* was published shortly after White's death in 1955.

—DENTON L. WATSON

WIDEMAN, JOHN EDGAR

John Edgar Wideman (June 14, 1941–), novelist. Born in Washington, D.C., John Edgar Wideman spent much of his early life first in Homewood, Pa., and then in Shadyside, an upper-middle-class area of Pittsburgh. In 1960 he received a scholarship to the University of Pennsylvania, where he proved himself equally outstanding in his undergraduate studies and on the basketball court. He graduated Phi Beta Kappa in 1963, and his athletic achievements led to his induction into the Big Five Basketball Hall of Fame. Upon graduation, Wideman became only the second African American to be awarded a Rhodes Scholarship (Alain Locke had received one almost fifty-five years earlier), an honor which allowed him to study for three years at Oxford University in England, where he earned a degree in eighteenth-century literature.

After returning to the United States in 1966 and attending the Creative Writing Workshop at the University of Iowa as a Kent Fellow, Wideman returned to the University of Pennsylvania, where he served as an instructor (and later, professor) of English. In 1967, at the age of twenty-six, he published his first novel, *A Glance Away.* The novel was well received by critics, and two years after its appearance Wideman published *Hurry Home* (1969), a novel that chronicled its protagonist's struggle to reconcile the past and the present. After publishing a third novel in 1973, a dense and technically complex work entitled *The Lynchers,* Wideman found his name was increasingly associated with a diverse set of literary forebears including James Joyce, William Faulkner, and Ralph Ellison.

During this period, Wideman served as the assistant basketball coach (1968–1972) at the Uni-

See also
Alain Locke

versity of Pennsylvania, as well as director of the Afro-American Studies Program (1971–1973). In 1975 he left Philadelphia to teach at the University of Wyoming in Laramie. Six years later he ended a long literary silence with the publication of two books: a collection of stories, *Damballah*, and *Hiding Place*, a novel. Both books focus on Wideman's Homewood neighborhood. And with the publication in 1983 of the third book in the trilogy, Wideman's reputation as a major literary talent was assured. *Sent for You Yesterday* won the 1984 P.E.N./Faulkner Award, winning over several more established writers.

At this point, Wideman was drawn (by circumstance rather than choice) into the world of nonfiction after his brother, Robbie, was convicted of armed robbery and sentenced to life imprisonment. At times angry, at others deeply introspective and brooding, *Brothers and Keepers* (1984) relates the paradoxical circumstances of two brothers: one a successful college professor and author, the other a drug addict struggling to establish an identity apart from his older, famous brother. Nominated for the 1985 National Book Award, the memoir set the stage for what arguably might be called Wideman's "next phase."

In 1986, after seeing his son, Jake, tried and convicted for the murder of a camping companion, Wideman moved back east to teach at the University of Massachusetts, Amherst. The following year saw the publication of his less than successful but nonetheless intriguing novel *Reuben*. Two years later, Wideman published a collection of stories, *Fever* (1989), and followed that in 1990 with a novel, *Philadelphia Fire*. Both of these works reflect Wideman's ability to interrogate his own experiences, even as his fiction takes up pertinent social issues. In the short stories and the novel, Wideman weaves fiction into the fabric of historical events (the former involves an outbreak of yellow fever in eighteenth-century Philadelphia, and the latter the aftermath of the confrontation with and subsequent bombing by Philadelphia police of the radical group Move). In 1992 Wideman brought out *The Stories of John Edgar Wideman* (1992), which contains ten new stories written especially for the collection, themselves entitled *All Stories Are True*. What distinguishes these ten stories is their extraordinary repositioning of the reader's attention, away from the source of the stories and toward the human issues they depict. As he works to make sense of his own assets and losses, one finds in Wideman's fiction a continuing engagement with the complexity of history as layered narrative and an ability to

articulate the inner essence of events that often elude us.

—HERMAN BEAVERS

WILKINS, ROY OTTOWAY

Roy Ottoway Wilkins (August 30, 1901–September 8, 1981), civil rights leader, laborer, and journalist. Born in a first-floor flat in a black section of St. Louis, Mo., Roy Wilkins got his middle name from the African-American physician who delivered him, Dr. Ottoway Fields. At age four, following his mother's death, Wilkins went to St. Paul, Minn. to live with his Aunt Elizabeth (Edmundson) and Uncle Sam Williams. The Williamses wrested legal guardianship of Roy, his brother, Earl, and sister, Armeda, from their absentee, footloose father, William.

After graduating from the University of Minnesota (1923) and following a stint as night editor of the college newspaper and editor of the black weekly, the *St. Paul Appeal*, Wilkins moved to Kansas City where he was editor of the *Kansas City Call* for eight years. In 1929 in Kansas City he married Aminda Badeau. In St. Paul and Kansas City, he was active in the local National Association for the Advancement of Colored People chapters during a period when the NAACP was waging a full-scale attack against America's Jim Crow practices. Under Wilkins's stewardship the *Call* gave banner headline coverage to NAACP (Acting) Executive Secretary Walter White's 1930 campaign to defeat President Herbert Hoover's nomination of Circuit Court Judge John J. Parker to the United States Supreme Court. Parker, in a race for North Carolina governor ten years earlier, had declared his antipathy toward blacks. The *Call* published Parker's photo alongside his quote during the campaign: "If I should be elected Governor . . . and find that my election was due to one Negro vote, I would immediately resign my office." The *Kansas City Call* editorialized that "for a man who would be judge, prejudice is the unpardonable sin. . . ." The NAACP's success in blocking Parker's ascension to the U.S. Supreme Court gave Walter White national prominence and a friendship was forged between White, in New York, and Wilkins, in Kansas City.

In 1931 White invited Wilkins to join the national staff of the NAACP in New York as assis-

While the local branches were largely staffed by African Americans, the national NAACP was a largely white group during its early days.

480

See also
Brown v. Board of Education of Topeka, Kansas
NAACP

tant secretary. Wilkins accepted the post with great excitement and anticipation, regarding the NAACP at the time as "the most militant civil rights organization in the country." Wilkins, in his autobiography, recalled that the NAACP during the 1920s and '30s, had "pounded down the South's infamous grandfather clauses, exposed lynchings, and pushed for a federal anti-lynching law" and had "exposed the spread of peonage among black sharecroppers in the South, prodded the Supreme Court into throwing out verdicts reached by mob-dominated juries, and blotted out residential segregation by municipal ordinance." The NAACP was overturning the racial status quo and Wilkins wanted to be involved.

But there was also dissent within the NAACP. In 1934, following a blistering public attack on Walter White's leadership and on the NAACP's integrationist philosophy from NAACP cofounder W. E. B. Du Bois, who subsequently resigned as editor of the NAACP's penetrating and influential magazine, *The Crisis,* Wilkins succeeded Du Bois as editor of *The Crisis* while he continued in his post as assistant secretary. Wilkins was editor of *The Crisis* for fifteen years (1934–1949).

Du Bois's open flirtation with voluntary segregation did not alter the NAACP's course; throughout the 1930s, '40s, and '50s, the NAACP continued to attack Jim Crow laws and to work on behalf of blacks' full integration into American society. But by 1950, Walter White's leadership was on the wane; in that year Wilkins was designated NAACP administrator. White lost key support because of a divorce and his remarriage to a white woman; failing health made him especially vulnerable to his detractors. Upon White's death in 1955, Wilkins became executive secretary of the NAACP in the wake of its momentous victory in *Brown* v. *Board of Education of Topeka, Kansas* (1954), where NAACP lawyers had successfully argued that racially separate public schools were *inherently* unequal.

Wilkins served as the NAACP's executive secretary/director for twenty-two years, longer than any other NAACP leader. His tenure characterized him as a pragmatist and strategist who believed that reasoned arguments, both in the courtroom and in public discourse, would sway public opinion and public officials to purposeful actions on behalf of racial equality. During the 1960s, Wilkins was widely regarded as "Mr. Civil Rights," employing the NAACP's huge nationwide membership of 400,000 and lawyers' network to back up the direct-action campaigns of

more fiery leaders like the Rev. Dr. Martin Luther King, Jr., and James Farmer. The NAACP supplied money and member support to the massive March on Washington in 1963. Always moderate in language and temperament, and lacking a charismatic personal style, Wilkins was most comfortable as a strategist and adviser, had meetings with presidents from Franklin D. Roosevelt to Jimmy Carter, and was a friend of President Lyndon B. Johnson. Major civil rights legislation was signed into law in Wilkins's presence, including the Civil Rights Act of 1964, the Voting Rights Act of 1965, and the Fair Housing Act of 1968.

As standard-bearer of integration, the NAACP during the turbulent 1960s and throughout the 1970s, was pilloried with criticism from black separatists and from whites who opposed school busing and affirmative action programs. Wilkins steered a steady course, however, eschewing racial quotas but insisting on effective legal remedies to purposeful and systemic racial discrimination that included race-conscious methods of desegregating schools, colleges, and the work place. He simultaneously took to task the exponents of black nationalism. During the height of the Black Power movement, in 1966, Wilkins denounced calls for black separatism, saying black power "can mean in the end only black death." Although one of America's most influential and well-known leaders, Wilkins refused to arrogate to himself the plaudits due him because of his successes. He was a frugal administrator and humble individual who routinely took the subway to work and back home.

By 1976, after forty-five years with the NAACP, Wilkins, at age seventy-five, was barely holding on to his post at the NAACP's helm. A year later, in failing health, he retired to his home in Queens, N.Y., where he spent his last years in the company of his wife. The winner of the NAACP's Spingarn Medal in 1964, and the recipient of many other awards, including over fifty honorary degrees, Wilkins died in September 1981. At his funeral in New York City hundreds of mourners, black and white, remembered him as a man who refused to bend to fashion.

—MICHAEL MEYERS

WILLIAMS, JOHN ALFRED

John Alfred Williams (1925–), writer, editor, and educator. Williams was born in Jackson, Miss., but raised in Syracuse, N.Y. After service in

See also

Education

BERT WILLIAMS

Performer Lights Up the Vaudeville Stage

Egbert Austin "Bert" Williams (ca. November 12, 1874–March 4, 1922), entertainer. It is likely, though unconfirmed, that Williams was born in Antigua, the West Indies, on November 12, 1874. In 1885 he moved with his parents, Fred and Julia, to Riverside, Calif., where his father became a railroad conductor. After high school, Bert moved to San Francisco, seeking an entertainment career. He sang in rough saloons, toured lumber camps in a small minstrel troupe, learned minstrel dialect, became a comedian, and in 1893 formed a partnership with George Walker that lasted sixteen years and brought them fame.

After years of trial and error, by 1896 they had evolved their act—the classic minstrel contrast of the "darky" and the "dandy." The large, light-skinned Williams used blackface makeup, ill-fitting clothes, heavy dialect, and a shuffle to play hapless bumblers while the smaller, darker Walker played well-dressed, cocky, nimble-footed hustlers. In 1899, they launched the first of a string of successful African-American musicals, *A Lucky Coon*. In 1903, *In Dahomey*, with exotic African elements, exciting chorus numbers, hard-luck songs and comedy for Williams, and snappy dances and a wise-guy role for Walker, brought them international acclaim, from appearances on Broadway to a command performance at Buckingham Palace in London. Their successes continued until Walker fell ill and retired in 1909.

Without Walker, Williams became a "single" in vaudeville and in 1910 was the first African American to perform in the *Ziegfeld Follies*. He was at the center of American show business, where he remained—in the *Follies* (1910–1912, 1914–1917, 1919), other top-notch revues and vaudeville (1913, 1918), and his own shows (1920–1922). A master of pantomime, pathos, understatement, and timing, he gave universal appeal to his poignant hit songs, such as "Nobody" and "I'm a Jonah Man," and his comedy sketches of sad-sack bellhops, gamblers, and porters, despite heavy dialect and caricatures. The critic Ashton Stevens in 1910 hailed Williams as "the Mark Twain of his color," whose "kindly, infectious human . . . made humans of us all."

Williams felt blackface and dialect liberated him as a comedian by letting him become "another person" onstage, but offstage this racially stereotyped minstrel mask stifled a man who longed to be accepted as a human being. "Bert Williams is the funniest man I ever saw," observed *Follies* veteran W. C. Fields, "and the saddest man I ever knew." Suffering discrimination and rejection everywhere except onstage and at home with his devoted wife, Lottie, whom he married in 1900, he became a heavy drinker plagued by depression. Despite failing health, he drove himself mercilessly onstage, where he was happiest. On February 25, 1922, weakened by pneumonia, he struggled through a matinee of his new show, *Under the Bamboo Tree*. During the performance that evening, he collapsed. He died a week later.

—ROBERT C. TOLL

White men in blackface had portrayed black people almost since the first contact of the races.

PAGE 456

the Navy in World War II, he returned to Syracuse, married, and fathered two sons. When his marriage ended in 1952, he turned to writing. With a degree in journalism and English from Syracuse University, he began a series of jobs in public relations, radio and television, and publishing. In the late 1950s and early 1960s he traveled the world as a correspondent for *Ebony, Holiday, Jet, Newsweek,* and other magazines, and completed two novels, one of which was published as *The Angry Ones.*

The diverse characters and plots of Williams's many novels are unified by an impulse to correct history and analyze American life from an uncompromisingly black perspective. His protagonists are African-American or African professionals with the courage to battle their weaknesses as human beings as well as their ambiguous status as blacks in a racist society. His narratives are always informed by the problems and possibilities of the human capacity to give and receive love.

Williams's novels are often grouped in three phases. In the first phase, an initial optimism balances a frank depiction of racial struggle. In *The Angry Ones* (1960), he establishes major themes: guilt, racial equity, institutionalized racism, black male-black female tensions, blacks in the military, and the mutual exploitation of interracial sex. In *Night Song* (1962), he evokes the Greenwich Village jazz environment with symbolic resonances between the white world of day and the black underworld of night. *Sissie* (1965) portrays a black family seeking refuge in success, but driven by memories of earlier hard times. A darker vision of

racial apocalypse runs through the middle novels. In *The Man Who Cried I Am* (1967), Williams juxtaposes the poisonous racism of the body politic on the larger scale with the cancer destroying Max Reddick's physical system, as the dying reporter struggles to complete the task laid on him by his murdered mentor and rival Harry Ames, who resembles Richard Wright. In *Sons of Darkness, Sons of Light* (1969), Williams dramatizes the plight of a decent man who can only put his own household in order, as the American social order explodes around him. *Captain Blackman* (1972) asserts the ubiquitous history of African Americans in the military, from the Revolutionary War to Vietnam, and extrapolates from that experience to an impending racial coup d'état.

Consciousness of an emerging black unity underlies the novels of Williams's third phase. In *Mothersill and the Foxes* (1975), the author takes the reader on a comic odyssey of social service and sexual adventurism that lurches past mass murder and suicide, to the verge of incest, but ends in domestic tranquillity. In *The Junior Bachelor Society* (1976) he portrays middle-class African Americans uniting to confront internal and external threats. In *!Click Song* (1982), Williams intertwines the careers of a black writer and a Jewish writer, affirming writing itself as one of the few instrumentalities of human possibility and hope.

Jacob's Ladder (1987) perhaps signals a new period in Williams's work, returning to the atmosphere of conspiracy and betrayal of the middle period but with the optimism of the first and the sense of emerging unity of the third phase. The powerful and innovative *The Man Who Cried I Am* is acclaimed as his masterpiece, placing him in the first rank of American novelists, although *!Click Song* is thought by some critics to be an even greater achievement. Yet Williams still is, as he was characterized in 1969 in the *New York Times Book Review*, "probably the most important—and least recognized—Negro writer in America" of his generation.

—JAMES DE JONGH

WINFREY, OPRAH GAIL

Oprah Gail Winfrey (January 29, 1954–), talk-show host, actress. Born on a farm in Kosciusko, Miss., to Vernita Lee and Vernon Winfrey, Oprah Winfrey was reared by her grandmother for the early part of her life. At age six, she was sent to live with her mother, who worked as a domestic, and two half brothers in Milwaukee. It was in Milwaukee that Winfrey began to display her oratorical gifts, reciting poetry at socials and teas. During her adolescence, Winfrey began to misbehave to such a degree that she was sent to live with her father in Nashville. Under the strict disciplinary regime imposed by her father, Winfrey started to flourish, distinguishing herself in debate and oratory. At sixteen, she won an Elks Club oratorical contest that awarded her a scholarship to Tennessee State University.

While a freshman in college, Winfrey won the Miss Black Nashville and Miss Black Tennessee pageants. As a result of this exposure, she received a job offer from a local television station and in her sophomore year became a news anchor at WTVF-TV in Nashville. After graduating in 1976, Winfrey took a job with WJZ-TV in Baltimore as a reporter and coanchor of the evening news. In 1977 she was switched to updates on local news, which appeared during the ABC national morning show *Good Morning America*. That same year she found her niche as a talk-show host, cohosting WJZ-TV's morning show, *Baltimore Is Talking*.

In 1984 Winfrey moved to Chicago to take over *A.M. Chicago*, a talk show losing in the ratings to Phil Donahue's popular morning program. Within a month Winfrey's ratings were equal to Donahue's. In three months she surpassed him. A year and a half later the show extended to an hour and was renamed *The Oprah Winfrey Show*. The show, which covers a wide range of topics from the lighthearted to the sensational or the tragic, was picked up for national syndication by King World Productions in 1986. By 1993 *The Oprah Winfrey Show* was seen in 99 percent of U.S. television markets and sixty-four countries. Since the show first became eligible in 1986, it has won Emmy awards for best talk show, or best talk-show hostess each year except one.

In 1985 Winfrey was cast as the strong-willed Sofia in the film version of Alice Walker's *The Color Purple*, for which she received an Oscar nomination. The following year she formed her own production company, HARPO Productions, to develop projects. In 1989 Winfrey produced and acted in a television miniseries based on Gloria Naylor's novel *The Women of Brewster Place*, and in 1993 she starred in and produced the television drama *There Are No Children Here*. That same year *Forbes* magazine listed Winfrey as America's richest entertainer based on her 1992 and 1993 earnings of approximately $98 million.

See also
Alice Walker

Winfrey's influence on the public became apparent when she introduced the Oprah Book Club in the fall of 1996. Sales of the books she chose increased by an average of 700,000 copies, causing a commotion in the publishing industry as Winfrey's selections created instant bestsellers. Her impact was further emphasized when she made a comment about her unwillingness to eat beef during an April 1996 show about mad cow disease. When the price of cattle futures dropped 10% the next day, a group of Texas cattlemen sued her for damages. She was cleared of liability in February of 1998.

—KENYA DILDAY

WOODRUFF, HALE ASPACIO

Hale Aspacio Woodruff (August 26, 1900– September 10, 1980), painter, educator. Born in Cairo, Ill., Hale Woodruff moved with his mother to Nashville, Tenn., where he attended public schools. In 1920, he moved to Indianapolis to study at the John Herron Art Institute while working part-time as a political cartoonist for the black newspaper the *Indiana Ledger*. In 1927, he traveled to Europe and lived in France for the next four years. He studied with the African-American painter Henry O. Tanner and at the

R&B reflected the confluence of jazz, blues, gospel, and vocal harmony group music that took place in cities such as New York, Detroit, Chicago, Memphis, Philadelphia, and New Orleans.

PAGE 592

STEVIE WONDER
Gifted Singer / Songwriter Redefines Motown

Stevie Wonder (Morris, Stevland) (May 13, 1950–), singer and songwriter. Born Stevland Morris on May 13, 1950, in Saginaw, Mich., Stevie Wonder has been blind since birth. He grew up in Detroit and by the age of nine had mastered the harmonica, drums, bongos, and piano. His early influences included rhythm-and-blues artists "B. B." King and Ray Charles. Once his youthful talent as a musician and composer was discerned, Berry Gordy signed him to Hitsville, U.S.A. (later known as Motown) in 1961. He was soon dubbed "Little Stevie Wonder" and in 1963 achieved the first of many number one pop singles with "Fingertips—Pt. 2," a live recording featuring blues-flavored harmonica solos. The album of the same year, *Twelve-Year-Old Genius,* was Motown's first number one pop album. From 1964 to 1971, Wonder had several top twenty hits, including "Uptight (Everything's Alright)" (1966), "Mon Cherie Amour" (1969), and "Signed, Sealed, Delivered I'm Yours" (1970), cowritten with Syreeta Wright, to whom he was married for eighteen months.

In 1971 at the age of twenty-one, Wonder obtained a release from his Motown contract that allowed him to break free of the strict Motown production sound. With his substantial earnings he employed the latest electronic technology, the ARP and Moog synthesizers, to record original material for future use, playing most of the instruments himself. That same year he negotiated a new contract with Motown for complete artistic control over his career and production. The album *Music in My Mind*

that followed was the first fruit of his new artistic freedom. In 1975, he renegotiated with Motown for an unprecedented $13 million advance for a seven-year contract.

Wonder's humanitarian interests have charged his music since the early 1970s. His material has consistently reflected an effort to incorporate contemporary musical trends (reggae and rap) and social commentary that has given a voice to the evolution of American black consciousness. This is demonstrated in "Living for the City" (1973), a ghetto-dweller's narrative; "Happy Birthday" (1980), the anthem for a nationwide appeal to honor the Rev. Dr. Martin Luther King, Jr.'s birthday as a national holiday; "Don't Drive Drunk" (1984); and "It's Wrong," (1985), a critique of South African apartheid. He also supported such causes as the elimination of world hunger (U.S.A. for Africa's recording "We Are the World"), AIDS research ("That's What Friends Are For" with singer Dionne Warwick and friends, 1987), and cancer research.

Wonder's popularity has been strengthened by his scores for various films including *The Woman in Red* (1984), which won an Oscar for Best Original Song ("I Just Called to Say I Love You") and *Jungle Fever* (1991), a film about interracial relationships by Spike Lee. Wonder has been the recipient of more than sixteen Grammys, eighteen gold records, five platinum records, and five gold albums. He was inducted into the Songwriters Hall of Fame in 1982.

—KYRA D. GAUNT

In 1973 Motown was the biggest black-owned company in the United States.

PAGE 469

Académie Scandinave and Académie Moderne in 1927 and 1928. Like other American artists who sought an education in the center of the art world, Woodruff spent his time recapitulating the succession of avant-garde art movements of the previous fifty years. His landscapes and figure paintings first synthesized elements of the late-nineteenth-century styles of impressionism and postimpressionism in their interest in the non-realistic shifts of color and the manipulation of the texture of the brushstroke. His key work of the period, *The Card Players* (1930; repainted in 1978), plays on the distortions of figure and space found in the work of Paul Cézanne and the cubists Pablo Picasso and Georges Braque. This work emphasizes Woodruff's debt to African art (which had also been a source for the cubists) in the masklike nature of the faces. Woodruff had first encountered African art in Indianapolis in the early 1920s, when he saw one of the first books on the subject. As it was written in German, he could not read it; but he was intrigued by the objects. Woodruff and the African-American philosopher and teacher Dr. Alain Locke visited flea markets in Paris where the artist bought his first works of African art.

In 1931, Woodruff returned to the United States to found the art department at Atlanta University. Through his pioneering efforts, the national African-American arts community developed the kind of cohesion that previously had been lacking. Woodruff himself taught painting, drawing, and printmaking. To teach sculpture, he recruited the artist Nancy Elizabeth Prophet. The works that came from the department's faculty and students came to be known as the "Atlanta School" because their subjects were the African-American population of that city. Fully representational with modernist nuances, they fall into the style of American regionalism practiced throughout the country at that time. The use of woodcuts and linoleum prints added a populist tone to these works, which dealt with everyday life. Besides teaching, he brought to Atlanta University exhibitions of a wide range of works, including those of historical and contemporary black artists and the Harmon Foundation exhibitions, providing a unique opportunity for the entire black Atlanta community, since the local art museum was then segregated. The year 1942 saw the initiation of the Atlanta University Annuals, a national juried exhibition for black artists that expanded opportunities for many who were frequently excluded from the American art scene. Woodruff's legacy can be seen in the re-markable list of his students—Frederick Flemister, Eugene Grigsby, Wilmer Jennings, and Hayward Oubré—and of the artists who showed in the Annuals, including Charles Alston, Lois Mailou Jones, Elizabeth Catlett, Claude Clark, Ernest Crichlow, Aaron Douglas, William H. Johnson, Norman Lewis, Hughie Lee-Smith, Jacob Lawrence, and Charles White. The exhibitions continued until 1970.

During this same period, Woodruff, as part of his efforts to present a populist art, produced a series of murals. Two of his inspirations were the murals placed in public buildings across the country by WPA artists, and the Mexican mural movement. Woodruff himself received a grant to study with Diego Rivera for six weeks in the summer of 1934, when he assisted in fresco painting. After completing two WPA murals, he painted the major work of this period, the *Amistad Murals* (1938–1939) at Talladega College (Alabama). Designed in the boldly figurative style associated with social realism, the murals depict the mutiny led by Cinqué aboard the slave ship *Amistad* in 1834 and the subsequent trial and repatriation of the Africans. Other mural projects included *The Founding of Talladega College* (1938–1939), murals at the Golden State Mutual Life Insurance Company (Los Angeles) on the contribution of blacks to the development of California (1948), and *The Art of the Negro* for Atlanta University (1950–1951).

In 1946, after receiving a two-year Julius Rosenwald Foundation Fellowship to study in New York (1943–1945), Woodruff moved to that city permanently to teach in the art education department of New York University. The move was not a rejection of the South, but came as an attempt by Woodruff to be part of the new art capital which had shifted from Paris to New York. Woodruff changed his style from that of a figurative painter of the American scene to a practitioner of the ideas of abstract expressionism. While employing the gestural spontaneity of that style, he incorporated design elements from the African art he had studied since his student days in Indianapolis. Worked into his compositions are motifs from a variety of African cultural objects, including Asante goldweights, Dogon masks, and Yoruba Shango implements—a kind of aesthetic pan-Africanism. This, the third major style of his career, demonstrates the adaptability of an artist always open to new currents in both the aesthetic and political worlds. He continued to be supportive of African-American artists by being one of the founders in 1963 of Spiral, a group of black New

See also

Romare Bearden

Jacob Lawrence

York artists (including Charles Alston, Emma Amos, Romare Bearden, Norman Lewis, and Richard Mayhew) who sought to weave the visual arts into the fabric of the civil rights struggle.

Woodruff received awards from the Harmon Foundation in 1926, 1928 and 1929, 1931, 1933, and 1935, and an Atlanta University Purchase Prize in 1955. He received a Great Teacher Award at NYU in 1966 and became professor emeritus in 1968.

—HELEN M. SHANNON

WOODS, ELDRICK "TIGER"

Eldrick "Tiger" Woods (December 30, 1975–), golfer. Tiger Woods is the most acclaimed golfer of African-American ancestry to compete on the Professional Golfers' Association (PGA) tour. His enormous success is attributable to his great talent and personal appeal, especially among young people. Woods' greatest achievement thus far is his 1997 victory in the prestigious Masters Tournament by a record margin of 12 strokes. He was the youngest Masters champion in history

Born and raised in Cypress, California, Woods became interested in golf at a young age. At 2 he putted against Bob Hope on the Mike Douglas Show. By 17 he had won three U.S. Junior Amateur Championships between (1991–1993). His come-from-behind victory at the 1996 U.S. Amateur Championship capped an impressive amateur career including the NCAA title and three successive U.S. Amateur victories.

Woods turned professional in August 1996, hoping to earn enough money in eight tournaments ($150,000) to qualify for the 1997 PGA Tour. He stunned the golf world by winning the Las Vegas Invitational and the Disney/Oldsmobile Classic, earning $790,594 and finishing twenty-fifth on the money list. He was PGA Tour's 1996 Rookie of the Year.

Apart from his Masters victory, Woods won another four tournaments in 1997 including the Mercedes Championships, the Asian Honda Classic in Thailand, the GTE Byron Nelson Classic, and the Motorola Western Open. He finished 1997 with a record $2,066,833—a PGA Tour record for single season earnings—and was selected 1997 Player of the Year by the PGA Tour, PGA of America, and Golf Writers Association of America. The Associated Press chose Woods as the 1997 Male Athlete of the Year.

Woods, whose father is black and mother is of Chinese-Thai ancestry, is conscious of the significance of his Masters win for minority golfers. He pays tribute to black golfers who have broken barriers in the sport including Calvin Peete and Charlie Sifford, and Lee Elder. Woods is expected to be a champion for years to come.

—JILL LECTKA

WOODSON, CARTER GODWIN

Carter Godwin Woodson (December 19, 1875–April 3, 1950), historian, educator. He was born in New Canton, in Buckingham County, Va. Woodson probably descended from slaves held by Dr. John Woodson, who migrated from Devonshire, England, to Jamestown, Va., in 1619. He was the first and only black American of slave parents to earn a Ph.D. in history. After the Civil War, Woodson's grandfather and father, who were skilled carpenters, were forced into sharecropping. After saving for many years, the family purchased land and eked out a meager living in the late 1870s and 1880s.

Although they were poor, James Henry and Anne Eliza Woodson instilled in their son high

CARTER WOODSON

Woodson founded the Association for the Study of Negro Life and History, and began the work that sustained him for the rest of his career. PHOTOGRAPHS AND PRINTS DIVISION, SCHOMBURG CENTER FOR RESEARCH IN BLACK CULTURE, THE NEW YORK PUBLIC LIBRARY, ASTOR, LENOX AND TILDEN FOUNDATIONS

743

WOODSON, CARTER GODWIN

morality and strong character through religious teachings and a thirst for education. One of nine children, the youngest boy and a frail child, Carter purportedly was his mother's favorite and was sheltered. He belonged to that first generation of blacks whose mothers did not have to curry favor with whites to provide an education for their children. As a boy Woodson worked on the family farm, and in his teens he was an agricultural day laborer. In the late 1880s the family moved to West Virginia, where Woodson's father worked in railroad construction and Woodson worked as a coal miner in Fayette County. In 1895, at the age of twenty, Woodson enrolled at Frederick Douglass High School. Perhaps because he was older than the rest of the students and felt that he needed to catch up, he completed four years of course work in two years and graduated in 1897. He then enrolled at Berea College in Berea, Ky., which had been founded by abolitionists in the 1850s for the education of ex-slaves. He briefly attended Lincoln University in Pennsylvania, but graduated from Berea College in 1903, just a year before Kentucky would pass the infamous "Day Law," which prohibited interracial education. Woodson then briefly taught at Frederick Douglass High School. Because of his belief in the uplifting power of education, and because of the opportunity to travel to another country to observe and experience its culture firsthand, he decided to accept a teaching post in the Philippines, remaining there from 1903 to 1907.

Experiences as a college student and high school teacher expanded and influenced Woodson's worldview and shaped his ideas about the ways in which education could transform society, improve race relations, and benefit the lower classes. Determined to obtain additional education, he enrolled in correspondence courses at the University of Chicago. By 1907 he was enrolled there as a full-time student and earned both a bachelor's degree and a master's degree in European history. His thesis examined French diplomatic policy toward Germany in the eighteenth century. He then attended Harvard University, matriculating in 1909 and earning his Ph.D. in history in 1912. He studied with Edward Channing, Albert Bushnell Hart, and Frederick Jackson Turner, the latter of whom had moved from the University of Wisconsin to Harvard in 1910. Turner influenced the interpretation Woodson advanced in his dissertation, which was a study of the events leading to secession in West Virginia after the Civil War broke out. Unfortunately, Woodson never published the dissertation.

Woodson taught in the Washington, D.C., public schools, at Howard University, and at the West Virginia Collegiate Institute. In 1915, in Chicago, he founded the Association for the Study of Negro Life and History, and began the work that sustained him for the rest of his career. Indeed, his life was given over to the pursuit of truth about the African and African-American pasts. He later founded the *Journal of Negro History,* the *Negro History Bulletin,* and the Associated Publishers; launched the annual celebration of Negro History Week in February 1926; and had a distinguished publishing career as a scholar of African-American history.

After the publication in 1915 of *The Education of the Negro Prior to 1861,* his first book, Woodson began a scholarly career that, even if judged by output alone, very few of his contemporaries or successors could match. By 1947, when the ninth edition of his textbook *The Negro in Our History* appeared, Woodson had published four monographs, five textbooks, five edited collections of source materials, and thirteen articles, as well as five sociological studies that were collaborative efforts. With his writings covering a wide array of subjects, Woodson's scholarly productivity and range were equally broad. He was among the first scholars to study slavery from the slaves' point of view, and to give attention to the comparative study of slavery as an institution in the United States and in Latin America. His work prefigured the interpretations of contemporary scholars of slavery by several decades. Woodson also noted in his work the African cultural influences on African-American culture.

One of the major objectives of his own research and the research program he sponsored through the Association for the Study of Negro Life and History was to correct the racism promoted in the work published by white scholars. Woodson and his assistants pioneered in writing the social history of black Americans, and used new sources and methods. They moved away from interpreting blacks solely as victims of white oppression and racism. Instead, blacks were viewed as major actors in American history. In recognition of his achievements, the National Association for the Advancement of Colored People (NAACP) in June 1926 presented Woodson with its highest honor, the prestigious Spingarn Medal. In the award ceremony, John Haynes Holmes, minister and interracial activist, cited Woodson's tireless labors to promote the truth "about Negro life and history."

See also

NAACP

Slavery

Woodson suffered a heart attack and died in his sleep on April 3, 1950, in his Washington, D.C., home. He had dedicated his life to the exploration and study of the African-American past. In view of the enormous difficulties he faced battling white racism and in convincing whites and blacks alike that his cause was credible and worthy of support, the achievement of so much seminal work in black history seems almost miraculous. Through his own scholarship and the programs he launched in the Association for the Study of Negro Life and History, Woodson made an immeasurable contribution to the advancement of black history.

—JACQUELINE GOGGIN

JAY WRIGHT

A Complex Poet Receives Critical Acclaim

Jay Wright (May 25, 1934–), poet. Jay Wright was born on May 25 in either 1934 or 1935 in Albuquerque, N.M., to Leona Dailey and George Murphy, a.k.a. Mercer Murphy Wright. He grew up in the care of a black Albuquerque, N.M., couple to whom his father left him at age three—Frankie Faucett, a cook, and his wife, Daisy. In his early teens Wright went to live with his father, a jitney driver and handyman, in Los Angeles and San Pedro, Calif., where he soon began to play both acoustic bass and minor-league baseball. From 1954 to 1957, he served in the Army. Being stationed in Germany gave him the opportunity to travel throughout Europe. After Wright graduated from the University of California at Berkeley in 1961, he spent a semester at Union Theological Seminary in New York and subsequently attended Rutgers University, where he completed all the requirements for a doctoral degree in comparative literature except the dissertation. In 1964 Wright spent a year in Mexico; he returned in 1968 for another three years, this time in the company of his wife, Lois Silber. His poems consistently return to this stay in Guadalajara and Xalapa. In 1971, Wright went to Scotland where he accepted a position as creative writing fellow at Dundee University in Scotland. Since 1975, he has taught at Yale, the universities of Utah, Kentucky, and North Carolina at Chapel Hill, and Dartmouth College. He received a MacArthur Fellowship in 1986.

The fact that his personal origins are a composite of uncertain and contradictory stories may explain why Wright has a "passion for what is hidden," which takes the shape of a ceaseless spiritual quest. From *The Homecoming Singer* (1971) to *Elaine's Book* (1988) and *Boleros* (1991), his autobiographical person, traversing far-flung geographies, assimilates a vast and heterogeneous body of historical and mythological knowledge and uncovers forgotten links between Western Europe, Africa, the Caribbean, North and South America, and Asia. Wright's poetry insists on continuities across, not just within, cultures. Though his poetic vision is firmly grounded in both African-American historical experience and African—particularly Akan and Dogon—religion, it is cross-cultural in that it seeks to restore to African-American literature a sense of the breadth, the complexity, and the coherence of its cultural, historical, social, artistic, intellectual, and spiritual resources. In that respect, Wright's poetics and cultural politics have more in common with those of Robert Hayden and even Melvin Tolson than with the black cultural nationalism many poets of his generation embraced in the late 1960s and early 1970s. The scope and depth of Wright's vision are due to extensive research in medieval and Renaissance literatures, music, anthropology, the history of religions, and the history of science. The texture of his poetry is as dense as his formal experiments are daring. A mixture of Italian, German, and Spanish often interspersed with Dogon, Bambara, and other ideograms, Wright's language is at times so unfamiliar that to call it "English" seems inadequate. The blues and jazz, as well as a host of Caribbean and Latin American song and dance forms, are as integral to his poetic endeavors as are splendid attempts at making English verse responsive to the "grammars" and metrics of other languages.

The book-length poems *Explications/Interpretations* (1984), *Dimensions of History* (1976), and *The Double Invention of Komo* (1980)—which, together with *Soothsayers and Omens* (1976), make up Wright's first poetic cycle—include notes that acknowledge some of the author's principal scholarly debts. Yet Wright remains adamant in his refusal to make his poetry more "accessible." Behind this refusal lies neither arrogance nor obscurantism, as some have assumed, but an abiding respect for the complexity and difficulty of the social, historical, and creative processes his poetry tries to represent and enact.

—VERA M. KUTZINSKI

See also

Blues

Jazz

WRIGHT, LOUIS TOMPKINS

Louis Tompkins Wright (July 23, 1891–October 8, 1952), physician and hospital administrator. Louis Tompkins Wright was born in LaGrange, Ga. Both his father, Ceah K. Wright, and his stepfather, William F. Penn, were physicians. Wright received a B.A. from Clark College in Atlanta in 1911. Four years later, he graduated from Harvard Medical School, finishing fourth in his class. During his Harvard obstetrics course he was told that he could not participate in the delivery of babies at Boston-Lying-In Hospital. Wright rallied his classmates to change this policy of racial discrimination. From 1915 to 1916, he completed his internship at Freedmen's Hospital in Washington, D.C. While there, he disproved the accepted medical belief that the Schick test for diphtheria was not useful on blacks because of their dark pigmentation. Wright devised new observational techniques that allowed physicians to detect the reddening of skin necessary to judge the test's results. Wright then returned to Atlanta and entered a medical practice with his stepfather, where he also worked as treasurer of a local branch of the NAACP.

During World War I, Wright entered the U.S. Army Medical Corp at Fort McPherson near Atlanta. Commissioned a first lieutenant, he served at the Colored Officers Training Camps in Iowa and New York. During his service years, Wright introduced the intradermal method of vaccination for smallpox that was adopted by the U.S. Army Medical Corps. Assigned to the 367th Infantry Regiment in France, he suffered permanent lung damage from a phosgene gas attack on the battlefield. The recipient of a Purple Heart, Wright rose to the rank of lieutenant colonel, but was forced to resign this commission because of his injuries. He moved to New York City in 1918, married Corrine Cooke and opened an office for the general practice of surgery.

In 1919 Wright was appointed clinical assistant visiting surgeon at New York's Harlem Hospital. The hospital, in a black community, was staffed and controlled by white physicians. Four doctors resigned in protest when Wright, the first black appointed to a municipal-hospital position in New York City, joined the staff. In 1928, he became the first African-American police surgeon in the city's history. Meanwhile, at Harlem Hospital he continued to succeed, becoming director of surgery in 1943 and president of the hospital's medical board in 1948.

Wright's interests went beyond his surgical specialty. He devised a splint for cervical fractures and a special plate for the repair of certain types of fractures of the femur bone. Using a mostly inert substance, the metal tantalum, he developed a procedure for repairing hernias. His chapter on "Head Injuries" in *The Treatment of Fractures* (1938), was one of the first contributions by an African American to a major medical text. Perhaps Wright's most significant contribution to clinical research involved the first tests on humans of the antibiotic Aureomycin. Aureomycin had been tested in laboratory mice but never on humans. After it was first isolated in the Lederle Laboratories by a former Harvard classmate in 1945, a sample was sent to Wright at Harlem Hospital to adminster to patients who had infections for which other treatments had not worked. The results of this 1947 test were positive, and he experimented with another antibiotic, Terramycin. From 1948 to 1952, Wright published some thirty papers on his trials with antibiotics. His work helped pave the way for these drugs to be approved by the Food and Drug Administration for subsequent manufacturing and widespread use.

In 1948 Wright entered the field of cancer research. Grants from the National Cancer Institute and the Damon Runyon Fund allowed him to establish the Harlem Hospital Cancer Research Foundation. Wright and his researchers, including his daughter, Jane Cooke Wright, pioneered the use of chemotherapy to destroy cancerous cells. He published fifteen papers detailing his investigations with drugs and hormones in treating cancer.

Throughout his career, Wright attacked racial prejudice and discrimination in medicine. In 1932 he opposed the establishment of a separate veteran's hospital for African Americans in the North and protested the inadequate medical care being received by black veterans. As chairman of the board of directors of the NAACP from 1935 to 1952, he established the National Medical Committee to oppose racial discrimination in medicine. The NAACP under his leadership pressed a dozen investigations into discriminatory medical training and care. As chairman, Wright often served in an advisory role to Walter White, the secretary and dominant figure of the NAACP. With speeches and writings, Wright held the powerful American Medical Association accountable for inequalities in medical care for African Americans across the country. In 1940 Wright was awarded the NAACP's Spingarn Medal for his work as a scientist, public servant, and activist.

See also
NAACP

Wright suffered a fatal heart attack in 1952. Before his death, a new medical library at Harlem Hospital was named after him. At the library dedication ceremony, Wright said, "Harlem Hospital represents the finest example of democracy at work in the field of medicine. Its policy of complete integration throughout the institution has stood the test of time."

—ROBERT C. HAYDEN

WRIGHT, RICHARD

Richard Wright (September 4, 1908–November 28, 1960), writer. Richard Wright was born near Roxie, Miss., the son of a sharecropper and a rural schoolteacher who supported the family when her husband deserted her. Wright's childhood, which he later described in his classic autobiography, *Black Boy* (1945), was horrific. His mother, Ella Wilson Wright, was never healthy, and she became completely paralyzed by the time her son was ten years old. Wright and his family were destitute, and their lives were sharply constricted by pervasive segregation and racism. Wright and his brother Leon moved several times to the homes of relatives in Natchez and in Memphis, Tenn., and then to their grandmother's house in Jackson. A staunch Seventh Day Adventist, Wright's grandmother discouraged his reading, destroyed a radio he had built, and unwittingly alienated him from religious practice. Wright had already had his first story published in a local newspaper, however, when he completed the ninth grade in 1925. He found employment in Memphis, where he discovered the work of H. L. Mencken. Mencken's essays spurred Wright's writing ambitions. Determined to escape the segregated South, which had plagued his childhood, Wright moved to Chicago in 1927.

Over the next several years, during the worst of the Depression, Wright supported himself and his family, which had joined him, through menial labor and at the post office, and wrote when he could find the time. He became acquainted with contemporary literature through Mencken's essays and through friends at the post office, and in 1932 he began meeting writers and artists, mostly white, at the communist-run John Reed Club. Impressed by Marxist theory, Wright became a leader of the Chicago Club and published revolutionary verse in *New Masses* and in small magazines like *Anvil, Left Front* (whose editorial board he joined), and *Partisan Review*. Recruited by communists eager to showcase African Americans in their movement, Wright became active in the party as much for literary reasons as for political ones. He wished, he later explained, to describe the real feelings of the common people and serve as the bridge between them and party theorists. Wright participated in party literary conferences, wrote poetry and stories, and gave lectures. Wright's first novel, *Lawd Today*, written during this period, was published posthumously, in 1963. In 1935, the same year he started as a journalist for *New Masses*, Wright joined the Federal Writers Project of the Works Progress Administration (WPA), helping to write a guide to Illinois, and was transferred to the local Negro Theater unit of the Federal Theater Project the next year. By this time, Wright was having doubts about the Communist party, which he believed to be promoting him only because of his skin color. He insisted on freedom from the party line for his creative work, but he remained publicly committed to the party. In 1937, eager to find a publisher for his work, Wright moved to New York, where he worked as Harlem reporter for the Communist party newspaper *The Daily Worker*, and wrote the Harlem section of the WPA's *New York City Guide* (1939).

In the Autumn 1937 issue of the leftist magazine *Challenge*, Wright wrote his influential "Blueprint for Negro Writing," in which he tried to assert and encourage black nationalism among writers, within a larger Marxist perspective. Wright called on black writers to make use of

INTERNATIONAL WRITER

Richard Wright appears at the Venice Film Festival in 1951 before a poster for the Argentinian film Sangre Negro, *an adaptation of his novel* Native Son. AP/WIDE WORLD PHOTOS

See also
St. Clair Drake

We live here and they live here. We black and they white. They got things and we ain't. They do things and we can't. It's just like living in jail.

RICHARD WRIGHT
NATIVE SON, 1940

folklore and oral tradition in their work, but also to pay attention to psychological and sociological data in framing their work. Wright's own short stories, whose unsparing treatment of racism and violence in the South was couched in poetic style, were winning competitions from *Story* magazine and others, and were collected under the title *Uncle Tom's Children* (1938). Though the work was a success, Wright was dissatisfied. He thought that while he had generated sympathy for victims of racism, he had not shown its effects on all of society.

Native Son (1940), Wright's first published novel, became a Book-of-the-Month Club selection and called national attention to his compelling talent, although his unrelenting depiction of racism aroused controversy. In fact, editors had already toned down controversial material (it was not until 1992 that the unexpurgated version of the novel was published). *Native Son* is the story of a ghetto youngster, Bigger Thomas. Trapped by white racism and his own fear, Bigger accidentally murders a white woman. While he tries to cover up his deed, he is arrested, put on trial, and sentenced to death. Bigger's white communist lawyer argues that he is not responsible for his crimes, but Bigger feels that his murder and cover-up were his first creative acts, through which he has found a new freedom. The book's success won Wright the NAACP's prestigious Spingarn Medal in 1941, and a dramatization by Wright and Paul Green was produced by Orson Welles. There were two film adaptations, one a Brazilian film, *Sangre Negra* (1950), in which Wright himself played the part of Bigger Thomas, and *Native Son* (1986), starring Victor Love, but both were commercially unsuccessful.

In 1941 Wright wrote a lyrical Marxist "folk history" of African Americans, *Twelve Million Black Voices*. The following year, he finally left the Communist party. Though still a Marxist, Wright felt that the communists were unrealistic, self-serving, and not truly interested in the liberation of African Americans. During the war years, Wright worked on *Black Boy* (1945), "a record of childhood and youth," which brought him money and international fame. In *Black Boy*, Wright gives a precise, unrelenting account of how he was scarred by the poisons of poverty and racism during his early years in Mississippi. *American Hunger* (1977), a version which included Wright's Chicago years, was published posthumously.

The same year *Black Boy* appeared, Wright wrote an introduction to *Black Metropolis*, the sociological study by St. Clair Drake and Horace

Cayton of African Americans in Chicago, in which he first expounded his major political theories. White American racism, Wright believed, was a symptom of a deeper general insecurity brought about by the dehumanizing forces of modernity and industrialization. He considered the condition of African Americans a model, and extreme example, of the alienation of the human individual by modern life.

Wright was invited to France by the French government in 1945, and during the trip he found himself lionized by French intellectuals as a spokesperson for his race. Wright had married a white woman, Ellen Poplar, in 1941, and the couple had had a daughter, Julia. They wished to escape America's racial discrimination. He was delighted by France's apparent freedom from racial prejudice and impressed by the central role that literature and thought enjoyed in French society. Wright decided to "choose exile," and moved to Paris permanently in 1947, although he kept his American passport.

While in France, Wright became friendly with the French existentialists, although he claimed his reading of Dostoyevsky had made him an existentialist long before he met Jean-Paul Sartre and the others. Wright's thesis novel, *The Outsider* (1953), explores the contemporary condition in existentialist terms while rejecting the ideologies of communism and fascism. A posthumously published novella Wright wrote during the period, *The Man Who Lived Underground* (1971), also makes use of existential ideas. Neither *The Outsider* nor Wright's next novel, *Savage Holiday* (1954), was well received.

Wright shared the French intellectuals' suspicion of America, and participated with Sartre and the existentialists in political meetings in 1948 with the idea of producing a "third way" to preserve European culture from the Cold War struggle between American industrial society and Soviet communism. Ironically, Wright was harassed for his leftist background in America, despite his repudiation of the communists. The hostility of the Communist party to Wright grew after he published his essay "I Tried to Be a Communist" in the important anticommunist anthology *The God That Failed* (1950).

Wright had been an original sponsor of the review *Présence Africaine* in 1946, and he turned his primary attention to anticolonial questions during the 1950s. After visiting the Gold Coast in 1954, he wrote *Black Power* (1954), "a record of reactions in a land of pathos," in which he approved Kwame Nkrumah's pan-Africanist policies but

stressed his own estrangement from Africa. Wright's introduction to George Padmore's *Pan-Africanism or Communism?* (1956) further disclosed his pan-African ideas. In *The Color Curtain* (1956) he reported on the First Conference of Non-Aligned Countries held in Bandung, Indonesia, in 1955, and explored the importance of race and religion in the world of politics. The same year, he helped organize, under *Présence Africaine*'s auspices, the First Conference of Black Writers and Intellectuals. Papers from the conference, along with texts from the numerous lectures on decolonization Wright gave in Europe, were published as *White Man, Listen!* in 1959.

Wright's last works include *Pagan Spain* (1958), a report on Franco's Spain which included a discussion of the Catholic impact on European culture; *The Long Dream* (1959), the first novel of an unfinished trilogy dealing with the lasting effects of racism; *Eight Men* (1960), a collection of short stories; and thousands of unpublished haiku on the Japanese model. Wright died unexpectedly, on November 28, 1960, in Paris, of a heart attack. He was under emotional and mental stress at the time, partly due to spying by U.S. intelligence agents on African Americans in Paris. His sudden death fostered lasting rumors that he had been poisoned by the CIA because of his persistent fight against racial oppression and colonialism.

Wright was the first African-American novelist of international stature, and his violent denunciation of American racism and the black deprivation and hatred it causes was uncompromising. Wright inspired both African-American novelists like Ralph Ellison and Chester Himes and foreign writers such as the novelists Peter Abrahams and George Lanning and the political theorist Frantz Fanon. Wright's legendary generosity to other writers was both moral and sometimes financial, through the grants and jobs he found them. Wright also created for himself a role as expatriate writer and international social critic. His strong intellectual interests and earnestness, through which he melded Freudian, Marxist, and pan-African perspectives, were matched by a deep spirituality—despite his rationalist suspicion of religion—and occasional humor and comedy in his works.

—MICHEL FABRE

See also

Literature

749

YOUNG, WHITNEY MOORE, JR.

Whitney Moore Young, Jr. (July 31, 1921–March 11, 1971), civil rights leader. Whitney M. Young, Jr., was born and raised in rural Lincoln Ridge, Ky., to Whitney, Sr., and Laura Ray Young. He grew up on the campus of Lincoln Institute, a vocational high school for black students where his father taught and later served as president. In this setting, Young, who attended the institute from 1933 to 1937, was relatively isolated from external racism. At the same time, he was surrounded by black people who held positions of authority and were treated with respect. In September 1937, Young enrolled at Kentucky State Industrial College in Frankfort; he graduated in June 1941. In college he met Margaret Buckner, whom he married in January 1944; the couple later had two daughters.

After serving in World War II, Young entered a master's program in social work at the University of Minnesota in the spring of 1946, which included a field placement with the Minneapolis chapter of the National Urban League (NUL). He graduated in 1947 and, in September of that year, he became industrial relations secretary of the St. Paul Urban League, where he encouraged employers to hire black workers. Two years later he was appointed to serve as executive secretary with the NUL's affiliate in Omaha, Neb.

During his tenure in Omaha, Young dramatically increased both the chapter's membership base and its operating budget. He fared less well, however, in his attempts to gain increased employment opportunities for African Americans; victories in this area continued to be largely symbolic, resulting primarily from subtle behind-the-scenes pressure exerted by Young himself. Through his Urban League experience, Young became adept at cultivating relationships with powerful white corporate and political leaders.

In early 1954 Young became dean of the Atlanta University School of Social Work. He doubled the school's budget, raised teaching salaries and called for enhanced professional development. With the 1954 *Brown* v. *Board of Education of Topeka, Kansas*, Supreme Court decision and the unfolding of civil rights activism, his activities became increasingly political. He served on the board of the Atlanta NAACP, and he played a leadership role in several other organizations committed to challenging the racial status quo, including the Greater Atlanta Council on Human Relations and the Atlanta Committee for Cooperative Action. Unlike some other black community leaders, Young supported and even advised students who engaged in sit-in demonstrations in 1960. Yet Young personally opted for a low-key approach characterized by technical support for the Civil Rights Movement rather than activism.

Young retained close ties with NUL, and in 1960 he emerged as a top candidate for executive director of the New York-based organization. Although by far the youngest of the contenders for the position, and the least experienced in NUL work, Young was selected to fill the national post effective October 1961. Since its founding in 1910–1911, NUL had been more concerned with social services than social change; its successes had long depended on alliance with influential white corporate and political figures. However, by the early 1960s it was clear that unless it took on a more active and visible role in civil rights, the organization risked losing credibility with the black community. It was Whitney Young who, in more ways than one, would lead NUL into that turbulent decade.

For years, local Urban League activists had lobbied for a more aggressive posture on racial issues. At Young's urging, NUL's leadership reluctantly resolved to participate in the Civil Rights Movement—but as a voice of "respectability" and restraint. In January 1962, Young declared that, while NUL would not engage actively in protests, it would not condemn others' efforts if they were carried out "under responsible leadership using legally acceptable methods." By helping to plan the 1963 March on Washington, Young simultaneously hoped to confirm NUL's new commitment and ensure that the march would pose no overt challenge to those in authority. Young also

See also
Brown v. *Board of Education of Topeka, Kansas*

Y

furthered NUL's moderate agenda by participating in the Council for United Civil Rights Leadership (CUCRL), a consortium founded in June 1963 to facilitate fundraising and information-sharing. (CUCRL was initiated by wealthy white philanthropists concerned with minimizing competition among civil rights organizations and tempering the movement's more militant elements.)

As "black power" gained currency within the movement, new tensions surfaced inside NUL itself. Students and other Urban League workers disrupted the organization's yearly conferences on several occasions, demanding the adoption of a more action-oriented strategy. Young continued to insist on the primacy of social service provision. But in June 1968, in an address at the Congress of Racial Equality's (CORE) annual meeting, he spoke favorably of self-sufficiency and community control. The NUL initiated a "New Thrust" program intended to strengthen its base in black neighborhoods and to support community organizing.

During his ten-year tenure, Young made his mark on NUL in other significant ways. He guided the development of innovative new programs meant to facilitate job training and placement, and he vastly increased corporate and foundation support for the organization. In the early and mid-1960s, as corporations (especially government contractors) came under fire for failing to provide equal employment opportunities, business leaders turned to the NUL and its affiliates for help in hiring black workers. At the same time, by aiding NUL financially, they hoped to demonstrate convincingly a commitment to nondiscriminatory policies.

Of the three U.S. presidents in office during Young's tenure with the League, Lyndon B. Johnson proved to be the closest ally; he drew on Young's ideas and expertise in formulating anti-poverty programs, tried to bring Young into the administration, and awarded him the Medal of Freedom in 1969. Although the relationship with Johnson was important for accomplishing NUL's goals, at times it constrained Young's own political positions. In mid-1966, Young clashed with the Rev. Dr. Martin Luther King, Jr., and other civil rights leaders who opposed the Vietnam War; Young insisted that communism must be stopped in Southeast Asia; and he disagreed that the military effort would divert resources away from urgent problems facing African Americans at home. A year later, he was no longer so sure. Nonetheless, at Johnson's request, he traveled to South Vietnam with an official U.S. delegation. Young did not speak publicly against the war until late 1969, when Richard M. Nixon was president.

In addition to overseeing NUL's "entry" into civil rights, Young heightened the organization's visibility to a popular audience. He wrote a regular column, "To Be Equal," for the *Amsterdam News,* which was syndicated through newspapers and radio stations nationwide. He published several books, including *To Be Equal* (1964), and *Beyond Racism* (1969). At the same time, Young continued to maneuver in the highest echelons of the corporate world; among other activities, he served on the boards of the Federal Reserve Bank of New York, the Massachusetts Institute of Technology, and the Rockefeller Foundation. He also remained a prominent figure in the social work profession, serving as president of the National Conference on Social Welfare in 1967 and acting as president of the National Association of Social Workers from June 1969 until his death.

In March 1971, Young traveled to Lagos, Nigeria, with a delegation of African Americans, in order to participate in a dialogue with African leaders. He died there while swimming, either from drowning or from a brain hemorrhage.

—TAMI J. FRIEDMAN

See also

Civil Rights Movement

Congress of Racial Equality

ZYDECO

Zydeco is a style of popular dance music played by African Americans of Francophone descent in the Gulf Coast region, particularly in the bayou country of southwestern Louisiana.

Despite its frenetic tempos, often led by a buoyant singer doubling on accordion, the term *zydeco* derives from the old Louisiana song "Les Haricots Sont Pas Salés," literally translated as "the green beans aren't salted," but commonly having the meaning "times aren't good."

The origins of zydeco go back to the popular dance tunes of French settlers, or Acadians, who were expelled from Nova Scotia by the British and arrived in Louisiana in the eighteenth century. They intermarried with African Americans and Native Americans of French and Spanish descent, and their European-derived string music absorbed Afro-Caribbean rhythmic elements. The first zydeco recordings, difficult to distinguish from other forms of Cajun music, are 1934 field recordings, including "Cajun Negro Fais Dos-Dos Tune," by Ellis Evans and Jimmy Lewis, and "Les Haricots Sont Pas Salés," by Austin Coleman and Joe Washington. Accordionist Amadé Ardoin was an important early zydeco musician whose "Les Blues de la Prison" (1934) shows a strong blues influence.

After World War II, rhythm and blues began to influence zydeco, a development clearly heard on Clarence Garlow's "Bon Ton Roula" (1950), which translates as "Let the Good Times Roll." During this time accordionist Clifton Chenier, perhaps the greatest of all zydeco musicians, came to prominence. Born in Opelousas, La., in 1925, he made his first recordings in the 1950s, and pioneered the use of the piano accordion—an accordion with a keyboard—in zydeco music. Among the many popular and important records, noted for their heavy dance rhythms, that Chenier made before his death from diabetes in 1987 are "Black Gal" (1965), "Jambalaya" (1975), and *Country Boy Now* (1984).

In Louisiana, zydeco is invariably performed for dancers, often at nightclubs, dance halls, churches, picnics, and house parties known as "fais-do-do." Zydeco bands are typically led by a singer, with lead accompaniment by fiddle, button or piano accordion, or guitar, and backed by a rhythm section of bass, piano, and drums. Harmonica, washboard, "frottoir" (a metal rubbing board played with household implements), and the "bas trang" (triangle), were often used earlier in the century, but today are often replaced by electric instruments. Zydeco is sung in the patois of Creole Louisiana, with lyrics ranging from narrative tales, love songs, and laments to simple invocations to dancing and good times.

Although for a century zydeco has been, along with jazz and blues, a mainstay of the secular music scene among the Creole-descended population along the Gulf Coast from Louisiana to Texas, in recent years zydeco has achieved international popularity, and its greatest exponents have become celebrities with prolific touring and recording schedules. In addition to Chenier, other important zydeco musicians include accordionist Boozoo Chavis ("Paper In My Shoe," 1984), singer Queen Ida (*Cookin' With Queen Ida,* 1989), Rockin' Sidney ("My Toot Toot," 1984), and Lawrence "Black" Ardoin ("Bayou Two Step," 1984). Important ensembles include the Lawrence Ardoin Band, Terrence Semiens and the Mallet Playboys, and Buckwheat Zydeco's Ils Sont Partis Band.

Although zydeco and Cajun music share many musical elements and have common sociocultural origins in the late nineteenth-century contact between Creoles and Acadians, they are distinct forms, representing two aspects of the complex, multiracial culture that also produced jazz. Zydeco tends toward faster tempos, a syncopated rhythmic structure, and a deemphasis of the melodic line. Cajun's rhythms are often more rigid two-step dances or waltzes emphasizing melody. Zydeco has been documented in such films as *Zydeco: Creole Music and Culture in Rural Louisiana* (1984), and *J'ai Eté au Bal* (1991).

—JONATHAN GILL

See also
Blues
Rhythm and Blues

753

Index

T

September is
Library Card
Sign-Up Month

Items are due on the   dates listed below:

Title: The African-American experience : selecti
ons from
Author: Salzman, Jack.
Item ID: 0000613941541
Date due: 10/2/2021,23:59

Euclid Public Library

Total Items: 1
Date Printed: 9/11/2021 3:19:24 PM

Euclid Public Library

216-261-5300
Adult Department press 3
Children's Department press 4
Renew Items press 2
Employee Directory press 9

Visit us on the web: www.euclidlibrary.org

CHARLES DICKENS

THE FRIENDLY WAITER AND I.

CHARLES DICKENS

❧

David Copperfield

VOLUME I

WITH ILLUSTRATIONS BY
HABLÔT KNIGHT BROWNE ('PHIZ')

❧

WALTER J. BLACK, INC.
NEW YORK

AFFECTIONATELY INSCRIBED

TO

THE HON. MR. AND MRS. RICHARD WATSON

OF

ROCKINGHAM, NORTHAMPTONSHIRE

PREFACES

I DO not find it easy to get sufficiently far away from this Book, in the first sensations of having finished it, to refer to it with the composure which this formal heading would seem to require. My interest in it, is so recent and strong; and my mind is so divided between pleasure and regret—pleasure in the achievement of a long design, regret in the separation from many companions—that I am in danger of wearying the reader whom I love, with personal confidences, and private emotions.

Besides which, all that I could say of the Story, to any purpose, I have endeavoured to say in it.

It would concern the reader little, perhaps, to know how sorrowfully the pen is laid down at the close of a two-years' imaginative task; or how an Author feels as if he were dismissing some portion of himself into the shadowy world, when a crowd of the creatures of his brain are going from him for ever. Yet, I have nothing else to tell; unless, indeed, I were to confess (which might be of less moment still) that no one can ever believe this Narrative, in the reading, more than I have believed it in the writing.

Instead of looking back, therefore, I will look forward. I cannot close this Volume more agreeably to myself, than with a hopeful glance towards the time when I shall again put forth my two green leaves once a month, and with a faithful remembrance of the genial sun and showers that have fallen on these leaves of David Copperfield, and made me happy.

LONDON, *October,* 1850.

CONTENTS

ILLUSTRATIONS

DAVID COPPERFIELD

DAVID COPPERFIELD

CHAPTER I

I AM BORN

WHETHER I shall turn out to be the hero of my own life, or whether that station will be held by anybody else, these pages must show. To begin my life with the beginning of my life, I record that I was born (as I have been informed and believe) on a Friday, at twelve o'clock at night. It was remarked that the clock began to strike, and I began to cry, simultaneously.

In consideration of the day and hour of my birth, it was declared by the nurse, and by some sage women in the neighbourhood who had taken a lively interest in me several months before there was any possibility of our becoming personally acquainted, first, that I was destined to be unlucky in life; and secondly, that I was privileged to see ghosts and spirits; both these gifts inevitably attaching, as they believed, to all unlucky infants of either gender, born towards the small hours on a Friday night.

I need say nothing here on the first head, because nothing can show better than my history whether that prediction was verified or falsified by the result. On the second branch of the question, I will only remark, that unless I ran through that part of my inheritance while I was still a baby, I have not come into it yet.

1

But I do not at all complain of having been kept out of this property; and if anybody else should be in the present enjoyment of it, he is heartily welcome to keep it.

I was born with a caul, which was advertised for sale, in the newspapers, at the low price of fifteen guineas. Whether sea-going people were short of money about that time, or were short of faith and preferred cork jackets, I don't know; all I know is, that there was but one solitary bidding, and that was from an attorney connected with the bill-broking business, who offered two pounds in cash, and the balance in sherry, but declined to be guaranteed from drowning on any higher bargain. Consequently the advertisement was withdrawn at a dead loss—for as to sherry, my poor dear mother's own sherry was in the market then—and ten years afterwards the caul was put up in a raffle down in our part of the country, to fifty members at half a crown a head, the winner to spend five shillings. I was present myself, and I remember to have felt quite uncomfortable and confused, at a part of myself being disposed of in that way. The caul was won, I recollect, by an old lady with a hand-basket, who, very reluctantly, produced from it the stipulated five shillings, all in halfpence, and twopence halfpenny short—as it took an immense time and a great waste of arithmetic, to endeavour without any effect to prove to her. It is a fact which will be long remembered as remarkable down there, that she was never drowned, but died triumphantly in bed, at ninety-two. I have understood that it was, to the last, her proudest boast, that she never had been on the water in her life, except upon a bridge; and that over her tea (to which she was extremely partial) she, to the last, expressed her indignation at the impiety of mariners and others, who had the presumption to go 'meandering' about the world. It was in vain to represent to her that some conveniences, tea perhaps included, resulted from this objectionable practice. She always returned, with greater emphasis and with an instinctive knowledge of the strength of her objection, 'Let us have no meandering.'

Not to meander myself, at present, I will go back to my birth.

I was born at Blunderstone, in Suffolk, or 'thereby,' as they say in Scotland. I was a posthumous child. My father's eyes had closed upon the light of this world six months, when mine opened on it. There is something strange to me, even now, in the reflection that he never saw me; and something stranger yet in the shadowy remembrance that I have of my first childish associations with his white gravestone in the churchyard, and of the indefinable compassion I used to feel for it lying out alone there in the dark night, when our little parlour was warm and bright with fire and candle, and the doors of our house were —almost cruelly, it seemed to me sometimes—bolted and locked against it.

An aunt of my father's, and consequently a great-aunt of mine, of whom I shall have more to relate by-and-by, was the principal magnate of our family. Miss Trotwood, or Miss Betsey, as my poor mother always called her, when she sufficiently overcame her dread of this formidable personage to mention her at all (which was seldom), had been married to a husband younger than herself, who was very handsome, except in the sense of the homely adage, 'handsome is, that handsome does'—for he was strongly suspected of having beaten Miss Betsey, and even of having once, on a disputed question of supplies, made some hasty but determined arrangements to throw her

out of a two pair of stairs' window.   These evidences
of an incompatibility of temper induced Miss Betsey
to pay him off, and effect a separation by mutual
consent.   He went to India with his capital, and
there, according to a wild legend in our family, he
was once seen riding on an elephant, in company with
a Baboon; but I think it must have been a Baboo—
or a Begum.   Anyhow, from India tidings of his
death reached home, within ten years.   How they affected my aunt, nobody knew; for immediately upon
the separation she took her maiden name again,
bought a cottage in a hamlet on the sea-coast a long
way off, established herself there as a single woman
with one servant, and was understood to live secluded,
ever afterwards, in an inflexible retirement.

My father had once been a favourite of hers, I believe; but she was mortally affronted by his marriage,
on the ground that my mother was 'a wax doll.'   She
had never seen my mother, but she knew her to be not
yet twenty.   My father and Miss Betsey never met
again.   He was double my mother's age when he
married, and of but a delicate constitution.   He died
a year afterwards, and, as I have said, six months
before I came into the world.

This was the state of matters on the afternoon of,
what I may be excused for calling, that eventful and
important Friday.   I can make no claim, therefore,
to have known, at that time, how matters stood; or to
have any remembrance, founded on the evidence of
my own senses, of what follows.

My mother was sitting by the fire, but poorly in
health, and very low in spirits, looking at it through
her tears, and desponding heavily about herself and
the fatherless little stranger, who was already welcomed by some grosses of prophetic pins in a drawer

upstairs, to a world not at all excited on the subject of his arrival; my mother, I say, was sitting by the fire, that bright, windy March afternoon, very timid and sad, and very doubtful of ever coming alive out of the trial that was before her, when, lifting her eyes as she dried them, to the window opposite, she saw a strange lady coming up the garden.

My mother had a sure foreboding at the second glance, that it was Miss Betsey. The setting sun was glowing on the strange lady, over the garden fence, and she came walking up to the door with a fell rigidity of figure and composure of countenance that could have belonged to nobody else.

When she reached the house, she gave another proof of her identity. My father had often hinted that she seldom conducted herself like any ordinary Christian; and now, instead of ringing the bell, she came and looked in at that identical window, pressing the end of her nose against the glass to that extent that my poor dear mother used to say it became perfectly flat and white in a moment.

She gave my mother such a turn, that I have always been convinced I am indebted to Miss Betsey for having been born on a Friday.

My mother had left her chair in her agitation, and gone behind it in the corner. Miss Betsey, looking round the room, slowly and inquiringly, began on the other side, and carried her eyes on, like a Saracen's head in a Dutch clock, until they reached my mother. Then she made a frown and a gesture to my mother, like one who was accustomed to be obeyed, to come and open the door. My mother went.

'Mrs. David Copperfield, I *think*,' said Miss Betsey; the emphasis referring, perhaps, to my mother's mourning weeds, and her condition.

'Yes,' said my mother, faintly.

'Miss Trotwood,' said the visitor. 'You have heard of her, I dare say?'

My mother answered she had had that pleasure. And she had a disagreeable consciousness of not appearing to imply that it had been an overpowering pleasure.

'Now you see her,' said Miss Betsey. My mother bent her head, and begged her to walk in.

They went into the parlour my mother had come from, the fire in the best room on the other side of the passage not being lighted—not having been lighted, indeed, since my father's funeral; and when they were both seated, and Miss Betsey said nothing, my mother, after vainly trying to restrain herself, began to cry.

'Oh, tut, tut, tut!' said Miss Betsey, in a hurry. 'Don't do that! Come, come!'

My mother couldn't help it notwithstanding, so she cried until she had had her cry out.

'Take off your cap, child,' said Miss Betsey, 'and let me see you.'

My mother was too much afraid of her to refuse compliance with this odd request, if she had any disposition to do so. Therefore she did as she was told, and did it with such nervous hands that her hair (which was luxuriant and beautiful) fell all about her face.

'Why, bless my heart!' exclaimed Miss Betsey. 'You are a very baby!'

My mother was, no doubt, unusually youthful in appearance even for her years; she hung her head, as if it were her fault, poor thing, and said, sobbing, that indeed she was afraid she was but a childish widow, and would be but a childish mother if she lived. In a short pause which ensued, she had a fancy that she felt Miss Betsey touch her hair, and that with no un-gentle hand; but, looking at her, in her timid hope, she found that lady sitting with the skirt of her dress tucked up, her hands folded on one knee, and her feet upon the fender, frowning at the fire.

'In the name of Heaven,' said Miss Betsey, sud-denly, 'why Rookery?'

'Do you mean the house, ma'am?' asked my mother.

'Why Rookery?' said Miss Betsey. 'Cookery would have been more to the purpose, if you had had any practical ideas of life, either of you.'

'The name was Mr. Copperfield's choice,' returned my mother. 'When he bought the house, he liked to think that there were rooks about it.'

The evening wind made such a disturbance just now, among some tall old elm-trees at the bottom of the garden, that neither my mother nor Miss Betsey could forbear glancing that way. As the elms bent to one another, like giants who were whispering secrets, and after a few seconds of such repose, fell into a violent flurry, tossing their wild arms about, as if their late confidences were really too wicked for their peace of mind, some weather-beaten ragged old rooks'-nests burdening their higher branches, swung like wrecks upon a stormy sea.

'Where are the birds?' asked Miss Betsey.

'The—?' My mother had been thinking of some-thing else.

'The rooks—what has become of them?' asked Miss Betsey.

'There have not been any since we have lived here,' said my mother. 'We thought—Mr. Copperfield thought—it was quite a large rookery; but the nests were very old ones, and the birds have deserted them a long while.'

'David Copperfield all over!' cried Miss Betsey.

'David Copperfield from head to foot! Calls a house a rookery when there's not a rook near it, and takes the birds on trust, because he sees the nests!'

'Mr. Copperfield,' returned my mother, 'is dead, and if you dare to speak unkindly of him to me—'

My poor dear mother, I suppose, had some momentary intention of committing an assault and battery upon my aunt, who could easily have settled her with one hand, even if my mother had been in far better training for such an encounter than she was that evening. But it passed with the action of rising from her chair; and she sat down again very meekly, and fainted.

When she came to herself, or when Miss Betsey had restored her, whichever it was, she found the latter standing at the window. The twilight was by this time shading down into darkness; and dimly as they saw each other, they could not have done that without the aid of the fire.

'Well?' said Miss Betsey, coming back to her chair, as if she had only been taking a casual look at the prospect; 'and when do you expect—'

'I am all in a tremble,' faltered my mother. 'I don't know what's the matter. I shall die, I am sure!'

'No, no, no,' said Miss Betsey. 'Have some tea.'

'Oh dear me, dear me, do you think it will do me any good?' cried my mother in a helpless manner.

'Of course it will,' said Miss Betsey. 'It's nothing but fancy. What do you call your girl?'

'I don't know that it will be a girl, yet, ma'am,' said my mother innocently.

'Bless the baby!' exclaimed Miss Betsey, unconsciously quoting the second sentiment of the pincushion in the drawer upstairs, but applying it to my mother instead of me, 'I don't mean that. I mean your servant.'

'Peggotty,' said my mother.

'Peggotty!' repeated Miss Betsey, with some indignation. 'Do you mean to say, child, that any human being has gone into a Christian church, and got herself named Peggotty?'

'It's her surname,' said my mother, faintly. 'Mr. Copperfield called her by it, because her Christian name was the same as mine.'

'Here, Peggotty!' cried Miss Betsey, opening the parlour-door. 'Tea. Your mistress is a little unwell. Don't dawdle.'

Having issued this mandate with as much potentiality as if she had been a recognised authority in the house ever since it had been a house, and having looked out to confront the amazed Peggotty coming along the passage with a candle at the sound of a strange voice, Miss Betsey shut the door again, and sat down as before; with her feet on the fender, the skirt of her dress tucked up, and her hands folded on one knee.

'You were speaking about its being a girl,' said Miss Betsey. 'I have no doubt it will be a girl. I have a presentiment that it must be a girl. Now child, from the moment of the birth of this girl—'

'Perhaps boy,' my mother took the liberty of putting in.

'I tell you I have a presentiment that it must be a girl,' returned Miss Betsey. 'Don't contradict. From the moment of this girl's birth, child, I intend to be her friend. I intend to be her godmother, and I beg you'll call her Betsey Trotwood Copperfield. There must be no mistakes in life with *this* Betsey Trotwood. There must be no trifling with *her* affections poor dear. She must be well brought up, and well guarded from reposing any foolish confidences where they are not deserved. I must make that *my* care.'

There was a twitch of Miss Betsey's head, after each of these sentences, as if her own old wrongs were working within her, and she repressed any plainer reference to them by strong constraint. So my mother suspected, at least, as she observed her by the low glimmer of the fire: too much scared by Miss Betsey, too uneasy in herself, and too subdued and bewildered altogether, to observe anything very clearly, or to know what to say.

'And was David good to you, child?' asked Miss Betsey, when she had been silent for a little while, and these motions of her head had gradually ceased. 'Were you comfortable together?'

'We were very happy,' said my mother. 'Mr. Copperfield was only too good to me.'

'What, he spoilt you, I suppose?' returned Miss Betsey.

'For being quite alone and dependent on myself in this rough world again, yes, I fear he did indeed,' sobbed my mother.

'Well! Don't cry!' said Miss Betsey. 'You were not equally matched, child—if any two people *can* be equally matched—and so I asked the question. You were an orphan, weren't you?'

'Yes.'

'And a governess?'

'I was nursery-governess in a family where Mr. Copperfield came to visit. Mr. Copperfield was very kind to me, and took a great deal of notice of me, and paid me a good deal of attention, and at last proposed to me. And I accepted him. And so we were married,' said my mother simply.

'Ha! Poor baby!' mused Miss Betsey, with her

frown still bent upon the fire. 'Do you know anything?'

'I beg your pardon, ma'am,' faltered my mother.

'About keeping house, for instance,' said Miss
Betsey.

'Not much, I fear,' returned my mother. 'Not so
much as I could wish. But Mr. Copperfield was
teaching me—'

('Much he knew about it himself!') said Miss
Betsey in a parenthesis.

—'And I hope I should have improved, being very
anxious to learn, and he very patient to teach, if the
great misfortune of his death'—my mother broke
down again here, and could get no farther.

'Well, well!' said Miss Betsey.

—'I kept my housekeeping-book regularly, and
balanced it with Mr. Copperfield every night,' cried
my mother in another burst of distress, and breaking
down again.

'Well, well!' said Miss Betsey. 'Don't cry any
more.'

—'And I am sure we never had a word of difference respecting it, except when Mr. Copperfield objected to my threes and fives being too much like each
other, or to my putting curly tails to my sevens and
nines,' resumed my mother in another burst, and
breaking down again.

'You'll make yourself ill,' said Miss Betsey, 'and
you know that will not be good either for you or for
my goddaughter. Come! You mustn't do it!'

This argument had some share in quieting my
mother, though her increasing indisposition had perhaps a larger one. There was an interval of silence,
only broken by Miss Betsey's occasionally ejacula-
ting 'Ha!' as she sat with her feet upon the fender.

'David had bought an annuity for himself with his

money, I know,' said she, by and by. 'What did he
do for you?'

'Mr. Copperfield,' said my mother, answering with
some difficulty, 'was so considerate and good as to
secure the reversion of a part of it to me.'

'How much?' asked Miss Betsey.

'A hundred and five pounds a year,' said my mother.

'He might have done worse,' said my aunt.

The word was appropriate to the moment. My
mother was so much worse that Peggotty, coming in
with the tea-board and candles, and seeing at a glance
how ill she was,—as Miss Betsey might have done
sooner if there had been light enough,—conveyed her
upstairs to her own room with all speed; and immediately despatched Ham Peggotty, her nephew, who
had been for some days past secreted in the house, unknown to my mother, as a special messenger in case
of emergency, to fetch the nurse and doctor.

These allied powers were considerably astonished,
when they arrived within a few minutes of each other,
to find an unknown lady of portentous appearance
sitting before the fire, with her bonnet tied over her
left arm, stopping her ears with jewellers' cotton.
Peggotty knowing nothing about her, and my mother
saying nothing about her, she was quite a mystery in
the parlour; and the fact of her having a magazine of
jewellers' cotton in her pocket, and sticking the article
in her ears in that way, did not detract from the
solemnity of her presence.

The doctor having been upstairs and come down
again, and having satisfied himself, I suppose, that
there was a probability of this unknown lady and himself having to sit there, face to face, for some hours,
laid himself out to be polite and social. He was the
meekest of his sex, the mildest of little men. He
sidled in and out of a room, to take up the less space.

He walked as softly as the Ghost in Hamlet, and
more slowly. He carried his head on one side, partly
in modest depreciation of himself, partly in modest
propitiation of everybody else. It is nothing to say
that he hadn't a word to throw at a dog. He couldn't
have *thrown* a word at a mad dog. He might have
offered him one gently, or half a one, or a fragment
of one; for he spoke as slowly as he walked; but he
wouldn't have been rude to him, and he couldn't have
been quick with him, for any earthly consideration.

Mr. Chillip, looking mildly at my aunt with his head
on one side, and making her a little bow, said, in allusion to the jewellers' cotton, as he softly touched his
left ear—

'Some local irritation, ma'am?'

'What?' replied my aunt, pulling the cotton out of
one ear like a cork.

Mr. Chillip was so alarmed by her abruptness—
as he told my mother afterwards—that it was a mercy
he didn't lose his presence of mind. But he repeated
sweetly—

'Some local irritation, ma'am?'

'Nonsense!' replied my aunt, and corked herself
again, at one blow.

Mr. Chillip could do nothing after this, but sit and
look at her feebly, as she sat and looked at the fire,
until he was called upstairs again. After some quarter of an hour's absence, he returned.

'Well?' said my aunt, taking the cotton out of the
ear nearest to him.

'Well, ma'am,' returned Mr. Chillip, 'we are—we
are progressing slowly, ma'am.'

'Ba—a—ah!' said my aunt, with a perfect shake on
the contemptuous interjection. And corked herself
as before.

Really—really—as Mr. Chillip told my mother, he

was almost shocked; speaking in a professional point
of view alone he was almost shocked. But he sat and
looked at her, notwithstanding, for nearly two
hours, as she sat looking at the fire, until he was
again called out. After another absence, he again
returned.

'Well?' said my aunt, taking out the cotton on that
side again.

'Well, ma'am,' returned Mr. Chillip, 'we are—we
are progressing slowly, ma'am.'

'Ya—a—ah!' said my aunt. With such a snarl at
him, that Mr. Chillip absolutely could not bear it. It
was really calculated to break his spirit, he said afterwards. He preferred to go and sit upon the stairs, in
the dark and a strong draught, until he was again
sent for.

Ham Peggotty, who went to the national school,
and was a very dragon at his catechism, and who may
therefore be regarded as a credible witness, reported
next day, that happening to peep in at the parlour-
door an hour after this, he was instantly descried by
Miss Betsey, then walking to and fro in a state of
agitation, and pounced upon before he could make his
escape. That there were now occasional sounds of
feet and voices overhead which he inferred the cotton
did not exclude, from the circumstance of his evidently
being clutched by the lady as a victim on whom to expend her superabundant agitation when the sounds
were loudest. That, marching him constantly up and
down by the collar (as if he had been taking too much
laudanum), she, at those times, shook him, rumpled
his hair, made light of his linen, stopped *his* ears as if
she confounded them with her own, and otherwise
touzled and maltreated him. This was in part con-

firmed by his aunt, who saw him at half-past twelve
o'clock, soon after his release, and affirmed that he
was then as red as I was.

The mild Mr. Chillip could not possibly bear malice
at such a time, if at any time. He sidled into the
parlour as soon as he was at liberty, and said to my
aunt in his meekest manner—

'Well, ma'am, I am happy to congratulate you.'

'What upon?' said my aunt sharply.

Mr. Chillip was fluttered again, by the extreme
severity of my aunt's manner; so he made her a little
bow, and gave her a little smile, to mollify her.

'Mercy on the man, what's he doing!' cried my
aunt, impatiently. 'Can't he speak?'

'Be calm, my dear ma'am,' said Mr. Chillip, in his
softest accents. 'There is no longer any occasion for
uneasiness, ma'am. Be calm.'

It has since been considered almost a miracle that
my aunt didn't shake him, and shake what he had to
say out of him. She only shook her own head at him,
but in a way that made him quail.

'Well, ma'am,' resumed Mr. Chillip, as soon as he
had courage, 'I am happy to congratulate you. All
is now over, ma'am, and well over.'

During the five minutes or so that Mr. Chillip
devoted to the delivery of this oration, my aunt eyed
him narrowly.

'How is she?' said my aunt, folding her arms with
her bonnet still tied on one of them.

'Well, ma'am, she will soon be quite comfortable, I
hope,' returned Mr. Chillip. 'Quite as comfortable
as we can expect a young mother to be, under these
melancholy domestic circumstances. There cannot be
any objection to your seeing her presently, ma'am.
It may do her good.'

'And *she*.   How is *she?*' said my aunt, sharply.

Mr. Chillip laid his head a little more on one side, and looked at my aunt like an amiable bird.

'The baby,' said my aunt.   'How is she?'

'Ma'am,' returned Mr. Chillip, 'I apprehended you had known.   It 's a boy.'

My aunt said never a word, but took her bonnet by the strings, in the manner of a sling, aimed a blow at Mr. Chillip's head with it, put it on bent, walked out, and never came back.   She vanished like a discontented fairy; or like one of those supernatural beings whom it was popularly supposed I was entitled to see; and never came back any more.

No.   I lay in my basket, and my mother lay in her bed; but Betsey Trotwood Copperfield was for ever in the land of dreams and shadows, the tremendous region whence I had so lately travelled; and the light upon the window of our room shone out upon the earthly bourne of all such travellers, and the mound above the ashes and the dust that once was he, without whom I had never been.

CHAPTER II

I OBSERVE

THE first objects that assume a distinct presence before me, as I look far back, into the blank of my infancy, are my mother with her pretty hair and youthful shape, and Peggotty, with no shape at all, and eyes so dark that they seemed to darken their whole neighbourhood in her face, and cheeks and arms so hard and red that I wondered the birds didn't peck her in preference to apples.

I believe I can remember these two at a little distance apart, dwafed to my sight by stooping down or kneeling on the floor, and I going unsteadily from the one to the other. I have an impression on my mind which I cannot distinguish from actual remembrance, of the touch of Peggotty's forefinger as she used to hold it out to me, and of its being roughened by needlework, like a pocket nutmeg-grater.

This may be fancy, though I think the memory of most of us can go farther back into such times than many of us suppose; just as I believe the power of observation in numbers of very young children to be quite wonderful for its closeness and accuracy. Indeed, I think that most grown men who are remarkable in this respect, may with greater propriety be said not to have lost the faculty, than to have acquired it; the rather, as I generally observe such men to retain a certain freshness, and gentleness, and capacity of being pleased, which are also an inheritance they have preserved from their childhood.

I might have a misgiving that I am 'meandering' in stopping to say this, but that it brings me to remark that I build these conclusions, in part upon my own experience of myself; and if it should appear from anything I may set down in this narrative that I was a child of close observation, or that as a man I have a strong memory of my childhood, I undoubtedly lay claim to both of these characteristics.

Looking back, as I was saying, into the blank of my infancy, the first objects I can remember as standing out by themselves from a confusion of things, are my mother and Peggotty. What else do I remember? Let me see.

There comes out of the cloud, our house—not new to me, but quite familiar, in its earliest remembrance. On the ground-floor is Peggotty's kitchen, opening into a back yard; with a pigeon-house on a pole, in the centre, without any pigeons in it; a great dog-kennel in a corner, without any dog; and a quantity of fowls that look terribly tall to me, walking about, in a menacing and ferocious manner. There is one cock who gets upon a post to crow, and seems to take particular notice of me as I look at him through the kitchen window, who makes me shiver, he is so fierce. Of the geese outside the side-gate who come waddling after me with their long necks stretched out when I go that way, I dream at night, as a man environed by wild beasts might dream of lions.

Here is a long passage—what an enormous perspective I make of it!—leading from Peggotty's kitchen to the front-door. A dark store-room opens out of it, and that is a place to be run past at night; for I don't know what may be among those tubs and jars and old tea-chests, when there is nobody in there with a dimly-burning light, letting a mouldy air come out at the door, in which there is the smell of soap, pickles, pepper, candles, and coffee, all at one whiff. Then there are the two parlours; the parlour in which we sit of an evening, my mother and I and Peggotty—for Peggotty is quite our companion, when her work is done and we are alone —and the best palour where we sit on a Sunday; grandly, but not so comfortably. There is something of a doleful air about that room to me, for Peggotty has told me—I don't know when, but apparently ages ago—about my father's funeral, and the company having their black cloaks put on. One Sunday night my mother reads to Peggotty and me in there, how Lazarus was raised up from the dead. And I am so frightened that they are afterwards obliged to take me out of bed, and show me the quiet churchyard out of the bedroom window, with the dead all lying in their graves at rest, below the solemn moon.

There is nothing half so green that I know anywhere, as the grass of that churchyard; nothing half so shady as its trees; nothing half so quiet as its tombstones. The sheep are feeding there, when I kneel up, early in the morning, in my little bed in a closet within my mother's room, to look out at it; and I see the red light shining on the sun-dial, and think within myself, 'Is the sun-dial glad, I wonder, that it can tell the time again?'

Here is our pew in the church. What a high-backed pew! With a window near it, out of which our house can be seen, and *is* seen many times during the morning's service, by Peggotty, who likes to make herself as sure as she can that it's not being robbed, or is not in flames. But though Peggotty's eye wanders, she is much offended if mine does, and frowns to me, as I stand upon the seat, that I am to look at the clergyman. But I can't always look at him—I know him without that white thing on, and I am afraid of his wondering why I stare so, and perhaps stopping the service to inquire—and what am I to do? It's a dreadful thing to gape, but I must do something. I look at my mother, but *she* pretends not to see me. I look at a boy in the aisle, and *he* makes faces at me. I look at the sunlight coming in at the open door through the porch, and there I see a stray sheep—I don't mean a sinner, but mutton—half making up his mind to come into the church. I feel that if I looked at him any longer, I might be tempted to say something out loud; and what would become of me then? I look up at the monumental tablets on the wall, and try to think of Mr. Bodgers late of this parish, and what the feelings of Mrs. Bodgers must have been, when affliction sore, long time Mr. Bodgers bore, and physicians were in vain. I wonder whether they called in Mr. Chillip, and he was in vain; and if so, how he likes to be reminded of it once a week. I look from Mr. Chillip, in his Sunday neckcloth, to the pulpit; and think what a good place it would be to play in, and what a castle it would make, with another boy coming up the stairs to attack it, and having the velvet cushion with the tassels thrown down on his head. In time my eyes gradually shut up; and, from seeming to hear the clergyman singing a drowsy song in the heat, I hear nothing, until I fall off the seat with a crash, and am taken out, more dead than alive, by Peggotty.

And now I see the outside of our house, with the latticed bedroom windows standing open to let in the sweet-smelling air, and the ragged old rooks'-nests still dangling in the elm-trees at the bottom of the front garden. Now I am in the garden at the back, beyond the yard where the empty pigeon-house and dog-kennel are—a very preserve of butterflies, as I remember it, with a high fence, and a gate and padlock; where the fruit clusters on the trees, riper and richer than fruit has ever been since, in any other garden, and where my mother gathers some in a basket, while I stand by, bolting furtive gooseberries, and trying to look unmoved. A great wind rises, and the summer is gone in a moment. We are playing in the winter twilight, dancing about the parlour. When my mother is out of breath and rests herself in an elbow-chair, I watch her winding her bright curls round her fingers, and straightening her waist, and nobody knows better than I do that she likes to look so well, and is proud of being so pretty.

That is among my very earliest impressions. That, and a sense that we were both a little afraid of Peggotty, and submitted ourselves in most things to her direction, were among the first opinions—if they may be so called—that I ever derived from what I saw.

Peggotty and I were sitting one night by the parlour fire, alone. I had been reading to Peggotty about crocodiles. I must have read very perspicuously, or the poor soul must have been deeply interested, for I remember she had a cloudy impression, after I had done, that they were a sort of vegetable. I was tired of reading, and dead sleepy; but having leave, as a high treat, to sit up until my mother came home from spending the evening at a neighbour's, I would rather have died upon my post (of course) than have gone to bed. I had reached that stage of sleepiness when Peggotty seemed to swell and grow immensely large. I propped my eyelids open with my two forefingers, and looked perseveringly at her as she sat at work; at the little bit of wax-candle she kept for her thread—how old it looked, being so wrinkled in all directions!—at the little house with a thatched roof, where the yard-measure lived; at her work-box with a sliding lid, with a view of St. Paul's Cathedral (with a pink dome) painted on the top; at the brass thimble on her finger; at herself, whom I thought lovely. I felt so sleepy, that I knew if I lost sight of anything, for a moment, I was gone.

'Peggotty,' says I, suddenly, 'were you ever married?'

'Lord, Master Davy,' replied Peggotty. 'What's put marriage in your head?'

She answered with such a start, that it quite awoke me. And then she stopped in her work, and looked at me, with her needle drawn out to its thread's length.

'But *were* you ever married, Peggotty?' says I. 'You are a very handsome woman, an't you?'

I thought her in a different style from my mother, certainly; but of another school of beauty, I considered her a perfect example. There was a red velvet footstool in the best parlour, on which my mother had painted a nosegay. The ground-work of that stool and Peggotty's complexion appeared to me to be one and the same thing. The stool was smooth, and Peggotty was rough, but that made no difference.

'Me handsome, Davy!' said Peggotty. 'Lawk, no, my dear. But what put marriage in your head?'

'I don't know!—You mustn't marry more than one person at a time, may you, Peggotty?'

'Certainly not,' says Peggotty, with the promptest decision.

'But if you marry a person, and the person dies, why then you may marry another person, mayn't you, Peggotty?'

'You MAY,' says Peggotty, 'if you choose, my dear. That's a matter of opinion.'

'But what is your opinion, Peggotty?' said I.

I asked her, and looked curiously at her, because she looked so curiously at me.

'My opinion is,' said Peggotty, taking her eyes from me, after a little indecision, and going on with her work, 'that I never was married myself, Master Davy, and that I don't expect to be. That's all I know about the subject.'

'You an't cross, I suppose, Peggotty, are you?' said I, after sitting quiet for a minute.

I really thought she was, she had been so short with me; but I was quite mistaken: for she laid aside her work (which was a stocking of her own), and opening her arms wide, took my curly head within them, and gave it a good squeeze. I know it was a good squeeze, because, being very plump, whenever she made any little exertion after she was dressed, some of the buttons on the back of her gown flew off. And I recollect two bursting to the opposite side of the parlour, while she was hugging me.

'Now let me hear some more about the Crorkindills,' said Peggotty, who was not quite right in the name yet, 'for I an't heard half enough.'

I couldn't quite understand why Peggotty looked so queer, or why she was so ready to go back to the crocodiles. However, we returned to those monsters, with fresh wakefulness on my part, and we left their eggs in the sand for the sun to hatch; and we ran away from them, and baffled them by constantly turning, which they were unable to do quickly, on account of their unwieldly make; and we went into the water after them, as natives, and put sharp pieces of timber down their throats; and in short we ran the whole crocodile gauntlet. *I* did, at least; but I had my doubts of Peggotty, who was thoughtfully sticking her needle into various parts of her face and arms all the time.

We had exhausted the crocodiles, and begun with the alligators, when the garden-bell rang. We went out to the door; and there was my mother, looking unusually pretty, I thought, and with her a gentleman with beautiful black hair and whiskers, who had walked home with us from church last Sunday.

As my mother stooped down on the threshold to take me in her arms and kiss me, the gentleman said I was a more highly privileged little fellow than a monarch—or something like that; for my later understanding comes, I am sensible, to my aid here.

'What does that mean?' I asked him, over her shoulder.

He patted me on the head; but somehow, I didn't like him or his deep voice, and I was jealous that his hand should touch my mother's in touching me—which it did. I put it away as well as I could.

'Oh, Davy!' remonstrated my mother.

'Dear boy!' said the gentleman. 'I cannot wonder at his devotion!'

I never saw such a beautiful colour on my mother's face before. She gently chid me for being rude; and, keeping me close to her shawl, turned to thank the gentleman for taking so much trouble as to bring her home. She put out her hand to him as she spoke, and, as he met it with his own, she glanced, I thought, at me.

'Let us say "good night," my fine boy,' said the gentleman, when he had bent his head—*I* saw him!—over my mother's little glove.

'Good night!' said I.

'Come! Let us be the best friends in the world!' said the gentleman, laughing. 'Shake hands!'

My right hand was in my mother's left, so I gave him the other.

'Why, that's the wrong hand, Davy!' laughed the gentleman.

My mother drew my right hand forward, but I was resolved, for my former reason, not to give it him, and I did not. I gave him the other, and he shook it heartily, and said I was a brave fellow, and went away.

At this minute I see him turn round in the garden, and give us a last look with his ill-omened black eyes, before the door was shut.

Peggotty, who had not said a word or moved a finger, secured the fastenings instantly, and we all went into the parlour. My mother, contrary to her usual habit, instead of coming to the elbow-chair by the fire, remained at the other end of the room, and sat singing to herself.

—'Hope you have had a pleasant evening, ma'am,' said Peggotty, standing as stiff as a barrel in the centre of the room, with a candlestick in her hand.

'Much obliged to you, Peggotty,' returned my mother in a cheerful voice, 'I have had a *very* pleasant evening.'

'A stranger or so makes an agreeable change,' suggested Peggotty.

'A very agreeable change, indeed,' returned my mother.

Peggotty continuing to stand motionless in the middle of the room, and my mother resuming her singing, I fell asleep, though I was not so sound asleep but that I could hear voices, without hearing what they said. When I half awoke from this uncomfortable doze, I found Peggotty and my mother both in tears, and both talking.

'Not such a one as this, Mr. Copperfield wouldn't have liked,' said Peggotty. 'That I say, and that I swear!'

'Good Heavens!' cried my mother, 'you 'll drive me mad! Was ever any poor girl so ill-used by her servants as I am! Why do I do myself the injustice of calling myself a girl? Have I never been married, Peggotty?'

'God knows you have, ma'am,' returned Peggotty.

'Then, how can you dare,' said my mother—'you know I don't mean how can you dare, Peggotty, but how can you have the heart—to make me so uncomfortable and say such bitter things to me, when you are well aware that I haven't, out of this place, a single friend to turn to?'

'The more's the reason,' returned Peggotty, 'for saying that it won't do. No! That it won't do. No! No price could make it do. No!'—I thought Peggotty would have thrown the candlestick away, she was so emphatic with it.

'How can you be so aggravating,' said my mother, shedding more tears than before, 'as to talk in such an unjust manner? How can you go on as if it was all settled and arranged, Peggotty, when I tell you over and over again, you cruel thing, that beyond the commonest civilities nothing has passed? You talk of admiration. What am I to do? If people are so silly as to indulge the sentiment, is it my fault? What am I to do, I ask you? Would you wish me to shave my head and black my face, or disfigure myself with a burn, or a scald, or something of that sort? I dare say you would, Peggotty. I dare say you'd quite enjoy it.'

Peggotty seemed to take this aspersion very much to heart, I thought.

'And my dear boy,' cried my mother, coming to the elbow-chair in which I was, and caressing me, 'my own little Davy! Is it to be hinted to me that I am wanting in affection for my precious treasure, the dearest little fellow that ever was?'

'Nobody never went and hinted no such a thing,' said Peggotty.

'You did, Peggotty!' returned my mother. 'You know you did. What else was it possible to infer from what you said, you unkind creature, when you know as well as I do, that on his account only last quarter I wouldn't buy myself a new parasol, though that old green one is frayed the whole way up, and the fringe is perfectly mangy? You know it is, Peggotty; you can't deny it.' Then, turning affec-

tionately to me, with her cheek against mine, 'Am
I a naughty mamma to you, Davy? Am I a nasty,
cruel, selfish, bad mamma? Say I am, my child;
say "yes," dear boy, and Peggotty will love you; and
Peggotty's love is a deal better than mine, Davy.
I don't love you at all, do I?'

At this, we all fell a crying together. I think I was
the loudest of the party, but I am sure we were all sincere about it. I was quite heart-broken myself, and
am afraid that in the first transports of wounded
tenderness I called Peggotty a 'beast.' That
honest creature was in deep affliction, I remember,
and must have become quite buttonless on the occasion; for a little volley of those explosives went off
when, after having made it up with my mother, she
kneeled down by the elbow-chair, and made it up with
me.

We went to bed greatly dejected. My sobs kept
waking me, for a long time; and when one very strong
sob quite hoisted me up in bed, I found my mother
sitting on the coverlet, and leaning over me. I fell
asleep in her arms, after that, and slept soundly.

Whether it was the following Sunday when I saw
the gentleman again, or whether there was any
greater lapse of time before he reappeared, I cannot
recall. I don't profess to be clear about dates. But
there he was, in church, and he walked home with us
afterwards. He came in, too, to look at a famous
geranium we had, in the parlour-window. It did
not appear to me that he took much notice of it, but
before he went he asked my mother to give him a
bit of the blossom. She begged him to choose it for
himself, but he refused to do that—I could not understand why—so she plucked it for him, and gave it
into his hand. He said he would never, never, part

with it any more; and I thought he must be quite a fool not to know that it would fall to pieces in a day or two.

Peggotty began to be less with us, of an evening, than she had always been. My mother deferred to her very much—more than usual, it occurred to me—and we were all three excellent friends; still we were different from what we used to be, and were not so comfortable among ourselves. Sometimes I fancied that Peggotty perhaps objected to my mother's wearing all the pretty dresses she had in her drawers, or to her going so often to visit at that neighbour's; but I couldn't, to my satisfaction, make out how it was.

Gradually, I became used to seeing the gentleman with the black whiskers. I liked him no better than at first, and had the same uneasy jealousy of him; but if I had any reason for it beyond a child's instinctive dislike, and a general idea that Peggotty and I could make much of my mother without any help, it certainly was not *the* reason that I might have found if I had been older. No such thing came into my mind, or near it. I could observe, in little pieces, as it were; but as to making a net of a number of these pieces, and catching anybody in it, that was, as yet, beyond me.

One autumn morning I was with my mother in the front garden, when Mr. Murdstone—I knew him by that name now—came by, on horseback. He reined up his horse to salute my mother, and said he was going to Lowestoft to see some friends who were there with a yacht, and merrily proposed to take me on the saddle before him if I would like the ride.

The air was so clear and pleasant, and the horse seemed to like the idea of the ride so much himself, as he stood snorting and pawing at the garden-gate, that I had a great desire to go. So I was sent upstairs to Peggotty to be made spruce; and, in the meantime Mr. Murdstone dismounted, and, with his horse's bridle drawn over his arm, walked slowly up and down on the outer side of the sweetbriar fence, while my mother walked slowly up and down on the inner, to keep him company. I recollect Peggotty and I peeping out at them from my little window; I recollect how closely they seemed to be examining the sweetbriar between them, as they strolled along; and how, from being in a perfectly angelic temper, Peggotty turned cross in a moment, and brushed my hair the wrong way, excessively hard.

Mr. Murdstone and I were soon off, and trotting along on the green turf by the side of the road. He held me quite easily with one arm, and I don't think I was restless usually; but I could not make up my mind to sit in front of him without turning my head sometimes, and looking up in his face. He had that kind of shallow black eye—I want a better word to express an eye that has no depth in it to be looked into—which, when it is abstracted, seems, from some peculiarity of light, to be disfigured, for a moment at a time, by a cast. Several times when I glanced at him, I observed that appearance with a sort of awe, and wondered what he was thinking about so closely. His hair and whiskers were blacker and thicker, looked at so near, than even I had given them credit for being. A squareness about the lower part of his face, and the dotted indication of the strong black beard he shaved close every day, reminded me of the wax-work that had travelled into our neighbourhood some half a year before. This, his regular eyebrows, and the rich white, and black, and brown, of his complexion—confound his complexion, and his memory!—made me think him, in spite of my misgivings, a very handsome man. I have no doubt that my poor dear mother thought him so too.

We went to an hotel by the sea, where two gentlemen were smoking cigars in a room by themselves. Each of them was lying on at least four chairs, and had a large rough jacket on. In a corner was a heap of coats and boat-cloaks, and a flag, all bundled up together.

They both rolled on to their feet, in an untidy sort of manner, when we came in, and said, 'Halloa, Murdstone! We thought you were dead!'

'Not yet,' said Mr. Murdstone.

'And who 's this shaver?' said one of the gentlemen, taking hold of me.

'That 's Davy,' returned Mr. Murdstone.

'Davy who?' said the gentleman. 'Jones?'

'Copperfield,' said Mr. Murdstone.

'What! Bewitching Mrs. Copperfield's incumbrance?' cried the gentleman. 'The pretty little widow?'

'Quinion,' said Mr. Murdstone, 'take care, if you please. Somebody 's sharp.'

'Who is?' asked the gentleman, laughing.

I looked up, quickly; being curious to know.

'Only Brooks of Sheffield,' said Mr. Murdstone.

I was quite relieved to find that it was only Brooks of Sheffield; for, at first, I really thought it was I.

There seemed to be something very comical in the reputation of Mr. Brooks of Sheffield, for both the gentlemen laughed heartily when he was mentioned, and Mr. Murdstone was a good deal amused also. After some laughing, the gentleman whom he had called Quinion said—

'And what is the opinion of Brooks of Sheffield, in reference to the projected business?'

'Why, I don't know that Brooks understands much about it at present,' replied Mr. Murdstone; 'but he is not generally favourable, I believe.'

There was more laughter at this, and Mr. Quinion said he would ring the bell for some sherry in which to drink to Brooks. This he did; and when the wine came, he made me have a little, with a biscuit, and, before I drank it, stand up and say, 'Confusion to Brooks of Sheffield!' The toast was received with great applause, and such hearty laughter that it made me laugh too; at which they laughed the more. In short, we quite enjoyed ourselves.

We walked about on the cliff after that, and sat on the grass, and looked at things through a telescope—I could make out nothing myself when it was put to my eye, but I pretended I could—and then we came back to the hotel to an early dinner. All the time we were out, the two gentlemen smoked incessantly—which, I thought, if I might judge from the smell of their rough coats, they must have been doing, ever since the coats had first come home from the tailor's. I must not forget that we went on board the yacht, where they all three descended into the cabin, and were busy with some papers. I saw them quite hard at work, when I looked down through the open skylight. They left me, during this time, with a very nice man, with a very large head of red hair and a very small shiny hat upon it, who had got a cross-barred shirt or waistcoat on, with 'Skylark' in capital letters across the chest. I thought it was his name; and that as he lived on board ship and hadn't a street-door to put his name on, he put it there instead; but when I called him Mr. Skylark, he said it meant the vessel.

I observed all day that Mr. Murdstone was graver and steadier than the two gentlemen. They were very gay and careless. They joked freely with one another, but seldom with him. It appeared to me that he was more clever and cold than they were, and that they regarded him with something of my own feeling. I remarked that, once or twice, when Mr. Quinion was talking, he looked at Mr. Murdstone sideways, as if to make sure of his not being displeased; and that once when Mr. Passnidge (the other gentleman) was in high spirits, he trod upon his foot and gave him a secret caution with his eyes, to observe Mr. Murdstone, who was sitting stern and silent. Nor do I recollect that Mr. Murdstone laughed at all that day, except at the Sheffield joke— and that, by the bye, was his own.

We went home early in the evening. It was a very fine evening, and my mother and he had another stroll by the sweetbriar, while I was sent in to get my tea. When he was gone, my mother asked me all about the day I had had, and what they had said and done. I mentioned what they had said about her, and she laughed, and told me they were impudent fellows who talked nonsense—but I knew it pleased her. I knew it quite as well as I know it now. I took the opportunity of asking if she was at all acquainted with Mr. Brooks of Sheffield, but she answered No, only she supposed he must be a manufacturer in the knife and fork way.

Can I say of her face—altered as I have reason to remember it, perished as I know it is—that it is gone, when here it comes before me at this instant, as distinct as any face that I may choose to look on in a crowded street? Can I say of her innocent and girlish beauty, that it faded, and was no more, when its breath falls on my cheek now, as it fell that night? Can I say she ever changed, when my remembrance brings her back to life, thus only; and,

truer to its loving youth than I have been, or man
ever is, still holds fast what it cherished then?

I write of her just as she was when I had gone to
bed after this talk, and she came to bid me good
night. She kneeled down playfully by the side of
the bed, and laying her chin upon her hands, and
laughing, said—

'What was it they said, Davy? Tell me again. I
can't believe it.'

' "Bewitching—" ' I began.

My mother put her hands upon my lips to stop me.

'It was never bewitching,' she said, laughing. 'It
never could have been bewitching, Davy. Now I
know it wasn't!'

'Yes it was. "Bewitching Mrs. Copperfield," ' I
repeated stoutly. 'And "pretty." '

'No, no, it was never pretty. Not pretty,' interposed my mother, laying her fingers on my lips
again.

'Yes it was. "Pretty little widow." '

'What foolish, impudent creatures!' cried my
mother, laughing and covering her face. 'What
ridiculous men! An't they? Davy dear—'

'Well, ma.'

'Don't tell Peggotty; she might be angry with
them. I am dreadfully angry with them myself; but
I would rather Peggotty didn't know.'

I promised, of course; and we kissed one another
over and over again, and I soon fell fast asleep.

It seems to me, at this distance of time, as if it
were the next day when Peggotty broached the striking and adventurous proposition I am about to mention; but it was probably about two months afterwards.

We were sitting as before, one evening (when my
mother was out as before), in company with the

stocking and the yard measure, and the bit of wax, and the box with Saint Paul's on the lid, and the crocodile book, when Peggotty, after looking at me several times, and opening her mouth as if she were going to speak, without doing it—which I thought was merely gaping, or I should have been rather alarmed—said coaxingly—

'Master Davy, how should you like to go along with me and spend a fortnight at my brother's at Yarmouth? Wouldn't *that* be a treat?'

'Is your brother an agreeable man, Peggotty?' I inquired, provisionally.

'Oh, what an agreeable man he is!' cried Peggotty, holding up her hands. 'Then there's the sea; and the boats and ships; and the fishermen; and the beach; and Am to play with—'

Peggotty meant her nephew Ham, mentioned in my first chapter; but she spoke of him as a morsel of English Grammar.

I was flushed by her summary of delights, and replied that it would indeed be a treat, but what would my mother say?

'Why then I'll as good as bet a guinea,' said Peggotty, intent upon my face, 'that she'll let us go. I'll ask her, if you like, as soon as ever she comes home. There now!'

'But what's she to do while we are away?' said I, putting my small elbows on the table to argue the point. 'She can't live by herself.'

If Peggotty were looking for a hole, all of a sudden, in the heel of that stocking, it must have been a very little one indeed, and not worth darning.

'I say! Peggotty! She can't live by herself, you know.'

'Oh bless you!' said Peggotty, looking at me again at last. 'Don't you know? She's going to stay for

a fortnight with Mrs. Grayper. Mrs. Grayper's
going to have a lot of company.'

Oh! If that was it, I was quite ready to go. I
waited, in the utmost impatience, until my mother
came home from Mrs. Grayper's (for it was that
identical neighbour), to ascertain if we could get
leave to carry out this great idea. Without being
nearly so much surprised as I expected, my mother
entered into it readily: and it was all arranged that
night, and my board and lodging during the visit
were to be paid for.

The day soon came for our going. It was such an
early day that it came soon, even to me, who was in
a fever of expectation, and half afraid that an earthquake or a fiery mountain, or some other great con-
vulsion of nature, might interpose to stop the expedition. We were to go in a carrier's cart, which departed in the morning after breakfast. I would have
given any money to have been allowed to wrap myself up overnight, and sleep in my hat and boots.

It touches me nearly now, although I tell it lightly,
to recollect how eager I was to leave my happy
home; to think how little I suspected what I did leave
for ever.

I am glad to recollect that when the carrier's cart
was at the gate, and my mother stood there kissing
me, a grateful fondness for her and for the old
place I had never turned my back upon before, made
me cry. I am glad to know that my mother cried
too, and that I felt her heart beat against mine.

I am glad to recollect that when the carrier began
to move, my mother ran out at the gate, and called
to him to stop, that she might kiss me once more. I
am glad to dwell upon the earnestness and love with
which she lifted up her face to mine, and did so.

As we left her standing in the road, Mr. Murd-

stone came up to where she was, and seemed to ex-
postulate with her for being so moved.   I was looking back round the awning of the cart, and wondered what business it was of his.   Peggotty, who
was also looking back on the other side, seemed anything but satisfied; as the face she brought back in
the cart denoted.

I sat looking at Peggotty for some time, in a reverie on this supposititious case: whether, if she were
employed to lose me like the boy in the fairy tale, I
should be able to track my way home again by the
buttons she would shed.

CHAPTER III

I HAVE A CHANGE

THE carrier's horse was the laziest horse in the world,
I should hope, and shuffled along, with his head down,
as if he liked to keep people waiting to whom the
packages were directed.   I fancied, indeed, that he
sometimes chuckled audibly over this reflection, but
the carrier said he was only troubled with a cough.

The carrier had a way of keeping his head down,
like his horse, and of drooping sleepily forward as he
drove, with one of his arms on each of his knees.   I
say 'drove,' but it struck me that the cart would have
gone to Yarmouth quite as well without him, for the
horse did all that; and as to conversation, he had no
idea of it but whistling.

Peggotty had a basket of refreshments on her knee,
which would have lasted us out handsomely, if we
had been going to London by the same conveyance.
We ate a good deal, and slept a good deal.   Peggotty   always   went   to   sleep   with   her   chin

upon the handle of the basket, her hold of which never relaxed; and I could not have believed unless I had heard her do it, that one defenceless woman could have snored so much.

We made so many deviations up and down lanes, and were such a long time delivering a bedstead at a public-house, and calling at other places, that I was quite tired, and very glad, when we saw Yarmouth. It looked rather spongy and soppy, I thought, as I carried my eye over the great dull waste that lay across the river; and I could not help wondering, if the world were really as round as my geography-book said, how any part of it came to be so flat. But I reflected that Yarmouth might be situated at one of the poles; which would account for it.

As we drew a little nearer, and saw the whole adjacent prospect lying a straight low line under the sky, I hinted to Peggotty that a mound or so might have improved it; and also that if the land had been a little more separated from the sea, and the town and the tide had not been quite so much mixed up, like toast and water, it would have been nicer. But Peggotty said, with greater emphasis than usual, that we must take things as we found them, and that, for her part, she was proud to call herself a Yarmouth Bloater.

When we got into the street (which was strange enough to me), and smelt the fish, and pitch, and oakum, and tar, and saw the sailors walking about, and the carts jingling up and down over the stones, I felt that I had done so busy a place an injustice; and said as much to Peggotty, who heard my expressions of delight with great complacency, and told me it was well known (I suppose to those who had the good fortune to be born Bloaters) that Yarmouth was, upon the whole, the finest place in the universe.

'Here's my Am!' screamed Peggotty, 'growed out of knowledge!'

He was waiting for us, in fact, at the public-house; and asked me how I found myself, like an old acquaintance. I did not feel, at first, that I knew him as well as he knew me, because he had never come to our house since the night I was born, and naturally he had the advantage of me. But our intimacy was much advanced by his taking me on his back to carry me home. He was, now, a huge, strong fellow of six feet high, broad in proportion, and round-shouldered; but with a simpering boy's face and curly light hair that gave him quite a sheepish look. He was dressed in a canvas jacket, and a pair of such very stiff trousers that they would have stood quite as well alone, without any legs in them. And you couldn't so properly have said he wore a hat, as that he was covered in atop, like an old building, with something pitchy.

Ham carrying me on his back and a small box of ours under his arm, and Peggotty carrying another small box of ours, we turned down lanes bestrewn with bits of chips and little hillocks of sand, and went past gas-works, rope-walks, boat-builders' yards, ship-wrights' yards, ship-breakers' yards, caulkers' yards, riggers' lofts, smiths' forges, and a great litter of such places, until we came out upon the dull waste I had already seen at a distance; when Ham said—

'Yon's our house, Mas'r Davy!'

I looked in all directions, as far as I could stare over the wilderness, and away at the sea, and away at the river, but no house could I make out. There was a black barge, or some other kind of superannuated boat, not far off, high and dry on the ground, with an iron funnel sticking out of it for a chimney and smoking very cosily; but nothing else in the way of a habitation that was visible to *me*.

'That's not it?' said I.   'That ship-looking thing?'

'That's it, Mas'r Davy,' returned Ham.

If it had been Aladdin's palace, roc's egg and all, I suppose I could not have been more charmed with the romantic idea of living in it.   There was a delightful door cut in the side, and it was roofed in, and there were little windows in it; but the wonderful charm of it was, that it was a real boat which had no doubt been upon the water hundreds of times, and which had never been intended to be lived in, on dry land.   That was the captivation of it to me.   If it had ever been meant to be lived in, I might have thought it small, or inconvenient, or lonely; but never having been designed for any such use, it became a perfect abode.

It was beautifully clean inside, and as tidy as possible.   There was a table, and a Dutch clock, and a chest of drawers, and on the chest of drawers there was a tea-tray with a painting on it of a lady with a parasol, taking a walk with a military-looking child who was trundling a hoop.   The tray was kept from tumbling down, by a bible; and the tray, if it had tumbled down, would have smashed a quantity of cups and saucers and a teapot that were grouped around the book.   On the walls there were some common coloured pictures, framed and glazed, of scripture subjects; such as I have never seen since in the hands of pedlars, without seeing the whole interior of Peggotty's brother's house again, at one view.   Abraham in red going to sacrifice Isaac in blue, and Daniel in yellow cast into a den of green lions, were the most prominent of these.   Over the little mantel-shelf, was a picture of the

Sarah Jane lugger, built at Sunderland, with a real little wooden stern stuck on to it; a work of art, combining composition with carpentry, which I considered to be one of the most enviable possessions that the world could afford. There were some hooks in the beams of the ceiling, the use of which I did not divine then; and some lockers and boxes and conveniences of that sort, which served for seats and eked out the chairs.

All this, I saw in the first glance after I crossed the threshold—child-like, according to my theory—and then Peggotty opened a little door and showed me my bedroom. It was the completest and most desirable bedroom ever seen—in the stern of the vessel; with a little window, where the rudder used to go through; a little looking-glass, just the right height for me, nailed against the wall, and framed with oyster-shells; a little bed, which there was just room enough to get into; and a nosegay of seaweed in a blue mug on the table. The walls were whitewashed as white as milk, and the patchwork counterpane made my eyes quite ache with its brightness. One thing I particularly noticed in this delightful house, was the smell of fish; which was so searching, that when I took out my pocket-handkerchief to wipe my nose, I found it smelt exactly as if it had wrapped up a lobster. On my imparting this discovery in confidence to Peggotty, she informed me that her brother dealt in lobsters, crabs, and crawfish; and I afterwards found that a heap of these creatures, in a state of wonderful conglomeration with one another, and never leaving off pinching whatever they laid hold of, were usually to be found in a little wooden outhouse where the pots and kettles were kept.

We were welcomed by a very civil woman in a white apron, whom I had seen curtseying at the door when

I AM HOSPITABLY RECEIVED BY MR. PEGGOTTY.

I was on Ham's back, about a quarter of a mile off. Likewise by a most beautiful little girl (or I thought her so), with a necklace of blue beads on, who wouldn't let me kiss her when I offered to, but ran away and hid herself. By and by, when we had dined in a sumptuous manner off boiled dabs, melted butter, and potatoes, with a chop for me, a hairy man with a very good-natured face came home. As he called Peggotty 'Lass,' and gave her a hearty smack on the cheek, I had no doubt, from the general propriety of her conduct, that he was her brother; and so he turned out—being presently introduced to me as Mr. Peggotty, the master of the house.

'Glad to see you, sir,' said Mr. Peggotty. 'You'll find us rough, sir, but you'll find us ready.'

I thanked him, and replied that I was sure I should be happy in such a delightful place.

'How's your ma, sir?' said Mr. Peggotty. 'Did you leave her pretty jolly?'

I gave Mr. Peggotty to understand that she was as jolly as I could wish, and that she desired her compliments—which was a polite fiction on my part.

'I'm much obleeged to her, I'm sure,' said Mr. Peggotty. 'Well, sir, if you can make out here, for a fortnut, 'long wi'' her,' nodding at his sister, 'and Ham, and little Em'ly, we shall be proud of your company.'

Having done the honours of his house in this hospitable manner, Mr. Peggotty went out to wash himself in a kettleful of hot water, remarking that 'cold would never get *his* muck off.' He soon returned, greatly improved in appearance; but so rubicund, that I couldn't help thinking his face had this in common with the lobsters, crabs, and crawfish—that it went into the hot water very black and came out very red.

After tea, when the door was shut and all was made snug (the nights being cold and misty now), it seemed to me the most delicious retreat that the imagination of man could conceive. To hear the wind getting up out at sea, to know that the fog was creeping over the desolate flat outside, and to look at the fire and think that there was no house near but this one, and this one a boat, was like enchantment. Little Em'ly had overcome her shyness, and was sitting by my side upon the lowest and least of the lockers, which was just large enough for us two, and just fitted into the chimney corner. Mrs. Peggotty, with the white apron, was knitting on the opposite side of the fire. Peggotty at her needlework was as much at home with Saint Paul's and the bit of wax-candle, as if they had never known any other roof. Ham, who had been giving me my first lesson in all-fours, was trying to recollect a scheme of telling fortunes with the dirty cards, and was printing off fishy impressions of his thumb on all the cards he turned. Mr. Peggotty was smoking his pipe. I felt it was a time for conversation and confidence.

'Mr. Peggotty!' says I.

'Sir,' says he.

'Did you give your son the name of Ham, because you lived in a sort of ark?'

Mr. Peggotty seemed to think it a deep idea, but answered—

'No, sir. I never giv him no name.'

'Who gave him that name, then?' said I, putting question number two of the catechism to Mr. Peggotty.

'Why, sir, his father giv it him,' said Mr. Peggotty.

'I thought you were his father!'

'My brother Joe was *his* father,' said Mr. Peggotty.

'Dead, Mr. Peggotty?' I hinted, after a respectful pause.

'Drowndead,' said Mr. Peggotty.

I was very much surprised that Mr. Peggotty was not Ham's father, and began to wonder whether I was mistaken about his relationship to anybody else there. I was so curious to know, that I made up my mind to have it out with Mr. Peggotty.

'Little Em'ly,' I said, glancing at her. 'She is your daughter, isn't she, Mr. Peggotty?'

'No, sir. My brother-in-law, Tom, was *her* father.'

I couldn't help it. '—Dead, Mr. Peggotty?' I hinted, after another respectful silence.

'Drowndead,' said Mr. Peggotty.

I felt the difficulty of resuming the subject, but had not got to the bottom of it yet, and must get to the bottom somehow. So I said—

'Haven't you *any* children, Mr. Peggotty?'

'No, master,' he answered, with a short laugh. 'I 'm a bacheldore.'

'A bachelor!' I said, astonished. 'Why, who 's that, Mr. Peggotty?' Pointing to the person in the apron who was knitting.

'That 's Missis Gummidge,' said Mr. Peggotty.

'Gummidge, Mr. Peggotty?'

But at this point Peggotty—I mean my own peculiar Peggotty—made such impressive motions to me not to ask any more questions, that I could only sit and look at all the silent company, until it was time to go to bed. Then, in the privacy of my own little cabin, she informed me that Ham and Em'ly were an orphan nephew and niece, whom my host had at different times adopted in their childhood, when they were left destitute; and that Mrs. Gummidge was the widow of his partner in a boat, who had died

very poor. He was but a poor man himself, said
Peggotty, but as good as gold and as true as steel
—those were her similes. The only subject, she
informed me, on which he ever showed a violent temper or swore an oath, was this generosity of his;
and if it were ever referred to, by any one of them,
he struck the table a heavy blow with his right hand
(had split it on one such occasion), and swore a
dreadful oath that he would be 'Gormed' if he didn't
cut and run for good, if it was ever mentioned again.
It appeared, in answer to my inquiries, that nobody
had the least idea of the etymology of this terrible
verb passive to be gormed; but that they all regarded
it as constituting a most solemn imprecation.

I was very sensible of my entertainer's goodness,
and listened to the woman's going to bed in another
little crib like mine at the opposite end of the boat,
and to him and Ham hanging up two hammocks for
themselves on the hooks I had noticed in the roof, in
a very luxurious state of mind, enhanced by my being
sleepy. As slumber gradually stole upon me, I
heard the wind howling out at sea and coming on
across the flat so fiercely, that I had a lazy apprehension of the great deep rising in the night. But I
bethought myself that I was in a boat, after all; and
that a man like Mr. Peggotty was not a bad person to
have on board if anything did happen.

Nothing happened, however, worse than morning.
Almost as soon as it shone upon the oyster-shell
frame of my mirror I was out of bed, and out with
little Em'ly, picking up stones upon the beach.

'You're quite a sailor, I suppose?' I said to Em'ly.
I don't know that I supposed anything of the kind,
but I felt it an act of gallantry to say something;
and a shining sail close to us made such a pretty lit-

tle image of itself, at the moment, in her bright eye, that it came into my head to say this.

'No,' replied Em'ly, shaking her head, 'I 'm afraid of the sea.'

'Afraid!' I said, with a becoming air of boldness, and looking very big at the mighty ocean. '*I* an't!'

'Ah! but it 's cruel,' said Em'ly. 'I have seen it very cruel to some of our men. I have seen it tear a boat as big as our house all to pieces.'

'I hope it wasn't the boat that—'

'That father was drownded in?' said Em'ly. 'No. Not that one. I never see that boat.'

'Nor him?' I asked her.

Little Em'ly shook her head. 'Not to remember!'

Here was a coincidence! I immediately went into an explanation how I had never seen my own father; and how my mother and I had always lived by ourselves in the happiest state imaginable, and lived so then, and always meant to live so; and how my father's grave was in the churchyard near our house, and shaded by a tree, beneath the boughs of which I had walked and heard the birds sing many a pleasant morning. But there were some differences between Em'ly's orphanhood and mine, it appeared. She had lost her mother before her father; and where her father's grave was no one knew, except that it was somewhere in the depths of the sea.

'Besides,' said Em'ly as she looked about for shells and pebbles, 'your father was a gentleman and your mother is a lady; and my father was a fisherman and my mother was a fisherman's daughter, and my uncle Dan is a fisherman.'

'Dan is Mr. Peggotty, is he?' said I.

'Uncle Dan—yonder,' answered Em'ly, nodding at the boat-house.

'Yes. I mean him. He must be very good, I should think?'

'Good?' said Em'ly. 'If I was ever to be a lady, I'd give him a sky-blue coat with diamond buttons, nankeen trousers, a red velvet waistcoat, a cocked hat, a large gold watch, a silver pipe, and a box of money.'

I said I had no doubt that Mr. Peggotty well deserved these treasures. I must acknowledge that I felt it difficult to picture him quite at his ease in the raiment proposed for him by his grateful little niece, and that I was particularly doubtful of the policy of the cocked hat; but I kept these sentiments to myself.

Little Em'ly had stopped and looked up at the sky in her enumeration of these articles, as if they were a glorious vision. We went on again, picking up shells and pebbles.

'You would like to be a lady?' I said.

Emily looked at me, and laughed and nodded 'yes.'

'I should like it very much. We would all be gentlefolks together, then. Me, and uncle, and Ham, and Mrs. Gummidge. We wouldn't mind then, when there come stormy weather.—Not for our own sakes, I mean. We would for the poor fishermen's, to be sure, and we'd help 'em with money when they come to any hurt.'

This seemed to me to be a very satisfactory, and therefore not at all improbable, picture. I expressed my pleasure in the contemplation of it, and little Em'ly was emboldened to say, shyly—

'Don't you think you are afraid of the sea, now?'

It was quiet enough to reassure me, but I have no doubt if I had seen a moderately large wave come tumbling in, I should have taken to my heels, with an awful recollection of her drowned relations.

However, I said 'No,' and I added, 'You don't seem
to be, either, though you say you are';—for she was
walking much too near the brink of a sort of old jetty
or wooden causeway we had strolled upon, and I was
afraid of her falling over.

'I'm not afraid in this way,' said little Em'ly.
'But I wake when it blows, and tremble to think of
uncle Dan and Ham, and believe I hear 'em crying
out for help. That's why I should like so much to
be a lady. But I'm not afraid in this way. Not a
bit. Look here!'

She started from my side, and ran along a jagged
timber which protruded from the place we stood upon,
and overhung the deep water at some height, without
the least defence. The incident is so impressed on
my remembrance, that if I were a draughtsman I
could draw its form here, I dare say, accurately as it
was that day, and little Em'ly springing forward to
her destruction (as it appeared to me), with a look
that I have never forgotten, directed far out to sea.

The light, bold, fluttering little figure turned and
came back safe to me, and I soon laughed at my fears,
and at the cry I had uttered; fruitlessly in any case,
for there was no one near. But there have been times
since, in my manhood, many times there have been,
when I have thought, Is it possible, among the possibilities of hidden things, that in the sudden rashness
of the child and her wild look so far off, there was
any merciful attraction of her into danger, any tempting her towards him permitted on the part of her dead
father, that her life might have a chance of ending
that day. There has been a time since when I have
wondered whether, if the life before her could have
been revealed to me at a glance, and so revealed as
that a child could fully comprehend it, and if her
preservation could have depended on a motion of my

hand, I ought to have held it up to save her. There has been a time since—I do not say it lasted long, but it has been—when I have asked myself the question, would it have been better for little Em'ly to have had the waters close above her head that morning in my sight; and when I have answered Yes, it would have been.

This may be premature. I have set it down too soon, perhaps. But let it stand.

We strolled a long way, and loaded ourselves with things that we thought curious, and put some stranded starfish carefully back into the water—I hardly know enough of the race at this moment to be quite certain whether they had reason to feel obliged to us for doing so, or the reverse—and then made our way home to Mr. Peggotty's dwelling. We stopped under the lee of the lobster-outhouse to exchange an innocent kiss, and went in to breakfast glowing with health and pleasure.

'Like two young mavishes,' Mr. Peggotty said. I knew this meant, in our local dialect, like two young thrushes, and received it as a compliment.

Of course I was in love with little Em'ly. I am sure I loved that baby quite as truly, quite as tenderly, with greater purity and more disinterestedness, than can enter into the best love of a later time of life, high and ennobling as it is. I am sure my fancy raised up something round that blue-eyed mite of a child, which etherealised, and made a very angel of her. If, any sunny forenoon, she had spread a little pair of wings, and flown away before my eyes, I don't think I should have regarded it as much more than I had had reason to expect.

We used to walk about that dim old flat at Yarmouth in a loving manner, hours and hours. The days sported by us, as if Time had not grown up him-

self yet, but were a child too, and always at play. I
told Em'ly I adored her, and that unless she confessed
she adored me I should be reduced to the necessity of
killing myself with a sword. She said she did, and I
have no doubt she did.

As to any sense of inequality, or youthfulness, or
other difficulty in our way, little Em'ly and I had no
such trouble, because we had no future. We made
no more provision for growing older, than we did for
growing younger. We were the admiration of Mrs.
Gummidge and Peggotty, who used to whisper of an
evening when we sat lovingly, on our little locker side
by side, 'Lor! wasn't it beautiful!' Mr. Peggotty
smiled at us from behind his pipe, and Ham grinned
all the evening and did nothing else. They had something of the sort of pleasure in us, I suppose, that they
might have had in a pretty toy, or a pocket model of
the Colosseum.

I soon found out that Mrs. Gummidge did not always make herself so agreeable as she might have been
expected to do, under the circumstances of her residence with Mr. Peggotty. Mrs. Gummidge's was
rather a fretful disposition, and she whimpered more
sometimes than was comfortable for other parties in
so small an establishment. I was very sorry for her;
but there were moments when it would have been more
agreeable, I thought, if Mrs. Gummidge had had a
convenient apartment of her own to retire to, and had
stopped there until her spirits revived.

Mr. Peggotty went occasionally to a public-house
called The Willing Mind. I discovered this, by his
being out on the second or third evening of our visit,
and by Mrs. Gummidge's looking up at the Dutch
clock, between eight and nine, and saying he was
there, and that, what was more, she had known in the
morning he would go there.

Mrs. Gummidge had been in a low state all day, and had burst into tears in the forenoon, when the fire smoked. 'I am a lone lorn creetur',' were Mrs. Gummidge's words, when that unpleasant occurrence took place, 'and everythink goes contrairy with me.'

'Oh, it 'll soon leave off,' said Peggotty—I again mean our Peggotty—'and besides, you know, it 's not more disagreeable to you than to us.'

'I feel it more,' said Mrs. Gummidge.

It was a very cold day, with cutting blasts of wind. Mrs. Gummidge's peculiar corner of the fireside seemed to me to be the warmest and snuggest in the place, as her chair was certainly the easiest, but it didn't suit her that day at all. She was constantly complaining of the cold, and of its occasioning a visitation in her back which she called 'the creeps.' At last she shed tears on that subject, and said again that she was 'a lone lorn creetur' and everythink went contrairy with her.'

'It is certainly very cold,' said Peggotty. 'Everybody must feel it so.'

'I feel it more than other people,' said Mrs. Gummidge.

So at dinner; when Mrs. Gummidge was always helped immediately after me, to whom the preference was given as a visitor of distinction. The fish were small and bony, and the potatoes were a little burnt. We all acknowledged that we felt this something of a disappointment; but Mrs. Gummidge said she felt it more than we did, and shed tears again, and made that former declaration with great bitterness.

Accordingly, when Mr. Peggotty came home about nine o'clock, this unfortunate Mrs. Gummidge was knitting in her corner, in a very wretched and miserable condition. Peggotty had been working cheerfully. Ham had been patching up a great pair of water-boots; and I, with little Em'ly by my side, had been reading to them. Mrs. Gummidge had never made any other remark than a forlorn sigh, and had never raised her eyes since tea.

'Well, mates,' said Mr. Peggotty, taking his seat, 'and how are you?'

We all said something, or looked something, to welcome him, except Mrs. Gummidge, who only shook her head over her knitting.

'What's amiss?' said Mr. Peggotty, with a clap of his hands. 'Cheer up, old mawther!' (Mr. Peggotty meant old girl.)

Mrs. Gummidge did not appear to be able to cheer up. She took out an old black silk handkerchief and wiped her eyes; but instead of putting it in her pocket, kept it out, and wiped them again, and still kept it out, ready for use.

'What's amiss, dame?' said Mr. Peggotty.

'Nothing,' returned Mrs. Gummidge. 'You've come from The Willing Mind, Dan'l?'

'Why yes, I've took a short spell at The Willing Mind to-night,' said Mr. Peggotty.

'I'm sorry I should drive you there,' said Mrs. Gummidge.

'Drive! I don't want no driving,' returned Mr. Peggotty, with an honest laugh. 'I only go too ready.'

'Very ready,' said Mrs. Gummidge, shaking her head, and wiping her eyes. 'Yes, yes, very ready. I am sorry it should be along of me that you're so ready.'

'Along o' you! It an't along o' you!' said Mr. Peggotty. 'Don't ye believe a bit on it.'

'Yes, yes, it is,' cried Mrs. Gummidge. 'I know what I am. I know that I am a lone lorn creetur', and not only that everythink goes contrairy with me, but that I go contrary with everybody. Yes, yes, I feel more than other people do, and I show it more. It's my misfortun'.'

I really couldn't help thinking, as I sat taking in all this, that the misfortune extended to some other members of that family besides Mrs. Gummidge. But Mr. Peggotty made no such retort, only answering with another entreaty to Mrs. Gummidge to cheer up.

'I an't what I could wish myself to be,' said Mrs. Gummidge. 'I am far from it. I know what I am. My troubles has made me contrairy. I feel my troubles, and they make me contrairy. I wish I didn't feel 'em, but I do. I wish I could be hardened to 'em, but I an't. I make the house uncomfortable. I don't wonder at it. I've made your sister so all day, and Master Davy.'

Here I was suddenly melted, and roared out, 'No, you haven't, Mrs. Gummidge,' in great mental distress.

'It's far from right that I should do it,' said Mrs. Gummidge. 'It an't a fit return. I had better go into the house and die. I am a lone lorn creetur', and had much better not make myself contrairy here. If things must go contrairy with me, and I must go contrairy myself, let me go contrairy in my parish. Dan'l, I'd better go into the house, and die and be a riddance!'

Mrs. Gummidge retired with these words, and betook herself to bed. When she was gone, Mr. Peggotty, who had not exhibited a trace of any feeling but the profoundest sympathy, looked round upon us, and nodding his head with a lively expression of that sentiment still animating his face, said in a whisper—

'She's been thinking of the old 'un!'

I did not quite understand what old one Mrs. Gummidge was supposed to have fixed her mind upon, until Peggotty, on seeing me to bed, explained that it was the late Mr. Gummidge; and that her brother always took that for a received truth on such occasions, and that it always had a moving effect upon him. Some time after he was in his hammock that night, I heard him myself repeat to Ham, 'Poor thing! She's been thinking of the old 'un!' And whenever Mrs. Gummidge was overcome in a similar manner during the remainder of our stay (which happened some few times), he always said the same thing in extenuation of the circumstance, and always with the tenderest commiseration.

So the fortnight slipped away, varied by nothing but the variation of the tide, which altered Mr. Peggotty's times of going out and coming in, and altered Ham's engagements also. When the latter was unemployed, he sometimes walked with us to show us the boats and ships, and once or twice he took us for a row. I don't know why one slight set of impressions should be more particularly associated with a place than another, though I believe this obtains with most people, in reference especially to the associations of their childhood. I never hear the name, or read the name, of Yarmouth, but I am reminded of a certain Sunday morning on the beach, the bells ringing for church, little Em'ly leaning on my shoulder, Ham lazily dropping stones into the water, and the sun, away at sea, just breaking through the heavy mist, and showing us the ships, like their own shadows.

At last the day came for going home. I bore up against the separation from Mr. Peggotty and Mrs. Gummidge, but my agony of mind at leaving little Em'ly was piercing. We went arm-in-arm to the public-house where the carrier put up, and I promised, on the road, to write to her. (I redeemed that promise afterwards, in characters larger than those in which apartments are usually announced in manuscript, as being to let.) We were greatly overcome at parting; and if ever, in my life, I have had a void made in my heart, I had one made that day.

Now, all the time I had been on my visit, I had been ungrateful to my home again, and had thought little or nothing about it. But I was no sooner turned towards it, than my reproachful young conscience seemed to point that way with a steady finger; and I felt, all the more for the sinking of my spirits, that it was my nest, and that my mother was my comforter and friend.

This gained upon me as we went along; so that the nearer we drew, and the more familiar the objects became that we passed, the more excited I was to get there, and to run into her arms. But Peggotty, instead of sharing in these transports, tried to check them (though very kindly), and looked confused and out of sorts.

Blunderstone Rookery would come, however, in spite of her, when the carrier's horse pleased—and did. How well I recollect it, on a cold grey afternoon, with a dull sky, threatening rain!

The door opened, and I looked, half laughing and half crying in my pleasant agitation, for my mother. It was not she, but a strange servant.

'Why, Peggotty!' I said, ruefully, 'isn't she come home?'

'Yes, yes, Master Davy,' said Peggotty. 'She's come home. Wait a bit, Master Davy, and I'll—I'll tell you something.'

Between her agitation, and her natural awkwardness in getting out of the cart, Peggotty was mak-

ing a most extraordinary festoon of herself, but I
felt too blank and strange to tell her so. When she
had got down, she took me by the hand; led me,
wondering, into the kitchen; and shut the door.

'Peggotty!' said I, quite frightened. 'What's the
matter?'

'Nothing's the matter, bless you, Master Davy,
dear!' she answered, assuming an air of sprightli-
ness.

'Something's the matter, I'm sure. Where's
mamma?'

'Where's mamma, Master Davy?' repeated Peggotty.

'Yes. Why hasn't she come out to the gate, and
what have we come in here for? Oh, Peggotty!'
My eyes were full, and I felt as if I were going to
tumble down.

'Bless the precious boy!' cried Peggotty, taking
hold of me. 'What is it? Speak, my pet!'

'Not dead, too! Oh, she's not dead, Peggotty?'

Peggotty cried out No! with an astonishing
volume of voice; and then sat down, and began to
pant, and said I had given her a turn.

I gave her a hug to take away the turn, or give
her another turn in the right direction, and then
stood before her, looking at her in anxious inquiry.

'You see, dear, I should have told you before now,'
said Peggotty, 'but I hadn't an opportunity. I
ought to have made it, perhaps, but I couldn't
azackly'—that was always the substitute for exactly,
in Peggotty's militia of words—'bring my mind to
it.'

'Go on, Peggotty,' said I, more frightened than
before.

'Master Davy,' said Peggotty, untying her bonnet with a shaking hand, and speaking in a breathless sort of way. 'What do you think? You have got a pa!'

I trembled, and turned white. Something—I don't know what, or how—connected with the grave in the churchyard, and the raising of the dead, seemed to strike me like an unwholesome wind.

'A new one,' said Peggotty.

'A new one?' I repeated.

Peggotty gave a gasp, as if she were swallowing something that was very hard, and, putting out her hand, said—

'Come and see him.'

'I don't want to see him.'

—'And your mamma,' said Peggotty.

I ceased to draw back, and we went straight to the best parlour, where she left me. On one side of the fire, sat my mother; on the other, Mr. Murdstone. My mother dropped her work, and arose hurriedly, but timidly I thought.

'Now, Clara my dear,' said Mr. Murdstone. 'Recollect! control yourself, always control yourself! Davy boy, how do you do?'

I gave him my hand. After a moment of suspense, I went and kissed my mother: she kissed me, patted me gently on the shoulder, and sat down again to her work. I could not look at her, I could not look at him, I knew quite well that he was looking at us both; and I turned to the window and looked out there at some shrubs that were drooping their heads in the cold.

As soon as I could creep away, I crept upstairs. My old dear bedroom was changed, and I was to lie a long way off. I rambled downstairs to find anything that was like itself, so altered it all seemed; and roamed into the yard. I very soon started back

from there, for the empty dog-kennel was filled up
with a great dog—deep-mouthed and black-haired
like Him—and he was very angry at the sight of me,
and sprang out to get at me.

CHAPTER IV

I FALL INTO DISGRACE

IF the room to which my bed was removed were a
sentient thing that could give evidence, I might appeal to it at this day—who sleeps there now, I wonder!—to bear witness for me what a heavy heart I
carried to it. I went up there, hearing the dog in
the yard bark after me all the way while I climbed
the stairs; and, looking as blank and strange upon the
room as the room looked upon me, sat down with my
small hands crossed, and thought.

I thought of the oddest things. Of the shape of
the room, of the cracks in the ceiling, of the paper on
the wall, of the flaws in the window-glass making rip-
ples and dimples on the prospect, of the washing-
stand being rickety on its three legs, and having a discontented something about it, which reminded me of
Mrs. Gummidge under the influence of the old one.
I was crying all the time, but, except that I was conscious of being cold and dejected, I am sure I never
thought why I cried. At last in my desolation I began to consider that I was dreadfully in love with
little Em'ly, and had been torn away from her to
come here where no one seemed to want me, or to
care about me, half as much as she did. This made
such a very miserable piece of business of it, that I
rolled myself up in a corner of the counterpane, and
cried myself to sleep.

I was awakened by somebody saying, 'Here he is!'
and uncovering my hot head. My mother and Peggotty had come to look for me, and it was one of
them who had done it.

'Davy,' said my mother. 'What's the matter?'

I thought it was very strange that she should ask
me, and answered, 'Nothing.' I turned over on my
face, I recollect, to hide my trembling lip, which answered her with greater truth.

'Davy,' said my mother. 'Davy, my child!'

I dare say no words she could have uttered would
have affected me so much, then, as her calling me her
child. I hid my tears in the bedclothes, and pressed
her from me with my hand, when she would have
raised me up.

'This is your doing, Peggotty, you cruel thing!'
said my mother. 'I have no doubt at all about it.
How can you reconcile it to your conscience, I wonder,
to prejudice my own boy against me, or against anybody who is dear to me? What do you mean by it,
Peggotty?'

Poor Peggotty lifted up her hands and eyes, and
only answered, in a sort of paraphrase of the grace
I usually repeated after dinner, 'Lord forgive you,
Mrs. Copperfield, and for what you have said this
minute, may you never be truly sorry!'

'It's enough to distract me,' cried my mother. 'In
my honeymoon, too, when my most inveterate enemy
might relent, one would think, and not envy me a
little peace of mind and happiness. Davy, you
naughty boy! Peggotty, you savage creature! Oh,
dear me!' cried my mother, turning from one of us to
the other, in her pettish, wilful manner. 'What a
troublesome world this is, when one has the most right
to expect it to be as agreeable as possible!'

I felt the touch of a hand that I knew was neither

hers nor Peggotty's, and slipped to my feet at the bedside. It was Mr. Murdstone's hand, and he kept in on my arm as he said—

'What's this? Clara, my love, have you forgotten?—Firmness, my dear!'

'I am very sorry, Edward,' said my mother. 'I meant to be very good, but I am so uncomfortable.'

'Indeed!' he answered. 'That's a bad hearing, so soon, Clara.'

'I say it's very hard I should be made so now,' returned my mother, pouting; 'and it is—very hard —isn't it?'

He drew her to him, whispered in her ear, and kissed her. I knew as well, when I saw my mother's head lean down upon his shoulder, and her arm touch his neck—I knew as well that he could mould her pliant nature into any form he chose, as I know, now, that he did it.

'Go you below, my love,' said Mr. Murdstone. 'David and I will come down together. My friend,' turning a darkening face on Peggotty, when he had watched my mother out, and dismissed her with a nod and a smile: 'do you know your mistress's name?'

'She has been my mistress a long time, sir,' answered Peggotty. 'I ought to it.'

'That's true,' he answered. 'But I thought I heard you, as I came upstairs, address her by a name that is not hers. She has taken mine, you know. Will you remember that?'

Peggotty, with some uneasy glances at me, curtseyed herself out of the room without replying; seeing, I suppose, that she was expected to go, and had no excuse for remaining. When we two were left alone, he shut the door, and sitting on a chair, and holding me standing before him, looked steadily into my eyes. I felt my own attracted, no less steadily, to his.   As I recall our being opposed thus, face to face, I seem again to hear my heart beat fast and high.

'David,' he said, making his lips thin, by pressing them together, 'if I have an obstinate horse or dog to deal with, what do you think I do?'

'I don't know.'

'I beat him.'

I had answered in a kind of breathless whisper, but I felt, in my silence, that my breath was shorter now.

'I make him wince, and smart.   I say to myself, "I 'll conquer that fellow"; and if it were to cost him all the blood he had, I should do it.   What is that upon your face?'

'Dirt,' I said.

He knew it was the mark of tears as well as I. But if he had asked the question twenty times, each time with twenty blows, I believe my baby heart would have burst before I would have told him so.

'You have a good deal of intelligence for a little fellow,' he said, with a grave smile that belonged to him, 'and you understood me very well, I see.   Wash that face, sir, and come down with me.'

He pointed to the washing-stand, which I had made out to be like Mrs. Gummidge, and motioned me with his head to obey him directly.   I had little doubt then, and I have less doubt now, that he would have knocked me down without the least compunction, if I had hesitated.

'Clara, my dear,' he said, when I had done his bidding, and he walked me into the parlour, with his hand still on my arm; 'you will not be made uncomfortable any more, I hope.   We shall soon improve our youthful humours.'

God help me, I might have been improved for my

whole life, I might have been made another creature perhaps, for life, by a kind word at that season. A word of encouragement and explanation, of pity for my childish ignorance, of welcome home, or reassurance to me that it *was* home, might have made me dutiful to him in my heart henceforth, instead of in my hypocritical outside, and might have made me respect instead of hate him. I thought my mother was sorry to see me standing in the room so scared and strange, and that, presently, when I stole to a chair, she followed me with her eyes more sorrowfully still—missing, perhaps, some freedom in my childish tread—but the word was not spoken, and the time for it was gone.

We dined alone, we three together. He seemed to be very fond of my mother—I am afraid I liked him none the better for that—and she was very fond of him. I gathered from what they said, that an elder sister of his was coming to stay with them, and that she was expected that evening. I am not certain whether I found out then or afterwards, that, without being actively concerned in any business, he had some share in, or some annual charge upon the profits of, a wine-merchant's house in London, with which his family had been connected from his great-grandfather's time, and in which his sister had a similar interest; but I may mention it in this place, whether or no.

After dinner, when we were sitting by the fire, and I was meditating an escape to Peggotty without having the hardihood to slip away, lest it should offend the master of the house, a coach drove up to the garden-gate, and he went out to receive the visitor. My mother followed him. I was timidly following her, when she turned round at the parlour-door, in the dusk, and taking me in her embrace as she had been used to do, whispered me to love my new father and be obedient to him. She did this hurriedly and secretly, as if it were wrong, but tenderly; and, putting out her hand behind her, held mine in it, until we came near to where he was standing in the garden, where she let mine go, and drew hers through his arm.

It was Miss Murdstone who was arrived, and a gloomy-looking lady she was, dark, like her brother, whom she greatly resembled in face and voice; and with very heavy eyebrows, nearly meeting over her large nose, as if, being disabled by the wrongs of her sex from wearing whiskers, she had carried them to that account. She brought with her two uncompromising hard black boxes, with her initials on the lids in hard brass nails. When she paid the coachman she took her money out of a hard steel purse, and she kept the purse in a very jail of a bag which hung upon her arm by a heavy chain, and shut up like a bite. I had never, at that time, seen such a metallic lady altogether as Miss Murdstone was.

She was brought into the parlour with many tokens of welcome, and there formally recognised my mother as a new and near relation. Then she looked at me, and said—

'Is that your boy, sister-in-law?'

My mother acknowledged me.

'Generally speaking,' said Miss Murdstone, 'I don't like boys. How d' ye do, boy?'

Under these encouraging circumstances, I replied that I was very well, and that I hoped she was the same; with such an indifferent grace, that Miss Murdstone disposed of me in two words—

'Wants manner!'

Having uttered which with great distinctness, she begged the favour of being shown to her room, which

became to me from that time forth a place of awe
and dread, wherein the two black boxes were never
seen open or known to be left unlocked, and where
(for I peeped in once or twice when she was out)
numerous little steel fetters and rivets, with which
Miss Murdstone embellished herself when she was
dressed, generally hung upon the looking-glass in
formidable array.

As well as I could make out, she had come for
good, and had no intention of ever going again.
She began to 'help' my mother next morning, and
was in and out of the store-closet all day, putting
things to rights, and making havoc in all the old
arrangements. Almost the first remarkable thing I
observed in Miss Murdstone was, her being constantly haunted by a suspicion that the servants had
a man secreted somewhere on the premises. Under
the influence of this delusion, she dived into the coal-
cellar at the most untimely hours, and scarcely ever
opened the door of a dark cupboard without clapping
it to again, in the belief that she had got him.

Though there was nothing very airy about Miss
Murdstone, she was a perfect Lark in point of getting up. She was up (and, as I believe to this hour,
looking for that man) before anybody in the house
was stirring. Peggotty gave it as her opinion that
she even slept with one eye open; but I could not concur in this idea; for I tried it myself after hearing the
suggestion thrown out, and found it couldn't be done.

On the very first morning after her arrival she was
up and ringing her bell at cock-crow. When my
mother came down to breakfast and was going to
make the tea, Miss Murdstone gave her a kind of
peck on the cheek, which was her nearest approach to
a kiss, and said—

'Now, Clara, my dear, I am come here, you know,

to relieve you of all the trouble I can.   You 're much too pretty and thoughtless'—my mother blushed but laughed, and seemed not to dislike this character—'to have any duties imposed upon you that can be undertaken by me.   If you 'll be so good as give me your keys, my dear, I 'll attend to all this sort of thing in future.'

From that time, Miss Murdstone kept the keys in her own little jail all day, and under her pillow all night, and my mother had no more to do with them than I had.

My mother did not suffer her authority to pass from her without a shadow of protest.   One night when Miss Murdstone had been developing certain household plans to her brother, of which he signified his approbation, my mother suddenly began to cry, and said she thought she might have been consulted.

'Clara!' said Mr. Murdstone sternly.   'Clara! I wonder at you.'

'Oh, it 's very well to say you wonder, Edward!' cried my mother, 'and it 's very well for you to talk about firmness, but you wouldn't like it yourself.'

Firmness, I may observe, was the grand quality on which both Mr. and Miss Murdstone took their stand.   However I might have expressed my comprehension of it at that time, if I had been called upon, I nevertheless did clearly comprehend in my own way, that it was another name for tyranny; and for a certain gloomy, arrogant, devil's humour, that was in them both.   The creed, as I should state it now, was this.   Mr. Murdstone was firm; nobody in his world was to be so firm as Mr. Murdstone; nobody else in his world was to be firm at all, for everybody was to be bent to his firmness.   Miss Murdstone was an exception.   She might be firm, but only by relationship, and in an inferior and tributary degree. My mother was another exception. She might be firm, and must be; but only in bearing their firmness, and firmly believing there was no other firmness upon earth.

'It's very hard,' said my mother, 'that in my own house—'

'*My* own house?' repeated Mr. Murdstone. 'Clara!'

'*Our* own house, I mean,' faltered my mother, evidently frightened—'I hope you must know what I mean, Edward—it's very hard that in *your* own house I may not have a word to say about domestic matters. I am sure I managed very well before we were married. There's evidence,' said my mother sobbing; 'ask Peggotty if I didn't do very well when I wasn't interfered with!'

'Edward,' said Miss Murdstone, 'let there be an end of this. I go to-morrow.'

'Jane Murdstone,' said her brother, 'be silent! How dare you to insinuate that you don't know my character better than your words imply?'

'I am sure,' my poor mother went on at a grievous disadvantage, and with many tears, 'I don't want anybody to go. I should be very miserable and unhappy if anybody was to go. I don't ask much. I am not unreasonable. I only want to be consulted sometimes. I am very much obliged to anybody who assists me, and I only want to be consulted as a mere form, sometimes. I thought you were pleased, once, with my being a little inexperienced and girlish, Edward—I am sure you said so—but you seem to hate me for it now, you are so severe.'

'Edward,' said Miss Murdstone, again, 'let there be an end of this. I go to-morrow.'

'Jane Murdstone,' thundered Mr. Murdstone, 'Will you be silent? How dare you?'

Miss Murdstone made a jail-delivery of her pocket-handkerchief, and held it before her eyes.

'Clara,' he continued, looking at my mother, 'you surprise me! You astound me! Yes, I had a satisfaction in the thought of marrying an inexperienced and artless person, and forming her character, and infusing into it some amount of that firmness and decision of which it stood in need. But when Jane Murdstone is kind enough to come to my assistance in this endeavour, and to assume, for my sake, a condition something like a housekeeper's, and when she meets with a base return—'

'Oh, pray, pray, Edward,' cried my mother, 'don't accuse me of being ungrateful. I am sure I am not ungrateful. No one ever said I was before. I have many faults, but not that. Oh, don't, my dear!'

'When Jane Murdstone meets, I say,' he went on, after waiting until my mother was silent, 'with a base return, that feeling of mine is chilled and altered.'

'Don't, my love, say that!' implored my mother very piteously. 'Oh, don't, Edward! I can't bear to hear it. Whatever I am, I am affectionate. I know I am affectionate. I wouldn't say it, if I wasn't certain that I am. Ask Peggotty. I am sure she 'll tell you I 'm affectionate.'

'There is no extent of mere weakness, Clara,' said Mr. Murdstone in reply, 'that can have the least weight with me. You lose breath.'

'Pray let us be friends,' said my mother, 'I couldn't live under coldness or unkindness. I am so sorry. I have a great many defects, I know, and it 's very good of you, Edward, with your strength of mind, to endeavour to correct them for me. Jane, I don't object to anything. I should be quite broken-hearted if you thought of leaving—' My mother was too much overcome to go on.

'Jane Murdstone,' said Mr. Murdstone to his sister, 'any harsh words between us are, I hope, uncommon. It is not my fault that so unusual an occurrence has taken place to-night. I was betrayed into it by another. Nor is it your fault. You were betrayed into it by another. Let us both try to forget it. And as this,' he added, after these magnanimous words, 'is not a fit scene for the boy—David, go to bed!'

I could hardly find the door, through the tears that stood in my eyes. I was so sorry for my mother's distress; but I groped my way out, and groped my way up to my room in the dark, without even having the heart to say good night to Peggotty, or to get a candle from her. When her coming up to look for me, an hour or so afterwards, awoke me, she said that my mother had gone to bed poorly, and that Mr. and Miss Murdstone were sitting alone.

Going down next morning rather earlier than usual, I paused outside the parlour-door, on hearing my mother's voice. She was very earnestly and humbly entreating Miss Murdstone's pardon, which that lady granted, and a perfect reconciliation took place. I never knew my mother afterwards to give an opinion on any matter, without first appealing to Miss Murdstone, or without having first ascertained by some sure means, what Miss Murdstone's opinion was; and I never saw Miss Murdstone, when out of temper (she was infirm that way), move her hand towards her bag as if she were going to take out the keys and offer to resign them to my mother, without seeing that my mother was in a terrible fright.

The gloomy taint that was in the Murdstone blood, darkened the Murdstone religion, which was austere and wrathful. I have thought, since, that its assuming that character was a necessary consequence of

Mr. Murdstone's firmness, which wouldn't allow him to let anybody off from the utmost weight of the severest penalties he could find any excuse for. Be this as it may, I well remember the tremendous visages with which we used to go to church, and the changed air of the place. Again the dreaded Sunday comes round, and I file into the old pew first, like a guarded captive brought to a condemned service. Again, Miss Murdstone, in a black velvet gown, that looks as if it had been made out of a pall, follows close upon me; then my mother; then her husband. There is no Peggotty now, as in the old time. Again, I listen to Miss Murdstone mumbling the responses, and emphasising all the dread words with a cruel relish. Again, I see her dark eyes roll round the church when she says 'miserable sinners,' as if she were calling all the congregation names. Again, I catch rare glimpses of my mother, moving her lips timidly between the two, with one of them muttering at each ear like low thunder. Again, I wonder with a sudden fear whether it is likely that our good old clergyman can be wrong, and Mr. and Miss Murdstone right, and that all the angels in heaven can be destroying angels. Again, if I move a finger or relax a muscle of my face, Miss Murdstone pokes me with her prayer-book, and makes my side ache.

Yes, and again, as we walk home, I note some neighbours looking at my mother and at me, and whispering. Again, as the three go on arm-in-arm, and I linger behind alone, I follow some of those looks, and wonder if my mother's step be really not so light as I have seen it, and if the gaiety of her beauty be really almost worried away. Again, I wonder whether any of the neighbours call to mind, as I do, how we used to walk home together, she and I;

and I wonder stupidly about that, all the dreary, dismal day.

There had been some talk on occasions of my going to boarding-school. Mr. and Miss Murdstone had originated it, and my mother had of course agreed with them. Nothing, however, was concluded on the subject yet. In the meantime I learnt lessons at home.

Shall I ever forget those lessons! They were presided over nominally by my mother, but really by Mr. Murdstone and his sister, who were always present, and found them a favourable occasion for giving my mother lessons in that miscalled firmness, which was the bane of both our lives. I believe I was kept at home for that purpose. I had been apt enough to learn, and willing enough, when my mother and I had lived alone together. I can faintly remember learning the alphabet at her knee. To this day, when I look upon the fat black letters in the primer, the puzzling novelty of their shapes, and the easy good-nature of O and Q and S, seem to present themselves again before. me as they used to do. But they recall no feeling of disgust or reluctance. On the contrary, I seemed to have walked along a path of flowers as far as the crocodile-book, and to have been cheered by the gentleness of my mother's voice and manner all the way. But these solemn lessons which succeeded those, I remember as the death-blow at my peace, and a grievous daily drudgery and misery. They were very long, very numerous, very hard—perfectly unintelligible, some of them, to me —and I was generally as much bewildered by them as I believe my poor mother was herself.

Let me remember how it used to be, and bring one morning back again.

I come into the second-best parlour after breakfast.

with my books, and an exercise-book, and a slate. My mother is ready for me at her writing-desk, but not half so ready as Mr. Murdstone in his easy-chair by the window (though he pretends to be reading a book), or as Miss Murdstone, sitting near my mother stringing steel beads. The very sight of these two has such an influence over me, that I begin to feel the words I have been at infinite pains to get into my head, all sliding away, and going I don't know where. I wonder where they *do* go, by the bye?

I hand the first book to mother. Perhaps it is a grammar, perhaps a history or geography. I take a last drowning look at the page as I give it into her hand, and start off aloud at a racing pace while I have got it fresh. I trip over a word. Mr. Murdstone looks up. I trip over another word. Miss Murdstone looks up. I redden, tumble over half a dozen words, and stop. I think my mother would show me the book if she dared, but she does not dare, and she says softly—

'Oh, Davy, Davy!'

'Now, Clara,' says Mr. Murdstone, 'be firm with the boy. Don't say, "Oh, Davy, Davy!" That's childish. He knows his lesson, or he does not know it.'

'He does *not* know it,' Miss Murdstone interposes awfully.

'I am really afraid he does not,' says my mother.

'Then, you see, Clara,' returns Miss Murdstone, 'you should just give him the book back, and make him know it.'

'Yes, certainly,' says my mother; 'that is what I intend to do, my dear Jane. Now, Davy, try once more, and don't be stupid.'

I obey the first clause of the injunction by trying once more, but am not so successful with the second, for I am very stupid. I tumble down before I get to the old place, at a point where I was all right before, and stop to think. But I can't think about the lesson. I think of the number of yards of net in Miss Murdstone's cap, or of the price of Mr. Murdstone's dressing-gown, or any such ridiculous problem that I have no business with, and don't want to have anything at all to do with. Mr. Murdstone makes a movement of impatience which I have been expecting for a long time. Miss Murdstone does the same. My mother glances submissively at them, shuts the book, and lays it by as an arrear to be worked out when my other tasks are done.

There is a pile of these arrears very soon, and it swells like a rolling snowball. The bigger it gets, the more stupid *I* get. The case is so hopeless, and I feel that I am wallowing in such a bog of nonsense, that I give up all idea of getting out, and abandon myself to my fate. The despairing way in which my mother and I look at each other, as I blunder on, is truly melancholy. But the greatest effect in these miserable lessons is when my mother (thinking nobody is observing her) tries to give me the cue by the motion of her lips. At that instant, Miss Murdstone, who has been lying in wait for nothing else all along, says in a deep warning voice—

'Clara!'

My mother starts, colours, and smiles faintly. Mr. Murdstone comes out of his chair, takes the book, throws it at me or boxes my ears with it, and turns me out of the room by the shoulders.

Even when the lessons are done, the worst is yet to happen, in the shape of an appalling sum. This is invented for me, and delivered to me orally by Mr. Murdstone, and begins, 'If I go into a cheesemonger's shop, and buy five thousand double-

Gloucester cheeses at fourpence-halfpenny each, present payment'—at which I see Miss Murdstone secretly overjoyed. I pore over these cheeses without any result or enlightenment until dinner-time, when, having made a mulatto of myself by getting the dirt of the slate into the pores of my skin, I have a slice of bread to help me out with the cheeses, and am considered in disgrace for the rest of the evening.

It seems to me, at this distance of time, as if my unfortunate studies generally took this course. I could have done very well if I had been without the Murdstones; but the influence of the Murdstones upon me was like the fascination of two snakes on a wretched young bird. Even when I did get through the morning with tolerable credit, there was not much gained but dinner; for Miss Murdstone never could endure to see me untasked, and if I rashly made any show of being unemployed, called her brother's attention to me by saying, 'Clara, my dear, there's nothing like work—give your boy an exercise'; which caused me to be clapped down to some new labour there and then. As to any recreation with other children of my age, I had very little of that; for the gloomy theology of the Murdstones made all children out to be a swarm of little vipers (though there *was* a child once set in the midst of the Disciples), and held that they contaminated one another.

The natural result of this treatment, continued, I suppose, for some six months or more, was to make me sullen, dull, and dogged. I was not made the less so, by my sense of being daily more and more shut out and alienated from my mother. I believe I should have been almost stupefied but for one circumstance.

It was this.   My father had left a small collection
of books in a little room upstairs, to which I had
access (for it adjoined my own) and which nobody
else in our house ever troubled.   From that blessed
little room, Roderick Random, Peregrine Pickle,
Humphrey Clinker, Tom Jones, the Vicar of Wake-
field, Don Quixote, Gil Blas, and Robinson Crusoe,
came out, a glorious host, to keep me company.   They
kept alive my fancy, and my hope of something beyond that place and time,—they, and the Arabian
Nights, and the Tales of the Genii,—and did me no
harm; for whatever harm was in some of them
was not there for me; *I* knew nothing of it.   It
is astonishing to me now, how I found time, in the
midst of my porings and blunderings over heavier
themes, to read those books as I did.   It is curious
to me how I could ever have consoled myself
under my small troubles (which were great troubles
to me), by impersonating my favourite characters
in them—as I did—and by putting Mr. and Miss
Murdstone into all the bad ones—which I did too.
I have been Tom Jones (a child's Tom Jones, a
harmless creature) for a week together.   I have
sustained my own idea of Roderick Random for a
month at a stretch, I verily believe.   I had a greedy
relish for a few volumes of Voyages and Travels—
I forget what, now—that were on those shelves;
and for days and days I can remember to have gone
about my region of our house, armed with the centre-
piece out of an old set of boot-trees—the perfect
realisation of Captain Somebody, of the Royal
British Navy, in danger of being beset by savages,
and resolved to sell his life at a great price.   The
captain never lost dignity, from having his ears
boxed with the Latin Grammar.   I did; but the captain was a captain and a hero, in despite of all the

grammars of all the languages in the world, dead or alive.

This was my only and my constant comfort. When I think of it, the picture always rises in my mind, of a summer evening, the boys at play in the churchyard, and I sitting on my bed, reading as if for life. Every barn in the neighbourhood, every stone in the church, and every foot of the church-yard, had some association of its own, in my mind, connected with these books, and stood for some locality made famous in them. I have seen Tom Pipes go climbing up the church-steeple; I have watched Strap, with the knapsack on his back, stop-ping to rest himself upon the wicket-gate; and I *know* that Commodore Trunnion held that club with Mr. Pickle, in the parlour of our little village ale-house.

The reader now understands, as well as I do, what I was when I came to that point of my youthful history to which I am now coming again.

One morning when I went into the parlour with my books, I found my mother looking anxious, Miss Murdstone looking firm, and Mr. Murdstone bind-ing something round the bottom of a cane—a lithe and limber cane, which he left off binding when I came in, and poised and switched in the air.

'I tell you, Clara,' said Mr. Murdstone, 'I have been often flogged myself.'

'To be sure; of course,' said Miss Murdstone.

'Certainly, my dear Jane,' faltered my mother, meekly. 'But—but do you think it did Edward good?'

'Do you think it did Edward harm, Clara?' asked Mr. Murdstone, gravely.

'That's the point,' said his sister.

To this my mother returned, 'Certainly, my dear Jane,' and said no more.

I felt apprehensive that I was personally interested in this dialogue, and sought Mr. Murdstone's eye as it lighted on mine.

'Now, David,' he said—and I saw that cast again as he said it—'you must be far more careful to-day than usual.' He gave the cane another poise, and another switch; and having finished his preparation of it, laid it down beside him, with an impressive look, and took up his book.

This was a good freshener to my presence of mind, as a beginning. I felt the words of my lessons slipping off, not one by one, or line by line, but by the entire page; I tried to lay hold of them; but they seemed, if I may so express it, to have put skates on, and to skim away from me with a smoothness there was no checking.

We began badly, and went on worse. I had come in, with an idea of distinguishing myself rather, conceiving that I was very well prepared; but it turned out to be quite a mistake. Book after book was added to the heap of failures, Miss Murdstone being firmly watchful of us all the time. And when we came at last to the five thousand cheeses (canes he made it that day, I remember), my mother burst out crying.

'Clara!' said Miss Murdstone, in her warning voice.

'I am not quite well, my dear Jane, I think,' said my mother.

I saw him wink, solemnly, at his sister, as he rose and said, taking up the cane—

'Why, Jane, we can hardly expect Clara to bear, with perfect firmness, the worry and torment that

David has occasioned her to-day. That would be stoical. Clara is getting strengthened and improved, but we can hardly expect so much from her. David, you and I will go upstairs, boy.'

As he took me out at the door, my mother ran towards us. Miss Murdstone said, 'Clara! are you a perfect fool?' and interfered. I saw my mother stop her ears then, and I heard her crying.

He walked me up to my room slowly and gravely —I am certain he had a delight in that formal parade of executing justice—and when we got there, suddenly twisted my head under his arm.

'Mr. Murdstone! Sir!' I cried to him. 'Don't! Pray don't beat me! I have tried to learn, sir, but I can't learn while you and Miss Murdstone are by. I can't indeed!'

'Can't you, indeed, David?' he said. 'We'll try that.'

He had my head as in a vice, but I twined round him somehow, and stopped him for a moment, entreating him not to beat me. It was only for a moment that I stopped him, for he cut me heavily an instant afterwards, and in the same instant I caught the hand with which he held me in my mouth, between my teeth, and bit it through. It sets my teeth on edge to think of it.

He beat me then, as if he would have beaten me to death. Above all the noise we made, I heard them running up the stairs, and crying out—I heard my mother crying out—and Peggotty. Then he was gone; and the door was locked outside; and I was lying, fevered and hot, and torn, and sore, and raging in my puny way, upon the floor.

How well I recollect, when I became quiet, what an unnatural stillness seemed to reign through the whole house! How well I remember, when my smart and passion began to cool, how wicked I began to feel!

I sat listening for a long while, but there was not a sound. I crawled up from the floor, and saw my face in the glass, so swollen, red, and ugly, that it almost frightened me. My stripes were sore and stiff, and made me cry afresh, when I moved; but they were nothing to the guilt I felt. It lay heavier on my breast than if I had been a most atrocious criminal, I dare say.

It had begun to grow dark, and I had shut the window (I had been lying, for the most part, with my head upon the sill, by turns crying, dozing, and looking listlessly out), when the key was turned, and Miss Murdstone came in with some bread and meat, and milk. These she put down upon the table without a word, glaring at me the while with exemplary firmness, and then retired, locking the door after her.

Long after it was dark I sat there, wondering whether anybody else would come. When this appeared improbable for that night, I undressed, and went to bed; and there, I began to wonder fearfully what would be done to me. Whether it was a criminal act that I had committed? Whether I should be taken into custody, and sent to prison? Whether I was at all in danger of being hanged?

I never shall forget the waking next morning; the being cheerful and fresh for the first moment, and then the being weighed down by the stale and dismal oppression of remembrance. Miss Murdstone reappeared before I was out of bed; told me, in so many words, that I was free to walk in the garden for half an hour and no longer; and retired, leaving the door open, that I might avail myself of that permission.

I did so, and did so every morning of my imprisonment, which lasted five days. If I could have seen my mother alone, I should have gone down on my knees to her and besought her forgiveness; but I saw no one, Miss Murdstone excepted, during the whole time—except at evening prayers in the parlour; to which I was escorted by Miss Murdstone after everybody else was placed; where I was stationed, a young outlaw, all alone by myself near the door; and whence I was solemnly conducted by my jailer, before any one arose from the devotional posture. I only observed that my mother was as far off from me as she could be, and kept her face another way, so that I never saw it; and that Mr. Murdstone's hand was bound up in a large linen wrapper.

The length of those five days I can convey no idea of to any one. They occupy the place of years in my remembrance. The way in which I listened to all the incidents of the house that made themselves audible to me; the ringing of bells, the opening and shutting of doors, the murmuring of voices, the footsteps on the stairs; to any laughing, whistling, or singing, outside, which seemed more dismal than anything else to me in my solitude and disgrace— the uncertain pace of the hours, especially at night, when I would wake thinking it was morning, and find that the family were not yet gone to bed, and that all the length of night had yet to come—the depressed dreams and nightmares I had—the return of day, noon, afternoon, evening, when the boys played in the churchyard, and I watched them from a distance within the room, being ashamed to show myself at the window lest they should know I was a prisoner—the strange sensation of never hearing myself speak—the fleeting intervals of something like cheerfulness, which came with eating and drinking, and went away with it—the setting in of rain one evening, with a fresh smell, and its coming down faster and faster between me and the church, until it and gathering night seemed to quench me in gloom, and fear, and remorse—all this appears to have gone round and round for years instead of days, it is so vividly and strongly stamped on my remembrance.

On the last night of my restraint, I was awakened by hearing my own name spoken in a whisper. I started up in bed, and putting out my arms in the dark, said—

'Is that you, Peggotty?'

There was no immediate answer, but presently I heard my name again, in a tone so very mysterious and awful, that I think I should have gone into a fit, if it had not occurred to me that it must have come through the keyhole.

I groped my way to the door, and putting my own lips to the keyhole, whispered—

'Is that you, Peggotty, dear?'

'Yes, my own precious Davy,' she replied. 'Be as soft as a mouse, or the Cat 'll hear us.'

I understood this to mean Miss Murdstone, and was sensible of the urgency of the case; her room being close by.

'How 's mamma, dear Peggotty? Is she very angry with me?'

I could hear Peggotty crying softly on her side of the keyhole, as I was doing on mine, before she answered. 'No. Not very.'

'What is going to be done with me, Peggotty dear? Do you know?'

'School. Near London,' was Peggotty's answer. I was obliged to get her to repeat it, for she spoke it the first time quite down my throat, in consequence of my having forgotten to take my mouth away from the keyhole and put my ear there; and though her

words tickled me a good deal, I didn't hear them.
'When, Peggotty?'

'To-morrow.'

'Is that the reason why Miss Murdstone took the
clothes out of my drawers?' which she had done,
though I have forgotten to mention it.

'Yes,' said Peggotty. 'Box.'

'Shan't I see mamma?'

'Yes,' said Peggotty. 'Morning.'

Then Peggotty fitted her mouth close to the keyhole, and delivered these words through it with as
much feeling and earnestness as a keyhole has ever
been the medium of communicating, I will venture
to assert: shooting in each broken little sentence in
a convulsive little burst of its own.

'Davy, dear. If I ain't been azackly as intimate
with you. Lately, as I used to be. It ain't because
I don't love you. Just as well and more, my pretty
poppet. It's because I thought it better for you.
And for some one else besides. Davy, my darling,
are you listening? Can you hear?'

'Ye—ye—ye—yes, Peggotty!' I sobbed.

'My own!' said Peggotty, with infinite compassion. 'What I want to say, is. That you must
never forget me. For I'll never forget you. And
I'll take as much care of your mamma, Davy. As
ever I took of you. And I won't leave her. The
day may come when she'll be glad to lay her poor
head. On her stupid, cross, old Peggotty's arm
again. And I'll write to you, my dear. Though I
ain't no scholar. And I'll—I'll—' Peggotty fell to
kissing the keyhole, as she couldn't kiss me.

'Thank you, dear Peggotty!' said I. 'Oh, thank
you! Thank you! Will you promise me one thing,
Peggotty? Will you write and tell Mr. Peggotty
and little Em'ly, and Mrs. Gummidge and Ham, that

I am not so bad as they might suppose, and that I sent 'em all my love—especially to little Em'ly? Will you, if you please, Peggotty?'

The kind soul promised, and we both of us kissed the keyhole with the greatest affection—I patted it with my hand, I recollect, as if it had been her honest face—and parted. From that night there grew up in my breast a feeling for Peggotty which I cannot very well define. She did not replace my mother; no one could do that; but she came into a vacancy in my heart, which closed upon her, and I felt towards her something I have never felt for any other human being. It was a sort of comical affection, too; and yet if she had died, I cannot think what I should have done, or how I should have acted out the tragedy it would have been to me.

In the morning Miss Murdstone appeared as usual, and told me I was going to school; which was not altogether such news to me as she supposed. She also informed me that when I was dressed, I was to come downstairs into the parlour, and have my breakfast. There I found my mother, very pale and with red eyes: into whose arms I ran, and begged her pardon from my suffering soul.

'Oh, Davy!' she said. 'That you could hurt any one I love! Try to be better, pray to be better! I forgive you; but I am so grieved, Davy, that you should have such bad passions in your heart.'

They had persuaded her that I was a wicked fellow, and she was more sorry for that, than for my going away. I felt it sorely. I tried to eat my parting breakfast, but my tears dropped upon my bread-and-butter, and trickled into my tea. I saw my mother look at me sometimes, and then glance at the watchful Miss Murdstone, and then look down or look away.

'Master Copperfield's box there!' said Miss Murdstone, when wheels were heard at the gate.

I looked for Peggotty, but it was not she; neither she nor Mr. Murdstone appeared. My former acquaintance, the carrier, was at the door; the box was taken out to his cart, and lifted in.

'Clara!' said Miss Murdstone, in her warning note.

'Ready, my dear Jane,' returned my mother. 'Good bye, Davy. You are going for your own good. Good bye, my child. You will come home in the holidays, and be a better boy.'

'Clara!' Miss Murdstone repeated.

'Certainly, my dear Jane,' replied my mother, who was holding me. 'I forgive you, my dear boy. God bless you!'

'Clara!' Miss Murdstone repeated.

Miss Murdstone was good enough to take me out to the cart, and to say on the way that she hoped I would repent, before I came to a bad end; and then I got into the cart, and the lazy horse walked off with it.

CHAPTER V

I AM SENT AWAY FROM HOME

WE might have gone about half a mile, and my pocket-handkerchief was quite wet through, when the carrier stopped short.

Looking out to ascertain for what, I saw, to my amazement, Peggotty burst from a hedge and climb into the cart. She took me in both her arms, and squeezed me to her stays until the pressure on my nose was extremely painful, though I never thought

of that till afterwards when I found it very tender.
Not a single word did Peggotty speak. Releasing
one of her arms, she put it down in her pocket to
the elbow, and brought out some paper bags of cakes
which she crammed into my pockets, and a purse
which she put into my hand, but not one word did she
say. After another and a final squeeze with both arms,
she got down from the cart and ran away; and my
belief is, and has always been, without a solitary button on her gown. I picked up one, of several that
were rolling about, and treasured it as a keepsake for
a long time.

The carrier looked at me, as if to inquire if she
were coming back. I shook my head, and said I
thought not. 'Then, come up,' said the carrier to
the lazy horse; who came up accordingly.

Having by this time cried as much as I possibly
could, I began to think it was of no use crying any
more, especially as neither Roderick Random, nor
that captain in the Royal British Navy had ever cried,
that I could remember, in trying situations. The
carrier seeing me in this resolution, proposed that
my pocket-handkerchief should be spread upon the
horse's back to dry. I thanked him, and assented;
and particularly small it looked, under those circumstances.

I had now leisure to examine the purse. It was a
stiff leather purse, with a snap, and had three bright
shillings in it, which Peggotty had evidently polished
up with whitening, for my greater delight. But its
most precious contents were two half-crowns folded
together in a bit of paper, on which was written, in
my mother's hand, 'For Davy. With my love.' I
was so overcome by this, that I asked the carrier to
be so good as to reach me my pocket-handkerchief

again; but he said he thought I had better do without it, and I thought I really had, so I wiped my eyes on my sleeve and stopped myself.

For good, too; though, in consequence of my previous emotions, I was still occasionally seized with a stormy sob. After we had jogged on for some little time, I asked the carrier if he was going all the way?

'All the way where?' inquired the carrier.

'There,' I said.

'Where's there?' inquired the carrier.

'Near London,' I said.

'Why that horse,' said the carrier, jerking the rein to point him out, 'would be deader than pork afore he got over half the ground.'

'Are you only going to Yarmouth, then?' I asked.

'That's about it,' said the carrier. 'And there I shall take you to the stage-cutch, and the stage-cutch that'll take you to—wherever it is.'

As this was a great deal for the carrier (whose name was Mr. Barkis) to say—he being, as I observed in a former chapter, of a phlegmatic temperament, and not at all conversational—I offered him a cake as a mark of attention, which he ate at one gulp, exactly like an elephant, and which made no more impression on his big face than it would have done on an elephant's.

'Did *she* make 'em, now?' said Mr. Barkis, always leaning forward, in his slouching way, on the footboard of the cart with an arm on each knee.

'Peggotty, do you mean, sir?'

'Ah!' said Mr. Barkis. 'Her.'

'Yes. She makes all our pastry and does all our cooking.'

'Do she though?' said Mr. Barkis.

He made up his mouth as if to whistle, but he didn't whistle. He sat looking at the horse's ears, as if he saw something new there; and sat so for a considerable time. By and by, he said—

'No sweethearts, I b'lieve?'

'Sweetmeats did you say, Mr. Barkis?' For I thought he wanted something else to eat, and had. pointedly alluded to that description of refreshment.

'Hearts,' said Mr. Barkis. 'Sweethearts; no person walks with her?'

'With Peggotty?'

'Ah!' he said. 'Her.'

'Oh, no. She never had a sweetheart.'

'Didn't she, though?' said Mr. Barkis.

Again he made up his mouth to whistle, and again he didn't whistle, but sat looking at the horse's ears.

'So she makes,' said Mr. Barkis, after a long interval of reflection, 'all the apple parsties, and does all the cooking, do she?'

I replied that such was the fact.

'Well. I'll tell you what,' said Mr. Barkis. 'P'raps you might be writin' to her?'

'I shall certainly write to her,' I rejoined.

'Ah!' he said, slowly turning his eyes towards me. 'Well! If you was writin' to her, p'raps you'd recollect to say that Barkis was willin'; would you?'

'That Barkis was willing,' I repeated, innocently. 'Is that all the message?'

'Ye—es,' he said, considering. 'Ye—es. Barkis is willin'.'

'But you will be at Blunderstone again to-morrow, Mr. Barkis,' I said, faltering a little at the idea of my being far away from it then, 'and could give your own message so much better.'

As he repudiated this suggestion, however, with a jerk of his head, and once more confirmed his previous request by saying, with profound gravity, 'Barkis is willin'. That's the message,' I readily undertook its transmission. While I was waiting for the coach in the hotel at Yarmouth that very afternoon, I procured a sheet of paper and an inkstand and wrote a .note to Peggotty, which ran thus: 'My dear Peggotty. I have come here safe. Barkis is willing. My love to mamma. Yours affectionately. P.S. He says he particularly wants you to know—*Barkis is willing.*'

When I had taken this commission on myself prospectively, Mr. Barkis relapsed into perfect silence; and I, feeling quite worn out by all that had happened lately, lay down on a sack in the cart and fell asleep. I slept soundly until we got to Yarmouth: which was so entirely new and strange to me in the inn-yard to which we drove, that I at once abandoned a latent hope I had had of meeting with some of Mr. Peggotty's family there, perhaps even with little Em'ly herself.

The coach was in the yard, shining very much all over, but without any horses to it as yet; and it looked in that state as if nothing was more unlikely than its ever going to London. I was thinking this, and wondering what would ultimately become of my box, which Mr. Barkis had put down on the yard-pavement by the pole (he having driven up the yard to turn his cart), and also what would ultimately become of me, when a lady looked out of a bow-window where some fowls and joints of meat were hanging up, and said—

'Is that the little gentleman from Blunderstone?'

'Yes, ma'am,' I said.

'What name?' inquired the lady.

'Copperfield, ma'am,' I said.

'That won't do,' returned the lady. 'Nobody's dinner is paid for here, in that name.'

'Is it Murdstone, ma'am?' I said.

'If you 're Master Murdstone,' said the lady, 'why do you go and give another name first?'

I explained to the lady how it was, who then rang a bell, and called out, 'William! show the coffee-room!' upon which a waiter came running out of a kitchen on the opposite side of the yard to show it, and seemed a good deal surprised when he was only to show it to me.

It was a large long room with some large maps in it. I doubt if I could have felt much stranger if the maps had been real foreign countries, and I cast away in the middle of them. I felt it was taking a liberty to sit down, with my cap in my hand, on the corner of the chair nearest the door; and when the waiter laid a cloth on purpose for me, and put a set of casters on it, I think I must have turned red all over with modesty.

He brought me some chops, and vegetables, and took the covers off in such a bouncing manner that I was afraid I must have given him some offence. But he greatly relieved my mind by putting a chair for me at the table, and saying very affably, 'Now, six-foot! come on!'

I thanked him, and took my seat at the board; but found it extremely difficult to handle my knife and fork with anything like dexterity, or to avoid splashing myself with the gravy, while he was standing opposite, staring so hard, and making me blush in the most dreadful manner every time I caught his eye. After watching me into the second chop, he said—

'There 's half a pint of ale for you. Will you have it now?'

I thanked him and said 'Yes.' Upon which he poured it out of a jug into a large tumbler, and held it up against the light, and made it look beautiful.

'My eye!' he said. 'It seems a good deal, don't it?'

'It does seem a good deal,' I answered with a smile. For it was quite delightful to me to find him so pleasant. He was a twinkling-eyed, pimple-faced man, with his hair standing upright all over his head; and as he stood with one arm akimbo, holding up the glass to the light with the other hand, he looked quite friendly.

'There was a gentleman here yesterday,' he said— 'a stout gentleman, by the name of Topsawyer—perhaps you know him?'

'No,' I said, 'I don't think—'

'In breeches and gaiters, broad-brimmed hat, grey coat, speckled choker,' said the waiter.

'No,' I said bashfully, 'I haven't the pleasure—'

'He came in here,' said the waiter, looking at the light through the tumbler, 'ordered a glass of this ale—*would* order it—I told him not—drank it, and fell dead. It was too old for him. It oughtn't to be drawn; that's the fact.'

I was very much shocked to hear of this melancholy accident, and said I thought I had better have some water.

'Why you see,' said the waiter, still looking at the light through the tumbler, with one of his eyes shut up, 'our people don't like things being ordered and left. It offends 'em. But *I*'ll drink it, if you like. I'm used to it, and use is everything. I don't think it'll hurt me, if I throw my head back, and take it off quick. Shall I?'

I replied that he would much oblige me by drinking it, if he thought he could do it safely, but by no means otherwise. When he did throw his head back, and take it off quick, I had a horrible fear, I confess, of seeing him meet the fate of the lamented Mr. Topsawyer, and fall lifeless on the carpet. But it didn't hurt him. On the contrary, I thought he seemed the fresher for it.

'What have we got here?' he said, putting a fork into my dish. 'Not chops?'

'Chops,' I said.

'Lord bless my soul!' he exclaimed, 'I didn't know they were chops. Why a chop's the very thing to take off the bad effects of that beer! Ain't it lucky?'

So he took a chop by the bone in one hand, and a potato in the other, and ate away with a very good appetite, to my extreme satisfaction. He afterwards took another chop, and another potato; and after that another chop and another potato. When he had done, he brought me a pudding, and having set it before me, seemed to ruminate, and to become absent in his mind for some moments.

'How's the pie?' he said, rousing himself.

'It's a pudding,' I made answer.

'Pudding!' he exclaimed. 'Why, bless me, so it is! What?' looking at it nearer. 'You don't mean to say it's a batter-pudding?'

'Yes, it is indeed.'

'Why, a batter-pudding,' he said, taking up a table-spoon, 'is my favourite pudding! Ain't that lucky? Come on, little 'un, and let's see who'll get most.'

The waiter certainly got most. He entreated me more than once to come in and win, but what with his table-spoon to my tea-spoon, his despatch to my despatch, and his appetite to my appetite, I was left far behind at the first mouthful, and had no chance with him. I never saw any one enjoy a pudding so much, I think; and he laughed, when it was all gone, as if his enjoyment of it lasted still.

Finding him so very friendly and companionable, it was then that I asked for the pen and ink and paper to write to Peggotty. He not only brought it immediately, but was good enough to look over me while I wrote the letter. When I had finished it, he asked me where I was going to school.

I said, 'Near London,' which was all I knew.

'Oh! my eye!' he said, looking very low-spirited, 'I am sorry for that.'

'Why?' I asked him.

'Oh, Lord!' he said, shaking his head, 'that's the school where they broke the boy's ribs—two ribs—a little boy he was. I should say he was—let me see —how old are you, about?'

I told him between eight and nine.

'That's just his age,' he said. 'He was eight years and six months old when they broke his first rib; eight years and eight months old when they broke his second and did for him.'

I could not disguise from myself, or from the waiter, that this was an uncomfortable coincidence, and inquired how it was done. His answer was not cheering to my spirits, for it consisted of two dismal words 'With whopping.'

The blowing of the coach-horn in the yard was a seasonable diversion, which made me get up and hesitatingly inquire in the mingled pride and diffidence of having a purse (which I took out of my pocket), if there were anything to pay.

'There's a sheet of letter-paper,' he returned. 'Did you ever buy a sheet of letter-paper?'

I could not remember that I ever had.

'It's dear,' he said, 'on account of the duty. Threepence. That's the way we're taxed in this country. There's nothing else, except the waiter. Never mind the ink. *I* lose by that.'

'What should you—what should *I*—how much

ought I to—what would it be right to pay the waiter, if you please?' I stammered, blushing.

'If I hadn't a family, and that family hadn't the cowpock,' said the waiter, 'I wouldn't take a sixpence. If I didn't support a aged pairint, and a lovely sister,' —here the waiter was greatly agitated—'I wouldn't take a farthing. If I had a good place, and was treated well here, I should beg acceptance of a trifle, instead of taking of it. But I live on broken wittles —and I sleep on the coals'—here the waiter burst into tears.

I was very much concerned for his misfortunes, and felt that any recognition short of ninepence would be mere brutality and hardness of heart. Therefore I gave him one of my three bright shillings, which he received with much humility and veneration, and spun up with his thumb, directly afterwards, to try the goodness of.

It was a little disconcerting to me, to find, when I was being helped up behind the coach, that I was supposed to have eaten all the dinner without any assistance. I discovered this, from overhearing the lady in the bow-window say to the guard, 'Take care of that child, George, or he'll burst!' and from observing that the women-servants who were about the place came out to look and giggle at me as a young phenomenon. My unfortunate friend the waiter, who had quite recovered his spirits, did not appear to be disturbed by this, but joined in the general admiration without being at all confused. If I had any doubt of him, I suppose this half-awakened it; but I am inclined to believe that with the simple confidence of a child, and the natural reliance of a child upon superior years (qualities I am very sorry any children should prematurely change for worldly wisdom), I had no serious mistrust of him on the whole, even then.

I felt it rather hard, I must own, to be made, without deserving it, the subject of jokes between the coachman and guard as to the coach drawing heavy behind, on account of my sitting there, and as to the greater expediency of my travelling by waggon. The story of my supposed appetite getting wind among the outside passengers, they were merry upon it likewise; and asked me whether I was going to be paid for, at school, as two brothers or three, and whether I was contracted for, or went upon the regular terms; with other pleasant questions. But the worst of it was, that I knew I should be ashamed to eat anything, when an opportunity offered, and that, after a rather light dinner, I should remain hungry all night—for I had left my cakes behind, at the hotel, in my hurry. My apprehensions were realised. When we stopped for supper I couldn't muster courage to take any, though I should have liked it very much, but sat by the fire and said I didn't want anything. This did not save me from more jokes, either; for a husky-voiced gentleman with a rough face, who had been eating out of a sandwich-box nearly all the way, except when he had been drinking out of a bottle, said I was like a boa-constrictor, who took enough at one meal to last him a long time; after which he actually brought a rash out upon himself with boiled beef.

We had started from Yarmouth at three o'clock in the afternoon, and we were due in London about eight next morning. It was midsummer weather, and the evening was very pleasant. When we passed through a village, I pictured to myself what the insides of the houses were like, and what the inhabitants were about; and when boys came run-

ning after us, and got up behind and swung there
for a little way, I wondered whether their fathers
were alive, and whether they were happy at home.
I had plenty to think of, therefore, besides my mind
running continually on the kind of place I was going
to—which was an awful speculation. Sometimes, I
remember, I resigned myself to thoughts of home
and Peggotty; and to endeavouring, in a confused
blind way, to recall how I had felt, and what sort of
boy I used to be, before I bit Mr. Murdstone: which
I couldn't satisfy myself about by any means, I
seemed to have bitten him in such a remote antiquity.

The night was not so pleasant as the evening, for
it got chilly; and being put between two gentlemen
(the rough-faced one and another) to prevent my
tumbling off the coach, I was nearly smothered by
their falling asleep, and completely blocking me up.
They squeezed me so hard sometimes, that I could
not help crying out, 'Oh, if you please!'—which they
didn't like at all, because it woke them. Opposite
me was an elderly lady in a great fur cloak, who
looked in the dark more like a haystack than a lady,
she was wrapped up to such a degree. This lady
had a basket with her, and she hadn't known what
to do with it, for a long time, until she found that,
on account of my legs being short, it could go underneath me. It cramped and hurt me so, that it made
me perfectly miserable: but if I moved in the least,
and made a glass that was in the basket rattle against
something else (as it was sure to do), she gave me
the cruellest poke with her foot, and said, 'Come,
don't *you* fidget. *Your* bones are young enough *I* 'm
sure!'

At last the sun rose, and then my companions
seemed to sleep easier. The difficulties under which
they had laboured all night, and which had found

utterance in the most terrific gasps and snorts, are
not to be conceived. As the sun got higher, their
sleep became lighter, and so they gradually one by
one awoke. I recollect being very much surprised
by the feint everybody made, then, of not having
been to sleep at all, and by the uncommon indignation with which every one repelled the charge. I
labour under the same kind of astonishment to this
day, having invariably observed that of all human
weaknesses, the one to which our common nature is
the least disposed to confess (I cannot imagine why)
is the weakness of having gone to sleep in a coach.

What an amazing place London was to me when
I saw it in the distance, and how I believed all the
adventures of all my favourite heroes to be constantly enacting and re-enacting there, and how I
vaguely made it out in my own mind to be fuller of
wonders and wickedness than all the cities of the
earth, I need not stop here to relate. We approached it by degrees, and got, in due time, to the
inn in the Whitechapel district, for which we were
bound. I forget whether it was the Blue Bull, or the
Blue Boar; but I know it was the Blue Something,
and that its likeness was painted upon the back of
the coach.

The guard's eye lighted on me as he was getting
down, and he said at the booking-office door—

'Is there anybody here for a yoongster booked in
the name of Murdstone, from Bloonderstone, Soof-
folk, to be left till called for?'

Nobody answered.

'Try Copperfield, if you please, sir,' said I, looking
helplessly down.

'Is there anybody here for a yoongster, booked in
the name of Murdstone, from Bloonderstone, Soof-
folk, but owning to the name of Copperfield, to be

left till called for?' said the guard. 'Come! *Is* there anybody?'

No. There was nobody. I looked anxiously around; but the inquiry made no impression on any of the bystanders, if I except a man in gaiters, with one eye, who suggested that they had better put a brass collar round my neck, and tie me up in the stable.

A ladder was brought, and I got down after the lady, who was like a haystack: not daring to stir, until her basket was removed. The coach was clear of passengers by that time, the luggage was very sooned cleared out, the horses had been taken out before the luggage, and now the coach itself was wheeled and backed off by some hostlers, out of the way. Still, nobody appeared, to claim the dusty youngster from Blunderstone, Suffolk.

More solitary than Robinson Crusoe, who had nobody to look at him, and see that he was solitary, I went into the booking-office, and, by invitation of the clerk on duty, passed behind the counter, and sat down on the scale at which they weighed the luggage. Here, as I sat looking at the parcels, packages, and books, and inhaling the smell of stables (ever since associated with that morning), a procession of most tremendous considerations began to march through my mind. Supposing nobody should ever fetch me, how long would they consent to keep me there? Would they keep me long enough to spend seven shillings? Should I sleep at night in one of those wooden bins, with the other luggage, and wash myself at the pump in the yard in the morning; or should I be turned out every night, and expected to come again to be left till called for, when the office opened next day? Supposing there was no mistake in the case, and Mr. Murdstone had devised this plan to get rid of me, what should I do? If they allowed me to remain there until my seven shillings were spent, I couldn't hope to remain there when I began to starve. That would obviously be inconvenient and unpleasant to the customers, besides entailing on the Blue Whatever-it-was, the risk of funeral expenses. If I started off at once and tried to walk back home, how could I ever find my way, how could I ever hope to walk so far, how could I make sure of any one but Peggotty, even if I got back? If I found out the nearest proper authorities, and offered myself to go for a soldier, or a sailor, I was such a little fellow that it was most likely they wouldn't take me in. These thoughts, and a hundred other such thoughts, turned me burning hot and made me giddy with apprehension and dismay. I was in the height of my fever when a man entered and whispered to the clerk, who presently slanted me off the scale, and pushed me over to him, as if I were weighed, bought, delivered, and paid for.

As I went out of the office hand-in-hand with this new acquaintance, I stole a look at him. He was a gaunt, sallow young man, with hollow cheeks, and a chin almost as black as Mr. Murdstone's; but there the likeness ended, for his whiskers were shaved off, and his hair, instead of being glossy, was rusty and dry. He was dressed in a suit of black clothes which were rather rusty and dry too, and rather short in the sleeves and legs; and he had a white neckerchief on, that was not over-clean. I did not, and do not, suppose that this neckerchief was all the linen he wore, but it was all he showed or gave any hint of.

'You 're the new boy?' he said.

'Yes, sir,' I said.

I supposed I was. I didn't know.

'I 'm one of the masters at Salem House,' *he* said.

I made him a bow and felt very much overawed. I was so ashamed to allude to a commonplace thing like my box, to a scholar and a master at Salem House, that we had gone some little distance from the yard before I had the hardihood to mention it. We turned back, on my humbly insinuating that it might be useful to me hereafter; and he told the clerk that the carrier had instructions to call for it at noon.

'If you please, sir,' I said, when we had accomplished about the same distance as before, 'is it far?'

'It 's down by Blackheath,' he said.

'Is *that* far, sir?' I diffidently asked.

'It 's a good step,' he said. 'We shall go by the stage-coach. It 's about six miles.'

I was so faint and tired, that the idea of holding out for six miles more was too much for me. I took heart to tell him that I had had nothing all night, and that if he would allow me to buy something to eat I should be very much obliged to him. He appeared surprised at this—I see him stop and look at me now—and after considering for a few moments said he wanted to call on an old person who lived not far off, and that the best way would be for me to buy some bread, or whatever I liked best that was wholesome, and make my breakfast at her house, where we could get some milk.

Accordingly we looked in at a baker's window, and after I had made a series of proposals to buy everything that was bilious in the shop, and he had rejected them one by one, we decided in favour of a nice little loaf of brown bread, which cost me three-pence. Then, at a grocer's shop, we bought an egg and a slice of streaky bacon; which still left what I thought a good deal of change, out of the second of the bright shillings, and made me consider London a very cheap place. These provisions laid in, we went on through a great noise and uproar that confused my weary head beyond description, and over a bridge which, no doubt, was London Bridge (indeed I think he told me so, but I was half asleep), until we came to the poor person's house, which was a part of some almshouses, as I knew by their look, and by an inscription on a stone over the gate, which said they were established for twenty-five poor women.

The Master at Salem House lifted the latch of one of a number of little black doors that were all alike, and had each a little diamond-paned window on one side, and another little diamond-paned window above; and we went into the little house of one of these poor old women, who was blowing a fire to make a little saucepan boil. On seeing the Master enter, the old woman stopped with the bellows on her knee, and said something that I thought sounded like 'My Charley!' but on seeing me come in too, she got up, and rubbing her hands made a confused sort of half-curtsey.

'Can you cook this young gentleman's breakfast for him, if you please?' said the Master at Salem House.

'Can I?' said the old woman. 'Yes can I, sure!'

'How 's Mrs. Fibbitson to-day?' said the Master, looking at another old woman in a large chair by the fire, who was such a bundle of clothes that I feel grateful to this hour for not having sat upon her by mistake.

'Ah she 's poorly,' said the first old woman. 'It 's one of her bad days. If the fire was to go out, through any accident, I verily believe she 'd go out too, and never come to life again.'

As they looked at her, I looked at her also

Although it was a warm day, she seemed to think of nothing but the fire. I fancied she was jealous even of the saucepan on it; and I have reason to know that she took its impressment into the service of boiling my egg and broiling my bacon, in dudgeon; for I saw her, with my own discomfited eyes, shake her fist at me once, when those culinary operations were going on, and no one else was looking. The sun streamed in at the little window, but she sat with her own back and the back of the large chair towards it, screening the fire as if she were sedulously keeping *it* warm, instead of it keeping her warm, and watching it in a most distrustful manner. The completion of the preparations for my breakfast, by relieving the fire, gave her such extreme joy that she laughed aloud—and a very unmelodious laugh she had, I must say.

I sat down to my brown loaf, my egg, and my rasher of bacon, with a basin of milk besides, and made a most delicious meal. While I was yet in the full enjoyment of it, the old woman of the house said to the Master—

'Have you got your flute with you?'

'Yes,' he returned.

'Have a blow at it,' said the old woman, coaxingly. 'Do!'

The Master, upon this, put his hand underneath the skirts of his coat, and brought out his flute in three pieces, which he screwed together, and began immediately to play. My impression is, after many years of consideration, that there never can have been anybody in the world who played worse. He made the most dismal sounds I have ever heard produced by any means, natural or artificial. I don't know what the tunes were—if there were such things in the performance at all, which I doubt—

but the influence of the strain upon me was, first, to make me think of all my sorrows until I could hardly keep my tears back; then to take away my appetite; and lastly, to make me so sleepy that I couldn't keep my eyes open. They begin to close again, and I begin to nod, as the recollection rises fresh upon me. Once more the little room, with its open corner cupboard, and its square-backed chairs, and its angular little staircase leading to the room above, and its three peacock's feathers displayed over the mantelpiece—I remember wondering when I first went in, what that peacock would have thought if he had known what his finery was doomed to come to—fades from before me, and I nod, and sleep. The flute becomes inaudible, the wheels of the coach are heard instead, and I am on my journey. The coach jolts, I wake with a start, and the flute has come back again, and the Master at Salem House is sitting with his legs crossed, playing it dolefully, while the old woman of the house looks on delighted. She fades in her turn, and he fades, and all fades, and there is no flute, no Master, no Salem House, no David Copperfield, no anything but heavy sleep.

I dreamed, I thought, that once while he was blowing into this dismal flute, the old woman of the house, who had gone nearer and nearer to him in her ecstatic admiration, leaned over the back of his chair and gave him an affectionate squeeze round the neck, which stopped his playing for a moment. I was in the middle state between sleeping and waking, either then or immediately afterwards; for, as he resumed—it was a real fact that he had stopped playing—I saw and heard the same old woman ask Mrs. Fibbitson if it wasn't delicious (meaning the flute), to which Mrs. Fibbitson replied, 'Ay, ay! yes!'

MY MUSICAL BREAKFAST.

and nodded at the fire: to which, I am persuaded, she gave the credit of the whole performance.

When I seemed to have been dozing a long while, the Master at Salem House unscrewed his flute into the three pieces, put them up as before, and took me away. We found the coach very near at hand, and got upon the roof; but I was so dead sleepy, that when we stopped on the road to take up somebody else, they put me inside where there were no passengers, and where I slept profoundly, until I found the coach going at a footpace up a steep hill among green leaves. Presently, it stopped, and had come to its destination.

A short walk brought us—I mean the Master and me—to Salem House, which was enclosed with a high brick wall, and looked very dull. Over a door in this wall was a board with SALEM HOUSE upon it; and through a grating in this door we were surveyed, when we rang the bell, by a surly face, which I found, on the door being opened, belonged to a stout man with a bull-neck, a wooden leg, over-hanging temples, and his hair cut close all round his head.

'The new boy,' said the Master.

The man with the wooden leg eyed me all over— it didn't take long, for there was not much of me— and locked the gate behind us, and took out the key. We were going up to the house, among some dark heavy trees, when he called after my conductor.

'Hallo!'

We looked back, and he was standing at the door of a little lodge, where he lived, with a pair of boots in his hand.

'Here! The cobbler 's been,' he said, 'since you 've been out, Mr. Mell, and he says he can't mend 'em any more. He says there ain't a bit of the original boot left, and he wonders you expect it.'

With these words he threw the boots towards Mr.
Mell, who went back a few paces to pick them up,
and looked at them (very disconsolately, I was
afraid) as we went on together. I observed then,
for the first time, that the boots he had on were a
good deal the worse for wear, and that his stocking
was just breaking out in one place, like a bud.

Salem House was a square brick building with
wings, of a bare and unfurnished appearance. All
about it was so very quiet, that I said to Mr. Mell
I supposed the boys were out; but he seemed surprised at my not knowing that it was holiday-time.
That all the boys were at their several homes. That
Mr. Creakle, the proprietor, was down by the sea-
side with Mrs. and Miss Creakle. And that I was
sent in holiday-time as a punishment for my mis-
doing. All of which he explained to me as we went
along.

I gazed upon the schoolroom into which he took
me, as the most forlorn and desolate place I had
ever seen. I see it now. A long room, with three
long rows of desks, and six of forms, and bristling
all round with pegs for hats and slates. Scraps of
old copy-books and exercises litter the dirty floor.
Some silkworms' houses, made of the same materials,
are scattered over the desks. Two miserable little
white mice, left behind by their owner, are running
up and down in a fusty castle made of pasteboard
and wire, looking in all the corners with their red eyes
for anything to eat. A bird, in a cage very little
bigger than himself, makes a mournful rattle now
and then in hopping on his perch, two inches high,
or dropping from it; but neither sings nor chirps.
There is a strange unwholesome smell upon the
room, like mildewed corduroys, sweet apples wanting air, and rotten books. There could not well be

more ink splashed about it, if it had been roofless
from its first construction, and the skies had rained
snowed, hailed, and blown ink through the varying
seasons of the year.

Mr. Mell having left me while he took his irreparable boots upstairs, I went softly to the upper end
of the room, observing all this as I crept along.
Suddenly I came upon a pasteboard placard, beautifully written, which was lying on the desk, and bore
these words: *Take care of him.   He bites.*

I got upon the desk immediately, apprehensive of
at least a great dog underneath.   But, though I
looked all around with anxious eyes, I could see
nothing of him.   I was still engaged in peering
about, when Mr. Mell came back, and asked me what
I did up there?

'I beg your pardon, sir,' says I, 'if you please, I 'm
looking for the dog.'

'Dog?' says he.   'What dog?'

'Isn't it a dog, sir?'

'Isn't what a dog?'

'That 's to be taken care of, sir; that bites?'

'No, Copperfield,' says he, gravely, 'that 's not a
dog.   That 's a boy.   My instructions are, Copperfield, to put this placard on your back.   I am sorry
to make such a beginning with you, but I must do
it.'

With that he took me down, and tied the placard,
which was neatly constructed for the purpose, on my
shoulders like a knapsack; and wherever I went
afterwards, I had the consolation of carrying it.

What I suffered from that placard nobody can
imagine.   Whether it was possible for people to see
me or not, I always fancied that somebody was reading it.   It was no relief to turn round and find nobody; for wherever my back was, there I imagined

somebody always to be. That cruel man with the wooden leg, aggravated my sufferings. He was in authority, and if he ever saw me leaning against a tree, or a wall, or the house, he roared out from his lodge-door in a stupendous voice, 'Hallo, you sir! You Copperfield! Show that badge conspicuous, or I 'll report you!' The play-ground was a bare gravelled yard, open to all the back of the house and the offices; and I knew that the servants read it, and the butcher read it, and the baker read it; that everybody, in a word, who came backwards and forwards to the house, of a morning when I was ordered to walk there, read that I was to be taken care of, for I bit. I recollect that I positively began to have a dread of myself, as a kind of wild boy who did bite.

There was an old door in this playground, on which the boys had a custom of carving their names. It was completely covered with such inscriptions. In my dread of the end of the vacation and their coming back, I could not read a boy's name, without inquiring in what tone and with what emphasis *he* would read, 'Take care of him. He bites.' There was one boy—a certain J. Steerforth—who cut his name very deep and very often, who, I conceived, would read it in a rather strong voice, and afterwards pull my hair. There was another boy, one Tommy Traddles, who I dreaded would make game of it, and pretend to be dreadfully frightened of me. There was a third, George Demple, who I fancied would sing it. I have looked, a little shrinking creature, at that door, until the owners of all the names—there were five-and-forty of them in the school then, Mr. Mell said—seemed to send me to Coventry by general acclamation, and to cry out, each in his own way, 'Take care of him. He bites!'

It was the same with the places at the desks and forms. It was the same with the groves of deserted bedsteads I peeped at, on my way to, and when I was in, my own bed. I remember dreaming night after night, of being with my mother as she used to be, or of going to a party at Mr. Peggotty's, or of travelling outside the stage-coach, or of dining again with my unfortunate friend the waiter, and in all these circumstances making people scream and stare, by the unhappy disclosure that I had nothing on but my little night-shirt, and that placard.

In the monotony of my life, and in my constant apprehension of the re-opening of the school, it was such an insupportable affliction! I had long tasks every day to do with Mr. Mell; but I did them, there being no Mr. and Miss Murdstone here, and got through them without disgrace. Before, and after them, I walked about—supervised, as I have mentioned, by the man with the wooden leg. How vividly I call to mind the damp about the house, the green cracked flagstones in the court, an old leaky water-butt, and the discoloured trunks of some of the grim trees, which seemed to have dripped more in the rain than other trees, and to have blown less in the sun! At one we dined, Mr. Mell and I, at the upper end of a long bare dining-room, full of deal tables and smelling of fat. Then, we had more tasks until tea, which Mr. Mell drank out of a blue tea-cup, and I out of a tin pot. All day long, and until seven or eight in the evening, Mr. Mell, at his own detached desk in the schoolroom, worked hard with pen, ink, ruler, books, and writing-paper, making out the bills (as I found) for last half-year. When he had put up his things for the night, he took out his flute, and blew at it, until I almost thought he would gradually blow his whole being into the

large hole at the top, and ooze away at the keys.
I picture my small self in the dimly-lighted rooms,
sitting with my head upon my hand, listening to the
doleful performance of Mr. Mell, and conning to-
morrow's lessons. I picture myself with my books
shut up, still listening to the doleful performance of
Mr. Mell, and listening through it to what used to
be at home, and to the blowing of the wind on Yarmouth flats, and feeling very sad and solitary. I
picture myself going up to bed, among the unused
rooms, and sitting on my bed-side crying for a comfortable word from Peggotty. I picture myself
coming downstairs in the morning, and looking
through a long ghastly gash of a staircase window
at the school-bell hanging on the top of an outhouse
with a weather-cock above it; and dreading the time
when it shall ring J. Steerforth and the rest to work.
Such time is only second, in my foreboding apprehensions, to the time when the man with the wooden
leg shall unlock the rusty gate to give admission to
the awful Mr. Creakle. I cannot think I was a very
dangerous character in any of these aspects, but in
all of them I carried the same warning on my back.

Mr. Mell never said much to me, but he was never
harsh to me. I suppose we were company to each
other, without talking. I forgot to mention that he
would talk to himself sometimes, and grin, and
clench his fist, and grind his teeth, and pull his hair in
an unaccountable manner. But he had these peculiarities. At first they frightened me, though I soon
got used to them.

CHAPTER VI

I ENLARGE MY CIRCLE OF ACQUAINTANCE

I HAD led this life about a month, when the man with the wooden leg began to stump about with a mop and a bucket of water, from which I inferred that preparations were making to receive Mr. Creakle and the boys. I was not mistaken; for the mop came into the schoolroom before long, and turned out Mr. Mell and me, who lived where we could, and got on how we could, for some days, during which we were always in the way of two or three young women, who had rarely shown themselves before, and were so continually in the midst of dust that I sneezed almost as much as if Salem House had been a great snuff-box.

One day I was informed by Mr. Mell, that Mr. Creakle would be home that evening. In the evening, after tea, I heard that he was come. Before bed-time, I was fetched by the man with the wooden leg to appear before him.

Mr. Creakle's part of the house was a good deal more comfortable than ours, and he had a snug bit of garden that looked pleasant after the dusty playground, which was such a desert in miniature, that I thought no one but a camel, or a dromedary, could have felt at home in it. It seemed to me a bold thing even to take notice that the passage looked comfortable, as I went on my way, trembling to Mr. Creakle's presence: which so abashed me, when I was ushered into it, that I hardly saw Mrs. Creakle or Miss Creakle (who were both there, in the parlour), or anything but Mr. Creakle, a stout gentleman with a bunch of watch-chain and seals, in an arm-chair with a tumbler and bottle beside him.

'So!' said Mr. Creakle. 'This is the young gentle-man whose teeth are to be filed! Turn him around.'

The wooden-legged man turned me about so as to exhibit the placard; and having afforded time for a full survey of it, turned me about again, with my face to Mr. Creakle, and posted himself at Mr. Creakle's side. Mr. Creakle's face was fiery, and his eyes were small, and deep in his head; he had thick veins in his forehead, a little nose, and a large chin. He was bald on the top of his head; and had some thin wet-looking hair that was just turning grey, brushed across each temple, so that the two sides interlaced on his forehead. But the circumstance about him which impressed me most, was, that he had no voice, but spoke in a whisper. The exertion this cost him, or the consciousness of talking in that feeble way, made his angry face so much more angry, and his thick veins so much thicker, when he spoke, that I am not surprised, on looking back, at this peculiarity striking me as his chief one.

'Now,' said Mr. Creakle. 'What's the report of this boy?'

'There's nothing against him yet,' returned the man with the wooden leg. 'There has been no opportunity.'

I thought Mr. Creakle was disappointed. I thought Mrs. and Miss Creakle (at whom I now glanced for the first time, and who were, both, thin and quiet) were not disappointed.

'Come here, sir!' said Mr. Creakle, beckoning to me.

'Come here!' said the man with the wooden leg, repeating the gesture.

'I have the happiness of knowing your father-in-law,' whispered Mr. Creakle, taking me by the ear; 'and a worthy man he is, and a man of a strong character. He knows me, and I know him. Do *you* know me? Hey?' said Mr. Creakle, pinching my ear with ferocious playfulness.

'Not yet, sir,' I said, flinching with the pain.

'Not yet? Hey?' repeated Mr. Creakle. 'But you will soon. Hey?'

'You will soon. Hey?' repeated the man with the wooden leg. I afterwards found that he generally acted, with his strong voice, as Mr. Creakle's interpreter to the boys.

I was very much frightened, and said I hoped so, if he pleased. I felt, all this while, as if my ear were blazing; he pinched it so hard.

'I'll tell you what I am,' whispered Mr. Creakle, letting it go at last, with a screw at parting that brought the water into my eyes. 'I'm a Tartar.'

'A Tartar,' said the man with the wooden leg.

'When I say I'll do a thing, I do it,' said Mr. Creakle; 'and when I say I will have a thing done, I will have it done.'

'—Will have a thing done, I will have it done,' repeated the man with the wooden leg.

'I am a determined character,' said Mr. Creakle. 'That's what I am. I do my duty. That's what *I* do. My flesh and blood,' he looked at Mrs. Creakle as he said this, 'when it rises against me, is not my flesh and blood. I discard it. Has that fellow,' to the man with the wooden leg, 'been here again?'

'No,' was the answer.

'No,' said Mr. Creakle. 'He knows better. He knows me. Let him keep away. I say let him keep away,' said Mr. Creakle, striking his hand upon the table, and looking at Mrs. Creakle, 'for he knows me. Now you have begun to know me too, my young friend, and you may go. Take him away.'

I was very glad to be ordered away, for Mrs. and

Miss Creakle were both wiping their eyes, and I felt as uncomfortable for them as I did for myself. But I had a petition on my mind which concerned me so nearly, that I couldn't help saying, though I wondered at my own courage—

'If you please, sir—'

Mr. Creakle whispered, 'Hah! What's this?' and bent his eyes upon me, as if he would have burnt me up with them.

'If you please, sir,' I faltered, 'if I might be allowed (I am very sorry indeed, sir, for what I did) to take this writing off, before the boys come back—'

Whether Mr. Creakle was in earnest, or whether he only did it to frighten me, I don't know, but he made a burst out of his chair, before which I precipitately retreated, without waiting for the escort of the man with the wooden leg, and never once stopped until I reached my own bedroom, where finding I was not pursued, I went to bed, as it was time, and lay quaking, for a couple of hours.

Next morning Mr. Sharp came back. Mr. Sharp was the first master, and superior to Mr. Mell. Mr. Mell took his meals with the boys, but Mr. Sharp dined and supped at Mr. Creakle's table. He was a limp, delicate-looking gentleman, I thought, with a good deal of nose, and a way of carrying his head on one side, as if it were a little too heavy for him. His hair was very smooth and wavy; but I was informed by the very first boy who came back that it was a wig (a second-hand one *he* said), and that Mr. Sharp went out every Saturday afternoon to get it curled.

It was no other than Tommy Traddles who gave me this piece of intelligence. He was the first boy who returned. He introduced himself by informing me that I should find his name on the right-hand corner of the gate, over the top bolt; upon that I said, 'Traddles?' to which he replied, 'The same,' and then he asked me for a full account of myself and family.

It was a happy circumstance for me that Traddles came back first. He enjoyed my placard so much, that he saved me from the embarrassment of either disclosure or concealment, by presenting me to every other boy who came back, great or small, immediately on his arrival, in this form of introduction, 'Look here! Here's a game!' Happily, too, the greater part of the boys came back low-spirited, and were not so boisterous at my expense as I had expected. Some of them certainly did dance about me like wild Indians, and the greater part could not resist the temptation of pretending that I was a dog, and patting and smoothing me, lest I should bite, and saying, 'Lie down, sir!' and calling me Towzer. This was naturally confusing, among so many strangers, and cost me some tears, but on the whole it was much better than I had anticipated.

I was not considered as being formally received into the school, however, until J. Steerforth arrived. Before this boy, who was reputed to be a great scholar, and was very good-looking, and at least half a dozen years my senior, I was carried as before a magistrate. He inquired, under a shed in the playground, into the particulars of my punishment, and was pleased to express his opinion that it was 'a jolly shame'; for which I became bound to him ever afterwards.

'What money have you got, Copperfield?' he said, walking aside with me when he had disposed of my affair in these terms.

I told him seven shillings.

'You had better give it to me to take care of,' he

said. 'At least, you can if you like. You needn't if you don't like.'

I hastened to comply with his friendly suggestion, and opening Peggotty's purse, turned it upside down into his hand.

'Do you want to spend anything now?' he asked me.

'No, thank you,' I replied.

'You can, if you like, you know,' said Steerforth. 'Say the word.'

'No, thank you, sir,' I repeated.

'Perhaps you'd like to spend a couple of shillings or so, in a bottle of currant wine by and by, up in the bedroom?' said Steerforth. 'You belong to my bedroom, I find.'

It certainly had not occurred to me before, but I said, Yes, I should like that.

'Very good,' said Steerforth. 'You'll be glad to spend another shilling or so, in almond cakes, I dare say?'

I said, Yes, I should like that, too.

'And another shilling or so in biscuits, and another in fruit, eh?' said Steerforth. 'I say, young Copperfield, you're going it!'

I smiled because he smiled, but I was a little troubled in my mind, too.

'Well!' said Steerforth. 'We must make it stretch as far as we can; that's all. I'll do the best in my power for you. I can go out when I like, and I'll smuggle the prog in.' With these words he put the money in his pocket, and kindly told me not to make myself uneasy; he would take care it should be all right.

He was as good as his word, if that were all right which I had a secret misgiving was nearly all wrong —for I feared it was a waste of my mother's two half-crowns—though I had preserved the piece of paper they were wrapped in: which was a precious saving. When we went upstairs to bed, he produced the whole seven shillings' worth, and laid it out on my bed in the moonlight, saying—

'There you are, young Copperfield, and a royal spread you 've got.'

I couldn't think of doing the honours of the feast, at my time of life, while he was by; my hand shook at the very thought of it. I begged him to do me the favour of presiding; and my request, being seconded by the other boys who were in that room, he acceded to it, and sat upon my pillow, handing round the viands—with perfect fairness, I must say—and dispensing the currant wine in a little glass without a foot, which was his own property. As to me, I sat on his left hand, and the rest were grouped about us, on the nearest beds and on the floor.

How well I recollect our sitting there, talking in whispers; or their talking, and my respectfully listening, I ought rather to say; the moonlight falling a little way into the room, through the window, painting a pale window on the floor, and the greater part of us in shadow, except when Steerforth dipped a match into a phosphorus-box, when he wanted to look for anything on the board, and shed a blue glare over us that was gone directly! A certain mysterious feeling, consequent on the darkness, the secrecy of the revel, and the whisper in which everything was said, steals over me again, and I listen to all they tell me with a vague feeling of solemnity and awe, which makes me glad that they are all so near, and frightens me (though I feign to laugh) when Traddles pretends to see a ghost in the corner.

I heard all kinds of things about the school and

all belonging to it. I heard that Mr. Creakle had not preferred his claim to being a Tartar without reason; that he was the sternest and most severe of masters; that he laid about him, right and left, every day of his life, charging in among the boys like a trooper, and slashing away, unmercifully. That he knew nothing himself, but the art of slash-ing, being more ignorant (J. Steerforth said) than the lowest boy in the school; that he had been, a good many years ago, a small hop-dealer in the Borough, and had taken to the schooling business after being bankrupt in hops, and making away with Mrs. Creakle's money. With a good deal more of that sort, which I wondered how they knew.

I heard that the man with the wooden leg, whose name was Tungay, was an obstinate barbarian who had formerly assisted in the hop business, but had come into the scholastic line with Mr. Creakle, in consequence, as was supposed among the boys, of his having broken his leg in Mr. Creakle's service, and having done a deal of dishonest work for him, and knowing his secrets. I heard that with the single exception of Mr. Creakle, Tungay considered the whole establishment, masters and boys, as his natural enemies, and that the only delight of his life was to be sour and malicious. I heard that Mr. Creakle had a son, who had not been Tungay's friend, and who, assisting in the school, had once held some remonstrance with his father on an occa-sion when its discipline was very cruelly exercised, and was supposed, besides, to have protested against his father's usage of his mother. I heard that Mr. Creakle had turned him out of doors, in consequence, and that Mrs. and Miss Creakle had been in a sad way ever since.

But the greatest wonder that I heard of Mr.

Creakle was, there being one boy in the school on whom he never ventured to lay a hand, and that boy being J. Steerforth. Steerforth himself confirmed this when it was stated, and said that he should like to begin to see him do it. On being asked by a mild boy (not me) how he would proceed if he did begin to see him do it, he dipped a match into his phosphorus-box on purpose to shed a glare over his reply, and said he would commence by knocking him down with a blow on the forehead from the seven-and-sixpenny ink-bottle that was always on the mantelpiece. We sat in the dark for some time, breathless.

I heard that Mr. Sharp and Mr. Mell were both supposed to be wretchedly paid; and that when there was hot and cold meat for dinner at Mr. Creakle's table, Mr. Sharp was always expected to say he preferred cold; which was again corroborated by J. Steerforth, the only parlour-boarder. I heard that Mr. Sharp's wig didn't fit him; and that he needn't be so 'bounceable'—somebody else said 'bumptious'—about it, because his own red hair was very plainly to be seen behind.

I heard that one boy, who was a coal-merchant's son, came as a set-off against the coal-bill, and was called, on that account, 'Exchange or Barter'—a name selected from the arithmetic-book as expressing this arrangement. I heard that the table-beer was a robbery of parents, and the pudding an imposition. I heard that Miss Creakle was regarded by the school in general as being in love with Steerforth; and I am sure, as I sat in the dark, thinking of his nice voice, and his fine face, and his easy manner, and his curling hair, I thought it very likely. I heard that Mr. Mell was not a bad sort of fellow, but hadn't a sixpence to bless himself with; and that there was no doubt that old Mrs. Mell, his mother, was as poor as Job. I thought of my breakfast then, and what had sounded like 'My Charley!' but I was, I am glad to remember, as mute as a mouse about it.

The hearing of all this, and a good deal more, outlasted the banquet some time. The greater part of the guests had gone to bed as soon as the eating and drinking were over; and we, who had remained whispering and listening half undressed, at last betook ourselves to bed, too.

'Good night, young Copperfield,' said Steerforth. 'I'll take care of you.'

'You're very kind,' I gratefully returned. 'I am very much obliged to you.'

'You haven't got a sister, have you?' said Steerforth, yawning.

'No,' I answered.

'That's a pity,' said Steerforth. 'If you had had one, I should think she would have been a pretty, timid, little, bright-eyed sort of girl. I should have liked to know her. Good night, young Copperfield.'

'Good night, sir,' I replied.

I thought of him very much after I went to bed, and raised myself, I recollect, to look at him where he lay in the moonlight, with his handsome face turned up, and his head reclining easily on his arm. He was a person of great power in my eyes; that was, of course, the reason of my mind running on him. No veiled future dimly glanced upon him in the moonbeams. There was no shadowy picture of his footsteps, in the garden that I dreamed of walking in all night.

CHAPTER VII

MY 'FIRST HALF' AT SALEM HOUSE

SCHOOL began in earnest next day. A profound impression was made upon me, I remember, by the roar of voices in the schoolroom suddenly becoming hushed as death when Mr. Creakle entered after breakfast, and stood in the doorway looking round upon us like a giant in a story-book surveying his captives.

Tungay stood at Mr. Creakle's elbow. He had no occasion, I thought, to cry out 'Silence!' so ferociously, for the boys were all struck speechless and motionless.

Mr. Creakle was seen to speak, and Tungay was heard, to this effect.

'Now, boys, this is a new half. Take care what you 're about, in this new half. Come fresh up to the lessons, I advise you, for I come fresh up to the punishment. I won't flinch. It will be of no use your rubbing yourselves; you won't rub the marks out that I shall give you. Now get to work, every boy!'

When this dreadful exordium was over, and Tungay had stumped out again, Mr. Creakle came to where I sat, and told me that if I were famous for biting, he was famous for biting, too. He then showed me the cane, and asked me what I thought of *that,* for a tooth? Was it a sharp tooth, hey? Was it a double tooth, hey? Had it a deep prong, hey? Did it bite, hey? Did it bite? At every question he gave me a fleshy cut with it that made me writhe; so I was very soon made free of Salem

House (as Steerforth said), and was very soon in tears also.

Not that I mean to say these were special marks of distinction, which only I received. On the contrary, a large majority of the boys (especially the smaller ones) were visited with similar instances of notice, as Mr. Creakle made the round of the schoolroom. Half the establishment was writhing and crying, before the day's work began; and how much of it had writhed and cried before the day's work was over, I am really afraid to recollect, lest I should seem to exaggerate.

I should think there never can have been a man who enjoyed his profession more than Mr. Creakle did. He had a delight in cutting at the boys, which was like the satisfaction of a craving appetite. I am confident that he couldn't resist a chubby boy, especially; that there was a fascination in such a subject, which made him restless in his mind, until he had scored and marked him for the day. I was chubby myself, and ought to know. I am sure when I think of the fellow now, my blood rises against him with the disinterested indignation I should feel if I could have known all about him without having ever been in his power; but it rises hotly, because I know him to have been an incapable brute, who had no more right to be possessed of the great trust he held, than to be Lord High Admiral, or Commander-in-Chief—in either of which capacities, it is probable, that he would have done infinitely less mischief.

Miserable little propitiators of a remorseless idol, how abject we were to him! What a launch in life I think it now, on looking back, to be so mean and servile to a man of such parts and pretensions!

Here I sit at the desk again, watching his eye—

humbly watching his eye, as he rules a ciphering-book for another victim whose hands have just been flattened by that identical ruler, and who is trying to wipe the sting out with a pocket-handkerchief. I have plenty to do. I don't watch his eye in idleness, but because I am morbidly attracted to it, in a dread desire to know what he will do next, and whether it will be my turn to suffer, or somebody else's. A lane of small boys beyond me, with the same interest in his eye, watch it too. I think he knows it, though he pretends he don't. He makes dreadful mouths as he rules the ciphering-book; and now he throws his eye sideways down our lane, and we all droop over our books and tremble. A moment afterwards we are again eyeing him. An unhappy culprit, found guilty of imperfect exercise, approaches at his command. The culprit falters excuses, and professes a determination to do better to-morrow. Mr. Creakle cuts a joke before he beats him, and we laugh at it,—miserable little dogs, we laugh, with our visages as white as ashes, and our hearts sinking into our boots.

Here I sit at the desk again, on a drowsy summer afternoon. A buzz and hum go up around me, as if the boys were so many bluebottles. A cloggy sensation of the lukewarm fat of meat is upon me (we dined an hour or two ago), and my head is as heavy as so much lead. I would give the world to go to sleep. I sit with my eye on Mr. Creakle, blinking at him like a young owl; when sleep overpowers me for a minute, he still looms through my slumber, ruling those ciphering-books, until he softly comes behind me and wakes me to plainer perception of him, with a red ridge across my back.

Here I am in the playground, with my eye still fascinated by him, though I can't see him. The

window at a little distance from which I know he
is having his dinner, stands for him, and I eye that
instead. If he shows his face near it, mine assumes
an imploring and submissive expression. If he looks
out through the glass, the boldest boy (Steerforth
excepted) stops in the middle of a shout or yell,
and becomes contemplative. One day, Traddles (the
most unfortunate boy in the world) breaks that
window accidentally with a ball. I shudder at this
moment with the tremendous sensation of seeing it
done, and feeling that the ball has bounded on to
Mr. Creakle's sacred head.

Poor Traddles! In a tight sky-blue suit that
made his arms and legs like German sausages, or
roly-poly puddings, he was the merriest and most
miserable of all the boys. He was always being
caned—I think he was caned every day that half-year,
except one holiday Monday when he was only ruler'd
on both hands—and was always going to write to
his uncle about it, and never did. After laying his
head on the desk for a little while, he would cheer
up somehow, begin to laugh again, and draw skeletons
all over his slate, before his eyes were dry. I used
at first to wonder what comfort Traddles found in
drawing skeletons; and for some time looked upon
him as a sort of hermit, who reminded himself by
those symbols of mortality that caning couldn't last
for ever. But I believe he only did it because they
were easy, and didn't want any features.

He was very honourable, Traddles was, and held
it as a solemn duty in the boys to stand by one
another. He suffered for this on several occasions;
and particularly once, when Steerforth laughed in
church, and the beadle thought it was Traddles, and
took him out. I see him now, going away in custody,
despised by the congregation. He never said who

was the real offender, though he smarted for it next day, and was imprisoned so many hours that he came forth with a whole churchyardful of skeletons swarming all over his Latin Dictionary. But he had his reward. Steerforth said there was nothing of the sneak in Traddles, and we all felt that to be the highest praise. For my part, I could have gone through a good deal (though I was much less brave than Traddles, and nothing like so old) to have won such a recompense.

To see Steerforth walk to church before us, arm-in-arm with Miss Creakle, was one of the great sights of my life. I didn't think Miss Creakle equal to little Em'ly in point of beauty, and I didn't love her (I didn't dare); but I thought her a young lady of extraordinary attractions, and in point of gentility not to be surpassed. When Steerforth, in white trousers, carried her parasol for her, I felt proud to know him; and believed that she could not choose but adore him with all her heart. Mr. Sharp and Mr. Mell were both notable personages in my eyes; but Steerforth was to them what the sun was to two stars.

Steerforth continued his protection of me, and proved a very useful friend, since nobody dared to annoy one whom he honoured with his countenance. He couldn't—or at all events he didn't—defend me from Mr. Creakle, who was very severe with me; but whenever I had been treated worse than usual, he always told me that I wanted a little of his pluck, and that he wouldn't have stood it himself; which I felt he intended for encouragement, and considered to be very kind of him. There was one advantage, and only one that I know of, in Mr. Creakle's severity. He found my placard in his way when he came up or down behind the form on which I sat.

and wanted to make a cut at me in passing; for this reason it was soon taken off, and I saw it no more.

An accidental circumstance cemented the intimacy between Steerforth and me, in a manner that inspired me with great pride and satisfaction, though it sometimes led to inconvenience. It happened on one occasion, when he was doing me the honour of talking to me in the playground, that I hazarded the observation that something or somebody—I forget what now—was like something or somebody in Peregrine Pickle. He said nothing at the time; but when I was going to bed at night, asked me if I had got that book?

I told him no, and explained how it was that I had read it, and all those other books of which I have made mention.

'And do you recollect them?' Steerforth said.

Oh, yes, I replied; I had a good memory, and I believed I recollected them very well.

'Then I tell you what, young Copperfield,' said Steerforth, 'you shall tell 'em to me. I can't get to sleep very early at night, and I generally wake rather early in the morning. We'll go over 'em one after another. We'll make some regular Arabian Nights of it.'

I felt extremely flattered by this arrangement, and we commenced carrying it into execution that very evening. What ravages I committed on my favourite authors in the course of my interpretation of them, I am not in a condition to say, and should be very unwilling to know; but I had a profound faith in them, and I had, to the best of my belief, a simple earnest manner of narrating what I did narrate; and these qualities went a long way.

The drawback was, that I was often sleepy at night, or out of spirits and indisposed to resume the story, and then it was rather hard work, and it must be done; for to disappoint or to displease Steerforth was of course out of the question. In the morning too, when I felt weary, and should have enjoyed another hour's repose very much, it was a tiresome thing to be roused, like the Sultana Scheherazade, and forced into a long story before the getting-up bell rang; but Steerforth was resolute; and as he explained to me, in return, my sums and exercises, and anything in my tasks that was too hard for me, I was no loser by the transaction. Let me do myself justice, however. I was moved by no interested or selfish motive, nor was I moved by fear of him. I admired and loved him, and his approval was return enough. It was so precious to me, that I look back on these trifles, now, with an aching heart.

Steerforth was considerate too, and showed his consideration, in one particular instance, in an unflinching manner that was a little tantalising, I suspect, to poor Traddles and the rest. Peggotty's promised letter—what a comfortable letter it was!—arrived before 'the half' was many weeks old, and with it a cake in a perfect nest of oranges, and two bottles of cowslip wine. This treasure, as in duty bound, I laid at the feet of Steerforth, and begged him to dispense.

'Now, I'll tell you what, young Copperfield,' said he: 'the wine shall be kept to wet your whistle when you are story-telling.'

I blushed at the idea, and begged him, in my modesty, not to think of it. But he said he had observed I was sometimes hoarse—a little roopy was his exact expression—and it should be, every drop, devoted to the purpose he had mentioned. Accordingly, it was locked up in his box, and drawn off by himself in a phial, and administered to me through a piece of

quill in the cork, when I was supposed to be in want
of a restorative. Sometimes, to make it a more sover-
eign specific, he was so kind as to squeeze orange-
juice into it, or to stir it up with ginger, or dissolve a
peppermint-drop in it; and although I cannot assert
that the flavour was improved by these experiments,
or that it was exactly the compound one would have
chosen for a stomachic, the last thing at night and the
first thing in the morning, I drank it gratefully, and
was very sensible of his attention.

We seem, to me, to have been months over Peregrine, and months more over the other stories. The
institution never flagged for want of a story, I am
certain, and the wine lasted out almost as well as the
matter. Poor Traddles—I never think of that boy
but with a strange disposition to laugh, and with tears
in my eyes—was a sort of chorus, in general, and affected to be convulsed with mirth at the comic parts,
and to be overcome with fear when there was any
passage of an alarming character in the narrative.
This rather put me out, very often. It was a great
jest of his, I recollect, to pretend that he couldn't
keep his teeth from chattering, whenever mention was
made of an Alguazil in connection with the adventures of Gil Blas; and I remember that when Gil Blas
met the captain of the robbers in Madrid, this unlucky
joker counterfeited such an ague of terror, that he
was overheard by Mr. Creakle, who was prowling
about the passage, and handsomely flogged for disorderly conduct in the bedroom.

Whatever I had within me that was romantic and
dreamy, was encouraged by so much story-telling in
the dark; and in that respect the pursuit may not have
been very profitable to me. But the being cherished
as a kind of plaything in my room, and the consciousness that this accomplishment of mine was bruited

about among the boys, and attracted a good deal of notice to me though I was the youngest there, stimulated me to exertion. In a school carried on by sheer cruelty, whether it is presided over by a dunce or not, there is not likely to be much learnt. I believe our boys were, generally, as ignorant a set as any schoolboys in existence; they were too much troubled and knocked about to learn; they could no more do that to advantage than any one can do anything to advantage in a life of constant misfortune, torment, and worry. But my little vanity, and Steerforth's help, urged me on somehow; and without saving me from much, if anything, in the way of punishment, made me, for the time I was there, an exception to the general body, insomuch that I did steadily pick up some crumbs of knowledge.

In this I was much assisted by Mr. Mell, who had a liking for me that I am grateful to remember. It always gave me pain to observe that Steerforth treated him with systematic disparagement, and seldom lost an occasion of wounding his feelings, or inducing others to do so. This troubled me the more for a long time, because I had soon told Steerforth, from whom I could no more keep such a secret than I could keep a cake or any other tangible possession, about the two old women Mr. Mell had taken me to see; and I was always afraid that Steerforth would let it out, and twit him with it.

We little thought, any one of us, I dare say, when I ate my breakfast that first morning, and went to sleep under the shadow of the peacock's feathers to the sound of the flute, what consequences would come of the introduction into those almshouses of my insignificant person. But the visit had its unforeseen consequences; and of a serious sort, too, in their way.

One day when Mr. Creakle kept the house from indisposition, which naturally diffused a lively joy through the school, there was a good deal of noise in the course of the morning's work. The great relief and satisfaction experienced by the boys made them difficult to manage; and though the dreaded Tungay brought his wooden leg in twice or thrice, and took notes of the principal offenders' names, no great impression was made by it, as they were pretty sure of getting into trouble to-morrow, do what they would, and thought it wise, no doubt, to enjoy themselves to-day.

It was, properly, a half-holiday; being Saturday. But as the noise in the playground would have disturbed Mr. Creakle, and the weather was not favourable for going out walking, we were ordered into school in the afternoon, and set some lighter tasks than usual, which were made for the occasion. It was the day of the week on which Mr. Sharp went out to get his wig curled; so Mr. Mell who always did the drudgery, whatever it was, kept school by himself.

If I could associate the idea of a bull or a bear with any one so mild as Mr. Mell, I should think of him, in connection with that afternoon when the uproar was at its height, as of one of those animals, baited by a thousand dogs. I recall him bending his aching head, supported on his bony hand, over the book on his desk, and wretchedly endeavouring to get on with his tiresome work, amidst an uproar that might have made the Speaker of the House of Commons giddy. Boys started in and out of their places, playing at puss-in-the-corner with other boys; there were laughing boys, singing boys, talking boys, dancing boys, howling boys; boys shuffled with their feet, boys whirled about him, grinning, making faces, mimicking him behind his back and before his eyes; mimicking his poverty, his boots, his coat, his mother, everything belonging to him that they should have had consideration for.

'Silence!' cried Mr. Mell, suddenly rising up, and striking his desk with the book. 'What does this mean? It's impossible to bear it. It's maddening. How can you do it to me, boys?'

It was my book that he struck his desk with; and as I stood beside him, following his eye as it glanced round the room, I saw the boys all stop, some suddenly surprised, some half afraid, and some sorry perhaps.

Steerforth's place was at the bottom of the school, at the opposite end of the long room. He was lounging with his back against the wall, and his hands in his pockets, and looked at Mr. Mell with his mouth shut up as if he were whistling, when Mr. Mell looked at him.

'Silence, Mr. Steerforth!' said Mr. Mell.

'Silence yourself,' said Steerforth, turning red. 'Whom are you talking to?'

'Sit down,' said Mr. Mell.

'Sit down yourself,' said Steerforth, 'and mind your business.'

There was a titter, and some applause; but Mr. Mell was so white, that silence immediately succeeded; and one boy, who had darted out behind him to imitate his mother again, changed his mind, and pretended to want a pen mended.

'If you think, Steerforth,' said Mr. Mell, 'that I am not acquainted with the power you can establish over any mind here'—he laid his hand, without considering what he did (as I supposed), upon my head— 'or that I have not observed you, within a few minutes, urging your juniors on to every sort of outrage against me, you are mistaken.'

'I don't give myself the trouble of thinking at all about you,' said Steerforth, coolly; 'so I 'm not mistaken, as it happens.'

'And when you make use of your position of favouritism here, sir,' pursued Mr. Mell, with his lip trembling very much, 'to insult a gentleman—'

'A what?—where is he?' said Steerforth.

Here somebody cried out, 'Shame, J. Steerforth! Too bad!' It was Traddles; whom Mr. Mell instantly discomfited by bidding him hold his tongue.

—'To insult one who is not fortunate in life, sir, and who never gave you the least offence, and the many reasons for not insulting whom you are old enough and wise enough to understand,' said Mr. Mell, with his lip trembling more and more, 'you commit a mean and base action. You can sit down or stand up as you please, sir. Copperfield, go on."

'Young Copperfield,' said Steerforth, coming forward up the room, 'stop a bit. I tell you what, Mr. Mell, once for all. When you take the liberty of calling me mean or base, or anything of that sort, you are an impudent beggar. You are always a beggar, you know; but when you do that, you are an impudent beggar.'

I am not clear whether he was going to strike Mr. Mell, or Mr. Mell was going to strike him, or there was any such intention on either side. I saw a rigidity come upon the whole school as if they had been turned into stone, and found Mr. Creakle in the midst of us, with Tungay at his side, and Mrs. and Miss Creakle looking in at the door as if they were frightened. Mr. Mell, with his elbows on his desk and his face in his hands, sat, for some moments, quite still.

'Mr. Mell,' said Mr. Creakle, shaking him by the arm; and his whisper was so audible now, that Tungay felt it unnecessary to repeat his words; 'you have not forgotten yourself, I hope?'

'No, sir, no,' returned the Master, showing his face, and shaking his head, and rubbing his hands in great agitation. 'No, sir, no. I have remembered myself, I—no, Mr. Creakle, I have not forgotten myself, I—I have remembered myself, sir. I—I—could wish you had remembered me a little sooner, Mr. Creakle. It—it—would have been more kind, sir, more just, sir. It would have saved me something, sir.'

Mr. Creakle, looking hard at Mr. Mell, put his hand on Tungay's shoulder, and got his feet upon the form close by, and sat upon the desk. After still looking hard at Mr. Mell from this throne, as he shook his head, and rubbed his hands, and remained in the same state of agitation, Mr. Creakle turned to Steerforth, and said—

'Now, sir, as he don't condescend to tell me, what *is* this?'

Steerforth evaded the question for a little while; looking in scorn and anger on his opponent, and remaining silent. I could not help thinking even in that interval, I remember, what a noble fellow he was in appearance, and how homely and plain Mr. Mell looked opposed to him.

'What did he mean by talking about favourites, then?' said Steerforth, at length.

'Favourites?' repeated Mr. Creakle, with the veins in his forehead swelling quickly. 'Who talked about favourites?'

'He did,' said Steerforth.

'And pray, what did you mean by that, sir?' demanded Mr. Creakle, turning angrily on his assistant.

'I meant, Mr. Creakle,' he returned in a low voice, 'as I said; that no pupil had a right to avail himself of his position of favouritism to degrade me.'

'To degrade *you?*' said Mr. Creakle. 'My stars! But give me leave to ask you, Mr. What's-your-name'; and here Mr. Creakle folded his arms, cane and all, upon his chest, and made such a knot of his brows that his little eyes were hardly visible below them; 'whether, when you talk about favourites, you showed proper respect to me? To me, sir,' said Mr. Creakle, darting his head at him suddenly, and drawing it back again, 'the principal of this establishment, and your employer.'

'It was not judicious, sir, I am willing to admit,' said Mr. Mell. 'I should not have done so, if I had been cool.'

Here Steerforth struck in.

'Then he said I was mean, and then he said I was base, and then I called him a beggar. If I had been cool, perhaps I shouldn't have called him a beggar. But I did, and I am ready to take the consequences of it.'

Without considering, perhaps, whether there were any consequences to be taken, I felt quite in a glow at this gallant speech. It made an impression on the boys, too, for there was a low stir among them, though no one spoke a word.

'I am surprised, Steerforth—although your candour does you honour,' said Mr. Creakle, 'does you honour, certainly—I am surprised, Steerforth, I must say, that you should attach such an epithet to any person employed and paid in Salem House, sir.'

Steerforth gave a short laugh.

'That's not an answer, sir,' said Mr. Creakle, 'to my remark. I expect more than that from you, Steerforth.'

If Mr. Mell looked homely, in my eyes, before the

handsome boy, it would be quite impossible to say how homely Mr. Creakle looked.

'Let him deny it,' said Steerforth.

'Deny that he is a beggar, Steerforth?' cried Mr. Creakle. 'Why, where does he go a begging?'

'If he is not a beggar himself, his near relation's one,' said Steerforth. 'It's all the same.'

He glanced at me, and Mr. Mell's hand gently patted me upon the shoulder. I looked up with a flush upon my face and remorse in my heart, but Mr. Mell's eyes were fixed on Steerforth. He continued to pat me kindly on the shoulder, but he looked at him.

'Since you expect me, Mr. Creakle, to justify myself,' said Steerforth, 'and to say what I mean,— what I have to say is, that his mother lives on charity in an almshouse.'

Mr. Mell still looked at him, and still patted me kindly on the shoulder, and said to himself in a whisper, if I heard right, 'Yes, I thought so.'

Mr. Creakle turned to his assistant, with a severe frown and laboured politeness—

'Now you hear what this gentleman says, Mr. Mell. Have the goodness, if you please, to set him right before the assembled school.'

'He is right, sir, without correction,' returned Mr. Mell, in the midst of a dread silence; 'what he has said is true.'

'Be so good then as declare publicly, will you,' said Mr. Creakle, putting his head on one side, and rolling his eyes round the school, 'whether it ever came to my knowledge until this moment?'

'I believe not directly,' he returned.

'Why, you know not,' said Mr. Creakle. 'Don't you, man?'

'I apprehend you never supposed my worldly circumstances to be very good,' replied the assistant. 'You know what my position is, and always has been here.'

'I apprehend, if you come to that,' said Mr. Creakle, with his veins swelling again bigger than ever, 'that you've been in a wrong position altogether, and mistook this for a charity school. Mr. Mell, we'll part, if you please. The sooner the better.'

'There is no time,' answered Mr. Mell, rising, 'like the present.'

'Sir, to you!' said Mr. Creakle.

'I take my leave of you, Mr. Creakle, and all of you,' said Mr. Mell, glancing round the room, and again patting me gently on the shoulder. 'James Steerforth, the best wish I can leave you is that you may come to be ashamed of what you have done to-day. At present I would prefer to see you anything rather than a friend, to me, or to any one in whom I feel an interest.'

Once more he laid his hand upon my shoulder; and then taking his flute and a few books from his desk, and leaving the key in it for his successor, he went out of the school, with his property under his arm. Mr. Creakle then made a speech, through Tungay, in which he thanked Steerforth for asserting (though perhaps too warmly) the independence and respectability of Salem House; and which he wound up by shaking hands with Steerforth, while we gave three cheers—I did not quite know what for, but I supposed for Steerforth, and so joined in them ardently, though I felt miserable. Mr. Creakle then caned Tommy Traddles for being discovered in tears, instead of cheers, on account of Mr. Mell's departure;

and went back to his sofa, or his bed, or wherever he had come from.

We were left to ourselves now, and looked very blank, I recollect, on one another. For myself, I felt so much self-reproach and contrition for my part in what had happened, that nothing would have enabled me to keep back my tears but the fear that Steerforth, who often looked at me, I saw, might think it unfriendly—or, I should rather say, considering our relative ages, and the feeling with which I regarded him, undutiful—if I showed the emotion which distressed me. He was very angry with Traddles, and said he was glad he had caught it.

Poor Traddles, who had passed the stage of lying with his head upon the desk, and was relieving himself as usual with a burst of skeletons, said he didn't care. Mr. Mell was ill used.

'Who has ill used him, you girl?' said Steerforth.

'Why, you have,' returned Traddles.

'What have I done?' said Steerforth.

'What have you done?' retorted Traddles. 'Hurt his feelings and lost him his situation.'

'His feelings!' repeated Steerforth disdainfully. 'His feelings will soon get the better of it, I'll be bound. His feelings are not like yours, Miss Traddles. As to his situation—which was a precious one, wasn't it?—do you suppose I am not going to write home, and take care that he gets some money? Polly?'

We thought this intention very noble in Steerforth, whose mother was a widow, and rich, and would do almost anything, it was said, that he asked her. We were all extremely glad to see Traddles so put down, and exalted Steerforth to the skies: especially when he told us, as he condescended to do, that what he

had done had been done expressly for us, and for
our cause, and that he had conferred a great boon
upon us by unselfishly doing it.

But I must say that when I was going on with a
story in the dark that night, Mr. Mell's old flute
seemed more than once to sound mournfully in my
ears; and that when at last Steerforth was tired, and
I lay down in my bed, I fancied it playing so sorrowfully somewhere, that I was quite wretched.

I soon forgot him in the contemplation of Steerforth, who, in an easy amateur way, and without any
book (he seemed to me to know everything by heart),
took some of his classes until a new master was
found. The new master came from a grammar-
school, and before he entered on his duties, dined in
the parlour one day, to be introduced to Steerforth.
Steerforth approved of him highly, and told us he
was a brick. Without exactly understanding what
learned distinction was meant by this, I respected
him greatly for it, and had no doubt whatever of his
superior knowledge: though he never took the pains
with me—not that *I* was anybody—that Mr. Mell
had taken.

There was only one other event in this half-year,
out of the daily school-life, that made an impression
upon me which still survives. It survives for many
reasons.

One afternoon, when we were all harassed into a
state of dire confusion, and Mr. Creakle was laying
about him dreadfully, Tungay came in, and called out
in his usual strong way: 'Visitors for Copperfield!'

A few words were interchanged between him and
Mr. Creakle, as, who the visitors were, and what
room they were to be shown into; and then I, who
had, according to custom, stood up on the announcement being made, and felt quite faint with astonish-

ment, was told to go by the back-stairs and get a clean frill on, before I repaired to the dining-room. These orders I obeyed, in such a flutter and hurry of my young spirits as I had never known before; and when I got to the parlour-door, and the thought came into my head that it might be my mother—I had only thought of Mr. or Miss Murdstone until then—I drew back my hand from the lock, and stopped to have a sob before I went in.

At first I saw nobody; but feeling a pressure against the door, I looked round it, and there, to my amazement, were Mr. Peggotty and Ham, ducking at me with their hats, and squeezing one another against the wall. I could not help laughing; but it was much more in the pleasure of seeing them, than at the appearance they made. We shook hands in a very cordial way; and I laughed and laughed, until I pulled out my pocket-handkerchief and wiped my eyes.

Mr. Peggotty (who never shut his mouth once, I remember, during the visit) showed great concern when he saw me do this, and nudged Ham to say something.

'Cheer up, Mas'r Davy bor'!' said Ham, in his simpering way. 'Why, how you have growed!'

'Am I grown?' I said, drying my eyes. I was not crying at anything particular that I know of; but somehow it made me cry, to see old friends.

'Growed, Mas'r Davy bor'? Ain't he growed?' said Ham.

'Ain't he growed?' said Mr. Peggotty.

They made me laugh again by laughing at each other, and then we all three laughed until I was in danger of crying again.

'Do you know how mamma is, Mr. Peggotty?' I said. 'And how my dear, dear, old Peggotty is?'

'Oncommon,' said Mr. Peggotty.

'And little Em'ly, and Mrs. Gummidge?'

'On—common,' said Mr. Peggotty.

There was a silence. Mr. Peggotty, to relieve it, took two prodigious lobsters, and an enormous crab, and a large canvas bag of shrimps, out of his pockets, and piled them up in Ham's arms.

'You see,' said Mr. Peggotty, 'knowing as you was partial to a little relish with your wittles when you was along with us, we took the liberty. The old mawther biled 'em, she did. Mrs. Gummidge biled 'em. Yes,' said Mr. Peggotty, slowly, who I thought appeared to stick to the subject on account of having no other subject ready, 'Mrs. Gummidge, I do assure you, she biled 'em.'

I expressed my thanks. Mr. Peggotty, after looking at Ham, who stood smiling sheepishly over the shell-fish, without making any attempt to help him, said—

'We come, you see, the wind and tide making in our favour, in one of our Yarmouth lugs to Gravesen'. My sister she wrote to me the name of this here place, and wrote to me as if ever I chanced to come to Gravesen', I was to come over and inquire for Mas'r Davy, and give her dooty, humbly wishing him well, and reporting of the fam'ly as they was oncommon toe-be-sure. Little Em'ly, you see, she 'll write to my sister when I go back as I see you, and as you was similarly oncommon, and so we make it quite a merry-go-rounder.'

I was obliged to consider a little before I understood what Mr. Peggotty meant by this figure, expressive of a complete circle of intelligence. I then thanked him heartily; and said, with a consciousness of reddening, that I supposed little Em'ly was altered too, since we used to pick up shells and pebbles on the beach.

'She's getting to be a woman, that's wot she's getting to be,' said Mr. Peggotty. 'Ask *him*.'

He meant Ham, who beamed with delight and assent over the bag of shrimps.

'Her pretty face!' said Mr. Peggotty, with his own shining like a light.

'Her learning!' said Ham.

'Her writing!' said Mr. Peggotty. 'Why, it's as black as jet! And so large it is, you might see it anywheres.'

It was perfectly delightful to behold with what enthusiasm Mr. Peggotty became inspired when he thought of his little favourite. He stands before me again, his bluff hairy face irradiating with a joyful love and pride for which I can find no description. His honest eyes fire up, and sparkle, as if their depths were stirred by something bright. His broad chest heaves with pleasure. His strong loose hands clench themselves, in his earnestness; and he emphasises what he says with a right arm that shows, in my pigmy view, like a sledge-hammer.

Ham was quite as earnest as he. I dare say they would have said much more about her, if they had not been abashed by the unexpected coming in of Steerforth, who, seeing me in a corner speaking with two strangers, stopped in a song he was singing, and said—'I didn't know you were here, young Copperfield!' (for it was not the usual visiting room) and crossed by us on his way out.

I am not sure whether it was in the pride of having such a friend as Steerforth, or in the desire to explain to him how I came to have such a friend as Mr. Peggotty, that I called to him as he was going away.

But I said, modestly—Good Heaven, how it all comes back to me this long time afterwards!—

'Don't go, Steerforth, if you please. These are two Yarmouth boatmen—very kind, good people—who are relations of my nurse, and have come from Gravesend to see me.'

'Aye, aye?' said Steerforth, returning. 'I am glad to see them. How are you both?'

There was an ease in his manner—a gay and light manner it was, but not swaggering—which I still believe to have borne a kind of enchantment with it. I still believe him, in virtue of this carriage, his animal spirits, his delightful voice, his handsome face and figure, and, for aught I know, of some inborn power of attraction besides (which I think a few people possess), to have carried a spell with him to which it was a natural weakness to yield, and which not many persons could withstand. I could not but see how pleased they were with him, and how they seemed to open their hearts to him in a moment.

'You must let them know at home, if you please, Mr. Peggotty,' I said, 'when that letter is sent, that Mr. Steerforth is very kind to me, and that I don't know what I should ever do here without him.'

'Nonsense!' said Steerforth, laughing. 'You mustn't tell them anything of the sort.'

'And if Mr. Steerforth ever comes into Norfolk or Suffolk, Mr. Peggotty,' I said, 'while I am there, you may depend upon it I shall bring him to Yarmouth, if he will let me, to see your house. You never saw such a good house, Steerforth. It's made out of a boat!'

'Made out of a boat, is it?' said Steerforth. 'It's the right sort of house for such a thorough-built boat-man.'

'So 'tis, sir, so 'tis, sir,' said Ham, grinning.

'You 're right, young gen'l'm'n. Mas'r Davy, bor',
gen'l'm'n 's right. A thorough-built boatman! Hor,
hor! That 's what he is, too!'

Mr. Peggotty was no less pleased than his nephew,
though his modesty forbade him to claim a personal
compliment so vociferously.

'Well, sir,' he said, bowing and chuckling, and tuck-
ing in the ends of his neckerchief at his breast: 'I
thankee, sir, I thankee! I do my endeavours in my
line of life, sir.'

'The best of men can do no more, Mr. Peggotty,'
said Steerforth. He had got his name already.

'I 'll pound it it 's wot you do yourself, sir,' said
Mr. Peggotty, shaking his head, 'and wot you do
well—right well! I thankee, sir. I 'm obleeged to
you, sir, for your welcoming manner of me. I 'm
rough, sir, but I 'm ready—least ways, I *hope* I 'm
ready, you unnerstand. My house ain't much for to
see, sir, but it 's hearty at your service if ever you
should come along with Mas'r Davy to see it. I 'm
a reg'lar Dodman, I am,' said Mr. Peggotty, by
which he meant snail, and this was in allusion to his
being slow to go, for he had attempted to go after
every sentence, and had somehow or other come back
again; 'but I wish you both well, and I wish you
happy!'

Ham echoed this sentiment, and we parted with
them in the heartiest manner. I was almost tempted
that evening to tell Steerforth about pretty little
Em'ly, but I was too timid of mentioning her name,
and too much afraid of his laughing at me. I remember that I thought a good deal and in an uneasy
sort of way, about Mr. Peggotty having said that she
was getting on to be a woman; but I decided that was
nonsense.

We transported the shell-fish, or the 'relish' as Mr.

Peggotty had modestly called it, up into our room unobserved, and made a great supper that evening. But Traddles couldn't get happily out of it. He was too unfortunate even to come through a supper like anybody else. He was taken ill in the night—quite prostrate he was—in consequence of crab; and after being drugged with black draughts and blue pills, to an extent which Demple (whose father was a doctor) said was enough to undermine a horse's constitution, received a caning and six chapters of Greek Testament for refusing to confess.

The rest of the half-year is a jumble in my recollection of the daily strife and struggle of our lives; of the waning summer and the changing season: of the frosty mornings when we were rung out of bed, and the cold, cold smell of the dark nights when we were rung into bed; of the evening schoolroom dimly lighted and indifferently warmed, and the morning schoolroom which was nothing but a great shivering-machine; of the alternation of boiled beef with roast beef, and boiled mutton with roast mutton; of clods of bread-and-butter, dog's-eared lesson-books, cracked slates, tear-blotted copy-books, canings, rulerings, hair-cuttings, rainy Sundays, suet puddings, and a dirty atmosphere of ink surrounding all.

I well remember though, how the distant idea of the holidays, after seeming for an immense time to be a stationary speck, began to come towards us, and to grow and grow. How from counting months, we came to weeks, and then to days; and how I then began to be afraid that I should not be sent for, and when I learnt from Steerforth that I *had* been sent for, and was certainly to go home, had dim forebodings that I might break my leg first. How the breaking-up day changed its place fast, at last, from

the week after next to next week, this week, the day
after to-morrow, to-morrow, to-day, to-night—when
I was inside the Yarmouth mail, and going home.

I had many a broken sleep inside the Yarmouth
mail, and many an incoherent dream of all these
things. But when I awoke at intervals, the ground
outside the window was not the playground of Salem
House, and the sound in my ears was not the sound
of Mr. Creakle giving it to Traddles, but was the
sound of the coachman touching up the horses.

CHAPTER VIII

MY HOLIDAYS. ESPECIALLY ONE HAPPY AFTERNOON

WHEN we arrived before day at the inn where the
mail stopped, which was not the inn where my friend
the waiter lived, I was shown up to a nice little bedroom, with DOLPHIN painted on the door. Very
cold I was, I know, notwithstanding the hot tea they
had given me before a large fire downstairs; and very
glad I was to turn into the Dolphin's bed, pull the
Dolphin's blankets round my head, and go to sleep.

Mr. Barkis the carrier was to call for me in the
morning at nine o'clock. I got up at eight, a little
giddy from the shortness of my night's rest, and was
ready for him before the appointed time. He received me exactly as if not five minutes had elapsed
since we were last together, and I had only been into
the hotel to get change for sixpence, or something of
that sort.

As soon as I and my box were in the cart, and the
carrier was seated, the lazy horse walked away with
us all at his accustomed pace.

'You look very well, Mr. Barkis,' I said, thinking he would like to know it.

Mr. Barkis rubbed his cheek with his cuff, and then looked at his cuff as if he expected to find some of the bloom upon it; but made no other acknowledgment of the compliment.

'I gave your message, Mr. Barkis,' I said: 'I wrote to Peggotty.'

'Ah!' said Mr. Barkis.

Mr. Barkis seemed gruff, and answered drily.

'Wasn't it right, Mr. Barkis?' I asked, after a little hesitation.

'Why, no,' said Mr. Barkis.

'Not the message?'

'The message was right enough, perhaps,' said Mr. Barkis; 'but it come to an end there.'

Not understanding what he meant, I repeated inquisitively: 'Came to an end, Mr. Barkis?'

'Nothing come of it,' he explained, looking at me sideways. 'No answer.'

'There was an answer expected, was there, Mr. Barkis?' said I, opening my eyes. For this was a new light to me.

'When a man says he's willin',' said Mr. Barkis, turning his glance slowly on me again, 'it's as much as to say, that man's a waitin' for a answer.'

'Well, Mr. Barkis?'

'Well,' said Mr. Barkis, carrying his eyes back to his horse's ears; 'that man's been a waitin' for a answer ever since.'

'Have you told her so, Mr. Barkis?'

'N—no,' growled Mr. Barkis, reflecting about it. 'I ain't got no call to go and tell her so. I never said six words to her myself. *I* ain't a goin' to tell her so.'

'Would you like me to do it, Mr. Barkis?' said I, doubtfully.

'You might tell her, if you would,' said Mr. Barkis, with another slow look at me, 'that Barkis was a waitin' for a answer. Says you—what name is it?'

'Her name?'

'Ah!' said Mr. Barkis, with a nod of his head.

'Peggotty.'

'Chrisen name? Or nat'ral name?' said Mr. Barkis.

'Oh, it's not her Christian name. Her Christian name is Clara.'

'Is it though?' said Mr. Barkis.

He seemed to find an immense fund of reflection in this circumstance, and sat pondering and inwardly whistling for some time.

'Well!' he resumed at length. 'Says you, "Peggotty! Barkis is a waitin' for a answer." Says she, perhaps, "Answer to what?" Says you, "To what I told you." "What is that?" says she. "Barkis is willin'," says you.'

This extremely artful suggestion, Mr. Barkis accompanied with a nudge of his elbow that gave me quite a stitch in my side. After that, he slouched over his horse in his usual manner; and made no other reference to the subject except, half an hour afterwards, taking a piece of chalk from his pocket, and writing up, inside the tilt of the cart, 'Clara Peggotty'—apparently as a private memorandum.

Ah, what a strange feeling it was to be going home when it was not home, and to find that every object I looked at, reminded me of the happy old home, which was like a dream I could never dream again! The days when my mother and I and Peggotty were all in all to one another, and there was no one to come between us, rose up before me so sorrowfully on the road, that I am not sure I was glad to be there—not sure but that I would rather have remained away, and forgotten it in Steerforth's company. But there I was; and soon I was at our house, where the bare old elm-trees wrung their many hands in the bleak wintry air, and shreds of the old rooks'-nest drifted away upon the wind.

The carrier put my box down at the garden-gate, and left me. I walked along the path towards the house, glancing at the windows, and fearing at every step to see Mr. Murdstone or Miss Murdstone lowering out of one of them. No face appeared, however; and being come to the house, and knowing how to open the door, before dark, without knocking, I went in with a quiet, timid step.

God knows how infantine the memory may have been, that was awakened within me by the sound of my mother's voice in the old parlour, when I set foot in the hall. She was singing in a low tone. I think I must have lain in her arms, and heard her singing so to me when I was but a baby. The strain was new to me, and yet it was so old that it filled my heart brimful; like a friend come back from a long absence.

I believed, from the solitary and thoughtful way in which my mother murmured her song, that she was alone. And I went softly into the room. She was sitting by the fire, suckling an infant, whose tiny hand she held against her neck. Her eyes were looking down upon its face, and she sat singing to it. I was so far right, that she had no other companion.

I spoke to her, and she started, and cried out. But seeing me, she called me her dear Davy, her own boy! and coming half across the room to meet me, kneeled down upon the ground and kissed me, and laid my head down on her bosom near the little creature that was nestling there, and put its hands up to my lips.

I wish I had died. I wish I had died then, with that feeling in my heart! I should have been more fit for heaven than I ever have been since.

'He is your brother,' said my mother, fondling me. 'Davy, my pretty boy! My poor child!' Then she kissed me more and more, and clasped me round the neck. This she was doing when Peggotty came running in, and bounced down on the ground beside us, and went mad about us both for a quarter of an hour.

It seemed that I had not been expected so soon, the carrier being much before his usual time. It seemed, too, that Mr. and Miss Murdstone had gone out upon a visit in the neighbourhood, and would not return before night. I had never hoped for this. I had never thought it possible that we three could be together undisturbed, once more; and I felt, for the time, as if the old days were come back.

We dined together by the fireside. Peggotty was in attendance to wait upon us, but my mother wouldn't let her do it, and made her dine with us. I had my own old plate, with a brown view of a man-of-war in full sail upon it, which Peggotty had hoarded somewhere all the time I had been away, and would not have had broken, she said, for a hundred pounds. I had my own old mug with David on it, and my own old little knife and fork that wouldn't cut.

While we were at table, I thought it a favourable occasion to tell Peggotty about Mr. Barkis, who, before I had finished what I had to tell her, began to laugh, and throw her apron over her face.

'Peggotty,' said my mother. 'What's the matter?'

Peggotty only laughed the more, and held her

apron tight over her face when my mother tried to pull it away, and sat as if her head were in a bag.

'What are you doing, you stupid creature?' said my mother, laughing.

'Oh, drat the man!' cried Peggotty. 'He wants to marry me.'

'It would be a very good match for you; wouldn't it?' said my mother.

'Oh! I don't know,' said Peggotty. 'Don't ask me. I wouldn't have him if he was made of gold. Nor I wouldn't have anybody.'

'Then, why don't you tell him so, you ridiculous thing?' said my mother.

'Tell him so,' retorted Peggotty, looking out of her apron. 'He has never said a word to me about it. He knows better. If he was to make so bold as say a word to me, I should slap his face.'

Her own was as red as ever I saw it, or any other face, I think; but she only covered it again, for a few moments at a time, when she was taken with a violent fit of laughter; and after two or three of those attacks, went on with her dinner.

I remarked that my mother, though she smiled when Peggotty looked at her, became more serious and thoughtful. I had seen at first that she was changed. Her face was very pretty still, but it looked careworn, and too delicate; and her hand was so thin and white that it seemed to me to be almost transparent. But the change to which I now refer was superadded to this: it was in her manner, which became anxious and fluttered. At last she said, putting out her hand, and laying it affectionately on the hand of her old servant—

'Peggotty, dear, you are not going to be married?'

'Me, ma'am?' returned Peggotty, staring. 'Lord bless you, no!'

'Not just yet?' said my mother, tenderly.

'Never!' cried Peggotty.

My mother took her hand, and said—

'Don't leave me, Peggotty. Stay with me. It will not be for long, perhaps. What should I ever do without you?'

'Me leave you, my precious!' cried Peggotty. 'Not for all the world and his wife. Why, what's put that in your silly little head?' For Peggotty had been used of old to talk to my mother sometimes, like a child.

But my mother made no answer, except to thank her, and Peggotty went running on in her own fashion.

'Me leave you? I think I see myself. Peggotty go away from you? I should like to catch her at it! No, no, no,' said Peggotty, shaking her head, and folding her arms; 'not she, my dear. It isn't that there ain't some Cats that would be well enough pleased if she did, but they shan't be pleased. They shall be aggravated. I'll stay with you till I am a cross cranky old woman. And when I'm too deaf, and too lame, and too blind, and too mumbly for want of teeth, to be of any use at all, even to be found fault with, then I shall go to my Davy, and ask him to take me in.'

'And, Peggotty,' says I, 'I shall be glad to see you, and I'll make you as welcome as a queen.'

'Bless your dear heart!' cried Peggotty. 'I know you will!' And she kissed me beforehand, in grateful acknowledgment of my hospitality. After that, she covered her head up with her apron again, and had another laugh about Mr. Barkis. After that, she took the baby out of its little cradle, and nursed it. After that, she cleared the dinner-table; after that, came in with another cap on, and her work-box, and the yard-measure, and the bit of wax-candle, all just the same as ever.

We sat round the fire, and talked delightfully. I told them what a hard master Mr. Creakle was, and they pitied me very much. I told them what a fine fellow Steerforth was, and what a patron of mine, and Peggotty said she would walk a score of miles to see him. I took the little baby in my arms when it was awake, and nursed it lovingly. When it was asleep again, I crept close to my mother's side, according to my old custom, broken now a long time, and sat with my arms embracing her waist, and my little red cheek on her shoulder, and once more felt her beautiful hair drooping over me—like an angel's wing as I used to think, I recollect—and was very happy indeed.

While I sat thus, looking at the fire, and seeing pictures in the red-hot coals, I almost believed that I had never been away; that Mr. and Miss Murdstone were such pictures, and would vanish when the fire got low; and that there was nothing real in all that I remembered, save my mother, Peggotty, and I.

Peggotty darned away at a stocking as long as she could see, and then sat with it drawn on her left hand like a glove, and her needle in her right, ready to take another stitch whenever there was a blaze. I cannot conceive whose stockings they can have been that Peggotty was always darning, or where such an unfailing supply of stockings in want of darning can have come from. From my earliest infancy she seems to have been always employed in that class of needle-work, and never by any chance in any other.

'I wonder,' said Peggotty, who was sometimes seized with a fit of wondering on some most unexpected topic, 'what 's become of Davy's great-aunt?'

'Lor, Peggotty!' observed my mother, rousing herself from a reverie, 'what nonsense you talk!'

'Well, but I really do wonder, ma'am,' said Peggotty.

'What can have put such a person in your head?' inquired my mother. 'Is there nobody else in the world to come there?'

'I don't know how it is,' said Peggotty, 'unless it's on account of being stupid, but my head never can pick and choose its people. They come and they go, and they don't come and they don't go, just as they like. I wonder what's become of her?'

'How absurd you are, Peggotty,' returned my mother. 'One would suppose you wanted a second visit from her.'

'Lord forbid!' cried Peggotty.

'Well, then, don't talk about such uncomfortable things, there's a good soul,' said my mother. 'Miss Betsey is shut up in her cottage by the sea, no doubt, and will remain there. At all events, she is not likely ever to trouble us again.'

'No!' mused Peggotty. 'No, that ain't likely at all—I wonder, if she was to die, whether she'd leave Davy anything?'

'Good gracious me, Peggotty,' returned my mother, 'what a nonsensical woman you are! when you know that she took offence at the poor dear boy's ever being born at all!'

'I suppose she wouldn't be inclined to forgive him now?' hinted Peggotty.

'Why should she be inclined to forgive him now?' said my mother, rather sharply.

'Now that he's got a brother, I mean,' said Peggotty.

My mother immediately began to cry, and wondered how Peggotty dared to say such a thing.

'As if this poor little innocent in its cradle had ever done any harm to you or anybody else, you jealous thing!' said she. 'You had much better go and marry Mr. Barkis, the carrier. Why don't you?'

'I should make Miss Murdstone happy, if I was to,' said Peggotty.

'What a bad disposition you have, Peggotty!' returned my mother. 'You are as jealous of Miss Murdstone as it is possible for a ridiculous creature to be. You want to keep the keys yourself, and give out all the things, I suppose? I shouldn't be surprised if you did. When you know that she only does it out of kindness and the best intentions! You know she does, Peggotty—you know it well.'

Peggotty muttered something to the effect of 'Bother the best intentions!' and something else to the effect that there was a little too much of the best intentions going on.

'I know what you mean, you cross thing,' said my mother. 'I understand you, Peggotty, perfectly. You know I do, and I wonder you don't colour up like fire. But one point at a time. Miss Murdstone is the point now, Peggotty, and you shan't escape from it. Haven't you heard her say, over and over again, that she thinks I am too thoughtless and too —a—a—'

'Pretty,' suggested Peggotty.

'Well,' returned my mother, half laughing, 'and if she is so silly as to say so, can I be blamed for it?'

'No one says you can,' said Peggotty.

'No, I should hope not, indeed!' returned my mother. 'Haven't you heard her say over and over again, that on this account she wishes to spare me a great deal of trouble, which she thinks I am not suited for, and which I really don't know myself that I *am* suited for; and isn't she up early and late, and going to and fro continually—and doesn't she do all sorts of things, and grope into all sorts of places, coal-holes and pantries and I don't know where, that can't be very agreeable—and do you mean to insinuate that there is not a sort of devotion in that?'

'I don't insinuate at all,' said Peggotty.

'You do, Peggotty,' returned my mother. 'You never do anything else, except your work. You are always insinuating. You revel in it. And when you talk of Mr. Murdstone's good intentions—'

'I never talked of 'em,' said Peggotty.

'No, Peggotty,' returned my mother, 'but you insinuated. That's what I told you just now. That's the worst of you. You *will* insinuate. I said, at the moment, that I understood you, and you see I did. When you talk of Mr. Murdstone's good intentions, and pretend to slight them (for I don't believe you really do, in your heart, Peggotty), you must be as well convinced as I am how good they are, and how they actuate him in everything. If he seems to have been at all stern with a certain person, Peggotty—you understand, and so I am sure does Davy, that I am not alluding to anybody present—it is solely because he is satisfied that it is for a certain person's benefit. He naturally loves a certain person, on my account; and acts solely for a certain person's good. He is better able to judge of it than I am; for I very well know that I am a weak, light, girlish creature, and that he is a firm, grave, serious man. And he takes,' said my mother, with the tears which were engendered in her affec-tionate nature, stealing down her face, 'he takes great pains with me; and I ought to be very thankful to him, and very submissive to him even in my thoughts;

and when I am not, Peggotty, I worry and condemn myself, and feel doubtful of my own heart, and don't know what to do.'

Peggotty sat with her chin on her foot of the stocking, looking silently at the fire.

'There, Peggotty,' said my mother, changing her tone, 'don't let us fall out with one another, for I couldn't bear it. You are my true friend, I know, if I have any in the world. When I call you a ridiculous creature, or a vexatious thing, or anything of that sort, Peggotty, I only mean that you are my true friend, and always have been, ever since the night when Mr. Copperfield first brought me home here, and you came out to the gate to meet me.'

Peggotty was not slow to respond, and ratify the treaty of friendship by giving me one of her best hugs. I think I had some glimpses of the real character of this conversation at the time; but I am sure, now, that the good creature originated it, and took her part in it, merely that my mother might comfort herself with the little contradictory summary in which she had indulged. The design was efficacious; for I remember that my mother seemed more at ease during the rest of the evening, and that Peggotty observed her less.

When we had had our tea, and the ashes were thrown up, and the candles snuffed, I read Peggotty a chapter out of the crocodile book, in remembrance of old times—she took it out of her pocket: I don't know whether she had kept it there ever since—and then we talked about Salem House, which brought me round again to Steerforth, who was my great subject. We were very happy; and that evening, as the last of its race, and destined evermore to close that volume of my life, will never pass out of my memory.

It was almost ten o'clock before we heard the sound

of wheels. We all got up then; and my mother said
hurriedly that, as it was so late, and Mr. and Miss
Murdstone approved of early hours for young people,
perhaps I had better go to bed. I kissed her, and
went upstairs with my candle directly, before they
came in. It appeared to my childish fancy, as I
ascended to the bedroom where I had been imprisoned, that they brought a cold blast of air into the
house which blew away the old familiar feeling like
a feather.

I felt uncomfortable about going down to breakfast in the morning, as I had never set eyes on Mr.
Murdstone since the day when I committed my
memorable offence. However, as it must be done, I
went down, after two or three false starts half-way,
and as many runs back on tiptoe to my own room,
and presented myself in the parlour.

He was standing before the fire with his back to
it, while Miss Murdstone made the tea. He looked
at me steadily as I entered, but made no sign of
recognition whatever.

I went up to him, after a moment of confusion,
and said—'I beg your pardon, sir. I am very sorry
for what I did, and I hope you will forgive me.'

'I am glad to hear you are sorry, David,' he replied.

The hand he gave me was the hand I had bitten.
I could not restrain my eye from resting for an instant on a red spot upon it; but it was not so red as
I turned, when I met that sinister expression in his
face.

'How do you do, ma'am?' I said to Miss Murdstone.

'Ah, dear me!' sighed Miss Murdstone, giving me
the tea-caddy scoop instead of her fingers. 'How
long are the holidays?'

'A month, ma'am.'

'Counting from when?'

'From to-day, ma'am.'

'Oh!' said Miss Murdstone. 'Then here's *one* day off.'

She kept a calendar of the holidays in this way, and every morning checked a day off in exactly the same manner. She did it gloomily until she came to ten, but when she got into two figures she became more hopeful, and, as the time advanced, even jocular.

It was on this very first day that I had the misfortune to throw her, though she was not subject to such weakness in general, into a state of violent consternation. I came into the room where she and my mother were sitting; and the baby (who was only a few weeks old) being on my mother's lap, I took it very carefully in my arms. Suddenly Miss Murdstone gave such a scream that I all but dropped it.

'My dear Jane!' cried my mother.

'Good Heavens, Clara, do you see?' exclaimed Miss Murdstone.

'See what, my dear Jane?' said my mother; 'where?'

'He's got it!' cried Miss Murdstone. 'The boy has got the baby!'

She was limp with horror; but stiffened herself to make a dart at me, and take it out of my arms. Then, she turned faint; and was so very ill, that they were obliged to give her cherry-brandy. I was solemnly interdicted by her, on her recovery, from touching my brother any more on any pretence whatever, and my poor mother, who, I could see, wished otherwise, meekly confirmed the interdict, by saying, 'No doubt you are right, my dear Jane.'

On another occasion, when we three were together, this same dear baby—it was truly dear to me, for our mother's sake—was the innocent occasion of Miss

Murdstone's going into a passion. My mother, who had been looking at its eyes as it lay upon her lap, said—

'Davy! come here!' and looked at mine.

I saw Miss Murdstone lay her beads down.

'I declare,' said my mother, gently, 'they are exactly alike. I suppose they are mine. I think they are the colour of mine. But they are wonderfully alike.'

'What are you talking about, Clara?' said Miss Murdstone.

'My dear Jane,' faltered my mother, a little abashed by the harsh tone of this inquiry, 'I find that the baby's eyes and Davy's are exactly alike.'

'Clara!' said Miss Murdstone, risingly angrily, 'you are a positive fool sometimes.'

'My dear Jane,' remonstrated my mother.

'A positive fool,' said Miss Murdstone. 'Who else could compare my brother's baby with your boy? They are not at all alike. They are exactly unlike. They are utterly dissimilar in all respects. I hope they will ever remain so. I will not sit here, and hear such comparisons made.' With that she stalked out, and made the door bang after her.

In short, I was not a favourite with Miss Murdstone. In short, I was not a favourite there with anybody, not even with myself; for those who did like me could not show it, and those who did not showed it so plainly that I had a sensitive consciousness of always appearing constrained, boorish, and dull.

I felt that I made them as uncomfortable as they made me. If I came into the room where they were, and they were talking together and my mother seemed cheerful, an anxious cloud would steal over her face from the moment of my entrance. If Mr.

Murdstone were in his best humour, I checked him. If Miss Murdstone were in her worst, I intensified it. I had perception enough to know that my mother was the victim always; that she was afraid to speak to me, or be kind to me, lest she should give them some offence by her manner of doing so, and receive a lecture afterwards; that she was not only ceaselessly afraid of her own offending, but of my offending, and uneasily watched their looks if I only moved. Therefore I resolved to keep myself as much out of their way as I could; and many a wintry hour did I hear the church-clock strike, when I was sitting in my cheerless bedroom, wrapped in my little great-coat, poring over a book.

In the evening, sometimes, I went and sat with Peggotty in the kitchen. There I was comfortable, and not afraid of being myself. But neither of these resources was approved of in the parlour. The tormenting humour which was dominant there stopped them both. I was still held to be necessary to my poor mother's training, and, as one of her trials, could not be suffered to absent myself.

'David,' said Mr. Murdstone, one day after dinner when I was going to leave the room as usual; 'I am sorry to observe that you are of a sullen disposition.'

'As sulky as a bear!' said Miss Murdstone.

I stood still, and hung my head.

'Now, David,' said Mr. Murdstone, 'a sullen obdurate disposition is, of all tempers, the worst.'

'And the boy's is, of all such dispositions that ever I have seen,' remarked his sister, 'the most confirmed and stubborn. I think, my dear Clara, even you must observe it?'

'I beg your pardon, my dear Jane,' said my mother, 'but are you quite sure—I am certain you 'll excuse me, my dear Jane—that you understand Davy?'

'I should be somewhat ashamed of myself, Clara,' returned Miss Murdstone, 'if I could not understand the boy, or any boy. I don't profess to be profound; but I do lay claim to common sense.'

'No doubt, my dear Jane,' returned my mother, 'your understanding is very vigorous.'

'Oh dear, no! Pray don't say that, Clara,' interposed Miss Murdstone, angrily.

'But I am sure it is,' resumed my mother; 'and everybody knows it is. I profit so much by it myself, in many ways—at least I ought to—that no one can be more convinced of it than myself; and therefore I speak with great diffidence, my dear Jane, I assure you.'

'We'll say I don't understand the boy, Clara,' returned Miss Murdstone, arranging the little fetters on her wrists. 'We'll agree, if you please, that I don't understand him at all. He is much too deep for me. But perhaps my brother's penetration may enable him to have some insight into his character. And I believe my brother was speaking on the subject when we—not very decently—interrupted him.'

'I think, Clara,' said Mr. Murdstone, in a low grave voice, 'that there may be better and more dispassionate judges of such a question than you.'

'Edward,' replied my mother, timidly, 'you are a far better judge of all questions than I pretend to be. Both you and Jane are. I only said—'

'You only said something weak and inconsiderate,' he replied. 'Try not to do it again, my dear Clara, and keep a watch upon yourself.'

My mother's lips moved, as if she answered 'Yes, my dear Edward,' but she said nothing aloud.

'I was sorry, David, I remarked,' said Mr. Murdstone, turning his head and eyes stiffly towards me, 'to observe that you are of a sullen disposition. This is not a character that I can suffer to develop itself beneath my eyes without an effort at improvement. You must endeavour, sir, to change it. We must endeavour to change it for you.'

'I beg your pardon, sir,' I faltered. 'I have never meant to be sullen since I came back.'

'Don't take refuge in a lie, sir!' he returned so fiercely, that I saw my mother involuntarily put out her trembling hand as if to interpose between us. 'You have withdrawn yourself in your sullenness to your own room. You have kept your own room when you ought to have been here. You know now, once for all, that I require you to be here, and not there. Further, that I require you to bring obedience here. You know me, David. I will have it done.'

Miss Murdstone gave a hoarse chuckle.

'I will have a respectful, prompt, and ready bearing towards myself,' he continued, 'and towards Jane Murdstone, and towards your mother. I will not have this room shunned as if it were infected, at the pleasure of a child. Sit down.'

He ordered me like a dog, and I obeyed like a dog.

'One thing more,' he said. 'I observe that you have an attachment to low and common company. You are not to associate with servants. The kitchen will not improve you, in the many respects in which you need improvement. Of the woman who abets you, I say nothing—since you, Clara,' addressing my mother in a lower voice, 'from old associations and long-established fancies, have a weakness respecting her which is not yet overcome.'

'A most unaccountable delusion it is!' cried Miss Murdstone.

'I only say,' he resumed, addressing me, 'that I disapprove of your preferring such company as Mistress Peggotty, and that it is to be abandoned.

Now, David, you understand me, and you know what will be the consequence if you fail to obey me to the letter.'

I knew well—better perhaps than he thought, as far as my poor mother was concerned—and I obeyed him to the letter. I retreated to my own room no more; I took refuge with Peggotty no more; but sat wearily in the parlour day after day looking forward to night, and bed-time.

What irksome constraint I underwent, sitting in the same attitude hours upon hours, afraid to move an arm or a leg lest Miss Murdstone should complain (as she did on the least pretence) of my restlessness, and afraid to move an eye lest she should light on some look of dislike or scrutiny that would find new cause for complaint in mine! What intolerable dulness to sit listening to the ticking of the clock; and watching Miss Murdstone's little shiny steel beads as she strung them; and wondering whether she would ever be married, and if so, to what sort of unhappy man; and counting the divisions in the moulding on the chimney-piece; and wandering away, with my eyes, to the ceiling, among the curls and corkscrews in the paper on the wall!

What walks I took alone, down muddy lanes, in the bad winter weather, carrying that parlour, and Mr. and Miss Murdstone in it, everywhere: a monstrous load that I was obliged to bear, a daymare that there was no possibility of breaking in, a weight that brooded on my wits, and blunted them!

What meals I had in silence and embarrassment, always feeling that there were a knife and fork too many, and those mine; an appetite too many, and that mine; a plate and chair too many, and those mine; a somebody too many, and that I!

What evenings, when the candles came, and I was

expected to employ myself, but not daring to read an entertaining book, pored over some hard-headed harder-hearted treatise on arithmetic; when the tables of weights and measures set themselves to tunes, as Rule Britannia, or Away with Melancholy; when they wouldn't stand still to be learnt, but would go threading my grandmother's needle through my unfortunate head, in at one ear and out at the other!

What yawns and dozes I lapsed into, in spite of all my care; what starts I came out of concealed sleeps with; what answers I never got, to little observations that I rarely made; what a blank space I seemed, which everybody overlooked, and yet was in everybody's way; what a heavy relief it was to hear Miss Murdstone hail the first stroke of nine at night, and order me to bed!

Thus the holidays lagged away, until the morning came when Miss Murdstone said: 'Here's the last day off!' and gave me the closing cup of tea of the vacation.

I was not sorry to go. I had lapsed into a stupid state; but I was recovering a little and looking forward to Steerforth, albeit Mr. Creakle loomed behind him. Again Mr. Barkis appeared at the gate, and again Miss Murdstone in her warning voice said: 'Clara!' when my mother bent over me, to bid me farewell.

I kissed her, and my baby brother, and was very sorry then; but not sorry to go away, for the gulf between us was there, and the parting was there, every day. And it is not so much the embrace she gave me, that lives in my mind, though it was as fervent as could be, as what followed the embrace.

I was in the carrier's cart when I heard her calling to me. I looked out, and she stood at the garden-gate alone, holding her baby up in her arms for me to

see. It was cold still weather; and not a hair on her
head, nor a fold of her dress, was stirred, as she looked
intently at me, holding up her child.

So I lost her. So I saw her afterwards, in my
sleep at school—a silent presence near my bed—looking at me with the same intent face—holding up her
baby in her arms.

CHAPTER IX

I HAVE A MEMORABLE BIRTHDAY

I pass over all that happened at school, until the anniversary of my birthday came round in March. Except that Steerforth was more to be admired than
ever, I remember nothing. He was going away at
the end of the half-year, if not sooner, and was more
spirited and independent than before in my eyes, and
therefore more engaging than before; but beyond
this I remember nothing. The great remembrance
by which that time is marked in my mind, seems to
have swallowed up all lesser recollections, and to exist alone.

It is even difficult for me to believe that there was
a gap of full two months between my return to Salem
House and the arrival of that birthday. I can only
understand that the fact was so, because I know it
must have been so; otherwise I should feel convinced
that there was no interval, and that the one occasion
trod upon the other's heels.

How well I recollect the kind of day it was! I
smell the fog that hung about the place; I see the hoar-
frost, ghostly, through it; I feel my rimy hair fall
clammy on my cheek; I look along the dim perspective of the schoolroom, with a sputtering candle here

and there to light up the foggy morning, and the breath of the boys wreathing and smoking in the raw cold as they blow upon their fingers, and tap their feet upon the floor.

It was after breakfast, and we had been summoned in from the playground, when Mr. Sharp entered and said—

'David Copperfield is to go into the parlour.'

I expected a hamper from Peggotty, and brightened at the order. Some of the boys about me put in their claim not to be forgotten in the distribution of the good things, as I got out of my seat with great alacrity.

'Don't hurry, David,' said Mr. Sharp. 'There's time enough, my boy, don't hurry.'

I might have been surprised by the feeling tone in which he spoke, if I had given it a thought; but I gave it none until afterwards. I hurried away to the parlour; and there I found Mr. Creakle, sitting at his breakfast with the cane and a newspaper before him, and Mrs. Creakle with an opened letter in her hand. But no hamper.

'David Copperfield,' said Mrs. Creakle, leading me to a sofa, and sitting down beside me. 'I want to speak to you very particularly. I have something to tell you, my child.'

Mr. Creakle, at whom of course I looked, shook his head without looking at me, and stopped up a sigh with a very large piece of buttered toast.

'You are too young to know how the world changes every day,' said Mrs. Creakle, 'and how the people in it pass away. But we all have to learn it, David; some of us when we are young, some of us when we are old, some of us at all times of our lives.'

I looked at her earnestly.

'When you came away from home at the end of the

vacation,' said Mrs. Creakle, after a pause, 'were they all well?' After another pause, 'Was your mamma well?'

I trembled without distinctly knowing why, and still looked at her earnestly, making no attempt to answer.

'Because,' said she, 'I grieve to tell you that I hear this morning your mamma is very ill.'

A mist rose between Mrs. Creakle and me, and her figure seemed to move in it for an instant. Then I felt the burning tears run down my face, and it was steady again.

'She is very dangerously ill,' she added.

I knew all now.

'She is dead.'

There was no need to tell me so. I had already broken out into a desolate cry, and felt an orphan in the wide world.

She was very kind to me. She kept me there all day, and left me alone sometimes; and I cried, and wore myself to sleep, and awoke and cried again. When I could cry no more, I began to think; and then the oppression on my breast was heaviest, and my grief a dull pain that there was no ease for.

And yet my thoughts were idle; not intent on the calamity that weighed upon my heart, but idly loitering near it. I thought of our house shut up and hushed. I thought of the little baby, who, Mrs. Creakle said, had been pining away for some time, and who, they believed, would die too. I thought of my father's grave in the churchyard, by our house, and of my mother lying there beneath the tree I knew so well. I stood upon a chair when I was left alone, and looked into the glass to see how red my eyes were, and how sorrowful my face. I considered, after some hours were gone, if my tears were really hard to flow now, as they seemed to be, what, in connection with my loss, it would affect me most to think of when I drew near home—for I was going home to the funeral. I am sensible of having felt that a dignity attached to me among the rest of the boys, and that I was important in my affliction.

If ever a child were stricken with sincere grief, I was. But I remember that this importance was a kind of satisfaction to me, when I walked in the playground that afternoon while the boys were in school. When I saw them glancing at me out of the windows, as they went up to their classes, I felt distinguished, and looked more melancholy, and walked slower. When school was over, and they came out and spoke to me, I felt it rather good in myself not to be proud to any of them, and to take exactly the same notice of them all, as before.

I was to go home next night; not by the mail, but by the heavy night-coach, which was called the Farmer, and was principally used by country-people travelling short intermediate distances upon the road. We had no story-telling that evening, and Traddles insisted on lending me his pillow. I don't know what good he thought it would do me, for I had one of my own; but it was all he had to lend, poor fellow, except a sheet of letter-paper full of skeletons; and that he gave me at parting, as a soother of my sorrows and a contribution to my peace of mind.

I left Salem House upon the morrow afternoon. I little thought then that I left it, never to return. We travelled very slowly all night, and did not get into Yarmouth before nine or ten o'clock in the morning. I looked out for Mr. Barkis, but he was not there; and instead of him a fat, short-winded, merry-looking, little old man in black, with rusty little bunches of ribbons at the knees of his breeches, black stockings, and a broad-brimmed hat, came puffing up to the coach-window, and said—

'Master Copperfield?'

'Yes, sir.'

'Will you come with me, young sir, if you please,' he said, opening the door, 'and I shall have the pleasure of taking you home?'

I put my hand in his, wondering who he was, and we walked away to a shop in a narrow street, on which was written, OMER, DRAPER, TAILOR, HABER-DASHER, FUNERAL FURNISHER, &c. It was a close and stifling little shop; full of all sorts of clothing, made and unmade, including one window full of beaver-hats and bonnets. We went into a little back-parlour behind the shop, where we found three young women at work on a quantity of black materials, which were heaped upon the table, and little bits and cuttings of which were littered all over the floor. There was a good fire in the room, and a breathless smell of warm black crape. I did not know what the smell was then, but I know now.

The three young women, who appeared to be very industrious and comfortable, raised their heads to look at me, and then went on with their work. Stitch, stitch, stitch. At the same time there came from a workshop across a little yard outside the window, a regular sound of hammering that kept a kind of tune: RAT—tat-tat, RAT—tat-tat, RAT—tat-tat, without any variation.

'Well,' said my conductor to one of the three young women. 'How do you get on, Minnie?'

'We shall be ready by the trying-on time,' she replied gaily, without looking up. 'Don't you be afraid, father.'

Mr. Omer took off his broad-brimmed hat, and sat down and panted. He was so fat that he was obliged to pant some time before he could say—

'That's right.'

'Father!' said Minnie, playfully. 'What a porpoise you do grow!'

'Well, I don't know how it is, my dear,' he replied, considering about it. 'I *am* rather so.'

'You are such a comfortable man, you see,' said Minnie. 'You take things so easy.'

'No use taking 'em otherwise, my dear,' said Mr. Omer.

'No, indeed,' returned his daughter. 'We are all pretty gay here, thank Heaven! Ain't we, father?'

'I hope so, my dear,' said Mr. Omer. 'As I have got my breath now, I think I'll measure this young scholar. Would you walk into the shop, Master Copperfield?'

I preceded Mr. Omer, in compliance with his request; and after showing me a roll of cloth which he said was extra super, and too good mourning for anything short of parents, he took my various dimensions, and put them down in a book. While he was recording them he called my attention to his stock in trade, and to certain fashions which he said had 'just come up,' and to certain other fashions which he said had 'just gone out.'

'And by that sort of thing we very often lose a little mint of money,' said Mr. Omer. 'But fashions are like human beings. They come in, nobody knows when, why, or how; and they go out, nobody knows when, why, or how. Everything is like life, in my opinion, if you look at it in that point of view.'

I was too sorrowful to discuss the question, which would possibly have been beyond me under any circumstances; and Mr. Omer took me back into the parlour, breathing with some difficulty on the way.

He then called down a little break-neck range of steps behind a door: 'Bring up that tea and bread-and-butter!' which, after some time, during which I sat looking about me and thinking, and listening to the stitching in the room and the tune that was being hammered across the yard, appeared on a tray, and turned out to be for me.

'I have been acquainted with you,' said Mr. Omer, after watching me for some minutes, during which I had not made much impression on the breakfast, for the black things destroyed my appetite, 'I have been acquainted with you a long time, my young friend.'

'Have you, sir?'

'All your life,' said Mr. Omer. 'I may say before it. I knew your father before you. He was five foot nine and a half, and he lays in five and twen-ty foot of ground.'

'Rat—tat-tat, rat—tat-tat, rat—tat-tat,' across the yard.

'He lays in five and twen-ty foot of ground, if he lays in a fraction,' said Mr. Omer, pleasantly. 'It was either his request or her direction, I forget which.'

'Do you know how my little brother is, sir?' I inquired.

Mr. Omer shook his head.

'Rat—tat-tat, rat—tat-tat, rat—tat-tat.'

'He is in his mother's arms,' said he.

'Oh, poor little fellow! Is he dead?'

'Don't mind it more than you can help,' said Mr. Omer. 'Yes. The baby's dead.'

My wounds broke out afresh at this intelligence. I left the scarcely tasted breakfast, and went and rested my head on another table in a corner of the little room, which Minnie hastily cleared, lest I should spot the mourning that was lying there with my tears. She was a pretty good-natured girl, and put my hair away from my eyes with a soft kind touch; but she was very cheerful at having nearly finished her work and being in good time, and was so different from me!

Presently the tune left off, and a good-looking young fellow came across the yard into the room. He had a hammer in his hand, and his mouth was full of little nails, which he was obliged to take out before he could speak.

'Well, Joram!' said Mr. Omer. 'How do *you* get on?'

'All right,' said Joram. 'Done, sir.'

Minnie coloured a little, and the other two girls smiled at one another.

'What! you were at it by candle-light last night, when I was at the club, then? Were you?' said Mr. Omer, shutting up one eye.

'Yes,' said Joram. 'As you said we could make a little trip of it, and go over together, if it was done, Minnie and me—and you.'

'Oh! I thought you were going to leave me out altogether,' said Mr. Omer, laughing till he coughed.

'—As you was so good as to say that,' resumed the young man, 'why I turned to with a will, you see. Will you give me your opinion of it?'

'I will,' said Mr. Omer, rising. 'My dear'; and he stopped and turned to me; 'would you like to see your—'

'No, father,' Minnie interposed.

'I thought it might be agreeable, my dear,' said Mr. Omer. 'But perhaps you 're right.'

I can't say how I knew it was my dear, dear mother's coffin that they went to look at. I had never heard one making; I had never seen one that I know of: but it came into my mind what the noise was, while it was going on; and when the young man entered, I am sure I knew what he had been doing.

The work being now finished, the two girls, whose names I had not heard, brushed the shreds and threads from their dresses, and went into the shop to put that to rights, and wait for customers. Minnie stayed behind to fold up what they had made, and pack it in two baskets. This she did upon her knees, humming a lively little tune the while. Joram, who I had no doubt was her lover, came in and stole a kiss from her while she was busy (he didn't appear to mind me, at all), and said her father was gone for the chaise, and he must make haste and get himself ready. Then he went out again; and then she put her thimble and scissors in her pocket, and stuck a needle threaded with black thread neatly in the bosom of her gown, and put on her outer clothing smartly, at a little glass behind the door, in which I saw the reflection of her pleased face.

All this I observed, sitting at the table in the corner with my head leaning on my hand, and my thoughts running on very different things. The chaise soon came round to the front of the shop, and the baskets being put in first, I was put in next, and those three followed. I remember it as a kind of half chaise-cart, half pianoforte-van, painted of a sombre colour, and drawn by a black horse with a long tail. There was plenty of room for us all.

I do not think I have ever experienced so strange a feeling in my life (I am wiser now, perhaps) as that of being with them, remembering how they had been employed, and seeing them enjoy the ride. I was not angry with them; I was more afraid of them, as if I were cast away among creatures with whom I had no community of nature. They were very cheerful.

The old man sat in front to drive, and the two young people sat behind him, and whenever he spoke to them leaned forward, the one on one side of his chubby face and the other on the other, and made a great deal of him. They would have talked to me too, but I held back, and moped in my corner; scared by their love-making and hilarity, though it was far from boisterous, and almost wondering that no judgment came upon them for their hardness of heart.

So, when they stopped to bait the horse, and ate and drank and enjoyed themselves, I could touch nothing that they touched, but kept my fast unbroken. So, when we reached home, I dropped out of the chaise behind, as quickly as possible, that I might not be in their company before those solemn windows, looking blindly on me like closed eyes once bright. And oh, how little need I had had to think what would move me to tears when I came back—seeing the window of my mother's room, and next it that which, in the better time, was mine!

I was in Peggotty's arms before I got to the door, and she took me into the house. Her grief burst out when she first saw me; but she controlled it soon, and spoke in whispers, and walked softly, as if the dead could be disturbed. She had not been in bed, I found, for a long time. She sat up at night still, and watched. As long as her poor dear pretty was above the ground, she said, she would never desert her.

Mr. Murdstone took no heed of me when I went into the parlour, where he was, but sat by the fireside, weeping silently, and pondering in his elbow-chair. Miss Murdstone, who was busy at her writing-desk, which was covered with letters and papers, gave me her cold finger-nails, and asked me, in an iron whisper, if I had been measured for my mourning.

I said, 'Yes.'

'And your shirts,' said Miss Murdstone; 'have you brought 'em home?'

'Yes, ma'am. I have brought home all my clothes.'

This was all the consolation that her firmness administered to me. I do not doubt that she had a choice pleasure in exhibiting what she called her self-command, and her firmness, and her strength of mind, and her common sense, and the whole diabolical catalogue of her unamiable qualities, on such an occasion. She was particularly proud of her turn for business; and she showed it now in reducing everything to pen and ink, and being moved by nothing. All the rest of that day, and from morning to night afterwards, she sat at that desk; scratching composedly with a hard pen, speaking in the same imperturbable whisper to everybody; never relaxing a muscle of her face, or softening a tone of her voice, or appearing with an atom of her dress astray.

Her brother took a book sometimes, but never read it that I saw. He would open it and look at it as if he were reading, but would remain for a whole hour without turning the leaf, and then put it down and walk to and fro in the room. I used to sit with folded hands watching him, and counting his footsteps, hour after hour. He very seldom spoke to her, and never to me. He seemed to be the only restless thing, except the clocks, in the whole motionless house.

In these days before the funeral, I saw but little of Peggotty, except that, in passing up or down stairs, I always found her close to the room where my mother and her baby lay, and except that she came to me every night, and sat by my bed's head while I went to sleep. A day or two before the burial—I think it was a day or two before, but I am conscious of confusion in my mind about that heavy time with nothing to mark its progress—she took me into the room. I only recollect that underneath some white covering on the bed, with a beautiful cleanliness and freshness all around it, there seemed to me to lie embodied the solemn stillness that was in the house; and that when she would have turned the cover gently back, I cried, 'Oh no! oh no!' and held her hand.

If the funeral had been yesterday, I could not recollect it better. The very air of the best parlour, when I went in at the door, the bright condition of the fire, the shining of the wine in the decanters, the patterns of the glasses and plates, the faint sweet smell of cake, the odour of Miss Murdstone's dress, and our black clothes. Mr. Chillip is in the room, and comes to speak to me.

'And how is Master David?' he says kindly.

I cannot tell him very well. I give him my hand, which he holds in his.

'Dear me!' says Mr. Chillip, meekly smiling, with something shining in his eye. 'Our little friends grow up around us. They grow out of our knowledge, ma'am?'

This is to Miss Murdstone, who makes no reply.

'There is a great improvement here, ma'am?' says Mr. Chillip.

Miss Murdstone merely answers with a frown and a formal bend; Mr. Chillip, discomfited, goes into a corner, keeping me with him, and opens his mouth no more.

I remark this, because I remark everything that happens, not because I care about myself, or have done since I came home. And now the bell begins to sound, and Mr. Omer and another come to make us ready. As Peggotty was wont to tell me, long ago, the followers of my father to the same grave were made ready in the same room.

There are Mr. Murdstone, our neighbour Mr. Grayper, Mr. Chillip, and I. When we go out to the door, the bearers and their load are in the garden; and they move before us down the path, and past the elms, and through the gate, and into the churchyard, where I have so often heard the birds sing on a summer morning.

We stand around the grave. The day seems different to me from every other day, and the light not of the same colour—of a sadder colour. Now there is a solemn hush, which we have brought from home with what is resting in the mould; and while we stand bareheaded, I hear the voice of the clergyman, sounding remote in the open air, and yet distinct and plain, saying, 'I am the Resurrection and the Life, saith the Lord!' Then I hear sobs; and, standing apart among the lookers-on, I see that good and faithful servant, whom of all the people upon earth I love the best, and unto whom my childish heart is certain that the Lord will one day say, 'Well done.'

There are many faces that I know, among the little crowd; faces that I knew in church, when mine was always wondering there; faces that first saw my mother, when she came to the village in her youthful bloom. I do not mind them—I mind nothing but my grief—and yet I see and know them all; and even in the background, far away, see Minnie looking on, and her eye glancing on her sweetheart, who is near me.

It is over, and the earth is filled in, and we turn to come away. Before us stands our house, so pretty and unchanged, so linked in my mind with the young idea of what is gone, that all my sorrow has been nothing to the sorrow it calls forth. But they take me on; and Mr. Chillip talks to me; and when we get home, puts some water to my lips; and when I ask his leave to go up to my room, dismisses me with the gentleness of a woman.

All this, I say, is yesterday's event. Events of later date have floated from me to the shore where all forgotten things will reappear, but this stands like a high rock in the ocean.

I knew that Peggotty would come to me in my room. The Sabbath stillness of the time (the day was so like Sunday! I have forgotten that) was suited to us both. She sat down by my side upon my little bed; and holding my hand, and sometimes putting it to her lips, and sometimes smoothing it with hers, as she might have comforted my little brother, told me, in her way, all that she had to tell concerning what had happened.

'She was never well,' said Peggotty, 'for a long time. She was uncertain in her mind, and not happy. When her baby was born, I thought at first she would get better, but she was more delicate, and sunk a little every day. She used to like to sit alone before her baby came, and then she cried; but afterwards she used to sing to it—so soft—that I once thought when I heard her, it was like a voice up in the air, that was rising away.

'I think she got to be more timid, and more frightened-like, of late; and that a hard word was like a blow to her. But she was always the same to me. She never changed to her foolish Peggotty, didn't my sweet girl.'

Here Peggotty stopped, and softly beat upon my hand a little while.

'The last time that I saw her like her own old self, was the night when you came home, my dear. The day you went away, she said to me, "I never shall see my pretty darling again. Something tells me so, that tells the truth, I know."

'She tried to hold up after that; and many a time, when they told her she was thoughtless and light-hearted, made believe to be so; but it was all a bygone then. She never told her husband what she had told me—she was afraid of saying it to anybody else—till one night, a little more than a week before it happened, when she said to him, "My dear, I think I am dying."

'"It's off my mind now, Peggotty," she told me, when I laid her in her bed that night. "He will believe it more and more, poor fellow, every day for a few days to come; and then it will be past. I am very tired. If this is sleep, sit by me while I sleep: don't leave me. God bless both my children! God protect and keep my fatherless boy!"

'I never left her afterwards,' said Peggotty. 'She often talked to them two downstairs—for she loved them; she couldn't bear not to love any one who was about her—but when they went away from her bedside, she always turned to me, as if there was rest where Peggotty was, and never fell asleep in any other way.

'On the last night, in the evening, she kissed me and said, "If my baby should die too, Peggotty, please let them lay him in my arms, and bury us together." (It was done; for the poor lamb lived but a day beyond her.) "Let my dearest boy go with us to our resting-place," she said, "and tell him that his mother, when she lay here, blessed him not once, but a thousand times."'

Another silence followed this, and another gentle beating on my hand.

'It was pretty far in the night,' said Peggotty, 'when

she asked me for some drink; and when she had taken it, gave me such a patient smile, the dear!—so beautiful!

'Daybreak had come, and the sun was rising, when she said to me, how kind and considerate Mr. Copperfield had always been to her, and how he had borne with her, and told her, when she doubted herself, that a loving heart was better and stronger than wisdom, and that he was a happy man in hers. "Peggotty, my dear," she said then, "put me nearer to you," for she was very weak. "Lay your good arm underneath my neck," she said, "and turn me to you, for your face is going far off, and I want it to be near." I put it as she asked; and oh Davy! the time had come when my first parting words to you were true—when she was glad to lay her poor head on her stupid cross old Peggotty's arm—and she died like a child that had gone to sleep!'

Thus ended Peggotty's narration. From the moment of my knowing of the death of my mother, the idea of her as she had been of late had vanished from me. I remembered her, from that instant, only as the young mother of my earliest impressions, who had been used to wind her bright curls round and round her finger, and to dance with me at twilight in the parlour. What Peggotty had told me now, was so far from bringing me back to the later period, that it rooted the earlier image in my mind. It may be curious, but it is true. In her death she winged her way back to her calm untroubled youth, and cancelled all the rest.

The mother who lay in the grave, was the mother of my infancy; the little creature in her arms, was myself, as I had once been, hushed for ever on her bosom.

CHAPTER X

I BECOME NEGLECTED, AND AM PROVIDED FOR

THE first act of business Miss Murdstone performed when the day of the solemnity was over, and light was freely admitted into the house, was to give Peggotty a month's warning. Much as Peggotty would have disliked such a service, I believe she would have retained it, for my sake, in preference to the best upon earth. She told me we must part, and told me why; and we condoled with one another, in all sincerity.

As to me or my future, not a word was said, or a step taken. Happy they would have been, I dare say, if they could have dismissed me at a month's warning too. I mustered courage once, to ask Miss Murdstone when I was going back to school; and she answered drily, she believed I was not going back at all. I was told nothing more. I was very anxious to know what was going to be done with me, and so was Peggotty; but neither she nor I could pick up any information on the subject.

There was one change in my condition, which, while it relieved me of a great deal of present uneasiness, might have made me, if I had been capable of considering it closely, yet more uncomfortable about the future. It was this. The constraint that had been put upon me, was quite abandoned. I was so far from being required to keep my dull post in the parlour, that on several occasions, when I took my seat there, Miss Murdstone frowned to me to go away. I was so far from being warned off from Peggotty's society, that, provided I was not in Mr. Murdstone's, I was never sought out or inquired for. At first I was in daily dread of his taking my education in hand again, or of Miss Murdstone's devoting herself to it; but I soon began to think that such fears were groundless, and that all I had to anticipate was neglect.

I do not conceive that this discovery gave me much pain then. I was still giddy with the shock of my mother's death, and in a kind of stunned state as to all tributary things. I can recollect, indeed, to have speculated, at odd times, on the possibility of my not being taught any more, or cared for any more; and growing up to be a shabby moody man, lounging an idle life away, about the village; as well as on the feasibility of my getting rid of this picture by going away somewhere, like the hero in a story, to seek my fortune; but these were transient visions, day dreams I sat looking at sometimes, as if they were faintly painted or written on the wall of my room, and which, as they melted away, left the wall blank again.

'Peggotty,' I said in a thoughtful whisper, one evening, when I was warming my hands at the kitchen fire, 'Mr. Murdstone likes me less than he used to. He never liked me much, Peggotty; but he would rather not even see me now, if he can help it.'

'Perhaps it's his sorrow,' said Peggotty, stroking my hair.

'I am sure, Peggotty, I am sorry too. If I believed it was his sorrow, I should not think of it at all. But it's not that; oh no, it's not that.'

'How do you know it's not that?' said Peggotty, after a silence.

'Oh, his sorrow is another and quite a different thing. He is sorry at this moment, sitting by the fireside with Miss Murdstone; but if I was to go in, Peggotty, he would be something besides.'

'What would he be?' said Peggotty.

'Angry,' I answered, with an involuntary imitation

of his dark frown. 'If he was only sorry, he wouldn't look at me as he does. *I* am only sorry, and it makes me feel kinder.'

Peggotty said nothing for a little while, and I warmed my hands, as silent as she.

'Davy,' she said at length.

'Yes, Peggotty?'

'I have tried, my dear, all ways I could think of— all the ways there are, and all the ways there ain't, in short—to get a suitable service here, in Blunderstone; but there's no such a thing, my love.'

'And what do you mean to do, Peggotty?' says I, wistfully. 'Do you mean to go and seek your fortune?'

'I expect I shall be forced to go to Yarmouth,' replied Peggotty, 'and live there.'

'You might have gone farther off,' I said, brightening a little, 'and been as bad as lost. I shall see you sometimes, my dear old Peggotty, there. You won't be quite at the other end of the world, will you?'

'Contrary ways, please God!' cried Peggotty, with great animation. 'As long as you are here, my pet, I shall come over every week of my life to see you. One day every week of my life!'

I felt a great weight taken off my mind by this promise; but even this was not all, for Peggotty went on to say—

'I'm a going, Davy, you see, to my brother's, first, for another fortnight's visit—just till I have had time to look about me, and get to be something like myself again. Now, I have been thinking, that perhaps, as they don't want you here at present, you might be let to go along with me.'

If anything, short of being in a different relation to every one about me, Peggotty excepted, could have given me a sense of pleasure at that time, it would have been this project of all others. The idea of being again surrounded by those honest faces, shining welcome on me; of renewing the peacefulness of the sweet Sunday morning, when the bells were ringing, the stones dropping in the water, and the shadowy ships breaking through the mist; of roaming up and down with little Em'ly, telling her my troubles, and finding charms against them in the shells and pebbles on the beach; made a calm in my heart. It was ruffled next moment, to be sure, by a doubt of Miss Murdstone giving her consent; but even that was set at rest soon, for she came out to take an evening grope in the store-closet while we were yet in conversation, and Peggotty, with a boldness that amazed me, broached the topic on the spot.

'The boy will be idle there,' said Miss Murdstone, looking into a pickle-jar, 'and idleness is the root of all evil. But, to be sure, he would be idle here—or anywhere, in my opinion.'

Peggotty had an angry answer ready, I could see; but she swallowed it for my sake, and remained silent.

'Humph!' said Miss Murdstone, still keeping her eye on the pickles; 'it is of more importance than anything else—it is of paramount importance—that my brother should not be disturbed or made uncomfortable. I suppose I had better say yes.'

I thanked her, without making any demonstration of joy, lest it should induce her to withdraw her assent. Nor could I help thinking this a prudent course, when she looked at me out of the pickle-jar, with as great an access of sourness as if her black eyes had absorbed its contents. However, the permission was given, and was never retracted; for when the month was out, Peggotty and I were ready to depart.

Mr. Barkis came into the house for Peggotty's boxes. I had never known him to pass the garden-gate before, but on this occasion he came into the house. And he gave me a look as he shouldered the largest box and went out, which I thought had meaning in it, if meaning could ever be said to find its way into Mr. Barkis's visage.

Peggotty was naturally in low spirits at leaving what had been her home so many years, and where the two strong attachments of her life—for my mother and myself—had been formed. She had been walking in the churchyard, too, very early; and she got into the cart, and sat in it with her handkerchief at her eyes.

So long as she remained in this condition, Mr. Barkis gave no sign of life whatever. He sat in his usual place and attitude, like a great stuffed figure. But when she began to look about her, and to speak to me, he nodded his head and grinned several times. I have not the least notion at whom, or what he meant by it.

'It's a beautiful day, Mr. Barkis!' I said, as an act of politeness.

'It ain't bad,' said Mr. Barkis, who generally qualified his speech, and rarely committed himself.

'Peggotty is quite comfortable now, Mr. Barkis,' I remarked, for his satisfaction.

'Is she, though?' said Mr. Barkis.

After reflecting about it, with a sagacious air, Mr. Barkis eyed her, and said—

'*Are* you pretty comfortable?'

Peggotty laughed, and answered in the affirmative.

'But really and truly, you know. Are you?' growled Mr. Barkis, sliding nearer to her on the seat, and nudging her with his elbow. 'Are you? Really

and truly, pretty comfortable? Are you? Eh?'
At each of these inquiries Mr. Barkis shuffled nearer
to her, and gave her another nudge; so that at last
we were all crowded together in the left-hand corner
of the cart, and I was so squeezed that I could hardly
bear it.

Peggotty calling his attention to my sufferings, Mr.
Barkis gave me a little more room at once, and got
away by degrees. But I could not help observing
that he seemed to think he had hit upon a wonderful expedient for expressing himself in a neat, agreeable, and pointed manner, without the inconvenience
of inventing conversation. He manifestly chuckled
over it for some time. By and by he turned to Peggotty again, and repeating, 'Are you pretty comfortable, though?' bore down upon us as before, until
the breath was nearly wedged out of my body. By
and by he made another descent upon us with the
same inquiry, and the same result. At length, I got
up whenever I saw him coming, and standing on the
footboard, pretended to look at the prospect; after
which I did very well.

He was so polite as to stop at a public-house, expressly on our account, and entertain us with broiled
mutton and beer. Even when Peggotty was in the
act of drinking, he was seized with one of those approaches, and almost choked her. But as we drew
nearer to the end of our journey, he had more to do
and less time for gallantry; and when we got on
Yarmouth pavement, we were all too much shaken
and jolted, I apprehend, to have any leisure for anything else.

Mr. Peggotty and Ham waited for us at the old
place. They received me and Peggotty in an affectionate manner, and shook hands with Mr. Barkis.

who, with his hat on the very back of his head, and a shamefaced leer upon his countenance, and pervading his very legs, presented but a vacant appearance, I thought. They each took one of Peggotty's trunks, and we were going away, when Mr. Barkis solemnly made a sign to me with his forefinger to come under an archway.

'I say,' growled Mr. Barkis, 'it was all right.'

I looked up into his face, and answered, with an attempt to be very profound, 'Oh!'

'It didn't come to a end there,' said Mr. Barkis nodding confidentially. 'It was all right.'

Again I answered, 'Oh!'

'You know who was willin',' said my friend. 'It was Barkis, and Barkis only.'

I nodded assent.

'It's all right,' said Mr. Barkis, shaking hands; 'I'm a friend of your'n. You made it all right first. It's all right.'

In his attempts to be particularly lucid, Mr. Barkis was so extremely mysterious that I might have stood looking in his face for an hour, and most assuredly should have got as much information out of it as out of the face of a clock that had stopped, but for Peggotty's calling me away. As we were going along, she asked me what he had said; and I told her he had said it was all right.

'Like his impudence,' said Peggotty, 'but I don't mind that! Davy dear, what should you think if I was to think of being married?'

'Why—I suppose you would like me as much then, Peggotty, as you do now?' I returned, after a little consideration.

Greatly to the astonishment of the passengers in the street, as well as of her relations going on before, the good soul was obliged to stop and embrace me on the spot, with many protestations of her unalterable love.

'Tell me what should you say, darling?' she asked again, when this was over, and we were walking on.

'If you were thinking of being married--to Mr. Barkis, Peggotty?'

'Yes,' said Peggotty.

'I should think it would be a very good thing. For then you know, Peggotty, you would always have the horse and cart to bring you over to see me, and could come for nothing, and be sure of coming.'

'The sense of the dear!' cried Peggotty. 'What I have been thinking of, this month back! Yes, my precious; and I think I should be more independent altogether, you see; let alone my working with a better heart in my own house, than I could in anybody else's now. I don't know what I might be fit for now, as a servant to a stranger. And I shall be always near my pretty's resting-place,' said Peggotty musing, 'and be able to see it when I like; and when I lie down to rest, I may be laid not far off from my darling girl!'

We neither of us said anything for a little while.

'But I wouldn't so much as give it another thought,' said Peggotty, cheerily, 'if my Davy was anyways against it—not if I had been asked in church thirty times three times over, and was wearing out the ring in my pocket.'

'Look at me, Peggotty,' I replied; 'and see if I am not really glad, and don't truly wish it!' As indeed I did, with all my heart.

'Well, my life,' said Peggotty, giving me a squeeze, 'I have thought of it night and day, every way I can, and I hope the right way; but I 'll think of it again, and speak to my brother about it, and in the

meantime we'll keep it to ourselves, Davy, you and
me. Barkis is a good plain creatur',' said Peggotty,
'and if I tried to do my duty by him, I think it would
be my fault if I wasn't—if I wasn't pretty comfortable,' said Peggotty, laughing heartily.

This quotation from Mr. Barkis was so appropriate,
and tickled us both so much, that we laughed again
and again, and were quite in a pleasant humour when
we came within view of Mr. Peggotty's cottage.

It looked just the same, except that it may, perhaps, have shrunk a little in my eyes; and Mrs. Gummidge was waiting at the door as if she had stood
there ever since. All within was the same, down to
the seaweed in the blue mug in my bedroom. I went
into the outhouse to look about me; and the very same
lobsters, crabs, and crawfish, possessed by the same
desire to pinch the world in general, appeared to be
in the same state of conglomeration in the same old
corner.

But there was no little Em'ly to be seen, so I asked
Mr. Peggotty where she was.

'She's at school, sir,' said Mr. Peggotty, wiping
the heat consequent on the porterage of Peggotty's
box from his forehead; 'she'll be home,' looking at
the Dutch clock, 'in from twenty minutes to half an
hour's time. We all on us feel the loss of her, bless
ye!'

Mrs. Gummidge moaned.

'Cheer up, mawther!' cried Mr. Peggotty.

'I feel it more than anybody else,' said Mrs. Gummidge; 'I'm a lone lorn creetur', and she used to be
a'most the only thing that didn't go contrairy with
me.'

Mrs. Gummidge, whimpering and shaking her
head, applied herself to blowing the fire. Mr. Peggotty, looking round upon us while she was so en-

gaged, said in a low voice, which he shaded with his hand: 'The old 'un!' From this I rightly conjectured that no improvement had taken place since my last visit in the state of Mrs. Gummidge's spirits.

Now, the whole place was, or it should have been, quite as delightful a place as ever; and yet it did not impress me in the same way. I felt rather disappointed with it. Perhaps it was because little Em'ly was not at home. I knew the way by which she would come, and presently found myself strolling along the path to meet her.

A figure appeared in the distance before long, and I soon knew it to be Em'ly, who was a little creature still in stature, though she was grown. But when she drew nearer, and I saw her blue eyes looking bluer, and her dimpled face looking brighter, and her whole self prettier and gayer, a curious feeling came over me that made me pretend not to know her, and pass by as if I were looking at something a long way off. I have done such a thing since in later life, or I am mistaken.

Little Em'ly didn't care a bit. She saw me well enough; but instead of turning round and calling after me, ran away laughing. This obliged me to run after her, and she ran so fast that we were very near the cottage before I caught her.

'Oh, it's you, is it?' said little Em'ly.

'Why, you knew who it was, Em'ly?' said I.

'And didn't *you* know who it was?' said Em'ly. I was going to kiss her, but she covered her cherry lips with her hands, and said she wasn't a baby now, and ran away, laughing more than ever, into the house.

She seemed to delight in teasing me, which was a change in her I wondered at very much. The teatable was ready, and our little locker was put out in its old place, but instead of coming to sit by me, she went and bestowed her company upon that grumbling Mrs. Gummidge: and on Mr. Peggotty's inquiring why, rumpled her hair all over her face to hide it, and would do nothing but laugh.

'A little puss it is!' said Mr. Peggotty, patting her with his great hand.

'So sh' is! so sh' is!' cried Ham. 'Mas'r Davy bor, so sh' is!' and he sat and chuckled at her for some time, in a state of mingled admiration and delight, that made his face a burning red.

Little Em'ly was spoiled by them all, in fact; and by no one more than Mr. Peggotty himself, whom she could have coaxed into anything by only going and laying her cheek against his rough whisker. That was my opinion, at least, when I saw her do it; and I held Mr. Peggotty to be thoroughly in the right. But she was so affectionate and sweet-natured, and had such a pleasant manner of being both sly and shy at once, that she captivated me more than ever.

She was tender-hearted, too; for when, as we sat round the fire after tea, an allusion was made by Mr. Peggotty over his pipe to the loss I had sustained, the tears stood in her eyes, and she looked at me so kindly across the table, that I felt quite thankful to her.

'Ah!' said Mr. Peggotty, taking up her curls, and running them over his hand like water, 'here 's another orphan, you see, sir. And here,' said Mr. Peggotty, giving Ham a back-handed knock in the chest, 'is another of 'm, though he don't look much like it.'

'If I had you for my guardian, Mr. Peggotty,' said I, shaking my head, 'I don't think I should *feel* much like it.'

'Well said, Mas'r Davy, bor!' cried Ham in an

ecstasy. 'Hoorah! Well said! Nor more you wouldn't! Hor! Hor!'—Here he returned Mr. Peggotty's back-hander, and little Em'ly got up and kissed Mr. Peggotty.

'And how 's your friend, sir?' said Mr. Peggotty to me.

'Steerforth?' said I.

'That 's the name!' cried Mr. Peggotty, turning to Ham. 'I knowed it was something in our way.'

'You said it was Rudderford,' observed Ham, laughing.

'Well!' retorted Mr. Peggotty. 'And ye steer with a rudder, don't ye? It ain't fur off. How is he, sir?'

'He was very well indeed when I came away, Mr. Peggotty.'

'There 's a friend!' said Mr. Peggotty, stretching out his pipe. 'There 's a friend, if you talk of friends! Why, Lord love my heart alive, if it ain't a treat to look at him!'

'He is very handsome, is he not?' said I, my heart warming with this praise.

'Handsome!' cried Mr. Peggotty. 'He stands up to you like—like a—why I don't know what he *don't* stand up to you like. He 's so bold!'

'Yes! That 's just his character,' said I. 'He 's as brave as a lion, and you can't think how frank he is, Mr. Peggotty.'

'And I do suppose, now,' said Mr. Peggotty, looking at me through the smoke of his pipe, 'that in the way of book-larning he 'd take the wind out of a'most anything?'

'Yes,' said I, delighted; 'he knows everything. He is astonishingly clever.'

'There 's a friend!' murmured Mr. Peggotty, with a grave toss of his head.

'Nothing seems to cost him any trouble,' said I.

'He knows a task if he only looks at it.   He is the best cricketer you ever saw.   He will give you almost as many men as you like at draughts, and beat you easily.'

Mr. Peggotty gave his head another toss, as much as to say, 'Of course he will.'

'He is such a speaker,' I pursued, 'that he can win anybody over; and I don't know what you 'd say if you were to hear him sing, Mr. Peggotty.'

Mr. Peggotty gave his head another toss, as much as to say: 'I have no doubt of it.'

'Then, he 's such a generous, fine, noble fellow,' said I, quite carried away by my favourite theme, 'that it 's hardly possible to give him as much praise as he deserves.   I am sure I can never feel thankful enough for the generosity with which he has protected me, so much younger and lower in the school than himself.'

I was running on, very fast indeed, when my eyes rested on little Em'ly's face, which was bent forward over the table, listening with the deepest attention, her breath held, her blue eyes sparkling like jewels, and the colour mantling in her cheeks.   She looked so extraordinarily earnest and pretty, that I stopped in a sort of wonder; and they all observed her at the same time, for as I stopped, they laughed and looked at her.

'Em'ly is like me,' said Peggotty, 'and would like to see him.'

Em'ly was confused by our all observing her, and hung down her head, and her face was covered with blushes.   Glancing up presently through her stray curls, and seeing that we were all looking at her still (I am sure I, for one, could have looked at her for hours), she ran away, and kept away till it was nearly bedtime.

I lay down in the old little bed in the stern of the boat, and the wind came moaning on across the flat as it had done before. But I could not help fancying now, that it moaned of those who were gone; and instead of thinking that the sea might rise in the night and float the boat away, I thought of the sea that had risen, since I last heard those sounds, and drowned my happy home. I recollect, as the wind and water began to sound fainter in my ears, putting a short clause into my prayers, petitioning that I might grow up to marry little Em'ly, and so dropping lovingly asleep.

The days passed pretty much as they had passed before, except—it was a great exception—that little Em'ly and I seldom wandered on the beach now. She had tasks to learn, and needlework to do; and was absent during a great part of each day. But I felt that we should not have had these old wanderings, even if it had been otherwise. Wild and full of childish whims as Em'ly was, she was more of a little woman than I had supposed. She seemed to have got a great distance away from me, in little more than a year. She liked me, but she laughed at me, and tormented me; and when I went to meet her, stole home another way, and was laughing at the door when I came back, disappointed. The best times were when she sat quietly at work in the doorway, and I sat on the wooden steps at her feet, reading to her. It seems to me at this hour, that I have never seen such sunlight as on those bright April afternoons; that I have never seen such a sunny little figure as I used to see, sitting in the doorway of the old boat; that I have never beheld such sky, such water, such glorified ships sailing away into golden air.

On the very first evening after our arrival, Mr.

Barkis appeared in an exceedingly vacant and awkward condition, and with a bundle of oranges tied up in a handkerchief. As he made no allusion of any kind to this property, he was supposed to have left it behind him by accident when he went away; until Ham, running after him to restore it, came back with the information that it was intended for Peggotty. After that occasion he appeared every evening at exactly the same hour, and always with a little bundle, to which he never alluded, and which he regularly put behind the door, and left there. These offerings of affection were of a most various and eccentric description. Among them I remember a double set of pigs' trotters, a huge pincushion, half a bushel or so of apples, a pair of jet earrings, some Spanish onions, a box of dominoes, a canary bird and cage, and a leg of pickled pork.

Mr. Barkis's wooing, as I remember it, was altogether of a peculiar kind. He very seldom said anything; but would sit by the fire in much the same attitude as he sat in his cart, and stare heavily at Peggotty, who was opposite. One night, being, as I suppose, inspired by love, he made a dart at the bit of wax-candle she kept for her thread, and put it in his waistcoat-pocket and carried it off. After that, his great delight was to produce it when it was wanted, sticking to the lining of his pocket, in a partially melted state, and pocket it again when it was done with. He seemed to enjoy himself very much, and not to feel at all called upon to talk. Even when he took Peggotty out for a walk on the flats, he had no uneasiness on that head, I believe; contenting himself with now and then asking her if she was pretty comfortable; and I remember that sometimes, after he was gone, Peggotty would throw her apron over her face, and laugh for half an hour.

Indeed, we were all more or less amused, except that miserable Mrs. Gummidge, whose courtship would appear to have been of an exactly parallel nature, she was so continually reminded by these transactions of the old one.

At length, when the term of my visit was nearly expired, it was given out that Peggotty and Mr. Barkis were going to make a day's holiday together, and that little Em'ly and I were to accompany them. I had but a broken sleep the night before, in anticipation of the pleasure of a whole day with Em'ly. We were all astir betimes in the morning; and while we were yet at breakfast, Mr. Barkis appeared in the distance, driving a chaise-cart towards the object of his affections.

Peggotty was dressed as usual, in her neat and quiet mourning; but Mr. Barkis bloomed in a new blue coat, of which the tailor had given him such good measure, that the cuffs would have rendered gloves unnecessary in the coldest weather, while the collar was so high that it pushed his hair up on end on the top of his head. His bright buttons, too, were of the largest size. Rendered complete by drab pantaloons and a buff waistcoat, I thought Mr. Barkis a phenomenon of respectability.

When we were all in a bustle outside the door, I found that Mr. Peggotty was prepared with an old shoe, which was to be thrown after us for luck, and which he offered to Mrs. Gummidge for that purpose.

'No. It had better be done by somebody else, Dan'l,' said Mrs. Gummidge. 'I 'm a lone lorn creetur' myself, and everythink that reminds me of creeturs that an't lone and lorn, goes contrairy with me.'

'Come, old gal!' cried Mr. Peggotty. 'Take and heave it.'

'No, Dan'l,' returned Mrs. Gummidge, whimpering and shaking her head. 'If I felt less, I could do more. You don't feel like me, Dan'l; thinks don't go contrairy with you, nor you with them; you had better do it yourself.'

But here Peggotty, who had been going about from one to another in a hurried way, kissing everybody, called out from the cart, in which we all were by this time (Em'ly and I on two little chairs, side by side), that Mrs. Gummidge must do it. So Mrs. Gummidge did it; and, I am sorry to relate, cast a damp upon the festive character of our departure, by immediately bursting into tears, and sinking subdued into the arms of Ham, with the declaration that she knowed she was a burden, and had better be carried to the House at once. Which I really thought was a sensible idea, that Ham might have acted on.

Away we went, however, on our holiday excursion; and the first thing we did was to stop at a church, where Mr. Barkis tied the horse to some rails, and went in with Peggotty, leaving little Em'ly and me alone in the chaise. I took that occasion to put my arm round Em'ly's waist, and propose that as I was going away so very soon now, we should determine to be very affectionate to one another, and very happy, all day. Little Em'ly consenting, and allowing me to kiss her, I became desperate; informing her, I recollect, that I never could love another, and that I was prepared to shed the blood of anybody who should aspire to her affections.

How merry little Em'ly made herself about it! With what a demure assumption of being immensely older and wiser than I, the fairy little woman said I was 'a silly boy'; and then laughed so charmingly that I forgot the pain of being called by that disparaging name, in the pleasure of looking at her.

Mr. Barkis and Peggotty were a good while in the church, but came out at last, and then we drove away into the country. As we were going along, Mr. Barkis turned to me, and said, with a wink,—by the bye, I should hardly have thought, before, that he *could* wink—

'What name was it as I wrote up in the cart?'

'Clara Peggotty,' I answered.

'What name would it be as I should write up now, if there was a tilt here?'

'Clara Peggotty, again?' I suggested.

'Clara Peggotty BARKIS!' he returned, and burst into a roar of laughter that shook the chaise.

In a word, they were married, and had gone into the church for no other purpose. Peggotty was resolved that it should be quietly done; and the clerk had given her away, and there had been no witnesses of the ceremony. She was a little confused when Mr. Barkis made this abrupt announcement of their union, and could not hug me enough in token of her unimpaired affection; but she soon became herself again, and said she was very glad it was over.

We drove to a little inn in a bye-road, where we were expected, and where we had a very comfortable dinner, and passed the day with great satisfaction. If Peggotty had been married every day for the last ten years, she could hardly have been more at her ease about it; it made no sort of difference in her: she was just the same as ever, and went out for a stroll with little Em'ly and me before tea, while Mr. Barkis philosophically smoked his pipe, and enjoyed himself, I suppose, with the contemplation of his happiness. If so, it sharpened his appetite; for I distinctly called to mind that, although he had eaten a good deal of pork and greens at dinner, and had finished off with a fowl or two, he was obliged to have cold boiled bacon for tea, and disposed of a large quantity without any emotion.

I have often thought, since, what an odd, innocent, out-of-the-way kind of wedding it must have been! We got into the chaise again soon after dark, and drove cosily back, looking up at the stars, and talking about them. I was their chief exponent, and opened Mr. Barkis's mind to an amazing extent. I told him all I knew, but he would have believed anything I might have taken it into my head to impart to him; for he had a profound veneration for my abilities, and informed his wife in my hearing, on that very occasion, that I was 'a young Roeshus'—by which I think he meant prodigy.

When we had exhausted the subject of the stars, or rather when I had exhausted the mental faculties of Mr. Barkis, little Em'ly and I made a cloak of an old wrapper, and sat under it for the rest of the journey. Ah, how I loved her! What happiness (I thought) if we were married, and were going away anywhere to live among the trees and in the fields, never growing older, never growing wiser, children ever, rambling hand in hand through sunshine and among flowery meadows, laying down our heads on moss at night, in a sweet sleep of purity and peace, and buried by the birds when we were dead! Some such picture, with no real world in it, bright with the light of our innocence, and vague as the stars afar off, was in my mind all the way. I am glad to think there were two such guileless hearts at Peggotty's marriage as little Em'ly's and mine. I am glad to think the Loves and Graces took such airy forms in its homely procession.

Well, we came to the old boat again in good time at night; and there Mr. and Mrs. Barkis bade us good-bye, and drove away snugly to their own home. I felt then, for the first time, that I had lost Peggotty. I should have gone to bed with a sore heart indeed under any other roof but that which sheltered little Em'ly's head.

Mr. Peggotty and Ham knew what was in my thoughts as well as I did, and were ready with some supper and their hospitable faces to drive it away. Little Em'ly came and sat beside me on the locker for the only time in all that visit; and it was altogether a wonderful close to a wonderful day.

It was a night tide; and soon after we went to bed, Mr. Peggotty and Ham went out to fish. I felt very brave at being left alone in the solitary house, the protector of Em'ly and Mrs. Gummidge, and only wished that a lion or a serpent, or any ill-disposed monster, would make an attack upon us, that I might destroy him, and cover myself with glory. But as nothing of the sort happened to be walking about on Yarmouth flats that night, I provided the best substitute I could by dreaming of dragons until morning.

With morning came Peggotty; who called to me, as usual, under my window, as if Mr. Barkis the carrier had been from first to last a dream too. After breakfast she took me to her own home, and a beautiful little home it was. Of all the moveables in it, I must have been most impressed by a certain old bureau of some dark wood in the parlour (the tile-floored kitchen was the general sitting-room), with a retreating top which opened, let down, and became a desk, within which was a large quarto edition of Foxe's Book of Martyrs. This precious volume, of which I do not recollect one word, I immediately discovered and immediately applied myself to; and I never visited the house afterwards, but I kneeled on a chair, opened the casket where this gem was enshrined, spread my arms over the desk, and fell to devouring the book afresh. I was chiefly edified, I am afraid, by the pictures, which were numerous, and represented all kinds of dismal horrors; but the Martyrs and Peggotty's house have been inseparable in my mind ever since, and are now.

I took leave of Mr. Peggotty, and Ham, and Mrs. Gummidge, and little Em'ly, that day; and passed the night at Peggotty's in a little room in the roof (with the crocodile book on a shelf by the bed's head), which was to be always mine, Peggotty said, and should always be kept for me in exactly the same state.

'Young or old, Davy dear, as long as I am alive and have this house over my head,' said Peggotty, 'you shall find it as if I expected you here directly minute. I shall keep it every day, as I used to keep your old little room, my darling; and if you was to go to China, you might think of it as being kept just the same, all the time you were away.'

I felt the truth and constancy of my dear old nurse, with all my heart, and thanked her as well as I could. That was not very well, for she spoke to me thus, with her arms round my neck, in the morning, and I was going home in the morning, and I went home in the morning, with herself and Mr. Barkis in the cart. They left me at the gate, not easily or lightly; and it was a strange sight to me to see the cart go on, taking Peggotty away, and leaving me under the old elm-trees looking at the house in which there was no face to look on mine with love or liking any more.

And now I fell into a state of neglect, which I cannot look back upon without compassion. I fell at once into a solitary condition,—apart from all friendly notice, apart from the society of all other boys of my own age, apart from all companionship but my own spiritless thoughts,—which seems to cast its gloom upon this paper as I write.

What would I have given, to have been sent to the hardest school that ever was kept?—to have been taught something, anyhow, anywhere? No such hope dawned upon me. They disliked me; and they sullenly, sternly, steadily, overlooked me. I think Mr. Murdstone's means were straitened at about this time; but it is little to the purpose. He could not bear me; and in putting me from him, he tried, as I believe, to put away the notion that I had any claim upon him—and succeeded.

I was not actively ill used. I was not beaten, or starved; but the wrong that was done to me had no intervals of relenting, and was done in a systematic, passionless manner. Day after day, week after week, month after month, I was coldly neglected. I wonder sometimes, when I think of it, what they would have done if I had been taken with an illness; whether I should have lain down in my lonely room, and languished through it in my usual solitary way, or whether anybody would have helped me out.

When Mr. and Miss Murdstone were at home, I took my meals with them; in their absence, I ate and drank by myself. At all times I lounged about the house and neighbourhood quite disregarded, except that they were jealous of my making any friends: thinking, perhaps, that if I did, I might complain to some one. For this reason, though Mr. Chillip often asked me to go and see him (he was a widower, having, some years before that, lost a little small light-haired wife, whom I can just remember connecting in my own thoughts with a pale tortoise-shell cat), it was but seldom that I enjoyed the happiness of passing an afternoon in his closet of a surgery; reading some book that was new to me, with the smell of the whole pharmacopœia coming up my nose, or pounding something in a mortar under his mild directions.

For the same reason, added no doubt to the old dislike of her, I was seldom allowed to visit Peggotty. Faithful to her promise, she either came to see me, or met me somewhere near, once every week, and never empty-handed; but many and bitter were the disappointments I had, in being refused permission to pay a visit to her at her house. Some few times, however, at long intervals, I was allowed to go there! and then I found out that Mr. Barkis was something of a miser, or, as Peggotty dutifully expressed it, was 'a little near,' and kept a heap of money in a box under his bed, which he pretended was only full of coats and trousers. In this coffer, his riches hid themselves with such a tenacious modesty, that the smallest instalments could only be tempted out by artifice; so that Peggotty had to prepare a long and elaborate scheme, a very Gunpowder Plot, for every Saturday's expenses.

All this time I was so conscious of the waste of any promise I had given, and of my being utterly neglected, that I should have been perfectly miserable, I have no doubt, but for the old books. They were my only comfort; and I was as true to them as they were to me, and read them over and over I don't know how many times more.

I now approach a period of my life, which I can never lose the remembrance of, while I remember anything; and the recollection of which has often, without my invocation, come before me like a ghost, and haunted happier times.

I had been out, one day, loitering somewhere, in the listless meditative manner that my way of life engendered, when, turning the corner of a lane near our house, I came upon Mr. Murdstone walking with a gentleman. I was confused, and was going by them, when the gentleman cried—

'What? Brooks?'

'No, sir, David Copperfield,' I said.

'Don't tell me. You are Brooks,' said the gentleman. 'You are Brooks of Sheffield. That's your name.'

At these words, I observed the gentleman more attentively. His laugh coming to my remembrance too, I knew him to be Mr. Quinion, whom I had gone over to Lowestoft with Mr. Murdstone to see, before—it is no matter—I need not recall when.

'And how do you get on, and where are you being educated, Brooks?' said Mr. Quinion.

He had put his hand upon my shoulder, and turned me about, to walk with them. I did not know what to reply, and glanced dubiously at Mr. Murdstone.

'He is at home at present,' said the latter. 'He is not being educated anywhere. I don't know what to do with him. He is a difficult subject.'

That old, double look was on me for a moment; and then his eye darkened with a frown, as it turned, in its aversion, elsewhere.

'Humph!' said Mr. Quinion, looking at us both, I thought. 'Fine weather.'

Silence ensued, and I was considering how I could

best disengage my shoulder from his hand, and go away, when he said—

'I suppose you are a pretty sharp fellow still? Eh, Brooks?'

'Ay! He is sharp enough,' said Mr. Murdstone, impatiently. 'You had better let him go. He will not thank you for troubling him.'

On this hint, Mr. Quinion released me, and I made the best of my way home. Looking back as I turned into the front garden, I saw Mr. Murdstone leaning against the wicket of the churchyard, and Mr. Quinion talking to him. They were both looking after me, and I felt that they were speaking of me.

Mr. Quinion lay at our house that night. After breakfast, the next morning, I had put my chair away, and was going out of the room, when Mr. Murdstone called me back. He then gravely repaired to another table, where his sister sat herself at her desk. Mr. Quinion, with his hands in his pockets, stood looking out of window: and I stood looking at them all.

'David,' said Mr. Murdstone, 'to the young this is a world for action; not for moping and droning in.'

'—As you do,' added his sister.

'Jane Murdstone, leave it to me, if you please. I say, David, to the young this is a world for action, and not for moping and droning in. It is especially so for a young boy of your disposition, which requires a great deal of correcting; and to which no greater service can be done than to force it to conform to the ways of the working world, and to bend it and break it.'

'For Stubbornness won't do here,' said his sister. 'What it wants is, to be crushed. And crushed it must be. Shall be, too!'

He gave her a look, half in remonstrance, half in approval, and went on—

'I suppose you know, David, that I am not rich. At any rate, you know it now. You have received some considerable education already. Education is costly; and even if it were not, and I could afford it, I am of opinion that it would not be at all advantageous to you to be kept at a school. What is before you, is a fight with the world; and the sooner you begin it, the better.'

I think it occurred to me that I had already begun it, in my poor way: but it occurs to me now, whether or no.

'You have heard "the counting-house" mentioned sometimes,' said Mr. Murdstone.

'The counting-house, sir?' I repeated.

'Of Murdstone and Grinby, in the wine trade,' he replied.

I suppose I looked uncertain, for he went on hastily—

'You have heard the "counting-house" mentioned, or the business, or the cellars, or the wharf, or something about it.'

'I think I have heard the business mentioned, sir,' I said, remembering what I vaguely knew of his and his sister's resources. 'But I don't know when.'

'It does not matter when,' he returned. 'Mr. Quinion manages that business.'

I glanced at the latter deferentially as he stood looking out of window.

'Mr. Quinion suggests that it gives employment to some other boys, and that he sees no reason why it shouldn't, on the same terms, give employment to you.'

'He having,' Mr. Quinion observed in a low voice,

and half turning round, 'no other prospect, Murdstone.'

Mr. Murdstone, with an impatient, even an angry gesture, resumed, without noticing what he had said—

'Those terms are, that you will earn enough for yourself to provide for your eating and drinking, and pocket-money. Your lodging (which I have arranged for) will be paid by me. So will your washing.'

'Which will be kept down to my estimate,' said his sister.

'Your clothes will be looked after for you, too,' said Mr. Murdstone; 'as you will not be able, yet awhile, to get them for yourself. So you are now going to London, David, with Mr. Quinion, to begin the world on your own account.'

'In short, you are provided for,' observed his sister; 'and will please to do your duty.'

Though I quite understood that the purpose of this announcement was to get rid of me, I have no distinct remembrance whether it pleased or frightened me. My impression is, that I was in a state of confusion about it, and, oscillating between the two points, touched neither. Nor had I much time for the clearing of my thoughts, as Mr. Quinion was to go upon the morrow.

Behold me, on the morrow, in a much-worn little white hat, with a black crape round it for my mother, a black jacket, and a pair of hard stiff corduroy trousers—which Miss Murdstone considered the best armour for the legs in that fight with the world which was now to come off—behold me so attired, and with my little worldly all before me in a small trunk, sitting, a lone lorn child (as Mrs. Gummidge might have said), in the post-chaise that was carrying Mr. Quinion to the London coach at Yarmouth! See, how our house and church are lessening in the distance; how the grave beneath the tree is blotted out by intervening objects; how the spire points upward from my old playground no more, and the sky is empty!

CHAPTER XI

I BEGIN LIFE ON MY OWN ACCOUNT, AND DON'T LIKE IT

I KNOW enough of the world now, to have almost lost the capacity of being much surprised by anything; but it is matter of some surprise to me, even now, that I can have been so easily thrown away at such an age. A child of excellent abilities, and with strong powers of observation, quick, eager, delicate, and soon hurt bodily or mentally, it seems wonderful to me that nobody should have made any sign in my behalf. But none was made; and I became, at ten years old, a little labouring hind in the service of Murdstone and Grinby.

Murdstone and Grinby's warehouse was at the water-side. It was down in Blackfriars. Modern improvements have altered the place; but it was the last house at the bottom of a narrow street, curving down hill to the river, with some stairs at the end, where people took boat. It was a crazy old house with a wharf of its own, abutting on the water when the tide was in, and on the mud when the tide was out, and literally overrun with rats. Its panelled rooms, discoloured with the dirt and smoke of a hundred years, I dare say; its decaying floors and staircase; the squeaking and scuffling of the old grey rats down in the cellars; and the dirt and rottenness of the place; are things, not of many years ago, in my mind, but of the present instant. They are all before me, just as they were in the evil hour when I went among them for the first time, with my trembling hand in Mr. Quinion's.

Murdstone and Grinby's trade was among a good many kinds of people, but an important branch of it was the supply of wines and spirits to certain packet-ships. I forget now where they chiefly went, but I think there were some among them that made voyages both to the East and West Indies. I know that a great many empty bottles were one of the consequences of this traffic, and that certain men and boys were employed to examine them against the light, and reject those that were flawed, and to rinse and wash them. When the empty bottles ran short, there were labels to be pasted on full ones, or corks to be fitted to them, or seals to be put upon the corks, or finished bottles to be packed in casks. All this work was my work, and of the boys employed upon it I was one.

There were three or four of us, counting me. My working place was established in a corner of the warehouse, where Mr. Quinion could see me, when he chose to stand up on the bottom rail of his stool in the counting-house, and look at me through a window above the desk. Hither, on the first morning of my so auspiciously beginning life on my own account, the oldest of the regular boys was summoned to show me my business. His name was Mick Walker, and he wore a ragged apron and a paper cap. He informed me that his father was a bargeman, and walked, in a black velvet headdress, in the Lord Mayor's Show. He also informed me that our principal associate would be another boy whom he introduced by the—to me—extraordinary name of Mealy

Potatoes. I discovered, however, that this youth had not been christened by that name, but that it had been bestowed upon him in the warehouse, on account of his complexion, which was pale or mealy. Mealy's father was a waterman, who had the additional distinction of being a fireman, and was engaged as such at one of the large theatres; where some young relation of Mealy's—I thing his little sister—did Imps in the Pantomimes.

No words can express the secret agony of my soul as I sunk into this companionship; compared these henceforth every-day associates with those of my happier childhood—not to say with Steerforth, Traddles, and the rest of those boys; and felt my hopes of growing up to be a learned and distinguished man crushed in my bosom. The deep remembrance of the sense I had, of being utterly without hope now; of the shame I felt in my position; of the misery it was to my young heart to believe that day by day what I had learned, and thought, and delighted in, and raised my fancy and my emulation up by, would pass away from me, little by little, never to be brought back any more; cannot be written. As often as Mick Walker went away in the course of that forenoon, I mingled my tears with the water in which I was washing the bottles; and sobbed as if there were a flaw in my own breast, and it were in danger of bursting.

The counting-house clock was at half-past twelve, and there was general preparation for going to dinner, when Mr. Quinion tapped at the counting-house window, and beckoned to me to go in. I went in, and found there a stoutish, middle-aged person, in a brown surtout and black tights and shoes, with no more hair upon his head (which was a large one, and very shining) than there is upon an egg, and with a very extensive face, which he turned full upon me. His clothes were shabby, but he had an imposing shirt-collar on. He carried a jaunty sort of a stick, with a large pair of rusty tassels to it; and a quizzing-glass hung outside his coat,—for ornament, I after-wards found, as he very seldom looked through it, and couldn't see anything when he did.

'This,' said Mr. Quinion, in allusion to myself, 'is he.'

'This,' said the stranger, with a certain condescend-ing roll in his voice, and a certain indescribable air of doing something genteel, which impressed me very much, 'is Master Copperfield. I hope I see you well, sir?'

I said I was very well, and hoped he was. I was sufficiently ill at ease, Heaven knows; but it was not in my nature to complain much at that time of my life, so I said I was very well, and hoped he was.

'I am,' said the stranger, 'thank Heaven, quite well. I have received a letter from Mr. Murdstone, in which he mentions that he would desire me to receive into an apartment in the rear of my house, which is at present unoccupied—and is, in short, to be let as a— in short,' said the stranger, with a smile and in a burst of confidence, 'as a bedroom—the young beginner whom I have now the pleasure to—' and the stranger waved his hand, and settled his chin in his shirt-collar.

'This is Mr. Micawber,' said Mr. Quinion to me.

'Ahem!' said the stranger, 'that is my name.'

'Mr. Micawber,' said Mr. Quinion, 'is known to Mr. Murdstone. He takes orders for us on commis-sion, when he can get any. He has been written to by Mr. Murdstone, on the subject of your lodgings, and he will receive you as a lodger.'

'My address,' said Mr. Micawber, 'is Windsor Terrace, City Road. I—in short,' said Mr. Micawber, with the same genteel air, and in another burst of confidence—'I live there.'

I made him a bow.

'Under the impression,' said Mr. Micawber, 'that your peregrinations in this metropolis have not as yet been extensive, and that you might have some difficulty in penetrating the arcana of the Modern Babylon in the direction of the City Road—in short,' said Mr. Micawber, in another burst of confidence, 'that you might lose yourself—I shall be happy to call this evening, and instal you in the knowledge of the nearest way.'

I thanked him with all my heart, for it was friendly in him to offer to take that trouble.

'At what hour,' said Mr. Micawber, 'shall I—'

'At about eight,' said Mr. Quinion.

'At about eight,' said Mr. Micawber. 'I beg to wish you good-day, Mr. Quinion. I will intrude no longer.'

So he put on his hat, and went out with his cane under his arm: very upright, and humming a tune when he was clear of the counting-house.

Mr. Quinion then formally engaged me to be as useful as I could in the warehouse of Murdstone and Grinby, at a salary, I think, of six shillings a week. I am not clear whether it was six or seven. I am inclined to believe, from my uncertainty on this head, that it was six at first and seven afterwards. He paid me a week down (from his own pocket, I believe), and I gave Mealy sixpence out of it to get my trunk carried to Windsor Terrace at night: it being too heavy for my strength, small as it was. I paid sixpence more for my dinner, which was a meat pie and a turn at a neighbouring pump; and passed the hour which was allowed for that meal, in walking about the streets.

At the appointed time in the evening, Mr. Micawber reappeared. I washed my hands and face, to do the greater honour to his gentility, and we walked to our house, as I suppose I must now call it, together; Mr. Micawber impressing the names of streets, and the shapes of corner houses upon me, as we went along, that I might find my way back, easily, in the morning.

Arrived at his house in Windsor Terrace (which I noticed was shabby like himself, but also, like himself, made all the show it could), he presented me to Mrs. Micawber, a thin and faded lady, not at all young, who was sitting in the parlour (the first floor was altogether unfurnished, and the blinds were kept down to delude the neighbours), with a baby at her breast. This baby was one of twins; and I may remark here that I hardly ever, in all my experience of the family, saw both the twins detached from Mrs. Micawber at the same time. One of them was always taking refreshment.

There were two other children; Master Micawber, aged about four, and Miss Micawber, aged about three. These, and a dark-complexioned young woman, with a habit of snorting, who was servant to the family, and informed me, before half an hour had expired, that she was 'a Orfling,' and came from St. Luke's workhouse, in the neighbourhood, completed the establishment. My room was at the top of the house, at the back: a close chamber; stencilled all over with an ornament which my young imagination represented as a blue muffin; and very scantily furnished.

'I never thought,' said Mrs. Micawber, when she came up, twin and all, to show me the apartment, and sat down to take breath, 'before I married, when I lived with papa and mamma, that I should ever find it necessary to take a lodger. But Mr. Micawber being in difficulties, all considerations of private feeling must give way.'

I said, 'Yes, ma'am.'

'Mr. Micawber's difficulties are almost overwhelming at present,' said Mrs. Micawber; 'and whether it is possible to bring him through them, I don't know. When I lived at home with papa and mamma, I really should have hardly understood what the word meant, in the sense in which I now employ it, but experientia does it—as papa used to say.'

I cannot satisfy myself whether she told me that Mr. Micawber had been an officer in the Marines, or whether I have imagined it. I only know that I believe to this hour that he *was* in the Marines once upon a time, without knowing why. He was a sort of town traveller for a number of miscellaneous houses, now; but made little or nothing of it, I am afraid.

'If Mr. Micawber's creditors *will not* give him time,' said Mrs. Micawber, 'they must take the consequences; and the sooner they bring it to an issue the better. Blood cannot be obtained from a stone, neither can anything on account be obtained at present (not to mention law expenses) from Mr. Micawber.'

I never can quite understand whether my precocious self-dependence confused Mrs. Micawber in reference to my age, or whether she was so full of the subject that she would have talked about it to the very twins if there had been nobody else to communicate with, but this was the strain in which she began, and she went on accordingly all the time I knew her.

Poor Mrs. Micawber! She said she had tried to

exert herself; and so, I have no doubt, she had. The centre of the street-door was perfectly covered with a great brass plate, on which was engraved 'Mrs. Micawber's Boarding Establishment for Young Ladies': but I never found that any young lady had ever been to school there; or that any young lady ever came, or proposed to come; or that the least preparation was ever made to receive any young lady. The only visitors I ever saw or heard of, were creditors. *They* used to come at all hours, and some of them were quite ferocious. One dirty-faced man, I think he was a bootmaker, used to edge himself into the passage as early as seven o'clock in the morning, and call up the stairs, to Mr. Micawber—'Come! You ain't out yet, you know. Pay us, will you? Don't hide, you know; that's mean. I wouldn't be mean if I was you. Pay us, will you? You just pay us, d'ye hear? Come!' Receiving no answer to these taunts, he would mount in his wrath to the words 'swindlers' and 'robbers'; and these being ineffectual too, would sometimes go to the extremity of crossing the street, and roaring up at the windows of the second floor, where he knew Mr. Micawber was. At these times, Mr. Micawber would be transported with grief and mortification, even to the length (as I was once made aware by a scream from his wife) of making motions at himself with a razor; but within half an hour afterwards, he would polish up his shoes with extraordinary pains, and go out, humming a tune with a greater air of gentility than ever. Mrs. Micawber was quite as elastic. I have known her to be thrown into fainting fits by the king's taxes at three o'clock, and to eat lamb chops breaded, and drink warm ale (paid for with two teaspoons that had gone to the pawnbroker's) at four. On one occasion, when an execution had just been put in, coming home through some chance as early as six o'clock, I saw her lying (of course with a twin) under the grate in a swoon, with her hair all torn about her face; but I never knew her more cheerful than she was, that very same night, over a veal-cutlet before the kitchen fire, telling me stories about her papa and mamma, and the company they used to keep.

In this house, and with this family, I passed my leisure time. My own exclusive breakfast of a penny loaf, and a pennyworth of milk, I provided myself, I kept another small loaf, and a modicum of cheese, on a particular shelf of a particular cupboard, to make my supper on when I came back at night. This made a hole in the six or seven shillings, I know well; and I was out at the warehouse all day, and had to support myself on that money all the week. From Monday morning until Saturday night, I had no advice, no counsel, no encouragement, no consolation, no assistance, no support, of any kind, from any one, that I can call to mind, as I hope to go to heaven!

I was so young and childish, and so little qualified —how could I be otherwise?—to undertake the whole charge of my own existence, that often, in going to Murdstone and Grinby's, of a morning, I could not resist the stale pastry put out for sale at half-price at the pastry-cooks' doors, and spent in that, the money I should have kept for my dinner. Then, I went without my dinner, or bought a roll or a slice of pudding. I remember two pudding-shops, between which I was divided, according to my finances. One was in a court close to St. Martin's Church—at the back of the church,—which is now removed altogether. The pudding at that shop was made of currants, and was rather a special pudding, but was dear, twopennyworth not being larger than a pennyworth of more ordinary pudding. A good shop for the latter was ın the Strand—somewhere in that part which has been rebuilt since. It was a stout pale pudding, heavy and flabby, and with great flat raisins in it, stuck in whole at wide distances apart. It came up hot at about my time every day, and many a day did I dine off it. When I dined regularly and handsomely, I had a saveloy and a penny loaf, or a fourpenny plate of red beef from a cook's shop; or a plate of bread and cheese and a glass of beer, from a miserable old public-house opposite our place of business, called the Lion, or the Lion and something else that I have forgotten. Once, I remember carrying my own bread (which I had brought from home in the morning) under my arm, wrapped in a piece of paper, like a book, and going to a famous alamode beef-house near Drury Lane, and ordering a 'small plate' of that delicacy to eat with it. What the waiter thought of such a strange little apparition coming in all alone, I don't know; but I can see him now, staring at me as I ate my dinner, and bringing up the other waiter to look. I gave him a halfpenny for himself, and I wish he hadn't taken it.

We had half an hour, I think, for tea. When I had money enough, I used to get half a pint of ready-made coffee and a slice of bread-and-butter. When I had none, I used to look at a venison-shop in Fleet Street; or I have strolled, at such a time, as far as Covent Garden Market, and stared at the pine-apples. I was fond of wandering about the Adelphi, because it was a mysterious place, with those dark arches. I see myself emerging one evening from some of these arches, on a little public-house close to the river, with an open space before it, where some coal-heavers were dancing; to look at whom I sat down upon a bench. I wonder what they thought of me!

I was such a child, and so little, that frequently

when I went into the bar of a strange public-house for a glass of ale or porter, to moisten what I had had for dinner they were afraid to give it me. I remember one hot evening I went into the bar of a public-house, and said to the landlord—

'What is your best—your *very best*—ale a glass?' For it was a special occasion. I don't know what. It may have been my birthday.

'Twopence-halfpenny,' says the landlord, 'is the price of the Genuine Stunning ale.'

'Then,' says I, producing the money, 'just draw me a glass of the Genuine Stunning, if you please, with a good head to it.'

The landlord looked at me in return over the bar, from head to foot, with a strange smile on his face; and instead of drawing the beer, looked round the screen and said something to his wife. She came out from behind it, with her work in her hand, and joined him in surveying me. Here we stand, all three, before me now. The landlord in his shirt-sleeves, leaning against the bar window-frame; his wife looking over the little half-door; and I, in some confusion, looking up at them from outside the partition. They asked me a good many questions; as, what my name was, how old I was, where I lived, how I was employed, and how I came there. To all of which, that I might commit nobody, I invented, I am afraid, appropriate answers. They served me with the ale, though I suspect it was not the Genuine Stunning: and the landlord's wife, opening the little half-door of the bar, and bending down, gave me my money back, and gave me a kiss that was half admiring, and half compassionate, but all womanly and good, I am sure.

I know I do not exaggerate, unconsciously and unintentionally, the scantiness of my resources or the difficulties of my life. I know that if a shilling were given me by Mr. Quinion at any time, I spent it in a dinner or a tea. I know that I worked from morning until night, with common men and boys, a shabby child. I know that I lounged about the streets, insufficiently and unsatisfactorily fed. I know that, but for the mercy of God, I might easily have been, for any care that was taken of me, a little robber or a vagabond.

Yet I held some station at Murdstone and Grinby's too. Besides that Mr. Quinion did what a careless man so occupied, and dealing with a thing so anomalous, could, to treat me as one upon a different footing from the rest, I never said, to man or boy, how it was that I came to be there, or gave the least indication of being sorry that I was there. That I suffered in secret, and that I suffered exquisitely, no one ever knew but I. How much I suffered, it is, as I have said already, utterly beyond my power to tell. But I kept my own counsel, and I did my work. I knew from the first, that, if I could not do my work as well as any of the rest, I could not hold myself above slight and contempt. I soon became at least as expeditious and as skilful as either of the other boys. Though perfectly familiar with them, my conduct and manner were different enough from theirs to place a space between us. They and the men generally spoke of me as 'the little gent,' or 'the young Suffolker.' A certain man named Gregory, who was foreman of the packers, and another named Tipp, who was the carman, and wore a red jacket, used to address me sometimes as 'David': but I think it was mostly when we were very confidential, and when I had made some efforts to entertain them, over our work, with some results of the old readings; which were fast perishing out of my remembrance. Mealy Potatoes uprose once, and rebelled against my being so distinguished; but Mick Walker settled him in no time.

My rescue from this kind of existence I considered quite hopeless, and abandoned, as such, altogether. I am solemnly convinced that I never for one hour was reconciled to it, or was otherwise than miserably unhappy; but I bore it; and even to Peggotty, partly for the love of her and partly for shame, never in any letter (though many passed between us) revealed the truth.

Mr. Micawber's difficulties were an addition to the distressed state of my mind. In my forlorn state I became quite attached to the family, and used to walk about, busy with Mrs. Micawber's calculations of ways and means, and heavy with the weight of Mr. Micawber's debts. On a Saturday night, which was my grand treat,—partly because it was a great thing to walk home with six or seven shillings in my pocket, looking into the shops and thinking what such a sum would buy, and partly because I went home early,—Mrs. Micawber would make the most heart-rending confidences to me; also on a Sunday morning, when I mixed the portion of tea or coffee I had bought overnight, in a little shaving-pot, and sat late at my breakfast. It was nothing at all unusual for Mr. Micawber to sob violently at the beginning of one of these Saturday night conversations, and sing about Jack's delight being his lovely Nan, towards the end of it. I have known him come home to supper with a flood of tears, and a declaration that nothing was now left but a jail; and go to bed making a calculation of the expense of putting bow-windows to the house, 'in case anything turned up,' which was his favourite expression. And Mrs. Micawber was just the same.

A curious equality of friendship, originating, I suppose, in our respective circumstances, sprung up between me and these people notwithstanding the ludicrous disparity in our years. But I never allowed myself to be prevailed upon to accept any invitation to eat and drink with them out of their stock (knowing that they got on badly with the butcher and baker, and had often not too much for themselves), until Mrs. Micawber took me into her entire confidence. This she did one evening as follows:—

'Master Copperfield,' said Mrs. Micawber, 'I make no stranger of you, and therefore do not hesitate to say that Mr. Micawber's difficulties are coming to a crisis.'

It made me very miserable to hear it, and I looked at Mrs. Micawber's red eyes with the utmost sympathy.

'With the exception of the heel of a Dutch cheese —which is not adapted to the wants of a young family'—said Mrs. Micawber, 'there is really not a scrap of anything in the larder. I was accustomed to speak of the larder when I lived with papa and mamma, and I use the word almost unconsciously. What I mean to express is, that there is nothing to eat in the house.'

'Dear me!' I said, in great concern.

I had two or three shillings of my week's money in my pocket—from which I presume that it must have been on a Wednesday night when we held this conversation—and I hastily produced them, and with heartfelt emotion begged Mrs. Micawber to accept of them as a loan. But that lady, kissing me, and making me put them back in my pocket, replied that she couldn't think of it.

'No, my dear Master Copperfield,' said she, 'far be it from my thoughts! But you have a discretion beyond your years, and can render me another kind of service, if you will; and a service I will thankfully accept of.'

I begged Mrs. Micawber to name it.

'I have parted with the plate myself,' said Mrs. Micawber. 'Six tea, two salt, and a pair of sugars, I have at different times borrowed money on, in secret, with my own hands. But the twins are a great tie; and to me, with my recollections of papa and mamma, these transactions are very painful. There are still a few trifles that we could part with. Mr. Micawber's feelings would never allow *him* to dispose of them; and Clickett'—this was the girl from the workhouse—'being of a vulgar mind, would take painful liberties if so much confidence was reposed in her. Master Copperfield, if I might ask you'—

I understood Mrs. Micawber now, and begged her to make use of me to any extent. I began to dispose of the more portable articles of property that very evening; and went out on a similar expedition almost every morning, before I went to Murdstone and Grinby's.

Mr. Micawber had a few books on a little chiffonier, which he called the library; and those went first. I carried them, one after another, to a bookstall in the City Road—one part of which, near our house, was almost all bookstalls and bird-shops then —and sold them for whatever they would bring. The keeper of this bookstall, who lived in a little house behind it, used to get tipsy every night, and to be violently scolded by his wife every morning. More than once, when I went there early, I had audience of him in a turn-up bedstead, with a cut in his forehead or a black eye, bearing witness to his excesses overnight (I am afraid he was quarrelsome in his drink), and he with a shaking hand, endeavouring to find the needful shillings in one or other of the pockets of his clothes, which lay upon the floor, while his wife, with a baby in her arms and her shoes down at heel, never left off rating him. Sometimes he had lost his money, and then he would ask me to call again; but his wife had always got some—had taken his, I dare say, while he was drunk—and secretly completed the bargain on the stairs, as we went down together.

At the pawnbroker's shop, too, I began to be very well known. The principal gentleman who officiated behind the counter, took a good deal of notice of me; and often got me, I recollect, to decline a Latin noun or adjective, or to conjugate a Latin verb, in his ear, while he transacted my business. After all these occasions Mrs. Micawber made a little treat, which was generally a supper; and there was a peculiar relish in these meals which I well remember.

At last Mr. Micawber's difficulties came to a crisis, and he was arrested early one morning, and carried over to the King's Bench Prison in the Borough. He told me, as he went out of the house, that the God of day had now gone down upon him—and I really thought his heart was broken and mine too. But I heard, afterwards, that he was seen to play a lively game at skittles, before noon.

On the first Sunday after he was taken there, I was to go and see him, and have dinner with him. I was to ask my way to such a place, and just short of that place I should see such another place, and just short of that I should see a yard, which I was to cross, and keep straight on until I saw a turnkey. All this I did; and when at last I did see a turnkey (poor little fellow that I was!), and thought how, when Roderick Random was in a debtors' prison, there was a man there with nothing on him but an old rug, the turnkey swam before my dimmed eyes and my beating heart.

Mr. Micawber was waiting for me within the gate, and we went up to his room (top story but one), and cried very much. He solemnly conjured me, I remember, to take warning by his fate; and to observe that if a man had twenty pounds a-year for his income, and spent nineteen pounds nineteen shillings and sixpence, he would be happy, but that if he spent twenty pounds one he would be miserable. After which he borrowed a shilling of me for porter, gave me a written order on Mrs. Micawber for the amount, and put away his pocket-handkerchief, and cheered up.

We sat before a little fire, with two bricks put within the rusted grate, one on each side, to prevent its burning too many coals; until another debtor, who shared the room with Mr. Micawber, came in from the bakehouse with the loin of mutton which was our joint-stock repast. Then I was sent up to 'Captain Hopkins' in the room overhead, with Mr. Micawber's compliments, and I was his young friend, and would Captain Hopkins lend me a knife and fork.

Captain Hopkins lent me the knife and fork, with his compliments to Mr. Micawber. There was a very dirty lady in his little room, and two wan girls, his daughters, with shock heads of hair. I thought it was better to borrow Captain Hopkins's knife and fork, than Captain Hopkins's comb. The captain himself was in the last extremity of shabbiness, with large whiskers, and an old, old brown great-coat with no other coat below it. I saw his bed rolled up in a corner; and what plates and dishes and pots he had, on a shelf; and I divined (God knows how) that though the two girls with the shock heads of hair were Captain Hopkins's children, the dirty lady was not married to Captain Hopkins. My timid station on his threshold was not occupied more than a couple of minutes at most; but I came down again with all this in my knowledge, as surely as the knife and fork were in my hand.

There was something gipsy-like and agreeable in the dinner, after all. I took back Captain Hopkins's knife and fork early in the afternoon, and went home to comfort Mrs. Micawber with an account of my visit. She fainted when she saw me return, and made a little jug of egg-hot afterwards to console us while we talked it over.

I don't know how the household furniture came to be sold for the family benefit, or who sold it, except that *I* did not. Sold it was, however, and carried away in a van; except the bed, a few chairs, and the kitchen-table. With these possessions we encamped, as it were, in the two parlours of the emptied house in Windsor Terrace; Mrs. Micawber, the children, the Orfling, and myself; and lived in those rooms night and day. I have no idea for how long, though it seems to me for a long time. At last Mrs. Micawber resolved to move into the prison, where Mr. Micawber had now secured a room to himself. So I took the key of the house to the landlord, who was very glad to get it; and the beds were sent over to the King's Bench, except mine, for which a little room was hired outside the walls in the neighbourhood of that Institution, very much to my satisfaction, since the Micawbers and I had become too used to one another, in our troubles, to part. The Orfling was likewise accommodated with an inexpensive lodging in the same neighbourhood. Mine was a quiet back-garret with a sloping roof, commanding a pleasant prospect of a timber-yard, and when I took possession of it, with the reflection that

Mr. Micawber's troubles had come to a crisis at last,
I thought it quite a paradise.

All this time I was working at Murdstone and
Grinby's in the same common way, and with the same
common companions, and with the same sense of
unmerited degradation as at first. But I never,
happily for me no doubt, made a single acquaintance,
or spoke to any of the many boys whom I saw daily
in going to the warehouse, in coming from it, and in
prowling about the streets at meal-times. I led the
same secretly unhappy life; but I led it in the same
lonely, self-reliant manner. The only changes I am
conscious of are, firstly, that I had grown more
shabby, and secondly, that I was now relieved of
much of the weight of Mr. and Mrs. Micawber's
cares; for some relatives or friends had engaged to
help them at their present pass, and they lived
more comfortably in the prison than they had lived
for a long while out of it. I used to breakfast with
them now, in virtue of some arrangement, of which
I have forgotten the details. I forget, too, at what
hour the gates were opened in the morning, admitting
of my going in; but I know that I was often
up at six o'clock, and that my favourite lounging-
place in the interval was old London Bridge, where
I was wont to sit in one of the stone recesses,
watching the people going by, or to look over the
balustrades at the sun shining in the water, and
lighting up the golden flame on the top of the Monument. The Orfling met me here sometimes, to be
told some astonishing fictions respecting the wharves
and the Tower; of which I can say no more than
that I hope I believed them myself. In the evening
I used to go back to the prison, and walk up and
down the parade with Mr. Micawber; or play casino
with Mrs. Micawber, and hear reminiscences of her

papa and mamma.   Whether Mr. Murdstone knew
where I was, I am unable to say.   I never told them
at Murdstone and Grinby's.

Mr. Micawber's affairs, although past their crisis,
were very much involved by reason of a certain
'Deed,' of which I used to hear a great deal, and
which I suppose, now, to have been some former
composition with his creditors, though I was so far
from being clear about it then, that I am conscious
of having confounded it with those demoniacal parch-
ments which are held to have, once upon a time, obtained to a great extent in Germany.   At last this
document appeared to be got out of the way, somehow; at all events it ceased to be the rock ahead it
had been; and Mrs. Micawber informed me that 'her
family' had decided that Mr. Micawber should apply
for his release under the Insolvent Debtors' Act,
which would set him free, she expected, in about six
weeks.

'And then,' said Mr. Micawber, who was present,
'I have no doubt I shall, please Heaven, begin to be
beforehand with the world, and to live in a perfectly
new manner, if—in short, if anything turns up.'

By way of going in for anything that might be
on the cards, I call to mind that Mr. Micawber, about
this time, composed a petition to the House of Commons, praying for an alteration in the law of imprisonment for debt.   I set down this remembrance here,
because it is an instance to myself of the manner in
which I fitted my old books to my altered life, and
made stories for myself, out of the streets, and out
of men and women; and how some main points in the
character I shall unconsciously develop, I suppose,
in writing my life, were gradually forming all this
while.

There was a club in the prison, in which Mr.

Micawber, as a gentleman, was a great authority. Mr. Micawber had stated his idea of this petition to the club, and the club had strongly approved of the same. Wherefore Mr. Micawber (who was a thoroughly good-natured man, and as active a creature about everything but his own affairs as ever existed, and never so happy as when he was busy about something that could never be of any profit to him) set to work at the petition, invented it, engrossed it on an immense sheet of paper, spread it out on a table, and appointed a time for all the club, and all within the walls if they chose, to come up to his room and sign it.

When I heard of this approaching ceremony, I was so anxious to see them all come in, one after another, though I knew the greater part of them already, and they me, that I got an hour's leave of absence from Murdstone and Grinby's, and established myself in a corner for that purpose. As many of the principal members of the club as could be got into the small room without filling it, supported Mr. Micawber in front of the petition, while my old friend Captain Hopkins (who had washed himself, to do honour to so solemn an occasion) stationed himself close to it, to read it to all who were unacquainted with its contents. The door was then thrown open, and the general population began to come in, in a long file: several waiting outside, while one entered, affixed his signature, and went out. To everybody in succession, Captain Hopkins said, 'Have you read it?'—'No.'—'Would you like to hear it read?' If he weakly showed the least disposition to hear it, Captain Hopkins, in a loud sonorous voice, gave him every word of it. The Captain would have read it twenty thousand times, if twenty thousand people would have heard him, one by one. I remember a certain luscious roll he gave to such phrases as 'The people's representatives in Parliament assembled,' 'Your petitioners therefore humbly approach your honourable house,' 'His gracious Majesty's unfortunate subjects,' as if the words were something real in his mouth, and delicious to taste; Mr. Micawber, meanwhile, listening with a little of an author's vanity, and contemplating (not severely) the spikes on the opposite wall.

As I walked to and fro daily between Southwark and Blackfriars, and lounged about at meal-times in obscure streets, the stones of which may, for anything I know, be worn at this moment by my childish feet, I wonder how many of these people were wanting in the crowd that used to come filing before me in review again, to the echo of Captain Hopkins's voice! When my thoughts go back now, to that slow agony of my youth, I wonder how much of the histories I invented for such people hangs like a mist of fancy over well-remembered facts! When I tread the old ground, I do not wonder that I seem to see and pity, going on before me, an innocent romantic boy, making his imaginative world out of such strange experiences and sordid things.

CHAPTER XII

LIKING LIFE ON MY OWN ACCOUNT NO BETTER, I FORM A GREAT RESOLUTION

In due time, Mr. Micawber's petition was ripe for hearing; and that gentleman was ordered to be discharged under the act, to my great joy. His creditors were not implacable; and Mrs. Micawber informed me that even the revengeful bootmaker had declared in open court that he bore him no malice, but that when money was owing to him he liked to be paid. He said he thought it was human nature.

Mr. Micawber returned to the King's Bench when his case was over, as some fees were to be settled, and some formalities observed, before he could be actually released. The club received him with transport, and held an harmonic meeting that evening in his honour; while Mrs. Micawber and I had a lamb's fry in private, surrounded by the sleeping family.

'On such an occasion I will give you, Master Copperfield,' said Mrs. Micawber, 'in a little more flip,' for we had been having some already, 'the memory of my papa and mamma.'

'Are they dead, ma'am?' I inquired, after drinking the toast in a wine-glass.

'My mamma departed this life,' said Mrs. Micawber, 'before Mr. Micawber's difficulties commenced, or at least before they became pressing. My papa lived to bail Mr. Micawber several times, and then expired, regretted by a numerous circle.'

Mrs. Micawber shook her head, and dropped a pious tear upon the twin who happened to be in hand.

As I could hardly hope for a more favourable opportunity of putting a question in which I had a near interest, I said to Mrs. Micawber—

'May I ask, ma'am, what you and Mr. Micawber intend to do, now that Mr. Micawber is out of his difficulties, and at liberty? Have you settled yet?'

'My family,' said Mrs. Micawber, who always said those two words with an air, though I never could discover who came under the denomination, 'my family are of opinion that Mr. Micawber should quit London, and exert his talents in the country. Mr.

Micawber is a man of great talent, Master Copperfield.'

I said I was sure of that.

'Of great talent,' repeated Mrs. Micawber. 'My
family are of opinion, that, with a little interest,
something might be done for a man of his ability in
the Custom House. The influence of my family
being local, it is their wish that Mr. Micawber should
go down to Plymouth. They think it indispensable
that he should be upon the spot.'

'That he may be ready?' I suggested.

'Exactly,' returned Mrs. Micawber. 'That he may
be ready in case of anything turning up.'

'And do you go too, ma'am?'

The events of the day, in combination with the
twins, if not with the flip, had made Mrs. Micawber
hysterical, and she shed tears as she replied—

'I never will desert Mr. Micawber. Mr. Micawber
may have concealed his difficulties from me in the
first instance, but his sanguine temper may have led
him to expect that he would overcome them. The
pearl necklace and bracelets which I inherited from
mamma, have been disposed of for less than half their
value; and the set of coral, which was the wedding
gift of my papa, has been actually thrown away for
nothing. But I never will desert Mr. Micawber.
No!' cried Mrs. Micawber, more affected than before,
'I never will do it! It's of no use asking me!'

I felt quite uncomfortable—as if Mrs. Micawber
supposed I had asked her to do anything of the sort!
—and sat looking at her in alarm.

'Mr. Micawber has his faults. I do not deny that
he is improvident. I do not deny that he has kept
me in the dark as to his resources and his liabilities,
both,' she went on, looking at the wall; 'but I never
will desert Mr. Micawber!'

Mrs. Micawber having now raised her voice into a perfect scream, I was so frightened that I ran off to the club-room, and disturbed Mr. Micawber in the act of presiding at a long table, and leading the chorus of

'Gee up, Dobbin,
Gee ho, Dobbin,
Gee up, Dobbin,
Gee up, and gee ho—o—o !'

—with the tidings that Mrs. Micawber was in an alarming state, upon which he immediately burst into tears, and came away with me with his waistcoat full of the heads and tails of shrimps, of which he had been partaking.

'Emma, my angel!' cried Mr. Micawber, running into the room; 'what is the matter?'

'I never will desert you, Micawber!' she exclaimed.

'My life!' said Mr. Micawber, taking her in his arms. 'I am perfectly aware of it.'

'He is the parent of my children! He is the father of my twins! He is the husband of my affections,' cried Mrs. Micawber, struggling; 'and I ne—ver—will—desert Mr. Micawber!'

Mr. Micawber was so deeply affected by this proof of her devotion (as to me, I was dissolved in tears), that he hung over her in a passionate manner, imploring her to look up, and to be calm. But the more he asked Mrs. Micawber to look up, the more she fixed her eyes on nothing; and the more he asked her to compose herself, the more she wouldn't. Consequently Mr. Micawber was soon so overcome, that he mingled his tears with hers and mine; until he begged me to do him the favour of taking a chair on the staircase, while he got her into bed. I would have taken my leave for the night, but he would not hear of my doing that until the strangers' bell should ring. So I sat at the staircase window, until he came out with another chair and joined me.

'How is Mrs. Micawber now, sir?' I said.

'Very low,' said Mr. Micawber, shaking his head; 'reaction. Ah, this has been a dreadful day! We stand alone now—everything is gone from us!'

Mr. Micawber pressed my hand, and groaned, and afterwards shed tears. I was greatly touched, and disappointed too, for I had expected that we should be quite gay on this happy and long-looked-for occasion. But Mr. and Mrs. Micawber were so used to their old difficulties, I think, that they felt quite shipwrecked when they came to consider that they were released from them. All their elasticity was departed, and I never saw them half so wretched as on this night; insomuch that when the bell rang, and Mr. Micawber walked with me to the lodge, and parted from me there with a blessing, I felt quite afraid to leave him by himself, he was so profoundly miserable.

But through all the confusion and lowness of spirits in which we had been, so unexpectedly to me, involved, I plainly discerned that Mr. and Mrs. Micawber and their family were going away from London, and that a parting between us was near at hand. It was in my walk home that night, and in the sleepless hours which followed when I lay in bed, that the thought first occurred to me—though I don't know how it came into my head—which afterwards shaped itself into a settled resolution.

I had grown to be so accustomed to the Micawbers, and had been so intimate with them in their distresses, and was so utterly friendless without them, that the prospect of being thrown upon some new shift for a lodging, and going once more among unknown people, was like being that moment turned adrift into my present life, with such a knowledge of it ready made, as experience had given me. All the sensitive feelings it wounded so cruelly, all the shame and misery it kept alive within my breast, became more poignant as I thought of this; and I determined that the life was unendurable.

That there was no hope of escape from it, unless the escape was my own act, I knew quite well. I rarely heard from Miss Murdstone, and never from Mr. Murdstone; but two or three parcels of made or mended clothes had come up for me, consigned to Mr. Quinion, and in each there was a scrap of paper to the effect that J. M. trusted D. C. was applying himself to business, and devoting himself wholly to his duties—not the least hint of my ever being anything else than the common drudge into which I was fast settling down.

The very next day showed me, while my mind was in the first agitation of what it had conceived, that Mrs. Micawber had not spoken of their going away without warrant. They took a lodging in the house where I lived, for a week; at the expiration of which time they were to start for Plymouth. Mr. Micawber himself came down to the counting-house, in the afternoon, to tell Mr. Quinion that he must relinquish me on the day of his departure, and to give me a high character, which I am sure I deserved. And Mr. Quinion, calling in Tipp the carman, who was a married man, and had a room to let, quartered me prospectively on him—by our mutual consent, as he had every reason to think; for I said nothing, though my resolution was now taken.

I passed my evenings with Mr. and Mrs. Micawber, during the remaining term of our residence under the

same roof; and I think we became fonder of one another as the time went on. On the last Sunday, they
invited me to dinner; and we had a loin of pork
and apple sauce, and a pudding. I had bought a
spotted wooden horse overnight as a parting gift to
little Wilkins Micawber—that was the boy—and a
doll for little Emma. I had also bestowed a shilling
on the Orfling, who was about to be disbanded.

We had a very pleasant day, though we were all
in a tender state about our approaching separation.

'I shall never, Master Copperfield,' said Mrs.
Micawber, 'revert to the period when Mr. Micawber
was in difficulties, without thinking of you. Your
conduct has always been of the most delicate and
obliging description. You have never been a lodger.
You have been a friend.'

'My dear,' said Mr. Micawber; 'Copperfield,' for
so he had been accustomed to call me of late, 'has a
heart to feel for the distresses of his fellow-creatures
when they are behind a cloud, and a head to plan,
and a hand to—in short, a general ability to dispose
of such available property as could be made away
with.'

I expressed my sense of this commendation, and
said I was very sorry we were going to lose one another.

'My dear young friend,' said Mr. Micawber, 'I am
older than you; a man of some experience in life, and
—and of some experience, in short, in difficulties, generally speaking. At present, and until something
turns up (which I am, I may say, hourly expecting),
I have nothing to bestow but advice. Still my advice
is so far worth taking that—in short, that I have
never taken it myself, and am the'—here Mr. Micawber, who had been beaming and smiling, all over his

head and face, up to the present moment, checked himself and frowned—'the miserable wretch you behold.'

'My dear Micawber!' urged his wife.

'I say,' returned Mr. Micawber, quite forgetting himself, and smiling again, 'the miserable wretch you behold. My advice is, never do to-morrow what you can do to-day. Procrastination is the thief of time. Collar him!'

'My poor papa's maxim,' Mrs. Micawber observed.

'My dear,' said Mr. Micawber, 'your papa was very well in his way, and Heaven forbid that I should disparage him. Take him for all in all, we ne'er shall —in short, make the acquaintance, probably, of anybody else possessing, at his time of life, the same legs for gaiters, and able to read the same description of print, without spectacles. But he applied that maxim to our marriage, my dear; and that was so far prematurely entered into, in consequence, that I never recovered the expense.'

Mr. Micawber looked aside at Mrs. Micawber, and added, 'Not that I am sorry for it. Quite the contrary, my love.' After which he was grave for a minute or so.

'My other piece of advice, Copperfield,' said Mr. Micawber, 'you know. Annual income twenty pounds, annual expenditure nineteen nineteen six, result happiness. Annual income twenty pounds, annual expenditure twenty pounds ought and six, result misery. The blossom is blighted, the leaf is withered, the God of day goes down upon the dreary scene, and—and in short you are for ever floored. As I am!'

To make his example the more impressive, Mr. Micawber drank a glass of punch with an air of great enjoyment and satisfaction, and whistled the College Hornpipe.

I did not fail to assure him that I would store these precepts in my mind, though indeed I had no need to do so, for, at the time, they affected me visibly. Next morning I met the whole family at the coach-office, and saw them, with a desolate heart, take their places outside, at the back.

'Master Copperfield,' said Mrs. Micawber, 'God bless you! I never can forget all that, you know, and I never would if I could.'

'Copperfield,' said Mr. Micawber, 'farewell! Every happiness and prosperity! If, in the progress of revolving years, I could persuade myself that my blighted destiny had been a warning to you, I should feel that I had not occupied another man's place in existence altogether in vain. In case of anything turning up (of which I am rather confident), I shall be extremely happy if it should be in my power to improve your prospects.'

I think, as Mrs. Micawber sat at the back of the coach, with the children, and I stood in the road looking wistfully at them, a mist cleared from her eyes, and she saw what a little creature I really was. I think so, because she beckoned to me to climb up, with quite a new and motherly expression in her face, and put her arm round my neck, and gave me just such a kiss as she might have given to her own boy. I had barely time to get down again before the coach started, and I could hardly see the family for the handkerchiefs they waved. It was gone in a minute. The Orfling and I stood looking vacantly at each other in the middle of the road, and then shook hands and said good-bye; she going back, I suppose, to St. Luke's workhouse, as I went to begin my dreary day at Murdstone and Grinby's.

But with no intention of passing many more weary days there. No. I had resolved to run away.—To go, by some means or other, down into the country, to the only relation I had in the world, and tell my story to my aunt, Miss Betsey.

I have already observed that I don't know how this desperate idea came into my brain. But, once there, it remained there; and hardened into a purpose than which I have never entertained a more determined purpose in my life. I am far from sure that I believed there was anything hopeful in it, but my mind was thoroughly made up that it must be carried into execution.

Again, and again, and a hundred times again, since the night when the thought had first occurred to me and banished sleep, I had gone over that old story of my poor mother's about my birth, which it had been one of my great delights in the old time to hear her tell, and which I knew by heart. My aunt walked into that story, and walked out of it, a dread and awful personage; but there was one little trait in her behaviour which I liked to dwell on, and which gave me some faint shadow of encouragement. I could not forget how my mother had thought that she felt her touch her pretty hair with no ungentle hand; and though it might have been altogether my mother's fancy, and might have had no foundation whatever in fact, I made a little picture, out of it, of my terrible aunt relenting towards the girlish beauty that I recollected so well and loved so much, which softened the whole narrative. It is very possible that it had been in my mind a long time, and had gradually engendered my determination.

As I did not even know where Miss Betsey lived, I wrote a long letter to Peggotty, and asked her, incidentally, if she remembered; pretending that I had heard of such a lady living at a certain place I named at random, and had a curiosity to know if it were the same. In the course of that letter, I told Peggotty that I had a particular occasion for half-a-guinea; and that if she could lend me that sum until I could repay it, I should be very much obliged to her, and would tell her afterwards what I had wanted it for.

Peggotty's answer soon arrived, and was, as usual, full of affectionate devotion. She enclosed the half-guinea (I was afraid she must have had a world of trouble to get it out of Mr. Barkis's box), and told me that Miss Betsey lived near Dover, but whether at Dover itself, at Hythe, Sandgate, or Folkestone, she could not say. One of our men, however, informing me on my asking him about these places, that they were all close together, I deemed this enough for my object, and resolved to set out at the end of that week.

Being a very honest little creature, and unwilling to disgrace the memory I was going to leave behind me at Murdstone and Grinby's, I considered myself bound to remain until Saturday night; and, as I had been paid a week's wages in advance when I first came there, not to present myself in the counting-house at the usual hour, to receive my stipend. For this express reason, I had borrowed the half-guinea, that I might not be without a fund for my travelling expenses. Accordingly, when the Saturday night came, and we were all waiting in the warehouse to be paid, and Tipp the carman, who always took precedence, went in first to draw his money, I shook Mick Walker by the hand; asked him, when it came to his turn to be paid, to say to Mr. Quinion that I had gone to move my box to Tipp's; and, bidding a last good night to Mealy Potatoes, ran away.

My box was at my old lodging over the water, and
I had written a direction for it on the back of one of
our address cards that we nailed on the casks: 'Master
David, to be left till called for, at the Coach Office,
Dover.' This I had in my pocket ready to put on
the box, after I should have got it out of the house;
and as I went towards my lodging, I looked about
me for some one who would help me to carry it to the
booking-office.

There was a long-legged young man with a very
little empty donkey-cart, standing near the Obelisk,
in the Blackfriars Road, whose eye I caught as I was
going by, and who, addressing me as 'Sixpenn'orth of
bad ha'pence,' hoped 'I should know him agin to
swear to'—in allusion, I have no doubt, to my staring
at him. I stopped to assure him that I had not done
so in bad manners, but uncertain whether he might
or might not like a job.

'Wot job?' said the long-legged young man.

'To move a box,' I answered.

'Wot box?' said the long-legged young man.

I told him mine, which was down that street there,
and which I wanted him to take to the Dover coach-
office for sixpence.

'Done with you for a tanner!' said the long-legged
young man, and directly got upon his cart, which was
nothing but a large wooden tray on wheels, and rattled
away at such a rate, that it was as much as I could
do to keep pace with the donkey.

There was a defiant manner about this young man,
and particularly about the way in which he chewed
straw as he spoke to me, that I did not much like;
as the bargain was made, however, I took him upstairs to the room I was leaving, and we brought the
box down, and put it on his cart. Now, I was unwilling to put the direction-card on there, lest any

of my landlord's family should fathom what I was doing, and detain me; so I said to the young man that I would be glad if he would stop for a minute, when he came to the dead-wall of the King's Bench Prison. The words were no sooner out of my mouth, than he rattled away as if he, my box, the cart, and the donkey, were all equally mad; and I was quite out of breath with running and calling after him, when I caught him at the place appointed.

Being much flushed and excited, I tumbled my half-guinea out of my pocket in pulling the card out. I put it in my mouth for safety, and though my hands trembled a good deal, had just tied the card on very much to my satisfaction, when I felt myself violently chucked under the chin by the long-legged young man, and saw my half-guinea fly out of my mouth into his hand.

'Wot?' said the young man, seizing me by my jacket collar, with a frightful grin. 'This is a pollis case, is it? You're a going to bolt, are you? Come to the pollis, you young warmin, come to the pollis!'

'You give me my money back, if you please,' said I, very much frightened; 'and leave me alone.'

'Come to the pollis!' said the young man. 'You shall prove it yourn to the pollis.'

'Give me my box and money, will you?' I cried, bursting into tears.

The young man still replied: 'Come to the pollis!' and was dragging me against the donkey in a violent manner, as if there were any affinity between that animal and a magistrate, when he changed his mind, jumped into the cart, sat upon my box, and, exclaiming that he would drive to the pollis straight, rattled away harder than ever.

I ran after him as fast as I could, but I had no breath to call out with, and should not have dared to call out, now, if I had. I narrowly escaped being run over, twenty times at least in half a mile. Now I lost him, now I saw him, now I lost him, now I was cut at with a whip, now shouted at, now down in the mud, now up again, now running into somebody's arms, now running headlong at a post. At length, confused by fright and heat, and doubting whether half London might not by this time be turning out for my apprehension, I left the young man to go where he would with my box and money; and, panting and crying, but never stopping, faced about for Greenwich, which I had understood was on the Dover road: taking very little more out of the world, towards the retreat of my aunt, Miss Betsey, than I had brought into it, on the night when my arrival gave her so much umbrage.

CHAPTER XIII

THE SEQUEL OF MY RESOLUTION

For anything I know, I may have had some wild idea of running all the way to Dover, when I gave up the pursuit of the young man with the donkey-cart, and started for Greenwich. My scattered senses were soon collected as to that point, if I had; for I came to a stop in the Kent Road, at a terrace with a piece of water before it, and a great foolish image in the middle, blowing a dry shell. Here I sat down on a doorstep, quite spent and exhausted with the efforts I had already made, and with hardly breath enough to cry for the loss of my box and half-guinea.

It was by this time dark; I heard the clocks strike ten, as I sat resting. But it was a summer night fortunately, and fine weather. When I had recovered my breath, and had got rid of a stifling sensation in my throat, I rose up and went on. In the midst of my distress, I had no notion of going back. I doubt if I should have had any, though there had been a Swiss snow-drift in the Kent Road.

But my standing possessed of only three-halfpence in the world (and I am sure I wonder how *they* came to be left in my pocket on a Saturday night!) troubled me none the less because I went on. I began to picture to myself, as a scrap of newspaper intelligence, my being found dead in a day or two, under some hedge; and I trudged on miserably, though as fast as I could, until I happened to pass a little shop, where it was written up that ladies and gentlemen's wardrobes were bought, and that the best price was given for rags, bones, and kitchen-stuff. The master of this shop was sitting at the door in his shirt-sleeves, smoking; and as there were a great many coats and pairs of trousers dangling from the low ceiling, and only two feeble candles burning inside to show what they were, I fancied that he looked like a man of a revengeful disposition, who had hung all his enemies, and was enjoying himself.

My late experiences with Mr. and Mrs. Micawber suggested to me that here might be a means of keeping off the wolf for a little while. I went up the next bye-street, took off my waistcoat, rolled it neatly under my arm, and came back to the shop-door. 'If you please, sir,' I said, 'I am to sell this for a fair price.'

Mr. Dolloby—Dolloby was the name over the shop-door, at least—took the waistcoat, stood his pipe on its head against the door-post, went into the shop, followed by me, snuffed the two candles with his fingers, spread the waistcoat on the counter, and looked at it there, held it up against the light, and looked at it there, and ultimately said—

'What do you call a price, now, for this here little weskit?'

'Oh! you know best, sir,' I returned, modestly.

'I can't be buyer and seller too,' said Mr. Dolloby. 'Put a price on this here little weskit.'

'Would eighteenpence be?'—I hinted, after some hesitation.

Mr. Dolloby rolled it up again, and gave it me back. 'I should rob my family,' he said, 'if I was to offer ninepence for it.'

This was a disagreeable way of putting the business; because it imposed upon me, a perfect stranger, the unpleasantness of asking Mr. Dolloby to rob his family on my account. My circumstances being so very pressing, however, I said I would take ninepence for it, if he pleased. Mr. Dolloby, not without some grumbling, gave ninepence. I wished him good night, and walked out of the shop, the richer by that sum, and the poorer by a waistcoat. But when I buttoned my jacket, that was not much.

Indeed, I foresaw pretty clearly that my jacket would go next, and that I should have to make the best of my way to Dover in a shirt and a pair of trousers, and might deem myself lucky if I got there even in that trim. But my mind did not run so much on this as might be supposed. Beyond a general impression of the distance before me, and of the young man with the donkey-cart having used me cruelly, I think I had no very urgent sense of my difficulties when I once again set off with my ninepence in my pocket.

A plan had occurred to me for passing the night, which I was going to carry into execution. This

was, to lie behind the wall at the back of my old
school, in a corner where there used to be a haystack.
I imagined it would be a kind of company to have
the boys, and the bedroom where I used to tell the
stories, so near me: although the boys would know
nothing of my being there, and the bedroom would
yield me no shelter.

I had had a hard day's work, and was pretty well
jaded when I came climbing out, at last, upon the
level of Blackheath. It cost me some trouble to
find out Salem House; but I found it, and I found
a haystack in the corner, and I lay down by it; having first walked round the wall, and looked up at
the windows, and seen that all was dark and silent
within. Never shall I forget the lonely sensation of
first lying down, without a roof above my head!

Sleep came upon me as it came on many other
outcasts, against whom house-doors were locked, and
house-dogs barked, that night—and I dreamed of
lying on my old school-bed, talking to the boys in
my room; and found myself sitting upright, with
Steerforth's name upon my lips, looking wildly at
the stars that were glistening and glimmering above
me. When I remembered where I was at that untimely hour, a feeling stole upon me that made me
get up, afraid of I don't know what, and walk about.
But the fainter glimmering of the stars, and the pale
light in the sky where the day was coming, reassured me: and my eyes being very heavy, I lay
down again, and slept—though with a knowledge in
my sleep that it was cold—until the warm beams
of the sun, and the ringing of the getting-up bell
at Salem House, awoke me. If I could have hoped
that Steerforth was there, I would have lurked
about until he came out alone; but I knew he must
have left long since. Traddles still remained, per-

haps, but it was very doubtful; and I had not sufficient confidence in his discretion or good luck, however strong my reliance was on his good-nature, to
wish to trust him with my situation. So I crept
away from the wall as Mr. Creakle's boys were getting up, and struck into the long dusty track which
I had first known to be the Dover Road when I was
one of them, and when I little expected that any
eyes would ever see me the wayfarer I was now,
upon it.

What a different Sunday morning from the old
Sunday morning at Yarmouth! In due time I
heard the church-bells ringing, as I plodded on; and
I met people who were going to church; and I passed
a church or two where the congregation were inside, and the sound of singing came out into the
sunshine, while the beadle sat and cooled himself in
the shade of the porch, or stood beneath the yew-
tree, with his hand to his forehead, glowering at me
going by. But the peace and rest of the old Sunday morning were on everything except me. That
was the difference. I felt quite wicked in my dirt
and dust, with my tangled hair. But for the quiet
picture I had conjured up, of my mother in her
youth and beauty, weeping by the fire, and my aunt
relenting to her, I hardly think I should have had
courage to go on until next day. But it always went
before me, and I followed.

I got, that Sunday, through three-and-twenty
miles on the straight road, though not very easily,
for I was new to that kind of toil. I see myself,
as evening closes in, coming over the bridge at
Rochester, footsore and tired, and eating bread that
I had bought for supper. One or two little houses,
with the notice, 'Lodging for Travellers,' hanging
out, had tempted me; but I was afraid of spending

the few pence I had, and was even more afraid of the vicious looks of the trampers I had met or overtaken. I sought no shelter, therefore, but the sky; and toiling into Chatham,—which, in that night's aspect, is a mere dream of chalk, and drawbridges, and mastless ships in a muddy river, roofed like Noah's arks, crept, at last, upon a sort of grassgrown battery overhanging a lane, where a sentry was walking to and fro. Here I lay down, near a cannon; and, happy in the society of the sentry's footsteps, though he knew no more of my being above him than the boys at Salem House had known of my lying by the wall, slept soundly until morning.

Very stiff and sore of foot I was in the morning, and quite dazed by the beating of drums and marching of troops, which seemed to hem me in on every side when I went down towards the long narrow street. Feeling that I could go but a very little way that day, if I were to reserve any strength for getting to my journey's end, I resolved to make the sale of my jacket its principal business. Accordingly, I took the jacket off, that I might learn to do without it; and carrying it under my arm, began a tour of inspection of the various slop-shops.

It was a likely place to sell a jacket in: for the dealers in second-hand clothes were numerous, and were, generally speaking, on the look-out for customers at their shop-doors. But, as most of them had, hanging up among their stock, an officer's coat or two, epaulettes and all, I was rendered timid by the costly nature of their dealings, and walked about for a long time without offering my merchandise to any one.

This modesty of mine directed my attention to the marine-store shops, and such shops as Mr. Dolloby's, in preference to the regular dealers. At last I

found one that I thought looked promising, at
the corner of a dirty lane, ending in an inclosure
full of stinging-nettles, against the palings of which
some second-hand sailors' clothes, that seemed to have
overflowed the shop, were fluttering among some cots,
and rusty guns, and oilskin hats, and certain trays
full of so many old dusty keys of so many sizes that
they seemed various enough to open all the doors in
the world.

Into this shop, which was low and small, and
which was darkened rather than lighted by a little
window, overhung with clothes, and was descended
into by some steps, I went with a palpitating heart;
which was not relieved when an ugly old man, with
the lower part of his face all covered with a stubbly
grey beard, rushed out of a dirty den behind it, and
seized me by the hair of my head. He was a dreadful old man to look at, in a filthy flannel waistcoat,
and smelling terribly of rum. His bedstead, covered with a tumbled and ragged piece of patchwork,
was in the den he had come from, where another little
window showed a prospect of more stinging-nettles,
and a lame donkey.

'Oh, what do you want?' grinned this old man, in
a fierce, monotonous whine. 'Oh, my eyes and
limbs, what do you want? Oh, my lungs and liver,
what do you want? Oh, goroo, goroo!'

I was so much dismayed by these words, and particularly by the repetition of the last unknown one,
which was a kind of rattle in his throat, that I could
make no answer; hereupon the old man, still holding me by the hair, repeated—

'Oh, what do you want? Oh, my eyes and limbs,
what do you want? Oh, my lungs and liver, what
do you want? Oh, goroo!'—which he screwed out of

himself, with an energy that made his eyes start in his head.

'I wanted to know,' I said, trembling, 'if you would buy a jacket.'

'Oh, let 's see the jacket!' cried the old man. 'Oh, my heart on fire, show the jacket to us! Oh, my eyes and limbs, bring the jacket out!'

With that he took his trembling hands, which were like the claws of a great bird, out of my hair; and put on a pair of spectacles, not at all ornamental to his inflamed eyes.

'Oh, how much for the jacket?' cried the old man, after examining it. 'Oh—goroo!—how much for the jacket?'

'Half-a-crown,' I answered, recovering myself.

'Oh, my lungs and liver,' cried the old man, 'no! Oh, my eyes, no! Oh, my limbs, no! Eighteen-pence. Goroo!'

Every time he uttered this ejaculation, his eyes seemed to be in danger of starting out; and every sentence he spoke, he delivered in a sort of tune, al-ways exactly the same, and more like a gust of wind, which begins low, mounts up high, and falls again, than any other comparison I can find for it.

'Well,' said I, glad to have closed the bargain, 'I 'll take eighteenpence.'

'Oh, my liver!' cried the old man, throwing the jacket on a shelf. 'Get out of the shop! Oh, my lungs, get out of the shop! Oh, my eyes and limbs —goroo!—don't ask for money; make it an ex-change.'

I never was so frightened in my life, before or since; but I told him humbly that I wanted money, and that nothing else was of any use to me, but that I would wait for it, as he desired, outside, and had no wish to hurry him. So I went outside, and sat down in the shade in a corner. And I sat there so many hours, that the shade became sunlight, and the sunlight became shade again, and still I sat there waiting for the money.

There never was such another drunken madman in that line of business, I hope. That he was well known in the neighbourhood, and enjoyed the reputation of having sold himself to the devil, I soon understood from the visits he received from the boys, who continually came skirmishing about the shop, shouting that legend, and calling to him to bring out his gold. 'You ain't poor, you know, Charley, as you pretend. Bring out your gold. Bring out some of the gold you sold yourself to the devil for. Come! It's in the lining of the mattress, Charley. Rip it open and let's have some!' This, and many offers to lend him a knife for the purpose, exasperated him to such a degree, that the whole day was a succession of rushes on his part, and flights on the part of the boys. Sometimes in his rage he would take me for one of them, and come at me, mouthing as if he were going to tear me in pieces; then, remembering me, just in time, would dive into the shop, and lie upon his bed, as I thought from the sound of his voice, yelling in a frantic way, to his own windy tune, the Death of Nelson; with an Oh! before every line, and innumerable Goroos interpersed. As if this were not bad enough for me, the boys, connecting me with the establishment, on account of the patience and perseverance with which I sat outside, half-dressed, pelted me, and used me very ill all day.

He made many attempts to induce me to consent to an exchange; at one time coming out with a fishing-rod, at another with a fiddle, at another with a cocked hat, at another with a flute. But I resisted all these overtures, and sat there in desperation; each time asking him, with tears in my eyes, for my money or my jacket. At last he began to pay me in half-pence at a time; and was full two hours getting by easy stages to a shilling.

'Oh, my eyes and limbs!' he then cried, peeping hideously out of the shop, after a long pause, 'will you go for twopence more?'

'I can't,' I said; 'I shall be starved.'

'Oh, my lungs and liver, will you go for three-pence?'

'I would go for nothing, if I could,' I said, 'but I want the money badly.'

'Oh, go—roo!' (it is really impossible to express how he twisted this ejaculation out of himself, as he peeped round the door-post at me, showing nothing but his crafty old head;) 'will you go for fourpence?'

I was so faint and weary that I closed with this offer; and taking the money out of his claw, not with-out trembling, went away more hungry and thirsty than I had ever been, a little before sunset. But at an expense of threepence I soon refreshed myself completely; and, being in better spirits then, limped seven miles upon my road.

My bed at night was under another haystack, where I rested comfortably, after having washed my blistered feet in a stream, and dressed them as well as I was able, with some cool leaves. When I took the road again next morning, I found that it lay through a succession of hop-grounds and orchards. It was sufficiently late in the year for the orchards to be ruddy with ripe apples; and in a few places the hop-pickers were already at work. I thought it all extremely beautiful, and made up my mind to sleep among the hops that night: imagining some cheerful companionship in the long perspective of poles, with the graceful leaves twining round them.

The trampers were worse than ever that day, and inspired me with a dread that is yet quite fresh in my mind. Some of them were most ferocious-looking ruffians, who stared at me as I went by; and stopped, perhaps, and called after me to come back and speak to them, and when I took to my heels, stoned me. I recollect one young fellow—a tinker, I suppose, from his wallet and brazier—who had a woman with him, and who faced about and stared at me thus; and then roared to me in such a tremendous voice to come back, that I halted and looked round.

'Come here, when you 're called,' said the tinker, 'or I 'll rip your young body open.'

I thought it best to go back. As I drew nearer to them, trying to propitiate the tinker by my looks, I observed that the woman had a black eye.

'Where are you going?' said the tinker, gripping the bosom of my shirt with his blackened hand.

'I am going to Dover,' I said.

'Where do you come from?' asked the tinker, giving his hand another turn in my shirt, to hold me more securely.

'I come from London,' I said.

'What lay are you upon?' asked the tinker. 'Are you a prig?'

'N—no,' I said.

'Ain't you, by G——? If you make a brag of your honesty to me,' said the tinker, 'I 'll knock your brains out.'

With his disengaged hand he made a menace of striking me, and then looked at me from head to foot.

'Have you got the price of a pint of beer about you?' said the tinker. 'If you have, out with it, afore I take it away!'

I should certainly have produced it, but that I met the woman's look, and saw her very slightly shake her head, and form 'No!' with her lips.

'I am very poor,' I said, attempting to smile, 'and have got no money.'

'Why, what do you mean?' said the tinker, looking so sternly at me, that I almost feared he saw the money in my pocket.

'Sir!' I stammered.

'What do you mean,' said the tinker, 'by wearing my brother's silk handkercher? Give it over here!' And he had mine off my neck in a moment, and tossed it to the woman.

The woman burst into a fit of laughter, as if she thought this a joke, and tossed it back to me, nodded once, as slightly as before, and made the word 'Go!' with her lips. Before I could obey, however, the tinker seized the handkerchief out of my hand with a roughness that threw me away like a feather, and putting it loosely round his own neck, turned upon the woman with an oath, and knocked her down. I never shall forget seeing her fall backward on the hard road, and lie there with her bonnet tumbled off, and her hair all whitened in the dust; nor, when I looked back from a distance, seeing her sitting on the pathway, which was a bank by the roadside, wiping the blood from her face with the corner of her shawl, while he went on ahead.

This adventure frightened me so, that, afterwards, when I saw any of these people coming, I turned back until I could find a hiding-place, where I remained until they had gone out of sight; which happened so often, that I was very seriously delayed.

But under this difficulty, as under all the other difficulties of my journey, I seemed to be sustained and
led on by my fanciful picture of my mother in her
youth, before I came into the world.   It always kept
me company.   It was there, among the hops, when I
lay down to sleep; it was with me on my waking in
the morning; it went before me all day.   I have associated it, ever since, with the sunny street of Canterbury, dozing as it were in the hot light; and with
the sight of its old houses and gateways, and the
stately, grey cathedral, with the rooks sailing round
the towers.   When I came, at last, upon the bare,
wide downs near Dover, it relieved the solitary aspect of the scene with hope; and not until I reached
that first great aim of my journey, and actually set
foot in the town itself, on the sixth day of my flight,
did it desert me.   But then, strange to say, when I
stood with my ragged shoes, and my dusty, sun-
burnt, half-clothed figure, in the place so long desired, it seemed to vanish like a dream, and to leave
me helpless and dispirited.

I inquired about my aunt among the boatmen first,
and received various answers.   One said she lived in
the South Foreland Light, and had singed her
whiskers by doing so; another, that she was made fast
to the great buoy outside the harbour, and could
only be visited at half-tide; a third, that she was
locked up in Maidstone Jail for child-stealing; a
fourth, that she was seen to mount a broom, in the
last high wind, and make direct for Calais.   The fly-
drivers, among whom I inquired next, were equally
jocose and equally disrespectful; and the shopkeepers, not liking my appearance, generally replied, without hearing what I had to say, that they had got
nothing for me.   I felt more miserable and destitute
than I had done at any period of my running away.

My money was all gone, I had nothing left to dispose of; I was hungry, thirsty, and worn out; and seemed as distant from my end as if I had remained in London.

The morning had worn away in these inquiries, and I was sitting on the step of an empty shop at a street-corner, near the market-place, deliberating upon wandering towards those other places which had been mentioned, when a fly-driver, coming by with his carriage, dropped a horse-cloth. Something good-natured in the man's face, as I handed it up, encouraged me to ask him if he could tell me where Miss Trotwood lived; though I had asked the question so often, that it almost died upon my lips.

'Trotwood,' said he. 'Let me see. I know the name, too. Old lady?'

'Yes,' I said, 'rather.'

'Pretty stiff in the back?' said he, making himself upright.

'Yes,' I said. 'I should think it very likely.'

'Carries a bag?' said he: 'bag with a good deal of room in it: is gruffish, and comes down upon you, sharp?'

My heart sank within me as I acknowledged the undoubted accuracy of this description.

'Why then, I tell you what,' said he. 'If you go up there,' pointing with his whip towards the heights, 'and keep right on till you come to some houses facing the sea, I think you'll hear of her. My opinion is, she won't stand anything, so here's a penny for you.'

I accepted the gift thankfully, and bought a loaf with it. Despatching this refreshment by the way, I went in the direction my friend had indicated, and walked on a good distance without coming to the houses he had mentioned. At length I saw some be-

fore me; and approaching them, went into a little
shop (it was what we used to call a general shop, at
home), and inquired if they could have the goodness
to tell me where Miss Trotwood lived. I addressed
myself to a man behind the counter, who was weighing some rice for a young woman; but the latter, taking the inquiry to herself, turned round quickly.

'My mistress?' she said. 'What do you want with
her, boy?'

'I want,' I replied, 'to speak to her, if you please.'

'To beg of her, you mean,' retorted the damsel.

'No,' I said, 'indeed.' But suddenly remembering
that in truth I came for no other purpose, I held my
peace in confusion, and felt my face burn.

My aunt's handmaid, as I supposed she was from
what she had said, put her rice in a little basket and
walked out of the shop; telling me that I could follow
her, if I wanted to know where Miss Trotwood lived.
I needed no second permission; though I was by this
time in such a state of consternation and agitation,
that my legs shook under me. I followed the young
woman, and we soon came to a very neat little cottage with cheerful bow-windows: in front of it, a
small square gravelled court or garden full of flowers,
carefully tended, and smelling deliciously.

'This is Miss Trotwood's,' said the young woman.
'Now you know; and that's all I have got to say.'
With which words she hurried into the house, as if to
shake off the responsibility of my appearance; and left
me standing at the garden-gate, looking disconsolately
over the top of it towards the parlour-window, where
a muslin curtain, partly undrawn in the middle, a
large round green screen or fan fastened on to the
window-sill, a small table, and a great chair, suggested to me that my aunt might be at that moment
seated in awful state.

My shoes were by this time in a woeful condition. The soles had shed themselves bit by bit, and the upper leathers had broken and burst until the very shape and form of shoes had departed from them. My hat (which had served me for a night-cap, too) was so crushed and bent, that no old battered handleless saucepan on a dunghill need have been ashamed to vie with it. My shirt and trousers, stained with heat, dew, grass, and the Kentish soil on which I had slept—and torn besides—might have frightened the birds from my aunt's garden, as I stood at the gate. My hair had known no comb or brush since I left London. My face, neck, and hands, from unaccustomed exposure to the air and sun, were burnt to a berry-brown. From head to foot I was powdered almost as white with chalk and dust, as if I had come out of a lime-kiln. In this plight, and with a strong consciousness of it, I waited to introduce myself to, and make my first impression on, my formidable aunt.

The unbroken stillness of the parlour-window leading me to infer, after a while, that she was not there, I lifted up my eyes to the window above it, where I saw a florid, pleasant-looking gentleman, with a grey head, who shut up one eye in a grotesque manner, nodded his head at me several times, shook it at me as often, laughed, and went away.

I had been discomposed enough before; but I was so much the more discomposed by this unexpected behaviour, that I was on the point of slinking off, to think how I had best proceed, when there came out of the house a lady with a handkerchief tied over her cap, and a pair of gardening gloves on her hands, wearing a gardening-pocket like a toll-man's apron, and carrying a great knife. I knew her immediately to be Miss Betsey, for she came stalking out of the house exactly as my poor mother had so often described her stalking up our garden at Blunderstone Rookery.

'Go away!' said Miss Betsey, shaking her head, and making a distant chop in the air with her knife. 'Go along! No boys here!'

I watched her, with my heart at my lips, as she marched to a corner of her garden, and stopped to dig up some little root there. Then, without a scrap of courage, but with a great deal of desperation, I went softly in and stood beside her, touching her with my finger.

'If you please, ma'am,' I began.

She started and looked up.

'If you please, aunt.'

'EH?' exclaimed Miss Betsey, in a tone of amazement I have never heard approached.

'If you please, aunt, I am your nephew.'

'Oh, Lord!' said my aunt. And sat flat down in the garden-path.

'I am David Copperfield, of Blunderstone, in Suffolk—where you came, on the night when I was born, and saw my dear mamma. I have been very unhappy since she died. I have been slighted, and taught nothing, and thrown upon myself, and put to work not fit for me. It made me run away to you. I was robbed at first setting out, and have walked all the way, and have never slept in a bed since I began the journey.' Here my self-support gave way all at once; and with a movement of my hands, intended to show her my ragged state, and call it to witness that I had suffered something, I broke into a passion of crying, which I suppose had been pent up within me all the week.

My aunt, with every sort of expression but wonder discharged from her countenance, sat on the gravel staring at me, until I began to cry; when she got up in a great hurry, collared me, and took me into the parlour. Her first proceeding there was to unlock a tall press, bring out several bottles, and pour some of the contents of each into my mouth. I think they must have been taken out at random, for I am sure I tasted aniseed water, anchovy sauce, and salad dressing. When she had administered these restoratives, as I was still quite hysterical, and unable to control my sobs, she put me on the sofa, with a shawl under my head, and the handkerchief from her own head under my feet, lest I should sully the cover; and then, sitting herself down behind the green fan or screen I have already mentioned, so that I could not see her face, ejaculated at intervals, 'Mercy on us!' letting those exclamations off like minute-guns.

After a time she rang the bell. 'Janet,' said my aunt, when her servant came in. 'Go upstairs, give my compliments to Mr. Dick, and say I wish to speak to him.'

Janet looked a little surprised to see me lying stiffly on the sofa (I was afraid to move lest it should be displeasing to my aunt), but went on her errand. My aunt, with her hands behind her, walked up and down the room, until the gentleman who had squinted at me from the upper window came in laughing.

'Mr. Dick,' said my aunt, 'don't be a fool, because nobody can be more discreet than you can, when you choose. We all know that. So don't be a fool, whatever you are.'

The gentleman was serious immediately, and looked at me, I thought, as if he would entreat me to say nothing about the window.

'Mr. Dick,' said my aunt, 'you have heard me mention David Copperfield? Now don't pretend not to have a memory, because you and I know better.'

'David Copperfield?' said Mr. Dick, who did not appear to me to remember much about it. '*David* Copperfield? Oh yes, to be sure. David, certainly.'

'Well,' said my aunt, 'this is his boy, his son. He would be as like his father as it 's possible to be, if he was not so like his mother, too.'

'His son?' said Mr. Dick. 'David's son? Indeed?'

'Yes,' pursued my aunt, 'and he has done a pretty piece of business. He has run away. Ah! His sister, Betsey Trotwood, never would have run away.' My aunt shook her head firmly, confident in the character and behaviour of the girl who never was born.

'Oh! you think she wouldn't have run away?' said Mr. Dick.

'Bless and save the man,' exclaimed my aunt, sharply, 'how he talks! Don't I know she wouldn't? She would have lived with her godmother, and we should have been devoted to one another. Where, in the name of wonder, should his sister, Betsey Trotwood, have run from, or to?'

'Nowhere,' said Mr. Dick.

'Well then,' returned my aunt, softened by the reply, 'how can you pretend to be wool-gathering, Dick, when you are as sharp as a surgeon's lancet? Now, here you see young David Copperfield, and the question I put to you is, what shall I do with him?'

'What shall you do with him?' said Mr. Dick, feebly, scratching his head. 'Oh! do with him?'

'Yes,' said my aunt, with a grave look, and her forefinger held up. 'Come! I want some very sound advice.'

'Why, if I was you,' said Mr. Dick, considering, and looking vacantly at me, 'I should—' The contemplation of me seemed to inspire him with a sudden idea, and he added, briskly, 'I should wash him!'

'Janet,' said my aunt, turning round with a quiet triumph, which I did not then understand. 'Mr. Dick sets us all right. Heat the bath.'

Although I was deeply interested in this dialogue, I could not help observing my aunt, Mr. Dick, and Janet, while it was in progress, and completing a survey I had already been engaged in making of the room.

My aunt was a tall, hard-featured lady, but by no means ill-looking. There was an inflexibility in her face, in her voice, in her gait and carriage, amply sufficent to account for the effect she had made upon a gentle creature like my mother; but her features were rather handsome than otherwise, though unbending and austere. I particularly noticed that she had a very quick, bright eye. Her hair, which was grey, was arranged in two plain divisions, under what I believe would be called a mob-cap; I mean a cap, much more common then than now, with side-pieces fastening under the chin. Her dress was of a lavender colour, and perfectly neat; but scantily made, as if she desired to be as little encumbered as possible. I remember that I thought it, in form, more like a riding-habit with the superfluous skirt cut off, than anything else. She wore at her side a gentleman's gold watch, if I might judge from its size and make, with an appropriate chain and seals; she had some linen at her throat not unlike a shirt-collar, and things at her wrists like little shirt-wristbands.

Mr. Dick, as I have already said, was grey-headed and florid: I should have said all about him, in saying so, had not his head been curiously bowed—not by age; it reminded me of one of Mr. Creakle's boys' heads after a beating—and his grey eyes prominent and large, with a strange kind of watery brightness in them that made me, in combination with his va-

cant manner, his submission to my aunt, and his childish delight when she praised him, suspect him of being
a little mad; though, if he were mad, how he came to
be there, puzzled me extremely. He was dressed like
any other ordinary gentleman, in a loose grey morning coat and waistcoat, and white trousers; and had
his watch in his fob, and his money in his pockets:
which he rattled as if he were very proud of it.

Janet was a pretty, blooming girl, of about nineteen or twenty, and a perfect picture of neatness.
Though I made no further observation of her at the
moment, I may mention here what I did not discover
until afterwards, namely, that she was one of a series
of protégées whom my aunt had taken into her service expressly to educate in a renouncement of mankind, and who had generally completed their abjura-
tion by marrying the baker.

The room was as neat as Janet or my aunt. As I
laid down my pen, a moment since, to think of it,
the air from the sea came blowing in again, mixed
with the perfume of the flowers; and I saw the old-
fashioned furniture brightly rubbed and polished, my
aunt's inviolable chair and table by the round green
fan in the bow-window, the drugget-covered carpet,
the cat, the kettle-holder, the two canaries, the old
china, the punch-bowl full of dried rose-leaves, the tall
press guarding all sorts of bottles and pots, and, wonderfully out of keeping with the rest, my dusty self
upon the sofa, taking note of everything.

Janet had gone away to get the bath ready, when
my aunt, to my great alarm, became in one moment
rigid with indignation, and had hardly voice to cry
out, 'Janet! Donkeys!'

Upon which, Janet came running up the stairs as
if the house were in flames, darted out on a little
piece of green in front, and warned off two saddle-

donkeys, lady-ridden, that had presumed to set hoof upon it; while my aunt, rushing out of the house, seized the bridle of a third animal laden with a bestriding child, turned him, led him forth from those sacred precincts, and boxed the ears of the unlucky urchin in attendance who had dared to profane that hallowed ground.

To this hour I don't know whether my aunt had any lawful right of way over that patch of green; but she had settled it in her own mind that she had, and it was all the same to her. The one great outrage of her life, demanding to be constantly avenged, was the passage of a donkey over that immaculate spot. In whatever occupation she was engaged, however interesting to her the conversation in which she was taking part, a donkey turned the current of her ideas in a moment, and she was upon him straight. Jugs of water, and watering-pots, were kept in secret places ready to be discharged on the offending boys; sticks were laid in ambush behind the door; sallies were made at all hours; and incessant war prevailed. Perhaps this was an agreeable excitement to the donkey-boys; or perhaps the more sagacious of the donkeys, understanding how the case stood, delighted with constitutional obstinacy in coming that way. I only know that there were three alarms before the bath was ready; and that on the occasion of the last and most desperate of all, I saw my aunt engage, single-handed, with a sandy-headed lad of fifteen, and bump his sandy head against her own gate, before he seemed to comprehend what was the matter. These interruptions were the more ridiculous to me, because she was giving me broth out of a table-spoon at the time (having firmly persuaded herself that I was actually starving, and must receive nourishment at first in very small quantities), and, while my mouth was yet open to receive the spoon, she would put it back into the basin, cry 'Janet! Donkeys!' and go out to assault.

The bath was a great comfort. For I began to be sensible of acute pains in my limbs from lying out in the fields, and was now so tired and low that I could hardly keep myself awake for five minutes together. When I had bathed, they (I mean my aunt and Janet) enrobed me in a shirt and a pair of trousers belonging to Mr. Dick, and tied me up in two or three great shawls. What sort of bundle I looked like, I don't know, but I felt a very hot one. Feeling also very faint and drowsy, I soon lay down on the sofa again and fell asleep.

It might have been a dream, originating in the fancy which had occupied my mind so long, but I awoke with the impression that my aunt had come and bent over me, and had put my hair away from my face, and laid my head more comfortably, and had then stood looking at me. The words, 'Pretty fellow,' or 'Poor fellow,' seemed to be in my ears, too; but certainly there was nothing else, when I awoke, to lead me to believe that they had been uttered by my aunt, who sat in the bow-window gazing at the sea from behind the green fan, which was mounted on a kind of swivel, and turned any way.

We dined soon after I awoke, off a roast fowl and a pudding; I sitting at table, not unlike a trussed bird myself, and moving my arms with considerable difficulty. But as my aunt had swathed me up, I made no complaint of being inconvenienced. All this time, I was deeply anxious to know what she was going to do with me; but she took her dinner in profound silence, except when she occasionally fixed her eyes on me sitting opposite, and said, 'Mercy upon us!' which did not by any means relieve my anxiety.

The cloth being drawn, and some sherry put upon
the table (of which I had a glass), my aunt sent up
for Mr. Dick again, who joined us, and looked as
wise as he could when she requested him to attend to
my story, which she elicited from me, gradually, by
a course of questions. During my recital, she kept
her eyes on Mr. Dick, who I thought would have
gone to sleep but for that, and who, whensoever he
lapsed into a smile, was checked by a frown from my
aunt.

'Whatever possessed that poor unfortunate Baby,
that she must go and be married again,' said my
aunt, when I had finished, '*I* can't conceive.'

'Perhaps she fell in love with her second husband,'
Mr. Dick suggested.

'Fell in love!' repeated my aunt. 'What do you
mean? What business had she to do it?'

'Perhaps,' Mr. Dick simpered, after thinking a little, 'she did it for pleasure.'

'Pleasure, indeed!' replied my aunt. 'A mighty
pleasure for the poor Baby to fix her simple faith
upon any dog of a fellow, certain to ill use her in some
way or other. What did she propose to herself, I
should like to know? She had had one husband.
She had seen David Copperfield out of the world, who
was always running after wax dolls from his cradle.
She had got a baby—oh, there were a pair of babies
when she gave birth to this child sitting here, that
Friday night!—and what more did she want?'

Mr. Dick secretly shook his head at me, as if he
thought there was no getting over this.

'She couldn't even have a baby like anybody else,'
said my aunt. 'Where was this child's sister, Betsey
Trotwood? Not forthcoming. Don't tell me!'

Mr. Dick seemed quite frightened.

'That little man of a doctor, with his head on one

side,' said my aunt, 'Jellips, or whatever his name was, what was *he* about? All he could do was to say to me, like a robin redbreast—as he *is*—"It's a boy." A boy! Yah, the imbecility of the whole set of 'em!'

The heartiness of the ejaculation startled Mr. Dick exceedingly; and me, too, if I am to tell the truth.

'And then, as if this was not enough, and she had not stood sufficiently in the light of this child's sister, Betsey Trotwood,' said my aunt, 'she marries a second time—goes and marries a Murderer—or a man with a name like it—and stands in *this* child's light! And the natural consequence is, as anybody but a baby might have foreseen, that he prowls and wanders. He's as like Cain before he was grown up, as he can be.'

Mr. Dick looked hard at me, as if to identify me in this character.

'And then there's that woman with the Pagan name,' said my aunt, 'that Peggotty, *she* goes and gets married next. Because she has not seen enough of the evil attending such things, *she* goes and gets married next, as the child relates. I only hope,' said my aunt, shaking her head, 'that her husband is one of those poker husbands who abound in the newspapers, and will beat her well with one.'

I could not bear to hear my old nurse so decried, and made the subject of such a wish. I told my aunt that indeed she was mistaken. That Peggotty was the best, the truest, the most faithful, most devoted, and most self-denying friend and servant in the world; who had ever loved me dearly, who had ever loved my mother dearly; who had held my mother's dying head upon her arm, on whose face my mother had imprinted her last grateful kiss. And my remembrance of them both, choking me, I broke down as I was trying to say that her home was my home, and that all she had was mine, and that I would have gone to her for shelter, but for her humble station, which made me fear that I might bring some trouble on her—I broke down, I say, as I was trying to say so, and laid my face in my hands upon the table.

'Well, well,' said my aunt, 'the child is right to stand by those who have stood by him.—Janet! Donkeys!'

I thoroughly believe that but for those unfortunate donkeys, we should have come to a good understanding; for my aunt had laid her hand on my shoulder, and the impulse was upon me, thus emboldened, to embrace her and beseech her protection. But the interruption, and the disorder she was thrown into by the struggle outside, put an end to all softer ideas for the present, and kept my aunt indignantly declaiming to Mr. Dick about her determination to appeal for redress to the laws of her country, and to bring actions for trespass against the whole donkey proprietorship of Dover, until tea-time.

After tea, we sat at the window—on the look-out, as I imagined, from my aunt's sharp expression of face, for more invaders—until dusk, when Janet set candles, and a back-gammon board, on the table, and pulled down the blinds.

'Now, Mr. Dick,' said my aunt, with her grave look, and her forefinger up as before, 'I am going to ask you another question. Look at this child.'

'David's son?' said Mr. Dick, with an attentive, puzzled face.

'Exactly so,' returned my aunt. 'What would you do with him, now?'

'Do with David's son?' said Mr. Dick.

'Ay,' replied my aunt, 'with David's son.'

'Oh!' said Mr. Dick. 'Yes. Do with—I should put him to bed.'

'Janet!' cried my aunt, with the same complacent triumph that I had remarked before. 'Mr. Dick sets us all right. If the bed is ready, we'll take him up to it.'

Janet reporting it to be quite ready, I was taken up to it; kindly, but in some sort like a prisoner; my aunt going in front, and Janet bringing up the rear. The only circumstance which gave me any new hope, was my aunt's stopping on the stairs to inquire about a smell of fire that was prevalent there; and Janet's replying that she had been making tinder down in the kitchen, of my old shirt. But there were no other clothes in my room than the odd heap of things I wore; and when I was left there, with a little taper which my aunt forewarned me would burn exactly five minutes, I heard them lock my door on the outside. Turning these things over in my mind, I deemed it possible that my aunt, who could know nothing of me, might suspect I had a habit of running away, and took precautions, on that account, to have me in safe keeping.

The room was a pleasant one, at the top of the house, overlooking the sea, on which the moon was shining brilliantly. After I said my prayers, and the candle had burnt out, I remember how I still sat looking at the moonlight on the water, as if I could hope to read my fortune in it, as in a bright book; or to see my mother with her child, coming from heaven, along that shining path, to look upon me as she had looked when I last saw her sweet face. I remember how the solemn feeling with which at length I turned my eyes away, yielded to the sensation of gratitude and rest which the sight of the white-curtained bed—and

how much more the lying softly down upon it, nestling in the snow-white sheets!—inspired. I remember how I thought of all the solitary places under the
night sky where I had slept, and how I prayed that
I never might be houseless any more, and never might
forget the houseless. I remember how I seemed to
float, then, down the melancholy glory of that track
upon the sea, away into the world of dreams.

CHAPTER XIV

MY AUNT MAKES UP HER MIND ABOUT ME

On going down in the morning, I found my aunt
musing so profoundly over the breakfast-table, with
her elbow on the tray, that the contents of the urn
had overflowed the tea-pot and were laying the whole
tablecloth under water, when my entrance put her
meditations to flight. I felt sure that I had been the
subject of her reflections, and was more than ever
anxious to know her intentions towards me. Yet I
dared not express my anxiety, lest it should give her
offence.

My eyes, however, not being so much under control as my tongue, were attracted towards my aunt
very often during breakfast. I never could look at
her for a few moments together but I found her
looking at me—in an odd thoughtful manner, as if I
were an immense way off, instead of being on the
other side of the small round table. When she had finished her breakfast, my aunt very deliberately leaned
back in her chair, knitted her brows, folded her arms,
and contemplated me at her leisure, with such a
fixedness of attention that I was quite overpowered
by embarrassment. Not having as yet finished my

own breakfast, I attempted to hide my confusion by proceeding with it; but my knife tumbled over my fork, my fork tripped up my knife, I chipped bits of bacon a surprising height into the air instead of cutting them for my own eating, and choked myself with my tea, which persisted in going the wrong way instead of the right one, until I gave in altogether, and sat blushing under my aunt's close scrutiny.

'Hallo!' said my aunt, after a long time.

I looked up, and met her sharp bright glance respectfully.

'I have written to him,' said my aunt.

'To ——?'

'To your father-in-law,' said my aunt. 'I have sent him a letter that I 'll trouble him to attend to, or he and I will fall out, I can tell him!'

'Does he know where I am, aunt?' I inquired, alarmed.

'I have told him,' said my aunt, with a nod.

'Shall I—be—given up to him?' I faltered.

'I don't know,' said my aunt. 'We shall see.'

'Oh! I can't think what I shall do,' I exclaimed, 'if I have to go back to Mr. Murdstone!'

'I don't know anything about it,' said my aunt, shaking her head. 'I can't say, I am sure. We shall see.'

My spirits sank under these words, and I became very downcast and heavy of heart. My aunt, without appearing to take much heed of me, put on a coarse apron with a bib, which she took out of the press; washed up the teacups with her own hands; and, when everything was washed and set in the tray again, and the cloth folded and put on the top of the whole, rang for Janet to remove it. She next swept up the crumbs with a little broom (putting on a pair of gloves first), until there did not appear to be one microscopic speck left on the carpet; next dusted and arranged the room, which was dusted and arranged to a hair's-breadth already. When all these tasks were performed to her satisfaction, she took off the gloves and apron, folded them up, put them in the particular corner of the press from which they had been taken, brought out her work-box to her own table in the open window, and sat down, with the green fan between her and the light, to work.

'I wish you 'd go upstairs,' said my aunt, as she threaded her needle, 'and give my compliments to Mr. Dick, and I 'll be glad to know how he gets on with his Memorial.'

I rose with all alacrity, to acquit myself of this commission.

'I suppose,' said my aunt, eyeing me as narrowly as she had eyed the needle in threading it, 'you think Mr. Dick a short name, eh?'

'I thought it was rather a short name, yesterday,' I confessed.

'You are not to suppose that he hasn't got a longer name, if he chose to use it,' said my aunt, with a loftier air. 'Babley—Mr. Richard Babley—that 's the gentleman's true name.'

I was going to suggest, with a modest sense of my youth and the familiarity I had been already guilty of, that I had better give him the full benefit of that name, when my aunt went on to say—

'But don't you call him by it, whatever you do. He can't bear his name. That 's a peculiarity of his. Though I don't know that it 's much of a peculiarity, either; for he has been ill-used enough, by some that bear it, to have a mortal antipathy for it, Heaven knows. Mr. Dick is his name here, and everywhere else, now—if he ever went anywhere else, which he don't. So take care, child, you don't call him anything *but* Mr. Dick.'

I promised to obey, and went upstairs with my message; thinking, as I went, that if Mr. Dick had been working at his Memorial long, at the same rate as I had seen him working at it, through the open door, when I came down, he was probably getting on very well indeed. I found him still driving at it with a long pen, and his head almost laid upon the paper. He was so intent upon it, that I had ample leisure to observe the large paper kite in a corner, the confusion of bundles of manuscript, the number of pens, and, above all, the quantity of ink (which he seemed to have in, in half-gallon jars by the dozen), before he observed my being present.

'Ha! Phœbus!' said Mr. Dick, laying down his pen. 'How does the world go? I'll tell you what,' he added, in a lower tone, 'I shouldn't wish it to be mentioned, but it's a—' here he beckoned to me, and put his lips close to my ear—'it's a mad world. Mad as Bedlam, boy!' said Mr. Dick, taking snuff from a round box on the table, and laughing heartily.

Without presuming to give my opinion on this question, I delivered my message.

'Well,' said Mr. Dick, in answer, 'my compliments to her, and I—I believe I have made a start. I think I have made a start,' said Mr. Dick, passing his hand among his grey hair, and casting anything but a confident look at his manuscript. 'You have been to school?'

'Yes, sir,' I answered; 'for a short time.'

'Do you recollect the date,' said Mr. Dick, looking earnestly at me, and taking up his pen to note it down, 'when King Charles the First had his head cut off?'

I said I believed it happened in the year sixteen hundred and forty-nine.

'Well,' returned Mr. Dick, scratching his ear with his pen, and looking dubiously at me. 'So the books say; but I don't see how that can be. Because, if it was so long ago, how could the people about him have made that mistake of putting some of the trouble out of *his* head, after it was taken off, into *mine?*'

I was very much surprised by the inquiry; but could give no information on this point.

'It 's very strange,' said Mr. Dick, with a despondent look upon his papers, and with his hand among his hair again, 'that I never can get that quite right. I never can make that perfectly clear. But no matter, no matter!' he said cheerfully, and rousing himself, 'there 's time enough! My compliments to Miss Trotwood, I am getting on very well indeed.'

I was going away, when he directed my attention to the kite.

'What do you think of that for a kite?' he said.

I answered that it was a beautiful one. I should think it must have been as much as seven feet high.

'I made it. We 'll go and fly it, you and I,' said Mr. Dick. 'Do you see this?'

He showed me that it was covered with manuscript, very closely and laboriously written; but so plainly, that as I looked along the lines, I thought I saw some allusion to King Charles the First's head again, in one or two places.

'There 's plenty of string,' said Mr. Dick, 'and when it flies high, it takes the facts a long way. That 's my manner of diffusing 'em. I don't know where they may come down. It 's according to circumstances, and the wind, and so forth; but I take my chance of that.'

His face was so very mild and pleasant, and had something so reverend in it, though it was hale and hearty, that I was not sure but that he was having a good-humoured jest with me. So I laughed, and he laughed, and we parted the best friends possible.

'Well, child,' said my aunt, when I went downstairs. 'And what of Mr. Dick, this morning?'

I informed her that he sent his compliments, and was getting on very well indeed.

'What do you think of him?' said my aunt.

I had some shadowy idea of endeavouring to evade the question by replying that I thought him a very nice gentleman; but my aunt was not to be so put off, for she laid her work down in her lap, and said, folding her hands upon it—

'Come! Your sister Betsey Trotwood would have told me what she thought of any one, directly. Be as like your sister as you can, and speak out!'

'Is he—is Mr. Dick—I ask because I don't know, aunt—is he at all out of his mind, then?' I stammered; for I felt I was on dangerous ground.

'Not a morsel,' said my aunt.

'Oh, indeed!' I observed faintly.

'If there is anything in the world,' said my aunt, with great decision and force of manner, 'that Mr. Dick is not, it's that.'

I had nothing better to offer than another timid 'Oh, indeed!'

'He has been *called* mad,' said my aunt. 'I have a selfish pleasure in saying he has been called mad, or I should not have had the benefit of his society and advice for these last ten years and upwards—in fact, ever since your sister, Betsey Trotwood, disappointed me.'

'So long as that?' I said.

'And nice people they were, who had the audacity

to call him mad,' pursued my aunt. 'Mr. Dick is a sort of distant connection of mine; it doesn't matter how; I needn't enter into that. If it hadn't been for me, his own brother would have shut him up for life. That's all.'

I am afraid it was hypocritical in me, but seeing that my aunt felt strongly on the subject, I tried to look as if I felt strongly too.

'A proud fool!' said my aunt. 'Because his brother was a little eccentric—though he is not half so eccentric as a good many people—he didn't like to have him visible about his house, and sent him away to some private asylum-place: though he had been left to his particular care by their deceased father, who thought him almost a natural. And a wise man *he* must have been to think so! Mad himself, no doubt.'

Again, as my aunt looked quite convinced, I endeavoured to look quite convinced also.

'So I stepped in,' said my aunt, 'and made him an offer. I said, "Your brother's sane—a great deal more sane than you are, or ever will be, it is to be hoped. Let him have his little income, and come and live with me. *I* am not afraid of him, *I* am not proud, *I* am ready to take care of him, and shall not ill-treat him as some people (besides the asylum-folks) have done." After a good deal of squabbling,' said my aunt, 'I got him; and he has been here ever since. He is the most friendly and amenable creature in existence; and as for advice! But nobody knows what that man's mind is, except myself.'

My aunt smoothed her dress and shook her head, as if she smoothed defiance of the whole world out of the one, and shook it out of the other.

'He had a favourite sister,' said my aunt, 'a good creature, and very kind to him. But she did what they all do—took a husband. And *he* did what they all do—made her wretched. It had such an effect upon the mind of Mr. Dick (*that's* not madness, I hope!) that, combined with his fear of his brother, and his sense of his unkindness, it threw him into a fever. That was before he came to me, but the recollection of it is oppressive to him even now. Did he say anything to you about King Charles the First, child?'

'Yes, aunt.'

'Ah!' said my aunt, rubbing her nose as if she were a little vexed. 'That's his allegorical way of expressing it. He connects his illness with great disturbance and agitation, naturally, and that's the figure, or the simile, or whatever it's called, which he chooses to use. And why shouldn't he, if he thinks proper?'

I said, 'Certainly, aunt.'

'It's not a business-like way of speaking,' said my aunt, 'nor a worldly way. I am aware of that; and that's the reason why I insist upon it, that there shan't be a word about it in his Memorial.'

'Is it a Memorial about his own history that he is writing, aunt?'

'Yes, child,' said my aunt, rubbing her nose again. 'He is memorialising the Lord Chancellor, or the Lord Somebody or other—one of those people, at all events, who are paid to *be* memorialised—about his affairs. I suppose it will go in, one of these days. He hasn't been able to draw it up yet, without introducing that mode of expressing himself; but it don't signify; it keeps him employed.'

In fact, I found out afterwards that Mr. Dick had been for upwards of ten years endeavouring to keep King Charles the First out of the Memorial: but he had been constantly getting into it, and was there now.

'I say again,' said my aunt, 'nobody knows what that man's mind is except myself; and he's the most amenable and friendly creature in existence. If he likes to fly a kite sometimes, what of that! Franklin used to fly a kite. He was a Quaker, or something of that sort, if I am not mistaken. And a Quaker flying a kite is a much more ridiculous object than anybody else.'

If I could have supposed that my aunt had recounted these particulars for my especial behoof, and as a piece of confidence in me, I should have felt very much distinguished, and should have augured favourably from such a mark of her good opinion. But I could hardly help observing that she had launched into them, chiefly because the question was raised in her own mind, and with very little reference to me, though she had addressed herself to me in the absence of anybody else.

At the same time, I must say that the generosity of her championship of poor harmless Mr. Dick, not only inspired my young breast with some selfish hope for myself, but warmed it unselfishly towards her. I believe that I began to know that there was something about my aunt, notwithstanding her many eccentricities and odd humours, to be honoured and trusted in. Though she was just as sharp that day, as on the day before, and was in and out about the donkeys just as often, and was thrown into a tremendous state of indignation, when a young man, going by, ogled Janet at a window (which was one of the gravest misdemeanours that could be committed against my aunt's dignity), she seemed to me to command more of my respect, if not less of my fear.

The anxiety I underwent, in the interval which necessarily elapsed before a reply could be received to her letter to Mr. Murdstone, was extreme; but I made an endeavour to suppress it, and to be as agreeable as I could in a quiet way, both to my aunt and Mr. Dick. The latter and I would have gone out to fly the great kite; but that I had still no other clothes than the anything but ornamental garments with which I had been decorated on the first day, and which confined me to the house, except for an hour after dark, when my aunt, for my health's sake, paraded me up and down on the cliff outside before going to bed. At length the reply from Mr. Murdstone came, and my aunt informed me, to my infinite terror, that he was coming to speak to her himself on the next day. On the next day, still bundled up in my curious habiliments, I sat counting the time, flushed and heated by the conflict of sinking hopes and rising fears within me; and waiting to be startled by the sight of the gloomy face, whose non-arrival startled me ever minute.

My aunt was a little more imperious and stern than usual, but I observed no other token of her preparing herself to receive the visitor so much dreaded by me. She sat at work in the window, and I sat by, with my thoughts running astray on all possible and impossible results of Mr. Murdstone's visit, until pretty late in the afternoon. Our dinner had been indefinitely postponed; but it was growing so late, that my aunt had ordered it to be got ready, when she gave a sudden alarm of donkeys, and to my consternation and amazement, I beheld Miss Murdstone, on a side-saddle, ride deliberately over the sacred piece of green, and stop in front of the house, looking about her.

'Go along with you!' cried my aunt, shaking her

head and her fist at the window. 'You have no business there. How dare you trespass? Go along!
Oh! you bold-faced thing!'

My aunt was so exasperated by the coolness with
which Miss Murdstone looked about her, that I really
believe she was motionless, and unable for the moment
to dart out according to custom. I seized the opportunity to inform her who it was; and that the
gentleman now coming near the offender (for the way
up was very steep, and he had dropped behind), was
Mr. Murdstone himself.

'I don't care who it is!' cried my aunt, still shaking her head, and gesticulating anything but welcome from the bow-window. 'I won't be trespassed
upon. I won't allow it. Go away! Janet, turn
him round. Lead him off!' and I saw, from behind
my aunt, a sort of hurried battle-piece, in which the
donkey stood resisting everybody, with all his four
legs planted different ways, while Janet tried to
pull him round by the bridle, Mr. Murdstone tried
to lead him on, Miss Murdstone struck at Janet with
a parasol, and several boys, who had come to see the
engagement, shouted vigorously. But my aunt, suddenly descrying among them the young malefactor
who was the donkey's guardian, and who was one of
the most inveterate offenders against her, though
hardly in his teens, rushed out to the scene of action,
pounced upon him, captured him, dragged him, with
his jacket over his head and his heels grinding the
ground, into the garden, and, calling upon Janet to
fetch the constables and justices, that he might be
taken, tried, and executed on the spot, held him at
bay there. This part of the business, however, did
not last long; for the young rascal, being expert
at a variety of feints and dodges, of which my aunt
had no conception, soon went whooping away, leav-

ing some deep impressions of his nailed boots in the flower-beds, and taking his donkey in triumph with him.

Miss Murdstone, during the latter portion of the contest, had dismounted, and was now waiting with her brother at the bottom of the steps, until my aunt should be at leisure to receive them. My aunt, a little ruffled by the combat, marched past them into the house, with great dignity, and took no notice of their presence, until they were announced by Janet.

'Shall I go away, aunt?' I asked, trembling.

'No, sir,' said my aunt. 'Certainly not!' With which she pushed me into a corner near her, and fenced me in with a chair, as if it were a prison or a bar of justice. This position I continued to occupy during the whole interview, and from it I now saw Mr. and Miss Murdstone enter the room.

'Oh!' said my aunt, 'I was not aware at first to whom I had the pleasure of objecting. But I don't allow anybody to ride over that turf. I make no exceptions. I don't allow anybody to do it.'

'Your regulation is rather awkward to strangers,' said Miss Murdstone.

'Is it?' said my aunt.

Mr. Murdstone seemed afraid of a renewal of hostilities, and interposing began—

'Miss Trotwood!'

'I beg your pardon,' observed my aunt with a keen look. 'You are the Mr. Murdstone who married the widow of my late nephew, David Copperfield, of Blunderstone Rookery? Though why Rookery, *I* don't know!'

'I am,' said Mr. Murdstone.

'You'll excuse my saying, sir,' returned my aunt, 'that I think it would have been a much better and happier thing if you had left that poor child alone.'

'I so far agree with what Miss Trotwood has remarked,' observed Miss Murdstone, bridling, 'that I consider our lamented Clara to have been, in all essential respects, a mere child.'

'It is a comfort to you and me, ma'am,' said my aunt, 'who are getting on in life, and are not likely to be made unhappy by our personal attractions, that nobody can say the same of us.'

'No doubt!' returned Miss Murdstone, though, I thought, not with a very ready or gracious assent. 'And it certainly might have been, as you say, a better and happier thing for my brother if he had never entered into such a marriage. I have always been of that opinion.'

'I have no doubt you have,' said my aunt. 'Janet,' ringing the bell, 'my compliments to Mr. Dick, and beg him to come down.'

Until he came, my aunt sat perfectly upright and stiff, frowning at the wall. When he came, my aunt performed the ceremony of introduction.

'Mr. Dick. An old and intimate friend. On whose judgment,' said my aunt, with emphasis, as an admonition to Mr. Dick, who was biting his forefinger and looking rather foolish, 'I rely.'

Mr. Dick took his finger out of his mouth, on this hint, and stood among the group, with a grave and attentive expression of face. My aunt inclined her head to Mr. Murdstone, who went on—

'Miss Trotwood. On the receipt of your letter, I considered it an act of greater justice to myself, and perhaps of more respect to you—'

'Thank you,' said my aunt, still eyeing him keenly. 'You needn't mind me.'

'To answer it in person, however inconvenient the journey,' pursued Mr. Murdstone, 'rather than by letter. This unhappy boy who has run away from his friends and his occupation—'

'And whose appearance,' interposed his sister, directing general attention to me in my indefinable costume, 'is perfectly scandalous and disgraceful.'

'Jane Murdstone,' said her brother, 'have the goodness not to interrupt me. This unhappy boy, Miss Trotwood, has been the occasion of much domestic trouble and uneasiness; both during the lifetime of my late dear wife, and since. He has a sullen, rebellious spirit; a violent temper; and an untoward, intractable disposition. Both my sister and myself have endeavoured to correct his vices, but ineffectually. And I have felt—we both have felt, I may say; my sister being fully in my confidence—that it is right you should receive this grave and dispassionate assurance from our lips.'

'It can hardly be necessary for me to confirm anything stated by my brother,' said Miss Murdstone; 'but I beg to observe, that, of all the boys in the world, I believe this is the worst boy.'

'Strong!' said my aunt, shortly.

'But not at all too strong for the facts,' returned Miss Murdstone.

'Ha!' said my aunt. 'Well, sir?'

'I have my own opinions,' resumed Mr. Murdstone, whose face darkened more and more, the more he and my aunt observed each other, which they did very narrowly, 'as to the best mode of bringing him up; they are founded, in part, on my knowledge of him, and in part on my knowledge of my own means and resources. I am responsible for them to myself, I act upon them, and I say no more about them. It is enough that I place this boy under the eye of a friend of my own, in a respectable business; that it does not please him; that he runs away from it;

makes himself a common vagabond about the country; and comes here, in rags, to appeal to you, Miss Trotwood. I wish to set before you, honourably, the exact consequences—so far as they are within my knowledge—of your abetting him in this appeal.'

'But about the respectable business first,' said my aunt. 'If he had been your own boy, you would have put him to it, just the same, I suppose?'

'If he had been my brother's own boy,' returned Miss Murdstone, striking in, 'his character, I trust, would have been altogether different.'

'Or if the poor child, his mother, had been alive, he would still have gone into the respectable business, would he?' said my aunt.

'I believe,' said Mr. Murdstone, with an inclination of his head, 'that Clara would have disputed nothing, which myself and my sister Jane Murdstone were agreed was for the best.'

Miss Murdstone confirmed this with an audible murmur.

'Humph!' said my aunt. 'Unfortunate baby!'

Mr. Dick, who had been rattling his money all this time, was rattling it so loudly now, that my aunt felt it necessary to check him with a look, before saying—

'The poor child's annuity died with her?'

'Died with her,' replied Mr. Murdstone.

'And there was no settlement of the little property —the house and garden—the what 's-its-name Rookery without any rooks in it—upon her boy?'

'It had been left to her, unconditionally, by her first husband,' Mr. Murdstone began, when my aunt caught him up with the greatest irascibility and impatience.

'Good Lord, man, there 's no occasion to say that.

Left to her unconditionally! I think I see David Copperfield looking forward to any condition of any sort or kind, though it stared him point-blank in the face! Of course it was left to her unconditionally. But when she married again—when she took that most disastrous step of marrying you, in short,' said my aunt, 'to be plain—did no one put in a word for the boy at that time?'

'My late wife loved her second husband, madam,' said Mr. Murdstone, 'and trusted implicitly in him.'

'Your late wife, sir, was a most unworldly, most unhappy, most unfortunate baby,' returned my aunt, shaking her head at him. 'That's what *she* was. And now, what have you got to say next?'

'Merely this, Miss Trotwood,' he returned. 'I am here to take David back; to take him back unconditionally, to dispose of him as I think proper, and to deal with him as I think right. I am not here to make any promise, or give any pledge to anybody. You may possibly have some idea, Miss Trotwood, of abetting him in his running away, and in his complaints to you. Your manner, which I must say does not seem intended to propitiate, induces me to think it possible. Now I must caution you that if you abet him once, you abet him for good and all; if you step in between him and me, now, you must step in, Miss Trotwood, for ever. I cannot trifle, or be trifled with. I am here, for the first and last time, to take him away. Is he ready to go? If he is not—and you tell me he is not; on any pretence; it is indifferent to me what—my doors are shut against him henceforth, and yours, I take it for granted, are open to him.'

To this address, my aunt had listened with the closest attention, sitting perfectly upright, with her hands folded on one knee, and looking grimly on the speaker.   When he had finished, she turned her eyes so as to command Miss Murdstone, without otherwise disturbing her attitude, and said—

'Well, ma'am, have *you* got anything to remark?'

'Indeed, Miss Trotwood,' said Miss Murdstone, 'all that I could say has been so well said by my brother, and all that I know to be the fact has been so plainly stated by him, that I have nothing to add except my thanks for your politeness.   For your very great politeness, I am sure,' said Miss Murdstone; with an irony which no more affected my aunt than it discomposed the cannon I had slept by at Chatham.

'And what does the boy say?' said my aunt.   'Are you ready to go, David?'

I answered no, and entreated her not to let me go. I said that neither Mr. nor Miss Murdstone had ever liked me, or had ever been kind to me.   That they had made my mamma, who always loved me dearly, unhappy about me, and that I knew it well, and that Peggotty knew it.   I said that I had been more miserable than I thought anybody could believe who only knew how young I was.   And I begged and prayed my aunt—I forget in what terms now, but I remember that they affected me very much then—to befriend and protect me, for my father's sake.

'Mr. Dick,' said my aunt; 'what shall I do with this child?'

Mr. Dick considered, hesitated, brightened, and rejoined, 'Have him measured for a suit of clothes directly.'

'Mr. Dick,' said my aunt triumphantly, 'give me your hand, for your common sense is invaluable.' Having shaken it with great cordiality, she pulled me towards her and said to Mr. Murdstone—

'You can go when you like; I'll take my chance with the boy.   If he's all you say he is, at least I can

do as much for him then, as you have done.   But I
don't believe a word of it.'

'Miss Trotwood,' rejoined Mr. Murdstone, shrug-
ging his shoulders, as he rose, 'if you were a gentleman—'

'Bah!   Stuff and nonsense!' said my aunt.   'Don't
talk to me!'

'How exquisitely polite!' exclaimed Miss Murdstone, rising.   'Overpowering, really!'

'Do you think I don't know,' said my aunt, turning
a deaf ear to the sister, and continuing to address
the brother, and to shake her head at him with infinite expression, 'what kind of life you must have led
that poor, unhappy, misdirected baby?   Do you think
I don't know what a woeful day it was for the soft little creature when *you* first came in her way—smirking
and making great eyes at her, I 'll be bound, as if
you couldn't say boh! to a goose!'

'I never heard anything so elegant!' said Miss
Murdstone.

'Do you think I can't understand you as well as if
I had seen you,' pursued my aunt, 'now that I *do* see
and hear you—which I tell you candidly, is anything
but a pleasure to me?   Oh yes, bless us! who so
smooth and silky as Mr. Murdstone at first!   The
poor, benighted innocent had never seen such a man.
He was made of sweetness.   He worshipped her.
He doted on her boy—tenderly doted on him!   He
was to be another father to him, and they were all to
live together in a garden of roses, weren't they?
Ugh!   Get along with you, do!' said my aunt.

'I never heard anything like this person in my life!'
exclaimed Miss Murdstone.

'And when you had made sure of the poor little
fool,' said my aunt—'God forgive me that I should
call her so, and she gone where *you* won't go in a

hurry—because you had not done wrong enough to
her and hers, you must begin to train her, must you?
begin to break her, like a poor caged bird, and wear
her deluded life away, in teaching her to sing *your*
notes?'

'This is either insanity or intoxication,' said Miss
Murdstone, in a perfect agony at not being able to
turn the current of my aunt's address towards herself; 'and my suspicion is that it's intoxication.'

Miss Betsey, without taking the least notice of the
interruption, continued to address herself to Mr.
Murdstone as if there had been no such thing.

'Mr. Murdstone,' she said, shaking her finger at him,
'you were a tyrant to the simple baby, and you broke
her heart. She was a lovely baby—I know that; I
knew it years before *you* ever saw her—and through
the best part of her weakness you gave her the wounds
she died of. There is the truth for your comfort,
however you like it. And you and your instruments
may make the most of it.'

'Allow me to inquire, Miss Trotwood,' interposed
Miss Murdstone, 'whom you are pleased to call, in a
choice of words in which I am not experienced, my
brother's instruments?'

Still stone-deaf to the voice, and utterly unmoved
by it, Miss Betsey pursued her discourse.

'It was clear enough, as I have told you, years before *you* ever saw her—and why in the mysterious
dispensations of Providence, you ever did see her, is
more than humanity can comprehend—it was clear
enough that the poor soft little thing would marry
somebody, at some time or other; but I did hope it
wouldn't have been as bad as it has turned out. That
was the time, Mr. Murdstone, when she gave birth
to her boy here,' said my aunt; 'to the poor child you
sometimes tormented her through afterwards, which

is a disagreeable remembrance, and makes the sight
of him odious now. Aye, aye! you needn't wince!'
said my aunt. 'I know it's true without that.'

He had stood by the door, all this while, observant of
her, with a smile upon his face, though his black
eyebrows were heavily contracted. I remarked now,
that, though the smile was on his face still, his colour
had gone in a moment, and he seemed to breathe as
if he had been running.

'Good day, sir,' said my aunt, 'and good-bye!
Good day to you, too, ma'am,' said my aunt, turning
suddenly upon his sister. 'Let me see you ride a donkey over *my* green again, and as sure as you have a
head upon your shoulders, I'll knock your bonnet off,
and tread upon it!'

It would require a painter, and no common painter
too, to depict my aunt's face as she delivered herself
of this very unexpected sentiment, and Miss Murdstone's face as she heard it. But the manner of the
speech, no less than the matter, was so fiery, that
Miss Murdstone, without a word in answer, discreetly
put her arm through her brother's, and walked
haughtily out of the cottage; my aunt remaining in
the window looking after them; prepared, I have no
doubt, in case of the donkey's reappearance, to carry
her threat into instant execution.

No attempt at defiance being made, however, her
face gradually relaxed, and became so pleasant, that
I was emboldened to kiss and thank her; which I did
with great heartiness, and with both my arms clasped
round her neck. I then shook hands with Mr. Dick,
who shook hands with me a great many times, and
hailed this happy close of the proceedings with repeated bursts of laughter.

'You'll consider yourself guardian, jointly with
me, of this child, Mr. Dick,' said my aunt.

'I shall be delighted,' said Mr. Dick, 'to be the guardian of David's son.'

'Very good,' returned my aunt, *that's* settled. I have been thinking, do you know, Mr. Dick, that I might call him Trotwood?'

'Certainly, certainly. Call him Trotwood, certainly,' said Mr. Dick. 'David's son's Trotwood.'

'Trotwood Copperfield, you mean,' returned my aunt.

'Yes, to be sure. Yes. Trotwood Copperfield,' said Mr. Dick, a little abashed.

My aunt took so kindly to the notion, that some ready-made clothes, which were purchased for me that afternoon, were marked 'Trotwood Copperfield,' in her own handwriting, and in indelible marking-ink, before I put them on; and it was settled that all the other clothes which were ordered to be made for me (a complete outfit was bespoke that afternoon) should be marked in the same way.

Thus I began my new life, in a new name, and with everything new about me. Now that the state of doubt was over, I felt, for many days, like one in a dream. I never thought that I had a curious couple of guardians, in my aunt and Mr. Dick. I never thought of anything about myself, distinctly. The two things clearest in my mind were, that a remoteness had come upon the old Blunderstone life —which seemed to lie in the haze of an immeasurable distance; and that a curtain had for ever fallen on my life at Murdstone and Grinby's. No one has ever raised that curtain since. I have lifted it for a moment, even in this narrative, with a reluctant hand, and dropped it gladly. The remembrance of that life is fraught with so much pain to me, with so much mental suffering and want of hope, that I have never had the courage even to examine how long I was doomed to lead it. Whether it lasted for a year, or more, or less, I do not know. I only know that it was, and ceased to be; and that I have written, and there I leave it.

CHAPTER XV

I MAKE ANOTHER BEGINNING

MR. DICK and I soon became the best of friends, and very often, when his day's work was done, went out together to fly the great kite. Every day of his life he had a long sitting at the Memorial, which never made the least progress, however hard he laboured, for King Charles the First always strayed into it, sooner or later, and then it was thrown aside, and another one begun. The patience and hope with which he bore these perpetual disappointments, the mild perception he had that there was something wrong about King Charles the First, the feeble efforts he made to keep him out, and the certainty with which he came in, and tumbled the Memorial out of all shape, made a deep impression on me. What Mr. Dick supposed would come of the Memorial, if it were completed; where he thought it was to go, or what he thought it was to do; he knew no more than anybody else, I believe. Nor was it at all necessary that he should trouble himself with such questions, for if anything were certain under the sun, it was certain that the Memorial never would be finished.

It was quite an affecting sight, I used to think, to see him with the kite when it was up a great height in the air. What he had told me, in his room, about his belief in its disseminating the statements pasted on

it, which were nothing but old leaves of abortive
Memorials, might have been a fancy with him sometimes; but not when he was out, looking up at the
kite in the sky, and feeling it pull and tug at his hand.
He never looked so serene as he did then. I used to
fancy, as I sat by him of an evening, on a green
slope, and saw him watch the kite high in the quiet
air, that it lifted his mind out of its confusion, and
bore it (such was my boyish thought) into the skies.
As he wound the string in, and it came lower and
lower down out of the beautiful light, until it fluttered to the ground, and lay there like a dead thing,
he seemed to wake gradually out of a dream; and I
remember to have seen him take it up, and look about
him in a lost way, as if they had both come down together, so that I pitied him with all my heart.

While I advanced in friendship and intimacy with
Mr. Dick, I did not go backward in the favour of
his staunch friend, my aunt. She took so kindly to
me, that, in the course of a few weeks, she shortened
my adopted name of Trotwood into Trot; and even
encouraged me to hope, that if I went on as I had
begun, I might take equal rank in her affections with
my sister Betsey Trotwood.

'Trot,' said my aunt one evening, when the back-
gammon-board was placed as usual for herself and
Mr. Dick, 'we must not forget your education.'

This was my only subject of anxiety, and I felt
quite delighted by her referring to it.

'Should you like to go to school at Canterbury?'
said my aunt.

I replied that I should like it very much, as it was
so near her.

'Good,' said my aunt. 'Should you like to go to-
morrow?'

Being already no stranger to the general rapidity of my aunt's evolutions, I was not surprised by the suddenness of the proposal, and said, 'Yes.'

'Good,' said my aunt again. 'Janet, hire the grey pony and chaise to-morrow morning at ten o'clock, and pack up Master Trotwood's clothes to-night.'

I was greatly elated by these orders; but my heart smote me for my selfishness, when I witnessed their effect on Mr. Dick, who was so low-spirited at the prospect of our separation, and played so ill in consequence, that my aunt, after giving him several admonitory raps on the knuckles with her dice-box, shut up the board, and declined to play with him any more. But, on hearing from my aunt that I should sometimes come over on a Saturday, and that he could sometimes come and see me on a Wednesday, he revived; and vowed to make another kite for those occasions, of proportions greatly surpassing the present one. In the morning he was down-hearted again, and would have sustained himself by giving me all the money he had in his possession, gold and silver too, if my aunt had not interposed, and limited the gift to five shillings, which, at his earnest petition, were afterwards increased to ten. We parted at the garden-gate in a most affectionate manner, and Mr. Dick did not go into the house until my aunt had driven me out of sight of it.

My aunt, who was perfectly indifferent to public opinion, drove the grey pony through Dover in a masterly manner; sitting high and stiff like a state coachman, keeping a steady eye upon him wherever he went, and making a point of not letting him have his own way in any respect. When we came into the country road, she permitted him to relax a little, however; and looking at me down in a valley of cushion by her side, asked me whether I was happy?

'Very happy indeed, thank you, aunt,' I said.

She was much gratified; and both her hands being occupied, patted me on the head with her whip.

'Is it a large school, aunt?' I asked.

'Why, I don't know,' said my aunt. 'We are going to Mr. Wickfield's first.'

'Does *he* keep a school?' I asked.

'No, Trot,' said my aunt. 'He keeps an office.'

I asked for no more information about Mr. Wickfield, as she offered none, and we conversed on other subjects until we came to Canterbury, where, as it was market-day, my aunt had a great opportunity of insinuating the grey pony among carts, baskets, vegetables, and hucksters' goods. The hair-breadth turns and twists we made, drew down upon us a variety of speeches from the people standing about, which were not always complimentary; but my aunt drove on with perfect indifference, and I dare say would have taken her own way with as much coolness through an enemy's country.

At length we stopped before a very old house bulging out over the road; a house with long low lattice-windows bulging out still farther, and beams with carved heads on the ends bulging out too, so that I fancied the whole house was leaning forward, trying to see who was passing on the narrow pavement below. It was quite spotless in its cleanliness. The old-fashioned brass knocker on the low arched door, ornamented with carved garlands of fruit and flowers, twinkled like a star; the two stone steps descending to the door were as white as if they had been covered with fair linen; and all the angles and corners, and carvings and mouldings, and quaint little panes of glass, and quainter little windows, though as old as the hills, were as pure as any snow that ever fell upon the hills.

When the pony-chaise stopped at the door, and my eyes were intent upon the house, I saw a cadaverous face appear at a small window on the ground floor (in a little round tower that formed one side of the house), and quickly disappear. The low arched door then opened, and the face came out. It was quite as cadaverous as it had looked in the window, though in the grain of it there was that tinge of red which is sometimes to be observed in the skins of red-haired people. It belonged to a red-haired person—a youth of fifteen, as I take it now, but looking much older —whose hair was cropped as close as the closest stubble; who had hardly any eyebrows, and no eyelashes, and eyes of a red-brown, so unsheltered and unshaded, that I remember wondering how he went to sleep. He was high-shouldered and bony; dressed in decent black, with a white wisp of a neckcloth; buttoned up to the throat; and had a long, lank, skeleton hand, which particularly attracted my attention, as he stood at the pony's head, rubbing his chin with it, and looked up at us in the chaise.

'Is Mr. Wickfield at home, Uriah Heep?' said my aunt.

'Mr. Wickfield's at home, ma'am,' said Uriah Heep, 'if you'll please to walk in there': pointing with his long hand to the room he meant.

We got out; and leaving him to hold the pony, went into a long low parlour looking towards the street, from the window of which I caught a glimpse, as I went in, of Uriah Heep breathing into the pony's nostrils, and immediately covering them with his hand, as if he were putting some spell upon him. Opposite to the tall old chimney-piece, were two portraits: one of a gentleman with grey hair (though not by any means an old man) and black eyebrows, who was looking over some papers tied together with red tape; the other, of a lady, with a very placid and sweet expression of face, who was looking at me.

I believe I was turning about in search of Uriah's picture, when, a door at the farther end of the room opening, a gentleman entered, at sight of whom I turned to the first-mentioned portrait again, to make quite sure that it had not come out of its frame. But it was stationary; and as the gentleman advanced into the light, I saw that he was some years older than when he had had his picture painted.

'Miss Betsey Trotwood,' said the gentleman, 'pray walk in. I was engaged for a moment, but you'll excuse my being busy. You know my motive. I have but one in life.'

Miss Betsey thanked him, and we went into his room, which was furnished as an office, with books, papers, tin boxes, and so forth. It looked into a garden, and had an iron safe let into the wall; so immediately over the mantel-shelf, that I wondered, as I sat down, how the sweeps got round it when they swept the chimney.

'Well, Miss Trotwood,' said Mr. Wickfield; for I soon found that it was he, and that he was a lawyer, and steward of the estates of a rich gentleman of the county; 'what wind blows you here? Not an ill wind, I hope?'

'No,' replied my aunt, 'I have not come for any law.'

'That's right, ma'am,' said Mr. Wickfield. 'You had better come for anything else.'

His hair was quite white now, though his eyebrows were still black. He had a very agreeable face, and, I thought, was handsome. There was a certain richness in his complexion, which I had been long accustomed, under Peggotty's tuition, to connect with port wine; and I fancied it was in his voice too, and referred his growing corpulency to the same cause. He was very cleanly dressed, in a blue coat, striped waistcoat, and nankeen trousers; and his fine frilled shirt and cambric neckcloth looked unusually soft and white, reminding my strolling fancy (I call to mind) of the plumage on the breast of a swan.

'This is my nephew,' said my aunt.

'Wasn't aware you had one, Miss Trotwood,' said Mr. Wickfield.

'My grand-nephew, that is to say,' observed my aunt.

'Wasn't aware you had a grand-nephew, I give you my word,' said Mr. Wickfield.

'I have adopted him,' said my aunt, with a wave of her hand, importing that his knowledge and his ignorance were all one to her, 'and I have brought him here, to put him to a school where he may be thoroughly well taught, and well treated. Now tell me where that school is, and what it is, and all about it.'

'Before I can advise you properly,' said Mr. Wickfield,—'the old question, you know. What's your motive in this?'

'Deuce take the man!' exclaimed my aunt. 'Always fishing for motives, when they're on the surface! Why, to make the child happy and useful.'

'It must be a mixed motive, I think,' said Mr. Wickfield, shaking his head and smiling incredulously.

'A mixed fiddlestick!' returned my aunt. 'You claim to have one plain motive in all you do yourself. You don't suppose, I hope, that you are the only plain dealer in the world?'

'Ay, but I have only one motive in life, Miss Trotwood,' he rejoined, smiling. 'Other people have dozens, scores, hundreds. I have only one. There's the difference. However, that's beside the question.

The best school! Whatever the motive, you want
the best?'

My aunt nodded assent.

'At the best we have,' said Mr. Wickfield, considering, 'your nephew couldn't board just now.'

'But he could board somewhere else, I suppose?'
suggested my aunt.

Mr. Wickfield thought I could. After a little discussion, he proposed to take my aunt to the school,
that she might see it and judge for herself; also, to
take her, with the same object, to two or three houses
where he thought I could be boarded. My aunt embracing the proposal, we were all three going out together, when he stopped and said—

'Our little friend here might have some motive, perhaps, for objecting to the arrangements. I think
we had better leave him behind?'

My aunt seemed disposed to contest the point; but
to facilitate matters I said I would gladly remain behind, if they pleased; and returned into Mr. Wickfield's office, where I sat down again, in the chair I had
first occupied, to await their return.

It so happened that this chair was opposite a narrow passage, which ended in the little circular room
where I had seen Uriah Heep's pale face looking out
of window. Uriah, having taken the pony to a
neighbouring stable, was at work at a desk in this
room, which had a brass frame on the top to hang
papers upon, and on which the writing he was making a copy of was then hanging. Though his face
was towards me, I thought, for some time, the writing being between us, that he could not see me; but
looking that way more attentively, it made me uncomfortable to observe that every now and then, his
sleepless eyes would come below the writing, like two

red suns, and stealthily stare at me for I dare say a whole minute at a time, during which his pen went, or pretended to go, as cleverly as ever. I made several attempts to get out of their way—such as standing on a chair to look at a map on the other side of the room, and poring over the columns of a Kentish newspaper—but they always attracted me back again; and whenever I looked towards those two red suns, I was sure, to find them, either just rising or just setting.

At length, much to my relief, my aunt and Mr. Wickfield came back, after a pretty long absence. They were not so successful as I could have wished; for though the advantages of the school were undeniable, my aunt had not approved of any of the boarding-houses proposed for me.

'It's very unfortunate,' said my aunt. 'I don't know what to do, Trot.'

'It *does* happen unfortunately,' said Mr. Wickfield. 'But I'll tell you what you can do, Miss Trotwood.'

'What's that?' inquired my aunt.

'Leave your nephew here, for the present. He's a quiet fellow. He won't disturb me at all. It's a capital house for study. As quiet as a monastery, and almost as roomy. Leave him here.'

My aunt evidently liked the offer, though she was delicate of accepting it. So did I.

'Come, Miss Trotwood,' said Mr. Wickfield. 'This is the way out of the difficulty. It's only a temporary arrangement, you know. If it don't act well, or don't quite accord with our mutual convenience, he can easily go to the right-about. There will be time to find some better place for him in the meanwhile. You had better determine to leave him here for the present!'

'I am very much obliged to you,' said my aunt; 'and so is he, I see; but—'

'Come! I know what you mean,' cried Mr. Wickfield. 'You shall not be oppressed by the receipt of favours, Miss Trotwood. You may pay for him, if you like. We won't be hard about terms, but you shall pay if you will.'

'On that understanding,' said my aunt, 'though it doesn't lessen the real obligation, I shall be very glad to leave him.'

'Then come and see my little housekeeper,' said Mr. Wickfield.

We accordingly went up a wonderful old staircase; with a balustrade so broad that we might have gone up that, almost as easily; and into a shady old drawing-room, lighted by some three of four of the quaint windows I had looked up at from the street: which had old oak seats in them, that seemed to have come of the same trees as the shining oak floor, and the great beams in the ceiling. It was a prettily furnished room, with a piano and some lively furniture in red and green, and some flowers. It seemed to be all old nooks and corners; and in every nook and corner there was some queer little table, or cupboard, or bookcase, or seat, or something or other, that made me think there was not such another good corner in the room; until I looked at the next one, and found it equal to it, if not better. On everything there was the same air of retirement and cleanliness that marked the house outside.

Mr. Wickfield tapped at a door in a corner of the panelled wall, and a girl of about my own age came quickly out and kissed him. On her face, I saw immediately the placid and sweet expression of the lady whose picture had looked at me downstairs. It seemed to my imagination as if the portrait had grown womanly, and the original remained a child. Although her face was quite bright and happy, there was a tranquillity about it, and about her—a quiet, good, calm spirit,—that I never have forgotten; that I never shall forget.

This was his little housekeeper, his daughter Agnes, Mr. Wickfield said. When I heard how he said it, and saw how he held her hand, I guessed what the one motive of his life was.

She had a little basket-trifle hanging at her side, with keys in it; and she looked as staid and as discreet a housekeeper as the old house could have. She listened to her father as he told her about me, with a pleasant face; and when he had concluded, proposed to my aunt that we should go upstairs and see my room. We all went together, she before us. A glorious old room it was, with more oak beams, and diamond panes; and the broad balustrade going all the way up to it.

I cannot call to mind where or when, in my childhood, I had seen a stained-glass window in a church. Nor do I recollect its subject. But I know that when I saw her turn round, in the grave light of the old staircase, and wait for us, above, I thought of that window; and I associated something of its tranquil brightness with Agnes Wickfield ever afterwards.

My aunt was as happy as I was, in the arrangement made for me, and we went down to the drawing-room again, well pleased and gratified. As she would not hear of staying to dinner, lest she should by any chance fail to arrive at home with the grey pony before dark; and as I apprehend Mr. Wickfield knew her too well, to argue any point with her; some lunch was provided for her there, and Agnes went back to her governess, and Mr. Wickfield to his office.

So we were left to take leave of one another without any restraint.

She told me that everything would be arranged for me by Mr. Wickfield, and that I should want for nothing, and gave me the kindest words and the best advice.

'Trot,' said my aunt in conclusion, 'be a credit to yourself, to me, and Mr. Dick, and Heaven be with you!'

I was greatly overcome, and could only thank her, again and again, and send my love to Mr. Dick.

'Never,' said my aunt, 'be mean in anything; never be false; never be cruel. Avoid those three vices, Trot, and I can always be hopeful of you.'

I promised, as well as I could, that I would not abuse her kindness or forget her admonition.

'The pony's at the door,' said my aunt, 'and I am off! Stay here.'

With these words she embraced me hastily, and went out of the room, shutting the door after her. At first I was startled by so abrupt a departure, and almost feared I had displeased her; but when I looked into the street, and saw how dejectedly she got into the chaise, and drove away without looking up, I understood her better, and did not do her that injustice.

By five o'clock, which was Mr. Wickfield's dinner-hour, I had mustered up my spirits again, and was ready for my knife and fork. The cloth was only laid for us two; but Agnes was waiting in the drawing-room before dinner, went down with her father, and sat opposite to him at table. I doubted whether he could have dined without her.

We did not stay there, after dinner, but came upstairs into the drawing-room again; in one snug corner of which, Agnes set glasses for her father, and a decanter of port wine. I thought he would have missed its usual flavour, if it had been put there for him by any other hands.

There he sat, taking his wine, and taking a good deal of it, for two hours; while Agnes played on the piano, worked, and talked to him and me. He was, for the most part, gay and cheerful with us; but sometimes his eyes rested on her, and he fell into a brooding state, and was silent. She always observed this quickly, I thought, and always roused him with a question or caress. Then he came out of his meditation, and drank more wine.

Agnes made the tea, and presided over it; and the time passed away after it, as after dinner, until she went to bed; when her father took her in his arms and kissed her, and, she being gone, ordered candles in his office. Then I went to bed too.

But in the course of the evening I had rambled down to the door, and a little way along the street, that I might have another peep at the old houses, and the grey cathedral; and might think of my coming through that old city on my journey, and of my passing the very house I lived in, without knowing it. As I came back, I saw Uriah Heep shutting up the office; and, feeling friendly towards everybody, went in and spoke to him, and at parting, gave him my hand. But oh, what a clammy hand his was! as ghostly to the touch as to the sight! I rubbed mine afterwards, to warm it, *and to rub his off*.

It was such an uncomfortable hand, that, when I went to my room, it was still cold and wet upon my memory. Leaning out of window, and seeing one of the faces on the beam-ends looking at me sideways, I fancied it was Uriah Heep got up there somehow, and shut him out in a hurry.

CHAPTER XVI

I AM A NEW BOY IN MORE SENSES THAN ONE

NEXT morning, after breakfast, I entered on school-life again. I went, accompanied by Mr. Wickfield, to the scene of my future studies—a grave building in a courtyard, with a learned air about it that seemed very well suited to the stray rooks and jackdaws who came down from the cathedral towers to walk with a clerkly bearing on the grass-plot—and was introduced to my new master, Doctor Strong.

Doctor Strong looked almost as rusty, to my thinking, as the tall iron rails and gates outside the house; and almost as stiff and heavy as the great stone urns that flanked them, and were set up, on the top of the red-brick wall, at regular distances all round the court, like sublimated skittles, for Time to play at. He was in his library (I mean Doctor Strong was), with his clothes not particularly well brushed, and his hair not particularly well combed; his knee-smalls unbraced; his long black gaiters un-buttoned; and his shoes yawning like two caverns on the hearth-rug. Turning upon me a lustreless eye, that reminded me of a long-forgotten blind old horse who once used to crop the grass, and tumble over the graves, in Blunderstone churchyard, he said he was glad to see me: and then he gave me his hand; which I didn't know what to do with, as it did nothing for itself.

But, sitting at work, not far off from Doctor Strong, was a very pretty young lady—whom he called Annie, and who was his daughter, I supposed —who got me out of my difficulty by kneeling down to put Doctor Strong's shoes on, and button his gaiters, which she did with great cheerfulness and quickness. When she had finished, and we were going out to the schoolroom, I was much surprised to hear Mr. Wickfield, in bidding her good morning, address her as 'Mrs. Strong'; and I was wondering could she be Doctor Strong's son's wife, or could she be Mrs. Doctor Strong, when Doctor Strong himself unconsciously enlightened me.

'By the bye, Wickfield,' he said, stopping in the passage with his hand on my shoulder; 'you have not found any suitable provision for my wife's cousin yet?'

'No,' said Mr. Wickfield. 'No. Not yet.'

'I could wish it done as soon as it *can* be done, Wickfield,' said Doctor Strong, 'for Jack Maldon is needy, and idle; and of those two bad things, worse things sometimes come. What does Doctor Watts say,' he added, looking at me, and moving his head to the time of his quotation, ' "Satan finds some mischief still, for idle hands to do." '

'Egad, Doctor,' returned Mr. Wickfield, 'if Doctor Watts knew mankind, he might have written, with as much truth, "Satan finds some mischief still, for busy hands to do." The busy people achieve their full share of mischief in the world, you may rely upon it. What have the people been about, who have been the busiest in getting money, and in getting power, this century or two? No mischief?'

'Jack Maldon will never be very busy in getting either, I expect,' said Doctor Strong, rubbing his chin thoughtfully.

'Perhaps not,' said Mr. Wickfield; 'and you bring me back to the question with an apology for digressing. No, I have not been able to dispose of Mr. Jack Maldon yet. I believe,' he said this with some hesitation, 'I penetrate your motive, and it makes the thing more difficult.'

'My motive,' returned Doctor Strong, 'is to make some suitable provision for a cousin, and an old playfellow, of Annie's.'

'Yes, I know,' said Mr. Wickfield, 'at home or abroad.'

'Ay!' replied the Doctor, apparently wondering why he emphasised those words so much. 'At home or abroad.'

'Your own expression, you know,' said Mr. Wickfield. 'Or abroad.'

'Surely,' the Doctor answered. 'Surely. One or other.'

'One or other? Have you no choice?' asked Mr. Wickfield.

'No,' returned the Doctor.

'No?' with astonishment.

'Not the least.'

'No motive,' said Mr. Wickfield, 'for meaning abroad, and not at home?'

'No,' returned the Doctor.

'I am bound to believe you, and of course I do believe you,' said Mr. Wickfield. 'It might have simplified my office very much, if I had known it before. But I confess I entertained another impression.'

Doctor Strong regarded him with a puzzled and doubting look, which almost immediately subsided into a smile that gave me great encouragement; for it was full of amiability and sweetness, and there was a simplicity in it, and indeed in his whole manner, when the studious, pondering frost upon it was got through, very attractive and hopeful to a young scholar like me. Repeating 'no,' and 'not the least,'

and other short assurances to the same purport, Doctor Strong jogged on before us, at a queer, uneven
pace; and we followed: Mr. Wickfield looking grave,
I observed, and shaking his head to himself, without
knowing that I saw him.

The school-room was a pretty large hall, on the
quietest side of the house, confronted by the stately
stare of some half-dozen of the great urns, and commanding a peep of an old secluded garden belonging
to the Doctor, where the peaches were ripening on
the sunny south wall. There were two great aloes,
in tubs, on the turf outside the windows; the broad
hard leaves of which plant (looking as if they were
made of painted tin) have ever since, by association, been symbolical to me of silence and retirement.
About five-and-twenty boys were studiously engaged at their books when we went in, but they rose
to give the Doctor good morning, and remained
standing when they saw Mr. Wickfield and me.

'A new boy, young gentlemen,' said the Doctor;
'Trotwood Copperfield.'

One Adams, who was the head-boy, then stepped
out of his place and welcomed me. He looked like
a young clergyman, in his white cravat, but he was
very affable and good-humoured; and he showed me
my place, and presented me to the masters, in a gentlemanly way that would have put me at my ease,
if anything could.

It seemed to me so long, however, since I had been
among such boys, or among any companions of my
own age, except Mick Walker and Mealy Potatoes,
that I felt as strange as ever I have done in all my
life. I was so conscious of having passed through
scenes of which they could have no knowledge, and
of having acquired experiences foreign to my age,

appearance, and condition as one of them, that I half believed it was an imposture to come there as an ordinary little school-boy. I had become, in the Murdstone and Grinby time, however short or long it may have been, so unused to the sports and games of boys, that I knew I was awkward and inexperienced in the commonest things belonging to them. Whatever I had learnt, had so slipped away from me in the sordid cares of my life from day to night, that now, when I was examined about what I knew, I knew nothing, and was put into the lowest form of the school. But, troubled as I was, by my want of boyish skill, and of book-learning too, I was made infinitely more uncomfortable by the consideration, that, in what I did know, I was much farther removed from my companions than in what I did not. My mind ran upon what they would think, if they knew of my familiar acquaintance with the King's Bench Prison? Was there anything about me which would reveal my proceedings in connection with the Micawber family—all those pawnings, and sellings, and suppers—in spite of myself? Suppose some of the boys had seen me coming through Canterbury, wayworn and ragged, and should find me out? What would they say, who made so light of money, if they could know how I had scraped my halfpence together, for the purchase of my daily saveloy and beer, or my slices of pudding? How would it affect them, who were so innocent of London life and London streets, to discover how knowing I was (and was ashamed to be) in some of the meanest phases of both? All this ran in my head so much, on the first day at Doctor Strong's, that I felt distrustful of my slightest look and gesture; shrunk within myself whensoever I was approached by one of my new schoolfellows; and hurried off, the minute school was over, afraid of committing myself in my response to any friendly notice or advance.

But there was such an influence in Mr. Wickfield's old house, that when I knocked at it, with my new school-books under my arm, I began to feel my uneasiness softening away. As I went up to my airy old room, the grave shadow of the staircase seemed to fall upon my doubts and fears, and to make the past more indistinct. I sat there, sturdily conning my books, until dinner-time (we were out of school for good at three): and went down, hopeful of becoming a passable sort of boy yet.

Agnes was in the drawing-room, waiting for her father, who was detained by some one in his office. She met me with her pleasant smile, and asked me how I liked the school. I told her I should like it very much, I hoped; but I was a little strange to it at first.

'*You* have never been to school,' I said, 'have you?'

'Oh yes! Every day.'

'Ah, but you mean here, at your own home?'

'Papa couldn't spare me to go anywhere else,' she answered, smiling and shaking her head. 'His housekeeper must be in his house, you know.'

'He is very fond of you, I am sure,' I said.

She nodded 'Yes,' and went to the door to listen for his coming up, that she might meet him on the stairs. But, as he was not there, she came back again.

'Mamma has been dead ever since I was born,' she said, in her quiet way. 'I only know her picture, downstairs. I saw you looking at it yesterday. Did you think whose it was?'

I told her yes, because it was so like herself.

'Papa says so, too,' said Agnes, pleased. 'Hark! That's papa now?'

Her bright calm face lighted up with pleasure as she went to meet him, and as they came in, hand in hand. He greeted me cordially; and told me I should certainly be happy under Doctor Strong, who was one of the gentlest of men.

'There may be some, perhaps—I don't know that there are—who abuse his kindness,' said Mr. Wickfield. 'Never be one of those, Trotwood, in anything. He is the least suspicious of mankind; and whether that's a merit, or whether it's a blemish, it deserves consideration in all dealings with the Doctor, great or small.'

He spoke, I thought, as if he were weary, or dissatisfied with something; but I did not pursue the question in my mind, for dinner was just then announced, and we went down and took the same seats as before.

We had scarcely done so, when Uriah Heep put in his red head and his lank hand at the door, and said—

'Here's Mr. Maldon begs the favour of a word, sir.'

'I am but this moment quit of Mr. Maldon,' said his master.

'Yes, sir,' returned Uriah; 'but Mr. Maldon has come back, and he begs the favour of a word.'

As he held the door open with his hand, Uriah looked at me, and looked at Agnes, and looked at the dishes, and looked at the plates, and looked at every object in the room, I thought,—yet seemed to look at nothing; he made such an appearance all the while of keeping his red eyes dutifully on his master.

'I beg your pardon. It's only to say, on reflection,' observed a voice behind Uriah, as Uriah's head was pushed away, and the speaker's substituted—'pray excuse me for this intrusion—that as it seems

I have no choice in the matter, the sooner I go abroad the better. My cousin Annie did say, when we talked of it, that she liked to have her friends within reach rather than to have them banished, and the old Doctor—'

'Doctor Strong, was that?' Mr. Wickfield interposed, gravely.

'Doctor Strong of course,' returned the other; 'I call him the old Doctor; it's all the same, you know.'

'I *don't* know,' returned Mr. Wickfield.

'Well, Doctor Strong,' said the other. 'Doctor Strong was of the same mind, I believed. But as it appears from the course you take with me that he has changed his mind, why there's no more to be said, except that the sooner I am off, the better. Therefore, I thought I'd come back and say, that the sooner I am off the better. When a plunge is to be made into the water, it's of no use lingering on the bank.'

'There shall be as little lingering as possible, in your case, Mr. Maldon, you may depend upon it,' said Mr. Wickfield.

'Thank 'ee,' said the other. 'Much obliged. I don't want to look a gift-horse in the mouth, which is not a gracious thing to do; otherwise, I dare say, my cousin Annie could easily arrange it in her own way. I suppose Annie would only have to say to the old Doctor—'

'Meaning that Mrs. Strong would only have to say to her husband—do I follow you?' said Mr. Wickfield.

'Quite so,' returned the other, '—would only have to say, that she wanted such and such a thing to be so and so; and it would be so and so, as a matter of course.'

'And why as a matter of course, Mr. Maldon?'

asked Mr. Wickfield, sedately eating his dinner.

'Why, because Annie's a charming young girl, and the old Doctor—Doctor Strong, I mean—is not quite a charming young boy,' said Mr. Jack Maldon, laughing. 'No offence to anybody, Mr. Wickfield. I only mean that I suppose some compensation is fair and reasonable in that sort of marriage.'

'Compensation to the lady, sir?' asked Mr. Wickfield gravely.

'To the lady, sir,' Mr. Jack Maldon answered, laughing. But appearing to remark that Mr. Wickfield went on with his dinner in the same sedate, immoveable manner, and that there was no hope of making him relax a muscle of his face, he added—

'However, I have said what I came back to say, and, with another apology for this intrusion, I may take myself off. Of course I shall observe your directions, in considering the matter as one to be arranged between you and me solely, and not to be referred to, up at the Doctor's.'

'Have you dined?' asked Mr. Wickfield, with a motion of his hand towards the table.

'Thank 'ee. I am going to dine,' said Mr. Maldon, 'with my cousin Annie. Good-bye!'

Mr. Wickfield, without rising, looked after him thoughtfully as he went out. He was rather a shallow sort of young gentleman, I thought, with a handsome face, a rapid utterance, and a confident bold air. And this was the first I ever saw of Mr. Jack Maldon; whom I had not expected to see so soon, when I heard the Doctor speak of him that morning.

When we had dined, we went upstairs again, where everything went on exactly as on the previous day. Agnes set the glasses and decanters in the same corner, and Mr. Wickfield sat down to drink, and drank a good deal. Agnes played the piano to him, sat by him, and worked and talked, and played some games at dominoes with me. In good time she made tea; and afterwards, when I brought down my books, looked into them, and showed me what she knew of them (which was no slight matter, though she said it was), and what was the best way to learn and understand them. I see her, with her modest, orderly, placid manner, and I hear her beautiful calm voice, as I write these words. The influence for all good, which she came to exercise over me at a later time, begins already to descend upon my breast. I love little Em'ly, and I don't love Agnes —no, not at all in that way—but I feel that there are goodness, peace, and truth, wherever Agnes is; and that the soft light of the coloured window in the church, seen long ago, falls on her always, and on me when I am near her, and on everything around.

The time having come for her withdrawal for the night, and she having left us, I gave Mr. Wick-field my hand, preparatory to going away myself. But he checked me and said, 'Should you like to stay with us, Trotwood, or to go elsewhere?'

'To stay,' I answered, quickly.

'You are sure?'

'If you please. If I may!'

'Why, it's but a dull life that we lead here, boy, I am afraid,' he said.

'Not more dull for me than Agnes, sir. Not dull at all!'

'Than Agnes,' he repeated, walking slowly to the great chimney-piece, and leaning against it. 'Than Agnes!'

He had drank wine that evening (or I fancied it), until his eyes were bloodshot. Not that I could see them now, for they were cast down, and shaded by his hand; but I had noticed them a little while before.

'Now I wonder,' he muttered, 'whether my Agnes tires of me? When should I ever tire of her? But that's different, that's quite different.'

He was musing, not speaking to me; so I remained quiet.

'A dull old house,' he said, 'and a monotonous life; but I must have her near me. I must keep her near me. If the thought that I may die and leave my darling, or that my darling may die and leave me, comes like a spectre, to distress my happiest hours, and is only to be drowned in—'

He did not supply the word; but pacing slowly to the place where he had sat, and mechanically going through the action of pouring wine from the empty decanter, set it down and paced back again.

'If it is miserable to bear when she is here,' he said, 'what would it be, and she away? No, no, no. I cannot try that.'

He leaned against the chimney-piece, brooding so long that I could not decide whether to run the risk of disturbing him by going, or to remain quietly where I was, until he should come out of his reverie. At length he aroused himself, and looked about the room until his eyes encountered mine.

'Stay with us, Trotwood, eh?' he said in his usual manner, and as if he were answering something I had just said. 'I am glad of it. You are company to us both. It is wholesome to have you here. Wholesome for me, wholesome for Agnes, wholesome perhaps for all of us.'

'I am sure it is for me, sir,' I said. 'I am so glad to be here.'

'That's a fine fellow!' said Mr. Wickfield. 'As long as you are glad to be here, you shall stay here.'

He shook hands with me upon it, and clapped me on the back; and told me that when I had anything to do at night after Agnes had left us, or when I wished to read for my own pleasure, I was free to come down to his room, if he were there, and if I desired it for company's sake, and to sit with him. I thanked him for his consideration; and, as he went down soon afterwards, and I was not tired, went down too, with a book in my hand, to avail myself, for half an hour, of his permission.

But, seeing a light in the little round office, and immediately feeling myself attracted towards Uriah Heep, who had a sort of fascination for me, I went in there instead. I found Uriah reading a great fat book, with such demonstrative attention, that his lank fore-finger followed up every line as he read, and made clammy tracks along the page (or so I fully believed) like a snail.

'You are working late to-night, Uriah,' says I.

'Yes, Master Copperfield,' says Uriah.

As I was getting on the stool opposite, to talk to him more conveniently, I observed that he had not such a thing as a smile about him, and that he could only widen his mouth and make two hard creases down his cheeks, one on each side, to stand for one.

'I am not doing office-work, Master Copperfield,' said Uriah.

'What work, then?' I asked.

'I am improving my legal knowledge, Master Copperfield,' said Uriah. 'I am going through Tidd's Practice. Oh, what a writer Mr. Tidd is, Master Copperfield!'

My stool was such a tower of observation, that as I watched him reading on again, after this rapturous exclamation, and following up the lines with his fore-finger, I observed that his nostrils, which were thin and pointed, with sharp dints in them, had a singular and most uncomfortable way of expanding and contracting themselves; that they seemed to twinkle instead of his eyes, which hardly ever twinkled at all.

'I suppose you are quite a great lawyer?' I said, after looking at him for some time.

'Me, Master Copperfield?' said Uriah. 'Oh, no! I 'm a very umble person.'

It was no fancy of mine about his hands, I observed; for he frequently ground the palms against each other as if to squeeze them dry and warm, besides often wiping them, in a stealthy way, on his pocket-handkerchief.

'I am well aware that I am the umblest person going,' said Uriah Heep, modestly; 'let the other be where he may. My mother is likewise a very umble person. We live in a umble abode, Master Copperfield, but have much to be thankful for. My father's former calling was umble. He was a sexton.'

'What is he now?' I asked.

'He is a partaker of glory at present, Master Copperfield,' said Uriah Heep. 'But we have much to be thankful for. How much have I to be thankful for in living with Mr. Wickfield!'

I asked Uriah if he had been with Mr. Wickfield long?

'I have been with him going on four year, Master Copperfield,' said Uriah; shutting up his book, after carefully marking the place where he had left off. 'Since a year after my father's death. How much have I to be thankful for, in that! How much have I to be thankful for, in Mr. Wickfield's kind intention to give me my articles, which would otherwise not lay within the umble means of mother and self!'

'Then, when your articled time is over, you 'll be a regular lawyer, I suppose?' said I.

'With the blessing of Providence, Master Copperfield,' returned Uriah.

'Perhaps you'll be a partner in Mr. Wickfield's
business, one of these days,' I said, to make myself
agreeable; 'and it will be Wickfield and Heep, or
Heep late Wickfield.'

'Oh no, Master Copperfield,' returned Uriah, shaking his head, 'I am much too umble for that!'

He certainly did look uncommonly like the carved
face on the beam outside my window, as he sat, in
his humility, eyeing me sideways, with his mouth
widened, and the creases in his cheeks.

'Mr. Wickfield is a most excellent man, Master
Copperfield,' said Uriah. 'If you have known him
long, you know it, I am sure, much better than I can
inform you.'

I replied that I was certain he was; but that I had
not known him long myself, though he was a friend
of my aunt's.

'Oh, indeed, Master Copperfield,' said Uriah.
'Your aunt is a sweet lady, Master Copperfield!'

He had a way of writhing when he wanted to
express enthusiasm, which was very ugly; and which
diverted my attention from the compliment he had
paid my relation, to the snaky twistings of his throat
and body.

'A sweet lady, Master Copperfield!' said Uriah
Heep. 'She has a great admiration for Miss Agnes,
Master Copperfield, I believe?'

I said, 'Yes,' boldly; not that I knew anything
about it, Heaven forgive me!

'I hope you have, too, Master Copperfield,' said
Uriah. 'But I am sure you must have.'

'Everybody must have,' I returned.

'Oh, thank you, Master Copperfield,' said Uriah
Heep, 'for that remark! It is so true! Umble as I

I RETURN TO THE DOCTOR'S AFTER THE PARTY.

am, I know it is *so* true! Oh, thank you, Master Copperfield!'

He writhed himself quite off his stool in the excitement of his feelings, and, being off, began to make arrangements for going home.

'Mother will be expecting me,' he said, referring to a pale, inexpressive-faced watch in his pocket, 'and getting uneasy; for though we are very umble, Master Copperfield, we are much attached to one another. If you would come and see us, any afternoon, and take a cup of tea at our lowly dwelling, mother would be as proud of your company as I should be.'

I said I should be glad to come.

'Thank you, Master Copperfield,' returned Uriah, putting his book away upon the shelf. 'I suppose you stop here, some time, Master Copperfield?'

I said I was going to be brought up there, I believed, as long as I remained at school.

'Oh, indeed!' exclaimed Uriah. 'I should think *you* would come into the business at last, Master Copperfield!'

I protested that I had no views of that sort, and that no such scheme was entertained in my behalf by anybody; but Uriah insisted on blandly replying to all my assurances, 'Oh, yes, Master Copperfield, I should think you would, certainly!' over and over again. Being, at last, ready to leave the office for the night, he asked me if it would suit my convenience to have the light put out; and on my answering 'Yes,' instantly extinguished it. After shaking hands with me—his hand felt like a fish, in the dark —he opened the door into the street a very little, and crept out, and shut it, leaving me to grope my way back into the house: which cost me some trouble and a fall over his stool. This was the proximate cause, I suppose, of my dreaming about him, for what appeared to me to be half the night; and dreaming, among other things, that he had launched Mr. Peggotty's house on a piratical expedition, with a black flag at the mast-head, bearing the inscription, 'Tidd's Practice,' under which diabolical ensign he was carrying me and little Em'ly to the Spanish Main, to be drowned.

I got a little the better of my uneasiness when I went to school next day, and a good deal the better next day, and so shook it off by degrees, that in less than a fortnight I was quite at home, and happy, among my new companions. I was awkward enough in their games, and backward enough in their studies; but custom would improve me in the first respect, I hoped, and hard work in the second. Accordingly, I went to work very hard, both in play and in earnest, and gained great commendation. And, in a very little while, the Murdstone and Grinby life became so strange to me that I hardly believed in it, while my present life grew so familiar that I seemed to have been leading it a long time.

Doctor Strong's was an excellent school; as different from Mr. Creakle's as good is from evil. It was very gravely and decorously ordered, and on a sound system; with an appeal, in everything, to the honour and good faith of the boys, and an avowed intention to rely on their possession of those qualities unless they proved themselves unworthy of it, which worked wonders. We all felt that we had a part in the management of the place, and in sustaining its character and dignity. Hence, we soon became warmly attached to it—I am sure I did for one, and I never knew, in all my time, of any other boy being otherwise—and learnt with a good will, desiring to do it credit. We had noble games out of hours, and plenty of liberty; but even then, as I remember, we were well spoken of in the town, and rarely did any disgrace, by our appearance or manner, to the reputation of Doctor Strong and Doctor Strong's boys.

Some of the higher scholars boarded in the Doctor's house and through them I learned, at second hand, some particulars of the Doctor's history. As, how he had not yet been married twelve months to the beautiful young lady I had seen in the study, whom he had married for love; for she had not a sixpence, and had a world of poor relations (so our fellows said) ready to swarm the Doctor out of house and home. Also, how the Doctor's cogitating manner was attributable to his being always engaged in looking out for Greek roots; which, in my innocence and ignorance, I supposed to be a botanical furore on the Doctor's part, especially as he always looked at the ground when he walked about, until I understood that they were roots of words, with a view to a new Dictionary which he had in contemplation. Adams our head-boy, who had a turn for mathematics, had made a calculation, I was informed, of the time this Dictionary would take in completing, on the Doctor's plan, and at the Doctor's rate of going. He considered that it might be done in one thousand six hundred and forty-nine years, counting from the Doctor's last, or sixty-second, birthday.

But the Doctor himself was the idol of the whole school; and it must have been a badly-composed school if he had been anything else, for he was the kindest of men; with a simple faith in him that might have touched the stone hearts of the very urns upon the wall. As he walked up and down that part of the courtyard which was at the side of the house, with the stray rooks and jackdaws looking after him with their heads cocked slyly, as if they knew how much more knowing they were in worldly affairs than he, if any sort of vagabond could only get near enough to his creaking shoes to attract his attention to one sentence of a tale of distress, that vagabond was made for the next two days. It was so notorious in the house, that the masters and head-boys took pains to cut these marauders off at angles, and to get out of windows, and turn them out of the courtyard, before they could make the Doctor aware of their presence; which was sometimes happily effected within a few yards of him, without his knowing anything of the matter, as he jogged to and fro. Outside his own domain, and unprotected, he was a very sheep for the shearers. He would have taken his gaiters off his legs, to give away. In fact, there was a story current among us (I have no idea, and never had, on what authority, but I have believed it for so many years that I feel quite certain it is true), that on a frosty day, one winter-time, he actually did bestow his gaiters on a beggar-woman, who occasioned some scandal in the neighbourhood by exhibiting a fine infant from door to door, wrapped in those garments, which were universally recognised, being as well known in the vicinity as the cathedral. The legend added that the only person who did not identify them was the Doctor himself, who, when they were shortly afterwards displayed at the door of a little second-hand shop of no very good repute, where such things were taken in exchange for gin, was more than once observed to handle them approvingly, as if admiring some curious novelty in the pattern, and considering them an improvement on his own.

It was very pleasant to see the Doctor with his pretty young wife. He had a fatherly, benignant way of showing his fondness for her, which seemed in itself to express a good man. I often saw them

walking in the garden where the peaches were, and
I sometimes had a nearer observation of them in the
study or the parlour. She appeared to me to take
great care of the Doctor, and to like him very much,
though I never thought her vitally interested in the
Dictionary: some cumbrous fragments of which work
the Doctor always carried in his pockets, and in the
lining of his hat, and generally seemed to be expound-
ing to her as they walked about.

I saw a good deal of Mrs. Strong, both because she
had taken a liking for me on the morning of my
introduction to the Doctor, and was always afterwards kind to me, and interested in me; and because
she was very fond of Agnes, and was often backwards and forwards at our house. There was a
curious constraint between her and Mr. Wickfield,
I thought (of whom she seemed to be afraid), that
never wore off. When she came there of an evening,
she always shrunk from accepting his escort home,
and ran away with me instead. And sometimes, as
we were running gaily across the cathedral-yard
together, expecting to meet nobody, we would meet
Mr. Jack Maldon, who was always surprised to see
us.

Mrs. Strong's mamma was a lady I took great
delight in. Her name was Mrs. Markleman; but our
boys used to call her the Old Soldier, on account of
her generalship, and the skill with which she marshalled great forces of relations against the Doctor.
She was a little, sharp-eyed woman, who used to
wear, when she was dressed, one unchangeable cap,
ornamented with some artificial flowers, and two
artificial butterflies supposed to be hovering above
the flowers. There was a superstition among us
that this cap had come from France, and could only
originate in the workmanship of that ingenious

nation: but all I certainly know about it is, that it always made its appearance of an evening, wheresoever Mrs. Markleman made *her* appearance; that it was carried about to friendly meetings in a Hindoo basket; that the butterflies had the gift of trembling constantly; and that they improved the shining hours at Doctor Strong's expense, like busy bees.

I observed the Old Soldier—not to adopt the name disrespectfully—to pretty good advantage, on a night which is made memorable to me by something else I shall relate. It was the night of a little party at the Doctor's, which was given on the occasion of Mr. Jack Maldon's departure for India, whither he was going as a cadet, or something of that kind: Mr. Wickfield having at length arranged the business. It happened to be the Doctor's birthday, too. We had had a holiday, had made presents to him in the morning, had made a speech to him through the head-boy, and had cheered him until we were hoarse, and until he had shed tears. And now, in the evening, Mr. Wickfield, Agnes, and I, went to have tea with him in his private capacity.

Mr. Jack Maldon was there, before us. Mrs. Strong, dressed in white, with cherry-coloured ribbons, was playing the piano, when we went in; and he was leaning over her to turn the leaves. The clear red and white of her complexion was not so blooming and flower-like as usual, I thought, when she turned round; but she looked very pretty, wonderfully pretty.

'I have forgotten, Doctor,' said Mrs. Strong's mamma, when we were seated, 'to pay you the compliments of the day: though they are, as you may suppose, very far from being mere compliments in my case. Allow me to wish you many happy returns.'

'I thank you, ma'am,' replied the Doctor.

'Many, many, many, happy returns,' said the Old Soldier. 'Not only for your own sake, but for Annie's and John Maldon's, and many other people's. It seems but yesterday to me, John, when you were a little creature, a head shorter than Master Copperfield, making baby love to Annie behind the gooseberry bushes in the back-garden.'

'My dear mamma,' said Mrs. Strong, 'never mind that now.'

'Annie, don't be absurd,' returned her mother. 'If you are to blush to hear of such things, now you are an old married woman, when are you not to blush to hear of them?'

'Old?' exclaimed Mr. Jack Maldron. 'Annie? Come?'

'Yes, John,' returned the Soldier. 'Virtually, an old married woman. Although not old by years—for when did you ever hear me say, or who has ever heard me say, that a girl of twenty was old by years!—your cousin is the wife of the Doctor, and, as such, what I have described her. It is well for you, John, that your cousin *is* the wife of the Doctor. You have found in him an influential and kind friend, who will be kinder yet, I venture to predict, if you deserve it. I have no false pride. I never hesitate to admit, frankly, that there are some members of our family who want a friend. You were one yourself, before your cousin's influence raised up one for you.'

The Doctor, in the goodness of his heart, waved his hand as if to make light of it, and save Mr. Jack Maldon from any further reminder. But Mrs. Markleham changed her chair for one next the Doctor's, and putting her fan on his coat-sleeve said—

'No, really, my dear Doctor, you must excuse me if I appear to dwell on this rather, because I feel so very strongly. I call it quite my monomania, it is such a subject of mine. You are a blessing to us. You really are a boon, you know.'

'Nonsense, nonsense,' said the Doctor.

'No, no, I beg your pardon,' retorted the Old Soldier. 'With nobody present, but our dear and confidential friend Mr. Wickfield, I cannot consent to be put down. I shall begin to assert the privileges of a mother-in-law, if you go on like that, and scold you. I am perfectly honest and outspoken. What I am saying, is what I said when you first overpowered me with surprise—you remember how surprised I was?—by proposing for Annie. Not that there was anything so very much out of the way, in the mere fact of the proposal—it would be ridiculous to say that!—but because, you having known her poor father and having known her from a baby six months old, I hadn't thought of you in such a light at all, or indeed as a marrying man in any way—simply that, you know.'

'Aye, aye,' returned the Doctor, good-humouredly. 'Never mind.'

'But I *do* mind,' said the Old Soldier, laying her fan upon his lips. 'I mind very much. I recall these things that I may be contradicted if I am wrong. Well! Then I spoke to Annie, and I told her what had happened. I said, "My dear, here's Doctor Strong has positively been and made you the subject of a handsome declaration and an offer." Did I press it in the least? No. I said, "Now, Annie, tell me the truth this moment; is your heart free?" "Mamma," she said, crying, "I am extremely young"—which was perfectly true—"and I hardly know if I have a heart at all." "Then, my dear," I said, "you may rely upon it, it's free. At all events, my love," said I, "Doctor Strong is in an agitated state of mind, and must be answered. He cannot be kept in his present state of suspense." "Mamma," said Annie, still crying, "would he be unhappy without me? If he would, I honour and respect him so much, that I think I will have him." So it was settled. And then, and not till then, I said to Annie, "Annie, Doctor Strong will not only be your husband, but he will represent your late father: he will represent the head of our family, he will represent the wisdom and station, and I may say the means, of our family; and will be, in short, a boon to it." I used the word at the time, and I have used it again to-day. If I have any merit it is consistency.'

The daughter had sat quite silent and still during this speech, with her eyes fixed on the ground; her cousin standing near her, and looking on the ground too. She now said very softly, in a trembling voice—

'Mamma, I hope you have finished?'

'No, my dear Annie,' returned the Soldier, 'I have not quite finished. Since you ask me, my love, I reply that I have *not*. I complain that you really are a little unnatural towards your own family; and, as it is of no use complaining to you, I mean to complain to your husband. Now, my dear Doctor, do look at that silly wife of yours.'

As the Doctor turned his kind face, with its smile of simplicity and gentleness, towards her, she drooped her head more. I noticed that Mr. Wickfield looked at her steadily.

'When I happened to say to that naughty thing the other day,' pursued her mother, shaking her head and her fan at her playfully, 'that there was a family circumstance she might mention to you—indeed, I think, was bound to mention—she said, that to mention it was to ask a favour; and that, as you were too generous, and as for her to ask was always to have, she wouldn't.'

'Annie, my dear,' said the Doctor. 'That was wrong. It robbed me of a pleasure.'

'Almost the very words I said to her!' exclaimed her mother. 'Now really, another time, when I know what she would tell you but for this reason, and won't, I have a great mind, my dear Doctor, to tell you myself.'

'I shall be glad if you will,' returned the Doctor.

'Shall I?'

'Certainly.'

'Well, then, I will!' said the Old Soldier. 'That's a bargain.' And having, I suppose, carried her point, she tapped the Doctor's hand several times with her fan (which she kissed first), and returned triumphantly to her former station.

Some more company coming in, among whom were the two masters and Adams, the talk became general; and it naturally turned on Mr. Jack Maldon, and his voyage, and the country he was going to, and his various plans and prospects. He was to leave that night, after supper, in a postchaise, for Gravesend; where the ship, in which he was to make the voyage, lay; and was to be gone—unless he came home on leave, or for his health—I don't know how many years. I recollect it was settled by general consent that India was quite a misrepresented country, and had nothing objectionable in it, but a tiger or two, and a little heat in the warm part of the day. For my own part, I looked on Mr. Jack Maldon as a modern Sinbad, and pictured him the bosom friend of all the Rajahs in the East, sitting under canopies, smoking curly golden pipes—a mile long, if they could be straightened out.

Mrs. Strong was a very pretty singer: as I knew, who often heard her singing by herself. But, whether she was afraid of singing before people, or was out of voice that evening, it was certain that she couldn't sing at all. She tried a duet, once, with her cousin Maldon, but could not so much as begin; and afterwards, when she tried to sing by herself, although she began sweetly, her voice died away on a sudden, and left her quite distressed, with her head hanging down over the keys. The good Doctor said she was nervous, and, to relieve her, proposed a round game at cards; of which he knew as much as of the art of playing the trombone. But I remarked that the Old Soldier took him into custody directly, for her partner; and instructed him, as the first preliminary of initiation, to give her all the silver he had in his pocket.

We had a merry game, not made the less merry by the Doctor's mistakes, of which he committed an innumerable quantity, in spite of the watchfulness of the butterflies, and to their great aggravation. Mrs. Strong had declined to play, on the ground of not feeling very well; and her cousin Maldon had excused himself because he had some packing to do. When he had done it, however, he returned, and they sat together, talking, on the sofa. From time to time she came and looked over the Doctor's hand, and told him what to play. She was very pale, as she bent over him, and I thought her finger trembled as she pointed out the cards; but the Doctor was quite happy in her attention, and took no notice of this, if it were so.

At supper, we were hardly so gay. Every one appeared to feel that a parting of that sort was an awkward thing, and that the nearer it approached, the more awkward it was. Mr. Jack Maldon tried to be very talkative, but was not at his ease, and made matters worse. And they were not improved, as it appeared to me, by the Old Soldier: who continually recalled passages of Mr. Jack Maldon's youth.

The Doctor, however, who felt, I am sure, that he was making everybody happy, was well pleased, and had no suspicion but that we were all at the utmost height of enjoyment.

'Annie, my dear,' said he, looking at his watch, and filling his glass, 'it is past your cousin Jack's time, and we must not detain him, since time and tide —both concerned in this case—wait for no man. Mr. Jack Maldon, you have a long voyage, and a strange country, before you; but many men have had both, and many men will have both, to the end of time. The winds you are going to tempt, have wafted thousands upon thousands to fortune, and brought thousands upon thousands happily back.'

'It's an affecting thing,' said Mrs. Markleham, 'however it's viewed, it's affecting, to see a fine young man one has known from an infant, going away to the other end of the world, leaving all he knows behind, and not knowing what's before him. A young man really well deserves constant support and patronage,' looking at the Doctor, 'who makes such sacrifices.'

'Time will go fast with you, Mr. Jack Maldon,' pursued the Doctor, 'and fast with all of us. Some of us can hardly expect, perhaps, in the natural course of things, to greet you on your return. The next best thing is to hope to do it, and that's my case. I shall not weary you with good advice. You have long had a good model before you, in your cousin Annie. Imitate her virtues as nearly as you can.'

Mrs. Markleham fanned herself, and shook her head.

'Farewell, Mr. Jack,' said the Doctor, standing up; on which we all stood up. 'A prosperous voyage out, a thriving career abroad, and a happy return home!'

We all drank the toast, and all shook hands with Mr. Jack Maldon; after which he hastily took leave of the ladies who were there, and hurried to the door, where he was received, as he got into the chaise, with a tremendous broadside of cheers discharged by our boys, who had assembled on the lawn for the purpose. Running in among them to swell the ranks, I was very near the chaise when it rolled away; and I had a lively impression made upon me, in the midst of the noise and dust, of having seen Mr. Jack Maldon rattle past with an agitated face, and something cherry-coloured in his hand.

After another broadside for the Doctor, and another for the Doctor's wife, the boy's dispersed, and I went back into the house, where I found the guests all standing in a group about the Doctor, discussing how Mr. Jack Maldon had gone away, and how he had borne it, and how he had felt it, and all the rest of it. In the midst of these remarks, Mrs. Markleham cried: 'Where 's Annie?'

No Annie was there; and when they called to her, no Annie replied. But all pressing out of the room, in a crowd, to see what was the matter, we found her lying on the hall floor. There was great alarm at first, until it was found that she was in a swoon, and that the swoon was yielding to the usual means of recovery; when the Doctor, who had lifted her head upon his knee, put her curls aside with his hand, and said, looking around—

'Poor Annie! She 's so faithful and tender-hearted! It 's the parting from her old playfellow

and friend, her favourite cousin, that has done this.
Ah! It's a pity! I am very sorry!'

When she opened her eyes, and saw where she was,
and that we were all standing about her, she arose
with assistance: turning her head, as she did so, to
lay it on the Doctor's shoulder—or to hide it, I don't
know which. We went into the drawing-room, to
leave her with the Doctor and her mother; but
she said, it seemed, that she was better than she had
been since morning, and that she would rather be
brought among us; so they brought her in, looking very white and weak, I thought, and sat her on a
sofa.

'Annie, my dear,' said her mother, doing something
to her dress. 'See her! You have lost a bow. Will
anybody be so good as find a ribbon; a cherry-coloured ribbon?'

It was the one she had worn at her bosom. We all
looked for it; I myself looked everywhere, I am certain; but nobody could find it.

'Do you recollect where you had it last, Annie?'
said her mother.

I wondered how I could have thought she looked
white, or anything but burning red, when she
answered that she had had it safe, a little while ago,
she thought, but it was not worth looking for.

Nevertheless, it was looked for again, and still not
found. She entreated that there might be no more
searching; but it was still sought for in a desultory
way, until she was quite well, and the company took
their departure.

We walked very slowly home, Mr. Wickfield,
Agnes, and I; Agnes and I admiring the moonlight,
and Mr. Wickfield scarcely raising his eyes from the
ground. When we, at last, reached our own door,
Agnes discovered that she had left her little reticule

behind.   Delighted to be of any service to her, I ran back to fetch it.

I went into the supper-room where it had been left, which was deserted and dark.   But a door of communication between that and the Doctor's study, where there was a light, being open, I passed on there, to say what I wanted, and to get a candle.

The Doctor was sitting in his easy-chair by the fireside, and his young wife was on a stool at his feet. The Doctor, with a complacent smile, was reading aloud some manuscript explanation or statement of a theory out of that interminable Dictionary, and she was looking up at him.   But, with such a face as I never saw.   It was so beautiful in its form, it was so ashy pale, it was so fixed in its abstraction, it was so full of a wild, sleep-walking, dreamy horror of I don't know what.   The eyes were wide open, and her brown hair fell in two rich clusters on her shoulders, and on her white dress, disordered by the want of the lost ribbon.   Distinctly as I recollect her look, I cannot say of what it was expressive.   I cannot even say of what it is expressive to me now, rising again before my older judgment.   Penitence, humiliation, shame, pride, love, and trustfulness, I see them all; and in them all, I see that horror of I don't know what.

My entrance, and my saying what I wanted, roused her.   It disturbed the Doctor too, for when I went back to replace the candle I had taken from the table, he was patting her head, in his fatherly way, and saying he was a merciless drone to let her tempt him into reading on; and he would have her go to bed.

But she asked him, in a rapid, urgent manner, to let her stay.   To let her feel assured (I heard her murmur some broken words to this effect) that she was in his confidence that night.   And, as she turned again towards him, after glancing at me as I left the room and went out at the door, I saw her cross her hands upon his knee, and look up at him with the same face, something quieted, as he resumed his reading.

It made a great impression on me, and I remembered it a long time afterwards, as I shall have occasion to narrate when the time comes.

CHAPTER XVII

SOMEBODY TURNS UP

It has not occurred to me to mention Peggotty since I ran away; but, of course, I wrote her a letter almost as soon as I was housed at Dover, and another and a longer letter, containing all particulars fully related, when my aunt took me formally under her protection.   On my being settled at Doctor Strong's I wrote to her again, detailing my happy condition and prospects.   I never could have derived anything like the pleasure from spending the money Mr. Dick had given me, that I felt in sending a gold half-guinea to Peggotty, per post, inclosed in this last letter, to discharge the sum I had borrowed of her: in which epistle, not before, I mentioned about the young man with the donkey-cart.

To these communications Peggotty replied as promptly, if not as concisely, as a merchant's clerk. Her utmost powers of expression (which were certainly not great in ink) were exhausted in the attempt to write what she felt on the subject of my journey. Four sides of incoherent and interjectional beginnings of sentences, that had no end, except blots, were inadequate to afford her any relief. But the blots were more expressive to me than the best composition; for they showed me that Peggotty had been crying all over the paper, and what could I have desired more?

I made out without much difficulty, that she could not take quite kindly to my aunt yet. The notice was too short after so long a prepossession the other way. We never knew a person, she wrote; but to think that Miss Betsey should seem to be so different from what she had been thought to be, was a Moral! That was her word. She was evidently still afraid of Miss Betsey, for she sent her grateful duty to her but timidly; and she was evidently afraid of me, too, and entertained the probability of my running away again soon; if I might judge from the repeated hints she threw out, that the coach-fare to Yarmouth was always to be had of her for the asking.

She gave me one piece of intelligence which affected me very much, namely, that there had been a sale of the furniture at our old home, and that Mr. and Miss Murdstone were gone away, and the house was shut up, to be let or sold. God knows I had no part in it while they remained there, but it pained me to think of the dear old place as altogether abandoned; of the weeds growing tall in the garden, and the fallen leaves lying thick and wet upon the paths. I imagined how the winds of winter would howl round it, how the cold rain would beat upon the window-glass, how the moon would make ghosts on the walls of the empty rooms, watching their solitude all night. I thought afresh of the grave in the churchyard, underneath the tree: and it seemed as if the house were dead too, now, and all connected with my father and mother were faded away.

There was no other news in Peggotty's letters.

Mr. Barkis was an excellent husband, she said, though still a little near; but we all had our faults, and she had plenty (though I am sure I don't know what they were); and he sent his duty, and my little bedroom was always ready for me. Mr. Peggotty was well, and Ham was well, and Mrs. Gummidge was but poorly, and little Em'ly wouldn't send her love, but said that Peggotty might send it, if she liked.

All this intelligence I dutifully imparted to my aunt, only reserving to myself the mention of little Em'ly, to whom I instinctively felt that she would not very tenderly incline. While I was yet new at Doctor Strong's, she made several excursions over to Canterbury to see me, and always at unseasonable hours: with the view, I suppose, of taking me by surprise. But, finding me well employed, and bearing a good character, and hearing on all hands that I rose fast in the school, she soon discontinued these visits. I saw her on a Saturday, every third or fourth week, when I went over to Dover for a treat; and I saw Mr. Dick every alternate Wednesday, when he arrived by stage-coach at noon, to stay until next morning.

On these occasions Mr. Dick never travelled without a leather writing-desk, containing a supply of stationery and the Memorial; in relation to which document he had a notion that time was beginning to press now, and that it really must be got out of hand.

Mr. Dick was very partial to gingerbread. To render his visits the more agreeable, my aunt had instructed me to open a credit for him at a cake-shop, which was hampered with the stipulation that he should not be served with more than one shilling's-worth in the course of any one day. This, and the reference of all his little bills at the county inn where he slept, to my aunt, before they were paid, induced me to suspect that he was only allowed to rattle his money, and not to spend it. I found on further investigation that this was so, or at least there was an agreement between him and my aunt that he should account to her for all his disbursements. As he had no idea of deceiving her, and always desired to please her, he was thus made chary of launching into expense. On this point, as well as on all other possible points, Mr. Dick was convinced that my aunt was the wisest and most wonderful of women; as he repeatedly told me with infinite secrecy, and always in a whisper.

'Trotwood,' said Mr. Dick, with an air of mystery, after imparting this confidence to me, one Wednesday; 'who's the man that hides near our house and frightens her?'

'Frightens my aunt, sir?'

Mr. Dick nodded. 'I thought nothing would have frightened her,' he said, 'for she's—' here he whispered softly, 'don't mention it—the wisest and most wonderful of women.' Having said which, he drew back, to observe the effect which this description of her made upon me.

'The first time he came,' said Mr. Dick, 'was—let me see—sixteen hundred and forty-nine was the date of King Charles's execution. I think you said sixteen hundred and forty-nine?'

'Yes, sir.'

'I don't know how it can be,' said Mr. Dick sorely puzzled and shaking his head. 'I don't think I am as old as that.'

'Was it in that year that the man appeared, sir?' I asked.

'Why, really,' said Mr. Dick, 'I don't see how it can have been in that year, Trotwood. Did you get that date out of history?'

'Yes, sir.'

'I suppose history never lies, does it?' said Mr. Dick, with a gleam of hope.

'Oh dear, no, sir!' I replied, most decisively. I was ingenuous and young, and I thought so.

'I can't make it out,' said Mr. Dick, shaking his head. 'There's something wrong, somewhere. However, it was very soon after the mistake was made of putting some of the trouble out of King Charles's head into my head, that the man first came. I was walking out with Miss Trotwood after tea, just at dark, and there he was, close to our house.'

'Walking about?' I inquired.

'Walking about?' repeated Mr. Dick. 'Let me see. I must recollect a bit. N—no, no; he was not walking about.'

I asked, as the shortest way to get at it, what he *was* doing.

'Well, he wasn't there at all,' said Mr. Dick, 'until he came up behind her, and whispered. Then she turned round and fainted, and I stood still and looked at him, and he walked away; but that he should have been hiding ever since (in the ground or somewhere), is the most extraordinary thing!'

'*Has* he been hiding ever since?' I asked.

'To be sure he has,' retorted Mr. Dick, nodding his head gravely. 'Never came out, till last night! We were walking last night, and he came up behind her again, and I knew him again.'

'And did he frighten my aunt again?'

'All of a shiver,' said Mr. Dick, counterfeiting that affection and making his teeth chatter. 'Held by the palings. Cried. But, Trotwood, come here,' getting me close to him, that he might whisper very softly; 'why did she give him money, boy, in the moonlight?'

'He was a beggar, perhaps.'

Mr. Dick shook his head, as utterly renouncing the suggestion; and having replied a great many times, and with great confidence, 'No beggar, no beggar, no beggar, sir!' went on to say, that from his window he had afterwards, and late at night, seen my aunt give this person money outside the garden rails in the moonlight, who then slunk away—into the ground again, as he thought probable—and was seen no more: while my aunt came hurriedly and secretly back into the house, and had, even that morning, been quite different from her usual self; which preyed on Mr. Dick's mind.

I had not the least belief, in the outset of this story, that the unknown was anything but a delusion of Mr. Dick's, and one of the line of that ill-fated Prince who occasioned him so much difficulty; but after some reflection I began to entertain the question whether an attempt, or threat of an attempt, might have been twice made to take poor Mr. Dick himself from under my aunt's protection, and whether my aunt, the strength of whose kind feeling towards him I knew from herself, might have been induced to pay a price for his peace and quiet. As I was already much attached to Mr. Dick, and very solicitous for his welfare, my fears favoured this supposition; and for a long time his Wednesday hardly ever came round, without my entertaining a misgiving that he would not be on the coach-box as usual. There he always appeared, however, grey-headed, laughing, and happy; and he never had anything more to tell of the man who could frighten my aunt.

These Wednesdays were the happiest days of Mr.

Dick's life; they were far from being the least happy of mine. He soon became known to every boy in the school; and though he never took an active part in any game but kite-flying, was as deeply interested in all our sports as any one among us. How often have I seen him, intent upon a match at marbles or peg-top, looking on with a face of unutterable interest, and hardly breathing at the critical times! How often, at hare and hounds, have I seen him mounted on a little knoll, cheering the whole field on to action, and waving his hat above his grey head, oblivious of King Charles the Martyr's head, and all belonging to it! How many a summer-hour have I known to be but blissful minutes to him in the cricket-field! How many winter days have I seen him, standing blue-nosed, in the snow and east wind, looking at the boys down the long slide, and clapping his worsted gloves in rapture!

He was a universal favourite, and his ingenuity in little things was transcendent. He could cut oranges into such devices as none of us had an idea of. He could make a boat out of anything, from a skewer upwards. He could turn crampbones into chessmen; fashion Roman chariots from old court cards; make spoked wheels out of cotton reels, and birdcages of old wire. But he was greatest of all, perhaps, in the articles of string and straw; with which we were all persuaded he could do anything that could be done by hands.

Mr. Dick's renown was not long confined to us. After a few Wednesdays, Doctor Strong himself made some inquiries of me about him, and I told him all my aunt had told me; which interested the Doctor so much that he requested, on the occasion of his next visit, to be presented to him. This ceremony I per-formed; and the Doctor begging Mr. Dick, whenso-

ever he should not find me at the coach-office, to come
on there, and rest himself until our morning's work
was over, it soon passed into a custom for Mr. Dick
to come on as a matter of course, and, if we were a
little late, as often happened on a Wednesday, to
walk about the courtyard, waiting for me. Here he
made the acquaintance of the Doctor's beautiful
young wife (paler than formerly, all this time; more
rarely seen by me or any one, I think; and not so
gay, but not less beautiful), and so became more and
more familiar by degrees, until, at last, he would come
into the school and wait. He always sat in a particular corner, on a particular stool, which was called
'Dick,' after him; here he would sit, with his grey
head bent forward, attentively listening to whatever
might be going on, with a profound veneration for
the learning he had never been able to acquire.

This veneration Mr. Dick extended to the Doctor,
whom he thought the most subtle and accomplished
philosopher of any age. It was long before Mr. Dick
ever spoke to him otherwise than bareheaded; and
even when he and the Doctor had struck up quite a
friendship, and would walk together by the hour,
on that side of the courtyard which was known
among us as The Doctor's Walk, Mr. Dick would
pull off his hat at intervals to show his respect for
wisdom and knowledge. How it ever came about,
that the Doctor began to read out scraps of the
famous Dictionary, in these walks, I never knew;
perhaps he felt it all the same, at first, as reading to
himself. However, it passed into a custom too; and
Mr. Dick, listening with a face shining with pride
and pleasure, in his heart of hearts, believed the Dictionary to be the most delightful book in the world.

As I think of them going up and down before those
schoolroom windows—the Doctor reading with his

complacent smile, an occasional flourish of the manuscript, or grave motion of his head; and Mr. Dick listening, enchained by interest, with his poor wits calmly wandering God knows where, upon the wings of hard words—I think of it as one of the pleasantest things, in a quiet way, that I have ever seen. I feel as if they might go walking to and fro for ever, and the world might somehow be the better for it. As if a thousand things it makes a noise about, were not one-half so good for it, or me.

Agnes was one of Mr. Dick's friends, very soon; and in often coming to the house, he made acquaintance with Uriah. The friendship between himself and me increased continually, and it was maintained on this odd footing: that, while Mr. Dick came professedly to look after me as my guardian, he always consulted me in any little matter of doubt that arose, and invariably guided himself by my advice; not only having a high respect for my native sagacity, but considering that I inherited a good deal from my aunt.

One Thursday morning, when I was about to walk with Mr. Dick from the hotel to the coach-office before going back to school (for we had an hour's school before breakfast), I met Uriah in the street, who reminded me of the promise I had made to take tea with himself and his mother: adding, with a writhe, 'But I didn't expect you to keep it, Master Copperfield, we 're so very umble.'

I really had not yet been able to make up my mind whether I liked Uriah or detested him; and I was very doubtful about it still, as I stood looking him in the face in the street. But I felt it quite an affront to be supposed proud, and said I only wanted to be asked.

'Oh, if that 's all, Master Copperfield,' said Uriah.

'and it really isn't our umbleness that prevents you, will you come this evening? But if it is our umbleness, I hope you won't mind owning to it, Master Copperfield; for we are all well aware of our condition.'

I said I would mention it to Mr. Wickfield, and if he approved, as I had no doubt he would, I would come with pleasure. So, at six o'clock that evening, which was one of the early office evenings, I announced myself as ready, to Uriah.

'Mother will be proud, indeed,' he said, as we walked away together. 'Or she would be proud if it wasn't sinful, Master Copperfield.'

'Yet you didn't mind supposing *I* was proud this morning,' I returned.

'Oh dear, no, Master Copperfield!' returned Uriah. 'Oh, believe me, no. Such a thought never came into my head! I shouldn't have deemed it at all proud if you had thought *us* too umble for you. Because we are so very umble.'

'Have you been studying much law lately?' I asked, to change the subject.

'Oh, Master Copperfield,' he said, with an air of self-denial, 'my reading is hardly to be called study. I have passed an hour or two in the evening, sometimes, with Mr. Tidd.'

'Rather hard, I suppose?' said I.

'He is hard to *me* sometimes,' returned Uriah. 'But I don't know what he might be, to a gifted person.'

After beating a little tune on his chin as he walked on, with the two forefingers of his skeleton right-hand, he added—

'There are expressions, you see, Master Copperfield—Latin words and terms—in Mr. Tidd, that are trying to a reader of my umble attainments.'

'Would you like to be taught Latin?' I said briskly. 'I will teach it you with pleasure, as I learn it.'

'Oh, thank you, Master Copperfield,' he answered, shaking his head. 'I am sure it's very kind of you to make the offer, but I am much too umble to accept it.'

'What nonsense, Uriah!'

'Oh, indeed you must excuse me, Master Copperfield! I am greatly obliged, and I should like it of all things, I assure you; but I am far too umble. There are people enough to tread upon me in my lowly state, without my doing outrage to their feelings by possessing learning. Learning ain't for me. A person like myself had better not aspire. If he is to get on in life, he must get on umbly, Master Copperfield.'

I never saw his mouth so wide, or the creases in his cheeks so deep, as when he delivered himself of these sentiments: shaking his head all the time, and writhing modestly.

'I think you are wrong, Uriah,' I said. 'I dare say there are several things that I could teach you, if you would like to learn them.'

'Oh, I don't doubt that, Master Copperfield,' he answered; 'not in the least. But not being umble yourself, you don't judge well, perhaps, for them that are. I won't provoke my betters with knowledge, thank you. I'm much too umble. Here is my umble dwelling, Master Copperfield!'

We entered a low, old-fashioned room, walked straight into from the street, and found there Mrs. Heep, who was the dead image of Uriah, only short. She received me with the utmost humility, and apologised to me for giving her son a kiss, observing that, lowly as they were, they had their natural affections, which they hoped would give no offence to any one. It was a perfectly decent room, half parlour and half kitchen, but not at all a snug room. The tea-things were set upon the table, and the kettle was boiling on the hob. There was a chest of drawers with an escritoire top, for Uriah to read or write at of an evening; there was Uriah's blue bag lying down and vomiting papers; there was a company of Uriah's books commanded by Mr. Tidd; there was a corner cupboard; and there were the usual articles of furniture. I don't remember that any individual object had a bare, pinched, spare look; but I do remember that the whole place had.

It was perhaps a part of Mrs. Heep's humility, that she still wore weeds. Notwithstanding the lapse of time that had occurred since Mr. Heep's decease, she still wore weeds. I think there was some compromise in the cap; but otherwise she was as weedy as in the early days of her mourning.

'This is a day to be remembered, my Uriah, I am sure,' said Mrs. Heep, making the tea, 'when Master Copperfield pays us a visit.'

'I said you 'd think so, mother,' said Uriah.

'If I could have wished father to remain among us for any reason,' said Mrs. Heep, 'it would have been, that he might have known his company this afternoon.'

I felt embarrassed by these compliments; but I was sensible, too, of being entertained as an honoured guest, and I thought Mrs. Heep an agreeable woman.

'My Uriah,' said Mrs. Heep, 'has looked forward to this, sir, a long while. He had his fears that our umbleness stood in the way, and I joined in them myself. Umble we are, umble we have been, umble we shall ever be,' said Mrs. Heep.

'I am sure you have no occasion to be so, ma'am,' I said, 'unless you like.'

'Thank you, sir,' retorted Mrs. Heep. 'We know our station and are thankful in it.'

I found that Mrs. Heep gradually got nearer to me, and that Uriah gradually got opposite to me, and that they respectfully plied me with the choicest of the eatables on the table. There was nothing particularly choice there, to be sure; but I took the will for the deed, and felt that they were very attentive. Presently they began to talk about aunts, and then I told them about mine; and about fathers and mothers, and then I told them about mine; and then Mrs. Heep began to talk about fathers-in-law, and then I began to tell her about mine; but stopped, because my aunt had advised me to observe a silence on that subject. A tender young cork, however, would have had no more chance against a pair of corkscrews, or a tender young tooth against a pair of dentists, or a little shuttlecock against two battledores, than I had against Uriah and Mrs. Heep. They did just what they liked with me; and wormed things out of me that I had no desire to tell, with a certainty I blush to think of: the more especially as, in my juvenile frankness, I took some credit to myself for being so confidential, and felt that I was quite the patron of my two respectful entertainers.

They were very fond of one another: that was certain. I take it, that had its effect upon me, as a touch of nature; but the skill with which the one followed up whatever the other said, was a touch of art which I was still less proof against. When there was nothing more to be got out of me about myself (for on the Murdstone and Grinby life, and on my journey, I was dumb), they began about Mr. Wickfield and Agnes. Uriah threw the ball to Mrs.

Heep, Mrs. Heep caught it and threw it back to Uriah, Uriah kept it up a little while, then sent it back to Mrs. Heep, and so they went on tossing it about until I had no idea who had got it, and was quite bewildered. The ball itself was always changing too. Now it was Mr. Wickfield, now Agnes, now the excellence of Mr. Wickfield, now my admiration of Agnes; now the extent of Mr. Wickfield's business and resources, now our domestic life after dinner; now, the wine that Mr. Wickfield took, the reason why he took it, and the pity that it was he took so much; now one thing, now another, then everything at once; and all the time, without appearing to speak very often, or to do anything but sometimes encourage them a little, for fear they should be overcome by their humility and the honour of my company, I found myself perpetually letting out something or other that I had no business to let out, and seeing the effect of it in the twinkling of Uriah's dinted nostrils.

I had begun to be a little uncomfortable, and to wish myself well out of the visit, when a figure coming down the street passed the door—it stood open to air the room, which was warm, the weather being close for the time of year—came back again, looked in, and walked in, exclaiming loudly, 'Copperfield! Is it possible?'

It was Mr. Micawber! It was Mr. Micawber, with his eye-glass, and his walking-stick, and his shirt-collar, and his genteel air, and the condescending roll in his voice, all complete!

'My dear Copperfield,' said Mr. Micawber, putting out his hand, 'this is indeed a meeting which is calculated to impress the mind with a sense of the instability and uncertainty of all human—in short, it is a most extraordinary meeting. Walking along the street, reflecting upon the probability of something turning up (of which I am at present rather sanguine), I find a young but valued friend turn up, who is connected with the most eventful period of my life; I may say, with the turning point of my existence. Copperfield, my dear fellow, how do you do?'

I cannot say—I really can*not* say—that I was glad to see Mr. Micawber there; but I was glad to see him too, and shook hands with him heartily, inquiring how Mrs. Micawber was.

'Thank you,' said Mr. Micawber, waving his hand as of old, and settling his chin in his shirt-collar. 'She is tolerably convalescent. The twins no longer derive their sustenance from Nature's founts—in short,' said Mr. Micawber, in one of his bursts of confidence, 'they are weaned—and Mrs. Micawber is, at present, my travelling companion. She will be rejoiced, Copperfield, to renew her acquaintance with one who has proved himself in all respects a worthy minister at the sacred altar of friendship.'

I said I should be delighted to see her.

'You are very good,' said Mr. Micawber.

Mr. Micawber then smiled, settled his chin again, and looked about him.

'I have discovered my friend Copperfield,' said Mr. Micawber genteelly, and without addressing himself particularly to any one, 'not in solitude, but partaking of a social meal in company with a widowed lady, and one who is apparently her offspring—in short,' said Mr. Micawber, in another of his bursts of confidence, 'her son. I shall esteem it an honour to be presented.'

I could do no less, under these circumstances, than make Mr. Micawber known to Uriah Heep and his mother; which I accordingly did. As they abased themselves before him, Mr. Micawber took a seat, and waved his hand in his most courtly manner.

'Any friend of my friend Copperfield's,' said Mr. Micawber, 'has a personal claim upon myself.'

'We are too umble, sir,' said Mrs. Heep, 'my son and me, to be the friends of Master Copperfield. He has been so good as take his tea with us, and we are thankful to him for his company; also to you, sir, for your notice.'

'Ma'am,' returned Mr. Micawber, with a bow, 'you are very obliging: and what are you doing, Copperfield? Still in the wine trade?'

I was excessively anxious to get Mr. Micawber away; and replied, with my hat in my hand, and a very red face, I have no doubt, that I was a pupil at Doctor Strong's.

'A pupil?' said Mr. Micawber, raising his eyebrows. 'I am extremely happy to hear it. Although a mind like my friend Copperfield's'; to Uriah and Mrs. Heep; 'does not require that cultivation which, without his knowledge of men and things, it would require, still it is a rich soil teeming with latent vegetation—in short,' said Mr. Micawber, smiling, in another burst of confidence, 'it is an intellect capable of getting up the classics to any extent.'

Uriah, with his long hands slowly twining over one another, made a ghastly writhe from the waist upwards, to express his concurrence in this estimation of me.

'Shall we go and see Mrs. Micawber, sir?' I said, to get Mr. Micawber away.

'If you will do her that favour, Copperfield,' replied Mr. Micawber, rising. 'I have no scruple in saying, in the presence of our friends here, that I am a man who has, for some years, contended against the pressure of pecuniary difficulties.' I knew he was certain to say something of this kind; he always would be so boastful about his difficulties. 'Sometimes I have risen superior to my difficulties. Sometimes my difficulties have—in short, have floored me. There have been times when I have administered a succession of facers to them; there have been times when they have been too many for me, and I have given in, and said to Mrs. Micawber in the words of Cato, "Plato, thou reasonest well. It's all up now. I can show fight no more." But at no time of my life,' said Mr. Micawber, 'have I enjoyed a higher degree of satisfaction than in pouring my griefs (if I may describe difficulties, chiefly arising out of warrants of attorney and promissory notes at two and four months, by that word) into the bosom of my friend Copperfield.'

Mr. Micawber closed this handsome tribute by saying, 'Mr. Heep! Good evening. Mrs. Heep! Your servant,' and then walking out with me in his most fashionable manner, making a good deal of noise on the pavement with his shoes, and humming a tune as he went.

It was a little inn where Mr. Micawber put up, and he occupied a little room in it, partitioned off from the commercial room, and strongly flavoured with tobacco-smoke. I think it was over the kitchen, because a warm greasy smell appeared to come up through the chinks in the floor, and there was a flabby perspiration on the walls. I know it was near the bar, on account of the smell of spirits and jingling of glasses. Here, recumbent on a small sofa, underneath a picture of a racehorse, with her head close to the fire, and her feet pushing the mustard off the dumb-waiter at the other end of the room, was Mrs. Micawber, to whom Mr. Micawber entered first, saying, 'My dear, allow me to introduce to you a pupil of Doctor Strong's.'

I noticed, by the bye, that although Mr. Micawber was just as much confused as ever about my age and standing, he always remembered, as a genteel thing, that I was a pupil of Doctor Strong's.

Mrs. Micawber was amazed, but very glad to see me. I was very glad to see her too, and, after an affectionate greeting on both sides, sat down on the small sofa near her.

'My dear,' said Mr. Micawber, 'if you will mention to Copperfield what our present position is, which I have no doubt he will like to know, I will go and look at the paper the while, and see whether anything turns up among the advertisements.'

'I thought you were at Plymouth, ma'am,' I said to Mrs. Micawber, as he went out.

'My dear Master Copperfield,' she replied, 'we went to Plymouth.'

'To be on the spot,' I hinted.

'Just so,' said Mrs. Micawber. 'To be on the spot. But, the truth is, talent is not wanted in the Custom House. The local influence of my family was quite unavailing to obtain any employment in that department, for a man of Mr. Micawber's abilities. They would rather *not* have a man of Mr. Micawber's abilities. He would only show the deficiency of the others. Apart from which,' said Mrs. Micawber, 'I will not disguise from you, my dear Master Copperfield, that when that branch of my family which is settled in Plymouth became aware that Mr. Micawber was accompanied by myself, and by little Wilkins and his sister, and by the twins, they did not receive him with that ardour which he might have expected, being so newly released from captivity.

In fact,' said Mrs. Micawber, lowering her voice,—
'this is between ourselves—our reception was cool.'

'Dear me!' I said.

'Yes,' said Mrs. Micawber. 'It is truly painful to
contemplate mankind in such an aspect, Master
Copperfield, but our reception was, decidedly, cool.
There is no doubt about it. In fact, that branch of
my family which is settled in Plymouth became quite
personal to Mr. Micawber, before we had been there
a week.'

I said, and thought, they ought to be ashamed of
themselves.

'Still, so it was,' continued Mrs. Micawber. 'Under such circumstances, what could a man of Mr.
Micawber's spirit do? But one obvious course was
left. To borrow of that branch of my family the
money to return to London, and to return at any
sacrifice.'

'Then you all came back again, ma'am?' I said.

'We all came back again,' replied Mrs. Micawber.
'Since then, I have consulted other branches of my
family on the course which it is most expedient for
Mr. Micawber to take—for I maintain that he must
take some course, Master Copperfield,' said Mrs.
Micawber, argumentatively. 'It is clear that a family of six, not including a domestic, cannot live upon
air.'

'Certainly, ma'am,' said I.

'The opinion of those other branches of my family,' pursued Mrs. Micawber, 'is, that Mr. Micawber
should immediately turn his attention to coals.'

'To what, ma'am?'

'To coals,' said Mrs. Micawber. 'To the coal
trade. Mr. Micawber was induced to think, on inquiry, that there might be an opening for a man of
his talent in the Medway Coal Trade. Then, as Mr.

Micawber very properly said, the first step to be taken clearly was, to come and *see* the Medway. Which we came and saw. I say "we," Master Copperfield; for I never will,' said Mrs. Micawber with emotion, 'I never will desert Mr. Micawber.'

I murmured my admiration and approbation.

'We came,' repeated Mrs. Micawber, 'and saw the Medway. My opinion of the coal trade on that river, is, that it may require talent, but that it certainly requires capital. Talent, Mr. Micawber has; capital, Mr. Micawber has not. We saw, I think, the greater part of the Medway; and that is my individual conclusion. Being so near here, Mr. Micawber was of opinion that it would be rash not to come on, and see the cathedral. Firstly, on account of its being so well worth seeing,. and our never having seen it; and secondly, on account of the great probability of something turning up in a cathedral town. We have been here,' said Mrs. Micawber, 'three days. Nothing has, as yet, turned up; and it may not surprise you, my dear Master Copperfield, so much as it would a stranger, to know that we are at present waiting for a remittance from London, to discharge our pecuniary obligations at this hotel. Until the arrival of that remittance,' said Mrs. Micawber with much feeling, 'I am cut off from my home (I allude to lodgings in Pentonville), from my boy and girl, and from my twins.'

I felt the utmost sympathy for Mr. and Mrs. Micawber in this anxious extremity, and said as much to Mr. Micawber, who now returned: adding that I only wished I had money enough, to lend them the amount they needed. Mr. Micawber's answer expressed the disturbance of his mind. He said, shaking hands with me, 'Copperfield, you are a true friend; but when the worst comes to the worst, no man is without a friend who is possessed of shaving materials.' At this dreadful hint Mrs. Micawber threw her arms round Mr. Micawber's neck and entreated him to be calm. He wept; but so far recovered, almost immediately, as to ring the bell for the waiter, and bespeak a hot kidney pudding and a plate of shrimps for breakfast in the morning.

When I took my leave of them, they both pressed me so much to come and dine before they went away, that I could not refuse. But, as I knew I could not come next day, when I should have a good deal to prepare in the evening, Mr. Micawber arranged that he would call at Dr. Strong's in the course of the morning (having a presentiment that the remittance would arrive by that post), and propose the day after, if it would suit me better. Accordingly I was called out of school next forenoon, and found Mr. Micawber in the parlour; who had called to say that the dinner would take place as proposed. When I asked him if the remittance had come, he pressed my hand and departed.

As I was looking out of the window that same evening, it surprised me, and made me rather uneasy, to see Mr. Micawber and Uriah Heep walk past, arm-in-arm: Uriah humbly sensible of the honour that was done him, and Mr. Micawber taking a bland delight in extending his patronage to Uriah. But I was still more surprised, when I went to the little hotel next day at the appointed dinnerhour, which was four o'clock, to find, from what Mr. Micawber said, that he had gone home with Uriah, and had drunk brandy-and-water at Mrs. Heep's.

'And I'll tell you what, my dear Copperfield,' said Mr. Micawber, 'your friend Heep is a young fellow who might be attorney-general. If I had known that young man, at the period when my difficulties came to a crisis, all I can say is, that I believe my creditors would have been a great deal better managed than they were.'

I hardly understood how this could have been, seeing that Mr. Micawber had paid them nothing at all as it was; but I did not like to ask. Neither did I like to say, that I hoped he had not been too communicative to Uriah; or to inquire if they had talked much about me. I was afraid of hurting Mr. Micawber's feelings, or, at all events, Mrs. Micawber's, she being very sensitive; but I was uncomfortable about it, too, and often thought about it afterwards.

We had a beautiful little dinner. Quite an elegant dish of fish; the kidney-end of a loin of veal, roasted; fried sausage-meat; a partridge, and a pudding. There was wine, and there was strong ale; and after dinner Mrs. Micawber made us a bowl of hot punch with her own hands.

Mr. Micawber was uncommonly convivial. I never saw him such good company. He made his face shine with the punch, so that it looked as if it had been varnished all over. He got cheerfully sentimental about the town, and proposed success to it; observing that Mrs. Micawber and himself had been made extremely snug and comfortable there, and that he never should forget the agreeable hours they had passed in Canterbury. He proposed me afterwards; and he, and Mrs. Micawber, and I, took a review of our past acquaintance, in the course of which, we sold the property all over again. Then I proposed Mrs. Micawber; or, at least, said, modestly, 'If you 'll allow me, Mrs. Micawber, I shall now have the pleasure of drinking *your* health, ma'am.' On which Mr. Micawber delivered an eulogium on Mrs. Micawber's character, and said she had ever been his guide, philosopher, and friend, and that he would recommend me, when I came to a marrying-time of life, to marry such another woman, if such another woman could be found.

As the punch disappeared, Mr. Micawber became still more friendly and convivial. Mrs. Micawber's spirits becoming elevated, too, we sang 'Auld Lang Syne.' When we came to 'Here's a hand, my trusty fiere,' we all joined hands round the table; and when we declared we would 'take a right gude willie-waught,' and hadn't the least idea what it meant, we were really affected.

In a word, I never saw anybody so thoroughly jovial as Mr. Micawber was, down to the very last moment of the evening, when I took a hearty fare-well of himself and his amiable wife. Consequently, I was not prepared, at seven o'clock next morning, to receive the following communication, dated half-past nine in the evening; a quarter of an hour after I had left him:—

'MY DEAR YOUNG FRIEND,

'The die is cast—all is over. Hiding the ravages of care with a sickly mask of mirth, I have not informed you, this evening, that there is no hope of the remittance! Under these circumstances, alike humiliating to endure, humiliating to contemplate, and humiliating to relate, I have discharged the pecuniary liability contracted at this establishment, by giving a note of hand, made payable fourteen days after date, at my residence, Pentonville, Lon-don. When it becomes due, it will not be taken up. The result is destruction. The bolt is impending, and the tree must fall.

'Let the wretched man who now addresses you, my dear Copperfield, be a beacon to you through life.

He writes with that intention, and in that hope. If he could think himself of so much use, one gleam of day might, by possibility, penetrate into the cheerless dungeon of his remaining existence—though his longevity is, at present (to say the least of it), extremely problematical.

'This is the last communication, my dear Copperfield, you will ever receive

'From
'The
'Beggared Outcast,
'WILKINS MICAWBER.

I was so shocked by the contents of this heartrending letter, that I ran off directly towards the little hotel with the intention of taking it on my way to Doctor Strong's, and trying to soothe Mr. Micawber with a word of comfort. But, half-way there, I met the London coach with Mr. and Mrs. Micawber up behind; Mr. Micawber, the very picture of tranquil enjoyment, smiling at Mrs. Micawber's conversation, eating walnuts out of a paper bag, with a bottle sticking out of his breast-pocket. As they did not see me, I thought it best, all things considered, not to see them. So, with a great weight taken off my mind, I turned into a by-street that was the nearest way to school, and felt, upon the whole, relieved that they were gone: though I still liked them very much, nevertheless.

CHAPTER XVIII

A RETROSPECT

My school-days! The silent gliding on of my existence—the unseen, unfelt progress of my life—from childhood up to youth! Let me think, as I look back upon that flowing water, now a dry channel overgrown with leaves, whether there are any marks along its course, by which I can remember how it ran.

A moment, and I occupy my place in the cathedral, where we all went together, every Sunday morning, assembling first at school for that purpose. The earthy smell, the sunless air, the sensation of the world being shut out, the resounding of the organ through the black and white arched galleries and aisles, are wings that take me back, and hold me hovering above those days, in a half-sleeping and half-waking dream.

I am not the last boy in the school. I have risen, in a few months, over several heads. But the first boy seems to me a mighty creature, dwelling afar off, whose giddy height is unattainable. Agnes says 'No,' but I say 'Yes,' and tell her that she little thinks what stores of knowledge have been mastered by the wonderful being, at whose place she thinks I, even I, weak aspirant, may arrive in time. He is not my private friend and public patron, as Steerforth was; but I hold him in a reverential respect. I chiefly wonder what he 'll be, when he leaves Doctor Strong's, and what mankind will do to maintain any place against him.

But who is this that breaks upon me? This is Miss Shepherd, whom I love

Miss Shepherd is a boarder at the Misses Nettin-galls' establishment. I adore Miss Shepherd. She is a little girl, in a spencer, with a round face and curly flaxen hair. The Misses Nettingalls' young ladies come to the cathedral too. I cannot look upon my book, for I must look upon Miss Shepherd. When the choristers chaunt, I hear Miss Shepherd. In the service I mentally insert Miss Shepherd's name; I put her in among the Royal Family. At home, in my own room, I am sometimes moved to cry out, 'Oh, Miss Shepherd!' in a transport of love.

For some time, I am doubtful of Miss Shepherd's feelings, but, at length, Fate being propitious, we meet at the dancing-school. I have Miss Shepherd for my partner. I touch Miss Shepherd's glove, and feel a thrill go up the right arm of my jacket, and come out at my hair. I say nothing tender to Miss Shepherd, but we understand each other. Miss Shepherd and myself live but to be united.

Why do I secretly give Miss Shepherd twelve Brazil nuts for a present, I wonder? They are not expressive of affection, they are difficult to pack into a parcel of any regular shape, they are hard to crack, even in room-doors, and they are oily when cracked; yet I feel that they are appropriate to Miss Shepherd. Soft, seedy biscuits, also, I bestow upon Miss Shepherd! and oranges innumerable. Once, I kiss Miss Shepherd in the cloak-room. Ecstasy! What are my agony and indignation next day, when I hear a flying rumour that the Misses Nettingall have stood Miss Shepherd in the stocks for turning in her toes!

Miss Shepherd being the one pervading theme and vision of my life, how do I ever come to break with her? I can't conceive. And yet a coolness grows between Miss Shepherd and myself. Whispers reach

me of Miss Shepherd having said she wished I
wouldn't stare so, and having avowed a preference for
Master Jones—for Jones! a boy of no merit whatever!
The gulf between me and Miss Shepherd widens. At
last, one day, I met the Misses Nettingalls' establishment out walking. Miss Shepherd makes a face as
she goes by, and laughs to her companion. All is
over. The devotion of a life—it seems a life, it is
all the same—is at an end; Miss Shepherd comes out
of the morning service, and the Royal Family know
her no more.

I am higher in the school, and no one breaks my
peace. I am not at all polite, now, to the Misses
Nettingalls' young ladies, and shouldn't dote on any
of them, if they were twice as many and twenty times
as beautiful. I think the dancing school a tiresome
affair, and wonder why the girls can't dance by themselves and leave us alone. I am growing great in
Latin verses, and neglect the laces of my boots.
Doctor Strong refers to me in public as a promising
young scholar. Mr. Dick is wild with joy, and my
aunt remits me a guinea by the next post.

The shade of a young butcher rises, like the apparition of an armed head in Macbeth. Who is this
young butcher? He is the terror of the youth of
Canterbury. There is a vague belief abroad, that the
beef suet with which he anoints his hair gives him
unnatural strength, and that he is a match for a man.
He is a broad-faced, bull-necked young butcher, with
rough red cheeks, an ill-conditioned mind, and an
injurious tongue. His main use of this tongue, is,
to disparage Doctor Strong's young gentlemen. He
says, publicly, that if they want anything he'll give it
'em. He names individuals among them (myself included), whom he could undertake to settle with one
hand, and the other tied behind him. He waylays the

smaller boys to punch their unprotected heads, and
calls challenges after me in the open streets. For
these sufficient reasons I resolve to fight the butcher.

It is a summer evening, down in a green hollow,
at the corner of a wall. I meet the butcher by appointment. I am attended by a select body of our
boys; the butcher, by two other butchers, a young
publican, and a sweep. The preliminaries are adjusted, and the butcher and myself stand face to face.
In a moment the butcher lights ten thousand candles
out of my left eyebrow. In another moment, I don't
know where the wall is, or where I am, or where anybody is. I hardly know which is myself and which
the butcher, we are always in such a tangle and tussle,
knocking about upon the trodden grass. Sometimes
I see the butcher, bloody but confident; sometimes
I see nothing, and sit gasping on my second's knee;
sometimes I go in at the butcher madly, and cut my
knuckles open against his face, without appearing
to discompose him at all. At last I awake, very queer
about the head, as from a giddy sleep, and see the
butcher walking off, congratulated by the two other
butchers and the sweep and publican, and putting on
his coat as he goes; from which I augur, justly, that
the victory is his.

I am taken home in a sad plight, and I have beef-
steaks put to my eyes, and am rubbed with vinegar
and brandy, and find a great white puffy place bursting out on my upper lip, which swells immoderately.
For three or four days I remain at home, a very ill-
looking subject, with a green shade over my eyes; and
I should be very dull, but that Agnes is a sister to me,
and condoles with me, and reads to me, and makes
the time light and happy. Agnes has my confidence
completely, always; I tell her all about the butcher,
and the wrongs he has heaped upon me; she thinks I

couldn't have done otherwise than fight the butcher, while she shrinks and trembles at my having fought him.

Time has stolen on unobserved, for Adams is not the head-boy in the days that are come now, nor has he been this many and many a day. Adams has left the school so long, that when he comes back, on a visit to Doctor Strong, there are not many there, besides myself, who know him. Adams is going to be called to the bar almost directly, and is to be an advocate, and to wear a wig. I am surprised to find him a meeker man than I had thought, and less imposing in appearance. He has not staggered the world yet, either; for it goes on (as well as I can make out) pretty much the same as if he had never joined it.

A blank, through which the warriors of poetry and history march on in stately hosts that seem to have no end—and what comes next! *I* am the head-boy, now! I look down on the line of boys below me, with a condescending interest in such of them as bring to my mind the boy I was myself, when I first came there. That little fellow seems to be no part of me; I remember him as something left behind upon the road of life—as something I have passed, rather than have actually been—and almost think of him as of some one else.

And the little girl I saw on that first day at Mr. Wickfield's, where is she? Gone also. In her stead, the perfect likeness of the picture, a child likeness no more, moves about the house; and Agnes, my sweet sister, as I call her in my thoughts, my counsellor and friend, the better angel of the lives of all who come within her calm, good, self-denying influence, is quite a woman.

What other changes have come upon me, besides

the changes in my growth and looks, and in the knowledge I have garnered all this while? I wear a gold watch and chain, a ring upon my little finger, and a long-tailed coat; and I use a great deal of bear's grease—which, taken in conjunction with the ring, looks bad. Am I in love again? I am. I worship the eldest Miss Larkins.

The eldest Miss Larkins is not a little girl. She is a tall, dark, black-eyed, fine figure of a woman. The eldest Miss Larkins is not a chicken; for the youngest Miss Larkins is not that, and the eldest must be three or four years older. Perhaps the eldest Miss Larkins may be about thirty. My passion for her is beyond all bounds.

The eldest Miss Larkins knows officers. It is an awful thing to bear. I see them speaking to her in the street. I see them cross the way to meet her, when her bonnet (she has a bright taste in bonnets) is seen coming down the pavement, accompanied by her sister's bonnet. She laughs and talks, and seems to like it. I spend a good deal of my own spare time in walking up and down to meet her. If I can bow to her once in the day (I know her to bow to, knowing Mr. Larkins), I am happier. I deserve a bow now and then. The raging agonies I suffer on the night of the Race Ball, where I know the eldest Miss Larkins will be dancing with the military, ought to have some compensation, if there be even-handed justice in the world.

My passion takes away my appetite, and makes me wear my newest silk neckerchief continually. I have no relief but in putting on my best clothes, and having my boots cleaned over and over again. I seem, then, to be worthier of the eldest Miss Larkins. Everything that belongs to her, or is connected with her, is precious to me. Mr. Larkins (a gruff old gentleman with a double chin, and one of his eyes immoveable in his head) is fraught with interest to me. When I can't meet his daughter, I go where I am likely to meet him. To say, 'How do you do, Mr. Larkins? Are the young ladies and all the family quite well?' seems so pointed, that I blush.

I think continually about my age. Say I am seventeen, and say that seventeen is young for the eldest Miss Larkins, what of that? Besides, I shall be one-and-twenty in no time almost. I regularly take walks outside Mr. Larkins's house in the evening, though it cuts me to the heart to see the officers go in, or to hear them up in the drawing-room, where the eldest Miss Larkins plays the harp. I even walk, on two or three occasions, in a sickly, spoony manner, round and round the house after the family are gone to bed, wondering which is the eldest Miss Larkins's chamber (and pitching, I dare say now, on Mr. Larkins's instead); wishing that a fire would burst out; that the assembled crowd would stand appalled; that I, dashing through them with a ladder, might rear it against her window, save her in my arms, go back for something she had left behind, and perish in the flames. For I am generally disinterested in my love, and think I could be content to make a figure before Miss Larkins, and expire. Generally, but not always. Sometimes brighter visions rise before me. When I dress (the occupation of two hours), for a great ball given at the Larkins's (the anticipation of three weeks), I indulge my fancy with pleasing images. I picture myself taking courage to make a declaration to Miss Larkins. I picture Miss Larkins sinking her head upon my shoulder, and saying, 'Oh, Mr. Copperfield, can I believe my ears!' I picture Mr. Larkins waiting on me next morning, and saying, 'My dear Copperfield, my daughter has told me all.

Youth is no objection. Here are twenty thousand
pounds. Be happy!' I picture my aunt relenting,
and blessing us; and Mr. Dick and Doctor Strong
being present at the marriage ceremony. I am a
sensible fellow, I believe—I believe, on looking back,
I mean—and modest I am sure; but all this goes on
notwithstanding.

I repair to the enchanted house, where there are
lights, chattering, music, flowers, officers (I am sorry
to see), and the eldest Miss Larkins a blaze of beauty.
She is dressed in blue, with blue flowers in her hair
—forget-me-nots. As if *she* had any need to wear
forget-me-nots! It is the first really grown-up party
that I have ever been invited to, and I am a little
uncomfortable; for I appear not to belong to anybody, and nobody appears to have anything to say
to me, except Mr. Larkins, who asks me how my
school-fellows are, which he needn't do, as I have not
come there to be insulted.

But after I have stood in the doorway for some
time, and feasted my eyes upon the goddess of my
heart, she approaches me—she, the eldest Miss Larkins!—and asks me pleasantly, if I dance?

I stammer, with a bow, 'With you, Miss Larkins.'

'With no one else?' inquires Miss Larkins.

'I should have no pleasure in dancing with any one
else.'

Miss Larkins laughs and blushes (or I think she
blushes), and says, 'Next time but one, I shall be
very glad.'

The time arrives. 'It is a waltz, I think,' Miss
Larkins doubtfully observes, when I present myself.
'Do you waltz? If not, Captain Bailey—'

But I do waltz (pretty well, too, as it happens),
and I take Miss Larkins out. I take her sternly
from the side of Captain Bailey. He is wretched.

I have no doubt; but he is nothing to me. I have been wretched, too. I waltz with the eldest Miss Larkins! I don't know where, among whom, or how long. I only know that I swim about in space, with a blue angel, in a state of blissful delirium, until I find myself alone with her in a little room, resting on a sofa. She admires a flower (pink camellia japonica, price half-a-crown), in my button-hole. I give it her, and say—

'I ask an inestimable price for it, Miss Larkins.'

'Indeed! What is that?' returns Miss Larkins.

'A flower of yours, that I may treasure it as a miser does gold.'

'You're a bold boy,' says Miss Larkins. 'There.'

She gives it me, not displeased; and I put it to my lips, and then to my breast. Miss Larkins, laughing, draws her hand through my arm, and says, 'Now take me back to Captain Bailey.'

I am lost in the recollection of this delicious interview, and the waltz, when she comes to me again, with a plain elderly gentleman, who has been playing whist all night, upon her arm, and says—

'Oh, here is my bold friend. Mr. Chestle wants to know you, Mr. Copperfield.'

I feel at once that he is a friend of the family, and am much gratified.

'I admire your taste, sir,' says Mr. Chestle. 'It does you credit. I suppose you don't take much interest in hops; but I am a pretty large grower myself; and if you ever like to come over to our neighbourhood—neighbourhood of Ashford—and take a run about our place, we shall be glad for you to stop as long as you like.'

I thank Mr. Chestle warmly, and shake hands. I think I am in a happy dream. I waltz with the eldest Miss Larkins once again. She says I waltz so well!

I go home in a state of unspeakable bliss, and waltz in imagination, all night long, with my arm round the blue waist of my dear divinity. For some days afterwards, I am lost in rapturous reflections; but I neither see her in the street, nor when I call. I am imperfectly consoled for this disappointment by the sacred pledge, the perished flower.

'Trotwood,' says Agnes, one day after dinner. 'Who do you think is going to be married to-morrow? Some one you admire.'

'Not you, I suppose, Agnes?'

'Not me!' raising her cheerful face from the music she is copying. 'Do you hear him, papa?—The eldest Miss Larkins.'

'To—to Captain Bailey?' I have just enough power to ask.

'No; to no Captain. To Mr. Chestle, a hop-grower.'

I am terribly dejected for about a week or two. I take off my ring, I wear my worst clothes, I use no bear's grease, and I frequently lament over the late Miss Larkins's faded flower. Being, by that time, rather tired of this kind of life, and having received new provocation from the butcher, I throw the flower away, go out with the butcher, and gloriously defeat him.

This, and the resumption of my ring, as well as of the bear's grease in moderation, are the last marks I can discern, now, in my progress to seventeen.

CHAPTER XIX

I LOOK ABOUT ME, AND MAKE A DISCOVERY

I AM doubtful whether I was at heart glad or sorry, when my school-days drew to an end, and the time came for my leaving Doctor Strong's. I had been very happy there, I had a great attachment for the Doctor, and I was eminent and distinguished in that little world. For these reasons I was sorry to go; but for other reasons, unsubstantial enough, I was glad. Misty ideas of being a young man at my own disposal, of the importance attaching to a young man at his own disposal, of the wonderful things to be seen and done by that magnificent animal and the wonderful effects he could not fail to make upon society, lured me away. So powerful were these visionary considerations in my boyish mind, that I seem, according to my present way of thinking, to have left school without natural regret. The separation has not made the impression on me, that other separations have. I try in vain to recall how I felt about it, and what its circumstances were; but it is not momentous in my recollection. I suppose the opening prospect confused me. I know that my juvenile experiences went for little or nothing then; and that life was more like a great fairy story, which I was just about to begin to read, than anything else.

My aunt and I had held many grave deliberations on the calling to which I should be devoted. For a year or more I had endeavoured to find a satisfactory answer to her often-repeated question, 'What I would like to be?' But I had no particular liking, that I could discover, for anything. If I could have been inspired with a knowledge of the science of navigation, taken the command of a fast-sailing expedition, and gone round the world on a triumphant voyage of discovery, I think I might have considered myself completely suited. But in the absence of any such miraculous provision, my desire was to apply myself to some pursuit that would not lie too heavily upon her purse; and to do my duty in it, whatever it might be.

Mr. Dick had regularly assisted at our councils, with a meditative and sage demeanour. He never made a suggestion but once; and on that occasion (I don't know what put it in his head), he suddenly proposed that I should be 'a brazier.' My aunt received this proposal so very ungraciously, that he never ventured on a second; but ever afterwards confined himself to looking watchfully at her for her suggestions, and rattling his money.

'Trot, I tell you what, my dear,' said my aunt, one morning in the Christmas season when I left school; 'as this knotty point is still unsettled, and as we must not make a mistake in our decision if we can help it, I think we had better take a little breathing-time. In the meanwhile, you must try to look at it from a new point of view, and not as a school-boy.'

'I will, aunt.'

'It has occurred to me,' pursued my aunt, 'that a little change, and a glimpse of life out of doors, may be useful, in helping you to know your own mind, and form a cooler judgment. Suppose you were to take a little journey now. Suppose you were to go down into the old part of the country again, for instance, and see that—that out-of-the-way woman with the savagest of names,' said my aunt, rubbing her nose, for she could never thoroughly forgive Peggotty for being so called.

'Of all things in the world, aunt, I should like it best!'

'Well,' said my aunt, 'that's lucky, for I should like it too. But it's natural and rational that you should like it. And I am very well persuaded that whatever you do, Trot, will always be natural and rational.'

'I hope so, aunt.'

'Your sister, Betsey Trotwood,' said my aunt, 'would have been as natural and rational a girl as ever breathed. You'll be worthy of her, won't you?'

'I hope I shall be worthy of *you,* aunt. That will be enough for me.'

'It's a mercy that poor dear baby of a mother of yours didn't live,' said my aunt, looking at me approvingly, 'or she'd have been so vain of her boy by this time, that her soft little head would have been completely turned, if there was anything of it left to turn.' (My aunt always excused any weakness of her own in my behalf, by transferring it in this way to my poor mother.) 'Bless me, Trotwood, how you do remind me of her!'

'Pleasantly, I hope, aunt?' said I.

'He's as like her, Dick,' said my aunt, emphatically, 'he's as like her, as she was that afternoon, before she began to fret. Bless my heart, he's as like her, as he can look at me out of his two eyes!'

'Is he, indeed?' said Mr. Dick.

'And he's like David, too,' said my aunt, decisively.

'He is very like David!' said Mr. Dick.

'But what I want you to be, Trot,' resumed my aunt, '—I don't mean physically, but morally; you are very well physically—is, a firm fellow. A fine firm fellow, with a will of your own. With resolution,' said my aunt, shaking her cap at me, and clenching her hand. 'With determination. With char-

acter, Trot.   With strength of character that is not to
be influenced, except on good reason, by anybody,
or by anything.   That's what I want you to be.
That's what your father and mother might both have
been, Heaven knows, and been the better for it.'

I intimated that I hoped I should be what she
described.

'That you may begin, in a small way, to have a
reliance upon yourself, and to act for yourself,' said
my aunt, 'I shall send you upon your trip, alone.   I
did think, once, of Mr. Dick's going with you; but,
on second thoughts, I shall keep him to take care of
me.'

Mr. Dick, for a moment, looked a little disappointed; until the honour and dignity of having to
take care of the most wonderful woman in the world,
restored the sunshine to his face.

'Besides,' said my aunt, 'there's the Memorial.'

'Oh, certainly,' said Mr. Dick, in a hurry, 'I intend,
Trotwood, to get that done immediately—it really
must be done immediately!   And then it will go in,
you know—and then—,' said Mr. Dick, after checking himself, and pausing a long time, 'there'll be a
pretty kettle of fish!'

In pursuance of my aunt's kind scheme, I was
shortly afterwards fitted out with a handsome purse of
money, and a portmanteau, and tenderly dismissed
upon my expedition.   At parting, my aunt gave me
some good advice, and a good many kisses; and said
that as her object was that I should look about me,
and should think a little, she would recommend me
to stay a few days in London, if I liked it, either on
my way down into Suffolk, or in coming back.   In a
word, I was at liberty to do what I would, for three
weeks or a month; and no other conditions were imposed upon my freedom than the before-mentioned

thinking and looking about me, and a pledge to write three times a week and faithfully report myself.

I went to Canterbury first, that I might take leave of Agnes and Mr. Wickfield (my old room in whose house I had not yet relinquished), and also of the good Doctor. Agnes was very glad to see me, and told me that the house had not been like itself since I had left it.

'I am sure I am not like myself when I am away,' said I. 'I seem to want my right hand, when I miss you. Though that's not saying much; for there's no head in my right hand, and no heart. Every one who knows you, consults with you, and is guided by you, Agnes.'

'Every one who knows me, spoils me, I believe,' she answered, smiling.

'No. It's because you are like no one else. You are so good, and so sweet-tempered. You have such a gentle nature, and you are always right.'

'You talk,' said Agnes, breaking into a pleasant laugh, as she sat at work, 'as if I were the late Miss Larkins.'

'Come! It's not fair to abuse my confidence,' I answered, reddening at the recollection of my blue enslaver. 'But I shall confide in you, just the same, Agnes. I can never grow out of that. Whenever I fall into trouble, or fall in love, I shall always tell you, if you'll let me—even when I come to fall in love in earnest.'

'Why, you have always been in earnest!' said Agnes, laughing again.

'Oh! that was as a child, or a schoolboy,' said I, laughing in my turn, not without being a little shamefaced. 'Times are altering now, and I suppose I shall be in a terrible state of earnestness one day or other. My wonder is, that you are not in earnest yourself, by this time, Agnes.'

Agnes laughed again, and shook her head.

'Oh, I know you are not!' said I, 'because if you had been, you would have told me. Or at least,' for I saw a faint blush in her face, 'you would have let me find it out for myself. But there is no one that I know of, who deserves to love *you*, Agnes. Some one of a nobler character, and more worthy altogether than any one I have ever seen here, must rise up, before I give *my* consent. In the time to come, I shall have a wary eye on all admirers; and shall exact a great deal from the successful one, I assure you.'

We had gone on, so far, in a mixture of confidential jest and earnest, that had long grown naturally out of our familiar relations, begun as mere children. But Agnes, now suddenly lifting up her eyes to mine, and speaking in a different manner, said—

'Trotwood, there is something that I want to ask you, and that I may not have another opportunity of asking for a long time, perhaps. Something I would ask, I think, of no one else. Have you observed any gradual alteration in papa?'

I had observed it, and had often wondered whether she had too. I must have shown as much, now, in my face; for her eyes were in a moment cast down, and I saw tears in them.

'Tell me what it is,' she said, in a low voice.

'I think—shall I be quite plain, Agnes, liking him so much?'

'Yes,' she said.

'I think he does himself no good by the habit that has increased upon him since I first came here. He is often very nervous, or I fancy so.'

'It is not fancy,' said Agnes, shaking her head.

'His hand trembles, his speech is not plain, and his eyes look wild. I have remarked that at those times, and when he is least like himself, he is most certain to be wanted on some business.'

'By Uriah,' said Agnes.

'Yes; and the sense of being unfit for it, or of not having understood it, or of having shown his condition in spite of himself, seems to make him so uneasy, that next day he is worse, and next day worse, and so he becomes jaded and haggard. Do not be alarmed by what I say, Agnes, but in this state I saw him, only the other evening, lay down his head upon his desk, and shed tears like a child.'

Her hand passed softly before my lips while I was yet speaking, and in a moment she had met her father at the door of the room, and was hanging on his shoulder. The expression of her face, as they both looked towards me, I felt to be very touching. There was such deep fondness for him, and gratitude to him for all his love and care, in her beautiful look; and there was such a fervent appeal to me to deal tenderly by him, even in my inmost thoughts, and to let no harsh construction find any place against him; she was, at once, so proud of him and devoted to him, yet so compassionate and sorry, and so reliant upon me to be so, too; that nothing she could have said would have expressed more to me, or moved me more.

We were to drink tea at the Doctor's. We went there at the usual hour; and round the study-fireside found the Doctor, and his young wife, and her mother. The Doctor, who made as much of my going away as if I were going to China, received me as an honoured guest; and called for a log of wood to be thrown on the fire, that he might see the face of his old pupil reddening in the blaze.

'I shall not see many more new faces in Trotwood's stead, Wickfield,' said the Doctor, warming his hands; 'I am getting lazy, and want ease. I shall relinquish all my young people in another six months, and lead a quieter life.'

'You have said so, any time these ten years, Doctor,' Mr. Wickfield answered.

'But now I mean to do it,' returned the Doctor. 'My first master will succeed me—I am in earnest at last—so you'll soon have to arrange our contracts, and to bind us firmly to them, like a couple of knaves.'

'And to take care,' said Mr. Wickfield, 'that you 're not imposed on, eh? As you certainly would be, in any contract you should make for yourself. Well! I am ready. There are worse tasks than that, in my calling.'

'I shall have nothing to think of, then,' said the Doctor, with a smile, 'but my Dictionary; and this other contract-bargain—Annie.'

As Mr. Wickfield glanced towards her, sitting at the tea-table by Agnes, she seemed to me to avoid his look with such unwonted hesitation and timidity, that his attention became fixed upon her, as if something were suggested to his thoughts.

'There is a post come in from India, I observe,' he said, after a short silence.

'By the bye! and letters from Mr. Jack Maldon!' said the Doctor.

'Indeed!'

'Poor dear Jack!' said Mrs. Markleham, shaking her head. 'That trying climate! Like living, they tell me, on a sand-heap, underneath a burning-glass! He looked strong, but he wasn't. My dear Doctor, it was his spirit, not his constitution, that he ventured on so boldly. Annie, my dear, I am sure you must perfectly recollect that your cousin never was strong, not what can be called *robust,* you know,' said Mrs. Markleham, with emphasis, and looking round upon us generally; 'from the time when my daughter and himself were children, together, and walking about, arm-in-arm, the livelong day.'

Annie, thus addressed, made no reply.

'Do I gather from what you say, ma'am, that Mr. Maldon is ill?' asked Mr. Wickfield.

'Ill!' replied the Old Soldier. 'My dear sir, he's all sorts of things.'

'Except well?' said Mr. Wickfield.

'Except well, indeed!' said the Old Soldier. 'He has had dreadful strokes of the sun, no doubt, and jungle fevers and agues, and every kind of thing you can mention. As to his liver,' said the Old Soldier resignedly, 'that, of course, he gave up altogether, when he first went out!'

'Does he say all this?' asked Mr. Wickfield.

'Say? My dear sir,' returned Mrs. Markleham, shaking her head and her fan, 'you little know my poor Jack Maldon when you ask that question. Say? Not he. You might drag him at the heels of four wild horses first.'

'Mamma!' said Mrs. Strong.

'Annie, my dear,' returned her mother, 'once for all, I must really beg that you will not interfere with me, unless it is to confirm what I say. You know as well as I do, that your cousin Maldon would be dragged at the heels of any number of wild horses— why should I confine myself to four! I *won't* confine myself to four—eight, sixteen, two-and-thirty, rather than say anything calculated to overturn the Doctor's plans.'

'Wickfield's plans,' said the Doctor, stroking his face, and looking penitently at his adviser. 'That is to say, our joint plans for him. I said myself, abroad or at home.'

'And I said,' added Mr. Wickfield gravely, 'abroad. I was the means of sending him abroad. It's my responsibility.'

'Oh! Responsibility!' said the Old Soldier. 'Everything was done for the best, my dear Mr. Wickfield; everything was done for the kindest and best, we know. But if the dear fellow can't live there, he can't live there. And if he can't live there, he'll die there, sooner than he'll overturn the Doctor's plans. I know him,' said the Old Soldier, fanning herself, in a sort of calm prophetic agony, 'and I know he'll die there, sooner than he'll overturn the Doctor's plans.'

'Well, well, ma'am,' said the Doctor cheerfully, 'I am not bigoted to my plans, and I can overturn them myself. I can substitute some other plans. If Mr. Jack Maldon comes home on account of ill health, he must not be allowed to go back, and we must endeavour to make some more suitable and fortunate provision for him in this country.'

Mrs. Markleham was so overcome by this generous speech (which, I need not say, she had not at all expected or led up to) that she could only tell the Doctor it was like himself, and go several times through that operation of kissing the sticks of her fan, and then tapping his hand with it. After which she gently chid her daughter Annie, for not being more demonstrative when such kindnesses were showered, for her sake, on her old playfellow; and entertained us with some particulars concerning other deserving members of her family, whom it was desirable to set on their deserving legs.

All this time, her daughter Annie never once spoke, or lifted up her eyes. All this time, Mr. Wickfield had his glance upon her as she sat by his own daughter's side. It appeared to me that he never thought of being observed by any one; but was so intent upon her, and upon his own thoughts in connection with her, as to be quite absorbed. He now asked what Mr. Jack Maldon had actually written in reference to himself, and to whom he had written it?

'Why, here,' said Mrs. Markleham, taking a letter from the chimney-piece above the Doctor's head, 'the dear fellow says to the Doctor himself—where is it? Oh!—"I am sorry to inform you that my health is suffering severely, and that I fear I may be reduced to the necessity of returning home for a time, as the only hope of restoration." That's pretty plain, poor fellow! His only hope of restoration! But Annie's letter is plainer still. Annie, show me that letter again.'

'Not now, mamma,' she pleaded in a low tone.

'My dear, you absolutely are, on some subjects, one of the most ridiculous persons in the world,' returned her mother, 'and perhaps the most unnatural to the claims of your own family. We never should have heard of the letter at all, I believe, unless I had asked for it myself. Do you call that confidence, my love, towards Doctor Strong? I am surprised. You ought to know better.'

The letter was reluctantly produced; and as I handed it to the old lady, I saw how the unwilling hand from which I took it, trembled.

'Now let us see,' said Mrs. Markleham, putting her glass to her eye, 'where the passage is. "The remembrance of old times, my dearest Annie"—and so forth—it's not there. "The amiable old Proctor"—who's he? Dear me, Annie, how illegibly your cousin Maldon writes, and how stupid I am! "Doctor," of course. Ah! amiable indeed!' Here she left off, to kiss her fan again, and shake it at the Doctor, who was looking at us in a state of placid satisfaction. 'Now I have found it. *"You* may not be surprised to hear, Annie,"—no, to be sure, knowing that he never was really strong; what did I say just now?—"that I have undergone so much in this distant place, as to have decided to leave it at all hazards; on sick leave, if I can; on total resignation, if that is not to be obtained. What I have endured, and do endure here, is insupportable." And but for the promptitude of that best of creatures,' said Mrs. Markleham, telegraphing the Doctor as before, and refolding the letter, 'it would be insupportable to me to think of.'

Mr. Wickfield said not one word, though the old lady looked to him as if for his commentary on this intelligence; but sat severely silent, with his eyes fixed on the ground. Long after the subject was dismissed, and other topics occupied us, he remained so; seldom raising his eyes, unless to rest them for a moment, with a thoughtful frown, upon the Doctor, or his wife, or both.

The Doctor was very fond of music. Agnes sang with great sweetness and expression, and so did Mrs. Strong. They sang together, and played duets together, and we had quite a little concert. But I remarked two things: first, that though Annie soon recovered her composure, and was quite herself, there was a blank between her and Mr. Wickfield which separated them wholly from each other; secondly, that Mr. Wickfield seemed to dislike the intimacy between her and Agnes, and to watch it with uneasiness. And now, I must confess, the recollection of what I had seen on that night when Mr. Maldon went away, first began to return upon me with a meaning it had never had, and to trouble me. The innocent beauty of her face was not as innocent to me as it had been; I mistrusted the natural grace and charm of her manner; and when I looked at Agnes by her side, and thought how good and true Agnes was, suspicions arose within me that it was an ill-assorted friendship.

She was so happy in it herself, however, and the other was so happy too, that they made the evening fly away as if it were but an hour.   It closed in an incident which I well remember.   They were taking leave of each other, and Agnes was going to embrace her and kiss her, when Mr. Wickfield stepped between them, as if by accident, and drew Agnes quickly away.   Then I saw, as though all the intervening time had been cancelled, and I were still standing in the doorway on the night of the departure, the expression of that night in the face of Mrs. Strong, as it confronted his.

I cannot say what an impression this made upon me, or how impossible I found it, when I thought of her afterwards, to separate her from this look, and remember her face in its innocent loveliness again. It haunted me when I got home.   I seemed to have left the Doctor's roof with a dark cloud lowering on it.   The reverence that I had for his grey head, was mingled with commiseration for his faith in those who were treacherous to him, and with resentment against those who injured him.   The impending shadow of a great affliction, and a great disgrace that had no distinct form in it yet, fell like a stain upon the quiet place where I had worked and played as a boy, and did it a cruel wrong.   I had no pleasure in thinking, any more, of the grave old broad-leaved aloe-trees which remained shut up in themselves a hundred years together, and of the trim smooth grass-plot, and the stone urns, and the Doctor's Walk, and the congenial sound of the cathedral bell hovering above them all. It was as if the tranquil sanctuary of my boyhood had been sacked before my face, and its peace and honour given to the winds.

But morning brought with it my parting from the old house, which Agnes had filled with her influence; and that occupied my mind sufficiently. I should be there again soon, no doubt; I might sleep again—perhaps often—in my old room; but the days of my inhabiting there were gone, and the old time was past. I was heavier at heart when I packed up such of my books and clothes as still remained there to be sent to Dover, than I cared to show to Uriah Heep: who was so officious to help me, that I uncharitably thought him mighty glad that I was going.

I got away from Agnes and her father, somehow, with an indifferent show of being very manly, and took my seat upon the box of the London coach. I was so softened and forgiving, going through the town, that I had half a mind to nod to my old enemy the butcher, and throw him five shillings to drink. But he looked such a very obdurate butcher as he stood scraping the great block in the shop, and moreover, his appearance was so little improved by the loss of a front tooth which I had knocked out, that I thought it best to make no advances.

The main object on my mind, I remember, when we got fairly on the road, was to appear as old as possible to the coachman, and to speak extremely gruff. The latter point I achieved at great personal inconvenience; but I stuck to it, because I felt it was a grown-up sort of thing.

'You are going through, sir?' said the coachman.

'Yes, William,' I said, condescendingly (I knew him); 'I am going to London. I shall go down into Suffolk afterwards.'

'Shooting, sir?' said the coachman.

He knew as well as I did that it was just as likely, at that time of year, I was going down there whaling; but I felt complimented, too.

'I don't know,' I said, pretending to be undecided, 'whether I shall take a shot or not.'

'Birds is got wery shy, I'm told,' said William.

'So I understand,' said I.

'Is Suffolk your county, sir?' asked William.

'Yes,' I said, with some importance. 'Suffolk's my county.'

'I'm told the dumplings is uncommon fine down there,' said William.

I was not aware of it myself, but I felt it necessary to uphold the institutions of my county, and to evince a familiarity with them; so I shook my head, as much as to say, 'I believe you!'

'And the Punches,' said William. 'There's cattle! A Suffolk Punch, when he's a good 'un, is worth his weight in gold. Did you ever breed any Suffolk Punches yourself, sir?'

'N—no,' I said, 'not exactly.'

'Here's a gen'l'm'n behind me, I'll pound it,' said William, 'as has bred 'em by wholesale.'

The gentleman spoken of was a gentleman with a very unpromising squint, and a prominent chin, who had a tall white hat on with a narrow flat brim, and whose close-fitting drab trousers seemed to button all the way up outside his legs from his boots to his hips. His chin was cocked over the coachman's shoulder, so near to me, that his breath quite tickled the back of my head; and as I looked round at him, he leered at the leaders with the eye with which he didn't squint, in a very knowing manner.

'Ain't you?' asked William.

'Ain't I what?' said the gentleman behind.

'Bred them Suffolk Punches by wholesale?'

'I should think so,' said the gentleman. 'There ain't no sort of orse that I ain't bred, and no sort of dorg. Orses and dorgs is some men's fancy. They're wittles and drink to me—lodging, wife, and children—reading, writing, and 'rithmetic—snuff, tobacker, and sleep.'

'That ain't a sort of man to see sitting behind a coach-box, is it though?' said William in my ear, as he handled the reins.

I construed this remark into an indication of a wish that he should have my place, so I blushingly offered to resign it.

'Well, if you don't mind, sir,' said William, 'I think it *would* be more correct.'

I have always considered this as the first fall I had in life. When I booked my place at the coach-office, I had had 'Box Seat' written against the entry, and had given the book-keeper half-a-crown. I was got up in a special great-coat and shawl, expressly to do honour to that distinguished eminence; had glorified myself upon it a good deal; and had felt that I was a credit to the coach. And here, in the very first stage, I was supplanted by a shabby man with a squint, who had no other merit than smelling like a livery stable, and being able to walk across me, more like a fly than a human being, while the horses were at a canter!

A distrust of myself, which has often beset me in life on small occasions, when it would have been better away, was assuredly not stopped in its growth by this little incident outside the Canterbury coach. It was in vain to take refuge in gruffness of speech. I spoke from the pit of my stomach for the rest of the journey, but I felt completely extinguished, and dreadfully young.

It was curious and interesting, nevertheless, to be sitting up there, behind four horses: well educated,

well dressed, and with plenty of money in my pocket;
and to look out for the places where I had slept on
my weary journey. I had abundant occupation for
my thoughts, in every conspicuous landmark on the
road. When I looked down at the tramps whom we
passed, and saw that well-remembered style of face
turned up, I felt as if the tinker's blackened hand
were in the bosom of my shirt again. When we
clattered through the narrow street of Chatham, and
I caught a glimpse, in passing, of the lane where the
old monster lived who had bought my jacket, I
stretched my neck eagerly to look for the place where
I had sat, in the sun and in the shade, waiting for my
money. When we came, at last, within a stage of
London, and passed the veritable Salem House where
Mr. Creakle had laid about him with a heavy hand,
I would have given all I had, for lawful permission
to get down and thrash him, and let all the boys out
like so many caged sparrows.

We went to the Golden Cross, at Charing Cross,
then a mouldy sort of establishment in a close neighbourhood. A waiter showed me into the coffee-room;
and a chambermaid introduced me to my small bed-
chamber, which smelt like a hackney-coach, and was
shut up like a family vault. I was still painfully
conscious of my youth, for nobody stood in any awe
of me at all: the chambermaid being utterly indifferent to my opinions on any subject, and the waiter
being familiar with me, and offering advice to my
inexperience.

'Well now,' said the waiter, in a tone of confidence,
'what would you like for dinner? Young gentlemen
likes poultry in general: have a fowl!'

I told him, as majestically as I could, that I wasn't
in the humour for a fowl.

'Ain't you?' said the waiter. 'Young gentlemen

is generally tired of beef and mutton: have a weal cutlet!'

I assented to this proposal, in default of being able to suggest anything else.

'Do you care for taters?' said the waiter, with an insinuating smile, and his head on one side. 'Young gentlemen generally has been overdosed with taters.'

I commanded him, in my deepest voice, to order a veal cutlet and potatoes, and all things fitting; and to inquire at the bar if there were any letters for Trotwood Copperfield, Esquire—which I knew there were not, and couldn't be, but thought it manly to appear to expect.

He soon came back to say that there were none (at which I was much surprised), and began to lay the cloth for my dinner in a box by the fire. While he was so engaged, he asked me what I would take with it; and on my replying 'Half a pint of sherry,' thought it a favourable opportunity, I am afraid, to extract that measure of wine from the stale leavings at the bottoms of several small decanters. I am of this opinion, because, while I was reading the news-paper, I observed him behind a low wooden partition, which was his private apartment, very busy pouring out of a number of those vessels into one, like a chemist and druggist making up a prescription. When the wine came, too, I thought it flat; and it certainly had more English crumbs in it, than were to be expected in a foreign wine in anything like a pure state; but I was bashful enough to drink it, and say nothing.

Being then, in a pleasant frame of mind (from which I infer that poisoning is not always disagree-able in some stages of the process), I resolved to go to the play. It was Covent Garden Theatre that I chose; and there, from the back of a centre box, 1 saw Julius Cæsar and the new Pantomime. To have all those noble Romans alive before me, and walking in and out for my entertainment, instead of being the stern taskmasters they had been at school, was a most novel and delightful effect. But the mingled reality and mystery of the whole show, the influence upon me of the poetry, the lights, the music, the company, the smooth stupendous changes of glittering and brilliant scenery, were so dazzling, and opened up such illimitable regions of delight, that when I came out into the rainy street, at twelve o'clock at night, I felt as if I had come from the clouds, where I had been leading a romantic life for ages, to a bawling, splashing, link-lighted, umbrella-struggling, hackney-coach-jostling, patten-clinking, muddy, miserable world.

I had emerged by another door, and stood in the street for a little while, as if I really were a stranger upon earth; but the unceremonious pushing and hustling that I received, soon recalled me to myself, and put me in the road back to the hotel; whither I went, revolving the glorious vision all the way; and where, after some porter and oysters, I sat revolving it still, at past one o'clock, with my eyes on the coffee-room fire.

I was so filled with the play, and with the past— for it was, in a manner, like a shining transparency, through which I saw my earlier life moving along— that I don't know when the figure of a handsome well-formed young man, dressed with a tasteful easy negligence which I have reason to remember very well, became a real presence to me. But I recollect being conscious of his company without having noticed his coming in—and my still sitting, musing, over the coffee-room fire.

At last I rose to go to bed, much to the relief of

the sleepy waiter, who had got the fidgets in his legs, and was twisting them, and hitting them, and putting them through all kinds of contortions in his small pantry. In going towards the door, I passed the person who had come in, and saw him plainly. I turned directly, came back, and looked again. He did not know me, but I knew him in a moment.

At another time I might have wanted the confidence or the decision to speak to him, and might have put it off until next day, and might have lost him. But, in the then condition of my mind, where the play was still running high, his former protection of me appeared so deserving of my gratitude, and my old love for him overflowed my breast so freshly and spontaneously, that I went up to him at once, with a fast-beating heart, and said—

'Steerforth! won't you speak to me?'

He looked at me—just as he used to look, sometimes—but I saw no recognition in his face.

'You don't remember me, I am afraid,' said I.

'My God!' he suddenly exclaimed. 'It's little Copperfield!'

I grasped him by both hands, and could not let them go. But for very shame, and the fear that it might displease him, I could have held him round the neck and cried.

'I never, never, never was so glad! My dear Steerforth, I am so overjoyed to see you!'

'And I am rejoiced to see you, too!' he said, shaking my hands heartily. 'Why, Copperfield, old boy, don't be overpowered!' And yet he was glad, too, I thought, to see how the delight I had in meeting him affected me.

I brushed away the tears that my utmost resolution had not been able to keep back, and I made a clumsy laugh of it, and we sat down together, side by side.

'Why, how do you come to be here?' said Steerforth, clapping me on the shoulder.

'I came here by the Canterbury coach, to-day. I have been adopted by an aunt down in that part of the country, and have just finished my education there. How do *you* come to be here, Steerforth?'

'Well, I am what they call an Oxford man,' he returned; 'that is to say, I get bored to death down there, periodically—and I am on my way now to my mother's. You 're a devilish amiable-looking fellow, Copperfield. Just what you used to be, now I look at you! Not altered in the least!'

'I knew *you* immediately,' I said; 'but you are more easily remembered.'

He laughed as he ran his hand through the clustering curls of his hair, and said gaily—

'Yes, I am on an expedition of duty. My mother lives a little way out of town; and the roads being in a beastly condition, and our house tedious enough, I remained here to-night instead of going on. I have not been in town half a dozen hours, and those I have been dozing and grumbling away at the play.'

'I have been at the play, too,' said I. 'At Covent Garden. What a delightful and magnificent entertainment, Steerforth!'

Steerforth laughed heartily.

'My dear young Davy,' he said, clapping me on the shoulder again, 'you are a very Daisy. The daisy of the field, at sunrise, is not fresher than you are! I have been at Covent Garden, too, and there never was a more miserable business. Halloa, you sir!'

This was addressed to the waiter, who had been very attentive to our recognition, at a distance, and now came forward deferentially.

'Where have you put my friend, Mr. Copperfield?' said Steerforth.

'Beg your pardon, sir?'

'Where does he sleep? What's his number? You know what I mean,' said Steerforth.

'Well, sir,' said the waiter, with an apologetic air. 'Mr. Copperfield is at present in forty-four, sir.'

'And what the devil do you mean,' retorted Steerforth, 'by putting Mr. Copperfield into a little loft over a stable?'

'Why, you see we wasn't aware, sir,' returned the waiter, still apologetically, 'as Mr. Copperfield was anyways particular. We can give Mr. Copperfield seventy-two, sir, if it would be preferred. Next you, sir.'

'Of course it would be preferred,' said Steerforth. 'And do it at once.'

The waiter immediately withdrew to make the exchange. Steerforth, very much amused at my having been put into forty-four, laughed again, and clapped me on the shoulder again, and invited me to breakfast with him next morning at ten o'clock—an invitation I was only too proud and happy to accept. It being now pretty late, we took our candles and went upstairs, where we parted with friendly heartiness at his door, and where I found my new room a great improvement on my old one, it not being at all musty, and having an immense four-post bedstead in it, which was quite a little landed estate. Here, among pillows enough for six, I soon fell asleep in a blissful condition, and dreamed of ancient Rome, Steerforth, and friendship, until the early morning coaches, rumbling out of the archway underneath, made me dream of thunder and the gods.

CHAPTER XX

STEERFORTH'S HOME

WHEN the chambermaid tapped at my door at eight o'clock, and informed me that my shaving-water was outside, I felt severely the having no occasion for it, and blushed in my bed. The suspicion that she laughed too, when she said it, preyed upon my mind all the time I was dressing; and gave me, I was conscious, a sneaking and guilty air when I passed her on the staircase, as I was going down to breakfast. I was so sensitively aware, indeed, of being younger than I could have wished, that for some time I could not make up my mind to pass her at all, under the ignoble circumstances of the case; but, hearing her there with a broom, stood peeping out of window at King Charles on horseback, surrounded by a maze of hackney-coaches, and looking anything but regal in a drizzling rain and a dark-brown fog, until I was admonished by the waiter that the gentleman was waiting for me.

It was not in the coffee-room that I found Steerforth expecting me, but in a snug private apartment, red-curtained and Turkey-carpeted, where the fire burnt bright, and a fine hot breakfast was set forth on a table covered with a clean cloth; and a cheerful miniature of the room, the fire, the breakfast, Steerforth, and all, was shining in the little round mirror over the sideboard. I was rather bashful at first, Steerforth being so self-possessed, and elegant, and superior to me in all respects (age included); but his easy patronage soon put that to rights, and made me quite at home. I could not enough admire the change he had wrought in the Golden Cross; or compare the

dull forlorn state I had held yesterday, with this
morning's comfort and this morning's entertainment.
As to the waiter's familiarity, it was quenched as if it
had never been.   He attended on us, as I may say,
in sackcloth and ashes.

'Now, Copperfield,' said Steerforth, when we were
alone, 'I should like to hear what you are doing, and
where you are going, and all about you.   I feel as
if you were my property.'

Glowing with pleasure to find that he had still this
interest in me, I told him how my aunt had proposed
the little expedition that I had before me, and whither
it tended.

'As you are in no hurry, then,' said Steerforth,
'come home with me to Highgate, and stay a day
or two.   You will be pleased with my mother—she
is a little vain and prosy about me, but that you can
forgive her—and she will be pleased with you.'

'I should like to be as sure of that, as you are kind
enough to say you are,' I answered, smiling.

'Oh!' said Steerforth, 'every one who likes me, has
a claim on her that is sure to be acknowledged.'

'Then I think I shall be a favourite,' said I.

'Good!' said Steerforth.   'Come and prove it.   We
will go and see the lions for an hour or two—it's
something to have a fresh fellow like you to show
them to, Copperfield—and then we'll journey out to
Highgate by the coach.'

I could hardly believe but that I was in a dream,
and that I should wake presently in number forty-
four, to the solitary box in the coffee-room and the
familiar waiter again.   After I had written to my
aunt and told her of my fortunate meeting with my
admired old schoolfellow, and my acceptance of his
invitation, we went out in a hackney-chariot, and saw
a Panorama and some other sights, and took a walk

through the Museum, where I could not help observing how much Steerforth knew, on an infinite variety of subjects, and of how little account he seemed to make his knowledge.

'You'll take a high degree at college, Steerforth,' said I, 'if you have not done so already; and they will have good reason to be proud of you.'

'*I* take a degree!' cried Steerforth. 'Not I! my dear Daisy—will you mind my calling you Daisy?'

'Not at all!' said I.

'That's a good fellow! My dear Daisy,' said Steerforth, laughing, 'I have not the least desire or intention to distinguish myself in that way. I have done quite sufficient for my purpose. I find that I am heavy company enough for myself as I am.'

'But the fame—' I was beginning.

'You romantic Daisy!' said Steerforth, laughing still more heartily; 'why should I trouble myself, that a parcel of heavy-headed fellows may gape and hold up their hands? Let them do it at some other man. There's fame for him, and he's welcome to it.'

I was abashed at having made so great a mistake, and was glad to change the subject. Fortunately it was not difficult to do, for Steerforth could always pass from one subject to another with a carelessness and lightness that were his own.

Lunch succeeded to our sight-seeing, and the short winter day wore away so fast, that it was dusk when the stage-coach stopped with us at an old brick house at Highgate on the summit of the hill. An elderly lady, though not very far advanced in years, with a proud carriage and a handsome face, was in the doorway as we alighted; and greeting Steerforth as 'My dearest James,' folded him in her arms. To this lady he presented me as his mother, and she gave me a stately welcome.

It was a genteel old-fashioned house, very quiet and orderly. From the windows of my room I saw all London lying in the distance like a great vapour, with here and there some lights twinkling through it. I had only time, in dressing, to glance at the solid furniture, the framed pieces of work (done, I supposed, by Steerforth's mother when she was a girl), and some pictures in crayons of ladies with powdered hair and bodices, coming and going on the walls, as the newly-kindled fire crackled and sputtered, when I was called to dinner.

There was a second lady in the dining-room, of a slight short figure, dark, and not agreeable to look at, but with some appearance of good looks too, who attracted my attention: perhaps because I had not expected to see her: perhaps because I found myself sitting opposite to her: perhaps because of something really remarkable in her. She had black hair and eager black eyes, and was thin, and had a scar upon her lip. It was an old scar—I should rather call it, seam, for it was not discoloured, and had healed years ago—which had once cut through her mouth, downward towards the chin, but was now barely visible across the table, except above and on her upper lip, the shape of which it had altered. I concluded in my own mind that she was about thirty years of age, and that she wished to be married. She was a little dilapidated—like a house—with having been so long to let; yet had, as I have said, an appearance of good looks. Her thinness seemed to be the effect of some wasting fire within her, which found a vent in her gaunt eyes.

She was introduced as Miss Dartle, and both Steerforth and his mother called her Rosa. I found that she lived there, and had been for a long time Mrs. Steerforth's companion. It appeared to me that she never said anything she wanted to say, outright; but hinted it, and made a great deal more of it by this practice. For example, when Mrs. Steerforth observed, more in jest than earnest, that she feared her son led but a wild life at college, Miss Dartle put in thus—

'Oh, really? You know how ignorant I am, and that I only ask for information, but isn't it always so? I thought that kind of life was on all hands understood to be—eh?'

'It is education for a very grave profession, if you mean that, Rosa,' Mrs. Steerforth answered with some coldness.

'Oh! Yes! That's very true,' returned Miss Dartle. 'But isn't it, though?—I want to be put right, if I am wrong—isn't it, really?'

'Really what?' said Mrs. Steerforth.

'Oh! You mean it's not!' returned Miss Dartle. 'Well, I'm very glad to hear it! Now, I know what to do! That's the advantage of asking. I shall never allow people to talk before me about wastefulness and profligacy, and so forth, in connection with that life, any more.'

'And you will be right,' said Mrs. Steerforth. 'My son's tutor is a conscientious gentleman; and if I had not implicit reliance on my son, I should have reliance on him.'

'Should you?' said Miss Dartle. 'Dear me! Conscientious, is he? Really conscientious, now?'

'Yes, I am convinced of it,' said Mrs. Steerforth.

'How very nice!' exclaimed Miss Dartle. 'What a comfort! Really conscientious? Then he's not—but of course he can't be, if he's really conscientious. Well, I shall be quite happy in my opinion of him, from this time. You can't think how it elevates him in my opinion, to know for certain that he's really conscientious!'

Her own views of every question, and her correction of everything that was said to which she was opposed, Miss Dartle insinuated in the same way: sometimes, I could not conceal from myself, with great power, though in contradiction even of Steerforth. An instance happened before dinner was done. Mrs. Steerforth speaking to me about my intention of going down into Suffolk, I said at hazard how glad I should be, if Steerforth would only go there with me; and explaining to him that I was going to see my old nurse, and Mr. Peggotty's family, I reminded him of the boatman whom he had seen at school.

'Oh! That bluff fellow!' said Steerforth. 'He had a son with him, hadn't he?'

'No. That was his nephew,' I replied; 'whom he adopted, though, as a son. He has a very pretty little niece too, whom he adopted as a daughter. In short, his house (or rather his boat, for he lives in one, on dry land) is full of people who are objects of his generosity and kindness. You would be delighted to see that household.'

'Should I?' said Steerforth. 'Well, I think I should. I must see what can be done. It would be worth a journey (not to mention the pleasure of a journey with you, Daisy), to see that sort of people together, and to make one of 'em.'

My heart leaped with a new hope of pleasure. But it was in reference to the tone in which he had spoken of 'that sort of people,' that Miss Dartle, whose sparkling eyes had been watchful of us, now broke in again.

'Oh, but really? Do tell me. Are they, though?' she said.

'Are they what? And are who what?' said Steer-forth.

'That sort of people. Are they really animals and clods, and beings of another order? I want to know *so* much.'

'Why, there's a pretty wide separation between them and us,' said Steerforth, with indifference. 'They are not to be expected to be as sensitive as we are. Their delicacy is not to be shocked, or hurt very easily. They are wonderfully virtuous, I dare say. Some people contend for that, at least; and I am sure I don't want to contradict them. But they have not very fine natures, and they may be thankful that, like their coarse rough skins, they are not easily wounded.'

'Really!' said Miss Dartle. 'Well, I don't know, now, when I have been better pleased than to hear that. It's so consoling! It's such a delight to know that, when they suffer, they don't feel! Sometimes I have been quite uneasy for that sort of people; but now I shall just dismiss the idea of them altogether. Live and learn. I had my doubts, I confess, but now they're cleared up. I didn't know, and now I do know, and that shows the advantage of asking—don't it?'

I believed that Steerforth had said what he had, in jest, or to draw Miss Dartle out; and I expected him to say as much when she was gone, and we two were sitting before the fire. But he merely asked me what I thought of her.

'She is very clever, is she not?' I asked.

'Clever! She brings everything to a grindstone,' said Steerforth, 'and sharpens it, as she has sharpened her own face and figure these years past. She has worn herself away by constant sharpening. She is all edge.'

'What a remarkable scar that is upon her lip!' I said.

Steerforth's face fell, and he paused a moment.

'Why, the fact is,' he returned, '*I* did that.'

'By an unfortunate accident!'

'No. I was a young boy, and she exasperated me, and I threw a hammer at her. A promising young angel I must have been!'

I was deeply sorry to have touched on such a painful theme, but that was useless now.

'She has borne the mark ever since, as you see,' said Steerforth; 'and she'll bear it to her grave, if she ever rests in one; though I can hardly believe she will ever rest anywhere. She was the motherless child of a sort of cousin of my father's. He died one day. My mother, who was then a widow, brought her here to be company to her. She has a couple of thousand pounds of her own, and saves the interest of it every year, to add to the principal. There's the history of Miss Rosa Dartle for you.'

'And I have no doubt she loves you like a brother?' said I.

'Humph!' retorted Steerforth, looking at the fire. 'Some brothers are not loved over much; and some love—but help yourself, Copperfield! We'll drink the daisies of the field, in compliment to you; and the lilies of the valley that toil not, neither do they spin, in compliment to me—the more shame for me!' A moody smile that had over-spread his features cleared off as he said this merrily, and he was his own frank, winning self again.

I could not help glancing at the scar with a painful interest when we went in to tea. It was not long before I observed that it was the most susceptible part of her face, and that, when she turned pale, that mark altered first, and became a dull, lead-coloured streak, lengthening out to its full extent, like a mark in invisible ink brought to the fire. There was a little altercation between her and Steerforth about a cast of the dice at backgammon, when I thought her, for one moment, in a storm of rage; and then I saw it start forth like the old writing on the wall.

It was no matter of wonder to me to find Mrs. Steerforth devoted to her son. She seemed to be able to speak or think about nothing else. She showed me his picture as an infant, in a locket, with some of his baby-hair in it; she showed me his picture as he had been when I first knew him; and she wore at her breast his picture as he was now. All the letters he had ever written to her, she kept in a cabinet near her own chair by the fire; and she would have read me some of them and I should have been very glad to hear them too, if he had not interposed, and coaxed her out of the design.

'It was at Mr. Creakle's, my son tells me, that you first became acquainted,' said Mrs. Steerforth, as she and I were talking at one table, while they played backgammon at another. 'Indeed, I recollect his speaking, at that time, of a pupil younger than himself who had taken his fancy there; but your name, as you may suppose, has not lived in my memory.'

'He was very generous and noble to me in those days, I assure you, ma'am,' said I, 'and I stood in need of such a friend. I should have been quite crushed without him.'

'He is always generous and noble,' said Mrs. Steerforth, proudly.

I subscribed to this with all my heart, God knows. She knew I did; for the stateliness of her manner already abated towards me, except when she spoke in praise of him, and then her air was always lofty.

'It was not a fit school generally for my son,' said

she; 'far from it; but there were particular circumstances to be considered at the time, of more importance even than that selection. My son's high spirit made it desirable that he should be placed with some man who felt its superiority, and would be content to bow himself before it; and we found such a man there.'

I knew that, knowing the fellow. And yet I did not despise him the more for it, but thought it a redeeming quality in him, if he could be allowed any grace for not resisting one so irresistible as Steerforth.

'My son's great capacity was tempted on, there, by a feeling of voluntary emulation and conscious pride,' the fond lady went on to say. 'He would have risen against all constraint; but he found himself the monarch of the place, and he haughtily determined to be worthy of his station. It was like himself.'

I echoed, with all my heart and soul, that it was like himself.

'So my son took, of his own will, and on no compulsion, to the course in which he can always, when it is his pleasure, outstrip every competitor,' she pursued. 'My son informs me, Mr. Copperfield, that you were quite devoted to him, and that when you met yesterday you made yourself known to him with tears of joy. I should be an affected woman if I made any pretence of being surprised by my son's inspiring such emotions; but I cannot be indifferent to any one who is so sensible of his merit, and I am very glad to see you here, and can assure you that he feels an unusual friendship for you, and that you may rely on his protection.'

Miss Dartle played backgammon as eagerly as she did everything else. If I had seen her, first, at the board, I should have fancied that her figure had got thin, and her eyes had got large, over that pursuit, and no other in the world. But I am very much mistaken if she missed a word of this, or lost a look of mine as I received it with the utmost pleasure, and, honoured by Mrs. Steerforth's confidence, felt older than I had done since I left Canterbury.

When the evening was pretty far spent, and a tray of glasses and decanters came in, Steerforth promised, over the fire, that he would seriously think of going down into the country with me. There was no hurry, he said; a week hence would do; and his mother hospitably said the same. While we were talking, he more than once called me Daisy; which brought Miss Dartle out again.

'But really, Mr. Copperfield,' she asked, 'is it a nickname? And why does he give it you? Is it— eh?—because he thinks you are young and innocent? I am so stupid in these things.'

I coloured in replying that I believed it was.

'Oh!' said Miss Dartle. 'Now I am glad to know that! I ask for information, and I am glad to know it. He thinks you young and innocent; and so you are his friend? Well, that's quite delightful!'

She went to bed soon after this, and Mrs. Steerforth retired too. Steerforth and I, after lingering for half an hour over the fire, talking about Traddles and all the rest of them at old Salem House, went upstairs together. Steerforth's room was next to mine, and I went in to look at it. It was a picture of comfort, full of easy-chairs, cushions and footstools, worked by his mother's hand, and with no sort of thing omitted that could help to render it complete. Finally, her handsome features looked down on her darling from a portrait on the wall, as if it were even something to her that her likeness should watch him while he slept.

I found the fire burning clear enough in my room by this time, and the curtains drawn before the windows and round the bed, giving it a very snug appearance. I sat down in a great chair upon the hearth to meditate on my happiness; and had enjoyed the contemplation of it for some time, when I found a likeness of Miss Dartle looking eagerly at me from above the chimney-piece.

It was a startling likeness, and necessarily had a startling look. The painter hadn't made the scar, but *I* made it; and there it was, coming and going: now confined to the upper lip as I had seen it at dinner, and now showing the whole extent of the wound inflicted by the hammer, as I had seen it when she was passionate.

I wondered peevishly why they couldn't put her anywhere else instead of quartering her on me. To get rid of her, I undressed quickly, extinguished my light, and went to bed. But, as I fell asleep, I could not forget that she was still there looking, 'Is it really, though? I want to know'; and when I awoke in the night, I found that I was uneasily asking all sorts of people in my dreams whether it really was or not—without knowing what I meant.

CHAPTER XXI

LITTLE EM'LY

THERE was a servant in that house, a man who, I understood, was usually with Steerforth, and had come into his service at the University, who was in appearance a pattern of respectability. I believe there never existed in his station, a more respectable-looking man. He was taciturn, soft-footed, very quiet in his manner, deferential, observant, always at hand when wanted, and never near when not wanted; but his great claim to consideration was his respectability. He had not a pliant face, he had rather a stiff neck, rather a tight smooth head with short hair clinging to it at the sides, a soft way of speaking, with a peculiar habit of whispering the letter S so distinctly, that he seemed to use it oftener than any other man; but every peculiarity that he had he made respectable. If his nose had been up-side-down, he would have made that respectable. He surrounded himself with an atmosphere of respectability, and walked secure in it. It would have been next to impossible to suspect him of anything wrong, he was so thoroughly respectable. Nobody could have thought of putting him in a livery, he was so highly respectable. To have imposed any derogatory work upon him, would have been to inflict a wanton insult on the feelings of a most respectable man. And of this, I noticed the women-servants in the household were so intuitively conscious, that they always did such work themselves, and generally while he read the paper by the pantry fire.

Such a self-contained man I never saw. But in that quality, as in every other he possessed, he only seemed to be the more respectable. Even the fact that no one knew his Christian name, seemed to form a part of his respectability. Nothing could be objected against his surname, Littimer, by which he was known. Peter might have been hanged, or Tom transported; but Littimer was perfectly respectable.

It was occasioned, I suppose, by the reverend nature of respectability in the abstract, but I felt particularly young in this man's presence. How old he was himself, I could not guess. And that again went to his credit on the same score; for in the calmness of respectability he might have numbered fifty years as well as thirty.

Littimer was in my room in the morning before I was up, to bring me that reproachful shaving-water, and to put out my clothes. When I undrew the curtains and looked out of bed, I saw him, in an equable temperature of respectability, unaffected by the east wind of January, and not even breathing frostily, standing my boots right and left in the first dancing position, and blowing specks of dust off my coat as he laid it down like a baby.

I gave him good morning, and asked him what o'clock it was. He took out of his pocket the most respectable hunting-watch I ever saw, and preventing the spring with his thumb from opening far, looked in at the face as if he were consulting an oracular oyster, shut it up again, and said, if I pleased, it was half-past eight.

'Mr. Steerforth will be glad to hear how you have rested, sir.'

'Thank you,' said I, 'very well indeed. Is Mr. Steerforth quite well?'

'Thank you, sir, Mr. Steerforth is tolerably well.' Another of his characteristics. No use of superlatives. A cool calm medium always.

'Is there anything more I can have the honour of doing for you, sir? The warning bell will ring at nine; the family take breakfast at half-past nine.'

'Nothing, I thank you.'

'I thank *you,* sir, if you please'; and with that, and with a little inclination of his head when he passed the bedside, as an apology for correcting me, he went out, shutting the door as delicately as if I had just fallen into a sweet sleep on which my life depended.

Every morning we held exactly this conversation: never any more, and never any less; and yet, invariably, however far I might have been lifted out of myself overnight, and advanced towards maturer years, by Steerforth's companionship, or Mrs. Steerforth's confidence, or Miss Dartle's conversation, in the presence of this most respectable man, I became, as our smaller poets sing, 'a boy again.'

He got horses for us; and Steerforth, who knew everything, gave me lessons in riding. He provided foils for us, and Steerforth gave me lessons in fencing—gloves, and I began, of the same master, to improve in boxing. It gave me no manner of concern that Steerforth should find me a novice in these sciences, but I never could bear to show my want of skill before the respectable Littimer. I had no reason to believe that Littimer understood such arts himself; he never led me to suppose anything of the kind, by so much as the vibration of one of his respectable eye-lashes; yet whenever he was by, while we were practising, I felt myself the greenest and most inexperienced of mortals.

I am particular about this man, because he made a particular effect on me at that time, and because of what took place thereafter.

The week passed away in a most delightful manner. It passed rapidly, as may be supposed, to one entranced as I was; and yet it gave me so many occasions for knowing Steerforth better, and admiring him more in a thousand respects, that at its close I seemed to have been with him for a much longer time. A dashing way he had of treating me like a plaything, was more agreeable to me than any behaviour he could have adopted. It reminded me of our old acquaintance; it seemed the natural sequel of it; it showed me that he was unchanged; it relieved me of any uneasiness I might have felt, in comparing my merits with his, and measuring my claims upon his friendship by any equal standard; above all, it was a familiar, unrestrained, affectionate demeanour that he used towards no one else. As he had treated me at school differently from all the rest, I joyfully believed that he treated me in life unlike any other friend he had. I believed that I was nearer to his heart than any other friend, and my own heart warmed with attachment to him.

He made up his mind to go with me into the country, and the day arrived for our departure. He had been doubtful at first whether to take Littimer or not, but decided to leave him at home. The respectable creature, satisfied with his lot whatever it was, arranged our portmanteaus on the little carriage that was to take us into London, as if they were intended to defy the shocks of ages; and received my modestly proffered donation with perfect tranquillity.

We bade adieu to Mrs. Steerforth and Miss Dartle, with many thanks on my part, and much kindness on the devoted mother's. The last thing I saw was Littimer's unruffled eye; fraught, as I fancied, with the silent conviction that I was very young indeed.

What I felt, in returning so auspiciously to the old familiar places, I shall not endeavour to describe. We went down by the mail. I was so concerned, I recollect, even for the honour of Yarmouth, that when Steerforth said, as we drove through its dark streets to the inn, that, as well as he could make out, it was a good, queer, out-of-the way kind of hole, I was highly pleased. We went to bed on our arrival (I observed a pair of dirty shoes and gaiters in connection with my old friend the Dolphin as we passed that door), and breakfasted late in the morning. Steerforth, who was in great spirits, had been strolling about the beach before I was up, and had made acquaintance, he said, with half the boatmen in the place.

Moreover, he had seen, in the distance, what he was sure must be the identical house of Mr. Peggotty, with smoke coming out of the chimney; and had had a great mind, he told me, to walk in and swear he was myself grown out of knowledge.

'When do you propose to introduce me there, Daisy?' he said. 'I am at your disposal. Make your own arrangements.'

'Why, I was thinking that this evening would be a good time, Steerforth, when they are all sitting round the fire. I should like you to see it when it's snug, it's such a curious place.'

'So be it!' returned Steerforth. 'This evening.'

'I shall not give them any notice that we are here, you know,' said I, delighted. 'We must take them by surprise.'

'Oh, of course! It's no fun,' said Steerforth, 'unless we take them by surprise. Let us see the natives in their aboriginal condition.'

'Though they *are* that sort of people that you mentioned,' I returned.

'Aha! What! you recollect my skirmishes with Rosa, do you?' he exclaimed with a quick look. 'Confound the girl, I am half afraid of her. She's like a goblin to me. But never mind her. Now what are you going to do? You are going to see your nurse, I suppose?'

'Why, yes,' I said, 'I must see Peggotty first of all.'

'Well,' replied Steerforth, looking at his watch. 'Suppose I deliver you up to be cried over for a couple of hours. Is that long enough?'

I answered, laughing, that I thought we might get through it in that time, but that he must come also; for he would find that his renown had preceded him, and that he was almost as great a personage as I was.

'I'll come anywhere you like,' said Steerforth, 'or

do anything you like. Tell me where to come to; and in two hours I'll produce myself in any state you please, sentimental or comical.'

I gave him minute directions for finding the residence of Mr. Barkis, carrier to Blunderstone and elsewhere; and, on this understanding, went out alone. There was a sharp bracing air; the ground was dry; the sea was crisp and clear; the sun was diffusing abundance of light, if not much warmth; and everything was fresh and lively. I was so fresh and lively myself, in the pleasure of being there, that I could have stopped the people in the streets and shaken hands with them.

The streets looked small, of course. The streets that we have only seen as children always do, I believe, when we go back to them. But I had forgotten nothing in them, and found nothing changed, until I came to Mr. Omer's shop. OMER AND JORAM was now written up, where OMER used to be; but the inscription, DRAPER, TAILOR, HABERDASHER, FUNERAL FURNISHER, &c., remained as it was.

My footsteps seemed to tend so naturally to the shop-door, after I had read these words from over the way, that I went across the road and looked in. There was a pretty woman at the back of the shop, dancing a little child in her arms, while another little fellow clung to her apron. I had no difficulty in recognising either Minnie or Minnie's children. The glass door of the parlour was not open; but in the workshop across the yard I could faintly hear the old tune playing, as if it had never left off.

'Is Mr. Omer at home?' said I, entering. 'I should like to see him, for a moment, if he is.'

'Oh yes, sir, he is at home,' said Minnie: 'this weather don't suit his asthma out of doors. Joe, call your grandfather!'

The little fellow, who was holding her apron, gave such a lusty shout, that the sound of it made him bashful, and he buried his face in her skirts, to her great admiration. I heard a heavy puffing and blowing coming towards us, and soon Mr. Omer, shorter-winded than of yore, but not much older-looking, stood before me.

'Servant, sir,' said Mr. Omer. 'What can I do for you, sir?'

'You can shake hands with me, Mr. Omer, if you please,' said I, putting out my own. 'You were very good-natured to me once, when I am afraid I didn't show that I thought so.'

'Was I though?' returned the old man. 'I 'm glad to hear it, but I don't remember when. Are you sure it was me?'

'Quite.'

'I think my memory has got as short as my breath,' said Mr. Omer, looking at me and shaking his head; 'for I don't remember you.'

'Don't you remember your coming to the coach to meet me, and my having breakfast here, and our riding out to Blunderstone together: you, and I, and Mrs. Joram, and Mr. Joram too—who wasn't her husband then?'

'Why, Lord bless my soul!' exclaimed Mr. Omer, after being thrown by his surprise into a fit of coughing, 'you don't say so! Minnie, my dear, you recollect? Dear me, yes; the party was a lady, I think?'

'My mother,' I rejoined.

'To—be—sure,' said Mr. Omer, touching my waistcoat with his forefinger, 'and there was a little child too! There was two parties. The little party was laid along with the other party. Over at Blunderstone it was, of course. Dear me! And how have you been since?'

Very well, I thanked him, as I hoped he had been too.

'Oh! nothing to grumble at, you know,' said Mr. Omer. 'I find my breath gets short, but it seldom gets longer as a man gets older. I take it as it comes, and make the most of it. That's the best way, ain't it?'

Mr. Omer coughed again, in consequence of laughing, and was assisted out of his fit by his daughter, who now stood close beside us, dancing her smallest child on the counter.

'Dear me!' said Mr. Omer. 'Yes, to be sure. Two parties! Why, in that very ride, if you'll believe me, the day was named for my Minnie to marry Joram. "Do name it, sir," says Joram. "Yes, do, father," says Minnie. And now he's come into the business. And look here! The youngest!'

Minnie laughed, and stroked her banded hair upon her temples, as her father put one of his fat fingers into the hand of the child she was dancing on the counter.

'Two parties, of course!' said Mr. Omer, nodding his head retrospectively. 'Ex-actly so! And Joram's at work, at this minute, on a grey one with silver nails, not this measurement'— the measurement of the dancing child upon the counter—'by a good two inches. Will you take something?'

I thanked him, but declined.

'Let me see,' said Mr. Omer. 'Barkis's the carrier's wife—Peggotty's the boatman's sister—she had something to do with your family? She was in service there, sure?'

My answering in the affirmative gave him great satisfaction.

'I believe my breath will get long next, my memory's getting so much so,' said Mr. Omer. 'Well, sir, we've got a young relation of hers here, under articles to us, that has as elegant a taste in the dress-making business—I assure you I don't believe there's a duchess in England can touch her.'

'Not little Em'ly?' said I, involuntarily.

'Em'ly's her name,' said Mr. Omer, 'and she's little too. But if you'll believe me, she has such a face of her own that half the women in this town are mad against her.'

'Nonsense, father!' cried Minnie.

'My dear,' said Mr. Omer, 'I don't say it's the case with you,' winking at me, 'but I say that half the women in Yarmouth, ah! and in five mile round, are mad against that girl.'

'Then she should have kept to her own station in life, father,' said Minnie, 'and not have given them any hold to talk about her, and then they couldn't have done it.'

'Couldn't have done it, my dear!' retorted Mr. Omer. 'Couldn't have done it! Is that *your* knowledge of life? What is there that any woman couldn't do, that she shouldn't do—especially on the subject of another woman's good looks?'

I really thought it was all over with Mr. Omer, after he had uttered this libellous pleasantry. He coughed to that extent, and his breath eluded all his attempts to recover it with that obstinacy, that I fully expected to see his head go down behind the counter, and his little black breeches, with the rusty little bunches of ribbons at the knees, come quivering up in a last ineffectual struggle. At length, however, he got better, though he still panted hard, and was so exhausted that he was obliged to sit on the stool of the shop-desk.

'You see,' he said, wiping his head, and breathing with difficulty, 'she hasn't taken much to any companions here; she hasn't taken kindly to any particular acquaintances and friends, not to mention sweethearts. In consequence, an ill-natured story got about, that Em'ly wanted to be a lady. Now, my opinion is, that it came into circulation principally on account of her sometimes saying at the school, that if she was a lady, she would like to do so-and-so for her uncle—don't you see?—and buy him such-and-such fine things.'

'I assure you, Mr. Omer, she has said so to me,' I returned eagerly, 'when we were both children.'

Mr. Omer nodded his head and rubbed his chin. 'Just so. Then out of a very little, she could dress herself, you see, better than most others could out of a deal, and *that* made things unpleasant. Moreover, she was rather what might be called wayward. I'll go so far as to say what I should call wayward myself,' said Mr. Omer; 'didn't know her own mind quite; a little spoiled; and couldn't, at first, exactly bind herself down. No more than that was ever said against her, Minnie?'

'No, father,' said Mrs. Joram. 'That's the worst, I believe.'

'So when she got a situation,' said Mr. Omer, 'to keep a fractious old lady company, they didn't very well agree, and she didn't stop. At last she came here, apprenticed for three years. Nearly two of 'em are over, and she has been as good a girl as ever was. Worth any six! Minnie, is she worth any six, now?'

'Yes, father,' replied Minnie. 'Never say I detracted from her!'

'Very good,' said Mr. Omer. 'That's right. And so, young gentleman,' he added, after a few moments' further rubbing of his chin, 'that you may not consider me long-winded as well as short-breathed, I believe that's all about it.'

As they had spoken in a subdued tone, while speaking of Em'ly, I had no doubt that she was near. On my asking now, if that were not so, Mr. Omer nodded yes, and nodded towards the door of the parlour. My hurried inquiry if I might peep in, was answered with a free permission; and, looking through the glass, I saw her sitting at her work. I saw her, a most beautiful little creature, with the cloudless blue eyes, that had looked into my childish heart, turned laughingly upon another child of Minnie's who was playing near her; with enough of wilfulness in her bright face to justify what I had heard; with much of the old capricious coyness lurking in it; but with nothing in her pretty looks, I am sure, but what was meant for goodness and for happiness, and what was on a good and happy course.

The tune across the yard that seemed as if it never had left off—alas! it was the tune that never *does* leave off—was beating, softly, all the while.

'Wouldn't you like to step in,' said Mr. Omer, 'and speak to her? Walk in and speak to her, sir! Make yourself at home!'

I was too bashful to do so then—I was afraid of confusing her, and I was no less afraid of confusing myself: but I informed myself of the hour at which she left of an evening, in order that our visit might be timed accordingly; and taking leave of Mr. Omer, and his pretty daughter, and her little children, went away to my dear old Peggotty's.

Here she was, in the tiled kitchen, cooking dinner! The moment I knocked at the door she opened it, and asked me what I pleased to want. I looked at her with a smile, but she gave me no smile in return. I had never ceased to write to her, but it must have been seven years since we had met.

'Is Mr. Barkis at home, ma'am?' I said, feigning to speak roughly to her.

'He's at home, sir,' returned Peggotty, 'but he's bad abed with the rheumatics.'

'Don't he go over to Blunderstone now?' I asked.

'When he's well he do,' she answered.

'Do *you* ever go there, Mrs. Barkis?'

She looked at me more attentively, and I noticed a quick movement of her hands towards each other.

'Because I want to ask a question about a house there, that they call the—what is it?—the Rookery,' said I.

She took a step backward, and put out her hands in an undecided frightened way, as if to keep me off.

'Peggotty!' I cried to her.

She cried, 'My darling boy!' and we both burst into tears, and were locked in one another's arms.

What extravagances she committed; what laughing and crying over me; what pride she showed, what joy, what sorrow that she whose pride and joy I might have been, could never hold me in a fond embrace; I have not the heart to tell. I was troubled with no misgiving that it was young in me to respond to her emotions. I had never laughed and cried in all my life, I dare say, not even to her, more freely than I did that morning.

'Barkis will be so glad,' said Peggotty, wiping her eyes with her apron, 'that it'll do him more good than pints of liniment. May I go and tell him you are here? Will you come up and see him, my dear?'

Of course I would. But Peggotty could not get out of the room as easily as she meant to, for as often as she got to the door and looked round at me, she came back again to have another laugh and another cry upon my shoulder. At last, to make the matter easier, I went upstairs with her; and having waited outside for a minute, while she said a word of preparation to Mr. Barkis, presented myself before that invalid.

He received me with absolute enthusiasm. He was too rheumatic to be shaken hands with, but he begged me to shake the tassel on the top of his night-cap, which I did most cordially. When I sat down by the side of the bed, he said that it did him a world of good to feel as if he was driving me on the Blunderstone road again. As he lay in bed, face upward, and so covered, with that exception, that he seemed to be nothing but a face—like a conventional cherubim—he looked the queerest object I ever beheld.

'What name was it as I wrote up in the cart, sir?' said Mr. Barkis, with a slow rheumatic smile.

'Ah! Mr. Barkis, we had some grave talks about that matter, hadn't we?'

'I was willin' a long time, sir?' said Mr. Barkis.

'A long time,' said I.

'And I don't regret it,' said Mr. Barkis. 'Do you remember what you told me once, about her making all the apples parsties and doing all the cooking?'

'Yes, very well,' I returned.

'It was as true,' said Mr. Barkis, 'as turnips is. It was as true,' said Mr. Barkis, nodding his night-cap, which was his only means of emphasis, 'as taxes is. And nothing's truer than them.'

Mr. Barkis turned his eyes upon me, as if for my assent to this result of his reflections in bed; and I gave it.

'Nothing's truer than them,' repeated Mr. Barkis; 'a man as poor as I am, finds that out in his mind when he's laid up. I'm a very poor man, sir?'

'I am sorry to hear it, Mr. Barkis.'

'A very poor man, indeed I am,' said Mr. Barkis.

Here his right hand came slowly and feebly from under the bed-clothes, and with a purposeless uncertain grasp took hold of a stick which was loosely tied to the side of the bed.   After some poking about with this instrument, in the course of which his face assumed a variety of distracted expressions, Mr. Barkis poked it against a box, an end of which had been visible to me all the time.   Then his face became composed.

'Old clothes,' said Mr. Barkis.

'Oh!' said I.

'I wish it was money, sir,' said Mr. Barkis.

'I wish it was, indeed,' said I.

'But it AIN'T,' said Mr. Barkis, opening both his eyes as wide as he possibly could.

I expressed myself quite sure of that, and Mr. Barkis, turning his eyes more gently to his wife, said—

'She's the usefullest and best of women, C. P. Barkis.   All the praise that any one can give to C. P. Barkis she deserves, and more!   My dear, you 'll get a dinner to-day, for company; something good to eat and drink, will you?'

I should have protested against this unnecessary demonstration in my honour, but that I saw Peggotty, on the opposite side of the bed, extremely anxious I should not.   So I held my peace.

'I have got a trifle of money somewhere about me, my dear,' said Mr. Barkis, 'but I 'm a little tired.   If you and Mr. David will leave me for a short nap, I 'll try and find it when I wake.'

We left the room, in compliance with this request. When we got outside the door, Peggotty informed me that Mr. Barkis, being now 'a little nearer' than he used to be, always resorted to this same device before producing a single coin from his store; and that he endured unheard-of agonies in crawling out of bed alone, and taking it from that unlucky box.   In effect, we presently heard him uttering suppressed groans of the most dismal nature, as this magpie proceeding racked him in every joint; but while Peggotty's eyes were full of compassion for him, she said his generous impulse would do him good, and it was better not to check it. So he groaned on, until he had got into bed again, suffering, I have no doubt, a martyrdom; and then called us in, pretending to have just woke up from a refreshing sleep, and to produce a guinea from under his pillow. His satisfaction in which happy imposition on us, and in having preserved the impenetrable secret of the box, appeared to be a sufficient compensation to him for all his tortures.

I prepared Peggotty for Steerforth's arrival, and it was not long before he came. I am persuaded she knew no difference between his having been a personal benefactor of hers and a kind friend to me, and that she would have received him with the utmost gratitude and devotion in any case. But his easy, spirited good-humour; his genial manner, his handsome looks, his natural gift of adapting himself to whomsoever he pleased, and making direct, when he cared to do it, to the main point of interest in anybody's heart; bound her to him wholly in five minutes. His manner to me, alone, would have won her. But, through all these causes combined, I sincerely believe she had a kind of adoration for him before he left the house that night.

He stayed there with me to dinner—if I were to say willingly, I should not half express how readily and gaily. He went into Mr. Barkis's room like light and air, brightening and refreshing it as if he were healthy weather. There was no noise, no effort, no consciousness, in anything he did; but in everything an indescribable lightness, a seeming impossibility of doing anything else, or doing anything better, which was so graceful, so natural, and agreeable, that it overcomes me, even now, in the remembrance.

We made merry in the little parlour, where the Book of Martyrs, unthumbed since my time, was laid out upon the desk as of old, and where I now turned over its terrific pictures, remembering the old sensations they had awakened, but not feeling them. When Peggotty spoke of what she called my room, and of its being ready for me at night, and of her hoping I would occupy it, before I could so much as look at Steerforth, hesitating, he was possessed of the whole case.

'Of course,' he said. 'You'll sleep here, while we stay, and I shall sleep at the hotel.'

'But to bring you so far,' I returned, 'and to separate, seems bad companionship, Steerforth.'

'Why, in the name of Heaven, where do you naturally belong!' he said. 'What is "seems," compared to that!' It was settled at once.

He maintained all his delightful qualities to the last, until we started forth, at eight o'clock, for Mr. Peggotty's boat. Indeed, they were more and more brightly exhibited as the hours went on; for I thought even then, and I have no doubt now, that the consciousness of success in his determination to please, inspired him with a new delicacy of perception, and made it, subtle as it was, more easy to him. If any one had told me, then, that all this was a brilliant game, played for the excitement of the moment, for the employment of high spirits, in the thoughtless love of superiority, in a mere wasteful careless course of winning what was worthless to him, and next minute thrown away: I say, if any one had told me such a lie that night, I wonder in what manner of receiving it my indignation would have found a vent!

Probably only in an increase, had that been possible, of the romantic feelings of fidelity and friendship with which I walked beside him, over the dark wintry sands, towards the old boat; the wind sighing around us even more mournfully than it had sighed and moaned upon the night when I first darkened Mr. Peggotty's door.

'This is a wild kind of place, Steerforth, is it not?'

'Dismal enough in the dark,' he said: 'and the sea roars as if it were hungry for us. Is that the boat, where I see a light yonder?'

'That's the boat,' said I.

'And it's the same I saw this morning,' he returned. 'I came straight to it, by instinct, I suppose.'

We said no more as we approached the light, but made softly for the door. I laid my hand upon the latch; and whispering Steerforth to keep close to me, went in.

A murmur of voices had been audible on the outside, and, at the moment of our entrance, a clapping of hands: which latter noise, I was surprised to see, proceeded from the generally disconsolate Mrs. Gummidge. But Mrs. Gummidge was not the only person there who was unusually excited. Mr. Peggotty, his face lighted up with uncommon satisfaction, and laughing with all his might, held his rough arms wide open, as if for little Em'ly to run into them; Ham, with a mixed expression in his face of admiration, exultation, and a lumbering sort of bashfulness that sat upon him very well, held little Em'ly by the hand, as if he were presenting her to Mr. Peggotty; little Em'ly herself, blushing and shy, but delighted with Mr. Peggotty's delight, as her joyous eyes expressed, was stopped by our entrance (for she saw us first) in the very act of springing from Ham to nestle in Mr. Peggotty's embrace. In the first glimpse we had of them all, and at the moment of our passing from the dark cold night into the warm light room, this was the way in which they were all employed: Mrs. Gummidge in the background, clapping her hands like a madwoman.

The little picture was so instantaneously dissolved by our going in, that one might have doubted whether it had ever been. I was in the midst of the astonished family, face to face with Mr. Peggotty, and holding out my hand to him, when Ham shouted—

'Mas'r Davy! It's Mas'r Davy!'

In a moment we were all shaking hands with one another, and asking one another how we did, and telling one another how glad we were to meet, and all talking at once. Mr. Peggotty was so proud and overjoyed to see us, that he did not know what to say or do, but kept over and over again shaking hands with me, and then with Steerforth, and then with me, and then ruffling his shaggy hair all over his head, and laughing with such glee and triumph, that it was a treat to see him.

'Why, that you two gent'lmen—gent'lmen growed —should come to this here roof to-night, of all nights in my life,' said Mr. Peggotty, 'is such a thing as never happened afore, I do rightly believe! Em'ly, my darling, come here! Come here, my little witch! There's Mas'r Davy's friend, my dear. There's the gent'lman as you've heerd on, Em'ly. He comes to see you, along with Mas'r Davy, on the brightest night of your uncle's life as ever was or will be, Gorm the t' other one, and horroar for it!'

After delivering this speech all in a breath, and with extraordinary animation and pleasure, Mr. Peggotty put one of his large hands rapturously on each side of his niece's face, and kissing it a dozen times, laid it with a gentle pride and love upon his broad chest, and patted it as if his hand had been a lady's.

Then he let her go; and as she ran into the little chamber where I used to sleep, looked round upon us, quite hot and out of breath with his uncommon satisfaction.

'If you two gent'lmen—gent'lmen growed now, and such gent'lmen—' said Mr. Peggotty.

'So th' are, so th' are!' cried Ham. 'Well said! So th' are. Mas'r Davy bor—gent'lmen growed—so th' are!'

'If you two gent'lmen, gent'lmen growed,' said Mr. Peggotty, 'don't ex-cuse me for being in a state of mind, when you understand matters, I 'll arks your pardon. Em'ly, my dear!—She knows I 'm a going to tell,' here his delight broke out again, 'and has made off. Would you be so good as look arter her, mawther, for a minute?'

Mrs. Gummidge nodded and disappeared.

'If this ain't,' said Mr. Peggotty, sitting down among us by the fire, 'the brightest night o' my life, I 'm a shell-fish—biled too—and more I can't say. This here little Em'ly, sir,' in a low voice to Steerforth, 'her as you see a blushing here just now—'

Steerforth only nodded; but with such a pleased expression of interest, and of participation in Mr. Peggotty's feelings, that the latter answered him as if he had spoken.

'To be sure,' said Mr. Peggotty, 'that 's her, and so she is. Thank 'ee, sir.'

Ham nodded to me several times, as if he would have said so too.

'This here little Em'ly of ours,' said Mr. Peggotty, 'has been, in our house, what I suppose (I 'm a ignorant man, but that 's my belief) no one but a little bright-eyed creetur *can* be in a house. She ain't my child; I never had one; but I couldn't love her more. You understand! I couldn't do it!'

'I quite understand,' said Steerforth.

'I know you do, sir,' returned Mr. Peggotty, 'and thank 'ee again. Mas'r Davy, he can remember what she was; you may judge for your own self what she is; but neither of you can't fully know what she has been, is, and will be, to my loving 'art. I am rough, sir,' said Mr. Peggotty, 'I am as rough as a sea porky-pine; but no one, unless, mayhap, it is a woman, can know, I think, what our little Em'ly is to me. And bewixt ourselves,' sinking his voice lower yet, '*that* woman's name ain't Missis Gummidge neither, though she has a world of merits.'

Mr. Peggotty ruffled his hair again with both hands, as a further preparation for what he was going to say, and went on, with a hand upon each of his knees—

'There was a certain person as had know'd our Em'ly, from the time when her father was drownded; as had seen her constant; when a babby, when a young gal, when a woman. Not much of a person to look at, he warn't,' said Mr. Peggotty, 'something o' my own build—rough—a good deal o' the sou'-wester in him—wery salt—but, on the whole, a honest sort of a chap, with his 'art in the right place.'

I thought I had never seen Ham grin to anything like the extent to which he sat grinning at us now.

'What does this here blessed tarpaulin go and do,' said Mr. Peggotty, with his face one high moon of enjoyment, 'but he loses that there 'art of his to our little Em'ly. He follers her about, he makes hisself a sort o' sarvant to her, he loses in a great measure his relish for his wittles, and in the long-run he makes it clear to me wot 's amiss. Now I could wish myself, you see, that our little Em'ly was in a fair way of being married. I could wish to see her, at all ewents, under articles to a honest man as had a right to defend her. I don't know how long I may live, or how soon I may die; but I know that if I was capsized, any night, in a gale of wind in Yarmouth Roads here, and was to see the town-lights shining for the last time over the rollers as I couldn't make no head aginst, I could go down quieter for thinking "There 's a man ashore there, iron-true to my little Em'ly, God bless her, and no wrong can touch my Em'ly while so be as that man lives."'

Mr. Peggotty, in simple earnestness, waved his right arm, as if he were waving it at the town-lights for the last time, and then, exchanging a nod with Ham, whose eye he caught, proceeded as before—

'Well! I counsels him to speak to Em'ly. He 's big enough, but he 's bashfuller than a little 'un, and he don't like. So *I* speak. "What? *Him?*" says Em'ly. *"Him* that I 've know'd so intimate so many years, and like so much. Oh, uncle! I never can have *him.* He 's such a good fellow!" I gives her a kiss, and I says no more to her than "My dear, you 're right to speak out, you 're to choose for yourself, you 're as free as a little bird." Then I aways to him, and I says, "I wish it could have been so, but it can't. But you can both be as you was, and wot I say to you is, Be as you was with her, like a man." He says to me, a shaking of my hand, "I will!" he says. And he was—honourable and manful—for two year going on, and we was just the same at home here as afore.'

Mr. Peggotty's face, which had varied in its expression with the various stages of his narrative, now resumed all its former triumphant delight, as he laid a hand upon my knee and a hand upon Steerforth's (previously wetting them both, for the greater emphasis of the action), and divided the following speech between us—

WE ARRIVE UNEXPECTEDLY AT MR. PEGGOTTY'S FIRESIDE.

'All of a sudden, one evening—as it might be to-night—comes little Em'ly from her work, and him with her! There ain't so much in *that,* you'll say. No, because he takes care on her, like a brother, arter dark, and indeed afore dark, and at all times. But this tarpaulin chap, he takes hold of her hand, and he cries out to me, joyful, "Look here! This is to be my little wife!" And she says, half bold and half shy, and half a laughing and half a crying, "Yes, uncle! If you please."—If I please!' cried Mr. Peggotty, rolling his head in an ecstasy at the idea; 'Lord, as if I should do anythink else!—"If you please, I am steadier now, and I have thought better of it, and I'll be as good a little wife as I can to him, for he's a dear, good fellow!" Then Missis Gummidge, she claps her hands like a play, and you come in. Theer! the murder's out!' said Mr. Peggotty—'You come in! It took place this here present hour; and here's the man that'll marry her, the minute she's out of her time.'

Ham staggered, as well he might, under the blow Mr. Peggotty dealt him in his unbounded joy, as a mark of confidence and friendship; but feeling called upon to say something to us, he said, with much faltering and great difficulty—

'She warn't no higher than you was, Mas'r Davy —when you first come—when I thought what she'd grow up to be. I see her grow up—gent'lmen—like a flower. I'd lay down my life for her—Mas'r Davy—Oh! most content and cheerful! She's more to me—gent'lmen—than—she's all to me that ever I can want, and more than ever I—than ever I could say. I—I love her true. There ain't a gent'lmen in all the land—nor yet sailing upon all the sea— that can love his lady more than I love her, though

there's many a common man—would say better—
what he meant.'

I thought it affecting to see such a sturdy fellow
as Ham was now, trembling in the strength of what
he felt for the pretty little creature who had won his
heart. I thought the simple confidence reposed in
us by Mr. Peggotty and by himself, was, in itself,
affecting. I was affected by the story altogether.
How far my emotions were influenced by the recollections of my childhood, I don't know. Whether I
had come there with any lingering fancy that I was
still to love little Em'ly, I don't know. I know that
I was filled with pleasure by all this; but, at first,
with an indescribably sensitive pleasure, that a very
little would have changed to pain.

Therefore, if it had depended upon me, to touch
the prevailing chord among them with any skill, I
should have made a poor hand of it. But it depended
upon Steerforth; and he did it with such address, that
in a few minutes we were all as easy and as happy
as it was possible to be.

'Mr. Peggotty,' he said, 'you are a thoroughly
good fellow, and deserve to be as happy as you are
to-night. My hand upon it! Ham, I give you joy,
my boy. My hand upon that, too! Daisy, stir the
fire, and make it a brisk one! and Mr. Peggotty, unless you can induce your gentle niece to come back
(for whom I vacate this seat in the corner), I shall
go. Any gap at your fireside on such a night—such
a gap least of all—I wouldn't make, for the wealth
of the Indies!'

So Mr. Peggotty went into my old room to fetch
little Em'ly. At first, little Em'ly didn't like to come,
and then Ham went. Presently they brought her to
the fireside, very much confused. and very shy,—but
she soon became more assured when she found how

gently and respectfully Steerforth spoke to her; how skilfully he avoided anything that would embarrass her; how he talked to Mr. Peggotty of boats, and ships, and tides, and fish; how he referred to me about the time when he had seen Mr. Peggotty at Salem House; how delighted he was with the boat and all belonging to it; how lightly and easily he carried on, until he brought us, by degrees, into a charmed circle, and we were all talking away without any reserve.

Em'ly, indeed, said little all the evening; but she looked, and listened, and her face got animated, and she was charming. Steerforth told a story of a dismal shipwreck (which arose out of his talk with Mr. Peggotty), as if he saw it all before him—and little Em'ly's eyes were fastened on him all the time, as if she saw it too. He told us a merry adventure of his own, as a relief to that, with as much gaiety as if the narrative were as fresh to him as it was to us—and little Em'ly laughed until the boat rang with the musical sounds, and we all laughed (Steerforth too), in irresistible sympathy with what was so pleasant and light-hearted. He got Mr. Peggotty to sing, or rather to roar, 'When the stormy winds do blow, do blow, do blow'; and he sang a sailor's song himself, so pathetically and beautifully, that I could have almost fancied that the real wind creeping sorrowfully round the house, and murmuring low through our unbroken silence, was there to listen.

As to Mrs. Gummidge, he roused that victim of despondency with a success never attained by any one else (so Mr. Peggotty informed me), since the decease of the old one. He left her so little leisure for being miserable, that she said next day she thought she must have been bewitched.

But he set up no monopoly of the general attention, or the conversation. When little Em'ly grew more courageous, and talked (but still bashfully) across the fire to me, of our old wanderings upon the beach, to pick up shells and pebbles; and when I asked her if she recollected how I used to be devoted to her; and when we both laughed and reddened, casting these looks back on the pleasant old times, so unreal to look at now; he was silent and attentive, and observed us thoughtfully. She sat, at this time, and all the evening, on the old locker in her old little corner by the fire, with Ham beside her, where I used to sit. I could not satisfy myself whether it was in her own little tormenting way, or in a maidenly reserve before us, that she kept quite close to the wall, and away from him; but I observed that she did so, all the evening.

As I remember, it was almost midnight when we took our leave. We had had some biscuit and dried fish for supper, and Steerforth had produced from his pocket a full flask of Hollands, which we men (I may say we men, now, without a blush) had emptied. We parted merrily; and as they all stood crowded round the door to light us as far as they could upon our road, I saw the sweet blue eyes of little Em'ly peeping after us, from behind Ham, and heard her soft voice calling to us to be careful how we went.

'A most engaging little beauty!' said Steerforth, taking my arm. 'Well! It's a quaint place, and they are quaint company; and it's quite a new sensation to mix with them.'

'How fortunate we are, too,' I returned, 'to have arrived to witness their happiness in that intended marriage! I never saw people so happy. How delightful to see it, and to be made the sharers in their honest joy, as we have been!'

'That's rather a chuckle-headed fellow for the girl; isn't he?' said Steerforth.

He had been so hearty with him, and with them all, that I felt a shock in this unexpected and cold reply. But turning quickly upon him, and seeing a laugh in his eyes, I answered, much relieved—

'Ah, Steerforth! It's well for you to joke about the poor! You may skirmish with Miss Dartle, or try to hide your sympathies in jest from me, but I know better. When I see how perfectly you understand them, how exquisitely you can enter into happiness like this plain fisherman's, or humour a love like my old nurse's, I know that there is not a joy or sorrow, not an emotion, of such people, that can be indifferent to you. And I admire and love you for it, Steerforth, twenty times the more!'

He stopped, and looking in my face, said, 'Daisy, I believe you are in earnest, and are good. I wish we all were!' Next moment he was gaily singing Mr. Peggotty's song, as we walked at a round pace back to Yarmouth.

CHAPTER XXII

SOME OLD SCENES, AND SOME NEW PEOPLE

STEERFORTH and I stayed for more than a fortnight in that part of the country. We were very much together, I need not say; but occasionally we were asunder for some hours at a time. He was a good sailor, and I was but an indifferent one; and when he went out boating with Mr. Peggotty, which was a favourite amusement of his, I generally remained ashore. My occupation of Peggotty's spare-room put a constraint upon me, from which he was free: for, knowing how assiduously she attended on Mr. Barkis all day, I did not like to remain out late at night; whereas Steerforth, lying at the inn, had nothing to consult but his own humour. Thus it came about, that I heard of his making little treats for the fishermen at Mr. Peggotty's house of call, 'The Willing Mind,' after I was in bed, and of his being afloat, wrapped in fishermen's clothes, whole moonlight nights, and coming back when the morning tide was at flood. By this time, however, I knew that his restless nature and bold spirits delighted to find a vent in rough toil and hard weather, as in any other means of excitement that presented itself freshly to him; so none of his proceedings surprised me.

Another cause of our being sometimes apart was, that I had naturally an interest in going over to Blunderstone, and revisiting the old familiar scenes of my childhood; while Steerforth, after being there once, had naturally no great interest in going there again. Hence, on three or four days that I can at once recall, we went our several ways after an early breakfast, and met again at a late dinner. I had no idea how he employed his time in the interval, beyond a general knowledge that he was very popular in the place, and had twenty means of actively diverting himself where another man might not have found one.

For my own part, my occupation in my solitary pilgrimages was to recall every yard of the old road as I went along it, and to haunt the old spots, of which I never tired. I haunted them, as my memory had often done, and lingered among them as my younger thoughts had lingered when I was far away. The grave beneath the tree, where both my parents lay—on which I had looked out, when it was my father's only, with such curious feelings of compassion, and by which I had stood, so desolate, when it was opened to receive my pretty mother and her baby —the grave which Peggotty's own faithful care had ever since kept neat, and made a garden of, I walked near, by the hour. It lay a little off the churchyard path, in a quiet corner, not so far removed but I could read the names upon the stone as I walked to and fro, startled by the sound of the church-bell when it struck the hour, for it was like a departed voice to me. My reflections at these times were always associated with the figure I was to make in life, and the distinguished things I was to do. My echoing footsteps went to no other tune, but were as constant to that as if I had come home to build my castles in the air at a living mother's side.

There were great changes in my old home. The ragged nests, so long deserted by the rooks, were gone; and the trees were lopped and topped out of their remembered shapes. The garden had run wild, and half the windows of the house were shut up. It was occupied, but only by a poor lunatic gentleman, and the people who took care of him. He was always sitting at my little window, looking out into the churchyard; and I wondered whether his rambling thoughts ever went upon any of the fancies that used to occupy mine, on the rosy mornings when I peeped out of that same little window in my night-clothes, and saw the sheep quietly feeding in the light of the rising sun.

Our old neighbours, Mr. and Mrs. Grayper, were gone to South America, and the rain had made its way through the roof of their empty house, and stained the outer walls. Mr. Chillip was married again to a tall, raw-boned, high-nosed wife; and they had a weazen little baby, with a heavy head that it couldn't hold up, and two weak staring eyes, with which it seemed to be always wondering why it had ever been born.

It was with a singular jumble of sadness and pleasure that I used to linger about my native place, until the reddening winter sun admonished me that it was time to start on my returning walk. But when the place was left behind, and especially when Steerforth and I were happily seated over our dinner by a blazing fire, it was delicious to think of having been there. So it was, though in a softened degree, when I went to my neat room at night; and, turning over the leaves of the crocodile book (which was always there, upon a little table), remembered with a grateful heart how blest I was in having such a friend as Steerforth, such a friend as Peggotty, and such a substitute for what I had lost as my excellent and generous aunt.

My nearest way to Yarmouth, in coming back from these long walks, was by a ferry. It landed me on the flat between the town and the sea, which I could make straight across, and so save myself a considerable circuit by the high-road. Mr. Peggotty's house being on that waste-place, and not a hundred yards out of my track, I always looked in as I went by. Steerforth was pretty sure to be there expecting me, and we went on together through the frosty air and gathering fog towards the twinkling lights of the town.

One dark evening, when I was later than usual— for I had, that day, been making my parting visit to Blunderstone, as we were now about to return home —I found him alone in Mr. Peggotty's house, sitting thoughtfully before the fire. He was so intent upon his own reflections that he was quite unconscious of my approach. This, indeed, he might easily have been if he had been less absorbed, for footsteps fell noiselessly on the sandy ground outside; but even my entrance failed to arouse him. I was standing close to him, looking at him; and still, with a heavy brow, he was lost in his meditations.

He gave such a start when I put my hand upon his shoulder, that he made me start too.

'You come upon me,' he said, almost angrily, 'like a reproachful ghost!'

'I was obliged to announce myself, somehow,' I replied. 'Have I called you down from the stars?'

'No,' he answered. 'No.'

'Up from anywhere, then?' said I, taking my seat near him.

'I was looking at the pictures in the fire,' he returned.

'But you are spoiling them for me,' said I, as he stirred it quickly with a piece of burning wood, striking out of it a train of red-hot sparks that went careering up the little chimney, and roaring out into the air.

'You would not have seen them,' he returned. 'I detest this mongrel time, neither day nor night. How late you are! Where have you been?'

'I have been taking leave of my usual walk,' said I.

'And I have been sitting here,' said Steerforth, glancing round the room, 'thinking that all the people we found so glad on the night of our coming down, might—to judge from the present wasted air of the place—be dispersed, or dead, or come to I don't know what harm. David, I wish to God I had had a judicious father these last twenty years!'

'My dear Steerforth, what is the matter?'

'I wish with all my soul I had been better guided!' he exclaimed. 'I wish with all my soul I could guide myself better!'

There was a passionate dejection in his manner

that quite amazed me. He was more unlike himself than I could have supposed possible.

'It would be better to be this poor Peggotty, or his lout of a nephew,' he said, getting up and leaning moodily against the chimney-piece, with his face towards the fire, 'than to be myself, twenty times richer and twenty times wiser, and be the torment to myself that I have been, in this devil's bark of a boat, within the last half-hour!'

I was so confounded by the alteration in him, that at first I could only observe him in silence, as he stood leaning his head upon his hand, and looking gloomily down at the fire. At length I begged him, with all the earnestness I felt, to tell me what had occurred to cross him so unusually, and to let me sympathise with him, if I could not hope to advise him. Before I had well concluded, he began to laugh—fretfully at first, but soon with returning gaiety.

'Tut, it's nothing, Daisy! nothing!' he replied. 'I told you at the inn in London, I am heavy company for myself, sometimes. I have been a nightmare to myself, just now—must have had one, I think. At odd dull times, nursery tales come up into the memory, unrecognised for what they are. I believe I have been confounding myself with the bad boy who "didn't care," and became food for lions—a grander kind of going to the dogs, I suppose. What old women call the horrors, have been creeping over me from head to foot. I have been afraid of myself.'

'You are afraid of nothing else, I think,' said I.

'Perhaps not, and yet may have enough to be afraid of too,' he answered. 'Well! So it goes by! I am not about to be hipped again, David; but I tell you, my good fellow, once more, that it would have been well for me (and for more than me) if I had had a steadfast and judicious father!'

His face was always full of expression, but I never saw it express such a dark kind of earnestness as when he said these words, with his glance bent on the fire.

'So much for that!' he said, making as if he tossed something light into the air, with his hand.

'"Why, being gone, I am a man again,"

like Macbeth. And now for dinner! If I have not (Macbeth-like) broken up the feast with most admired disorder, Daisy.'

'But where are they all, I wonder!' said I.

'God knows,' said Steerforth. 'After strolling to the ferry looking for you, I strolled in here and found the place deserted. That set me thinking, and you found me thinking.'

The advent of Mrs. Gummidge with a basket, explained how the house had happened to be empty. She had hurried out to buy something that was needed, against Mr. Peggotty's return with the tide; and had left the door open in the meanwhile, lest Ham and little Em'ly, with whom it was an early night, should come home while she was gone. Steerforth, after very much improving Mrs. Gummidge's spirits by a cheerful salutation and a jocose embrace, took my arm, and hurried me away.

He had improved his own spirits, no less than Mrs. Gummidge's, for they were again at their usual flow, and he was full of vivacious conversation as we went along.

'And so,' he said, gaily, 'we abandon this buccaneer life to-morrow, do we?'

'So we agreed,' I returned. 'And our places by the coach are taken, you know.'

'Ay! there's no help for it, I suppose,' said Steerforth. 'I have almost forgotten that there is any-

thing to do in the world but to go out tossing on the
sea here.   I wish there was not.'

'As long as the novelty should last,' said I, laughing.

'Like enough,' he returned; 'though there's a sar-
castic meaning in that observation for an amiable
piece of innocence like my young friend.   Well! I
dare say I am a capricious fellow, David.   I know
I am; but while the iron *is* hot, I can strike it vigorously too.   I could pass a reasonably good examination already, as a pilot in these waters, I think.'

'Mr. Peggotty says you are a wonder,' I returned.

'A nautical phenomenon, eh?' laughed Steerforth.

'Indeed he does, and you know how truly; knowing
how ardent you are in any pursuit you follow, and
how easily you can master it.   And that amazes me
most in you, Steerforth—that you should be contented with such fitful uses of your powers.'

'Contented?' he answered, merrily.   'I am never
contented, except with your freshness, my gentle
Daisy.   As to fitfulness, I have never learnt the art
of binding myself to any of the wheels on which the
Ixions of these days are turning round and round.
I missed it somehow in a bad apprenticeship, and now
don't care about it.—You know I have bought a boat
down here?'

'What an extraordinary fellow you are, Steerforth!'
I exclaimed, stopping—for this was the first I had
heard of it.   'When you may never care to come
near the place again!'

'I don't know that,' he returned.   'I have taken a
fancy to the place.   At all events,' walking me
briskly on, 'I have bought a boat that was for sale—a
clipper, Mr. Peggotty says; and so she is—and Mr.
Peggotty will be master of her in my absence.'

'Now I understand you, Steerforth!' said I, exultingly. 'You pretend to have bought it for yourself, but you have really done so to confer a benefit on him. I might have known as much at first, knowing you. My dear kind Steerforth, how can I tell you what I think of your generosity?'

'Tush!' he answered, turning red. 'The less said, the better.'

'Didn't I know?' cried I, 'didn't I say that there was not a joy, or sorrow, or any emotion of such honest hearts that was indifferent to you?'

'Aye, aye,' he answered, 'you told me all that. There let it rest. We have said enough!'

Afraid of offending him by pursuing the subject when he made so light of it, I only pursued it in my thoughts as we went on at even a quicker pace than before.

'She must be newly rigged,' said Steerforth, 'and I shall leave Littimer behind to see it done, that I may know she is quite complete. Did I tell you Littimer had come down?'

'No.'

'Oh yes! came down this morning, with a letter from my mother.'

As our looks met, I observed that he was pale even to his lips, though he looked very steadily at me. I feared that some difference between him and his mother might have led to his being in the frame of mind in which I had found him at the solitary fireside. I hinted so.

'Oh no!' he said, shaking his head, and giving a slight laugh. 'Nothing of the sort! Yes. He is come down, that man of mine.'

'The same as ever?' said I.

'The same as ever,' said Steerforth. 'Distant and quiet as the North Pole. He shall see to the boat being fresh named. She's the Stormy Petrel now.

What does Mr. Peggotty care for Stormy Petrels!
I'll have her christened again.'

'By what name?' I asked.

'The Little Em'ly.'

As he had continued to look steadily at me, I took
it as a reminder that he objected to being extolled for
his consideration. I could not help showing in my
face how much it pleased me, but I said little, and he
resumed his usual smile, and seemed relieved.

'But see here,' he said, looking before us, 'where
the original little Em'ly comes! And that fellow
with her, eh? Upon my soul, he's a true knight.
He never leaves her!'

Ham was a boat-builder in these days, having improved a natural ingenuity in that handicraft, until
he had become a skilled workman. He was in his
working-dress, and looked rugged enough, but manly
withal, and a very fit protector for the blooming little
creature at his side. Indeed, there was a frankness
in his face, an honesty, and an undisguised show of
his pride in her, and his love for her, which were, to
me, the best of good looks. I thought, as they came
towards us, that they were well matched even in that
particular.

She withdrew her hand timidly from his arm as we
stopped to speak to them, and blushed as she gave
it to Steerforth and to me. When they passed on,
after we had exchanged a few words, she did not
like to replace that hand, but, still appearing timid
and constrained, walked by herself. I thought all
this very pretty and engaging, and Steerforth seemed
to think so too, as we looked after them fading away
in the light of a young moon.

Suddenly there passed us—evidently following
them—a young woman whose approach we had not
observed, but whose face I saw as she went by, and

thought I had a faint remembrance of. She was lightly dressed, looked bold, and haggard, and flaunting, and poor; but seemed, for the time, to have given all that to the wind which was blowing, and to have nothing in her mind but going after them. As the dark distant level, absorbing their figures into itself, left but itself visible between us and the sea and clouds, her figure disappeared in like manner, still no nearer to them than before.

'That is a black shadow to be following the girl,' said Steerforth, standing still; 'what does it mean?'

He spoke in a low voice that sounded almost strange to me.

'She must have it in her mind to beg of them, I think,' said I.

'A beggar would be no novelty,' said Steerforth; 'but it is a strange thing that the begger should take that shape to-night.'

'Why?' I asked him.

'For no better reason, truly, than because I was thinking,' he said, after a pause, 'of something like it, when it came by. Where the devil did it come from, I wonder!'

'From the shadow of this wall, I think,' said I, as we emerged upon a road on which a wall abutted.

'It's gone!' he returned, looking over his shoulder. 'And all ill go with it. Now for our dinner!'

But, he looked again over his shoulder towards the sea-line glimmering afar off; and yet again. And he wondered about it, in some broken expressions, several times, in the short remainder of our walk; and only seemed to forget it when the light of fire and candle shone upon us, seated warm and merry, at table.

Littimer was there, and had his usual effect upon me. When I said to him that I hoped Mrs. Steer-

forth and Miss Dartle were well, he answered respectfully (and of course respectably), that they were
tolerably well, he thanked me, and had sent their compliments. This was all; and yet he seemed to me to
say as plainly as a man could say, 'You are very
young, sir; you are exceedingly young.'

We had almost finished dinner, when taking a step
or two towards the table, from the corner where he
kept watch upon us, or rather upon me, as I felt, he
said to his master—

'I beg your pardon, sir. Miss Mowcher is down
here.'

'Who?' cried Steerforth, much astonished.

'Miss Mowcher, sir.'

'Why, what on earth does *she* do here?' said Steerforth.

'It appears to be her native part of the country, sir.
She informs me that she makes one of her professional visits here, every year, sir. I met her in the
street this afternoon, and she wished to know if she
might have the honour of waiting on you after dinner,
sir.'

'Do you know the giantess in question, Daisy?'
inquired Steerforth.

I was obliged to confess—I felt ashamed, even of
being at this disadvantage before Littimer—that Miss
Mowcher and I were wholly unacquainted.

'Then you shall know her,' said Steerforth, 'for she
is one of the seven wonders of the world. When Miss
Mowcher comes, show her in.'

I felt some curiosity and excitement about this
lady, especially as Steerforth burst into a fit of laughing when I referred to her, and positively refused to
answer any question of which I made her the subject.
I remained, therefore, in a state of considerable expectation until the cloth had been removed some half

an hour, and we were sitting over our decanter of wine before the fire, when the door opened, and Littimer, with his habitual serenity quite undisturbed, announced—

'Miss Mowcher!'

I looked at the doorway and saw nothing. I was still looking at the doorway, thinking that Miss Mowcher was a long while making her appearance, when, to my infinite astonishment, there came waddling round a sofa which stood between me and it, a pursy dwarf, of about forty or forty-five, with a very large head and face, a pair of roguish grey eyes, and such extremely little arms, that, to enable herself to lay a finger archly against her snub-nose as she ogled Steerforth, she was obliged to meet the finger half-way and lay her nose against it. Her chin, which was what is called a double-chin, was so fat that it entirely swallowed up the strings of her bonnet, bow and all. Throat she had none; waist she had none; legs she had none, worth mentioning; for though she was more than full-sized down to where her waist would have been, if she had had any, and though she terminated, as human beings generally do, in a pair of feet, she was so short that she stood at a common-sized chair as at a table, resting a bag she carried on the seat. This lady; dressed in an off-hand, easy style; bringing her nose and her forefinger together, with the difficulty I have described; standing with her head necessarily on one side, and, with one of her sharp eyes shut up, making an uncommonly knowing face; after ogling Steerforth for a few moments, broke into a torrent of words.

'What! My flower!' she pleasantly began, shaking her large head at him. 'You're there, are you! Oh, you naughty boy, fie for shame, what do you do so far away from home? Up to mischief, I'll be bound. Oh, you 're a downy fellow, Steerforth, so you are, and I 'm another, ain't I? Ha, ha, ha! You 'd have betted a hundred pound to five, now, that you wouldn't have seen me here, wouldn't you? Bless you, man alive, I 'm everywhere. I 'm here, and there, and where not, like the conjuror's half-crown in the lady's hankercher. Talking of han-kerchers—*and* talking of ladies—what a comfort you are to your blessed mother, ain't you, my dear boy, over one of my shoulders, and I don't say which?'

Miss Mowcher untied her bonnet, at this passage of her discourse, threw back the strings, and sat down, panting, on a footstool in front of the fire—making a kind of arbour of the dining-table, which spread its mahogany shelter above her head.

'Oh my stars and what 's-their-names!' she went on, clapping a hand on each of her little knees, and glancing shrewdly at me. 'I 'm of too full a habit, that 's the fact, Steerforth. After a flight of stairs, it gives me as much trouble to draw every breath I want, as if it was a bucket of water. If you saw me look-ing out of an upper window, you 'd think I was a fine woman, wouldn't you?'

'I should think that, wherever I saw you,' replied Steerforth.

'Go along, you dog, do!' cried the little creature, making a whisk at him with the handkerchief with which she was wiping her face, 'and don't be impudent! But I give you my word and honour I was at Lady Mithers's last week—*there 's* a woman! How *she* wears!—and Mithers himself came into the room where I was waiting for her—*there 's* a man! How *he* wears! and his wig too, for he 's had it these ten years—and he went on at that rate in the compli-mentary line, that I began to think I should be obliged to ring the bell. Ha! ha! ha! He's a pleasant wretch, but he wants principle.'

'What were you doing for Lady Mithers?' asked Steerforth.

'That's tellings, my blessed infant,' she retorted, tapping her nose again, screwing up her face, and twinkling her eyes like an imp of supernatural intelligence. 'Never *you* mind! You'd like to know whether I stop her hair from falling off, or dye it, or touch up her complexion, or improve her eyebrows, wouldn't you? And so you shall my darling—when I tell you! Do you know what my great grandfather's name was?'

'No,' said Steerforth.

'It was Walker, my sweet pet,' replied Miss Mowcher, 'and he came of a long line of Walkers, that I inherit all the Hookey estates from.'

I never beheld anything approaching to Miss Mowcher's wink, except Miss Mowcher's self pos-ession. She had a wonderful way too, when listening to what was said to her, or when waiting for an answer to what she had said herself, of pausing with her head cunningly on one side, and one eye turned up like a magpie's. Altogether I was lost in amazement, and sat staring at her, quite oblivious, I am afraid, of the laws of politeness.

She had by this time drawn the chair to her side, and was busily engaged in producing from the bag (plunging in her short arm to the shoulder, at every dive) a number of small bottles, sponges, combs, brushes, bits of flannel, little pairs of curling-irons, and other instruments, which she tumbled in a heap upon the chair. From this employment she suddenly desisted, and said to Steerforth, much to my confusion—

'Who's your friend?'

'Mr. Copperfield,' said Steerforth; 'he wants to know you.'

'Well then, he shall! I thought he looked as if he did!' returned Miss Mowcher, waddling up to me, bag in hand, and laughing on me as she came. 'Face like a peach!' standing on tiptoe to pinch my cheek as I sat. 'Quite tempting! I'm very fond of peaches. Happy to make your acquaintance, Mr. Copperfield, I'm sure.'

I said that I congratulated myself on having the honour to make hers, and that the happiness was mutual.

'Oh, my goodness, how polite we are!' exclaimed Miss Mowcher, making a preposterous attempt to cover her large face with her morsel of a hand. 'What a world of gammon and spinnage it is, though, ain't it!'

This was addressed confidentially to both of us, as the morsel of a hand came away from the face, and buried itself, arm and all, in the bag again.

'What do you mean, Miss Mowcher?' said Steerforth.

'Ha! ha! ha! What a refreshing set of humbugs we are, to be sure, ain't we, my sweet child?' replied that morsel of a woman, feeling in the bag with her head on one side, and her eye in the air. 'Look here!' taking something out. 'Scraps of the Russian Prince's nails. Prince Alphabet turned topsy-turvy, *I* call him. for his name's got all the letters in it, higgledy-piggledy.'

'The Russian Prince is a client of yours, is he?' said Steerforth.

'I believe you, my pet,' replied Miss Mowcher. 'I keep his nails in order for him. Twice a week! Fingers *and* toes.'

'He pays well, I hope?' said Steerforth.

'Pays as he speaks, my dear child—through the nose,' replied Miss Mowcher. 'None of your close shavers the Prince ain't. You'd say so, if you saw his moustachios. Red by nature, black by art.'

'By your art, of course,' said Steerforth.

Miss Mowcher winked assent. 'Forced to send for me. Couldn't help it. The climate affected *his* dye; it did very well in Russia, but it was no go here. You never saw such a rusty prince in all your born days as he was. Like old iron!'

'Is that why you called him a humbug, just now?' inquired Steerforth.

'Oh, you 're a broth of a boy, ain't you?' returned Miss Mowcher, shaking her head violently. 'I said, what a set of humbugs we were in general, and I showed you the scraps of the Prince's nails to prove it. The prince's nails do more for me in private families of the genteel sort, than all my talents put together. I always carry 'em about. They 're the best introduction. If Miss Mowcher cuts the Prince's nails, she *must* be all right. I give 'em away to the young ladies. They put 'em in albums, I believe. Ha! ha! ha! Upon my life, "the whole social system" (as the men call it when they make speeches in Parliament) is a system of Prince's nails!' said this least of women, trying to fold her short arms, and nodding her large head.

Steerforth laughed heartily, and I laughed too. Miss Mowcher continuing all the time to shake her head (which was very much on one side), and to look into the air with one eye, and to wink with the other.

'Well, well!' she said, smiting her small knees, and rising, 'this is not business. Come, Steerforth, let's explore the polar regions, and have it over.'

She then selected two or three of the little instruments, and a little bottle, and asked (to my surprise) if the table would bear. On Steerforth replying in the affirmative, she pushed a chair against it, and begging the assistance of my hand, mounted up, pretty nimbly, to the top, as if it were a stage.

'If either of you saw my ankles,' she said, when she was safely elevated, 'say so, and I 'll go home and destroy myself.'

'*I* did not,' said Steerforth.

'*I* did not,' said I.

'Well then,' cried Miss Mowcher, 'I 'll consent to live. Now, ducky, ducky, ducky, come to Mrs. Bond and be killed.'

This was an invocation to Steerforth to place himself under her hands; who, accordingly, sat himself down, with his back to the table, and his laughing face towards me, and submitted his head to her inspection, evidently for no other purpose than our entertainment. To see Miss Mowcher standing over him, looking at his rich profusion of brown hair through a large round magnifying glass, which she took out of her pocket, was a most amazing spectacle.

'*You 're* a pretty fellow!' said Miss Mowcher, after a brief inspection. 'You 'd be as bald as a frair on the top of your head in twelve months, but for me. Just half a minute, my young friend, and we 'll give you a polishing that shall keep your curls on for the next ten years!'

With this, she tilted some of the contents of the little bottle on to one of the little bits of flannel, and, again imparting some of the virtues of that preparation to one of the little brushes, began rubbing and scraping away with both on the crown of Steerforth's head in the busiest manner I ever witnessed, talking all the time.

'There 's Charley Pyegrave, the duke's son,' she

said. 'You know Charley?' peeping round into his face.

'A little,' said Steerforth.

'What a man *he* is! *There's* a whisker! As to Charley's legs, if they were only a pair (which they ain't), they'd defy competition. Would you believe he tried to do without me—in the Life-Guards, too?'

'Mad!' said Steerforth.

'It looks like it. However, mad or sane, he tried,' returned Miss Mowcher. 'What does he do, but, lo and behold you, he goes into a perfumer's shop, and wants to buy a bottle of the Madagascar Liquid.'

'Charley does?' said Steerforth.

'Charley does. But they haven't got any of the Madagascar Liquid.'

'What is it? Something to drink?' asked Steerforth.

'To drink?' returned Miss Mowcher, stopping to slap his cheek. 'To doctor his own moustachios with, you *know*. There was a woman in the shop—elderly female—quite a Griffin—who had never even heard of it by name. "Begging pardon, sir," said the Griffin to Charley, "it's not—not—not ROUGE, is it?" "Rouge," said Charley to the Griffin. "What the unmentionable to ears polite, do you think I want with rouge?" "No offence, sir," said the Griffin; "we have it asked for by so many names, I thought it might be." Now that, my child,' continued Miss Mowcher, rubbing all the time as busily as ever, 'is another instance of the refreshing humbug I was speaking of. *I* do something in that way myself—perhaps a good deal—perhaps a little—sharp's the word, my dear boy—never mind!'

'In what way do you mean? In the rouge way?' said Steerforth.

'Put this and that together, my tender pupil,' returned the wary Mowcher, touching her nose, 'work it by the rule of Secrets in all trades, and the product will give you the desired result. I say *I* do a little in that way myself. One Dowager, *she* calls it lip-salve. Another, *she* calls it gloves. Another, *she* calls it tucker-edging. Another, *she* calls it a fan. *I* call it whatever *they* call it. I supply it for 'em, but we keep up the trick so, to one another, and make believe with such a face, that they'd as soon think of laying it on, before a whole drawing-room, as before me. And when I wait upon 'em, they'll say to me sometimes—*with it on*—thick, and no mistake—"How am I looking, Mowcher? Am I pale?" Ha! ha! ha! ha! Isn't *that* refreshing, my young friend!'

I never did in my days behold anything like Mowcher as she stood upon the dining-table, intensely enjoying this refreshment, rubbing busily at Steerforth's head, and winking at me over it.

'Ah!' she said. 'Such things are not much in demand herabouts. That sets me off again! I haven't seen a pretty woman since I've been here, Jemmy.'

'No?' said Steerforth.

'Not the ghost of one,' replied Miss Mowcher.

'We could show her the substance of one, I think?' said Steerforth, addressing his eyes to mine. 'Eh, Daisy?'

'Yes, indeed,' said I.

'Aha?' cried the little creature, glancing sharply at my face, and then peeping round at Steerforth's. 'Umph?'

The first exclamation sounded like a question put to both of us, and the second like a question put to Steerforth only. She seemed to have found no answer to either, but continued to rub, with her head on one side and her eye turned up, as if she were looking for an answer in the air, and were confident of its appearing presently.

'A sister of yours, Mr. Copperfield?' she cried, after a pause, and still keeping the same look-out. 'Aye, aye?'

'No,' said Steerforth, before I could reply. 'Nothing of the sort. On the contrary, Mr. Copperfield used—or I am much mistaken—to have a great admiration of her.'

'Why, hasn't he now?' returned Miss Mowcher. 'Is he fickle? oh, for shame! Did he sip every flower, and change every hour, until Polly his passion requited? Is her name Polly?'

The elfin suddenness with which she pounced upon me with this question, and a searching look, quite disconcerted me for a moment.

'No, Miss Mowcher,' I replied. 'Her name is Emily.'

'Aha?' she cried exactly as before. 'Umph? What a rattle I am! Mr. Copperfield, ain't I volatile?'

Her tone and look implied something that was not agreeable to me in connection with the subject. So I said, in a graver manner than any of us had yet assumed—

'She is as virtuous as she is pretty. She is engaged to be married to a most worthy and deserving man in her own station of life. I esteem her for her good sense, as much as I admire her for her good looks.'

'Well said!' cried Steerforth. 'Hear, hear, hear! Now I'll quench the curiosity of this little Fatima, my dear Daisy, by leaving her nothing to guess at. She is at present apprenticed, Miss Mowcher, or articled, or whatever it may be, to Omer and Joram, Haberdashers, Milliners, and so forth, in this town.

Do you observe? Omer and Joram. The promise of which my friend has spoken, is made and entered into with her cousin; Christian name, Ham; surname, Peggotty; occupation, boat-builder, also of this town. She lives with a relative; Christian name, unknown; surname, Peggotty; occupation, seafaring; also of this town. She is the prettiest and most engaging little fairy in the world. I admire her—as my friend does —exceedingly. If it were not that I might appear to disparage her intended, which I know my friend would not like, I would add, that to *me* she seems to be throwing herself away; that I am sure she might do better; and that I swear she was born to be a lady.'

Miss Mowcher listened to these words, which were very slowly and distinctly spoken, with her head on one side, and her eye in the air, as if she were still looking for that answer. When he ceased she became brisk again in an instant, and rattled away with surprising volubility.

'Oh, and that's all about it, is it?' she exclaimed, trimming his whiskers with a little restless pair of scissors, that went glancing round his head in all directions. 'Very well: *very* well! Quite a long story. Ought to end "and they lived happy ever afterwards"; oughtn't it? Ah! What's that game at forfeits? I love my love with an E, because she's enticing: I hate her with an E, because she's engaged. I took her to the sign of the exquisite, and treated her with an elopement; her name's Emily, and she lives in the east? Ha! ha! ha! Mr. Copperfield, ain't I volatile?'

Merely looking at me with extravagant slyness, and not waiting for any reply, she continued, without drawing breath—

'There! If ever any scapegrace was trimmed and touched up to perfection, you are, Steerforth. If I understand any noddle in the world, I understand yours. Do you hear me when I tell you that, my darling? I understand yours,' peeping down into his face. 'Now you may mizzle, Jemmy (as we say at Court), and if Mr. Copperfield will take the chair I 'll operate on him.'

'What do you say, Daisy?' inquired Steerforth, laughing, and resigning his seat. 'Will you be improved?'

'Thank you, Miss Mowcher, not this evening.'

'Don't say no,' returned the little woman, looking at me with the aspect of a connoisseur; 'a little bit more eyebrow?'

'Thank you,' I returned, 'some other time.'

'Have it carried half a quarter of an inch towards the temple,' said Miss Mowcher. 'We can do it in a fortnight.'

'No, I thank you. Not at present.'

'Go in for a tip,' she urged. 'No? Let 's get the scaffolding up, then, for a pair of whiskers. Come!'

I could not help blushing as I declined, for I felt we were on my weak point, now. But Miss Mowcher, finding that I was not at present disposed for any decoration within the range of her art, and that I was, for the time being, proof against the blandishments of the small bottle which she held up before one eye to enforce her persuasions, said she would make a beginning on an early day, and requested the aid of my hand to descend from her elevated station. Thus assisted, she skipped down with much agility, and began to tie her double-chin into her bonnet.

'The fee,' said Steerforth, 'is—'

'Five bob,' replied Miss Mowcher, 'and dirt cheap, my chicken. Ain't I volatile, Mr. Copperfield?'

I replied politely: 'Not at all.' But I thought she was rather so, when she tossed up his two half-crowns like a goblin pieman, caught them, dropped them in her pocket, and gave it a loud slap.

'That 's the till!' observed Miss Mowcher, standing at the chair again, and replacing in the bag a miscellaneous collection of little objects she had emptied out of it. 'Have I got all my traps? It seems so. It won't do to be like long Ned Beadwood, when they took him to church "to marry him to somebody," as he says, and left the bride behind. Ha! ha! ha! A wicked rascal, Ned, but droll! Now, I know I 'm going to break your hearts, but I am forced to leave you. You must call up all your fortitude, and try to bear it. Good-bye, Mr. Copperfield! Take care of yourself, Jockey of Norfolk! How I *have* been rattling on! It 's all the fault of you two wretches. *I* forgive you! "Bob swore!"—as the Englishman said for "Good-night," when he first learnt French, and thought it so like English. "Bob swore," my ducks!'

With the bag slung over her arm, and rattling as she waddled away, she waddled to the door; where she stopped to inquire if she should leave us a lock of her hair. 'Ain't I volatile?' she added, as a commentary on this offer, and, with her finger on her nose, departed.

Steerforth laughed to that degree, that it was impossible for me to help laughing too; though I am not sure I should have done so, but for this inducement. When we had had our laugh quite out, which was after some time, he told me that Miss Mowcher had quite an extensive connection, and made herself useful to a variety of people in a variety of ways. Some people trifled with her as a mere oddity, he said; but she was as shrewdly and sharply observant as any one he knew, and as long-headed as she was short-armed. He told me that what she had said of being here, and there, and everywhere, was true enough; for she made little darts into the provinces, and seemed to pick up customers everywhere, and to know everybody. I asked him what her disposition was: whether it was at all mischievous, and if her sympathies were generally on the right side of things: but, not succeeding in attracting his attention to these questions after two or three attempts, I forebore or forgot to repeat them. He told me instead, with much rapidity, a good deal about her skill, and her profits; and about her being a scientific cupper, if I should ever have occasion for her service in that capacity.

She was the principal theme of our conversation during the evening: and when we parted for the night Steerforth called after me over the banisters, 'Bob swore!' as I went downstairs.

I was surprised, when I came to Mr. Barkis's house, to find Ham walking up and down in front of it, and still more surprised to learn from him that little Em'ly was inside. I naturally inquired why he was not there too, instead of pacing the streets by himself?

'Why, you see, Mas'r Davy,' he rejoined in a hesitating manner, 'Em'ly, she's talking to some 'un in here.'

'I should have thought,' said I, smiling, 'that that was a reason for your being in here too, Ham.'

'Well, Mas'r Davy, in a general way, so 't would be,' he returned; 'but look 'ee here, Mas'r Davy,' lowering his voice, and speaking very gravely. 'It's a young woman, sir—a young woman, that Em'ly knowed once, and doen't ought to know no more.'

When I heard these words, a light began to fall upon the figure I had seen following them, some hours ago.

'It's a poor wuren, Mas'r Davy,' said Ham, 'as

is trod underfoot by all the town. Up street and down street. The mowld o' the churchyard don't hold any that the folk shrink away from, more.'

'Did I see her to-night, Ham, on the sands after we met you?'

'Keeping us in sight?' said Ham. 'It's like you did, Mas'r Davy. Not that I know'd then, she was theer, sir, but along of her creeping soon arterwards under Em'ly's little winder, when she see the light come, and whisp'ring "Em'ly, Em'ly, for Christ's sake, have a woman's heart towards me. I was once like you!" Those was solemn words, Mas'r Davy, fur to hear!'

'They were indeed, Ham. What did Em'ly do?'

'Says Em'ly, "Martha, is it you? Oh, Martha, can it be you?"—for they had sat at work together, many a day, at Mr. Omer's.'

'I recollect her now!' cried I, recalling one of the two girls I had seen when I first went there. 'I recollect her quite well!'

'Martha Endell,' said Ham. 'Two or three year older than Em'ly, but was at the school with her.'

'I never heard her name,' says I. 'I didn't mean to interrupt you.'

'For the matter o' that, Mas'r Davy,' replied Ham, 'all's told a'most in them words, "Em'ly, Em'ly, for Christ's sake have a woman's heart towards me. I was once like you!" She wanted to speak to Em'ly. Em'ly couldn't speak to her theer, for her loving uncle was come home, and he wouldn't—no, Mas'r Davy,' said Ham, with great earnestness, 'he couldn't, kind-natur'd, tender-hearted as he is, see them two together, side by side, for all the treasures that's wrecked in the sea.'

I felt how true this was. I knew it, on the instant, quite as well as Ham.

'So Em'ly writes in pencil on a bit of paper,' he pursued, 'and gives it to her out o' window to bring here. "Show that," she says, "to my aunt, Mrs. Barkis, and she'll set you down by her fire, for the love of me, till uncle is gone out, and I can come." By and by she tells me what I tell you, Mas'r Davy, and asks me to bring her. What can I do? She doen't ought to know any such, but I can't deny her, when the tears is on her face.'

He put his hand into the breast of his shaggy jacket, and took out with great care a pretty little purse.

'And if I could deny her when the tears was on her face, Mas'r Davy,' said Ham, tenderly adjusting it on the rough palm of his hand, 'how could I deny her when she gave me this to carry for her—knowing what she brought it for? Such a toy as it is!' said Ham, thoughtfully looking on it. 'With such a little money in it, Em'ly my dear!'

I shook him warmly by the hand when he had put it away again—for that was more satisfactory to me than saying anything—and we walked up and down, for a minute or two, in silence. The door opened then, and Peggotty appeared, beckoning to Ham to come in. I would have kept away, but she came after me, entreating me to come in too. Even then, I would have avoided the room where they all were, but for its being the neat-tiled kitchen I have mentioned more than once. The door opening immediately into it, I found myself among them, before I considered whither I was going.

The girl—the same I had seen upon the sands— was near the fire. She was sitting on the ground, with her head and one arm lying on a chair. I fancied, from the disposition of her figure, that Em'ly had but newly risen from the chair, and that the forlorn head might perhaps have been lying on her lap. I saw but little of the girl's face, over which her hair fell loose and scattered, as if she had been disordering it with her own hands; but I saw that she was young, and of a fair complexion. Peggotty had been crying. So had little Em'ly. Not a word was spoken when we first went in; and the Dutch clock by the dresser seemed, in the silence, to tick twice as loud as usual.

Em'ly spoke first.

'Martha wants,' she said to Ham, 'to go to London.'

'Why to London?' returned Ham.

He stood between them, looking on the prostrate girl with a mixture of compassion for her, and of jealousy of her holding any companionship with her whom he loved so well, which I have always remembered distinctly. They both spoke as if she were ill; in a soft, suppressed tone that was plainly heard, although it hardly rose above a whisper.

'Better there than here,' said a third voice aloud— Martha's, though she did not move. 'No one knows me there. Everybody knows me here.'

'What will she do there?' inquired Ham.

She lifted up her head, and looked darkly round at him for a moment; then laid it down again, and curved her right arm about her neck, as a woman in a fever, or in an agony of pain from a shot, might twist herself.

'She will try to do well,' said little Em'ly. 'You don't know what she has said to us. Does he—do they—aunt?'

Peggotty shook her head compassionately.

'I 'll try,' said Martha, 'if you 'll help me away. I never can do worse than I have done here. I may

MARTHA.

do better. Oh!' with a dreadful shiver, 'take me out of these streets, where the whole town knows me from a child!'

As Em'ly held out her hand to Ham, I saw him put in it a little canvas bag. She took it, as if she thought it were her purse, and made a step or two forward; but finding her mistake, came back to where he had retired near me, and showed it to him.

'It's all yourn, Em'ly,' I could hear him say. 'I have nowt in all the wureld that ain't yourn, my dear. It ain't of no delight to me, except for you!'

The tears rose freshly in her eyes, but she turned away and went to Martha. What she gave her, I don't know. I saw her stooping over her, and putting money in her bosom. She whispered something, as she asked was that enough? 'More than enough,' the other said, as she took her hand and kissed it.

Then Martha arose, and gathering her shawl about her, covering her face with it, and weeping aloud, went slowly to the door. She stopped a moment before going out, as if she would have uttered something or turned back; but no word passed her lips. Making the same low, dreary, wretched moaning in her shawl, she went away.

As the door closed, little Em'ly looked at us three in a hurried manner, and then hid her face in her hands, and fell to sobbing.

'Doen't, Em'ly!' said Ham, tapping her gently on the shoulder. 'Doen't, my dear! You doen't ought to cry so, pretty!'

'Oh, Ham!' she exclaimed, still weeping pitifully, 'I am not as good a girl as I ought to be! I know I have not the thankful heart, sometimes, I ought to have!'

'Yes, yes, you have, I'm sure,' said Ham.

'No! no! no!' cried little Emily, sobbing, and shaking her head. 'I am not as good a girl as I ought to be. Not near! not near!'

And still she cried, as if her heart would break.

'I try your love too much. I know I do!' she sobbed. 'I'm often cross to you, and changeable with you, when I ought to be far different. You are never so to me. Why am I ever so to you, when I should think of nothing but how to be grateful, and to make you happy!'

'You always make me so,' said Ham, 'my dear! I am happy in the sight of you. I am happy, all day long, in the thoughts of you.'

'Ah! that's not enough!' she cried. 'That is because you are good; not because I am! Oh, my dear, it might have been a better fortune for you, if you had been fond of some one else—of some one steadier and much worthier than me, who was all bound up in you, and never vain and changeable like me!'

'Poor little tender-heart,' said Ham, in a low voice. 'Martha has overset her, altogether.'

'Please, aunt,' sobbed Em'ly, 'come here, and let me lay my head upon you. Oh, I am very miserable to-night, aunt! Oh, I am not as good a girl as I ought to be. I am not, I know!'

Peggotty had hastened to the chair before the fire. Em'ly, with her arms around her neck, kneeled by her, looking up most earnestly into her face.

'Oh, pray, aunt, try to help me! Ham, dear, try to help me! Mr. David, for the sake of old times, do, please, try to help me! I want to be a better girl than I am. I want to feel a hundred times more thankful than I do. I want to feel more, what a blessed thing it is to be the wife of a good man, and to lead a peaceful life. Oh me, oh me! Oh my heart, my heart!'

She dropped her face on my old nurse's breast, and, ceasing this supplication, which in its agony and grief was half a woman's, half a child's, as all her manner was (being, in that, more natural, and better suited to her beauty, as I thought, than any other manner could have been), wept silently, while my old nurse hushed her like an infant.

She got calmer by degrees, and then we soothed her; now talking encouragingly, and now jesting a little with her, until she began to raise her head and speak to us. So we got on, until she was able to smile, and then to laugh, and then to sit up, half-ashamed; while Peggotty recalled her stray ringlets, dried her eyes, and made her neat again, lest her uncle should wonder, when she got home, why his darling had been crying.

I saw her do, that night, what I had never seen her do before. I saw her innocently kiss her chosen husband on the cheek, and creep close to his bluff form as if it were her best support. When they went away together, in the waning moonlight, and I looked after them, comparing their departure in my mind with Martha's, I saw that she held his arm with both her hands, and still kept close to him.

CHAPTER XXIII

I CORROBORATE MR. DICK, AND CHOOSE A PROFESSION

When I awoke in the morning I thought very much of little Em'ly, and her emotion last night, after Martha had left. I felt as if I had come into the knowledge of those domestic weaknesses and tendernesses in a sacred confidence, and that to disclose them, even to Steerforth, would be wrong. I had no gentler feeling towards any one than towards the pretty creature who had been my playmate, and whom I have always been persuaded, and shall always be persuaded, to my dying day, I then devotedly loved. The repetition to any ears—even to Steerforth's—of what she had been unable to repress when her heart lay open to me by an accident, I felt would be a rough deed, unworthy of myself, unworthy of the light of our pure childhood, which I always saw encircling her head. I made a resolution, therefore, to keep it in my own breast; and there it gave her image a new grace.

While we were at breakfast, a letter was delivered to me from my aunt. As it contained matter on which I thought Steerforth could advise me as well as any one, and on which I knew I should be delighted to consult him, I resolved to make it a subject of discussion on our journey home. For the present we had enough to do, in taking leave of all our friends. Mr. Barkis was far from being the last among them, in his regret at our departure; and I believe would even have opened the box again, and sacrificed another guinea, if it would have kept us eight-and-forty hours in Yarmouth. Peggotty and all her family were full of grief at our going. The whole house of Omer and Joram turned out to bid us good-bye; and there were so many seafaring volunteers in attendance on Steerforth, when our portmanteaus went to the coach, that if we had had the baggage of a regiment with us, we should hardly have wanted porters to carry it. In a word, we departed to the regret and admiration of all concerned, and left a great many people very sorry behind us.

'Do you stay long here, Littimer?' said I, as he stood waiting to see the coach start.

'No, sir,' he replied; 'probably not very long, sir.'

'He can hardly say, just now,' observed Steerforth, carelessly. 'He knows what he has to do, and he'll do it.'

'That I am sure he will,' said I.

Littimer touched his hat in acknowledgment of my good opinion, and I felt about eight years old. He touched it once more, wishing us a good journey; and we left him standing on the pavement, as respectable a mystery as any pyramid in Egypt.

For some little time we held no conversation, Steerforth being unusually silent, and I being sufficiently engaged in wondering, within myself, when I should see the old places again, and what new changes might happen to me or them in the meanwhile. At length Steerforth, becoming gay and talkative in a moment, as he could become anything he liked at any moment, pulled me by the arm—

'Find a voice, David. What about the letter you were speaking of at breakfast?'

'Oh!' said I, taking it out of my pocket. 'It's from my aunt.'

'And what does she say, requiring consideration?'

'Why, she reminds me, Steerforth,' said I, 'that I came out on this expedition to look about me, and to think a little.'

'Which, of course, you have done?'

'Indeed I can't say I have, particularly. To tell you the truth, I am afraid I had forgotten it.'

'Well! look about you now, and make up for your negligence,' said Steerforth. 'Look to the right, and you'll see a flat country, with a good deal of marsh in it; look to the left, and you'll see the same. Look to the front, and you'll find no difference; look to the rear, and there it is still.'

I laughed, and replied that I saw no suitable profession in the whole prospect; which was perhaps to be attributed to its flatness.

'What says our aunt on the subject?' inquired Steerforth, glancing at the letter in my hand. 'Does she suggest anything?'

'Why, yes,' said I. 'She asks me, here, if I think I should like to be a proctor? What do you think of it?'

'Well, I don't know,' replied Steerforth, coolly. 'You may as well do that as anything else, I suppose!'

I could not help laughing again, at his balancing all callings and professions so equally; and I told him so.

'What *is* a proctor, Steerforth?' said I.

'Why, he is a sort of monkish attorney,' replied Steerforth. 'He is, to some faded courts held in Doctors' Commons—a lazy old nook near St. Paul's Churchyard—what solicitors are to the courts of law and equity. He is a functionary whose existence, in the natural course of things, would have terminated about two hundred years ago. I can tell you best what he is, by telling you what Doctors' Commons is. It 's a little out-of-the-way place, where they administer what is called ecclesiastical law, and play all kinds of tricks with obsolete old monsters of Acts of Parliament, which three-fourths of the world know nothing about, and the other fourth supposes to have been dug up, in a fossil state, in the days of the Edwards. It 's a place that has an ancient monopoly in suits about people's wills and people's marriages, and disputes among ships and boats.'

'Nonsense, Steerforth!' I exclaimed. 'You don't mean to say that there is any affinity between nautical matters and ecclesiastical matters?'

'I don't, indeed, my dear boy,' he returned; 'but I mean to say that they are managed and decided by the same set of people, down in that same Doctors' Commons. You shall go there one day, and find them blundering through half the nautical terms in Young's Dictionary, apropos of the "Nancy" having run down the "Sarah Jane," or Mr. Peggotty and the Yarmouth boatmen having put off in a gale of wind with an anchor and cable to the "Nelson" Indiaman in distress; and you shall go there another day, and find them deep in the evidence, pro and con., respecting a clergyman who has misbehaved himself; and you shall find the judge in the nautical case, the advocate in the clergyman's case, or contrariwise. They are like actors: now a man's a judge, and now he is not a judge; now he's one thing, now he's another; now he's something else, change and change about; but it's always a very pleasant profitable little affair of private theatricals, presented to an uncommonly select audience.'

'But advocates and proctors are not one and the same?' said I, a little puzzled. 'Are they?'

'No,' returned Steerforth, 'the advocates are civilians—men who have taken a doctor's degree at college —which is the first reason of my knowing anything about it. The proctors employ the advocates. Both get very comfortable fees, and altogether they make a mighty snug little party. On the whole, I would recommend you to take to Doctors' Commons kindly, David. They plume themselves on their gentility there, I can tell you, if that's any satisfaction.'

I made allowance for Steerforth's light way of treating the subject, and, considering it with reference to the staid air of gravity and antiquity which I associated with that 'lazy old nook near St. Paul's Churchyard,' did not feel indisposed towards my aunt's suggestion; which she left to my free decision, making no scruple of telling me that it had occurred to her, on her lately visiting her own proctor in Doctors' Commons for the purpose of settling her will in my favour.

'That's a laudable proceeding on the part of our aunt, at all events,' said Steerforth, when I mentioned it; 'and one deserving of all encouragement. Daisy, my advice is that you take kindly to Doctors' Commons.'

I quite made up my mind to do so. I then told Steerforth that my aunt was in town awaiting me (as I found from her letter), and that she had taken lodgings for a week at a kind of private hotel in Lincoln's Inn Fields, where there was a stone staircase, and a convenient door in the roof; my aunt being firmly persuaded that every house in London was going to be burnt down every night.

We achieved the rest of our journey pleasantly, sometimes recurring to Doctors' Commons, and anticipating the distant days when I should be a proctor there, which Steerforth pictured in a variety of humorous and whimsical lights, that made us both merry. When we came to our journey's end, he went home, engaging to call upon me next day but one; and I drove to Lincoln's Inn Fields, where I found my aunt up, and waiting supper.

If I had been round the world since we parted, we could hardly have been better pleased to meet again. My aunt cried outright as she embraced me; and said, pretending to laugh, that if my poor mother had been alive, that silly little creature would have shed tears, she had no doubt.

'So you have left Mr. Dick behind, aunt?' said I. 'I am sorry for that. Ah, Janet, how do you do?'

As Janet curtsied, hoping I was well, I observed my aunt's visage lengthened very much.

'I am sorry for it, too,' said my aunt, rubbing her

nose. 'I have had no peace of mind, Trot, since I have been here.'

Before I could ask why, she told me.

'I am convinced,' said my aunt, laying her hand with melancholy firmness on the table, 'that Dick's character is not a character to keep the donkeys off. I am confident he wants strength of purpose. I ought to have left Janet at home, instead, and then my mind might perhaps have been at ease. If ever there was a donkey trespassing on my green,' said my aunt, with emphasis, 'there was one this afternoon at four o'clock. A cold feeling came over me from head to foot, and I *know* it was a donkey!'

I tried to comfort her on this point, but she rejected consolation.

'It was a donkey,' said my aunt; 'and it was the one with the stumpy tail which that Murdering sister of a woman rode, when she came to my house.' This had been, ever since, the only name my aunt knew for Miss Murdstone. 'If there is any donkey in Dover, whose audacity it is harder to me to bear than another's, that,' said my aunt, striking the table, 'is the animal!'

Janet ventured to suggest that my aunt might be disturbing herself unnecessarily, and that she believed the donkey in question was then engaged in the sand-and-gravel line of business, and was not available for purposes of trespass. But my aunt wouldn't hear of it.

Supper was comfortably served and hot, though my aunt's rooms were very high up—whether that she might have more stone stairs for her money, or might be nearer to the door in the roof, I don't know —and consisted of a roast fowl, a steak, and some vegetables, to all of which I did ample justice, and which were all excellent. But my aunt had her own ideas concerning London provision, and ate but little.

'I suppose this unfortunate fowl was born and brought up in a cellar,' said my aunt, 'and never took the air except on a hackney coach-stand. I *hope* the steak may be beef, but I don't believe it. Nothing's genuine in the place, in my opinion, but the dirt.'

'Don't you think the fowl may have come out of the country, aunt?' I hinted.

'Certainly not,' returned my aunt. 'It would be no pleasure to a London tradesman to sell anything which was what he pretended it was.'

I did not venture to controvert this opinion, but I made a good supper, which it greatly satisfied her to see me do. When the table was cleared, Janet assisted her to arrange her hair, to put on her night-cap, which was of a smarter construction than usual ('in case of fire,' my aunt said), and to fold her gown back over her knees, these being her usual preparations for warming herself before going to bed. I then made her, according to certain established regulations from which no deviation, however slight, could ever be permitted, a glass of hot white wine and water, and a slice of toast cut into long thin strips. With these accompaniments we were left alone to finish the evening, my aunt sitting opposite to me drinking her wine and water; soaking her strips of toast in it, one by one, before eating them; and looking benignantly on me, from among the borders of her night-cap.

'Well, Trot,' she began, 'what do you think of the proctor plan? Or have you not begun to think about it yet?'

'I have thought a good deal about it, my dear aunt, and I have talked a good deal about it with Steerforth. I like it very much indeed. I like it exceedingly.'

'Come,' said my aunt. 'That's cheering.'

'I have only one difficulty, aunt.'

'Say what it is, Trot,' she returned.

'Why, I want to ask, aunt, as this seems, from what I understand, to be a limited profession, whether my entrance into it would not be very expensive?'

'It will cost,' returned my aunt, 'to article you, just a thousand pounds.'

'Now, my dear aunt,' said I, drawing my chair nearer, 'I am uneasy in my mind about that. It's a large sum of money. You have expended a great deal on my education, and have always been as liberal to me in all things, as it was possible to be. You have been the soul of generosity. Surely there are some ways in which I might begin life with hardly any outlay, and yet begin with a good hope of getting on by resolution and exertion. Are you sure that it would not be better to try that course? Are you certain that you can afford to part with so much money, and that it is right that it should be so expended? I only ask you, my second mother, to consider. Are you certain?'

My aunt finished eating the piece of toast on which she was then engaged, looking me full in the face all the while; and then setting her glass on the chimneypiece, and folding her hands upon her folded skirts, replied as follows—

'Trot, my child, if I have any object in life, it is to provide for your being a good, a sensible, and a happy man. I am bent upon it—so is Dick. I should like some people that I know to hear Dick's conversation on the subject. Its sagacity is wonderful. But no one knows the resources of that man's intellect except myself!'

She stopped for a moment to take my hand between hers, and went on—

'It 's in vain, Trot, to recall the past, unless it works some influence upon the present. Perhaps I might have been better friends with your poor father. Perhaps I might have been better friends with that poor child your mother, even after your sister Betsey Trotwood disappointed me. When you came to me, a little runaway boy, all dusty and wayworn, perhaps I thought so. From that time until now, Trot, you have ever been a credit to me and a pride and a pleasure. I have no other claim upon my means; at least'—here to my surprise she hesitated, and was confused—'no, I have *no* other claim upon my means —and you are my adopted child. Only be a loving child to me in my age, and bear with my whims and fancies; and you will do more for an old woman whose prime of life was not so happy or conciliating as it might have been, than ever that old woman did for you.'

It was the first time I had heard my aunt refer to her past history. There was a magnanimity in her quiet way of doing so, and of dismissing it, which would have exalted her in my respect and affection, if anything could.

'All is agreed and understood between us now, Trot,' said my aunt, 'and we need talk of this no more. Give me a kiss, and we 'll go to the Commons after breakfast to-morrow.'

We had a long chat by the fire before we went to bed. I slept in a room on the same floor with my aunt's, and was a little disturbed in the course of the night by her knocking at my door as often as she was agitated by a distant sound of hackney-coaches or market-carts, and inquiring 'if I heard the engines?' But towards morning she slept better, and suffered me to do so too.

At about midday, we set out for the office of Messrs. Spenlow and Jorkins, in Doctors' Commons. My aunt, who had this other general opinion in reference to London, that every man she saw was a pickpocket, gave me her purse to carry for her, which had ten guineas in it and some silver.

We made a pause at the toy-shop in Fleet Street, to see the giants of Saint Dunstan's strike upon the bells—we had timed our going, so as to catch them at it, at twelve o'clock—and then went on towards Ludgate Hill and St. Paul's Churchyard. We were crossing to the former place, when I found that my aunt greatly accelerated her speed and looked frightened. I observed, at the same time, that a lowering ill-dressed man who had stopped and stared at us in passing, a little before, was coming so close after us, as to brush against her.

'Trot! My dear Trot!' cried my aunt, in a terrified whisper, and pressing my arm. 'I don't know what I am to do.'

'Don't be alarmed,' said I. 'There's nothing to be afraid of. Step into a shop, and I'll soon get rid of this fellow.'

'No, no, child!' she returned. 'Don't speak to him for the world. I entreat, I order you!'

'Good Heaven, aunt!' said I. 'He is nothing but a sturdy beggar.'

'You don't know what he is!' replied my aunt. You don't know who he is! You don't know what you say!'

We had stopped in an empty doorway, while this was passing, and he had stopped too.

'Don't look at him!' said my aunt, as I turned my

head indignantly, 'but get me a coach, my dear, and wait for me in St. Paul's Churchyard.'

'Wait for you?' I repeated.

'Yes,' rejoined my aunt. 'I must go alone. I must go with him.'

'With him, aunt? This man?'

'I am in my senses,' she replied, 'and I tell you I *must*. Get me a coach!'

However much astonished I might be, I was sensible that I had no right to refuse compliance with such a peremptory command. I hurried away a few paces, and called a hackney-chariot which was passing empty. Almost before I could let down the steps, my aunt sprang in, I don't know how, and the man followed. She waved her hand to me to go away, so earnestly, that, all confounded as I was, I turned from them at once. In doing so, I heard her say to the coachman, 'Drive anywhere! Drive straight on!' and presently the chariot passed me, going up the hill.

What Mr. Dick had told me, and what I had supposed to be a delusion of his, now came into my mind. I could not doubt that this person was the person of whom he had made such mysterious mention, though what the nature of his hold upon my aunt could possibly be, I was quite unable to imagine. After half an hour's cooling in the churchyard, I saw the chariot coming back. The driver stopped beside me, and my aunt was sitting in it alone.

She had not yet sufficiently recovered from her agitation to be quite prepared for the visit we had to make. She desired me to get into the chariot, and to tell the coachman to drive slowly up and down a little while. She said no more, except, 'My dear child, never ask me what it was, and don't refer to it,' until she had perfectly regained her composure when she told me she was quite herself now, and we might get out. On her giving me her purse, to pay the driver, I found that all the guineas were gone, and only the loose silver remained.

Doctors' Commons was approached by a little low archway. Before we had taken many paces down the street beyond it, the noise of the city seemed to melt, as if by magic, into a softened distance. A few dull courts and narrow ways brought us to the sky-lighted offices of Spenlow and Jorkins; in the vestibule of which temple, accessible to pilgrims without the ceremony of knocking, three or four clerks were at work as copyists. One of these, a little dry man, sitting by himself, who wore a stiff brown wig that looked as if it were made of ginger-bread, rose to receive my aunt, and show us into Mr. Spenlow's room.

'Mr. Spenlow's in Court, ma'am,' said the dry man; 'it's an Arches day; but it's close by, and I'll send for him directly.'

As we were left to look about us while Mr. Spenlow was fetched, I availed myself of the opportunity. The furniture of the room was old-fashioned and dusty; and the green baize on the top of the writing table had lost all its colour, and was as withered and pale as an old pauper. There were a great many bundles of papers on it, some indorsed as Allegations, and some (to my surprise) as Libels, and some as being in the Consistory Court, and some in the Arches Court, and some in the Prerogative Court, and some in the Admiralty Court, and some in the Delegates' Court; giving me occasion to wonder much, how many courts there might be in the gross, and how long it would take to understand them all. Besides these, there were sundry immense manuscript Books of Evidence taken on affidavit, strongly bound, and tied together in massive sets, a set to each cause, as if every cause were a history in ten or twenty volumes. All this looked tolerably expensive, I thought, and gave me an agreeable notion of a proctor's business. I was casting my eyes with increasing complacency over these and similar objects, when hasty footsteps were heard in the room outside, and Mr. Spenlow, in a black gown trimmed with white fur, came hurrying in, taking off his hat as he came.

He was a little light-haired gentleman, with undeniable boots, and the stiffest of white cravats and shirt-collars. He was buttoned up mighty trim and tight, and must have taken a great deal of pains with his whiskers, which were accurately curled. His gold watch-chain was so massive, that a fancy came across me, that he ought to have a sinewy golden arm, to draw it out with, like those which are put up over the gold-beater's shops. He was got up with such care, and was so stiff, that he could hardly bend himself; being obliged, when he glanced at some papers on his desk, after sitting down in his chair, to move his whole body, from the bottom of his spine, like Punch.

I had previously been presented by my aunt and had been courteously received. He now said—

'And so, Mr. Copperfield, you think of entering into our profession? I casually mentioned to Miss Trotwood, when I had the pleasure of an interview with her the other day,'—with another inclination of his body—Punch again—'that there was a vacancy here. Miss Trotwood was good enough to mention that she had a nephew who was her peculiar care, and for whom she was seeking to provide genteelly in life. That nephew, I believe, I have now the pleasure of'—Punch again.

I bowed my acknowledgments, and said, my aunt had mentioned to me that there was that opening, and that I believed I should like it very much. That I was strongly inclined to like it, and had taken immediately to the proposal. That I could not absolutely pledge myself to like it, until I knew something more about it. That although it was little else than a matter of form, I presumed I should have an opportunity of trying how I liked it, before I bound myself to it irrevocably.

'Oh surely! surely!' said Mr. Spenlow. 'We always, in this house, propose a month—an initiatory month. I should be happy, myself, to propose two months—three—an indefinite period, in fact—but I have a partner. Mr. Jorkins.'

'And the premium, sir,' I returned, 'is a thousand pounds.'

'And the premium, stamp included, is a thousand pounds,' said Mr. Spenlow. 'As I have mentioned, to Miss Trotwood, I am actuated by no mercenary considerations; few men are less so, I believe; but Mr. Jorkins has his opinions on these subjects, and I am bound to respect Mr. Jorkins's opinions. Mr. Jorkins thinks a thousand pounds too little, in short.'

'I suppose, sir,' said I, still desiring to spare my aunt, 'that it is not the custom here, if an articled clerk were particularly useful, and made himself a perfect master of his profession'—I could not help blushing, this looked so like praising myself—'I suppose it is not the custom, in the later years of his time, to allow him any—'

Mr. Spenlow, by a great effort, just lifted his head far enough out of his cravat, to shake it, and answered, anticipating the word 'salary.'

'No. I will not say what consideration I might

give to that point myself, Mr. Copperfield, if I were unfettered. Mr. Jorkins is immoveable.'

I was quite dismayed by the idea of this terrible Jorkins. But I found out afterwards that he was a mild man of a heavy temperament, whose place in the business was to keep himself in the background, and be constantly exhibited by name as the most obdurate and ruthless of men. If a clerk wanted his salary raised, Mr. Jorkins wouldn't listen to such a proposition. If a client were slow to settle his bill of costs, Mr. Jorkins was resolved to have it paid; and however painful these things might be (and always were) to the feelings of Mr. Spenlow, Mr. Jorkins would have his bond. The heart and hand of the good angel Spenlow would have been always open, but for the restraining demon Jorkins. As I have grown older, I think I have had experience of some other houses doing business on the principle of Spenlow and Jorkins!

It was settled that I should begin my month's probation as soon as I pleased, and that my aunt need neither remain in town nor return at its expiration, as the articles of agreement of which I was to be the subject, could easily be sent to her at home for her signature. When we had got so far, Mr. Spenlow offered to take me into Court then and there, and show me what sort of place it was. As I was willing enough to know, we went out with this object, leaving my aunt behind; who would trust herself, she said, in no such place, and who, I think, regarded all Courts of Law as a sort of powder-mills that might blow up at any time.

Mr. Spenlow conducted me through a paved courtyard formed of grave brick houses, which I inferred, from the Doctors' names upon the doors, to be the official abiding places of the learned advocates of whom Steerforth had told me; and into a large dull room, not unlike a chapel to my thinking, on the left hand. The upper part of this room was fenced off from the rest; and there, on the two sides of a raised platform of the horseshoe form, sitting on easy old-fashioned dining-room chairs, were sundry gentlemen in red gowns and grey wigs, whom I found to be the Doctors aforesaid. Blinking over a little desk like a pulpit-desk, in the curve of the horseshoe, was an old gentleman, whom, if I had seen him in an aviary, I should certainly have taken for an owl, but who, I learned, was the presiding judge. In the space within the horseshoe, lower than these, that is to say on about the level of the floor, were sundry other gentlemen of Mr. Spenlow's rank, and dressed like him in black gowns with white fur upon them, sitting at a long green table. Their cravats were in general stiff, I thought, and their looks haughty; but in this last respect, I presently conceived I had done them an injustice, for when two or three of them had to rise and answer a question of the presiding dignitary, I never saw anything more sheepish. The public, represented by a boy with a comforter, and a shabby-genteel man secretly eating crumbs out of his coat pockets, was warming itself at a stove in the centre of the Court. The languid stillness of the place was only broken by the chirping of this fire and by the voice of one of the Doctors, who was wandering slowly through a perfect library of evidence, and stopping to put up, from time to time, at little road-side inns of argument on the journey. Altogether, I have never, on any occasion, made one at such a cosey, dosey, old-fashioned, time-forgotten, sleepy-headed little family party in all my life; and I felt it would be quite a soothing opiate to belong to it in any character—except perhaps as a suitor.

Very well satisfied with the dreamy nature of this retreat, I informed Mr. Spenlow that I had seen enough for that time, and we rejoined my aunt; in company with whom I presently departed from the Commons, feeling very young when I went out of Spenlow and Jorkins's, on account of the clerks poking one another with their pens to point me out.

We arrived at Lincoln's Inn Fields without any new adventures, except encountering an unlucky donkey in a costermonger's cart, who suggested painful associations to my aunt. We had another long talk about my plans, when we were safely housed; and as I knew she was anxious to get home, and between fire, food, and pickpockets, could never be considered at her ease for half an hour in London, I urged her not to be uncomfortable on my account, but to leave me to take care of myself.

'I have not been here a week to-morrow, without considering that too, my dear,' she returned. 'There is a furnished little set of chambers to be let in the Adelphi, Trot, which ought to suit you to a marvel.'

With this brief introduction, she produced from her pocket an advertisement, carefully cut out of a newspaper, setting forth that in Buckingham Street in the Adelphi there was to be let furnished, with a view of the river, a singularly desirable and compact set of chambers, forming a genteel residence for a young gentleman, a member of one of the Inns of Court, or otherwise, with immediate possession. Terms moderate, and could be taken for a month only, if required.

'Why, this is the very thing, aunt!' said I, flushed with the possible dignity of living in chambers.

'Then come,' replied my aunt, immediately resuming the bonnet she had a minute before laid aside. 'We'll go and look at 'em.'

Away we went.   The advertisement directed us to apply to Mrs. Crupp on the premises, and we rung the area bell, which we supposed to communicate with Mrs. Crupp.   It was not until we had rung three or four times that we could prevail on Mrs. Crupp to communicate with us, but at last she appeared, being a stout lady with a flounce of flannel petticoat below a nankeen gown.

'Let us see these chambers of yours, if you please, ma'am,' said my aunt.

'For this gentleman?' said Mrs. Crupp, feeling in her pocket for her keys.

'Yes, for my nephew,' said my aunt.

'And a sweet set they is for sich!' said Mrs. Crupp. So we went upstairs.

They were on the top of the house—a great point with my aunt, being near the fire-escape—and consisted of a little half-blind entry where you could see hardly anything, a little stone-blind pantry where you could see nothing at all, a sitting-room, and a bedroom.   The furniture was rather faded, but quite good enough for me; and, sure enough, the river was outside the windows.

As I was delighted with the place, my aunt and Mrs. Crupp withdrew into the pantry to discuss the terms, while I remained on the sitting-room sofa, hardly daring to think it possible that I could be destined to live in such a noble residence.   After a single combat of some duration they returned, and I saw, to my joy, both in Mrs. Crupp's countenance and in my aunt's, that the deed was done.

'Is it the last occupant's furniture?' inquired my aunt.

'Yes, it is, ma'am,' said Mrs. Crupp.

'What 's become of him?' asked my aunt.

Mrs. Crupp was taken with a troublesome cough,

in the midst of which she articulated with much difficulty. 'He was took ill here, ma'am, and—ugh! ugh!
ugh! dear me!— and he died!'

'Hey! What did he die of?' asked my aunt.

'Well, ma'am, he died of drink,' said Mrs. Crupp,
in confidence. 'And smoke.'

'Smoke? You don't mean chimneys?' said my
aunt.

'No, ma'am,' returned Mrs. Crupp. 'Cigars and
pipes.'

'*That's* not catching, Trot, at any rate,' remarked
my aunt, turning to me.

'No, indeed,' said I.

In short, my aunt, seeing how enraptured I was
with the premises, took them for a month, with leave
to remain for twelve months when that time was out.
Mrs. Crupp was to find linen, and to cook; every other
necessary was already provided; and Mrs. Crupp expressly intimated that she should always yearn towards me as a son. I was to take possession the day
after to-morrow, and Mrs. Crupp said, thank Heaven
she had now found summun she could care for!

On our way back, my aunt informed me how she
confidently trusted that the life I was now to lead
would make me firm and self-reliant, which was all
I wanted. She repeated this several times next day,
in the intervals of our arranging for the transmission of my clothes and books from Mr. Wickfield's;
relative to which, and to all my late holiday, I wrote
a long letter to Agnes, of which my aunt took charge,
as she was to leave on the succeeding day. Not to
lengthen these particulars, I need only add, that she
made a handsome provision for all my possible wants
during my month of trial; that Steerforth, to my
great disappointment and hers too, did not make his
appearance before she went away; that I saw her

safely seated in the Dover coach, exulting in the coming discomfiture of the vagrant donkeys, with Janet at her side; and that when the coach was gone, I turned my face to the Adelphi, pondering on the old days when I used to roam about its subterranean arches, and on the happy changes which had brought me to the surface.

CHAPTER XXIV

MY FIRST DISSIPATION

It was a wonderfully fine thing to have that lofty castle to myself, and to feel, when I shut my outer door, like Robinson Crusoe, when he had got into his fortification, and pulled his ladder up after him.   It was a wonderfully fine thing to walk about town with the key of my house in my pocket, and to know that I could ask any fellow to come home, and make quite sure of its being inconvenient to nobody, if it were not so to me.   It was a wonderfully fine thing to let myself in and out, and to come and go without a word to any one, and to ring Mrs. Crupp up, gasping, from the depths of the earth, when I wanted her —and when she was disposed to come.   All this, I say, was wonderfully fine; but I must say, too, that there were times when it was very dreary.

It was fine in the morning, particularly in the fine mornings.   It looked a very fresh, free life, by daylight: still fresher, and more free, by sunlight.   But as the day declined the life seemed to go down too. I don't know how it was; it seldom looked well by candle-light.   I wanted somebody to talk to, then. I missed Agnes.   I found a tremendous blank, in the place of that smiling repository of my confidence.

Mrs. Crupp appeared to be a long way off. I thought about my predecessor, who had died of drink and smoke; and I could have wished he had been so good as to live, and not bother me with his decease.

After two days and nights, I felt as if I had lived there for a year, and yet I was not an hour older, but was quite as much tormented by my own youthfulness as ever.

Steerforth not yet appearing, which induced me to apprehend that he must be ill, I left the Commons early on the third day, and walked out to Highgate. Mrs. Steerforth was very glad to see me, and said that he had gone away with one of his Oxford friends to see another who lived near St. Albans, but that she expected him to return to-morrow. I was so fond of him, that I felt quite jealous of his Oxford friends.

As she pressed me to stay to dinner, I remained, and I believe we talked about nothing but him all day. I told her how much the people liked him at Yarmouth, and what a delightful companion he had been. Miss Dartle was full of hints and mysterious questions, but took a great interest in all our proceedings there, and said, 'Was it really though?' and so forth, so often, that she got everything out of me she wanted to know. Her appearance was exactly what I have described it, when I first saw her; but the society of the two ladies was so agreeable, and came so natural to me, that I felt myself falling a little in love with her. I could not help thinking, several times in the course of the evening, and particularly when I walked home at night, what delightful company she would be in Buckingham Street.

I was taking my coffee and roll in the morning, before going to the Commons—and I may observe in this place that it is surprising how much coffee Mrs. Crupp used, and how weak it was, considering—when

Steerforth himself walked in, to my unbounded joy.

'My dear Steerforth,' cried I, 'I began to think I should never see you again!'

'I was carried off by force of arms,' said Steerforth, 'the very next morning after I got home. Why, Daisy, what a rare old bachelor you are here!'

I showed him over the establishment, not omitting the pantry, with no little pride, and he commended it highly. 'I tell you what, old boy,' he added, 'I shall make quite a town-house of this place, unless you give me notice to quit.'

This was a delightful hearing. I told him if he waited for that, he would have to wait till doomsday.

'But you shall have some breakfast!' said I, with my hand on the bell-rope, 'and Mrs. Crupp shall make you some fresh coffee, and I'll toast you some bacon in a bachelor's Dutch-oven that I have got here.'

'No, no!' said Steerforth. 'Don't ring! I can't. I am going to breakfast with one of these fellows who is at the Piazza Hotel, in Covent Garden.'

'But you'll come back to dinner?' said I.

'I can't, upon my life. There's nothing I should like better, but I *must* remain with these two fellows. We are all three off together to-morrow morning.'

'Then bring them here to dinner,' I returned. 'Do you think they would come?'

'Oh! they would come fast enough,' said Steerforth; 'but we should inconvenience you. You had better come and dine with us somewhere.'

I would not by any means consent to this, for it occurred to me that I really ought to have a little house-warming, and that there never could be a better opportunity. I had a new pride in my rooms after his approval of them, and burned with a desire to develop their utmost resources. I therefore made him promise positively in the names of his two friends, and we appointed six o'clock as the dinner-hour.

When he was gone, I rang for Mrs. Crupp, and acquainted her with my desperate design. Mrs. Crupp said, in the first place, of course it was well known she couldn't be expected to wait, but she knew a handy young man, who she thought could be prevailed upon to do it, and whose terms would be five shillings, and what I pleased. I said, certainly we would have him. Next, Mrs. Crupp said it was clear she couldn't be in two places at once (which I felt to be reasonable), and that 'a young gal' stationed in the pantry with a bed-room candle, there never to desist from washing plates, would be indispensable. I said, what would be the expense of this young female, and Mrs. Crupp said she supposed eighteen-pence would neither make me nor break me. I said I supposed not; and *that* was settled. Then Mrs. Crupp said, Now about the dinner.

It was a remarkable instance of want of forethought on the part of the ironmonger who had made Mrs. Crupp's kitchen fire-place, that it was capable of cooking nothing but chops and mashed potatoes. As to a fish-kittle, Mrs. Crupp said, well! would I only come and look at the range? She couldn't say fairer than that. Would I come and look at it? As I should not have been much the wiser if I *had* looked at it, I declined, and said, 'Never mind fish.' But Mrs. Crupp said, Don't say that; oysters was in, and why not them? So *that* was settled. Mrs. Crupp then said what she would recommend would be this. A pair of hot roast fowls—from the pastry-cook's; a dish of stewed beef, with vegetables—from the pastry-cook's; two little corner things, as a raised pie and a dish of kidneys—from the pastry-cook's; a tart, and (if I liked) a shape of jelly—from the pastry-cook's. This, Mrs. Crupp said, would leave her at full liberty to concentrate her mind on the potatoes, and to serve up the cheese and celery as she could wish to see it done.

I acted on Mrs. Crupp's opinion, and gave the order at the pastry-cook's myself. Walking along the Strand, afterwards, and observing a hard mottled substance in the window of a ham and beef shop, which resembled marble, but was labelled 'Mock Turtle,' I went in and bought a slab of it, which I have since seen reason to believe would have sufficed for fifteen people. This preparation, Mrs. Crupp, after some difficulty, consented to warm up; and it shrunk so much in a liquid state, that we found it what Steerforth called 'rather a tight fit' for four.

These preparations happily completed, I bought a little dessert in Covent Garden Market, and gave a rather extensive order at a retail wine-merchant's in that vicinity. When I came home in the afternoon, and saw the bottles drawn up in a square on the pantry-floor, they looked so numerous (though there were two missing, which made Mrs. Crupp very uncomfortable), that I was absolutely frightened at them.

One of Steerforth's friends was named Grainger, and the other Markham. They were both very gay and lively fellows; Grainger, something older than Steerforth; Markham, youthful-looking, and I should say not more than twenty. I observed that the latter always spoke of himself indefinitely, as 'a man,' and seldom or never in the first person singular.

'A man might get on very well here, Mr. Copperfield,' said Markham—meaning himself.

'It 's not a bad situation,' said I, 'and the rooms are really commodious.'

'I hope you have both brought appetites with you?' said Steerforth.

'Upon my honour,' returned Markham, 'town seems to sharpen a man's appetite. A man is hungry all day long. A man is perpetually eating.'

Being a little embarrassed at first, and feeling much too young to preside, I made Steerforth take the head of the table when dinner was announced, and seated myself opposite to him. Everything was very good; we did not spare the wine; and he exerted himself so brilliantly to make the thing pass off well, that there was no pause in our festivity. I was not quite such good company during dinner as I could have wished to be, for my chair was opposite the door, and my attention was distracted by observing that the handy young man went out of the room very often, and that his shadow always presented itself, immediately afterwards, on the wall of the entry, with a bottle at its mouth. The 'young gal' likewise occasioned me some uneasiness: not so much by neglecting to wash the plates, as by breaking them. For being of an inquisitive disposition, and unable to confine herself (as her positive instructions were) to the pantry, she was constantly peering in at us, and constantly imagining herself detected; in which belief, she several times retired upon the plates (with which she had carefully paved the floor), and did a great deal of destruction.

These, however, were small drawbacks, and easily forgotten when the cloth was cleared, and the dessert put on the table; at which period of the entertainment the handy young man was discovered to be speechless. Giving him private directions to seek the society of Mrs. Crupp, and to remove the 'young gal' to the basement also, I abandoned myself to enjoyment.

I began, by being singularly cheerful and light-hearted; all sorts of half-forgotten things to talk about, came rushing into my mind, and made me hold forth in a most unwonted manner. I laughed heartily at my own jokes, and everybody else's; called Steerforth to order for not passing the wine; made several engagements to go to Oxford; announced that I meant to have a dinner-party exactly like that, once a week until further notice; and madly took so much snuff out of Grainger's box, that I was obliged to go into the pantry, and have a private fit of sneezing ten minutes long.

I went on, by passing the wine faster and faster yet, and continually starting up with a corkscrew to open more wine, long before any was needed. I proposed Steerforth's health. I said he was my dearest friend, the protector of my boyhood, and the companion of my prime. I said I was delighted to propose his health. I said I owed him more obligations than I could ever repay, and held him in a higher admiration than I could ever express. I finished by saying, 'I'll give you Steerforth! God bless him! Hurrah!' We gave him three times three, and another, and a good one to finish with. I broke my glass in going round the table to shake hands with him, and I said (in two words) 'Steerforth, you're-theguidingstarofmyexistence.'

I went on, by finding suddenly that somebody was in the middle of a song. Markham was the singer, and he sang, 'When the heart of a man is depressed with care.' He said, when he had sung it, he would give us 'Woman!' I took objection to that, and I couldn't allow it. I said it was not a respectful way of proposing the toast, and I would never permit that toast to be drunk in my house otherwise than as 'The Ladies!' I was very high with him, mainly I think because I saw Steerforth and Grainger laughing at me—or at him—or at both of us. He said a man was not to be dictated to. I said a man *was*. He said a man was not to be insulted, then. I said he was right there—never under my roof, where the Lares were sacred, and the laws of hospitality paramount. He said it was no derogation from a man's dignity to confess that I was a devilish good fellow. I instantly proposed his health.

Somebody was smoking. We were all smoking. *I* was smoking, and trying to suppress a rising tendency to shudder. Steerforth had made a speech about me, in the course of which I had been affected almost to tears. I returned thanks, and hoped the present company would dine with me to-morrow and the day after—each day at five o'clock, that we might enjoy the pleasures of conversation and society through a long evening. I felt called upon to propose an individual. I would give them my aunt. Miss Betsey Trotwood, the best of her sex!

Somebody was leaning out of my bed-room window, refreshing his forehead against the cool stone of the parapet, and feeling the air upon his face. It was myself. I was addressing myself as 'Copperfield,' and saying, 'Why did you try to smoke? You might have known you couldn't do it.' Now, somebody was unsteadily contemplating his features in the looking-glass. That was I too. I was very pale in the looking-glass; my eyes had a vacant appearance; and my hair—only my hair, nothing else— looked drunk.

Somebody said to me, 'Let us go to the theatre, Copperfield!' There was no bed-room before me, but again the jingling table covered with glasses; the lamp; Grainger on my right hand, Markham on my left, and Steerforth opposite—all sitting in a mist, and a long way off. The theatre? To be sure. The very thing. Come along! But they must excuse me if I saw everybody out first, and turned the lamp off—in case of fire!

Owing to some confusion in the dark, the door was gone. I was feeling for it in the window-curtains, when Steerforth, laughing, took me by the arm and led me out. We went downstairs, one behind another. Near the bottom, somebody fell, and rolled down. Somebody else said it was Copperfield. I was angry at that false report, until finding myself on my back in the passage, I began to think there might be some foundation for it.

A very foggy night, with great rings round the lamps in the streets! There was an indistinct talk of its being wet. I considered it frosty. Steerforth dusted me under a lamp-post, and put my hat into shape, which somebody produced from somewhere in a most extraordinary manner, for I hadn't had it on before. Steerforth then said, 'You are all right, Copperfield, are you not?' and I told him, 'Neverberrer.'

A man, sitting in a pigeon-hole place, looked out of the fog, and took money from somebody, inquiring if I was one of the gentlemen paid for, and appearing rather doubtful (as I remember in the glimpse I had of him) whether to take the money for me or not. Shortly afterwards, we were very high up in a very hot theatre, looking down into a large pit, that seemed to me to smoke; the people with whom it was crammed were so indistinct. There was a great stage, too, looking very clean and smooth after the streets; and there were people upon it, talking about something or other, but not at all intelligibly. There was an abundance of bright lights, and there was music, and there were ladies down in

the boxes, and I don't know what more. The whole
building looked to me, as if it were learning to swim;
it conducted itself in such an unaccountable manner,
when I tried to steady it.

On somebody's motion, we resolved to go downstairs to the dress-boxes, where the ladies were. A
gentleman lounging, full dressed, on a sofa, with an
opera-glass in his hand, passed before my view, and
also my own figure at full length in a glass. Then I
was being ushered into one of these boxes, and found
myself saying something as I sat down, and people
about me crying 'Silence!' to somebody, and ladies
casting indignant glances at me, and—what! yes!—
Agnes, sitting on the seat before me, in the same box,
with a lady and gentleman beside her, whom I didn't
know. I see her face now, better than I did then, I
dare say, with its indelible look of regret and wonder
turned upon me.

'Agnes!' I said, thickly, 'Lorblessmer! Agnes!'

'Hush! Pray!' she answered, I could not conceive
why. 'You disturb the company. Look at the
stage!'

I tried, on her injunction, to fix it, and to hear
something of what was going on there, but quite in
vain. I looked at her again by and by, and saw her
shrink into her corner, and put her gloved hand to her
forehead.

'Agnes!' I said. 'I'mafraidyou'renorwell.'

'Yes, yes. Do not mind me, Trotwood,' she returned. 'Listen! Are you going away soon?'

'Amigoarawaysoo?' I repeated.

'Yes.'

I had a stupid intention of replying that I was
going to wait, to hand her downstairs. I suppose I
expressed it somehow; for, after she had looked at me

attentively for a little while, she appeared to understand, and replied in a low tone—

'I know you will do as I ask you, if I tell you I am very earnest in it. Go away now, Trotwood, for my sake, and ask your friends to take you home.'

She had so far improved me, for the time, that though I was angry with her, I felt ashamed, and with a short 'Goori!' (which I intended for 'Goodnight!') got up and went away. They followed, and I stepped at once out of the box-door into my bedroom, where only Steerforth was with me, helping me to undress, and where I was by turns telling him that Agnes was my sister, and adjuring him to bring the corkscrew, that I might open another bottle of wine.

How somebody, lying in my bed, lay saying and doing all this over again, at cross-purposes, in a feverish dream all night—the bed a rocking sea that was never still! How, as that somebody slowly settled down into myself, did I being to parch, and feel as if my outer covering of skin were a hard board; my tongue the bottom of an empty kettle, furred with long service, and burning up over a slow fire; the palms of my hands, hot plates of metal which no ice could cool!

But the agony of mind, the remorse, and shame I felt, when I became conscious next day! My horror of having committed a thousand offences I had forgotten, and which nothing could ever expiate—my recollection of that indelible look which Agnes had given me—the torturing impossibility of communicating with her, not knowing, beast that I was, how she came to be in London, or where she stayed—my disgust of the very sight of the room where the revel had been held—my racking head—the smell of smoke, the sight of glasses, the impossibility of going out, or even getting up! Oh, what a day it was!

Oh, what an evening, when I sat down by my fire to a basin of mutton broth, dimpled all over with fat, and thought I was going the way of my predecessor, and should succeed to his dismal story as well as to his chambers, and had half a mind to rush express to Dover and reveal all! What an evening, when Mrs. Crupp, coming in to take away the broth-basin, produced one kidney on a cheese-plate as the entire remains of yesterday's feast, and I was really inclined to fall upon her nankeen breast, and say, in heartfelt penitence, 'Oh, Mrs. Crupp, Mrs. Crupp, never mind the broken meats! I am very miserable!'—only that I doubted, even at that pass, if Mrs. Crupp were quite the sort of woman to confide in!

CHAPTER XXV

GOOD AND BAD ANGELS

I was going out at my door on the morning after that deplorable day of headache, sickness, and repentance, with an odd confusion in my mind relative to the date of my dinner-party as if a body of Titans had taken an enormous lever and pushed the day before yesterday some months back, when I saw a ticket-porter coming upstairs, with a letter in his hand. He was taking his time about his errand, then; but when he saw me on the top of the staircase, looking at him over the banisters, he swung into a trot, and came up panting as if he had run himself into a state of exhaustion.

'T. Copperfield, Esquire,' said the ticket-porter touching his hat with his little cane.

I could scarcely lay claim to the name: I was so

disturbed by the conviction that the letter came from Agnes. However, I told him I was T. Copperfield, Esquire, and he believed it, and gave me the letter, which he said required an answer. I shut him out on the landing to wait for the answer, and went into my chambers again, in such a nervous state that I was fain to lay the letter down on my breakfast-table, and familiarise myself with the outside of it a little, before I could resolve to break the seal.

I found, when I did open it, that it was a very kind note, containing no reference to my condition at the theatre. All it said was, 'My dear Trotwood. I am staying at the house of papa's agent, Mr. Waterbrook, in Ely Place, Holborn. Will you come and see me to-day, at any time you like to appoint? Ever yours affectionately, AGNES.'   . .

It took me such a long time to write an answer at all to my satisfaction, that I don't know what the ticket-porter can have thought, unless he thought I was learning to write. I must have written half a dozen answers at least. I began one, 'How can I ever hope, my dear Agnes, to efface from your remembrance the disgusting impression'—there I didn't like it, and then I tore it up. I began another, 'Shakespeare has observed, my dear Agnes, how strange it is that a man should put an enemy into his mouth'—that reminded me of Markham, and it got no farther. I even tried poetry. I began one note, in a six-syllable line, 'Oh, do not remember'—but that associated itself with the fifth of November, and became an absurdity. After many attempts, I wrote, 'My dear Agnes. Your letter is like you, and what could I say of it that would be higher praise than that? I will come at four o'clock. Affectionately and sorrowfully, T. C.' With this missive (which I was in twenty minds at once about recalling, as soon as it was out of my hands), the ticket-porter at last departed.

If the day were half as tremendous to any other professional gentleman in Doctors' Commons as it was to me, I sincerely believe he made some expiation for his share in that rotten old ecclesiastical cheese. Although I left the office at half-past three, and was prowling about the place of appointment within a few minutes afterwards, the appointed time was exceeded by a full quarter of an hour, according to the clock of St. Andrew's, Holborn, before I could muster up sufficient desperation to pull the private bell-handle let into the left-hand door-post of Mr. Waterbrook's house.

The professional business of Mr. Waterbrook's establishment was done on the ground floor, and the genteel business (of which there was a good deal) in the upper part of the building. I was shown into a pretty but rather close drawing-room, and there sat Agnes, netting a purse.

She looked so quiet and good, and reminded me so strongly of my airy fresh school days at Canterbury, and the sodden, smoky, stupid wretch I had been the other night, that, nobody being by, I yielded to my self-reproach and shame, and—in short, made a fool of myself. I cannot deny that I shed tears. To this hour I am undecided whether it was upon the whole the wisest thing I could have done, or the most ridiculous.

'If it had been any one but you, Agnes,' said I, turning away my head, 'I should not have minded it half so much. But that it should have been you who saw me! I almost wish I had been dead, first.'

She put her hand—its touch was like no other hand —upon my arm for a moment; and I felt so befriended and comforted, that I could not help moving it to my lips, and gratefully kissing it.

'Sit down,' said Agnes, cheerfully. 'Don't be unhappy, Trotwood. If you cannot confidently trust me, whom will you trust?'

'Ah, Agnes!' I returned. 'You are my good Angel!'

She smiled rather sadly, I thought, and shook her head.

'Yes, Agnes, my good Angel! Always my good Angel!'

'If I were, indeed, Trotwood,' she returned, 'there is one thing that I should set my heart on very much.'

I looked at her inquiringly; but already with a foreknowledge of her meaning.

'On warning you,' said Agnes, with a steady glance, 'against your bad Angel.'

'My dear Agnes,' I began, 'if you mean Steerforth—'

'I do, Trotwood,' she returned.

'Then, Agnes, you wrong him very much. He my bad Angel, or any one's! He, anything but a guide, a support, and a friend to me! My dear Agnes! Now, is it not unjust, and unlike you, to judge him from what you saw of me the other night?'

'I do not judge him from what I saw of you the other night,' she quietly replied.

'From what, then?'

'From many things—trifles in themselves, but they do not seem to me to be so, when they are put together. I judge him, partly from your account of him, Trotwood, and your character, and the influence he has over you.'

There was always something in her modest voice that seemed to touch a chord within me, answering to that sound alone. It was always earnest; but when it was very earnest, as it was now, there was a thrill in it that quite subdued me. I sat looking at her as she cast her eyes down on her work; I sat seeming still to listen to her; and Steerforth, in spite of all my attachment to him, darkened in that tone.

'It is very bold in me,' said Agnes, looking up again, 'who have lived in such seclusion, and can know so little of the world, to give you my advice so confidently, or even to have this strong opinion. But I know in what it is engendered, Trotwood,—in how true a remembrance of our having grown up together, and in how true an interest in all relating to you. It is that which makes me bold. I am certain that what I say is right. I am quite sure it is. I feel as if it were some one else speaking to you, and not I, when I caution you that you have made a dangerous friend.'

Again I looked at her, again I listened to her after she was silent, and again his image, though it was still fixed in my heart, darkened.

'I am not so unreasonable as to expect,' said Agnes, resuming her usual tone, after a little while, 'that you will, or that you can, at once, change any sentiment that has become a conviction to you; least of all a sentiment that is rooted in your trusting disposition. You ought not hastily to do that. I only ask you, Trotwood, if you ever think of me—I mean,' with a quiet smile, for I was going to interrupt her, and she knew why, 'as often as you think of me—to think of what I have said. Do you forgive me for all this?'

'I will forgive you, Agnes,' I replied, 'when you come to do Steerforth justice, and to like him as well as I do.'

'Not until then?' said Agnes.

I saw a passing shadow on her face when I made

this mention of him, but she returned my smile, and we were again as unreserved in our mutual confidence as of old.

'And when, Agnes,' said I, 'will you forgive me the other night?'

'When I recall it,' said Agnes.

She would have dismissed the subject so, but I was too full of it to allow that, and insisted on telling her how it happened that I had disgraced myself, and what a chain of accidental circumstances had had the theatre for its final link. It was a great relief to me to do this, and to enlarge on the obligation that I owed to Steerforth for his care of me when I was unable to take care of myself.

'You must not forget,' said Agnes, calmly changing the conversation as soon as I had concluded, 'that you are always to tell me, not only when you fall into trouble, but when you fall in love. Who has succeeded to Miss Larkins, Trotwood?'

'No one, Agnes.'

'Some one, Trotwood,' said Agnes, laughing, and holding up her finger.

'No, Agnes, upon my word! There is a lady, certainly, at Mrs. Steerforth's house, who is very clever, and whom I like to talk to—Miss Dartle—but I don't adore her.'

Agnes laughed again at her own penetration, and told me that if I were faithful to her in my confidence she thought she should keep a little register of my violent attachments, with the date, duration, and termination of each, like the table of the reigns of the kings and queens, in the History of England. Then she asked me if I had seen Uriah.

'Uriah Heep?' said I. 'No. Is he in London?'

'He comes to the office downstairs, every day,' returned Agnes. 'He was in London a week before me. I am afraid on disagreeable business, Trotwood.'

'On some business that makes you uneasy, Agnes, I see,' said I. 'What can that be?'

Agnes laid aside her work, and replied, folding her hands upon one another, and looking pensively at me out of those beautiful soft eyes of hers—

'I believe he is going to enter into partnership with papa.'

'What? Uriah? That mean, fawning fellow, worm himself into such promotion!' I cried, indignantly. 'Have you made no remonstrance about it, Agnes? Consider what a connection it is likely to be. You must speak out. You must not allow your father to take such a mad step. You must prevent it, Agnes, while there's time.'

Still looking at me, Agnes shook her head while I was speaking, with a faint smile at my warmth; and then replied—

'You remember our last conversation about papa? It was not long after that—not more than two or three days—when he gave me the first intimation of what I tell you. It was sad to see him struggling between his desire to represent it to me as a matter of choice on his part, and his inability to conceal that it was forced upon him. I felt very sorry.'

'Forced upon him, Agnes! Who forces it upon him?'

'Uriah,' she replied, after a moment's hesitation, 'has made himself indispensable to papa. He is subtle and watchful. He has mastered papa's weaknesses, fostered them, and taken advantage of them, until—to say all that I mean in a word, Trotwood—until papa is afraid of him.'

There was more that she might have said; more

that she knew, or that she suspected; I clearly saw. I could not give her pain by asking what it was, for I knew that she withheld it from me to spare her father. It had long been going on to this, I was sensible: yes, I could not but feel, on the least reflection, that it had been going on to this for a long time. I remained silent.

'His ascendancy over papa,' said Agnes, 'is very great. He professes humility and gratitude—with truth, perhaps: I hope so—but his position is really one of power, and I fear he makes a hard use of his power.'

I said he was a hound, which, at the moment, was a great satisfaction to me.

'At the time I speak of, as the time when papa spoke to me,' pursued Agnes, 'he had told papa that he was going away; that he was very sorry and unwilling to leave, but that he had better prospects. Papa was very much depressed then, and more bowed down by care than ever you or I have seen him; but he seemed relieved by this expedient of the partnership, though at the same time he seemed hurt by it and ashamed of it.'

'And how did you receive it, Agnes?'

'I did, Trotwood,' she replied, 'what I hope was right. Feeling sure that it was necessary for papa's peace that the sacrifice should be made, I entreated him to make it. I said it would lighten the load of his life—I hope it will!—and that it would give me increased opportunities of being his companion. Oh, Trotwood!' cried Agnes, putting her hands before her face, as her tears started on it, 'I almost feel as if I had been papa's enemy, instead of his loving child. For I know how he has altered, in his devotion to me. I know how he has narrowed the circle of his sympathies and duties, in the concentration of his whole mind upon me. I know what a multitude of things he has shut out for my sake, and how his anxious thoughts of me have shadowed his life, and weakened his strength and energy, by turning them aways upon one idea. If I could ever set this right! If I could ever work out his restoration, as I have so innocently been the cause of his decline!'

I had never before seen Agnes cry. I had seen tears in her eyes when I had brought new honours home from school, and I had seen them there when we last spoke about her father, and I had seen her turn her gentle head aside when we took leave of one another; but I had never seen her grieve like this. It made me so sorry that I could only say, in a foolish, helpless manner, 'Pray, Agnes, don't! Don't, my dear sister!'

But Agnes was too superior to me in character and purpose, as I know well now, whatever I might know or not know then, to be long in need of my entreaties. The beautiful, calm manner, which makes her so different in my remembrance from everybody else, came back again, as if a cloud had passed from a serene sky.

'We are not likely to remain alone much longer,' said Agnes; 'and while I have an opportunity, let me earnestly entreat you, Trotwood, to be friendly to Uriah. Don't repel him. Don't resent (as I think you have a general disposition to do) what may be uncongenial to you in him. He may not deserve it, for we know no certain ill of him. In any case, think first of papa and me!'

Agnes had no time to say more, for the room-door opened, and Mrs. Waterbrook, who was a large lady —or who wore a large dress: I don't exactly know which, for I don't know which was dress and which was lady—came sailing in. I had a dim recollection of having seen her at the theatre, as if I had seen her in a pale magic lantern; but she appeared to remember me perfectly, and still to suspect me of being in a state of intoxication.

Finding by degrees, however, that I was sober, and (I hope) that I was a modest young gentleman, Mrs. Waterbrook softened towards me considerably, and inquired, firstly, if I went much into the parks, and secondly, if I went much into society. On my replying to both these questions in the negative, it occurred to me that I fell again in her good opinion; but she concealed the fact gracefully, and invited me to dinner next day. I accepted the invitation, and took my leave, making a call on Uriah in the office as I went out, and leaving a card for him in his absence.

When I went to dinner next day, and, on the street-door being opened, plunged into a vapour-bath of haunch of mutton, I divined that I was not the only guest, for I immediately identified the ticket-porter in disguise, assisting the family servant, and waiting at the foot of the stairs to carry up my name. He looked, to the best of his ability, when he asked me for it confidentially, as if he had never seen me before; but well did I know him, and well did he know me. Conscience made cowards of us both.

I found Mr. Waterbrook to be a middle-aged gentleman, with a short throat, and a good deal of shirt collar, who only wanted a black nose to be the portrait of a pug-dog. He told me he was happy to have the honour of making my acquaintance; and when I had paid my homage to Mrs. Waterbrook, presented me, with much ceremony, to a very awful lady in a black velvet dress, and a great black velvet hat, whom I remember as looking like a near relation of Hamlet's—say his aunt.

Mrs. Henry Spiker was this lady's name; and her

husband was there too: so cold a man, that his head, instead of being grey, seemed to be sprinkled with hoar-frost. Immense deference was shown to the Henry Spikers, male and female; which Agnes told me was on account of Mr. Henry Spiker being solicitor to something or to somebody, I forget what or which, remotely connected with the Treasury.

I found Uriah Heep among the company, in a suit of black, and in deep humility. He told me, when I shook hands with him, that he was proud to be noticed by me, and that he really felt obliged to me for my condescension. I could have wished he had been less obliged to me, for he hovered about me in his gratitude all the rest of the evening; and whenever I said a word to Agnes, was sure, with his shadowless eyes and cadaverous face, to be looking gauntly down upon us from behind.

There were other guests—all iced for the occasion, as it struck me, like the wine. But, there was one who attracted my attention before he came in, on account of my hearing him announced as Mr. Traddles! My mind flew back to Salem House; and could it be Tommy, I thought, who used to draw the skeletons?

I looked for Mr. Traddles with unusual interest. He was a sober, steady-looking young man of retiring manners, with a comic head of hair, and eyes that were rather wide open; and he got into an obscure corner so soon, that I had some difficulty in making him out. At length I had a good view of him, and either my vision deceived me, or it was the old unfortunate Tommy.

I made my way to Mr. Waterbrook, and said, that I believed I had the pleasure of seeing an old schoolfellow there.

'Indeed!' said Mr. Waterbrook, surprised. 'You

are too young to have been at school with Mr. Henry Spiker?'

'Oh, I don't mean him!' I returned. 'I mean the gentleman named Traddles.'

'Oh! Aye, aye! Indeed!' said my host, with much diminished interest. 'Possibly.'

'If it's really the same person,' said I, glancing towards him, 'it was at a place called Salem House where we were together, and he was an excellent fellow.'

'Oh yes. Traddles is a good fellow,' returned my host, nodding his head with an air of toleration. 'Traddles is quite a good fellow.'

'It's a curious coincidence,' said I.

'It is really,' returned my host, 'quite a coincidence, that Traddles should be here at all: as Traddles was only invited this morning, when the place at table, intended to be occupied by Mrs. Henry Spiker's brother, became vacant, in consequence of his indisposition. A very gentlemanly man, Mrs. Henry Spiker's brother, Mr. Copperfield.'

I murmured an assent, which was full of feeling, considering that I knew nothing at all about him; and I inquired what Mr. Traddles was by profession.

'Traddles,' returned Mr. Waterbrook, 'is a young man reading for the bar. Yes. He is quite a good fellow—nobody's enemy but his own.'

'Is he his own enemy?' said I, sorry to hear this.

'Well,' returned Mr. Waterbrook, pursing up his mouth, and playing with his watch-chain, in a comfortable, prosperous sort of way. 'I should say he was one of those men who stand in their own light. Yes, I should say he would never, for example, be worth five hundred pound. Traddles was recommended to me, by a professional friend. Oh yes. Yes. He has a kind of talent, for drawing briefs, and stating a case in writing, plainly. I am able to throw something in Traddles's way, in the course of the year; something—for him—considerable. Oh yes. Yes.'

I was much impressed by the extremely comfortable and satisfied manner in which Mr. Waterbrook delivered himself of this little word 'Yes,' every now and then. There was wonderful expression in it. It completely conveyed the idea of a man who had been born, not to say with a silver spoon, but with a scaling ladder, and had gone on mounting all the heights of life one after another, until now he looked, from the top of the fortifications, with the eye of a philosopher and a patron, on the people down in the trenches.

My reflections on this theme were still in progress when dinner was announced. Mr. Waterbrook went down with Hamlet's aunt. Mr. Henry Spiker took Mrs. Waterbrook. Agnes, whom I should have liked to take myself, was given to a simpering fellow with weak legs. Uriah, Traddles, and I, as the junior part of the company, went down last, how we could. I was not so vexed at losing Agnes as I might have been, since it gave me an opportunity of making myself known to Traddles on the stairs, who greeted me with great fervour: while Uriah writhed with such unobtrusive satisfaction and self-abasement, that I could gladly have pitched him over the banisters.

Traddles and I were separated at table, being billeted in two remote corners: he in the glare of a red velvet lady: I, in the gloom of Hamlet's aunt. The dinner was very long, and the conversation was about the Aristocracy—and Blood. Mrs. Waterbrook repeatedly told us, that if she had a weakness, it was Blood.

It occurred to me several times that we should have

got on better, if we had not been quite so genteel. We were so exceedingly genteel, that our scope was very limited. A Mr. and Mrs. Gulpidge were of the party, who had something to do at second-hand (at least, Mr. Gulpidge had), with the law business of the Bank; and what with the Bank, and what with the Treasury, we were as exclusive as the Court Circular. To mend the matter, Hamlet's aunt had the family failing of indulging in soliloquy, and held forth in a desultory manner, by herself, on every topic that was introduced. These were few enough, to be sure; but as we always fell back upon Blood, she had as wide a field for abstract speculation as her nephew himself.

We might have been a party of ogres, the conversation assumed such a sanguine complexion.

'I confess I am of Mrs. Waterbrook's opinion,' said Mr. Waterbrook, with his wine-glass at his eye. 'Other things are all very well in their way, but give me Blood!'

'Oh! There is nothing,' observed Hamlet's aunt, 'so satisfactory to one! There is nothing that is so much one's *beau-ideal* of—of all that sort of thing, speaking generally. There are some low minds (not many, I am happy to believe, but there are *some*) that would prefer to do what *I* should call bow down before idols. Positively idols! Before services, intellect, and so on. But these are intangible points. Blood is not so. We see Blood in a nose, and we know it. We meet with it in a chin, and we say, "There it is! That's Blood!" It is an actual matter of fact. We point it out. It admits of no doubt.'

The simpering fellow with the weak legs, who had taken Agnes down, stated the question more decisively yet, I thought.

'Oh, you know, deuce take it,' said this gentleman,

looking round the board with an imbecile smile, 'we can't forego Blood, you know. We must have Blood, you know. Some young fellows, you know, may be a little behind their station, perhaps, in point of education and behaviour, and may go a little wrong, you know, and get themselves and other people into a variety of fixes—and all that—but deuce take it, it's delightful to reflect that they've got Blood in 'em! Myself, I'd rather at any time be knocked down by a man who had got Blood in him, than I'd be picked up by a man who hadn't!'

This sentiment, as compressing the general question into a nutshell, gave the utmost satisfaction, and brought the gentleman into great notice until the ladies retired. After that, I observed that Mr. Gulpidge and Mr. Henry Spiker, who had hitherto been very distant, entered into a defensive alliance against us, the common enemy, and exchanged a mysterious dialogue across the table for our defeat and overthrow.

'That affair of the first bond for four thousand five hundred pounds has not taken the course that was expected, Gulpidge,' said Mr. Henry Spiker.

'Do you mean the D. of A.'s?' said Mr. Spiker.

'The C. of B.'s?' said Mr. Gulpidge.

Mr. Spiker raised his eyebrows, and looked much concerned.

'When the question was referred to Lord—I needn't name him,' said Mr. Gulpidge, checking himself—

'I understand,' said Mr. Spiker, 'N.'

Mr. Gulpidge darkly nodded—'was referred to him, his answer was, "Money, or no release."'

'Lord bless my soul!' cried Mr. Spiker.

'Money or no release,' repeated Mr. Gulpidge,

firmly. 'The next in reversion—you understand me?'

'K.,' said Mr. Spiker, with an ominous look.

'—K. then positively refused to sign. He was attended at Newmarket for that purpose, and he point-blank refused to do it.'

Mr. Spiker was so interested, that he became quite stony.

'So the matter rests at this hour,' said Mr. Gulpidge, throwing himself back in his chair. 'Our friend Waterbrook will excuse me if I forbear to explain myself generally, on account of the magnitude of the interests involved.'

Mr. Waterbrook was only too happy, as it appeared to me, to have such interests, and such names, even hinted at, across his table. He assumed an expression of gloomy intelligence (though I am persuaded he knew no more about the discussion than I did), and highly approved of the discretion that had been observed. Mr. Spiker, after the receipt of such a confidence, naturally desired to favour his friend with a confidence of his own; therefore the foregoing dialogue was succeeded by another, in which it was Mr. Gulpidge's turn to be surprised, and that by another in which the surprise came round to Mr. Spiker's turn again, and so on, turn and turn about. All this time we, the outsiders, remained oppressed by the tremendous interests involved in the conversation; and our host regarded us with pride, as the victims of a salutary awe and astonishment.

I was very glad indeed to get upstairs to Agnes, and to talk with her in a corner, and to introduce Traddles to her, who was shy, but agreeable, and the same good-natured creature still. As he was obliged to leave early, on account of going away next morning for a month, I had not nearly so much conversation with him as I could have wished; but we exchanged addresses, and promised ourselves the pleasure of another meeting when he should come back to town. He was greatly interested to hear that I knew Steerforth, and spoke of him with such warmth that I made him tell Agnes what he thought of him. But Agnes only looked at me the while, and very slightly shook her head when only I observed her.

As she was not among people with whom I believed she could be very much at home, I was almost glad to hear that she was going away within a few days, though I was sorry at the prospect of parting from her again so soon. This caused me to remain until all the company were gone. Conversing with her, and hearing her sing, was such a delightful reminder to me of my happy life in the grave old house she had made so beautiful, that I could have remained there half the night; but, having no excuse for staying any longer, when the lights of Mr. Waterbrook's society were all snuffed out, I took my leave very much against my inclination. I felt then, more than ever, that she was my better Angel; and if I thought of her sweet face and placid smile, as though they had shone on me from some removed being, like an Angel, I hope I thought no harm.

I have said that the company were all gone; but I ought to have excepted Uriah, whom I don't include in that denomination, and who had never ceased to hover near us. He was close behind me when I went downstairs. He was close beside me, when I walked away from the house, slowly fitting his long skeleton fingers into the still longer fingers of a great Guy Fawkes pair of gloves.

It was in no disposition for Uriah's company, but

in remembrance of the entreaty Agnes had made to me, that I asked him if he would come home to my rooms and have some coffee.

'Oh, really, Master Copperfield,' he rejoined,—'I beg your pardon, Mister Copperfield, but the other comes so natural,—I don't like that you should put a constraint upon yourself to ask an umble person like me to your ouse.'

'There is no constraint in the case,' said I. 'Will you come?'

'I should like to, very much,' replied Uriah, with a writhe.

'Well, then, come along!' said I.

I could not help being rather short with him, but he appeared not to mind it. We went the nearest way, without conversing much upon the road; and he was so humble in respect of those scarecrow gloves, that he was still putting them on, and seemed to have made no advance in that labour, when we got to my place.

I led him up the dark stairs, to prevent his knocking his head against anything, and really his damp cold hand felt so like a frog in mine, that I was tempted to drop it and run away. Agnes and hospitality prevailed, however, and I conducted him to my fireside. When I lighted my candles, he fell into meek transports with the room that was revealed to him; and when I heated the coffee in an unassuming blocktin vessel in which Mrs. Crupp delighted to prepare it (chiefly, I believe, because it was not intended for the purpose, being a shaving-pot, and because there was a patent invention of great price mouldering away in the pantry), he professed so much emotion, that I could joyfully have scalded him.

'Oh, really, Master Copperfield,—I mean Mister Copperfield,' said Uriah, 'to see you waiting upon me

is what I never could have expected! But, one way
and another, so many things happen to me which I
never could have expected, I am sure, in my umble
station, that it seems to rain blessings on my ed.
You have heard something, I des-say, of a change in
my expectations, Master Copperfield,—*I* should say,
Mister Copperfield?'

As he sat on my sofa, with his long knees drawn
up under his coffee-cup, his hat and gloves upon the
ground close to him, his spoon going softly round
and round, his shadowless red eyes, which looked as
if they had scorched their lashes off, turned towards
me without looking at me, the disagreeable dints I
have formerly described in his nostrils coming and
going with his breath, and a snaky undulation pervading his frame from his chin to his boots, I decided
in my own mind that I disliked him intensely. It
made me very uncomfortable to have him for a guest,
for I was young then, and unused to disguise what
I so strongly felt.

'You have heard something, I des-say, of a change
in my expectations, Master Copperfield,—I should
say, Mister Copperfield?' observed Uriah.

'Yes,' said I, 'something.'

'Ah! I thought Miss Agnes would know of it!'
he quietly returned. 'I 'm glad to find Miss Agnes
knows of it. Oh, thank you, Master—Mister Copperfield!'

I could have thrown my bootjack at him (it lay
ready on the rug), for having entrapped me into the
disclosure of anything concerning Agnes, however
immaterial. But I only drank my coffee.

'What a prophet you have shown yourself, Mister
Copperfield!' pursued Uriah. 'Dear me, what a
prophet you have proved yourself to be! Don't you
remember saying to me once, that perhaps I should

be a partner in Mr. Wickfield's business, and perhaps it might be Wickfield and Heep? *You* may not recollect it; but when a person is umble, Master Copperfield, a person treasures such things up!'

'I recollect talking about it,' said I, 'though I certainly did not think it very likely then.'

'Oh! who *would* have thought it likely, Mister Copperfield!' returned Uriah, enthusiastically. 'I am sure I didn't myself. I recollect saying with my own lips that I was much too umble. So I considered myself really and truly.'

He sat, with that carved grin on his face, looking at the fire, as I looked at him.

'But the umblest persons, Master Copperfield,' he presently resumed, 'may be the instruments of good. I am glad to think I have been the instrument of good to Mr. Wickfield, and that I may be more so. Oh, what a worthy man he is, Mister Copperfield, but how imprudent he has been!'

'I am sorry to hear it,' said I. I could not help adding, rather pointedly, 'on all accounts.'

'Decidedly so, Mister Copperfield,' replied Uriah. 'On all accounts. Miss Agnes's above all! You don't remember your own eloquent expressions, Master Copperfield; but *I* remember how you said one day that everybody must admire her, and how I thanked you for it! You have forgot that I have no doubt, Master Copperfield?'

'No,' said I, drily.

'Oh, how glad I am you have not!' exclaimed Uriah. 'To think that you should be the first to kindle the sparks of ambition in my umble breast, and that you've not forgot it! Oh!—Would you excuse me asking for a cup more coffee?'

Something in the emphasis he laid upon the kindling of those sparks, and something in the glance he

directed at me as he said it, had made me start as if I
had seen him illuminated by a blaze of light. Recalled by his request, preferred in quite another tone
of voice, I did the honours of the shaving-pot; but
I did them with an unsteadiness of hand, a sudden
sense of being no match for him, and a perplexed
suspicious anxiety as to what he might be going to
say next, which I felt could not escape his observation.

He said nothing at all. He stirred his coffee round
and round, he sipped it, he felt his chin softly with
his grisly hand, he looked at the fire, he looked about
the room, he gasped rather than smiled at me, he
writhed and undulated about, in his deferential servility, he stirred and sipped again, but he left the
renewal of the conversation to me.

'So, Mr. Wickfield,' said I, at last, 'who is worth
five hundred of you—or me'; for my life, I think, I
could not have helped dividing that part of the sentence with an awkward jerk; 'has been imprudent,
has he, Mr. Heep?'

'Oh, very imprudent indeed, Master Copperfield,'
returned Uriah, sighing modestly. 'Oh, very much
so! But I wish you 'd call me Uriah, if you please.
It 's like old times.'

'Well! Uriah,' said I, bolting it out with some
difficulty.

'Thank you!' he returned, with fervour. 'Thank
you, Master Copperfield! It 's like the blowing of
old breezes or the ringing of old bellses to hear *you*
say Uriah. I beg your pardon. Was I making any
observation?'

'About Mr. Wickfield,' I suggested.

'Oh! Yes, truly,' said Uriah. 'Ah! Great im-
prudence, Master Copperfield. It 's a topic that I
wouldn't touch upon, to any soul but you. Even to

you I can only touch upon it, and no more. If any one else had been in my place during the last few years, by this time he would have had Mr. Wickfield (oh, what a worthy man he is, Master Copperfield, too!) under his thumb. Un—der—his thumb,' said Uriah, very slowly, as he stretched out his cruel-looking hand above my table, and pressed his own thumb down upon it, until it shook, and shook the room.

If I had been obliged to look at him with his splay foot on Mr. Wickfield's head, I think I could scarcely have hated him more.

'Oh dear, yes, Master Copperfield,' he proceeded, in a soft voice, most remarkably contrasting with the action of his thumb, which did not diminish its hard pressure in the least degree, 'there's no doubt of it. There would have been loss, disgrace, I don't know what all. Mr. Wickfield knows it. I am the umble instrument of umbly serving him, and he puts me on an eminence I hardly could have hoped to reach. How thankful should I be!' With his face turned towards me, as he finished, but without looking at me, he took his crooked thumb off the spot where he had planted it, and slowly and thoughtfully scraped his lank jaw with it, as if he were shaving himself.

I recollect well how indignantly my heart beat, as I saw his crafty face, with the appropriately red light of the fire upon it, preparing for something else.

'Master Copperfield,' he began—'but am I keeping you up?'

'You are not keeping me up. I generally go to bed late.'

'Thank you, Master Copperfield! I have risen from my umble station since first you used to address me, it is true; but I am umble still. I hope I never shall be otherwise than umble. You will not think the worse of my umbleness, if I make a little confidence to you, Master Copperfield? Will you?'

'Oh no,' said I, with an effort.

'Thank you!' He took out his pocket-handkerchief, and began wiping the palms of his hands. 'Miss Agnes, Master Copperfield—'

'Well, Uriah?'

'Oh, how pleasant to be called Uriah, spontaneously!' he cried; and gave himself a jerk, like a convulsive fish. 'You thought her looking very beautiful to-night, Master Copperfield?'

'I thought her looking as she always does: superior, in all respects, to every one around her,' I returned.

'Oh, thank you! It's so true!' he cried. 'Oh, thank you very much for that!'

'Not at all,' I said, loftily. 'There is no reason why you should thank me.'

'Why that, Master Copperfield,' said Uriah, 'is, in fact, the confidence that I am going to take the liberty of reposing. Umble as I am,' he wiped his hands harder, and looked at them and at the fire by turns, 'umble as my mother is, and lowly as our poor but honest roof has ever been, the image of Miss Agnes (I don't mind trusting you with my secret, Master Copperfield, for I have always overflowed towards you since the first moment I had the pleasure of beholding you in a pony-shay) has been in my breast for years. Oh, Master Copperfield, with what a pure affection do I love the ground my Agnes walks on!'

I believe I had a delirious idea of seizing the red-hot poker out of the fire, and running him through with it. It went from me with a shock, like a ball fired from a rifle: but the image of Agnes, outraged by so much as a thought of this red-headed animal's, remained in my mind (when I looked at him, sitting all awry as if his mean soul griped his body), and made me giddy. He seemed to swell and grow before my eyes; the room seemed full of the echoes of his voice; and the strange feeling (to which, perhaps, no one is quite a stranger) that all this had occurred before, at some indefinite time, and that I knew what he was going to say next, took possession of me.

A timely observation of the sense of power that there was in his face, did more to bring back to my remembrance the entreaty of Agnes, in its full force, than any effort I could have made. I asked him, with a better appearance of composure than I could have thought possible a minute before, whether he had made his feeling known to Agnes.

'Oh no, Master Copperfield!' he returned; 'oh dear, no! Not to any one but you. You see I am only just emerging from my lowly station. I rest a good deal of hope on her observing how useful I am to her father (for I trust to be very useful to him indeed, Master Copperfield), and how I smooth the way for him, and keep him straight. She's so much attached to her father, Master Copperfield (oh what a lovely thing it is in a daughter!), that I think she may come, on his account, to be kind to me.'

I fathomed the depth of the rascal's whole scheme, and understood why he laid it bare.

'If you'll have the goodness to keep my secret, Master Copperfield,' he pursued, 'and not, in general, to go against me, I shall take it as a particular favour. You wouldn't wish to make unpleasantness. I know what a friendly heart you've got; but having only known me on my umble footing (on my umblest, I should say, for I am very umble still), you might, unbeknown, go against me rather, with my Agnes. I call her mine, you see, Master Copperfield.

There's a song that says, "I'd crowns resign, to call her mine!" I hope to do it, one of these days.'

Dear Agnes! So much too loving and too good for any one that I could think of, was it possible that she was reserved to be the wife of such a wretch as this!

'There's no hurry at present, you know, Master Copperfield,' Uriah proceeded, in his slimy way, as I sat gazing at him, with this thought in my mind. 'My Agnes is very young still; and mother and me will have to work our way upwards, and make a good many new arrangements, before it would be quite convenient. So I shall have time gradually to make her familiar with my hopes, as opportunities offer. Oh, I'm so much obliged to you for this confidence! Oh, it's such a relief, you can't think, to know that you understand our situation, and are certain (as you wouldn't wish to make unpleasantness in the family) not to go against me!'

He took the hand which I dared not withhold, and having given it a damp squeeze, referred to his pale-faced watch.

'Dear me!' he said, 'it's past one. The moments slip away so, in the confidence of old times, Master Copperfield, that it's almost half-past one!'

I answered that I thought it was later. Not that I had really thought so, but because my conversational powers were effectually scattered.

'Dear me!' he said, considering. 'The ouse that I am stopping at—a sort of a private hotel and boarding ouse, Master Copperfield, near the New River ed—will have gone to bed these two hours.'

'I am sorry,' I returned, 'that there is only one bed here, and that I—'

'Oh, don't think of mentioning beds, Master Copperfield!' he rejoined ecstatically, drawing up one leg. 'But *would* you have any objections to my laying down before the fire?'

'If it comes to that,' I said, 'pray take my bed, and I 'll lie down before the fire.'

His repudiation of this offer was almost shrill enough, in the excess of its surprise and humility, to have penetrated to the ears of Mrs. Crupp, then sleeping, I suppose, in a distant chamber, situated at about the level of low water-mark, soothed in her slumbers by the ticking of an incorrigible clock, to which she always referred me when we had any little difference on the score of punctuality, and which was never less than three-quarters of an hour too slow, and had always been put right in the morning by the best authorities. As no arguments I could urge, in my bewildered condition, had the least effect upon his modesty in inducing him to accept my bedroom, I was obliged to make the best arrangements I could, for his repose before the fire. The mattress of the sofa (which was a great deal too short for his lank figure), the sofa pillows, a blanket, the table-cover, a clean breakfast-cloth, and a great-coat, made him a bed and covering, for which he was more than thankful. Having lent him a night-cap, which he put on at once, and in which he made such an awful figure, that I have never worn one since, I left him to his rest.

I never shall forget that night. I never shall forget how I turned and tumbled; how I wearied myself with thinking about Agnes and this creature; how I considered what could I do, and what ought I to do; how I could come to no other conclusion than that the best course for her peace, was to do nothing, and to keep to myself what I had heard. If I went to sleep for a few moments, the image of Agnes with her tender eyes, and of her father looking fondly on her, as I had so often seen him look, arose before me with appealing faces, and filled me with vague terrors. When I awoke, the recollection that Uriah was lying in the next room, sat heavy on me like a waking nightmare; and oppressed me with a leaden dread, as if I had had some meaner quality of devil for a lodger.

The poker got into my dozing thoughts besides, and wouldn't come out. I thought, between sleeping and waking, that it was still red-hot, and I had snatched it out of the fire, and run him through the body. I was so haunted at last by the idea, though I knew there was nothing in it, that I stole into the next room to look at him. There I saw him, lying on his back, with his legs extending to I don't know where, gurglings taking place in his throat, stoppages in his nose, and his mouth open like a post-office. He was so much worse in reality than in my distempered fancy, that afterwards I was attracted to him in very repulsion, and could not help wandering in and out every half-hour or so, and taking another look at him. Still, the long, long night seemed heavy and hopeless as ever, and no promise of day was in the murky sky.

When I saw him going downstairs early in the morning (for, thank Heaven! he would not stay to breakfast), it appeared to me as if the night was going away in his person. When I went out to the Commons, I charged Mrs. Crupp with particular directions to leave the windows open, that my sitting-room might be aired, and purged of his presence.

CHAPTER XXVI

I FALL INTO CAPTIVITY

I saw no more of Uriah Heep until the day when Agnes left town. I was at the coach-office to take leave of her and see her go; and there was he, returning to Canterbury by the same conveyance. It was some small satisfaction to me to observe his spare, short-waisted, high-shouldered, mulberry-coloured great-coat perched up, in company with an umbrella like a small tent, on the edge of the back-seat on the roof, while Agnes was, of course, inside; but what I underwent in my efforts to be friendly with him, while Agnes looked on, perhaps deserved that little recompense. At the coach-window, as at the dinner-party, he hovered about us without a moment's intermission, like a great vulture: gorging himself on every syllable that I said to Agnes, or Agnes said to me.

In the state of trouble into which his disclosure by my fire had thrown me, I had thought very much of the words Agnes had used in reference to the partnership: 'I did what I hope was right. Feeling sure that it was necessary for papa's peace that the sacrifice should be made, I entreated him to make it.' A miserable foreboding that she would yield to, and sustain herself by, the same feeling in reference to any sacrifice for his sake, had oppressed me ever since. I knew how she loved him. I knew what the devotion of her nature was. I knew from her own lips that she regarded herself as the innocent cause of his errors, and as owing him a great debt she ardently desired to pay. I had no consolation in seeing how different she was from this detestable Rufus with the mulberry-coloured great-coat, for I felt that in the very difference between them, in the self-denial of her pure soul and the sordid baseness of his, the greatest danger lay. All this, doubtless, he knew thoroughly, and had, in his cunning, considered well.

Yet, I was so certain that the prospect of such a sacrifice afar off, must destroy the happiness of Agnes; and I was so sure, from her manner, of its being unseen by her then, and having cast no shadow on her yet; that I could as soon have injured her, as given her any warning of what impended. Thus it was that we parted without explanation: she waving her hand and smiling farewell from the coach-window; her evil genius writhing on the roof, as if he had her in his clutches and triumphed.

I could not get over this farewell glimpse of them for a long time. When Agnes wrote to tell me of her safe arrival, I was as miserable as when I saw her going away. Whenever I fell into a thoughtful state, this subject was sure to present itself, and all my uneasiness was sure to be redoubled. Hardly a night passed without my dreaming of it. It became a part of my life, and as inseparable from my life as my own head.

I had ample leisure to refine upon my uneasiness: for Steerforth was at Oxford, as he wrote to me, and when I was not at the Commons, I was very much alone. I believe I had at this time some lurking distrust of Steerforth. I wrote to him most affectionately in reply to his, but I think I was glad, upon the whole, that he could not come to London just then. I suspect the truth to be, that the influence of Agnes was upon me, undisturbed by the sight of him; and that it was the more powerful with me, because she had so large a share in my thoughts and interest.

In the meantime, days and weeks slipped away.

I was articled to Spenlow and Jorkins. I had ninety pounds a year (exclusive of my house-rent and sundry collateral matters) from my aunt. My rooms were engaged for twelve months certain: and though I still found them dreary of an evening, and the evenings long, I could settle down into a state of equable low spirits, and resign myself to coffee; which I seem, on looking back, to have taken by the gallon at about this period of my existence. At about this time, too, I made three discoveries: first, that Mrs. Crupp was a martyr to a curious disorder called 'the spazzums,' which was generally accompanied with inflammation of the nose, and required to be constantly treated with peppermint; secondly, that something peculiar in the temperature of my pantry, made the brandy-bottles burst; thirdly, that I was alone in the world, and much given to record that circumstance in fragments of English versification.

On the day when I was articled, no festivity took place, beyond my having sandwiches and sherry into the office for the clerks, and going alone to the theatre at night. I went to see 'The Stranger' as a Doctors' Commons sort of play, and was so dreadfully cut up, that I hardly knew myself in my own glass when I got home. Mr. Spenlow remarked on this occasion, when we concluded our business, that he should have been happy to have seen me at his house at Norwood to celebrate our becoming connected, but for his domestic arrangements being in some disorder, on account of the expected return of his daughter from finishing her education at Paris. But, he intimated that when she came home he should hope to have the pleasure of entertaining me. I knew that he was a widower with one daughter, and expressed my acknowledgments.

Mr. Spenlow was as good as his word. In a week or two, he referred to this engagement, and said, that if I would do him the favour to come down next Saturday, and stay till Monday, he would be extremely happy. Of course I said I *would* do him the favour; and he was to drive me down in his phaeton, and to bring me back.

When the day arrived, my very carpet-bag was an object of veneration to the stipendiary clerks, to whom the house at Norwood was a sacred mystery. One of them informed me that he had heard that Mr. Spenlow ate entirely off plate and china; and another hinted at champagne being constantly on draught, after the usual custom of table beer. The old clerk with the wig, whose name was Mr. Tiffey, had been down on business several times in the course of his career, and had on each occasion penetrated to the breakfast-parlour. He described it as an apartment of the most sumptuous nature, and said that he had drank brown East India sherry there, of a quality so precious as to make a man wink.

We had an adjourned cause in the Consistory that day—about excommunicating a baker who had been objecting in a vestry to a paving-rate—and as the evidence was just twice the length of Robinson Crusoe, according to a calculation I made, it was rather late in the day before we finished. However, we got him excommunicated for six weeks, and sentenced in no end of costs; and then the baker's proctor, and the judge, and the advocates on both sides (who were all nearly related), went out of town together, and Mr. Spenlow and I drove away in the phaeton.

The phaeton was a very handsome affair; the horses arched their necks and lifted up their legs as if they knew they belonged to Doctors' Commons. There was a good deal of competition in the Commons on all points of display, and it turned out some very choice equipages then; though I always have considered, and always shall consider, that in my time the great article of competition there was starch: which I think was worn among the proctors to as great an extent as it is in the nature of man to bear.

We were very pleasant, going down, and Mr. Spenlow gave me some hints in reference to my profession. He said it was the genteelest profession in the world, and must on no account be confounded with the profession of a solicitor: being quite another sort of thing, infinitely more exclusive, less mechanical, and more profitable. We took things much more easily in the Commons than they could be taken anywhere else, he observed, and that sets us, as a privileged class, apart. He said it was impossible to conceal the disagreeable fact, that we were chiefly employed by solicitors; but he gave me to understand that they were an inferior race of men, universally looked down upon by all proctors of any pretensions.

I asked Mr. Spenlow what he considered the best sort of professional business? He replied, that a good case of a disputed will, where there was a neat little estate of thirty or forty thousand pounds, was, perhaps, the best of all. In such a case, he said, not only were there very pretty pickings, in the way of arguments at every stage of the proceedings, and mountains upon mountains of evidence on interrogatory and counter-interrogatory (to say nothing of an appeal lying, first to the Delegates, and then to the Lords); but, the costs being pretty sure to come out of the estate at last, both sides went at it in a lively and spirited manner, and expense was no consideration. Then, he launched into a general eulogium on the Commons. What was to be particularly admired (he said) in the Commons, was its compactness. It was the most conveniently organised place in the world. It was the complete idea of snugness. It lay in a nut-shell. For example: You brought a divorce case, or a restitution case, into the Consistory. Very good. You tried it in the Consistory. You made a quiet little round game of it, among a family group, and you played it out at leisure. Suppose you were not satisfied with the Consistory, what did you do then? Why, you went into the Arches. What was the Arches? The same court, in the same room, with the same bar, and the same practitioners, but another judge, for there the Consistory judge could plead any court-day as an advocate. Well, you played your round game out again. Still you were not satisfied. Very good. What did you do then? Why, you went to the Delegates. Who were the Delegates? Why, the Ecclesiastical Delegates were the advocates without any business, who had looked on at the round game when it was playing in both courts, and had seen the cards shuffled, and cut, and played, and had talked to all the players about it, and now came fresh, as judges, to settle the matter to the satisfaction of everybody! Discontented people might talk of corruption in the Commons, closeness in the Commons, and the necessity of reforming the Commons, said Mr. Spenlow solemnly, in conclusion; but when the price of wheat per bushel had been highest, the Commons had been busiest; and a man might lay his hand upon his heart, and say this to the whole world,—'Touch the Commons, and down comes the country!'

I listened to all this with attention; and though, I must say, I had my doubts whether the country was quite as much obliged to the Commons as Mr. Spenlow made out, I respectfully deferred to his opinion. That about the price of wheat per bushel, I modestly felt was too much for my strength, and quite settled the question. I have never, to this hour, got the better of that bushel of wheat. It has re-appeared to annihilate me, all through my life, in connection with all kinds of subjects. I don't know now, exactly, what it has to do with me, or what right it has to crush me, on an infinite variety of occasions; but whenever I see my old friend the bushel brought in by the head and shoulders (as he always is, I observe), I give up a subject for lost.

This is a digression. *I* was not the man to touch the Commons, and bring down the country. I submissively expressed, by my silence, my acquiescence in all I had heard from my superior in years and knowledge; and we talked about 'The Stranger' and the Drama, and the pair of horses, until we came to Mr. Spenlow's gate.

There was a lovely garden to Mr. Spenlow's house; and though that was not the best time of the year for seeing a garden, it was so beautifully kept, that I was quite enchanted. There was a charming lawn, there were clusters of trees, and there were prospective walks that I could just distinguish in the dark, arched over with trellis-work, on which shrubs and flowers grew in the growing season. 'Here Miss Spenlow walks by herself,' I thought. 'Dear me!'

We went into the house, which was cheerfully lighted up, and into a hall where there were all sorts of hats, caps, great-coats, plaids, gloves, whips, and walking sticks. 'Where is Miss Dora?' said Mr. Spenlow to the servant. 'Dora!' I thought. 'What a beautiful name!'

We turned into a room near at hand (I think it was the identical breakfast-room, made memorable by the brown East India sherry), and I heard a voice say, 'Mr. Copperfield, my daughter Dora, and

my daughter Dora's confidential friend!'   It was, no
doubt, Mr. Spenlow's voice, but I didn't know it, and
I didn't care whose it was.   All was over in a moment.
I had fulfiled my destiny.   I was a captive and a
slave.   I loved Dora Spenlow to distraction!

She was more than human to me.   She was a Fairy,
a Sylph, I don't know what she was—anything that
no one ever saw, and everything that everybody ever
wanted.   I was swallowed up in an abyss of love in
an instant.   There was no pausing on the brink; no
looking down, or looking back; I was gone, headlong, before I had sense to say a word to her.

'I,' observed a well-remembered voice, when I had
bowed and murmured something, 'have seen Mr.
Copperfield before.'

The speaker was not Dora.   No; the confidential
friend, Miss Murdstone!

I don't think I was much astonished.   To the best
of my judgment, no capacity of astonishment was
left in me.   There was nothing worth mentioning
in the material world, but Dora Spenlow, to be astonished about.   I said, 'How do you do, Miss Murdstone?   I hope you are well?'   She answered, 'Very
well.'   I said, 'How is Mr. Murdstone?'   She replied, 'My brother is robust, I am obliged to you.'

Mr. Spenlow, who, I suppose, had been surprised
to see us recognise each other, then put in his word.

'I am glad to find,' he said, 'Copperfield, that you
and Miss Murdstone are already acquainted.'

'Mr. Copperfield and myself,' said Miss Murdstone, with severe composure, 'are connections.   We
were once slightly acquainted.   It was in his childish
days.   Circumstances have separated us since.   I
should not have known him.'

I replied that I should have known her, anywhere.
Which was true enough.

'Miss Murdstone has had the goodness,' said Mr. Spenlow to me, 'to accept the office—if I may so describe it—of my daughter Dora's confidential friend. My daughter Dora having, unhappily, no mother, Miss Murdstone is obliging enough to become her companion and protector.'

A passing thought occurred to me that Miss Murdstone, like the pocket-instrument called a life-preserver, was not so much designed for purposes of protection as of assault. But as I had none but passing thoughts for any subject save Dora, I glanced at her, directly afterwards, and was thinking that I saw, in her prettily pettish manner, that she was not very much inclined to be particularly confidential to her companion and protector, when a bell rang, which Mr. Spenlow said was the first dinner-bell, and so carried me off to dress.

The idea of dressing one's self, or doing anything in the way of action, in that state of love, was a little too ridiculous. I could only sit down before my fire, biting the key of my carpet-bag, and think of the captivating, girlish, bright-eyed, lovely Dora. What a form she had, what a face she had, what a graceful, variable, enchanting manner!

The bell rang again so soon that I made a mere scramble of my dressing, instead of the careful operation I could have wished under the circumstances, and went down stairs. There was some company. Dora was talking to an old gentleman with a grey head. Grey as he was—and a great-grandfather into the bargain, for he said so—I was madly jealous of him.

What a state of mind I was in! I was jealous of everybody. I couldn't bear the idea of anybody knowing Mr. Spenlow better than I did. It was torturing to me to hear them talk of occurrences in which I had had no share. When a most amiable person, with a highly polished bald head, asked me across the dinner-table, if that were the first occasion of my seeing the grounds, I could have done anything to him that was savage and revengeful.

I don't remember who was there, except Dora. I have not the least idea what we had for dinner, besides Dora. My impression is, that I dined off Dora entirely, and sent away half a dozen plates untouched. I sat next to her. I talked to her. She had the most delightful little voice, the gayest little laugh, the pleasantest and most fascinating little ways, that ever led a lost youth into hopeless slavery. She was rather diminutive altogether. So much the more precious, I thought.

When she went out of the room with Miss Murdstone (no other ladies were of the party), I fell into a reverie, only disturbed by the cruel apprehension that Miss Murdstone would disparage me to her. The amiable creature with the polished head told me a long story, which I think was about gardening. I think I heard him say, 'my gardener,' several times. I seemed to pay the deepest attention to him, but I was wandering in a garden of Eden all the while, with Dora.

My apprehensions of being disparaged to the object of my engrossing affection were revived when we went into the drawing-room, by the grim and distant aspect of Miss Murdstone. But I was relieved of them in an unexpected manner.

'David Copperfield,' said Miss Murdstone, beckoning me aside into a window. 'A word.'

I confronted Miss Murdstone alone.

'David Copperfield,' said Miss Murdstone, 'I need not enlarge upon family circumstances. They are not a tempting subject.'

'Far from it, ma'am,' I returned.

'Far from it,' assented Miss Murdstone. 'I do not wish to revive the memory of past differences, or of past outrages. I have received outrages from a person—a female, I am sorry to say, for the credit of my sex—who is not to be mentioned without scorn and disgust; and therefore I would rather not mention her.'

I felt very fiery on my aunt's account; but I said it would certainly be better, if Miss Murdstone pleased, *not* to mention her. I could not hear her disrespectfully mentioned, I added, without expressing my opinion in a decided tone.

Miss Murdstone shut her eyes, and disdainfully inclined her head; then, slowly opening her eyes, resumed—

'David Copperfield, I shall not attempt to disguise the fact, that I formed an unfavourable opinion of you in your childhood. It may have been a mistaken one, or you may have ceased to justify it. That is not in question between us now. I belong to a family remarkable, I believe, for some firmness; and I am not the creature of circumstance or change. I may have my opinion of you. You may have your opinion of me.'

I inclined my head, in my turn.

'But it is not necessary,' said Miss Murdstone, 'that these opinions should come into collision here. Under existing circumstances, it is as well on all accounts that they should not. As the chances of life have brought us together again, and may bring us together on other occasions, I would say, let us meet here as distant acquaintances. Family circumstances are a sufficient reason for our only meeting on that footing, and it is quite unnecessary that either of us should make the other the subject of remark. Do you approve of this?'

'Miss Murdstone,' I returned, 'I think you and Mr. Murdstone used me very cruelly, and treated my mother with great unkindness. I shall always think so, as long as I live. But I quite agree in what you propose.'

Miss Murdstone shut her eyes again, and bent her head. Then just touching the back of my hand with the tips of her cold, stiff fingers, she walked away, arranging the little fetters on her wrists and round her neck: which seemed to be the same set, in exactly the same state, as when I had seen her last. These reminded me, in reference to Miss Murdstone's nature, of the fetters over a jail-door; suggesting on the outside, to all beholders, what was to be expected within.

All I know of the rest of the evening is, that I heard the empress of my heart sing enchanted ballads in the French language, generally to the effect that, whatever was the matter, we ought always to dance, Ta ra la, Ta ra la! accompanying herself on a glorified instrument resembling a guitar. That I was lost in a blissful delirium. That I refused refreshment. That my soul recoiled from punch particularly. That when Miss Murdstone took her into custody and led her away, she smiled and gave me her delicious hand. That I caught a view of myself in a mirror, looking perfectly imbecile and idiotic. That I retired to bed in a most maudlin state of mind, and got up in a crisis of feeble infatuation.

It was a fine morning, and early, and I thought I would go and take a stroll down one of those wire-arched walks, and indulge my passion by dwelling on her image. On my way through the hall I encountered her little dog, who was called Jip—short for

Gipsy. I approached him tenderly, for I loved even him; but he showed his whole set of teeth, got under a chair expressly to snarl, and wouldn't hear of the least familiarity.

The garden was cool and solitary. I walked about, wondering what my feelings of happiness would be, if I could ever become engaged to this dear wonder. As to marriage, and fortune, and all that, I believe I was almost as innocently undesigning then, as when I loved little Em'ly. To be allowed to call her 'Dora,' to write to her, to dote upon and worship her, to have reason to think that when she was with other people she was yet mindful of me, seemed to me the summit of human ambition—I am sure it was the summit of mine. There is no doubt whatever that I was a lackadaisical young spooney; but there was a purity of heart in all this still, that prevents my having quite a contemptuous recollection of it, let me laugh as I may.

I had not been walking long, when I turned a corner, and met her. I tingle again from head to foot as my recollection turns that corner, and my pen shakes in my hand.

'You—are—out early, Miss Spenlow,' said I.

'It's so stupid at home,' she replied, 'and Miss Murdstone is so absurd! She talks such nonsense about its being necessary for the day to be aired, before I come out. Aired!' (She laughed, here, in the most melodious manner.) 'On a Sunday morning, when I don't practise, I must do something. So I told papa last night I *must* come out. Besides, it's the brightest time of the whole day. Don't you think so?'

I hazarded a bold flight, and said (not without stammering) that is was very bright to me then, though it had been very dark to me a minute before.

'Do you mean a compliment?' said Dora, 'or that the weather has really changed?'

I stammered worse than before, in replying that I meant no compliment, but the plain truth; though I was not aware of any change having taken place in the weather. It was in the state of my own feelings, I added bashfully: to clench the explanation.

I never saw such curls—how could I, for there never were such curls!—as those she shook out to hide her blushes. As to the straw hat and blue ribbons which was on the top of the curls, if I could only have hung it up in my room in Buckingham Street, what a priceless possession it would have been!

'You have just come home from Paris,' said I.

'Yes,' said she. 'Have you ever been there?'

'No.'

'Oh! I hope you'll go soon! You would like it so much!'

Traces of deep-seated anguish appeared in my countenance. That she should hope I would go, that she should think it possible I *could* go, was insupportable. I depreciated Paris; I depreciated France. I said I wouldn't leave England, under existing circumstances, for any earthly consideration. Nothing should induce me. In short, she was shaking the curls again, when the little dog came running along the walk to our relief.

He was mortally jealous of me, and persisted in barking at me. She took him in her arms—oh my goodness!—and caressed him, but he persisted upon barking still. He wouldn't let me touch him, when I tried; and then she beat him. It increased my sufferings greatly to see the pats she gave him for punishment on the bridge of his blunt nose, while he winked his eyes, and licked her hand, and still growled within himself like a little double-bass. At length he was quiet—well he might be with her dimpled chin upon his head!—and we walked away to look at a greenhouse.

'You are not very intimate with Miss Murdstone, are you?' said Dora. 'My pet.'

(The last two words were to the dog. Oh if they had only been to me!)

'No,' I replied. 'Not at all so.'

'She is a tiresome creature,' said Dora, pouting. 'I can't think what papa can have been about, when he chose such a vexatious thing to be my companion. Who wants a protector? I am sure *I* don't want a protector. Jip can protect me a great deal better than Miss Murdstone,—can't you, Jip, dear?'

He only winked lazily, when she kissed his ball of a head.

'Papa calls her my confidential friend, but I am sure she is no such thing—is she, Jip? We are not going to confide in any such cross people, Jip and I. We mean to bestow our confidence where we like, and to find out our own friends, instead of having them found out for us—don't we, Jip?'

Jip made a comfortable noise, in answer, a little like a tea-kettle when it sings. As for me, every word was a new heap of fetters, riveted above the last.

'It is very hard, because we have not a kind mamma, that we are to have, instead, a sulky, gloomy old thing like Miss Murdstone, always following us about—isn't it, Jip? Never mind, Jip. We won't be confidential, and we 'll make ourselves as happy as we can in spite of her, and we 'll teaze her, and not please her—won't we, Jip?'

If it had lasted any longer, I think I must have gone down on my knees on the gravel, with the probability before me of grazing them, and of being presently ejected from the premises besides. But, by good fortune the greenhouse was not far off, and these words brought us to it.

It contained quite a show of beautiful geraniums. We loitered along in front of them, and Dora often stopped to admire this one or that one, and I stopped to admire the same one, and Dora, laughing, held the dog up childishly, to smell the flowers; and if we were not all three in Fairyland, certainly *I* was. The scent of a geranium leaf, at this day, strikes me with a half-comical, half-serious wonder as to what change has come over me in a moment; and then I see a straw hat and blue ribbons, and a quantity of curls, and a little black dog being held up, in two slender arms, against a bank of blossoms and bright leaves.

Miss Murdstone had been looking for us. She found us here; and presented her uncongenial cheek, the little wrinkles in it filled with hair powder, to Dora to be kissed. Then she took Dora's arm in hers, and marched us in to breakfast as if it were a soldier's funeral.

How many cups of tea I drank, because Dora made it, I don't know. But, I perfectly remember that I sat swilling tea until my whole nervous system, if I had had any in those days, must have gone by the board. By and by we went to church. Miss Murdstone was between Dora and me in the pew; but I heard her sing, and the congregation vanished. A sermon was delivered—about Dora, of course—and I am afraid that is all I know of the service.

We had a quiet day. No company, a walk, a family dinner of four, and an evening of looking over books and pictures; Miss Murdstone with a homily before her, and her eye upon us, keeping guard vigilantly. Ah! little did Mr. Spenlow imagine, when he sat opposite to me after dinner that

day, with his pocket-handkerchief over his head, how
fervently I was embracing him, in my fancy, as his
son-in-law! Little did he think, when I took leave
of him at night, that he had just given his full consent
to my being engaged to Dora, and that I was invoking blessings on his head!

We departed early in the morning, for we had a
salvage case coming on in the Admiralty Court, requiring a rather accurate knowledge of the whole
science of navigation, in which (as we couldn't be
expected to know much about those matters in the
Commons) the judge had entreated two old Trinity
Masters, for charity's sake, to come and help him out.
Dora was at the breakfast-table to make the tea
again, however; and I had the melancholy pleasure
of taking off my hat to her in the phaeton, as she
stood on the door-step with Jip in her arms.

What the Admiralty was to me that day; what
nonsense I made of our case in my mind, as I listened to it; how I saw 'DORA' engraved upon the
blade of the silver oar which they lay upon the table,
as the emblem of that high jurisdiction; and how I
felt when Mr. Spenlow went home without me (I
had had an insane hope that he might take me back
again), as if I were a mariner myself, and the ship
to which I belonged had sailed away and left me
on a desert island; I shall make no fruitless effort
to describe. If that sleepy old Court could rouse
itself, and present in any visible form the day-dreams
I have had in it about Dora, it would reveal my
truth.

I don't mean the dreams that I dreamed on that
day alone, but day after day, from week to week,
and term to term. I went there, not to attend to
what was going on, but to think about Dora. If
ever I bestowed a thought upon the cases, as they

dragged their slow length before me, it was only to
wonder, in the matrimonial cases (remembering
Dora), how it was that married people could ever be
otherwise than happy; and, in the Prerogative cases,
to consider, if the money in question had been left
to me, what were the foremost steps I should immediately have taken in regard to Dora. Within
the first week of my passion, I bought four sumptuous waistcoats—not for myself; I had no pride in
them; for Dora—and took to wearing straw-coloured
kid gloves in the streets, and laid the foundations
of all the corns I have ever had. If the boots I
wore at that period could only be produced and
compared with the natural size of my feet, they
would show what the state of my heart was, in a
most affecting manner.

And yet, wretched cripple as I made myself by this
act of homage to Dora, I walked miles upon miles
daily in the hope of seeing her. Not only was I soon
as well known on the Norwood Road as the postmen
on that beat, but I pervaded London likewise. I
walked about the streets where the best shops for
ladies were, I haunted the Bazaar like an unquiet
spirit, I fagged through the Park again and again,
long after I was quite knocked up. Sometimes, at
long intervals and on rare occasions, I saw her. Perhaps I saw her glove waved in a carriage-window;
perhaps I met her, walked with her and Miss Murdstone a little way, and spoke to her. In the latter
case I was always very miserable afterwards, to think
that I had said nothing to the purpose; or that she
had no idea of the extent of my devotion, or that she
cared nothing about me. I was always looking out,
as may be supposed, for another invitation to Mr.
Spenlow's house. I was always being disappointed,
for I got none.

Mrs. Crupp must have been a woman of penetration; for when this attachment was but a few weeks old, and I had not had the courage to write more explicitly even to Agnes, than that I had been to Mr. Spenlow's house, 'whose family,' I added, 'consists of one daughter';—I say Mrs. Crupp must have been a woman of penetration, for, even in that early stage, she found it out. She came up to me one evening, when I was very low, to ask (she being then afflicted with the disorder I have mentioned) if I could oblige her with a little tincture of cardamums mixed with rhubarb, and flavoured with seven drops of the essence of cloves, which was the best remedy for her complaint;—or, if I had not such a thing by me, with a little brandy, which was the next best. It was not, she remarked, so palatable to her, but it was the next best. As I had never even heard of the first remedy, and always had the second in the closet, I gave Mrs. Crupp a glass of the second, which (that I might have no suspicion of its being devoted to any improper use) she began to take in my presence.

'Cheer up, sir,' said Mrs. Crupp. 'I can't abear to see you so, sir: I'm a mother myself.'

I did not quite perceive the application of this fact to *myself,* but I smiled on Mrs. Crupp, as benignly as was in my power.

'Come, sir,' said Mrs. Crupp. 'Excuse me. I know what it is, sir. There's a lady in the case.'

'Mrs. Crupp?' I returned, reddening.

'Oh, bless you! Keep a good heart, sir!' said Mrs. Crupp, nodding encouragement. 'Never say die, sir! If She don't smile upon you, there's a many as will. You're a young gentleman to *be* smiled on, Mr. Copperfull, and you must learn your walue, sir.'

Mrs. Crupp always called me Mr. Copperfull: firstly, no doubt, because it was not my name; and secondly, I am inclined to think, in some indistinct association with a washing-day.

'What makes you suppose there is any young lady in the case, Mrs. Crupp?' said I.

'Mr. Copperfull,' said Mrs. Crupp, with a great deal of feeling, 'I'm a mother myself.'

For some time Mrs. Crupp could only lay her hand upon her nankeen bosom, and fortify herself against returning pain with sips of her medicine. At length she spoke again.

'When the present set were took for you by your dear aunt, Mr. Copperfull,' said Mrs. Crupp, 'my remark were, I had now found summun I could care for. "Thank Ev'in!" were the expression, "I have now found summun I can care for!"—You don't eat enough, sir, nor yet drink.'

'Is that what you found your supposition on, Mrs. Crupp?' said I.

'Sir,' said Mrs. Crupp, in a tone approaching to severity, 'I've laundressed other young gentlemen besides yourself. A young gentleman may be over-careful of himself, or he may be under-careful of himself. He may brush his hair too regular, or too un-regular. He may wear his boots much too large for him, or much too small. That is according as the young gentleman has his original character formed. But let him go to which extreme he may, sir, there's a young lady in both of 'em.'

Mrs. Crupp shook her head in such a determined manner, that I had not an inch of 'vantage-ground left.

'It was but the gentleman which died here before yourself,' said Mrs. Crupp, 'that fell in love—with a barmaid—and had his waistcoats took in directly, though much swelled by drinking.'

'Mrs. Crupp,' said I, 'I must beg you not to connect the young lady in my case with a barmaid, or anything of that sort, if you please.'

'Mr. Copperfull,' returned Mrs. Crupp, 'I'm a mother myself, and not likely. I ask your pardon, sir, if I intrude. I should never wish to intrude where I were not welcome. But you are a young gentleman, Mr. Copperfull, and my adwice to you is, to cheer up, sir, to keep a good heart, and to know your own walue. If you was to take to something, sir,' said Mrs. Crupp, 'if you was to take to skittles, now, which is healthy, you might find it divert your mind, and do you good.'

With these words, Mrs. Crupp, affecting to be very careful of the brandy—which was all gone—thanked me with a majestic curtsey, and retired. As her figure disappeared into the gloom of the entry, this counsel certainly presented itself to my mind in the light of a slight liberty on Mrs. Crupp's part; but, at the same time, I was content to receive it, in another point of view, as a word to the wise, and a warning in future to keep my secret better.

CHAPTER XXVII

TOMMY TRADDLES

IT may have been in consequence of Mrs. Crupp's advice, and, perhaps, for no better reason than because there was a certain similarity in the sound of the word skittles and Traddles, that it came into my head, next day, to go and look after Traddles. The time he had mentioned was more than out, and he lived in a little street near the Veterinary College at Camden Town, which was principally tenanted, as one of our clerks who lived in that direction informed me, by gentlemen students, who bought live donkeys, and made experiments on those quadrupeds in their private apartments. Having obtained from this clerk a direction to the academic grove in question, I set out, the same afternoon, to visit my old schoolfellow.

I found that the street was not as desirable a one as I could have wished it to be, for the sake of Traddles. The inhabitants appeared to have a propensity to throw any little trifles they were not in want of, into the road: which not only made it rank and sloppy, but untidy too, on account of the cabbage-leaves. The refuse was not wholly vegetable either, for I myself saw a shoe, a doubled-up saucepan, a black bonnet, and an umbrella, in various stages of decomposition, as I was looking out for the number I wanted.

The general air of the place reminded me forcibly of the days when I lived with Mr. and Mrs. Micawber. An indescribable character of faded gentility that attached to the house I sought, and made it unlike all the other houses in the street—though they were all built on one monotonous pattern, and looked like the early copies of a blundering boy who was learning to make houses, and had not yet got out of his cramped brick-and-mortar pothooks—reminded me still more of Mr. and Mrs. Micawber. Happening to arrive at the door as it was opened to the afternoon milkman, I was reminded of Mr. and Mrs. Micawber more forcibly yet.

'Now,' said the milkman to a very youthful servant-girl. 'Has that there little bill of mine been heerd on?'

'Oh, master says he 'll attend to it immediate,' was the reply.

'Because,' said the milkman, going on as if he had received no answer, and speaking, as I judged from his tone, rather for the edification of somebody within the house, than of the youthful servant—an impression which was strengthened by his manner of glaring down the passage—'because that there little bill has been running so long, that I begin to believe it's run away altogether, and never won't be heerd of. Now, I'm not a going to stand it, you know!' said the milkman, still throwing his voice into the house, and glaring down the passage.

As to his dealing in the mild article of milk, by the bye, there never was a greater anomaly. His deportment would have been fierce in a butcher or a brandy-merchant.

The voice of the youthful servant became faint, but she seemed to me, from the action of her lips, again to murmur that it would be attended to immediate.

'I tell you what,' said the milkman, looking hard at her for the first time, and taking her by the chin, 'are you fond of milk?'

'Yes, I likes it,' she replied.

'Good,' said the milkman. 'Then you won't have none to-morrow. D' ye hear? Not a fragment of milk you won't have to-morrow.'

I thought she seemed, upon the whole, relieved, by the prospect of having any to-day. The milkman, after shaking his head at her, darkly, released her chin, and with anything rather than good-will opened his can, and deposited the usual quantity in the family jug. This done, he went away, muttering, and uttered the cry of his trade next door, in a vindictive shriek.

'Does Mr. Traddles live here?' I then inquired.

A mysterious voice from the end of the passage

replied 'Yes.' Upon which the youthful servant replied 'Yes.'

'Is he at home?' said I.

Again the mysterious voice replied in the affirmative, and again the servant echoed it. Upon this, I
walked in, and in pursuance of the servant's directions walked upstairs; conscious, as I passed the back
parlour-door, that I was surveyed by a mysterious
eye, probably belonging to the mysterious voice.

When I got to the top of the stairs—the house was
only a story high above the ground floor—Traddles
was on the landing to meet me. He was delighted
to see me, and gave me welcome, with great heartiness, to his little room. It was in the front of the
house, and extremely neat, though sparely furnished.
It was his only room, I saw; for there was a sofa-bed-
stead in it, and his blacking-brushes and blacking
were among his books—on the top shelf, behind a
dictionary. His table was covered with papers, and
he was hard at work in an old coat. I looked at nothing, that I know of, but I saw everything, even to
the prospect of a church upon his china inkstand, as
I sat down—and this, too, was a faculty confirmed in
me in the old Micawber times. Various ingenious
arrangements he had made, for the disguise of his
chest of drawers, and the accommodation of his boots,
his shaving-glass, and so forth, particularly impressed
themselves upon me, as evidences of the same Traddles who used to make models of elephants' dens in
writing-paper to put flies in; and to comfort himself
under ill-usage, with the memorable works of art I
have so often mentioned.

In a corner of the room was something neatly
covered up with a large white cloth. I could not
make out what that was.

'Traddles,' said I, shaking hands with him again,

after I had sat down, 'I am delighted to see you.'

'I am delighted to see *you*, Copperfield,' he returned. 'I am very glad indeed to see you. It was because I was thoroughly glad to see you when we met in Ely Place, and was sure you were thoroughly glad to see me, that I gave you this address instead of my address at chambers.'

'Oh! You have chambers?' said I.

'Why, I have the fourth of a room and a passage, and the fourth of a clerk,' returned Traddles. 'Three others and myself unite to have a set of chambers— to look business-like—and we quarter the clerk too. Half-a-crown a week he costs me.'

His old simple character and good-temper, and something of his old unlucky fortune also, I thought, smiled at me in the smile with which he made this explanation.

'It's not because I have the least pride, Copperfield, you understand,' said Traddles, 'that I don't usually give my address here. It's only on account of those who come to me, who might not like to come here. For myself, I am fighting my way on in the world against difficulties, and it would be ridiculous if I made a pretence of doing anything else.'

'You are reading for the bar, Mr. Waterbrook informed me?' said I.

'Why, yes,' said Traddles, rubbing his hands, slowly over one another, 'I am reading for the bar. The fact is, I have just begun to keep my terms, after rather a long delay. It's some time since I was articled, but the payment of that hundred pounds was a great pull. A great pull!' said Traddles, with a wince, as if he had had a tooth out.

'Do you know what I can't help thinking of, Traddles, as I sit here looking at you?' I asked him.

'No,' said he.

'That sky-blue suit you used to wear.'

'Lord, to be sure!' cried Traddles, laughing. 'Tight in the arms and legs, you know? Dear me! Well! Those were happy times, weren't they?'

'I think our schoolmaster might have made them happier, without doing any harm to any of us, I acknowledge,' I returned.

'Perhaps he might,' said Traddles. 'But dear me, there was a good deal of fun going on. Do you remember the nights in the bedroom? When we used to have the suppers? And when you used to tell the stories? Ha, ha, ha! And do you remember when I got caned for crying about Mr. Mell? Old Creakle! I should like to see him again, too!'

'He was a brute to you, Traddles,' said I, indignantly; for his good-humour made me feel as if I had seen him beaten but yesterday.

'Do you think so?' returned Traddles. 'Really? Perhaps he was, rather. But it's all over, a long while. Old Creakle!'

'You were brought up by an uncle, then?' said I.

'Of course I was!' said Traddles. 'The one I was always going to write to. And always didn't, eh! Ha, ha, ha! Yes, I had an uncle then. He died soon after I left school.'

'Indeed!'

'Yes. He was a retired—what do you call it?— draper—cloth-merchant—and had made me his heir. But he didn't like me when I grew up.'

'Do you really mean that?' said I. He was so composed, that I fancied he must have some other meaning.

'Oh dear yes, Copperfield! I mean it,' replied Traddles. 'It was an unfortunate thing, but he didn't like me at all. He said I wasn't at all what he expected, and so he married his housekeeper.'

'And what did you do?' I asked.

'I didn't do anything in particular,' said Traddles. 'I lived with them, waiting to be put out in the world, until his gout unfortunately flew to his stomach—and so he died, and so she married a young man, and so I wasn't provided for.'

'Did you get nothing, Traddles, after all?'

'Oh dear yes!' said Traddles. 'I got fifty pounds. I had never been brought up to any profession, and at first I was at a loss what to do for myself. However, I began, with the assistance of a son of a professional man, who had been to Salem House— Yawler, with his nose on one side. Do you recollect him?'

No. He had not been there with me; all the noses were straight in my day.

'It don't matter,' said Traddles. 'I began, by means of his assistance, to copy law writings. That didn't answer very well; and then I began to state cases for them, and make abstracts, and do that sort of work. For I am a plodding kind of fellow, Copperfield, and had learnt the way of doing such things pithily. Well! That put it in my head to enter myself as a law student; and that ran away with all that was left of the fifty pounds. Yawler recommended me to one or two other offices, however—Mr. Waterbrook's for one—and I got a good many jobs. I was fortunate enough, too, to become acquainted with a person in the publishing way, who was getting up an Encyclopædia, and he set me to work; and, indeed' (glancing at his table), 'I am at work for him at this minute. I am not a bad compiler, Copperfield,' said Traddles, preserving the same air of cheerful confidence in all he said, 'but I have no invention at all; not a particle. I suppose there never was a young man with less originality than I have.'

As Traddles seemed to expect that I should assent to this as a matter of course, I nodded; and he went on, with the same sprightly patience—I can find no better expression—as before.

'So, by little and little, and not living high, I managed to scrape up the hundred pounds at last,' said Traddles; 'and thank Heaven that's paid—though it was—though it certainly was,' said Traddles, wincing again as if he had had another tooth out, 'a pull.   I am living by the sort of work I have mentioned, still, and I hope, one of these days, to get connected with some newspaper: which would almost be the making of my fortune.   Now, Copperfield, you are so exactly what you used to be, with that agreeable face, and it's so pleasant to see you, that I shan't conceal anything.   Therefore you must know that I am engaged.'

Engaged!   Oh Dora!

'She is a curate's daughter,' said Traddles; 'one of ten, down in Devonshire.   Yes!'   For he saw me glance, involuntarily, at the prospect on the inkstand. 'That's the church!   You come round here, to the left, out of this gate,' tracing his finger along the inkstand, 'and exactly where I hold this pen, there stands the house—facing, you understand, towards the church.'

The delight with which he entered into these particulars, did not fully present itself to me until afterwards; for my selfish thoughts were making a ground-plan of Mr. Spenlow's house and garden at the same moment.

'She is such a dear girl!' said Traddles; 'a little older than me, but the dearest girl!   I told you I was going out of town?   I have been down there. I walked there, and I walked back, and I had the most delightful time!   I dare say ours is likely to be a rather long engagement, but our motto is "Wait and hope!" We always say that. "Wait and hope," we always say. And she would wait, Copperfield, till she was sixty—any age you can mention—for me!'

Traddles rose from his chair, and, with a triumphant smile, put his hand upon the white cloth I had observed.

'However,' he said; 'it 's not that we haven't made a beginning towards housekeeping. No, no; we have begun. We must get on by degrees, but we have begun. Here,' drawing the cloth off with great pride and care, 'are two pieces of furniture to commence with. This flower-pot and stand, she bought herself. You put that in a parlour window,' said Traddles, falling a little back from it to survey it with the greater admiration, 'with a plant in it, and—and there you are! This little round table with the marble top (it 's two feet ten in circumference), I bought. You want to lay a book down, you know, or somebody comes to see you or your wife, and wants a place to stand a cup of tea upon, and—and there you are again!' said Traddles. 'It 's an admirable piece of workmanship—firm as a rock!'

I praised them both, highly, and Traddles replaced the covering as carefully as he had removed it.

'It 's not a great deal towards the furnishing,' said Traddles, but it 's something. The table-cloths, and pillow-cases, and articles of that kind, are what discourage me most, Copperfield. So does the ironmongery—candle-boxes, and gridirons, and that sort of necessaries—because those things tell, and mount up. However, "wait and hope!" And I assure you she 's the dearest girl!'

'I am quite certain of it,' said I.

'In the meantime,' said Traddles, coming back to

his chair; 'and this is the end of my prosing about myself, I get on as well as I can. I don't make much, but I don't spend much. In general, I board with the people downstairs, who are very agreeable people indeed. Both Mr. and Mrs. Micawber have seen a good deal of life, and are excellent company.'

'My dear Traddles!' I quickly exclaimed. 'What are you talking about?'

Traddles looked at me, as if he wondered what *I* was talking about.

'Mr. and Mrs. Micawber!' I repeated. 'Why, I am intimately acquainted with them!'

An opportune double-knock at the door, which I knew well from old experience in Windsor Terrace, and which nobody but Mr. Micawber could ever have knocked at that door, resolved any doubt in my mind as to their being my old friends. I begged Traddles to ask his landlord to walk up. Traddles accordingly did so, over the banister; and Mr. Micawber, not a bit changed—his tights, his stick, his shirt-collar, and his eye-glass, all the same as ever—came into the room with a genteel and youthful air.

'I beg your pardon, Mr. Traddles,' said Mr. Micawber, with the old roll in his voice, as he checked himself in humming a soft tune. 'I was not aware that there was any individual, alien to this tenement, in your sanctum.'

Mr. Micawber slightly bowed to me, and pulled up his shirt-collar.

'How do you do, Mr. Micawber?' said I.

'Sir,' said Mr. Micawber, 'you are exceedingly obliging. I am *in statu quo.*'

'And Mrs. Micawber?' I pursued.

'Sir,' said Mr. Micawber, 'she is also, thank God, *in statu quo.*'

'And the children, Mr. Micawber?'

'Sir,' said Mr. Micawber, 'I rejoice to reply that they are, likewise, in the enjoyment of salubrity.'

All this time, Mr. Micawber had not known me in the least, though he had stood face to face with me. But now, seeing me smile, he examined my features with more attention, fell back, cried, 'Is it possible? Have I the pleasure of again beholding Copperfield?' and shook me by both hands with the utmost fervour.

'Good Heaven, Mr. Traddles!' said Mr. Micawber, 'to think that I should find you acquainted with the friend of my youth, the companion of earlier days! My dear!' calling over the banisters to Mrs. Micawber, while Traddles looked (with reason) not a little amazed at this description of me. 'Here is a gentleman in Mr. Traddles's apartment, whom he wishes to have the pleasure of presenting to you, my love!'

Mr. Micawber immediately reappeared, and shook hands with me again.

'And how is our good friend the Doctor, Copperfield?' said Mr. Micawber, 'and all the circle at Canterbury?'

'I have none but good accounts of them,' said I.

'I am most delighted to hear it,' said Mr. Micawber. 'It was at Canterbury where we last met. Within the shadow, I may figuratively say, of that religious edifice, immortalised by Chaucer, which was anciently the resort of pilgrims from the remotest corners of— in short,' said Mr. Micawber, 'in the immediate neighbourhood of the cathedral.'

I replied that it was. Mr. Micawber continued talking as volubly as he could; but not, I thought, without showing, by some marks of concern in his countenance, that he was sensible of sounds in the next room, as of Mrs. Micawber washing her hands, and hurriedly opening and shutting drawers that were uneasy in their action.

'You find us, Copperfield,' said Mr. Micawber, with one eye on Traddles, 'at present established, on what may be designated as a small and unassuming scale; but, you are aware that I have, in the course of my career, surmounted difficulties, and conquered obstacles. You are no stranger to the fact, that there have been periods of my life, when it has been requisite that I should pause, until certain expected events should turn up; when it has been necessary that I should fall back, before making what I trust I shall not be accused of presumption in terming— a spring. The present is one of those momentous stages in the life of man. You find me, fallen back, *for* a spring; and I have every reason to believe that a vigorous leap will shortly be the result.'

I was expressing my satisfaction, when Mrs. Micawber came in; a little more slatternly than she used to be, or so she seemed now, to my unaccustomed eyes, but still with some preparation of herself for company, and with a pair of brown gloves on.

'My dear,' said Mr. Micawber, leading her towards me. 'Here is a gentleman of the name of Copperfield, who wishes to renew his acquaintance with you.'

It would have been better, as it turned out, to have led gently up to his announcement, for Mrs. Micawber, being in a delicate state of health, was overcome by it, and was taken so unwell, that Mr. Micawber was obliged, in great trepidation, to run down to the water-butt in the back-yard, and draw a basinful to lave her brow with. She presently revived, however, and was really pleased to see me. We had half an hour's talk, all together; and I asked her about the twins, who, she said, were 'grown great creatures';

and after Master and Miss Micawber, whom she described as 'absolute giants,' but they were not produced on that occasion.

Mr. Micawber was very anxious that I should stay to dinner. I should not have been averse to do so, but that I imagined I detected trouble, and calculation relative to the extent of the cold meat, in Mrs. Micawber's eye. I therefore pleaded another engagement; and observing that Mrs. Micawber's spirits were immediately lightened, I resisted all persuasion to forego it.

But I told Traddles, and Mr. and Mrs. Micawber, that before I could think of leaving, they must appoint a day when they would come and dine with me. The occupations to which Traddles stood pledged, rendered it necessary to fix a somewhat distant one; but an appointment was made for the purpose, that suited us all, and then I took my leave.

Mr. Micawber, under pretence of showing me a nearer way than that by which I had come, accompanied me to the corner of the street; being anxious (he explained to me) to say a few words to an old friend, in confidence.

'My dear Copperfield,' said Mr. Micawber, 'I need hardly tell you that to have beneath our roof, under existing circumstances, a mind like that which gleams —if I may be allowed the expression—which gleams —in your friend Traddles, is an unspeakable comfort. With a washerwoman, who exposes hard-bake for sale in her parlour-window, dwelling next door, and a Bow-street officer residing over the way, you may imagine that his society is a source of consolation to myself and to Mrs. Micawber. I am at present, my dear Copperfield, engaged in the sale of corn upon commission. It is not an avocation of a remunerative description—in other words, it does *not* pay—and some temporary embarrassments of a pecuniary nature have been the consequence. I am, however, delighted to add that I have now an immediate prospect of something turning up (I am not at liberty to say in what direction), which I trust will enable me to provide, permanently, both for myself and for your friend Traddles, in whom I have an unaffected interest. You may, perhaps, be prepared to hear that Mrs. Micawber is in a state of health which renders it not wholly improbable that an addition may be ultimately made to those pledges of affection which— in short, to the infantine group. Mrs. Micawber's family have been so good as to express their dissatisfaction at this state of things. I have merely to observe, that I am not aware it is any business of theirs, and that I repel that exhibition of feeling with scorn, and with defiance!'

Mr. Micawber then shook hands with me again, and left me.

CHAPTER XXVIII

MR. MICAWBER'S GAUNTLET

UNTIL the day arrived on which I was to entertain my newly-found old friends, I lived principally on Dora and coffee. In my love-lorn condition, my appetite languished; and I was glad of it, for I felt as though it would have been an act of perfidy towards Dora to have a natural relish for my dinner. The quantity of walking exercise I took, was not in this respect attended with its usual consequence, as the disappointment counteracted the fresh air. I have my doubts, too, founded on the acute experience acquired at this period of my life, whether a sound enjoyment of animal food can develop itself freely in any human subject who is always in torment from tight boots. I think the extremities require to be at peace before the stomach will conduct itself with vigour.

On the occasion of this domestic little party, I did not repeat my former extensive preparations. I merely provided a pair of soles, a small leg of mutton, and a pigeon-pie. Mrs. Crupp broke out into rebellion on my first bashful hint in reference to the cooking of the fish and joint, and said, with a dignified sense of injury, 'No! No, sir! You will not ask me sich a thing, for you are better acquainted with me than to suppose me capable of doing what I cannot do with ampial satisfaction to my own feelings!' But, in the end, a compromise was effected; and Mrs. Crupp consented to achieve this feat, on condition that I dined from home for a fortnight afterwards.

And here I may remark, that what I underwent from Mrs. Crupp, in consequence of the tyranny she established over me, was dreadful. I never was so much afraid of any one. We made a compromise of everything. If I hesitated, she was taken with that wonderful disorder which was always lying in ambush in her system, ready, at the shortest notice, to prey upon her vitals. If I rang the bell impatiently, after half a dozen unavailing modest pulls, and she appeared at last—which was not by any means to be relied upon—she would appear with a reproachful aspect, sink breathless on a chair near the door, lay her hand upon her nankeen bosom, and become so ill, that I was glad, at any sacrifice of brandy or anything else, to get rid of her. If I objected to having my bed made at five o'clock in the afternoon—which I *do* still think an uncomfortable arrangement—one motion of her hand towards the same nankeen region

of wounded sensibility was enough to make me falter
an apology. In short, I would have done anything in
an honourable way rather than give Mrs. Crupp offence; and she was the terror of my life.

I bought a second-hand dumb-waiter for this
dinner-party, in preference to re-engaging the handy
young man; against whom I had conceived a prejudice, in consequence of meeting him in the Strand,
one Sunday morning, in a waistcoat remarkably like
one of mine, which had been missing since the former
occasion. The 'young gal' was re-engaged; but on
the stipulation that she should only bring in the
dishes, and then withdraw to the landing-place, beyond the outer door; where a habit of sniffing she
had contracted would be lost upon the guests, and
where her retiring on the plates would be a physical
impossibility.

Having laid in the materials for a bowl of punch,
to be compounded by Mr. Micawber; having provided a bottle of lavender-water, two wax candles, a
paper of mixed pins, and a pincushion, to assist Mrs.
Micawber in her toilette, at my dressing-table; having
also caused the fire in my bed-room to be lighted for
Mrs. Micawber's convenience; and having laid the
cloth with my own hands, I awaited the result with
composure.

At the appointed time, my three visitors arrived
together. Mr. Micawber with more shirt-collar than
usual, and a new ribbon to his eye-glass; Mrs. Micawber with her cap in a whity-brown paper parcel;
Traddles carrying the parcel, and supporting Mrs.
Micawber on his arm. They were all delighted with
my residence. When I conducted Mrs. Micawber
to my dressing-table, and she saw the scale on which
it was prepared for her, she was in such raptures,
that she called Mr. Micawber to come in and look.

'My dear Copperfield,' said Mr. Micawber, 'this is luxurious. This is a way of life which reminds me of the period when I was myself in a state of celibacy, and Mrs. Micawber had not yet been solicited to plight her faith at the Hymeneal altar.'

'He means, solicited by him, Mr. Copperfield,' said Mrs. Micawber, archly. 'He cannot answer for others.'

'My dear,' returned Mr. Micawber with sudden seriousness, 'I have no desire to answer for others. I am too well aware that when, in the inscrutable decrees of Fate, you were reserved for me, it is possible you may have been reserved for one, destined, after a protracted struggle, at length to fall a victim to pecuniary involvements of a complicated nature. I understand your allusion, my love. I regret it, but I can bear it.'

'Micawber!' exclaimed Mrs. Micawber, in tears. 'Have I deserved this? I, who never have deserted you; who never *will* desert you, Micawber!'

'My love,' said Mr. Micawber, much affected, 'you will forgive, and our old and tried friend Copperfield will, I am sure, forgive, the momentary laceration of a wounded spirit, made sensitive by a recent collision with the Minion of Power—in other words, with a ribald turncock attached to the waterworks— and will pity, not condemn, its excesses.'

Mr. Micawber then embraced Mrs. Micawber, and pressed my hand; leaving me to infer from this broken allusion that his domestic supply of water had been cut off that afternoon, in consequence of default in the payment of the company's rates.

To divert his thoughts from this melancholy subject, I informed Mr. Micawber that I relied upon him for a bowl of punch, and led him to the lemons. His recent despondency, not to say despair, was gone in a moment. I never saw a man so thoroughly enjoy himself amid the fragrance of lemon-peel and sugar, the odour of burning rum, and the steam of boiling water, as Mr. Micawber did that afternoon. It was wonderful to see his face shining at us out of a thin cloud of these delicate fumes, as he stirred, and mixed, and tasted, and looked as if he were making, instead of punch, a fortune for his family down to the latest posterity. As to Mrs. Micawber, I don't know whether it was the effect of the cap, or the lavender-water, or the pins, or the fire, or the wax-candles, but she came out of my room, comparatively speaking, lovely. And the lark was never gayer than that excellent woman.

I suppose—I never ventured to inquire, but I suppose—that Mrs. Crupp, after frying the soles, was taken ill. Because we broke down at that point. The leg of mutton came up very red within, and very pale without: besides having a foreign substance of a gritty nature sprinkled over it, as if it had had a fall into the ashes of that remarkable kitchen fire-place. But we were not in a condition to judge of this fact from the appearance of the gravy, forasmuch as the 'young gal' had dropped it all upon the stairs—where it remained, by the bye, in a long train, until it was worn out. The pigeon-pie was not bad, but it was a delusive pie: the crust being like a disappointing head, phrenologically speaking: full of lumps and bumps, with nothing particular underneath. In short, the banquet was such a failure that I should have been quite unhappy—about the failure, I mean, for I was always unhappy about Dora—if I had not been relieved by the great good-humour of my company, and by a bright suggestion from Mr. Micawber.

'My dear friend Copperfield,' said Mr. Micawber,

'accidents will occur in the best-regulated families;
and in families not regulated by that pervading influence which sanctifies while it enhances the—a—I
would say in short, by the influence of Woman, in
the lofty character of Wife, they may be expected
with confidence, and must be borne with philosophy.
If you will allow me to take the liberty of remarking
that there are few comestibles better, in their way,
than a Devil, and that I believe, with a little division
of labour, we could accomplish a good one if the
young person in attendance could produce a gridiron,
I would put it to you, that this little misfortune may
be easily repaired.'

There was a gridiron in the pantry, on which my
morning rasher of bacon was cooked. We had it in,
in a twinkling, and immediately applied ourselves to
carrying Mr. Micawber's idea into effect. The division of labour to which he had referred was this:—
Traddles cut the mutton into slices; Mr. Micawber
(who could do anything of this sort to perfection)
covered them with pepper, mustard, salt, and cay-
enne; I put them on the gridiron, turned them with
a fork, and took them off, under Mr. Micawber's
direction; and Mrs. Micawber heated, and continually
stirred, some mushroom ketchup in a little saucepan.
When we had slices enough done to begin upon, we
fell-to, with our sleeves still tucked up at the wrists,
more slices sputtering and blazing on the fire, and our
attention divided between the mutton on our plates,
and the mutton then preparing.

What with the novelty of this cookery, the excellence of it, the bustle of it, the frequent starting up
to look after it, the frequent sitting down to dispose
of it as the crisp slices came off the gridiron hot and
hot, the being so busy, so flushed with the fire, so
amused, and in the midst of such a tempting noise

and savour, we reduced the leg of mutton to the bone. My own appetite came back miraculously. I am ashamed to record it, but I really believe I forgot Dora for a little while. I am satisfied that Mr. and Mrs. Micawber could not have enjoyed the feast more, if they had sold a bed to provide it. Traddles laughed as heartily, almost the whole time, as he ate and worked. Indeed we all did, all at once; and I dare say there never was a greater success.

We were at the height of our enjoyment, and were all busily engaged, in our several departments, endeavouring to bring the last batch of slices to a state of perfection that should crown the feast, when I was aware of a strange presence in the room, and my eyes encountered those of the staid Littimer, standing hat in hand before me.

'What's the matter?' I involuntarily asked.

'I beg your pardon, sir, I was directed to come in. Is my master not here, sir?'

'No.'

'Have you not seen him, sir?'

'No; don't you come from him?'

'Not immediately so, sir.'

'Did he tell you you would find him here?'

'Not exactly so, sir. But I should think he might be here to-morrow, as he has not been here to-day.'

'Is he coming up from Oxford?'

'I beg, sir,' he returned respectfully, 'that you will be seated, and allow me to do this.' With which he took the fork from my unresisting hand, and bent over the gridiron, as if his whole attention were concentrated on it.

We should not have been much discomposed, I dare say, by the appearance of Steerforth himself, but we became in a moment the meekest of the meek before his respectable serving-man. Mr. Micawber, humming a tune, to show that he was quite at ease, subsided into his chair, with the handle of a hastily concealed fork sticking out of the bosom of his coat, as if he had stabbed himself. Mrs. Micawber put on her brown gloves, and assumed a genteel languor. Traddles ran his greasy hands through his hair, and stood it bolt upright, and stared in confusion on the table-cloth. As for me, I was a mere infant at the head of my own table; and hardly ventured to glance at the respectable phenomenon, who had come from Heaven knows where, to put my establishment to rights.

Meanwhile he took the mutton off the gridiron, and gravely handed it round. We all took some, but our appreciation of it was gone, and we merely made a show of eating it. As we severally pushed away our plates, he noiselessly removed them, and set on the cheese. He took that off, too, when it was done with; cleared the table; piled everything on the dumb-waiter; gave us our wine-glasses; and, of his own accord, wheeled the dumb-waiter into the pantry. All this was done in a perfect manner, and he never raised his eyes from what he was about. Yet, his very elbows, when he had his back towards me, seemed to teem with the expression of his fixed opinion that I was extremely young.

'Can I do anything more, sir?'

I thanked him and said, No; but would he take no dinner himself?

'None, I am obliged to you, sir.'

'Is Mr. Steerforth coming from Oxford?'

'I beg your pardon, sir?'

'Is Mr. Steerforth coming from Oxford?'

'I should imagine that he might be here to-morrow, sir. I rather thought he might have been here to-day, sir. The mistake is mine, no doubt, sir.'

'If you should see him first—' said I.

'If you 'll excuse me, sir, I don't think I shall see him first.'

'In case you do,' said I, 'pray say that I am sorry he was not here to-day, as an old schoolfellow of his was here.'

'Indeed, sir!' and he divided a bow between me and Traddles, with a glance at the latter.

He was moving softly to the door, when, in a forlorn hope of saying something naturally—which I never could, to this man—I said—

'Oh! Littimer!'

'Sir!'

'Did you remain long at Yarmouth, that time?'

'Not particularly so, sir.'

'You saw the boat completed?'

'Yes, sir. I remained behind on purpose to see the boat completed.'

'I know!' He raised his eyes to mine respectfully. 'Mr. Steerforth has not seen it yet, I suppose?'

'I really can't say, sir. I think—but I really can't say, sir. I wish you good night, sir.'

He comprehended everybody present, in the respectful bow with which he followed these words, and disappeared. My visitors seemed to breathe more freely when he was gone; but my own relief was very great, for besides the constraint, arising from that extraordinary sense of being at a disadvantage which I always had in this man's presence, my conscience had embarrassed me with whispers that I had mistrusted his master, and I could not repress a vague uneasy dread that he might find it out. How was it, having so little in reality to conceal, that I always *did* feel as if this man were finding me out?

Mr. Micawber roused me from this reflection, which was blended with a certain remorseful apprehension of seeing Steerforth himself, by bestowing many encomiums on the absent Littimer as a most respectable fellow, and a thoroughly admirable servant. Mr. Micawber, I may remark, had taken his full share of the general bow, and had received it with infinite condescension.

'But punch, my dear Copperfield,' said Mr. Micawber, tasting it, 'like time and tide, waits for no man. Ah! it is at the present moment in high flavour. My love, will you give me your opinion?'

Mrs. Micawber pronounced it excellent.

'Then I will drink,' said Mr. Micawber, 'if my friend Copperfield will permit me to take that social liberty, to the days when my friend Copperfield and myself were younger, and fought our way in the world side by side. I may say, of myself and Copperfield, in words we have sung together before now, that

> "We twa' hae run about the braes
> And pu'd the gowans fine"

—in a figurative point of view—on several occasions. I am not exactly aware,' said Mr. Micawber, with the old roll in his voice, and the old indescribable air of saying something genteel, 'what gowans may be, but I have no doubt that Copperfield and myself would frequently have taken a pull at them, if it had been feasible.'

Mr. Micawber, at the then present moment, took a pull at his punch. So we all did: Traddles evidently lost in wondering at what distant time Mr. Micawber and I could have been comrades in the battle of the world.

'Ahem!' said Mr. Micawber, clearing his throat, and warming with the punch and with the fire. 'My dear, another glass?'

Mrs. Micawber said it must be very little; but we couldn't allow that, so it was a glassful.

'As we are quite confidential here, Mr. Copperfield,' said Mrs. Micawber, sipping her punch, 'Mr. Traddles being a part of our domesticity, I should much like to have your opinion on Mr. Micawber's prospects. For corn,' said Mrs. Micawber argumentatively, 'as I have repeatedly said to Mr. Micawber, may be gentlemanly, but it is not remunerative. Commission to the extent of two and ninepence in a fortnight cannot, however limited our ideas, be considered remunerative.'

We were all agreed upon that.

'Then,' said Mrs. Micawber, who prided herself on taking a clear view of things, and keeping Mr. Micawber straight by her woman's wisdom, when he might otherwise go a little crooked, 'then I ask myself this question. If corn is not to be relied upon, what is? Are coals to be relied upon? Not at all. We have turned our attention to that experiment, on the suggestion of my family, and we find it fallacious.'

Mr. Micawber, leaning back in his chair with his hands in his pockets, eyed us aside, and nodded his head, as much as to say that the case was very clearly put.

'The articles of corn and coals,' said Mrs. Micawber, still more argumentatively, 'being equally out of the question, Mr. Copperfield, I naturally look round the world, and say, "What is there in which a person of Mr. Micawber's talent is likely to succeed?" And I exclude the doing anything on commission, because commission is not a certainty. What is best suited to a person of Mr. Micawber's peculiar temperament is, I am convinced, a certainty.'

Traddles and I both expressed, by a feeling mur-

mur, that this great discovery was no doubt true of
Mr. Micawber, and that it did him much credit.

'I will not conceal from you, my dear Mr. Copperfield,' said Mrs. Micawber, 'that *I* have long felt the
brewing business to be particularly adapted to Mr.
Micawber. Look at Barclay and Perkins! Look at
Truman, Hanbury, and Buxton! It is on that extensive footing that Mr. Micawber, I know from my
own knowledge of him, is calculated to shine; and
the profits, I am told, are e-NOR—mous! But if
Mr. Micawber cannot get into those firms,—which decline to answer his letters, when he offers his services
even in an inferior capacity—what is the use of dwelling upon that idea? None. I may have a conviction that Mr. Micawber's manners—'

'Hem! Really, my dear,' interposed Mr. Micawber.

'My love, be silent,' said Mrs. Micawber, laying her
brown glove on his hand. 'I may have a conviction,
Mr. Copperfield, that Mr. Micawber's manners pe-
culiarly qualify him for the banking business. I may
argue within myself, that if *I* had a deposit at a banking-house, the manners of Mr. Micawber, as representing that banking-house, would inspire confidence,
and must extend the connection. But if the various
banking-houses refuse to avail themselves of Mr.
Micawber's abilities, or receive the offer of them with
contumely, what is the use of dwelling upon *that*
idea? None. As to originating a banking business,
I may know that there are members of my family
who, if they chose to place their money if Mr. Micawber's hands, might found an establishment of that
description. But if they do *not* choose to place their
money in Mr. Micawber's hands—which they don't—
what is the use of that? Again I contend that we
are no farther advanced than we were before.'

I shook my head, and said, 'Not a bit.' Traddles also shook his head, and said, 'Not a bit.'

'What do I deduce from this?' Mrs. Micawber went on to say, still with the same air of putting a case lucidly. 'What is the conclusion, my dear Mr. Copperfield, to which I am irresistibly brought? Am I wrong in saying, it is clear that we must live?'

I answered 'Not at all!' and Traddles answered 'Not at all!' and I found myself afterwards sagely adding, alone, that a person must either live or die.

'Just so,' returned Mrs. Micawber. 'It is precisely that. And the fact is, my dear Mr. Copperfield, that we can *not* live without something widely different from existing circumstances shortly turning up. Now I am convinced, myself, and this I have pointed out to Mr. Micawber several times of late, that things cannot be expected to turn up of themselves. We must, in a measure, assist to turn them up. I may be wrong, but I have formed that opinion.'

Both Traddles and I applauded it highly.

'Very well,' said Mrs. Micawber. 'Then what do I recommend? Here is Mr. Micawber with a variety of qualifications—with great talent—'

'Really, my love,' said Mr. Micawber.

'Pray, my dear, allow me to conclude. Here is Mr. Micawber, with a variety of qualifications, with great talent—*I* should say, with genius, but that may be the partiality of a wife.'

Traddles and I both murmured 'No.'

'And here is Mr. Micawber without any suitable position or employment. Where does that responsibility rest? Clearly on society. Then I would make a fact so disgraceful known, and boldly challenge society to set it right. It appears to me, my dear Mr. Copperfield,' said Mrs. Micawber, forcibly, 'that what Mr. Micawber has to do, is to throw down the gauntlet to society, and say, in effect, "Show me who will take that up. Let the party immediately step forward." '

I ventured to ask Mrs. Micawber how this was to be done.

'By advertising,' said Mrs. Micawber—'in all the papers. It appears to me, that what Mr. Micawber has to do, in justice to himself, in justice to his family, and I will even go so far as to say in justice to society, by which he has been hitherto overlooked, is to advertise in all the papers; to describe himself plainly as so-and-so, with such and such qualifications, and to put it thus: "*Now* employ me, on remunerative terms, and address, post-paid to *W. M.* Post Office, Camden Town." '

'This idea of Mrs. Micawber's, my dear Copperfield,' said Mr. Micawber, making his shirt-collar meet in front of his chin, and glancing at me sideways, is, in fact, the Leap to which I alluded, when I last had the pleasure of seeing you.'

'Advertising is rather expensive,' I remarked dubiously.

'Exactly so!' said Mrs. Micawber, preserving the same logical air. 'Quite true, my dear Mr. Copperfield! I have made the identical observation to Mr. Micawber. It is for that reason especially, that I think Mr. Micawber ought (as I have already said, in justice to himself, in justice to his family, and in justice to society) to raise a certain sum of money—on a bill.'

Mr. Micawber, leaning back in his chair, trifled with his eye-glass, and cast his eyes up at the ceiling; but I thought him observant of Traddles, too, who was looking at the fire.

'If no member of my family,' said Mrs. Micawber,

'is possessed of sufficient natural feeling to negotiate that bill—I believe there is a better business term to express what I mean—'

Mr. Micawber, with his eyes still cast up at the ceiling, suggested 'Discount.'

'To discount that bill,' said Mrs. Micawber, 'then my opinion is, that Mr. Micawber should go into the City, should take that bill into the Money Market, and should dispose of it for what he can get. If the individuals in the Money Market oblige Mr. Micawber to sustain a great sacrifice, that is between themselves and their consciences. I view it, steadily, as an investment. I recommend Mr. Micawber, my dear Mr. Copperfield, to do the same; to regard it as an investment which is sure of return, and to make up his mind to *any* sacrifice.'

I felt, but I am sure I don't know why, that this was self-denying and devoted in Mrs. Micawber, and I uttered a murmur to that effect. Traddles, who took his tone from me, did likewise, still looking at the fire.

'I will not,' said Mrs. Micawber, finishing her punch, and gathering her scarf about her shoulders, preparatory to her withdrawal to my bedroom: 'I will not protract these remarks on the subject of Mr. Micawber's pecuniary affairs. At your fireside, my dear Mr. Copperfield, and in the presence of Mr. Traddles, who, though not so old a friend, is quite one of ourselves, I could not refrain from making you acquainted with the course *I* advise Mr. Micawber to take. I feel that the time is arrived when Mr. Micawber should exert himself and—I will add—assert himself, and it appears to me that these are the means. I am aware that I am merely a female, and that a masculine judgment is usually considered more competent to the discussion of such questions;

still I must not forget that, when I lived at home with my papa and mamma, my papa was in the habit of saying, "Emma's form is fragile, but her grasp of a subject is inferior to none." That my papa was too partial, I well know; but that he was an observer of character in some degree, my duty and my reason equally forbid me to doubt.'

With these words, and resisting our entreaties that she would grace the remaining circulation of the punch with her presence, Mrs. Micawber retired to my bedroom. And really I felt that she was a noble woman—the sort of woman who might have been a Roman matron, and done all manner of heroic things, in times of public trouble.

In the fervour of this impression, I congratulated Mr. Micawber on the treasure he possessed. So did Traddles. Mr. Micawber extended his hand to each of us in succession, and then covered his face with his pocket-handkerchief, which I think had more snuff upon it than he was aware of. He then returned to the punch, in the highest state of exhilaration.

He was full of eloquence. He gave us to understand that in our children we lived again, and that, under the pressure of pecuniary difficulties, any accession to their number was doubly welcome. He said that Mrs. Micawber had latterly had her doubts on this point, but that he had dispelled them, and reassured her. As to her family, they were totally unworthy of her, and their sentiments were utterly indifferent to him, and they might—I quote his own expression—go to the devil.

Mr. Micawber then delivered a warm eulogy on Traddles. He said Traddles's was a character, to the steady virtues of which he (Mr. Micawber) could lay no claim, but which, he thanked Heaven, he could admire. He feelingly alluded to the young lady, unknown, whom Traddles had honoured with his affection, and who had reciprocated that affection by honouring and blessing Traddles with *her* affection. Mr. Micawber pledged her. So did I. Traddles thanked us both, by saying, with a simplicity and honesty I had sense enough to be quite charmed with, 'I am very much obliged to you indeed. And I do assure you, she 's the dearest girl!—'

Mr. Micawber took an early opportunity, after that, of hinting, with the utmost delicacy and ceremony, at the state of *my* affections. Nothing but the serious assurance of his friend Copperfield to the contrary, he observed, could deprive him of the impression that his friend Copperfield loved and was beloved. After feeling very hot and uncomfortable for some time, and after a good deal of blushing, stammering, and denying, I said, having my glass in my hand, 'Well, I would give them D.!' which so excited and gratified Mr. Micawber, that he ran with a glass of punch into my bedroom, in order that Mrs. Micawber might drink D., who drank it with enthusiasm, crying from within, in a shrill voice, 'Hear, hear! My dear Mr. Copperfield, I am delighted. Hear!' and tapping at the wall, by way of applause.

Our conversation, afterwards, took a more worldly turn; Mr. Micawber telling us that he found Camden Town inconvenient, and that the first thing he contemplated doing, when the advertisement should have been the cause of something satisfactory turning up, was to move. He mentioned a terrace at the western end of Oxford Street, fronting Hyde Park, on which he had always had his eye, but which he did not expect to attain immediately, as it would require a large establishment. There would probably be an interval, he explained, in which he should content himself with the upper part of a house, over some respectable place of business—say in Piccadilly,—which would be a cheerful situation for Mrs. Micawber; and where, by throwing out a bow window, or carrying up the roof another story, or making some little alteration of that sort, they might live, comfortably and reputably, for a few years. Whatever was reserved for him, he expressly said, or wherever his abode might be, we might rely on this—there would always be a room for Traddles, and a knife and fork for me. We acknowledged his kindness; and he begged us to forgive his having launched into these practical and business-like details, and to excuse it as natural in one who was making entirely new arrangements in life.

Mrs. Micawber, tapping at the wall again, to know if tea were ready, broke up this particular phase of our friendly conversation. She made tea for us in a most agreeable manner; and, whenever I went near her, in handing about the tea-cups and bread-and-butter, asked me, in a whisper, whether D. was fair, or dark, or whether she was short, or tall: or something of that kind; which I think I liked. After tea, we discussed a variety of topics before the fire; and Mrs. Micawber was good enough to sing us (in a small, thin, flat voice, which I remembered to have considered, when I first knew her, the very table-beer of acoustics) the favourite ballads of 'The Dashing White Serjeant,' and 'Little Tafflin.' For both of these songs Mrs. Micawber had been famous when she lived at home with her papa and mamma. Mr. Micawber told us, that when he heard her sing the first one, on the first occasion of his seeing her beneath the parental roof, she had attracted his attention in an extraordinary degree; but that when it came to Little Tafflin, he had resolved to win that woman or perish in the attempt.

It was between ten and eleven o'clock when Mrs. Micawber rose to replace her cap in the whity-brown paper parcel, and to put on her bonnet. Mr. Micawber took the opportunity of Traddles putting on his great-coat, to slip a letter into my hand, with a whispered request that I would read it at my leisure. I also took the opportunity of my holding a candle over the banisters to light them down, when Mr. Micawber was going, first leading Mrs. Micawber, and Traddles was following with the cap, to detain Traddles for a moment on the top of the stairs.

'Traddles,' said I, 'Mr. Micawber don't mean any harm, poor fellow; but if I were you, I wouldn't lend him anything.'

'My dear Copperfield,' returned Traddles, smiling, 'I haven't got anything to lend.'

'You have got a name, you know,' said I.

'Oh! You call *that* something to lend?' returned Traddles with a thoughtful look.

'Certainly.'

'Oh!' said Traddles. 'Yes, to be sure? I am very much obliged to you, Copperfield; but—I am afraid I have lent him that already.'

'For the bill that is to be a certain investment?' I inquired.

'No,' said Traddles. 'Not for that one. This is the first I have heard of that one. I have been thinking that he will most likely propose that one, on the way home. Mine's another.'

'I hope there will be nothing wrong about it,' said I.

'I hope not,' said Traddles. 'I should think not, though, because he told me, only the other day, that it was provided for. That was Mr. Micawber's expression. "Provided for."'

Mr. Micawber looking up at this juncture to where

we were standing, I had only time to repeat my caution. Traddles thanked me, and descended. But I was much afraid, when I observed the good-natured manner in which he went down with the cap in his hand, and gave Mrs. Micawber his arm, that he would be carried into the Money Market neck and heels.

I returned to my fireside, and was musing, half gravely and half laughing, on the character of Mr. Micawber and the old relations between us, when I heard a quick step ascending the stairs. At first, I thought it was Traddles coming back for something Mrs. Micawber had left behind; but as the step approached, I knew it, and felt my heart beat high, and the blood rush to my face, for it was Steerforth's.

I was never unmindful of Agnes, and she never left that sanctuary in my thoughts—if I may call it so—where I had placed her from the first. But when he entered, and stood before me with his hand out, the darkness that had fallen on him changed to light, and I felt confounded and ashamed of having doubted one I loved so heartily. I loved her none the less; I thought of her as the same benignant, gentle angel in my life; I reproached myself, not her, with having done him an injury; and I would have made him any atonement, if I had known what to make, and how to make it.

'Why, Daisy, old boy, dumfoundered!' laughed Steerforth, shaking my hand heartily, and throwing it gaily away. 'Have I detected you in another feast, you Sybarite! These Doctors' Commons fellows are the gayest men in town, I believe, and beat us sober Oxford people all to nothing!' His bright glance went merrily round the room, as he took the seat on the sofa opposite to me, which Mrs. Micawber had recently vacated, and stirred the fire into a blaze.

'I was so surprised at first,' said I, giving him welcome with all the cordiality I felt, 'that I had hardly breath to greet you with, Steerforth.'

'Well, the sight of me *is* good for sore eyes, as the Scotch say,' replied Steerforth, 'and so is the sight of you, Daisy, in full bloom. How are you, my Bacchanal?'

'I am very well,' said I; 'and not at all Bacchanalian to-night, though I confess to another party of three.'

'All of whom I met in the street, talking loud in your praise,' returned Steerforth. 'Who's our friend in the tights?'

I gave him the best idea I could, in a few words, of Mr. Micawber. He laughed heartily at my feeble portrait of that gentleman, and said he was a man to know, and he must know him.

'But who do you suppose our other friend is?' said I in my turn.

'Heaven knows,' said Steerforth. 'Not a bore, I hope? I thought he looked a little like one.'

'Traddles!' I replied, triumphantly.

'Who's he?' asked Steerforth in his careless way.

'Don't you remember Traddles? Traddles in our room at Salem House?'

'Oh! That fellow!' said Steerforth, beating a lump of coal on the top of the fire, with the poker. 'Is he as soft as ever? And where the deuce did you pick *him* up?'

I extolled Traddles in reply, as highly as I could; for I felt that Steerforth rather slighted him. Steerforth, dismissing the subject with a light nod, and a smile, and the remark that he would be glad to see the old fellow too, for he had always been an odd fish, inquired if I could give him anything to eat? During most of this short dialogue, when he had not been speaking in a wild vivacious manner, he had sat idly beating on the lump of coal with the poker. I observed that he did the same thing while I was getting out the remains of the pigeon-pie, and so forth.

'Why, Daisy, here's supper for a king!' he exclaimed, starting out of his silence with a burst, and taking his seat at the table. 'I shall do it justice, for I have come from Yarmouth.'

'I thought you came from Oxford?' I returned.

'Not I,' said Steerforth. 'I have been seafaring—better employed.'

'Littimer was here to-day, to inquire for you,' I remarked, 'and I understood him that you were at Oxford; though, now I think of it, he certainly did not say so.'

'Littimer is a greater fool than I thought him, to have been inquiring for me at all,' said Steerforth, jovially pouring out a glass of wine, and drinking to me. 'As to understanding him, you are a cleverer fellow than most of us, Daisy, if you can do that.'

'That's true, indeed,' said I, moving my chair to the table. 'So you have been at Yarmouth, Steerforth!' interested to know all about it. 'Have you been there long?'

'No,' he returned. 'An *escapade* of a week or so.'

'And how are they all? Of course, little Emily is not married yet?'

'Not yet. Going to be, I believe—in so many weeks, or months, or something or other. I have not seen much of 'em. By the bye'; he laid down his knife and fork, which he had been using with great diligence, and began feeling in his pockets; 'I have a letter for you.'

'From whom?'

'Why, from your old nurse,' he returned, taking

some papers out of his breast-pocket. ' "J. Steer-forth, Esquire, debtor, to the Willing Mind"; that 's not it. Patience, and we 'll find it presently. Old what 's-his-name 's in a bad way, and it 's about that, I believe.'

'Barkis, do you mean?'

'Yes!' still feeling in his pockets, and looking over their contents: 'it 's all over with poor Barkis, I am afraid. I saw a little apothecary there—surgeon, or whatever he is—who brought your worship into the world. He was mighty learned about the case, to me; but the upshot of his opinion was, that the carrier was making his last journey rather fast.—Put your hand into the breast-pocket of my great-coat on the chair yonder, and I think you 'll find the letter. Is it there?'

'Here it is!' said I.

'That 's right!'

It was from Peggotty; something less legible than usual, and brief. It informed me of her husband's hopeless state, and hinted at his being 'a little nearer' than heretofore, and consequently more difficult to manage for his own comfort. It said nothing of her weariness and watching, and praised him highly. It was written with a plain, unaffected, homely piety that I knew to be genuine, and ended with 'my duty to my ever darling'—meaning myself.

While I deciphered it, Steerforth continued to eat and drink.

'It 's a bad job,' he said, when I had done; 'but the sun sets every day, and people die ever minute, and we mustn't be scared by the common lot. If we failed to hold our own, because that equal foot at all men's doors was heard knocking somewhere, every object in this world would slip from us. No! Ride on! Rough-shod if need be, smooth-shod if that will do, but ride on! Ride on over all obstacles, and win the race!'

'And win what race?' said I.

'The race that one has started in,' said he. 'Ride on!'

I noticed, I remember, as he paused, looking at me with his handsome head a little thrown back, and his glass raised in his hand, that though the freshness of the sea-wind was on his face, and it was ruddy, there were traces in it, made since I last saw it, as if he had applied himself to some habitual strain of the fervent energy which, when roused, was so passionately roused within him. I had it in my thoughts to remonstrate with him upon his desperate way of pursuing any fancy that he took—such as this buffeting of rough seas, and braving of hard weather, for example—when my mind glanced off to the immediate subject of our conversation again, and pursued that instead.

'I tell you what, Steerforth,' said I, 'if your high spirits will listen to me—'

'They are potent spirits, and will do whatever you like,' he answered, moving from the table to the fireside again.

'Then I tell you what, Steerforth. I think I will go down and see my old nurse. It is not that I can do her any good, or render her any real service; but she is so attached to me that my visit will have as much effect on her, as if I could do both. She will take it so kindly, that it will be a comfort and support to her. It is no great effort to make, I am sure, for such a friend as she has been to me. Wouldn't you go a day's journey, if you were in my place?'

His face was thoughtful, and he sat considering a little before he answered, in a low voice, 'Well! Go. You can do no harm.'

'You have just come back,' said I, 'and it would be in vain to ask you to go with me?'

'Quite,' he returned. 'I am for Highgate to-night. I have not seen my mother this long time, and it lies upon my conscience, for it's something to be loved as she loves her prodigal son.—Bah! Nonsense!— You mean to go to-morrow, I suppose?' he said, holding me out at arm's length, with a hand on each of my shoulders.

'Yes, I think so.'

'Well, then, don't go till next day. I wanted you to come and stay a few days with us. Here I am, on purpose to bid you, and you fly off to Yarmouth!'

'You are a nice fellow to talk of flying off, Steerforth, who are always running wild on some unknown expedition or other!'

He looked at me for a moment without speaking, and then rejoined, still holding me as before, and giving me a shake—

'Come! Say the next day, and pass as much of to-morrow as you can with us! Who knows when we may meet again, else? Come! Say the next day! I want you to stand between Rosa Dartle and me, and keep us asunder.'

'Would you love each other too much, without me?'

'Yes; or hate,' laughed Steerforth; 'no matter which. Come! Say the next day!'

I said the next day; and he put on his great-coat and lighted his cigar, and set off to walk home. Finding him in this intention, I put on my own great-coat (but did not light my own cigar, having had enough of that for one while) and walked with him as far as the open road; a dull road, then, at night. He was in great spirits all the way; and when we parted, and I looked after him going so gallantly and airily homeward, I thought of his saying, 'Ride on over all obstacles, and win the race!' and wished, for the first time, that he had some worthy race to run.

I was undressing in my own room, when Mr. Micawber's letter tumbled on the floor. Thus reminded of it, I broke the seal and read as follows. It was dated an hour and a half before dinner. I am not sure whether I have mentioned that, when Mr. Micawber was at any particularly desperate crisis, he used a sort of legal phraseology: which he seemed to think equivalent to winding up his affairs.

'Sir—for I dare not say my dear Copperfield,

'It is expedient that I should inform you that the undersigned is Crushed. Some flickering efforts to spare you the premature knowledge of his calamitous position, you may observe in him this day; but hope has sunk beneath the horizon, and the undersigned is Crushed.

'The present communication is penned within the personal range (I cannot call it the society) of an individual, in a state closely bordering on intoxication, employed by a broker. That individual is in legal possession of the premises, under a distress for rent. His inventory includes, not only the chattels and effects of every description belonging to the undersigned, as yearly tenant of this habitation, but also those appertaining to Mr. Thomas Traddles, lodger, a member of the Honourable Society of the Inner Temple.

'If any drop of gloom were wanting in the overflowing cup, which is now "commended" (in the language of an immortal Writer) to the lips of the undersigned, it would be found in the fact, that a friendly acceptance granted to the undersigned, by the before-mentioned Mr. Thomas Traddles, for the sum of £23, 4s. 9½d. is overdue, and is NOT provided for. Also, in the fact, that the living responsibilities clinging to the undersigned, will, in the course of nature, be increased by the sum of one more helpless victim; whose miserable appearance may be looked for—in round numbers—at the expiration of a period not exceeding six lunar months from the present date.

'After premising this much, it would be a work of supererogation to add, that dust and ashes are for ever scattered

'On

'The

'Head

'Of

'WILKINS MICAWBER.'

Poor Traddles! I knew enough of Mr. Micawber by this time, to foresee that *he* might be expected to recover the blow; but my night's rest was sorely distressed by thoughts of Traddles, and of the curate's daughter, who was one of ten, down in Devonshire, and who was such a dear girl, and who would wait for Traddles (ominous praise!) until she was sixty, or any age that could be mentioned.

CHAPTER XXIX

I VISIT STEERFORTH AT HIS HOME, AGAIN

I MENTIONED to Mr. Spenlow in the morning, that I wanted leave of absence for a short time; and as I was not in the receipt of my salary, and consequently was not obnoxious to the implacable Jorkins, there was no difficulty about it. I took that opportunity, with my voice sticking in my throat, and my sight failing as I uttered the words, to express my hope that Miss Spenlow was quite well; to which Mr. Spenlow replied, with no more emotion than if he had been speaking of an ordinary human being, that he was much obliged to me, and she was very well.

We articled clerks, as germs of the patrician order of proctors, were treated with so much consideration, that I was almost my own master at all times. As I did not care, however, to get to Highgate before one or two o'clock in the day, and as we had another little excommunication case in court that morning, which was called The office of the Judge promoted by Tipkins against Bullock for his soul's correction, I passed an hour or two in attendance on it with Mr. Spenlow very agreeably. It arose out of a scuffle between two church-wardens, one of whom was alleged to have pushed the other against a pump; the handle of which pump projecting into a school-house, which school-house was under a gable of the church-roof, made the push an ecclesiastical offence. It was an amusing case; and sent me up to Highgate, on the box of the stage-coach, thinking about the Commons, and what Mr. Spenlow had said about touching the Commons, and bringing down the country.

Mrs. Steerforth was pleased to see me, and so was Rosa Dartle. I was agreeably surprised to find that Littimer was not there, and that we were attended by a modest little parlour-maid, with blue ribbons in her cap, whose eye it was much more pleasant, and much less disconcerting, to catch by accident, than the eye of that respectable man. But what I particularly observed, before I had been half an hour in the house, was the close and attentive watch Miss

Dartle kept upon me; and the lurking manner in which she seemed to compare my face with Steerforth's, and Steerforth's with mine, and to lie in wait for something to come out between the two. So surely as I looked towards her, did I see that eager visage, with its gaunt black eyes and searching brow, intent on mine; or passing suddenly from mine to Steerforth's; or comprehending both of us at once. In this lynx-like scrutiny she was so far from faltering when she saw I observed it, that at such a time she only fixed her piercing look upon me with a more intent expression still. Blameless as I was, and knew that I was, in reference to any wrong she could possibly suspect me of, I shrunk before her strange eyes, quite unable to endure their hungry lustre.

All day, she seemed to pervade the whole house. If I talked to Steerforth in his room, I heard her dress rustle in the little gallery outside. When he and I engaged in some of our old exercises on the lawn behind the house, I saw her face pass from window to window, like a wandering light, until it fixed itself in one, and watched us. When we all four went out walking in the afternoon, she closed her thin hand on my arm like a spring, to keep me back, while Steerforth and his mother went on out of hearing: and then spoke to me.

'You have been a long time,' she said, 'without coming here. Is your profession really so engaging and interesting as to absorb your whole attention? I ask because I always want to be informed, when I am ignorant. Is it really, though?'

I replied that I liked it well enough, but that I certainly could not claim so much for it.

'Oh! I am glad to know that, because I always like

to be put right when I am wrong,' said Rosa Dartle. 'You mean it is a little dry, perhaps?'

'Well,' I replied; 'perhaps it *was* a little dry.'

'Oh! and that's a reason why you want relief and change—excitement, and all that?' said she. 'Ah! very true! But isn't it a little—Eh?—for him; I don't mean you?'

A quick glance of her eye towards the spot where Steerforth was walking, with his mother leaning on his arm, showed me whom she meant; but beyond that, I was quite lost. And I looked so, I have no doubt.

'Don't it—I don't say that it *does,* mind I want to know—don't it rather engross him? Don't it make him, perhaps, a little more remiss than usual in his visits to his blindly-doting—eh?' With another quick glance at them, and such a glance at me as seemed to look into my innermost thoughts.

'Miss Dartle,' I returned, 'pray do not think—'

'I don't!' she said. 'Oh dear me, don't suppose that I think anything! I am not suspicious. I only ask a question. I don't state any opinion. I want to found an opinion on what you tell me. Then, it's not so? Well, I am very glad to know it.'

'It certainly is not the fact,' said I, perplexed, 'that I am accountable for Steerforth's having been away from home longer than usual—if he has been: which I really don't know at this moment, unless I understand it from you. I have not seen him this long while, until last night.'

'No?'

'Indeed, Miss Dartle, no!'

As she looked full at me, I saw her face grow sharper and paler, and the marks of the old wound lengthen out until it cut through the disfigured lip, and deep into the nether lip, and slanted down the face. There was something positively awful to me in this, and in the brightness of her eyes, as she said, looking fixedly at me—

'What is he doing?'

I repeated the words, more to myself than her, being so amazed.

'What is he doing?' she said, with an eagerness that seemed enough to consume her like a fire. 'In what is that man assisting him, who never looks at me without an inscrutable falsehood in his eyes? If you are honourable and faithful, I don't ask you to betray your friend. I ask you only to tell me, is it anger, is it hatred, is it pride, is it restlessness, is it some wild fancy, is it love, *what is it,* that is leading him?'

'Miss Dartle,' I returned, 'how shall I tell you, so that you will believe me, that I know of nothing in Steerforth different from what there was when I first came here? I can think of nothing. I firmly believe there is nothing. I hardly understand even what you mean.'

As she still stood looking fixedly at me, a twitching or throbbing, from which I could not dissociate the idea of pain, came into that cruel mark; and lifted up the corner of her lip as if with scorn, or with a pity that despised its object. She put her hand upon it hurriedly—a hand so thin and delicate, that when I had seen her hold it up before the fire to shade her face, I had compared it in my thoughts to fine porcelain—and saying, in a quick, fierce, passionate way, 'I swear you to secrecy about this!' said not a word more.

Mrs. Steerforth was particularly happy in her son's society, and Steerforth was, on this occasion, particularly attentive and respectful to her. It was very interesting to me to see them together, not only on account of their mutual affection, but because of the strong personal resemblance between them, and the manner in which what was haughty or impetuous in him was softened by age and sex, in her, to a gracious dignity. I thought, more than once, that it was well no serious cause of division had ever come between them; or two such natures—I ought rather to express it, two such shades of the same nature— might have been harder to reconcile than the two extremest opposites in creation. The idea did not originate in my own discernment, I am bound to confess, but in a speech of Rosa Dartle's.

She said at dinner—

'Oh, but do tell me, though, somebody, because I have been thinking about it all day, and I want to know.'

'You want to know what, Rosa?' returned Mrs. Steerforth. 'Pray, pray, Rosa, do not be mysterious.'

'Mysterious!' she cried. 'Oh! really? Do you consider me so?'

'Do I constantly entreat you,' said Mrs. Steerforth, 'to speak plainly, in your own natural manner?'

'Oh! then this is *not* my natural manner?' she rejoined. 'Now you must really bear with me, because I ask for information. We never know ourselves.'

'It has become a second nature,' said Mrs. Steerforth, without any displeasure; 'but I remember, —and so must you, I think,—when your manner was different, Rosa; when it was not so guarded, and was more trustful.'

'I am sure you are right,' she returned; 'and so it is that bad habits grow upon one! Really? Less guarded and more trustful? How *can* I, imperceptibly have changed, I wonder? Well, that 's very odd! I must study to regain my former self.'

'I wish you would,' said Mrs. Steerforth, with a smile.

'Oh! I really will, you know!' she answered. 'I will learn frankness from—let me see—from James.'

'You cannot learn frankness, Rosa,' said Mrs. Steerforth quickly—for there was always some effect of sarcasm in what Rosa Dartle said, though it was said, as this was, in the most unconscious manner in the world—'in a better school.'

'That I am sure of,' she answered, with uncommon fervour. 'If I am sure of anything, of course, you know, I am sure of that.'

Mrs. Steerforth appeared to me to regret having been a little nettled; for she presently said, in a kind tone—

'Well, my dear Rosa, we have not heard what it is that you want to be satisfied about?'

'That I want to be satisfied about?' she replied, with provoking coldness. 'Oh! it was only whether people, who are like each other in their moral constitution—is that the phrase?'

'It 's as good a phrase as another,' said Steerforth.

'Thank you:—whether people, who are like each other in their moral constitution, are in greater danger than people not so circumstanced, supposing any serious cause of variance to arise between them, of being divided angrily and deeply?'

'I should say yes,' said Steerforth.

'Should you?' she retorted. 'Dear me! Supposing then, for instance—any unlikely thing will do for a supposition—that you and your mother were to have a serious quarrel.'

'My dear Rosa,' interposed Mrs. Steerforth, laughing good-naturedly, 'suggest some other supposition! James and I know our duty to each other better, I pray Heaven!'

'Oh!' said Miss Dartle, nodding her head thoughtfully. 'To be sure. *That* would prevent it? Why, of course it would. Ex-actly. Now, I am glad I have been so foolish as to put the case, for it is so very good to know that your duty to each other would prevent it! Thank you very much.'

One other little circumstance connected with Miss Dartle I must not omit; for I had reason to remember it thereafter, when all the irremediable past was rendered plain. During the whole of this day, but especially from this period of it, Steerforth exerted himself with his utmost skill, and that was with his utmost ease, to charm this singular creature into a pleasant and pleased companion. That he should succeed, was no matter of surprise to me. That she should struggle against the fascinating influence of his delightful art—delightful nature I thought it then—did not surprise me either; for I knew that she was sometimes jaundiced and perverse. I saw her features and her manner slowly change; I saw her look at him with growing admiration; I saw her try, more and more faintly, but always angrily, as if she condemned a weakness in herself, to resist the captivating power that he possessed; and finally, I saw her sharp glance soften, and her smile become quite gentle, and I ceased to be afraid of her as I had really been all day, and we all sat about the fire, talking and laughing together, with as little reserve as if we had been children.

Whether it was because we had sat there so long, or because Steerforth was resolved not to lose the advantage he had gained, I do not know; but we did not remain in the dining-room more than five minutes after her departure. 'She is playing her harp,' said Steerforth, softly, at the drawing-room door, 'and nobody but my mother has heard her do that, I believe, these three years.' He said it with a curious smile, which was gone directly; and we went into the room and found her alone.

'Don't get up,' said Steerforth (which she had already done); 'my dear Rosa, don't! Be kind for once, and sing us an Irish song.'

'What do you care for an Irish song?' she returned.

'Much!' said Steerforth. 'Much more than for any other. Here is Daisy, too, loves music from his soul. Sing us an Irish song, Rosa! and let me sit and listen as I used to do.'

He did not touch her, or the chair from which she had risen, but sat himself near the harp. She stood beside it for some little while, in a curious way, going through the motion of playing it with her right hand, but not sounding it. At length she sat down, and drew it to her with one sudden action, and played and sang.

I don't know what it was, in her touch or voice, that made the song the most unearthly I have ever heard in my life, or can imagine. There was something fearful in the reality of it. It was as if it had never been written, or set to music, but sprung out of the passion within her; which found imperfect utterance in the low sounds of her voice, and crouched again when all was still. I was dumb when she leaned beside the harp again, playing it, but not sounding it, with her right hand.

A minute more, and this had roused me from my trance:—Steerforth had left his seat, and gone to her, and had put his arm laughingly about her, and had said, 'Come, Rosa, for the future we will love each other very much!' And she had struck him, and had thrown him off with the fury of a wild cat, and had burst out of the room.

'What is the matter with Rosa?' said Mrs. Steerforth, coming in.

'She has been an angel, mother,' returned Steerforth, 'for a little while; and has run into the opposite extreme, since, by way of compensation.'

'You should be careful not to irritate her, James. Her temper has been soured, remember, and ought not to be tried.'

Rosa did not come back; and no other mention was made of her, until I went with Steerforth into his room to say Good-night. Then he laughed about her, and asked me if I had ever seen such a fierce little piece of incomprehensibility.

I expressed as much of my astonishment as was then capable of expression, and asked if he could guess what it was that she had taken so much amiss, so suddenly.

'Oh, Heaven knows,' said Steerforth. 'Anything you like—or nothing! I told you she took everything, herself included, to a grindstone, and sharpened it. She is an edge-tool, and requires great care in dealing with. She is always dangerous. Goodnight!'

'Good-night!' said I, 'my dear Steerforth! I shall be gone before you awake in the morning. Goodnight!'

He was unwilling to let me go; and stood, holding me out, with a hand on each of my shoulders, as he had done in my own room.

'Daisy,' he said with a smile—'for though that's not the name your godfathers and godmothers gave you, it's the name I like best to call you by—and I wish, I wish, I wish, you could give it to me!'

'Why, so I can, if I choose,' said I.

'Daisy, if anything should ever separate us, you must think of me at my best, old boy. Come! Let us make that bargain. Think of me at my best, if circumstances should ever part us!'

'You have no best to me, Steerforth,' said I, 'and no worst. You are always equally loved, and cherished in my heart.'

So much compunction for having ever wronged him, even by a shapeless thought, did I feel within me, that the confession of having done so was rising to my lips. But for the reluctance I had, to betray the confidence of Agnes, but for my uncertainty how to approach the subject with no risk of doing so, it would have reached them before he said, 'God bless you, Daisy, and good-night!' In my doubt, it did *not* reach them; and we shook hands, and we parted.

I was up with the dull dawn, and, having dressed as quietly as I could, looked into his room. He was fast asleep; lying, easily, with his head upon his arm, as I had often seen him lie at school.

The time came in its season, and that was very soon, when I almost wondered that nothing troubled his repose, as I looked at him. But he slept—let me think of him so again—as I had often seen him sleep at school; and thus, in this silent hour, I left him.

—Never more, oh, God forgive you, Steerforth! to touch that passive hand in love and friendship. Never, never more!